HOW GOVERNMENT WORKS

HOW GOVERNMENT WORKS

SELECTIONS FROM

The Encyclopedia of the United States Congress

The Encyclopedia of the American Presidency

Encyclopedia of the American Judicial System

MACMILLAN LIBRARY REFERENCE USA

New York

Interior Design by Kevin Hanek
Cover Design by Judy Kahn

Macmillan Library Reference USA
1633 Broadway, 7th Floor
New York, NY 10019

Manufactured in the United States of America

Printing number
1 2 3 4 5 6 7 8 9 10

Library of Congress Cataloging-in-Publication Data

How government works : selections from the Encyclopedia of the United States Congress, the Encyclopedia of the American presidency, and the Encyclopedia of the American judicial system.
p. cm. — (Macmillan compendium)
Includes bibliographical references and index.
ISBN 0-02-864975-3 (hc. : alk. paper)
1. United States—Politics and government. I. Series.
JK271.H74 1999
320.473—dc21 98-49352
CIP

This paper meets the requirements of ANSI/NISO Z39.48-1992 (Permanence of Paper).

Contents

Part One: Legislative Branch

F

G

H

I

J

K

M

O

P

Q

R

Part Two: Executive Branch

Part Three: Judicial Branch

Preface

Origins

> "It is, sir, the people's Constitution, the people's government, made for the people, made by the people and answerable to the people."
>
> Daniel Webster
> U.S. Senate, January 26, 1830

The Constitution, which has served as the basic frame of government of the republic of the United States for over two hundred years, was the work of a constitutional convention held in Philadelphia during the summer and early fall of 1787. The framers of the Constitution set forth a national government "in order to form a more perfect Union, establish Justice, insure domestic Tranquility, provide for the common defence, promote the general Welfare, and secure the Blessings of Liberty to ourselves and our Posterity." The three-tiered federal structure included the Legislature (Article I), the Executive (Article II), and the Judiciary (Article III).

How Government Works, the latest volume in the Macmillan Compendium series, introduces the three branches of the U.S. government by combining core articles from three prestigious encyclopedias published by Macmillan Library Reference. Part One, the Legislative Branch, is drawn from *The Encyclopedia of the United States Congress*; Part Two, the Executive Branch, comes from *The Encyclopedia of the American Presidency*; and Part Three, the Judicial Branch, is excerpted from *Encyclopedia of the American Judicial System* with additional articles from the *Encyclopedia of the American Constitution.*

Students, library patrons, historians, and political scientists have indicated a need for a single-volume overview of the United States government. The Macmillan Compendium, *How Government Works* is designed to fulfill that need.

Each section of *How Government Works* begins with several articles that introduce the core players or institutions within each branch of government. For example, Part One begins with the articles "Legislative Branch," "Representative," and "Senator." The section then continues with "A" and retains the alphabetical structure of the classic volumes from which it is derived. The need to distill the vast workings of the Congress, the Presidency, and the Judiciary into a single volume necessitated some compromises. By and large the principal articles from each set were selected to present a basic overview of the nuts and bolts of the federal government. Readers who want to explore the U.S. Congress, the Presidency, and the Judiciary in depth are encouraged to consult the more comprehensive *Encyclopedia of the United States Congress*, the *Encyclopedia of the American Presidency*, and *Encyclopedia of the American Judicial System.*

As in the original volumes, bibliographies and comprehensive cross-references appear at the end of each article.

Features

To add visual appeal and enhance the usefulness of the volume, the page format was designed to include the following helpful features.

- Call-Out Quotations: These relevant, often provocative quotations are highlighted in order to promote exploration and add visual appeal to the page.
- Cross-References: Appearing at the end of most articles, cross-references will encourage further research.
- Photographs: Chosen to complement the text, the photo program is designed to further engage the reader.

There is also an extensive index at the end of the compendium, which provides ample opportunities for further exploration.

Acknowledgments

How Government Works contains over one hundred illustrations. Acknowledgments of sources for illustrations can be found within the captions.

The articles herein were written for the *Encyclopedia of the United States Congress*, edited by Donald C. Bacon, a Washington-based journalist specializing in the Congress, Roger H. Davidson, Professor of Government and Politics at the University of Maryland, and Morton Keller, Spector Professor of History at Brandeis University; the *Encyclopedia of the American Presidency*, edited by Leonard W. Levy, Andrew W. Mellon All-

Claremont Professor of the Humanities, Emeritus at the Claremont Graduate School, and Louis Fisher of the Congressional Research Service; *Encyclopedia of the American Judicial System*, edited by the late Robert J. Janosik, Professor of Politics at Occidental College; and the *Encyclopedia of the American Constitution*, edited by Leonard W. Levy and Kenneth L. Karst, Professor of Law, UCLA. Leading authorities at work in political science, government, history, public administration, economics, and law, as well as distinguished congressional staff members and journalists contributed to the original sets.

We are grateful to all of these scholars and experts for their contributions to these important reference works. We would also like to thank the in-house staff whose hard work and creativity made this book possible.

Editorial Staff
Macmillan Library Reference

PART ONE

Legislative Branch

LEGISLATIVE BRANCH

One of the three branches of the federal government of the United States, the legislative branch includes the United States Congress and several research and administrative agencies that provide support services to the Congress.

The legislative branch functions within a system of checks and balances prescribed by the Constitution and designed to keep power from becoming concentrated in any one person or any one branch of government. Most basically, Article I of the Constitution provides for a legislative branch, the Congress, to make the laws; Article II provides for an executive branch, the president, to enforce the laws; and Article III provides for a judicial branch, the Supreme Court, to interpret questions about the law.

The legislative branch has several unique powers that separate it from the executive and judicial branches.

The legislative branch has several unique powers that separate it from the executive and judicial branches. These include the power to collect taxes, pay debts, and provide for the general welfare of the United States; to borrow money; to coin money and regulate its value; to regulate commerce; to establish a postal system; to declare war; to maintain the armed forces; to enact patent and copyrights laws; and to establish federal courts below the Supreme Court.

In practice, however, powers of the three branches sometimes overlap and are shared rather than separated. For example, in addition to listing specific powers, the Constitution also provides Congress with generalized authority to make all the laws that are necessary to carry out its specified powers. This "elastic clause" may be broadly interpreted to justify a wide range of congressional activity.

There are a number of additional ways in which the three branches share powers and are interdependent. For example, the Supreme Court can declare unconstitutional a law enacted by Congress; the vice president of the United States acts as president of the Senate; and the president can veto congressional legislation.

Organizationally, Congress is a bicameral institution; that is, it is divided into two distinct chambers, the House of Representatives and the Senate. The two chambers have very different characteristics. The House has 435 members who serve two-year terms; the Senate has 100 members who serve six-year terms. In the House, states are represented according to their population; they may have one representative, as does Alaska, or fifty-two representatives, as does California. In the Senate, each state is represented by two senators, regardless of population.

The House and Senate have equal legislative power; both bodies write and pass laws and have executive oversight responsibilities. However, each chamber also has some specific responsibilities the other chamber does not have. Only the Senate can approve treaties and presidential appointments. The House of Representatives alone has the authority to initiate tax bills.

In addition to the House and the Senate, the legislative branch includes the following congressional support agencies: the Congressional Budget Office, the Library of Congress, the General Accounting Office, the Office of Technology Assessment, the Government Printing Office, the Architect of the Capitol, the United States Botanic Garden. Although these support agencies are a part of the legislative branch and exist primarily to support Congress, some perform wider service. For example, the Government Printing Office is responsible for all federal printing, the Library of Congress registers all copyrights, and the General Accounting Office sets governmentwide accounting standards and resolves disputed claims by or against the United States.

[See also (I) House of Representatives; (II) Congress, White House Influence on, Senate. For further discussion of congressional support agencies, see (I) Congressional Budget Office, General Accounting Office, Library of Congress.]

BIBLIOGRAPHY

Congressional Quarterly Inc. "Origins and Development of Congress." In *Congressional Quarterly's Guide to Congress.* 4th ed. Edited by Mary Cohn. 1991.

Silbey, Joel H., ed: *The First Branch of American Government: The United States Congress and Its Relations to the Executive and Judiciary, 1789–1989.* 1991.

– MARY ETTA BOESL

REPRESENTATIVE

A person selected, most commonly through an election, to act on behalf of a larger number of people in a decision-making body is called a representative. Representatives are expected to be typical of their constituents, and a representative chamber is expected to be a condensation of the nation.

The House of Representatives, with its 435 members and two-year terms, was designed to be the legislative chamber with closer ties to popular opinion. As such, its members are called "representatives." This was not the initial expectation for senators, who were originally appointed for six-year terms to shield them from the public's shifting ideas.

Is representation simply a matter of following constituency preferences on all issues, or should representatives exercise independent judgment?

Usually the links between representatives and their constituents depend on policy agreement. Some people also demand symbolic representation, in which politically important groups are represented by one of their own. In this view, blacks can best represent blacks, women can best represent women. Some political systems even reserve seats for designated groups in decision-making bodies. The Democratic party initiated quotas in order to ensure inclusion of blacks, women, and young people in its convention in 1972. Symbolic representation does not inevitably result in better policy congruence between leaders and their constituents.

Both policy-based and symbolic representation must confront the issue of whom representatives should represent. Must legislators pay attention to their entire constituencies or only to those who voted for them? Is representation simply a matter of following constituency preferences on all issues, or should representatives exercise independent judgment? These are all controversial issues in the study of representation that have no ready answers.

[See also (I) Senator.]

BIBLIOGRAPHY

Dexter, Lewis Anthony. "The Representative and His District." In *New Perspectives on the House of Representatives.* 2d ed. Edited by Robert L. Peabody and Nelson W. Polsby. 1969.

Pitkin, Hanna Fenichel. *The Concept of Representation.* 1967.

– ERIC M. USLANER

SENATOR

The term *senator* (which in Latin means "old man") derives from ancient Rome, whose senators were at first elected by patricians and later appointed to posts that combined legislative and administrative duties. Article I, section 3, paragraph 3 of the Constitution requires that a senator be thirty years of age, a U.S. citizen for nine years, and an inhabitant of the state from which he or she is chosen. Under the terms of one of the entrenched clauses of the Constitution (Article V), each state is guaranteed two senators, a right that cannot be taken away without the state's consent.

The Constitution also specifies that the Senate be divided into three classes and that one-third of the Senate be chosen every second year. This provides a six-year term for each senator and accounts for the continuity of the Senate, that is, the fact that two-thirds of its membership carries over from one Congress to the next.

The popular election of senators was established in 1913 with the ratification of the Seventeenth Amendment. (Before that, senators were named be their respective state legislatures.) Unlike members of the House of Representatives, senators may be appointed by governors when vacancies occur because of death, resignation, or disqualification. No senator may be appointed during his or her term to any other civil office in the United States.

Senators have every legislative power available to members of the House of Representatives except the power to originate revenue bills, and they have the additional power to "advise and consent" on nominations and treaties. Further, senators sit in judgment on impeachments voted by the House of Representatives.

BIBLIOGRAPHY

Davidson, Roger H., and Oleszek, Walter J. *Congress and Its Members.* 2d ed. 1985

– ROBERT B. DOVE

A

ADJOURNMENT AND RECESS

In the House

A simple motion to adjourn is highly privileged in the House, and thus, with certain restrictions, is in order whenever the floor can be secured. The motion to adjourn, however, cannot take another member who has the floor from his feet and is not in order in the Committee of the Whole. The motion is nondebatable and does not require a quorum for adoption.

Under clause 4 of Rule XVI, the Speaker has discretion to entertain "at any time" a motion that when the House adjourns *on that day* it stand adjourned to a day and time certain within three calendar days. When the Speaker exercises his discretion, the motion is of equal privilege with the simple motion to adjourn.

A simple motion to adjourn is highly privileged in the House.

Under Article I, section 5 of the Constitution, neither house may adjourn for more than three days (not counting Sundays) without the consent of the other. Adjournment for more than three days (often called a "recess" or a "district work period") is provided by concurrent resolution, which must also be adopted by the Senate; the concurrent resolution is privileged and is nondebatable. In recent years such concurrent resolutions have often contained "recall" provisions authorizing the joint House and Senate leaderships to reconvene the two houses prior to the end of the recess.

Provision for final adjournment (sine die) is made by concurrent resolution, which is also privileged.

Adjourning terminates the legislative day. The House (unlike the Senate) normally adjourns at the conclusion of business each calendar day, thus concluding the legislative day each day.

Under a new clause 12 of Rule I, adopted in the 103d Congress, the Speaker may suspend the business of the House by declaring a short recess at any time as long as no question is pending. Furthermore, under clause 4 of Rule XVI, the Speaker has discretion to entertain "at any time" a motion authorizing the Speaker to declare a recess. As with the motion to adjourn to a day and time certain, this motion is of equal privilege with the simple motion to adjourn when the Speaker exercises his discretion.

In committees, the motion to recess from day to day is highly privileged under clause 1 of Rule XI.

[See also (I) House of Representatives.]

BIBLIOGRAPHY

U.S. House of Representatives. *Constitution, Jefferson's Manual, and Rules of the House of Representatives, 103d Congress.* Compiled by William Holmes Brown. 102d Cong., 2d sess., 1992. H. Doc. 102-405.

– CHARLES W. JOHNSON

In the Senate

The Senate can end its daily session either by adjourning or recessing, but the recess is by far the more common. On average, the Senate adjourns three or four times during any legislative month, preferring to recess on all other days.

Generally, if the Senate wants to expedite its proceedings, recessing carries a number of advantages over adjourning. When the Senate reconvenes after a recess, it continues its activities at precisely the point at which it recessed. This provides maximum flexibility for the majority leader.

The procedural requirements for a recess are simple, but the Standing Rules of the Senate stipulate a number of time-consuming activities that must follow an adjournment. These procedures, known as the *morning hour,* were originally designed to consume the first two hours of a session following an adjournment. With one exception, these procedures can only be dispensed with by unanimous consent.

THE MORNING HOUR. During the morning hour, the Senate Rules require that senators approve or correct the journal, conduct morning business, consider resolutions that have been objected to, and consider bills and resolutions on the Senate calendar.

The Constitution requires that the Senate maintain a journal of its proceedings, and the Rules provide that it be read and corrected "if any mistakes be made" as the first item of business following an adjournment. Avoiding this requires either unanimous consent or a nondebatable motion. In practice, the Senate journal is seldom read and a vote on approving it is seldom taken. Unanimous consent is normally granted, allowing the Senate simply to approve the journal.

During the conduct of morning business, several things can happen. Petitions and memorials from private citizens or state legislatures may be presented; the Senate may receive reports from committees (Senate committees report several hundred bills during a congressional session); bills and joint resolutions may be introduced (more than two thousand bills and joint resolutions are introduced by individual senators during each Congress); and concurrent or simple resolutions may be submitted (simple resolutions involve only the Senate; concurrent resolutions involve both houses of Congress).

During the morning hour, the Senate is also required to consider resolutions that have been objected to on a previous day. The Senate must also consider bills and resolutions on the Senate Calendar; these bills and resolutions are laid before the Senate in the order in which they appear, and debate on each question is limited to five minutes.

REASONS FOR ADJOURNMENT. Despite adjournment's cumbersome requirements, on occasion the Senate finds it necessary to adjourn rather than recess. Some procedures can only be accomplished through adjournment. For example, the Rules provide that it is "not in order" to move to consideration of any piece of legislation on the Senate Calendar that has not been on the calendar for one legislative day. The only way to begin a new legislative day is to adjourn. The rules do not require that bills or joint resolutions be referred to a Senate committee. They can be placed directly on the Senate Calendar through a procedure contained in Rule XIV, but this procedure can only be invoked if the Senate adjourns rather than recesses.

[See also (I) Senate.]

BIBLIOGRAPHY

Riddick, Floyd M. *Senate Procedure.* 1981.

Tiefer, Charles. *Congressional Practice and Procedure.* 1989.

– ROBERT B. DOVE

AMENDING

Amending is the process by which members attempt to change the content of legislation as it is considered in committee markup sessions and during House and Senate floor sessions. Introducing a bill begins a process of informal review and formal consideration that can last for the entire length of a two-year Congress. Only under extraordinary circumstances would Congress pass a major bill without first making changes in it. These changes are made during the course of the amending process which, for this reason, is at the heart of the legislative process in Congress.

The legislative process permits a bill to be amended at as many as seven different stages: when it is considered by a subcommittee of the House, by the parent committee of that subcommittee, and by the full House; when it is considered by a subcommittee and committee of the Senate and by the Senate itself; and when the House and Senate try to reach final agreement on the bill's content, either in a conference committee or by a formal exchange of amendments between the two houses. In some cases, one or more of these stages is bypassed; for example, the House and Senate sometimes pass noncontroversial bills without first considering them in formal committee and subcommittee meetings. In other cases, stages are added to the process; for example, some bills are considered by one House or Senate committee only after having been debated and amended by another committee of that house.

AMENDMENTS IN COMMITTEE. Major bills usually are considered first by a subcommittee of the House or Senate. Identical, or "companion," bills frequently are introduced in both houses, so that House and Senate subcommittees can begin to act on the same subject at the same time. After one or more days of public hearings on the bill's merits, the subcommittee decides whether to consider amendments to it at a "markup" session. The text of the bill is marked up (figuratively, at least) as the subcommittee decides to make additions, deletions, or substitutions in its text. Members propose these changes in the form of amendments that specify precisely what alterations in the bill they wish to make. After an amendment has been proposed, members may debate it before voting to accept or reject it. They also may amend the amendment before deciding whether to approve it in its amended form. Ultimately, the subcommittee votes to report the bill, with the amendments it has adopted, to its parent committee, which then may repeat this process.

Much the same process takes place in Senate subcommittees and committees, and the process in both houses generally follows the rules of the full House or Senate for amending legislation on the floor. However, the smaller size of committees and subcommittees usually makes it possible for their markup process to be less formal and structured than the amending process on the floor. There is one other important difference between the amending process in committee and the process as it takes place on the floor. Only the full House and Senate actually may make changes in the text of a bill. Committees and subcommittees only recommend changes in the form of amendments. The full House and Senate then must approve these committee amendments before they actually are incorporated into the bill.

FLOOR AMENDMENTS. When the House or Senate begins to consider the bill on the floor, it acts first on any committee amendments. Members can offer amendments to each committee amendment before voting to accept or reject it, but they usually cannot offer their own amendments to the bill itself until after disposing of all committee amendments. An important exception arises when a committee reports a bill to either house with a single amendment that proposes an entirely different text for the bill. In that case, members generally direct their floor amendments to that committee amendment, often called an "amendment in the nature of a substitute," not to the text of the bill as it was originally introduced. When members eventually agree to the committee substitute, as amended, that completes the amending process because the bill now has been totally amended; the House or Senate then votes on passing the bill as amended by the substitute.

Each amendment must be in writing and read on the floor before members begin to debate it.

Each amendment must be in writing and read on the floor before members begin to debate it. An amendment to change the text of a measure is known as a "first-degree" amendment. Before the House or Senate votes on that amendment, members may offer amendments to it; an amendment to an amendment is a "second-degree" amendment. Amendments may add (insert) additional language into a bill, strike language from the bill, or replace (strike and insert) language in the bill. For some purposes, it also can be important to distinguish between "perfecting" amendments, which propose to make a limited change in a bill or first-degree amendment, and substitute amendments, which propose to completely replace the text of the bill or first-degree amendment. Once the House or Senate has approved an amendment, it no longer can be amended. Also, members cannot offer amendments that only propose to amend some language that already has been amended. For example, once the House amends a bill by changing a dollar amount from, say, $1 million to $2 million, an amendment is not in order if it proposes only to make another change in the same dollar amount.

CHAMBER DIFFERENCES. In these respects, the amending processes on the House and Senate floor are similar. In other respects, however, there are important differences in how the two houses amend legislation. The amending process in the House usually is systematic; members offer amendments to each section or title of a bill in sequence. Senators may offer their amendments to any portion of the bill in any order. Representatives usually may debate each amendment for only five minutes each; senators can debate an amendment at length and even filibuster an amendment they strongly oppose. In the House, each amendment must be germane to the provision or amendment it proposes to change. The Senate requires amendments to be germane only under limited circumstances: for example, senators' amendments to most appropriations and budget measures must be germane as must all amendments that are offered when the Senate has invoked cloture to limit debate. At all other times, senators are free to offer amendments that are totally unrelated to the subject of the bill the Senate is considering.

Representatives and senators do not have the same ability to amend each bill and resolution they consider on the floor. Each house can invoke procedures that limit or even foreclose members' amending opportunities. For example, the House considers many measures under the procedure known as "suspension of the rules," which precludes all amendments except for amendments that are incorporated in the motion to suspend the rules and pass the bill. The House normally considers more important and controversial bills by transforming itself into a Committee of the Whole (formally, a Committee of the Whole House on the State of the Union), which follows procedures that are more convenient for offering and debating amendments. Before the House debates and amends a bill in Committee of the Whole, however, it normally adopts a resolution, known as a "special rule," reported by its Rules Committee to propose special procedures for acting on that particular bill. These procedures may include restrictions on the amendments to the bill that members can offer. A "closed" rule typically prohibits all floor amendments except committee amendments. A "modified open" or "modified closed" rule precludes some but not all amendments; frequently, such a restrictive rule will specifically identify the relatively small number of floor amendments that members can propose. The House must adopt each special rule by majority vote before it takes effect.

In the Senate, members' freedom to offer amendments can be limited by invoking *cloture* to limit further debate on a measure. The effect of cloture, which usually requires support from at least sixty senators, is to permit the Senate to continue considering the measure for no more than thirty more hours, during which senators can only propose germane amendments that were submitted to the Senate in writing before the cloture vote. Alternatively, the Senate sometimes agrees by unanimous consent to limit debate on one or all amendments to a bill. A unanimous consent agreement also may prohibit all amendments to the bill except those identified in the agreement itself. On the other hand, unanimous consent agreements in the Senate and special rules in the House can allow senators or representatives to propose amendments that would not otherwise be in order.

After both houses have passed different versions of the same bill, they again resort to an amending process to resolve the differences between their two versions. The House and Senate must pass a bill in precisely the same form before it can be presented to the president for his approval or disapproval. So after the Senate passes a House bill with one or more amendments, or after the House amends and passes a Senate bill, they must reach agreement on each of these amendments before the legislative process is completed. They may do so through a process by which, for example, the House amends each Senate amendment and the Senate then amends that House amendment. The alternative is for both houses to create a conference committee to report a package settlement of the disagreements that both houses vote to accept or reject without further amendment.

THE IMPORTANCE OF AMENDING. The amending process on the House and Senate floors presents members with the opportunity to shape public policy on subjects that are not within the jurisdictions of the committees on which they serve. Strictly in policy terms, the votes on floor amendments can be considered the most important votes that members cast. During the 95th and 96th Congresses (1977–1981), the House passed 3,013 bills and resolutions and defeated 72; senators rejected only 8 of the 2,634 measures that reached a vote on final passage in that body. Thus, the two houses defeated fewer than 1.5 percent of the measures on which they completed floor action. Each bill must survive the vote on final passage, of course, but these data illustrate that the critical question to be asked of House or Senate floor action on a bill is not whether the bill will pass, but what provisions it will contain when it does pass.

The answer depends on the bill that the standing committee (or committees) brings before the House or Senate for debate, amendment, and passage. This establishes the basic policy approach and framework that chamber will consider. Equally important, however, is how that approach and framework is changed during its floor consideration as a result of the amendments that individual members propose and a majority of their colleagues support. Proposals that members advocate unsuccessfully in subcommittee or committee markup may be presented again as floor amendments in that house, and proposals that are not approved in one house may be revived as floor amendments in the other. The final version of a bill cannot be predicted with confidence until all the stages at which it can be amended have been completed.

Especially in the House of Representatives, the amending process on the floor has become even more important since the House began in 1970 to make organizational and procedural changes. On balance, the effect of many of these reforms has been to reduce the influence of committees and their chairmen. The ability of chairmen to control the agendas and decisions of their committees was reduced at the same time that the House exposed its proceedings to greater public scrutiny and influence. One consequence was to encourage members to offer floor amendments that challenged committee recommendations and for members to support those amendments, especially when they benefited important constituency interests.

As a result, more floor amendments were proposed and adopted, creating greater uncertainty about what would happen to legislation on the floor. Woodrow Wilson's classic dictum that the floor sessions of the House and Senate are merely "Congress on public exhibition," the real work being done in committee rooms, is not nearly as true as it may have been a century ago. In the contemporary Congress, there is no more important aspect of lawmaking than the amending process.

[See also (I) Committees, article on Markups, Conference Committees.]

BIBLIOGRAPHY

Bach, Stanley. "Parliamentary Strategy and the Amendment Process: Rules and Case Studies of Congressional Action." *Polity* 15 (1983): 573–592.

Smith, Steven S. *Call to Order: Floor Politics in the House and Senate.* 1989.

U.S. House of Representatives. *Deschler's Precedents of the United States House of Representatives,* by Lewis Deschler. 94th Cong., 2d sess., 1977. H. Doc. 94-661. Vol. 9.

U.S. Senate. *Senate Procedure, Precedents, and Practices,* by Floyd M. Riddick. 97th Cong., 1st sess., 1981. S. Doc. 97-2. Pp. 22–113.

– STANLEY BACH

APPORTIONMENT AND REDISTRICTING

The boundaries of congressional districts in all but the smallest states are redrawn at the beginning of every decade to equalize their populations. The need for such adjustment stems from the constitutional requirement that congressional districts have equal populations, together with a constantly shifting U.S. population. The alteration of old district lines to achieve new ideal populations is the essence of redistricting, or, as it is sometimes called, reapportionment.

The first step in congressional redistricting is called apportionment.

The first step in congressional redistricting is called apportionment. Using a modified proportional representation formula derived by Edward Huntingdon, the Census Bureau calculates each state's share of congressional districts when the decennial census is finished. The second step is to adjust congressional boundaries within each state's border to achieve near equality in district populations. The result of this two-stage process is that district populations are made equal within states but, by strict standards, remain relatively unequal across states. In 1980, Nevada, with its population of 787,000, and Maine, with its population of 1,125,000, were each apportioned two seats, while South Dakota, with 690,000, got only one, producing districts of very unequal size. Congressional districts in Maine had an ideal population of 563,000, in Nevada 393,000, and in South Dakota 690,000.

The authority for congressional apportionment is constitutional. Article I, section 2 states that "Representatives shall be apportioned among the states according to their numbers." In the beginning, Congress expanded its membership to accommodate new states and population increases, but since 1910, House membership has been kept at 435. In 1790, there was one member for each 33,000 people and 106 members total. By 1990, the average ratio was one seat per 570,000 people.

The method of congressional apportionment has changed five times since 1790. The differences between these methods are slight, all of them tending to produce roughly similar and proportionate outcomes. But the small differences associated with the choice of a particular formula mean a lot to states that lose a seat under one method and keep it under another. Some critics, for instance, maintain that the Huntingdon formula, which has been used since 1950, favors small states over large. But for the most part, the Huntingdon method has been widely accepted for its fairness to all states.

Shifting population trends within the United States have caused some enormous variations in the sizes of state delegations over time. New York had ten House seats in 1790, forty in 1830, twenty-one in 1860, forty-five in 1930, and thirty-one in 1990. California, by contrast, grew steadily from eleven seats in 1930 to fifty-two seats in 1990. The original thirteen states had 100 percent of the seats in Congress in 1790, 42 percent in 1870, and 33 percent in 1990. Between 1949 and 1992, nearly sixty seats shifted from the frostbelt to the sunbelt states.

EQUAL POPULATION DOCTRINE AND CONGRESS. In a number of legislative actions taken prior to the "one person, one vote" judicial decisions of *Baker v. Carr* and *Reynolds v. Sims,* Congress clearly demonstrated its support for the principle of redistricting in favor of districts of equal population. In 1842, Congress legislated that representatives should be "elected by districts of contiguous territory equal in number" with "no district electing more than one representative." Thirty years later, the Reapportionment Act of 1872 also declared that districts should contain "as nearly as possible an equal number of inhabitants." Because Congress had already put itself on a straight and narrow course toward equally populated districts, congressional malapportionment was relatively moderate in 1960. All but 40 of the 435 congressional districts were within 15 percent of the national average.

Prior to 1962, the Supreme Court repeatedly refused to tackle the problem of malapportionment. In *Wood v. Brown* (287 U.S. 1, 8 [1932]), the Supreme Court decided not to overturn a Mississippi law that created unequal congressional districts. In 1946, the Court was given another chance to intervene when a Northwestern University political scientist brought suit against the state of Illinois, arguing that the gross disparities in district populations violated the equal protection clause of the Fourteenth Amendment. As before, the Court refused by a vote of 4 to 3 to take up the case of *Colgrove v. Green* (328 U.S. 549 [1946]), because the issue was, in Justice Felix Frankfurter's words, "of a peculiarly political nature and therefore not meant for judicial interpretation."

The Court's approach changed dramatically with its ruling in *Baker v. Carr* (369 U.S. 186 [1962]). The plaintiffs had argued that the malapportionment of the Tennessee state assembly violated both the state and federal constitutions. The Supreme Court, by a vote of 6 to 2, decided that it had jurisdiction, despite Frankfurter's objection that this would "catapult the Courts into a mathematical quagmire." In *Wesberry v. Sanders* (376 U.S. 1 [1964]) and *Reynolds v. Sims* (377 U.S. [1964]), the Court applied its "one person, one vote" principle to congressional and state legislative districts, holding in essence that the right to vote is not equal if people vote in unequally sized districts. In particular, according to the logic of malapportionment, a vote in a large district has less value than one in a small district, because a vote's weight varies inversely with an electorate's size. After the initial ruling that malapportionment was justiciable, many of the subsequent cases focused on the issue of how equal new district populations had to be in order to meet the Court's expectations. The congressional standard is that, "as nearly as practicable," one person's vote should be worth as much as another's. The Supreme Court held in *Kirkpatrick v. Priesler* (394 U.S. 526 [1969]) that states should make a good faith effort to achieve exact mathematical equality, and in *White v. Weiser* (412 U.S. 783 [1973]), it struck down the Texas legislature's proposal for a congressional redistricting plan because one with smaller deviations was available. The rejected plan had population deviations from the ideal of less than 5 percent. A decade later, the Court in effect made the equal population requirement even stricter when in *Karcher v. Daggett* (426 U.S. 725 [1983]) it turned down a New Jersey congressional plan with trivial population differences (0.69 percent) in favor of a plan with even smaller deviations.

VOTE DILUTION AND THE EVOLVING CONCEPT OF EQUITY. The first meaning of redistricting equity is described by the principle of "one person, one vote"; namely, that every eligible voter has the right to an equally weighted vote. When districts vary in size, people voting in the larger districts have in a purely mathematical sense less voice in and influence over the outcome of an election than those in smaller districts. In addition, malapportionment gives more representation to some areas of a political jurisdiction than to others.

With the passage of the Voting Rights Act of 1965 and the growing clamor over political gerrymandering, a second sense of redistricting equity emerged—the right to a meaningful or undiluted vote. The logic of a vote-dilution claim is as follows: even if an individual has a right to an equally weighted vote, the exercise of that right can be frustrated if district lines are drawn in such a manner as to dilute the votes of one group and enhance the electoral prospects of another.

There are two distinct types of vote-dilution claims—partisan and racial. The first points to partisan or political gerrymandering, in which districting arrangements can unfairly favor a particular political party over another (usually the majority over the minority party) or favor incumbents over challengers (the so-called bipartisan or incumbent gerrymander problem). Historically, the Court has been reluctant to involve itself deeply in partisan gerrymandering issues. Indeed, until its ruling in *Davis v. Bandemer* (478 U.S. 109 [1986]), there was no clear indication that it regarded partisan gerrymandering as even a justiciable issue.

In considering the allegation by Indiana's Democrats in *Davis* that the Republican-controlled legislature diluted their voting strength and caused disproportionate gains for Republican candidates, the Supreme Court ruled 6 to 3 that a political gerrymandering claim was justiciable. At the same time, however, the Court cast considerable doubt on whether the potential justiciability of gerrymandering would mean anything of practical significance by overruling the lower court's decision to strike down the Indiana legislature's plan. Some interpret this decision as meaning that a partisan gerrymander claim can only be won by political parties who are able to show that they have suffered exclusion and discrimination comparable to that experienced by racial minorities, and that this threshold virtually rules out any claims by the two major American political parties, the Democrats and Republicans.

At the end of the decade, the Supreme Court further indicated its intention to keep a high threshold for political gerrymandering cases when it affirmed a lower court ruling in *Badham v. Eu* (109 U.S. 829 [1989]). The Court refused to overturn the infamous Burton congressional redistricting plan, holding that Republicans had many avenues of political redress (including the initiative and referendum process) and could not be said to be in a position of political exclusion since they had held a number of statewide offices throughout the 1980s.

In addition to the issue of political vote dilution, there is the equally controversial question of racial- and ethnic-group vote dilution.

Another form of political gerrymandering is the so-called bipartisan or incumbent protection gerrymander. Relative to partisan gerrymandering, the courts have taken a more benign view of explicitly bipartisan plans. In *Burns v. Richardson* (384 U.S. 73 [1966]) and *White v. Weiser* (412 U.S. 783 [1973]), the Court held that drawing lines to minimize contests between sitting incumbents does not in and of itself establish "invidiousness." And in *Gaffney v. Cummings* (412 U.S. 735 [1973]), the Court upheld a purposely political plan that attempted to create proportionate shares of districts for the two political parties based on voting results in the previous three elections. With the growing clamor over the incumbency advantage, however, the Court may find it harder to bless bipartisan gerrymanders in the future.

In addition to the issue of political vote dilution, there is the equally controversial question of racial- and ethnic-group vote dilution. The critical legislation in this regard is the Voting Rights Act (VRA) of 1965 and its subsequent amendments. Although most VRA litigation challenges the use of multi-member districts, sections 2 and 5 also apply to the arrangements of constituency boundaries in single-member district jurisdictions. Areas of the country that are covered by section 5 of the VRA must clear any changes in district boundaries with the Justice Department or the district court of the District of Columbia. The critical issue in clearance is whether any proposed changes in the procedures and rules governing elections in areas with a history of vote discrimination and low voting participation cause retrogression in the voting power of protected minority groups.

Areas that are not covered by section 5 still must meet the standards of section 2, which states: "No voting qualification or prerequisite to voting, or standard, practice, or procedure shall be imposed or applied by any State or political sub-division to deny or abridge the right of any citizen of the United States to vote on account of race or color." Prior to 1982, section 2 was interpreted to mean only the intentional dilution of disadvantaged minority votes (*Bolden v. City of Mobile,* 446 U.S. 55 [1980]). The act was amended in 1982 to cover rules and procedures that had the effect of diluting minority votes regardless of intentions. In *Thornburg v. Gingles* (478 U.S. 30 [1986]), a case involving state legislative districts in North Carolina, the Court singled out three criteria as most important in deciding whether a jurisdiction had complied with the provisions of the VRA: Is a minority group sufficiently large and compact enough to constitute a majority of a district? Is it politically cohesive? Is there evidence of racially polarized voting against minority candidates?

At a minimum, the protection afforded by the VRA prevents the exclusion of groups from the opportunity to elect representatives of their own choice. However, a number of critics maintain that the VRA is being interpreted more expansively by some plaintiffs as a right to proportional representation, a right which the Supreme Court has on several occasions explicitly denied.

More generally, the right to an undiluted vote is problematic in a system that employs single member, simple plurality (SMSP) rules. The logic of such a system is that it exaggerates the share of seats won by the party with the most votes and minimizes that share of seats the other parties get. This is touted by SMSP proponents as an advantage over proportional representation systems because it eases the task of creating a governing a majority in the legislature. If the right to an undiluted vote is interpreted to mean anything more than the right to nonexclusion, it puts the courts in the uncomfortable position of enforcing remedies for a right (namely, proportional representation for racial or political groups) that the VRA explicitly denies.

COMMON CRITERIA FOR REDISTRICTING. Broadly speaking, people commonly apply two types of criteria when assessing the quality and fairness of a redistricting: considerations of form and considerations of outcome. The most important considerations of form are equal population, natural communities of interest, and compactness or contiguity. Equal population has already been discussed. It is sometimes referred to as one of the primary criteria, meaning that considerations of population equality must be satisfied absolutely even if they conflict with other considerations of fairness.

By comparison, respect for natural communities of interest is not one of the primary criteria. In the broadest sense, this term encompasses many meanings, including agricultural areas, mountainous counties, desert regions, coastal land, and the like. The political interests associated with these geographical areas may be occupational (e.g., farming), sociological (e.g., areas within one media market), or policy oriented (e.g., the predilection of coastal areas toward environmentalism). The implicit assumption is that district boundaries should respect these natural community boundaries so that important social and economic interests are clearly articulated within the representative body. Opponents of a community-of-interest approach worry that districts so drawn encourage parochialism and factionalism.

A variant of the communities-of-interest criterion is respect for city, county, and local government boundaries. Prior to the "one person, one vote" decisions, several states required that state legislative districts follow county boundary lines exactly. The equal population standard requires that district boundaries stray from local government jurisdictions when necessary to achieve the target population figure. Assuming the satisfaction of the "one person–one vote" principle, a number of states mandate that districting arrangements minimize the splitting of city and county boundary lines to the degree feasible.

The last of the so-called formal criteria is compactness or contiguity. Contiguity means that all parts of the district must be connected at a point or, in other words, that a district cannot consist of unconnected tracts or "islands" surrounded by tracts from another district. However, contiguity can sometimes mean contiguous at a point in the water, as when offshore islands are grouped with an onshore district. Contiguity, rarely violated, is also a primary criterion.

By contrast, compactness is not a primary criterion and is often violated. Compactness can be measured in a variety of technical ways, but the essential notion behind any compactness measure is that districts should have relatively geometrical shapes, without many branches, dips, or jagged edges. At a minimum, compactness is thought to be a virtue because it constrains attempts to gerrymander by means of contorted shapes drawn to favor one party, group, or candidate over another. But some proponents of compactness also believe that it better protects political interests stemming from geographic propinquity. In reality, however, districts are often noncompact, sometimes because it better serves particular political interests, but frequently because compactness conflicts with other redistricting values, such as protecting communities of interest or complying with the VRA.

In sum, the so-called formal criteria—population equality, communities of interest, and compactness or contiguity—focus on the size, shape, and geography of ideal districts, but not on their desired political and ethnic makeup. These latter considerations are covered by outcome criteria, such as fairness between the political parties and fairness to racial and ethnic groups and competitive districts.

At a minimum, fairness between the parties means that the party receiving a majority of the votes should also receive a majority of the seats. With the elimination of gross malapportionment, this so-called majoritarian condition is rarely violated by even the most outrageous partisan gerrymanders. More often, what people mean by partisan fairness is something beyond the violation of the majority principle—namely, that a party's share of seats should match as closely as possible to its share of votes, a condition of at least rough proportionality.

There are a number of problems with this standard. To begin with, SMSP district systems do not yield proportional outcomes in most situations. One of the characteristic features of SMSP systems is that they on average exaggerate the seat share of the majority party and diminish the seat share of minority parties. So even if a redistricting plan is free of any attempt to gerrymander for partisan advantage, it will likely lead to nonproportional seat allocations. Second, the Court and Congress have explicitly acknowledged that there is no right, per se, to proportional representation, so that popular expectations of fairness and legal requirements are at odds with one another. Finally, the best way to achieve proportional outcomes would be to abandon the existing system of single-member districts for some form of proportional or semiproportional rules. While there is evidence of a limited degree of experimentation with such systems (i.e., in certain southern jurisdictions under the threat of voting rights litigation), there has historically been little enthusiasm in the United States for European-style electoral systems.

In response to this dilemma, political scientists have tried to develop alternative ways of measuring fairness in SMSP systems. For instance, some contend that fairness really consists of symmetry between the parties: if party A gets a given share of the seats for a given share of the votes, then party B in a symmetric system would get an identical share of seats given the same share of votes. In other words, a fair system treats the parties in the same way even if it does not yield proportional outcomes. Conceptually, this notion of partisan fairness is much closer to the spirit of SMSP systems than is "proportionality." Unfortunately, it is difficult to implement since it requires knowledge of counterfactual conditions—namely, what seat share a party would have received had it won a different share of the votes.

The idea that redistricting should be fair to all or as many political parties as possible seems intuitively appealing. Unfortunately, it is difficult to implement the concept of partisan fairness in the U.S. electoral system. The same difficulty underlies the concept of racial and ethnic fairness. As with partisan fairness, there are two approaches. At a minimum, racial fairness means that significantly sized minority groups should not be excluded from representation in the political system. A stronger and more widely held version of racial and ethnic fairness is that there should be rough proportionality between population strength and a group's share of elected officials—in short, proportional descriptive representation.

Nongeographical groups, such as women or left-handed people, cannot usually hope to win representation by being a majority of the voters in a district.

The critical factor for the electoral success of racial and ethnic groups under an SMSP system is numbers large enough and sufficiently concentrated to constitute a viable voting bloc in a given district. At best, the treatment of groups in an SMSP system is arbitrary. Groups that are optimally concentrated (i.e., neither too dispersed nor too packed together) and of sufficient size will tend to be treated more advantageously by the electoral system. Nongeographical groups, whose members are distributed throughout the population randomly (such as women or left-handed people), cannot usually hope to win representation by virtue of constituting a majority of the voters in a particular district. Quasi-geographical groups are loosely clumped by population and can be formed into districts by sensitive drawing of perimeters. Much of the current dispute over racial and ethnic gerrymandering centers on the quasi-geographical category. In essence, how far does the legal obligation of the state legislature or other redistricting body extend under the VRA to draw boundaries that unite geographically disparate minority neighborhoods into minority districts?

In a series of decisions prior to 1982, the courts ruled that electoral rules and institutions, including redistrictings, could not intentionally dilute the voting strength of minority communities. Jurisdictions covered under section 5 of the 1965 VRA had to submit proposed new district boundaries for approval to the Justice Department or the district court of the District of Columbia. In 1982, the language of section 2 of the VRA was amended to cover redistrictings that may not have had the intent to discriminate but had the effect of denying protected minority groups (i.e., blacks, Latinos, and Asians) the equal opportunity to elect a representative of their own choice. The meaning of this was elaborated in the Supreme Court's 1986 decision *Thornburg v. Gingles.* If a protected group can show that it is sufficiently numerous in a given area to constitute a majority of a congressional seat, if it can demonstrate that it tends to act as a politically cohesive force, and if it can demonstrate a pattern of racially polarized voting against it, then districting lines that divide its neighborhoods may be invalidated under this law. Proponents of the VRA proudly point to the significant increase in black and Latino elected officials as a result of VRA litigation. Opponents point out that it has created a special right to proportional representation for some racial and ethnic groups but not others, and they further argue that descriptive representation does not necessarily serve minority communities well.

The third and last of the outcome criteria is competitiveness—the idea that districts should be created to be as competitive as possible, which in effect means maximizing the number of marginal seats where candidates from either party have a chance to win. This is also referred to in political science literature as responsiveness. A responsive system is one in which small changes in the vote result in relatively large changes in seat shares.

Competitiveness is valued as a redistricting goal because it means that changes in voter preferences between elections can be translated into changes in policy. For example, if support for more social spending increases in the period between two elections, then in a responsive system candidates who support those policies should do better in the second election than those who do not. Changes in policy preference should ideally lead to changes in the partisan and ideological composition of the government.

In reality, while the competitiveness of districts is certainly shaped by redistricting, a number of other factors are also important. Disparities in the financial resources or name recognition of candidates, for example, often dampen the responsiveness of elections to shifting public opinion. In principle, however, districts could be drawn to make the underlying distribution of partisanship as even as possible, so that on average districts are more competitive. The chief problem with implementing this criterion is the difficulty of securing agreement from the concerned parties over how to measure and define a competitive seat. Should it be measured by using party-registration data or averages of previous statewide or district races? What are the thresholds that define the difference between competitive and safe districts? An inability to answer these basic questions has reduced competitiveness to a goal toward which much lip service is paid but on behalf of which there is little real effort.

These are the most frequently considered criteria for assessing redistricting plans. Redistricting is so contentious as a political issue because these criteria frequently conflict, forcing those who draw the lines to make difficult choices. Trade-offs between competing values require an implicit or explicit ordering of these values, and, to some degree, the courts have provided guidance in this regard. Equal population, contiguity, the VRA, and the provisions of the Fourteenth Amendment form the primary criteria—none can be violated for the sake of other criteria. Moreover, while it might be possible to do better with respect to one of the primary criteria by violating another, they are treated as forming binding constraints on one another. Thus, districts that satisfy the VRA must be equally populated and contiguous even though in theory many unequally populated and discontiguous districts might better comply with the VRA.

As for the nonprimary criteria, the examples of potential and real conflicts between them are too numerous to enumerate completely. The most common problems arise between fairness of outcome and formal criteria. In some cases, there is simply no logical connection between the two. In some circumstances, they are compatible, and in others, they are not. For instance, compactly drawn districts can produce politically "fair" or "unfair" districts, lessen or increase the number of minority-controlled districts, and discourage or promote political competitiveness. Compactness, for instance, might serve the cause of one criterion or the other in a particular political jurisdiction, but have the opposite effect in another jurisdiction due to different political and demographic circumstances.

THE PROCESS OF REDISTRICTING. The collection of the decennial census triggers the subsequent redrawing of congressional, state legislative, and local district boundaries. The Census Bureau is directed by law to make its national enumeration as of 1 April in the first year of a decade and to complete it in nine months, reporting the results to the president of the United States by 31 December of the census year. The allocation of congressional seats based on the census data is a purely mechanical exercise based on a "method of equal proportions" that ranks each state's priority of seat assignment by population share.

In recent years the accuracy of the census has been questioned by cities, states, and ethnic and racial groups who believe that they have received less than their fair share of congressional representation and federal spending. In particular, the Census Bureau acknowledges that every decade there is a differential undercount of blacks, Latinos, and, to a somewhat lesser degree, American Indians and Asians. In the 1990 census, for instance, blacks and Latinos were undercounted by approximately 5 percent.

The differential undercount lowers the apportioned share of congressional seats in states with high minority populations and causes malapportionment in inner-city minority districts, as compared to suburban or rural nonminority districts. In anticipation of another undercount in 1990, the Census Bureau designed and tested a postenumeration survey for the purpose of adjusting the enumerated figures to correct for the undercount bias. The Commerce Department sought to end the funding of the postenumeration survey in 1987. In July 1991, Secretary Robert Mosbacher overturned the Census Bureau director's recommendation in favor of adjustment. It seems likely, however, that future censuses will utilize samples and statistical techniques to improve on the data collected by enumeration alone.

Once the apportionment of congressional districts across states is completed, the second phase—the adjustment of boundaries within states—can occur. The Commerce Department secretary is required by law to give to the states by 1 April of the year after the census population counts at the census-tract and census-block level. A critical aspect of this second phase of the reapportionment cycle is the limited timetable in which states must complete their task. In large states especially, this means that a complex process must be completed quickly so that the lines can be in place for the primary elections the following year. For the most part, redistricting remains a state action, although the state's autonomy in these matters has been diminished significantly by three decades of court decisions. States are still free to decide such matters as whether to let legislators draw their own lines or give the task to a commission, whether to use majority or supermajority rules on redistricting bills, and whether to apply additional criteria beyond those mandated by the courts. These choices inevitably affect the nature of redistricting politics that ensues.

A unique feature of the American system is that while most state legislators draw their own district boundaries, members of the U.S. Congress never do. This most sensitive task is in all but three instances delegated to state officeholders. In the typical redistricting procedure in the states, the redrawing of district boundaries is treated like any other piece of legislation. Legislative leaders, including the chairs of committees with jurisdiction over election law and reapportionment, fashion a plan after consultation with some or all incumbent members of Congress, interested state legislators, and sometimes critical interest groups such as the Mexican-American Legal Defense Fund and the National Association for the Advancement of Colored People Legal Defense Fund. They then fashion one or more proposals.

A redistricting plan usually consists of either "metes and bounds" (i.e., detailed, street-by-street descriptions of district boundaries) or a list of census tracts and blocks composing each district. In addition, the legislature will usually produce maps of the new lines and supporting data that give the ethnic and racial breakdowns as well as district populations. Where available, states may also provide party registration figures and data from past elections that give some indication of the likely competitiveness of the district. The redistricting bills are reported out of committee like any other piece of legislation and onto the floor of the two houses of the legislature, where they are debated, sometimes amended, and then sent to the governor's office for approval. The governor can either sign or veto the bill, and in the event of the latter, his or her decision has to be overridden with a supermajority legislative vote. There are some variations in this model of legislative redistricting, but this describes the model process.

The governor's veto is a varying threat. In North Carolina, for instance, there is no gubernatorial veto on any legislative matter, and in New York, it cannot be applied to a redistricting plan. The supermajority vote needed to override the governor's veto is a critical barrier to a majority party's attempt to draw partisan district lines. Except in areas of one-party dominance, such as the South, the majority party will normally lack the votes to override the veto. So if the minority party can gain control of the governor's office, it can force a better deal from the legislature or cause the matter to be resolved by the courts. After *Baker v. Carr,* a number of states sought to escape from the inevitable controversies by referring redistricting to a commission or some other neutral agency. Three states now have pure commission systems: Hawaii, Montana, and Washington give their commissions both the original and final right to decide congressional district boundaries. In Connecticut, redistricting is given to a nine-member commission, but only in the event that an eight-member legislative commission, drawn evenly from both parties, cannot come to agreement. Iowa gives the tasks of changing congressional boundaries to its nonpartisan Legislative Services Bureau, although final approval is reserved to the legislature.

A redistricting plan usually consists of either "metes and bounds" or a list of census tracts and blocks composing each district.

The courts are involved in redistricting in several ways. They sometimes have to take over the process because of a political impasse at the state level. This is most likely to occur when control of a state is split between the two parties. It is commonly assumed that the party that appointed the judges to the bench will get a more favorable plan than the other party. In fact, it often works the other way. In Illinois during the 1981 redistricting, for instance, the task was given over to a three-judge panel that included two Republican appointees; yet, to the dismay of Illinois Republicans, the court chose a plan devised by the Illinois House Democratic leader. When the courts assume the responsibility of drawing district boundaries themselves, it is hard to predict what they will do and whom they will favor.

In a majority of instances, however, the courts are simply asked to review the constitutionality of district lines that are drawn by a state legislature. Several kinds of cases come up frequently. The most common involve claims of racial or ethnic minority vote dilution, usually under the provisions of the VRA. During the 1980 redistrictings, the courts overturned parts of the legislatures' redistricting plans for the states of Georgia, Louisiana, and Mississippi, in order to strengthen the electoral power and representation of black constituents. Latinos also obtained victories in the courts, most notably in Texas.

The courts in the 1980s also overturned several redistricting plans that had excessively large population deviations (e.g., New Jersey). The evolution of these cases, as discussed earlier, has been toward an increasingly strict application of "one person, one vote," especially in cases where deviations from exact equality seem to be coupled with political unfairness.

The least frequent form of constitutional review involves claims of partisan gerrymandering. The definitive statement of the Court on this subject to date is the decision in *Davis v. Bandemer* (1986), a case involving Indiana's state legislative districts. Whether this case signals a more activist posture by the courts in this area is a subject of some controversy.

In the end, however, it may not matter what the courts do. A number of recent studies indicate that there is no evidence of systematic partisan bias in congressional elections. This is not to deny that the parties in control of redistricting seek and gain local advantage through redistricting; it is only to say that the net effect is neutral over the country as a whole. The most common measure of electoral bias used by political scientists is the share of seats a party would receive if it were to get 50 percent of the vote. By this standard, according to one estimate, the Democrats would have received 52.1 percent of the congressional seats with 50 percent of the vote between 1946 and 1964, and 53.9 percent between 1966 and 1988. Correcting for the inflated percentages that result from uncontested seats, the Democrats would be predicted to get 42.8 percent of the congressional seats with 50 percent of the vote before 1966 and 50.6 percent after 1966. Another study concluded that only four of the twenty-six congressional losses the Republicans sustained in 1982 could be attributed to redistricting.

Nonetheless, the quest for a better way to redistrict continues. Reformers frequently argue that it is an unacceptable conflict of interest to allow state legislators to vote on their own district lines. Some point to the success of the Australians, Canadians, and British in removing redistricting from politics, but others point out that this is easier to achieve in parliamentary systems where there is no residency requirement, the civil service and the judiciary are less politicized, and incumbency matters less.

The inability to agree on a better process occurs at a time when expectations about redistricting are rising. Minority groups look for redistricting to remedy decades of underrepresentation. Political parties seek to use redistricting to restore single-party control of the government and to break the logjam of divided government. Good-government advocates envision better redistricting as a means of lessening the incumbency advantage. All of this ensures that redistricting will remain a matter of controversy.

[See also (I) Census, Districts, Elections, Congressional, Gerrymandering.]

BIBLIOGRAPHY

Baker, Gordon E. *The Reapportionment Revolution. 1967.*

Balinski, Michael L., and H. Peyton Young. *Fair Representation: Meeting the Ideal of One Man, One Vote.* 1982.

Browning, Robert X., and Gary King. "Seats, Votes and Gerrymandering: Estimating Representation and Bias in State Legislative Redistricting." *Law and Policy* 9 (1987): 305–322.

Cain, Bruce E. "Assessing the Partisan Effects of Redistricting." *American Political Science Review* 79 (1985): 320–333.

Cain, Bruce E. *The Reapportionment Puzzle.* 1984.

Davidson, Chandler, ed. *Minority Vote Dilution.* 1984.

Dixon, Robert. *Democratic Representation: Reapportionment in Law and Politics.* 1968.

Erikson, R. S. "Malapportionment, Gerrymandering and Party Fortunes." *American Political Science Review* 66 (1972): 1234–1245.

Ferejohn, John A. "On the Decline of Competitive Congressional Elections." *American Political Science Review* 7 (1977): 166–176.

Guinier, Lani. *The Tyranny of the Majority: Fundamental Fairness and Representative Democracy.* 1994.

McCubbins, M. D., and Thomas Schwartz. "Congress, the Courts, and Public Policy: Consequences of the One Man, One Vote Rule." *American Journal of Political Science* 32 (1988): 388–415.

Polsby, Nelson W., ed. *Reapportionment in the 1970s.* 1971.

– BRUCE E. CAIN

AWARDS AND PRIZES

Military as well as civilian awards are periodically authorized by Congress. Recipients of these prizes have been as diverse as the nation itself. Initially, both the Continental Congress and the U.S. Congress approved individually struck medals as tributes for military exploits. Following the outbreak of the Civil War, the contributions of private citizens also began to attract congressional attention. Standardized medals for particular types of actions, contributions, initiatives, and service were first authorized late in the nineteenth century.

Military as well as civilian awards are periodically authorized by Congress.

The first awards—individually struck gold medals—were for unique contributions to the fight for American independence. Less distinguished but still notable accomplishments occasionally prompted the awarding of silver and bronze medals and ceremonial swords. Only gold medals, however, have been continuously awarded to the present day. They have been bestowed upon prominent as well as relatively unknown individuals in the arts, athletics, aviation, diplomacy, exploration, politics, medicine, science, and entertainment. Although Congress has approved legislation that stipulates specific requirements for numerous other awards and decorations, there are no permanent statutory authority provisions that relate to the creation of congressional gold medals. When such an award has been deemed appropriate, Congress, by special action, has provided for the creation of a personalized medal to be given in its name to show the approbation of a grateful nation in each instance.

MILITARY AWARDS. Throughout its history, Congress has approved a variety of different military awards. Brevet promotions (honorary rank) were authorized for gallant action or meritorious conduct from 1812 to 1870. Certificates of Merit for extraordinary service were given under the direction of Congress from 1854 until the Civil War. Congress next approved the Medal of Honor (Navy, 1861; Army, 1862), which would become the keystone of the military medal system that Congress would enact into law. Current military decorations authorized by Congress are:

Distinguished Service Cross for extraordinary heroism not justifying the award of the Medal of Honor.

Distinguished Service Medal for exceptionally meritorious service to the United States.

Silver Star for gallantry in action not warranting a Medal of Honor or Distinguished Service Cross.

Distinguished Flying Cross for heroism and extraordinary achievement while participating in an aerial flight.

Soldier's Medal, Navy and Marine Corps Medal, Coast Guard Medal, and Airman's Medal for heroism involving voluntary risk of life under conditions other than those of conflict with an enemy.

Legion of Merit (first U.S. decoration created specifically for award to citizens of other nations) for exceptionally meritorious conduct in the performance of outstanding service to the United States since 8 September 1939.

Good Conduct Medal (Air Force) for exemplary behavior, efficiency, and fidelity during a three-year period of service.

Prisoner of War Medal for prisoners of war held captive after 5 April 1917, during World War I, World War II, the Korean War, and the Vietnam War.

Congress also approved decorations to honor the officers and men who participated in the

Indian Wars, 1865–1898 (Indian War Medals).

Spanish American War, 1898 (Cárdenas Medal of Honor, Manila Bay [Dewey] Medal, Specifically Meritorious Service Medal, West Indies Naval Campaign [Sampson] Medal).

Philippine Insurrection, 1899–1913 (Philippine Service Medal).

Mexican War, 1911–1917 (Mexican Border Service Medal).

World War I (Army of Occupation of Germany Medal).

World War II (World War II Victory Medal, Merchant Marine Distinguished Service Medal, Atlantic War Zone Bar, Mediterranean–Middle East War Bar, Pacific Zone Bar; Combat Bar, Merchant Marine Victory Medal, Mariner's Medal).
Berlin Airlift (Medal of Humane Action).
Korean War (Service Bar).

During the twentieth century, Congress authorized a national trophy and medals for military personnel (1901, 1918). Congress awarded the Medal of Honor to the Unknown Soldiers of World War I from Great Britain, France, Italy, and the United States; to the American Unknown Soldiers of World War II, the Korean War, and the Vietnam conflict; and to the city of Verdun, France, for its assistance during World War I. In commemoration of the fiftieth anniversary of World War II, Congress authorized a Congressional Medal for the Attack on Pearl Harbor.

On several occasions from the 1930s to the 1960s, Congress approved private bills authorizing certain members of Congress, as well as other U.S. government personnel, to accept and wear the decorations tendered to them by foreign nations. In August 1958, Congress authorized more than four hundred retired federal personnel to accept such awards.

PRESIDENTIAL AND OTHER AWARDS. Seventeen awards currently presented by either the president or a member of the cabinet are authorized by Congress.

Young American Medal for Bravery and Young American Medal for Service (1950) recognizes young Americans, eighteen years and younger, who exhibit exceptional courage in a lifesaving effort.
Presidential Cash Awards to Federal Employees (1954) rewards federal employees whose job performance and ideas have benefited the government and are substantially above normal job requirements.
Enrico Fermi Award (1954) recognizes meritorious contribution to the development, use, or control of atomic energy.
National Medal of Science (1959) recognizes individuals who have made outstanding contributions in physical, biological, mathematical, and engineering sciences.
Congressional Space Medal (1969) honors astronauts whose contributions have been exceptionally meritorious.
President's Award for Outstanding Public Safety Service (1974) recognizes public safety officers for extraordinary valor in the line of duty or for outstanding contribution to public safety.
Presidential Rank Awards for the Senior Executive Service (1978) recognize career members of the Senior Executive Service for outstanding contributions. Recipients are awarded the rank of either meritorious or distinguished executive.
National Technology Medal (1980) recognizes outstanding contributions to the promotion of technology or technological manpower for the improvement of the economic, environmental, or social well-being of the United States.
President's Foreign Affairs Medal (1980) recognizes distinguished, meritorious service to the nation, including extraordinary valor in the face of danger to life or health by members of the Foreign Service.
Presidential Awards for the Senior Foreign Service (1980) recognizes members of the Senior Foreign Service for having performed especially meritorious or distinguished service in the conduct of U.S. foreign policy.
Presidential Award for Cost Savings Disclosures (1981) recognizes federal employees whose disclosure of waste, fraud, or mismanagement results in substantial savings to the federal government.
Presidential Rank Award for the Senior Cryptologic Executive Service (1982) recognizes outstanding service by civilian personnel in the National Security Agency and the Defense Intelligence Agency.
National Medal of Arts (1984) recognizes individuals or groups for outstanding contributions to the excellence, growth, support, and availability of the arts in the United States.
Presidential Award of Excellence in Science and Mathematics Teaching (1984) recognizes annually two teachers from each state, the District of Columbia, and Puerto Rico who specialize in science and mathematics for grades seven through twelve.
Presidential Award for Outstanding Private Sector Involvement in Job Training Programs (1986) recognizes individuals and organizations who have demonstrated outstanding achievement in planning and administering job training partnership programs or contributed to the success of job training partnership programs.
Malcolm Baldrige National Quality Award (1987) recognizes companies and organizations that have substantially benefited the economic or social well-being of the United States through improvements in the quality of their goods and services resulting from the effective practices of quality management.
Presidential Awards for Teaching Excellence in Foreign Languages (1988) recognizes annually one elementary school teacher and one secondary school teacher from each state, the District of Columbia, Puerto Rico, the Trust Territories of the Pacific Islands, the Northern Mariana Islands, and other commonwealths, territories, and possessions of the United States, and from the United States Department of Defense Dependents' School who have demonstrated outstanding teaching ability in foreign languages.

Civilian awards approved by Congress include Gold and Silver Lifesaving Medals for rescue attempts in U.S. waters (1874), a Selective Service Medal (1945) awarded for faithful and loyal service during World War II, medals for meritorious service by the District of Columbia police and fire departments, and a heroism medal for courageous young Americans. Medals of various types have also been bestowed in recognition of the contributions of those involved in exploration expeditions such as Adm. Robert E. Peary (Polar expedition of 1908–1909) and Adm. Richard E. Byrd (Antarctic expeditions of 1928–1930, 1933–1935, 1939–1941, 1946–1947).

In 1979, Congress created the Congressional Award Program to promote initiative, achievement, and excellence among youths who dedicated specific amounts of time to public service, personal development, physical fitness, and expeditions. Any youth from fourteen through twenty-three years of age who satisfies the standards of achievement designated for these activities can earn gold, silver, or bronze medals. Medal recipients are also eligible for scholarships. The program is operated by the Congressional Award Board, which established a private, nonprofit corporation, the Congressional Award Foundation, to carry out daily operations. The foundation serves as the national office for local and statewide councils. Prior to December 1987, the program was financed totally from private sector sources.

A Civic Achievement Award Program in Honor of the Speaker of the House of Representatives was approved in 1987 to recognize achievement in civic literacy by students, classes, and schools throughout the nation in grades 5 through 8. The Civic Award Program, administered under the direction of the librarian of Congress, is conducted by the Close Up Foundation in cooperation with the National Association of Elementary School Principals. Annual awards, in the form of certificates signed by the Speaker of the House, are given annually to individuals, classes, and schools.

[See also (I) Congressional Medal of Honor; (II) Medals, Presidential.]

BIBLIOGRAPHY

Kerrigan, Evans E. *American War Medals and Decorations.* 1971.

McDowell, Charles P. Military *and Naval Decorations of the United States.* 1984.

Stathis, Stephen W. "Congressional Gold Medals." *Numismatist* 104 (July 1991): 1064–1070, 1109–1112.

– STEPHEN W. STATHIS

B

BARGAINING

When individuals seek to achieve goals that require the cooperation of others but cannot compel cooperation by either violence or authority, they must bargain. Because Congress is a largely nonhierarchical organization, bargaining is a pervasive phenomenon. Typically this means that members of Congress must exchange favors, benefits, or other resources they control to induce cooperation from others. Members of Congress bargain to influence votes in committee and on the floor, to get committees to consider bills they favor, to persuade the leadership to schedule a floor vote, and to keep other members from offering obnoxious amendments. They bargain with interest groups to overcome objections to legislation. The House and Senate must bargain with one another to resolve differences between House and Senate versions of bills. To head off vetoes, Congress bargains with the president as bills work their way through the legislative process. This list, which could be extended indefinitely, suggests the importance of bargaining in the work of Congress.

To understand congressional bargaining, one must first comprehend the resources possessed by senators, representatives, and the president. The basic power that all members of Congress have is to say no—that is, to vote on the floor against legislation favored by others or to block it in committee. Committee and subcommittee chairmen have a more powerful "no" than most members by virtue of their influence over the agendas of committees and subcommittees. Members of the majority party leadership also have extraordinary bargaining power because of their control over the floor schedule. The rules of the Senate grant individuals exceptional power to block legislation by filibustering or objecting to unanimous consent requests. Insistent senators thus have the ability to "blackmail" the rest of the Senate by threatening to block popular legislation unless some provision they find objectionable is removed or modified, or a benefit for their state is included. Unless the demand is truly outrageous the Senate may have no practical choice but to submit to such "holdups." The veto provides the president with an extremely powerful tool with which to influence legislation; provided he has the support of a third of either chamber of Congress, he can single-handedly stop any bill. Thus Congress must normally consult carefully with the executive branch as a bill moves toward enactment, and serious objections must be accommodated.

To get a bill through the House or the Senate, one must persuade a majority of members to vote for it. How can they be induced to do so? Many votes will be won on the basis of ideological agreement or common interest. Where these factors fail to produce enough votes, however, other kinds of persuasion are required. Representatives trying to gather votes for their bill may trade their votes, promising to support other legislation in the future in exchange for a vote for their bill today. An interesting vote trade was the so-called corn-for-porn swap of 1991, in which supporters of farmers and of the National Endowment for the Arts (which was being hamstrung by censorship efforts) agreed to help each other's legislation. It is impossible to determine how much explicit vote-trading occurs, but it is undoubtedly a powerful element in congressional bargaining. Implicit vote-trading is also important. Some legislators reportedly will vote for any legislation favored by other members provided that it is not terribly expensive or offensive to their own constituents, expecting that favors will be returned someday.

Members of Congress must exchange favors, benefits, or other resources they control to induce cooperation from others.

In high-stakes issues where legislators are unwilling to trust that a favor will be returned, a useful tactic is "logrolling." Representatives bundle two or more legislative proposals that appeal to largely different constituencies and produce an enthusiastic majority coalition. This accounts for the marriage of farm price supports to food stamps at a time when agricultural assistance was threatened by dwindling rural representation. To obtain the votes of urban liberals who might otherwise have voted against farm subsidies, food stamps were added to the bill, creating an unbeatable combination.

What distribution of benefits will legislative bargaining produce? William Riker conjectured that rational legislators ought to form "minimum winning coalitions"—coalitions that distribute benefits to just over half of all districts and that are funded by all districts. While attractive on a theoretical level, this notion has found little empirical support. Far more often researchers have found patterns of universalism, whereby benefits are distributed very widely. Why do legislators not employ more cutthroat tactics? This question has not been answered definitively, but it is likely that the shifting, unstable nature of congressional coalitions leaves legislators unsure of the future, uncertain whether they might be in the minority on the next bill. Because one never knows whose assistance will be needed to pass a bill next week or next year, legislators are understandably reluctant to make enemies. Consequently, benefits are more commonly distributed according to norms of universalism.

The idea of a *reversion point* helps in understanding many kinds of bargaining, including much that occurs in Congress. A reversion point is the policy that will obtain should no agreement be reached and no legislation passed. The more odious a negotiator finds the reversion point, the greater his or her incentive to reach an agreement. If one side is disproportionately harmed by the reversion, it will naturally have less bargaining power and be forced to accept a bad bargain. In policy disputes where neither side finds the reversion point particularly objectionable, the incentive to compromise is scant, and it is likely that no agreement will be reached. Such was the situation surrounding the budget deficit in the 1980s. The enactment of the Gramm-Rudman-Hollings law to balance the budget was an innovative effort to shift the reversion point in budget politics to a policy universally regarded as disastrous—massive, across-the-board spending reductions—and thereby to inspire compromise. It did not work, mostly because in the process of enactment the reversion point was shifted from a policy that was unimaginable to one that was merely unpleasant.

BIBLIOGRAPHY

Ferejohn, John. "Logrolling in an Institutional Context: A Case Study of Food Stamp Legislation." In *Congress and Policy Change.* Edited by Gerald Wright, Leroy Rieselbach, and Lawrence Dodd. 1986.

Riker, William. *The Theory of Political Coalitions.* 1962.

– JOHN B. GILMOUR

BICAMERALISM

The United States Congress, like most of the world's legislatures, is a bicameral institution, that is, composed of two chambers. The U.S. Congress consists of a House of Representatives, whose members represent small districts and serve two-year terms, and a Senate, whose members are elected by statewide constituencies and serve six-year terms. Seats in the House are apportioned among the states on the basis of population, but each state, regardless of population, is represented by two senators. Unlike the chambers of bicameral legislatures in most other countries, the House and the Senate are essentially equal in power. Neither can enact laws on its own; the consent of both chambers is required for all legislation. There are, though, some differences in their powers; revenue legislation must originate in the House, and the Senate alone ratifies treaties and approves appointments of federal officials and judges.

Unlike the chambers of bicameral legislatures in other countries, the house and senate are essentially equal in power.

That Congress would have a bicameral structure was barely a subject of debate at the Constitutional Convention, although the precise details of the arrangement were discussed extensively. Bicameralism was a foregone conclusion because it served three important goals, each subscribed to by most Convention delegates.

The first goal was to recognize the federal structure that was to be created by the new Constitution. By providing each state with equal representation in the Senate, the concept of the new nation as a union of federating states was emphasized. Further, the interests of the smaller states would have greater protection than they would receive in the House, where representation was to be based on population. Finally, the selection of senators by state legislatures suggested that the Senate represented the state governments themselves, with the people represented in the House.

A second goal of bicameralism was to protect against what many of the Founders believed to be the dangers of a legislature elected by the people. Such a body, James Madison wrote, draws "all powers into its impetuous vortex," is disposed "to sacrifice the aggregate interest to the local views of their constituents," and tends to disregard "the rules of justice and the rights of the minor party." Therefore, the power of the House needed to be checked, and bicameralism, along with a presidency electorally independent of Congress, were to be the primary checks. It was inevitable, said Madison, that the legislature would dominate in a republican form of government, but "the remedy for this inconvenience is to divide the legislature into different branches." Thus, Edmund Randolph promised, the unelected Senate would provide a cure for the "evils" that arose from "the turbulence and follies of democracy."

A third goal of bicameralism was to increase the likelihood of better government. Not only would the Senate protect against the democratic excesses of the House, but as Madison said, the Senate would act with "more coolness, with more system, and with more wisdom than the popular branch." It would be wiser because its members would not be elected by the public at large, but rather by state legislators who presumably would pick men of stature. Its small size would make it less chaotic than the larger House—more like a king's privy council than a legislature, some believed—thereby facilitating sober deliberation. Its members would serve six-year rather than two-year terms and would therefore be more able than members of the House to resist the pressures of public opinion. And senators would likely be men of substance, people who, in Gouverneur Morris's words, would "have great personal property" and exhibit "aristocratic pride." Better government decisions would result because, as George Washington suggested, the Senate would function in a manner analogous to the saucer into which one poured one's coffee; the saucer cools the hot coffee as the Senate would cool the hot passions of the House.

Of the two chambers, the role of the Senate has changed most dramatically over the years. Contrary to the hopes of the Founders, the Senate in its early days was clearly inferior to the House, primarily because it lacked democratic legitimacy. The principle of appointment of senators by state legislatures began to erode as early as the 1830s, however, and by 1913, when popular election of the Senate was constitutionally mandated, more than half of the states had already adopted procedures that provided the functional equivalent. Also, the end of the United States' geographic isolation in the beginning of the twentieth century brought a greatly enhanced role to the Senate because of its special powers over foreign policy. And, as the responsibilities of the federal government increased, the Senate's role in the appointment process became more significant as well. Finally, modern mass media increased the public importance of the Senate. Because there are fewer senators than representatives, members of the Senate were more visible than their House counterparts and could more readily be turned into national figures by the media.

Although the Senate has come to be as democratic as the House, important distinctions between the two chambers persist, distinctions attributable primarily to the smaller size of the Senate, the longer terms that its members serve, and the larger constituencies that they usually represent. Because of its size, the Senate has procedures that enhance the power of its individual members. Unlimited debate is only one example of Senate procedures that allow a minority of senators to bring the legislative process to a halt. The House, in contrast, has a more complex and rigid set of procedures that curbs the autonomy of its individual members. Because of its large size, the House also depends heavily on its committee system and is more likely to be characterized by strong party leadership. Senators, in contrast, demonstrate an extreme reluctance to be led, either by their committees or their party leaders.

Popular election has made the Senate as electorally volatile as the House and, as a result, senators have become more attentive to constituency and electoral pressures than in the past. Nonetheless, there is reason to believe that long electoral cycles and large constituencies enhance the capacity of senators to think and act on the basis of long-term policy considerations and with a national perspective.

But there is no evidence that the Senate in particular provides the braking action on unwise or controversial legislation that the Founders had anticipated. Rather, it is bicameralism itself—with its requirement that both chambers approve of legislation—that slows down, inhibits, moderates, and often prevents government action. More positively, it can be argued that the dual consideration required by bicameralism enhances the deliberative nature of the Congress by providing more opportunities for the gathering of information and the detection of errors. In that case, bicameralism would produce, as the Founders hoped, better—albeit slower—government decision making.

[See also (I) House of Representatives, Representative, Senate, Senator.]

BIBLIOGRAPHY

Baker, Ross K. *House and Senate.* 1989.

Carmines, Edward G., and Lawrence C. Dodd. "Bicameralism in Congress: The Changing Partnership." In *Congress Reconsidered.* 3d ed. Edited by Lawrence C. Dodd and Bruce I. Oppenheimer. 1985.

Fenno, Richard F., Jr. *The United States Senate: A Bicameral Perspective.* 1982.

Longley, Lawrence D., and Walter J. Oleszek. *Bicameral Politics: Conference Committees in Congress.* 1989.

Page, Benjamin I. "Cooling the Legislative Tea." In *American Politics and Public Policy.* Edited by Walter Dean Burnham and Martha Wagner Weinberg. 1978.

– MICHAEL L. MEZEY

BILL OF RIGHTS

The first ten amendments to the U.S. Constitution were fowarded to the states by the First Congress in 1789 and ratified two years later by the necessary number of states to become "the supreme law of the land." The events preceding their ratification form an essential part of the history of human rights in the British colonies that in 1776 became the United States.

The first ten amendments to the U.S. Constitution were forwarded to the states by the First Congress in 1789 and ratified to become "the supreme law of the land."

BACKGROUND. Although there is mention in the Magna Carta of 1215 of curbs on the use of arbitrary power, the common law of England was long the chief protector of an Englishman's right to hold property and live peaceably. Common law as it evolved assumed the right of an accused person to have a jury trial, to have counsel, and to be protected against excessive fines and bails. But in most cases, the way a prisoner was treated and the punishment meted out by the court was often a matter of local circumstances and the quality of the legal counsel.

The history of English law is essentially the story of a society's gradual transition from a feudal condition to modernity. This means that for many centuries little change took place. But by 1640, a clash between Charles I and Parliament resulted in civil war; the central issues of the conflict were an Englishman's right to his liberty of person, his right to own and keep property, and his right to express himself on public matters. The Petition of Right (1628) had forced Charles to acknowledge that no freeman could lose his life, liberty, or property without the due process of law; illegal and arbitrary demands for money were to end; and the obnoxious practice of quartering sailors and soldiers in private households was forbidden.

Charles clashed with Parliament and with the New Army led by Oliver Cromwell, and the king forfeited his life. Out of the tumult of civil war that followed, the Glorious Revolution of 1688 created an atmosphere that allowed an ordinary Englishman more personal freedom than the citizen of any other country enjoyed. Within two decades the encrusted arbitrary machinery of government had been overhauled to eliminate the Star Chamber (with its secrecy, arbitrary arrests, and torture), and defendants in criminal trials were granted the right to remain silent or at least not give self-incriminating testimony.

Other important concessions were wrung from Charles II and James II. The Toleration Act helped end strife between Protestants and Catholics, and in the 1689 Bill of Rights Parliament laid down certain principles for the future governance of England: the royal authority was limited and citizens were guaranteed the right to bail, freedom from cruel or unusual punishments, and the right to petition against grievances. These were specific guarantees, proclaimed by Parliament to be the supreme law of England, and their enactment showed the huge gulf between medieval law and the concern for a citizen's rights that had emerged from the battle between headstrong monarchs and the elected representatives serving in Parliament. A series of common law decisions emerged at the same time to make the bailing of prisoners held in custody (habeas corpus) a routine rather than an unusual circumstance to ensure that trials were held in the vicinity of the alleged crime, and to protect people from being tried twice for the same offense (double jeopardy).

British colonists in North America accepted the protection of the new laws; in some cases they themselves had dealt with similar matters earlier on. In colony after colony, laws were enacted by the colonial assemblies to provide a broad spectrum of personal liberties. Some curbs on the rights of Catholics remained on the statute books, but when the Stamp Act crisis erupted in 1765, most of the British colonies in North America had laws conferring on colonial subjects the same rights they would have possessed as native-born Englishmen.

When Parliament began searching for new sources of tax revenues after the expensive French and Indian War, a clash with American lawmakers brought an unexpected wave of dissension that rocked the established order. An informal body, the Stamp Act Congress of 1765, met to form a protest addressed to George III and "both Houses of Parliament." Resolutions were passed to warn Parliament that Americans believed their most fundamental liberties were involved, and among the jeopardized rights they catalogued were trial by jury, the right of petition, and the "full and free enjoyment of their rights and liberties."

The aftermath of the Boston Tea Party brought on a crisis that was resolved only by the outbreak of fighting in April 1775. Before those first shots of the American Revolution were fired, colonial leaders had reacted to British oppression by calling for a Continental Congress to give voice to their protests against the usurpations of Parliament.

One firebrand who served in the Continental Congress, Samuel Adams, pushed his colleagues for a propaganda weapon that would focus on human rights. "Should America hold up her own Importance to the

Congress OF THE United States,

begun and held at the City of New-York, on
Wednesday the Fourth of March, one thousand seven hundred and eighty nine.

THE Convention of a number of the States, having at the time of their adopting the Constitution, expressed a desire, in order to prevent misconstruction or abuse of its powers, that further declaratory and restrictive clauses should be added: And as extending the ground of public confidence in the Government, will best ensure the beneficent ends of its institution

RESOLVED by the Senate and House of Representatives of the United States of America, in Congress assembled, two thirds of both Houses concurring, that the following Articles be proposed to the Legislatures of the several States, as amendments to the Constitution of the United States, all, or any of which Articles, when ratified by three fourths of the said Legislatures, to be valid to all intents and purposes, as part of the said Constitution; viz.

ARTICLES in addition to, and Amendment of the Constitution of the United States of America, proposed by Congress, and ratified by the Legislatures of the several States, pursuant to the fifth Article of the original Constitution.

Article the first... After the first enumeration required by the first article of the Constitution, there shall be one Representative for every thirty thousand, until the number shall amount to one hundred, after which the proportion shall be so regulated by Congress, that there shall be not less than one hundred Representatives, nor less than one Representative for every forty thousand persons, until the number of Representatives shall amount to two hundred, after which the proportion shall be so regulated by Congress, that there shall not be less than two hundred Representatives, nor more than one Representative for every fifty thousand persons.

Article the second... No law, varying the compensation for the services of the Senators and Representatives, shall take effect, until an election of Representatives shall have intervened.

Article the third... Congress shall make no law respecting an establishment of religion, or prohibiting the free exercise thereof; or abridging the freedom of speech, or of the press, or the right of the people peaceably to assemble, and to petition the Government for a redress of grievances.

Article the fourth... A well regulated militia, being necessary to the security of a free State, the right of the people to keep and bear arms, shall not be infringed.

Article the fifth... No Soldier shall, in time of peace be quartered in any house, without the consent of the Owner, nor in time of war, but in a manner to be prescribed by law.

Article the sixth... The right of the people to be secure in their persons, houses, papers, and effects, against unreasonable searches and seizures, shall not be violated, and no Warrants shall issue, but upon probable cause, supported by Oath or affirmation, and particularly describing the place to be searched, and the persons or things to be seized.

Article the seventh... No person shall be held to answer for a capital, or otherwise infamous crime, unless on a presentment or indictment of a Grand Jury, except in cases arising in the land or naval forces, or in the Militia, when in actual service in time of War or public danger; nor shall any person be subject for the same offence to be twice put in jeopardy of life or limb; nor shall be compelled in any criminal case to be a witness against himself, nor be deprived of life, liberty, or property, without due process of law; nor shall private property be taken for public use without just compensation.

Article the eighth... In all criminal prosecutions, the accused shall enjoy the right to a speedy and public trial, by an impartial jury of the State and district wherein the crime shall have been committed, which district shall have been previously ascertained by law, and to be informed of the nature and cause of the accusation; to be confronted with the witnesses against him; to have compulsory process for obtaining witnesses in his favor, and to have the assistance of Counsel for his defence.

Article the ninth... In suits at common law, where the value in controversy shall exceed twenty dollars, the right of trial by jury shall be preserved, and no fact tried by a jury shall be otherwise re-examined in any Court of the United States, than according to the rules of the common law.

Article the tenth... Excessive bail shall not be required, nor excessive fines imposed, nor cruel and unusual punishments inflicted.

Article the eleventh... The enumeration in the Constitution, of certain rights, shall not be construed to deny or disparage others retained by the people.

Article the twelfth... The powers not delegated to the United States by the Constitution, nor prohibited by it to the States, are reserved to the States respectively, or to the people.

ATTEST,

Frederick Augustus Muhlenberg, Speaker of the House of Representatives

John Adams, Vice-President of the United States, and President of the Senate.

John Beckley, Clerk of the House of Representatives.

Sam. A. Otis Secretary of the Senate

Bill of Rights. Facsimile of the first page as sent to the states in 1789. (Library of Congress)

Body of the Nation and at the same Time agree in one general Bill of Rights," Adams suggested, "the Dispute might be settled on the Principles of Equity and Harmony restored between Britain and the Colonies." In October 1774 Congress had issued a "Declaration of Rights" that listed royal or parliamentary errors and enumerated the rights claimed by British Americans. Ten in number, these rights included the right "to life, liberty, and property"; the safeguards provided by the common law for accused persons; the right "peaceably to assemble"; and the right to petition for redress of grievances. With an echo from the Glorious Revolution in England, the delegates also insisted that "the keeping [of] a standing army in these colonies, in times of peace . . . is against the law."

Leaders from all of the thirteen colonies met in Philadelphia again in 1775. While the Continental Congress debated the next move, all the colonies used their legislatures to keep a semblance of government in place. In Virginia, a convention had replaced the old House of Burgesses, and its elected members met in May 1776 at Williamsburg. With what now seems to be blinding speed, the convention called for a complete break with Great Britain and the establishment of an independent nation. It appointed a committee to draft a constitution and declaration of rights for the "free state of Virginia." George Mason, a Virginia planter and patriot, drafted a plan that was soon enacted and broadcast to other states, with a prefatory declaration of rights and a constitution calling for a republic with executive, legislative, and judicial branches.

Formally proclaimed on 12 June 1776, the Virginia Declaration of Rights set the tone and format for all subsequent bills of rights. Mason's list of sixteen rights, which was reported by a committee and passed by the makeshift legislature, began with the statement "that all men are by nature free and independent" and cannot be deprived of their lives or liberties or the means of "pursuing and obtaining happiness and safety." The declaration went on to call for free elections of representatives, to repeat the safeguards for accused persons embedded in the common law, and to call for trial by jury, a free press, a ban on standing armies in peacetime, and "the free exercise of religion." James Madison, a fledgling delegate, helped broaden the scope of the article on religious freedom and thus established his credentials as a libertarian.

Copies of the Virginia Bill of Rights were printed in newspapers from Georgia to Massachusetts, and as the last tie with Great Britain was legally severed in July 1776, most of the new "free and independent" states passed laws similar to those Mason and his committee had written. By 1781 nearly all the former colonies either had explicit laws creating bills of rights or prefaces to their constitutions embodying those principles regarded as basic human liberties.

THE CONSTITUTION AND THE FIRST CONGRESS. This lawmaking process was completed by 1781, and the war ended in 1783, but the United States of America was a new nation moving in uncharted waters. Farm prices fell, taxes went unpaid, and commerce languished when England imposed punishing duties on American commodities. Searching for a solution to the new nation's dilemma, the Virginia legislature issued a call for all states to meet in Philadelphia in May 1787 to consider ways of revising the Articles of Confederation, which had provided a loose-knit interim government for thirteen "sovereign" states. Virginia sent a strong delegation, headed by George Washington and guided by Madison, who had devised a plan for a republican form of government that he thought could cure the ills afflicting the country. Madison's plan, which dealt with the specific shortcomings of the makeshift confederation, did not mention a bill of rights.

The debates at the Constitutional Convention lasted until mid September, when a final draft was in preparation. Some delegates had mentioned the rights of accused persons, and in piecemeal form the ban on bills of attainder and ex post facto laws were added, along with a prohibition on religious tests for officeholders. The writ of habeas corpus was not to be suspended except when "the public safety may require it."

James Madison confronted critics who said a bill of rights was not needed by insisting that such rights would have "a salutary effect against the abuse of power."

On 12 September George Mason, perhaps with lingering memories of May 1776, called for the addition of a bill of rights, observing that "it would give great quiet to the people." Impatient delegates quickly squelched Mason's motion, which lost by a unanimous vote. Over the next few days, Mason and several other delegates tried to insert provisions for a free press and civil jury trials, but their overall strategy failed. When the delegates signed the engrossed Constitution on 17 September 1787, Mason and two others abstained despite last-minute efforts to persuade them that a bill of rights was unnecessary.

The ensuing contest for the Constitution's ratification proved closer than its supporters had reckoned.

Mason wrote his *Objections to this Constitution* before he left Philadelphia, and its opening phrase became the tocsin of the opposition. "There is no Declaration of Rights," Mason began, and his phrase became the battle cry of Anti-Federalists who wanted either to alter the Constitution or to reject it outright. Early in 1788, Federalists supporting ratification realized their tactical error and began talking about the enactment of a bill of rights once the Constitution had been ratified. Madison not only joined Alexander Hamilton and John Jay in writing *The Federalist* to counteract dissension but was forced to concede that a bill of rights might be needed to calm apprehension. At the Virginia ratifying convention, Madison made his compromise explicit, and the Constitution was narrowly ratified by Virginia and the other key state, New York.

When the contest was settled, Madison heard from his friend Thomas Jefferson, then in Paris, who assured him that a bill of rights was needed. "I hope . . . a bill of rights will be formed to guard the people against the federal government, as they are already guarded against their state governments in most instances," Jefferson observed.

Madison got the point and acknowledged the promised bill of rights when he campaigned for a seat in the First Congress. Opposed by James Monroe, Madison promised voters in his district that he would work for "such amendments as will . . . guard essential rights, and will render certain vexatious abuses of power impossible." To erase all doubt, Madison said that he would seek amendments protecting "the rights of Conscience in the fullest latitude, the freedom of the press, trials by jury, security against general warrants &c."

Voters reacted by electing him by a comfortable margin, and Madison went to the First Congress prepared to fulfill his campaign promise. But he soon learned that most other members gave a bill of rights a low priority. Since debates in the House of Representatives were printed in newspapers, Madison soon learned of the impatience in his district and elsewhere because there had been no mention of amendments encompassing a bill of rights. On 25 May 1789 Madison announced on the House floor that he would soon be offering the promised amendments. Despite some grumbling, he kept his word, and on 8 June he presented amendments covering all the personal liberties brought forward during the ratification struggle.

Madison's proposed list added to the usual provisions—for a free press and freedom of speech and of religion—the right to petition, key provisions relating to justice for accused criminals, and two amendments to increase congressional representation and prohibit members of Congress from raising their salaries. He confronted critics who said a bill of rights was not needed by insisting that such rights would have "a salutary effect against the abuse of power. If they are incorporated into the constitution, independent tribunals of justice will consider themselves in a peculiar manner the guardians of those rights."

Madison had an easier time convincing the general public that a bill of rights was needed than he did his fellow members of Congress. His original idea was to place the amendments into the Constitution as part of the original plan, but this proposal was soon dropped. A committee was appointed 21 July to draft the amendments; the committee reported a week later, and the debate over each proposed amendment began. A list of seventeen amendments survived. The fourteenth, which Madison said he valued above all others, provided that "no State shall infringe the right of trial by Jury in criminal cases, nor the rights of conscience, nor the freedom of speech, or of the press."

On 24 August 1789 the House of Representatives sent the seventeen amendments to the Senate. Extensive debate and and even more extensive nit-picking led to the dropping of Madison's favorite fourteenth proposal, which made states responsible for personal rights, and the melding together of the several articles into one amendment dealing with personal liberties with the prefatory clause "Congress shall make no law," which clarified the federal government's role in preserving a citizen's personal liberty. A joint conference worked out a compromise that left twelve amendments, and by 28 September both houses had passed this trimmed-down version, keeping the first two to deal with congressional matters, and the proposed amendments were sent to the state legislatures for ratification.

More than two years were required to complete the business of ratifying the Bill of Rights. Former opponents of the Constitution (such as George Mason) were won over by the proposals, but a segment of the Anti-Federalist opposition dismissed the amendments as "good for nothing." Sen. William Grayson of Virginia held that view, writing in a letter to Patrick Henry, "I believe as many others do, that they will do more harm than benefit." Henry was all-powerful in the Virginia legislature, and his faction managed to argue over the amendments until all but one of the necessary states had ratified.

North Carolina and Rhode Island, both of which had so far remained outside the Union because of their delayed ratifications, finally accepted the Constitution together with the amendments. Meanwhile, however, Vermont had been admitted as a state, which meant that eleven states were required to adopt the amendments before they became law. The first two amendments were dropped in the ratifying process, so that what had been the third amendment now became the first in the renumbering that took place in Secretary of State Jefferson's office. Jefferson decided that the ten amendments became effective on the date of the Virginia ratification, 15 December 1791. (Three states that had never acted on the proposals made a ceremonial gesture of ratification in 1941, and the "lost" amendment dealing with congressional salaries was revived and finally ratified in 1992.)

In a sense the whole ratification process had been ceremonial, for in 1791 the Bill of Rights was more symbol than reality. Before the decade was over, Congress had passed the Sedition Act proscribing freedom of speech and shackling newspapers during the Quasi-War with France of 1798–1800. Vigorous prosecutions of dissident editors led to jail sentences. Jefferson and Madison responded with the Kentucky and Virginia resolutions, hoping that state legislatures would call the obnoxious law unconstitutional through "interposition." They knew that the Federalist judges would deny their claim that the law was clearly in violation of the First Amendment. But they found few state lawmakers eager to tackle these thorny constitutional problems. The laws expired, untested in the courts.

SLAVERY, THE CIVIL WAR, AND RECONSTRUCTION. Through the nineteenth century, citizens' rights remained tied to local circumstances. The Supreme Court held in *Barron v. Baltimore* (1833) that the Bill of Rights was binding only on the federal government, not the states—a ruling that made the Bill of Rights a dormant relic. The slavery crisis worsened, but Congress by its "gag rule" ignored antislavery petitions between 1836 and 1844; state and local officials banned abolitionist newspapers; Mormons were persecuted by mobs and denounced by state officers; and Indian tribes were pushed around by federal troops, with no public mention that the Bill of Rights was being violated. During the Civil War President Abraham Lincoln suspended the writ of habeas corpus and citizens suspected of disloyalty were thrown into Northern prisons, often without a formal charge or hearing. Preoccupied with winning the war, Congress overlooked these arbitrary acts.

After the Confederate surrender at Appomattox the nation attempted to address the problems faced by the new citizens created when the former slaves were freed. Three constitutional amendments ending slavery and trying to guarantee the civil and political rights of the freed slaves were passed by Congress and ratified between 1865 and 1870. Although their intent now seems clear, at the time the efforts to make former (male) slaves free men with all the rights of citizenship, including suffrage, led to much constitutional confusion. Southern states adopted various strategies to deny blacks full status as citizens, and in the North there was deep reluctance to accept blacks as social equals.

Change came slowly. In 1873 the Supreme Court in the *Slaughterhouse Cases* narrowly defined the meaning of the Fourteenth Amendment's guarantee of the "privileges and immunities of citizens." Instead of declaring the protection of the substantive and procedural rights that form the heart of the Bill of Rights as due to all citizens, the Court refused to erase important distinctions between state and national citizenship, in effect allowing states to enact laws that left southern blacks as second-class citizens. A hammer blow to full rights for blacks came in the Court's decision in *Plessy v. Ferguson* (1896), in which the Court gave its seal of approval to the growing number of laws that mandated "separate but equal" public facilities for blacks and whites. The effect was firmly to implant a Jim Crow society throughout the South—a society in which blacks were denied access to public restaurants, hotels, theaters, railroad passenger cars, and even seats on trolleys.

Congress chose to ignore the situation, even after the Supreme Court reinforced the *Slaughterhouse* decision with more restrictive rulings between 1900 and 1908 (although in 1907 Justice John Marshall Harlan had taken a minority position and suggested that free speech and freedom of the press were rights now protected by the due process clause of the Fourteenth Amendment).

VIOLATIONS OF CIVIL LIBERTIES. More setbacks came in the wave of hysteria that followed America's entry into World War I in April 1917. Congress passed the Espionage Act in 1917, which gave the imprimatur of statutory approval to a powerful crackdown on those who criticized or dissented from the war effort. And in *Schenck v. United States* (1919), the Supreme Court for the first time handed down a ruling on the claim that an act of Congress per se was a violation of the First Amendment guarantee of freedom of expression. Charles Schenck, a secretary of the Socialist party, had helped distribute leaflets urging young men to resist the draft for military service. His counsel pleaded that the Espionage Act violated a citizen's right to speak freely, even in wartime. The act was upheld, but a warning signal was hoisted by Justice Oliver Wendell Holmes, who said that the test was whether such expressions presented "a clear and present danger that they will bring about the substantive evils that Congress has a right to prevent."

An even tougher law, the Sedition Act of 1918, held that "disloyal, profane, scurrilous, or abusive language about the form of government, the Constitution, soldiers and sailors, flag or uniform of the armed forces" could be punished. More arrests were made, and the statute was upheld by the Supreme Court.

A legal breakthrough came in 1925 when the Court declared in *Gitlow v. New York* "that freedom of speech and of the press—which are protected by the First Amendment from abridgment by Congress—are among the fundamental personal rights and 'liberties' protected by the due process clause of the Fourteenth Amendment from impairment by the States." Then in 1931 the Court began opening an umbrella of protection for all First Amendment rights, and a generation later the work was virtually completed. In a series of decisions that were not always popular, the Court decided that the First Amendment protected schoolchildren from having to salute the flag or to pray in the classroom. The "wall of separation" that Thomas Jefferson yearned to erect between church and state was fitted firmly in place to prevent public expenditures for parochial schools. New tests of "symbolic speech" permitted protest groups to burn the American flag without fear of arrest. And to thwart censorship the Supreme Court liberally interpreted the rights of free speech in art and literature as well as in political discussion.

By 1969 the whole catalogue of personal liberties made the Bill of Rights a shield against unconstitutional acts by both federal and state officials.

The Court persistently used the due process and equal protection clauses of the Fourteenth Amendment to resurrect the First through the Ninth Amendments. Not only Congress but state governments and their officers likewise were forbidden to interfere with citizens' personal rights. By 1969 the whole catalog of personal liberties, including guaranteed rights for accused persons, made the Bill of Rights a shield against unconstitutional acts by both federal and state officials. Only in the murky areas of obscenity and pornography did doubts remain as to where Congress might wander without abridging a citizen's personal liberty; the Supreme Court was still trying to define those limits as the twentieth century entered its final decade.

One of the major fields of contention had finally closed with the end of the Cold War between the Western democracies and the former Soviet Union. Fears of the Bolsheviks translated into legislative efforts to stifle activities of the Communist party in the post–World War I era, as many states passed syndicalism laws covering a broad range of activities that were considered subversive. Congress remained aloof until 1940, when the Alien Registration Act (Smith Act) was passed to provide the federal government with a legal weapon to trap communists who plotted or advocated the overthrow of the government by force. The McCarran Internal Security Act of 1950 went further, and came close to outlawing the Communist party. But a generation after the red scares and the brief flurry of McCarthyism (when Congress had been used as a forum to cast aspersions on left-wing bureaucrats and scholars) there were few memories of the hysteria of the 1950s. Indeed, by 1992 the Soviet Union had disbanded and Congress was approving laws that provided aid for the republics that had once constituted that "Evil Empire."

CIVIL RIGHTS. As the spotlight shifted away from personal rights, the scope of the Bill of Rights broadened with public concern over racially motivated segregation. President Harry S Truman ordered the integration of the armed forces in 1947, despite outspoken protests by congressional critics from the South. State laws that prevented voting by blacks were challenged, as were the segregated school systems in southern public schools and colleges. First to go were the state laws separating white and black college students, and in 1954 the Supreme Court threw away the 1896 *Plessy* concept, ruling in *Brown v. Board of Education* that segregated public-supported schools were unconstitutional. Enforcement of the decision proved a long and arduous process, but the nation's commitment to "equal protection" was beyond doubt.

Except for passing the Civil Rights Act of 1960, which attempted to protect the rights of black citizens to vote in both state and federal elections, Congress was a reluctant participant in the desegregation process until after the assassination of President John F. Kennedy in 1963. National attention increasingly focused on the remnants of the old schemes of segregated facilities and racial discrimination still permitted by state codes. The resulting Civil Rights Act of 1964 created commissions to handle grievances, barred discrimination in public facilities, and made voting registration accessible to all citizens. Civil rights law was strengthened with another Civil Rights Act in 1968, which struck at segregated housing practices and acknowledged the civil rights of Native Americans. Congress passed legislation in 1980 to tighten enforcement procedures and accelerate the process of creating a color-blind social order.

Modern congressional responses to equal rights have taken the form of legislation directed toward a redress of old grievances suffered by minorities. Meanwhile, the Supreme Court has carried forward its traditional role of redefining and expanding the Bill of Rights. Thus the First Amendment has been broadly interpreted to strike down the use of public land or funds to erect a Christmas nativity scene (*City of Birmingham v. ACLU,* 1986) but to permit newspapers to attack elected officials with extreme charges so long as there is no "malice aforethought" (*New York Times v. Sullivan,* 1971). The flag-burning cases (*Texas v. Johnson,* 1989) provoked much public outrage and even a call for a constitutional amendment to punish such acts, but the furor dissipated with the passage of time.

In 1991 Americans celebrated the bicentennial of the Bill of Rights with public displays and ceremonies in every state of the Union. A visit to view the original manuscript deposited in the National Archives had become a kind of pilgrimage for thousands of citizens. Over two hundred years the public perception of government's role in preserving a citizen's rights had become manifest in the calendar of the Supreme Court rather than in the Congress. Madison, Jefferson, and others present when the Bill of Rights was created had predicted that the courts—not the legislature—would be the ultimate guardians of the people's liberties. More than two hundred years later, their judgment was confirmed in every Supreme Court term.

The role of Congress in protecting a citizen's right of privacy or the right to fair treatment in the marketplace remained controversial in the 1990s. The vexing matters of a woman's right to have an abortion or an African American's claim of job discrimination were thorny issues debated in Congress and the nation. In a country of more than 250 million people, where freedom is at the heart of most human problems, the Bill of Rights was a part of every lawmaker's consciousness. Legislators, judges, and juries were aware, as Justice William J. Brennan, Jr., once remarked, that the Bill of Rights exists because it is in the interest of the whole nation "that justice shall be done." The Bill of Rights had become the nation's conscience as well as "the supreme law of the land."

[See also (I) Constitution.]

BIBLIOGRAPHY

Abraham, Henry. *Freedom and the Court. Civil Right and Liberties in the United States.* 5th ed. 1988.

Brant, Irving. *The Bill of Rights: Its Origin and Meaning.* 1965.

Cox, Archibald. *The Court and the Constitution.* 1987.

Hickok, Eugene W., Jr., ed. *The Bill of Rights: Original Meaning and Current Understanding.* 1991.

Levy, Leonard. *Constitutional Opinions: Aspects of the Bill of Rights.* 1986.

Levy, Leonard. *Original Intent and the Framers' Constitution.* 1988.

Rutland, Robert A. *The Birth of the Bill of Rights, 1776–1791.* 1991.

Schwartz, Bernard, ed. *The Bill of Rights: A Documentary History.* 2 vols. 1971.

Smolla, Rodney A. *Free Speech in an Open Society.* 1992.

– ROBERT A. RUTLAND

BILLS

One of the four forms of legislation considered in the House and the Senate, bills are designated by chamber of origin (with "H.R." or "S.") and number. When a bill is passed by both chambers in identical form, it is enrolled and presented to the president for his signature. By statute, all bills begin with the following enacting clause: "Be it enacted by the Senate and House of Representatives of the United States of America in Congress assembled."

Current rules allow bills to be introduced by any member of Congress on any subject, and they are then generally referred to the appropriate committee or committees of jurisdiction for consideration. In the Senate, it has been a longstanding practice to allow multiple sponsorship of legislation. Limited cosponsorship was introduced in the House only in 1967, however, and just since 1979 has Rule XXII allowed for an unlimited number of House members to cosponsor legislation.

The early rules of both chambers carried over provisions inherited from English practice and the Continental Congress that restricted members' freedom to introduce bills. It was the expectation that committees would draft legislation, and motions for leave for individual members to introduce bills were not common and often were debated extensively. During the nineteenth century, the practice of requiring motions for leave fell into disuse, but as late as 1876 the House refused to receive a bill introduced without leave. A vestigial restriction remains in Senate Rule XIV, which refers to measures introduced "on leave," although modern practice makes no such requirement.

[For comprehensive discussion of how a bill becomes a law, see Lawmaking.]

BIBLIOGRAPHY

Cooper, Joseph, and Cheryl D. Young. "Bill Introduction in the Nineteenth Century: A Study of Institutional Change." *Legislative Studies Quarterly* 14 (February 1989): 67.

U.S. House of Representatives. *Constitution, Jefferson's Manual, and Rules of the House of Representatives, 103d Congress.* Compiled by William Holmes Brown. 102d Cong., 2d sess., 1992. H. Doc. 102-405. Rule XXII.

U.S. House of Representatives. *Hinds' Precedents of the House of Representatives of the United States,* by Asher C. Hinds. 59th Cong., 2d sess., 1907. Vol. 4, chap. 91.

U.S. Senate. *Senate Procedure, Precedents, and Practices,* by Floyd M. Riddick. 97th Cong., 1st sess., 1981. S. Doc. 97-2.

– JAMES V. SATURNO

BLUE RIBBON COMMISSIONS

Blue ribbon commissions are temporary advisory bodies, usually established to find broadly acceptable solutions to contentious problems. Because commissions lack the power to implement the recommendations they make, they are influential only to the extent that Congress or the president heeds their advice.

There is great variety in commissions, which can be uniquely crafted to meet the needs of the moment. They are created by presidential decree, by statute, or informally by the mutual consent of Congress and the president. They normally consist of prominent individuals representing a wide range of opinion whose findings will command respect—experts, prominent private citizens, and politicians. Although commissions were used sporadically throughout the nineteenth century, they did not come into common usage until the presidency of Theodore Roosevelt.

Blue ribbon commissions are temporary advisory bodies, usually established to find broadly acceptable solutions to contentious problems.

Among the best known and most effective was the National Commission on Social Security Reform, established by presidential order in 1981 to deal with a crisis in the funding of social security and medicare. Its report was issued in 1983. Representing a wide range of opinion from both parties, the commissioners joined in nearly unanimous support of the recommendations, which President Ronald Reagan and House Speaker Thomas P. (Tip) O'Neill, Jr., also embraced. Soon after, Congress adopted the commission's proposals with few changes. In this notable case, a commission transformed what had been the most partisan, contentious issue in American politics into a most tractable one. Summit negotiations between members of Congress and senior White House advisers helped to produce bipartisan agreements on budget deficit reduction in both 1987 and 1990.

Sharply divided reports do little or nothing to resolve problems. The National Economic Commission (1988–1989), modeled on the Social Security Commission, was intended to produce bipartisan recommendations on how to reduce the budget deficit. Its members divided along partisan lines and issued a majority report accompanied by a sharp dissent from the minority. The result was a continuation of previous conflict. The Pepper Commission (named for Rep. Claude Pepper [D-Fla.], an advocate for the elderly) was designed to produce a consensus on reform of the American health care system. Its members could not reach a consensus and issued a divided report, which did nothing to promote either consensus or action in Congress.

Countless politicians, pressed to make decisions that could prove unpopular however they are made, have taken the easy way out by appointing a commission. This time-honored practice encourages a cynical view that politicians create commissions mostly to fob off unwanted responsibilities. But commissions can help elected officials make difficult decisions by providing an ostensibly disinterested, expert justification. Moreover, research indicates that most commission recommendations are accepted and implemented. At the very least, appointing a commission can shift responsibility from government officials for a year or so while its members deliberate.

At their most effective, commissions allow Congress to realize purposes its members could not endorse directly. A 1967 law established a quadrennial Commission on Executive, Legislative, and Judicial Salaries, and instructed it to issue a recommendation for salary levels for the three branches of government. Because the proposal would take effect automatically unless Congress voted to oppose it, the use of the commission helped insulate members of Congress from the political hazards of voting for their own pay increase.

As the use of commissions increased in the 1980s, so did criticism of them, principally on the ground that elected officials were abdicating their responsibilities, but also on the ground that decisions were being made behind closed doors. There is some basis for these arguments, but it is the elected officials who must decide whether or not to adopt commission recommendations. Thus it is they who accept ultimate responsibility.

[See also (II) Commissions, Presidential.]

BIBLIOGRAPHY

Flitner, David. *The Politics of Presidential Commissions: A Public Policy Perspective.* 1986.

Light, Paul. *Artful Work: The Politics of Social Security Reform.* 1985.

Wolanin, Thomas R. *Presidential Advisory Commissions.* 1975.

– JOHN B. GILMOUR

BROADCASTING OF CONGRESSIONAL PROCEEDINGS

The relationship between Congress and radio and television is rooted in the earliest days of American broadcasting. In 1922—only two years after the first U.S. radio station became operational—Rep. Vincent M. Brennan (R-Mich.) introduced the first bill to authorize a radio service to broadcast congressional proceedings. The measure failed, but the idea persisted. By the late 1940s, television's displacement of radio as America's preeminent electronic mass medium had begun to change attitudes toward the broadcasting of congressional proceedings. Even House and Senate members who firmly opposed televising chamber deliberations welcomed television coverage of committee hearings.

TELEVISED COMMITTEE PROCEEDINGS. Television cameras first were admitted to congressional hearing rooms in 1948, to cover Senate Armed Services Committee hearings. Soon they were covering House Un-American Activities Committee hearings on the spread of communism. The small number of households with television sets during the period, however, meant that few Americans were able to watch the hearings. Television sets had become more numerous by the early 1950s, when the hearings of the Senate Special Committee to Investigate Organized Crime in Interstate Commerce were broadcast. The so-called Kefauver Crime Committee, named for its chairman, Estes Kefauver (D-Tenn.), conducted hearings in fourteen U.S. cities as it investigated the spread of organized crime in the United States. Kefauver Crime Committee testimony was televised locally in a number of these cities, but when the committee moved to New York City and Washington, D.C., its televised hearings caused a sensation when millions of people interrupted jobs and household chores alike to watch them.

On March 19, 1979, the House inaugurated live television coverage of its chamber proceedings.

Televised hearings led by Sen. Joseph R. McCarthy to investigate alleged communist infiltration of the U.S. armed forces generated even greater public attention than the Kefauver committee hearings. Senator McCarthy used his position as chairman of the Senate Committee on Government Operations' permanent investigations subcommittee to conduct thirty-six days of hearings lasting from 22 April to 17 June 1954. The ABC and Dumont television networks provided live coverage of all 187 hours of what came to be known as the Army-McCarthy hearings. The NBC television network carried only the first two days of the hearings live before it joined CBS in providing viewers with only filmed highlights of each day's proceedings. An opening-day estimated television audience of some thirty million people leveled off to an average of nine to ten million per day as the Army-McCarthy hearings wore on.

Viewer reaction to what they saw of the Army-McCarthy hearings centered on the demeanor of Senator McCarthy. Whereas some saw the senator as a courageous American, many of McCarthy's colleagues regarded his hearing tactics as intimidating and voted to censure him shortly after the Army-McCarthy hearings ended.

Nearly twenty years passed before televised congressional hearings again so thoroughly seized public attention. By the summer of 1973, when the Senate Select Committee on Presidential Campaign Activities—known as the Ervin committee after its chairman, Samuel J. Ervin, Jr. (D-N.C.)—opened its hearings on the Watergate affair to television cameras, practically every U.S. household had one or more television sets. An estimated 85 percent of these households tuned in to watch at least some portion of the Ervin committee hearings. Evidence of presidential misdeeds uncovered by the Ervin committee was eventually transferred to the House Judiciary Committee. During several days of high drama in July 1974, television viewers watched the committee initiate impeachment proceedings against President Richard M. Nixon. Nixon's resignation saved the nation from the trauma of an impeachment trial, but, had a trial occurred, television would have been there: both houses of Congress had already established ground rules to allow full coverage.

More recent hearings have also attracted extended television coverage. When the House Select Committee to Investigate Covert Arms Transactions with Iran and the Senate Select Committee on Secret Military Assistance to Iran and the Nicaraguan Opposition conducted joint hearings in 1987 on the Iran-contra affair, television cameras were there. And more drama than was anticipated accompanied televised coverage of the Senate Judiciary Committee's confirmation hearings for U.S. Supreme Court nominee Clarence Thomas in 1991. The routine hearings that supposedly had concluded in September were reconvened in October, when the Judiciary Committee was forced to consider charges of sexual harrassment leveled against Thomas.

TELEVISED CHAMBER PROCEEDINGS. In 1973 the Joint Committee on Congressional Operations returned House and Senate attention to the possibility of televising chamber proceedings. The committee's purpose was twofold: to explore ways in which Congress could better communicate its role to the American public, and to explore ways that Congress might compete with the extensive media attention given the president.

The joint committee's eventual recommendation that Congress test the televising of chamber proceedings won only a lukewarm reception in the Senate. The House showed more enthusiasm, forming a special broadcasting subcommittee to explore implementation of the joint committee's recommendation. One of the most controversial issues with which the subcommittee had to grapple pertained to the ultimate authority over a House television system. The subcommittee preferred a system controlled by the television networks, whereas Speaker Carl B. Albert (D-Okla.) insisted that ultimate control should reside with the Speaker.

Efforts to resolve the dispute over the system's control delayed further action on televising House proceedings until the 95th Congress, when the new Speaker, Thomas P. (Tip) O'Neill, Jr. (D-Mass.), surprised colleagues by announcing that a ninety-day test to judge the feasibility of a House television system would commence in March 1977. Remote-control cameras would provide various House offices with daily closed-circuit coverage of chamber activity. House members surveyed at the conclusion of the ninety-day experiment appeared pleased with chamber television. Few noted any of the feared adverse effects on House conduct or procedures.

The successful ninety-day test was followed by the introduction of legislation to make House television permanent. In October 1977, the House voted 342 to 44 to approve the measure in principle. Implementation of a House television system, however, had to await a final decision regarding who would control the television cameras. Advocates of network control claimed that House leaders could easily censor whatever they did not want the public to see, but advocates of a House-controlled system argued that network news managers could do the same.

The House Rules Committee considered the matter thoroughly and recommended that the House maintain control over its own television system. The recommendation was approved by a vote of 235 to 150 in June 1978, and on 19 March 1979, the House inaugurated live television coverage of its chamber proceedings. Rep. Albert A. Gore, Jr. (D-Tenn.), briefly noted the significance of the occasion before the House returned to routine business. The Public Broadcasting Service (PBS) and the Cable-Satellite Public Affairs Network (C-SPAN) were the only networks to carry the proceedings in their entirety.

The Senate's interest in televising its proceedings was slow to take hold, but by April 1981 the Senate Rules Committee had begun hearings on a measure, introduced by Sen. Howard H. Baker (R.-Tenn.), providing for continuous televised coverage of Senate chamber proceedings. Arguments on the issue were similar to ones voiced earlier in the House. Those who favored televising Senate chamber proceedings felt that it could help restore public esteem for the body. Opponents argued that it would encourage grandstanding and that the intricacies of Senate debate would confuse television viewers. The Baker bill won the approval of the Senate Rules Committee but encountered strong opposition on the Senate floor. A powerful block of senators, led by Russell B. Long (D-La.), successfully stymied any chance for televising Senate proceedings in the foreseeable future.

Sen. Robert C. Byrd (D-W.Va.) assumed retired senator Baker's advocacy role in 1985, introducing legislation calling once more for implementation of a Senate chamber television system. Senators' recognition of the success of House television had improved chances for Senate television, and Senator Long's pending retirement significantly diminished the strength of Senate television opponents.

Like the House, the Senate requires that television and radio signals originating from the Senate chamber be undiluted and not used for political purposes.

A Rules Committee recommendation that the Senate commence testing of a closed-circuit television system was approved by the full Senate by a vote of 67 to 21 on 27 February 1986. Live television coverage of Senate chamber proceedings began on a temporary basis in June 1986, continuing through July while senators judged its effectiveness. They were satisfied enough to vote on 29 July 1986 to make television a permanent Senate fixture. Television cameras attached to gallery railings (as in the House) covered chamber activity as the Senate inaugurated its television system on 2 June. C-SPAN arranged a satellite feed (separate from its House feed) to carry Senate proceedings to interested cable-television systems nationwide. Several senators, including then–majority leader Bob Dole (R-Kan.) delivered brief remarks commemorating the occasion.

RULES FOR BROADCAST OF COMMITTEE PROCEEDINGS. Senate rules regulating television and radio coverage of committee hearings began evolving in the 1950s, when such coverage was first instituted. The Kefauver Crime Committee hearings that generated so much interest in 1952 also raised questions concerning the proper conduct of hearings in general. Some critics argued that televised interrogation abused the due process and privacy rights of witnesses. Others claimed that the bulky cameras and bright lights that were required for TV broadcasts in television's early days disrupted hearing-room decorum. Efforts by several senators to create formal codes for conducting televised hearings proved unsuccessful. Rather than to create blanket rules, the Senate instead decided to allow each committee to adopt its own procedures. Current Senate rules specify that television and radio may be allowed to cover committee and subcommittee hearings that are open to the public in accordance with whatever rules a committee or subcommittee has set for that coverage.

Some committees empower their chairmen with authority to determine the proper conduct of hearings covered by television and radio; others require that the chairman share that authority with the committee's ranking minority member; and still others require that decisions pertaining to television and radio coverage of hearings be made by majority vote of the committee. Where specific rules exist, they generally require that the chairman order that television and radio coverage be interrupted at the request of any committee witness who objects to having his or her testimony broadcasted. Other rules require that television cameras, microphones, and lighting be unobtrusive and that television and radio personnel in the hearing room conduct themselves in an orderly fashion and forbid commercial sponsorship of committee hearings.

In the early 1950s, House members shared their Senate colleagues' concern and interest in developing a code to regulate televised hearings. That concern became moot, though, when House Speaker Sam Rayburn (D-Tex.) ruled in 1952 to prohibit television and radio coverage of House committee hearings. Speaker Joseph W. Martin, Jr., had allowed the broadcast of selected hearings during his tenure, but Speaker Rayburn took a narrower view. He held in 1952 and reaffirmed in 1955 that committees were bound by the same House rules that, as he interpreted their silence on the issue, barred broadcasts of House proceedings. House Rule XI spe-

Televised proceedings. A congressman watching floor proceedings from his office. (Library of Congress)

cifically extended the rules of the House to committees, and Rayburn announced on 24 January 1955 that until the rules were changed, he could not permit broadcast or photographic coverage of committee hearings, whether they were held in Washington or elsewhere. Some observers felt that the prohibition was due to the Speaker's general distrust of the media coupled with his particular reservations over the conduct of the televised Kefauver committee hearings. Whatever the reasons, the Rayburn ban remained virtually undisturbed until the 1970 Legislative Reorganization Act once again opened House committee room doors to television and radio.

Current rules for television and radio coverage of House committee hearings resemble Senate rules in that their intentions are to protect witnesses' rights and to preserve the decorum of committee proceedings. But the House provides a more precise and extensive list of blanket rules applying to all House committees than does the Senate. For instance, the House requires that committee hearings be open to television and radio coverage for the benefit of the public, that they be covered in an impartial fashion, and that coverage not be used for partisan or campaign-related purposes. A majority vote of committee members is required to allow television and radio coverage of the committee's hearings, and each House committee may determine its own procedural rules for such coverage as long as these rules contain provisions prohibiting commercial sponsorship of the coverage, forbidding television and radio coverage of witnesses upon their request, guaranteeing fair access to accredited news organizations that request television and radio coverage of committee hearings, prohibiting the removal of television and radio apparatus while hearings are in progress, forbidding excessive lighting, and requiring that television and radio personnel conduct themselves with dignity.

RULES FOR BROADCAST OF PROCEEDINGS OF FULL CHAMBER. Rules for television and radio coverage of House chamber proceedings are likewise more precise than are rules for such coverage in the Senate chamber. The Speaker of the House has clear authority to oversee operation of the House television and radio system. The Speaker controls the manner in which chamber proceedings are covered and approves the distribution of House-oriented television and radio signals to authorized media representatives. House rules stipulate that coverage, as it originates, be unedited, that it not be used for political purposes, and that it not be used in commercial advertisements.

One House rule stipulated that television cameras be allowed to focus only on members as they addressed their colleagues from lecterns in or near the well of the House. Speaker Tip O'Neill modified this particular rule in 1984 in response to his political opponents' use of so-called special order speeches. (Special orders are reserved for members wishing to speak on topics of their choice at the conclusion of daily legislative business.) Several conservative Republican representatives took advantage of the special orders privilege in 1984 to criticize the Speaker and his political agenda. Speaker O'Neill decided to embarrass his antagonists by ordering television cameras to pan the nearly empty House chamber. Although criticized for what Republicans cited as a breach of authority, O'Neill nonetheless refused to reverse the new rule allowing panning of the chamber.

Rules for television and radio coverage of Senate chamber proceedings are enforced by a less centralized authority than in the House. The Senate Rules and Administration Committee has the ultimate authority over the use of television and radio in the Senate chamber. Operation of the television and radio systems themselves are under the authority of the Senate sergeant at arms. Like the House, the Senate requires that the television and radio signals originating from the Senate chamber be unedited and that they not be used for political campaign purposes. Television cameras must focus on senators whenever they speak (and wherever they are speaking from) and are prohibited from panning the chamber, except during roll-call votes.

CONGRESSIONAL TELEVISION'S IMPACT. The amount and kind of television coverage given House and Senate activity can affect public policy. Television can influence the legislative conduct of individual members of Congress and, ultimately, their chances for reelection.

Some members of Congress have been known to seek committee assignments based on the amount of television exposure a particular committee is expected to receive and to participate actively in committee hearings only when television cameras are present. Regardless of whether a member of Congress seeks television exposure or prefers to work far from the camera's eye, any senator or representative may be thrust into the television limelight and achieve celebrity by virtue of his or her participation in newsworthy committee hearings. This is especially true of committee chairs.

No less affected by their television appearances are noncongressional House and Senate hearing participants. Attorney Anita Hill, for instance, became known to millions when she testified before the Senate Judiciary Committee's confirmation hearings for Supreme Court nominee Clarence Thomas. It was Hill's charges of sexual harrassment against the nominee that called into doubt his qualifications to serve on the Court. Another attorney—Joseph N. Welch—had achieved similar fame many years before. Welch had been appointed special counsel to represent the U.S. Army during the 1954 Army-McCarthy hearings. He not only defended the army successfully, but his mild-mannered and gentlemanly rebuff of Sen. Joseph McCarthy won him the respect of practically everyone who witnessed his performance. Welch continued to practice law after concluding his special counsel duties, but he also was in demand for television appearances to discuss legal matters.

The presence of television cameras in the House chamber has not appreciably changed legislative proceedings, although the House leadership has lost some control over younger House members who have used television to build public recognition and to increase their influence on colleagues and constituents alike. Television has been blamed for increasing partisan rhetoric in the House chamber, particularly during special order speeches (as noted above) and "one-minute" speeches delivered prior to the beginning of daily legislative business.

Senate chamber proceedings have not experienced any major departure from tradition as a result of television. Senate special order speeches increased when television first entered the chamber, but their number has since returned to a pretelevision level. Some observers contend that television actually has led to a more disciplined Senate, with senators making better, shorter, and more substantive remarks.

Self-policing has held grandstanding in both the Senate and House chambers to a minimum, and members of Congress have become more sensitive to what they say, and how they say it, because of their constituents' ability to view them on television. More important, a speaker's opponents may videotape his or her floor remarks for use in political campaigns. Although incumbent members of Congress are prohibited from such use of videotapes, nonincumbents are not.

Indirect effects of congressional television have included the improved appearance of senators and representatives: men, especially, are now taking more care to outfit themselves with telegenic suits and accessories, and some have reportedly resorted to makeup and hairpieces to improve their looks. Members have also become more proficient in the use of visual aids during debate. Outside the congressional chambers, members of Congress have found office television monitors an excellent means of keeping up with chamber debate and of becoming better informed about legislative matters.

The self-censorship that television network news organizations thought would happen unless they controlled House and Senate chamber television has not materialized. Nonetheless, networks give scant airtime to the televised proceedings, in part because of union rules that prohibit the networks from carrying more than a few minutes of programming originated by nonunion personnel. As a result of the limited time provided by the networks, members of Congress have become experts at producing comments that can easily fit into thirty-second sound bites.

There is no indication that public esteem for either the House or the Senate has improved as a result of television, but there is plenty of evidence that the public has benefited from televised House and Senate proceedings. Congressional television has increased awareness of particular issues, allowed the public to hear a wide spectrum of views on these issues, and instructed viewers in the fundamentals of the legislative process.

[See also (II) Committees, article on Committee Hearings.]

BIBLIOGRAPHY

Bates, Stephen, ed. *The Media and the Congress.* 1987.

Clark, Timothy B. "The House on Cable." *The Journal of the Institute for Socioeconomic Studies* 9 (Summer 1984): 12–22.

Crain, W. Mark, and Brian Goff. *Televised Legislatures: Political Information Technology and Public Choice.* 1988.

Garay, Ronald. *Congressional Television: A Legislative History.* 1984.

Hess, Stephen. *Live from Capitol Hill! Studies of Congress and the Media.* 1991.

– RONALD GARAY

BUDGET PROCESS

The power of the purse granted to Congress in Article I of the Constitution has long been an essential element of Congress's role as a policymaker. In recent years, the budget process has become the central feature of the internal operations of Congress. It affects the relative power of committees, the resources of majority party leaders, the rules and floor procedures, and Congress's ability to negotiate with the president.

Three important factors help explain the evolution of the congressional budget process and judgments about its performance. First, congressional budget reforms were in part spurred by basic changes in the nature of the budget itself. From the 1960s on, as outlays became dominated by entitlements and mandatory spending, discretionary spending shrank as a share of total outlays. The budget became increasingly sensitive to macroeconomic changes. Taxing and spending decisions were no longer strictly annual choices but increasingly encompassed multiyear commitments. The traditional authorization-appropriations process, which considered the budget in parts rather than as a whole, proved inadequate to the task of managing relatively inflexible budget figures. In short, the experimentation in congressional budgeting since the late 1960s reflects legislative attempts to adapt to a rapidly changing budgetary, economic, and political environment.

Second, the development of the congressional budget process reflects the constitutional separation of powers and institutional combat between the executive and legislative branches. Interbranch conflict was exacerbated in the late twentieth century by the prevalence of divided government. For example, the 1974 Budget Act was adopted not only to increase Congress's ability to control the budget but to check President Richard M. Nixon's power and ability to thwart congressional priorities. In the 1980s, the sharp divisions between President Ronald Reagan and congressional Democrats were reflected in the recurrence of chronic budget deficits. The major changes in the budget process after 1982 in large part occurred in response to growing deficits, procedural attempts to resolve prolonged institutional conflict, and divergent policy preferences.

Even when Congress imposes strict rules on itself to control spending, members use gimmicks, tricks, and "blue smoke and mirrors" to avoid fiscal discipline.

Third, apparent inconsistencies in Congress's budgeting performance reflect the tension between two basic roles of members of Congress: that of responsible national policymakers versus that of local district representatives concerned about reelection and oriented toward providing tangible benefits for constituents. Wishes that are rational and desirable for each individual member may make it difficult for Congress to demonstrate collective responsibility. This tension makes the necessary tasks of increasing taxes and cutting spending to reduce deficits much more difficult than spending for (albeit worthy) programs in education, health, defense, and other policy areas. As a result, even when Congress imposes strict rules and requirements on itself to control spending, members use gimmicks, tricks, and "blue smoke and mirrors" to avoid fiscal discipline. While many other forces have shaped the congressional budget process, structural changes in the budget, legislative-executive conflict, and divergent legislative roles help explain the unusual path that the budgeting process has taken.

CONGRESSIONAL BUDGETING BEFORE 1974. The congressional budget process has evolved through a number of stages over two hundred years. The House Ways and Means Committee initiated both taxing and spending bills until the Civil War. In 1865, the House created the Appropriations Committee to consider expenditures, and the Senate followed suit two years later, leaving the Ways and Means Committee and the Senate Finance Committee with jurisdiction over taxes. The process became more fragmented over the ensuing decades as standing committees gained control over various money bills. The Budget and Accounting Act of 1921 created the executive budget, strengthening the president's role, but Congress continued to use the decentralized authorization-appropriations process. The president's power in budgeting increased dramatically during the New Deal and World War II as part of a larger and more activist executive branch.

Following World War II, Congress attempted to improve its budget process. The 1946 Legislative Reorganization Act included provisions that provided for a legislative budget; a Joint Committee on the Budget was established to review the president's requests and report a legislative budget to both houses. But jurisdictional struggles, partisanship, and tension between the White House and Congress doomed efforts to make the congressional budget process more comprehensive. Although a number of solutions were attempted, efforts to create a legislative budget had ceased by 1950.

The authorization-appropriations process functioned adequately through much of the 1960s, when the economy was robust, and growing revenues made it possible gradually to increase the size and scope of programs. By the late 1960s, however, both the process and congressional control over the budget were deteriorating. Congress attempted to enact legislation to cap expenditures in five out of the six years from 1967 to 1972. With a frustrated Congress seemingly unable to stem the tide of rising expenditures, President Nixon attacked Congress's lack of discipline and impounded (refused to spend) funds appropriated by Congress. The expansion of federal programs and the escalating conflict between Congress and the president created the environment for major budget reform.

BUDGET AND IMPOUNDMENT CONTROL ACT OF 1974. The Joint Study Committee on Budget Control issued a report in 1973 stressing the importance of developing procedures that would allow Congress to take an overview of the budget, coordinate spending and revenues, and integrate separate spending bills. During the committee's year-long deliberations, various political and committee interests were represented. As a result, instead of instituting an entirely new process, the Budget Impoundment and Control Act created an additional set of procedures that was layered on top of the old system.

Budget committees. The act created new committees in both the House and Senate. The Senate Budget Committee (SBC) was established as a regular standing committee with sixteen members, subject to the same principles of committee assignments, seniority, and rules that applied to other Senate committees. Membership on the House Budget Committee (HBC), however, was defined and limited. Of the HBC's twenty-five members, five came from the Ways and Means Committee and five from the Appropriations Committee; House Republican and Democratic leadership supplied one member each. (Both the HBC and SBC have subsequently been enlarged.) Service on the HBC was limited to four years out of any ten (subsequently six years out of ten). These provisions were designed to keep the new panel broad in perspective and representative of the House, but they also left the HBC in a secondary position in relation to the existing money committees.

Congressional Budget Office. To help provide analytical support and better budget data, Title II of the act created the Congressional Budget Office (CBO). This nonpartisan agency was given responsibility for monitoring the economy and its effect on the budget, improving budgetary information, and providing cost estimates of legislation.

Budget resolutions. The congressional budget was to be specified in a series of resolutions to be reported by the budget committees. Concurrent resolutions were the chosen vehicle, since they were binding only on Congress, did not require the president's signature, and did not in themselves provide the authority to spend funds. The Budget Act required enactment of a first resolution, which established targets, by 15 May and a second resolution, which set binding totals, by 15 September. Each resolution would specify: (1) total budget authority (BA) and outlays, (2) budget authority and outlays for fifteen functional subtotals (e.g., function 050, national defense, or function 350, agriculture), (3) total revenues, (4) resulting surplus or deficit, and (5) resulting public debt.

Timetable. To help ensure that the new process would work, the law included a strict timetable. The original timetable, which has been revised on a number of occasions since, is summarized in table 1.

Using the president's budget, CBO analysis, the views and estimates of other committees, and testimony from economists and budget experts, each of the Budget committees was to draw up the first resolution and report it to its chamber by 15 April. By 15 May a single budget resolution was to be passed by both the House and Senate and all authorizing bills were to be reported by committees. After passage of the first resolution, the Budget committees translated the functional totals into committee allocations, informing the spending committees how much budget authority and outlays they could provide under the resolution. The Appropriations committees further subdivided the totals for their subcommittees. By September, all spending bills were to be passed. The Budget committees, reviewing these bills in light of current economic conditions, were to draft and report a second concurrent resolution by 15 September. It was to contain binding totals and subtotals, and once it was enacted, any legislation violating the totals would be ruled out of order. If the spending bills and the second resolution did not agree, a reconciliation bill ordering adjustments in the individual spending bills was to be passed by 25 September. Because the new fiscal year (FY) began on 1 October, a three-month transition quarter, from 1 July to 30 September 1976, was created to facilitate the change.

TABLE 1

CONGRESSIONAL BUDGET TIMETABLE, 1975

Action to be completed	On or before
President submits annual budget message to Congress	15 days after Congress meets
Congressional committees make recommendations to Budget committees	15 March
Congressional Budget Office reports to Budget committees	1 April
Budget committees report first budget resolution	15 April
Congress passes first budget resolution	15 May
Legislative committees complete reporting of authorizing legislation	15 May
Congress passes all spending bills	Seven days after Labor Day
Congress passes second budget resolution	15 September
Congress passes budget reconciliation bill	25 September
Fiscal year begins	1 October

Impoundment. The Budget and Impoundment Control Act moved to prevent the president from thwarting Congress's wishes by refusing to spend appropriated moneys. Congress did recognize the need for some executive discretion, however, and created two new processes: deferral and rescission. The president requests a *deferral* to delay temporarily the spending of money appropriated by Congress. Deferrals are automatically effective unless either house passes a disapproval resolution. The president requests a *rescission* to eliminate spending authority permanently. To take effect, rescissions must be approved by an affirmative vote of both the House and Senate within forty-five days of the request.

Passage of the legislation. Despite the many significant changes encompassed in the Budget Impoundment and Control Act and the many compromises it reflected, there was strong bipartisan support for the legislation in both houses. The House passed it 401 to 6 and the Senate 75 to 0. President Richard Nixon, in part the target of the legislation, signed the bill in July 1974, only weeks before he would resign the presidency. The consensus on final passage belied members' widely differing goals and expectations, however. Liberal Democrats saw it as opening an opportunity to debate national spending priorities for the first time—for example, to make explicit comparisons between amounts going to defense versus money spent on domestic programs. Conservative Republicans saw the legislation as providing a method for restraining spending and reducing deficits, since for the first time members would be accountable should they vote for an unbalanced budget. Because of these conflicting interpretations, the consensus over the new procedures, which had been designed to improve the policy performance of Congress and to check the president's power, crumbled as soon as real budget choices were faced.

IMPLEMENTING THE CONGRESSIONAL BUDGET PROCESS, 1975 TO 1980. During its first five years of operation, the new budget process inspired sharp partisan disputes in the House of Representatives, often to the point where many members feared the process would collapse. In the Senate, bipartisan support for the budget process was much greater and the new system seemed stronger and more secure.

In the first-year trial run in 1975, House Republicans objected to proposed changes in President Gerald R. Ford's budget and refused to cooperate. House Budget Committee chairman Brock Adams (D-Wash.) worked with the Democratic leaders in the House to fashion a slim majority. The first resolution in 1975 passed by a narrow margin of 200 to 196, with Democrats supporting it 197 to 68 and Republicans opposing it 3 to 128. This partisan voting pattern on budget resolutions would remain remarkably consistent over the next five years, as shown in table 2. Because Republicans and the more conservative Democrats opposed the budget resolutions, the Democratic leaders had to appeal to their party's liberal wing to gain a majority. As a result, budget resolution figures in the House tended to be higher on social spending and lower on defense than in the Senate.

As table 2 also shows, the process was more bipartisan and more secure on the Senate side. Some observers suggested that the six-year terms in the Senate insulated senators from the intense reelection pressure faced by House members, making it easier for senators to vote for budget resolutions. Furthermore, since the SBC was a regular Senate standing committee, its members had more incentive to restrain partisanship as a means of protecting the prestige and influence of the committee. Also, the Senate Budget Committee, in the eyes of many analysts, benefited from enlightened leadership. SBC chairman Edmund S. Muskie (D-Maine) and ranking minority member Henry L. Bellmon (R-Okla.) worked closely together to present a united front on the Senate floor to promote and strengthen the process.

The congressional budget process made some important changes in the way Congress handled taxing and spending decisions. In 1976, for the first time in years, all thirteen regular appropriations bills were enacted before the start of the fiscal year. Congress showed that it could use the process to modify the president's budget, as it did with Ford's budgets in 1975 and 1976. Congress also demonstrated that it could accommodate the plans of a new president when it enacted a third budget resolution in 1977 at the request of President Jimmy Carter. The CBO's reports and analyses raised the level of budget-related information available to Congress. Yet after five years most participants and observers were disappointed with the performance of the congressional budget process.

The congressional budget process made some important changes in the way Congress handled taxing and spending decisions.

Despite the changes that had followed in the wake of the Budget Impoundment and Control Act—the two Budget committees, the new voting coalitions, and the exacerbated partisanship in the House—there was no great shift in budget policy after 1975. The new budget process had survived, and Congress for the first time was approving budget totals and functional subtotals, but the process appeared to have little overall effect on fiscal policy or national priorities. Scholars who have studied the congressional budget process of the late 1970s agree that the second budget resolutions were little more than the sum of the actions of the spending committees. Rather than creating top-down influence on subsequent budget choices, the Budget committees—referred to by one observer as "adding machine committees"—largely accommodated the desires of the authorizing and appropriations committees.

TABLE 2

VOTES ON FIRST BUDGET RESOLUTIONS, 1975–1980

	Date	Total Vote Yes/No	Republicans Yes/No	Democrats Yes/No
House				
	1975	200–196	3–128	197–68
	1976	221–155	13–111	208–44
	1977	213–179	7–121	206–58
	1978	201–197	3–136	198–61
	1979	220–184	9–134	211–50
	1980	225–193	22–131	203–62
Senate				
	1975	69–22	19–18	50–4
	1976	62–22	17–16	45–6
	1977	56–31	15–17	41–14
	1978	64–27	16–19	48–8
	1979	64–20	20–15	44–5
	1980	68–28	19–22	49–6

There was little evidence of priorities being restructured or spending being restrained, and the deficits continued to mount. The tension between the congressional roles of delivering benefits to constituents and of imposing overall budgetary discipline was reflected in many of the debates and deals struck during the late 1970s. In most cases, spending prevailed over restraint.

The reconciliation process, one of the most potent creations of the Budget Act, was simply ignored in the 1970s. In 1979, efforts to use reconciliation were rejected by a coalition of committees. After the 1980 election, however, congressional leaders reported a reconciliation bill that reduced spending by some $8 billion. Significantly, it had both Democratic and Republican support and established an important precedent for the use of reconciliation in 1981.

REAGAN, DEFICITS, AND BUDGET PROCESS, 1981 TO 1985. The 1980 elections resulted in a shakeup in both the legislative and executive branches. Republicans regained control of the presidency after a four-year hiatus and took control of the Senate for the first time since 1955. The size of the Democratic majority in the House was reduced from 117 to 51. This meant that House Republicans had to attract only twenty-six Democratic defectors to create a majority. With Republicans replacing Democrats as Senate chairmen, Pete V. Domenici (R-N.Mex.) became chairman of the Senate Budget Committee. James R. Jones (D-Okla.), who was narrowly elected chairman of the House Budget Committee, had a more conservative perspective than his predecessor, Robert N. Giaimo (D-Conn.).

In his 1980 campaign, Ronald Reagan had promised three general changes in budgetary priorities: a rapid increase in defense spending, a significant reduction in taxes, and large cuts in domestic spending and entitlements. Led by Office of Management and Budget director David Stockman, the administration moved quickly, presenting revised budget proposals to Congress within weeks of taking office. An extremely important change in the congressional budget process assisted Reagan in accomplishing his "revolution" in U.S. government: the decision to move reconciliation from the end to the beginning of the budget process. A reconciliation bill instructed committees and subcommittees to make cuts in the programs under their jurisdiction, reconciling individual authorizations and appropriations with totals in the budget resolution. This was achieved using the so-called elastic clause of the 1974 Budget Act, which allowed Congress to change "such other matters relating to the budget as may be appropriate to carry out the purposes of this Act." In 1980, Congress had established that reductions in authorizations would count toward reconciliation totals. This meant that reconciliation instructions could mandate a wide range of cuts in appropriations, entitlements, borrowing and contract authority, and authorizations.

With solid support in the Senate, the Reagan administration still needed to win the backing of conservative, southern House Democrats commonly referred to as boll weevils. The initial confrontation took place over the first concurrent resolution on the budget for fiscal year 1982. HBC chair Jones reported a resolution that, while giving the president much of what he wanted, did not satisfy the administration. Representatives Phil Gramm (D-Tex.) and Delbert L. Latta (R-Ohio) drafted a substitute reflecting the president's wishes. In May, the substitute, dubbed Gramm-Latta I, was adopted 253 to 176. Republicans supported the substitute budget resolution 190 to 0, while 63 of the 229 Democrats voting defected to the president. The Senate adopted the resolution 78 to 20, with a majority of both parties supporting the president.

Despite the defeat, House Democrats believed that they could derail the administration's plans when the crucial reconciliation bill was considered in June. Once again, the Democratic version included most of the president's requests, cutting $39 billion from the budget for fiscal year 1982. The Rules Committee reported a rule for the bill that allowed the cuts to be voted on in six parts, greatly increasing the chances that many of the cuts would be rejected. However, on 25 June the Republican–boll weevil alliance narrowly defeated the rule 217 to 210, substituting instead a single yes-or-no vote on the entire package of cuts. This victory virtually assured the coalition the margin it needed to defeat the Democratic leadership on the reconciliation bill itself. The Republican substitute, the Budget and Reconciliation Act (known as Gramm-Latta II), was hurriedly drafted overnight and passed the next day by a six-vote margin. The third and final key vote occurred a month later, when the House and Senate, by large margins, approved the Economic Recovery Tax Act (ERTA), which slashed income taxes by 25 percent across the board.

The events of 1981 had lasting effects on budgeting for several reasons. First, when combined with the recession that began late in the year, the tax cuts and defense increases (which were not compensated for by domestic cuts) resulted in historically large, chronic budget deficits. These deficits would become the driving force for additional reforms and changes in the congressional budget process. Second, reconciliation at the beginning of the process became an integral part of congressional budgeting even though it was extremely unpopular with many members. Third, the process in 1981 demonstrated that the second budget resolution played no meaningful role in overall budget control, and it was effectively dropped after 1982. Because the budget process itself remained unpopular, many of the changes were adopted informally, an approach that avoided the necessity of opening up the 1974 act to revision on the House and Senate floors.

The 1982 elections resulted in Democratic gains in the House and effectively ended the ability of Republicans and conservative Democrats to create a majority coalition. Table 3 examines voting alignments in the House and Senate on the first budget resolution votes between 1981 and 1985. Only in 1981 and 1982, when they were able to build a majority coalition, did Republicans vote for a budget resolution. After 1982, the House reverted to voting patterns similar to those of the 1970s. On the Senate side, bipartisanship in voting disappeared after 1981. With the exception of 1983, Senate Democrats and Republicans divided sharply over the budget, matching the partisanship of the House.

TABLE 3

VOTES ON BUDGET RESOLUTIONS, 1981–1985

	Date	Total Vote Yes/No	Republicans Yes/No	Democrats Yes/No
House				
	1981	253–176	190–000	63–176
	1982	219–206	156–32	63–174
	1983	229–196	4–160	225–36
	1984	250–168	21–139	229–29
	1985	258–170	24–155	234–15
Senate				
	1981	78–20	50–2	28–18
	1982	49–43	46–2	3–41
	1983	50–49	21–32	29–17
	1984	41–34	40–3	1–31
	1985	50–49[1]	48–4	1–45

[1]Vice President George Bush cast the tie-breaking vote.

Deficits continued to rise in the early 1980s, hitting a record $208 billion in fiscal year 1983, with the deficit representing 6.3 percent of gross domestic product (GDP). Although several deficit reduction measures, which raised taxes and cut spending, were passed, the deficits remained at more than 5 percent of GDP through 1987. As had been true before 1975, some appropriations bills were not enacted by the start of the fiscal year; continuing resolutions were frequently needed when spending bills were not ready by 1 October. On several occasions when agreement could not be reached, the federal government had to shut down nonessential operations. Increasingly, both authorizations and appropriations were lumped together in "mega-bills." This must-pass legislation became the target for nongermane amendments of every description. A growing number of appropriations were enacted without authorizing legislation, a violation of House and Senate rules. Supplemental appropriations to restore cuts or avoid discipline were more frequent. Procedural controls and enforcement mechanisms weakened, while waivers to the Budget Act increased in frequency. These changes in the budget process, given the context of the large budget deficits, created the impetus to revise the Budget Act in 1985.

BALANCED BUDGET AND EMERGENCY DEFICIT CONTROL ACT, 1985. In December 1985, Congress made the most dramatic changes in its budgetary process in a decade when it enacted the Balanced Budget and Emergency Deficit Control Act, better known as Gramm-Rudman-Hollings after its Senate co-sponsors Phil Gramm (who had switched to the Republican party and gone to the Senate), Warren B. Rudman (R-N.H.), and Ernest F. Hollings (D-S.C.). The main thrust of the legislation was to create a mechanism for making across-the-board cuts in outlays should deficit targets not be met. Although the legislation was originally greeted with skepticism and derision, members frustrated with the inability to break the deadlock over deficits proved willing to sign on to almost anything that promised deficit reduction. The cosponsors forced congressional action by linking the deficit plan to the statutory debt-limitation legislation that had to pass for the government to operate and pay its bills. For several months, House and Senate negotiators tried to hammer out a compromise version of the mandatory deficit reduction plan. Finally, when Republicans agreed that half the automatic cuts would come from defense, a final agreement was reached. Expressing some misgivings, President Reagan signed the bill.

Gramm-Rudman-Hollings established maximum allowable federal deficits over a five-year period: $172 billion for fiscal year 1986, $144 billion for fiscal year 1987, $108 billion for fiscal year 1988, $72 billion for fiscal year 1989, and $36 billion for fiscal year 1990. The budget was to be balanced in fiscal year 1991 and beyond. The act mandated that the president submit a budget with deficits that met the targets. It required that the Office of Management and Budget and the Congressional Budget Office issue estimates each August of the deficits for the coming year. If the deficits exceeded the targets, the General Accounting Office (GAO) would list the amounts that needed to be cut to reach the deficit targets. The president would then have to issue a sequestering order making mandatory cuts. Congress would have until 15 October to either raise taxes or cut spending to meet the target and avoid sequestration. Under the Gramm-Rudman-Hollings rules, the sequester would impose half of all cuts on defense and half on domestic spending. However, the law exempted many categories of spending, including Social Security, interest on the federal debt, Medicaid, food stamps, veterans' benefits, existing contracts, and several other welfare and child nutrition programs. Provisions of the mandatory plan could be waived only during war or a recession.

Gramm-Rudman-Hollings also revised the congressional budget process, accommodating the new deficit plan, advancing the timetable, and attempting to strengthen enforcement procedures. It advanced the date by which the president had to submit his budget to Congress, although this requirement was dropped two years later. It moved up the date for CBO reports, the views and estimates of standing committees, and the budget resolution, and it formally dropped the second budget resolution. Perhaps the most important changes were the 15 June deadline for reconciliation and the 30 June deadline for appropriations bills.

In addition, Gramm-Rudman-Hollings attempted to strengthen enforcement procedures. First, totals and subtotals in the budget were made binding rather than mere targets. Second, committees were given ten days to publish their internal allocation of outlays, budget authority, and entitlements among their subcommittees. Third, no legislation providing new spending authority could come to the House or Senate floor unless a budget resolution had been passed. Fourth, any resolution that exceeded the Gramm-Rudman-Hollings deficit targets would be ruled out of order. Fifth, any committee or subcommittee that exceeded its allocations was subject to a point of order on the floor. Finally, all waivers of these provisions in the Senate and most in the House needed a three-fifths majority to be granted.

The act appeared to expand the scope of the budget process and strengthen the power of the Budget committees and party leaders at the expense of the other spending committees. As in the past, however, members and committees would prove creative in avoiding the discipline imposed by the budget rules. Under the compromise that allowed the passage of Gramm-Rudman-Hollings, a limited sequester for fiscal year 1986—which was already in progress—was ordered in early 1986. When all exempt programs were removed from the calculations, only around 25 percent of outlays were subject to sequestration. Through a complex formulation, the cuts amounted to 4.9 percent in defense accounts and 4.3 percent in domestic accounts. Gramm-Rudman-Hollings affected congressional budgeting in other ways. In particular, the new rules meant that amendments to taxing or spending legislation had to be revenue neutral; that is, any tax reduction or spending increase had to be offset or would be ruled out of order. This in particular affected the procedures surrounding Senate consideration of the Tax Reform Act of 1986.

In December 1985, Congress made the most dramatic changes in its budgetary process in a decade.

The revised timetable proved impossible for Congress to meet as it struggled to reach the $144 billion deficit target for the fiscal year 1987 budget. In July 1986, the Supreme Court in *Bowsher v. Synar* struck down the mechanism that triggered automatic cuts. The Court ruled that because the GAO is an agent of Congress, it could not instruct the president to order sequestration without violating the constitutional doctrine of separation of powers. Nonetheless, both Republicans and Democrats in Congress agreed that it was essential to meet the deficit target. When Congress returned in August, CBO and OMB revealed that the deficit projections had suddenly gotten worse. The difficult cuts that had already been agreed to were now nearly $20 billion short of reaching the deficit target of

$144 billion. Members agreed, however, that sequestration must be avoided at all costs.

To meet the target, the House and Senate used a variety of budgetary tricks and gimmicks to avoid across-the-board cuts. First, because Gramm-Rudman-Hollings allowed a $10 billion cushion, budgetmakers simply shot for $154 billion rather than $144 billion. Second, they used devices such as unrealistic economic assumptions, the proposed sale of government assets, and the elimination of an unspecified amount of government waste to reach the target. Even so, the process remained deadlocked through October, when an omnibus spending bill of $576 billion was enacted.

The experience of 1986 revealed some fundamental flaws in the Gramm-Rudman-Hollings process. Despite the new timetable, members would not know how big the deficit would be until August, which eliminated any incentives to make hard choices earlier in the year. Congress was chasing a moving target; most of the deficit increases between February and August stemmed from changes in the economy or technical errors in estimating revenues and outlays, not from the actions of Congress. As a result, Congress resorted to any expedient to get a short-term fix rather than the long-term solution to deficits that Gramm-Rudman-Hollings had promised. If it had not done so, the sequester would have had disastrous consequences on the outlays that were not exempt from cuts.

BALANCED BUDGET AND EMERGENCY DEFICIT CONTROL REAFFIRMATION ACT, 1987. Through 1986, Congress was unable to agree on how to fix the constitutional flaw in Gramm-Rudman-Hollings. In 1987, however, it enacted the Balanced Budget and Emergency Deficit Control Reaffirmation Act, dubbed Gramm-Rudman II, which gave the OMB rather than the GAO the power to order across-the-board cuts. It had become clear to members of both parties that the original deficit targets were unrealistic. Therefore, the date for balancing the budget was extended from 1991 to 1993, the targets were revised, and the ambitious timetable was relaxed. The new targets were as follows: $144 billion for fiscal year 1988, $136 billion for fiscal year 1989, $100 billion for fiscal year 1990, $64 billion for fiscal year 1991, $28 billion for fiscal year 1992, and a balanced budget thereafter. While mandatory cuts continued to be divided equally between defense and domestic programs, Gramm-Rudman II gave the president more flexibility in determining where cuts in defense could be made. In an attempt to reduce budget gimmickry, the revised law restricted what could be counted as savings and limited Congress's ability to use unrealistic economic assumptions in order to show deficit reduction. Gramm-Rudman II also disallowed items that increased outlays in future years, made it harder to waive the budget rules, and called for an experiment with biennial budgeting in certain agencies.

Abandonment of the original deficit targets only two years after they were adopted sent a negative signal to the financial markets about Congress's commitment to deficit reduction. On 19 October 1987, U.S. securities markets plunged, losing 23 percent of their value in a single day, the largest one-day drop in history. The crash had a chilling effect on Congress and the Reagan administration, and they agreed to meet in a summit to work out budget differences. In December 1987, an agreement covering fiscal years 1988 and 1989 was reached that was designed to meet the deficit targets through the beginning of the next administration.

Reacting to the eight years of partisan interbranch warfare over the budget, President George Bush promised a more constructive engagement with the Congress. In April 1989—the earliest that the two branches had reached such an accord—Bush and congressional leaders announced that they had come to tentative agreement on the budget for fiscal year 1990. Unfortunately, the agreement for the most part merely papered over lingering differences concerning taxes, social programs, and defense. By autumn, the agreement had unraveled as Congress and the president battled over the administration's proposal for a reduction in the capital gains tax. But the major budget crisis in the Bush administration would not occur until 1990, when once again the deficit targets were scrapped and yet another approach to congressional budgeting was adopted.

BUDGET SUMMIT AGREEMENT AND BUDGET ENFORCEMENT ACT, 1990. The path toward a balanced budget took a tortuous turn in 1990. In February; Bush submitted a budget for fiscal year 1991 that projected a deficit of $64 billion, which met the Gramm-Rudman II target. But six months later, an economic downturn, technical errors in forecasting revenues, and larger-than-anticipated outlays for a bailout of the savings and loan industry combined to leave the projected deficit near $250 billion. A sequester of nearly $200 million—which would gut more than 50 percent of domestic and defense discretionary spending—was unthinkable. Once again, the deficit targets would have to be scrapped and a new solution found.

On 30 September 1990, after five months of work, a summit composed of top congressional and White House leaders reached agreement on a five-year, $500 billion deficit reduction package and revised budget process. The plan both raised taxes and cut spending, with approximately one-third of the projected net savings from tax increases, one-third from defense cuts, and one-third from domestic spending cuts. Both sides compromised: Bush agreed to new taxes despite his "no new taxes" pledge during the 1988 presidential campaign, and congressional Democrats accepted large cuts in domestic programs such as Medicare. Both President Bush and Democratic leaders in Congress endorsed the plan, but restive members voted the measure down. Within weeks, however, a revised version encompassing most of the basic framework was adopted. The Omnibus Budget Reconciliation Act (OBRA) of 1990 not only was the largest deficit reduction package ever but also included a major revision of the congressional budget process in the Budget Enforcement Act (BEA).

The budget agreement embodied a number of important policy and procedural changes. Two of the most crucial were the suspension for three years of Gramm-Rudman-Hollings and the creation of separate appropriations caps for discretionary spending. Under Gramm-Rudman-Hollings, Congress had been held responsible for budget changes that were not of its own making. The new process eliminated fixed deficit targets and shifted the emphasis from deficit reduction to spending control, focusing on maintaining budgetary discipline in those areas where Congress actually has the power to determine how much taxes are raised and how much money is spent.

The Budget Enforcement Act divided discretionary appropriations into three categories with separate outlay and budget authority limits for fiscal years 1991 to 1993. For 1994 and 1995, the three discretionary caps were to be merged and a single discretionary appropriation cap imposed. The shares of domestic, defense, and international spending were fixed for three years; but in years four and five, trade-offs among the three components would be possible. The caps would be enforced by a new set of rules. Under Gramm-Rudman-Hollings, budget resolutions covered a single year, allowing spending increases and tax cuts to be shifted ahead. Under the Budget Enforcement Act, the resolutions cover five years and limits must be maintained for that period.

If any of the caps is exceeded, excess spending is eliminated by a minisequester within the offending category. For example, if international program spending should exceed allowable budget authority, an across-the-board cut would be assessed on all programs within the category. Before 1 July, the sequester takes place fifteen days after the cap is broken. After 1 July, a "look back" sequester is assessed in the next fiscal year. Under OBRA, the assumptions and targets were to be reassessed in early 1993. If the process was maintained as originally written in 1990, the Gramm-Rudman-Hollings process was to be reactivated to enforce the totals in 1994 and 1995.

The other major change in budget enforcement concerned the treatment of entitlements and revenues in the budget. Under the old system, a sequester of discretionary programs could be triggered by revenue shortfalls or increases in entitlement spending due to greater utilization or higher inflation. Under the Budget Enforcement Act, both revenues and entitlements were put on a pay-as-you-go basis. Any action to increase entitlement eligibility or reduce revenues had to be offset by spending cuts or tax increases elsewhere in the budget. These provisions affected the total of all legislation in a given year, not individual measures.

Increases in entitlement spending were to be compensated for by a sequester across certain entitlement categories. Reconciliation procedures were extended to revenues for the first time to enforce the pay-as-you-go rules. The Budget committees were given power to issue reconciliation instructions to the House Ways and Means or Senate Finance committees to mandate an offset for a revenue loss. Social Security was exempted from the pay-as-you-go requirement, and what the act called a "firewall" was created to protect the Social Security trust fund from legislation that would expand benefits or reduce payroll taxes.

Unlike appropriations caps, which focused on spending control, these entitlement provisions focused on deficit neutrality. Any discretionary or entitlement spending determined by both the president and Congress to be necessitated by an emergency was exempted from the requirement. In general, OBRA represented a dramatic change from past efforts to eliminate deficits because it retreated from fixed deficit targets. The deficit could increase because of economic changes, reestimation, or emergencies without triggering spending reductions. The revised process was more flexible and realistic than earlier efforts in its assertion of discipline over the aspects of budgeting that Congress actually controls: discretionary spending, entitlement expansion, and tax reductions.

The path toward a balanced budget took a tortuous turn in 1990.

Even with the critical changes in both policy and process that OBRA rendered, the deficit problem would not simply disappear. Despite the spending cuts and tax increases, the deficit increased in the early 1990s because of a recession, the savings and loan bailout, and spiraling Medicare and Medicaid costs. After Bill Clinton became president, projections showed that the deficits would remain in the range of $300 to $560 billion through the year 2000 without further policy changes. As a result, Clinton proposed a controversial five-year, $500 billion deficit reduction package in 1993. This suggests that Congress will continue to innovate and improvise with its budget procedures in an effort to find the means to assert fiscal discipline.

When the authorization-appropriations process was judged to be inadequate, Congress embarked on a quest to develop a budget process that could serve both the needs of individual members to serve their constituencies and the duty of Congress as a whole to set responsible national policy. The growth of entitlements and other inflexible mandatory spending and the decline of discretionary spending helped change the very nature of budgeting. In 1974, legislators developed a system intended to provide greater overall coordination and control and to allow Congress to compete more effectively with the president. Some wanted the budget process to restrain spending, but others wanted it to reallocate or rationalize greater spending. With the onset of chronic deficits and the recurring deadlock between congressional Democrats and the White House, the process was oriented almost exclusively to spending restraint and deficit reduction. Yet this did not reduce the members' interest in pursuing various policy goals and protecting pet programs and projects.

Scholars and observers have come to different conclusions about the performance of the congressional budget process. Some argue that it has been an unmitigated disaster that has failed to deal constructively with budget deficits. They criticize devices such as Gramm-Rudman-Hollings for making mindless cuts and restricting the options of both Congress and the president. Some see the instability and improvisational nature of the congressional budget process as a sign of weakness.

Yet many of the criticisms are based on unrealistic expectations of the process. In some ways, Congress has made extraordinary changes. It has emerged with stronger leadership and more centralized policy-making mechanisms. It is better equipped to compete with the president when priorities collide or to cooperate when priorities coincide. Reconciliation has proved to be a potent weapon in shaping the budget. Despite the repeated failure to reduce deficits, in 1982, 1987, 1990, and other years Congress made many hard, responsible choices that prevented the deficits from being significantly larger than they might have grown to be.

Congress's budgeting-performance problems are more a reflection of underlying conflicts in national government than of an inherent institutional inability to manage the budget effectively. The congressional budget process has been so unstable in part because of the divergent policy preferences of legislative and executive branches and the partisanship that has often dominated their relationship. Rules, procedures, and processes play an important role in shaping the context of congressional behavior and in influencing policy outcomes, but they cannot on their own resolve fundamental political and ideological conflicts.

[See also (I) Congressional Budget Office, General Accounting Office; (II) Budget Policy.]

BIBLIOGRAPHY

Gilmour, John B. *Reconcilable Differences? Congress, the Budget Process, and the Deficit.* 1990.

Haas, Lawrence J. *Running on Empty: Bush, Congress, and the Politics of a Bankrupt Government.* 1990.

Ippolito, Dennis. *Congressional Spending.* 1981.

Kettl, Donald E. *Deficit Politics: Public Budgeting in Its Institutional and Historical Context.* 1992.

LeLoup, Lance T. *The Fiscal Congress: Legislative Control of the Budget.* 1980.

Makin, John H., Norman J. Ornstein, and David Zlowe, eds. *Balancing Act: Debt, Deficit, and Taxes.* 1990.

Mills, Gregory B., and John Palmer. *Federal Budget Policy in the 1980s.* 1984.

Penner, Rudolph G., and Alan J. Abramson. *Broken Purse Strings: Congressional Budgeting, 1974—88.* 1988.

Savage, James D. *Balanced Budgets and American Politics,* 1988.

Schick, Allen. *The Capacity to Budget.* 1990.

Schick, Allen. *Congress and Money.* 1980.

White, Joseph, and Aaron Wildavsky. *The Deficit and the Public Interest: The Search for Responsible Budgeting in the 1980s.* 1989.

– LANCE T. LELOUP

BUREAUCRACY

One of the clearest of all clauses in the U.S. Constitution is the provision in Article II, section 1 that states with stark simplicity that "executive power shall be vested in a President of the United States." In awarding the president such preeminent authority over an executive branch that would in time become a vast and complex bureaucratic establishment with authority extending throughout the land, the Framers of the Constitution rejected a variety of proposals that would have required the chief executive to share that power with other government officials. They feared that dispersion of executive authority would weaken both the presidential office and the ability of the public to hold all government officials accountable for their decisions.

But even as the Framers were giving the president this exclusive title to executive authority, they also granted Congress the right to establish and empower all the agencies that might thereafter lie within the domain of the executive branch, along with the ability to determine how much financial support they would receive to carry out the tasks they might be assigned.

Here indeed was a prime example not of the separation of powers for which the Constitution is so famous, but of what Richard Neustadt was later to describe in *Presidential Power* (1992) as "separate institutions sharing power." Under the terms of the written Constitution, executive officials high and low would have to defer to the president as the head of their sphere of government, but Congress rather than the chief executive would ultimately determine both the scope of their power and the extent of their resources.

Over the years, both the president and Congress have sought an advantageous answer to the question inherent in the design of the Constitution: Whose executive branch is this, anyway? For its part, Congress has used the authority granted it to define the duties of each agency in the executive branch and to spell out in what is sometimes seen as excruciating detail how the agency should carry out its responsibilities. The legislature has done so both by statute and through a variety of informal ways for communicating its preferences and priorities to the bureaucracy.

Historical Development

Very early in American history, attempts were made to stake out the claim that Congress rather than the president had lawful authority to issue commands to at least some agencies in the executive branch. During the presidency of Andrew Jackson, for example, Whig party leaders argued that the national legislature had legal authority over the affairs of the Treasury Department, since Treasury, unlike the Department of State, did not perform functions that were inherently executive in character but derived its role in government from its responsibility for handling congressional appropriations.

These Whigs argued that the right to provide such appropriations was a central feature of the authority granted Congress under the Constitution, as well as a fiscal responsibility that historically had been at the heart of all legislative power. Consequently, it would be entirely proper for the secretary of the Treasury to take his instructions on the disposition of government funds from Congress rather than the president.

CONGRESSIONAL DOMINATION OF THE BUREAUCRACY. The president's legislative opponents could draw some support for their position from the decisions Congress made at the beginning of the Republic when it established executive departments. At that time, as Lloyd Short put it (*The Development of National Administrative Organization in the United States,* 1923), the

> secretaries of War and Foreign Affairs were made solely responsible and subordinate to the President, and only a general indication was made as to the scope of their duties. On the contrary, the Secretary of the Treasury, although he was also responsible to the President, was more minutely controlled and directed in the discharge of the specific duties assigned to him by Congress. (p. 100)

This attempt to wrest control over the Treasury Department from the president did not succeed. Jackson simply removed the Treasury secretary who had complied with the legislature and replaced him with an official who would submit to his control. Disputes over the proper extent of Congress's role in such matters as the appointment and removal of executive officials continued to surface, however. President Andrew Johnson's defiance of congressional restrictions on his appointment power brought him to the brink of impeachment in the years immediately following the Civil War.

But while Johnson was able to dodge the legislative bullet in his impeachment trial, the bureaucracy was not. As Richard M. Pious has noted (*The American Presidency,* 1979):

> By the time the House voted its impeachment, control of the departments already rested in the hands of congressional leaders. They instituted a system of congressional supremacy, involving a close connection between department secretaries and committee chairs, which remained in effect for the remainder of the century. . . . Woodrow Wilson made his academic reputation as a political scientist with a description of how congressional committees controlled departments, and urged adoption of cabinet government to bring order out of the chaos the rival committees had created. (p. 74)

Thus, in the nineteenth and early twentieth centuries, the chief impact of congressional involvement in the affairs of the bureaucracy was to decentralize power within the executive branch, with each of its major segments coming under the strong influence of a different set of legislative masters. In this way, the executive power that the Constitution had so carefully centered in the presidency was eventually spread among many hands. Agency executives found that their success in Washington depended less on staying on good terms with the White House than on their ability to get along well with Congress. While the Framers had sought to create unity within the executive through their provisions on presidential power, they had sown the seeds of disunity through the equally important clauses they included on legislative power.

Congress thus became a dominant presence in the lives of executive agencies very early on in U.S. history through its ability to define agency missions and to measure out agency appropriations. As it developed an elaborate committee structure, Congress also acquired the capacity to keep itself better informed on how well its instructions were being carried out, a process that eventually came to be known as congressional oversight of the bureaucracy.

Throughout U.S. history, Congress exercised enormous influence over what is now called "state-building," an area of research in which Stephen Skowronek has pioneered (1982). Over the years Congress has approved the establishment of a variety of bureaucratic organizations designed to give the American state the muscle needed to handle an expanding set of responsibilities.

The legislature has been criticized for the slowness with which it acted, but the most remarkable aspect of congressional involvement in state-building is the extent to which it served to keep the character of American bureaucracy in tune with the democratic character of the country. The establishment of organizations such as the Agriculture, Commerce, and Labor departments occurred not as a result of needs originated or defined in highly placed government circles, as might ordinarily be expected in Europe, but in response to pressures from within American society itself.

The Department of Labor, for example, was born in 1913, before the national government itself had assumed any significant responsibilities in this field (Francis E. Rourke, "The Department of Labor and the Trade Unions," *Western Political Quarterly* 7 [1954]: 656–672). Like the departments of Agriculture and Commerce (and later Veterans' Affairs and Housing and Urban Development), Labor was a department created to assure a significant sector of the population that it too had a voice in the affairs of government. Thus, "creating a bureaucracy that looks like America" is one of the major legislative contributions to state-building in the United States.

CONGRESS VERSUS THE PRESIDENT. Inevitably, the performance of each of these roles brought Congress into conflict with the White House, as neither was able to resist the invitation the Constitution had issued to vie for control over the bureaucracy. But it is important to note that, while the efforts of the rival branches of government to manage the affairs of executive bureaucracies did produce conflict, such efforts also led to a great deal of constructive constitutional innovation. This occurred as these separate institutions searched for political compromises to reconcile their conflicting legal authority over the operation of the national government's executive machinery.

As a result, the struggle for control over bureaucracy has been a powerful force for change in the way in which both the presidency and Congress now function. Because it is a written document, the Constitution has sometimes had the appearance of a fundamental law that is highly resistant—if not totally impervious—to change. In the case of the congressional relationship with the bureaucracy, however, the record suggests that the Constitution can also be viewed as a set of governing arrangements that have largely been invented as the country's history unfolded. In this area of governmental operations, the Constitution has revealed its great flexibility and capacity for adaptation.

Over the years, both the president and Congress have sought an advantageous answer to the question: Whose executive branch is this, anyway?

Executive Privilege. For example, U.S. presidents have always insisted that they alone have the ultimate right to determine whether information in the hands of executive officials should be released beyond the executive branch when, in their view, such disclosure might adversely affect vital national interests or the effective operation of the executive branch. The validity of this claim of executive privilege to withhold information from Congress was challenged at the very beginning of the Republic when President George Washington sought to withhold information about an unsuccessful military expedition against the Indians and about the negotiations preceding a peace treaty with Great Britain. Here Washington eventually compromised, supplying Congress information it requested on the military expedition but denying access to executive records on treaty negotiations.

Presidential assertion of executive privilege continued to plague the relationship between legislative committees and the chief executive. Not until the presidency of Richard M. Nixon was the legal issue finally resolved when in 1974 the Supreme Court held, in *United States v. Nixon,* that presidents did indeed enjoy such a privilege, although in this dispute Nixon's own claims of prerogative were disallowed.

The Court's decision in the *Nixon* case did not, however, alter the long-standing preference of Congress and the White House for negotiating a political solution to the legal conflicts that arose whenever the legislature sought access to information that an executive-branch organization refused to disclose. These legal disputes have customarily been settled by political bargains. Usually, the information requested by Congress is eventually released, with executive officials perhaps deleting particularly sensitive material. Too, access to the material is frequently confined to those legislators with an unmistakable "need to know."

Shaping Structural Change in the Bureaucracy. Such constitutional innovation has also been necessary when changes in the organizational structure of the bureaucracy are contemplated. For a very long time, decisions regarding structural change were shaped almost entirely by congressional statutes. This led to a great deal of organizational rigidity within the executive branch. Presidents who wanted to shift programs from one agency to another or otherwise to alter patterns of authority within their executive household usually had to persuade Congress to pass laws permitting such changes. These statutes were difficult to enact, since the agencies affected could easily rally the groups they served or their supporters in Congress to block such reorganizations. Legislative opponents of reorganization feared that it could shrink their influence over agency policies from which they or their constituents benefited.

So from the 1930s to the 1990s, the two branches of government made frequent use of a mutually satisfactory arrangement. By statutory enactment, modern presidents have generally been given the right to reorganize the executive branch at their own initiative, but their reorganization plans go into effect only if, within a specified period of time, the legislature has not chosen to pass a resolution vetoing the change. It was here that the legislative veto first came into prominent use as a means of breaking deadlocks between Congress and the president.

This legislative veto system puts the burden on the opposition to defeat the president's plans rather than requiring the White House to overcome the roadblocks in congressional procedures that ordinarily impede new legislation. Indeed, the obstacles posed by congressional procedures increase the likelihood that the president's reorganization plans will go into effect, since the legislative veto system converts them into impediments that opponents of reorganization (rather than its supporters) must surmount. As Peri E. Arnold has shown in *Making the Managerial Presidency: Comprehensive Reorganization Planning, 1905–1980* (1986), a great deal of executive reorganization has been accomplished as a result of this arrangement, under which, in contrast to the ordinary constitutional process, Congress exercises the power of veto.

The Role of Partisanship. It can therefore fairly be said that cooperation has characterized the various efforts by Congress and the White House to control the development and operation of American bureaucracy as often as has conflict. The compromises that have emerged are generally the product of a willingness of members of both political parties in Congress to modify what are often deemed to be its institutional prerogatives in order to produce some desired result. Conflict, on the other hand, is often rooted in the jockeying for partisan or ideological advantage that is an inevitable feature of legislative life. Congressional Democrats and Republicans alike have usually been inclined to allow the White House much more leeway in running the bureaucracy when a member of their party is president.

Thus, in the 1960s, congressional Democrats who had been highly critical of administrative secrecy within the executive branch while Republican Dwight D. Eisenhower held the presidency became strangely quiet about this issue when Democrat John F. Kennedy moved into the White House. Through most of the 1970s and 1980s, Republicans in Congress were highly supportive of grants of extensive discretion to executive agencies as their party began to win presidential elections with great regularity, reversing their strong opposition to this practice during the long period of Democratic ascendancy.

The divided government that emerged in the 1950s and generated growing conflict in the 1980s tended to heighten competition between Congress and the president for control over the bureaucracy. The Democrats, who held a majority in both houses of Congress during much of this period, were highly supportive of measures designed either to narrow the power of bureaucrats or to enhance the ability of the courts and groups outside government to challenge the decisions of executive agencies. These steps were triggered by Democratic fears that Republican presidents had saturated the bureaucracy with political appointees who were shifting agency policies in directions Congress never intended to go.

On the other hand, Republicans in the White House or at the head of executive agencies in this era of divided government were no less outspoken in their criticism of what they regarded as the efforts of Democratic legislators to micromanage administrative decisions. Their heaviest fire was directed at legislative efforts to intervene in foreign policy decisions that they viewed as entirely within the president's constitutional authority.

Congressional Acquiescence. Political combat has not been the only factor shaping the relationship between Congress and bureaucracy in modern times. As *United States v. Nixon* suggests, Supreme Court rulings have also had a major impact. In 1935, the Court handed down a decision in *Humphrey's Executor v. the United States* that effectively carved out a sphere of autonomy for the various independent regulatory agencies that had been created by Congress to prevent the abuse of economic power in broad sectors of the American society, beginning with the establishment of the Interstate Commerce Commission in 1887. In this case, the Court decided that these agencies administered functions that were not truly executive responsibilities but were, in the justices' view, quasi-legislative or quasi-judicial in character.

Cooperation has characterized the efforts by Congress and the White House to control the development and operation of American bureaucracy as often as has conflict.

As a result of this ruling, independent regulatory commissions were entitled to greater immunity from presidential control and subjected to a larger degree of congressional supervision than other organizations within the bureaucracy. In *Humphrey's Executor,* the Court upheld a congressional statute that set limits on the president's right to remove the chief officials of a regulatory agency, although the Court had previously ruled that, as chief executive, the president enjoyed an unlimited power to fire heads of executive organizations.

The *Humphrey's Executor* decision, however, can be regarded as part of a losing effort that was mounted in the 1930s to hold back the tide of growing presidential ascendancy within the executive branch. This effort was visible also in a 1939 Brookings Institution study that reflected the views of conservatives in Congress. It argued that "the departments and agencies constituted an administrative branch set up by acts of Congress and were therefore under the Congress rather than the President" (Don K. Price, *America's Unwritten Constitution,* 1983, p. 125). However, Congress eventually took its cue from the President's Committee on Administrative Management (which reported to Franklin D. Roosevelt in 1937) rather than from the Brookings Institution study, and in 1939 it approved a set of reorganization proposals that greatly strengthened presidential authority over the bureaucracy.

Thus, neither Supreme Court decisions nor isolated pockets of congressional resistance could prevent the onset of change in the New Deal era. As the number and power of federal agencies swelled, it became apparent in Congress and elsewhere that an increasingly complicated executive structure needed some kind of centralized, hierarchical direction and control and that such management could only come from the White House. In the end, therefore, presidential ascendancy within the executive branch came about with congressional acquiescence as the need for greater efficiency, effectiveness, and economy in the executive branch's operation became a matter of urgent necessity for legislative as well as executive officials.

BICAMERALISM. Another way in which the Constitution has affected the congressional relationship with the bureaucracy is the division of legislative power between the House and the Senate. This bicameral arrangement has had some negative consequences for bureaucracy, since it subjects executive agencies to a kind of double jeopardy. Agencies' policies and activities must pass muster with both houses of the legislature—both powerful and often very different. This situation is without parallel in other highly industrialized societies. But the bicameral system has also had one positive aspect for bureaucracy: it has enabled executive agencies to win reversals in one chamber of unfavorable decisions in the other.

Congressional Committees as Channels of Interaction

The relationship between Congress and the bureaucracy is primarily an encounter between individual executive agencies and the small number of legislative committees with which these organizations are obliged to interact. It is to such committees that both the House and the Senate ordinarily delegate the cutting edge of their legislative power, and it is only with them that agencies are required to have an ongoing connection.

The interests of executive agencies and the congressional committees with which they deal can be seen as either conflicting or converging. The conventional image of the relationship is one of confrontation. Framed by the traditional view of the Congress as the overseer of the bureaucracy, this view sees legislative committees as subjecting the executive agencies under their jurisdiction to vigorous and unrelenting scrutiny to determine how well or poorly they are carrying out their assigned duties.

Many studies of the legislative-bureaucratic relationship have drawn a quite different picture, however. Consensus rather than conflict is perceived to prevail as each party discovers that the other can generously serve its interests in many ways. The easiest and safest conclusion to draw from these contrasting images of the tie between Congress and the bureaucracy is that, as with many other relationships in human affairs, it can generate conflict while also providing comfort for the parties involved.

ADVERSARIAL RELATIONS WITH CONGRESS. The image of the relationship as adversarial is prominent in studies of Congress that focus on its ability to cut agency appropriations, strip executive organizations of major programs, or threaten agencies with reprisals unless they make major changes in their policies. This image of conflict is also prominent in studies of the Senate's use of its confirmation power. While Senate committees often appear willing to give routine approval to a president's nominees, the confirmation power can be used as a potent instrument of congressional control over bureaucracy. It enables the legislature to send strong signals to a newly appointed agency executive of its dissatisfaction with an organization's past performance.

SYMBIOSIS WITH CONGRESS. There is strong support in both the political arena and academic analysis, however, for the view that the interests of Congress and the bureaucracy more often converge than conflict. Public interest groups have led the way in criticizing what they perceive as the indulgent attitude of congressional committees toward the programs and activities of executive organizations. Witness the heavy fire directed at congressional intelligence committees with jurisdiction over the activities of the Central Intelligence Agency when it was revealed in the post-Vietnam years that they had often failed to detect or censure questionable CIA activities.

Academic studies of congressional behavior lend strong support to the view that the interests of Congress and the bureaucracy dovetail more often than they conflict. For example, Morris Fiorina's analysis of the bureaucratic-legislative relationship describes the connection between the two institutions as a cozy partnership from which each party derives substantial benefits (*Congress: Keystone of the Washington Establishment,* 2d ed., 1989).

According to Fiorina, this partnership provides members of Congress with the opportunity to gain political favor in their own districts by helping voters obtain information or benefits they need from executive agencies. It also allows legislators to intervene in their constituents' behalf with agencies that are imposing regulations that voters find objectionable. Such favors enable members to build coalitions of support within their own constituencies that transcend party lines and so to convert their districts into safe seats.

The bureaucracy benefits from this partnership as well, since members of Congress inevitably develop a vested interest in maintaining the health of executive organizations whose activities provide them with so many opportunities to serve their constituencies. In the modern U.S. administrative state, the hand of bureaucracy is everywhere, and, as Fiorina notes, "The more decisions the bureaucracy has an opportunity to make, the more opportunities there are for the congressman to build up credits" (p. 46).

Fiorina was by no means the first observer to note the presence of such symbiosis in the relationship between Congress and the bureaucracy. A number of earlier studies of policy-making in the United States highlighted how executive agencies and legislative committees could enter into alliances in the pursuit of common interests. Arthur Maass's *Muddy Waters* (1951), a study of the relationship between the U.S. Army Corps of Engineers and the House and Senate Public Works committees, was a pioneer investigation of how an executive agency and the committees that were expected to patrol its activities could instead organize into a mutual benefit society.

The Iron Triangle. In *The Political Process: Executive Bureau–Legislative Committee Relations* (1965), J. Leiper Freeman generalized this relationship into a model of policy-making designed to apply throughout the entire political system. He argued that executive agencies responsible for running particular government programs commonly forged close ties with both the legislative committee responsible for enacting the statutes on which their authority rested and the clientele groups served by their programs and policies. This "iron triangle" or "subgovernment" model of U.S. policy-making ultimately became (with some fine-tuning over the years) the dominant paradigm for explaining the way government policy is shaped in modern American democracy.

Each segment of the triangle, or subgovernment, is expected to serve its own interests by supporting the goals of both other participants in the policy-making system. The most salient characteristic of such an alliance is the fact that it is a closed system of decision making. Members of Congress not on the committee included in the triangle and segments of the population not part of the agency's clientele are excluded from effective participation in policy decisions in the many policy-making areas in which subgovernments have long held the reins of power.

THE EVOLUTION OF LEGISLATIVE-BUREAUCRATIC RELATIONSHIPS. There are thus two competing views of the relationship between Congress and the bureaucracy: one that sees their interests as diverging and another that sees them as converging. But it must be remembered that what is perceived may depend on the vantage point. White House officials who have difficulty imposing their policy preferences on an executive agency may come to view it as being in cahoots with the legislative committees with which it deals even as officials at that same agency may see those committees as trying to impose detailed and misguided controls over their organization's programs.

It should also be noted that the relationships between executive agencies and legislative committees are far from static. Developments in the environment in which they operate exert constant pressure for change in these relationships as in other aspects of the political system. For a number of reasons, for example, it has become increasingly difficult for both the committees and the agencies to prevent "outsiders" from invading the enclaves of public policy over which they maintained such close and exclusive control in the heyday of the iron triangle system.

For one thing, a proliferation of subcommittees is now characteristic of congressional organization as a result of various efforts the legislature has made to reform its operation since World War II. By reducing the number of committees, these reforms spawned an increasing number of subcommittees and provided additional points of entry through which legislators not part of traditional iron triangles could gain a voice in areas of policy-making over which subgovernment cartels once held exclusive power. By the early 1970s, as Steven S. Smith and Christopher J. Deering point out (*Committees in Congress,* 1990), "Few members considered deference to committee recommendations a viable norm" (p. 180). Moreover, by the 1980s a new vehicle for the expression of dissenting opinion had emerged in Congress: the special interest caucus. Made up of legislators who seek to promote the interests of a single group or region of the country, more than a hundred of these congressional caucuses seek to enact legislation or to tilt government agencies toward actions or decisions favorable to their constituencies.

The domination of policy formulation by iron triangles has also been weakened by another development. Today, executive agency jurisdictions increasingly overlap, with the external effects of one agency's decisions reverberating in other policy settings. Environmental groups, for example, have shown growing interest in the activities of a great many executive agencies other than those specifically concerned with environmental affairs. When these groups suspect that a government construction project will have an adverse impact on the environment, the responsible agency may suddenly discover that a new set of environmentally conscious legislators has become very interested in its activities and that these legislators are not at all reluctant to launch strong attacks on the agency. As a result, a once-harmonious relationship between an executive agency and its congressional network begins to show increasing signs of friction.

Morris Fiorina's analysis of the bureaucratic-legislative relationship describes the connection between the two institutions as a cozy partnership from which each derives substantial benefits.

Activist groups in other policy areas, such as civil rights and consumer issues, have also opened opportunities for greater participation in systems of policymaking previously closed to outsiders. The net effect of these various aspects of "movement politics" has thus been to make the relations between legislative committees and executive agencies much less predictable. When the National Endowment for the Arts was charged in the late 1980s and early 1990s with having provided financial support for "pornography," its activities, which had formerly been of interest only to the appropriate specialized committees, suddenly caught the attention of every member of Congress.

One major effect of these changes is that agency executives in the 1990s often discover that it is not enough to be working diligently toward the achievement of their organizations' programmatic goals, such as transportation or public works. To avoid criticism and possible retaliation from Congress, they must now be able to show that their agencies work out of buildings that provide easy access for the handicapped, avoid projects that will have an adverse impact on the environment, and otherwise comport themselves in ways that meet the expectations of the activist movements across the political spectrum that have become so conspicuous a feature of contemporary American political life.

It is, however, much too early to say that the iron triangle is a spent force. Symbiosis still characterizes the relationship between agencies and committees. Agencies cannot survive or prosper without the support they receive from the legislative committees concerned with their affairs. Nor can members of Congress ignore the fact that these agencies commonly provide services that are highly prized by their many constituents or can impose restrictions that will anger voters in their districts.

It thus becomes difficult for Congress or its committees to penalize a bureaucratic organization without imposing burdens on the voters on whom the legislators depend for reelection. Aware of this fact, agencies have become quite adept at making it more difficult for legislators to impose sanctions on them. For instance, agencies may respond, or threaten to respond, to cuts in appropriations by eliminating or cutting back on services that are especially cherished or badly needed by constituents in a great many congressional districts. Thus, Congress and the bureaucracy are bound together not only by the favors they exchange but also by the reprisals they can visit on one another.

The Growth of Congressional Staff

Also of great importance to legislative-bureaucratic relationships has been the proliferation of expertise throughout the political system on a growing number of subjects for which executive agencies are now charged with responsibility. Congress is one of the chief beneficiaries of this diffusion of expertise. Highly skilled professional staff organizations now serve all members, and legislative committees and many congressional offices have acquired their own stables of experts. These developments have greatly enhanced the ability of Congress to second-guess the decisions and policies of executive agencies. To be sure, the system of committee government already described has for a long time generated a great deal of legislative expertise, and participation in the work of such committees has allowed many members to acquire specialized knowledge.

Hugh Heclo has suggested that the term *issue network* describes the setting in which government policies are now forged better than does the traditional notion of the iron triangle. But, according to Heclo, participation in such a network is only open to those who are qualified by virtue of their expertise to discuss the policy issues salient to the network. To hold its own in this new setting, Congress has had to upgrade its own professional capacities. This development has led Lawrence C. Dodd to describe the modern Congress as a technocracy in which power has come increasingly to be centered in the hands of "technical experts" (Richard A. Harris and Sidney M. Milkis, eds., *Remaking American Politics,* 1989, pp. 89–111).

The growth in the size and skill of its professional staff has had a number of effects on Congress's relationship with the bureaucracy. It has saved legislators from having to deal with executive officials who are better informed than they on the finer points of policy issues. Closing the expertise gap has created a more level playing field in the policy debate that often characterizes the relationship between Congress and the executive branch.

The presence of a professional staff has also given Congress a much greater capacity for continuity in its involvement in the affairs of executive agencies. Staff members have both the time and knowledge to track decision making within the executive branch much more closely than can the members of Congress for whom they work, since the legislators must focus so much of their attention on getting reelected.

Mathew D. McCubbins and Thomas Schwartz have made the persuasive argument that Congress can pursue two strategies in overseeing the work of executive agencies ("Congressional Oversight Overlooked: Police Patrols Versus Fire Alarms," *American Journal of Political Science* 2 [1984]: 165–179). The first is a continuous process of legislative surveillance that they describe as a "police patrol" system. Under this arrangement, Congress undertakes to keep itself continuously informed on how well executive agencies are performing the various tasks that the legislature has given them. The other strategy open to the legislature is a system of "fire alarm" oversight. Congress leaves it to others, including the courts and various groups affected by an agency's decisions, to patrol each organization's activities on an ongoing basis. The legislature intervenes only when these other oversight mechanisms prove inadequate.

McCubbins and Schwartz conclude that, in view of various factors that limit their time and attention, legislators cannot police every executive agency and that fire-alarm oversight is therefore a rational option for them. But it can also be argued that the growth of legislative staff allows Congress to follow both strategies simultaneously. Members can confine themselves to dealing with the infrequent crises that trigger "fire alarms," while the legislative staff patrols the activities of executive agencies in an ongoing way.

Lawrence C. Dodd describes the modern Congress as a technocracy in which power has come increasingly to be centered in the hands of "technical experts."

Its ability to draw on the resources of a professional staff provides Congress with another asset as well: the legislature can look ahead and anticipate policy issues that may not yet have appeared on the congressional agenda. The Office of Technology Assessment (OTA) now plays this role for Congress. Fire-alarm oversight allows the legislature to become involved in policy problems only after they have assumed major proportions; OTA's expertise permits Congress to anticipate some fires beforehand. Of course, given the number of immediate issues that crowd the everyday congressional agenda, problems that are on the horizon always face an uphill struggle for legislative attention.

Finally, it should be noted that the steady expansion in the size and functions of legislative staff is one of the chief ways in which Congress has responded to the emergence of the national bureaucracy as a major force in the American political system. The United States was the last of the major industrial powers to accept the necessity of such a bureaucratic establishment. One "exceptional" feature of its political institutions—in which Americans long took great pride—was the fact that bureaucracy played a very small role in the national government. But a national bureaucracy came to Washington with a vengeance in the middle of the twentieth century. Its arrival forced both the executive and Congress to bureaucratize themselves in order to cope with the presence and the power of what soon came to be called a fourth branch of government. Beginning in the 1930s, a complex staff structure employing highly skilled professionals began to evolve in and around the White House, and Congress has since followed suit by spawning its own wide-ranging legislative staff system.

It used to be said in the Progressive era that the cure for the ills of democracy was more democracy. In the 1990s the United States confronts the irony that the cure for the ills of bureaucracy seems to be more bureaucracy in both the presidency and Congress.

[See also (I) Bicameralism, Oversight; (II) Executive Power, Executive Privilege.]

BIBLIOGRAPHY

Aberbach, Joel D. *Keeping a Watchful Eye: The Politics of Congressional Oversight.* 1990.

Davidson, Roger H., and Walter J. Oleszek. *Congress and Its Members.* 1981.

Dodd, Lawrence C., and Richard L. Schott. *Congress and the Administrative State.* 1979.

Fisher, Louis. *The Politics of Shared Power: Congress and the Executive.* 1987.

Foreman, Christopher H., Jr. *Signals from the Hill: Congressional Oversight and the Challenge of Social Regulation.* 1988.

Harris, Joseph P. *Congressional Control of Administration.* 1964.

Maass, Arthur. *Congress and the Common Good.* 1983.

Malbin, Michael J. *Unelected Representatives: Congressional Staff and the Future of Representative Government.* 1980.

Ogul, Morris. *Congress Oversees the Bureaucracy: Studies in Legislative Supervision.* 1976.

Rourke, Francis E. *Bureaucracy, Politics, and Public Policy.* 1984.

Skowronek, Stephen. *Building a New American State: The Expansion of National Administrative Capacities, 1877–1920.* 1982.

– FRANCIS E. ROURKE

C

CALENDARS

A chamber's calendar is essentially a list of the matters available for floor consideration; procedurally, to say a measure is "on the calendar" is to say that it is available for consideration. (Most measures reach this status by being reported from committee.) Such lists are printed daily for each chamber when in session. Committees also publish calendars, but usually in only two editions per Congress. The Senate Calendar lists only pending matters, but the House Calendar and those of most committees are cumulative and contain indexes and legislative histories of measures that have been on the calendar, making the final editions for each Congress valuable historical records.

House Calendar System

The House has five formal calendars: the House Calendar, the Union Calendar (also known as the Calendar of the Committee of the Whole House on the State of the Union), the Private Calendar (Calendar of the Committee of the Whole House), the Consent Calendar, and the Discharge Calendar (Calendar of Motions to Discharge Committees). Every measure reported is routinely placed on one of the first three.

This system reflects the House's establishment of separate procedures for considering different kinds of measures; each calendar carries measures governed by a distinct procedure. The heart of these distinctions is House Rule XXIII, clause 3, which provides that all matters "involving a . . . charge upon the people . . . be first considered in a Committee of the Whole." In the House, procedure in the Committee of the Whole is that which most fully secures the opportunity for amendment. Accordingly, this provision helps ensure the ability of the House to exercise the powers of the purse that the Constitution assigns it, as the institution of government whose members' short terms and (comparatively) small electorates tie it most closely to the people. Such a provision has been part of the rules since 1794.

Under this rule, not only tax measures but all measures appropriating funds or authorizing appropriations, as well as congressional budget resolutions, are to be considered in the Committee of the Whole and are accordingly, when reported, placed on its calendar, the Union Calendar. Private bills go to the Private Calendar. Measures falling into neither category may be considered "in the House, under the one-hour rule," and therefore go to the House Calendar.

Under House Rule XIII, clause 4, any member may have any bill on the House or Union Calendar placed on the Consent Calendar. On first and third Mondays, measures on this calendar are called up in order of their placement thereon. Any measure to which one member objects is postponed until the next call; if three members then object, the measure is stricken from this calendar. Each party appoints official objectors to monitor the Consent Calendar and to object to measures they find inappropriate thereunder. If no sufficient objection occurs at either stage, the measure is considered "in the House as in Committee of the Whole," a procedure permitting debate only under the five-minute rule. A measure pending on the Consent Calendar, or defeated when considered from that calendar, may still also be considered from its original calendar.

The Discharge Calendar, in order on second and fourth Mondays, contains only measures on which discharge petitions have received the requisite 218 signatures.

The original premise of the House calendar system was that measures on each calendar be in order at a specified time and be considered in order of their placement on that calendar. Because this system early showed itself too inflexible in handling major legislation, the House also developed the concept of privilege, which in this sense means a measure's right to consideration in preference over the otherwise prescribed order of business. Although the calendar on which a measure is placed indicates the procedure under which it may be considered, it can receive actual consideration only through obtaining privilege.

The rules distribute privilege among measures both by making certain calendars privileged on specified days and by making certain measures privileged over others on the same calendar. The Private, Consent, and Discharge calendars are privileged on specified days, and measures on these calendars come up in the order of their placement thereon. Among Union Calendar measures, general appropriations bills and measures under the Budget Act are privileged, as imperative legislation. Among those on the House Calendar, privilege extends to special rules, disciplinary resolutions, committee funding resolutions, and certain other housekeeping measures (House Rule XI, clause 4[a]). The committee reorganization of 1974–1975 abolished the privilege of several other categories of measure.

Certain other House procedures, which are also in order only on designated days, are sometimes called "calendars" as well. The "suspension calendar" is really just a list issued by the majority whip that announces which measures the leadership intends to call up by motions to suspend the rules, in order on Mondays and Tuesdays. The "District calendar" refers to measures that the Committee on the District of Columbia calls up pursuant to its privilege to do so on second and fourth Mondays. To be eligible for consideration on Calendar Wednesday, a measure must already be on the House or Union Calendar and cannot be otherwise privileged.

Since 1911, rules have required the daily printing of the House Calendar.

Measures belonging to no privileged category may obtain privilege in several ways. They may be called up on suspension, on the Consent Calendar, or on Calendar Wednesday. More significantly, a special rule, itself privileged, may grant privilege to the measure; this possibility underlies the key role of special rules in managing the House floor agenda.

DEVELOPMENT OF HOUSE CALENDARS. The House brought together the essentials of today's calendar system in its rules recodifications of 1880 and 1890, associated with Thomas B. Reed (R-Maine, Speaker 1889–1891 and 1895–1899). These rules, conceived with the objective of permitting the House "to go at once to any measure upon its calendars," consolidated control of the floor agenda by the Speaker, acting for the majority party.

At first, special orders granting privilege to otherwise nonprivileged measures were adopted by suspension of the rules (then in order only on first and third Mondays); only later did the Rules Committee begin reporting such resolutions as privileged. After 1890, a "Morning Hour" permitted committees in rotation to call up nonprivileged House Calendar measures. Although this provision persists today, it was soon vitiated by the continual intervention of more privileged business.

The House refined this system until the Speaker's virtually absolute control of access to the floor led to the 1910 "revolt" against Speaker Joseph G. Cannon (R-Ill.; Speaker 1903–1911). Reforms of 1909 instituted the Consent Calendar and Calendar Wednesday; the revolt itself resulted in the first discharge rule. The Consent Calendar was designed to permit members to secure consideration for bills of individual interest; Calendar Wednesday, which was modeled on the Morning Hour call of committees but given high privilege, was designed to allow committees to bring their measures to the floor. For securing consideration of otherwise nonprivileged measures, the use of both Calendar Wednesday and the Consent Calendar remained common through the 1920s, but declined thereafter, when Speaker Sam Rayburn (D-Tex.; Speaker 1940–1946, 1949–1952, 1955–1961) recentralized control of the floor. More recently, such measures have instead been increasingly considered under suspension of the rules, and in the 1970s the days on which that procedure is in order were increased.

THE PRINTED HOUSE CALENDAR. Since 1911, rules have required the daily printing of the House Calendar. It lists measures pending on each of the five formal calendars and provides legislative histories of the measures that have been on them, including short title, committee referral, calendar reported to, and subsequent actions, with dates. It also lists bills in conference and bills through conference, identifying conferees from both chambers. Lists indicate unfinished business and correlate measure numbers with private or public law numbers. Tables display dates of reporting and further action on key appropriations and other measures. Discharge petitions filed are listed, oddly, only in the index, under "Discharge."

The index to the House Calendar appears only on Mondays. Since 1988, the list of "Measures through Conference" and certain inactive legislative histories have also appeared only on Mondays. Since 1983 the calendar has also listed measures sequentially referred, and since 1979 a calendar in the everyday sense has displayed the days on which House sessions have occurred. The House Calendar no longer lists pending special orders (including special order speeches), committees called on Calendar Wednesdays, or titles of measures enacted into law or vetoed, as it formerly did.

Senate Calendar System

The Senate has not found it necessary to develop as elaborate a system of calendars as has the House, but it too arrived at the foundations of its present system in the late nineteenth century. A measure generally reaches the Senate floor, by motion or unanimous consent request that the Senate proceed to consider it, from a single Calendar of General Orders. Nominations and treaties submitted by the president for the advice and consent of the Senate are carried on separate calendars of executive business, however.

Ever since 1789, Senate rules have required one day's notice of introducing a bill and two readings before referral, on separate legislative days. Normally, measures are introduced, immediately read twice, and referred, all by unanimous consent. Under rules originating in 1877, however, if objection is raised after the second reading, the bill goes directly to the Calendar of General Orders.

Corresponding procedures apply to simple and concurrent resolutions, which the Senate normally either refers when submitted or considers immediately by unanimous consent. Under the procedures from 1877, though, any objection puts off consideration for one legislative day; the measure is then listed in the calendar as having been laid "Over, Under the Rule." It may then be laid before the Senate at a specified point in the Morning Hour that, under rules rooted in the recodifications of 1877 and 1884, is to begin each legislative day.

In the Morning Hour, after disposition of several categories of "morning business," the Calendar of General Orders is to be called, and measures not objected to are taken up under rules limiting each senator to five minutes' debate. This call may be interrupted, however, on any day except Monday by a nondebatable motion to consider some other measure. These Morning Hour procedures were still in active use at least into the 1950s and remain in the rules, but today the Morning Hour occurs only rarely and is used chiefly to make possible a nondebatable motion to consider some measure. This possibility is important because, outside the Morning Hour, a motion to proceed to consider a measure is normally debatable, and so can be filibustered.

The Senate reaches its executive business by a nondebatable motion to go into executive session. Executive or legislative matters to which no objection will be made may also be disposed of by routinized unanimous consent procedures.

PRINTED SENATE CALENDARS. The bulk of the printed Senate Calendar consists of the Calendar of General Orders, which gives measure numbers, sponsors, titles, committees of referral, senators reporting, and dates reported; a separate list correlates measure numbers with calendar numbers. Besides "Resolutions and Motions Over, Under the Rule" and "Bills and Joint Resolutions Read the First Time," the document also lists "Subjects on the Table," which are placed under this heading by unanimous consent and can come up by motion but not by calendar call. Also set forth are texts of unanimous consent agreements currently in effect that govern consideration of specific measures; "Bills in Conference," paralleling the list in the House Calendar; and "Motions for Reconsideration" entered but not yet acted on. Finally, there are lists of Senate and Senate committee members, a table of action on appropriation bills, and, nowadays, a literal calendar showing days on which the Senate has been in session. The document is not indexed, and few collected sets appear to exist.

The Senate's Executive Calendar, published separately, contains only lists of treaties and nominations reported and pending. It does not appear to be widely distributed.

PRINTED COMMITTEE CALENDARS. Most committees have published calendars since the 80th Congress (1947–1949), and a few published before then. These generally set forth committee membership, subcommittees, jurisdiction, and (sometimes) rules. The heart of a committee calendar is a list of measures referred, showing sponsors, official titles, and dates of action; these are often indexed by topic and by sponsor, and are sometimes supplemented with information about subcommittee referral or subsequent action.

Committee calendars also generally include lists of hearings held or printed and of reports and other committee documents published, sometimes cross-indexed to measures; lists of memorials, petitions, and executive communications received; and, in the Senate, lists of nominations received and action thereon. Some calendars list such additional matters as committee legislation enacted and measures over which the committee asserts jurisdiction. They may also summarize committee activities, legislation reported, or historical background, or they may set forth statistical summaries or excerpts from pertinent laws and executive orders.

[See also (I) Calendar Wednesday, Committee of the Whole, Discharge Rules, Five-Minute Rule, House of Representatives, article on Daily Sessions of the House.]

BIBLIOGRAPHY

Haynes, George H. *The Senate of the United States.* 1938. Pp. 339–379.

Oleszek, Walter J. *Congressional Procedures and the Policy Process.* 3d ed. 1989. Chaps. 5–8.

Riddick, Floyd M. *The United States Congress: Organization and Procedure.* 1949.

U.S. House of Representatives. *Cannon's Precedents of the House of Representatives of the United States,* by Clarence Cannon. 8 vols. 74th Cong., 1st sess., 1935. Vol. 6, chap. 210; vol. 7, chaps. 211–215; vol. 8, chaps. 237–241.

U.S. House of Representatives. *Deschler's Precedents of the United States House of Representatives,* by Lewis Deschler. 94th Cong., 2d sess., 1977. H. Doc. 94-661. Vol. 7, chap. 22, "Calendars."

U.S. House of Representatives. *Hinds' Precedents of the House of Representatives of the United States,* by Asher C. Hinds. 5 vols. 59th

Cong., 2d sess, 1907. Vol. 4, chaps. 87–89, 107–110; vol. 5, chap. 111.

U.S. Senate. *Riddick's Senate Procedure, Precedents, and Practices,* by Floyd M. Riddick and Alan S. Frumin. 101st Cong., 2d sess., 1992. S. Doc. 101-28. Pp. 253–267.

– RICHARD S. BETH

CALENDAR WEDNESDAY

The Calendar Wednesday procedure in the House of Representatives was adopted in 1909. Republican and Democratic progressives charged that the Speaker, then also the chairman of the Rules Committee, effectively blocked House floor action on bills reported from legislative committees. The Calendar Wednesday procedure was offered by Rep. John J. Fitzgerald (D-N.Y.) as a compromise aimed at opening up House procedures while preserving the Speaker's role in major legislation.

Under the current form of the rule (Rule XXIV, cl. 7), any bill on the House Calendar or the Union Calendar (lists of major public bills awaiting chamber action) may be called up for consideration on Wednesdays on a motion by the committee chairman or by a member of the committee authorized to do so. Committees are called alphabetically, and a committee not answering the call is passed over. After the House adjourns its Calendar Wednesday business, the call of committees begins the next time Calendar Wednesday occurs where it left off. Privileged measures, including general appropriations bills and rules from the Rules Committee, may not be called up through Calendar Wednesday.

Under the Calendar Wednesday procedures, bills on the Union Calendar must be considered in Committee of the Whole under the five-minute rule, with no more than two hours of general debate time. Matters on the House Calendar are considered under the one-hour rule. Calendar Wednesday can be set aside only by a two-thirds vote of the House or by unanimous consent. The Rules Committee is prohibited from reporting a rule that would directly or indirectly prevent action under Calendar Wednesday. Except in rare circumstances, Calendar Wednesday has not been proven to be a generally effective procedure for bringing bills to the floor.

[See also (I) Calendars.]

BIBLIOGRAPHY

Baker, John D. "The Character of the Congressional Revolution of 1910." *Journal of American History* 60 (December 1973): 679–691.

U.S. House of Representatives. *Constitution, Jefferson's Manual, and the Rules of the House of Representatives of the United States, 103d Congress.* Compiled by William Holmes Brown. 102d Cong., 2d sess., 1992. H. Doc. 102-405, Sec. 897.

– PAUL S. RUNDQUIST

CALL SYSTEM

A system of electronic bells and corresponding lights throughout the Capitol and in all the House and Senate office buildings is used to summon members to the floor when their presence is required. During a day of session, members must balance the need for their presence on the floor with competing demands from their committees, visiting constituents, and office staff. Televised floor proceedings, personal beepers, and portable telephones are used by many members to keep track of when they must go to the floor. Official notification, however, comes via a call system that is referred to by many names: bells and lights, legislative buzzers and signal lights, electric bell signals.

The call system sounds throughout the Capitol and the House and Senate office buildings. Simultaneously, a corresponding set of lights—usually in the shape of stars—is illuminated. The lights are either installed as part of a clock face or are mounted directly on the wall. While not every room in the Capitol complex contains them, most member offices and committee hearing rooms clearly display such lights.

Although frequently called "bells," the sound is more like that of an electronic buzzer. It is loud, intrusive, and is meant to interrupt the meetings, conversations, and phone calls that create the constant din of noise heard throughout the halls of Congress.

Prior to the introduction of electricity to the Capitol, pages and other employees were sent throughout the building to let members know they were needed on the floor. A direct-current bell system was first installed in the Capitol about 1891. In 1957, the then-new Dirksen Senate Office Building was the first to receive electronic clocks and buzzers. The call system throughout the Capitol complex has been modernized and upgraded several times since.

A system of electronic bells and lights throughout the Capitol and in all the House and Senate office buildings is used to summon members to the floor.

The call system uses different types of rings with different meanings. Each house of Congress employs a code unique to that chamber. Since the House and Senate officially share only one room in the Capitol, there is no chance that members will confuse the two separate codes; in the shared room the signal lights for the House are on the east side of the room, those for the Senate are on the west side.

Senate clock. With call lights. (Office of the Curator, U.S. Senate)

The signals used in the Senate and their meanings are as follows:

One long continuous ring indicates the Senate is convening.
One ring indicates a yea and nay vote.
Two rings indicate a quorum call.
Three rings indicate a call for the absentees.
Four rings indicate the adjournment or recess of that day's session.
Five rings indicate that seven and one-half minutes remain on a yea and nay vote.
Six rings indicate that morning business has concluded (if all lights are cut off), or that the Senate is in a short recess (if the lights remain on).

The signals used in the House are as follows:

One long continuous ring indicates the House is convening.
One ring indicates a teller vote.
One long continuous ring followed by three brief rings indicates a notice quorum call (terminated when 100 members appear on the floor.)
One long continuous ring indicates the termination of a notice quorum call.
Two rings indicate an electronic recorded vote.
Two rings followed by a pause followed by two rings indicate a manual roll-call vote.
Two rings followed by a pause followed by five rings indicate the first vote of a series of clustered votes postponed from earlier consideration.
Three rings indicate a recorded quorum call.
Three rings followed by a pause followed by three rings indicate a manual recorded quorum call.
Three rings followed by a pause followed by five rings indicate a quorum call in Committee of the Whole, to be immediately followed by a five-minute recorded vote.
Four rings indicate adjournment of the House.
Five rings indicate a five-minute electronic recorded vote.
Six rings indicate a recess of the House.
Twelve rings indicate a civil defense warning.

[See also (I) Quorum Call.]

BIBLIOGRAPHY

Bassett, Isaac. Papers. Office of the Curator of Arts and Antiquities, U.S. Senate, Washington, D.C. Unpublished memoirs of the nineteenth-century Senate.

Brown, Glenn. *History of the United States Capitol.* 1900. Repr. 1970.

U.S. House of Representatives. Committee on Public Buildings and Grounds. *Electric Lights and Call-Bells for House Wing, Rotunda and Tholus of the Capitol.* 50th Cong., 2d sess., 1889. H. Rept. 3699.

– ILONA B. NICKELS

CAMPAIGN FINANCING

Prior to 1972 the only restrictions on congressional campaign finance were the Tillman Act (1907) and the Taft-Hartley Labor-Management Relations Act (1947), which prohibited candidates from accepting contributions from corporate and union treasury funds, respectively. While the Federal Corrupt Practices Act of 1925 required disclosure of campaign receipts and expenditures, it was so poorly written and enforced that there was in practice no disclosure. Consequently, while academic and journalistic accounts provide some insights into the financing of presidential campaigns prior to 1972, little is known about the financing of congressional elections. With no effective disclosure of campaign receipts and expenditures, sources of congressional campaign funds were unknown prior to 1972. It was not until January of 1972, when the Federal Election Campaign Act of 1971 was passed, that meaningful disclosure of campaign finance contributions occurred.

In 1972 Congress passed the first of three campaign finance reform bills that would determine the way congressional elections are financed. The Federal Election Campaign Act of 1971 required a political committee or candidate to disclose receipts and expenditures in excess of $100 and required all political committees with receipts in excess of $1,000 to file a statement of organization. The act also required candidates to file regular reports of contributions and expenditures and to provide the names, addresses, and occupations of their contributors.

In 1974 the Federal Election Campaign Act (F.E.C.A.) was amended to limit both contributions and spending in congressional elections. Contributions by individuals were limited to $1,000 per candidate per election, with a total aggregate annual contribution limit of $25,000. Political and party committees were limited to $5,000 per election, but, unlike individuals, there was no aggregate limit placed on contributions. Senators and their families could contribute no more than $35,000 to their own campaigns; for House members and their families the limit was $25,000. Finally, independent expenditures on behalf of a candidate were limited to $1,000.

Spending by House candidates was limited to $70,000 in primary elections and another $70,000 in the general election. Senate candidates could spend up to $100,000 or eight cents per eligible voter, whichever was greater, in primary elections and $150,000 or twelve cents per eligible voter, whichever was greater, in general elections. Spending by the national political parties was limited to $10,000 for House candidates and $20,000 or two cents per eligible voter, whichever was greater, for Senate candidates. Spending limits were indexed to the Consumer Price Index.

The Federal Election Campaign Act of 1974 also established a Federal Election Commission to administer the act. The commission was to consist of six members, two appointed by the president, two by the Speaker of the House, and two by the president pro tempore of the Senate.

The constitutionality of the 1974 amendments was challenged in federal court soon after they were passed. The resulting Supreme Court case, *Buckley v. Valeo* (424 U.S. 1 [1976]), upheld the constitutionality of the contribution limits, but struck down the constitutionality of the spending limits; struck down limits on spending by House and Senate candidates; held that there could be no limits on independent expenditures; and ordered that all six members of the Federal Election Commission be appointed by the president.

In response to the Supreme Court's decision the F.E.C.A. was again amended in 1976. These amendments required that the Federal Election Commission consist of six members, three Democrats and three Republicans, appointed by the president and confirmed by the Senate. The amendments also limited contributions by individuals to political action committees (PACs) to $5,000 per year and to a political party to $20,000 per year. The individual contribution limits of $1,000 per candidate per election and the aggregate individual contribution limit of $25,000 per year remained in effect. The F.E.C.A. amendments of 1976 limited contributions from multicandidate committees to no more than $15,000 to a national party committee and limited the amount the senatorial campaign committees could give to Senate candidates to $17,500 per year. Finally, the 1976 amendments established that, for contribution purposes, all PACs created by a corporation, membership organization, or union would be considered one PAC.

The final changes to F.E.C.A. occurred in 1979, when Congress amended the act to promote "party building" activities. This allowed individuals to contribute unlimited amounts of money to the Democratic and Republican parties for activities such as registration and get-out-the-vote drives. This so-called soft money has been used primarily in presidential campaigns but also plays a role in congressional campaigns.

CAMPAIGN FINANCE LAWS. The contribution limits enacted in 1974 continue to apply to congressional campaigns. Individuals may contribute $1,000 to a candidate per election (i.e., $1,000 in the primary election and $1,000 in the general election), up to $20,000 to a national party committee, and $5,000 to any other political committee (e.g., a PAC), but the total contributions an individual may give to candidates for federal office may not exceed $25,000 in any one calendar year. Political action committees may give up to $5,000 per candidate per election (i.e., $5,000 in the primary election and $5,000 in the general election), up to $15,000 to a national political party committee per year, and up to $5,000 to any other political committee per year, but there is no aggregate limit on the amount of money PACs may give to candidates.

Political parties give money to congressional candidates in two ways: through direct contributions to the candidates and through indirect, or coordinated, expenditures. Coordinated expenditures are funds spent by the national and state party committees to help a candidate, but the expenditures are made by the party committee. For example, a party committee could commission a poll or media ad for a candidate, and the costs would be paid by the committee, not by the candidate's campaign.

The national party committees (the Democratic National Committee and the Republican National Committee), the Senate campaign committees (the Democratic Senatorial Campaign Committee and the National Republican Senatorial Committee), and the House campaign committees (the Democratic Congressional Campaign Committee and the National Republican Congressional Committee) may each contribute $10,000 to House candidates. In addition, the state party committees may contribute $10,000 to House candidates. The national party committees and the Senate campaign committees may together contribute $17,500 to Senate candidates, and the House campaign committees and the state party committees may each contribute $10,000 to Senate candidates.

The coordinated expenditure limits are the limits set in 1974 and then indexed for inflation. The coordinated expenditure limit for House races is $10,000, plus a cost-of-living increase. For the 1994 election cycle the coordinated expenditure limit for House candidates was $29,300, except for states with only one congressional candidate, where the limit was $58,600. For Senate elections the coordinated expenditure limit is two cents times the state voting-age population and then adjusted for inflation or $20,000 plus a cost-of-living adjustment, whichever is higher. In 1994 the coordinated expenditure for the least populous states was $58,600, the same as the coordinated expenditure limit for House candidates who ran statewide, while the coordinated expenditure limit for California, the most populous state, was $1,325,415. The state party committees have the same coordinated expenditure limits as the national party committees. The state party committees may make their own coordinated expenditures or give that authority to the national party committees, thus doubling the amount of money the national party committees control for House and Senate elections.

While there are limits on what individuals, political parties, and PACs may contribute to congressional candidates, there are no limits on what a candidate may spend on his or her own race, nor are there limits on individual or PAC independent expenditures. Independent expenditures are those made by an individual or PAC to support or oppose someone's candidacy, but there can be no consultation or communication between the candidate and his or her campaign and the individual or group making independent expenditures. While individuals rarely make individual expenditures of any size, some PACs have used independent expenditures to influence congressional elections. For example, in 1992 the National Rifle Association spent more than $100,000 on independent expenditures in an ultimately successful effort to unseat Rep. Beryl Anthony (D-Ark.). Altogether PACs spent $6 million dollars on independent expenditures in congressional elections in 1992.

There are no limits on what a candidate may spend on his or her own campaign.

SOURCES OF FUNDS. Congressional candidates receive campaign contributions from three sources: individual contributors, political action committees, and the party committees. The relative importance of these three groups depends in large part upon a candidate's status (incumbent, challenger, or open seat), party affiliation, and the office for which the candidate is running (House or Senate). Senate candidates, regardless of status, receive more than half of their campaign contributions from individuals. The same is true for House Republicans, but for House Democrats PACs are an important and, in some cases, major source of campaign funds.

Incumbents are more likely to receive contributions from PACs than are challengers and candidates for open seats. Party contributions, while less important for most candidates than contributions from PACs and individuals, are more important, or at least a larger percentage of total contributions, for Republicans than for Democrats.

Although Senate incumbents receive approximately two-thirds of their campaign contributions from individuals and between one-quarter and one-third of their contributions from PACs, House incumbents are much more dependent on PAC contributions. House Republican incumbents receive approximately 40 percent of their campaign contributions from PACs, while House Democratic incumbents receive over 50 percent of their campaign contributions from PACs.

For challengers and open-seat candidates, the campaign finance picture is quite different. Of challengers for a House seat, Democrats receive approximately one-third of their campaign funds from PACs, while Republicans receive only about 10 percent. Figures for Senate challengers are similar to those for House Republican challengers; in the Senate the difference between PAC receipts of Republican and Democratic challengers is much less than in the House. Open-seat candidates in both parties and in both the House and Senate generally receive more money from PACs than do challengers, but still considerably less than incumbents.

EXPENDITURES OF FUNDS. While the Federal Election Campaign Act requires extensive disclosure of campaign contributions, its requirements for disclosure of campaign expenditures are much less strict. While campaign expenditures exceeding $200 must be reported to the Federal Election Commission, F.E.C.A. requires only that the name, address, date, amount, and purpose of the expenditure be disclosed. Because describing the purpose of the expenditure is left up to the candidate, there is no uniformity in the reporting of expenditures.

Following the 1989 to 1990 election cycle, two *Los Angeles Times* reporters and their colleagues analyzed the expenditure reports of candidates who ran for Congress in 1990. In *The Handbook of Campaign Spending: Money in the 1990 Congressional Races* (1992), Sara Fritz and Dwight Morris grouped congressional expenditures into eight major categories, several with subcategories.

Fritz and Morris's efforts to categorize and compare campaign expenditures by congressional candidates illustrate the difficulty in tracing expenditures in House and Senate elections. Their research led to two very interesting findings. First, contrary to popular opinion, electronic media, particularly television, is not the primary expenditure for most congressional candidates. Senate candidates spent 35 percent of their resources on radio and television, House candidates 23 percent. The difference in the relative amounts spent on broadcast media is not surprising because in many House districts television and, to a lesser extent, radio are not efficient advertising mechanisms. However, the fact that only one-third of Senate spending was for radio and television was a surprise, since the common assumption had been that nearly two-thirds of all Senate campaign expenditures were for television advertising.

The second interesting finding was how little total spending was directed at traditional campaign activities such as voter contact. Fritz and Morris estimated that in House races over half of all campaign expenditures were unrelated to contacting voters. For Senate campaigns a larger percentage of expenditures was directed to voter contact, due in large part to the greater percentage of Senate expenditures on electronic media and direct mail.

CAMPAIGN FINANCE REFORM. While the Federal Election Campaign Act was a reform of campaign finance laws when it was initially passed in 1972, and amended in 1974, 1976, and 1979, the act was little more than a decade old when the first efforts to reform congressional campaign finance laws began anew. In 1985 Senators David Boren and Barry Goldwater introduced an amendment to limit the amount of money candidates for Congress could accept from PACs: $100,000 for House candidates and between $175,000 and $750,000 for Senate candidates (depending on the size of the state); and to reduce individual PAC contributions to $3,000 per candidate per election. The Boren-Goldwater amendment passed the Senate in December 1985, but because it was a nongermane amendment to a nuclear waste bill, and because there was no enforcement mechanism included in the bill, the amendment was merely symbolic of renewed interest in campaign finance reform in the U.S. Congress.

The attention that the Boren-Goldwater amendment received, however, began a debate on campaign finance reform that continued throughout the 1980s and into the 1990s. In 1987, prior to the start of the 100th Congress, Senators David Boren, Robert Byrd (the majority leader), George Mitchell, and Alan Cranston (the majority whip) were all at work on campaign finance legislation. Soon after the start of the Congress, Senator Byrd called together the other three senators, as well as Sen. Wendell Ford, the chairman of the Senate Rules Committee, to try to create a campaign finance bill that was acceptable to all of them.

Senate Bill 2 (S. 2, the Senatorial Election Campaign Act of 1987), the legislation drafted by the Senate leadership, established a state-by-state general election spending limit based on the voting-age population of the state and limited spending in primary elections to two-thirds of the general election limit. A candidate who raised 20 percent of the state general election spending in amounts of $250 or less received a grant of public funds equal to 80 percent of the general election spending limit. While individual PAC contribution limits were not changed, candidates could accept no more than 30 percent of the state primary spending limit from all PACs during the six-year election cycle. S. 2 also limited the amount the party committees could receive from PACs, placed restrictions on bundling (the practice of an organization collecting individual checks and then giving them to a candidate in a bundle, thereby enabling the organization to get credit for raising the funds), required disclosure of soft money, and provided additional public funds to candidates who had independent expenditures made against them.

Senate Republicans offered their own campaign finance reform bill. Senators Mitch McConnell and Bob Packwood introduced legislation to prohibit direct contributions from PACs to candidates, require disclosure of soft money, and require full disclosure by party committees of all receipts, expenditures, and soft money.

During the summer and fall of 1987 and into the winter of 1988, Republicans filibustered Democratic efforts to debate campaign finance reform. There were a record eight cloture votes on S. 2, but the Democratic leadership was unable to cut off the filibuster.

During the 101st (1989–1991) and 102d (1991–1993) Congresses campaign finance continued to be debated. In 1990 campaign finance bills passed both the House and Senate, but conferees never met to work out differences in the legislation. In 1992 legislation passed both the House and Senate, only to be vetoed by President George Bush in May 1992. The 1992 bill established spending limits in both House and Senate elections, further restrictions on PAC contributions, and public funding (in different forms) for House and Senate candidates.

The 1992 legislation established a spending limit of $600,000 for House elections and a limit of between $636,500 and $8.9 million for Senate elections. The lower amount would have applied to the least populous states; the limit of $8.9 million applied to California. Spending limits in each state for Senate elections were based on the voting-age population of the state. The limits on PAC contributions also differed for House and Senate candidates. House candidates could accept no more than $5,000 from any one PAC and no more than $200,000 from all PACs. Senate candidates could accept no more than $2,500 from any one PAC and no more than 20 percent of their general election spending limit from PACs. A House candidate who qualified for public funding by winning the primary and raising $60,000 in contributions of $250 or less, and who had an opponent in the general election, would receive $200 in federal matching funds for each $200 in individual contributions received, up to a limit of $200,000. Senate candidates, like their House counterparts, also had to win a primary and have a general election opponent. In addition, Senate candidates had to raise $250,000 or 10 percent of the general election spending limit, whichever was less, in amounts of $250 or less, and half of those $250 contributions had to come from within the state.

When the 103d Congress convened in January 1993, campaign finance reform was once again on the legislative agenda, but the probability of reform was considerably higher. Unlike in prior years, reform advocates in 1993 had the support of the president, Bill Clinton, who had pledged support for campaign finance reform legislation during his campaign and who had mentioned campaign finance reform as a priority of his administration during his State of the Union address. During the 100th, 101st, and 102d Congresses there was little likelihood that campaign finance legislation passed by Congress would be signed by Presidents Ronald Reagan and George Bush. Thus some members of Congress viewed a vote for campaign finance reform as a win-win vote; they could support reform, and thus be perceived as on the progressive side of the issue in the minds of both their constituents and special interest groups such as Common Cause, and yet not fear that they would actually have to run under the proposed changes in the law. In contrast, in 1993, reformers could be fairly confident that President Clinton would sign a campaign finance bill, and thus the provisions of that bill needed careful thought.

During the winter and spring of 1993 the Senate Rules Committee held hearings on Senate Bill 3 (S. 3, the Congressional Campaign Spending Limit and Election Reform Act), the same campaign finance reform bill that had been vetoed by President Bush a year earlier. In May 1993 President Clinton announced his proposals for campaign finance reform: spending limits in House and Senate campaigns, communications vouchers for candidates who accepted spending limits, further limits on the amount of money House and Senate candidates could accept from political action committees, and the elimination of soft money in presidential and congressional elections.

In June of 1993, following three weeks of intensive debate on the Senate floor, campaign finance reform legislation once again passed the Senate. The Senate legislation established spending limits in the general election of between $1.2 and $5.5 million, depending on a state's population, and limited spending in primary elections to 67 percent of the general election spending limit or $2.75 million, whichever was less. The bill also prohibited candidates from accepting PAC contributions, prohibited candidates for federal office from raising soft money, and severely curtailed the use of soft money by national party committees. What distinguished the bill that passed the Senate in 1993 from previous bills considered or passed by the Senate was that it did not include the public funding provisions included in earlier Senate legislation. While 1993 differed from 1987 and 1988 in that the president supported campaign finance reform, in 1993, just as in 1987 and 1988, the Democrats in the Senate still needed some bipartisan support for campaign finance reform legislation to avoid a Republican filibuster. To gain enough support to avoid a filibuster, Democrats in the Senate dropped federally funded communications vouchers for candidates who agreed to spending limits, thus passing a bill with spending limits but no public funding.

Unlike in prior years, campaign finance reform advocates in 1993 had the support of the president, Bill Clinton.

In November 1993 the House of Representatives passed its campaign finance bill. The House bill, H.R. 3, also called the Congressional Campaign Spending Limit and Reform Act of 1993, established spending limits of $600,000 for House candidates but indexed the spending limits to inflation. House candidates who accepted spending limits would receive up to $200,000 in federal communications vouchers, which could be used for paid media, postage, and other forms of voter contact, such as brochures, bumper stickers, and campaign buttons. The legislation also limited the aggregate amount of money House candidates could accept from PACs. All House candidates, whether or not they accepted spending limits, could accept no more than $200,000 from PACs. H.R. 3, like its Senate counterpart, also sharply restricted soft money. What H.R. 3 did not do, however, was provide a funding mechanism to pay for the federal communications vouchers. That mechanism was to be included in future legislation.

Well into 1994, campaign finance reform remained elusive. Representatives and senators continued to differ on the role of PACs in congressional elections: senators wanted to ban PACs; representatives, to continue to allow PAC contributions of $5,000 per election. A second contentious issue was public funding. Members of the House and Senate differed over whether campaign finance legislation should include partial public funding and, if so, where the revenues to support public funding would come from.

The debate over campaign finance reform presents a conflict between self-interest and philosophical interest for Democrats and Republicans, and House and Senate members, and the conflict was particularly brought to the fore with the election of a Democratic, reform-minded president. The three most controversial issues in the debate over congressional campaign finance reform continue to be spending limits, public funding, and political action committees. Because of differences in costs of campaigns, sources of funds, and House and Senate rules and procedures, partisan and institutional differences within Congress make agreement on campaign finance reform extremely difficult.

For example, the debate over spending limits is viewed differently by House and Senate members and by Republicans and Democrats. Because Senate races are more expensive than House races, on average, Senators spend more time raising money; thus limits on spending, and thus on the time spent raising money, are more important to senators than to representatives. At the same time, however, Republicans, in the minority, in both the House and Senate, fear that any spending limits will preclude them from ever becoming the majority party in either the House or the Senate, because nonincumbent candidates often need to spend more than incumbents to overcome the inherent advantages of incumbency.

Similar conflicts exist over the issue of public funding. For nonincumbent candidates, particularly for the House, public funding would provide seed money to build a campaign organization, achieve initial name recognition, and attract campaign contributions from PACs, individuals, and the party committees. The group of candidates who would most benefit from public funding are those who are most underfunded in the current system, namely, Republican nonincumbents seeking election to the House. However, because Republicans philosophically oppose government funding of congressional elections, Republicans oppose what likely is in the best interests of their candidates.

Political action committees are also targets for campaign finance reform. They are viewed by some advocates of reform as the epitome of special interest influence over congressional behavior, and proposals to further restrict PAC contributions to members of Congress, or to ban PACs entirely, are touted as a means to remove this influence. However, enthusiasm for further restricting or banning PACs varies from chamber to chamber and from one political party, to the other. Senators receive less than one-third of their campaign contributions from PACs, so restrictions on PACs would not significantly change their sources of campaign funds. Further, because business-related PACs, despite their general philosophical alignment with Republicans, tend to give almost one-half of their contributions to influential majority-party Democrats, Republican senators do not receive as many contributions from groups whose interests they support and thus have been the most vocal in the call for banning PAC contributions.

House members, however, are much more dependent on PAC contributions than are their Senate colleagues. Because House members receive over 40 percent of their campaign contributions from PACs, and House Democratic incumbents receive over half of all their campaign contributions from PACs, House members, particularly House Democrats, are much less enthusiastic than their Senate colleagues about banning or further restricting PAC contributions.

While spending limits, public funding, and restrictions on PACs are the most contentious issues in the debate over campaign finance reform, other issues also raise controversy. For example, while there is general agreement that soft money needs to be curtailed, the political parties want to ensure that the programs supported by soft money continue. Similarly, proposals to restrict bundling by individuals and PACs abound, but the parties want to create legislation that exempts organizations whose bundling helps their candidates. For instance, EMILY's List, a PAC that supports Democratic women candidates who favor abortion rights, raised $6.2 million dollars in 1992, and candidates who were the recipients of those dollars want to pass reform legislation that enables the bundling practices of EMILY's List to continue.

The debate over congressional campaign finance reform that began in earnest in 1987 continued into the 1990s. The issues first addressed in the original Senate bill (S. 2) continued to be the issues that plagued members of Congress in the 1990s, and the positions of the two parties and two chambers changed little. The difference between the late 1980s and early 1990s was the presence of a pro-reform president, a difference that influenced the debate over campaign finance reform.

Congressional campaign finance is an issue that increasingly pits the haves against the have-nots. As members of Congress have become increasingly adept at raising money under the provisions of the Federal Election Campaign Act, the disparity between the amount of money raised and spent by incumbents and challengers increases. After the flurry of open seats created in 1992 by redistricting and retirements, the 1990s will likely be another decade of high reelection rates for incumbents, helped in large part by their spending advantage over their generally underfunded challengers.

[See also (I) Elections, Congressional; (II) Campaign Finances.]

BIBLIOGRAPHY

Fritz, Sara, and Dwight Morris. *The Handbook of Campaign Spending: Money in the 1990 Congressional Races.* 1992.

Herrnson, Paul S. *Party Campaigning in the 1980s.* 1988.

Jackson, Brooks. *Honest Graft: Big Money and the American Political Process.* 1988.

Johannes, John R., and Margaret Latus Nugent. *Money, Elections, and Democracy: Reforming Congressional Campaign Finance.* 1990.

Magleby, David B., and Candice J. Nelson. *The Money Chase: Congressional Campaign Finance Reform.* 1990.

Mutch, Robert E. *Campaigns, Congress, and the Courts: The Making of Federal Campaign Finance Law.* 1988.

Sorauf, Frank J. *Inside Campaign Finance: Myths and Realities.* 1992.

Sorauf, Frank J. *Money in American Elections.* 1988.

Stern, Philip M. *The Best Congress Money Can Buy.* 1988.

– CANDICE J. NELSON

CENSUS

The United States Census is the foundation of the American statistical system, providing much of the demographic information on which Congress depends in making domestic policy. Although the census is required by the Constitution, the data that it collects are also important to state and local governments and private enterprise.

The census is not just an information-gathering activity. As with most activities of government, it is also political. The form, contents, and length of the questionnaires are intensely debated and negotiated within the executive and legislative branches. Most questions are designed to provide information used in federal programs, but the fundamental purpose of the census—the apportionment of representatives among the states and the resulting redistricting within states—remains a primary focus for Congress.

APPORTIONING REPRESENTATIVES AND TAXES. The apportionment concept is central to understanding the census as it relates to Congress. Two sections of the Constitution pertain to using the census to apportion representatives and taxes. Article 1, section 2 (subsequently modified by the Fourteenth Amendment) provided that

> Representatives and direct Taxes shall be apportioned among the several States which may be included within this Union, according to their respective Numbers, which shall be determined by adding to the whole Number of free Persons, including those bound to Service for a Term of Years, and excluding Indians not taxed, three fifths of all other Persons.

The Fourteenth Amendment removed the references to free persons and the rule providing that three-fifths of all other persons would be counted for apportionment. What remained was the concept that both representation in the House and taxation would be apportioned among the states according to their populations. As Margo Anderson (1988) points out, the concept was an example of constitutional checks and balances. More representation in the House was to carry a price—more taxes allocated to the state. This carrot-and-stick was intended to prevent states from inflating their populations for the census, but the importance of the stick faded along with attempts to impose "direct taxes." A national property tax, for example, failed as a revenue source in the late 1790s, was not very successful in the 1810s, and failed again during the Civil War. Thus, with exception of a successful Civil War income tax, throughout the nineteenth century most revenue for the federal government was obtained from duties and other fees. The Sixteenth Amendment (1913) removed the constitutional requirement that all taxes be apportioned among the states based on the census.

DETERMINING THE FORM, CONTENTS, AND METHOD. How the census is to be conducted is left to Congress. Article 1, section 2 of the Constitution provides that "the actual Enumeration shall be made within three Years after the first Meeting of the Congress of the United States, and within every subsequent Term of ten Years, in such Manner as they shall by Law direct."

The phrase "in such Manner as they shall by Law direct" has given Congress wide latitude to specify census form and contents. The first censuses asked relatively few questions, but in the late nineteenth century the scope and complexity of the questionnaires increased to include information from a wide variety of sources, including schools, farms, and industries. During the twentieth century, the questions relating to education, agriculture, and manufacturing were separated from the decennial census and put into separate surveys and censuses.

CHANGING COUNTING METHODS. The first census takers were federal marshals. The marshals and their assistants conducted the census until 1880, but the census has always required mobilization of a large temporary labor force. In 1990, for example, the Census Bureau hired approximately 300,000 temporary staff members.

The census is not strictly a head count. In fact, arguably, the census is basically (with some exceptions) a count of housing units, and the people are among the characteristics of the housing units. Census forms are sent to housing units, and one person in each unit is asked to fill out the form for all the others living there. Although every U.S. household receives a census questionnaire containing a core of basic questions, slightly fewer than a fifth of the households get a much longer questionnaire, from which much of the detailed information in the census is derived.

The census is not just an information-gathering activity; it is also political.

How the census is taken has changed in two centuries, and the methods changed significantly after 1960. The 1960 census was the last one for which enumerators visited every U.S. household. In 1970, 60 percent of the nation's households were asked to complete their census forms themselves and mail them back for processing. These households were contacted by enumerators only if they failed to return their forms or if the forms contained errors. Enumerators visited the remaining 40 percent of households. The 1980 census expanded the mail-based census to cover approximately 90 percent of the nation's households, and 1990 mail coverage extended to nearly all households.

CONTINUING CONTROVERSY: CENSUS ERROR. The Census Bureau has always had to control costs while attempting to count everyone in the country. The costs of enumerating a household have risen substantially, from $6.85 in 1970 to $12.10 in 1980, and to $17 in 1990 (figures in constant 1980 dollars). As costs have risen, increasing attention has been paid to the issue of miscounts. Postcensus research has shown that certain minority groups are more difficult to count than whites; while overall population coverage of the census has generally improved (from 94.4 percent in 1940 to an estimated 98 percent in 1990), the differential undercount between blacks and whites (the difference between the white under- or overcount and the black undercount) has improved little if at all (it was 5.2 percent in 1940 and again in 1980, with fluctuations during the intervening decades). The tendency for large segments of the minority population to settle in specific regions of the country and in certain large cities has politicized the undercount issue. Some cities and states see themselves as victims of census miscounts. Because representation in legislative bodies (at the federal, state, and local level) is allocated by population, and federal funds are distributed in part on the basis of population, those areas that believe they have been undercounted have sought redress in Congress and the courts.

At issue are the methods used to take the census and whether the census should be adjusted using statistical methods. As the U.S. population becomes more heterogeneous, traditional census-taking techniques may not work as well as in the past. The mailed census form was developed in part to reduce costs and speed up enumeration. The development of the technique coincided with the increase of women in the work force and a consequently smaller pool of potential part-time census workers, on whom the Census Bureau had relied during much of the twentieth century. Because the mail-based census requires an accurate address list and a cooperative population, changing living patterns and attitudes toward government could negatively affect the census.

As the twentieth century waned, nontraditional living patterns threatened the mail-based census. The 1990 census takers found a homeless population living either on the streets or in shelters. Portions of the large immigrant population (both legal and illegal) were perceived to be living in crowded conditions that might discourage compliance with the census, from fear that illegal immigrants would be found out or that landlords would find lease requirements being violated. People dependent on public assistance were believed to be similarly less likely to cooperate with the census, if they were violating rules that would affect their eligibility for continued assistance. As the 1990 census was analyzed, these concerns suggested that the mail-based census might not be a good technique for enumerating hard-to-count populations.

Early planning for the year 2000 census had to take into account the competing needs of producing better information about the U.S. population and finding a way to be fair to all the different groups in U.S. society. Should the census be a head count, or should the Census Bureau use statistical techniques (based on postcensus surveys) to adjust the counts to even out differential coverage? Given the apparent problems of getting people to respond to a mailed census questionnaire, either because people were less willing to provide personal information to the government or because the questionnaires were lost in a sea of direct mail, should the entire process be rethought? Should the census questionnaire count only that information necessary for reapportionment and redistricting and leave the rest of the questions for a sample survey? Should the entire census be a large-sample survey? These questions and others faced Congress and the Census Bureau as they planned for the 2000 census.

[See also (I) Apportionment and Redistricting.]

BIBLIOGRAPHY

Anderson, Margo J. *The American Census: A Social History.* 1988.

Halacy, Daniel Stephen. *Census: 190 Years of Counting America.* 1980.

U.S. Senate. Committee on Governmental Affairs. *The Decennial Census: An Analysis and Review.* 96th Cong., 2d sess., 1980. Committee Print.

– DAVID C. HUCKABEE

CLERK OF THE HOUSE

When the House of Representatives reached its initial quorum on 1 April 1789, the second order of business after the election of a Speaker was the appointment of a clerk. In naming John Beckley of Virginia as the first clerk, the representatives were fulfilling their constitutional authority "to chuse their Speaker and other Officers." The clerk was to serve the House as the chief administrator of the legislative process, much as the secretary of Congress had acted in the Continental Congress and clerks had assisted the colonial assemblies before independence.

The First Congress assigned the clerk duties that still define the office. His first action was to receive and certify the credentials of newly elected members, a responsibility the clerk has had ever since. From the First Congress, the clerk also has kept the Journal of House Proceedings, as required by the Constitution. In a resolution that gave the clerk's office a unique procedural importance in the House, the First Congress declared that the clerk should remain in office until a successor was appointed. The clerk thus has served as the formal means of maintaining continuity between Congresses. The resolution, similar to those passed at the closing of each succeeding Congress, also gave the clerk authority to preside over the opening of the next Congress before the election of a Speaker. Normally, the clerk plays a largely ceremonial role at the opening of a new Congress, but on several occasions in the decades preceding the Civil War, such as the opening of sessions in 1839, 1849, 1855, and 1859, he served as presiding officer for weeks as a factionalized House attempted to elect a Speaker. On each such occasion, however, the sitting clerk declined to rule on points of order and refused to settle contested elections.

The House elects the clerk at the opening of the first session of each Congress, generally as the first order of business following election of the Speaker. The vote is usually by resolution, and election requires approval by a majority of representatives assembled. Although the clerk bears no official party designation, the holder of the office is the candidate of the majority party. The clerk serves until the election of a successor, unless the House votes by resolution to remove the clerk from office for misconduct.

The clerk has served as the formal means of maintaining continuity between Congresses.

As the complexity of the work before the House increased, so too did the legislative responsibilities of the clerk. The officer is today responsible for furnishing the Daily Digest, recording and printing all bills and reports, certifying engrossed bills, affixing the seal of the House to all formal documents issued by the body, certifying bills and resolutions approved by the House, and sending and receiving messages from the president and the Senate. This legislative work is carried out through a staff of bill clerks, journal clerks, tally clerks, enrolling clerks, reading clerks, and recorders of debates. The clerk operates the House Library, which holds official records issued by the House since 1789.

In the twentieth century, with an increased membership and staff in the House, the clerk became responsible not only for the processing of legislation but also for providing the principle administrative support for the institution. Chief among these duties has been the operation of the Office of Finance, which prepares budgets for legislative operations and disburses House funds for all expenses except members' salaries. The clerk also manages the distribution of office supplies and furnishings, the printing services of the House, and various personnel services. In April 1992, the House approved a resolution transferring most financial and administrative duties from the clerk's office to a newly created position of director for nonlegislative and financial affairs.

Since 1789, thirty individuals have served as clerk of the House. Thirteen clerks have been former members of the House.

[See also (I) Parliamentarian, article on House Parliamentarian, Secretary of the Senate.]

BIBLIOGRAPHY

DePauw, Linda Grant, ed. *Documentary History of the First Federal Congress of the United States of America.* Vol. 3: *House of Representatives Journal.* 1977.

U.S. House of Representatives. Office of the Clerk. *Office of the Clerk, U.S. House of Representatives.* Prepared under the direction of Donnald K. Anderson. 1991.

– BRUCE A. RAGSDALE

CLOTURE

The U.S. Senate has two means for ending debate available to it. One is a unanimous consent agreement, and the other is a petition for cloture. Because its smaller size allows for less restrictive procedural rules than those placed on the House of Representatives and because of the value placed on free debate and deliberation, the Senate has been reluctant to limit the opportunities of members to speak on the floor. Until 1917, debate could be ended only if the Senate adopted a unanimous consent request to close debate. A single senator or a group of senators could prevent a bill from coming to a vote by objecting to unanimous consent requests and extending the debate. This tactic is known as a filibuster.

Although filibusters were relatively rare and successful only under certain conditions, some senators sought to reform the rules to provide another means for bringing debate to a close. During the 64th Congress (1915–1917), twelve progressives engaged in a filibuster against President Woodrow Wilson's bill to arm merchant ships; they succeeded in preventing a vote on it. When the new Senate convened it adopted a substitute amendment to Rule XXII that established cloture.

Under the cloture procedure, any senator may circulate a petition calling for an end to debate on a particular bill, resolution, or motion. After sixteen senators have signed the petition, it may be filed with the presiding officer of the Senate. On the second calendar day after such a petition is filed, the Senate votes on whether to end debate by invoking cloture. As originally established, at least two-thirds of those senators "present and voting" had to vote in favor of cloture for it to be successful. If the cloture motion was defeated, debate would continue.

Rule XXII changed very little between 1917 and 1975. In 1949, the requirements for invoking cloture changed to two-thirds of the Senate membership instead of two-thirds of those present and voting. In 1959, the Senate changed the provision back to two-thirds of those present and voting and allowed motions to change the Senate rules also to be subject to cloture.

Between 1917 and 1937 the cloture procedure was used rarely, on a diffuse group of issues, and with limited success; its use was uncontroversial. From 1937 until the early 1960s, cloture votes, though still infrequent, were primarily taken when southern Democratic senators engaged in filibusters of civil rights bills. In every instance cloture was defeated. Senate liberals and reformers sought to reduce the cloture vote requirement to three-fifths or to a simple majority of senators. Efforts to reduce the cloture requirements in 1957, 1963, 1965, and again in 1967 were defeated.

One interesting aspect of the issue involved limitations on debate on motions to change Senate rules. Reformers argued that because the Senate started anew with each Congress, preexisting Senate rules were not in effect and a simple majority vote could end debate on a motion to adopt a set of rules. The other side contended that the Senate was a continuing body because two-thirds of its membership automatically carried over from one Congress to the next. Prior to 1959 such an interpretation meant that debates on changing Senate rules could only end by unanimous consent, and even after 1959 ending such debates was subject to the two-thirds provision of Rule XXII.

Under the cloture procedure, any senator may circulate a petition calling for an end to debate on a particular bill, resolution, or motion.

By 1975, changes in the Senate had made possible an alteration of the cloture requirements. The filibuster was a growing problem. With the growing legislative workload, Senate sessions were running nearly year round; no longer could the Senate afford the luxury of unlimited debate. And because of the increased time pressures, the filibuster became a more effective tactic, more easily forcing legislative concessions. Thus there were both more filibusters and more cloture votes. In the forty-four years from 1917 to 1960, there were twenty-one cloture votes. In the following ten years, from 1961 to 1970, there were twenty-six cloture votes. And in the less than five years from 1971 until Rule XXII was altered in 1975, there were fifty-four cloture votes. Filibusters were no longer limited to southern Democrats trying to prevent action on civil rights bills. They were used by diverse senators and against diverse kinds of legislation.

The Senate voted in 1975 to change the cloture requirement from two-thirds of those present and voting to three-fifths of the Senate membership. (Only motions to change the Senate rules remained under the two-thirds cloture requirement.) Efforts to invoke cloture in the Senate were more successful after this change. But another effect was the development of the so-called post-cloture filibuster. Once cloture was invoked Senate rules allowed each member to speak for one hour on the bill or any amendments to it, up to a total of one hundred hours. In addition, procedural motions and votes could be used to extend the process well beyond that period. In reaction to post-cloture filibusters, the Senate in 1979 placed all activity following cloture under the one-hundred-hour limit. In 1986, as part of the legislation allowing television coverage of the Senate floor, the Senate restricted all post-cloture activity to thirty hours.

[See also (I) Filibuster.]

BIBLIOGRAPHY

Oleszek, Walter J. *Congressional Procedures and the Policy Process.* 3d ed. 1989.

Smith, Steven S. *Call to Order.* 1989.

– BRUCE I. OPPENHEIMER

COMMITTEE OF THE WHOLE

Known as the Committee of the Whole, the Committee of the Whole House on the State of the Union is the House of Representatives meeting as if it were a committee on which each member of the House serves. (The procedural device is employed frequently in the House but has been abandoned by the Senate.) This alternative debate forum is utilized to take advantage of more expeditious rules of procedure. The Committee of the Whole continues to meet in the same chamber, but other changes signal the shift.

When the House transforms itself into the Committee, the mace is moved to a lower position on the rostrum. The Speaker leaves the chair and a majority party member is instead designated to preside over the Committee. Members seeking recognition from the chair change the form of address from "Mister (or Madam) Speaker" to "Mister (or Madam) Chairman."

The most significant changes are procedural. First, the quorum requirement in the Committee is only 100 members, whereas 218 are needed to constitute a quorum in the House. Second, obtaining a recorded vote in the Committee requires a sufficient second of 25 members. In the House, one-fifth of those present must approve taking a vote for the record. If a quorum is present, the sufficient second is 44, rising even higher when more than 218 members are on the floor.

Third, consideration of a measure is more flexible in the Committee of the Whole. The one-hour rule of debate governs in the House, permitting up to one hour per question. In the Committee, however, general debate is provided for by the unanimous consent of the House or pursuant to a special rule from the House Rules Committee. It can range from one hour to several hours in length. Overall, the Committee spends most of its time in the amending process, where the five-minute rule prevails: five minutes for the proponents, five for the opponents. On controversial questions, the period for debate and amending is frequently extended by unanimous consent or by offering of pro forma amendments, which are amendments in form only, that is, their only purpose is to obtain debate time.

The use of the Committee of the Whole has been accepted House practice since 1789. The purpose behind its use has changed considerably over time, however. Its antecedents were found in the English parliamentary practice of concealing proceedings from the Speaker, who was viewed with suspicion as a conduit to the Crown. Many colonial legislatures as well as the Continental Congress utilized a committee of the whole to provide members with a temporary forum in which debate could be exercised in a freer manner. Until the early 1800s, the House of Representatives used the Committee of the Whole to work out the broad outlines of a legislative proposal, which would then be sent to a select committee for further refinement. After the select committee completed its work, the Committee of the Whole would again meet to debate and amend the measure before the House would vote on it. In modern House practice, use of the Committee is limited to this final stage of consideration: debate and amending up to the point of final passage. In the Senate, the use of Committee of the Whole for the consideration of legislative measures was abolished in 1930, and its use for the consideration of treaties ended in 1986.

[See also (I) Amending, Five-Minute Rule.]

BIBLIOGRAPHY

Alexander, De Alva Stanwood. *History and Procedure of the House of Representatives.* 1916. Pp. 256–272.

Nickels, Ilona B. *Committee of the Whole: An Introduction.* Congressional Research Service, Library of Congress. CRS Rept. 85-943. 1985.

U.S. House of Representatives. *Deschler's Precedents of the United States House of Representatives,* by Lewis Deschler. 94th Cong., 2d sess., 1977. H. Doc. 94-661. Vol. 5, chap. 19, pp. 39–286.

– ILONA B. NICKELS

COMMITTEES

An Overview

Committees and parties are the central organizational features of the U.S. Congress. The entire jurisdiction of each house of Congress is divided among a set of committees. Most legislative details are drafted in committee, and most investigations are conducted by committees. Further, committees provide most members of Congress their most important base of power.

ORGANIZATION OF THE MODERN COMMITTEE SYSTEMS. The U.S. Constitution makes no provision for committees, except to allow each house to devise its own rules to govern procedure. House and Senate rules list the standing committees, specify their jurisdictions, and prescribe certain features of committee procedure and organization. The two chambers have adopted rules affecting committees that differ in important ways. Committee activity is also regulated by a variety of statutes, party rules, and informal practices.

Joint committees are permanent but lack legislative authority.

Modern committees have two basic functions: (1) collecting information through hearings and investigations and (2) drafting and reporting legislation. Committees are the primary means for formally receiving the testimony of representatives of the executive branch, organized interest groups, and the general public. The vast majority of legislation introduced by members is routinely referred to the committee or committees of appropriate jurisdiction. And most of the details of legislation are scrutinized or written in committee markups. Various types of committees perform these informational and legislative functions.

Standing committees have legislative authority and permanent status. Their jurisdictions are specified in chamber rules and precedents, and they may write and report legislation on any matter within their jurisdictions. In the House, which must approve its rules at the start of each Congress, the jurisdictions of standing committees are routinely reapproved every two years. In the Senate, all rules remain in force until they are changed. Table 1 lists the standing committees in the 103d Congress (1993–1995).

Ad hoc committees may be created and appointed to consider and report legislation, but they are temporary and usually dissolve upon reporting legislation or at a specified date. Since 1975 the Speaker of the House has been permitted to appoint ad hoc committees, with House approval, but this authority has been used on only a few occasions.

Joint committees are permanent but lack legislative authority. Composed of members from both houses, with the chairmanships rotating between members of the two chambers, these committees conduct investigations, issue the results of studies, and recommend legislative action. Bills are not referred to them, and they cannot report legislation directly to the floor. The Joint Economic and Joint Taxation committees house sizable staffs and conduct newsworthy hearings from time to time. The Library and Printing committees, by contrast, perform the more ministerial duties of overseeing the operations of the Library of Congress and the Government Printing Office.

Select or special committees are, in principle, temporary committees without legislative authority. They

TABLE 1

STANDING COMMITTEES OF THE HOUSE AND SENATE, 1993–1994

House	Membership
Agriculture	45
Appropriations	57
Armed Services	52
Banking, Finance, and Urban Affairs	51
Budget	35
District of Columbia	11
Education and Labor	34
Energy and Commerce	43
Foreign Affairs	43
Government Operations	39
House Administration	21
Judiciary	35
Merchant Marine and Fisheries	43
Natural Resources	37
Post Office and Civil Service	23
Public Works and Transportation	50
Rules	13
Science, Space, and Technology	49
Small Business	44
Standards of Official Conduct	12
Veterans' Affairs	34
Ways and Means	36

Senate	Membership
Agriculture, Nutrition, and Forestry	19
Appropriations	29
Armed Services	20
Banking, Housing, and Urban Affairs	21
Budget	23
Commerce, Science, and Transportation	20
Energy and Natural Resources	19
Environment and Public Works	16
Finance	20
Foreign Relations	19
Governmental Affairs	14
Judiciary	14
Labor and Human Resources	16
Rules and Administration	16
Small Business	19
Veterans' Affairs	11

may be used to study problems falling within the jurisdiction of several standing committees, to symbolize Congress's commitment to key constituencies, or simply to reward particular legislators. Unfortunately, committee nomenclature can be misleading. For example, without eliminating the word *select* from their names, the House and Senate have made their intelligence committees permanent and granted them the power to report legislation. Some select committees are routinely re-created at the beginning of a new Congress.

In addition, the House and Senate jointly create conference committees to resolve the differences between their versions of legislation. The Constitution requires that legislation be approved by both houses in identical form before it is sent to the president. For important, complex legislation, the task of resolving differences often is difficult and time-consuming. While there are other ways to resolve interchamber differences, conference committees are named for most important legislation. These committees have wide but not unlimited discretion to redesign legislation in their efforts to gain House and Senate approval. When a majority of House conferees and of Senate conferees agree, a conference committee issues a report that must be approved by both houses. Conference committees dissolve as soon as one house takes an action on the conference report.

The committees of greatest interest are the standing committees. In the modern Congress, standing committees originate most legislation and their members manage the legislation on the floor and dominate the conference committee dedicated to it. The organization and role of standing committees in the two chambers is the further subject of this essay.

THE LEGISLATIVE POWER OF MODERN COMMITTEES. Committees have no power that is not granted to them by the parent chambers and parties. While the parent chambers approve committee assignments and budgets and must approve committee legislation, it is the parties that construct the committee lists routinely ratified by the chambers. This function gives the parties a source of leverage with committee members and allows the parties to regulate the behavior of committee members through formal and informal rules. In the main, committees must function in a procedural fashion and with a substantive effect that is consistent with the interests of their parent chambers and parties.

Nevertheless, committees exercise real power in the modern Congress. Their power stems in part from the indifference of the two parties and most members as to the details of legislation. Parties and their leaders focus on the few issues each year that are likely to affect party reputations and electoral prospects. The average member does not and could not take an interest in the details of most of the legislation that is considered on the floor. Party and member indifference varies from jurisdiction to jurisdiction, as well as over time, but it is common for the vast majority of measures that Congress processes.

When members are not indifferent, committees still have advantages that give their members disproportionate influence over policy outcomes. If committees abuse their advantages, it is yet often difficult to mount credible challenges to their power. Threats to strip a committee of jurisdiction, funding, or parliamentary privileges, or to retract members' committee assignments, usually are not credible, if for no other reason than that such actions might set precedents that members of other committees would not like to have established. The most practical means for keeping committees in check is to reject their policy recommendations.

Committee power comes in two forms. Negative power is the ability of committees to block legislation favored by others; positive power is the ability of committees to gain approval of legislation opposed by others. On both counts, committees have substantial advantages over rank-and-file members of the parent chambers and parties. Indeed, modern congressional committees have sources of negative and positive power that committees lack in most other national legislatures.

Negative power rests in committees' ability to control newly introduced legislation and obstruct alternative routes to the floor. This is accomplished more effectively under House rules than under Senate rules. In the House, such "gatekeeping" power is supported by rules that give committees near-monopoly control over newly introduced legislation and make it very difficult to circumvent them. Since 1880, all legislation relating to a committee's jurisdiction must be referred to that committee. Prior to 1975, this meant that the committee with the most relevant jurisdiction received the referral. Since then, the Speaker has been able to refer legislation to each committee with relevant jurisdiction. Short-circuiting the bill referral rule and bringing legislation directly to the floor requires either that the rules be suspended by a two-thirds vote or that a resolution from the Rules Committee be approved by majority vote.

House and Senate committees are granted wide latitude on most legislation that is referred to them. They may simply refuse to act, hold hearings but take no legislative action, amend the legislation in any way, or accept it without change. Or they may write their own legislation. They may vote to report legislation with a recommendation that it pass, with no recommendation, or with a recommendation that it be rejected.

Circumventing House committees is difficult but not impossible under current rules. The House operates under a germaneness rule that requires a floor amendment to be relevant to the section of the bill or resolution it seeks to modify. Thus, it is difficult to bring to the floor as an amendment a policy proposal whose subject has not been addressed in legislation reported by a committee. The germaneness rule can be waived, but only if the Rules Committee approves a resolution (a special rule) to this effect and the resolution is approved by a majority on the House floor. House rules provide other means for bringing legislation to the floor—a motion to suspend the rules, a special rule, and a petition to discharge a measure from committee—but these are difficult to employ and are used infrequently.

Each congressional party

has its own Committee on Committees.

House committees' blocking power is further enhanced by their members' domination of conference committees. House-Senate differences on complex legislation are usually resolved in conference, and conferees usually are named from the membership of the committees that originated the legislation. The power of these conferees rests in their wide latitude in negotiating with the Senate conferees and in a rule that prohibits amendments to the conference report. The House must usually accept or reject the entire report. This process gives conferees substantial discretion in designing the final form of legislation as long as they can gain the support of the Senate conferees and of the majority in both houses.

The situation in the Senate is very different. Although measures are routinely referred to Senate committees upon introduction, it is easy to object to a referral and keep a measure on the calendar for floor consideration. Furthermore, the Senate lacks a germaneness rule for most measures, allowing senators to circumvent committees by offering whole bills as amendments to unrelated legislation. Senators often hesitate to bypass committees in this way but do so much more frequently than in the House. And most conference reports are subject to filibusters, giving Senate minorities a source of bargaining leverage with conferees that does not exist in the House. In sum, the Senate's rules combine to create only very weak blocking power for its committees.

Committees depend on majority floor support for their policy proposals. Most positive power results from general indifference to the issues and details of specific legislation. Yet committees do have ways to gain the support of interested members who are adverse to committee legislation. By threatening to use their blocking power, for example, committees may gain bargaining leverage with members who want something from them on this or another matter. And committees may force their chambers to enact certain policy positions by giving them ultimatums in the form of conference reports.

Committee proposals benefit from the body's extra-procedural resources. Committees gain a tactical edge over opponents, for example, through their advantages in political and policy information. After sitting through hearings and after their previous experience with the issues, committee members are usually better informed than other members about the political and policy implications of their recommendations. Committees' large, expert staffs and their extensive networks of allies in the executive branch and in the interest-group community further enhance their informational advantage.

THE INVESTIGATIVE POWER OF MODERN COMMITTEES. Committees monitor or investigate the activities of the executive and judicial branches, as well as private activity that is or might be the subject of public policy. Congress's power to compel cooperation with its investigations, courts have ruled, is implicit in its constitutional functions of legislating and appropriating funds. Without broad powers to investigate and compel cooperation, Congress and its committees would not be able to act knowledgeably on public policy or authorize the use of public moneys. Beginning with the Legislative Reorganization Act of 1946, committees have been assigned the duty of maintaining "continuous watchfulness" over executive branch activities within their jurisdictions.

Oversight appears to have become an increasingly important part of committee activity in recent decades. According to Joel Aberbach's count in *Keeping a Watchful Eye* (Brookings, 1990), the number of days of oversight hearings conducted by House and Senate committees increased from 159 in 1961, to 290 in 1973, to 587 in 1983. The proportion of committee meetings and hearings devoted to oversight grew from less than 10 percent to more than 25 percent. The surge in the 1970s appears to be the product of several factors: the new independence of subcommittee chairs to pursue oversight at their discretion; a general expansion of committee activity made possible by larger staffs; the frequency of split party control of Congress and the White House; and a generally more assertive Congress.

COMMITTEE ASSIGNMENTS. At the start of each Congress, freshman members are named to committees and nonfreshmen may attempt to transfer from one committee to another. Nonfreshmen who do not seek to transfer are routinely reappointed to their committees.

The majority party in each chamber holds a majority of the seats on most committees, roughly in proportion to its size in the chamber as a whole. The exceptions are the House Appropriations, Budget, Rules, and Ways and Means committees, crucial committees on which House Democrats have reserved a disproportionate number of seats for themselves, and the House and Senate ethics committees, on which there are equal numbers of majority and minority party members. The specific size of committees is negotiated by majority and minority party leaders, with the majority leaders having the upper hand because of their ability to win a vote for the resolutions providing for committee sizes. Over the last few decades committee sizes have grown to accommodate members' requests for desirable assignments.

Each congressional party has its own Committee on Committees. Party leaders chair these committees, although the degree to which they dominate the proceedings varies. Assignments are constrained by the availability of vacancies, the number of members competing for assignments, and certain rules on the number and type of assignments each member may hold, to which exemptions are frequently granted. Only for Senate Republicans is seniority a decisive consideration in choosing among competitors for coveted assignments. Democrats and House Republicans consider seniority among many other factors, such as party loyalty, electoral needs, and geographic balance. Since the 1950s both Senate parties have granted every senator who seeks one a seat on one of the top four committees before any senator gets two such seats.

Distinct patterns are observable in committee assignments. A committee's appeal to members and importance to a party varies widely according to its jurisdiction, its active policy agenda, and its general political environment. The money committees (House Appropriations, Budget, and Ways and Means; Senate Appropriations and Finance) and certain other committees with large and important jurisdictions (for example, House Energy and Commerce and Senate Armed Services) have wide appeal and are considered vital to the parties' policy interests. There is intense competition for assignments to these committees, and party leaders exercise care in making appointments to them. Other committees attract only the few members whose constituencies are most affected by policy under their jurisdictions. Party leaders have little interest in these committees and seek to accommodate members requesting seats on them.

Scholars have ranked committees according to their attractiveness, as indicated by the balance of transfers to and from each committee. Table 2 lists House committees according to this measure of attractiveness (recent ratings are not available for the Senate). The table also indicates what research shows to be the distinctive political motivation for seeking assignment to each committee. Committees noted for their influence within the House are the most attractive. Committees with jurisdictions concerning which members have personal policy interests tend to be more attractive than committees that draw members because of their relevance to particular types of constituencies. A few committees attract the interest of virtually no members because of their limited jurisdiction or focus on housekeeping matters.

COMMITTEE LEADERSHIP. Both the majority and minority parties designate formal leaders for each com-

TABLE 2

HOUSE COMMITTEES RANKED BY ATTRACTIVENESS, WITH MEMBER GOALS

Name and Ranking	Goals
1. Ways and Means	prestige, influence
2. Appropriations	prestige, influence
3. Rules	prestige, influence
4. Energy and Commerce	policy
5. Armed Services	constituency
6. Foreign Affairs	policy
7. Budget	prestige, influence
8. Interior and Insular Affairs	constituency
9. Banking, Finance, and Urban Affairs	policy
10. Agriculture	constituency
11. Education and Labor	policy
12. Government Operations	policy
13. Small Business	constituency
14. Science, Space, and Technology	constituency
15. Merchant Marine and Fisheries	constituency
16. Post Office and Civil Service	constituency
17. Judiciary	policy
18. Veterans' Affairs	constituency
19. Public Works and Transportation	constituency

Note: Three committees are not included: the District of Columbia and House Administration committees attract very few members; members generally do not take the initiative to request seats on Standards of Official Conduct but rather are solicited by party leaders.

Source: The attractiveness rating is an updated transfer ratio for the 95th–99th Congresses, as reported in Michael Munger, "Allocation of Desirable Committee Assignments," *American Journal of Political Science* 32 (May 1988), p. 325; member goals are based on freshmen's motives for committee requests in the 100th and 101st Congresses, as reported in Steven S. Smith and Christopher J. Deering, *Committees in Congress* (Washington, D.C.: CQ Press, 1990), Chap. 3.

mittee and subcommittee. The majority party names the chairmen of all committees and subcommittees, and the minority party appoints a ranking minority member for every committee and subcommittee. The seniority norm dictates that the member with the longest continuous service on the committee serve as chairman, although there are limitations on the number and type of chairmanships a member may hold. Subcommittee chairmen and ranking minority members are chosen, in most cases, on the basis of committee seniority as well. Accruing seniority toward leadership posts is one reason members are reluctant to transfer to other committees, where they must start at the bottom of the seniority ladder.

Compared with the rules of House committees, most Senate committees' rules are very brief.

In the last two decades, the seniority norm has been checked in both houses by new party rules that require a secret-ballot election of full committee chairs and ranking minority members. House Democrats led the way by requiring that all committee chairs and the chairmen of the Appropriations Committee subcommittees stand for election in the Democratic caucus at the start of each Congress. Three full committee chairs were deposed in 1975, another was defeated in 1985, two were defeated in 1990, and an Appropriations subcommittee chairman was replaced in 1977.

Subcommittee chairmen traditionally were appointed by the full committee chairman, who could thereby manipulate subcommittee activity. That procedure also was made more egalitarian in the 1970s. House Democratic rules require that committee Democrats bid for subcommittee chairmanships in order of seniority and that their choices be ratified by a majority vote of the committee's party members. While seniority generally is observed, party members on a committee have the right to reject the most senior member and elect someone else, as has happened more than a dozen times since the mid-1970s. House Republicans leave the appointment process to each committee's ranking minority member, but in practice Republicans also select most of their subcommittee ranking members by committee seniority. Both Senate parties also allow committee members to select their subcommittee chairmanships or ranking positions in order of seniority.

Restrictions on chairmanships were developed in the 1970s to spread the chairmanships among more members. The House Democratic caucus rules limit members to one full committee and one subcommittee chairmanship. Full committee chairmen may chair only one subcommittee, and that within the full committee they chair. This rule, along with the increasing number of subcommittees, greatly increased the number of members holding subcommittee chairmanships—more than half of the House Democrats now hold a subcommittee chairmanship, up from one quarter in 1955.

Senate rules permit a member to hold only one chairmanship—the full committee chairmanship or a subcommittee chairmanship—on each committee on which he or she sits. Because most senators are limited to three standing committee assignments, they can have up to three subcommittee chairmanships, in addition to a full committee chairmanship of one of those standing committees. Nearly all majority party members hold at least one subcommittee-chairmanship today, and more than half of the majority party Democrats hold two or three subcommittee chairmanships.

On most full committees, the chairman is the most powerful member. The chairman controls the committee's agenda; schedules meetings and hearings of the fall committee and influences the scheduling of subcommittees' meetings and hearings; benefits from years of dealing with the committee's policy problems and constituencies; normally names conferees; controls the committee budget; supervises a sizable full committee staff; and often serves as a spokesperson for the committee and party on issues that fall under the committee's jurisdiction. Consequently, the committee chairman's support is critical to bill sponsors or opponents. That is as true today as it was thirty or forty years ago.

Nevertheless, compared with their predecessors of the 1950s and 1960s, committee chairmen now are more accountable to their party colleagues and face more effective competition for control over policy choices. This is due in part to changes in the formal rules limiting chairmen's discretion on a variety of procedural matters, particularly in the House, and in part to the acquisition of resources by other members who may not share the chairs' policy views.

The House and the House Democratic caucus adopted rules in the 1970s to reduce the influence of full committee chairmen over the decisions of their committees. Chairmen were required to stand for election by the Democratic caucus at the start of each Congress; subcommittees were required on committees with fifteen or more members and were empowered with written jurisdictions and staffs; proxy voting was restricted; the minority party contingents on committees were guaranteed staff; committees were required to open their meetings to the public unless a majority of committee members agreed to close them; a procedure for committee majorities to call meetings was created so the chairs could no longer refuse to hold meetings; and chairmen were required to promptly report legislation to the floor that had been approved by their committees.

The ability of committee chairmen to delay the referral of legislation to subcommittees or to delay the reporting of committee-approved legislation to the floor was curtailed. And House Democrats adopted a self-selection procedure for subcommittee assignments so that full committee chairmen could no longer stack important subcommittees with their supporters.

Like the House, the Senate adopted rules to provide guidelines for the conduct of committee meetings, hearings, and voting and required committees to publish additional rules governing committee procedure. In both houses, committee meetings were required to be held in public session, except by a recorded majority vote of the committee, making all committee members, including chairmen, more accountable to outside colleagues and constituents. And in both houses a majority of committee members may call and set the agenda for committee meetings if chairmen refuse to do so on their own authority.

But, unlike the House, Senate chamber and party rules do not specify internal committee organization in any detail and are silent on the functions of subcommittees. Compared with the rules of House committees, most Senate committees' rules are very brief, usually not even mentioning the structure, jurisdiction, or function of subcommittees. In most cases, committee chairmen are assumed to have great discretion, although even that

Senate Committee Room. Photographed in 1902. (Office of the Architect of the Capitol)

is left unstated. The referral of legislation to subcommittees, the discharge of legislation from subcommittees, and the distribution of legislation between the full committee and subcommittees remain under the formal control of nearly all Senate committee chairmen. Thus, Senate chairmen are granted more discretion in designing the internal decision-making processes of their committees than House chairs, and Senate subcommittee chairs enjoy less autonomy than their House counterparts.

It is in the House, then, that the full committee chairmen's control of committee decisions by procedural means has declined most in recent decades. Even their ability to keep issues off the agenda was undermined by the empowerment of subcommittees. House chairmen must be responsive to the demands of the Democratic caucus or risk losing their posts in the future, and they must tolerate independent subcommittees with professional staffs. Senate chairmen enjoy greater freedom in the internal affairs of their committees but must tolerate and anticipate more frequent and successful efforts to circumvent their committees altogether.

SUBCOMMITTEES. Subcommittees became more important on many committees after the Legislative Reorganization Act of 1946 consolidated committee jurisdictions and reduced the number of standing committees in both chambers. The number of subcommittees grew after World War II and continued to grow into the 1970s as individual committees responded to new policy problems and to demands from members for their own subcommittees. By the early 1990s, there were more than 130 House subcommittees and more than 90 Senate subcommittees. Currently, of the committees with authority to report legislation, only the House Budget and Standards of Official Conduct committees and the Senate Budget, Rules and Administration, Ethics, Indian Affairs, and Veterans' Affairs committees lack standing subcommittees.

In the House, the resistance of some full committee chairmen to efforts to create legislative subcommittees was eventually overcome by a 1974 rule that requires that "each standing committee . . . , except the Committee on the Budget, that has more than twenty members shall establish at least four subcommittees." Later, problems associated with the growth in the number of House subcommittees—jurisdictional squabbles among subcommittees, scheduling difficulties, the burden of subcommittee hearings on executive officials—led the Democratic caucus to limit the number of subcommittees. The 1981 caucus rule limits large committees (at least thirty-five members) to eight subcommittees, with the exception of Appropriations, and small committees to six subcommittees.

Neither the Senate nor its parties have a formal rule on the number of subcommittees any committee may have, although restrictions on the number of subcommittee assignments that individual senators may hold effectively limit the number of subcommittees that can be created. The stricter enforcement of limits on subcommittee assignments in 1985 led five committees to eliminate one or more subcommittees after a few senators were forced to give up one of their subcommittee chairmanships. On other committees, enforcement of the rule meant that not enough members were able and willing to take subcommittee assignments, forcing the abolition of some subcommittees. A total of ten Senate committees were compelled or chose to eliminate at least one subcommittee that year.

Subcommittees have gained great importance in committee decision making in the House. As noted above, the House adopted rules in the early 1970s that substantially weakened the ability of full committee chairs to control subcommittees. The net result is that decision-making processes within House committees are now more decentralized than they were in the 1950s and 1960s. Most legislation originates in subcommittees, the vast majority of hearings are held in subcommittees, about half of all committee staff are allocated to subcommittees, and subcommittee leaders usually serve as the floor managers for legislation originating in their subcommittees. The pattern in the House has led some observers to label House decision making "subcommittee government."

"Subcommittee government" is a more appropriate description of the internal decision-making processes of House committees than of Senate committees.

The empowerment of House subcommittees greatly increased the importance of subcommittee chairmen. One indication of the change is increased contention for subcommittee chairmanship: several House members in line for a chairmanship by virtue of their seniority have been rejected by committee colleagues in favor of competitors. The few systematic studies of intracommittee decision making since the reforms of the 1970s indicate that subcommittee chairmen, full committee chairmen, and ranking minority members are the most influential members of their committees. Because of their limited jurisdiction, most subcommittee chairmen are not as powerful as many full chairmen were in the 1950s and 1960s, but their independence of action makes them central players on most legislation.

In the Senate, subcommittee appointment practices are much like those of the House. Committee rules often guarantee members a first (or second) subcommittee choice before any other member receives a second (or third) choice, and all party contingents operate in this way even in the absence of a formal rule. Consequently, committee members are no longer dependent on the full committee chair for desirable subcommittee assignments. But the lack of formal rules empowering subcommittees in the Senate has produced great variation among committees in their reliance on subcommittees. Several Senate committees hold very few hearings in subcommittee, and only a few Senate committees use subcommittees to write legislation. The concept of "subcommittee government" does not fit decision-making processes in most Senate committees.

In addition to standing subcommittees, committees occasionally create other subunits. Most but not all committees allow their chair to create ad hoc subcommittees to handle matters that fall under the jurisdiction of more than one subcommittee. Unfortunately, there is no reliable record of how frequently such ad hoc arrangements are employed, but the relative ease of altering subcommittee jurisdictions keeps the number very small. Committee rules generally imply that the ad hoc subcommittees dissolve upon completing action on the specific matters assigned to them.

COMMITTEE STAFF. The size of committee staffs increased steadily between 1946 and the early 1980s. The Legislative Reorganization Act of 1946 granted each standing committee authority to hire four professional staff assistants and six clerical aides, and the 1970 act increased to six the number of professional assistants each committee could hire. In 1974 the House increased the number to eighteen professional assistants and twelve clerical aides, where it remains today. The 1970 act guaranteed minority party selection of at least two professional staff assistants on each committee, and both chambers later adopted rules guaranteeing even larger staffs to the minority party. The House now gives the minority party control over one third of professional and clerical staffs, and the Senate requires that staff be allocated to the minority party in proportion to the number of minority party members on each committee. Since the early 1980s, budget constraints have caused many committees to reduce staff sizes somewhat, and there has been little overall growth.

Staffing has buttressed committee power and altered the distribution of power within committees. In rules adopted in the early 1970s, the House allowed both the chair and ranking minority member of each standing subcommittee to appoint at least one staff member. Unless the House authorizes additional staff, subcommittee staff positions come out of the allocation guaranteed to the full committee and so directly reduce the number of staff under the control of the full committee chairman and the ranking minority member. This rule dramatically altered staffing patterns in House committees. Between 1969 and 1985, the proportion of all committee staff assigned to subcommittees grew from about 23 percent to nearly 46 percent. Some House subcommittee staffs have grown far beyond the minimum required by House rules, to levels as high as fifteen to twenty aides in a handful of particular cases.

In the Senate, where no rule guaranteeing subcommittee staff was adopted, subcommittee staff has made up about 40 percent of all committee staff. Indeed, while the total number of House committee staff more than tripled between 1969 and 1979, due primarily to the expansion of subcommittee staffs, Senate committee staff grew by only 80 percent or so.

House committees, operating under requirements that committee staff be shared with subcommittees and the minority party, now have very similar distributions of staff between full committee and subcommittees. In some cases, most notably Ways and Means, the full committee chairman, through the senior full committee staff, exercises substantial control over at least the majority party staff of the committee and subcommittees. Senate committees, because they are not constrained by chamber or party rules requiring separate subcommittee staffs, continue to vary widely in the manner in which they staff subcommittee activities.

COMMITTEE DECENTRALIZATION. The extent of decentralization in the decision-making processes found within House and Senate committees is indicated in an index of "subcommittee orientation." The higher the index score, the more the committee relies on subcommittees. The greater the reliance on subcommittees, the more decentralized the committee's decision-making process is said to be.

Table 3 lists House and Senate committees according to the degree of decentralization found in the 100th Congress (1987–1989). House committees were more decentralized than Senate committees. House committees had an average subcommittee orientation of 47 percent from 1969 to 1971, 62 percent from 1979 to 1981, and 57 percent from 1987 to 1989. In contrast, the respective levels for the Senate were 26 percent, 25 percent, and 20 percent. Compared to the situation in the late 1960s, all but one of the fourteen House committees examined became more subcommittee oriented

TABLE 3

HOUSE AND SENATE COMMITTEES RANKED BY SUBCOMMITTEE ORIENTATION (MOST DECENTRALIZED TO LEAST DECENTRALIZED), 1987–1988

1. House Energy and Commerce
2. House Science, Space, and Technology
3. House Judiciary
4. House Banking, Finance, and Urban Affairs
5. House Government Operations
6. House Interior and Insular Affairs
7. House Public Works and Transportation
8. House Education and Labor
9. House Agriculture
10. House Merchant Marine and Fisheries
11. House Foreign Affairs
12. House Armed Services
13. House Veterans' Affairs
14. Senate Judiciary
15. Senate Commerce, Science, and Transportation
16. House Small Business
17. Senate Governmental Affairs
18. Senate Environment and Public Works
19. House Ways and Means
20. Senate Labor and Human Resources
21. Senate Energy and Natural Resources
22. Senate Banking, Housing, and Urban Affairs
23. Senate Armed Services
24. Senate Agriculture, Nutrition, and Forestry
25. Senate Finance
26. Senate Rules and Administration
27. Senate Foreign Relations
28. Senate Small Business
29. Senate Veterans' Affairs
30. House Budget
31. Senate Budget

Note: The index is the mean of the following measures: (1) the percentage of measures considered on the floor that are managed by a subcommittee chair, (2) the percentage of measures reported to the floor that were referred to a subcommittee or on which a subcommittee hearing was held, (3) the percentage of meetings (primarily markups) that were subcommittee meetings, and (4) the percentage of staff specifically allocated to subcommittees. Data not available for House Appropriations, House Rules, and Senate Appropriations. Excludes three minor House committees: House Administration, Standards of Official Conduct, and District of Columbia.

Source: Adapted from Steven S. Smith and Christopher J. Deering, *Committees in Congress* (1990), pp. 157–158.

by the late 1970s. In sharp contrast, eight of the twelve Senate committees for which complete data are available became less subcommittee oriented during the 1970s.

"Subcommittee government" clearly is a more appropriate description of the internal decision-making processes of House committees than of Senate committees. House subcommittees have developed a more thoroughly institutionalized role. This role is established not only in the rules of the House and the Democratic caucus, but also in the interests of individual representatives. Representatives with sufficient seniority to chair a subcommittee ordinarily chair only one. That chairmanship gives them additional staff, control over hearings on matters under their subcommittee's jurisdiction, and the power to initiate or block legislation in the absence of actions by the full committee.

In contrast, a typical majority party senator chairs two or three subcommittees. A senator is not very dependent on any one subcommittee or subcommittee chairmanship for his or her legislative livelihood. The tremendous demands on senators' time make senators less likely to insist that their subcommittees be active, effective decision-making units. As a result, Senate subcommittees vary more in importance. On several Senate committees, subcommittees play no formal role in writing legislation. And over the last decade or so, reliance on subcommittees has declined on some Senate committees. Rather than developing a central role in Senate policy making, Senate subcommittees have proved to be one component of a very individualistic decision-making process.

FORCES SHAPING THE POWER OF COMMITTEES. The decision-making processes of the House and Senate represent an interaction of committees, parties, and the parent chambers. The relationship among the three varies through time, as does the relative importance of each in shaping public policy. Committees have been used since Congress's first session in 1789, but their functions and influence have changed as the chambers, parties, and their political environment have evolved.

The potential importance of committees can be seen in three contrasting models of committee power. Each model is a highly stylized view of what congressional decision making could be like. The models highlight the advantages and disadvantages of the modern committee systems and provide a basis for specifying the conditions that shape the role of committees.

In the autonomous committee model, members of each committee determine policy within their jurisdiction, irrespective of the policy preferences of the parent chamber and parties. That is, committees have monopoly control over both setting the agenda for their parent chamber and making policy choices.

In the party-dominated committee model, committee members are agents of their parties. The parties have the capacity to shape the composition and policy outlook of their committee contingents because they control appointments to committees. Committee members take direction from their party leaders on what issues to consider and what policy choices to make.

In the chamber-dominated committee model, committee members are agents of their parent chambers.

Committees are created to meet the needs of the chamber for a division of labor, the development of expertise, the acquisition of information, and the organization of a supporting staff. Committees must obtain majority support on the floor for their legislation and so tailor their proposals to the expectations of floor majorities.

Each of the three models has attractive features. Autonomous committees allow Congress to manage a large work load by providing a division of labor and encourages the development of expertise among committee members, who know that their work will be respected and approved by others. A party-dominated system allows for the emergence of strong party leadership, which can supervise the development of coherent, timely policy and makes it possible to hold a party accountable for congressional decisions. A chamber-dominated system seems quite democratic because it preserves the equality of all members, regardless of their committee assignments or party affiliation, and allows all members to have an active voice in important decisions.

The fit of these models to actual House and Senate practices has varied over time in response to several sets of factors: the character of Congress's policy agenda, the distribution of policy preferences, and the institutional context. The effects of these factors can be summarized in several propositions.

Issue agenda. The larger the agenda, the more separable the issues, the more issues recur frequently, and the less salient the issues, the more Congress relies on committees to make policy choices. Large agendas require a division of labor to handle the work load, and a system of powerful committees provides such a division of labor. If the issues are easily separable into distinct categories, then committees with distinct jurisdictions work well. If issues recur frequently, then committee jurisdictions can be fixed without concern that some committees will become superfluous over time. Moreover, if most issues concern only a few members, committees can make decisions without serious challenge on the floor. Over its two-hundred-year history, Congress's expanding policy agenda has produced a nearly continuous elaboration of its committee systems, which provide the basic means for dividing labor and increasing Congress's capacity to process legislation.

Alignment of policy preferences. The more issues are salient to most members and the more cohesive the majority party, the more Congress relies on the majority party to make policy choices. When more issues are salient to most members and the majority party lacks cohesiveness, however, Congress relies more on the chamber floor to make policy choices. When most members take an active interest in policy decisions, they will not tolerate autonomous committees that do not share their policy views. If members' policy preferences reflect partisan alignments so that the majority party is cohesive, the majority party will have both the incentive and the capacity to control committees. Party leaders will be encouraged to see to it that committees either have little influence over outcomes or are stacked with friendly members. If issues are salient to most members, preferences are not aligned by party, and the majority party lacks sufficient cohesiveness, coalitions cutting across the parties—perhaps different coalitions on different issues—may assert themselves on the floor and determine policy outcomes. Historically, the partisanship of policy alignments has varied greatly.

Institutional context. The more chamber rules and practices preserve the right of individual members to debate and offer amendments at will on the floor, the less autonomy committee members and party leaders will have. The House and Senate are very different institutions. There is greater need for a strong presiding officer and for observance of formal rules in the larger, more unwieldy House. In the Senate, there is greater tolerance of individual initiative and greater resistance to committee- or party-imposed policy choices. That tolerance is represented in Senate rules that protect the individual member's right to offer amendments on any subject and conduct extended debate. Such rules preserve individual senators' bargaining leverage with committee and party leaders.

Committee power has come under attack during the past two decades.

The critical feature of past procedural and structural choices is that they limit the range of feasible institutional arrangements for the future. Neither house has the time or capacity to completely reconstitute its decision-making processes. Elaboration of existing procedures and structures is the common response to new demands. Different institutional arrangements in the House and Senate are likely to cause different responses to similar changes in issue agendas and policy alignments. In general, the committee autonomy and party-dominated committee models generally fit the Senate less well than the House.

RECENT TRENDS. Committee power has come under attack during the past two decades. While committees continue to draft the details of nearly all legislation and their members remain central players in nearly all congressional policy decisions, they no longer operate as autonomously as they once did. Change has been most dramatic in the House of Representatives, where committees traditionally dominated policy-making more completely than they did in the Senate. But both houses have become less committee centered.

Changes in both the policy agenda and political alignments have led to a decline in committee autonomy in recent decades. In the 1960s and 1970s, many new issues, like energy, the environment, and consumer protection, were interconnected and fell under the jurisdiction of several committees. The agenda became less predictable and recurrent. In the 1980s, concern about the federal budget deficit began to dominate policy-making. Most other domestic policy issues were set aside or reinterpreted in terms of their budgetary consequences. The agenda contracted and the remaining issues, all seen as connected to fiscal policy, concerned nearly all members.

These changes stimulated intercommittee conflict, which has sometimes been fueled by multiple referrals. Noncommittee members have more frequently challenged committee recommendations. Floor amending activity increased in the last two decades, and demands for recorded votes on committee and conference recommendations have increased. And in the area of budgeting, a number of procedures to limit committee discretion and order committee action have been imposed.

While the agenda fluctuated, the political alignments among members shifted. Due to electoral changes and a new agenda, the party coalitions proved far more cohesive in the 1980s. Party leaders and caucuses became more assertive in structuring the agenda and formulating policy on important issues.

The decline of committee autonomy is most apparent in the House, where committees had more to lose than in the Senate. House committees recovered to some extent in the 1980s, by the more creative use of special rules to limit amendments, but the fact that restrictive special rules are necessary indicates how much committee autonomy has declined in the House.

Committees are integral to a remarkably complex congressional decision-making process. For most of the past century, the basic structure of the committee systems has remained stable, reflecting fundamental features of Congress itself—a large, diverse agenda, weak parties, and the great variation in the salience of issues among members. Nevertheless, the House and Senate committee systems are not rigid and fixed. They have demonstrated substantial variability in their place in the policy-making process and will continue to do so in the future.

[See also (I) Subcommittees.]

BIBLIOGRAPHY

Davidson, Roger H. "Subcommittee Government: New Channels for Policy Making." In *Congress Reconsidered,* 3d ed. Edited by Lawrence C. Dodd and Bruce L. Oppenheimer. 1985.

Evans, C. Lawrence. *Leadership in Committee.* 1991.

Fenno, Richard F., Jr. *Congressmen in Committees.* 1973.

Fenno, Richard F., Jr. *The Power of the Purse: Appropriations Politics in Congress.* 1966.

Goodwin, George. *The Little Legislatures.* 1970.

Huitt, Ralph K. "The Congressional Committee: A Case Study." *American Political Science Review* 48 (1954): pp. 340–365.

Kiewiet, D. Roderick, and Mathew D. McCubbins. *The Logic of Delegation.* 1991.

Krehbiel, Keith. *Information and Legislative Organization.* 1991.

Manley, John F. *The Politics of Finance.* 1970.

Matthews, Donald R. *U.S. Senators and Their World.* 1960.

Parker, Glenn R., and Suzanne L. Parker. *Factions in House Committees.* 1985.

Price, David E. *Who Makes the Laws?* 1972.

Shepsle, Kenneth A., and Barry Weingast. "The Institutional Foundations of Committee Power." *American Political Science Review* 81 (1987): pp. 85–105.

Smith, Steven S. *Call to Order.* 1989.

Smith, Steven S., and Christopher J. Deering. *Committees in Congress.* 2d ed. 1990.

Strahan, Randall. *New Ways and Means.* 1990.

– STEVEN S. SMITH

Assignment of Members

Members of both chambers generally seek assignment to committees with certain jurisdictions: those that relate to their own professional background (e.g., former teachers to the panels that have responsibility for education issues); those that reflect the demographic complexion of their district or state (e.g., members from farm states to the Agriculture committees, the type often referred to as "constituency committees"); or those involved in policy areas of particular personal interest (e.g., tax-policy specialists to the tax writing committees). Some seek influence through assignments to so-called power or prestige committees. Once members are assigned to committees, it is fairly uncommon for them to change assignments, although given the opportunity to serve on a prestige committee, such as Appropriations, very few members elect not to seek the appointment. Therefore, the committee assignment process largely determines committee membership, especially since that membership is usually very stable.

SENATE. Many key regulations affecting committee assignments are included in the rules of the Senate. The political parties in the chamber make their initial decisions regarding committee sizes following an election and then include those provisions in the Senate rules changes adopted early in the new Congress. Obviously, changes to those rules require a majority vote in the chamber in addition to agreement within one of the party conferences.

Senate Rule XXV contains the basic elements of the committee assignment process. The assignment portion of the rule, substantially rewritten in 1977 and modified in 1984, is traditionally adjusted at the beginning of each Congress to reflect the party ratios in the chamber and to determine the size and ratio of each committee. If changes in Senate membership occur during the course of a Congress, the ratios also may be altered. Despite the periodic changes, the rule still serves as the preeminent determinant of committee membership.

Rule XXV divides Senate committees into three categories, designated "A," "B," and "C." Included in the "A" category are the standing committees on Agriculture, Nutrition, and Forestry; Appropriations; Armed Services; Banking, Housing, and Urban Affairs; Commerce, Science, and Transportation; Energy and Natural Resources; Environment and Public Works; Finance; Foreign Relations; Governmental Affairs; Judiciary; and Labor and Human Resources. In the "B" category are the remaining standing committees—Budget, Rules and Administration, Small Business, and Veterans' Affairs—the permanent select committees on Aging and Intelligence, and the Joint Economic Committee. In the "C" category are the remaining select and joint committees.

Each member is required to serve on two A committees, may serve on one B committee, and can serve on as many C committees as he or she desires and the parties agree to. Many members serve on more committees than the rules allow. This is done by including a waiver, called a grandfather provision, approved by the party caucus and included in Rule XXV for that Congress. The waiver basically says that the particular senator may serve on a specific committee notwithstanding the rule that would otherwise limit such service. Numerous members have such waivers.

The rule also lists the size of each committee for each Congress. The ratio of majority to minority party members on the committee approximates the ratio of majority to minority party members in the full chamber, within the confines of the committee's size as determined by Rule XXV. In order to accommodate the political orientation of the members and majority party control of committees, the rule provides for a so-called working majority, which in effect allows an additional member to serve on the majority side if there are majority party members who frequently vote with the other party on committee business. Committee sizes usually remain fairly constant from Congress to Congress, and it is the ratios that change as party strength in the chamber varies. For sizes to change, amendment of Rule XXV is required.

Once committee sizes and ratios are determined, usually at organization meetings in early December after the November election, each of the parties begins the assignment process. (If a member is elected to the Senate from a party other than the Democratic or Republican party, that member selects which of the two parties he will associate, or caucus, with for assignment purposes.) Each party maintains a committee that is responsible for committee assignments, called the Committee on Committees. This entity reviews the members' requests for assignments and tries to match those requests with available slots. Also, this panel is responsible for internal party rules relating to committee assignments. For example, both parties try to discourage senators from the same party and the same state from serving on the same committee. This is usually accomplished, although there have been exceptions. Further, each party designates "exclusive" committees within the A category and tries to limit members to service on only one such exclusive panel. Regional and philosophical balance also serve as variables that the parties weigh in making assignments. Finally, although waivers (called grandfathers) are included in Rule XXV, each party caucus determines which senators will receive such waivers.

Senators are limited to one full committee chairmanship, although such a chairman can also chair a joint committee whose jurisdiction is directly related to that of his standing committee; for instance, the Finance Committee chairman can chair the Joint Committee on Taxation. Exceptions to this limitation are rare. Ranking minority slots are usually also limited to one per member, although the application of this restriction depends on the party ratio and the number of minority slots that need to be filled.

Generally, senators are limited to service on three subcommittees on each of their class A committees and two subcommittees on their class B committee. There is no limitation on subcommittee service on class C committees. Senators with full committee assignment waivers are entitled to corresponding additional subcommittee assignments. Regarding subcommittee chairmanships, senators are usually limited to one such chairmanship on each full committee on which they serve, although waivers can be granted to exceed this limit.

HOUSE OF REPRESENTATIVES. Unlike the Senate, which incorporates some committee assignment procedures in chamber rules, the House of Representatives invests almost all of the assignment process in its party machinery, especially that of the majority party. In addition, the party decisions never appear in House rules and occasionally do not appear in writing at all.

As the Democrats have been the majority party all but four years between 1931 and 1993, most of the committee assignments have rested with that party and are handled by the Democratic caucus and its Steering and Policy Committee. The Democratic caucus manual details the specific rules and regulations guiding committee assignment procedures for the Democrats; it is modified as necessary each Congress, and occasionally during the Congress, to reflect shifts in party strength.

Committees are divided into three basic categories: exclusive, major, and nonmajor (with general agreement that the divisions in the latter two categories do not carry value judgments regarding the importance of the committees, although the former are the most desirable). Exclusive committees are Appropriations, Rules, and Ways and Means. Major committees are Agriculture; Armed Services; Banking, Finance, and Urban Affairs; Education and Labor; Foreign Affairs; Energy and Commerce; Judiciary; and Public Works and Transportation. Nonmajor committees are Budget; District of Columbia; Government Operations; House Administration; Interior and Insular Affairs; Merchant Marine and Fisheries; Post Office and Civil Service; Science, Space, and Technology; Small Business; and Veterans' Affairs.

Once committee sizes and ratios are determined, each of the parties begins the assignment process.

Select, special, and joint committees are not included in the categorization, and indeed, assignments to these panels are made outside the limitations discussed below. Select and special committee membership procedures are either included in the resolution creating the panel or made by the Speaker of the House. Joint committee membership is generally drawn from the corresponding standing committee.

Sizes of committees are determined by the Democratic caucus, with ratios usually reflecting majority-to-minority party strength in the chamber. In a few cases, ratios do not reflect party strength (e.g., the Rules Committee has a 2-to-1 plus 1 ratio, and the Committee on Standards of Official Conduct has an equal number of Democrats and Republicans). Also, sizes are often altered to reflect interest in a panel; that is, sizes can be raised to accommodate members' requests, or limited to deny assignment. It is rare for sizes to be decreased in order to eliminate members already serving on the panel.

Democratic members are generally limited to service on one exclusive committee, or one major and one nonmajor committee, or two nonmajor committees. However, members often receive waivers to serve on more than the requisite number of major and nonmajor panels. Waivers most often result from assignments to those committees that are perceived to be less desirable and thus are more difficult to fill. In addition, for some committees, such as Budget and Standards of Official Conduct, the Democratic caucus limits the terms a member can serve and these committees therefore have what has been called a rotating membership. They are also outside the assignment limitations. For the Budget Committee, some members are appointed because of their other committee assignments; for instance, some members represent the Appropriations Committee, others the Ways and Means Committee, and so forth. Finally, waivers regarding the exclusive committees are rare.

The Democratic caucus rules state that the chairman of an exclusive or major committee may not serve on any other exclusive, major, or nonmajor committee. Further, a full committee chairman may not serve as a chairman of any other full committee without a waiver from the caucus. Finally, no committee chairman can serve as a member of the Committee on Standards of Official Conduct.

Generally, members are limited to service on a total of five subcommittees among their standing committee assignments. Members usually bid for three subcommittee assignments on their major committee and two on their nonmajor committee, although there is no rule governing this selection. However, because of the numerous waivers discussed above, some members exceed the five subcommittee limit. The caucus rules also limit members to election to one subcommittee chairmanship on their legislative committees. Because of their unique nature, the subcommittees of the Appropriations and Ways and Means Committees have a distinct set of assignment guidelines, which basically provide more authority to the full Democratic caucus, rather than to the Democrats on the committee.

Because the majority party determines committee sizes and ratios, assignment decisions by the Republican party's Committee on Committees must wait until the Democrats have completed their initial assignment processes. Accordingly, the Republican rules and practices are much more flexible, much less formal, and rarely found in writing. However, they do categorize committees as "red," "white," and "blue," a categorization roughly the same as the Democrats', the major difference being that Energy and Commerce is a red committee. Generally, most Republican members serve on only one standing committee, with some limited exceptions. Members are limited to service as a ranking member (often called vice chairman) on only one full committee, and as a ranking member on only two subcommittees.

As in the Senate, members from third parties receive their committee assignments through one of the two party caucuses, although past practice has been inconsistent regarding how these members are counted toward committee size, ratio, and other seniority questions.

[See also (I) Congress, article on Politics and Influence in Congress, Seniority.]

BIBLIOGRAPHY

Schneider, Judy. *Senate Rules and Practices on Committees, Subcommittees, and Chairmanship Assignment Limitations as of October 31, 1992.* Congressional Research Service, Library of Congress. CRS Rept. 92-780. 1992.

Shepsle, Kenneth A. *The Giant Jigsaw Puzzle.* 1978.

Smith, Steven S., and Bruce A. Ray. "The Impact of Congressional Reform: House Democratic Committee Assignments." *Congress and Presidency* 10 (Autumn 1983).

Smith, Steven S. and Christopher J. Deering. *Committees in Congress.* 1990.

– JUDY SCHNEIDER

Committee Hearings

Scholars have differed as to the role committees play in the legislative process. The traditional view is found in Joseph Chamberlain's classic *Legislative Processes* (1936) and Arthur Maass's *Congress and the Common Good* (1983). By this view committees are tools used by the larger chamber to arrive at the "common good" of the larger society. The committee acts as the guardian of the general public interest after hearing from special-interest advocates who appear before it. From this perspective, committee hearings take on features of a legislative court where members decide what to do based upon the evidence of law and fact brought before them by the interested parties. These open hearings at the same time act as a public forum where the public interest will emerge from the clamor of competing special interests.

By a second view, first proposed in 1908 by Arthur Bentley in *The Process of Government* but not popularized until the publication of David Truman's *The Governmental Process* in 1951, the legislative process is but a struggle between competing groups, none of whom are concerned with a guiding abstraction like the "common good." Public policy emerges from the push and pull of competing groups, each seeking its own interests. In this process, individual legislators act as advocates of these parochial interests and not as neutral judges seeking the general good. Committee hearings are not neutral legislative fact-finding courts but vehicles to further the interests of members.

Truman argues that committee hearings serve three purposes. First, the hearings allow for the transmission of information from the various interest groups to the committee. Second, because committee members are not acting in the role of neutral judges, the hearings are used as a propaganda platform by the interest groups, with little thought given to a meaningful debate on the subject at hand. Third, the hearings act as a safety valve whereby group conflicts can be adjusted before they become explosive.

The most recent view to emerge takes the group concept one step further by relying upon econometric research to focus upon the economic calculus of individuals and thus to explain committee activity. A laudable attempt to summarize in a nonmathematical manner the two classes of formal theory that make up much of this literature is Keith Krehbiel's *Information and Legislative Organization* (1991).

AUTHORITY TO HOLD HEARINGS. The authority of committees to hold hearings rests on the constitutionally granted power to legislate, which includes the power to conduct inquiries and investigations (*Kilbourn v. Thompson,* 103 U.S. 168 [1881]; *McGrain v. Daugherty,* 273 U.S. 135 [1927]; *Watkins v. United States,* 354 U.S. 178 [1957]; *Barenblatt v. United States,* 360 U.S. 109 [1959]). Both chambers of Congress have developed sets of rules to guide their conduct based upon the power to legislate. Rule X of the Rules of the House of Representatives and Rule XXV of the Standing Rules of the Senate provide for the establishment and jurisdiction of standing committees. Rule XI, clause 1 (a) (2) (b) of the House rules stipulates, "Each committee is authorized at any time to conduct such investigations and studies as it may consider necessary or appropriate in the exercise of its responsibilities under Rule X. . . ." Furthermore, clause 2 (m) (1) of Rule XI authorizes committees or their subcommittees to hold hearings and require, by subpoena or otherwise, the attendance and testimony of such witnesses and the production of such records or documents as it deems necessary.

Authority for Senate committees to hold hearings is found in Rule XXVI, clause 1 of the Senate rules. This provision states:

> Each standing committee, including any subcommittee of any such committee, is authorized to hold such hearings, to sit and act at such times and places during the sessions, recesses, and adjourned periods of the Senate,

> to require by subpoena or otherwise the attendance of such witnesses and the production of such correspondence, books, papers, and documents, to take such testimony . . . as may be authorized by resolutions of the Senate. Each such committee may make investigations into any matter within its jurisdiction. . . .

Besides the Standing Rules, the authority for committee action may also be found in statutes or in chamber rules and resolutions not specifically focusing on developing the committee's basic charter. The Senate has simplified the process of determining the rights of individuals subpoenaed or otherwise called to appear before a committee by publishing a document that identifies the authority and rules of Senate committees (S. Doc. No. 102-6). Here can be found the authority for matters including provisions for the administration of oaths to witnesses; the payment of witnesses' expenses; the criminal and civil enforcement of Senate subpoenas; immunity for witnesses; the preservation and disclosure of Senate records; and authorization of testimony.

HEARING PROCESS. Roger Davidson and Walter Oleszek in *Congress against Itself* (1977) describe most committee hearings as being conducted with little fanfare, with participation usually confined to the persons giving testimony, a rotating cast of committee or subcommittee members, and a sprinkling of observers, generally interest-group representatives. Witnesses usually give testimony from prepared texts while committee members occasionally follow along. More often than not, members will use this time to review their correspondence or consult with staff. When the testimony ends, the questioning begins, with committee members most often proceeding in order of seniority. There is little interchange between members at this point, and, since witnesses usually appear alone, there is no opportunity for them to exchange views on the subject.

The authority of committees to hold hearings rests on the constitutionally granted power to legislate.

It would be a mistake, however, to believe that committee hearings are used solely for the purpose of collecting information. Various interests vie with one another in the legislative arena to decide public policy, and it should come as no surprise to see the committee hearing process used as a tool in that struggle.

Legislation ultimately needs majority support to be successful. Legislators need to know what the various positions are on an issue before proceeding, and the hearing process can serve the purpose of legislative coalition building by providing a forum for the public discussion of issues. The support of the administration on an issue, for example, might be necessary before members sign on to a bill, or, conversely, presidential opposition might be enough to doom any serious consideration of the proposal.

Hearings, in the hands of a skillful full or subcommittee chairman, can also be used to promote or retard the chances of proposed legislation. For example, scheduling friendly or critical witnesses early in the hearing process when outside interest may be high might be critical to the subsequent success or failure of the legislation. Badgering opposition witnesses or setting up and coaching friendly witnesses can also have an impact on the outcome of a proposal.

Before the Legislative Reform Act of 1970 forced Congress to open up its process, over a third of all committee hearings were closed to the public. Today virtually all hearings are open with many now televised, primarily by C-SPAN (Ornstein et al., 1992). The televised proceedings of the nomination hearings of Robert Bork and Clarence Thomas riveted millions of viewers to their television sets and gave many a revealing look at just how the process is used by legislators to further aims other than the elucidation of an issue.

INVESTIGATIVE HEARINGS. The hearing most familiar to the average person is the investigative hearing. From the very beginning of the Republic, when the House of Representatives in 1792 appointed a select committee to inquire into the St. Clair expedition, to present-day concerns over government malfeasance, congressional investigations have captured the nation's attention in a manner not possible with other forms of legislative activity.

The power to investigate is not one of the powers expressly granted to Congress, but the Supreme Court has ruled that it can be exercised as an implied power (*McGrain v. Daugherty*, 1927). There is little controversy over whether Congress has or needs the power to investigate in order to meet its obligation to enact legislation, to oversee the administration of its enactments, and to inform the public. Criticism has, for the most part, focused on the extent of the legislature's power and the manner in which investigations are carried out. Initially, the courts attempted to limit the scope of congressional investigations by insisting that they be related to some legislative purpose (*Kilbourn v. Thompson*, 1881). The modern Court, however, has come to take a much less restrictive position: "To be a valid legislative inquiry there need be no predictable end result" (*East-*

land v. United States Serviceman's Fund, 421 U.S. 491, 509 [1975]).

Primarily because of the abuses of investigative power by such individuals as Sen. Joseph R. McCarthy and by the House Un-American Activities Committee (later known as the Committee on Internal Security) in the 1950s, Congress has adopted procedures to assure fairness in committee investigations (Fisher, 1990). The courts have also moved to define the scope and proper authorization for congressional hearings (*United States v. Rumely,* 345 U.S. 41 [1953]; *Gojack v. United States,* 384 U.S. 702 [1966]).

FUTURE OF HEARINGS. The extent to which hearings are utilized by committees depends upon the number of committees and the level of their workloads. The trend since the early 1950s (for which the first reliable figures are available) reveals, first, a dramatic increase in overall levels of congressional activity including committee hearings. This activity peaked in the mid-1970s and has been followed by a slow but steady decline in all levels of committee activity, but not to the levels of the 1950s. The total number of committees in the House and Senate peaked at 385 in the 94th Congress (1975–1977) and then began a steady decline of almost one-third, reaching a total of 284 in the 102d Congress (1991–1993). Likewise, the number of Senate committee and subcommittee meetings grew from 2,607 in the 84th Congress (1955–1957) to a high of 4,265 in the 94th Congress (1975–1977) and then declined to 2,340 in the 101st Congress (1989–1991). The House peaked in the 95th Congress (1977–1979) at 7,896 meetings, up from a total of 3,210 meetings in the 84th Congress. The House then declined, but not as precipitously as the Senate, to a total of 5,305 meetings in the 101st Congress (Ornstein et al., 1992).

HEARING PUBLICATIONS. Because one of the primary purposes of hearings is to gather opinions and information regarding proposed legislation, much valuable information is contained in the hearing publications. This information may range from a full transcript of the proceedings, to statistical analyses, texts of related reports, and expert testimony.

The Congressional Information Service's *U.S. Congressional Committee Hearings Index* (1981, pp. vii–ix) explains that committee hearings began to be recorded and printed only when committees became an important part of the legislative process. Well into the late 1800s, committee hearings were published only sporadically, and as late as the 1930s, committees viewed their hearings as internal documents for their own use and not as public documents. As a consequence, many hearings were never printed. Since that time, however, there has been a more systematic effort to preserve these valuable records.

Through the years committee publications have been stored in a number of places, including the U.S. Senate Library, the Library of Congress, congressional committee collections, and the Supreme Court Library, as well as a number of libraries maintained by major federal departments and private organizations. Many of these facilities are not open to the public.

In 1975 a project was completed that included placing on microfiche more than twenty-seven thousand congressional committee hearings publications held by the U.S. Senate Library, as well as an index and checklist of hearings held before 1935 that had been compiled from major sources outside the U.S. Senate collection.

One can refer to congressional committee hearings by consulting the indexes of the Congressional Information Service (CIS), which cover materials from the early 1800s through the first session of the 91st Congress. Subsequent Congresses are covered through CIS five-, four-, and one-year indexes.

The National Archives are another source of committee hearings. Committees have periodically turned over their records to the National Archives for storage and safe keeping. The extent of each committee's records held in the National Archives has been documented in two companion volumes compiled by the Archives staff (S. Doc. No. 100-42; H. Doc. No. 100-245).

[See also (I) Investigations, Subpoena Power, Witnesses, Rights of.]

BIBLIOGRAPHY

Bentley, Arthur F. *The Process of Government.* 1908. Repr. 1967.
Chamberlain, Joseph P. *Legislative Processes: National and State.* 1936. Repr. 1969.
Congressional Information Services, Inc. *U.S. Congressional Committee Hearings Index* (1833–1969). 1981.
Davidson, Roger H., and Walter J. Oleszek. *Congress against Itself.* 1977.
Fisher, Louis. *American Constitutional Law.* 1990.
Krehbiel, Keith. *Information and Legislative Organization.* 1991.
Maass, Arthur. *Congress and the Common Good.* 1967.
Ornstein, Norman J., Thomas E. Mann, and Michael J. Malbin. *Vital Statistics on Congress, 1991–1992.* 1992.
Truman, David B. *The Governmental Process: Political Interests and Public Opinion.* 1951.

– JOSEPH K. UNEKIS

Committee Jurisdictions

Committee jurisdiction is a complex matter, determined by a number of factors. Paramount among these are House Rule X and Senate Rule XXV, which designate the subject matter within the purview of each standing committee. The rules list jurisdictions in broad topical terms rather than narrowly drawn language or programmatic references.

Select and special committee jurisdiction is generally included in the resolution authorizing a panel. Select committees usually do not have legislative jurisdiction and therefore cannot have measures referred to them. In the case of select or special committees, therefore, *jurisdiction* usually refers to investigative responsibility.

Within each chamber, some standing committees' jurisdictions overlap those of other committees, and the parallel yet distinctive House and Senate committee systems distribute policy responsibilities in somewhat different ways. Major analogous jurisdictional clusters can be identified, however, many of which correspond with committee names. (Table 1, adapted from Steven S. Smith and Christopher J. Deering [1990], identifies these jurisdictional clusters.)

All the areas over which a standing committee has jurisdiction cannot necessarily be inferred from the committee's name, however. Because of the complexity of issues, jurisdictional divisions and matchups often seem arbitrary. For example, child nutrition falls within the purview of the Agriculture Committee in the Senate, where it is viewed as a food-related issue, but under the Education and Labor Committee's jurisdiction in the House, where it is viewed as an education-related issue.

Subcommittee jurisdictions further delineate these broad topical areas. Subcommittee jurisdictions are determined not by chamber rules but by the individual full committees and are often defined in committee rules. The level of specificity of subcommittee jurisdiction varies widely from committee to committee. In fact, some Senate subcommittee jurisdictions are designated solely by the name of the subcommittee, while other Senate committees merely number their subcommittees, giving the chairman (often on behalf of the full committee) the authority to determine the panels' responsibilities. House subcommittee jurisdiction is usually more formally defined.

Both House Rule X and Senate Rule XXV are broad and largely the products of an era in which governmental activity was not so extensive and relations between policies not so complex as now. Most of Rule X and Rule XXV was drawn from nineteenth- and early-twentieth-century precedents and codified in the Legislative Reorganization Act of 1946. Although both rules underwent modest revision in the 1970s (the Senate rule once and the House rule three times), there are legislative topics still omitted from the purview of any specified jurisdiction, as well as unclear and overlapping jurisdictions among those specified.

Accordingly, the formal provisions of the rules are supplemented by an intricate series of precedents and informal agreements governing the referral of legislation. In general, once a measure has been referred to a given committee, it remains the responsibility of that committee; if the measure is enacted into law, amendments to the law are presumed to be within the originating committee's responsibility. Relatedly, bills that are more comprehensive than the measure they amend or supersede are presumed to be within the jurisdiction of the committee reporting the more comprehensive measure. Therefore, policy areas considered in a broad manner may enable a committee to attain jurisdiction; if a more narrow approach were taken, this might not occur. The resultant procedural accretions of responsibility greatly expand the range and scope of subjects assigned to each committee.

In considering jurisdictional overlap, a distinction needs to be made between legislative and oversight responsibility. The former entails the authority to report measures to the full chamber; the latter, the authority to review or investigate. Although oversight jurisdiction may be given by a specific legislative enactment, it also accrues when committees accept responsibilities for broad topical areas. Hence, there are more likely to be broader and more frequent overlaps in oversight jurisdiction than in legislative jurisdiction. Legislative jurisdiction, however, is usually the occasion of the majority of overt conflicts between standing committees.

Committee jurisdiction is a complex matter, determined by a number of factors.

Several other factors are at work in fixing committee jurisdiction, although these are not formal or even acknowledged in rules or precedents. First, when determining the appropriate referral of a bill, the Speaker of the House and the House and Senate parliamentarians may take into account the committee assignments and generally acknowledged policy expertise of a measure's sponsor. This is especially true if the sponsor is a committee or subcommittee chairman or ranking minority member. Similarly, members may draft bills in such a manner as to possibly influence the referral to committee, especially in the Senate, where predominant jurisdiction is the controlling factor in referrals.

Second, the timing of a measure's introduction may also affect which committee receives a bill referral. For example, if a member introduces a bill following hearings on or press coverage of a subject in which that

TABLE 1

STANDING CONGRESSIONAL COMMITTEES AND THEIR JURISDICTIONS

Senate Committee	House Committee	Jurisdiction
Agriculture, Nutrition, and Forestry	Agriculture	Agriculture and forestry development and conservation; farm credit and farmer assistance programs; nutrition programs, including food stamps; in House, rural electrification
Appropriations	Appropriations	House and Senate appropriations of money for government agencies and federal programs and activities
Armed Services	Armed Services	Military and defense matters, including human resources and weapons research and development
Banking, Housing, and Urban Affairs	Banking, Finance, and Urban Affairs	Regulation of banking industry and other financial institutions; money supply and its control; public and private housing; urban development; aspects of international finance and foreign trade; in Senate, mass transit
Budget	Budget	Setting annual spending targets and priorities for broad categories of governmental functions—health, education, defense, and so on—and reconciling revenues with expenditures
Commerce, Science, and Transportation	Energy and Commerce Merchant Marine and Fisheries Science, Space, and Technology	Coast Guard; Merchant Marine; science and technology; nonmilitary aeronautics and space sciences; communications; coastal zone management; interstate commerce; regulation of interstate transportation, including railroads; in Senate, also ships, pipelines, and civil aviation; in House, national energy policy generally; energy research and development; securities and exchanges; health care; consumer affairs and protection; Panama Canal
Energy and Natural Resources	Interior and Insular Affairs	Mining; national parks; wilderness areas and historic sites; territorial possessions of the United States; public lands; in Senate, regulation, conservation, research and development of all forms of energy (Energy and Commerce in House); in House, regulation of domestic nuclear energy industry
Environment and Public Works	Public Works and Transportation	Environmental protection; water resources and flood control; watershed development; rivers and harbors; public works and buildings; highways; noise pollution; in House, surface transportation, except railroads, and civil aviation
Finance	Ways and Means	Taxation; Social Security; tariffs; in House, health care programs financed through payroll taxes
Foreign Relations	Foreign Affairs	Foreign relations and foreign policy; United Nations; in Senate, treaties; in House, international trade and economic policy
Governmental Affairs	District of Columbia Government Operations Post Office and Civil Service	Organization and reorganization of executive branch; intergovernmental relations; in Senate, municipal affairs of District of Columbia, civil service, postal service, census, while in individual committees in House; in House, revenue sharing (Government Operations)
Judiciary	Judiciary	Federal courts; appointment of judges (Senate only); constitutional amendments; crime; drug control and policy: immigration and naturalization; antitrust and monopolies; patents, trademarks, and copyrights; impeachment; in House, presidential succession
Labor and Human Resources	Education and Labor	Education; labor, including vocational rehabilitation, minimum wages; in Senate, public welfare and health (Energy and Commerce and Ways and Means in House); in House, school lunch program (Agriculture in Senate)
Rules and Administration	Rules House Administration Standards of Official Conduct	Rules of chamber, administration and management of chamber; federal elections; Smithsonian Institution; Library of Congress; in Senate, presidential succession
Select Indian Affairs (has legislative jurisdiction)	Interior and Insular Affairs Education and Labor	Indians generally, including land management and trust responsibilities, education, health, special services, claims against the United States
Select Intelligence (has legislative jurisdiction)	Select Intelligence (has legislative jurisdiction)	Intelligence activities and programs
Small Business	Small Business	Small business generally and Small Business Administration
Veterans' Affairs	Veterans' Affairs	Veterans' affairs, including pensions, medical care, life insurance, education, and rehabilitation

member was involved, there could be an implicit understanding that the sponsor wants the bill referred to his committee.

Third, even if a committee did not originally consider a measure, representation from its membership at the conference on the measure could be used to argue that the committee has an implicit claim on the measure's subject. The committee might thus begin to accrue jurisdictional prerogatives.

Fourth, on some occasions committee jurisdiction over specific authorizing legislation has been influenced or, arguably, specifically determined by which subcommittee of the Appropriations Committee considers appropriations requests for the programs authorized. Too, even though the rules of the House forbid legislating in an appropriations bill (i.e., making policy decisions in a bill limited to making monetary choices), the Appropriations Committee occasionally does make legislative policy in in annual, supplemental, or continuing appropriations bill that has not been considered by the appropriate authorizing committee of jurisdiction. Relatedly, since passage of the Budget and Impoundment Control Act of 1974, budget reconciliation measures (which, in mandating budget cuts, may effect program changes) have had potential influence on committee jurisdiction. For example, when the Budget Committee directs a particular committee to respond to reconciliation instructions (especially in an area of overlapping jurisdictions) or when a committee traditionally considers programs under specific budget functions, these circumstances can be used to support a committee's jurisdictional claims. (It should not be assumed, however, that legislative committees deliberately use the Appropriations Committee or Budget Committee, or the appropriations or budget reconciliation process generally, to avoid jurisdictional disputes, although these options are always open.)

In 1974, with the adoption of the Committee Reform Amendments (H. Res. 988, reported by the Select Committee on Committees chaired by Rep. Richard W. Bolling and modified by a Democratic caucus panel chaired by Rep. Julia Butler Hansen), the House authorized the referral of measures to more than one committee. House Rule X, clause 5(c) invested in the Speaker the authority to refer measures in a joint, split, or sequential manner. Multiple referrals have since been used frequently, often to acknowledge overlapping jurisdictions and often to avoid choosing among committees' jurisdictional prerogatives. The effect has been to further broaden committee jurisdictions and further fragment policy and program responsibility.

In the Senate, multiple referrals are possible but rarely used. Unanimous consent is often difficult to obtain, and a motion to make multiple referrals, granted to the leadership in 1977 (pursuant to recommendations reported by the Select Committee on Committees chaired by Sen. Adlai E. Stevenson III), has not yet been invoked.

[See also (I) Subcommittees.]

BIBLIOGRAPHY

Smith, Steven S., and Christopher J. Deering. *Committees in Congress.* 2d ed. 1990.

U.S. House of Representatives. Select Committee on Committees. *Monographs on the Committees of the House of Representatives.* 93d Cong., 2d sess., 1974.

U.S. Senate. Temporary Select Committee to Study the Senate Committee System. *The Senate Committee System: Jurisdictions, Referrals, Numbers and Sizes, and Limitations on Membership.* 94th Cong., 2d sess., 1976.

– JUDY SCHNEIDER

Markups

Markups are sessions held by a congressional committee during which the text of a bill is discussed and revised. The term *markup* is derived from the practice of literally marking up the original text of the bill to reflect the committee's proposed changes. Bills may be examined and revised by the committee line-by-line, paragraph-by-paragraph, section-by-section, or title-by-title. Alternatively, a complete substitute text for the entire bill may be offered. Committees also may decide not to alter the original bill at all, although this is rare.

Markups are sessions held by a congressional committee during which the text of a bill is discussed and revised.

The measure used for purposes of discussion and revision in committee is usually a previously introduced bill that had been referred to the committee. However, sometimes an informal draft, which has never been introduced, is used instead. The bill or draft, typically presented by the chairman to the committee for consideration, is known as "the chairman's mark." The decision of which bill or draft to use for the markup session is an important strategic choice because it is generally simpler to defend existing language than it is to form the consensus necessary to alter it.

Markup sessions are held at either the subcommittee or full committee level, or both. The full committee may choose to accept the subcommittee's modifications or may decide to repeat the entire markup process.

Markups normally follow the completion of hearings, but committees need not have held hearings prior to holding a markup session on a bill. Conversely, not every bill on which hearings were held is guaranteed a markup. Many measures receive some committee consideration but do not complete the committee process for political or policy reasons.

Markup practices vary among the legislative committees of the House and Senate. Most committees follow formal parliamentary procedure, which requires that proposed changes to the text under review be offered as motions, known as amendments. These amendments modify or strike out existing language or insert new text. They are discussed, then adopted or rejected by a majority vote. Some committees, however, utilize a more informal procedure. Their members discuss and negotiate any changes to the text, reach a consensus, and defer to the committee staff the responsibility for drafting the precise language to reflect their agreements.

Markup sessions may end with a vote on whether or not to report the committee version of the bill to the floor for further consideration. Or a committee may choose to wait for all its members to have an opportunity to examine the marked up version of the bill, taking the vote on reporting the measure to the floor in a subsequent session. In both the House and Senate, the decision to report must be made by majority vote, with a quorum physically present, or the vote may be challenged on the floor.

In 1973, the House changed its rules to encourage committees and subcommittees to open markup sessions to the press and public. The Senate followed suit in 1975. Committees in both chambers retain the right to close any particular session if a majority of its members so vote. While open sessions remain the general practice, markups on appropriations, tax, defense, and national security bills are frequently closed.

[See also (I) Amending.]

BIBLIOGRAPHY

Calmes, Jacqueline. "Fading Sunshine Reforms: Few Complaints Are Voiced As Doors Close on Capitol Hill." *Congressional Quarterly Weekly Report,* 23 May 1987, pp. 1059–1060.

Oleszek, Walter J. *Congressional Procedures and the Policy Process.* 3d ed. 1989. Pp. 101–103.

Tiefer, Charles. *Congressional Practice and Procedure.* 1989. Pp. 167–170.

– ILONA B. NICKELS

Committee Reports

Since 1880, the House has required its committees to issue a written report accompanying each bill sent to the floor for consideration. In the Senate, however, committee reports are voluntary. Committee reports explain committee actions on a bill and present the case to the full chamber for passage of the legislation.

Reports must contain a section-by-section analysis of the measure and describe the changes recommended by the committee to the original introduced version of the bill. In addition, reports must contain a side-by-side comparison with existing law to show how the proposed measure would alter it. This requirement for a current law comparison is termed the *Ramseyer Rule* in the House and the *Cordon Rule* in the Senate, after the lawmakers who first proposed it in each house (Rep. C. William Ramseyer [R-Iowa] and Sen. Guy Cordon [R-Oreg.]). Roll-call votes taken in committee also must be listed in committee reports. Other content requirements include cost estimates of implementing the legislation, a regulatory impact statement, and an analysis of the impact on the inflation rate. Executive comments received from federal agencies on the proposed legislation are frequently included in the report as well, although these are not mandatory.

Select and special committees are temporary, ad hoc study panels that function without legislative authority.

Committee members may also insert in the report their own views on the proposed measure. If they are essentially in agreement with the viewpoint expressed in the committee report, their statements are included as "supplemental" or "additional" views. The statements of individual members in opposition to the committee's perspective are termed "minority" or "dissenting" views. These individual views often forecast possible future floor amendments and dissent.

Committee reports serve as an essential part of a bill's legislative history. Should the measure be enacted into law, federal agencies responsible for its implementation will turn to the committee report for guidance regarding congressional intent when the language is not clear. If the measure is ever challenged legally, courts of law may refer to the committee report as an aid in interpreting the text. It is because of this value to the legislative history of a measure that most Senate committees choose to issue reports, even though they are not required to do so.

At times, however, the press of legislative business makes expediting the normal reporting procedure necessary, especially if time constraints would make preparation of a committee report difficult prior to its scheduled floor consideration. While Senate committees can simply choose to send a measure to the floor without a report, House committees must use special procedures to circumvent the written report requirement. One procedure used in the House for this purpose is "suspension of the rules." Because all rules of the House are waived when a bill is under suspension, no point of order can be lodged against its consideration on the grounds that a committee report is not available. House committees may also arrange for a friendly floor motion or unanimous consent request to discharge themselves from further consideration of a specific measure. The effect of discharging obviates the requirement for a written report.

[See also (I) Bills.]

BIBLIOGRAPHY

Tiefer, Charles. *Congressional Practice and Procedure.* 1989. Pp. 180–186.

U.S. House of Representatives. *Procedure in the U.S. House of Representatives,* by Lewis Deschler and William Holmes Brown. 4th ed. 97th Cong., 2d sess., 1982. Chap. 17, secs. 39–45.

U.S. Senate. *Riddick's Senate Procedure, Precedents, and Practices,* by Floyd M. Riddick and Alan S. Frumin. 101st Cong., 2d sess., 1992. S. Doc. 101-28. Pp. 1176–1201.

– ILONA B. NICKELS

Standing Committees

Standing committees are primarily responsible for crafting the legislative proposals that are subsequently debated on the floor of the U.S. House of Representatives or U.S. Senate. Standing committees are characterized by their permanence and legislative authority: standing committees continue from Congress to Congress, and they have the power to receive and report legislation.

The House and Senate have independently developed parallel standing committee systems; each body has organized its committees to correspond roughly to the responsibilities of executive branch departments. Most standing committees in both bodies have further divided their work into subcommittees. In modern Congresses there have been slightly fewer than twenty standing committees in the Senate and slightly more than twenty in the House.

Standing committees serve as Congress's issue specialists. When members believe a problem requires a legislative remedy, the committee considers policy options and writes a legislative proposal to address the issue. Measures agreed to by a majority of committee members are reported from committee and may then be debated by the entire House and the entire Senate and enacted into law.

In addition to processing legislation, standing committees plan and conduct public hearings and other fact-finding activities. Committees also review, or oversee, the progress of programs administered by federal agencies.

Legislators tend to remain on the same committees throughout their congressional careers. Standing committees are an integral part of the legislative process, and their activities can and often do shape legislative decision making.

[See also (I) Subcommittees.]

BIBLIOGRAPHY

Davidson, Roger H., and Walter J. Oleszek. *Congress and Its Members.* 3d ed. 1990.

Smith, Steven S., and Christopher J. Deering. *Committees in Congress.* 2d ed. 1990.

– MARY ETTA BOESL

Select and Special Committees

Select and special committees are temporary, ad hoc study panels that function without legislative authority. Both the U.S. Senate and U.S. House of Representatives usually set specific boundaries within which each select or special committee must operate. House or Senate rules that create the panels specify the length of time a committee will exist and the specific policy issue it will investigate.

Traditionally, select committee members were appointed by the Senate or the House, and special committee members were appointed by the leadership. In modern Congresses, the traditional distinction is no longer valid in either the House or the Senate. Both select and special committees are authorized by a resolution passed by a majority vote and are provided with operating budgets, staff, and office space. Members are assigned to both select and special committees by their respective political party organizations.

Generally select and special committees exist for one or two Congresses and are then disbanded. Only a few have continued over several Congresses. In the 103d Congress (1993–1995) select and special committees

SELECT AND SPECIAL COMMITTEES OF THE 103D CONGRESS

Permanent Select Committee on Intelligence (House)
Select Committee on Ethics (Senate)
Select Committee on Intelligence (Senate)
Special Committee on Aging (Senate)

Source: U.S. Congress. Joint Committee on Printing. *Congressional Directory, 1993–1994.* 1993.

came under fire as wasteful expenditures that could no longer be afforded in the era of federal budget cutbacks, and the House of Representatives consequently eliminated all four of its ad hoc committees.

The House and Senate have created select and special committees in response to a variety of situations. Some have been investigative panels. An example is the House Select Committee to Investigate Covert Arms Transactions with Iran (the Iran-contra Committee), organized in 1987. Select or special committees have also been appointed when a necessary study would cross the jurisdictions of several standing committees, as with the Senate Select Committee to Study the Senate Committee System (1984). Other select and special committees have been formed around highly visible public policy issues or particular interest groups, such as the Senate Special Committee on Aging, created in 1977, and the House Select Committee on Children, Youth, and Families, first organized in 1983.

The House Permanent Select Committee on Intelligence and the Senate Select Committees on Intelligence, which function as standing committees in spite of their names, represent a special case. Created in the mid-1970s to study federal intelligence issues, these panels were later given legislative and budget authority.

[See also (I) Committees, article called An Overview.]

BIBLIOGRAPHY

Congressional Quarterly. "The Committee System." In *Congressional Quarterly's Guide to Congress.* 4th ed. Edited by Mary Cohn. 1991.

Smith, Steven S., and Christopher J. Deering. *Committees in Congress.* 2d ed. 1990.

– MARY ETTA BOESL

Joint Committees

Joint committees are permanent legislative panels organized by and responsible to both the U.S. House of Representatives and the U.S. Senate. Joint committee membership is equally divided between senators and representatives. The chairmanship of joint committees is rotated between the Senate and the House in alternating Congresses.

Congress now rarely grants legislative authority to joint committees; the last to have such authority was the Joint Committee on Atomic Energy, which disbanded in 1977. Many scholars attribute this reluctance to permanent standing committees' fears that a joint committee might infringe on their jurisdictions and an unwillingness on the part of the two houses to closely share the development of legislative proposals.

However, joint committees do provide important options to Congress, and their value is reflected by the five panels that exist in the 103d Congress (1993–1995). First, joint committees have traditionally been utilized for shared administrative housekeeping tasks. The Joint Committee on the Library oversees the Library of Congress, and the Joint Committee on Printing oversees the Government Printing Office.

Second, panels such as the Joint Economic Committee and the Joint Committee on Taxation provide Congress with an additional layer of staff specialists on the complex issues of the national economy and the federal tax laws. Staffs of both joint committees work closely with individual members and with the House and Senate standing committees that do write legislation. These panels also provide Congress with additional opportunities to focus and mold legislative decision making through the use of studies and public hearings on selected policy issues.

[See also (I) Library Committee, Taxation Committee.]

BIBLIOGRAPHY

LeLoup, Lance T. "Congress and the Dilemma of Economic Policy." In *Making Economic Policy in Congress.* Edited by Allen Schick. 1983. Pp. 6–37.

Smith, Steven S., and Christopher J. Deering. *Committees in Congress.* 2d ed. 1990.

– MARY ETTA BOESL

CONCURRENT POWERS

Concurrent powers are those exercised simultaneously by both national and state governments. Taxation is an example of a concurrent power, which falls under national as well as state authority.

Concurrent powers were created to promote the independent exercise of national and state governance—what James Madison called a "compound republic" of two sovereignties. Yet concurrent powers have not yielded wholly independent governments. As the "supremacy clause" of Article VI and the "necessary and proper clause" of Article I of the Constitution intended, the doctrine of national preemption has generally governed. When a conflict of authority arises, even in the presence of a concurrent power such as taxation, the federal government is said to prevail over the state. Early disputes over concurrent powers to tax (*McCulloch v. Maryland,* 1819) and to regulate commerce (*Gibbons v. Odgen,* 1824) were resolved decidedly in favor of the national government in decisions by Chief Justice John Marshall. This occurred despite the Tenth Amendment's grant of reserved powers to the states in the face of federal preemptive authority. Significantly, the idea of concurrent powers was cited only once in the Constitution: in the Eighteenth Amendment's enforcement clause (1919), later repealed by the Twenty-first Amendment (1933).

The political significance of concurrent powers and the preemption doctrine have remained a critical part of constitutional law. Congressional authority is said to preempt state action when the legislature intends to "occupy a field" exclusively. The case of *Pennsylvania v. Nelson* (1956) illustrates such a point. Even in the face of the Tenth Amendment's promise of state police power to govern the welfare of its citizens, the Supreme Court stated that Congress intended to occupy the field of sedition with the passage of the 1940 Smith Act. The state's sedition act was declared unconstitutional, thus weakening the concurrent power of the state to regulate so-called repugnant speech. A more recent controversy over environmental regulation of the nuclear industry has dominated the debate over concurrent powers, the preemption doctrine, and the Tenth Amendment.

[See also (I) Implied Powers; (III) Jurisdiction.]

BIBLIOGRAPHY

Ducat, Craig, and Harold Chase. *Constitutional Interpretation: Powers of Government.* 1974.

Fisher, Louis. *American Constitutional Law.* 1990.

– JANIS JUDSON

CONFERENCE COMMITTEES

The United States legislative branch is divided into two separate and equal chambers, the House of Representatives and the Senate. Constitutionally, the House and Senate must each pass measures with absolutely identical language before they can be sent to the White House for presidential consideration. The issue, then, is how to unite what the Constitution divides when each chamber passes different versions of the same bill.

Because the Constitution is silent, Congress has devised three techniques for achieving agreement. First, many bills are enacted into law when one chamber simply accepts the other's version. One chamber's deference to the other house's bill has various explanations, ranging from lack of controversy to political necessity because time is running out in a legislative session. Second, the House and Senate can motion—or "ping-pong"—measures back and forth between them until substantive disagreements are ironed out. In this case, each chamber agrees to some of the other's amendments or amends the other's amendments until both agree to identical language for all provisions of the legislation. Members and staff aides from each chamber consult frequently to facilitate the compromise. There is a parliamentary limit, however, to the number of times measures may be sent between the two bodies.

Finally, the House and Senate may agree to establish a conference committee, composed of selected senators and representatives charged with reconciling the items of disagreement. Only a relatively small number of public laws passed by a Congress (15 to 25 percent by one estimate) reach the conference stage, but these measures are often the most controversial and important. Moreover, recent decades have witnessed an even more important role—reconciliation—for these bicameral panels, sometimes dubbed the "third house of Congress."

Several factors account for the heightened significance of these committees. First, institutional rivalry between the House and Senate is long-standing. Then, during the 1980s, another factor increased the competition: split party control. For the first time in twenty-six years the Senate went Republican after the November 1980 elections, staying in Republican hands for the next six years while the House remained Democratic. Conference committees during this period reconciled not only bicameral policy differences but sharp partisan disagreements as well.

Second, a new form of policy-making emerged on Capitol Hill: bills of massive size and scope. These "megabills" (called omnibus bills and sometimes thousands of pages long) cut across the jurisdictions of many standing committees. As a result, omnibus bills are commonly referred to more than one standing committee for simultaneous or sequential consideration. When conference committees are convened to deal with megabills, they frequently involve hundreds of lawmakers. The biggest conference in history—more than 250 conferees from the House and Senate—met on the Omnibus Reconciliation Act of 1981 to reconcile hundreds of matters in bicameral disagreement. Big conferences regularly shape the final content of these massive and major instruments of national policy-making.

Finally, before the 1970s junior lawmakers rarely served on conference committees. Instead, senior leaders of House and Senate committees dominated the conferences. Today, participatory democracy characterizes lawmaking in both chambers, with entrepreneurial members active in all phases of congressional policy-making. As scores of committees, subcommittees, task forces, and ad hoc groups strive to shape policies, it is often harder for Congress to act coherently. Thus, conference committees can function as important centralizing forces, capable of producing integrated policies from a more fragmented legislature.

Once the House and Senate agree to establish a conference committee, several major steps ensue: the selection of conferees (or managers, as they are sometimes called), conference negotiations, and House-Senate action on the conference report (the product of the bicameral negotiations). Each merits discussion.

SELECTION OF CONFEREES. Selection of conferees is regulated by rules and precedents in both chambers. Each time a bill is sent to conference, the House Speaker and the presiding officer of the Senate formally appoint the respective conferees. In fact, both chambers usually rely on selections made by the chairman and ranking minority member of the committee or committees that originally considered and reported the bill. Some committees have their own rules or customs that influence conferee selection, such as naming subcommittee members as conferees. Rules of the House Democratic caucus obligate committee chairmen to ensure that conference delegations reflect the distribution of majority and minority members on the full committee. House and Senate committee leaders also name as conferees lawmakers who have special knowledge of the subject or whose states or districts are affected by the matters at hand.

The House Speaker does not simply rubber-stamp the committee leaders' list. The Speaker may choose conferees in addition to those the committee chairman has proposed or even veto some who offend the Speaker's personal or political sensibilities. In both chambers party support is sometimes especially critical in conferee selection. House and Senate leaders will seek to name conferees whose work is likely to reflect the goals and preferences of the Democratic or Republican leadership and who are skilled and shrewd negotiators.

Recent decades have witnessed an even more important role—reconciliation—for these bicameral panels, sometimes dubbed the "third house of Congress."

Rules and precedents in both chambers require that a majority of conferees have "generally supported" the bill under discussion. Adhering to this standard is not always easy. Usually, for purposes of selection to a conference committee, a lawmaker's floor vote on final consideration is taken as evidence of an overall position on the measure.

Both the House and Senate may select as many conferees as they want. Neither chamber gains an edge over the other by naming more conferees because the respective delegations vote as a unit. The two chambers have one vote each, with a majority in each delegation deciding how its vote is to be cast on the various issues in bicameral disagreement. This feature facilitates compromise.

Although the size of conference delegations does not affect the bargaining authority of either chamber, it does have several consequences. The more conferees from each chamber, the more time and effort are invariably required to resolve bicameral differences. Moreover, size affects the mechanics of decision making. Large conferences regularly and of necessity divide into smaller groups, which means that size can affect the pace of decision making. Simply scheduling negotiating sessions for many conferees is sometimes difficult.

BARGAINING IN CONFERENCE. Bargaining strategies and tactics used in the conference committee are shaped to a considerable extent by several preconference considerations, such as the unity of each chamber's delegation, the amount of tradable material that each side brings to the negotiating table, and whether a chamber's conferees have been instructed by their parent body to insist on a certain provision, although such instructions are not always followed. Bargaining in conference is a process based on a carefully planned strategy and the skilled use of resources and opportunities during bargaining.

House-Senate conferences typically operate in an informal, agreement-oriented context. As professional politicians, conferees are accustomed to the personal give-and-take, bargains, and trade-offs that foster bicameral accord. Their objectives are to fashion an agreement acceptable to at least a majority of each chamber's conferees and to create an agreement (compromise legislation) that will attract majority support in the House and Senate. As conferees strive to achieve these broad objectives, only a few formal rules guide the bargaining. One rule specifies that conferees are to consider only the items in disagreement; they may not reconsider provisions approved in identical form by both houses. Even these few rules are sometimes waived by the House or Senate when conferees submit their completed product (the conference report) to their respective chambers. House and Senate rules also state that conference committees are to meet in open session, unless specific steps are taken to close them for a reason such as national security. Nonetheless, much conference bargaining occurs in secret as various individual legislators, small groups, or key leaders privately discuss how to iron out differences.

Conference bargaining can best be viewed as multilateral rather than bicameral. Although constituted in terms of House versus Senate negotiating teams, conference bargaining usually involves other participants. Lobbyists, executive branch officials, and White House aides regularly attend conference deliberations and influence the shape of the final compromises.

When at least a majority of the conferees from each chamber has reached agreement, committee staffers prepare the appropriate documents, such as the conference report and the accompanying joint explanatory statement. Preparing these documents might take several weeks, especially when the legislation is controversial and complex or requires intensive, round-the-clock work to meet tight deadlines. House-Senate agreement is reached when at least a majority of each chamber's conferees signs the conference report. When that is done, the conference committee has concluded its work. Its negotiated settlement must now be considered by the House and Senate.

CHAMBER CONSIDERATION OF THE CONFERENCE REPORT. By custom, the chamber that requested a conference acts second on the conference report, but this is not an inviolable practice. The first chamber to act has three options: to adopt the conference report, reject it, or recommit it—that is, return it to the conferees for further deliberation. When the first chamber adopts the conference report, the conference committee is automatically dissolved and the other chamber is faced with only two options, to accept or reject.

Conference reports are seldom rejected or recommitted to conference by either house, largely because there are procedural and political incentives for their adoption. For one thing, conference reports are "privileged" business in each chamber, which means that they can be brought to the floor at almost any time, sometimes even when key opponents are out of town. They are usually not open to amendment; "take it or leave it" is the rule at this stage of the legislative process. Members understand, too, that the defeat of a conference report is likely to subject the legislation to further arduous and lengthy negotiations.

The conference floor managers in the House and Senate, usually the senior majority conferees, are key actors in developing the strategy for winning enactment of the bicameral accord. Consultations with party leaders, executive branch officials, and affected interest groups, among others, are standard elements of the coalition-building process both before and during floor deliberations. On the floor, the floor managers' primary concerns are to promote and defend their handiwork and to ensure that there are enough votes to adopt the conference report. Once both chambers agree to the conference report, the bill as finally approved by Congress is transmitted to the White House for presidential consideration.

Conference committees make crucial policy decisions. They are often the most important lawmaking forums on Capitol Hill. House and Senate members understand that many bills will end up in conference. Hence, they purposefully plan how they can enhance their leverage with the other body. This feature of congressional policy-making underscores how legislatively locked the House and Senate are, despite their constitutional separation. Conference committees epitomize bicameralism in action and are centrally important in uniting what the Constitution divides.

[See also (I) Amending, Bargaining, Bicameralism.]

BIBLIOGRAPHY

Longley, Lawrence D., and Walter J. Oleszek. *Bicameral Politics: Conference Committees in Congress.* 1989.

McCown, Ada C. *The Congressional Conference Committee.* 1927.

Pressman, Jeffrey L. *House vs. Senate: Conflict in the Appropriations Process.* 1966.

Steiner, Gilbert. *The Congressional Conference Committee.* 1951.

Vogler, David J. *The Third House: Conference Committees in the U.S. Congress.* 1971.

– WALTER J. OLESZEK

CONGRESS

Powers of Congress

As the first branch of government, Congress has powers that are broader and more profound than is indicated by a mere reading of the constitutional document. In Article I, section 8 and in the enforcement clauses of many of the amendments, there are specific, formal grants of power, but these are enhanced by the fact that the Constitution leaves much to Congress in constituting the other branches of government and in regulating their powers, and Congress has authority both to expand and to contract the scope of state powers.

CONGRESS'S INSTITUTIONAL POWERS. Each house of Congress has the internal powers of any legislative body: to determine its rules, to determine contests over who has been elected to it, to police its members, and to discipline those who violate its standards of conduct. It determines its internal procedures, largely free of outside forces, although the courts do at times review and sometimes set aside decisions. For example, the decision to exclude a member-elect was voided because the Supreme Court held in *Powell v. McCormack* (1969) that the House of Representatives had added to the constitutional listing of qualifications. Lawmaking procedures have been evaluated to determine, for instance, whether a revenue-raising measure was initiated in the Senate rather than in the House, although the latter has a procedure to police the violation of its privileges. Generally, the political-question doctrine, under which the courts determine that some issues are not suitable for judicial resolution, enables judges to leave many otherwise litigable questions to Congress and the president.

At the conclusion of Article I, section 8, the Constitution in clause 18 authorizes Congress to make all laws that may be "necessary and proper" for executing its granted powers. Chief Justice John Marshall, writing for the Court in *McCulloch v. Maryland* (1819), interpreted this clause as an enlargement of Congress's powers rather than as a constriction. That is, Congress need not show that a law is strictly necessary; rather, Congress may select any means it thinks reasonable to effectuate its granted powers. It is not a judicial function to review whether a particular exercise is "necessary" or "proper," except within the context of the limitations the Constitution imposes, such as in the Bill of Rights. This discretion as to means is critical to the scope of congressional legislation.

Congress has powers that are broader and more profound than is indicated by a mere reading of the constitutional document.

The power to investigate to determine whether legislation is needed and how existing laws are being implemented is one of the most important, although unenumerated, powers of Congress. Sometimes abused, it is critical to Congress's role.

Congress also has initiated all twenty-seven amendments to the Constitution, and while Article V authorizes state initiation as well, Congress would play a significant oversight role there.

CONGRESS AND THE STATES. The core of the formal grants of power to Congress is in section 8 of Article I, but only some of these are of signal importance. As in so many provisions of the Constitution, these grants serve a dual purpose. Many were intended to demarcate the scope of authority delegated to the national government. Under the supremacy clause (Article VI, clause 2), congressional exercises of these powers are the supreme law of the land, and state law, even state constitutional law, is subordinate to federal law. However, the mere grant of a power does not deny the states the authority to legislate. States may, for instance, enact debtor-creditor legislation despite the grant to Congress in Article I, section 8, clause 4 of the power to enact bankruptcy legislation. Even when Congress acts, the states do not necessarily lose their authority. If Congress expressly provides for federal exclusivity, as for example in copyright law, enacted pursuant to Article I, section 8, clause 4, that concludes the matter. Congress may expressly permit some state role, but if Congress does not specify, then the courts, which have developed an elaborate set of standards to do so, determine whether state law must yield, because it conflicts with the federal law or interferes with the federal plan or regulates some activity Congress wished to leave free, or whether the state law may coexist in whole or in part with the federal scheme.

Under the Articles of Confederation, Congress lacked the power to impose taxes, and it could not regulate interstate commerce to prevent state discrimination. The grants of these two powers, Article I, section 8, clauses 1 and 3, made national governance possible in the beginning; since then, especially in the twentieth century, they have been the principal engines of federal dominance of the states.

The ability to raise money by direct levy on individuals in the states meant that Congress could obtain the resources necessary for federal functions. Especially with the confirmation of the power to impose income taxes by ratification of the Sixteenth Amendment, Congress also obtained the ability to compete fully with states for all available moneys, to the fiscal detriment of the states, because national legislation was supreme. When combined with the power to spend tax revenues for the general welfare (clause 2), the execution and significance of these two powers cannot be overstated. Beginning in the 1920s but increasingly since, numerous federal programs have been created that offer money to the states if they will administer the programs in accordance with federal standards and subject to federal conditions. Social security programs such as unemployment compensation and assistance to the poor, highway programs, and educational programs are examples. Utilization of state administration is important to the national government, but just as important is Congress's ability to set conditions (often of minimal connection to the purposes of the spending), which gives to the national legislature a regulatory function that it often exercises. For example, the minimum age at which alcoholic beverages can be purchased and the maximum speed limit are two cases in which Congress set national policy through highway expenditures. Conditions of nondiscrimination imposed on the receipt and use of federal moneys are another. (The imposition of mandates on the states to do certain things, but absent federal moneys to cover the costs, is a more recent feature of national legislation; this accompanies the deficit-imposed shortage of federal moneys.)

The growth of an interrelated national economy and judicial latitude in permitting regulation of even *de minimis* activities affecting commerce have transformed

Congress's role from overseeing the rules of how interstate business is done to exercising a national police power in the areas of crime, consumer protection, rules of nondiscrimination, protection of the environment, and many others.

Initially, the Supreme Court permitted Congress to regulate only the use of interstate facilities and the crossing of state boundaries. The production of goods for interstate commerce was an intrastate transaction, as was the sale or other disposal at the other end (*Kidd v. Pearson* [1988], *United States v. E. C. Knight Co.* [1895], *Oliver Iron Co. v. Lord* [1923], *Carter v. Carter Coal Co.* [1936]). Now, Congress may regulate the entire stream of commerce from production to disposal (*National Labor Relations Board v. Jones & Laughlin Steel Corp.* [1937], *United States v. Darby* [1941]). It may also reach local activities that involve no state lines but that Congress has determined have an "effect," even a minimal one, on interstate commerce (*Wickard v. Filburn* [1942], *Fry v. United States* [1975], *Hodel v. Indiana* [1981]). It has been permitted to aggregate individual transactions into a class of like transactions that "affect" interstate commerce (*Perez v. United States* [1971], *Russell v. United States* [1985]). Judicial review is negligible; it is limited to ascertaining that Congress is rational.

An exception exists in instances in which Congress seeks to regulate the governmental activities of the states, with the Supreme Court continuing to be inconsistent with respect to limits. Thus in *Maryland v. Wirtz* (1968), the Court held that Congress could impose federal wage and hour laws on state and local employees, but in *National League of Cities v. Usery* (1976), it overruled *Wirtz* and held that such regulation violated the Constitution. Then, in *Garcia v. San Antonio Metropolitan Transit Authority* (1985), the Court overruled *Usery* and held that congressional application of wage and hour laws to state employees violated no provision of the Constitution and that states had to use their political resources in Congress to defend themselves. Most recently, in *New York v. United States* (1992), the justices held that Congress could not compel the states to enforce and implement a program of radioactive waste disposal and that Congress could not "commandeer" state legislative and administrative assistance.

The result is that instead of debates about Congress's ability to prescribe standards of labor-management relations in large or small industries, the constitutional debates at present are whether Congress can declare gun-free zones around local schools and punish possession of firearms in those areas, whether it can set specific punishments for local carjackings, and whether it can bar racial discrimination in a small restaurant that purchases a significant amount of its food from interstate sources.

As has been noted, conferral of a power on Congress does not deny the states the power to act on the same subject. Thus the states have always had the authority to tax and to regulate interstate commerce, subject to congressional dispossession. Although the commerce clause in its terms is only an authorization for congressional action, the Supreme Court has interpreted it as imposing some limits on state authority, even absent congressional action, making it "negative" on some state laws. The result is that states may not discriminate against interstate commerce (on behalf of local businesses, for example), and if they burden interstate commerce too severely by nondiscriminatory taxation or regulation, the courts can set aside such state legislation (*Brown-Forman Distillers Corp. v. New York State Liquor Authority* [1986], *Quill Corp. v. North Dakota* [1992], *Fort Gratiot Sanitary Landfill v. Michigan Natural Resources Department* [1992], *Barclays Bank v. California Franchise Tax Board* [1994]). It is important to note that Congress may authorize the states to enact measures the courts have disapproved or would disapprove because it is congressional power that is overriding; this permits Congress to enlarge as well as contract state power (*Prudential Insurance Co. v. Benjamin* [1946], *South Central Timber Development v. Wunnicke* [1984]).

Another means by which Congress regularly enlarges state power is its approval of interstate compacts, pursuant to Article I, section 10, clause 3. States often come together to work on a common problem (e.g., pollution of a river that passes through more than one state, or cooperation in extraditing criminals), but because these agreements affect important issues of federalism, they are permissible only by congressional consent.

Conferral of a power on Congress does not deny the states the power to act on the same subject.

Adoption of the Reconstruction Amendments following the Civil War further strengthened Congress relative to the states. New constraints were imposed—on the power to regulate suffrage and on the power to deny privileges and immunities of citizenship, due process, and equal protection—and with these restraints came authorization to Congress to enforce them. Remedial legislation in the nineteenth century failed, but the civil rights struggle energized Congress beginning in the 1960s, leading to new protections of the franchise. Congress turned from merely banning discrimination in voting, a largely failed initiative, to affirmatively guaranteeing ballot access, fair apportionment and districting, and general effectuation of the right to a valid ballot. In the course of this movement, Congress sought and the Supreme Court approved a power, not yet fully defined, both to enforce discrimination bans and also to define, free of all but the most restrained judicial review, what conduct and acts were in fact discriminatory. Under this exercise, minority voting and districting that enhanced minority power were legislated and enforced. However, the *Shaw v. Reno* (1993) decision and a pending 1994 case suggest that this power may be more limited than was previously thought.

Similarly, Congress has acted under the Fourteenth Amendment, especially the equal protection clause, to bar states and local governments from discriminating in a large number of areas. Congress's ability to interpret the meaning of the amendment contrary to what the judiciary has decided means that it can, for example, engage in more far-reaching affirmative action than the states can, and it may be able to authorize the states to act more broadly to establish affirmative action programs than they could without such authorization.

Inasmuch as it was through the Fourteenth Amendment's due process clause that the Supreme Court applied most of the provisions of the Bill of Rights, which originally limited only the national government, Congress may define and enforce these constraints against the states.

That the Union would be enlarged through the addition of new states was clear to the Framers, who specifically provided in Article IV, section 3 for the admission of new states, subject to limits on breaking up existing states. An unexpressed command of this provision, recognized in the first and subsequent admissions and enforced by the judiciary, is that each new state comes into the Union on an "equal footing," a condition of equality with the states already forming the Union. In framing the provisions for the admission of new states, the Convention looked to the example of the Northwest Territory, which would later be formed into states and for which the Continental Congress was providing a government through the Northwest Ordinance (passed as the Convention was meeting and repassed during the First Congress). Thus, in section 3, the Framers coupled the statehood clause, granting Congress the power to admit new states, with the clause authorizing Congress to provide governments for the territories. Implicit in this section was the power to acquire new territories by conquest, by treaty, or otherwise. This power remained relatively uncontroversial, save for the intrusion of the slavery debate, until overseas colonies (the Philippines, Puerto Rico, and others) were acquired at the end of the nineteenth century.

SEPARATION OF POWERS. The terms *separation of powers* and *checks and balances* do not appear in the Constitution, but they are implicit throughout the document. The first three articles disperse the legislative, executive, and judicial powers. Yet the Framers recognized that paper boundaries would not deter abuse of powers; only individuals and institutions would be able to resist incursions. The experience of the Framers following the Revolution and the creation of state governments had demonstrated that popularly elected legislatures were threats to liberties, and Congress was constructed to reduce that danger. A bicameral body, a popularly elected House, a Senate elected by the state legislatures, combined with the presidential veto and constitutional judicial review (not set out expressly but acknowledged by all Framers who spoke about it) were intended to suppress the opportunities for abuse.

Surprisingly, therefore, it was in Congress that the Framers reposed much of the power to structure, and necessarily to restructure from time to time, the other two branches of the national government. Article II creates the office of the president (and vice president), but the powers set out are general and the system in which he is to operate is sketchy. Congress must, and did from the beginning, legislate to create executive departments and offices, to disperse authority, and to establish qualifications and terms for officeholders. It has lodged authority in executive offices subject to presidential direction, but it also has created numerous independent agencies (independent in the sense of limits on the ability of the president to remove officers and thus to direct them) charged with the execution of national laws. Recently, in upholding the creation of independent counsels in the executive branch, the Court in *Morrison v. Olson* (1988) altered the understanding of the president's removal power to give to Congress some limited discretion in restricting the removal of many of those who hold executive office. The judiciary as envisioned in Article III consists of a Supreme Court of unspecified size (headed by a chief justice) and of inferior courts that Congress may from time to time create, revise, or abolish. The entire appellate jurisdiction of the Supreme Court appears to depend upon congressional sufferance, since Article III, section 2, clause 2 authorizes Congress to make exceptions and regulations to the Court's appellate jurisdiction. Only the Court's original jurisdiction, a tiny part of its entire jurisdiction, is constitutionally immune from congressional defeasance. Even determining when the Supreme Court is to convene requires congressional legislation.

In part, the power proceeds from direct grants—that is, the authority to constitute courts inferior to the Supreme Court (Article I, section 8, clause 9 and Article III, section 1)—but the most important grant flows from the necessary and proper clause (Article I, section 8, clause 18), which empowers Congress not only to legislate to carry out its own powers but also to carry into execution "all other powers vested in this Constitution in the Government of the United States, or in any department or officer thereof." From this language stems the congressional ability to organize and to structure the executive and judicial branches and to structure much of the exercise of power in those branches.

The Constitution also bars the expenditure of any money from the Treasury except pursuant to appropriations (Article I, section 9, clause 7), giving to Congress the power to determine not only whether money may be or may not be spent for something but also the right to impose conditions under which such moneys may be spent. The money power is a potent force in setting policy and structuring execution.

Congressional authority today is much more circumscribed than what is described here; it is limited by political constraints associated primarily with presidential leadership but also by judicial interpretation that, accepting congressional delegations of power to the other two branches, resolutely stands against attempted congressional policing of that delegation and of other activity in those branches. The Court in its opinions continues to refer to the dangers flowing from legislative predominance (*Immigration and Naturalization Service v. Chadha* [1983], *Bowsher v. Synar* [1986], *Metropolitan Airports Authority v. Citizens for the Abatement of Aircraft Noise* [1991]). The result is that the executive and judiciary may legislate through rules and regulation, the former may adjudicate, and the latter may execute, but Congress may act outside its own walls only through the processes of legislation set out in the Constitution.

Congress is the only entity thoroughly described and empowered in the Constitution.

Other grants in section 8 involve Congress closely in the exercise of powers that are exclusive to the executive in other governmental systems. The texts of Article I, section 8, clauses 11–16 and of Article II, section 2, and the sparse debates in the Convention, disclose a conscious blending across the two branches of the great powers of war and peace. The president is the commander in chief of the armed forces of the United States, but the Framers probably viewed this grant as little more than giving control of the military to the president. In modern practice, begun under Abraham Lincoln and accelerated in the last half of the twentieth century, the power extends beyond simple control to the sole conduct of national and foreign policy in war and peacetime. The Framers intended that the nation ordinarily should go to war only under a declaration of war by Congress and that peace should be restored again through a treaty negotiated by the president and ratified by the Senate.

However, two world wars, regional conflicts, and the long period of the Cold War in effect validated an expansive theory of presidential dominance. Congress reasserted itself in the War Powers Resolution of 1973, defining the terms of presidential use of military forces abroad in the absence of a declaration of war. A combination of presidential assertiveness and congressional acquiescence has minimized the effects of the resolution; although President George Bush sought and obtained congressional approval for the 1991 Persian Gulf War, the president claimed the right to proceed absent any approval. Congress has also, with somewhat more success, sought to rein in the use of executive agreements, in contrast with treaties, and the enhancement of executive powers through declarations of national emergencies.

Here, too, the congressional power of the purse has force. The president needs money to conduct military operations and other activities abroad. Congress successfully required the withdrawal of troops from Indochina through the conditioning of funds; yet the effort to change U.S. policy in Central America by conditions on funds resulted in presidential evasion and led to the Iran-contra controversy.

Finally, the power to impeach and upon conviction to remove from office the president, justices and judges, and high civil officers is one lodged solely in the legislative branch.

CONCLUSION. Congress is the only entity thoroughly described and empowered in the Constitution. Its internal structure is minutely detailed. Its powers are affirmatively conveyed, and the language defines the relationships between and among the other two branches of the national government and between the federal government and the states. Most important, Congress is given the discretion to determine largely for itself how it should legislate to effectuate its powers, both express and implied.

Congress in the late twentieth century is different from what the Framers envisioned. It is more powerful in that it has more plenary powers vis-à-vis the states than the Framers intended; but it is less powerful in that its role in developing and implementing national policy has increasingly eroded before the power of a chief executive, who, in fact, if not strictly in constitutional terms, is the only nationally elected officeholder and the most visible embodiment of the national government.

[See also (I) Concurrent Powers, Emergency Powers, Implied Powers, Subpoena Power.]

BIBLIOGRAPHY

Mikva, Abner J. *The American Congress: The First Branch.* 1983.
Shane, Peter M., and Harold H. Bruff. *The Law of Presidential Power: Cases and Materials.* 1988.
Thompson, Kenneth W., ed. *The Presidency, the Congress, and the Constitution: Deadlock or Balance of Powers?* 1991.
Tribe, Lawrence H. *American Constitutional Law.* 2d ed. 1988. Pp. 297–400. See also chapters 2, 4, and 6.
Van Alstyne, William. "The Role of Congress in Determining Incidental Powers of the President and of the Federal Courts: A Comment on the Horizontal Effect of 'the Sweeping Clause.' " *Ohio State Law Journal* 36 (1975): 788–825.

– JOHNNY H. KILLIAN

Congressional Workload

Although the workload of Congress traditionally focuses on Congress's lawmaking function, it embraces such other responsibilities as overseeing the executive branch, providing a forum for constituencies to be heard, and participating in its shared responsibilities with the president. The various components of legislative workload offer some measure of the activities of members of the House and Senate in lawmaking and representation. By considering the different aspects of legislative workload, we can follow their chronology during the life of a bill or resolution, from introduction to final passage.

THE PROPOSAL STAGE. At the proposal stage, a number of different activities can be used to measure the productivity of members of Congress. One common gauge is the number of bills or resolutions introduced by members of the House and Senate. Roger H. Davidson (1986) shows that bill introduction in the House rose dramatically from 1947 to the early 1970s, from a low of 7,611 in the 80th Congress (1947–1949) to a high of 22,060 in the 90th Congress (1967–1969). After 1970, the numbers dropped off to a new postwar low of 6,263 in the 100th Congress (1987–1989), as reported by Norman J. Ornstein, Thomas E. Mann, and Michael J. Malbin (1992). By contrast, the numbers in the Senate remained fairly flat, with bill introductions averaging four thousand bills a year during the post–World War II era. During this period, the high point was 4,867 Senate introductions during the 91st Congress (1969–1971). The lowest figure, 3,325, occurred in the 100th Congress (1987–1989). While this provides a rough measure of workload, some problems attend its use. First, it does not address the content of bills. In fact, most measures of workload do not consider the relative importance of legislation. This way of counting workload would give the same weight to a bill making the monarch butterfly the national insect, for example, as to a tax bill.

Second, this measure does not count the changing levels of activity of specific members of the House or Senate. The number of bills or resolutions introduced can easily be affected by the activities of a single member or a small group of members. Also, the seeming hyperactivity of the House compared to the apparently lower activity of the Senate can be corrected by examining the mean number of bills and resolutions sponsored by each member. In the prolific 1960s, House members were sponsoring, on average, forty-two bills or joint resolutions per Congress, a figure comparable to that in the Senate. By the 1980s, House members' activity had substantially lessened to about sixteen bills or resolutions per member. At the same time, the average number of bills introduced by each senator also decreased, to thirty-four. When using such sponsorship data, one must be careful to acknowledge that the rules for sponsorship of legislation have changed over time. For most of the history of the House of Representatives, a piece of legislation could be introduced only by a single member. Beginning in the 1960s, however, a series of rules changes eventually allowed a House bill to have an unlimited number of sponsors. Davidson (1986) links the decline in bill sponsorship in the House partly to this factor, but this still leaves the uniform decline in bill introduction by both the House and the Senate in the 1980s unexplained.

Third, measuring workload by the number of bills introduced may not address how the meaning of proposing legislation changes over time. Joseph Cooper and Cheryl Young, in a 1989 article in *Legislative Studies Quarterly,* note that before the 1870s House members were not freely allowed to introduce their own legislation. During the House's early history, most legislation was initially discussed in the Committee of the Whole and was then introduced in the House. Bill introduction by a single member was seen as usurping the judgment of the House. In addition, David Mayhew (1974) and other writers have noted that during the recent history of the House, representatives seem often to introduce legislation solely in order to claim credit for doing so. In other words, legislation is introduced not so that it may be passed but to let constituents or groups know that their representative supports their cause.

In addition to looking at the number of bills and resolutions introduced, scholars who study Congress during its first century examine the number of petitions introduced. In Congress's early years, petitions provided the link between constituent demands and legislative activity; often, petitions would lead to the development of a bill in the Committee of the Whole. Through petitions, constituents would advise members of the House or Senate of their position on an issue; ask that some subject matter be addressed; or ask that some wrong—whether caused by nature, other citizens, other nations, or the government—be redressed. Whether or not a petition was ultimately transformed into a piece of legislation, such pleas for action from constituents were ultimately presented to the entire chamber. Finally, measures of nineteenth-century workload not only must include petitions but must accommodate the unusual circumstances that obtained the gag rule that prohibited the introduction of abolitionists' petitions from the 23d through the 28th Congresses (1833–1845).

COMMITTEE WORKLOAD. As Woodrow Wilson declared in *Congressional Government* (1885), "It is not far from the truth to say that Congress in session is Congress on public exhibition, whilst Congress in its committee-rooms is Congress at work." What Wilson wrote more than a century ago seems still to be true today. After a bill is introduced, it is automatically referred to a standing committee. One way to measure committee workload is to examine the number of bills referred to and reported by committees (Davidson, 1986). Of course, such counts must, again, be used carefully, because the same problems mentioned in the previous section also apply here. For example, a committee is dependent on the introduction of bills for it to consider. Thus, there is a supply problem. More importantly, the subject matter of bills referred to and reported by committees varies widely.

Other measures can also be used to examine the effort expended in committees. When looking at these other factors, one must recognize that committee output is not limited to producing bills and resolutions. The most important of committees' other tasks is the oversight of executive agencies. The workload involved in this function cannot be monitored by examining the number of bills or resolutions considered or passed. Instead, one must look, for example, at the number and length of committee hearings and reports devoted to the oversight function. These measures might also be used comparatively, to judge the amount of time and effort a committee spends in developing legislation.

Besides oversight, one might also consider the number and length of hearings that the Senate holds in order to give its advice and consent on presidential nominations of judges and other appointees. These hearings may take a great deal of time and require much effort by the senators involved.

FLOOR ACTIVITY. After a bill or resolution has been considered in committee and the committee votes in favor of it, it is sent to the floor of the House or Senate. Here again, one may use the number of bills referred to the floor and the number of bills passed as simple measures of legislative productivity. Both the House and the Senate showed a tremendous decline in the number of bills passed between the 1950s and the 1980s. In the 1950s, the average number of bills and joint resolutions passed per Congress was 2,039 and 2,102 in the House and the Senate, respectively. In the 1980s, the averages had dropped by half, to 937 and 887 (Davidson, 1986; Ornstein et al., 1992). Many cite this decline as evidence of the so-called gridlock of the Reagan-Bush administrations. But interpreting the decline is not that simple since the 1980s also saw an increase in the number of bills consolidated into catchall omnibus bills. Thus the change in how bills were packaged was reflected in the decline in total numbers of bills.

It is not far from the truth to say that Congress in session is Congress on public exhibition, whilst Congress in its committee-rooms is Congress at work.

Alternative ways of examining legislative productivity at the floor level are available. Almost all important legislation makes its way to the floor of the House and the Senate through, respectively, a special rule or a unanimous consent agreement. By examining the number of special rules passed in the House and the number of unanimous consent agreements used in the Senate, one can create a rough measure of the amount of important legislation considered.

Alternatively, one might count the length of legislative sessions, either by days or, for a more accurate measure, by the number of hours the House and Senate spend in session considering legislation (Davidson and Hardy, 1987a, 1987b). Other possible measures of floor activity are the number of amendments proposed and the number of roll-call votes taken in each chamber. These methods are time-bound since reforms in the 1970s increased members' access to the floor and relaxed requirements for roll-call votes.

Some measures of legislative activity are applicable only to the Senate. For instance, one might want to consider the number of filibusters pursued in the Senate. As with petitions in the nineteenth-century House, filibusters in the modern Senate represent a different form of legislative "work," in which the interests of a political minority are expressed. As in other cases, counts would have to account for changes over time; regarding filibusters, these changes concern rules of recognition and cloture. Yet rules changes also reflect changing perceptions of what constitutes appropriate use of legislative floor time and thus reflect changes in legislators' "work" roles. Counting the number of cloture votes may also be a method of helping to determine workload, but the same caveats apply.

There are still other measures of floor workload that one may want to consider. If House and Senate disagree on provisions in one another's versions of a bill, they may form a conference committee to resolve their differences. Also, because presidents may veto legislation, it would be helpful to know the proportion of bills vetoed and to measure the effort expended on trying to have those vetoes overriden.

THE FINAL PRODUCT. Finally, attention must be given to the amount of legislation passed and then enacted into law. Public laws are the end product of the system. Donald L. Eilenstine, David L. Farnsworth, and James S. Fleming (1978) identified three distinct eras by the number of bills passed by Congress: a limited Congress before 1860; the more active Congress of the industrial era of 1860 to 1921; and the much more active Congress of the era from 1928 through 1957. Since the late 1950s, the steady decline in the number of bills passed by Congress is reflected in the number of public laws. As has been discussed, one problem of measuring workload during the later decades of the twentieth century has to do with bills being packaged into large omnibus bills covering many subjects. Certainly, the number of pages per statute increased more than threefold from the 1950s through the 1990s. Focusing only on this output, however, presents a biased picture of the work of Congress. Activities such as legislative oversight and the consideration of executive nominations should not be neglected. Likewise, focusing solely on output allows no consideration of time spent developing legislation at the committee and floor stages. Nor does it consider the time spent working on legislation that never becomes law because of disagreements within or between chambers or between Congress and the president.

Numerous activities contribute to legislative workload. To measure Congress's workload accurately, one must cast a wide net, looking at all aspects of the work performed by the House and Senate. One can never disregard, however, the tried and true measures: the number of bills introduced and passed per chamber, the number of public laws enacted, and the number of days in the session. Each of these gauges of legislative activity has stayed relatively constant over the last five to six Congresses.

[See also (I) Legislative Day.]

BIBLIOGRAPHY

Davidson, Roger H. "The Legislative Workload of Congress." Paper presented at the annual meeting of the American Political Science Association, Washington, D.C., 28–31 August 1986.

Davidson, Roger H., and Carol Hardy. *Indicators of House of Representatives Workload and Activity.* Congressional Research Service, Library of Congress. CRS Rept. 87-497 S. 1987.

Davidson, Roger H., and Carol Hardy. *Indicators of Senate Activity and Workload.* Congressional Research Service, Library of Congress. CRS Rept. 87-492 S. 1987.

Eilenstine, Donald L., David L. Farnsworth, and James S. Fleming. "Trends and Cycles in the Legislative Productivity of the United States Congress, 1789–1976." *Quality and Quantity* 12 (1978): 19–44.

Mayhew, David. *Congress: The Electoral Connection.* 1974.

Ornstein, Norman J., Thomas E. Mann, and Michael J. Malbin. *Vital Statistics on Congress, 1991–1992.* 1992.

Wilson, Woodrow. *Congressional Government: A Study in American Politics.* 1885. Repr. 1981.

– EVELYN C. FINK
BRIAN D. HUMES

Politics and Influence in Congress

Who is influential in the U.S. Congress? Why? To understand influence, one needs to know on what it is based, where it is located, how it is exercised, and how to define and measure it.

BASES OF INFLUENCE. Influence has three fundamental bases: (1) information and expertise; (2) reciprocity or exchange of favors; and (3) the power to command. In Congress there is a great deal of the first two and very little of the third.

Information. There is much truth in the old saying that "information is power." Some members of Congress are more influential than others simply because they have a greater store of information and a greater expertise. These attributes give them a considerable advantage in persuading their colleagues to cast a favorable vote in committee or on the floor or to take some other form of favorable action.

One incentive for developing such expertise, or for using expertise that predates the member's arrival in Washington, lies in the structure of Congress. Unlike most state legislatures or foreign parliaments, Congress is highly specialized. Its committee system divides the legislative work load, and so command of a subject is prized, while being active in an area without knowing much about it is discouraged. In order to make a mark, a member finds a kind of policy niche—a topic about which he or she becomes expert. Many members develop a genuinely impressive level of knowledge.

However, it is legislative staff who have the most detailed and thorough command of information. Through the 1950s, Congress was not highly staffed, but during the 1960s and 1970s, staffing increased dramatically. Since then, there has been a substantial bureaucracy on the Hill, including the personal staffs of members, committee and subcommittee staffs, and staff agencies like the Congressional Budget Office. Some of this bureaucracy is occupied with clerical duties, constituency service, and reelection efforts. A part of it, though, comprises an impressive source of public policy information internal to Congress and independent of the executive branch or other outside influences.

Because information is power, these centers of staffing figure prominently in drafting bills and amendments, affecting policy outcomes both in committee and on the floor, mounting persuasive efforts internal to the Congress, and mobilizing support outside of the Congress.

Reciprocity. The second of the three fundamental bases of power is exchange. One of the principal norms of Congress is reciprocity: "You do a favor for me, and I'll do a favor for you." Reciprocity, of course, is a norm of social relations in general. Without some expectation that a favor begets a favor in return, most forms of cooperation, including the workings of the legislative process, would collapse.

One of the principal norms of Congress is reciprocity: "You do a favor for me, and I'll do a favor for you."

Some members of Congress are in a better position than others to do favors. A committee or subcommittee chairman, for example, is in a position to see to it that an amendment favored by a non-committee member is inserted into a bill being marked up by the committee. The chair of a party's campaign committee is able to funnel funds into politicians' campaigns. Those members best situated to do favors can be quite influential in the legislative process, since they can expect favors in return. If a committee chairman helps a member with a provision in one bill, for instance, that member is likely to express appreciation by voting with the chairman on some other bill. If the member does not, he or she will not be able to count on the future cooperation of that particular chairman.

These exchanges occasionally take the form of an explicit quid pro quo. Most of the time, however, the exchanges are implicit and unspoken. Members who do favors for others build up a kind of bank of credit on which they can draw when necessary. But just as with a bank, one can draw down the account, and it needs replenishing from time to time by granting more favors.

The power to command. The third base of influence is the power to command. There are a few cases of that sort of power in the Congress. An elected member, for instance, directs his or her own personal staffers. He or she is in a position to hire and fire them at will, to decide which subjects they will work on, and to direct their activities. Most of the time, of course, that kind of command is not invoked, and the relationships between staffers and their bosses are wholly two-way, compatible, and cooperative. The growth of the Hill bureaucracy, indeed, has led some observers to worry that the elected members are not sufficiently in control. The entire relationship of a member to his or her own personal staff, however, is set in an understanding on both sides that the ultimate power in the situation rests with the elected member.

However, there are hardly any other such examples of command authority on the Hill. Certainly, party leaders are in no position simply to command the troops to follow them. Senators and representatives are elected and returned to office by their own constituents. They do not owe their membership in the body to the sufferance of the party leaders, and everybody understands that fact. Similarly, committee chairs cannot simply command that one type of bill be reported to the floor rather than another version. These leaders are important and influential, to be sure, but their influence does not rest on their power to command committee members. Instead, it is very much linked to expertise and reciprocity. They possess either a fund of information that is hard to match, an ability to do favors for others and profit from the exchange, or both.

LOCATIONS OF INFLUENCE. It is very difficult to identify locations of power and influence in the U.S. Congress. In many ways, it is a remarkably decentralized institution. Its 100 senators and 435 representatives, together with their staffs, make up a body of 535 autonomous enterprises. Far from commanding them, the most that leaders can hope for is some modicum of coordination, and even that is usually quite weak. There is nothing like the hierarchy of superiors and subordinates that one finds in the pyramidal organization charts of business firms or executive branch agencies. Compared to most other legislative bodies, furthermore, the party discipline in Congress is extraordinarily weak.

House-Senate differences. There are some differences between the House and Senate regarding the distribution of influence. First, senators have somewhat more autonomy than House members. When floor business is scheduled, for instance, the Senate majority leader engages in an elaborate process of negotiating among the involved senators regarding when a given bill will be scheduled and how long the debate will take. He then proposes a unanimous consent agreement to schedule the bill, which can in principle be scuttled by the objection of any single senator. Debate in the Senate is unlimited unless cloture is imposed by a vote of sixty senators or a unanimous consent agreement imposes limits. Nongermane amendments are often introduced, debated, and even passed.

The House, by contrast, schedules its business by a majority vote on a rule for a given bill that is proposed by the Rules Committee. The rule limits debate and often allows only specified amendments to be offered. House members are allowed somewhat less autonomy, in part because the House is bigger and hence potentially more unwieldy. Even House members, however, have greater autonomy than members of parliament in most other democracies.

Another difference between House and Senate involves expertise and hence the distribution of information-based influence. Partly because of the size of the body, senators are spread thinner than House members. The Senate has all of the work of the House, plus the handling of confirmations and treaties, and less than one-fourth the membership. Therefore, more of the detail of legislative business devolves onto staff than in the House. And since information is power, staffers are somewhat more influential on the Senate side of the Capitol.

Formal positions. There are two families of influential formal positions in the Congress: the committee and subcommittee leaders and the party leaders. The committee and subcommittee leaders include the chairmen and the ranking minority members. The party leaders include the majority and minority leaders; the whips on both sides; the chairmen of the party caucuses; the senatorial or congressional campaign chairmen of each party; and, in the House, the Speaker (the top majority party leader, selected by vote of the majority party members).

Committee and subcommittee chairmen derive their influence partly through their expertise and partly through their prerogatives. First, many of them are highly expert in the subject matter of their committees. They have dealt with it for years and know the policy issues, the legislative histories, and the important players in the system surrounding their committees' jurisdictions. Second, their prerogatives are useful in the exchange of favors discussed above. Chairs schedule the meetings and decide what will be taken up and what will be shelved. They direct the majority staff of the committees or subcommittees. So if another member would like a hearing scheduled on a favorite bill, the help of staff members in drafting an amendment, a timely good word from the chairman in favor of a pet proposal, or an endorsement for reelection from a visible colleague, a chairman is in a position to decide whether to help or not.

Party leaders also have a number of resources at their disposal. First, they influence the agenda—which bills will be taken up, when, and under what conditions. Second, the whip system places party leaders at the center of a communications network. That network conducts counts of members for, against, and undecided on a given issue, coordinates campaigns for or against key amendments or bills, and attempts to persuade party members of the virtues of the leadership's position. Third, the party leadership influences the committee assignments of their party's members. Since committee assignments are central to members' careers in the Congress, this prerogative gives leaders an important ability to reward friends and punish enemies and to do favors for new members that build credit. Fourth, the role of party leaders in campaign finance provides another means of building indebtedness that can be used in legislative battles of various kinds. Fifth, party leaders enjoy a publicity advantage over other members, because they are constantly interviewed and featured in the media. Finally, the party leaders of the president's party use the resources of the presidency as well as their own resources.

As noted above, however, the influence of party leadership in Congress is quite limited, especially in comparison with other legislatures. If members cross party leaders, the leaders do not have much redress, especially if the members already hold the committee assignments they want. There is actually a fairly high degree of party cohesion in Congress, but not through the ability of leaders to whip party members into line that one finds in most parliaments. Cohesion, rather, is a result of constituency and coalition differences between the parties, ideological differences between the parties, and the resultant intraparty patterns of communication. Party leaders are overwhelmingly brokers, persuaders, and negotiators. There are very few occasions for command.

Informal influence. An inventory of formal positions of power in Congress does not by any means exhaust the locations of influence. Some senators and representatives are influential beyond their formal positions. They develop reputations among their colleagues for their good judgment, their political savvy, and their expertise. Members have a great many opportunities to observe and to interact with their colleagues. They see each other daily in committee sessions, in floor debate, in informal conversations, on social occasions, and even in the House gym. Thus, their opinions about their colleagues are based on a rich fund of information.

Also, some members who hold formal positions are not as influential as those positions would suggest. They have not developed reputations for very effective use of their resources. They may not be seen as knowledgeable, tenacious, or skillful. Since members have many opportunities to make judgments about their formal leaders' performance and to differentiate among them, formal position does not necessarily translate directly into influence. Some holders of formal positions are not particularly influential, and some members are influential beyond their positions.

FORMS AND EXERCISE OF INFLUENCE. The forms of influence have two general aspects: individual and institutional.

Individual influence: cue taking. One important way in which members of Congress decide how to vote on the floor, and to some extent even in committee, is by taking cues from each other. Members must cast so many votes that they cannot possibly study each issue with care. They simply do not have sufficient time, and their staffs are occupied with many other matters. So on any particular bill or amendment, they take their cue from a colleague or set of colleagues whose judgment they trust, sometimes following them quite blindly. These cues may take the form of floor speeches, "Dear Colleague" letters, brief conversations with the cue givers, staffs' calls to other staffs, or even the yea or nay lights of cue givers on the electronic display in the chamber. By taking these shorthand cues, members believe they can make the same decisions that they would have made had they studied the issue themselves.

By what criteria do they choose colleagues from whom to take cues? When voting on the floor, they tend to rely heavily on cues from specialists, colleagues with some claim to expertise. These fellow members are overwhelmingly from the committees and subcommittees that considered the legislation. Deciding members also pick cue givers whose judgment they trust and who are likely to come to the same positions they would have had they studied the issue. That criterion for choice implies two things. First, they pick people whose policy positions or philosophies of government are like their own. Second, they pick people whose political judgment is similar to theirs; who are in similar electoral situations; and who share their views about major interest groups, coalition supporters, partisan opponents, and reelection strategies.

These criteria have two major implications. First, most cue taking takes place within parties, not across parties. There may be a regional component to the pattern, with southern Democrats following other southern Democrats or with members following colleagues from within their own state party delegations. One occasionally observes patterns of leading and following across party lines, but it is rare. This intraparty communication pattern is one major reason for the degree of party cohesion that exists in Congress, and it derives from similarities of constituencies, supporting coalitions, and electoral experiences within the parties.

When voting on the floor, members of Congress tend to rely heavily on cues from specialists.

The second and even more important implication of the pattern of cue taking is that, fundamentally, ideology drives voting. Members of Congress choose to follow colleagues whose worldviews, policy attitudes, or ideologies are like theirs. Because they are free to choose whomever they like, this criterion of philosophical agreement with the cue giver means that ideology drives the legislative process to a considerable degree. This implication is quite different from notions about the legislative process that emphasize politicians' efforts to win reelection, buy off pressure groups, or promote their careers through delivering benefits for their districts and angling for favorable media coverage. They do all of those things, to be sure, but the stress on such activities misses the importance of ideas about public policy in the legislative process. It is not that ideas run counter to politics. In fact, because voters tend to elect politicians whose views are not totally unlike their own, elected officials often do both the expedient and principled things at once.

Institutional influence: committee-chamber relations. It follows from the congressional emphasis on expertise that committees and subcommittees are important in the legislative process and in the making of public policy. As discussed above, senators and representatives prize specialization and turn to committee and subcommittee members for cues as they vote on the floor. Thus, the committee system is set up to give an institutional advantage to expertise. Committees also use the influence base of reciprocity to exchange favors with each other. Thus, the pattern, "You help my committee and I'll help yours," also contributes to committee power.

The patterns of cue taking raise a series of critical institutional questions: What is the relationship between committees and the chambers (House or Senate) of which they are a part? Do committees dictate to the floor? What power does the parent chamber have over its committees? Does it make a difference where power rests, or would the outcomes be similar whether committees or parent chambers dominate the legislative process?

Scholars debate whether committees are representative microcosms of their parent chambers or biased subsets of those chambers. Much depends on the answer. If committees are fundamentally representative of their parent chambers, then lodging power in the committees does not produce outcomes very different from those that would be produced if matters resolved in committees were instead decided by votes in the chambers. But if they are unlike their chambers in important ways, then their power raises normative questions concerning whether committee outcomes violate the will of the majority in the parent chamber. Some scholars (e.g., Krehbiel, 1991) assert that committees are not systematically biased, or to the extent that they are, they still must tailor their bills to the wishes of the parent chamber to muster majority votes for passage. Other scholars (e.g., Shepsle, 1978) argue that the committee assignment process, by which members express their preferences for committees and are assigned to one committee rather than another, systematically biases committees away from being representative of the parent chamber.

Probably the best way to reconcile these positions is first to observe that some committees are more representative than others. The Agriculture committees of both houses, for instance, are dominated by farm state members who respond most clearly to farm and agribusiness interests, making them systematically unlike the parent chambers. Second, some types of actions raise concerns about representativeness more than oth-

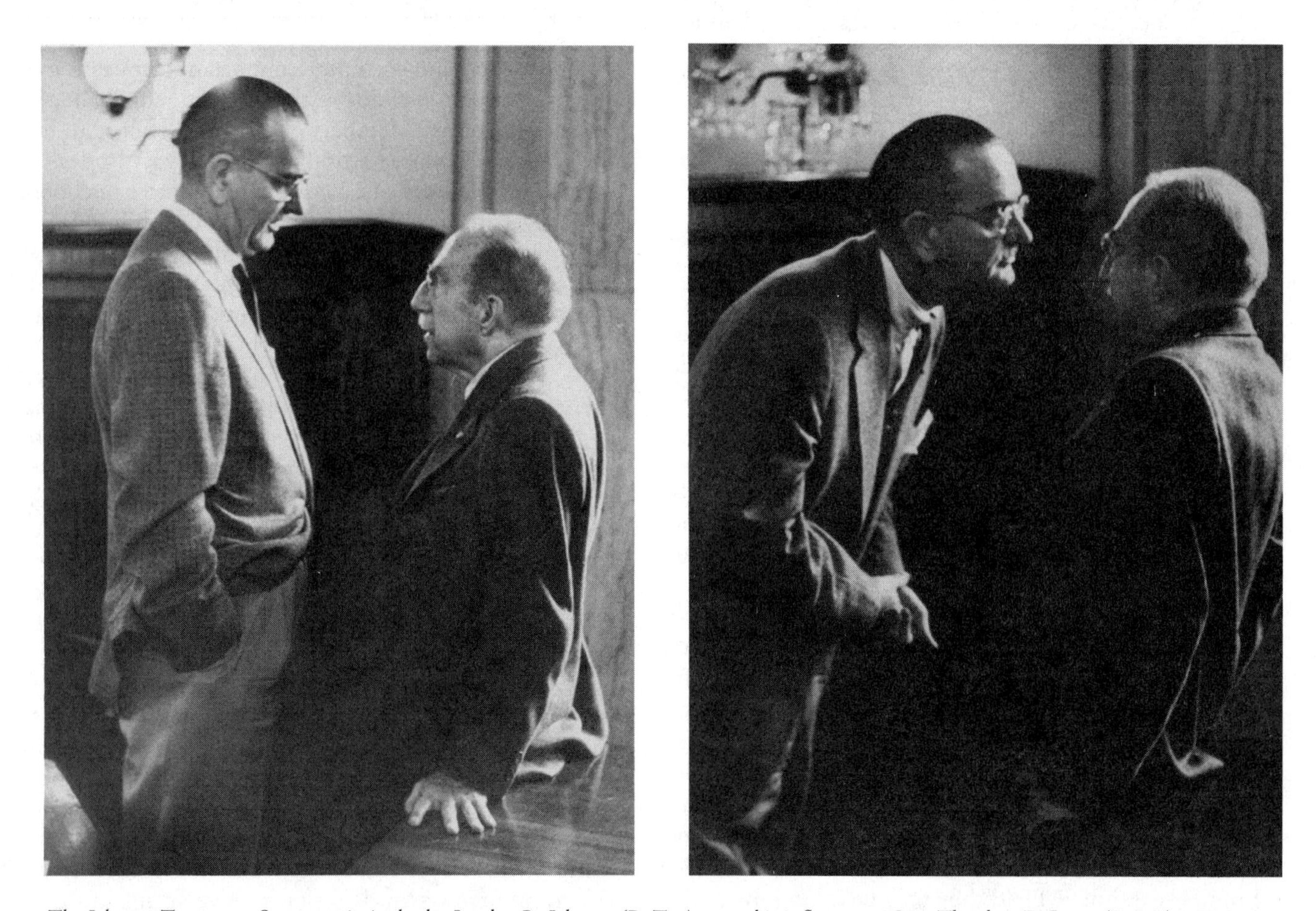

The Johnson Treatment. Senate majority leader Lyndon B. Johnson (D-Tex.) exerts his influence on Sen. Theodore F. Green (D-R.I.), 1957. Johnson was the most forceful majority leader to hold that office. Understanding the issues that were important to each senator, Johnson was usually able to persuade his colleagues to vote with him on a given bill. Uncooperative senators faced the so-called Johnson Treatment, in which the majority leader would praise, coax, needle, and threaten his colleagues. In 1955, through his influence, Johnson was able to usher the passage of over thirteen hundred bills, almost two hundred more than in the previous Congress. (George Tames, New York Times*)*

ers. For instance, committees are better able to block than to pass legislation without taking much account of chamber majorities, because passage requires floor approval and blocking does not.

One way to think of the committee-parent chamber relationship (Kingdon, 1989) is to picture the parent chamber as setting boundaries for each committee. On matters where most noncommittee members care little about a given provision of a bill, the committee has a great deal of discretion. On matters where most members care a great deal about a provision, committees have less discretion. These patterns of chamber attention, and hence of the boundaries the chamber sets for the committee, may vary from one committee to another, from one bill to another, and over time.

The importance of selection processes. Many of these observations about flows of influence point to the importance of the selection processes by which officials come to the positions they hold. Members of Congress often make their judgments straightforwardly according to their own attitudes about what constitutes good public policy. That being the case, the processes by which some people rather than others are selected to hold positions critically drive outcomes.

Those selection processes start with nomination and election of members back in individual constituencies and states. More than anything, the larger contours of outcomes in the House and Senate are structured by the distribution of parties and ideologies in the two chambers. Thus, the processes by which these members, rather than their actual or conceivable competitors, are selected to represent their districts and states, go a long way to explaining why the legislative process produces one outcome rather than another.

The ways in which some members rather than others become leaders within the Congress further highlight the importance of these selection processes. To the extent that committees are powerful, for instance, the biases that are built into the committee assignment process fundamentally affect policy outcomes. And to the extent that committee and subcommittee chairs and party leaders affect the workings of Congress, the process for choosing these leaders affects the orientations and ideologies that drive the institution.

MEASUREMENT AND CONCEPTUALIZATION. Robert Dahl's (1957) classic definition of power states: "A has power over B to the extent that he can get B to do something that B would not otherwise do." While this is a sensible statement of what we mean when we say that one individual or agent influences or has power over another, it indicates how difficult the measurement of influence is. We need to determine what B would otherwise have done. The problem is that the world often does not hold still long enough for us to do that satisfactorily. At the same time that A is trying to influence B, many other things are happening to B, so it is extremely difficult to isolate the effects of A's activities. It is also extremely difficult to say what B would have done in the absence of A's activities, since determining what might have happened, but did not, must be speculative. Finally, one does not want to commit the fallacy of assuming that just because B acted after A's activities, B's actions were the result of A's activities.

A frequent approach to measurement in legislative studies often is the computation of some sort of agreement score. If legislators vote together, for instance, one might say that they affected each other. But agreement does not tell us the direction of influence; A may have affected B, but B might as easily have affected A. Actually, agreement does not even tell us whether there has been any influence; both A and B might have been affected by some third factor, and the agreement between A and B in that case is unconnected to any relationship between them.

Measurement of influence is also plagued by the problem of anticipated reactions. If one would like to know how much a given president affected Congress, for instance, one might calculate how often Congress passed that president's legislative proposals. But one president might anticipate congressional reaction and scale down his proposals to get them passed, generating a high box score; another president might push for a much more ambitious program and get less of it passed. In that case, one might conclude not that the first president was more successful in getting what he wanted, but only that he tailored his proposals to congressional wishes more skillfully. In fact, one might well argue that he obtained little and that Congress actually ruled the relationship.

The same consideration applies to measures of committee success on the floor. Some committees and committee chairs look tremendously influential because they get their legislation passed intact on the floor. But if they have anticipated floor reaction and tailored their proposals accordingly, then it is the parent chamber that actually controls legislative content, and the committee's surface power is illusory.

The best general solution is not to rely on any one measure. One might want to use agreement scores, combined with interviews, participant observation, analysis of contemporary documents, examination of confidential memoranda and letters, and other indicators. As is often the case, some sort of multimethod design gets better results than any single approach.

[See also (I) Bargaining, Committees, article on Assignment of Members, Leadership, Seniority.]

BIBLIOGRAPHY

Dahl, Robert. "The Concept of Power." *Behavioral Science* 2 (1957): 201–215.

Fenno, Richard. *Congressmen in Committees.* 1973.

Kingdon, John. *Congressmen's Voting Decisions.* 3d ed. 1989.

Krehbiel, Keith. *Information and Legislative Organization.* 1991.

Matthews, Donald. *U.S. Senators and Their World.* Rev. ed. 1973.

Matthews, Donald, and James Stimson. *Yeas and Nays: Normal Decision-Making in the U.S. House of Representatives.* 1975.

Shepsle, Kenneth. *The Giant Jigsaw Puzzle: Democratic Committee Assignment in the Modern House.* 1978.

– JOHN W. KINGDON

Customs and Mores of Congress

The United States Congress comprises some 540 independent actors, counting 100 senators, 435 representatives, the 4 delegates from the District of Columbia and the territories and 1 resident commissioner from Puerto Rico. Each of these men and women has been elected in his or her own right, and they reach the Congress owing their election to many people: mentors, sponsors, contributors, local political bosses, and the voters of their district or state. They owe very little of their success to each other. Once elected to Congress, of course, members of their party may help them with fund-raising and on rare occasions with campaign appearances, but even this assistance is based largely upon self-interest, such as the desire to further one's advancement within the party hierarchy.

The fact that these men and women are in one sense independent of one another yet depend upon each other to pass legislation means that the way the Congress operates has to do as much with the personal relationships that develop between members and the customs, mores, and rituals of the Congress as with the elaborate written rules and regulations that govern their conduct as individuals and as members of the collective body. Over the two hundred years since the First Congress met in 1789, there have been many changes in the way in which members behave toward each other. Verbal slights and insults, for example, no longer merit challenges to meet on the Bladensburg dueling ground at sunrise. But there has also been continuity in the way members of Congress have treated each other, based largely upon their independence, equality within their respective bodies (with the exception of the nonstate House members, who can vote only in committee), their shared election experience (analogous to the fraternity pledge's "hell week" in terms of building camaraderie, except that it may be a "hell year"—or longer—in the case of a congressional election), and their mutual desire for reelection.

It is difficult to determine which of these factors weighs most heavily in the development of congressional mores and customs. They all have their part in the building of the traditions of Capitol Hill, and together they create a congressional culture that transcends the political and ideological differences that divide the membership.

Some may dispute the notion that there is a culture on Capitol Hill.

Some may dispute the notion that there is a culture on Capitol Hill. Actually, there are two cultures: one on the House side of the Hill, and one on the Senate side. They are similar in some ways—being developed and driven by the same forces—but they are different also, just as the House and the Senate are different bodies with different histories and different constitutional responsibilities and expectations. Some of these customs have become clichés, such as Speaker Sam Rayburn's admonition to the members of the House of Representatives: "To get along, go along." But other customs unique to the federal legislative bodies are more subtle and relate to the fact that this is indeed an exclusive club, with two distinct parts.

JOINING THE CLUB. Getting elected to Congress is seldom an easy affair. With the exception of those lucky few individuals who are appointed to office to fill an unexpired term, many members run and are defeated several times before finally being granted the grand prize. They are generally successful, well-known men and women, with a drive and desire for public recognition and acclaim that exceeds anything that most people can understand. There is the occasional member who is genuinely self-effacing, but most members necessarily have egos that rival the Washington Monument in size, even if they keep them well hidden most of the time. Given what it takes to put oneself forward to be accepted or rejected publicly by hundreds of thousands—perhaps millions—of one's fellow citizens, it could hardly be otherwise. And once elected they have often discovered that reaching Capitol Hill does not immediately make them members of the club.

Twenty years ago curmudgeonly House members like Wayne L. Hays (D-Ohio)—infamous for his dalliance with his secretary, Elizabeth Ray—were reputed to rail at new members with such endearing terms as "potato head," "mush head," and "scum." In the Senate the rites were more sophisticated, such as Henry M. Jackson's mispronunciation of the name of the new senator from Massachusetts: "Tongas," ignoring the "s" that followed the initial "t" in the name. It is barely possible, of course, that the distinguished senator from Washington State might simply have been ignorant of the way Paul E. Tsongas's name was pronounced, but not likely.

As late as the 1940s and 1950s, and perhaps into the 1960s, it could reasonably be said that new members were expected to serve a silent apprenticeship. Donald Matthews reported in his *U.S. Senators and Their World* (1960) that even laudatory remarks praising the service of one of the senior colleagues were discouraged when they came from a new member of the Senate. Indeed, the tradition of learning one's specialty before taking an active role in the affairs of the legislative body seems to have been fairly well observed.

Likewise, the tradition that Speaker Sam Rayburn (D-Tex.) observed of inviting new Democratic members of the House to his Capitol "Board of Education" room, where they would sip bourbon and branch water and learn the rituals of the body from their more senior colleagues, died out with the passing of "Mr. Sam." New members of the House are now given an orientation that includes presentations by members of the Harvard University faculty, but it is just not the same.

Observation since the 1980s suggests that there is little if any humiliation involved in the initiation of new members. Indeed, it is unlikely that any member of the Congress would allow himself or herself to be abused by a bully like Hays. Returning members seem to strive to welcome their new colleagues and begin a relationship with them that might prove mutually advantageous. Such a relationship is not enhanced by deliberately insulting someone or implying that they should learn the business of legislation by observing, not by doing.

COURTESIES AND CONVENTIONS. Both the Senate and the House are bodies of elaborate ritual and formality, probably second only to the British Parliament in their historical ceremony. In neither house, for example, do members address each other directly in debate, and neither do they refer to each other by name. In the House all remarks are addressed to the Speaker; in the Senate the president (whoever is presiding at the time) is the addressee. A member wishing to refer to or address a remark to Sen. Ernest F. Hollings, for example, would refer to him as "the senator from South Carolina," leaving it to the listener to determine whether it is to Hollings or to Sen. Strom Thurmond that the remarks are addressed. The *Congressional Record* for that day would make clear who was intended by placing the name of the member in parentheses.

Likewise, in the House the member might refer to "the gentleman from Massachusetts," as if there were only one such in the body. This indirect method of address is customarily observed in both House and Senate, except that in the heat of debate a member will occasionally slip and begin speaking directly to another member. It then falls to the presiding officer to remind the member that all remarks are to be addressed to the chair.

There are also customs as to what can and cannot be uttered on the floor of either body. Members of the House, for example, do not usually refer to the Senate by name, calling it "the other body" or "some other body," when it is found necessary to mention it at all, thereby bringing to mind a homicide detective discussing a multiple killing. Congressional speech when delivered on the floor of the House or Senate is constitutionally protected (Article I, section 6), but this protection does not mean that members can say anything they wish and not be called to account.

The custom of the Congress is that a member is not supposed to attack another member personally. Today's verbal attacks are rather tame affairs when compared with the rough-and-tumble fights—both verbal and physical—that characterized the nineteenth-century Congress. Still, House Speaker Thomas P. (Tip) O'Neill, Jr. (D-Mass.) discovered in 1984 that there are certain limits beyond which even a Speaker cannot venture with impunity.

Speaker O'Neill was provoked when Rep. Newt Gingrich of Georgia, a conservative Republican, uttered words that O'Neill took as disparaging the patriotism of Democratic members of the House. The imposing Speaker immediately left the presiding position—which a Speaker rarely does—and took Gingrich to task, declaring that the Republican's statement was "the lowest thing I have ever seen in my thirty-two years in Congress." At that point another Republican challenged O'Neill's phrasing, and demanded that the words "be taken down," or stricken from the record. The parliamentarian of the House ruled that O'Neill had indeed violated the prohibition against personal insult, and for the first time since 1797 a Speaker was chastised for his language.

Nineteenth-century members of both bodies would undoubtedly be astonished that language as mild as O'Neill's would bring an official rebuke. An examination of the record of the first hundred years of the Congress reveals that words spoken in the chamber were often the cause of duels, beatings, and fistfights.

In 1838, for example, Rep. Jonathan Cilley of Maine delivered a speech that criticized a New York City newspaper editor. Another member, William J. Graves, attempted to deliver a note to Cilley demanding an explanation. When Cilley refused the note, Graves challenged Cilley to a duel. Though pistols were the usual dueling instrument, these two members chose rifles, and Cilley's death was the result. The House appointed a committee to look into the matter, but decided against expulsion or censure of either Graves or the House members who had served as seconds in the duel.

Neither has the Senate been spared violence arising out of floor debate. In one example, tempers routinely flared during the height of controversy over the great compromise on slavery that had been fashioned by Henry Clay and others in 1850. On 17 April 1850, for instance, Henry S. Foote of Mississippi drew his pistol—there were no rules preventing the well-armed member from entering the Senate chamber—and aimed it at Thomas Hart Benton as the Missouri senator advanced toward him. Benton was unafraid and challenged Foote: "Let him fire! Stand out of the way! Let the assassin fire!" Both men were restrained by others in the chamber, and there was no further breach of protocol that day. But it was abundantly clear, as other members—notably Sen. Charles Sumner of Massachusetts, whose assault on the floor of the Senate by Rep. Preston S. Brooks of South Carolina became a pre–Civil War cause célèbre—discovered throughout the remaining years of the nineteenth century, words could provoke a physical retaliation from another member of Congress.

Sometimes a member does not display the proper courtesy toward his colleagues.

The standards of today have led to changed mores within the Congress as well, so that it is only on the rarest of occasions when a member physically assaults another. Just such an occasion occurred in the House chamber in March 1985. According to reliable reports, Rep. Thomas J. Downey, a liberal New York Democrat, accosted Rep. Robert K. Dornan, a conservative California Republican. Downey allegedly grabbed Dornan by the shoulder and spun him around, demanding to know whether Dornan had called him a "draft-dodging wimp" in a recent speech. Dornan took offense at Downey's hands-on approach and grabbed the New York representative by the necktie, hoisting him partway off the floor. As others intervened, Dornan released Downey's tie, explaining that he "only wanted to straighten the knot."

For the most part, senators do not today engage in such unseemly behavior. Indeed, the elaborate rituals and courtesies of the U.S. Senate might make the courtiers of Louis XVI feel quite at home. A member is hardly ever just "the gentleman from South Dakota." He is "the distinguished gentleman from South Dakota." He or she is "the able Senator from Nebraska" or the "learned Senator from Alabama." All of this is done with the straightest of faces, even if the speaker knows that the member being referred to is in reality dumb as a tree stump. As Sen. Alben W. Barkley of Kentucky was reputed to have said, "If you think your colleague is stupid, refer to him as 'the able, learned, and distinguished Senator.' If you know he is stupid, refer to him as 'the very able, learned and distinguished Senator.' " It is sometimes difficult to maintain the front. As one member said, "I know he is a dumb SOB; everyone else knows he is a dumb SOB. But we must keep up the charade."

Sometimes a member does not display the proper courtesy toward his colleagues, and other than the disdain of his fellows, there is not usually much that can be done about it. Occasionally, though, such a member will leave the Senate and then come back in another capacity, perhaps seeking confirmation for an important post within the executive branch. Consideration of a former member is ordinarily a time for senatorial courtesies to be put on fullest display, and most such nominations sail through without much delay. One such nomination in 1989, however, proved the exception.

John G. Tower, the former senator from Texas, was nominated by President George Bush to be secretary of Defense. Even before credible allegations that touched on Tower's qualifications to be Defense secretary had surfaced, astute observers of the process discerned that there might be some problem with the Tower confirmation. Tower's ego and his prickliness were legendary, even by Senate standards, and during his three-plus terms in the Senate he had apparently aggravated many of his colleagues. Tower's potential difficulty was corroborated when a Republican senator—someone who eventually voted for Tower—was heard to mutter to one of his staff, "I wonder if the little [expletive] expects this to be easy." It was not easy, and Tower was ultimately rejected by the Senate in which he had served for over twenty-three years. It was a rare departure from senatorial norms.

THE TYRANNY OF THE MINORITY. The legislative courtesies of the Senate are much more necessary than are those of the House of Representatives, primarily because of the rules of the two bodies. As more than one observer has noted, the rules of the House are designed to allow the majority to work its will; the rules of the Senate are designed to protect the minority, even if that minority consists of only one member. The minority in the House of Representatives can often do little more than engage in guerrilla warfare and snipe at the majority, while in the Senate a minority can effectively derail the legislative train by objecting to the usual method by which the Senate does business.

Most of the business of the Senate is conducted by means of what are called "unanimous consent agreements," or "UCs." Unless a member objects, the Senate can violate its own rules with impunity, and the rules are routinely violated every time a bill is called up for floor action. If a member does not want to allow such latitude it is easy enough for him or her to object to the terms of a unanimous consent agreement when it is offered by the majority leader or other sponsor of the bill, and such objections are not uncommon. Through what is called the "hold" system, however, it is possible for a member to indicate his objection even before the UC stage is reached.

To do so, he tells his leader—Republican or Democrat—that he wants to be consulted before a bill is brought up for consideration and that he is placing a "hold" on the bill. This indicates to the leadership that there is no point in seeking a unanimous consent agreement, because the member has a particular problem with that particular piece of legislation. Holds may remain secret for a time, though they are almost inevitably revealed if they are kept in place for longer than a few days. A hold is in many instances an indication that the member wants the sponsor of the bill to accommodate an amendment, but it may signal that a unanimous consent agreement will be objected to no matter what "sweeteners" are offered. As a result, the majority leader or his designee will not generally attempt to bring up for floor action a bill that is the subject of a hold.

Students of the hold system do not know precisely how long it has operated, but it goes back to the 1960s at least. By the 1970s it had developed into the system as it operates now: a powerful brake on the operations of the Senate. The person placing the hold is usually known to the members of his own party, but it can be difficult for a member of the opposite party to discover the identity of the culprit. Both Democrats and Republicans deplore the practice of placing anonymous holds on bills, but members of both parties admit to using holds themselves. It is simply one of the tools of the Senate, and it is one that owes its existence purely to courtesy and tradition.

The unanimous consent agreement also owes its effectiveness to the courtesies and comity of the Senate. A perfectly naive newcomer, learning about the routine use of such agreements to transact Senate business, might say, "Then that's the answer. If there is anything coming up that I do not like, I will just object to its consideration." That might be within the rules, and if you did not care what your colleagues thought of you, and you never wanted to get anything passed yourself, then this would certainly be a way to delay the passage of objectionable legislation. If one person did it, however, it is a certainty that others would do the same, and the Senate would quickly come to a screeching halt. Senatorial courtesy would have been breached, and the entire nature of the body would change.

The Senate found out in 1957 just what the reaction would be if someone attempted to depart from the norms of the Senate and violate the usual customs and courtesies. According to the *New York Times,* Sen. H. Styles Bridges (R-N.H.) sought the routine permission of the Senate to insert into the *Record* a speech he had delivered some fifteen years earlier. The *Congressional Record* is filled with this sort of drivel, and upon hearing such a request the presiding officer drones almost automatically that "without objection, it is so ordered."

Suddenly, the new (two months in the Senate) member from Ohio, Frank J. Lausche, lodged an objection. Mouths fell open, and there was a dead silence in the chamber. Bridges indicated that if there was to be an objection to his routine request, then he would do the same to others. The Senate leadership could see the cloth unraveling; without such routine comity, the Senate could not function. Majority Leader Lyndon B. Johnson thereupon stepped in; Lausche withdrew his objection; Bridges inserted his speech; and the wheels of the Senate turned freely again.

The same courtesy occurs when a member requests a speaker to yield to him for a question. This is sometimes done for the purpose of helping the speaker make a point, but at other times the purpose is hostile. In both instances the member holding the floor normally yields, but if there is a limitation on his time and he knows the question will be a hostile one, he will sometimes refuse the request to "yield for a question."

It is also part of the courtesy of Senate debate to allow each member to have his say on a bill or amendment before moving to table. "Tabling" a bill or amendment effectively kills the measure, and since the motion to table is nondebatable, offering that motion cuts off debate and causes an immediate vote on the issue at hand. In the normal partisanship of many legislative bodies, such a move would be regarded as a fair and appropriate tactic. In the Senate, though, a member who attempts to shut off debate before each interested senator has had the opportunity (within reason) to have his say will bring down upon him the wrath of his fellows. It has sometimes occurred that someone moves to table an amendment, a member objects that he has not been allowed to be heard on the issue, and the one who moved to table thereupon withdraws his motion.

SENIORITY. It may come as some surprise to learn that the seniority system, by which the chairmanship and ranking position on a congressional committee or subcommittee are largely determined, is purely a matter of custom and is not a part of the Senate or House rules. Seniority in the Congress is based on (1) length of continuous service within the body (House or Senate), followed by (2) total service in the one body, including noncontinuous service, followed by (3) service in the other body of Congress, followed by (4) service as a state governor. It may also be further determined by alphabetical order.

This system was never as strong in the House as in the Senate, where it still holds sway. A rigid seniority system for committee chairmanships in the House was a fairly recent phenomenon, developing only in the late 1940s and 1950s. Prior to that time the Speaker of the House could influence the committee vote regarding appointments of committee chairmen, and even as recently as 1943 eleven of thirty-four House committees were chaired by other than the most senior member.

Going further back, in the early years of the nineteenth century even presidents got into the act. John Quincy Adams, for example, met with Speaker of the House John W. Taylor in 1825 to discuss the appointment of committee chairmen "so that justice may be done as far as practicable to the Administration." Seniority was not even a consideration in Adams's time.

In the modern House of Representatives Democrats who become chairmen of committees are elected by the Democratic caucus, and a chairman who takes his position for granted may find himself ousted, as occurred in the 1970s with the chairmen of Ways and Means, Agriculture, Armed Services, and Banking and Currency. The days of the all-powerful committee chairman in the House seem gone for good, and it was a sign of the times that the members of the House class of 1992 interviewed the committee chairmen even as they themselves jockeyed for assignments to coveted committees.

In the Senate the seniority system is much more strictly observed. Democratic committee chairmen or ranking members are nominated by the Steering Committee, a part of the Democratic leadership, and these nominations are invariably made by seniority. If 20 percent of the Democratic membership of the Senate wishes to challenge the nominations, the caucus decides the issue by secret ballot. This has not happened, but such a vote theoretically could occur.

On the other side of the aisle, the Republican members of each committee elect the chairman or ranking member, the choice being subject to confirmation by the Republican conference. Seniority has generally been the rule in such selections, and the conference has even overturned the wishes of a committee in order to preserve seniority. Such was the case in 1987, for example, when Jesse Helms (R-N.C.) decided to assert his seniority and bump Richard G. Lugar (R-Ind.) from the ranking position on the Foreign Relations Committee. Republicans on Foreign Relations wanted to keep Lugar, who had chaired the committee during the previous Congress. Helms, however, prevailed in the Republican conference, where even some of those philosophically opposed to the conservative Helms voted with an eye toward the integrity of the seniority system, an example of custom and tradition prevailing over ideological commitment or political compatibility.

DRESS. The advent of C-SPAN, the Cable Satellite Public Affairs Network, has allowed the typical voter to see for the first time just how a member of Congress dresses while representing him or her in the halls of Congress. For some voters it is probably quite a shock. For male members, coats and ties are de rigueur for entry onto the House or Senate floor, but beyond that bare code very little else is applicable. Senators generally dress in a conservative fashion, and there is a certain amount of peer pressure to conform to a "Brooks Brothers" look. House members, on the other hand, are all over the place sartorially. Loud plaids and other outrageous patterns are a constant for some members, such that one staffer, in response to a representative's flamboyant attire, was heard to remark that he had "wondered what happened to Pinky Lee's wardrobe," referring to the 1950s children's television star.

The advent of C-SPAN has allowed the typical voter to see for the first time just how a member of Congress dresses while in the halls of Congress.

There is no actual rule requiring that a male member wear a necktie or even a jacket or suit, but these are traditions that have been hallowed by the years. Rep. Ben Nighthorse Campbell (D-Colo.), an American Indian, broke one precedent when he wore his bolo tie onto the House floor, but even in the 1970s no member is known to have attempted to pass into the House chamber wearing a polyester double knit leisure suit.

FORMER MEMBERS. Many members who retire or are defeated decide—particularly if they have spent a considerable period of time in the Congress—that they do not really want to go back to Montana or Louisiana or wherever. Instead, they settle into law firms and lobbying operations in the nation's capital and use to great advantage their knowledge of the way legislation is made, the friendships they made while serving in the House or Senate, and the courtesies that are afforded them as former members.

These courtesies are considerable, and they offer the ex-member a distinct advantage as a lobbyist. The former member, for example, has the privileges of the floor, meaning that he can go into the House or Senate chamber while the legislative body is in session and chat with his former colleagues. Both Senate and House tradition prohibits actual lobbying while on the floor, and the House rules even prohibit the presence on the floor of an ex-member who has an interest in pending legislation. But there are few who believe that the presence of a former member who is known to be representing a particular side of an issue goes unnoticed and does not inure to the benefit of his client.

A recent example of the benefits of having an ex-member on a lobbying team comes from the Senate at the close of the second session of the 102d Congress, when Russell B. Long, former chairman of the Finance Committee, ventured into the chamber where he had served for some thirty-seven years. Long was not at that moment lobbying his former colleagues on behalf of the biotech firm that had developed a new and promising possible AIDS vaccine; he had already done his work along those lines. Long was there just to show the flag, so to speak, and his presence was noted by Sen. John W. Warner. Warner affirmed that Long was not there as a lobbyist, but the presence of the former colleague, said Warner, "connoted the importance of the amendment" the Senate was then considering. This amendment proposed $20 million for the Defense Department to conduct clinical trials of the vaccine, and it passed with ease.

Former members are also afforded additional perks that other lobbyists cannot approach, such as the right to enter the "members only" dining rooms in the Capitol, a nice place for schmoozing with one's former colleagues. Former senators qualify for other, lesser privileges, too, ranging from a permanent identification card from the Senate sergeant at arms (which allows unfettered access to the Capitol, including those parts that are off-limits to the general public) to parking in the Senate parking lots (a considerable convenience given the difficulty of parking on Capitol Hill). Some of these privileges, states the *Congressional Handbook,* are derived from statute and Senate rules, "but most are traditional courtesies." There is no publication of the House of Representatives that offers a comparable list of courtesies afforded former members, but knowledgeable insiders suggest ex-representatives are treated about the same as ex-senators.

EQUALITY OF MEMBERS. All members, with the exception of the nonstate members of the House of Representatives, are equal, whether one is a junior Republican or the Democratic chairman of the Appropriations Committee. This does not mean, of course, that everyone enjoys the same power, prestige, or esteem, but within their own offices they are equally king or queen, or equally despots.

A member can hire and fire staff for no reason at all—even on a momentary whim—and though there are both House and Senate rules that say that a member should not discriminate against his or her staff on the basis of race, color, religion, sex, or national origin, there is little if any enforcement mechanism to ensure that if such discrimination occurs there is real consequence for the member or relief for the victim.

This reluctance among members to involve themselves in one another's domain is perhaps best exemplified in the congressional reaction to allegations of ethics violations by their colleagues, including allegations of sexual misconduct or harassment of staff. Each house of Congress has an ethics committee, and service on it—a duty in which one is compelled to judge one's fellow House or Senate members—is anything but a sought-after assignment. House minority leader Robert H. Michel, for example, described such an assignment as "dirty, dirty duty" and suggested that anyone who served on the ethics committee would fairly much be able to name his or her next committee assignment.

Senators and members of the House have been disciplined for violation of the rules of the body. The extreme reluctance of the membership to recognize and consider accusations against one of their own, however, only reinforces the notion that there is a "congressional protective society" that turns its collective face away from all but the most egregious violations. It has been suggested that even when the Congress acts against an unethical member; it does so only against conduct that is clearly criminal or in the face of mounting publicity that threatens the body itself. After all, as is a common saying on the Hill, "what goes around comes around," and no member wants to be deprived of the freedom to run his own office and treat his own staff the way he sees fit.

The way in which the Senate and the House conduct their business is the result of some two hundred years of practice, precedent, and tradition. Many of these rules have been codified by the two bodies, beginning with the manual of procedure developed by Thomas Jefferson while he served as vice president of the United States. But many other rules are not written down in any official handbook of the Congress. They are nevertheless just as applicable and operate just as surely as those that have been sanctified by codification. These traditions, mores, folkways, and customs are part and parcel of the Congress, and it is impossible to understand these two legislative bodies without both acknowledging them and accepting their place in the culture of the Hill.

[See also (I) Freshmen, Seniority.]

BIBLIOGRAPHY

Baker, Richard A. *The Senate of the United States: A Bicentennial History.* 1989.

Currie, James T. *The United States House of Representatives.* 1989.

Davidson, Roger, and Walter J. Oleszek. *Congress and Its Members.* 3d ed. 1990.

Jones, Rochelle, and Peter Woll. *The Private World of Congress.* 1979.

MacNeil, Neil. *Forge of Democracy: The House of Representatives.* 1963.

Matthews, Donald R. *U.S. Senators and Their World.* 1960.

Weatherford, J. McIver. *Tribes on the Hill: The U.S. Congress, Rituals and Realities.* 1985.

– JAMES T. CURRIE

CONGRESSIONAL BUDGET OFFICE

Created by the Congressional Budget Act of 1974 (Title I–IX, P.L. 93-344; 88 Stat. 297), the Congressional Budget Office (CBO) started operations on 24 February 1975 with the appointment of its first director, Alice M. Rivlin. Compared with the other congressional support agencies—the Congressional Research Service, the General Accounting Office, and the Office of Technology Assessment—CBO has a narrow mission. It provides economic and budgetary information for the congressional budget and legislative processes. CBO's work covers a wide range of activities, however, in keeping with the diversity and scope of the federal budget. Before CBO existed, only the president had a complete source of data on the budget and the economy. With CBO, Congress has its own source of budgetary information, knowledge that can be used to make policy decisions or to challenge presidential information.

CBO has three primary responsibilities in assisting Congress with the budget process: monitoring the economy and estimating its impact on government actions; improving the flow and quality of budgetary information to members and committees; and analyzing the costs and effects of alternative budgetary choices. The Congressional Budget Act directs CBO to produce an annual report "with respect to fiscal policy taking into account projected economic factors," "national budget priorities," and "alternative allocations of budgetary resources." In carrying out these responsibilities, CBO has been instrumental in preserving a nonpartisan, professional reputation, which has enhanced the credibility of its budget estimates and analysis.

CBO meets these responsibilities by providing analysis and data to the Senate and House Budget committees, analytic assistance to the Appropriations, Ways and Means, and Finance committees; and similar services, to a limited degree, to other committees and members. Prior to CBO's creation, Congress had no unit comparable to the Office of Management and Budget (OMB) of the Executive Office of the President. Through its director, CBO is authorized to obtain data, estimates, statistical analyses, and other information from executive branch agencies, departments, and commissions. It also allows Congress to be more independent of the president and the executive branch in determining final budget figures.

CBO spends a great deal of its time (about 40 percent) on program and budgetary analysis for the two Budget committees and other money committees of Congress. The Budget Act requires CBO to prepare an annual report analyzing the president's budget recommendations, economic conditions, and budget policy. This report, considered essential to the congressional budget process, focuses on fiscal policy, five-year budget projections, and deficit reduction. CBO is also required to prepare five-year cost projections on every piece of legislation reported out of committee. It spends approximately 25 percent of its time providing these five-year projections. Additionally, CBO helps committees determine the cost of programs proposed in pending legislation (20 percent of its time). "Scorekeeping," which takes about 15 percent of CBO's time, consists of periodically informing Congress of the impact of legislation on the spending limits in its most recent budget resolution. This function gives Congress information that can lead to significant budgetary control.

Congress has assigned additional responsibilities to CBO since 1974. CBO was given a major role in the sequestration process established by the Balanced Budget and Emergency Deficit Control Act of 1985, more popularly called the Gramm-Rudman-Hollings Act. Under Gramm-Rudman-Hollings, CBO and OMB initially played equal roles in calculating whether the annual deficit targets specified by the act were met and, if not, in determining the amounts and percentages of budgetary resources that would be cut to meet the deficit target. In *Bowsher v. Synar* (1986), however, the Supreme Court ruled that in allowing the comptroller general to make the final determination on the amount of required spending reductions, the act had delegated the executive's responsibility to carry out the law to a legislative branch official. Consequently, in 1987 the Gramm-Rudman-Hollings Act was amended to give

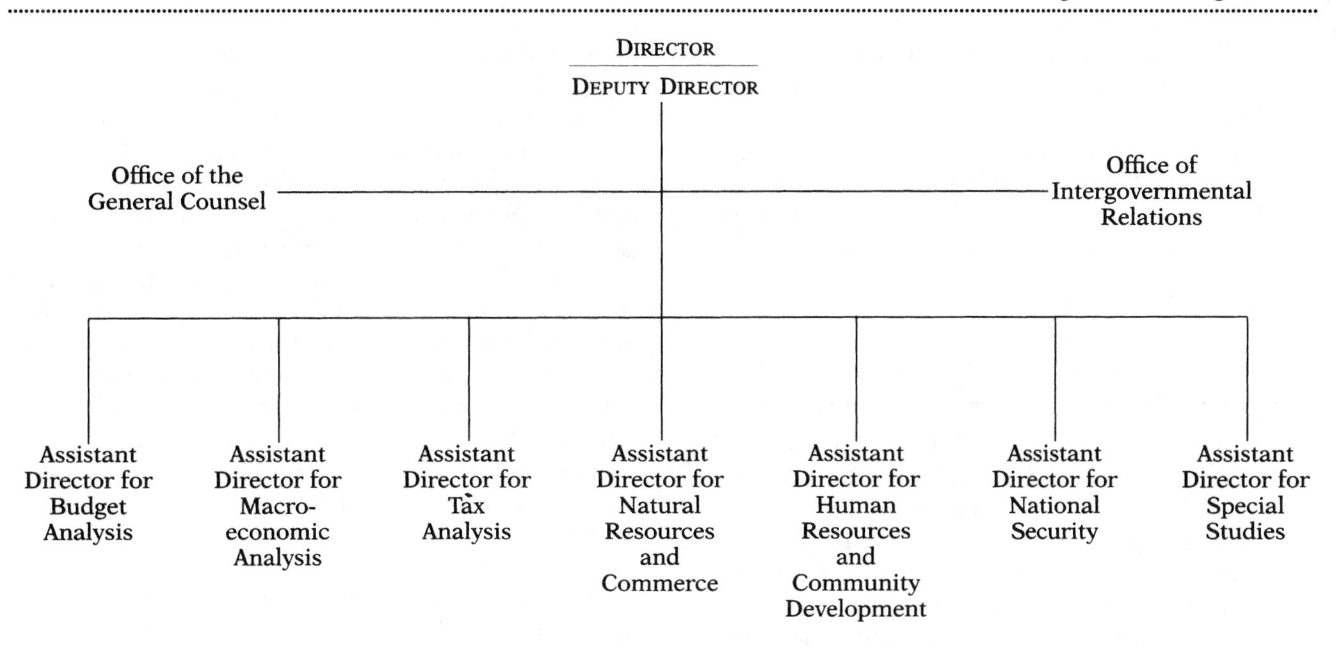

Organization of the Congressional Budget Office. (Congressional Budget Office. Responsibilities and Organization of the Congressional Budget Office. *1993)*

the responsibility for determining whether a sequester should occur to OMB, and CBO's role was reduced to providing advisory reports.

In 1981, CBO's original responsibility was expanded when it was directed to estimate the costs that state and local governments would incur in complying with proposed federal legislation. Congress also may direct CBO to undertake specific studies on various subjects, such as the costs of including coverage of outpatient prescription drugs under Medicare, the outlook for farm-commodity program spending, and the cost of curbing acid rain. These policy-analysis reports are widely used and highly respected. The influence of many CBO reports has extended well beyond Capitol Hill, helping to shape public debate on many issues.

The most widely used CBO publication is its annual report to the budget committees. This report has evolved over time, and in 1993 consists of two volumes. One makes economic and budget projections for the next five years, and the other (first issued in 1982) suggests spending and revenue options for reducing the budget deficit. The economic and budget volume also includes an excellent discussion of fiscal policy and the implications of federal deficits for economic growth. The Budget Act requires that this two-volume annual report be submitted by 15 February; it is customarily updated by mid-August of each year.

Another highly respected and popular CBO report is the annual analysis of the president's budget, prepared at the request of the Senate Appropriations Committee. The executive's budget is recast using CBO's economic assumptions and estimating techniques, thus allowing Congress to see how CBO's baseline estimates would be affected by the president's revenue and spending projections. The CBO analysis has often shown that the president has underestimated the size of the deficit. For example, in nine of the ten years from 1982 to 1992, CBO estimated that adoption of the president's budgetary proposals would result in baseline deficits much higher—averaging $22 billion higher—than those estimated by the administration.

CBO also prepares cost estimates for every public bill reported by congressional committees to show how these legislative proposals will affect spending or revenues over the following five years. The number of cost estimates prepared by CBO each year varies depending on the amount of legislation being considered and reported by committees, but the number has tended to increase: for example, CBO produced 553 such reports in 1980 and 861 in 1989.

One of CBO's most important functions is "scorekeeping," or keeping track of all spending and revenue legislation that is considered each year. Score-keeping helps Congress know whether or not it is acting within the limits set by the annual budget resolutions, bringing more discipline to the budget process. Scorekeeping can be quite controversial. There are no written rules, and the conventions are frequently challenged by committees that feel pinched by the limits set in the annual budget resolutions. The two budget committees are the ultimate scorekeepers for Congress; they often settle disputes by political compromises rather than using a formal written rule.

CBO is structured along lines of production and responsibility. In 1993 CBO's organizational structure remained almost identical to that established in 1975.

CBO has three primary responsibilities in assisting Congress with the budget process.

The number of employees at CBO, which is limited by its annual appropriations, rose from 193 in fiscal year 1976 to 226 positions in 1993. CBO's director is appointed jointly by the Speaker of the House and the president pro tempore of the Senate after considering recommendations from the two budget committees. The director's term is four years, with no limit on the number of terms he or she may serve. As of late 1993, there had been three directors, each a prominent economist with knowledge of the federal budget process. Rivlin served two terms, from 1975 to 1983; Rudolph G. Penner served one term, from 1983 to 1987; and Robert D. Reischauer became the third director in March 1989. The process of jointly appointing the CBO director has proved difficult. It took seven months after passage of the 1974 Budget Act for the two budget committees to agree on the Rivlin appointment, eight months for them to agree on the Penner appointment, and more than two years to agree on the Reischauer appointment.

[See also (I) Budget Process; (II) Budget Policy.]

BIBLIOGRAPHY

Schick, Allen. *Congress and Money: Budgeting, Spending, and Taxing.* 1980.

Thurber, James A. "The Evolving Role and Effectiveness of the Congressional Research Agencies." In *The House at Work.* Edited by Joseph Cooper and Calvin MacKenzie. 1981. Pp. 292–315.

U.S. Congress. Congressional Budget Office. *A Profile of the Congressional Budget Office.* 1990.

U.S. Congress. Congressional Budget Office. *Responsibilities and Organization of the Congressional Budget Office.* 102d Cong., 2d sess., 1993.

– JAMES A. THURBER

CONGRESSIONAL DIRECTORY

The *Congressional Directory* is the official almanac of Congress. Early predecessors of the modern *Directory,* compiled and printed in very small numbers by private firms, were little more than lists of members of the House of Representatives and the Senate. Produced as broadsides and pamphlets, they were temporary documents that were readily discarded at the end of each Congress or when a new issue was published.

Over time, new details were added to the directories. When Congresses first began arriving in Washington, D.C., members were listed by boardinghouse groups. By 1814, the compilation included the postal address of each legislator, and the next version contained a list of the principal officers of the government and their residences. Issues for the 14th Congress (1815–1817) first specified the American ministers serving abroad and the foreign diplomats stationed in the United States, followed by an enumeration of the standing committees of each house. For the period from 1801 to 1840, directories grew from seven to sixty-nine pages, with an average of forty-five pages.

The *Directory* for the first session of the 30th Congress (1847), compiled and published by the postmaster of the House of Representatives, is generally considered to be the initial official edition because it was the first to be ordered and paid for by Congress. The Joint Committee on Printing began supervising the production of the *Directory* in 1864.

When biographical sketches of legislators were added in 1867, the *Directory* had essentially attained its modern format. Today, the *Directory* is published at the outset of each Congress. Its contents, totaling 1,314 pages in 1992, include lists of all individuals currently serving in Congress (with biographical information supplied by members); the principal officials and entities supporting and assisting Congress; the existing congressional committees, boards, and commissions; the committee assignments of legislators; the primary entities and leaders of the executive branch, the judicial branch, and the government of the District of Columbia; U.S. diplomatic offices; international organizations of which the United States is a member; and journalists accredited to the congressional press galleries. It also includes certain congressional statistical data, historical information on and floor plans of the Capitol, and current congressional district maps. The *Directory* may be purchased from the Government Printing Office and is available in many public libraries.

BIBLIOGRAPHY

Goldman, Perry M., and James S. Young, eds. *The United States Congressional Directories, 1789–1840.* 1973.

– HAROLD C. RELYEA

CONGRESSIONAL MEDAL OF HONOR

Among the most enduringly popular misnomers in American English, the term *Congressional Medal of*

Honor reflects a long-standing confusion regarding two entirely separate awards: the special medals presented by Congress from time to time for distinguished achievements (generally known as congressional gold medals or, simply, Congressional Medals); and the highest of all military awards for valor, officially designated as the Medal of Honor.

The Medal of Honor, authorized in 1862, has been, awarded to some thirty-four hundred persons, nearly half of them for "gallantry in action" during the Civil War. More than seven hundred additional awards were made over the following half century, in connection with the Indian campaigns and various U.S. ventures in the Philippines, China, Mexico, and elsewhere. The large number of Medals of Honor given prior to World War I was due to the absence, until the war, of any other medals for valor.

The inception in 1918 of several new awards raised the Medal of Honor to its present exalted and unique stature: it is to be given only for actions involving actual conflict with an enemy, distinguished by "gallantry and intrepidity at the risk of life above and beyond the call of duty." Consequently, awards became far less common following World War I; only about 430 were made for all of World War II, roughly 130 for the Korean War, and about 240 for the Vietnam War. In addition, there have been a handful of "special legislation" awards by Congress, such as that made in 1927 to Charles Lindbergh, to whom Congress also awarded a Congressional Medal the following year.

Under existing law, the Medal of Honor is presented by, or by the direction of, the president, following a set of procedures for nomination, investigation, verification, endorsements, approvals, and so on, all governed by the regulations of the respective armed services. While Congress plays no part in the selection of recipients or other aspects of the process (except in the rare instances of the special legislation awards mentioned above), the medal is presented "in the name of Congress" (10 U.S.C. 3741)—probably the main reason for the widespread use of the term *Congressional* Medal of Honor. Although this remains the award's popular name and occasionally appears even in the text of federal laws and other documents, the correct, official designation has been "Medal of Honor" since 1905, when the matter was the subject of a ruling by the War Department.

[See also (I) Awards and Prizes; (II) Medals, Presidential.]

BIBLIOGRAPHY

Editors of Boston Publishing Company. *Above and Beyond: A History of the Medal of Honor from the Civil War to Vietnam.* 1985.

U.S. Senate. Committee on Veterans' Affairs. *Medal of Honor Recipients 1863–1978.* 96th Cong., 1st sess., 1979. Committee Print 3.

— E. RAYMOND LEWIS

CONGRESSIONAL RECORD

The *Congressional Record* is the primary written source for a daily account of the floor proceedings of the House and Senate. The courts and federal agencies rely on it to interpret legislative intent, and scholars use it to compile a bill's legislative history. However, much more than legislative matters such as roll-call votes, texts of bills, amendments, conference reports, and floor debates appear in its pages. A regular reader of the *Congressional Record* might well qualify for a liberal arts degree, for he or she would be exposed to an astounding variety of material: articles reprinted from newspapers and magazines, speeches on a broad variety of topics, copies of correspondence between federal officials, tributes to athletic teams, eulogies to the departed, renditions of local and regional concerns and celebrations, and even occasional attempts at poetry and humor.

The official records of House and Senate proceedings, as mandated by Article I, section 5, clause 3 of the Constitution, are the House and Senate journals. The journals, akin to the minutes of a meeting, describe only briefly the procedural actions and votes that occurred on a given day and do not contain the text of the debates surrounding them or any extraneous material. Therefore, although not the official account, the *Congressional Record* remains the more complete source of legislative activity and debate.

The *Congressional Record* is not, however, a word-for-word account of all that is spoken on the floors of the two chambers. Rather, the *Record* is required to be only a "substantially verbatim" rendition of chamber action. The expectation of a more verbatim account grew simultaneously with technological innovations such as audio amplification and phonetic shorthand, which made more accurate reporting possible. Omissions and errors in the reporting of debates were commonplace in earlier years due to the poor acoustics within the chambers and a necessary reliance on longhand. As a result, members often took the opportunity to revise, expand upon, and edit words they spoke on the floor, a tradition that remains the practice today.

In addition to revising their remarks, many members also "extend" them by inserting supplementary material into the *Congressional Record.* This includes items such as newspaper or magazine articles, scholarly essays, constituents' letters, and research studies. The daily practice of revising and extending remarks means that the *Con-*

gressional Record is not a perfectly verbatim record of the floor proceedings of Congress.

Each daily edition of the *Congressional Record* is divided into four separately numbered sections. The "H" pages signify the House floor proceedings for that day; the "S" pages, the Senate's. The "E" pages denote the "Extensions of Remarks" section, which is used almost exclusively by House members to insert material not spoken on the floor. The "D" pages designate the "Daily Digest," which appears at the back of each issue and serves as a combined index and table of contents. It summarizes legislative action that occurred in each chamber by giving capsule descriptions of bills and amendments considered. It also lists committee meetings held, often including the names of the witnesses who testified. Future floor and committee schedules are also published when announced.

The *Congressional Record* presents other significant legislative information in addition to the daily renditions of congressional proceedings. Periodically, the editors of the *Congressional Record* include a "Résumé of Congressional Activity" that provides useful legislative statistics, such as the numbers of measures introduced, reported, and passed by each chamber, as well as the number of hours and days each chamber has been in session. Lists of registered lobbyists and the policy issues they contact legislators about are also periodically published in the *Congressional Record.* In addition, the text of all conference reports and floor amendments are printed in the *Record* when submitted. Sometimes the text of newly introduced legislation also is provided, but this is not a consistent practice. More often only the fact of introduction, along with the names of the sponsor and any cosponsors, and the committee of referral are noted. The *Congressional Record* does not contain any text of committee proceedings on legislation. Committee information is limited to announcements of scheduled hearings and markups and daily summaries of those committee meetings that were actually held.

After each two-year Congress ends, the Government Printing Office issues a hardbound edition of the *Congressional Record* for that Congress. This becomes the permanent edition maintained by depository libraries across the nation, and most discard the softcover daily edition when the permanent edition is published. There are discrepancies between the two editions, however. In the permanent edition, pages are numbered consecutively within each volume, and the separate "H," "S," "E," and "D" page indicators are removed. In addition, members routinely receive permission from their colleagues to correct, revise, and extend their remarks for the permanent edition, even after the original version of those remarks has already been published in the daily edition.

Highly skilled reporters, known as the "Official Reporters of Debate," most using stenographic machines, but some still using shorthand, take down each word spoken on the House and Senate floor for shifts of approximately ten to fifteen minutes each. A new reporter takes over while the first transcribes the notations just taken. Computer technology is used to hasten the process and to begin the electronic printing of the *Congressional Record* while floor proceedings continue to unfold. The daily edition is kept open until midnight so that all the revisions and extensions from members can be received. Any floor proceedings held after midnight are published separately in the subsequent day's edition. The first printed copies of the *Congressional Record* are ready for distribution by about 6 A.M. the following morning.

The House and Senate differ somewhat in their editorial practices for their respective sections of the *Congressional Record.* For example, the House provides time blocs, while the Senate does not. The House editors insert square indicators approximately every ten to twenty minutes using the military time style (e.g., "1400 hours" for 2 P.M.). Members find this indicator useful for identifying the point at which they might wish to obtain videotape of that portion of the day's session. Researchers have used the indicators to estimate the time spent on specific legislative actions on the floor. The Senate, however, provided time blocs only in the late 1980s and then dropped them. The start-and-stop nature of Senate sessions (due largely to quorum calls and other delays) contributed to this decision.

In recent years, the average length of the Congressional Record *has been about 218 pages per issue.*

In another difference between the two chambers, text inserted but not spoken is designated in the House proceedings with a unique type face that visually separates such inserted material from the spoken word. On the Senate side, black dots, referred to as bullets, are used at the beginning and at the end of inserted material. However, the Senate practice is more casual than that of the House. Senators routinely obtain unanimous consent to have their remarks appear "as if spoken." Although this material is never fully delivered on the floor, no bullets appear when such permission has been granted.

Congress controls the reporting and editing of the content of the *Congressional Record;* the Government Printing Office is responsible for printing and distribution. This division of responsibility goes back to 1873. The House and Senate first began to take direct responsibility for the recording of their debates in 1855 by hiring the reporters of debates as congressional employees. Then in 1872 Congress decided to publish the debates as well as supervise their reporting, first assigning the work to the Congressional Printer and in the following year, to the Government Printing Office.

From 1789 to 1848, the floor proceedings of Congress were recorded by private entrepreneurs, mostly journalists. In addition to leading newspapers, which sometimes carried accounts of congressional floor proceedings, several commercial publications dedicated to floor coverage appeared, although none lasted for any length of time. Among them were *Lloyd's Congressional Register, Carpenter's American Senator, Callender's Political Register,* and *The Congressional Reporter.*

The first issue of the *Congressional Record* appeared on 4 March 1873. Its predecessors were the *Annals of Congress* (1789–1824), the *Register of Debates* (1824–1837), and the *Congressional Globe* (1833–1873). However, many of these earlier volumes had been compiled well after the fact, relying on news accounts, private journals, and the recollections of members of Congress and their employees. Over the course of the history of Congress, the recording of congressional proceedings has progressed from mere notations of floor actions to reconstructed abstracts, to admittedly flawed transcripts, to substantially verbatim accounts.

The *Congressional Record* is still published by the Government Printing Office under the supervision of the Joint Committee on Printing. The "Laws and Rules for Publication of the Congressional Record" appear on an unnumbered page near the back of every daily edition. These guidelines combine the mandates of the Joint Committee on Printing with the applicable provisions of public law (82 Stat. 1255–1256.)

In recent years, the average length of the *Congressional Record* has been about 218 pages per issue; the average printing cost has been about $485 per page. Printing costs are influenced not only by the length of daily floor sessions, but also by fluctuating prices of newsprint, technical equipment, and personnel. Approximately twenty thousand issues are distributed to the offices of members of Congress, congressional committees, and private subscribers per year. The subscription cost in 1994 was $225 annually, although members of Congress receive three free subscriptions for their office use and twenty-five free subscriptions for designated constituents, most of whom are depository libraries.

[See also (I) Records of Debate.]

BIBLIOGRAPHY

Amer, Mildred. The *Congressional Record. Content, History, and Issues.* Congressional Research Service, Library of Congress. CRS Rept. 93-60. 1993.

Block, Bernard A. The *Congressional Record.* Serials Review, January–March 1980, pp. 23–28.

McPherson, Elizabeth Gregory. "Reporting the Debates of Congress." *Quarterly Journal of Speech* 28 (April 1942): 141–148. (Reprinted in the *Congressional Record,* 10 June 1942, pp. A2182–2185.)

– ILONA B. NICKELS

CONSTITUENCY OUTREACH

Constituency outreach (or, to be more precise, attention to one's constituency) refers to the ways in which legislators serve and at the same time cultivate their constituencies, often with the objective of impressing voters back home and quelling their fears about the latitude that their legislators exercise away from the watchful eyes of constituents. Attention to one's constituents has always been a recognized activity of legislators, but it wasn't until Richard Fenno's classic *Home Style* (1978), a study of the behavior of members of Congress in their constituencies, that scholars began to appreciate the significance of constituency attention. For one thing, few realized the extent to which members were preoccupied with constituent matters; an even smaller number of scholars could boast of anything but a peripheral understanding of what legislators hoped to accomplish through their constituency activities. This is not to say that legislative scholars dismissed the constituency behavior of representatives and senators as unimportant; rather, the emphasis on the behavior of legislators while in Washington led researchers to focus on the study of congressional policy-making and institutions, to the exclusion of research on the activities of legislators that are directly related to constituents. What Fenno accomplished was to move critical questions about the constituency activities of representatives and senators to a more prominent position within legislative research. Fenno achieved this by introducing a rich conceptualization of the constituency behavior of legislators, the varieties of which he called "home styles," and suggesting how such activity was linked to their behavior while in Washington. There are three main expressions or categories of constituency outreach: casework, pork barreling, and constituent communication.

CASEWORK. In casework, legislators help constituents deal with the federal bureaucracy. It would be a rare day in a congressional office that passed without letters, visits, or calls from constituents requesting the assistance of their legislator. The range of items on which constituents seek help is broad. Sometimes a government check is late in arriving, or some ambiguity in a federal regulation applicable to local businesses stimulates constituents to appeal to their representative or senator for help. In general, legislator-constituent contact occurs as incumbents seek to resolve or redress constituent grievances. When these problems involve the operations of the federal bureaucracy, the incumbent performs the role of legislative ombudsman. At other times, constituents contact their legislator to receive information or to express opinions.

Members actually spend little time themselves on casework problems; rather, their staffs bear the brunt of the daily casework. The legislator's personal involvement in casework normally is triggered only when staff are unsuccessful in resolving the problem or when the incumbent has a special interest in the case (e.g., a district dam or water project). Nevertheless, incumbents respond to constituent inquiries as if they were personally involved in resolving them. For instance, newsletters to constituents often point to the personal intercession of the senator or representative in resolving relatively minor constituent problems; responses to constituent inquiries carry the member's name in a smearable ink (to impress the truly skeptical), although probably few incumbents read or sign them. In this way, senators and representatives cultivate the image that they are personally involved in serving their constituents.

The key word here is "personally." Incumbents' personal involvement in such service is often exaggerated. Yet even if their personal involvement in casework is less than they would like their constituents to believe, members of Congress do allocate a large proportion of their staffs' time—only the legislator's own time is a more valuable resource—to constituent affairs. In addition to several staffers designated specifically as caseworkers, most legislative assistants, press aides, personal secretaries, and others without explicit constituent responsibilities also engage in casework from time to time.

The volume of casework processed in congressional offices is difficult to gauge, but one of the best estimates of the casework load is provided by John Johannes's survey of members and their staffs. Johannes asked about a number of issues regarding the processing of constituent requests; he then estimated that each week the average office in the Senate processed about 302 cases, and the average House office about 115 cases (Johannes, 1980, p. 519). Moreover, the casework load apparently was increasing, as 71 percent of the 193 staff surveyed by Johannes perceived an increase in the volume of casework reaching their offices, and more constituents were writing to their representatives and senators than in the past (Parker, 1986).

Pork-barreling is one way in which legislators look after the interests of the constituents.

Members of Congress and their staffs cite different reasons for the growth in casework: the legislators point to growth in government, while their staffs attribute it to the efforts of legislators to stimulate casework. There is an indisputable logic to the members' argument: legislators have always engaged in casework, but the expansion of government programs resulting from Great Society legislation passed in the 1960s created more laws, regulations, bureaucracies, paperwork, and problems with government. Members found themselves besieged by constituents who were now more dependent than ever upon government action.

Despite the logic of the argument, incumbents must bear a significant proportion of the responsibility for the rise in casework, since senators and representatives clearly have exploited the resources of their offices to increase casework. Staffs and offices in the home district or state have expanded their operations, and mobile offices—vans equipped with office furniture—have become increasingly popular with legislators. Newsletters constantly remind constituents to bring their problems to their congressional representative; community forums and councils are encouraged to do the same. Johannes (1981) estimates that about half of members exploit at least two sources of contact with constituents to solicit casework.

PORK-BARRELING. The processes through which members of Congress divert federal funds to their districts and states are known collectively as "pork-barreling." What better way to demonstrate concern for the district or state than to bring home the bacon! And the opportunities to do so have never been greater. There is a variety of "pork" to be found in the federal budget: grants to local governments and universities, federal aid for specific constituent groups (e.g., subsidies for certain agricultural products), federal buildings and installations (e.g., military bases), and federal dollars in the form of contracts to local business for government work are just a few of the standard items available at the pork barrel.

Pork-barreling is one way in which legislators look after the interests of their constituents, ensuring that their districts and states receive their "fair share" of the federal pork barrel. Within their committees, in their interactions with agency officials, and on the floor of Congress, representatives and senators seek to further the interests of their constituents in a material fashion; federal projects, contracts, grants, installations, and federal office buildings bring money and jobs to the district or state—two benefits that most constituents appreciate. The value of a district or state project to constituents—rather than its efficiency, necessity, or worth to society—is the major consideration prompting legislators to raid the federal budget. Some may accuse members of expending too much effort procuring such benefits, but many members believe that such activity is what their constituents want and expect. And, indeed, constituents do expect their legislators to be on the watch for opportunities to further constituency interests. As a consequence, incumbents create and seize opportunities to benefit their constituencies. Their efforts often meet with remarkable success.

Another way in which legislators materially benefit their constituents is through their intercessions with federal agencies. For example, in the past members have used both legislative and extralegislative methods to assure that military bases or federal offices in their districts and states remain open. Notwithstanding the force of legislative imperatives, incumbents often need not resort to this drastic approach to assure that their constituents benefit from administrative decisions; phone calls, personal visits, political exchanges, and the exploitation of contacts within an agency may be equally successful. The main reason for the effectiveness of legislators in bureaucratic intercessions is that they are the ones who can provide what bureaucrats value most: higher budgets and program expansion. Agencies cannot even survive, much less thrive, without congressional support, since Congress controls the purse strings, authorizes new programs, and reauthorizes existing programs.

CONSTITUENT COMMUNICATION. The two forms of constituent communication are personal contact with constituents and legislator (mass) mailings. How members of Congress allocate time between Washington and the district or state reveals a lot about their priorities, since time is the scarcest and most valuable resource at a legislator's command. If there is one perennial complaint among legislators, the lack of time is surely it. Incumbents jealously guard their own time, often erecting barriers of staff to protect them from claims on it; activities that squander a member's time are avoided—unless they involve constituents. Protecting their own time has become such a preoccupation of members that concerted efforts have been taken to reduce work loads. For instance, congressional leaders have frequently justified increases in legislative staff as a means of coping with demands made on the time of legislators. But while staff perform many constituency-related functions, their efforts only supplement those of their bosses. The personal time of the incumbent is often one resource without substitutes; for many constituents there is no adequate replacement for the personal attention of the member, and some things can only be done personally by the incumbent, like meeting with influential constituents or addressing large gatherings at home.

The personal time of the representative or senator is also a resource that is less divisible than the time of staff. Staff can be distributed between the Washington and home offices without disrupting either the lawmaking or constituency service responsibilities of congressional offices. Not so with the time of members. The allocation of time to constituent affairs poses a dilemma for most members of Congress, since the time spent in the constituency (or with constituents at any location) could also be spent in legislative activities that might enhance the realization of members' more personal goals. Thus there is a potential "zero-sum" relationship between the desire to attend to legislative business and the need to spend time on district and state matters. Most representatives and senators would rather devote their time to legislative business, and many see constituency matters as actually interfering with the performance of legislative responsibilities. Yet members willingly allocate large proportions of their personal time to constituent affairs.

John Saloma estimated that more than one-quarter (28 percent) of a representative's average workweek in Washington is devoted to constituency affairs and that a similar amount (25 percent) of the legislator's staff time is also spent on constituency matters (1969, pp. 184–185). More recent data suggest an even higher percentage of time may be devoted to constituency affairs, since a large proportion of a member's time in Washington and in the district or state is devoted to constituency matters. In Washington, about one-third of the average day of senators is spent dealing with constituent mail or talking with constituents and groups (U.S. Senate, 1976, p. 28), and representatives devote a similar proportion of time to district affairs while in their Washington offices (U.S. House of Representatives, 1977, pp. 18–19). In the district or state, almost all of a legislator's time is occupied with presentations to constituents, and incumbents spend considerable time there; in 1980, representatives spent about one of every three days in their districts, while senators spent one of every four days in their states (Parker, 1986).

In addition to personal contact, legislators express their attention to constituent problems and district or state interests through mass mailings sent to voters. Despite restrictions, a wide range of material qualifies for use of the congressional frank (free postage for mass mailings), such as newsletters, questionnaires, biographical material, federal laws and regulations, and nonpartisan election information (e.g., voter registration dates and places). These types of printed matter are exploited both to serve constituents and to promote the image that the incumbent is attentive to district or state interests. These two functions are almost impossible to separate.

MESSAGES TO CONSTITUENTS: CONTENT AND INTENT. The attentiveness that legislators shower upon their constituents conveys several messages that influence how members of Congress are perceived by voters. These messages are conveyed through the behavior and statements of legislators while in their constituencies and they can be both explicit and implicit. For example, a legislator may demonstrate concern for constituents by "bringing home" district projects, or by issuing statements designed to elicit voter trust; both actions convey the same message. In most instances, legislators rely upon both statements and actions, thereby serving to reinforce the messages they consider critical to their longevity in office. These messages present an image of a concerned representative, explain actions in Congress, and generally serve as self-promotion for the member. Legislators spend considerable time and effort in promulgating these messages, and their efforts seem to pay off, since voters tend to perceive legislators in terms of the images they project.

Presentations. Incumbents believe that support at home is won by the kind of individual self they portray, and they are not the least reluctant to manipulate their presentations of themselves. "So members of Congress go home," according to Fenno "to present themselves as a person and to win the accolade: 'he's a good man,' 'she's a good woman!' " (1975, p. 55). Fenno lists three personal characteristics that legislators emphasize: qualification, identification, and empathy. Every legislator creates the impression that he or she is qualified to hold office, that he or she can identify with the attitudes and beliefs of constituents, and that he or she can empathize with the problems of constituents. These personal characteristics are transmitted at each and every opportunity that a legislator has to communicate with constituents: newsletters, constituent mailings, meetings in the constituency, personal visits. The more personal and pervasive the contact, the greater the probability that the message will be retained. Incumbents make considerable use of these presentations to convey the image that they care about constituents, their problems, and their frustrations.

Explanations. Members of Congress also justify their Washington activities to constituents; Fenno (1978) refers to this as "explanations of Washington activities." Explanations are the mechanisms through which incumbents describe, interpret, and legitimize legislative pursuits, especially the two major preoccupations of senators and representatives: power and policy. The pursuit of power, for example, can be justified by claiming that influence is used to further district or state interests within Congress.

Even though they probably have little to fear from electoral reprisals for one or two unpopular votes, incumbent legislators make a point of explaining their votes and policy positions to their constituents when they are called upon to do so. Since most constituents are unaware of the specific votes and perceive their representative as voting in line with constituent sentiment (Parker, 1989), explaining roll-call votes generally creates few problems for incumbents. A string of "wrong" votes could pose problems, but most members avoid creating such patterns in their votes by developing a good sense of the policy stands that are likely to produce adverse constituent reaction. In fact, since there is always some uncertainty as to what votes a member may be called upon to explain, legislators tend to "stockpile" more explanations than they actually need.

The fact that members frequently make themselves available to voters reinforces constituent trust.

It is impossible for constituents to keep tabs on their legislators, especially when they are in Washington; hence, voters are largely uninformed about the behavior of their representatives and senators. But while the actions of incumbents may be invisible to their constituents, the incumbents themselves are not. Constituents normally find their legislators willing and prepared to explain their Washington activities, and their frequent appearances within their constituencies provide ample opportunities to question them about these activities. The fact that members frequently make themselves available to voters reinforces constituent trust, thereby assuring incumbents some measure of latitude in their Washington activities.

Self-promotion. John Saloma (1969) analyzed printed matter sent to constituents by representatives and senators (newsletters, news releases, form letters, and policy statements) during the first session of the 89th Congress. Saloma found that more than one-half of the representatives (55 percent) and senators (63 percent) used their written communications to enhance their own personal image and to advance their private interests (reelection). Three activities associated with such self-promotion have been identified: advertising, credit claiming, and position taking (Mayhew, 1974). Advertising activities are designed to disseminate a legislator's name widely among constituents and to associate it with a positive image. Credit-claiming activities involve the efforts of incumbents to create the belief that constituency benefits are solely attributable to their unique efforts. The notion of constituency benefits generally conjures images of the legislative pork barrel, but, in fact, a large proportion of the benefits that members funnel to their constituents do not even involve legislative action; rather, casework forms the bulk of the particularized benefits distributed to voters. Finally, position taking characterizes the efforts of incumbents to take policy stands that are pleasing to their constituents. There is no better way for a legislator to endear himself to his constituents than by publicly voicing policy positions that are strongly supported in the district or state.

These home activities are not entirely self-serving, since they meet legitimate representational responsibilities. Constituents expect to be kept informed about issues that are relevant to their concerns, and incumbents oblige them by providing such information while also taking the opportunity to further their own interests through these communications. Diana Yiannakis's study (1982) of the newsletters and press releases produced by a sample of members during the first six months of both the 94th and 95th Congresses demonstrates exactly how adept incumbents are at fulfilling these dual objectives. Yiannakis found that 42 percent of the paragraphs in these newsletters and press releases were devoted to explaining the incumbents' stands on national issues, and less than 10 percent were devoted to national or local information of a more general sort—an amount of space smaller than that allocated to claiming credit for particularized district benefits (11.6 percent).

Constituent perceptions. Since representatives and senators work exceedingly hard to promote the image that they care about their districts and states, it should not be too surprising to find that constituents see them in exactly these terms. Table 1 presents data describing the content of what voters liked or disliked about their representatives and senators in 1988 and 1990. It is clear from this table that constituency outreach was mentioned frequently by voters in evaluating their representative but considerably less often in voter evaluations of senators. This was the major difference in constituent

TABLE 1

VOTER PERCEPTIONS OF HOUSE AND SENATE INCUMBENTS, 1988 AND 1990[1]

Content of Likes/Dislikes	1988 Representatives				1990 Representatives				1988 Senators				1990 Senators			
	Likes		Dislikes		Likes		Dislikes		Likes		Dislikes		Likes		Dislikes	
	No.	%	No.	%	No.	%	No.	%	No.	%	No.	%	No.	%	No.	%
Leadership	10	1	9	5	25	2	8	2	42	3	21	4	79	2	47	4
Experience	78	11	7	4	176	14	10	3	226	14	19	3	623	19	20	2
Constituency Attention	192	28	19	11	343	27	43	11	260	17	50	9	585	18	128	12
Trust	71	10	20	12	126	10	76	19	242	15	71	12	420	13	155	14
Personal Characteristics	68	10	11	6	144	11	25	6	174	11	26	5	280	9	51	5
Party	25	4	26	15	67	5	57	14	46	3	91	16	145	4	168	15
Ideology	64	9	24	14	70	6	41	10	171	11	99	17	233	7	149	13
Domestic Issues	66	10	19	11	164	13	63	16	181	12	97	17	449	14	199	16
Foreign Policy Issues	10	1	5	3	11	1	12	3	33	2	24	4	67	2	46	4
Group Support	59	9	14	8	92	7	19	5	103	7	34	6	175	5	57	5
Miscellaneous	49	7	17	10	54	4	42	11	87	6	43	7	183	6	92	8

[1] Voters were asked: Was there anything in particular you liked or disliked about the incumbent candidate? Poll group sizes varied. The candidates were running in elections involving both House and Senate incumbents.

Source: National Election Studies, 1988–1990 (University of Michigan)

perceptions of representatives and senators. This should not be construed, however, to suggest that the constituency service provided by senators cannot rival the level or quality of district service; few constituents had anything negative to say about the constituency behavior of senators. We should not ignore the fact that while constituency attention was mentioned less frequently in evaluations of senators than representatives, it remained a central ingredient in the images of both. The other important conclusion that can be derived from this table is that constituents rarely saw their legislators in terms of political issues. This is even more surprising because of the degree to which senators talk about public policies. No matter how much senators talk about political issues, however, voters were no more likely to mention issues in their evaluations of senators than they did in evaluating their representative. In both cases, the images carried only a wisp of issue content.

Why are the popular images of senators less colored by constituency outreach? The differing responsibilities and representational arrangements of representatives and senators, such as length of term, may make constituency attention less central to voter perceptions of senators. Or, perhaps, senators have more to "lose" by spending time with constituents than do representatives, in the sense that they possess and exercise greater power than the average representative; the lawmaking activities that must be given up are more valuable to senators than to representatives. Since constituency outreach requires more of a sacrifice on the part of senators, they might be expected to devote less time to it. In any event, senators do spend less time with constituents than do representatives, and it shows in their images among voters.

One reason why constituency service may be important to constituents is that they do not perceive representatives and senators, in general, as devoting a great deal of time to district or state affairs. It seems clear, therefore, that legislators can create a sacred place for themselves in the minds of their constituents by being attentive to constituency matters. It is a good way to distinguish oneself from others in Congress who are perceived to spend more of their time on legislative business than on constituency affairs. This may explain why over one-third of the reasons given by respondents in a national survey (U.S. House, 1977, p. 820) for believing their representative to be better than most other incumbents made mention of some aspect of his or her service to the district (communicates with constituents, cares about constituents, tries to solve constituent problems, obtains federal funds for the district). It is easy to understand why attentive legislators are so popular with their constituents: they are spending time on activities that are important to constituents but are perceived as generally getting too little attention.

IMPACT OF OUTREACH. One of the basic motivations of legislators is the desire to be reelected; no other goal (e.g., attaining a position of congressional leadership) can be entertained without first assuring reelection. Given the amount of time that legislators devote to constituency outreach activity, we might expect such actions to yield clearly identifiable reelection benefits. Indeed, many of the outreach activities that legislators engage in are designed to help them get reelected; the empirical evidence, however, remains inconclusive. Regardless of the electoral effects of constituency attention, there is less uncertainty about the effects of outreach efforts in promoting the efficiency and effectiveness of congressional oversight of federal programs: constituent contact provides legislators with valuable feedback about the operation of bureaucratic agencies and the programs they implement.

Electoral effects. Many of the services that members provide to constituents, such as mass mailings, fulfill representational obligations. A newsletter is one means through which constituents can learn about the activities of their representative or senator and about the impact of national policies on the district or state. On the other hand, fulfilling such a representational obligation may simultaneously satisfy electoral needs; the same newsletter that keeps constituents informed about government can be packaged to convey images that have electoral appeal. For instance, claiming credit for a federal project or advertising one's record of constituency service can be easily integrated with less political information. Government-subsidized travel to the state or district helps incumbents maintain contact with their constituents, but meetings with constituents also provide legislators with a ubiquitous channel for disseminating the types of messages that elicit voter support. The similarity of the member's messages between and during congressional campaigns testifies to the dual objectives that these incumbent resources serve—it is precisely the intertwining of electoral and representational purposes in their use that makes it difficult to regulate usage effectively without impairing representational responsibilities. The constituent contact that results from the utilization of most of these resources provides opportunities for incumbents to engage in electioneering. Incumbents use these contacts to enhance their visibility among constituents, to project electorally rewarding homestyle images, and to mobilize supporters for an approaching election.

Senators face more obstacles than representatives in exploiting their contacts with their constituents for electoral advantage. One obstacle is that senators exercise less control over the dissemination of information about themselves than do representatives; for example, the higher levels of "free" (e.g., media supplied) information in Senate elections make challengers far more visible to voters than in House elections. This is not to say that senators gain less from the exploitation of office resources; rather, the nature of the office—the greater prestige, power, competitiveness, and campaign costs—makes senators more vulnerable to forces beyond their control.

Newsletters, trips to the state or district, and the use of other office resources do more than increase constituent contact and, therefore, voter support. These resources also discourage competitive challenges by influencing perceptions of vulnerability. If an incumbent can convince potential opponents, and those who would financially support their candidacies, that he or she is unbeatable, few formidable challenges will be made by the opposition party. It is difficult to recruit a candidate to run against a popular incumbent; often the activity degenerates into recruiting "losers" rather than highly qualified candidates. Thus, by maintaining extensive contact with voters, incumbents are able to weaken the opposition they face in primaries or at the next election.

The empirical link between constituency attention and electoral safety has stirred considerable research and controversy. Some constituency activities appear to influence elections, while others seem to have little or no effect; in still other instances, constituency activities and their impact on electoral safety remain an issue for debate. For example, the effects of mass mailings on electoral margins seem weak, if at all apparent. John Ferejohn (1977) found no evidence that an increase in mass mailings increased the visibility of incumbents, thereby giving them an electoral edge; an ingenious quasi-experimental study of the distribution of baby books to new parents by one representative found an immediate, but not a lasting, effect on the incumbent's electoral support (Cover and Brumberg, 1982). There is also no evidence that pork-barreling increases electoral safety; Paul Feldman and James Jondrow (1984) report that bringing government employment and money to the district appears to have no pronounced effect in increasing an incumbent's vote support.

Personal visits to the district and state, however, appear to increase electoral safety; representatives and senators who secured their previous reelection with a small margin of victory in states electorally dominated by the opposition party increased their election margins as they increased the time they spent in their constituencies (Parker, 1986). The results are less definitive with respect to casework. Morris Fiorina (1977) contends that legislators seize upon bureaucratic errors of omission and commission to curry favor with voters; resolving constituent grievances in a manner favorable to one's constituents impresses voters and solidifies electoral support within the district or state. Diana Yiannakis's study (1982) supports Fiorina's hypothesis; she found that levels of voter satisfaction with an incumbent's service to constituents was related to voter choice, especially among partisans of the challenger's party. John Johannes and John McAdams (1981), in contrast, contend that casework fails to affect an incumbent's reelection because constituents fully expect their legislators to render such service. Perhaps the issue is not whether constituency outreach affects electoral support, but what facets of such attention are most effective in doing so.

The same newsletter that keeps constituents informed about government can be packaged to convey images that have electoral appeal.

Oversight. Representatives and senators devote time and resources (staff) to addressing constituent problems, and they are quite effective in these efforts. Legislators intervene between constituents and bureaucrats in a whole range of matters—disagreements over a regulation, delays in federal grants (e.g., welfare), absence of administrative action, and others. In some instances, the incumbent may actually serve as a lobbyist for special interests within the constituency vis-à-vis his or her committees and the federal bureaucracy. These "errand boy" activities, as they are unflatteringly called, are viewed by members and constituents as basic elements of the job.

One result of the emphasis on pursuing constituent complaints is that oversight of the executive branch is provided on a continuous and timely basis. Casework sometimes even leads directly to formal oversight hearings or to the introduction of remedial legislation. Constituent reaction to agency programs and regulations may be the quickest way to alert agency officials and committee leaders to problems involved in the administration of a policy or program. It provides the type of scrutiny that neither Congress nor its administration watchdog, the General Accounting Office, can supply. Since legislative goals are stated so vaguely in legislation, it is difficult to determine whether any violation has occurred unless some citizen or group registers a complaint; the large number of constituents affected by a program ensures that any violation that seriously harms an organized group will be identified. Such a system of decentralized "alarms" may serve as an efficient check on the great authority that Congress has delegated to executive agencies:

> Although Congress may, to some extent, have allowed the bureaucracy to make law, it may also have devised a reasonably effective and non-costly way to articulate and promulgate its own legislative goals—a way that depends on the fire-alarm oversight system. It is convenient for Congress to adopt broad legislative mandates and give substantial rule-making authority to the bureaucracy. The problem with doing so, of course, is that the bureaucracy might not pursue Congress's goals. But citizens and interest groups can be counted on to sound an alarm in most cases in which the bureaucracy has arguably violated Congress's goal. Then Congress can intervene to rectify the violation. (McCubbins and Schwartz, 1984, pp. 174–175).

Constituency outreach involves the ways in which incumbent legislators serve and at the same time cultivate their constituencies with the aim of improving their standing among constituents and reducing voter fears about the latitude their representatives and senators exercise in Washington. There are three categories of constituency attention: casework (helping constituents dealing with the federal bureaucracy); pork-barreling (bringing federal funds to the district or state); and constituent communication (personal and impersonal contacts with constituents). These "services" to constituents are designed to convey images that win voter approval, justify Washington behavior such as legislative votes, and promote one's standing within the constituency by advertising on-the-job accomplishments, claiming credit for constituency benefits (e.g., federal contracts), and taking policy positions that voters strongly favor. These activities and the messages they contain leave an indelible mark on voter evaluations and perceptions of their legislators—and the imprint is likely to create positive images of incumbent legislators. Constituency attention can be linked to the electoral safety of incumbents, though the relationship appears to vary by constituency activity (e.g., personal visits, mass mailings, casework, pork-barreling) and the effectiveness of legislative oversight of the federal bureaucracy.

[See also (I) Broadcasting of Congressional Proceedings, Constituency Service, Pork Barrel.]

BIBLIOGRAPHY

Cain, Bruce, John Ferejohn, and Morris Fiorina. *The Personal Vote.* 1987.

Cover, Albert, and Bruce Brumberg. "Baby Books and Ballots: The Impact of Congressional Mail on Constituent Opinion." *American Political Science Review* 76 (June 1982): 347–359.

Dodd, Lawrence C. "Congress and the Quest for Power." In *Studies of Congress.* Edited by Glenn R. Parker. 1985. Pp. 489–520.

Feldman, Paul, and James Jondrow. "Congressional Elections and Local Federal Spending." *American Journal of Political Science* 28 (May 1984): 147–163.

Fenno, Richard F. *Home Style.* 1978.

Ferejohn, John. "On the Decline of Competition in Congressional Elections." *American Political Science Review* 71 (March 1977): 166–176.

Fiorina, Morris P. *Congress. Keystone of the Washington Establishment.* 1977.

Johannes, John R. "Casework in the House." In *The House at Work.* Edited by Joseph Cooper and G. Calvin MacKenzie. 1981. Pp. 78–96.

Johannes, John R., and John C. McAdams. "The Congressional Incumbency Effect: Is It Casework, Policy Compatibility, or Something Else?" *American Journal of Political Science* 25 (August 1981): 512–542.

Kingdon, John. *Congressmen's Voting Decisions.* 1973.

Mayhew, David R. *Congress: The Electoral Connection.* 1974.

McCubbins, Matthew, and Thomas Schwartz. "Congressional Oversight Overlooked: Police Patrols Versus Fire Alarms." *American Journal of Political Science* 28 (February 1984): 165–179.

Parker, Glenn R. *Characteristics of Congress.* 1989.

Parker, Glenn R. *Homeward Bound.* 1986.

Saloma, John S., III. *Congress and the New Politics.* 1969.

U.S. House of Representatives. *Final Report of the Commission on Administrative Review.* 95th Cong., 1st sess., 1977. H. Doc. 95-276.

U.S. Senate. Commission on the Operation of the Senate. *Toward A More Modern Senate.* 94th Cong., 2d sess., 1976. S. Doc. 94-278.

Yiannakis, Diana E. "House Members Communication Styles: Newsletters and Press Releases." *Journal of Politics* 44 (November 1982): 1049–1071.

– GLENN R. PARKER

CONSTITUENCY SERVICE

From the first meeting of the First Congress, senators and representatives have been attending to the needs, requests, and demands of their constituents for help in dealing with governmental problems. Over time, such constituency service has become a regular feature of the congressional landscape. Demands have grown; the process for handling constituent requests has become institutionalized; and controversies have arisen over the utility and consequences of the practice.

THE NATURE OF CONSTITUENCY SERVICE. The range of constituency service is immense. Legislators routinely secure White House tour tickets for visitors, mail out pamphlets and government documents on a host of topics, answer constituents' questions about government policies or regulations, expedite the purchase of flags that have flown over the Capitol, help job seekers, and select young men and women for the

Raising and Lowering Flags. Constituents often request a flag that has flown at the U.S. Capitol. (Office of the Architect of the Capitol)

armed service academies. More importantly, they engage in individual casework and federal projects assistance.

Individual ("low-level") casework involves intervening on behalf of citizens or, occasionally, resident aliens who feel aggrieved by or need assistance in dealing with federal (and sometimes state or local) agencies. Usually such people come to Congress after having failed to get what they want from the appropriate executive source, although a noticeable proportion go directly to Congress before exhausting administrative remedies. They may want to know what is holding up their applications or claims, for example, or be demanding explanations for denials, asking for help in expediting requests, or complaining about poor treatment at the hands of bureaucrats. Although no federal agency or program is immune to citizens' dissatisfaction, the most common cases involve social security, health insurance, and pension claims; military and veterans' affairs; job-related matters; immigration and visa issues; housing; and taxes. At times the petitioner is a group of constituents seeking, perhaps, a transfer of federal property or aid for a community project.

Federal projects assistance, sometimes called high-level casework, involves helping states and localities to win grants from federal departments and agencies. Because most federal funding for state and local governments is determined by statutory formulas, the amount of discretionary funding controlled by the executive branch is limited; thus congressional intervention becomes important to state and local governments that want to tap the federal "pork barrel." These projects rarely constitute more than 7 or 8 percent of the requests coming into congressional offices, but because of their importance and complexity, they may take up to a quarter or more of the time a legislative office devotes to constituency service.

Although throughout the nineteenth century senators and representatives complained of the excessive burden that petitioning citizens laid upon them, the volume of casework increased greatly after the New Deal establishment of new agencies and programs in the 1930s and then again after the explosion of Great Society programs in the 1960s. Both the New Deal and Great Society dramatically increased government benefits and regulations. National public-opinion surveys begun in 1978 have revealed that about 15 percent of Americans claim that they or their families have contacted their senators or representatives and that about two-fifths to one-half that number did so to request help. The others wrote or called to express opinions or seek information.

Precise numbers of case requests coming to Congress are hard to pin down, because until the onset of the computer age accurate records were seldom kept and because cases pour into both Washington and home-state or district congressional offices. The most accurate counts available come from surveys taken in 1977–1978 and 1982 by John R. Johannes and John C. McAdams. In the 95th Congress, the mean number of new requests received by 136 House offices was 108 per week (with a median of 100), about 90 percent of which were individual cases; in 53 Senate offices studied, the average was 302, but the median was only 175. By the 97th Congress, 204 House offices reported an average of 103 cases (again, 90 percent of which were "low-level" casework items), but the median fell to 70. The 28 Senate offices surveyed averaged 175 cases.

Explanations of who asks for casework help and why fall into two categories. One focuses on the demand side, picturing the legislator as an agent of the state or district, with the demand for casework services primarily determined by objective constituency needs, expectations, and abilities. The other, "supply-side," view sees senators and representatives as active entrepreneurs, urging their constituents to seek their services. Both explanations have some validity. Research (mostly on the House) indicates that senior representatives from constituencies with generally lower levels of education (and, presumably, higher need) are more likely to receive large numbers of casework requests. Members representing districts with concentrations of very highly educated citizens and large numbers of government employees—in other words, constituents, who are very capable of making demands—also attract heavy case loads. Finally, constituencies in regions of the country that share what Daniel Elazar terms a "traditionalistic" political culture (paternalistic, antibureaucratic, focusing on "friends and neighbors" politics) tend to make greater demands; conversely, those in "moralistic" (issue-oriented, "clean government") regions are distinctly less likely to do so.

The supply-side explanation also stands up to analysis. One of the clearest predictors of heavy caseloads is member seniority. Constituents also seem more inclined to seek help from representatives with whom they have come into contact. Thus, for example, in late 1981 and 1982, members who made the most trips back home were more likely to have heavy caseloads than those making fewer trips to their districts, all other factors being equal.

The range of constituency service is immense.

Contact need not always be in person, of course, and legislators have accordingly devised all sorts of tactics to advertise their services: newsletters; general or targeted mailings; personal appearances that include reminders of their willingness to help constituents; mobile offices; special seminars with local government officials or major constituency groups; staff members generously sprinkled in local offices; radio, television, and newspaper advertisements; and even matchbook covers and billboards—all are part of the casework "hustling" enterprise. By 1982, only 3 percent of the offices surveyed claimed to do nothing to solicit cases and projects; more than half the representatives employed four or more distinct devices (Johannes and McAdams, 1987). Younger representatives developed and deployed many of these aggressive tactics in the 1970s, but no matter when or by whom they were introduced, they have become standard fare in the House and, to a lesser degree, in the Senate. There is little doubt that they are at least somewhat effective.

A legislator's reputation for successful casework service is likely to bring in additional cases. Word-of-mouth advertising is considered by congressional staff assistants to be one of the best techniques for generating more case requests. (Scholarly research has only begun to test this claim.)

Decades of increased constituency service have created a strong set of casework expectations on the part of constituents and legislators alike, and local governments positively bank on cooperation from, and often leadership by, their Washington representatives in the search for federal dollars. Surveys conducted biennially by the University of Michigan's Center for Political Studies as well as those commissioned in 1977 by the House Commission on Administrative Review (the Obey commission) have revealed the extent to which the public believes that constituency service is important. For example, 37 percent of respondents in the Obey commission's poll responded to an open-ended question about what things were most important for representatives to do by pointing to district service; 70 percent agreed that it was "very important" for Congress to provide people with a direct link to the federal government. Ninety percent thought it very or fairly important for their representatives to help people in their districts who have problems with the government, and 94 percent said the same about getting a fair share of money for the district. A quarter to a third of respondents to the Center for Political Studies poll have told interviewers that if they have a problem with the government, they expect their representatives to be very helpful in resolving it; only about one in ten anticipate little or no help. Members of Congress understand what all this means: when the Obey commission asked members what sorts of duties they thought they were expected to perform, four-fifths mentioned the constituent service role.

Members themselves see casework and projects as important, though not so important as legislative and policy-related duties. Their reasons include the obvious implications constituency service has for reelection and the attendant freedom to pursue policies that might otherwise find little support in their districts, but their reasoning goes further than this. Members of Congress are probably as compassionate as other Americans, and, as politicians, they are naturally sensitive to others; they genuinely care about their constituents and want to help them when they can. There are simply too many electorally safe or retiring senators and representatives who work diligently on constituency service without any electoral incentive to believe otherwise. Moreover, some members believe that casework carries other payoffs: inspiring ideas for legislation, for example, or strengthening congressional oversight of the executive branch. Some members harbor a deep-seated disdain for bureaucrats; several believe that casework prevents public alienation and cynicism or has symbolic importance; and a few see casework as a link to the "real world" outside Washington. Finally, almost all perceive casework as part of a legislator's job. Studies of legislatures around the world show that such views are almost universal. In short, motives for and the importance of constituency service are complex; no single reason can adequately explain why case and projects work has become "big business" in Washington.

THE CASEWORK SYSTEM. Casework and federal projects assistance have become institutionalized in a routine and substantially bureaucratized system of exchanges. Constituents, in effect, are perceived to barter votes for congressional help with their problems, and executive agencies scurry to provide timely responses and, if possible, favorable decisions for congressional offices in return for legislative support for their programs.

All but a tiny portion of constituency service work is performed by the personal staffs of senators and representatives. Between the mid-1950s and 1980, these staffs roughly tripled in size, and staff positions became more specialized. Among those specializations is constituency service. Today a senator from a large state commonly has twenty or more aides doing little more than handling cases and projects, while a representative may assign half of his or her entire staff to such chores.

Led by the newest cohorts of legislators, especially those from urban areas and electorally marginal districts, members in the 1970s placed increasing portions of their staffs in offices located in their states and districts precisely to handle casework and, to a lesser extent, projects work. According to *Vital Statistics on Congress, 1991–1992,* the proportion of House staff in district offices jumped from about 23 percent in 1972 to more than 41 percent in 1990, while the increase in Senate staff in home-state offices went from 12 to 35 percent. Doing casework and projects work back home is a mixed blessing, since staff members must often contact executive agencies in Washington; conversely, Capitol Hill staffs frequently need to deal with local or regionally based executive officials. Over time, a variety of elaborate schemes for coordination have developed.

Casework staffs tend to be young, well educated, and female. Because constituency service is emotionally fatiguing and often perceived as the first step on the staff career ladder, there is considerable turnover. By and large, however, these women and men are dedicated to their work and share a great variety of casework-related motivations and attitudes, as do their employers.

Members of Congress see casework and projects as important, though not so important as legislative and policy-related duties.

The executive-branch casework bureaucracy is equally well developed. Almost all departments and agencies have congressional relations offices, whose primary functions include handling requests and inquiries from congressional staffs. Most of these offices are located in Washington; but congressional caseworkers frequently bypass them, going directly to agencies' regional and local offices around the country. Both sides perceive advantages in bringing cases to a successful resolution and maintaining good working relationships with their counterparts. However, rivalry and resentment do appear, especially when House and Senate staffs push harder for a particular resolution than agency people deem warranted or when a congressional staffer treats an agency official improperly.

In short, the casework process has become routinized at both ends, with clear expectations, standard operating procedures, and behavioral norms in place. So long as congressional staff are polite and sincere, and provided they don't push agencies to violate laws or administrative rules, executive officials will take care of their Capitol Hill counterparts by expediting the process of review. The interbranch politics of constituency service has its ups and downs, but most participants realize that they must get along with each other.

ISSUES IN CONSTITUENCY SERVICE. Four overriding and often controversial issues surround constituency service: Does it work? Is it fair? Does it help or hinder the primary congressional duty of policy making? Does it pay off in votes and thus contribute to keeping legislators in office?

Effectiveness. Congressional interventions on behalf of constituents usually (but far from always) are effective in moving their questions, requests, and complaints through the executive bureaucracy more quickly than would otherwise happen and in getting the agencies involved to take a more thorough look at the cases, often at higher bureaucratic levels. The rule in agency offices is to settle cases as soon as possible. Occasionally, however, a congressional inquiry can actually delay the processing of a request, since the time devoted to giving special attention to the matter and replying to Congress might exceed the normal processing period.

Congressional staff estimates place the proportion of cases in which the original executive decision is modified in the range of 30 to 50 percent. In almost all cases, such changes are simply the result of taking a second and closer look at a constituent's problem and seeing that an error had been made, that new information is available to alter the original decision, or that there is in fact enough leeway in the relevant law or regulation to be more accommodating than was originally believed. Many of these cases probably would have been decided in the same fashion without congressional intervention if the constituent had made the appeal directly to the agency involved. Considering that perhaps as many as one-fifth of all cases are utterly lacking in merit (and are usually instantly recognized as such by both congressional and executive participants), the overall success rate is rather high.

Not all casework staffs and not all congressional offices are equally successful. Clearly, some staff members are more experienced and skillful at getting along with their executive counterparts. Personal intervention by senators and representatives is relatively rare, occurring when cases are particularly delicate or important or, more often, when the staff faces strong resistance from executive officials. Sometimes such personal intervention by the member makes a difference; at other times it does not. Much depends on the case, the executive official handling it, and the legislator's skills and influence.

Fairness, equity, and ethics. On the whole, relatively few outright violations of the equity principle seem to occur. Legislators and their staffs seldom ask agency personnel to break a law or a regulation (though they do ask that regulations be stretched), and only rarely do executive actors comply with such requests. The primary reason is that professional casework teams in both Congress and the executive branch are sensitive to the fairness issue and share a sense of casework ethics; legislators and their staffs also fear that public revelations of improper pressure will backfire and prove politically embarrassing.

Such was the case in the Charles H. Keating, Jr., affair of the 1980s. Keating, chairman of Lincoln Savings and Loan Association, had made substantial campaign contributions and other political donations to five senators, as well as loans and gifts to their family members and staff assistants. These senators were discovered to have held meetings with Federal Home Loan Bank Board regulators on behalf of Lincoln Savings. In November 1991, after two years of investigations and hearings, the Senate Select Ethics Committee publicly and formally reprimanded Sen. Alan Cranston (D-Calif.) for his involvement in the scandal. Cranston and the four other senators involved defended their actions as merely helping a constituent in need.

Such spectacular cases are relatively rare. Still, several questions deserve attention. At a superficial level, casework can be unfair because congressional or executive staffs might act arbitrarily, because a constituent might get away with a lie, or because only citizens who ask for help are likely to get it. Even among those who are being helped, not all receive the same quality of attention. Many of those involved in casework operations report that a legislator's friends, relatives, major contributors, and other VIPs occasionally receive special treatment, although most contend that they seek to treat all similar cases—certainly all routine cases—alike, regardless of the petitioner. Partisanship plays no significant role. Agency officials also admit to providing faster and more careful service to important senators and representatives (such as those on key committees), but even here there is some disagreement.

The real question is whether congressional intervention affects the substance, rather than the speed or care, of an agency's response. The best available evidence suggests that the answer is yes, but only rarely, and that this applies more to federal projects than to individual citizens' requests. In short, to the extent that there is unfairness or inequity in casework, it is not systematic in ways that might be expected. Rather, lack of perfect equity can be attributed as much to personalities and the peculiar nature of a given case as to partisanship and politics.

The Keating scandal is not unique. Anytime a senator or representative intervenes in the administrative process on behalf of a constituent, there arises the possibility of some impropriety, whether bribery (usually in the form of campaign financing), illegal gratuities, conflicts of interest, or even extortion or conspiracy to defraud. The courts have had to handle a number of such cases, and the House and Senate ethics committees have issued rules, ethics codes, and principles bearing on the problem. In all instances, however, the burden of judgment rests on the office of the member who is assisting constituents. In the vast majority of cases, no problems emerge, but constituency service sometimes crosses into a gray area of congressional ethics.

Policy-making implications. One common view of constituency service is that it is a necessary evil, a burden to be endured so that senators and representatives can remain in office to attend to the important work of legislation and oversight. Arguments in support of this thesis focus on the time spent by legislators on constituency service, the dedication of staff resources to casework, and the disruption to the administrative process that occurs when agencies must review cases already decided and respond to congressional staffs. Although there is truth to all these charges, they are exaggerated.

Anytime a senator or representative intervenes in the administrative process on behalf of a constituent, there arises the possibility of some impropriety.

The fact is that senators and representatives spend relatively little time on cases and projects per se; they do, of course, spend endless hours with their constituencies explaining their positions, building political support, raising funds, and campaigning. Studies by the House Commission on Administrative Review (1977), Robert Klonoff (1979), and John R. Johannes (1984) have shown that the vast majority of members spend less, often far less, than 10 percent of their time pursuing case and project results for constituents. Their involvement typically comes when they meet constituents back in the state or district and pick up numerous requests for help or when they contact agencies directly because their staffs have come up against resistance. Legislators from highly educated districts, where voters are more concerned with policy issues, and those in leadership positions are less involved than others.

An estimated 40 percent or more of the average member's staff time and resources is dedicated to constituency service, and home-based staff devote virtually all their time to serving constituent needs. These facts raise three questions: (1) Is such resource allocation excessive or wasteful? (2) Does constituency work detract from legislative or oversight work staff might otherwise do? (3) Would these staff positions exist at all were it not for the enormous growth in casework? Obviously, if the staff positions existed and if constituency service volume were low, there would be more time for policy matters. These, of course, are hypothetical questions that cannot be answered empirically. What is known is that staffing is generally perceived as adequate, even though some legislators could clearly use more help.

Casework and projects work play a significant and costly role in departments and agencies. Thus it may be surprising that agency personnel take a benign or, frequently, positive view of the process, sharing the view that citizens often deserve a second chance. As for disruption to administrative procedures and efficiency, the results of a survey of executive personnel (Johannes, 1984) are surprising: for every official agreeing that casework disrupted his or her agency or detracted from more important things, nearly three disagreed. Four-fifths of legislators and their staffs disagreed as well. In terms of their own jobs, only one-fifth of the agency officials surveyed viewed handling cases as an interference or a problem. Their primary complaint concerned the time involved; other complaints involved cost, potential loss of respect for executive agencies, and damage to morale.

Dealing with constituent grievances and inquiries contributes positively to congressional oversight of the bureaucracy, to the legislative function, and to internal executive branch oversight. Hearing from constituents provides much of the raw data for oversight. Casework allows ad hoc correction of bureaucratic error, impropriety, and laxity, and can lead a senator or representative to consider changes in laws because of particularly flagrant or persistent problems that casework staffs have discovered. Cases provide opportunities for legislators to raise issues at hearings, and they are cited in speeches on the floors of the House and Senate. Johannes's 1984 survey revealed that about one-third of representatives regularly reviewed cases with their staffs, whereas only about one-fifth said they never did so.

But casework proves less effective and useful than it might be in terms of systematic use of its data for formal committee-based oversight. There are several reasons for this. One has to do with the volume and type of cases received. Frequently the weekly deluge of cases does not allow caseworkers sufficient time to do anything more than passively process constituent requests and complaints; most cases, moreover, are routine and do not raise issues relevant to oversight or legislation.

A second problem concerns how staffs are structured. Although congressional offices are now more able to rely on computers to keep track of cases, the separation of casework staff from policy staff in most offices means that caseworkers have little incentive to think in terms of overall policy or oversight when handling particular problems or requests. Records are kept, but systematic searches—especially searches across a number of House or Senate offices—are rare. Rather, staff members take an anecdotal approach and rely on their memories to identify recurring problems, unusually troublesome executive agencies, or apparent flaws in laws or agency regulations. Most congressional casework staff members, at least in Washington, claim that they generalize from specific cases to broader issues, but their frequent inability to attract the attention of the legislative staff or administrative assistants constrains the efficacy of their efforts. Obviously, the problem is compounded when casework is done in district or state offices. Conversely, when staffers handle both casework and legislation on a particular topic, the prospects increase for using casework for policy making.

Finally, to make the linkage between citizen problems and oversight or legislation requires active involvement at the subcommittee and committee level, where yet another cadre of legislators and staffers, with their own interests and priorities, holds sway. Only when a committee member or aide is intrigued by the information provided via casework experience and is in a position to employ it actively can casework contribute systematically to oversight or the legislative process.

Casework's greatest impact on policy may occur not through congressional procedures but through internal executive-agency responses to congressional interventions. In a survey of 212 executive officials, two-thirds indicated that congressional inquiries helped to highlight problems, and one-third indicated that some sort of systematic attempts were made to utilize them to examine agency policies and operations (Johannes, 1984, p. 171). Granted, the frequency of such use is minimal in most agencies, and often the problems being addressed are already known to agency officials, but even a low level of attention can be useful to police an agency's operations, reevaluate procedures, reconsider rules and regulations, or observe particular bureaucrats' behavior. All things considered, therefore, constituency service often contributes positively, if only rarely in a profound fashion, to Congress's legislative function and to both congressional and internal administrative oversight.

Electoral impact. One of the most important phenomena in American politics is the extremely high frequency with which representatives and, to a lesser extent, senators are able to return to Congress after each election. House reelection rates in the 95-to-98-percent range have been common since the 1960s or before. Documenting this phenomenon is easy; explaining it has proved a greater challenge. In addition to partisan and economic factors, presidential popularity, and particular national and local policy issues, a major explanatory factor is the "personal vote." In a 1987 book that takes its title from this term, Bruce Cain, John Ferejohn, and Morris Fiorina articulated better than anyone else the commonly accepted argument that legislator visibility and constituency service produce enough votes to win close elections or to turn marginal congressional seats into electorally safe ones. That legislators and staffs believe this is beyond dispute, as is the proposition that electorally threatened members are the most aggressive in courting their constituencies and advertising their casework, federal projects, and pork-barrel expertise. Scholars, however, are in disagreement; nearly all concede the logic of the argument, but many dispute the evidence.

Although it has many variants, the argument essentially runs as follows. Citizens seeking help from their representatives and senators are given excellent treatment, even if their requests cannot be granted. They are highly satisfied with what senators and representatives do for them. Constituents observe how diligently their representatives attend to the district (by means of frequent visits and staff allocations), remember what the legislators have done for them, their friends, or the constituency generally, and then come to believe firmly that, should they have difficulties in the future, they can depend on their senators and representatives for help. Voters' satisfaction with and favorable evaluations of legislator constituency service positively affect how they view their representatives' policy positions and actions and contribute to an overall positive job rating. All these factors together—partisanship, name recognition, expectation of helpfulness, favorable job rating, high levels of district service—make voters inclined to cast their ballots for incumbents. Furthermore, the reputation for excellent constituency service will deter challengers and weaken their chances of attracting financial and electoral support.

Legislator visibility and constituency service produce enough votes to win close elections or to turn marginal congressional seats into electorally safe ones.

In the words of Morris Fiorina, "Pork barrelling and casework . . . are basically pure profit" (1977, p. 45). Fiorina goes a step further, suggesting that Congress's inability or unwillingness to legislate clearly and carefully allows and perhaps causes bureaucratic imprecision and error, which triggers the citizen requests that lead to support for incumbents.

The primary means used to prove the case are sophisticated "multivariate" analyses of national election survey data, bolstered by some district-level information on legislator resource allocation and casework effort. If one accepts as valid the questions and the coding of the national election surveys conducted by the University of Michigan's Center for Political Studies, and if one agrees with the models and methodologies employed, the Fiorina thesis stands up to analysis.

Some scholars, however, dispute the validity of the data as well as the methodology employed to support the hypothesis. In one dissenting view John C. McAdams and John R. Johannes (1988) have argued that if the long chain of linkages (that casework for oneself or a friend brings satisfaction, which causes an expectation of helpfulness, which in turn produces a favorable evaluation that leads to a vote for the incumbent) holds, then one should be able to demonstrate a direct causal effect between casework and the vote. But such a link has yet to be demonstrated.

Critics argue that survey responses are often invalid or represent generalized affect toward incumbents rather than careful assessments of them. Analysts always run the risk of confusing correlation with causality, and the surveys on which analyses are based do not determine which came first: exposure to legislators' constituency service, voters' contacts with incumbents, expectations of helpfulness, or positive attitudes toward the incumbents. Faced with such uncertainties, scholars have attempted to use aggregate data—actual casework loads, dollars of federal spending, district election results, legislative resource allocation, and so on—rather than relying on individual survey data to tackle the problem. Again, results are mixed; the casework effect cannot be clearly demonstrated or even carefully measured.

FUTURE POSSIBILITIES. Without doubt, constituency service will remain a major occupation of senators, representatives, and their staffs, and it probably will grow somewhat in complexity, if not in volume. For several reasons—because it is so time consuming, because ethical considerations occasionally loom large, and because of the possibility of systematically using casework for oversight purposes—some legislators have advocated centralizing the function and even turning the function over to a specialized congressional staff, a sort of congressional ombudsman. Arguments in favor of establishing such a central casework operation include greater ease of access for constituents, higher quality service from better-trained professional assistants, reduction of workload, elimination of many ethical problems, and enhanced use of casework for legislative and oversight purposes. Objections include the loss of the personal touch, loss of possible electoral benefits, and higher costs. To date, none of the bills introduced to establish such an institution have been successful, most likely because senators and representatives perceive a need to remain in the business of helping their constituents "fight city hall."

[See also (I) Constituency Outreach.]

BIBLIOGRAPHY

Cain, Bruce E., John A. Ferejohn, and Morris P. Fiorina. *The Personal Vote: Constituency Service and Electoral Independence.* 1987.

Fiorina, Morris P. *Congress: The Keystone of the Washington Establishment.* 1977.

Johannes, John R. *To Serve the People: Congress and Constituency Service.* 1984.

Johannes, John R., and John C. McAdams. "The Congressional Incumbency Effect: Is it Casework, Policy Compatibility, or Something Else?" American Journal of Political Science 25 (1981): 512–542.

Johannes, John R., and John C. McAdams. "Entrepreneurs or Agents: Congressmen and the Distribution of Casework in the House: 1977–1978." *Western Political Quarterly* 40 (1987): 535–553.

Klonoff, Robert. "The Congressman as Mediator between Citizens and Government Agencies: Problems and Prospects." *Harvard Journal on Legislation* 16 (1979): 701–734.

McAdams, John C., and John R. Johannes. "Congressmen, Perquisites, and Elections." Journal of Politics 50 (1988): 412–439.

U.S. House of Representatives. Commission on Administrative Review. *Final Report.* 2 vols. 95th Cong., 1st sess., 1977.

– JOHN R. JOHANNES

CONSTITUTION

Congress in the Constitution

The existence of a Congress in America predates the Constitution. The first Continental Congress was formed in 1774 as an assembly of delegates from the American colonies. By 1775 the Continental Congress had assumed governmental responsibilities, and in 1776 it declared the United States of America independent from Great Britain.

In 1777 Congress proposed the Articles of Confederation, which the states approved over the next four years. The Articles provided for governance of the new confederacy by "[t]he United States in Congress assembled." During and following the Revolutionary War, defects in the Articles became apparent. Congress lacked power to levy taxes or to regulate commerce among the states or with foreign countries, and laws, which required the approval of nine of the thirteen states represented in Congress, and amendments to the Articles, which required the unanimous approval of state legislatures, were difficult to adopt. Also, the Articles established no executive independent of Congress.

In 1787 Congress agreed to organize a convention to consider and report proposed revisions to the Articles of Confederation. Meeting throughout the summer of 1787 in Philadelphia, the convention reported to Congress a draft of a new Constitution instead of limited revisions to the Articles. Congress submitted the new Constitution for state approval. Following ratification by eleven states, Congress passed a resolution in September 1788 initiating the new government under the Constitution.

The Constitution established three separate branches of government: Congress, the executive, and the judiciary. The most important provisions for Congress are concentrated in Article I, which establishes Congress, makes rules for its election and governance, and assigns it legislative powers. Because the Constitution establishes a system of mutually checking (as well as separated) powers among the branches, succeeding articles of the Constitution govern congressional interaction with the executive and judicial branches. Provisions throughout the Constitution and its amendments limit Congress's powers.

ELECTION AND GOVERNANCE OF THE CONGRESS. The Constitution establishes rules for the election and governance of the Congress. It addresses the structure, membership, and election of Congress; its officers, meeting, and operations; and the compensation and privileges of its members.

Structure, membership, and election. Article I, section 1 creates "a Congress of the United States, which shall consist of a Senate and House of Representatives. In *Federalist* 51, James Madison explained that "the weight of the legislative authority" made it necessary "to divide the legislature into different branches; and to render them, by different modes of election and different principles of action, as little connected with each other as the nature of their common functions and their common dependence on the society will admit."

Initially, members of the House of Representatives were popularly elected (Art. I, sec. 2, cl. 1), while senators were chosen by the state legislatures (Art. I, sec. 3, cl. 1). By 1913, dissatisfaction with legislatures' selection of senators and support for popular enfranchisement led to ratification of the Seventeenth Amendment, which provided that senators, too, would be popularly elected.

The original idea that members of the House were direct representatives of the people was manifested by the requirement, preserved in the Fourteenth Amendment, that "Representatives shall be apportioned among the several States according to their respective numbers," except that each state was entitled to at least one representative (Amend. XIV, sec. 2, superseding Art. I, sec. 2, cl. 3). The Supreme Court ruled in *Wesberry v. Sanders* (1964) that each state's congressional districts must include as equal a number of inhabitants as is practical.

In contrast, the Senate consists of two members from every state (Amend. XVII, superseding Art. I, sec. 3, cl, 1). The determination that the House would be apportioned by population, while the Senate would represent the states equally, regardless of size, is known as the Great Compromise of the Constitutional Convention and was key to the Constitution's ratification. Equal state representation was so basic to the plan that no constitutional amendment may deprive a state of equal representation in the Senate without its consent (Art. V).

Because the more representative body of Congress "should have an immediate dependence on, and an intimate sympathy with, the people" (*Federalist* 52), representatives are chosen every two years (Art. I, sec. 2). Senators are elected for six-year terms (Amend. XVII, superseding Art. I, sec. 3, cl. 1), after initially having been divided as evenly as possible into three groups so that one-third of them are selected every two years (Art. I, sec. 3, cl. 2). Congressional terms begin and end at noon on 3 January (Amend. XX, sec. 1).

Constitutional amendments bar Congress or the states from denying voting rights on grounds of race, sex, nonpayment of poll or other taxes, or age, for people eighteen or older.

The Constitution established the House initially at sixty-five members, allocated among the states by population. It required an "actual Enumeration," or population census, within three years and every ten years thereafter, to reapportion seats. The Constitution did not permanently fix the House's size, except to stipulate that there not be more than one representative per thirty thousand people (Art. I, sec. 2, cl. 3).

For the House of Representatives, special elections, called by the state governors, are the sole method of choosing members to fill unexpired terms (Art. I, sec. 2, cl. 4). No temporary representatives are appointed pending a special election.

The Constitution also authorizes governors to call elections for filling vacancies in the Senate. However, unlike House vacancies—and even though the election of senators by state legislatures was replaced by direct popular election under the Seventeenth Amendment—the Constitution permits state legislatures to empower governors to fill vacancies temporarily until special elections are held (Amend. XVII, superseding Art. I, sec. 3, cl. 2). The states may act quickly, therefore, to assure equality of state representation in the Senate.

The Constitution specifies only a few uniform qualifications for service in each house. A member of Congress must, at the time of election, be an inhabitant of the state from which he or she is elected (Art. I, sec. 2, cl. 2; Art, I, sec. 3, cl. 3). Representatives and senators must also meet age and length of citizenship requirements before taking office. A representative must be at least twenty-five years of age and a citizen for at least seven years (Art. I, sec. 2, cl. 2); a senator must be a minimum of thirty years old and a citizen for at least nine years (Art. I, sec. 3, cl. 3). Madison justified these distinctions "by the nature of the senatorial trust, which . . . requir[es the] greater extent of information and stability of character" that comes with age, and which, because of the Senate's foreign affairs role, warrants greater distance "from the prepossessions and habits incident to foreign birth and education" (*Federalist* 62). Members also must take an "Oath or Affirmation, to support this Constitution" (Art. VI, sec. 3).

The Framers' rejection of other qualifications expressed their democratic conviction that "under these reasonable limitations, the door of this part of the federal government is open to merit of every description, whether native or adoptive, whether young or old, and without regard to poverty or wealth, or to any particular profession or religious faith" (*Federalist* 52). The Supreme Court ruled in *Powell v. McCormack* (1969) that Congress may not add to the qualifications in the Constitution.

In addition, the Constitution establishes disqualifications for federal legislators. The incompatibility clause prohibits members from simultaneously holding judicial or executive office: "no Person holding any Office under the United States, shall be a Member of either House during his Continuance in Office" (Art. I, sec. 6, cl. 2). There are also two disqualifications applying to government officials generally. Thus, "no person shall be a Senator or Representative in Congress, . . . who, having previously taken an oath, as a . . . [federal or state official], to support the Constitution of the United States, shall have engaged in insurrection or rebellion against the same, or given aid or comfort to the enemies thereof," unless both houses vote by two-thirds majorities to waive this provision (Amend. XIV, sec. 3). Further, officers who have been convicted on impeachment charges may be disqualified from ever holding "any Office of honor, Trust, or Profit under the United States" (Art. I, sec. 3, cl. 7).

The Framers believed that qualifications for service in Congress were "more susceptible of uniformity" than qualifications for voting for Congress (*Federalist* 52). Therefore, the Constitution states only that "the Electors in each State shall have the Qualifications requisite for Electors of the most numerous Branch of the State Legislature" (Art. I, sec. 2, cl. 1). In accordance with Madison's belief that "the right of suffrage is very justly regarded as a fundamental article of republican government" (*Federalist* 52), constitutional amendments bar Congress or the states from denying voting rights on grounds of race (Amend. XV), sex (Amend. XIX), nonpayment of poll or other taxes (Amend. XXIV), or age, for people eighteen or older (Amend. XXVI).

Although the Constitution gives Congress no power to enlarge qualifications for congressional office, Congress has reserved plenary power over the congressional election process and final authority over election results. The Constitution provides that state legislatures may prescribe the "Time, Places and Manner" of holding congressional elections (Art. I, sec. 4, cl. 1). However, fearful that granting exclusive power over national elections to the states "would leave the existence of the Union entirely at their mercy" (*Federalist* 59), the Framers authorized Congress to "make or alter such Regulations, except as to the Places of chusing Senators" (Art. I, sec. 4, cl. 1).

After elections, the elections or qualifications clause provides that "each House shall be the Judge of the Elections, Returns, and Qualifications of its own Members" (Art. I, sec. 5, cl. 1). The Supreme Court held in *Roudebush v. Hartke* (1972) that Congress's power to determine winners of its elections is final.

Power to discipline members of Congress is similarly reserved to each house, which may "punish its Members for disorderly Behaviour, and, with the Concurrence of two thirds, expel a Member" (Art. I, sec. 5, cl. 2). Members are not subject to recall, nor, as the Senate established in 1799 in the case of Sen. William Blount, to impeachment. Blount was the first member of Congress to be expelled. Subsequently, during the Civil War, fourteen senators and three representatives were expelled for rebellion, and one representative was expelled in 1980 for criminal misconduct.

Officers, meeting, and operation. The Constitution grants each house of Congress broad power to "determine the Rules of its Proceedings" (Art. I, sec. 5, cl. 2). The Supreme Court has stated that Congress "may not by its rules ignore constitutional restraints or violate fundamental rights," but "within these limitations all matters of method are open to the determination of the house" (*United States v. Ballin* [1892]). The Constitution prescribes a few specific requirements as to Congress's officers, meetings, and business.

Regarding Congress's leadership, the Constitution creates one House and two Senate officers and grants both houses authority to appoint other officers. "The House of Representatives shall chuse their Speaker and other Officers" (Art. I, sec. 2, cl. 5), but the Constitution also specifies that the vice president is to be president of the Senate (Art. I, sec. 3, cl. 4). The vice president is without a vote except in case of a tie. The Constitution authorizes the Senate to choose other officers, including a president pro tempore, to serve when the vice president is either absent or serving as president of the United States" (Art. I, sec. 3, cl. 5). Both houses have appointed other officers, and each party's members have selected leaders in each house.

The Constitution sets specifications for Congress's meeting, establishment of a quorum, and adjournment. The Constitution requires Congress to "assemble at least once in every Year" (Art. I, sec. 4, cl. 2; Amend. XX, sec. 2). Originally, the Constitution directed annual assembly "on the first Monday in December, unless they shall by Law appoint a different Day" (Art. I, sec. 4, cl. 2). In 1933, the Constitution was amended, in conjunction with moving presidential inaugurations to 20 January, so that 3 January became the date for the annual convening of Congress, unless Congress should legislate a different day (Amend. XX, sec. 2).

Beyond stipulating the reach of Congress's legislative authority, the Constitution also specifies the procedures for making laws.

The only other time that Congress is required to assemble is when the president uses the power "on extraordinary Occasions, [to] convene both Houses, or either of them" (Art. II, sec. 3). This power has been used only rarely. The Constitution also directs the president "from time to time [to] give to the Congress Information of the State of the Union, and recommend to their Consideration such Measures as he shall judge necessary and expedient" (Art. II, sec. 3). Although the first two presidents addressed Congress on the state of the Union in person, subsequent chief executives communicated in writing, until President Woodrow Wilson returned to the original practice in 1913. President Harry S Truman initiated the current formal State of the Union address in 1947.

Regarding Congress's day-to-day meetings, a majority of each house "shall constitute a Quorum to do Business" (Art. I, sec. 5, cl. 1). The congressional majority may not, by absenting itself, prevent either house from functioning, as "a smaller Number may adjourn from day to day, and may be authorized to compel the Attendance of absent Members, in such Manner, and under such Penalties as each House may provide" (Art. I, sec. 5, cl. 1).

Longer adjournments are regulated by the restriction that "neither House, during the Session of Congress, shall, without the Consent of the other, adjourn for more than three days, nor to any other Place than that in which the two Houses shall be sitting" (Art. I, sec. 5, cl. 4). Although the power has never been used, the president may, when the houses cannot agree on the time of adjournment, "adjourn them to such Time as he shall think proper" (Art. II, sec. 3).

The Constitution imposes two other general requirements on Congress's operations. The publications or journal clause provides that "Each House shall keep a Journal of its Proceedings, and from time to time publish the same, excepting such Parts as may in their Judgment require Secrecy; and the Yeas and Nays of the Members of either House on any question shall, at the Desire of one fifth of those Present, be entered on the Journal" (Art. I, sec. 5, cl. 3). Also, when Congress votes on overriding a presidential veto, the Constitution requires that "the Votes of both Houses shall be determined by yeas and Nays, and the Names of the Persons voting for and against the Bill shall be entered on the Journal of each House respectively" (Art. I, sec. 7, cl. 2).

Each House acts by majority vote, except where the Constitution specifies a two-thirds vote. The two-thirds provision applies to both houses for overrides of presidential vetoes (Art. I, sec. 7, cl. 2–3), proposals of constitutional amendments (Art. V), and declarations of presidential disability (Amend. XXV, sec. 4); to either house's expulsion of members (Art. I, sec. 3, cl. 6); and to the Senate's impeachment conviction (Art. I, sec. 5, cl. 2) and consent to ratification of treaties (Art. II, sec. 2, cl. 2).

Compensation and privileges. The Constitution guarantees that senators and representatives will be paid, but leaves the amount to be determined by legislation, with the compensation to be disbursed from the U.S. Treasury (Art. I, sec. 6, cl. 1). In 1992, the states ratified an amendment, which the First Congress had proposed with the Bill of Rights in 1789, regulating the timing of congressional pay legislation. It states that no legislation changing the compensation of senators and representatives shall take effect until after the next election of representatives (Amend. XXVII).

The Constitution provides members of Congress with two legal privileges. The arrest clause states that "Senators and Representatives . . . shall in all Cases, except Treason, Felony and Breach of the Peace, be privileged from Arrest during their Attendance at the Session of their respective Houses, and in going to and returning from the same (Art. I, sec. 6, cl. 1). The arrest clause is of limited contemporary significance because arrests in civil suits, its intended target, are no longer common. The arrest clause offers no protection against arrest on criminal charges.

Of more lasting importance is the speech or debate clause, which provides that "for any Speech or Debate in either House, [senators and representatives] shall not be questioned in any other Place" (Art. I, sec. 6, cl. 1). To ensure legislative independence from the judiciary and executive, the clause protects members and their staffs from civil or criminal liability or compulsory testimony for their actions within the legislative sphere, including speeches, debates, voting on the floor or in committee, committee reports, and resolutions. The Supreme Court reads the speech or debate clause broadly and has held that, where applicable, its protection is absolute (*United States v. Johnson* [1966]; *Gravel v. United States* [1972]; *Eastland v. United States Servicemen's Fund* [1974]). The Court has also ruled, however, that the clause does not protect nonlegislative activities, including press relations, constituent service, and lobbying executive agencies (*Hutchinson v. Proxmire* [1979]).

CONGRESS'S LEGISLATIVE POWERS. Article I, section 1, vests "all legislative Powers herein granted . . . in a Congress of the United States." Although the federal legislative power is defined and limited by the Constitution, it consists of a formidable complex of powers enumerated in Article I and elsewhere and implied from the enumerated powers. The supremacy clause makes the "Constitution, and the Laws of the United States which shall be made in Pursuance thereof; and all Treaties made . . . the supreme Law of the Land" (Art. VI, cl. 2). Beyond stipulating the reach of Congress's legislative authority, the Constitution also specifies the procedures for making laws.

Enumerated powers. Congress's primary legislative authority is detailed in Article I, section 8, which empowers Congress, most significantly,

"To lay and collect Taxes . . . , to pay the Debts and provide for the common Defence and general Welfare of the United States" (cl. 1)
"To borrow Money" (cl. 2)
"To regulate Commerce with foreign Nations, and among the several States, and with the Indian tribes" (cl. 3)
"To establish an uniform Rule of Naturalization, and uniform Laws on . . . Bankruptcies" (cl. 4)
"To coin Money" (cl. 5)
"To establish Post Offices and post Roads" (cl. 7)
To grant patents and copyrights (cl. 8)
"To declare War" (cl. 11)
"To raise and support Armies" and a Navy (cl. 12–13)
"To exercise exclusive Legislation in all Cases whatsoever" over the District of Columbia (cl. 17).

The final clause of the section, known as the necessary and proper clause, authorizes Congress "To make all Laws which shall be necessary and proper for carrying into Execution the foregoing Powers, and all other Powers vested by this Constitution in the Government of the United States, or in any Department or Officer thereof" (Art. I, sec. 8, cl. 18).

The relationship between Congress's specifically enumerated powers and the necessary and proper clause was the first great issue raised about Congress's legislative authority. Defending the clause from attack, Alexander Hamilton stated that "the constitutional operation of the intended government would be precisely the same" without the clause, as it was "only declaratory of a truth which would have resulted by necessary and unavoidable implication from the very act of constituting a federal government, and vesting it with certain specified powers" (*Federalist* 33). Madison affirmed that "without the substance of this power, the whole Constitution would be a dead letter" (*Federalist* 44).

In 1819, the Supreme Court upheld an expansive reading of the necessary and proper clause in *McCulloch v. Maryland.* Rejecting a challenge to Congress's chartering of a national bank based on the argument that Article I, section 8, did not specifically grant power to do so, the Court held that the necessary and proper clause gives Congress broad authority to implement the enumerated powers: "Let the end be legitimate, let it be within the scope of the constitution, and all means which are appropriate, which are plainly adapted to that end, which are not prohibited, but consist with the letter and spirit of the constitution, are constitutional."

Throughout U.S. history, the significance of Congress's individual enumerated powers has fluctuated with the nation's particular needs. Two powers—to tax and spend for the general welfare and to regulate interstate and foreign commerce—have figured critically in all stages of the nation's domestic development. Not coincidentally, the powers to tax and to regulate commerce were the two principal subjects of legislative authority that had been lacking under the Articles of Confederation.

Hamilton believed taxation was the most significant power given to Congress (*Federalist* 33) and stated that "As revenue is the essential engine by which the means of answering the national exigencies must be procured, . . . the federal government must of necessity be invested with an unqualified power of taxation in the ordinary modes" (*Federalist* 31).

Although Madison viewed the taxing power as limited by the purposes enumerated in Article I, section 8 (*Federalist* 41), the Supreme Court in *United States v. Butler* (1936) ultimately adopted Hamilton's broader understanding that the taxing and spending clause "confers a power separate and distinct from those later enumerated, is not restricted in meaning by the grant of them, and Congress consequently has a substantive power to tax and to appropriate, limited only by the requirement that it shall be exercised to provide for the general welfare of the United States." The potency of Congress's "power of the purse" is reinforced by the express confirmation of Article I, section 9, clause 7 that the executive has no independent spending power: "No Money shall be drawn from the Treasury, but in Consequence of Appropriations made by Law."

The other enumerated power that proved central to national development is the authority to regulate interstate commerce (Art. I, sec. 8, cl. 3). The eventual dominance of Supreme Court decisions broadly interpreting interstate commerce sustained congressional regulation of a vast array of activities with a "substantial economic effect on interstate commerce" (*Wickard v. Filburn* [1942]; *National Labor Relations Board v. Jones & Laughlin Steel Corporation* [1937]; *Gibbons v. Ogden* [1824]).

The Constitution also assigns Congress critical responsibilities over national security, but by designating the president as "Commander in Chief of the Army and Navy" (Art. II, sec. 2, cl. 1), it divides war powers between Congress and the president. Congress is given power to declare war and to raise, support, and regulate military forces (Art. I, sec. 8, cl. 11–14). Congress has formally declared five wars: the War of 1812, the Mexican War, the Spanish-American War, and the two world wars. Congress has also periodically authorized use of armed force against hostile foreign powers without declaring war.

The Supreme Court has stated in *United States v. Curtiss-Wright Export Corporation* (1936) that war powers stand on a different footing from the federal government's enumerated domestic powers, because "the investment of the federal government with the powers of external sovereignty did not depend upon the affirmative grants of the Constitution. The powers to declare and wage war . . . if they had never been mentioned in the Constitution, would have vested in the federal government as necessary concomitants of nationality."

Clauses other than Article I, section 8 grant Congress legislative power. Article IV, section 3, clauses 1 and 2, for example, empower Congress to admit states into the Union and to make "all needful Rules and Regulations respecting the Territory or other Property belonging to the United States." The territory clause, the Supreme Court has declared in *Simms v. Simms* (1899), gives Congress "entire dominion and sovereignty, national and local, Federal and state, and . . . full legislative power over all subjects upon which the legislature of a State might legislate within the State."

Several constitutional amendments have expanded Congress's lawmaking authority by empowering Congress to enforce rights guaranteed by the amendments through "appropriate legislation." Thus, Congress has legislative power to enforce freedom from slavery (Amend. XIII), due process of law and equal protection of the laws (Amend. XIV), and voting rights (Amend. XV, XIX, XXIV, XXVI). Coupled with the commerce power, these grants give Congress broad authority over civil rights in employment, housing, public accommodations, education, and voting.

Implied powers and lawmaking procedures. In addition to the legislative powers expressly granted in the Constitution, Congress possesses implied powers essential to the exercise of the express powers, such as the power to investigate, which includes power to compel testimony. The investigatory power inheres in the power to make laws, as a "legislative body cannot legislate wisely or effectively in the absence of information respecting the conditions which the legislation is intended to affect or change" (*McGrain v. Daugherty* [1927]).

The Constitution vests Congress not only with legislative power, but also with several controls over, and shared responsibilities with, the other government branches.

Along with vesting substantive legislative power in Congress, Article I prescribes procedures for lawmaking. Either house may initiate legislation, except for the origination clause's proviso: "All Bills for raising Revenue shall originate in the House of Representatives; but the Senate may propose or concur with Amendments as on other Bills" (Art. I, sec. 7, cl. 1). The House's prerogative to initiate revenue legislation derives from the Framers' conception of that chamber as being closer to the people. By custom, general spending and borrowing bills also originate in the House.

Article I, section 7, clause 2 provides that laws must be passed by both houses of Congress and presented to the president for signature or, if vetoed, repassed by two-thirds of each house. The president must return the bill to the originating house within ten days (excluding Sundays) or it becomes law without signature, unless under the pocket veto clause, "Congress by their Adjournment prevent its Return, in which Case it shall not be a Law" (Art. I, sec. 7, cl. 2).

The president's veto, or "qualified negative," accomplishes two purposes: it "serves as a shield to the Executive" and "furnishes an additional security against the enaction of improper laws" (*Federalist* 73). The Supreme Court has stated that this process of bicameral action and presentation reflects "the Framers' decision that the legislative power of the Federal Government be exercised in accord with a single, finely wrought and exhaustively considered, procedure" (*Immigration and Naturalization Service v. Chadha* [1983]).

Congress has broad power to delegate legislative power to the executive and judicial branches so long as it prescribes in legislation the terms of the delegation. The Supreme Court last invalidated acts of Congress on undue delegation grounds early in the New Deal (*Panama Refining Company v. Ryan* [1935]; *A.L.A. Schechter Poultry Corporation v. United States* [1935]). The Court has upheld every challenged delegation of power since then, including laws granting the president very broad regulatory discretion.

The Constitution does not grant the president inherent lawmaking power. In *Youngstown Sheet and Tube Company v. Sawyer* (1952), the Supreme Court stated, "The Founders of this Nation entrusted the lawmaking power to the Congress alone in both good and bad times." Justice Robert Jackson, in a concurring opinion, stated that presidential power is strongest when supported by congressional authorization and weakest when "incompatible with the expressed or implied will of Congress."

CONGRESS'S RELATIONSHIP WITH THE OTHER BRANCHES. The Constitution vests Congress not only with legislative power but also with several controls over, and shared responsibilities with, the other government branches, including a role in selecting, retaining, and compensating officers of the other branches; a role in treaty making; and various duties regarding the judicial branch.

In *Federalist* 48, Madison reconciled this system of mutually checking powers with the principle of a strict separation of powers by explaining that "unless these departments be so far connected and blended as to give to each a constitutional control over the others, the degree of separation which the maxim requires, as essential to a free government, can never in practice be duly maintained."

Appointment and removal. The question of who should appoint judges and high executive officials occupied much attention at the Constitutional Convention. Some delegates thought presidential appointment would ensure "responsibility"; others thought the power too important for one individual. The Framers ultimately divided the power, providing that the president "shall nominate, and by and with the Advice and Consent of the Senate, shall appoint" judges and principal executive officers, including "Ambassadors, other public Ministers and Consuls" (Art. II, sec. 2, cl. 2). The appointments clause achieves both responsibility, because only one person selects officers, and security, because the Senate can block the president's choice. As Hamilton explained in *Federalist* 76, Senate confirmation is "an excellent check upon a spirit of favoritism in the President, and would tend greatly to prevent the appointment of unfit characters." Furthermore, before any officer may be appointed, Congress must establish the office by law.

For lesser officers, Congress may forgo Senate confirmation and vest appointment "in the President alone, in the Courts of Law, or in the Heads of Departments" (Art. II, sec. 2, cl. 2). The Supreme Court has ruled that, in selecting among these appointing authorities, Congress has significant discretion, needing to avoid only "incongruous" interbranch appointments (*Morrison v. Olson* [1988]). The Court has also held that because Congress is not itself a listed appointing authority, Congress may not appoint nonlegislative officers (*Buckley v. Valeo* [1976]).

Article II, section 2, clause 3 authorizes the president to make temporary appointments to fill vacant offices when the Senate is adjourned. Such "recess appointments" last only through the next congressional session.

Other than through impeachment, the Constitution is silent on removal of officers. When the First Congress established the original cabinet positions (Foreign Affairs, War, and the Treasury) in 1789, it decided that only the president, not the Senate, could remove executive officers. Citing this decision, the Supreme Court has held that the Senate may not participate in the president's decision to dismiss cabinet officers (*Myers v. United States* [1926]) but that Congress may limit the president's discretion to remove other officers (*Humphrey's Executor v. United States* [1935]; *Morrison v. Olson* [1988]).

Impeachment. Impeachment is the only constitutional mechanism through which Congress can remove federal judges, who serve "during good Behaviour" (Art. III, sec. 1), and top executive officers. Because officers are impeachable only for serious misconduct, "high Crimes and Misdemeanors," impeachment is infrequent. Although the Framers drew upon English parliamentary practice in drafting impeachment provisions, they departed from English experience by limiting impeachment to offenses by government officers and barring the use of impeachment for criminal punishment.

Article II, section 4 provides that "the President, Vice President and all civil Officers of the United States, shall be removed from Office on Impeachment for, and Conviction of, Treason, Bribery, or other high Crimes and

Misdemeanors." Hamilton explained in *Federalist* 65 that impeachment is "a method of national inquest" into the conduct of public officials for "the abuse or violation of some public trust." He described impeachment "as a bridle in the hands of the legislative body upon the executive servants of the government."

To prevent misuse, impeachment is divided between the two houses. The House of Representatives alone may initiate charges, or impeach, by majority vote (Art. I, sec. 2, cl. 5). Only the Senate may try impeachments—that is, determine guilt after receiving evidence on the charges (Art. I, sec. 3, cl. 6). On conviction, which requires concurrence of two-thirds of those senators present, the guilty official automatically loses his or her office (Art. I., sec. 3, cl. 7). The Senate also may disqualify convicted officers from holding future office but may not impose any further sanction. The Supreme Court has determined that the Senate's impeachment trial procedures are not subject to judicial review (*Nixon v. United States* [1993]).

In all, the House has impeached fifteen officers, seven of whom (all judges) were convicted. In addition to eleven lower-court judges, the House has impeached President Andrew Johnson, Supreme Court Justice Samuel Chase, Secretary of War William W. Belknap, and Senator Blount, although the Senate ruled that senators cannot be impeached but only expelled by the Senate. President Richard M. Nixon resigned while the House was preparing to impeach him.

Tenure and compensation. The Constitution regulates the compensation of officers to preserve the balance among the branches. As Hamilton stated in *Federalist* 79, "a power over a man's subsistence amounts to a power over his will." To safeguard judicial independence, the Constitution stipulates that the compensation of judges is not to be reduced while they are in office (Art. III, sec. 1). The Constitution likewise guarantees the president "a Compensation, which shall neither be encreased nor diminished during the Period for which he shall have been elected" (Art. II, sec. 1, cl. 7).

To "guard . . . against the danger of executive influence upon the legislative body" (*Federalist* 76) through inducements, the ineligibility and incompatibility clauses provide that

> No Senator or Representative shall, during the Time for which he was elected, be appointed to any civil Office under the Authority of the United States, which shall have been created, or the Emoluments whereof shall have been encreased during such time; and no Person holding any Office under the United States, shall be a Member of either House during his Continuance in Office. (Art. I, sec. 6, cl. 2)

Foreign affairs. The Constitution divides responsibility for foreign affairs between the Senate and the president through several provisions aside from those conferring the legislative and war powers on the House and Senate jointly. The power to make treaties is distributed much like the appointing power. The president is assigned the initial role, subject to Senate approval by a two-thirds majority (Art. II, sec. 2, cl. 2). Hamilton explained that the power to make "agreements between sovereign and sovereign . . . seems to form a distinct department, and to belong, properly, neither to the legislative nor to the executive" (*Federalist* 75). The Framers authorized the president to negotiate treaties so that he could act with "secrecy and despatch" (*Federalist* 64); they required Senate approval to ensure caution, steadiness, and conformity with law (*Federalist* 75).

The Framers also split the responsibility for appointing those officers who communicate between the United States and foreign governments. The power to appoint the nation's representatives abroad is divided under the appointments clause, with the president nominating and the Senate approving them (Art. II, sec. 2, cl. 2).

The Constitution gives to the president alone the duty to "receive Ambassadors and other public Ministers" from foreign countries (Art. II, sec. 3). Along with Madison, Hamilton initially viewed this function as unimportant (*Federalist* 69). However, Hamilton subsequently relied on this duty as a source of presidential authority in foreign affairs, and the provision has come to be cited as a constitutional basis for presidential power over recognizing foreign governments and the president's role as the nation's sole organ in communicating with them.

Presidential election and succession. Congress has an important, but rarely triggered, role in the selection of the president. If no presidential candidate is supported by a majority of the electoral college, the House of Representatives selects the president from the three top candidates (Amend. XII, superseding Art. II, sec. 1, cl. 2). Each state delegation has one vote, and a majority is necessary to select a president. Similarly, if the electors do not cast a majority for a vice-presidential candidate, the Senate chooses one of the top two candidates as vice president. This procedure elected the president in 1800 and 1824 and the vice president in 1836.

The Constitution initially addressed the prospect of a vacancy in the presidency only by authorizing Congress to legislate the order of succession after the vice president (Art. II, sec. 1, cl. 6). Under this authority, Congress has mandated succession by the Speaker of the House, then the president pro tempore of the Senate, and then through the cabinet. The Twenty-fifth

Amendment additionally provides that, if the vice presidency is vacant, the president nominates a vice president subject to approval by a majority vote of both houses. This provision was used in 1973, when Gerald Ford was selected to fill the vacancy caused by Vice President Spiro T. Agnew's resignation, and in 1974, when Nelson A. Rockefeller replaced Ford as vice president after Ford became president on Richard M. Nixon's resignation.

The Twenty-fifth Amendment also establishes procedures in the event of presidential disability. If the vice president and a majority of the cabinet determine "that the President is unable to discharge the powers and duties of his office, the Vice President shall immediately assume the powers and duties of the office as Acting President." The president resumes his or her powers on declaring in writing that he or she is not disabled, unless the vice president and a majority of the cabinet disagree, in which case Congress makes the final decision. The president resumes his or her duties unless two-thirds of both houses determine that he or she is unable to function.

Courts and constitutional amendments. In addition to confirmation and impeachment, the Constitution grants Congress three powers affecting the courts. First, Congress has the duty to establish all courts inferior to the Supreme Court, which is the only court established in the Constitution (Art. III, sec. 1). Second, Congress has authority to regulate the Supreme Court's exercise of appellate jurisdiction over cases filed in the inferior courts (Art. III, sec. 2, cl. 2). The Supreme Court held in *Marbury v. Madison* (1803) that Congress may not add to the original jurisdiction that the Constitution assigns to the Supreme Court. By invalidating a law expanding its original jurisdiction, the Court established in that case the principle of judicial review regarding the constitutionality of acts of Congress.

In addition to confirmation and impeachment, the Constitution grants Congress three powers affecting the courts.

Third, Article V grants Congress a role in overruling constitutional decisions of the Supreme Court or otherwise altering the Constitution by empowering Congress to propose amendments to the Constitution. In addition to a never-used mechanism for calling a constitutional convention, the Constitution provides that, by two-thirds vote of both houses, Congress may propose amendments, which become effective if ratified by three-fourths of the states. The Constitution has been amended twenty-seven times this way, including the ten amendments in the Bill of Rights.

LIMITATIONS ON CONGRESSIONAL POWER. Congress's broad legislative powers are limited by several specific restrictions. Because of states' dissatisfaction with the paucity of limitations in the original text, the Bill of Rights was added to the Constitution to ensure additional limits on federal power.

Original constitutional limitations. Two important original limitations on congressional power were temporary. First, the Constitutional Convention compromised its bitter disagreement over the slave trade by providing that "the Migration or Importation of such Persons as any of the States now existing shall think proper to admit, shall not be prohibited by the Congress prior to the Year one thousand eight hundred and eight" (Art. I, sec. 9, cl. 1). In 1807 Congress passed a law banning the slave trade as of 1 January 1808, and slavery was abolished by the Thirteenth Amendment in 1865.

Another key original limitation on congressional power survived until this century. Article I, section 9, clause 4 provided that "no Capitation, or other direct, Tax shall be laid, unless in Proportion to the Census or Enumeration herein before directed to be taken." Following the Supreme Court's decision that this provision barred income taxes (*Pollock v. Farmers' Loan and Trust Company* [1895]), the Sixteenth Amendment was adopted in 1913 to permit direct levying of income taxes, irrespective of apportionment or population.

The Constitution also imposes restrictions on legislative authority that remain in force. Article I guarantees open and nondiscriminatory trade by the states with each other and with foreign countries by providing that "no Tax or Duty shall be laid on Articles exported from any State" and "no Preference shall be given by any Regulation of Commerce or Revenue to the Ports of one State over those of another" (Art. I, sec. 9, cl. 5–6).

Even prior to the Bill of Rights, the Constitution limited legislative action in order to safeguard individual liberty. Article I guarantees that "the Privilege of the Writ of Habeas Corpus shall not be suspended, unless when in Cases of Rebellion or Invasion the public Safety may require it" (Art. I, sec. 9, cl. 2). Habeas corpus has been suspended four times in American history, most notably during the Civil War.

Article I also bars bills of attainder and ex post facto laws (Art. I, sec. 9, cl. 3). The Supreme Court ruled in *United States v. Lovett* (1946) that laws which "apply either to named individuals or to easily ascertainable members of a group in such a way as to inflict punishment on them without a judicial trial are bills of attainder prohibited by the Constitution." The Court has defined an ex post facto law as a criminal law "that makes an action done before the passing of the law, and which was innocent when done, criminal; and punishes such action," or "aggravates a crime, or makes it greater than it was, when committed," or "inflicts a greater punishment, than the law annexed to the crime, when committed" (*Calder v. Bull* [1798]). Article III guarantees that "the trial of all Crimes, except in Cases of Impeachment, shall be by Jury" (Art. III, sec. 2, cl. 3). Article III also limits legislative power over the crime of treason by defining the offense, prescribing the evidence required for conviction, and limiting punishment (Art. III, sec. 3, cl. 1–2). Finally, the Constitution provides that "no religious Test shall ever be required as a Qualification to any Office or public Trust under the United States" (Art. VI, cl. 3).

The Bill of Rights and subsequent amendment. The omission of a formal bill of individual rights was one of the most controversial aspects of the proposed Constitution. Notwithstanding Hamilton's insistence that the restrictions enumerated in the text sufficed and that a more general bill of rights was "not only unnecessary in the proposed Constitution, but would even be dangerous" (*Federalist* 84), the lack of a bill of rights generated potent criticism. Several state conventions coupled ratification with proposed amendments guaranteeing individual rights or conditioned ratification on the addition of a bill of rights.

Following an election campaign dominated by controversy over amending the Constitution, the First Congress proposed the Bill of Rights in 1789. As ratified, it comprises ten amendments limiting federal power. Only the First Amendment specifically restricts Congress. It declares that "Congress shall make no law respecting an establishment of religion, or prohibiting the free exercise thereof; or abridging the freedom of speech, or of the press; or the right of the people peaceably to assemble, and to petition the Government for a redress of grievances."

The balance of the Bill of Rights likewise guarantees individual rights against governmental intrusion. Worded as general limitations on government power, the amendments restrict legislative actions, as well as those of the other branches. These amendments guarantee procedural rights for persons accused in criminal cases (Amend. VI); the right to jury trial in civil cases (Amend. VII); rights against unreasonable searches and seizures (Amend. IV); rights against double jeopardy, compelled self-incrimination, deprivation of life, liberty, or property without due process of law or the taking of private property without just compensation (Amend. V); and rights against excessive bail and cruel and unusual punishment (Amend. VIII).

Further extension of individual rights by constitutional amendment after the Civil War also limited legislative power by guaranteeing "the equal protection of the laws" (Amend. XIV, sec. 1), which is applied to the federal government through the due process clause of the Fifth Amendment.

[See also (I) Delegation of Powers, Emergency Powers, Implied Powers; (II) Executive Orders, Executive Power.]

BIBLIOGRAPHY

Elliot, Jonathan, ed. *The Debates in the Several State Conventions on the Adoption of the Federal Constitution.* 1974.

Farrand, Max, ed. *The Records of the Federal Convention of 1787.* 1974.

Fisher, Louis. *Constitutional Conflicts between Congress and the President.* 3d ed. 1991.

Henkin, Louis. *Foreign Affairs and the Constitution.* 1975.

Kurland, Philip B., and Ralph Lerner, eds. *The Founders' Constitution.* 1987.

Story, Joseph. *Commentaries on the Constitution of the United States.* Edited by Ronald D. Rotunda and John E. Nowak. 1987.

U.S. House of Representatives. *Constitution, Jefferson's Manual, and Rules of the House of Representatives, 103d Congress.* 102d Cong., 2d sess., 1993. H. Doc. 102–405.

U.S. House of Representatives. *Documents Illustrative of the Formation of the Union of the American States,* edited by Charles C. Tansill. 69th Cong., 1st sess., 1927. H. Doc. 398.

U.S. Senate. *The Constitution of the United States of America,* edited by Johnny H. Killian. 99th Cong., 1st sess., 1987. S. Doc. 16. Supplemented by *1990 Supplement.* 101st Cong., 2d sess., 1990. S. Doc. 36.

Wood, Gordon S. *The Creation of the American Republic,* 1776–1787. 1969.

Wright, Benjamin F., ed. *The Federalist.* 1961.

– MICHAEL DAVIDSON, MORGAN J. FRANKEL, AND CLAIRE M. SYLVIA

Congressional Interpretation of the Constitution

Throughout its history, Congress has played an integral part in interpreting the meaning of the Constitution. Amendments to the Constitution represent one opportunity for congressional influence, but the principal way in which Congress defines constitutional values is through the regular statutory process. Congress is constantly engaged in balancing constitutional interests when it legislates on commerce, criminal law, federalism, the separation of powers, and other matters that require legislative attention. It is thus superficial to believe that the Supreme Court exercises some kind of monopoly on constitutional interpretation. In the U.S. system, all three branches are intimately involved in protecting and defending the Constitution.

EARLY PRECEDENTS. When members of the First Congress assembled, they had a clean slate for interpretation of the Constitution. The Supreme Court was not yet functioning, and it would be many years before the Court explored the constitutional issues that members of Congress had to grapple with in 1789. To the best of their ability, members studied the constitutional text and the intent of the Framers without judicial rulings to guide them. During the Republic's first decade, the scope of confronting Congress that required interpretation of the Constitution was impressive: they included judicial review, the president's power to remove executive officials, federalism, the Bank of the United States, treaties and foreign relations, war-making powers, interstate commerce, slavery, and the power of Congress to investigate executive activities. The reader of the *Annals of Congress* for 1789 finds a constitutional debate by members of Congress that was intense, informed, and diligent.

Throughout its history, Congress has played an integral part in interpreting the meaning of the Constitution.

Independent legislative judgments of the Constitution were needed for two reasons. One was practical: members of Congress had constitutional questions thrown at them that they had to field as best they could. The second reason was constitutional in nature. Members of Congress, under Article VI, clause 3, are constitutionally required to take an oath "to support the Constitution." As later elaborated by statute (5 U.S.C. 3331), members "solemnly swear [to] support and defend the Constitution of the United States against all enemies, foreign and domestic; [to] bear true faith and allegiance to the same; [to] take this obligation freely, without any mental reservation or purpose of evasion; and [to] well and faithfully discharge the duties [of their office]."

Members have a duty to debate constitutional questions when a bill is under consideration or when the president threatens to operate outside constitutional boundaries. Although many members happen to be lawyers, that is irrelevant to this duty, for they all swear or affirm to defend the Constitution "without any mental reservation or purpose of evasion." Because Article I, section 9 mandates that "No Bill of Attainder or ex post facto Law shall be passed," they need to address those issues before a bill passes, not after. The First Amendment commands that Congress "shall make no law" respecting an establishment of religion, prohibiting the free exercise of religion, or abridging the freedom of speech or of the press. Congress is not at liberty to legislate on those subjects blindly, hoping that the president or the judiciary will catch any infringement of the Constitution. As Sen. Slade Gorton (R-Wash.) told his colleagues during debate in 1984: "You swore an oath, as I did, when you became Members of this body to uphold the Constitution of the United States. You cannot hide behind the fact that the Supreme Court of the United States has final authority on constitutional questions. . . . It is your duty to make a judgment as to whether or not this amendment is constitutional."

When Congress in 1789 created the first executive departments—Foreign Affairs, War, and Treasury—it had to decide whether the president had the implied power to remove the heads of those departments. The debates on this issue take up several hundred pages of the *Annals of Congress* and constitute an exceptionally penetrating examination of the doctrine of implied powers. Although some members argued that the Senate should participate with the president in the removal of executive officials, others believed that these officials could be removed only through the constitutional process of impeachment. A third camp argued that since Congress creates an office, it may attach to that office any condition it deems appropriate for tenure and removal. A fourth school insisted that the power of removal belonged exclusively to the president as a function of his executive power.

Should Congress have submitted this constitutional question to the courts for resolution? James Madison, who led the implied powers debate, refused to defer to the judiciary. He strongly rejected the advice of those who said that "it would be officious in this branch of the Legislature to expound the Constitution, so far as it relates to the division of power between the President and the Senate." To Madison it was "incontrovertibly of as much importance to this branch of the Government as to any other, that the Constitution should be preserved entire. It is our duty, so far as it depends upon us, to take care that the powers of the Government be preserved entire to every department of Government." He continued:

> But the great objection drawn from the source to which the last arguments would lead us is, that the Legislature itself has no right to expound the Constitution; that wherever its meaning is doubtful, you must leave it to take its course, until the Judiciary is called upon to declare its meaning. I acknowledge, in the ordinary

> course of Government, that the exposition of the laws and Constitution devolves upon the Judiciary. But I beg to know, upon what principles it can be contended, that any one department draws from the Constitution greater powers than another, in marking out the limits of the powers of the several departments? The Constitution is the charter of the people to the Government; it specifies certain great powers as absolutely granted, and marks out the departments to exercise them. If the Constitutional boundary of either be brought into question, I do not see that any one of these independent departments has more right than another to declare their sentiments on that point.

After extensive debate, Congress agreed that the president had the power to remove the heads of the executive departments. The statutes creating those departments provided that the subordinate officers would have charge and custody of all records whenever the secretary "shall be removed from office by the President of the United States." At the same time, it recognized some constitutional limitations on the president's removal power. When Congress debated the formation of the Treasury Department, Madison noted that the tenure of the comptroller required independence from presidential control because the properties of that office were not "purely of an Executive nature." It seemed to Madison that the comptroller exercised duties partly of "a Judiciary quality" and thus needed protection from presidential removals. That insight by Madison would later apply to other agency officials who exercised adjudicative duties. In particular, it applied to the comptroller general of the United States, created in 1921 as the successor to the comptroller.

In 1792, Congress had to decide by itself whether it possessed the constitutional power to investigate the executive branch. Just as the Constitution has no mention of the president's power of removal, so is it silent on the power of Congress to investigate the executive branch. When the House of Representatives learned that the troops of Maj. Gen. Arthur St. Clair had suffered heavy losses during an Indian attack, it first considered a resolution to request the president to institute an inquiry. The resolution was defeated by a vote of 35 to 21. The House then passed a resolution to empower a committee to inquire into the causes of the military failure and "to call for such persons, papers, and records, as may be necessary to assist their inquiries." According to the account of Thomas Jefferson, who at that time was secretary of State, President George Washington convened the cabinet to consider the extent to which the House could call for papers. The cabinet debated the issue and agreed,

> first, that the House was an inquest, and therefore might institute inquiries. Second, that it might call for papers generally. Third, that the Executive ought to communicate such papers as the public good would permit, and ought to refuse those, the disclosure of which would injure the public: consequently were to exercise a discretion. Fourth, that neither the committee nor House had a right to call on the Head of a Department, who and whose papers were under the President alone; but that the committee should instruct their chairman to move the House to address the President.

The cabinet concluded that there was not a paper "which might not be properly produced." The committee examined papers furnished by the executive branch, including papers and accounts furnished by the Treasury and the War departments, and listened to explanations from the heads of those departments and from other witnesses. St. Clair supplied the committee with written remarks on the expedition. The cabinet's advice that the House could call on the heads of departments only through the president was a formality that has long since been abandoned.

Although Congress exercised its investigative power on numerous occasions after 1792, it was not until *McGrain v. Daugherty* (1927) that the Supreme Court acknowledged the constitutional power of Congress to investigate activities in the executive branch. The Court had no alternative. It could not at that time, or even earlier, deny that such power existed. It could merely give its blessing to a power already recognized as legitimate by Congress and the president.

Congress again established precedents for its attention to constitutional issues in 1796, when President Washington notified the House of Representatives that Jay's Treaty had been ratified. Rep. Edward Livingston of New York offered a resolution requesting the president to transmit to the House a copy of the instructions that had been given to the American minister who had negotiated the treaty, together with correspondence and other related documents. The resolution was later modified to permit the president to withhold any papers that existing negotiations might render improper to disclose. In support of the resolution, Livingston argued that the House possessed "a discretionary power of carrying the Treaty into effect, or refusing it their sanction." In other words, agreement to a treaty by the president and the Senate did not compel the House to furnish funds or enact legislation to implement it. Rep. Albert Gallatin of Pennsylvania argued that this was particularly true when the Constitution gave certain powers, such as the authority to regulate foreign commerce or to establish tariffs, to both houses of Congress.

After weeks of debate, the Livingston resolution passed by a vote of 62 to 37. At that point Washington denied the request for papers and documents, citing the need for caution and discretion in foreign negotiations and maintaining the exclusive role of the Senate in the treaty-making process. (This controversy is wrongly characterized as an example of the president exercising "executive privilege" in withholding documents from Congress. Washington did not withhold papers from the Senate but only from the House.) The House adopted a resolution, sponsored by Rep. Thomas Blount of North Carolina, conceding the House's exclusion from the treaty-making process. But the resolution noted

> that when a Treaty stipulates regulations of any of the subjects submitted by the Constitution to the power of Congress, it must depend, for its execution, as to such stipulations, on a law or laws to be passed by Congress. And it is the Constitutional right and duty of the House of Representatives, in all such cases, to deliberate on the expediency or inexpediency of carrying such Treaty into effect, and to determine and act thereon, as, in their judgment, may be most conducive to the public good.

Over the years, the House has blocked certain treaties that required appropriations, two examples being the Gadsden purchase treaty with Mexico in 1853 and the 1867 treaty with Russia that effected the U.S. purchase of Alaska. It is now commonplace for treaties expressly to recognize that their effectiveness depends on legislative consent by both houses.

CONSTITUTIONAL AMENDMENTS. Whenever two-thirds of both houses of Congress deem it necessary, they may propose amendments to the Constitution. On four occasions Congress has used the amendment process to reverse Supreme Court decisions. The Eleventh Amendment was passed in response to *Chisholm v. Georgia* (1793), in which the Court decided that a state could be sued in federal court by a plaintiff from another state. To protect states from a flood of costly citizen suits, Congress quickly passed a constitutional amendment declaring that "the Judicial power of the United States shall not be construed to extend to any suit in law or equity, commenced or prosecuted against one of the United States by Citizens of another State, or by Citizens or Subjects of any foreign States."

The Civil War amendments—the Thirteenth, Fourteenth, and Fifteenth—nullifed the Court's Dred Scott decision of 1857, which held that Congress could not prohibit slavery in the territories and that blacks as a class were not citizens protected under the Constitution. The Thirteenth Amendment abolished slavery; the Fourteenth Amendment provided that all persons born or naturalized in the United States "are citizens of the United States and of the State wherein they reside"; and the Fifteenth Amendment gave black men the right to vote. Before these amendments were ratified (in 1865, 1868, and 1870), Congress had already passed legislation in 1862 prohibiting slavery in the territories.

The Sixteenth Amendment overruled *Pollock v. Farmers' Loan and Trust Company* (1895), which struck down a federal income tax. In 1909, the Senate debated whether to reenact an income tax and let the Supreme Court reconsider the issue. Other senators cautioned that a confrontation with the Court might lead either to the Court yielding, and thereby losing the confidence of the people, or reaffirming its ruling and creating a breach between the judiciary and the legislature. To avert either outcome, Congress chose to pass a constitutional amendment in 1909, which was ratified in 1913. The Sixteenth Amendment gives Congress the power "to lay and collect taxes on incomes, from whatever source derived, without apportionment among the several States, and without regard to any census or enumeration."

Whenever two-thirds of both houses of Congress deem it necessary, they may propose amendments to the Constitution.

The Twenty-sixth Amendment, ratified in 1971, overturned *Oregon v. Mitchell* (1970), a Supreme Court decision that voided a congressional effort to lower the minimum voting age in state elections to eighteen. The Court held that Congress could fix the voting age for national elections but not for state contests. Within a matter of months the states had ratified the amendment, which reads, "The right of citizens of the United States, who are eighteen years of age or older, to vote shall not be denied or abridged by the United States or any State on account of age."

On a number of other occasions Congress has challenged Court decisions first by passing new legislation and, when that has failed, by attempting to amend the Constitution. A child labor law enacted in 1916, relying on the commerce power of Congress, was declared unconstitutional by the Court in *Hammer v. Dagenhart* (1918). Congress refused to accept that verdict. In 1919 it enacted another child labor statute, this time based on its power to tax. Congress was criticized for trying to evade the Supreme Court by doing indirectly what could not be done directly. Sen. Henry Cabot Lodge (R-Mass.) countered that child labor was such a "great evil" that Congress could legitimately act by whatever means were at its disposal. Nevertheless, the Court struck down the second statute in *Bailey v. Drexel Furniture Company* (1922).

Undaunted, Congress passed a constitutional amendment in 1924 to give it the power to regulate child labor. By 1937, only twenty-eight of the necessary thirty-six states had ratified the amendment. By that time, however, the composition of the Supreme Court had begun to change, and Congress included a child labor provision in the Fair Labor Standards Act of 1938. The issue was taken to the Supreme Court, which in *United States v. Darby* (1941) unanimously upheld the child labor provision.

In general, over the course of the twentieth century Congress increasingly came to question narrow judicial constructions adopted during the century's early decades, and in such contests Congress is likely to prevail. As the Court later admitted in *Prudential Insurance Company v. Benjamin* (1946), "The history of judicial limitation of congressional power over commerce, when exercised affirmatively, has been more largely one of retreat than of ultimate victory." After retiring from the Court in 1945, Justice Owen Roberts explained why the Court chose to back off in the face of congressional efforts to regulate the economy: "Looking back, it is difficult to see how the Court could have resisted the popular urge for uniform standards throughout the country—for what in effect was a unified economy."

STATUTORY ACTION. Interpretation of constitutional text, constitutional amendments, and judicial rulings on constitutional questions are of undeniable importance, but the principal road to constitutional change is statutory action. Congress constantly addresses constitutional issues when it legislates, and the president considers constitutional issues when deciding to sign or veto a bill. A major function of the Supreme Court is statutory construction, and through that function it interacts with other branches of government in a process that refines the meaning of the Constitution.

When judicial decisions are restricted to the meaning of a congressional statute, Congress may overturn the ruling simply by passing a new statute that clarifies legislative intent. This process is called statutory reversal. The private sector often uses Congress as an "appellate court" to reverse judicial interpretations of a statute. Corporations, trade unions, environmental groups, and other organizations come to Congress every year, urging it to pass legislation that will nullify judicial decisions. Although in a technical sense these are statutory and not constitutional interpretations, that distinction is largely meaningless. Many congressional statutes, such as those covering civil rights, pronounce constitutional values of great moment.

For example, a statute concerning the rights of women, enacted shortly after the Civil War, illustrates how the regular legislative process can redefine constitutional rights. In *Bradwell v. State* (1873), the Supreme Court denied that women had a constitutional right under the privileges and immunities clause of the Fourteenth Amendment to practice law. Concurring in that judgment, Justice Joseph P. Bradley reflected traditional judicial doctrines by arguing that the "paramount destiny and mission of women are to fulfil the noble and benign offices of wife and mother. This is the law of the Creator." Elsewhere in his concurrence Bradley gave other reasons, including "the divine ordinance," for excluding women from engaging in professional work. Other judicial opinions by the Supreme Court and state courts were based on similar arguments.

Although women won the right to practice law in some states, a rule adopted by the U.S. Supreme Court prohibited women from arguing there. In 1878, the House of Representatives began debate on a bill to authorize women to practice before the Court. The bill passed the House easily, 169 to 87, but was held up when the Senate Judiciary Committee reported the bill adversely, preferring to leave the question to the discretion of the Court. A year later, the Senate passed the bill by the vote of 39 to 20. It provided that any woman who was a member of the bar of the highest court of any state or territory or of the Supreme Court of the District of Columbia for at least three years, and was a person of good moral character, should be admitted to practice before the U.S. Supreme Court.

Sen. Aaron A. Sargent (R-Calif.) delivered a powerful statement that broke free from judicial stereotypes and drew on principles established by the Declaration of Independence. Calling attention to the progress of women in the medical and legal professions, he said that men had no right to circumscribe the ambitions of women in any way: "The enjoyment of liberty, the pursuit of happiness in her own way, is as much the birthright of woman as of man. In this land man has ceased to dominate over his fellow—let him cease to dominate over his sister; for he has no higher right to do the latter than the former."

During this period, Congress was ahead of the judiciary in many areas of constitutional rights. Congress passed legislation in 1875 to guarantee blacks equal access to public accommodations. The preamble of the statute also reflected the philosophy of the Declaration of Independence, beginning with the phrase, "Whereas, it is essential to just government we recognize the equality of all men before the law." The debate over the bill reveals an eloquent commitment on the part of Congress to provide for basic constitutional rights that would not have been protected by many of the states or by the courts. Much of the 1875 statute was declared unconstitutional by the Supreme Court in the *Civil Rights Cases* (1883).

The constitutional rights of African Americans remained in a constitutional backwater for decades, until the Supreme Court in the 1930s and 1940s began to invalidate many state laws that segregated blacks from whites, especially in universities and law schools. These decisions culminated in *Brown v. Board of Education* (1954), which represented a giant step forward in the establishment of civil rights for blacks. In important ways, it aroused the public conscience and articulated fundamental constitutional values. By itself, however, the decision did little to integrate public schools. As late as 1964, the Court complained in its decisions that there had been too much deliberation and not enough speed in enforcing *Brown*.

What finally turned the tide was a series of congressional enactments, including the Civil Rights Act of 1964, the Voting Rights Act of 1965, and the Fair Housing Act of 1968. The struggle against racial discrimination required a bipartisan consensus within Congress and the strong leadership of President Lyndon B. Johnson. In upholding these statutes, the Court recognized that much of constitutional law depends on fact-finding, which is a particular strength of Congress. The Court adopted a broad interpretation of the power of Congress "to enforce, by appropriate legislation," the provisions of the Fourteenth Amendment.

For example, section 4(e) of the Voting Rights Act of 1965 prohibited New York's literacy requirement as a precondition for voting. Congress provided that no person who had completed the sixth grade in Puerto Rico could be denied the right to vote in any election because of an inability to read or write in English. Upholding that law in *Katzenbach v. Morgan* (1966), the Court noted that fact-finding was a legislative, not a judicial, responsibility.

> It was for Congress, as the branch that made this judgment, to assess and weigh the various conflicting considerations—the risk of pervasiveness of the discrimination in governmental services, the effectiveness of eliminating the state restriction on the right to vote as a means of dealing with the evil, the adequacy or availability of alternative remedies, and the nature and significance of the state interests that would be affected by the nullification of the English literacy requirement as applied to residents who have successfully completed the sixth grade in a Puerto Rican school. It is not for us to review the congressional resolution of these factors. It is enough that we be able to perceive a basis upon which the Congress might resolve the conflict as it did.

The Civil Rights Act of 1964 included a title that gave African Americans equal access to public accommodations, reopening an issue that had lain dormant since the *Civil Rights Cases* of 1883. That decision, in fact, had never been overturned and raised the danger of a confrontation between the Court and Congress. The framers of the Civil Rights Act of 1964 saw a way to defuse the issue, and in so doing to give the Court a graceful retreat. They offered two constitutional arguments in support of equal access: the Fourteenth Amendment (at issue in the *Civil Rights Cases*) and the commerce clause. In *Heart of Atlanta Motel v. United States* (1964), the Court held that Congress had "ample power" under the commerce clause to enact the equal access provision. On this fundamental issue of giving blacks equal access to public accommodations, the guardians of minority rights and constitutional liberties were Congress and the president, not the courts. Once again, as for nearly a century, congressional persistence and ingenuity triumphed over judicial obstacles. Interestingly, majoritarian branches driven by majoritarian pressures took the lead in defending the constitutional rights of minorities, who are supposed to look to the courts for protection.

The power of Congress under the commerce clause was also at issue in a legislative-judicial conflict over federal minimum-wage legislation in the 1970s. In *National League of Cities v. Usery* (1976), the Supreme Court struck down a congressional statute that extended federal wage and hour provisions to almost all state employees. Although Congress had justified the legislation under the commerce clause, the Court held in a vote of 5 to 4 that the statute threatened the independent existence of the states. The fifth vote was supplied by Justice Harry Blackmun, who admitted, however, that he was "not untroubled by certain possible implications of the Court's opinion." If he decided in later years to swing to the other side, the Court's ruling could be easily overturned.

Justice Blackmun had the opportunity to do precisely that in a case involving local mass transit systems, which the Department of Labor considered a "nontraditional" state function and therefore within the reach of federal legislation. The San Antonio Metropolitan Transit Authority (SAMTA) challenged the department's interpretation, while several SAMTA employees brought suit against SAMTA for overtime pay under the Fair Labor Standards Act. During oral argument, the Justice Department conceded that mass transit was not a traditional function and was therefore subject to the commerce power of Congress.

In *Garcia v. San Antonio Metropolitan Transit Authority* (1985), Justice Blackmun abandoned the majority of 1976 and voted to overturn the *National League* decision, which he now regarded as having proved itself too impractical and abstract to apply in the lower courts. He also emphasized that the essential safeguard for federalism was not the judiciary but rather the political dynamics that operate within Congress: "[T]he principal and basic limit on the federal commerce power is that inherent in all congressional action—the built-in restraints that our system provides through state participation in federal governmental action. The political process ensures that laws that unduly burden the States will not be promulgated."

In the 1980s and 1990s, several cases have illustrated the constant interaction between Congress and the courts in defining and recognizing constitutional rights. In *Grove City College v. Bell* (1984), the Supreme Court interpreted the meaning of Title IX of the Education Amendments of 1972, which prohibits sex discrimination in any education program or activity that receives federal funds. The specific issue before the Court was whether the statute required federal funds to be terminated only for specific programs—or for the entire educational institution—in which discrimination was found to exist. The Court decided that the narrower interpretation should apply. Within four months, the House of Representatives, voting 375 to 32, passed legislation to overturn the decision. Action on the Senate side was delayed for several years because of disputes over the extent to which the issue involved abortion and the separation of church and state. In 1988, however, Congress passed legislation to reverse the *Grove City* decision. President Ronald Reagan vetoed the bill, but both houses overrode him, reasserting Congress's commerce power and its application to sex discrimination.

Another face-off between Congress and the Supreme Court, this time involving religious freedom, occurred in 1986 when the Court, in *Goldman v. Weinberger,* upheld a U.S. Air Force regulation that prohibited an officer from wearing a yarmulke indoors while on duty. The officer, an Orthodox Jew and an ordained rabbi, had worn a yarmulke for years without incident, until he appeared at a military trial and testified against the U.S. Air Force. When the case appeared before the Supreme Court, the Court ruled by a vote of 5 to 4 that the air force regulation was justified because the military services required discipline, unity, and order. In a dissenting opinion, Justice William J. Brennan rebuked the Court for abdicating "its role as primary expositor of the Constitution and protector of individual liberties [and lending its support to] credulous deference to unsupported assertions of military necessity." Later in his dissent he acknowledged that other institutions of government, including Congress, are available to protect individual liberties.

Congress mobilized its forces to overturn the Court's decision. Each year Congress passes an authorization bill for the Defense Department. Just one year after the *Goldman* decision Congress attached an amendment to this bill to require the air force to change its regulation. Congress now permitted military personnel to wear conservative, unobtrusive religious apparel indoors, provided that the apparel does not interfere with their military duties. Thus basic rights unavailable from the courts were successfully secured by congressional action.

On the fundamental issue of giving blacks equal access to public accommodations, the guardians of minority rights and constitutional liberties were Congress and the president.

In another dialogue between Congress and the Court, Congress passed the Civil Rights Act of 1991, overturning or modifying nine Supreme Court decisions. The ruling that provoked legislative action was *Wards Cove Packing Company v. Atonio* (1989), which shifted the burden to employees to prove that racial disparities resulted from employment practices and were not justified by business needs. Earlier judicial doctrines, dating back to 1971, appeared to require an employee to demonstrate only disparate results, not intent.

To overturn this decision and several others that gave a narrow interpretation of constitutional civil rights, Congress passed legislation in 1990. President George Bush vetoed the bill, claiming that it would require employers to institute quotas for racial minorities to avoid expensive and time-consuming litigation. In 1991, Congress again pushed for the legislation, this time with what appeared to be sufficient votes for both houses to override a Bush veto. With only minor changes in the bill's language, and with the knowledge that his override-free record was in jeopardy, Bush signed the bill. Congressional initiatives once again were effective in securing the rights of members of racial minorities and of women.

The sometimes tenuous relationship between judicial decisions and congressional practices is borne out by the history of the legislative veto. In the prominent case of *Immigration and Naturalization Service v. Chadha* (1983), the Supreme Court held that legislative vetoes are an invalid form of congressional control over the executive branch. Not only did the Court strike down one-house vetoes (for violating the principle of bicameralism), it also ruled legislative vetoes unconstitutional because they are not presented to the president for his signature or veto. The broad principles announced by the Court nullified all existing legislative vetoes, which covered such diverse areas as executive reorganization, rule making, impoundment, foreign trade, and national emergencies. In his dissent, Justice Byron White claimed that the Court in "one fell swoop" struck down provisions in more laws enacted by Congress than the Court had cumulatively invalidated in its entire history.

Nevertheless, from the moment of the *Chadha* decision, on 23 June 1983 to the end of the 103d Congress in 1995, Congress continued to rely on the legislative veto to control agency actions. Over that period of time, Congress created more than two hundred *new* legislative vetoes, and Presidents Reagan and Bush signed them into law. Instead of acting through the full legislative process required by *Chadha* (action by both houses and the presentment of a bill to the president), these new statutes enable Congress to rely on controls short of passing a public law. The usual method is to require committee or subcommittee approval of agency proposals. This practice continued under President Bill Clinton.

This record may appear to be one of congressional contempt for a judicial decision, but the institutional dynamics are more complex than that. A better explanation is that the Court reached too far and failed to understand the practical needs that led Congress and the executive branch to adopt the legislative veto in the first place. Those needs existed before the *Chadha* decision and persist after it.

Following the Court's ruling, Congress amended a number of statutes by deleting legislative vetoes and replacing them with joint resolutions (which must pass both houses and be presented to the president). The statutes that were changed to comply with *Chadha* include the District of Columbia Home Rule Act as well as laws dealing with executive reorganization, national emergencies, export administration, and federal pay. But Congress also added language to statutes requiring the executive branch to obtain the approval of specified committees. Congress no longer attempted to use one-house or two-house resolutions to control agency actions. The effect of *Chadha* was thus to drive legislative vetoes underground, operating at the committee and subcommittee level.

Executive agencies accepted this committee oversight because they understood the risks of challenging Congress on the constitutionality of legislative vetoes. Pushed on this question, Congress was willing to repeal the committee vetoes and, at the same time, repeal discretionary authority it had granted to the agencies over the years. Instead of agency officials having to obtain the approval of designated committees for these discretionary actions, they would have to approach Congress and seek what the Court in *Chadha* demanded: action by both houses on a bill that is presented to the president. The committee veto represents a much less taxing procedure.

This accommodation between congressional committees and executive agencies is unlikely to be challenged in the courts. It is difficult to imagine who would have the standing necessary to bring suit. Plaintiffs would have an uphill battle in convincing the judiciary that the committee veto constituted an injury to them. Judges, sensing that lawsuits of this sort would be more on the order of academic or abstract exercises, would refuse to hear them. Courts now have a more sophisticated understanding of the complexities and varieties of executive-legislative relations and the practical limits of judicial directives.

CONSTITUTIONAL DIALOGUES. It is simplistic to believe that the judiciary is peculiarly equipped to protect individual and minority rights. That thesis was advanced in 1937, at the time of President Franklin D. Roosevelt's effort to pack the Supreme Court with six additional justices. Opponents condemned his plan as a threat to the independence of the judiciary, which was widely described as the guardian of individual rights. Roosevelt's proposal was soundly rejected, but Henry W. Edgerton, who later became a federal appellate judge, wrote an article at that time that examined the proposition that judicial supremacy is necessary to restrain Congress from infringing on personal liberty. Edgerton studied the Court's record and found little evidence to show that the judiciary was especially sensitive to individual and minority rights. With few exceptions, from 1789 to the time of Edgerton's study, the Supreme Court consistently favored governmental power over individual rights, lent support to harmful business practices, deprived African Americans of protection, upheld business interests over labor interests, and defended private wealth against taxation. For most of that period, individual rights were more likely to be protected by Congress and the president.

The interests of constitutional law and the political process are best served when members of Congress form independent judgments about constitutional issues. Most of these issues are comprehensible to members, whether or not they have legal training. Constitutional issues often turn not so much on technical legal points but on a balancing of competing political and social interests. Collisions occur between congressional regulation and federalism, states' rights and civil rights, government regulation and individual privacy, a free press and the right to a fair trial, congressional investigation and executive privilege, and other questions of constitutional priorities. Congress has adequate resources to analyze those issues. Although members should form their judgments with an awareness of what courts have decided, there is no need to follow those rulings in mechanical fashion. Legislators should not behave like district judges. That congressional interpretations or understandings of the Constitution differ from those of the Supreme Court is hardly reason for concluding that Congress ignores the Constitution—a charge that imputes bad faith.

The interests of constitutional law and the political process are best served when members of Congress form independent judgments about congressional issues.

Even after courts hand down a decision, there are opportunities for Congress to test the soundness of the decision by passing new legislation and supporting further litigation. The Supreme Court often makes room for congressional involvement by deciding an issue on statutory, not constitutional, grounds. This strategy invites Congress to reenter the arena and modify judicial decrees.

No single institution, including the judiciary, has the final word on constitutional questions. All citizens have a responsibility to review what judges decide. It is not true, as Justice Robert H. Jackson once remarked, that justices of the Supreme Court "are not final because we are infallible, but we are infallible only because we are final." The Court is neither final nor infallible. Judicial decisions rest undisturbed only to the extent that Congress, the president, and the general public find the rulings convincing, reasonable, and acceptable.

The courts therefore find themselves engaged in what Alexander Bickel once called a "continuing colloquy" with political institutions and with society at large, a process in which constitutional principle is "evolved conversationally, not perfected unilaterally." This process of give and take and mutual respect permits judges—who are appointed, not elected—to function and survive in a democratic society. The rough-and-tumble character of political debate lacks some of the amenities and dignity of the judicial process, but legislative products are not for that reason inferior to court rulings. The historical record provides convincing evidence that the collective wisdom of Congress, working in concert with the president and the executive branch, is often superior to judicial decisions.

Each decision by a court is subject to scrutiny and rejection by private citizens and public officials. What is final at one stage of judicial proceedings may be reopened by Congress at a later date, leading to revisions, fresh interpretation, and reversals of Supreme Court decisions. Members of Congress have both the authority and the capacity to participate constructively in constitutional interpretation. Their duty to support and defend the Constitution is not erased or nullified by doubts about personal or institutional competence. Much of constitutional law depends on fact-finding and the balancing of competing values, areas in which Congress justifiably can claim substantial expertise.

[See also (III) The Supreme Court of the United States.]

BIBLIOGRAPHY

Agresto, John. *The Supreme Court and Constitutional Democracy.* 1984.

Andrews, William G., ed. *Coordinate Magistrates: Constitutional Law by Congress and the President.* 1969.

Brest, Paul. "The Conscientious Legislator's Guide to Constitutional Interpretation." *Stanford Law Review* 27 (1975): 585–601.

Cox, Archibald. "The Role of Congress in Constitutional Determinations." *University of Cincinnati Law Review* 40 (1971): 199–261.

Fisher, Louis. *American Constitutional Law.* 2d ed. 1995.

Fisher, Louis. "Constitutional Interpretation by Members of Congress." *North Carolina Law Review* 63 (1985): 707–747.

Fisher, Louis. "The Curious Belief in Judicial Supremacy." *Suffolk University Law Review* 25 (1991): 85–116.

Mikva, Abner J. "How Well Does Congress Support and Defend the Constitution?" *North Carolina Law Review* 61 (1983): 587–611.

Morgan, Donald G. *Congress and the Constitution.* 1966.

Murphy, Walter F. "Who Shall Interpret: The Quest for the Ultimate Constitutional Interpreter." *Review of Politics* 48 (1986): 401–423.

Pritchett, C. Herman. *Congress versus the Supreme Court.* 1961.

Schmidhauser, John R., and Larry L. Berg. *The Supreme Court and Congress.* 1972.

Stumpf, Harry P. "Congressional Response to Supreme Court Rulings: The Interaction of Law and Politics." *Journal of Public Law* 14 (1965): 377–395.

– LOUIS FISHER

CONTEMPT OF CONGRESS

Contempt of Congress is an act of disrespect or disobedience to an official congressional body. Holding a party in contempt of Congress was once deemed an inherent and summary power, but since 1857 the offense has been defined by statute (11 Stat. 155), now in 2 U.S. Code (1958). Typical acts punished as contempt of Congress are refusing to testify or to submit documents ordered by a committee, or misbehavior before a legislative body.

Historically, the congressional contempt power derives from the judicial contempt of court power. The reason is that American law is rooted in English common law, under which Parliament originally was deemed to be exercising quasi-judicial functions as well as legislative powers. The king could do no wrong under English common law, and courts and Parliament were administrators of the king's will. Nowadays, the House of Lords exercises these quasi-judicial powers, while Commons carries out the purely legislative role.

The rationale for a contempt power is necessity as well as custom. The reasoning is that without such a power a legislative body could not function; there would be no way to deter disrespect or to encourage cooperation. So essential has it seemed that it has been deemed an inherent power of any legislature by scholars, historians, and judges.

The American colonies adopted many common-law procedures, and contempt of the legislature was one. State assemblies early exercised the contempt power to compel testimony and to protect their dignity. The federal Constitution is silent on the subject of congressional contempt; according to some commentators, it was deemed axiomatic that the power was inherent and thus did not need to be explicitly listed.

In any event, Congress always believed it had a contempt power, whatever its source and legal basis. As early as 1795 a House committee summarily imprisoned a nonmember for contempt. During the next fifty years the House and Senate did so regularly. The power of Congress to summarily punish contempt was first adjudicated and upheld in 1821 in *Anderson v. Dunn* (19 U.S. [6 Wheat] 204), though the power was later questioned in a landmark case, *Kilbourn v. Thompson* (103 U.S. 168 [1880]).

To clarify the confusion caused by reliance on dated English common law and conflicting American cases concerning the summary contempt power, Congress passed a law in 1857 authorizing punishment for contempt of Congress, but only after indictment and trial. Presently, when a congressional committee decides it has been offended by contempt, the Speaker of the House or the president of the Senate must certify this contempt to the attorney general, who then proceeds to prosecute the case as he would any other criminal offense.

In the mid-twentieth century the congressional contempt statute has been used frequently, often in contentious cases. Congressional committees have actively investigated crime, subversion, and security cases, for example, and they have resorted to contempt proceedings as a means of retribution. So the nature of the use of the congressional contempt power has evolved, as have its source and its procedural implementation. In the ninety-two years between 1857 and 1949, 113 witnesses were cited for contempt of Congress, while from 1950 to 1952, 117 witnesses were cited.

Has Congress been more active, or have witnesses become more obstinate? Between 1789 and 1925 Congress authorized 285 investigations, while between 1950 and 1952 it authorized 225. It is interesting to consider how the courts have disposed of congressional contempt cases. In the District of Columbia, where most contempt of Congress cases arise, between 1950 and 1959 there were 83 indictments for contempt of Congress, while grand juries refused to indict in 17 proposed cases. Of those indicted, 30 defendants were convicted and 47 were acquitted. Of the 30 convictions, 15 were reversed on appeal.

In the late twentieth century, resort to the congressional contempt power has decreased. The wrong itself has come to be regarded as an ordinary criminal offense to be treated no differently from other offenses.

[See also (I) Investigations, Witnesses, Rights of; (II) Investigations, Congressional.]

BIBLIOGRAPHY

Aiyar, Krishna Jagavisa. *The Law of Contempt of Court, Parliament and Public Servants.* 1949.

Beck, Carl. *Contempt of Congress: A Study of the Prosecutions Initiated by the Committee on Un-American Activities, 1945–1947.* 1959.

Galloway, George Barnes. *Congress and Parliament: Their Organization and Operation in the U.S. and the U.K.* 1955.

Goldfarb, Ronald L. *The Contempt of Power.* 1971.

– RONALD GOLDFARB

CONTINUING RESOLUTION

Congress normally funds federal agencies for a fiscal year by annual enactment of thirteen general appropriation bills. If Congress fails to complete action on one or more of these bills before the start of a fiscal year, it enacts a joint resolution specifying that appropriations continue at some specified rate.

First enacted in 1876, continuing resolutions were intended to provide the funding necessary for the orderly continuation of government between the expiration of one fiscal year's appropriations and the delayed enactment of new appropriations. These measures are usually of a specific, limited duration and restrict funding to a specified rate of operations—usually the previous year's rate, the rate set by either the House or Senate version of the pertinent regular appropriation act for the upcoming fiscal year, or possibly the lowest of these alternatives. Congress is criticized, both inside and outside of its ranks, for also using continuing resolutions as a means of enacting one or more regular annual appropriations measures by specifying new levels and new objects of expenditure and extending their availability for the entire fiscal year.

The House treats continuing resolutions as a class apart from general appropriations and thus allows different procedural rules to govern their consideration. (For example, the prohibitions in Rule XXI against unauthorized appropriations and legislation in general appropriation bills do not apply.) Although the rules of the Senate do not make this distinction, their greater flexibility in general reduces the need for such.

BIBLIOGRAPHY

Keith, Robert A. *An Overview of the Use of Continuing Appropriations.* Congressional Research Service, Library of Congress. CRS Rept. 1980.

U.S. Congress. General Accounting Office. *Principles of Federal Appropriations Law.* GAO Doc. OGC-92-13. 2d ed. 1992. Vol. 2, chap. 8, "Continuing Resolutions."

U.S. House of Representatives. *Deschler's Precedents of the United States House of Representatives,* by Lewis Deschler. 94th Cong., 2d sess., 1977. H. Doc. 94-661. Vol. 7, chap. 25.

– JAMES V. SATURNO

D

DELEGATES, NONVOTING

Nonvoting delegates to Congress were authorized by the Continental Congress in the Ordinance of 1784. The ordinance provided for the political organization of territories outside of the original thirteen states and authorized these territories, once a territorial government had been established, to "keep a member in Congress, with a right of debating, but not of voting." The 1784 measure was restated in the Northwest Ordinance of 1787, which recognized the status of territorial legislatures in the Northwest Territory to "elect a delegate to Congress, who shall have a seat in Congress, with a right of debating but not of voting." In 1789, one of the earliest acts of the First Congress under the Constitution was to reenact the provisions of the Northwest Ordinance. The position of territorial delegate has been recognized continuously since then.

Nonvoting delegates to Congress were authorized by the Continental Congress in the Ordinance of 1784.

Initially, organized territories were clearly on the road to ultimate admission to statehood, but with the United States' acquisition of noncontiguous overseas territories (Hawaii, Puerto Rico, and the Philippines) in the 1890s, and other territories (e.g., the U.S. Virgin Islands and Guam) at later dates, territories came to be distinguished as either "incorporated" or "unincorporated"; the former were clearly likely to become states and the latter had a less clearly determined status. Congress created the post of resident commissioner for these indeterminate-status territories; the Philippines (until 1946) and Puerto Rico were granted representation status through commissioners whose formal duties were identical to those of delegates with the exception that commissioners were chosen for four-year terms while delegates served two-year terms.

House historical records are unclear, but it appears that delegates were permitted to vote in the House committees to which they were assigned at least until the 1840s. Thereafter, the practice evidently ended (a proposal was offered in 1884 to allow delegates committee-voting rights, but it was not acted on). At the time of that proposal, delegates and resident commissioners were assigned only to committees concerned with territorial affairs and not panels with broader jurisdictions. Delegates never accrued seniority on the committees and were not counted in determining the party ratios on panels.

During consideration of the Legislative Reorganization Act of 1970, the House agreed by voice vote to an amendment by Resident Commissioner Jorge Cordova of Puerto Rico to elect the commissioner (then, the only House delegate) to standing committees in the same manner as other members and "to possess in such committees the same powers and privileges as the other Members." Through this language, delegates were permitted to accrue seniority, to chair committees and subcommittees, to serve on conference committees, and to vote in committee.

Later that year, the House authorized the post of delegate from the District of Columbia. In 1972 delegates from Guam and the Virgin Islands were authorized in law, and a delegate from American Samoa was authorized in 1980. The resident commissioner from Puerto Rico is still elected for a four-year term, while the other delegates are chosen for two-year terms. Each receives the same salary, staffing allowance, and other benefits as members of the House. Since 1980, proposals have been offered to authorize nonvoting delegates to represent American Indians and Americans residing abroad, but these proposals have not been acted upon.

In 1993, the House changed its rules to allow delegates to vote on issues (primarily amendments to bills) considered in the Committee of the Whole. Complex procedures were adopted to ensure that delegate votes would not affect the ultimate outcome of Committee of the Whole votes. House Republicans charged that the new rules were unconstitutional, but the U.S. District Court and the U.S. Court of Appeals for the Washington, D.C. circuit denied the lawsuit.

[See also (I) Shadow Senators.]

BIBLIOGRAPHY

Berkhofer, Robert F. "Jefferson, the Ordinance of 1784, and the Origins of the American Territorial System." *William and Mary Quarterly* 29 (April 1972): 231–262.

Harlow, Ralph V. *History of Legislative Methods before 1824.* 1917.

U.S. House of Representatives. *Cannon's Precedents of the House of Representatives of the United States,* by Clarence Cannon. 74th Cong., 1st sess., 1935. Vol. 6, ch. 73.

U.S. House of Representatives. *Constitution, Jefferson's Manual, and Rules of the House of Representatives, 103d Congress.* Compiled by William Holmes Brown. 102d Cong., 2d sess., 1992. H. Doc. 102–405.

U.S. House of Representatives. *Hinds' Precedents of the House of Representatives of the United States,* by Asher C. Hinds. 59th Cong., 2d. sess., 1907. Vol 2, chap. 43.

– PAUL S. RUNDQUIST

DELEGATION OF POWERS

Following the political philosophy of John Locke, as exemplified by the U.S. constitutional system of separate powers, it is thought that a power originally given cannot be delegated away. This nondelegation doctrine would appear to limit Congress's authority to transfer power to another branch of government. In reality, however, Congress has been forced to delegate to accomplish the breadth of its policy-making tasks, so that "the exertion of legislative power does not become a futility."

Historically, the Supreme Court has given a variety of interpretations to the delegation doctrine. The Court first approved congressional delegation to the executive in *The Brig Aurora v. United States* (1813). Then, in 1935, the Court invalidated legislative delegation in two domestic cases involving the National Industrial Recovery Act (NIRA): *Panama Refining Co. v. Ryan* and *Schechter Poultry Corp. v. United States.* Delegating to the president the right to take statutory action under NIRA to alter prices, production, and competition, the Court ruled that the transfer of power was too broad a delegation of independent authority. It would leave the executive branch virtually "unfettered" in its authority to regulate trade and industry.

Only one year after the *Panama* and *Schechter* cases, the Court sustained a congressional delegation of authority to the executive branch in the area of foreign affairs. In *United States v. Curtiss-Wright Corp.* (1936), Congress had given the president permission to ban the sale of arms to two South American countries involved in armed conflict. More than half a century later, during the 1987 Iran-contra hearings, several individuals testified that actions taken under the Reagan administration in the area of foreign affairs could be traced to the delegation of power articulated and upheld in *Curtiss-Wright.* The Iran-contra committee (the House Select Committee to Investigate Covert Arms Transactions with Iran), however, rejected such a "blanket endorsement of plenary presidential power" in the area of a delegated foreign policy. Although the *Curtiss-Wright* decision was not used to justify action in the Iran-contra controversy, the decision did represent the Court's firm commitment to validating legislative delegation in the majority of its future cases.

Congress has continued to use its power to delegate to administrative agencies the authority to implement certain public policies. For example, in *Skinner v. Mid-American Pipelines* (1989), Congress delegated to the Department of Transportation the right to establish fees for pipeline users, and in *Mistretta v. United States* (1989), the Supreme Court upheld legislative delegation to the U.S. Sentencing Commission of the responsibility to formulate guidelines for federal judges in establishing sentences for federal offenses. Although delegation of legislative authority remains a significant part of the U.S. constitutional system, compelling questions remain. For example, what are the limits of delegated authority? How does Congress monitor the power it delegates and, finally, how are administrative agencies held accountable for the authority they are delegated? These will remain important concerns for the Supreme Court as it continues to interpret the delegation doctrine.

[See also (II) The Supreme Court of the United States.]

BIBLIOGRAPHY

Corwin, Edward, and Jack Peltason. *Understanding the Constitution.* 1991.

Rossum, Ralph, and Alan Tarr. *American Constitutional Law.* 1991.

– JANIS JUDSON

DILATORY MOTIONS

Dilatory motions are proposed by representatives and senators solely or primarily to delay legislative action, not to achieve a constructive policy or procedural effect.

Dilatory motions are proposed by representatives and senators solely or primarily to delay legislative action.

Clause 10 of House Rule XVI directs that "[n]o dilatory motion shall be entertained by the Speaker." The House first adopted this rule in 1890 to codify the principle that members should not be able to make motions that are intended only to prevent the House from working its will. This principle is especially important in the House because the general theory underlying its procedures is that a majority of its members should be able to control their legislative agenda and the amount of time they devote to debating each matter they consider.

The Senate has no comparable rule. Since the late 1970s, however, the Senate has established several precedents that permit the presiding officer to rule amendments, motions, and other actions out of order as being dilatory after cloture has been invoked on a matter. The rationale for these precedents is that dilatory actions are incompatible with the purpose of cloture, which is to enable the Senate to vote on a matter by limiting further consideration of it while still giving senators ample opportunities to debate seriously and to amend it.

There are no fixed criteria for determining when a proposed action is dilatory. The decision necessarily involves a subjective judgment. The Speaker and the Senate's presiding officer rule actions to be dilatory only under what they consider to be extreme and obvious circumstances.

[See also (I) Cloture.]

BIBLIOGRAPHY

U.S. House of Representatives. *Deschler's Precedents of the United States House of Representatives,* by Lewis Deschler. 94th Cong., 2d sess., 1977. H. Doc. 94-661. Vol. 7, pp. 77–84.

– STANLEY BACH

DISCHARGE RULES

Especially in the House, congressional committees play a gatekeeping role, because introduced measures are normally referred to committee and cannot receive floor consideration unless reported. Discharge circumvents this obstacle by taking an unreported measure from the committee charged with it.

The Senate has no explicit discharge rule, but permits a discharge motion. Senators seldom move discharge on a measure, because they can more readily place an identical measure directly on the calendar or offer its text as a nongermane amendment. Discharge occasionally occurs on nominations, where those alternatives are unavailable because only the president can initiate nominations.

The House discharge rule originated from the 1910 revolt against Speaker Joseph G. Cannon's total control of floor action. Though amended several times before 1931, this rule remained vulnerable to dilatory tactics, so that the leadership was able to prevent any measure passing the House by discharge, notably in a session-long blockage of railway labor arbitration (1924–1925). Since 1931, a more effective rule framed by Charles R. Crisp (D-Ga.; former House parliamentarian) has been in effect.

House Rule XXVII, clause 3 today permits a discharge petition to be filed at the clerk's desk on any measure (except a private bill) that a committee has held for thirty legislative days. If half the House membership (218) then signs this petition, the motion is "entered" on a special discharge calendar. On any second or fourth Monday falling at least seven legislative days later, any signer may move discharge. After twenty minutes debate, a majority vote may adopt the motion. The measure then goes to the appropriate calendar unless a nondebatable motion to consider is then offered and agreed to. If this happens, the measure comes up under the general rules of the House (i.e., money bills in Committee of the Whole; others under the one-hour rule). If the discharge motion is rejected, no further discharge action on the same subject can be taken during that session of Congress.

The rule also permits a second method of discharge, designed as the principal one, in which the petition is filed not on the measure itself, but on a special rule for considering it. If supporters of an unreported measure introduce such a rule, and the Rules Committee does not report it within seven legislative days, the supporters may file a petition to discharge that committee. If discharge succeeds and the rule is adopted, the underlying measure comes to the floor under the terms of the special rule rather than the general rules. (Until 1991, a special rule coming up by discharge was neither debatable nor amendable.)

The Rules Committee under conservative coalition control (ca. 1937–1960) often declined to report special rules for considering reported measures, especially New Deal and racial equality legislation. The House often attempted to discharge the committee from special rules on these reported measures. Discharge attempts for special rules on unreported measures were largely forgotten until the 1960s. The Rules Committee then began to supersede such attempts by reporting alternative special rules that set the Committee's own terms for considering the measure. By the 1990s, some discharge proponents succeeded in forestalling this response and securing adoption of their own special rules.

Only by discharge can the House consider a measure without cooperation from either the committee of jurisdiction, the Speaker, or the Rules Committee. Yet success by this procedure is difficult. The signature requirement exceeds the majority normally needed for passage. Proponents must hold their majority through several complicated stages. Committee and floor leaders generally oppose discharge as infringing their prerogatives and disruptive, and have several opportunities to recover control of the floor.

Consequently, of 447 petitions filed from 1935 to 1992, only thirty-three were entered, and only two measures became law through use of the rule. Yet discharge may be more successful as a threat. Over the same years, discharge was attempted on twenty-six measures that then came up through other procedures. Of these, twenty-two passed the House and fifteen received final approval.

From 1931 through 1934, only one-third of the House had to sign a discharge petition. Petitions were filed on forty-three measures and entered on eleven (including the veterans' bonus and repeal of prohibition), but only two passed the House. The change to a higher requirement reflected leadership desires to keep from the floor measures that could not pass. Since 1970, discharge has been attempted disproportionately on proposed constitutional amendments (e.g., school busing, school prayer, balanced budget), which require greater support to pass than to discharge.

Discharge petition signatures used to be considered confidential until the full required number signed, with the intent of protecting members from pressure to sign. Nevertheless, signatures to at least five petitions were revealed without authorization, notably on the 1960 civil rights bill. In the 1980s the argument gained strength that abolishing confidentiality would foster accountability, and in 1993, discharge was attempted on a resolution for this purpose. After signatures to this petition were disclosed, the required number were obtained, and the House adopted the rules change.

BIBLIOGRAPHY

U.S. House of Representatives. *Cannon's Precedents of the House of Representatives of the United States,* by Clarence Cannon. 74th Cong., 1st sess., 1935. Vol. 7, secs. 1007–1023.

U.S. House of Representatives. Committee on Rules. Subcommittee on Rules of the House. *Discharge Petition Disclosure.* 103d Cong., 1st sess., 1993. Hearing.

U.S. House of Representatives. *Deschler's Precedents of the United States House of Representatives.* 94th Cong., 2d sess., 1977. H. Doc. 94-661. Vol. 5, chap. 18.

– RICHARD S. BETH

DISTRICTS

A congressional district is a legally defined and delimited geographic area in which all qualified voters have the right to select a representative to the U.S. House of Representatives. From the First Congress to the present, the vast majority of representatives elected to the House have been selected by single-member, geographically defined districts. Over congressional history, however, several other methods have also been used to select representatives.

The first in a series of laws requiring the district method of election appeared in the Apportionment Act of 1842, which stated that for the extent of the law (ten years) members of the House were to be "elected by districts composed of contiguous territory equal in number to the representatives to which said state may be entitled" (5 Stat. 491). Although alternative methods of election were used before and after this statute, the act began the legal precedent that codified the single-member, geographically defined congressional district as part of the American political system. The most recent law (as of 1992) mandating House elections by district was passed on 14 December 1967 (81 Stat. 581). This statute, as well as court rulings in the 1960s against malapportionment, mandates that all states having two or more representatives must divide into districts of somewhat equal population after each decennial reapportionment. After the apportionment of the 1990 census, six states were assigned one representative apiece and the remaining 429 members of the House were elected from states that were subdivided into districts.

A congressional district is a legally defined and delimited geographic area in which all qualified voters have the right to select a representative to the U.S. House of Representatives.

ORIGIN OF POLITICAL REPRESENTATION BY GEOGRAPHIC AREA. The origin of political representation by geographic area can be traced back through Western civilization, the British heritage of the American political system, and the American colonial experience. Ancient tribal councils, royal tribunals, Greek and Roman assemblies, and councils of the Middle Ages are in a sense the precursors of modern democratic legislatures. The medieval assemblies of Europe represented class and corporate interests and were, of course, dominated by an absolute ruler. During the Middle Ages, membership in these assemblies also gradually began to be drawn from towns or other settled areas—the genesis of the idea of representation by place rather than by rank, status, or class.

In medieval England, representation on the king's assembly was generally divided between nobility, clergy, and townsmen. Parliamentary representation by geographic area evolved with the gradual emergence of constitutional government. Eventually, a bicameral parliament emerged, with the House of Lords representing class interests and the House of Commons representing the various towns, boroughs, and counties from which its members were selected. The American tradition of colonial legislative assemblies whose members were elected by geographic area undoubtedly derives from this British heritage. The House of Burgesses, the first American colonial legislature, convened in Jamestown, Virginia in 1619. As Virginia expanded the burgesses were selected by and represented the various plantations and towns of the European-settled portion of Virginia. As other North American colonies were established by England, they also instituted assemblies that followed the British and Virginian traditions of representation by geographical area.

During the latter colonial period, the assemblies were often arenas for debate over economic and political freedom, and their existence became a point of contention between leading citizens and the royal appointed governor. After the Revolution, the Constitutional Convention of 1787 grappled with the meaning of democracy and how the concerns of the people should be represented through elected assemblies. The Connecticut Compromise established a bicameral national legislature composed of the Senate and the House of Representatives. The Senate consisted of two members from each state regardless of population, elected by the state legislature. The House consisted of state delegations apportioned according to population. The Constitution, however, does not state that House members are to be elected by districts. Despite this omission, there is evidence in the Constitution, in the proceedings of the Constitutional Convention, and in political writings of the day to support the assertion that the Framers intended the House to be elected by districts, as was the custom in the colonial assemblies.

ALTERNATIVES TO SINGLE-MEMBER DISTRICTS. Because the Framers determined that the number of representatives from each state should be roughly proportional to a state's population relative to the total population of the nation, they probably intended that each state be divided into districts whose boundaries would be drawn according to the same proportional idea. The first five federal apportionment laws (1792–1832), however, simply provided the apportionment ratio and the resultant specific number of representatives for each state. After reapportionment the task of devising the electoral procedures for electing House members was up to the respective states. This created a situation in which individual states could, and did, elect representatives to the House of Representatives in different ways. Although single-member, geographically defined district representation was dominant, the lack of legal precedent and guidance from the Constitution spawned three other electoral and representative formats: statewide election of the entire delegation (general tickets, multimember geographically defined districts (plural districts), and a combination format, in which some members of a state delegation were elected by single-member, geographically defined districts and some members by statewide election (at-large representation).

General ticket representation. In spite of custom and the probable intentions of the Framers, a number of states in the 1790s and the early nineteenth century did not divide into congressional districts. These states elected their entire House delegations through statewide elections—that is, all the eligible voters of the state voted for all the seats in Congress from that state. This type of election is called a general ticket election to differentiate it from the at-large election, discussed below. One political effect of general ticket representation is that geographic areas of a state that are not in political agreement with the majority have their political power diluted. If a state is divided into congressional districts, such areas can elect representatives of political persuasions different from those of the statewide majority. General ticket elections hit their peak in the Third Congress (1793–1795), when nearly a third of House members (33 out of 105) were elected by this method. In the first fifty years of Congress an average of 10 to 20 percent of the House was elected by general ticket. General ticket elections were first discouraged by the district provisions of the 1842 apportionment law, but they were in use through the 91st Congress (1969–1971), until the 1967 law mandating districts.

Plural district representation. Plural, or multimember, district representation occurs when one geographically defined district elects more than one person. Over the first fifty years of congressional history there were plural districts that elected two, three, or even four members to the House. This type of election ended after the Apportionment Act of 1842. In the plural district method one populous county or group of counties usually comprised one district. In most cases this was an attempt to keep the county unit as the entity of legal description while recognizing urban areas that deserved greater representation. Plural districts were extensively used in New York, Pennsylvania, and Maryland, states with areas of high population density and other vast areas of virtual wilderness. For example, in the 14th Congress (1815–1817) New York elected 12 out of 27, Pennsylvania 14 out of 23, and Maryland 2 out of 9 representatives by way of plural districts. Although plural district elections kept the county unit intact, abuses similar to the potential abuses of general ticket elections were possible. Several representatives could in effect be elected by a city, diluting the power of other areas, which might elect a representative of a different political persuasion under a single-member-district scheme.

At-large representation. The term *at-large election* refers to cases in which the majority of a state congressional delegation is elected from single-member, geographically defined districts but one, two, three, or four additional representatives are elected statewide. Representatives elected statewide are labeled *at-large representatives* when the majority of a state delegation is elected by districts. It is important to differentiate this method from the general ticket, in which the entire delegation is elected statewide.

The federal courts have also played a role in the drawing of congressional districts.

The first at-large representative was elected from Mississippi to the 33d Congress (1853–1855); the last three were elected from Maryland, Ohio, and Texas to the 89th Congress (1965–1967). At-large representation was most often used after a decennial reapportionment by states that were given a greater number of House seats. At-large representation usually occurred when the state legislature either (1) could not convene in time to perform redistricting, (2) could not agree on a new redistricting plan, (3) used this representative method in its new redistricting plan, or (4) decided not to redistrict. Again, partisan advantage could be attained by the majority party by the election of several representatives statewide. In many cases, the majority-party congressional delegation did not want to redistrict because its members were satisfied and did not want to tamper with existing, "safe" districts. The 63d Congress (1913–1915), elected immediately after the 1910 census apportionment, had the greatest number of at-large representatives, with twelve states electing twenty-one members at-large.

FEDERAL PROVISIONS CONCERNING CONGRESSIONAL DISTRICTS. To achieve the Framers' intentions—electoral equity within states and a systematic form of representation—Congress passed a series of provisions, usually included in apportionment laws, mandating single-member districts as the method by which members of the House should be elected. Over time, the establishment of single-member districts eliminated the general ticket, plural district, and at-large methods of election. In addition, Congress has historically given directives to the states with respect to the actual drawing of district boundaries. For example, the precedent-setting Apportionment Act of 1842 not only mandated single-member districts but also directed that, for the time the law was in force, congressional districts must be "contiguous" (5 Stat. 491). This temporarily slowed the practice of creating districts with geographically separate portions. The 1872 apportionment law was the first to direct that each district contain "as nearly as practicable an equal number of inhabitants" (17 Stat. 192). And the 1901 apportionment law, besides specifying that districts should be contiguous, also prescribed that each district be a "compact territory" (31 Stat. 733). This stipulation targeted the practice of gerrymandering, that is, the drawing of congressional districts with odd or peculiar shapes, so as to favor the party or group in power, with results that seem to defy geography. Again, these provisions were in effect for the ten-year period of the particular law. Because the general Apportionment Act of 1929 (46 Stat. 21) and later apportionment laws did not carry provisions concerning compactness, contiguity, or equal population, numerous examples of malapportioned, gerrymandered, and even split districts occurred in the latter portion of the twentieth century.

The federal courts have also played a role in the drawing of congressional districts. In the 1960s the Supreme Court ruled that malapportionment, the drawing of districts of significantly unequal population, is unconstitutional. In the 1970s the Court ruled that gerrymandering to deprive or dilute minority representation is unconstitutional. In the 1980s the Court ruled in *Davis et al. v. Bandemer et al.* that even partisan gerrymanders were subject to judicial review and possible alteration.

CONGRESSIONAL REDISTRICTING PROCESS. The original purpose of holding a census every ten years was to reallocate House seats to the states and, ideally, to allow the states to redraw congressional districts according to population changes. This has not always been the result. The longest interval without a new redistricting law was in New Hampshire, where the congressional district law of 19 February 1881 remained in effect until 3 July 1969. The Supreme Court rulings in malapportionment cases of the 1960s now ensure that after each decennial census states must pass redistricting laws to alter boundaries to reflect population changes even when a state's number of representatives remains the same.

Although some redistricting guidance has historically been given by Congress, the state legislatures finally define and draw district boundaries. The congressional redistricting process is usually accomplished by a law passed by both chambers of a state legislature and signed by the governor. Of course, if the same political party controls both chambers and the governorship it completely controls the redistricting process.

Historically, state legislatures have used given political entities to construct congressional districts. The county (in New England, the town) has been the basic building block of congressional districts and congressional redistricting statutes. In densely populated urban areas the counterpart to the county, the ward, was used extensively, especially in the 150 years after the First Congress. Many times these common political units were divided by gerrymanders to achieve majority-party objectives. As metropolitan areas became larger and more complex, streets became common boundaries dividing the expanding cities into congressional districts. The stringent Supreme Court equal-population rulings of the 1960s necessitated using numerous other fine divisions (census tracts, precinct boundaries, etc.) to draw district boundaries, resulting in increasingly complicated and lengthy districting laws. Many states have codes regulating congressional redistricting, including directives for compactness and contiguity and using current boundaries of counties, cities, and other political units where possible.

DISTRICTS AND POLITICAL REPRESENTATION. States can be subdivided into congressional districts in many ways. Even when boundaries are drawn in a nonpartisan way, different schemes for creating compact districts will yield different political results, though the district populations remain equal. Even when performed most fairly, the district method of representation carries an inherent electoral bias. Under a bad, gerrymandered districting, the results can be significantly skewed in favor of the party in power.

Virtually all Western-style democratic national legislatures elect representatives by district. In most parliamentary systems, however, the elected members view themselves as representatives of the party and agents in the promotion of its platform and ideology. Within these parliaments, voting virtually always follows party lines. In the parliamentary model, election by district only occasionally affects representative behavior. Additionally, numerous parliamentary election laws have integrated proportional representation schemes with voting districts to produce a more representative electoral result and lessen the need for gerrymandering since seats are distributed to political parties based upon the percentage of the total vote. In the United States the representative philosophy of the House is quite different. Representatives partly view their role as that of agents of their districts and see themselves as charged with the promotion of local concerns. The freedom of roll-call voting in the U.S. Congress is unsurpassed in the world. In the U.S. model, concern for district affairs has a great effect on the behavior and actions of representatives. The election of House members by district is therefore fundamental to understanding the functioning of Congress and representative democracy in the United States.

[See also (I) Apportionment and Redistricting, Gerrymandering.]

BIBLIOGRAPHY

Grofman, Bernard, ed. *Political Gerrymandering and the Courts.* 1990.

Hacker, Andrew. *Congressional Districting.* 1963.

Luce, Robert. *Legislative Principles.* 1930.

Martis, Kenneth C. *The Historical Atlas of United States Congressional Districts,* 1789–1983. 1982.

Morrill, Richard L. *Political Redistricting and Geographic Theory.* 1981.

Pitkin, Hanna E. *The Concept of Representation.* 1967.

– KENNETH C. MARTIS

DRAFTING

The terms *legislative drafting* and *bill drafting* are often used to describe the act of sitting down and committing legislative language to paper. More accurately, however, they describe the entire multifaceted process of converting raw ideas into legislative language that will effectively carry them out. Actually writing the words is merely the last stage in this process, although it is obviously a critical stage, and one that differs in a number of important respects from other literary activities.

Legislative language requires an unusually high degree of accuracy and precision; it cannot tolerate the minor ambiguities that are common in everyday speech and in most other kinds of writing. Because a bill is meant to become law it must be written with careful attention to how it and existing laws will interrelate. It must be cast in a form and style that is highly specialized yet varies from setting to setting, and its passage often depends on a maze of procedural and parliamentary questions that can only be guessed at in advance.

A legislative proposal starts on its way because someone—the sponsor—believes there is a problem that should be addressed by legislation and calls upon a drafter for assistance. Whoever originates this legislative idea is the sponsor during the preliminary drafting, but a legislator must take over this sponsoring function once the product is ready for introduction.

Legislative drafting is a highly pragmatic operation,

not an academic exercise.

The drafter's job is to help put into legislative form what the sponsor envisions. In many cases, however, the sponsor's ideas are imperfectly formed; he or she often provides no more than a set of general objectives that must be refined before a practical means for achieving them can be devised or may have no appreciation of the collateral problems that the proposal might raise.

The sponsor's initial generalities must be converted into specifics: problems, gaps, inconsistencies, or ambiguities in the proposal must be identified and dealt with; substantive, legal, administrative, and technical questions that may arise along the way must be anticipated; and an arrangement of the bill's various elements that will effectively communicate its message to the intended audience must be found. The drafter's efforts in these areas often constitute the best way—sometimes the only way—of identifying those aspects of the sponsor's policy that need modification or further refinement.

The final product must be cast in language that is clear, consistent, legally effective, technically sound, administrable, enforceable, and constitutional; be correct in terms of form and style; be as readable as possible; and not create unintended any side effects.

Producing a bill that is objectively correct in terms of form and style is complicated by the fact that four different drafting styles (with occasional variants) are currently used in federal legislation: (1) the older or "traditional" style, which has the fewest arbitrary requirements and is the least demanding in a technical sense; (2) "Code" style, which is used in the positive-law titles of the United States Code; (3) revenue style, which is used in all tax laws, has many formal requirements, and is the most demanding; and (4) a modified version of revenue style that incorporates most of the features of that style while avoiding its extremes. Any bill could be written in any of these styles, although in most cases the drafter will feel constrained to conform with the style of existing law in the field or to accommodate the stylistic preferences of the committees that will consider the bill. Revenue style is increasingly becoming the style of choice in federal legislation when no such constraints are present.

Language that can be easily comprehended by readers is always desirable, but bills that are inescapably complex or deal with highly technical subjects cannot be couched in the language of everyday speech and frequently cannot be made "readable" at all. In any event, most important federal legislation today is addressed to an audience of administrators or specialists rather than to ordinary people, even if ordinary people are the ones who will ultimately benefit or suffer under it.

Legislative drafting is a highly pragmatic operation, not an academic exercise. The drafter's overriding objective with any bill is to develop a full understanding of the underlying problem and the sponsor's policy for solving it and then to give expression to that policy clearly and accurately. All other drafting rules and principles, though they are normally quite consistent with and supportive of that objective, are secondary; stylistic deviations and lack of readability become virtues (or at least are forgivable) when they are unavoidable consequences of the effort to achieve it.

[See also (I) Bills, Lawmaking, Public Law, Resolutions.]

BIBLIOGRAPHY

Dickerson, Reed. *The Fundamentals of Legal Drafting.* 1965.

Filson, Lawrence E. *The Legislative Drafter's Desk Reference.* 1992.

Hirsch, Donald. *Drafting Federal Law.* Published for the Department of Health and Human Services, 1980. Revised for the use of the Office of the Legislative Counsel, U.S. House of Representatives, 1989.

– LAWRENCE E. FILSON

E

ELECTIONS, CONGRESSIONAL

Theory and Law

Any electoral system represents decisions made about voters' eligibility (whether suffrage will be exclusive or inclusive), the size of the geographic areas that will be represented (whether representatives will be elected from small districts or larger regions such as states or provinces or the nation as a whole), and the number of representatives that will be chosen from a given electoral area. Different electoral systems weigh votes differently, allow voters to name their preferences in different ways, and use different rules for determining who wins and who loses an election. These differing choices have consequences for a given system's fairness and equitability, affecting how voters vote and determining whom representatives represent.

Like all election systems, the American congressional election system is grounded in law and precedent.

VOTING ELIGIBILITY. In congressional elections in the United States, suffrage is regulated by both federal and state law. The U.S. Constitution allows the states to determine their eligible electorates, but with a few caveats: a state must apply the same suffrage rules in U.S. congressional elections as it applies in elections to the most numerous house of its state legislature, and a state cannot pass suffrage laws that are discriminatory or that in any other way violate the U.S. Constitution. (State suffrage laws applied only to U.S. House elections until 1913, when the Seventeenth Amendment to the U.S. Constitution provided for direct election of U.S. senators as well.) The Constitution also provides that elections be held every two years for all members of the House of Representatives and every two years for one-third of the members of the U.S. Senate.

Early state suffrage laws were exclusive rather than inclusive. Suffrage was restricted along lines of race, sex, and class. Blacks, women, and men without certain landed or personal property could not vote. Suffrage was soon extended to white male taxpayers, and by 1860 most states had achieved universal white male suffrage. The Fifteenth Amendment (1870) to the Constitution allowed black men to vote. Several states allowed women to vote in the period from 1890 to 1919, but it took the passage of the Nineteenth Amendment in 1920 to give women throughout the country the right to vote—which thereby established universal suffrage. Throughout the nineteenth century, then, voting for U.S. representatives was based on restricted suffrage, and the elected representatives reflected this fact: all were white males of the upper or middle class. As states expanded their suffrage, nonwhite, female, and lower-class interests were expressed in congressional voting, and candidates reflecting their areas' demographic characteristics had a better chance of being elected to congressional office.

NUMBER OF REPRESENTATIVES. Determining a state's eligible voters is one component of an electoral system; determining the number of representatives to be elected is another. The Constitution (Article I, section 2) stipulates that the number of U.S. representatives from any state is to be based on that state's population relative to other states' populations and that the figure is to be revised every ten years according to the results of the federal census. Each decade, the U.S. Congress passes apportionment laws detailing the apportionment formula used and giving the total number of representatives in the House of Representatives and the number of representatives each state receives. The Constitution (Article I, section 3) also stipulates that each state shall have the same number of senators: that is, two.

AREA OF REPRESENTATION. The Constitution is silent on whether representatives should be elected by districts or statewide or whether, if election is by district, how many should be elected from each district. The Constitution specifies only that representatives (and senators) must be inhabitants of their states. Today, Americans take for granted that representatives are elected in single-member districts, but this has not always been the case. Because of the ambiguity in the U.S. Constitution, during the early part of the nation's history states used four different methods: electing one member per district (single-member district), electing several members per district (plural or multimember district), electing some members from single-member districts and some statewide (mixed single-member district and at-large system), and electing all members statewide (completely at-large system). In 1842, a congressional apportionment law called for the election of representatives by the single-member district system, bringing an end to plural-member districts. At-large systems were discouraged, but some states continued to use mixed at-large systems until 1967 and completely at-large systems until 1970. A congressional act in 1967 declared these two types of at-large systems invalid. This act allowed only two exceptions: New Mexico and Hawaii could retain their completely at-large systems. However, New Mexico passed a law in 1968 adopting the single-member district system and, in 1970, Hawaii followed suit. The year 1970 marked the universal acceptance of the popular single-member district system of representation in the United States.

HOW ARE VOTES CAST? How one's vote is counted is also determined by state law. Throughout American history, states have weighted votes equally in congressional and other elections. No one's vote is counted more than once nor is any person allowed to vote more than once. Of course, vote fraud did occur and was particularly prevalent throughout the nineteenth century in large urban areas that did not have secret ballots or personal registration systems to prevent people from voting more than once. The passage by most states of personal registration laws in the period from 1890 to 1920 and the passage of secret ballot acts in the period from 1888 to 1896 eliminated much of the corrupt voting.

Americans' preference for unweighted voting also means that state laws prohibit voters from transferring their votes to other candidates for the same office on the ballot. Nor can voters rank their candidate preferences for an office on the ballot. In a congressional race, a voter can vote for only one candidate in his or her district. In essence, Americans have single-preference, unweighted voting: each voter selects only one candidate per office, and that vote is counted only once in the vote tabulation.

Among the various rules governing congressional elections, Americans are most used to the plurality (winner-take-all) voting rule for determining winners and losers. All states adopted this rule on entry into the Union. Basically, plurality voting means that the candidate who receives the most votes wins the contest; if candidate A receives one more vote than candidates B, C, D, etc., candidate A wins the congressional seat. This rule is easy to apply in a single-member district system. When, as sometimes happened in the earlier part of the nation's history, a state had a plural-member district or at-large election system, the rule extended to the number of congressional seats at stake: if, for example, four seats were in contention, then the four candidates with the highest vote totals would be declared winners. Most scholars believe that the plurality voting rule in single-member districts sustains and reinforces a two-party system in congressional elections. These and other election laws make it very difficult for third parties to compete for congressional seats.

COMPARATIVE VOTING SYSTEMS. The electoral systems of the United States and other democracies have much in common. There is a shared belief in universal suffrage, the secret ballot, and some form of voter registration. Most democratic nations have followed the same historical progression in extending suffrage from upper-class males to middle- and then lower-class males and finally to women. Some other democracies (e.g., England, Canada, India, New Zealand) even have plurality voting rules and single-member districts similar to those in the United States. But in many parliamentary democracies, voting rules are very different from those in U.S. congressional elections. Some democracies, particularly in continental Europe, use party lists for voting, multimember or plural districts, and proportional representation. A few of these countries also permit votes to be transferred and have runoff elections. A few of these countries once permitted plural voting as well. This practice allowed certain individuals in a country to vote more than once on election day; for example, from 1918 to 1948, England allowed university graduates and occupants of most business premises to vote both in the election districts of their places of residence and their places of graduation or business.

The electoral systems of the United States and other democracies have much in common.

Proportional representation is the central feature of many European voting systems. Parties are represented in legislatures in proportion to the numbers of voters supporting them. In an ideal system, a party's share of seats in parliament would exactly correspond to the proportion of the vote it receives. While in a few countries (e.g., the Netherlands) the entire nation is a single constituency, most countries use proportional representation at the district level, leading to results that only approximate the ideal. Proportional representation only works at the district level if each district sends multiple members to the legislature; otherwise, not all votes would be represented.

An example will illustrate how proportional representation works. If a given district has ten seats in its country's parliament, party A receives four of these seats if it wins 40 percent of the district's vote; Party B receives three seats if it wins 30 percent of the district's vote; and so on. In proportional representation systems, the focus is on voting for a political party; choice of a particular candidate is considered less important and, in some countries, is not even permitted. Parties prepare party lists at election time to facilitate voting along party lines. In closed-list countries, the voter can vote only for the party of his or her choice. In open-list countries, the voter must first vote for a party but then can exercise the option to vote for particular candidates printed on the party list. Under either system, the order in which the candidates are placed on the list by the party organization determines which party members get elected unless candidate-preference voting is large enough to counteract the party organization's ranking of candidates. The only way all candidates of a given party can be elected in a district is if the party receives close to 100 percent of the district's vote.

Norway, in its 1814 constitution, was the first to use proportional representation with multimember districts. Today the majority of the world's democracies use proportional representation. These countries define the quotas of votes needed to obtain parliamentary seats by various mathematical formulas; still other mathematical formulas are used to set rules regarding how seats are allocated among parties when the breakdown of votes for the various parties is not exactly proportional to the number of seats in a district.

Some countries have also legislated variants to the basic proportional representation voting system. A prime example is Ireland, which allows voters to rank in order of preference candidates so that when one candidate is successfully elected in the district, his or her surplus votes go to the second-ranked choice of voters, and so on. (The last-place candidate also has his or her votes transferred to the second-ranked preference in the same way.) This concept of transferring or rank-ordering votes stands in direct contrast to the American system and to most proportional representation systems, which allow only a single preference vote (i.e., one vote for a legislative candidate or party in a given district). The transferable (or alternative) vote is also used in elections for the lower house of the Australian parliament, but in a voting system more reminiscent of congressional voting in the United States: single-member districts with a majority (not plurality) voting rule. In this case, only the second preferences of the last-place candidate's votes are transferred until one candidate has a majority vote. France, with a single-member district system similar to Australia's, has at times in its history used a second ballot runoff election for parliament if no candidate has received a majority vote in the district in the first election. Some of these voting schemes seem to weaken the party voting that is a basic feature of the proportional representation voting system.

COMPARATIVE EFFECTS OF VOTING SYSTEMS. The differences between the American system of congressional elections and these other voting systems have implications not only for legislative representation but for candidate campaign strategies and voter psychology as well. The American single-member district is a narrow territorial base that has a political life of its own. This may lead congressional candidates to stress local issues, pork-barrel projects, and service to the district to the detriment of national issues and national party policy. It may also lead congressional candidates to stress individual personality more than their European counterparts do. On the other hand, party-list ballots and proportional representation in multi-member districts can lead to a too-great focus on party, with a correspondingly lopsided emphasis on national party platforms and national issues. Such differences are a matter of degree rather than absolute, but the kind of electoral system that is used does influence voter psychology and affects how campaign strategies are developed.

Historically, nations that were more culturally and ethnically homogeneous tended to adopt plurality-based voting systems for legislative elections. Countries that were more socially heterogeneous seemed to adopt proportional representation systems so that the many, diverse opinions in their societies might be represented. These diverse opinions often crystalized into intense and formidable political cleavages; the histories of many European countries, for example, show major ethnic, religious, cultural, and social conflicts.

Whether a nation adopts a plurality or a proportional representation voting system also influences the system of political parties that develops, which in turn reflects the social homogeneity or heterogeneity of that society. Plurality voting is usually associated with two-party systems in more homogeneous societies, proportional representation voting with multiparty systems in more heterogeneous societies. Two parties seem able to represent most opinions in a homogeneous society, for the large mass of political opinion in such societies (e.g., the United States) is often moderate or centrist in character. Plurality voting reinforces the two-party system by mandating that only one candidate can be a winner in a political race. Translated into the context of U.S. congressional elections, this means that only two parties will field candidates that can meaningfully compete for a congressional seat in a single-member district. Both candidates will often take moderate views on many issues, reflecting majority opinion in their district. By contrast, in a socially heterogeneous society more extreme views on the left and right of the ideological spectrum need to be taken into account. Proportional representation encourages many parties to compete for political office since they will receive seats in parliament roughly proportional to the votes cast for them in each district. No votes are wasted and no votes (beyond a minimum vote threshold required by law) go unrepresented because there is never only one winner in a legislative race in any district. Given this incentive to sustain multiparty competition for parliamentary seats, political parties are encouraged to run party slates, which cumulatively reflect the diversity of opinion in society.

The modern American tendency toward candidate-oriented voting fits well with locally based plurality voting in congressional elections.

Advocates of plurality voting in congressional elections argue that it leads to clear-cut results and that government is made more stable because one party often controls Congress. They also argue that plurality voting reflects the moderate ideological stance of most Americans. (Others argue instead that it reflects the natural duality of opinion on issues in American politics.) Advocates further stress that plurality, district-based voting allows for stronger representation of vital local interests, issues, and constituencies. Supporters of proportional representation in parliamentary elections contend, however, that their system of voting permits many different points of view to be represented. They also assert that the political focus in such systems is on national issues, national party policy, and party responsibility in government. They do concede that clear-cut results are often difficult to obtain, since coalition governments are the likely electoral outcome. Most important, advocates of proportional representation emphasize that their system allows virtually every voter to be represented, unlike the American plurality system, in which all votes for the losing congressional candidate are wasted and, hence, all those voters go unrepresented. Supporters of proportional representation also believe that the American election system leads to an overrepresentation of parochial concerns to the detriment of the national interest.

Each system of elections reflects and serves the culture and society that uses it. Europeans and others with proportional representation systems want to represent diversity of opinion and minority interests in their parliaments. Given their cultural history, proportional representation was the way to achieve these goals. Americans in their early history formulated election laws to ensure local or geographic representation in congressional elections. They balanced this with the establishment of a presidential system representing the national interest. Plurality, single-member-district voting rules also ensured the maintenance of a two-party system in what was then a reasonably homogeneous society. It may be that the sharply dualistic nature of political opinion in early American history was the original motivation for plurality voting, but the more moderate views of most Americans today still make this same system of voting suitable for congressional elections. Also, the modern American tendency toward candidate-oriented voting fits well with locally based plurality voting in congressional elections. Plurality voting does not produce correspondences between voting and party-seat allocation as accurately as does proportional representation, but the benefits of the plurality system seem to outweigh the disadvantages for the American experience.

[See also (I) Apportionment and Redistricting, Districts, Gerrymandering.]

BIBLIOGRAPHY

Bogdanor, Vernon, and David Butler. *Democracy and Elections: Electoral Systems and their Political Consequences.* 1983.

Katz, Richard S. *A Theory of Parties and Electoral Systems.* 1980.

Lijphart, Arend, and Bernard Grofman, eds. *Choosing an Electoral System: Issues and Alternatives.* 1984.

Mackie, Thomas T., and Richard Rose. *The International Almanac of Electoral History.* 3d ed. 1991.

Martis, Kenneth C. *The Historical Atlas of United States Congressional Districts, 1789–1983.* 1982.

Rae, Douglas W. *The Political Consequences of Electoral Laws.* Rev. ed. 1971.

Rusk, Jerrold G. "The American Electoral Universe: Speculation and Evidence." *American Political Science Review* 68 (September 1974): 1028–1049.

Rokkan, Stein. *Citizens, Elections, Parties.* 1970.

Taagepera, Rein, and Matthew Shugart. *Seats and Votes: The Effects and Determinants of Electoral Systems.* 1989.

– JERROLD G. RUSK

Becoming a Candidate

Who runs for Congress, and why? Of people who are similarly situated in society, why do some enter politics while others do not? Approximately 150 million Americans could run for Congress every two years, but only about one thousand run in a typical year, and only a fraction of those conduct serious campaigns. (The average number of challengers for House races in the years 1972 to 1988 was 1,017; this figure excludes incumbents as well as the approximately one hundred people who run for Senate seats in a given election year.) This winnowing of the politically active from the inactive, and of the potential candidate from the political observer, is known to scholars as the process of recruitment, or "candidate emergence." Two approaches have been used to examine the process: one proceeds at the individual level, the other at the institutional level.

INDIVIDUAL-LEVEL THEORIES. Individual-level approaches include the following: an approach that focuses on psychological dispositions and personality traits as the basis for explaining political motivation and behavior; the traditional sociological approach that points to the importance of occupation, social status, and social mobility; and the rationalist approach that views potential candidates as rational actors who assess the costs and benefits of running for office.

Psychological approach. Proponents of the psychological approach argue that people with certain personality types are most likely to enter politics. The pioneer of this approach, Harold Lasswell, believed that because politics involves the quest for and exercise of power, the successful political personality must be power-centered (Lasswell, 1948). The pursuit of power was seen as a basis for overcoming low self-esteem, either by changing the traits of the self or altering the environment in which the person lives. To support this theory of political motivation, Lasswell examined individual life histories to discover the traumatic experiences that create the power-centered personality. Early childhood experiences and indoctrination by parents were generally viewed in the psychological literature as central in forming the political personality.

Though the theory is appealing, practical and theoretical problems limit the applicability of the approach. First, it is difficult to get high-level politicians to take the personality tests (such as the thematic apperception tests) required to assess the theories. In fact, no member of Congress has ever subjected himself or herself to such tests, although research at the state and local levels shows that politicians do not have a distinctive concern for power or affiliation. Second, the interpretation of behavior and the methods for determining important personality traits are not agreed upon. Even Lasswell backed away from his early focus on power-centered personalities, recognizing that such people were not likely to be effective in politics, and proposed a natural selection process that weeds out the intensely power-oriented person because his or her personality precludes the flexible give-and-take that is required in politics.

Sociological approach. Do elected officials differ from the people they represent? Are certain groups or classes of people advantaged in the pursuit of a seat in Congress? Not surprisingly, the upper and upper-middle classes are heavily overrepresented in the top levels of elected public office. At the federal level, almost no politicians have working-class or blue-collar backgrounds. Nearly half of all members of Congress are lawyers, and the next largest percentage comes from business and banking. Also, members of Congress are mostly male and white. In the 103d Congress (1993–1995), there were only 6 women in the Senate and 48 in the House (11 percent of the latter chamber's membership). There was only one African American in the Senate and 38 in the House (8.7 percent; if one includes Eleanor Holmes Norton, the District of Columbia's nonvoting delegate, there were 39). That members of Congress are not cut from the same cloth as the broader public is well established, but the link between background variables and behavior has been more difficult to determine. In fact, there is virtually no link between background variables and behavior in office, once other factors, such as constituency, are controlled. For most issues there are not even correlations between background and behavior, so trying to establish actual causation has not been an issue in the research. Indeed, the weakness of any such links has led most scholars to reject the sociological approach.

The most important aspect of occupational data is whether or not the congressional aspirant is a current officeholder. This is a key variable in the rational approach outlined below, but it is not emphasized in the social-background research, which tends to focus on occupations at the time of entry into politics. The sociological approach makes sense for studies of lower-level offices, most of whose occupants enter politics from other careers. But most new members of Congress are being "promoted" rather than recruited—that is, they enter Congress from some lower office. Thus, to understand why most candidates run for Congress, the rational calculations of career politicians must be examined.

Rational approach. The rational approach to studying recruitment to Congress looks at the costs and benefits associated with the decision to run for higher office. While those who work from this perspective recognize that psychological and background differences may be important, they do not see them as central. The costs and benefits approach is relatively new, though it had become dominant by the early 1980s, coincident with a change in the nature of congressional elections. In the 1960s, scholars noted the advent of candidate-centered campaigns and the declining role of political parties. By the 1980s, the notion that contemporary congressional elections were dominated by candidates rather than parties had become conventional wisdom. Once political campaigns were viewed in these terms, it made analytical sense to focus on the rational calculations of the individual political entrepreneur. If, indeed, the candidate bore the "risks, rewards, and pains" of campaigns, then the specification and measurement of those factors should be made from an individual-level perspective.

Research looking at individual-level influences on the strategic calculations of politicians was extended and formalized by David Rohde in 1979 with his article on risk bearing and progressive ambition (that is, the desire to move from a lower to a higher office). Rohde moved toward predicting who would run for Congress by focusing on the decision to run for higher office rather than on the initial decision to enter politics. The first formal statement of an ambitious politician's decision calculus reads: $Uo = PB - R$ where

Uo = utility of the target office O
P = probability of winning election to office O
B = value of office O
R = risk of running

This equation has two important implications. First, it states that ambitious politicians will always aspire to higher office if expected net benefits are positive (i.e., $PB > R$). In making strategic calculations, a potential candidate for Congress who already holds a lower office will consider the probability of winning a House (or Senate) race and the chances of winning reelection to his or her current office, times the benefits of the respective offices, minus the costs associated with running. The benefits of holding office include the power and prestige of the office and the excitement of being in the public limelight.

The costs of running are both financial and personal. Fund-raising is the most demeaning and difficult task to be performed in running for Congress. The cost of mounting a strong challenge to an incumbent or running for an open seat in the House started at about $500,000 in 1992. Fund-raising can easily consume a majority of the candidate's time. The personal costs are also high. The lack of privacy and the pressures on families that come with being a member of Congress deter many potential candidates from running. Furthermore, politicians must consider the opportunity costs associated with a campaign for Congress—that is, the value of the political office or other job they would have to give up to serve in Congress.

The second implication of this simple calculation is also important; the greater the risk of running, the greater the probability of winning must be before a politician would decide to run for Congress. This observation illuminates an important distinction between amateur and experienced candidates. Candidates who already hold political office have many advantages over inexperienced candidates in seeking higher office, but they also have more to lose if they are not elected. Thus, experienced politicians attempt to time their campaigns for higher office with periods when there is a higher probability of winning, while amateurs may not be as sensitive to electoral goals. Therefore, experienced candidates are less likely to challenge a sitting incumbent and are more likely to attempt to gain higher office when the seat is open (by a ratio of more than two to one from 1972 to 1990). They are also sensitive to national economic conditions and various district-level variables. Amateurs, on the other hand, are more likely to be motivated by nonelectoral concerns such as a sense of duty to the party and policy goals, though many "ambitious amateurs" are also motivated by electoral goals (Canon, 1990).

Two historical patterns in the political backgrounds of House candidates are worthy of brief mention. First, consistent with the rational calculus outlined above, experienced Democratic challengers were far more likely to run in 1974 and 1982 (because of Watergate and the recession, respectively) than in other elections over the period 1972 to 1988, while experienced Republican challengers were more likely to run in 1972. For example, 30.5 percent of Democratic challengers in 1982 had previous elective experience, compared to an average of only 17.3 percent during the entire period 1972 to 1988. Second, there was a general trend toward fewer challengers with previous elective experience through the 1980s (dropping from 22.3 percent of all challengers to incumbents in 1982, to 13.4 percent in 1984, to 11.5 percent in 1986, to 8.5 percent in 1988). Not surprisingly, about 98 percent of all incumbents who ran for reelection in 1986 and 1988 were reelected. These trends, however, are generally cyclical. In 1992 about 14 percent of all challengers had some previous elective experience—a figure nearly identical to the average of all challengers during the years 1972 to 1988.

INSTITUTIONAL THEORIES. The institutional approach to studying political recruitment examines the context of the decision to run for Congress rather than individual motivations or backgrounds. It points to the importance of political-career structures, the rules of the game, and political parties.

Career structure. One central aspect of this context is the nature of the political-career structure—the tiering of local, state, and national offices with thousands of opportunities at the bottom of the pyramid and only a handful at the top. In general, this career structure charts out the path of least resistance because it indicates to aspiring politicians which lower office is most likely to serve as a stepping-stone to a higher office. (For example, in many states, a majority of U.S. House members previously served in the state legislature.) There is, however, great variation in the nature of these paths. In some districts, politicians must serve long apprenticeship in lower-level offices or in the party organization. In others, the career structure is more open to amateurs who attempt to make Congress their initial public office.

The theoretical contribution of this perspective was its focus on the importance of political ambition and political careers. Joseph Schlesinger (1966) built a theory of ambition on the notion that political opportunities were structured by ambitious people looking to further their political careers. When a series of challengers uses a state legislative seat as a stepping-stone to the House, it becomes more firmly entrenched as the preferred route or, as he calls it, the "manifest office." The use of manifest offices for the House and Senate has undergone significant changes since 1960. More House members have been elected from state legislatures (slightly more than half in the years 1980–1992, compared with 30 percent in the 1930s and 1940s), while fewer senators have used the common stepping-stone of holding a governorship before running for the Senate (13.7 percent between 1960 and 1987, compared with 23.2 percent between 1913 and 1959).

Fund-raising is the most demeaning and difficult task to be performed in running for Congress.

Candidates with previous political experience, especially in the manifest office, have many advantages in running for Congress: an existing voter base, which enhances name recognition; a campaign organization and fund-raising network in place from previous races; and greater attention from the media, which are more likely to treat their candidacies seriously. Survey research indicates that voters value political experience in candidates for public office. Of some thirty desirable qualities for political candidates ranked in various polls, ranging from youth and good health to courage and intelligence, political experience was the only one consistently mentioned as the most important characteristic. Given this public attitude, previous political experience is typically viewed as a necessary requirement for serving in Congress.

Aggregate-level results provide some evidence for the link between experience and votes. On the average, experienced challengers received 7 percent more of the two-party vote than inexperienced candidates from 1972 to 1978 (Jacobson and Kernell, 1983, p. 31). Some of the experienced candidates' relative success may be explained by their tendency to challenge vulnerable incumbents (that is, experienced challengers may not receive more votes in elections because they are better candidates than amateurs but because they run against incumbents who are not very popular). Even after controlling for other variables that would reduce the incumbent's vote, however, the relationship between previous experience and votes remains very strong. It has been shown that a highly experienced challenger receives 10 percent more of the vote than a complete amateur, even after controlling for the candidates' relative ability to raise campaign money.

A majority of those who make it to Congress have climbed their way up the political ladder, but a sizable number of amateurs do not follow the typical path. These amateurs are at a disadvantage for several reasons: the absence of prior campaign experience, low name recognition (celebrities are the exception), and a general preference among voters for candidates with prior experience. But these obstacles are not insurmountable. The successful campaigns of Senators Herb Kohl (D-Wis.) and Frank R. Lautenberg (D-N.J.) and former representative Ed Zschau (R-Calif.), among many others, indicate that large expenditures on consultants, staff, and advertising can permit amateurs to overcome initial deficits. The careers of some celebrities, such as astronaut John Glenn (D-Ohio), basketball players Bill Bradley (D-N.J.) and Tom McMillen (D-Md.), football player Jack Kemp (R-N.Y.), and actor Fred Grandy (R-Iowa), demonstrate that name recognition from careers outside politics can be parlayed into a House or Senate seat. Overall, about one-fourth of the members of the U.S. Congress do not have prior elective experience.

A 1990 study found that more amateurs are elected during periods of generally increased political opportunity, such as the 1930s were for the Democrats or 1980 was for the Republicans (Canon, 1990, chap. 3). In such elections, amateurs take advantage of a desire for political change and exploit the relative openness of the career structure in the United States. Compared to nations with stronger party systems, the United States requires little in the way of party or office apprenticeship, even for the highest offices. Furthermore, all voters do not necessarily prefer experience. The suspicions many Americans hold about career politicians and the long-standing tradition of "running against Washington" can be exploited by amateurs who can credibly claim that they are not part of the power structure.

Rules governing elections. The rules of the game set the boundaries and guide the ambitions of politicians, amateurs, and experienced politicians alike. Two types of rules are central: those that define office availability and term restrictions (if any) and those that define electoral conditions. Provisions that establish the number of elective offices define the number of opportunities to run for office at various levels of government. These rules shape political careers by ensuring that the outlets for initial political ambitions are usually at the local level, where opportunities are the most numerous. Term restrictions also direct ambition. An office with a one- or two-term limit does not arouse the same ambition as an office in which one could make a career. Thus, congressional office is a more likely outlet for those wishing to establish a long-term career (though this would obviously change if term limits were imposed).

While office availability and term restrictions must be accepted as givens by ambitious politicians, one factor that helps define the nature of political opportunities is subject to manipulation: the drawing of district lines. Gerrymandering, the practice of tinkering with district lines for partisan advantage, can create substantial distortions in the geographic distribution of votes. The courts throw out the most blatant cases, but in many states the decennial practice of redistricting can affect the strategic calculations of candidates for office.

The second set of rules of the game defines the electoral conditions. Runoff primaries in the South have often discriminated against blacks, while third parties have never taken hold in the United States, largely because of single-member districts and winner-take-all elections. Both the transition from the party ballot to the secret ballot and the implementation of the direct primary had significant impact on the party's control over general elections and nominations. The Seventeenth Amendment, which provided for the direct election of U.S. senators, took their selection away from the party elite and gave it to the public. Both of these changes opened up the political process to a broader range of candidates. On the other hand, closed primaries, in which only members of a given party can vote, still serve as a tool, albeit a limited one, for maintaining some party control over who runs for office.

Political parties. Political parties influence who runs for Congress by structuring competition through the two-party system and by nominating political candidates, minimally through supplying them with a party label and more substantially through participating in their recruitment and selection. The two-party system's profound impact on the field of candidates has several dimensions. Most basically, having a two-party system means that third parties do not compete realistically for public office; few candidates have an actual chance of winning without the Democratic or Republican label. Each party's competitive standing in a given congressional district further defines potential candidates' ambitions and careers. Republicans considering a career in politics face a different set of opportunities on the south side of Chicago than in the suburbs of Dallas. The competitive positions of the parties at the national level also affect the types of candidates who are elected in a given year. Thus 1932, 1964, and 1974 were years in which many Democratic candidates were swept into office; in 1980, some Republicans who formerly would not have had much of a chance found themselves in Washington.

The rules of the game set the boundaries and guide the ambitions of amateur and experienced politicians alike.

Parties also influence the career structure through nominations for political office. It is obviously in the party's interest to field the strongest possible candidate for the general election. Ideally, this is done by grooming, candidates as they work their way up through party ranks. Parties also like to control politicians' ambitions and so act to stop or inhibit challengers to the strongest candidate in a primary race. Preprimary endorsements can provide an effective means of choking off outside candidacies. In 1986, for example, 99 percent of those endorsed by the Minnesota Democratic-Farmer-Labor party (the Democratic party in Minnesota) won in open seat and incumbent primary races (373 of 377). The closed primary—in which voters must be registered members of a party to vote in that party's primary—is another minimally effective but widely used step for exerting some party control. Parties have recently attempted to play a larger role in candidate recruitment through aggressive recruitment and candidate training schools. An expanding resource base enhances the party's role in recruitment. In the 1989–1990 election cycle, the various Democratic party committees raised $86.7 million, while the Republicans raised $207.2 million, compared with only $16.1 million and $44.1 million for the two parties, respectively, in the 1975–1976 cycle.

While parties clearly have some impact on the types of candidates who emerge in congressional elections, their role can be overstated. Studies of recruitment consistently reveal that the party does not play a central role in a candidate's decision to run for office. Candidates usually seek the blessing of the party organization, but, with a few exceptions, nominations are not rewards handed out to the party faithful.

The various perspectives discussed here offer insights into how people become candidates for Congress. The psychological and sociological approaches best explain initial recruitment (why someone chooses politics as a career). For example, early studies of the social backgrounds of political leaders demonstrated that the opportunity to enter politics is strongly skewed toward highly educated, upper-middle-class professionals. On the other hand, social backgrounds do not help predict which lower-level politicians will seek higher office. Thus, social background analysis provides little analytical leverage in explaining patterns of advancement to the U.S. Congress. The rational and institutional approaches have the opposite strengths and weaknesses: they do an excellent job of explaining the logic behind promotion to higher office, but they provide little assistance in helping explain which of the eligible millions will enter politics. A comprehensive understanding of who becomes a candidate for Congress must combine the several approaches.

BIBLIOGRAPHY

Canon, David T. *Actors, Athletes, and Astronauts: Political Amateurs in the United States Congress.* 1990.

Jacobson, Gary C., and Samuel Kernell. *Strategy and Choice in Congressional Elections.* 1983.

Lasswell, Harold D. *Power and Personality.* 1948.

Matthews, Donald R. "Legislative Recruitment and Legislative Careers." *Legislative Studies Quarterly* 9 (1984): 547–585.

Matthews, Donald R. *U.S. Senators and Their World.* 1960.

Rohde, David W. "Risk Bearing and Progressive Ambition: The Case of Members of the United States House of Representatives." *American Journal of Political Science* 23 (1979): 1–26.

Schlesinger, Joseph A. *Ambition and Politics: Political Careers in the United States.* 1966.

– DAVID T. CANON

Nomination to Candidacy

When machines dominated American politics, one of the most important aspects of their control was the ability to control political nominations. As Boss Tweed of Tammany Hall is reported to have claimed, "I don't care who does the electing, just so I do the nominating." Machines no longer dominate congressional and senatorial nominations as they once did, but what has replaced them?

This question can be answered in a number of ways. The fifty states have fifty different sets of laws that govern nominations. Normally, the procedures governing congressional and senatorial nominations parallel those for other partisan offices within the state. In the vast majority of the states, nomination is by direct primary election, but primaries vary according to who may run, who may vote, the role played by formal party organizations, and what is necessary to win. In the remaining states, party organization plays a more determinative role in deciding nominations.

When are nominations contested? When are they hotly contested? What difference do nomination contests make for the general election prospects of winners? No incumbent U.S. senator and only seven incumbent U.S. representatives lost primary elections between 1982 and 1990. In 1992 primaries played a more significant role, in part because of redistricting, in part because of the House bank scandal, and in part because of an anti-incumbent mood in the electorate. Whether this election represents an aberration or the breaking of a long pattern remains in doubt. Given the success of incumbents in other years, seeking reelection, it might be asked: do those who oppose them necessarily represent the challengers who would provide the most competition? If not, why are the best challengers not nominated? An understanding of the legal mechanisms of party nomination for the House and Senate and of the political ramifications of the nominating process will point toward answers to all these questions.

THE LEGAL ENVIRONMENT. States with strong party organizations and intense two-party competition were among the last to adopt the direct primary as a means of nominating candidates for office. But by 1955, when Connecticut adopted a challenge primary as a means for contesting the party organization's convention- or caucus-nominated candidate through a primary, all states had instituted some form of primary for statewide offices and thus for congressional nominations. In several southern states, however, parties are given the option of nominating either by primaries or by convention. In Virginia, for instance, each party has used the convention system on occasion.

Within the framework of the primary nominating system, there are differences among legal environments in the states. State primary systems are distinguished from one another by the formal role played by political parties, by the definition of the electorate, and by provisions regarding how the winner is determined.

Eight states (Colorado, Connecticut, Delaware, New Mexico, New York, North Dakota, Rhode Island, and Utah) permit political parties formally to endorse candidates before primary elections. In each case, the endorsee has certain advantages in the primary itself—for example, automatic placement on the ballot or a preferred ballot position. A number of other states have informal endorsement procedures, but these do not have the impact of those specified by law. Endorsed candidates in those states with legal provisions for expression of party preference are rarely challenged for nominations, and when challenged they are rarely defeated, except for the seemingly aberrant cases of the Democrats in New York and the Republicans in Utah.

The most frequently noted legal distinction among primary systems is how the electorate is defined. The question is whether a citizen must be enrolled in a political party to vote in that party's primary. Twelve states

(California, Connecticut, Kentucky, Maine, Maryland, Nebraska, Nevada, New Hampshire, New Jersey, New Mexico, New York, Oklahoma) hold closed primaries, that is, primaries in which a citizen must enroll in a party some time well in advance of the primary election to be eligible to vote in that primary. Typically, public records of partisan involvement are available to candidates and others, and citizens wishing to change their affiliation must do so long before the primary election. Fifteen additional states (Arizona, Colorado, Delaware, Florida, Iowa, Kansas, Massachusetts, North Carolina, Ohio, Oregon, Pennsylvania, Rhode Island, South Dakota, West Virginia, Wyoming) have closed primaries in which the rules are more flexible: either the record of affiliations is not published, or switches are permitted right up to primary day. In some of these states, independents can enroll in either party on primary day, but partisans cannot switch from one party to the other.

Twenty states (Alabama*, Arkansas*, Georgia*, Hawaii, Idaho, Illinois*, Indiana*, Michigan, Minnesota, Mississippi*, Missouri*, Montana, North Dakota, South Carolina*, Tennessee*, Texas*, Utah, Vermont, Virginia*, and Wisconsin) have open primaries, that is, primary elections in which any registered voter can vote in either party's primary. Among these states there is some variation. In eleven of them (those marked with an asterisk in the list above), mostly in the South, the choice of party must be made publicly though no permanent record is kept. In the remaining states, the choice is made in the secrecy of the voting booth.

Alaska and Washington employ a variation of the open primary called the blanket primary, a system in which citizens can vote in the Republican primary for some offices and the Democratic primary for other offices on the same ballot (but not in both primaries for the same office). Finally, Louisiana has a unique nonpartisan primary in which candidates for both parties appear on the same ballot. A runoff is held between the top two finishers, regardless of party affiliation, unless one candidate achieves a majority of the votes cast on primary day, in which case that candidate is declared the winner without opposition at the general election.

State nominating systems also vary according to the percentage of votes needed to win a primary. Normally, primaries are won by the candidate with a plurality of the votes, that is, more votes than any other candidate. However, in a number of states (mostly southern and border states, for example, Georgia and North Carolina) in order to win a primary a candidate must win a majority of the votes; if no candidate wins a majority, a runoff is held between the top two finishers. This procedure has engendered a good deal of criticism from activists who claim it disadvantages African-American candidates in the South, but it has been defended by others who refute that claim.

THE POLITICAL ENVIRONMENT. The most important element in the political environment for the nominating process is the presence or absence of an incumbent. Incumbent representatives and senators are rarely defeated. More to the point, they are rarely challenged in primaries. In the congressional elections from 1982 through 1990, 69.5 percent of the incumbents running for reelection to the House of Representatives were nominated without any opposition. In the majority of the other cases, opposition has been only token. Incumbent senators are challenged more frequently; 43.3 percent were challenged during the 1982 through 1990 elections, and many more of those challenges than House challenges were significant.

The differences between the positions of House and Senate incumbents are significant. First, Senate seats are seen as more prestigious than are House seats. In addition, these seats come up only once every six years rather than every other year. But just as important, representatives are perceived to be nearly invulnerable; they build up positive name recognition and, barring personal moral or ethical problems, are rarely harshly criticized in the press. Senators, on the other hand, because they represent larger constituencies (except in the case of those senators from states with only one representative), build up less of a personal relationship with their constituents; also, they are viewed more as national figures and so as more legitimate targets for criticism on policy stands. Challengers—and particularly serious challengers—are more likely to appear when the prize is more valued and when the chances for success seem higher.

The most frequently noted legal distinction among primary systems is how the electorate is defined.

The following theme is a constant no matter how one looks at the politics of House nominations: incumbents are less likely to be challenged in their own party if the party has legal endorsing powers. That is, if the party is strong and backs the incumbent, challengers are even less likely to emerge than otherwise. If one turns to the party of the challenger, the norm is for the nomination to go by default to a self-starter, an ambitious politician who thinks he or she has the key to beating the incumbent. Few find that key. The role of a political party organization is frequently to find a challenger; in fact, over the past five elections, an average of more than fifty seats per election have had no major party opposition to the incumbent; the nomination, viewed as of little value, went begging.

In cases where incumbents are viewed as vulnerable—perhaps because of scandal or advancing age or a close race in the preceding general election—contested primaries in the other party are more common. Of the few challengers who beat incumbent representatives, most do so after having won a contested primary. In contested primaries, the definition of the electorate becomes important. Obviously, political strategists have an easier time in states with closed primaries, because they know who is eligible and likely to vote in the primary. On the other hand, in open primary states, strategists can appeal to those in the other party who favor their candidates.

Other challengers have beaten incumbents without having to contest for the party nomination. In some cases, strong party organizations, often armed with legal endorsement procedures, have dissuaded those who would oppose the anointed challenger. In other cases, an incumbent's vulnerability was not apparent when nomination contests were planned. A challenger with a free ride through the nominating process has the advantage of a united party, though some argue that such challengers are disadvantaged because contested primaries enhance name recognition.

Most Senate challengers do face primary elections, because a Senate seat is viewed as having more value than a House seat and as more likely to turn over. Prospective candidates are more difficult to dissuade, because their turn will not come up again very soon. Thus, not only are more senators challenged in primaries than is true of representatives, but more Senate challengers have to win primary contests to garner nominations than is true of House challengers. Again, some of these are divisive primaries that harm general election chances; others are less divisive and serve to enhance the challenger's name recognition throughout the state.

Finally, the same pattern appears in a more exaggerated form in open seats. When House or Senate incumbents retire, ambitious politicians see an all-too-infrequent opportunity to win a seat in Congress. For open seats, the norm is contested primaries in both parties. The exceptions to this rule prove the point. Nominations go uncontested—and on rare occasion even begging—only when they are viewed as not having much worth, for instance in the minority party in a strong one-party area.

The congressional nominating process is highly significant because a responsive legislature depends on competitive elections, and competitive elections depend on high-quality nominees. At least since the 1970s, few congressional elections have been very competitive. One reason is that few nominees have been capable of running serious races, and the reason is that high-quality challengers have decided to forego congressional races.

The nominating process all but guarantees this result. For the most part, except in those few states with strong party organizations and formal endorsement procedures, congressional and senatorial nominees are self-starters, ambitious politicians who want to move into the national legislature or to "promote" themselves from the House to the Senate. And ambitious politicians only run when they think they stand a good chance for victory. Thus, incumbent representatives are rarely challenged, incumbent senators are rarely defeated for nomination, and challengers frequently are nominated by default. Only when elections are viewed as potentially winnable, as when incumbents appear vulnerable or seats are vacated, do the strongest candidates put themselves forth and compete for congressional nominations.

[See also (I) Political Parties.]

BIBLIOGRAPHY

Jacobson, Gary C. *The Politics of Congressional Elections.* 3d ed. 1992.

Jewell, Malcolm E., and David M. Olson. *Political Parties and Elections in American States.* 3d ed. 1988.

Key, V. O., Jr. *American State Parties: An Introduction.* 1956.

Maisel, L. Sandy, Linda L. Fowler, Ruth S. Jones, and Walter J. Stone. "The Naming of Candidates: Recruitment or Emergence?" In *The Parties Respond: Changes in the American Party System.* Edited by L. Sandy Maisel, 1990. Pp. 137–159.

– L. SANDY MAISEL

Congressional Campaigns

Modern congressional campaigns can be characterized as "candidate-centered." Party organizations no longer play a major role in the nomination and election of candidates; candidates are typically self-starters who were not recruited by political parties. These candidates raise the bulk of their campaign funds from their own direct contacts with contributors, are responsible for the conduct and content of their own campaigns, and generate their own publicity and advertising. In presenting themselves to the voters, they may choose to emphasize or to deemphasize their party affiliation, depending on what kind of strategy they believe will enable them to win the election.

PARTY LOYALTIES. Although party organizations are no longer as involved in congressional campaigns as they used to be, most voters still identify with one of the two major parties, and party identification is the single best predictor of how a citizen will vote. For these reasons, candidates representing the majority party in a

Campaign badge. For Matthew S. Quay's race for a U.S. Senate seat from Pennsylvania in 1893. Lavish badges and ribbons were often employed in campaigns around the end of the nineteenth century. (Library of Congress)

district generally choose to emphasize their party affiliation, while those representing the minority party usually deemphasize it. In some states and congressional districts, one party has such a strong advantage in party affiliation among voters that candidates of the minority party have little or no chance of winning elections. Still, in most states and districts, there are enough voters without a party identification, or willing to vote contrary to their party identification, to elect a candidate from either party.

Voters who reject the simple cue of voting based on party may consider a variety of factors in their ballot decisions. Although national issues and candidates' ideologies can be important, they clearly do not dominate some other dimensions of voter choice, such as candidates' personal qualities. Certainly, it is difficult for candidates to communicate complex messages about issues in the brief time or space available in advertisements. Furthermore, commentators and journalists tend to focus their attention on the personal attributes of the candidates or on the closeness of the race, factors that, they argue, are of more interest to citizens. For these reasons, much of the information that citizens receive about candidates has little issue content.

INCUMBENTS AND CHALLENGERS. Incumbents themselves are nonetheless responsible for much of the content of campaigns. Over his or her term of office, an incumbent seeks to build constituent support in various ways. The incumbent serves constituents by voting for popular legislation, by sponsoring and promoting legislation that meets the particular needs and interests of constituents, and by acting as an intermediary between constituents and the federal government.

Service to their constituents has become a much more prominent part of a representative's job. Starting with Lyndon B. Johnson's Great Society, the federal government vastly expanded the level of services it provided to state and local governments and to individuals. This expanded federal role gave representatives a greater opportunity to intervene with the government on behalf of constituents. Constituents came to expect that a representative would not just vote to represent their opinions in Congress but would actually help them in their dealings with the federal government, in ways ranging from aiding them in getting disability benefits, for example, to securing a tax exemption for a small business.

Morris Fiorina (1977) argues that House members have taken such advantage of these opportunities for constituency service that their reelection prospects have been noticeably enhanced. In the 1980s, an average of 92.2 percent of all House races involved an incumbent seeking reelection, and 94.8 percent of these incumbents were successful.

The high reelection rates of House incumbents are not a result simply of their constituency work in Congress but also of their success in advertising their accomplishments. The franking privilege allows representatives to send postage-free mailings to constituents. This is a tremendously valuable resource enabling incumbents to inform constituents of their activities. In addition, representatives seek as much newspaper and television coverage of their work as possible. Thus, by the time an election campaign begins, an incumbent generally has a substantial name-recognition advantage over any challenger, and the campaign itself seldom redresses this imbalance. Surveys have established that, by election day, voters are much more likely to recognize or to recall the names of incumbents than of their challengers.

Modern congressional campaigns can be characterized as "candidate-centered."

Although senators and House members have similar opportunities to serve their constituents and to publicize their service, senators do not achieve the same security of reelection. During the 1980s, an average of 87.5 percent of all Senate races involved an incumbent seeking reelection, and of those incumbents, 82.5 percent were successful.

There are several explanations for the greater advantage of House incumbency. One focuses on the different expectations citizens have of senators as compared to House members. Surveys indicate that citizens, especially in the larger states, believe national issues are a more important part of the job of a senator than of a House member. Senators themselves give greater emphasis to national issues in their public activities and reelection campaigns than do House members. Such emphasis is a response to constituent expectations and also contributes to the formation of their future expectations.

Senators' reelection prospects are more closely tied than are House members' prospects to swings of national opinion on the major issues of the day, and senators are more likely to be held accountable for failures of national public policy. In contrast, House members are more likely to be evaluated in terms of local service. Unlike major national policy issues, local service is generally not controversial. Helping a Democratic constituent who has a problem with the government does not preclude helping a Republican who also has a problem. Both constituents will be grateful, but one may decide to cross party lines and vote for the helpful House member at election time. Similarly, local public works projects are generally popular among constituents regardless of party affiliation.

A second, related explanation for the more favorable reelection prospects of House members focuses on differences in the constituencies of House members and of Senators. The populations of House members' districts are about equal, and with the exception of a few states with small populations, House members represent fewer constituents than do senators. In fact, the average senator represents about nine times as many constituents as the average House member. Thus, it is much easier for individual House members to meet and serve individual constituents and to build support on that basis. This further reinforces the differences in expectations that constituents have of a House member compared to a senator and illustrates how House members can more easily build support based on constituency service than can senators.

House and Senate constituencies also differ in terms of partisan competition. House districts are more likely than states to be dominated by one party. When a large majority of citizens identifies with one party, it is much less likely that other factors will be strong enough to override this partisan imbalance and affect the outcome of an election. Thus, many House districts often reelect the candidate representing the majority party again and again, contributing to the higher reelection rate of House members as compared to senators.

Finally, the quality of challengers in House and Senate races differs sharply. Only high-quality challengers are at all likely to defeat incumbents. A challenger must be considered competitive from the start in order to get the media attention and campaign contributions necessary to mount a strong challenge. One characteristic common to good challengers is prior elective office. A successful run for election in the district, albeit for another office, helps give the challenger the visibility, experience, and fund-raising contacts necessary to wage an effective campaign.

Few such high-quality challengers choose to run against incumbents in House races. By contrast, Senate races more often involve a challenger of high caliber. Because the Senate term is six years long, as opposed to two for the House, a Senate challenger has much more time to raise funds and wage an effective campaign than does a House challenger. House seats and statewide elective offices are logical stepping-stones, providing a ready pool of potentially interested candidates with the visibility and other resources needed to run for the Senate.

The relative lack of high-quality challengers in House races compared to Senate races is more a consequence than a cause of the apparent safety of House incumbents. Challengers, whatever their qualifications, must choose to enter a race. The greater a potential challenger's belief that he or she can win, the more likely he or she is to enter the race. Incumbents, of course, use the resources at their disposal to convince prospective challengers of the futility of a challenge. House incumbents generally succeed at this more often than do Senate incumbents.

For all these reasons, House members have a greater advantage in retaining office than do senators. Recent studies have estimated the incumbency advantage to be worth about 8.5 percent of the vote in House elections (Jacobson, 1990) and between 3 and 4 percent of the vote in Senate elections (Erikson, 1991).

LEVELS OF COMPETITIVENESS. Despite the difficulties and long odds of a successful challenge, most races for the House and Senate are contested. Strong challengers are more likely to enter the race when they perceive the incumbent to be vulnerable. Such vulnerability is often a product of the incumbent's real or supposed personal failings and may reflect scandal, such as the 1991 House banking scandal, or an inattention to the wishes of the district. A close election result in the most recent prior election may suggest that an incumbent is vulnerable, even if there are no other obvious signs of trouble.

The quality of challengers in House and Senate races differs sharply.

Factors beyond the incumbent's control can also increase vulnerability. Changes in House district partisanship or geographic composition may make a district more competitive. The outcome of a House or Senate election may also be influenced by voters' approval or disapproval of the president's program or by their views on other national issues, most often the state of the economy. Quality challengers are more likely to enter races when they judge that national or local constituency factors favor their party.

While there clearly are difficulties in mounting a challenge to a House or Senate incumbent, many challengers nevertheless enter these races. Those that choose to run against incumbents seek to negate the advantages of incumbency during the course of the election campaign. Their disadvantages in this regard, however, are tremendous, because so little is generally known about them and what is known about the incumbent tends to be quite favorable, since it is based largely on the incumbent's own publicity efforts.

THE MONEY FACTOR. Challengers also begin their campaigns with severe disadvantages in organization and fund-raising ability. Fund-raising is essential; the cost of a congressional campaign almost quadrupled between 1976 and 1990. In 1976, the average cost of a House campaign was $73,316; in 1990, it was $284,257. The Senate has seen a similar increase in the cost of campaigning. In 1976, the average cost of a Senate campaign was $595,449; in 1990, it was $2,574,868. These averages include noncompetitive as well as competitive races; competitive races cost even more.

Funds are raised from several sources, but primarily from individual contributors and political action committees. Parties play a very small financial role in both House and Senate races; in 1990, they provided only 4 percent of the total funds for House races and 7 percent of the total funds in Senate races (Ornstein, Mann, and Malbin, 1992).

Money is especially crucial for challengers because of their lack of name recognition, for which they must compensate through television, radio, and newspaper advertisements and campaign flyers and pamphlets. While an incumbent is guaranteed a certain amount of publicity by virtue of his or her office, the challenger has to buy that same publicity.

The importance of money in congressional campaigns is well documented. Gary Jacobson (1990) has demonstrated the importance of campaign contributions in reinforcing the disparities between incumbents and challengers. Incumbents can raise much more money than challengers because of their established contacts with constituents and interest groups. Furthermore, they are, as the numbers show, good bets to win reelection, and there is more to be gained from giving to a winner than to a loser. Challengers are likely to be able to raise enough money to mount a strong campaign only if they can convince others that they have a good chance of winning, and this is a difficult task at the start of a campaign.

Interestingly, though, if a challenger manages to raise sufficient funds, every dollar he or she spends is worth more votes than the dollar spent by an incumbent (Jacobson, 1990). Given the electorate's relative unfamiliarity with the challenger, spending by the challenger has a greater effect than spending by the incumbent in increasing voters' familiarity.

Money is crucial to waging a campaign not only for the advertising it buys, but also because it is needed to build an organization that will coordinate additional campaign activities, such as fund-raising, polling, and turning out the vote. In the past, a representative could rely on the local party organization to carry out many of these tasks; the party informed the majority of voters about its candidates through publicity and personal contact with the voters. David Olson (1978) has documented how, more recently, representatives have developed their own personal organizations independent of local parties. Furthermore, as an incumbent's seniority increases, he or she becomes better known in the district and has less need for party assistance.

CONTACTING CONSTITUENTS. Part of the ability of representatives to develop their own organizations must be attributed directly to television. Starting with the 1952 presidential race, television permanently changed the face of American political campaigns. With television, voters could see candidates for themselves and listen to their messages instead of relying on the parties to deliver those messages.

Generally, television and other direct means of communicating with the voter, such as newspaper or radio, are most effective if the media market closely fits the constituency of the candidate. One study has shown that voters are more familiar with House candidates when the House constituency closely matches a natural community boundary (Niemi, Powell, and Bicknell, 1986). Voters are less likely to be confused about which district they live in because in such communities everyone lives in the same House district. Furthermore, since all media coverage is devoted to a single House district news attention is directed toward only one district and purchased advertising time is cost-effective.

In contrast, a large city may contain many House districts. In such cities, voters are likely to be confused about which district they live in and who their representative is. The news media seldom devote much attention to candidates in any one district, because only a small portion of their audience is interested in any single district, and purchased advertising is relatively expensive because it generally must be aimed at a citywide audience larger than the district. Television is the most expensive of advertising media, and for this reason its use is not practical in some House districts. Challengers are at a particular disadvantage in such fragmented communities; although incumbents are somewhat less well known in fragmented than in single-district communities, challengers are *much* less well known in fragmented communities. Thus, incumbents have a bigger net familiarity advantage in fragmented communities.

Surveys of constituents are another form of direct contact between candidate and constituent. Beginning in the 1970s, the use of these surveys became common, especially in Senate campaigns. This was only one aspect of the increasing professionalism of campaigns. In the past, campaign staff consisted mostly of volunteers from the district who made phone calls and personally contacted voters. Today, most members of campaign staffs are still volunteers, but candidates, especially Senate candidates, often hire professionals for advice on campaign strategy, media, and polling (Herrnson, 1988).

Parties have begun to reassert themselves in this area of professional campaign services. Both the Republican and Democratic parties have Senate and House campaign committees. While they help raise funds for candidates, the bulk of their contribution lies in providing polling and advertising advice and, in some cases, the recruitment of candidates. While these national party organizations do not constitute the primary campaign organizations for candidates, they have become more and more involved, especially in House races (Herrnson, 1988).

Open seat races (in which the incumbent does not seek reelection) are typically more competitive than races with incumbents running for reelection.

Open seat races, that is, races in which the incumbent does not seek reelection, are typically more competitive than races with incumbents running for reelection. Nonetheless, studies have shown that in House elections, the outcome in open seat races is strongly influenced by the partisan composition of the district and the popularity of the former incumbent. Thus, although candidates whose party has not held the seat have a much better chance of winning, on average, in open seat races, the incumbent's party typically retains the seat. In 203 open seat races in the 1980s only 49 were won by the opposing party. In the Senate, the outcome of the race seems to depend more on the quality of the two candidates. Of the 25 open seats in the 1980s, 12 changed party hands, a much higher proportion than for the House.

Open seat races by definition result in the election of new members. The disproportionately large number of open seats in 1992 resulted from three factors: redistricting reduced the electoral security of some members; the House banking scandal threatened the electoral prospects of House incumbents, especially the forty-six incumbents with one hundred or more overdrafts; and, finally, 1992 was the last year in which an incumbent could retire and retain for personal use moneys collected for political campaigns. Although twenty House and Senate incumbents were defeated in primaries in 1992, the large number of freshmen members in the 103d Congress was primarily a result of retirements, not electoral defeats of incumbents. Contrary to popular belief, H. Ross Perot's presidential campaign—and all the anti-incumbent fervor that accompanied it—was of little importance in the general election, where the typical party and incumbency factors worked much as usual.

The consequences of "candidate-centered" campaigns are clear. Incumbents in both House and Senate races have a distinct advantage because of the resources that incumbency provides. Over time, they can build support by virtue of their service to their constituents, an opportunity challengers do not have. District service translates into campaign contributions and publicity that in turn build further support. These advantages frequently deter strong challengers from entering a race, and those who do run seldom win. House members, by virtue of their smaller constituencies and the more particular expectations that voters have of them, are better able to use these resources to establish electoral safety than are senators. In the absence of any major change in the electoral system, these patterns are likely to persist.

[See also (I) Campaign Financing.]

BIBLIOGRAPHY

Erikson, Robert S. "Incumbency and U.S. Senators." Paper presented at Stanford Conference on Senate Elections. 1991.

Fiorina, Morris. *Congress: Keystone of the Washington Establishment.* 1977.

Herrnson, Paul. *Party Campaigning in the 1980's.* 1988.

Jacobson, Gary. *Electoral Origins of Divided Government.* 1990.

Niemi, Richard G., Linda W. Powell, and Patricia L. Bicknell. "The Effects of Congruity between Community and District on Salience of U.S. House Candidates." *Legislative Studies Quarterly* 11 (1986): 187–201.

Olson, David. "U.S. Congressmen and Their Diverse Congressional District Parties." *Legislative Studies Quarterly* 3 (1978): 239–264.

Ornstein, Norman J., Thomas E. Mann, and Michael J. Malbin. *Vital Statistics on Congress, 1991–1992.* 1992.

– LYNDA W. POWELL
WENDY SCHILLER

Voting

"Few die and none retire" was the adage applied to incumbent members of the House of Representatives in the 1950s. Only in the Democratic landslide of 1958 did fewer than 90 percent—89.9 percent—of incumbents fail to win reelection during that decade. Senators were not quite so fortunate; only in 1956 were more than three-quarters of incumbent senators successful in winning new terms. Reelection rates to the House fell slightly during the turbulent 1960s but crept back over the 90 percent mark in the 1970s. By the mid-to-late 1980s, it seemed that only a scandal could unseat an incumbent representative. Not only were reelection rates high, but the margins of victory had become ever larger. Senators continued to have a more difficult time achieving reelection, but by the 1980s incumbents had become more secure than they had been in decades.

The incumbency advantage in the House is a twentieth-century phenomenon. For most of the nineteenth century representatives were not career politicians. Henry Clay served as Speaker of the House in his first term. Reelection rates began to rise in the mid-nineteenth century as more members became career politicians, peaking in 1920 before falling again. Prior to the 1960s, reelection rates tracked the fortunes of the president's party. Since then, incumbents have increasingly won new terms regardless of national tides.

Twentieth-century House elections have become less competitive over time, while contests for the Senate have become slightly more competitive. The post–World War II House incumbency reelection rates have increased more steadily over time than those for the Senate. Not only have fewer Senate incumbents won reelection than their House counterparts (76 percent compared to 92 percent in the postwar era), but Senate elections have demonstrated considerably more volatility. The standard deviation for Senate incumbency victories is almost three times as large as that for the House (12.9 compared to 4.7). The fortunes of Senate incumbents can change quickly, even as House incumbents remain relatively insulated from national trends. Incumbent senators' success rates plummeted in 1958, only to rise to near record levels two years later. Barely more than half of incumbent senators won reelection in 1980, yet more than 90 percent won just two years later. Some of the variation in Senate reelection rates is attributable to the peculiar cycle in which just one-third of senators face the electorate every two years, but the wide swings over time suggest that other, more systematic factors are also at work.

House and Senate elections are fundamentally different from each other. The aggregate correlation between House and Senate incumbent reelection rates in the twenty-three postwar elections is just .31. House contests are marked by weak challengers who have had little prior experience and have difficulty raising enough money to compete with well-funded incumbents. Senators face much stronger challengers, often House members or governors, with widespread name recognition and the ability to raise substantial amounts of money. Representatives come from more homogenous constituencies, which limits the role of issues in elections. Senators' more heterogenous constituencies highlight the controversial policy stands that legislators are expected to take in the "world's greatest deliberative body." Most House districts are more compact than states, so representatives can establish personal relationships with their constituents. Senators are forced to rely mostly on the media to reach voters; they cannot establish the same trusting relationship with constituents that comes from one-on-one contact.

The decline of parties made voters more likely to support incumbents. Presidents could no longer carry large majorities of their partisans into Congress, but they were also less likely to lose many seats in the midterm "referenda" on the president's popularity. Weaker partisanship made House incumbents more secure, but not senators.

Students of congressional elections agree that senators have greater difficulty winning reelection than members of the House.

Students of congressional elections agree that senators have greater difficulty winning reelection than members of the House. Yet that is one of the few assertions about congressional elections that is unchallenged. There are few disputes over what drives Senate elections, but largely because they have not been studied in great detail. The sources of the incumbency advantage for the House remain controversial. Indeed, it is not even clear whether House incumbents became safer in the 1970s and early 1980s. From 1946 to 1964, 61 percent of House incumbents won more than 60 percent of the vote in their reelection bids; from 1966 to 1984, 73 percent achieved this measure of security. Yet Gary Jacobson (1991) demonstrates that incumbents elected with supposedly secure margins of between 60 and 65 percent of the vote in the 1970s were just as likely to lose the next time around as members who garnered from 55 to 60 percent of the vote in the 1950s. Not until 1986 and 1988 did increased vote margins bring greater short-term security. Ten percent fewer incumbents won by more than 60 percent in 1990 than in 1986 and 1988, presaging the high retirement and defeat rates of 1992.

Ironically, the members who supposedly were most secure—those with the longest tenure—were more likely to lose than they had been in the era when seniority equaled power in the House. Freshman members, in contrast, became more secure than they had once been. The "sophomore surge," the boost in votes from an initial victory to the first reelection campaign, tripled from the 1960s to the 1970s and has remained high. Currently there is both more uniformity and greater volatility in House contests. The seniority of members is not so strongly related to their prospects of victory.

Voters are becoming more fickle in House races as well as in Senate contests. Members with "safe" margins can no longer rest assured of victory. Voters now shift their loyalties in less predictable ways than before. What has saved many incumbents from defeat in light of these trends is a decrease in the "swing ratio," a measure of how many seats change for every percentage of aggregate vote change. In races involving incumbents, the House swing ratio was cut in half from the period between 1946 and 1964 to the period between 1966 and 1986. Higher vote margins protected incumbents from being swept out of office when national tides went against their party. Even large swings in the national two-party vote would not spell defeat for the increasing share of members who had won by comfortable margins. Senators, who usually won by smaller margins than their House counterparts, were less insulated from national trends, as the elections of 1958, 1980, and 1986 indicate.

The elections of 1984 through 1988 signaled a sharp increase in the electoral security of House members. While only fifteen incumbents were defeated in the 1990 general elections—still two and a half times as many as in 1986 or 1988—sitting members' vote shares declined to just under two-thirds of the vote, the lowest average since 1974. The average vote shares dropped for members of both parties, although more precipitously for Republicans than for Democrats. Thus, 1990 set the stage for the sea change of 1992, which began setting a record for retirements as sixty-five House members decided not to seek new terms. Historically, representatives have had long-established auras of invincibility, especially in comparison to their Senate counterparts. What kept them so secure for so long and why did their advantages atrophy so quickly?

HOUSE INCUMBENCY ADVANTAGES. A range of interrelated factors has made House incumbents more secure since the 1960s. They include (1) the waning of party identification; (2) the correspondent deemphasizing of issues in House elections; (3) legislators' development of "home styles" designed to enhance reelection prospects; (4) increasing perquisites of office that help members develop nonpartisan home styles; (5) spending patterns that strongly favor incumbents over challengers; and (6) weaker challengers with less political experience and feeble party support. Overall, incumbents now run largely on their own merits and demerits. Weaker parties rob challengers of auxiliary campaign organizations. They eviscerate the ties between presidential popularity and party-line voting, thus insulating incumbents from trends that would harm their party nationally. Legislators are now free to develop their own style, deemphasizing issues and highlighting the delivery of services and personal style. The more popular members are, the more money they can raise—and the less money challengers can amass. Faced with very popular incumbents who can raise a lot of money, the strongest challengers are likely to opt out and leave weaker candidates as the sole contestants in House races.

Party identification. Party identification has become less central to American politics since the 1970s. Americans no longer identify as strongly with parties as they did in the 1950s and 1960s. The percentage of those without party identification doubled—from approximately 10 percent to about 20 percent—in House and Senate elections from the 1950s to the 1980s. From the 1940s through 1952, about 20 percent of congressional districts split their partisan tickets between the presidency and the House; by the 1970s and 1980s, approximately one-third of the districts regularly did so, with that portion rising to 44 percent in the presidential landslides of 1972 and 1984. Even when national trends strongly favored one party, incumbents won approximately 90 percent of their contests.

Issues and home style. As partisanship became less important in House races, sitting legislators increasingly relied on their own resources to win new terms. Representatives sought to develop home styles that downplayed controversial issues and highlighted the bonds of trust between legislators and their constituents. Members told voters that they were primarily concerned with looking out for local interests. Some studies (e.g., Johannes, 1984) show that policy agreement between legislators and constituents does affect incumbents' reelection success.

The development of a successful home style usually, though not always, depends on a representative's ability to sidestep controversial issues. If members want to appeal to a sufficient number of voters to take 70 percent of the vote, then they must avoid contention. Jacobson (1992) shows why incumbents should avoid issues and focus on the personal contact that is essential to establishing trust between voters and members. In 1988, 19 percent of respondents to the American National Election Study said that they liked the incumbents' ideology and policy positions, while 35 percent disliked their members' stands on issues. Given this two-to-one balance against issues, incumbents try to shift attention away from ideology. If a district is homogenous, so the range of ideological positions is not wide, members may be able to benefit from highlighting issues. The more diverse the district—or if the incumbent represents the disadvantaged party—the more the incumbent will steer the campaign away from issues.

Development of a successful home style requires being known and liked. Throughout the 1980s an average of 92 percent of constituents recognized their incumbent's name, compared to 54 percent name-recognition for challengers. Half of the respondents who recognized the incumbent's name liked something about the member; only 12 percent disliked anything. By contrast, only 21 percent of those who recognized the challenger's name liked something about the candidate, while 14 percent disliked something (Jacobson, 1992).

Incumbents have a presence that challengers lack. More than twice as many voters report some contact with the incumbent compared to the challenger in House races. Almost all voters (91 percent) report some contact with the incumbent. About two-thirds received mail from their legislator, compared to just 15 percent from the challenger. On the specific dimensions of contact—personal, attending a meeting, talking to staff, read about in newspaper, saw on television, heard on radio, or indirect contact through family or friends—incumbents' advantages ranged from 2 to 1 to 10 to 1. The better known and liked incumbents are, the more votes they get, especially from people who identify with the opposition party. Contact develops both name recognition and likability; more critically, it develops positive evaluations of the incumbent's job performance and reputation for helpfulness (Jacobson, 1992).

Perquisites. Incumbents grant themselves a wide array of perquisites, estimated to be worth up to $1.5 million over a two-year term, to increase their name recognition and likability. Members have unlimited mailing ("franking") privileges to their districts and very generous office expenditures that permit them to travel back to their districts as often as they wish, to make unlimited long-distance phone calls (and to receive them on toll-free numbers), to send newsletters to their constituents, and to maintain office staffs considerably larger than those of any other legislature in the world. Both the House and Senate have television studios in which members can produce programs and relay them via satellite to stations in their districts without charge.

Members of Congress have always paid attention to their constituents. The new era of powerful incumbents has been marked by a sharp increase in perquisites. There was a tenfold increase in the volume of congressional mailings from the 1950s to the 1970s and a further doubling over the next decade. The initial big spurt occurred in the 1970s, as incumbent vote shares shot up. The number of House employees jumped from 1,440 in 1947 to 7,569 in 1989. More critically, an ever-increasing number of legislators—in the Senate as well as the House—shifted office staff to their constituencies. By 1990, 42 percent of House staff (and 35 percent of Senate staff) were constituency-based. Most of the district staff handles mail, constituents' requests, and casework designed to resolve peoples' problems with the government.

Perquisites enhance name recognition. They also buy likability at relatively little cost. Casework and publicity are noncontroversial. They appeal to voters across partisan and ideological lines, whereas stances on issues are more divisive. Do perquisites attract votes? The evidence is mixed. Johannes (1984) finds that the volume of casework done by a congressional office has little impact on the member's vote margin and that voters are moved more by a legislator's policy positions than by specific benefits. Few constituents, after all, ask members for help in casework. Yet even if casework does not directly produce votes, it does lead to a reputation for helpfulness, which generates support for incumbents.

Do perquisites attract votes? The evidence is mixed.

LEGISLATIVE SPENDING. Incumbents also use legislative spending to build coalitions. The increasing incumbency advantage has been traced in part to the growing expenditures on pork-barrel projects that often provide more political than economic benefit. Legislators like such projects—a new dam, a post office—because they are visible. The electoral impact of the pork barrel is unclear, however. The amount of money spent on such programs does not seem to affect the share of the votes incumbents receive. Rather, a member's reputation for helping the district seems more important than actual dollars spent, and reputations do not seem to have suffered in the mid-1980s, when funds for such projects were severely limited. Morris P. Fiorina (1991) argues that it is not pork-barrel spending on specific projects that matters. Much more important, he claims, is the overall increase, beginning in the 1960s and 1970s, in government expenditures on a wide range of social programs. This spending changed people's expectations of government. Members of Congress can claim credit for these entitlement programs and offer constituents real assistance in getting benefits—thus securing votes from a grateful electorate.

Campaign funding and spending. The greatly expanded role of the federal government has led to the proliferation of new interest groups seeking to influence policy. These organizations not only lobby; they increasingly have formed political action committees (PACs) to influence the outcome of congressional elections. PACs burgeoned after the enactment of the Federal Election Campaign Act of 1974, which sought to curb the accountability-free cash campaign contributions that had figured so importantly in the Watergate scandal. The number of political action committees rose from 608 in 1974 to more than 4,000 by 1990. PAC contributions to House candidates rose from $30 million in 1974 to $147.9 million in 1988 (both in 1988 dollars). PAC contributions rose from 17 percent of all House receipts in 1974 to 43 percent in 1988. The largest source of campaign funds was still individuals, but their share nevertheless declined from 60 percent to 49 percent during the same period. Most PAC contributions go to incumbents. Even business-oriented PACs usually pursue a pragmatic strategy of rewarding those who hold power and so give more money to Democratic than to Republican incumbents.

Congressional campaigns have become very expensive. The average House incumbent spent $79,000 in 1976 but almost $400,000 in 1990. Challengers were reasonably competitive in 1976, spending $51,000; but by 1990 they had fallen to just $109,000. Challengers need money to buy name recognition. Their name recognition increases with spending, although the rate of increase tapers off as spending goes up and stops increasing altogether after a plateau of about $500,000 is reached. Increased expenditures bring votes, so the amount a challenger spends is one of the most important, if not the most important, determinant of whether the incumbent or the challenger wins in a House election.

There was a long-standing debate about the effect of incumbent expenditures. For all the money that sitting members raised, there appeared to be little payoff. The more incumbents spend, the *worse* they do—a most anomalous result. Members who spend the most face the strongest challenges; they must react in turn. Incumbents garner large war chests to scare off high-quality challengers. There is now agreement that incumbent spending does lead to at least some increment in vote shares for the sitting member. Sitting members who spend virtually nothing already start with virtually universal name recognition—greater than even the highest spending challenger can hope to achieve. Therefore, the impact of incumbent spending is bound to be less than it is for challengers.

As the gap between challenger and incumbent spending increases, incumbents' advantages grow. Most challengers from 1972 to 1990 spent under $100,000 (1990 dollars); this level of spending gave them just a 1 percent chance of unseating an incumbent. Even the best-funded challengers—the 14 percent who spend more than $300,000 (1990 dollars)—stood only a one-in-four chance of besting the incumbent.

Challenger quality. Most challengers are amateurs, with no background in politics. High-quality challengers, who have previously held elective office, are experienced in running campaigns and begin with greater name recognition. Jacobson (1991) finds that from 1946 to 1988, 17.3 percent of experienced challengers defeated incumbents, compared to a mere 4.3 percent of amateurs. A high-quality challenger can, on average, expect to win an additional 3 percent of the vote against an incumbent. Beyond that, high-quality challengers are also able to raise more money, so that their competitive advantage over amateur challengers is magnified. Yet the quality of challengers—especially Republicans—declined markedly in the late 1980s and in 1990. The share of incumbents who ran unopposed rose sharply.

SENATORS' LOWER INCUMBENCY ADVANTAGE. Senators have fared less well than representatives in winning reelection because they do not have some of the latter's incumbency advantages. The decline of partisanship benefits incumbents in both chambers, but senators do not gain as much from it as House members, because they are not as sheltered by nonpartisan, constituency-oriented activities. Issues play a greater role in Senate elections than in House contests. Voters expect senators to take more prominent roles than representatives in debates on national policy. Also, the six-year term encourages senators to take greater risks on policy issues.

Senators have different home styles than representatives. Their constituencies are usually larger and more diverse. They cannot—or will not—engage in the personal contact that House members do. Senators are less likely than are House members to meet constituents personally. They go home less often. They pay less attention to constituents in the middle years of their terms and have less direct contact with them during election campaigns. When they campaign, they are more likely to do so through the media. Here they are at a disadvantage, because they cannot control what television or newspapers report about them. Senators also find it more difficult to claim credit for legislative accomplishments than do representatives.

Most critically, senators face stronger and better-financed challengers than do representatives. About two-thirds of Senate challengers in the 1970s and 1980s have held prior elective office—often serving in the House or as governor—while still others have achieved celebrity status as, for example, astronauts or athletes. While Senate incumbents are slightly more likely than their House counterparts to be recognized by constituents (97 compared to 92 percent), Senate challengers are substantially more likely to be known than are House challengers (78 percent compared to 54 percent). While Senate challengers are about as well liked as their House counterparts, more voters know who they are. Incumbent senators are not as well liked as representatives, perhaps because they do not perform the wide array of constituent service functions that House members do. Senators are more likely to face primary challenges—and to lose them—than are House members.

Most voters still cast ballots consistent with party identification.

Senate elections are far more expensive to mount than House campaigns. Incumbent expenditures rose from $623,000 in 1976 to $3.55 million in 1990. Challengers spent $452,000 in 1976 and $1.7 million in 1990. The spending gap between incumbents and challengers has widened, reflecting the somewhat greater security senators had in the early 1990s as compared to the 1970s and early 1980s. Yet the gap is far narrower than in House races. Strong challengers need not match incumbent spending. They need only spend enough to gain widespread name recognition. Challenger spending, according to Alan I. Abramowitz (1988), is the most important factor in Senate elections, followed by the closeness of a primary challenge, the ideology and partisanship of the state, and the voters' judgment of which party can best handle national problems.

Yet all Senate constituencies are not alike. As Mark C. Westlye (1991) shows, only 48 percent of the Senate elections between 1968 and 1984 fit the category of hard-fought races. The remainder are very much like House contests, with little competition and moderate amounts of money spent. There are two distinct types of Senate incumbents: the vulnerable (mostly in large, heterogenous, competitive states) and the relatively safe (mostly in small, homogenous, one-party states).

NATIONAL PARTY TRENDS. Even though partisanship has waned, party identification still exerts a strong pull on individual voting behavior in congressional elections. Most voters still cast ballots consistent with party identification. When a president and his party become unpopular—most often on account of a weak economy—do voters take out their frustrations on his congressional party? There is substantial historical evidence for such "retrospective" voting. In five midterm elections from 1874 to 1938, the president's party lost seventy or more seats. Since 1950, no House election has cost either party even fifty seats. Yet Senate elections remain volatile and more subject to national trends than contemporary House contests.

There is stronger evidence for retrospective voting in aggregate studies of vote and seat shifts than in voters' motivations as expressed through survey research. Voters now punish presidents for their mistakes when they come up for reelection and are less likely to take out their frustrations on the president's partisans in the House. On the other hand, they are also less likely to reward the chief executive with sizable majorities in presidential election years. Coattails are substantially less important than they were before partisan ties atrophied. Dwight D. Eisenhower's 55 percent victory in 1952 brought him a Republican Congress; George Bush's slightly smaller victory in 1988 saw the Democrats pad their majority by three House seats.

Even though more modest, there are still partisan shifts in the House and Senate that track presidential popularity and the national economy, as in the elections of 1974, 1980, 1982, and 1986. Because many analyses had failed to find any direct link between evaluations of the president and the economy and voters' choices for Congress, Jacobson and Kernell (1983) suggested that it was candidates, not voters, who behaved strategically. Better quality candidates run during their party's "good years." Donors are more likely to contribute to the campaigns of these high-quality challengers. Even though voters do not behave strategically, candidates and donors do, thus creating the impression that voters respond to the political and economic environment.

While House elections are more insulated from national trends than they were in the nineteenth century and the first half of the twentieth, at least some voters do respond to presidential popularity and the state of the economy. In the 1974 referendum on Watergate and a weak economy, voters who backed Republican candidates in 1972 cast their ballots retrospectively, while those who had voted for the Democrats two years earlier logically continued to back their own party (Uslaner and Conway, 1985). Senate elections suggest the weakness of the "strategic politicians" thesis. In several postwar elections (1946, 1958, 1980, 1986), Senate turnover has appeared far more responsive to national trends than House results. Yet there is far less variation in challenger quality for the Senate than for the House. There is still the potential for retrospective voting, even if party ties no longer bring about the massive seat changes that marked earlier elections.

WHAT HAPPENED TO THE INCUMBENCY ADVANTAGE? The first crack in the House incumbency advantage came in 1990, when incumbents' vote shares dropped precipitously in both chambers. Yet few House incumbents lost, and Senate turnover set a postwar low (one incumbent defeated, three retired). We know that weak challengers who were poorly funded saved many House incumbents (Jacobson, 1992). (Senate incumbents, especially Democrats, did face strong challengers—including some of the Republicans' best and brightest House members.)

Incumbents in both chambers possessed all the advantages of previous campaigns, yet their vote shares fell. Something was happening. Congress and the president were stymied over the federal budget deficit in 1990; the confrontation proved embarrassing to both, and confidence in the government fell. The level of the public's confidence in government has, however, borne an inconsistent relationship to electoral outcomes for Congress. Discontent in 1974 and 1980 produced massive partisan shifts, first toward the Democrats and then toward the Republicans. Yet similarly high levels of distrust had no measurable effect in 1976 or 1978.

In 1990 and again in 1992, confidence in leaders plummeted after having recovered to some degree. For most of the 1980s, confidence in government had been higher than during the 1970s. In 1990 it fell sharply, right before the election. It rose in 1991 with the Persian Gulf War but then slid rapidly throughout 1992. These dips resembled the 1974 decline, but with a difference. The Watergate-inspired fall let voters take out their frustration on one party. The 1990 and 1992 declines were directed at both parties. In 1990, Republican House incumbents lost more races than did Democratic incumbents. The House bank scandal and the independent presidential candidacy of H. Ross Perot in 1992 encouraged stronger challengers in both parties. With Democrats holding substantial majorities, they had more to lose.

Democratic incumbents lost twice as many seats (16 compared to 8) as Republicans in 1992. Nevertheless, the net partisan swing was small. The electorate took out its frustrations on both parties. The success rate of House incumbents running for reelection fell to 88.3 percent, the lowest level since 1974. Senate victory rates are more volatile, so 1992 did not stand out. For both chambers, incumbents' share of the vote plummeted—to the lowest level for the House since 1974 and for the Senate since 1980. Rising distrust of government, the anti-incumbent theme that resonated from Ross Perot's campaign, and a sharp rise in the quality of challengers (especially for the House) all contributed to the weakening of the incumbency advantage. Even incumbents tried to campaign as outsiders. Legislators worried whether the electoral security of the 1980s would give way to increased volatility in the 1990s and in the twenty-first century, which might look more like the nineteenth century than the twentieth.

BIBLIOGRAPHY

Abramowitz, Alan I. "Explaining Senate Election Outcomes." *American Political Science Review* 82 (1988): 385–404.

Canon, David T. *Actors, Athletes, and Astronauts.* 1990.

Fenno, Richard F., Jr. *Home Style.* 1978.

Fenno, Richard F., Jr. *The United States Senate: A Bicameral Perspective.* 1982.

Fiorina, Morris P. *Congress. Keystone of the Washington Establishment.* 2d ed. 1991.

Green, Donald Philip, and Jonathan S. Krasno. "Salvation for the Spendthrift Incumbent." *American Journal of Political Science* 32 (1988): 884–907.

Gross, Donald, and David Breaux. "Historical Trends in U.S. Senate Elections, 1912–1988." *American Politics Quarterly* 19 (1991): 284–309.

Jacobson, Gary C. *The Electoral Origins of Divided Government.* 1991.

Jacobson, Gary C. *The Politics of Congressional Elections.* 3d ed. 1992.

Jacobson, Gary C., and Samuel Kernell. *Strategy and Choice in Congressional Elections.* 2d ed. 1983.

Johannes, John R. *To Serve the People: Congress and Constituency Service.* 1984.

Uslaner, Eric M., and M. Margaret Conway. "The Responsible Congressional Electorate." *American Political Science Review* 79 (1985): 788–803.

Westlye, Mark C. *Senate Elections and Campaign Intensity.* 1991.

– ERIC M. USLANER

EMERGENCY POWERS

Federal law makes available to the president a variety of powers for use in crises or emergency conditions threatening the nation. This authority is not limited to military or war situations. Some of these powers, deriving from the Constitution or statutory law, are continuously available to the president, with little or no qualification. Others—statutory delegations from Congress—exist on a standby basis and remain dormant until the president formally declares a national emergency. Using the powers delegated by such statutes, the president may seize property and commodities, organize and control the means of production, assign military forces abroad, institute martial law, seize and control all transportation and communication, regulate the operation of private enterprise, and restrict travel.

There are, however, limits and restraints on the president in his exercise of emergency powers. With the exception of the habeas corpus clause, the Constitution makes no allowance for the suspension of any of its provisions during a national emergency. Disputes over the constitutionality or legality of the exercise of emergency powers are subject to judicial review. Indeed, the courts and Congress can restrain the president regarding emergency powers, as can public opinion. Certainly Congress may modify, rescind, or render dormant its delegations of emergency authority.

Until World War I, U.S. presidents utilized emergency powers at their own discretion. However, during and after the war, chief executives had available to them a growing body of standby emergency law, which became operative upon the proclamation of a national emergency. Sometimes these proclamations confined the matter of crisis to a specific policy sphere, such as during the banking crisis of 1933; at other times, such as in the general proclamation of 1950, they placed no limitation on the pronouncement.

Disputes over the constitutionality or legality of the exercise of emergency powers are subject to judicial review.

These activations of standby emergency authority remained acceptable until the era of the Vietnam War. In 1976, Congress curtailed this practice with the passage of the National Emergencies Act (90 Stat. 1255). This act grew out of the recommendations of the Senate Special Committee on National Emergencies and Delegated Emergency Powers, a temporary study panel. According to the statute's procedures, the president, when declaring a national emergency, must specify the standby authorities he is activating. Congress may negate this action through a resolution disapproving the emergency declaration or the activation of a particular statutory power. The act was amended in 1985 (99 Stat. 448) to require the use of a joint resolution in this regard, which must be approved through the constitutionally provided legislative process. Originally, a so-called legislative veto could be effected via a concurrent resolution approved by both houses of Congress.

Any national emergency declared by the president that is not previously terminated by Congress expires automatically on the anniversary of the declaration, unless the president, within the ninety-day period prior to each anniversary date, gives notice to Congress and in the *Federal Register* that the emergency is to continue in effect. In practice, Congress did not find it necessary to rescind the national emergencies subsequently declared by Presidents Jimmy Carter, Ronald Reagan, and George Bush.

[See also (II) Emergency Powers.]

BIBLIOGRAPHY

U.S. Senate. Committee on Government Operations and Special Committee on National Emergencies and Delegated Emergency

Powers. *The National Emergencies Act (Public Law 94-412)—Source Book: Legislative History, Texts, and Other Documents.* 94th Cong., 2d sess., 1976. Committee Print.

U.S. Senate. Special Committee on National Emergencies and Delegated Emergency Powers. *A Brief History of Emergency Powers in the United States.* 93d Cong., 2d sess., 1974. Committee Print.

– HAROLD C. RELYEA

ENACTING CLAUSE

Every bill begins with an enacting clause, and every resolution with a resolving clause, as a formal declaration that the substantive language that follows has been duly adopted in accordance with the constitutionally mandated procedures. The exact form of these clauses was first prescribed by statute in 1871 and is at present set forth in Title 1 of the United States Code.

The enacting clause reads as follows:

> Be it enacted by the Senate and House of Representatives of the United States of America in Congress assembled, . . .

The resolving clause in a joint resolution uses the single word *Resolved* in place of *Be it enacted* with *two thirds of each House concurring therein* inserted before the final comma if the resolution is one proposing a constitutional amendment. In either case, the Senate is always mentioned first, regardless of where the measure originates.

In a concurrent resolution the clause reads *Resolved by the House of Representatives (the Senate concurring)* (with the names of the two houses reversed if it originates in the Senate). In a simple resolution it consists of the single word *Resolved.*

In the early days of the Republic, it was thought necessary to give every subdivision of a bill its own separate enacting clause, and the sections were not numbered. This practice gradually disappeared, and today Title 1 of the Code provides that "no enacting or resolving clause shall be used in any section of an Act or resolution of Congress except the first."

[See also (I) Bills, Resolutions.]

BIBLIOGRAPHY

Filson, Lawrence E. *The Legislative Drafter's Desk Reference.* 1992.

U.S. House of Representatives. Law Revision Counsel. *How Our Laws Are Made.* Published periodically.

– LAWRENCE E. FILSON

ENFORCEMENT

The U.S. constitutional system permits change through the amendment process, but such change does not come easily. After Congress or the states have proposed an amendment, it must be ratified by three-fourths of the state legislatures or by a national convention composed of representatives from three-fourths of the states. Since the Civil War amendments, Congress has been given the dubious task of ensuring the enforcement of the substance of these respective amendments. For example, although section 1 of the Thirteenth Amendment abolished slavery, section 2 was written to ensure that the actual burdens of slavery would be permanently eliminated—"Congress shall have the power to enforce this article by appropriate legislation." And while the Fourteenth Amendment's section 1 promised equal protection under the laws, section 5—"Congress shall have the power to enforce, by appropriate legislation, the provisions of this article"—was necessary to guarantee those very protections. In the case of the Fourteenth Amendment, however, Congress's enforcement power was often weakened by the Supreme Court's narrow interpretation of the enforcement clause. For example, Congress passed the Civil Rights Act of 1875, which intended to secure for all people the "full and equal enjoyment" of public accommodations, such as inns or theaters. Yet the Supreme Court found that act unconstitutional. The law, the Court argued, attempted to control, for example, the private discriminatory action of innkeepers, and that limit was not intended to be within the scope of the Fourteenth Amendment. Only state action that discriminated was limitable under the amendment.

Congress's enforcement power under the Thirteenth Amendment actually received a more generous reading by the Court, but not until the 1968 decision of *Jones v. Alfred H. Mayer Co.* At issue in *Jones* was a modern legislative act (42 U.S.C. 1982) based on the older Civil Rights Act of 1866, an act that attempted to ensure that all citizens enjoy the right to sell, lease, or purchase real and personal property. This time the Court interpreted Congress's enforcement power in a way that would permit the antidiscrimination act. The law could be used to reach private as well as state and public conduct, a result the Court had refused to consider in its reading of the Civil Rights Act of 1875. By broadly interpreting 42 U.S.C. 1982 to protect the right of all people to purchase property, the Court had expanded the very meaning of the enforcement clause under the Thirteenth Amendment. Eliminating the badges of slavery in 1865 meant obliterating any obstacles to the acquisition of property in 1968.

Congress's enforcement power of the Fifteenth Amendment has also had a slow and protracted history. Before the Voting Rights Act of 1965, which was extended in 1970, 1975, and 1982, Congress rarely used its power to enforce voting rights. But with the 1965 legislation firmly in place, Congress has used a variety of procedures such as bilingual elections and changes in state residence requirements to guarantee the right to vote and to prevent the "dilution" of minority voting power. Critics of the Voting Rights Act argue that it has encouraged federal intervention in state and local voting matters: Yet even the Supreme Court has upheld an expansive view of Congress's authority, under the enforcement clause, to implement and secure voting rights. It remains to be seen how well Congress achieves its commitment to equality as it aggressively utilizes its enforcement powers to guarantee the protections of all the Civil War amendments.

BIBLIOGRAPHY

Peltason, Jack W. *Understanding the Constitution.* 1994.

Rossum, Ralph, and Alan Tarr. *American Constitutional Law.* 1991.

– JANIS JUDSON

ETHICS AND CORRUPTION IN CONGRESS

In American society, distrust of politics and politicians is a deeply ingrained cultural feature. Many people assume that members of Congress cannot be trusted and that "political ethics" is a contradiction in terms.

That assumption has constituted a staple of humorists at least since Mark Twain wrote that there is no criminal class in America—except Congress. Although popular cynicism about political ethics has not stopped people from running for Congress or from getting elected and reelected, it has added to the natural tension within the political system over how congressional standards and ethics are set and enforced.

Whatever the definition of graft and corruption, they have always existed in government to some extent.

According to the U.S. Constitution, Article I, section 5, Congress has the unique power of governing itself and its members: "Each House may determine the Rules of its Proceedings, punish its Members for disorderly Behavior, and with the concurrence of two thirds, expel a Member." This constitutional power serves as the basis for the congressional system of ethics. It means, obviously, that Congress has the responsibility to police itself, even though members of Congress are still subject to the dictates of criminal law and, except for official responsibilities and speech and debate, to civil proceedings as well. At the same time, lawmakers are judged individually every two or six years by the voters.

The self-regulatory aspect of Congress has fueled public suspicion; it has also produced within Congress substantial tension and frustration—a frustration compounded by the reality that standards of official conduct regularly change as overall standards and ethics evolve. Because of the contradictory nature of representative government, establishing sound ethical guidelines that balance the public interest against the private concerns of representatives has proved complex. Members of Congress must live with this inherent tension, and the ethics codes and standards intended to guide congressional behavior often simply add to their frustration.

Nonetheless, ethical standards and a system of oversight and discipline are necessary if Congress is to maintain its institutional legitimacy. To be sure, ethical standards are constantly changing as society changes; what would clearly be considered corruption today was perfectly acceptable in an earlier era. For example, in 1833, Sen. Daniel Webster argued vigorously in the Senate for the protection of Nicholas Biddle's Bank of the United States against attack from President Andrew Jackson. Subsequently, he wrote to Biddle, "If it is wished that my relation to the Bank should be continued, it may be well to send me the usual retainers." Webster ultimately received $32,000 for his efforts on behalf of the bank.

Whatever the definition of graft and corruption, however, they have always existed in government to some extent. The onset of organized interest group lobbying in the 1830s has often been credited with bringing more extensive corruption, more bribery, and monumental conflicts of interest. Industrialization in the 1850s expanded lobbying and group involvement, thereby augmenting congressional corruption. Popular gambling houses of the time, such as Edward Pendleton's Palace of Fortune, worked closely with lobbyists. If a legislator fell into debt with a house, the manager could steer his vote on a piece of legislation by threatening exposure or demanding payment. Lobbyists reciprocated managers' efforts through patronage as well as special gifts. One wealthy industrialist arrived at Pendleton's offering a team of horses. If such events occurred frequently, they could still generate public outrage whenever they were uncovered and reported.

Lobbying, and attendant corruption, grew steadily until the Grant administration of the early 1870s, an era particularly marked by political debauchery. The most famous scandal during this period was one involving Crédit Mobilier, a joint stock company controlled by Union Pacific Railroad. Rep. Oakes Ames (R-Mass.), also a director of Crédit Mobilier and Union

Pacific, bribed his fellow congressmen with stock to guarantee federal subsidies to the railroad. The exposure of the scheme in 1872 revealed a list of eighteen current or former legislators in both parties who allegedly received stock. Although Congress officially censured only two representatives, Ames and Democratic leader James Brooks of New York, the event fomented strong public distrust in the institution.

Soon after the Crédit Mobilier incident, Congress made a bad situation worse when it voted itself a pay raise, increasing legislators' remuneration from $5,000 to $7,000 per year. The public might have grudgingly accepted the raise in itself, but it became outraged when Congress voted to apply it retroactively, granting members back pay for that Congress even though the measure was passed on the last day of the session and more than half of those who benefited were lame ducks.

In other scandals of the era, Secretary of War William W. Belknap was impeached for selling Indian trading posts to the highest bidders, and a number of candidates or their supporters were accused of bribing voters for support or intimidating them from going to the polls at all. There were also sex scandals, including one involving Senators Roscoe Conkling (R-N.Y.) and William Sprague (R-R.I.) and Sprague's wife, that caught public attention and intensified the sense of corruption inside government.

Periodically throughout American history, scandals or allegations of scandal have erupted to reinforce public outrage over Washington's illicit politics; examples include the Whiskey Ring of 1875, the Teapot Dome scandal of 1922–1923, the Internal Revenue Service scandal of 1950–1951, Watergate and "Koreagate" in the 1970s, and Abscam and the savings and loan scandals in the 1980s. There followed the House bank and post office scandals, accusations of misconduct against Speaker James C. Wright, Jr. (D-Tex.), and scandals involving members under fire for allegations ranging from sexual misconduct to personal use of government funds. In several cases, ethics or lobbying reforms en-

Senate Select Committee on Investigation of Charges against Burton K. Wheeler. Left to right at the table, Senators William E. Borah (R-Idaho), chairman, Claude A. Swanson (D-Va.), Thaddeus H. Caraway (D-Ark.), Charles L. McNary (R-Oreg.), and Thomas Sterling (R-S.Dak.), 1924. (Library of Congress)

sued. These scandals contributed to the delegitimation of Congress and its self-policing mechanisms and helped shape the system that exists today.

Understanding the present system involves reviewing the historical precedents, evaluating the structural and legal approaches adopted through the years, and outlining the current set of ethical codes and standards. Furthermore, because reform has often evolved in response to some scandal or case of ethical wrongdoing, a few examples can furnish valuable insight into the conduct of members of Congress and the rationale behind the system they have devised.

EXPULSION AND CENSURE. In its original form Article I, section 5 did not include the phrase "with the concurrence of two thirds." This was added at the suggestion of James Madison during debate at the Constitutional Convention of 1787. Madison asserted that the right of expulsion was "too important to be exercised by a bare majority of a quorum, and in emergencies might be dangerously abused."

Belying Madison's concerns, Congress has exercised its disciplinary powers sparingly through the years. Lawmakers have been reluctant to punish their own, and when possible they have adopted less stringent and often symbolic forms of punishment. By 1993, only fifteen senators and four representatives had been expelled in the history of Congress. Expulsion is the most severe form of punishment and has traditionally been reserved for cases involving criminal abuse of the office or disloyalty. All but two cases of expulsion occurred during the tumultuous years of the Civil War, when some Southern members were charged with supporting a rebellion. At one point ten Senators were expelled in a single day, 11 July 1861, though one expulsion was later annulled. Of the two remaining cases, one involved a charge of conspiracy in 1797, and the other, expelling Rep. Michael O. Myers (D-Pa.), involved personal corruption and bribery in the Abscam scandal of the late 1970s and early 1980s.

Unsuccessful attempts at expelling members of Congress have arisen from charges such as assault on a fellow member, killing another member in a duel, sedition, corruption, and even Mormonism. In the case of the duel, the surviving member was not even subjected to censure, a less severe form of punishment than expulsion. In 1838, Rep. Jonathan Cilley, a Democrat from Maine, was fatally wounded by Rep. William J. Graves, a Whig from Kentucky. While a majority of the investigating committee recommended that Graves be expelled, their report was never taken up by the full House. Apparently dueling among members was not infrequent and had commonly gone unremarked.

The more lenient punishment, censure, requires only a majority vote, as opposed to the two-thirds required for a vote of expulsion. The House and Senate differ somewhat in their approaches to censure. In the Senate, members may speak before the chamber in their own behalf, whereas in the House, members come before the Speaker and are formally denounced without any opportunity to defend themselves. Some of the offenses that have warranted censure in the House include insulting the Speaker or another representative, assaulting a senator, treasonable and offensive utterances, corruption, and financial misconduct.

Over time, the House has censured a total of twenty-two members; the Senate has censured (or "denounced" or "condemned") nine. The first formal House censure was in 1832, issued to Rep. William Stanbery, an Ohio anti-Jacksonian, for what was considered unacceptable and offensive language. He had said, "The eyes of the Speaker [Andrew Stevenson] are too frequently turned from the chair you occupy toward the White House."

Senators have been censured for breach of confidence, assault, bringing the Senate into disrepute, obstruction of the legislative process, and financial misconduct. One of the more notorious cases of censure in the Senate involved Sen. Joseph R. McCarthy (R-Wis.). In 1954, McCarthy was disciplined by his Senate colleagues for failing to cooperate with the Subcommittee on Privileges and Elections in their investigation of his behavior, for obstructing the constitutional process by harassing the members of that committee, and for generally bringing the Senate into disrepute. Although McCarthy went on record as having been censured, the actual term used by the Senate was *condemned.*

Another important case was that of Sen. Thomas J. Dodd (D-Conn.) in 1967. Dodd was censured for using campaign funds to cover personal expenses and for fraudulently billing travel costs to the government. His was the first case taken on by the newly established Select Committee on Standards and Conduct.

In the late 1980s, both the House and the Senate witnessed cases of censure and denouncement that involved financial wrongdoing. This trend primarily reflected the increasing importance of money in the campaign process and Congress's inability to devise an adequate system of codes and standards to guide members in handling their congressional finances. Many members accused of financial wrong-doing have pleaded their own uncertainty over the boundaries of propriety in serving constituents.

In addition to expulsion and censure Congress has through the years come up with lesser forms of punishment, such as reprimand, condemnation, and loss of chairmanship or seniority. These penalties are largely symbolic and are designed to quell public anxiety without ruining a member's political career.

EVOLUTION OF ETHICAL STANDARDS. The institutionalization of ethical standards and practices in Congress has been an evolutionary process. In early Congresses, the rules were loose and often inconsistently applied. The establishment of House and Senate ethics committees in the 1960s represented a major step toward uniformity. These committees were formed in the wake of a series of scandals in the early 1960s, highlighted by revelations about Robert G. "Bobby" Baker. As secretary to the Democratic majority in the Senate, Baker was accused of influence peddling and bribery; his actions tarnished the entire Senate leadership.

The institutionalization of ethical standards and practices in Congress has been an evolutionary process.

The Senate Ethics Committee, established in 1964, was originally called the Select Committee on Standards and Conduct. It was given the task of drawing up a code of conduct and was authorized to receive complaints and recommend disciplinary action. Members hoped that the bipartisan composition of the committee would shield it against the charges of prejudice and partisanship that had marred ethics investigations in the past. As already mentioned, the committee's first official action involved an inquiry into the activities of Senator Dodd.

The Powell case. In the House, the Committee on Standards of Official Conduct gained permanent status and was given investigative and enforcement powers in 1968. The committee was formed largely in reaction to the case of Rep. Adam Clayton Powell, Jr. (D-N.Y.). Within the scope of congressional ethics, the Powell case remains significant because it resulted in a precedent-setting Supreme Court ruling that limited Congress's power to exclude recalcitrant members.

Powell, who was first elected to Congress in 1944 and served as chairman of the Education and Labor Committee from 1961 to 1967, was widely considered the most powerful African American of his time. He got into trouble with the Internal Revenue Service and was indicted on a charge of tax evasion. He was also involved in two civil suits, one in which he was sued for libel by a constituent and the other involving the fraudulent transfer of property.

Many members, upset by Powell's behavior and blatant disregard for the law, sought to take action against him. First, the House Democratic Caucus removed him as chairman of the Education and Labor Committee (the last time a committee chairman had been deposed was in 1925). This occurred in January 1967, after Powell's Harlem constituents had elected him to a twelfth term in Congress.

In March 1967, against the recommendation of a select committee established to investigate Powell's "qualifications," the full House adopted a resolution to exclude him from the 90th Congress—the first such exclusion since 1919. Because Powell had not yet been seated, a simple majority of the House was able to vote to exclude him; had he been seated, only a vote for expulsion—requiring a two-thirds majority—could have removed him from office. The final resolution to exclude Powell was adopted by a vote of 307 to 116.

Powell filed suit against the House, and the proceedings eventually reached the Supreme Court. With his case pending before the Court, Powell entered his name in the special election held to fill his own vacant seat. He won the election but never applied to the House to be seated. Powell ran again in 1968 and again was victorious. In January 1969, he was sworn in as a member of the 91st Congress, after a two-year exile (during which his district went unrepresented). Later that year, the Court ruled that because Powell met the constitutional requirements for membership, the House had wrongly excluded him. Powell's case made clear that the House needed to develop some form of internal discipline—a code of conduct and a means of enforcing it.

The original codes of conduct established by the House and Senate ethics committees were general in nature and vague in content. Congress intended them largely to restore public confidence, eroded by certain ethical scandals of the mid-1970s.

The Hays scandal. One impropriety with significant consequences involved Rep. Wayne L. Hays, a Democrat from Ohio, and his employee-mistress, Elizabeth Ray. Although Hays resigned from the House before being officially disciplined, his case marked an important turning point in the level of scrutiny given to the personal lives of members of Congress. The scandal was uncovered by a pair of *Washington Post* reporters. Because of the ground swell of attention and publicity generated by the story, similar charges of sexual scandals involving other members of Congress and top government officials readily surfaced. Ben Bradlee, the *Post's* executive editor, likened the Hays affair to Watergate: it brought public and especially press attention to congressional abuses and excesses, just as Watergate had for the executive branch.

This and subsequent scandals seemed to affect the behavior of many members of Congress profoundly.

More caution was evident in their handling of financial and personnel issues, and many were more discreet in their personal affairs.

Strengthening the codes. Pressure built both within and outside Congress to toughen the ethics codes. In 1976 the House formed a fifteen-member bipartisan group—the Commission on Administrative Review, commonly known as the Obey Commission—to draft a new code of ethics that would address a whole host of issues, including congressional perquisites, acceptance of outside gifts and favors, financial disclosure, and limits on campaign financing. To no one's surprise, opinions among House members conflicted. Ultimately the commission came up with a series of proposals that would substantially change procedures and regulations regarding members' financial accountability. The proposals included a ban on office accounts; a limitation on outside earned income, including fees or honoraria; limitations on acceptance of gifts, use of the frank (or free postage), and reimbursed travel; and a more rigorous system of financial disclosure.

The commission's proposals survived the scrutiny of three separate House committees and were adopted in March 1977, nearly intact. The most controversial issue was the proposed limit on earned income. Because the limitation did not apply to unearned income derived from financial investments such as stocks and bonds, opponents argued that it would unduly burden less wealthy members. In the end Speaker Thomas P. (Tip) O'Neill, Jr. (D-Mass.), reminded his colleagues that the credibility of the institution was at stake and urged that all members would have to make sacrifices toward restoring public confidence in Congress.

In 1977 the Senate set about devising its own official code of ethics by establishing the Special Committee on Official Conduct. The committee came up with a plan that, in general terms, greatly resembled that of the House. One difference was that the Senate code extended many of its provisions to cover key staff members. In addition, the Senate code forbade all lobbying activities of former Senators and Senate employees for a specified period after leaving the Senate, prohibited certain kinds of employment discrimination by senators in hiring their staffs, and required that the Senate ethics committee publicly justify all decisions regarding allegations against members or staff.

The final vote of 86 to 9 in support of the code's passage in no way reflected the depth of conflict that characterized the debate. Many senators voted to institute the code mainly because they feared the political ramifications of voting against it. Arguments against limitations on earned income echoed those in the House. In the end, the new Senate code was a clear improvement over the previous one, which had been largely symbolic, offering little guidance, few means of enforcement, and many gaps and inconsistencies.

Adoption of these new ethics codes in both the House and Senate was closely tied to a congressional pay raise that took effect in February 1977. Members knew that in order to make a pay raise more palatable to the public, they would have to clean up their act, so to speak. In fact the commission that recommended the pay raise in 1976 issued a strong statement warning that a new code of ethics represented "the indispensable prelude to a popular acceptance of a general increase in executive, legislative and judicial salaries."

Ethics in Government Act (1978). With each house having passed its own new code of conduct, Congress moved to draft a comprehensive code of ethics that could be enacted into law. The Ethics in Government Act was signed into law in October 1978. It mandated detailed financial disclosure by federal officials and placed new restrictions on the license of former federal officials (not including members of Congress and their staffs) to lobby their former agencies. In addition, the bill encompassed most of the major elements of the House and Senate ethics codes. It did not refer only to Congress, though, as it was in part a response to the Watergate scandal of the mid-1970s, which had cast a dark shadow over the executive branch. In fact, one important provision of the bill set up an Office of Government Ethics to oversee financial disclosures and possible conflicts of interest within the executive branch.

Although prosecutorial independence had generally been maintained, the power wielded by independent counsels had been politicized and in some cases abused.

Another important provision of the 1978 law authorized special prosecutors to investigate and prosecute high-ranking executive-branch officials, separate and apart from the activities of the attorney general's office. Supporters of the provision aimed to eliminate the conflict inherent in a system in which the attorney general might be responsible for investigating the president who appointed him or her. The position of special prosecutor—or independent counsel, as it was renamed in 1983—was devised to operate outside the reach of executive-branch coercion. The 1978 law was also intended to restore public confidence in the political system, particularly in the wake of the Watergate scandal.

In the early 1990s a great debate was raging over whether the law had served its purpose or had become a blunt weapon for Congress and ambitious, unchecked prosecutors to use against executive-branch officials for political purposes. Although prosecutorial independence had generally been maintained, the power wielded by independent counsels had been politicized and in some cases abused. Critics of the office further claimed that it reflected a double standard: if the executive branch cannot be trusted to police its own, neither can Congress, so the independent counsel law should have applied to the legislature as well.

That argument suffers from two problems. First, the Framers specifically charged Congress with policing itself, believing that voters would prove the ultimate judges of elected officials. Appointed officials are treated by a different standard. Second, Congress is in fact policed by others, including executive-branch prosecutors—as occurred in the Abscam case, discussed below. In addition, the attorney general can choose to appoint a special counsel to investigate wrongdoing by members of Congress. Attorney General William Barr exercised this prerogative to investigate overdrafts by representatives from the House bank in 1992, when he appointed retired federal judge Malcolm Wilkey to take over the investigation from the U.S. attorney in Washington.

Even though some criticism might have been overstated or misguided, the independent counsel law still had problems. Some analysts believe that the law contributed in the long run to the culture of scandal pervading Washington in the late twentieth century. They argue further that Congress wielded an inordinate amount of power over the executive branch and that this power threatened the traditional integrity of the system of checks and balances.

The Iran-contra scandal and subsequent legal proceedings have been cited by some as evidence of the current system's inadequacy. Independent counsel Lawrence Walsh came for many to symbolize a process in which tens of millions of taxpayer dollars were spent on political prosecutions that some considered abusive and ultimately obstructive of the normal functioning of the criminal justice system. Furthermore, critics of the system express doubt that Justice Earl Warren's support of Congress's investigative powers for the "furtherance of a legislative purpose" was intended to generate what they perceive as political harassment, character assassination, and partisan bickering.

The creation of the independent counsel can be linked in large part to the Watergate scandal of 1972–1974. Watergate really ushered in the modern era of ethics reform, not only because it brought into question the standard of ethical behavior proper for public officials, but also because of the instrumental role the media played in uncovering the scandal. In the past, reporters had hesitated to publicize allegations concerning ethics abuses by elected officials; the Watergate affair paved the way for more active and aggressive involvement. In essence the press adopted a much more assertive role as watchdog over the government establishment, heightening public awareness of and interest in the ethical behavior of government officials.

DEVELOPMENTS DURING THE 1980S. The development of congressional codes of conduct and the passage of the Ethics in Government Act were indeed important steps toward developing a system of responsible and ethical government. As a series of ethical scandals during the 1980s demonstrated, however, inherent weaknesses remained in the system. Evidently members of Congress either failed to comprehend the regulations and standards laid out in their own codes of conduct or assumed that fellow members would show leniency in enforcing those codes, especially because ethical indiscretions by individual members often reflect poorly on the institution as a whole. In addition, with campaign costs escalating in the 1980s, members were under increasing pressure to solicit new donors and maintain large campaign funds. Simultaneously, the public was becoming increasingly cynical about Congress as an institution.

During the 1980s little was accomplished in the way of ethics reform. At the same time there were many scandals and investigations involving members of Congress, perhaps indicating the need for reform and clarification of the standards established in the late 1970s. That only a small percentage of these investigations resulted in any real disciplinary action caused many to question the effectiveness of the system. During the 1980s, in the view of many, there was not much a member of Congress could do short of criminal indictment to incur expulsion or even censure. As a result, Congress was criticized for failing to punish its members adequately for ethical infractions.

Abscam. The new decade was ushered in by what may have been the biggest scandal in congressional history. The incident, commonly known as Abscam, involved six representatives and one senator and resulted in the expulsion of one House member and the resignation of three. The three other lawmakers escaped congressional discipline when they were defeated at the polls before their investigations could be completed.

The scandal arose out of an undercover operation in which FBI agents disguised as businessmen and Arab sheiks enticed several members of Congress into accepting bribes in return for certain legislative and political favors. Five of the seven members implicated were actually videotaped accepting cash or stocks, and those videotapes were seen widely by TV viewers throughout the country. In the end, seven members of Congress were convicted of criminal wrongdoing.

The speed and severity of Congress's action in dealing with the Abscam scandal contrasted with its usual disposition of ethical scandals. Perhaps actual criminal wrongdoing provided an unmistakable motivation. Congress has had more difficulty in dealing with infractions that fall within the written law but outside the boundaries of what is popularly accepted as proper behavior for public officials.

Sex scandals. In 1982 the media played a prominent role in bringing to light allegations concerning a sex and drug ring that involved members of Congress and teenage congressional pages. Assertions of misconduct were aired on TV and printed in the papers before any official inquiry had been made. The ethics committee found the claims to be without merit, and it was later revealed that several of the allegations made by former pages had been exaggerations or outright lies. This incident raised important questions about press coverage of ethical scandals. Many members of Congress felt that the media had no business reporting unsubstantiated accusations, which could significantly damage the reputations of members of Congress and the body as a whole.

In 1983 it became apparent that not all the allegations of sexual misconduct had been unfounded. Two members of the House, Daniel B. Crane (R-Ill.) and Gerry E. Studds (D-Mass.), were censured for sexual misconduct with congressional pages, marking the first time any member had been censured for a sexual offense. Although the ethics committee had recommended a reprimand, the House chose the more severe form of discipline.

Attempts at ethics reform. During the late 1980s a good deal of concern was brewing over government ethics. First came the Iran-contra scandal, which implicated members of the executive branch and also cast a spotlight on Congress, where a select committee was given the task of investigating the incident and making recommendations. In addition, questions were being raised, both within Congress and repeatedly by the press, about illegal office accounts, free travel provided by lobbyists and interest groups, and large sums of money paid to members for speeches made to interest groups.

Finally, two major attempts at ethics reform in Congress emerged from other highly publicized investigations into wrongdoing by prominent members of Congress. One reform attempt was successful and one was not. During an investigation into the Speaker of the House Jim Wright, when a general feeling of unease prevailed among members about the rules governing financial disclosure, Congress attempted to broaden the reach of the 1978 Ethics in Government Act. That act restricted lobbying by certain executive-branch employees after they left the government; the 1988 bill would have extended those restrictions to members of Congress and high-ranking staff members. Many felt that such legislation was necessary to counter the public perception of a revolving door between government and the world of lobbyists and interest groups. In the end the bill was pocket vetoed by President Ronald Reagan; many members breathed a sigh of relief, having voted for the bill less because they supported its provisions than because they were afraid to go on record as being against ethics reform.

The other major attempt at ethics reform came in 1989. The House passed and the president signed into law a combination ethics and pay-raise package. This law came on the heels of the resignation of Speaker Wright, who had been under investigation for questionable financial dealings. Never before had a Speaker resigned in midterm; in fact, no previous Speaker had ever been formally charged with violating House ethics rules. Wright's troubles and eventual resignation seemed to act as catalysts for reform. Wright himself, in his resignation speech, called for an overhaul of the entire ethics process and the outright abolition of honoraria.

A task force had been created in January 1988 to review ethics standards and make recommendations for reform. In the following months, not only had the Speaker resigned, but the majority whip had also resigned, one member had been convicted in a state court of sexual misconduct, another had admitted to involvement with a male prostitute, and still another had been tried for bribery. In the Senate, the public focus on the so-called Keating Five—senators who had helped savings and loan magnate Charles Keating by intervening with regulatory offices—had further put congressional ethics under scrutiny and attack. The new Speaker of the House, Thomas S. Foley (D-Wash.), made ethics legislation one of his top priorities and, on assuming the role of Speaker, directed the task force to report on its findings within ninety days.

Passage of HR 3660, the ethics-pay package, in November 1989 resulted in significant changes in the congressional codes of ethics. The bill effectively overhauled the 1978 Ethics in Government Act. It included a pay raise for members of the House, federal judges, and top executive-branch officials. At the same time it prohibited House members, staff, and some other federal officials from keeping any honoraria, effective January 1991; in lieu of paying honoraria, organizations could make charitable contributions of up to $2,000. The amount of honoraria senators would be allowed to keep was lowered from 40 percent of their salary to 27 percent.

The bill also imposed further restrictions on members' earned income and tightened existing restrictions on gifts and travel. In addition, more detail was required in financial disclosure statements, and the ban on lobbying activities after leaving office was extended to members of Congress and their staffs.

While the propriety of lobbying activities has often been questioned, the lobbying system has proven difficult to regulate.

In the end, many praised Congress's efforts in coming up with this latest ethics reform package. Even Common Cause, a citizens' group usually quite critical of Congress, hailed the bill, saying that it "could well spell the beginning of the end of the anything-goes ethics era that dominated Washington during the 1980s."

The 1989 bill by no means resolved the troublesome issues involved in congressional ethics, but many argue that a real change in congressional behavior followed the 1989 reforms. In fact, after the bill was passed many members gave up accepting honoraria altogether, although the new law banning honoraria was not scheduled to take effect until 1991 and even then would apply only to House members.

LOBBYING. One important aspect of congressional politics that further complicates the ethical equation is lobbying, which has a powerful—many would say corrupting—effect on the legislative process. Lobbyists representing a whole host of special interests exert significant influence over both individual legislators and the content of legislation.

While the propriety of lobbying activities has often been questioned, the lobbying system has proven difficult to regulate. Because the right to "lobby" falls under the rubric of the rights of free speech and petition, it is very hard to draw the line between influence peddling and these constitutional freedoms.

The only comprehensive law to affect lobbying was passed in 1946. The Federal Regulation of Lobbying Act required lobbyists to register, indicate their legislative interests, and report on how much money they spend in pursuing those interests. This legislation was intended to expose the pressures brought to bear on public policy. Because the law is vaguely worded and has been narrowly interpreted by the Supreme Court, however, its effectiveness has often been questioned and there have been numerous attempts to reform it.

Later efforts aimed at regulating the lobbying industry focused on the need to create a uniform code for lobby registration. Reformers maintain that such a code would encourage more compliance and allow for a more effective means of enforcement. In addition, there have been calls to tighten the requirements for financial disclosure. Both initiatives have been met with opposition from lobbyists themselves.

Lobbyists gain access and influence through many channels, including financial ones. While corporations and labor unions are barred from making direct campaign contributions, they can collect, aggregate, and distribute contributions through political action committees (PACs). Campaign contributions to members of Congress serve the dual purpose of keeping "friendly" members in power and ensuring access to lawmakers when they consider important pieces of legislation. While this strategy has worked well for the lobbyists, it has exacerbated the ethical problems and dilemmas faced by members of Congress. Often members have difficulty in putting a safe distance between the money they receive from special interests and the actions they take on behalf of those interests.

The issues and controversies surrounding lobbying are closely tied to the debate over campaign finance. As long as money continues to play so important a part in campaigns and elections, it will remain a powerful tool for the organized groups that come to Washington to pursue specific legislative interests and broad policy goals.

Despite the recurring preoccupation with congressional ethics and ethics reform, public and press unhappiness with Congress and its standards has, if anything, increased. Ironically, this disillusionment has been fed by the reforms themselves—notably, by the many ensuing disclosures concerning unsavory congressional activity and campaign contributions. As more reports of PAC contributions, congressional travel, and gifts received are made public, more media stories appear on the subjects and more public outrage is expressed—regardless of the extent of corruption, contributions, or trips, which may actually have declined. As a matter of fact, in the early 1990s, many veteran observers of Washington and Congress believed that, in part because of ethics reform, the level of personal corruption had declined sharply since the period from 1940 to 1970.

THE "KEATING FIVE" CASE. In the late 1980s, the continuing problems and confusion that plague the congressional ethics system were epitomized by the highly publicized example of the so-called Keating Five. This case illustrated how the world of political fund-raising had become a veritable minefield for many politicians. The five senators involved collectively accepted some $1.5 million in political contributions from a savings and loan executive named Charles H. Keating, Jr. In return Keating asked the senators to intervene on his behalf with the federal regulators who were investigating the failing Lincoln Savings and Loan Bank of California. Eventually the government was forced to seize the bank, and the subsequent bailout cost taxpayers an estimated $2 billion.

The central question faced by the committee investigating this case concerned the extent to which members of Congress can properly intercede with federal agencies for campaign contributors while actively soliciting and accepting donations from these same contributors.

In the end, two senators, John McCain (R-Ariz.) and John Glenn (D-Ohio), were found guilty only of exercising poor judgment. Two other senators, Donald W. Riegle, Jr. (D-Mich.), and Dennis DeConcini (D-Ariz.), were held in slightly stronger reproach by the Senate Ethics Committee. The committee concluded that the senators had indeed acted improperly and that their actions could not be condoned. Ultimately, however, it determined that no formal punishment could be warranted for any of the four under existing ethics codes.

The congressional ethics system operating in the late twentieth century retains many gaps and inconsistencies.

The fifth senator, Alan Cranston (D-Calif.), was found to have violated the Senate's general rule against improper behavior. Following a formal investigation, Cranston was reprimanded by the ethics panel. This punishment represented a new form of discipline, with the committee's reprimand falling somewhere between a committee rebuke and a full censure. The committee's findings and ultimate determination were presented to the full chamber as a fait accompli; the full Senate did not vote on the matter.

In the end, speaking before his Senate colleagues, Cranston maintained that although his behavior might have appeared improper to some, at no time had he violated the established norms of behavior in the Senate. He suggested that virtually all senators were at risk because they all had at one time or another engaged in similar behavior. Cranston's comments angered many of his colleagues, illustrating the lack of consensus within the Senate regarding standards of behavior. Without clear guidelines, disciplinary measures must remain difficult to impose and enforce.

The details of the Keating case are less important than its broader implications for congressional ethics. One of the most critical questions raised by this case involved the proper boundaries of constituent service: How far should senators go in helping their constituents? Over time many senators have complained of unclear standards in this area. The Ethics Committee had the important task of clarifying these standards. While the committee members conceded that the relevant written guidelines were less than adequate, it stopped short of redrawing those guidelines, leaving that duty for yet another task force.

The Keating Five investigation also brought out the need for campaign finance reform. Clearly, a system in which special interests contribute money and expect favors in return will inevitably generate conflicts of interest. The ethics panel stated that senators can indeed intervene on behalf of contributors when such action will promote the public interest, but that campaign contributions should not be a factor. This left most senators just as bewildered about operating within the standards of proper behavior as they had been prior to the Keating case. One area of confusion arose from the absence of PAC money in the Keating case; the contributions Keating gave to the senators took the form of personal money or so-called soft money—contributions not to individual senators but to state parties for get-out-the-vote or voter registration efforts.

Even before the Keating deliberations had been concluded, both the Senate and the House began work on new guidelines for campaign finance. Similar efforts were under way in 1990, but a comprehensive bill was never passed. Regulating campaign finance is a tricky business, in part because certain constitutional protections—free speech and freedom of association—guarantee individuals the right to raise money for and contribute to politicians.

Many members of Congress believe that avoiding such scandals in the future will necessitate instituting a system of public finance, although significant partisan differences exist on this subject. While Democrats favor spending limits and public financing, Republicans oppose both. Furthermore, the House and Senate differ in their approaches to reform. For example, in the 1992 Senate version of campaign finance reform, PAC contributions had been banned, while most House incumbents who relied heavily on PAC contributions strongly opposed any such stricture.

While some had hoped that the Keating Five scandal would provide just the spark needed to bring about some compromise on campaign finance reform, it was not clear in 1993 whether the lessons learned would translate into any real change in the system. The Ethics Committee clearly passed the buck on establishing a more stringent set of standards. The House and Senate subsequently came up with their own respective proposals for reform. In addition a certain degree of public pressure must be brought to bear on legislators if substantive reform is to be achieved. If the past is any indication, an atmosphere of increased public scrutiny, usually present in the wake of some highly publicized scandal, is often conducive to the reevaluation and rewriting of old standards.

UNRESOLVED ISSUES. The congressional ethics system operating in the late twentieth century retains many gaps and inconsistencies. Some have suggested that the problem lies more with the system of enforcement than with the ethics codes themselves, pointing out that members must be willing to punish their colleagues in order to deter future transgressions. Certainly standards need to be made clear, but beyond that, many believe that members must have some incentive—if only a negative incentive—to adhere to even the broadest guidelines for proper behavior.

While House and Senate ethics committees composed of sitting lawmakers from their respective chambers have generally been conscientious at evaluating charges of ethical violations by their colleagues, the simple fact that sitting members are charged with evaluating their colleagues carries a built-in suspicion of unfairness—either that members will more harshly punish their colleagues for political advantage or will try to soft-pedal allegations to protect their friends.

Given the constitutional requirement that Congress police itself, many members of the 1993 Joint Committee on the Organization of Congress made the following suggestion: that Congress create ethics committees consisting of former members of Congress—people with sensitivity to the requirements of a legislative, inherently political, body but without the inherent conflicts of judging their current peers. Any findings from their investigations, or requirements for action, could then be referred to the appropriate committee or chamber for action by the full House or Senate as the Constitution mandates.

Furthermore, while critical examination of the congressional ethics system is indisputably worthwhile, any heightened awareness of and focus on the personal and professional lives of members of Congress creates a certain danger—namely, that such a focus could dissuade people from entering public life.

It seems we have reached the point now where the press and the public have come to believe that every detail of a government official's life ought to be available for public consumption and considered relevant to his or her job. Certainly any behavior that impinges on an official's job or ability to carry out his or her duties is relevant and should be treated with a certain degree of scrutiny.

Most people would agree that elected officials are bound to some degree by the public trust, and perhaps the standards to which they are held ought to be higher than those of the average citizen. There is an increased risk, however, that if the most qualified individuals feel their talents and abilities will be taken into consideration only after they have passed some sort of ethical litmus test, they will likely take those talents and abilities elsewhere. It seems obvious that without the best minds at work in government, we have little hope of solving the many public policy crises we face, crises which by far surpass this issue of ethics reform in terms of their urgency and gravity.

[See also (I) Campaign Financing, House Bank, Interest Groups, Lobbying, Members, article on Qualifications.]

BIBLIOGRAPHY

Association of the Bar of the City of New York. Special Committee on Congressional Ethics. *Congress and the Public Trust.* 1970.
Beard, Edmund, and Stephen Horn. *Congressional Ethics: The View from the House.* 1975.
Berg, Larry, et al. *Corruption in the American Political System.* 1976.
Clark, Marion, and Rudy Maxa. *Public Trust, Private Lust.* 1977.
Congressional Quarterly. *Congressional Ethics.* 1980.
Congressional Quarterly. *Guide to Congress.* 3d ed. 1982.
Douglas, Paul H. *Ethics in Government.* 1952.
Garment, Suzanne. *Scandal—The Culture of Mistrust in American Politics.* 1991.
Getz, Robert. *Congressional Ethics—The Conflict of Interest Issue.* 1966.
Jennings, Bruce, and Daniel Callahan. *Representation and Responsibility: Exploring Legislative Ethics.* 1985.
Simmons, Charlene Wear. "Thoughts on Legislative Ethics Reform and Representation." *PS: Political Science & Politics* 24 (June 1991): 193–200.
Thompson, Margaret Susan. *The "Spider Web": Congress and Lobbying in the Age of Grant.* 1985.
Weeks, Kent M. *Adam Clayton Powell and the Supreme Court.* 1971.

– NORMAN J. ORNSTEIN

EXPEDITED CONSIDERATION

Expedited consideration stems from procedures established to ensure that a measure moves from introduction to conclusive floor action within a short or definite time frame. Expedited procedures are usually included in statutes as rule-making provisions, enacted pursuant to the constitutional authority of each chamber to "determine the rules of its proceedings."

Historically, expedited procedures have often been enacted as part of legislative veto provisions. Expedited procedures have also been enacted for consideration of recurring legislation, such as concurrent resolutions on the budget and reconciliation bills in the Congressional Budget Act of 1974, and for special purpose measures such as consideration of the North American Free Trade Agreement in 1993 or the recommendations of the Commission on Base Realignment and Closure established in the Base Closure and Realignment Act of 1988.

Typically, expedited procedures provide a time limit for a committee to report the specified legislation and a means of discharging the committee if it fails to report. This discharge mechanism can be either automatic or a privileged motion with little or no debate allowed. There is also generally a method for the measure to reach the floor for prompt consideration, such as making it privileged. These provisions are more important in the House, where control of the agenda rests with the chamber and committee leadership, than in the Senate.

Often these procedures prohibit amendments, even committee amendments, to the measure and impose a time limit on its consideration. These characteristics are more important in the Senate, due to its greater vulnerability to dilatory tactics.

BIBLIOGRAPHY

Nickels, Ilona. *Fast-Track and the North American Free Trade Agreement.* Congressional Research Service, Library of Congress. CRS Rept. 93–116. 1993.

U.S. House of Representatives. *Constitution, Jefferson's Manual, and Rules of the House of Representatives, 103d Congress.* Compiled by William Holmes Brown. 102d Cong., 2d sess., 1992. H. Doc. 102–405.

U.S. House of Representatives. Committee on Rules. *Legislative Veto after Chadha.* 98th Cong., 2d sess., 1984. See Stanley Bach, "Statement on Expedited Procedures."

— JAMES V. SATURNO

EXPUNGEMENT

Adopted from the practices of the British House of Commons and Colonial legislatures, *expungement* is the legislative process by which specific words are struck from the record of proceedings of either the Senate or the House of Representatives. Expungement is tied to traditions of congressional decorum and helps to promote order during debate. Rules governing debate in both the House and the Senate require members to observe proper protocol. For example, members may be critical of legislation but may not engage in personal attacks.

Disorderly, derogatory, and unparliamentary language of any form may be expunged. Most typically, language expunged consists of words spoken on the floor. But words inserted into the *Congressional Record* from letters, telegrams, or charts may also be expunged. A motion to expunge may be made by the individual who entered the words, by the target of the offending remarks, or by a third party not directly involved.

When a senator or representative wishes to have material struck from the record, that member objects to the words and makes a motion that they be expunged. The motion may be accepted by unanimous consent, or a vote on the motion may be held. If the motion carries, the words are crossed out of the record by the clerk.

Words may be expunged immediately after they are spoken or well after the fact. For example, language uttered in 1834 that censured President Andrew Jackson was not expunged until 1837.

[See also (I) Congressional Record.*]*

BIBLIOGRAPHY

Luce, Robert. *Legislative Procedure.* 1922. Pp. 527–534.

U.S. House of Representatives. *Deschler's Precedents of the United States House of Representatives,* by Lewis Deschler. 94th Cong., 2d sess., 1977. H. Doc. 94–661. Vol. 1, chap. 29.

— MARY ETTA BOESL

EXTENSIONS OF REMARKS

The section of each day's *Congressional Record* that follows the proceedings of the House and Senate is known as the Extensions of Remarks. It is primarily used by members of the House to include the text of bills and additional legislative statements not delivered on the House floor as well as matters not germane to the proceedings, such as speeches delivered outside Congress, letters from and tributes to constituents, and published

The section of each day's Congressional Record *that follows the proceedings of the House and Senate is known as the Extensions of Remarks.*

articles. A member must get permission from the House to have an item published in the Extensions of Remarks.

Although the laws and rules for publication of the *Record* provide direction for the use of this section by the Senate as well, it is only on rare occasions that remarks by senators are included here. Their so-called extraneous remarks are found in the Senate portion of the *Record* under the heading Additional Statements.

Until 1968 (90th Cong., 2d sess.), what is now known as the Extensions of Remarks section was called the Appendix. The Appendix formed part of both the daily and permanent editions of the *Record.* Beginning in 1941 (77th Cong., 1st sess.), each page number was preceded by the designation "A." Beginning in 1954 (83d Cong., 2d sess.), the Appendix pages were omitted from the permanent editions of the *Record* and could only be found in the daily editions. However, material from the Appendix considered germane to legislation was inserted in the permanent *Record* at the point where the legislation was under discussion.

Since 1968 the Extensions of Remarks have replaced the Appendix and been published in both the daily and permanent editions. At the same time the *Record* began publishing on the last page of each daily edition an alphabetical listing of members whose Extensions of Remarks appear in that issue. All of these actions were at the direction of the Joint Committee on Printing.

[See also (I) Congressional Record.*]*

BIBLIOGRAPHY

U.S. Congress. Joint Committee on Printing. "Laws and Rules for Publication of the *Congressional Record.*" (Appears periodically in editions of the *Congressional Record* following the Extensions of Remarks.)

U.S. House of Representatives. *Deschler's Precedents of the United States House of Representatives,* by Lewis Deschler. 94th Cong., 2d sess., 1977. H. Doc. 94-661. Vol. 1, pp. 407–430.

– MILDRED LEHMANN AMER

F

FILIBUSTER

A word of Dutch and Spanish origin meaning *freebooter*, *filibuster* was first used in a legislative context in the mid-nineteenth century in reference to delaying tactics employed to prevent a vote on a legislative matter that would pass if a vote were allowed. Such obstructive tactics predate the application of the term, however. There is evidence of their employment, for example, in American colonial legislatures; and in the First Congress, what became known as a filibuster was used in the House of Representatives against a bill to establish the nation's permanent capital.

Currently, the term is primarily applied to tactics used in the U.S. Senate. Originally, however, it was also applicable to practices that were a common feature of House activity. As the House grew in size, it adopted rules changes that restricted the opportunities for filibuster. These included the use of a previous-question motion whereby a House majority could end debate, limitations on the time members are allowed to speak during general debate and on amendments, and enforcement of a rule of germaneness requiring that members speak to the subject under consideration. Although obstructive and delaying tactics still exist in the House, the vehicles are far more limited and less effective than in the Senate.

The Senate's smaller size allowed it the luxury of a tradition of unlimited debate and thus an environment favorable to filibusters. Until 1917, Senate debate could only be ended by unanimous consent. If a single senator objected to a request to end debate and vote on a measure, that request was denied and debate continued.

From the 1840s until the 1880s filibusters in the Senate were common but rarely successful. Underlying the filibuster strategy was an assumption that the filibuster not only prevented a vote on the item of legislation under consideration but also delayed the disposal of other matters on the Senate floor. Thus, senators concerned to move these other matters forward might be willing to make concessions to those filibustering in order to break the logjam. A filibuster's success depended on the presence of one of two conditions: either a sizable minority of the Senate had to be so intensely opposed to the bill under consideration that it could sustain debate indefinitely or the filibuster had to occur near the end of a session, when a handful of senators or even a single senator could threaten the completion of other legislative business.

In the late nineteenth century, with party divisions in the Senate more equal in number, the frequency, intensity, and success of filibusters increased. Debate was extended not only through filibusters but also through use of a range of parliamentary delaying tactics, such as frequent votes and quorum calls. Efforts to change Senate rules to allow for cloture, a formal means whereby the Senate could vote to end debate, failed.

In the late 1960s and 1970s filibuster use rose again, dramatically, and new means had to be developed to manage Senate business.

Although several modest changes in Senate rules in the early years of the twentieth century placed curbs on obstructionism, it was not until 1917 that the Senate adopted its first cloture rule. During the lame-duck session of the 64th Congress (1915–1917), eleven senators successfully filibustered a bill to arm merchant ships favored by the administration of Woodrow Wilson. Wilson then called the Senate into special session and demanded that it change its rules, which it did with Rule XXII. As adopted, Rule XXII provided that sixteen senators could submit a cloture petition requesting a vote on ending debate on a matter before the Senate. Two days after the filing a vote would be taken, and if two-thirds or more of the senators present and voting supported the cloture motion, further debate would then be limited to one hour for each senator.

If cloture votes are used as an indicator of the frequency of filibusters, Rule XXII appears to have had the desired impact. From 1917 to 1960 only twenty-three cloture votes occurred. Clearly, there were more than twenty-three filibusters during this time, but the threat of cloture had somewhat changed the nature of the tactic itself. In some cases senators engaged in individual filibusters intended to dramatize an issue rather than to defeat a bill. In 1957, for example, after other southerners had decided against trying to block a modest civil rights bill, Strom Thurmond, then a Democratic senator from South Carolina, held the floor for a record twenty-four hours and eighteen minutes. In other instances, no cloture vote took place, either because a compromise was reached or because the Senate surrendered to the filibuster.

With the adoption of a cloture rule, then, the filibuster became a less effective weapon and its use declined. On occasion, the filibuster could still be a valued tactic, as at the end of a session, or when a sizable number of members were vehement in their opposition to a bill (as southern Democrats were to most civil rights legislation from 1937 through the 1960s) and thus there were likely insufficient votes to invoke cloture.

The adoption of Rule XXII also signaled a change in Senate norms regarding the use of the filibuster. It became accepted practice that the filibuster would be reserved for only the most major issues. It was understood that to employ the filibuster for relatively trivial matters would result in new efforts to put restrictions on debate. In addition, as civil rights votes began to dominate filibusters and cloture efforts, civil rights advocates became reluctant to engage the tactic. The pro–civil rights senators realized that were they to engage in filibusters themselves, they would be deprived of a major ground for criticizing civil rights opponents in the Senate.

In the late 1960s and 1970s filibuster use rose again, dramatically, and new means had to be developed to manage Senate business. The primary reason for the filibuster's increased use was that it had again become an effective tactic. Senate workload had grown significantly and Senate sessions started to run year-round; time pressure became severe. Under these conditions, a filibuster—or even the threat of one—took on important implications. The floor time needed to indulge those wanting to filibuster and still assure completion of other business had simply disappeared. Moreover, the threat of a filibuster from an individual senator was often enough to bring concessions. In addition, the filibuster was now used by others besides southern Democrats and against initiatives other than civil rights bills.

In an effort to manage floor business in this changed environment, Senate leaders developed new methods of dealing with the filibuster. A traditional method had been to keep the Senate in session day and night. This not only wears down the filibusterers but also gives other senators, who are inconvenienced by around-the-clock sessions, a strong incentive to vote for cloture. This tactic was used successfully to pass the 1964 Civil Rights Bill. Understandably, Senate leaders are reluctant to resort to this strategy frequently.

Two now more commonly used methods, the "track system" and "holds," came into use in the early 1970s under Majority Leader Mike Mansfield (D-Mont.). Under the track system an agreement is reached with those filibustering that part of each day will be devoted to the legislation being filibustered and part of the day to other legislation. This allows the Senate to complete other business while the filibuster proceeds. It does help the leadership manage the Senate's work, but it also takes pressure off those engaging in the filibuster.

Sen. Hugh Scott (R-Pa.). Resting on a makeshift bed during the filibuster against the Civil Rights Act of 1964. (Office of the Historian of the U.S. Senate)

The hold is a more informal way for party leaders to respond to a filibuster threat. A senator or a group of senators may place a hold on a piece of Senate business by making a request of the leadership. This means that no action will be taken until the hold is released. It allows senators to work out disagreements over legislation before tying up the Senate floor with a filibuster. In 1983, Senate leaders of both parties agreed to restrict the use of holds and refused to guarantee them for indefinite periods.

These tactics for coping with the filibuster did not reduce its frequency. From 1961 to 1970, there were sixteen cloture votes, from 1971 until 1975, when Rule XXII was changed, there were twenty-four cloture votes. With use of the filibuster getting out of hand, the Senate was forced to make cloture easier. In 1975, Rule XXII was amended to require that three-fifths of the total membership of the Senate—instead of two-thirds of those present and voting—be required to end debate.

Two major effects have ensued from this change. First, efforts to invoke cloture have been more successful. Prior to the change, cloture was successfully voted 22 percent of the time, but from 1975 through 1987 cloture was voted 41 percent of the time. Second, senators resurrected another form of filibuster, the post-cloture filibuster. By appending hundreds of amendments to a bill, demanding that the amendments be read, requesting roll-call votes, and through other tactics, a filibuster could be extended long after cloture. Sen. James B. Allen (D-Ala.) was the first to uncover the post-cloture filibuster strategy, and others soon followed his lead. In response, the Senate has twice restricted Senate debate after cloture. In 1979, the rules were amended to limit all Senate activity following cloture to one hundred hours, and in 1986, as part of the effort to allow for the televising of Senate floor proceedings, post-cloture activity was reduced to thirty hours.

Although the changes in the cloture rule may have slowed the growth of filibusters and filibuster threats, they had not led to an overall decline in their use. In the 100th Congress (1987–1989), forty-three cloture votes were taken. Despite efforts to control its excesses and its lower rate of success, the filibuster remains a tactic with which any senator can derail the schedule of business.

[See also (I) Cloture, Extensions of Remarks, Previous Question.]

BIBLIOGRAPHY

Oppenheimer, Bruce I. "Changing Time Constraints on Congress: Historical Perspectives on the Use of Cloture." In *Congress Reconsidered,* 3d ed. Edited by Lawrence C. Dodd and Bruce I. Oppenheimer. 1985. Pp. 393–413.

Smith, Steven S. *Call to Order.* 1989.

– BRUCE I. OPPENHEIMER

FIVE-MINUTE RULE

The five-minute rule in clause 5(a) of the House of Representatives Rule XXIII governs the reading of bills for amendment when the House resolves into the Committee of the Whole. The provision of five minutes in which to explain an amendment was adopted by the House in 1847. The provision of five minutes to speak in opposition was adopted in 1850. Five-minute debate also occurs in the House as in Committee of the Whole on any motion to recommit a bill or joint resolution with instructions pursuant to clause 4 of Rule XVI and in committee proceedings.

Through pro forma amendments, five-minute debate theoretically may continue until each member has spoken. The right to explain or oppose an amendment has precedence over motions to amend it. Recognition typically alternates between members of the majority and minority parties, but priority is accorded to members of a reporting committee. Debate must be confined to the pending subject. Time may not be yielded or reserved. Debate on the pending text and its amendments may be limited by nondebatable motion after one speech, however brief. This motion is amendable but may not allocate time.

A preferential motion to rise and report a recommendation to strike the enacting clause is debated under the five-minute rule: the proponent may not reserve time, and an opponent is not recognized until the proponent has spoken. Five-minute debate on an appeal in Committee of the Whole continues at the discretion of the chairman.

BIBLIOGRAPHY

U.S. House of Representatives. *Constitution, Jefferson's Manual, and Rules of the House of Representatives, 103d Congress.* Compiled by William Holmes Brown. 102d Cong., 2d sess., 1992. H. Doc. 102–405.

– JOHN V. SULLIVAN

FRESHMEN

The status of freshmen members of Congress differs according to whether they are in the House or Senate and has varied dramatically over the course of American history.

IN THE HOUSE. In the nineteenth century, freshmen House members assumed such positions as Speaker of the House and other prominent posts. But as the House became institutionalized and the seniority system became more important, the status of the freshman declined significantly. By the mid-twentieth century, it was common to hear such admonitions as "Freshmen should be seen and not heard" and "To get along you go along." It was expected that freshmen members would serve a period of apprenticeship in which they sat back and learned the ropes. Freshmen were given the less desirable committee assignments and were discouraged from being too active and visible in the legislative process.

By the 1960s and 1970s, the tradition of apprenticeship had been substantially weakened. Although freshmen were still at a disadvantage vis-à-vis their more senior colleagues, they moved more rapidly than before into significant House roles. These changes occurred for a number of reasons. Certainly, the large influxes of new members chosen in the 1964, 1966, and 1974 elections were a factor. Also, societal pressures on Congress and its members made it more difficult for a newcomer to serve an apprenticeship and more difficult for senior members to keep them down. As the public's expectations for congressional action on a large number of domestic problems grew, freshmen members became more active, sometimes in response to the perceived inaction of senior members, many of whom were conservative, from the South, and hostile toward governmental problem-solving. Moreover, all House members, freshmen included, increasingly recognized that they controlled their own fate, and, as incumbents became more and more confident of reelection, the most meaningful sanctions they faced resided in their districts and their constituents—not in the party or Congress. The dramatic reforms adopted in 1975 resulted in the decentralization of power in the House, giving many more members a stake in the action, particularly through the enhancement of the subcommittee system. As freshmen with ambitions for higher office realized that positive media coverage and public recognition would facilitate their careers, they became much bolder in seeking the limelight. Since the 1970s, the seniority system has been further eroded and opportunities for freshmen have continued to open up.

The status of freshmen members of Congress differs according to whether they are in the House or Senate.

Nevertheless, freshmen members still face some hurdles. They are put toward the back of the line for desired committee assignments and receive the smallest House offices. Most freshmen are at a natural disadvantage because of their unfamiliarity with House rules and procedures. Furthermore, since freshmen are less entrenched than their more senior colleagues, they will undoubtedly continue to devote the bulk of their efforts to ensuring their reelection.

According to *Congressional Quarterly,* in the post-World War II era up to 1992, the total turnover in the House has ranged from a high of 118 in 1948 to a low of 34 in 1988. The number of incumbents defeated in general elections has ranged from a high of 68 in 1948 to a low of 6 in 1986 and 1988. With the substantial turnover in 1992 due to the resignation or defeat of incumbent members, the opportunities for the freshmen of the 103d Congress to play an important role in the reform of the U.S. House were unusually great, although at the end of that Congress's first session it appeared that new members' impact would be less than originally thought. If the movement to limit members' terms continues to flourish, freshmen members of Congress may move even more quickly to become active and influential participants in the legislative process.

IN THE SENATE. Writing about the Senate of the 1950s, Donald Matthews (1960) discussed the norm of apprenticeship as it applied to freshmen senators. Even then, Matthews quoted senior senators bemoaning the weakening of the apprenticeship norm. Since that time, apprenticeship has practically vanished from the Senate. Norman J. Ornstein and his coauthors (1993) argue that the apprenticeship norm died out because it had served the interests of only those conservative senators, in both parties, who had dominated the Senate in the 1950s. As this conservative domination weakened in the 1960s, 1970s, and 1980s, in large part because of the influx of new members who, generally, preferred a more activist Congress, the apprenticeship norm declined. Moreover, senators are now more likely to fashion their careers independently of their parties and are therefore less dependent on moving up the party ladder. Added to this is the fact that, increasingly, senators come to Congress from backgrounds in business, the military, or other non-political occupations—and such newcomers are simply unwilling to sit back and take a passive role.

[See also (I) Members, article on Tenure and Turnover.]

BIBLIOGRAPHY

Davidson, Roger H. *The Postreform Congress.* 1992.

Mann, Thomas E., and Norman J. Ornstein. *The New Congress.* 1981.

Matthews, Donald R. *U.S. Senators and Their World.* 1960.

Ornstein, Norman J., Robert L. Peabody, and David W. Rohde. "The U.S. Senate in an Era of Change." In *Congress Reconsidered.* Edited by Lawrence C. Dodd and Bruce J. Oppenheimer. 5th ed. 1993.

– HERB ASHER

G

GAG RULE

Since the late eighteenth century, in both the United States and Great Britain, the term *gag rule* has referred to formal restrictions on political speech. Then, as now, use of the word *gag* has implied a constraint that exceeded accepted rules of debate or violated established rights of free speech. Congressional critics of the Sedition Act of 1798 called the legislation a *gag law*. Within the first decade of the nineteenth century, American political writers used *gag rule* to refer to congressional limitations on floor debate.

The most notorious gag rule was that passed by the House of Representatives on 26 May 1836 in response to a petition campaign demanding the abolition of slavery and the slave trade in the District of Columbia. House Rule XXI ordered that all petitions dealing with slavery were to be laid on the table without printing or referral. The House renewed some form of the gag rule in each ensuing Congress until 3 December 1844, when John Quincy Adams's motion for repeal finally won approval. The Senate in March 1836 rejected John C. Calhoun's motion to refuse all antislavery petitions but approved James Buchanan's compromise motion that ostensibly affirmed the right of petition by allowing the Senate to receive antislavery petitions that would then be rejected without referral or consideration. Throughout the antebellum period, gag rule applied to any attempt to restrict debate on slavery.

In more recent years, gag rule has applied to unusual limits on the debate and amendment of legislation before the House of Representatives. One example is closed rules that allow only committee amendments.

BIBLIOGRAPHY

Peterson, Merrill D. *The Great Triumvirate: Webster, Clay, and Calhoun.* 1987.

– BRUCE A. RAGSDALE

GALLERIES

Ringing the House and Senate chambers, galleries allow the public and media to view congressional floor proceedings. Although the Constitution did not mandate open sessions, the popularly elected House opened its gallery in Federal Hall in New York City to the public on 8 April 1789, two days after establishing its first quorum. Upstairs on the second floor the smaller Senate chamber contained no gallery. Even after moving to Congress Hall in Philadelphia, the Senate met in closed session until 9 December 1795, when construction of a gallery was completed, and even then opened only its legislative proceedings. Until 1929 the Senate routinely emptied the galleries during executive sessions dealing with treaties and nominations.

As a symbol of democratic government, the galleries remain open, day or night, whenever the Senate and House are in session.

Doorkeepers under the supervision of the House and Senate sergeants at arms regulated traffic into the galleries and enforced the rules of each chamber. Nineteenth-century citizens and foreign visitors showed such interest in congressional debates that they packed the galleries to capacity. "Never were the amphitheaters of Rome more crowded by the highest ranks of both sexes than the Senate chamber," Margaret Bayard Smith wrote during the Webster-Hayne debate of 1830. "Every seat, every inch of ground, even the steps, were *completely* filled." Tickets to the public galleries were first issued in 1868 to meet the immense demand for admittance to the Senate's impeachment trial of President Andrew Johnson. Thereafter, visitors received gallery tickets from their senators and representatives.

In the 1850s, construction of new chambers provided greatly expanded gallery seating. Galleries to the left of the chair were assigned to women and their male escorts, while galleries to the right of the chair were open to men only. The central gallery above the chair was reserved for the press. Later, galleries were set aside for diplomats, staff, and members' families and guests. Although the galleries were never officially segregated by race, when segregation became common in Washington the doorkeepers tacitly steered African-American visitors to separate seating.

Rules require that members of Congress neither address the galleries nor introduce special visitors in the galleries. During dramatic debates and votes, presiding officers often admonish the galleries against applause or other demonstrations and sometimes threaten to clear the galleries following outbursts. Gallery visitors may not read, write, or take photographs. These rules have arisen because of the long lines of visitors waiting for available seats in the galleries and the desire to prevent any disturbance to the floor proceedings. In 1916, when President Woodrow Wilson addressed a joint session of Congress, suffragists unfurled a banner over the gallery railing with the message: "Mr. President, What Will You Do for Woman Suffrage?" Since then, rules have restricted visitors from placing any items on the railings or from leaning over them.

After Puerto Rican nationalists fired shots from the House gallery and wounded several representatives in 1954, some members talked of installing glass partitions between the galleries and the chambers. Congress rejected these proposals, but in later years metal screening devices outside the gallery entrances helped augment security.

As a symbol of democratic government, the galleries remain open, day or night, whenever the Senate and House are in session. Only during rare executive sessions dealing with highly classified information is the public excluded from the congressional galleries.

BIBLIOGRAPHY

Byrd, Robert C. *The Senate, 1789–1989: Addresses on the History of the United States Senate.* Vol. 2. 1991.

Smith, Margaret Bayard. *The First Forty Years of Washington Society.* 1906.

– DONALD A. RITCHIE

GENERAL ACCOUNTING OFFICE

With 4,900 employees (as of 1993), the General Accounting Office (GAO) is the largest of the congressional support agencies. Created in 1921 by the Budget and Accounting Act, the GAO attempts to ferret out waste, fraud, and abuse in the management of federal programs. In addition, the GAO offers advice to Congress on a wide variety of policy-relevant topics.

The GAO differs from other congressional support agencies in several respects: it is much larger (twenty times larger than the Congressional Budget Office); it relies more heavily on regional offices (located in fourteen cities); it is more independent, thanks to a comptroller general who is appointed for a fifteen-year term; it is more controversial, because it routinely attacks federal agencies and federal programs; it is more visible, because its reports often generate considerable media publicity; and it has governmentwide duties, acting, in effect, as the audit agency of the federal government. Like other congressional support agencies, however, the GAO is guided by congressional moods and by specific congressional requests. The GAO is also subject to formal congressional oversight and to Congress's power of the purse.

EVOLUTION OF THE GAO. Until the mid-1960s the GAO focused primarily on audits of federal agencies. To perform these tasks, the GAO hired accountants. Its work, though useful, received little attention in the mass media and was often taken for granted on Capitol Hill. This began to change in the mid-1960s, when Congress asked the GAO to evaluate new federal programs, especially antipoverty programs associated with Lyndon B. Johnson's Great Society. Although the GAO often focused on program implementation rather than program results, the latter received some attention.

The GAO's program-evaluation role became further institutionalized in 1970, when the Legislative Reorganization Act required the GAO to "review and analyze the results of Government programs and activities carried on under existing law, including the making of cost benefit studies." The Congressional Budget and Impoundment Control Act of 1974 expanded the GAO's program-evaluation role and required the GAO to set up a program review and evaluation office. This office eventually became the Program Evaluation and Methodology Division (PEMD), which hired social science academics to conduct increasingly sophisticated evaluations of federal programs.

At the same time, the GAO was placing less emphasis on traditional audits. The General Accounting Act of 1974 transferred some of the GAO's audit functions to the General Services Administration, thus relieving the GAO of these time-consuming responsibilities. Such steps transformed the GAO from a low-profile auditing agency into a highly visible source of policy advice.

THE GAO'S AGENDA. Congressional interest in the GAO and its work heightened as a result of two developments. The first was the GAO's growing capacity for policy analysis and program evaluation. The second was Congress's growing interest in legislative oversight of the bureaucracy. The latter played to the GAO's strengths as a "counterbureaucracy"—that is, an agency required by law to monitor and report wrongdoing by other government agencies.

As a result of these changes, GAO reports proliferated. At the same time, congressional committees took a more active interest in the subject and content of GAO reports. When Elmer Staats took over as comptroller general in 1966, less than 10 percent of the GAO's reports were requested by members of Congress. In 1992, Comptroller General Charles Bowsher reported that 80 percent of the GAO's reports were requested by members of Congress, usually congressional

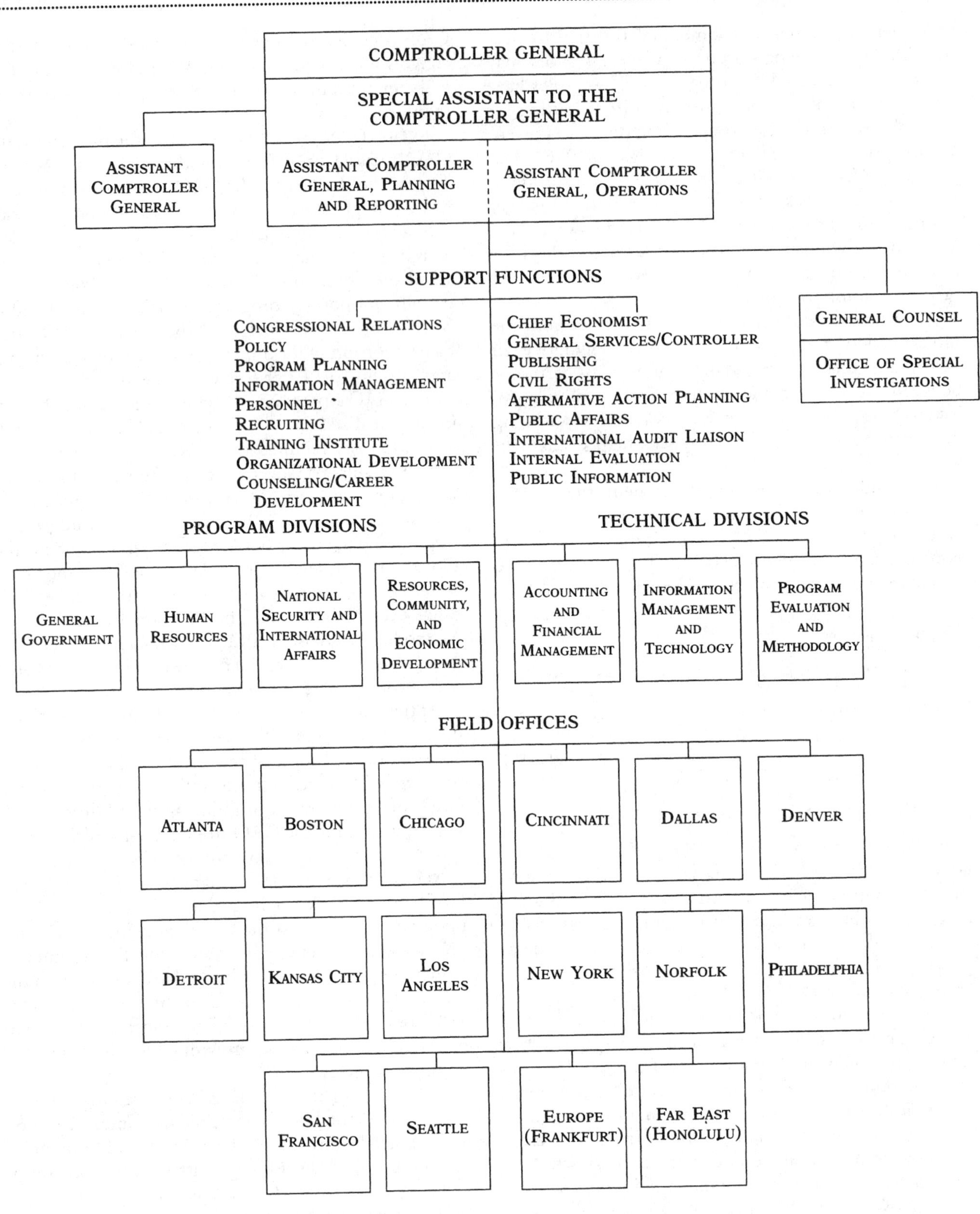

Organization of the General Accounting Office. (U.S. Government Manual)

committee or subcommittee chairmen. Although the importance of the distinction between requested and unrequested reports can be overdrawn, there has clearly been a trend toward more requested reports.

GAO reports encompass a wide range of topics, from defense procurement to transportation to environmental protection to welfare reform. In general, GAO reports reflect the current preoccupations of Congress. For example, in 1991 and 1992 the GAO issued numerous reports on health policy—a reflection of growing congressional interest in health care reform. Less visible issues receive less attention. By virtue of its size, however, the GAO can devote at least some attention to such obscure topics as Census Bureau methodology, Social Security Administration computers, and the spread of the Western spruce budworm.

STRATEGIES AND TACTICS. The GAO serves Congress primarily by scrutinizing and criticizing federal administrative agencies. Most GAO reports are critical of federal agencies, and most include recommendations for administrative reform. Clearly, the GAO takes its role as a counterbureaucracy seriously.

Increasingly, the GAO has been willing to advise Congress directly, and GAO testimony on Capitol Hill has increased dramatically. In 1985, GAO officials testified on Capitol Hill a total of 117 times. In 1990, GAO officials testified a total of 306 times, more often than any other agency except for the Department of Defense.

Under Comptroller General Bowsher, the GAO has also made a concerted effort to offer policy recommendations. Bowsher also initiated an unusual series of transition reports, issued just after the 1988 presidential election. These reports, which aroused considerable interest and controversy, criticized the federal government's lack of progress in a number of policy areas and made explicit recommendations for reform.

POLICY IMPACT. The GAO's impact on public policy has not been systematically evaluated. One recent study did find, however, that GAO reports are frequently cited by congressional staff members as examples of public policy reports with which they are personally familiar. Indeed, of eighty-three evaluation studies cited, 71 percent were GAO reports.

The impact of GAO reports on policy depends in part on the timeless of their release. Recognizing this, the GAO attempts to issue reports without delay. Often, however, it is impossible to release a report as quickly as Congress would like. The clarity of GAO reports also seems to make a difference. With this in mind, the GAO has in recent years stressed readability and accessibility, achieved through crisply written summaries, the use of clearer typefaces, and improved graphics.

Beyond these factors, congressional committees are likely to differ in their receptiveness to GAO reports. Constituency committees, with well-established commitments to programs that benefit constituents, may be less receptive to GAO reports (which often criticize such programs) than are policy committees, whose members are less constrained by constituents. Thus the House Public Works and Transportation Committee might be less responsive to GAO reports than the House Energy and Commerce Committee. This generality has not, however, been fully investigated.

ROLE CONFLICTS. Like other congressional support agencies, the GAO sometimes experiences role conflicts. The GAO is called on to decide whether to pursue its own agenda or the agenda of congressional committee chairs, whether to criticize administrative agencies or Congress itself, and whether to be drawn into partisan debates or remain aloof. These conflicts are not easily resolved.

The General Accounting Office assists Congress in several different ways—through formal reports, prepared testimony, briefing sessions, and informal advice.

The most frequent conflict is between professionalism, on the one hand, and responsiveness, on the other. The GAO has hired large numbers of highly skilled auditors and analysts, whose professional norms structure their response to work assignments. At the same time, the GAO is extremely aware of its responsibilities to Congress. When members of Congress define the GAO's responsibilities in parochial or particularistic terms, problems may arise. For example, Sen. Christopher S. Bond (R-Mo.) became upset when, in 1992, the GAO conducted a study of the Missouri River basin and reached conclusions inimical to the interests of Bond's "downstream" constituents. Although Bond focused on methodological flaws in the GAO's research procedures, he appeared to be concerned above all with the GAO's conclusions and their implications for his state. Ironically, the GAO got embroiled in this controversy by acceding to a request for a report from two members of Congress who represented states "upstream" of Missouri.

Some of the most bitter disputes over the GAO's role arise during periods of divided government, when the legislative and executive branches are controlled by different political parties. By deferring to congressional committee chairs, the GAO inadvertently defers to members of one political party. If its reports are highly critical of the executive branch, the GAO may be accused of partisanship, even though it carried out its assignment in good faith. Thus, responsiveness may be mistaken for partisanship.

The General Accounting Office assists Congress in several different ways—through formal reports, prepared testimony, briefing sessions, and informal advice. Members of Congress, in turn, utilize GAO input in a variety of ways—to support positions they have already taken, to anticipate emerging problems, to fine-tune legislative proposals, and even to rethink fundamental assumptions. Although most GAO reports focus on administrative failures, some reports identify legislative mistakes and recommend legislative remedies. Moreover, the GAO's strong administrative oversight role seems fully consistent with renewed congressional interest in the oversight function. In this respect, as in many others, the GAO's activities seldom deviate very far from congressional expectations.

[See also (I) Oversight; (II) General Accounting Office.]

BIBLIOGRAPHY

Boyer, John, and Laura Langbein. "Factors Influencing the Use of Health Evaluation Research in Congress." *Evaluation Review* 15, no. 5 (1991):507–532.

Mosher, Frederick. *A Tale of Two Agencies: A Comparative Analysis of the GAO and the OMB.* 1984.

Weiss, Carol. "Congressional Committees as Users of Analysis." *Journal of Policy Analysis and Management* 8, no. 3 (1989):411–431.

– WILLIAM T. GORMLEY, JR.

GERRYMANDERING

The procedure of dividing a political unit into election districts with the objective of giving one group the greatest advantage in the largest number of districts is called *gerrymandering.* Gerrymandering most often results in oddly or peculiarly shaped districts, which may appear artificially elongated, protruded, fragmented, or perforated. A skillful gerrymander, however, may have the appearance of geographic symmetry but the real effect of culling out votes in one area or adding votes in another. Gerrymandering can be practiced on many different levels—in the creation of city council districts, county commissioner districts, state legislative districts, and U.S. congressional districts.

The most common form of this practice is the *partisan gerrymander,* in which one political party intentionally draws electoral districts to dilute or eliminate the electoral power of the opposition party. Also common is the *racial gerrymander,* in which the majority racial group draws electoral districts to dilute or eliminate the electoral power of minority voters, who are often geographically concentrated in certain areas. There have also been cases of gerrymandering against linguistic, religious, and ethnic groups and where urban-rural power conflicts exist.

ORIGIN OF THE TERM The technique of drawing congressional district boundaries to favor a particular individual or party goes back to the First Congress and probably has roots in colonial assemblies. The term *gerrymander* originated with the Massachusetts congressional redistricting law enacted after the 1810 census apportionment. This law was passed by the Democratic-Republican majority in the Massachusetts legislature specifically to dilute the power of the formerly majority Federalists. The statute was signed into law on 11 February 1812 by Democratic-Republican governor Elbridge Gerry. To reduce Federalist electoral power the law contained a number of districts that divided counties and had peculiar shapes. One particularly unusual configuration was the Essex (2d) district. This elongated district stretched north from Boston and then east along the New Hampshire border. Federalist politicians ridiculed the shape of the Essex district, saying it resembled an animal or monster. The "salamander"-shaped district was dubbed a *gerrymander* after Governor Gerry. The first appearance of *gerrymander* in print was probably in the Boston *Gazette* of 26 March 1812. The newspaper published a political cartoon by artist Elkanah Tisdale that showed a map of the Essex district embellished with the trappings of a prehistoric monster. The cartoon's caption was "Gerrymander," and Federalist newspapers throughout New England and the United States began using the term to describe the process of drawing legislative districts for partisan advantage.

THE PROCESS OF GERRYMANDERING. The goal of the partisan congressional gerrymander is the enhancement of electoral power, leading to the election of representatives in numbers substantially greater than would otherwise result, given the gerrymandering party's share of the total statewide vote. This goal can be accomplished in either of two basic ways. The first gerrymandering method is "packing," that is, concentrating the voting strength of the opposition in as few electoral districts as possible. This puts a large surplus of votes in these districts, wasting opposition votes in the winner-take-all, one-member-to-a-district system of congressional representation (see table 1). The second gerrymandering method is "cracking," or splitting—that is, defusing or spreading out the opposition vote by dividing the opposition areas and placing small portions in a number of different districts so as to deny the

TABLE 1

DISTRICTS, ELECTION METHODS, AND ELECTORAL RESULTS: STATEWIDE ELECTION RESULTS[1]

Method and Type	Reapportionment, if Any	Election Results	
I General Ticket	—	4 Republicans	0 Democrats
II Proportional Representation	—	2 Republicans	2 Democrats[2]
III Gerrymandered Districts with Democrats Split	District 1: 50,000 Republican 48,750 Democrat District 2: 50,000 Republican 48,750 Democrat District 3: 50,000 Republican 48,750 Democrat District 4: 50,000 Republican 48,750 Democrat	3 Republicans	1 Democrat
IV Gerrymandered Districts with Republicans Packed	District 1: 80,000 Republican 18,750 Democrat District 2: 40,000 Republican 58,750 Democrat District 3: 40,000 Republican 58,750 Democrat District 4: 40,000 Republican 58,750 Democrat	1 Republican	3 Democrats
V Possible Fair and Competitive Districts, or Possible Bipartisan Gerrymander	District 1: 52,000 Republican 46,750 Democrat District 2: 52,000 Republican 46,750 Democrat District 3: 48,000 Republican 50,750 Democrat District 4: 48,000 Republican 50,750 Democrat	2 Republicans	2 Democrats

[1] Concerning the election of four representatives. Statewide vote total: 200,000 Republican, 195,000 Democrat.

[2] Results depend upon the method and formula used.

opposition a majority in any district. Packing and cracking are used together, depending on the geographic distribution of opposition voters.

Congressional redistricting laws are usually statutes passed by the state legislature and signed by the governor. A party's ability to gerrymander, then, first relies on its having control of both chambers of the state legislature and the governorship. If the opposition controls one of the three key actors, then it has the power to influence or stop the redistricting process. In such states, compromise redistricting laws are the norm. In many instances such compromise laws contain *bipartisan gerrymanders* that draw district boundaries to preserve the districts of incumbents of both parties or to gain or lose seats in proportion to the current partisan ratio of representatives (see table 1). These are *incumbent gerrymanders* of the *inclusionary* type. An *intraparty gerrymander* occurs when the party in power tampers with or eliminates the district of an unwanted incumbent because of a reduction in a state's number of House seats or because of intraparty fighting. These are also incumbent gerrymanders, but of the *exclusionary* type.

The art and science of gerrymandering relies on detailed knowledge of voter-registration statistics and historic voting patterns in precincts, wards, cities, and counties. The typical partisan congressional gerrymander manifests one or more of the following characteristics: (1) shaping districts in bizarre or unusual ways, (2) dividing well-known political entities (e.g., wards, cities, counties) between different districts, (3) splitting known communities of interest between different districts, (4) packing known communities of interest into a few districts, (5) placing the residences of opposition incumbents in new districts, and (6) dividing up the old districts of opposition incumbents and distributing the pieces among adjacent districts.

Historically, gerrymanders were hand-drawn maps painstakingly put together using voting statistics and arithmetic. Since the 1980s large census and voting databases and geographic information technologies have enabled computers to quickly calculate and draw a myriad of possible district configurations with different political-demographic characteristics.

REFORMING THE CONGRESSIONAL REDISTRICTING PROCESS. The first national electoral provision addressing the practice of unusually configured congressional districts was the Apportionment Act of 1842 (5 Stat. 581), which mandated congressional districts of "contiguous" territory, thereby temporarily banning the physical splitting of a district into two or more geographically separated areas. The 1901 (31 Stat. 733) and 1911 (37 Stat. 13) apportionment laws specifically addressed gerrymandering by adding the word *compact* to the stipulation of contiguity. These prescriptions did not appear in the general census apportionment law of 1929 or in subsequent acts or amendments. Before and since the 1930s numerous gerrymandered and even split districts have appeared in congressional redistricting.

Historically, malapportionment and the gerrymander were practiced hand-in-hand to give the greatest possible advantage to the partisan political cartographer. Supreme Court rulings of the 1960s eliminated population malapportionment. The case against malapportionment has sound legal standing, and abuses can easily be identified and rectified. Gerrymandering, on the other hand, poses much tougher legal questions and involves courts in the partisan political process. However, the Court has ruled on certain gerrymander cases, and guidelines for measuring the practice have been developed.

RACIAL GERRYMANDERING. Evidence of racial gerrymandering can be found in the post-Reconstruction South and in northern cities during the first half of the twentieth century. The disenfranchisement of African Americans in the South in the late nineteenth century lessened this practice, but after the voting rights acts of the 1960s, the practice of diluting minority votes surfaced again, mainly in the form of racial gerrymandering and at-large elections. Racial gerrymanders split highly concentrated urban and rural black populations between two or more election districts, making black voters the minority in each district. Similar cases of gerrymandering to dilute the power of Hispanic voters have also been demonstrated. In the 1970s court challenges were made to obvious, deliberate racial gerrymanders, mostly in the southern states. The courts ruled that conspicuous and premeditated gerrymandering against groups that had previously suffered discrimination was unconstitutional. The most famous case of racial gerrymandering on the statewide congressional-district level was that involving the Mississippi congressional redistrictings of 1966, 1972, and 1981, which split the concentration of African-American voters in the Mississippi Delta region of the state. This and similar occurrences on the local and state levels prompted a 1982 amendment to the Voting Rights Act (96 Stat. 131) obligating election districts at all levels to be fashioned in such a way that racial or linguistic minorities would have the potential power to elect representatives. These so-called minority-majority districts in 1992 led to the election of more minority representatives to Congress. To accomplish the minority representation goal, however, some districts were drawn with erratic boundaries to connect minority concentrations, thereby packing minority groups into the same district. The exclusionary gerrymander of the past gave way to this type of inclusionary gerrymander.

CONTINUING JUDICIAL ISSUES. Reformers of the redistricting process consider both partisan and racial gerrymandering inherently unfair, biased, and, because they weaken voter choice, inherently undemocratic. As mentioned, the courts have ruled racial gerrymandering unconstitutional. In 1984 the courts went one step further in an Indiana congressional redistricting case, *Bandemer v. Davis* (603 F. Supp. 1479), ruling that partisan gerrymandering was not only subject to judicial review but also unconstitutional. Although the Supreme Court ruled against the specifics in the Indiana case, the way was opened for judicial review of the intentional partisan gerrymander.

If the partisan gerrymander is justiciable (i.e., open to challenge in court), then defining criteria to prove the presence of the practice become important. Such proof is important in the case of either *intentional gerrymander* or *innocent gerrymander.* The most obvious test is the geographic compactness of the district. Geographers and mathematicians have developed formulas for measuring the spatial compactness of areas as well as models for dividing a given geographical space (for example, a state) into a certain number of districts in the most compact way. But a state may be divided into compact districts in a number of different ways, and even the most compact division may either intentionally or innocently pack or split votes.

Criteria other than shape are therefore also important in establishing a fair and unbiased redistricting. Three other geographic factors are (1) consideration of the boundaries of established political units, (2) recognition of geographic concentrations of communities of interest, and (3) correlation of new districts with previous district boundaries. These geographic considerations are quantifiable and can give objective, substantive evidence vital to the judicial review of redistricting.

A number of political criteria have also been considered in the analysis of gerrymandering, including (1) political fairness (that is, that the ratio of elected members of both parties is roughly in proportion to the total partisan breakdown of a given region over several elections; see table 1), (2) electoral responsiveness (that is, that districts are competitive enough to react to electoral swings and the possible selection of new representatives), and (3) the intention of the lawmakers to establish a partisan advantage.

Reformers of the redistricting process consider both partisan and racial gerrymandering inherently unfair, biased, and undemocratic.

Some states have considered creating nonpartisan (or at least bipartisan) electoral commissions to draw congressional districts. Even under the best conditions, however, the district method of election carries an inherent electoral bias. Referring to table 1, a case can be made that Method III is actually a fair (and certainly a competitive) districting, even though skillfully gerrymandered for partisan advantage. Some observers say that this and like examples suggest that, without proof of intent, the gerrymander may be a political problem without judicial solution. Enough geographical and political standards do seem available, however, to establish initial criteria before the drawing of electoral districts and to judge their fairness after they have been drawn.

[See also (I) Apportionment and Redistricting.]

BIBLIOGRAPHY

Davidson, Chandler, ed. *Minority Vote Dilution.* 1984.

Griffith, Elmer C. *The Rise and Development of the Gerrymander.* 1907.

Grofman, Bernard, ed. *Political Gerrymandering and the Courts.* 1990.

Morrill, Richard L. *Political Redistricting and Geographic Theory.* 1981.

Musgrove, Philip. *The General Theory of Gerrymandering.* 1977.

U.S. Senate. Committee on Government Affairs. *Congressional Anti-Gerrymandering Act of 1979, Hearings.* 91st Cong., 1st sess., 1979.

– KENNETH C. MARTIS

GOVERNMENT PRINTING OFFICE

Statutorily established in 1860, the Government Printing Office (GPO) provides public printing for the entire federal government through its own facilities and the procurement of commercial services. An agency of the legislative branch, GPO is headed by the public printer, who is appointed by the president subject to the approval of the Senate.

During the initial meetings of Congress in 1789, many members recognized the practical need for printed documents to assist each chamber with the performance of its duties and responsibilities. If nothing more, printing would allow legislators to work with legible documents and would provide multiple copies of records. Members also appreciated the civic value served by the publication of government documents—informing the sovereign citizenry. Consequently, early Congresses quickly provided for the printing and distribution of both laws and treaties. Similar action was taken regarding the House and Senate journals in 1813. Publication of congressional floor proceedings was begun in 1824, and, later, in 1846, Congress provided for the routine printing of congressional reports, special documents (including executive branch material), and legislative proposals. All this work was performed by private printers under contract to Congress.

By the time of the Jefferson administration, if not earlier, public printing had become an instrument for patronage. Those receiving contracts were political friends (often newspaper publishers) who owned printing machinery. Both an administration press (faithful to the president) and a party press (loyal to congressional leaders) were developing in Washington, D.C. The ability of heads of executive branch agencies to procure printing was usually controlled by the president. To meet printing needs and to bestow patronage, the president might turn to House or Senate contract printers or to both. These congressional printers were selected on a partisan basis and according to their ability to publish a newspaper that would function as a party organ. Such printers produced a large volume of the printing required by each house, and they frequently received smaller amounts of executive-branch printing from the president. It was a profitable business for the printers and one that rapidly became corrupt.

A congressional investigation in 1840 revealed that printers utilized by Congress had made profits of almost $470,000 during the previous seven years. Similar revelations by other inquiries in 1846, 1852, and 1860 contributed to growing embarrassment and outcry over the deplorable ethics and the graft of the public printing industry.

The reform response was the establishment of GPO to produce all public printing, either using its own facilities or through the competitive procurement of commercial services. Additional aspects of government-wide printing and publication were set with the Printing Act of 1895, still the source of much of the basic policy found in the printing chapters of the U.S. Code. This statute also transferred to GPO a program begun in

1813 for distributing selected government publications to certain depository libraries throughout the country.

The Printing Act also relocated the superintendent of documents, previously an Interior Department official, to GPO, giving him responsibility for managing document sales and preparing periodic catalogs of federal publications. The sale stock available to the superintendent derived entirely from materials provided for this purpose by the departments and agencies or returned from depository libraries. In 1904, the superintendent was authorized to reprint any departmental publication, with the consent of the pertinent secretary, for public sale. Congress legislated comparable discretion to reproduce its documents in 1922.

When the Printing Act became law, GPO relied on electrically powered rotary presses with hand-set type. This technology was subsequently replaced by linotype composition, which eventually gave way to computer-assisted composition and printing. Paper copies of documents came to be supplemented by microform, computer tapes, and diskettes. Since the mid-1980s, electronic formats have been introduced in both fixed modes, such as CD-ROMs, and in on-line services.

When GPO was established, it came under the immediate scrutiny of an existing special oversight panel. The Joint Committee on Public Printing, mandated in 1846, continues to monitor GPO management and operations. Through the exercise of remedial powers, the joint committee sets government printing and binding regulations. Its ten members are drawn equally from the chairs and ranking members of the Committee on House Administration and the Senate Committee on Rules and Administration, which have legislative jurisdiction over GPO and matters pertaining to it, but the joint committee itself has no actual legislative authority. GPO must seek funding annually from the appropriations committees of both houses, and it is subject to audit by the General Accounting Office, another legislative branch agency.

[See also (II) Executive Departments.]

BIBLIOGRAPHY

Stathis, Stephen W. "The Evolution of Government Printing and Publishing in America." *Government Publications Review* 7A (1980):377–390.

U.S. Government Printing Office. *100 GPO Years, 1861–1961.* 1961.

U.S. Government Printing Office. *GPO/2001: Vision for a New Millennium.* 1992.

– HAROLD C. RELYEA

GRANT-IN-AID

Grants-in-aid are a leading technique of intergovernmental relations in the U.S. federal system. Congress uses grants to state and local governments as instruments of national policy. They are typically given for a specified purpose, with conditions attached, and not just to redistribute public revenues.

Grants initially took the form of lands, although in one noteworthy measure in 1836 Congress distributed revenue that had been realized from land sales. Over the course of the nineteenth century, Congress made massive grants to state governments from the federal domain. By far the greatest amount, over eighty-one million acres, was for common schools. Far surpassing what was needed for school sites, this land was to be leased or sold, with the proceeds going to education. The statements of purpose accompanying grants were usually very general.

Grants-in-aid as a systematic technique of federal-state relations, applying to all states and employing a reasonably specific statement of purpose, are usually traced to the Morrill Land-Grant College Act (1862), which gave each state thirty thousand acres for each of its senators and representatives in Congress to endow colleges in the agricultural and mechanic arts. States that contained no public lands were given scrip.

Grants-in-aid financed out of appropriations followed, and they were well-established by the early twentieth century. Examples included the Hatch Act of 1887 (agricultural experiment stations); a second Morrill Act, in 1890 (annual appropriations for the land-grant colleges); the Weeks Act of 1911 (forest fire protection); the Smith-Lever Act of 1914 (agricultural and home economics extension work); the Federal Aid Highway Act of 1916; the Smith-Hughes Act of 1917 (vocational education); and the Sheppard-Towner Act of 1921 (maternal and infant hygiene).

Massachusetts challenged the constitutionality of the Sheppard-Towner Act, arguing that it lay beyond the scope of Congress's spending power. In *Massachusetts v. Mellon* (1923), the Supreme Court declined to rule on the merits, holding that a state is not entitled to a remedy in the courts against an allegedly unconstitutional appropriation of national funds.

Federal grants prior to the New Deal amounted to less than 10 percent of states' revenue from their own sources. With the Social Security Act (1935), which initiated grants for public assistance, the figure rose precipitously. With the Interstate Highway Act of 1956, which authorized a mammoth public works program, it jumped again. During the Johnson administration in the mid-1960s, Congress enacted scores of grant programs to combat poverty and inequality. Medicaid, providing medical care for the needy, and aid for elementary and secondary education, benefiting especially the poorest states and school districts having a high proportion of poor children, were passed in 1965. The election of Republican presidents did not slow the growth of grants. In particular, enactment of sewage treatment system grants in 1972 gave spending yet another big push. By 1978, federal grant programs numbered close to five hundred and totaled $79 billion, which approached a third of state and local governments' general revenues from their own sources and a fourth of federal domestic outlays. They had become pervasive.

Most grants are distributed by formula, and much of the politics of grant-in-aid programs is linked to the construction of the formulas.

Until the New Deal, federal grants went almost exclusively to state governments. With the enactment of aid for public housing in 1937 and urban redevelopment in 1949, grants to cities became routine. However, they remained a minor share of local revenues until the explosion of grant spending in the 1960s and 1970s, of which local governments were the principal beneficiaries.

Grants are allocated among recipient governments either by statutory formulas (formula grants) or at the discretion of federal administrators who pass judgment on applications (project grants). Most grants are distributed by formula, and much of the politics of grant-in-aid programs is linked to the construction of the formulas. While many formulas contain equalizing elements intended to compensate for interjurisdictional disparities in taxable wealth and socioeconomic composition, the normal tendency of grant politics is toward wide geographic dispersion of aid.

In the State and Local Fiscal Assistance Act of 1972, Congress enacted a program of grants-in-aid unrestricted by purpose. Called "general revenue sharing," this program was a radical departure, but after the federal government began to experience severe fiscal shortages at the end of the 1970s it was discontinued. Congress reverted to prescribing the purposes of grants. However, initiatives by Presidents Richard M. Nixon and Ronald Reagan led to the emergence of "broad-based" or "block" grants, which provided funds on relatively general and permissive terms. They were created by consolidating and simplifying clusters of related categorical grants, most importantly in regard to community development and employment and training.

Largely through such consolidations, the number of grant programs fell to 435 (422 "categorical" and 13 "block") by 1987. However, even as revenue sharing reached a peak and block grants took effect, categorical grants continued to predominate in terms of dollars.

The tendency over time, despite the introduction of block grants, has been for conditions to become more numerous, exacting, and varied. Included are sweeping prohibitions against discrimination on the basis of race, color, national origin, gender, age, and handicapped status, all products of the rights revolution of the 1960s and 1970s. Also, as grants exploded, Congress began threatening to withhold all or part of the biggest grants (e.g., for highways and medicaid) in order to influence actions of the states, sometimes in ways having no connection to the purpose of the grant. Thus, federal grants gradually have become more coercive, their conditions perceived by state and local governments as "mandates." This trend continued even as, after 1978, they began to decline as a share of federal domestic outlays and state and local expenditures.

It is not necessarily the case that conditioned grants-in-aid produce uniform policy. Interjurisdictional differences are reduced but not eliminated by this type of federal intervention. Gaps in federal laws and limits on the supervisory capacities of federal agencies leave room for the play of state and local politics and policy traditions.

The states' appeals to federal courts for relief from grant conditions have been futile. Courts have granted standing to challenge such conditions but invariably have found that they are not coercive because states are technically free to refuse the grants and that Congress has power to set the terms on which federal funds are disbursed. The precedent-setting case was *Oklahoma v. Civil Service Commission* (330 U.S. 127 [1947]). Additionally, after the late 1960s, federal judicial readings of the Constitution and federal statutes often specified the states' obligations in grant programs, especially in the field of welfare. Courts have admitted claims of private individuals against state governments under grant-in-aid statutes.

BIBLIOGRAPHY

Advisory Commission on Intergovernmental Relations. *Significant Features of Fiscal Federalism.* Published annually.

Advisory Commission on Intergovernmental Relations. *Regulatory Federalism: Policy, Process, Impact, and Reform.* 1984.

Clark, Jane Perry. *The Rise of a New Federalism.* 1938.

– MARTHA DERTHICK

H

HOUSE BANK

For a century and a half, the House bank was a facility in the Capitol where the pay of representatives was deposited into accounts and could be redeemed by them for cash. During the mid-twentieth century, a practice developed at the bank of allowing representatives to write checks on their bank accounts with little regard for whether their account balances were sufficient to cover their drafts. In 1991, the news media took note that members had been writing thousands of overdrafts on the bank, triggering a sensational scandal that led to abolition of the facility on 31 December 1991.

The affair, which began in September 1991 and raged intermittently throughout 1992, shook the House more severely than any previous scandal, with the possible exception of the 1972 Abscam affair. It is widely believed to have forced at least twenty-five representatives from office, through either retirement or defeat at the polls.

The banking facility's history and traditions of operation, in the view of many, made the final catastrophe inevitable. The bank originated as an informal operation of the House sergeant at arms in the early 1800s, when the Speaker charged that office with disbursing salaries. Sometime between 1830 and 1889, the sergeant at arms began allowing representatives to keep their pay on deposit rather than receive it all at once (though no interest was ever paid). Thus, the office of the sergeant at arms almost inadvertently became a sort of bank, although its informal evolution prevented the establishment of traditional banking practices at the facility, including regular audits.

The lack of common banking controls led to a series of thefts at the House bank over the next century and a half, the first of which occurred in 1889, when a cashier absconded with some $50,000. In 1947, a new scandal erupted over the bank when Kenneth Romney, the previous sergeant at arms, was convicted of lying to General Accounting Office investigators to hide two decades of embezzlement.

Regular GAO audits were first mandated in the aftermath of the Romney scandal, but controls remained weak overall. Around the same time, a practice developed at the bank routinely allowing House members to write overdrafts—in effect, taking short-term, no-interest loans—funded with the deposits of other representatives.

Beginning in 1954 and possibly even earlier, the General Accounting Office periodically voiced concerns about the overdrafts in reports to the House, but House leaders paid little heed. On 18 September 1991, however, the GAO published an unusually detailed report about the overdraft practice, stating that in a one-year period (from mid-1989 to mid-1990), a total of 8,331 overdrafts had been written, and that a group of 134 members had written 581 overdraft checks with face amounts of $1,000 or more. Questions about possible administrative and financial abuses by Sergeant at Arms Jack Russ were also raised. Press coverage of the report, which occurred in a climate of escalating controversy over other congressional perquisites and alleged ethical lapses, quickly touched off a tempest. On 3 October the House passed a resolution ordering the bank abolished and an investigation launched.

The investigation by the House Committee on Standards of Official Conduct ultimately led to a vote by the House on 13 March 1992 in favor of public disclosure of the number of overdrafts written by each House

House scandals. Following the discovery of two decades of embezzlement from the House bank by former sergeant at arms Kenneth Romney, a new congressional scandal emerged concerning theft from the House stationery room. The political cartoon depicts the recurring Berryman figure John Q. Public offering brooms to Speaker Joseph W. Martin, Jr. (R-Mass.), so he can clean up the House. Clifford K. Berryman, Washington Evening Star, *23 January 1947. (U.S. Senate Collection, Center for Legislative Archives)*

member in the two years prior to October 1991. Release of this information forced dozens of members to explain their seemingly irresponsible banking practices to hostile constituents who did not enjoy similar penalty-free banking privileges. Many members saw their perceived transgressions as too great a political liability and chose not to seek reelection. At least a dozen other members with records of significant numbers of overdrafts were defeated in primaries or in the November general election.

Amid the furor following release of the committee report in the spring of 1992, U.S. Attorney General William P. Barr appointed a prosecutor to probe possible criminal wrongdoing in the affair. The prosecutor promptly sought legally to compel the House to provide him its bank records, touching off a new controversy. Some representatives, including Speaker Thomas S. Foley, opposed providing the records on the ground that such an act would jeopardize the independence of the legislative branch. On 30 April, however, the House voted overwhelmingly to comply with the demand, and subsequent court challenges to that decision, on separation-of-powers grounds, were rejected. The prosecutor was ultimately unable to establish wrongdoing in the vast majority of cases. On 6 October 1993 former sergeant at arms Russ pleaded guilty to wire fraud and false statement charges related to misuse of House bank funds. He was later sentenced to two and a half years in prison. One congressman defeated in 1992, Carroll Hubbard, Jr., was convicted on 6 April 1994 of financial crimes uncovered during the bank probe and was later sentenced to prison.

The most significant effects of the House bank scandal were the heavy turnover in House membership that it fueled and the boost it gave to the movement for congressional reform and higher standards of ethical conduct. Some reforms, such as reduced patronage in the House bureaucracy and appointment of a professional administrator to oversee House affairs, were enacted almost immediately, while others were taken up in the 103d Congress (1993–1995).

BIBLIOGRAPHY

Kuntz, Phil. "The History of the House-Bank: Scandal Waiting to Happen." *Congressional Quarterly Weekly Report,* 8 February 1992, pp. 282–289.

Simpson, Glenn R. "In the End, Over Half Members with More Than 100 Overdrafts Won't Be Back in 1993." *Roll Call,* 5 November 1992, p. 5.

U.S. House of Representatives. Committee on Standards of Official Conduct. *Inquiry into the Operation of the Bank of the Sergeant at Arms of the House of Representatives.* 102d Congress, 2d sess., 1992. H. Rept. 102-452.

– GLENN R. SIMPSON

HOUSE OF REPRESENTATIVES

An Overview

In his notes on the Constitutional Convention of 1787, James Madison called the proposed House of Representatives "the grand repository of the democratic principle of government." The House was designed to be the institution of national government most responsive to popular sentiment. Its members were given two-year terms, shorter than the six-year terms of senators and the four-year terms of presidents, and seats in the House were allocated to states based on population. Unlike the Senate, the presidency, and the Supreme Court, the House was to be directly elected by the people.

For more than a century, the House grew as the nation grew, maintaining a low ratio of representatives to constituents but creating a rapidly expanding legislative body. The House, which had sixty-five members in the First Congress, added seats every ten years, following the national census, to reflect population growth and the addition of new states. In 1911, when the House had 435 seats, Congress decided to halt the body's expansion and instead to reapportion seats among the states every ten years based on changes in relative population, while ensuring that each state had at least one seat. Nonvoting delegates have been added from American Samoa, the District of Columbia, Guam, and the Virgin Islands; a nonvoting resident commissioner represents Puerto Rico.

The House is assigned one special constitutional prerogative—the power to originate all legislation on taxation—in order to protect the people from a confiscatory, self-aggrandizing central government. The House soon assumed the power to originate all appropriations (spending) legislation as well.

The "grand repository" was not fully trusted by the framers of the Constitution. It was feared that the House, with its short terms and direct mode of election, would react impulsively to shifting public opinion and parochial pressures and would not be a reliable judge of the general welfare. As Madison put it, the House "was liable to err . . . from fickleness and passion." Bicameralism and separation of powers were devised, in part, to make it difficult for the transient public passions registered in the House to be translated into public law. And the House was excluded from certain functions—ratification of treaties and confirmation of presidential nominees for the courts, diplomatic posts, and high government positions—that were given to the Senate.

These fundamental institutional features—term of office, constituency, size, and constitutional prerogatives and constraints—continue to shape the modern House. For example, the size of the House makes it difficult for the typical member to contribute much on most legislation. Indeed, there is a limit to how much collegial exchange and deliberation is feasible in the House. Policy-making responsibilities must be shouldered by smaller groups, whether committees, party leaders, or ad hoc task forces. When the House relies on committees, policy-making takes on a decentralized cast; when the majority party and its leaders dominate policy-making, it takes on a centralized look. The history of the House has often been characterized as oscillating between centralized and decentralized control.

The House of Representatives was designed to be the institution of national government most responsive to popular sentiment.

Reliance on committees and subcommittees has, however, been the general tendency. Only occasionally, on important, highly partisan issues and when powerful people have held positions, have majority party leaders directed the process with a strong hand. The inclination toward a decentralized, committee-oriented process is partly a result of the need for a division of labor to manage a large work load. This system also meets the needs of individual members, who enjoy a process that enables them to contribute meaningfully to public policy, at least within certain policy areas, and to exercise special influence in areas of particular interest to themselves or their constituencies.

THE MODERN HOUSE. The basic institutional features of the House, as well as its tendency toward a decentralized process, are reflected in its modern rules, internal distribution of power, media attention, policy-making role, and capacity to change.

Rules and procedures. The House and its rules are recreated every two years. In early January, following each election, the House elects a new Speaker and adopts a set of rules. The last Speaker of the House, if he or she is reelected and his or her party remains in the majority, is routinely reelected to the position. The rules of the last Congress, usually with a few changes, are adopted again. Both the vote on the Speaker and the vote on the rules are party-line votes, as the two major parties nominate their own leaders for Speaker and usually differ over the content of the rules.

The rules of the modern House are more elaborate than those of the Senate. Because of its size, the House cannot afford unlimited debate and unrestricted amending activity, so its rules carefully limit and structure debate, and bar nongermane amendments. Floor debate and amending action on most important legislation occurs in the Committee of the Whole, where debate is severely limited but where business may be conducted with a quorum of only one hundred members. Generally, important legislation is brought to the floor and considered in the Committee of the Whole by special rules, written by the Rules Committee and supported by majority votes. Special rules allow the majority to impose its agenda and further structure or limit debate and amendments. And, unlike the Senate, the House has a previous question rule that allows a majority to bring debate to an end and force a vote.

The potential unwieldiness of the large House has led to the emergence of a powerful presiding officer. The Speaker, who gains the post by virtue of leading the majority party, refers legislation to committees, controls the recognition of members to speak or offer motions from the floor, makes parliamentary rulings, and appoints conference committee delegations in addition to exercising numerous powers within his or her party caucus. No other member of Congress, House or Senate, enjoys formal powers as great as those of the Speaker.

The strong speakership, along with rules allowing simple majorities to overcome procedural obstacles that minorities may place in their way, gives the House a strongly majoritarian character. The majority party and its leaders usually exercise control over the agenda. The minority party, small factions, and individual representatives have no effective options when facing a cohesive majority party. This stands in sharp contrast to the Senate, where minorities and individual senators have the means to obstruct rapid action by offering amendments and conducting extended debate.

Yet the full potential of majoritarian rule is seldom realized in the House. Divisions within the majority party often limit its ability to devise policy and push it through the House. Majority party leaders usually rely on committees to initiate legislative action and draft the details of legislation. Much of the central leaders' effort is devoted to facilitating the work of committees and managing the flow of legislation from committees and through the House floor. The House seems to operate most smoothly when committees and the majority party leadership operate in collaboration or partnership.

House rules and precedents reinforce the power of standing committees. The rules make it difficult to circumvent a committee by bringing a measure directly to the floor or by attaching the measure as an amendment to some other legislation. House committees are granted a great deal of deference. Committee bill managers are granted advantages on the floor, and committee members dominate conference committee delega-

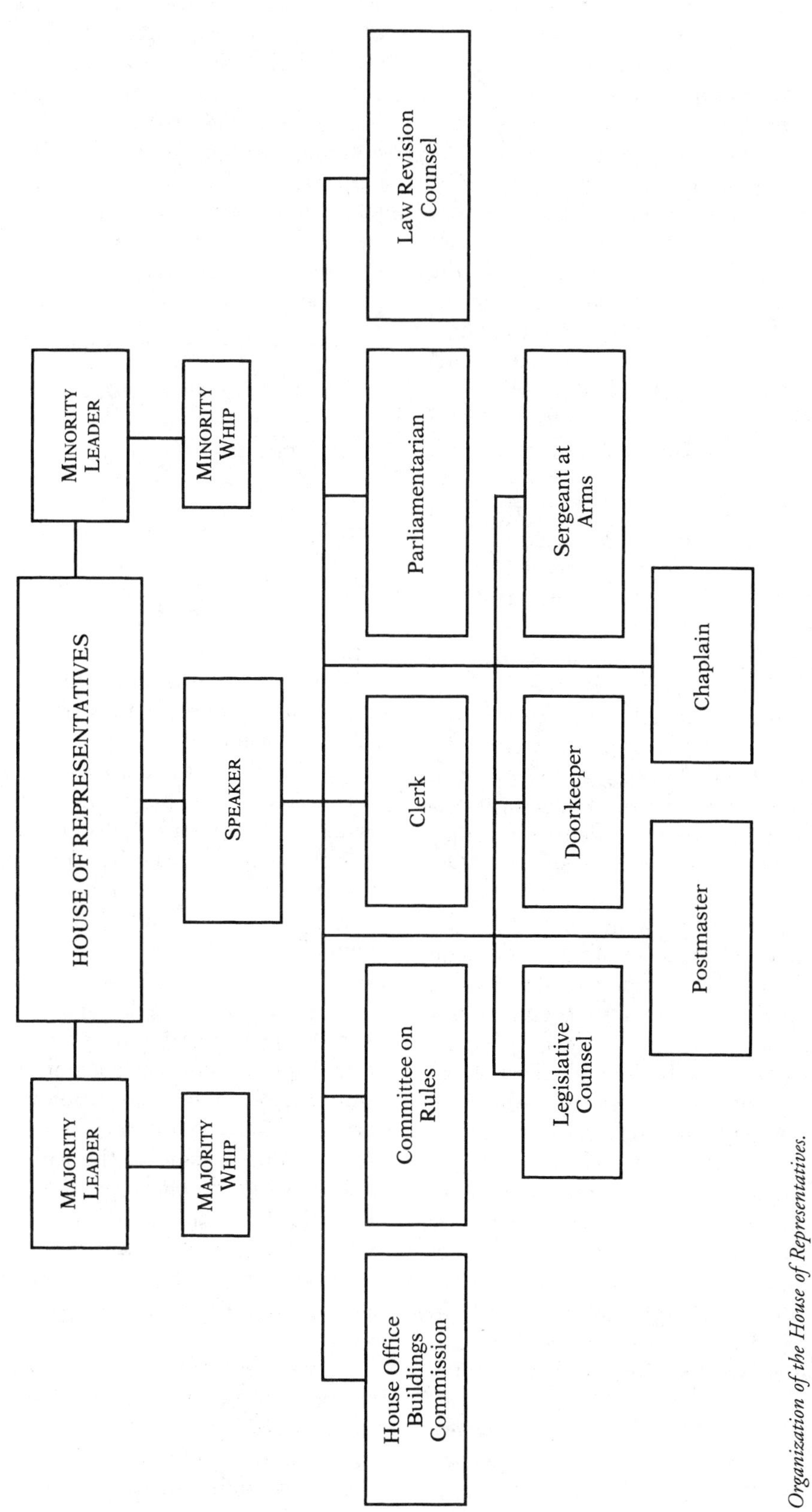

Organization of the House of Representatives.

tions. Committees also are advantaged by the expertise their members acquire through years of service, their relationships with interest groups and executive agencies, and their large professional staffs.

Media coverage. The typical representative lacks the influence and media visibility of the typical senator. The sheer size of the House reduces the formal power of the average representative. Majoritarian rules minimize the opportunities for individuals or factions to attract attention by employing obstructionist tactics. And the committee-centered process removes much of the action from the House floor to committee rooms, where legislative markups seldom draw the attention of visitors, print journalists, or the electronic media.

A study of television news coverage in the mid-1980s demonstrated that senators averaged six times as much attention as representatives. One reason for the differential is that few presidential candidates emerge from the House. The Senate is the home of a larger number of potential, current, and former presidential candidates, whose national visibility makes them attractive subjects for TV news and feature programs. Representatives are less frequently seen as the leading spokespersons for a point of view or cause. And the fact that senators typically make a greater effort to attract media attention plays a role as well. Senators, who generally face more sharply contested elections, must appeal to larger constituencies. Because they are frequently seeking to build a national base for a presidential bid, they work harder to appear on television news and interview programs.

In the middle decades of the twentieth century, the low-visibility, decentralized character of House decision making gave the House a technocratic flavor. The House, as Nelson Polsby noted in a 1970 essay, was a "highly specialized instrument for processing legislation." Policy-making was quietly dominated by senior members, particularly committee chairmen, who were disproportionately southern and conservative. Individual members were specialists in the subject matter of their committees and tended to be more expert than their counterparts in the Senate. They gained power by accruing seniority and waiting their turn to chair subcommittees and full committees. During this period, partisanship was muted in the House, particularly in the field of foreign policy, where the Cold War consensus after World War II kept the House in line with the president on most matters.

CHANGES SINCE THE 1960S. But the House is not immutable. To the contrary, important and dramatic change has occurred since the late 1960s. Perhaps most conspicuously, more representatives now seek to use television as a tool for generating attention for themselves and their causes. Though still a small proportion of the House, a number of representatives now have national visibility as leaders of certain factions or crusades. Recent House party leaders have hired media specialists, more aggressively sought to influence public opinion through the mass media, and sometimes incorporated explicit media strategies into their legislative plans. And spicy debates in televised floor sessions occasionally generate network news coverage. The House still lacks the coverage given the Senate, but it is not the nearly invisible institution it was at midcentury.

The typical representative lacks the influence and media visibility of the typical senator.

Below the surface of media coverage, the neatly decentralized, committee-oriented policy-making of the past has given way to a more fluid process. In the early 1970s, the grip of full committee chairs on committee action was loosened. Most committees were required for the first time to create subcommittees with guaranteed jurisdictions, bill referral, and staff. Committee chairs faced biennial election by the Democratic Caucus; between 1974 and 1990, six chairmen lost bids to be reelected to their posts. Since 1974, committee chairs have been less obstructionist and more sensitive to the preferences of the majority party caucus. Furthermore, new sunshine rules required committees to open most meetings to the public and required committees to maintain a public record of committee actions and voting.

At the same time, the Speaker gained new formal powers. He acquired new discretion to refer legislation to multiple committees, the ability to set deadlines for committee consideration in some circumstances, more influence over committee assignments, and firm control over the membership of the Rules Committee. Moreover, rank-and-file members gained more opportunities to participate thanks to the revitalization of the Democratic Caucus and rules changes that made it possible to record votes on floor amendments and that encouraged the Speaker to appoint larger conference delegations.

At first, the reforms of the 1970s appeared to have a strongly decentralizing effect. Committee government was replaced by subcommittee government, observers argued, and the House's ability to enact coherent legislation in a timely manner declined. Norms restraining participation among junior members and committee outsiders were weakened, and floor amendments to committee bills multiplied. The Speakers of the 1970s, Carl B. Albert (D-Okla.) and Thomas P. (Tip) O'Neill, Jr. (D-Mass.), did not exploit their new powers. The predictability and efficiency of midcentury gave way to a more fragmented, seemingly disorderly process.

Conditions changed in the 1980s and early 1990s. Tolerance of the chaos on the House floor wore thin. The legislative work load moderated as the policy agenda shifted to resolving serious fiscal problems. Democrats, who had suffered deep regional divisions in the 1960s and early 1970s, became more cohesive. The majority party Democrats of the House were thrown on the defensive as Republicans gained control of the White House (1981–1993) and Senate (1981–1987). Divided party control of the major institutions intensified conflict between the legislative and executive branches. Policy stalemate on fiscal, civil rights, environmental, and other issues was common. And attributing and avoiding blame for policy stalemate became a dominant strategy of both parties.

In response, the House became more partisan, more centralized, and more dependent on flexible special rules. Speaker O'Neill became more assertive in the 1980s, and his successor, James C. Wright, Jr. (D-Tex.), aggressively shaped the agenda of the House. These Speakers, along with Wright's successor, Thomas S. Foley (D-Wash.), more frequently sought special rules to limit and structure floor amendments. Budget rules and negotiations among top leaders on budget matters reduced the autonomy of committees and their subcommittees. Partisanship and the cohesiveness of the House Democrats further diminished the policy contributions of minority party Republicans, who, out of the majority since the years 1953 to 1955, became increasingly frustrated. The House of the 1980s and early 1990s looked so different from the decentralized one predicted in the 1970s that some observers began to refer to the "postreform" House.

In the postreform House, the decision-making process looks more flexible than it did in the tidy, committee-oriented process of midcentury. The Speaker uses multiple referral power more frequently to shape committee action on major legislation. The Speaker often appoints task forces of Democrats to design policy and generate support for the party. The task forces are extracommittee entities, composed of members and nonmembers of the committees with formal jurisdiction. Furthermore, the content of legislation is more frequently negotiated among contending factions and committees after a committee has reported the measure but before it is taken to the floor. Such negotiations, usually conducted under the direction of the Speaker, often lead the Rules Committee to structure floor action so as to advantage the negotiated product.

Many of these changes were reflected in the policy-making role of the House. The House, once less liberal and assertive than the Senate, became more liberal and assertive in the 1970s and 1980s. In the 1970s, liberated subcommittee chairs and rank-and-file members, bolstered by enlarged staffs, assumed more initiative in generating policy ideas. More House members ran for president, cultivated national constituencies, and became recognized policy leaders. The House became a more important source of policy ideas in both the domestic and foreign policy fields. Indeed, the House often led the Senate in challenging the foreign policies of Republican presidents. No longer is the House merely a "specialized instrument for processing legislation."

ESSENTIAL ELEMENTS OF HOUSE POLITICS. The record of recent decades illustrates several properties of House politics. First, House decision-making processes are quite malleable. They respond to external forces, particularly the nature of policy problems, electoral forces, and relations with the president and the Senate, and to internal factors, such as the expectations of a changing membership, the distribution of policy views within and between the parties, the personal style of individual Speakers, and inherited procedures and structures.

Second, the House is majoritarian. House policy majorities, particularly when a policy majority can be created from within the majority party, are usually able to gain House approval of their legislation. Generally, a cohesive majority party can establish rules and pass legislation that suit its needs. Cross-party majority coalitions face greater difficulty when they are opposed by the majority party leadership or committee leaders, who enjoy substantial parliamentary advantages. But even a determined cross-party majority coalition can eventually force action on its legislation or even impose new procedures. Many of the new budget procedures created in the 1980s and 1990s were the work of cross-party coalitions.

Third, floor decision making in the House is structured by formal rules. The House relies on its standing rules—and increasingly on special rules that supplant or supplement the standing rules—to guide virtually all floor action on legislation. In contrast, the Senate lacks detailed rules to order floor debate or limit floor amendments and must instead rely on unanimous consent agreements, which are negotiated on a case-by-case basis, to order floor activity.

The House's malleability, majoritarianism, and formality are related. In contrast to the Senate, where large minorities can block changes in the rules, the House may change its rules by simple majority vote. This allows House majorities to adjust the rules frequently to meet changing conditions, and it allows House majorities to grant procedural advantage to their own proposals by imposing special rules of their choosing.

Fourth, party considerations structure House decision-making processes. In both houses, the two major parties make committee assignments, sit on opposite sides of the center aisle on the floor, and usually serve as the basis for organizing floor debate. The House goes further by granting to the leader of the majority party the wide powers of the speakership. Consequently, the majority party leadership has the ability to set the agenda of the House without meaningful consultation with the minority.

The House's malleability, majoritarianism, and formality are related.

Finally, the House is constrained by the demands of the rank-and-file membership. Party structure and majoritarianism might appear to be a formula for rule by central majority party leaders. Yet party leaders are severely constrained by the tolerance of the rank and file. House members know that the next election is never far away, and they realize that their reelection prospects turn on what they do for their constituencies. These considerations uncouple many members from their own party leaders. To be sure, the House is not as individualistic as the Senate, but it is far more individualistic than most other national legislatures. Its leaders and committees must, and usually do, operate within bounds acceptable to the majority of members.

House politics, then, usually represents some balance among competing pressures for centralization, decentralization, and a more collegial process. The size and workload of the House require the delegation of power to subgroups of members. The interests of individual members limit the extent to which power devolves to small groups of central leaders or committee members. House members have created a maze of formal rules and insisted on majority rule in order to limit the exercise of arbitrary power by advantaged groups.

[See also (I) House of Representatives, articles on Daily Sessions of the House, House Rules and Procedures.]

BIBLIOGRAPHY

Bach, Stanley, and Steven S. Smith. *Managing Uncertainty in the House of Representatives.* 1988.

Davidson, Roger H., and Walter J. Oleszek. *Congress against Itself.* 1977.

Fenno, Richard F., Jr. "The Internal Distribution of Influence: The House." In *The Congress and America's Future,* edited by David B. Truman. 1965.

Jacobson, Gary. *The Politics of Congressional Elections.* 1987.

Madison, James. *Notes of Debates in the Federal Convention of 1787.* 1969.

Ornstein, Norman. "The House and Senate in a New Congress." In *The New Congress,* edited by Thomas Mann and Norman Ornstein. 1981.

Polsby, Nelson. "Strengthening Congress in National Policy Making." *Yale Review* (Summer 1970): 481–497.

Price, David E. *The Congressional Experience.* 1992.

Sinclair, Barbara. *Majority Leadership in the U.S. House.* 1983.

– STEVEN S. SMITH

Daily Sessions of the House

A typical day in the House of Representatives begins with the opening of the cloakroom doors. The sergeant at arms enters the House chamber carrying the mace, an ebony and silver rod symbolizing his authority and that of the institution. He is followed by the Speaker of the House, who ascends the rostrum. The various clerks take their places at the lower two tiers. With the bang of the Speaker's gavel, the House convenes.

Normally the House convenes at noon, although the press of business may dictate an earlier, or occasionally a later, hour. The chaplain of the House, or a guest chaplain, delivers a prayer. The Speaker then announces his approval of the House Journal (the official record of the proceedings of the House) from the last day of session. At times, members may ask for a vote on the Speaker's approval of the Journal, a vote that is used more to discover who is present for that day's deliberations than actually to approve the Journal. Next, the Speaker chooses a member to lead the House in the Pledge of Allegiance.

One-minute speeches follow, alternating between majority and minority members. These speeches are popular for their value in publicizing a wide variety of subjects, both to constituents and to colleagues. How many one-minute speeches are permitted on any particular day depends on the Speaker's judgment of how pressing the day's agenda appears.

The House then turns to routine—that is, uncontroversial or minimally controversial—business. On the first and third Mondays of each month, the clerk will call the Consent Calendar. Uncontroversial bills expected to clear the House by unanimous consent with little or no debate are scheduled under this procedure. In addition to the 2 percent of all measures considered under the Consent Calendar procedure, the House calls up another 33 percent of its measures for consideration with a simple unanimous consent request, again with virtually no debate.

On the second and fourth Tuesdays of the month, the clerk calls the Private Calendar. About 4 percent of bills that reach the floor affect the welfare of private individuals only, and not the nation as a whole. They are considered with very little debate, and usually passed by voice vote.

Every Monday and every Tuesday of every week are considered "suspension days." Under the suspension procedure, it is in order to move to suspend the Rules of the House and pass legislation whether the measure is still in committee, pending on the calendar, or being held at the House desk. A motion to suspend limits debate on a measure to forty minutes and prohibits floor amendments. Adoption of a motion to suspend the rules and pass a bill requires two-thirds of those present to vote in the affirmative. The suspension procedure is used for approximately 35 percent of all measures that receive floor consideration. From the majority perspective, this method is popular because the committee version of the bill is protected from any further modification on the floor. From the minority perspective, the prohibition against amendments is a drawback, although the minority does gain the advantage of being able to defeat a measure with only one-third of the House in opposition, rather than the one-half normally required.

The House considers another 19 percent of legislation on the floor as "privileged matter." Under this procedure, debate is normally restricted to one hour and amendments are permitted only if the House defeats a motion calling for the previous question, a rare event.

In the early afternoon the House considers that day's planned agenda. The main piece of legislation chosen undoubtedly has some controversy attached to it, and amendments are expected. Or it may contain language that either raises or spends public money. For any of these reasons, the House considers the measure in a special legislative forum—the Committee of the Whole House on the State of the Union, better known simply as the Committee of the Whole. The House transforms itself into the committee through two simple steps. First, the Speaker leaves the rostrum and appoints a majority-party member to serve as the presiding officer in his stead. Second, the sergeant at arms lowers the mace. Both actions signal that the House is no longer meeting but has resolved into the Committee of the Whole. Although the chamber and membership stay the same, the more expeditious rules of debate and amendment utilized by committees can now govern.

Most significant and controversial measures considered in the Committee of the Whole are considered under the auspices of a "special rule," a resolution reported out of the House Committee on Rules, which must then be adopted by the House. It acts as a blueprint, setting the terms for debate and amendment of a specific bill. Some 7 percent of all measures are considered according to the provisions of a special rule.

The presiding officer, now addressed as "Mister [or Madam] Chairman," directs the clerk to designate the bill before the Committee. A period of general debate on the legislation then follows. Time for debate is evenly divided between the majority and minority sides. A majority and minority floor manager control and allocate the time for debate on their respective sides of the aisle.

After all time for general debate has been either utilized or yielded back to the chair, the clerk designates the first section of the bill as open for amendment. An amendment—a proposal to change the text of the bill—must be formally offered as either a motion to insert language, a motion to delete language, or a motion to strike out language and insert new text in that same place.

When all amendments have been disposed of, the Committee of the Whole disbands via a motion to rise and then resolves itself back into the House. The chairman leaves the rostrum and the Speaker returns. The mace is returned to its original position. The measure debated and amended in the Committee is now before the House for a vote on final passage. If desired, a minority member may at this point move to recommit the bill to the committee that originally had reported it to the House. The motion may be an indirect attempt to defeat the measure or, if it contains instructions, may be a final attempt to amend the bill. Once the recommittal motion has been disposed of, the House takes the vote on final passage of the measure.

It is now late afternoon or early evening. The majority leader and minority leader often engage in a short dialogue to inform the members about the remaining agenda for the week. Members may begin to leave the chamber and head for official dinners, receptions, or home knowing that no more votes will occur that day.

The House completes the day with a series of special order speeches. These speeches can be on any subject a member wishes. They vary in length from five minutes to the maximum time allowed, one hour. Members must get the unanimous consent of the House prior to delivering a special order speech. Because these speeches are considered nonlegislative debate and no votes are involved, the member giving the special order usually speaks to an empty chamber—but live television cameras in the chamber continue to ensure that there will be an audience. The last motion of the day—the motion to adjourn—is usually made by the member giving the last special order of the day. The Speaker pro tempore (substitute Speaker) and the clerks then leave the rostrum, and the day is over.

[See also (I) Amending, Calendars, Committee of the Whole.]

BIBLIOGRAPHY

Congressional Quarterly. *Congress A to Z.* 1988. P. 189.
Green, Alan. *Gavel to Gavel: A Guide to the Televised Proceedings of Congress.* 1991.

– ILONA B. NICKELS

House Rules and Procedures

The procedures followed by the House of Representatives are derived from several sources. First, the U.S. Constitution, while giving each house the authority to determine the rules of its proceedings, establishes certain basic requirements to which those rules must conform. Article I, section 5 provides that a quorum (a majority of each house) is necessary to do business. The yeas and nays may be demanded by one-fifth of those present, and votes so taken must be "entered on the Journal," that is, made a matter of public record.

The second source of House procedure is the Rules of the House, adopted by the body for each Congress. Many of these rules are readopted when each new Congress convenes in the January following its election. In the 103d Congress the House had fifty-one adopted rules. Some individual rules contain disparate and independent concepts so that in reality almost two hundred different precepts are expressed in the Rules. Of these, about thirty have their origins in the First Congress.

Some of the rules deal with the organization of the House. The duties of the five elected officers of the House (the Speaker, clerk, doorkeeper, sergeant at arms, and chaplain) are set forth. The number, jurisdiction, and oversight responsibilities of the House's twenty-two standing committees are specified.

Another category of rules is perhaps best termed administrative, or regulatory: prescribing how the House chamber and the galleries of the House may be used, providing for services of the House (how, for instance, its proceedings are to be recorded and broadcast), establishing a code of conduct for members and employees, and delineating how expenses of members and committees are to be accounted for.

Finally, there are rules that deal with the passage of legislation: detailing the motions to be utilized in the conduct of business on the floor and in committees, establishing the scope and time for debate and the amendment process, dealing with amendments made by the Senate, and reconciling differences between the content of House and Senate legislation.

One House rule specifically makes the provisions of Jefferson's Manual applicable to and binding on the House where its concepts are not inconsistent with the adopted rules. The Manual, compiled by Jefferson when he was vice president of the United States and thus president of the Senate and its presiding officer, is a restatement of the procedure of the British House of Commons during the period. Many of the principles set forth in the Manual, particularly those dealing with the conduct of debate in the House and the relationship between House and Senate, are followed today.

Finally, many statutes contain explicit rules for the conduct of certain types of legislative activity. The Legislative Reorganization acts of 1946 and 1970 and the Congressional Budget Act of 1974 are examples of laws that contain rules governing House and Senate consideration of certain legislation.

Undergirding these four sources of rules are the decisions of the Speakers and other presiding officers of the House (precedents of the House) interpreting the specific written rules. The House follows precedent when points of order or parliamentary inquiries are raised on the floor. The decisions rendered by the House itself (by its vote on an appeal) or by various presiding officers in ruling on points of order or answering parliamentary inquiries have been recorded, annotated, and published. *Hinds' Precedents, Cannon's Precedents, Deschler's Precedents,* and Deschler and Brown's *Procedure in the United States House of Representatives* are such works. The compilation process is a continuous one, and the number of precedents created by rulings of the chair grows annually. Finding the applicable precedents to guide the chair in a contemporary ruling is one of the main tasks of the parliamentarian's office.

STEPS IN THE LEGISLATIVE PROCESS. Rules and procedures affect all the stages in the legislative process: (1) introduction and referral of legislation; (2) committee consideration and reporting to the House; (3) consideration, debate, and passage; (4) action on Senate amendments, including conference consideration; and (5) transmittal of bills to the president, and action if the president vetoes a bill.

Introduction and referral. Legislative measures may be introduced by placing them in the "hopper," a receptacle placed at the rostrum of the House when it is in session (Rule XXII, clause 4). They may be introduced by one member, but public bills may be cosponsored.

Bills are referred by the Speaker (Rule XXII, clause 4) to the appropriate committees of jurisdiction. (The jurisdiction of the twenty-two standing committees is spelled out in Rule X, clause 1). The Speaker is required to refer a bill to all committees having jurisdiction (Rule

X, clause 5). Measures may be referred to a single committee, to several concurrently, or to several in sequence (clause 5). The Speaker's authority (under clause 5) permits the division of a bill for reference (for example, by giving Title 1 to committee A, Title 2 to committee B, and so on) or, with the permission of the House, a bill's referral to a select committee that the Speaker would then appoint.

Certain committees are authorized to originate legislation without having it referred to them. Rule XI, clause 4, gives this privilege to the committees on Appropriations, Budget, House Administration, Rules, and Standards of Official Conduct. Bills that originate in this manner and are then reported to the House can be considered on the floor as "privileged" and do not have to be given a floor slot by the Committee on Rules (see Rule XI, clause 4[b]) or by some other scheduling mechanism such as suspension of the rules. Intervention of the Committee on Rules may be sought if the appropriation bill, for instance, requires protection from points of order, or if there is a desire to structure the process by which the bill may be amended.

Committee consideration and reporting to the House. Committee hearings, consideration, and amendment of bills are conducted in accordance with procedures broadly outlined in Rule XI, clause 2. In the interrogation of witnesses before committees and in the markup (amendment process) of bills, the five-minute rule is applied: each member recognized is entitled to five minutes to ask questions or to offer or debate an amendment. A committee can establish the quorum required for taking testimony as being as few as two members. For preliminary legislative steps (voting on amendments and other motions in markup), the quorum may be as low as one-third of the committee membership. For reporting a bill to the House, however, a majority of the members must be present. Proxies may be used for certain actions in committees, pursuant to committee-adopted rules, which must be consistent with the overall House rule on the subject (see Rule XI, clause 2[f]).

When all committees to which a measure has been referred have reported, the bill is assigned by the Speaker to one of the calendars of the House—the Union Calendar (or, more precisely and accurately, the calendar of the Committee of the Whole House on the State of the Union), the House Calendar, or the Private Calendar (see Rule XIII, clause 1). Measures that raise revenue, directly or indirectly spend money, or dispose of property go to the Union Calendar and must be considered in a Committee of the Whole (Rule XXIII, clause 3). The House Calendar is the repository of all other public measures.

Private bills, for the relief of an individual or a corporation, go to the Private Calendar. Bills on the House Calendar or Union Calendar that are thought to have no opposition can, at the request of a member, be placed on the Consent Calendar. Both the Private and Consent calendars are "called," that is, the bills on these calendars are considered without objection in the order on the calendars. The Consent Calendar is called on the first and third Mondays of each month (Rule XIII, clause 4), and the Private Calendar on the first and third Tuesdays (Rule XXIV, clause 6). If there is an objection to consideration of a bill on the Consent or Private calendar, other procedures must be employed to obtain floor consideration.

Consideration, debate, and passage. Rules exist that provide for calling bills on the House and Union calendars, but they are seldom utilized in modern practice. Calendar Wednesday (Rule XXIV, clause 7) does provide a mechanism for considering bills on the Union Calendar: the standing committees are called alphabetically and, when a bill is reached in the call, the chairman may call it up. House Calendar bills are eligible for consideration under Rule XXIV, clause 4 (the "morning hour" rule), but since there are more efficient ways to secure their consideration, this rule is not used.

The procedures followed by the House of Representatives are derived from several sources.

The rules also set aside special days for the consideration of measures under suspension of the rules. On each Monday and Tuesday the Speaker has authority to recognize motions to suspend the rules (Rule XXVII, clause 1). Such motions require a two-thirds vote for adoption (two-thirds of those present and voting, a quorum being present) and can be used for a variety of legislative purposes: a bill may be brought directly to the floor, avoiding committee consideration, or any rule of the House that impedes passage can be circumvented. The motion may be to suspend the rules and pass a bill; to agree to Senate amendments to a House bill; or to suspend a measure and agree to a conference report on it. Debate is limited to forty minutes (twenty in favor, twenty opposed). When pending, the motion is not subject to amendment; although the proponent may include an amendment in the motion, as, for instance, "I move to suspend the rules and pass the reported bill with a further amendment that is at the desk." As a session of the House proceeds and committees have reported measures to the House, this mechanism is used to gain consideration and passage of a large proportion of House business. However, because of the supermajority required to adopt the motion, it is obviously not suited for the consideration of controversial legislation.

Finally, Rule XXIV, clause 8, permits the Committee on the District of Columbia to seek recognition on the second and fourth Mondays of the month to call up measures dealing with the District and reported by that committee.

Legislative measures in the House take several forms: most are introduced as House bills (noted in the *Congressional Record* and other documents as H.R., followed by an identifying number). Where the use of a preamble is necessary, the proper legislative vehicle is the House joint resolution (H.J. Res.). Both of these, when enacted, are sent to the president for his approval and become laws of the United States when so approved. Matters internal to the House, such as authorizing printing of a document for use by the House, can be in the form of House resolutions (H. Res.). If the concurrence of the Senate is necessary (e.g., to provide for an adjournment of the Congress or of either house for more than three days), the proper vehicle is the House concurrent resolution (H. Con. Res.). The Senate has similar nomenclature (S., S.J. Res.) for measures originating in that body.

The rules set aside special days for the consideration of measures under suspension of the rules.

Voting in the House can be by voice ("Those in favor will say 'Aye'; those opposed, 'No.' "); by division ("Those in favor will stand and remain standing until counted; those opposed will rise . . ."); by the yeas and nays (if supported by one-fifth of those present); or by recorded vote (if ordered by one-fifth of a quorum). (See Rule I, clause 5[a]; U.S. Constitution, Article I, section 5). The House uses electronic voting for taking the yeas and nays and record votes. On certain types of questions the Speaker has the authority to postpone the votes to a later time on the same or the next legislative day (see Rule I, clause 5[b]). This authority is customarily used on rules-suspension days, when roll-call votes (if ordered) on motions entertained and debated on Monday or Tuesday are postponed to and taken at an announced time within the next two legislative days. Votes then come in sequence without intervening debate, and can be reduced to five minutes each.

While there is a rule for the order of business on any legislative day (Rule XXIV, clause 1), the House, after prayer by the chaplain and approval of the Journal (see Rule XXIV, clause 1), normally interrupts that order to consider business that is privileged under other House rules. While appropriation bills and concurrent resolutions of the budget are often considered under the rule giving them privilege (Rule XI, clause 4), most major bills are brought to the floor pursuant to resolutions reported from the Committee on Rules, providing special orders for their consideration (see Rule XI, clause 4[b]). A typical special order will provide for consideration of the measure in the House or in Committee of the Whole, whichever is appropriate; specify a length of time for general debate on the bill; waive any points of order that would otherwise inhibit consideration of the measure; address the amendment process by making specific amendments in order or by prohibiting certain (or all) amendments; and provide that, at the conclusion of the amendment process, the bill shall be reported back to the House, where the previous question is considered as ordered to final passage (thereby prohibiting further debate or amendment in the House) except for one motion to recommit.

There are numerous patterns for these special orders. The design of a rule will depend on the legislative complexity of the subject, the political battleground anticipated, and the amount of floor time available in the House schedule. "Open" rules permit all germane amendments to be offered, whereas "closed" rules may prohibit all amendments except those offered by direction of the committee reporting the measure; variations on these forms are referred to as "modified open" or "modified closed" rules. Some rules, especially those that inhibit amendments or curtail the right of the minority in the House to offer a motion to recommit, may be opposed by factions of the House. An effort may be made to defeat the previous question on the rule in order to offer an amendment to it and change the procedures recommended by the Committee on Rules or to defeat the rule.

A special order of this character may be reported, as privileged, from the Committee on Rules (Rule XI, clause 4[b]). When called up for consideration, the resolution is debated for up to one hour, with time customarily divided equally between the member of the Committee on Rules calling up the resolution and a minority member of the Rules Committee. If the resolution is adopted, the House has thereby established a procedural framework for the consideration of the bill in question.

Without the discipline imposed by a special rule, consideration of a bill would be under the general rules of the House. Debate could conceivably proceed for up to 435 hours (if each member exercised his or her right to speak for one hour, the maximum time permitted). Following debate, the bill would be "read for amendment," that is, considered by section or paragraph for amendment, and any germane amendment could be offered.

The germaneness rule (Rule XVI, clause 7) is an important discipline that the House has imposed on itself since 1789. While parliamentary law at that time did not require that an amendment relate to the text under consideration (see *Hinds' Precedents,* V, section 5825), the House determined that such a rule was essential for orderly legislative procedure. The rule applies to whatever text is pending: a first-degree amendment must be germane to the bill under consideration, and a second-degree amendment must be germane to the primary or first-degree amendment. Hundreds of germaneness rulings have been made since 1789, and the chair, in ruling on a point of order, attempts to follow the applicable precedent. Several general principles emerge from the germaneness precedents: one individual proposition is not germane to another; a specific subject may not be amended by an amendment that is general in scope; an individual or specific addition or subtraction may be in order to a general proposition. The germaneness of an amendment must be determined from its text and not from some abstract "purpose." The rule is applied in House committees during markup and on the House floor when the bill is read for amendment; it is sometimes also applied to have a separate vote on a Senate amendment not germane to a House bill, as well as on nongermane Senate amendments agreed to by conferees.

The Committee of the Whole House is a useful parliamentary fiction that permits business to be expedited. To an observer in the gallery, there is little discernible change when the House resolves into the Committee of the Whole. The Speaker appoints a member to preside over the deliberations of the Committee, the mace is lowered from its pedestal, and debate is directed to "Mr. (or Madam) Chairman," not to the Speaker. But the "invisible" changes in procedure are substantial: the quorum required in the full House is a majority of those members elected, sworn, and still living whose membership has not been terminated by resignation or action of the House. (See U.S. Constitution, Article I, section 5.) In a "full" House, a quorum is 218. But in Committee, under Rule XXIII, clause 2(a), the quorum is reduced to 100.

Debate in the Committee is of two types: general debate, during which each member can theoretically speak for one hour, and debate on amendments under the five-minute rule. The general debate is invariably limited to a reasonable period, either by a unanimous consent agreement entered into before the House resolves into Committee or by the terms of a special order reported from the Committee on Rules and adopted by the House. The five-minute rule (Rule XXIII, clause 5) permits any person offering an amendment to speak for five minutes in favor of it. A member opposed can have the same time to speak in opposition. Debate in this mode can be continued beyond the ten minutes by use of a pro forma amendment to "strike out the last word," which permits an additional ten minutes of debate. Pro forma amendments are normally considered as withdrawn after the debate thereon, so another can be offered, allowing more debate (in blocks of ten minutes) on a pending primary amendment.

In the Committee, the constitutional right for one-fifth of those present to demand the yeas and nays (U.S. Constitution, Article I, section 5) is not applicable, but a "record" vote (also taken by roll call or electronic device) can be demanded by twenty-five members (Rule XXIII, clause 2[b]). When the Committee of the Whole finishes the amendment process, it reports its work back to the full House, where separate votes may be demanded on those amendments adopted in the Committee, and where the vote on final passage occurs.

Pending the vote on final passage, one motion to recommit the bill is in order. This motion, recognition for which is the right of someone who is opposed to the bill (Rule XVI, clause 4), is an important tool for the minority in the House, since it provides a last opportunity to shape the bill to its liking. If the motion is to recommit (to any committee) with instructions (that is, to amend or direct the committee to take certain further legislative action), it may be debated for ten minutes (five on each side), if demanded. A "straight" motion, without instructions, is not debatable.

The rules specify the motions that can be entertained, as a matter of right, at appropriate times during sessions of the House and the Committee of the Whole.

The rules of the House specify the motions that can be entertained, as a matter of right, at appropriate times during sessions of the House and of the Committee of the Whole. When a question is under debate, the permissible motions, in their order of precedence, are the following: to adjourn (with its variations of equal privilege—the motion that when the House adjourns, it stand adjourned to a day and time certain, and the motion to authorize the Speaker to declare a recess); to lay on the table; to move for the previous question; to postpone to a day certain; to amend; to refer; and to postpone indefinitely. The first three of these motions—to adjourn, to table, and to move for the previous question—are not debatable. Understanding the precedence of the motions in Rule XVI, clause 4, is essential. If the House adopts a motion to adjourn, obviously no further actions on the matter under debate can be taken until the next legislative day. If the motion to table is adopted, the matter is thereby adversely disposed of, without debate. If the previous question is ordered, amendments and the other motions of lesser precedence are no longer in order. Knowing when to apply these various motions and using them to accomplish a legislative purpose is the essence of legislative strategy.

The *motion to lay on the table* is used in the House to dispose of a matter adversely, without debate. It is in order whenever a motion is pending that is either debatable or subject to amendment, but it is not used in the Committee of the Whole. It is useful in reaching a quick decision on a matter; an appeal from the decision of the chair, which is subject to debate in the House, is often laid on the table to get an immediate decision on the question of order. Privileged business, if presented unexpectedly, is often tabled (or referred) so that the House can continue its announced schedule.

The *motion for the previous question* is used to cut off debate and amendments and bring the House to an immediate vote on the underlying motion or question. For example, when a resolution providing for printing a document for the House is under debate, the member in charge will customarily move the previous question when he feels there has been sufficient explanation. If carried, no further debate is in order and the House then immediately has before it the question on the adoption of the resolution. If defeated, the manager loses the floor; a member opposing the previous question is entitled to recognition and can offer an amendment and have an hour to debate it. At the conclusion of that hour, the previous question can again be moved, and in this manner the House determines when a majority is ready to vote on the underlying resolution, without further amendment.

The two *motions to postpone*—to a day or time certain, and indefinitely—have quite different uses. The first obviously allows the House to influence its agenda. An example of its use can be found in the manner of dealing with a presidential veto. When the president vetoes a bill and returns it to the house of origin, the Constitution requires the house to "proceed to reconsider it" (Article I, section 7). This does not mean that the house has to vote immediately on the reconsideration ("the question is, shall the bill pass, the objections of the President to the contrary notwithstanding"); it can refer the matter to committee or postpone consideration indefinitely or to a day certain. Such motions are debatable under the hour rule.

The *motion to amend* is one of the most important legislative tools offered in Rule XVI. House rules permit one amendment at a time to be offered to pending text. But that amendment (the primary, or first-degree, amendment) can be amended, either by a second-degree amendment or by a substitute amendment. The substitute itself (which is not considered to be in the second degree) may also have one amendment offered to it. The "amendment tree," as it is called, can then have four components. When all these amendments are pending, the "tree" is fully developed; no further amendment is in order since it would be in the "third degree," which is specifically prohibited. Jefferson's Manual governs the order of voting on these amendments. When one of the second-degree amendments is adopted or rejected, another amendment can be offered to fill its place on the tree. In the House the motion to amend is debatable under the hour rule. In the Committee of the Whole the five-minute rule applies.

The parliamentary *motion to refer* is recognized in several House rules. When a matter is "under debate," the motion to refer has the precedence indicated above and is debatable within narrow limits: the debate must be focused on the question of referral and not on the merits of the underlying proposition. The motion can direct referral to any committee or committees. This motion is used by the House when a matter is before the body that has not had prior committee consideration. For instance, if a resolution is offered from the floor that raises a question of privilege of the House, the motion to refer is one of the preferred options. Likewise, when the president returns a vetoed bill, the House often refers the measure back to the committee from which it came rather than voting immediately on whether to override the president's veto.

The same rule (Rule XVI, clause 4) provides for a variation on the motion to refer after the previous question is ordered on a bill or joint resolution to final passage. One *motion to recommit* is guaranteed at this point, and the Speaker is instructed to recognize a member opposed to the measure to offer the motion. Debate on a simple or straight motion to recommit at this stage is precluded by the operation of the previous question on the bill "to final passage," but if the motion is to recommit with instructions, ten minutes of debate are specifically guaranteed, which can be extended to one hour if the manager of the bill so demands.

Rule XVII provides for a *motion to commit* or recommit pending the motion for the previous question or after it has been ordered, and the broader language of this form of the motion to refer covers resolutions as well as bills. The motion under this rule can be applied to Senate amendments and various other motions pending in the House.

The minority party in the House views the motion to recommit (after the previous question is ordered on a bill or joint resolution) as one of its basic protections. It is often used to state a party position, and when the motion includes "instructions" to the committee to report back to the House "forthwith" with a specified amendment, the manager of the bill does so immediately and the House then has the opportunity to vote on the amendment. The proposed amendment must be germane to the bill in its perfected form, as shaped by the action of amendments previously adopted in the Committee of the Whole or in the House. The rules otherwise restrict the use of the motion: a motion to recommit with instructions cannot change an amendment already adopted by the House. Hence, if a bill under consideration has been amended by a complete amendment in the nature of a substitute, the motion to recommit cannot further amend; for this reason, a special order addressing the consideration of a measure reported from a standing committee with an amendment in the nature of a substitute may specify that the motion may be "with or without instructions." The inclusion of this language, commonly utilized where the adoption of an amendment in the nature of a substitute is anticipated, is a further guarantee of the minority's use of the motion.

The *motion to reconsider* (Rule XVIII) may be made by a member who has been recorded on the prevailing side on a matter on the same or succeeding day. (If the vote is not of record, any member can make the motion). The motion is rarely utilized, however, and is customarily laid on the table following the vote on passage of a matter, thus assuring the finality of the vote. The chair normally states that "the bill is passed and without objection, a motion to reconsider is laid on the table." The measure or matter can then proceed to the next legislative step.

Action on Senate amendments. When a House measure is passed by the House, it is then sent to the Senate, which, using its own procedures, can consider and amend the House proposal. When the Senate sends the bill back to the House in amended form, the House must then act on the Senate amendments: it may accept or concur in the actions of the Senate (thus enabling the bill to be enrolled and sent to the president), or it may amend the Senate language and return it to the Senate. If the House does not approve or amend, it can either send its latest proposal back to the Senate or request a conference on the disagreeing votes.

The precedence of the various motions used in the House with respect to Senate amendments—the motions to amend, concur, disagree and request a conference, or disagree (motions in order before the stage of disagreement), and the motions to recede (from disagreement) and concur, to amend, to insist and request a conference, or to insist (motions in order after the stage of disagreement)—are set forth in Jefferson's Manual (section XLV; House Rules and Manual, section 528).

When all items in disagreement have been resolved,

the bill is enrolled, signed by the Speaker

and the president of the Senate,

and sent to the president for consideration.

If the Senate agrees to the request for a conference, the Speaker (under Rule X, clause 6[f]) has the authority to appoint managers to represent the House at the conference. The conferees or managers from the two houses must stay within the differences submitted to them. Simply put, if the House has authorized a million dollars for a project, and the Senate two million, the conferees can accept the high or low figure or anything in between; but they cannot go outside these parameters. If they do, their report is subject to a point of order when called up in the House. Most conferences involve far more complex compromises than this illustration, but the same principle of the "scope of conference" applies (Rule XXVIII, clause 3).

When the conference report is filed in the House, it may be called up for consideration after it is printed and has been available for three days (Rule XXVIII, clause 2[a]). A conference report is debatable for an hour and must be adopted by a majority vote. If the House is acting first on the report, a motion to recommit the report to the committee of conference is in order prior to the vote on adoption. Since a conference report is in the nature of a contract between House and Senate, it cannot be amended, but the House managers can be "instructed" to attempt to preserve or compromise the House position.

On occasion, particularly when dealing with appropriations, the Senate may have added numerous amendments to the House bill, and the conferees may agree to some Senate amendments, compromise others, but remain in true (or technical) disagreement with respect to the remainder. When this occurs, it is often necessary to report a partial conference agreement. In this event, the conference report embodies those items on which agreement has been reached; items still in disagreement are brought up in the House for disposition after the conference report has been adopted. The House may recede from its disagreement and concur in the Senate amendment or recede and concur with a further amendment; or it can insist on its original position and see if the Senate will recede. If the Senate insists, a further conference may be required.

Transmittal of bills to the president. When all items in disagreement have been resolved, the bill is enrolled, signed by the Speaker and the president of the Senate, and sent to the president for consideration. If the president vetoes the bill (returns it to the house of origin without his signature), that house can address the question of reconsideration by using the permissible motions discussed above.

POINTS OF ORDER. The Speaker decides all questions of order, subject to appeal to the House (Rule I, clause 4); in the Committee of the Whole, the chair fulfills this responsibility. A point of order can be raised against any motion or procedure that violates a House rule, but it must be raised in a timely manner, at the appropriate stage in the proceedings. Questions of order that the chair is frequently called on to decide include the following: (1) that an offered amendment is not germane (Rule XVI, clause 7); (2) that a provision in an appropriation bill or an amendment thereto changes existing law (often referred to as "legislating on an appropriation bill," prohibited by Rule XXI, clause 2), or that the appropriation is unauthorized (that is, that there is no law to support the appropriation, as required by Rule XXI, clause 2); (3) that a bill or amendment violates a requirement of the Congressional Budget Act; (4) that debate is proceeding in an unparliamentary manner; (5) that a bill reported from a committee other than Ways and Means carries a tax or tariff provision (prohibited by Rule XXI, clause 5[b]); and (6) that conferees have exceeded their authority by reporting matters not in disagreement between the House and Senate (Rule XXVIII, clause 3). Debate on a point of order is within the discretion of the chair. Appeals in the House are debatable but are subject to the motion to lay on the table. In the Committee of the Whole they are decided without debate, but the motion to table cannot be used in the Committee.

[See also (I) Bills, Committees.]

BIBLIOGRAPHY

Luce, Robert. *Legislative Procedure.* 1922.

U.S. House of Representatives. *Cannon's Precedents of the House of Representatives of the United States,* by Clarence Cannon. 8 vols. 74th Cong., 1st sess., 1935.

U.S. House of Representatives. *Constitution, Jefferson's Manual, and Rules of the House of Representatives, 103d Congress.* Compiled by William Holmes Brown. 102d Cong., 2d sess., 1992. H. Doc. 102-405.

U.S. House of Representatives. *Hinds' Precedents of the House of Representatives of the United States,* by Asher C. Hinds. 5 vols. 59th Cong., 2d sess., 1907.

U.S. House of Representatives. *Procedure in the United States House of Representatives,* by Lewis Deschler and William Holmes Brown. 4th ed. 97th Cong., 2d sess., 1982.

– WILLIAM HOLMES BROWN

I

IMPLIED POWERS

Congress may make any law it deems necessary and proper to implement its enumerated powers (Article I, section 8 of the U.S. Constitution). The Framers' notion of implied powers provided the broad-scale authority required by the new legislative branch of government.

Implied powers gained credibility with the 1819 Supreme Court decision of *McCulloch v. Maryland* (17 U.S. [4 Wheat.] 316 [1819]). Maryland had placed a tax on the Baltimore branch of the Bank of the United States, objecting that the bank's charter was not expressly stated in the Constitution and arguing simultaneously for a limited interpretation of congressional power. The bank refused to comply on several grounds: Congress had the implied power to create the bank, and a state had no authority to tax an institution of the federal government. The Supreme Court upheld the bank's claims in an eloquent defense of national power written by Chief Justice John Marshall. Creating a bank, Marshall argued, was reasonable to accommodate such enumerated powers as regulating currency or encouraging interstate commerce. As Marshall wrote, "Let the end be legitimate, let it be within the scope of the Constitution, and all means which are appropriate . . . , which are not prohibited, . . . are constitutional."

The political controversy surrounding implied powers has been evident ever since. States' rights advocates have warned that Congress may expand its powers too far, so as to intrude upon the powers that are reserved for the states. Another facet of the controversy occurs over the precise means to achieve legislative ends or goals. For example, when Congress has the express constitutional power to raise and support armies and navies, does this imply that a draft policy is the most appropriate means to provide for national defense? The heart of the dilemma is thus the debate over the proper scope and means of implied legislative powers.

[See also (II) Implied Powers.]

BIBLIOGRAPHY

Ducat, Craig, and Harold Chase. *Constitutional Interpretation: Powers of Government.* 1974.

Peltason, Jack W. *Understanding the Constitution.* 1994.

– JANIS JUDSON

INCUMBENCY

The dominant fact about elections to the House of Representatives is that incumbents who seek reelection almost always win. The high reelection rate (94 percent in the period from 1982 to 1992) has important consequences for congressional careers. Not only do incumbents generally win, but likely victory is an incentive to keep trying. Incumbents generally keep seeking reelection until presented with a compelling reason not to. In a typical election year, less than 10 percent of sitting House members actually retire. Those who voluntarily leave often do so to run for another office or to become lobbyists. Some quit because of illness or old age. Rarely do members leave because they prefer to abandon politics. Almost all representatives are, to use a pejorative term, "career politicians."

The incumbency advantage does not accrue automatically.

While several factors account for House incumbents' electoral success, attention tends to focus on one simple reason; incumbents exploit their advantage of incumbency over potential opponents. Incumbents can accrue an electoral advantage over potential challengers by utilizing their many perquisites of office, such as free mailing privileges (franking), generous travel allowances, and large staffs primarily devoted to servicing constituent needs. Also, incumbents have greater access than their opponents to publicity and campaign funds. As a result, incumbents have the wherewithal to generate favorable images for themselves among their constituents, while their opponents must fight an uphill battle for even minimal visibility.

Technically, "incumbency advantage" is the added increment to the vote margin that a candidate gains by virtue of being the incumbent. Or, put another way, incumbency advantage is the causal effect of incumbency on the vote. The best way to measure the advantage is to calculate the size of the "sophomore surge," that is, the percentage of the vote that candidates gain from their first victory (as nonincumbents) to their first reelection attempt (as incumbents). Adjusted for the national partisan trend, the average sophomore surge is a simple but accurate measure of the typical vote share gained from incumbency. In the 1970s and 1980s, the surge averaged about seven percentage points. That is, their incumbency status gave new incumbents about seven percentage points more than they otherwise would have won.

The seven-point sophomore surge represented an increase from a value of only about two percentage points in the 1950s. This growth occurred in part because of the decline of partisanship in the United States. As voters became more inclined to vote on the basis of the candidates themselves rather than on simple party affiliation, incumbency mattered more. Simultaneously, by increasing their own perquisites of office, House members kept themselves more in the public spotlight.

The incumbency advantage does not, however, accrue automatically. To earn it, incumbents must invest in the sort of activities that please their constituencies. Representatives who were elected by a slim margin have the most incentive to please their districts, and they are the ones who attend most carefully to district interests. As a result, they are the ones who earn the largest reward, in terms of added vote share, from being incumbents.

The incumbency advantage is not the only reason incumbents generally win. Even if incumbency offered no special electoral edge, most incumbent candidates would win reelection. First, and most obviously, many incumbents are almost guaranteed to win because they represent the majority party in their district. Every constituency has a particular partisan makeup, tilting to some degree to either the Democratic or Republican party. In districts where the majority always supports one party, the incumbent need do nothing special to stay elected other than to stay nominated. (Of course, this is not true of all districts; some are competitive.)

One overlooked reason incumbents win is that incumbency status is, in effect, earned at the ballot box. Beyond district partisanship or any national partisan trend, elections are won on the basis of which party can field the stronger candidate. Strong candidates tend to win, and by winning become incumbents. After winning, they survive until they falter or lose to even stronger candidates. But strong candidates tend to draw weak challengers. Politicians who are electorally strong tend to run for election to a new office when their prospects of victory are strongest—when there is an open seat, a weak incumbent, or the anticipation of a favorable electoral tide. When incumbents are strong candidates in their own right, they scare off strong challenges even without exploiting the added leverage of incumbency. When they do exploit the perquisites of incumbency, the chance that a strong challenge will arise is reduced even further.

Although the incumbency advantage is usually discussed in the context of House elections, it also plays some role in Senate elections. Incumbent senators are slightly more vulnerable to defeat (with an 87-percent reelection rate for 1982–1992) than House incumbents. Senators enjoy only a modest incumbency advantage, with an average sophomore surge of only about two percentage points. One possible reason for the relative weakness of the Senate incumbency advantage is that senatorial challengers achieve electoral visibility more easily than do House challengers. A senator can rarely win simply because he or she represents a state that is safe for his or her party. Unlike congressional districts, all states are to some extent competitive. Like House members, however, senators earn their incumbency at the ballot box. Most senators achieve reelection for no other reason than that they retain the electoral strengths that allowed them to win their first election as nonincumbents.

The 1992 election campaign was marked by an unusual surge of anti-incumbent and anti-Congress sentiment among the electorate. Still, when the primary and general elections were over, 88 percent of House incumbent candidates (and 82 percent from the Senate) had survived to serve another term. As always, it seemed that voters hate Congress but love their local representatives. But not to be ignored is 1992's high number of congressional retirements (15 percent in the House, 20 percent in the Senate). The retirement rate was highest (approaching one third) among incumbents connected to the "rubbergate" scandal involving bounced checks from the House bank. Incumbents of the 1990s appear to be less certain about making Congress their career. They must worry that if the voters do not get them directly, then maybe the movement for term limitations will.

[See also (I) Members, article on Tenure and Turnover.]

BIBLIOGRAPHY

Alford, John R., and David W. Brady. "Personal and Partisan Advantage in U.S. Congressional Elections." In *Congress Reconsidered.* 5th ed. Edited by Lawrence C. Dodd and Bruce I. Oppenheimer. 1993.

Erikson, Robert S., and Gerald C. Wright. "Voters, Candidates, and Issues, in U.S. Congressional Elections." In *Congress Reconsidered.* 5th ed. Edited by Lawrence C. Dodd and Bruce I. Oppenheimer. 1993.

Mayhew, David W. "Congressional Elections: The Case of the Vanishing Marginals. *Polity* 6 (1974): 295–317.

– ROBERT S. ERIKSON

INSPECTOR GENERAL OF THE HOUSE

The Office of Inspector General is one of two House offices created in the aftermath of the post office and house bank scandals of 1992, the other being the director of Non-Legislative and Financial Services. The inspector general's office was established by House Rule VI, clause 2 (103d Cong.), pursuant to the House Administrative Reform Resolution of 1992 (H. Res. 423, 102d Cong.), which provides that the inspector general be appointed by the Speaker, the majority leader, and the minority leader of the House, acting jointly.

The duties of the inspector general, subject to oversight by the Subcommittee on Administrative Oversight of the Committee on House Administration, include conducting periodic audits of the financial functions of the offices of Non-Legislative and Financial Services, Clerk, Sergeant at Arms, and Doorkeeper. Reports of such audits are submitted to the Speaker, majority leader, minority leader, and the chairman and ranking member of the Subcommittee on Administrative Oversight. The purposes of the audits are to ensure that financial functions are efficient, reliable, and in compliance with laws and regulations and to prevent and detect fraud and abuse. The first inspector general, John W. Lainhart IV, was appointed on 14 November 1993.

BIBLIOGRAPHY

U.S. House of Representatives. *Constitution, Jefferson's Manual, and Rules of the House of Representatives, 103d Congress.* Compiled by William Holmes Brown. 102d Cong., 2d sess., 1992. H. Doc. 102-405.

– RAYMOND W. SMOCK

INTEREST GROUPS

The intimate connection between interest groups and Congress becomes immediately evident to an observer taking a simple walk around Capitol Hill. The hallways of the House and Senate office buildings, the sidewalks between the offices and the Capitol, the hearing rooms, the corridors outside the chambers of the two houses—all are filled with an admixture of members, staff, and lobbyists. Capitol Hill is as much the home and workplace of lobbyists as it is of lawmakers and their staffs.

Interest groups and lobbyists have been viewed alternately—sometimes simultaneously—as staples of the American legislative process, protected by the Constitution, and as pernicious indicators of the kind of corruption and influence-peddling that is always a danger, and frequently a reality, in the political system.

The legitimacy of lobbying is set in the First Amendment to the U.S. Constitution, which guarantees all citizens the right to free speech and the right to petition the government for redress of grievances. Taken together, these rights have for centuries legitimized the actions of individuals and groups as they have pursued their own interests within the political system, often at the expense of the interests of others. At the same time, James Madison, in *Federalist* 10, both warns of the "mischiefs of factions" (groups less than the whole citizenry) and yet acknowledges the necessity of their existence and their activity. Indeed, Madison says that the only way to limit the mischief is to allow the growth and activity of groups to check and balance one another.

TYPES OF INTEREST GROUPS. In the nineteenth century, the range of groups represented in the corridors of Congress was quite limited, and their activity was highly directed. Lobbyists of the time represented commercial, business, and trust interests in areas from banking to railroads to armaments and agriculture—all in keeping with the limited number of areas, such as tariffs, government finance, and territorial expansion, in which Congress and the federal government were involved. As the twentieth century unfolded, however, the range in number and types of groups expanded dramatically.

Business Groups. Business groups with representatives in Washington range from small local firms seeking a federal subcontract, to a national business interest seeking a particular government benefit or tax break, to a large multinational corporation that maintains permanent representation in the capital. Business groups generally aim their lobbying activity as much toward regulatory agencies and the federal bureaucracy as toward Congress. Rather than set up a Washington office or use their own personnel, many businesses hire Washington law firms for their representation and lobbying. Many others do both, while also relying on one or more trade associations and umbrella groups for broader business issues.

Capitol Hill is as much the home and workplace of lobbyists as it is of lawmakers and their staffs.

Traditionally, the two largest and best-known umbrella groups representing business interests have been the U.S. Chamber of Commerce and the National Association of Manufacturers. In recent years, smaller, more narrowly focused groups such as the Business Roundtable (representing larger corporations), the American Business Conference (representing entrepreneurial, fast-growth businesses), and the National Federation of Independent Business (representing smaller businesses) have also come into their own.

In addition, Washington is filled with hundreds of industry-specific trade associations, including the American Petroleum Institute, the National Association of Broadcasters and the National Cable Television Association, and lobbying offices of individual firms, from General Motors and General Electric to General Dynamics and General Mills. Large companies like General Motors have on their lobbying staffs substantial numbers of engineers and scientists, who mainly interact with the Defense Department, the Highway Traffic Safety Administration, and the Environmental Protection Agency, along with people who track policy developments and legislation and others whose jobs involve lobbying members of Congress and staff on legislative proposals and bills.

Labor. Labor interests are also represented en masse in Washington, even if the role and influence of organized labor has diminished significantly over the years. Some unions have their main headquarters in Washington, while others have established legislative offices in the capital whose sole purpose is to represent the views of the union's members on Capitol Hill.

The American Federation of Labor and Congress of Industrial Organizations (AFL-CIO) is the largest and most powerful labor organization in the country. The AFL-CIO is an umbrella organization that represents nearly one hundred affiliated unions with a total of fourteen million dues-paying members. It has a variety of interrelated internal components, operates through a large and hierarchical organization, and is housed in an impressive headquarters only two blocks from the White House. The United Auto Workers, Teamsters, United Mine Workers, and other unions are also represented in Washington. Labor has been an active and visible player in Congress for many decades, although since the late 1980s it has had little success with its basic legislative agenda, from labor law reform to legislation banning replacement workers during strikes.

Public interest groups. Groups that seek policy goals (and often governmental reform) without regard for the material benefits of their members have been present in Washington in one form or another since the progressive, prohibitionist, and suffragist movements at the turn of the century. But the expansion in the numbers and activity of so-called public interest groups is really a phenomenon of the 1970s. The two groups that have come to epitomize the goals and strategies of interest groups in general are Common Cause and Ralph Nader's Public Citizen.

Common Cause, founded in 1970 by John Gardner, has approximately 275,000 members and an annual operating budget of more than $11 million. Common Cause has fought for such causes as ending the Vietnam War, reforming Congress and the campaign finance system, and tightening government ethics codes.

Public Citizen, a mass-membership organization modeled on Common Cause, is part of a conglomerate of public interest groups headed by Ralph Nader, which include groups directed toward consumer, environmental, health, science, regulatory reform, energy, and other orientations. These groups conduct research, lobby, publish books and reports, and generally attempt to influence the course of public policy. Norman Lear's People for the American Way has become another major player in the broad public interest field. Both Nader's and Lear's groups raise a substantial part of their funds through direct-mail solicitations.

The multitude of public interest groups that exist in the 1990s include groups representing the interests of women, children, and the elderly and groups concentrating on legal and health issues as well as on social welfare and urban problems. Initially, public interest groups seemed to have largely a liberal coloration. But in recent years a number of more conservative public interest groups have been formed or have expanded their focus and influence, partly in reaction to their liberal counterparts. These include organizations such as Accuracy in Media, Americans United for Life, Citizens against Government Waste, the National Taxpayers' Union, and the Washington Legal Foundation.

Environmental groups. The number and stature of environmental groups have grown since the 1980s as environmental issues have risen in importance on the legislative agenda. These groups include several older, established conservation organizations such as the Sierra Club, the National Audubon Society, and the National Wildlife Federation. Newer groups, organized in the late 1960s and early 1970s when *ecology* became a common term in the political lexicon, include Environmental Action, Friends of the Earth, and the Environmental Defense Fund.

Since the late 1980s, a community-based environmental movement has begun to take hold at the state and local levels. At the same time, with increasing multilateral action to deal with global environmental problems such as global warming and the deterioration of the ozone layer, environmental groups have had to broaden their focus beyond Congress and the states.

Civil rights groups. For most of the twentieth century, civil rights groups have been a factor in the policymaking process. The National Association for the Advancement of Colored People (NAACP) was established in 1910 to promote the interests of African Americans. Along with the National Urban League and other organizations, including some representing Hispanics, Asians, and women, these groups have lobbied on behalf of black Americans and other minority groups on issues such as educational opportunity, voting rights, equal employment, and fair housing. An umbrella organization, the Leadership Conference on Civil Rights, headed by Ralph Neas, played a particularly prominent role in the 1990–1991 struggle over a new civil rights act and in the controversial Senate confirmation hearings on the Supreme Court nominations of Robert Bork in 1987 and Clarence Thomas in 1991.

Foreign lobbying. Foreign lobbying has been controversial at least since the 1930s, when questions were raised about foreign agents lobbying Congress and the White House on behalf of Germany as American hostility toward Adolf Hitler's Nazi government grew. Here, American ambivalence about the legitimate political role of interests takes on yet another aspect: how far do Constitutional protections extend to foreign interests?

Literally thousands of groups are active in Washington, tracking congressional action and lobbying Congress.

Lobbying on behalf of foreign interests or for U.S. interests whose concern is foreign policy is nonetheless an important and growing part of the political scene in Washington. In the 1990s, virtually every foreign nation of significant size has a lobbying agent or agents operating in Washington. Many foreign agents are prominent political figures; they lobby Congress and the State Department on a variety of issues. In recent years, lobbying by domestic groups on foreign policy has clearly increased, with the American-Israel Public Affairs Committee (AIPAC) and the newer Arab-American Institute being two examples. At the same time, business and labor groups lobby frequently for tariff protection, trade provisions, or other policies on behalf of foreign interests.

If foreign lobbying has always been a sensitive subject, it has grown even more controversial. A book by Pat Choate, *Agents of Influence* (1990), decries the growing influence of Japanese interests in the United States, focusing on the number of prominent Americans who receive compensation, in one form or another, from groups in Japan, suggesting that their views are being bought and that they are giving unwitting legitimacy to a point of view that is inimical to U.S. national interests. While many observers do not share this alarmist view, additional, tougher regulation of the representation of foreign interests is on the congressional policy agenda, and is likely to be passed in coming years.

This list is by no means complete. Literally thousands of groups are active in Washington, tracking congressional action and lobbying Congress. Some of the most consequential are not encompassed by the categories mentioned above. These include, for instance, the American Association of Retired Persons (AARP) and the National Committee to Preserve Medicare and Social Security, two groups that represent elderly Americans and have wide influence in the debate over entitlements; the National Rifle Association (NRA), which has had enormous influence over gun control policy; the American Legion, one of many organizations active in policy affecting veterans; and the U.S. Catholic Conference, one of many religious organizations with a base in Washington, which has been active in many areas of social policy but particularly in the antiabortion movement. For every large trade association like the American Petroleum Institute, there are dozens of small specialty associations representing, for example, independent gas stations, fig growers, natural gas pipeline producers, oil pipeline manufacturers, wine growers, or ball-bearing makers.

As power has become increasingly decentralized in Washington and the points of entry into the system have multiplied, the number of interest groups has mushroomed and groups have become more and more specialized—and the sources they use to lobby on their behalf have become more specialized and numerous as well.

THEORIES ABOUT GROUPS. Early research and literature on lobbying and interest groups focused on the origins and dynamics of groups themselves. Through the years many theories have been propounded about the impact and desirability of groups in the U.S. political system—some positive and some negative.

In general, the various theories about groups that have been offered have centered on three questions. First and most broadly, are interest groups good or bad forces in American politics and society? Second, do groups, in the sum of their actions and interactions, provide some approximation of the public interest, or is the public interest ignored or shortchanged by group behavior in the political process? And, third, do interest groups reflect a basic bias in favor of monied, upper-class or business-oriented segments of the society, or are they a fair cross section of all interests in the society?

Most of the group theories that have emerged tend to reinforce the ambivalent attitude most Americans hold toward groups in politics and society; that is, while most Americans decry the insidious influence groups seem to have over politicians, they jump at the chance to influence the system as members of a group in pursuit of their own goals and interests.

James Madison was probably the earliest American "group theorist." John C. Calhoun, writing in the mid-

1800s, turned Madison's notion of factional checks and balances on its head. Calhoun's theory of the "concurrent majority" posited that, because the existence of varying group views and positions is vital to the nation, each of the various interest groups in the society should be allowed a veto power over any major policy proposition that affected it. Conversely, a "concurrent majority" of all interest groups would have to support a policy proposal for it to be adopted.

The most important aspect of Calhoun's theory was that it focused attention on the notion of a broad community interest—a public interest—that exists and is independent of the views of particular factions. To Calhoun, the various factions were the community interests and should be treated as such by allowing them veto powers.

In the early twentieth century, the debate over the role of groups in U.S. politics took on a new coloration as political science entered the arena. The focus of academic political science shifted away from the legal-institutional framework and toward the interplay of groups, or nongovernmental forces, in the U.S. political system. From Arthur F. Bentley's *The Process of Government,* published in 1908, through David Truman's *The Governmental Process,* some forty years later, theorists used groups to explore the entire political process, examining their overlapping membership, access to decision makers, and role as catalyst in the democratic governmental process.

Truman's book fit in well with the emerging stream of political science research in the 1950s and early 1960s, which emphasized "objective" analysis of how things worked in the political arena rather than speculating on how they ought to work. In general, these political scientists viewed groups positively, seeing them mainly as the central vehicle through which individuals participated in the political system.

Still, some observers questioned the benignity of interest groups. E. E. Schattschneider identified what he saw as a pattern of undue influence whereby interest groups gained access to politicians through campaign contributions and inside connections. Echoing Schattschneider's warnings and criticisms, more recent critics, such as Theodore Lowi, take the argument one step further by suggesting that the existence and acceptance of interest groups in the political system have contributed to an erosion of government authority.

In recent years the focus of much of the literature on groups has shifted away from the study of groups per se to focus more closely on specific types of groups and their impact on the political system. Narrowly focused special interest groups, it is argued, can have a major influence on government and policy in a system of divided power, where political parties are of very little significance and constituent influences hold a great deal of sway over politicians.

GROUP FUNCTIONS. Why do groups form, how do they persist, and how are they able to use their resources to influence the course of public policy? Groups can serve several functions for members, ranging from the symbolic to the instrumental. The function a group performs will have a direct effect on how that group impacts the political process, because it will determine the motivation of the group members and the nature of the political action the group will take.

The strategies a group employs are dictated in part by the resources that the group can draw on.

Some groups provide symbolic benefits for their members, allowing individuals to express certain values or interests without pursuing them in a concrete manner. For example, membership or activity in a religious interest group may be undertaken to reinforce one's identification in that group rather than to promote a particular goal or policy.

Some groups are in business solely to promote economic interests. Groups that are economically based or motivated may function to advance the economic interests of a broad class of individuals or institutions, or they may act more narrowly, to protect an individual entity.

Still other groups may perform ideological functions for their members. These types of groups may adopt far-reaching political ideologies (e.g., liberal, conservative, socialist) covering all policy areas or more narrow ideologies that reflect deep feelings about a single issue such as abortion or gun control.

Another important group function is to provide valuable information or data to its members, to the public, or to members of Congress. In fact, most U.S. interest groups have as part of their function the collection, analysis, and dissemination of information.

In addition to these four primary functions, groups share instrumental goals. Instrumental functions involve concrete and immediate goals that often involve legislative or government decisions. Groups organized to support or condemn U.S. involvement in Central America in the 1980s fit into this category, as do groups that lobby for increased funding for the AIDS epidemic.

ROLE OF INTEREST GROUPS. The American Association of Retired Persons, or AARP, exists and thrives primarily as a service organization for Americans over fifty—providing discounts on prescription drugs, hotels and airlines, and supplemental health insurance, as well as a glossy magazine and other benefits. But it also plays a major role in the political process, working on the range of issues affecting the elderly.

While some groups target all or most of their efforts toward the executive branch and others direct their energies at the judicial branch, most lobbying activity takes place within the halls of Congress. In general, groups attempt to monitor governmental activity that might affect them, to initiate governmental action to promote their interests, and to block action that would work to their detriment. Each of these areas of activity requires, above all else, access—access to information on what the government is doing or is about to do and access to key decision makers.

One important role of lobbyists and interest groups is to monitor political activity. A group must keep track of, digest, analyze, and disseminate all the information relevant to its particular interests. Often, in order to have a political effect, a group must go beyond monitoring to take action, such as testifying at congressional hearings, drafting amendments to legislation, or notifying members of Congress of its support or opposition to a bill or amendment.

Besides monitoring political activity, groups may seek avenues for promoting their interests through governmental action. This can involve initiating a new program, increasing congressional appropriations, or awarding a government contract, among other things. Conversely, groups may seek to oppose government action in an effort to protect their own interests. In fact, because of the slow and complex nature of the U.S. political system, groups often find they have a better chance of blocking government action than of spurring it.

Interest groups' primary weapons are the incentives they can offer politicians and the sanctions they can use against them. Finding successful ways of deploying these resources is the key to effective lobbying. Lobbying can be a mutually beneficial process in which both the interests of the group and those of the politician are served. Sometimes even the public stands to gain from these relationships.

GROUP RESOURCES AND STRATEGIES. The strategies a group employs are dictated in part by the resources that the group can draw on. There are various types of group resources, and each group has its own mix, depending on its membership base and primary function. The combination of a group's goals, focus of activity, motivation, mix of resources, and skill at using them determines the political influence of the group.

Physical resources. Money is perhaps the most important resource for influencing public policy because it can be used to attract many other resources, including substantive expertise, political and leadership skill, and public relations talent. Another important resource is sheer membership size. Members are voters, and politicians pay attention to voters. If its membership is spread across the country, that means that a group has a presence in more congressional districts, which in itself can bring greater influence. Membership works best when it is intensely interested and motivated; if lawmakers think that a group or its lobbyist represents people who care deeply about an issue, are united, are paying attention, and are motivated to vote on that basis, they will pay much more attention to the group. The National Rifle Association, to take one example, has had extraordinary influence because of the intense motivation of its members on gun control issues.

Organizational resources. To be effective, any group must have the ability to mobilize its membership for political action. Members must be informed, often very quickly, of impending congressional action, must be told how to respond, and must have their responses channeled to the appropriate places. The U.S. Chamber of Commerce and the AFL-CIO, to choose two examples, have begun to use teleconferencing as a way of effectively communicating with and mobilizing members. Leadership skill and substantive expertise are important components of a strong organization. Common Cause cleverly developed a strong and sophisticated team to analyze campaign finance information from the Federal Election Commission; the group's information about campaign contributions and political activity has become the most widely used and credible information available, adding to Common Cause's leverage in the campaign reform debate.

Political resources. Knowledge of the political process is vital to a group's legislative success, which is why many groups hire former members of Congress or former congressional staffers. In addition, a group's political reputation is a crucial element in its political success. If lawmakers believe a group is effective, knowledgeable, and trustworthy, it will tend to win greater trust and hence be more effective.

Strategies. How do groups use their resources? One major outlay is campaign support. While corporations and labor unions are barred by law from contributing directly to campaigns for federal office, they do manage to channel a significant amount of money to the candidates of their choice through political action committees (PACs). PACs grew significantly in number and influence in the 1980s. From 1978 to 1991 the number of registered PACs increased by more than 150 percent, and the amount of money PACs contributed to congressional campaigns more than quadrupled—although this can mean only that more groups now counter each other in the policy process.

Aside from campaign support there is, of course, direct lobbying of members of Congress and their staffs. In general, lobbyists seek out like-minded legislators. While lobbying is, in a sense, a practice of persuasion, the relationships that develop are often friendly and mutually beneficial. Access is obviously a major factor here, for lobbyists must have access to members of Congress to get their message across.

In order to maximize access and enhance their "inside" contacts, interest groups frequently employ former members of Congress, former staff aides, or "old Washington hands." Washington-based representatives cultivate relationships with members and their staffs by taking them to lunch, stopping by offices to chat, and providing whatever help and useful information members might need.

Controversies remain over the role of interest groups in Washington.

In addition to direct lobbying techniques and strategies, lobbyists use a multitude of indirect methods to influence legislators and the policy-making process. Indirect strategies, often featuring mass media campaigns, are designed to drum up grassroots support for a particular measure or movement. Utilizing modern communications technologies, interest groups have been able to reach more and more people with computer-based direct-mail campaigns, satellite links, and teleconferencing, in addition to public service messages on local and cable television stations.

By mobilizing grassroots support, groups are able to gain public support for their interests. The public, in turn, applies pressure on members of Congress; for obvious reasons, members often respond (especially when the pressure is coming directly from their constituents).

The ability to influence public opinion and to mobilize grassroots support has been at a premium in recent years, leading to the growth of firms that specialize in these areas. Public relations firms such as Hill & Knowlton and Ogilvy & Mather have expanded their Washington operations sharply to provide interests with public relations support. PR firms have not only helped business and commercial clients: the Roman Catholic church, for example, hired Hill & Knowlton to improve its communications on the abortion issue when that issue began to move from the courts to the legislatures in the 1990s.

Often different interest groups come together and work collectively on major pieces of legislation. This increasingly common practice is called coalition lobbying. While these coalitions have the advantage of sheer numbers, they are often difficult to control and navigate because of conflicting views within the coalition. Many analysts believe that, because there are now so many diverse and specialized interests represented in Washington, the influence and clout of the larger, more encompassing groups has been undercut. In the 1990s most legislation involves a variety of interests, and as a result more often than not coalitions of interests (sometimes competing interests) are necessary to get measures passed.

THE CHANGING WORLD OF GROUP INFLUENCE. If the basic relationships between interest groups, their representatives in Washington, and Congress have remained fundamentally the same since Madison wrote *Federalist* 10, almost everything else that affects their interactions has changed. The change has been particularly marked since the late 1960s and early 1970s.

In particular, the landmark series of congressional reforms during the 1970s revolutionized the legislative process and ushered in the modern era of interest group politics. Congress was sharply decentralized and democratized, spreading power downward and outward from committees to subcommittees and rank-and-file members. Staffs were expanded sharply for individual members and subcommittees, and the legislative process was opened up dramatically to public, press, and group scrutiny—in the recording of members' votes on amendments on the floor, in the opening of previously closed committee meetings and mark-up sessions, and through the advent of televised proceedings via C-SPAN.

The deep divisions in Congress over the Vietnam War provided the catalyst for many of these reforms. Groups such as Common Cause were formed at this time in response to the demand for governmental reform. The origins of other public interest groups, including environmental, consumer, and antidefense groups, also date to this period since, as Congress changed, more and more points of access to the legislative process opened up, providing entry to more and more groups.

The reforms unleashed a large number of activist entrepreneurial lawmakers and staff looking for ideas to promote, bills to sponsor, and amendments to offer. They found natural allies in group representatives who had ideas and political skills to complement the insiders' needs. For many such groups, substantial sums of money or vast memberships were not required; sometimes a small storefront office and a copying machine could suffice.

As these ideas generated new legislation and regulations, they bred counterlobbying by business groups and others affected by the policies that were being implemented. The result was a veritable explosion in the number of groups, trade associations, and Washington offices throughout the 1970s and early 1980s.

All these changes altered the art of lobbying in fundamental ways. The need for up-to-date intelligence on congressional activity increased sharply; the decentralized, more fluid legislative process was less predictable than the old process had been and required more constant vigilance. New technologies were necessary for lobbyists to reach a broader range of lawmakers, meaning that more sophisticated direct-mail and teleconferencing techniques, among others, were needed.

Specialized lobbying became more prominent, along with a growing number of outside professionals selling their services to an expanding range of clients. Lawyers, specialized lobbyists, public relations firms, legislative strategy groups, direct-mail specialists, media consultants, grassroots organizers, and advertising agencies all mushroomed in Washington during the 1970s and 1980s.

By the 1990s, their growth had slowed, although it had not stopped, and additional questions about the role and focus of groups in the American political process were being raised. For instance, just as questions had long been raised concerning how an elected legislator could represent his or her constituents—as a "trustee" or as a "delegate"—questions increasingly were raised about how an unelected group official or lobbyist could represent an affinity group.

The American Association of Retired Persons was actively involved in 1987 and 1988 in the congressional debate and negotiations that led to passage of catastrophic-illness health insurance for the elderly; AARP's leadership actively supported the bill when it passed. But strong subsequent opposition from a core of affluent elderly put the organization's leadership on the defensive and eventually caused the group to disavow much of its earlier action. At the same time, the National Committee to Preserve Social Security and Medicare, an organization with a small national staff and none of the support services provided by AARP, mobilized vigorous opposition to the catastrophic-illness plan through dire warnings in direct-mail appeals to the elderly, but survey evidence suggested that most elderly people polled viewed the issue in a very different way.

Just as much of the political debate in 1992 revolved around whether Washington elites in elective office were out of touch with the American public "outside the beltway," some debate began over whether interest group elites in Washington pursued agendas that were out of touch with their constituencies. Controversies remain over the role of interest groups and lobbies in Washington.

[See also (I) Lobbying; (II) Primaries, Presidential.]

BIBLIOGRAPHY

Bentley, Arthur F. *The Process of Government.* 1949.

Calhoun, John C. "A Disquisition on Government." In *Source Book of American Political Theory.* Edited by Benjamin F. Wright. 1929.

Judis, John B. "The Pressure Elite." *The American Prospect* 9 (Spring 1992): 15–29.

Lowi, Theodore. *The End of Liberalism.* 1969.

Olson, Mancur. *The Logic of Collective Action: Public Good and the Theory of Groups.* 1965.

Ornstein, Norman J., and Shirley Elder. *Interest Groups: Lobbying and Policymaking.* 1978.

Ornstein, Norman J., and Mark Schmitt. "The New World of Interest Politics. *The American Enterprise* 1 (January–February 1990): 47–51.

Peterson, Paul. "The Rise and Fall of Special Interests." *Political Science Quarterly* 105 (1990–1991): 539–556.

Rauch, Jonathan. "The Parasite Economy." *National Journal,* 25 April 1992.

Salisbury, Robert H. "An Exchange Theory of Interest Groups." *Midwest Journal of Political Science* 13 (February 1969): 1–32.

Schattschneider, E. E. *The Semisovereign People.* 1960.

Truman, David. *The Governmental Process.* 1971.

– NORMAN J. ORNSTEIN

INTERSTATE COMPACTS

The Framers of the Constitution gave Congress authority to approve compacts among the states in order to prevent the states from organizing to wrest power from the federal government. Article I, section 10 provides that "No State shall, without the Consent of Congress, . . . enter into any Agreement or Compact with another State.

Compacts are formal agreements among states somewhat akin to treaties among nations. Ordinarily, they are approved by the legislatures of the states concerned and then submitted to Congress for its approval. They are binding on all the citizens of the signatory states, protecting their rights as individuals as well as rights of the public as a whole. States cannot escape their financial obligations under these agreements since compacts are protected by the contract clause of the Constitution. The U.S. Supreme Court has original jurisdiction over their enforcement. Congress also can compel compliance.

Despite the constitutional requirement, some compacts are not submitted to Congress. A few, such as the

Southern Regional Education Compact, operate without congressional approval. No precise line separates compacts requiring congressional consent and those that have taken effect without it; the U.S. Supreme Court has made the final determination in each instance. The Court held in *Virginia v. Tennessee* (1893) that express congressional consent was not required in every instance but could be implied. A 1978 case, *U.S. Steel v. Multistate Tax Corporation,* identified interstate agreements that increase the political power of the states or encroach on the supremacy of the United States as ones requiring specific approval.

Until the 1930s, Congress rather routinely consented to compacts. Since that time Congress has occasionally refused approval or given it for a limited time period. Congress has also stipulated that it could amend, alter, or repeal compacts or could require compact agencies to provide information about the agreements; the Supreme Court has yet to determine the enforceability of such limitations.

Only thirty-six compacts were ratified before 1920. Subsequently, with population growth and mobility and technological advancement, the pace of adoption accelerated. The Council of State Governments estimated that more than 150 compacts were in effect in 1992. All states have signed the Interstate Compact on the Supervision of Parolees and Probationers and the Interstate Compact on Juveniles. The typical state is a signatory to at least twenty agreements.

Early compacts were agreements between two states, but today they frequently include several states and occasionally Canadian provinces. The federal government has become a signatory to as well as the ratifier of a few compacts, including the Delaware River Basin Development Compact and the Susquehanna River Basin Compact, and engages actively in their administration.

States use compacts to solve intractable jurisdictional problems and to avoid service duplication. From oil regulation to water rights, these devices allay sibling rivalry among the states. They facilitate the settlement of disputes, although they sometimes elevate private controversies to the state level (as has happened in river basin development). Compacts help maintain state power in the federal system by blocking federal action, by disrupting direct federal-local relations, and by preventing the transfer of state functions to the national government.

Critics have attacked interstate compacts for the lack of attention they receive, both at adoption and during administration; for operating in improper spheres; for the possibility that compact commissions will be responsive to special interests and unresponsive to state control; and for their unrepresentativeness, since each signatory usually has only one member on a compact commission regardless of the state's size. Moreover, critics point out that Congress does not perform systematic reviews of interstate compacts.

BIBLIOGRAPHY

Barton, Weldon V. *Interstate Compacts in the Political Process.* 1967.

Glendening, Parris N., and Mavis M. Reeves. *Pragmatic Federalism.* 2d ed. 1984.

Ridgeway, Marian E. *Interstate Compacts: A Question of Federalism.* 1971.

– MAVIS MANN REEVES

INVESTIGATIONS

Congress conducted its first formal investigation in 1792. The subject was Maj. Gen. Arthur St. Clair's disastrous expedition against Native Americans in the Ohio Territory. Ever since, rarely has a session of Congress gone by without a formal inquiry by one or another of its committees or subcommittees.

THE OBJECTIVES OF A CONGRESSIONAL INVESTIGATION. The topics for investigation selected by members of Congress have been as plentiful as the problems faced by the nation. The wide range of subjects has included the migration of African Americans from the South to the North after the Civil War; the immigration of foreign contract labor during the 1800s; strikebreaking in the railroad industry; western land reclamation; grain speculation; the stock exchange (following the onset of the Great Depression); the munitions industry (on the eve of World War II); the unfairness of monopolies; the surprise attack on Pearl Harbor; communists in the federal government; mismanagement of the Atomic Energy Commission; the Internal Revenue Service; a suspected lag in U.S. nuclear missile production; the use of lie detectors by federal agencies; a criminal cover-up in the White House (the infamous Watergate scandal of the Nixon administration); illegal domestic operations carried out by the Central Intelligence Agency (CIA); and the covert sale of weapons to Iran with diversion of the profits to support a secret CIA war in Nicaragua (the Iran-contra scandal of the Reagan administration).

Congress has resorted to investigations for five primary purposes. First, investigations have proved useful in gathering information for the drafting of legislation. Second, investigations have been important instruments for the legislative supervision of agencies within the executive branch—the oversight or review function of Congress urged by James Madison in *Federalist* 51. Third, investigations have provided a highly visible means (especially since the advent of television) by which legislators can inform and educate the citizenry on the pressing issues of the day. Fourth, investigations have been used by legislators to police themselves through the congressional ethics committees or to improve their internal organization and procedures by way of ad hoc reform committees. And, fifth, an investigation can serve the subtle purpose of defusing potentially divisive issues in the nation, working them out in the hearing rooms of Congress rather than in the streets.

Fairly or not, investigations have often been criticized as exercises in self-promotion by legislators.

This last, the "safety-valve" function, was important in 1951, for example, when the controversy over President Harry S Truman's firing of Gen. Douglas MacArthur threatened to stir a national donnybrook between the political parties. A congressional inquiry, led by Sen. Richard B. Russell (D-Ga.), managed to deflate the rising anger by allowing a thorough airing of the issue in public hearings. During this inquiry, many of America's other leading generals testified in support of the president's dismissal of MacArthur. The public became convinced that the general had overstepped the boundaries of civilian supremacy over the military, a well-established principle in the United States.

Although congressional investigations serve many purposes, at the heart of most inquiries is a search for information that can guide legislators in their lawmaking duties. A noted member of Congress, J. William Fulbright (D-Ark.), the longtime chairman of the Senate Foreign Relations Committee, looked upon the congressional investigation as "primarily a search for information which it is believed is needed in order to solve a governmental problem."

INVESTIGATIONS GOOD AND BAD. The authority for legislative inquiries, although nowhere explicitly mentioned in the nation's founding document, has been generally upheld in the courts by virtue of the Constitution's "elastic clause." This clause affirms the right of Congress "to make all Laws which shall be necessary and proper for carrying into Execution the foregoing Powers" (Article I, section 8). If legislators were to be granted the right to make laws, by implication they would also have to have a way to ensure that the laws were faithfully executed. So long as Congress has remained loyal to this purpose of improved lawmaking, the courts have granted broad—but not unlimited—discretion to investigators (*McGrain v. Daugherty,* 273 U.S. 135 [1927]; *Watkins v. United States,* 354 U.S. 178 [1957]).

This is not to say that Congress's investigative powers have been free of controversy. They have long had articulate proponents and opponents. In their favor, Woodrow Wilson once opined that the "informing function of Congress should be preferred even to its legislative function" (*Congressional Government,* 1885). Other proponents have applauded legislators for defending freedom in the United States by asking pointed questions of executive bureaucrats, admirals and generals, cabinet members, and presidential advisers during formal investigative hearings. In contrast, opponents have looked with disdain upon the investigation as a dangerous weapon often misused by legislators in an attack on the civil liberties of the accused.

Most observers agree that throughout the history of this nation congressional investigative committees have ranged in quality and professionalism (as gauged by their adherence to the goal of improving legislation) from the egregious to the exemplary. By all accounts, the worst investigative committee ever assembled on Capitol Hill was the Joint Committee on the Conduct of the [Civil] War, which trampled extensively on the rights and reputations of its witnesses. A more recent example was the notorious McCarthy inquiry of 1954, an anticommunist witch-hunt into alleged communist influences in the U.S. Army, led by Joseph R. McCarthy, the junior Republican senator from Wisconsin, who chaired the Senate Government Operations Committee and the Permanent Subcommittee on Investigations. In the course of his "investigating," Senator McCarthy tossed out the window any semblance of preserving the rights of witnesses; instead, he engaged in smear tactics and innuendo against individual citizens inside and outside the government.

By consensus, one of the best congressional inquiries was the Senate's Special Committee to Investigate the National Defense Program (1941–1948). Its careful marshaling of evidence and fair treatment of witnesses drew extensive praise—and catapulted one of its chairmen, an obscure senator from Missouri by the name of Truman, into national prominence and soon thereafter the vice presidency.

Fairly or not, investigations have often been criticized as exercises in self-promotion by legislators, turning relatively unknown personalities into household names—Senators Truman, McCarthy, Richard M. Nixon (R-Calif.), Estes Kefauver (D-Tenn.), and Samuel J. Ervin, Jr. (D-N.C.), among others. And, as McCarthy found out, they can destroy as well as make a career. The line between a legislator's trying to publicize an inquiry in order to attract public support for legislative reform in one instance, and his or her self-promotion in another instance, can often be thin and hard to distinguish. The chairman of an investigative committee will find it difficult to muster public support for proposed remedial legislation without at the same time jumping into the limelight. Whether political ambition (and the phototropism it induces, bending legislators toward the television lights) or a sincere desire to inform the public of the need for new legislation is the more powerful consideration for the chairman is a matter that may fall beyond the competence of even a close observer to judge with assurance. In the best of cases, when a legislator is strongly driven by a sense of the public good, the two motivations are most likely intertwined in complicated ways—although self-interested grandstanding can become so transparent that it is easily seen through by observers (as McCarthy learned).

THE PHASES OF A CONGRESSIONAL INVESTIGATION. A congressional investigation must normally go through six major phases: start-up, discovery, interrogation, presentment, reform, and follow-through. Once stimulated to establish an investigative committee (say, by indications of corruption in an executive agency; by a major societal problem outside the government, such as widespread failures in the banking industry; or by an international controversy, such as the CIA's covert-action disaster in 1961 at the Bay of Pigs in Cuba), Congress must sort out in its start-up phase a series of key decisions that will guide its probe.

Start-up. Congressional leaders must determine the precise mandate to give their investigative committee, ascertain the extent of resources (time, money, staff) that they are willing to make available for the inquiry, and select the committee members (who then select the staff).

Each decision is laden with implications for the course of the investigation. In the absence of a specific mandate, along with clear rules of conduct and a manifest legislative intent, investigators may flounder, because they lack a sense of direction. Inadequate time, money, or staff can similarly dim the prospects for a thorough inquiry. In particular, time is rarely on the side of congressional investigators. They are expected to show results quickly, often to the drumbeat of media hungry for dramatic revelations and bored by a methodical search for facts, however essential to a complete and fair inquiry.

The nature of the committee's membership is also vital. Have impartial individuals been appointed? Are they senior legislators, with extensive experience and wide respect in the chamber and the country? Do the members exhibit a wide disparity in ideological orientations, or are they a relatively cohesive group? Are would-be presidential aspirants—notoriously eager for publicity—among the members? Decisions on staffing are critical as well. Are the staff aides chiefly lawyers, social scientists, political aides (or, in some instances, political hacks)? Each brings a different, and sometimes clashing, set of cultural norms and investigative approaches to an inquiry.

Discovery. Once the committee is in place (which can take months), the next step is gathering evidence about the subject the committee is investigating. The most reliable evidence usually comes in the form of documents, broadly defined to include memoranda, minutes of meetings, letters, tapes, diaries, notes, appointment calendars, and other records. In the lexicon of law (and Capitol Hill), the gathering of documents is known as *discovery.* The staff of an investigative committee is expected first to lay out the chronology of the event under probe, then to substantiate this record with documentary sources.

Discovery can be a difficult undertaking. The required documents may be classified, posing special problems of access. Those individuals being investigated may do their best to stymie access through legal maneuvering. During the Watergate inquiry, President Nixon, citing executive privilege, tried to bar investigators from his papers—a move partially rebuffed by the Supreme Court in the celebrated case of *United States v. Nixon* (418 U.S. 283, [1974]). Or those under investigation may employ less overt actions. A key portion of taped White House conversations was mysteriously—suspiciously—erased by Nixon's secretary in the midst of the Watergate inquiry. During congressional investigations into the CIA and other intelligence agencies in 1975, one ploy used by an executive agency to slow and discourage discovery was to send literally truckloads of documents to investigators—almost all of which proved worthless. (The ruse was used fifty years earlier by the executive branch during the Teapot Dome investigation.) As Congress's Iran-contra investigation moved forward in 1986 and 1987, the White House shredding machines worked overtime, and some documents were surreptitiously removed from the premises.

As weapons against stalling ("stonewalling," in Washington argot), members of Congress sometimes resort to subpoenas and votes of contempt, which can carry stiff penalties, including imprisonment. Often, threats from Congress that these instruments of punishment will be used prove sufficient to gain compliance.

Interrogation. Once an investigative committee has collected enough documentation to understand the essential facts related to the subject of inquiry (again, a process that can take months), its members and staff

"Suggestion for a New Dome on the Capitol." Political cartoon commenting on the Teapot Dome affair, a Harding administration scandal involving the improper leasing of government oil reserves in Wyoming and California. The investigation into the affair, launched by the Senate Committee on Public Lands and headed by Sen. Thomas J. Walsh (D-Mont.), resulted in the conviction and imprisonment of Warren G. Harding's secretary of the Interior, former senator Albert B. Fall. Billy Borne, Ashville Citizen, *21 February 1924. (Library of Congress)*

augment the record by interviewing knowledgeable individuals, the interrogation phase. And frequently some early interviewing will take place as part of the discovery process—particularly attempts to learn about the existence and location of key documents.

Investigative staffs (and the few legislators who may wish to become involved in the proceedings at this early stage) use a range of approaches to interviews. At the less formal end of the continuum are friendly conversations with people who may know about the subject—for instance, individuals who have worked in the government for decades and have a deep understanding of the agency under investigation. The approach in this instance is to be nonthreatening and cordial, in hopes of ferreting out information helpful to the probe. At the opposite end of the interview continuum is the full-blown—and sometimes hostile—interrogation, with the witness testifying under oath (at risk of perjury and usually accompanied by counsel) and a verbatim record kept of the proceedings.

The softer data obtained through interviews can be less reliable than documentary evidence. It was the still-extant White House tapes that established Nixon's involvement in the Watergate cover-up—the "smoking gun" of hard, culpable fact that investigators dream of in the discovery phase. Officials widely known for their intellectual acuity suddenly can be struck by profound bouts of amnesia regarding key points of evidence—especially if they are under investigation for wrongdoing. Nixon went so far as to explicitly advise his aides to resort to amnesia during the Watergate probe. And sometimes officials flatly mislead, even under oath and in executive (closed) session, as did former CIA director Richard Helms before investigators on the Senate Foreign Relations Committee during the Vietnam War. Another senior CIA official conceded before an investigative committee that in earlier testimony before the House Permanent Select Committee on Intelligence, he had been "technically correct, [but] specifically evasive"—bureaucratic gobbledygook meaning he had intentionally sidestepped the House committee's attempts to probe the improper diversion of funds to the Contras in Nicaragua, in violation of the law. These problems are not limited to investigations of government agencies. Probes into private-sector misconduct have been plagued by evasiveness as well—as recently exemplified by inquiries into the operations of some savings and loan companies.

Yet, a committee cannot always expect to find a rich documentary trail (let alone a smoking gun), especially in the modern era, when shredding machines are ubiquitous and government officials are leery of writing down sensitive information. Interviews become an important means for filling in the inevitable gaps.

Presentment. The purpose of discovery and interrogation is to build a solid record of evidence for public presentation, on the road to legislative remedy. Presumably, public understanding and support will encourage legislators in the full Congress to support corrective measures. The centerpiece of the presentment phase is the hearing. Ideally, the hearing is held in public, to help build citizen support for the investigative findings and recommendations; sometimes, the hearing must be held in executive session, if the inquiry involves a topic that must be kept classified in order to protect sensitive national security information or the identity of endangered witnesses.

During this phase, members of the investigative panel may resort to political combat, attacking or protecting witnesses during the hearings, arguing among themselves (although usually with the veneer of Capitol Hill collegiality), emphasizing different sets of documents to make their point, and advancing their own brand of legislative remedies (or countering those proposed by adversaries)—all shaped by the partisan, philosophical, and constituency leanings of the individual committee members. Insiders already have seen these political stresses, for they immediately became apparent in member and staff selection during the committee's start-up phase, throughout the period of document requests and witness selection, and with all the other decisions an investigative panel must make in its early workings.

Investigative committees can also be quite cohesive. Often they are less divided by the forces of partisanship, ideology, or constituency—politics—than they are united by a desire to expose and correct wrongdoing; by a common sense of dismay over the mistakes, excesses, or crimes of government officials; and by institutional pride, especially when the executive branch is perceived as having affronted the constitutional prerogatives of Congress.

A committee cannot always expect to find a rich documentary trail (let alone a smoking gun).

Of particular importance during the presentment phase is the development of public support for the investigative committee's work and recommendations. Without public interest (outrage directed against those being investigated is even better, from the committee's perspective), it becomes difficult to garner support among the plenary assembly of legislators for new laws or regulations designed to ameliorate the conditions that stimulated the investigation.

Reform. The success or failure of a congressional investigation is typically judged by whether it produces tangible reforms. This benchmark can be spurious, for sound and fury alone can lead to important changes, as bureaucrats (or other targets of investigation) correct their ways without further and more formal prodding from Congress, the institution upon which they depend for future funding. As government bureaucrats and private-sector officials anticipate the negative reactions that wrongdoing will bring on Capitol Hill, this latent check helps to keep potential miscreants in line. This so-called law of anticipated reactions is often subtle and difficult for the outside observer to detect, but it can be all important.

Explicit manifestations of reform provide, however, the most persuasive evidence of a committee's success—most visibly in the guise of new statutes (for example, the sweeping and widely supported National Security Act of 1947, which followed a legislative investigation into the Pearl Harbor attack and the nation's inadequate security and readiness). More frequent, the result of an inquiry is likely to be not so much new law as a fresh understanding between Congress and the executive agencies about expected behavior. Beyond a tacit sense of "anticipated reactions," the understanding may acquire official or semi-official status through an exchange of letters, by way of a legislative record (frequently a colloquy among members on the floor), by updated executive regulations insisted upon by key legislators (holders of the purse strings), or simply by informal verbal agreements.

While the informal arrangements often succeed, they lack the permanence of law. Like sand castles, they can wash away with the incoming tide of a new administration or even with the retirement of a key legislator, a change in staff, or secret executive codicils to public documents. Herein lies the attraction of formal statutes for those who seek more lasting protection against the abuse that initially triggered an investigation. A further hazard in the reform phase is that legislators will propose unneeded change. They may feel compelled to justify their long (and expensive) inquiry with new law, however unnecessary.

Follow-through. The best legislative reforms may be to little avail if they are never properly implemented. When the investigative committee has filed its report, passed its legislation, and (unless it is a permanent panel) disbanded its staff and dismantled its offices, who is left to see that the malfeasance that led to the inquiry will not occur again? Indeed, the mistake, crime, or scandal might well happen again. Government officials are like other human beings; they may err once more. They may even decide to ignore Congress in deference to a "higher law" spelled out by a president or some other lofty executive official (as one conspirator testified before Congress's Iran-contra investigators). So follow-through is necessary.

Part of the follow-through phase is to conduct periodic probes—especially oversight hearings, with or without immediate cause—into the same agencies and policies that have caused problems in the past. Legislators can also be more thorough in their confirmation hearings for high officials, guarding at the outset against the placement of dubious individuals in positions of authority. The avoidance of crime and scandal depends in part on the quality of government officials; the greater their integrity, the less likely it is that a formal investigation into their activities will prove necessary.

Others, including the media and the courts, as well as inspectors general and legal counsels within the agencies, have an important role in curbing malfeasance before it becomes scandalous. Most important among these checks are the standing committees of Congress, with their control over the budget, their subpoena powers, and other points of leverage. In their day-to-day interaction with men and women of power—ever liable to abuse in human hands, Madison warned—the standing committees are in a good position to guard against violations of the public trust.

Studies of congressional oversight indicate, however, that the devotion of legislators to this aspect of their duties has often been uneven. Failure to conduct serious routine legislative review of government programs ironically may be the most important trigger of congressional investigations, as legislators are finally forced to confront a full-blown scandal that the preventive of careful systematic oversight might have scotched.

[See also (I) Witnesses, Rights of; (II) Investigations, Congressional.]

BIBLIOGRAPHY

Cohen, William, and George Mitchell. *Men of Zeal.* 1989.

Davidson, Roger H. "The Political Dimensions of Congressional Investigations." *Capitol Studies* 5 (1977): 41–63.

Fulbright, J. W. "Congressional Investigations: Significance for the Legislative Process." *University of Chicago Law Review* 18 (1950–1951): 440–448.

Johnson, Loch K. *A Season of Inquiry: The Senate Intelligence Investigation.* 1985.

Rovere, Richard. *Senator Joe McCarthy.* 1959.

Schlesinger, Arthur M., Jr., and Roger Bruns, eds. *Congress Investigates, 1792–1974.* 1975.

– LOCH K. JOHNSON

J

JOINT SESSIONS AND MEETINGS

Joint sessions and joint meetings of Congress occur when members of the House and Senate gather together to transact congressional business or to receive addresses from the president or other dignitaries. The first such gathering was a joint session held on 6 April 1789 to count electoral votes for the nation's first president and vice president.

Of the two types of gatherings, a joint session is the more formal and occurs upon adoption of a concurrent resolution passed by both houses of Congress. Congress holds joint sessions to receive the president's annual State of the Union address and other presidential addresses, and to count electoral votes for president and vice president every four years.

A joint meeting, on the other hand, occurs after both houses, by unanimous consent or by resolution, declare themselves in recess for such a joint gathering in the Hall of the House of Representatives. Because the Hall of the House of Representatives has more seats than the Senate chamber, both joint sessions and joint meetings have nearly always been held in the Hall of the House. Congress holds joint meetings for such matters as receiving addresses from dignitaries (e.g., foreign heads of state and famous Americans such as astronauts and military leaders) and for commemorating major events. The Speaker of the House of Representatives usually presides over joint sessions and meetings; however, the president of the Senate presides over counts of the electoral votes, as required by the Constitution.

Between 1913 and 1993, every president from Woodrow Wilson to Bill Clinton has delivered an annual State of the Union address before Congress. During this period presidents gave over 120 addresses before Congress. These included Woodrow Wilson's 1917 request for a declaration of war against Germany and his request for Senate approval of the Versailles treaty in 1919; Franklin D. Roosevelt's 1934 speech on the 100th anniversary of Lafayette's death and the 1941 declaration of war; Harry S Truman's submission of the United Nations charter in 1945 and his speech on the railroad strike in 1946; Lyndon B. Johnson's voting rights speech in 1965; Richard M. Nixon's Vietnam policy address in 1969; Jimmy Carter's Middle East speech in 1978; Ronald Reagan's U.S.-Soviet summit address in 1985; George Bush's speech on the invasion of Kuwait by Iraq in 1990; and Bill Clinton's address on health reform in 1993.

According to Seymour H. Fersh, "With President Roosevelt taking advantage of radio, the annual address more than ever before was directed at a national and world audience, rather than merely to Congress." Using the broadcast media of first radio and then television, presidents have been able to deliver their messages not just to Congress, but directly to the voters.

Of the two types of gatherings, a joint session is the more formal and occurs upon adoption of a concurrent resolution passed by both houses of Congress.

The Marquis de Lafayette, French hero of the American Revolution, in 1824 became the first foreign dignitary to address a joint meeting of Congress. More than seventy-five foreign dignitaries have since addressed joint meetings. Sir Winston Churchill addressed three joint meetings (in 1941, 1943, and 1952), the most by a non-American. Congress upon occasion has declined requests by foreign dignitaries to address a joint meeting because of the volume of such requests, a busy legislative schedule, or differences of opinion surrounding the proposed speaker. Among the more controversial requests were those by Soviet leaders Nikita Khrushchev (1959) and Mikhail S. Gorbachev (1987), who were never invited to address a joint meeting of Congress. However, with the collapse of the Union of Soviet Socialist Republics, Boris Yeltsin, president of Russia, addressed a joint meeting of Congress in 1992.

For a foreign dignitary to address Congress, a formal agreement must be reached by the Senate and House. The Speaker then sends a formal letter of invitation to the foreign dignitary. Parallel to these formalities, however, informal efforts are usually undertaken to prepare the way for extending the formal invitation.

After the two chambers have recessed, the senators and representatives assemble in the House in a joint meeting to receive the foreign dignitary's address. When the House next convenes after a joint meeting, it usually agrees to a unanimous consent request by the majority leader or his designee permitting the proceedings and remarks of the foreign dignitary made during the recess to be printed in the Congressional Record.

From the first joint meeting to receive Lafayette's address to the present time, the process has been simplified. Congress typically approves the unanimous consent request, thus eliminating the need to bring the matter up by resolution, joint resolution, public bill, or appropriation. When the matter is controversial, however, or involves the expenditure of public funds, a joint resolution or public bill is the legislative vehicle used.

Other American citizens below the level of U.S. president also address the Congress in joint meeting, or in the Senate or House separately. These speakers have included Generals Douglas MacArthur and Norman Schwarzkopf, astronauts, and others.

BIBLIOGRAPHY

Byrd, Robert C. *The Senate, 1789–1989.* Vol. 4: *Historical Statistics, 1789–1992.* 1992.

Kerr, Mary Lee, ed. *Foreign Visitors to Congress: Speeches and History.* 2 vols. 1989.

Pontius, John Samuels. *Addresses by Foreign Dignitaries, 1789–1986.* Congressional Research Service, Library of Congress. 1986.

Wellborn, Clay. *Joint Sessions and Joint Meetings of Congress.* Congressional Research Service, Library of Congress, CRS Rept. 87-244. 1987.

– JOHN SAMUELS PONTIUS

JOURNALS

The Constitution (Art. 1, sec. 5) provides that "Each House shall keep a Journal of its Proceedings, and from time to time publish the same, excepting such Parts as may in their Judgment require Secrecy." The House maintains one Journal and the Senate keeps two: the *Journal of the Senate of the United States of America,* which reports Senate legislative action, and the *Executive Journal,* which records Senate actions on matters requiring the Senate's advice and consent (i.e., treaties and nominations). Actions taken by the Senate in secret session or when it sits as a court of impeachment are kept separate and are published only by Senate order as separate journals.

The journals are the formal, official record of House or Senate action. They differ from the *Congressional Record* in that the journals do not include transcripts of floor debate prepared by the official reporters of debate. The journals merely summarize chamber activity: the number and title of bills, the sponsors and texts of floor amendments, the results of all yea-and-nay votes in the chamber, and the text of resolutions and conference reports. Any discrepancies between a journal and the *Congressional Record* are decided in favor of the journal. The House *Journal* does not include detailed descriptions of actions taken in the Committee of the Whole (or indeed in any committee) because technically these actions do not occur in the House. In early Congresses, the journals were kept personally by the Clerk of the House or the Secretary of the Senate, but journal clerks in both houses now prepare the journals under the supervision of the Clerk or Secretary.

Approval and correction of these documents is accorded high parliamentary standing. In earlier years, approving the journal in the House and Senate caused substantial delay because members could demand the reading of the journal in full. During the Jackson administration, the Senate passed a resolution censuring President Andrew Jackson for removing government funds from the Bank of the United States; later, the Senate voted to expunge the resolution from the original, handwritten *Journal,* and a black box was then drawn around the offending language with an inscription noting the later action to expunge the censure resolution.

Under current House and Senate rules, the journal is not read. In the House, the Speaker announces that he has found the *Journal* for the previous day to be accurate. In the Senate, the majority leader offers a nondebatable motion to approve the journal. Votes on approving the journal in the House or Senate are usually attendance checks by the parties and not serious attempts to reject the journal.

[*See also* (I) Congressional Record.]

BIBLIOGRAPHY

Byrd, Robert C. *The Senate, 1789–1989: Addresses on the History of the United States Senate.* Vol. 1, chap. 8. 1988.

Tiefer, Charles. *Congressional Practice and Procedure: A Reference, Research, and Legislative Guide.* 1989.

– PAUL S. RUNDQUIST

JUDICIAL REVIEW

The Supreme Court and the lower federal courts have the power to review any federal or state legislation or other official governmental action and to invalidate it if they deem it inconsistent with the Constitution or federal law. The constitutional language (Article III) simply provides that "the judicial Power of the United States, shall be vested in one supreme Court, and in such inferior Courts as the Congress may from time to time ordain and establish." Aside from the enumeration of the kinds of cases and controversies that the Court may hear on original jurisdiction, the judiciary's power is not further defined. Instead, Article III gives Congress the authority to define the Court's appellate jurisdiction and the structure of, as well as the types of cases to be heard by, the lower federal courts.

Congress's power to define the Court's appellate jurisdiction and the kinds of cases that may be raised in federal courts significantly conditions the exercise of judicial review. The Judiciary Act of 1789 initially defined the Supreme Court's appellate jurisdiction and created the basic structure of the federal judiciary: federal district courts are the trial courts of the federal judicial system, and situated between them and the Supreme Court are the circuit, or regional, courts of appeals. But Congress did not authorize any appellate court judgeships in 1789. Rather, Supreme Court justices were required to "ride circuit," sitting with district court judges as circuit courts of appeals. Appellate court judgeships were not authorized until the Circuit Court of Appeals Act of 1891. In response to growing caseloads, Congress subsequently increased the number of circuit courts of appeals from three to thirteen and the number of district courts to ninety-four, together staffed by more than seven hundred judges.

The business of the federal judiciary also changed as a result of congressional legislation. Congress greatly expanded the jurisdiction of all federal courts by extending it to include civil rights, questions of federal law decided by state courts, and all suits of more than five hundred dollars arising under the Constitution or federal legislation. In the post–World War II era, Congress enacted major legislation regulating health, safety, and the environment as well as greatly expanding federal criminal law. That legislation in turn dramatically increased the number of administrative appeals and regulatory and criminal cases confronting the federal judiciary.

SHAPING THE SUPREME COURT'S CASELOAD. Besides defining federal courts' jurisdiction, congressional legislation indirectly affects the work of the federal judiciary. During its first decade, the Supreme Court had little of importance to do. Over 40 percent of its business consisted of admiralty and prize cases (disputes over captured property at sea). About 50 percent raised issues of common law, and the remaining 10 percent dealt with matters such as equity. But in the early years of the Republic, Congress did not undertake to broadly regulate social and economic conditions. When it began regulating railroads, corporations, and working conditions in the late nineteenth century, the Court's business evolved with challenges to that legislation. The number of admiralty cases dwindled to less than 4 percent by 1882. Almost 40 percent of the Court's decisions still dealt with either disputes of common law or questions of jurisdiction and procedure. More than 43 percent, however, involved interpreting congressional statutes. The increase in statutory interpretation registered the impact of the Industrial Revolution and growing regulation of social and economic relations. In the 1990s, about 47 percent of the cases annually decided by the Court involve matters of constitutional law. Another 40 percent deal with the interpretation of congressional legislation. The remaining cases involve issues of administrative law, taxation, patents, and claims.

As the Court's caseload grew, its discretionary jurisdiction was expanded by Congress. Congress thus enabled the Court not only to manage its workload but to set its substantive agenda for exercising judicial review. In its first few decades, the Court annually heard fewer than one hundred cases. Its docket then steadily grew throughout the late nineteenth and twentieth centuries. Whereas in 1920 there were only 565 cases on its docket, the number rose to more than 1,300 by 1950, 2,300 by 1960, 4,200 by 1970, to more than 5,000 cases a year in the 1980s. By 1990, the Court docket annually exceeded 6,000 cases.

Major confrontations between Congress and the Court have occurred a number of times over the exercise of judicial review.

For most of the nineteenth century, Congress required the Court to decide every appeal. But because the Court could not stay abreast of its caseload, Congress incrementally enlarged the Court's discretionary jurisdiction by eliminating mandatory rights of appeal in narrow though important areas. Then, in the Judiciary Act of 1925, Congress basically established the jurisdiction of the modern Court. That act replaced many provisions for mandatory review of appeals with discretionary review of petitions for writs of certiorari (requests that the Court review the record and judgment of a lower court), which the Court may deny. In 1988, the Act to Improve the Administration of Justice eliminated virtually all of the Court's remaining nondiscretionary appellate jurisdiction. As a result, the Court has virtually complete discretion over what cases it reviews and how it exercises its power of judicial review.

THE SUPREME COURT AND CONGRESSIONAL STATUTES. Because judicial review is not expressly defined in Article III, the Court was initially reluctant to assert that power. Chief Justice John Marshall provided the classic justification for judicial review in the landmark ruling in *Marbury v. Madison* (1803). There, the Court struck down a section of the Judiciary Act of 1789 that Marshall in his opinion construed as having unconstitutionally expanded the Court's original jurisdiction under Article III by giving it the power to issue writs of mandamus—court orders directing a government official to take some action. While that decision was controversial, the Marshall Court further legitimated its power of judicial review by overturning a number of state laws, although it did not again challenge Congress's power. Indeed, the Court did not strike down another act of Congress until *Scott v. Sandford* (1857), which invalidated the Missouri Compromise of 1820.

Since the late nineteenth century, the Court has more frequently asserted its power to overturn congressional legislation.

Note, though, that when invalidating a congressional statute, the Court sometimes throws into question many other statutes as well. In *Immigration and Naturalization Service v. Chadha* (1983), for instance, the Court struck down a provision for a one-house legislative veto in the Immigration and Naturalization Act and effectively declared all legislative vetoes unconstitutional. While *Chadha* is counted as a single declaration of the unconstitutionality of a statute, more than two hundred provisions for legislative vetoes were affected by the Court's decision.

Major confrontations between Congress and the Court have occurred a number of times over the exercise of judicial review. The Marshall Court generally approved the expansion of national governmental power, but because of the states' opposition to the Court's rulings Congress in the 1820s and 1830s threatened to remove the Court's jurisdiction over disputes involving states' rights. After the Civil War, Congress repealed the Court's jurisdiction over certain denials of writs of habeas corpus—orders commanding that a prisoner be brought before a judge and that cause be shown for his imprisonment. In *Ex parte McCardle* (1869), the Court upheld that repeal of its jurisdiction, thereby avoiding a controversial case attacking Reconstruction legislation.

CONGRESSIONAL RESTRAINTS ON THE COURT. Progressives in Congress unsuccessfully sought to pressure the economically conservative Court at the turn of the century. They proposed requiring a two-thirds vote by the justices when striking down federal statutes and permitting Congress to overrule the Court's decisions by a two-thirds majority. The confrontation escalated with the Court's invalidation of much of the early New Deal program in the 1930s. The Senate refused to go along with President Franklin D. Roosevelt's Court-packing plan to increase the number of justices from nine to fifteen; but in order to secure a majority on the bench in support of the New Deal, Congress passed legislation allowing justices to retire with full rather than half salary, thus making retirement more financially attractive to the sitting justices and giving Roosevelt openings to appoint justices who shared his political philosophy.

Congress may pressure the Court in a number of ways. It has tried to do so when setting the Court's terms and size and when authorizing appropriations for salaries, law clerks, secretaries, and office technology. Only once, in 1802, in repealing the Judiciary Act of 1801 and abolishing one year's session, did Congress actually set the Court's term in order to delay and influence a particular decision.

The size of the Court is not constitutionally ordained, and changes in the number of justices generally reflect congressional attempts to influence the Court's exercise of judicial review. The Jeffersonian Republicans' quick repeal of the act passed by the Federalists in 1801, an act that reduced the number of justices, was the first of several such attempts to influence the Court. Presidents James Madison, James Monroe, and John Adams all claimed that the country's geographical expansion warranted enlarging the size of the Court. But Congress refused to do so until the last day of Andrew Jackson's term in 1837. During the Civil War, the number of justices was increased to ten, ostensibly because of the creation of a tenth circuit in California. This gave Abraham Lincoln his fourth appointment and a pro-Union majority on the bench. Antagonism toward Andrew Johnson's Reconstruction policies led to a reduction from ten to seven justices. After General Ulysses S. Grant was elected president, Congress again authorized nine justices, the number that has prevailed.

Under Article III, Congress is authorized "to make exceptions" to the Court's appellate jurisdiction. That authorization has been viewed as a way of denying the Court review of certain kinds of cases. Although Congress once succeeded in doing so, with the 1868 repeal of jurisdiction over writs of habeas corpus, Court-curbing legislation has generally failed to win passage. Furthermore, the Court has suggested that it would not approve repeals of its jurisdiction that are merely attempts to dictate how particular kinds of cases should be decided.

Reversal by constitutional amendment. Congress has had somewhat greater success in reversing the Court by constitutional amendment. Four decisions have prompted this approach. *Chisholm v. Georgia* (1793), holding that citizens of one state could sue another state in federal courts, was reversed in 1795 by the Eleventh

Amendment, which guaranteed sovereign immunity for states from suits by citizens of other states. In 1865 and 1868, the Thirteenth and Fourteenth Amendments abolished slavery and made African Americans citizens of the United States, thereby overturning *Scott v. Sandford.* With the ratification in 1913 of the Sixteenth Amendment, Congress reversed *Pollock v. Farmers' Loan & Trust Company* (1895), which had invalidated a federal income tax. In 1970, an amendment to the Voting Rights Act of 1965 lowered the voting age to eighteen years for all elections. But within six months, the Court held in *Oregon v. Mitchell* (1970) that Congress had exceeded its power by lowering the voting age for state and local elections. Less than a year later, the Twenty-sixth Amendment was ratified, extending the franchise to eighteen-year-olds in all elections.

In addition, two other amendments effectively overrode two prior rulings. In 1920, the Nineteenth Amendment extended voting rights to women and basically nullified *Minor v. Happersett* (1874), which had rejected the claim that women could not be prohibited from voting under the Fourteenth Amendment's equal protection clause. The Twenty-fourth Amendment, ratified in 1964, prohibits the use of poll taxes as a qualification for voting. It technically invalidated the Court's rejection of a challenge to poll taxes in *Breedlove v. Suttles* (1937).

The Court may invite Congress to reverse its rulings when legislation appears ambiguous.

Finally, several leaders in the Reconstruction Congress maintained that the Fourteenth Amendment would override *Barron v. Baltimore* (1833) and apply the Bill of Rights to the states as well as to the federal government. Shortly after that amendment's ratification, however, the Court rejected that interpretation of the amendment in the *Slaughterhouse Cases* (1873). Yet in the twentieth century, the Court selectively incorporated the major guarantees of the first eight amendments into the Fourteenth Amendment and applied them to the states.

Reversals by statute. More successful than amending the Constitution have been congressional revisions of legislation in response to Court rulings. For example, the Court held in *Pennsylvania v. Wheeling and Belmont Bridge Company* (1852) that a bridge built across the Ohio River obstructed interstate commerce and violated a congressionally approved state compact. Congress immediately passed a statute declaring that the bridge did not obstruct interstate commerce.

Congressional reversals usually relate to nonstatutory matters involving administrative policies. But in *Zurcher v. The Stanford Daily* (1978), the Court held that there was no constitutional prohibition against police searching newsrooms without a warrant for "mere evidence" (in this case, photographs) of a crime. Congress reversed that ruling by passing the Privacy Protection Act of 1980 and prohibiting warrantless searches of newsrooms.

Congressional reversals of the Court's statutory interpretations are less frequent, since Congress is usually constrained by the lobbying efforts of beneficiaries of the Court's rulings. Still, the modern Congress has tended to reverse a growing number of the federal judiciary's statutory decisions. The Civil Rights Act of 1991, for instance, reversed twelve rulings of the Court. Between 1967 and 1990, Congress overrode 121 of the Court's statutory decisions; by contrast, between 1945 and 1957 only twenty-one rulings were overridden. Moreover, Congress has increasingly overruled lower federal court decisions.

Notably, 73 percent of the decisions overturned were handed down by the Court less than ten years earlier. Almost 40 percent were conservative rulings while 20 percent were liberal holdings, and in slightly over 40 percent there was no clean liberal-conservative split. The decisions reversed by Congress most commonly involved civil rights, followed by criminal law, antitrust law, bankruptcy, federal jurisdiction, and environmental law.

The Court may invite Congress to reverse its rulings when legislation appears ambiguous. It suggested as much in *Tennessee Valley Authority v. Hill* (1978) when holding that a TVA dam could not be put into operation because it would destroy the only habitat of a tiny fish, the snail darter, protected under the Endangered Species Act of 1973. Congress later modified the act by authorizing a special board to decide whether to allow federally funded public works projects when they threaten endangered species.

Defying the Court. Congress cannot overturn the Court's interpretations of the Constitution by mere legislation. But Congress can enhance or thwart compliance with the Court's rulings. After the Warren Court's landmark decision in *Gideon v. Wainwright* (1963) that indigents have a right to counsel, Congress provided attorneys for indigents charged with federal offenses. By contrast, in the Crime Control and Safe Streets Act of 1968, Congress permitted federal courts to use evidence obtained from suspects who had not been read their rights under *Miranda v. Arizona* (1966) if their testimony appeared voluntary based on the "totality of the circumstances" surrounding their interrogation. In 1977 Congress passed the so-called Hyde Amendment, sponsored by Republican representative Henry J. Hyde of Illinois. That amendment registered opposition to the Court's abortion ruling in *Roe v. Wade* (1973) and to federal funding of abortions. The Hyde Amendment to appropriations bills bars Medicaid coverage of abortions except where the life of the mother would be endangered were the fetus carried to full term.

Congress may openly defy the Court in other ways. After *Chadha,* Congress passed no fewer than two hundred new provisions for legislative vetoes, in direct defiance of *Chadha.* Congress indubitably has the power to delay and undercut implementation of the Court's rulings. For example, Congress delayed implementation of the Court's watershed school desegregation ruling in *Brown v. Board of Education* (1954) by not authorizing the executive branch to enforce the decision until the Civil Rights Act of 1964. Then, by cutting back on appropriations for the departments of Justice and of Health, Education and Welfare, Congress registered the growing opposition to busing and other attempts to achieve integrated public schools.

In sum, on major issues of public policy, Congress is likely to prevail or at least to temper the impact of the Court's rulings and its exercise of judicial review.

[See also (I) Constitution, article on Congress in the Constitution, Judiciary and Congress; (III) Judicial Review.]

BIBLIOGRAPHY

Craig, Barbara. *Chadha: The Story of An Epic Constitutional Struggle.* 1988.

Eskridge, William N., Jr. "Overriding Supreme Court Statutory Interpretation Decisions." *Yale Law Journal* 101 (1991):331–445.

Fisher, Louis. *Constitutional Conflicts between Congress and the President.* 3d ed. 1991.

Katzman, Robert, ed. *Judges and Legislators: Toward Institutional Comity.* 1988.

Keynes, Edward, with Randall K. Miller. *The Court vs. Congress: Prayer, Busing and Abortion.* 1989.

O'Brien, David M. *Constitutional Law and Politics: Struggles for Power and Governmental Accountability.* 1991.

– DAVID M. O'BRIEN

JUDICIARY AND CONGRESS

The federal judiciary has become a critical element in the legislative process because what the courts decide can have significant consequences for Congress. At the same time, Congress affects in vital ways the structure, function, composition, and well-being of the judiciary (Katzmann, 1986). Indeed, the character of relations between the two branches has ramifications not only for each, but for the shape and development of policy (Shapiro, 1988; Melnick, 1985; Katzmann, 1988a).

THE CONSTITUTION. Article III, section 1 of the Constitution states that "the judicial Power of the United States, shall be vested in one supreme Court, and in such inferior Courts as the Congress may from time to time ordain and establish." The article further asserts that "the Judges, both of the supreme and inferior Courts, shall hold their Offices during good Behaviour, and shall, at stated Times, receive for their Services, a Compensation, which shall not be diminished during their Continuance in Office." Apart from establishing the Supreme Court, the Constitution says nothing about the subject of federal court organization; that matter is left to Congress.

Congress's power to punish individual members of the judiciary is limited, but recent impeachment proceedings reaffirm that all federal judges are "civil officers of the United States" within the meaning of Article II, section 4 of the Constitution and can be removed from office for the commission of "high crimes and misdemeanors" in the constitutional sense. Commission of, and conviction for, a criminal offense are not preconditions for impeachment (Kastenmeier and Remington, 1988, p. 56).

With respect to the classes of cases and controversies to which the judicial power of the United States extends, Article III, section 2 delineates nine categories, including controversies between citizens of different states and cases arising under the Constitution and federal laws. In cases affecting ambassadors, public ministers, and consuls, and those in which a state is a party, the Supreme Court has original jurisdiction. In all other cases, the Supreme Court has appellate jurisdiction, both as to law and as to fact, with such exceptions and under such regulations as the Congress shall make. Article VI declares that the Constitution, treaties, and laws of the United States shall be "the supreme Law of the Land" and that "the Judges in every State shall be bound thereby, any Thing in the Constitution or Laws of any State to the Contrary notwithstanding."

With regard to the selection of the federal bench, the Constitution states that the president shall nominate, "and by and with the Advice and Consent of the Senate" shall appoint judges of the Supreme Court and all other officers of the United States "whose Appointments are not herein otherwise provided for, and which shall be established by Law."

Article I, the legislature's guide, provides in section 8 that "Congress shall have the Power . . . To constitute Tribunals inferior to the supreme Court." In accordance with that article, Congress, beginning with the creation of the Court of Claims shortly before the Civil War, has established many specialized courts. These tribunals, known as legislative courts, which include the bankruptcy courts, the Tax Court and the Court of Military Appeals, do not provide judges with lifetime tenure. Congress thus has the flexibility to "modify or abolish the tribunal at any time in response to changing societal, legal, or political conditions" (Kastenmeier and Remington, 1988, p. 58).

HOW THE JUDICIARY AFFECTS CONGRESS. The judiciary affects Congress when it passes on the constitutionality of laws and interprets statutes.

Judging constitutionality. The Framers of the Constitution, having established the fundamental ground rules for the evolution of the new republic, left for succeeding generations the task of developing the character of relationships among institutions. Alexander M. Bickel wrote that

> Congress was created very nearly full blown by the Constitution itself. The vast possibilities of the presidency were relatively easy to perceive and soon, inevitably materialized. But the institution of the judiciary needed to be summoned up out of the constitutional vapors, shaped and maintained. And the Great Chief Justice, John Marshall—not singlehanded, but first and foremost—was there to do it and did. (Bickel, 1962)

Accordingly, the Supreme Court soon settled the question of whether it could invalidate an act of Congress.

In *Marbury v. Madison* (5 U.S. [1 Cranch] 137 [1803]), William Marbury asked the justices to order Secretary of State James Madison to deliver to him his commission as a justice of the peace for the District of Columbia. Marbury had been appointed to the position by outgoing president John Adams, but acting secretary of State John Marshall failed to deliver the commission before the Adams administration left office at midnight on 3 March. Marbury filed suit, asking that the Supreme Court issue a writ of mandamus to Secretary of State James Madison of the new Jefferson administration, pursuant to the Judiciary Act of 1789. Chief Justice Marshall recognized that the Jefferson administration was virtually certain to ignore any order directing Madison to deliver the commission, and such a consequence would undoubtedly have been ruinous for the Court. Thus, as Louis Fisher says: "Marshall chose a tactic he used in future years. He would appear to absorb a short-term defeat in exchange for a long-term victory" (Fisher, 1983, p. 55). The Court held that Marbury was entitled to his commission, but that it lacked authority to order its delivery. Chief Justice Marshall concluded that section 13 of the Judiciary Act of 1789 expanded the original jurisdiction of the Court, and thus violated Article III of the Constitution. The highest tribunal held that Congress could change only the appellate jurisdiction of the court. Asserting that the law conflicted with the Constitution, and that judges took an oath to support the Constitution, the chief justice wrote that the Court had the power to declare such an act void. The opinion, Robert G. McCloskey observes, is a "masterwork of indirection, a brilliant example of Marshall's capacity to sidestep danger while seeking to court it, to advance in one direction, while his opponents are looking in another" (McCloskey, 1960, p. 40).

Since 1803, the Supreme Court, according to one account, has voided, in whole or in part, some 120 pieces of legislation. Of these, several have figured especially prominently in U.S. history (Baum, 1985). For instance, in the Dred Scott case (60 U.S. [19 How.] 393 [1857]), the Court struck down provisions of the Missouri Compromise of 1820 having to do with slavery in the territories; in *Hammer v. Dagenhart* (247 U.S. 251 [1918]) and *Bailey v. Drexel Furniture Co.* (259 U.S. 20 [1922]), the Court invalidated laws designed to protect child labor; the Court overturned New Deal legislation in such decisions as *Carter v. Carter Coal Co.* (298 U.S. 238 [1936]) and *Schechter Poultry Corp. v. United States* (295 U.S. 495 [1935]); in *Buckley v. Valeo,* (424 U.S. 1 [1976]), the Court invalidated provisions

Replacing Oliver Wendell Holmes. This political cartoon, which appeared shortly after Justice Holmes announced his retirement on 12 January 1932, ridicules progressive Republican senators, who expressed doubts about all the leading contenders to replace Holmes. Bearing Who's Who in America, *the billygoat, cartoonist Clifford K. Berryman's symbol for the insurgents, suggests to President Hoover that nobody rises to the progressives' ideal.* Washington Evening Star, *January 1932. (Library of Congress)*

of the Federal Election Campaign Act relating to campaign financing; in its 1982 decision *Northern Pipeline Construction Co. v. Marathon Pipe Line Company* (458 U.S. 50 [1982]), it declared unconstitutional the bankruptcy court system Congress had created in 1978; and in *Immigration and Naturalization Service v. Chadha* (462 U.S. 919 [1983]), as well as some other related cases decided in 1983, the Court struck down the legislative veto.

On average, the Court overturns legislation, in whole or in part, more than once every two years (Baum, 1985, p. 169). In one sense, that activity affects only a fraction of the more than sixty thousand pieces of legislation Congress has enacted. In another sense, the real measure is the significance of the legislation under review and the consequences of the Court's action.

Lawrence Baum has reviewed historical patterns of judicial review and has identified periods in which the Court has been in "major" conflict with Congress as a legislator. The most conflictual period lasted from 1918 to 1936, when the Court overturned twenty-nine laws. That time period included the attack on the New Deal, which lessened with the Court's retreat in 1937. "Only in a single period, then, has the Court's power to review federal legislation been used to disturb a major line of federal policy" (Baum, 1985, p. 172).

Interpreting statutes. The judiciary touches the legislative branch not only when it renders a constitutional decision, but also when it interprets statutes in the quest to discern legislative intent (a subject to which we will later return). Indeed, in this age of statutes, the task of interpreting statutes has become a critical part of the legislative process (Mikva, 1987; Eskridge and Frickey, 1988). The courts are called upon to reach such decisions on matters of varying significance, ranging from the Standard Apple Barrel Act (1912), which set the dimensions for a standard barrel of apples and provided for penalties recoverable in federal court, to major legislation that affects every facet of American life, such as civil rights, the economy, and air and water pollution. Apart from diversity cases, Congress has vested jurisdiction in federal courts in legislation covering over three hundred subjects.

HOW CONGRESS AFFECTS THE JUDICIARY. Just as the judiciary affects Congress, so the legislature touches the courts in a variety of ways.

Confirmation. The president "shall nominate, and by and with the Advice and Consent of the Senate, shall appoint . . . Judges of the supreme Court." With these words, Article II of the Constitution sets forth the formal order of the appointment process, but little else. The charter of nationhood is silent about the bases for nomination and approval and about the balance of authority between the president and Congress in the confirmation process. Nor has the nation since prescribed exactly what criteria a nominee must meet to guarantee approval. Throughout the two-hundred-year history of the United States, the standards for confirmation have been the assertions of the Senate at the particular moment it considers a nominee. Altogether, twenty-eight nominees to the Supreme Court—nearly one out of five—have been rejected or have otherwise failed to take their seats on the Court (Katzmann, 1988b; Abraham, 1992).

Although the Senate has a formal role in the confirmation of all federal judges, the influence of individual senators is perhaps greatest in the choice of district court nominees. Appointments to the lower court are made following discussions between the executive branch and individual senators who belong to the same political party as the president, from the state where the appointment is being made. Senatorial courtesy allows a senator from the president's party to block a nomination. Senators from a particular state also can reach some agreement between them as to the allocation of appointments. For example, in New York, where the senators are of different parties, Daniel Patrick Moynihan (D) and Alfonse M. D'Amato (R) agreed that the senator whose president is in power has responsibility for recommending three out of every four nominees; the other senator makes the fourth recommendation (although the White House has not felt bound to follow that recommendation). The president exercises more authority over appellate judgeships, and even more over Supreme Court nominees. Even there, however, the White House consults with key senators and takes into account the likelihood of confirmation when making nominations.

Controversy surrounding confirmations is not a new development, nor is change in the confirmation process itself. Although the confirmation hearing is a standard practice today, it was not until 1925 that a Supreme Court nominee—Harlan Fiske Stone—testified before the Senate Judiciary Committee. Fourteen years and five confirmation proceedings elapsed before Felix Frankfurter became the second nominee to testify. As late as 1949, a nominee, Sherman Minton, could refuse to appear, asserting that his "record speaks for itself," and still be confirmed.

However standard the hearings have become, it was, at least until the 1987 hearings on Robert L. Bork, generally considered inappropriate to probe into a nominee's views about specific areas and doctrines. Since the Bork proceedings, senators have viewed ideology as an acceptable subject for questioning. The Bork nomination involved a change not only in the nature of the hearings, but also in lobbying techniques. In addition to trying to influence senators directly, several groups sought to mobilize public opinion. To defeat his nomination, Bork's opponents undertook an extensive media campaign that included advertisements on radio and television and in the newspapers.

Structure, function, procedure, and institutional health. The legislative branch not only has a role in determining who becomes a judge; it also shapes the structure of the judiciary. That has been true since the passage of the Judiciary Act of 1789 (24 September), which established a three-tier system: apart from the constitutionally created Supreme Court, it consisted of district courts and intermediate appellate bodies (circuit courts). Supreme Court justices and district court judges were the members of the intermediate courts. Little more than a century passed before Congress enacted the Evarts Act (1891), which established regional courts of appeals, with full-time judges. Congress has created thirteen circuits—twelve are regional; the other, the Court of Appeals for the Federal Circuit, has special jurisdiction over such cases as patents and government contracts.

On average, the Court overturns legislation, in whole or in part, more than once every two years.

Congress also sets the number of judges in the federal judiciary. In 1994, in addition to the 9 Supreme Court judges, there are 168 circuit judges, 575 district judges, 284 bankruptcy judges, and 280 magistrates. In expanding the judiciary, Congress generally responds to the requests of the judicial branch through its Judicial Conference, the policy-making arm of the courts. The Judicial Conference is an outgrowth of the Judiciary Act of 1922 (which in no small measure bore the imprint of Chief Justice William Howard Taft).

Congress not only affects the structure and size of the judiciary, but also has the power to regulate practice and procedure in the federal courts. The legislature in the first instance delegates to the courts the power to prescribe rules that regulate evidence, bankruptcy, appellate proceedings, and criminal and civil procedures, but retains the authority to veto those rules. Through its appropriations power, Congress has a significant effect on the financial health of the judiciary (in 1994, the judicial branch represented about 0.1 percent of the federal budget). Congress, through its legislative committees and the authorizations, oversight, and investigation processes, directly affects the administration of justice (Kastenmeier and Remington, 1988, pp. 65–70). The Judicial Conduct and Disability Act of 1980, the Speedy Trial Act of 1974, the Judicial Improvements and Access to Justice Act of 1988, and the Judicial Improvements Act of 1990 are examples of such legislative activity. The first created mechanisms within the judicial branch to assess complaints against judges; the second regulated the conduct of trials; the third (among other things) established within the Judicial Conference a Federal Courts Study Committee to study and report on the future of the federal judiciary; and the fourth created a national commission to examine judicial discipline and removal.

Legislation that affects judicial administration is the product of the Judiciary committees, in particular their subcommittees: the House Subcommittee on Intellectual Property and Judicial Administration and the Senate Subcommittee on Courts. The two Judiciary panels receive more bills and resolutions than any other committees in the House and Senate (Davidson, 1988, pp. 104–105), but interest in judicial administration tends to be restricted to the two subcommittees. Despite the fact that virtually all legislation affects the courts charged with interpreting statutes, few committees are cognizant of the consequences on the judiciary.

Congress is, of course, central to the determination of judicial pay, survivors' annuities, and travel expenses. With respect to salaries, the Commission on Executive, Legislative, and Judicial Salaries makes its report to the president by 15 December every four years, and the president then accepts, changes, or rejects its proposals. The president's recommendations take effect unless disapproved by a joint resolution of Congress, not later than thirty days following the transmittal of the recommendations.

Congressional responses to judicial decisions. In response to judicial decisions, Congress can take a variety of actions (Fisher, 1988, pp. 200–230). Four times, the legislative branch was a partner in the effort to overturn the Court through constitutional amendments. The Eleventh Amendment sought to reverse *Chisolm v. Georgia* (2 U.S. [2 Dall.] 419 [1793]), which held that a state could be sued in federal court by out-of-state plaintiffs; the Thirteenth, Fourteenth, and Fifteenth Amendments overturned *Scott v. Sandford* (60 U.S. [19 How.] 393 (1857]), which ruled that blacks as a class were not citizens protected by the Constitution; the Sixteenth Amendment overturned *Pollock v. Farmers' Loan and Trust Co.* (157 U.S. 429 [1895]), which voided a federal income tax; and the Twenty-sixth Amendment reversed a court decision, *Oregon v. Mitchell* (400 U.S. 112 [1970]), which had nullified a congressional attempt to lower the minimum voting age in state elections to eighteen.

Congress also occasionally passes legislation in reaction to judicial interpretations of its statutes (Henschen, 1983; Mikva and Bleich, 1991). Between 1967 and 1990, Congress overrode 121 of the Court's statutory decisions, compared with only 21 such reversals between 1945 and 1957 (Eskridge, 1991). One such example was legislation, passed over President Reagan's veto, responding to *Grove City College v. Bell* (464 U.S. 555 [1984]). In that case, the Supreme Court ruled that Title IX of the Education Amendments of 1972, which prohibited sex discrimination in any education program or activity that received federal financial assistance, applied only to those specific programs tainted by the discrimination. Congress's 1988 legislation essentially holds that federal funds would be terminated for the entire institution, not simply the specific program.

In another important instance, Congress overturned twelve rulings of the Court with the Civil Rights Act of 1991. Thus, it reversed *Wards Cove Packing, Inc. v. Atonio* (490 U.S. 642 [1989]) and returned the burden to employers (sued for discrimination) of proving that their hiring practices are "job-related to the position in question and consistent with business necessity." Congress, in that same act, reversed eight other decisions that had made it more difficult for women and African Americans to prove discrimination in employment—*Crawford Fitting Co. v. J. T. Gibbons, Inc.* (482 U.S. 437 [1987]); *Price Waterhouse v. Hopkins* (490 U.S. 228 [1989]); *West Virginia University Hospitals v. Casey* (111 S. Ct. 1138 [1991]); *Independent Federation of Flight Attendants v. Zipes* (491 U.S. 754 [1989]); *Evans v. Jeff D.* (474 U.S. 717 [1986]); and *Marek v. Chesney* (473 U.S. 1 [1985])—and less difficult for whites to challenge court-ordered affirmative-action programs—*Lorance v. AT&T* (490 U.S. 900 [1989]) and *Martin v. Wilks,* (490 U.S. 755 [1989]). Congress broadened the coverage of the 1866 Civil Rights Act to forbid discrimination in all phases of employment, not only in hiring practices, as the Rehnquist Court ruled in *Patterson v. McClean Credit Union* (485 U.S. 617 [1988]). Overturning *Equal Employment Opportunity Commission v. Arabian American Oil* (111 S.Ct. 1227 [1991]), Congress provided protection against discrimination based on race, religion, gender, and national origin to employees of American companies who are stationed abroad. Last, Congress overrode a 1986 decision, *Library of Congress v. Shaw* (478 U.S. 310 [1986]), to allow winning parties in cases against the federal government to recover interest payments as compensation for delays in securing awards for past discrimination. Through these various means, Congress thus engages in what Louis Fisher has called a "dialogue" (Fisher, 1988), or as Alexander Bickel put it, "a continuing colloquy" (Bickel, 1962, p. 240; Murphy, 1986, p. 401). Some in Congress have attempted to remove the Supreme Court from the decision-making process by withdrawing the Court's jurisdiction to hear appeals in such cases as school prayer, abortion, and school busing, but these endeavors have thus far failed.

PRESENT AND FUTURE STATE OF RELATIONS. If Congress and the judiciary affect each other in fundamental ways, each also feels that the other needs to better understand its institutional workings. From the judiciary's perspective, Congress seems often unaware of the courts' institutional needs. In this view, the legislative branch consistently adds to the judiciary's burdens without concomitant resources. Apart from the Judiciary committees and Appropriations committees of Congress, the sense is that few in the legislative branch focus on the problems of the courts. From the legislature's vantage point, the judiciary often seems unattuned to the critical nuances of the legislative process. Using strong words, Judge Frank M. Coffin, a former House member, described the state of affairs between the branches as one of "estrangement." Former Rep. Robert W. Kastenmeier and Judiciary Committee staff member Michael Remington commented that "as participants in the legislative process, we are struck by the simple fact that few in Congress know much about or pay attention to the third branch of government" (Kastenmeier and Remington, 1988, p. 54). Judge Deanell R. Tacha lamented that the "complexities of the law-making and law-interpreting tasks in the third century of this republic cry out for systematic dialogue between those who make and those who interpret legislation" (Tacha, 1991, p. 281). Yet many in each branch are uncertain about how and under what conditions they can interact with members of the others.

To some extent, the judiciary is hesitant to maintain a greater presence because of constitutional barriers against rendering advisory opinions and the need to avoid prejudging issues that might come before it. Even regarding nonadjudicatory matters, some of which directly affect the administration of justice, there is unease that Congress might view such involvement as improper. To be sure, the perception that the courts are above the political fray reinforces the judiciary's legitimacy, although such a stance is not without costs.

Members of Congress might be more sensitive to the problems of the courts if they were more knowledgeable about the courts' problems. In addition, Congress generally does not draw upon judicial experience when it revises laws. Courts that have had to grapple with statutes may have something useful to contribute when

Congress considers changing them; they may, for example, be able to identify parts of legislation that need legislative review. The gap between the branches, however, has inhibited such input.

Even more fundamentally, perhaps, distance has fostered among some on Capitol Hill a feeling of hostility toward the "Third Branch." Judges, according to this view, are unelected, imperial beings who mangle legislation to impose their preferences on society. But this perception ignores the irony that judicial action is often a function of legislative directives. Not infrequently, Congress passes the buck to the courts to avoid controversial choices and then blames judges for rendering decisions that it in fact mandated.

Congress also occasionally passes legislation in reaction to judicial interpretations of its statutes.

In recent years, efforts have been made by the judiciary and by some in Congress to bridge the gulf between the branches. The Administrative Office of the U.S. Courts, the Federal Judicial Center, and some of the committees of the Judicial Conference, particularly the Committee on the Judicial Branch, have all devoted attention to improving relations between the branches. More generally, Chief Justice William Rehnquist focused on improving interbranch relations as the theme of his 1992 end-of-the-year report. Within Congress, the Subcommittee on Intellectual Property, Civil Liberties, and the Administration of Justice of the House Committee on the Judiciary, and the Joint Committee on the Organization of Congress, have held hearings on problems of interbranch relations. Private organizations such as the Brookings Institution and the Governance Institute have also sought to work with both branches in an attempt to increase understanding between Congress and the courts. At the invitation of the U.S. Judicial Conference Committee on the Judicial Branch, the Governance Institute has undertaken a major project with two principal themes. The first examines the sorts of ground rules for communication and patterns of relationships that are proper. The second explores how the judiciary can better understand the legislative process and legislative history, how Congress can better signal the intent of its legislation, and how the courts can make the legislature better understand its decisions that interpret statutes. The objective is to devise or refine mechanisms to ameliorate relations between the branches. One product of that effort is a pilot project, begun with the participation of both chambers of Congress, in which the opinions of various courts of appeals, which identify problems in statutes, are sent to the legislative branch for consideration. This is but one more step that could help bridge the gulf between Congress and the courts.

No one should harbor any illusions about the ease with which some of the problems in judicial-congressional relations can be resolved. Indeed, some may simply be an inevitable part of the political system. But to the extent that one branch better appreciates the processes of the other, unnecessary tensions may be avoided.

[See also (I) Constitution, Judicial Review, Legislative Courts, Legislative Intent; (III) The Judiciary.]

BIBLIOGRAPHY

Abraham, Henry J. *Justices and Presidents.* 3d ed. 1992.

Baum, Lawrence. *The Supreme Court.* 1985.

Bickel, Alexander M. *The Least Dangerous Branch.* 1962.

Davidson, Roger H. "What Judges Ought to Know about Lawmaking in Congress." *In Judges and Legislators.* Edited by Robert A. Katzmann. 1988.

Eskridge, William N., Jr. "Overriding Supreme Court Statutory Interpretation Decisions." *Yale Law Journal* 101 (1991):331, 338.

Eskridge, William N., Jr., and Philip Frickey. *Cases and Materials on Legislation: Statutes and the Creation of Public Policy.* 1988.

Fisher, Louis. *Constitutional Dialogues: Interpretation as Political Process.* 1988.

Henschen, Beth. "Statutory Interpretations of the Supreme Court: Congressional Response." *American Political Quarterly* 11 (1983): 441.

Kastenmeier, Robert W., and Michael S. Remington. "A Judicious Legislator's Lexicon to the Federal Judiciary." In *Judges and Legislators.* Edited by Robert A. Katzmann. 1988.

Katzmann, Robert A. "Approaching the Bench: Judicial Confirmation in Perspective." *Brookings Review* 6 (Spring 1988): 42–46.

Katzmann, Robert A. *Institutional Disability: The Sage of Transportation Policy for the Disabled.* 1986.

Katzmann, Robert A. *Judges and Legislators: Toward Institutional Comity.* 1988.

McCloskey, Robert G. *The American Supreme Court.* 1960.

Melnick, R. Shep. "The Politics of Partnership." *Public Administration Review* 45 (November 1985): 653–660.

Mikva, Abner J. "Reading and Writing Statutes." *University of Pittsburgh Law Review* 48 (1987): 627.

Mikva, Abner J., and Jeff Bleich. "When Congress Overrides the Court." *California Law Review* 79 (1991): 729.

Murphy, Walter F. "Who Shall Interpret? The Quest for the Ultimate Constitutional Interpreter." *Review of Politics* 48 (1986): 401.

Shapiro, Martin M. *Who Guards the Guardians? Judicial Control of Administration.* 1988.

Tacha, Deanell. "Judges and Legislators: Renewing the Relationship." *Ohio State Law Journal* 52 (1991): 279, 281.

– ROBERT A. KATZMANN

L

LAME DUCK SESSION

The term *lame duck session* refers to the time Congress is in session between the November congressional elections and the convening of the new Congress following those elections. The defeated members of Congress who remain in office during this time are the lame ducks. Lame duck, which has British origins in the early nineteenth century, originally described a bankrupt businessman. The expression found application in politics, where it is used to describe a defeated officeholder or a political party, or the time period between an incumbent's defeat at the polls and the beginning of the successor's term. Its usage in the United States dates from the 1830s according to some authorities. While the term can apply to state and local politics, most often it is used to characterize a president or a Congress.

The Continental Congress set 4 March 1789 as the date the First Federal Congress under the new Constitution would meet. In an age when the nation was largely agricultural and when transportation and communication over long distances consumed considerable time, the length of time between the fall elections and a 4 March beginning date did not seem particularly long. Furthermore, Congress, with some exceptions, convened a new session in December of the year following the elections, which meant that newly elected members had to wait thirteen months before taking office.

The ratification of the Twentieth Amendment of the Constitution (sometimes called the lame duck amendment) on 23 January 1933 addressed both the problem of shortening the time period between the election and the assumption of office and the long time period between election and the beginning of a new session of Congress, calling for Congress to convene on 3 January (unless another date close to this is selected by law). It also stipulates that the terms of the president and vice president begin on 20 January.

Prior to the adoption of the Twentieth Amendment critics pointed to the potential mischief of the lame duck session. On the rare occurrences when the House of Representatives was called upon to select a president, lame ducks took part in the process. Some questioned whether a lame duck could remain an effective member of Congress and represent the wishes of his or her district if they were more interested in voting to improve their chances for a job with the new administration or in private life.

BIBLIOGRAPHY

Safire, William. *Safire's Political Dictionary.* 1980.

U.S. Congress. *Congressional Record.* 69th Cong., 2d sess., 3 March 1927. See Emanuel Celler, "Lame Ducks: Exclusively American," pp. 5673–5678.

– RAYMOND W. SMOCK

LAWMAKING

The legislative process in practice is a complex maze through which measures must wind their way. The efficient assembly line portrayed in a typical legislative process flow chart may be true for some noncontroversial issues, but for more significant measures, a game of chess is a more accurate analogy. Most legislative moves can be met with a countermove. What is lost at one stage of the process can be reclaimed at another. The reverse is also true. Victory in an earlier phase may turn into defeat later. Until the stage of public law is reached, no game of legislative chess is truly over. A bill may clear the entire legislative labyrinth, only to be vetoed by the president. Conversely, there are instances in which bills are enacted without passing through all of the earlier legislative stages. Therefore, while the narrative that follows describes the usual route most measures travel, it does not encompass all the possible procedural side roads the legislative process permits.

Moreover, legislation is not processed solely in a procedural context. The need for a political consensus and the complexities of policy disputes also contribute to a measure's progress along the legislative path. Those measures that become public law reach that end only through a combination of political, policy, and procedural factors.

DEVELOPMENT AND INTRODUCTION. While only members of the House or Senate may introduce a bill, the idea for the measure can come from many different sources. The president, federal department or agency officials, state governors or legislatures, interest groups, lobbyists, constituents, or congressional staff may contribute to a member's decision to initiate a specific proposal.

The primary motive for introducing a bill is enactment into law. However, a bill may also be introduced

How a Bill Becomes a Law

This illustration shows the most typical way in which proposed legislation is enacted into law. There are more complicated as well as simpler routes, and most bills never become law. The process is illustrated with two hypothetical bills, House bill No. 1 (H.R. 1) and Senate bill No. 2 (S. 2). Bills must be passed by both houses in identical form before they can be sent to the president. The path of H.R. 1 is traced by a solid line, that of S. 2 by a dotted line. In practice, most bills begin as similar proposals in both houses.

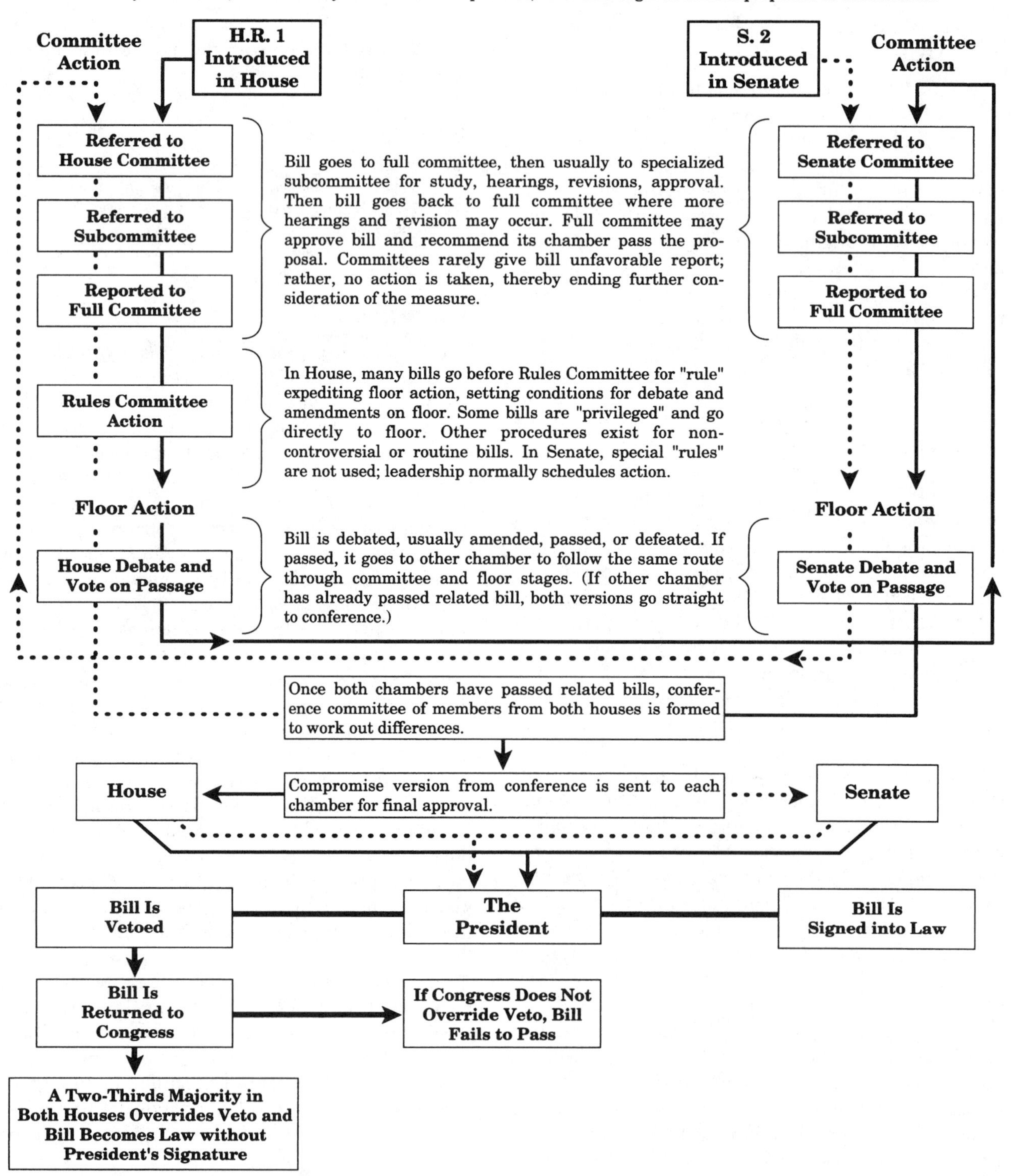

(Congressional Quarterly, Inc.)

for other reasons: for example, to establish a member's political position on an issue; to spur desired executive or judicial action; to serve as a basis for policy development; or as a vehicle to heighten public awareness of an issue.

The member who introduces a measure is known as that bill's sponsor. Other members who wish to associate themselves with the proposal are known as its cosponsors. Members strive to collect a large number of cosponsors prior to introducing a bill in the hopes that it will signal that the proposal has significant support and merits priority consideration. In the House chamber, members introduce their bills by dropping them into a deep wooden box located on the Speaker's dais, known as the hopper. In the Senate chamber, bills are handed to a clerk at the rostrum. The bills are printed and copies distributed to all members. Copies of bills are also available to the public through the House or Senate document rooms or the Government Printing Office.

Both the House and Senate provide the services of nonpartisan legislative counsels to assist members in drafting the legal language necessary to transform their legislative proposal into the text of a bill. Members may also choose to accept draft language for a bill from interest groups, or assign the drafting responsibility to their own staff.

The term *bill* is commonly used interchangeably with the term *measure* to refer to any piece of legislation. However, there are clear distinctions between bills, joint resolutions, and concurrent and simple resolutions. Measures designed to become public law must technically take the form of bills or joint resolutions. House bills are expressed as "H.R. 1000" (the actual numbers vary), while those that originate in the Senate are numbered "S. 1000." House joint resolutions are labeled "H.J. Res. 100," while those in the Senate are marked "S.J. Res. 100." While no rule stipulates whether a proposed law be drafted as a bill or a joint resolution, some traditions apply. For example, proposals to amend the Constitution are normally drafted as joint resolutions, as are some appropriation bills and commemorative measures. Bills and joint resolutions must pass both chambers and receive the president's approval or survive his veto to become law.

Concurrent resolutions do not make law but are used to take an action on behalf of the Congress as a whole, or to express congressional opinion on a matter. The House version is tagged "H. Con. Res. 100," while the Senate label is "S. Con. Res. 100." Concurrent resolutions must pass both chambers, but are not presented to the president.

Simple resolutions take action on behalf of one chamber alone, or express the opinion of only that body. They are classified as either "H. Res. 100" or "S. Res. 100." Because these proposals affect only one chamber, they are sent neither to the other body nor to the president.

The life span of a measure is limited to the two-year Congress in which it is introduced. Measures die at the end of a Congress unless they are enacted prior to its final adjournment. If passed by Congress and approved by the president, bills become either public or private law. Proposals that affect the nation at large become public laws, while proposals that seek relief for only one individual or legal entity become private laws.

REFERRAL TO COMMITTEE. After introduction, most measures are referred to a legislative committee for review. House and Senate rules establish the specific subject matter areas, known as jurisdiction, of each chamber's standing committees. In the House, the Speaker makes the referral decision based on advice from the House parliamentarian, a nonpartisan employee of the chamber. In the Senate, the presiding officer refers measures pursuant to the recommendations of its parliamentarian. In making their referral decisions, the parliamentarians rely on their chambers jurisdiction rule, as well as past historical practice, known as precedents.

Some measures encompass subject matter that may fall within the purview of more than one legislative committee. Referral to more than one committee, known as multiple referral, is possible in both chambers. Multiple referrals come in three varieties. A "joint" referral sends an entire bill to two or more committees simultaneously. A "sequential" referral sends an entire bill first to one committee, and subsequently to a second or more committees. A "split" referral sends most of the measure to one committee but splits off a provision, usually an entire title, and sends just the designated portion to another committee. If a bill has been multiply referred, it is not eligible for floor consideration until all the committees involved have completed their work. As a result, a multiple referral tends to reduce a bill's chances of reaching the floor. The complexities of coordinating disparate political perspectives and committee schedules inherent in a multiple referral are sometimes enough to halt a measure's progress. At times, however, the presiding officer may impose a time deadline on each committee involved in a multiple referral. In such cases, a measure's progress may actually be speeded up.

Because most legislation that fails to become law fails to clear the committee process, the decision on committee referral can be crucial. Members sometimes employ creative drafting techniques to ensure that a bill is referred to a committee inclined to give it favorable consideration.

COMMITTEE HEARINGS. Once a committee receives a measure it may keep it at the full committee level for processing, or it may refer it to one of its subcommittees. Individual committee rules, which differ, govern this practice. Hearings on a measure are usually first held at the subcommittee level, although this is not mandatory. The full committee may accept the views developed during the subcommittee's review, or choose to hold its own hearings, which must be open to the public unless the committee, in open session, votes to close further proceedings. This is rarely done except in cases where national security issues or pending court cases are involved. Most hearings are held in Washington, D.C., although so-called field hearings are sometimes scheduled in localities across the country.

The legislative process in practice is a maze through which measures must wind their way.

Hearings serve a variety of purposes. They may be planned to help a committee gain specific information and advice from expert witnesses in order to perfect the policies and the language of the legislation under consideration. Some hearings are designed to explore whether or not legislation in a given area is even necessary. Hearings can be devised to increase public awareness of an issue, or to simply provide a forum for interested individuals and groups to express their views or frustrations with certain federal policies. Hearings are also structured to investigate problems or to conduct a review of executive branch performance or programs, known as oversight.

Each committee has its own rules governing various aspects of hearing procedure, such as quorum requirements, calling of witnesses, scheduling, and order of recognition. Copies of a committee's rules can be obtained from the committee or from the *Congressional Record.* Hearings usually consist of committee members making opening remarks, listening to prepared statements offered by witnesses, and posing questions to those witnesses. Witnesses are most frequently federal agency or department officials, members of Congress, representatives of interest groups or trade associations, technical specialists, or academic experts.

Committees are required to keep a verbatim transcript of hearings held, and these may be examined by the public. Most committees eventually publish a full record of the hearing, including the texts of witness statements not delivered and other related material inserted for the record. The hearing record becomes a part of a measure's legislative history, although it reflects only the preliminary explorations of that panel and does not necessarily indicate the entire chamber's perspective on the issue.

Hearings are a good, but not final, indicator that a measure will receive further legislative action. Legislative enactment is not the motivation behind all hearings; conversely, some legislation is enacted even though it was never the subject of committee hearings.

COMMITTEE MARKUP. Markups are committee meetings held to discuss and often revise the text of a particular bill. The term is derived from the practice of literally marking up the original text of the bill to reflect changes adopted by the committee. Committees may also decide not to alter the original bill at all, although this rarely happens.

Markups can be held on bills previously introduced and referred to the committee, or on informal drafts of bills not yet introduced. Such drafts are commonly referred to as the "chairman's mark" because it is the chairman of the committee who typically initiates the proposed text.

Markups are held at either the subcommittee or full committee level, or both. The full committee may choose to accept the subcommittee's proposed changes, or it may decide to revise the text further. Markups usually follow the completion of hearings, although hearings are not a required prerequisite to holding a markup. Markups are usually open to the public, but a committee or subcommittee may decide by majority vote to close a particular session, usually done if national or international security issues are involved.

Committees vary in their reliance on parliamentary procedure during a markup. Some panels require that proposals to change text be offered as formal amendments, each of which must receive a vote. Other committees prefer a more informal approach. Changes to the text are discussed and negotiated and committee staff are delegated the task of drafting the precise language to reflect these agreements. Committees may report a bill with one amendment that substitutes an entire new text for the original, or with a series of amendments that make lesser changes throughout the bill. At times, committees choose to report an entirely new measure, written in committee, for the original text. These are known as clean bills in the House, and original bills in the Senate.

Markup sessions normally end with a vote on whether or not to report the revised version to the House or Senate floor with a recommendation for passage by the chamber. This vote must be taken at the full committee level, with a quorum present, or the measure may later be ruled out of order.

COMMITTEE REPORTS. Committee reports explain the committee's actions on a bill and present the case for passage to the full chamber. Committee reports are required in the House, but are optional in the Senate. They accompany a reported bill to the floor and are filed along with it.

Reports must contain a section-by-section analysis of the measure and describe the changes the committee recommends to the original text. Reports must also contain a comparison with the text of existing law to show how the committee version proposes to alter it. Other content requirements include roll-call votes taken in committee, cost estimates of implementing the legislation, and regulatory impact statements, among others. Frequently comments received from federal agencies on the proposed legislation, known as executive comments, are included.

Committee members may also place their own individual views in the report. Statements essentially in agreement with the viewpoint expressed in the report are inserted as "supplemental" or "additional" views. Statements in opposition to the committee's perspective are incorporated as "minority" or "dissenting" views. These individual statements often signal possible floor amendments and debating points.

Hearings are a good, but not final, indicator that a measure will receive further legislative action.

Committee reports serve as an essential part of a bill's legislative history. If the measure is enacted into law, the federal agencies responsible for its implementation will turn to the committee report for guidance on congressional intent. Courts of law also consult committee reports to aid in interpreting the meaning of the text.

Procedures exist in both the House and Senate that permit the chamber to consider a bill not yet reported from committee. When time constraints make expediting the legislative process necessary, committees often arrange for a friendly floor motion or a unanimous consent request to be discharged from further consideration of a measure. The effect of discharging a committee also supplants the House requirement for a committee report.

GETTING TO THE FLOOR. Legislation reported from a House committee is placed on one of two primary calendars (House or Union) or on one of three specialized calendars (Consent, Private, or District of Columbia). In the Senate, all legislation is placed on the Calendar of General Orders (known as the Legislative Calendar). Executive branch business (nominations or treaties) reported from a Senate committee are placed on the Executive Calendar. Placement on a calendar, however, does not guarantee that an item will receive floor consideration. The majority leadership in both chambers selects the floor agenda, basing their choices on a variety of political, procedural, and scheduling factors.

Once the decision has been made to turn to a specific measure, the chamber's leadership chooses from among several procedures available to call up a bill for floor consideration. The choice of procedure is crucial because it also determines the conditions under which the bill will be debated and amended. Some procedures allow for open-ended debate and amending, while others severely restrict the opportunity for legislators to discuss or change the measure before them.

House leaders call up most bills under a set of restrictions known as the "suspension of the rules" procedure. As its name connotes, the suspension procedure waives the regular rules of order. Measures brought up under the suspension procedure are debated for no more than forty minutes and may not be amended from the floor. Therefore, the vote on final passage occurs on the unaltered committee version of a bill.

Moreover, because the suspension procedure waives all normal rules of procedure, points of order against a measure are prohibited. This concept extends to the committee reporting requirements. Measures brought up under suspension of the rules need not have been formally reported by their committee of jurisdiction, nor is a committee report necessary. The suspension procedure is also useful for the consideration of conference reports that may contain rules violations. In a measure brought up under suspension, the fact that conferees may have inserted new language that was not in either the original House or Senate version or may have taken out language that appeared in both versions is not subject to challenge.

The most controversial measures in the House are called up under the auspices of a "special rule" from the House Rules Committee. A special rule temporarily replaces the regular rules of order, serving as a blueprint for a bill's consideration. It imposes upon the chamber uniquely crafted debate and amending conditions for the specified measure, taking into account the political factions and policy disputes that affect that particular bill. However, before it can take effect, a special rule must be adopted by a majority vote of the House.

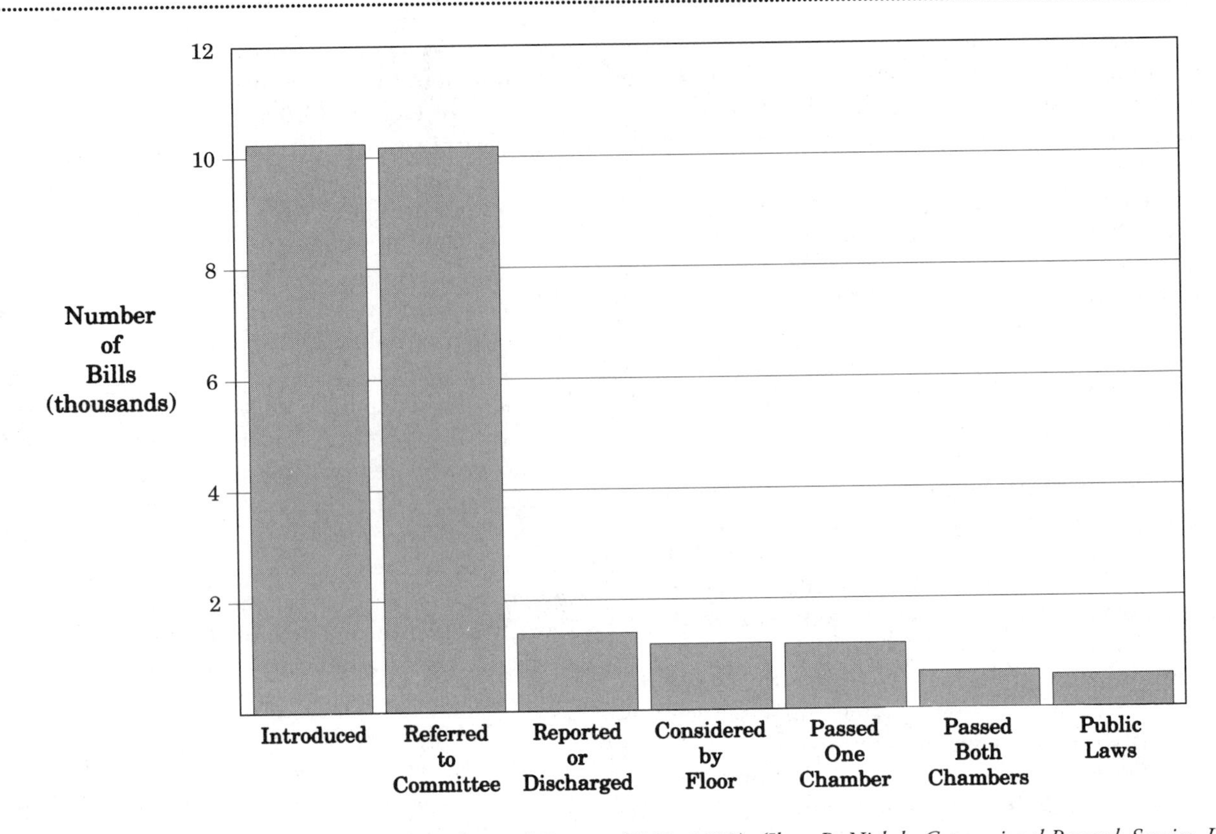

From Bill to Law: House and Senate Statistics[1] from the 102d Congress (1991–1993). (Ilona B. Nickels, Congressional Research Service, Library of Congress, Washington, D.C.)

[1]Statistics represent only measures that can become public law (i.e., bills and joint resolutions). Simple resolutions, concurrent resolutions, and private bills are excluded.

Special rules typically have four routine provisions. The first makes it in order to call up the bill for consideration. The second provision sets a time limit on general debate and allocates that time between the majority and minority parties. The third structures the amending process by either allowing all amendments (a so-called open rule), no amendments except those reported by the committee (a closed rule), some amendments but only by specified individuals (a modified closed rule), or all amendments except those to certain portions of the bill protected from change (a modified open rule). In its final provision, a special rule may prohibit points of order, which means that technical violations in the text of the bill or in a designated floor amendment may not be challenged.

Special rules are frequently controversial and the subject of intense debate. Members of the majority party see special rules as a method of establishing priorities among the legislative agendas of 435 members, and of streamlining the consideration of conflicting policy perspectives. However, minority party members often view special rules as unduly restricting lawmaking by overly curtailing debate and excessively limiting amendments.

The House leadership calls up the least controversial bills under unanimous consent practices. In most instances, these measures attract little attention and receive no debate, no amendments, and passage "without objection" or by voice vote.

Finally, a very small number of bills are called up under either the Private, Consent, or District of Columbia calendars. Measures on those calendars are called up for floor consideration during two specified days per month, under the particular procedures prescribed by the individual rules governing that calendar.

In the Senate, measures most often are brought up by a simple request to turn to a specified bill's immediate consideration. If the request meets no objection, the Senate debates and amends the bill without any restrictions. A second method is a unanimous consent agreement, negotiated in advance by the Senate majority and minority leaders among all interested senators on their respective side of the aisle. Often called time agreements, these contracts for a bill's consideration impose time limitations on debate, restrict the offering of amendments and motions, and sometimes provide for a "vote certain" on final passage. The agreement takes effect unless an objection is registered at the time it is formally proposed by the majority leader on the Senate floor.

A motion to proceed to the consideration of a bill is the final method by which a measure can be raised for floor consideration in the Senate. The motion requires a simple majority vote for adoption. However, it is fully debatable and is often subjected to a filibuster. Ending a filibuster requires sixty votes, a super-majority. If the filibuster is ended and the motion to proceed is adopted, the measure called up is itself subject to another filibuster. Therefore, unless assured of the support of at least sixty senators, the Senate majority leader uses the motion to proceed sparingly.

DEBATE AND AMENDING. The normal debate rule of the House is the "one-hour rule," which provides one hour of debate, equally divided between the majority and minority party, for any measure or matter brought up in the House. However, special rules or the suspension of the rules procedure frequently supersede the one-hour rule.

The House conducts debate on the most significant measures in another forum, the *Committee of the Whole,* the term used to describe the House when it meets as the Committee of the Whole House on the State of the Union. Debate is still conducted in the House chamber, with the full membership of the House, but under different procedures. To signal the change of forum, the Speaker leaves the podium and appoints a majority party member as chairman to preside over the Committee of the Whole. The mace is removed by its keeper, the sergeant at arms. When members wish to address the chair, they now forsake "Mr. or Madame Speaker" in favor of "Mr. or Madame Chairman." With these symbolic changes, the House has resolved itself into the Committee of the Whole.

The rules of procedure employed in the Committee of the Whole expedite the consideration of bills. As a result, it is the favored forum for all measures to which numerous amendments are expected. Instead of the one-hour rule, the five-minute rule operates in the Committee of the Whole. It provides for five minutes for the proponents and five minutes for the opponents of any amendment offered. However, the time for debate is frequently extended on more controversial amendments through unanimous consent or parliamentary devices known as pro forma amendments.

At the end of general debate on a bill, the Committee of the Whole begins the amending process. The bill is normally presented to the chamber for amendment section by section, and amendments must be offered at the right time in the sequence, or they will be ruled out of order. Amendments must also be germane, or relevant, to the subject matter of the bill. When all allowed amendments are disposed of, the Committee of the Whole "rises," transforming itself back into the House. Amendments adopted by the Committee of the Whole must also be approved by the House. Usually they are endorsed as a package with one vote. However, at times a member will insist on a separate vote on one or more of the amendments agreed to in the Committee of the Whole. As the parent chamber, the House has the last word, and, at times, has reversed the decision of the Committee of the Whole on an amendment.

The Senate's rules governing debate and amendment are in sharp contrast to the strictly regulated debate period and the sequential and orderly amending process in the House. The regular order in the Senate places no restrictions on debate time nor on the number or nature of amendments. As a result, it is always difficult to predict for how long the Senate will consider a particular measure. This emphasis in the Senate on deliberation, not on efficiency, is in keeping with the Founders' original concept for a bicameral Congress. The ability to force deliberation in the Senate was viewed as a check on decisions that might be taken too hastily and with insufficient examination by a House eager to respond to popular opinion.

Once recognized, senators may speak for as long as they wish on a bill. It is this right to extend debate that allows a senator to conduct a filibuster, the Senate's term for speaking at length to prohibit the chamber from coming to a vote on final passage. At times senators voluntarily cede their rights to unlimited debate by agreeing to a unanimous consent agreement that sets debate limitations.

The House leadership calls up the least controversial bills under unanimous consent practices.

Amendments in the Senate may be offered when any senator so desires. Bills are open to amendment at any point, and no chronological sequence is observed. In most circumstances, amendments in the Senate need not be germane to the subject matter of the bill under consideration. This allows senators the ability to bring to the floor of the Senate subject matter of their own choosing. Nongermane amendments, known as riders, are frequently offered with motives other than passage in mind. They may be used as devices to focus the attention of the Senate, and in dramatic cases, of the nation, upon topics a senator feels merit immediate attention. Nongermane amendments are integral to the concept of minority rights in the Senate. Such amendments serve as a method by which the decisions of the majority party concerning the agenda can be supplemented or even circumvented.

In the interests of hastening the legislative process, senators sometimes do permit unanimous consent agreements to establish a germaneness requirement for amendments. In a few specified circumstances, Senate procedure also requires amendments to be germane. However, these restrictions are often set aside. As a result, the amending process in the Senate is often complex in nature and extensive in reach.

FINAL PASSAGE AND VOTING PROCEDURES. The House may dispose of the question of final passage by one of four voting methods. The bill may pass "without objection" or by unanimous consent. If even one objection is heard, the chair will put the question of final passage to a voice vote. The yeas and nays are shouted aloud and the chair declares his or her judgment as to which side prevailed. Any member dissatisfied with the opinion of the chair may demand a division vote, a standing vote in which members are counted as they stand in support or opposition to the bill.

The final method of voting is the record vote, and it alone places members on record. A record vote requires a sufficient second. If it is ordered, members in the House vote by electronic device. Members are issued plastic identification cards, which are inserted into voting stations on the House floor. They press a button for their chosen position and their vote is instantly displayed on the chamber's vote tally board. Each record vote is also printed in the *Congressional Record.* The House has three forms of record votes: the yeas and nays, an automatic roll-call, and a recorded vote. They are each obtained differently, but all are conducted in the same way and have the same result—a member's position becomes a matter of public record.

In the Senate, the same four methods of voting are used. However, the Senate has only one form of record vote, known as the yeas and nays. No electronic machinery exists. Instead, a clerk reads each senator's name aloud and waits for a response. The call of the roll is repeated; thereafter, senators are recognized out of sequence as they appear in the chamber to signal their position. In both chambers, the period for a vote is established at a minimum of fifteen minutes. Sufficient time is allowed to give members the ability to reach the chamber from their offices and committee rooms. Bells ring throughout the Capitol complex to signal a vote. In addition, many members carry beepers to alert them of a pending vote. Often the voting period is held open in order to convince undecided members to change their votes when the margin is close.

RESOLVING DIFFERENCES BETWEEN THE HOUSES. The House and Senate each must pass identical versions of a bill before it can proceed to the president for his signature or veto. Because the two chambers so often enact differing versions of the same bill, the differences must be fully resolved before the bill can progress. The two chambers use one of two methods to reconcile their versions: a conference committee or a procedure known as amendments between the houses. Although conferences are the better known method, more measures are reconciled using the amendments between the houses procedure.

In the latter method the House and Senate exchange the text of a bill back and forth, each further amending the changes last made by the other. The ping-pong match continues until one chamber concurs with the last amendment of the other body, making no further changes. The differences in text are thus resolved and the measure is cleared for the White House. This method is favored when the number of members interested in the final text of the measure is minimal, when no written reports are needed or required, or when time deadlines make it difficult to convene a conference committee.

The conference process begins when members of the House and Senate are appointed by their presiding officer to serve as their chamber's representatives on a conference committee. Known as conferees, they come primarily from the standing committees that initially reported the bill. The conference committee's responsibility is to negotiate a compromise text from the two differing versions. Their final agreement is known as the conference report. The conference report must be adopted by a majority in both the House and Senate. If one chamber defeats the conference report, the other body takes no action on it. Once the report has passed both the House and Senate, it is presented to the president for his review.

PRESIDENTIAL ACTION. The final version of a bill is prepared for formal presentation to the president by the enrolling clerk of the chamber where the measure originated. The president is given ten days to review the proposed law, not counting Sundays or the day on

RESOLVING HOUSE AND SENATE DIFFERENCES, 102D CONGRESS

Method of Resolving Differences	Percent of Laws	Number of Laws
Adoption of measure without change by second chamber	68	404
Exchange of amendments between the houses	20	118
Conference committees	12	68

which the measure was received by the White House. Four options are available to the president. First, the president can sign the measure into law. Second, the president can permit the bill to become law without his signature, which occurs when ten days pass without his taking action, but only if Congress is in session. Third, the president can "pocket veto" the bill. If ten days pass and the president takes no action, the measure does not become law, but only if Congress *is not* in session due to an adjournment. Fourth, the president can veto the bill. If Congress is still in session, he may return the measure to the chamber that originated it with a veto message expressing his objections to the bill. Two-thirds of that chamber, with a quorum present, must vote to again pass the bill "the President's objections notwithstanding." If the vote (known as a veto override) is successful, the bill is sent to the other body, which also must pass the bill over the president's objections with a two-thirds vote of those present. If both chambers are able to override the veto, the bill becomes law.

The complexities of parliamentary procedure make it far simpler to block the progress of a bill than to secure its passage.

The complexities of parliamentary procedure make it far simpler to block the progress of a bill than to secure its passage. Only those measures aggressively promoted and with sufficient political appeal will reach the ultimate goal of public law. In recent years, no more than 7 percent of all the legislation introduced in each Congress has become public law. This statistic reveals that the legislative process is truly "Darwinian," permitting only the survival of the fittest.

[See also (I) Amending, Bills, Committees, Subcommittees; (II) Veto, Pocket, Veto, Regular.]

BIBLIOGRAPHY

Congressional Quarterly Inc. *How Congress Works.* 2d ed. 1991.

Green, Alan. *Gavel to Gavel: A Guide to the Televised Proceedings of Congress.* C-SPAN and the Benton Foundation. 1986.

U.S. House of Representatives. *How Our Laws are Made.* 101st Cong., 2d sess., 1990. H. Doc. 101-139.

– ILONA B. NICKELS

LEADERSHIP

House Leadership

In 1959, political scientist David Truman described the complexity of congressional leadership: "Everyone knows something of leaders and leadership of various sorts, but no one knows very much. Leadership, especially in the political realm, unavoidably or by design often is suffused by an atmosphere of the mystic and the magical, and these have been little penetrated by systematic observation" (Truman, 1959, p. 94). House leadership remains a complex concept, but it has been defined more clearly and more systematically in the years since Truman's observation.

An explanation and evaluation of House leadership should incorporate at least four key elements: (1) the functions of the House of Representatives; (2) the context, or conditions under which those functions are performed; (3) a description of the various formal and informal leadership positions; and (4) the individual leaders themselves.

GENERAL CONSIDERATIONS. A general concept of House leadership can be developed with reference to the functions of the House, the conditions that affect House politics, and the role of individual leaders. After taking a look at these overarching considerations, the remaining sections of this article describe the tasks, styles, and strategies pursued by three types of House leaders: party, committee, and informal leaders.

Functions. All institutions are designed to perform certain functions, and leaders are expected to assist in those functions. The primary functions of the House of Representatives are lawmaking and representation; leadership can be defined in terms of those functions. "Leadership is an organizational condition facilitating the expression [i.e., representation] and integration [i.e., lawmaking] of opinions, facts, and conclusions among the extended membership (to include staff) at different stages of the lawmaking process" (Charles O. Jones, "House Leadership in an Age of Reform," in Mackaman, 1981, p. 119). Thus, a conception of House leadership should identify the specific tasks, strategies, and styles that leaders pursue as they attempt to facilitate lawmaking and representation.

Context. The actions of House leaders are influenced partly by the context, or the conditions under which the House attempts to make laws and represent interests. Ideally, leaders seek to facilitate both representation and lawmaking, but circumstances often limit their capacity to do so. Some conditions are conducive to lawmaking, while others favor representation. Under some circumstances neither representation nor lawmaking is easily served, making leadership extremely difficult. Political scientists are interested in understanding how the particular set of conditions at any given time affects the tasks, styles, and strategies of House leaders.

Context is defined by three categories of factors: institutional, political, and issue-agenda factors. Institutional factors include the organization, rules, and procedures of the House and the constitutional arrangements (bicameralism, separation of powers, and checks and balances) that define the House's role in the political system. Political factors include the outcomes of elections and the strength of political parties. Elections determine the relative numbers of Democrats and Republicans in the House and Senate as well as the party represented by the president. House leadership also depends on the strength of party organizations—specifically, their capacity to nominate candidates for office—and party unity within the Congress. The issue agenda consists of the policy issues debated and deliberated in the committees and on the floor of the House.

The variety of conditions that affect how leaders attempt to facilitate lawmaking and representation confirms the notion that House leadership is a complex phenomenon. While some conditions are very stable (e.g., bicameralism), others change occasionally with institutional reforms (e.g., reforms of the committee system) and still others change periodically (e.g., electoral outcomes). Thus, leadership depends on the enduring conditions that shape the general patterns of lawmaking and representation as well as the changing conditions that alter leadership tasks, styles, and strategies.

Enduring conditions support at least three general, complementary propositions about House leadership. Each proposition will necessarily be refined to fit specific leadership positions and particular circumstances, but together they provide a general framework for the concept of House leadership.

First, since leaders are elected by House members, leadership requires the leaders to pay attention to members' goals. The most difficult questions are determining what the members want and how their preferences relate to those of the leaders—questions that can be answered only by reference to specific leadership positions under a given set of conditions.

Second, there are limitations to strong, centralized leadership in the House of Representatives. Speaker of the House Joseph G. Cannon (R-Ill.) and Rules Committee Chairman Howard W. Smith (D-Va.) both exceeded the acceptable bounds of authority in the eyes of most members (see Jones, 1968). Although the degree of centralized power in the House has varied over time, there are always limitations to the power a leader can exercise.

Finally, leadership style typically, though not always, involves bargaining with other members and accommodating their preferences. With few exceptions, House leaders have lacked the power to dictate policy or procedure to the members.

These general tendencies of leadership stem from three relatively stable conditions that have defined representation and lawmaking in the House: constituency representation, weak parties, and a fragmented committee system. Perhaps the most enduring feature of House politics from the standpoint of leadership is that members are obliged to pursue the interests of their constituents. A second important condition for understanding party leadership is that, with the exception of a brief period at the turn of the twentieth century, congressional parties generally have been weak, and party leaders have lacked the power to discipline members. The combination of strong constituency representation and weak parties normally gives members a certain degree of autonomy from leaders. And since leaders are ultimately selected by the members, they must be responsive to the members' goals and preferences. A third prevailing feature of House politics is its decentralized committee system. Except for the period of strong parties (1890–1910), power in the House has traditionally been dispersed among numerous committees. There have been circumstances under which members have tolerated centralized party leadership, but members accept such leadership only if it helps them satisfy their political and policy goals.

Personality. A third critical aspect of House leadership is the individual leader. Whereas political scientists tend to emphasize the context within which leaders operate, journalists and the leaders themselves tend to view leadership from the perspective of individual personalities. Biographies by journalists (e.g., John Barry's book on Speaker James C. Wright, Jr. [D-Tex.], *The Ambition and the Power,* 1989) and autobiographies by political leaders (e.g., Speaker Thomas R. [Tip] O'Neill, Jr.'s book, *Man of the House,* 1987) furnish rich insights into the personalities of individual leaders. These studies describe a leader's upbringing and personal experiences as they relate to leadership style. By definition, biographical studies furnish the least general theoretical claims about House leadership, since their central purpose is to account for the peculiarities of individuals and their influence on the House. Most biographies of House leaders have focused on Speakers, and they are too numerous to list here (see Donald Kennon's *Speaker of the U.S. House of Representatives: A Bibliography, 1789–1984,* 1986). Perhaps the most thoroughly developed biography of a Speaker is *Rayburn: A Biography* by D. B. Hardeman and Donald C. Bacon (1987).

Some studies conceptualize leadership in terms of both context and personal factors (see Peters, 1990; Rohde, 1991; and Palazzolo, 1992). These studies argue that institutional, political, and issue-agenda conditions set the constraints within which leaders operate, but leaders can define their styles within those constraints. For example, both Speakers Tip O'Neill and Jim Wright acted under roughly similar conditions during the 1980s, but Wright pursued a more aggressive leadership style.

In sum, institutional functions, context, and individual personalities are all essential to understanding House leadership. In general, leaders operate within a context that places limitations on power, demands responsiveness to House members, and typically requires leaders to bargain with members and accommodate their preferences. Yet these general propositions take us only so far in understanding the complex phenomenon of House leadership: even relatively stable conditions are subject to change, which in turn may create new opportunities for leadership or place greater constraints on leaders. Institutional reforms have occasionally altered the committee system, legislative procedures, and the formal powers of leaders. Changes in the party system have at times strengthened and at other times weakened the powers of party leaders. Furthermore, individual leaders have made special contributions to House leadership. The general conception of leadership will be elaborated here by assessing the evolution of specific leadership positions in the House.

Institutional functions, context, and individual personalities are all essential to understanding House leadership.

PARTY LEADERS. House leadership by party differs according to whether the party is in the majority or the minority. Also, the styles and strategies employed by party leaders in the House have changed over time.

Majority party leadership. The majority party leadership is headed by the Speaker of the House, who fills the only constitutionally mandated leadership position in the House. In addition to representing a congressional district, the Speaker essentially performs two leadership roles: leader of the majority party and presiding officer of the House. As presiding officer, the Speaker is expected to administer the rules and procedures of the House in a fair, impartial, and consistent manner. The Speaker also refers bills to committees and is in charge of allocating office space to members. As party leader, the Speaker aims to advance the priorities of the majority party in the House. His role depends partly on the president. If the president is of the same party, the Speaker's primary task is to build coalitions in support of the president's legislative priorities. If the president is of the opposing party, the Speaker acts as the leading spokesperson of the majority party and will more likely be involved in setting the party's legislative priorities. In both roles—presiding officer and party leader—the Speaker is responsible for managing conflict in the House. Conflict can be managed in a variety of ways: from helping to draft fair rules for floor debate, to appointing members to special committees or task forces, to building camaraderie among members.

The Speaker's role as party leader is shared by several other party leaders. Barbara Sinclair (1983) divides the party leadership into two groups: the core leadership and the extended leadership. The core leadership includes the majority leader (who assists the Speaker with scheduling legislation, conducting business on the floor, and mediating intraparty conflict) and the majority whip (who is in charge of collecting and distributing information about member preferences and plotting strategy to build coalitions in support of the leadership). From the late 1970s to the early 1990s, the chief deputy whip and the chairman of the Democratic Caucus were also considered part of the core leadership. The extended leadership refers to the auxiliary resources the party leadership uses to carry out its basic functions: the whip system, the party's steering and policy committee, and the House Rules Committee.

Minority party leadership. The House minority party is headed by the minority leader, the minority whip, the party caucus (or conference) chairman, and the steering and policy committee chairman. Like majority leaders, minority leaders seek to manage intraparty conflict and to build coalitions, a task that includes attempting to win the support of some members in the majority party. Minority party leadership may also involve obstructing the majority party from advancing its agenda, though obstructive tactics became less common after the late 1800s and early 1900s. In the late twentieth century, minority party leaders were more likely to offer alternative programs to the majority party or to help members of their party initiate programs. A common strategy of Republican minority leaders in the 1980s was to blame the Democratic party for policy failures and procedural unfairness.

History of party leadership. The styles and strategies of party leadership have varied with conditions and the individuals occupying formal positions. At least five conceptions of party leadership have evolved over time: (1) parliamentary, (2) centralized party leadership, (3) leadership by commission, (4) middleman leadership, and (5) conditional party leadership. In her 1896 work *The Speaker of the House,* Mary Parker Follett found that the Speaker had always been a parliamentary and party leader. The Speaker had the power to appoint committees and committee chairmen and to recognize members on the floor. Yet, as Ronald Peters (1990) argues, conditions before the Civil War prevented Speakers from exercising strong party leadership. The federal government had a limited role in American society, the nation was divided over the slavery issue, and the House was just beginning to develop as a representative and lawmaking institution. Under those conditions, the Speaker concentrated primarily on the tasks associated with the presiding officer role. The speakership was not a highly sought-after position and was generally occupied by "second rate men," according to Follett.

Henry Clay of Kentucky (Speaker, 1811–1814, 1815–1820, and 1823–1825) represented the one major exception to the parliamentary leadership model of the pre–Civil War era. Clay made several unique contributions to the status and power of the Speaker's office. He added a third component to the Speaker's theretofore twofold role of party leader and presiding officer—that of exercising the privileges of a House member (specifically, participating in floor debate and regularly casting roll-call votes). As Peters points out, Clay was popular and famous for his oratory skills; he was one of the only Speakers in history to be elected on the basis of the programs he advocated; and he was instrumental in developing the committee system in the House.

After the Civil War, the Speaker's office developed into a strong party leadership position. By the end of the nineteenth century, House leadership was virtually defined by the centralized power wielded by the Speaker. From 1890 to 1910, the House saw the rise of "boss," or "czar," Speakers. Two notable Republican Speakers of this period—Thomas B. Reed (R-Maine, 1889–1891 and 1895–1899) and Joseph G. Cannon (R-Ill., 1903–1911)—epitomized strong, centralized party leadership. In addition to appointing committees, the Speaker chaired a five-person Rules Committee, which controlled the scheduling of bills for debate on the floor and the length of floor debate. The Speaker also had unprecedented power on the House floor, including the ability to recognize members and suspend House rules.

The Speaker's vast power was supported by conditions that encouraged strong, centralized party leadership. A stable and cohesive party system enabled the Speaker to set the congressional agenda and discipline members. State and local party organizations controlled nominations for office and encouraged party loyalty and conformity to the Speaker's demands. Most important, the members within each party were unified on most issues because they represented similar constituencies and therefore shared many interests (Cooper and Brady, 1981). Finally, the seniority rule had not yet developed as the standard for career development. Thus, the Speaker could use committee assignments to sanction or reward members, depending on their loyalty to the party's position on issues that came to the House for a vote.

Although centralized party leadership expedited lawmaking, it limited representation in the House. Ultimately, members concluded that Speaker Cannon had abused his powers and too greatly restricted their ability to participate in the process. The period of centralized party leadership ended in 1910 with the famous revolt against Speaker Cannon. A faction of progressive Republicans coalesced with Democrats to pass a resolution that called for enlarging the Rules Committee from five to fifteen members, electing the Rules Committee's members by House vote, removing the Speaker from the committee, and having the members of the committee select its chairman. The revolt against Cannon demonstrated the limitations to centralized leadership in the House (see Jones, 1968).

After 1910, centralized party leadership was never fully restored to the Speaker. The concept of leadership evolved in important ways, however, as conditions changed and new leaders defined their roles. For a brief period, until 1916, party leadership continued under the auspices of a highly disciplined party caucus. As Chang-wei Chiu observed (*The Speaker of the House of Representatives since 1896,* 1928), in contrast to the strong centralized leadership exercised by the czar Speakers, caucus government relied more on leadership by "commission"—a group of leaders who collaborated on strategy. The commission typically included the Speaker, majority floor leader, chairmen of the Rules and Appropriations committees, and the chairman and members of the Ways and Means Committee. The Democrats were the majority party during the period of caucus government, and Oscar W. Underwood (D-Ala.), floor leader and chairman of the Ways and Means Committee, emerged as a prominent figure.

After only a few years, though, party factionalism undermined the binding caucus and the House proceeded through a long period of "committee government." Powerful, autonomous committee chairmen, protected by seniority, emerged as the leaders of a fragmented committee structure. As noted in the following section, committee chairmen wielded most of the lawmaking power and exercised constraints on representation. While party leadership was not totally ineffectual, it was undermined by weak parties and the dispersion of power among the committees. The Speaker continued to exercise scheduling powers, participated in committee assignments, and could extend small favors to members, but his primary function was to act as a mediator of the various factions within the majority party.

According to Truman (1959) the conditions of the committee government era were conducive to a "middleman" concept of party leadership. The middleman concept comes from the nature of the congressional party itself, which lacked sufficient cohesion to formulate and enact a party program. Party leaders were expected to be ideological moderates who avoided siding with any factions in the party and acted as brokers of competing interests within the party. Sam Rayburn, Speaker of the House for eighteen years during the committee government era (1940–1947, 1949–1953, and 1955–1961), skillfully implemented the middleman style of leadership. Lacking the formal powers of the czar Speakers, Rayburn developed informal relationships with committee chairmen and led by bargaining, compromise, and persuasion.

Conditional party leadership is rooted in the peculiar mix of institutional reforms passed during the 1970s.

Finally, "conditional party leadership," a term developed by David Rohde (1991), reflected the role of party leaders in the period following the extensive reforms passed by the House in the 1970s. Although party leaders in the late twentieth century lacked the power of the czar Speakers, they did have the resources to exercise strong leadership on issues that enjoyed a consensus among party members. In fact, the key condition of "conditional" party leadership was consensus among party members: when members of the majority party agreed on an issue, they wanted leaders to exercise the authority to advance the party's interests.

Conditional party leadership is rooted in the peculiar mix of institutional reforms passed during the 1970s, which seemed to serve contradictory purposes. Some reforms aimed toward decentralization—weakening the power of committee chairmen and enhancing opportunities for all members to participate in the policy process. Others sought to centralize power in the Speaker, who was given the authority to refer bills to more than one committee, appoint members to the Rules Committee, and chair the party's steering and policy committee, which has responsibility for nominating members to appointments on standing committees.

The reforms make sense from the perspective of members who wanted to improve Congress's capacity to perform the functions of lawmaking and representation. The reforms created a context within which members of the majority party could pursue their individual interests but also bind together when they agreed on specific issues. The first impulse of party leaders in the reform period was to involve members in the policy process as much as possible and to accommodate the diverse preferences of party members (Sinclair, 1983). In the 1980s, members continued to participate actively in the policy process, but with increased party unity. House Democrats enjoyed a greater consensus—greater than at any other time since the turn of the twentieth century—on many issues because the preferences of their constituents were more alike. Strong party unity combined with the reforms that strengthened the party leadership enabled party leaders to exert strong leadership when members thought it was necessary for collective action.

COMMITTEE LEADERS. Committee chairmen also hold important leadership positions in the House. The workload of the House is divided up by standing committees, which have traditionally served as the primary source of deliberation and lawmaking in the House of Representatives. Each committee has jurisdiction over a particular set of policy issues: agricultural, armed services, foreign affairs, and the like. Almost all committees further divide up their work by subcommittees. Committee leadership involves the actions taken by the chairman of each committee and each subcommittees. Conceptions of committee leadership evolved as the committee system developed and as political scientists conducted more systematic study of committees.

Woodrow Wilson gave the first description of committee leadership in *Congressional Government* (1885). He argued that if Congress possessed any leadership at all, it resided in the standing committees. House leadership reflected the incoherent, fragmented committee system, which produced a "multiplicity of leaders"—the committee chairmen.

> There are in Congress no authoritative leaders who are recognized spokesmen of their parties. Power is nowhere concentrated; it is rather deliberately and of set policy scattered amongst many small chiefs. It is divided up, as it were, into forty-seven seigniories, in each of which a Standing Committee is the court-baron and its chairman lord-proprietor. (Wilson, p. 92)

The feudal nature of this initial conception of committee leadership suggested a general lack of leadership in the House as a whole. The committee chairmen were "petty barons," despotic in their narrow spheres of policy-making but incapable of acting responsibly on behalf of the House as an institution. The committees were autonomous and unconnected, and their leaders were generally selfish, unruly, and uncooperative. In Wilson's view, the committee system's supposed virtues of limiting centralized power and permitting members to become experts on specific policies were outweighed by the "irresponsible" leadership that inevitably surfaces when power is divided. The emergence of seniority in the post–World War I period reinforced the general conception of the narrow-minded, all-powerful, despotic committee chairmen described in Wilson's account of the late 1800s. Seniority made committee chairmen even more powerful, enshrining them as the permanent leaders of their respective committees and giving them a sense of invincibility.

Analysts eventually challenged the generalizations about committee politics and refined the concept of committee leadership. Later studies found that committees and committee chairmen were not all alike. Those studies also drew distinctions between "power" and "influence" in the exercise of committee leadership. A description of Chairman Wilbur D. Mills (D-Ark.) of the Ways and Means Committee (1958–1974) underscores the notion that committee leadership encompasses far more than the simplified conception of chairmen as "petty barons" (Manley, 1969). While formal power was indeed centralized in the chairman of the Ways and Means Committee, Mills's personal leadership style was very informal. Mills was not a dictator who sought to advance a particular policy agenda but was, in fact, an ideological moderate who worked to build consensus on the committee and to ensure that the committee's bills would be approved by large margins on the House floor. Such leadership required compromise and bargaining. Thus, belying the notion that committee chairmen ruled by intimidation and coercion, members of Ways and Means praised Mills as a cooperative, fair, and persuasive leader.

Richard E. Fenno (*Congressmen in Committees,* 1978) develops a broader theoretical context for committee leadership in his comparative study of six House committees (Appropriations, Education and Labor, Foreign Affairs, Interior and Insular Affairs, Post Office and Civil Service, and Ways and Means) from the 84th through the 89th Congresses (1955–1967). Fenno argues that committee leadership, as with committee decision making, will differ according to several variables: member goals, external constraints (the expectations of external groups), and strategies for pursuing member goals within the context of external constraints.

Committee leadership has also changed as a result of institutional reforms. Reforms passed in the 1970s further decentralized committee power and encouraged wider participation by junior members. Specifically, reforms increased the number of subcommittees and enhanced their autonomy, opened committee hearings to the public, facilitated floor amendments to committee bills, and empowered the party caucus to elect committee chairmen. Of course, Fenno's central argument still held in the 1990s—leadership continued to vary from one committee to the next. But committee chairmen generally had less control over subcommittees; the chairmen were more responsive to members preferences; and they depended more upon party leaders to pass bills on the floor.

INFORMAL LEADERSHIP. Besides the formally designated party and committee leaders, House leadership includes "informal leaders"—leaders who lack formal authority in the House. Informal leaders typically are characterized as independent, hardworking policy experts. Yet, as Roger H. Davidson indicates, informal leaders perform a wide variety of roles: as "procedural experts," who are skillful at facilitating or delaying action with parliamentary tactics; as "brokers," or mediators, among competing interests; as ideologues or publicists, who use the media to try to build external support; as leaders of regions or special caucuses; and as "policy entrepreneurs," who formulate and build support for specific issues ("Congressional Leaders as Agents of Change," in Mackaman, 1981). Susan Hammond divides informal leaders into two categories: leaders with portfolio and leaders without portfolio ("Committee and Informal Leaders in the U.S. House of Representatives," in Kornacki, 1990). Leaders with portfolio include all formal leaders plus informal leaders who act on behalf of an informal organization (a caucus or discussion group). Leaders without portfolio are members who act individually or without any organizational base.

The number and type of informal leaders increased under the conditions of the House prevailing in the late twentieth century. Informal leadership was promoted by the expanded subcommittee system, changes in rules and informal norms that encouraged members to participate more actively in the policy process, and increases in staff and information sources (the Congressional Budget Office, the Congressional Research Service, and the Office of Technology Assessment). As Burdett Loomis illustrates in *The New American Politician* (1988), many members who came to the House in the 1970s exercised informal leadership. Unwilling to wait patiently for a formal leadership position in order to affect policy decisions, these members built their own informal enterprises through caucuses or personal staffs. Eventually, many informal leaders expanded their influence through formal subcommittee chairmanships, and came to constitute the group from which committee chairmen and party leaders were recruited.

Of course, in any institution there are clear limitations to influence without a formal position of power. Still, the ambitious, independent, entrepreneurial style of informal leaders broadened the concept of House leadership and placed particular emphasis on representation. As Loomis warns, however, the rise of the new American politician may undermine prospects of collective leadership and lawmaking with respect to the nation's most pressing problems. Since the informal leaders of yesterday and today are the formal leaders of tomorrow, the future of House leadership—specifically, the capacity of leaders to balance lawmaking and representation—will depend on how the self-styled politicians of the 1990s respond to the conditions of the future.

[See also (I) Cannon Revolt, Clerk of the House, Speaker of the House.]

BIBLIOGRAPHY

Cooper, Joseph, and David W. Brady. "Institutional Context and Leadership Style: The House from Cannon to Rayburn." *American Political Science Review* 75 (1981): 411–425.

Follett, Mary Parker. *The Speaker of the House of Representatives.* 1896.

Jones, Charles O. "Joseph G. Cannon and Howard W. Smith: An Essay on the Limits of Leadership in the House of Representatives." *Journal of Politics* 30 (1968): 617–646.

Jones, Charles O. *The Minority Party in Congress.* 1970.

Kornacki, John J., ed. *Leading Congress: New Styles, New Strategies.* 1990.

Mackaman, Frank H., ed. *Understanding Congressional Leadership.* 1981.

Manley, John F. "Wilbur Mills: A Study in Congressional Influence." *American Political Science Review* 63 (1969): 442–464.

Palazzolo, Daniel J. *The Speaker and the Budget.* 1992.

Peabody, Robert L. *Leadership in Congress.* 1976.

Peters, Ronald M., Jr. *The American Speakership.* 1990.

Ripley, Randall B. *Party Leaders in the House of Representatives.* 1967.

Rohde, David W. *Parties and Leaders in the Postreform House.* 1991.

Sinclair, Barbara. *Majority Leadership in the U.S. House.* 1983.

Truman, David. *The Congressional Party.* 1959.

– DANIEL J. PALAZZOLO

Senate Leadership

The Senate leadership refers collectively to the top Democratic and Republican leaders, called the "majority leader" or "minority leader," depending on which party controls the Senate. Both are elected to their position for every new Congress by their party's caucus. Both the majority leader and the minority leader are responsible for developing their party's procedural and political strategy, typically in collaboration with their top lieutenants (e.g., the whips and committee leaders), and for acting as their party's chief spokesperson, both on the Senate floor and with the press and media. Because the Senate's procedures and practices grant large influence to individual senators, the majority leader's fundamental prerogative of agenda setting is done in consultation with the minority leader.

In June 1990, one Democratic senator described Majority Leader George J. Mitchell thusly: "This poor guy who gets here before us in the morning and leaves after we are all back home at night in our pajamas . . . is supposed to keep on standing here subject to all this abuse." Mitchell, the Senate's top institutional and party leader, was in this instance struggling to speed up the pace of Senate business.

The Senate leadership refers collectively to the top Democratic and Republican leaders, called the "majority leader" or "minority leader," depending on which party controls the Senate.

Mitchell, a Maine Democrat, faced a common dilemma, because the Senate is unique among legislative assemblies worldwide. The principle of minority rule undergirds the Senate's rules; its customs grant large authority to every senator, with each lawmaker having the right of unlimited debate (filibuster) and of offering unlimited and even nongermane floor amendments to legislation. No wonder Senate leaders find it difficult to set firm schedules or to move legislation, especially near the end of a legislative session, when time is at a premium. Only in the Senate and "only in the last few days of a session," stated Majority Leader Mitchell, "can 85 Senators vote one way: Yes, for this bill; 12 Senators vote another way, No, against the bill—and the noes prevail." The noes prevailed because there were so many opportunities for opponents to filibuster the measure and insufficient time to bring them all to an end.

From virtually the beginning, senators recognized that two "rules" broadly characterize their chamber's deliberative processes: unanimous consent and exhaustion. In 1893, for example, Sen. Orville H. Platt (R-Conn.) said, "There are just two ways under our rules by which a vote can be obtained. One is by getting unanimous consent—the consent of each Senator—to take a vote at a certain time. Next comes what is sometimes called 'sitting it out,' that is for the friends of a bill to remain in continuous session until the opponents of it are so physically exhausted that they can not struggle any longer." Daily, Senate leaders confront something akin to institutionalized anarchy: the reality or threat (the "silent" filibuster) of talkathons that can frustrate decision making. To be sure, the right to engage in endless debate gives a minority protection against majority steamrollers, but it also gives the minority a steamroller power of its own.

Although the modern Senate has Rule XXII, the cloture rule, to curtail filibusters, cloture requires an extraordinary majority of sixty votes to invoke. There are also many informal ways to achieve compromises and accommodations that facilitate the lawmaking process, yet the Senate's emphasis on freedom of expression and individual prerogative means that Senate leaders dread hearing the words "I object" to their unanimous consent requests. Such an objection may forecast blocking action. Patience, persistence, and perseverance are among the important qualities of Senate leaders; these virtues are essential to the leadership's ability to overcome frustrating circumstances and to guide and manage the chamber's legislative business.

EMERGENCE OF SENATE LEADERSHIP. Leadership in a formal sense came belatedly to the Senate. During the nineteenth century, Senate leadership was informal and individual. The Senate's small size and its tradition of viewing members as "ambassadors" from sovereign states promoted a style of leadership linked to the personal talents and abilities of individual lawmakers. Scores of senators were regarded as "leaders": some were sectional or factional leaders; some were committee leaders (by the 1840s committees and their chairmen had become important centers of power); and still others (Henry Clay, Daniel Webster, John C. Calhoun) exercised wide influence because of their special political, oratorical, or intellectual gifts. As late as 1885, Woodrow Wilson could write in *Congressional Government,* "No one is *the* Senator. . . . No one exercises the special trust of acknowledged leadership."

This situation changed, however. By the late nineteenth and early twentieth centuries, officially designated party leaders began to take charge of the Senate's business. They emerged because senatorial parties became more coherent, stable, structured, and active. Party caucuses assumed important roles in debating legislation and promoting party unity. Caucus committees were created to assign party members to committees and to assist in scheduling the Senate's business. Called by various names—Policy Committee, Steering Committee, or Committee on Committees—these caucuses' descendants still exist today. The senators who chaired the partisan gatherings acquired levers of authority, shaped the Senate's agenda, and mobilized party majorities behind issues. By the early 1900s, the official position of floor (majority or minority) leader had evolved from the post of caucus leader.

Not every floor leader is automatically the "real" leader of his or her party. The majority leadership has had its ups and downs since the office came into formal existence at the turn of the twentieth century. Democrat Scott W. Lucas of Illinois, who served as floor leader (1949–1951) of fifty-four Democrats during the Truman administration, was often blocked in trying to enact the president's programs by a shifting coalition of Republicans and southern Democrats. After his one term as majority leader of a "paper" majority, Illinois voters ended Lucas's political career. His successor, Ernest W. McFarland of Arizona, met the same fate, losing his reelection bid after serving only two years (1951–1953) as majority leader.

The majority leader is the head of his or her party in the Senate, its leader on the floor, and the leader of the Senate.

Many members by this time viewed the majority leader's position more as a liability than an asset. All this changed when Republican Robert A. Taft of Ohio became majority leader in 1953 and Democrat Lyndon B. Johnson of Texas assumed the leadership of his party, first as minority leader (1953–1955) and then as majority leader (1955–1961).

Until 1953, Taft had dominated his party behind the scenes through the force of his character, his intellect, his partisan zeal, and his chairmanship of the Republican Policy Committee. After losing the presidential nomination to Dwight D. Eisenhower in 1952, Taft decided to run for the leadership post and was unanimously elected majority leader at the beginning of the 83d Congress. He died less than a year after becoming majority leader, but his occupancy of that office enhanced its stature and underscored its potential as an independent source of authority.

Johnson was elected minority leader in 1953 after only four years of Senate service. Supported by Sen. Richard B. Russell of Georgia, the de facto leader of the Democratic party, Johnson possessed a winning combination of personal attributes that helped him gain the top party office. "He doesn't have the best mind on the Democratic side," remarked Russell. "He isn't the best orator; he isn't the best parliamentarian. But he's the best combination of all of these qualities." Johnson transformed the Democratic leadership post into one of immense authority and prestige and made it the influential office that it has remained.

The styles of party leaders are broadly shaped by personal inclinations and institutional context. Factors such as leaders view of their roles, their colleagues expectations, the size of their party's (or the other's) majority in the Senate, whether the White House is controlled by the opposition party, workload demands, and the national mood define leadership opportunities and constraints.

DUTIES OF THE MAJORITY LEADER. Elected, not formally by the Senate, but by partisan colleagues at closed party caucuses that meet prior to the start of a new Congress, the majority leader is the head of his or her party in the Senate, its leader on the floor, and the leader of the Senate. Several important functions are part of the floor leader's responsibilities. How the leader conducts these diverse responsibilities and employs available resources influences both the effectiveness of leadership and legislative decision making. Other Senate leaders—the minority leader, the party whips, and committee chairmen—have a hand in carrying out or influencing the majority leader's functions, such as scheduling floor business, promoting party unity, conducting liaison with the White House, consulting with House leaders, and managing the leader's senatorial party.

Scheduling floor business. Scheduling is the bedrock on which the majority leader's authority rests. The Senate's floor activities are essentially scheduled by the majority leader in consultation with the minority leader. The majority leader, by using scheduling power aggressively, can transform this procedural responsibility into one with significant programmatic overtones. Legislation can be scheduled to suit party or White House initiatives, to expedite policies supported by the bipartisan leadership, to coordinate policy-making, or to dramatize the majority party's differences from the minority.

Each party's policy committee might help identify legislative priorities and formulate strategies and tactics appropriate to each measure's consideration on the floor: when it should be taken up, what amendments might be offered, or who should offer them. The leadership may also try to accommodate the personal scheduling preferences of individual lawmakers. Scheduling involves other elements as well, such as formulating the annual calendar of recesses and adjournments.

Promoting party unity. The majority leader tries to persuade colleagues to support priority legislation and to mobilize winning coalitions. With the assistance of the whip and other senators, the leader works to ascertain how lawmakers might vote on given pieces of legislation and to make sure that senators who favor the leadership's views are on the floor at the right time. Being on the winning side enhances a leader's reputation, while too many losses may tarnish his or her record. Careful use of resources—scheduling an important colleague's favorite bill, for example, or helping someone win a coveted committee assignment—can strengthen the leader's persuasive abilities.

Liaison with the White House. Traditionally, the majority leader is the central person communicating Senate views to the president and, conversely, informing members of executive preferences and intentions. At least since the days of President Franklin D. Roosevelt, House and Senate leaders have collectively or individually met regularly with the presidents to discuss a wide range of policy and political issues. If the majority leader and the president are of the same party, it is expected that the Senate leader will assist the president whenever their policy views coincide.

Consulting with House leaders. House and Senate party leaders commonly communicate and cooperate closely on legislative and political matters. The preeminent examples of such cooperation during the mid-twentieth century were the close personal relationship between Speaker Sam Rayburn (D-Tex.) and Senate Democratic leader Lyndon B. Johnson and the "Ev and Charlie Show" of Senate minority leader Everett M. Dirksen (R-Ill.) and House minority leader Charles A. Halleck (R-Ind.). House and Senate leaders, as well as their key aides, meet regularly and keep in touch on important matters so that interchamber efforts can be coordinated and unnecessary delays avoided.

Managing the party organization. Leaders help to organize, manage, and guide their senatorial party. They can appoint members to party committees, facilitate the election of other party leaders, choose administrative officers, revamp party rules, influence the assignment of party colleagues to committees, and appoint party task forces to study and recommend substantive changes to legislation or procedural changes to Senate rules. In 1992, for example, Majority Leader Mitchell appointed the Democratic Defense Transition Task Force to identify ways to ease defense employment disruptions in the post–Cold War era. Two years earlier, Minority Leader Bob Dole (R-Kans.) had named the Republican Health Care Task Force to study and develop health care reform legislation. And in the 102d Congress both leaders appointed a bipartisan task force to clarify acceptable constituent service by members to people who contribute to their campaigns. Majority Leader Mitchell named Majority Whip Wendell Ford (D-Ky.) to chair the bipartisan task force. Party leaders may also use task forces or their party conferences (once called caucuses) to develop an agenda highlighting their parties' substantive goals or identifying areas of potentially fruitful cooperation between the Senate and White House.

A variety of resources augments the majority leader's influence in the legislative process. By custom, law, and Senate rules, the leaders have gained a number of useful prerogatives: they occupy a front row, center aisle seat; they are accorded priority in recognition by the presiding officer, which better enables them to control floor actions; they are recognized first at the beginning of each day's session; they possess additional staff resources and office space; they usually offer the motion to recess or adjourn each daily session; and they may, with the concurrence of minority leaders, waive certain Senate rules.

The Senate leaders also participate in committee work while discharging their leadership duties. Several Senate majority and minority leaders have made notable, substantive policy contributions: Lyndon Johnson on space policy, Mike Mansfield (D-Mont.) on international affairs, Bob Dole on tax policy, and George Mitchell on environmental protection.

THE MINORITY LEADER. Minority leaders, like their majority party counterparts, are the principal spokespersons on the floor for their political parties. They, or their designees, are always on or near the Senate floor to protect the party's substantive and political interests or to take the floor to address important issues. By longstanding custom, the minority leader receives preferential recognition (after the majority leader) from the presiding officer, which facilitates the minority leader's ability to advance party priorities on the floor.

Minority leaders possess an array of formal and informal prerogatives that mirror those of majority leaders. Formally, for example, Senate rules prohibit most standing committees from meeting after the first two hours of a daily session. The majority leader and minority leader are authorized jointly to waive that rule. Informally, the Senate operates largely through the unanimous consent of the membership. The minority leader plays an instrumental role in advancing the Senate's business by securing, with the assistance of key staff aides, the consent of party colleagues to move legislative issues. To be sure, the minority leader is strategically positioned to block legislation as well. Depending on issues and circumstances, then, the minority leader may function in diverse capacities: to oppose the majority party, to promote alternatives to majority party initiatives, or to cultivate a cooperative relationship with the majority leader to maximize the Senate's legislative performance.

An important determiner of the minority leader's job is the president. If the president is of the same party, the minority leader typically defends the administration from partisan attacks and mobilizes support for presidential initiatives. By contrast, if the president is of the opposite party, the minority leader has leeway to function between two poles: partisan critic or presidential ally. Of utmost concern to the minority leader is devising legislative and political strategies to win the Senate back for the party.

SETTING AND PERSONALITY: TWO CASES OF LEADERSHIP. Different circumstances produce different kinds of Senate leaders. Donald Matthews, the noted scholar of the 1950s Senate (*U.S. Senators and Their World,* 1960), wrote that "Democrats incline toward a highly personalized rule by the floor leader." Matthews was referring to Sen. Lyndon Johnson, whose persuasive techniques and manipulative skill as Democratic leader are legendary. Mike Mansfield, Johnson's successor as floor leader, had a very different personal style and operated under contrasting circumstances. Table 1, which lists but a few characteristics of the Senate during Johnson's time and Mansfield's time, illuminates how different were the environments in which they worked.

Different circumstances produce different kinds of Senate leaders.

Table 1 shows not only that Johnson and Mansfield operated in dissimilar political environments but that each had a different conception of the majority leader's role. Johnson utilized every fragment of power (scheduling, committee assignments, office space) to run the Senate personally. He had an extensive intelligence-gathering network of trusted aides and colleagues. As a result, he was better informed about more issues than any other senator. The power of persuasion was Johnson's forte, and he was famous for the face-to-face method dubbed the "Johnson treatment." As Rowland Evans and Robert Novak described it in their book *Lyndon B. Johnson: The Exercise of Power* (1966),

> The Treatment could last ten minutes or four hours. It came, enveloping its target, at the LBJ Ranch swimming pool, in one of LBJ's offices, in the Senate cloakroom, on the floor of the Senate itself—wherever Johnson might find a fellow Senator within his reach. Its tone could be supplication, accusation, cajolery, exuberance, scorn, tears, complaint, the hint of threat. It

TABLE 1

THE SENATE UNDER JOHNSON AND UNDER MANSFIELD

Under Lyndon B. Johnson (1955–1961)	Under Mike Mansfield (1961–1977)
Southern Democrats dominate	Northern and midwestern Democrats dominate
Small Democratic majorities (until 1959)	Large Democratic majorities
Opposition party controls the White House	Democratic and Republican presidents
Power centralized in majority leader	Majority leader viewed as first among equals
Senate activities dominated by majority leader	Majority leader encouraged participation of all senators on an equal basis
Aggressive leadership style	Relaxed leadership style
Staff resources concentrated in senior members	More staff resources available to all senators
Contained workload	Expanded workload
Senate passive in relation to the president	Senate assertive in relation to the president

was all of these together. It ran the gamut of human emotions. Its velocity was breathtaking, and it was all in one direction. Interjections from the target were rare. Johnson anticipated them before they could be spoken. He moved in close, his face a scant millimeter from his target, his eyes widening and narrowing, his eyebrows rising and falling. From his pockets poured clippings, memos, statistics. Mimicry, humor, and the genius of analogy made the Treatment an almost hypnotic experience and rendered the target stunned and helpless. (p. 104)

Reinforcing the effectiveness of the Johnson treatment was an "inner club" of powerful senior senators as well as an internal, informal system of norms that rewarded rank-and-file deference to "club" leaders. Johnson also enjoyed the solid backing of more than twenty southern Democrats. This regional group, many members of which held committee chairmanships, often voted as a bloc. Johnson could usually count on them for solid, consistent support.

Johnson's effectiveness as majority leader was also facilitated by the opposition party's control of the White House. Under no obligation to support President Eisenhower's legislative program, Johnson could pick which policies to favor and choose the strategies to get them enacted. He had the luxury of independence, discretion, and a small Democratic majority for most of his tenure. In sum, Johnson's dominating personality, persuasive skills, and mastery of both details and broad strategies, centralized his control over practically every phase of senatorial policy-making.

Mansfield exercised his leadership in a completely different way. He worked diligently to decentralize authority, sharing power with colleagues and committees. He encouraged greater participation by junior senators and substantially did away with the informal norm of apprenticeship. New senators were not expected to sit back for months, listening to their elders, before they became actively involved in the Senate's business. As one freshman of that period, Sen. William D. Hathaway (D-Maine), explained to his colleagues in 1973:

> Being a freshman senator in 1973 is very different from being a freshman senator in 1953. The freshmen of that year were expected to listen and learn, but not to be heard. That ancient tradition no longer holds. Freshmen are encouraged to speak out, to play an active and vocal role in formulating legislation and policy. Indeed, one freshman was mildly chastised by Mike Mansfield, the majority leader, for not speaking up and making his views known at a Democratic caucus.

Unlike Johnson, Mansfield limited his role as majority leader. He permitted his colleagues a larger piece of the action. A number of party groups—the Conference, the Policy Committee, and the Steering Committee—were revamped, granted genuine responsibility, and utilized more frequently. Majority Leader Mansfield worked quietly behind the scenes, permitting floor managers and individual Senators to handle substantive issues on their own and to take public credit when measures were enacted. He relied heavily on Majority Whip Robert C. Byrd of West Virginia to manage floor activities. For example, Byrd refined and expanded the use of unanimous consent agreements designed to impose debate limitations on amendments and motions and to bring more control and predictability into floor sessions.

The power of individual senators was enhanced as a result. Members found it easier to exercise initiative in legislation and oversight, to have their amendments adopted on matters reported by other committees, to influence the scheduling of measures, and in general to participate more equally and widely in all Senate and party activities. None of these developments occurred overnight, yet their cumulative effect wrought fundamental changes in the Senate and on its leadership.

TABLE 2

SENATE MAJORITY AND MINORITY LEADERS

Majority			Minority		
Congress	**(Dates)**	**Leader**	**Congress**	**(Dates)**	**Leader**
63d	(1913–1915)	John Worth Kern, D-Ind.	63d	(1913–1915)	Jacob H. Gallinger, R-N.H.
64th	(1915–1917)	John Worth Kern, D-Ind.	64th	(1915–1917)	Jacob H. Gallinger, R-N.H.
65th	(1917–1919)	Thomas S. Martin, D-Va.	65th	(1917–1918)	Jacob H. Gallinger, R-N.H.
				(1918–1919)	Henry Cabot Lodge, R-Mass
66th	(1919–1921)	Henry Cabot Lodge, R-Mass.	66th	(1919)	Thomas S. Martin, D.-Va.
				(1920–1921)	Oscar W. Underwood, D-Ala.
67th	(1921–1923)	Henry Cabot Lodge, R-Mass.	67th	(1921–1923)	Oscar W. Underwood, D-Ala.
68th	(1923–1924)	Henry Cabot Lodge, R-Mass.	68th	(1923–1925)	Joseph T. Robinson, D-Ark.
	(1924–1925)	Charles Curtis, R-Kans.			
69th	(1925–1927)	Charles Curtis, R-Kans.	69th	(1925–1927)	Joseph T. Robinson, D-Ark.
70th	(1927–1929)	Charles Curtis, R-Kans.	70th	(1927–1929)	Joseph T. Robinson, D-Ark.
71st	(1929–1931)	James E. Watson, R-Ind.	71st	(1929–1931)	Joseph T. Robinson, D-Ark.
72d	(1931–1933)	James E. Watson, R-Ind.	72d	(1931–1933)	Joseph T. Robinson, D-Ark.
73d	(1933–1935)	Joseph T. Robinson, D-Ark.	73d	(1933–1935)	Charles L. McNary, R-Oreg.
74th	(1935–1937)	Joseph T. Robinson, D-Ark.	74th	(1935–1937)	Charles L. McNary, R-Oreg.
75th	(1937)	Joseph T. Robinson, D-Ark.	75th	(1937–1939)	Charles L. McNary, R-Oreg.
	(1937–1939)	Alben W. Barkley, D-Ky.			
76th	(1939–1941)	Alben W. Barkley, D-Ky.	76th	(1939–1941)	Charles L. McNary, R-Oreg.
77th	(1941–1943)	Alben W. Barkley, D-Ky.	77th	(1941–1943)	Charles L. McNary, R-Oreg.
78th	(1943–1945)	Alben W. Barkley, D-Ky.	78th	(1943–1945)	Charles L. McNary, R-Oreg.
79th	(1945–1947)	Alben W. Barkley, D-Ky.	79th	(1945–1947)	Wallace H. White, Jr., R-Maine
80th	(1947–1949)	Wallace H. White, Jr., R-Maine	80th	(1947–1949)	Alben W. Barkley, D-Ky.
81st	(1949–1951)	Scott W. Lucas, D-Ill.	81st	(1949–1951)	Kenneth S. Wherry, R-Nebr.
82d	(1951–1953)	Ernest W. McFarland, D-Ariz.	82d	(1951)	Kenneth S. Wherry, R-Nebr.
				(1952–1953)	H. Styles Bridges, R-N.H.
83d	(1953)	Robert A. Taft, R-Ohio	83d	(1953–1955)	Lyndon B. Johnson, D-Tex.
	(1953–1955)	William F. Knowland, R-Calif.			
84th	(1955–1957)	Lyndon B. Johnson, D-Tex.	84th	(1955–1957)	William F. Knowland, R-Calif.
85th	(1957–1959)	Lyndon B. Johnson, D-Tex.	85th	(1957–1959)	William F. Knowland, R-Calif.
86th	(1959–1961)	Lyndon B. Johnson, D-Tex.	86th	(1959–1961)	Everett M. Dirksen, R-Ill.
87th	(1961–1963)	Mike Mansfield, D-Mont.	87th	(1961–1963)	Everett M. Dirksen, R-Ill.
88th	(1963–1965)	Mike Mansfield, D-Mont.	88th	(1963–1965)	Everett M. Dirksen, R-Ill.
89th	(1965–1967)	Mike Mansfield, D-Mont.	89th	(1965–1967)	Everett M. Dirksen, R-Ill.
90th	(1967–1969)	Mike Mansfield, D-Mont.	90th	(1967–1969)	Everett M. Dirksen, R-Ill.
91st	(1969–1971)	Mike Mansfield, D-Mont.	91st	(1969)	Everett M. Dirksen, R-Ill.
				(1969–1971)	Hugh Scott, R-Pa.
92d	(1971–1973)	Mike Mansfield, D-Mont.	92d	(1971–1973)	Hugh Scott, R-Pa.
93d	(1973–1975)	Mike Mansfield, D-Mont.	93d	(1973–1975)	Hugh Scott, R-Pa.
94th	(1975–1977)	Mike Mansfield, D-Mont.	94th	(1975–1977)	Hugh Scott, R-Pa.
95th	(1977–1979)	Robert C. Byrd, D-W.Va.	95th	(1977–1979)	Howard H. Baker, Jr., R-Tenn.
96th	(1979–1981)	Robert C. Byrd, D-W.Va.	96th	(1979–1981)	Howard H. Baker, Jr., R-Tenn.
97th	(1981–1983)	Howard H. Baker, Jr., R-Tenn.	97th	(1981–1983)	Robert C. Byrd, D-W.Va.
98th	(1983–1985)	Howard H. Baker, Jr., R-Tenn.	98th	(1983–1985)	Robert C. Byrd, D-W.Va.
99th	(1985–1987)	Bob Dole, R-Kans.	99th	(1985–1987)	Robert C. Byrd, D-W.Va.
100th	(1987–1989)	Robert C. Byrd, D-W.Va.	100th	(1987–1989)	Bob Dole, R-Kans.
101st	(1989–1991)	George J. Mitchell, D-Maine	101st	(1989–1991)	Bob Dole, R-Kans.
102d	(1991–1993)	George J. Mitchell, D-Maine	102d	(1991–1993)	Bob Dole, R-Kans.
103d	(1993–1995)	George J. Mitchell, D-Maine	103d	(1993–1995)	Bob Dole, R-Kans.
104th	(1995–1997)	Bob Dole, R-Kans., Trent Lott, R-Miss.	104th	(1995–1997)	Tom Daschle, D-S. Dak.
105th	(1997–1999)	Trent Lott, R-Miss.	105th	(1997–1999)	Tom Daschle, D-S. Dak.

Mansfield bequeathed to the party leaders who followed him a Senate that was more democratic, more assertive, more independent, and more open to public view. It became an institution where individualism and freedom of action were widely shared norms and where there was wider participation in the many phases of policy-making. The Senate was transformed from being a clublike institution to an individualistic legislative body in which senators' personal agendas must be accommodated if the collective enterprise is to achieve its goals and deadlines. Senate leaders must constantly negotiate with their colleagues—on both sides of the aisle—if they are to achieve their objectives with reasonable dispatch. As congressional scholar Richard F. Fenno put it:

> The relevant distinction in [a Senator's life] is not between the Senate and the rest of the political world but between himself (plus his staff) and everything else. With the help of the media, he knows he can cultivate a visible national image for himself. With the help of the Senate's formal rules, he knows he can bring the collective business to a halt. He can be a force to be reckoned with whenever he wants to be. Among these prima donnas there are always leaders, people who think about the collectivity and tend to its common business. But they lead only so long as they indulge the individualism of their colleagues and obtain unanimous consent for their actions. (1986)

CURRENT AND FUTURE LEADERSHIP CHALLENGES. Scores of diverse developments influence the activities and functions of Senate leaders. Some of these changes are beyond the floor leader's control (the country's mood, technological breakthroughs, and so on), yet they affect his fundamental responsibilities of agenda-setting and coalition-building. For example, today's video politics (C-SPAN began to televise the Senate's floor proceedings gavel-to-gavel in 1986) has added another requirement to leadership: the ability to project well on television and to articulate Senate and party positions to the viewing public. To illuminate how contemporary circumstances have altered the floor leader's work, three trends are discussed below. They reflect the outside dimensions (changes in the electorate), electoral perspectives (pursuit of campaign funds), and institutional dimensions (floor amendment activity) that affect how the floor leader operates.

Changes in the electorate. Many interests compete for influence on Capitol Hill, but *constituents*—not the president, the party, or the congressional leadership—are the ones who grant and can take away a senator's job. A lawmaker who is popular back home can defy the president, the party, and the leadership in ways unthinkable in a parliamentary system, where the executive, the party, and the legislative leadership are the same.

To maintain popularity back home is not always easy, however. Lobbyists and their political action committees (PACs) employ sophisticated techniques to generate grassroots pressure campaigns; they can combine with other state-based groups to form potent electoral coalitions. Further, senatorial actions are subject to close scrutiny by the press and media. The intensity of such pressures means that the majority leader encounters more difficulty in brokering necessary compromises because senators may be unable or unwilling to change or modify their positions once they have expressed them publicly.

Constituents are better informed than ever before. Voters learn about their senators largely from media accounts. Political parties no longer act as the main mediators between elected officials and voters. Senators make up their minds about constituency opinion not simply on what local political leaders say but on what their statewide polls and surveys reveal. Small wonder, then, that senators create their own personal party organizations back home. Like House members, senators travel to their states frequently to meet with constituents: most senators now go home nearly every weekend of the year. The consequence of this trend is some loss of collegiality, which complicates the floor leader's job of coalition-building.

Heightened attentiveness to constituents and the almost permanent campaign that senators now engage in to ensure their reelection affect the floor leader's scheduling responsibilities in many ways. Senate leaders must regularly resolve conflicting demands as they strive to process the Senate's essential business yet accommodate senators who may want votes delayed or business postponed or who must leave the chamber by a certain time. The conflicting pressures of working on legislation and handling constituents' needs even prompted a scheduling innovation. The majority leader, with the concurrence of the other Senators, established a "three-week, one-week" scheduling system in which the Senate is in session three weeks (Monday through Friday) every month and then off for one week. Senators can thus plan with greater certainty and conduct their constituency-related business without fear they will miss votes.

The money chase. It costs a lot to win and hold a Senate seat. Election expenditures have escalated enormously (inflation and the cost of television ads account for part of these increases). In 1976 the winner of a Senate seat spent an average of $610,000 on his or her campaign; by 1992 the average cost was more than $4 million. This financial reality affects the majority leader's job in several connected ways.

First, it influences the scheduling of the Senate's business. Members' fund-raising activities take up more of their time and have increasingly led to scheduling conflicts. Members cannot "chase money" and debate and vote on measures at the same time. Floor leaders, as a result, commonly provide windows in the Senate schedule—periods when no votes will be taken. These windows often occur from around 6:00 P.M. to 8:00 P.M. to allow senators to attend fund-raising events near Capitol Hill. Some senators worry that they are becoming part-time legislators and full-time fund-raisers.

A lawmaker who is popular back home can defy the president, the party, and the leadership in ways unthinkable in a parliamentary system.

The ongoing need to raise funds affects the party leader's job in another important way. To the qualities of intelligence, parliamentary shrewdness, and so on that influence who is chosen party leader can be added fund-raising capability. Party leaders are expected to raise money for their partisan colleagues. They and other senators often establish their own personal political action committees and distribute financial contributions to party office-holders. It is worth noting that Majority Leader Mitchell headed the Democrats' campaign committee in 1986, before he became floor leader. He reportedly won the support of many Democrats elected that year, and he succeeded in his bid for the job of majority leader in the 101st Congress. According to the *Washington Post,* Senator Mitchell "became an overnight Democratic hero when he led the 1986 campaign that resulted in his party regaining Senate control."

Floor amendments. Given the contemporary Senate's individualistic and entrepreneurial culture, it should come as no surprise that the floor has become a more active arena for decision making. In the 1950s, most Senators specialized in their own committee work and generally deferred to other committee experts on the floor. "The [floor] consideration of matters not previously studied by a committee," Donald Matthews wrote of the 1950s Senate, "is frowned upon." Today, it is commonplace for senators who are not members of the committees originally evaluating legislation to offer floor amendments. Scores of such amendments may be offered, immensely compounding the floor leader's problems in processing senatorial business. Because the Senate has no general germaneness rule, extraneous issues are often raised on the floor. "We seem to create amendments," remarked one senator, "by reading yesterday's headlines so that we can write today's amendments so that we can gather tomorrow's headlines."

Scheduling is no easy assignment for the majority leader when senators are increasingly willing to offer amendments to whatever appropriate "vehicle" is pending on the floor. Not only do many senators want to be involved in scores of issues; they are often under pressure from outsiders (interest groups, the White House, the media, and so on) to employ their resources to shape or frustrate the Senate's agenda. Floor amendments are offered not only to affect policy changes but for a variety of other purposes, such as making friends in outside constituencies and embarrasing partisan foes. When Democrats recaptured control of the Senate following the 1986 elections, assistant Republican leader Alan K. Simpson of Wyoming told the *New York Times,* "We'll be standing there with our little score cards, waiting for them to jump over the cliff." Party leaders must be ready to respond quickly to partisan amendments and statements, especially now that Senate floor proceedings are televised.

The connection between lawmaking and campaigning adds to the majority leader's responsibilities. Inevitably, members' reelection concerns affect their decisions. "Don't make us vote on that or it will kill me" is a refrain party leaders regularly hear. Thus, decisions may sometimes be postponed if Senators fear electoral retribution. Or leaders may innovate, for example, by encouraging the use of megabills (legislation that may be thousands of pages in length), outside commissions, ad hoc panels, or legislative-executive summits to provide political cover for colleagues and to diffuse sensitive political issues, such as changes in Social Security eligibility or benefits. Matching good politics with effective governance is an ever-present challenge for leaders in today's individualistic Senate.

Howard H. Baker (R-Tenn.), who served as majority leader from 1981 to 1985, once said: "Every majority leader reinvents the role. He does it in his own image." Both George Mitchell and Bob Dole, the Democratic and Republican leaders of the Senate in the early 1990s, were forced to reinvent their roles when divided government ended after the 1992 election. As leader of the opposition, Minority Leader Dole lacked the leverage provided by a Republican president and was now forced to decide whether and on what issues to cooperate with or to confront Democratic president Bill Clinton and to strategize about how to advance and publicize Republican policy alternatives now that his party had been deprived of the "bully pulpit" of the White House. Majority Leader Mitchell, too, faced a new situation; he had to develop a new relationship with the White

House and determine how best to advance President Clinton's agenda in the Senate.

It is plain that its unique method of operation makes it difficult for anyone to "lead" the Senate. Given the large authority accorded every Senator, the ever-present partisan and ideological divisions, and the participatory nature of senatorial decision making, Senate leaders must work constantly to achieve compromise, to gain consensus, and to forge winning coalitions. Their tasks have become even more arduous in an era of fiscal scarcity and growing complexity of policy issues. Ironically, as issues have become more intricate and globally interdependent, the Senate's hectic schedule gives senators less time to study and think about policy matters. "There is no shortage of information," declared Majority Leader Mitchell. "There is a shortage of time."

Senate leaders are expected to meet the needs and expectations of their colleagues (leadership, after all, depends on followership) and to process and structure the Senate's business with reasonable dispatch and coherence. These objectives often conflict. How to reconcile the tension between individual senators' prerogatives and institutional obligations is something that confronts Senate leaders virtually every day. As Senate Republican leader Everett Dirksen (1959–1969) so aptly put it, "There are one hundred diverse personalities in the U.S. Senate. O Great God, what an amazing and dissonant one hundred personalities they are! What an amazing thing it is to harmonize them. What a job it is." Ultimately, the Senate leaders are responsible for focusing and framing the actions of these "one hundred diverse personalities."

[See also (I) President Pro Tempore of the Senate, Secretary of the Senate.]

BIBLIOGRAPHY

Baker, Richard A., and Roger H. Davidson. *First among Equals: Outstanding Senate Leaders of the Twentieth Century.* 1991.

Davidson, Roger H. "The Senate: If Everybody Leads, Who Follows?" In *Congress Reconsidered.* 4th ed. Edited by Lawrence Dodd and Bruce Oppenheimer. 1989. Pp. 275–305.

Ehrenhalt, Alan. "In the Senate of the '80s, Team Spirit Has Given Way to the Rule of Individuals." *Congressional Quarterly Weekly Report,* 4 September 1982, pp. 2175–2182.

Evans, Rowland, and Robert Novak. *Lyndon B. Johnson: The Exercise of Power.* 1966.

Fenno, Richard F. "Adjusting to the U.S. Senate." In *Congress and Policy Change.* Edited by Gerald Wright et. al. 1986. Pp. 123–147.

Foley, Michael. *The New Senate.* 1980.

Kornacki, John J. *Leading Congress: New Styles, New Strategies.* 1990.

Mackaman, Frank. *Understanding Congressional Leadership.* 1981.

Matthews, Donald. *U.S. Senators and Their World.* 1960.

Peabody, Robert L. *Leadership in Congress.* 1976.

Sinclair, Barbara. *The Transformation of the U.S. Senate.* 1989.

Stewart, John G. "Two Strategies of Leadership: Johnson and Mansfield." In *Congressional Behavior.* Edited by Nelson W. Polsby. 1971. Pp. 61–92.

Smith, Steven S. *Call to Order. Floor Politics in the House and Senate.* 1989.

– WALTER J. OLESZEK

LEGISLATIVE COURTS

The Constitution plainly vests the judicial power of the United States in independent courts staffed by judges with security of tenure and compensation. But early on—in an 1828 opinion by Chief Justice John Marshall—the Supreme Court approved giving judicial power to bodies not having that security. At times, the practice was based on necessity, providing courts for the territories, the District of Columbia, and the military, but the broadest justification is in the doctrine of public rights. Tracing to an 1856 opinion, the doctrine holds that in matters involving the enforcement of statutory rights and benefits—whether between government and individual or between individuals—Congress may recognize tribunals other than those set forth in Article III, which describes the judicial branch. Judicial bodies owing their provenance to the doctrine are the Tax Court, Court of Veterans Appeals, Court of Military Appeals, Court of Federal Claims, bankruptcy courts (adjuncts of federal district courts), and local courts in the District of Columbia and the territories. Congress has also given judicial powers to executive branch and independent regulatory agencies, such as the Federal Trade Commission and the Interstate Commerce Commission, so that they may adjudicate certain matters within their jurisdiction.

The Supreme Court has intermittently sought to limit the power of courts established by Congress. Could the values intended to be protected by Article III—generally, the rule of law—be undermined when Congress gives jurisdiction to unprotected entities that may bend to the popular will? Subjecting these entities to review by Article III courts is the only security against abuse, and it is not yet established that the Constitution requires Congress to provide such review.

[See also (III) The Federal Court System.]

BIBLIOGRAPHY

Fallon, Richard S. "Of Legislative Courts, Administrative Agencies, and Article III." *Harvard Law Review* 101 (1988): 916.

Bator, Paul. "The Constitution as Architecture: Legislative and Administrative Courts under Article III." *Indiana Law Journal 65* (1990): 233.

Young, Gordon. "Public Rights and the Federal Judicial Power: From *Murray's Lessee* through *Crowell* to *Schor.*" *Buffalo Law Review* 35 (1986): 765.

– JOHNNY H. KILLIAN

LEGISLATIVE DAY

In the Senate a legislative day is the period beginning with Morning Hour and ending with adjournment. It may involve one or more calendar days; in an extreme case, one legislative day ran for 162 calendar days (from 3 January to 12 June 1980). Alternatively, two legislative days may occur within a single calendar day.

At the end of each calendar day, the Senate adjourns or recesses pursuant to either a unanimous consent request or a motion. The decision of whether to adjourn or to recess is significant because Senate Rule VII provides for a two-hour period called Morning Hour at the beginning of each legislative day, during which routine morning business is transacted before any unfinished business may be considered. If the Senate recesses, the legislative day remains the same and the Senate may turn immediately to any unfinished business. In addition, the general practice of the Senate is to interpret the use of the word *day* in the rules to mean legislative day (unless calendar day is specified), as in the requirement under Rule XVII that committee reports lie over one day or in the prohibition against speaking more than twice on the same question during a legislative day under Rule XIX.

This distinction between legislative and calendar days is not as significant in the House.

This distinction between legislative and calendar days is not as significant in the House, where the motion to recess is not highly privileged and the practice accordingly is to adjourn at the end of each day's session. On occasion, however, the House has had two legislative days on a single calendar day by reconvening immediately after an adjournment to comply with the requirement that resolutions reported by the Rules Committee lie over for one day.

[See also (I) Adjournment and Recess.]

BIBLIOGRAPHY

U.S. Senate. *Precedents, Decisions on Points of Order with Phraseology in the United States Senate.* Compiled by Henry H. Gilfry. 61st Cong., 1st sess., 1909. S. Doc. 129.

U.S. Senate. *Senate Procedure, Precedents, and Practices,* by Floyd M. Riddick. 97th Cong., 1st sess., 1981. S. Doc. 97-2.

– JAMES V. SATURNO

LEGISLATIVE INITIATIVE

During the 101st Congress (1989–1991), members of the House of Representatives introduced 6,683 bills and joint resolutions, averaging more than fifteen legislative initiatives per member. Although the Senate introduced fewer (3,669), senators were individually more active, submitting an average of nearly thirty-seven initiatives each. In past Congresses members of both chambers were often even more prodigious, averaging as many as fifty initiatives per member (Norman J. Ornstein, Thomas E. Mann, and Michael J. Malbin, eds., *Vital Statistics on Congress, 1991–1992,* 1991, pp. 151–153). What is the source of such active legislative initiative in Congress, intending everything from the most modest adjustments in existing law to sweeping reforms of the nation's economic, health care, welfare, educational, environmental, and defense establishments?

First, these numbers admittedly overstate the actual amount of independent legislative activity. Numerous initiatives are "companion" bills introduced in both chambers with nearly or completely identical wording. Dozens of bills in the same house may share quite similar themes or approaches. Indeed, on Capitol Hill, legislative plagiarism is the highest form of flattery, as whole paragraphs, sections, and parts of previously introduced initiatives are mixed and matched for inclusion in another member's "new" proposal. Further, a significant number of bills entail routine and recurring legislative business, from reauthorizations of expiring programs to mandatory annual appropriations. However, even discounting companion legislation, common frameworks, word-for-word copying, and repetitive routines, Congress displays a striking propensity to initiate legislation. This activity requires a close examination of the contributions made by presidents and their administrations, members of Congress themselves aided by their staffs, interest groups, constituents, and policy entrepreneurs.

PRESIDENTS AND THEIR ADMINISTRATIONS. Ever since George Washington took the oath of office in 1789, presidents have demonstrated the capacity to be legislative initiators. It was not until early in the twentieth century, however—when Theodore Roosevelt forged national policy on railroads and conservation and Woodrow Wilson developed the first systematic party program—that the chief executive of the Constitution became identified in common practice as the "chief legislator" (under the Constitution, the president cannot formally introduce bills; actual submission must be done by a sympathetic representative or senator). By the time of Franklin D. Roosevelt's New Deal in the 1930s, actual legislative language was routinely drafted by the executive, and the president's announced policy agenda became the primary legislative agenda of Congress. As Dwight D. Eisenhower entered office in 1953, law and custom, as well as congressional expectations, granted enduring institutional means for presidents to identify and convey a formal program of legislative initiatives to Congress. The Constitution provided for the State of the Union address; the Budget and Accounting Act of 1921 mandated a unified federal budget under executive leadership as expressed in the president's annual budget message; the Employment Act of 1946 required the president's annual economic report; and the practice of sending special messages to Congress to transmit additional administration proposals had become fully accepted. Eisenhower added a formalized White House office of congressional liaison to help further the president's legislative interests.

The president in the modern era has emerged as the single most influential agenda setter in Congress, although the executive's clout over what issues the legislature deliberates is far greater than over which particular policy alternatives it enacts. The vast majority of bills introduced in Congress do not receive serious legislative attention. In the House, almost seven times as many bills are submitted as enacted; in the Senate, more than three bills are introduced for every one that passes. A mere fraction survive in both chambers and make it to the statute books. But three-quarters of the legislative initiatives proposed by presidents from Eisenhower to Reagan, for example, and 85 percent of their most consequential initiatives, were acted upon by Congress. Over half were passed into law. Successful legislative initiative in Congress is closely associated with legislative initiative by the president.

Policies that presidents propose, therefore, have particular significance. Where do they come from? Presidents may have ideas of their own for legislative initiatives, and their campaigns for office often identify issues of priority for their administrations, but U.S. chief executives most often select ideas and alternatives from the reservoir of options generated by others inside and outside of government. Since Harry S Truman standardized the process by which the Bureau of the Budget (now the Office of Management and Budget, OMB) solicits legislative recommendations from federal departments and agencies, political appointees and career officials in the executive branch have customarily participated in shaping legislation sponsored by the president. However, because presidents typically become frustrated by the perceived inertia and absence of imagination in the bureaucracy, and fear the lack of responsiveness by the permanent government to their own political needs, they often turn to more reliable and creative sources of ideas. Major legislative initiatives are frequently drafted by trusted aides in the Executive Office of the President, or White House personnel coordinate policy alternatives that are developed by presidentially appointed task forces and commissions composed of specially selected external policy experts, group representatives, administration officials, and possibly members of Congress and civil servants. At times, the ideas of outside policy entrepreneurs find their way into the president's legislative initiatives. In making their legislative choices, presidents and their staffs generally also keep a watchful eye on current events, public opinion, and the media.

Where do members of Congress get their ideas?

The most important source of ideas for presidential legislative initiatives, however, is Capitol Hill. Dozens of careful qualitative and quantitative studies of legislative initiatives, beginning with Lawrence Chamberlain's classic work, *The President, Congress, and Legislation* (1946), reveal the extent to which even the most important presidential proposals can be traced to bills previously introduced in Congress. Only rarely are presidential proposals truly new legislative initiatives. For example, core facets of Franklin D. Roosevelt's New Deal and many of the social welfare programs of the Kennedy and Johnson administrations (such as Medicare) all were derived from legislation in play on Capitol Hill before these presidents entered the White House. The 1981 income tax cuts of Ronald Reagan's economic recovery plan began as the Kemp-Roth bill, which was defeated in 1980. Chief executives usually choose policy options that comport with their policy preferences, and the presidential imprimatur unquestionably transforms the politics of initiatives, but as Nelson Polsby put it: Congress, especially the Senate, is an "incubator" of policy ideas.

CONGRESS AS INITIATOR. Congress is quite unlike legislatures in parliamentary systems, where the cabinet, representing the majority party or multiparty coalition, develops almost all legislative initiatives and individual members of the parliament possess little of the institutional resources necessary to formulate, or even evaluate, complex policy proposals. With its constitutional separation from the executive (reinforced by the absence of strong party organizations with clear policy agendas), independent electoral base, decentralized structure, powerful committee and subcommittee system, vast professional staffs, and analytically mature support agencies, the U.S. Congress provides its entrepreneurial members with myriad opportunities to nurture the ideas that ultimately appear in presidential initiatives and to grant independent judgment to recurring program reauthorizations and appropriations. Congress also affords members the discretionary resources needed to challenge presidential initiatives and to fill in proactively the policy gaps not addressed by presidential agendas. Despite the well-recognized rise of the president as chief legislator, empirical research by Lawrence Chamberlain and subsequent scholars has consistently found that Congress is responsible for most proposed legislation and a large share of enacted programs, either on its own or working in conjunction with the president.

Where do members of Congress get their ideas? Sometimes they arise from personal experience—their own or that of constituents. Members also react to and build upon the previous legislative efforts of others, especially those programs that trigger popular expansions of federal activity. Usually congressional staff operating within the guidelines established by their bosses, particularly the committee and subcommittee professional staff, are instrumental in generating (sometimes), receiving, soliciting, shaping, and advocating various policy options. Issue and program evaluation reports distributed by the Congressional Budget Office (CBO), General Accounting Office (GAO), and Office of Technology Assessment (OTA) commonly furnish ready-made proposals that are picked up and introduced by members.

Innumerable external sources of ideas are also directed at Congress, primarily through this conduit of congressional staff. In the complex, intermixed world of legislative initiative, a major source of ideas for members of Congress, usually those in the president's party, are the broader reaches of the executive branch. Federal agencies constantly generate legislative proposals that are not included in the president's agenda but that are determined by OMB to be "in accordance" (i/a) with administration policy and available for introduction. On occasion, too, executive-branch officials take proposals that were rejected by the administration and surreptitiously promote their introduction by agency supporters in Congress.

Interest groups and their lobbyists, both individually and in coalitions, enjoy far more open access to the legislature than to the executive and are another significant source of policy options. As representatives of important constituent groups, distributors of campaign financing, and disseminators of valuable policy information, they are uniquely situated to provide legislators with needed political intelligence and technical expertise.

Academics, independent policy specialists, and members of think tanks and consulting firms also contribute ideas for legislative initiatives through both the circulation of their writings and personal contact with members of Congress and their staffs. Taken together, in any given policy area Congress taps into a broad network of idea merchants and managers in the executive and legislative branches of government, the interest group community, the business world, as well as universities and other research settings.

[See also (II) Congress, White House Influence on.]

SOURCES OF IDEAS FOR THE PRESIDENT'S DOMESTIC AGENDA

Sources Mentioned	Percentage of Respondents
External Sources	
Congress	52
Events and crises	51
Executive branch	46
Public opinion	27
Party	11
Interest groups	7
Media	4
Internal Sources	
Campaign and platform	20
President	17
Staff	16
Task forces	6

Note: Respondents were 118 officials who had served in the Executive Office of the President from the Kennedy through the Carter administrations. They were asked the following question: "Generally speaking, what would you say were the most important sources of ideas for the domestic agenda?"
Source: Paul C. Light, *The President's Agenda: Domestic Policy Choice from Kennedy to Carter* (1982), p. 86.

BIBLIOGRAPHY

Chamberlain, Lawrence C. *The President, Congress and Legislation.* 1946.

Kingdon, John W. *Agendas, Alternatives, and Public Policies.* 1984.

Light, Paul C. *The President's Agenda: Domestic Policy Choice from Kennedy to Carter.* 1982.

Neustadt, Richard E. "The Presidency and Legislation: Planning the President's Program." *American Political Science Review* 49 (1955): 980–1021.

Peterson, Mark A. *Legislating Together: The White House and Capitol Hill from Eisenhower to Reagan.* 1990.

Polsby, Nelson W. *Political Innovation in America: The Politics of Policy Initiation.* 1984.

– MARK A. PETERSON

LEGISLATIVE INTENT

Legislative intent is the meaning that Congress imbues in a statute as a guide to its purposes and direction. How that intent is to be discerned has been the subject of ongoing debate. What should the balance of authority be between those political institutions, the agencies and the courts, charged with interpreting legislative intent? What should constitute the materials by which legislative intent is divined? How should the courts, the ultimate interpreters of legislative intent, approach their task?

The first question, the balance to be struck between agencies and courts in determining legislative intent, goes to the heart of power relations in an administrative state. In the case of *Chevron v. Natural Resources Defense Council, Inc.* (467 U.S. 837 [1984]), the Supreme Court determined that if Congress has not spoken directly to an issue, courts should defer to an agency's interpretation of a statute if it is based on a permissible construction. The effect of that ruling, in the view of many, has been to shift power to the executive branch in administrative policy.

Ultimately, courts become involved in a large number of cases that seek to ascertain legislative intent. In this age of statutes, interpretation has become for courts an increasingly significant, difficult, and time-consuming duty. Consider the typical pattern. Congress passes a law; the statute becomes the subject of legal action. The court must interpret the meaning of the words of the statute. But the language is often unclear. As the judiciary looks for clues to congressional intent, it delves into the legislative history—the basis on which judges have traditionally sought to interpret statutory meaning. In so doing, the court must first determine what constitutes legislative history and how to assess its various parts—such as committee reports, conference committee reports, floor debates, and votes. It may have to delve into layers of rules and procedures. At times, the legislative history is virtually nonexistent. In other situations, the legislative history is ambiguous. To be sure, in particular cases Congress may deliberately not deal with difficult issues. In other circumstances, the legislature might well have chosen to deal with the issue if it had been made aware of the problem.

Sometimes, the problem results not from legislative ambiguity but from silence: Congress simply has not addressed the issue. The court is then asked to fill in the gaps, not only with respect to the meaning of statutory language but also with regard to a whole host of commonly overlooked issues—for example, those bearing on preemption, attorney's fees, civil statutes of limitation, constitutional severability provisions, private right of action, exhaustion of administrative remedies, and the nature of the administrative proceedings.

The difficulty of discerning the legislative will has increased as Congress has changed. In some ways, fragmentation has increased—staffs have grown substantially, subcommittees have proliferated—and the opportunities for legislative entrepreneurship, in ways unobserved by the entire house, have expanded as well.

Courts have traditionally relied on the "canons of statutory construction" in interpreting statutes (Sutherland, 1972, p. 5). The canons allow courts to use generic rules to resolve cases. Whatever their utility, the canons, as Karl Llewellyn wrote, are not definitive guides to construction. Equal and opposite canons may be invoked to support virtually every outcome possible. No canon exists for ranking or choosing among canons.

Other approaches, based on assumptions about how the legislative process works, seek to provide judges with more direction as they interpret statutes. One influential perspective—a "public interest" approach, advocated by Henry Hart and Albert Sacks (1958), among others—claims that "every statute and every doctrine of unwritten law developed by the decisional process has some kind of purpose or objective" (pp. 166–167). Thus, a judge who seeks to understand unclear wording identifies the purpose and policy it embraces and then deduces the result most consonant with that purpose or policy. This approach, much like the vision of James Madison, assumes that the legislative process and legislative decisions are deliberative, informed, and efficient.

The perspective provides an important antidote to the canons of statutory construction. Its thrust is to try to understand the meaning of statutes in context, with appropriate resort to the process that produced the law, which encompasses relevant legislative history. The flexible nature of the inquiry means that judges can extend the underlying rationale of the policies of the statute to cover new circumstances, even those not envisioned when the legislature enacted the law.

Other perspectives deny the validity of the public interest conceptions, offering startlingly different assumptions about the way Congress works, although not necessarily a shared view about how courts should interpret statutes. One such challenge, the public-choice school, uses principles of market economics to explain decision making. Like many schools, its scholars are not all of one mind and cannot be characterized simply. Generally, however, its proponents depict the legislative process as driven by rational, egoistic legislators whose primary motivation is to be returned to office. Legislators will pass laws that tend to transfer wealth and reduce efficiency, at the expense of society, to satisfy cohesive special interest groups that lobby the legislature. Laws that benefit the public will be scarce, because of the "collective action" problem—that is, the difficulty of mobilizing the wider public not directly affected by a policy.

But public-choice theory hardly explains the universe of the legislative process. The motivations of legislators are complex and cannot be reduced to simple formulas. The view that legislators simply respond to interest groups, that their behavior, votes, and agenda are dictated by those interest groups, and that they simply transfer wealth to those groups in return for campaign support is askew. As studies have shown, Congress can respond without much interest-group support and often despite powerful and intense interest-group opposition. To be sure, legislators are responsive to the need to be reelected. But they are also affected by a desire to affect policy in ways that they think are in the public interest. The twentieth century saw a wide variety of legislation to protect the environment, health, and safety of the public—legislation that the various economic theories of regulation would not have predicted.

Even if the theories of public choice succeeded in explaining legislative outcomes, they do not—indeed, could not—lead to a single prescriptive view about how judges should construe statutes. Any theory of statutory interpretation inevitably is based upon some conception of the judicial role in society, a subject not central to most public-choice explanations.

Still another conception of how to discern legislative intent maintains that judges should generally restrict themselves to the words of the statute, to the "plain meaning" of the statute. This "textualist approach" regards legislative history as susceptible to distortion and manipulation. Supreme Court Justice Antonin Scalia is the most prominent proponent of this view, and thus what was once an argument conducted in the halls of academia has become a viable assault on traditional modes of statutory construction that draw upon legislative history.

Legislators are affected by a desire to affect policy in ways that they think are in the public interest.

Intellectually, at least three prongs appear to underlie the textualist attack on legislative history. The first is the idea that the only appropriate law, according to the Constitution, is that which both houses of Congress and the president have approved (or in some cases enacted over the chief executive's veto). It is a perspective that draws strength from the Supreme Court's interpretation of Article I, section 7 in *Immigration and Naturalization Service v. Chadha* (462 U.S. 919 [1983]), in which the high tribunal struck down legislative vetoes, because they effectively legislated without securing the affirmation of both legislative chambers and the president. According to this view, because it is unlikely that all members of Congress are familiar with the hearings, floor debates, and committee reports surrounding a bill, those documents cannot be thought of as dispositive of legislative intent.

A second prong of this critique is that when judges rely on legislative history, they perforce increase their discretion at the expense of elected representatives. The textualists argue that when judges go beyond the words of the statute and choose from a wide range of (often conflicting) materials that comprise legislative history, they increase their capacity, however unconsciously, to enforce their own policy preferences. According to this view, the responsibility for making policy belongs to those in the elected branches, not to usurping jurists.

A final prong holds that focusing attention on the words of a statute will compel legislators to do their jobs with greater care—to write laws with precision and with a clarity that would offer direction to the executive and judicial branches.

Textualists have quite rightly pointed to some of the excesses of legislative history. But to acknowledge the value of their challenge is not necessarily to accept their analyses of the problem or their prescriptions. As to the causes of the problem, it is undoubtedly true that at times laws are ambiguous because of sloppy drafting; certainly, one can point to examples of a conscious strategy of drafters to put the contentious aspects of statutory meaning in committee reports in order to obscure controversy. However, it is also the case that legislation is often ambiguous because the problems confronted are not simply defined and Congress lacks the expertise to resolve them; given the complexities and uncertainties that the problem presents, it might be more prudent to cast the legislation in more general terms and leave difficulties to administrative agencies to resolve. The committee reports can thus provide important policy guidance for agencies as they seek to implement legislative intent. That Congress does not foresee problems arising from the statutory scheme may not always be a failure of legislative will or precision; sometimes it is too much to expect Congress to foresee all manner of developments. In such situations, exhorting the legislative branch to write unambiguous legislation will have little effect.

It is not at all clear, moreover, that a judiciary that refrains from using legislative history is less likely to impose its preferences. If the courts simply stick to the statutory text, and if that text is ambiguous, arguably courts will have considerable discretion to interpret the statute, perhaps in ways that Congress did not intend.

Context thus becomes important, particularly when it takes into account the legitimate historical record. The task, given some of the criticisms of legislative history, is to find ways to make the legislative history more authoritative, to find ways that Congress can more clearly signal its meaning and the judiciary better interpret statutes.

Clarifying statutory meaning has at least three parts. The first is in some sense preventative; that is, it seeks to anticipate potential difficulties and to deal with them before a bill becomes a law. As such, it goes to the heart of the drafting process. The second component focuses on the materials that constitute legislative history and is geared toward finding ways for Congress to signal its meaning more clearly. The third part entails developing routinized means so that, after the enactment of legislation, courts that have experience with particular statutes can transmit their opinions to Congress, identifying problems for legislative consideration. In fact, a major project, sponsored by the Governance Institute with the support of representatives of both branches, was under way in the mid-1990s; it sought to bridge the gap between legislators who make legislative history and those who digest it.

BIBLIOGRAPHY

Eskridge, William N., Jr. *Statutory Interpretation. Virginia Law Review* 74 (1988): 275, 320.

Eskridge, William N., Jr., and Philip P. Frickey. "Legislation Scholarship and Pedagogy in the Post-Legal Era." *University of Pittsburgh Law Review* 48, no. 3 (Spring 1987): 691–731.

Hart, Henry M., Jr., and Albert Sacks. *The Legal Process: Basic Problems in the Making and Application of Law.* 1958.

Katzmann, Robert A. "Bridging the Statutory Gulf between Courts and Congress: A Challenge for Positive Political Theory." *Georgetown Law Journal* 87 (1992): 653–669.

Katzmann, Robert A., ed. *Judges and Legislators.* 1988.

Landis, James. "A Note on Statutory Interpretation." *Harvard Law Review* 43 (1930): 886–901.

Llewellyn, Karl N. *The Common Law Tradition: Deciding Appeals.* 1960.

Llewellyn, Karl N. "Remarks on the Theory of Appellate Decision and the Rules or Canons about How Statutes Are to Be Construed." *Vanderbilt Law Review* 3 (1950): 395–410.

Sutherland, J. G. *Statutes and Statutory Construction.* 4th ed. 1972.

– ROBERT A. KATZMANN

LIBRARIES OF THE HOUSE AND SENATE

As early as the Second Congress, meeting in Philadelphia in 1791 and 1792, both the Senate and House of Representatives adopted resolutions directing each of their respective officers "to procure, and deposit in his office, the laws of the several states" for the use of members. These actions are regarded as the foundation of the present-day libraries of the two chambers, which serve primarily as legislative libraries.

The modern United States Senate Library was formally established as a department under the jurisdiction of the secretary of the Senate in 1870 and 1871, when a suite of rooms in the Capitol was designated for such use and a Senate librarian was appointed. Since then, the library's collections and range of services have gradually expanded to include comprehensive sets of congressional, governmental, legal, and periodical materials as well as both traditional and technology-based information resources. Its staff specializes in compiling legislative histories and in answering legislative and general reference inquiries from the chamber during debates and from senators' and committee offices. In addition to its normal hours of daily operation, the library is open whenever the Senate is in session. Its core holdings are a complete collection of the printed documents of the Senate and House of Representatives that have been produced from the earliest Congresses to the present time. As a government depository library, it also has an extensive collection of publications of the executive branch. Its book holdings consist primarily of political biographies and the published papers of senators, presidents, and other key political figures, along with works of history, political science, international relations, economics, and general reference.

The Library of the House of Representatives, in part because of its physical proximity to the Library of Congress, is a smaller facility than its Senate counterpart. Its collection, while similar to that of the Senate Library, is confined for the most part to materials generated by the House itself. It has few commercially published works and only a limited number of Senate documents. It is oriented specifically toward directly supporting the House's legislative activities, both those related to the ongoing preparation and development of legislation and those involving the immediate needs of floor, committee, and other legislative operations. The House library is by far the older of the two, as it has evidently been in continuous existence since its origin in 1792; it is known to have been burned by the British in 1814, and a designated librarian has been on the rolls since at least 1824. It is under the jurisdiction of the clerk of the House of Representatives.

Both the Senate and House libraries act as the official internal libraries of record of their respective houses and as such are reserved for the exclusive use of the members of the two chambers and their staffs, committees, and leadership and administrative offices. Both are also distinct from and independent of the Library of Congress, although they often work in close cooperation with the latter's Congressional Research Service.

BIBLIOGRAPHY

DeMaggio, Janice A., ed. *Directory of Special Libraries and Information Centers.* Vol. 1, pt. 2. 1991.

Lewis, E. Raymond. "The House Library." *Capitol Studies* 3 (1975): 107–128.

— ROGER K. HALEY
E. RAYMOND LEWIS

LIBRARY COMMITTEE, JOINT

The Joint Committee on the Library is one of five joint committees in the 103d Congress. The panel is a permanent committee that continues to exist from one Congress to the next, but it does not have legislative authority.

Membership on the Joint Committee on the Library includes an equal number of legislators from the House and from the Senate. In the 103d Congress (1993–1995) five senators and five representatives serve on the joint committee. The chairmanship of the committee is rotated; a senator is the committee chair in one Congress, and a member of the House of Representatives is the chair in the next Congress. The committee also has a vice chairman, who is a member of the legislative body that does not hold the chairman position in that Congress.

Congress organized temporary library committees as early as 1800. A permanent Joint Committee on the Library was established on 7 December 1843 and was given the authority to manage the Library of Congress.

In modern times, the Joint Committee on the Library remains an administrative unit that handles routine internal housekeeping matters. Much of the work of both the librarian of Congress and the architect of the Capitol falls under the general direction of the committee.

Senate Library at the Capitol. Left to right, Senators Harold H. Burton (R-Ohio) and Carl Heyden (D-Ariz.) studying in the library in 1945. (Library of Congress)

The jurisdiction of the committee in the 103d Congress includes: (1) management of the Library of Congress; (2) development and maintenance of the Botanic Gardens; (3) receipt of gifts for the benefit of the Library of Congress; and (4) matters related to receiving and placing statues and other works of art in the U.S. Capitol.

BIBLIOGRAPHY

U.S. House of Representatives. Commission on Information and Facilities. *Organizational Effectiveness of the Congressional Research Service.* 95th Cong., 1st sess., 1977. See Paul S. Rundquist, "Congressional Committee Jurisdiction over the Library of Congress," pp. 108–115.

– MARY ETTA BOESL

LIBRARY OF CONGRESS

A unit of the legislative branch of the federal government, the Library of Congress is also the national library of the United States. While not designated as the national library by law, it has attained this position through almost two centuries of growth of its collections, facilities, functions, and services.

The library's fundamental mission is to assemble, organize, maintain, and promote access to and use of a general collection of information and human expression. Its collection of materials in 1992 consisted of 101,395,257 items, including 15,700,905 classified books; 41,467,185 manuscripts; 15,744,298 visual materials, including photographs, posters, prints and drawings, moving images (motion pictures, videotapes, and videodiscs), and other visual media; 9,350,504 microforms; and 4,156,896 maps. The collection contains materials in 470 languages. The library also registers claims to copyrights in the United States filed by individual authors, artists, and composers and by the motion picture, music, computer software, and other industries. In 1992, 605,322 claims were filed.

In addition, the library provides extensive services to many local, national, and international clients. Services include processing and preservation of material; organization and dissemination of information and references; consultation and technical assistance; education; and conduct of artistic, cultural, and ceremonial events. These functions can be classified into eight categories by the primary constituency served:

1. Providing materials, information, research, and technical assistance and consultation to members and committees of the Congress in support of their legislative, oversight, and representational functions, particularly through the Congressional Research Service, a department of the library;
2. Operating reference centers in House and Senate office buildings for the public, twenty-two public reading rooms in the library's three buildings on Capitol Hill, and the public Performing Arts Library at the John F. Kennedy Center for the Performing Arts in Washington, D.C.;
3. Providing books and other informational materials to the executive and judicial branches of the federal government and to state and local governments on request or under cooperative agreements and contracts;
4. Exercising leadership in the professional library community and providing services and assistance to other libraries through the establishment of national and international cataloging standards, original cataloging of books and other materials in systems used by other libraries, distribution of cataloging and reference data, and other methods;
5. Administering the National Library Service for the Blind and Handicapped, a national program serving 750,000 people with more than twenty million materials in braille or recorded form available through a network of 160 affiliated libraries in 1993;
6. Conducting educational and cultural activities through The Center for the Book, the American Folk Life Center, the Global Library Project, and the American Memory project;
7. Responding to requests for reference material from organizations and the public at large through the National Reference Service and other services, requests that totaled 1,362,490 in 1991;
8. Conducting international activities, such as acquisition and exchange of informational materials with other countries, in which are involved permanent offices in Rio de Janeiro, Cairo, New Delhi, Karachi, Jakarta, Nairobi, and Moscow, as well as providing limited-term assistance to institutions in other countries, including the emerging democratic parliaments and libraries in Central and Eastern Europe in the early 1990s.

In addition to these functions, the library pursues innovation in information technology to improve access to its collections and to data held by other organizations. It promotes the development of electronic networks among organizations, such as the Linked Systems Project, a computer-to-computer system that is a cooperative effort between the Library of Congress and other research libraries. The library also undertakes special initiatives with congressional approval, as when it assisted the library of the Russian Academy of Sciences in Saint Petersburg in preserving materials damaged by a disastrous fire in 1988.

The library provides extensive services to many local, national, and international clients.

ORIGINS AND DEVELOPMENT. The Library of Congress was created as a unit of Congress by the law establishing Washington, D.C., as the site of the federal government. The law, signed by President John Adams in 1800, provided "$5000 for the purchase of such books as may be necessary for the use of Congress . . . and for fitting up a suitable apartment for containing them."

From its inception, many factors have affected the library's development. These have included the person-

Librarian of Congress
Deputy Librarian of Congress
Associate Librarian of Congress

MANAGEMENT SERVICES
Affirmative Action Office
Equal Employment Opportunity Complaints Office
Women's Program Office
Automated Systems Office
Central Services Division
Financial Management Office
Library Support Services Office
Personnel and Labor Relations Office
Photoduplication Service
Procurement and Supply Division

OFFICE OF THE LIBRARIAN
Office of the Librarian
Office of the Deputy Librarian
Office of the Associate Librarian
Center for the Book
Collections Development Office
Council of Scholars
Internal Audit Office
Legislative Liaison Office
Library Environment Resources Office
Office of Planning and Development
Office of the General Counsel
Personnel Security Office

CONGRESSIONAL RESEARCH SERVICE
Office of the Associate Director for Research Coordination
Office of the Assistant Director for Policy
Office of the Assistant Director for Operations
Office of the Assistant Director for Special Programs
American Law Division
Congressional Reference Division
Economics Division
Education and Public Welfare Division
Environment and Natural Resources Policy Division
Foreign Affairs and National Defense Division
Government Division
Library Services Division
Science Policy Research Division

COPYRIGHT OFFICE
Cataloging Division
Deposits and Acquisitions Division
Examining Division
Information and Reference Division
Licensing Division
Records Management Division

LAW LIBRARY
American-British Law Division
European Law Division
Far Eastern Law Division
Hispanic Law Division
Near Eastern and African Law Division

NATIONAL PROGRAMS
American Folklore Center
Children's Literature Center
Educational Liaison Office
Exhibits Office
Federal Library and Information Center Committee
Information Office
National Library Service for the Blind and Physically Handicapped
Publishing Office

PROCESSING SERVICES
Acquisitions and Overseas Operations
Cataloging in Publication Division
Exchange and Gift Division
Order Division
Overseas Operations Division
Cataloging
Decimal Classification Division
Descriptive Cataloging Division
MARC Editorial Division
Office for Descriptive Cataloging Policy
Shared Cataloging Division
Special Materials Cataloging Division
Subject Cataloging Division
Bibliographic Products and Services
Automation Planning and Liaison Office
Catalog Management and Publication Division
Cataloging Distribution Service
Serial Record Division

RESEARCH SERVICES
Performing Arts Library
Area Studies
African and Middle Eastern Division
Asian Division
European Division
Hispanic Division
General Reference
Collections Management Division
Federal Research Division
General Reading Rooms Division
Loan Division
National Referral Center
Science and Technology Division
Serial and Government Publications Division
Special Collections
Geography and Map Division
Manuscript Division
Motion Picture Broadcasting and Recorded Sound Division
Music Division
Prints and Photographs Division
Rare Book and Special Collections Division
Preservation Office

Collections Services
Library Collections (Manual or electronic, remote or on-site, accessed by subject)
Library Collections (maintained by format)
Manu-scripts
Books
Rare books
Microforms
Films
Prints and photos
Maps
Music
Recorded sound
Machine readable
Serials

Organization of the Library of Congress (Library of Congress)

alities and leadership qualities of the thirteen librarians of Congress; the changing needs and priorities of Congress; the interests of members serving on the principal congressional committee with jurisdiction over the library, the Joint Committee on the Library of Congress, established early in the library's history; developments in the library profession and the community of libraries in the United States and abroad; and changing national needs and priorities in domestic and international affairs.

The early period of the library's history (1800–1864) was marked by notable advances and notable disasters. The disasters included fires in 1814, 1825, and 1851 that destroyed many of the library's holdings, then housed in rooms of the Capitol. The 1814 fire resulted from the British attack on Washington. The most notable advance in this period was the acquisition in 1815 of Thomas Jefferson's library of 6,487 volumes (many of which were destroyed in the fire of 1851). Jefferson's cataloging system was used by the library throughout the nineteenth century. The second major advance was the appropriation by Congress in 1853 of $150,000 to replace the books destroyed by the 1851 fire and to construct extensive space and facilities for the library on the west side of the Capitol.

The second period of development, from 1864 to 1897, was a time of extensive expansion of library holdings and facilities. Librarian Ainsworth Rand Spofford dramatically shaped the library during this thirty-three-year period. Spofford, a Cincinnati publisher and writer, was serving as first assistant librarian when he was appointed librarian of Congress by President Abraham Lincoln in 1864. A lover of books, he also proved to be an adept politician and institution builder. With Congress's support, he transformed the library from a small government agency into an important national institution.

During Spofford's tenure, the library was assigned copyright functions by law. Laws required the deposit in the library of free copies of each copyrighted work, greatly increasing the library's holdings. In 1866, the Smithsonian Institution transferred its approximately forty-thousand-volume library to the Library of Congress, and in 1867 the Library of Congress purchased the collection of Peter Force, a Washington publisher, which consisted of 22,529 books on the early history of the United States. In 1886, legislation was enacted authorizing the construction of a library building adjacent to the Capitol grounds, and the building was completed in 1897, the last year of Spofford's term. (He was succeeded by John Russell Long, who served as librarian from 1897 to 1899.)

The massive Italian Renaissance–style building was designed by John L. Smithmeyes and Paul J. Pelz. Dozens of skilled craftsmen and artisans worked on the project, creating one of the most ornate and majestic structures in Washington. Its centerpiece is the dome of the main reading room, 125 feet high and 100 feet in diameter. Now renamed the Thomas Jefferson Building, it was extensively renovated in the late 1980s and early 1990s. An annex, now called the John Adams Building, was opened in 1939, and a third building, the James Madison Building, was added in 1980. The Madison Building contains a total of 1,560,582 square feet of floor space, making it the third-largest building of the federal government and the largest library building in the world.

Daniel Boorstein emphasized making the library accessible to readers and researchers.

While the second era of the library was marked by expansion of holdings and facilities, the third period (1899–1939) was distinguished by increased professional leadership of the library community; systemization and professionalization of cataloging and other operations; extension of services to the Congress and others; and diversification of holdings to include musical manuscripts, musical instruments, many additional rare documents and books, and other items.

In this period of consolidation, further expansion, and diversification, the library was led by Herbert Putnam, who served as librarian of Congress from 1899 to 1939. Putnam, a lawyer, was director of the Boston Public Library before he took office on 5 April 1899. He replaced the Jeffersonian classification system with an alphanumeric system (e.g., world history is classified under the letter *D,* and, under that general category, modern history is classified under the numerals 204 to 725). This system is still used by large libraries in the United States. Putnam exercised strong leadership in the library community by developing centralized services for other libraries, such as the printing and selling of catalog cards at cost and a program of interlibrary loans.

To meet Congress's increasing needs for information and technical, legal, and other services, Putnam worked with interested members in developing the Legislative Reference Service, which was formally established as a department of the library in 1915.

Putnam also attracted more gifts from private donors than did his predecessors, and he proposed creating the

Library of Congress Trust Fund to receive them. Congress enacted this proposal into law in 1925. The largest gift received was from Elizabeth Sprague Coolidge, who donated funds to construct an auditorium for the performance of chamber music. Gertrude Clarke Whittall provided perhaps the most unusual gift—five Stradivarius instruments, with an endowment to cover the cost of concerts using the instruments. In this period, the Hispanic Division reading room was donated to the library by the Hispanic Society of America and its president, Archer M. Huntington. Putnam initiated several special divisions, such as the program for acquisition of American folk songs, now part of the library's American Folk Life Center. He also was the first librarian to name a consultant in poetry to the library. This position was the predecessor to the poet laureate.

In the most recent period, 1939 to 1992, five librarians provided leadership that especially emphasized increasing service to Congress and strengthening the library's national and international roles. Archibald MacLeish (1939–1945) developed a strong fiscal and administrative structure. Luther Evans (1945–1953) stressed increased foreign acquisitions and established the Science Division. L. Quincy Mumford (1954–1974) developed automation in cataloging. One of his most notable accomplishments was his defense of the location of the library in the legislative branch against an effort by the Kennedy administration to transfer the library to the executive and to designate it officially the National Library of the United States. In 1970 he oversaw conversion of the Legislative Reference Service into the Congressional Research Service (CRS) through the Legislative Reorganization Act of 1970.

Daniel Boorstein (1975–1987) emphasized making the library accessible to readers and researchers. He created the Council of Scholars to advise the library on developments in scholarship and was instrumental in establishing The Center for the Book, which promotes public interest in the history and culture of the book. James H. Billington (1987–) has emphasized the potential of technology to make the Library of Congress a "library without walls." In Billington's vision, the library will expand its service to people nationwide through electronic links to local libraries and other initiatives.

GOVERNANCE AND ORGANIZATION. As a unit of the legislative branch, the Library of Congress is governed by the Congress through the Joint Committee on the Library. The committee consists of five representatives and five senators. Appropriations are made by the legislative branch subcommittees of the House and Senate Appropriations committees. Other committees, such as the Joint Committee on Printing, also oversee certain aspects of the library's operations.

The librarian of Congress is nominated by the president and confirmed by the Senate. The librarian submits an annual report, which constitutes an official record of the activities of the library, to the president of the Senate and the Speaker of the House. The Trust Fund of the library is overseen by a board composed of the librarian of Congress, the secretary of the Treasury, the chairman of the Joint Committee on the Library, and ten private citizens (two appointed by the U.S. president, four by the House Speaker, and four by the Senate majority leader).

In 1990, the Library of Congress established the James Madison Council, the library's first general-purpose private-sector advisory body. The council's mission is to support the library's outreach efforts to the public, which include conferences, exhibits, and fellowships. In 1991, the fifty council members each made contributions of $10,000 to $100,000 to the library's public outreach efforts. The National Film Preservation Board advises the librarian on the selection each year of twenty-five films for the National Film Registry, designed to preserve prints of notable films at least ten years after their release. An eight-member board of trustees oversees the American Folk Life Center, and other committees and individuals advise the library from time to time on other aspects of its operations.

Following his 1987 appointment as librarian of Congress, James Billington initiated a broad strategic management and planning review process to examine the library's goals, objectives, and operations on a continuing basis and to develop a dynamic and flexible approach to the library's structure and operations. Billington's initiatives are designed to make the library a future-oriented institution open to opportunities for organizational, technological, and other forms of change in the twenty-first century.

As of 1992, the Library of Congress employed 5,050 people. For fiscal year 1992, the Library of Congress received appropriations that totaled $322,228,000; this

LIBRARIANS OF CONGRESS

John Beckley, 1802–1807
Patrick Magruder, 1807–1815
George Watterston, 1815–1829
John Silva Meehan, 1829–1861
John C. Stephenson, 1861–1864
Ainsworth Rand Spofford, 1864–1897
John Russell Young, 1897–1899
Herbert Putnam, 1899–1939
Archibald MacLeish, 1939–1944
Luther Harris Evans, 1945–1953
Lawrence Quincy Mumford, 1954–1974
Daniel J. Boorstein, 1975–1987
James H. Billington, 1987–

represented a 9 percent increase over 1991. Appropriated funds are supplemented by reimbursements and receipts for goods and services, gifts, trusts, service fees, and other funds resulting in a total of almost $400 million under the library's control in 1992.

With pressure on the federal budget generated by the deficit, the library in the 1990s has struggled to resolve competing claims for allocations of the limited increases in its funding. These claims included reductions in backlogs of unprocessed materials; modernization of the library's computer systems; installation of new technologies to improve and enlarge its data base; and special initiatives in response to congressional concerns, such as increasing the library's resources on the relationship of science and technology to business.

ASSESSMENT. The competing demands and pressures faced by the Library of Congress are a product not of failure but of its success in responding to and initiating change over two centuries. The diversity and plurality of the library's operations are an expression of the pluralistic nature of American democracy, the rate and magnitude of changes in information technology, and the changing role of the United States in the international economic and political order. Somewhat ironically, the implicit tension between the library's role in serving Congress and its role as a national library has increased its influence in national life. The materials, information, analysis, research, and consultation and advice the library provides Congress through the CRS are indispensable to the national legislature. Because Congress appropriates funds and authorizes agency activities, the library has benefited from Congress's involvement and support. This support has allowed the institution to remain responsive to shifting historical currents, sometimes at the cost of orderly development. At the same time, the library's development as a national institution with ties to the community of libraries, scholars, publishers, and artistic and cultural groups has deepened its expertise and capacity to serve Congress, other clients, and the public.

The strength of the Library of Congress lies in the plurality as well as in the expertise of its operations. In a period of budget constraints, tension from competing priorities—assembling, processing, and preserving knowledge; serving Congress; and serving other constituencies—will persist. This tension has strengthened the library for almost two centuries.

[See also (I) Library Committee, Joint.]

BIBLIOGRAPHY

Annual Report of the Librarian of Congress. 1991.

Cole, John Y. *For Congress and the Nation: A Chronological History of the Library of Congress.* 1979.

Dalrymple, Helen. *The Library of Congress.* 1992.

Goodrum, Charles A. *Treasures of the Library of Congress.* 1991.

Goodrum, Charles A., and Helen W. Dalrymple. *The Library of Congress.* 1982.

Library of Congress. *Librarians of Congress: 1802–1974.* 1977.

Nelson, Josephus, and Judith Farley. *Full Circle: Ninety Years of Service in the Main Reading Room.* 1991.

Simpson, Andrew. *The Library of Congress.* 1989.

Small, Herbert. *The Library of Congress: Its Architecture and Decoration.* 1982.

– JAMES D. CARROLL

LOBBYING

Lobbying is a technique in the political process of advocacy and persuasion. As applied to Congress it is the practice of convincing individual members or groups of members to take a particular course of action to the benefit of the interest or interests represented by the lobbyist.

Perhaps the most important feature of lobbying in the American system is its status as a constitutionally protected freedom. The First Amendment guarantees every citizen the rights of free speech and assembly, and the right "to petition the Government for redress of grievances." Court decisions have consistently upheld this principle, but have also determined that lobbying is not a totally unfettered right and is subject to certain prohibitions, limitations, and disclosures.

Because lobbying is both protected under the Constitution and encouraged by the democratic nature of American politics and society, the role of interest groups and lobbyists has been pivotal in the history of the republic. The Founders considered as a matter of first importance the question of balancing self-interested "factions" with what would be best for the new nation. Lobbyists were prominent in the economic expansion of the new nation and in the social upheavals of the late nineteenth and mid-twentieth centuries, and they are conspicuous in the current era of postindustrial change.

A number of considerations make it important to understand the role of interest groups and lobbyists today. First, the interest group system has grown extremely large and shows no signs of slowing down (although this does not mean that lobbyists are more effective or successful); more diverse and different types of interests are represented than ever before; and the techniques of interest representation have multiplied, causing confusion for policymakers, who struggle to separate the honest voices from the clamor. Second, attitudes and beliefs among leaders and the public about lobbying are complex and paradoxical; some blame the interests for policy stalemate or even national decline. Third, federal regulation of lobbying appears to have gained ground as a strategy to mitigate the stresses caused by interest group activities. Finally, the explosion of interest group activity does not seem to be a uniquely American occurrence: other democracies are now considering strategies to contend with special interest pressures.

ORIGINS. The term *lobbying* is English in origin. Its common usage dates from the mid-seventeenth century and derives from the large public room off the floor of the House of Commons where members of Parliament could be approached by special pleaders.

In the United States, the political and philosophical justification for interest group lobbying can be traced to the nation's formative years. In *Federalist* 10, James Madison discussed how the new Constitution proposed to treat the role of "faction"—today, the term is *interests*—in the new democracy. Factions, he wrote disapprovingly, "are united and actuated by some common impulse of passion, or of interest, adverse to the rights of other citizens, or to the permanent and aggregate interests of the community." In one respect, he believed that factions should be constrained because they represent only the interests of the few at the expense of the larger common good. But in another respect, they are a natural and unavoidable part of democratic governance; to constrain them would be to deny them their liberty, an unacceptable consequence. Control of the "mischief of faction" in a democratic republic, Madison concluded, could best be accomplished by promoting competition among groups and by devising a system of procedural checks and balances to reduce the power of any single group, majority or minority.

The Founders' concerns were realized as the new Constitution was implemented: factional groups within Congress coalesced almost immediately, soon leading to an embryonic party system. So, too, individuals and groups appeared at the convening of the First and all subsequent Congresses to press their claims, causes, and interests before the legislature.

Indeed, Madison, Alexander Hamilton, George Washington, and their Federalist colleagues had themselves orchestrated one of the most successful lobbying campaigns in American history. They promoted the idea of a revised national charter, guided the deliberations of the Philadelphia Convention of 1787, and secured state ratification of the Constitution in a campaign that would have been the envy of any modern lobbyist.

LOBBYING IN THE NINETEENTH CENTURY. Early lobbying activities had several features. Lobbying was usually conducted by individuals or ad hoc coalitions established for specific purposes and carried forward for a limited duration. Most lobbyists represented commercial or business interests: Congress had the ability to grant concessions, to enact tariffs on foreign goods, to extend patents, to grant railroad right-of-ways, to grant subsidies, licenses, and charters, and in general to encourage commercial and industrial growth. Lobbying techniques included familiar methods of advocacy: legal and technical arguments, the planting of news stories (some reporters were hired by lobbyists or combined the two vocations), the pursuit of personal contacts with influential lawmakers, and appearances at committee proceedings.

By standards that today would be found intolerable, lobbyists offered and lawmakers accepted—and sometimes solicited—money and gifts as bribes.

By standards that today would be found intolerable, lobbyists offered and lawmakers accepted—and sometimes solicited—money and gifts as bribes and payments for services rendered. One of the better-known cases involved Sen. Daniel Webster of Massachusetts and his relationship with Nicholas Biddle, president of the second Bank of the United States. In 1833, when the question of rechartering the bank was before Congress, Webster was in Biddle's employ. His letter to Biddle soliciting the "usual retainers" to ensure his support is often cited in criticisms of lobbying.

In the explosion of economic and industrial growth following the Civil War, individual lobbyists—who could be retained to promote any bill—began to be replaced by permanent representatives of established interests. In addition to the rail lobby, industrialists' agents successfully lobbied for high tariffs on imported manufactures (a basic element of Republican party platforms) and veterans' organizations sought to expand Civil War pension coverage. Likewise, the Women's Christian Temperance Union and similar groups launched a persistent, and ultimately successful, campaign for prohibition.

Abuses and ethical improprieties, especially during and just following the Grant administration—the Gilded Age—were common during this period, depicting a view of Washington as scandalous, corrupt, and decadent. The poet Walt Whitman characterized "lobbyers" as "crawling serpentine men, the lousy combings and born freedom sellers of the earth." In 1873, an author of a Washington exposé wrote of lobbyists: "Their plan is to rob the public treasury." An 1888 *Dictionary of American Politics* defined *The Lobby* as "a term applied collectively to men that make a business of corruptly influencing legislators."

Although political corruption and lobbying abuses were significant features of late-nineteenth-century politics, recent scholarship (for example, Margaret Susan Thompson, *The "Spider Web": Congress and Lobbying in the Age of Grant,* 1985) suggests that the depiction of lobbyists as a principal cause of governmental ineptitude does not tell the whole story. In the post–Civil War era, both Congress and the executive branch struggled to cope with an ever greater work load caused by increasing responsibilities undertaken by the government. The institutional mechanisms of both branches, however, were still better suited to the less complicated days of the antebellum period. Lobbyists' knowledge of substance and process, this interpretation argues, helped focus legislators' attention on demands that might otherwise have gone unnoticed in a legislature characterized by clogged agendas, obsolete procedures, amateurism, and a lack of professional staff.

PROGRESSIVE REACTION. By the latter part of the century, the excesses of the Gilded Age gave way to the reforms of the Progressive Era, which included among its aims a frontal assault on lobbying. One element of this assault consisted of the work of the "muckrakers," journalists and writers who exposed social, economic, and political corruption and injustice. Their exposés were enormously influential, and many of them targeted the power of special interests in Washington.

A second point of attack came from reform-minded politicians, the best known of whom was President Theodore Roosevelt. Roosevelt's drive against big corporate interests—oil, railroads, banking, and drugs (at the time, patent medicine manufacturers whose products often did more harm than good)—was one of the hallmarks of his presidency and helped account for his enormous popularity. As president, Woodrow Wilson also clashed with the industrial and commercial interests; as early as 1885, in his classic *Congressional Government,* he had warned against "the power of corrupt lobbyists to turn legislation to their own purposes."

In 1913, the Senate launched the first full-scale investigation of lobbying ever undertaken by either house. The impetus was the disclosure in a New York newspaper that a lobbyist for the National Association of Manufacturers (NAM) had his own office in the Capitol, had the chief House page in his employ, and influenced appointments to House committees and subcommittees. Senate Judiciary Committee hearings disclosed a pattern of abuses by Washington lobbyists. The investigators eventually recommended passage of a bill requiring registration of all lobbyists with the clerk of the House. The bill passed the House of Representatives but failed in the Senate. This investigation, however, set the pattern for Congress's treatment of egregious lobbying abuses—investigation, recommendations for remedial legislation, most often in the form of disclosure requirements, and eventual collapse of the legislative initiative.

The years of the Wilson administration also witnessed an accelerating trend toward institutionalized interest group representation. When the United States entered World War I in 1917, the federal government faced an unprecedented challenge of mobilizing the private sector to participate in the war effort. Federal agencies officially requested the establishment of trade associations in many industries that had not previously been served by such groups. Organized to promote cooperative planning and standardization of products during wartime, new associations, such as the National Coal Association, were established in many segments of American society and remained in existence after 1918, acquiring the peacetime mandate of promoting the interests of their members.

The number of interest groups grew as government became increasingly occupied with the lives of its citizens. As programs were enacted, as statutes created classes of citizens entitled to special treatment, as industries and sectors of the economy fell under governmental regulation, groups arose to monitor governmental actions and to seek to influence governmental decisions. For example, the American Farm Bureau Federation, established in 1919, was energized by laws passed to improve food production during World War I. The United States Chamber of Commerce found itself responding to a number of measures, such as a 1921 law to prevent unfair trade practices in the livestock, poultry, and dairy industries. Hostility toward the interests, especially those engaged in commerce and industry, increased. In 1927, Sen. Thaddeus Caraway, the sponsor of a lobby regulation bill, noted that "nearly every activity of the human mind has been capitalized by some grafter with headquarters established for this activity in Washington."

The growth of government activity created by the New Deal brought a legion of lobbyists to Washington. Before the decade of the 1930s was over, Congress had investigated and passed laws regulating lobbying by public utility holding companies, shipping firms, and propagandists for the fascist and Nazi cause. By 1936, as the result of an investigation by Alabama senator Hugo Black (later a Supreme Court justice), the House and Senate both passed broad lobbying disclosure bills, but attempts to reconcile differences between the bills failed in conference.

In 1946, with the support of President Harry S Truman—who as a senator had chaired an investigation into waste and mismanagement in wartime production and so had firsthand experience with the lobbying efforts of defense contractors—Congress passed a broad lobby disclosure bill, which came under almost immediate criticism and was rendered generally ineffective a few years later. A 1954 Supreme Court decision, *United States v. Harriss* (347 U.S. 612), found the 1946 Federal Regulation of Lobbying Act to be vague and overly broad. The Court's narrow interpretation has meant that reports filed under the act rarely portray an accurate picture of lobbying.

Grassroots lobbying campaigns, when undertaken, were generally unsophisticated letter writing, telephone, or telegraph campaigns.

INTEREST GROUP EXPLOSION. Prior to the mid-1960s, the Washington interest group community was relatively limited in numbers and in scope, "a closed-door marketplace of political influence by a few established interests," observed Norman J. Ornstein and Mark Schmidt ("The New World of Interest Politics," in *Governing,* edited by Roger H. Davidson and Walter J. Oleszek, 1991). Most trade associations were headquartered in New York City, and few corporations kept Washington offices. On broad public policy matters business relied on the presence of the United States Chamber of Commerce and the National Association of Manufacturers. For specific representation, they called on their own legal departments or Washington law firms. Labor and agriculture had several large pressure groups. Other interests included veterans' groups, churches and religious organizations, and professional groups like the American Medical Association (AMA).

Congressional operations at the time favored insider lobbying. Power was centralized in the committee chairmen, the "barons"; staffs, who might act as a buffer between members and lobbyists, were small. Lobbyists were thus able to concentrate their efforts on a few individuals. Grassroots lobbying campaigns, when undertaken, were generally unsophisticated letter-writing, telephone, or telegraph campaigns. Many interests, especially those inexperienced or with few resources, were either underrepresented or not represented at all. Individuals could make large campaign donations with little or no accountability.

Interest representation during this period could be viewed as "iron triangles" of interest groups, congressional subcommittees, and government regulatory agencies. The cast of political and policy actors was limited and stable, the policy debates contained, and the outcomes largely predictable. Organizations had a relatively limited and manageable set of policy concerns, and could participate effectively in a narrow range of institutional arenas.

In a few years, this changed dramatically. The size of government continued to grow into the 1980s, but more important, the scope of government involvement expanded; even during Nixon's administration, the Democratic Congress enacted and the Republican president signed legislation—for example, creating a Consumer Product Safety Commission—that invested the national government with new and far-reaching responsibilities. To an unprecedented degree, Washington came to be seen as a place where, if one's interests involved a government component, a physical presence was essential.

Congress changed as the result of procedural reforms, and the locus of policy-making expanded from the committees to the subcommittees and to the floor. Lobbyists had to increase their activities to cover the large number of members who could influence legislative outcomes. Open-meeting rules lowered some of the barriers that separated members of Congress from group pressures, and lobbyists were permitted to attend markup sessions and conference committee sessions that used to be held behind closed doors.

Political parties also changed. No longer did they act to mediate and aggregate citizen and interest group demands; they left that for the interest groups. The relative rise in national affluence and education meant that Americans had more opportunities for social and economic mobility, and luxury of choice about ideas and values that were often expressed in political terms, that is, in the number and types of organizations people joined. Advances in technology, especially in telecommunications, allowed rapid mobilization of group resources, including capabilities for soliciting contributions and directing communications to the offices of government officials.

While the power of the political parties and the power of the vote declined in this period, direct involvement in political decision making in the form of interest group membership grew. Beginning in the 1950s, civil rights groups, groups who protested the Vietnam War, and environmental, consumer, and public interest groups all became components of the new interest group universe. Many protest groups, for example, were transformed from loosely knit gatherings concerned with short-term goals through the use of confrontational techniques to legitimized, permanent interests with long-term goals whose lobbying strategies and techniques were indistinguishable from those of their more established counterparts.

Groups continued to use protests and demonstrations as a tactic for getting a point across, attracting media attention, and promoting group cohesion. Various groups have massed on the steps of the Capitol, protesting issues such as abortion policy or U.S. intervention abroad. In one notable demonstration in 1979, farmers who were unhappy with U.S. agriculture policy drove their tractors to Washington, paraded in "tractorcades" around the Capitol, camped on the Mall, and announced their intention to stay until Congress passed the legislation they sought. Confrontations with police and property damage to the Mall in excess of a million dollars turned the protest into a public relations disaster; the farmers eventually left without achieving their goals.

By 1993, interest group and lobbying activity had exploded. For example, the membership of the American Association of Retired Persons (AARP)—a group with an interest in protecting old-age benefits such as Social Security and Medicare—grew from 4.5 million in 1973 to 33 million in 1993. This made the AARP twice the size of the AFL-CIO and, after the Roman Catholic Church, the nation's largest organization.

The number of organizations with an interest in health care policy and with Washington offices grew from slightly more than one hundred in 1979 to more than seven hundred in 1991. The proportion of national trade and professional associations headquartered in Washington rose from 19 percent to 32 percent between 1971 and 1990. The total number of national associations grew from 4,900 in 1956, to 8,900 in 1965, to 12,900 in 1975, and to 23,000 by 1989, in effect doubling every fifteen years. Further, the number of registered, active lobbyists increased from slightly more than 3,000 in 1976 to more than 8,500 in 1992, although because of flaws in the lobbyist registration statute, this number greatly underestimates the total number of Washington lobbyists.

The increase in the diversity of interests is also striking, in large part the result of technological achievements and scientific advancements in the late twentieth century. An example is the system of interest groups that developed around public policy issues of organ transplantation. In the early 1980s, development of the drug cyclosporine greatly mitigated the problem of organ rejection, and transplant success rates improved dramatically. Thus, transplantation of organs other than kidneys became possible and practical, and in 1984 Congress enacted the National Organ Transplant Act (which established the Division of Organ Transplantation within the Department of Health and Human Services to administer programs under the act) to encourage donation and to regulate the allocation of donor organs. As the field of organ transplantation experienced rapid growth, a network of groups (including National Transplant Action, the Transplant Foundation, and others) emerged to represent interests within the field and to participate in setting government policies.

Another recent distinguishing characteristic of lobbying since the 1980s is the growth of foreign interest activity, especially foreign corporate and commercial lobbying. In 1994, about 750 individuals or organizations representing about 1,400 foreign governments, political parties, or private interests were registered with the Department of Justice as foreign agents under a 1938 statute meant originally to disclose the activities of fascist propagandists in the United States. These numbers, however, underestimate the actual degree of activity because, like other lobbyist disclosure rules, the 1938 act is ineffective in reliably portraying lobbying activities.

The growth in foreign interest lobbying can be attributed, in addition to the forces discussed above, to the trend toward economic and trade globalization. In the last twenty years, international trade has become a major element in the U.S. economy. Congress's passage of the 1988 Omnibus Trade and Competitiveness Act, the 1988 Canada Free Trade Agreement and Implementation Act, and the 1993 North American Free Trade Agreement (NAFTA) are an indication of the changing relationship of the United States and its trading partners. For some, who perceive the lobbying activities of countries such as Japan to be overly aggressive, this growth is a cause for apprehension. Similarly, analysts are troubled by the so-called revolving door by which U.S. government officials leave federal service to work on behalf of foreign interests.

Responding to these concerns in one of his first actions after taking office in 1993, President Bill Clinton issued an executive order that added to and expanded upon postemployment restrictions for certain high-level political appointees in the executive branch. The Clinton rules expanded the one-year ban on working for a foreign entity to five years. High executive-branch officials were barred for life from employment as lobbyists for foreign governments or political parties (but, significantly, were not excluded from foreign corporations or other private entities). Similar rules to cover members of Congress have been introduced in legislation. A new lobby disclosure law under consideration in 1994 would provide more effective reporting of foreign lobbying activities, and Congress was also considering legislation to prohibit foreign interest lobbyists from providing members and staff with gifts such as vacations, tickets to sporting events, and expensive dinners. Finally, in 1993

Congress ended the tax breaks available to lobbyists for lobby-related expenses.

While traditional lobbying techniques—testifying at hearings, meeting with members of Congress and their staff, drafting legislation, making campaign contributions, and activating letter-writing campaigns—show no signs of becoming outdated, modern communications technology provides new avenues for access to congressional offices. In recent years, interest groups have delivered video tapes, have created computer-generated letters designed to look as though they were personally written by group members, and have set up free "800" telephone numbers that connect directly with a member of Congress's office or the Capitol switchboard. As a result it is increasingly difficult to tell the difference between manufactured public opinion and genuine expressions of popular sentiment.

One of the most controversial techniques used by interest groups is that of giving financial contributions to political campaigns, seen by many as a form of institutional bribery. According to this view, political action committees (PACs), the legally established organizations that funnel interest group money into political campaigns, heavily favor incumbents and put challengers at a disadvantage; moreover, contributions make legislators more beholden to contributors than to their constituents. Defenders of PACs, on the other hand, argue that campaign contributions encourage participation and broaden the base of the political system. In 1976, the Supreme Court decided (*Buckley v. Valeo,* 424 U.S. 1) that campaign contributions comprised a form of protected free speech. Where detractors claim that PAC contributions influence legislators' voting decisions, other analysts point out that legislators make voting decisions for a multiplicity of reasons, including ideology, party, constituency, and individual conscience. The many issues associated with political money, especially the question of whether moneyed special interests benefit unfairly, continue to confound reformers in and out of Congress, and the search for a solution that satisfies the diversity of opinions remains elusive.

THE CASE AGAINST AND THE CASE FOR LOBBYING. Madison's belief that interest groups (factions) were an inherently disruptive force in society remains a compelling theme. It surfaces in attitudes reflected in public opinion surveys, in attacks on lobbyists by governmental officials and others, and in journalistic accounts.

Public attitudes toward lobbying are complex and often paradoxical. Opinion surveys consistently indicate that people believe government officials and institutions are beholden to special interests. But responses are different when people are asked about interests to which they belong or in which they have a personal stake. For example, an older American may decry the power of the special interests in general, but also may see no contradiction in supporting the public policy objectives of the AARP.

Congress's attitudes are similarly complex. It is often both a willing suitor and an unhappy victim of pressure groups. Depending upon time, place, and circumstance, it welcomes the assistance that groups provide, such as research and political support, or it assails them for selfishness and obstructionism. Likewise, government leaders see no contradiction in assailing lobbyists while seeking their support for favored policies. For example, in 1993 and 1994, the Clinton administration, with one hand, conducted an aggressive campaign against the special interests, and with the other hand, solicited from the same interests campaign contributions and support for its budget, jobs program, and other policies, including campaign finance reform.

One of the most controversial techniques is giving financial contributions to political campaigns, seen by many as a form of institutional bribery.

From the muckrakers to the present, journalists have found special interest lobbying a fertile field. Often, their focus is on the shady, dubious aspects of lobbying. The introduction to *Wall Street Journal* reporter Jeffrey Birnbaum's book *The Lobbyists* (1992) is illustrative: "[This book] is an insider's glimpse at a process that is usually cloaked in darkest secrecy. It will attempt to shed light on the trials and triumphs, the foibles and failings of a little understood but increasingly important group. It lays bare the brazen manipulation of both lawmakers and the public by the entire lobbying industry."

Arguments against lobbying are easily summarized: groups exercise influence far beyond the numbers of their membership; their influence runs counter to what is perceived as the public interest; their activities are conducted in secret and are unavailable to public scrutiny; their techniques, involving campaign contributions and social relationships with officials, are unsavory if not improper or illegal; and their activities undermine public confidence in the institutions of government. Issues surrounding campaign contributions and the belief of many that this type of political giving and spending is corrupt has cast particular doubt on the political activities of groups.

These perceptions have been bolstered by the research of some political scientists and analysts who have found that lobby groups tend to represent the interests of the well-to-do at the expense of the poor, that campaign contributions have influenced policy-makers' decisions, and that interest groups in general are an inherently divisive force in society.

The arguments that lobbying is an important, necessary, and useful force can also be summarized: significantly, lobbying is a tangible manifestation of the First Amendment freedom of petition for redress of grievances. Lobbyists bring information to the government and take away information from the government; in this way, they facilitate the flow of knowledge and understanding. Lobbying is a check on governmental power; without the input lobbyists provide, decisions would be based entirely on the information developed by government officials—information that may or may not be sufficient, accurate, complete, or fair. Lobbying is a representational activity that supplements the electoral process. It permits citizen participation not only in legislative affairs but also in administrative matters. Lobbying legitimizes emerging groups; the move from protest group to interest group signifies political maturity and commitment. Lobbying contributes to political socialization by educating group members about government and keeping them informed about governmental decisions. More often than not, lobbying is a self-regulating activity; when a group arises to support or oppose an issue, another group appears to take the opposite position.

The debate on whether interest groups and their lobbyists are harmful or helpful turns, in part, on how successful they are judged in shaping legislation to their own benefit. As in other facets of this subject, informed observers disagree sharply. Some cases demonstrate that interest group pressure is effective; many of these depend on showing a relationship between political campaign contributions and decision making. Other cases demonstrate the power of grassroots action. For example, in 1988, Congress passed the Medicare Catastrophic Coverage Act, a plan developed with the endorsement of the AARP. But a year later, Congress was forced to repeal the act after a grassroots uprising among AARPs' membership objected to the higher Medicare premiums some senior citizens would be required to pay.

Other observers contend that interest groups are not very powerful, are concerned more with information gathering and monitoring government activities than with influencing them, and that when they do seek to influence policymakers, they are only marginally effective. A 1972 study by Harmon L. Zeigler and G. Wayne Peak concluded that most lobbyists accomplish little except to convince their own membership to continue payment of dues. A large-scale study, reported in 1993 (Heinz, et al.), found that the contemporary system of interest representation presented a paradox: although attempts to shape national policy were at a historic high, there was little tangible evidence to show that these efforts were successful.

Disagreement over the effectiveness of lobbying raises a broader question about its ultimate objectives. Lobbyists themselves argue that the techniques of influence—from straightforward activities such as testifying at hearings (a technique that lobbyists rank as one of their most important) to campaign contributions to social relationships—are meant to help gain access to decision makers in order to present information. The degree to which legislators are influenced or persuaded by lobbyists depends primarily, according to practitioners, on both the merits of the case presented and the skill of the presenter—not on a sinister capacity to cloud the minds of decision makers. To others, "access," "influence," and "persuasion" are synonymous, especially in cases where moneyed interests are perceived to dominate interests that cannot draw competitively on similar resources, either financial or political. In this view, access is influence, since only one side of the issue will reach the decision maker.

IMPACT OF SIZE. Of perhaps greater significance than lobbyist effectiveness is the impact of the expanding size of the interest group system. As the number of interest groups has increased, groups with similar concerns have sought to position themselves in the marketplace of ideas, and Congress must now contend with a dynamic of intergroup competition. Entrepreneurial leadership groups—formed from the top down, often with little or no rank-and-file membership—also contribute to Congress's difficult task of sorting out who speaks for what and for whom. Finally, the rate of interest group growth suggests that in the future Congress may need to develop new strategies to manage interest group demands.

Beyond the narrow problem of how Congress manages its relations with this large system are the broad social and political implications of the interest group explosion. Three perspectives can be identified. At one extreme are theorists who believe the interest group system dooms Congress to gridlock and the nation to decline. These theorists (Olson, 1982) argue that in a stable democracy interests develop and accumulate over time; their long-term effect is to inhibit economic innovation and growth, and further stifle the economy through permanent subsidy arrangements with government. These beliefs are popular with those who see the

United States in a broad period of decline. But the theory is also controversial, and analysts have produced research that questions its assumptions and conclusions.

Another view is held by those who, far from conceding the certainty of decline, view the proliferation of interests as a positive indication of the vitality of pluralism in American society. However, the vast array of political choices available bring with them certain social consequences, namely that the traditional institutions and support systems one looks to for stability in an era of rapid change are themselves subject to the same laws of change responsible for the benefits of pluralism. The result, according to Nelson W. Polsby (1984), is that "we are doing better and feeling worse."

The rate of interest group growth suggests that Congress may need to develop new strategies to manage interest group demands.

Finally, a middle perspective between the extremes are those who worry that the interest group explosion has introduced "a potentially dysfunctional particularism into national politics." But they acknowledge, as James Madison articulated, that restraints on interest groups as a remedy are more pernicious than the cure for the disease. The interests, no matter how difficult they may make life for Congress and other governmental decision makers, conclude Kay Lehman Schlozman and John T. Tierney (1986), are the price of a free society. Other analysts such as Jeffrey Berry (1984) take a more reformist position, emphasizing the need for renewal of the party system and the usefulness of campaign reform as one way to level the playing field between well-represented and underrepresented interests.

REGULATION AS A COPING MECHANISM. In 1993 and 1994, statutory regulation of lobbying seemed to be the strategy chosen by Congress and the Clinton White House to reduce the stress of the interests on the political system. In addition to the overarching dynamic of the interest group explosion, the immediate antecedents for this effort were several: the tradition, articulated by all three candidates in the 1992 presidential campaign, of blaming the interest groups for the failures of government; reformist unhappiness with present laws controlling interests—especially campaign finance laws but also postemployment and lobbyist disclosure laws; and the public perception of the Reagan-Bush years as a period when lobbyists, especially those representing corporate and foreign interests, were able to hold sway over policies that ran counter to the public interest.

The 1993 and 1994 offensive against the interests included the following elements: by executive order, postemployment rules were changed to require a five-year wait before a senior executive-branch official could become a lobbyist; and senior executive-branch officials were barred entirely from ever becoming lobbyists for foreign political or business interests. Legislation was introduced to make similar standards apply to members of Congress and senior staff. Congress considered a measure to rewrite several lobby disclosure laws and fold them into a single statute; its sponsors hoped this new law would provide more useful information about lobbying activities. President Clinton's deficit reduction package ended the policy of allowing businesses to deduct lobbying expenses. Campaign reform legislation proposed prohibiting political contributions by lobbyists. Other legislation would bar members of Congress from accepting gifts from lobbyists and others.

These initiatives could provide a measure of relief from the perception that lobbyists have undue influence over the governmental process, although some may have to survive a constitutional challenge first. Restoring the political parties' former role of mediating interest group demands would also reduce some of the pressure. But the structural dilemma of growing numbers of interests, expanding varieties, and increasing demands from all will remain. In whatever way they are regulated, interest groups and their lobbyists will continue to be major actors in governmental decision making; the debate as to their merit will not diminish; and government policymakers will seek new strategies to curb their perceived excesses.

[See also (I) Interest Groups.]

BIBLIOGRAPHY

Berry, Jeffrey M. *The Interest Group Society.* 1984.

Birnbaum, Jeffrey H. *The Lobbyists: How Influence Peddlers Get Their Way in Washington.* 1992.

Cigler, Allan J., and Burdett A. Loomis. *Interest Group Politics.* 3d ed. 1991.

Crawford, Kenneth G. *The Pressure Boys: The Inside Story of Lobbying in America.* 1939.

Deakin, James. *The Lobbyists.* 1966.

Heinz, John P., Edward O. Laumann, Robert L. Nelson, and Robert H. Salisbury. *The Hollow Core: Private Interests in National Policy Making.* 1993.

Herring, Pendleton. *Group Representation before Congress.* 1928.

Olson, Mancur. *The Rise and Decline of Nations.* 1982.

Ornstein, Norman J., and Mark Schmidt. "The New World of Interest Politics. In *Governing.* Edited by Roger H. Davidson and Walter J. Oleszek. 1991.

Polsby, Nelson W. "Prospects for Pluralism in the American Federal System: Trends in Unofficial Public-Sector Intermediation." In *The Costs of Federalism.* Edited by Robert T. Golembiewski and Aaron Wildavsky. 1984.

Rauch, Jonathan. *Demosclerosis: The Silent Killer of American Government.* 1994.

Salisbury, Robert H. *Interests and Institutions: Substance and Structure in American Politics.* 1992.

Schlozman, Kay Lehman, and John T. Tierney. *Organized Interests and American Democracy.* 1986.

Thompson, Margaret Susan. *The "Spider Web": Congress and Lobbying in the Age of Grant.* 1985.

U.S. Senate. Committee on Governmental Affairs. Subcommittee on Intergovernmental Relations. *Congress and Pressure Groups: Lobbying in a Modern Democracy.* 99th Cong., 2d sess., 1986. 5. Prt. 99-161.

Zeigler, L. Harmon, and G. Wayne Peak. *Interest Groups in American Society.* 1972.

– RICHARD C. SACHS

M

MANAGERS

Managers are members of Congress who serve as floor leaders during a bill's consideration, as negotiators during conference deliberations, or as prosecutors during an impeachment trial.

The chairman and ranking minority member of the committee (or subcommittee) that reported a measure act as its floor managers. The majority floor manager has the responsibility to defend the committee text, while the minority floor manager seeks to either alter the bill's language prior to passage or to defeat the bill altogether. Floor managers explain their party's position on the measure and control the debate time allotted their party. They take the lead in defending against or offering amendments to the bill, and are responsible for handling the parliamentary motions or points of order that may arise.

Members who represent their chamber in conference committee negotiations seek to resolve the differences between House and Senate versions of a bill. Although officially known as managers on the part of the House or Senate, they are more commonly called "conferees." Conferees are expected to uphold their chamber's version to the maximum extent possible without jeopardizing the ultimate goal of achieving agreement with the other body. They are appointed by their chamber's presiding officer, upon the recommendation of the chairman or ranking member of the original committee(s) of jurisdiction.

House members serve as the managers in an impeachment proceeding and are elected by House resolution. They present to the Senate the articles of impeachment against the accused official and conduct the prosecution during the Senate trial.

[See also (II) Impeachment.]

BIBLIOGRAPHY

Beth, Richard. *Senate Floor Managers: Functions and Duties.* Congressional Research Service, Library of Congress. CRS Rept. 87-328. 1987.

Oleszek, Walter. *Congressional Procedures and the Policy Process.* 3d ed. 1989. Pp. 148–151, 246–252.

U.S. House of Representatives. *Deschler's Precedents of the United States House of Representatives,* by Lewis Deschler. 94th Cong., 2d sess. 1977. H. Doc. 94-661. Vol. 3, chap. 14.

– ILONA B. NICKELS

MAVERICKS

The term *maverick* first arose in the 1840s, initially referring to an unbranded stray, after a Texas rancher named Samuel Maverick who did not brand his cattle. By the Civil War, however, it had begun to be used more generally as a description for an independent person. Although the term may refer to a person in any walk of life, its most common usage has been political. As the power of political parties grew throughout the nineteenth century, the label *maverick* was applied to some legislators who resisted the constraints that partisanship imposes on individual judgment. The label reflected admiration for a frontier-style independence that seemed to be vanishing as the decades passed.

No single political style can be identified as maverick. Some mavericks, such as Rep. John Quincy Adams of Massachusetts in the 1840s and Sen. Wayne L. Morse of Oregon a century later, have been genuinely intellectual. Others, like New Deal senator Huey D. Long (D-La.), have been noted for thumbing their noses at staid Washingtonians. Still others, such as Sen. Joseph R. McCarthy (R-Wis.) in the 1950s, won fame for belligerence and invective. Whatever the style, however, maverick politicians have always been outspoken and often stridently individualistic in their rhetoric.

Maverick politicians have always been outspoken and often stridently individualistic in their rhetoric.

No common ideology unites maverick politicians. Behind some have stood constituencies with goals unpopular in the mainstream. Others have been pioneers for new values. Before the Civil War, many mavericks took extreme sectional stances, exacerbating tensions that divided the major parties. Ohio representative Joshua R. Giddings, for example, was expelled by the House for his radical antislavery tactics. In the decades after the Civil War, mavericks were associated with troubled groups such as western farmers or industrial workers. On the other hand, the mugwumps, dissident elite Republicans of the 1880s, were also described as mavericks.

By the early twentieth century, as more regular organization of the procedures for lawmaking gave parties—or the powerful groups within them—still greater control over legislation, the term increasingly conveyed the image of someone outside the machinery of the government as well as of parties. A case in point is Sen. William Proxmire (D-Wis.), for many years portrayed as the conscience of a bloated executive and a profligate Congress. As government has steadily grown in size, the image of maverick has become a political asset deliberately cultivated by men and women who may be privately at ease with partisanship.

The studied individualism of maverick politicians can be politically effective. By appealing to the spirit of principled independence, the politician may be able to move the legislature to action. Interested constituencies or influential outsiders may be persuaded to exert pressure in support of a maverick's position. Yet maverick politicians can also become destructive. In his essay "Civil Disobedience," perhaps the most famous personal declaration of independence ever written in the United States, Henry David Thoreau attacked legislators who could not see beyond the procedures and policies of the Congress, and he urged right-thinking men to "stop the machine" of government. In a pluralistic society, mavericks who follow the dictates of conscience and disdain the practical methods that reconcile differences within the Congress may stop government when it needs to act. Whether seen as heroes or villains, however, maverick politicians seem inseparable from the consensus politics that has dominated the United States since the rise of the two-party system.

BIBLIOGRAPHY

Huitt, Ralph K. "The Outsider in the Senate: An Alternative Role." In *Congress: Two Decades of Analysis.* Edited by Ralph K. Huitt and Robert L. Peabody. 1969.

Shields, Johanna Nicol. *The Line of Duty: Maverick Congressmen and the Development of American Political Culture, 1836–1860.* 1985.

– JOHANNA NICOL SHIELDS

MEMBERS

Daily Life and Routine in the House

Long, unpredictable days are a fact of life for all members of Congress, representatives and senators alike. Time constraints are a constant source of difficulty for those with families as well as for those single members who would simply like their lives to have some semblance of normalcy. In fact, the lack of free time is one of the commonest reasons leading some members to decide after a few terms to return to private life. "I need to spend more time with my family" is the reason lawmakers give most often when announcing they will not seek reelection.

Being a member of Congress not only means working long days in Washington, D.C., when the House and Senate are in session; it also means having to travel back home at least several times a month to keep in touch with constituents. Dividing their time between Washington and their home districts frequently undermines members' family life. Some members leave their spouses and children back home and visit them on weekends and holidays. Ironically, many of those who move their families to Washington so that they can be close to them find that their duties back in their home districts cause them to be away too often. There is, in fact, no perfect solution to the dilemma.

Of course, the conflict between private life and public duty is only one of the multiple conflicts a member faces, day in and day out. Each day presents its own wealth of pressures. A good idea of how a member of the House spends a legislative day can be gained by following a typical representative through that day. The legislator, in this case study, was Rep. Robert T. Matsui (D-Calif.). The day was 29 July 1992—one of the final days of the 102d Congress.

MORNING. When Representative Matsui showed up for work at 8:00 A.M. on the morning of 29 July 1992, he knew he was in for a long day. His schedule listed a dozen appointments. He did not anticipate, however, that his day would not end until 12:08 A.M. the following morning, when the House finally recessed. Matsui's sixteen-hour workday included at least a dozen private meetings, fifteen recorded floor votes, a committee markup session, several minor crises, numerous telephone conversations, a fund-raiser for a House colleague, and a banquet.

Like most of his colleagues, Matsui knew well the inconveniences and occasional heartache caused by the crowded, hectic nature of congressional life. When Matsui had first moved to Washington after his 1978 election, he and his wife, Doris, were the parents of a six-year-old boy, Brian. He moved his family into a house in the Washington suburbs but had to spend many long weekends by himself back in their hometown of Sacramento. Now, thirteen years later, Brian Matsui was attending college in California, and his father was still regretting how much his enjoyment of his son's childhood years had been diminished by the strenuous demands of his own political career.

And just a year before, in 1991, Matsui had been sadly forced to choose between politics and family obligations. He had already committed himself to a campaign for the Senate when he learned that his father was dying of cancer. His duties as a House member and the frantic fund-raising schedule for his Senate campaign left him no time to spend with his ailing father, whom he loved dearly, so Matsui quit the Senate race, deciding to remain a House member for the foreseeable future.

On 29 July, as Matsui began his marathon sixteen-hour day, family matters had weighed heavily on him as he had driven to the Capitol from his home in Chevy Chase, Maryland. Doris was in California, visiting her sick father, and Matsui found himself making mental contingency plans to return to California himself if Doris's father were to take a turn for the worse. He was also planning a memorial service for his own father, who had died a few weeks after Matsui dropped out of the Senate race in 1991. As usual, he also found himself missing Brian, who was attending summer school in California.

Competing with these personal thoughts were concerns about a number of pressing political matters. As cochairman for finance of the Democratic National Committee, Matsui was deeply involved in raising money for presidential candidate Bill Clinton, and he hoped to arrange his schedule to allow him to be on hand when Clinton visited California on 15 August. Also on his mind was his commitment to winning repeal of a Civil War–era law establishing what is known as the Special Occupational Tax on Alcohol, levied against businesses that manufacture, distribute, or sell alcohol. In addition, he was one of many House Democrats involved in intensive efforts to fashion a Democratic proposal for health-care reform in the upcoming 103d Congress.

Finding sufficient time to do necessary reading is difficult.

Like most energetic members of Congress, Matsui became involved in numerous issues and political causes. But he insisted that he had become better at focusing his energy than he had been during earlier stages of his congressional career. He claimed to have learned how to say no to interest groups pressing him to champion their cause in Congress: "I've learned to take on just a few big issues that I want to develop and to say to people who come to me with other matters, 'I may be sympathetic, I will vote for you, but I'm not going to carry your water,' " he said.

Matsui had little reason to be concerned about his own chances in the upcoming November election. (His Republican opponent, Robert Dinsmore, ultimately received less than 25 percent of the vote.) But other members of Congress were growing anxious about getting home to campaign. It was, after all, late July, and many incumbents were facing tough challenges mounted by candidates trying to capitalize on the anti-incumbent sentiment among voters across the nation. As July wore on, the House was meeting for longer hours each day in an effort to adjourn as early as possible.

On the small printed scheduled that Matsui received from his staff when he arrived at the office on 29 July were twelve scheduled events, beginning at 8:00 A.M. and ending at 8:00 P.M. he was aware that there were several other tentatively scheduled meetings that he might be called on to attend as the day progressed.

"The most difficult part of this job is the competing scheduling demands," confided Matsui. "For each scheduled appointment, there are usually five [others] that come in."

Members of Congress seldom strictly adhere to the schedules that their staffs work so hard to prepare. Perhaps because members tend to overbook themselves, many find it necessary—or simply desirable—to skip even some scheduled appointments throughout the day. Indeed, Matsui began this day by deciding to skip the first three meetings on his printed schedule: a breakfast with the California delegation, a Democratic budget study group meeting led by Majority Leader Richard A. Gephardt of Missouri to discuss health-care legislation, and a smaller meeting of Democratic members on the health-care issue. He instead decided to remain in his office and catch up on reading and letters that had accumulated during a recent trip to California.

Finding sufficient time to do necessary reading is difficult. Members accumulate piles of reading material each day and often take it home to read in the evening. Many members use airplane travel time to catch up on newspapers. It is hardly unusual to see a member of Congress boarding an airplane carrying a huge shopping bag of unread periodicals.

As Matsui learned later in the day, the early-morning health-care meetings he missed had actually been canceled because too many other members, with their own pressing and overbooked schedules, had also decided not to attend.

Matsui particularly hated to miss the weekly California delegation breakfast, because its members often used that occasion to make important decisions affecting the whole group. He vividly remembered how unhappy some of his fellow Californians had been after missing a similar meeting a year earlier—and finding out afterward that the group had decided that each member would contribute $25,000 from his or her campaign fund to win a state reapportionment plan favorable to the Democrats. Despite the absent members' complaints, that decision was never reversed.

After a brief meeting with five members of his staff, who reviewed the issues that he was likely to encounter that day, Matsui headed off to a House Ways and Means Committee markup accompanied by Dianne Sullivan, his adviser on tax and trade issues. By design, Matsui arrived at the committee room at 10:15, fifteen minutes after the markup had been scheduled to begin. Since most members do not arrive at markups on time, it is a waste of time to be punctual. As it turned out, though, Matsui was still early; the committee meeting did not convene until 10:25. For congressional workaholics, late-convening hearings and meetings inflict enormous frustration. Many complain bitterly that they waste too much time waiting for their colleagues to show up for meetings, hearings, and floor votes. The irony is that these complainers are often the very same people who regularly show up late.

The meeting finally got under way, and while the committee marked up a minor bill on international trade—the last piece of legislation the committee would report out during the 102d Congress—Matsui talked privately with a number of other members, including Representatives J. J. (Jake) Pickle (D-Tex.) and Don J. Pease (D-Ohio), hoping to secure their support for repeal of the special occupational tax on alcohol. It is not unusual for a member of Congress to use a committee meeting as a place to conduct other business. In most cases, every member of the committee knows in advance how the voting will come out, so they often pay only scant attention to the formal proceedings.

The Ways and Means Committee adjourned at 10:45 A.M., and members were summoned to a vote on the House floor. On the way to the Capitol from the committee room, Matsui encountered Rep. Barbara B. Kennelly (D-Conn.), who pleaded with him to relinquish a room that he controlled adjacent to her office suite. The two had discussed this subject many times before.

"Tip gave that to me," said Matsui, referring to former House Speaker Thomas P. O'Neill, Jr.

"I understood why you didn't want to give it up during your Senate race," Kennelly countered. "But now, you don't use it."

"My staff doesn't want to give it up," Matsui replied.

With the proliferation of staff over the past few decades, office space available to members of the House is now at a premium. House staffers often work in very cramped quarters, and members are constantly on the lookout for ways to gain more space.

While casting his vote, Matsui did what House members regularly do during floor votes: he cornered a number of members and asked for their support on a matter of special concern, in his case the repeal of the occupational alcohol tax. Among others, he persuaded Ed Jenkins (D-Ga.) to talk to other House members about it. It is always easier to contact a member on the floor than to reach him or her on the telephone during a busy legislative day.

Back in his office at 11:12 A.M., Matsui sat down with a group of lobbyists representing child welfare agencies to discuss the dubious fate of certain provisions of the Family Preservation Act. It was a short meeting, the first of a series of face-to-face encounters with lobbyists during the day. Matsui expressed support for the child welfare legislation and promised to contact several of the Democratic leaders on its behalf.

At 11:30 A.M., Matsui welcomed an old friend, lobbyist Howard Paster, into his office. Paster, who worked for the lobbying firm of Timmons & Co., was accompanied by a new client, Maura Melley, vice president of Phoenix Home Mutual. Melley was concerned about how her firm would fare under health-care reform legislation. During the discussion, Paster bluntly noted that Matsui had received financial support for his campaign from Phoenix Home Mutual.

AFTERNOON. At 12:20 P.M., traveling to the Capitol on the congressional subway, Matsui ran into Rep. Robert A. Roe (D-N.J.), chairman of the Committee on Public Works and Transportation, and Rep. Vic Fazio (D-Calif.), Matsui's colleague from Sacramento. Matsui and Fazio seized the opportunity to lobby Roe on behalf of a local project, the Auburn Dam. Roe listened, but he gave them no encouragement that the dam would be approved by his committee.

After a quick lunch in the House dining room, Matsui returned to his office to chair a meeting of lobbyists favoring repeal of the Special Occupational Tax on Alcohol. The group included representatives of grocers, truck-stop operators, distillers, vintners, and convenience store owners. Although the measure was scheduled to appear on the suspension calendar, the lobbyists feared that House members might balk and demand a recorded vote on what might appear to be a special interest tax break. Matsui pledged to redouble his efforts on their behalf.

Matsui's 3:00 P.M. meeting with Richard G. Austin, administrator of the General Services Administration (GSA), was delayed. Therefore, Matsui agreed to meet briefly with Joyce Ride, mother of astronaut Sally Ride, who had come to encourage Matsui to continue using summer interns from Santa Monica College on his staff.

On his way to another floor vote, Matsui was briefed by an aide in preparation for his meeting with Austin, which began at 3:43 P.M. Matsui wanted to persuade the GSA to build a new federal courthouse in Sacramento rather than at a possible site outside the city, and, in inviting Austin to his office, Matsui was trying to smooth over a dispute between the GSA and local officials.

His next visitors, arriving at about 4:15 P.M., were lobbyists from two big insurance companies, Aetna and CIGNA, who wanted to explain their views on health-care reform. At about 4:45 P.M., he received a visit from two lobbyists for Pacific Telesis who had come to urge him to oppose a bill to prevent telephone companies from getting into the information services business. Matsui made no commitment to either the insurance or the telephone company lobbyists.

Between meetings, Matsui was on the telephone with the office of Majority Leader Gephardt in an effort to determine when his tax-repeal bill would appear on the House calendar.

After his last scheduled meeting of the day, Matsui learned from an aide that although the House had been scheduled to recess at 6:15 P.M., floor proceedings were likely to stretch late into the evening. Matsui observed that although many members go to the House gym around 5:00 P.M., he cannot. "I can't imagine putting on a gym outfit at this time of day," he said.

EVENING. At 6:00 P.M., Matsui walked down New Jersey Avenue to the Democratic Club, where he attended a fund-raiser for Rep. William J. Coyne (D-Pa.). Matsui seldom accepted evening invitations, preferring to go straight home when his work was done. But with Mrs. Matsui in California tending to her father, there was no reason to reject Coyne's invitation. And, as it turned out, he could not have left Capitol Hill anyway, because the House was still in session.

After Coyne's party, Matsui stopped by the annual House Gym Dinner, which was attended by President George Bush. Matsui had earlier told the organizers of the dinner that he did not intend to come, but it proved to be something for him to do between floor votes.

As the evening wore on and the House continued to meet, Matsui stayed on the House floor, chatting with friends and continuing to ask colleagues to support repeal of the alcohol tax (which later was defeated on the House floor). It was past midnight when the House finally adjourned, and Matsui was exhausted as he drove home through the empty Washington streets.

Never once during his sixteen-hour day did Matsui ever sit down at the massive mahogany desk that dominated his office. As his day demonstrates, being a member of Congress is not a desk job. "If you're working at your desk," he observed, "you are not really working."

[See also (I) Congress, article on Congressional Workload.]

BIBLIOGRAPHY

Miller, Clem. *Member of the House: Letters of a Congressman.* Edited by John W. Baker. 1962.

Price, David E. *The Congressional Experience: A View from the Hill.* 1992.

Tacheron, Donald G., and Morris K. Udall. *The Job of the Congressman.* 2d ed. 1970.

– SARA FRITZ

Daily Life and Routine in the Senate

The Framers of the Constitution conceived of the Senate as a reservoir for deliberation and reflection. Public opinion was to play little or no role in shaping the institution or its members' activities, for under Article I, section 3 senators were to be appointed by state legislatures, not elected by the public. Further shielded by its members' staggered six-year terms, the Senate was perpetually to have a majority that would not be standing for reappointment.

Because of its representational structure,

daily life in the Senate

was destined to be filled with crosspressures.

These provisions, placing the Senate at arm's length from the popularly elected, shorter-termed House, were clearly designed to protect the institution from a volatile public. Daily life in the Senate was to be centered on the great debates of the day, leavening the popular instincts of the House. And so it was for much of the nation's first century, with senators witnessing great debates led by orators like Daniel Webster and Henry Clay and having ample time for deliberation.

CHANGING CLIMATE OF SENATE LIFE. Yet because of its representational structure, daily life in the Senate was destined to be filled with crosspressures. As political scientist Richard Hall suggests, "Elected from larger and more heterogeneous areas, senators must represent a wider range of interests; they receive greater media and interest group attention; and, given the relative size of the two chambers, individual senators face both greater obligations and greater opportunities for legislative involvement" (Dodd and Oppenheimer, 1989, p. 203). These organizational pressures have existed from the beginning, but, in addition, five more recent political factors have reshaped the daily life of the Senate, transforming it into an arena of nearly unending stress.

Electoral pressure. First, senators now face immense electoral pressure. Directly elected since the ratification of the Seventeenth Amendment in 1913, senators have lost much of the protection from public passions that they once enjoyed. The decision to expose one-third of the body to electoral scrutiny every two years has taken its toll, forcing the Senate to accustom itself to increasingly expensive, highly visible campaigns. In contrast to the local issues that dominate House races, Senate contests are now national in nature, with better-funded challengers; thus, senators have lower reelection rates than representatives. Senators therefore invest great amounts of time and energy planning for future contests, reserving large blocks of their days for campaign-oriented efforts. With spending for the average Senate race reaching almost $6 million in 1992—more than ten times the cost of the average House campaign—fund-raising is a major component of that activity. Even spread over six years, an average senator must now raise almost $3,000 every day to meet the average spending level.

Workload. Second, the 100 members of the Senate must handle the same workload as the 435 members of the House—all thirteen annual appropriations bills, all reauthorizations, and so on—with arguably less institutional support. Although the Senate has fewer committees than the House (16 versus 22 in 1989–1990) and subcommittees (86 versus 138 in 1989–1990), it actually produces a larger number of bills introduced per member (33 versus 14 in 1987–1988). Even though the total number of bills introduced in the Senate has declined from 4,500 in the late 1950s to just over 3,300 in 1989–1990, the average length of each bill has increased substantially. Personal staffs are larger in the Senate (50 staff members versus 17 in 1987), but so, in most cases, is the geographic area that a senator must cover back home.

Further, as senators have engaged in more casework for their constituents, this time-honored source of incumbency advantage has come to occupy a significant portion of the average day. Moreover, because senators serve on nearly twice as many committees and subcommittees as their House colleagues (11.1 versus 6.8 in 1989–1990), and because these committees have somewhat broader jurisdictions than the corresponding bodies in the House, senators spend more time shuttling between hearings and legislative markups and cover a wider agenda. Every day therefore begins with the need to make choices between competing priorities and opportunities.

Floor debate. Third, Senate floor debate is rife with opportunities for the consideration of new and old issues alike; every bill is a potential vehicle for amendment. Unlike the House, whose Rules Committee structures and limits debate, the Senate can be in session longer and offer more conduits for indirect influence. This greater flexibility is a product of the natural individualism of the Senate. According to political scientist Steven Smith's 1989 analysis of floor politics in the House and Senate, "Senators view deliberation as central to their chamber's collegial process, with its minimal restraints on floor participation and relatively weak procedural safeguards for committee recommendations." Floor amendments have become more likely in the Senate than the House as the norms of apprenticeship and deference to committees have evaporated. Vigilance is therefore the watchword, as senators must dedicate significant amounts of staff and personal energy just to monitor the unpredictable course of each legislative day.

Presidential ambitions. Fourth, the Senate has long been an incubator of future candidates for the presidency. Although the vice presidency has more recently become the preeminent launching post for successful party nominees (nine out of the eighteen nominees between 1960 and 1992 were sitting or former vice presidents), the Senate is still a time-honored institution for producing presidential candidates.

The fact that a large number of senators may harbor presidential ambitions clearly shapes the institution's daily routines. Many senators maintain crushingly heavy speaking agendas, traveling widely outside their home states in search of national exposure and potential campaign financing.

Thus, as the number of print and electronic journalists covering Congress roughly doubled over the 1960–1990 period, members had more outlets for their stories. Further, as the number of political action committees (PACs) that provide campaign dollars grew from roughly 600 in the mid-1970s to 4,500 plus today, so, too, did the number of contact points for senators, for both incoming lobbying and outgoing fund-raising. Members had to find time on the daily schedule for these new lobbyists, too. As a result of PACs, writes political scientist Gary Jacobsen in *Congress Reconsidered,* "More time and attention is devoted to politics outside the institution, and outside influences on internal politics have become stronger and more pervasive." Whether or not those PACs have undue influence in the Senate, they have certainly reshaped daily life in the body, demanding an increasing share of a finite commodity, time.

Decline of consensus. Fifth, like the House, the Senate has experienced growing difficulty in achieving consensus on policy. Facing an unyielding budget deficit, tempers have flared more frequently as the once-contemplative Senate has struggled to balance its entrepreneurial instincts with budget realities. Senators have noted the decline in comity among members, reporting that their greatest frustration is with the budget process and its series of seemingly meaningless votes.

This growing anger over sessions that are too long and too often crowded with trivia, coupled with the election of increasingly younger members—who come to Washington with their young families—has led the Senate leadership to promise shorter sessions and, consequently, more time for family life. Despite that promise, the average Senate day remains frenetic, driven by endless scheduling conflicts, comings and goings, and nearly interminable waiting.

It is hardly surprising that daily life in the Senate is extraordinarily stressful.

Overlong days, fragmented schedules, and member frustration have resulted in increasing committee truancy, as Richard Hall characterizes it. Absenteeism became such a serious obstacle to legislative productivity in the mid-1980s that the Senate created a select committee to hold hearings on possible reforms. It was therefore rather ironic when nine of this select committee's twelve members had scheduling conflicts during the first two days of hearings. Only three attended both days of the opening hearings, while five never appeared at all.

SENATORS' MAJOR ACTIVITIES. The average day in the Senate has become increasingly fractured as electoral pressures, a growing casework burden, constant media scrutiny, and an increasingly complex policy agenda threaten to overwhelm members. Although every day has its own contours—the days at the beginning of a session, for example, being vastly different and more relaxed than the days just before adjournment—most senators divide their time between four sometimes competing kinds of activity.

Constituent service and contact. Senators invest significant amounts of time in traditional casework and constituent contact, amounts that appear to be relatively constant across the six-year term. According to a 1988 study, senators not running for reelection were almost as likely as those who were running to make contact with voters through mail, television, radio, print media, or personal meetings. All of these points of contact with constituents must be squeezed into a schedule already crowded with the normal legislative business of the Senate. Although most Senate casework is performed by staff, whether in Washington, D.C., or back in the home state, senators must be kept posted; furthermore, they occasionally intercede on particularly difficult or visible issues.

Publicity seeking and credit claiming. Media interviews present senators with opportunities to claim credit for the public service they have performed and the benefits their work has created, both in their home states and, when a senator has presidential ambitions, in the key states of an upcoming presidential campaign. A senator's ability to claim credit for a particular piece of legislation, however, depends on a long trail of actions: his or her work in shaping an appropriations bill, for example, or participation in an oversight hearing or in fashioning new rules for a federal agency, or the committed way in which he or she backed a presidential initiative. That is, to claim credit, a senator has to have done a lot of work. True, staff often lay the groundwork, but there is no substitute for the kind of individual, personal lobbying that only a senator can perform. And no matter what form that personal contact takes—composing a note, making a phone call, arranging for a face-to-face meeting—the senator must clear the time needed to do it. Added to this time pressure is the fact that a senator must often personally lobby the media to make sure that he or she gets the credit due.

Agenda setting and policy advancement. Ultimately, senators may care the most about setting the policy agenda. Becoming known as a national expert and spokesperson on an issue such as health care is one route to a presidential candidacy. Thus, the Senate's role as a presidential incubator has long gone hand in hand with its role as an incubator of policy agendas. Individual senators often invest great energy in developing ideas that bear their mark and that ultimately become statutes. No matter how pressured by the exigencies of the budget deficit or other time-consuming matters, many senators make sure they reserve at least a portion of each day to learn more about the policy areas in which they have chosen to become experts.

Enterprise management. Finally, all senators must dedicate time merely to keeping track of their staffs, staff assignments, and schedules. Although this management function is often overlooked when the sources of constraint are enumerated, a significant portion of an average day is dedicated to making choices regarding how time will be allocated. The calendar itself can be a source of conflict among staffers representing different concerns, such as constituent demands, publicity seeking, and policy development. Some senators resolve this pressure by appointing strong chiefs of staff; others reserve the adjudicatory role for themselves. At least one recent senator has handled the problem electronically, setting up a command center in his Senate hideaway office from which he monitored his personal staff by phone and electronic mail.

THE STRESSES OF AN AVERAGE DAY. Given all these activities, it is hardly surprising that daily life in the Senate is extraordinarily stressful. The average day starts long before the opening prayer by the Senate chaplain.

Usually, it begins with an early breakfast, then continues with the first of several committee and subcommittee appearances. These are normally marked by quick opening statements, which can be inserted for the record, and short rounds of questions and answers for particularly important witnesses. More often than not, several hearings are scheduled simultaneously, so senators conduct a good deal of business as they run from one to the other and back again. Such is a normal morning when Congress is in session.

The already frantic day continues with trips to the Senate television studio for short interviews and longer satellite feeds to television stations back home, speeches to and meetings with assorted lobbying groups, occasional stops at Capitol hideaway offices, subway rides to and from the Senate office buildings, staff briefings, quorum calls and votes on the Senate floor, constituent contacts, quick lunches and dinners, caucus meetings, interviews with local and national reporters, strategy sessions, scheduling conferences to sort out invitations, and further business until late into the evening. Now that Senate floor debate is televised, rare is the senator who does not make at least one appearance a day to speak on the floor. Although every senator's schedule is different, it is safe to say that the average day allows little or no time for reflection and debate as meetings and quick contacts merge into a strobe light of activity. The schedule rarely eases, even during the most contentious floor debates (which merely make the day longer).

Ironically, the greater collegiality of the Senate as compared to the House can actually contribute to the frustrations of the daily routine. Senators do possess a much greater potential to exert individual influence than do their House colleagues, but the atmosphere in which conversation and dealings go on has a claustrophobic, small-townish intensity. Senators strive to keep personal conflict at a minimum through, for example, the time-honored practice of seeking unanimous consent for all business. But while the search for unanimity does smoothe the rough edges of policy disputes, it also often delays progress, adding to the time needed for passing even the most routine legislation. The sources of delay are many and varied—ranging from the full-blown filibuster to personal requests for delays on pending legislation—and they are available to even the most junior member.

In the search for ways to resolve disputes, individual senators, particularly committee chairmen, have few of the levers that allow for quick action in the House. The norm of committee deference is long forgotten, and committee chairmen may find that even the most strongly supported committee measure can be all too easily replaced on the floor by an alternative crafted by a single member. Such unpredictability adds to the demands on already pressured members, who must allocate time for scouting the potential opposition and for crafting the bargains that will make progress possible.

A HOUSE IN SENATE CLOTHING? The notion that the Senate has become a House of Representatives in more collegial, less rule-bounded clothing has clear implications for daily life. Unanimous consent does provide at least some semblance of predictability in the daily floor schedule, but the rest of the process, including floor amending, is often anything but predictable. The Senate's lack of the tight rules that guide procedure in the House, combined with the ever-greater electoral tension felt by all its members, have made the Senate the antithesis of what the Framers envisioned—at least in terms of the daily routine. Tune to think and reflect has become exceedingly rare.

[See also (I) Congress, article on Customs and Mores of Congress.]

BIBLIOGRAPHY

Davidson, Roger H., ed. *The Post-Reform Congress.* 1992.
Deering, Christopher. *Congressional Politics.* 1989.
Dodd, Lawrence, and Bruce I. Oppenheimer. *Congress Reconsidered.* 4th ed. 1989.
Light, Paul. *Forging Legislation.* 1992.
Loomis, Burdette. *The New American Politician: Ambition, Entrepreneurship, and the Changing Face of Political Life.* 1988.
Sinclair, Barbara. *Transformation of the U.S. Senate.* 1989.
Smith, Steven. *Call to Order: Floor Politics in the House and Senate.* 1989.

– PAUL C. LIGHT

Qualifications

The Constitution clearly and starkly enumerates the qualifications for serving in the House of Representatives and the Senate. In the qualifications clauses (Article I, sections 2 and 3), the basic requirements of age, citizenship, and residency are set out. House members must be twenty-five years old, U.S. citizens for at least seven years, and inhabitants of the state (not the district) that they represent. Senators must be thirty years old, citizens for at least nine years, and inhabitants of their states.

A series of court rulings and two hundred years of congressional decisions have established that these constitutional criteria represent an exclusive list of qualifications for members of Congress. States have been barred from imposing additional requirements; for example, ex-felons cannot be barred, nor can those rare individuals who reside outside the congressional districts in which they run and are elected.

Still, the two houses have traditionally served as the judges of the qualifications of their own memberships. In the past, the chambers have excluded members-elect on the basis of polygamy and disloyalty. Like the Senate, the House has the uncontested capacity to expel one of its members for actions committed after election, but this power has been exercised only four times in its history, three times in the 1860s in connection with members from border states who were accused of treason and in 1981 in connection with one representative found guilty of accepting bribes in the Abscam corruption case. On occasion, members have resigned rather than face possible expulsion, as did two other members involved in the Abscam affair. But there is no question that actions committed prior to their election cannot be used to bar members-elect from taking their seats.

In 1969 the Supreme Court clarified the qualifications criteria with its landmark decision in *Powell v. McCormack.* In 1967 the House voted to deny Rep. Adam Clayton Powell, Jr. (D-N.Y.), the seat he had won in the 1968 election. Powell stood accused of the misuse of official funds and unauthorized travel by staff members; in addition, he had refused to pay a judgment in a highly publicized libel case. After the Democrats stripped him of his Education and Labor Committee chairmanship, the full House refused to seat him. Powell sued the House, and the Supreme Court somewhat surprisingly agreed to hear the case. Powell's congressional seat remained vacant through 1968, and he once again won the office in the 1968 election. In January 1969 he was seated, although he had been stripped of his seniority. But the 1967 House decision remained before the Court, which ruled in June 1969 that the House had exceeded its constitutional limits by imposing additional qualifications for its membership. Only a constitutional amendment could impose further restrictions.

Directly related to the question of qualifications is that of contested elections. While the qualifications issue has rarely generated much internal congressional turmoil, this has not been the case with contested elections. Almost six hundred such cases have come before the House and its Elections Committee (or, after 1947, a subcommittee of the House Administration Committee). In the nineteenth century, highly partisan decisions were regularly rendered; more recently, however, the winner of a contested seat has generally been decided on the merits of the case, as a substantial body of precedent has been established. Still, only very rarely have contested elections turned on matters of formal qualification. For example, one issue of residence was resolved in 1807 when the House decided that the current residence in Maryland of representative-elect William McCreery met the inhabitancy qualification and that the state could not require a twelve-month residence for eligibility.

Advocates of term limitations contest past rulings and congressional practice; they argue that there is no explicit constitutional prohibition of such state-imposed limits. With Colorado leading the way in 1990 by mandating twelve-year limits for both U.S. senators and representatives (1991 counted as the first year), and with many other states having since passed similar requirements, this argument will surely come before the Supreme Court, unless a constitutional amendment renders the issue moot.

Supporters of term limits want a legislature that is as good as the American People; opponents want one that is better.

There have been some apparent state limitations on would-be candidates. Some defeated congressional primary candidates have been refused ballot access as independents in the general election. When write-in votes have been permitted, this restriction has not generally been interpreted as an additional qualification; rather, the states have been seen as carrying out their constitutional duty to conduct the elections of senators and representatives. More common have been various states' attempts to regulate ballot access to independents and to sitting state officeholders. Independents can be forced to comply with stringent provisions for gaining ballot status. Current state officeholders can be forced to resign their positions in order to run for the Congress; the Ninth District Court of Appeals ruled in an Arizona case (*Joyner v. Mofford* [1983]) that such restrictions are within the state's province of regulating state officials. *Joyner* ruled that no new qualifications are considered to have been imposed on such individuals; rather, they are being required to comply with the conditions of service that apply to the state offices they hold.

In sum, the constitutional qualifications of age, citizenship, and residency have stood solidly as the major formal restrictions on congressional service. In the wake of the *Powell* decision, other prior qualifications have little chance of standing up to the scrutiny of the House, the Senate, or the Supreme Court. The term limitation movement, while presenting the most serious set of qualifications issues in more than two hundred years, will probably need a constitutional amendment to triumph in its attempt to restrict congressional service.

[See also (I) Elections, Congressional, Ethics and Corruption in Congress.]

BIBLIOGRAPHY

Benjamin, Gerald, and Michael Malbin, eds. *Limiting Legislative Terms.* 1992.
Galloway, George B. *History of the House of Representatives.* 1961.
Jacobs, Andrew. *The Powell Affair: Freedom Minus One.* 1973.

– BURDETT A. LOOMIS

Tenure and Turnover

As applied to Congress, tenure and turnover are closely related concepts. Tenure refers to the length of time members serve in the House of Representatives or Senate. Turnover refers to the rate at which the membership "turns over," or changes. Tenure is usually reported as the mean number of years the current membership has served. Turnover is usually measured as the percent of the membership entering the body for the first time. Tenure and turnover are thus different ways of measuring the relative stability of the congressional membership. A stable membership is one in which new members rarely enter, because those already in the body are willing and able to stay. This results in small entering classes, a lengthy mean tenure, and a relatively consistent and experienced membership.

DESIRABILITY OF LONG TENURES. Historically, there has been much discussion of the optimal length of congressional service. Under the Articles of Confederation, the length of a stay in Congress was limited to "only three out of every six years." But during the summer of 1787, when the current U.S. Constitution was being debated, mandatory limits on length of service were proposed (in the Virginia Plan) and then rejected. It seems clear from several sources that most of the delegates assumed that congressional service, even without formal limits, would be brief. In recent years, the idea of limiting the tenure of senators and representatives has resurfaced. States have passed laws limiting service, and amendments to the Constitution have been floated. Public opinion polls indicate that approximately 70 percent of the American people feel term limits are a good idea. The most commonly mentioned figure is twelve years (two six-year terms) in the Senate and eight years (four two-year terms) in the House.

The debate over limits on length of service reveals deep differences as to the ideal nature of a legislature. Supporters of term limits prefer representatives to serve briefly and never lose sight of the views possessed by ordinary citizens. Opponents of term limits prefer representatives who are sophisticated and experienced in complex public issues and the nature of the legislative process. Supporters want a legislature that is a mirror of the American people, opponents a prism. Supporters want a legislature that is as good as the American people; opponents want a legislature that is better than the American people. Thus, squabbles over the proper length of congressional service can quickly turn into fundamental disagreements over approaches to governance.

ACTUAL TENURE. The absence of a restriction on length of congressional service was of little consequence for quite some time. In the early days of the Republic few members of either the House or the Senate were eager to stay for more than a year or two. Indeed, members often did not even serve out their terms, instead choosing to resign before a session was complete. Even in the 1830s the membership was surprisingly fluid. Of the 242 members in the 24th Congress (1835–1837), 128 were not in the 25th Congress. Gradually, however, the mean length of stay in the House and the Senate increased and the number of first-termers diminished. Still, the pace of change should not be overstated. As recently as one hundred years ago, the mean length of service in the House was approximately five years. In 1893, 44 percent of the House membership were new to their positions.

Why, in the nineteenth century, did members leave Congress so quickly? Most of the turnover was voluntary (that is, members were not defeated in an election but instead simply decided to quit). The federal government did not then have nearly the clout it does now. Many state legislatures were more important than Congress, and Washington was viewed by some politicians as a mosquito-infested outback. In addition, some states followed a tradition of rotation, whereby after a few years of congressional service the incumbent would step aside to make room for someone else. In a restricted sense, then, departures for reasons other than electoral defeat may not all have been entirely voluntary. Finally, there was a high level of electoral volatility. Partisan tides would occasionally sweep out large numbers of members. In 1874, for example, the Republicans lost 96 seats in the House, and in 1894 the Democrats lost 116.

All this combined to create substantial turnover. In the first half of the twentieth century, however, things began to settle down. The United States was becoming a world power; the New Deal expanded the domestic role of the federal government; Washington was becoming more livable (some say the introduction of air-conditioning was a factor here); and the custom of rotation had long since faded. As a result, the rate at which members of Congress were retiring voluntarily declined sharply and by the 1960s had reached very low levels; only eighty people left the House voluntarily (and did not pursue another political office) during that decade.

Electoral volatility also diminished. The previously mentioned partisan swings in the range of one hundred seats were replaced by swings in the range of ten, twenty, or perhaps, in an unusual election year, forty to fifty. Incumbent senators and, especially, incumbent representatives became much more adept at winning reelection. On average, in the last thirty years, nearly 95 percent of all House incumbents and 80 percent of all Senate incumbents who wanted to secure reelection were able to do so. Most of these incumbents won quite easily. During the late 1960s, the mean percentage of the vote received by incumbents went up more than 5 percent. Thus, since 1970 not only have 95 percent of House incumbents won, but they have also received on average two votes to every one for the increasingly outgunned challengers.

In the 1970s, although incumbents continued to do well electorally, there was an increase in voluntary retirements, due largely to an improved pension plan and congressional reforms which devalued the seniority of older members who were already predisposed to voluntary retirement. But by the 1980s both the desire and the ability of incumbents to secure reelection were present in force. In percentage terms, fewer new members entered the Congress in the 1980s than in any previous decade. Each new Congress of the decade (in other words, every two years) brought in less than fifty new representatives, or only about 12 percent of the House.

Compared to two hundred years ago, congressional tenure has increased and congressional turnover has decreased.

In light of this, it may not be surprising that some recent careers in Congress have been remarkably long. Carl Vinson (D-Ga.) served for fifty consecutive years in the House of Representatives before retiring in 1965. Emanuel Celler (D-N.Y.) also served five full decades in the House before he was defeated in 1972. And in January of 1992 Jamie L. Whitten (D-Miss.) passed both of them by beginning his fifty-first consecutive year of House service. In terms of combined House and Senate service, the record is held by Carl Hayden (D-Ariz.) who served fifteen years in the House and forty-two years in the Senate prior to 1969.

While intriguing, these record-length careers are not typical. The average stay is about twelve years in the House and eleven years in the Senate. As of 1990, nearly 60 percent of the congressional membership had begun their service sometime in the 1980s and thus had served less than ten years. In the 102d Congress (1991–1993) there were as many representatives who had served less than four years as had served more than twenty, and about one-third of all senators were in their first terms. The atypically high House turnover in the 1992 elections (110 new members) lowered the mean length of service even more. Nevertheless, congressional career length is longer than it has ever been, on average, but is still not as long as some people imagine—and it is not as long as average length of service in many other national legislatures.

Still, the low (by historical standards) current level of membership turnover has prompted concern. As happened fleetingly in the 1960s, much was written in the late 1980s about a stale, ossified, and out-of-touch Congress. By the early 1990s such concerns had coalesced around the issue of term limitations. Highly visible failures in dealing with budget matters, unpopular pay raises that members had voted themselves, and various scandals and revelations about congressional barbershops, restaurants, and banks all contributed to the sentiment.

Of course, the key feature in the debate over the merits of congressional experience is whether senior legislators are assets or liabilities. Advocates of term limits feel that senior members are susceptible, to "Potomac fever"—that their concerns shift from the home district to Washington—and that they become too chummy with interest groups and big contributors. Opponents of term limits are more likely to see the value of expertise and experience and to worry about the tendencies of inexperienced junior members (whose numbers would increase under term limits) to rely on unelected staffers and bureaucrats and to put forward an unfocused and unrealistic legislative agenda.

EVOLVING BICAMERALISM. One of the more instructive changes in turnover rates over the years has to do with the relationship of the House and the Senate. The authors of the Constitution clearly intended for the Senate to be less influenced by short-term changes in personnel and political mood. The six-year term, staggered elections, and indirect elections were designed to put a little distance between senators and the people. The House was to be more electorally sensitive. But something unexpected happened as the years passed. In recent decades, the House has become the less changeable body, largely due to the overwhelming advantage of House incumbents over their challengers. The Senate once had a much more stable membership than the House, but around the time of World War I the patterns merged, and during some recent periods the stability of House membership has actually exceeded that of the Senate. Even though individual terms are three times longer in the Senate, careers in the Senate are not currently any longer than careers in the House. For the most part, Senate tenure and turnover are about equal to House tenure and turnover.

This new bicameral equality of tenure was underlined recently when the partisan majority in the Senate switched twice (in 1980 and 1986) while the House remained dominated by the same party (the Democrats). Senate membership has become every bit as fluid as House membership, and U.S. politics may even have experienced an inversion of the bicameral relationship intended by the Framers. This situation makes it less likely the Senate will serve as the "saucer" that cools the passions of the House. Whether this is ultimately for the better or the worse is a question beyond the scope of this essay.

Three points about congressional tenure and turnover are worth underscoring. First, compared to two hundred years ago, congressional tenure has increased and congressional turnover has decreased. The changes are substantial. By 1990, the annual infusion of new members constituted, on average, about 6 percent of the overall membership (or 12 percent every two years) and the average representative or senator had been in the body a little over eleven years. The range of service ran from a few months to fifty years. Second, Senate turnover is now virtually equal to House turnover despite the Framers' desire for the Senate to be the more stable and sedate body (*Federalist* 62). Finally, as the ongoing debate over term limits would point up, changes in levels of turnover and length of tenure have serious political implications. Views as to the optimal level of each are generally determined by larger convictions about the kind of legislators most desirable as the U.S. political system enters the next century.

[See also (I) Elections, Congressional, article on Voting, Incumbency.]

BIBLIOGRAPHY

Hibbing, John R. *Congressional Careers: Contours of Life in the U.S. House of Representatives.* 1991.

Matthews, Donald R. *U.S. Senators and Their World.* 1960.

Polsby, Nelson W. "The Institutionalization of the U.S. House of Representatives." *American Political Science Review* 62 (1968): 144–168.

Price, H. Douglas. "The Congressional Career: Then and Now." In *Congressional Behavior.* Edited by Nelson W. Polsby. 1971.

– JOHN R. HIBBING

MOTIONS

In the House

The term *motion* refers generally to any formal proposal made before a deliberative assembly. However, its use here is confined only to the general and more frequently used motions, called *secondary motions,* which are used to dispose of the main proposition under consideration.

Secondary motions are outlined in clause 4 of Rule XVI of the House Rules, where they are given the following order of priority: to adjourn, to lay on the table, for the previous question, to postpone to a specified day (day certain), to refer, to amend, and to postpone indefinitely.

The motion to adjourn not only has the highest precedence when a question is under consideration but, with certain restrictions, has the highest privilege under all other conditions. The motion to lay on the table is used in the House for a final, adverse disposition of a matter.

The motion for the previous question, explained in Rule XVII, is used to close debate or to foreclose further amendments and bring the pending matter to a vote. Defeat of this motion not only throws the main question open for further consideration but also transfers the right of recognition to those members who opposed the motion.

There are two distinct, debatable motions to postpone: to postpone to a day certain and to postpone indefinitely. The adoption of a motion to postpone indefinitely constitutes a final, adverse disposition of the underlying measure.

There are four motions to refer, which send a measure to a specific committee or committees, with or without instructions as to the actions the committee is to take: the ordinary motion to refer when a question is "under debate" (clause 4 of Rule XVI), the motion to recommit after the previous question has been ordered on a bill or joint resolution to final passage (clause 4 of Rule XVI), the motion to commit pending the motion for or after the ordering of the previous question (clause 1 of Rule XVII), and the motion to refer pending a vote in the House on the motion to strike the enacting clause (clause 7 of Rule XXIII). The terms *refer, commit,* and *recommit* are sometimes used interchangeably; when used in the precise manner contemplated in each rule, they reflect certain procedural differences.

The motion to amend (under Rule XIX and under Section XXXV of Jefferson's Manual) and motions to dispose of amendments between the houses (under Section XLV of Jefferson's Manual) are discussed elsewhere in this work.

[See also (I) Previous Question, Recommital.]

BIBLIOGRAPHY

U.S. House of Representatives. *Constitution, Jefferson's Manual, and Rules of the House of Representatives, 103d Congress.* Compiled by William Holmes Brown. 102d Cong., 2d sess., 1992. H. Doc. 102–405.

U.S. House of Representatives. *Deschler's Precedents of the United States House of Representatives,* by Lewis Deschler. 94th Cong., 2d sess., 1977. H. Doc. 94-661. Vol. 7, Chap. 23.

– MUFTIAH MCCARTIN

In the Senate

The Senate operates largely by unanimous consent of its members. When that fails, there are a number of motions that can be used to avoid the requirement of unanimous consent. The two most commonly used motions are the motion to proceed and the motion to invoke cloture.

It is in order to move to proceed to bills on the calendar if the bill has complied with the requirement of being on the calendar for one legislative day and a written report on the bill has been printed and available for forty-eight hours. The motion to proceed is a prerogative of the majority leader. Such a motion is debatable, however. While it is pending, Rule XXII allows senators to make a second motion that would end debate on the motion to proceed. The second motion is a motion to invoke cloture, or limit debate. Cloture motions are also the prerogative of the majority leader.

A motion to invoke cloture is automatically voted on after one intervening day of session. Unlike the motion to proceed, which is carried by a majority vote, a cloture motion requires a three-fifths majority of the total membership. Under the rules of the Senate, thirty hours of consideration are allowed once a cloture motion passes.

If a motion to proceed is agreed to, several other motions are in order under Rule XXII. For example, it is then in order to move that the pending matter be referred to a Senate committee. It is also in order to move to postpone a pending matter either to a certain day or indefinitely (this latter is a "killing" motion).

All these motions are debatable in the Senate. Several other kinds of motions, however, must be decided without debate. The motion to table, which is commonly used when amendments are pending, is not a debatable motion, and, if it is adopted, it kills the item that is tabled. Certain procedural motions are also not debatable under Rule XXII. These include motions to recess and adjourn.

With rare exceptions, motions in the Senate do not require seconding. The motion to go into closed session does require one senator to second the motion, and the motion to discharge a particular kind of bill—the so-called rescission bill—requires a second by one-fifth of the members. A senator's request that a vote be a recorded vote also requires a second by one-fifth of the members.

[See also (I) Cloture.]

BIBLIOGRAPHY

Tiefer, Charles. *Congressional Practice and Procedure.* 1989.

U.S. Senate. *Riddick's Senate Procedure, Precedents, and Practices,* by Floyd M. Riddick and Alan S. Frumin. 101st Cong., 2d sess., 1992. S. Doc. 101-28.

– ROBERT B. DOVE

O

OATH OF OFFICE

Article VI, clause 3 of the U.S. Constitution requires that senators and representatives take an oath of office to support the Constitution. The language of the oath is set by statute (5 U.S.C. 3331) and has changed several times since 1789. In 1994 it reads:

> I do solemnly swear that I will support and defend the Constitution of the United States against all enemies, foreign and domestic; that I will bear true faith and allegiance to the same; that I take this obligation freely, without any mental reservation or purpose of evasion, and that I will well and faithfully discharge the duties of the office on which I am about to enter. So help me God.

The oath is administered to members-elect on the opening day of each new Congress. In the House, the most senior member (the "Dean" of the House) first administers the oath to the Speaker, who then administers it to all other members in the chamber en masse. Prior to 1929, the oath was administered by state delegation.

In the Senate, the oath is administered by the president of the Senate or a designated senator in his stead. Since 1927, senators have come forward to take the oath in alphabetical order in groups of four.

Members must be sworn before they can take their seats (2 U.S.C. 21, 25). Both chambers have at times authorized a member of Congress, one of their officers, or a justice to administer the oath to members necessarily absent on opening day.

BIBLIOGRAPHY

U.S. House of Representatives. *Deschler's Precedents of the United States House of Representatives,* by Lewis Deschler. 94th Cong., 2d sess., 1977. H. Doc. 94-661. Vol. 1, chap. 2.

U.S. Senate. *Riddick's Senate Procedure, Precedents, and Practices,* by Floyd M. Riddick and Alan S. Frumin. 101st Cong., 2d sess., 1992. S. Doc. 101-28, Pp. 699–710.

– ILONA B. NICKELS

OBJECTORS

Objectors are members of the House of Representatives appointed to screen legislation considered under expedited floor procedures permitting passage with only minimal debate and no recorded vote. So that such measures are not adopted without some review, the majority and minority leaders appoint six members, three from each party, to serve as "official objectors" responsible for examining measures placed on the Consent Calendar. Another six members serve as objectors for Private Calendar measures.

Bills on the Private Calendar benefit one individual or entity, and do not become public law. Bills on the Consent Calendar must be so routine that they elicit no more than two objections to their passage.

During each new Congress, the official objectors issue criteria that legislation must meet to avoid an objection. The objectors are present on the House floor when Consent Calendar legislation is considered on the first and third Mondays of each month, and on the first and third Tuesdays when Private Calendar bills are called. The objectors decide if the legislation violates the announced criteria for their respective calendars, or is otherwise unacceptable. While other members are free to lodge an objection during these proceedings, the official objectors are responsible for doing so on behalf of their party.

The official objector system was first proposed in 1932, although several House members had been operating informally as objectors on their own initiative for years before that. The Senate abandoned objectors in the 1970s. The responsibility for reviewing routine legislation in the Senate now belongs to staff members of the two party policy committees.

[See also (I) Calendars.]

BIBLIOGRAPHY

Congressional Quarterly Inc. *How Congress Works.* 2d ed. 1991. Pp. 46–48.

U.S. House of Representatives. *Deschler's Precedents of the United States House of Representatives,* by Lewis Deschler. 94th Cong., 2d sess., 1977. H. Doc. 94-661. Vol. 7, chap. 22.

– ILONA B. NICKELS

OFFICE OF TECHNOLOGY ASSESSMENT (OTA)

During the years following World War II, technology increasingly became both the source of and the answer to public policy problems. The Office of Technology Assessment was created in response to this emergence of technology as a major force in twentieth-century society. By 1972, when the OTA was established, Congress was confronted with three immediate and compelling issues. First, it had become clear that technological innovation had unexpected environmental consequences—for example, the ecological devastation that had accompanied the widespread use of the insecticide DDT. Second, federal expenditures on technological research and development amounted to more than eighteen billion dollars, expenditures widely recognized as essential investments in the future. Third, struggles between President Richard M. Nixon and Congress over such issues as super-sonic jet transport had convinced many members of Congress of the necessity of a specially designated source of scientific technical advice.

In retrospect, it is clear that Congress hoped that the OTA would act as an objective organization that could provide both Congress and the public with scientific and technical assessments in layman's terms. The OTA was seen as a body that could provide early identification of so-called second-order consequences of technology, such as negative environmental impacts. The OTA was intended as a support organization that could identify policy alternatives but that would not seek to substitute its judgments for those of the members of Congress.

In pursuit of these goals, Congress established a unique governance and advisory structure for the OTA. It is governed by the twelve-member Technology Assessment Board (TAB), divided equally between the House and the Senate and between the Democratic and Republican parties. In addition the Technology Assessment Advisory Council (TAAC), which is composed of eminent leaders from across the nation, the comptroller general of the United States, and the director of the Congressional Research Service, provides general advice. The OTA's director is chosen by the TAB and appointed for six years.

The OTA was a center of controversy throughout the tenure of its first two directors, Emilio Q. Daddario and Russell Petersen. During Daddario's term, some critics raised questions about perceived patronage on the part of TAB members in hiring OTA staff. The OTA was also seen by some as being too responsive to the short-term concerns of Congress (that is, its studies were too responsive to current legislative initiatives) and not concerned enough about major long-range issues, such as global warming. Some members of the press accused the OTA of being a research arm for the anticipated presidential campaign of Sen. Edward M. Kennedy (D-Mass.), who was TAB's first chairman. When Petersen took over as director, he had sole control over hiring; thus, any suspicion of patronage was eliminated. He also moved the OTA away from concern with short-term congressional interests toward what he perceived to be long-term issues. In so doing, however, he created the impression of being unresponsive to the needs of Congress.

John Gibbons's appointment, in June 1979, as OTA's third director was widely viewed as the OTA's last chance. Under Gibbons the OTA became what many believe to be Washington's most competent, unbiased, and valuable policy research organization concerned with science and technology issues. No longer a focus of controversy, the OTA was now a source of information, analysis, and insight used by a broad range of interests in the policy debates of the nation. Thus, when OTA's fourth director, Roger C. Herdman, was appointed in May 1993, he took over a highly regarded, well-established organization.

Over the years, the range of issues studied by the OTA has included the Strategic Defense Initiative (SDI), lie detector testing, and the preservation of books in the Library of Congress, as well as more general technological and environmental concerns. Key to the OTA's reputation is its ability to present clear characterizations of the uncertainty and controversy that frequently surround scientific and technical information relevant to public policy.

The OTA was seen as a body that could provide early identification of so-called second-order consequences of technology, such as negative environmental impacts.

Recent OTA studies illustrate the diversity of its work. In a report entitled *Complex Cleanup,* OTA investigated the environmental management of nuclear waste materials stored at Department of Energy facilities. It noted that at some facilities technical solutions are not available and that for all sites there is a major need for establishing procedures that provide public credibility for the cleanup activities. The OTA has also devoted major attention to the health area recently. Reports have ranged from a focus on the efficacy and economics of various health-related technologies to the challenge posed by drug-resistant strains of tuberculosis.

Studies in the energy area have given particular attention to the many possibilities for increasing energy efficiency and within that focus have looked at the role that more efficient technologies might play in helping the new free-market economies of Eastern Europe. Studies in the international security area have ranged from reports on satellite-based remote sensing to reports on the proliferation of nuclear- and chemical-warfare capability. The diversity of topics treated by OTA reports is illustrated by, for example, an investigation of the efficacy of computers in improving American education and a report on crop substitution as a way to stop South American farmers from growing coca, the plant from which cocaine is made.

Many people believe the OTA's success is tied to its small size and the manifold expertise of its staff. It has less than two hundred employees and a budget of roughly $20 million. The OTA has a unique ability to tap diverse experts and interested parties through its contracting authority and its advisory panels.

The OTA's major studies have advisory panels of from twelve to twenty people, chosen to represent both the range of expert opinion and the range of interested parties. OTA advisory panel meetings sometimes contribute to the evolution of a consensus since they serve as a neutral meeting ground for such varied interests and experts.

The OTA uses outside expertise more than other congressional support organizations. OTA reports are written by the agency's staff, but it has great flexibility in contracting for specific expert support. Under Daddario, an effort was made to have all studies contracted out. Both because of the unique character of the OTA's assessments and the need to be sensitive to Congress's desires, the contracting approach failed.

OTA studies are normally completed in one to two years. The OTA responds only to study requests from committee chairmen, from the TAB, or from its own director. The OTA's relatively small size and budget means that it must do less than is requested and thus must negotiate with the requesting committees in establishing its priorities. This has resulted in a pattern of careful study development. Frequently, studies are defined in ways that serve the needs of multiple committees.

Information generated by the OTA flows to the Congress in a number of ways. OTA staff maintain informal (e.g., briefings) and formal (e.g., testimony and interim publications) contact with committee staff during the studies. The OTA produces highly readable reports that are of importance not only to Congress but to the research and policy community nationwide. Thus, information flows back to the Congress through interested parties who use the OTA's work.

For those who have observed the evolution of the OTA, there is a consensus that it is a striking success story. As scientific and technical issues become ever more important to U.S. policy-making, it seems clear that the OTA will continue to play a key role.

BIBLIOGRAPHY

Burby, Jack. "OTA Comes of Age." *Los Angeles Times,* 1 November 1987.

Jenkins, Chris. "The Office of What?" *San Diego Union,* 24 November 1992.

U.S. Congress. Office of Technology Assessment. *An Experiment in Technology Policy-Making: Fifteen Years of the U.S. Office of Technology Assessment,* by Mary Proctor. 100th Cong., 1st sess., 1987.

Walters, Rhodri. "The Office of Technology Assessment of the United States Congress: A Model for the Future?" *Government and Opposition* 27 (1992): 89–108.

Wood, Fred B. "The Status of Technology Assessment: A View from the Congressional Office of Technology Assessment." *Technological Forecasting and Social Change* 22 (1982):211–222.

– DON E. KASH

ONE-MINUTE SPEECHES

At the start of each day of session in the House of Representatives, members are normally recognized to address the House for one-minute on any subject they wish. These speeches are not a right accorded members under the Rules of the House of Representatives. Rather, they are a privilege granted under accepted House tradition. In order to give a one-minute speech, a member must first gain recognition by the chair and then must ask and receive the unanimous consent of the House to address it for one minute.

Members who wish to give a one-minute speech sit in the front row of seats on their respective party's side of the main aisle. The Speaker recognizes members in order from his right to his left. A majority member is recognized first, followed by a minority member, in an alternating pattern. There is no guarantee that each member seated will receive the opportunity to give a one-minute speech that day. The Speaker may decline to hold any one-minute speeches at all on a day when legislative business is pressing, or he may decide to hold only a minimal number.

One-minute speeches provide members with an outlet for expression and commentary, without the usual requirement to make only remarks relevant to pending legislative matters. In practice, members devote almost half these speeches to either national or international issues and approximately one-third to pending legislation, followed in descending order of frequency by eulogies or special tributes, items of local interest to their districts, commentary on internal House operations and procedures, and humorous topics.

One-minute speeches are very popular because of their brevity and variety. They are well suited for use as videotaped news releases to constituents and are widely viewed by congressional colleagues and staff. This makes them effective publicity tools for legislative initiatives.

Only a small number of members—less than 10 percent of any given Congress—choose to give no one-minute speeches at all. Invariably, one or two members gain reputations for giving many more one-minute speeches than their colleagues. The vast majority of members, whether they be majority, minority, junior or senior in tenure, fall between these extremes, giving occasional one-minute speeches.

The first one-minute speech was given in the House on 2 August 1937. By 1940, the strict one-minute limitation had been established as accepted practice, having been institutionalized by then-Speaker Sam Rayburn. In 1980, party leaders agreed that one-minute speeches would occur at the start of each day's proceedings unless advance notice is given that they will be shifted to a later time of day. In 1984, the Speaker instituted the practice of alternating recognition for one-minute speeches between majority and minority members. One-minute speeches are unquestionably an integral and valued part of House procedure.

[See also (I) House of Representatives, article on Daily Sessions of the House.]

BIBLIOGRAPHY

Nickels, Ilona B. *One-Minute Speeches: House Practice and Procedure.* Congressional Research Service, Library of Congress. CRS Rept. 90-47 GOV. 1990.

Tiefer, Charles. *Congressional Practice and Procedure.* 1989. Pp. 237–238.

U.S. House of Representatives. *Deschler's Precedents of the United States House of Representatives,* by Lewis Deschler. 94th Cong., 2d sess., 1977. Vol. 6, chap. 21, pp. 127–136.

– ILONA B. NICKELS

ORDERS

Orders grant authority for floor actions in both the House and Senate. Orders are used to govern a wide range of activities, from elaborately structuring a bill's consideration to simply permitting speeches not otherwise in order. Several specific types of orders exist.

A regular order consists of the normal standing rules of the chamber, taken together with its precedents (previous interpretive rulings of the chair). The regular order governs unless expressly waived.

A special order supplants the regular order, but usually only on a temporary basis. It is given the same respect as a standing rule while it is in force. A special order is also necessary to undertake an action on the floor on which the regular order is silent. In both chambers, special orders are most often agreed to by unanimous consent.

In the House, special orders are also created when the Rules Committee drafts a resolution establishing a procedure for floor action that does not otherwise fall within the regular order. Before this special resolution can become governing authority, the House must adopt it by majority vote. The Rules Committee has reported special orders as temporary authority for House floor actions since 1883.

Orders grant authority for floor actions in both the House and Senate.

In both chambers, a motion to suspend the rules and take a specified action implicitly creates a special order. If adopted by a two-thirds vote, the effect of a rules suspension is to temporarily waive the regular order for the purposes stated.

In the House special orders also mean those speeches delivered at the end of the day by members who have reserved time for this purpose in advance. Special order speeches may be given on any subject desired, and may range in length from five minutes to one hour. These speeches are not part of the regular order and unanimous consent is required for them to take place.

A standing order is a special order that applies for a specified duration of time. In the Senate, this is usually for the length of a two-year Congress but also can be for an open-ended period, with the order governing until retired or replaced. In the House, standing orders are quite infrequent, and usually govern only for the duration of one session.

In the Senate, the chamber will routinely agree to a list of requests for standing orders offered by its majority leader on the first day of a new Congress. For example, the majority and minority leaders are each granted ten minutes of floor time under their personal control on each day the Senate is in session. This so-called leader time occurs under the authority of a standing order, and is not addressed in the standing rules of the Senate. In the House, the chamber designates the hour of its daily meeting time by standing order on a yearly basis.

BIBLIOGRAPHY

U.S. House of Representatives. *Constitution, Jefferson's Manual, and Rules of the House of Representatives, 103d Congress.* Compiled by William Holmes Brown. 102d Cong., 2d sess., 1992. H. Doc. 102-405.

U.S. Senate. *Riddick's Senate Procedure, Precedents, and Practices,* by Floyd M. Riddick and Alan S. Frumin. 101st Cong., 2d sess., 1992. S. Doc. 101-28. P. 956.

– ILONA B. NICKELS

OVERSIGHT

Congress is vested with the power not only to make laws but also to ensure that these laws are effectively executed. Thus the obligation to oversee—that is, to supervise and to monitor the bureaucracy—stems from the lawmaking function of Congress. Constitutional provisions reinforce this logic: the basic structure of the executive branch is determined by Congress; important policies concerning executive branch personnel are established in Congress; the money that the executive branch spends is appropriated by Congress; the laws that the bureaucracy applies come from Congress.

From a historical perspective, the task of overseeing the executive flows from an obligation to monitor the spending of money raised through the votes of the legislative assembly. From a more contemporary perspective, oversight results from the realization that public policy is created not only in the text of laws but also during the process of implementing them. Congressional interest in bureaucratic activity then emerges from a general sense of obligation to make certain that laws are faithfully carried out and from specific concerns with implementation of particular policies. The former motive is general and diffuse; its impact is less than comprehensive. The latter motive is specific and pointed. Its power to stimulate oversight is considerable.

Congress has conducted oversight of the bureaucracy throughout U.S. history. There were congressional investigations of the conduct of war against the Indian tribes in 1792. Congress looked into the conduct of the Civil War. There were legislative inquiries into the Teapot Dome scandals in the 1920s. More recently, Congress investigated executive conduct in the Iran-contra scandal during the Reagan administration. Yet historically such oversight has not been frequent, comprehensive, or systematic.

The modern age of legislative oversight can be said to have begun in 1946, when Congress converted an assumed, traditional obligation to oversee into an explicit legal requirement. The Legislative Reorganization Act of 1946 required standing committees of the Congress to "exercise continuous watchfulness of the execution by the administrative agencies concerned of any laws, the subject of which is within the jurisdiction of such committee." Although this mandate seems all-inclusive, Congress has continued to write into law additional oversight authority, as in the Legislative Reorganization Act of 1970 and the Congressional Budget and Impoundment Control Act of 1974.

The legal mandate for oversight is substantial enough to permit Congress to look into just about any policy matter it desires. Therein lies the problem; the assigned task presents a broad agenda indeed. Moreover, oversight is only one of many congressional obligations. Because they are burdened with so many important tasks, members of Congress are constantly confronted with hard choices. Some of their obligations are given careful attention, some are generally attended to, and some are necessarily slighted. Members of Congress usually deny that any of their obligations are slighted, but the reality is clear. Where does oversight of the bureaucracy fit into the legislative workload?

Members of Congress set priorities in relation to their motives, the most prominent of which is the quest for reelection. Motivation for oversight of the bureaucracy soars if such activity leads to publicity for the member or benefits his or her constituency or persons, groups, or causes of special concern. Since much oversight involves hard, unglamorous work yielding little media attention and few direct benefits to the constituency, oversight tends not to be a high priority for members. Other motives are less prominent but surely relevant to oversight: the general desire to implement good policy and the desire to gain respect from one's peers. Members do not systematically oversee the bureaucracy because the law requires them to do so. If that were the dominant motive the quantity, and quality of oversight would be vastly different than at present.

After motivation, resources are important. How much oversight is accomplished relates to the resources available. Adequately staffed committees and subcommittees with substantial investigative budgets can better oversee the bureaucracy when motivated to do so. Committees and subcommittees with inadequate resources are more predisposed to slight their obligations. In Congress, resources are largely adequate to support major, sustained oversight efforts. In some state legislatures, this is not the case. In Congress, staff numbers and committee budgets have been regularly augmented and auxiliary staff agencies, such as the Congressional Research Service, the General Accounting Office, the Office of Technology Assessment, and the Congressional Budget Office, provide significant additional support for oversight efforts.

So how is oversight conducted, and to what effect? The former question is amenable to extended discussion and serious analysis. Answers to the latter are fewer and less reliable.

OVERSIGHT TECHNIQUES. Congress conducts legislative oversight of the bureaucracy through a variety of techniques. Most obvious is the committee or subcommittee investigation where a particular program, agency, or policy area is subject to a formal on-the-record study. Congress may also require executive units to file periodic reports detailing their activities in specified areas. The assumption is that these reports will provide a solid base of information on which oversight can be built. Congress, more precisely the Senate, is called upon to confirm high-level executive branch appointments. Confirmation hearings may provide occasion for questions about departmental and agency behavior. To facilitate oversight, some congressional committees, about fifteen, have created subcommittees primarily dedicated to this task.

The legal mandate for oversight is substantial enough to permit Congress to look into just about any policy matter it desires.

If oversight were limited to such formal procedures as investigations and reports, the oversight record would be easier to establish. In fact, much oversight occurs indirectly, as members of Congress pursue other tasks. Thus, in hearings held on proposed legislation, questions concerning what has been done before, by whom, and how well may arise. In appropriations hearings, how money previously requested was spent may become an issue. In pursuing casework (constituents' problems with the bureaucracy) congressional offices may identify patterns of abuse that require attention beyond solving the individual constituent's problem. Telephone calls, informal meetings, and luncheon sessions between congressional committee staff members and persons from the executive branch provide many occasions for the exchange of information and gossip useful for oversight.

In general, most members and staff persons prefer informal and unobtrusive methods of oversight. Regular communications removed from the public eye are commonplace. In fact, formal investigations sometimes signal that normal, informal methods have failed.

Each method, formal and informal, provides an opportunity for oversight. Not all opportunities are effectively pursued, however. For example, while Congress requires the president and executive departments and agencies to file annually thousands of reports detailing their activities, there is scant evidence that these reports are seriously attended to or even read. At times, report requirements are added to legislation simply to draw bureaucratic attention to specific constituent problems. While much daily casework takes place in Congress as members pursue constituents' requests, little attention is given to identifying from this activity patterns of problems that might require congressional attention. Confirmation hearings, an apt setting for oversight, are not often used for that purpose. Such sessions are often perfunctory, symbolic exercises.

CONDITIONS FOR OVERSIGHT. Calculating the amount of oversight is difficult also because the degree of activity is not historically constant. Scholarly studies asserted in the 1950s and 1960s that little systematic oversight was being conducted, while more recent research argues that more congressional oversight is being conducted. While it is possible that some of these studies were simply wrong, it is more likely that the amount of oversight conducted did vary with time and context. If so, then what elements explain this variation?

Joel Aberbach has identified several possibilities. In eras when money is especially scarce, members of Congress may become more concerned with oversight partly because they lack resources to establish new programs and partly because of heightened concern with how scarce resources are actually used. Congressional staffs, grown larger over the years and not tied up in creating legislation, seek outlets for their creativity and energy and are on the prowl for good publicity vehicles for their members. Increased investigative journalism in the aftermath of the Watergate scandals has brought more information to Congress and has alerted members to new problems. Extended periods of divided government, where one political party controls the Congress and the other the executive, may also add incentive.

If congressional oversight has increased in recent years, attempts to assess the significance of the change generate controversy. Some scholars continue to suggest that Congress simply does not do its job of systematically and comprehensively overseeing the bureaucracy very well, even if it now does more than in the past. For others, the increase in oversight is seen as significant. Comprehensive and systematic oversight, they argue, is simply an unrealizable ideal. The fact that Congress is doing more is central. For still another group, any focus on comparative quantity is misplaced. What is central for these writers is how well members of Congress are using available time and energy. From this perspective, to oversee all bureaucratic activity or to try to do so is a waste of resources. What Congress should do and what it does is essentially to respond to problems. If programs are running well, why monitor them closely? If problems arise, look into them. Sometimes referred to as the "fire alarm model," this approach applauds the good sense of members of Congress in using their resources efficiently.

IMPACT. Even more difficult to assess firmly is the impact of congressional oversight. The clearest evidence is scattered and anecdotal, hardly a reliable base. Yet clearly specific efforts have resulted in changes in programs and bureaucratic behavior. Most bureaucratic units, most bureaucrats, and most programs are rarely the direct object of formal oversight. If oversight is effective it is not because it is comprehensive. It is more likely due to the possibility of its exercise.

The impact of the "law of anticipated reactions" is inordinately difficult to demonstrate. The argument here is that while comprehensive formal oversight is rarely conducted, much informal oversight does take place, and any executive branch structure, program, policy, or person is in principle an appropriate subject for inquiry. Thus the possibility of oversight, rather than its actual execution, may be the more potent congressional weapon. Executive units and members may be pressured to rethink what they might want to do by the threat of having to answer for their behavior in subsequent congressional investigations. Pushing the executive branch to anticipate possible questions from Congress and to be able to defend their actions and policies may be the most useful consequence of congressional oversight.

POLITICAL CONSIDERATIONS. The ostensible goal of oversight—more effective and responsible public policy and bureaucratic behavior—is not always attained. Abuse of congressional power is always possible. Members of the executive are not always wrong, and members of Congress are not always correct in executive-legislative disputes arising from oversight efforts. Executive departments are sometimes as capable as Congress of a broad perspective, just as members of Congress may adopt a parochial outlook. The ways in which the executive branch implements law may be more effective than the alternative actions pushed by Congress.

Moreover, the line between vigorous oversight and influence peddling is sometimes blurred. An apt illustration from the early 1990s is the case of the so-called Keating Five; it was charged that the efforts of several members of Congress, acting on behalf of substantial campaign contributors, were unduly vigorous in attempting to influence how regulators treated some savings and loan associations. What gave these legislative efforts particular clout was the potential for legislative reaction against nonresponsive regulators. The issue here is not whether the senators involved abused their power but rather that the power and influence legislators had may have led to questionable behavior by apprehensive bank regulators. Whether specific examples of legislative oversight, either formal or informal, promote efficient and responsible behavior and policy is always an open question.

One could argue that the executive branch should welcome congressional oversight in the hopes of improving performance and policy. This is, in fact, sometimes the case. More often, fears of congressional overmanagement, apprehensions concerning the clout of vested interests in Congress, and concerns over whether members of Congress have sufficient expertise usefully to challenge what the executive is doing probably predominate.

At the heart of the issue is the fact that oversight seldom concerns mere technical problems of management but more often is part of a wider process of building support or opposition to programs or agencies. This larger context is essentially political. Executive departments and agencies will react well to supportive oversight efforts from the Congress, just as committee members who largely agree with what an executive agency is doing are less likely to push oversight. When oversight is designed to support executive actions, there will be no resistance, only full cooperation, on the executive side.

When, as is more frequently the case, formal oversight results from someone in Congress thinking that something is wrong in the executive branch, guarded reactions from the executive are the norm. Delays and evasions are common in such circumstances. Few persons in or out of the executive branch gain joy in the exposure of their own errors of judgment, in revelations of failures to act expeditiously, or in disclosures seeming to show that they protected vested interests.

EXECUTIVE PRIVILEGE. Perhaps the most extreme example of resistance comes when the doctrine of executive privilege is invoked. From the beginning of the republic, presidents and their subordinates have, at times, balked at congressional requests for information. Presidents argue that the advice they are given by assistants and some executive files should not be revealed to congressional investigators. In contrast, congressional committees regularly assert that, given their constitutional powers, they should be entitled access to any bureaucratic activity they find of interest. Neither position is totally without vested interest. Members of Congress may be trying to embarrass the president for partisan reasons. Assertions of executive privilege may relate to desires to hide ties to specific interests or to mask questionable decisions.

How, when, and by whom executive privilege can be invoked has never been resolved authoritatively. The Constitution is silent on this question. For most of U.S.

history the courts have avoided grappling with the question of executive privilege. Only in the context of the Watergate incidents, subsequent court trials, and the strong possibility of the impeachment of President Richard M. Nixon did the Supreme Court directly confront the legality of the executive privilege doctrine. What the Court decided in *United States v. Nixon* (1974) was that there was a legal basis for the existence of the doctrine but that the limits of executive privilege were not to be decided by the president alone. In essence, this decision provides an astute political resolution of the problem cast in legal terms. Similarly, most disputes over executive privilege are resolved politically through intense negotiations and bargaining. Both executive and legislative positions are argued publicly in constitutional and legal terms. These conflicts are often resolved politically because problems with manifest political dimensions lend themselves to political solutions.

The line between vigorous oversight and influence peddling is sometimes blurred.

Congressional oversight of the bureaucracy is only one of many methods of promoting bureaucratic responsiveness. The personal values and professional norms of bureaucrats may stimulate responsive behavior. Presidents and their immediate associates try to impose on bureaucrats their view of what is appropriate. Interest groups monitor the executive just as they attempt to influence Congress. The courts on occasion impose standards of behavior on the bureaucracy. The executive branch, then, is accountable to institutions and groups other than Congress.

Moreover, Congress itself is not a single force when it comes to oversight. Oversight efforts normally come from committees and subcommittees in Congress. The fragmented nature of the congressional committee system is well known. Committees may work at cross-purposes. Some committees may be supportive of particular agencies or programs while others are hostile. What then does Congress want? The question almost answers itself. On many matters of legislative oversight of the bureaucracy, there is no single congressional voice. This fact further reinforces the proposition that an effective and responsive bureaucracy cannot be created by Congress alone.

[See also (I) Bureaucracy, President and Congress, Veto; (II) Executive Privilege.]

BIBLIOGRAPHY

Aberbach, Joel D. *Keeping a Watchful Eye: The Politics of Congressional Oversight.* 1990.

Dodd, Lawrence C., and Richard L. Schott. *Congress and the Administrative State.* 1979.

Foreman, Christopher H., Jr. *Signals from the Hill: Congressional Oversight and the Challenge of Social Regulation.* 1988.

Harris, Joseph P. *Congressional Control of Administration.* 1964.

Ogul, Morris S. *Congress Oversees the Bureaucracy: Studies in Legislative Supervision.* 1978.

Ripley, Randall B., and Grace A. Franklin. *Congress, the Bureaucracy, and Public Policy.* 5th ed. 1991.

– MORRIS S. OGUL

P

PAGES

A group of high school juniors, known as pages, serve as messengers for members of the U.S. Congress. Numbering about one hundred young men and women, they come from all areas of the United States. Several current and former members and officials of Congress began their careers as pages.

Although the Senate employed older messengers from its beginning in 1789, it is believed that Sen. Daniel Webster arranged for the appointment of the first Senate page in 1829. The earliest record of pages in the House of Representatives dates from 1842. Not until 1971, however, were women first appointed as pages.

In 1983, following allegations of misconduct by pages and members of Congress, unfavorable press accounts of the system, and a desire to reform the program, Congress offered supervised housing near the Capitol for all pages, established a common age requirement, and made changes in the education provided.

The House page program is administered by the doorkeeper of the House and supervised by the House Page Board, composed of House members and officers. There were sixty-six House pages in 1992, all chosen through the patronage system administered by the majority party, then the Democrats.

In the Senate, both party secretaries supervise page appointments consistent with patronage positions given senior senators. The Senate sergeant at arms is in charge of the overall operation of the Senate page program. The Senate usually has thirty pages at a time. Customarily, members of Congress appoint pages from the areas they represent.

Pages are paid about one thousand dollars per month. Their salaries, which are subject to taxation, are expected to cover transportation costs to Washington, their living expenses, and uniforms.

Until 1983, when both houses required pages to be high school juniors (generally age sixteen or seventeen), ages had varied considerably and had been debated in and out of Congress. In the nineteenth century the youngest House and Senate pages were ten and twelve years old, respectively. For most of the twentieth century, however, they ranged in age from fourteen to eighteen.

Pages' duties have changed considerably over the years. Today, they no longer have ink boxes to fill or candles to light on members' desks, nor must they ride horseback to deliver urgent messages to the executive branch. Instead, the pages now serve principally as messengers on Capitol Hill, carrying documents between members' offices, committees, and the Library of Congress. They also help prepare the congressional chambers for each day's business, and they are present during sessions, seated near the members or in cloakrooms nearby, waiting to be summoned.

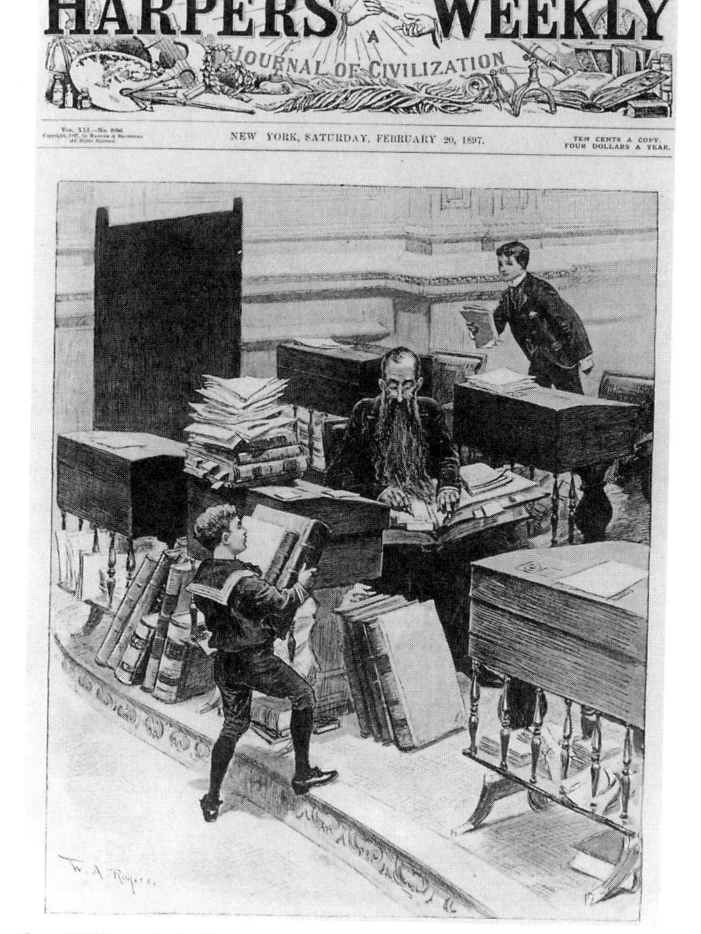

IMPORTANT ARTICLE FROM MADRID IN THIS NUMBER.

HARPER'S WEEKLY

A JOURNAL OF CIVILIZATION

NEW YORK, SATURDAY, FEBRUARY 20, 1897.

TEN CENTS A COPY. FOUR DOLLARS A YEAR.

Sen. William A. Peffer (Prog.-Kans.). Shown preparing an "oratorical eruption" for the Senate with the aid of two pages. Cover of Harper's Weekly, *20 February 1897. (Office of the Historian of the U.S. Senate)*

Pages live in housing provided by Congress and supervised by proctors and a full-time director. Since

1926, Congress has provided for the education of pages who serve during the school year. Since 1983, the House and Senate have had separate school facilities located in the Library of Congress. The Senate Page School is operated by the District of Columbia school system, and the House operates and provides the staff for its school. Both facilities offer college preparatory courses and extracurricular activities unique to the Washington, D.C., area.

Today, pages no longer have ink boxes to fill or candles to light on members' desks, nor must they ride horseback to deliver urgent messages to the executive branch.

Prospective pages request appointment by contacting their representatives or senators. Members' eligibility to appoint pages is based primarily on the patronage system. While selection procedures vary in the House and Senate, all pages must be American citizens and are expected to have good scholastic records.

BIBLIOGRAPHY

"Groundless Page Sex Charges Prompt Reforms." *Congressional Quarterly Almanac* 38 (1982): 528–529.

Severn, Bill. *Democracy's Messengers.* 1975.

Springer, William. "Congressional Pages, Their Work and Schooling." In *We Propose a Modern Congress.* 1966. Pp. 183–184.

"Two Members Censured." *Congressional Quarterly Almanac* 39 (1983): 580–583.

– MILDRED LEHMANN AMER

PAIRING

Pairing is a procedure available to members of Congress who wish to indicate their position with respect to a question even though they are not present when the vote is taken. In the House of Representatives, a pair is an agreement between members on opposite sides not to vote on a specified question or during a stipulated time. While pairing is authorized by clause 2 of Rule VIII and clause I of Rule XV, neither the House nor the Speaker exercises jurisdiction over pairs, and any interpretation of the terms of a pair rests with the contracting members. A member with a "live pair" with another member will first cast his vote on the question, and then withdraw the vote and vote "present" after announcing his agreement with an absent colleague who would have voted on the opposite side of the issue. This is the only type of pair that affects the outcome of a vote. An "definite" or "for and against" pair will appear in the *Congressional Record* immediately following the vote and will reflect specific instructions as to the preferences left by the contracting members that terminate automatically after the vote. An "indefinite" or "until further notice" pair does not indicate how either member would have voted if present. On constitutional amendments and other questions requiring a two-thirds vote it is customary to pair two affirmative votes with one negative.

Although its use is well established in the Senate, pairing is not mentioned in the Senate rules and therefore has no official standing. A senator who has a "live pair" merely refrains from voting and announces that he or she is paired with another senator who is absent. The process is not as simple as in the House because senators must have an acceptable excuse for not voting on a roll call, and pairing, about which the rules are silent, does not automatically qualify as an excuse. In practice, the Senate deals with this problem by ignoring it. The clerk and the presiding officer take no notice when pairs are announced and ignore them in calculating the results of a roll call. By custom, however, pairs are listed for informational purposes at the bottom of the roll-call tabulation.

BIBLIOGRAPHY

U.S. House of Representatives. *Constitution, Jefferson's Manual, and Rules of the House of Representatives, 103d Congress.* Compiled by William Holmes Brown. 102d Cong., 2d sess., 1992. H. Doc. 102-405.

U.S. House of Representatives. *Cannon's Procedure in the United States House of Representatives,* by Clarence Cannon. 87th Cong., 2d sess., 1963. H. Doc. 87-610.

U.S. Senate. *Riddick's Senate Procedure, Precedents, and Practices,* by Floyd M. Riddick and Alan S. Frumin. 101st Cong., 2d sess., 1992. S. Doc. 101-28.

– THOMAS G. DUNCAN

PARLIAMENTARIAN

House Parliamentarian

The important office of the House parliamentarian has evolved from several earlier incarnations. In 1857 Speaker James L. Orr of South Carolina appointed Thaddeus Morrice as "Messenger." Morrice was an adept young man whose memory for House precedents and other decisions of the Speaker quickly made him indispensable to the Speaker in his role as presiding officer of the House. When Morrice died in 1864, the position was continued, its title changed to clerk to the Speaker, then to clerk at the Speaker's Table, and finally in 1927 to House parliamentarian. Only seventeen in-

PARLIAMENTARIANS OF THE HOUSE AND THEIR PREDECESSORS

Name	Dates of Service	Congress	Title
Thaddeus Morrice	1857–1864	34th–38th	Messenger to the Speaker
William D. Todd	1865–1968	38th, 2d sess.–40th, 2d sess.	Messenger to the Speaker
William D. Todd	1869	40th, 3d sess.	Clerk to the Speaker
John M. Barclay	1869–1875	41st, 1st sess.	Clerk at the Speaker's Table
William H. Scudder	1875–1877	44th–45th, 1st sess.	Clerk at the Speaker's Table
J. Randolph Tucker, Jr.	1877–1879	45th, 2d and 3d sess.–46th, 1st sess.	Clerk at the Speaker's Table
George P. Miller	1879–1880	46th, 2d sess.	Clerk at the Speaker's Table
Michael Sullivan	1880–1881	46th, 3d sess.	Clerk at the Speaker's Table
J. Guilford White	1881–1882	47th, 1st sess.	Clerk at the Speaker's Table
J. Guilford White; Michael Sullivan	1882–1883	47th, 2d sess.	Clerk at the Speaker's Table
Nathaniel T. Crutchfield	1883–1890	48th–51st, 1st sess.	Clerk at the Speaker's Table
Edward F. Goodwin	1890–1891	51st, 2d sess.	Clerk at the Speaker's Table
Charles R. Crisp	1891–1895	52d–53d	Clerk at the Speaker's Table
Asher C. Hinds	1895–1911	54th–61st	Clerk at the Speaker's Table
Charles R. Crisp	1911–1913	62d	Clerk at the Speaker's Table
Bennett C. Clark	1913–1917	63d–65th, 1st sess.	Clerk at the Speaker's Table
Clarence C. Cannon	1917–1919	65th, 2d and 3d sess.–66th, 1st sess.	Clerk at the Speaker's Table
Lehr Fess	1919–1927	66th, 2d sess.–69th	Clerk at the Speaker's Table
Lehr Fess; Lewis Deschler	1927–1928	70th, 1st sess.	Parliamentarian
Lewis Deschler	1928–1974	70th, 2d sess.–93d, 2d sess.	Parliamentarian
William Holmes Brown	1974–1994	93d, 2d sess.–103d, 2d sess.	Parliamentarian
Charles W. Johnson	1994–	103d, 2d sess.–	Parliamentarian

dividuals have held the position since its inception in 1857. The first person to be called by the title of parliamentarian was Lehr Fess, who served from 1927 to 1928. Lewis Deschler served as parliamentarian from 1928 to 1974 and was the author of the multi-volume work *Deschler's Precedents of the United States House of Representatives.* His successor, William Holmes Brown, continued the practice of compiling and publishing volumes of House precedents, upon which many of the Speakers' parliamentary rulings are based.

The parliamentarian, or a member of his staff, sits or stands to the right of the Speaker when the House is in session and advises the Speaker or chairman of the Committee of the Whole on parliamentary procedure. A good portion of the parliamentarian's time is taken up by reading and referring, on behalf of the Speaker, the thousands of bills, resolutions, and executive communications that are introduced into the House in each session. The referral of bills to one or more committees of the House is often a routine matter, but in some instances it is a crucial step in the legislative process. The parliamentarian is also available for consultation with all members of the House on matters of procedure and legislative details related to the introduction or passage of a bill or resolution. The office functions in a nonpartisan manner, providing its services in an impartial manner to members of both political parties. The parliamentarian's office, just off the House chamber near the Speaker's lobby, can be a beehive of activity on a busy legislative day.

The parliamentarian also oversees a small operation known as the Precedents Office, which edits and publishes the precedents of the House, as well as the *Rules of the House of Representatives,* which is published every two years with each new Congress.

[See also (I) House of Representatives, article on House Rules and Procedures.]

BIBLIOGRAPHY

Tiefer, Charles. *Congressional Practice and Procedure: A Reference, Research, and Legislative Guide.* 1989.

U.S. Congress. *Hearings before the Joint Committee on the Organization of Congress.* 103d Cong., 1st sess., 1993. S. Hrg. 103-119.

U.S. House of Representatives. *Deschler's Precedents of the United States House of Representatives,* by Lewis Deschler. 94th Cong., 2d sess., 1977. H. Doc. 94-661.

— RAYMOND W. SMOCK

Senate Parliamentarian

The parliamentarian of the Senate is responsible for advising the presiding officer of the Senate on all matters affecting Senate procedure. The parliamentarian's role is most evident when the presiding officer must rule on formal points of order or give responses to informal parliamentary inquiries. Less evident, though equally important, is the parliamentarian's responsibility for ensuring that the consideration of all bills, resolutions,

SENATE PARLIAMENTARIANS

Name	Dates
Charles L. Watkins	1937–1964
Floyd M. Riddick	1965–1974
Murray Zweben	1975–1980
Robert B. Dove	1981–1986
Alan S. Frumin	1987–

treaties, nominations, and trials of impeachment comply with the rules of the Senate and the applicable provisions of the Constitution and public law.

In the name of the presiding officer, the parliamentarian refers to the committee of jurisdiction all bills and resolutions introduced in the Senate or passed by the House of Representatives, all nominations and other communications received from the president, and all communications from other officers of the executive branch, as well as all communications to the Senate from state legislatures or from private citizens. The parliamentarian also advises senators and their staffs, the staffs of the Senate's committees, officers of the other branches of the federal government, state and local government officials, members of the press, and the general public on questions concerning Senate procedure.

The parliamentarian helps Senate leaders to formulate and interpret the numerous unanimous consent agreements that are indispensable to the daily operation of the Senate. When time for debate is limited by such agreements or by rule or statute, the parliamentarian serves as the Senate's official timekeeper. The parliamentarian is responsible for determining what amendments are in order at any given time, whether they are properly drafted, and whether they are subject to any points of order.

Another important part of the parliamentarian's job is to analyze all Senate proceedings and to maintain the precedents that are set, periodically publishing these in book form. Precedents were first published in their current format in 1958 as *Senate Procedure, Precedents, and Practices;* revised editions were published in 1964, 1974, and 1981. The current edition, which contains the Senate's precedents through the end of the 101st Congress, is entitled *Riddick's Senate Procedure, Precedents, and Practices,* in honor of the author of the previous three editions.

The parliamentarian frequently prepares replies on behalf of senators or other officers of the Senate to letters regarding the Senate's rules, precedents, and practices. The parliamentarian also participates in the orientation of newly elected senators and addresses groups interested in learning more about how the Senate operates.

The position of Senate parliamentarian was first recognized on 1 July 1935, when the title of the incumbent Senate journal clerk, Charles L. Watkins, was changed to that of parliamentarian and journal clerk. On 1 July 1937, the two positions were separated, and Watkins became the first parliamentarian of the U.S. Senate.

The parliamentarian is appointed by, and serves at the pleasure of, the secretary of the Senate. Every person who has become Senate parliamentarian has first served a lengthy apprenticeship as an assistant Senate parliamentarian. The parliamentarian or an assistant parliamentarian is always on duty when the Senate is in session, sitting just below and slightly to the right of the presiding officer.

[See also (I) Senate, article on Senate Rules and Procedures.]

BIBLIOGRAPHY

U.S. Senate. *Riddick's Senate Procedure, Precedents, and Practices,* by Floyd M. Riddick and Alan S. Frumin. 101st Cong., 2d sess., 1992. S. Doc. 101-28.

U.S. Senate. Committee on Rules and Administration. *Senate Manual, Containing the Standing Rules, Orders, Laws, and Resolutions Affecting the Business of the United States Senate.* 102d Cong., 1st sess., 1992. S. Doc. 102-1.

– ALAN S. FRUMIN

POINTS OF ORDER

A point of order is a claim from the floor by a member that a pending action violates a chamber rule or is procedurally improper in a specified way. Generally, the chair must entertain the point, at least if the member may be recognized, but no point of order may be raised against certain decisions of the chair or after the challenged action has been completed. The chair rules on the point of order (nowadays, on the basis of consultation with the parliamentarian); if the point is sustained, the proposed action is prohibited. Any debate on the point occurs for the information of the chair, who therefore controls it; under cloture in the Senate, no debate is permitted.

Any member may appeal the chair's ruling. The appeal is a debatable question, decided by vote; it may be viewed as an exercise of the body's constitutional power to say what its rules are. Rulings on points of order make precedents; those by the full body are held to be the most authoritative. Only the chamber, and not the chair, may decide a point of order raised on constitutional grounds.

In the House today, appeals are rare and reversals of the chair virtually unheard of, although before about 1930 the House seems to have addressed such questions more freely. The full Senate often settles points of order not only on appeal, but also by tabling, by waiving, by practices requiring it to do so, and, seldom nowadays, by suspending the rules. Some of these actions are available only on specific points of order, and some require a three-fifths or two-thirds majority.

In both chambers, points of order are frequently directed against amendments.

In both chambers, points of order are frequently directed against amendments; perhaps the most common point raised is that an amendment to an appropriations bill constitutes legislation. In the House a point of order on an amendment must be raised (or reserved) before debate on the amendment begins.

[See also (I) Amending.]

BIBLIOGRAPHY

U.S. House of Representatives. *Procedure in the United States House of Representatives,* by Lewis Deschler and William Holmes Brown. 4th ed. 97th Cong., 2d sess., 1982. Chap. 31, secs. 1–8, "Points of Order."

U.S. Senate. *Riddick's Senate Procedure, Precedents, and Practices,* by Floyd M. Riddick and Alan S. Frumin. 101st Cong., 2d sess., 1992. S. Doc. 101-28. Pp. 987–996.

– RICHARD S. BETH

POLITICAL PARTIES

Political parties in the United States are unique social institutions whose adherents are not normally formal card-carrying or dues-paying members. Party organization is highly decentralized, with power scattered among party officials, candidates' organizations, elected officials, fund-raisers, consultants, and professional staffs. In addition, American parties lack strong ideological and policy coherence and hence do not fit well under the often-quoted definition provided by the eighteenth-century English philosopher Edmund Burke, who described political parties as bodies "of men united, for promoting by their joint endeavors the national interest, upon some particular principle in which they are all agreed." Indeed, American political parties are in reality three-part social structures composed of the party in the electorate (voters with a sense of attachment to the party), the party organization (party officers, staff, and volunteer workers), and the party in government (party candidates and public officeholders).

The essence of political parties in the United States has been captured by Leon D. Epstein (*Political Parties in Western Democracies,* 1967), who defined parties as "any group, however loosely organized, seeking to elect governmental officeholders under a given label." This definition reflects the preoccupation of American parties with electoral activity and the fact that only parties nominate and run candidates under their own labels. The definition also allows for American parties' frequent disunity on policy and lack of hierarchical organization.

Unlike parties, other politically involved organizations, such as interest groups, do not have politics as their exclusive concern. Even the most politically active interest groups usually have significant nonpolitical activities. For example, labor unions engage in collective bargaining and manage pension funds. American parties also exhibit a level of durability and persistence that is not matched by cliques, campaign organizations, and most interest groups. Parties are also distinguished by the degree to which they serve as emotional symbols of voter loyalty. For millions of Americans, the party label is a potent cue in determining how they will vote on election day. Indeed, studies of voting behavior have determined that a voter's party identification is the single most important determinant of voter choice.

EVOLUTION OF POLITICAL PARTIES. The drafters of the Constitution deplored parties and factions and believed that by including provisions for federalism, separation of powers, and bicameralism they could prevent parties from dominating the government order. Initially, their goal of partyless politics seemed possible. The first national balloting under the Constitution (1788–1789) did not involve political parties. There was no formal nomination of candidates for president or Congress; George Washington was virtually the unanimous choice for president. Because the right to vote was restricted to property owners, electoral participation was low—only 5 to 8 percent of white males. As a result, there was little need for party organizations to mobilize masses of voters to contest elections.

The first party system: the emergence of parties (1790–1824). Parties began to emerge between 1790 and 1800 as Secretary of the Treasury Alexander Hamilton, a dominating figure in the Washington administration, proposed a controversial legislative program that called for funding of state debts, instituting a protective tariff, and creating a national bank. To gain congressional support for his program Hamilton called a legislative caucus of supporters, who called themselves "Federalists." Thomas Jefferson, a member of Washington's cabinet who opposed much of Hamilton's program, allied himself with other so-called Republican leaders in Congress, led by Rep. James Madison of Virginia.

Differences over foreign policy also fueled the development of partisan alliances within Congress. A major source of contention was Jay's treaty (narrowly ratified in 1796), designed to resolve differences between the United States and England arising from the treaty that had ended the Revolutionary War. Federalists and Republicans also divided over whether to support England or France in those nations' ongoing power struggle.

The early parties thus developed within Congress amid deep controversies over national, not state, policy issues, with Hamilton and Jefferson leading the two major clusters of interest. It was Jefferson's followers who first sought to broaden their operations by recruiting and endorsing candidates for Congress and presidential electors. The Republicans later ran slates of candidates for state offices. The Federalists were forced to follow the Republican example and compete for support within an electorate that was expanding as property restrictions on voting were eased. Reflecting their somewhat elitist orientation toward politics, the Federalists proved to be reluctant and less effective grassroots party organizers than their rivals.

Through aggressive local organizing efforts, the followers of Jefferson, operating under the Democratic-Republican label, swept the elections of 1800 as Jefferson won the presidency and his followers took control of Congress. After their disastrous defeat in 1800, the Federalists went into a precipitous decline and by 1816 disappeared as a party capable of contesting the presidency.

With the demise of the Federalists, partisan competition ceased, and the nation entered a period of partyless politics, characterized by factionalism within the dominant Democratic-Republican party. Thus, in 1811, House Speaker Henry Clay of Kentucky, leader of the party's War Hawks, sought to assert the power of the speakership and the supremacy of Congress over the other branches of government while pressuring President James Madison to declare war on Britain. Continuing intraparty factionalism during the administration of President James Monroe (1817–1825)—when most elected officials were members of one party—made it impossible for the president to exercise discipline over Congress; coherent policy-making suffered.

Intraparty factionalism within the dominant Democratic-Republican party also caused the downfall of the congressional caucus system for presidential nominations. In 1824, the congressional caucus nominated William H. Crawford for president, thereby bypassing the party's more prominent figures—John Quincy Adams, Andrew Jackson, and Clay. Each of these men then challenged Crawford in the general election, creating a four-way presidential race. When no candidate won a majority of votes in the Electoral College, the election was thrown into the House of Representatives, which chose Adams as president. Adams's administration was characterized by intense intraparty conflicts within Congress and between Congress and the president. The battles between the administration and the Jackson faction brought the first party system to a close.

The second party system: Democrats versus Whigs (1828–1854). Unlike the first party system, which emerged from the conflicts between the followers of Hamilton and Jefferson, the second party system was not closely linked to divisions within Congress nor was it the result of polarization on specific public policy issues. Rather, it developed between 1824 and 1840 out of successive contests for the presidency. And unlike the first party system after 1816, it did not lapse into one-partyism or partyless politics. Instead, two-party politics became a continuing feature of the American political system.

The second party system arose during a period in which politics was being democratized.

The election of Andrew Jackson in 1828 and 1832 marked a transitional period of bi-factional politics within the Democratic-Republican party, though by 1832 Jackson's faction was labeling itself the Democratic party. In 1834, midway through Jackson's second term, a loose amalgam of anti-Jackson forces (eastern manufacturers, southern planters, and westerners supporting higher outlays for internal improvements) sufficiently coalesced to form a new opposition party, the Whig party. For more than two decades between the 1830s and 1850s the Democrats and Whigs engaged in relatively close electoral competition. Both were truly national parties, though the Democrats were electorally the stronger of the two (the Whigs controlled both houses of Congress only during the 27th Congress, 1841–1843). The absence of highly salient national issues and the party leaders' skill in balancing diverse interests enabled the parties to compete in all regions. However, when the sectional conflicts between the North and the South intensified and slavery issues reached crisis proportions, the Whig party was eclipsed in the North by the new Republican party, and the Democrats, like the country as a whole, split along a North-South axis in the election of 1860.

The second party system arose during a period in which politics was being democratized: slates of presidential electors were being popularly elected, property restrictions on voting were being lifted, participation in elections was increasing, and party conventions were replacing caucuses as the means by which candidates were nominated. In this increasingly participatory environment, Democratic and Whig party organizations grew up across the country. Their development reflected the need for a way to mobilize the expanding electorate.

The third party system: Republicans emerge to challenge the Democrats (1856–1896). In the mid-1850s' sectional turmoil over slavery, the Republican party emerged to contest both congressional and presidential elections and established itself as the Democrats' principal electoral opposition. In 1854 and again in 1858 the Republican party won control of the House; in 1860 it elected its first president, Abraham Lincoln. The new Republican party was composed of abolitionists, members of the old Free Soil party, and dissident northern Whigs and Democrats.

Between 1864 and 1874 the Republican party was electorally dominant, controlling both Congress and the presidency. The Civil War identified the party—at least in the North—with the Union, patriotism, and emancipation. The Republican electoral coalition was, however, broadly based. It gained rural voters for its support of the Homestead Act, which granted free land in the West, and it appealed to both business and labor with its high protective tariff policies.

During the immediate post–Civil War years the Republicans controlled the presidency and both congressional chambers, where their leaders exerted a dominating influence over policy-making. The House in particular was characterized by strong party leadership. For example, Speaker James G. Blaine of Maine (1869–1875) appointed loyal lieutenants to key committee posts, thereby controlling the flow of bills and producing a flood of Republican-sponsored probusiness legislation.

In the 1868 and 1872 elections, the Republicans swept the northern states, and with the benefit of Reconstruction, won the electoral votes of most of the southern states. The end of Reconstruction in 1874, however, enabled the Democrats to gain ascendency in the South, while the GOP's electoral support was confined to the North and West. The legacy of the war and of Reconstruction, along with regional economic differences, thus created a politics of sectionalism. Each party had its own sectional base of electoral strength. After 1874, the Republicans and Democrats competed nationally on a more even basis than in the immediate post–Civil War period, and they alternated control of the presidency and Congress.

During the post–Civil War era patronage-based party organizations (machines) emerged in many cities and states, particularly in the Northeast and Midwest. These organizations were capable of controlling the caucuses and conventions by which parties made nominations for elective offices. They also demonstrated a remarkable ability to mobilize voters. Indeed, party organizations of the period have been described as "militarist" (in Walter Dean Burnham's *Critical Elections and the Mainsprings of American Politics,* 1970) in the sense that they emphasized drill-like mobilization of their supporters. It is estimated, for example, that in Republican William McKinley's 1896 "front porch" campaign for the presidency, 750,000 people (13 percent of the total Republican vote) visited the candidate in his hometown of Canton, Ohio.

The fourth party system: continuing Republican ascendancy and Progressive reforms (1896–1928). By the turn of the century, the United States had been transformed from an agrarian society into an industrialized and urban nation. The ethnic makeup of the country had also been changed by waves of immigrants from non-English-speaking European nations. The economic and social hardships caused by these changes reverberated through the party system. Agrarian protest movements spawned a major third-party movement, the People's party, or Populist party, of 1892. The discontent of urban workers in the new industrial order stimulated the labor unions. Initially, neither the Republican party nor the Democratic party was responsive to these protest movements. However, in 1896 the Democratic party convention was captured by the populist forces of agrarian discontent, and their champion, William Jennings Bryan, became the party's presidential nominee.

Bryan appropriated many of the policy positions of the 1892 Populists by advocating free and unlimited coinage of silver along with a downward revision of the tariff. In contrast, McKinley, the Republican nominee, campaigned with a slogan advocating "Prosperity, Sound Money, Good Markets and Employment for Labor" while opposing calling for unlimited coinage of silver and retention of the gold standard and the maintenance of a high protective tariff.

The 1896 election, which the Republicans won, caused a major realignment of the electorate, which gave the Republican party an infusion of adherents, especially among urban residents of the Northeast. Indeed, this election so weakened the Democratic party that it was able to elect only one president, Woodrow Wilson, between 1896 and 1928, and his initial election was made possible by the 1912 split within the Republican party. The Republicans also controlled Congress from the election of 1896 until 1911, a period during which both the House and Senate were characterized by centralized and hierarchical partisan leadership. Both parties were internally homogeneous, with constituency interests in line with party policy. Republicans largely represented northern industrial constituencies and favored tariffs to protect domestic industries, the gold standard, and expansion of American interests abroad; the Democrats represented rural and southern areas and favored freer trade, coinage of silver at a ratio of 16 to 1 with gold, and an isolationist foreign policy. Strong party leadership was further enforced by machinelike organizations in many states, which sent to Congress loyal partisans prepared to bow to the wishes of congressional leaders.

Roosevelt's New Deal forged a powerful electoral coalition of southern whites, blue-collar workers and union members, Catholics, Jews, urban dwellers, and African Americans.

It was during the fourth party system that the Progressive movement, with its emphasis on direct citizen control of the government, developed. Progressive-era reforms of the political system took root and weakened the capacity of party organizations to control nominations and mobilize voters. The most important of these reforms was probably the direct primary—the nomination of candidates via elections rather than by party conventions or caucuses. Presidential primaries were first instituted during this period. Parties also came under government regulation as states enacted primary laws that often contained provisions regulating the organization, operations, and financing of parties and campaigns.

The Progressive movement and the split it created within the Republican party between the conservative "stalwarts" and the Progressives had major consequences for the parties in Congress. In the House, the split within the Republican party led to a progressive Republican-Democratic revolt against Speaker Joseph G. Cannon of Illinois in 1910 and 1911 that deprived the Speaker of his membership on the Rules Committee and of the authority to appoint committees. The split also led to procedures (Calendar Wednesday and the Discharge Petition) that bypassed the leadership in scheduling legislation. The revolt against Cannon resulted in a severely weakened speakership as the constituencies represented by the two parties became less homogeneous and both parties became less cohesive in roll-call voting.

The fifth party system: from the New Deal to candidate-centered politics (1932–1992). The stock market crash of 1929 and Depression of the 1930s ended the era of Republican electoral dominance and made possible Franklin D. Roosevelt's 1932 election as president and the overwhelming Democratic majorities in the House and Senate. Roosevelt's New Deal program of economic reform and government social welfare programs, which Congress initially embraced with enthusiasm, forged a powerful electoral coalition composed of southern whites, blue-collar workers and union members, Catholics, Jews, urban dwellers, and African Americans. This electoral coalition gave the Democratic party electoral ascendancy from 1932 to 1964, except for 1952 and 1956, when the Republicans nominated a presidential candidate, Gen. Dwight D. Eisenhower, whose appeal extended beyond partisanship.

Ironically, Roosevelt's elections and his New Deal social welfare programs had long-term party-weakening consequences for the urban political organizations that had helped put him in office. New social programs (such as social security and unemployment compensation) and grant-in-aid programs, which emphasized professionalism in their administration, undermined the patronage base of the urban machines and robbed them of their traditional function of providing welfare services to deprived urban populations. Even so, the Democrats maintained their dominance of House and Senate elections. Between 1932 and 1995, the Republicans controlled both chambers only in the 82d Congress (1951–1953).

By the late 1960s, America had entered a post–New Deal political era. The electoral alignments of that period were still visible, but the New Deal Democratic coalition was suffering defections, particularly among white southerners, Catholics, and blue-collar workers.

The defection from the Democrats of white southerners was particularly significant because it helped the Republican party win five of six presidential elections between 1968 and 1988 and dramatically changed the composition of the congressional parties. As elections in the South became more competitive, Republicans began winning significant numbers of House and Senate seats in the region, making southerners a significant force within the Republican ranks in Congress. By 1993, for example, southerners constituted 23 percent of Senate Republican membership and 27 percent of House Republican members. This growth of southern influence gave the congressional Republicans a more conservative policy orientation. At the same time, the congressional Democratic party became less southern and less internally divided on policy.

Republican victories in presidential elections between 1968 and 1988 were not matched in elections to Congress and state offices, where the Democrats remained dominant. Instead of a major realignment and the emergence of a new Republican electoral majority, what seemed a partial realignment occurred. White southerners shifted to the Republicans, as did many Catholics, but the Democrats retained a plurality among those voters who identified themselves as belonging to a party and gained an overwhelming level of support among blacks.

Another major change was the tendency of voters to be less guided by partisan cues and to engage in substantial ticket-splitting in their votes for president and Congress. American politics had become more candidate centered, and as a result divided government became commonplace. Thus, between 1969 and 1992, one party controlled both the presidency and Congress only during the four years of the Carter administration, from 1977 to 1980. United party control of the executive and legislature was not restored until Bill Clinton's election as president in 1992.

TWO-PARTY DOMINANCE. While there have been transitional periods of one-party factionalism (e.g., 1824–1832, 1910–1912) and elections in which third parties or independent candidacies have constituted significant electoral forces (Progressives of 1912, Dixiecrats of 1948, George C. Wallace in 1968, John B. Anderson in 1980, and H. Ross Perot in 1992), the American political system has predominantly been a two-party system. Even when one party has disintegrated, as the Whigs did in the 1850s, the two-party character of the system has reestablished itself.

Causes of the two-party system. Political scientist V. O. Key, Jr., in *Politics, Parties, and Pressure Groups* (1964), offered three explanations for the creation and maintenance of the two-party system in the United States. The first focused on the institutional arrangements used to elect public officials. National and state legislators are elected from single-member constituencies, with the candidate who receives a plurality of the vote being declared the winner. Unlike a proportional representation system, which rewards each serious party with a share of the legislative seats equal to its share of the popular vote, the single-member system is a winner-take-all arrangement. Such a system encourages the formation of broadly based parties that are capable of winning pluralities in a large number of districts. The single-member system tends to condemn third and minor parties to perpetual defeat—hardly a prescription for long-term political viability. The Electoral College system of electing the president also encourages two-party politics by requiring an absolute majority in the electoral vote (270 votes of 538) and by allocating individual states' electoral votes on a winner-take-all basis.

Key also noted that special historical circumstances played a role in producing the two-party system in the United States. The initial lines of political cleavage were built on a dualism of interests that prevailed when the economic and social structure of the country was far less complex than it is today. There was a split between agriculture and the interests of the mercantile and financial community.

The absence in American society of blocs of people irreconcilably attached to a particular ideology, creed, or class consciousness has also helped make two-party politics possible. Religious, racial, ethnic, and economic groups have not generally tended toward separatism. Most have found a niche in society. As a result of the broad consensus that exists regarding such fundamentals as maintenance of the constitutional order and a predominantly market-oriented economy, it is possible for one party to be slightly to the right and the other slightly to the left of center and still gain widespread voter support. Thus, while both the Democrats and Republicans have core support groups, both maintain a sufficiently centrist orientation to compete effectively for the votes of the majority of Americans who consider themselves moderates or middle-of-the-roaders.

While the American system is accurately described as a two-party system, that phrase masks substantial variation in the actual extent of inter-party electoral competition. Two-party competition for the presidency clearly is intense, as it is in most states for major statewide offices such as governor or U.S. senator. In smaller and more socially homogeneous districts, however, such as those for members of the House and state legislatures, one party is frequently dominant, and meaningful interparty competition is therefore the exception rather than the rule.

One of the most striking features of electoral competition since 1856 has been the domination of electoral competition by the same two parties, the Democrats and Republicans. Only Democrats and Republicans have occupied the White House during this time, and only Republicans and Democrats have controlled the House and Senate.

In *Political Parties in American Society* (1982), Samuel Eldersveld attributed the persistence of Republican-Democratic electoral dominance to the parties' ideological eclecticism or nondoctrinaire approach to issues and changing conditions. This ideological flexibility makes it possible for both parties to harbor within their ranks leaders of widely varying policy viewpoints. In addition, both parties have exhibited an ability to attract significant levels of support from virtually every element of society.

Although American politics has since the 1830s been characterized by two-party competition, third parties have at times had a major impact.

The Republican and Democratic parties have also shown a capacity to absorb protests. Major third-party protest movements have arisen periodically since 1856, but none has been able to attract sustained voter, organizational, or financial support. Each has bloomed briefly and then withered as its remnants were absorbed into one or both major parties. Thus, the Populists of 1892 were taken over by the Democrats in 1896 through the nomination of Bryan, and the Progressive parties of Theodore Roosevelt (1912) and Robert M. La Follette, Sr. (1924), were absorbed back into the Republican fold.

The Republican and Democratic parties' success in absorbing protests owes much, in Leon D. Epstein's view (*Political Parties in the American Mold,* 1986), to the direct primary as the principal method of nominating congressional and state candidates. This uniquely American nominating procedure permits insurgents outside the ranks of the established party leadership to use an intraparty route to gain influence and public office, including seats in the U.S. Congress. By contesting and winning primaries, insurgents can gain access to the general election ballot without having to organize third parties. The availability of the direct primary as a means of achieving political change from within the major parties thereby reduces the incentive to create third parties.

Epstein has further observed that the direct primary contributes to Republican-Democratic dominance because voters become accustomed to participating in party primaries and choosing among people competing for their party's nomination. Voters' partisan attachments are further encouraged by the requirement in most states that voters in a primary publicly declare their party affiliations or even register as Republicans or Democrats in order to participate in primary elections.

Federal campaign finance laws also work to the advantage of the two major parties. Under the Federal Election Campaign Act of 1974, the Republican and Democratic parties, the only parties that qualify as major parties under the law, receive the following governmental benefits: public funding for national conventions ($11.048 million in 1992), authority for national party committees to make expenditures in support of their presidential nominees ($10.332 million in 1992), public matching funds for candidates seeking presidential nominations, and public funding of general election campaigns for president ($55.240 million in 1992).

THIRD AND MINOR PARTIES. Although American politics has since the 1830s been characterized by two-party competition, third parties have at times had a major impact. The emerging Republican party, for example, helped focus national attention on the slavery issue and caused deep schisms within the Whig and Democratic parties during the 1850s. Third parties do not normally become major parties, but they can affect election outcomes and electoral alignments. The significant third-party movements in the twentieth century have been splinter parties—offshoots of the major parties—formed to protest policies of a party's dominant faction. Thus, Theodore Roosevelt's Progressive (Bull Moose) party reflected a split within the Republican party between the stalwart conservatives and the progressives. It caused the Republican vote in 1912 to be divided between Roosevelt and the Republican nominee, William H. Taft, enabling Democrat Woodrow Wilson to gain the presidency with less than a majority of the popular vote. In 1968 George C. Wallace, the antiestablishment, populist, and segregationist Democratic governor of Alabama, ran on the American Independent ticket and siphoned 13.5 percent of the popular vote from the major-party candidates, causing one of the closest elections in American history.

More significant, even, than Wallace's challenge was that mounted by H. Ross Perot in 1992. By capturing 19 percent of the presidential vote (though no electoral votes), he drew a larger share of the popular vote than any third-party or independent candidate since Theodore Roosevelt in 1912. Perot took votes from both major-party nominees, enabling Democrat Bill Clinton to be elected with 43 percent of the popular vote.

Third-party movements and major independent candidacies like Perot's are normally an indication of substantial voter discontent. When faced with such evident voter unrest and potential threats to their power, at least one of the major parties has usually sought to accommodate the protest group within its ranks.

Despite their occasional influence on presidential elections, third parties have not played a major role in congressional politics during the twentieth century. This was particularly evident during the century's last few decades. Between 1970 and 1992, only two people were elected to the House who were not Democrats or Republicans, and only one senator was elected on a third-party ticket. These numbers reflect the inability of third parties to overcome the problems associated with recruiting and running candidates in a sufficient number of constituencies to have even a chance of electing a bloc of representatives or senators. In a few states, however, third-party movements like Wisconsin's La Follette Progressives and the Farmer-Labor party of Minnesota were able briefly in the 1930s and 1940s to elect both senators and representatives. National political forces, however, caused these state-based parties to merge with the major parties.

PARTY ORGANIZATION. Party organization at the national level illustrates the decentralized nature of party organizations in the United States. The national Republican and Democratic party organizations are composed of three major units—the national committees, the House campaign committees, and the Senate campaign committees.

National committees. National committees developed in the mid-1800s with the creation of the Democratic National Committee (DNC) in 1848 and the Republican National Committee (RNC) in 1856. They were created to serve as interim agents of the parties' supreme governing bodies, the national conventions. During the post–Civil War era, their principal function was the management of presidential campaigns. As a result, they were active for only a few months every four years. Not until the chairmanship of Will Hayes (1918–1921) did the RNC establish a year-round national headquarters with a full-time paid staff. The DNC followed the Republicans' example in 1928. Staffing through the 1930s and 1940s continued, however, to have a rather ad hoc quality, with party notables brought in temporarily to help with campaigns.

Gradually, the national committees became more institutionalized, with expanded full-time staffs that were characterized by specialization and professionalism. By the mid-1970s and 1980s the national committees had become highly sophisticated operations engaged in ongoing, large-scale fund-raising, research, campaign training and consulting, and public relations. With multimillion-dollar budgets, the national committees provide technical and financial assistance to state and local party organizations across the country and to candidates. The national committees, however, do not manage presidential, congressional, senatorial, or gubernatorial campaigns. In America's candidate-centered system, campaigns are directed by the personal organizations of the nominees.

Presidents usually exert a dominating influence over the activities of the national committee of their party through designation of the national chairman and close liaison and supervision by the White House staff. For the "out" party, the national committee constitutes the party's most inclusive organization, and it is therefore an important intra-party force. The national committees tend to have a presidential and state-party focus. As a result, they involve themselves only limitedly in congressional and senatorial campaigns and operate quite autonomously from the party organizations within Congress. The autonomy of the national committees and the congressional parties reflects the effect of the constitutional separation-of-powers system and the electoral reality that representatives and senators are ultimately responsible for their own reelection.

Hill committees. On Capitol Hill, both Democrats and Republicans operate House and Senate campaign organizations; their official names are the Democratic Congressional Campaign Committee (DCCC), the Democratic Senatorial Campaign Committee (DSCC), the National Republican Congressional Committee (NRCC), and the National Republican Senatorial Committee (NRSC). These campaign units are organizationally autonomous from each other and the national committees. The so-called Hill committees are composed of incumbent representatives and senators, but the actual work of the committees is carried out by professional staffs. As their names suggest, the congressional (House) and senatorial campaign committees focus their efforts on holding their parties' marginal seats in Congress, assisting challengers with a realistic chance of being elected, and winning open-seat contests.

Although the national committees and Hill committees are separate and distinct entities, a good deal of interaction takes place between them. Coordination is encouraged by party expenditure limits imposed by the Federal Election Campaign Act, which restricts the amount that can be spent by Washington-based party committees in support of House and Senate candidates. The linked series of competitive races for president, senator, representative, and governor within each state also encourages coordination of activities. Relationships between a party's national-level committees, however, are not necessarily always harmonious because they compete for funds, professional staff, and the services of political consultants. Tensions also arise from the national-level committees' differing constituencies and electoral priorities. The national committees have as their principal constituencies the state party organizations, the president, and presidential candidates. They therefore tend to be primarily concerned with presidential politics and with assisting state organizations. By contrast, the Hill committees are composed of incumbent representatives and senators and therefore give priority to congressional and senatorial elections.

State parties. Each state has a state-level party committee, often operating under a title such as the Republican (or Democratic) State Central Committee. These state party groups, organizationally separate from the national parties, have tended to give priority to elections for state constitutional offices, especially the governorship and state legislature, rather than to U.S. House or Senate campaigns. Increasingly, however, state-party activities have been integrated into the programs of the national-level party committees. As the national committees have become more institutionalized and capable of raising larger and larger amounts of money, they have increasingly provided technical and financial assistance to their state affiliates. By transferring money to state parties for voter registration and get-out-the-vote drives, research, polling, fund-raising, and candidate recruitment, the national-level committees have strengthened the state parties while using them to achieve national party objectives. For example, the House and Senate party committees channel assistance to those states where there are highly competitive Senate or House races while largely ignoring other state parties. Similarly, in presidential election years the resources of the national committees flow primarily to states deemed critical to gaining an Electoral College majority for the party's presidential nominee.

In most states, there are state legislative campaign committees operating with autonomy from the state central committees. Legislative campaign committees, which are composed of incumbent legislators and operate in both the upper and lower legislative chambers, have become the principal party-support organizations for legislative candidates. These committees tend to focus their resources—money and technical services—upon competitive races and hence follow a strategy of seeking to maximize their parties' seats in legislative chamber. Because of their ability to raise campaign funds, legislative campaign committees in a number of instances have become the most effective party organizations in the state.

THE CONGRESSIONAL PARTIES. While political parties in the United States emerged initially during the first Washington administration, the substantial organizational apparatus that now characterizes the congressional parties developed gradually. It was not until the twentieth century that an array of permanent party leadership positions, independent of the standing committee system, was established.

House party leadership. With the emergence of competing political parties in Congress, control of the position of Speaker of the House became a source of partisan contention. The early Speakers, however, were not party leaders. Instead, Federalist party leadership was in the hands of Treasury Secretary Hamilton until he left office in 1795. Similarly, Jefferson's Treasury secretary, Albert Gallatin, guided administration bills through the party caucus and House. During the Jefferson administration executive control of the congressional party even extended to the president's picking the chairman of the Ways and Means Committee as his floor leader and spokesman.

The era of executive dominance of the House ended during the Madison administration with Clay's election as Speaker in 1811. As leader of the War Hawks faction of the Democratic-Republican party, Clay eventually pushed a reluctant President Madison into war with England in 1812. Clay was a strong leader who stacked House standing committees with supporters of his policies. Clay's tenure marked the first time that the Speaker's prerogative to appoint committee members had been used independent of the president's designs. Clay also used his powers of recognition to limit the influence of his opponents.

It was not until the twentieth century that an array of permanent party leadership positions, independent of the standing committee system, was established.

For most of the nineteenth century, party leadership in the House, aside from the Speaker, was largely informal. The majority party floor leaders were informally designated for indefinite tenures. Often, the chairman of the Ways and Means Committee functioned as the chief lieutenant of the Speaker, though the chairman of the Committee on Appropriations occasionally assumed this role. It was not until the 1880s to early 1900s that the majority and minority leadership positions, along with the party whips, were established on a permanent basis.

The most elaborate leadership apparatus is found in the House of Representatives. Each party is ultimately governed by a party caucus (Republicans prefer the term *conference*) composed of all party members within the chamber. The caucus elects party leaders and determines party rules.

The House's most powerful figure is the Speaker, who serves as the leader of the majority party. Besides serving as the chamber's presiding officer, the Speaker influences committee assignments within the majority party, nominates party members to the Rules Committee, and refers bills to committee. Working with the majority party members of the Rules Committee, the

Speaker is able to influence profoundly the agenda of the House and to structure the conditions under which bills are considered on the House floor—conditions that frequently give advantage to the position of the Speaker's party.

The second-ranking leadership position in the House is the majority floor leader, who schedules bills, handles floor strategy, and serves as the principal party spokesperson on the floor. Assisting the Speaker and majority floor leader is a whip organization headed by a chief whip. The whip organization notifies members when key votes will occur, conducts head counts of members' sentiment on controversial issues, and attempts to whip up support for the party position on important roll-call votes.

Within the minority party, the highest-ranking official is the minority floor leader, who acts as its principal strategist and spokesperson. Like the majority floor leader, the minority leader has a whip organization to assist in measuring party sentiment and maintaining unity.

In addition to these formal leadership positions, both parties have a series of committees with specialized responsibilities. The Democratic Steering and Policy Committee assigns Democrats to standing committees and also discusses and endorses party policy positions. The Republicans divide these responsibilities between a Committee on Committees and a Policy Committee.

Senate party leadership. As in the House of Representatives, party leadership of the Senate emanated largely from the executive branch from the Washington through the Jefferson administration, with individual senators temporarily assuming the mantle of leadership. The vice president, an outsider imposed on the Senate by the Constitution, never served as its leader. Rather, in accordance with the precedent set by the first vice president, John Adams, the vice president served solely as a presiding officer. Throughout most of the nineteenth century, the Senate lacked strong, formal party leadership. It was, in the words of Sen. Daniel Webster (W-Mass.), a chamber "of equals" whose members "knew no master." Similarly, Woodrow Wilson observed in his classic treatise *Congressional Government* (1885) that in the Senate "no one exercises the special trust of acknowledged leadership."

Not until the 1890s did modern party leadership make its appearance in the Senate, when Republican William B. Allison of Iowa, the Senate Appropriations Committee chairman, was elected chairman of the Republican caucus and that group assumed control of the chamber. By the end of the nineteenth century parties had assumed a dominant role in the Senate's deliberations. The parties named members to committees, made initial decisions on proposed legislation, and determined which bills would be considered for floor consideration. In the early 1900s the formal positions of majority and minority leader had been created.

In the Senate, an institution characterized by a high level of member independence and individualism, the formal powers of the party leaders are less extensive than in the House, and leaders are forced to rely more heavily on their skills of persuasion and negotiation.

The principal party leadership positions in the Senate are the majority and minority floor leaders, who are elected by their respective caucuses every two years at the beginning of each new Congress. Although the formal powers of the majority leader are limited, the leader does derive influence from the position's responsibility for scheduling legislative business in the Senate. As in the House, both parties have specialized committees. Each has a committee on committees (called the Steering Committee by the Democrats), which makes committee assignments, and a policy committee, which considers party positions on legislation. In the case of the Democrats the policy committee assists the floor leader in scheduling bills for floor consideration.

In both the House and Senate, party policy committees function mainly as mechanisms for gauging members' sentiment regarding legislation and for providing guidance on the party's position on an issue. The policy committees do not have the power to bind party members to support a particular position. They tend to enter the legislative process after bills have been considered in standing committee and hence do not function as agents for developing a party program.

Although virtually all representatives and senators are elected as Republicans or Democrats and also belong to a collegial entity in the House and Senate bearing one of those labels, the congressional environment is not usually conducive to high levels of intraparty unity or strong policy leadership by the parties. Party leaders in Congress are forced to adapt to the fact that their partisans are individually responsible for their own nomination and reelection. Since the congressional party cannot guarantee renomination, electoral safety in the general election, or extensive campaign resources to even its most able and loyal members, members frequently adopt relatively independent and constituency-oriented policy stances when voting on legislation. Party influence is also limited by decentralization of power through the standing committee system, which is Congress's principal means of ensuring specialized consideration of legislation.

Partisanship in Congress. Despite electoral forces and institutional arrangements that limit party influence, the congressional party is the primary integrative mechanism in both chambers and the primary means of achieving majority decision-making. Evidence of partisanship abounds in Congress.

Congress is organized on a partisan basis. Members of the majority party hold the most powerful leadership posts in each chamber—Speaker of the House, House majority leader, and Senate majority leader. A chamber's majority party controls all committee and subcommittee chairmanships and holds the majority on all the standing committees. With control of key leadership posts, a majority in the chamber, and the majority membership on committees, the dominant party's leadership largely determines which bills will be considered for floor action and under what conditions they will be considered.

Partisan influence is also apparent in House and Senate roll-call voting. Neither party is monolithic, and by the standards of most European parties the congressional Republican and Democratic parties are anything but unified. Even so, partisan influences on roll-call voting behavior are substantial. Since 1954 the level of unity in either party on roll calls has rarely dipped below 70 percent per session. Party unity is most commonly measured by computing the average number of party members voting with their party on roll calls that pit a majority of Democrats against a majority of Republicans.

By the late 1980s and early 1990s, party unity had increased in response to changes in the party system that affected each party's congressional membership. As the once solidly Democratic South gradually became more competitive between the parties and the Republicans came to win a significant share of the southern seats in the House and Senate, the composition of the parties within Congress underwent a substantial change. Republicans increasingly won election in many of the conservative districts of the region. This helped to create a more southern- and conservative-oriented Republican party in both chambers. At the same time, Democratic House and Senate candidates became increasingly dependent on African American and moderate-to-liberal white voters in both the primaries and general elections in the South. The Democrats who emerge from this milieu tend to be "national Democrats" whose policy views and constituencies have much more in common with their northern and western colleagues than was true in the 1950s and 1960s. The result has been heightened party unity in both parties, especially in the House, and a greater willingness on the part of the majority Democrats to accept firm leadership control of the policy agenda (David W. Rohde, *Parties and Leaders in the Postreform House,* 1991).

Partisanship also affects the relationship between the president and Congress. Presidents' success in achieving their legislative programs is heavily dependent on the number of their partisans serving in the House and Senate. Single-party control of both the White House and Congress does not ensure passage of a president's legislative program, but it can make the president's congressional leadership task substantially easier. Indeed, party leaders in Congress usually act as congressional spokespersons for the president's policies, and the president tends to work through them in seeking passage of policy initiatives.

The parties' role in Congress and the governing process is paradoxical.

The parties' role in Congress and the governing process is paradoxical. Party influence on the organization of Congress is pervasive, and partisan affiliation has been shown to be the best single predictor of how representatives and senators will vote on congressional roll calls. Shared partisanship can help bridge the gap between the president and Congress created by the constitutional separation of powers, just as divided partisan control of the executive and legislative branches tends to intensify conflict. Yet despite the evidence of strong party influence, there are constant reminders of the parties' limited capacity to control policy-making in government institutions like Congress. Given a committee system that makes coordinated party policy development difficult and given that senators and representatives are individually responsible for their own electoral survival, the congressional parties cannot impose strict discipline on their members. They periodically fragment on critical roll-call votes, and cross-party coalitions constantly form to pass legislation that either advances or impedes the president's program. Yet for all their weaknesses, which are so often on display in Congress, the American political parties have shown a remarkable capacity for adaptability, durability, and influence.

[See also (I) Leadership; (II) Executive Power.]

BIBLIOGRAPHY

Beck, Paul Allen, and Frank J. Sorauf. *Party Politics in America.* 7th ed. 1992.

Bibby, John F. *Politics, Parties, and Elections in America.* 2d ed. 1992.

Chambers, William Nisbet. *Political Parties in a New Nation.* 1963.

Epstein, Leon D. *Political Parties in the American Mold.* 1986.

Herrnson, Paul S. *Party Campaigning in the 1980s.* 1988.

Key, V. O., Jr. *Politics, Parties and Pressure Groups.* 5th ed. 1964.

Maisel, L. Sandy, ed. *Political Parties and Elections in the United States: An Encyclopedia.* 1991.
Mayhew, David R. *Placing Parties in American Politics.* 1986.
Reichley, A. James. *The Life of the Parties: A History of American Political Parties.* 1992.
Rohde, David W. *Parties and Leaders in the Postreform House.* 1991.
Rosenstone, Steven J., Roy L. Behr, and Edward H. Lazarus. *Third Parties in America: Citizen Response to Major Party Failure.* 1984.

– JOHN F. BIBBY

PORK BARREL

Pork barrel refers to the appropriation of public money for geographically defined projects that would not be funded in the absence of strong support from their local representatives. Such projects typically provide visible benefits to the geographic areas in which they are built while distributing their less visible costs across the entire nation. The term has its origins in the practice on southern plantations of distributing rations of salt pork to the slaves from large wooden barrels. The earliest known citation to a political use of the term was in 1863, but not until the turn of the century did pork barrel became a common political expression.

For some scholars the notion of pork barrel is reserved for projects that are inefficient, meaning that the costs outweigh the benefits. The term is used more generally to refer to a local project that is chosen because of the strong support of a local legislator rather than because it is the best way to achieve some national purpose. Pork barrel projects are part of a broader class known as particularized benefits (Mayhew, 1974), or benefits awarded to a specific individual, group, or geographic constituency in a case-by-case manner. The ad hoc nature of their distribution allows legislators to claim credit for obtaining these benefits, since unlike entitlement benefits, they are not awarded automatically.

Pork barrel arises because legislators are elected from geographically defined constituencies and are constantly looking for ways to demonstrate how effectively they serve their constituents' interests. "Bringing home the bacon" is a universal favorite among legislators because it involves few political risks. Most constituents consider federal spending a good thing; it stimulates the local economy and generates employment. Since most of the benefits of a project are locally concentrated, while most of the costs are incurred outside the district, on election day a legislator usually faces the beneficiaries of a local project rather than those who pay the costs.

The classic pork barrel program is rivers and harbors, a program that promotes water navigation and flood control by constructing a series of dams, levees, locks, and waterways across the nation. Legislators propose individual projects for their districts. These projects compete for funds in the House and Senate Public Works and Appropriations committees and again on the two floors; the funded projects are then constructed by the U.S. Army Corps of Engineers. Committees regularly obtain large supporting majorities for this program on the two floors, awarding virtually every representative and senator a project now and then. Legislators vote for rivers and harbors bills to guarantee that their districts will obtain their share of pork.

The standard criticism of rivers and harbors projects is that they are economically inefficient: they cost more to construct than they will deliver in benefits. For example, Congress approved and the corps constructed a $2 billion project to connect the Tennessee River to the Gulf of Mexico through Alabama (saving barge owners from taking the more natural route down the Mississippi), despite estimates that the project would yield only thirty-nine cents on the dollar. Congress has also built dams to control flooding when it would have been cheaper to buy all the land in the floodplain. Although some rivers and harbors projects fail to satisfy standard cost-benefit criteria, many projects do achieve that standard. They are still considered pork barrel projects, however, because they are chosen for political reasons rather than on the basis of the best use of national transportation funds.

Congress makes decisions about the geographic allocation of benefits for only a few programs, most notably the construction of large federal facilities and large transportation projects. Most decisions about geographic allocation are made by bureaucrats in federal agencies. However, the fact that Congress delegates direct authority over geographic allocation to agencies does not diminish legislators' interest in these allocations. The record shows that legislators work hard to obtain geographic benefits for their districts and that bureaucrats respond to their pressure. Bureaucrats work simultaneously to broaden the geographic distribution of benefits, and thereby attract the support of as many legislators as possible, and to concentrate generous shares in the districts of crucial supporters, most notably the members of the committees that oversee a program's funding. A famous example is the model cities program, which began as an effort to concentrate federal funds in a handful of large, troubled cities but quickly evolved into a program that spread funds among 150 cities. Some of the model cities were actually small villages that had the good fortune to be represented in Congress by influential legislators.

Journalists and scholars disagree about how much pork exists in the federal budget. Many journalists find pork everywhere they look and delight in recounting the worst examples. Most scholars conducting empirical studies find more modest amounts. Part of the reason for this disparity is that some journalists confuse correlation with causation. For example, after finding an association between representation on the military committees and military spending in the districts that are represented on the military committees, they presume that the former causes the latter. Most scholarly studies suggest that causation runs in the opposite direction; legislators seek to serve on the military committees because their districts already contain large military facilities. A second reason is that journalists often focus their attention on notorious pork barrel programs such as rivers and harbors and then incorrectly assume that this tiny part of the federal budget is representative of the whole. In actuality over half of the federal budget consists of interest on the national debt and transfer payments to individuals—expenditures unconnected to geographic concerns. Of the remaining programs, most geographic benefits are allocated by formula or in competitions where merit clearly dominates.

Most experts conclude that pork barrel spending constitutes a tiny and declining portion of the federal budget. Charles Schultze, former chairman of the Council of Economic Advisers, estimates that the amount of pork in the 1988 federal budget was "no more than $10 billion," less than 1 percent of annual expenditures (Ellwood and Patashnik, 1993). Pork barrel spending continues to decline as a share of federal spending because it is being squeezed by the steady growth in entitlement programs. Each year the federal government spends less and less on construction projects and more and more on health care, social security, and other transfer payments.

[See also (I) Bargaining.]

BIBLIOGRAPHY

Arnold, R. Douglas. *Congress and the Bureaucracy.* 1979.
Ellwood, John W., and Eric M. Patashnik. "In Praise of Pork." *The Public Interest* 110 (1993): 19-33.
Hird, John. "The Political Economy of Pork." *American Political Science Review* 85 (1991): 429-456.
Mayer, Kenneth. *The Political Economy of Defense Contracting.* 1991.
Mayhew, David. *Congress: The Electoral Connection.* 1974.

– R. DOUGLAS ARNOLD

POSTAL SERVICE

Article I, section 8 of the Constitution states: "The Congress shall have Power . . . To establish Post Offices and post Roads." For more than two centuries the application of this grant of authority has had significant consequences for the nation's economic and social development. From the first, its importance made the operation of the postal service a highly political matter, subject to strong economic, regional, and patronage interests. At the same time it is the most personal and universal of government services, daily touching almost every citizen. Yet it was assumed from the outset that the postal service would be a revenue-producing government activity. The resulting conflicts involving special interests, the general demand for universal and efficient delivery of the mail, and the pressure for economy have shaped the often turbulent history of congressional postal policy.

CREATION AND DEVELOPMENT. In 1782 the Continental Congress made an effort to consolidate the scattered and disparate postal services that had developed during the colonial and revolutionary periods. For the first time a single set of regulations governed postal management, organization, routes, rates, and penalties for related offenses. The Continental Congress made it clear that the central government would have authority over both interstate and intrastate postal systems.

Although the federal legislature established the United States Post Office in 1789, it did not provide permanency of the service or define the place of the Post Office in the new government beyond prescribing a loose constituent relationship of the Post Office to the Treasury Department.

Congressional acts in 1792 and 1794 further consolidated the authority and responsibility of the service and established the Post Office as a permanent organization in the federal government. Its independence as a government department evolved gradually through changes in bureaucratic practice. Postmaster General John McLean began to report directly to the president instead of to the secretary of the Treasury in 1825 and to label his correspondence as coming from the "Post Office Department," instead of the "General Post Office." Andrew Jackson was the first president to include the postmaster general in the cabinet. Congress in 1873 finally recognized the Post Office formally as an executive department.

Over time Congress frequently enacted legislation affecting postal services. But the system established in the late 1790s was the basic framework for the organization until its decentralization in the 1950s.

POLITICS. The very nature of the postal service invites political association and involvement. The Post Office employed 78 percent of federal employees in 1816, 56 percent in 1881, and 57 percent in 1901. There were more than seventy-six thousand post offices in 1900, and the appointment of postmasters was the largest single source of party patronage in the nineteenth century. The Senate had to confirm appointments to some of the more important postmasterships, and members of the House assumed that they would be consulted on appointments in their districts.

Building post roads involved Congress not only in the appropriations for their construction but in the determination of locale and routes. Selection of those sites was the subject of intense debate. Post roads were the tracks over which the mail was carried from city to city, and they became the foundation for much of the country's early permanent highways. In later years, as railroads and airlines began to replace road carriers, lobbying for mail contracts was intense.

PERSONNEL. For two hundred years Congress had considerable say over the numbers, pay, and working conditions of postal personnel. The legislature established categories of jobs such as postmasters, postal clerks, and letter carriers. Members of this work force became a constituency with considerable influence.

Congress on several occasions responded to pressures to establish a merit system in the postal service. Most positions other than postmaster were covered by the Pendleton Act of 1883. The Ramspeck-O'Mahoney Act of 1938 replaced postmasters' terms with lifetime appointments (dependent on good behavior). One consequence was an increasing number of appointments of postmasters from the career ranks.

FINANCES. From 1836 until 1971 Congress required that all postal revenues be deposited in the general treasury, that the postmaster general submit itemized budget estimates for the coming year, and that the Post Office secure annual congressional appropriations. These requirements were a serious source of friction between the Post Office and the legislature, because they enabled Congress to exert considerable influence over the policies of the department.

The setting of rates, levels of service balanced against revenue and deficits, and the issue of service priorities versus business practices are major themes in the rich history of Congress's relations with the Post Office. The legislature occasionally increased rates only to see revenues fall, because people were not using the service. Congress then would lower the rates, and revenues would increase, sometimes because service had expanded to new territories.

Post Office accounting methods became the subject of legislation. The Kelly Act (1930) provided for the separation of the expenses of direct postal services from ancillary activities such as private carrier subsidies, franked mail for government agencies (and Congress), the conduct of unemployment censuses, and the sale of migratory bird stamps.

SERVICES. In its long history the Post Office has offered a variety of services, initiated either by or with the support of Congress. The Pony Express (1860) was a particularly dramatic example, although it was in place only for eighteen months. Other innovations have been postal money orders (1864), special delivery (1885), rural free delivery (1893, 1896), parcel post (1912), postal savings (1910–1966), and air mail (1918). Congress has imposed a number of other duties on the service, including the mail distribution and collection of census schedules.

CONGRESS AND THE CORPORATION. The Postal Reorganization Act of 1970 converted the U.S. Postal Service into a government corporation. A nine-member board of governors, appointed by the president with the advice and consent of the Senate, elects the postmaster general. The Postal Rate Commission, established in 1970, is responsible for recommending postage rate adjustments. The salaries of postal service employees are established through collective bargaining. In short, Congress has divested itself of most of its traditionally close and highly political control over rates, personnel, and other management issues. Still, the postal service has not achieved full fiscal autonomy: Congress continues to legislate an annual subsidy through the Treasury, the Post Office, and general government appropriations acts. And Congress retains its constitutional prerogative in that it can legislate at any time to change the structure and duties of the system.

BIBLIOGRAPHY

Cullinan, Gerald. *The United States Postal Service.* 1973.

Daniel, Edward G. *United States Postal Service and Postal Policy, 1789–1860.* 1941.

Stewart, Alva W. *The U.S. Postal Service: Problems and Prospects.* 1985.

Tierney, John T. *The U.S. Postal Service: Status and Prospects of a Public Enterprise.* 1988.

– SHARON STIVER GRESSLE

PRECEDENTS

House Precedents

The prefaces to Asher C. Hinds's, Clarence Cannon's, and Lewis Deschler and William Holmes Brown's Precedents of the U.S. House of Representatives all recite the overriding importance of precedent in assuring the stability of parliamentary bodies and protection of the rights of its various components: the majority, the minority, individual members, and the entire membership. Hinds describes the great majority of the rules of all parliamentary bodies as "unwritten law; they spring up by precedent and custom and are to this day the chief law of both Houses of Congress." However, he, Cannon, Deschler, and Brown all recognized the need to publish the precedents, not only to expedite the routine business of the House, but to enhance the concept of parliamentary equity and the prestige of the legislative branch of government.

The precedents of the House, while comprising the "unwritten law" in that they are not prescripted as standards of general applicability in advance of their establishment, fall into three main categories: (1) the rulings or decisions of the Speaker or chairman or Committee of the Whole, which are generally made in resolving a point of order or parliamentary inquiry (as distinguished from a situation that merely lurks in the *Record* and is never brought to the chair's attention); (2) the decisions or conclusions, express or implied, that emanate from the House itself without objection being made; and (3) precedents sub silento, that is, practices or procedures of the House that are never specifically ruled on but that have a tacit conceptual underpinning of procedural correctness and are thus more than mere "instances" or procedural aberrations. The definition of "precedent" as represented by these categories is to be distinguished from a routine substantive result that does not illuminate the procedure of the House, such as the regularity with which the House may vote for or against a particular bill.

A decision by the Speaker or chairman is a precedent in subsequent procedural dispute where the same point is again in controversy. Before applying a precedent, however, the chair must first be convinced that the pending factual situation—for example, the pending relationship between the underlying text and amendment offered thereto in the case of a germaneness question—does indeed comprise the same point.

On the theory that a government of laws is preferable to a government of men and women, the House has repeatedly recognized the importance of following its precedents and obeying its well-established procedural rules. In so doing, the House is applying a doctrine known to appellate courts as stare decisis, under which a judge in making a decision will look to earlier cases involving the same question of law. Determination of the will of the majority in an orderly and predictable way is to be desired, and thus parliamentary law as "common law" has come to be recognized as binding on the assembly and its members (except as it may be varied by the adoption by the membership of special rules).

BIBLIOGRAPHY

U.S. House of Representatives. *Cannon's Precedents of the House of Representatives of the United States,* by Clarence Cannon. 8 vols. 74th Cong., 1st sess., 1935.

U.S. House of Representatives. *Deschler's Precedents of the United States House of Representatives,* by Lewis Deschler. 10 vols. 94th Cong., 2d sess., 1977. H. Doc. 94-661.

U.S. House of Representatives. *Hinds' Precedents of the House of Representatives of the United States,* by Asher C. Hinds. 5 vols. 59th Cong., 2d sess., 1907.

U.S. House of Representatives. *Procedure in the United States House of Representatives,* by Lewis Deschler and William Holmes Brown. 4th ed. 97th Cong., 2d sess., 1982.

– CHARLES W. JOHNSON

Senate Precedents

Since its Standing Rules provide only a skeletal framework for procedure, the U.S. Senate relies on recorded precedents to clarify and preserve its legislative practices. The historical development of Senate procedure has tended to enhance the legislative rights of individual senators and political minorities.

The U.S. Senate relies on recorded precedents to clarify and preserve its legislative practices.

The absence of fundamental procedural constraints in the rules is striking. The rules do not, for example, impose a general germaneness requirement on amendments. Similarly, there is no limit to the time senators may consume in debate. Senators may, therefore, raise nonrelevant issues almost at will. Extensive, even exhaustive, debate may follow, often in face of the will of a large majority. Such freedoms dramatically affect the Senate's day-to-day consideration of legislation. The body has thus necessarily developed a mass of precedents addressing every conceivable aspect of procedure, and these have become essential to the Senate's ability to conduct business in an orderly manner. The precedents are the road signs on the Senate's legislative map.

Precedents are established in a variety of ways. The manner in which a precedent arises dictates its procedural weight in future Senate practice. The precedents of the greatest probative value are created when the Senate votes on a procedural question. In rare instances, such a vote occurs when the chair (the vice president, the president pro tempore, or a senator acting as presiding officer) submits a point of order to the Senate for consideration. More commonly, the Senate votes on an appeal from a ruling by the chair in response to a point of order. The Senate may vote to sustain or to reverse any ruling by the chair. A precedent is created regardless of the ultimate outcome of the vote.

Precedents of lesser weight are established when the chair rules on a point of order raised by a senator from the floor. The majority of the Senate's precedents are created in this manner. The chair's rulings, based on interpretation of Senate rules, precedents, and relevant statutes, are controlling in the Senate unless an appeal is taken.

Precedents of relatively limited probative value arise when the chair responds to a parliamentary inquiry from the Senate floor on some question of procedure. Responses to parliamentary inquiries are advisory opinions and are not necessarily dispositive statements of Senate practice or procedure. They do, however, provide guidance to the chair in the absence of precedents of greater weight.

Precedents occasionally arise when the chair itself calls a senator to order. This practice often springs from interpretations of the Senate's cloture rule. Cloture is the process by which the Senate determines, by supermajority vote, to limit debate on a question. Precedents initiated by the chair reflect the extraordinary significance of cloture within Senate procedure. The Senate always retains the right to reject the chair's rulings. Historically, the Senate has shown great deference to the chair within the cloture context.

Senate precedents are compiled and maintained by the Office of the Parliamentarian, a nonpartisan arm of the Office of the Secretary of the Senate.

[See also (I) Cloture.]

BIBLIOGRAPHY

U.S. Senate. Committee on Rules and Administration. *Standing Rules of the Senate.* 1990. S. Doc. 101-25.

U.S. Senate. *Riddick's Senate Procedure, Precedents, and Practices,* by Floyd M. Riddick and Alan S. Frumin. 101st Cong., 2d sess., 1992. S. Doc. 101-28.

U.S. Senate. Committee on Rules and Administration. *Congressional Handbook.* 1990. S. Prt. 101-103.

– JAMES P. WEBER

PRESIDENT AND CONGRESS

One of the enduring conflicts in U.S. government is that between Congress and the presidency. At times Congress has been dominant; at other times the presidency has been in control; and at still other times the two branches have been roughly in balance. The Framers of the Constitution established the conflict in 1787 when they devised a government with Congress as the preeminent branch and the president as secondary to, but independent of, the legislature.

The Framers intensified the conflict when they combined a system of checks and balances with that of separation of powers. The Framers knew that separation of powers was a misnomer. The Constitution separates the three branches of government (legislative, executive, and judicial), but it fuses their functions, as each branch shares in the powers of another branch. For instance, Congress has the legislative power but the president has the power to veto congressional legislation. The Framers further magnified the conflict by providing for a bicameral legislature. Friction arises not simply between the president and Congress but among the House, the Senate, and the president.

That the three institutions have separate electoral bases and terms of office makes matters worse. Presidents often face a Congress in which one or both houses are controlled by the opposite party. In seventeen of the forty-six Congresses from 1900 to 1994—thirty-four years—the majority party in one or both houses has been the party opposing the president. The Framers thus guaranteed an ongoing struggle between successive Congresses and presidents attempting to direct government action.

THEORIES OF PRESIDENTIAL AND CONGRESSIONAL POWER. Three theories of power—one concerning congressional power and two concerning presidential power—have guided the conflict between Congress and the president. In the Constitution, the Framers offered a theory of congressional activism in which Congress, acting on behalf of the people, defines the scope and policies of the national government. "In republican government," wrote James Madison in *Federalist* 51, "the legislative authority necessarily predominates." The Congress enjoys a series of enumerated and implied powers that place it in charge of the very stuff of government: the authority to raise, borrow, coin, and spend money; the power to regulate the nation's interstate and foreign commerce; and the authority to oversee the national defense by declaring war, maintaining the army and the navy, and placing state militias in the service of the United States.

The Framers conceived of a theory of presidential restraint to complement their theory of congressional activism. Under this conception, the president acts as a true executive—carrying out the wishes of Congress and not initiating government action. The Framers did not wish the executive to be as powerful as the one they had known in the British monarchy, but they did wish to give the executive sufficient "energy" to counteract any congressional excesses. In the Constitution, the president has a series of enumerated powers, less developed than those given to Congress, which include treaty making, appointing government officials, serving as military commander in chief, vetoing legislation, and executing the laws. By the logic of presidential restraint, the president acts only according to specified constitutional powers or others found in federal law.

The Framers' theory of congressional activism, coupled with that of presidential restraint, directed government action throughout most of the nineteenth century. After the turn of the century, however, two progressive presidents, Republican Theodore Roosevelt (1901–1909) and Democrat Woodrow Wilson (1913–1921), propounded a theory of presidential activism to replace the Framers' theory of presidential restraint. Roosevelt offered a twofold definition of presidential activism. First, in the absence of any specific prohibitions in the Constitution or in law, the president has an inherent grant of executive power to do whatever he feels is necessary to act in the public interest. Second, the president makes such claims, in Roosevelt's words, as the "steward of the people," or the people's representative. Wilson extended Roosevelt's claims of public leadership, maintaining that the link between the president and the public was the most significant feature of the office and not merely, as Roosevelt had maintained, a significant aspect of presidential power. Presidential activism turns presidential restraint on its head and makes the president at least as powerful as Congress.

With the introduction of presidential activism, the theory of congressional activism was not replaced by one of congressional restraint. Instead, throughout the twentieth century, as demands on government grew, both the president and Congress relied on notions of activism. These combinations of theories—congressional activism and presidential restraint in the nineteenth century and congressional activism and presidential activism in the twentieth century—have set the tone for the conflict between Congress and the president in four areas of power: legislation, war, executive action, and diplomacy.

LEGISLATION. Most nineteenth-century presidents followed the lead of George Washington (1789–1797), who believed that the president's role was to execute the laws of Congress faithfully, not actively initiate legislation. Thomas Jefferson (1801–1809) proved an exception when he developed a disciplined party organization of Jeffersonian Republicans in Congress with the president as its leader. Yet, mindful of the precedent set by Washington that the president should not directly guide the course of congressional events, Jefferson privately funneled proposals to Republican members of Congress. When Jefferson left office, the party apparatus he had established became a congressional, not an executive, tool. With the exceptions of Andrew Jackson

View of the Capitol. From the White House, c. 1840. Engraving by H. Wallis from a sketch by W. H. Bartlett, in Bartlett's History of America. *(Library of Congress)*

(1829–1837), James K. Polk (1845–1849), and Abraham Lincoln (1861–1865), the remaining nineteenth-century presidents endorsed presidential restraint in legislation. Congress handled issues of slavery, western expansion, Reconstruction, tariffs, and industrialization with little help from presidents.

Not until the progressives championed the view that innovation should be expected from the president did presidential activism in legislative affairs emerge and remain. Theodore Roosevelt sent Congress his Square Deal initiatives, which included antitrust action, railroad regulation, consumer protection, civil service reform, and conservation. Woodrow Wilson's New Freedom crafted Progressivism to the traditions of the Democratic party, pushing for lower tariffs, an overhaul of the banking system, agricultural reform, and the adoption of a federal income tax. Although Warren G. Harding (1921–1923), Calvin Coolidge (1923–1929), and Herbert Hoover (1929–1933) were not as active as Roosevelt or Wilson, they presented or supported initiatives before Congress on several occasions, thus continuing to move beyond the bounds of the nineteenth-century presidency. For instance, Harding endorsed the Budget and Accounting Act of 1921, which instituted a central comprehensive budget under presidential control.

Franklin D. Roosevelt (1933–1945) raised the legislative agenda-setting power of Theodore Roosevelt and Wilson to two new levels. First, the sheer quantity of his initiatives surpassed earlier presidential activism. New Deal legislation was adopted on a wide range of topics, including banking, securities, direct relief to states and localities, industrial codes, labor practices, farm relief, and social security. Second, much of the legislation required the delegation of power from Congress to the president to implement the programs. Roosevelt not only asserted power to propose programs but gained from Congress discretionary power to implement the programs. Presidents since Roosevelt have continued to offer policy packages. Harry S Truman (1945–1953) announced the Fair Deal; John F. Kennedy (1961–1963) heralded the New Frontier; Lyndon B. Johnson (1963–1969) called for the Great Society; and Richard M. Nixon (1969–1974) announced the New Federalism. The initiatives of Ronald Reagan (1981–1989) were never officially titled because the nickname "Reaganomics" stuck so well.

To sell their legislative programs, presidents must "hit the ground running"—that is, they must present major policy initiatives with great public fanfare in the first months of their term. The honeymoon with the press, the public, and Congress, which almost all presidents enjoy upon taking office, provides presidents with the greatest opportunity to get what they want. To achieve success, presidents engage in three strategies: personally lobbying members of Congress, relying on the White House liaison staff to lobby Congress, and making appeals to the American public, which will itself lobby Congress.

Presidential activism turns presidential restraint on its head and makes the president at least as powerful as Congress.

Personal lobbying. Presidents can be their own best (or worst) liaison officers with congressional members. They use various mixes of accommodationist, combative, and detached legislative styles as events, bills, and members dictate. In adopting an accommodationist style, a president builds coalitions through bargaining and give-and-take. Lyndon Johnson frequently played the accommodationist by getting as many members of Congress as possible involved in legislation, keeping tabs on support, using personal persuasion, and granting personal and political favors to convince members to join the coalition. Adopting the combative style, a president builds coalitions through threats and intimidation. Although Johnson often employed an accommodationist style, he also displayed a combative style by withdrawing support from a member's favorite bill if the member did not support the presidential initiative. In adopting a detached style, a president removes himself from lobbying efforts as much as possible and relies heavily on the formal congressional liaison staff to build a coalition. President Jimmy Carter (1977–1981), who had campaigned as a Washington outsider, adopted a detached style and did not personally court the Democratic leadership or membership. As criticism mounted, Carter's style began to shift to a more accommodationist approach.

White House liaison. Presidents since Dwight D. Eisenhower (1953–1961) have also relied on a staff of legislative liaisons to monitor the progress of their programs and other legislation through Congress. (Today, the liaison staff numbers nearly twenty people in the Office of Legislative Affairs.) Presidents Kennedy, Johnson, Nixon, Gerald R. Ford (1974–1977), Reagan, George Bush (1989–1993), and Bill Clinton (1993-) organized their liaison offices around key blocs in Congress, based on combinations of geography, ideology, and party. Some liaison staff members were assigned conservative Democrats; others courted their more liberal colleagues; still other staffers were assigned to Republicans. Carter initially reorganized the liaison office along issue lines because he felt members would support an issue on its merits. When members of Congress told Carter that he did not understand congressional factions, Carter switched to the approach taken by the other presidents.

Public appeals. Presidents also seek support for presidential programs before Congress by taking their case to the people. Theodore Roosevelt summed up this approach: "I achieved results only by appealing over the heads of the Senate and House leaders to the people, who were the masters of both of us." Presidents gamble that they will gain popular support by making public appearances throughout the country, delivering national radio and television addresses, and holding news conferences. If they are successful, they will use this new public support in bargaining with members of Congress.

Success and vetoes. How well have presidents done in Congress? Analyses of roll-call votes examine whether a majority of members concur with presidents' public stands on bills. Although this indicator is often referred to as presidential success, *presidential-congressional concurrence* is a better term. The measure merely shows the number of times presidents and Congresses agree on bills. It does not say anything about who influenced whom. Members of both parties will overwhelmingly support many roll-call votes regardless of whether the president has a position. The results show that the president and a majority of members of Congress often agree on legislation, especially early in the president's term, when the president and the Congress are of the same party and when the president's public approval is high.

This concurrence should not mask the difficulties many presidents have in getting their top-priority programs through Congress. Although people remember the early days of Roosevelt's New Deal, Johnson's Great Society, and Reagan's budget and tax cuts, some presidents have encountered problems in getting Congress to pass the main items on their policy agenda. In 1961, only one of Kennedy's high-priority items—rural development—was enacted; Nixon was unable to get his welfare reform plan through Congress intact; Ford's economic initiatives failed to win passage, as did Bush's capital gains tax proposal; Carter had difficulties with his energy, environment, and hospital-cost containment plans; and Clinton encountered opposition to his economic stimulus plan and health care reform. Members of Congress typically have their own ideas about what are major problems and how to solve them.

As the Framers intended, presidents do well in vetoing legislation. Woodrow Wilson observed in *Congressional Government* (1885) that a president's "power of veto . . . is, of course, beyond all comparison, his most formidable prerogative." Strategically, however, presidents recognize that vetoes are negative powers: by vetoing legislation a president stops what he does not want, but he does not get what he does want. According to the Constitution, a presidential veto automatically prevents a bill passed by both houses from becoming law unless two-thirds of both houses vote to override the veto. Getting two-thirds of all members of Congress to agree on a controversial action such as an override is almost always a herculean task. Congress has overridden presidents' vetoes just over one hundred times in more than two hundred years—a mere seven-tenths of 1 percent of all vetoes. This statistic applies only to regular vetoes. Congress cannot override so-called pocket vetoes, which occur when Congress adjourns before the elapse of the ten-day period that the Constitution gives the president to make up his mind. Between 1789 and 1991, presidents used the regular veto on 1,447 bills and the pocket veto on 1,055 bills. Actual vetoes are important items in a president's legislative bag of tricks, but veto threats may be just as compelling. Because overrides are usually unsuccessful, a president may exact compromises from Congress by threatening a veto. Congressional activism and presidential activism are pronounced in the legislative arena.

WAR. The Framers felt that the president's designation as commander in chief merely established that a civilian head would be in charge of the military. The commander would have the power to respond to surprise attacks but not to do much more without congressional authorization. Congress was expressly given the power to declare war and provide for the armed forces. Although Lincoln did not concur, all other nineteenth-century presidents acted as commanders in chief under the theory of presidential restraint. Jefferson made two requests to Congress to engage in offensive actions (against Tripoli in 1801 and Spain in 1805), both of which Congress denied. Although President Polk asked for and received a congressional declaration of war against Mexico in 1846, Congress, not the president, led the country to war against England in the War of 1812 and against Spain in the Spanish-American War of 1898.

Lincoln, however, asserted presidential activism in military affairs. He acted unilaterally during a three-month period at the outset of the Civil War when Congress was not in session to, among other things, call out state militias, expand the army and navy, spend $2 million from the Treasury without congressional appropriation, and issue the first Emancipation Proclamation. Congress approved some of the decisions (not all) after the fact.

Presidents' powers in the two declared total wars of the twentieth century—World War I and World War II—were as vast as those claimed by Lincoln and extended over the whole U.S. economy and social order, but Congress delegated many of these powers to the president. For instance, Congress gave Wilson the power to take over factories and railroads, fix prices in certain industries, declare certain exports unlawful, censor foreign communications, and operate the telephone and telegraph systems. Similarly, Congress gave Franklin Roosevelt the authority to establish and staff numerous emergency boards; to negotiate with other countries the sale, lease, or exchange of various items related to defense; and to evacuate and confine seventy thousand American citizens of Japanese descent residing on the West Coast.

Since World War II, presidents have effectively devised their own war-making power by expanding their authority as commander in chief and preempting Congress's power to declare war. This presidential war-making power involves presidents' ability to unilaterally commit U.S. troops anywhere on the globe. Presidents have unilaterally committed U.S. forces in two types of restricted military interventions: limited wars and emergency interventions.

Limited wars. So-called limited wars are limited in resources and goals. They involve specific initial commitments of troops, although the numbers have typically increased incrementally as such wars have gone on. The goal of a limited war often falls short of all-out victory. U.S. objectives have been to prevent communism in a vulnerable nation, for example, or to stop an aggressive dictator, not necessarily to bring the enemy to its knees. Limited wars are defensive military efforts confined to one country or one region. Today, however, because the United States is a world military and economic power, a president can determine that almost any nation at any moment in some way impinges on the security of the United States. Presidents have conducted three limited wars in the twentieth century: the Korean War, the Vietnam War, and the Persian Gulf War.

Truman took the most expansive view of the president's power to conduct limited war. When a senator asked Truman to seek a congressional resolution to authorize the U.S. intervention in Korea, Truman replied that he did not need one but instead could use his constitutional powers as commander in chief. As the war went on, Truman consistently relied on the commander-in-chief power to add more men, expand the theater of war into North Korea, and threaten the use of nuclear weapons.

Johnson agreed with Truman that the president already had full constitutional authority to send troops to foreign soil, but, unlike Truman, Johnson sought a resolution from Congress to support his decision to commit major ground troops in Vietnam after a reported attack on two U.S. destroyers by North Vietnamese gunboats in the Gulf of Tonkin in late July 1964. On 7 August 1964, Congress passed what became known as the Gulf of Tonkin Resolution, which read: "The Congress approves and supports the determination of the President, as Commander in Chief, to take all necessary measures to repel any armed attack against the forces of the United States and to prevent further aggression." In 1967, Johnson remarked, "We did not think the resolution was necessary to do what we did and what we're doing." Johnson sought the resolution as a matter of political insurance: through the resolution Congress gave the president full power to direct the war but it shared responsibility for the war in case something went wrong. When the Vietnam War turned ugly and Congress repealed the Gulf of Tonkin Resolution in January 1971, Nixon returned to Truman's exclusive reliance on the commander-in-chief power.

According to the Constitution, a presidential veto automatically prevents a bill passed by both houses from becoming law unless two-thirds of both houses vote to override the veto.

Congress attempted to reassert its war-making role with the War Powers Resolution of 1973. Passed over President Nixon's veto, the act requires that within forty-eight hours after committing U.S. troops into actual or "imminent" hostilities, the president must submit a report to Congress describing the reasons and the constitutional authority for the action. Once the notification has been given, a clock starts ticking. The president has sixty days to complete the military action, although he may request a thirty-day extension. The operation, however, must be completed in that ninety-day period unless Congress declares war or supplies specific authorization for the use of U.S. armed forces. The War Powers Resolution looks good on paper as a device by which Congress might reclaim some control over U.S. military efforts, yet presidents since Ford have brushed its requirements aside.

After Iraq invaded Kuwait in August 1990, Bush asserted that he had the sole authority to send first 120,000, then 200,000, and ultimately 560,000 men and women from all branches of the armed forces to fight Iraq. Bush, like Johnson, asked Congress to pass a resolution sanctioning the use of force. Bush, like Johnson, insisted that he had the authority to deploy troops without the resolution. "I don't think I need it," he said. The resolution was consistent with a United Nations declaration that asked member nations to use "all necessary means" to force Iraq out of Kuwait unless it ended its occupation by 15 January 1991. Several days before the deadline, a sharply divided Congress passed Bush's resolution. With the resolution in hand, Bush saw no need to follow the requirements of the War Powers Resolution.

Emergency interventions. Since the Vietnam War, presidents have favored the use of emergency interventions—the engagement of small numbers of troops for short periods of time in situations that purportedly involve threats to American lives. Emergency interventions are often the symbolic flexing of American military muscle that do not risk the large-scale entanglements of limited wars.

The Constitution instructs the president to take care that the laws be faithfully executed and to appoint executive officers to help in that execution.

Presidents have consistently circumvented the requirements of the War Powers Resolution in ordering emergency interventions. They are loathe to have their hands tied by the act's consultation and report procedures. When Ford ordered the marines and navy to rescue a U.S. merchant ship, the *Mayaguez,* seized by Cambodia in May 1975, he did not report to Congress. Similarly, Carter did not tell Congress beforehand of the secret, ultimately unsuccessful, helicopter mission in March 1980 to try to free Americans held hostage in Iran. In October 1983, Reagan and Congress worked out a complex compromise regarding U.S. Marines in Lebanon. For the first time, a president invoked the imminent hostilities provision of the War Powers Resolution, but Congress gave Reagan eighteen months to complete the Lebanese mission (rather than the ninety-day maximum called for in the War Powers Resolution). In a separate letter, Reagan refused to recognize the constitutionality of the War Powers Resolution. In October 1985, Reagan informed congressional leaders that he was sending nineteen hundred troops to Grenada to protect the lives of American students on the island. But he expressly refused to comply with the notification requirements of the War Powers Resolution. Bush followed Reagan's lead when he ordered the invasion of Panama in December 1990. Truman had summed up presidential thinking about consulting Congress long before the War Powers Resolution was passed: "I do not have to unless I want to. But of course I am polite and I usually always consult them." Yet Truman did not consult Congress, nor have most presidents, with or without the War Powers Resolution.

Restricted military action, whether in the form of limited wars or emergency interventions, provides presidents unique opportunities to expand presidential activism. Congress today, weary because of Vietnam and wary of what many members perceive as a diminution of congressional activism, is plainly aware of this pattern. As the debates before the Persian Gulf War attested, Congress is no longer likely to be the silent partner of military affairs that presidents prefer. Instead, it will act as a watchdog. Its best weapon is not the War Powers Resolution but its appropriations power—its ability to give presidents money and to take it away. Although congressional efforts are often reactive and sporadic, post–Vietnam Congresses have consciously sought to avoid losing congressional power to activist presidents.

EXECUTIVE ACTION. The Constitution instructs the president to take care that the laws be faithfully executed and to appoint executive officers to help in that execution. Ambiguities in these stipulations of the Constitution have, however, led to yet other conflicts between the legislative and executive branches.

Removal power. During the nineteenth century, the central debate in the arena of executive action stemmed from the Constitution's ambiguity concerning how executive officers can be removed from office. Although the Constitution gave the president the authority to make appointments with the advice and consent of the Senate, it was silent on the removal of such appointees. Congress narrowly defeated a bill opposed by Washington that would have made removal subject to Senate consent. As political parties grew, so did the practice of patronage whereby presidents gave government jobs to loyal party members. To maintain party unity, presidents accepted the names of job applicants from members of Congress, who took more and more interest in presidential appointments and, consequently, in presidential removals.

In 1867, Congress passed over Andrew Johnson's (1865–1869) veto the Tenure of Office Act, which required Senate consent for the president's removal of any executive official previously confirmed by the Senate, thus codifying presidential restraint. Johnson's resistance to the act led to his impeachment and near conviction. Congress denied President Ulysses S. Grant (1869–1877) his request to repeal the Tenure of Office Act. Presidents Rutherford B. Hayes (1877–1881) and James A. Garfield (1881) fought against congressional efforts to block presidential nominations. After an eighteen-month battle, Hayes felt he had beaten top Senate leaders: "The contest has been a bitter one. It has exposed me to attack, opposition, misconstruction, and the actual hatred of powerful men. But I have had great success. No member of either house now attempts even to dictate appointments. My sole right to make appointments is now tacitly conceded." But senators continued to block executive appointments and removals until 1887, when Congress repealed the Tenure of Office Act. After a struggle of two decades, presidents regained their control over executive appointments and removals. Yet the victory did little more than recapture old ground. Presidents gained control of the executive action, but the action was decidedly restricted.

Congressional delegation and executive orders. In the twentieth century, the debate over executive power shifted from executive removals to congressional delegation of power. Congress has provided a dramatic expansion of executive power by its delegation of power to the president in two ways. First, Congress specifies that a law goes into effect when the president determines an event has occurred or a set of conditions has been met. Second, Congress gives the president authority to issue executive orders to carry out the substance of legislation. Executive orders carry the weight of law but do not require the approval of Congress. Executive orders allow presidents to act as legislators and in effect create a presidential lawmaking power.

Presidents since Franklin Roosevelt have used executive orders to shape policy. On civil rights, Roosevelt established the Fair Employment Practices Commission in 1943 to prevent discrimination in hiring by government agencies and military suppliers. Truman ended segregation in the armed services by executive order. Eisenhower and Kennedy issued executive orders to enforce school desegregation in Arkansas, Mississippi, and Alabama. In 1965, Johnson signed an executive order that required affirmative action (the active seeking of qualified minority applicants) in hiring by the federal government and government contractors. Reagan, who opposed affirmative action, sought to "repeal" Johnson's order, but public controversy swelled and he dropped the idea.

Reagan signed, and Bush continued, an executive order that prohibited federally funded family planning clinics from informing their clients about abortion. The Supreme Court in *Rust v. Sullivan* (1991) upheld the order. Congress tried several times to pass legislation that would have negated the executive order, but Bush vetoed one such attempt and threatened to veto others. Congress was unable to rally the two-thirds vote of both houses needed to override the Bush veto, and in October 1992 the executive order went into full effect. It did not last long. Also acting by executive order, President Clinton overturned this Reagan-Bush "gag order" as one of his first acts in office.

In an attempt to control presidential lawmaking, Congress has fashioned the so-called legislative veto. By means of this device, Congress may disapprove of executive orders designed to enforce legislation. In the most typical instance, Congress requires that the proposed executive action lie before Congress for a specified period of time. If, during the time period, either house disapproves the measure, it is void. In 1983, the Supreme Court held in *Immigration and Naturalization Service v. Chadha* that the legislative veto is unconstitutional because it is a violation of separation of powers. The Supreme Court's ruling against legislative vetoes has done little, however, to eliminate them as statutory and informal devices. In the year immediately following the Chadha case, Congress placed fifty-three legislative vetoes into bills that Reagan signed. As with legislation and war, congressional activism and presidential activism rival each other in matters of executive action.

DIPLOMACY. Although in legislation, war, and executive action, presidential restraint directed the actions of nineteenth-century presidents, presidents beginning with George Washington took an activist role in diplomacy and never lost the advantage to Congress. Although the Framers saw foreign relations as a joint presidential-senatorial venture, Washington moved the Senate to a subordinate role. He asserted that the negotiation of treaties was under the exclusive purview of the executive and that the president had a monopoly on the right to communicate with foreign governments. Members of Congress were willing to accept the president's central position in foreign affairs. The president was, according to Rep. John Marshall (later the chief justice of the United States), "the sole organ of the nation in its external relations, and its sole representative with foreign nations." In dicta the Supreme Court ratified the sole-organ doctrine in *United States v. Curtiss-Wright Export Corp.* (1936), stating that the president's power as the sole organ did "not require as a basis for its exercise an act of Congress."

Twentieth-century presidents have expanded their foreign policy role by the use of what are known as executive agreements. These are international agreements entered into by presidents; unlike treaties they do not require Senate consent. Presidents since Truman have entered into roughly seven times as many executive agreements as treaties. Truman both started and ended U.S. involvement in the Korean War by executive agreement, and Johnson and Nixon made key decisions to escalate the Vietnam War in the same way.

Treaties, however, have not been abandoned as a form of diplomatic exchange. In some instances, the importance of a diplomatic effort mandates a treaty, as did the creation of the North Atlantic Treaty Organization (NATO) after World War II and several Strategic Arms Limitation Talks (SALT) beginning in the Nixon administration. Presidents see political advantages to having the Senate on board. In other cases, tradition dictates that a treaty rather than an executive agreement be adopted. But presidents have few difficulties even with treaties. To be sure, presidents must keep an eye on Congress, especially the Senate, in negotiating treaties. Provisions of important treaties frequently evolve through informal consultation with senators. Senate ratification is usually pro forma, however. Since 1949, presidents have won approval of all but two treaties submitted to the Senate. If a treaty is in trouble, a president is more likely to withdraw it rather than face its defeat. In addition, the Supreme Court has held that presidents may unilaterally break treaties. The sole-organ doctrine espoused by presidents and approved by the Court gives presidents a broad, inherent claim of diplomatic power and plenty of room for unilateral action.

The presidents immediately before and after the Civil War are often depicted as prosaic, unhappy men unable to champion the office in which they served. In this view, they were too shy, too lazy, too inept, or too stupid to live up to the office's potential. Yet personality and talent hardly seem to explain why twenty of the twenty-five presidents during the eighteenth and nineteenth centuries were lords of passivity. Only Washington, Jefferson, Jackson, Polk, and Lincoln are clear exceptions to the nineteenth-century rule of presidential restraint. Nor does it seem possible that the restraint resulted from the charisma, energy, cunning, and intelligence of members of Congress. What stood in the way of nineteenth-century presidents were the ideas that the Framers had fashioned years before. The Framers offered a scheme of government dominated by Congress and characterized by presidential restraint. For the most part, the nineteenth-century presidency and Congress followed the Framers' philosophy. Woodrow Wilson declared in 1885 that "unquestionably, the predominant and controlling force, the center and source of all motive and all regulative power, is Congress."

Of the seventeen U.S. presidents of the twentieth century, only William Howard Taft (1909–1913) vigorously fought presidential activism. All the other presidents of this century have advanced, or at least have not opposed, activism in at least one, and often more than one, of the four areas of power. Helping twentieth-century presidents in their advocacy of presidential activism were different ideas, in part drawn from progressivism, that called for an expanded role of government and looked on the president as a representative of the people. Imbued with a public mandate and saddled with a government required to do more and more things for that public, the president's role expanded.

Presidents realize that setting the agenda and getting one's way are two different things.

Yet congressional activism has not faded. While presidents today are far more active in the legislative process than any of their nineteenth-century (or even early twentieth-century) predecessors, the legislative process nevertheless remains firmly in congressional hands. The work of congressional committees and subcommittees, the power and autonomy of senior members, the electoral safety of many incumbents, and a complex budget process make it difficult for presidents to dominate Congress. Presidents realize that setting the agenda and getting one's way are two different things. Presidents may dominate, even determine, what problems are discussed, but they may have little control over the solutions that Congress takes seriously or the policy choices that are finally made. Similarly, presidents' command of television, the public's fascination with the president, and weak ties between the president and his party on Capitol Hill prohibit Congress from dominating the presidency. The twentieth-century conflict is not a zero-sum game in which one side wins and the other loses. Although in certain areas of policy, notably war and diplomacy, presidential influence has arguably grown at the expense of Congress, the overall influence of Congress on public affairs has not necessarily diminished. The conflict established by the Framers more than two hundred years ago is still a lively one.

[See also (II) Accountability, Presidential, Chief Executive, Executive Power, War, Declaration of.]

BIBLIOGRAPHY

Davis, Eric. "Congressional Liaison: The People and the Institutions." In *Both Ends of the Avenue.* Edited by A. King. 1983. Pp. 59–95.

Fisher, Louis. *The Politics of Shared Power.* 3d ed. 1992.

King, Gary, and Lyn Ragsdale. *The Elusive Executive: Discovering Statistical Patterns in the Presidency.* 1988.
Light, Paul. *The President's Agenda.* Revised 1991.
Milkis, Stanley, and Michael Nelson. *The American Presidency: Origins and Development, 1776–1990.* 1990.
Ragsdale, Lyn. *Presidential Politics.* 1993.
Roosevelt, Theodore. *Theodore Roosevelt: Autobiography.* 1913.
Schlesinger, Arthur, Jr. *The Imperial Presidency.* 1973.
Shull, Steven, ed. *The Two Presidencies.* 1991.
Wayne, Stephen. *The Legislative Presidency.* 1978.
Wilson, Woodrow. *Congressional Government.* 1885. Repr. 1973.

– LYN RAGSDALE

PRESIDENT PRO TEMPORE OF THE SENATE

The Constitution designates the vice president of the United States as the president of the Senate and further provides that in the vice president's absence, the Senate may choose a president pro tempore to perform the duties of the chair. On 6 April 1789 the Senate elected New Hampshire senator John Langdon as its first president pro tempore. Langdon served until 21 April, when John Adams arrived to take his oath as vice president.

During the Senate's first century, vice presidents presided routinely, and the Senate chose a president pro tempore only for the limited periods when the vice president was ill or otherwise absent. Consequently, the Senate frequently elected several presidents pro tempore during a single session. Those individuals were selected on the basis of their personal characteristics, popularity, and reliability.

In 1890 the Senate established the policy, which continues today, of having its president pro tempore hold office continuously until the election of a successor, rather than just for the period of the vice president's absence. Since the end of World War II, the Senate has customarily elected the senior member of its majority party as president pro tempore.

That the Senate, from its earliest days, took the post of president pro tempore seriously can be seen in the Presidential Succession Act of 1792. Should the offices of president and vice president both become vacant, the president pro tempore would then succeed to the presidency, followed by the Speaker of the House. The potentially serious consequences of this arrangement became clear after President Abraham Lincoln's assassination.

When Vice President Andrew Johnson succeeded him, the president pro tempore, Benjamin F. Wade of Ohio, became next in line for the White House. Had the Senate voted to remove Johnson during his impeachment trial in 1868, Senator Wade would have become president of the United States. Wade voted for conviction and President Johnson, after his acquittal, objected to placing the president pro tempore in the line of succession because he would therefore be "interested in producing a vacancy." In 1886 Congress removed the president pro tempore and Speaker of the House from the line of succession—only to return them in 1947. However, the Speaker of the House was placed ahead of the president pro tempore in order of succession.

The responsibilities of the office have changed significantly over the past two centuries. Between 1823 and 1863, presidents pro tempore appointed members of the Senate's standing committees, either indirectly or directly. Since 1820 the president pro tempore has had the power to name other senators to perform the duties of the chair in his absence. Various laws assign the president pro tempore authority to make appointments to an assortment of national commissions, usually with the advice of the appropriate party floor leader. In the absence of the vice president, the president pro tempore may administer all oaths required by the Constitution, may sign legislation, and may fulfill all other obligations of the presiding officer. Also, in the absence of the vice president, the president pro tempore jointly presides with the Speaker of the House when the two houses sit together in joint sessions or joint meetings.

The election of a senator to the office of the president pro tempore has always been considered one of the highest honors offered to a senator by the Senate as a body. That honor has been bestowed upon a colorful and significant group of senators during the past two centuries—men such as Richard Henry Lee (Va.), John Tyler (R-Va.), Arthur H. Vandenberg (R-Mich.), Carl Hayden (D-Ariz.), and Richard B. Russell (D-Ga.)—who stamped their imprint on the office and on their times.

[See also (I) Presiding Officer.]

BIBLIOGRAPHY

Byrd, Robert C. *The Senate, 1789–1989: Addresses on the History of the United States Senate.* Vol. 2. 1991.

– ROBERT C. BYRD

PRESIDING OFFICER

The presiding officer of the Senate is the vice president of the United States, an appointment imposed by Article I, section 3 of the Constitution. The Constitution further provides that in the absence of the vice president, the Senate elect a president pro tempore, usually the senior senator of the majority party, to carry out the duties of the chair. Given their numerous other responsibilities, neither the vice president nor the president pro tempore spends much time presiding over the Senate. In daily practice, the duties of the chair are carried out by the acting president pro tempore, usually first-term senators who rotate in the chair for shifts of one hour each. Since 1977, only majority party senators have been appointed to serve in the chair.

As a member of the executive branch, the vice president's role as presiding officer is viewed warily by the Senate, which has severely limited the powers of the position. For example, the presiding officer may not debate unless given the unanimous consent of the Senate, he may not vote except to break a tie, and he is instructed by the standing rules of the Senate to recognize the first senator addressing the chair, even without knowing the purpose for which the senator seeks recognition. (By precedent, however, the majority leader is given priority recognition over any other senator.) The presiding officer's procedural rulings in response to points of order are subject to appeal, and it is not unusual for the chair's rulings to be overturned by vote of the Senate. As a result, the duties of the chair in the Senate have become minimal, consisting mostly of preserving order and decorum, answering parliamentary inquiries, ruling on points of order, and enforcing voting and amending procedures.

The presiding officer of the Senate is assisted in performing his duties by the Senate parliamentarian, a nonpartisan employee of the chamber who is an expert on the Senate's rules, precedents, and procedures. The parliamentarian is always on duty when the Senate is in session, seated just below the presiding officer.

[See also (I) Parliamentarian, article on Senate Parliamentarian, President Pro Tempore of the Senate.]

BIBLIOGRAPHY

U.S. Senate. *Riddick's Senate Procedure, Precedents, and Practices,* by Floyd M. Riddick and Alan S. Frumin. 101st Cong., 2d sess., 1992. S. Doc. 101-28. Pp. 1025–1033.

U.S. Senate. *The United States Senate,* 1787–1801, by Roy Swanstrom. 100th Cong., 1st sess., 1988. S. Doc. 100-31. Pp. 253–260.

– ILONA B. NICKELS

PREVIOUS QUESTION

The "previous question" is a motion used by the House of Representatives to end a debate and bring the House to a vote on the pending matter. This motion is not in order in the Senate.

Typically, the majority floor manager of a bill or resolution moves the previous question after the first hour of debate on it, but only if the House is considering the measure under its general rules. The motion to order the previous question is not debatable and requires a majority vote for adoption. If the motion is adopted, the measure is not subject to further debate or amendments. The House often proceeds to an immediate vote on the measure, although a motion to recommit may intervene. The previous question is not in order in the Committee of the Whole.

The most important practical effect of the previous question is to preclude amendments to a measure considered under the general rules of the House. Under these rules, the majority floor manager controls the first hour of debate, during which no other member can offer an amendment; only the member controlling the time for debate can propose an amendment to the measure. A member wishing to propose an amendment first must convince the House to vote against the previous question. If the motion to order the previous question is rejected, the Speaker then recognizes an opponent of the measure (in its present form) to control a second hour of debate, during which that member can offer an amendment to it.

[See also (I) Amending, Bills.]

BIBLIOGRAPHY

U.S. House of Representatives. *Deschler's Precedents of the United States House of Representatives,* by Lewis Deschler. 94th Cong., 2d sess. 1977. H. Doc. 94-661, Vol. 7, pp. 114–176.

U.S. House of Representatives. *Constitution, Jefferson's Manual, and Rules of the House of Representatives, 102d Congress.* Compiled by William Holmes Brown. 101st Cong., 2d sess., 1990. H. Doc. 101-256. Pp. 577–582.

– STANLEY BACH

PUBLIC LANDS

The making of public land policy may not rank among the most glamorous subjects in the history of Congress. Who but the most specialized scholar knows that the famous 1830 Webster-Hayne debate in the Senate had to do with a proposal for the elimination of the General Land Office's post of surveyor general? Yet the historyof congressional policy toward the public lands touches on important themes ranging over the past two centuries of American life, including national attitudes toward the West, the environment, and Native Americans.

The public domain consists of federally owned land and as of 1994 makes up more than a quarter of the land area of the fifty states. It once comprised the entirety of all the states except for the original thirteen and Vermont, Kentucky, Tennessee, Texas, and Hawaii. In all, nearly two billion acres were at one time owned by the United States. The job of Congress in setting public land policy has been to decide what to do with this magnificent patrimony.

Public lands and public land policy make up one of the longest index entries to the *Congressional Record* and its predecessor the *Congressional Globe.* Early on, both houses found it necessary to have standing committees on the public lands, the House in 1805 and the Senate in 1816. These committees necessarily worked closely with the executive department charged with administering the public lands, starting with the Treasury Department and, after 1812, the more specialized General Land Office. In 1849 Congress removed the General Land Office from Treasury and placed it in the newly created Interior Department.

Congress itself has helped write the history of its own public land policies by authorizing periodic Public Lands Review commissions, the first in 1879 and the most recent in 1968. The commissions were created at times of national debate about land policy and the future of the public lands. Each commission has included among its documents a historical perspective on policymaking. The first such effort, Thomas Donaldson's massive *The Public Domain* (1881), contained every imaginable summary statistic about the survey and disposition of the public domain.

Paul W. Gates, the leading modern historian of U.S. public land policy, writing for the 1968 Review Commission, suggested a basic periodization for U.S. public land history, one that is generally accepted by modern historians. Policy was driven from the 1790s to the Great Depression of the 1930s by the desire to promote settlement and growth in the American West. This was best accomplished, Congress reasoned, by transferring the public lands to millions of private farmers. At times this central goal was modified by other congressional needs. For example, during the first fifty years of congressional policy-making, according to Gates, there was a strong countertendency to use the public lands to generate revenue to help pay the public debt. From the 1840s through the Civil War, Congress made frequent use of the public domain to promote the interests of certain parties, ranging from veterans of past wars to newly organized railroad companies. Gates found that the postbellum era was characterized by an "incongruous" land policy. Congress passed a homestead measure during the Civil War, but at the same time maintained a cash sales policy and promoted corporate ownership of land. Congress took important conservation measures in the Progressive era, but the basic imperative toward western growth and development did not come to a close until the Great Depression. Writing from the vantage point of 1968, Gates cautiously characterized the decades since the New Deal as a period of multiple-purpose use of the public domain.

THE PUBLIC LANDS AND THE PUBLIC DEBT. One of the lasting achievements of the federal government under the Articles of Confederation was the establishment of the public domain, first by general agreement of the states to give up their western land claims and then by the passage of the two Northwest Ordinances. The first ordinance, enacted in 1785, provided the basis for future public land administration. It specified the rectangular survey system of townships and ranges, and defined the section of 640 acres (one square mile) as the basic unit of public land. Public land surveying followed this principle from the Ohio River lands bordering Pennsylvania all the way to the Pacific Ocean, heedless of the vagaries of terrain. In today's age of air travel people look down from the sky on the fruits of the rectangular survey when they see the distinctive checkerboard pattern of the land.

One of the lasting achievements of the federal government under the Articles of Confederation was the establishment of the public domain.

The Confederation Congress faced two basic problems of land policy that would engage future congresses over the next century: what should be the price, if any, for public land, and what should be the amount sold or donated? Congress decided against a policy of free land in 1785, despite the precedent of "headrights" from some of the old southern colonies. Instead, it decided to sell the public domain to individuals for a minimum of one dollar an acre. In practice, this amounted to just a penny or two an acre in coin, because Congress allowed purchasers to pay with the severely depreciated Continental paper currency. Other noteworthy features of the Northwest Ordinance of 1785 included a provision that land should first be surveyed and then offered for sale at a public auction, and that one section from each township should be reserved for the benefit of local public education. The minimum tract for purchase was set at 640 acres.

The legislature established under the federal Constitution initially reaffirmed the land policy of the Confederation Congress. Not until 1796 did the new Congress change its land policy in any significant way. In that year Albert Gallatin led a move to change the minimum price to two dollars an acre, with a provision allowing buyers up to a year's credit to complete their purchases. This meant a significant rise in land prices, given the fact that the value of federal currency had risen dramatically during the Washington administration. The Land Act of 1796 may be seen in retrospect as the high point for a policy that sought to maximize revenue from public land sales. Both the Treasury faction of Federalists around Alexander Hamilton and the opposition party led by Jefferson and Madison agreed that the public lands must be safeguarded as collateral for the national debt.

THE PROMOTION OF INDIVIDUAL WESTERN SETTLEMENT AND GROWTH. Public land legislation in the century and a quarter after the Land Act of 1796 may best be characterized as a series of measures designed to promote the changing needs of individual and family farms and ranches. Thomas Jefferson is often identified with the ideal of using the public domain to maintain Americans as individual farmers, but this policy was widely approved by Congress throughout the nineteenth century. Settlers were pouring into the Northwest Territory, especially Ohio, after 1800 and soon began a clamor to amend some of the provisions of the 1796 Land Act. Some complained that the price of land was too high, while others petitioned Congress to reduce the minimum tract for purchase from 640 acres to a lesser figure. Still others noted that the federal credit term of one year did not leave sufficient time for a settler to pay his debt. Congress acted on all these complaints over the next few years. Much of the legislative history of public land law in the early republic was a matter of tinkering with the Land Act of 1796.

Congress continued to make homesteading more attractive in the first decade of the twentieth century by increasing the maximum acreage that a settler could claim.

In 1800, for example, the tract size was reduced to 320 acres and credit was extended over a five-year period. The Land Act of 1800 also provided for the establishment of land offices in Ohio staffed by federal officials, where purchasers could scrutinize the records of the official surveys without having to go to Philadelphia to conduct their land business. Here was the origin of the American phrase "doing a land-office business," signifying a booming market. In 1804 the minimum acreage for purchase was again halved to a quarter-section, 160 acres. The price, credit, and quantity limits remained constant until 1820, when in an effort to reduce land speculation, the minimum tract size was again halved to eighty acres, credit sales were abolished, and the price was reduced to $1.25 an acre. Congress now insisted that prospective buyers pay cash at the land office.

The figure of $1.25 an acre stood as what Congress called the "cash-entry" price until cash sales were halted in 1890. Yet cash sales at $1.25 an acre were declining in relative importance in the alienation of the public lands as early as the 1840s. Congressional land grants for various purposes, as discussed below, accounted for part of the shift. Another reason for the move away from cash-entry sales at $1.25 an acre was a policy implemented in 1854 called "graduation." This was an attempt by Congress to set prices by matching supply and demand. Congress and the General Land Office set the supply by determining when new tracts of land should be surveyed and declared open to public entry.

Slowing or speeding the process of offering new lands had an indirect effect on the demand for public land already offered; as several recent studies have shown, the demand for public land was driven mainly by the level of commodity prices and not just by the supply of public land offered by the General Land Office. Congress and several Democratic administrations had encouraged the rapid opening of new land districts, so that by the advent of the Pierce administration in 1853, some 25 million acres of offered public land remained unsold. To encourage more rapid sales, the General Land Office was instructed by Congress to reduce the price on unsold land by a fifth for every five years that a tract remained on the market. The effect of graduated land prices was most evident in the South, where millions of acres in Alabama, Mississippi, Louisiana, and Arkansas had their prices reduced to as low as twelve and a half cents an acre.

During the 1820s and 1830s the House and Senate committees on public lands received numerous petitions from western settlers requesting congressional permission to occupy without charge parcels on the public domain for short periods of time, in effect, postponing the time when they had to pay for their claims. This practice, known as preemption or more derisively as "squatting," was illegal and took up a great deal of congressional time. Only the U.S. Army could enforce the law against illegal occupation of the public domain and prevent preemptors from occupying their parcels without payment. The army had no desire to make war on settlers, but from time to time troops were dispatched to remove squatters.

Congress periodically passed special bills forgiving trespassing in various land districts and finally in 1830 enacted a statute forgiving all prior preemptions, provided that the preemptors paid what they owed. After several extensions of this law, Congress passed a more general bill in 1841 legalizing future preemptions but only on land surveyed by the General Land Office. The law allowed settlers to preempt their parcels for up to fifteen months before they had to make payment, provided they could show or "prove up" evidence that they had made rudimentary improvements to the tract. The Preemption Act of 1841 left out another class of preemptors seeking congressional forgiveness, those who "squatted" on unsurveyed land, particularly Indian land where title had not yet passed to the United States. The strength of sentiment behind preemptors was sufficient for Congress to grant even this right in 1853, so that preemptors could legally become pioneers, staking a claim to 160 acres before the surveyor had even arrived. The basic proof statement specified by the Preemption Act of 1841 required a description of the house built by the preemptor as well as an account of the land cleared and brought into production.

The same approach to settlers and public land administration informed the congressional crafting of the greatest of all land laws, the Homestead Act of 1862. The act had a long gestation period in Congress before becoming law. Earlier versions had been proposed in the 1840s and were seriously debated and voted on during the Pierce administration. A homestead bill actually passed Congress in the Buchanan administration but was vetoed by the president. Homestead might be regarded as the ultimate reform of the old 1796 Land Act in that the minimum purchase price was eliminated entirely. But as in the Preemption Act of 1841, Congress very much wanted the General Land Office to keep an eye on the activities of the settlers before letting title pass from the federal government to private owners. Over seventy years after the passage of the Homestead Act, settlers filed more than one million homestead claims to public land parcels totaling over 200 million acres. The peak years for homestead entries were just before World War I, when for several years over 10 million acres were claimed.

Although the Homestead Act became the central feature of land policy through the end of the nineteenth century, Congress adopted several supplementary policies as well. In 1873 it passed the Timber Culture Act to encourage homesteaders to enter an additional quarter section with the provision that the entrant had to plant forty acres in trees. The Desert Land Act of 1877 granted tracts of 640 acres to those who pledged to construct irrigation works that brought water to previously dry land. Both acts were less than successful in execution, and in the 1890–1891 winter session Congress halted entries under the Timber Culture Act and also ended cash sales and preemptions.

At the same time Congress formulated a policy of using the public domain to increase mining output. The Mining Act of 1872 set prices of $2.50 an acre for placer-mined lands and $5.00 an acre for lode mining. Fraud and evasion flourished under the Mining Act, as they did under the Timber Act, and Congress moved in 1909 and 1910 to separate the surface use of public land from subsoil mining use.

Congress continued to make homesteading more attractive in the first decade of the twentieth century by increasing the maximum acreage that a settler could claim. Nebraskans were first allowed to claim up to 640 acres in 1904 under the Kincaid Act, and in 1909 a similar privilege was extended to nine other western states under the Enlarged Homestead Act.

In the western Great Plains and intermountain states, much of the public domain was used by ranchers who grazed their livestock for free on the public lands. Congress sought to turn much of this remaining land into private property when it passed the Stock Raising Homestead Act of 1916, granting 640-acre homesteads to Great Plains ranchers. This was the last of the great legislative acts designed to grant public lands to individuals who wished to become self-supporting farmers or ranchers. The agricultural downturn of the 1920s, and especially the Great Depression, permanently changed the old Jeffersonian notion. In 1934 and 1935 most of the public domain was withdrawn from further entries under the various land laws. The era in which the public domain was used primarily to promote new farms and ranches came to an end.

CONGRESS AS LANDED PROPRIETOR. The goal of turning public land into private property was shared by most in Congress throughout the nineteenth century, but there was much room for disagreement over how to bring about this end. Congress continually faced conflicts over how best to manage the public domain. Should the public lands be administered largely for the benefit of prospective western settlers and landowners? Or should the older, nonpublic land states receive some benefit, too? These questions dominated much of the public land debate between Andrew Jackson's Democrats and Henry Clay's Whigs. The latter group fought long and hard, but ultimately without much success, to have a portion of the revenue from land sales "distributed" back to the states. Clay engineered a distribution bill through both houses in the 1832–1833 session, but President Jackson vetoed it. When the Whigs finally came to power in 1841, the newly sworn-in president, John Tyler, signed a distribution bill into law, but it was repealed the next year when the public debt rose sufficiently to convince the Whigs that federal revenues could not stand such an outflow to the states.

Within the larger context of using the public lands to promote western settlement, Congress did come to see the public lands as a substitute for making actual expenditures. Proponents of "proprietorship" argued that Congress could make grants of the public lands to achieve desired goals of national policy. Congress used this power sparingly in the early decades of the nineteenth century, primarily to increase enlistments in the army during times of national emergency. It resorted to such a policy before and during the War of 1812: some 29,000 men took advantage of the bounty and at the war's end claimed over 4 million acres of public land, mainly in western Illinois.

When war with Mexico broke out in 1846, Congress repeated the procedure in the Ten Regiments Act of February 1847. In all, about 90,000 men received 13 million acres of public land. The terms of their land grants were more generous than those given to the army and militia veterans of the War of 1812. As many as 475,000 men had seen some federal service against the British and their Indian allies, and many among the great majority who did not receive land bounties were jealous of the treatment accorded the Mexican War soldiers. Therefore in 1850, 1852, and 1855 Congress passed acts that redressed the inequity and granted more than 47 million new acres in land bounties, most of which went to the now elderly veterans of the War of 1812 and to their widows and minor children. One study estimates that 95 percent chose to sell their land warrants in a secondary market. Warrant brokers in turn sold discounted warrants to frontier bankers and settlers for use in the West.

The unprecedented size of the grants to veterans unleashed a flood of new requests for Congress to act in its proprietor role. Why not make grants of land directly with the express purpose of resale? In 1854 the House and Senate passed the so-called Dix bill, named after the Massachusetts reformer Dorothea Dix and designed to grant 10 million acres of public land for the benefit of the indigent insane. President Pierce vetoed the bill, but after the Republicans came to power in 1861, Congress passed similar legislation granting land for purposes other than the direct promotion of western settlement. The Morrill Land-Grant College Act of 1862 used public lands for the benefit of all the states. Here was an updated version of Henry Clay's old distribution idea: allot acreage, not the proceeds of land sales, on the basis of a state's population, and let the states do with public land grants what they wanted, so long as the proceeds were used to create agricultural colleges. The result was that New York, the state with the largest population, got the most public land. New York in turn entrusted its land grants to the upstate financier Ezra Cornell, who located millions of acres in the pine forests of northern Wisconsin, holding many valuable tracts until they rose in market value to ten and twenty times the land office price of $1.25 an acre. The profits from this sale led to a sizable endowment for New York State's agricultural college, named in Cornell's honor by a grateful legislature.

The most extensive and enduring application of congressional proprietorship of the public domain was the land grants in the 1850s and 1860s for the promotion of internal improvements, most notably railroads. Illinois Democrat Stephen A. Douglas put together the legislation authorizing land grants to aid the construction of a railroad from Chicago to Mobile in 1850. Hard on the heels of his triumphant legislative maneuvering of the Compromise of 1850, Douglas sought to bind up the nation with railroads built with federal land assistance. The Chicago-Mobile line, later known as the Illinois Central, set the pattern for later railroad land grants: alternating sections within a strip of land several miles wide on each side of the projected line. The lands reserved by the General Land Office were doubled in price to $2.50 an acre, which in effect insured the government against any loss of revenue. Congress intended the land to be resold to raise money for construction costs, and railroads like the Illinois Central opened offices to encourage emigration to railroad-owned lands.

By the close of the nineteenth century, most of the public domain suitable for family farming had been alienated into private ownership.

The Illinois Central land grant was soon followed by other land grants for internal improvements in the 1850s, including one for constructing a canal and locks around the St. Mary's River, running from Lake Superior to Lake Huron at Sault Sainte Marie, Michigan. More than 25 million acres of public land were donated to various internal improvement projects in the 1850s, when Democrats controlled both House and Senate. Yet the biggest grants came after the outbreak of the Civil War, when the Republicans controlled Congress. Congress gave over 90 million acres to aid in the construction of transcontinental railroads between 1861 and 1871. The largest beneficiary by far was the Northern Pacific Railway, intended to run from Duluth to Tacoma, which received a land grant of 38 million acres in its 1864 enabling act.

CONGRESS, THE PUBLIC LANDS, AND INDIAN AFFAIRS. Textbook maps of the expansion of the United States usually show acquisitions from negotiations with European nations or by conquest, starting with the Peace of Paris in 1783, continuing through the purchase of the Louisiana Territory, Florida, and the Mexican Cession of 1848, ending with the purchase of Alaska and the acquisition of Hawaii. The general claim of sovereignty, however, did not give clear title; that remained to be negotiated with the hundreds of American Indian nations that occupied the land. The numerous treaties signed between the United States and assorted American Indian nations between 1790 and 1871 provided the essential basis for legal title to the public lands, and the subsequent basis of private ownership of the land.

The general sequence of events in the history of the American West for a century after the 1790s was as follows: peace treaties with Native American landholders; land cession treaties granting title to the United States; Indian removal or reservation agreements; General Land Office surveys; land district auctions and sales; in-migration of new settlers; and finally, territorial governments leading to statehood. Sometimes, particularly in Kansas, this idealized sequence of events became jumbled, with the settlers preceding the army and the treaty makers. But the essential point remains that new additions to the supply of the public domain came primarily from a host of treaties and agreements between the United States and American Indians.

The pace of treaty making and Indian land cessions expanded considerably after the War of 1812, led in large part by the actions of Gen. Andrew Jackson in negotiating agreements with the Five Civilized Nations of the South. Jackson's postwar actions became general congressional policy in 1830 with the passage of the Indian Removal Act. The rash of treaties entered into under that act often included assorted grants of public lands to interested parties. Sometimes the treaty interpreters received land grants for their troubles, and in some cases, as with the Mississippi Choctaws and the Lake Superior Chippewas, mixed-blood tribal members were granted quarter sections of public land if they chose to remain in the ceded territory.

The intended land grants reflected long-standing notions of reformers that if American Indians were granted land in fee simple ownership, then old tribal loyalties would be cast aside and a new Indian man would emerge, similar to the American yeoman farmer. For much of the nineteenth century this was an article of faith for "friends of the Indian," and in 1887 the idea was made official federal Indian policy in the General Allotment Act, also known as the Dawes Severalty Act. This legislation granted 160 acres to every head of household (in itself, an inexact representation of the complexity of American Indian family structure), with lesser acreage awarded to minors and dependents. The Dawes Act also had the foreseen consequence of separating over 120 million acres of what was once Indian reservation land and bringing it into the public domain, where it was entered by homesteaders and ranchers under other land laws. What had started as an idealistic, if misguided, attempt to reform the personality of Indian people degenerated into little more than a grab of the tribal land base throughout the West.

CONGRESS AND CONSERVATION: THE RESERVING OF THE PUBLIC LANDS. In the twentieth century, Congress has used the public lands once again as a proprietor, not only to promote the aggressive immediate development of natural resources, but also for their long-term conservation and use. Economic development has remained the primary congressional goal, but in a more planned and less unregulated manner. By the close of the nineteenth century, most of the public domain suitable for family farming had been alienated into private ownership. What remained was and lands on the western Great Plains and in the intermountain region, as well as considerable timberland that had not yet been logged. Starting in 1891, Congress gave the president the right to withdraw land from the public domain and reserve it for future forest use. More than 40 million acres were withdrawn in the 1890s, and after Theodore Roosevelt's accession to the presidency in 1901, another 150 million acres were taken from the public domain and transformed into national forests under the administration of the Department of Agriculture.

In addition to reserving timberland for future production, Congress passed a series of measures in the first two decades of the twentieth century designed to use the public domain for irrigation and hydroelectric power generation. The Reclamation Act of 1902, sponsored by the aptly named Francis G. Newlands (D-Nev.), aimed to promote the construction of irrigation works by the Bureau of Reclamation, to be funded by the fees and commissions received by the General Land Office. It was expected that the irrigation projects would be remunerative to the federal government, because the arid lands brought into production would generate new land-office fees and water-use payments. The Reclamation Act even had a Jeffersonian clause limiting the beneficiaries under the act to landowners holding no more than 160 acres. In practice the act was soon evaded by large corporate landowners, and the Bureau of Reclamation grew into an empire unto itself, with its single-minded goal of transforming the West into an agricultural domain.

The best-known public lands are the national parks, administered by the Department of the Interior. Starting with Yellowstone National Park in 1872, the National Park Service has grown in the size and scope of its mission. Most, although not all, national parks and national monuments consist of lands withdrawn from the public domain. Yellowstone, with more than 8 million acres, is still the largest of the forty-eight national parks, but the National Park Service also maintains sites such as the comparatively tiny one at Hot Springs, Arkansas. A separate category of public lands is the acreage classified as wilderness areas under the Wilderness Act of 1964 and the Alaska Wilderness Act of 1980.

Congressional public land policy of the later twentieth century has been characterized by a vigorous debate between those who want a more rapid development of the natural resources on the public lands and those who wish to see more land designated as wilderness areas. The Public Land Law Review Commission that operated in the late 1960s acknowledged that the public domain would never be opened up to widespread private alienation, as in the nineteenth and early twentieth centuries, but not until 1976 did Congress finally repeal most of the old nineteenth-century land laws. The Federal Land Policy and Management Act of that year directed the Bureau of Land Management (the reorganized General Land Office) to determine by 1991 the extent of acreage that should be withdrawn from grazing use and declared wilderness areas. Some of the bitterest political disputes of the 1980s over land policy arose because of conflict between the Interior Department and Congress over implementing the 1976 statute. Congress had asked the Bureau of Land Management to study 25 million acres of public land for inclusion in the National Wilderness Preservation System. Interior secretaries James Watt and William Clarke wanted none of the land taken from ranchers and only grudgingly allowed the transfer of 300,000 acres from grazing land to wilderness.

A review of congressional policy toward the public lands reveals the alternating and sometimes conflicting goals of promoting both individual land ownership and other social policies. Landmark legislation such as the Homestead Act of 1862 and the Reclamation Act of 1902 came after decades of debate over the terms and intent of public land disposal to private ownership. This does not mean that congressional policy has been constant or unchanging in such broad areas as western regionalism, environmentalism, and Indian affairs. Rather, looking at congressional public land policy within this framework helps the modern policymaker and student better understand the mix of idealism and expediency that has characterized the past.

[See also (I) Oversight.]

BIBLIOGRAPHY

Donaldson, Thomas C. *The Public Domain: Its History with Statistics.* 1881.
Feller, Daniel. *The Public Lands in Jacksonian Politics.* 1984.
Gates, Paul Wallace. *History of Public Land Law Development.* 1968.
Hibbard, Benjamin Horace. *History of the Public Land Policies.* 1924.
Oberly, James W. *Sixty Million Acres: American Veterans and the Public Lands before the Civil War.* 1990.
Opie, John. *The Law of the Land.* 1987.
Robbins, Roy. *Our Landed Heritage.* 1942.
Rohrbough, Malcom. *The Land Office Business.* 1968.
Worster, Donald. *Rivers of Empire.* 1986.
Zaslowsky, Dyan. *These American Lands: Parks, Wilderness, and the Public Lands.* 1986.

— JAMES W. OBERLY

PUBLIC LAW

Every measure that completes the lawmaking process prescribed by the Constitution is thereby enacted into law. Except for private measures, every enacted bill or joint resolution becomes a *public law.* By contrast, concurrent and simple resolutions, if adopted, do not make law. Also, joint resolutions proposing constitutional amendments do not become law but go to the states for ratification.

The format of acts of Congress, which include bills and joint resolutions passed by Congress, is prescribed by law. The enacting clause of a bill reads, "Be it enacted by the Senate and House of Representatives of the United States of America in Congress Assembled"; the resolving clause of a joint resolution replaces the first three words by "Resolved." Statute also prescribes that this clause appear only once, at the beginning, and that the measure be divided into numbered sections, each containing "as nearly as may be, a single proposition or enactment." Appropriations, especially in general appropriations bills, are usually set forth in captioned paragraphs rather than numbered sections. In long measures, sections are often grouped into titles, and sometimes into parts, chapters, or other divisions.

The lawmaking process is completed on the date when (1) the president signs, (2) the period expires during which he may veto, or (3) Congress completes action to override a veto. On that date the law is enacted and, unless otherwise specified in law, takes effect. It is sent to the Archivist of the United States for publication, initially in pamphlet form as a "slip law"; an annual volume, *United States Statutes at Large,* compiles all public laws enacted during a session of Congress (and, under separate headings, private laws, concurrent resolutions adopted, treaties, presidential proclamations, and certain presidential recommendations on which Congress may act). Between 1930 and 1984, these functions were carried out by the General Services Administration, and before that by the State Department.

The *Statutes* identify public laws by date of enactment and number them by Congress and order of enactment within the Congress (e.g., P.L. 91-510). Before the 85th Congress (i.e., before 1957), laws were numbered only within a Congress and commonly cited by date of enactment and *Statutes* chapter number. Public laws are also cited by *Statutes* volume and page number (e.g., 84 Stat. 1410).

New law often amends or repeals provisions of previous public law. Under the direction of the House Law Revision Counsel, most new public laws are codified as revisions or additions to the *United States Code,* organized topically under fifty titles, some of which have been reenacted as statutes in their codified form. Codified provisions of law may be cited to the *Code* (e.g., 2 U.S.C. § 166). The first edition of the *Code* was released in 1926. Federal law had been comprehensively revised and reenacted in the *Revised Statutes* of 1875 and 1878, and some current law still traces to these revisions.

BIBLIOGRAPHY

1 U.S. Code, chap. 2.

– RICHARD S. BETH

Q

QUORUM

The Constitution specifies in Article I that "a majority of each House shall constitute a quorum to do business." (When in Committee of the Whole, the House is not bound by this requirement, and the quorum is set at one hundred in Rule XXIII.) The question of what constitutes a "house" in this context—all of the members provided for by statute or some lesser number determined by circumstance—remained open for some time.

During the Civil War, the seceding states did not choose representatives, and in 1861 House Speaker Galusha A. Grow ruled that a quorum consisted of "a majority of those chosen" rather than simply a majority of the total seats provided for by statute. In 1890 this was clarified by Speaker Thomas B. Reed to mean all members "chosen and living." The current interpretation was established in 1903, when Speaker Joseph G. Cannon ruled that "a quorum consists of a majority of those Members chosen, sworn, and living, whose membership has not been terminated by resignation or by the action of the House."

In the Senate, the path to the current interpretation was quicker. Although originally reluctant to embrace the House's view, in 1864 the Senate formally adopted a rule stating that a quorum consisted of "a majority of the Senators duly chosen." A revision of the Senate rules in 1868 amended this to read "a majority of the Senators duly chosen and sworn."

Both the House and Senate operate under the general assumption that a quorum is present unless demonstrated otherwise. In the House, whether operating as the House or in Committee of the Whole, the rules discourage raising points of order questioning the presence of a quorum. Another factor in House practice is the provision in Rule XV that allows the Speaker to direct the clerk to record the names of members who do not vote in determining the presence of a quorum. This change was Speaker Reed's response to "disappearing quorums," caused when members refused to respond to quorum calls to delay or prevent the House from conducting business. House rules also greatly restrict the applicability of such points of order in the House and in Committee of the Whole. Quorum calls are rarely permitted except in conjunction with a recorded vote.

In the Senate, however, quorum calls are quite common, and that body's rules and practices allow senators to suggest the absence of a quorum at virtually any time; furthermore, the chair has no power to count for a quorum (except under cloture). This has led to the distinction between a "live" quorum call—designed to ascertain the presence of an actual quorum, in response to a point of order—and "constructive delay"—when a quorum call is designed as a means of suspending proceedings to accomplish some other action.

When the absence of a quorum is determined, no business can be transacted except a call of the House or Senate, a motion to secure a quorum, or a motion to adjourn (although a motion to recess is also in order in the Senate if pursuant to a prior order or unanimous consent agreement).

Committees are given great flexibility in establishing the size of a quorum.

Committees are given great flexibility in establishing the size of a quorum. A majority of the panel's membership is necessary to make a quorum to report a measure, but for other action it can be set by committee rules as low as one-third the membership. A quorum in committees needs to be established by the physical presence of the members. Proxies or other means of polling the members do not count in determining a quorum. Both Senate and House committees, however, sometimes use what is called a "rolling quorum" by which the members may record their presence on a ledger, so that a quorum may not necessarily be physically present at all times. For a hearing, Senate rules allow for a quorum of less than one-third, and the House specifically allows for quorums as small as only two.

[See also (I) Quorum Call.]

BIBLIOGRAPHY

U.S. House of Representatives. *Constitution, Jefferson's Manual, and Rules of the House of Representatives, 103d Congress.* Compiled by William Holmes Brown. 102d Cong., 2d sess., 1993. H. Doc. 102-405. Rules XI, XV, XXIII.

U.S. House of Representatives. *Hinds' Precedents of the House of Representatives of the United States,* by Asher C. Hinds. 59th Cong., 2d sess., 1907. Vol. 4, chap. 86.

U.S. Senate. *Senate Procedure, Precedents, and Practices,* by Floyd M. Riddick. 97th Cong., 1st sess., 1981. S. Doc. 97-2.

– JAMES V. SATURNO

QUORUM CALL

In the House

There are two calls of the House that can be used to ascertain the presence of a quorum (usually 218 members): (1) the call ordered on motion and (2) the automatic call. A point of no quorum may not be entertained unless the pending question has been put to a vote, but the Speaker may, at his discretion, recognize a member for a motion for a quorum call of the House at any time. If the motion is agreed to, the roll is called until a quorum answers or until the House adjourns.

The automatic call ensues when a quorum fails to vote on any question that requires a quorum, a quorum is not present, and objection is made for that reason. Following the announcement of a voice or division vote, if the Speaker sustains a point of no quorum from the floor, the yeas and nays are considered as ordered on the pending question. Members vote and thereby indicate their presence as part of the same action.

In the Committee of the Whole, the first time the Committee finds itself without a quorum (one hundred members) on any day, the chairman invokes a quorum call. The chairman may refuse to entertain a point of order that a quorum is not present during general debate only. After a quorum has been established once on that measure during a day, the chairman has put the pending question to a vote. At that point, the chair may use either a regular quorum call or a "notice" quorum call, whereby the call is "vacated" as soon as one hundred members are present.

[See also (I) Quorum.]

BIBLIOGRAPHY

U.S. House of Representatives. *Deschler's Precedents of the United States House of Representatives,* by Lewis Deschler. 94th Cong., 2d sess., 1977. H. Doc. 94-661. Vol. 5.

U.S. House of Representatives. *Constitution, Jefferson's Manual, and Rules of the House of Representatives, 103d Congress.* Compiled by William Holmes Brown. 102d Cong., 2d sess., 1992. H. Doc. 102-405.

– THOMAS G. DUNCAN

In the Senate

The practice of the quorum call is based on the constitutional requirement that a majority of the Senate must be present for the Senate to transact business. While quorum calls were originally used to require senators' presence on the Senate floor, they have assumed a different character in the modern legislative process. In practice, quorum calls are used to fill the time between transactions of business and are primarily a delaying mechanism.

Quorum calls are a typical feature of any extended debate in the Senate. They allow Senators to negotiate and discuss pending items away from the Senate floor. There is no limit on the length of a quorum call, and during contentious debates quorum calls have been known to last several hours.

A quorum call begins when any senator who has the floor states to the presiding officer, "I suggest the absence of a quorum." A quorum call can be brought to an end by unanimous consent to "dispense with the calling of the roll." However, such consent must come before the chair announces that a quorum is not present. When a quorum call goes to completion and the chair announces that a quorum is not present, a majority of the Senate must appear or the Senate must adjourn. Because unanimous consent is required to suspend a quorum call, a single senator can force the attendance of a majority of senators on the Senate floor.

[See also (I) Quorum.]

BIBLIOGRAPHY

U.S. Senate. *Senate Procedure, Precedents, and Practices,* by Floyd M. Riddick. 97th Cong., 1st sess., 1981. S. Doc. 97-2.

– ROBERT B. DOVE

R

RECOGNITION

The Speaker of the House's power of recognition derives from clause 2 of House Rule XIV, which states, "When two or more Members rise at once, the Speaker shall name the Member who is first to speak. . . ." This rule was adopted in 1789, the first year of Congress; and its origins may be traced to Section XVII of Thomas Jefferson's *Manual of Parliamentary Practice.*

In the early days of the House, following adoption of clause 2 of Rule XIV, business proceeded upon recognition by the Speaker of individual members. During this time, the Speaker simply recognized the first member to rise to his feet. In the early nineteenth century, as the membership and work load of the House increased, it became necessary to establish and adhere to a fixed order of business. Rule XXIV, adopted in 1811, was an early attempt by the House to establish a schedule for House business. Rule XXIV necessarily affects recognition practice, requiring that the Speaker recognize certain types of business before others. Nevertheless, in practice, Rule XXIV does not bind the House to a daily routine and, in fact, allows the House considerable freedom to schedule matters it deems most important.

As legislation in the nineteenth and twentieth centuries continued to grow in volume and complexity, the House Committee on Rules evolved as the primary tool of the House democratic leadership to schedule legislation. The Rules Committee makes certain legislation in order and establishes procedures governing its consideration by reporting to the House a special order of business. The Speaker has a close relationship to the Rules Committee, recommending Rules Committee nominees directly to the Democratic caucus and suggesting to the Rules Committee which measures to make in order. Furthermore, the Speaker retains authority to schedule a measure because clause 1 of Rule XXIII gives the Speaker discretion to determine when to proceed to the consideration of a measure recommended to be made in order by the Rules Committee (after the recommendation is adopted by the House). Thus, the Speaker's power of scheduling is derived not only from his Rule XIV power of recognition but also from his close relationship to the Rules Committee and his ability to schedule measures made in order by the House.

While the Senate has a rule similar to Rule XIV of the House governing recognition (Paragraph 1 [a] of Rule XIX), the presiding officer of the Senate does not have the Speaker's comparable power to schedule legislation. In the Senate, whose Rules Committee has no comparable scheduling role, the schedule and procedures governing consideration of legislation are normally established by unanimous consent agreement negotiated by the party leaders.

While recognition rests with the Speaker's discretion and is not subject to appeal, the Speaker's authority ordinarily is constrained by the House rules and longstanding practices of the House. For example, the Speaker is obliged to recognize a member who represents a committee reporting a bill for allowable motions to expedite the bill and must recognize a member proposing to offer a motion of higher privilege. Similarly, during the amendment process under the five-minute rule, the chairman of the Committee of the Whole is constrained to alternate recognition between majority and minority party members, giving priority to members of the reporting committee.

In some situations, however, the Speaker's discretion on recognition is not constrained. Absolute discretion extends, for example, to motions to suspend the rules, which are in order on Monday and Tuesday of each week. The Speaker may also decline to recognize a member not proceeding under the Consent Calendar (a calendar reserved for noncontroversial bills under clause 4 of House Rule XIII) who desires to ask unanimous consent to set aside the rules in order to consider a bill not otherwise in order. Similarly, recognition for one-minute speeches by unanimous consent and the order of such recognition are entirely within the discretion of the Speaker; and when the House has a heavy legislative schedule, the Speaker may refuse to recognize members for such speeches until the completion of legislative business.

So that members are on notice, the Speaker has announced several policies by which he confers recognition in those situations where his discretion is absolute. For example, the Speaker has declared a policy (first enunciated on 15 December 1981) of conferring recognition upon members to call up unreported bills and resolutions by unanimous consent only when the measures are cleared by the majority and minority floor and committee leadership. Similarly, the Speaker has declared a policy (first enunciated on 8 August 1984) for recognition of one-minute and special-order speeches: recognition alternates between majority and minority members, and speeches of five minutes or less are recognized first before longer special-order speeches.

The Speaker only recognizes a member with respect to a particular matter and such recognition does not extend to a motion relating to another matter.

On the other hand, the Speaker in some situations has declined to curtail or limit his discretion and does not announce in advance whom he will recognize if a certain parliamentary situation develops. For example, pending a vote on ordering the previous question, the Speaker has declined to indicate who might be recognized if the motion ordering the previous question was defeated.

Finally, the Speaker only recognizes a member with respect to a particular matter and such recognition does not extend to a motion relating to another matter. For that reason, the Speaker will first inquire, "for what purpose does the Gentleman [or Gentlewoman] rise?" Such an inquiry does not confer recognition; rather ultimate recognition will be granted to the member seeking recognition only for a stated purpose. Similarly, if the recognized member yields to another member for presentation of other business, the member loses the floor, as, for example, when the member in charge of a pending resolution in the House yields to another member to offer an amendment.

[See also (I) House of Representatives, article on House Rules and Procedures.]

BIBLIOGRAPHY

U.S. House of Representatives. *Constitution, Jefferson's Manual, and Rules of the House of Representatives, 103d Congress.* Compiled by William Holmes Brown. 102d Cong., 2d sess., 1992. H. Doc. 102-405.

U.S. Senate. *Riddick's Senate Procedure, Precedents, and Practices,* by Floyd M. Riddick and Alan S. Frumin. 101st Cong., 2d sess., 1992. S. Doc. 101-28.

– MUFTIAH MCCARTIN

RECOMMITTAL

The motion to recommit, one of several variations of the parliamentary motion to refer, has a significant place in House procedure. The motion often provides the final political confrontation on a measure before the vote is taken on passage. House Rule XVI, clause 4 specifies that after the previous question is ordered on passage, one motion to recommit is in order, and priority in recognition goes to a member opposed to the bill. The motion may be with or without instructions. A "straight" motion (which, if adopted, sends the bill back to the reporting committee) is not debatable. If instructions are included, ten minutes of debate are permitted, divided equally between the proponent and a member opposed, usually the floor manager of the bill. The instructions can be to amend the measure ("The committee is instructed to report the bill forthwith with the following amendment: . . ."). The amendments proposed by the motion must be germane to the bill, but if one motion is ruled out as improper, another may be entertained. If the House recommits, the bill manager immediately responds ("Pursuant to the instructions of the House, I report the bill with the following amendment: . . ."). The question is then put on the amendment; if adopted, it becomes part of the bill to be engrossed (put in its perfected form, with all adopted amendments added to the introduced text). After the third reading the question recurs on passage.

The importance of the motion is demonstrated by the fact that the Committee on Rules is precluded from reporting a special order that prevents its being offered (Rule XI, clause 4). Given the modern tendency to expedite the amendment process by adopting closed or modified closed rules for the consideration of many pieces of legislation, the motion has gained renewed significance as one of the options available to the minority to establish its legislative record. The minority in the House has by various parliamentary maneuvers resisted attempts to limit the free and full use of the motion.

The special recommittal motion in Rule XVI applies only to bills and joint resolutions, but Rule XVII extends the motion to commit (or recommit) to any measure, including resolutions and conference reports. This rule, however, provides no guarantee of the right of the minority to recognition. Precedents dictate that such recognition is appropriate when a measure reported from a committee is regularly before the House, but when an unreported matter is called up as privileged, recognition does not depend on party affiliation. When a conference report is before the House, a minority member who qualifies as being opposed is entitled to recognition to move to recommit. Recommittal of a conference report is only in order in the house first acting on the report, since adoption of the report in either body dissolves the conference committee.

In the Senate the motion to recommit is not a "minority" motion, but it is sometimes used by supporters to salvage a bill after it has become weighed down with amendments. It is also applied to conference reports when the Senate wishes to dispose of the report adversely.

[See also (I) House of Representatives, article on House Rules and Procedures.]

BIBLIOGRAPHY

U.S. House of Representatives. *Constitution, Jefferson's Manual, and Rules of the House of Representatives, 103d Congress.* Compiled by William Holmes Brown. 102d Cong., 2d sess., 1992. H. Doc. 102-405.

U.S. House of Representatives. *Deschler's Precedents of the United States House of Representatives,* by Lewis Deschler. 94th Cong., 2d sess., 1977. H. Doc. 94-661.

– WILLIAM HOLMES BROWN

RECONCILIATION

Established in section 310 of the Congressional Budget Act of 1974, reconciliation is a procedure in which House and Senate committees are instructed in a budget resolution to recommend changes in spending and revenue laws within their jurisdiction. It has been used under current practices since 1980, exclusively for the purpose of deficit reduction.

Reconciliation begins with instructions in the concurrent resolution on the budget. House and Senate committees with jurisdiction over mandatory spending (principally entitlements) or revenue laws are instructed in the budget resolution to recommend changes in those laws to bring spending and revenue levels in line with the totals set forth in the resolution. The committees' recommendations are forwarded to the House and Senate Budget committees, which normally combine the proposals into an omnibus measure for House and Senate action. The Congressional Budget Act establishes expedited procedures in the House and Senate for consideration of reconciliation legislation, and in the Senate prohibits the inclusion of so-called "extraneous matter" (provisions unrelated to deficit reduction) in reconciliation measures.

Reconciliation is not used to change discretionary spending (spending controlled by the Appropriations committees). Other enforcement procedures, based on points of order (objections raised under House or Senate rules to the consideration of legislation), are used to make annual appropriations measures conform to the budget resolution.

Reconciliation legislation has been the principal legislative vehicle for congressional action to reduce the deficit since 1980. In particular it has been used to implement broad deficit reduction agreements between the president and congressional leaders.

BIBLIOGRAPHY

U.S. House of Representatives. Committee on the Budget. *A Review of the Reconciliation Process.* 98th Cong., 2d sess., 1984. Committee Print 9.

U.S. House of Representatives. Committee on the Budget. *The Whole and the Parts: Piecemeal and Integrated Approaches to Congressional Budgeting.* Report prepared by Allen Schick. 100th Cong., 1st sess., 1987. Committee Print 3.

– EDWARD DAVIS

RECONSIDER, MOTION TO

In the House

The motion to reconsider a question may be offered by a member of the majority in voting thereon. It may be offered on the same day the question is decided or on the succeeding day for the consideration of that type of business, but the motion may not be repeated. It has been used in the House of Representatives since 1789 and was first stated in the standing rules in 1802.

The motion to reconsider is not admitted in the Committee of the Whole. The "majority" means the prevailing side in a vote. On a tie vote, all those voting "no" qualify to offer a motion to reconsider. On an unrecorded vote, all those voting qualify. In standing committees, all those voting in person qualify. Any member may object to the chair's customary statement that by unanimous consent a motion to reconsider is laid on the table, in which case a qualifying member may offer a formal motion to reconsider.

The motion to reconsider is subject to the motion to lay on the table. It may not be applied to negative votes on adjournment, recess, resolving into the Committee of the Whole, the question of consideration, suspension of the rules, or overriding a veto. It may not be applied to a partially executed order of the previous question. In modern practice, adoption of a motion to reconsider a question on which the previous question has been ordered does not render the question debatable or amendable unless the vote on the previous question is separately reconsidered.

BIBLIOGRAPHY

U.S. House of Representatives. *Constitution, Jefferson's Manual, and Rules of the House of Representatives, 103d Congress.* Compiled by William Holmes Brown. 102d Cong., 2d sess., 1992. H. Doc. 102-405.

– JOHN V. SULLIVAN

In the Senate

A single motion to reconsider is in order following almost any vote of the Senate. The purpose of the motion is to provide senators with an opportunity to change their minds about their vote. It can be made or entered only by a senator who voted with the prevailing side or who did not vote, and only on the day of the vote or one of the next two days of session. In practice, motions to reconsider are routinely tabled, that is, killed immediately following any vote. The typical scenario following a vote involves an immediate motion to reconsider that is then followed immediately by a motion to table the motion to reconsider. The motion to table is routinely adopted by unanimous consent.

It is extremely rare for senators to use the motion to reconsider for the purpose for which it was created. On those rare occasions when it is allowed to follow its course, however, it can be extremely important. For example, in 1987, President Ronald Reagan's veto of the Highway bill was sustained in the Senate by one vote. The following day a motion to reconsider was entered and the Senate voted again. One senator changed his vote and the veto was overridden.

BIBLIOGRAPHY

U.S. Senate. *Senate Procedure, Precedents, and Practices,* by Floyd M. Riddick. 97th Cong., 1st sess., 1981. S. Doc. 97-2.

– ROBERT B. DOVE

RECORDS OF DEBATE

During its first century, Congress gradually came to endorse and then direct the compilation of a systematic and comprehensive record of debate. The constitutional requirement that the House of Representatives and Senate keep journals of their proceedings included no provision for a record of debate in the legislative chambers; earlier legislatures in Great Britain and America provided few precedents. The British Parliament and colonial assemblies generally discouraged the printing of any debates. Although the British Parliament ceased to prosecute printers after the 1770s, that body failed to provide an official record of debate until 1909. The Continental Congress and the Constitutional Convention met in secret sessions, and the former published only a journal of official proceedings. When early state governments and ratification conventions opened their sessions, however, printers were quick to meet the public demand for summaries of debates.

Early in the First Congress, the House voted to open sessions to the public, thereby making debates accessible to reporters. Several newspapers printed accounts of House debates, and one short-lived publication, Thomas Lloyd's *Congressional Register,* was devoted exclusively to summaries of proceedings in the House. Without officially commissioning any publication of records, the House, in the interest of greater accuracy, soon provided reporters with seats on the floor of the chamber. The Senate met in secret session until December 1795, after which reporters also printed summaries of debates in that body. Following the relocation of the government to Washington, D.C., the Senate chamber could not accommodate reporters, and no record of debate survives for 1800 to 1802. Thereafter, the District's *National Intelligencer,* a thrice-weekly newspaper, printed accounts of debates in both bodies of Congress. Other newspapers periodically printed their own summaries of debates.

Beginning with the session of 6 December 1824, Joseph Gales, Jr., and William Seaton, congressional printers and the editors of the *National Intelligencer,* initiated the *Register of Debates,* a forerunner of the *Congressional Record.* The Register, issued after the close of each session, presented regular summaries of debates in a dedicated publication. In an effort to recover the record of debate from the First Congress through the conclusion of the first session of the 18th Congress on 27 May 1824, Gales and Seaton also published the *Annals of Congress,* which reconstructed debates from various published sources, the stenographers' notes from the *National Intelligencer,* and the House and Senate journals. Gales and Seaton published two volumes of the *Annals* in 1834 but suspended work until 1849, when a congressional subscription allowed them to prepare forty more volumes; they completed publication in 1856.

The Register, *issued after the close of each session, presented regular summaries of debates in a dedicated publication.*

The record of debate in the *Annals of Congress* and the *Register of Debates,* like the newspaper reports that preceded them, were summaries of speeches and floor action rather than a verbatim record of debates in the House and Senate. Deficiencies in recording methods, omission of entire speeches, political biases, and the editors' limited access to sources compromised the accuracy and reliability of the debate summaries. Some members of Congress presented printers with texts of their remarks that may or may not have reflected their spoken words, while others revised speeches after delivering them on the floor. Any researcher seeking a complete record of debates from these years must consult the various sources used by Gales and Seaton.

Beginning with the opening session of the 23d Congress in 1833, Francis Blair and John C. Rives, who replaced Gales and Seaton as official printers of Congress, began publication of the *Congressional Globe* in direct competition with the *Register of Debates.* The two publications coexisted until 16 October 1837, when Gales and Seaton discontinued the *Register of Debates.* The *Congressional Globe* continued to publish summaries of debates that were recorded by reporters of the *Globe* newspaper owned by Blair and Rives; the record suffers from the same omissions, political bias, and deficiencies of earlier publications. After the *Globe* newspaper failed in 1845, however, the *Congressional Globe* achieved greater accuracy in its reporting.

In the first official endorsements of a printed record of debate, the Senate in 1848 and the House in 1850 contracted with local newspapers and the *Congressional Globe* to publish a record of debate in the respective bodies. The contracts were also the beginning of efforts to compile a verbatim record of debate. Aided by the development of Pitman shorthand, reporters were able to transcribe more accurate records and avoid the frequent charges of political motivation in the inclusion or exclusion of speeches. In 1855, Congress moved a step closer to official sponsorship of compiling the record when it agreed to pay *Congressional Globe* reporters; in 1863, it appropriated money for reporting debates. In 1865, it required the *Congressional Globe* to begin daily printing of debates.

The government funding of reporters of debate, the desire for a more accurate record, and the establishment of the Government Printing Office in 1860 convinced Congress to oversee directly the printing of its debates after the *Congressional Globe*'s contract expired in 1873. Under the title of *Congressional Record,* Congress initiated its own reporting with the proceedings for 4 March 1873, at the opening of the 43d Congress. The format remained the same as the *Congressional Globe*'s for nearly seventy years, and both House and Senate retained the *Globe* reporters for compilation of the *Congressional Record.*

The inception of the *Congressional Record* did not end the prolonged debate over the compilation of a verbatim record. According to a statute of 12 January 1895, the *Congressional Record* is supposed to publish a "substantially verbatim report of the proceedings." Government direction of the publication and improved methods of recording debate solved many of the problems of earlier publications, but members still may revise and extend their remarks and submit for publication remarks not spoken in the chambers.

[See also (I) Congressional Record.*]*

BIBLIOGRAPHY

Amer, Mildred. *The Congressional Record: Content, History, and Issues.* Congressional Research Service, Library of Congress. CRS Rept. 93-60. 1993.

McPherson, Elizabeth Gregory. "The History of Reporting the Debates and Proceedings of Congress." Ph.D. diss., University of North Carolina, 1940.

Springer, Michelle M. "The *Congressional Record:* Substantially a Verbatim Report?" *Government Publications Review* 13 (May–June 1986): 371–378.

– BRUCE A. RAGSDALE

REORGANIZATION OF CONGRESS

Conventional wisdom to the contrary, Congress renews itself regularly; at the start of each session, it inevitably adopts some institutional changes, most often minor and perhaps merely cosmetic, but occasionally fundamental. The accretion of change—any shift, intended or inadvertent, gradual or abrupt, in Congress's method of procedure—dramatically alters the contours of the legislative institution but does so in a more-or-less random or unobtrusive fashion over extended periods.

Reform—more conscious efforts to reshape institutional structures and processes—occurs less frequently, most often in response to members' perceptions that their assembly is an ineffective policy-maker or that it is at risk of losing the public approbation necessary to sustain its legitimacy. The years 1910 to 1911 and 1970 to 1977 saw notable manifestations of the reform impulse. More rarely still, reform is embodied in a major statute, a legislative reorganization act, such as those enacted in 1946 and 1970.

Whatever form it takes, change continually alters Congress. The committee-centered institution of the 1980s was a far cry from the party-dominated legislature of the early twentieth century, and the 1990s promise significant change as Congress reels under the burden of both ineffective policy-making and a series of scandals that have undermined its popular standing.

PERSPECTIVES ON CHANGE AND REFORM. Self-conscious change—reform and reorganization—most often reflects events in Congress's environment, in the form of international or domestic crises that raise new issues to the top of the legislative agenda and demand efficient organizational forms for effective resolution. In addition, membership turnover may bring new people with different backgrounds, experiences, and perspectives to Congress; newcomers may require new modes of action to achieve their legislative goals. Alternatively, events and new issues may induce incumbent members to reassess their views, leading, among other things, to reorganization of Congress.

The problem confronting would-be reformers is to construct a set of institutional forms that implement their vision of an improved legislature. Several images of the ideal Congress exist, but none has generated consensus or broadly energized law-makers. At one extreme is an executive-force theory that envisions a Congress subordinate to the president, the only person capable of providing the nation with the leadership it needs. An alternative answer to an immobilized and obstructionist Congress is a responsible political party system. Disciplined, cohesive congressional parties could pass programs with dispatch, either supporting the executive or imposing legislative priorities. Adherents of the "literary" theory revere the tradition of checks and balances and separation of powers they see embedded in the text of the Constitution; they look to Congress to check the power-seeking president and to deter radical policy initiatives. Finally, congressional supremacists (reflecting the Whig tradition of the mid-nineteenth century) envision a dominant first branch of government as the prime mover in national politics, able to set policy and to oversee its implementation.

In the 1960s, reformers focused on the House Rules Committee, the "traffic cop" that manages the flow of legislation to the House floor.

These broad visions of an altered Congress have inspired little interest beyond academic circles; rather, reform and reorganization have proceeded more pragmatically, more incrementally, in response to contemporary political pressures. One strand of change has sought to make Congress more responsible, more capable of enacting effective policy with dispatch. A responsible legislature resolves policy problems successfully and efficiently. A second set of changes has emphasized responsiveness, the capacity of Congress to consider carefully and act in accordance with the expressed preferences of those—citizens, organized groups, local and state governments, and presidents and federal bureaucrats—whom its actions will affect. There is a tension between responsibility and responsiveness: a responsible Congress will act rapidly and decisively; a responsive assembly will move slowly, waiting for those with opinions to voice them and for some basic agreement to emerge. A third focus of change has been accountability, the ability of citizens to discover what Congress and its members have done and to hold them to account what they have, or have not, accomplished. Responsibility, responsiveness, and accountability—concepts narrower than the broad philosophic visions—offer benchmarks against which to assess Congress's performance.

REORGANIZATION AND REFORM, 1946–1992. Recent reformers have sought to improve congressional performance in each of these three areas. A major effort has been made to enhance the legislature's decision-making prowess, that is, to make Congress more responsible. Earlier reforms, beginning with the 1910–1911 revolt against the domineering Speaker of the House, Joseph G. Cannon (R-Ill.), brought down a centralized party apparatus and led to the emergence of a fragmented, atomized institution where individual members enjoyed considerable freedom to pursue their own career interests from positions of strength within independent committees and subcommittees. The lessons of the Depression and World War II suggested that a more efficient Congress was in order.

Thus, the Legislative Reorganization Act of 1946 sought to streamline a chaotic committee system, paring the number of House committees to nineteen (from forty-eight) and of Senate panels to fifteen (from thirty-three) and rationalizing their jurisdictions. Recognizing that Congress (following the procedures of the 1921 Budget and Accounting Act) had not handled its fiscal responsibilities competently, the act called for a legislative budget, an omnibus bill that would treat revenues and expenditures in unified fashion. Finally, the act provided Congress with vastly enlarged information resources and analytic capacity in the form of professional personal and committee staff and a bigger and better Legislative Reference Service in the Library of Congress. The reformers, following the recommendations of a Joint Committee on the Organization of Congress, hoped to make Congress better able to address effectively the nation's pressing policy problems.

The 1946 legislation was less than a total success. Changes in the legislative agenda and members' career interests led to the creation of new committees (four in the House, one in the Senate) and, more significantly in the long term, to the proliferation of subcommittees. The new budget process did not work; here, too, the goals of individualistic, election-oriented members prevailed over the need for efficiency, and budgeting almost immediately reverted to its previous form, with fiscal decisions parceled out among thirteen virtually autonomous Appropriations subcommittees. Only the increase in information resources endured; Congress continues to call on its own expertise to buttress its policy-making efforts.

In the 1960s, reformers focused on the House Rules Committee, the "traffic cop" that, among other things,

TABLE 1

LANDMARKS OF LEGISLATIVE REORGANIZATION

1910–1911	"Revolt" against Speaker of the House Joseph G. Cannon (R-Ill.). Stripped the Speaker of the ability to manage House affairs through control of powerful political parties; marked the advent of the modern committee-centered Congress.
1921	Budget and Accounting Act (42 Stat. 20–27). Assigned the president the task of submitting a unified executive budget to Congress; initiated contemporary budget practices.
1946	Legislative Reorganization Act of 1946 (60 Stat. 812–852). Sought to restructure the committee system, create a comprehensive budget process, and provide Congress with improved information resources.
1961	House Rules Committee enlarged.
1970–1977	Major postwar reform era, beginning formally with passage of the Legislative Reorganization Act of 1970 (84 Stat. 1140–1204). Simultaneously decentralized the congressional process, strengthened the political parties, and opened congressional deliberations to public scrutiny.
1985	Balanced Budget and Emergency Deficit Control (Gramm-Rudman-Hollings) Act (99 Stat. 1038). Revised the budget process significantly.
1990	Budget Enforcement Act (P.L. 101–508). Major revision of the budget process.
1992–	Revival of interest in broad congressional reform. Creation of a Joint Committee on the Organization of Congress.

manages the flow of legislation to the House floor. In the previous decade, two conservative southern Democrats, including the chairman, voted frequently with the four Rules Republicans, all conservatives, to deadlock the twelve-member committee at 6 to 6, thus preventing the majority Democrats' policy initiatives from reaching the floor. Following the 1960 election, the liberal bloc in the House narrowly (217 to 212) won a difficult fight to enlarge the committee to fifteen members, ostensibly giving the majority an 8 to 7 working margin. In the 1970s, the Democrats empowered the Speaker, subject to caucus approval, to nominate Rules members; they set the ratio of members from the majority and minority parties at "2 to 1 plus 1" (currently nine Democrats and four Republicans). In the 89th Congress (1965–1967), the Democrats adopted a "twenty-one-day rule" that in effect prevented the committee from holding up bills for more than three weeks. (The ensuing Congress, however, repealed the rule.) Overall, the reformers succeeded in harnessing the sometimes defiant Rules Committee to the party leadership, smoothing the flow of legislation to the House floor.

In the mid-1960s and after, learning from its inability to exert its collective influence with respect to the war in Vietnam and the Watergate scandals, Congress launched a new effort to enhance institutional responsibility. As a consequence of agitation for change from the Democratic Study Group (an informal caucus of liberal Democrats) and the recommendations of a new Joint Committee on the Organization of Congress, the Legislative Reorganization Act of 1970 inaugurated an unprecedented period of reform. In the ensuing years, the House Democratic Caucus adopted a wide variety of other changes; reform in the Senate was considerably more restrained. Efforts to make Congress more responsible followed two tracks: reclaiming traditional authority ceded unwisely to the president and instituting a more efficient decision-making process.

To resist executive domination, Congress enacted the War Powers Resolution in 1973. Passed over Richard M. Nixon's veto, the act circumscribed the commander in chief's ability to commit the armed forces to combat by empowering Congress to compel the president to withdraw troops sent into the field at any time, or within sixty days of deployment if Congress did not declare war or extend the sixty-day period by law. Also, to regain control over federal expenditures, the legislature enacted the Congressional Budget and Impoundment Control Act of 1974. The law was designed to allow Congress to produce a coherent, comprehensive budget that compared revenues and expenditures, thus offering a clear picture of the deficit. The act also created new procedures that permitted Congress to curb the president's capacity to impound—refuse to spend—duly authorized and appropriated funds. The act did not stem the flow of red ink—members found creative ways to evade its strictures—and Congress modified it with the Gramm-Rudman-Hollings Balanced Budget Act (1985) and the Budget Enforcement Act (1990). The former exacted automatic spending cuts if the deficit exceeded prescribed levels; the latter abandoned a focus on the deficit and sought instead to impose spending limits (caps) on domestic, military, and international outlays. Third, building on the precedent of the 1946 Reorganization Act, Congress gave itself new staff and support agency information resources to enable it to countervail the executive with its own expertise.

A second dimension of the attempt to enhance responsibility was to make the policy-making process less fragmented. To that end, the House Democratic Caucus (in a Democratic-controlled Congress) sought to limit the independence of individual committee chairs. It decreed that seniority (length of committee service) would no longer automatically determine who would preside in the committee room; it empowered its Steering and Policy Committee to recommend chairs using other criteria and retained the right to vote to reject that panel's nominations. The Speaker of the House won new authority to control the Steering and Policy Committee; to nominate, subject to caucus approval, members of the Rules Committee and thus to exercise some influence over the conditions under which bills were considered on the House floor; to regulate the flow of legislation to and from committee (through the prerogative to refer bills to several panels); and to create ad hoc committees and task forces to facilitate systematic treatment of complex policy issues. These changes, reformers hoped, would give the majority party improved capacity to centralize congressional operations and enact policy more efficiently.

In the Senate, the major effort to advance responsibility was a limitation of the minority's capacity to filibuster—to use unlimited debate to tie up the chamber and defeat or substantially weaken controversial legislation (such as civil rights bills). Until 1975, a two-thirds majority of those present and voting (sixty-seven votes if all senators were in attendance) was required to invoke cloture (end debate). After that year, a constitutional three-fifths majority (sixty votes) could force Senate action.

In the 1970s, Congress also put in place significant reforms for responsiveness, reflecting the desire of dissatisfied lawmakers for greater participation and influence on policy. Substantial pieces of committee power were reallocated to the rank and file. The consolidation of full committees under the 1946 Legislative Reorganization Act led to the proliferation of subcommittees—to facilitate Congress's division of labor and to provide senior members with positions of influence. At the time of the act, there were approximately 97 House subcommittees; by the 94th (1975–1977) Congress there were 151; by the 103d (1993–1995), the number declined to 120. In the Senate, there were roughly 34 subcommittees in 1946; the number peaked at 140 in the 94th Congress, but fell back to 86 in the 103d.

New rules reined in the full committee chairs, limited the committee and subcommittee chairmanships that any individual could hold, and established procedures that enabled more members to attain desirable subcommittee assignments. A "subcommittee bill of rights" required that subcommittees have fixed jurisdictions and that legislation within their jurisdictions be referred automatically to them; it also authorized subcommittees to meet at the pleasure of their members, to write their own rules, and to manage their own budgets and staffs. In 1975, the Democratic Caucus mandated that all House committees with more than twenty members create a minimum of four subcommittees. These reforms democratized the House; more members, responding to more diverse constituency and group interests, occupied positions from which they could exercise some influence over some parts of the legislative agenda. But the reforms also made responsible decision making more problematic: the increased number of players with greater ability to influence policy made forging coalitions to enact meaningful legislation more difficult.

Another route to reorganization and reform led toward increased accountability. To restore its popular standing, damaged by policy failure and a series of highly publicized scandals, the legislature enacted a set of reforms designed to expose its operations to citizens' scrutiny. Members were to conduct the public's business in public: committees were to meet in open session; votes in committee and on the floor were to be recorded; and proceedings were made available for live television coverage on the C-SPAN network. Both the House and Senate adopted codes of ethics, including financial disclosure provisions, intended to deter or expose conflicts of interest. The Federal Election Campaign Act (1971), as interpreted by the Supreme Court in *Buckley v. Valeo* (1976) and amended subsequently by Congress, set up an election finance system that limited contributors' donations but not candidates' expenditures. Moreover, it stipulated that candidates report in detail the sources—individuals and political action committees (PACs)—of their funds and the uses to which they put the money; the Federal Election Commission, which administers the campaign act, publishes this data. Both the ethics codes and the campaign statute aim to permit concerned citizens to discover to whom, if anyone, senators and representatives are financially beholden and to assess whether members' personal or political interests impinge on matters about which they must vote or otherwise act. Dissatisfied voters can exact retribution at the ballot box.

These reforms of the 1970s failed to revive Congress's flagging reputation. A series of new revelations further undercut public support for the legislature: charges of ethical improprieties led to the resignations in 1989 of House Speaker James C. Wright, Jr. (D-Tex.) and Majority Leader Tony Coelho (D-Calif.); more than three hundred members wrote overdrafts on the House bank; a group of senators, the so-called Keating five, were chastised for ethically dubious relations with a savings and loan executive; and the public became aware of members' perquisites (e.g., subsidized meals and beauty services and free [franked] mail) that made the lawmakers appear to be a pampered elite.

Further reforms ensued in 1991 and 1992. As a quid pro quo for a sizable salary increase, the House and Senate gave up honoraria paid to members by various interests for speeches and articles. The House Bank was shut down, the franking privilege limited, and other perquisites eliminated or reduced; professional administrators, particularly a director of Non-Legislative and Financial Services, assumed responsibility, for day-to-day House operations. Again, the intent of these changes was to demonstrate that Congress acts openly and aboveboard and thus to rekindle public confidence in the legislature.

THE IMPACT OF REORGANIZATION AND REFORM. In the short term, reform favored responsiveness (fragmentation) over responsibility (centralization) while simultaneously enlarging the potential for (if not the reality of) accountability. On balance, Congress has neither often reclaimed authority from, nor regularly imposed its programmatic judgments on, the executive. The War Powers Act has not enabled the legislature to impose its will systematically on the president. Reshaping the budget process—in the 1974 act and with the Gramm-Rudman-Hollings experiment with automatic spending cuts or the efforts of 1990 and after to cap spending—has not reduced outlays or the growth of the deficit. Even enlarged legislative expertise has produced mixed results. Congress does have greater access to more and better data with which to propose legislative alternatives to executive initiatives, but politically motivated lawmakers often have little incentive to use policy analysis or, if they do, may find themselves overwhelmed with a surfeit of data.

Nor has the House majority party's new authority—control over committee chairs, the Speaker's enhanced influence over committee assignments and the Rules Committee, and the multiple referral power—consistently produced cohesive partisan majorities. To be sure, a curious concatenation of events at the end of the 1980s—increased party polarization stemming from divided government and greater ideological homogeneity among the Democrats, coupled with Speaker Jim Wright's aggressive use of the full panoply of leadership powers—led to somewhat greater party cohesion among members, who came to recognize the need to pull together to enact party programs. Whether such centralization and its attendant party discipline will continue under Speaker Thomas S. Foley (D-Wash.) and his successors remains questionable.

More significantly, recent legislative change has made Congress more responsive. The breach of the seniority tradition, the allocation of leadership positions among a wider array of more junior members, the devolution of authority to independent subcommittees at the expense of full committee chairs, and the provision of greater staff and analytic resources have, especially in the House, afforded more members, responding to more interests, a piece of the policy-making action. Enhanced responsiveness, however, has not been without cost. Responsibility, or policy-making efficiency, has suffered. Specialization and expertise have declined; fewer members have the capacity to formulate coherent and effective policies on any given subject. With more participants possessing influence, assembling coalitions at the multiple stages of the lawmaking process becomes more difficult, requiring more negotiation and compromise among more interests and reducing the possibilities for truly innovative programs.

The contemporary Congress is more accountable, but this also is not necessarily an unmixed blessing. In principle, the campaign and financial disclosure rules make the public better able to ferret out members' potential ethical and economic conflicts of interest; in reality, there is little evidence that citizens are inclined to do so. There has been no diminution in charges of ethical and campaign malfeasance, as the House bank and post office scandals and the Keating five affair amply illustrate. Moreover, the necessity of acting openly, in public, forces members to protect their political flanks; with lobbyists, journalists, and administrative officials monitoring their behavior, they may be reluctant to take the political risks that responsible policy-making entails.

Yet incumbents have continued to win reelection in overwhelming numbers. In 1992, 88 percent of incumbents seeking reelection retained their seats, down only slightly from the rates of over 90 percent that characterized the 1980–1990 decade. Electoral margins, however, decreased significantly in both 1990 and 1992, and 67 retirements in the latter year coupled with the defeat of 43 incumbents brought 110 new members to the House. Eighty-two percent of incumbent senators seeking new terms (twenty-two out of twenty-seven seeking reelection) won in 1992; newcomers to the 103d Senate totaled fourteen. Although more vulnerable, incumbents continue to win in impressive numbers.

REORGANIZATION AND REFORM IN THE 1990S. Reorganization and reform have thus changed the nature of congressional responsibility, responsiveness, and accountability incrementally, but sometimes with unexpected results. In consequence, a number of items remain on the reform agenda, and Congress has established another Joint Committee on the Reorganization of Congress to explore them. Some attention will go to improving legislative responsibility. Recognizing that a decentralized decision-making process contributes substantially to congressional policy-making immobilism, senior members proposed another joint committee to tackle such issues as simplification of the tangled and overlapping committee jurisdictions, reducing the excessive use of subcommittees, streamlining the complicated budget process, and strengthening the position of party leaders in relation to the committees and their chairs. Such changes would move Congress toward party-based centralization, reducing responsiveness to parochial constituency interests and enabling the legislature to move policy initiatives forward more efficiently. Term limitations—barring members from serving more than twelve years in Congress or more than six or eight years as committee chairs—would, proponents argue, concentrate member attention on policy and the national interest rather than on reelection concerns.

The House Bank was shut down,

the franking privilege limited,

and other perquisites eliminated or reduced.

Greater attention will likely be given to accountability. Campaign finance and congressional ethics seem certain to be subjects of intensive and extensive debate. High reelection rates for incumbents, achieved with the help of campaign contributions from political action committees, are inviting targets. Career-oriented legislators, critics allege, place electoral above other concerns and make concessions to special interests to gain financial support for excessively and increasingly expensive media-driven campaigns; they vote themselves abundant perquisites to the same end, it is said. Spending limits, restrictions on PAC contributions, and public funding of campaigns emerge as possible remedies, but consensus has proved elusive. Minority Republicans reject spending caps and public finance as inimical to their efforts to unseat Democratic incumbents. Sitting Democrats are disinclined to limit PACs, a significant source of their contributions.

Continuing controversy over legislative ethics—highlighted by the House bank and Keating five scandals, among others—has spawned a host of reform issues. Most significant is the need to define "proper" constituency service. When does a legitimate effort to serve residents of the members' states or districts become a self-serving exercise of policy-making power or unwarranted interference in administrative matters? Limitation of member perquisites is likely to proceed apace, salary increases and use of franked mail will be difficult to sustain, and staff resources will not grow and may even be reduced. Pressure to ensure coverage of Congress under worker safety and antidiscrimination laws, from which it has exempted itself, will not diminish. The legislature will face increasing demands to organize and display its activities in ways that promote the public's ability to evaluate the propriety of congressional performance.

Congress, in short, has changed and continues to change. Reorganization and reform proceed, sometimes dramatically in response to singular events, more often quietly and in evolutionary rather than revolutionary fashion. The institution tries, haltingly and incrementally in most instances, to balance its needs to be responsible, responsive, and accountable. On the whole, these efforts produce a mixed record of success and failure, guaranteeing that reorganization and reform will continue to animate at least some members of Congress as well as attentive observers of the national legislature.

[See also (I) House Bank.]

BIBLIOGRAPHY

Center for Responsive Politics. *"Not for the Short Winded": Congressional Reform, 1961–1986.* 1986.

Davidson, Roger H. "The Advent of the Modern Congress: The Legislative Reorganization Act of 1946." *Legislative Studies Quarterly* 15 (1990): 357–373.

Davidson, Roger H., David M. Kovenock, and Michael K. O'Leary. *Congress in Crisis: Politics and Congressional Reform.* 1966.

Davidson, Roger H., and Walter J. Oleszek. *Congress against Itself.* 1977.

Kravitz, Walter. "The Advent of the Modern Congress: The Legislative Reorganization Act of 1970." *Legislative Studies Quarterly* 15 (1990): 375–399.

Magleby, David B., and Candice J. Nelson. *The Money Chase: Congressional Campaign Finance Reform.* 1990.

Ornstein, Norman J., ed. *Congress in Change: Evolution and Reform.* 1975.

Rieselbach, Leroy N. *Congressional Reform.* 1986.

Rohde, David W. *Parties and Leaders in the Postreform House.* 1991.

Sheppard, Burton D. *Rethinking Congressional Reform: The Reform Roots of the Special Interest Congress.* 1985.

– LEROY N. RIESELBACH

RESOLUTIONS

Resolutions are one of the two general types of measures on which the House of Representatives and Senate act. There are three forms of resolutions: simple, concurrent, and joint. Each may originate in either house. Simple resolutions are designated as "H. Res." or "S. Res.," concurrent resolutions as "H. Con. Res." or "S. Con. Res.," and joint resolutions as "H.J. Res." or "S.J. Res."—all followed by an identifying number.

In contrast to bills, simple and concurrent resolutions do not become law, even after being approved by one or both houses of Congress. These resolutions usually address questions concerning the internal operations of Congress or express a nonstatutory opinion of one or both houses. Like bills, joint resolutions do become law once signed by the president or enacted without his signature or over his veto. Traditionally, constitutional amendments also take the form of joint resolutions but are not submitted for presidential approval.

Simple resolutions of the House or Senate relate only to the house of Congress in which they are proposed and require no action by the other house. Many simple resolutions address "housekeeping" questions and other matters of internal organization and procedure. The House establishes its rules at the beginning of each Congress by adopting a simple House resolution, and either house may change its rules at any time by adopting simple resolutions. By simple resolutions, the House and Senate assign members to their committees and determine committee budgets. Questions concerning the conduct of members also are decided by votes on simple resolutions of the House or Senate.

The most common and important simple resolutions are House resolutions affecting its order of business on the floor. These resolutions, also known as special orders or special rules, are reported by the House Rules Committee and recommend procedures for debating and amending individual measures on the floor. Each house also adopts simple resolutions to express "the sense of the House" or "the sense of the Senate." These are expressions of opinion or preference that may be intended to influence actions by the president or executive branch officials, but they have no binding force.

The Senate also acts on executive resolutions, especially resolutions of ratification by which it gives its advice and consent to the ratification of treaties the president has submitted. The House occasionally considers resolutions of inquiry asking the president or an executive branch official to provide it with certain facts or documents that the House determines it needs in order to fulfill its constitutional responsibilities.

When the House or Senate adopts a simple resolution, the other house is not even officially informed because it may take no action on the resolution. By contrast, concurrent resolutions require adoption by both houses. The House and Senate must pass the same concurrent resolution and reach complete agreement on its text before they have successfully completed legislative action on it.

Concurrent resolutions are used to express "the sense of Congress," instead of the opinion of only one house. These resolutions also can be used for organizational questions affecting both houses: for example, joint committees may be created and abolished by concurrent resolutions. Similarly, concurrent resolutions are used to fix the date and time at which both houses will adjourn for more than three days and at the end of each session of Congress. In addition, budget resolutions take the form of concurrent resolutions because they are not intended to become law. They only prescribe a budget plan that is supposed to guide both houses during their subsequent consideration of revenue, appropriations, and other spending bills.

In their potential effect, joint resolutions are indistinguishable from bills. Like a bill, a joint resolution requires passage by both houses, which must reach complete agreement on its text. Also like a bill, almost every joint resolution that Congress passes is presented to the president for his approval or disapproval.

Joint resolutions often are considered more appropriate than bills when the statutory purpose to be achieved is limited or temporary. For example, joint resolutions are used to continue the availability of appropriations temporarily until annual appropriations bills are enacted. These are called continuing resolutions. On the other hand, some major, permanent laws have taken the form of joint resolutions, such as the War Powers Resolution of 1973, which attempted to establish conditions and procedures relating to presidential decisions to use U.S. armed forces without first securing a declaration of war from Congress. The fact that this law was enacted by Congress as a joint resolution instead of a bill did not enhance or diminish its statutory force once both houses approved it over President Richard M. Nixon's veto. Unlike bills, joint resolutions (and other resolutions) may include preambles, stating the facts or reasons prompting Congress to approve them.

Congress also acts on constitutional amendments in the form of joint resolutions. Once approved by both houses, a joint resolution for this purpose is not presented to the president. Instead, it is submitted directly to the states for them to consider for ratification.

[See also (I) Bills.]

BIBLIOGRAPHY

U.S. House of Representatives. *Deschler's Precedents of the United States House of Representatives,* by Lewis Deschler. 94th Cong., 2d sess., 1977. H. Doc. 94-661. Vol. 7, pp. 323–425.

U.S. Senate. *Senate Procedure, Precedents, and Practices,* by Floyd M. Riddick. 97th Cong., 1st sess., 1981. S. Doc. 97-2. Pp. 367–373, 975–985.

– STANLEY BACH

RIDERS

Riders are amendments, or sometimes provisions of bills, that are unrelated to the bills' principal subjects and purposes. *Rider* is an unofficial term, not recognized in the rules or precedents of either house of Congress, that sometimes is used imprecisely to refer to legislative proposals that can be presented to one house or the other in several different ways.

Congressional committees may write bills containing provisions on any subjects within their respective jurisdictions. If a committee includes a provision on one subject in a bill that primarily addresses another subject, some members and observers might call that provision a rider. Most often, however, *rider* refers to House or Senate floor amendments that either are not germane to the bill being considered or are so-called legislative or limitation amendments proposed during consideration of an appropriations bill.

GERMANENESS. The House rules generally require that each amendment be germane to the text it would amend. Germaneness is related to relevance and pertinence, but it is a more technical requirement that the House interprets and applies by reference to a large and complex body of published precedents. No nongermane amendment may be considered if a point of order is made and sustained against it. However, the Rules Committee may report a resolution, or special rule, for considering a particular measure that also waives clause 7 of Rule XVI, the germaneness rule, so that one or more nongermane amendments can be offered to it.

The Senate has no such general germaneness requirement. Senate floor amendments must be germane only if offered to a general appropriations or budget measure, if offered under cloture, or if offered under a unanimous consent agreement or a statutory provision that permits only germane amendments to a particular measure or class of measures. At all other times, senators are free to offer nongermane amendments to the bills the Senate considers on the floor. In this way, a senator can compel the Senate to consider, debate, and cast a vote concerning any policy proposal that he or she considers sufficiently important and timely to propose as a nongermane amendment. This right also makes the Senate floor schedule rather unpredictable because of the possibility that senators will offer unexpected nongermane amendments on subjects unrelated to the pending measure.

Members and observers sometimes have nongermane amendments, especially those originating in the Senate, in mind when they speak of riders. Such an amendment is thought to be riding, or perhaps even enjoying a free ride, on the bill to which it is attached. At other times, however, the rider at issue is what is more formally known as a legislative or limitation amendment to a general appropriations bill.

APPROPRIATIONS AMENDMENTS. The general purpose and effect of House and Senate rules is to separate decisions about the funding levels for federal programs from decisions about what federal programs should be established and funded and how those programs should operate. To this end, House rules preclude bills that create programs or change their operating authority from also including the appropriations to pay for them. The same rule also protects appropriations bills from "legislative" provisions and amendments—those that are intended to change the existing law that the bill's appropriations will implement. Like the germaneness requirement, however, this proscription may be waived as part of the Rules Committee's "order of business resolution," or special rule, which the House may adopt before considering an appropriations bill.

In addition, House procedures can permit members to propose amendments to appropriations bills that limit the purposes for which the appropriated funds may be used without making permanent changes in federal programs and authorities. Examples of limitation amendments were those offered to appropriations bills, especially for the Department of Health, Education, and Welfare (later Health and Human Services), to prohibit the funds appropriated in such bills from being used to pay for or encourage abortions. Senators also can propose limitation amendments, and they can effectively decide by a simple majority vote to circumvent the prohibition in their rules against considering a legislative amendment to an appropriations bill.

The effect of riders, whether as nongermane amendments or as legislative or limitation amendments to appropriations bills, can be to delay the legislative process and to distract members from concentrating on the purposes of the bill to which the riders are attached. On the other hand, offering riders sometimes has been the only way in which members have been able to present critical policy issues for votes on the House or Senate floor.

[See also (I) Bills, Committees.]

BIBLIOGRAPHY

Bach, Stanley. "Germaneness Rules and Bicameral Relations in the U.S. Congress." *Legislative Studies Quarterly* 7 (1982): 341–357.

U.S. House of Representatives. *Deschler's Precedents of the United States House of Representatives,* by Lewis Deschler. 94th Cong., 2d sess. 1977. H. Doc. 94-661. Vol. 8.

U.S. Senate. *Senate Procedure: Precedents and Practices,* by Floyd M. Riddick. 97th Cong., 1st sess., 1981. S. Doc. 97-2. Pp. 119–170.

– STANLEY BACH

RULE, SPECIAL

Also known as a special order, order of business resolution, or rule, a special rule is a simple resolution of the House of Representatives, usually reported by the

Committee on Rules, to permit the immediate consideration of a legislative measure, notwithstanding the usual order of business, and to prescribe conditions for its debate and amendment. The authority of the Rules Committee to report special rules can be traced to 1883. Prior to that time, bills could not be considered out of their order on the calendars of the House except by unanimous consent or under a suspension of the rules, which required a two-thirds vote. Since special rules reported from the Rules Committee required only a majority vote in the House, the new practice greatly facilitated the ability of the majority leadership to depart from the regular order of business and schedule major legislation according to the majority's priorities.

A special rule establishes the amount of time for general debate on a bill and how that time is to be allocated.

In addition to giving a bill privileged status for consideration at any time after the rule's adoption, a special rule establishes the amount of time for general debate on the bill and how that time is to be allocated. Usually the time is equally divided between the chairman and ranking minority member of the committee or committees reporting the bill.

Special rules also provide for the type of amendment process to be followed once general debate has been concluded. Under an open rule, any member may offer germane amendments. Under a closed rule, no amendments are permitted. Between open and closed rules are modified open and modified closed rules, which limit the amendment process to only those amendments referred to in the rule. The text of such amendments, who may offer them, and how long they may be debated are often contained in the Rules Committee's report on the resolution.

Studies have documented a significant increase, beginning in the 1980s, in the frequency of special rules that restrict the amendment process. This trend has been variously attributed to increasing legislative complexity, member independence, member partisanship, and leaders' desire for predictable results.

Special rules are also used to waive points of order against bills or amendments and thereby permit their consideration notwithstanding their violation of House rules. In this regard, special rules are often necessary to waive points of order for matters that would otherwise be privileged for floor consideration without a rule, such as appropriations bills and conference reports.

Special rule resolutions are subject to one hour of debate in the House, controlled by the majority party manager for the Rules Committee. Half this time is traditionally yielded to the minority. The resolutions may not be considered by the House on the same day they are reported from the Rules Committee except by a two-thirds vote of the House. They may not be amended unless the majority manager offers an amendment or yields to another member for that purpose, or unless the previous question (the motion to end debate and proceed to a final vote) is defeated. If the previous question is defeated, its leading opponent is recognized for one hour of debate and the right to amend the rule in a similar fashion.

[See also (I) Previous Question.]

BIBLIOGRAPHY

Bach, Stanley, and Steven S. Smith. *Managing Uncertainty in the House of Representatives: Adaptation and Innovation in Special Rules.* 1988.

U.S. House of Representatives. *Deschler's Precedents of the United States House of Representatives,* by Lewis Deschler. 94th Cong., 2d sess., 1976. H. Doc. 94-661. Vol. 6.

– DONALD R. WOLFENSBERGER

S

SECRECY OF CONGRESS

The Continental Congress and the Constitutional Convention met in secret, and the Senate, in writing its first rules, never considered opening its sessions to the public. Most senators believed that the body's role in providing advice and consent to the executive branch and in acting as a "council of revision" for measures coming over from the House compelled it to conduct its business behind closed doors. The absence of a gallery in the Senate chamber in the building in New York City where the Senate first met no doubt contributed to this viewpoint as well.

Not until 1794 did the Senate agree to open its legislative sessions to the public. The initial impetus for this decision was public interest in the challenge to seating Senator-elect Albert Gallatin. The Senate opened its sessions to the public during debate on Gallatin's credentials, and later acted to open its legislative sessions to the public beginning in December 1794.

The Senate kept its doors closed during consideration of so-called executive business (debate on treaties and presidential nominations). Although these sessions were not open to the press or public, and debate transcripts were released to the public much later, senators frequently passed information about the proceedings to the press. In June 1929, at the suggestion of Sen. Robert M. La Follette, Jr. (R-Wis.), the Senate rules were changed to require that executive business be conducted in public session, while preserving the right of any senator to move for a closed-door session subject to approval by a Senate majority.

In June 1929 the Senate rules were changed to require that executive business be conducted in public session.

The Senate generally receives testimony in impeachment trials in public session, according to a rule dating from the impeachment trial of Justice Samuel Chase in 1805, but the Senate amended the rule before the trial of President Andrew Johnson in 1868 to permit closed-door sessions during deliberations only. During the 1980s, the Senate met in secret session six times to deliberate on verdicts in the impeachment trials of federal judges Harry Claiborne, Alcee L. Hastings, and Walter Nixon.

From the time public sessions on nominations and treaties began in 1929, the Senate has met in secret on all or part of forty-one days, including 25 February 1992, when it considered President George Bush's proposal to grant most-favored-nation trading status to the People's Republic of China. Thirty of these secret sessions occurred after 1970, reflecting an increasingly assertive Senate role in policy matters concerning national security. Since 1986, the Senate has held secret sessions in the Old Senate Chamber in the Capitol; the presence of television cameras and other electronic equipment in the Senate chamber can compromise secrecy, so for closed sessions the Senate has returned to this chamber, which it last regularly used in 1859.

The House has a long tradition of holding public sessions. Although it was common for the House to clear its galleries of outsiders to receive a confidential message from the president or some other executive-branch official, closed sessions ceased being commonplace after the War of 1812. The last nineteenth-century House secret session occurred on 27 May 1830, and the House did not meet in secret again until 1979. On 19 July 1983, it met in secret to consider portions of the intelligence authorization bill prohibiting U.S. support for the Contra rebels in Nicaragua.

Under House Rule XXIX, a representative claiming to hold confidential information may move that the House conduct a secret session. The Speaker may permit debate for up to one hour on this motion. If the House concurs in the motion, the galleries are cleared, electronic equipment is turned off, and superfluous staff are excluded from the chamber. Remaining staff are sworn to secrecy until such time as the House should vote to divulge the substance of the secret session. Under an alternative rule (Rule XLVII), the Intelligence Committee may move that the House hold a secret session to determine whether to divulge classified information held by the Intelligence Committee.

Allowing committees routinely to meet in secret session was a long-standing practice of Congress. Committee actions are not official until ratified by the parent chamber, and the feeling was that the preliminary deliberation and action could and generally should be done privately. Also, during the nineteenth century, committee meeting rooms were generally not designed to accommodate an audience. By the early twentieth century, with the construction of the first congressional office buildings, committee rooms became larger, and evidence suggests that more hearings were opened to the public. Business meetings and markup sessions remained closed, however.

In the 1970s, as part of a general movement to open government meetings to public scrutiny at the local, state, and federal levels, proposals were offered in Congress to require that committee hearings and meetings, including markup sessions, be open to the public. However, a committee could vote publicly (in open session, with a quorum present) to close the session for national security or other reasons specified in House and Senate rules.

In a series of rules changes beginning in the House in 1973 and the Senate in 1975, progressively stronger language was added to both chambers' rules to ensure that most committee work would be done in public. The House went even further, requiring that the full House grant its approval before a conference committee could vote to close its meetings. By the end of the 1970s virtually all committee meetings and hearings, except for those dealing with national security issues, ongoing criminal investigations, or matters that might defame an individual, were open to the public. Beginning in the mid-1980s, however, there were press reports that some in Congress were using creative devices to evade the open-meeting requirement, choosing meeting rooms too small to accommodate observers, using only committee staff to conduct preliminary committee activities, or holding private informal gatherings of members.

BIBLIOGRAPHY

Calmes, Jacqueline. "Few Complaints Are Raised as Doors Close on Capitol Hill." *Congressional Quarterly Weekly Report,* 23 May 1987, pp. 1059–1060.

Eckhardt, Bob. "The Presumption of Committee Openness under House Rules." *Harvard Journal of Legislation* 11 (February 1974): 279–302.

"Open Committee Trend in House and Senate." *Congressional Quarterly Weekly Report,* 11 January 1975, pp. 81–82.

Ornstein, Norman J. "The Open Congress Meets the President." In *Both Ends of the Avenue.* Edited by Anthony King. 1983.

Vaden, Ted. "Senate Votes Sunshine Rules for Committees." *Congressional Quarterly Weekly Report,* 8 November 1975, pp. 2413–2414.

– PAUL S. RUNDQUIST

SECRETARY OF THE SENATE

The secretary of the Senate, one of five elected Senate officers, is that body's chief administrative official. The first secretary was elected on 8 April 1789, two days after the Senate achieved its first quorum for business, and from the start the secretary was responsible for keeping the minutes and records of the Senate and purchasing supplies. As the Senate grew, numerous other duties were assigned to the secretary, whose jurisdiction came to encompass clerks, curators, and computers; disbursement of payrolls; acquisition of stationery supplies; training of Senate pages; and maintenance of public records.

The first secretary purchased quill pens, ink, and parchment needed by eighteenth-century senators; modern secretaries are responsible for a multimillion-dollar office supply operation.

The first secretary purchased quill pens, ink, and parchment needed by eighteenth-century senators, while modern secretaries have responsibility for the Senate Stationery Room, whose multimillion-dollar retail operations keep senators' offices supplied. The first secretary took minutes of Senate proceedings, a function today continued by the journal clerk and executive clerk. After the *Congressional Record* evolved into an official publication, the secretary came to supervise the Senate's reporters of debates, as well as those who prepare the *Congressional Record's* Daily Digest. Among other members of the Senate floor staff who report to the secretary are the parliamentarian, bill clerk, legislative clerk, and enrolling clerk. To answer both the immediate and the historical interest in Senate bills, resolutions, hearings, reports, and original records, the secretary oversees the Office of Printing Services, the Senate Document Room, the Office of Senate Security (which maintains classified documents), the Senate Library, the Office of Senate Curator, and the Senate Historical Office.

The secretary maintains the Office of Interparliamentary Services to assist senators participating in international legislative conferences, and the Office of Public Records to collect and provide documents relating to campaign finance, financial ethics, foreign travel, and lobbying. The secretary serves as a member of the Federal Election Commission and keeps senators informed about current election laws and filing requirements.

A seat beside the presiding officer is reserved for the secretary, who examines and signs every act of the Senate. In certain parliamentary circumstances, the secretary may preside. The last such occasion occurred in 1947, when the offices of vice president and Senate president pro tempore were vacant.

This post has attracted a long line of distinguished individuals. Samuel Allyne Otis, the first secretary and a former member of the Continental Congress, served for twenty-five years, never missing a day that the Senate was in session. Two former senators, Walter Lowrie of Pennsylvania and Charles Cutts of New Hampshire, have held the post. In 1985, Jo-Anne L. Coe became the first woman to serve as secretary of the Senate. In 1994 Martha S. Pope became the second woman to hold the office and, as a former sergeant at arms, the first person to have held the Senate's two major administrative posts.

It has not been unusual for secretaries to devote their entire careers to the Senate. Several secretaries began as pages, including Edwin A. Halsey, who served throughout the New Deal years; Leslie Biffle, a confidant of President Harry S Truman; Carl A. Loeffler and J. Mark Trice, secretaries during the Republican majorities of the 80th (1947–1949) and 83d (1953–1955) Congresses; and Walter J. Stewart, secretary from 1987 to 1994.

With a budget of $13 million (fiscal year 1992), the secretary directs a staff of approximately 225 persons. In 1991, Congress established the annual salary of Senate officers, including the secretary, at $123,000.

[See also (I) Pages, Parliamentarian, article on Senate Parliamentarian.]

BIBLIOGRAPHY

Byrd, Robert C. *The Senate, 1789–1989: Addresses on the History of the United States Senate.* Vol. 2. 1991.

U.S. Senate. *Report of the Secretary of the Senate* (semiannual, 1823–).

– WALTER J. STEWART

SENATE

An Overview

The very first provision of the U.S. Constitution states: "All legislative powers herein granted shall be vested in

Secretaries of the Senate. From 1945 through 1965. Left to right, J. Mark Trice, Leslie Biffle, Felton M. Johnston, and Carl A. Loeffler. (Library of Congress)

a Congress of the United States which shall consist of a Senate and a House of Representatives." Those "legislative powers," as they have been elaborated, interpreted, exercised, and preserved, have made Congress the most powerful national legislature in the world. It is bicameral in structure, with its lawmaking power equally divided between House and Senate. Each chamber, acting separately, must approve of each piece of legislation before it can become law. The equality of the Senate within the bicameral arrangement has made it—from the start—independent and powerful as a legislative institution.

In its basic institutional features, the Senate reflects the circumstances of its origins. The Framers of the Constitution were in total and early agreement that there should be two chambers—distinct, different, and equal. After all, eleven of the thirteen state legislatures already had a bicameral arrangement, and nine of the eleven had labeled one chamber its "Senate." This bicameral agreement of 1787 was grounded in a philosophy widely shared among the Framers that power ought not to be concentrated anywhere in government, especially not within that institution of government most likely to predominate—the legislature.

As James Madison explained during the ratification debate (in *Federalist* 51),

> In republican government, the legislative authority necessarily predominates. The remedy for this inconveniency is to divide the legislature into different branches; and to render them, by different modes of election and different principles of action, as little connected with each other as the nature of their common functions and their common dependence on the society will admit.

The debate at the Constitutional Convention over the exact content of those differences, however, was lengthy, bitter, and nearly fatal for the new constitution.

Four Basic Institutional Features.

Having agreed that members of the House should be apportioned among the states according to population, the Framers became deadlocked, in Madison's words, by "the opposite pretensions of large and small states" regarding their representational strength in the Senate. The ultimate compromise provided that two senators would be apportioned to each state, regardless of population. Voting equality in the Senate was the price the large states paid to get what they wanted—a new union.

The apportionment decision was a victory for the small states. It fixed two basic institutional features of the Senate—both of which gave advantages to the small states. First, every senator was given a statewide constituency. While these Senate constituencies might vary widely in population, the voting strength of the smallest state would equal that of the largest state. In 1990, senators from the twenty-six smallest states represented only 18 percent of the nation's population, yet they held a majority of the votes in the Senate. Conversely, the nine largest states contained a majority of the nation's population but held only 18 percent of the Senate's votes.

The equality of the Senate within the bicameral arrangement has made it independent and powerful as a legislative institution.

The apportionment decision also guaranteed a second institutional feature: that the Senate would be relatively small in size—twenty-two members at the beginning, one hundred members today. For nearly a century, the Senate has been only one-quarter the size of the House. In the smaller body, each member has a greater opportunity to be heard. And successive generations of senators have nurtured an array of parliamentary procedures to guarantee that opportunity.

The Framers of the Constitution had certain other ideas about the Senate, and they translated them, too, into permanent features of the institution. They pictured the more popularly elected House as especially liable to succumb to transient public passions and to be in need, therefore, of another body, whose members would provide a brake, a second look, a longer-run view, and a well-deliberated decision. "The use of the Senate," said Madison in his *Notes on Debates in the Federal Convention of 1787,* "is to consist in its proceeding with more coolness, with more system and with more wisdom, than the popular branch."

In the most famous anecdote about the Senate, Thomas Jefferson asks George Washington why he consented to the idea of a Senate. "Why did you pour that coffee into your saucer?" asks Washington. "To cool it," replies Jefferson. "Even so," replies Washington, "we pour legislation into the senatorial saucer to cool it." In Madison's words, that saucer would consist of "enlightened citizens, whose limited number and firmness might reasonably interpose against impetuous councils."

From this set of views came two other fundamental institutional features of the Senate. To promote "coolness" and to ensure the election of "proper characters,"

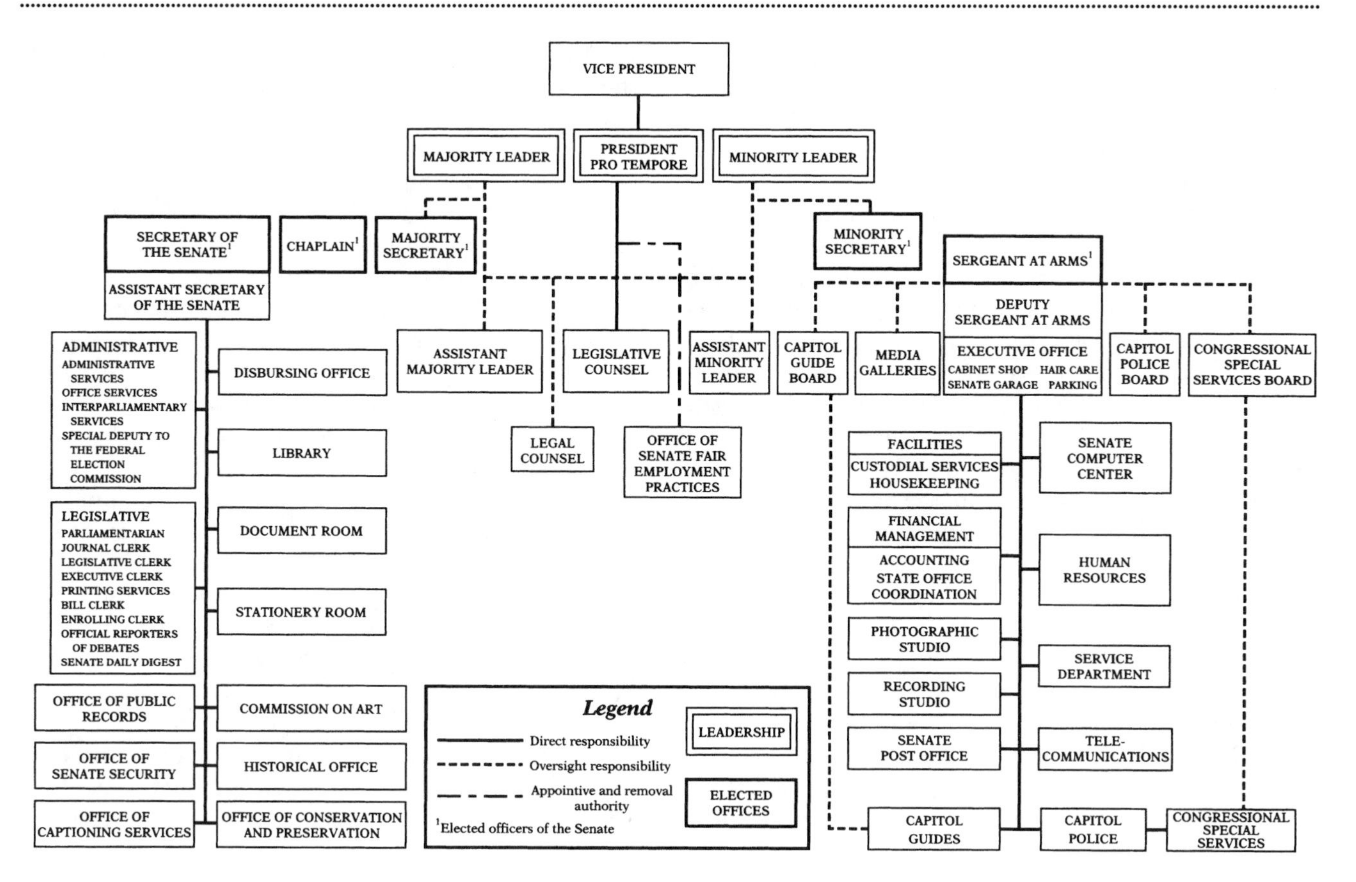

Organization of the Senate.

the Framers provided some electoral insulation from the popular mood. Senators would be elected for six-year terms. Their terms would be staggered, with only one-third of the membership up for election under one single set of circumstances and pressures. And they would be chosen by their state legislatures. This latter piece of insulation was removed—gradually in practice, and formally in 1913—when the Seventeenth Amendment to the Constitution mandated the popular election of senators.

The staggered six-year terms still provide some continuity. But the longevity of senators has become every bit as tenuous—in fact, more so—at the hands of the electorate as that of House members. And such "coolness" as Congress exhibits is more the result of the two-chamber lawmaking sequence than of any especially dispassionate steadiness on the part of the Senate.

In the expectation, however, that the Senate would be a calm, deliberative body, the Framers gave to the Senate a set of special policy prerogatives. In foreign policy, they granted the Senate the power to ratify treaties and to confirm the appointment of ambassadors. The wise and stable Senate, they believed, would be the best guardian of the nation's reputation in foreign affairs. They also bestowed on the Senate the power of "advice and consent" to presidential nominations of top-level executive department officials and to the federal judiciary. These various provisions placed the Senate uniquely in a position to exercise an extra increment of influence over the executive and judicial branches.

Each of these four basic institutional features—statewide constituency, small size, six-year terms, special policy prerogatives—differentiates the Senate from the House of Representatives. Taken together, they constitute the starting point for any understanding of the Senate; all of the characteristic properties or behaviors now associated with the modern Senate are the derivatives of one or more of the original four.

Constituency makeup and small size combine, for example, to make the Senate a uniquely favorable arena for small states to band together to protect their common interests. At various points in U.S. history, slave states in the South, agricultural states in the Midwest, and water-poor states in the Far West have relied upon their disproportionate voting strength in the Senate to protect their interests. But more broadly and more importantly, today the Senate's special body of internal rules and procedures grants the same institutional advantages to all sorts of minority interests and diverse viewpoints—provided only that some senator gives voice to them.

For this development, the small size of the Senate has been crucial. It permitted the early acceptance of a less formal, more flexible set of rules than was possible in the larger House—rules conferring no prerogatives upon a presiding officer, no previous question rule to shut off debate, no germaneness rule to prevent irrelevant or pernicious attachments to legislation. Senate party leaders have far fewer procedural resources with which to promote the orderly processing of business than do their counterparts in the House. Taken together, these procedural features guarantee individual senators a high degree of independence in advancing their personal goals.

Above all, the Senate's rules preserve the right of every individual senator or small group of senators to talk at length and at will—to filibuster—so as to stop all activity and kill legislation they oppose. It was not until 1914 that the Senate imposed upon itself a cloture rule to make it possible to stop debate. But the procedures related to its imposition, and the extra majority (now three-fifths of the membership) required to invoke it, have made cloture difficult to carry out.

The cloture rule, as it protects the right of every individual senator to talk or threaten to talk or to exact a price for silence, is the quintessential procedural bulwark of the modern Senate. It is every member's ultimate weapon. And its presence has necessitated a whole series of ad hoc devices to keep Senate business flowing—unanimous consent agreements and multitrack scheduling, for example. The Framers of the Constitution got what they wanted—a deliberative legislative body. But subsequent procedural developments within their small-sized, state-based institution have sometimes produced deliberation unto obstructionism unto paralysis.

Media Spotlight on the Senate.

A fifth distinctive feature of the Senate—institutional in its impact and permanence—must be added to the original four. It is the amount and the kind of media attention that senators attract. By every measure, senators command more media attention than House members—more on the nightly newscasts, more in the national press, more during their campaigns at home, and more on weekend talk shows in Washington. Two years after the House had begun to televise its floor proceedings, the Senate in 1986 followed suit. Given the advent of a new communications technology that has made possible mass media attention to public figures, the phenomenon of media attention to senators and their business can be seen as a derivative of the four basic features previously discussed.

As a matter of logistics, the relatively small size of the body makes it more tempting, if not easier, for reporters to cover than the House. Furthermore, in the smaller body personalities stand out, and the media—especially television—prefer to deal with personalities rather than with the numerology of coalition building so essential to understanding the House. A senator's six-year term gives members of the press an added incentive to invest their time in establishing contacts with the chamber's newcomers.

Because of their huge work load and small numbers, senators tend to spread themselves across numerous committees, subcommittees, and policy areas. While this means that they specialize less than House members, it also means they are better prepared to talk to the press about a wide range of subjects. And the Washington-based press has an insatiable appetite for commentary on all subjects of the moment. In addition, their statewide constituencies have forced most senators to concern themselves with the fullest range of national policy problems. Their election campaigns, too, tend to demand more of an emphasis on national policy matters than do House campaigns.

Because of their huge work load and small numbers, senators tend to spread themselves across numerous committees, subcommittees, and policy areas.

Finally, by virtue of their special prerogatives, senators get propelled into the national spotlight whenever foreign policy matters or presidential appointments are matters of dispute. From Woodrow Wilson and the Versailles treaty or Lyndon B. Johnson and Vietnam on the foreign policy side, to Ronald Reagan and Robert Bork or George Bush and Clarence Thomas on the nominations side, the Senate has frequently found itself at the center of national controversy. Some such controversies have been highly partisan, some not. But in all cases, Senate investigations, debates, and votes have been widely publicized and intensively followed. And a few senators have become prominent media figures in the process.

This media-Senate attraction is fully mutual. From the senator's point of view, media attention is a resource to manipulate in order to achieve their own goals. Most of them want media attention and they work hard to get it. They hire staff people whose only job is to get it for them. Most prominent among the publicity seekers are senators with presidential or vice presidential ambitions. For almost all of its history, the Senate has been a major incubator of presidential candidacies. Ambitions for higher office can always be found in various stages of development within the Senate, most actively among members of whichever party lacks an incumbent president eligible for reelection.

As presidential nominations have become tied increasingly to public participation in primaries, media attention has become the indispensable ingredient of senatorial success in pursuit of higher office ambitions. Estes Kefauver pioneered this path by parlaying his televised hearings on organized crime into a string of primary victories in 1956. In every election since, one or more senators have turned media attention into a bid for the presidential nomination. Typically, this attention comes by way of some highly publicized senatorial performance (Howard H. Baker, Edward M. Kennedy), a leadership role in the senatorial party (Lyndon B. Johnson, Bob Dole), or association in the Senate with an issue of absorbing national concern (Barry Goldwater, George McGovern).

The opportunity to publicize one's issue positions and to be recognized by the media on a given issue is, of course, available to all senators as they work to fulfill other personal goals—reelection, making good policy, or developing a reputation for effectiveness in the Senate. Committee or subcommittee chairmanships and party leadership positions provide the greatest opportunities in this respect. At any point in time, therefore, a minority of senators will figure prominently in the public eye. Their presence, as it focuses the media's attention on the Senate, enhances the opportunity for other members to take their turn in the spotlight.

THE CHANGING SENATE. Our addition of media attention to the four original features of the institution indicates that the Senate has changed as the national context has changed. Historians have charted its ups and downs as a national force. In the earliest years, it struggled to achieve functional parity with the House. And in the pre-Civil War period, it enjoyed what has been called its "golden era," the time when the institution best lived up to the Framers' idea of a deliberative assembly. In that time of national peril, conflicting philosophies and strategies were articulated and debated, at length and single-mindedly, by senators of exceptional talent. Their ability has been memorialized by their successors, with John C. Calhoun, Henry Clay, and Daniel Webster being named by the Senate as three of its five "outstanding senators."

While there is, among today's senators, some nostalgia for that era of great debate—and occasional traces of the deliberative impulse—the modern Senate does not command any such superlatives. But it has maintained its parity within the bicameral system. As such, it remains the most powerful second legislative chamber in the world.

In the contemporary period, there have been two dominant characterizations of the Senate as an institution. The Senate of the 1950s and 1960s has been described in largely *communitarian* terms—as a club or small town, as self-contained, self-regulating, inward looking. The Senate of the 1970s and 1980s has been described in largely *individualistic* terms—as a gathering of prima donnas or movie stars, as entrepreneurial, publicity seeking, outward looking. The differences are, of course, matters of degree. But they are measurable. And they are both distinctively senatorial descriptions. Neither would serve very well to describe the House.

In the communitarian Senate, behavior was heavily influenced by informal, member-to-member understandings about apprenticeship for newcomers, committee-based specialization for everyone, and self-restraint in the use of procedural advantages for obstructive purposes on the Senate floor. These norms helped to restrict participation, regulate the internal distribution of influence, and dampen internal conflict. They made members sensitive to the benefits of collegial approval and, thereby, helped to buffer and modulate the divisive impact of external influences. It was an arrangement that tended to keep the legislative policy agenda small, and for that reason, it was kept in place by policy conservatives.

In the individualistic Senate, the basic understanding among members is that everyone plays whenever, wherever, and however he or she wishes. And all senators now have the necessary resources to become players. Every senator holds a position of leadership on at least one subcommittee, in addition to which the jurisdictional lines separating subcommittees are more easily breached. Senate staffs, which exploded in size from 1,115 in 1957 to 3,593 in 1979, have made possible a greater breadth of participation and a greater independence for each senator. And publicity opportunities have, as noted, increased apace. With these resources at hand, collegial approval has lost the importance it once had. Senators who wish to pursue reputations and cultivate constituencies outside the Senate are enabled and encouraged to do so.

This atomized and hyperactive Senate is much more difficult to lead than the more collegial one that preceded it, and recent majority leaders have found it impossible to duplicate the 1950s success of Johnson. The

Senate floor, the special province of the party leadership, has become more important as a decision-making arena and, at the same time, a more unruly cockpit. The decline of self-restraint in exploiting Senate rules for individual or partisan advantage is symbolic of the institutional change that has taken place in the last quarter of a century.

This change can be explained as the indirect result of changes in the external context and as the direct result of changes in Senate membership. Among the changes in context that had indirect effects, we would include: a change in the policy agenda that brought issues like civil rights, environmentalism, consumerism, and women's rights to the fore; an explosion of private special interest groups battling for or against these causes; the revolution in communications and the onset of public relations politics; the Watergate scandal and the resulting clamor for openness in government; the decline of party organizational influence in controlling nominations and the subsequent rise of self-starting candidates; and the increased costs of electioneering and the nationalization of campaign financing. Taken together, these changes encouraged greater issue activism and more highly personalized coalition-building methods both electorally and legislatively.

The Senate remains an ever-changing institution within an ever-changing context.

More directly, however, the Senate changed when new members were elected to it, bringing with them from the outside new policy commitments and new values with regard to their participation in policymaking. The modern turning point was the Senate election of 1958, which brought an especially large cohort of activist, liberal Democrats into the chamber. It took several more elections, bringing in some activist Republicans as well as Democrats, plus the sixteen years of benign, egalitarian leadership by Mike Mansfield (1961–1977), to make the individualistic pattern secure and to register—as in the field of civil rights—some distinctive changes in national policy.

Within the constraints fixed by its five basic institutional features, we can expect the Senate to change whenever new, politically relevant external conditions arise and whenever elections produce a new group of senators large enough and committed enough to make changes in chamber procedures or policies. The Senate remains distinctive and identifiable in its core characteristics. But it also remains an ever-changing institution within an ever-changing context.

[See also (II) Appointment Power, Treaty-making Power, Vice President.]

BIBLIOGRAPHY

Baker, Ross. *Friend and Foe in the U.S. Senate.* 1980.

Byrd, Robert C. *The Senate, 1789–1989: Addresses on the History of the United States Senate.* 2 vols. 1988, 1991.

Evans, Lawrence. *Leadership in Committee: A Comparative Analysis of Leadership Behavior in the U.S. Senate.* 1991.

Fenno, Richard. *The United States Senate: A Bicameral Perspective.* 1982.

Hibbing, John, ed. *The Changing World of the U.S. Senate.* 1990.

Matthews, Donald. *U.S. Senators and Their World.* 1960.

Sinclair, Barbara. *The Transformation of the United States Senate.* 1989.

– RICHARD F. FENNO, JR.

Daily Sessions of the Senate

Prior to the sound of the bells that signal the start of a Senate session, reporters huddle around the majority leader's desk on the Senate floor in the morning ritual known as the dug-out to receive his briefing on that day's anticipated floor action. The Senate is then called to order by its presiding officer, officially the vice president of the United States, but in his frequent absence, the president pro tempore. That position is held by the most senior majority-party senator, although in his absence other majority-party senators also serve as presiding officer, rotating approximately every hour throughout the day.

After the prayer offered by the Senate chaplain, the majority leader and minority leader each receive ten minutes of "leader time." The majority leader usually announces the planned agenda for the day during his allotment of time; the minority leader may react to the agenda or may address other pertinent legislative or political issues. Sometimes the leaders reserve their time for use later in the day or yield it to other senators.

The Senate will then normally go into a period of "morning business," during which bills are introduced, committee reports are filed, messages are received, and senators may be granted unanimous consent to give "morning business speeches," usually five minutes in length, on any topic they wish. The duration of the morning business period on any given day varies widely, ranging from a few minutes to an hour or more.

The Senate will then take up a piece of legislation or an item of executive business, such as a nomination or a treaty. Whether legislative or executive business, the Senate must first agree to call a matter up before the matter can receive consideration. This is usually done through prior negotiation, and then agreed to by the unanimous consent of all present on the floor at the time. Alternatively, when negotiations to obtain unanimous consent to take up the matter have failed, the majority leader may make a motion to proceed to the consideration of a bill or executive item. The motion to proceed may precipitate extensive debate, even a filibuster, if the measure itself is strongly opposed. If a vote does occur on the motion to proceed, a simple majority suffices for adoption.

Once a measure is before the Senate, the debate on the legislation and the amendments that may be offered to it are normally unlimited. Except in certain parliamentary circumstances, amendments to a bill in the Senate need not be relevant, or germane, to the content of the bill. Therefore, it is usually difficult to predict the length of time the Senate will spend in consideration of a specific measure. The majority and minority leaders strive to mitigate this uncertainty by negotiating unanimous consent agreements that restrict the debate time and structure the number and nature of amendments to be offered. These agreements, commonly referred to as "u.c." or "time" agreements, provide the blueprint for a bill's consideration.

When legislation is considered on the Senate floor without a unanimous consent agreement, attempts might be made during its consideration to negotiate terms for the remainder of the debate and amending process. Most often these negotiations take place in the cloakrooms or in the leaders' offices. Quorum calls are used to permit senators to leave the floor and participate in the negotiations. The clerk of the Senate reads the call of the roll quite slowly, an indicator that the purpose of the quorum call is not to command the actual presence of a majority of Senators on the floor, but rather to suspend formal action while the process continues informally, off the floor. It is a common pattern to have the Senate's proceedings punctuated with the interruption of frequent quorum calls. When senators are ready to resume floor action, the quorum call is "rescinded" or withdrawn.

Voting on final passage of a bill or an amendment can either be by the "yeas and nays" or by voice vote. If the yeas and nays are ordered, the clerk of the Senate reads each senator's name in alphabetical order and each vote is recorded. In a voice vote, the judgment of the chair determines the outcome, and no names or positions are recorded.

No day in the Senate is truly typical. The Senate may work on one bill for most of a day and well into the evening, it may temporarily suspend a bill's consideration and turn to another piece of legislation, or it may switch back and forth among several measures during the same day. This flexibility reflects the Senate's emphasis on arranging business through informal negotiations that can accommodate the schedules of the senators who are key to the legislation under consideration. It also allows the opportunity to mediate political conflicts as they arise.

The Senate's floor schedule is also difficult to predict because each senator recognized to speak has the right to extend debate and keep the floor for as long as desired, thus preventing or delaying a vote. Senators also enjoy the right to offer "non-germane" amendments. Known as "riders," such amendments allow a single senator to introduce subject matter for floor consideration, sometimes contrary to the wishes of the party leaders. Both extended debate (which may become filibusters) and non-germane amendments are an integral part of the Senate's tradition of offering individual senators considerable procedural autonomy.

After the vote on final passage of the measure, or after the majority leader in consultation with the minority leader has concluded that no more progress can be made on legislation that day, the Senate turns to a series of routine actions known as the wrap-up. This might include a recitation of a series of unanimous consent requests for minor internal procedural arrangements (e.g., permission for committees to meet while the Senate is in session). Noncontroversial bills that have been cleared for passage through both party cloakrooms then are called off the calendar by the clerk of the Senate, and passed by unanimous consent or voice vote, usually with little or no debate. Finally, a motion is made by the majority leader or his designee to either recess or adjourn the Senate until its next scheduled meeting time, thus ending the daily session.

[See also (II) Vice President.]

BIBLIOGRAPHY

Congressional Quarterly Inc. *How Congress Works.* 2d ed. 1991.

Green, Alan. *Gavel to Gavel. A Guide to the Televised Proceedings of Congress.* 1991.

Oleszek, Walter J. *Congressional Procedures and the Policy Process.* 1989. Pp. 177–238.

– ILONA B. NICKELS

Senate Rules and Procedures

The U.S. Senate has forty-two standing rules that have been adopted to control its day-to-day functions. These brief rules are supplemented by thousands of precedents filling several dozen volumes and dating back to the 1800s. In current practice, the rules are often waived by unanimous consent. These unanimous consent agreements themselves, however, rely on the precedents for interpretation. As a result, the actions that the Senate has previously taken are often more important than the actual rules in determining procedure.

Moreover, the evolution of the positions of majority and minority leaders, a twentieth-century development, has made the rules less relevant. Because they have the prerogative of introducing unanimous consent agreements, these leaders, especially the majority leader, set the pace and course of floor action in the Senate. Despite this centralization of power, a single senator who knows the rules of the Senate and chooses to use them can significantly affect Senate action.

HISTORY OF THE RULES. In April 1789, one day after a quorum of the Senate had first been achieved, a special committee to prepare a system of rules was created. The committee was composed of some of the new Senate's most experienced legislators: one committee member, Richard Henry Lee of Virginia, had been president of the Continental Congress; another, Caleb Strong of Massachusetts, had been a delegate to the Constitutional Convention.

The twenty "standing rules" finally adopted by the Senate in 1789 were similar to the 1778 rules of the Continental Congress. Debate over the rules was intense. William Maclay of Pennsylvania, for instance, proposed a rule that would have allowed four senators to force a vote on any question on which debate was becoming "tedious." The Senate rejected this course, moving instead toward a set of rules allowing unlimited debate.

The Senate has remained organized with its rules in force without interruption since 1789. Because only a third of the Senate is newly elected every two years, it is considered a continuing body whose rules require no readoption from one Congress to the next. As a result the Senate's standing rules have been subjected to fewer and less dramatic changes over time than have the House rules, which have been held not binding on a newly elected House unless readopted, frequently with certain revisions—usually but not always a perfunctory procedure.

The person who had the most influence on Senate rules and procedures was Thomas Jefferson of Virginia. As vice president of the United States, Jefferson served also as president of the Senate (1797–1801), and it fell to him to interpret the newly adopted standing rules. He created a manual of precedents, *The Manual of Parliamentary Practice,* to guide the Senate in implementing the rules. His publication, which is still used today, contained fifty-three sections covering the range of Senate activities, from the order of business to motions for debate, and even included information on such esoteric areas as impeachment. Jefferson prefaced his manual with the following observation: "It is much more material that there be a rule to go by than what that rule is. . . . It is very material that order, decency, and regularity be preserved in a dignified public body."

During the nineteenth century, the Senate continued to revise and expand its rules, recodifying them in 1806, 1820, 1828, 1868, 1877, and 1884. The Senate did not adopt another new codification until 1979, when it incorporated many provisions of the legislative reorganization acts of 1946 and 1970 into its rules. One of the primary thrusts of the 1979 recodification was to provide detailed new provisions that took into account the greatly expanded Senate committee structure.

The Senate's standing rules have been subjected to fewer and less dramatic changes over time than the House rules.

THE SENATE AS A DELIBERATIVE BODY. Through all their changes and permutations, the rules have always been designed, first and foremost, to allow the Senate to be a deliberative body. The rules protect the rights of the minority to debate and delay. Many bills have been killed through the use of the filibuster—that is, the technique of debating a bill endlessly to prevent its coming to a vote. Prior to the adoption, in 1917, of Rule XXII, which allows two-thirds of the Senate to invoke cloture or limit debate, a single senator could filibuster and defeat a bill. Despite this change in the rules, a minority of the Senate—two-fifths of its members—can still prevent a majority from working its will. This emphasis on minority rights differentiates the Senate rules from those of the House of Representatives, where a simple majority of the members can vote to end debate.

INTERPRETING RULES AND PRECEDENTS. As the rules and precedents of the Senate became more complex, the Senate established the office of parliamentarian. Charles L. Watkins was named the first parliamentarian in 1937; he served until 1964. The Senate parliamentarian is charged with maintaining the precedents and advising the chair on procedural matters. The parliamentarian sits below the presiding officer and whispers advice, which is then repeated by the chair. The parliamentarian is appointed by the secretary of the Senate after consultation with the majority leader.

COMMITTEE RULES AND PROCEDURES. The major change in the Senate rules in the second half of the twentieth century was the 1979 inclusion of many specific rules controlling committee activities. Among its other provisions, Rule XXVI allows the committees to adopt their own rules and procedures as long as they are consistent with the standing rules of the Senate. Rule XXVI has, however, only one enforceable stipulation involving committee procedures: the requirement that a physical quorum be present when any measure or matter is reported. Under the rule, the presence of such a quorum is "deemed to be a ratification by the Committee of all previous action." The presence of a quorum means that no point of order can be raised against the measure on the Senate floor based on any previous action by the committee. Thus, despite their detail, Rule XXVI and the committee rules themselves are nonbinding.

Committees usually have regular meeting days, but a committee may meet at the call of its chair or, at other times, on the request of a majority of its members. Matters on the committee calendar are usually the order of business during a committee meeting, but any matter within the committee's jurisdiction may be considered. Most committees have standing subcommittees to which they may refer pending bills. Ad hoc subcommittees are frequently appointed to study and report on particular bills or subjects of interest. The chairman, or some designated member of the committee, reports bills to the Senate, where they are placed on the Senate calendar of business unless unanimous consent is given for immediate consideration.

In practice, most committees reflect the interests and temperaments of the chairman, who is usually selected by virtue of seniority. The style of the chairman, rather than the rules, often establishes the procedures of the committee.

FLOOR PROCEDURES. Generally speaking, procedures on the Senate floor are controlled not by the rules but by the majority and minority leaders. Although designed to establish a regime for handling legislation, nominations, and treaties—the three major responsibilities of the Senate—the rules are routinely ignored. Instead, legislative business usually is considered under ad hoc unanimous consent agreements.

The majority and minority leaders implement and direct the Senate's legislative schedule and program. Most measures are passed on the call of the calendar or by unanimous consent procedure. The more significant and controversial bills are usually considered under a unanimous consent agreement limiting debate and controlling the introduction of amendments. These agreements allow the Senate to transact its business under rules that provide for unlimited debate.

First and second readings. The Senate rules require that, before passage, every bill and joint resolution must have three readings, each on a different legislative day. Two of these readings must occur before the bill or resolution is referred to committee. Bills are seldom read in full, however, since all bills and resolutions are available in printed form. These readings are most commonly dispensed with by unanimous consent. The requirement that readings occur on different legislative days is rarely invoked and usually only when there are procedural conflicts. This requirement, however, can still be forced on the Senate by a single senator. After the second reading of a bill, it is referred by the presiding officer to that standing committee that in his or her judgment has jurisdiction of the subject matter. The Senate rules require action by the joint leadership or unanimous consent to refer a bill jointly or sequentially to two or more committees.

Once a bill has been introduced or reported by a committee, it is placed on the Senate calendar. Placement on the calendar does not guarantee consideration by the full Senate, however, and this is the point where an understanding of the rules and procedure can be very significant. A bill may be brought to the floor by a simple majority vote if it has been on the calendar for one legislative day. Again, it is the majority leader who normally makes the motion to proceed to consideration of a bill. Since the motion to proceed is a debatable motion, it is usually made after negotiation with possible opponents and when a unanimous consent agreement has been successfully formulated.

On very controversial matters, the Senate frequently has to resort to cloture, or limiting debate, to work its will. Under Rule XXII, three-fifths of the Senate (sixty senators) can vote to limit debate. Once cloture is invoked, debate is limited to one hour for each senator, with a maximum of thirty hours unless that time limit is increased by a three-fifths vote.

Amendments. Once a bill or resolution is before the Senate, it is subject to amendment, both by the committee reporting it and by individual senators. With one exception, committee amendments take priority over those introduced by individual senators and are considered in the order they appear in the printed copy of the measure before the Senate. Once the committee amendments have been disposed of, any senator may propose amendments to any part of the bill not already amended. While such an amendment (called an amendment in the first degree) is pending, an amendment to that amendment (an amendment in the second degree) is in order. Much of the action on controversial bills involves the amending process, and the procedure can be very technical, involving amendments in the first and second degree. Each of these procedures has its own set of rules and governing precedents, which differ from those of the House of Representatives. Moreover, there are special procedures for amendments to certain types of bills—general appropriations and budget bills, for example. Nongermane amendments are prohibited in certain cases—for example, general appropriations bills, bills upon which cloture has been voted, and concurrent resolutions considered under the Congressional Budget and Impoundment Control Act of 1974. Otherwise, there is no requirement of germaneness.

Most bills are passed by a voice vote only, although any senator can request a roll-call vote.

In most instances proposed amendments need not be germane to pending legislation. The right of every senator to offer nongermane amendments, except as noted above or unless constrained by a unanimous consent agreement, has long been a distinguishing feature of Senate procedure. It provides individual senators, or groups of senators, a range of options through the amending process. A senator may introduce nongermane amendments to (1) alter dramatically or effectively kill legislation proposed by a committee, (2) bypass committees entirely by bringing new issues directly before the Senate, or (3) prolong debate and thus deter a final vote as a statement of opposition to pending legislation.

Third reading and vote. When all committee amendments and individual floor amendments have been disposed of, a bill is ordered "engrossed" and is read for a third time. This reading is by title only. The senators then vote on the bill, which is passed by majority vote. Even at this point, senators can use certain procedures to kill or avoid further proceedings on a bill. For example, at any time before final passage, a bill can be "laid on the table," or postponed indefinitely. It can be referred back to committee (or to another committee). It can even be displaced by a majority vote to move action to another bill.

Most bills are passed by a voice vote only, although any senator can request a roll-call vote. A roll-call vote is taken if one-fifth of the senators demand it. Even after passage of a bill, a senator who voted with the majority or did not vote can move to "reconsider" the bill. A majority vote determines questions of reconsideration. It is extremely unusual for the Senate to reconsider a vote, and these motions are routinely tabled by unanimous consent.

UNFINISHED BUSINESS. Congress measures itself by *sessions* of varying duration, up to one year, and *Congresses,* which last for two years. Bills and resolutions started on their way to enactment but left unfinished at the end of one session of a Congress are carried over to the next session. Bills pending at the end of a final session of a Congress, however, do not carry over and must be reintroduced if they are to be considered again.

EXECUTIVE MATTERS. In addition to its legislative responsibilities, the Senate is charged with the executive functions of providing "advice and consent" on nominations and treaties. These functions are handled separately from legislative business, and executive business is governed by unique rules and procedures.

Treaties. To discuss treaties, the Senate moves into executive session—a special period during which the Senate considers those matters that it shares only with the executive branch of government and not with the House of Representatives. The Senate may decide to consider a treaty in closed or secret session, and it has sometimes done so when classified material was being discussed. Most often, however, treaties are considered in open session.

Rule XXX, which governs the procedures involving treaties, requires a two-thirds majority to ratify a treaty. Unlike ordinary legislation and nominations, treaties do not die at the end of a Congress. For example, the Genocide treaty was submitted by President Harry S Truman in 1949 and remained before the Senate for thirty-seven years until it was finally ratified in 1986.

Nominations. A presidential nomination requiring advice and consent must be approved by a majority vote of the Senate. After a nomination is received, it is referred to the appropriate committee, which holds hearings and votes to recommend or reject confirmation. If approved by the committee, the nomination is reported back to the Senate for debate and vote. If the nomination is confirmed, a resolution of confirmation is transmitted to the White House and the appointment is then signed by the president.

Presidential nominations may be made during Senate recesses. The Constitution authorizes the president to "fill up" vacancies that may occur during such recesses "by granting Commissions which shall expire at the end of the next session." Such nominations are thus valid only for the current session of the Senate and must be renewed again with full advice and consent when the session ends. The use of recess appointments to the Supreme Court troubled senators enough that on 29 August 1960 they passed a sense of the Senate resolution stating that "such appointments . . . should not be made except under unusual circumstances and for the purpose of preventing or ending a demonstrable breakdown in the administration of the Court's business."

Unlike treaties, nominations that are not acted on in a session die and must be resubmitted to the Senate at the next session. Nominations that are not confirmed before a recess of more than thirty days are also returned to the president and must be resubmitted.

[See also (II) Appointment Power.]

BIBLIOGRAPHY

Haynes, George H. *The Senate of the United States: Its History and Practice.* 1938.

Oleszek, Walter J. *Congressional Procedures and the Policy Process.* 2d ed. 1984.

Rothman, David J. *Politics and Power: The United States Senate, 1869–1901.* 1966.

Tiefer, Charles. *Congressional Practice and Procedure.* 1989.

U.S. Senate Committee on Rules and Administration. *Rules and Manual of the United States Senate.* 102d Cong., 1st sess., 1992. S. Doc. 102-1.

U.S. Senate. *Senate Procedure, Precedents, and Practices,* by Floyd M. Riddick. 97th Cong., 1st sess., 1981. S. Doc. 97-2.

Wilson, Woodrow. *Congressional Government.* 1885.

– ROBERT B. DOVE

SENIORITY

The rank of a member of Congress is determined by seniority. Although seniority is not part of formal chamber or party rules, it is a well-established tradition in both houses of Congress. Rank in the House or Senate chamber is known as *chamber seniority;* rank on a committee—based on length of service on that panel—is called *committee seniority.*

CHAMBER SENIORITY. The formal starting date of a member's service—usually 3 January, the official beginning of a new Congress—determines his or her chamber seniority. When a senator fills an unexpired term, the date of appointment, certification, or swearing in determines the official date. In the House, the date of the new member's election determines the starting date.

For members sworn in on the same date, prior experience is a factor in determining seniority. In the Senate, prior Senate, House, and gubernatorial service, in that order, count toward seniority. The most senior member of the Senate of the majority party is usually designated the president pro tempore. In the House, only prior House service counts toward seniority. In both chambers, if members still have equal rank, seniority is determined by listing members alphabetically. Until 1980, a senator could gain several days' seniority if his or her predecessor resigned before the end of his or her term and the new member was then sworn in early. In that year, both parties eliminated the practice of giving these new senators an edge in seniority for obtaining committee assignments.

Chamber seniority is important in bidding for room assignments, gaining access to patronage appointments, and, in the House, floor recognition. Seniority is also vital to the committee assignment process and therefore to the selection of committee and subcommittee chairmen.

COMMITTEE SENIORITY. Most scholars agree that committee seniority became evident in the Senate by the 1840s, seems to have been followed more strictly in both chambers after the Civil War, and was firmly entrenched in the House by 1910. Prior to 1840, seniority was relatively unimportant, in part because of the high turnover among members that reflected a widely held belief in the concept of the "citizen legislator" (espoused since the earliest days of the nation) as well as the difficulty in traveling to and staying in Washington, D.C., during the congressional session and the relative weakness of political parties. After the Civil War, however, tenure became longer as members began making legislative service a career and political parties gained increased influence. Accordingly, the seniority system gained strength, a development that reflected also the evolution of committees as powerful and autonomous entities and the concomitant growing importance of committee chairmen.

In the House, the year 1910 marks an entrenchment of the seniority system, in part related to the overthrow of Speaker Joseph G. Cannon (R-Ill.). Members made it clear that they wanted stronger adherence to seniority in the selection of committee chairmen, as opposed to allowing the Speaker continued wide discretion in making such appointments. Speaker Cannon, especially, had often bypassed more senior members in selecting committee chairmen in order to appoint members who agreed with his conservative philosophy.

Despite growing adherence to the system, there were some major departures from seniority during its early period in both the House and the Senate. For example, in 1859, Sen. Stephen A. Douglas (D-Ill.) was removed as chairman of the Committee on Territories when he refused to support President James Buchanan on the issue of slavery in the territories. In 1866, three Senate Republican committee chairmen were dropped to the bottom of their committees for failing to vote with the Radical Republicans on overriding a presidential veto of a civil rights bill. In 1871, Sen. Charles Sumner (R-Mass.) was removed as chairman of the Committee on Foreign Relations because of his disagreement with President Ulysses S. Grant over annexation of the Dominican Republic. In 1913, Sen. Benjamin R. Tillman (D-S.C.) was denied the chairmanship of the Appropriations Committee.

In 1882, Sen. Wilkinson Call (D-Fla.) made an unsuccessful attempt to limit members to service on one major committee. In 1919, following the lead of former senator Call, Sen. George W. Norris (R-Nebr.), who earlier had led the revolt in the House against Speaker Cannon, unsuccessfully sought to limit members to seats on two major committees. In 1924, with Republicans in the majority, Sen. Albert B. Cummins (R-Iowa) lost the chairmanship of the Interstate Commerce Committee because he was also president pro tempore. The next-ranking Republican, Robert M. La Follette of Wisconsin, was also passed over. In a rare move, the chairmanship was granted to Democrat Ellison D. Smith (S.C.). In 1925, Rep. John M. Nelson (R-Wis.), chairman of the House Committee on Elections; Rep. Florian Lampert (R-Wis.), chairman of the Committee on Patents; and nine other Wisconsin members were stripped of their seniority and dropped to the bottom of their committees or moved to less influential committees for supporting La Follette's 1924 Progressive Party presidential bid.

With the adoption of the Legislative Reorganization Act of 1946, some committees were abolished or consolidated, giving some of the surviving committees wider jurisdictions. Accordingly, committee chairmen gained greater power and authority. In addition, in the years following World War II, lower turnover among members strengthened the already powerful seniority system, in particular by entrenching Democratic committee chairmen from southern states.

The first assault on the seniority system occurred in the Senate, when in 1953 the Democrats enacted the Johnson Rule (named after Minority Leader Lyndon B. Johnson of Texas), which provided that all Democratic senators be given a seat on a major committee before any Democrat be assigned a second seat on a major committee. The Republican conference informally adopted the Johnson Rule in 1959 and formally adopted it in 1965.

Despite the strong hold of the seniority system, exceptions to it continued to be made. For example, in 1965, the House Democratic caucus censured and stripped of seniority Representatives John Bell Williams of Mississippi and Albert W. Watson of South Carolina for having supported Republican presidential nominee Barry Goldwater the previous year. Both were dropped to the bottom of their committees. For Representative Williams, who ranked second on the Commerce Committee and fifth on the District of Columbia Committee, it was a severe blow.

In 1967, following prolonged ethical and legal battles, the House excluded Rep. Adam Clayton Powell, Jr. (D-N.Y.), from the 90th Congress. The following session, after winning reelection, Powell was seated in the House but was removed as chairman of the Education and Labor Committee and made the lowest-ranking Democrat on the panel.

In 1969, the Democratic caucus stripped Rep. John R. Rarick (La.) of his seniority on the Agriculture Committee for having supported third-party candidate George Wallace in his 1968 presidential bid. (Representative Rarick was the lowest-ranking member of the Agriculture Committee, so the impact was minimal.)

Despite the strong hold of the seniority system, exceptions to it continued to be made.

CHANGES IN THE SENIORITY SYSTEM. The 1970s saw numerous congressional reforms enacted. Many were aimed at decentralizing power to give the large influx of junior Democratic, often liberal, members more of a voice in the workings of their chambers. These new members targeted the seniority system because they believed that limiting its influence was one way they could quickly obtain greater power over the mostly southern and conservative committee chairmen. Electing chairmen by secret ballot and putting limits on the number of chairmanships a member could hold weakened the seniority system and held members more accountable to junior rank-and-file members. Most of the changes made during this period, and indeed after, were made to the respective party rules rather than to chamber rules, since party leaders believed that, were changes to seniority made through legislative vehicles, a bipartisan coalition could hinder the majority's control of the legislative agenda.

In 1970, the House rejected two floor amendments to the Legislative Reorganization Act of 1970 relating to the seniority system. By a teller vote of 160 to 73, the House rejected an amendment offered by Rep. Henry S. Reuss (D-Wis.) that provided that seniority need not be the sole criterion for the selection of chairmen. A second amendment, by Rep. Fred Schwengel (R-Iowa), was rejected 196 to 28. This amendment would have provided that chairmen be selected by committee majority members from among the three most senior members.

In 1971, House Democratic caucus rules were changed so that, first, the Committee on Committees (then composed of Democratic members of the Ways and Means Committee) could recommend chairmen regardless of seniority, and, second, no member could chair more than one legislative subcommittee. Obviously, the latter change especially affected more senior members, forcing them to relinquish such chairmanships. These changes were recommended by the newly formed Democratic caucus Committee on Organization, Study, and Review, created in 1970 to examine party organization and the seniority system. Simultaneously, House Republicans were changing Republican conference rules to allow votes on nominations for ranking minority members, thereby not relying solely on seniority. This change was the product of the Conference Task Force on Seniority headed by Rep. Barber B. Conable of New York.

In 1971 the Senate Democratic caucus modified its rules to allow a caucus meeting to be called by any member and to allow any senator to challenge any Steering Committee chairmanship nomination. In the same year, Senate Republican conference rules were modified to allow members to serve as ranking member on only one standing committee. Also in that year, both parties established panels to study the seniority system; three Democrats and five Republicans on their two respective partisan panels were charged with the task. On 16 March 1971, however, the Senate tabled a resolution—thereby effectively killing it—that would have permitted committee chairmen to be selected on bases other than seniority.

Notwithstanding the changes discussed, during the 92d Congress (1971–1973), all chairmanships and ranking minority slots in both chambers were held by the committees' senior members. In 1973, the Senate Republicans did make a change affecting the seniority system when they adopted a conference rule that permitted Republican members of each standing committee to elect the ranking Republican and not use seniority as the sole criterion for selection. During the first selection after the change, several senior Republicans were challenged, but none of the challenges were successful.

In October 1974, the House adopted numerous changes to the committee system recommended by the Select Committee on Committees (the Bolling Committee), as modified by the Democratic caucus Committee on Organization, Study, and Review (the Hansen Committee). One month later, with the election of 1974, the so-called Watergate class came to Congress, many of whom had their eyes set on changing the institution, especially the House. More than seventy new Democratic members were elected, and one of their first targets was the seniority system within the new committee structure.

In the House, several changes were made to party rules when the early organizational meetings (authorized by the Bolling Committee) convened to plan for the new Congress. By a relatively close vote of 147 to 116 Democratic caucus rules were changed to make all Appropriations Committee subcommittee chairmen subject to a full caucus vote rather than just a vote of Appropriations Committee Democrats, as had previously been the case. (In 1992, caucus rules were changed again to extend the same requirement to the Ways and Means Committee subcommittee chairmen). An attempt to authorize the caucus to vote on all subcommittee chairmen was, however, rejected. The caucus also voted to authorize a secret ballot on all chairmanship' nominations. Also, the new caucus rules allowed competitive nominations if the original Steering and Policy Committee's nominee were defeated.

Perhaps the greatest triumph of the incoming class was the overthrow of three sitting committee chairmen: William R. Poage (Tex.) of Agriculture, F. Edward Hébert (La.) of Armed Services, and Wright Patman (Tex.) of Banking and Currency, all of whom the younger members perceived as too old and out of touch. It is interesting to note that the next-senior members of the Agriculture and Armed Services committees became their chairmen, while the fourth-ranking Democrat, Henry Reuss of Wisconsin, assumed the chairmanship of the Banking Committee. It is also worth noting, and ironic, that the Armed Services chair went to Charles M. Price of Illinois, who lost his chairmanship ten years later to a member then seventh in seniority. Also in 1975, two House committee chairmen were denied subcommittee chairs despite their seniority. This instituted a trend toward removal of chairmen of committees, and especially subcommittees, without regard to seniority that continued to the early 1990s. Other recommendations considered by the caucus were defeated, including one to impose an age limit of seventy on committee chairmen and another to limit the length of time a member could serve as a committee chair to no more than three consecutive Congresses.

Seniority in most cases is still the preeminent factor in determining chairmanships.

The Senate in 1975 adopted no major-party rules changes expressly related to seniority. However, one Democratic change that year—allowing any senator to call a caucus meeting to challenge a nominated chairman—has been interpreted as making committee leaders more accountable.

In 1977, the Senate effected a major reorganization of its committee system that, among other things, opened up many more committee leadership slots to junior members. The committee and subcommittee assignment process was also altered by limiting the number of slots a member could occupy, further diluting the power of the seniority system. Also in 1977, a sitting

House Appropriations subcommittee chairman, Rep. Robert L. F. Sikes of Florida, who chaired the Military Construction Subcommittee, was rejected by the Democratic caucus, 189 to 93, following a House reprimand of him the previous year. Two years later, three subcommittee chairmen on the House Commerce and House Government Operations committees were removed and replaced by less senior members.

LATER DEVELOPMENTS. The reforms of the 1970s democratized the process for selecting committee chairmen and allowed the selection to be based on criteria other than just seniority. Nevertheless, seniority in most cases is still the preeminent factor in determining chairmanships.

Yet in the 1980s several additional nominations for House subcommittee chairman were rejected in favor of more junior members. For example, in 1981, two subcommittee chairmen were rejected and replaced by more junior members. The Senate, however, fervently adhered to the seniority system, even during the six years when the Republicans were in the majority. In 1987, Republican senators Richard G. Lugar of Indiana and Jesse Helms of North Carolina vied for the ranking minority slot on the Foreign Relations Committee. Senator Lugar had chaired Foreign Relations during the previous Congress, but, although they had joined the committee the same day, Senator Helms had served in the Senate longer than Senator Lugar. The position was therefore given to Helms despite the misgivings of many members concerning the latter's policy views.

A number of proposed new caucus rules were defeated during the 1980s. An attempt to impose an age limit of seventy for all chairmen was rejected, as was limiting service to three consecutive terms.

In 1985, Charles Price of Illinois, chairman of the House Armed Services Committee, was unseated at the Democratic caucus meeting. The seventh-ranked Democrat, Les Aspin of Wisconsin, won the chairmanship even though the caucus had nominated the next most senior Democrat, Charles E. Bennett of Florida.

In 1990, two House chairmen, Glenn M. Anderson (Calif.) of the Public Works and Transportation Committee and Frank Annunzio (Ill.) of the House Administration Committee, were deposed, in part because they were perceived as weak, ineffective leaders not protective enough of their committee's jurisdictional prerogatives. Each was replaced by the most senior Democrat available for service.

PROPOSED ADJUSTMENTS OR ALTERNATIVES. Over the years, adjustments in or alternatives to the seniority system have been proposed by organizations calling for reform, by individual members, and by congressional scholars. Some of the most notable options were presented by the liberal Democratic Study Group in 1970. They and others since have suggested the following changes to House rules and practices:

Use the seniority system to nominate chairmen, subject to majority approval by the party caucus (very similar to current practice but not always bowing to seniority)

Have the caucus elect committee chairmen from among the three most senior members of each committee

Authorize the Speaker to nominate chairmen, subject to approval of a majority of the caucus

Authorize the majority members of each committee to nominate the chairmen, subject to caucus approval

Authorize both majority and minority party members of each committee to select the chairmen, subject to full House approval

Establish a special committee to nominate chairmen, subject to majority caucus approval

Impose an age limitation on committee chairmen

Impose a limit on the number of years members can serve as chairmen

Rotate the chairmanships among the three most senior members every two years.

Despite continuing concerns about the seniority system and the recommended changes, Congress still retains it. Perhaps the views of Emanuel Celler (D-N.Y.), former dean of the House during the 92d Congress, are illustrative. He stated that the system survives in part because it is "the least objection-able of all systems for elevation of men to chairmanships."

[See also (I) Committees, article on Assignment of Members, Leadership.]

BIBLIOGRAPHY

Aboam, Michael, and Joseph Cooper. "The Rise of Seniority in the House of Representatives." *Polity* 1 (Fall 1968): 52–84.

Goodwin, George. "Seniority System in Congress." *American Political Science Review* 53 (1959): 412–436.

Hinckley, Barbara. *The Seniority System in Congress.* 1971.

Polsby, Nelson W., Miriam Gallaher, and Barry S. Rundquist. "Growth of the Seniority System in the U.S. House of Representatives." *American Political Science Review* 63 (1969):787–807.

Wolanin, Thomas R. "Committee Seniority and the Choice of House Subcommittee Chairmen: 80th–91st Congresses." *Journal of Politics* 36 (1974):687–702.

– JUDY SCHNEIDER

SESSIONS OF CONGRESS

Each Congress meets for a two-year period that coincides with the two-year terms of representatives. To satisfy its constitutional duty to meet at least once a year, Congress has divided its two-year life into sessions. Since adoption of the Twentieth Amendment in 1933, each session corresponds roughly to the calendar year.

Prior to 1934 the terms of the president, vice president, representatives, and senators started on 4 March

DATES OF CONGRESSIONAL SESSIONS

Congress	Session	Term
1st	1	4 March 1789–29 September 1789
	2	4 January 1790–12 August 1790
	3	6 December 1790–3 March 1791
2d	1	24 October 1791–8 May 1792
	2	5 November 1792–2 March 1793
3d	1	2 December 1793–9 June 1794
	2	3 November 1794–3 March 1795
4th	1	7 December 1795–1 June 1796
	2	5 December 1796–3 March 1797
5th	1	15 May 1797–10 July 1797
	2	13 November 1797–16 July 1798
	3	3 December 1798–3 March 1799
6th	1	2 December 1799–14 May 1800
	2	17 November 1800–3 March 1801
7th	1	7 December 1801–3 May 1802
	2	6 December 1802–3 March 1803
8th	1	17 October 1803–27 March 1804
	2	5 November 1804–3 March 1805
9th	1	2 December 1805–21 April 1806
	2	1 December 1806–3 March 1807
10th	1	26 October 1807–25 April 1808
	2	7 November 1808–3 March 1809
11th	1	22 May 1809–28 June 1809
	2	27 November 1809–1 May 1810
	3	3 December 1810–3 March 1811
12th	1	4 November 1811–6 July 1812
	2	2 November 1812–3 March 1813
13th	1	24 May 1813–2 August 1813
	2	6 December 1813–18 April 1814
	3	19 September 1814–3 March 1815
14th	1	4 December 1815–30 April 1816
	2	2 December 1816–3 March 1817
15th	1	1 December 1817–20 April 1818
	2	16 November 1818–3 March 1819
16th	1	6 December 1819–15 May 1820
	2	13 November 1820–3 March 1821
17th	1	3 December 1821–8 May 1822
	2	2 December 1822–3 March 1823
18th	1	1 December 1823–27 May 1824
	2	6 December 1824–3 March 1825
19th	1	5 December 1825–22 May 1826
	2	4 December 1826–3 March 1827
20th	1	3 December 1827–26 May 1828
	2	1 December 1828–3 March 1829
21st	1	7 December 1829–31 May 1830
	2	6 December 1830–3 March 1831
22d	1	5 December 1831–16 July 1832
	2	3 December 1832–2 March 1833
23d	1	2 December 1833–30 June 1834
	2	1 December 1834–3 March 1835
24th	1	7 December 1835–4 July 1836
	2	5 December 1836–3 March 1837
25th	1	4 September 1837–16 October 1837
	2	4 December 1837–9 July 1838
	3	3 December 1838–3 March 1839
26th	1	2 December 1839–21 July 1840
	2	7 December 1840–3 March 1841
27th	1	31 May 1841–13 September 1841
	2	6 December 1841–31 August 1842
	3	5 December 1842–3 March 1843
28th	1	4 December 1843–17 June 1844
	2	2 December 1844–3 March 1845
29th	1	1 December 1845–10 August 1846
	2	7 December 1846–3 March 1847
30th	1	6 December 1847–14 August 1848
	2	4 December 1848–3 March 1849
31st	1	3 December 1849–30 September 1850
	2	2 December 1850–3 March 1851
32d	1	1 December 1851–31 August 1852
	2	6 December 1852–3 March 1853
33d	1	5 December 1853–7 August 1854
	2	4 December 1854–3 March 1855
34th	1	3 December 1855–18 August 1856
	2	21 August 1856–30 August 1857
	3	1 December 1856–3 March 1857
35th	1	7 December 1857–14 June 1858
	2	6 December 1858–3 March 1859
36th	1	5 December 1859–25 June 1860
	2	3 December 1860–28 March 1861
37th	1	4 July 1861–6 August 1861
	2	2 December 1861–17 July 1862
	3	1 December 1862–3 March 1863
38th	1	7 December 1863–4 July 1864
	2	5 December 1864–3 March 1865
39th	1	4 December 1865–28 July 1866
	2	3 December 1866–3 March 1867
40th	1	4 March 1867–2 December 1867
	2	2 December 1867–10 November 1868
	3	7 December 1868–3 March 1869
41st	1	4 March 1869–10 April 1869
	2	6 December 1869–15 July 1870
	3	5 December 1870–3 March 1871
42d	1	4 March 1871–20 April 1871
	2	4 December 1871–10 June 1872
	3	2 December 1872–3 March 1873
43d	1	1 December 1873–23 June 1874
	2	7 December 1874–3 March 1875
44th	1	6 December 1875–15 August 1876
	2	4 December 1876–3 March 1877
45th	1	15 October 1877–3 December 1877
	2	3 December 1877–20 June 1878
	3	2 December 1878–3 March 1879
46th	1	18 March 1879–1 July 1879
	2	1 December 1879–16 June 1880
	3	6 December 1880–3 March 1881
47th	1	5 December 1881–8 August 1882
	2	4 December 1882–3 March 1883
48th	1	3 December 1883–7 July 1884
	2	1 December 1884–3 March 1885
49th	1	7 December 1885–5 August 1886
	2	6 December 1886–3 March 1887
50th	1	5 December 1887–20 October 1888
	2	3 December 1888–3 March 1889
51st	1	2 December 1889–1 October 1890
	2	1 December 1890–3 March 1891
52d	1	7 December 1891–5 August 1892
	2	5 December 1892–3 March 1893
53d	1	7 August 1893–3 November 1893
	2	4 December 1893–28 August 1894
	3	3 December 1894–3 March 1895

DATES OF CONGRESSIONAL SESSIONS *(CONTINUED)*

Congress	Session	Term
54th	1	2 December 1895–11 June 1896
	2	7 December 1896–3 March 1897
55th	1	15 March 1897–24 July 1897
	2	6 December 1897–8 July 1898
	3	5 December 1898–3 March 1899
56th	1	4 December 1899–7 June 1900
	2	3 December 1900–3 March 1901
57th	1	2 December 1901–1 July 1902
	2	1 December 1902–3 March 1903
58th	1	9 November 1903–7 December 1903
	2	7 December 1903–28 April 1904
	3	5 December 1904–3 March 1905
59th	1	4 December 1905–30 June 1906
	2	3 December 1906–3 March 1907
60th	1	2 December 1907–30 May 1908
	2	7 December 1908–3 March 1909
61st	1	15 March 1909–5 August 1909
	2	6 December 1909–25 June 1910
	3	5 December 1910–3 March 1911
62d	1	4 April 1911–22 August 1911
	2	4 December 1911–26 August 1912
	3	2 December 1912–3 March 1913
63d	1	7 April 1913–1 December 1913
	2	1 December 1913–24 October 1914
	3	7 December 1914–3 March 1915
64th	1	6 December 1915–8 September 1916
	2	4 December 1916–3 March 1917
65th	1	2 April 1917–6 October 1917
	2	3 December 1917–21 November 1918
	3	2 December 1918–3 March 1919
66th	1	19 May 1919–19 November 1919
	2	1 December 1919–5 June 1920
	3	6 December 1920–3 March 1921
67th	1	11 April 1921–23 November 1921
	2	5 December 1921–22 September 1922
	3	20 November 1922–4 December 1922
	4	4 December 1922–3 March 1923
68th	1	3 December 1923–7 June 1924
	2	1 December 1924–3 March 1925
69th	1	7 December 1925–3 July 1926
	2	6 December 1926–3 March 1927
70th	1	5 December 1927–29 May 1928
	2	3 December 1928–3 March 1929
71st	1	15 April 1929–22 November 1929
	2	2 December 1929–3 July 1930
	3	1 December 1930–3 March 1931
72d	1	7 December 1931–16 July 1932
	2	5 December 1932–3 March 1933
73d	1	9 March 1933–15 June 1933
	2	3 January 1934–18 June 1934
74th	1	3 January 1935–26 August 1935
	2	3 January 1936–20 June 1936
75th	1	5 January 1937–21 August 1937
	2	15 November 1937–21 December 1937
	3	3 January 1938–16 June 1938
76th	1	3 January 1939–5 August 1939
	2	21 September 1939–3 November 1939
	3	3 January 1940–3 January 1941
77th	1	3 January 1941–2 January 1942
	2	5 January 1942–16 December 1942
78th	1	6 January 1943–21 December 1943
	2	10 January 1944–19 December 1944
79th	1	3 January 1945–21 December 1945
	2	14 January 1946–2 August 1946
80th	1	3 January 1947–19 December 1947
	2	6 January 1948–31 December 1948
81st	1	3 January 1949–19 October 1949
	2	3 January 1950–2 January 1951
82d	1	3 January 1951–20 October 1951
	2	8 January 1952–7 July 1952
83d	1	3 January 1953–3 August 1953
	2	6 January 1954–2 December 1954
84th	1	5 January 1955–2 August 1955
	2	3 January 1956–27 July 1956
85th	1	3 January 1957–30 August 1957
	2	7 January 1958–24 August 1958
86th	1	7 January 1959–15 September 1959
	2	6 January 1960–1 September 1960
87th	1	3 January 1961–27 September 1961
	2	10 January 1962–13 October 1962
88th	1	9 January 1963–30 December 1963
	2	7 January 1964–3 October 1964
89th	1	4 January 1965–23 October 1965
	2	10 January 1966–22 October 1966
90th	1	10 January 1967–15 December 1967
	2	15 January 1968–14 October 1968
91st	1	3 January 1969–23 December 1969
	2	19 January 1970–2 January 1971
92d	1	21 January 1971–17 December 1971
	2	18 January 1972–18 October 1972
93d	1	3 January 1973–22 December 1973
	2	21 January 1974–20 December 1974
94th	1	14 January 1975–19 December 1975
	2	19 January 1976–1 October 1976
95th	1	4 January 1977–15 December 1977
	2	19 January 1978–15 October 1978
96th	1	15 January 1979–3 January 1980
	2	3 January 1980–16 December 1980
97th	1	5 January 1981–16 December 1981
	2	25 January 1982–23 December 1982
98th	1	3 January 1983–18 November 1983
	2	23 January 1984–12 October 1984
99th	1	3 January 1985–20 December 1985
	2	21 January 1986–18 October 1986
100th	1	6 January 1987–22 December 1987
	2	25 January 1988–22 October 1988
101st	1	3 January 1989–22 November 1989
	2	23 January 1990–28 October 1990
102d	1	3 January 1991–3 January 1992
	2	3 January 1992–9 October 1992
103d	1	5 January 1993–26 November 1993
	2	25 January 1994–1 December 1994
104th	1	4 January 1995–3 January 1996
	2	3 January 1996–4 October 1996
105th	1	3 January 1997–7 January 1998
	2	7 January 1998–

of the year following their election, but sessions of Congress usually began later. Since 1934, representatives and senators take office at noon on 3 January following election, and the president and vice president at noon on 20 January, as prescribed in the Twentieth Amendment. This amendment also changed the convening date of a new Congress to correspond with the commencement of members' terms, unless Congress by law determines otherwise. Before that year, sessions usually started in December, although among the 169 sessions between 1789 and 1935, 40 began in a month other than December. Since the Twentieth Amendment took effect, Congress has convened in January, except for two three-session Congresses (the 75th and 76th Congresses, 1937–1941).

Before 1935 Congress often held more than two sessions. Of the seventy-three Congresses between 1789 and 1935, fifty had two sessions, twenty-two held three, and one had four. From the adoption of the Twentieth Amendment through the 102d Congress, all but the two noted have been two-session Congresses.

Prior to the Twentieth Amendment, the Senate met thirty-one times for brief periods in special session following the election of a president to advise and consent on the president's cabinet and other significant nominees. The Senate also held eleven special sessions to consider other executive nominations and four to consider treaties.

The Constitution empowers presidents to call Congress into extraordinary session. John Adams first invoked this clause in 1797 to ask Congress to debate suspension of relations with France; it was most recently done by Harry S Truman in 1948 to deal with stalled domestic legislation. Of the twenty-seven such sessions thus far, seven dealt with foreign affairs, three with war, eight with revenues, including tariffs, three with appropriations, and six with domestic policy. Extraordinary sessions have become less common because of the practice of Congress in uncertain circumstances to adjourn subject to the recall of its chamber leaders.

There are also joint sessions, meetings, or gatherings of Congress. These rarely last longer than part of a day and include such activities as counting the electoral vote, inauguration of the president and vice president, the president's annual state of the union and other major addresses, state funerals, addresses by visiting foreign dignitaries or distinguished Americans, ceremonies, and the bestowal of awards. (A complete list of all sessions and meetings of Congress appears in the "Statistical" section of the *Congressional Directory.*)

During the early nineteenth century, representatives and senators (the latter of whom were elected by state legislatures until 1914) were elected at various times during the course of an election cycle (the first Tuesday after the first Monday in November did not become the uniform day for election of representatives until 1876). To accommodate these variable election dates and to allow time for members to travel from their states to Washington (transportation being arduous and time consuming) regular sessions did not commence until December of the year following the election of a new Congress.

A consequence of this delay was the so-called lame-duck session that occurred after each congressional set of elections but before the commencement of terms (as opposed to commencement of sessions) for the new Congress the following March. Complaints about lame-duck sessions were instrumental in passage of the Twentieth Amendment.

Nowadays congressional leaders set a target date for adjournment of each session and also schedule intrasession recesses, which aid members in planning for trips back to their districts and states. This scheduling also helps chairs and leaders to plan committee and floor work during each session.

[See also (I) Adjournment and Recess.]

BIBLIOGRAPHY

Galloway, George. *The Legislative Process in Congress.* 1953.

Luce, Robert. Legislative Assemblies. 1924. Repr. 1974. Chap. 7

U.S. Senate. Senate Historical Office. "Extraordinary Sessions of Congress." Typescript.

– FREDERICK H. PAULS

SHADOW SENATORS

The concept of a shadow senator dates to 1796, when legislators in the Southwest Territory, now Tennessee, elected Gov. William Blount and William Cocke to the U.S. Senate. The men reached Philadelphia only to find that Tennessee had not yet been admitted to the Union. They were, however, permitted on the Senate floor as observers. From their status came the term *shadow senator.* Even after Tennessee was granted statehood, Congress would not seat the two men until they were reelected by the Tennessee General Assembly.

The Senate deviated from the Tennessee Plan in the case of shadow senators from the areas that became Michigan (1837), California (1850), and Minnesota (1858). One of Michigan's shadow senators was already the state's territorial delegate to the House of Representatives; the Senate allowed him and his colleague to occupy "privileged seats" as observers without voting privileges until the state was admitted. In the case of California, the question of privileges for shadow senators was overshadowed by southern hostility to the state's admission as a free state. The same reason may have sparked opposition to observer status for Minnesota's lone shadow senator. The immediate seating of these men after their states gained admission marked another departure from the Tennessee Plan and riled Southerners. No such dispute engulfed the shadow senators elected by the Oregon legislature in mid-1858, eight months before that territory became the thirty-third state.

Alaska chose Ernest Gruening and William A. Egan to the Senate in 1956, three years before the territory attained statehood. Gruening and Egan occupied seats in the diplomatic gallery until Alaska's star was added to the flag; then they, too, had to stand for reelection. Whether they were welcome observers before statehood or seat takers afterward, a majority of shadow senators maintained a low profile while lobbying for their territory's admission to the Union.

The shadow-senator concept was revived in 1990. In that year, District of Columbia voters selected Jesse Jackson to be their agent in promoting statehood for the District.

BIBLIOGRAPHY

Grayson, George W. "Casting D.C.'s Shadows: Statehood-Seeking 'Senators' Are as Old as the Republic." *Washington Post,* 11 November 1990, p. B-5.

Quattannens, Jo Anne McCormick. "Shadow Senators." Paper prepared by the Historical Office, U.S. Senate. 1990. Mimeo.

– GEORGE W. GRAYSON

SPEAKER OF THE HOUSE

Drawing on British and colonial precedent, the Framers created the position of the Speaker of the House of Representatives as that body's presiding officer. For

The Speaker is elected by a majority vote of members and need not be a member of the House.

many centuries British Speakers were under the influence of the monarchy. In 1376 Peter de la Mare became the first Speaker to have been elected by the Commons, but it was not until the seventeenth century that the British speakership emerged from crown control. When the colonial governments were established in the seventeenth century, colonial speakers were under the influence of royal governors. By the century's end, they too had emerged as the voice of the legislative body, playing an independent political role in addition to serving as presiding officers. It was this hybrid political and parliamentary, model that shaped the Founders' perceptions of the office. Consequently, the American speakership has always been a political and a parliamentary office, and it remains so today.

FORMAL DUTIES. The Speaker is elected by a majority vote of members and need not be a member of the House. His constitutional responsibility is to preside over the House. He is empowered by the rules of the House to administer the oath of office to members, to call the House to order, to maintain order and decorum, to recognize members for the purpose of speaking or making motions, to rule upon the propriety of motions under the Constitution and the Rules of the House, to refer bills to committee, to put questions to a vote of members, to declare a quorum, to count and declare all votes, to receive and transmit formal messages to the Senate and to the president, to appoint all select and conference committees, to appoint House members to conferences, and to sign all bills passed by the House. Such formal duties define the Speaker's role while the House of Representatives is in session, that is, on the House "floor." When the House meets in the Committee of the Whole, the Speaker does not preside but names a member to chair the Committee of the Whole. In addition, the Speaker may appoint a member as Speaker pro tempore during floor sessions.

POLITICAL FUNCTIONS. These formal duties pertinent to the legislative process capture the main aims of the Framers but only hint at the meaning of the office as it has developed over time. From its earliest days, the speakership has been an irreducibly political office. While its parliamentary role continued and, especially prior to the Civil War, predominated, the speakership evolved as one of the most powerful political offices in the nation. The political role of the Speaker of the House results from the fact that the speakership is controlled by the political party that controls a majority of seats in the House. The Speaker is, therefore, the leader of his congressional party and has further powers deriving from party rules. While the rules of the Democratic and Republican parties vary somewhat, in general the Speaker participates in making his party's standing-committee assignments, influences the flow of legislation to the floor (currently by nominating the chairman and majority members of the Rules Committee), makes recommendations on legislation to the party caucus, can authorize members' travel, appoints members to party task forces, makes political appearances on behalf of members, and in recent times has been influential in raising and distributing campaign funds.

ADMINISTRATIVE DUTIES. To the Speaker's parliamentary and political functions has been added, especially in modern times, a vital role as chief administrator

Speaker James Beauchamp (Champ) Clark (D-Mo.). Although the powers of the Speaker were curtailed after the 1910 revolt against Speaker Joseph G. Cannon, the position was still viewed as a path to the White House. As the cartoonist predicted, Clark did make a run for the presidency, seeking the Democratic nomination for the 1912 presidential election. He lost to Woodrow Wilson, then governor of New Jersey. Clifford K. Berryman, Washington Evening Star, *c. April 1911. (U.S. Senate Collection, Center for Legislative Archives)*

of the House. The Speaker is responsible for the offices of sergeant at arms, clerk, doorkeeper, House counsel, House parliamentarian, and the Capitol Police on the House side of the Hill. He is responsible for office assignments, all travel not delegated to individual members or to committees, and appointments to special boards and commissions. These administrative duties place the office under a heavy burden and are often sources of institutional stress. They have, however, expanded the Speaker's leverage over members and hence his power. In 1992 the House, in response to scandals in the House Bank and House Post Office, created the positions of Director of Non-Legislative and Financial Services and House Auditor and Inspector General. These offices are to be filled on recommendation of the Speaker and the majority and minority leaders. These employees are accountable to the House Administration Committee and are removable by the Speaker alone. In 1993 these new offices were being implemented and the extent to which they will affect the Speaker's power is yet to be determined. One result of the expansion of the Speaker's administrative powers in the post–World War II era has been a dramatic expansion in the Speaker's staff. Whereas Speaker Sam Rayburn had a personal staff numbering fewer than a dozen people in the 1950s, Speakers Thomas P. (Tip) O'Neill, Jr., James C. Wright, Jr., and Thomas S. Foley have had staffs numbering in the dozens in the 1980s and 1990s. This bureaucratization of the speakership brought about fundamental change in the office, with more and more responsibility delegated to core staff. It seems unlikely that the new administrative offices created in 1992 will lessen the Speaker's need to rely on staff.

The political role accorded Speakers by their party membership greatly enhances the powers given to the office under the Constitution and House Rules, and the political and institutional powers work reciprocally to strengthen the Speaker's hand. At the same time, the dual role of presiding officer (requiring fairness) and party leader (requiring political commitment) creates a tension in the office that has provided its distinctive character. Although the Speaker need not be a member of the House, all Speakers to date have been. Thus, Speakers have obligations as representatives of their constituencies that place further claims on their loyalty. The speakership is, then, a multifaceted office that appears somewhat splintered to observers from parliamentary regimes in which the speakership has become a nonpolitical office.

HISTORY OF THE OFFICE. The evolving character of the speakership has meant that Speakers of different periods have played different roles. During the pre–Civil War period, for example, the party system was unstable and often fragmented, and so the Speaker of the House could not easily emerge as a powerful party leader. The most famous antebellum Speaker was Henry Clay of Kentucky, who was elected to the office on his first day in the House as the leader of the congressional War Hawks. Clay was a charismatic national leader who used the speakership to further his presidential ambitions. While no student of parliamentary procedure, he used the power of recognition to his own political purposes and won the respect of members by his firm command from the chair. His parliamentary encounters with his nemesis, John Randolph of Roanoke, were notorious, yet the House backed Clay in all of his rulings from the chair. He served off and on as Speaker from 1811 until 1824, when he moved to the Senate. Other Speakers of this period served much shorter tenures, and none could be said to have been a national leader in the Clay mold, although one, James

K. Polk of Tennessee, was later elected president, something Clay never achieved.

Peak of power. After the Civil War, the United States welcomed a strong two-party system. During the fifty years following the war, Congress was relatively strong, the presidency relatively weak, and the Republican party mostly predominant. The speakership reached its peak of power, and both Republican and Democratic Speakers were strong party leaders and major players on the national stage. Among Democratic Speakers, the two most effective were Samuel J. Randall of Pennsylvania, who was responsible for the adoption of major rules reforms in 1880, including the creation of the Rules Committee, and John G. Carlisle of Kentucky, who later served as a U.S. senator and as secretary of the Treasury in the second administration of Grover Cleveland. These two Democrats were not as effective, however, as the best of the Republican Speakers of this period, including James G. Blaine of Maine, the "Plumed Knight" who led his party for almost two decades; Thomas B. Reed of Maine, who revolutionized the House by the adoption of the Reed Rules in 1890; and Joseph G. (Uncle Joe) Cannon of Illinois, who ruled the House with an iron hand from 1903 until his power was undermined by the great revolution of 1910 in which the Speaker lost control over the Rules Committee.

These Republican Speakers distinguished themselves in several ways. Each was responsible for major innovations in House Rules. Blaine developed the "Speaker's list" for floor recognition and used the power of committee appointment to maintain control over the House agenda. Reed broke the back of the disappearing quorum and dilatory motion, clearing the way for majority governance in the House for the first time. Cannon gathered the various reins of power into his hands and demonstrated how they could be used. He stood toe to toe with Presidents Theodore Roosevelt and William Howard Taft and made the House the dominant force in the government. All three Republicans were serious presidential candidates. Blaine left the House for the Senate, and as senator he competed for the presidential nomination in 1884. Reed was the main rival of William McKinley for the Republican nomination in 1896. Cannon sought the nomination in 1908.

The "feudal" House. After the revolt against Cannon in 1910, the speakership began its slow transformation to a new and very different kind of office. Beginning at the turn of the century, membership tenure began steadily to lengthen, especially among southern Democrats. The power that had been taken away from the speakership devolved upon the standing committees and their chairmen. Over time the committees became the real locus of power in the House. The Democrats flirted with caucus governance during the speakership of James Beauchamp (Champ) Clark of Missouri (1911–1918), and the Republicans offered a reasonably strong speakership under Nicholas Longworth of Ohio (1925–1931). But by the time of the Great Depression and New Deal, the committee barons had taken full control of the House. Since the Democrats controlled the House for all but two Congresses between 1933 and 1970 (the year when average congressional tenure reached its peak), they most shaped this system; and since the most senior Democrats were from the deep South, it was the southern wing of the party that gained most of its benefits. Committee appointments on the Democratic side were made by the Democratic members of the Ways and Means Committee, which was typically controlled by senior southerners. The path of legislation to the floor passed through the standing committees, which met at the call of chairmen, who were typically southern Democrats. From there, legislation went to the Rules Committee, chaired by southern Democrats and controlled by a coalition of southern Democrats and Republicans. By controlling the legislative process the Conservative Coalition was able to throttle liberal legislation. While the southern wing of the Democratic party had always had influence due to its size and seniority, it was only after President Franklin D. Roosevelt's Court-packing scheme in 1937 and the retribution he sought against some southern Democrats in the 1938 elections that the Coalition emerged as a regular voting block. With southern Democrats controlling most major committees, with the Rules Committee in the hands of the Coalition, and with the Coalition active on the floor, the liberal Democratic political agenda was placed in abeyance until the Lyndon B. Johnson administration and its Great Society.

By far the strongest Speaker of this period was Sam Rayburn of Texas, who led the Democrats from his first election as Speaker in 1941 until his death in 1961, a period interrupted by Republican control of the 80th (1947–1949) and 83d (1953–1955) Congresses. Many regard Rayburn as the most powerful Speaker in the history of the House, but he was never as powerful as his late-nineteenth-century predecessors. Instead, he was a man whose personality and political circumstances were ideally suited to the conditions of the House during its "feudal" era. Rayburn had been an effective chairman of the Committee on Interstate and Foreign Commerce during the 1930s, and as Speaker he respected the prerogatives of the committees and their chairmen. He made himself the broker among these titans rather than seek power over them. In this way, he positioned himself so that his stature enhanced his ability to influence events when it was important to him to do so. Because the arrangements of the baronial House suited his purposes well, he resisted any change in them until 1961, when he led the successful effort to "pack" the Rules Committee in order to break the back of the conservative coalition's control over it. That victory and Rayburn's death heralded the end of an era in the history of the House and its speakership.

Reforms. The 1960s and 1970s were a time of tremendous change in the House. The liberal wing of the Democratic party was pressing for social and economic legislation that was resisted by conservative Democrats and Republicans. To enact their programs, the liberal Democrats sought to change the rules that permitted conservative control of the congressional agenda. Led in the House by the liberal Democratic Study Group, the reformers sought further to abridge the power of the committee chairmen, to open up the legislative process to public scrutiny, to redistribute power from committees to subcommittees, and to strengthen the office of Speaker, which liberal Democrats expected to control. The Legislative Reform Act of 1970 and subsequent reforms adopted by the Democratic caucus transformed the House. Among the most significant changes were those that provided for recorded (later electronic) votes, opened committee meetings to the public, empowered committee majorities to call meetings, required caucus votes to approve committee chairs, transferred the power of committee assignments to the Democratic Steering and Policy Committee from the Ways and Means Democratic caucus, and gave the Speaker the power to nominate Democratic members of the Rules Committee. Especially significant was the adoption of a "subcommittee bill of rights," which provided staffing and required all legislation to be referred to subcommittee before being considered by the full committee. These changes revolutionized the House, diffused power within it, and greatly strengthened the office of Speaker. The two Speakers who presided over these changes were Democrats John W. McCormack of Massachusetts (1962–1971) and Carl B. Albert of Oklahoma (1971–1976). These Speakers confronted the most difficult period in the history of the House since before the Civil War, as the country was torn apart by domestic strife over the civil rights movement and the Vietnam War. Both were protégés of Rayburn. Of the two, Speaker Albert was more receptive to the changes that followed in the wake of political upheaval.

The "post-reform" House of the period since 1975 has suffered from a malady that is both similar to and different from the malady of the old House. In the "prereform" House, conservatives controlled the parliamentary machinery and used that control to thwart the liberal agenda. When Congress failed to act, it was often because those in control did not want action. In the post-reform Congress, legislation has frequently bogged down even when everyone has agreed that legislation is needed. Power has been so diffused that it is difficult to forge consensus. The inherent difficulty in gaining agreement among 435 autonomous members was exacerbated by divided government. Except during the administration of Jimmy Carter (1977–1981), Republicans were in control of the White House and Democrats in control of at least one house of Congress from 1969 through 1992 (Republicans did control the Senate from 1981 through 1986, during Republican Ronald Reagan's presidency). This condition contributed to a paralysis in public policy.

Many regard Sam Rayburn as the most powerful Speaker in the history of the House, but he was never as powerful as his late nineteenth-century predecessors.

Under these circumstances, the speakership of the House changed again. Democratic Speakers emerged as public spokesmen for their party and as policy leaders in ways not seen since the turn of the twentieth century. As his party's highest elected officeholder, Speaker Tip O'Neill of Massachusetts (1977–1986) was especially prominent in leading the Democratic opposition to the policies of President Reagan. His successor, Jim Wright of Texas, sought to use the powers of the speakership to forge a legislative program in both domestic and foreign policy. His heavy-handed tactics caused disgruntlement within the ranks of his own party and attacks from Republicans, notwithstanding his considerable legislative success in the 100th Congress. When, in the 101st Congress, ethics charges were brought against him, he lacked the legislative support to survive and was forced to resign. Speaker Tom Foley of Washington (1989–1995), assumed a much more conciliatory role.

Thus, the speakership of the House is, on the one hand, defined by its parliamentary, administrative, representative, and partisan roles, which have evolved over time; on the other, the speakership's character has changed with the changing character of the party system, the distribution of power between the two major parties, and the character of individual Speakers. It is unique among all American political creations, reflecting as it does the fragmentation of power under the

Constitution and the diversity of the American political system.

[See also (I) Congress.]

BIBLIOGRAPHY

Cheney, Richard B., and Lynne V. Cheney. *Kings of the Hill: Power and Personality in the House of Representatives.* 1983.

Follett, Mary Parker. *The Speaker of the House of Representatives.* 1896.

Kenon, Donald R., ed. *The Speakers of the U.S. House of Representatives, 1798–1984.* 1986.

Peters, Ronald M., Jr. *The American Speakership: The Office in Historical Perspective.* 1990.

Sinclair, Barbara. *Majority Party Leadership in the U.S. House.* 1983.

– RONALD M. PETERS, JR.

SPECIAL ELECTIONS

Special elections to Congress are used to fill vacant seats in both the Senate and House of Representatives. Voter participation in these elections usually falls well below normal levels, except when they are held concurrently with regular general elections. Special elections occasionally produce prominent figures, particularly in the contemporary Senate, where Democrats Edward M. Kennedy (Mass.) and Sam Nunn (Ga.) and Republicans Ted Stevens (Alaska) and Strom Thurmond (S.C.) first gained their seats through special elections.

For Senate vacancies, the Constitution authorizes state legislatures to empower governors to make temporary appointments "until the people fill the vacancies by election as the legislature may direct." Forty-nine states provide for temporary appointments, but Arizona requires special elections for all Senate vacancies. Most states provide for nomination by primary or party convention, and they usually require that special elections be held at the next statewide election, unless the seat becomes vacant after a statewide election but before the end of the term, in which case the appointee serves until the term expires.

All House vacancies are filled by special elections, with authority over scheduling and nomination procedures delegated to the states. Most states provide for nomination by primary or other party action. For House vacancies that occur during a Congress's first session, all states mandate a special election; for second-session vacancies, the special election is usually held at the same time as the regularly scheduled election for the seat. Some states do not provide for a special election under these circumstances: the seat remains vacant until the next Congress convenes.

BIBLIOGRAPHY

Sigelman, Lee. "Special Elections to the U.S. House: Some Descriptive Generalizations." *Legislative Studies Quarterly* (1981): 577–588.

Studlar, Donley T., and Lee Sigelman. "Special Elections: A Comparative Perspective." *British Journal of Political Science* 17 (1987): 247–256.

– THOMAS H. NEALE

SPEECH OR DEBATE CLAUSE

The speech or debate clause of the Constitution, Article I, section 6, clause 1, confers immunity upon members of Congress with the words: "For Speech or Debate in either House, they [the Senators and Representatives] shall not be questioned in any other Place." That clause covers both what members of Congress do on the floor of the House or Senate—debating, motions, and voting—and what they do in other areas of the legislative process, such as bill preparation, investigations, committee work, and oversight of departments and agencies. It protects members from criminal prosecutions or civil suits against them and from being questioned as witnesses in suits against others. Thus, for example, when a senator prepares and offers an amendment to a tax bill in committee to confer a benefit on a particular company, his preparation and his offering of the amendment could not be questioned in a civil case or even in a criminal indictment. Speech or debate immunity gives protection against depositions and subpoenas, which are frequent in modern civil cases. The immunity protects congressional staff when they function as the "alter egos" of members on legislative matters.

This speech or debate immunity serves as a pillar of the government's separation of powers by keeping disputes about Congress out of the courts and by requiring executive officials and private individuals alike to deal with members of Congress politically rather than through legal assault. Speaking broadly, since World War II, presidents have often been of one political party while one or both houses of Congress have had a majority of the other political party. Yet during this time presidents have not generally attempted to use Justice Department prosecutions or civil lawsuits to fight issues with Congress because the speech or debate clause prevents such lawsuits. When President Ronald Reagan tried to file such a lawsuit in 1983, entitled *United States v. House of Representatives,* the court agreed with lawyers for the House that the case had to be dismissed. Charges by the president or anyone else against Congress, and disputes within Congress that concern legislative matters, must be settled through political processes and at the ballot box rather than in court.

Originally, the Framers of the Constitution modeled the speech or debate clause on the traditional immunity enjoyed by members of the British Parliament and by members of colonial and state legislatures. As cases arose, U.S. courts up to the Supreme Court have interpreted the clause to demarcate its meaning in the evolving work of Congress. In *Kilbourn v. Thompson* (1881), the Supreme Court decided that the immunity protected members of a committee who had voted to arrest a resisting witness; the Court decided that the committee process was part of the whole legislative process and deserving of the speech or debate protection. However, the Court held that the immunity did not protect the House sergeant at arms, who had carried out the actual arrest of the witness. One of the great twentieth-century cases, *Gravel v. United States* (1972), decided that the immunity protected Sen. Mike Gravel from prosecution for reading documents into a committee record that revealed the secret history of decisions leading to the Vietnam War. The immunity was complete, even though by placing those documents in the public record, Senator Gravel disclosed records bearing national security classifications of a high secrecy level.

Potentially, the speech or debate immunity could make it difficult to prosecute members of Congress for corruption, but Congress has acted in ways that ensure policing of its conduct. It has enacted ethics codes with comprehensive financial disclosure requirements to which immunity does not apply. Additionally, both the Senate and the House have created internal ethics committees. Because the clause only prevents members from being "questioned in any other Place" than Congress, it does not protect members in any way from being questioned or disciplined by the House or Senate through their internal ethics process.

Moreover, the Supreme Court held, in *United States v. Brewster* (1972), that the Justice Department could indict and prosecute a senator for taking a bribe. However, immunity requires that the prosecution not offer evidence about whether the member who received a bribe then actually performed particular legislative acts such as voting, which are protected by immunity. Instead, the prosecution offers proof that the member received a bribe and proof of what he said when arranging to receive it.

In general, the Supreme Court has interpreted the immunity expansively to preserve Congress's independence in modern conditions. However, in *Hutchinson v. Proxmire* (1979), the Court decided that speech or debate immunity does not protect members when they talk to the press, even when they are informing their constituents about public affairs. This deters Congress from performing what Woodrow Wilson called its "informing function."

BIBLIOGRAPHY

Cella, Alexander J. "The Doctrine of Legislative Privilege of Speech or Debate: The New Interpretation as a Threat to Legislative Coequality." *Suffolk University Law Review* 8 (1974): 1019–1905.

"Evidentiary Implications of the Speech or Debate Clause." *Yale Law Journal* 88 (1979): 1280–1298.

Wittke, Carl. *The History of English Parliamentary Privilege.* 1970.

– CHARLES TIEFER

SPONSORSHIP

Members of Congress express their endorsement of legislation by associating their name with it in a formal act known as sponsorship. The member who introduces the bill, resolution, or amendment is known as the measure's sponsor. Only a member of Congress can sponsor legislation. Therefore, when the term *by request* appears along with the sponsor's name, it is an indication that the member introduced the measure as a courtesy on behalf of an individual or organization outside the Congress (e.g., the president). However, such sponsorship by request does not necessarily imply endorsement by the sponsor.

Members of Congress express their endorsement of legislation by associating their name with it in a formal act known as sponsorship.

Members who simultaneously or subsequently affiliate themselves with a proposal upon its introduction are known as cosponsors. The primary reason for cosponsorship in both the House and Senate is for members to have a concrete proposal to point to, a proposal that expresses their position on an issue and demonstrates their political support for its concept. Gaining cosponsors is accomplished by personal lobbying and by soliciting them through internal letters known as "Dear Colleagues."

In the House, the original sponsor frequently seeks cosponsors for the legislative initiative prior to introducing it. In a body of 435, one way members have found to distinguish their measure from all the rest, and thus encourage its progress, is to accumulate a large number of cosponsors.

Only those members who agree to become cosponsors prior to a measure's introduction will have their name printed on the face of the legislation. Members may cosponsor the measure subsequent to its introduction but, while their names will be noted in the *Congressional Record,* they will not appear on the face of the bill. There is no limitation on how many cosponsors a measure may have, and in practice the number ranges widely. Amendments, however, are rarely cosponsored by more than one or two individuals.

The House, in 1967, adopted a change to House Rule XXII, which allows members to have up to twenty-five cosponsors per measure. Prior to this change, members frequently introduced hundreds of identical proposals, thus incurring substantial printing costs. A further change was made to Rule XXII in 1979 to permit an unlimited number of members to cosponsor a measure upon its introduction and up until it is reported from committee.

In the Senate, cosponsorship does not play as significant a role as in the House. The smaller size of the Senate decreases the need for large numbers of cosponsors to distinguish one senator's proposal from the next. There has been no limitation on how many senators can cosponsor a measure since at least 1937. Cosponsorship practice in the Senate differs somewhat from the House when it comes to its timing. Rather than signing on to a measure when it is introduced, senators will more frequently ask unanimous consent to cosponsor a measure or an amendment during its floor consideration, often just moments before the vote on final passage.

Cosponsorship can be withdrawn in both chambers, but only by unanimous consent.

[See also (I) Bills.]

BIBLIOGRAPHY

Briscoe, Cynthia. *Co-sponsorship of Bills and Resolutions in the House of Representatives.* Congressional Research Service, Library of Congress. CRS Rept. 76-237G.1976.

Overby, Peter. "Is There a Co-sponsor in the House?" *Washington Post,* 6 January 1991, p. C4.

U.S. House of Representatives. Committee on Science, Space, and Technology. *Legislative Manual.* 5th ed. 102d Cong., 1st sess., 1991. Committee Print.

– ILONA B. NICKELS

STAFFING

The end of the nineteenth century and the beginning of the twentieth brought enduring changes in the type and amount of Congress's work; with this workload expansion came the need to augment staff resources. During most of the nineteenth century, Congress neither needed nor authorized appropriations for staff for itself, with two exceptions. First, under the direction of each chamber's officers was a small cadre of employees who performed security, maintenance, postal, and administrative tasks; as late as 1918, this group numbered fewer than 700 employees (compared with more than 5,000 today). Second, starting in the 1840s, Congress hired a handful of clerks, messengers, and janitors for its committees; these "clerk hires" (the term remains part of congressional lingo to this day) totaled fewer than 150 as late as 1890 and about 400 in 1920 (compared with almost 4,000 today).

Several reasons account for Congress's lack of need for staff assistance during the nineteenth century; they include the limited number and kinds of issues on Congress's agenda; the short duration of congressional sessions; a belief in a relatively short rotation in office—the citizen legislator concept—that largely prevailed until the end of the nineteenth century; a lack of office space; minimal constituent demand on members other than by those seeking patronage appointments to federal jobs; and a commitment to limited government, including a laissez-faire attitude toward economic and social regulation.

Growth of Congressional Staff

It is likely that the large number of Senate committees that existed until their consolidation in 1947 existed in part to provide personal staff for senators. The extent to which individual members of both chambers paid for personal staff from their own pockets between 1789 and 1885 or thereafter remains unrecorded, though debate on legislative appropriations through the first half of the twentieth century was punctuated by claims from members that they had to dip into their private funds to supplement the public funding provided to them for staff. Currently members may use only public funds to pay for their staffs.

In 1990, the size of senators' staffs ranged from twenty-four to seventy-three, with forty-one on the average.

PERSONAL STAFF. The Senate system for funding personal staff is more complicated than that in the House. Moneys for personal office staffing were appropriated first in the Senate, then in the House. In 1885 the Senate authorized a clerk for each senator not entitled to one "under the rules" as chairman of a committee—a practice that, though later modified, continued in the Senate until 1947 but that the House followed for less than a decade (1893–1902).

Senate. In earlier years, because of the large number of standing and select committees, some senators would chair more than one committee but could use committee staff as personal staff on only one of the committees they chaired. For example, in 1891 there were 88 senators and 55 Senate committees, including 13 select committees, but because of multiple chairmanships,

TABLE 1

CONGRESSIONAL COMMITTEES: 1891, 1914, 1924, 1930, 1946, 1947

	House		Senate			
Year	Standing	Select	Standing	Select	Joint	Total
1891	49	13	42	13	0	117
1914	58	0	73	0	4	135
1924	61	4	34	0	5	104
1930	47	0	33	0	9	89
1946	48	7	33	11	9	108
1947	19	3	15	3	6	46

Source: Author's count from the *Congressional Directory* for the years indicated: 15 January 1891, 2d ed., 51st, 2d; February 1914, 2d ed., 63d, 2d; May 1924, 3d ed., 68th, 1st; 18 January 1930, 2d ed., 71st, 2d; 29 March 1946, 2d ed., 79th, 2d; and 11 January 1947, 2d ed., 80th, 1st.

TABLE 2

HOUSE PERSONAL STAFF AUTHORIZATION INCREASES: 1893–1992

Year	Authorized Staff	Staff for Districts over 500,000
1893	1–2	NA
1919	2	NA
1940	3	NA
1945	6	NA
1949	7	NA
1954	8	NA
1955	9	10 (1956)
1961	10	11
1965	11	12
1966	12	13
1969	13	14
1971	15	16
1972	16	NA
1975	18	NA
1979	22	NA

Note: Eighteen permanent and four nonpermanent staff were authorized as of 1979; there have been no increases since that year.
Source: U.S. House of Representatives. Legislative Branch Appropriations Subcommittee. *Legislative Branch Appropriation Bill: Fiscal Year 1992.* 1991. P. 27 (as corrected by author).

only 49 senators were staffed through their committees, while 39 senators were authorized a clerk for their personal office.

The Senate practice of funding chairmen through one of the committees they chaired while funding non-chairmen through their personal offices lasted with some variation for fifty years, until 1935, when the Senate passed a resolution (S. Res. 144) authorizing an additional clerk for all ninety-six senators. Approximately twenty-five years before, however, the Senate had begun to deviate from the practice of funding chairmen only through the committees they chaired, with anywhere from seven to eleven chairmen in any year being entitled to one or more personal clerks in addition to staff they received through their positions as chairs of Senate committees. The public record does not explain why this occurred.

By 1930, for example, Senate membership and the number of committees had stabilized at 96 and 33, respectively. Yet 70, not just 63, senators were authorized to have personal staff even though all committees were staffed and no senator chaired more than one committee.

Table 1 illustrates the fluctuation in the number of House and Senate committees from 1891 until the modern committee system was established in 1947. On the Senate side, these variable counts affected the number of senators during any session who were not chairmen of a committee and thus entitled to personal staff.

In 1940 the Senate commenced a practice that evolved into the current method for funding personal staff. In the Third Deficiency Appropriation Act of that year, senators from states with populations of three million or more were authorized to have one more clerk than were senators from states with populations under three million. With the passage of time additional adjustments based on population were made.

Seven years later, because of the Legislative Reorganization Act of 1946 (P.L. 79-601), the Senate stopped distinguishing between chairmen and non-chairmen in the allocation of personal staff. This occurred because section 202 of that law forbade use of committee staff for any purpose other than committee business. In 1946 each senator was authorized to hire an administrative assistant in addition to any other clerks.

In 1947 the Senate eliminated its practice of specifying in legislative-branch appropriation bills the exact number of clerks to be hired by senators—and, for that matter, by committees—as well as the maximum salary

TABLE 3

SENATE AND HOUSE PERSONAL STAFF: 1891–1991

Year	House	Senate	Total	Average per Representative	Average per Senator
1891	0	39	39	0	1
1914	435	72	507	1	3
1930	870	280	1,150	2	4
1947	1,440	590	2,030	3	6
1957	2,441	1,115	3,556	6	12
1967	4,055	1,749	5,804	9	17
1977	6,942	3,554	10,496	16	35
1987	7,584	4,075	11,659	17	41
1991	c. 8,000	c. 4,100	12,100	18	41

Sources: *Vital Statistics on Congress, 1991–1992,* p. 126, for 1891–1987, based on data through 1967 from Fox and Hammond, *Congressional Staffs,* 1977, p. 171; author's data for House for 1914 and House and Senate for 1991.

each could be paid. Over the next several years, the Senate gradually replaced these specifications with a personal staffing system based on state population categories (at one time there were as many as twenty-nine categories), which prescribed differing annual allotments of money for each population category, putting restrictions on the minimum and maximum salaries payable to personal and committee staff rather than limiting their numbers.

Since 1992 there have been twenty-four such categories, ranging from states with fewer than five million inhabitants to states with a population of twenty-eight million and above. In 1993, seventy-four of the one hundred senators fell into the lowest category and thus were eligible for $1.4 million a year for personal staff through their combined administrative-clerical and legislative assistance allowance. By contrast, senators from California, the most populous state, were entitled to $2.3 million each. In 1990, the size of senators' staffs ranged from twenty-four to seventy-three, with forty-one as the average.

House. The House developed a more straightforward way of funding personal staff. It could do so because, for the most part, representatives have constituencies of roughly the same size, which, of course, is not the case for senators. In 1893, at the outset of House personal staffing, the House copied the Senate by giving fifty-six chairmen authorization for combined personal and committee staff, while the 269 members who were not chairmen were each authorized $100 per month to hire one clerk while the House was in session. Three years hence the House removed the "in session" limitation and the next year granted chairmen the same clerk-hire privilege as nonchairmen when the House was out of session. Five years later, in 1902, the House abandoned the distinction between chairmen and nonchairmen and granted all representatives the right to a personal staff.

TABLE 4

STANDING COMMITTEE STAFF: 1891–1989

Year	House	Senate	Total
1891	65	73	138
1914	120	239	359
1924	129	139	268
1930	122	172	294
1947	246	300	546
1950	440	470	910
1967	589	621	1,210
1970	702	635	1,337
1980	1,917	1,191	3,108
1989	1,986	1,013	2,999

Note: To arrive at total committee staffing, the number of staff for joint and House and Senate select and special committees must be factored in. For 1980, for example, add 400 to the "Total" column; for 1989, add 500.

Sources: *Vital Statistics on Congress, 1991–1992,* p. 130, 1930–1967 based on data from Fox and Hammond, *Congressional Staffs,* 1977, p. 171; author's count from *U.S. Statutes* for 1891, 1914, and 1924.

Table 2 indicates the years (beginning in 1893) in which increases were made in the number of staff authorized for representatives. In 1992, each representative was authorized up to $515,760 annually to pay for the eighteen permanent and four temporary personal staff to which each was entitled. Members, however, seldom use all the money available for this purpose.

Table 3 shows that on average the number of personal staff per representative did not reach double-digit figures until around 1970—even though each representative was allowed ten as of 1965. While senators reached an average of ten or more personal staff in the 1950s, the growth in personal staff, for senators did not surge until the 1970s.

TABLE 5

CONGRESSIONAL STAFF: 1991 (APPROXIMATE)

House		Senate		Support Agencies		Joint		Congress	
Leaders	150	Leaders, incl. vice pres.	190	CRS	800	Architect	980	All leaders	340
Officers	1,180	Officers	1,500	CBO	220	Capitol police	1,350	All officers	5,040
Committees	2,400	Committees	1,400	GAO (30% of workforce)	1,530	Attending physician	30	All committees	3,940
Personal	8,000	Personal	4,100	OTA	150	Committees	140	All personal	12,100
								All support agencies	2,700
Total House	11,730	Total Senate	7,190	Total support	2,700	Total joint	2,500	Total Congress	24,120

Sources: Compiled by the author from hearings, reports, and prints issued by the House or Senate Legislative Branch Appropriations subcommittees, the *Report of the Clerk*, and the *Report of the Secretary of the Senate*.

TABLE 6

CONGRESSIONAL STAFFING: 1918

Category	Senate	House	Joint	Total
Leaders, incl. vice pres.	4	5	NA	9
Personal	72	870	NA	942
Committees	248	132	3	383
Officers	224	308	134	666
Totals	548	1,315	137	2,000

Source: Author's count from H. Rept. 65-346, Legislative, Executive, and Judicial Appropriation Bill (1918).

COMMITTEE STAFF. A parallel development occurred with committee staff, as documented in Table 4 which shows modest staffing until 1947, the year that marks the beginning of the modern committee system in Congress. Numbers of committee staff almost doubled within three years thereafter, nearly tripling by 1970 and more than quintupling by 1980, when they peaked. They have since leveled off. The growth in the number of committee staff since 1947 is only partially attributable to growth in the number of committees and subcommittees (230 in 1947 and 284 in 1991, an increase of roughly 25 percent).

TOTAL STAFF, 1918 AND 1991. Table 5 reports the approximate number of staff worked for Congress in 1991; Table 6 shows comparable data for 1918. Included in the 1991 totals are not only personal and committee staff but also employees of party leaders, the several officers of the House and Senate, the Architect of the Capitol, the Capitol police, and employees of the four agencies that provide policy research and information assistance to Congress (the Congressional Budget Office, the Congressional Research Service, a portion of the General Accounting Office, and the Office of Technology Assessment—none of which existed in 1918 as they are known today).

Staff numbered 2,000 in 1918, but more than 24,000 in 1991. For each year, nearly 70 percent were staff for members, leaders, or committees. In 1918 only three buildings were needed to house the entire congressional staff (the Capitol, and the Longworth and Russell buildings), but by 1991 congressional staff were scattered among sixteen buildings on or near Capitol Hill or in one of twelve hundred district and state offices.

The legislature of no other nation comes close to matching the staff available to the U.S. Congress. In part this is because most other democracies are of the parliamentary type, in which the government's leaders come from the legislature and so can draw on ministry staff—that is, the executive bureaucracy—for assistance. By contrast, the U.S. Congress is a coequal and separate branch of government, which has come zealously to guard its independence from the executive, including the independence of its staff and information resources.

Professionalization of Congressional Staff

Congressional staff have become increasingly credentialed and professionalized since the end of World War II. For committee staff, this professionalization was mandated by law; for other offices it has resulted from the increasingly diverse and sophisticated needs of Congress and from ever-expanding reliance on a range of new technologies.

PERSONAL STAFF. Until the middle of the twentieth century, personal staff were basically what their generic title implied: clerks. Indeed, not until 1970 did the House authorize variable titles for personal staff, although the Senate had begun doing so piecemeal and in largely informal fashion in 1947.

Before the days of typewriters—let alone computers and modern printing, copying, recording, and communications equipment—everything had to be handwritten. Accordingly, even well into the twentieth century members needed secretarial and stenographic assistance, especially as their correspondence and legislative work loads increased. With the advent of electronic communications technologies, however, the number of secretaries on personal and committee staffs dwindled to insignificance, with secretaries being replaced by computer operators and other technically skilled staff.

Developments in personal staffing since World War II have included the hiring of administrative assistants (now also called chiefs of staff), legislative assistants, press aides, constituent-service staff, and technical and support staff. Because senators average twice the number of staff of representatives, senators' staffs include more of each type of worker.

Neither chamber has yet established detailed hiring, firing, or other employment rules and regulations—although of late both the House and Senate have accorded employees protection against arbitrary and capricious actions by their employers. Nor have they agreed on formal position descriptions or official job titles. (The existing descriptions and titles, while sometimes technically accurate, are something of an art form.) Working within the prescribed limits on numbers of staff persons they can have, the ceilings on the amount of money they can spend on staff, and the minimum (around $1,500) and maximum (more than $100,000) they can pay in individual salaries, members hire, promote, terminate, pay, and assign work to personal staff as they wish with minimal guidance or interference from their respective chambers. Traits that members look for and value in their staffs include intelligence, trustworthiness, loyalty, enterprise, good judgment, political astuteness, and energy.

Types and titles. Personal office staff can be categorized as follows: administrative, executive, and political; technical, clerical, and support; legislative and research; constituent-related; and media.

The first category includes the administrative assistant, usually the most powerful staffperson; office manager; legal counsel; scheduling assistants; personal, executive, or special counsels, advisers, or assistants; state, regional, or local office directors; and appointment and personal secretaries. Technical, clerical, and support employees have titles such as systems administrator; computer or entry operator; mailroom coordinator, supervisor, or clerk; files supervisor or clerk; secretary; typist; receptionist; and just plain clerk.

There are several titular variants for legislative assistants, the most commonly used title among legislative and research staff. These include legislative director, often the senior legislative assistant overseeing the others; legislative aide; legislative correspondent, the lowliest legislative assistant but also the workhorse of office operations; policy-specific assistants, advisers, or counselors (frequently correlated with a member's committee assignments); research director or assistant; special assistant; and staff assistant (a title also used for many state and district office employees).

Constituent-related staff, mostly housed in state or district offices, bear the titles of caseworker, constituent-service or field representative, specialist, liaison, project assistant, state or district assistant, and the ubiquitous staff assistant.

Media staff have titles such as director or coordinator of communications and press secretary. Senators may have two or three media staff; representatives rarely employ more than one, with some members either serving as their own press spokespersons or delegating these responsibilities to, for instance, their administrative assistants.

Duties. Collectively these staff perform the numerous tasks associated with the operation of a member's office, which, despite increasing formalization, is still apt to be run more like a small business than a bureaucracy. Although lines of authority exist, the atmosphere of a congressional office is frequently informal, and teamwork is essential to the routine daily work load. Because Murphy's Law frequently seems at play in congressional life, everyone must be ready to adapt and respond to whatever crises the day may bring. The amount and kind of interplay between a member and the staff is still largely a function of the member's style.

Office management and support services. Besides making sure that an office runs as smoothly as possible, administrative staff, particularly the administrative assistant and the schedulers, see to political business. Political business includes organizing and coordinating the member's busy schedule, which comprises legislative obligations in committee and on the floor, meeting with constituents and others interested in conferring with him or her, and political appearances in Washington and at home.

The administrative assistant is often called on to meet with important constituents, make and take critical calls, orchestrate reelection activity (a continuous task for House members), stand in for the member as needed, and in other ways serve as the member's alter ego. The administrative assistant frequently hires, evaluates, dismisses, and sets the pay of all other staff, subject, of course, to the member's approval.

Increasingly, scheduling staff operate from district and state offices, from which vantage they survey the mood of their members' constituents and of the electorate in general. Caseworkers, who are mostly quartered in district and state offices, have become additional sources of the people's concerns and their problems with government.

Support and technical staff perform the myriad tasks of office operations, including mail intake and outflow, filing and archiving, computer operations, receiving calls and visitors, and secretarial assistance to the member and high-ranking staffpersons.

Media staff have titles such as director or coordinator of communications and press secretary.

Mail. One major office enterprise is responding to the mail that floods members' offices. Virtually all staff are to some extent involved in this work, although legislative correspondents are specifically charged with the responsibility of assembling letters of response to inquiries about legislative and political issues.

While there is no exact measure of the amount of mail requiring written response, the total amount of mail coming into the House approaches 300 million pieces a year; the Senate receives more than 40 million pieces. But, as in every American household, a portion of this mail is composed of magazines, newspapers, books, and junk mail and therefore requires no response.

The extent to which the amount of outgoing mail reflects the volume of incoming mail is also unknown, because members send out unsolicited letters and engage in mass mailings—to "postal patron" or specifically targeted audiences—in addition to responding to correspondence.

Generally, members receive greater volumes of mail in election years than in nonelection years. In the House, where all members must stand for reelection every second year, outgoing mail totals around 400 million pieces in a nonelection year and more than 500 million in an election year. Because only one-third of the Senate stands for reelection at a time, the volume of its outgoing mail is not so closely tied to the electoral cycle and in fact has fluctuated considerably from year to year: for example, the Senate's outgoing mail totaled 156 million pieces in 1987, 256 million the next year, 226 million in 1989, but only an estimated 116 million in 1990. It rose sharply in 1991, however, to more than 230 million pieces. Since 1989 steps have been taken to restrict the types and amount of "franked" mail—the mail that senators and representatives can send out at no cost to themselves.

Another factor that makes generalizing about mail a complicated affair is that members vary widely in their mailing practices; some mail a lot, others little, and still others a lot or a little, depending on whether it is an election year. Newer members tend to mail more than senior members, and those in competitive election contests more than incumbents whose seats are relatively safe.

Whatever the numbers, mail operations have grown increasingly sophisticated and efficient in order to keep pace with volume. The days when members could peruse much of their mail and craft individual responses have vanished; now most responses are generated using computerized methods. Nowadays administrative, legislative, and press staff draft position statements on the issues that constituents inquire about most frequently. After review and approval by the member or a key staffer, this boilerplate is stored in computers and retrieved as needed for composing letters.

Constituent assistance. Letters, calls, or visits by constituents seeking a member's assistance with a federal agency or foreign government are handled individually, although standardized letters of acknowledgment and interim responses (progress reports) are customary. Members place a high premium on this kind of work, fervently believing that assisting and intervening on behalf of their constituents is both an important service and sound politics. So important is this service that as late as the 1940s members themselves frequently accompanied constituents to meetings with federal agencies. In the 1990s their busy schedules permit this, or other forms of personal intervention on behalf of constituents, only on rare occasions. Most often it falls to staff to perform the crucial task of acting as liaison for constituents and intervening with agencies and governments.

Constituents seek help from their members of Congress mostly as a last resort, and members know this. Accordingly, when requests for assistance arrive, staff spring into action, learning why a constituent has experienced difficulty—if this is the case—and ascertaining what a constituent must do in order to obtain relief. Constituents seek a variety of kinds of assistance, from claiming benefits they think are due them (casework), to requesting federal funds for businesses or local governmental bodies (project work), to needing fair decisions on matters of special consideration. While member intervention cannot always guarantee an outcome that will satisfy the supplicant, the assistance is frequently helpful and almost invariably appreciated.

Legislative work. Another nucleus of staff assists members with legislative work. Many members tie most of their legislative work to their committee assignments.

Some, however, introduce legislation across a wide range of policy areas.

The number of legislative staff and the amount of work they do varies according to the aims and activities of the member they serve. Their duties include identifying policy options and gathering and analyzing information and views on these alternatives; helping the member to determine a position on pending legislation; and assisting the member in defining the scope and substance of legislative proposals he or she is considering or planning to sponsor. If the member is introducing legislation, staff make sure that policy ideas are transformed into properly worded bills by the expert legal staff of the House or Senate Office of Legislative Counsel. Staff are responsible for devising legislative strategies and guiding legislation through the many wickets that lie between submission and enactment. They assist at committee hearings and meetings and help with committee and floor statements or floor management of a bill if that task falls to their member. Beyond these jobs, legislative staff perform various other tasks related to a member's legislative and representational duties—including assisting in drafting letters to explain the member's policy choices and assisting in obtaining information for or drafting portions of the member's speeches.

This component of personal staffing has swollen in numbers and risen in influence since the 1960s. Over time, members have come to rely on these staffers for legislative intelligence and networking with other members' offices and with committees—in other words, they serve as members' eyes and ears.

Media relations. Press staff assist members in communicating with voters through the media—a task that, in the years before World War II, was almost entirely handled by members themselves.

Gaining media coverage—and thus being able to highlight activities, goals, positions, and proposals—is easier for congressional party leaders and chairs of important committees than it is for new members or members who lack positions of authority. Senators are likely to command more coverage than representatives.

The House and Senate press and radio and television galleries, with more than forty-five hundred accredited print or electronic journalists, are regularly populated by a handful of correspondents of the so-called prestige press, that is, radio and television network reporters and reporters for newspapers such as the *Washington Post* and *New York Times* and wire services such as the Associated Press and United Press International. Of necessity, the prestige press is highly selective about what and whom it covers.

Network television and the wire services—along with syndicated Washington columnists—constitute the major source of news about Congress and its members for most local stations and newspapers. Their coverage focuses on policy actions, leadership announcements, and news about the institution itself—especially scandals and executive-legislative relations and tensions—rather than on the work of individual members of Congress. Accordingly, members must cultivate and promote coverage in home-state and home-district newspapers, television, and radio. They do so by taking reporters' calls, soliciting media coverage through press interviews or comments on presidential initiatives and congressional actions, holding press conferences when warranted, issuing traditional press releases, and appearing on radio or television either in interviews—for instance, on news talk shows—or in prepared audio or video feeds for satellite broadcast to local stations serving their constituency.

Relatedly, the advent and spread of cable television, including the public affairs and news channels C-SPAN and CNN, have led to greater television coverage of committee hearings and thus have expanded members' "electronic visibility." The House authorized gavel-to-gavel television coverage of daily floor proceedings in 1979 and the Senate followed suit in 1986. Both House and Senate proceedings are carried by C-SPAN and available in more than fifty million homes, meaning that members now get a degree of public exposure heretofore unavailable. At the same time, network television news increasingly uses clips from floor and committee telecasting for stories on legislative activity, thus providing additional notice for members.

Credentials, age, tenure, and pay. Most professional and some clerical personal staff have had some higher education. Studies by the Congressional Management Foundation, a Washington-based nonprofit educational organization, show that 76 percent of those who work in House offices and almost 80 percent of those in Senate ones have at least a bachelor's degree, as compared with 35 percent of federal civilian employees and 17 percent of the general U.S. adult population. In the House, only 13 percent of personal staff have not gone beyond high school, while in the Senate less than 7 percent fall into this category. Members want bright and informed people working for them.

These same studies show that the average age of Senate and House personal staff is less than thirty-five, which is about two years below the median age of the U.S. labor force and seven years below the average age of federal civilian employees. In large measure this is the result of short tenure and the attendant high turnover. (Among Senate staffers, the average tenure on the

Hill is less than six years; in the House, five, with average tenure in a given position running about three and one-half years in the Senate and just under three years in the House.)

Studies show that the average age of Senate and House personal staff is less than thirty-five.

Few staff make a career of working for members, in part because, on average, members serve only ten years (five terms) in the House and twelve years (two terms) in the Senate. People also leave congressional staff jobs because of personal ambition and the low pay—salaries average about $30,000 in the House and $33,000 in the Senate, compared with almost $34,000 for all federal workers and $42,000 for Washington-based federal workers. Comparable workers in the private sector earn anywhere from 28 to 35 percent more.

COMMITTEE STAFF. Congressional committee staff now number about four thousand. Their principal job is to provide information of various sorts to help the committees meet their several responsibilities, which include exploring the need, feasibility, consequences, risks, benefits, and political consensus for policy change and innovation; authorizing and reauthorizing government programs and activities, appropriating money to pay for them, and raising revenue to fund the government; inquiring into foreign policy and foreign governments and evaluating treaties with other nations and international organizations; overseeing federal programs, agencies, and expenditures to ensure they are administered in ways that are economical, effective, equitable, and efficient; investigating wrongdoing, malfeasance, or chicanery; and, in the Senate, conducting inquiries into executive, judicial, and ambassadorial nominees as part of the confirmation process.

These dedicated men and women must be familiar with their committees' jurisdictions and the programs and activities for which they have sole or shared responsibility. They must be highly informed, intelligent, and savvy and possessed of good political judgment and negotiating skills. While data on the education, experience, tenure, and age of committee staff (comparable to those for personal staff) are not available, it is known that in all these characteristics committee staff match or exceed personal staff. Because their work is far more concentrated—that is, program- and agency-specific—and because their relationships with agencies are closer and endure longer than those of personal staff, professional committee staff tend to be better informed, more experienced, and more influential than personal staff. When allegations are made that congressional staff have become overly powerful, critics are usually referring to committee staff. Top committee staffers make more than $100,000 annually.

ADMINISTRATIVE AND HOUSEKEEPING STAFF. Congress also has the basic need to keep its physical plant operating. Congressional administrative and housekeeping staff include engineers, architects, maintenance workers, postal clerks, restaurant and dining room workers, police, computer specialists, bill drafters, people who help with the floor operations in each chamber, and employees who see that checks are written and financial and other records are maintained.

LEADERSHIP STAFF. This small complement of staff, numbering fewer than 350, assists party leaders in each chamber—the Speaker of the House, the vice president, the president pro tempore of the Senate, and the majority and minority leaders and whips of the House and Senate—with the many chores that accompany framing and promoting party policy programs, scheduling and managing floor business, rounding up votes, and maintaining party coordination and communication. Such staff are usually party loyalists who are mentally agile and politically astute.

SUPPORT AGENCY STAFF. Finally, each of the four congressional support agencies has its own staff. Together, these staffs number about three thousand and represent a pooled resource for members and committees.

The Congressional Budget Office, established in 1974, principally provides neutral and competent economic, fiscal, and budgetary analysis and information. Its major clients are the budget committees, appropriating committees, and finance committees in each house.

The Office of Technology Assessment, established in 1972, provides a limited number of in-depth studies each year on the impact of technology on society, the economy, and the ecosystem. A major information resource for congressional committees, these reports evaluate existing or proposed policies and programs across a spectrum of issues—education, health, defense, the environment, energy, foreign policy, and so forth.

The General Accounting Office, established in 1921, assists committees with their oversight activities. It is also the principal agency in the government vested with authority to conduct audits of programs and activities to ascertain whether they are being managed effectively and in accordance with law.

The Congressional Research Service, a separate department in the Library of Congress since 1914, serves all members and committees equally by quickly providing them with information, research, and analysis on virtually any topic or issue of interest to them.

ISSUES IN STAFFING. The growth of congressional staff has elicited concerns and criticisms in and outside Congress. Worth noting is that some of these concerns have been voiced since the late nineteenth century, when Congress inaugurated the modern system of staffing. As Fox and Hammond pointed out in *Congressional Staffs,* six themes have recurred in congressional staffing debates: (1) managing increases in work load; (2) improving economy and efficiency in government—including congressional—operations; (3) the cost of increased staffing; (4) members' concerns about adverse public reaction to the growth in Congress's operating costs; (5) minority party concerns that their members be given adequate committee staff and that there be equitable distribution of committee staff resources between minority and majority party members; and (6) the effect of institutional reform on staffing.

Other concerns have arisen as congressional staffs have grown to current levels. These concerns have centered on, among other things, the need to arrive at an appropriate balance between staff allocated to members and staff allocated to committees; members' judgment in hiring the right mix of staff and members' ability to use their staffs with maximum effectiveness; and the Hill's idiosyncratic, highly autonomous employment practices, including the lack of systematic rules regarding hiring and firing and the absence of meaningful job protections for some employees. Concerns have also been expressed about the increasingly rapid turnover of congressional staff, particularly in the House, resulting in staffs that are inexperienced and unseasoned, and about how staff salaries are set. Current practice allows for a host of salary inequities: between House and Senate staff, between committee and personal staff in each house, and between men and women in identical positions. The ease with which members and committees raid one another's staffs and the propensity of congressional staffers to "job hop" are blamed on these inequities. The crowded conditions under which congressional staffers too often work have also been assailed.

Beyond these complaints, there is the reiterated criticism that congressional staff have come to wield too much influence and to exercise powers that should belong to members alone.

The history of congressional staffing suggests that over time these issues and concerns will be addressed and to some extent remedied. Despite repeated calls for substantial cuts in staff, need and work load appear to make unfeasible any significant reduction in the number of congressional staff.

BIBLIOGRAPHY

Chaleff, Ira, et al. *Setting Course: A Congressional Management Guide.* 3d ed. 1988.

Congressional Quarterly, Inc. *Congressional Pay and Perquisites: History, Facts, and Controversy.* 1992.

Cooper, Joseph, and G. Calvin Mackenzie, eds. *The House at Work.* 1981.

Fox, Harrison, and Susan Webb Hammond. *Congressional Staffs: The Invisible Force in American Lawmaking.* 1977.

Hammond, Susan Webb. "Legislative Staffs." *Legislative Studies Quarterly* 9 (1984): 271–317.

Heaphey, James J., ed. "Public Administration and Legislatures." *Public Administration Review* 35 (1975).

Johannes, John R. *To Serve the People: Congress and Constituency Service.* 1984.

Kofmehl, Kenneth. *Professional Staff of Congress.* 3d ed. 1977.

Malbin, Michael J. *Unelected Representatives: Congressional Staff and the Future of Representative Government.* 1980.

Pauls, Frederick H. *Clerk Hire Authorizations for Senators and Representatives. Congressional Research Service, Library of Congress.* CRS Rept. 93-595 S. 1993.

Pauls, Frederick H., ed. "Congress and the Bureaucracy." *The Public Manager* (summer 1992). A special issue, with articles on constituency service, congressional office operations, leaders, and congressional oversight.

Rundquist, Paul, Judy Schneider, and Frederick H. Pauls. *Congressional Staff: An Analysis of Their Roles, Functions, and Impacts.* Congressional Research Service, Library of Congress. CRS Rept. 92-905. 1992.

– FREDERICK H. PAULS

SUBCOMMITTEES

The smallest, most specialized, and most accessible panels on Capitol Hill are the subcommittees. They are the point of entry for most citizen activists, bureaucrats, and professional lobbyists who track legislation through Congress. Like their parent committees, subcommittees vary in their attractiveness to members, their visibility to constituents, their legislative activity, and their autonomy. Since the 1950s, the number of subcommittees has ranged from 83 to 135 in the House and 85 to 140 in the Senate. Over the past three decades the number of House subcommittees has been fairly stable at around 130, but the Senate number has been more erratic, in the early 1990s hovering in the high eighties. In accordance with a 1993 initiative to reduce the number of subcommittees in Congress, the figure now stands at 115 sub-committees in the House and 86 in the Senate. This represents an average of five panels per parent committee, with a range of zero (Senate Veterans Affairs) to thirteen (House and Senate Appropriations).

Subcommittees are products not of the U.S. Constitution but of procedural rules, individual ambition, and the political temperament of different periods. They emerged in the early 1900s to establish a comprehensible division of labor that would spread the responsibilities as well as the political fortunes associated with policy-making. They burgeoned after the Legislative Reorganization Act of 1946 consolidated the full committees, paradoxically encouraging the formation of new subcommittees—some along the lines of committees that had been eliminated. Another major boost came in 1973 with the "Subcommittee Bill of Rights." This and other reforms of the day diffused power, allowing congressional newcomers to hold positions of authority on subcommittees with definable jurisdictions and staff.

With few exceptions a bill is considered first in subcommittee, where it undergoes a public hearing and preliminary markup. It takes a majority of subcommittee members to report a bill for full committee review. Usually, the full committee bases its assessment on the preliminary evidence established in subcommittee. Because subcommittee members are the first to pass judgment on bills, they and their staffers are the first to be pressured by interested outsiders. For some powerful subcommittee chairmen the job does not end there. Subcommittee sponsors often champion their bills throughout the legislative cycle, amassing supporters along the way in terms of staff and colleagues at the full committee level.

The responsibilities for creating, renewing, and overseeing governmental intervention are dispersed among subcommittees in such a way that some panels have more appeal than others. The most highly sought-after subcommittees are those that pertain to Congress's role in taxing and spending or have jurisdiction over broad public concerns. These are also the subcommittees that afford their chairs media exposure and recognition that translate into campaign support—money and votes. Other subcommittees are consistently avoided either because they have narrow jurisdictions of interest to few citizens or because they arouse conflict and certain vulnerability at the polls. Subcommittee variations can be explained by (1) the political milieu; (2) procedural rules, precedent, and norms; and (3) their members' individual ambitions.

POLITICAL MILIEU. Unprecedented demands on Congress elevated the prestige and accompanying attractiveness of office in the wake of the Civil War, and for the first time legislators began to view their work as having real career potential. Changed expectations increased the value of committee seats, so new seats were created. The reforms of the 1970s also followed tumultuous change in the country. This time, public cynicism over the protracted war in Vietnam and the dirty-tricks politics of Watergate contributed to an extraordinary number of electoral upsets. The new and aggressive class of first-year members entering Congress in 1975 promised and delivered change, generally weakening the seniority system, democratizing the committee assignment process, and dispersing power. Ninety percent of members from the majority party in the Senate, for example, chair at least one committee or subcommittee. Although the figure is much lower in the House, the increase is dramatic, from 27.2 percent in 1955 to 48.7 percent in 1992.

STRUCTURE AND RULES. Whereas the House controls proliferation of the number of subcommittees with rules limiting standing committees to six or eight each, depending on their size, the Senate creates de facto ceilings by limiting the number of panels on which any one senator may participate.

Subcommittee staff resources also vary within and across chambers. While all subcommittee positions are funded at the behest of the full committee leadership, staff allocations are more distinct and routine in the House. Note, for example, that seven of the fourteen standing committees in the Senate centralize all staff at the full committee level and dispatch personnel as needed to the subcommittees; only two House committees engage in this practice. Comparing the fortunes of the two political parties in terms of their share of staff resources, House subcommittee members of the controlling party hire from one to seventeen professional aides, with an average of four per panel. The Senate range is from one to twelve aides, with an average of four. Members of the minority party hire roughly one-third this number of assistants.

The most highly sought-after subcommittees are those that pertain to Congress's role in taxing and spending or have jurisdiction over broad public concerns.

The increase in the autonomy of House subcommittees relative to their parent committees gives meaning to the phrase "subcommittee government." In the Senate the role of subcommittees is much more ambiguous. The differences are striking. Eighty percent of House bills go to a subcommittee first, and only if they pass this initial screening are they forwarded to a full committee for a vote. Senate subcommittees perform this function only half as often. A larger proportion of House public hearings are held at the subcommittee level as well—95 percent, as compared with 64 percent in the Senate (1990 figures). Furthermore, bills' sponsors typically defend their initiatives from hostile amendments on the floor of the House, with subcommittee leaders fulfilling the role three times as often as full committee chairmen. The majority party leader in the Senate, who does not sit on either full committees or subcommittees, manages nearly 60 percent of the bills that reach the floor for debate in that chamber.

MEMBERSHIP. Because of their widely differing jurisdictions, committees and subcommittees attract members with differing ambitions, and the bidding for subcommittee assignments, while competitive, is highly responsive to members' preferences. Entrepreneurial chairmen, with the consent of their members, can modify a subcommittee's focus to address emerging policy concerns. The varying composition of subcommittees and the varying ambitions of subcommittee leaders help explain the different levels of activity and productivity between panels.

As a result of the increased division of labor created by subcommittees, more individuals share the work and the fortunes of lawmaking. The screening process through which issues pass is more rigorous as more members and staff participate in new levels of review. Democratizing the policy-making process within Congress serves also to expand the institution's accessibility to interested parties outside Congress. Increased opportunities for involvement and representation are not without costs, however. As the number of players expands, so too does the likelihood of indecision and stalemate.

[See also (I) Committees.]

BIBLIOGRAPHY

Davidson, Roger H. *The Postreform Congress.* 1992.

Deering, Christopher J. "Subcommittee Government in the U.S. House: An Analysis of Bill Management." *Legislative Studies Quarterly* 7 (1982): 533–546.

DeGregorio, Christine. "Leadership Approaches in Congressional Committees Hearings." *Western Politics Quarterly* 45 (1992): 971–983.

Evans, Lawrence, and Richard L. Hall. "The Power of Subcommittees." *Journal of Politics* 52 (1990): 335–355.

Smith, Steven S., and Christopher J. Deering. *Committees in Congress.* 1990.

– CHRISTINE DEGREGORIO

UNITED STATES OF AMERICA

Congress of the United States

Richard Whitney, Individually and as President of

To NEW YORK STOCK EXCHANGE,

11 Wall Street, New York City.

, Greeting:

Pursuant to lawful authority, YOU ARE HEREBY COMMANDED to appear before the Committee on Banking & Currency of the Senate of the United States, on February 13th, 1934 at 10:00 o'clock A. m., at their Committee Room 301 Senate Office Building, Washington, D.C., then and there to testify what you may know relative to the subject matters under consideration by said Committee. AND YOU, the said RICHARD WHITNEY, bring with you all records, reports and writings filed with the NEW YORK STOCK EXCHANGE pursuant to Section 6, of Chapter 15, of Rules of the New York Stock Exchange.

Hereof fail not, as you will answer your default under the pains and penalties in such cases made and provided.

To Stuart C. Ross.

to serve and return.

Given under my hand, by order of the Committee, this 3rd day of February, in the year of our Lord one thousand nine hundred and Thirty-four.

Chairman, Committee on Banking & Currency
U. S. Senate

Subpoena served on Richard Whitney. Whitney, president of the New York Stock Exchange, was subpoenaed to appear before the Senate Committee on Banking and Currency on 13 February 1934, during an investigation of stock market practices. (National Archives)

SUBPOENA POWER

The authority to issue subpoenas—to require the testimony of witnesses or the production of records, documents, and other materials for congressional inquiries—is granted by the House and Senate to all their standing committees and subcommittees. Special or select committees must be specifically delegated this authority when they are established (by a resolution of the House or the Senate). The Legislative Reorganization Act of 1946 granted subpoena power to all Senate standing committees but not to standing committees of the House because of opposition from Speaker Sam Rayburn (D-Tex.) and House minority leader Joseph W. Martin, Jr. (R-Mass.). It was not until 3 January 1975 that all House standing committees were granted subpoena power (H. Res. 988, 93d Cong.).

First issued in 1792, during the House's inquiry into Gen. Arthur St. Clair's military defeat, subpoenas have apparently been issued with increasing frequency in modern times. The subpoena authority is an integral part of Congress's investigative and oversight powers. Nonetheless, subpoenas must be directly connected with the issuing panel's authority and jurisdiction and may be challenged by claims of executive privilege. Because the subpoena is a legal order, a witness who refuses it can be cited for contempt of Congress and prosecuted in federal court.

Although the Constitution does not expressly grant Congress the power to issue subpoenas, the Supreme Court has recognized an implied subpoena power on several notable occasions. In *McGrain v. Daugherty* (1927) the Court held that "the power of inquiry—with process to enforce it—is an essential and appropriate auxiliary to the legislative function." The Court reaffirmed this principle in *Eastland v. U.S. Servicemen's Fund* (1975), stating, "The issuance of a subpoena pursuant to an authorized investigation is . . . an indispensable ingredient of lawmaking."

[See also (I) Oversight.]

BIBLIOGRAPHY

Grabow, John C. *Congressional Investigations: Law and Practice.* 1988.

Hamilton, James. *The Power to Probe: A Study of Congressional Investigations.* 1976.

U.S. Congress. Joint Committee on Congressional Operations. *Leading Cases on Congressional Investigatory Power.* 94th Cong., 2d sess., 1976. Committee Print.

– FREDERICK M. KAISER

SUSPENSION OF THE RULES

Suspension of the rules refers to procedures by which the House of Representatives acts expeditiously on matters enjoying widespread support among its members.

A bill or resolution considered under suspension of the rules is debated by all members for no more than forty minutes, after which a two-thirds vote is required to pass it. The Speaker may postpone the vote until a later time or the following day. Members cast a single vote on suspending the rules and passing the measure. The bill or resolution may not be amended during its consideration, although the member making the motion to pass the measure under suspension of the rules may include amendments to the measure in that motion.

As time pressures on the House have grown, these procedures have become increasingly popular, and the House rules have been amended to permit suspension motions to be made more often. Once in order only on two Mondays of each month, these motions now may be made on Monday and Tuesday of each week and during the closing days of each congressional session. Toward the end of a session, the House may act on ten or more suspension motions in a single day. However, the Speaker has the authority to determine whether a suspension motion may be offered and, therefore, whether a bill or resolution may be considered in this way. In recent Congresses, the House has used these procedures to act on between one-third and one-half of the measures it has passed.

[See also (I) Rule, Special.]

BIBLIOGRAPHY

Bach, Stanley. "Suspension of the Rules, the Order of Business, and the Development of Congressional Procedure." *Legislative Studies Quarterly* 15 (1990): 49–63.

U.S. House of Representatives. *Deschler's Precedents of the United States House of Representatives,* by Lewis Deschler. 94th Cong., 2d sess., 1977. H. Doc. 94-661. Vol. 6, pp. 165–265.

– STANLEY BACH

T

TABLING

The motion to lay a proposition on the table, if successful, is equivalent to final adverse disposition of that matter without debate in both the House and Senate.

In the Senate the motion to table a matter is in order any time a question is pending before the Senate, unless that question is more privileged than the motion to table itself (i.e., a motion to adjourn, recess, or proceed to consideration of executive business). If successful, the motion does not carry with it, or prejudice, the underlying question as well. This means, for example, that tabling an amendment will not cause the underlying bill to be tabled with it. As a result of this convention, and the fact that the motion is decided upon without debate, the Senate has developed the practice of using the motion for a variety of purposes, including to dispose of a matter immediately, as a vote to test support for an amendment, as a means of avoiding a direct yes-or-no vote on a matter, or to counter dilatory tactics. An important exception is that the motion is not applicable during a period of debate specified in a unanimous consent agreement.

In the House, however, the use of the motion is restricted by the fact that when a proposed amendment is laid on the table, the underlying measure goes there also. It is not in order in a number of circumstances, including with regard to motions to adjourn, to suspend the rules, or to recommit; motions relating to the order of business; or generally motions that are neither debatable nor amendable. It is also not applicable to demands for the previous question, or once the previous question has been ordered, or to motions to resolve into Committee of the Whole; in addition, when the House is operating in Committee of the Whole, the motion to table is not in order at all. Therefore, the chief use of tabling is against matters brought up as privileged that the leadership wishes to remove from consideration.

[See also (I) Bills.]

BIBLIOGRAPHY

U.S. House of Representatives. *Deschler's Precedents of the United States House of Representatives,* by Lewis Deschler. 94th Cong., 2d sess., 1977. H. Doc. 94-661. Vol. 7, chap. 23.

U.S. House of Representatives. *Hinds' Precedents of the House of Representatives of the United States,* by Asher C. Hinds. 59th Cong., 2d sess., 1907. Vol. 5, chap. 119.

U.S. Senate. *Senate Procedure, Precedents, and Practices,* by Floyd M. Riddick. 97th Cong., 1st sess., 1981. Doc. 97-2.

U.S. House of Representatives. *Constitution, Jefferson's Manual, and Rules of the House of Representatives, 102d Congress.* Compiled by William Holmes Brown. 101st Cong., 2d sess., 1990. H. Doc. 101-256.

– JAMES V. SATURNO

TREATIES

Under international law, a treaty means any legally binding agreement between nations. In the United States, the term *treaty* is reserved for those international agreements submitted to the Senate for its advice and consent. Other international agreements, often called executive agreements in the United States, are not treaties in U.S. parlance but are considered treaties under international law and are legally binding on the United States.

Treaties submitted to the Senate are the most formal international undertakings and commitments of the United States. Past treaties provide a history of U.S. foreign policy. For example, the Treaty of Ghent with Great Britain of 24 December 1814 provided for settlement of issues after the War of 1812. In the Treaty of Paris of 10 December 1898, Spain ceded Puerto Rico, Guam, and the Philippines to the United States. The Hay-Pauncefote Treaty of 18 November 1901 gave the United States the right to build a canal across the Isthmus of Panama, and the Panama Canal Treaty of 7 September 1977 provided for Panama's assuming total control of the canal after 31 December 1999. The United States did not become a member of the League of Nations because President Woodrow Wilson and the Senate disagreed on reservations to the Versailles Treaty of 1919, while ratification of the United Nations Charter of 1945 and the North Atlantic Treaty in 1949 launched a new period of international involvement and leadership.

Because the treaty power is divided or shared under the Constitution, numerous controversies have arisen between the Senate and the president over the proper roles of each branch.

CONSTITUTIONAL PROVISIONS. The Articles of Confederation, which formed the basis of the relationship among the thirteen states from 1776 to 1789, vested the treaty power in the Congress, the only central organ, and required nine states for assent to a treaty.

During the Constitutional Convention, the Virginia and New Jersey plans, representing the views of the large and small states, respectively, did not specify how treaties were to be made, both apparently assuming that Congress would continue to make them. On 18 June 1787, Alexander Hamilton presented a plan under which the chief executive "with the advice and approbation of the Senate" would have the power to make treaties, and similar language was ultimately adopted. Article II, section 2, clause 2 of the Constitution provides that the president "shall have Power, by and with the Advice and Consent of the Senate, to make Treaties, provided two-thirds of the Senators present concur."

Three other provisions of the Constitution complete the framework for U.S. law on treaties. Article I, section 10 restricts the states from entering into any treaty or compact without the consent of Congress, making treaties solely the responsibility of the federal government. Article II, section 2, clause 1 provides that the judicial power extend to all cases arising under the Constitution or U.S. laws and treaties. Article VI, section 2 provides that treaties be the supreme law of the land, along with the Constitution and laws.

The Senate has approved approximately 90 percent of the treaties submitted to it.

The Constitution thus created the dilemma in which treaties are part of the supreme law of the land but are not formed by the regular legislative process. Some Framers of the Constitution objected to having instruments with the status of law concluded without the concurrence of the House of Representatives. The view prevailed, however, that the necessity for secrecy precluded referring treaties to the entire Congress.

EVOLUTION TO MODERN PRACTICE. The original intention of the Framers was that the Senate and the president share the treaty-making process and that the sharing begin early, with the proposal to enter negotiations and the appointment and instruction of negotiators. The Senate was to serve as a council advising the president. On 22 August 1789, in one of the first treaty actions, President George Washington came into the Senate chamber to present a proposal for a treaty with specific questions; he returned two days later for votes on additional questions related to the treaty. Both the president and the Senate were dissatisfied with that encounter, however, and Washington did not again visit the Senate to consult on a treaty. On occasion he sought advice by written message to the Senate before opening negotiations, but by the end of his administration, Washington was informing the Senate about a proposed treaty for the first time when he sought approval of a negotiator, and was submitting the negotiating instructions with the completed treaty.

By 1816, the practice became established that the Senate's role was to approve, to approve with reservations or other conditions, or to disapprove treaties after they had been negotiated by the president or his emissary. In the European monarchies prior to that time, it had been considered obligatory for a monarch to ratify a treaty if his emissary had stayed within his instructions and no practice existed of making reservations to parts of a treaty, but gradually the American practice was accepted. After considering Jay's Treaty of 19 November 1794 with Great Britain, the Senate approved it on 24 June 1795, with the condition that the twelfth article be amended, and the amendment was accepted by President Washington and Great Britain. In the Treaty with Tunis of 1797, the Senate gave its advice and consent subject to renegotiation of an article; the article was renegotiated and the Senate subsequently approved the treaty. The King-Hawksbury Convention of 12 May 1803 became the first treaty not to enter into force because the other party, in this case Great Britain, would not accept an amendment by the Senate.

U.S. TREATY PROCESS. The negotiation of a treaty is undertaken solely by the president and executive branch officials, although members of Congress frequently suggest ideas for negotiations and sometimes participate as observers or advisers. The president or his representatives decide whether to sign a treaty and when to submit it to the Senate for advice and consent. Once submitted to the Senate, the treaty is referred to the Foreign Relations Committee. If the committee decides to report the treaty to the Senate, it proposes a resolution of ratification that may contain various conditions. Conditions may include amendments (changes in the text of a treaty), reservations (qualifications that change obligations under the treaty), understandings (an interpretation or elaboration clarifying the treaty), and declarations, provisos, or other statements (statements of policy relating to the subject of a treaty but not necessarily affecting its provisions). The important distinction among various kinds of conditions is the legal effect. Whatever a condition is named, if the president considers that it constitutes an amendment or reservation that changes a treaty obligation, he is obligated to transmit it to the other party for a decision on whether to accept the condition, reject the treaty, or seek renegotiation.

After the treaty is reported from the committee, the leadership determines when it will be considered by the full Senate. The Senate first considers any proposed conditions or amendments to the treaty to be placed in the resolution of ratification; in 1868 the Senate changed its rules to permit adoption of such amendments by a simple majority vote. The final resolution of ratification must be adopted by a two-thirds majority. The Senate procedure has been simplified since 1986, when the Senate amended Senate Rule XXX to eliminate a step in which the Senate met "as in Committee of the Whole" to consider amendments to the treaty.

After the Senate adopts the resolution of ratification, if the president wants the treaty to enter into force and accepts any conditions added by the Senate, he signs a document called the instrument of ratification. He then exchanges the instrument of ratification with the other party to a bilateral treaty or deposits it with a depository in the case of a multilateral treaty. When the ratifications are exchanged or the required number of ratifications deposited, the treaty enters into force (becomes legally binding internationally) and the president signs a proclamation publicizing that fact domestically. If the president objects to any of the Senate conditions, he does not sign the ratification, and if the other party objects, it does not exchange ratifications, and the treaty does not enter into force.

USE OF THE SENATE TREATY POWER. Normally the Senate gives its advice and consent to treaties without conditions. The Senate has approved approximately 90 percent of the treaties submitted to it, and most of these have been approved without conditions.

The requirement for its advice and consent is a powerful tool for the Senate in foreign affairs because it gives the Senate a veto power over treaties. The requirement for a two-thirds majority enables a minority of one-third plus one, or thirty-four senators, to cast that veto. The Senate veto power over treaties has been recognized as permissible by the Supreme Court. In *Immigration and Naturalization Service v. Chadha* (1983), which held many legislative vetoes unconstitutional, the Court cited the Senate's "unreviewable power to ratify treaties negotiated by the President" as one of only four provisions in the Constitution by which "one House may act alone with the unreviewable force of law, not subject to the President's veto."

Outright rejection of a treaty by Senate vote is rare. Fewer than twenty treaties have been brought to a vote by the full Senate and have subsequently failed to receive the required two-thirds majority. The Treaty with Wabash and Illinois Indians of 27 September 1792 was the first treaty defeated by the Senate. The Treaty with Colombia on Suppression of the Slave Trade, concluded 10 December 1824, was rejected by the Senate on 9 March 1825. The most famous rejection was that of the Treaty of Versailles, signed 28 June 1919, containing the Covenant of the League of Nations. The Senate attached such conditions that, although President Wilson had negotiated the treaty, he requested his supporters in the Senate to vote against the final resolution of ratification because he believed that the reservations nullified rather than ratified the treaty. The treaty finally failed on 19 March 1920 with a vote of 49 in favor to 35 opposed, falling short of the required two-thirds majority.

When the Senate defeats a treaty, it usually employs means other than a direct rejection by vote. The most frequent of these is lack of action. If the Senate Foreign Relations Committee opposes a treaty or believes that it lacks adequate support, the committee does not report the treaty to the Senate. Alternatively, the Senate may choose not to vote on a treaty that has been reported favorably because the leadership believes that the treaty does not have a two-thirds majority, and the treaty is returned to the Foreign Relations Committee calendar. More than one hundred treaties have failed because the Senate did not act on them. Such treaties may be withdrawn, may be renegotiated and resubmitted, or may remain pending on the Senate Foreign Relations Committee calendar.

Sometimes the president makes known that he does not wish the Senate to act on a treaty. An example was the treaty with the Soviet Union on the limitation of strategic offensive arms, known as the SALT II Treaty, signed 18 June 1979. The Foreign Relations Committee reported the treaty with various conditions on 19 November 1979. After the Soviet invasion of Afghanistan in December 1979, President Jimmy Carter asked the Senate to delay consideration. The treaty was referred back to the Foreign Relations Committee calendar, and President Ronald Reagan did not ask for further action.

Some treaties fail because the Senate approves them with conditions that are subsequently refused by the president or other countries. The Department of State has attributed the failure of at least forty treaties to Senate reservations or amendments not acceptable to the president or the countries party to the treaty. For example, in January 1926 the Senate approved adherence to the Permanent Court of International Justice with five reservations, but other members would not accept the reservation that the court should never entertain a request for an advisory opinion on a dispute affecting the United States without the consent of the United States. (The Senate defeated a revised version on 29 January 1935. The United States became a member of the new International Court of Justice as part of its acceptance of the United Nations Charter, approved by the Senate on 28 July 1945.) A series of arbitration treaties signed in the early 1900s failed because of Senate conditions, as did several income tax treaties after 1965.

Even if the Senate gives its advice and consent unconditionally, it can exert influence on a treaty. Throughout the negotiation of a treaty the president is aware that the completed agreement must obtain the approval of a two-thirds majority, and he is commensurately alert to Senate views. On several occasions when the Senate has approved a treaty without formal conditions, senators prior to the approval have insisted on assurances about various concerns. In considering the Limited Nuclear Test Ban Treaty in 1963, for instance, the Senate turned down a reservation stating that the treaty did not inhibit the use of nuclear weapons in armed conflict, but it insisted on written assurances on this issue. Subsequently, on 23 September 1963, President John E. Kennedy wrote to Senate leaders that the treaty in no way limited the authority of the commander in chief to use nuclear weapons for defense of the United States or its allies, should such a need arise, and that such a decision would be made in accordance with American constitutional processes.

TREATIES IN INTERNATIONAL LAW. Under international law an international agreement is considered a treaty—and therefore binding on the parties under international law—if it meets four criteria: (1) it is intended to be legally binding and subject to international law, (2) it concerns significant matters, (3) it clearly and specifically describes the legal obligations of the parties, and (4) its form indicates an intention to conclude a legally binding agreement. International undertakings not intended to be legally binding, such as joint communiqués and final acts of conferences, are not considered treaties, but other international agreements that are intended to be legally binding, such as executive agreements, are considered treaties under international law.

On 23 May 1969, a United Nations conference of 110 nations adopted the Vienna Convention on the Law of Treaties, codifying international law on treaties. Although the United States signed the Vienna Convention on 24 April 1970, it had not ratified the convention by 1993 and so was not a party for which the treaty was in force. Nevertheless the executive branch considered that the convention reflected customary international law and generally followed its provisions. President Richard M. Nixon submitted the convention to the Senate on 22 November 1971, but the Senate Committee on Foreign Relations had not, by 1993, reported the convention to the Senate. The committee was concerned primarily because of the differing usage of the term *treaty* in the convention and in U.S. parlance. In 1972 the committee sought executive branch agreement on an interpretation and understanding stating that it is a rule of internal U.S. law that no treaty is valid unless the Senate has given its advice and consent or the terms have been approved by law; the Department of State, however, opposed the wording. Twenty years later the convention remained pending on the committee's calendar, reflecting the differing institutional interests of the legislative and executive branches.

TREATIES IN DOMESTIC LAW. Intermittently throughout U.S. history some have expressed concern that the president or Senate might use the treaty power to impose something as the law of the land without going through the legislative process. The treaty power is broad, extending to all matters considered proper for negotiation with foreign countries, but there are limitations. One is that the power does not extend to rights reserved to the states, except the unspecified reserved rights under the Tenth Amendment. Another limitation concerns participation in certain kinds of international judicial tribunals because of the final appellate jurisdiction of the Supreme Court and other constitutional concerns. Still another concerns subjects that lie within congressional delegated powers, such as foreign commerce, in which implementing legislation may be necessary for an agreement to become effective as domestic law. Some treaties expressly call for implementing legislation or clearly require additional congressional action, such as the appropriation of funds or enactment of domestic penal provisions.

The average number of treaties per year has leveled off at about fifteen to twenty.

Treaties that do not require implementing legislation are called self-executing treaties and become part of domestic law as soon as they enter into force. When a treaty is deemed self-executing, it overrides any conflicting provision of the law of an individual state. Courts try to harmonize domestic and international obligations, but if a treaty conflicts with a federal law, the one enacted later prevails.

During the 1950s some senators became concerned that treaties or executive agreements might be used as instruments of domestic legislation, and Sen. John W. Bricker (R-Ohio) proposed a series of constitutional amendments dealing with treaties and executive agreements. In 1953 he and sixty cosponsors introduced Senate Joint Resolution 1, which would have amended the Constitution to make a treaty effective as internal law only through the enactment of appropriate legislation, and to permit executive agreements only to the extent to be prescribed by law. As amended before being voted on, the resolution stated that any provision of a treaty that conflicted with the Constitution would be of no effect, and an international agreement other than a treaty would become effective as international law only by act of Congress. On 26 February 1954, the vote on the resolution, as amended, was 60 yeas to 31 nays. Since a two-thirds vote was required for a constitutional amendment, the resolution failed by one vote.

GROWTH IN INTERNATIONAL AGREEMENTS. Since the end of World War II, tremendous growth has occurred in international agreements concluded by the United States, reflecting increased U.S. involvement in the world, the growing number of sovereign states, and the interdependence of those states.

In the first fifty years of U.S. history (1789–1839), the United States concluded approximately sixty treaties and twenty-seven executive agreements; in the second fifty years (1839–1889), more than two hundred treaties and a slightly higher number of executive agreements; in the third fifty years (1889–1939), more than five hundred treaties and more than nine hundred executive agreements; and in the fourth fifty years (1939–1989), more than seven hundred treaties and almost eleven thousand executive agreements. The average number of treaties per year has leveled off at about fifteen to twenty, while the average number of executive agreements per year has soared to three or four hundred.

The growth in the number of international agreements has not brought a corresponding growth in the importance of the Senate role primarily because of the ever-increasing proportion of executive agreements—that is, international agreements that are not submitted to the Senate for its advice and consent. Such agreements have the same standing as treaties under international law, although not necessarily in domestic law. Many legal authorities hold that some executive agreements, which might be called congressional-executive agreements because they have been specifically authorized or approved by law, are virtually interchangeable with treaties. The domestic legal effect of executive agreements made pursuant to treaties and especially those concluded solely by the president on his own authority remains controversial.

The greater use of executive agreements reflects the ease of that mode of agreement making compared with the process of ratification, in which a Senate minority of one-third plus one can defeat a treaty. When laws authorize the conclusion of agreements in a field, such as postal services or space cooperation, or the president believes that he has adequate authority from a treaty or his own executive powers, the agreements receive no further congressional action. On some occasions presidents choose the congressional-executive agreement form by submitting an agreement to both houses of Congress rather than to the Senate alone. A president may want to involve the House of Representatives, or he may believe that an agreement can obtain the support of a majority of both houses but not a two-thirds majority of the Senate. This is what happened, for example, with the annexation of Texas. A treaty with the Republic of Texas providing for annexation concluded 12 April 1844 was defeated in the Senate on 8 June 1844. The next year, on 1 March 1845, at the request of the president, Texas was admitted into the Union by joint resolution. Similarly, the St. Lawrence Waterway Treaty with Canada of 18 July 1932 was rejected by a Senate vote of 46 to 42 on 14 March 1934. On 13 May 1954, Congress approved the Saint Lawrence Seaway by public law.

On other occasions, Congress through legislation directs the procedure for making international agreements in certain fields. Legislation has established special procedures for making and approving agreements in trade, nuclear cooperation, international fishery, and social security.

GROWTH IN MULTILATERAL TREATIES. Although the United States participated in relatively few multilateral agreements prior to the twentieth century, such agreements have become common since World War II. They have comprised some of the most important U.S. commitments, such as membership in the United Nations and Organization of American States. Because of its importance, the likelihood of a multilateral agreement being submitted to the Senate as a treaty is much higher than in the case of a bilateral agreement. Of the almost one thousand international multilateral agreements the United States entered through 1992, approximately one-third were treaties and two-thirds were executive agreements.

Multilateral treaties pose special problems for the Senate because they are often negotiated by many nations in large international organizations over a long time period. The result frequently constitutes an intricate package that the Senate must accept or reject as a whole. Although amendments to the treaty are discouraged because renegotiation would be so difficult, the Senate, often at the request of the president, sometimes places reservations or other conditions on its approval of a multilateral treaty.

To enhance the prospects of Senate approval of a treaty, especially a multilateral treaty in which renegotiation of a completed treaty is impracticable, presidents have on some occasions appointed senators or representatives as delegates or observers to the negotiations. Of the eight members of the official U.S. delegation to the San Francisco Conference that in 1945 adopted the United Nations Charter, four were members of Congress: Senators Tom T. Connally (D-Tex.) and Arthur H. Vandenberg (R-Mich.) and Representatives Sol Bloom (D-N.Y.) and Charles A. Eaton (R-N.J.). One issue is whether appointment of senators or representatives to serve on a delegation violates the separation of powers or creates a conflict of interest because they will later be called on to pass judgment on the completed treaty. A compromise solution has been to appoint members of Congress as advisers or observers, rather than as members of the delegation.

OTHER TREATY ISSUES. The Constitution makes no mention of the interpretation, amendment, or termination of treaties, and each of these processes has from time to time been disputed by the two branches.

While U.S. termination of a treaty ideally occurs through the same procedure as the original treaty was made, in practice a wide variety of methods have been used. The president has terminated treaties pursuant to prior authorization or direction of Congress or of the Senate alone, without prior authorization but with subsequent approval, or without any authorization or approval. On 15 December 1978, without any authorization from the Senate or Congress, President Carter gave notice of termination of the 1954 Mutual Defense Treaty with Taiwan. In *Goldwater v. Carter* (1979) Sen. Barry Goldwater (R-Ariz.) attempted to force a judicial resolution of the issue of whether the president could terminate the treaty without the advice and consent of the Senate or the approval of both houses of Congress. The Supreme Court dismissed the complaint, vitiating any precedent-setting value of earlier court rulings in the cases and leaving the issue unresolved.

Similarly, the general rule holds that an amendment to a prior international agreement should be made, domestically, in the same way as the original agreement. Thus an executive agreement may be modified by another executive agreement, but a modification of a treaty that received the advice and consent of the Senate should also be submitted to the Senate. In this case the president submits the formal amendment, often called a protocol, to the Senate as if it were a new treaty. On occasion, however, treaties have been modified through executive action or interpretation, by tacit understanding, or by legislation.

Treaty reinterpretation became an issue after 1985, when the Reagan administration announced a new interpretation of the 1972 Anti-Ballistic Missile (ABM) Treaty that would have permitted virtually unrestricted research and development of the Strategic Defense Initiative. The reinterpretation raised sharp debate in the Senate in 1987 about whether the president could interpret a treaty differently from the way it had been presented to or understood by the Senate at the time the Senate gave its advice and consent to ratification. State Department legal adviser Abraham Sofaer contended that the president was not bound to the original interpretation because the Senate had not been informed of some relevant aspects of the negotiating record and there was no formal record of the Senate's understanding of the issues. As a result of the controversy, in 1987 Sen. Sam Nunn (D-Ga.) requested the entire negotiating record of the Intermediate Nuclear Force (INF) Treaty with the Soviet Union, and the State Department supplied the documents. When the Senate gave its advice and consent to the INF Treaty on 27 May 1988, it did so with the condition, among others, that the United States would interpret the treaty in accordance with the common understanding shared by the president and the Senate at the time it gave its advice and consent, and that the United States would not adopt a different interpretation except pursuant to Senate advice and consent or the enactment of a statute. In 1993 the Clinton administration made clear it had returned to the traditional interpretation of the ABM Treaty.

[See also (II) Treaty-making Power.]

BIBLIOGRAPHY

American Law Institute. *Restatement of the Law First, Second, and Third. The Foreign Relations Law of the United States.* 1987. Part 3, "International Agreements."

Dangerfield, Royden J. *In Defense of the Senate: A Study in Treaty-Making.* 1933.

Fleming, Denna Frank. *The Treaty Veto of the American Senate.* 1930.

Glennon, Michael J. "The Senate Role in Treaty Ratification." *American Journal of International Law* 77 (1983): 257–280.

Hayden, Ralston. *The Senate and Treaties, 1789–1817.* 1920.

Holt, W. Stull. *Treaties Defeated by the Senate.* 1964.

U.S. Department of State. Office of the Legal Adviser. *Treaties in Force: A List of Treaties and Other International Agreements of the United States in Force on January 1, 1993.* 1993.

U.S. Senate. Committee on Foreign Relations. *Legislative Activities Report; 102d Congress, January 3, 1991–October 8, 1992.* 103d Cong., 1st sess, 1993. S. Rept. 103-35.

U.S. Senate. Committee on Foreign Relations. *Treaties and Other International Agreements: The Role of the United States Senate.* 98th Cong., 2d sess., 1984. S. Rept. 98-205. Includes annotated bibliography.

– ELLEN C. COLLIER

U

UNANIMOUS CONSENT

Members of both the House and Senate regularly use unanimous consent to request permission from their colleagues to set aside the normal rules of procedure or to take a procedural action not expressly provided for in the rules. Unanimous consent is used for a wide variety of actions, ranging from adopting legislation, amendments, or motions to more routine matters such as extending debate time.

The use of unanimous consent provides the House and Senate with flexibility to set aside formal procedures in order to facilitate the business at hand. Yet it preserves the standing rules of each chamber by setting them aside only temporarily. Thus any single member can call upon the full protection of the regular order if necessary.

A unanimous consent request must receive the approval of every member present on the floor at the time it is made; a single objection will block its implementation. Agreement to a unanimous consent request does not require a vote. Instead, the presiding officer can ask if there is an objection to the request. Without objection, action proceeds as outlined in the request.

There is a difference between unanimous consent requests and unanimous consent agreements. Requests are routinely offered in both chambers by any member, and normally receive immediate consideration. Agreements are more extensive and cover a broader range of procedural activity (e.g., setting terms for calling up, debating, amending, and voting on a bill). They require extensive negotiations and are usually proposed only by a member of the chamber's leadership.

In the Senate, unanimous consent has been common practice since 1789 and is expressly provided for by Rule V. In the House, regular use began around 1832. Although not specifically authorized by any House rule, unanimous consent is addressed in House precedents and remains unchallenged as standard operating procedure.

[See also (I) House of Representatives, article on House Rules and Procedures, Senate, article on Senate Rules and Procedures.]

BIBLIOGRAPHY

Nickels, Ilona B. *Unanimous Consent: A Study of Its Use in House and Senate Practice from 1979–1984.* Congressional Research Service, Library of Congress. CRS Rept. 23 November 1984.

U.S. Senate. *Committees and Senate Procedures: A Compilation of Papers Prepared for the Commission on the Operation of the Senate.* 94th Cong., 2d sess., 1977. Committee Print. See especially Robert Keith, "The Use of Unanimous Consent in the Senate," pp. 140–168.

– ILONA B. NICKELS

V

VACANCY

Vacancies in the U.S. Senate or House of Representatives occur when incumbent members die, resign, or are expelled or excluded by the action of either house. Historically, the reasons for exclusion and expulsion have included conviction for a felony, serious misconduct, election fraud or irregularities, and treason. The Constitution makes each house the ultimate judge of the elections, returns, and qualifications of its members and also authorizes both houses to expel an incumbent for any reason by a two-thirds vote of that house's members. Exclusion and expulsion were more common in the nineteenth century than afterward; in the late twentieth century, vacancies almost invariably occurred as the result of the death or resignation of senators or representatives.

The Constitution outlines basic requirements for filling vacancies in Congress but leaves the states considerable leeway in establishing detailed procedures. The Constitution authorizes state governors to call for special elections to fill a Senate vacancy, while also authorizing state legislatures to empower the governor to make temporary appointments to fill the vacancy until an election is scheduled. In practice, forty-nine of the fifty states provide their governors with this appointment power; Arizona is the sole exception, requiring a special election to fill any Senate vacancy. In the event a senator resigns, members of the incumbent's staff continue to be compensated for a period not exceeding ninety days, performing their duties under direction of the secretary of the Senate.

Governors have wide discretion in appointing senators to fill vacancies, although some states require that the appointee be either a registered voter or a member of the same political party of the former incumbent.

Nomination procedures are established by state law and most frequently provide for a primary election or state party action, such as a convention. Scheduling for special elections varies by state, but all require that they be held at the next statewide general election (which can, for example, be for state elected officials for statewide local elections). Senators appointed to fill a vacancy falling between a statewide election and the end of the incumbent's term generally serve the balance of the term. Historically, appointed senators have had a mixed record of electoral success. From 1939 to 1992 there were 101 appointed senators, of whom sixty-five subsequently ran in special elections. Of these, only twenty-six (40 percent) were elected.

Procedures governing the House differ from the Senate primarily in that all House vacancies are filled by special election, with no provision for temporary appointments. The Constitution authorizes state governors to issue writs calling for special elections in such cases. Members of the staff of a deceased or resigned representative are compensated until a successor is elected; in the interim, they perform their duties under the direction of the clerk of the House.

Special election nominations for filling House vacancies vary according to state requirements. Nomination can be by petition, primary election, or party action such as a convention or caucus. Some states do not provide for a primary and require all candidates to compete in the general election, with a majority of the vote in the first round necessary for election. In the event no candidate receives a majority, the two candidates receiving the most votes, regardless of party affiliation, compete in a runoff. This procedure sometimes leads to first-round special elections in which several candidates from each of the major parties compete with minor-party and independent nominees, and such elections frequently require a runoff to determine the winner.

House vacancies that occur during the first session of a Congress are invariably filled by a special election that coincides, if possible, with a regularly scheduled election in the affected district. Procedures differ from state to state for vacancies that occur within six months of the expiration of a previous incumbent's term: in the interest of convenience and economy, many states require special House elections to be held on the date regularly scheduled for elections to the next Congress. In these cases, voters in affected districts simultaneously elect both a representative to fill the seat for the balance of the term and a representative to the next Congress. Often these may be the same person. In other states they simply elect a representative to the new Congress, with the seat remaining vacant until the new Congress convenes.

Winners of special House elections held late in a Congress are frequently not sworn in, Congress having usually adjourned sine die before election day. They are, however, accorded the status of incumbent representatives for the purposes of seniority, office selection, and staff hiring.

The incidence of vacancies during the life of a particular Congress depends largely on circumstance and tends to fluctuate. Since 1971, Senate vacancies have been one or two per Congress, while those in the House have ranged from a low of four (98th Congress, 1983–1985) to a high of ten (92d Congress, 1971–1973, and 101st Congress, 1989–1991), for an average of seven per Congress.

Vacancies in Congress occur when members die, resign, or are expelled or excluded by the action of either house.

Special elections to fill vacancies in both houses are often observed as indicators of the popularity of an incumbent president and his party. For example, as the Watergate scandal developed in 1973 and 1974, Republican losses in several special elections appeared to indicate declining public support for the administration of Richard M. Nixon. Similarly, a 1991 election held to fill the vacancy created by the death a Pennsylvania Republican senator was widely characterized as a referendum on the presidency of George Bush: the election of an appointed Democratic senator Harris Wofford, over better-known Republican challenger Richard Thorn-burgh, who had resigned as U.S. attorney general to run for the seat, embarrassed the Bush administration.

General theories concerning the predictive value of special elections are disputed by many observers, however. A wide range of factors, including local economic conditions, comparative candidate name recognition, and the level of party and special interest group efforts, are cited to argue against the validity of determining an incumbent president's popularity through observation of special elections.

[See also (I) Elections, Congressional, article on Nomination to Candidacy.]

BIBLIOGRAPHY

Feigert, Frank B., and Pippa Norris. "Do By-Elections Constitute Referenda?" *Legislative Studies Quarterly* 15 (May 1990): 183–200.

Morris, William D., and Roger H. Marz. "Treadmill to Oblivion: The Fate of Appointed Senators." *Publius* 11 (Winter 1981): 65–80.

Sigelman, Lee. "Special Elections to the U.S. House: Some Descriptive Generalizations." *Legislative Studies Quarterly* 6 (November 1981): 577–588.

Studlar, Donley T., and Lee Sigelman. "Special Elections: A Comparative Perspective." *British Journal of Political Science* 17 (April 1987): 247–256.

– THOMAS H. NEALE

VETO

Presidential Veto

The presidential power to veto legislation is one of the few explicitly granted powers that formally involves the chief executive in legislative affairs. Described in Article I, section 7 of the Constitution, the veto is the final leg of the legislative gauntlet a bill must run before it becomes law.

When presented with a bill passed by Congress, the president faces four possible choices. First, he may approve the bill by signing it into law; second, he may exercise the regular, or return, veto by returning the bill to the house of origin with a statement of objections; third, he may do nothing, in which case the bill automatically becomes law after ten days (Sundays excepted); and fourth, if Congress adjourns within ten days of having presented a bill to the president and the president does nothing, the bill is pocket-vetoed if, according to the Constitution, "Congress by their Adjournment prevent its [the bill's] Return." (The Constitution requires no written statement accompanying pocket vetoes, but traditionally presidents have issued "memorandums of disapproval.") A return veto is subject to override by a two-thirds vote of both houses of Congress. A pocket veto is not.

The veto power is indisputably a presidential power, yet its location in Article I, the article otherwise devoted to the legislative branch, points to an important fact: the power is a legislative one possessed by the executive, and thus it reflects a sharing of powers between the branches of government.

THE FRAMERS' CONCERNS. Fears of the baneful consequences of a strong executive motivated the country's early leaders to create a governing system, under the Articles of Confederation, that had no independent executive branch. But by the time the Constitution's Framers met in 1787, the prevailing sentiment was toward an independent executive. Even though many still remembered the oppressive veto practices of the British king and his appointed colonial governors before the Revolutionary War, there was little disagreement that the new president should have a qualified veto power. The Framers were adamant, however, that the president's veto not be absolute, as was that of the British monarchs.

A central reason for granting the president this power was the Framers' concern that the executive would need it to protect the executive branch against legislative encroachments on executive power, a tendency observed in many state governments during the time the nation was governed by the Articles of Confederation. The Framers expected that the veto would be used to block legislation that was hastily conceived, unjust, or of dubious constitutionality. In addition, the power was not considered purely negative. Often called the "revisionary power," the veto was conceived as a creative, positive device whereby the president could bring a bill back to Congress for a final round of debate and consideration.

INCREASING USE. Early presidents used the veto power cautiously and sparingly, giving rise to claims that the Constitution somehow countenanced restrictions on numbers or kinds of bills vetoed. Neither claim is substantiated by the Constitution itself or the debates of the Framers. President George Washington, who had presided over the Constitutional Convention, used the veto twice in his two terms—once for constitutional reasons, and once for policy reasons. President Andrew Jackson aroused deep antipathy by invoking the veto twelve times. His veto of a national bank bill in 1832 infuriated his foes and also served as the pivotal issue for that year's presidential election. Jackson's sweeping reelection victory was viewed at least in part as a referendum on the bank veto. Some of Jackson's vetoes also focused attention on another major issue of the time—government involvement in public works projects and other internal improvements.

Of the early presidents, John Tyler faced the greatest difficulties in connection with his use of the veto. During his almost four years in office, he vetoed a total of ten bills. While Tyler's political problems sprang primarily from his maladroit political leadership, controversy surrounding his use of the veto contributed directly to the effort to impeach him in 1843. Indeed, the two central impeachment charges brought against him focused on his allegedly improper use of the veto. In 1845, Tyler became the first president to have a veto successfully overridden by Congress.

Veto use exploded after the Civil War. From the first veto to 1868, presidents vetoed 88 bills. From that time to 1992, over 2,300 bills were vetoed. Most of these vetoes were attributable to the proliferation of private pension and related private relief bills, by which members of Congress sought to obtain relief for specific individuals seeking pensions or other private benefits that only Congress could authorize. Many such bills involved dubious claims.

Franklin D. Roosevelt holds the record for most vetoes, blocking a total of 635 bills in his four terms. On a per-year basis, Roosevelt falls second, behind Grover Cleveland, who averaged 73 vetoes per year, with a total of 584 vetoes. Most of their vetoes involved private bills.

As use of the veto increased, its importance ironically seemed to recede, as presidents acquired a wide array of political powers that enabled them to influence virtually every aspect of the legislative process. Yet the veto remained a key means whereby presidents inserted themselves into the legislative process. Early in the nineteenth century, many members of Congress considered it improper for presidents to express public opinions about legislation pending before Congress; they feared that such expressions might taint or alter the deliberations of Congress. Yet as veto use increased, Congress openly solicited the opinions of presidents concerning whether they might be planning a veto. These informal inquiries opened the door to more formal requests that the president submit to Congress a statement of his legislative preferences, a process that now takes the form of extensive legislative agendas submitted to Congress annually by the president.

CONSEQUENCES OF VETO USE. Although use of the veto has expanded the power of the presidency, the delicate politics associated with it are demonstrated by the fact that vigorous veto use has usually been politically detrimental to presidents. This is because the veto is viewed as a negative, reactive measure in contrast to the assertive, positive leadership for which Americans have come to reward presidents. Cleveland's prolific veto use certainly contributed to his defeat in his first bid for reelection in 1888. Franklin Roosevelt's presidency might seem an anomaly, given his high veto use, yet his use of the power was symptomatic of a powerful president who felt free to use all of the tools at his disposal. Moreover, most of his vetoes involved bills of little importance.

In more recent times, President Gerald R. Ford found reliance on a true veto strategy to be both necessary and damaging to his presidency. Appointed vice president by President Richard M. Nixon after the resignation of Spiro T. Agnew in 1973, Ford suddenly found himself sitting in the Oval Office when Nixon resigned the following year. The new president had neither won an electoral mandate nor had time to develop a legislative program of his own. As a result, Republican Ford and his aides felt compelled to rely heavily on the veto to try to control the actions of a headstrong post-Watergate Democratic Congress. Thus, in his two and one-half years in office, Ford vetoed sixty-six bills. Taken together, these vetoes helped encourage the attitude that Ford was unable to engage in affirmative governance and the kind of positive leadership the country had come to expect, an attitude that contributed to his defeat in 1976.

President George Bush also suffered some criticism for overreliance on the veto and for an apparent failure to produce more positive policy alternatives. Yet Bush was also careful in his veto use. In his four years in office, he vetoed 45 bills. Only one of those bills, a measure to regulate cable television rates, was enacted into law over the veto (in October 1992).

In 1845, John Tyler became the first president to have a veto successfully overridden by Congress.

For presidents, one appealing trait of the veto is its effectiveness. Of the 1,447 regular vetoes applied by presidents from 1789 to 1992, only 7.2 percent were overridden. When that figure is broken down between public and private bills, the record is somewhat less impressive for important legislation: 19.3 percent of public bill vetoes and 0.8 percent of private bill vetoes were overridden. Still, a presidential success rate of greater than 80 percent for public bills poses a daunting challenge for anyone seeking to overturn a veto.

Presidents are more likely to use a veto when the executive and legislative branches are controlled by different parties, when the president lacks congressional experience, when the president's public standing is low, and during the second and fourth years of a presidential term. Congress is more likely to override a veto when party control is split between the two branches, when the president's popular support is low, after a midterm election, and in times of economic crisis. In short, a veto is most potent when it is least needed by presidents—at the beginning of a term.

HANDLING VETOES. Presidents rarely act alone in making important decisions, and since Washington they have sought advice on whether to veto bills. Washington often solicited opinions from his cabinet members, especially Alexander Hamilton and Thomas Jefferson, and from members of Congress, especially James Madison. As the presidency became institutionalized in the twentieth century, so too did the way veto decisions were handled.

Until the early twentieth century, when an enrolled bill (one passed by Congress but not yet signed into law) reached the White House, a presidential aide would decide which agencies would be affected, have the bill delivered to them, and then wait for their replies. This process yielded a number of inadequate, ill-considered veto decisions in the nineteenth century. But the growing volume of legislation, combined with the constitutionally mandated ten-day period within which the veto decision must be made, spurred a more formal institutionalization of the process.

The effort to deal more systematically with enrolled bills began with the creation of the Bureau of the Budget (known as the Office of Management and Budget, or OMB, after 1970) in 1921. The Budget Bureau was asked to render its views of enrolled appropriations bills as part of the larger effort to enhance executive authority over the budget process. Naturally, this led to occasional veto recommendations from the bureau. The examination of enrolled bills was expanded by Franklin D. Roosevelt in 1934 to include private bills. By 1938, the Budget Bureau was assessing all enrolled bills, a process that included contacting affected departments and compiling views on the bills under scrutiny. Since the 1930s, these procedures have not changed significantly, except that ever more attention has been focused on the president's priorities, as distinct from the independent opinions of affected agencies.

THE POCKET VETO. Early concerns about the pocket veto centered on two principles that weighed heavily on the Constitution's Framers. First, it was thought important that presidents have adequate time to consider the legislation sent to them. The pocket veto would come into play at the end of a congressional session, when Congress would likely present the president with a rush of last-minute bills. The pocket veto ensured that presidents would not be forced into signing imprudent legislation. The Framers also wanted to ensure that Congress would have time to consider and, if it chose, to override the president's objections. Obviously, the pocket veto does not allow for any reconsideration or override; thus, the return veto was the preferred option, if circumstances allowed.

Persisting ambiguities have surrounded the pocket veto power. For example, several court cases have addressed the question of when a congressional adjournment prevents a bill's return. In 1972, Sen. Edward M. Kennedy (D-Mass.) filed suit challenging a 1970 pocket veto by President Nixon that occurred during a Christmas recess. The U.S. Court of Appeals ruled that the president had not been prevented from returning the bill to Congress, voiding the pocket veto and ordering the enactment of the law (*Kennedy v. Sampson,* 511 F. 2d 430 [D.C. Cir. 1974]). Further, the ruling cast doubt on any pocket veto during such adjournments as long as Congress designated an agent to receive veto messages, a practice Congress has maintained for several decades. The Nixon administration declined to appeal the case to the Supreme Court. Presidents Gerald Ford and Jimmy Carter followed the practice of using the pocket veto only when Congress adjourned *sine die* at the end of a two-year Congress, using the return veto in all other instances.

President Ronald Reagan argued, however, that pocket vetoes between congressional sessions (that is, between sessions of the same Congress) should be allowed. Reagan applied such a veto to a bill between the first and second sessions of the 98th Congress in November 1983. The pocket veto was challenged in court by members of Congress from both parties. A federal district court upheld the pocket veto, but the Court of Appeals ruled it unconstitutional on appeal. The Supreme Court declared the case moot, dismissing the suit and avoiding a ruling on the issues, in *Burke v. Barnes* (491 U.S. 361 [1987]). President George Bush went even further, arguing that a pocket veto was justified after any congressional recess longer than three days (as long as the bill's tenth day fell during the break). In his four years, however, Bush never attempted such a pocket veto, and the idea garnered little support.

[See also (II) Veto, Pocket; Veto, Regular.]

BIBLIOGRAPHY

Jackson, Carleton. *Presidential Vetoes, 1792–1945.* 1967.

Mason, Edward C. *The Veto Power.* 1890.

Spitzer, Robert J. *The Presidential Veto: Touchstone of the American Presidency.* 1988.

U.S. House of Representatives. Rules Committee. Subcommittee on the Legislative Process. *Hearings on H.R. 849: A Bill to Clarify the Law Surrounding the President's Use of the Pocket Veto.* 101st Cong., 1st sess., 1989.

– ROBERT J. SPITZER

WITNESSES, RIGHTS OF

Congressional investigations offer the most vivid and vital dramas in which high officials appear before the people's representatives to account for their conduct in office or their role in scandals. Such investigations serve national democracy as its laboratory for finding truth, its arena for combat, and its theater. Yet congressional investigations pose the potential danger, as during the McCarthy era, of injuring the reputations of witnesses through unfair tactics and accusations. This dichotomy has led to the evolution of witnesses' rights as a way of ensuring that Congress has the power to obtain the evidence it needs while minimizing abuses to the witnesses it calls.

Committees and witnesses often have sharp legal disputes, such as when President Richard M. Nixon withheld tape recordings from the Senate Select Committee on Presidential Campaign Activities (Senate Watergate Committee) in 1973, claiming executive privilege, or when Assistant Secretary of State Elliott Abrams made false statements to committees about the Iran-contra affair. Abrams later pleaded guilty to lying to Congress but was pardoned by President George Bush. Because of the "speech or debate" clause of the Constitution, witnesses cannot initiate lawsuits against a congressional committee to block its questions or to dispute its procedures. Witnesses can have a court decide whether their rights were violated only if they block an investigation and are prosecuted for contempt, or, in the case of some fundamental rights, if they lie and are prosecuted for making false statements. Then, as part of defending the contempt or false statement prosecution, the witness can raise issues challenging the validity of the committee's procedures. Hence, such trials as Oliver North's in 1989—on charges (among others) that he lied to Congress—turn into unusual occasions for courts to resolve issues about witnesses' rights.

In general, a witness's rights include being accompanied by a lawyer who may provide advice, which sometimes produces exciting confrontations between skilled courtroom-style lawyers and dogged members of Congress. Witnesses usually can read an opening statement that tells their story the way they see it but then have to respond to whatever questions the members or the committee counsel ask them. The committee determines whether to hear a witness in public or in a closed ("executive") session, although the witness may voice a preference. Witnesses have few grounds for general refusal to answer questions, except a claim under the Fifth Amendment that by answering they would incriminate themselves. However, they may require the committee to state the pertinency of the question to the subject of the inquiry. Individual House and Senate committees have rules that may provide further rights, such as defining the minimum number of members—the quorum—that must attend the hearing.

There has always been controversy over televising witnesses.

There has always been controversy over televising witnesses. In a famous 1951 incident, the Kefauver Committee (the Senate Special Committee to Investigate Organized Crime in Interstate Commerce) summoned New York City racketeer Frank Costello. Costello objected to being televised and, to the agitation of the watching public, the live television coverage of the hearings showed only his hands, which twisted and clenched as he was subjected to tough questioning. The House has a rule that witnesses who appear pursuant to a compulsory subpoena can require that their testimony not be broadcast at all.

Important congressional investigations may raise questions about a witness's claims of the right to withhold particular information. For example, a lawyer who had handled transactions on behalf of Philippines ruler Ferdinand Marcos attempted to assert attorney-client privilege. Congressional committees have broad discretion whether to accept or reject such an assertion of privilege. The committee rejected that particular assertion, noting that the lawyer had acted as a realtor locating investment properties for Marcos rather than as an adviser on pure legal questions. A witness employed in a business such as pharmaceutical manufacture may ask not to be required to reveal trade secrets to an inquiry about profits. While congressional committees have the power to overrule such claims, they typically weigh them carefully, both to decide well and to visibly provide fair procedures in the inquiry.

[See also (I) Investigations.]

BIBLIOGRAPHY

Grabow, John C. *Congressional Investigations: Law and Practice.* 1988.

Hamilton, James. *The Power to Probe: A Study of Congressional Investigations.* 1976.

– CHARLES TIEFER

PART TWO
Executive Branch

EXECUTIVE DEPARTMENTS

In designing the organization for the government they were creating, the Framers of the Constitution did not rely on classical political philosophy nor on the example of Great Britain or France, the two great nation-states of the period. Instead, the Framers relied largely upon their own experience in trying to wage the Revolutionary War against a global power and in attempting to manage the national confederation of states after the close of hostilities in 1781. Their personal experiences became the crucible for political thought.

Organization of the Executive Branch

While questions regarding how best to organize the executive branch were raised at the Constitutional Convention, the Constitution itself is nearly silent on organizational matters. There are only two indirect references to the question of administrative organization in the Constitution, namely, that the President "may require the Opinion, in writing, of the principal Officer in each of the executive Departments, upon any Subject relating to the Duties of their respective Offices" and that "the Congress may by Law vest the Appointment of such inferior Officers, as they think proper, in the President alone, in the Courts of Law, or in the Heads of Departments" (Article II, Section 2, clauses 1 and 2).

The paucity of language in the Constitution respecting organizational matters should not be interpreted, however, as showing lack of interest or concern on the part of the Framers. Quite to the contrary, there was lively concern for organizational matters. The Framers were influenced by eighteenth-century Enlightenment philosophy rather than nineteenth-century social-revolutionary philosophy. Enlightenment philosophy stressed reason, and reason embraced scientific methodology. Alexander Hamilton was articulate in his arguments that public administration was a "science" and that the United States could organize a government that was at once efficient and representative. Writing in *Federalist* 9, Hamilton states,

> The science of politics, however, like most other sciences, has received great improvement. The efficacy of various principles is now well understood, which was either not known at all or imperfectly known to the ancients. The regular distribution of power into distinct departments; the introduction of legislative balances and checks; the institution of courts composed of judges holding their offices during good behavior; the representation of the people in the legislature by deputies of their election; these are wholly new discoveries, or have made their principal progress toward perfection during modern times

The important point is that the Framers believed that it was possible to create a rational and democratically accountable administrative structure. They believed that there were principles of organization that ought to be followed and that deviation from these principles should require the promoters to meet a higher standard of proof. The role of historical and legal precedent in the evolution of the federal executive establishment came into play during the First Congress. Much that takes place today in the field of organizational management can be traced back in origin to the very first years of the Republic.

One of the first orders of business for the new Congress in 1789 was the establishment of executive departments.

One of the first orders of business for the new Congress in 1789 was the establishment of executive departments. Three "organic" statutes were passed creating three great departments: Treasury, State, and War. A problem arose with respect to the numerous domestic activities of government that did not fit neatly into these three departments. The First Congress made an attempt to establish a "Home Department," such as existed in England, to which these domestic functions might be assigned. Opposition to this proposal arose from several sources. There was concern that such a department would lead to a diminution of the states and their responsibilities for providing basic services to the citizenry. Also, Congress was wary of creating another department under the President's authority. The rejection of the Home Department proposal led to the parceling out of many domestic activities among the three departments and the creation of some long-standing anomalies.

Just a few of these anomalies are worth noting. The State Department was given responsibility for conducting the census and for supervising the Mint. The Treasury Department was assigned the Coast Survey, the General Land Office, and the Revenue Cutter Service, later to be the U.S. Coast Guard. And the War Department was assigned responsibility for supervising Indian affairs and for national construction projects (Army Corps of Engineers).

EXECUTIVE BRANCH

Executive Departments

Department of Agriculture
Department of Commerce
Department of Defense
  Joint Chiefs of Staff
Department of Education
Department of Energy
Department of Health and Human Services
  Social Security Administration
Department of Housing and Urban Development
Department of the Interior
Department of Justice
  Attorney General
  Solicitor General
  Office of Legal Counsel
  Federal Bureau of Investigation
  Office of the Pardon Attorney
Department of Labor
Department of State
Department of Transportation
  Saint Lawrence Seaway Development Corporation
Department of the Treasury
  United States Secret Service
Department of Veterans Affairs

Independent Commissions

Commodity Futures Trading Commission (CFTC)
Consumer Product Safety Commission (CPSC)
Federal Communications Commission (FCC)
Federal Election Commission (FEC)
Federal Energy Regulatory Commission (FERC)
Federal Maritime Commission (FMC)
Federal Mine Safety and Health Review Commission
Federal Reserve System, Board of Governors of the Federal Trade Commission (FTC)
Interstate Commerce Commission (ICC)
National Labor Relations Board (NLRB)
Nuclear Regulatory Commission (NRC)
Occupational Safety and Health Review Commission
Postal Rate Commission
Securities and Exchange Commission (SEC)
U.S. International Trade Commission (ITC)

Government Corporations

African Development Foundation
Export-Import Bank of the United States
Farm Credit Administration
Federal Deposit Insurance Corporation (FDIC)
Federal Housing Finance Board
Inter-American Foundation
Legal Services Corporation
National Railroad Passenger Corporation (Amtrak)
Pennsylvania Avenue Development Corporation
Pension Benefit Guaranty Corporation
Resolution Trust Corporation
Tennessee Valley Authority (TVA)

Other Agencies and Boards

ACTION
Administrative Conference of the U.S.
Central Intelligence Agency (CIA)
Commission on the Bicentennial of the U.S. Constitution
Commission on Civil Rights
Defense Nuclear Facilities Safety Board
Environmental Protection Agency (EPA)
Equal Employment Opportunity Commission (EEOC)
Federal Emergency Management Agency (FEMA)
Federal Labor Relations Authority
Federal Mediation and Conciliation Service
Federal Retirement Thrift Investment Board
General Services Administration
Merit Systems Protection Board (MSPB)
National Aeronautics and Space Administration (NASA)
National Archives and Records Administration
National Capitol Planning Commission
National Credit Union Administration
National Foundation on the Arts and the Humanities
National Mediation Board
National Science Foundation
National Transportation Safety Board
Office of Government Ethics
Office of Personnel Management
Oversight Board for the Resolution Trust Corporation
Peace Corps
Railroad Retirement Board
Selective Service System
U.S. Arms Control and Disarmament Agency (ACDA)
U.S. Information Agency (USIA)
U.S. International Development Cooperation Agency
    Agency for International Development (AID)
U.S. Office of Special Cousel
U.S. Postal Service

The underlying concepts behind the executive branch structure were that it should be a unitary organizational structure and that departments should be headed by a single individual, not a committee. Both George Washington and Hamilton were opposed to a plural executive in any form. Some dispute arose as to the supervision of these departments. While Congress accepted the premise that foreign affairs and national defense were essentially executive functions and therefore properly the responsibility of the President, they did not accept the view that national finances were an executive function. Congress, since the earliest days of the Continental Congress, had kept the supervision of the Treasury and the appointment of its officers within its orbit. Under the Constitution, Congress agreed to share the supervision of the new Treasury, but only up to a point.

Unlike the departments of State and War, Treasury was not styled an executive department, and many in Congress anticipated that the Secretary of the Treasury and lesser statutorily designated officials (e.g., the Comptroller) would be "agents" of Congress. Hamilton, as the first Secretary of the Treasury, relished his special relationship with Congress, but he disappointed those in Congress who hoped he would be satisfied with an agent's role. Hamilton held himself accountable first and foremost to the President.

Expansion of the Departments

President Washington assembled his department secretaries for advice and counsel, and in 1793 this informal group became popularly known as the Cabinet. In addition to the three secretaries (after 1798 there was a fourth secretary representing the new Department of the Navy), the Attorney General was considered a member of the Cabinet. The Attorney General was initially a private lawyer on retainer ($1,500 annually) to the federal government. Only later did the Attorney General become a full-time officer of the United States, finally becoming the head of the newly created Department of Justice in 1870. The Postmaster General, though head of the Post Office, was not a member of the Cabinet until 1829. The Post Office became an executive department in 1872, a status it held until 1971, when it was redesignated by Congress as "an independent establishment of the executive branch."

The first major new addition to the list of executive departments was the Department of the Interior, created in 1849. Transferred to this department were the already existing General Land Office, Office of Indian Affairs, Pension Office, Patent Office, and census activities. Over succeeding decades the role of the department evolved, with Interior eventually becoming the custodian of the nation's natural resources and parks.

As functions were assumed by the federal government, they were assigned to new or existing departments. Before 1860, only four permanent "detached agencies" were created: the Library of Congress, the Smithsonian Institution, the Botanical Gardens, and the Government Printing Office. For the first hundred years or so of the Republic, the executive branch, with few exceptions, consisted of departments headed by single administrators under the authority of the President.

Supervision: Competing Claims

The Constitution and political customs of the United States provide the basis for a continuing struggle between the President and Congress over who should be the primary supervisor of the administrative agencies. Many of the complex issues involving statutory authority, lines of accountability, tenure, and organizational management were first aired in the dispute over the President's right to remove officers of the executive branch. This dispute and its resolution have come down to us in history as the decision of 1789.

Soon after Washington's inauguration, a major crisis loomed. In proposing legislation to establish the departments of Foreign Affairs (later State), War, and Treasury, James Madison included language providing that the secretaries of these departments would be "removable by the President." Many members of Congress objected to this provision, arguing that the Constitution's silence concerning where the removal power would reside indicated that removals were to be guided by the same authority as that specified in the appointment clause, which required Senate approval of all appointments. According to this reasoning, removals, other than by the impeachment process, would require Senate confirmation as well.

Washington and Madison strongly disagreed with this argument and the interpretation of the Constitution it reflected. They contended that the power of removal belonged exclusively with the President and is incident to the President's general executive power under the Constitution. The debate in both houses of Congress was sophisticated in its theoretical nuances and in its evaluation of the likely practical consequences that would follow if a particular choice were made. At one point Madison concluded, "Vest [the removal power] in the Senate jointly with the President, and you abolish at once that great principle of unity and responsibility in the Executive department which was intended for the security of liberty and the public good."

The final vote on the removal issue favored Washington's and Madison's position that the President should have the exclusive right to remove department heads and, with a few exceptions, all officers of the executive branch. Although the issue appeared resolved, it was not. Congress has sought on several occasions to limit the President's power to remove executive-branch officials. Additionally, the Supreme Court in several cases has approved limitations on the authority of the President to remove officers (e.g., *Humphrey's Executor* v. *United States* [1935]).

Congress has sought on several occasions to limit the President's power to remove executive-branch officials.

The Federalist period (1789–1801) was a period of extraordinary achievement in many fields, not the least being organizational design and management. The decision to establish a unitary administrative structure, an innovation much admired at the time, was designed by the Federalists to complement their more comprehensive theory of government. Although the main lines of Federalist philosophy of organizational management would remain in place throughout the Jeffersonian period (1801–1829), the institutional presidency gradually declined in power vis-à-vis Congress. Congress began to assert its authority over executive agencies more energetically with each passing year, forcing nineteenth-century Presidents, with several notable exceptions, to rely heavily on the appointment power, the removal power, the veto, and personal persuasion to exert whatever influence they might have over the course of administrative affairs.

The period between 1829 and 1900 was a period of congressional dominance over the presidency, a period characterized by a devolution of authority and of responsibility for the administration of the United States government. The once-small departments were required by rapidly escalating demands for services to devolve their authorities and capacities to subunits. The creation within departments of bureaus marked by specialization of personnel and tasks was a dominant feature of the nineteenth century. Often these bureaus developed their own cultures and sets of loyalties that were at odds with the objectives of departmental secretaries.

The movement toward bureaus within departments and the development of field structures to bring services directly to the people highlighted the issue of to whom these bureaus were accountable. Initially, Congress resisted the creation of bureaus because it associated bureaus with increased expenditures. Later, however, Congress tended to encourage their creation since bureaus could serve the interests of their constituents more directly and were also more amenable to congressional intervention.

The idea that the President ought to be an active manager of the executive branch was not one of the burning issues of the nineteenth century. Presidents tended to be jealous of their institutional and legal prerogatives and on occasion would fight tenaciously for some particular administrative or managerial concept. By and large, however, Presidents tended to be deferential to Congress on organizational management questions. Congress had control over the purse-strings, and thus Congress was the initiator of most reorganizations and changes in administrative practices.

The dominance of Congress in matters of administrative oversight notwithstanding, the earlier appeal of the unitary executive branch retained its persuasiveness throughout the nineteenth century. The first substantial break with departmentalism, and with the idea of a single administrative head for each bureau, did not occur until the 1880s, with the creation of the Civil Service Commission (1883) and the Interstate Commerce Commission (1887). This break was associated in many respects with the newly triumphant movement for civil-service reform and with a growing recognition by Congress that it was institutionally unable to oversee the growing body of regulatory activities. Thus, Congress was increasingly sympathetic to the idea of delegating some of its managerial and regulatory authority to the President and executive agencies, but not necessarily to department secretaries.

The problem, however, was that the institutionalized presidency was unable to substantially enhance either its political or managerial leverage over the executive departments. The President had virtually no staff, no budgetary authority over departments, and few general management laws through which the departments and agencies could be supervised collectively. The situation was ripe for change.

The President as Chief Manager

The new century ushered in new opportunities for American Presidents to exert their leadership skills. Government institutions were growing rapidly not only in size but in their resource requirements. The executive branch needed new organizational forms and a skilled manager, and the President was looked upon to furnish this leadership.

Under the banner of Progressivism, the doctrines of "scientific management" were promoted for application in the executive branch. With respect to organizational management, Progressives, by and large, favored four reforms: reorganization of the executive branch into functional departments and agencies, promotion of the President's authority to manage a unified executive branch, introduction of an executive budget, and development of a neutrally competent management class for departmental leadership. Progressives believed that progress was not only possible but inevitable if certain sound principles of organizational management were followed.

Under the Progressives' scheme, the President was to be the chief manager of the executive branch, which was to be reorganized as an integrated structure with strict lines of responsibility and accountability leading to the President. Reorganization of the executive departments and agencies was viewed as a critical precondition for effective governance.

Throughout the twentieth century a large number of commissions have been established by Congress, the President and, on occasion, jointly to study the organization and management of the executive branch and to make recommendations for change. Several of these commissions have achieved landmark status—most notably the Brownlow Committee (1937), the first of the Hoover Commissions (1949), and the Ash Council (1970). For the most part, at least through the Ash Council, the commissions' reports recommended a stronger institutionalized presidency and greater reliance on departments rather than independent agencies. Collectively, the three commissions noted above promoted a group of organizational management concepts that came to be known as the orthodox theory of federal organization. A brief review of the recommendations of these commissions is useful for understanding the present status of executive departments.

BROWNLOW COMMITTEE. As his second term approached, President Franklin D. Roosevelt sought to develop a comprehensive organizational strategy that would enhance his capacity to manage the executive branch. He named a three-member committee headed by Louis Brownlow to provide him with organizational recommendations. The Brownlow Committee recommended the creation of two additional departments (of public works and of social welfare) and the reintegration into the departmental structure of most existing independent agencies, regulatory commissions, and government corporations. The committee's report was particularly critical of the independent regulatory commissions, referring to them as the "headless fourth branch of government."

The Brownlow report has been characterized as the "high noon of orthodoxy" because of its advocacy of clear lines of accountability, departmentalism, and the doctrine that responsibility for making policy and setting standards ought to reside in the President and departmental secretaries rather than being devolved to the agency level. Congress did not accept the 1937 legislation that would have implemented much of the report's recommendations in part because its timing coincided with Roosevelt's ill-fated Court-packing plan. Roosevelt had to be satisfied with the achievement, in 1939, of a law establishing the Executive Office of the President and the assignment of some reorganization power to the President.

FIRST HOOVER COMMISSION. In the immediate aftermath of World War II, there was a fairly broad consensus favoring governmental "retrenchment." Congress enacted and President Harry S Truman signed a bill creating a commission headed by former President Herbert Hoover to comprehensively review the entire organizational management of the federal government. The premise underlying the Hoover Commission recommendations was similar to the orthodox approach of the earlier Brownlow Committee. The commission made proposals to strengthen the President as manager and secretaries as administrative chiefs of their departments. The commission criticized the tendency toward dispersing functions to independent agencies and called for a renewed, hierarchical administrative structure. "The unity of administration of the executive branch as planned by the Constitution must be restored," said the commission report, which called for grouping agencies "as nearly as possible by major purposes." Concerning departmental secretaries, the Commission stated, "Under the President, the heads of departments must hold full responsibility for the conduct of their departments. There must be a clear line of authority reaching down through every step of the organization and no subordinate should have authority independent from that of his superior."

The consensus that the President should be the chief manager of the executive branch and that he should have the necessary legal and organizational resources to perform these responsibilities permitted the passage of a number of far-reaching laws providing generic management direction for the departments and agencies. Two large, functionally based departments were created (Department of Defense, 1949; Department of Health, Education, and Welfare, 1953) in part as a consequence of Hoover Commission recommendations.

ASH COUNCIL. A third commission worth highlighting was the Ash Council, which submitted its report to President Richard M. Nixon in 1970. The council's objective was to provide the President with a comprehensive reorganization proposal that would improve the President's capacity to manage—even control—the executive branch while rationalizing the structure of the executive branch to reflect new service demands being placed on government.

The Hoover Commission criticized the tendency toward dispersing functions to independent agencies and called for a renewed, hierarchical administrative structure.

The council recommended more centralized and politically responsible lines of authority within the executive branch. It advocated a package approach to reorganization that combined various elements of the New Federalism (e.g., revenue sharing) with executive-branch reorganization. In proposing its restructuring of the executive branch, the council recommended a move away from the narrow, constituency-oriented traditional departments toward broader functional departments. In March 1971, Nixon sent four bills to Congress that had as their intent the reorganization of seven existing departments and various independent agencies into four large super departments of Human Resources, Community Development, Natural Resources, and Economic Affairs.

It was a dramatic proposal, the logical conclusion of the orthodox public administration values embodied in the earlier Brownlow Committee and Hoover Commission reports. Policy directions and lines of accountability to the department secretaries would be strengthened while administrative functions (e.g., awarding of grants) would be decentralized, often to standardized regional offices. In short, the four pieces of legislation embodied a comprehensive conceptual approach, yet Congress was not persuaded. No action was forthcoming.

With the failure of Nixon's comprehensive strategy to reorganize the executive branch according to orthodox principles, the commission and report approach to organizational management fell into disrepute. President Jimmy Carter initiated a large reorganization effort—but one without a commission, without a report, and without, according to its executive director, a distinctive theoretical basis, orthodox or otherwise. Two new departments were created during Carter's tenure, Energy and Education, but these two constituency-based departments represented a further fragmentation of the executive branch, not a return to administrative unity.

President Ronald Reagan, noting the relative failure of his predecessor in structuring a comprehensive organizational strategy, rejected the commission approach to reorganizing government and relied instead on the budget and regulatory review processes as tools for management. The one substantial commission during the Reagan years, the Grace Commission (1984), was principally concerned with program management and control and did not recommend the creation or abolition of any departments.

The appeal of the commission approach, despite the negative opinions of late-twentieth-century Presidents, remains high in Congress, and it is a rare session in which there is not some legislation considered for a new commission of some sort. In 1988, for instance, legislation to establish a National Commission on Executive Organization based on the Hoover Commission model was passed. The key provision was that the new President in 1989 would have the discretion to convene such a commission. The newly elected President, George Bush, decided for various reasons that such a commission was not needed.

The Executive Branch in the 1990s

By 1992 there were fourteen departments in the executive branch, the most recent department to be established being the Department of Veterans Affairs (1988). The others (and the dates of their creation or reorganization) are as follows: Department of Agriculture (1889), Department of Commerce (1903; 1913), Department of Defense (1789; 1949), Department of Education (1979), Department of Energy (1977), Department of Health and Human Services (1953; 1980), Department of Housing and Urban Development (1965), Department of the Interior (1849), Department of Justice (1870), Department of Labor (1903; 1913), Department of State (1789), Department of Transportation (1966), and Department of the Treasury (1789). In addition to these departments, the executive branch includes more than fifty independent agencies, regulatory commissions, government corporations, and quasi-governmental units.

With the exception of portions of several commission reports discussed above, there is very little in the literature of government on the subject of institutional types. The absence of principles to guide the choice of institutions for performance of functions results in decisions that are based more on intuition than on experience. There are no general laws defining the structure, powers, and immunities of the several categories of institutions. A department, for instance, has only those powers assigned in its enabling act. Other attributes of a department singularly or of departments as a class are determined by custom, precedent, judicial interpretation, congressional agreement, and subsequent laws amending the original legislation.

The strength of departments as a class of organization lies largely in their potential to bring leadership initiatives into play to address complex policy issues. A department does provide the organizational context and limits within which budgetary and personnel decisions can be made. Department secretaries are able to deal with one another on reasonable parity, thus providing a channel of communications and policy accommodation between constituent agencies, but agencies that are not in departments may find themselves without a high-level defender in the inevitable bureaucratic wars of government. When the President meets with the Cabinet, most of the executive branch is represented, and some (often quite modest) degree of administrative coherence, moving the administration in a single direction, is achieved in these meetings.

The case for departmentalism, while retaining much of its persuasiveness, is no longer the dominant political thrust of organizational management in the executive branch. Following congressional rejection of Nixon's 1971 proposals for four super departments, a fundamental shift in organizational philosophy occurred. Presidents, by and large, retreated from the view that having a comprehensive organizational strategy is a necessary basis for political leadership. The integrated, unitary executive branch was no longer an ideal worth expending political capital to achieve.

Disaggregation, not integration, became the primary motivating force behind most reorganizations. Although Congress might give lip service to the principles of departmentalism enunciated by the first Hoover Commission, in practice Congress sought to increase political and administrative leverage at the expense of department leadership. Increasingly, agencies in departments (e.g., the Federal Aviation Administration in the Department of Transportation, the Office of Thrift Supervision in the Department of the Treasury) were assigned their authority directly by statute, bypassing the secretaries in the process. Additionally, more functions, including functions of a governmental character, were being assigned to third-party contractors because of budgetary and personnel limitations placed on departments.

Congress, in the absence of the interest or leadership of the President or the Office of Management and Budget (OMB), has increasingly intervened in organizational management issues traditionally viewed as the province of the executive branch. Agencies and programs that might once have been assigned to departments are now given almost routinely to bodies of deliberately ambiguous legal status that function in a "twilight zone" between the governmental and private sectors. Bodies such as the Resolution Trust Corporation, the National Endowment for Democracy, and the Federal National Mortgage Association ("Fannie Mae") are products of this retreat from departmentalism.

There is little doubt that if the Federalists and the Progressives were permitted a return visit, they would be disappointed with the state of organizational management in the executive branch. They would be displeased with the loss of presidential will and capacity to enunciate and promote a comprehensive organizational management strategy. The erosion of a unified departmental structure would, in all likelihood, be a cause for their special concern as more and more activities have been assigned to nondepartmental bodies. Reorganizations of executive agencies and programs continued apace in the early 1990s (e.g., the proposal to establish a Department of Environmental Affairs) but without any discernible theoretical basis. Executive reorganizations tend to be influenced most by immediate political considerations, with structural options simply becoming chips in the political game.

Executive reorganizations tend to be influenced most by immediate political considerations, with structural options simply becoming chips in the political game.

The future of departments as a class of organization in the executive branch is not in danger. They will not disappear; indeed, there are likely to be more rather than fewer departments. But the mission of departments as centers for political and administrative leadership has become less clear. In the 1980s and 1990s, laws creating departments and agencies were distinguished by their length, detail, regulatory emphasis, and conflicting lines of accountability. The exciting action in government has tended to move away from departments and toward other categories of organization. The big challenge, therefore, to those who seek to reorient and reinvigorate the federal government to confront both domestic and international problems more effectively is to rethink the role and structure of departments. The organizational structure and management of departments is a critical factor to any successful comprehensive political strategy in the third century of the Republic.

TABLE 1

PRESIDENTS: PERSONAL INFORMATION

No.	President	Birthdate	Age at Election	First Lady
1	George Washington, 1789–1797	22 Feb 1732	57	Martha Dandridge Custis Washington
2	John Adams, 1797–1801	30 Oct 1735	61	Abigail Smith Adams
3	Thomas Jefferson, 1801–1809	13 Apr 1743	57	Widower
4	James Madison, 1809–1817	16 Mar 1751	57	Dolley Payne Todd Madison
5	James Monroe, 1817–1825	28 Apr 1758	58	Elizabeth Kortright Monroe
6	John Quincy Adams, 1825–1829	11 Jul 1767	57	Louisa Johnson Adams
7	Andrew Jackson, 1829–1837	15 Mar 1767	61	Widower
8	Martin van Buren, 1837–1841	5 Dec 1782	54	Widower
9	William Henry Harrison, 1841	9 Feb 1773	68	Anna Symmes Harrison
10	John Tyler, 1841–1845	29 Mar 1790	51	Letitia Christian Tyler; Julia Gardiner Tyler
11	James Knox Polk, 1845–1849	2 Nov 1795	49	Sarah Childress Polk
12	Zachary Taylor, 1849–1850	24 Nov 1784	64	Margaret Mackall Smith Taylor
13	Millard Fillmore, 1850–1853	7 Jan 1800	50	Abigal Powers Fillmore
14	Franklin Pierce, 1853–1857	23 Nov 1804	48	Jane Means Appleton Pierce
15	James Buchanan, 1857–1861	23 Apr 1791	65	Never married
16	Abraham Lincoln, 1861–1865	12 Feb 1809	52	Mary Todd Lincoln
17	Andrew Johnson, 1865–1869	29 Dec 1808	56	Eliza McCardle Johnson
18	Ulysses S. Grant, 1869–1877	27 Apr 1822	46	Julia Dent Grant
19	Rutherford B. Hayes, 1877–1881	4 Oct 1822	54	Lucy Webb Hayes
20	James A. Garfield, 1881	19 Nov 1831	49	Lucretia Rudolph Garfield
21	Chester A. Arthur, 1881–1885	5 Oct 1830	50	Widower
22	Grover Cleveland, 1885–1889	18 Mar 1837	47	Frances Folsom Cleveland
23	Benjamin Harrison, 1889–1893	20 Aug 1833	55	Caroline Scott Harrison
24	Grover Cleveland, 1893–1897	18 Mar 1837	55	Frances Folsom Cleveland
25	William McKinley, 1897–1901	29 Jan 1843	54	Ida Saxton McKinley
26	Theodore Roosevelt, 1901–1909	27 Oct 1858	42	Edith Kermit Carow Roosevelt
27	William Howard Taft, 1909–1913	15 Sep 1857	51	Helen Herron Taft
28	Woodrow Wilson, 1913–1921	28 Dec 1856	56	Ellen Louise Axson Wilson; Edith Bolling Galt Wilson
29	Warren G. Harding, 1921–1923	2 Nov 1865	55	Florence Kling De Wolfe Harding
30	Calvin Coolidge, 1923–1929	4 Jul 1872	51	Grace Goodhue Coolidge
31	Herbert C. Hoover, 1929–1933	10 Aug 1874	54	Lou Henry Hoover
32	Franklin D. Roosevelt, 1933–1945	30 Jan 1882	51	Anna Eleanor Roosevelt Roosevelt
33	Harry S Truman, 1945–1953	8 May 1884	60	Elizabeth Wallace ("Bess") Truman
34	Dwight D. Eisenhower, 1953–1961	14 Oct 1890	62	Mamie Doud Eisenhower
35	John F. Kennedy, 1961–1963	29 May 1917	43	Jacqueline Bouvier Kennedy
36	Lyndon B. Johnson, 1963–1969	27 Aug 1908	55	Claudia Alta Taylor ("Lady Bird") Johnson
37	Richard M. Nixon, 1969–1974	9 Jan 1913	56	Thelma Catherine ("Pat") Ryan Nixon
38	Gerald Ford, 1974–1977	14 Jul 1913	61	Betty Bloomer Warren Ford
39	Jimmy Carter, 1977–1981	1 Oct 1924	52	Rosalynn Smith Carter
40	Ronald Reagan, 1981–1989	6 Feb 1911	69	Nancy Davis Reagan
41	George Bush, 1989–1993	12 Jun 1924	64	Barbara Pierce Bush
42	Bill Clinton, 1993–	19 Aug 1946	46	Hillary Rodham Clinton

[See also (II) Commerce, Department of; Defense, Department of; State, Department of; Treasury, Department of.]

BIBLIOGRAPHY

Arnold, Peri E. *Making the Managerial Presidency: Comprehensive Managerial Reorganization Planning, 1905–1980.* 1986.

Fairlie, John A. *The National Administration of the United States.* 1905.

Fisher, Louis. *Constitutional Conflicts between Congress and the President.* 3d rev. ed. 1991.

Moe, Ronald C. "Traditional Organizational Principles and the Managerial Presidency: From Phoenix to Ashes." *Public Administration Review* 50 (1990): 129–140.

Seidman, Harold, and Robert S. Gilmour. *Politics, Position, and Power: From the Positive to the Regulatory State.* 4th rev. ed. 1986.

Short, Lloyd M. *The Development of National Administrative Organization in the United States.* 1923.

U.S. Commission on the Organization of the Executive Branch of Government (First Hoover Commission). *The Hoover Commission Report.* 1949.

U.S. Office of Management and Budget (Ash Council). *Papers Relating to the President's Departmental Reorganization Program.* 1971.

U.S. President's Committee on Administrative Management (Brownlow Committee). *Report with Special Studies.* 1937.

Wallace, Schuyler C. *Federal Departmentalization: A Critique of Theories of Organization.* 1941.

– RONALD C. MOE

EXECUTIVE POWER

Article II of the Constitution stipulates that all executive power resides in the hands of the President. Article II defines formal executive power, but like many constitutional provisions it is a framework, not a blueprint. While the President may initially define his own executive powers under the Constitution, his interpretations may be challenged before the Supreme Court and by Congress. For example, President Harry S Truman, citing his constitutional authority as Chief Executive and Commander in Chief, seized the steel mills in 1952 to prevent a crippling strike during the Korean War. However, in the *Steel Seizure Cases* (1952), the Supreme Court held that the President had exceeded his constitutional powers.

Overview

The Framers of the Constitution, while recognizing the importance of the presidency, did not foresee the vast expansion of presidential power that eventually occurred. Article II states that "the executive Power shall be vested in a President" and that "the President shall be Commander in Chief of the Army and Navy of the United States, and of the Militia." Aside from providing that the President "shall take Care that the Laws be faithfully executed" and that "he may require the Opinion, in writing, of the principal Officer in each of the executive Departments," the Constitution does not specify how "executive" power is to be exercised.

Under the checks and balances system, the Constitution specifies that certain executive powers are subject to senatorial advice and consent: the treaty-making power and the power to "appoint Ambassadors, other public Ministers and Consuls, Judges of the supreme Court, and all other Officers of the United States whose Appointments are not herein otherwise provided for." But, "Congress may by Law vest the Appointment of such inferior Officers, as they think proper, in the President alone, in the Courts of Law, or in the Heads of Departments."

Article II gives the President direct and indirect legislative powers and responsibilities. He may veto congressional legislation, and his action can be overridden only by a two-thirds vote in the House and the Senate. Article II also provides that the President is, from time to time, to recommend legislation to Congress and give Congress a state of the union message. The President can also convene either or both houses of Congress on "extraordinary occasions."

Article II makes the President the ceremonial head of state, by providing, for example, that he must "receive Ambassadors and other public Ministers." The President represents that nation at home and abroad, and his ceremonial role enhances his informal powers by making him in a sense both a king and a prime minister.

Chief Executive

The Constitution provides that the President shall "take Care that the Laws be faithfully executed." This simple provision makes the President the nation's Chief Executive, and he alone exercises primary executive power. The executive branch is an extension of the presidency, and the President may "require the Opinion, in writing, of the principal Officer in each of the executive Departments, upon any subject relating to the Duties of their respective offices."

The Framers envisioned a small and easily controllable executive branch performing the essential executive functions of defense, foreign relations, revenue raising, law enforcement, the post office, control over patents, regulation of navigation, territorial administration, and a few other miscellaneous responsibilities. Aside from 6,479 military personnel, 1,223 collectors of revenue, and 947 deputy postmasters, the entire executive branch in 1802 consisted of 588 persons. That figure contrasts with the over 2.5 million federal employees in the 1990s. Clearly the President's ability to control the modern executive branch is severely limited by its size, complexity, and vast responsibilities.

Regardless of changes in the scope and character of the executive branch over the years, the President's role as Chief Executive is firmly embedded in the Constitution. Alexander Hamilton in *Federalist* 72, recognized that one of the most important presidential duties was to be leader of the executive branch. He argued that since the President would appoint, albeit with the advice and consent of the Senate, members of the executive branch they should be considered as his assistants and "subject to his superintendence." Article II, coupled with Hamilton's arguments in the *Federalist,* support presidential control over the executive branch.

GROWTH OF THE FEDERAL BUREAUCRACY. The President had little difficulty in supervising executive activities until the growth of the federal bureaucracy in the twentieth century, most notably during President Franklin D. Roosevelt's administration in the 1930s. The Hamiltonian theory that backed presidential domination of the executive branch surfaced during Roosevelt's presidency to support measures that would shore up the President's role as Chief Executive. Most important, the Report of the President's Committee on Administrative Management (Brownlow Committee) in 1937 recommended that the President's staff be increased to give him the upper hand over the burgeoning New Deal bureaucracy that threatened to run out of control completely. The committee, which Roosevelt had selected, supported his view that it was not only the constitutional responsibility of the President to be "Chief Administrator," but also that democracy and efficiency required the President to pay strict attention to his responsibilities as Chief Executive. In 1939, Roosevelt created the Executive Office of the President as a direct result of the committee's report, into which he placed the White House staff and the then Bureau of the Budget (the Office of Management and Budget) as central components.

Roosevelt's attempts to solidify the President's power as Chief Executive faced formidable opposition in departments and agencies that often were beholden to clientele groups and congressional committees for political support and appropriations. Presidents after Roosevelt continued attempts to buttress their powers as Chief Executive, only to find that White House control of the federal bureaucracy remained an elusive goal.

GROWTH OF THE PRESIDENTIAL BUREAUCRACY. After Roosevelt, Democratic and Republican Presidents alike turned to their own bureaucracy, the Executive Office of the President, to help them deal with the regular bureaucracy, which had its own political constituencies separate from the President and much of which civil service rules protected from presidential removal. Both Lyndon B. Johnson and Richard M. Nixon, although from opposite sides of the political spectrum, agreed that presidential control of the bureaucracy was essential. To achieve this end both men expanded the Executive Office of the President and set the precedent of a powerful White House staff at the center of an increasingly institutionalized presidency. Later Presidents, Jimmy Carter, Ronald Reagan, and George Bush, agreed that the size and power of the federal bureaucracy was a major problem, and they kept the President's bureaucracy intact and expanded its power.

Future Presidents will undoubtedly continue to face obstacles as they strive to be effective Chief Executives. While the Constitution delegates the executive power to the President, it also creates a checks and balances system that often limits presidential power. Congress cannot directly exercise executive power, but it possesses major constitutional authority over the executive branch. Congress alone creates executive departments and agencies, unless through legislation it permits the President to do so. Congress also determines agency powers, and whether or not the courts will have the authority to review administrative decisions. Congress may create "independent" agencies that are mostly outside of presidential control. From the vantage point of Capitol Hill, the executive branch is an extension of Congress as much as of the President.

The presidency of Franklin Roosevelt, which centralized power in the White House, marked the beginning of an ascendant presidency with a comprehensive legislative agenda.

POLITICAL LIMITS. Formal constitutional prescriptions are only one component of presidential power. As the President seeks to carry out his role as Chief Executive his success depends as much upon his political skills as upon his constitutional powers. In the end, as Richard Neustadt pointed out in his famous work, *Presidential Power,* executive power depends more upon the President's responsibility to persuade others that their interests coincide with his than upon his formal powers. Departments and agencies are linked to powerful political constituencies and congressional committees that may combine to override presidential initiatives. In Neustadt's view, the Constitution makes the President a clerk, not a king. But a politically astute President can turn his clerkship into a powerful Chief Executive.

Chief Legislator

The role of the President as chief legislator, initially based on Article II, has vastly expanded in the twentieth century beginning with Roosevelt's administration. The President's constitutional responsibilities to recommend legislation to Congress and to inform the legislature about the state of the union from time to time, and most particularly his power to veto legislation, give him an important legislative role. But, with the exception of the veto authority, these constitutional provisions pale in comparison to important political changes that have occurred that support the President's power of legislative leadership.

Outside of the Constitution, the President derives his legislative role from his position as political party leader. Although presidential parties are loosely knit confederations of diverse interests that often cannot agree with each other, they do have party platforms and represent interests that back public policies in many areas. Presidents have little influence on the platforms, and rarely even read them or know their contents. But they are sensitive to party interests. In the broadest sense the two major parties represent different national economic and social goals. Presidents stand at the head of their parties and derive a legislative role from the position.

The political mantle Presidents wear as head of their parties is further enhanced from the broad electoral base of the presidency that makes it the focus of democratic aspirations and the popularly chosen instrument for political change. This aspect of presidential power is in sharp contrast to the intentions of the Framers of the Constitution who envisioned the President as an indirectly elected statesman, not a down-to-earth politician.

POWER LIMITS. The President's power as chief legislator is even more limited than as Chief Executive. The Constitution makes the President Chief Executive, while it only indirectly gives him a legislative role, albeit an important one. The presidency of Franklin Roosevelt, which centralized power in the White House, marked the beginning of an ascendant presidency with a comprehensive legislative agenda. But presidential domination of the legislative sphere requires, both under the Constitution and politically, congressional assent that Presidents more often than not find elusive. The failure of parties to bridge the constitutional gap between the President and Congress is a major restraint on presidential power in the legislative arena.

DELEGATION OF LEGISLATIVE AUTHORITY. While Congress exercises the primary legislative authority under the Constitution, it may and often does delegate important legislative power to the President and executive departments and agencies. The executive branch's role in policy implementation gives it an important voice in defining legislation. The executive fills in the details of often vaguely worded and ambiguous legislation. This is particularly true in the regulatory sphere where Congress usually cannot go very far beyond directing the executive to heed the public interest, convenience, and necessity in implementing regulatory policy and programs. By filling in legislative details under such circumstances the executive more than Congress gives legislation its true meaning.

Commander in Chief

Article II provides that the President "shall be Commander in Chief of the Army and Navy of the United States, and of the Militia of the several states, when called into the actual Service of the United States." The President is, in Hamilton's words, the first general and admiral of the confederacy. The President's role as Commander in Chief has assumed great proportions in times of crisis, such as during the Civil War and the wars of the twentieth century. As the power has evolved, the President makes war, even though the Constitution delegates to Congress the authority to declare war [*see* war, declaration of].

The Framers of the Constitution made the President Commander in Chief for two reasons. First, they wanted unequivocally to establish civilian control over the military, a principle that is essential to the preservation of constitutional democracy. Second, they found it only logical to make the President Commander in Chief as the presidency was the only office that was unified and could act with dispatch. Moreover, the Commander in Chief power is clearly executive in nature.

As Commander in Chief the President exercises executive prerogative power. Congress, however, checks the President. Congress alone has the power to declare war, to raise and support armies, and to determine the organization of the military and its appropriations. Presidents may claim prerogative power, but Congress may decide otherwise.

In the aftermath of the Vietnam War, which its opponents saw as an abuse of presidential discretion, Congress enacted a wide range of checks upon executive power in foreign and military affairs, requiring the President to inform Congress before taking action in many areas, such as the sale of arms abroad. Congress also passed the War Powers Resolution of 1973, which technically required the President to gain congressional approval before committing American troops abroad for a time period longer than sixty days. Congress intended the resolution to limit the President's Commander in Chief powers that had grown so enormously in the twentieth century, although many saw the law ironically as a recognition for the first time of the constitutional authority of the President to make war. The resolution has had virtually no impact upon the President's extensive powers as Commander in Chief.

Leader in Foreign Affairs

So extensive is presidential power in making foreign policy that one political scientist, Aaron Wildavsky, has written that there are two presidencies, one in foreign and the other in domestic affairs. When Harry Truman said categorically, "I make foreign policy," few disagreed. The two presidencies emerged after World War II and Roosevelt's administration, which marked the beginning of an imperial presidency in foreign affairs.

During Roosevelt's administration Congress willingly delegated broad authority to the President as diplomat in chief to make foreign policy. In a historic decision, *United States* v. *Curtiss-Wright* (1936), the Supreme Court held that Congress could delegate far broader legislative authority to the President to make foreign policy than it could to make domestic policy. The *Curtiss-Wright* opinion contrasted with a prior case, *Schechter Poultry Corp.* v. *United States* (1935), in which the Court announced the Schechter Rule, which held that in the domestic sphere the Constitution required Congress, not the President, to exercise legislative power. Congress could not delegate its exclusive authority to legislate to the President or to the executive branch. However, in the *Curtiss-Wright* case, the Court found that the Constitution gave to the President primary foreign-policy making power that supported broad congressional delegations of authority to the executive in the foreign-policy sphere.

Presidential authority to conduct foreign policy is derived from his constitutional powers in Article II: to make treaties; nominate ambassadors and consuls; receive foreign ambassadors; and command the military forces.

Presidents are not expected simply to exercise narrow executive power, but to overcome the constitutional limits set by the checks and balances system.

The extent to which the President becomes personally involved in the conduct of foreign policy depends upon his style and the times. Foreign crises require personal presidential attention. The growth of the White House staff in the modern presidency, which includes the important post of national security adviser, has enabled the White House to dominate the Secretary of State and his bureaucracy in foreign affairs.

Presidential power even over the area of foreign affairs, however, can never be absolute. Congress through legislation has restricted presidential authority in many areas and has delegated not only to the State Department but to more than forty administrative agencies the authority to make foreign-policy decisions. No President, even with a foreign-policy staff, can hope to control the bureaucratic maze that exists in foreign policy.

Moreover, the Constitution provides for the sharing of important foreign-policy making between the President and the Senate. The Founding Fathers envisioned a major role for the Senate and as a minimum a sharing of foreign-policy making responsibilities between the President and the Senate in the then important treaty-making area.

During much of the nineteenth century Congress and the President were equal partners in making foreign policy, with the Congress often dominant. But World War II marked at least a temporary end of important congressional power over foreign affairs. President Franklin D. Roosevelt had firmly established presidential supremacy with a cooperative Congress. Even in the area of treaty making, Presidents, starting with Franklin D. Roosevelt with an acquiescent Congress, have essentially turned to the use of executive agreements over which the President has virtually complete discretion in dealing with foreign nations.

Throughout United States history the President's power over foreign affairs has ebbed and flowed, but mostly flowed. As Justice George Sutherland wrote in his opinion in *Curtiss-Wright:*

> In the vast external realm [of foreign affairs] with its important, complicated, delegate and manifold problems, the President alone has the power [under the Constitution] to speak or listen as a representative of the nation. He *makes* treaties with the advice and consent of the Senate; but he alone negotiates. Into the field of negotiation the Senate cannot intrude; and Congress itself is powerless to invade it.

Chief of State

The President is the nation's chief of state by default. He exercises the ceremonial functions of the head of government, making him a king and prime minister. In Great Britain the monarch performs the ceremonial head-of-state role, but the President must carry out this demanding and time-consuming task in the United States. Being ceremonial head of state is not a "power" in the sense that being Chief Executive and Commander in Chief is, but it greatly adds to the strength of the presidency as he assumes a nonpolitical and symbolic mantle that places him above the crowd, and, particularly in times of foreign crises, helps to immunize him from political criticism. An attack upon the President under such circumstances can be viewed as unpatriotic.

As ceremonial chief of state the President represents the nation abroad as he travels, for example, to summit meetings and trade conferences. At home the President receives foreign ambassadors in elaborate ceremonies on the South Lawn of the White House, and presides over state dinners for foreign leaders. The President's ceremonial responsibilities extend far beyond activities relating to foreign affairs, and include such activities as receiving the Boy Scouts of America, Olympic athletes and other sports champions, lighting the national Christmas tree on the Washington Mall, proclaiming national holidays, and delivering messages supporting

John Adams, one of the Framers of the Constitution, helped establish that all executive power resides in the hands of the President. (Library of Congress, Prints and Photographs Division)

charities of all kinds. The President also must sign all bills, treaties, and certification of many appointments.

As ceremonial chief the President is also the voice of the American people. For example, President Franklin Roosevelt in 1941 expressed before a joint session of Congress the outrage of the American people at the Japanese attack on Pearl Harbor. President George Bush similarly expressed popular outrage at the Iraq invasion of Kuwait that led to the Gulf War in 1991.

Ceremonial functions are an important ingredient of presidential power. Presidents adopt different styles as they carry out their ceremonial role, stressing more or less White House glamour and glitz. All Presidents have recognized that being ceremonial "kings" adds to their power.

The Reality of Presidential Power

Popular expectations that the President is the person in charge and capable of changing the nation's course mark the modern presidency. Presidents are not expected simply to exercise narrow executive power, but to overcome the constitutional limits set by the separation-of-powers and checks-and-balances system. After Roosevelt, Presidents, regardless of affiliation, accepted the Roosevelt model of the presidency as the dominant political force.

CONTRASTING VIEWS OF EXECUTIVE POWER. The ambiguity of Article II about many aspects of executive power left problems of definition to the future. The Framers of the Constitution themselves saw executive power differently and their contrasting views are best summarized by Alexander Hamilton on the one hand and James Madison on the other.

The Hamiltonian model. Hamilton wrote in *Federalist* 70 that "energy in the executive is a leading character in the definition of good government." Hamilton told the Constitutional Convention that what he preferred was an "elected monarch for life," something no other delegate would accept. Hamilton happily settled for the unified and independent presidency the Framers created. He viewed the separation of powers not as a limit on the executive but, because it created a presidency separate from Congress, a support for a strong even an "imperial" executive. The Constitution supported Hamilton's view by giving the President prerogative powers in Article II and a separate political constituency from that of the legislature. Ironically, from a Hamiltonian perspective, the very separation-of-powers system designed ostensibly to limit the President actually strengthened the office vis-à-vis Congress.

The Madisonian model. James Madison's view of executive power was the exact opposite of that of Hamilton. Madison saw the separation-of-power and checks-and-balances system as a strong limit upon the President who would be forced to carry out his responsibilities under a watchful and powerful Congress.

The history of executive power is cyclical, reflecting at different times the Hamiltonian and Madisonian models. The Hamiltonian executive prevails mostly in foreign affairs, while the weaker Madisonian executive characterizes domestic politics. Presidential ascendancy is never guaranteed.

PRESIDENTIAL STRENGTHS. The Constitution, when viewed from a Hamiltonian perspective, supports a strong executive. Political and economic changes, particularly in the twentieth century, have made the presidency the focus of national leadership, and both constitutional and political factors strengthen the executive.

Unified office. Unlike the plural executives of parliamentary countries, the American presidency is a single executive. Alexander Hamilton wrote in *Federalist* 70: "That unity is conducive to energy will not be disputed, decision, activity, secrecy, and dispatch, will generally characterize the proceedings of one man, in a much more eminent degree than the proceedings of any greater number; and in proportion as the number is increased, these qualities will be diminished." Inevitable internal dissention in a plural executive would "tincture the exercise of the executive authority with the spirit of habitual feebleness and dilatoriness." Moreover a plural executive would tend "to conceal faults, and destroy responsibility. . . . It often becomes impossible, amidst mutual accusations, to determine on whom the blame or the punishment of a pernicious measure . . . ought really to fall." The unified presidency has been particularly important to effective executive power in the American political system, which is characterized by political pluralism and the lack of disciplined parties. The centripetal force of the presidency has helped to aggregate diverse political interests by giving them an incentive to form national political parties to capture the presidency.

Fixed four-year term. Unlike prime ministers, who can lose their office upon a parliamentary vote of no confidence, Presidents have a constitutionally guaranteed four-year term subject only to the highly unlikely possibility of impeachment. The Twenty-second Amendment prevents the President from serving more than two terms, but while they are in office Presidents have some decision-making leeway. Alexander Hamilton wrote in *Federalist* 71: "Duration in office has been mentioned as the second requisite to energy of the executive authority."

Independent constituency. Another source of executive strength is the President's independent electoral constituency—the Electoral College. The Framers of the Constitution considered but rejected a plan to have Congress choose the President. Alexander Hamilton recognized that a strong and independent executive required an electoral constituency separate from that of Congress, which would both enable the President and give him an incentive to check Congress. Different electoral constituencies for the executive and legislature were central to the theory and practice of the separation-of-powers and checks-and-balances system. The President and Congress do not depend upon each other because they do not draw from the same base of electoral support. The President's constituency is far more national than that of the House or the Senate.

Independent powers. The President's prerogative powers as Chief Executive and Commander in Chief and his authority to veto legislation make the executive a powerful independent force. Executive initiatives do not depend upon legislative majorities as they do in parliamentary systems. Extreme presidential actions have occasionally been challenged in the courts, but with only a few important exceptions the judiciary has exercised self-restraint and refused to overturn presidential initiatives.

Growth of executive responsibilities. Franklin D. Roosevelt made the presidency the focus of leadership. The Roosevelt presidency assumed wide-ranging responsibilities to deal with the Great Depression. For the first time the President became the "Manager of Prosperity," to use Clinton Rossiter's apt phrase in his classic work *The American Presidency* (1956). Congress strengthened the executive's capacity to make economic policy by creating the Council of Economic Advisers in 1946 and putting it directly under presidential control in the Executive Office of the President. Simultaneously Congress formed a Joint Economic Committee that was to work closely with the executive in economic policy.

Woodrow Wilson used the metaphor "feudal barons" to describe the chairmen of Congress's standing committees.

World War II helped to solidify the President's powers as Commander in Chief and leader in foreign affairs. Responsibilities help to create power but do not guarantee it. Nevertheless, by the time of the Nixon administration, which began in 1968 and ended in disgrace with the President's resignation in 1974, critics of the executive described it as the "imperial presidency." Presidential power ebbed somewhat in the 1970s as Congress attempted to curb executive discretion to make war and foreign policy, but the constitutional and political forces that have supported executive dominance, particularly in foreign affairs, remain intact.

EXECUTIVE LIMITS. Both the Constitution and politics limit executive power. Ironically, the President's chosen instruments, the Cabinet and the executive branch, restrain the President because they have both legal powers and political constituencies independent of the White House.

Constitutional restraints. Under the checks-and-balances system of shared powers the executive must gain congressional approval for executive appointments and treaties. However, these are not the most important constitutional powers the legislature has over the executive. Far more significant is the authority of Congress to control many aspects of the executive branch through authorization and appropriations legislation. Congress authorizes executive programs and determines the departments and agencies that will administer them and how they will be implemented. The legislature sets policies for the executive branch. After authorizations the House and Senate appropriations committees determine how much money will be spent on executive programs. By separating the legislature from the executive the Constitution requires the President to deal with Congress as one of his political constituencies, seeking and sometimes even pleading for congressional support.

The President has no automatic power over Congress, and in relation to Congress the executive is indeed more a clerk than a king.

Although not part of the original Constitution, the Supreme Court's power to review executive decisions when they are challenged in appropriate cases and controversies also constitutes a restraint, albeit a remote one.

Political limits. While the Constitution explicitly makes Congress a check upon the executive, Presidents also must heed a variety of other political constituencies to be effective leaders. Political pluralism complicates the President's task.

First, Presidents must deal not only with Congress as a whole, but separately with the House and the Senate and within those bodies with the numerous committees that control public policy and appropriations. Washington insider and former *New York Times* bureau chief Hedrick Smith, in his book *The Power Game* (1988), characterizes congressional committee chairs as "Prime Ministers." A century before, Woodrow Wilson, then a young scholar, used the metaphor "feudal barons" to describe the chairmen of Congress's standing committees who had emerged as one of the most powerful forces in national politics. Congressional "prime ministers" have their own political constituencies independent not only of the President but of their own party chiefs, which requires the President to deal separately with committee chairs as he tries to persuade them to follow him.

Presidential attempts to wield executive power require him to confront a pluralistic and often independent executive branch. Executive departments and agencies are beholden to their own independent political constituencies as they strive to maintain a balance of political support over opposition. Departments, such as Labor, Commerce, and Agriculture, may put client interests above those of the President. In other areas political iron triangles, which define collusion among congressional committees, administrative agencies, and special interests, impede presidential control. Finally, congressionally imposed civil-service rules protect most of the federal bureaucracy from presidential removal.

Other political limits upon the President come from his own party as he strives to compromise diverse interests in order to maintain party support. Although more difficult to pinpoint, the media and public opinion may also put limits on presidential initiatives for no Chief Executive wants to be perceived as being outside of mainstream America.

The American presidency is a uniquely powerful and democratic institution that has become the focus of national leadership. Popular expectations require the President to set the domestic as well as the foreign agenda. The growth of presidential responsibilities has not always been accompanied by a commensurate increase in executive power, which in the future will require particularly skillful politicians in the White House to fulfill the demands of the modern presidency.

[See also (II) Chief Executive, Commander in Chief, Executive Prerogative, Treaty-Making Power.]

BIBLIOGRAPHY

Barber, James D. *The Presidential Character: Predicting Performance in the White House.* 3d ed. 1985.

Corwin, Edward S. *The President: Office and Powers.* 4th ed. 1957.

Cronin, Thomas E. *The State of the Presidency.* 2d ed. 1980.

Greenstein, Fred, ed. *Leadership in the Modern Presidency.* 1988.

Milkis, Sidney M., and Michael Nelson. *The American Presidency: Origins and Development, 1776–1990.* 1990.

Nelson, Michael, ed. *The Presidency and the Political System.* 3d ed. 1990.

Neustadt, Richard. *Presidential Power.* 1980.

Rossiter, Clinton. *The American Presidency.* 2d ed. 1960.

Schlesinger, Arthur M., Jr. *The Imperial Presidency.* 1973.

Sorenson, Theodore C. *Decision-Making in the White House.* 1963.

Wildavsky, Aaron. "The Two Presidencies." In *American Government: Readings and Cases.* Edited by Peter Woll. 1993.

– PETER WOLL

A

ACCOUNTABILITY, PRESIDENTIAL

The concept of presidential accountability has several dimensions: *electoral accountability,* which requires the President or his party's nominee to defend his performance in the next election; *executive accountability,* which places the ultimate responsibility for actions by presidential appointees with the President himself; and, finally, *legal and constitutional accountability,* which holds the President responsible for the discharge of his own statutory and constitutional duties. There are no provisions for mechanisms of presidential accountability in the Constitution of 1787. The Framers concentrated on separation of powers to increase the efficiency of government, provisions of reelection to ensure dependence on the people's will; and checks and balances to guard against abuses of power. Attempts to increase presidential accountability inevitably run up against, and require trade-offs with, these higher constitutional values.

The Framers provided for electoral accountability based on the state legislatures, which controlled the Electoral College. In the early nineteenth century Presidents also became accountable to their congressional parties through congressional nominating caucuses, but by the 1830s congressional influence gave way to state parties that controlled both the national nominating conventions and the Electoral College vote. The modern transformation of conventions into a registering device for the preferences of a party's electorate in the presidential primaries, combined with public financing of campaigns and candidate-centered campaign organizations, has loosened the bonds between President and party leaders, which in turn has created a plebiscitary presidency. To the extent that there is electoral accountability it is to the primary voters during the renomination contest and then to that part (about half) of the eligible electorate that actually votes in the general election. But the Twenty-second Amendment has eliminated presidential electoral accountability in the second term and proposals for a six-year presidential term with no reeligibility would have the effect of eliminating altogether this aspect of accountability.

Presidential electoral accountability has also been lessened because divided government rather than party government has been the prevailing partisan pattern in the twentieth century. Only during the administrations of Theodore Roosevelt, Warren G. Harding, Calvin Coolidge, Franklin D. Roosevelt, John F. Kennedy, and Lyndon Baines Johnson were Congresses always controlled by the party that occupied the White House. Since the 1950s Republican Presidents have first railed and then run against "do-nothing" or "irresponsible" Congresses that have refused to pass their programs while Democratic congressional leaders have blamed the Republican Presidents for inaction or ineptitude. Those arguing that a presidential election mandate should be respected have proposed to amend the Constitution so that one chamber by a two-thirds vote should be able to pass a bill to be sent to the President, even if the other house fails to pass the measure. Another idea is that the Senate should consent to treaties by a three-fifths rather than a two-thirds vote. Such reforms would allow Presidents to get their way with Congress more easily, increasing the electoral accountability of the President at the expense of checks and balances.

Presidents have argued that their accountability is strengthened when the chain of command runs down through the executive branch without legislative or judicial interference.

Another proposal is to provide Presidents with automatic congressional majorities, for instance, by the automatic election of an at-large slate of candidates for the House of Representatives sufficient to ensure the winning presidential candidate a majority in that chamber. Or the weak presidential coattails could be strengthened if House and Senate members had four-year terms and there were party tickets so that a single ballot cast for President would also automatically be cast for the local House and Senate candidates of the President's party. While maximizing the prospects for responsible party government and electoral accountability, these reforms would also erode the independence of the congressional parties and the effectiveness of checks and balances.

Several proposals borrowed from parliamentary systems would increase the influence of Congress at the expense of the presidency. In 1974, Representative Henry Reuss of Wisconsin proposed a constitutional amendment that would have permitted three-fifths of the members of each chamber of Congress to vote a resolution of no confidence in the President. Congress would then fix a date to call special elections for President, Vice President, Representatives, and Senators. Cabinet government has also been proposed. In 1879, Senator George Pendleton offered a bill providing that "the principal officers of each of the Executive Departments may occupy seats on the floor of the Senate and House of Representatives" and participate in debates, and in the 1880s Gamaliel Bradford suggested that Cabinet secretaries be subject to question periods. Similar proposals were endorsed by President William Howard Taft in his last message to Congress in 1913 and by President Harding in 1921. The fullest exposition of the doctrine of Cabinet government was developed by Woodrow Wilson, who as a senior at Princeton University in 1879 proposed in an article submitted to the *International Review* (accepted for publication by its editor, Henry Cabot Lodge) that the President select members of his Cabinet from the legislature. They would retain their seats in Congress and have the power to initiate legislation and would be prepared to resign should Congress reject their programs.

Most proposals since Wilson's have called for some sort of joint council of legislators and Cabinet secretaries to coordinate government policies. Edward Corwin, a Princeton University professor of constitutional law, in 1940 called for an advisory joint cabinet consisting of all the departmental secretaries as well as the chairs of appropriate standing legislative committees. In 1945 Thomas Finletter, Secretary of the Air Force, called for a "joint cabinet of Congress" consisting of nine committee chairs in each chamber; nine of these chairs along with nine cabinet secretaries would constitute a "joint executive-legislative cabinet." A constitutional amendment would provide the President with power to dissolve the government in case of deadlock between Congress and the joint cabinet. In 1979 Henry Reuss proposed a constitutional amendment to permit members of Congress to serve in key executive-branch offices. Section 1 of his amendment proposed that "Congress shall have the power by law to designate officers of the Executive Branch, not to exceed 50 in number, to which Members of the Senate and the House of Representatives would be eligible for nomination and appointment . . . without being required to vacate their offices in the Senate or House of Representatives." All these ideas would make Presidents and their Cabinets more accountable to Congress; at the same time, joint executive-legislative decision making would erode institutional lines of responsibility and make it even more difficult for the electorate to hold a President accountable for public policy during his term of office. All, it should be added, would be unworkable in periods of divided government.

Presidents have argued that their accountability is strengthened when the chain of command in the bureaucracy runs from the Oval Office down to subordinates in "the executive branch" without legislative or judicial interference. Not surprisingly, presidential study commissions such as the Commission on Economy and Efficiency in the Taft administration, the Brownlow Committee in the Franklin Roosevelt presidency, and the two Hoover Commissions in the Harry S Truman and Dwight D. Eisenhower presidencies, have all endorsed this view. Presidential budgeting, legislative and regulatory clearance, and management oversight have all increased at the expense of departmental autonomy. The Supreme Court has accepted presidential separation-of-powers claims over congressionalist arguments based on checks and balances in cases such as *Myers* v. *United States* (1926), which recognized presidential removal power; *INS* v. *Chadha* (1983), which invalidated legislative vetoes of administrative acts; *Buckley* v. *Valeo* (1976), in which the Court refused to recognize rule-making powers of officials not appointed

President William Howard Taft's Commission on Economy and Efficiency found that presidential accountability is strengthened when there is no interference in the executive chain of command. (Library of Congress, Prints and Photographs Division)

in conformity with the appointments clause; and *Bowsher* v. *Synar* (1986), which limited the power of the Comptroller General to instruct the President to make certain expenditure cuts that might be required by a statute. While the High Court required judicial in camera inspection of presidential claims of executive privilege in *United States* v. *Nixon* (1974), a lower court sustained the claim of executive privilege against a congressional committee investigating crimes associated with the Watergate affair.

At times Congress has passed framework statutes that require the executive to report and wait before taking action (in matters such as arms sales) or that require presidential consultation with Congress before action is taken (as in the use of armed forces in hostilities). Alternatively, to ensure that lines of accountability are clear in national security matters, the laws can require presidential findings so that Presidents cannot later deny that actions (such as schemes to assassinate foreign leaders or destabilize and overthrow foreign governments) were taken without their knowledge. The finding requirement is designed to end the practice of plausible deniability, which shields top members of the administration from having to take responsibility for the consequences of their actions. Unfortunately, in many instances Presidents have not complied with either the spirit or the letter of framework legislation. They have argued that the War Powers Resolution (1973) is unconstitutional and have evaded its provisions. In the Iran-contra affair the Intelligence Oversight Act (1980) was flouted: President Ronald Reagan issued findings orally or even retroactively, and no notification was ever given to Congress by the Director of Central Intelligence or the President that arms were being sold to Iran, leaving presidential accountability for major decisions in the affair subject to plausible deniability.

In spite of numerous attempts by Congress to legislate frameworks that provide for both collaborative decision making and procedures to prevent abuses of power, presidential legal and constitutional accountability remains weak. The Ethics in Government Act (1978) provides for the appointment of an independent counsel to investigate and prosecute high-level government officials where it appears the Department of Justice might have a conflict of interest. The Attorney General conducts a preliminary investigation and then may request appointment of independent counsel by a special panel of federal judges. The statute itself came under attack by Colonel Oliver North in the Iran-contra affair but was upheld by the Supreme Court in *Morrison* v. *Olson* (1988). But the difficulty in bringing presidential subordinates to justice was underlined by the dismissal of North's conviction by an appeals court on the grounds that his right to a fair trial had been prejudiced by congressional hearings into the Iran-contra affair. The effort to ensure the political accountability of the President before Congress and the American public had interfered with the subsequent attempts to provide for the legal accountability of the President's agents, and this pattern is likely to be repeated.

"All the officers of the government, from the highest to the lowest, are creatures of the law and are bound to obey it," Justice Samuel F. Miller said in *United States* v. *Lee* (1882). But while in office a President's accountability to the courts is minimal. Presidents take the language of Article I, Section 5, clause 7—that "judgment in cases of impeachment shall not extend further than to removal from Office"—to mean that a President must be impeached and removed from office before he is subject to judicial sanctions. While federal judges can be indicted prior to being removed from office it is doubtful that such a precedent would apply to the President (unless he were charged with something like murder). The Watergate grand jury wished to indict President Richard M. Nixon for obstruction of justice, but special prosecutor Leon Jaworski thought it might not be upheld by the courts and had the jury settle instead for naming Nixon an unindicted co-conspirator.

While in office a President's accountability to the courts is minimal.

In civil cases presidential immunity from suit is absolute. The Supreme Court in *Nixon* v. *Fitzgerald* (1982) ruled that the President has absolute immunity from civil damages liability for his official acts, an immunity that goes well beyond the qualified or functional immunity granted to other government officials. In its sweeping language the Court held that immunity attaches to the office of President, extends to the outer perimeters of the powers of that office, and includes all official acts, whether constitutionally mandated or not. Lawsuits, Chief Justice Warren Burger held, would violate separation of powers.

The impeachment clause makes the President accountable to Congress for "Treason, Bribery, and other High Crimes and Misdemeanors." The impeachment of Andrew Johnson involved a debate about the meaning of "High Crimes and Misdemeanors," with Republicans arguing that abuse of power could be the standard for conviction and Democrats insisting that conviction required proof that laws of the United States had been violated. The same issues were revisited in the impeachment proceedings against Nixon, but this time the party positions switched: Democrats insisted that "usurpation or abuse of power or a serious breach of trust" would be an impeachable offense while Republicans followed Nixon, who argued that "a criminal offense on the part of the President is the requirement for impeachment." Nixon's resignation prior to impeachment by the House left these issues unsettled, though it seems in both cases that "abuse of power" was a sufficient standard to initiate impeachment proceedings.

The political and executive models of accountability, in which an energetic chief executive takes decisive action and then holds himself accountable to the electorate, prevailed through most of the twentieth century. The model of constitutional accountability, which emphasizes protection against presidential abuses of power, seemed outdated until the Watergate crisis, when it became clear that some of the executive's decisive actions were designed to subvert electoral accountability itself, thus requiring what James Madison would have termed auxiliary precautions. Since then, reformers have divided, with some continuing to emphasize electoral and administrative accountability and doctrines of party and Cabinet government while others concentrate on strengthening institutional checks and balances and providing improved framework legislation to promote collaborative decision making, especially in national security affairs. Neither group, it should be noted, as yet has had much success.

[See also (II) Cabinet, Executive Privilege, Separation of Powers.]

BIBLIOGRAPHY

Committee on the Constitutional System. *Report and Recommendations of the Committee on the Constitutional System: A Bicentennial Analysis of the American Political Structure.* 1987. Pp. 1–20.

Cutler, Lloyd N. "To Form a Government." *Foreign Affairs* 59 (1980): 126–143.

Danielson, George. "Presidential Immunity from Criminal Prosecution." *Georgetown Law Journal* 63 (1975): 1065–1069.

Harriger, Katy J. *Independent Justice: The Federal Special Prosecutor in American Politics.* 1992.

Lindbeck, Kathryn. "Presidential Immunity—Supreme Court Attaches Absolute Immunity to the Presidential Office, *Nixon* v. *Fitzgerald,* 102 S. Ct. 2690." *Southern Illinois University Law Journal* (1983): 109–126.

Petracca, Mark P. "Proposals for Constitutional Reform: An Evaluation of the Committee on the Constitutional System." *Presidential Studies Quarterly* 20 (1990): 503–532.

Robinson, Donald, ed. *Reforming American Government: The Bicentennial Papers of the Committee on the Constitutional System.* 1985.

Wilson, Woodrow. "Cabinet Government in the United States." *International Review* 7 (1879): 146–163.

– RICHARD M. PIOUS

ACT OF STATE DOCTRINE

The Supreme Court expressed the act of state doctrine in *Underhill* v. *Hernandez* (1897) as follows:

> Every sovereign State is bound to respect the independence of every other sovereign State, and the courts of one country will not sit in judgment on the acts of the government of another done within its own territory. Redress of grievances by reason of such acts must be obtained through the means open to be availed of by sovereign powers as between themselves.

The Court restated the doctrine and gave it new vigor in 1964 in *Banco Nacional de Cuba* v. *Sabbatino.* In that case the Court gave effect to a nationalization by Cuba of properties of U.S. nationals without just compensation, though the expropriation was alleged to be in violation of international law.

In its effect, the act of state doctrine may be seen as a special principle of the law governing the conflict of laws. In circumstances in which a court in the United States would ordinarily apply and give effect to foreign law, the court is generally free not to do so where the foreign law contravenes U.S. (or local) public policy. The act of state doctrine, where it applies, requires the court to give effect to the laws of the foreign state regardless of any domestic public policy.

The Supreme Court established the act of state doctrine on its own authority, under an inherent judicial power to make rules for the guidance of the courts. The Court also declared the doctrine to be a federal principle binding on the courts of the states of the United States.

In *Sabbatino,* the Court identified the constitutional underpinnings of the doctrine as reflecting "a basic choice regarding the competence and function of the Judiciary and the National Executive in ordering our relationships with other members of the international community" and in making "decisions in the area of international relations." The Court saw the act of state doctrine as an expression of judicial deference to executive diplomacy [*see* diplomat in chief] and a reflection of doubt as to the competence of the judiciary to address issues of possible diplomatic sensitivity. For these reasons courts have commonly honored a "Bernstein letter" (deriving its appellation from *Bernstein* v. *Van Heyghen Freres, S.A.* [1947, 1949, 1954]), in which the executive branch declares that it has no objection to the court's refusing effect to an act of a foreign state in the particular case. However, in *First National City Bank of New York* v. *Banco Nacional de Cuba* (1972), a majority of the Justices declared that the doctrine was judicial policy and that the judiciary was not bound to follow executive dictate in the matter.

Lower courts have been unanimous in refusing to give effect to an act of a foreign state applied outside its territory. In 1984, the executive branch supported another exception asking the court not to apply the doctrine where the act of the foreign state violated a provision in a treaty with the United States; a court of appeals adopted that exception in *Kalamazoo Spice Extraction Co.* v. *Provisional Military Government of Socialist Ethiopia* (1984) but it has not been considered by the Supreme Court. Courts have also refused to apply the doctrine to acts of torture or other gross violations of human rights by foreign officials as in *Filartiga* v. *Pena Irala* (1980) and *Forti* v. *Suarez-Mason* (1987). In *Alfred Dunhill of London, Inc.* v. *Republic of Cuba* (1976), four Justices of the Supreme Court suggested that the act of state doctrine should not apply to acts of state of a commercial character, an exception akin to that recognized in the application of the doctrine of state sovereign immunity.

The act of state doctrine requires the court to give effect to the laws of the foreign state regardless of any domestic public policy.

The act of state doctrine applies not only to legislative acts of foreign states but also to other state policies and state involvements. It applies only to acts of the state, not to those of foreign private persons or other entities. In *Kirkpatrick & Co.* v. *Environmental Tectonics Corp.* (1990), a case involving allegations of bribery in the awarding of Nigerian government contracts, the Supreme Court held that the act of state doctrine does not apply where the U.S. court is not required to rule directly on the validity of an act of state even if adjudication may require the court to impute improper motives to foreign officials and to establish that foreign officials had made an illegal contract.

The act of state doctrine is sometimes confused with the principle of state sovereign immunity. Both are based on considerations of respect for the independence and equality of states, but the doctrines are independent of each other and differ in important ways. Sovereign immunity is an undisputed principle of customary international law; the act of state doctrine is not a principle of international law but only of the law of the United States (though some other states have also adopted such a doctrine). By the principle of sovereign immunity, a state cannot be sued in and is otherwise immune from the jurisdiction of courts of another state; the act of state doctrine applies whether or not the foreign state is itself a party to the case before the court. Act of state does not deny the court's jurisdiction but limits the scope of judicial inquiry and may direct the court as to how to decide the case or an issue before it.

The act of state doctrine has been a subject of controversy. At the time of *Sabbatino* (1964), the Johnson administration appeared to favor the act of state doctrine. Later administrations, however, tended to favor limitations and exceptions to the doctrine in response to business interests that wanted the opportunity to challenge the validity of foreign acts of state in U.S. courts rather than be relegated to the fruits of diplomatic negotiations. Some segments of the business community and of the bar have favored the doctrine, apparently fearing that its abolition would create uncertainty in trade and financial markets. Immediately after *Sabbatino,* Congress in the second Hickenlooper Amendment declared the doctrine inapplicable to foreign acts confiscating properties of U.S. nationals without the required compensation unless the President determined that application of the doctrine in a particular case was required by the national interest. By implication Congress thereby gave legislative support to the judge-made act of state doctrine for all cases where the Hickenlooper Amendment does not apply.

BIBLIOGRAPHY

American Law Institute. *Restatement (Third) of the Foreign Relations Law of the United States* 1987. Secs. 443–444.

Mooney, Eugene F. *Foreign Seizures: Sabbatino and the Act of State Doctrine* 1967.

– LOUIS HENKIN

AGRICULTURE, DEPARTMENT OF

The U.S. Department of Agriculture (USDA) is the sixth-largest Cabinet department, with about ninety-five thousand permanent, full-time employees. Organizationally, it has forty-two separate agencies reporting to nine assistant secretaries and other subcabinet officials. During most administrations agricultural policy has been considered a specialized issue, receiving less White House attention than some others. This has left Secretaries of Agriculture with relatively large discretion in formulating policy.

Early History

USDA was established as an independent agency in 1862, during the presidency of Abraham Lincoln. It was the first department of the federal government devoted to a particular economic interest. Previously, most federal assistance to farmers had been indirect, for example, through the rapid sale of federal lands and transportation subsidies. In 1839, Patent Office commissioner Oliver Ellsworth obtained a small appropriation to assist in distributing seeds to farmers from promising crop varieties collected by diplomats overseas. The appropriation also provided for the collection of agricultural statistics. Subsequent Patent Office reports became compendiums of agricultural information from voluntary reporters in different states. Scientific work began with a small propagating garden in Washington, D.C. By the 1850s pressure was growing, both in Congress and in the newly formed United States Agricultural Society, to establish a formal agriculture department. This, along with the creation of the land-grant college system and the Homestead Act, which provided 160 acres of free land those who would farm it, became possible after the southern states withdrew from Congress during the Civil War. On 15 May 1862 Lincoln signed the act creating a separate Department of Agriculture with nine employees headed by a commissioner.

The new department continued the seed-distribution and information work that had been done by the Patent Office. The first commissioner, Isaac Newton, soon expanded the government's research to include plants, animals, soils, and fertilizers. Statistics were systematized and collected on a more rigorous basis. During the department's first quarter-century it expanded rapidly, reaching 488 employees by 1889. That year, USDA's significant role was recognized in the granting of Cabinet status. President Grover Cleveland appointed Norman J. Colman to be the first secretary.

By the turn of the century the Department of Agriculture was reaching out into a number of new areas. It began regulatory work, including the inspection and grading of food, the quarantining of foreign animals, and the investigation of adulterated food. It began to assist farmers in marketing crops at home and abroad, forecasted the weather, took charge of the nation's forest reserves, and between 1893 and 1939 served as the government's road-building agency. Research expanded greatly after the Hatch Experiment Station Act of 1887 began sponsoring cooperative federal-state experiment stations at land-grant colleges. Influential new research began on nutrition and diet. Statistical activities also improved, and the department began to hire economists to analyze the data. During this period the department's organization developed, with bureaus covering such scientific disciplines as soil, chemistry, entomology, and plant and animal industry. By 1900, USDA had 3,128 employees.

By 1914 the department had begun to look for a more efficient means of delivering the results of its research to farmers. That year the Smith-Lever Act set up the USDA Extension Service, which put extension agents in nearly every county in the nation to bring the latest in research information directly to farmers. The department's combination of local, state, and federal initiative and funding became a model of federalism. World War I brought new, though temporary, regulatory powers to USDA to control prices and encourage production of food for the war effort. In this period USDA also began to regulate futures trading and stockyards and to provide long-term credit for farmers.

A sharp decline in commodity prices in 1920, following the collapse of wartime demand, led to a long-term depression in agriculture and to demands for direct government intervention in the agricultural economy to support farm prices. American farmers were able to produce considerably more than they could sell domestically or overseas. Congressional efforts to do this in the 1920s were vetoed by President Calvin Coolidge. The Federal Farm Board was created in 1929 to buy surplus production but found the problem too big to solve with its limited resources.

The New Deal and After

With the full-scale depression that followed the stock market crash of 1929, demands for action by the government grew more urgent. Farm prices fell to a low point in 1932, sending many farmers into bankruptcy. After Franklin D. Roosevelt's election in 1932, the new administration saw agricultural relief as a means of stimulating the whole economy. During the New Deal USDA attained its modern form, undertaking many new programs and expanding its work force four times by 1940.

During most administrations agricultural policy has been considered a specialized issue, receiving less White House attention than some others.

The New Deal's first agricultural priority under Secretary Henry A. Wallace was to raise farm prices and remove burdensome surpluses from the market. The Agricultural Adjustment Acts of 1933 and 1938 and their amendments inaugurated government price-support and acreage-reduction programs, encouraged farmers to practice proper soil conservation, and began export subsidies, import quotas, and crop insurance. Food relief assisted the unemployed. To improve the quality of rural life, USDA subsidized rural electric power cooperatives and stepped up road-building activities. Many farmers on drought-stricken or other marginal land were resettled in more productive areas. Laboratories were built to find new uses for farm products. Several new rural credit programs appeared. Most of these programs spawned new agencies to administer them.

During World War II the department was given even more emergency control over agriculture than it had had during the previous war. Through such agencies as the War Food Administration, USDA helped ration food, stimulated production, allocated scarce resources needed by farmers, encouraged gardening, established labor importation programs, and educated the public on food conservation and other wartime themes. The department's research emphasized finding agricultural alternatives to scarce products that could no longer be imported. High price supports kept production near record levels.

Following World War II the department returned to its peacetime orientation. New Deal programs, which had often originated as reform ideas, entered the mainstream, except for some of the more unconventional plans, such as farmer resettlement and greenbelt towns. Farming went through a major transformation in the two decades after the war. Farms became larger, more specialized, more heavily capitalized, and fewer in number. With the growing use of chemical fertilizers and pesticides, productivity soared. Fearing that the return of farm surpluses would lead to a price collapse like that which had occurred after World War I, the department grappled with ways to use or dispose of excess commodities. Marketing received renewed emphasis from the Agricultural Market Act of 1946. Beginning in 1954, the Food for Peace (P.L. 480) program sought to combine assistance to hungry nations with a reduction in surplus commodities. The Dwight D. Eisenhower administration began a rural development program to revitalize rural communities that lost population as farm families left for the cities.

From Kennedy to Bush

The administrations of John F. Kennedy and Lyndon B. Johnson put new emphasis on alleviating hunger. The Food Stamp Act of 1964 was joined by school lunch subsidies and other assistance targeted to poor children and mothers. The department cooperated in enforcing the Civil Rights Act of 1964, an assignment made difficult by the persistence of racist mores in many local USDA offices. Rural development was expanded nationwide in cooperation with other agencies active in Johnson's War on Poverty. In the 1960s many older price-support programs were replaced with a voluntary system of relatively low supports supplemented by income payments.

In the 1970s farmers enjoyed a period of prosperity stimulated by a rapid increase in exports of major field crops such as wheat, corn, and soybeans. Rural development activities were enhanced by the Rural Development Act of 1972. Food programs expanded to become the major item in the USDA budget. Many nonagricultural groups became interested in USDA programs, encouraging the department to place greater emphasis on consumer issues such as food safety.

American agriculture suffered another reversal in the 1980s. Exports peaked in 1981 and then fell because of a rising dollar and lower foreign demand. Farm prices followed. Many farmers had gone deeply into debt in order to expand their operations. When commodity and farmland prices began to decline in the early 1980s, many farmers suffered financial hardship. The Ronald Reagan administration proposed sharp cuts in farm programs to stem their rising costs. Congress sustained the programs, but the administration did succeed in cutting back in some areas. The 1985 Food Security Act stimulated exports with lower price supports and export subsidies while the administration's General Agreement on Tariffs and Trade (GATT) proposals in the Uruguay round of negotiations attempted to eliminate subsidies from world trade. The 1985 act also showed a new interest in conservation with its provision for a conservation reserve to remove erodible land from production. The 1990 Food, Agriculture, Conservation, and Trade Act continued in the same direction, with strong conservation provisions. In the 1980s, USDA also took a more important role on other environmental issues, such as organic farming and pollution from agricultural chemicals.

Following World War II New Deal programs, which had often originated as reform ideas, entered the mainstream.

The Department of Agriculture remains active in its traditional areas of research, forestry, marketing, inspection, disease control, and price supports. But its mandate now covers much more than agriculture per se. About 90 percent of its employees are in field locations.

BIBLIOGRAPHY

Baker, Gladys L. et al. *Century of Service: The First 100 Years of the United States Department of Agriculture.* 1963.

Fite, Gilbert C. *American Farmers: The New Minority.* 1981.

Gaus, John M., and Leon O. Wolcott. *Public Administration and the United States Department of Agriculture.* 1940.

Harding, T. Swann. *Some Landmarks in the History of the Department of Agriculture.* Rev. ed 1951.

Rasmussen, Wayne D., and Gladys L. Baker. *The Department of Agriculture.* 1972.

Saloutos, Theodore. *The American Farmer and the New Deal.* 1982.

– DOUGLAS E. BOWERS

AIR FORCE

Following the important contribution by the U.S. Army Air Forces to victory in World War II, the Congress and President Harry S Truman advocated "air parity," that is, an independent air force coequal with the army and navy. The Senate and House Armed Services committees held hearings in late 1946 and 1947 at which leading military and civilian officials testified. On 5 June 1947, the Senate Committee on Armed Services approved the so-called unification bill (S.758) with amendments. The Senate and the House approved the legislation in July by voice vote. On 26 July 1947, President Truman approved the unification legislation known as the National Security Act. The act created the National Military Establishment, headed by a civilian secretary of Defense who exercised control over the executive departments of the Army, Navy, and Air Force, each headed by a civilian secretary.

The National Security Act established the United States Air Force under the Department of the Air Force. However, because of roles and missions clashes during 1947–1949, especially between the air force and the navy, Congress passed amendments to the act in 1949. This legislation began the long process of centralizing authority within the office of the secretary of Defense. Under the 1949 act, the Department of Defense was designated as an executive department; the army, navy, and air force were relegated to military departments; and the service secretaries were removed as statutory members of the National Security Council.

These amendments of 1949 failed to end the roles and missions dispute between the navy and the air force, which centered on the issue of which service would hold responsibility for the strategic atomic mission. Secretary of State James V. Forrestal's "Functions Paper" of April 1948 delineated the functions of the services, giving the air force primary responsibility for conducting strategic air warfare. The severity of the controversy was heightened by the defense budget restraints imposed by the Truman administration—an almost equal three-way split of the defense funding between the services, limiting the funds available to each. During this bitter dispute, Secretary Forrestal resigned and subsequently committed suicide; Secretary of the Navy John L. Sullivan also resigned; and Chief of Naval Operations Adm. Louis E. Denfeld was fired by Truman.

The controversy, known as the "revolt of the admirals," broke out into a rancorous public dispute in hearings before the House Armed Services Committees, then chaired by Rep. Carl Vinson (D-Ga.), in the late summer and autumn of 1949. Two separate hearings were convened, the first focusing on charges that the fledgling air force, and its secretary, Stuart Symington, were guilty of fraud in the procurement of the B-36 bomber, and the second featuring a review of national security strategy and the policy of strategic deterrence.

Chairman Vinson absolved the air force of irregularities in its B-36 procurement. The House Armed Services Committee issued a report in March 1950 that reaffirmed that the air force held primary responsibility for strategic bombing and yet deplored the manner in which the navy's flush-deck aircraft carrier was canceled, which had ignited the navy-air force clash. When the aircraft carrier, the centerpiece of the navy's drive to gain a share of the strategic mission, was canceled by the Truman administration, the navy alleged it had not been given the opportunity properly to present the case for building the carrier. Although the committee's report did not settle the services' struggle over roles and missions, it did recommend ways to ameliorate service rivalry within the structure of the Joint Chiefs of Staff.

In addition to solving issues of roles and missions, the fledgling air force needed to codify its internal structure. The National Security Act gave the new service great latitude in structuring itself, but the air force had not been granted a specific authorized strength. The Army and Air Force Authorization Act of 10 July 1950 stipulated that the air force would be composed of a regular air force of 502,000 officers and airmen, divided into seventy groups and whatever separate squadrons were required. The act also provided for an air national guard of 150,000 personnel and an air force reserve totaling 100,000 personnel.

More than a year later, under the impetus provided by House Military Affairs Committee chairman Vinson, the organization of U.S. Air Force headquarters was codified by the Air Force Organization Act of 1951. The headquarters would be composed of an air staff and not more than five deputy chiefs of staff under the chief of staff of the air force. The act provided for a chief of staff who would command the three combat commands—Strategic Air Command, Tactical Air Command, and Air Defense Command—and supervised all other air force activities. It also provided for a presidentially appointed judge advocate general to provide comprehensive legal services in support of air force operations.

Following the important contribution by the U.S. Army Air Forces in World War II, Truman advocated an independent air force coequal with the army and navy.

In 1953, President Dwight D. Eisenhower came to power determined to centralize authority in the office of the secretary of Defense. Eisenhower's Reorganization Plan No. 6 of June 1953, which became law when Congress failed either to amend or disapprove it, abolished a number of boards and staff agencies and replaced them with six new assistant secretaries of Defense. This trend toward centralizing power in the hands of the secretary of Defense culminated in Eisenhower's Department of Defense Reorganization Act of 1958, which stated that the operational chain of command no longer included the service secretaries but rather ran from the President to the secretary of Defense and through the Joint Chiefs of Staff to the unified theater commands and the Strategic Air Command—the latter being a "specified" command, that is, a command having an overall strategic mission not confined to any special geographic theater of operations. Thus the act repealed the legislative authority for the service chiefs of staff to command their respective services. Now, unified and specified commanders would carry out specific military missions with service forces assigned under the operational control of the unified commanders. The 1958 reorganization act survived for almost thirty years without major change.

The Goldwater-Nichols Reorganization Act of 1986 was the most comprehensive revision of the joint military establishment since the 1958 reorganization. The Goldwater-Nichols act gave the air force more responsibility for the military's role in the space program; concentrated more authority in the chairman of the Joint Chiefs of Staff; and directed reviews of the mission, responsibilities, and force structures of the unified and specified commands. This review created the United States Transportation Command in 1987 to supervise joint deployment for land, sea, and air components of the military. The 1986 law also strengthened the authority of the combatant commanders and confirmed the 1958 legislation specifying that the chain of command ran from the President to the secretary of Defense to the combatant commanders.

In the almost half century since Congress established the U.S. Air Force, the evolution of weapons technology and clashes over service roles and missions had led inexorably to the centralization of power and authority in the office of the secretary of Defense. The Goldwater-Nichols Reorganization Act confirmed this drive, gave more power to the chairman of the Joint Chiefs of Staff, and spurred the ongoing trend toward the joint application of doctrine, planning, and strategy supportive of joint operations.

[See also (II) Defense, Department of; National Security Council.]

BIBLIOGRAPHY

Caraley, Demetrios. *The Politics of Military Unification: A Study of Conflict and the Policy Process.* 1966.

Maurer, Maurer. "The Constitutional Basis of the United States Air Force." *Air University Review* 16 (1965): 63–68.

Wolf, Richard I. *USAF Basic Documents on Roles and Missions.* 1987.

Wolk, Herman S. *Planning and Organizing the Postwar Air Force, 1943–1947.* 1984.

– HERMAN S. WOLK

AMBASSADORS, RECEIVING AND APPOINTING

The President's authority to receive and appoint ambassadors is an important part of his foreign affairs powers. Article II, Section 2, of the Constitution says that the President "shall nominate, and by and with the Advice and Consent of the Senate, shall appoint Ambassadors, other public Ministers and Consuls." Article II, Section 3, says that the President "shall receive Ambassadors and other public Ministers." Hence, the presidential power to appoint ambassadors is subject to senatorial oversight, while the power to receive ambassadors is not. The reception and appointment of ambassadors helps the executive branch to communicate with other nations and to supervise the United States' international relations. In modern times, the power to appoint and receive ambassadors has not, standing alone, been as controversial as some of the President's other international powers (e.g., the treaty-making power and the power to command the armed forces). But when combined with all the President's express and implied international powers, the authority to receive and appoint ambassadors is enmeshed in the larger separation of powers dispute between the executive and legislative branches over the governance of foreign affairs.

Appointing Ambassadors

The United States sends one ambassador to most of the foreign governments it recognizes. An ambassador serves as the nation's highest ranking diplomat, representing the United States in its regular dealings with the other country. The United States also sends an ambassador to the United Nations. Presidential nominations of these individuals normally fall into one of three categories: the nomination of a career diplomat, that is, someone who has dedicated his or her professional life to foreign service and normally has been educated for the position and moved up through the diplomatic ranks; the nomination of someone with more domestic government experience, that is, a Washington insider, who may be chosen due to the current circumstances in a particular country and for an ability to deal successfully with that specific situation; and, finally, the nomination of a significant political benefactor, that is, someone with neither foreign affairs nor government expertise, who has contributed a large sum of money to or helped to manage the President's successful campaign for the White House. Unfortunately, Presidents have recently nominated as ambassadors more and more individuals who fall into this final category, putting presidential politics above the nation's foreign affairs needs. The Senate and the public have sometimes criticized Presidents for making such nominations, although virtually all of these nominees have been confirmed; perhaps such nominations are relatively harmless if the ambassador is appointed to a smaller and less significant foreign country. Sometimes an ambassador will continue to serve the United States even when a new President takes over. Ambassadors have no particular tenure in office and may resign or be recalled by the President at any time without senatorial approval being necessary.

Foreign ambassadors usually have immunity from prosecution if they violate the United States' laws.

Under Article II of the Constitution, the Senate's consent is necessary not only when the President nominates an ambassador, but also when he nominates a consul. A consul's diplomatic duties are more narrow than an ambassador's. An ambassador may carry the President's message to the foreign sovereign on a panoply of issues and may also assume ceremonial functions; but a consul's primary job historically has been to represent the commercial interests of United States citizens in a foreign country. Apart from ambassadors and consuls, however, Presidents have traditionally appointed lesser and temporary diplomats without seeking the Senate's consent. For example, in 1791 President George Washington authorized Gouverneur Morris of New York to negotiate with the British government concerning both the treaty of peace and the potential for a new commercial treaty. In doing so, Washington acted upon the counsel of Thomas Jefferson, who advised that the President did not need senatorial consent except when nominating ambassadors and consuls. President Washington and his successors often unilaterally appointed diplomatic agents to further a particular foreign relations goal or to draft a treaty with another nation. Presidents occasionally have even conferred the ambassadorial rank on someone temporarily, without the Senate's approval. In 1917, for instance, President Woodrow Wilson unilaterally named Elihu Root as ambassador to Russia on a special mission. The legislative branch has tried to control the President's enlargement of his diplomatic cadre, requiring congressional authorization of new ministerial posts and regulating the diplomatic corps' expenditures. But where confidentiality or dispatch is needed—as when President Grover Cleveland sent J. H. Blount to Hawaii in 1893—Presidents have regularly prevailed in sending their private envoys abroad with little senatorial oversight. In his renowned study *The President,* Edward Corwin refers to the executive's "long . . . conceded right to employ in the discharge of his diplomatic function so-called 'special,' 'personal,' or 'secret' agents in whose designation the Senate has no voice."

Receiving Ambassadors

The President's control over foreign affairs also derives from his reception of ambassadors and other ministers from foreign countries. Diplomatic relations are generally reciprocal in nature, so that the executive receives an ambassador from any country to which he has appointed an ambassador. The President and his delegatees may have regular contact with foreign diplomats who reside in embassies in Washington, D.C. Such contacts may range from being ceremonial in nature to being very significant in times of international exigency. Under international law, foreign ambassadors should abide by the United States' laws and regulations; but they nevertheless usually have immunity from prosecution if they violate the United States' laws. In such instances, the executive branch has the authority to declare that the foreign ambassador is no longer welcome in the United States and must return to his or her own country (hopefully to be prosecuted there). Such scenarios may lead to diplomats being recalled by both nations and to strained foreign relations. The Senate has no say in these matters.

In *Federalist* 69, Alexander Hamilton downplayed the significance of the President's power to receive ambassadors. He called it "more a matter of dignity than of authority." Viewing this executive power to be merely ceremonial in nature, Hamilton said that "it was far more convenient that it should be arranged in this manner than that there should be a necessity of convening the legislature, or one of its branches, upon every arrival of a foreign minister, though it were merely to take the place of a departed predecessor." Hamilton, however, was interested in allaying fears that the executive branch would become too powerful; and he probably was incorrect so to demean the President's power to receive ambassadors. First, the executive branch's communications with foreign dignitaries have become an integral part of the President's growing domination of foreign affairs within the federal government; the legislative branch is not part of such communications and its influence and expertise in foreign affairs suffer as a result.

The power of the President to recognize a foreign government has been inferred from the President's power to receive ambassadors.

Second, the power to receive ambassadors has helped to establish the President's important authority to recognize foreign governments. It is now established that the President has the authority to decide whether to recognize a foreign government, whether that government is part of a new country or is competing with another regime for an older country's governance. The Constitution does not explicitly give the President the recognition power. Instead, the recognition power has been inferred from the President's power to receive ambassadors. By implication, if the President has the ability to receive a foreign diplomat, he impliedly also has the power to decide from which foreign governments he will receive those diplomats. Hence, the reception of ambassadors has become a power more important than Hamilton had originally indicated; Hamilton himself recognized this point when later arguing against James Madison and in favor of presidential supremacy in foreign affairs.

[See also (II) Recognition Power, Separation of Power.]

BIBLIOGRAPHY

Corwin, Edward S. *The President.* 5th ed. 1984.

Henkin, Louis. *Foreign Affairs and the Constitution.* 1972. Chapter 2.

Stein, Bruce. "Justiciability and the Limits of Presidential Foreign Policy Power." *Hofstra Law Review* 11(1982): 413, 463–466.

Taft, William Howard. *The President and His Powers.* 1916. Chapter 3.

– KENNETH C. RANDALL

AMNESTY

Amnesty is an act of mercy that exempts a group of persons from the punishment the law inflicts for the commission of what is typically a political offense against the state. The Supreme Court has acknowledged that there may be a "philological" difference between amnesties, which overlook or forget offenses, and pardons, which repeal or remit sanctions. Amnesty exhibits characteristics of a legislative act rather than of an executive act since it applies to a defined class of persons and not to a particular individual. In spite of these differences, the terms have been treated as synonyms in judicial decisions and scholarly discourse. Amnesty may be issued anytime after an offense has been committed, either before legal proceedings have been commenced or after conviction and judgment, and it may be conferred absolutely or conditionally, provided the conditions are constitutional. Under the Constitution, the President shares with Congress the power to grant amnesties, a power that is limited to offenses against the United States. The Court has held that the presidential pardon power includes the authority to issue amnesties. Congress may grant general amnesties pursuant to its authority under the necessary and proper clause.

There is no doubt that the Constitutional Convention intended to vest the President with authority to issue general amnesties. In the context of their debate on the issue of whether the President should be empowered to confer pardons for treasonous activities, the Framers were persuaded to do so, as Alexander Hamilton explained in the *Federalist* 74 by the argument that such a power might be critical to halting rebellions and restoring domestic tranquillity. Without the offer of a general amnesty, rebels might choose to die in the battlefields rather than at the gallows.

In 1795, President George Washington initiated the use of the power when he issued a proclamation of amnesty to participants in the Whiskey Rebellion. President Thomas Jefferson granted amnesty in 1801 to persons convicted or charged under the Alien and Sedition Acts. During the Civil War and its aftermath, some two hundred thousand Southern rebels benefitted from amnesties issued by Presidents Abraham Lincoln and An-

President Jimmy Carter responded to renewed calls for amnesty to draft dodgers when he gave an unconditional pardon to draft evaders in 1977. (Library of Congress, Prints and Photographs Division)

drew Johnson. But Congress was concerned about the exercise of the power and sought to limit it through legislation. In 1862, Congress passed a statute that "authorized" the President to issue amnesties. But since Lincoln and Johnson believed the Constitution empowered the President to issue amnesties, they regarded the act as meaningless and made no reference to it in granting clemency. In 1867, Congress responded by enacting legislation that annulled the political benefits of the pardons already extended by denying recipients the rights to vote, hold office, and own property. The conflict hinged on the severity of punishment to be inflicted on the Confederates, and it required the intervention of the Supreme Court. In 1867, in the *Test Oath Cases,* the Court declared the law unconstitutional on the grounds that the President's pardon power may not be restricted by legislation. Presidents Franklin D. Roosevelt and Harry S Truman issued general amnesties to classes of convicts and deserters.

The end of the Vietnam War brought renewed calls for amnesty for draft-law violators. On 16 September 1974, President Gerald R. Ford issued a conditional amnesty to military deserters and draft evaders of the war. The Presidential Clemency Board was established to direct applicants to alternative public service for up to a period of two years. On 21 January 1977, one day after his inaugural address, President Jimmy Carter granted an unconditional pardon to draft evaders. However, deserters from the armed services were not affected by the amnesty and were to be considered on a case-by-case basis.

[See also (II) Pardon Power.]

BIBLIOGRAPHY

Corwin, Edward S. *The President: Office and Power. 1787–1984: A History and Analysis of Practice and Opinion* 5th rev. ed. 1984.

Dorris, Jonathan T. *Pardon and Amnesty under Lincoln and Johnson* 1953.

Duker, William. "The President's Power to Pardon: A Constitutional History." *William and Mary Law Review* 18 (1977): 475–535.

Humbert, W. H. *The Pardoning Power of the President.* 1941.

Kurland, Philip. *Watergate and the Constitution.* 1978.

– DAVID GRAY ADLER

APPOINTMENT POWER

Disagreement prevailed among the framers of the Constitution over the proper manner of selecting federal judges, ambassadors, and executive-branch officials. Some of them, like Alexander Hamilton and James Wilson, believed that this was inherently an executive function and ought to be assigned to the President alone. In their view, this would minimize intrigue and cabal in the selection process and focus accountability on the person solely responsible for selection.

Others, including John Rutledge and Luther Martin, disagreed, arguing that personnel selection was too important to be left to one person. To prevent an undesirable concentration of power, in their view, it was necessary to assign appointment responsibility to the legislature, whose members would have a broad acquaintance with the leading citizens of the country and whose debates would ensure careful consideration of qualifications.

When neither view prevailed, the Constitutional Convention resolved the disagreement with the compromise that came to reside in Article II, Section 2, of the Constitution: the President "shall nominate, and by and with the Advice and Consent of the Senate, shall appoint Ambassadors, other public Ministers and Consuls, Judges of the supreme Court, and all other Officers of the United States, whose Appointments are not herein otherwise provided for, and which shall be established by Law." The President and the Senate would share the appointment power.

Historical Overview

And so they have, with varying degrees of formality and informality, comity and hostility. The constitutional language was only a starting point in this long relationship. It did not envision the emergence of political parties before the end of the eighteenth century, the development of standing congressional committees in the nineteenth, or the vast growth of the executive and judicial branches in the twentieth. Nor could it possibly have envisioned the extended period of divided party control of the federal government in the years since World War II. All these changes have added new dimensions and new strains to the appointment process.

Over time, there has been remarkably little litigation to alter or interpret the constitutional limits on the appointment power. In 1932, in *United States* v. *Smith,* the Supreme Court decided that the Senate could not revoke its consent to a nomination once an appointee had been installed in office. In 1976, in *Buckley* v. *Valeo,* the Court found unconstitutional a provision of the 1974 federal campaign act amendments that provided for the appointment of four of the six members of the Federal Election Commission by the president pro tempore of the Senate and the Speaker of the House. The Court held that because this commission was an administrative agency with significant authority to make and enforce rules, its members had to be appointed by the President as specified in Article II.

Greater confusion has resulted from the recess appointments clause of Article II. The language states that "The President shall have Power to fill up all Vacancies that may happen during the Recess of the Senate, by granting Commissions which shall expire at the End of the next Session." For much of the early history of the country, congressional sessions lasted only a few months, and Presidents often made recess appointments during the long periods when Congress was in recess or adjournment. This raised technical questions about such matters as when a recess actually occurred and whether a recess appointee could continue to serve even after his or her appointment was rejected by the Senate. Congress has enacted legislation to restrict the President's use of recess appointments.

Over time, there has been remarkably little litigation to alter or interpret the constitutional limits on appointment power.

A separate issue concerns vacancies that result from the death, absence, or sickness of the heads of executive departments. Such vacancies can occur throughout the year, whether the Senate is in session or in recess, and require the President to make temporary appointments subject to restrictions placed in the Vacancies Act.

Through much of American history, the selection by the President of nominees for executive or judicial positions was a process without much structure and often without much rationality. For most of the thousands of positions that came to be presidential appointments, Presidents relied on their parties to propose nominees. Most of these were patronage appointments such as local postmasters, customs collectors, and revenue agents. They commanded little presidential attention. In the vast majority of cases, in fact, Presidents nominated candidates suggested by Senators of their own party from the state in which the position was located. This practice quickly acquired the veneer of custom when the Senate rejected George Washington's appointment of Benjamin Fishbourn to be naval officer for the port of Savannah, Georgia. Fishbourn was fully qualified for the post, but the two Senators from Georgia preferred another candidate and succeeded in convincing their colleagues to reject the Fishbourn nomination. Hence was born the concept of senatorial courtesy by which Senators are granted significant influence over presidential appointments within their home states. When parties later emerged, the courtesy was usually granted only to Senators of the President's party.

For higher-level positions in the executive branch and for appointments to the Courts of Appeal and the Supreme Court, Presidents often selected personal acquaintances or leading federal or state office-holders in their party. It was a common practice up through the early decades of the twentieth century, for example, for presidential Cabinets to include representatives of all of the major factions of the President's party.

The Senate, for its part, adopted a dual posture toward presidential appointments. It expected to be consulted, and in most cases deferred to, on appointments to lower-level positions operating within the home states of individual Senators. Over positions of this sort, it is fair to say, the Senate dominated. On the other hand, the Senate—with a few notable exceptions—usually acquiesced to the President's choices on Cabinet and other top-level positions in the executive branch. From 1789 to 1993, only nine Cabinet nominees were rejected by the Senate. The consensus in the Senate throughout much of American history was that the President was entitled to work closely with people of his own choosing.

The one set of positions about which the President and the Senate did disagree with some frequency was appointments to the Supreme Court. Recognizing that such appointees often served for very long terms and that their decisions directly affected the shape of public policy, the Senate objected to Supreme Court nominations more than to any others. From 1789 through 1991, 106 individuals served on the Supreme Court. In that same period, the Senate rejected 27 nominees for the Court, more than 1 in 5 overall.

The Early Twentieth Century

In the first third of the twentieth century the appointment process varied little from what it had been in the second half of the nineteenth. The positions outside the civil service were filled by a process in which political parties played an important role, and appointments were viewed as a reward for political services.

This is not to suggest that all presidential appointees lacked substantive qualifications for federal service. Many of those who had been party activists had also built impressive records of public service and would have merited high-level positions even without party sponsorship. Names like Charles Evans Hughes and William Jennings Bryan would have appeared on most lists of highly qualified eligibles for Cabinet or other top positions in government. And Presidents also retained the latitude to select some appointees who had no significant record of party service, whose primary qualification was their talent or experience. In this category were people like Josephus Daniels and Andrew W. Mellon.

But partisan pressures in the appointment process were ever-present. In putting together their Cabinets, for example, Presidents felt constrained to select people who represented different factions or regional elements in their party. In this sense, Woodrow Wilson's Cabinet was not very different from Abraham Lincoln's. Though strong-willed and independent leaders, both felt compelled to respect partisan concerns in staffing the top positions in their administrations.

Throughout this period, the national party organizations played an important role in identifying candidates for presidential appointments. It was quite common, in fact, for the head of the President's party to hold a position in the Cabinet, usually as Postmaster General. This made sense, not only because the Post Office Department was the principal source of patronage appointments, but also because a Cabinet post provided a vantage point from which the party leader could work with the President and other Cabinet secretaries to ensure a steady flow of partisan loyalists into federal posts throughout the government.

The party role was critical to the functioning of the government because there was at the time no alternative source of candidates for appointment. Each Cabinet secretary had his own acquaintances and contacts, but few of them knew enough politicians to fill all the available positions in their departments with people who would be loyal to the administration, pass muster with appropriate members of Congress, and satisfy the political litmus tests of party leaders in the states and cities where they might serve. The party could help with all of that.

If some of those the parties brought forward to fill appointive positions were unqualified political hacks—and some surely were—the parties performed valuable functions as well. Many of the appointees who came through the party channel were skilled and qualified. More important, partisan control of this process usually guaranteed the construction of an administration that was broadly representative of the elements of the President's party and thus, in some important ways, in touch with the American people it was intended to serve. Equally important, the parties served as an employment agency upon which the government was heavily reliant. They provided a steady stream of politically approved candidates for federal offices. That was a function of no small significance in a government that lacked any other tested means of recruitment for positions outside the civil service.

The New Deal seemed to spawn new agencies and programs almost daily.

Following the pattern of his predecessors, Franklin Roosevelt appointed James A. Farley, the leader of the Democratic Party, to serve as Postmaster General and superintend the selection of lower-level appointments in the first Roosevelt administration. Farley directed a patronage operation that bore close resemblance to those of the previous half century.

New Deal Transformations

Despite the familiar look of Roosevelt's patronage operation, however, three changes were set in motion by the New Deal that would have lasting consequences for staffing presidential administrations. The first was the very nature of the politics of the New Deal. The coalition that brought Franklin Roosevelt to office was composed of a broad divergence of groups and views. It provided him a sweeping victory by drawing support from Americans who disagreed with each other about important matters yet agreed on the need to elect a President of their own party. But the New Deal coalition soon proved as useless for running a government as it had been useful for winning elections. Even with the most delicate kind of balancing act, it was no small task to construct an administration of intellectuals and union members, northern liberals and southern conservatives, progressives and racists. The task was complicated all the more by the intensity of the new administration's efforts, not merely to redirect, but to reconstruct public policy in the United States. It simply could not be reliably assumed that Democratic appointees would fully support all the dimensions of the President's program.

Hence Roosevelt and his senior advisers began increasingly to evade the Democratic Party patronage system in filling key positions in the government. More and more the people closest to the President—James Rowe, Louis McHenry Howe, Harry Hopkins, and others—began to operate their own recruitment programs. Typically they would identify bright young people already serving in government or anxious to do so and cultivate them with the kind of ad hoc assignments that prepared them for more important managerial positions. While these were either life-long or recently converted Democrats, they tended not to be people with any history of party activism. It was the passions of the time and their commitment to the New Deal that inspired their interest in politics, not a pattern of service to local or state political machines.

Before the New Deal years Presidents had to rely on their party's patronage operation because they lacked the staff to run a personnel recruitment operation.

The need for such people grew increasingly apparent as the consequence of a second change wrought by the New Deal. The government was growing. Total federal employment was 604,000 in 1933. It nearly doubled by the end of that decade. The New Deal seemed to spawn new agencies and programs almost daily. This created a voracious need not merely for people to fill newly created slots, but for skilled managers and creative program specialists to attend to problems at least as complicated as any the federal government had ever before tackled. This, too, had the effect of diminishing the importance of the party patronage system as a source of appointees. It became increasingly apparent that the party faithful did not always include the kinds of people required to operate technical agencies like the Securities and Exchange Commission and the Agriculture Adjustment Administration. So Roosevelt turned to other sources, even occasionally risking the wrath of party leaders in so doing.

A third change in the New Deal years fed the momentum of the first two. That was the growing importance of the White House staff. As the energy of the federal government came to be centered in the President—and it did dramatically during the New Deal—the need for more support for the President became increasingly apparent. In 1936, Roosevelt appointed a committee headed by his friend Louis Brownlow to study the organization of the executive branch and make recommendations. The report of the Brownlow Committee described the need for vigorous executive leadership to make a modern democracy work. But it also pointed out that "the President needs help" in this enterprise. It went on to recommend the creation of an Executive Office of the President (EOP) and the creation of presidential authority to appoint a small personal staff to assist in the management of the government. In 1939, the Congress acted affirmatively on most of the recommendations of the Brownlow Committee.

Presidents had previously had little choice but to rely on their party's patronage operation because they lacked the staff necessary to run a personnel recruitment operation of their own. With the creation of the EOP that began to change. Embedded in the recommendations of the Brownlow Committee was a philosophy of public management that also threatened the importance of party patronage. Political control of the government, in the view of Brownlow and his many supporters in the schools of public administration, had come to mean policy control, not merely party control. It was no longer enough for a President to staff his administration with members of his own party and let them work with copartisans in Congress to superintend the routines of government. Instead, the President needed managerial support through broader control of the budget, government organization, and personnel selection to move public policy in the direction that he set and that had earned the endorsement of the American electorate.

This gradual evolution in management philosophy clearly suggested the need for the President and his personal staff to play a larger role in recruiting appointees who supported his policy priorities and who possessed the skills and creativity necessary to develop and implement them. In that scheme, government jobs could not be viewed primarily as rewards for party loyalty, and recruitment could not be left primarily to party patronage operations.

None of these changes took place overnight, but they slowly found their way into the operations of the presidency. Loyal Democrats continued to claim positions in the Roosevelt and later the Truman administration. The pressure to fill vacancies with the party faithful did not abate. The Democratic National Committee continued to operate a full-service employment agency. But few of the appointments to important positions came via this route any longer.

The strains on the patronage operation grew more acute after Roosevelt's death. The enormous expansion that the New Deal and World War II wrought in the size and responsibility of the government put new pressures on the appointment process. With more departments and agencies to staff, Presidents could no longer rely on personal acquaintances for their nominees. And, when political parties went into decline, they were no longer the useful pipeline of candidates for appointment they had once been. In response, Presidents began to construct new sets of procedures for identifying, recruiting, clearing, and nominating candidates for appointment. The creation of the EOP in 1939 also gave Presidents, for the first time, resources of their own to use in taking fuller command of the appointment power.

The White House Personnel Office

Harry S Truman was the first President to assign one staff member, Donald Dawson, to work nearly full time on appointments and to serve as his administration's principal overseer for recruitment. In the administration of Dwight D. Eisenhower, more staff members were added to this function, and by 1958 Eisenhower had created an Office of Special Assistant for Executive Appointments that formalized the personnel function in the EOP.

John F. Kennedy came to office promising to establish a "ministry of talent," and realizing the need for a more sophisticated personnel operation than ever before existed. He assigned to Dan H. Fenn, Jr., responsibility for assessing presidential needs and for setting up a White House personnel office to supply the administration with a steady stream of talented candidates for appointment. Under Fenn—and later in the administration of Lyndon B. Johnson under the leadership of John W. Macy, Jr.—the personnel office in the White House developed procedures for identifying candidates from many sources, some traditional and political, others not. The office took the lead in recruiting candidates and managed the politically necessary task of clearing potential appointees with leading figures in the states and in Congress before their nominations were announced. From 1958 to 1970 the personnel selection process in the White House became increasingly formalized and institutionalized.

The administration of Richard M. Nixon was committed to getting control of the federal bureaucracy, many of whose employees it thought to be burdened by enduring loyalties to the Democratic Party. The Nixon administration regarded firm and efficient control of the appointment power as a critical part of its efforts. Only by recruiting and appointing people who were loyal to the President and sufficiently competent to impose Nixon's policy preferences on recalcitrant bureaucrats could the Nixon imprimatur be placed on public policy.

In 1970, Frederic V. Malek was brought from the subcabinet to the White House to analyze and then reorganize the White House personnel operation. What emerged was a comparatively large (more than sixty people at its peak), segmented, and functionally specialized professional recruiting operation. When a vacancy occurred, a position profile was prepared describing the functions of the office and the kinds of skills and experience it required. A staff of professional personnel recruiters would then reach out through carefully woven networks of contacts to identify candidates for the position. When this list was shortened, one or more of the candidates would be contacted and asked about their interest in serving. When a favorite was identified, his or her name would be circulated in the White House and among relevant members of Congress to ensure that there were no strong objections to going forward with the nomination. After successful clearance and approval by the President and his top aides (see below), the nomination would be announced.

From 1958 to 1970 the personnel selection process in the White House became increasingly formalized and institutionalized.

This process, with minor variations, has remained essentially intact since the early 1970s. The Office of Presidential Personnel is now a regular component of the White House Office and its director is usually an assistant to the President, the highest rank among presidential aides.

Prenomination Clearances

In 1993 the President has direct appointment authority for slightly more than four thousand positions. Some of these require the consent of the Senate and are usually designated as PAS (presidential appointment with Senate confirmation) positions; others do not require confirmation and are called PA (presidential appointment) positions. Cabinet secretaries, ambassadors, and the members of independent regulatory commissions are examples of PAS positions. Part-time members of most of the federal advisory boards and commissions are examples of PA positions. As of 4 March 1992, the totals in each category within the executive branch (not including military appointments) were: PAS full time, 1,971; PAS part time, 505; PA full time, 24; and PA part time, 1,584. In addition to these 4,084 appointees, 438 members of the White House staff serve at the pleasure of the President.

Once the President has designated a candidate of choice for a position in his administration, and once that candidate has agreed to serve if appointed, a series of clearances is initiated to ensure the candidate's fitness for the job. In most cases, these clearances are completed before the formal announcement of the nomination. They include a congressional clearance, a Federal Bureau of Investigation full field investigation, and an examination of the potential nominee's background and personal finances by the Office of the Counsel to the President.

CONGRESSIONAL CLEARANCE. Congress is a prominent feature on any President's political landscape, and the selection of appointees is an important component of presidential-congressional relations. Sensitivity to congressional concerns in the appointment process can often strengthen the President's working relations with important congressional leaders. Hence routine efforts are made to inform members of Congress of the progress of a personnel search and to allow them opportunities to express their reactions to the candidates under consideration. Among those most often consulted on appointments are: the leaders of the President's party in the House and Senate, the Senators and influential Representatives from the candidate's home state who are members of the President's party, and the leaders of the committees and subcommittees with jurisdiction over the agency in which the nominee will serve.

Most of the contact with members of Congress on appointment matters is handled by the White House Office of Congressional Relations, the presidential aides who work with Congress every day. Members of Congress generally recognize that the appointment power belongs to the President and that by "clearing" a nomination with them, the White House is not offering an opportunity for a veto, only for a reaction. This is essentially a process of information exchange and, except in a few cases, not much more. It would normally require a major objection, strongly expressed by a member of Congress, to stop a nomination at this point. In reality, the vast majority of congressional clearances result in pro forma approval.

FBI FULL FIELD INVESTIGATION. The full field investigation is a comprehensive inquiry designed to turn up information that might disqualify a candidate from holding high office or that might embarrass the President were it to become public. The requirement for a full field investigation on all candidates for presidential appointment originated with President Eisenhower's Executive Order 10450 in 1953.

Most full field investigations are conducted by a unit of the Criminal Investigation Division of the FBI that handles special inquiries from the White House, the so-called SPIN Unit. SPIN investigations are given high priority by FBI special agents. The thrust of the investigation is summarized by the acronym CARL: character, associations, reputation, loyalty. The background investigation covers the candidate's entire adult life with emphasis on the recent past. Those interviewed by FBI agents are told that the candidate is being considered for a government position, but the position is not identified. In some cases, the FBI may not know what the position is.

If the FBI develops information of alleged misconduct or obtains unfavorable information about a potential nominee, the FBI, after contact with the White House, may arrange for an interview with the nominee in an attempt to resolve suitability or access issues or to make as part of an official record that person's response to the allegations. The FBI also makes a significant effort to uncover any evidence that exculpates the candidate. Both sides of the allegation are fully explored and reported. The FBI does not evaluate the information it uncovers. Its role is to furnish as complete a record as possible to the White House, where the actual judgments are made.

The thrust of the FBI full field investigation is summarized by the acronym CARL: character, associations, reputation, loyalty.

Full field investigations are scheduled for completion in twenty-five to thirty-five days, but may take substantially longer if there are delays in receipt of records and reports from other agencies, if the need arises for follow-up inquiries after the first level of interviews and review, or for other reasons that may be difficult to anticipate or predict. Once completed, the results of the full field investigation are sent to the White House Counsel for evaluation. Routine and favorable information is summarized by the FBI and sent to the White House, but the complete results of interviews of individuals who provide derogatory information are included so that the White House can make its own assessment. The counsel usually examines the file and reports the general results to the Presidential Personnel Office. Only if there is reason for particular concern does the President or his top aides examine the contents of the file.

The records of the full field investigation are protected by the Privacy Act and are generally exempt from release under the Freedom of Information Act. The results are provided only to the White House. With the President's authorization, the record may also be shared with specific Senators and staff members on the committee responsible for confirmation of the appointment.

PERSONAL BACKGROUND REVIEW. The third clearance that takes place before a nomination is announced is a thorough examination of the potential nominee's personal background and financial situation, supervised by the Office of the Counsel to the President.

This begins with the completion by the nominee of a personal data statement, a lengthy list of questions on such matters as the previous involvement of the candidate in criminal or civil litigation, the candidate's business associations, controversial public statements made by the candidate, and any other information that, if made public, might prove harmful or embarrassing to the nominee or the President. All this information is for internal White House use only; none of it is made public. Once this statement has been completed, it is submitted to the counsel's office, where it is subject to careful review. The candidate may well be asked to clarify any information that seems incomplete or potentially troublesome.

The counsel's office also works with nominees to help them complete a draft of SF 278, the Executive Personnel Financial Disclosure Report. This allows the counsel's office to determine whether the potential nominee is likely to encounter serious conflict-of-interest problems and to begin the process of resolving those problems before the nomination is announced.

If each of these clearances is completed without producing information that causes a reconsideration of the President's choice, there soon follows a formal announcement. If the position requires Senate confirmation, the nomination is transmitted to the Senate. If the President is the sole appointing authority, a certificate is issued and the appointee's service begins.

New Burdens on the Appointment Power

Changes in the laws affecting presidential appointees and in the public environment in the early 1990s have made it increasingly difficult for Presidents to recruit the individuals they prefer for positions in the executive branch. Each passing year, in fact, seems to add more encumbrances to the task of the executive recruiters who work for the President of the United States. Especially notable among those are relatively low government salaries, an increasingly intrusive press, and ever more rigid conflict-of-interest restrictions.

There have been few, if any, times in American history when the salaries paid to executives in the federal government equaled those for equivalent work in the private sector. Since the early 1970s, however, the gap has expanded. Salary levels for the five executive ranks in the federal pay structure have grown slowly over time. At the same time, the salaries of corporate executives, partners in large law firms, medical and technical specialists, and professors have grown dramatically.

For most of the people the Presidential Personnel Office seeks to recruit, acceptance of a position in government requires a financial sacrifice. Some students of this process suggest that the sacrifice is short-term, and that government executives return to the private sector in more prestigious jobs at higher salaries than the ones they held before entering government. While that is true in some cases, experiences differ widely. Many departing government executives find that their federal service has added little to their employability in the private sector, especially if the President they served has been replaced by one from the opposition party. And some government jobs—like arms-control negotiation or management of welfare programs—have few analogs in private industry where high salaries are most available.

Many private-sector leaders look with trepidation on the visibility of executive jobs in government. Even those who have run large corporations are unlikely to have had the experience in dealing with the communications media, special-interest groups, and congressional committees that are part of the daily routines of many government executives.

The visibility attendant to public life is two-edged. It has made some people famous and added to their reputations. But others have had less happy experiences, their reputations diminished or destroyed while the nation watched. Investigative reporting has been very much a growth industry since the 1970s. In many ways, it has helped to improve the integrity and accountability of government. But it has not been without excess or cost. And its costs are felt most fully by the President's executive recruiters in their efforts to overcome the fears that many potential appointees hold about risking their reputations and their futures in the glare of the public eye.

One of the largest impediments that presidential personnel officers face is the burden of educating the people they are trying to recruit about the growing body of federal ethics law. There were good reasons for many of these laws, and they provide some important new safeguards against conflicts of interest, but they have made it harder to recruit people to government from the private sector. Part of the problem is simply misunderstanding. Many of those outside of government believe the ethics laws more restrictive than they are in fact. But the impediment to recruiting is not just perceptual. Compliance with conflict-of-interest legislation has required a number of new government executives to rearrange their personal finances, sometimes at significant cost.

To many potential government executives, one of the most troubling aspects of the ethics laws is the financial-disclosure requirement. Under the Ethics in Government Act of 1978, all senior government executives must, at the time of their appointment and annually thereafter, make full public disclosure of their personal finances: sources and amounts of income (within broad categories), assets, investments, and significant liabilities. In addition, much of this information must be disclosed for the executive's spouse and minor children. Some of those whom Presidents have sought to recruit have declined appointments simply because they thought the public disclosure requirement too great an intrusion into their personal lives.

Many private-sector leaders look with trepidation on the visibility of executive jobs in government.

The appointment power has become an increasingly important tool of presidential leadership in the second half of the twentieth century. With many large and complex enterprises to run in the federal government, modern Presidents require lots of talented help. As it has become more important, however, the appointment process has become more formal, more institutionalized, more conflictual, and more burdened by rules and procedural constraints. The appointment power has become simultaneously a more valuable and a more cumbersome instrument of executive leadership.

[See also (II) Executive Departments, Federal Election Commission.]

BIBLIOGRAPHY

Fenno, Richard F. *The President's Cabinet.* 1959.

Fisher, Louis. *Constitutional Conflicts between Congress and the President.* 3d ed 1991.

Heclo, Hugh. *A Government of Strangers.* 1977.

Mackenzie, G. Calvin, ed. *The In and Outers.* 1987.

Mackenzie, G. Calvin. "Partisan Presidential Leadership: The President's Appointees." In *The Parties Respond: Changes in the American Party System.* Edited by L. Sandy Maisel. 1990.

Mackenzie, G. Calvin. *The Politics of Presidential Appointments.* 1981.

Mann, Dean E. *The Assistant Secretaries: Problems and Processes of Appointment.* 1965.

Pfiffner, James P. *The Strategic Presidency: Hitting the Ground Running.* 1988.

Twentieth Century Fund. *Judicial Roulette: The Report of the Twentieth Century Fund Task Force on the Appointment of Federal Judges.* 1988.

— G. CALVIN MACKENZIE

ARMS CONTROL AND DISARMAMENT AGENCY

The U.S. Arms Control and Disarmament Agency (ACDA) was established by Congress as an independent agency in the executive branch of the U.S. government. President John F. Kennedy signed the ACDA Act into law on 26 September 1961 in New York City. Before then, except for two years (1955–1957) when there was an Office of the Special Assistant to the President for Disarmament in the White House, the Department of State had responsibility for arms control and disarmament matters.

The ACDA Act stipulated that the agency's Director would serve as the principal adviser to the Secretary of State and the President on arms control and disarmament and, under the direction of the Secretary of State, would have primary responsibility for those matters.

The Committee of Principals during the Kennedy-Johnson administrations (1961–1969) and the National Security Council (NSC) and its various committees since then have been the administrative bodies through which ACDA's Director has advised the President and Secretary of State (and the heads of other government agencies). In 1975, the Director became the principal adviser on arms control and disarmament to the NSC, and in 1983 was designated to be in attendance at its meetings involving not only arms control and disarmament matters but also weapons procurement, arms sales, and the defense budget.

The ACDA Act also charged the agency with preparing for and managing U.S. participation in international negotiations, conducting research, and disseminating public information on arms control and disarmament. Amendments to the act have charged the agency with preparation of various reports and studies, including an annual report on compliance with arms control agreements that the President submits to the Congress.

ACDA has been involved with many international negotiating forums. During the 1960s, an international body meeting in Geneva called the Eighteen Nation Disarmament Committee (ENDC) was the only one.

It still functions as the principal forum for multilateral negotiations. Having been enlarged and having changed its name three times, it is now known as the Conference on Disarmament (CD) and has thirty-nine members.

The following international agreements were negotiated in whole or in part in the ENDC-CD: the Limited Test Ban Treaty (1963), the Nuclear Non-Proliferation Treaty (1968), the Seabed Arms Control Treaty (1971), the Biological Weapons Convention (1972), the Environmental Modification Convention (1977), and the Chemical Weapons Convention (1992). This last agreement had been under negotiation there since the late 1960s. In 1984, then Vice President George Bush submitted to the conference a draft convention that was used thereafter as the basis for negotiations.

Since 1969, other forums have been used as well. Bilateral talks between the United States and the Soviet Union have reached agreements limiting strategic arms: the Anti-Ballistic Missile Treaty (1972), the Interim Agreement on Strategic Offensive Arms (1972), the Strategic Arms Limitation Treaty (1979), and the Strategic Arms Reduction Treaty (1991). They produced agreements limiting underground nuclear tests (1974, 1976, 1990). They achieved the Intermediate-Range Nuclear Forces Treaty (1987) that eliminated an entire class of nuclear missiles. They resulted in a series of agreements designed to reduce the risk of war by accident, among them the three hot-line agreements (1963, 1971, and 1984) establishing and then modernizing direct communications links between Washington and Moscow. They also led to a bilateral agreement to destroy chemical weapons stocks (1990).

Multilateral negotiations begun in Helsinki in 1973 among thirty-three states of Europe plus the United States and Canada have led to a series of agreements on confidence- and security-building measures (in 1975, 1986, 1990, and 1992), such as advance notice of military maneuvers and movements, to reduce the likelihood of military attack, particularly by surprise. Negotiations in 1989 and 1990 among the twenty-two nations of NATO and the former Warsaw Pact led to the Treaty on Conventional Armed Forces in Europe (1990) reducing various types of conventional weapons—tanks, armored personnel vehicles, artillery, and certain types of aircraft and helicopters. Succeeding negotiations produced agreements in 1992 providing for an aerial inspection regime to promote openness and transparency in military activities and for reductions in conventional forces personnel.

Significantly, these arms-control agreements have included increasingly intrusive verification provisions, agreed to at U.S. insistence and designed to create confidence in compliance by deterring cheating and detecting it before it threatens security. Also important have been their provisions for review conferences and for the creation, beginning with the first strategic-arms-limitations agreements (1972), of a series of commissions, consisting of representatives of the parties to the agreements, charged with considering questions of compliance and proposals for increasing the agreements' viability.

NATO and the former Warsaw Pact produced agreements in 1992 providing for an aerial inspection regime to promote openness and transparency in military activities.

ACDA representatives have been on the U.S. delegations to these disarmament negotiations. Some delegation leaders have been ACDA officials. For many delegations, ACDA has supplied a significant portion of the diplomatic, advisory, and administrative personnel. It has also chaired or played a leading role in the day-to-day interagency committees in Washington that have supported the delegations.

In discharging its research function, ACDA has sponsored an external research program, which in some of the earliest years accounted for half of its budget and now amounts to about $1.5 million annually. To inform the public about its activities, ACDA has issued annual reports, collections of documents, data on world military expenditures and arms transfers, and other information items. Its officials have given numerous interviews to journalists and spoken before many groups of interested citizens.

Since the end of the cold war, the United States has been shifting emphasis from measures to obtain military balance to measures to further reduce levels of weapons, prevent the proliferation of weapons of mass destruction, and promote regional arms control.

Most ACDA offices have been located in the Department of State building in the Foggy Bottom section of Washington, D.C. The ACDA staff has usually numbered some 200 to 250 people. In addition to its Director and Deputy Director, ACDA's four bureau heads are presidential appointees.

BIBLIOGRAPHY

United States Arms Control and Disarmament Agency. *Annual Report to the Congress.* Annual. 1961–.

United States Arms Control and Disarmament Agency. *Arms Control and Disarmament Agreements: Texts and Histories of Negotiations.* 6th ed. 1990.

United States Arms Control and Disarmament Agency. *Documents on Disarmament.* Issued by ACDA annually, 1961–1986.

United States Arms Control and Disarmament Agency. *The U.S. Control and Disarmament Agency: Thirty Years Promoting a Secure Peace.* 1991.

United States Arms Control and Disarmament Agency. *World Military Expenditures and Arms Transfers.* Issued by ACDA periodically, 1968–1989.

– R. WILLIAM NARY

ARMY

Empowered by Article I, section 8 of the Constitution to make laws and allocate money to the land forces of the United States, Congress has exercised its responsibilities with persistent interest in the affairs of the U.S. Army and the various land-force reserve components, now split between the Army Reserve and Army National Guard (the latter the descendant of the state militias). Congress created a Military Affairs Committee and a Naval Affairs Committee in the House of Representatives and in the Senate to deal with the War Department and Navy Department, but it merged these committees in 1947 into two new Armed Services committees, which deal with all four military services, the three service departments (Army, Navy, Air Force), and the Department of Defense. In addition, the Appropriations committees of both houses have always had subcommittees to deal with military budgets, and the chairs of these subcommittees have often wielded substantial power over land-forces policy. The House and Senate Government Operations committees have occasionally been a third focal point of congressional interest in the Army.

Congress examines the Army's policies and practices on an annual basis through the appropriations and authorization process, and it often dictates policy through the budget bill. It also considers and passes major legislation for the Army, much of which is now incorporated in Title 10 of the U.S. Code. Individual senators and representatives often intercede with the Army on behalf of service constituents and their dependents on individual problems; the Army's congressional liaison office and the Army staff take these concerns very seriously, regardless of their merit.

Land-Force Structure and Recruitment Policy

From its first session Congress focused on the size and structure of the U.S. land forces. It supported a regular army only because it believed such a standing force had two legitimate peacetime missions: patroling the Indian frontier and manning the coastal fortifications built to deter maritime raiders. These two different functional branches of the U.S. Army would presumably provide the professional cadre to train and command a wartime army of citizen-soldiers, whether volunteers or conscripts. In the two Militia Acts of 1792, Congress determined that the War Department would have little influence on the state militias until they were formally called into federal service, which the president could do for up to ninety days per year. The Militia Acts began a struggle over control of the reserve forces that has gone on ever since, with the War Department (after 1947, the Department of the Army) gradually increasing its control over the peacetime organization, recruitment, and training of the militia, now known as the Army National Guard.

Nineteenth-century militia reform left the states in substantial control of their state armies. Congress encouraged the states (with scant success) to improve their militias by offering arms, purchased by special appropriations in 1808. During the Civil War, Congress inched toward conscription by calling for better state management in 1862, but it finally enacted draft legislation the next year, after militia reform and the bounty system had failed to produce an adequate number of recruits. To compensate for militia problems, Congress had allowed the U.S. Army, which it expanded in wartime and reduced in peacetime, to maintain its officers, commissioned and noncommissioned, at wartime regimental strength, a plan first advocated in 1819 by Secretary of War John C. Calhoun. The "expansible army," presumably to be filled by wartime volunteers, would be the first force into action, a policy that worked well in the Mexican War (1846–1848) but that set limits on the size of the wartime army. New units of state and federal volunteers became the norm in the Civil War and the Spanish-American War (1898). In a crisis, Congress sided with the states' rights position on mobilization—that is, that the existing militia be mobilized and manned first and its officers given preferred treatment. The inherent inefficiencies in this system, however, led to the adoption of the Militia Act of 1903 and the Militia Act of 1908 (the so-called Dick Acts), which gave the War Department more control over the peacetime National Guard. The laws, however, did not give clear enough constitutional authorization to use the Guard beyond the continental United States (a new problem after 1898) for extended periods of time.

Congress then accepted the Army's argument that it required a second land-forces reserve completely under federal control. First authorized in the National Defense Act of 1916, the Army Reserve received even stronger endorsement in the National Defense Act of 1920, which profited from the Army's successful experience with a second wartime draft (the Conscription Act of 1917) and continued wartime problems with ineffective National Guard officers. The War Department and Congress embraced the concept of university-based peacetime officer training with the creation of the Reserve Officer Training Corps (ROTC) through both these acts. It did not, however, reject the Guard, which received additional support for federal training. In return, the National Guard Association, the Guard's lobby, accepted a revision of the law that made it clear that a federally supported Guard recognized no constitutional limits to its federal service since it was now considered the National Guard of the United States.

Nineteenth-century militia reform left the states in substantial control of their state armies.

Congress also took the lead in introducing peacetime conscription, first established in 1940 and reinstituted in 1947 when the Army could not meet its requirements with volunteers. Then Congress, in the Universal Military Training and Service Act of 1951 and the Reserve Forces Act of 1956, attempted to rationalize the relationship between conscripts and volunteers in every portion of the active and reserve Army. The latter act further strengthened regular Army control over its reserve components. Even when conscription ended in the early 1970s, Congress remained concerned that the Army "total force" of regulars and reservists provide ample training and professional opportunities for Army reservists, and it remained the champion of the Army National Guard.

Army Procurement and Construction

From the early nineteenth century on, Congress expected the Army to provide engineering services for national development and to spend its money in ways that would encourage "infant industry." The Army embraced the role as a way to build its popularity in a society not predisposed to value standing armies. By midcentury the Army Corps of Engineers had become the Army's elite and the primary beneficiary of the U.S. Military Academy (founded 1802); the academy itself was a darling of Congress, which assumed the major responsibility for appointing cadets. The Corps of Engineers built coastal fortifications, provided civil engineers to survey and build turnpikes under federal sponsorship (the most notable being the east-west National Road), and supplied expertise for the earliest stages of commercial railroad development. In 1824 Congress passed the Rivers and Harbors Act, giving the Corps the task of developing the nation's seaports and inland waterways. This mission shifted from canal building to flood control in the twentieth century, which in turn led to the creation of great inland reservoirs for city water supplies and recreation. No member of Congress would deny the benefits a Corps project might bring to a home district. The Corps also provided the pioneer project managers for construction of the Capitol building and the Manhattan Project of World War II, as well as the development of the Army's massive base system during the two world wars. Military construction still interests Congress. In fiscal year 1993, for example, Congress approved $28 million for construction in the state of Ohio, $17 million more than the Department of Defense had requested.

Until the twentieth century the Army did not have much impact on American industry, but that changed with the world wars and continued into the Cold War. Except during wartime, the nineteenth-century Army built cannon and firearms in its own armory system; most of its other logistical purchases (clothing, animals, food, forage, fuel, and wagons) came from contractors who also had civilian clients, and these could be readily procured in a rural, agricultural economy. The only consistent industrial recipients of Army dollars were the great firearms companies of New England, but they usually entered the market during wartime expansions. In the twentieth century, the War Department, with congressional support, contributed to the early development of the automotive and aviation industries, especially the latter. The attractiveness of funneling federal aid to commercial aviation through the War Department ensured congressional favor for the Army Air Corps, which received a disproportionate share of the Army budget for planes and bases between the world wars. Congress also approved of growing ties between the Army and industry when it gave the War Department the task of planning for wartime economic regulation and industrial mobilization in the National Defense Act of 1920.

Command of the Army

After the Civil War, Army reformers argued that the United States needed a centralized general staff system to focus the entire Army's effort on wartime mobilization. Fearing that a general staff, viewed as a creation of autocratic Germany, would lead to militarism and reduce congressional influence, Congress rejected the concept in the 1870s. After the confusions of the war with Spain and the inadvertent creation of an insular empire, Congress approved the General Staff Act of

1903 backed by Secretary of War Elihu Root. With the President's and its own constitutional powers intact, Congress felt safe enough to allow a central planning agency in the War Department.

Congress may have been more comfortable, however, with an Army run by lawyers, engineers, and accountants rather than by warriors, for it continued its informal, horizontal relationships with the department and bureau chiefs who spent the Army's money. It was also wary of ambitious Army chiefs of staff who might use their office for political advancement; three such officers—Leonard Wood, Douglas MacArthur, and Dwight D. Eisenhower—had presidential ambitions. The chief of staff of greatest historical significance, George C. Marshall, set the tone for the office, that of an apolitical professional adviser to the political leadership of both branches of government as well as unchallenged commander of the entire Army. Until the Goldwater-Nichols Defense Reorganization Act of 1986, Congress supported the concept that the Army chief of staff should have no internal rival in determining the Army's business, but the new law gave the chairman of the Joint Chiefs of Staff and the unified and specified commanders in the field unparalleled influence over the Army. Ironically, the reform conformed with the traditional Army view that greater centralization of authority means more efficient and timely defense decision making, especially if it is done by professional officers. Although Congress rejected this assumption in the National Security Act of 1947—which led to greater agency proliferation and civilianization—it came to prefer a chairman of the Joint Chiefs almost coequal with the secretary of Defense, a relationship that also appeals to the Army.

Investigations

In April 1792 Congress, with the cooperation of the Washington administration, investigated the conduct of military policy by the War Department, asserting its constitutional authority to review the execution of the laws it had passed and the money it had appropriated. This first use of the investigatory power—on any issue—followed an Indian victory over an Army expedition in the Ohio Territory, the worst such defeat (657 U.S. soldiers died) in the nation's history. The investigation proved inconclusive, though the quartermaster department was shown to have been negligent, forcing the resignation of Quartermaster General Samuel Hodgdon. The expedition's commander, Maj. Gen. Arthur St. Clair, also resigned at Washington's urging at the beginning of the proceedings. Congress concluded that he deserved praise, not censure, but did not order him reinstated. Secretary of War Henry Knox emerged from the inquiry with the taint of ineptness, but his close relationship with Washington ensured that he would remain in office. Although the special House committee of inquiry did not recommend legislation, it showed that it could exercise influence over the War Department outside the normal legislative process.

The St. Clair affair started a tradition of investigatory activism affecting the Army. The most memorable example was the Joint Committee on the Conduct of the War (37th Congress, 1861), which decided that it should review the generalship of the Union army. The joint committee, dominated by "hard war" Republicans, tended to see competence and agreement with its political views as inseparable, and it forced President Abraham Lincoln and Secretary of War Edwin M. Stanton to relieve or reassign generals who fell from congressional favor. The careers of George B. McClellan, Charles P. Stone, William B. Franklin, and Fitzjohn Porter, among others, were blighted by the committee. Lincoln and Stanton managed to hold the committee at bay most of the time, but its enthusiasm for headlines made it a nuisance until war's end. In 1899 Congress (both the 56th and 57th Congresses) established a Senate Committee on the Philippines, which subsequently held hearings on the Army's suppression of the Filipino insurgency. The hearings turned up ample evidence of troop indiscipline and atrocities, although the Senate could not decide whether the criminal behavior had had official approval. Nevertheless, congressional interest ensured that the War Department would investigate suspect officers and enlisted men and discipline the guilty—which won Congress few admirers in the Army.

In 1953, McCarthy established an investigating subcommittee to continue his witch-hunts for "communists" in the executive branch, including the Army.

Responding to complaints by constituents after World War I, Congress conducted an investigation of the administration of the Articles of War in the wartime army. It was aided by the acting judge-advocate, Gen. Samuel Ansell, a liberal legal reformer who shared Congress's concern that the Army gave inordinate weight to command interest in its prosecutions of errant soldiers. Completing its work in 1920, Congress revised the Articles of War to protect soldier-defendants. The next congressional assault on the Army's internal management had far less justification. Acting as chairman of the Senate Government Operations Committee, Sen. Joseph R. McCarthy (R-Wis.) in 1953 established a permanent investigating subcommittee, which he also chaired, to continue his witch-hunts for "communists" and "fellow travelers" in the executive branch, including the Army. His irresponsible actions in the Army-McCarthy hearings led to the first successful resistance to his tactics of fear, and in 1954 his fellow senators and the Eisenhower administration collaborated to both discredit and disempower him through censure. McCarthy's abuse of the investigatory option did not, however, end congressional investigations of the military. Congress has since examined officer education, weapons procurement, recruiting, property management, opportunities for advancement for women and members of racial minorities, and the administration of military justice.

Congress and the land forces of the United States share a common vision: they believe they are an expression of the broadest popular will in regional, class, ethnic, and religious terms, uncontaminated by elitism, false privilege, or excessive wealth. Such hallowed assumptions are truer of the Army than of Congress, but Congress insists that its populism remains intact when it hectors the Army career officer corps for mismanagement and political insensitivity. It champions the Army reserve forces, whose military utility falls short of their numbers and budgets. The ambivalent relationship of Congress and the Army during the Cold War was due in part to the issue of conscription (in the painful wars in Korea and Vietnam, Army infantry represented the majority of casualties) and in part to the reduced influence of the Army in high-dollar defense contracting, a dubious honor now held by the Air Force and Navy. It also in part reflects the professionalization of the Army officer corps and its strong behavioral norms, which predispose it to view politicians and the media with contempt. How the relationship of Congress and the post–Cold War Army will develop is uncertain—except that the Constitution requires that there be such a relationship.

[See also (I) Congress, article on Powers of Congress; (II) Defense, Department of; War, Department of.]

BIBLIOGRAPHY

Hagan, Kenneth J., and William R. Roberts. *Against All Enemies: Interpretations of American Military History from Colonial Times to the Present.* 1986.

Kolodziej, Edward A. *The Uncommon Defense and Congress, 1945–1963.* 1966.

Mahon, John K. *History of the Militia and National Guard.* 1983.

Millett, Allan R. *The American Political System and Civilian Control of the Military: A Historical Perspective.* 1979.

Millett, Allan R., and Peter Maslowski. *For the Common Defense: A Military History of the United States of America.* 1983.

Schlesinger, Arthur M., Jr., and Roger Bruns, eds. *Congress Investigates, 1792–1974.* 1975.

Weigley, Russell F. *History of the United States Army.* 1967.

– ALLAN R. MILLETT

ATOMIC ENERGY COMMISSION

The atomic age thrust itself upon a largely unsuspecting world when the United States detonated two atomic bombs on the Japanese cities of Hiroshima and Nagasaki in August of 1945. These weapons of unprecedented explosive force were the creation of the Manhattan Engineer District (the Manhattan Project), the United States' secret program for the creation of an atomic bomb. The devastating explosions ended World War II and at the same time catalyzed a debate over the future of atomic energy. The military possibilities of nuclear fission had been dramatically demonstrated; but a potential for peaceful use of it was also apparent. With the specific mission of the Manhattan Engineer District accomplished, it was clear that the United States needed to develop a more comprehensive program to oversee the development and use of atomic energy.

President Harry S Truman urged Congress in October 1945 to create an atomic energy commission to control the development and use of atomic energy. (Library of Congress, Prints and Photographs Division)

On 3 October 1945, President Harry S Truman sent a special message to Congress on the subject of atomic energy. Truman urged Congress to create an atomic energy commission, the purpose of which would be "to control all sources of atomic energy and all activities connected with its development and use in the United States." Among other things the commission would promote scientific investigation and the development of practical applications for the use of atomic energy. The President's message also informed Congress that he intended to open discussions with foreign nations regarding the international control of atomic energy, particularly with respect to nuclear weapons.

An intense debate ensued. From a national security perspective, the need for strict secrecy and control over the secrets of atomic energy seemed evident; from the academic perspective, the importance of uninhibited scientific research and free dissemination of information seemed equally evident. A number of leading scientists also argued for complete disclosure of all scientific discoveries in order to ensure and promote international control over atomic energy. The result of this debate was the Atomic Energy Act of 1946, which President Truman signed into law on 1 August 1946.

The act created the Atomic Energy Commission, a five-person board appointed by the President with the advice and consent of the Senate. The commission was vested with broad authority to oversee the development and production of atomic energy, including research and development of military applications. To this end, ownership of Manhattan Engineer District production facilities and laboratories was transferred to the commission. The express purpose of the commission was to encourage scientific progress, to promote and control the dissemination and reciprocal sharing of scientific and technical information, and to oversee governmental research and development, all with an eye toward safeguarding "the common defense and security." In addition, the commission was to oversee and control the production, ownership and use of all fissionable material, later defined as special nuclear material, within the United States. A fundamental premise of the act was that the authority of the commission would be limited by any subsequent international agreements regarding atomic energy entered by the United States.

The rapid development of nuclear physics over the next few decades, as well as the international proliferation of nuclear technology, led to various amendments to the act. These amendments were designed to enhance security over sensitive data, to keep the commission's authority abreast of current developments in nuclear physics, and to promote more aggressively the development of peaceful uses of nuclear energy. Eventually, the commission was also given the authority to license and regulate privately owned nuclear power plants. In addition, between the years 1946 and 1974, the commission oversaw a wide-ranging program of weapons testing and development. Not coincidentally, the vast network of commission-owned production facilities and laboratories expanded dramatically during that period.

The Atomic Energy Commission was abolished by the Energy Reorganization Act of 1974. The licensing and regulatory functions of the commission were transferred to the newly created Nuclear Regulatory Commission. The research and development functions, including both military and nonmilitary uses, were transferred to the Energy Research and Development Administration. During the administration of President Jimmy Carter, the research and development functions were placed in the newly created Department of Energy.

[See also (II) Energy, Department of.]

BIBLIOGRAPHY

Hewlett, Richard G., and Oscar E. Anderson, Jr. *The New World, 1939/1946. A History of the United States Atomic Energy Commission,* vol. 1. 1962.

Hewlett, Richard G. and Francis Duncan. *Atomic Shield, 1947/1952. A History of the United States Atomic Energy Commission,* vol. 2. 1969.

Miller, Richard L. *Under the Cloud: The Decades of Nuclear Testing.* 1986.

Truman, Harry S *Public Papers of the Presidents (1945).* 1961.

– ALLAN IDES

ATTORNEY GENERAL

The chief law officer of the national government, a key presidential adviser, a member of the Cabinet since 1792, and the head of the Department of Justice since its creation in 1870, the Attorney General is appointed by the President with the advice and consent of the Senate. Hearings on the Attorney General's confirmation are held by the Senate Judiciary Committee. Edmund Randolph, the first Attorney General, joined the Washington administration in 1790. The burdens on the incumbent have increased heavily since then, significantly so since the 1940s as executive branch responsibilities, federal legislation, and court activity have increased.

Functions

The oldest function of the office is to represent the government in court, a function that dates from fourteenth-century England. Originally, the U.S. Attorney General argued cases before the Supreme Court, a task now delegated to the Solicitor General. In the lower federal courts, U.S. attorneys represent the government. The Solicitor General, working with the Attorney General, determines what cases will be appealed to the Supreme Court or other appellate courts and what position (if any) the government will take as an amicus curiae ("friend of the court") in cases to which it is not a party. Generally, the Attorney General expresses broad administration perspectives in making these decisions. On occasion, however, the Justice Department has clashed with the White House over Supreme Court litigation issues.

Periodically Attorneys General have been charged with manipulating their legal opinions to suit political needs.

The Attorney General's second most venerable function—with antecedents in seventeenth-century England and the American colonies—is to provide legal advice to the Chief Executive. By defining the scope and meaning of the law, the Attorney General assists the President in fulfilling his constitutional obligation to "take care that the laws be faithfully executed." This advisory role has been widely regarded as quasi-judicial. Today, much of the responsibility for writing opinions is delegated to the Office of Legal Counsel (OLC). As a legal adviser, the Attorney General faces competition from other persons and agencies in government, particularly the White House Counsel and the legal staffs in the various executive departments.

The third function of the Attorney General is to administer the large bureaucracy of the Department of Justice. The Attorney General supervises much of the government's legal work, overseeing the department's six divisions involved in litigation (antitrust, civil, criminal, civil rights, tax, and environment and natural resources), the Solicitor General's office, the ninety-five U.S. attorneys, and the Office of Legal Counsel. In addition, the Attorney General supervises several nonlawyering offices, including the Immigration and Naturalization Service, the Bureau of Prisons, the U.S. Parole Commission, and the U.S. Marshals Service. The Federal Bureau of Investigation (FBI), created in 1924 out of a small detective staff formed in 1908, also falls within the Attorney General's administrative jurisdiction. Another investigative unit, the Drug Enforcement Administration, was added to the Justice Department in 1973.

Besides providing legal counsel, the Attorney General often serves as a political adviser to the President, offering policy and political advice in three capacities. First, as a department head the Attorney General is constitutionally required to provide policy advice to the President on matters relating to the Justice Department, including departmental priorities, policies, and budget requests. The Attorney General participates in formulating legislation related to the Justice Department and the federal court system, and testifies before Congress. The Attorney General assists the President in recommending and screening nominees to the federal bench [*see* judges, appointment of].

Secondly, as a Cabinet member, the Attorney General may be involved in policy decisions that reach beyond the Justice Department—for example, decisions affecting education policy or national security. He or she may be required to lobby Congress on measures that are only tangentially related (if at all) to the Justice Department. Whether the Attorney General plays this role depends on how the President uses the Cabinet.

Finally, some Attorneys General have been friends and political allies of their Presidents. As such, they have helped to plan campaign strategy, to organize partisan activities, and to frame broad administration policy goals. A minority have become trusted presidential advisers on a wide range of issues.

Unlike his or her colleagues in the executive branch, the Attorney General has responsibilities that are distinctly legal in character. On one hand, he or she is the chief law officer of the nation and an officer of the court. Yet he or she is also a political actor, an appointed official who is accountable to an elected chief executive. This legal-political duality makes his or her position a singular one. Obligated to serve the President, who is, in a sense, his or her client, the Attorney General must also exhibit "a proper loyalty . . . to the idea of law itself," as former Attorney General and legal scholar Edward Levi put it during his 1975 Senate confirmation hearings. These dual responsibilities, while not necessarily conflicting, create the potential for tension between loyalty to the law and loyalty to the President. Many Attorneys General have experienced little difficulty responding to these dual demands. Some have defined their office primarily as that of the President's advocate; others have stressed its quasi-judicial character. But, periodically, Attorneys General have been charged with manipulating their legal opinions to suit political needs. Among the legal opinions that have been cited as examples of politics prevailing over law are Robert Jackson's support for Franklin D. Roosevelt's destroyers for bases exchange in the early days of World War II, and Robert F. Kennedy's interpretation of the Cuban quarantine during the 1962 Cuban missile crisis as an act short of war, an interpretation that ran contrary to international law.

Public sensitivity to the dual nature of the office may be heightened because most Attorneys General have been politically active prior to appointment. Many have held elective office on state and national levels. A few have had presidential ambitions, although as of 1993 none had become President or Vice President. A further factor is that Presidents tend to name partisans and political campaigners to the post. With the exception of Lyndon B. Johnson, Gerald Ford, Jimmy Carter, and George Bush, every President from 1933 to 1992 named either a campaign manager, campaign aide, or national party chairman as Attorney General sometime during his administration. Notable examples include Robert Kennedy in the John F. Kennedy administration, John Mitchell in the Richard M. Nixon administration, and Edwin Meese III in the Ronald Reagan administration. Nonpolitical law officers have been appointed on occasion, but they are the exception, generally chosen by Presidents who, in the wake of predecessors' scandals, are under pressure by Congress or the public to select law officers from outside politics. Both Ford and Carter felt constrained in their choices by the need to rebuild public confidence in the Justice Department in the wake of the Watergate affair. Bill Clinton may have felt a similar pressure when he named Janet Reno as Attorney General. For one thing, controversy about the Attorney General's political role resurfaced during the Reagan-Bush years. Further, Clinton's earlier nominees—Zoe Baird and Kimba Wood—were unsuccessful precisely because of legal and/or ethical questions. Reno, in contrast, has been highly praised for her integrity during her fifteen years as Miami's top prosecutor, a quality that is essential to public confidence. Clinton's choices of Baird, Wood, and Reno may also reflect a new dynamic constraining presidential Cabinet selections, as women's groups put pressure on the White House to name a woman to Justice, one of the top four Cabinet positions.

Until 1853, Attorneys General were encouraged to maintain a private law practice as a means of honing legal skills and keeping abreast of the law.

[See also (II) Cabinet; Justice, Department of.]

BIBLIOGRAPHY

Baker, Nancy V. *Conflicting Loyalties: Law and Politics in the Attorney General's Office, 1789–1990.* 1992.

Bell, Griffin. *Taking Care of the Law.* 1982.

Clayton, Cornell. *The Politics of Justice: The Attorney General and the Making of Legal Policy.* 1992.

Cummings, Homer, and Carl McFarland. *Federal Justice: Chapters in the History of Justice and the Federal Executive.* 1937; rpt. 1970.

Huston, Luther. *The Department of Justice.* 1967.

Learned, Henry B. *The President's Cabinet.* 1912.

Meador, Daniel J. *The President, the Attorney General, and the Department of Justice.* 1980.

– NANCY V. BAKER

B

BENEFITS, PRESIDENTIAL

In addition to a salary of $200,000 per year, the President of the United States and his family are eligible for benefits that confer security and ease the burdens of office. Of these benefits, only one is monetary: an annual, taxable allowance of $50,000. There are no constraints on spending this allowance, other than that it be used for expenses.

The White House is the official residence of the President. The second-floor family quarters are largely furnished, though each First Family brings its personal touches to these rooms. The family is required to provide the food eaten by its members and personal guests, as well as to pay for services such as personal long-distance telephone calls and laundry. Most of the White House staff is employed by the government. The President must pay the salary of any personal service staff, however. The White House itself and the grounds are often changed, to varying degrees, to fit the needs and desires of the incumbent. In addition to the major restoration and remodeling of 1952, there have been additions such as a swimming pool, tennis courts, a movie theater, a putting green, a horseshoe pit, and, within weeks of Bill Clinton's taking office, a jogging track, which was privately funded.

Most First Families have considered the White House a constraining environment in which to live, despite its comfort. Because the White House is a public building and a workplace, the President's family has little privacy, unlike the families of most heads of government. Security considerations severely restrict the movements of the President and all members of the First Family outside the White House.

Personal security for the President and his family is provided by the U.S. Secret Service. The size of the detail depends on whether the President is traveling or in Washington.

Camp David, a naval facility in the Catoctin Mountains of Maryland, has served several Presidents as a rustic retreat. The U.S. Marine Corps provides security and the Navy Corps of Engineers administers, maintains, and services the facility. Camp David has several guest cabins, making it possible to use the site for meetings. The level of use has varied from administration to administration.

The Secret Service and the General Services Administration are responsible for altering the President's personal home site(s) to make it, or them, acceptable in terms of security and communication access. Whenever possible, these alterations are not permanent, and the homes are returned to to their previous condition when the President leaves office.

Most First Families have considered the White House a constraining environment in which to live, despite its comfort.

The President is eligible to enroll in the contributory Federal Employees Health Benefits program. However, a personal physician, selected by the President, maintains an office in the White House. The White House medical office is staffed by military medical personnel, and the President and the immediate family are eligible for medical care in military hospitals, a benefit available to the President as Commander in Chief of the armed forces.

The communication system available to the President is one of the most sophisticated in the world. Regardless of location, the President can be in voice communication with almost anywhere in the world within a matter of seconds.

The President travels principally by automobile, airplane, and helicopter. Several presidential limousines have been customized for security and comfort and are used for short local trips. Often when the President travels, one of the limousines is flown to the destination for his ground transportation.

The President is transported by helicopter to and from Camp David and Andrews Air Force Base just outside Washington, D.C. (Rarely is a motorcade used for these purposes.) The helicopter in which the President flies is designated Marine One.

Air Force One is the radio designation given to any aircraft on which the President flies. Generally, Air Force One is either of two Boeing 747 aircraft that in 1990 replaced the 707s. These presidential aircraft are supported by the 89th Military Airlift Wing and are based at Andrews Air Force Base. Air Force One is equipped with state-of-the-art electronics for operation and communications and incorporates sophisticated safeguards against attack. On board are the President's quarters, two galleys, several bathrooms, and seating and accommodations for a crew of twenty-three and seventy passengers. The plane's office facilities include conference rooms, computers, copy machines, and banks of communications equipment.

Under statute, the President has $100,000 available to him for travel expenses. In reality, that amount comes nowhere near answering the costs of presidential travel. Most of the vehicle-related expenses are covered in the budgets of the agencies responsible for maintaining and operating the vehicles. The actual total cost of the support of the President of the United States is probably not calculable. Although the annual cost of operating the White House physical plant can be determined by reading the U.S. government budget, there are many hidden costs. The military services, the National Park Service, and the General Services Administration bear much of the responsibility and costs for the support provided to the White House. The Navy and the Marine Corps do not publish the costs of maintaining and operating Camp David, largely because of the security involved. Most of the other security cots are borne by the Department of the Treasury, the parent agency of the Secret Service.

[See also (II) Executive Office of the President.]

BIBLIOGRAPHY

Aikman, Lonnelle. *The Living White House.* 1991.
Boyd, Betty. *Inside the White House.* 1992.
Ter Horst, J. F., and Ralph Albertazzie. *The Flying White House.* 1979.

– SHARON STIVER GRESSLE

BENEFITS TO FORMER PRESIDENTS

To what extent should a former President be required to earn a living after having served in the highest office in the nation? Are there occupations or activities that would be considered inappropriate or unseemly for a former President of the United States? For decades these questions were intermittently raised as former Presidents who did not have significant personal wealth left office with no pension provision and the necessity of "earning" a living.

Congress addressed these questions in 1873 when it voted to increase the presidential salary from $25,000 to $50,000. The support for the increase reflected the opinion that there should be sufficient financial provision while in office to preclude the necessity of seeking money-making pursuits after serving as President. Several of the nineteenth-century former Presidents died in various stages of poverty.

The Former Presidents Act of 1958 (72 Stat. 838) established a systematic pension payment for former Presidents, as well as other benefits. As amended, the provisions now require that each former President be paid an annual taxable pension, which is equal to the salary rate paid at Executive level I (Cabinet-level positions) of the executive salary schedule. Widows of Presidents or former Presidents are paid a pension of $20,000 per annum.

For the purposes of the act, a former President is defined as "an individual who shall have held the office of President of the United States, whose service in such office shall have been terminated other than by removal pursuant to section 4 Article II, of the Constitution" (3 U.S. C. 102, note). Thus, although he left office by resigning, Richard M. Nixon remained eligible for all benefits available to former Presidents.

A former President is eligible to receive funds under the Presidential Transitions Effectiveness Act of 1988 (102 Stat. 985). Up to $1.5 million may be appropriated for the use of the outgoing President and Vice President. There are provisions for a diminution of that amount if the outgoing Vice President is the newly elected President. Unused funds are to be returned to the general treasury. The General Services Administration (GSA) is authorized to provide the President with adequate services and facilities to be available from one month prior to, and for a period of six months from the date of, the expiration of the term of office.

To what extent should a former President be required to earn a living after having served in the highest office of the nation?

The GSA in addition to administering the Former Presidents Act pension provisions is authorized to provide the former President with staff. The annual compensation for such staff may not exceed $150,000 during the initial thirty-month period and thereafter, the aggregate staff compensation is limited to $96,000 per annum. A former President may supplement staff hire and compensation through nonfederal funds. The statute also requires that the GSA shall provide for each former President furnished office space at a location within the United States chosen by the former President.

As a general rule, travel funds are available through the GSA support activities for the former President and no more than two staff members. The GSA provides to the oversight committees, upon request, information on those travel expenses.

The former Presidents and the surviving spouses may use the franking privilege. Nonpolitical mail may be sent within the United States, its territories, and possessions. To some extent nonpolitical mail may also be sent internationally at no fee.

Former Presidents, their spouses, widows, and minor children hold the status of secretarial designees with regard to eligibility for care in military service health facilities. They receive care on a minimally reimbursable basis. These same individuals are eligible to enroll in and contribute to the group health plans available to federal employees.

Secret Service protection is available to former Presidents and to their families. Originally, in 1962, it was available to former Presidents only for a period of six months. In 1963 the Secret Service was authorized to protect the widow and minor children of President John F. Kennedy. Since 1965, Secret Service protection has been extended to include lifetime protection for former Presidents and their spouses. Surviving spouses are covered until remarriage and minor children receive protection until age sixteen. Congress determined, in 1984, that former Presidents or their dependents should be allowed to decline protective services. Former President and Mrs. Richard M. Nixon declined the Secret Service protection pursuant to that statute.

Presidential libraries serve as the depositories for the papers and historical materials related to specific presidencies. These institutions are becoming important centers for scholarly research. Presidential libraries, while planned, developed, and constructed with private funds, must meet certain federal guidelines. The subsequent maintenance of the libraries is a federal responsibility.

[See also (II) Benefits, Presidential.]

BIBLIOGRAPHY

Hecht, Marie B. *Beyond the Presidency.* 1976.

U.S. House of Representatives. Committee on the Judiciary. *Salaries of Executive, Judicial, and Legislative Officers.* 42d Cong., 3d Sess. 1873. H. Rep. No. 59.

U.S. House of Representatives. Committee on Post Office and Civil Service. *Retirement, Staff Assistants, and Mailing Privileges for Former Presidents and Annuities for Widows of Former Presidents.* 85th Cong., 2d sess. 1958. H Rept. 2200.

U.S. Senate. Committee on the Judiciary. *Providing Continuing Authority for the Protection of Former Presidents.* 89th Cong., 1st sess. 1965. S. Rept. 89–611.

U.S. Senate. Subcommittees of the Committee on Appropriations and Committee on Governmental Affairs. *Cost of Former Presidents to U.S. Taxpayers.* 96th Cong., 1st sess. 1980. Hearings.

– SHARON STIVER GRESSLE

BOXSCORES, PRESIDENTIAL

Designed to indicate the level of presidential support in Congress, presidential boxscores reveal the extent to which members of Congress take the same position as the President when they vote on legislation. The most frequently cited boxscore is the *Congressional Quarterly's* presidential support score. These scores, which the *Congressional Quarterly* has calculated since 1953, measure the percentage of time each member of Congress votes in accordance with the stated position of the President. The *Quarterly* aggregates such scores for the entire Congress for each session, by voting blocs within the Congress (primarily by section—southern and nonsouthern—and by party), and by the legislation's subject (foreign and domestic) to indicate how effective the President has been in attracting congressional support.

Overall congressional support scores have ranged from a high of 93 percent in 1965, when Lyndon B. Johnson was President, to a low of 43.5 percent in 1987, when Ronald Reagan was President. The average score for a single session of Congress from 1953 through 1991 was 69.6 percent.

In addition to determining presidential support scores, the *Congressional Quarterly* also devised a measure called a presidential boxscore. It was designed to measure the percentage of presidentially initiated legislative proposals that were enacted into law during each session of Congress. The journal, however, discontinued computing the boxscore after 1975 because this measure was not sensitive to the time it takes to enact legislation, which is usually longer than a single session of Congress. Also, the measure did not reflect the modifications that are frequently made to the President's proposals during the course of congressional deliberations, and the boxscores were often misleading, giving cautious, programmatically conservative Presidents higher "batting averages" because they introduced fewer new proposals than more legislatively active Presidents.

The presidential support score has also been subject to considerable criticism as an indicator of presidential influence in Congress. One problem has to do with its failure to discriminate between roll calls. All votes on all substantive bills on which the President has taken a position are counted equally. (Procedural bills and appropriations bills are generally excluded from the tally.) Thus priority presidential issues are weighted the same as trivial and unimportant ones; similarly, unanimous, near unanimous, and controversial roll-call votes are lumped together. This system of measurement ignores the fact that, with a limited amount of time, energy, and political capital available, Presidents naturally focus their attention on major legislation and on the controversial votes in which their intervention can make a difference.

To overcome this problem, the *Congressional Quarterly* has also begun to calculate presidential support on key votes. However, this measure includes only a small number of votes, and the range of issues covered by these votes may be very narrow, particularly if more than one of these key votes concerns the same issue. Generalizing on the basis of these key votes can also be hazardous.

There are other problems. The presidential support score will not be sensitive to individualized presidential efforts. Aggregate analysis is not likely to detect the exercise of legislative skills by individual Presidents. Nor is the measure sensitive to other situational variables, such as presidential popularity, that might help explain congressional voting.

The average level of presidential support in Congress for a single session from 1953 through 1991 was 69.6 percent.

Finally, roll-call voting occurs at the final stage of the legislative process, but presidential influence is often exerted earlier. This early influence may be very important to the final disposition and composition of the legislation. Moreover, a vote has to be recorded for it to be analyzed, which means that the method misses voice voting, which the Senate utilizes far more often than the House. Thus, any generalization about presidential influence in Congress made on the basis of presidential support scores must be seen as being limited to recorded votes at the final stage of the legislative process.

Given these limitations, why are presidential support scores employed so frequently by political scientists? There are several reasons. They are easy to compute. They are based on quantitative data that are available in sufficiently large numbers to yield testable hypotheses. Moreover, they enable scholars to take a longitudinal perspective and compare presidential success over time.

One of the most sophisticated studies to utilize presidential support scores is George C. Edwards III's *At the Margins* (1989). Edwards examines presidential support in Congress from 1953 to 1986 by computing the support each member of Congress gave the President during this period on all recorded votes, on all nonunanimous votes, on the most important nonunanimous votes, and on the key votes. He concludes that party and, to a much lesser extent, popularity contribute to a President's effectiveness in Congress, but that Presidents' legislative skills have been over-rated as a critical factor affecting congressional voting.

Another important quantitative study is Jon R. Bond and Richard Fleisher's *The President in the Legislative Arena* (1990), in which the authors analyze conflictual and important roll-call votes to examine the conditions in which Presidents succeed in congressional floor votes. They reach similar conclusions to Edwards's, finding that members' party and ideology are more strongly related to presidential success than are the legislative skills of individual Presidents. Members are more influenced by their own dispositions and attitudes than by the President's actions. Bond and Fleisher did not, however, find presidential popularity to have a major impact on legislative success.

A third study, Mark A. Peterson's *Legislating Together* (1990), attempts to overcome the shortcomings of the boxscores by refining the *Congressional Quarterly*'s technique. Peterson examines new presidential domestic proposals to Congress from 1953 to 1984, determines what happens to them, and then tries to explain this outcome on the basis of the "contexts" of congressional decision making. He concludes that these contexts are influenced by the institutional, political, and economic settings in which they occur as well as by the kind of policy proposal made. Nevertheless, he did find that Presidents can have an impact—that their exercise of legislative skills does matter.

Roll-call votes cannot reveal the scope of the President's legislative involvement, measure the extent of his legislative influence, nor evaluate the effectiveness of his leadership in Congress. They only indicate how successful Presidents are at the final stage of voting and which members are most and least supportive of the President on these votes.

[See also (II) Polls and Popularity.]

BIBLIOGRAPHY

Bond, Jon R., and Richard Fleisher. *The President in the Legislative Arena.* 1990.

Edwards, George C. III. *At the Margins: Presidential Leadership of Congress.* 1989.

King, Gary, and Lyn Ragsdale. *The Elusive Executive.* 1988.

Peterson, Mark A. *Legislating Together.* 1990.

Wayne, Stephen J. *The Legislative Presidency.* 1978. Pp. 168–172.

– STEPHEN J. WAYNE

BUDGET POLICY

Since 1921, one of the most important powers of the presidency has been the formulation of the budget of the United States and its submission to Congress, a process that involves both symbol and substance. The budget is a plan for the nation's finances and therefore a statement of national priorities. As such, it dictates how much money goes to defense or domestic needs and whether or not taxes should be raised or lowered, all the while being balanced or in deficit. The budget provides an opportunity to influence the nation's economy, adjusting taxing and spending to spur growth or restrain inflationary surges. Symbolically, the budget reflects a President's values and leadership abilities, whether in proposing bold new spending initiatives, offering sweeping tax cuts, or resolving to reduce the budget deficit.

Despite its importance for the presidency, budget policy also presents difficult, often intractable problems to an administration. The President does not operate alone under the constitutional system on matters of taxing and spending; the Constitution grants Congress the greater share of taxing and spending powers. Since 1974, with the passage of the Congressional Budget and Impoundment Control Act, Congress has been particularly assertive and able to compete with the President as a coequal partner in determining budget policy. Budgets have become increasingly inflexible in recent decades, reducing presidential control. Most budget outlays are mandatory because of previous commitments such as social security, Medicare, federal retirement, or interest on the national debt. Since the 1980s, chronic budget deficits have constrained the presidency in terms of policy options. Because the budget is built on estimates and assumptions, it is vulnerable to external factors such as the performance of the economy or increases in health care costs. For example, the deficit can increase by as much as $30 billion if unemployment rises only a single percentage point higher than was estimated. Finally, the President is constrained by other liabilities of the federal government, such as loan guarantees and government insurance programs. When savings and loan institutions failed in large numbers, the President had no choice but to ask for hundreds of billions of additional monies to reimburse depositors. While the budget offers some potential for presidential leadership, it also is fraught with political pitfalls.

Components of Budget Policy

To understand both the opportunities and the potential problems that budgeting presents the President, it is necessary to identify the budget numbers that Presidents and the public watch most closely and to examine the composition of spending.

BUDGET TOTALS. Presidents are frequently most concerned with the overall budget aggregates that will often be the basis for judging their requests to Congress. Particularly important are total outlays, total revenues, and the size of the deficit—the amount that spending exceeds tax receipts in a given year. Total spending indicates the size and scope of government, particularly when measured as a proportion of gross domestic product (GDP). For example, in late 1963 President Lyndon B. Johnson retired to his Texas ranch to make cuts so he would not be the first President to send a $100 billion budget to Congress. In 1974, President Gerald Ford did the same thing to keep total spending below $400 billion. In more recent years, Presidents have been as concerned with the deficit as with total spending. Also of concern to budget makers is the size of the public debt, the sum total of the budget deficits over the years. All Presidents must be concerned with controlling spending, but controlling spending is more difficult with certain categories of outlays than others.

ENTITLEMENTS. The largest and fastest-growing component of federal outlays consists of mandatory spending for entitlements, that is, statutory guarantees that benefits will be paid to all those who qualify for them. The largest entitlement program is Social Security, followed by Medicare, Medicaid, and civilian and military retirement programs. These programs cannot be cut by appropriating less money but only by changing the law that defines eligibility. In 1960, entitlements made up less than a quarter of the budget. By 1990, they approached half of all outlays.

The budget provides an opportunity to influence the nation's economy, adjusting taxing and spending to spur growth or restrain inflationary surges.

DEFENSE SPENDING. Historically, defense has been one of the largest and most important components of federal spending. During wartime, as much as 85 percent of the budget has gone to defense. By the early 1990s, it had approached 20 percent of annual outlays. Determining how much to spend on national defense is a critical question for the President, but it takes many years to expand or reduce the size of the military establishment. In the post-cold war era, pressures have increased to reduce defense spending in favor of other needs.

INTEREST ON THE NATIONAL DEBT. This expense, representing the third-largest component of spending in the early 1990s, is the most uncontrollable since the credit of the federal government depends on meeting its borrowing obligations.

DOMESTIC DISCRETIONARY SPENDING. This category, although smaller than the other three, often consumes the most time and attention by the administration and Congress. It includes hundreds of programs in health, education, agriculture, environmental protection, housing, and a host of other activities.

REVENUES. A budget includes an accounting of where the money will come from as well as where it will go. Decisions on raising or lowering taxes are among the most important policy decisions a President and Congress make. The largest source of federal revenue is the individual income tax, followed by social insurance payroll taxes, corporate income taxes, and excise taxes.

Making Budget Policy

The Budget and Accounting Act of 1921 created the national budget and gave the President responsibility for submitting requests from agencies and departments in a single package. To help accomplish this task, the Bureau of the Budget (BOB) was created within the Department of the Treasury. Although Congress did not intend to abdicate its constitutional authority in taxing and spending, the Budget and Accounting Act shifted budgetary power toward the President. This budgetary authority became even more important in the 1930s under President Franklin D. Roosevelt, as the government took a more active role in managing the economy. Under the Keynesian economic theory employed by the Roosevelt administration, the budget became the primary tool for stimulating or restraining the economy. Reflecting its growing importance, BOB was moved in 1939 to the newly created Executive Office of the President (EOP), where BOB was directly responsible to the President and took a leading role in formulating budget policy. The BOB grew in importance in the ensuing decades and became responsible for assembling the President's legislative program. In 1970, President Richard M. Nixon reorganized the BOB into the Office of Management and Budget (OMB), giving the new agency both management and budgetary functions. In the 1980s, President Ronald Reagan gave OMB additional responsibilities in reviewing federal regulations.

Despite the importance of the President's budget office, many other executive-branch officials play key roles in making budget policy. The budget involves literally thousands of large and small decisions, from individual salaries to the amount going to national defense. The executive budget is actually a compendium of budget requests for the government's departments, agencies, bureaus, and public corporations. The federal fiscal year runs from 1 October through 30 September, three months ahead of the calendar year. The executive budget process begins almost eighteen months before the start of the fiscal year, when agencies and departments review their spending needs for the coming years. The busiest time of the year is the fall, when OMB examiners review agency requests and begin to assemble the massive budget document. The President gives the budget director broad guidelines concerning priorities, new initiatives, and areas to cut. Because agencies usually seek additional funding for their programs, OMB generally reduces their requests in order to control spending.

The process involves much more than paring and assembling agency requests, however, since discretionary spending now constitutes a relatively small share of total outlays. The President's budget, built on a series of estimates and projections, is shaped by the data of various administration officials. First, revenues and entitlements will rise or fall automatically depending on the performance of the economy during the fiscal year. The President's Council of Economic Advisers prepares economic projections of GDP, unemployment, inflation, and interest rates. These will determine estimates of tax revenues and spending on unemployment compensation, welfare, and other automatic programs. The Treasury Department estimates revenues under existing tax laws and the consequences of any changes the President may propose in the budget. OMB works with agencies such as the Department of Health and Human Services to estimate changes in the number of eligible recipients, healthcare cost increases, and other factors that determine outlays. This information is reviewed by the President, the Cabinet, and a handful of close advisers in late December as the budget nears final preparation. The budget is printed and delivered to Capitol Hill in late January, eight months before the start of the fiscal year.

Presidents' involvement in budgeting varies, but in most cases the President enters the process only at the highest levels of decision making. Most Presidents are particularly active in their first year in office as they try to leave their imprint on the nation's most important policy document. Because the budget has important political consequences as well as policy implications, Presidents must consider the potential outcomes of their budget requests. Within these overall bounds, some Presidents take a more active role in making budget policy, depending on their interests and abilities. President Jimmy Carter, for example, spent a great deal of time early in his administration on the details of the budget. He reviewed massive briefing books summarizing hundreds of policy decisions throughout the federal government. In contrast, President Reagan avoided detail altogether, issuing broad instructions and delegating the implementation to the staff. Excessive attention to detail is extremely time consuming for a President and can obscure the big picture. Conversely, an overly detached approach can result in serious miscalculations by subordinates and can obscure accountability.

Whatever the President's personal role in developing the executive budget, it bears his name and represents his vision of the country's needs for the coming year. The President has various means to develop political support for his budget proposals as they wend their way through Congress. The first is the message that accompanies the budget when it is submitted to Congress. Directed to both Congress and the American public, the budget message is a political appeal that the administration's proposals are best for the country. The state of the union message, delivered close to the same time, gives the President another chance to lobby for his budget priorities. The Economic Report of the President explains the administration's economic assumptions and explains how the budget requests relate to the nation's fiscal and monetary policy. Throughout the year, the President may deliver special messages to Congress, introduce new tax packages, or hold press conferences to lobby for budget proposals. At critical junctures, the President may address the nation to argue for the program. In 1981, for example, President Reagan successfully went on television to build public support for his defense buildup, tax cut, and domestic spending reductions. In 1990, President George Bush similarly took to the airwaves but was unable to convince a restive Congress to pass the bipartisan budget agreement that had been worked out with Democratic congressional leaders.

From the 1980s on, as controversy over the budget and the deficit increased, budget summits between the executive and legislative branch became more important in determining final budget numbers. These involved closed-door negotiations and lobbying between the President's surrogates and top legislative leaders. In addition to negotiations and lobbying by the President and key administration officials, the President may take direct actions to affect budget policy. Before 1974, Presidents could impound funds—that is, refuse to spend monies appropriated by Congress on the grounds that such spending was not necessary. Because of large impoundments by President Nixon, Congress banned impoundment by enacting the Congressional Budget and Impoundment Control Act of 1974. Instead of impoundment, the President may request a deferral to temporarily delay spending; this action takes effect unless Congress votes not to accept it. The President may also request a rescission to eliminate spending permanently; this action does not take effect unless Congress

President Ronald Reagan sought item veto power, which would allow him to veto parts of a proposed budget without rejecting the entire spending bill. (Library of Congress, Prints and Photographs Division)

votes to affirm it within forty-five days. Finally, the President may veto appropriations bills, tax bills, or other legislation that affects spending. This does not guarantee that the administration's proposals will be adopted, but it does send Congress back to the drawing board. Dissatisfied with their budgetary powers, Presidents Reagan, Bush, and Clinton requested a constitutional amendment for an item veto, a power enjoyed by most state governors, that would allow the President to veto parts of a spending bill without rejecting the entire bill.

When the budget is finally approved, the executive branch is responsible for the execution of the budget. OMB and the Treasury work together to disburse monies to various agencies and programs and to coordinate tax collection and borrowing. The executive branch is also responsible for managing programs and auditing various agencies. The General Accounting Office, an arm of Congress, also has responsibility for auditing federal spending.

Trends in Budget Policy

The nature of federal budgeting and the composition of revenues and expenditures have changed dramatically since World War II. Yet some themes, such as balancing the budget or choosing the proper balance between defense and domestic spending have remained constant. Total outlays were slashed in half as the nation demobilized in the 1940s, but by the early 1950s, defense spending still constituted more than half of the budget. President Dwight D. Eisenhower was willing to use the budget to help stimulate the economy, but balancing the budget remained his highest budgetary principle. Eisenhower had a balanced budget three out of eight years—the last President to do so more than once. His efforts to balance the budget during an economic downturn, however, worsened the recession, and Richard Nixon believed those policies hurt his campaign for the presidency in 1960.

Defense spending first declined in real terms following the end of the Korean War, then leveled off after 1955. Despite Eisenhower's military background, John F. Kennedy during the 1960 presidential campaign accused the Eisenhower administration of creating a missile gap with the Soviet Union. But defense spending did not begin to rise significantly again until after Lyndon Johnson assumed the presidency and the United States became more deeply involved in the Vietnam War.

Most Presidents are particularly active in making budget policy during their first year in office.

Other budget policy issues that dominated the Kennedy-Johnson era included taxes and domestic spending initiatives. Enacted in 1964, a tax cut designed to stimulate the economy was widely acclaimed: unemployment was low, economic growth was robust, and inflation was modest. This provided a fiscal dividend to support new government programs, particularly the Johnson administration's war on poverty and Great Society programs. As spending increased because of the Vietnam War and new social programs, budgetary problems began to increase. Inflation heated up and budget deficits became more troublesome. The Johnson administration was forced to opt for guns over butter and to propose a tax increase, finally enacted in 1968, to curb inflation.

The budget itself began to change under Presidents Nixon, Ford, and Carter. New entitlements such as Medicare, Medicaid, and food stamps, all enacted in the mid-to-late 1960s, commanded a larger share of budget outlays. Increases in Social Security benefits, by as much as 20 percent in a single year, sharply increased the cost of that program. At the same time, economic growth did not match its performance in the 1960s, resulting in revenues that were not growing as fast as expenditures. The post-Vietnam reductions in defense spending from 1970 to 1980 freed some money for domestic uses, but not enough to balance the budget. The last balanced budget occurred in 1969, during the Nixon administration. During the 1970s, total federal spending rose to around 22 percent of GDP, up from 18 percent in 1965. The composition of the budget changed as well. In 1970, defense constituted 43 percent of spending and entitlements 28 percent. By 1980, defense had fallen to 23 percent while entitlements shot up to 42 percent of outlays. Presidents Ford and Carter struggled with stagflation—simultaneously high levels of unemployment and inflation—as well as growing budget deficits. These developments set the stage for the 1980 election of Ronald Reagan, who would make the most dramatic changes in budget policy in a generation.

Reagan campaigned on a platform that defense spending had grown dangerously low, that domestic spending was too high, and that taxes needed to be cut. In 1981, the administration was successful in getting its sweeping budget proposals adopted. A rapid defense buildup—of $1.8 trillion over five years—was initiated. Income taxes were cut 25 percent across the board. Domestic spending was cut, but not enough to compensate for additional defense spending and reduced revenues. The result was an explosion of budget deficits that would become the dominant constraint on budget policy. Defense spending increased to 25 percent of outlays and entitlements to 45 percent, but the largest increase was in interest payments on the growing debt: 15 percent of all outlays by 1990. The category that fell most sharply was discretionary domestic spending, which dropped from 26 percent of the budget to 15 percent.

Taxes have been a crucial element of budget policy in recent years. The 1981 Reagan tax cut lowered the top marginal tax rate to 50 percent; the rate on the wealthiest taxpayers had been as high as 90 percent in the 1950s. Rates fell again in 1986 when President Reagan and Congress adopted the landmark Tax Reform Act that lowered the top marginal rate to 31 percent. Taxes and the deficit were key elements of budget controversies during the administration of President George Bush. Despite the 1985 adoption of the Gramm-Rudman-Hollings Act, a mandatory deficit reduction plan, by 1990 deficits stood at record levels. After a divisive summit with congressional Democrats, the President broke his 1988 campaign promise ("Read by lips, no new taxes") agreeing to raise taxes to help cut the deficit. Despite the package of tax increases and spending cuts, however, deficits continued to run as high as $300 billion annually. When he took office, President Bill Clinton proposed a massive deficit reduction package of nearly $500 billion over five years that included an increase in the top marginal income tax rate for wealthier households.

Budget policy remains one of the most critical challenges of the American presidency. Making the budget involves extremely difficult choices between competing goals: keeping taxes low and providing adequate spending for domestic and defense needs while trying to reduce large deficits and keep the economy out of recession. The President faces many constraints in trying to manage the nation's budget from a powerful Congress to the continued rapid growth of entitlements. Yet despite the obstacles, the budget will continue to be the most important policy statement of government and a challenge to presidential leadership.

[See also (I) Budget Process, General Accounting Office; (II) Treasury, Department of.]

BIBLIOGRAPHY

Fisher, Louis. *Presidential Spending Power.* 1975.

Ippolito, Dennis S. *Uncertain Legacies: Federal Budget Policy from Roosevelt through Reagan.* 1990.

Kettl, Donald E. *Deficit Politics: Public Budgeting in its Institutional and Historical Context.* 1992.

LeLoup, Lance T. *Budgetary Politics.* 1988.

Schick, Allen. *The Capacity to Budget.* 1990.

– LANCE T. LELOUP

C

CABINET

The United States generally insists on having a constitutional rationale to justify public actions, so it is odd that the Cabinet is not mentioned in the Constitution. The only reference to a cabinet is the provision that the President "may require the Opinion, in writing, of the principal Officer in each of the executive Departments, upon any Subject relating to the Duties of their respective Offices" (Article II, Section 2, clause 1). But this reference is to the individuals who serve as secretaries of the executive departments, not to a collective entity, or cabinet, in which the secretaries would come together as a group to discuss and help formulate public policies. The Framers of the Constitution did not question that the President would need advice, but they did not consider that these advisers might come together in formal body from which to offer that advice.

Defining the Cabinet

There are two ways to define the Cabinet. The first focuses on the people who direct the executive departments, the departmental secretaries. These persons are nominated by the President, subject to Senate confirmation, and serve only through the duration of the administration and at the pleasure of the President. (Legally, Cabinet secretaries may serve for one month after a President leaves office, to smooth the transition for the new department secretary. In practice, Cabinet secretaries tender their resignations just prior to the outgoing President's departure from office.)

The second way of defining the Cabinet focuses on the Cabinet as a collective body, that is, the group formed when the Cabinet secretaries meet formally together. Because the Cabinet lacks constitutional or statutory foundation, there has been confusion over its membership, as officials who do not head departments may attend Cabinet meetings. For instance, the Attorney General was not initially accorded secretarial status. The Department of Justice was not elevated to departmental status until 1870, and therefore it was not until that year that the Attorney General's salary reached the level of the department secretaries' pay. Nevertheless, the Attorney General was recognized as a member of George Washington's Cabinet.

In recent years, other officials who are not departmental heads have also attended Cabinet meetings. It is now common practice for the Vice President and the Director of the Central Intelligence Agency (CIA), neither of whom is a departmental head, to attend Cabinet sessions, although the CIA Director's attendance is usually limited to meetings concerning national security issues.

Abraham Lincoln felt compelled to call Cabinet meetings but did not feel obligated to heed the advice of the Cabinet secretaries.

Creating even more conceptual confusion is the idea of a kitchen cabinet. Andrew Jackson, who often ignored the departmental secretaries, was the first to employ a kitchen cabinet. Jackson's kitchen cabinet was composed of close personal friends and advisers, people he felt he could trust and rely on. All Presidents have had some type of informal group of close advisers who have played such a role. The limitations and weaknesses of the Cabinet, detailed below, have given rise to kitchen cabinets and other kinds of non-Cabinet presidential advisory systems.

Weakness of the Cabinet

The Cabinet's weakness stems partly from its lack of a constitutional foundation. As a result, it has little institutional authority and cannot issue binding group decisions. While the modern Cabinet does possess some institutional resources, such as a secretary, a modest staff, and a record of meetings, only the forces of tradition and expectation give the Cabinet power.

The Cabinet is totally reliant on the President and subject to each President's preference concerning how to employ it. At best it is only advisory to the President; at worst it will be completely ignored. Moreover, the Cabinet's utility to the President is limited by the fact that others, particularly Congress and interest groups, have some influence over who is named a Cabinet secretary.

Each President decides for himself how to use the Cabinet. For example, meetings are called at the discretion of the President. Some Presidents, like Dwight D. Eisenhower, have called meetings frequently and relied on the advice generated at such meetings. Others, like John F. Kennedy, have found little utility in the collective Cabinet. Still others, like Abraham Lincoln, have felt compelled to call meetings but have not felt obligated to heed the advice of their secretaries. In one famous story, Lincoln called a vote of the Cabinet. The result was a unanimous "nay," which Lincoln overrode with his solitary "aye."

Creation of the Cabinet

Two constitutional decisions affect the Cabinet: first, the system of separation of powers and checks and balances and, second, the decision to have a unitary and strong presidency. Other factors also influenced the Framers ideas about a cabinet, including the United States' British heritage, the experience of the Continental Congress during the Revolutionary War, and the congressional experience during the Articles of Confederation period.

BRITISH HERITAGE. The word *cabinet* was first used in seventeenth-century Britain. The king would consult with members of the privy council, but, because that body's membership was quite numerous, the king would often retreat with a select number of counselors to a smaller room, adjacent to the king's room, called the cabinet. Thus the "cabinet council" to the king was established.

The cabinet council, soon simply referred to as the cabinet, was initially only advisory, but by the late nineteenth century it had evolved into the modern British cabinet system, with the cabinet as a decision-making body with strong ties to the majority party in Parliament. In effect, the new, more powerful British cabinet became the seat of government.

The British cabinet influenced American thinking, but the American Cabinet is not a direct copy of the British one. When the U.S. Constitution was being written, the British governmental model was still developing, and the American Cabinet came more to resemble the earlier, advisory, less-powerful cabinet rather than the parliamentary cabinet that was to emerge later.

PRECONSTITUTIONAL AMERICAN EXPERIENCES. The Continental Congress's experience with executive departments during the Revolutionary War also helped set a foundation for the American Cabinet. At first, the Congress conducted affairs through committees of its members. Among the most important of these were the committees of correspondence to agents of several of the colonies, then in England. These early agents, through their contact with the Continental Congress, in effect became the seeds of the Foreign Service and diplomatic corps. In time, these committees were reorganized as the Committee of Foreign Affairs.

In 1781, the Congress found it necessary to have a formal channel for conducting foreign affairs and created the first Department of Foreign Affairs. Importantly, that department was headed by a single secretary, which the Congress felt to be an improvement over the past practice, administration by committee. Soon after, three more executive offices were created: the Superintendent of Finance, the Secretary of War, and the Secretary of Marine. By this time, the idea of executive offices headed by a single executive had been firmly planted, setting a precedent for the later Cabinet departments. During the period of the Articles of Confederation, these departments operated under congressional supervision and direction because the government under the Articles did not include an executive.

IMPACT OF CONSTITUTIONAL DESIGN. The decisions of the Constitutional Convention to provide for a unitary, strong presidency and the system of separations and checks and balances had lasting impact on the Cabinet.

A unitary executive. The decision to create a unitary executive with relatively strong powers stifled any effort at institutionalizing an advisory body, such as a cabinet, in the executive branch. The Framers feared that creating an advisory council in the executive branch could not only give the President a group to hide behind but could potentially dissipate presidential powers. It might become an alternative power center in the executive, dividing the executive and depriving it of the "energy," "unity," and "vigor" that Alexander Hamilton, the major proponent of a strong executive, sought. Executive responsibility was to lie solely with the President. Thus, no collective advisory body or cabinet was created.

Separation of powers. The second important constitutional decision was the formal separation of government institutions, which, in turn, are bound together through the system of checks and balances. The separation-of-powers system drove a wedge between the executive and legislative branches. One consequence of this system was that incumbents of one branch could not sit in the other. Thus, no parliamentary-style cabinet could develop, and this separation limited the interaction between an executive cabinet and Congress as well. Discussion arose in early Congresses about allowing (or requiring) departmental secretaries to sit in Congress and participate in floor deliberations. Legislators decided, however, that such participation would violate the spirit of the Constitution's wall of separation between the branches.

Lastly, the separation between the branches obstructed President Washington's early attempts to seek

CABINET DEPARTMENTS, 1789–1993

1789	1798	1829	1849	1862	1870	1889	1903	1913
State	State	State	State	State	State	State	State	State
Treasury	Treasury	Treasury	Treasury	Treasury	Treasury	Treasury	Treasury	Treasury
War	War	War	War	War	War	War	War	War
	Navy	Navy	Navy	Navy	Navy	Navy	Navy	Navy
Attorney General	Attorney General	Attorney General	Attorney General	Attorney General	Justice[a]	Justice	Justice	Justice
(Postmaster General)[b]	(Postmaster General)	Postmaster General	Postmaster General	Postmaster General	Postmaster General	Postmaster General	Postmaster General	Postmaster General
			Interior	Interior	Interior	Interior	Interior	Interior
				(Agriculture)[c]	(Agriculture)	Agriculture	Agriculture	Agriculture
							Commerce and Labor	Commerce
								Labor

[a] The Attorney General became head of the Justice Department when the department was created in 1870.

[b] Positions in parentheses are heads of departments but not members of the Cabinet. The Postmaster General was not added to the Cabinet until 1829; the Postmaster General was dropped from the Cabinet in 1971, when the United States Postal Service replaced the United States Post Office.

[c] The Department of Agriculture was created in 1862; the Secretary of Agriculture was added to the Cabinet in 1889.

personal counsel and advice from both the legislative and judicial branches.

This turn of events occurred very early on, in 1789. Washington was trying to fashion a treaty with the Indians. At first he sought advice from the Senate, but the Senate rebuffed his attempt to establish the Senate as a consultative body. Then he turned for legal advice to the Supreme Court, then headed by John Jay, who like Washington, was a Federalist. Jay also refused to extend advice. With both the legislative and judicial branches personally unapproachable, Washington turned to his Cabinet secretaries for policy advice and to his Attorney General for legal counsel, although he continued to consult with Congress in writing.

Checks and balances. The system of checks and balances raised questions of how much and in what ways the Congress and the Cabinet would interact. Three issues stood out. First, the Senate was constitutionally empowered to confirm presidential nominations for departmental secretaries, giving the Senate the power to deny the President his choices. The second issue was whether the Congress could remove a secretary from office. The third was whether Congress could question Cabinet secretaries, and, if so, in what ways. The last two issues remained unsettled at the Constitutional Convention and required resolution at a later date. In the case of the removal power, that resolution came nearly a century later.

The removal debate. Congress was cautious about its power to remove Cabinet secretaries from office. In the act creating the Department of State, Congress laid no claim to removal, allowing that power to reside with the

CABINET DEPARTMENTS, 1789–1993 (CONTINUED)

1947	1953	1965	1966	1971	1977	1979	1980	1988
State	State	State	State	State	State	State	State	State
Treasury	Treasury	Treasury	Treasury	Treasury	Treasury	Treasury	Treasury	Treasury
Defense	Defense	Defense	Defense	Defense	Defense	Defense	Defense	Defense
Justice	Justice	Justice	Justice	Justice	Justice	Justice	Justice	Justice
Postmaster General	Postmaster General	Postmaster General	Postmaster General					
Interior	Interior	Interior	Interior	Interior	Interior	Interior	Interior	Interior
Agriculture	Agriculture	Agriculture	Agriculture	Agriculture	Agriculture	Agriculture	Agriculture	Agriculture
Commerce	Commerce	Commerce	Commerce	Commerce	Commerce	Commerce	Commerce	Commerce
Labor	Labor	Labor	Labor	Labor	Labor	Labor	Labor	Labor
						Education	Education	Education
	Health, Education, & Welfare	Health, Education, & Welfare	Health, Education, & Welfare	Health, Education, & Welfare	Health, Education, & Welfare		Health and Human Services	Health and Human Services
		Housing and Urban Development	Housing and Urban Development	Housing and Urban Development	Housing and Urban Development	Housing and Urban Development	Housing and Urban Development	Housing and Urban Development
			Transportation	Transportation	Transportation	Transportation	Transportation	Transportation
					Energy	Energy	Energy	Energy
								Veterans Affairs

President. It acknowledged the same presidential removal power over the Secretary of the Treasury and the Secretary of War.

The proponents of exclusive presidential power to remove secretaries cited executive control over personnel as critical to the constitutional operation of the executive office. Without this power, they maintained, the President would have limited ability to direct the bureaucracy and would not be able to "faithfully execute the laws," as the Constitution mandated. Advocates of a congressional role, however, cited the congressional power to investigate, its power to impeach, and the fact that each department was a creation of Congress. They contended that if Congress could eliminate a department through legislative action—which would have the effect of removing the secretary from office—then it also should possess the power to remove a secretary from office without having to dismantle the department.

Cabinet interactions with Congress. The other unresolved issue, concerning congressional interaction with Cabinet secretaries, arose from the congressional power to investigate. Early congressional actions established that Cabinet secretaries could not sit in the halls of Congress but could be questioned by Congress—and that they should answer Congress in writing, not in person. Furthermore, though President Washington and some of his secretaries felt that all queries should be submitted through the President, Secretary of the Treasury Hamilton's position carried the day. Hamilton wanted to allow direct communication, though written inquiry, from Congress to a secretary without presidential mediation. Hamilton, who had a very active style as secretary, found this direct contact useful in promoting his economic policies in Congress.

Development of the Cabinet

The Cabinet continued to evolve long after the Constitution was ratified and early precedents were established. Importantly, the Cabinet began to take on a collective identity through meetings with the President.

The issue of congressional power over the suspension and removal of secretaries from office finally came to a head during the Andrew Johnson administration. And throughout the nineteenth and twentieth centuries the Cabinet expanded as particular interests pressed for representation at the highest levels of the executive branch.

EVOLUTION OF CABINET MEETINGS. Early in his administration George Washington named several people to serve as departmental secretaries: Thomas Jefferson as Secretary of State, Alexander Hamilton as Secretary of the Treasury, Henry Knox as Secretary of War, Edmund Randolph as Attorney General, and Samuel Osgood as Postmaster General.

The separation between the branches obstructed President Washington's early attempts to seek personal counsel and advice from both the legislative and judicial branches.

The idea of holding meetings in which all departmental secretaries would convene commenced in 1791, when Washington suggested that the Vice President and the departmental secretaries should meet during Washington's absence from the capital city. Such a meeting did take place, but without the Attorney General, presumably because he was not yet of Cabinet rank.

Thereafter, such meetings (with Washington present) became more common. During the spring of 1793, a period of political crisis, the secretaries met with Washington almost daily. This frequency led James Madison to call the group a cabinet, the first time the term was specifically applied in the American context.

Washington quickly learned the limited usefulness of such meetings, however. His primary problem was the political battle between the Federalist Secretary of the Treasury, Hamilton, and the Democratic-Republican Secretary of State, Jefferson. Their conflict undermined the utility of Cabinet meetings, and Washington increased the political stakes and tensions by calling for Cabinet votes. Washington seems to have been bent on using Cabinet votes to decide policy, perhaps to depersonalize the presidency and build a sense of collective governing. It was not long, however, before Hamilton and Jefferson left the Cabinet and Washington's voting innovation was dropped. The political incompatibility of secretaries would plague other Presidents, undermining their Cabinets' utility as well.

THE REMOVAL POWER CONTROVERSY. The impeachment of Andrew Johnson was precipitated in part by the unresolved issue of the power of Congress to monitor and control the removal of Cabinet secretaries. In 1867, Congress passed the Tenure of Office Act, which required that the Senate had to confirm a successor before the President could remove a Cabinet secretary from office. Moreover, the act granted the President the power to suspend a secretary while the Senate was in recess, requiring the President to report to the Senate the evidence and reasons for the suspension once its session recommenced. If the Senate concurred with the suspension, the secretary would be removed, while the secretary would resume his official duties if the Senate refused to concur. In effect, the Senate could keep a secretary in office over presidential objections by refusing to confirm a new nominee. The political intention behind the act was to ensure that Johnson would follow the dictates of congressional Radical Republicans with respect to Reconstruction policy.

Johnson's Secretary of War, Edwin M. Stanton, who was aligned with the congressional Republicans, was authorized to administer the Reconstruction program. A bitter dispute between Johnson and Stanton erupted, whereupon Johnson suspended Stanton. The Senate refused to concur with the suspension once it reconvened. Johnson countered by removing Stanton from office, an action that increased tensions with the Senate. Johnson's tactic failed, however, as Stanton regained his office. Soon thereafter, Congress initiated impeachment proceedings against Johnson, spurred on very much by the Stanton incident.

For the twenty years after its enactment, every President urged repeal of the law every year in his state of the union message. In 1887, Congress repealed the act, giving the President sole power to remove Cabinet secretaries from office and settling the issue of the President's removal power at the Cabinet level.

EXPANSION AND POLITICAL REPRESENTATION. Though the Cabinet was not able to develop into a decision-making body whose actions were binding, it did acquire some political importance for the President. The President could use Cabinet appointments to build support coalitions and repay past supporters for their backing. In effect, the Cabinet became a place in the administration for the representation of important political interests.

The push to represent particular interests on the Cabinet has come in several waves. In the first wave, departments generally considered to be concerned with a single economic interest were added to the Cabinet. The second wave saw Cabinet status for departments concerned with multiple interests, often social in nature. A third wave of Cabinet expansion in the 1970s and 1980s embraced both patterns.

Thus, in 1849 the Interior Department was created at the behest of interests concerned with development of the west and control of native populations. In 1889, agricultural interests gained representation in the newly formed Agriculture Department, and in 1903 business interests were recognized with establishment of the Department of Commerce and Labor. Ten years later, labor interests secured a seat when commerce and labor concerns were separated into two new departments, the Department of Labor and the Department of Commerce.

The multipurpose Cabinet departments that constitute the second wave, which began after World War II, included the Department of Health, Education, and Welfare (HEW), established in 1953, the Department of Housing and Urban Development (1966) and the Department of Transportation (1967).

A third wave of Cabinet expansion occurred in the late 1970s and 1980s. First, as a consequence of the energy crises of the 1970s, energy-related programs and agencies were consolidated into the Department of Energy in 1977. Next, HEW was reorganized in 1979 by separating education from health and welfare programs, thus creating two new departments, the Department of Education and the Department of Health and Human Services. Finally, in 1988, the Veterans Administration was elevated to Cabinet rank as the Department of Veterans Affairs.

Other Cabinet Developments

Beginning in the 1930s, the already institutionally weak Cabinet began a trend of further decline. This came about because of the growth of government, the shift of public expectations and government power to the presidency, and the institutionalization of a presidential advisory system separate from the Cabinet.

Public expectations about government and the presidency underwent a fundamental transformation during the 1930s. The ethic of limited government gave way to a push for greater government involvement in directing the economy. The President played the leading role in this expansion.

This increase in presidential policy responsibility and leadership could have transformed the Cabinet into an important policy adviser to the President, since, at the time, it was the only government institution that could have played this role. Instead, the Cabinet's weaknesses, its lack of collective responsibility, and its sensitivity to the demands of special interest groups and other nonpresidential interests (e.g., Congress) motivated the President to develop policy advisement along a different path.

The President institutionalized advice through the Executive Office of the President (EOP), created in 1939. In time, EOP developed units to provide advice free of, or at least less encumbered with, interest-group demands. In time, three of these units—the Council of Economic Advisers, the National Security Adviser, and the Domestic Policy Group—assumed the primary presidential advisement role. The Bureau of the Budget (later the Office of Management and Budget) also came to take on a major policy advising role, sometimes eclipsing the three EOP staffs in importance. This development pushed the Cabinet further away from the President, lessening its policy influence.

Eisenhower attempted to reverse the Cabinet's decline by providing it with some institutional resources, such as a secretary, and by calling frequent and regular meetings, but the Cabinet continued its decline under Kennedy, who rarely called Cabinet meetings. But the increasing complexity of government and the perceived failure of government effectively to implement its many programs led some later Presidents to try to integrate the Cabinet into the policy-making process at the White House.

The Executive Office of the President created units to provide advice to the President that was free of, or less encumbered with, interest-group demands.

Richard M. Nixon made the first major reform proposal in 1971 with his plan to create four new "super-departments" of human resources, community development, natural resources, and economic affairs from the more numerous existing departments responsible for those activities. Nixon wanted to reorganize the Cabinet around functional rather than interest-group lines, hoping that this would both tie the Cabinet more closely to the policy-making process at the White House and weaken the bonds between the departments and interest groups. As expected, Congress balked at the plan because it would have disrupted established networks among Congress, the departments, and important interest groups. The Watergate affair eventually destroyed Nixon's position with Congress as he sought the reorganization.

The second major attempt at Cabinet–White House integration came during the 1980s under the Ronald Reagan administration. Close attention to the appointment process and the creation of Cabinet councils were the devices that Reagan used. In paying close mind to the appointment process, Reagan wanted to ensure that Cabinet secretaries would be loyal to him. Extensive background checks were conducted prior to nomination, and, once appointed, the new secretaries were taught about their jobs and departments by White House staff rather than by career departmental personnel. The aim was to create a sense of identification with the administration and to loosen secretaries' ties to their departments and to the long-serving bureaucrats and special-interest groups.

The second aspect of Reagan's approach involved the establishment and use of Cabinet councils. In 1981 and 1982, seven Cabinet councils were created: Economic Affairs, Commerce and Trade, Food and Agriculture, Human Resources, Natural Resources and the Environment, Legal Policy, and Management and Administration. Membership on the councils was composed of departmental secretaries and their aides, as well as White House personnel responsible for particular policy areas. Staff worked up policy proposals, which were later refined at the secretarial level, and finally a meeting, sometimes with the President attending, culminated the policy decision process.

For the first two years of the Reagan administration, the councils were quite active, but they quickly fell into disuse. Again, the lack of a firm institutional sanction, either constitutional or statutory, probably accounts for the decline of the Cabinet council system.

Nixon's proposal to reorganize the Cabinet and Reagan's use of Cabinet councils were the most important attempts at Cabinet–White House integration. Both attempts failed in the end, but they probably herald a trend in presidential management of the White House, the Cabinet, and the policy process in which the Cabinet will take on a more important advisory and policy-making role in the highest chambers of the executive.

[See also (II) Individual articles on each of the 14 Cabinet departments.]

BIBLIOGRAPHY

Cohen, Jeffrey E. *The Politics of the U.S. Cabinet: Representation in the Executive Branch, 1789–1984.* 1988.

Fenno, Richard F. *The President's Cabinet: An Analysis of the Period from Wilson to Eisenhower.* 1959.

Hart, James. *The American Presidency in Action 1789.* 1948.

Hinsdale, Mary L. *A History of the President's Cabinet.* 1911.

Horn, Stephen. *The Cabinet and Congress.* 1960.

Learned, Henry B. *The President's Cabinet.* 1912.

Smith, William Henry. *History of the Cabinet of the United States.* 1925.

– JEFFREY E. COHEN

CAMPAIGN FINANCES

Presidential campaigns have become vast spectacles. Modern presidential campaigns contrast with the view of John Quincy Adams, who wrote in 1828, "The presidency of the United States was an office neither to be sought nor declined. To pay money for securing it, directly or indirectly, was in my opinion incorrect in principle." Despite Adams's lofty sentiment, candidates in every election since George Washington first assumed the office in 1789 have spent money to secure the presidency. From torchlight parades to television presentations, someone has had to pay the expenses.

The substantial—and ever-increasing—expense of running for President results from a variety of factors, many of which have evolved since the Republic was founded: the development of competitive political parties; the democratization of the presidency; the extension of suffrage; the introduction of national nominating conventions and presidential primaries; and the development of costly communications media and campaign technologies, with their attendant hosts of expensive political consultants.

Many Americans now worry that the escalating costs and greater reliance on mass media are having a deleterious effect on the presidential selection process. In response to periodic public concern, federal law has sought ways to reduce the perceived influence of monied interests, while also seeking to protect the democratic ideals of free speech and assembly.

Early Presidential Elections

Since the Republic's founding, the cost of printing has been the most basic campaign expense. In 1791, Thomas Jefferson started the *National Gazette,* the subsidized organ of the Anti-Federalists. The Federalist Party had been financing its own paper, the *Gazette of the United States,* with money from Alexander Hamilton and Rufus King and from printing subsidies. Newspapers vilified candidates mercilessly, and various factions spun off their own papers. During the early 1800s, books, pamphlets, and even newspapers were handed from person to person until they were no longer readable.

By 1840, pictures, buttons, banners, and novelty items had appeared. William Henry Harrison's campaign that year arranged for conventions and mass meetings; scheduled parades and processions with banners and floats; produced long speeches on the log-cabin theme, log-cabin song books and log-cabin newspapers; distributed Harrison pictures; and introduced Tippecanoe handkerchiefs and badges. Each item and activity cost money, though some brought revenues to the campaign.

Presidential candidates did not always actively campaign. Andrew Jackson retired to his home, the Hermitage, after he was nominated, although his supporters held torchlight parades and hickory-pole raisings.

Stephen A. Douglas decided to barnstorm the country in his 1860 campaign against Abraham Lincoln, a practice not tried again until 1896, when William Jennings Bryan traveled eighteen thousand miles giving some six hundred speeches to a total of at least five million people. By contrast, his opponent, William McKinley, sat on his front porch and let the people come to him; special trains were run to his hometown of Canton, Ohio, with the railroads cooperating by cutting fares. McKinley did not have to travel because his friend, the wealthy industrialist and Republican national committee chairman Marcus A. Hanna, organized fourteen hundred surrogates to speak on his behalf. Hanna also spent money to publish and distribute more than 120 million pieces of McKinley campaign literature.

Twentieth-Century Developments

In the twentieth century, broadcasting became the most effective means by which candidates could get their messages across to voters. Presidential and other federal candidates first used radio broadcasts in the 1924 campaign. Ever since, candidates have devoted more and more time and money to honing their campaign messages to fit the broadcasting formats. Presidential contenders started using televised advertising in 1952. Generally, such advertising is used minimally during the early prenomination period, which is marked by retail politics and small-state campaigning, but expands dramatically in larger states and in the general election period. Over time, the microphone and the camera came to be the main means through which presidential candidates conveyed their messages.

Television has added new dimensions to campaigning by encouraging presidential debates and forums among candidates and also by focusing campaign strategy, influencing campaign managers to seek out photo opportunities and coverage on free news broadcasts. The costly national nominating conventions are now timed to reach the largest possible audiences.

As the size of the U.S. population expanded and the technology of campaigning became increasingly complex, the costs of campaigning for political office grew correspondingly. In 1860, Lincoln's victorious general election campaign was said to have cost about $100,000, while the cost of his opponent Douglas's campaign was reportedly $50,000. One hundred years later, the leading two presidential candidates—John F. Kennedy and Richard M. Nixon—spent nearly $20 million to finance their hotly contested race, one of the most competitive in U.S. history.

The 1988 presidential contest was the fourth in which public funds were provided to cover part of the campaign costs. No incumbent was running, and costs were especially high in both major party campaigns. In the general election campaign, the Republican ticket of George Bush and Dan Quayle spent (and had spent on its behalf) about $93.7 million, including a public grant of $46.1 million. Democratic Party candidates Michael Dukakis and Lloyd Bentsen spent (and had spent on their behalf) about $106.5 million, also including a public grant of $46.1 million. The 1988 campaign marked the first time in the twentieth century that the Republicans and their allies were outspent by the Democrats and their allies.

John Quincy Adams wrote in 1828,

"The presidency of the United States was an office

neither to be sought nor declined."

The price of electing a President—some $500 million altogether—represented about 20 percent of the $2.7 billion Americans spent on all politics at the federal, state, and local levels in the 1987–1988 election cycle. When calculated for each phase of the presidential selection process, the costs were approximately $234 million in the prenomination period, $40 million for the conventions, and $208 million in the general election. Of course, candidates seeking nomination are entrepreneurs, building their own fund-raising, organizational and media campaigns; some spending on their behalf by organized labor, delegates, and independent individuals and groups is factored into the calculations. Once a candidate has been nominated, significant supplemental roles are played in the general election by the political parties and their allies. Amounts spent in party support, "soft money," communication costs, parallel labor spending, and independent expenditures during the post-nomination period are included in the figures that indicate the amounts spent by the presidential candidates, on their behalf, or in support of party tickets.

In the early days of presidential campaigning, funds were raised through collections from candidates and assessments from officeholders. The money raised through these two sources was at first sufficient, but as campaign costs escalated, candidates had to find other sources.

In the early nineteenth century, candidates began raising money by rewarding campaign contributors with favors and government jobs—the spoils system of patronage. The system proved increasingly productive for candidates by the end of the Civil War in 1865, when corporations and wealthy individuals began paying a major portion of presidential campaign costs. After Congress enacted the Civil Service Act of 1883, contributions from corporations and from wealthy individuals became an even larger source of presidential campaign funds. The act prohibited officers and employees of the United States, with some exceptions, from seeking or receiving political contributions from one another.

In the hotly contested 1896 campaign between Republican candidate McKinley and Democrat-Populist candidate Bryan, for example, Mark Hanna, the manager of McKinley's campaign, collected $3.5 million for the general election campaign effort, mainly from the largesse of corporations, such as the Standard Oil Company, which gave $250,000. In that race, several banks agreed to give McKinley campaign donations in amounts equal to a quarter of 1 percent of their capital.

As restrictions on funding sources mounted, political candidates were forced to devise new methods of raising money and to rely more heavily on particular sources of campaign gifts. When corporate gifts were banned in 1907, candidates responded by seeking more contributions from wealthy individuals, including many corporate stockholders and executives. Some candidates' families were generous; for example, Charles P. Taft contributed more than $200,000 to his brother William Howard Taft's campaign in 1912. And when the Hatch Act of 1939 and its 1940 amendment restricted the size of contributions to political committees, candidates and political parties began to find other ways of raising funds, including holding fund-raising dinners and events. When labor gifts were banned, PACs (political action committees) were established to solicit voluntary contributions from members and their families; later, corporations and ideological groups also established PACs.

Candidates also have tried to raise big money in small sums from a great number of individual contributors, but their efforts have not been uniformly successful. In 1964, Republican candidate Barry Goldwater raised large amounts from small contributions solicited through the use of direct mail. Other candidates who had success with direct-mail solicitations include independent candidate George Wallace in 1968, Democratic nominee George McGovern in 1972, and Republican Ronald Reagan in his 1976 and 1980 prenomination campaigns. All these candidates who successfully built large financial constituencies were factional party leaders or outside the mainstream of American politics; direct mail has not been notably productive for centrist candidates. In 1992, Edmund G. (Jerry) Brown, Jr., a contender for the Democratic nomination, received a generous response to appeals for contributions not exceeding $100 each, utilizing an "800" (toll-free) telephone number.

An incumbent President is normally the biggest attraction in political fund raising. If not raising funds for reelection, the President, as party leader, usually devotes considerable amounts of time to speaking at political-party events and at dinners and events on behalf of party candidates throughout the country.

Efforts at Reform

Following civil-service reform, growing public concern led Congress to enact a number of electoral reform laws that were designed to lessen any undue influence of large donations in presidential and other federal election campaigns.

In 1907, Congress passed the first law, the Tillman Act, that made it illegal for any corporation or national bank to make a "money contribution in connection with any election" of candidates for federal office.

The first laws requiring House and Senate candidates to file campaign finance disclosure reports were enacted in 1910 and 1911. The latter act extended disclosure to include primary, convention, and preelection financial statements. While neither law specified authority over presidential campaigns, the House committee report accompanying the 1910 bill stated that because presidential electors were elected at the same time as representatives, they were presumed to be covered by the law.

In 1925, Congress codified and revised all previous campaign finance legislation by enacting the Federal Corrupt Practices Act, which remained basic federal campaign law until 1972. The act required all Senate and House candidates and certain political committees to disclose their campaign receipts and expenditures. It also required any political committees conducting their activities in two or more states (mainly national party committees and committees seeking to influence the election of presidential electors) to file disclosure reports. Presidential candidates were not covered until the 1971 Federal Election Campaign Act (FECA).

The Hatch Act of 1939 imposed further constraints on government employees by extending restrictions on political activity to all but about four thousand top policy-making employees in the executive branch of the federal government. The act, along with its 1940 amendments, also sought to reduce the influence of wealthy individuals by limiting the amount that could be contributed to $5,000; multiple contributions up to $5,000 could, however, be contributed to a series of committees supporting the same candidate. This system was ended following the Watergate affair, when it was revealed that the Nixon campaign in 1972 had benefited from contributions as high as $2 million from a single individual, though distributed among numerous supporting committees. The financing of the 1972 election was investigated thoroughly by a Senate committee and special counsel, so more was learned about the financing of that campaign than had been known about any previous campaign.

In the early nineteenth century, candidates began raising money by rewarding campaign contributors with favors and government jobs—the spoils system of patronage.

In 1943, the Smith-Connally War Labor Disputes Act prohibited labor unions from making contributions to federal election campaigns, just as corporate contributions had been banned in 1907. That law was codified by the Taft-Hartley Act of 1947.

Public Funding

The 1970s witnessed a resurgence of the political reform movement, which was the impetus for a wide array of campaign finance laws passed at both the federal and state levels. At the federal level, these reform efforts were embodied in the Federal Election Campaign Act of 1971, the Revenue Act of 1971, and the FECA Amendments of 1974, 1976, and 1979. The 1971 and 1974 laws contained special provisions relating to presidential elections, providing public financing (starting in 1976) and limiting the amounts that could be contributed and spent. The newly established Federal Election Commission administered the law and certified the disbursement of the public funds. Public funds are government subsidies provided for presidential campaigns and derived from a federal income tax checkoff. The checkoff had started in 1972; amounts were aggregated over a four-year period, and the first payouts in the public-funding program were made in 1976, representing a dramatic departure from the entirely privately funded campaigns up to that time.

Three kinds of public funding are available for different phases of a presidential campaign. During the prenomination period, matching funds are provided for qualifying candidates seeking the nomination for President; expenditure limits (adjusted for inflation) are imposed for the entire prenomination period and for spending in each primary and caucus state. Grants (adjusted for inflation) are made to each of the major parties to arrange for and hold their national nominating conventions. Lesser amounts can be provided for qualifying minor party conventions, but, as of 1992, none had ever proved eligible. For the general election period, a flat grant (adjusted for inflation) is given to each major party candidate; the amount also serves as the candidates' expenditure limit. Smaller amounts are available for minor party or independent candidates if they receive 5 percent or more of the vote; in 1980, independent candidate John Anderson qualified for such a grant.

Federal election law provides optional public funds only for presidential candidates who agree to abide by expenditure limitations. To qualify for matching funds during the prenomination period, candidates must raise $5,000 in contributions of $250 or less in each of twenty states. The federal government then matches each contribution made by an individual to a qualified candidate, up to a limit of $250 per contributor. The federal subsidies may not exceed half the prenomination campaign spending limit, which was $27.6 million in 1992. As noted, the federal government also finances the national nominating conventions of the two major political parties. In 1992, each of the parties received $11 million for this purpose.

The major party presidential candidates also are eligible to receive public treasury grants to fund their general election campaigns; $55.2 million was given to each major party candidate in 1992.

The intentions behind public funding are to help supply serious candidates with the money they need to present themselves and their qualifications, to help keep the process competitive, to diminish or eliminate candidates' need to solicit contributions from wealthy donors and interest groups, and to encourage candidates for nomination to broaden their bases of support by requiring them to seek out large numbers of small individual contributions.

Since its inception, public financing of presidential campaigns has been dependent on taxpayers' willingness to earmark a small portion of their tax liabilities—$1 for individual returns and $2 for married persons filing jointly—for the Presidential Election Campaign Fund. Through the 1992 election, the checkoff system has been adequate to cover the costs of providing public financing. The Federal Election Commission certified a total of $70.9 million in public funds for the presidential selection process in 1976, $100.6 million in 1980, $133.1 million in 1984, and $177.8 million in 1988. Thus the federal government became the largest contributor to presidential campaigns.

As of 1992, Congress had not increased the $1 federal income tax checkoff even though the value of the U.S. dollar had eroded since public financing was established in 1971. Tax checkoff participation reached its peak in 1981, when about 29 percent of all Americans filing personal federal income tax returns supported the income tax checkoff. By 1990, that amount of support had diminished to just under 20 percent of taxpayers. Unless remedied, the diminishing support for the checkoff meant that the fund would face a deficit by the 1996 election.

There are several legal ways that private funds can be spent to influence the outcome of a presidential election.

Along with public financing, Congress enacted legislation imposing contribution and expenditure limits on all federal election campaigns. In 1976, however, the Supreme Court ruled in *Buckley* v. *Valeo* that spending limits are permissible only in publicly financed campaigns. Since presidential election contests are the only federal elections in which public funds are available to candidates, spending limits pertain only to presidential candidates and their election committees. The law also limits to $50,000 per election the amount of personal funds that publicly financed presidential candidates and their immediate families may use for their own campaigns. A presidential candidate, such as H. Ross Perot in 1992, can spend unlimited amounts of money in his or her campaign if he or she does not choose public funding and the accompanying expenditure limits.

Continuing Financing Controversies

Even though public funding and its related expenditure limits attempt to control presidential campaign spending, there are still several legal ways that private funds can be spent to influence the outcome of a presidential election. For example, under the *Buckley* v. *Valeo* decision, individuals and groups can make unlimited independent expenditures in presidential and other federal campaigns to advocate the election or defeat of any particular candidate, so long as the spending takes place without the consultation or coordination of the candidate's campaign committee.

Individuals and groups also may contribute to elections by making donations to political parties, which, in turn, may spend the money on behalf of their parties' presidential tickets. Some direct spending by the national party is permitted by law, but some so-called soft money expenditures have become controversial because federal election law allows state and local political parties (if permitted by state law) to raise money for such party-building activities as voter registration and get-out-the-vote campaigns from sources that are normally barred from making contributions to federal elections, such as labor unions and corporations. And because these soft-money contributions are not counted against a candidate's expenditure limit and are not subject to federal law, their prevalence in presidential campaigns has become controversial.

Although labor organizations are prohibited from making contributions to presidential campaigns in general election campaigns, their PACs make notable contributions through parallel campaigning among their membership. In addition, labor groups conduct voter registration and get-out-the-vote drives of their own.

The challenge and potential conflict in regulating political finance is to protect the integrity of the election process, usually by limiting or restricting certain monies or activities, while also respecting the rights of free speech and association guaranteed by the First Amendment to the Constitution. Federal election law and its attendant regulations have not been able to curb spending increases in presidential campaigns. The current system of presidential campaign financing is an experiment that, like the system of American democracy itself, is subject to change. It is likely to be further modified in the years to come.

[See also (I) Campaign Financing; (II) Federal Election Commission; Primaries, Presidential.]

BIBLIOGRAPHY

Alexander, Herbert E., and Monica Bauer. *Financing the 1988 Election.* 1991.
Heard, Alexander. *The Costs of Democracy.* 1960.
Overacker, Louise. *Money in Elections.* 1932.
Roseboom, Eugene. *A History of Presidential Elections.* 1957.
Shannon, Jasper B. *Money and Politics.* 1959.

– HERBERT E. ALEXANDER

CAUCUSES, PRESIDENTIAL

Caucuses have long been a fixture in American presidential selection politics. From 1796 until 1824, presidential nominees were chosen in congressional party caucuses. Even after the rise of national nominating conventions in 1832, most national convention delegates were hand-picked in closed caucus-convention meetings by local and statewide party leaders; rank-and-file party supporters had little or no effective opportunity to influence the choice of their state's convention delegates. Since the 1970s, both Republican and Democratic party rules have required that caucuses and conventions be open to all interested party supporters. Modern caucus meetings typically begin with local (usually precinct) caucus meetings scheduled on a specific date to select delegates for later district and state conventions.

Although presidential primaries receive the bulk of media attention, candidates' personal time, and campaign dollars, caucus-convention states remain an important part of the presidential nomination process. In 1988, some nineteen state Democratic parties and seventeen state Republican parties relied on the caucus-convention system to select part or all their national convention delegates. Smaller, less populous, less urban states more often use the caucus-convention, versus presidential primary system. In 1988 and 1992, almost one-fifth of all national party convention delegates in either party were chosen in caucus-convention states. As a result, no serious presidential contender can afford to ignore the caucus-convention states, which differ from primary states in turnout, media coverage, momentum, costs, and occasionally, representation.

Presidential contenders should not expect a heavy turnout in most caucus-convention states. On the average, only 4 percent of voting-age adults attend local caucus meetings in caucus-convention states—compared to nearly 24 percent of voting-age Americans who vote in states with a presidential primary. Although turnout in caucus-convention states is typically low, considerable variation occurs from one state to another. In 1988, for example, the best-attended, first-in-the-nation Iowa caucuses drew 11 percent of that state's voting-age public. By contrast, barely 1 percent of the voting-age public attended the 1988 Hawaii, Nevada, or Wyoming local caucuses. Turnout in caucus-convention states typically rises when the first-round meetings are early and well-publicized, when candidates spend personal time in the state, when the nominations contest is close and competitive, and when the candidates differ considerably in their policy and ideological views. Although one-third to one-half of first-round caucus attenders may be first-time participants, caucus attenders are more often long-term party supporters, strongly committed candidate supporters, or interest group members.

Until the 1980s, caucus-convention states were typically less costly, delegate-for-delegate, than presidential primary states. Campaign costs were usually lower in caucus-convention states because radio and television ads were unnecessary, and because party loyalists and interest group members were easier and cheaper to target.

In 1976, for example, the three major GOP and Democratic contenders (Gerald Ford, Ronald Reagan, and Jimmy Carter) reported spending only 27 percent as much, per delegate available, in caucus-convention states as in presidential primary states. Over time, however, this difference shrank. By 1980 and 1984, seven major GOP and Democratic contenders averaged 62 percent as much, per delegate available, in caucus-convention states as in primary states. By 1988, the three major contenders (George Bush, Michael Dukakis, and Jesse Jackson) spent slightly more (102 percent as much), per delegate available, in caucus-convention states. These spending changes may have resulted from the early scheduling of first-round caucus meetings.

Caucus-convention states rarely produce the media attention and resulting momentum that come from a well-covered presidential primary state win. Caucus-convention states are more difficult for journalists to cover because vote tallies are often slow to be reported and the delegates themselves are not allocated until district or state conventions, usually held several weeks after the first-round precinct caucuses. During the 1970s and 1980s, caucus-convention states won far less media attention than did primary states.

A well-publicized victory in a caucus-convention state can boost a presidential contender's nationwide poll standings just as a well-publicized primary win does.

When a caucus-convention state is well-covered, however, a well-publicized victory can boost a presidential contender's nationwide poll standings just as a well-publicized primary win does. After the 1976 Iowa caucuses, for example, Jimmy Carter's first-place plurality win led to an 8 percent jump among Democrats in the national polls. Similarly, in 1980, George Bush's first-place Iowa caucus finish led to a nearly 20 percent jump among Republicans in the national polls.

Presidential candidates usually find that caucus-convention attenders are generally more affluent, better educated, and more loyal to their party than nonattending party supporters. Overall, caucus-state attenders may represent their state party's rank-and-file identifiers slightly less well than do presidential primary voters in those states. At recent national party conventions, caucus-convention state delegates have seldom voted very differently from presidential primary state delegates—controlling for a state's urban-rural, racial, regional, and liberal-conservative differences. In a few instances (such as the 1988 Democratic national convention) these differences may be larger if a well-organized, ideologically extreme, or charismatic candidate can turn out supporters at otherwise little-attended caucuses. Overall, however, there is little evidence that holding a caucus-convention system, versus a presidential primary, made large differences in the quality of grass-roots representation during the 1970s and 1980s.

[See also (II) Electoral College; Primaries, Presidential.]

BIBLIOGRAPHY

Abramowitz, Alan, and Walter Stone. *Nomination Politics: Party Activists and Presidential Choice.* 1984.

Marshall, Thomas R. "Measuring Reform in the Presidential Nomination Process." *American Politics Quarterly* 7 (1979). 155–174.

———. *Presidential Nominations in a Reform Age.* 1981.

– THOMAS R. MARSHALL

CENTRAL INTELLIGENCE AGENCY (CIA)

In the midst of two hundred well-guarded acres of forested land in Langley, Virginia, twelve miles from Washington, D.C., along the Potomac River, stands the headquarters of the Central Intelligence Agency. Known more informally by insiders as the Pickle Factory, the Company, or simply the Agency, the CIA is the United States' premier secret intelligence agency, founded by the National Security Act of 1947 (with key strengthening amendments in 1949).

Organization

Organizationally, the CIA is divided into six major divisions: the Office of the Director and, beneath that office, five directorates. The Director wears two hats, serving both as Director of the CIA (DCIA) and as Director of Central Intelligence (DCI). As the DCIA, the Director is the chief executive officer for the Central Intelligence Agency, with all the managerial and planning responsibilities that attend the top position in an executive agency. The CIA chief is assisted by a Deputy Director of the Central Intelligence Agency (DDCIA), the second-in-command and for all practical purposes the top day-to-day administrator at the agency.

DIRECTOR OF CENTRAL INTELLIGENCE. As the DCI, the Director is in charge of the National Foreign Intelligence Program, which in addition to the CIA and its operations includes all satellite and airplane reconnaisance programs and other remote surveillance operations; intelligence codemaking and codebreaking activities; strategic intelligence programs carried out by intelligence entities in the departments of State, Defense, Treasury, Energy, and Justice (which, together with the CIA, comprise the so-called intelligence community); and the overseas counterintelligence responsibilities of the Department of Defense. Above the DCI in the chain of command is the nation's primary decision-making forum for national security and intelligence policy—the National Security Council (NSC), whose key statutory members include the President, the Vice President, and the secretaries of State and Defense.

The vast majority of all intelligence-policy proposals recommended to the NSC originate with the CIA. These proposals, approved by the President on the advice and counsel of the other NSC members and the DCI, take the form of National Security Council Intelligence Directives (NSCIDs, pronounced "n-skids"). These are the broad marching orders for important intelligence operations; the operational specifics are worked out by CIA officials at Langley and at the CIA's stations around the world.

Assisting the DCI is a series of subsidiary units within the Office of the Director at CIA Headquarters: the Office of General Counsel, home of the agency's litigants; the Public Affairs Office, the public relations branch of the CIA; the Office of Congressional Affairs to handle relations with Congress; the Comptroller's Office for budgetary control; and the Office of Inspector General, expected to investigate major allegations of unlawfulness or impropriety by agency officials. Also reporting to the DCI is the National Intelligence Council (NIC), home to the sixteen National Intelligence Officers (NIOs) who work hand in hand with senior analysts throughout the community to prepare major analytic papers, on which policymakers often base their decisions regarding how the United States should react to world developments.

The DCI is further assisted by the Intelligence Community Staff (ICS), an organization designed to assist in the coordination of the various intelligence agencies. Several key ICS interagency committees have been established to aid the DCI in this work of coordination, including panels on human intelligence (i.e., classic espionage); signals intelligence, a generic term for the interception and analysis of communications intelligence as well as other electronic intelligence and telemetry intelligence (chiefly missile emissions); counterintelligence; photographic intelligence; long-range intelligence community planning; and budget coordination.

The DCI is expected not only to run the CIA but also to coordinate and generally supervise every other major intelligence agency in the community—a total of eleven other organizations. Indeed, the budget of the CIA accounts for less than 15 percent of the community's total personnel and annual expenditures (some $30 billion).

DIRECTOR OF THE CIA. The DCIA runs the CIA chiefly through its five directorates. The largest and most controversial of these is the Directorate of Operations (DO), home to what insiders refer to as the "spooks"—the Agency's spy-handlers and officers responsible for "dirty tricks" (covert operations) abroad. Roughly two-thirds of the personnel in the Directorate of Operations are involved in espionage, counterintelligence, and liaison relations with intelligence services in allied nations. The rest are engaged in some form of covert action, such as mounting paramilitary operations or secretly financing friendly politicians overseas. One unit of the DO, the National Collection Division (NCD), operates inside the United States to gather information from foreign visitors and to debrief selected American travelers on their return to the United States. Another DO unit, the Foreign Resources Division (FRD), attempts to recruit foreigners living or traveling in the United States as agents (i.e., spies).

About 75 percent of the information gathered by the CIA has tended to come from public sources (scientific magazines, for instance).

The Directorate of Operations is also subdivided into geographic units (the former Soviet republics, Near East, Europe, East Asia, Africa, and the Western Hemisphere) and other specialized staffs, among them the Covert Action Staff, the Counterintelligence Staff, the Counternarcotics Staff, and the Counterterrorism Staff. Out in the field, the top CIA person in each foreign nation is called the chief-of-station (COS). Beneath the COS are the agency's "case officers," each of whom is in charge of a team of native spies.

The Directorate of Science and Technology (DS&T) is devoted to the improved application of technology to espionage, notably through spy satellites and airplanes. It works closely with the National Reconnaissance Office (NRO), an independent agency that coordinates America's high-altitude spying and reports directly to the DCI. Among other units, the Foreign Broadcast Information Service (FBIS) is lodged in this directorate; the FBIS is responsible for monitoring foreign radio and television broadcasts. The Office of Technical Assistance (OTA), one of the most well-hidden units in the CIA, is also a part of DS&T, providing clandestine eavesdropping capability for the U.S. government overseas. Occasionally, the capabilities of OTA have been misused, as in the Watergate affair, when the "burglars" obtained their disguises from OTA for the infamous attempted theft of documents from the Democratic National Committee headquarters, an action authorized by officials in the Nixon administration.

The Directorate of Administration (DA) handles the CIA's housekeeping, hiring, training, computer processing, worldwide communications, and logistics. It also houses the Office of Security (OS), which is responsible for the physical protection of agency facilities and personnel at home and abroad. This directorate has also been misused on occasion. At the request of White House officials, the surveillance skills of its officers were turned against U.S. antiwar protesters during the Vietnam War era; these activities, called Operation CHAOS, were in violation of the agency's statutory prohibition against spying on U.S. citizens.

The Directorate for Planning and Coordination (DPC), established in 1989, is the newest of the directorates. Its purpose is to conduct long-range planning for the CIA and the broader intelligence community. Its instructions are to map out U.S. intelligence agencies' responses to the new international situation following the end of the cold war.

Finally, the Directorate of Intelligence (DI) is where the agency's research is conducted—the refining, sorting, and interpretation of data from around the world that constitute the essence of the intelligence mission. The CIA has the largest analytic staff of any of the agencies in the intelligence community. Its reports to policymakers, warning them about dangers confronting the United States, represent the primary reason that the CIA and the other intelligence agencies were created in the first place—above all, to guard the nation against another surprise attack like the Japanese bombing of Pearl Harbor on 7 December 1941.

Purposes and Tasks

The core purpose of this elaborate organizational apparatus has been—and will continue to be in the post–cold war era—the collection, analysis, coordination, and dissemination of information about threats and opportunities affecting the United States abroad (this objective is called collection-and-analysis, for short).

About 75 percent of the information gathered by the CIA and the other intelligence agencies has tended to come from public sources (scientific magazines, for instance). The remaining 25 percent has been obtained through secret sources and methods (though this percentage has shrunk as the Soviet Union has disappeared and its republics have become more open to outside scrutiny). The secret collection of information abroad depends, first, on modern (and expensive) surveillance devices, such as satellites and reconnaisance airplanes—so-called intelligence platforms. These machines, which function at astonishingly high levels of scientific competence, are the key components of the United States' National Technical Means (NTM)—the technical component of intelligence collection. Second, collection continues to rely on more old-fashioned and less costly approaches to espionage—the human intelligence component.

The attack on Pearl Harbor taught the United States the danger of blindness to foreign threats and provided the rationale for the creation of the CIA. In the post-cold war era, almost 90 percent of the CIA's resources are devoted to collection-and-analysis. This represents a significant increase over earlier decades, when this task often took a back seat to counterintelligence and covert action.

The term *counterintelligence* (CI) refers to a range of methods designed to protect the United States against aggressive operations perpetrated by foreign intelligence agencies, including attempts by foreign nations to infiltrate U.S. intelligence agencies through the use of double agents, penetration agents (moles), and false defectors. Counterintelligence employs two approaches: security and counterespionage. Security is the defensive side of counterintelligence—physically guarding U.S. personnel, installations, and operations against hostile nations and terrorist groups. Among the defenses employed by CIA security officers are codes, alarms, watchdogs, fences, document classifications, polygraphs, and restricted areas. Counterespionage represents the more aggressive side of counter intelligence, involving, for instance, infiltrating (penetrating) a foreign intelligence service with a U.S. agent.

Covert action, known more euphemistically as special activities, is the most controversial of the operations carried out by the CIA. It consists of aiming secret propaganda at foreign nations, as well as using political, economic, and paramilitary operations to influence, disrupt, or even overthrow their governments (as in Iran in 1953 and Guatemala in 1954). The objective of covert action is secretly to mold events overseas (insofar as possible) in support of U.S. foreign-policy goals. Since the late 1980s, less than 5 percent of the CIA's resources have been earmarked for covert action. This represents a decrease from the roughly 20 percent allocated during the early years of the Reagan administration, and a steep decline from the 1960s, when a majority of the agency's budget was expended in support of the robust use of covert actions against communist regimes (notably in Southeast Asia).

Supervision

The supervision of the CIA and the other intelligence agencies has presented congressional oversight committees with a difficult challenge. In response to abuses of power by the CIA (Operation CHAOS foremost among them), legislators have created an exceptional approach to the problem of restraining the United States' secret agencies—an approach characterized by an openness that most other nations (even other democracies) find astonishing and inappropriate.

From 1947 until 1975, the CIA, like other intelligence agencies throughout the world, enjoyed almost complete freedom from serious external review. Reports of CIA abuses (Operation CHAOS and other transgressions) in the *New York Times* in December 1974 abruptly altered this situation. The House and Senate, as well as President Gerald Ford, created investigative committees to examine the charges.

These probes culminated in the creation of intelligence oversight committees in both chambers of Congress as well as new instruments of accountability within the executive branch (including an Intelligence Oversight Board in the White House). After decades of isolation from the rest of the government, the CIA and the other intelligence agencies—accustomed to operating on the dark side of U.S. foreign policy—suddenly found themselves, to their great discomfort, bathed in torchlight from Capitol Hill. Since 1975, both branches have struggled to find the proper balance between legislative supervision, on the one hand, and executive discretion, on the other. With the deeply troubling exception of the Iran-contra affair (when in the mid 1980s the Reagan administration chose to violate the new intelligence oversight rules), the Congress and the CIA seemed to have arrived at a workable balance between the two important values of accountability and security.

[See also (I) Oversight; (II) National Security Council.]

BIBLIOGRAPHY

Colby, William, and Peter Forbath. *Honorable Men: My Life in the CIA.* 1978.

Jeffreys-Jones, Rhodri. *The CIA and American Democracy.* 1989.

Johnson, Loch K. *America's Secret Power: The CIA in a Democratic Society.* 1989.

Ranelagh, John. *The Agency: The Rise and Decline of the CIA.* 1986.

Ransom, Harry Howe. *The Intelligence Establishment.* 1970.
Smist, Frank J., Jr. *Congress Oversees the United States Intelligence Community, 1947–1989.* 1990.
Treverton, Gregory F. *Covert Action: The Limits of Intervention in the Postwar World.* 1987.
Turner, Stansfield. *Secrecy and Democracy: The CIA in Transition.* 1985.

– LOCH K. JOHNSON

CHIEF EXECUTIVE

One of the most important roles of the President is that of Chief Executive. The President's executive role is grounded in Article II of the Constitution. In ambiguous language the Constitution vests "the executive Power" in the President and directs him to "take Care that the laws be Faithfully executed." He may also "require the Opinion, in writing, of the principal Officer in each of the executive Departments" and "grant reprieves and pardons." He derives substantial power from his designation as "Commander in Chief of the Army and Navy." Modern Presidents have tended to interpret these constitutional provisions broadly and have derived from them substantial additional powers. In addition to their constitutionally based powers, Presidents have received extensive delegations of authority from Congress.

Most modern Presidents, however, have encountered difficulty in their efforts to direct the executive branch. President Franklin D. Roosevelt complained about the independence of the navy, President John F. Kennedy lamented the inertia of the State Department, and President Ronald Reagan made his campaign attack on an overgrown federal bureaucracy one of the enduring themes of his presidency.

The effectiveness of the political leadership the President provides depends on the personality and values of the President as well as on external events.

There is an apparent paradox in, on the one hand, the President's considerable formal legal powers and his position as head of a vast, complex bureaucracy and, on the other hand, his limited ability to direct that bureaucracy toward the achievement of his policy goals. That paradox results, at least in part, from the constitutional relationship of the presidency to the legislative and judicial branches of government and the nature of the federal bureaucracy and the President's relationship to it.

The Constitution not only created the executive branch, with the President as its head, but also established the legislative and judicial branches and prescribed a sharing of powers among those separate institutions. The President is dependent on congressional cooperation to carry out his executive responsibilities. Only Congress can authorize government programs, establish administrative agencies to implement them, and appropriate funds to finance them. There are also occasions when the exercise of presidential power must be approved by the judiciary, as when the Supreme Court in 1952 disallowed President Harry S Truman's seizure of U.S. steel mills to forestall a strike during the Korean War (*Youngstown Sheet & Tube Co.* v. *Sawyer*). The point is that presidential power is not self-executing and it is subject to restraint.

The President's task as the nation's Chief Executive is much more, therefore, than issuing commands. Nor is the job mainly that of finding ways to bring a large and complex bureaucracy under his operational control. Rather, he must secure congressional cooperation while suppressing the executive branch's natural tendencies toward conflict with the legislative branch, and he must give direction to the bureaucracy.

Ideally, Presidents should use the White House staff and other units of the Executive Office of the President to help them define their objectives, convert them into operating programs, allocate resources to the agencies that administer the programs, and coordinate the implementation of programs within the federal government and among federal, state, and local governments. Department executives should direct the work of career civil servants, coordinate the operations of their component bureaus, and develop and maintain links with other federal departments and agencies and with state and local governments. Presidents discover, however, that the reality of their relations with the federal bureaucracy bears little resemblance to the idealized vision just described.

Dealing with the Bureaucracy

There is an inherent tension between the White House, which favors centralized presidential control, and the bureaucracy, which strives for autonomy, that has been present in every modern administration. It exists, at least in part, because of the difference between political leadership of the bureaucracy and bureaucratic power. The direction and effectiveness of the political leadership the President provides depend on the personality, leadership style, and values of the President as well as on external events and conditions. In contrast, bureaucratic power is relatively permanent and does not depend on personalities and transitory political and environmental factors.

At least five general factors contribute to bureaucratic power and present obstacles to presidential control of the federal bureaucracy: the size, complexity, and dispersion of the executive branch; bureaucratic inertia and momentum; the personnel of the executive branch; the legal position of the executive branch; and the susceptibility of executive branch units to external political influence.

SIZE. By 1993 the federal budget reached $1.5 trillion and there were more than 2.9 million civilian and 2.5 million military employees. The domestic activities of the federal government extended into every community of the nation and touched the lives of individuals from birth to death. Considerations of national security projected U.S. military and foreign policy activities around the world. Providing leadership and direction to the federal bureaucracy is a difficult task.

The multiplicity of agencies and programs creates an additional obstacle to presidential leadership of the executive branch. The complexity that results from overlapping jurisdictions leads to duplication of efforts and complicates the President's job. It places a premium on coordination by the presidency. Bureaucratic complexity also stems from the interdependence of many federal activities. Policy goals in one area are often affected by objectives in other areas. The difficult trade-off between energy policy and environmental policy, which became acute in the 1970s, illustrates policy interdependence. Efforts to conserve energy and reduce foreign oil imports were at variance with attempts to reduce air and water pollution.

The great size of the federal bureaucracy further frustrates presidential efforts at direction and control because its activities are so widely dispersed. Presidents are at the center of government. The people who operate programs, deliver services to individuals, and regulate the conduct of businesses and other organizations are at the periphery. These people, almost all of whom are civil servants, were there when the President and his staff took office, and they will be there after the political executives have departed. They control many of the resources, human and material, that are needed to implement programs successfully. Their position, at the point of delivery, is the source of much of their power.

INERTIA. Because of bureaucratic inertia it is hard to get a new government activity started, and once under way, it is even more difficult to stop or significantly change the activity. Two important factors contributing to bureaucratic inertia are organizational routines: prescribed operating procedures that have worked successfully in the past and the support of interest groups for programs that benefit them and in which they have a material stake.

The aspect of bureaucratic inertia primarily responsible for presidential frustration is the momentum of ongoing programs. The degree of that momentum is revealed in the number of activities to which the government is committed by public laws, the amount of money allocated for those activities in annual appropriations, and the number of employees who carry out the activities. "Uncontrollable" expenditures that the government was obligated to make constituted about 75 percent of President George Bush's proposed 1993 budget. The principal uncontrollable items include interest on the national debt; entitlement programs such as social security, Medicare and Medicaid, Food Stamps, federal retirement and veterans' benefits; and contractual obligations to pay for such things as weapons systems and public facilities. Even the "controllable" portion of the budget is highly resistant to cuts because of support from groups that benefit from those expenditures. Presidents can influence the shape of the federal budget, but major changes usually require several years to be implemented. From one year to the next, Presidents tend to be limited to incremental changes. [*See* budget policy.]

PERSONNEL. The large number of career federal employees also commits the President to maintain ongoing programs. Major reductions in personnel or redirection of their activities are economically and politically costly. People will oppose actions that threaten to deprive them of their jobs or require them to move, or reduce their sense of security and importance. Most Presidents can make only modest adjustments in the size and mission of the federal workforce.

The personnel—political and career officials—upon whom Presidents depend to operate the bureaucracy are the third aspect of bureaucratic power that impedes presidential control of the executive branch. Political executives often are amateurs in the precarious world of Washington politics. They often lack the political knowledge and substantive skills needed to perform their jobs effectively. They quickly discover their dependence on career executives and other lower-ranking civil servants for the information and advice they need. That support comes at a price: loyalty to the agency and support for its programs within the administration, before Congress, and with the public.

Political executives in the bureaucracy are torn between looking upward to the President for support and direction and downward to the permanent government for support and services. In such a position they are imperfect instruments for presidential control of the bureaucracy. They can best serve the President by winning

President Woodrow Wilson tested his power to remove top-level political officials when he removed the postmaster from his post without senatorial consent. (Library of Congress, Prints and Photographs Division)

the trust of the careerists who compose the permanent government, but to do so they find it expedient to maintain a considerable degree of independence from the White House.

Career executives and other civil servants provide the institutional resources, such as political experience, substantive knowledge, and technical competence, required to accomplish an agency's mission. They are aware of political problems the agency faces and of its political resources. They have established links with its clientele and with the congressional committees that oversee it through legislative and appropriations powers. They also have a vested interest in their agencies and their programs. Their loyalties are based on norms of bureaucratic and occupational professionalism. They recognize the legitimacy of the President's position and of the claims of political executives for the support, but they will not hesitate to use their substantial capacity to resist the directives of their political superiors.

LEGAL POSITION. The legal position of the executive branch is ambiguous. All departments and agencies are established by Congress and derive their authority to operate from statutes. Although Presidents act through subordinates, they do so principally through persuasion because of the nature and source of their legal authority and that of their subordinates.

Although the Constitution requires the President to "take care" that the laws are faithfully executed, his legal position as Chief Executive is somewhat unclear because Congress has—with presidential approval—delegated authority to and imposed duties directly on various administrative officials. In some cases, such as independent regulatory commissions, the President has no formal power to direct agency actions or set agency policy. His influence upon these units is based on his budgetary and appointment powers and on his persuasive abilities. For Cabinet members, heads of independent agencies, and other political executives with operating authority to whom Congress has directly delegated power, the situation is not clearly defined. The Supreme Court long ago ruled that the President may not interfere with the performance of a "purely ministerial" duty that does not involve the exercise of discretion or judgment (*Kendall* v. *United States* [1838]).

EXTERNAL INFLUENCE. Susceptibility to external influence and pressure derives in part from the inability of American political parties to provide administrative units with political support and to link party programs with the pursuit of presidential goals. If partisan and presidential support for an agency is lacking, the agency must look elsewhere for help in maintaining its authority, funding, and personnel. It looks for support particularly to the individuals and groups who are affected by its programs and to the congressional committees or subcommittees with jurisdiction over its legislative authorizations and appropriations. An agency without support from such entities is in a precarious position. But to the extent that agencies succeed in the quest for external support presidential control is frustrated.

Presidential Powers

However, Presidents are not without resources to cope with the obstacles to their control of the executive branch. They have substantial powers granted by the Constitution, delegated by Congress, and derived from the nature of their office. The most important are the appointment power and the removal power, the power to issue executive orders, and the power to prepare the annual federal budget and regulate expenditures.

APPOINTMENTS AND REMOVAL. As critical as the appointment and removal powers are to the President's executive responsibilities, they are subject to limitation by Congress. The Constitution makes high-ranking officials subject to senatorial confirmation and Congress determines whether an appointment must be confirmed by the Senate. In addition, it can narrow the President's discretion in making appointments by establishing detailed qualifications for various offices. Congress cannot, however, give itself the power to appoint executive officials that have enforcement or adjudicatory duties. (*Buckley* v. *Valeo* [1976]). The President's appointive powers also are constrained by political considerations and practices, such as senatorial courtesy whereby the President gives the Senators of his own party a veto over certain administrative and judicial appointments in the states.

The Senate generally has given Presidents considerable leeway in the appointment of top-level political executives, but confirmation is not automatic, and the Senate has used rejections to express disapproval of specific individuals or particular practices. Since the Watergate affair of 1972–1974, the Senate has tended to be more careful and procedurally consistent in examining the backgrounds, qualifications, and relevant policy views of presidential nominees. However, the confirmation process has become more demanding and time-consuming for the nominees.

The removal power is the logical complement of the appointment power. The ability to remove subordinate officials on performance or policy grounds is fundamental to presidential control of the executive branch. Without the removal power, the President cannot be held fully responsible for the actions of his subordinates or for failure of departments and agencies to achieve his objectives. The Constitution is silent, however, concerning the removal of executive officials other than through impeachment, a cumbersome process that is limited to instances of "Treason, Bribery, or other high Crimes and Misdemeanors."

The Supreme Court has dealt directly with the removal power in a decision involving a challenge to President Woodrow Wilson's summary removal of a postmaster. In *Myers* v. *United States* (1926), the Court invalidated an 1876 law that required senatorial consent for the removal of postmasters. It held that the Constitution gave the removal power to the President and that Congress could not place restrictions on its exercise. Nine years later, however, the Court upheld the provisions of the Federal Trade Commission Act, which limited the grounds for removal of its members. In *Humphrey's Executor* v. *United States* (1935), the Court ruled that the President's unqualified power of removal is limited to "purely executive offices" and that Congress may prescribe conditions for the removal of officials performing "quasi-legislative" and "quasi-judicial" functions. However, the Court has not clarified fully the meaning of those terms.

Although there are some statutory and judicial restrictions on the removal power, its precise limits remain somewhat undefined. Moreover, the President may be able through informal means to force officials from office for reasons other than statutory cause. The President can call publicly for an official's resignation, or he may revoke authority he has delegated to an official as a means of indicating displeasure and lack of confidence.

LEGISLATIVE POWER. Under a strict interpretation of the separation of powers, the President has no direct legislative authority. Established practice, however, based on liberal interpretations of the Constitution by Presidents and the Supreme Court, has vested substantial authority in him to issue executive orders that have the force of law. From the beginnings of the Republic, Presidents have issued orders and directives on the basis of Article II. Executive orders have been a primary means of exercising this broad presidential prerogative power. Presidents also have used them in making public policy in crucial areas such as civil rights, economic stabilization, and national security.

It is generally recognized that executive orders must find their authority in the Constitution or in an act of Congress. The Supreme Court has upheld delegations of legislative power to the executive branch provided Congress establishes "intelligible" standards to guide administrative officials in the exercise of their authority in *Hampton & Co.* v. *United States* (1928). In reviewing challenges to statutory delegations, however, the Court has consistently adopted a presumption in favor of statutes authorizing executive action by order or rule.

FINANCIAL POWERS. Presidents have substantial financial powers, delegated by Congress, which they use in their efforts to control the bureaucracy. The most important of these powers is the budget, which is an annual plan for spending by federal departments and agencies. The budget also establishes the President's spending priorities, sets the timing of program initiatives, and distributes rewards to and imposes sanctions on executive branch units. By controlling the total amount of the budget, the President can attempt to influence the performance of the economy.

Presidential use of the executive budget is a twentieth-century development. The Budget and Accounting Act of 1921 made the President responsible for compiling department and agency estimates and for submitting them annually to Congress in the form of a budget. The departments and agencies were prohibited from submitting their requests directly to Congress as they had done previously.

The initial emphasis in the development of the budget process was on the control of expenditures and the prevention of administrative abuses. The focus of the budget was on objects of expenditure, that is, personnel, supplies, and equipment. During the New Deal period, in the 1930s, the emphasis shifted from control to management. The budget became a means of evaluating and improving administrative performance. The focus of the budget shifted from objects of expenditure to the work and activities of departments and agencies. The third stage in the development of budgeting is its orientation toward planning, which began in the 1960s. This stage has featured attempts to link annual budgeting, geared to the appropriations process in Congress, to long-range planning of government objectives. The focus is on the relationship of long-term policy goals to current and future spending decisions.

The limited utility of the budget as a means of incorporating planning in presidential decision making stems from the incremental nature of the budget process and from restrictions and conditions imposed by Congress. Budgeting is inherently incremental because it is done annually. Decision makers in Congress and the executive branch are concerned primarily with how large an increase or decrease will be made in a department's or an agency's budget and they focus on spending for the forthcoming fiscal year. Pressures are intense, and the stakes are high. There is little opportunity for consideration of long-range objectives and costs or for examining the effects of different spending levels for specific activities.

It has been almost an article of faith among political leaders that executive reorganization can increase presidential power over the bureaucracy.

In addition to budgeting, Presidents have certain discretionary spending powers that increase their leverage over the bureaucracy. They have substantial nonstatutory authority, based on understandings with congressional appropriations committees, to shift funds within an appropriation and from one program to another. Presidents also have exercised some degree of expenditure control through the practice of impounding or returning appropriated funds to the Treasury. Since George Washington, Presidents have routinely impounded funds as a means of saving when expenditures fall short of appropriations. They have also withheld funds when authorized to do so by Congress and have, on occasion, impounded funds that Congress had added, over their objections, to various appropriations.

Managerial Tools

Beyond their formal powers, modern Presidents have relied on managerial tools in their efforts to coordinate and direct executive-branch operations. Three major tools—staffing, reorganization, and planning—have been employed with mixed results. The limited success of presidential efforts to manage the federal bureaucracy more effectively stems primarily from the political character of the administration of the executive branch. The President must rely more on persuasion than command to achieve his objectives, and departments and agencies have substantial autonomy. This is not to argue that the public sector is inhospitable to modern management techniques, but to suggest that their use is significantly affected by political forces.

STAFF AND CABINET. The presidency has grown steadily as Presidents have turned to staff support as a means of discharging their many roles and of directing the executive branch. The roles of presidential staff in program implementation and of the Cabinet in advising the President have varied in recent administrations, but the tendency has been toward reliance on a strong, sizable, and centralized White House staff to protect the political interests of the President, to act as his principal policy advisers, and to direct (as opposed to monitor and coordinate) the implementation of his priorities by the bureaucracy. Critics of this structure argue that it has undercut the advisory potential of the Cabinet, narrowed the President's perspective on policy choices, and inhibited effective and responsive bureaucratic performance. Experience under President Richard M. Nixon, in the Watergate scandal, and President Ronald Reagan, in the Iran-contra affair, indicates that excessive reliance on staffing can be disastrous. Yet, both Presidents Gerald Ford and Jimmy Carter tried a decentralized model of White House staffing and abandoned it in favor of hierarchical arrangements, which President George Bush also utilized. Increasingly, the demands and expectations that Presidents confront lead them to rely on a centralized White House staff run by a strong White House Chief of Staff.

REORGANIZATION. It has been almost an article of faith among political leaders and public administration theorists that executive reorganization can increase presidential power over the bureaucracy. Organizational structure and administrative arrangements are significant because they reflect values and priorities and because they affect access to decision makers. The location and status of an administrative unit—as a department, an independent agency, or a component of a department—symbolize the importance of its goals and the interests it serves. Administrative arrangements also can contribute to or frustrate the achievement of accountability to Congress and the public. Reorganizing, however, does not necessarily result in increased efficiency of operation, greater program effectiveness, or enhanced public accountability. This is true because there is no ideal form for a government agency or a consistent set of prescriptions for organizing the executive branch. Experience has shown that although the rationale for reorganization is couched in the rhetoric of economy and efficiency, the crucial factors in decisions to reorganize and the results of reorganizations are power, policy, and symbolic significance.

PLANNING. Planning is current action designed to achieve future conditions. It is a rational process that operates on the assumption that objectives are known and accepted. The task is to select the best means appropriate to the achievement of the desired ends. Conflict and disagreement do not interfere because the planners know what is desired. However, planning takes place in an uncertain world. Planners do not have adequate knowledge of the future and their predictions often are fallible.

In addition to the intellectual limitations of all planning, public planning is limited by politics. Public planners do not have the power to command acceptance of their choices. Public choices are made on the basis of the preferences of individuals and groups through a process of bargaining and compromise. The agreements reached in the process of political decision making determine the objectives of public planners. There is no correct result because political preferences are continually changing. As a consequence, political planners shorten their time frames (usually extending them no further into the future than the next election), thus reducing the need for prediction, and offer their plans as proposals or suggestions rather than as directives. The result is that political factors tend to dominate planning and planning tends to blend with regular political decision making. Presidents have engaged in long-range planning with only limited success.

Can the President lead the executive branch? There are reasons to doubt that he can. It is apparent that although the President has substantial formal powers and managerial resources, he is by no means fully in control of his own branch of government. His capacity to direct its many departments and agencies in the implementation of his policies is constrained by bureaucratic complexity and fragmentation, conflict between the presidency and the bureaucracy, congressional and other external pressures and influences on the bureaucracy, and the extreme difficulty of establishing an effective management system within the government.

[See also (I) Legislative Branch; (II) Commander in Chief; Executive Power; Immunity, Presidential.]

BIBLIOGRAPHY

Arnold, Peri E. *Making the Managerial Presidency.* 1986.

Berman, Larry. *The Office of Management and Budget and the Presidency.* 1979.

Campbell, Colin. *Managing the Presidency: Carter, Reagan, and the Search for Executive Harmony.* 1986.

Cohen, Jeffrey E. *The Politics of the U.S. Cabinet: Representation in the Executive Branch, 1789–1984.* 1988.

Cronin, Thomas E. *The State of the Presidency.* 2d ed. 1980.

Fisher, Louis. *Constitutional Conflicts between Congress and the President.* 3d ed., rev. 1991.

Hart, John. *The Presidential Branch.* 1987.

Hess, Stephen. *Organizing the Presidency.* 2d ed. 1988.

Mackenzie, G. Calvin. *The Politics of Presidential Appointments.* 1981.

Mackenzie, G. Calvin, ed. *The In-and-Outers* 1987.

Nathan, Richard P. *The Administrative Presidency.* 1983.

Pfiffner, James P. *The Strategic Presidency.* 1988.

Seidman, Harold, and Robert Gilmour. *Politics, Position, and Power.* 4th ed. 1986.

Wildavsky, Aaron. *The New Politics of the Budgetary Process.* 2d ed. 1992.

– NORMAN C. THOMAS

CIVIL SERVICE

In the United States, "civil service" is not a precise legal category or political term. It generally refers to civilian employees, who are not politically appointed officers, in the executive branch of government. The term may also encompass employees of legislative agencies, such as the General Accounting Office, and some judicial employees. Legislative staff and judicial clerks are generally not considered civil servants. Further, the term typically connotes white-collar employment, although police and fire fighters are within its purview and public school teachers and public university professors usually are not. In some contexts, "civil service" is used to distinguish employees working under a merit system and enjoying formal job security from temporary, conditional, and politically appointed public employees.

Even if "civil service" is not precisely defined, the development of large and politically influential civil services has been of great importance to governments throughout the world. Civil services are repositories of expertise on which governments depend in formulating and executing public policy. In some countries, including France, Germany, and at times, China, the civil service enjoys considerable prestige. Elsewhere, as in the United States, it is often derided for inefficiency and incompetence. Virtually everywhere there is concern with the influence of the civil service on policy and the potential or reality of corruption within it.

Historically the U.S. federal government has faced difficulty in fully integrating the civil service into the separation of powers and the dominant political culture. The constitutional scheme places the President at the head of the executive branch but makes the civil service highly dependent on Congress. Not only must the creation of all offices and the disbursement of all appropriations be pursuant to law, but Congress has constitutional authority to determine how civil servants will be appointed. In practice, Congress delegates considerable legislative authority to executive-branch agencies in establishing their missions. Overall, the legislature is deeply involved in the organization, staffing, and funding of the civil service and in overseeing its performance.

In the United States, civil service is often derided for inefficiency and incompetence.

At various times, the model for the civil service has been one of responsiveness to executive leadership, politically neutral competence, or representativeness of the people. There tends to be a trade-off between managerial and political values in the civil service that thus far has not been resolved. The management approach emphasizes efficiency, economy, and effective hierarchical control, whereas the political approach values responsiveness, representativeness, and accountability to external bodies, such as the legislature. The tensions inherent in these approaches have been complicated since the 1970s by far greater judicial involvement in public administration. The courts have required that civil-service procedures and the actions of civil servants incorporate appropriate constitutional rights and values, such as due process and equal protection. For example, in *Rutan* v. *Republican Party of Illinois,* the Supreme Court held that the First and Fourteenth Amendments prohibited the use of partisanship in the vast majority of ordinary civil-service hirings, promotions, transfers, and other personnel actions.

Organizing Concepts in the Past

Historians agree that by the early twentieth century the United States had developed three distinct organizing concepts for the civil service in three different periods.

FIRST PERIOD. From 1789 until 1829, federal civil servants were selected and retained primarily on the basis of fitness of character. They were recruited from the upper class, and consequently, the period is generally referred to as the era of "gentlemen." For the most part, the civil service was the arm of the elite who controlled national politics. Some concern with civil servants' political leanings developed in the administration of John Adams and became more pronounced in the early years of Thomas Jefferson's presidency, but the service was characterized more by political stability than by change. Executive leadership was a pronounced organizing value.

SECOND PERIOD. The period from 1829 until the early 1870s was a reaction to the first. The inauguration of President Andrew Jackson ushered in a fundamentally different concept of the civil service. In his inaugural address, Jackson argued that reform was necessary because the upper-class basis of the civil service, coupled with the long incumbency of civil servants, had made the service indifferent to the public interest. He proposed that civil servants be selected from the broad spectrum of the white male population and that they be rotated in and out of office relatively rapidly. In other words, the civil service was to be socially and politically representative of the public. Although Jackson's own record in implementing such reforms was modest in comparison with his successors, he is generally credited with establishing the spoils system because he provided a compelling rationale for it.

By the 1840s, when the system was at its height, the civil service was best considered the arm of the political party (or faction) in office. Wholesale rotation of civil servants occurred upon the inaugurations of new Presidents. Superfluous positions were created to satisfy the demand for patronage. Tenure was short, business methods were haphazard, the separation between political parties and the government was blurred, and corruption was rife. The spoils system is generally credited with fostering the development of mass-based, competitive political parties and with breaking the upper class's dominance of the national government.

THIRD PERIOD. The period from the 1870s to the 1920s was a reaction to the excesses of the spoils system. Three civil-service reform movements combined to organize the civil service according to a third set of concepts—merit, political neutrality, and scientific management. Early merit reforms were introduced in the 1870s, but it was not until the enactment of the Civil Service Act (1883) that the merit system became a permanent organizing concept of the federal civil service. The act placed only about 10 percent of all federal civil-service positions under the merit system, but it authorized the President to extend such coverage. By 1919, at least 70 percent of the civil service was in the competitive classified civil service (organized on the basis of merit). The act also sought to eliminate partisan coercion and partisanship generally from the civil service. Enforcement was by an independent Civil Service Commission, consisting of a chairperson and two members appointed by the President with the advice and consent of the Senate. No more than two of the commissioners could be of the same political party.

Civil-service reformers had long favored taking the civil service out of politics and politics out of the civil service. The idea of a politically neutral civil service dates back at least to Jefferson's first administration. Additional limited efforts to restrict the political activities of federal civil servants were made in the 1840s and from the 1870s through the 1890s. But it was not until the Progressive Era that the first successful federal restrictions on the partisan activities of civil servants took hold. President Theodore Roosevelt amended Civil Service Rule I so that those in the competitive classified service were prohibited from taking an active part in political management or campaigns. Rule I was superseded by the Hatch Act (1939), which placed similar restrictions on a statutory basis.

The reformers and Progressives valued civil-service reform for the efficiency and higher public morality it would bring. However, it was also instrumental to their larger interests in making fundamental political change. They sought to destroy the machine-based, spoils-oriented political leadership and culture that had developed in the period after the Civil War. Depriving the political bosses of patronage and the use of the civil service for partisan purposes was central to their objectives.

In order to make their case regarding depoliticization of the civil service, however, the reformers and Progressives had to convince the public and their elected representatives that the civil service should be organized on the principle of politically neutral expertise. To do so, they presented two main arguments. First, they argued that public administration and politics were separate endeavors and that, therefore, it was unnecessary (or even undesirable) for the civil service to be organized according to executive leadership or representativeness. Administrative questions were matters of business, not politics. Second, they argued that there was a developing body of administrative expertise that could efficiently, economically, and effectively replace the haphazard practices of the past. In making the latter argument, the Progressives were aided immensely by the advent of Frederick Taylor's scientific-management movement.

Taking the perspective of engineering, in the early 1900s Taylor argued that there was an applied science of job design, work flow, and employee selection and motivation. He reported tremendous successes in improving efficiency and productivity in a variety of manual-labor jobs. The scientific-management movement attracted adherents and interest worldwide partly because of its promise of greater efficiency and partly because it presented a blueprint for redistributing authority in the workplace. At the core of Taylorism was the belief that the functions of management should be enlarged to include job design and work flow. In the past, workers had determined how jobs would be performed, thereby giving them considerable leverage vis-à-vis management. Under scientific management, managers would take over the responsibility of structuring jobs and work flow. They would use science, rather than past practices or the workers' rule of thumb, as the basis for assuring the highest level of efficiency. Although it was not a necessary outcome, Taylorism in fact led to the "de-skilling" of jobs, thereby reducing the value of what workers had to sell in the labor market and making them more or less interchangeable. Hence, management gained greater control of workers.

The Progressives benefited doubly from scientific management in promoting their organizing principles for the civil service. On the one hand, they could present much of public administration—employee selection, job design, position classification, and pay plans—as a science, rather than a set of practices to be established according to changing political or popular preferences. On the other hand, many of the Progressives, including such leaders as Woodrow Wilson, were deeply concerned that the very large influx of immigrants during the 1890s and 1910s could corrupt the Anglo-American political culture if that influx were not channeled in appropriate directions. Immigrants and political bosses had established symbiotic relationships based on patronage and personal loyalty. Scientific management offered the same excellent prospect in the public sector as in private industry for making workers, many of whom were immigrants, thoroughly dependent on managers, who were much more likely to be well assimilated into the dominant political culture. Indeed, early merit examinations often asked questions about civic organization and history that were seemingly irrelevant to the jobs at hand. In the Progressives' view, however, civil servants should be concerned about the public and imbued with civic virtue, which included knowledge about the structure and operation of government.

Aside from the merit system and political neutrality, the organizing concepts developed by the reformers, Progressives, and scientific managers included position classification. By 1920, the federal civil service was thoroughly organized according to positions rather than around individuals, collective bargaining units, or work teams. Among the leading principles of position classification were the following: Positions, not individuals, should be classified (thus, rank has overwhelmingly been in the position, not the person). Positions should be classified according to the duties and responsibilities they require. The duties and responsibilities should determine the educational, experiential, and other qualifications required of applicants. The individual characteristics of incumbent employees have no bearing on the classification of positions. Persons holding positions with the same classification should be considered interchangeable. Today, the civil service includes several classification systems. The main one is the General Schedule, which includes most white-collar occupations and ranges from grade 1 (low) to grade 18. The U.S. Postal Service, Foreign Service, some other agencies, and blue-collar workers are under separate classification systems.

Although the organization of state and local civil services varied considerably, the spoils system and the reform period left their mark throughout the nation. By the mid-twentieth century, merit, political neutrality, and position classification had become the dominant ideal, if not the actual reality, almost everywhere in the nation.

Organization after 1978

The federal civil service was substantially reorganized by the Civil Service Reform Act (1978) (92 Stat. L. 1111).

IMPETUS FOR THE 1978 REFORM ACT. In some respects, the act was a delayed outgrowth of political developments that occurred during the New Deal. The size of the civil service had grown from about 610,000 in 1931 to 1,438,000 in 1941. In the 1990s it employed some three million personnel. This rapid growth placed considerable strains on the organization derived from the reform-Progressive period. The independent Civil Service Commission was no longer able to perform most personnel functions on a centralized basis. More and more authority for personnel had to be delegated to the departments and agencies, with the commission engaging in audits, investigations, and other policing functions. Increasingly this policing role, which was appropriate according to the neutral-competence model, was viewed as a barrier to strong executive leadership. A dynamic President appointed department and agency heads to develop and implement policies, only to see their work frustrated by civil-service rules and procedures designed for an earlier time in which spoils was perceived as a preeminent problem. In 1937 Roosevelt appointed the President's Committee on Administrative Management (also known as the Brownlow Committee after its chair, Louis Brownlow). Among many other recommendations, the committee called for the elimination of the Civil Service Commission in favor of an office of personnel under more direct presidential control. Although this proposal made little headway, the reformers of the 1970s looked at similar problems and reached similar conclusions.

The immediate impetus for the 1978 civil-service reform was threefold. First, public confidence in government had been severely shaken by the Watergate Affair, culminating in President Richard M. Nixon's resignation in 1974. The Civil Service Commission had been tainted during the Nixon years by illegally favoring the applications of persons having White House backing. It had long been considered ineffective in helping the President to exert executive leadership, and by the mid 1970s it seemed to fail at policing as well. Second, the relatively clear-cut organizing principles of the earlier reform-Progressive period were challenged by new concerns and practices, including the growing importance of efforts to achieve equal employment opportunity and the development of widespread collective bargaining throughout most of the civil service. For instance, merit examinations, such as the Federal Service Entrance Examination and, later, the Professional and Administrative Careers Examination, had a disparate (and harsh) impact on the employment interests of African Americans and Hispanics. The pronounced managerial authority that was partly a legacy of scientific management, and position-classification practices, reduced the scope of bargaining available to unionized federal civil servants. Third, President Jimmy Carter strongly believed that the federal bureaucracy was bloated, inefficient, and badly in need of reform.

The idea of a politically neutral civil service dates back at least to Jefferson's first administration.

PROVISIONS OF THE 1978 REFORM ACT. The Civil Service Reform Act included the following changes:

1. The Civil Service Commission was abolished. Its legal successor is the Merit Systems Protection Board (MSPB). The board consists of a chairperson and two members, appointed to seven-year terms by the President with the advice and consent of the Senate. No more than two of these appointees may be of the same political party. The MSPB is considered the watchdog of the merit system. It is responsible for ensuring that merit principles, laws, and regulations are not violated. It hears employee appeals of adverse actions, such as dismissals and demotions, and has specific authority to protect whistle-blowers, who expose waste, fraud, abuse, or gross mismanagement, against reprisals. Adjudicatory decisions by the MSPB can be appealed to the Court of Appeals for the Federal Circuit, which has upheld its decisions in about 90 percent of the cases. The MSPB also has responsibility for conducting special studies of aspects of federal personnel administration.

2. A Special Counsel was established, which was initially attached to the MSPB, appointed to a five-year term by the President with the advice and consent of the Senate. The Special Counsel is now an independent entity responsible for investigating allegations of violations of personnel laws, rules, and regulations. The Special Counsel can bring cases before the MSPB for adjudication. It reports suspected criminal violations to the Attorney General.

3. An Office of Personnel Management (OPM) was created to take over most of the Civil Service Commission's managerial functions. It is headed by a director, appointed to a four-year term by the President with the advice and consent of the Senate. OPM is considered the President's arm for personnel management and is more directly responsible to him than was the commission. Its responsibilities include operating the retirement system, training, position classification, examining, and developing and overseeing merit pay procedures for upper-level federal managers.

4. The act included a section on labor-management relations (Title VII), which placed labor relations affecting most of the civil service on a comprehensive statutory basis for the first time. Title VII establishes a Federal Labor Relations Authority (FLRA), consisting of a chair and two members appointed by the President with the advice and consent of the Senate for five-year overlapping terms. No more than two appointees to the authority may be of the same political party. The FLRA has general responsibility for oversight of the federal labor-relations program, including employee representational matters, determination of bargaining units, grievances, unfair labor practices, and definition of the scope of bargaining. Title VII provides for a relatively narrow scope of bargaining, which does not include pay and many personnel matters such as hiring, promotion, and position classification. A Federal Service Impasses Panel works under the authority's general direction in trying to aid employee organizations and management to resolve disputes. Title VII does not cover the Postal Service and several smaller agencies, including the General Accounting Office, the Federal Bureau of Investigation (FBI), the Central Intelligence Agency (CIA), and the Tennessee Valley Authority (TVA). FLRA relies overwhelmingly on adjudication, as opposed to rule making, in carrying out its mission. Its decisions can be appealed to the federal Circuit Courts of Appeals, in which it prevailed in less than half the cases brought from 1979 to 1987. The authority's failure to do better in court resulted from a number of factors ranging from the competence of its decision makers to the difficulty it, the agencies, unions, and courts have in interpreting Title VII.

5. A Senior Executive Service (SES) was created out of positions in grades GS 16 to 18 (previously called supergrades). The SES is predominantly composed of top-level, career civil servants, though by law 10 percent of the positions in it may be filled with political appointees. The SES is a kind of higher civil service long thought desirable for the federal government. It reflects the beliefs that first, there is a body of skill or professionalism called public management that can be transferred from agency setting to agency setting; second, it is politically desirable for top federal managers to move among bureaus and agencies in order to develop a more comprehensive view of the public interest; and third, political executives need greater flexibility in assigning and directing top, career civil servants. The SES differs from most of the federal civil service in that rank is essentially vested in the person, not the position. Consequently, reassignments, transfers, and changes in the content of their jobs are not treated as promotions or demotions subject to complicated personnel rules or adverse-action procedures. However, involuntary transfers between agencies are prohibited. Members of the SES are eligible for bonuses and cash awards based on performance. They retain fallback rights to positions at the GS 15 level.

6. A minority recruitment program was established within OPM. Unlike earlier equal-opportunity measures, which were mostly based on executive orders, the reform act included the policy that the federal work force should reflect the nation's diversity and be drawn from all segments of society. It established the principle that there should be no "underrepresentation" of minority groups in any category of federal employment. Although not part of the act, the Civil Service Commission's adjudicatory functions and some oversight authority for equal employment opportunity within the civil service were transferred to the Equal Employment Opportunity Commission in 1979.

7. The Office of Personnel Management was given authority to suspend many personnel regulations in order to permit the development and implementation of personnel research and demonstration projects. These can involve up to five thousand employees and last up to five years.

8. The civil service was to make greater use of performance-appraisal systems and merit pay. The latter was for those in management positions in GS 13 to 15 (subsequently labeled "GM" positions). These provisions reflected the belief that the civil-service system was inadequate at motivating employees and punishing them for poor performance. Both performance appraisal and merit pay have been difficult to implement,

however, and they have undergone almost continual revision.

Issues of Concern

The civil service has always been a matter of political concern. With some three million federal civil servants and approximately fourteen million state and local government employees in the 1990s, the size and cost of the civil service are constant issues. Efforts to control taxes and budget deficits often focus on reducing the size of the civil service and making it operate more efficiently. One leading strategy for so doing has been to "privatize" civil-service functions by contracting them out to private firms. Reducing government functions, either through deregulation or some other means, is a complementary approach.

President Jimmy Carter strongly believed that the federal bureaucracy was bloated, inefficient, and badly in need of reform.

The appropriate roles for legislatures, elected executives, and courts in regulating or directing the civil service is also an issue. In exercising its clear constitutional authority to oversee the executive branch, Congress can become deeply involved in civil-service decisions. When congressional oversight seems to be interference in legitimate agency decisions, it is often called micromanagement. For instance, a member of Congress, chairing a committee or subcommittee of strategic importance to an agency, may try to convince the agency to relocate many of its employees to his or her district.

The President can also seem to overstep the legitimate bounds of his authority over the civil service. For example, during the first administration of Ronald Reagan, there were well-publicized cases of members of the SES being involuntarily transferred geographically for political rather than administrative purposes. The number of political appointees within the executive branch also increased, and it was alleged that they were taking on functions that had previously been exercised by career civil servants.

Judicial decisions have had a major impact on civil-service examinations, hiring procedures, and dismissals. The courts have held that where civil-service rules provide job protection to civil servants they have a "property interest" in their jobs that is protected by constitutional due process, for example, *Cleveland Board of Education* v. *Loudermill* (1985). Examinations, hiring processes, and promotions are currently regulated by court decisions interpreting not only a variety of statutes but also the Constitution's equal-protection clause, for example, *United States* v. *Paradise* (1987).

Finally, the overall quality of the civil service has become an issue in the last few years. According to the National Commission on the Public Service (called the Volcker Commission, after its chair, Paul Volcker), the federal civil service is in need of "rebuilding." The main concern has been that after years of criticism by politicians and the press, low pay increases, limited training opportunities, and inability to recruit the talent it requires, the civil service has lost the capacity to serve the public interest as well as it should. Similar concerns, however, have often developed in the past. As a result, the civil service is almost always undergoing a variety of incremental reforms and has been subject to major reorganizations when these prove insufficient.

[See also (I) Bureaucracy, Separation of Powers.]

BIBLIOGRAPHY

Ingraham, Patricia, and David H. Rosenbloom. *The Promise and Paradox of Civil Service Reform.* 1992.

Mosher, Frederick. *Democracy and the Public Service.* 2d ed. 1982.

Shafritz, Jay, Norma Riccucci, David H. Rosenbloom, and Albert Hyde. *Personnel Management in Government.* 4th ed. 1992.

Skowronek, Stephen. *Building a New American State.* 1982.

Van Riper, Paul. *History of the United States Civil Service.* 1958.

— DAVID H. ROSENBLOOM

CLASSIFIED INFORMATION

Classified information encompasses a massive and continually growing amount of official secrets of the federal government. The classification system is designed to prevent the unauthorized disclosure of information that could cause damage to national security, broadly defined as the national defense and foreign relations of the United States. The contemporary system began in World War II and expanded during the cold war. Throughout much of the Reagan administration, the number of classification actions escalated dramatically. As of 1991, there were approximately seven million classification actions annually.

Secrecy in American History

The system has been dominated by the executive branch through a succession of executive orders. Ronald Reagan's 1982 Executive Order 12356 governs the system. In addition, a number of public laws support it both directly—by requiring protection for specific types of information and by funding the system—and indirectly, by providing penalties for espionage and related crimes. The inherent tension between official secrecy and democratic values, along with problems in the classification system itself, has resulted in major conflicts between the government and the press, among others, and between the executive and the legislature. With the end of the cold war, efforts to reduce the amount of classified information and change the system emerged in the executive, Congress, and the public.

Official secrecy has existed throughout the history of the United States. Presidents and other executive officials, particularly with regard to military matters and foreign diplomacy, have controlled access to national defense and foreign relations information based on constitutional authority, custom and experience, and perceived practical necessity. In discussing the President's power to negotiate treaties, for instance, John Jay wrote in *Federalist* 64 that "So often and so essentially have we heretofore suffered from the want of secrecy and dispatch that the Constitution would have been inexcusably defective if no attention had been paid to those objectives."

The inherent power of the President to classify information for national security purposes was affirmed by the Supreme Court in 1988: "The President, after all, is the 'Commander in Chief of the Army and Navy of the United States'. . . . His authority to classify and control access to information bearing on national security . . . flows primarily from this constitutional investment of power in the President and exists quite apart from any explicit congressional grant" (*U.S. Navy* v. *Egan*).

The inherent tension between official secrecy and democratic values has resulted in major conflicts between the government and the press.

The contemporary system for controlling national security information, which began with Franklin Roosevelt during World War II, is more formalized and institutionalized than its predecessors. It was established and revised by executive orders issued by Presidents: Franklin D. Roosevelt (E.O. 8381 in 1940); Harry S Truman (E.O. 10104 in 1950 and E.O. 10290 in 1951); Dwight D. Eisenhower (E.O. 10501 in 1953); Richard M. Nixon (E.O. 11652 in 1972); Jimmy Carter (E.O. 12065 in 1978); and Ronald Reagan (E.O. 12356 in 1982). The Bush and Clinton administrations also considered a revision but, as of mid 1992, had not issued a new order. These actual and contemplated revisions reflect differences in the Presidents' philosophies with regard to official secrecy, changes in the international environment, fluctuations in presidential-congressional relations, and competing pressures in the domestic arena coming from government agencies and private organizations.

Agencies and Categories

In addition to the executive controls, the classification system relies upon various public laws that require the protection of certain types of information, such as "restricted data," referring to nuclear weapons and special nuclear material (42 U.S.C. 2161–2169 and 2274). The National Security Act of 1947, which created the Central Intelligence Agency, moreover, requires the Director of the CIA to protect "intelligence sources and methods from unauthorized disclosure" (50 U.S.C. 403(d)(3)). The Freedom of Information Act (FOIA) also lends support to the system, by recognizing an exemption for matters that are "to be kept secret in the interest of national defense or foreign policy" and are properly classified (5 U.S.C. 552(b)). The operational files of the CIA, furthermore, may also be exempted from FOIA by the CIA Director (50 U.S.C. 431).

Other statutes reinforce the system indirectly, by setting requirements and penalties related to the unauthorized disclosure of classified information. These are found in laws dealing with the theft of government property, espionage, and other unauthorized disclosures (e.g., 18 U.S.C. 792–799). Incidentally, although Congress is frequently blamed for leaks to the press and inadvertent disclosures of classified information, the overwhelming majority of them, according to studies, are attributable to the executive branch, particularly high-ranking personnel.

The information security system is presently implemented by about eighty federal agencies that classify and handle national security information. Based on fiscal year 1991 data, original classification—that is, an initial determination that the information requires protection—accounts for only about 7 percent of the 7.1 million classification actions, while derivative classification, which results in a new form of classified information based on original classified materials, for nearly 93 percent. Nearly all the classified information is generated by four agencies, led by the Department of Defense, which, in fiscal year 1991, accounted for 61 percent (higher than the previous year's 50 percent because of the Persian Gulf War). The Department of Defense was followed by the Central Intelligence Agency, accounting for 26 percent; the Justice Department, 9 percent; and the State Department, 3 percent. Other organizations and entities that handle classified information range from the National Security Council

(NSC) to the Peace Corps, from the Office of National Drug Control Policy to the Marine Mammal Commission, and from the Department of Energy, which is responsible for the development of nuclear weapons, to the Department of Education. All follow classification and declassification directives from the Information Security Oversight Office (ISOO). ISOO, in turn, receives its policy and program direction from the NSC, a part of the Executive Office of the President.

National security information is to be controlled and safeguarded at three successively higher levels under E.O. 12356: "confidential" covers information whose unauthorized disclosure could cause damage to the national security; "secret," if it could cause serious damage to the national security; and "top secret," if it could cause exceptionally grave damage to the national security. Of the 7.1 million classification actions in fiscal year 1991, "confidential" accounted for 20 percent, "secret" for 73 percent, and "top secret" for 7 percent.

Specialized categories of classified information also exist. One of the most important is sensitive compartmented information (SCI), which covers intelligence sources and methods and is governed by a directive from the Director of the CIA. Another separate category encompasses special access programs (SAPs), which refer to military programs and weapons systems and collectively account for an estimated 24 percent of the military budget. Within SAPs are "black" programs, regarded as so sensitive that their very existence and purpose are classified.

Individual access to classified information is controlled by two basic means: First, the appropriate security clearance (or clearances for special categories, such as SCI) determines eligibility to a level and category of information; second, the need-to-know principle governs immediate access to specific information for individuals with the appropriate clearance; they are to demonstrate a legitimate need to know the information.

Amount of Classified Information

The precise amount of classified information is unknown. Even annual data are based only on estimates of classification actions and not on a direct count of the actual amount of information that is classified. Each classification action can vary from covering a single word, a name, or a sentence to covering a paragraph, a page, or an entire document. Consequently, the resulting statistics may be misleading. It is possible that the actual amount of classified information may increase from one year to the next even though the number of classification actions holds steady or even declines.

The increase in classified information was, in part, attributable to the size and growth of national security programs, reflected in the dramatic escalation of the defense and intelligence budgets in the 1980s. Because such spending has since declined or held constant, the amount of classified information generated by it has also stabilized. President Reagan's executive order, moreover, expanded the standards and criteria for classifying information and made declassification more difficult, compared to previous executive orders.

The precise amount of classified information is unknown.

In addition, the confidential level has long been criticized for being too vague, allowing for the classification of nonsensitive information. Another seemingly permanent condition—overclassification—adds to the amount of classified information and introduces its own set of problems. Since it refers to unwarranted or unnecessary classification in violation of the provisions of the executive orders, overclassification not only results in more information being classified than should be, but it also perverts the classification system, by using it to hide administrative defects, policy disputes and misjudgments, and even unethical or illegal activities. Some of these problems were exposed in the famous 1971 Pentagon Papers case, dealing with the publication of documents connected with the Vietnam War; inquiries in the mid 1970s into intelligence community abuses; and investigations of the 1985–1986 Iran-contra affair. Finally, a failure to declassify information on any set schedule contributes to the total amount of classified information continuing at an unnecessarily high level.

[See also (I) Secrecy of Congress; (II) Executive Orders.]

BIBLIOGRAPHY

Abel, Elie. *Leaking: Who Does It? Who Benefits? At What Cost?* 1987.

Edgar, Harold, and Benno C. Schmidt, Jr. "*Curtiss-Wright* Comes Home: Executive Power and National Security Secrecy." *Harvard Civil Rights—Civil Liberties Review* 21 (1986): 349–408.

Kaiser, Frederick M. "The Amount of Classified Information: Causes, Consequences, and Correctives of a Growing Concern." *Government Information Quarterly* 6 (1989): 247–266.

Relyea, Harold, ed. Symposium on "Protecting National Security Information: An Overview of Federal Policy and Practice." *Government Information Quarterly* 1 (1984): 113–208.

Rourke, Francis E. *Secrecy and Publicity: Dilemmas of Democracy.* 1966.

Shattuck, John, and Muriel Morisey Spence. *Government Information Controls Implications for Scholarship, Science and Technology.* 1987.

U.S. House of Representatives. Committee on Government Operations. *Security Classification Policy and Executive Order 12356.* H.R. 97-731. 97th Cong., 2d Sess. 1982.

U.S. Information Security Oversight Office. *Annual Reports.* 1978–present.

– FREDERICK M. KAISER

COAST GUARD

The United States Coast Guard has undergone substantial evolution in both name and functions since it began in 1790 as the Revenue Cutter Service (also known as the Revenue Marine Service) within the Department of the Treasury. Initially, its only responsibility was to collect revenues for the Customs Service. However, since its founding, the Coast Guard and its missions have been gradually broadened through many statutes that reflect Congress's and the country's strong commitment to this agency.

In 1790, the Department of the Treasury was authorized by the First Congress to acquire not more than ten cutters, which were to be used for the collection of "the duties imposed by law on goods, wares and merchandise imported into the United States, and on the tonnage of ships or vessels." In 1797, with a war against France threatening, Congress expanded the Revenue Cutter Service's responsibilities to include authority, at the direction of the President, "to defend the sea coast and to repel any hostility to their vessels." Thereafter, until an enlarged Coast Guard was formed in 1915, the missions assigned to the Revenue Cutter Service grew to include many of the traditional missions that the Coast Guard currently exercises, including interdiction of illegal immigrants, rescue at sea, fisheries enforcement, enforcement of navigation regulations, and service as part of the military force protecting the U.S. coastline.

Several proposals were put forward in the 1790s to transfer the Revenue Cutter Service to the navy. Although none were adopted, Congress in 1799 enacted legislation that placed the Coast Guard under the navy's control during a declaration of war. In both world wars, the Coast Guard was transferred to the navy by executive order of the President. In addition, although not officially transferred to the navy, the Coast Guard played an important role in the Korean, Vietnam, and Persian Gulf wars.

Apart from the Revenue Cutter Service, a separate lifesaving service existed from 1837 until its merger into the Coast Guard in 1915. It began as a series of lighthouses, with later appropriations for rescue boats. In 1878 an act was passed providing for the appointment of a general superintendent of the Life-Saving Service, a separate appointment of a gulf coast superintendent, rates of compensation and duties, the schedule of times when lifesaving stations would be open, and support for the service.

In 1915 Congress officially established the Coast Guard under its current designation. The Revenue Cutter Service was merged with the Life-Saving Service in the new Coast Guard, which was in the Department of the Treasury. The president retained the authority to transfer the Coast Guard to the navy in time of war. When the Department of Transportation was established in 1967, the Coast Guard was transferred to that agency because of the Coast Guard's important role in maritime transportation.

In recent years, the Coast Guard's duties have been expanded to encompass a broad array of domestic law-enforcement missions, search-and-rescue functions, military readiness operations, marine environmental protection responsibilities, the maintenance of aids for safe navigation, and many more.

Congress exercises legislative and oversight control of the Coast Guard through several standing committees. Authorization bills are the jurisdiction of the House Merchant Marine and Fisheries Committee, through its Subcommittee on Coast Guard and Navigation, and of the Senate Committee on Commerce, Science, and Transportation, through its National Ocean Policy Study Subcommittee. Funding proposals for the Coast Guard must go through the House Appropriations Subcommittee on Transportation and Related Agencies.

Major acts giving additional responsibilities to the Coast Guard under the Department of Transportation include:

Natural Gas Pipeline Safety Act of 1968
Recreational Boating Fund Act, as amended by the Federal Boat Safety Act of 1971
Ocean Dumping Act of 1972
Ports and Waterways Safety Act of 1972
Trans-Alaska Pipeline Authorization Act of 1973
Deepwater Port Act of 1974
Intervention on the High Seas Act of 1974
Hazardous Materials Transportation Act of 1975
Fishery Conservation and Management Act of 1976 (Magnuson Fishery Conservation and Management Act)
Federal Water Pollution Control Act Amendments of 1977
Outer Continental Shelf Lands Act Amendments of 1978
Port Tanker Safety Act of 1978
Hazardous Liquid Pipeline Safety Act of 1979
An Act to Prevent Pollution from Ships of 1980
Maritime Drug Law Enforcement Act of 1980
Omnibus Diplomatic Security and Antiterrorism Act of 1986
Anti-Drug Abuse Act of 1986
Marine Plastic Pollution Research and Control Act of 1987
Anti-Drug Abuse Amendments Act of 1988
Oil Pollution Act of 1990

Abandoned Barge Act of 1992
Passenger Vessel Safety Act of 1993

[See also (II) Transportation, Department of.]

BIBLIOGRAPHY

U.S. House of Representatives. *Report on the Activities of the Merchant Marine and Fisheries Committee.* 102d Cong., 1992. H. Rep. 102–1092.

U.S. Senate. Committee on Commerce, Science, and Transportation. *The U.S. Coast Guard.* 97th Cong., 2d sess., 1982.

– ELIZABETH R. MEGGINSON

COMMANDER IN CHIEF

Article II, Section 2, of the Constitution provides that "the President shall be Commander in Chief of the Army and Navy of the United States, and of the Militia of the several States, when called into the actual Service of the United States." In *Youngstown Sheet & Tube Co.* v. *Sawyer* (1952), Justice Robert H. Jackson condemned as "sinister and alarming" the invocation of the Commander in Chief clause as a source of presidential "power to do anything, anywhere, that can be done with an army or navy." While stated in the context of reviewing President Harry S Truman's invocation of the clause to support his seizure of the steel mills, Jackson's observations certainly anticipated the claims of later executives, from Lyndon B. Johnson to George Bush, who carelessly invoked the provision as justification for their military adventures. The clause also has become the principal pillar for those commentators who hope to vest the constitutional power of war and peace in the President. The title of Commander in Chief, however, confers no warmaking power whatever, nor does it afford the President any general foreign policy powers. Understood by the Framers of the Constitution in narrow terms, the title vests in the President only the authority to repel sudden attacks on the United States and to conduct war when so authorized by Congress. In this capacity, the President is responsible for directing those forces placed at his command by an act of Congress, which is vested by the Constitution with the sole and exclusive power to decide for war.

Separation of Powers

The Constitutional Convention severed the authority to decide for war from the power to conduct it. The Framers' decision to withhold from the President the power to commence war signaled a marked departure from the existing models of government that placed the war power, indeed virtually all foreign affairs powers, in the hands of the executive. In *The Second Treatise of Government* (1690), John Locke had described three branches of government: legislative, executive, and federative. According to Locke, the federative power, or what we today refer to as the power to conduct foreign affairs, encompassed "the power of war and peace, leagues and alliances, and all the transactions with all persons and communities without the commonwealth." The power, moreover, was "almost always united" with the executive. The separation of the executive and federative powers, Locke warned, would bring "disorder and ruin." Similarly, Sir William Blackstone, in his distinguished *Commentaries on the Laws of England* (1765–1769), had explained that the king enjoyed absolute power over foreign affairs and war: the authority to send and receive ambassadors, make treaties and alliances, make war or peace, issue letters of marque and reprisal, command the military, raise and regulate fleets and armies, and represent the nation in its intercourse with foreign governments.

James Madison and other Framers of the Constitution decided to withhold from the President the power to commence war. (Library of Congress, Prints and Photographs Division)

Despite their familiarity with the English scheme of governance, the Framers granted Congress most of the nation's foreign affairs powers. Congress was vested with the sole and exclusive authority to initiate war. The Constitution withheld from the President the sole power to make treaties, making him share that power with the Senate. James Madison and Alexander Hamilton referred to this combination as a "fourth branch" of government, which they expected would manage most of the country's foreign policy responsibilities. The President was granted the authority to receive ambassadors, an act that entails important international legal obligations. But the founding trio of Hamilton, Madison, and Thomas Jefferson did not view the reception or "recognition" clause as a font of discretionary executive power to decide whether the United States would have relations with other nations or to determine unilaterally the tone and temper of those relations. Rather, the Framers understood the recognition power as a narrow, clerklike function or duty imposed as a matter of convenience on the President, rather than Congress, to carry out the nation's obligation under international law to receive ambassadors from sovereign countries. The President was granted the authority to send ambassadors abroad but only after the Senate approved his nominations. He was not vested with the monarchical power to issue letters of marque and reprisal; that power was granted to Congress. Nor was he given the authority to raise and regulate fleets and armies. That power, too, was left with Congress. Finally, Congress was also granted plenary authority over foreign commerce.

The Debate over the War Power

The Framers' decision to grant Congress the war power is illuminated by the debates at the Constitutional Convention. An early draft reported by the Committee of Detail vested Congress with the power to "make war." This bore sharp resemblance to the Articles of Confederation, which had placed the "sole and exclusive right and power of determining on peace and war" in the Continental Congress. Charles Pinckney, who expected Congress to meet only once a year, objected to the plan because he thought the legislative proceedings "were too slow" to protect the security interests of the nation. The draft also proved unsatisfactory to Madison and Elbridge Gerry. In a joint resolution, they moved to substitute "declare" for "make," "leaving to the Executive the power to repel sudden attacks." The meaning of the motion is unmistakable. Congress was granted the power to make—that is, to initiate—war; the President, for obvious reasons, would be empowered to act immediately to repel sudden attacks without authorization from Congress. There was no quarrel whatever with respect to the sudden attack provision, but there was some question as to whether the substitution of "declare" for "make" would effectuate the intention of Madison and Gerry. Roger Sherman of Connecticut thought the joint motion "stood very well," saying, "The Executive shd. be able to repel and not commence war. 'Make' better than 'declare' the latter narrowing the power [of the legislature] too much." Virginia's George Mason "was agst. giving the power of war to the Executive, because [he was] not [safely] to be trusted with it; or to the Senate, because [it was] not so constructed as to be entitled to it. He was for clogging rather than facilitating war; but for facilitating peace. He preferred 'declare' to 'make.' " The Madison-Gerry proposal was adopted by a vote of 7 to 2. When Rufus King explained that the word "make" might be understood to authorize Congress to initiate as well as conduct war, Connecticut changed its vote so that the word "declare" was approved, eight states to one.

The debates and the vote on the war power make it clear that Congress alone possesses the authority to initiate war. The war-making power was specifically withheld from the President; he was given only the authority to repel sudden attacks. James Wilson, who played a role only slightly less important than Madison's in the Constitutional Convention, told the Pennsylvania ratifying convention: "This system will not hurry us into war; it is calculated to guard against it. It will not be in the power of a single man . . . to involve us in such distress; for the important power of declaring war is vested in the legislature at large." Similar assurances were provided to other state ratifying conventions.

The Constitutional Convention's rejection of prevailing governmental models for foreign affairs is attributable to two principal factors. First, the Framers were attached to republican ideology, the core principle of which was collective decision making in domestic as well as foreign affairs. Second, the founding generation, influenced by its own experience under King George III and by its understanding of history, lived in fear of a powerful executive and was adamantly opposed to a President's unilateral control of foreign policy. History had its claims. In *Federalist* 75 Hamilton stated, "The history of human conduct does not warrant that exalted opinion of human virtue which would make it wise in a nation to commit interests of so delicate and momentous a kind, as those which concern its intercourse with the rest of the world, to the sole disposal of . . . a President." In a letter to Jefferson in 1798, Madison observed "The constitution supposes, what the History of all Govts demonstrates, that the Ex. is the branch of power most interested in war, & most prone to it. It has accordingly with studied care, vested the question of war in the Legisl." The Framers' decision to create a radically new blueprint for the conduct of foreign affairs justified Wilson's remark that it was incorrect to consider "the Prerogatives of the British Monarch as a proper guide in defining the Executive powers. Some of these prerogatives were of a Legislative nature. Among others that of war & peace."

The separation of the power to initiate war from the power to conduct it reflected the interplay of different values. The decision to commence war requires the most solemn, deliberative debate. It emphasizes the values of collective decision making. But the decision actually to conduct a war, to determine strategy and tactics, pivots on a different value, that of efficiency. In *Federalist* 74, Hamilton adduced the basic reason for making the President Commander in Chief: the direction of war "most peculiarly demands those qualities which distinguish the exercise of power by a single hand." The power of directing war and emphasizing the common strength "forms a usual and essential part in the definition of the executive authority."

The English and Colonial Legacy

While the Framers rejected the Locke-Blackstone model for foreign affairs, they nevertheless drew their concept of the Commander in Chief directly from English history. As Francis D. Wormuth observed, "The office of commander in chief has never carried the power of war and peace, nor was it invented by the framers of the Constitution." The title of Commander in Chief was introduced by King Charles I in 1639 and was always used as a generic term referring to the highest officer in a particular chain of command. With the eruption of the English civil wars, both the king and Parliament appointed commanders in chief in various theaters of action. The ranking commander in chief, purely a military post, was always under the command of a political superior, whether appointed by the king, Parliament or, with the development of the cabinet system in the eighteenth century, by the secretary of war.

England transplanted the title to America in the eighteenth century by appointing a number of commanders in chief and by the practice of entitling colonial governors as commanders in chief (or occasionally as vice admirals or captains general). The appointment of General Thomas Gage as commander in chief from 1763 to 1776 caused the colonists grave concern, for he proceeded to interfere in civil affairs and acquired considerable influence over Indian relations, trade, and transportation. The bitter memory of his decision to quarter troops in civilians' homes spawned the Third Amendment to the Constitution. These activities and others prompted the colonists in the Declaration of Independence to complain of King George III that he had "affected to render the Military Independent of and superior to the Civil Power."

But the colonists had no reason to fear the governors who were given the title commander in chief, even though they controlled the provincial forces, since the colonial assemblies claimed and asserted the right to vote funds for the militia as well as to call it into service. In fact, grievances came from the governors, who complained of the relative impotence of their positions. The colonists' assemblies' (and later, the states') assertions of the power of the purse as a check on the commander in chief reflected an English practice that was instituted in the middle of the seventeenth century. By 1665, Parliament, as a means of maintaining political control of the military establishment, had inaugurated the policy of making annual military appropriations lasting but one year. This practice sharply emphasized the power of Parliament to determine the size of the army to be placed under the direction of the commander in chief.

The practice had a long influence, for, under its constitutional power to raise and support armies and to provide a navy, Congress acquired the right that the colonial and state assemblies had had to vote funds for the armed forces. An additional historical parallel in the Article I, Section 8, clause 13 provides that "no Appropriation of Money to that Use shall be for a longer Term than two Years." The requirement of legislative approval for the allocation of funds to raise troops underscores the principle of political superiority over military command. It also constitutes a sharp reminder that a Commander in Chief is dependent on the legislature's willingness to give him an army to command.

Most of the early state constitutions followed the colonial practice of making the governor commander in chief under the authority of state legislatures. For example, article VII of the Massachusetts constitution of 1780 provided that the governor would be "commander in chief of the army and navy." In carefully circumscribing his power, the governor was to "repel, resist [and] expel" attempts to invade the commonwealth, and was vested "with all these and other powers incident to the offices of captain general . . . to be exercised agreeably to the rules and regulations of the Constitution and the laws of the land, and not otherwise."

Early Presidents often refused to initiate hostilities without prior authorization from Congress.

The Continental Congress continued the usage of the title in 1775, when it unanimously decided to appoint George Washington as general. His commission named him "General and Commander in Chief, of the Army of the United Colonies." He was required to comply with orders and directions from Congress, which did not hesitate to instruct the commander in chief on military and policy matters.

The practice of entitling the office at the apex of the military hierarchy as commander in chief and of subordinating the office to a political superior, whether a king, a parliament, or a congress, had thus been firmly established for a century and a half and was thoroughly familiar to the Framers when they met in Philadelphia. Perhaps this settled historical usage accounts for the fact that there was no debate on the Commander in Chief clause at the Convention.

In the plan he read to the convention on 29 May 1787, South Carolinian Charles Pinckney introduced the title of President and proposed, "He shall, by Virtue of his Office, be Commander in Chief of the Land Forces of U.S. and Admiral of their Navy." Presumably, Pinckney had drawn on the traditional usage of the title employed in the South Carolina constitution of 1776, which had provided for a "president and commander-in-chief," and that of 1778, which had included a provision for a "governor and commander in chief." There was no such provision in the Randolph (or Virginia) Plan, which was read to the convention on the same day. On 15 June William Paterson submitted the New Jersey Plan, which called for a plural executive. It provided that "the Executives . . . ought . . . to direct all military operations; provided that none of the persons composing the federal executive shall at any time take command of any troops, so as personally to conduct any enterprise as General, or in other capacity." The qualifying clause was meant to discourage a military takeover of the government. When Hamilton submitted a plan to the convention on 18 June he probably did not propose the title Commander in Chief, but he undoubtedly had it in mind when he said the President was "to have the direction of war when authorized or begun."

Hamilton's speech summarized the essence of the President's powers as Commander in Chief: when war is "authorized or begun," the President is to command the military operations of American forces. He elaborated on this theme and sharply distinguished the powers of the king and those of the President in *Federalist* 69. While the power of the king includes the power to declare war and to raise and regulate fleets and armies, those powers, explained Hamilton, would be vested in Congress "by the Constitution under consideration." The President, as Commander in Chief, was to be "first General and admiral" in the "direction of war when authorized or begun." But all political authority remained in Congress, as it had under the Articles of Confederation.

Nineteenth-Century Practice

Nineteenth-century presidential practice and judicial decisions reaffirmed this understanding of the war power and the President's role as Commander in Chief. Early Presidents often refused to initiate hostilities without prior authorization from Congress. In 1792 and 1793, President Washington received urgent requests for the use of military force from governors who feared impending attacks by Indians. Washington stated that he had no authority to order an attack and deferred the issue to Congress, "who solely are vested with the powers of war." Contrary to the charge that President John Adams acted unilaterally in the Quasi-War with France of 1798–1800, Congress, in fact, passed some twenty laws to authorize the war. In *Bas* v. *Tingy* (1800), the Supreme Court held that those statutes had authorized imperfect, or limited, war. In *Talbot* v. *Seeman* (1801), a case that involved issues raised by the quasi-war, Chief Justice John Marshall held that since the "whole powers of war" are "vested in Congress," it is for that body alone to authorize perfect or imperfect war. In *Little* v. *Barreme* (1804), Marshall emphasized that the President, as Commander in Chief, is subject to statutory restriction. One of the statutes passed by Congress during the Quasi-War with France authorized the President to seize vessels that sailed *to* French ports. But President Adams ordered American ships to capture vessels that sailed *to or from* French ports, and, in his opinion for the Court, Marshall held that Adams's order had violated the statute. Subsequent judicial rulings have reiterated that the Commander in Chief may be controlled by statute.

President Thomas Jefferson understood the limitations of the Commander in Chief clause. In 1801, in his first annual message to Congress, he reported the arrogant demands made by Joseph Caramanly, the pasha of Tripoli. Unless the United States paid tribute, the pasha threatened to seize American ships and citizens. In response, Jefferson sent a small squadron to the Mediterranean to protect against the threatened attack. He then asked Congress for further guidance, since he was "unauthorized by the Constitution, without the sanction of Congress, to go beyond the line of defense." It was left to Congress to authorize "measures of offense." Jefferson's understanding of the war clause underwent no revision. Like Jefferson, President James Madison was aggrieved by the punishment and harassment inflicted on United States vessels. In 1812, he expressed to Congress his extreme resentment of the British practices of seizing American ships and seamen and inducing Indian tribes to attack the United States. Madison complained but said the question of "whether the United States shall remain passive under these progressive usurpations and these accumulating wrongs, or, opposing force, to force in defense of their national rights" is "a solemn question which the Constitution wisely confides to the legislative department of the Government." Following his 1823 announcement of what has become known as the Monroe Doctrine, President James Monroe was confronted with international circumstances that seemed to invite the use of force, but Monroe repeatedly disclaimed any constitutional power to initiate hostilities, since, he maintained, that authority was granted to Congress. President James K. Polk may well have initiated war with Mexico in 1846, when he ordered an army into a disputed area on the Texas-Mexico border. But Polk understood the constitutional dimensions of the war power and offered the rationale that Mexico had invaded the United States, which, if true, would justify a response by the Commander in Chief. It is noteworthy that he did not adduce a presidential power to initiate war. None of President Abraham Lincoln's actions in the Civil War involved a claim to a presidential power to initiate war. In the Prize Cases (1863), the Supreme Court upheld Lincoln's blockade against the rebellious Confederacy as a constitutional response to sudden invasion, which began with the attack on Fort Sumter. In the opinion for the Court, Justice Robert Grier stated that, as Commander in Chief, the President "has no power to initiate or declare war either against a foreign nation or a domestic State."

Presidential Warmaking

Until 1950, no President departed from this understanding of the parameters of the Commander in Chief clause. But to justify President Truman's unilateral decision to introduce troops into the Korean War, revisionists purported to locate in the President a broad discretionary authority to commence hostilities. Emboldened by Truman's claim, subsequent Presidents have likewise unilaterally initiated acts of war, from the Vietnam War to the incursions in Grenada and Panama. But this claim is cut from whole cloth. It ignores the origins and development of the title, the clear understanding of the Constitution's Framers, the nineteenth-century record, and the history of judicial interpretation. The Supreme Court has never held that the Commander in Chief clause confers power to initiate war. In *United States* v. *Sweeny* (1895), Justice Henry Brown wrote for the Court that the object of the clause was to give the President "such supreme and undivided command as would be necessary to the prosecution of a successful war." In 1919, Senator George Sutherland, who later became an Associate Justice of the Supreme Court, wrote, "Generally speaking, the war powers of the President under the Constitution are simply those that belong to any commander-in-chief of the military forces of a nation at war. The Constitution confers no war powers upon the President as such."

While the Supreme Court has held that the President may not initiate hostilities and that he is authorized only to direct the movements of the military forces placed by law at his command, it has been contended that the existence of a standing army provides the President with broad discretionary authority to deploy troops on behalf of foreign-policy goals. Although the intrusion of a public force into a foreign country may well entangle the United States in a war, Presidents have often manipulated troop deployments so as to present Congress with a fait accompli. Given the broad range of war powers vested in Congress, including the authority to provide for the common defense, to raise and support armies, and to decide, in Madison's words, whether "a war ought to be commenced, continued or concluded," it seems clear that Congress may govern absolutely the deployment of forces outside U.S. borders. As a practical measure, Congress may choose, within the confines of the delegation doctrine, to vest the President with some authority to send troops abroad, but there is nothing inherent in the Commander in Chief clause that yields such authority.

[See also (I) Congress, article on Powers of Congress; (II) Declaration of War.]

BIBLIOGRAPHY

Adler, David Gray. "The Constitution and Presidential Warmaking: The Enduring Debate." *Political Science Quarterly* 103 (1988): 1–36.

Berger, Raoul. *Executive Privilege: A Constitutional Myth.* 1974.

Fisher, Louis. *Constitutional Conflicts between Congress and the President.* 3d rev. ed. 1991.

Henkin, Louis. *Foreign Affairs and the Constitution.* 1972.

Keynes, Edward. *Undeclared War: Twilight Zone of Constitutional Power.* 2d. ed 1991.

Koh, Harold. *The National Security Constitution: Sharing Power after the Iran-Contra Affair.* 1990.

Robinson, Donald L. *To the Best of My Ability: The Presidency and the Constitution.* 1987.

Schlesinger, Arthur, Jr. *The Imperial Presidency.* 1973.

Wormuth, Francis D., and Edwin B. Firmage. *To Chain the Dog of War: The War Power of Congress in History and Law.* 1986.

– DAVID GRAY ADLER

COMMERCE, DEPARTMENT OF

The modern Department of Commerce was established under the administration of President William Howard Taft on 4 March 1913. Signed on Taft's last day in office, the act establishing the department was one of the final actions of his presidency. After more than a century of debate and deliberation, which consumed the thought and energy of Presidents from George Washington on, the commerce and manufacturing sectors in the United States finally had an executive department they could call their own.

At the Constitutional Convention,

a recommendation was made

that there be a secretary of commerce to promote

the commercial interests of the United States.

Yet it was not a President in office but a President-to-be, Herbert Hoover, who, during his tenure as Secretary of Commerce in the 1920s, saw the potential of the post and of the department to have wide-ranging and significant impact on U.S. domestic and international policy. The Commerce Department, which became the primary government entity responsible for fostering and promoting U.S. agendas for international trade, economic growth, and technological advancement was molded into the vehicle for doing so through the vision and actions of the "domestic dynamo" Hoover.

Origins

As early as 1787, at the Constitutional Convention, a recommendation was made that there be a secretary of commerce and finance to help the new government and new national executive administer and promote the commercial interests of the United States. This followed on the heels of Alexander Hamilton's proposition, cosigned by James Madison and Edmund Randolph at a historical meeting in Annapolis, that matters of trade and commerce be addressed comprehensively by the federal government.

The importance of commerce to the maturation of a young nation was clearly recognized. The Framers cited the promotion of the general welfare—in part another way of saying the promotion of commercial interests—as essential to the formation of a more perfect union. Washington, in his first inaugural address, said, "The advance of agriculture, commerce and manufactures by all proper means will not, I trust, need recommendation." Yet the question remained which department within the federal government should handle the new nation's commercial affairs. Ultimately, the charge went to the Treasury Department, while a committee of commerce and manufacturing was established by the House of Representatives in 1795. It was not until almost a century later that substantive action was taken toward creating a formal department expressly devoted to commerce.

Largely owing to President William McKinley's policy of actively promoting exports (exports exceeded $1 billion for the first time during McKinley's presidency), Theodore Roosevelt was able to recommend and accomplish the creation of a combined Department of Commerce and Labor. On 14 February 1903, Congress approved legislation creating such a department, with Roosevelt nominating his personal secretary, George B. Cortelyou, as the first secretary. The Department survived in its combined form through the Taft term, but with markets expanding at home and abroad, and with labor interests demanding a department of their own the formulation of a separate and distinct Department of Commerce was accomplished.

The new restructured department, which Woodrow Wilson then presided over, was composed of the following entities: the Coast and Geodetic Survey; the Steamboat Inspection Service; and the bureaus of Corporations, Census, Lighthouses, Standards, Navigation, Fisheries, and Foreign and Domestic Commerce. The bureaus within the department were almost completely different by the time of the presidency of Bill Clinton, exemplifying both the growth of government and the commercial changes that the United States had undergone during the previous six decades. In 1993 the department comprised the Office of Secretary and the following units: the Bureau of the Census, the Bureau of Economic Analysis, the Bureau of Export Administration, the Economic Development Administration, the International Trade Administration, the Minority Business Administration, the National Oceanic and Atmospheric Administration, the National Telecommunications and Information Administration, the Patent and Trademark Office, the National Institute of Standards and Technology, the National Technical Information Service, and the U.S. Tourism Administration.

The Hoover Era

By far the most substantive changes to the department occurred during Hoover's years as Commerce Secretary. In 1924, Hoover summarized his ultimate goal as the restructuring of the department "to change the attitude of government relations with business from that of interference to that of cooperation." Believing that government should not meddle in corporate affairs and thus make itself a burden to business, Hoover saw in the Commerce Department a vehicle for promoting and encouraging commercial activity. He saw the department as a service center, with U.S. business as its primary customer.

Hoover's tenure at Commerce showcased many of his talents. Though he would, as President, be criticized for inaction and indecisive leadership in the face of the Great Depression, Hoover's Commerce years showed him to be a man of progressive ideas capable of engineering change. Always searching for "a middle way . . . between monopoly and state socialism," Hoover used the Commerce Department to experiment with the optimum bureaucratic structure ("associationalism") for the post–World War I environment.

The first change Hoover accomplished was to gain President Warren G. Harding's promise to give the Commerce Secretary a voice not just in matters of commerce but in all economic issues of importance. From this beginning, Hoover worked to elevate the stature of the department further. Recognizing that the scope of the department's activities was dictated by the size of its budget, Hoover lobbied for and received a larger share of the budgetary pie. Between 1921 and 1928, at a time when other departmental budgets were shrinking, Commerce's budget increased from $860,000 to more than $38 million. Staff rolls swelled as well, as Hoover hired more than three thousand new employees.

Hoover worked to limit red tape and the duplication of duties. Further, he filled posts with experts who understood the postwar situation. This new blood is credited with turning the Census Bureau into a first-rate statistical bureau and for enabling Commerce to carry out extensive public education programs. Hoover and his staff put forward a steady stream of ideas, both radical and practical. In recognition of Hoover's impact, the central Department of Commerce building, located between 14th and 15th Streets and Pennsylvania and Constitution Avenues in Washington, D.C., was renamed the Herbert Clark Hoover Building in 1982.

Retrenchment and Constant Revision

Under Hoover's presidency, the high-profile activities of the Department of Commerce continued, but Franklin D. Roosevelt's defeat of Hoover brought about a drastic reduction in department activities. Because the department was almost a Hoover invention, there was even talk during the beginning of the Roosevelt administration of abolishing it altogether, but, instead, Roosevelt transferred primary responsibility for his business recovery programs to other areas of government, effectively breaking up the bureaucratic empire that Hoover had organized. The Bureau of Air Commerce was transferred to the Civil Aeronautics Authority; the Bureau of Lighthouses was made part of the Coast Guard, under the authority of the Treasury Department; and Domestic Commerce was even transferred to the Department of State.

Roosevelt's and subsequent administrations continued the constant shifting of bureaus from one Cabinet-level department to another. In 1940, the Weather Service became a Commerce entity; the Civil Aeronautics Authority (renamed the Civil Aeronautics Administration) bounced back from its short-term home at Treasury. Under Harry S Truman, the Bureau of Public Roads was moved to Commerce; the Maritime Administration followed in 1950. It was the Commerce Department that implemented Dwight D. Eisenhower's plan for an interstate highway system in the 1950s, but by the end of the 1960s highways and other land transportation had been moved to the newly created Department of Transportation. The Civil Rights Act of 1964 installed a Community Relations Service as part of the department, but two years later the agency was shifted to the Department of Justice. In the early 1970s, Commerce claimed control of the National Fire Prevention and Control Administration, but in 1979 control of that agency shifted to the newly created Federal Emergency Management Administration (FEMA).

Both the Reagan and Bush administrations were champions not only of free trade, but of fair trade with other nations.

During the Nixon administration the department saw another period of significant change, with greater emphasis being placed on international issues, and fervent cultivation of commercial opportunities abroad. This period also saw Commerce initiate a minority business program and establish an ombudsman for business.

The Department's role in international trade and domestic economic affairs was again pushed into the limelight during the Reagan administration, under the direction of Secretary Malcomb Baldridge. An extremely capable administrator, Baldridge championed quality in U.S. business. He was determined to keep America competitive internationally and used the Commerce Department to that end. He chaired a Cabinet-level Trade Strike Force to deal with unfair trade practices, and he made the department the lead player in supporting and implementing the Export Trading Company Act of 1982. Both the Reagan and George Bush administrations were champions not only of free trade, but of fair trade with other nations, painstakingly negotiating with the world community to exact a trade agenda that would be satisfactory to U.S. commercial interests in an increasingly global economy.

BIBLIOGRAPHY

Ambrose, Stephen B. *Nixon, Ruin and Recovery 1973–1990.* 1991.
Bartley, Robert L. *The Seven Fat Years.* 1992.
Bowers, Helen. *From Lighthouses to Lasers: A History of the U.S. Department of Commerce.* 1988.
Kennedy, Paul. *The Rise and Fall of the Great Powers.* 1987.
Smith, Richard Norton. *An Uncommon Man: The Triumph of Herbert Hoover.* 1984.
Wilson, Joan Hoff. *Herbert Hoover, Forgotten Progressive.* 1975.

– PETER CHANDLER

COMMISSIONS, PRESIDENTIAL

The need for impartial information for policy making and political judgment has been a constant thread throughout the history of the presidency, and advisory commissions have been a part of the process of gathering information.

Commissions in History

President George Washington appointed a commission to investigate and attempt to mediate settlement of the Whiskey Rebellion, a revolt of western Pennsylvania farmers against a federal tax on spirits. The fact that the commission was unsuccessful in settling the situation neither deterred Washington from praising the body's efforts nor kept future Presidents from turning to commissions for guidance.

President Martin Van Buren sent commissions to study European postal systems and armies, and President Andrew Jackson appointed a commission to investigate the Navy Department. When President John Tyler appointed a commission to examine the New York customhouse, in 1841, Congress challenged his action. Tyler claimed constitutional authority for the appointment of commissions under Article II, Section 3, which states that the President shall "take Care that the Laws be faithfully executed" and "give to the Congress Information of the State of the Union, and recommend to their Consideration such Measures as he shall judge necessary and expedient."

Early in the twentieth century Theodore Roosevelt imparted a visibility and vitality to the use of commissions, contributing to their evolution as a tool for policy development and public education. His commissions on conservation, public lands, inland waterways, and country life focused national attention on the intelligent use of natural resources. Roosevelt actually participated in some commission activities and vigorously promoted commission reports. In response to his appointment of extralegal, unsalaried commissions to study social and economic issues, Congress passed legislation in 1909 that prohibited the appointment of commissions that lacked legislative authority (35 Stat. 1023).

The administrations of Presidents Franklin D. Roosevelt, Harry S Truman, and Dwight D. Eisenhower saw the appointment of noteworthy commissions on government management and organization, with former President Herbert Hoover chairing the two Hoover Commissions, under Truman and Eisenhower, respectively.

The 1960s and early 1970s—a period of profound change, turmoil, and social questioning in the United States—saw the employment of commissions in the examination of deeply troubling national issues under the administrations of Lyndon B. Johnson and Richard M. Nixon. Some commission reports became, themselves, part of the national debate and influenced national thinking. The President's Commission on the Assassination of President Kennedy (referred to as the Warren Commission, after its chairman, Chief Justice Earl Warren), the National Advisory Commission on Civil Disorders (known as the Kerner Commission, for its chairman, Otto Kerner, governor of Illinois), and the President's Commission on Campus Unrest (the Scranton Commission, for chairman William Scranton, former governor of Pennsylvania) exemplified the highly visible, volatile nature of the commissions' subjects and their times. Other prominent commissions of the period explored crime, violence, obscenity and pornography, population growth, and drug abuse. In many cases these commissions offered unexpectedly provocative and controversial recommendations and critiques.

Controversy notwithstanding, use of commissions proceeded apace in subsequent decades, achieving attention during the Ronald Reagan presidency with investigations of the disastrous launch of the space shuttle *Challenger,* the Iran-contra affair (the Tower Commission), and the Presidential Commission on the Human Immunodeficiency Virus Epidemic (AIDS Commission).

Forms and Functions

Presidential advisory bodies take many forms, from specialized executive-level permanent committees and councils to task forces, White House conferences, and commissions. Presidential commissions are best known as investigatory bodies, established by the President or by Congress for the President's appointment, which within a defined area of inquiry seek out all relevant information, subject it to scrutiny and review, and arrange it in a written report containing considered recommendations for presidential, legislative, and/or social reform.

Commissions may be seen in a typological sense as situation-oriented, crisis-oriented, or procedure-oriented. Situation-oriented groups are directed at social conditions or phenomena, widely dispersed and of general relevance, for which new perspectives may be required. The President's Commission on Law Enforcement and the Administration of Justice (established 1965), the Commission on Population Growth and the American Future (1970), and the Commission on Obscenity and Pornography (1967) fall within this category.

Commissions offer a means of symbolic reassurance to the public that the President takes something seriously and is willing to listen.

Crisis- or event-oriented commissions are occasioned by specific, highly charged developments that may or may not reflect longer-term issues but that are seen as requiring immediate exploration. The Warren Commission (1963), the National Advisory Commission on Civil Disorders (1967), and the commission on the *Challenger* disaster (1986) are examples.

Procedure-oriented commissions are intended to evaluate the operation of extant organizations and agencies and make recommendations with respect to policy and procedure. They are generally of more limited scope and lower profile. The aforementioned Herbert Hoover–chaired Commissions on the Organization of the Executive Branch of the Government exemplified this category, which may also include bodies assigned a specific task such as arranging the celebration of the American Revolution bicentennial.

Presidents (and Congresses) appoint commissions to achieve four general goals, any combination of which may be at play in a specific case: commissions provide symbolic reassurance; they are a part of the process of policy development; they overcome organizational complexity; and they permit delay.

The modern presidency is expected to respond to virtually any situation of national political or social consequence. Often, Presidents may be under significant pressure—externally or from within—to act when it is not at all certain what, in fact, should be done. For example, the 1968 assassinations of Martin Luther King, Jr., and Robert F. Kennedy raised disturbing questions for many Americans, including President Johnson, of why U.S. society is so violent. One response was appointment of the National Commission on the Causes and Prevention of Violence. Commissions are a high-visibility mechanism for demonstrating concern, awareness, and intent to address a subject. They offer a means of symbolic reassurance to the public that the President takes something seriously and is willing to listen.

Commissions may provide an informational foundation for the construction of national policy. They may increase public and governmental awareness and perspective on a wide scale. Their mission, in this respect, was best expressed by President Johnson's charge to the Kerner Commission: "Let your search be free. Let it be untrammeled by what has been called the 'conventional wisdom.' As best you can, find the truth, the whole truth, and express it in your report." Presidents may hope for commissions to lend an underpinning of legitimacy or confirmation to policy that has already been developed. And, as part of the policy process, a commission may represent a response to a specifically concerned group, for example, the Commission on Wartime Relocation and Internment of Civilians, which dealt (in the 1980s) with the treatment of Japanese Americans interned during World War II.

Commissions generally focus investigative energies and attention in a single vehicle and avoid duplication or overlapping efforts by competing bodies. The ad hoc nature of some commissions not only allows for greater efficiency and clarity of perspective outside organizational norms, but also permits investigations unburdened by the appearance of conflict of interest.

Finally, commission appointments may afford delay, a cooling-off period in an environment of turmoil during which conflict may be guided toward legitimate channels. Here there is a real potential for abuse, that is, for presidential evasion of substantive response and the dismissal by pundits of commissions as reflective of cynical presidential motives. While this has undoubtedly been the case, in certain instances, it is the exception rather than the rule. Most often, with respect to crises or superheated issues, commissions provide time for defusing tension, marshaling resources, and coalescing attention in an organized search for answers.

Creation and Procedures

Most high-level commissions follow relatively similar procedures. They require membership, staff, and funding; they must conduct investigations; and they must prepare reports. Presidents are involved primarily in the initial stages of a commission's existence and, in widely varying degrees, in responding to commission findings and recommendations.

Advisory commissions are created either by presidential executive order or by legislation. Operating funds have come from any number of executive branch sources, for example, emergency funds or executive agencies, or from congressional appropriations.

For the most part, commissioners are appointed by the President. In the case of commissions established by Congress, appointment authority may be shared by the two branches, with legislation requiring balance of partisanship or points of view among appointees. The designation *blue-ribbon commission* reflects the tendency for commissioners to be individuals with records of distinction in the public or private sectors who lend credibility to commission efforts. Persons with well-known proclivities in the area of commission inquiry are generally to be avoided although proportion is often sought through appointments from various racial, geographic, and ideological groups. Commission memberships range from as few as three to more than twenty members.

Of particular importance is the selection of the commission chair. Presidents give serious attention to this position, which sets the tone for and communicates the importance of the commission's task. This is a role for individuals of integrity, fairness, high intelligence, administrative skills, and objectivity. When commission work becomes contentious—and it often does—the chair is the person, above all others, who may make the difference between confrontation and conciliation. Chief Justice Earl Warren, Governor Otto Kerner, Johns Hopkins University president emeritus Milton Eisenhower, and Senator John Tower were all, in their time, examples of high-profile chairmen capable of lending stature to commissions.

While diversity of membership is considered an asset in pursuit of measured inquiry, trouble may arise from what may be called a partisan temptation on the part of the President, that is, a desire to influence the direction of a commission via the appointment of partisan commissioners. An egregious, albeit rare, instance took place on the Commission on Obscenity and Pornography, whose members were appointed by President Lyndon B. Johnson and were still at work when Richard M. Nixon took office. When a vacancy occurred in the commission membership President Nixon chose to fill it with an antipornography crusader, Charles H. Keating, Jr. While the commission made efforts to accommodate its new member he nonetheless embarked on a campaign of obstruction and sabotage of commission work. Impartial inquiry is dependent, in the first instance, on presidential motivation.

Once a staff is selected and office space is procured a commission's work begins. Commissions may divide themselves into study areas or task forces to focus their efforts. Ad hoc commissions face time constraints (mandates vary from a few months to two or three years) and commissions often work with the knowledge that their independence may collide with the interests of the President and other relevant political actors. Depending on the nature and scope of a commission's subject, it may use any combination of investigative tools: information from government agencies, social-scientific consultation, contracted special reports, survey research, travel for on-site examination of situations, public hearings (open or closed), and specially sponsored conferences.

As data are gathered, examined, and disseminated by the staff, and then as full commission meetings are held, commissioners may go through a process of intellectual growth. In-depth exposure to information and new perspectives may significantly alter preconceptions and lead to commissioners' advocacy of positions they would previously have opposed.

Generally, commissions meet for a few days on several occasions. During the final stages of work the report must be compiled. At this point compromise and consensus are sought; provision must be made, if necessary, for concurring and dissenting statements; decisions are made regarding the primary audience for the report; and choices are faced as to the strength and specificity of language to be used in the presentation of findings. Although appointed by the President, a commission may aim its conclusions and recommendations in many social and political directions, recognizing that the President's political imperatives—not to mention his personal opinions—may limit his response.

Final commission reports are presented to the President and, often, Congress. They are printed by the government and, in the case of commissions that have dealt with subjects of significant public interest, commercial publishers may release editions.

Goals and Milieus

The Federal Advisory Committee Act of 1972 establishes standards for the operation of advisory committees, inventories all such existing bodies, and requires a presidential response to reports. Prior to this legislation there was no such requirement, and, of course, nothing guarantees the quality of a response.

Presidents may welcome commission reports and seek implementation of their recommendations. In this respect lower-key procedure-oriented commissions and advisory committees may more successfully yield policy and organizational adjustments at the executive level, facilitated by the less contentious nature of their subjects and recommendations. Certain factors, however, militate against a warm executive welcome, particularly in the case of high-visibility situation- and crisis-oriented commissions.

The goals and milieus of commissions and Presidents are different and, not surprisingly, are not always compatible. The President's response is shaped largely by sensitivity to his own political needs and to the realities of the political environment. During the Johnson administration, recommendations of the President's Commission on Law Enforcement and the Administration of Justice were incorporated in the Safe Streets Act of 1968. Yet Johnson was deeply frustrated by the report of the National Advisory Commission on Civil Disorders, with its calls for massive federal outlays at a time of congressional resistance to spending and its strong language condemning the behavior of white society.

Considerations of personality also condition responses. The President may be limited in the degree to which he is intellectually or emotionally capable of entertaining ideas contrary to—or critical of—his own. This seemed to play a role in the response of the Nixon administration to the Commission on Campus Unrest, among others.

In addition, a commission that is appointed by one President and that survives his term and reports to his successor risks a limited response due to partisan and policy differences and the unlikelihood of a new administration wanting to pass much credit to its predecessor.

President Lyndon B. Johnson was frustrated by a commission's call for large budget appropriations to deal with civil disorder at a time of spending cutbacks. (Library of Congress, Prints and Photographs Division)

Cabinet- and agency-level responses may occur, on a less publicized basis, that reflect commission recommendations even in the case of commissions that have not received a presidential endorsement. And, beyond the presidency, at times quite strong responses may come from Congress, the states, public and private organizations and institutions, and the press.

The lasting value of high-visibility blue-ribbon advisory commissions must be seen in their role as instruments of public education. Commissions affect the social climate: they help redefine issues, increase awareness, demythologize loosely held but unexamined theories, legitimize new or out-of-the-mainstream ideas, speak to the national conscience, and inspire. While not empowered, by themselves, to change anything, commissions contribute to attitudinal shifts in what is socially and politically acceptable. In the context of its own place and time, a commission may advocate and lend credibility to points of view that exceed anything coming from other bodies of government. Commissions have shown a flexibility and an openness to the exploration of new ideas and the possibilities of intellectual growth as a result of exposure to information that is both rare in the conduct of public affairs and essential to the health of democracy.

[See also (I) Blue Ribbon Commission.]

BIBLIOGRAPHY

Bledsoe, W. Craig. "Presidential Commissions." In *Guide to the Presidency.* Edited by Michael Nelson. 1989.

Flitner, David, Jr. *The Politics of Presidential Commissions.* 1986.

Marcy, Carl. *Presidential Commissions.* 1945, repr. 1973.

Popper, Frank. *The President's Commissions.* 1970.

Wolanin, Thomas R. *Presidential Advisory Commissions.* 1975.

– DAVID FLITNER, JR.

CONGRESS, WHITE HOUSE INFLUENCE ON

The notion of the dominant President who moves the country and Congress through strong, effective leadership has deep roots in American political culture. Those chief executives whom Americans revere, such as George Washington, Abraham Lincoln, and Theodore and Franklin D. Roosevelt, have taken on mythic proportions as leaders. Yet every President bears scars from his battles with the legislature. Many of the proposals from the White House fail to pass Congress, while legislators champion initiatives to which the President is opposed.

The peculiar sharing of powers by the two institutions established by the Constitution prevents either from acting unilaterally on most important matters. As a result, the political system virtually compels the President to attempt to influence Congress.

Contemporary processes, such as the preparation of an elaborate legislative program in the White House, have evolved in response to the system's need for centralization. Yet such changes only provide instruments for Presidents to employ as they seek support from the legislature. They carry no guarantee of success and are no substitute for influence.

The right to make proposals to Congress and to veto legislation are the only formal legislative powers given to the President by the Constitution. Since the veto is rarely overridden, even the threat of one can be an effective tool for persuading Congress to give more weight to Presidents' views. Yet the veto is an inherently negative resource. It is most useful for preventing legislation. Much of the time, however, Presidents are more interested in passing their own legislation. Here they must marshal their political resources to obtain positive support for their programs.

The three most useful sources of influence for Presidents in Congress are their party leadership, public support, and their own legislative skills.

Party Leadership

Presidents are dependent upon their party to move their legislative programs. Despite the pull of party ties, all Presidents experience substantial slippage in the support of their party in Congress. Presidents can count on their own party members for support no more than two-thirds of the time, even on key votes.

The primary obstacle to party unity is the lack of consensus among party members on policies, especially in the Democratic Party; members of Congress are more likely to vote with their constituents, to whom they must return for reelection. To create goodwill with congressional party members, the White House provides them with many amenities, ranging from photographs with the President to rides on Air Force One. Yet, party members expect such courtesies from the White House and are unlikely to be especially responsive to the President as a result. Despite the resources available to the President, if party members wish to oppose the White House, there is little the President can do to stop them. Political parties have become highly decentralized and national party leaders do not control those aspects of politics that are of vital concern to members of Congress: nominations and elections.

The President's party is often in the minority in Congress; moreover, the President cannot depend on his own party for support and must solicit help from the opposition party. Although the opposition is generally not fertile ground for seeking support, the President may receive enough votes to ensure passage of a piece of legislation.

Public Support

One of the President's most important resources for leading Congress is public support. Presidents with the backing of the public have an easier time influencing Congress. Presidents with low approval ratings in the polls find the going tougher. Members of Congress and others in Washington closely watch two indicators of public support for the President: approval in the polls and mandates in presidential elections.

PUBLIC APPROVAL. Members of Congress anticipate the public's reactions to their support for or opposition to Presidents and their policies. They may choose to be close to or independent from the White House—depending on the President's standing with the public, as shown by his public ratings—to increase their chances for reelection. Representatives and Senators may also use the President's standing in the polls as an indicator of the ability to mobilize public opinion against presidential opponents.

Public approval also makes other leadership resources more efficacious. If the President is high in the public's esteem, the President's party is more likely to be responsive, the public is more easily moved, and legislative skills become more effective. Thus public approval is the political resource that has the most potential to turn a situation of stalemate between the President and Congress into one supportive of the President's legislative proposals.

One of the President's most important resources for leading Congress is public support.

Public approval operates mostly in the background and sets the limits of what Congress will do for or to the President. Widespread support gives the President leeway and weakens resistance to presidential policies. It provides a cover for members of Congress to cast votes to which their constituents might otherwise object. They can defend their votes as support for the President rather than support for a certain policy alone.

Lack of public support strengthens the resolve of those inclined to oppose the President and narrows the range in which presidential policies receive the benefit of the doubt. In addition, low ratings in the polls may create incentives to attack the President, further eroding an already weakened position. Disillusionment is a difficult force for the White House to combat.

The impact of public approval or disapproval on the support the President receives in Congress is important, but it occurs at the margins of the effort to build coalitions behind proposed policies. No matter how low presidential standing dips, the President still receives support from a substantial number of Senators and Representatives. Similarly, no matter how high approval levels climb, a significant portion of the Congress will still oppose certain presidential policies. Members of Congress are unlikely to vote against the clear interests of their constituencies or the firm tenets of their ideology out of deference to a widely supported Chief Executive. Public approval gives the President leverage, not control.

In addition, Presidents cannot depend on having the approval of the public, and it is not a resource over which they have much control. Once again it is clear that Presidents' leadership resources do not allow them to dominate Congress.

MANDATES. The results of presidential elections are another indicator of public opinion regarding Presidents. An electoral mandate—the perception that the voters strongly support the President's character and policies—can be a powerful symbol in American politics. It accords added legitimacy and credibility to the newly elected President's proposals. Moreover, concerns for both representation and political survival encourage members of Congress to support new Presidents if they feel the people have spoken.

More important, mandates change the premises of decision. Ronald Reagan's victory in 1980 placed a stigma on big government and exalted the unregulated marketplace and large defense efforts. Reagan had won a major victory even before the first congressional vote.

Although presidential elections can structure choices for Congress, merely winning an election does not provide Presidents with a mandate. Every election produces a winner, but mandates are much less common. Even large electoral victories, such as Richard Nixon's in 1972 and Ronald Reagan's in 1984, carry no guarantee that Congress will interpret the results as mandates from the people to support the President's programs, especially if the voters also elect majorities in Congress from the other party (of course, the winner may claim a mandate anyway).

Legislative Skills

Presidential legislative skills come in a variety of forms. Some, such as bargaining, personal appeals, and consultation, are oriented toward what might be termed the tactical level. In other words, the President and his aides attempt to obtain one or a few votes at a time. Other times Presidents may employ skills such as setting priorities, exploiting political honeymoons, and structuring votes in an attempt to influence most or all members of Congress at the same time.

BARGAINING. Presidents often bargain in the form of trading support on two or more policies or providing specific benefits for Representatives and Senators. Yet the White House does not wish to encourage this process, and there is a scarcity of resources with which to bargain, especially in an era of large budget deficits. In addition, the President does not have to bargain with every member of Congress to receive support. On controversial issues on which bargaining may be useful, the President almost always starts with a sizable core of party supporters and may add to this group those of the opposition party who provide support on ideological or policy grounds. Others may support the President because of relevant constituency interests or strong public approval. Thus the President needs to bargain only if this coalition does not provide a majority (two-thirds on treaties and veto overrides), or, if this is not the case, the President needs to bargain only with enough people to provide that majority.

PERSONAL APPEALS. The President's personal efforts at persuading members of Congress take several forms, including telephone calls and private meetings in the Oval Office. Appeals to fellow partisans can be useful, but the President operates under rather severe constraints in employing his persuasive skills to lobbying one-on-one: appeals often fail; members of Congress often exploit appeals in attempts to obtain quid pro quos; the uniqueness of appeals must be maintained to preserve their usefulness; some Presidents dislike and therefore avoid making personal appeals; making appeals is time-consuming for the President. As a result, one-on-one lobbying by the President is the exception rather than the rule. The White House conserves appeals for obtaining the last few votes on issues of special significance to it. In addition, the White House is hesitant to employ the President when defeat is likely because it risks incurring embarrassing political damage.

CONSULTATION. Members of Congress appreciate advance warning of presidential proposals, especially those that affect their constituencies directly. In addition, consultation can provide the White House with early commitments of support if members of Congress have had a role in formulating a bill, or it may help the White House anticipate and preempt congressional objections. At the very least, members of Congress will feel that they have had an opportunity to voice their objections.

Despite these advantages, presidential consultation with Congress is often nothing more than a public relations effort that follows the White House's initiation of a bill rather than preceding it. Consultation with Congress does not normally have a significant impact on a President's proposals.

SETTING PRIORITIES. An important aspect of a President's legislative strategy can be the establishment of priorities among legislative proposals in order to set Congress's agenda. The President does not want his high priority proposals to become lost in the complex and overloaded legislative process, and Presidents and their staff can lobby effectively for only a few bills at a time. The President's political capital is inevitably limited, and it is sensible to focus it on the issues he cares about most.

First year presidential proposals have a considerably better chance of passing Congress than do those sent to the Hill later in an administration.

There are, however, fundamental obstacles to focusing congressional attention on a few items of high priority. First, the White House can put off dealing with the full spectrum of national issues for several months at the beginning of a new President's term, but it cannot do so for four years: eventually it must make decisions. By the second year the President's agenda is full and more policies are in the pipeline, as the administration attempts to satisfy its constituencies and responds to unanticipated or simply overlooked problems. Moreover, the President himself will inevitably be a distraction from his own priorities. There are so many demands on the President to speak, appear, and attend meetings that it is impossible to organize his schedule for very long around his major goals, especially if he has been in office for long.

Second, Congress is quite capable of setting its own agenda. The public expects Congress to take the initiative, and members of Congress have strong electoral incentives to respond. Finally, Presidents may not want to set priorities and concentrate attention on a few items. Lyndon B. Johnson, for example, was more concerned with moving legislation through Congress rapidly to exploit the favorable political environment.

MOVING FAST. Being ready to send legislation to the Hill early in the first year of a new President's term to exploit the favorable atmosphere that typically characterizes this honeymoon period is related to the setting of priorities. First-year proposals have a considerably better chance of passing Congress than do those sent to the Hill later in an administration. Yet the President may not be able to turn to a well-established party program and thus may have to take a long time to draft complex legislation. Alternatively, the President can choose simply to propose a policy without thorough analysis, as appears to have been the strategy of Ronald Reagan's White House regarding the budget cuts passed by Congress in 1981 and Lyndon Johnson's legislation to establish the War on Poverty in 1964.

STRUCTURING CHOICE. Framing issues in ways that favor the President's programs may set the terms of the debate on his proposals and thus the premises on which members of Congress cast their votes. Usually this involves emphasizing consensual features of a policy other than its immediate substantive merits. For example, federal aid to education had been a divisive issue for years before President Johnson proposed the Elementary and Secondary Education Act in 1965. To blunt opposition, he successfully changed the focus of debate from teachers' salaries and classroom shortages to fighting poverty, and from the separation of church and state to aiding children.

Although the structuring of choices can be a useful tool for the President, there is no guarantee that he will succeed. In addition, the White House must advocate the passage of many proposals at roughly the same time, further complicating its strategic position. Finally, opponents of the President's policies are unlikely to defer to his attempts to structure choices on the issues.

In general Presidents are limited in their ability to obtain support from Senators and Representatives. A President operates in a legislative forum that is outside his control.

Conditions for Success

The conditions for successful presidential leadership of Congress are interdependent. Strength in only one resource is seldom enough to sustain leadership efforts. Congressional party cohorts and public support are the principal underpinnings of presidential leadership of Congress. Whereas the party composition of Congress is relatively stable, public approval of the President may be quite volatile. When both are in the President's favor, he may accomplish a great deal, but in the absence of such fortuitous circumstances, stalemate is the most likely relationship with Congress. Party loyalty is not sufficiently strong to overcome public skepticism of the President, and members of the opposition party will only move so far in the President's direction in response to public support for the White House.

The interdependence of resources extends beyond the need for a sizable party base in Congress and public support. For example, public support makes the use of legislative skills more effective. A President high in the polls or who is viewed as having a mandate will find members of Congress more responsive to his personal appeals for support. When he is lower in the polls, he is less likely even to seek votes in such a manner. Similarly, only if the President has strong public approval is it sensible to employ the strategies of moving rapidly to exploit this resource or of structuring congressional decisions in terms of support for or opposition to the President.

A President who already has strong public approval is also likely to find it easier to move the public to support specific policies, and efforts to mobilize the public are likely to be most effective when the party and White House organize private sector interests that will communicate with Congress. In turn, constituent groups are most enthusiastic about applying pressure on behalf of the White House when the President is high in the polls.

A favorable environment makes some potential resources less effective and others more so. If a President is skilled at bargaining but enjoys a large majority of supporters in Congress, he will have less need to engage in exchanges. Similarly, legislative skills will have less utility if the President emphasizes mobilizing the public to move Congress rather than dealing more directly with legislators. Thus resources such as legislative skills have more relevance in some situations than in others.

Clearly, the conditions for successful presidential leadership of Congress are contingent, and the President's strategic position uncertain. If circumstances are not serendipitous, the potential for leadership is diminished. In such a context it becomes all the more necessary for the President to take advantage of whatever opportunities do appear.

[See also (I) Congress; (II) Executive Powers.]

BIBLIOGRAPHY

Bond, Jon R., and Richard Fleisher. *The President in the Legislative Arena.* 1990.

Edwards, George C., III. *At the Margins: Presidential Leadership of Congress.* 1989.

———. *Presidential Influence in Congress.* 1980.

Fisher, Louis. *Constitutional Conflicts between the Congress and the President.* 3d ed., rev. 1991.

Jones, Charles O. *The Trusteeship Presidency.* 1988.

Light, Paul C. *The President's Agenda.* Rev. ed. 1991.

Peterson, Mark A. *Legislating Together.* 1990.

– GEORGE C. EDWARDS III

COUNCIL OF ECONOMIC ADVISERS (CEA)

The Council of Economic Advisers to the President was established by the Employment Act of 1946. The council is composed of three members appointed by the President with the advice and consent of the Senate. One member is designated by the President to serve as chair. The act specifies that each member should be "exceptionally qualified" to (1) analyze and interpret economic developments, (2) evaluate programs and activities of the government in light of the policy objectives declared in the act, and (3) formulate and recommend economic policies to the President to promote the achievement of maximum employment, production, and purchasing power.

The council assists in the preparation of the Economic Report of the President and makes a report on the economy, both of which are transmitted annually to the Congress within sixty days after the beginning of each regular session. It also gives testimony on the Economic Report before the Joint Economic Committee and is often invited to give testimony before other committees of Congress on legislative matters of importance to economic policy.

In addition to advising the President, the council and its staff of economists work closely with other government agencies and departments, particularly the Departments of the Treasury, Labor, Commerce, and Agriculture, and the Office of Management and Budget (OMB).

Over the years the chair of the council has participated in meetings with the Secretary of the Treasury and the Director of OMB—the so-called Troika—to discuss economic issues. Occasionally, the Federal Reserve Board chair has participated in these sessions. In the 1950s the process was relatively informal, but it became more structured in the early 1960s. The weekly meetings of the group have played an important role in the formulation and management of economic policy ever since.

The CEA has played both advisory and advocacy roles to the administration.

Among the three members of the council, the chair has traditionally acted as the principal adviser to the President. The chair's advice on economic matters is given both in regular meetings with the President and in brief memoranda. The other two members work closely with the chair and provide important input in the advisory process. Moreover, they function as specialists in certain policy areas, such as macroeconomic analysis, microeconomic and sectoral analysis, international trade, regulation, and agriculture.

In recent years, the council staff has consisted of about ten senior and seven junior economists. The senior economists are primarily professors of economics recruited from many of the nation's leading universities. They are usually granted one- or two-year leaves from their positions to serve as staff experts on a wide variety of economic topics, such as macroeconomics, public finance, financial markets, banking, insurance, labor markets, agriculture, international trade, regulation, and energy. The seven junior economists are typically advanced graduate students who spend a one- or two-year internship at the CEA. In addition to performing economic research for the council, the staff participate in agency and interagency groups formed to study economic issues that may or may not be resolved at this level. A council member or a senior staff economist participates in these deliberations on issues requiring attention at the sub-Cabinet level. Topics that require higher-level attention or possible presidential action are referred to Cabinet-level bodies. The CEA chair participates in sessions that include Cabinet officials from those departments that have a particular interest in the economic topic being considered.

Legislatively, the council's mandate and responsibilities have changed very little since 1946. In its early years, there was some confusion about its policy role. One view held that its functions should be limited to providing professional economic advice to the President. Others believed that it was appropriate for the council to be an advocate of administration economic policies in public statements and testimony before congressional committees. This issue continued unresolved into the early 1950s, with some in Congress advocating the abolishment of the CEA. Nonetheless, in the early days of his administration, President Eisenhower was successful in averting such action, and the council has played both advisory and advocacy roles ever since.

The CEA assumed an additional responsibility when the Full Employment and Balanced Growth Act (P.L. 95-523) was enacted in 1978. This legislation requires the President to include five-year economic forecasts in the Economic Report for employment, unemployment, production, real income, productivity, and prices. Such forecasts are also included in the President's annual budget. Because these macroeconomic forecasts have an important bearing on the administration's estimates for revenues and budget expenditures, the council works in close consultation with the Treasury Department and OMB in preparing its forecasts.

Ultimately, all administration policies affecting the economy are the responsibility of the President. In developing and implementing these policies, the President, in addition to receiving advice from the CEA chair, draws extensively on the advice of the Secretary of the Treasury and the Director of OMB. Heads of other federal agencies also provide economic counsel when the need arises.

Over the years it has been difficult to gauge the influence of the chair and the other council members on the policy-making process. Much depends on the extent to which the President is receptive to the views of the chair. For example, the chair played a visible and highly influential role in developing and promoting the adoption of a tax-cut strategy to promote economic growth during the Kennedy and Johnson administrations. In contrast, when the Reagan administration in early 1981 unveiled its economic program to promote economic growth, reduce unemployment and inflation, and balance the budget, the principal design work for the program was done during the latter stages of the 1980 presidential campaign. Moreover, in the early months of the administration, the Director of OMB and the Secretary of the Treasury were the most influential advisers and spokespersons for the program. The council chair, in this instance, did not appear to play a prominent role in the process.

Despite these different experiences, the CEA has always possessed the potential to offer influential economic advice to the President and to perform an important educational and analytical role in deliberations on economic issues at all levels of policy making within the administration. The council's influence, nonetheless, depends on the receptiveness of those government officials who have the power to shape economic policy, particularly the President.

[See also (II) Office of Management and Budget.]

BIBLIOGRAPHY

Feldstein, Martin. "The Council of Economic Advisers and Economic Advising in the United States." *The Economic Journal* 102 (September 1992): 1223–1234.

Hargrove, Erwin C., and Samuel A. Morley, eds. *The President and the Council of Economic Advisers: Interviews with CEA Chairmen.* 1984.

Naveh, David. "The Political Role of Academic Advisers: The Case of the U.S. President's Council of Economic Advisers, 1946–1976." *Presidential Studies Quarterly* 7 (Fall): 492–510.

Porter, Roger B. "Economic Advice to the President: From Eisenhower to Reagan." *Political Science Quarterly* 98, 3 (Fall 1983): 403–426.

Zwicker, Charles H. "The President's Council of Economic Advisers." In *The Presidency and the Economy.* Edited by James P. Pfiffner and R. Gordon Hoxie. 1989.

– EDWARD KNIGHT

CRISIS MANAGEMENT

The word *crisis* is applied to a situation that occurs suddenly, heightens tensions, carries a high level of threat to a vital interest, provides only limited time for making

President John F. Kennedy wanted to avoid the mistakes that led to World War I in managing the Cuban missile crisis. (Library of Congress, Prints and Photographs Division)

decisions, and possesses an atmosphere of uncertainty. Crisis management involves both precrisis planning and the handling of the situation during a crisis.

In normal times, the checks and balances of the U.S. political system can be quite formidable, severely limiting presidential initiatives. But in a political crisis, most of these checks evaporate, and the President is given wide discretionary leeway in the exercise of executive prerogative or emergency powers. While the Constitution contains no explicit provisions for government during a crisis, in an emergency a President can invoke emergency statutes or merely assume power and become the nation's crisis manager in chief (as did Abraham Lincoln in the Civil War, Franklin D. Roosevelt during the Great Depression, and John F. Kennedy during the Cuban missile crisis).

As Alexander George points out, "Optimal strategy for crisis management is extremely context-dependent. While all crises share some characteristics in common, the precise configuration of each crisis varies in ways that have different implications for the selection of an approach strategy. In consequence, there is no single dominant strategy that is equally suitable for managing every crisis" (*Avoiding War,* p. 378). But there are lessons to be derived from past crises, do's and don't's that can help guide decision makers. Successful crisis management requires the President's capacity to manage crises, an effective process for making decisions, and policies for avoiding capitulation or war.

One of the most important features of crisis management relates to the personality of the President. In a crisis, everything is heightened: stress, intensity of feelings, sense of loss of control, and feelings of powerlessness. All these have an impact on the decision maker. Thus the President's personality, style, interaction with senior staff, manner of processing information, and way of thinking are of great importance. In crisis situations, the combination of uncertainty, high stakes, shortness of time, high levels of stress, lack of sleep, and so on make for intense pressure. These pressures may lead to a variety of dysfunctional forms of behavior. Some Presidents have tended to overpersonalize events (during the Cuban missile crisis, Kennedy is reported to have exclaimed, "How could he [Khrushchev] do this to *me?*"), often leading to inappropriate judgments and actions.

Given the shortness of time and the perceived need to respond quickly, Presidents may rush to judgment, acting without adequate information, making too-limited a review of options, or overreacting by seeing the adversary's actions as a personal challenge. Likewise, high levels of stress may cause fatigue and inhibit the ability of the President to make realistic judgments. While, at the early stages of a crisis, stress can heighten concentration, as time goes by stress inhibits performance and may lead to perceptual problems, exaggerated coping and defense mechanisms, fear, aggressiveness, cognitive processing problems, premature decision making, and rigidity. Robert F. Kennedy noted the impact of prolonged stress on the members of the EXCOMM (Executive Committee) during the Cuban missile crisis: "For some there were only small changes, perhaps varieties of a single idea. For others, there were continuous changes of opinion each day; some, because of the pressures of events, even appeared to lose their judgment and stability."

During crises, Presidents tend to screen out information that does not fit their preconceptions: new information is often not processed or is fit into preexisting mental constructs, and outright misperception is likely, leading to decisional problems. As Secretary of State Henry Kissinger noted, "During fast moving events those at the center of decisions are overwhelmed by floods of reports compounded by conjecture, knowledge, hope and worry. . . . Only rarely does a coherent picture emerge; in a sense, coherence must be imposed on the events by the decision-maker."

During crises, Presidents are likely to feel powerless or victimized. They are likely to have an exaggerated view of the control an adversary has over events and to overestimate the adversary's hostility and capabilities.

How a President copes with this wide range of pressures will vary based on personality factors, but the tendency of crises to evoke dysfunctional individual response is clearly powerful.

The characteristics of the decision-making process also play a significant role in managing crisis. Each President will choose a crisis-management structure with which he is comfortable (e.g., Kennedy and EXCOMM, George Bush and a small group of advisers), but it is clear that there are several potential structural hazards that may impair decision making during the fog of crisis. How a President organizes and interacts with top staff during a crisis matters greatly. The first presidential decision involves whom to bring into the inner decision circle. There are a wide range of options, but it is important that the President solicit a wide range of ideas and opinions, avoid yes-men or groupthink, and insist on the presence of a devil's advocate within the proximate decision-making structure.

Good decisions require good information that is properly presented and clearly understood. Given the time pressures in a crisis, such information is extremely difficult to come by. It is hard to check the validity of information, difficult to wait for more information, easy for bias and misperception to replace information. Quantity of information can easily overwhelm quality and may lead to information overload and decisional paralysis. Decisional processes are prone to several common errors: omission of alternatives, confusion regarding objectives, failure to assess risks, reliance on poor information, bias in processing information, failure to examine choices critically, and weakness in implementing and monitoring decisions.

While bureaucratic routines and roadblocks are reduced in a crisis, Presidents must still be cognizant of problems that may arise if the President's decisions are not fully implemented. No policy gets implemented automatically, and during a crisis it is especially important that the President's orders are clearly communicated and faithfully executed. Additionally, it is wise for a President to use senior civil servants as part of his core decision group because it is so important to maintain institutional memory in crisis situations. As Presidents are only temporary holders of power, an ability to tap the memory of people who were there during past crises can be especially useful.

It is vitally important to give the decision makers as much time as possible to make decisions. Therefore, Presidents must attempt to slow the pace of crises, creating pauses and giving both sides time to collect their thoughts. The perception that there is no time is one of the leading causes of misjudgments during crises.

In deciding which policy to pursue, a President must first assess the situation and threat facing the nation. What has happened? Does it threaten a vital or a secondary national interest? What can the President realistically hope to achieve and how can he best pursue his goals? As Presidents attempt to solve crises, there is a tendency for short-term needs to drive out long-term considerations. In their need to devise policies that avoid both war and U.S. capitulation, Presidents must always calibrate decisions against the likely response of an adversary. Crisis decisions are not made in a vacuum, and the President must therefore be sensitive to a variety of complex factors when developing crisis policies.

Given the complexity of crisis management, what steps should a President take to improve the quality of crisis decision making? While there is no solution that applies to all cases, there are things a President can do to make sound decision making more likely. First, Presidents must be aware of the traps a crisis may contain. Crises produce pathological responses against which Presidents must be on guard. President Kennedy, having read the historian Barbara Tuchman's book *The Guns of August* just prior to the Cuban missile crisis, was determined not to repeat the mistakes that led to World War I.

Second, several precrisis steps can be taken. Good anticipation, prediction, and intelligence skills are required so that the country is not caught by surprise. Presidents and their top staff should study past crises, engage in simulations of crises, learn about negotiation, and become familiar with the crisis-control mechanisms of government.

While precrisis preparation is useful, once a crisis begins it is important to introduce pauses wherever possible to give leaders more time to think. Presidents must also limit their crisis means and objectives and avoid taking excessively threatening postures or making ultimatums. Presidents must also engage in other-shoes exercises, seeing the crisis from the adversary's perspective, and must always give the adversary a "golden road" to retreat on, never sealing off the escape route but offering opportunities to disengage. Also, Presidents must be ever cautious about information received, options discussed, and decisions made. It is vital for a President to view every assumption, every piece of information, and every bit of advice with skepticism. Presidents must also keep all lines of communication with the adversary open. And it is often useful to bring an outside third party into negotiations.

A President bears a heavy burden during a crisis. While there is no magic formula for successful resolution of crises, Presidents can take steps that will make war or U.S. capitulation less likely.

[See also (II) Executive Powers, Executive Prerogative.]

BIBLIOGRAPHY

Allison, Graham. *Essence of Decision: Explaining the Cuban Missile Crisis.* 1971.

Fisher, Roger, and William Ury. *Getting to Yes: Negotiating Agreement without Giving In.* 1981.

Genovese, Michael A. "Presidential Leadership and Crisis Management." *Presidential Studies Quarterly* 16 (1986): 300–309.

———. "Presidents and Crisis: Developing a Crisis Management System in the Executive Branch." *International Journal on World Peace* 4 (1987): 81–101.

George, Alexander L. *Presidential Decision-making in Foreign Policy: The Effective Use of Information and Advice.* 1980.

———. *Avoiding War: Problems of Crisis Management.* 1991.

Janus, Irving L. *Crucial Decisions: Leadership in Policymaking and Crisis Management.* 1989.

Rossiter, Clinton. *Constitutional Dictatorship: Crisis Government in the Modern Democracies.* 1963.

– MICHAEL A. GENOVESE

D

DEFENSE, DEPARTMENT OF

The Department of Defense (DOD) grew out of two major events of the mid-twentieth century—World War II and the emergence of the cold war. When World War II ended in August 1945, the armed forces of the United States totaled over 12 million men and women. Although demobilization occurred rapidly, the U.S. experience in the conflict demonstrated the necessity for teamwork among the services and with allies.

Creation of the Department

Congressional action in 1947 creating a new national security system resulted from an intense debate about service "unification" during the latter stages of World War II. At President Harry S Truman's insistence, the secretaries of War and Navy agreed on a plan that became the basis for the National Security Act of 1947. Title II created the National Military Establishment (NME), composed of the departments of the army, navy, and air force, and several other agencies, including the Joint Chiefs of Staff. Heading the NME was a civilian secretary of defense, with power to "establish general direction, authority, and control" over the services. The law established other new organizations, including the National Security Council and the Central Intelligence Agency (CIA).

A compromise between full unification and no change, the act fashioned a confederation—the military departments would be separate executive departments, retaining "all powers and duties . . . not specifically conferred upon the Secretary of Defense." President Truman selected as the first Secretary of Defense James V. Forrestal, who immediately faced a succession of challenges in 1948—a Soviet-supported communist coup in Czechoslovakia, the Berlin blockade, the Arab-Israeli War, passage of the Marshall Plan, and the creation of the North Atlantic Treaty Organization (1949). Sharp disagreements among the military services over roles and missions also preoccupied Forrestal.

Based on his proposals, which were supported by Truman, Congress amended the National Security Act in August 1949. The NME became the Department of Defense; the army, navy, and air force became military departments without cabinet status; and the Secretary of Defense gained "direction, authority, and control" over the military departments.

Three other men served as Secretary of Defense under Truman—Louis A. Johnson (1949–1950), Gen. George C. Marshall (1950–1951), and Robert A. Lovett (1951–1953). Truman brought in General Marshall to provide leadership in the Korean War and the long-term buildup of the armed forces. Under Marshall the defense budget skyrocketed ($57 billion for fiscal year 1952) and the size of the armed forces doubled, to over 3 million. Marshall supported Truman's controversial dismissal of Gen. Douglas MacArthur, who wanted to broaden the conflict by bombing military installations in China. Marshall worked to improve the national security structure—by promoting NATO and new mutual-security treaties with the Philippines, Japan, and Australia and New Zealand. One of Lovett's major contributions was a series of defense reorganization proposals that later influenced President Dwight D. Eisenhower.

McNamara brought to the Pentagon a civilian group who used systems analysis in decision making.

Eisenhower was his own Secretary of Defense, but three men formally held the office during his term—Charles E. Wilson (1953–1957), Neil H. McElroy (1957–1959), and Thomas S. Gates, Jr. (1959–1961). Eisenhower's defense reorganization plan (1953) abolished some existing agencies and replaced them with six new assistant secretaries. The services worried about Wilson's efforts to control the defense budget and about what their roles would be in the use of air power and missiles.

Because of these emerging issues, the Department of Defense passed through difficult times during the first Eisenhower administration. Under McElroy, the department had to respond to the first satellite launching by the Soviet Union (October 1957) and charges of a missile gap. McElroy ordered a speedup in development and production of intermediate range ballistic missiles and their deployment in England and Europe. Charges of a missile gap persisted, and later, although erroneous, played a role in the presidential campaign of 1960.

Supporting President Eisenhower's interest, McElroy presided over another reorganization of the Defense Department in 1958. He created the Advanced Research Projects Agency, responsible for antimissile and satellite projects. The Defense Reorganization Act replaced the military secretaries in the chain of command with the Joint Chiefs of Staff (JCS) and strengthened the role of the JCS chairman. The act continued the trend toward centralization of power in the Secretary of Defense and diminishment of the roles of the service secretaries.

Gates further improved DOD organization by instituting regular meetings with the JCS, and he sought to eliminate disputes over control of strategic weapons between the air force and the navy. During Gates's term intercontinental and submarine-launched ballistic missiles became operational.

Dealing with Vietnam

Upon his election in 1960, John F. Kennedy chose Robert S. McNamara, the president of Ford Motor Company, to be Secretary of Defense. During his seven-year tenure, McNamara worked closely with Presidents Kennedy and Lyndon B. Johnson in a difficult period for the Department of Defense, marked by involvement in the Vietnam War. McNamara was an active manager who carried further the centralization of authority, much to the discontent of the military. He brought to the Pentagon a civilian group who used systems analysis in decision making. McNamara canceled the B-70 bomber and the Skybolt missile projects but supported the controversial TFX (F-111) aircraft. Because of McNamara's reliance on civilian advisers and decisions the services considered detrimental to their interests, his relationship with them deteriorated.

McNamara played a major role in developing defense policy, advising the President, and directing U.S. military forces in a series of crises—the Bay of Pigs invasion of Cuba (1961), the Cuban missile crisis (1962), the conflict in the Dominican Republic (1965), and above all, the Vietnam War. While publicly supporting President Johnson's escalation of U.S. involvement in Southeast Asia, including rapid increases in U.S. combat forces and a bombing campaign against North Vietnam, McNamara became skeptical about the President's approach. As domestic opposition to the war increased after 1965, McNamara and the Pentagon became central targets for criticism of the administration's approach. He left the Defense Department in February 1968.

President Johnson then chose Clark Clifford to become Secretary of Defense. The war preoccupied Clifford during his eleven months at the Pentagon. He approved the last increase in U.S. troop strength in Vietnam, to 549,000, but he eventually adopted McNamara's final position—a halt to troop increases and the bombing in North Vietnam, and gradual disengagement from the war. Clifford appears to have strongly influenced President Johnson to adopt a deescalation strategy by the time the President left office in January 1969.

Elected in 1968 after a campaign in which he promised a solution to the war in Southeast Asia, Richard M. Nixon chose Rep. Melvin R. Laird to preside over the Pentagon. Laird developed Vietnamization, a gradual shift of the burden of fighting to South Vietnamese troops, as a way to achieve the President's goal of "peace with honor." Although the war reached some critical moments during this period, Laird steadily withdrew U.S. troops, cutting the total to under 70,000 by May 1972. Continued negotiations with the enemy led to a settlement in January 1973, providing for the liberation of U.S. prisoners held by North Vietnam and the withdrawal of U.S. fighting forces. Laird immediately announced the end of the controversial draft and the creation of an all volunteer force.

Nixon later brought to the Pentagon James R. Schlesinger, an economist who had been a member of the Atomic Energy Commission since 1971. Schlesinger had to deal with several crises with military implications for the United States—the Arab-Israeli War of October 1973, the Turkish invasion of Cyprus in July 1974, the final collapse of South Vietnam in April 1975, and the Mayaguez incident with Cambodia a month later. Schlesinger wanted to build up U.S. conventional forces, which had declined gradually since the 1950s, as well as NATO's conventional forces. He had the support of President Nixon, but his relationship with Nixon's successor, Gerald R. Ford, deteriorated, especially over the issue of defense funding. His outspoken advocacy of budget increases irritated both Congress and the President, who dismissed him in November 1975.

Donald H. Rumsfeld, the next Secretary of Defense, accepted Schlesinger's strategic-policy initiatives and moved ahead with the development of new weapon systems, including the B-1 bomber, the Trident nuclear submarine, and the MX intercontinental ballistic missile. Ford supported Rumsfeld's priorities, including budget increases. Congress cooperated to an extent, but still the fiscal year 1977 budget was in constant dollars only a little over the 1956 level.

Reorganization, Buildup, and the End of the Cold War

President Jimmy Carter's Secretary of Defense, Harold Brown (1977–1981), instituted significant organizational change, including the full integration of women into the army. Supporting Carter's interest in controlling defense costs, Brown worked hard both to strengthen NATO and persuade its members to increase their defense spending, and he also pressured major allies such as Japan and South Korea to share more of the defense burden. Responding to crises in 1979, in Iran and Afghanistan, Brown and Carter began a defense buildup.

During the 1980 presidential campaign, Ronald Reagan spoke widely about the deterioration of the U.S. defense posture in the 1970s and the need for a significant defense buildup. His first secretary of defense, Caspar W. Weinberger, supported Reagan's effort to increase the defense budget, with particular emphasis on improving the strategic capabilities of the United States, including production of B-1 bombers and MX missiles and development of a Stealth bomber and a new submarine-launched ballistic missile. Weinberger got big increases, although Congress never agreed to as much as Reagan wanted.

Weinberger's successor, Frank C. Carlucci (1987–1989), carried on his policy emphases but showed a willingness to adapt defense policy to the changing world situation. Dick Cheney, appointed Secretary of Defense by President George Bush in 1989, faced the task of downsizing the military forces following the breakup of the Soviet empire and the diminishment of the nuclear threat. In spite of new military challenges, including an invasion of Panama in 1989 to unseat a dictator hostile to the United States, and the Gulf War in 1991, brought on by Iraq's seizure of Kuwait in 1990, the pressure to cut the military establishment and the defense budget continued apace. A massive budget deficit, which settled on the United States during the 1980s, contributed significantly to this pressure.

After its establishment in 1947, it was almost inevitable that the Department of Defense would become one of the most important units of the federal government. The United States was increasingly concerned about its security as the cold war developed. U.S. military involvement in conflicts, such as the Korean War and the struggle in Vietnam, seemed to require the maintenance of large standing military forces, typically over 2 million in the 1980s, supported by a civilian staff of 1 million. The Defense Department, with the support of the Presidents, consumed a major portion of the federal dollar.

[See also (II) Central Intelligence Agency, National Security Council.]

BIBLIOGRAPHY

Caraley, Demetrios. *The Politics of Military Unification: A Study of Conflict and the Policy Process.* 1966.

Cole, Alice C., et al., eds. *The Department of Defense: Documents on Establishment and Organization, 1944–1978.* 1978.

Hammond, Paul Y. *Organizing for Defense: The American Military Establishment in the Twentieth Century.* 1961.

Huntington, Samuel P. *The Common Defense: Strategic Programs in National Politics.* 1961.

Rearden, Steven L. *History of the Office of the Secretary of Defense,* Vol. I: *The Formative Years, 1947–1950.* 1984.

Rees, John C. *The Management of Defense: Organization and Control of the U.S. Armed Services.* 1964.

Trask, Roger R. *The Secretaries of Defense: A Brief History, 1947–1985.* 1985.

– ROGER R. TRASK

DEPARTMENTAL SECRETARIES

The departmental secretary is the highest ranking appointive position in the executive branch, being referred to in the Constitution as "the principal Officer in each of the executive Departments." In 1789 the Congress established the first three departments, the State Department, the War Department, and the Treasury Department. Congress also provided for an attorney general, although the Justice Department was not created until 1870. In 1793 President George Washington began to meet with his department heads collectively, and the group came to be referred to as the President's Cabinet.

President James Polk relied heavily upon his departmental secretaries for advice. He convened with them 350 times during his one presidential term. (Library of Congress, Prints and Photographs Division)

The distinction must be made between the role of departmental secretaries in the United States and the role of cabinet ministers in parliamentary forms of government. In a parliamentary system cabinet ministers are members of the parliament, and the role of prime minister is that of first among equals. In the U.S. system of separation of powers, however, the executive power rests with the President, and departmental secretaries serve at his pleasure. Cabinet ministers have independent status and formal powers in parliament and their political parties that U.S. departmental secretaries do not have.

The Cabinet

Throughout the nineteenth century Presidents used their departmental secretaries as sources of advice as well as the administrators of the major departments of the government. The practices of individual Presidents, however, varied. President Andrew Jackson did not meet with his departmental secretaries collectively for the first two years of his administration, preferring to rely on his informal kitchen cabinet for advice. On the other hand, President James Polk convened his departmental secretaries 350 times during his one term. Some Presidents weighed very heavily the consensus among their departmental secretaries in Cabinet meetings, carefully polling the judgment of each member on major issues. President Abraham Lincoln, however, summed up the constitutional relationship of the President to departmental secretaries when he announced the vote in a cabinet meeting: "Seven nays and one aye, the ayes have it."

In the twentieth century the Cabinet has been expanded to include fourteen department heads who hold the civil service rank of Executive Level I, the highest-ranking appointive executive branch positions. Occasionally the President may include other officials in his Cabinet, such as the Director of the Office of Management and Budget or the U.S. Representative to the United Nations; occasionally others may hold Executive Level I positions. But the Cabinet secretaries traditionally constitute the President's Cabinet, though it is not established in law or the Constitution.

The role of departmental secretary is Janus-like in that secretaries must face the President as the person who appoints them and to whom they report, but also each must face downward to his or her department, the people whom they must lead. Thus Cabinet secretaries are often caught in a bind: they must prove themselves loyal to the President and carry out his policies, but in order to be effective leaders they must also be advocates for the agencies and employees in the department and the programs they operate. Cabinet secretaries must also be attentive to the constituencies of their departments and programs for political support for themselves and for help with presidential priorities in Congress.

The Secretaries' Role

The role of departmental secretary is a complex one. Each must be a skilled manager of the department's many bureaus and programs, an effective campaigner for the President's reelection, an effective lobbyer with Congress for the administration's programs, a leader of the career and political officials in the department, and a visible symbol of the President's commitment to the policy area he or she represents. The role of the secretary within his or her department is to act as the general manager of what often amounts to a holding company of separate bureaus and agencies. The role calls for adept political use of budgetary, organizational, and personnel skills by the secretary. At times these levers are sufficient, but in other cases bureaus have ties to sympathetic members of Congress independent of the secretary that enable them to pursue bureau priorities that may be at odds with their departmental secretary's agenda. Secretarial authority can also be undercut by the White House, which in recent administrations has centralized budget and personnel decisions formerly exercised by department secretaries.

A distinction is often made between the "inner" Cabinet secretaries of State, Defense, Treasury, and the Attorney General. These original four departments cover the core of the functions of the national government, were the first to be created, and their heads are often the closest political advisers to the President. This inner core is often contrasted with the more recent additions to the Cabinet: the Department of the Interior and the Department of Agriculture created in the nineteenth century, and in the twentieth the Department of Commerce (1913), Department of Labor (1913), Department of Health and Human Services (1953), Department of Housing and Urban Development (1965), Department of Transportation (1966), Department of Energy (1977), Department of Education (1979), and the Department of Veterans Affairs (1989).

The "outer" departmental secretaries have the disadvantage that they are often not as close to the President personally, and they are subject to the pulls of powerful interest groups whose interests their departments serve. Part of the tension between secretaries and the White House is that secretaries are often seen by interest groups as their advocates inside the administration, and they are often chosen by Presidents because of their appeal to these interest groups. When they act as advocates, however, they are often seen as disloyal to the President.

The selection of Cabinet secretaries by Presidents is one of the first official acts of a new President and sends important symbolic signals about the nature of the new administration. Thus secretaries are often chosen not merely because they are loyal to the President but also to represent presidential political values. In addition to loyalty, Presidents often consider sexual balance, racial mix, geographical distribution, religious representation, or ideological balance.

Part of the tension between departmental secretaries and the White House is that secretaries are often seen by interest groups as their advocates inside the administration.

Because of the pressures from departmental constituencies and the need to administer their programs, secretaries are sometimes charged with "going native," that is, putting their departmental interests before their loyalty to the President. But this is understandable if one considers that the reason that many are chosen to head departments is that they have spent their careers becoming experts in the policy areas they are now administering. In addition, they want to perform well during their secretarial tenure, and in order to do a good job for the administration they need the resources of money and personnel. It is thus quite understandable they should be advocates for their departments. Charles G. Dawes, Calvin Coolidge's Vice President and the first director of the Bureau of the Budget, said: "Cabinet secretaries are vice presidents in charge of spending, and as such are the natural enemies of the President." This absence of absolute loyalty to the President is also inherent in the U.S. constitutional system, because departmental secretaries are legally bound to carry out the law and can be called to report to Congress on the policies their departments are carrying out.

Thus the centripetal forces pulling departmental secretaries toward the President are often counterbalanced by centrifugal forces in the political system. But it may also be in the President's best interest for departmental secretaries to act as advocates for their departments. They may win the support of their interest groups as well as their own employees when they appear to be advocates for the programs and policies within their jurisdictions. This support may help the President politically.

The White House Staff

But these understandable forces that pull departmental secretaries away from the President are also part of the reason for the rise of the White House staff in the modern presidency. In the nineteenth century and first half of the twentieth, cabinet members were the primary advisers to Presidents; in the last half of the twentieth century that function has been largely taken over by the White House staff. The organizational apparatus of the presidency has been greatly expanded since the report of the Brownlow Committee in 1937 and the establishment of the Executive Office of the President in 1939.

The reason for the rise of the White House staff is that top-level White House staffers are chosen only for their loyalty to the President and not for the symbolic reasons mentioned above. They do not answer to Congress, have no independent political standing, and have no client other than the President. In addition they enjoy proximity and access to the President, and they can respond immediately to his demands. They have no other legal obligations and are not responsible for the managing of programs. So it is no wonder that the White House staff has grown and become more powerful as the rest of the executive branch has become more fragmented.

The dominance of the White House staff has become institutionalized in several ways: on the foreign policy side by the development of the National Security Council (NSC) and its staff and on the domestic side by the domestic policy staff and Cabinet councils. The NSC was created in 1947 as a coordinating mechanism for foreign and defense policy, but it was not until the Assistant to the President for National Security Affairs became the President's primary adviser in the 1970s that the NSC staff came to eclipse the departments of State and Defense. Henry A. Kissinger's role in the Nixon Administration overshadowed Secretary of State William Rogers and Secretary of Defense Melvin R. Laird. Control of national security initiatives was centralized in the White House. The dominance of the White House staff was evident when President Reagan ignored the advice of his secretaries of State and Defense when he chose to sell arms to Iran in trying to get U.S. hostages released. The NSC staff's supplanting of cabinet secretaries went to the extreme when the profits from the sales of arms to Iran were diverted to the contras in Nicaragua by the NSC staff without the knowledge of the Secretaries of State or Defense.

The domestic-policy staff, led by the domestic-policy adviser, grew out of the Domestic Policy Council created in 1970 and has played an important role in domestic-policy development in each presidency since then. The rise of the White House domestic-policy capacity has led to frequent conflict between departmental secretaries and White House staffers. Part of this is necessary when disagreements between departmental secretaries have to be settled. Not every dispute can be settled by the President, and only top level White House staffers have the perspective to settle disagreements short of the President.

One way to mitigate this conflict is a policy development device known as Cabinet councils. Ad hoc groups of departmental secretaries and White House staffers had been used in several presidencies but the Reagan administration institutionalized the arrangement by creating seven Cabinet councils in its first term. The intention was to bring together White House staffers and departmental secretaries in the policy areas that each was concerned with. In President Reagan's second term the seven-council structure was deemed to be too unwieldy and was replaced with two councils, one for economic policy and one for domestic policy. These two councils, in addition to the National Security Council, continued into the Bush administration.

Cabinet Government

Presidents from Nixon on have campaigned for office promising Cabinet government, by which they meant that they intended to use their departmental secretaries actively, solicit their collective advice, and delegate significant authority to them. As candidates they were critical of the centralization of power in the White House that had occurred since the Kennedy administration and intended to return to President Eisenhower's manner of actively using his departmental secretaries. But these hopes and promises have been uniformly dashed on the rocks of the reality of the modern presidency.

President Nixon began his first term intending to delegate domestic policy to his secretaries, but ended up replacing many of them and centralizing power in his White House staff, particularly H. R. Haldeman and John Ehrlichman. In reacting against the centralized Nixon administration both candidates Ford and Carter promised Cabinet government and tried to be their own chiefs of staff. Each was soon disillusioned and named a White House Chief of Staff while increasing the authority of their White House staffs. The Reagan campaign also promised a Cabinet approach to government as had been used in California by Governor Reagan. But after winning the election the White House staff systematically took control of budget, political personnel, and policy development. The Reagan administration had one of the most dominant White House staffs in history.

The fragmenting forces in American politics have increased with the growth of the scope and size of government. The modern presidency has dealt with this fragmentation by increasing the size and power of the White House staff. Regardless of campaign promises, the reality of the modern presidency is that the White House staff will continue to compete with and often overshadow departmental secretaries.

[See also (II) Cabinet, Executive Power.]

BIBLIOGRAPHY

Cohen, Jeffrey E. *The Politics of the U.S. Cabinet.* 1988.
Fenno, Richard F. *The President's Cabinet.* 1959.
Hess, Stephen. *Organizing the Presidency.* 2d ed. 1988.
Laski, Harold J. *The American Presidency.* 1940.
Patterson, Bradley H., Jr. *The Ring of Power.* 1988.
Pfiffner, James P. *The Strategic Presidency.* 1988.
Polsby, Nelson W. *Consequences of Party Reform.* 1983.
Seidman, Harold. *Politics, Position, and Power.* 4th ed. 1989.

— JAMES P. PFIFFNER

DIPLOMAT IN CHIEF

Of the manifold functions of the President one of the more important is that of serving as diplomat in chief. In this role of managing foreign relations, he determines fundamental national goals and concrete objectives, defines the nation's vital interests, frames and assesses optional courses of action to achieve them, refines policy precepts, wins congressional support and popular consensus, and supervises diplomatic representation to and negotiation with foreign governments.

Each President, though, is selective regarding the specific manner and degree of his involvement. Reasons for variation include their individual predispositions; the respective amounts of emphasis given to internal and external issues; technological developments in travel and communication; and the changing role of the United States in world affairs. Whereas Presidents' personal diplomatic activities were limited in the nineteenth century, with the emergence of the United States as a major power (and subsequently a superpower), they have come to pursue active, if not decisive, summit careers, at times even serving as their own Secretaries of State and ambassadors.

Since the days of George Washington, American Presidents have not only formulated and proclaimed foreign policy and directed the negotiation of treaties; they also have engaged in five summit diplomatic processes, which include: communicating directly with foreign chiefs of state and heads of government; sending special emissaries (private envoys) to consult personally with them as his personal surrogates; receiving foreign leaders on official visits to the United States; visiting and conferring with them abroad; and participating in summit meetings and conferences.

Written Communications

When Washington sent a message to the Sultan of Morocco in 1789, only seven months after the birth of the Republic, he set an important diplomatic precedent. The transmittal of written communications—at the presidential level, and bearing his signature—has since become well-established American practice.

> *Presidents have come to pursue active summit careers, at times even serving as their own Secretaries of State and ambassadors.*

Congratulatory, condolatory, and other ceremonial messages have proliferated with the expansion of nations. Mediatory messages, whereby the President assumes the mantle of peacemaker, are exemplified by those of Theodore Roosevelt during the Russo-Japanese War, Woodrow Wilson during World War I, Franklin Roosevelt during the Sudetenland and Danzig crises in the 1930s, and late-twentieth-century Presidents in the Cyprus, Israeli-Arab, inter-American, and other international disputes.

Some twentieth-century exchanges warrant special attention, such as the more than twenty-five hundred World War II messages generated by Roosevelt and the British, Chinese, and Soviet leaders that focused on defeating the Axis powers. The Eisenhower-Kremlin "correspondence diplomacy" from 1955 to 1960, featuring seventy-two communications of more than 100,000 words, dealt with arms reduction and summit conferencing. Published immediately, they tended to amount to little more than diplomatic speechifying. On the other hand, the five Kennedy-Khrushchev "eyeball-to-eyeball" summit notes during the Cuban missile crisis constituted the diplomatic nexus for defusing nuclear confrontation in 1962.

Initially, presidential messages were communicated by written instruments transmitted via traditional diplomatic channels or oral statements conveyed by special emissaries. Telegraphy and transoceanic cables expedited transmission. During World War II President Roosevelt, in communicating with Prime Minister Churchill, introduced the use of teleconferences; and after 1940 he had a direct phone line to Churchill. Following the Cuban missile crisis, these techniques were supplemented with direct White House–Kremlin contact, established by the 1963 hot-line agreement and first used during the Six-Day War in the Middle East in 1967. Dozens of summit communications may be sent and received by the President each year. They bypass the normal bureaucracy and diplomatic channels, and reflect the degree to which the President is disposed to become his own ambassador.

Travel

In an age of rapid travel, it is not surprising to see heads of government crisscrossing the globe to meet, consult, and bargain with one another as they ply their statecraft. The earliest summit visit to the United States, in 1806, brought the Bashaw of Tunis to negotiate a claims settlement for the depredations of Barbary pirates, and in 1874 King Kalakaua of Hawaii came to the United States on an informal visit for twelve days. His stay was technically the first summit visit to this country.

Foreign leaders come for a variety of official and unofficial reasons. Whereas only twenty-three such visits occurred prior to Franklin Roosevelt's term, since then visits have increased, annually averaging approximately twenty, but numbering more than thirty-five per year during the 1980s and 1990s and occasionally mounting to forty-five to fifty. Summit visitors have come from some 150 nations on more than a thousand visits. The countries with the largest number of summit visitors are the United Kingdom, neighboring Canada and Mexico, West Germany, Israel, Italy, and, in the Far East, Australia, Japan, and New Zealand.

Matters of timing, intent, ceremony, agenda, presidential protocol, and mechanics of individual visits are designed in advance by mutual agreement. Visits serve various purposes, ranging from purely ceremonial and formal state visits to informal consultation, working sessions, and deliberative meetings concerned with major issues of public policy. Usually, foreign guests focus on Washington, D.C., for one or two days, but sometimes they tour other parts of the country and remain as long as ten to twelve days. If a President hosts twenty-five to thirty such visits per year and each visitor averages two days in Washington, this time may amount to 20 percent of the President's normal workdays. Moreover, as the quantity increases, there is the risk that they become so routine that government leaders and the American people tire of them. Techniques are devised, therefore, to give key visits some air of individuality.

Early tradition established the precedent that the President should not leave American territory during his incumbency. Theodore Roosevelt was the first to break with tradition by visiting Panama in 1906. After World War I President Wilson headed the American delegation to the Paris Peace Conference and was lionized in Paris, Brussels, London, and Rome. To the time of Franklin Roosevelt, only five Presidents set foot on foreign soil but, with the exception of Herbert Hoover, all Presidents since 1918 have visited foreign lands, with the frequency of these visits accelerating substantially during and since World War II. For example, Roosevelt went abroad fourteen times on thirty-six visits, including his wartime meetings with Winston Churchill, Joseph Stalin, and other Allied leaders. Harry S Truman was the first to be received abroad on formal state visits (Mexico and Brazil, 1947).

Other firsts include Dwight D. Eisenhower's participation in multipartite East-West conferences convened abroad (Geneva, 1955, and Paris, 1960) and the introduction of the grand tour ("Quest for Peace" mission to Asia and Europe, 1959); Lyndon B. Johnson's attendance at the Manila Conference and sweep of seven Far Eastern allies (1966) and his circumnavigation of the globe (1967); Richard M. Nixon's historic trips to Beijing and Moscow (1972 and 1974); Gerald R. Ford's participation in the first annual conclave of the leaders of the major industrial powers (Rambouillet, 1975); Jimmy Carter's trip to Panama to exchange Panama Canal Treaty ratifications (1978); and Ronald Reagan's attendance at the North-South conclave at Cancun (1981).

Presidential trips abroad were commonplace by the early 1990s. Nearly 60 percent have been to a single country. In a half century Presidents made approximately 100 trips consisting of some 235 separate visits—an average of four to five per year. Some were formal state visits, 40 percent were devoted to informal consultation, and less than one-fourth entailed international conferencing.

The consequences of presidential trips vary with the objectives sought. Aside from purely ceremonial and formal state visits there are many goodwill and conferral missions, some negotiatory conclaves, and occasional limited-purpose ventures. The issue is not whether the President will go abroad on summit trips, but whether a particular visit is best suited to achieve his objectives and those of the nation.

Summits

The form of presidential diplomacy that receives the greatest amount of popular, journalistic, and official attention is the summit meeting and conference. Although such gatherings were not untried previously, presidential involvement in conferencing began with Theodore Roosevelt's indirect role as mediator in the Portsmouth Conference during the Russo-Japanese War in 1905, followed by Wilson's participation in the Paris Peace Conference.

Since then every President has become involved personally in some conferencing capacity, ranging from purely ceremonial functions—such as Coolidge's address to an inter-American conference at Havana (1928) and Truman's address to the San Francisco Conference convened to produce the United Nations Charter (1945)—to serious deliberation and negotiation. To illustrate the latter, during World War II Presidents Roosevelt and Truman confined their conferencing primarily to solidifying policy alignments with the leaders of five friendly countries: Australia, Canada, China, and especially the United Kingdom and the Soviet Union. Roosevelt engaged in twenty-one summit gatherings in less than six years from 1940 to 1945, including those at Casablanca, Cairo, Tehran, and Yalta; Truman continued this series at Potsdam in 1945.

In a half century Presidents made approximately 100 trips consisting of some 235 separate visits—an average of four to five per year.

Subsequent Presidents have engaged extensively in summit conferencing, largely of a bilateral nature. These meetings include periodic East-West summits with the leaders of the Soviet Union and China, and frequent meetings with the leaders of Britain, Mexico, and other allied countries and friendly nations. However, one in four meetings has been multilateral, such as the Western four-power conferences (including the United States, Britain, France, and Germany) to align policy on the German and Berlin questions and East-West relations, occasional NATO sessions, the seven-nation Manila Conference concerned with Southeast Asia (1966), several inter-American gatherings and, since 1975, the annual conclaves of the major industrial powers.

Official publications and the media describe such conferencing as "discussions," "conversations," "exchange of views," "conferral," or just plain "talks." All these descriptions denote face-to-face oral exchanges. Normally, the President explicates United States objectives and policies, solicits understanding of American interests, and seeks agreement on basic principles. Occasionally, serious negotiation is necessary, but rarely is the President subjected to the tortuous hammering out of the details of an important treaty or agreement. This work usually is delegated to foreign ministers and diplomats.

Presidential participation in summit conferencing has become an expanding, though controlled, technique of American diplomacy. Generally the President avoids formal multilateral conferences that entail detailed bargaining. He prefers those meetings that are intended to establish unity of purpose embodied in an impelling "spirit" or a declaration of mutual policy. Presidents favor smaller, less ostentatious, usually bilateral meetings or businesslike "working sessions" to exchange views, align positions, achieve understanding, or defuse a crisis.

Since World War II, such presidential personal involvement in summitry has become an accepted, highly visible, vital, and potentially expedient component of contemporary diplomatic practice. In part, America's central role in world affairs, which may require leadership as well as rapid and significant accommodation at the highest level, appears to justify, if not require, diplomacy at the summit; it is a viable supplement to—not replacement for—traditional and ministerial diplomacy.

Presidents generally prefer to communicate and confer rather than to negotiate in detail at summits. They realize that summitry—enriching and personally gratifying though it may be—is no substitute for sound policy and patient, skillful diplomacy. A few Presidents are historically remembered for their concrete contributions to the initiation, development, and utilization of summitry. As the first President, Washington employed the summit techniques available at the time. In the twentieth century the two Roosevelts, Wilson, Truman, Eisenhower, and Nixon contributed most to the expansion and refinement of presidential participation in summit practices.

The functioning of the President as diplomat in chief, although time-tested, widespread and newsworthy, is by no means a magic cure-all for international differences, problems, and crises. It is but one of several alternative diplomatic processes, is limited in potentiality, entails inherent costs and possible risks, and can be overemployed. Like other institutions and procedures, its value is determined by the willingness of the President and other world leaders to make it succeed in achieving mutual national objectives and ameliorating or resolving difficulties. Still, it needs to be wisely employed lest it lose its impact, and care needs to be exercised that it does not become a popular fetish or become an end in itself.

[See also (I) Treaties; (II) Peace Corps, Treaty-Making Powers.]

BIBLIOGRAPHY

Eubank, Keith. *The Summit Conferences, 1919–1960.* 1966.

McDonald, John W., Jr., ed. *U.S.-Soviet Summitry: Roosevelt through Carter.* 1987.

Plischke, Elmer. *Diplomat in Chief: The President at the Summit.* 1986.

———. *Presidential Diplomacy: A Chronology of Summit Visits, Trips, and Meetings.* 1986.

———. "The President's Right to Go Abroad." *ORBIS* 15 (1971):755–783.

———. "Rating Presidents and the Diplomats in Chief." *Presidential Studies Quarterly* 15 (1985):725–742.

Putnam, Robert D., and Nicholas Bayne. *Hanging Together: The Seven-Power Summits.* 1984.

Weihmiller, Gordon R. *U.S.-Soviet Summits: An Account of East-West Diplomacy at the Top, 1955–1985.* 1986.

– ELMER PLISCHKE

DOMESTIC POLICY ADVISER

Each President has used either formal or informal advisers on domestic policy. The variegated nature of domestic policy issues and their changing priority on the political agenda, as well as differing presidential management styles, have resulted in various roles and forms of domestic advising. Ad hoc advisers, often Cabinet officials or friends of the President, were standard into the early twentieth century. As domestic policy became an increasing concern of the modern presidency, however, the position of domestic policy adviser began to emerge.

In the Harry S Truman White House, domestic policy coordination was associated with the Special Counsel—Samuel Rosenman, Clark Clifford and, later, Charles Murphy—working in cooperation with the Bureau of the Budget. Under Dwight D. Eisenhower, domestic policy advice became more diffuse, drawing on Cabinet members and various White House staff and channeling information through the White House Chief of Staff, Sherman Adams. President John F. Kennedy turned to his friend and Special Counsel, Theodore Sorensen.

President Lyndon B. Johnson initially relied on presidential assistant Bill Moyers to coordinate the development of Hooveresque task forces on domestic policy issues [*see* Hoover Commissions]. After 1965, Joseph Califano established the first distinct and stable domestic policy operation within the White House, setting the stage for the establishment of the Domestic Council (DC) under President Richard M. Nixon and Nixon's formal appointment of an Assistant to the President for Domestic Affairs in the person of John Ehrlichman. Ehrlichman used the Domestic Council apparatus to oversee domestic policy formulation, coordination, and implementation for the President, at times dominating even Cabinet members [*see* Office of Policy Development (OPD)].

President Gerald Ford named Nelson A. Rockefeller vice chairman of the DC and placed the council staff under his direction, with an expectation that the Vice President would serve as the primary domestic policy adviser. Delays in Rockefeller's confirmation helped to impede this plan, however.

Stuart Eizenstadt, President Jimmy Carter's Assistant for Domestic Affairs, served as an information broker in the domestic policy area, collecting and assessing domestic policy information and advice from many sources and then analyzing and passing it on to the president.

The variegated nature of domestic policy issues and their changing priority on the political agenda have resulted in various roles and forms of domestic advising.

Under President Ronald Reagan the domestic policy adviser lost influence and access and faced stiff competition from other presidential staff and offices. Instead of dealing directly with the President, the domestic policy adviser reported through Presidential Counselor Edwin Meese III. Chief of staff James A. Baker III coordinated legislative strategy aspects while David Stockman, director of the Office of Management and Budget (OMB), essentially set the pace for domestic policy as part of the budget process.

While President George Bush continued Reagan's pattern of reliance on Cabinet officials for advice, he also relied on White House advisers, notably Roger Porter and Richard Darman. Porter had the knowledge, access, and experience to serve as a focal point for administration policy making, and he chaired a number of working groups and councils on domestic policy issues. But the budget office generally took the lead in domestic policy via the budget process, with the domestic agenda having less presidential priority than foreign affairs.

The initial indications for the Clinton presidency suggest that there will not be a primary domestic policy adviser. Rather, the President seems likely to turn to various officials to take the lead in specific domestic-policy areas, using a variety of advisory structures. For example, he has relied on department heads, such as Secretary of Education Richard Riley to articulate the administration's education policy, and Secretary of Labor Robert Reich to take the lead on labor policy. Alternatively, he has asked Vice President Al Gore to form a six-month National Performance Review task force, while the First Lady, Hillary Rodham Clinton, orchestrates a comprehensive health-care task force.

BIBLIOGRAPHY

Burke, John. *The Institutional Presidency.* 1992.

Cronin, Thomas E. *Presidents and Domestic Policy Advice.* 1975.

Moe, Ronald. "The Domestic Council in Perspective." *The Bureaucrat* 5 (1976): 251–272.

Wyszomirski, Margaret Jane. "The Roles of a Presidential Office of Domestic Policy: Three Models and Four Cases." In *The Presidency and Public Policy Making.* Edited by George Edwards III, Steven Shull, and Norman Thomas. 1985.

– MARGARET JANE WYSZOMIRSKI

E

EDUCATION, DEPARTMENT OF

The history of the U.S. Department of Education mirrors the growth of federal involvement in setting public education policy. From an agency that was created mainly to collect statistics on education, the department has grown to oversee an increasing number of federal programs representing a multibillion-dollar chunk of the federal budget. This involvement has developed despite the lack of a clear constitutional mandate for federal responsibility for education.

The idea of a federal agency to oversee education dates back to 1800. President Thomas Jefferson seconded a proposal for a national council on education and proposed it to Congress, but the concept received scant support. It was revived in 1838 by Henry Barnard, a secretary of schools in Connecticut. Barnard petitioned Washington for what he termed a "permanent statistical bureau . . . which would present an annual report on the educational statistics and progress of the country." Thirty years elapsed, however, before Barnard could secure its creation. Ohio Congressman and future President James A. Garfield introduced a bill in 1866 to create a federal educational agency. Garfield was especially education-minded, having been a college teacher and college president.

Garfield's bill passed both Houses and in 1867 President Andrew Johnson signed it into law. The act established a U.S. department of education, with a commissioner but without Cabinet status. Its function was informational in nature. Two years later, the new department became an "office" of education and was relegated to the Department of the Interior. In 1939 the agency was transferred to the Federal Security Agency, and in 1953 the office was placed under the jurisdiction of the newly created Department of Health, Education and Welfare. There it remained until 1979, when it became a department with Cabinet rank at the urging of President Jimmy Carter. By that time the agency had outgrown its original informational purpose to oversee innumerable government programs.

Expanding Its Function

By the 1880s the office was assigned the responsibility of administering the education portion of the Morrill Land Grant Act. Gradually the office was given more responsibility over federal education laws.

By the 1930s, the office oversaw some eighty federal education programs. After the Soviet Union's launch of the spacecraft *Sputnik* in 1957, President Dwight D. Eisenhower successfully lobbied for passage of the National Defense Education Act to improve science education. President Lyndon B. Johnson's Great Society programs sought to improve the education of the poor. Under Johnson, some sixty education bills were enacted, creating programs to help African Americans and other minorities, women, disabled people, and non-English speaking students.

Without the support of the conservatives in the Reagan administration, Education Secretary Bell published the study, A Nation at Risk: The Imperative for Educational Reform.

In the 1860s the Department of Education consisted of four staff members and had a budget of $15,000. In 1965, the Office of Education was staffed by more than two thousand employees and had a budget of $1.5 billion. In fiscal 1992, the U.S. Department of Education had some forty-five hundred employees and a budget of $32.3 billion.

The department still collects data and supervises federal education research, but it also focuses on national education issues, oversees federal education programs, and enforces federal statutes prohibiting discrimination in federally funded programs.

Although the responsibilities of the U.S. Department of Education have been increasing, the monies allocated to states and localities through federal programs are relatively small. The federal portion of national education costs was approximately 6 percent in 1992, down from a high of 10 percent during the Johnson administration.

Achieving Cabinet Status

By the twentieth century, interest had grown in making the Office of Education into a Cabinet-rank department. Seventy bills to create such a department were introduced into Congress between 1918 and 1925. In 1929, President Herbert Hoover commissioned the National Advisory Committee on Education, which recommended, among other things, the establishment of a Cabinet-level education department. In 1943, President Franklin D. Roosevelt's policy arm, the National Resources Planning Board, recommended that the office of education take a larger role to "offer educational leadership to the nation." But it was not until the mid 1970s that interest was renewed in creating a department of education. The drive was led by the National Education Association (NEA), and the issue became that teachers' union's litmus test for supporting any presidential candidate. The NEA, with some two million members, had become the chief representative of the education lobby. In 1976, the organization decided to support a presidential candidate for the first time. It lent its considerable resources, both financial and human, to Democratic candidate Jimmy Carter when he agreed to create a department of education should he be elected.

The rationale of the NEA leaders was that a department of education would provide both a symbolic and substantive role for education. NEA leaders argued that the United States was the only major industrial nation without a national education department or ministry. Granting Cabinet status, they felt, would give education a national focus. Moreover, it would better coordinate the many education programs that were strewn over innumerable government agencies. Some sixty other educational organizations supported the move.

Opposition to a new department came from a number of sectors. Many feared further centralization of government. Others felt that another layer of needless bureaucracy would be created. Much of the opposition came from the old coalition of labor, education, and civil rights. Some believed the department was unnecessary and others contended that it should be created only when needed to execute a major policy. Even President Carter's Secretary of Health, Education and Welfare, Joseph Califano, Jr., was against the plan.

Carter wavered. But renewed pressure from NEA leaders compelled Carter to honor his campaign pledge. Passage of the bill establishing the department was not easy, however. It barely received the endorsement of the Government Operations Committee and passed the House with a mere four-vote margin. On 17 October 1979, President Carter signed the bill. He appointed a federal judge from California, Shirley Hufstedler, as the first secretary of the department.

An Ideological Department

No sooner did President Carter establish the new department than an attack aiming to dismantle it began. In the presidential campaign of 1980, Ronald Reagan pledged to eliminate what he considered an unnecessary bureaucratic agency. Moreover, Reagan wanted to diminish federal involvement in education. As President, Reagan had difficulty in choosing a Secretary of Education who would preside over the department's liquidation. He finally chose Terrel H. Bell, a former commissioner of the Office of Education under Presidents Richard M. Nixon and Gerald Ford. Bell, a moderate, had hoped to convince Reagan of the need to promote education.

Without the support of the conservatives in the Reagan administration, Bell authorized a study of the status of American education. Published in April 1983, the department's study, *A Nation at Risk: The Imperative for Educational Reform,* galvanized the nation for educational reform. The study decried the state of American education as lagging behind that of other developed nations. Alarmist and political in tone, *A Nation at Risk* ushered in "excellence" reform with these provocative words: "If an unfriendly foreign power had attempted to impose on America the mediocre performance that exists today we might have viewed it as an act of war."

The essence of excellence reform was the raising of academic standards. It was cost-neutral and appealed to President Reagan as a solution to America's economic decline in the face of strenuous foreign competition, especially from Japan. Reagan became a leading advocate of excellence reform and reversed his position on abolishing the new department.

President George Bush inherited the Reagan education agenda. He augmented excellence reform by advocating national standards, national testing, and a choice plan that would provide federal-government vouchers that, theoretically, would enable all students to select from among private, parochial, and public schools. The Department of Education thus promoted a conservative education program to the nation, and its influence on American education was strong.

[See also (I) Cabinet.]

BIBLIOGRAPHY

Berube, Maurice R. *American Presidents and Education.* 1991.

Lapati, Americo D. *Education and the Federal Government: A Historical Record.* 1975.

Stickney, Benjamin D., and Lawrence R. Marcus. *The Great Education Debate: Washington and the Schools.* 1984.

— MAURICE R. BERUBE

ELECTORAL COLLEGE

The body of electors empowered under the Constitution to select a President is popularly known as the Electoral College. Article II, Section 1 provides: "Each State

Rutherford B. Hayes was one of the few to lose the popular vote but win the presidential election based on votes in the Electoral College. (Library of Congress, Prints and Photographs Division)

shall appoint in such manner as the Legislature thereof may direct, a Number of Electors, equal to the whole Number of Senators and Representatives to which the State may be entitled in the Congress," with the proviso that no Senator or Representative or officer of the U.S. government may be an elector. The census, performed every ten years, determines the size of a state's membership in the House of Representatives and therefore the number of its electors in the Electoral College.

The Institution

Although in the early years of the Republic state legislatures frequently chose the electors themselves, every state now provides for popular election. To succeed, a presidential candidate must receive a majority in the Electoral College, which in 1992 was 270 out of 538 votes. Formally, voters choose a slate of state electors who are pledged to support a particular candidate's election in the Electoral College. Rarely do the names of the electors appear on the ballot. The total electoral vote of a state accrues to the winner of the popular vote.

By law, the electors meet in their respective state capitals on the first Monday after the second Wednesday in December and cast their votes for President and Vice President. A certified copy of the state results is dispatched to the president of the U.S. Senate. On 6 January, in a joint session of Congress, he opens the certificates and announces the result.

Despite the formally indirect method of election, the result basically reflects the popular will. But the popular will is expressed in a distinctive pattern—state by state rather than by a national referendum. This "federalized" mode of choosing a President is the heart of the Electoral College election process.

If no candidate gains a majority in the Electoral College, the Constitution prescribes a contingency procedure: the House of Representatives, voting by state delegations rather than by individual Representatives, selects the President from the three candidates (originally five) who earned the highest number of electoral votes. Only twice, in 1800 and in 1824, has the House been called upon to decide. If no vice presidential candidate receives a majority in the Electoral College the Senate chooses from the top two candidates in the college. Only once, in 1837, has the Senate made that choice.

Origins

What prompted the Framers to adopt such a complex system of election? The progressive historians J. Allen Smith and Charles Beard claim that the complicated, indirect method reflected the Framers' deep distrust of democracy. This thesis was rejected by the political scientist John P. Roche, who argued that the Electoral College was simply a last-minute compromise designed to allow the Constitutional Convention to wind up its business. It was, according to Roche, merely a "jerry-rigged improvisation."

More recent scholarship, based on a close reading of the Constitutional Convention records, suggests a third explanation. The Electoral College system did have a clear design and purpose, but antimajoritarianism did not inspire its adoption. According to this thesis, the Electoral College emerged at Philadelphia as a second chapter of the Connecticut Compromise to resolve the fundamental dispute between large and small states at the convention.

Both the Virginia and New Jersey plans, the documents on which the Constitution was based, advocated election of the executive by the legislature, the practice most common in the states. But this method, it was felt, would violate the principle of the separation of powers and compromise the executive's independence. To avoid these undesirable consequences it was at first decided to limit the President to one rather lengthy term of office (seven years). Some delegates, however, objected to the bar on reeligibility. They advocated moving the choice from the legislature to the people since popular election would avoid undue influence on the executive by the legislature and remove any barrier to reeligibility. Many delegates, including James Madison, Gouverneur Morris, and James Wilson, strongly supported the idea of popular elections. But two groups objected to removing the choice from the legislature. The smaller states had gained a distinct advantage in the upper house (ultimately the Senate) after the Connecticut Compromise secured equality for them in that body. The slave states had gained an increment in voting power in the lower house (ultimately the House of Representatives) by virtue of the rule that made a state's representation in the House proportional to its white population plus three-fifths of its black population, although only the white population would vote. Transferring the choice from the legislature to the public at large would eliminate the built-in advantages that these two groups of states had secured in the legislature. Those favoring election by Congress and those favoring popular election remained locked in battle until practically the end of the Convention.

At the last minute, the Brearley Committee on Unfinished Parts proposed the Electoral College scheme, which successfully preserved the advantages of the small and slave states without compromising the executive's independence. Since each state would be entitled in the Electoral College to the same number of votes that it would enjoy in a joint session of Congress, both small and slave states were amenable to transferring the task of selecting a president from the real Congress to this ad hoc single-purpose congress. Since the electors would never assemble together at one national site but would meet to vote "in their respective States" and immediately thereafter disband, there was no danger of corruption, plotting, or cabal. To help prevent the larger states from dominating the selection process, each elector was to vote for two persons, one of whom, at least, would not be a citizen of his own state. At the same time, since a majority was required for selection of the President, no elector would be prone to throw away his second vote. Thus a national figure would likely be chosen at the first round. If no candidate received an absolute majority in the Electoral College, the House of Representatives would choose the President from the five candidates receiving the highest totals in the Electoral College.

The delegates saw the Electoral College scheme as an equitable system for electing a President and one that reserved considerable influence for the states. This influence was reflected not only in the composition of the Electoral College but also in the states' power to determine the manner of appointment of the electors and in the contingency arrangements granting the House of Representatives, voting by states, the ultimate choice. An incidental by-product of the new scheme was the emergence of the office of Vice President, designed to take care of the electors' second vote.

The Electoral College, a one-purpose congress, was a well-wrought compromise, blending national and federal elements in the selection of a President. Thus Alexander Hamilton, in *Federalist* 68, could declare with pride that if "the mode of appointment of the Chief Magistrate is . . . not perfect it is at least excellent."

Operation

Not surprisingly, the Electoral College worked smoothly in the first two presidential elections, those of 1788 and 1792. Since George Washington was the unanimous choice of the electors both times, the only issue dividing them was how to cast their second vote in choosing a Vice President. On both occasions John Adams was chosen.

By 1796, however, the advent of political parties radically transformed the Electoral College from a conclave of independent-minded men of "information and discernment" (as Hamilton had envisaged) engaged in a search for the most qualified executive, into a body of committed politicians pledged to cast their votes in accordance with prearranged instructions. The double ballot for President, designed to give the smaller states a chance to land a President and to preclude a straight-out vote for favorite sons, could lead to highly undesirable results, as events proved.

Two parties were now vying for control of the government—the Federalist Party, which advocated federal supremacy, and the Democratic-Republicans, who espoused greater state autonomy. The 1796 race was closely fought, and a split result ensued: Federalist John Adams captured the presidency (71 votes), and Democratic-Republican Thomas Jefferson gained the vice presidency (68 votes). In 1800, when every Democratic-Republican elector faithfully cast his two votes for the party's nominees—Jefferson for President and Aaron Burr for Vice President—the result was that both received exactly the same number of votes (73) in the Electoral College, thereby propelling the final choice into the House of Representatives. Federalists predominated in the House, and many were intent on punishing Jefferson by awarding the presidency to Burr. Only the strong intervention of Hamilton swung the election to Jefferson after six days of debate and thirty-six ballots.

This situation revealed yet a further danger. Had Burr conspired with the Federalists, he would assuredly have become President. The double vote to which each elector was entitled in the College opened the way for the minority party to connive with the majority party's vice presidential candidate to make him President. The only solution was to separate the Electoral College vote for President from the vote for Vice President. This was effected by adoption of the Twelfth Amendment to the Constitution in 1804. (Additionally, the amendment prescribed that the election of a Vice President in the College required a majority vote, not just a plurality, and that in the contingency procedure the House would choose the President from the top three candidates, not from the top five, as previously.) The large state–small state dichotomy that, in large measure, had prompted the adoption of the Electoral College, had now been attenuated by the emergence of political parties.

The politicization of the election process also affected the pattern of state voting in the Electoral College. By 1836, all states except South Carolina had instituted popular election of electors. Likewise, all the states had adopted the general ticket system, with the winner taking all. The dominant political party in each state preferred this system since it magnified the party vote in the college. James Madison himself gave the greatest spur to the general ticket system. In 1800, realizing that Democratic-Republican candidate Jefferson faced a close contest to win the presidency from Federalist Adams, Madison induced the Virginia state legislature to abandon the district system, which previously operated in that state, and to switch to the general ticket system. This effectively shut out the Federalists from any share in Virginia's electoral vote.

The Electoral College was a well-wrought compromise, blending national and federal elements in the selection of a President.

This general ticket system, which has prevailed with only rare exceptions, has had profound consequences for the course of American political history. On the one hand, it has been responsible, in no small measure, for the existence of a two-party system in the United States. Since a political party must be capable of capturing a plurality in an entire state in order to score in the Electoral College, third parties have invariably fallen by the wayside in their endeavor to make in-roads in the presidential sweepstakes. Even where a regional third party has arisen, as has happened on occasion in the South, it has never gained sufficient strength to modify the outcome of an election. Ideological parties have never made headway in the United States since they have never succeeded even in capturing a state's electoral vote much less securing a majority in the college. The end result is that the United States is dominated by two large political parties, each of which is a conglomerate of different interests and ideologies.

The general ticket system has also influenced the nature of the political campaign in presidential elections. Since the winner takes all, candidates have tended to concentrate their efforts on the states with the highest number of electoral votes. In recent times this has sometimes led political parties to exhibit particular sensitivity in their platforms to the needs of the ethnic minorities concentrated in the large, populous urban centers.

Moreover, the system has operated to magnify the winner's margin of victory in the Electoral College. Even a razor-thin popular victory, such as that won by John F. Kennedy over Richard M. Nixon in 1960 (49.5 percent to 49.3 percent) produced an unequivocal Electoral College vote of 303 to 219. In short, the general ticket system helps convert even a modest victory into a decisive and categorical verdict.

By the same token, a winning candidate in the Electoral College may well be a minority President and may even receive a smaller popular vote than his chief rival. In sixteen elections (1824, 1844, 1848, 1856, 1860, 1876, 1880, 1884, 1888, 1892, 1912, 1916, 1948, 1960, 1968, 1992) a candidate gained a majority in the Electoral College without commanding a majority of the popular vote. The most notable instance of a minority President is Abraham Lincoln in 1860, who garnered just under 40 percent in the popular vote. Twice, the loser in the popular-vote contest has prevailed in the Electoral College. In 1876 Democrat Samuel J. Tilden polled 4,287,670 votes against 4,035,924 for Republican Rutherford B. Hayes. In the Electoral College Tilden scored 184 votes to Hayes's 165, with a further 20 electoral votes, mainly from Southern states still under Reconstruction, in dispute. A majority in the College consisted of 185; thus Tilden was one vote short of outright victory. An electoral commission set up by Congress ultimately ruled that all 20 disputed votes accrued to Hayes, who thereby prevailed by 185 votes to 184. Hayes's promise to the Democrats to end Reconstruction and remove federal troops from the South induced them to accept the results. In 1888 Democrat Grover Cleveland, the incumbent, received 5,540,309 votes, about 95,000 votes more than Republican Benjamin Harrison (5,444,337). Nonetheless, Cleveland lost the election because Harrison scored 233 electoral votes to Cleveland's 168.

The politicization of the Electoral College process has also given rise to the unexpected problem of the maverick, or wayward, elector who refuses to vote as pledged. In contrast to the independence electors were initially expected to possess, electors were now bidden to adhere faithfully to the choice of those who appointed them. To act otherwise constituted a betrayal of trust. Fortunately, the number of electors who have presumed to act independently over the years has been miniscule and their impact nil. Between 1820 and 1988 more than eighteen thousand electoral votes were cast for President, but only seven of these can categorically be said to constitute misvotes. Nonetheless, complaints about potentially unfaithful electors has fueled criticism of the Electoral College system as presently constituted. A number of states have adopted legislation (of doubtful constitutionality) requiring electors to abide by their party commitment.

Adoption in 1961 of the Twenty-third Amendment to the Constitution, allotting Washington, D.C., the same number of electors to which the least populous state is entitled, confirmed the attenuation of state influence in the Electoral College process.

Proposals for Reform

No provision of the Constitution has drawn so much criticism over the years nor provoked so many constitutional amendments as has the Electoral College clause. Whatever the considerations of the Framers in creating the College, many believe that its retention under a democratic form of government is an anachronism. In truth, the real target of the criticism of the Electoral College is less the college itself than an incidental aspect of the scheme—the general ticket system. Critics maintain that, by awarding the winner in a state the entire electoral vote of that state, the system distorts the popular vote nationally and robs nearly half of the electorate of its say in the selection of a President. Four reform schemes have been proposed.

THE AUTOMATIC PLAN. This is the least-innovative scheme since it retains the College and keeps the general ticket system intact while eliminating the role of elector. The state's electoral vote would automatically go to the victor in the popular vote, and no unfaithful electors could disturb the result. For most reformers the automatic plan constitutes no reform at all since it would furnish constitutional fiat to the general ticket system, which at present is based on custom.

THE DISTRICT PLAN. The Electoral College would be retained in this scheme, but each state would be divided into electoral districts in accordance with its electoral vote. The people in each district would choose one elector and the national totals would faithfully reflect the measure of national support accorded each candidate. While the district plan would not promote ideological splinter parties it would be open to gerrymandering by state legislatures. Moreover, it would not preclude a minority President or even recourse to the House of Representatives under the Constitution's contingency procedures.

THE PROPORTIONAL PLAN. In this plan, the Electoral College as an institution would be eliminated, but electoral votes would continue to be distributed among the states as at present. The assignment of a state's votes to the candidates, however, would not be on the basis of winner-take-all but would be proportionate to the percentage of the popular vote each candidate has scored. Gerrymandering would become pointless, and every voter's ballot would count. Tallying up the national vote of each candidate would be a simple matter of aggregating the electoral vote scored in each state. To be elected, a candidate would have to receive at least 40 percent of the electoral vote. If no candidate received that percentage of the national vote there would be a contingency procedure, with members of Congress, in joint session, voting as individuals to select the President from the top two candidates or alternatively a runoff election.

This plan was proposed several times in Congress, most notably in the late 1940s and early 1950s, when it was strongly promoted by Senator Henry Cabot Lodge of Massachusetts and Congressman Ed Gossett of Texas. The major criticism of the so-called Lodge-Gossett Plan was that it would encourage the emergence of splinter parties and, given the narrowness of most victories, would fail to provide a President with a categorical mandate.

THE DIRECT VOTE PLAN. This plan would eliminate the Electoral College entirely and provide for direct election of the President by the national electorate. Under some variations of the plan, winning a plurality would be sufficient to be elected, eliminating the need for any contingency arrangement. Under another variation the victor would have to receive at least 40 percent of the popular vote to be pronounced winner; if no candidate received 40 percent, there would either be a runoff election between the two top contenders or the Congress, in joint session, would choose between them. The great advantage of direct popular election of the President is that it serves as a true national referendum; the primary criticism is that it would encourage splinter parties and would not produce a categorical result.

Denying the need for reform, numerous commentators have extolled the virtues of the Electoral College as at present constituted, claiming that the College continues to fulfill a vital federal function. The United States remains a nation of states, as reflected in the continuing requirement of equality in state representation in the Senate—a requirement that cannot be modified under the Constitution. Furthermore, although the Supreme Court has endorsed the rule of "one person, one vote" in the formulation of electoral districts for state and national elections, the Court in 1966 refused to entertain an action by Delaware and other states against New York that alleged that these states were disadvantaged by the winner-take-all arrangement of the Electoral College system (*Delaware* v. *New York*). The argument that the Electoral College system is not consistent with a democratic system of government is simply a non sequitur since the very existence of a constitution represents a bar on absolute majority rule. Proponents say that the Electoral College operates to ensure that a President will be elected only on the basis of a special kind of majority—a federative one—and that the result will reflect a wide consensus in the national choice.

Supporters maintain that the Electoral College has stood the test of time, successfully providing the nation with Chief Executives for more than two centuries without any major upheavals. The last time the contingency procedure was invoked was in 1824. To attempt to radically modify a system that has operated so flawlessly is to take a leap in the dark, not knowing what lies at the other end. If the presidential sweepstakes tends to advantage larger states and to give a premium to urban centers and their ethnic minorities, this serves to balance the rural influence dominant in Congress. Whatever adverse consequences arise under the Electoral College scheme should be balanced against the great benefits accruing from this set-up, including the two-party system, the forestalling of splinter parties, the stability that derives from the nonideological character of American political parties, and a categorical rendering of the outcome of the election so that no matter how narrow the margin of victory the decision is clear-cut, giving the winner an unchallengeable mandate to govern. The broad national consensus that a victor must command in the Electoral College is said by some to constitute the foremost prescription for sound government.

While in recent years the demand for reform has been quiescent, if a runner-up in the popular vote is elected, or if the contingency procedure involving the House of Representatives is brought into operation because of the candidacy of a third party, the nation may once again reverberate with the call to reform the Electoral College system.

BIBLIOGRAPHY

Best, Judith. *The Case against Direct Election of the President.* 1975.

Bickel, Alexander. *Reform and Continuity: The Electoral College, the Convention and the Party System.* 1968.

Diamond, Martin. *The Electoral College and the American Idea of Democracy.* 1977.

Pierce, Neal R., and Lawrence D. Longley. *The People's President: The Electoral College in American History and the Direct Vote Alternative.* Rev. ed. 1981.

Sayre, Wallace S., and Judith H. Parris. *Voting for President: The Electoral College and the American Political System.* 1970.

Slonim, Shlomo. "The Electoral College at Philadelphia: The Evolution of an Ad Hoc Congress for the Selection of a President." *Journal of American History* 73 (1986): 35–58.

Wilmerding, Lucius, Jr. *The Electoral College.* 1958.

Zeidenstein, Harvey. *Direct Election of the President.* 1973.

– SHLOMO SLONIM

EMERGENCY POWERS

In the context of the U.S. governmental system, emergency powers are those authorities and controls—deriving in varying degrees from the Constitution, the statutes, or a concept of executive prerogative—used to address an emergency. While there can be varying understandings of what constitutes an emergency, its characteristics generally are sudden and unforseen occurrence, endangerment of life and well-being, and requirement of an immediate response, which rule and law may not always provide. In the midst of the crisis of the Great Depression, the majority opinion of the Supreme Court in *Home Building and Loan Association* v. *Blaisdell* (1934), for example, described an emergency in terms of urgency and relative infrequency of incidence as well as equivalence to a public calamity resulting from fire, flood, or like disaster not reasonably subject to anticipation.

Almost five centuries ago, Niccolo Machiavelli warned of the necessity for republics, when in imminent danger, to have recourse to a dictatorship to avoid ruin.

The Political Theory of Emergency Powers

The necessity of having some special arrangements to preserve a state in the face of an emergency has long been recognized in political theory. Almost five centuries ago, the Italian political realist Niccolo Machiavelli warned in his *Discourses on Titus Livy* of the necessity for republics, when in imminent danger, to have recourse to dictatorship or some form of authority analogous to it to avoid ruin. Similarly, the seventeenth-century English philosopher, John Locke—a preeminent exponent of government by law and not by men—

argued in his *Second Treatise of Civil Government* that occasions may arise when the executive must exert a broad discretion in meeting special exigencies or "emergencies" for which the legislative power has provided no relief and existing law grants no necessary remedy.

THE FOUNDERS. During the course of the Constitutional Convention of 1787, emergency powers, as such, failed to attract much attention. In its aftermath, Alexander Hamilton addressed one obvious emergency issue in *Federalist* 23. There he argued against "constitutional shackles" on "authorities essential to the care of the common defense" because, in his view, "it is impossible to foresee or to define the extent and variety of national exigencies, and the correspondent extent and variety of the means which may be necessary to satisfy them." It appears, however, that little else was offered on the matter of emergencies by Hamilton or his *Federalist* coauthors. Nonetheless, the Constitution does contain some obvious emergency powers, such as congressional authority to declare war or call forth the militia to execute the laws, suppress insurrections, and repel invasions; congressional power to suspend habeas corpus when public safety is endangered by rebellion or invasion; presidential authority to call special sessions of Congress; and the guarantee to the states of protection against invasion or domestic violence. These are explicit or enumerated constitutional powers that have pertinence for a condition of emergency.

Through the tradition of interpretive derivation of implied constitutional authority have come other emergency powers. From time to time, for example, Presidents have relied generally upon the Commander in Chief clause or the faithful execution clause to exercise police powers relative to an emergency.

STATUTORY GRANTS OF POWER. Apart from the Constitution but resulting from its prescribed procedures and provisions of legislative authority, there are statutory grants of power—both explicit and implied—for emergency conditions. Sometimes these laws are only temporary, such as the Economic Stabilization Act (1970), which mandated presidential imposition of wage and price controls for about three years before it eventually expired in 1974.

Many of these laws, however, are permanent and readily available for presidential use in responding to an emergency. The Defense Production Act (1950), for example, gives the executive authority for prioritizing and regulating the manufacture of military goods and materiel. Others have been enacted on a stand-by basis and delegate to the President certain powers that become available with a formal declaration of the existence of a national emergency.

PREROGATIVE. Finally, Presidents have occasionally exercised powers in response to an emergency by relying on a concept of executive prerogative. Locke had counseled that the executive, faced with an emergency for which neither the legislature nor available law afforded counteraction, must exert a broad discretion in responding. Assertion of independent prerogative in this regard was sufficient if the exercise might advance the "public good." Theodore Roosevelt's stewardship theory of the presidency was consistent with Locke's concept of executive prerogative. In his *Autobiography* (1913) the former Chief Executive contended that it was not only the President's right "but his duty to do anything that the needs of the Nation demanded unless such action was forbidden by the Constitution or by the laws."

A rather different understanding of executive prerogative in time of emergency guided the actions of President Abraham Lincoln. By the time of his inauguration, seven states of the lower South had announced their secession; the Confederate provisional government had been established; Jefferson Davis had been elected and installed as president of the Confederacy; and an army was being mobilized by the secessionists. When Lincoln assumed office, Congress was not in session. He delayed calling a special meeting of the legislature and ventured into its constitutional domain. Without making a declaration of war or asking for one, he took the legally suspect step of blockading the ports of the secessionist states, ordered the addition of nineteen vessels to the navy, extended the blockade, and ordered increases in armed forces personnel. In his July message to the newly assembled Congress, Lincoln suggested that his recent emergency actions, "whether strictly legal or not, were ventured upon under what appeared to be a popular and a public necessity, trusting then, as now, that Congress would readily ratify them. It is believed," he wrote, "that nothing has been done beyond the constitutional competency of Congress." Congress did, indeed, give its approval, and did so again concerning some other questionable emergency actions. Clearly, the President had made a quick unilateral response to the emergency at hand—the rebellion and secession of the southern states. Congress, for reasons of partisan politics and popular approval, gave post factum sanction to these assertions of executive prerogative, as Lincoln had anticipated.

Partisan political controversy arose concerning emergency actions taken by Presidents Woodrow Wilson and Franklin D. Roosevelt. Both men exercised extensive emergency powers with regard to world hostilities; Roosevelt also used emergency authority to deal with the Great Depression. Their emergency actions, however, were largely supported by statutory delegations and a high degree of public approval.

PROCLAMATIONS. Furthermore, it was during the Wilson and Roosevelt presidencies that a major procedural change came about in the exercise of emergency powers—the use of a proclamation to declare a national emergency, which activated all stand-by statutory provisions that delegated authority to the President during such an emergency. The first such proclamation was issued by President Wilson in February 1917 (39 Stat. 1814), pursuant to a statute establishing the United States Shipping Board (39 Stat. 728). It was statutorily terminated along with a variety of other wartime measures in March 1921 (41 Stat. 1359).

The next such proclamations were promulgated by Roosevelt with regard to the Great Depression and the oncoming war. A March 1933 proclamation declared the famous "bank holiday" (48 Stat. 1689), which closed banks until they were certified that they were able to comply with the new emergency banking law (48 Stat. 1).

Later, in September 1939, Roosevelt declared a "limited" national emergency, though the qualifying term really was legally insignificant (54 Stat. 2643). Almost two years later, in May 1941, he issued a proclamation of "unlimited" national emergency (55 Stat. 1647). While it did not make any significant new powers available, it served to apprise the American people symbolically of the worsening conflict in Europe and growing tensions in Asia.

Truman's 1950 national-emergency proclamation continued long after actual conditions prompting its issuance had disappeared.

Both the war-related proclamations remained operative until 1947, when certain of the provisions of law they had activated were statutorily rescinded (61 Stat. 449). After Congress terminated the declaration of war against Germany in 1951 (65 Stat. 451) and a treaty of peace with Japan was ratified the following year, legislation was required to keep certain emergency provisions in effect (66 Stat. 54, 96, 137, 296, and 330; 67 Stat. 18 and 131). President Harry S Truman terminated the 1939 and 1941 proclamations in April 1952 (66 Stat. c 31), supposedly leaving operative those emergency authorities continued by statutory specification.

Truman's 1952 termination, however, specifically exempted a December 1950 proclamation of national emergency, which he had issued in response to hostilities in the Korean War (64 Stat. A454). Furthermore, two other national-emergency proclamations resulted before Congress once again returned to these matters. Faced with a postal strike, President Richard M. Nixon declared a national emergency in March 1970, which permitted him to use ready reserve military units to move the mail (84 Stat. 2222). He issued another proclamation in August 1971 to control balance-of-payments difficulties by temporarily suspending certain trade agreement provisos and imposing supplemental duties on some imported goods (85 Stat. 926).

Controlling Emergency Powers

In the years following the conclusion of U.S. armed forces' involvement in active conflict in Korea, expressions of concern regarding the continued existence of Truman's 1950 national-emergency proclamation, long after actual conditions prompting its issuance had disappeared, were occasionally heard in Congress. There was some annoyance that the President retained extraordinary delegated powers intended only for times of genuine emergency, and there was a feeling that the continued failure of the Chief Executive to terminate the declared national emergency was thwarting the legislative intent of Congress. However, no immediate corrective action was taken.

CONGRESSIONAL INTEREST. Several years later, growing public and congressional displeasure with presidential exercise of war powers and deepening U.S. involvement in hostilities in the Vietnam War prompted interest in a variety of related matters. One of these was the exercise of statutory emergency powers that remained available to the President as a consequence of the unrescinded 1950 national-emergency proclamation. In response, the Senate created a special committee to study and investigate the termination of this proclamation and "to consider problems which might arise as the result of the termination and to consider what administrative or legislative actions might be necessary." Initially chartered in June 1972 as the Special Committee on the Termination of the National Emergency, the panel did not begin operations before the end of the year.

Reconstituted by the 93d Congress in 1973, the panel soon found its mission to be more complex and more burdensome than its creators had originally thought it would be. Staff research revealed that there was not just one proclamation of national emergency in effect but four—those issued in 1933, 1950, 1970, and 1971. The country was in a condition of national emergency four times over, and with each proclamation, the whole collection of statutorily delegated emergency powers was activated. Consequently, in 1974, the study panel was rechartered as the Special Committee on National Emergencies and Delegated Emergency Powers.

The panel produced several studies, including one identifying 470 provisions of federal law delegating extraordinary authority to the executive in time of national emergency. Not all of them required a declaration of national emergency to become operative, but they were, nevertheless, extraordinary grants. Furthermore, there was no ready procedure for terminating the four outstanding national-emergency proclamations. Consequently, the panel began developing corrective legislation for the situation. The resulting reform bill was unanimously recommended in a July 1974 committee report and was introduced in the Senate by the panel's chairman late in the following month. Scheduling complications in the House, however, delayed consideration of the measure; it was reintroduced in the next Congress in early 1975. Eventually, the legislation received final congressional approval during this summer of 1976 and was signed into law in September by President Gerald Ford.

LEGISLATION. As enacted, the National Emergencies Act (90 Stat. 1255) generally returned all stand-by statutory delegations of emergency power activated by an outstanding declaration of national emergency to a dormant state two years after the date of the law's approval. The statute did not actually cancel the 1933, 1950, 1970, and 1971 emergency proclamations because of their issuance by the President pursuant to Article II of the Constitution. Nevertheless, it rendered them ineffective by returning to dormancy the stand-by statutory authorities they had made operational, thereby necessitating a new declaration for any reactivation. Also, some provisions of emergency law were amended and others were repealed.

According to the procedural provisions of the act, the President, when declaring a national emergency, must specify the stand-by authorities he is activating. Congress may negate this action with a resolution disapproving the emergency declaration or the activation of a particular statutory power. The statute was amended in 1985 (99 Stat. 448) to require the use of a joint resolution in this regard, which must be approved through the constitutionally provided legislative process. Originally, a so-called legislative veto could be effected with a concurrent resolution approved by both chambers of Congress. Any national-emergency declaration that is not previously terminated by the President or Congress expires automatically on the anniversary date of the declaration, unless the President, within the ninety-day period prior to each anniversary date, gives notice to Congress and in the *Federal Register* that the emergency is to continue in effect. The act also sets certain reporting and accounting requirements for each national-emergency declaration.

Aftermath

In the years immediately following the enactment of the National Emergencies Act, a few emergency-powers statutes were modified, but no sweeping changes were made. One of the most ambitious of these was the division of the President's international economic regulatory authority between the Trading with the Enemy Act of 1917 and the new International Emergency Economic Powers Act of 1977 (91 Stat. 1626).

In subsequent years, several matters identified in the Senate special committee's final report received slight congressional attention. These included investigation of emergency-preparedness efforts conducted by the executive branch, attention to congressional preparations for an emergency and continual review of emergency law, halting open-ended grants of authority to the executive, investigation and institution of stricter controls over delegated powers, and improving the accountability of executive decision making.

The procedures of the National Emergencies Act were first used for a presidential declaration of national emergency in 1979. In November, President Jimmy Carter issued Executive Order 12170 blocking the Iranian government's access to its property within U.S. jurisdiction in response to the seizure of American citizens as hostages in Teheran during the Iranian hostage crisis. Five months later, Carter issued Executive Order 12211, which declared another national emergency and set further prohibitions on economic and commercial transactions with Iran. Similar emergency declarations were made in 1985 regarding Nicaragua (E.O. 12513) and South Africa (E.O. 12532), in 1986 regarding Libya (E.O. 12543), in 1988 regarding Panama (E.O. 12635), in 1990 regarding Iraq (E.O. 12722), and in 1991 regarding Haiti (E.O. 12775). National emergencies also were declared in 1980 (E.O. 12211), 1983 (E.O. 12444), and 1990 (E.O. 12735) to continue export-control regulations when the Export Administration Act, failing to be congressionally reauthorized, automatically expired. Finally, in November 1990, President George Bush declared a national emergency (E.O. 12735) with regard to the international proliferation of chemical and biological weapons. Generally, Congress concurred in these actions. Thus, while the presidential exercise of emergency powers is somewhat more regulated as a consequence of the National Emergencies Act, a variety of functional and geographic crises continue to be addressed.

BIBLIOGRAPHY

Rankin, Robert S., and Winfried R. Dallmayr. *Freedom and Emergency Powers in the Cold War.* 1964.

Rossiter, Clinton L. *Constitutional Dictatorship.* 1963.

Smith, J. Malcolm, and Cornelius P. Cotter. *Powers of the President during Crisis.* 1960.

U.S. Senate. Special Committee on National Emergencies and Delegated Emergency Powers. *A Brief History of Emergency Powers in the United States.* 93d Cong., 2d sess., 1974. Committee Print.

U.S. Senate. *National Emergencies and Delegated Emergency Powers.* 94th Cong., 2d sess., 1976. S. Rept. 94–922.

U.S. Senate. Special Committee on the Termination of the National Emergency. *Emergency Powers Statutes.* 93d Cong., 1st sess., 1973. S. Rept. 93–549.

— HAROLD C. RELYEA

ENERGY, DEPARTMENT OF

On 1 October 1977 the Department of Energy (DOE) became the twelfth Cabinet-level agency, fulfilling President Carter's campaign promise to bring together the patch-work of existing federal energy programs and to implement a more concerted national energy policy.

Congress was more deliberate and less accommodating in its consideration of Carter's energy policy than it was in establishing DOE.

America's fragmented energy policy was a legacy of the government's traditional focus on, and limited intervention in, markets for specific energy resources. However, a broader concept of energy policy began to emerge in the early 1970s as the nation recognized that its energy resources were limited. The Arab oil embargo in 1973–1974 and the natural gas shortages of 1976–1977 shocked energy markets, disrupted daily life, and riveted the nation's attention on the "energy crisis."

Creation

The creation of DOE was a major step in a succession of federal responses to the crisis. As an outgrowth of President Nixon's efforts to coordinate federal energy policy and to respond to the embargo, Congress created the Federal Energy Administration (FEA) to address what many thought was a temporary crisis. After the oil embargo was lifted in March 1974, President Ford approved the creation of the Energy Research and Development Administration (ERDA), bringing together parts of the Atomic Energy Commission (AEC), the Department of the Interior, and other scattered programs to pursue technological avenues to energy independence. ERDA also inherited the nuclear weapons research and production complex.

In the summer of 1977, Carter's energy reorganization plan eased through the Democratic Congress after the natural gas shortages revived public anxiety over energy. Meanwhile, James Schlesinger, Director of the White House Energy Policy and Planning Office, sought passage of Carter's national energy plan, which was to be implemented by DOE. The plan was a blueprint for increased federal management of energy resources, with an emphasis on conservation. Carter signed the Department of Energy Organization Act on 4 August 1977, creating a new department that would merge ERDA and FEA with energy programs from nine other departments or commissions. Schlesinger, who as AEC chairperson under Nixon had expanded research into broader energy fields, became the first Secretary of Energy. Rather than follow patterns set by the organizations inherited by DOE, Schlesinger structured the core DOE offices in accordance with Carter's plan to manage energy resources through various developmental stages, from basic research to commercialization. The Energy Information Administration collected and disseminated energy-related data. The nearly autonomous Federal Energy Regulatory Commission inherited the regulatory functions of the Federal Power Commission and shared responsibility for regulating petroleum with the department's Economic Regulatory Administration. The Office of Defense Programs oversaw the nuclear weapons complex and controlled one-third of the department's budget.

Congress was more deliberate and less accommodating in its consideration of Carter's energy policy than it was in establishing DOE. Schlesinger concentrated on working toward passage of Carter's policy and on the difficulties of reshaping existing bureaucracies into a new organization. The National Energy Act of 1978, signed in November, consisted of about half of the program originally proposed by Carter. Two months later Iranian oil exports were cut off, and Americans experienced another disruption of petroleum markets. While Carter renewed his call for stricter conservation measures, gradual decontrol of oil prices, and a windfall profits tax, DOE officials from the Economic Regulatory Administration stepped up efforts to enforce price and allocation controls. As the crisis eased in the summer of 1979, Schlesinger resigned, and Carter named Charles Duncan as the new Secretary of Energy. Duncan abandoned Schlesinger's organizational structure in favor of a more traditional arrangement of DOE offices by fuel or technology. At the close of Carter's term, DOE's emphasis on conservation and energy security was evident in reduced oil consumption and imports.

The Reagan Administration

President Reagan promised to abolish DOE, reduce government intervention in energy markets, and strengthen the nation's security. The efforts of his first Energy Secretary, James Edwards, to dismantle the department met with congressional resistance. Reagan succeeded in shrinking DOE's involvement in energy markets by implementing further deregulation, eliminating many conservation programs, and cutting back the department's efforts to commercialize new energy technologies. Reagan's focus on national security led to a continued commitment to DOE's research and development of energy technologies and increased funding for the nuclear weapons complex.

After the Gulf War, America's leaders sought to encourage cleaner, more efficient energy production and consumption without resorting to renewed federal energy management.

Reagan's second Secretary of Energy, Donald Hodel, began a massive research effort in support of the President's SDI (Strategic Defense Initiative). Soon after his confirmation in February 1985, John Herrington, Reagan's third Energy Secretary, focused his attention on the nuclear weapons complex, where he found facilities and environmental problems dating back to the Manhattan Project. By late 1988, the nuclear weapons complex had come under intense public criticism. Herrington proposed costly long-term programs to clean up and modernize the complex.

President Bush, Reagan's successor, assured employees that he would not dismantle DOE and appointed James Watkins as the sixth Secretary of Energy. Watkins moved quickly to cultivate "a new culture of accountability" at DOE by stressing its environmental, safety, and health responsibilities. He also established an Office of Environmental Restoration and Waste Management to coordinate clean-up efforts and opened the department to increased oversight by other agencies. Watkins backed off from Herrington's weapons complex modernization plans as the cold war came to end. These efforts to transform the culture and composition of the weapons complex did not entirely overcome bureaucratic inertia and congressional skepticism.

Continued concern for energy security and a growing interest in the environmental impact of energy development led Watkins to draft a national energy strategy based on broad DOE, interagency, and public input. The Persian Gulf crisis brought on by Iraq's invasion of Kuwait in 1990 interrupted this process. DOE helped stabilize petroleum prices and supplies by providing accurate information about the status of oil supplies and drawing down the Strategic Petroleum Reserve in cooperation with other nations to mitigate the loss of embargoed Iraqi and Kuwaiti oil. When America's leaders considered DOE's national energy strategy after the Gulf War, they had a renewed concern for the nation's energy security. The strategy sought to encourage cleaner, more efficient energy production and consumption without resorting to renewed federal energy management. Just before the 1992 election, Congress incorporated key elements of Bush's energy strategy in the first comprehensive energy legislation passed in over a decade.

BIBLIOGRAPHY

Department of Energy. *National Energy Strategy: Powerful Ideas for America.* 1st ed. 1991.

General Accounting Office. *Nuclear Weapons Complex: Major Safety, Environmental, and Reconfiguration Issues Facing DOE.* 1992.

Goodwin, Craufurd D., ed. *Energy Policy in Perspective: Today's Problems, Yesterday's Solutions.* 1980.

– BRIAN WELLS MARTIN

EXECUTIVE AGREEMENTS

An executive agreement is a U.S. international agreement other than a treaty, but is similarly binding on the U.S. government as a matter of international law. Executive agreements are concluded without Senate advice and consent. Although State Department parlance seeks to limit the term to mean those presidential agreements that rest entirely on inherent powers conferred on the President by the Constitution, the term is also commonly used to cover nontreaty international agreements that are authorized by legislation or by prior treaties.

The Constitution does not mention executive agreements, explicitly authorizing only treaties, which are negotiated by the President and approved by the Senate, for the formalization of U.S. international commitments. Nonetheless, historians have variously identified the first such agreement as being either a 1792 postal agreement with the British colonies in Canada or the 1817 United States–Great Britain agreement to limit their naval forces on the Great Lakes.

Executive agreements represent the predominant form of international agreement for the United States, with more than six thousand in force as compared to roughly one thousand treaties. Most cover routine military or diplomatic matters. Congress in 1972 implicitly ratified the general constitutionality of the executive-agreement process by enacting the Case Act, which requires the Secretary of State to transmit the text of agreements other than treaties to each house of Congress for informational purposes within sixty days of their taking effect. Moreover, the trend toward increasing their use is manifest. Between 1945 and 1980, roughly 95 percent of U.S. international agreements were in the form of executive agreements, as compared to about 50 percent a century earlier.

Treaties may authorize subsequent executive agreements relative to their implementation. An example is the NATO Treaty, which has been regarded as authorizing hundreds of agreements on the status of military forces and other matters.

Congressional Authorization

Congress may also authorize executive agreements through statutes. Areas in which Congress has authorized the President to negotiate executive agreements include postal relations, trade matters, and foreign assistance. Congress has also authorized the President to conclude certain agreements that have already been negotiated, as in the case of the Headquarters Agreement with the United Nations and various multilateral agreements establishing international organizations, for example, the United Nations Relief and Rehabilitation Administration, the International Bank for Reconstruction and Development, the International Monetary Fund, and the International Refugee Organization.

Except for the subject of foreign trade, explicitly assigned by the Constitution to Congress as part of its regulatory authority, the source of power for Congress to legislate on international matters is unclear. Theoretical uncertainties, however, have not at all impeded the use of legislatively authorized executive agreements (sometimes called congressional-executive agreements). In large part, this is because virtually all these agreements represent commitments that international law recognizes as within the sovereign power of the United States. So long as Congress and the President concur in these commitments, the often difficult question of domestic law—that is, the question as to which branch is the actual repository of that power—need not be faced. Like a treaty, such an agreement becomes the law of the land, superseding inconsistent state laws as well as inconsistent provisions in earlier treaties, other international agreements, or acts of Congress.

Legislatively authorized executive agreements afford the President two advantages over treaties in international relations. Because such agreements may be approved by a simple majority of both houses, the Senate cannot veto an executive agreement by the one-third-plus-one vote sufficient to defeat a treaty. Thus, for example, after anti-expansionist Democrats and others from sugar-growing southern states blocked a treaty for the annexation of Hawaii, President William McKinley successfully sought statutory authorization for annexation by executive agreement, which was accomplished in 1898. (President John Tyler had made the identical move in order to bring about the annexation of Texas.) Also, including the House of Representatives in the process helps assure that the House will not resist any later presidential effort to secure whatever legislative implementation, including appropriations, may be required to put an international agreement into effect.

Unilateral Agreements

Agreements that rest entirely on presidential authority (so-called unilateral agreements) are less numerous—perhaps only 2 to 3 percent of the total—but more controversial, though they are often of great diplomatic significance. The State Department's traditional position has been that the President's foreign affairs powers,

President William McKinley used executive agreement to authorize the annexation of Hawaii after anti-expansionist Democrats and others in Congress blocked a treaty for its annexation. (Library of Congress, Prints and Photographs Division)

role as Commander in Chief, law enforcement powers, and generalized executive power may all legitimate an executive agreement lacking congressional authorization. The Commander-in-Chief power, for example, supports armistice agreements and, arguably, wartime commitments on territorial and political issues for a postwar era, such as at the Yalta Conference and Potsdam Conference. The President also has sole exercise of the recognition power, and the Supreme Court held in *United States* v. *Belmont* (1937) that this power is sufficient to authorize unilateral executive agreements to settle issues that are necessary to establish diplomatic relations.

The danger of according the President unlimited discretion to make unilateral executive agreements on any foreign relations matter is that such a doctrine would not only obliterate Article II's express check of Senate consent to treaties but would substantially weaken any legislative check on U.S. international commitments. Any such commitments that did not require subsequent legislative implementation, for example, would never be reviewed by either the House or Senate. It is historically clear that the motivation behind certain congressional-executive agreements was precisely to circumvent the Senate two-thirds-majority requirement for treaties, but it is less certain to what degree, if any, circumventing Congress altogether has been an impetus to unilateral agreements. A possible example is Franklin D. Roosevelt's 1940 agreement to lend Great Britain fifty overage destroyers, arguably breaching the obligations of the United States as a neutral in the conflict with Germany at a time when the American public still substantially favored neutrality as national policy.

To recognize this danger, however, is not to suggest any solution. Neither courts nor commentators have been able to articulate any clear, principled line dividing those initiatives for which the President may properly rely on exclusive and inherent powers and those that, if taken unilaterally, would trespass on the Senate's role. The Supreme Court has not yet held any executive agreement ultra vires (beyond the scope of presidential authority) for lack of Senate consent, nor has it given other guidelines that might define the President's power to act alone. The State Department's foreign affairs manual specifies criteria to be considered in deciding whether to proceed by treaty or nontreaty agreement but offers no rule other than an instruction to the department's Legal Adviser to seek appropriate consultations with Congress on difficult cases. The criteria to be considered include the degree to which an anticipated agreement would affect the nation as a whole, whether the agreement would be intended to affect state laws, whether subsequent legislative action would be needed for implementation, past practice on similar agreements, Congress's preferences with regard to a particular category of agreement, the desired level of formality, the proposed duration and need for prompt conclusion of an agreement, and general international practice with respect to the sort of agreement in question.

In 1981 the Supreme Court in *Dames & Moore* v. *Regan* evaded this difficult set of issues with respect to a very common use of executive orders, namely, their use to settle international claims disputes. The agreement at issue—facilitating the end of the Iranian hostage crisis—had not been congressionally authorized and did not fall within any category of unilateral agreement already approved by the Court. The Court's majority, however, upheld the agreement based on Congress's implicit authorization, evidenced largely by a consistent history of ratifying prior claims-settlement agreements through implementing legislation.

It is possible to identify at least two likely limitations on the unilateral executive-agreement power that would not apply to treaties or congressional-executive agreements. First, courts are unlikely to treat unilateral executive agreements as overriding prior statutes. In *United States* v. *Guy W. Capps* (1953), a federal circuit court refused to give effect to an executive agreement regulating the export of potatoes from Canada to the United States. The court regarded the agreement, effecting a regulation of interstate and foreign commerce, as lying not only within presidential authority, but also within Congress's power to regulate such trade. Because the agreement conflicted with provisions of the Agricultural Act of 1948, the court held that the agreement was invalid; the President's inherent foreign affairs powers were insufficient to permit him to override Congress's determinations as to trade.

The requirement that Presidents respect prior statutes does not necessarily prohibit a President from making an executive agreement regarding a matter on which Congress could legislate but has not. Unilateral executive agreements would seem to be unlawful, however, in any area for which the courts have determined that affirmative legislative authority is a prerequisite to government initiative. An important example is extradition. The Supreme Court held in *Valentine* v. *United States* (1936) that extradition, "albeit a national power, is not confined to the executive in the absence of treaty or legislative provision." It would seem to follow that an extradition pursuant to a unilateral executive agreement would be unlawful.

Federal courts have struck down executive agreements that violate constitutional rights. In *Seery* v. *United States* (1955) the Court of Claims invalidated an executive agreement insofar as it denied a woman compensation that she was entitled to receive under the Fifth Amendment. Two years later, in *Reid* v. *Covert* (1957), the Supreme Court declared an executive agreement invalid because it permitted American military courts in Great Britain to use trial by court-martial for offenses committed by dependents of American military personnel, depriving them of the constitutional right to trial by jury.

If an executive agreement is within the President's power, there are no formal requirements as to how it must be made. It may be signed by the President or on his behalf; it can be made by the Secretary of State, an ambassador, or a lesser authorized official; in fact, there is no reason why it must be formal or even written.

It is not clear to what degree, if any, Congress may legislatively proscribe unilateral executive agreements. The Bricker Amendment of 1953, a proposed comprehensive limit on such agreements, failed to be enacted. To the extent, however, that the War Powers Resolution of 1973 purports to limit the President's authority to deploy U.S. military forces, it prohibits his use of executive agreements to promise such deployment as well. The Arms Control and Disarmament Act of 1962 prohibits arms limitation or reduction agreements except through treaties or as legislatively authorized. The Fishery Conservation and Management Act of 1972 provides that no international fishery agreement may take effect until sixty days after its transmission to Congress, during which time Congress reserves authority to prohibit the agreement by statute.

[See also (I) Treaties; (II) Treaty-Making Power.]

BIBLIOGRAPHY

American Law Institute. *Restatement of the Law: Foreign Relations Law of the United States.* 1965. Rev. Tentative Draft No. 1. 1980.

Bloom, Evan. "The Executive Claims Settlement Power: Constitutional Authority and Foreign Affairs Applications." *Columbia Law Review* 85 (1985): 155–189.

Byrd, Elbert. *Treaties and Executive Agreements of the United States.* 1960.

Fisher, Louis. *Constitutional Conflicts between Congress and the President.* 3d ed. 1991.

Gilbert, Amy M. *Executive Agreements and Treaties, 1946–1973: Framework of the Foreign Policy of the Period.* 1973.

Glennon, Michael J. *Constitutional Diplomacy.* 1990.

Henkin, Louis. *Foreign Affairs and the Constitution.* 1972.

McClure, Wallace. *International Executive Agreements: Democratic Procedure under the Constitution of the United States.* 1967.

— PETER M. SHANE

EXECUTIVE OFFICE OF THE PRESIDENT (EOP)

The Executive Office of the President, created in 1939, houses the President's staff. It was formally established by President Franklin D. Roosevelt through Reorganization Plan No. 1 and Executive Order 8248 in 1939, under the authority granted to the President by the Reorganization Act of 1939.

EXECUTIVE OFFICE OF THE PRESIDENT

- White House Office
- Office of Management and Budget
- Council of Economic Advisers
- National Security Council
- Office of Policy Development
- Council on Environmental Quality
- Office of National Drug Control Policy
- Office of Administration
- Office of the U.S. Trade Representative
- Office of Science and Technology Policy
- National Critical Materials Council
- National Economic Council

Establishment

The proposal to establish an Executive Office of the President originated in the report of the President's Committee on Administrative Management (the Brownlow Report) of January 1937. In its attempt to strengthen presidential leadership of the executive branch, the Brownlow Committee proposed to bring the principal managerial units of government firmly under presidential control by housing those agencies concerned with budgeting, efficiency research, personnel, and planning in the proposed EOP along with the White House office, home of the President's immediate and intimate personal staff. "The canons of efficiency," said the committee, "require the establishment of a responsible and effective chief executive as the center of energy, direction, and administrative management."

Initially, the EOP functioned primarily as a managerial institution, consistent with the Brownlow blueprint. In addition to the White House office, Executive Order 8248 placed four presidential agencies within the EOP: the Bureau of the Budget, the National Resources Planning Board, the Liaison Office for Personnel Management, and the Office of Government Reports. All of these agencies were new except the Bureau of the Budget, which had hitherto been located in the Department of the Treasury. The executive order also provided for the establishment of an emergency management office in the EOP in the event of a national emergency and, within a year, President Roosevelt had utilized this authority to create the first of several but vitally important management agencies to coordinate the war effort. Long before Franklin Roosevelt came to the presidency, managing the activities of a rapidly expanding executive branch had grown beyond the capabilities of one person. The establishment of the Executive Office was a significant attempt to match the President's managerial responsibilities with managerial capacity.

Divisions

The agencies established within the EOP are not necessarily permanent. They can be disbanded when they have outlived their usefulness and new presidential staff units, serving different purposes, can be added when needed. A variety of agencies, more than forty in all, have been housed in the Executive Office of the President since 1939 and only a small proportion have survived the administration that created them.

Divisions of the EOP can be created and disbanded by statute, by a reorganization plan (when presidential reorganization authority has been granted by Congress), or by executive order. The President, therefore, is not the sole determinant of the structure of the EOP and, on more than one occasion, Congress has demonstrated its capacity to shape the presidential staff system by adding or removing staff units from the executive office irrespective of whether or not the President at the time approves of its decisions. For example, two of the most important divisions currently in the EOP, the National Security Council and the Council of Economic Advisers, were devised in the corridors of Congress rather than the White House, and it was Congress, not the President, that decided to terminate the existence of one of the major original agencies, the National Resources Planning Board, after just four years.

Currently, the Executive Office of the President consists of twelve divisions (with the date of inclusion in the EOP in parentheses): White House Office (1939); Bureau of the Budget/Office of Management and Budget (1939/1970); Council of Economic Advisers (1946); National Security Council (1949); Council on Environmental Quality (1969); Office of Special Representative for Trade Negotiations/Office of the United States Trade Representative (1974); Office of Science and Technology Policy (1976); Domestic Policy Staff/Office of Policy Development (1977); Office of Administration (1977); National Critical Materials Council (1984); Office of National Drug Control Policy (1988); and National Economic Council (1993).

The EOP has an annual budget in excess of $200 million and a full-time staff conservatively estimated at sixteen hundred. Because of the large staff, a number of EOP staff have offices some distance from the Oval Office.

Politicization

Over the course of its development since 1939 the EOP has also gradually outgrown the Brownlow blueprint. Presidential staff in the EOP operates in a much broader range of government activity than the Brownlow Report originally planned. Whereas Brownlow's EOP was intended to be an agency for centralized administrative management and coordination, today's executive office is very much involved in policy advice, policy making, policy implementation, and political strategy, in addition to the management and coordination of executive branch activities. Furthermore, some of the major functions that Brownlow did intend the EOP to perform, particularly long-term resource planning and personnel management, have never figured prominently in the work of the executive office.

Because the reach of the EOP now extends across the whole range of public policy, it often overlaps, second-guesses, and conflicts with the work done in the executive-branch departments and agencies. This, together with the budgetary control exercised by the Office of Management and Budget, is the principal source of the generally adversarial relationship between the EOP and the executive branch, a relationship that Brownlow had never intended to encourage but that has become a recurring pattern in post–World War II presidencies. By the mid 1980s, political scientist Nelson W. Polsby felt compelled to suggest that perhaps the most interesting political development of the postwar period "is the emergence of a presidential branch of government separate and apart from the executive branch."

The deinstitutionalization of the executive office has been criticized by many experts on the presidency, particularly in the post-Watergate era.

The most significant deviation from the spirit and ethos of the Brownlow Report is the preeminence of the White House Office, which has become the directing force and the most powerful division within the EOP. To a great extent, the major EOP agencies operate as satellites of the White House Office with key political appointees directing the work of the various staffs. As a consequence, the distinction made in the Brownlow Report between an institutional staff for the presidency and the President's personal staff has been substantially eroded over the years. The EOP is no longer a permanent, professional, nonpartisan, expert staff serving the presidency irrespective of who holds the office at any one time. The senior echelons of the executive office are now filled by noncareer, highly partisan presidential loyalists, many of whom lack professional expertise in government or even prior experience in the executive branch. In that sense, the EOP has become politicized or, as some political scientists would say, "deinstitutionalized."

The deinstitutionalization of the executive office has been criticized by many experts on the presidency, particularly in the post-Watergate era. Politicization, together with the growing power and expanding size of the EOP, were seen as major defects in the system of government and a significant contributor to the events of the Watergate affair. There was a widely shared feeling that the presidential staff system was out of control, that the growth of the EOP should be curtailed, that staff should be made more accountable, that the Cabinet ought not to be neglected, and that the flow of power from the departments to the EOP should be reversed. The post-Watergate literature was especially critical of the practice of placing loyal presidential appointees in those key EOP posts originally intended to be occupied by career professionals. It cost the presidency the benefits of expertise, professionalism, objectivity, continuity and institutional memory. Advocates of reform have urged future Presidents to think institutionally, to consider the long-term organizational interests of the presidency and to restore the values of neutral-competence to the executive office. Almost all of the post-Watergate critics of the EOP have urged a return to the fundamentals of the Brownlow Report.

Notwithstanding the events of Watergate and the Iran-contra affair, both of which were generated from within the EOP, post-Watergate Presidents have been unresponsive to the post-Watergate reform agenda. The size of the executive office has not been reduced significantly, nor has its power, nor has there been any meaningful attempt to restore policy-making responsibility and authority to the Cabinet and, through it, to the departments and agencies. Neither has there been any effort to depoliticize the EOP. The classical textbook virtues of neutral-competence, institutional continuity, and objective, nonpartisan, professional advice have had little appeal for post-Watergate Presidents.

Some literature has suggested that these classic textbook virtues are found only in textbooks and have little relevance to the real world of the presidency and the highly political framework within which any contemporary President has to work. The evidence since the 1970s does seem to indicate that what Presidents really want, and think they need, is a staff unit that is primarily politically sensitive and politically responsive and that they are better served by expanding the responsibilities of their staff, by centralizing decision making in the EOP, and by politicizing what was meant to be an institutional arm of the presidency. Indeed, Presidents might wonder why they are being criticized for not thinking institutionally with regard to the role and function of the EOP when, from their point of view, it is the advocates of reform who ought to be criticized for not thinking politically.

An Assessment

The Executive Office of the President is a very significant innovation in American government. As Clinton Rossiter once argued, it was a vital creation that had helped to save the presidency from paralysis and the Constitution from oblivion, and it enabled future Presidents to cope with the exigencies of the modern state. But, like many other reforms in post–World War II American politics, the creation of the EOP has had unintended consequences, and, in the aftermath of Watergate, it appeared to many commentators that the EOP was yet another reform gone wrong.

Any assessment of the performance of the EOP would have to recognize that the EOP's mission to help the President coordinate and manage the activities of the executive branch of government has been interpreted as a mandate to control the executive branch and, in establishing control, the EOP has set itself up as a counterbureaucracy and a separate presidential branch of government. It has interposed itself between the President and the executive branch and has upset what was the traditional relationship between the Chief Executive and his top political executives in the departments and agencies. As a consequence, the nature of decision making in American government has changed since 1939 with a marked decline in the status and authority of the members of the Cabinet.

The EOP has not only challenged the power of the executive branch, but it has also challenged the constitutional prerogatives of the legislative branch by frustrating its attempts to intervene in and oversee the policy-making process. A large, powerful, and highly developed presidential staff system reduces the President's dependency on the executive branch for advice, information, and policy initiatives and so renders the legislature's ties with the departments and agencies less potent than they once were.

The EOP was originally designed as an administrative-management entity but has evolved into a political body competing for power at the very center of government in a highly fragmented and pluralistic political system. The consequences of this evolution have been mixed. The EOP has undoubtedly enhanced the capacity of the President to do the things that the President wants to do, but its record in helping Presidents do what Presidents ought to do is much less obvious. Enhanced management of the executive branch has been achieved at the cost of a seemingly permanent adversarial relationship between the President and the bureaucracy, and, while it is difficult to generalize about the quality of public policy that has emerged from the EOP over the years, it is far from proved that centralization of decision making in the EOP has been, even on balance, a beneficial development (see Walter Williams for a critique of the policy performance of the EOP). Good public policy can never be guaranteed by any institutional innovation in government. The rise of the EOP to center stage of political decision making has been largely unchecked and unconstrained, even after the Watergate and Iran-contra affairs. Thus there can be no certainty that presidential staff in a future EOP will not produce their own version of Watergate or Iran-contra in the name of the President whom they have been appointed to serve.

[See also (II) Executive Orders.]

BIBLIOGRAPHY

Burke, John P. *The Institutional Presidency.* 1992.

Graham, George A. "The Presidency and the Executive Office of the President." *Journal of Politics* 12 (1950): 599–621.

Hart, John. *The Presidential Branch.* 1987.

Moe, Terry. "The Politicized Presidency." In *The New Direction in American Politics.* Edited by John E. Chubb and Paul E. Peterson. 1985.

Rossiter, Clinton. "The Constitutional Significance of the Executive Office of the President." *American Political Science Review* 43 (1949): 1206–1217.

Williams, Walter. *Mismanaging America: The Rise of the Anti-Analytic Presidency.* 1990.

– JOHN HART

EXECUTIVE ORDERS

Presidents have long made legally binding policy without the participation of Congress by issuing executive orders that command government officials to take or refrain from taking some kind of action. These orders have been used to craft foreign policy actions, like the order in 1992 directing the Coast Guard to return Haitian refugees found at sea to Haiti without a refugee claims assessment in a neutral location. Executive orders have also been used to make domestic policy, as in the case of the much debated Executive Order 12291 (1981) authorizing the Office of Management and Budget (OMB) to use wide-ranging powers of review over agency issuance of regulations.

The Numbering System

By the time Ronald Reagan left office in 1989, there had been approximately 12,667 executive orders promulgated. The number is approximate because the exact number of orders is unknown. The present numbering system was based upon an effort to backtrack in history to find the earliest executive order clearly delineated as such, which is taken to have been one issued by Abraham Lincoln, and numbering forward. However, because Presidents have historically issued the equivalent of executive orders that may have been called by other names and because there was no uniform process for publishing such orders until the passage of the Federal Register Act in 1935, the current numbering system is little more than a useful approximation that is accepted as a matter of convention.

Although the Federal Register Act mandated publication of orders in the *Federal Register* and attempted to impose some degree of uniformity on the format in which they are promulgated, its provisions are very general. The more specific guideline for the issuance of executive orders is itself an executive order, E.O. 11030 (1962). However, even that order does little more than describe the general format and routing for the development of drafts and final publication. Security-classified orders are not published at all.

Because of the problems of access to documentation and the late adoption of rules for uniform publication, a codification of all executive orders that would present all currently valid orders has been difficult to develop. After considerable effort, the Office of the Federal Register has published a codification of orders and proclamations promulgated since the end of World War II.

Types and Legal Force

Executive orders issued on a valid assertion of constitutional or statutory authority are legally binding. Courts have held that the legislature may ratify an executive order after its issuance. The failure of the Congress to take any kind of action with respect to an order that is consequently permitted to stand for an extended period is taken as evidence of approval. This is the so-called acquiescence doctrine.

Presidents have long made legally binding policy without the participation of Congress by issuing executive orders.

However, the President may not promulgate an executive order that violates a valid statute or usurps the constitutional authority of a coordinate branch of government. On that ground, Congress may nullify an executive order unless the President can demonstrate an independent basis of constitutional authority in Article II to support it.

The legal force of presidential action does not depend upon labeling it an executive order. The Supreme Court has held that there is no meaningful legal distinction between, for example, a presidential proclamation and an executive order. As a matter of form, a proclamation is generally directed to persons outside of government while an executive order governs actions by government officials and agencies. Proclamations are most often used for hortatory purposes like the declaration of a national day of celebration for a group or historical figure. However, they have been used for very important actions, like President George Washington's Proclamation of Neutrality.

In truth, the effort to distinguish between internal and external effect is not helpful, since orders directed to executive-branch officials or agencies are often aimed at commanding them to carry out policy governing all citizens in a certain way. Thus, orders directed at officers involved in immigration and refugee administration plainly affect asylum seekers. Similarly, orders like E.O. 12291 and Executive Order 12498—mandating regulatory review by the Office of Management and Budget and President Bush's moratorium on agency rulemaking, while specifically directed to administrative agencies, affect the implementation of a wide variety of major policies and therefore clearly have an impact upon state and local governments as well as individual citizens.

Beyond the use of proclamations, Presidents have employed a variety of other formats to issue what are, in effect, executive orders. Thus President Bush's order in 1992 for executive agencies to impose a ninety-day moratorium on the issuance of new regulations and to review existing regulations to determine which ones could be eliminated or modified to be less burdensome, was issued in the form of a presidential memorandum (Memorandum for Certain Department and Agency Heads on the Subject of "Reducing the Burden of Government Regulations" 1992). Indeed, although E.O. 12291 was the basis for the Reagan administration's creation of the Vice President's Task Force on Regulatory Relief as part of the regulatory review process when George Bush was Vice President, later President Bush did not see the need for a new or amended executive order when he created the Vice President's Council on Competitiveness under Vice President Dan Quayle, which effectively replaced the Task Force on Regulatory Relief and gave the new body much greater power than that exercised by its predecessor.

Some Presidents have avoided reference to executive orders in part because there is no specific requirement for publication of other kinds of documents. For example, there has been considerable tension between the White House and Congress over the use of national security directives (NSDs). In a number of cases, the contents of these directives, issued by the President to various executive agencies, have not even been disclosed to Congress.

Tensions with Congress

Where there is no clear order or proclamation, as in the case of the Quayle commission, or where there are devices such as NSDs in use that are not disclosed, the possibilities for tensions between the President and Congress may be particularly high.

Similarly, where an order is issued unilaterally by the White House without much open public discussion or informal exchange with key figures in the Congress and if it concerns particularly important questions, the potential for conflict may be great. Thus, the issuance of E.O. 12356 (1982) governing security classifications during the Reagan administration caused noticeable frustration on Capitol Hill. Although there is legislation prohibiting disclosure of classified information, the definition of security classification and government policy in the handling of classified material have historically been addressed by executive orders. The Carter administration revised the entire system in its executive order on security classification, E.O. 12065 (1978), through a relatively open and participative process, to reduce the amount of classified material and move toward as much declassification of existing material as possible. The Reagan replacement took a much more restrictive approach and did not involve conversations with the participants involved in the earlier version. The result was substantial strain in presidential-congressional relations.

History suggests that the significant use of executive orders by Presidents since Lyndon B. Johnson, and in particular Jimmy Carter and his successors, has been both a cause and effect of presidential-congressional tensions. Johnson promulgated Executive Order 11246 (1965), which laid the basis for what came to be known, during the Nixon administration, as the Philadelphia Plan, requiring affirmative action in government contracting in part because he could not move the same policy through the Congress. Others have taken action that they thought was implied in more or less expansive terms by prior statutes. Presidents Richard M. Nixon and Carter both took significant action based in part on the assertion that existing legislation authorized their decisions. In August 1971, President Nixon issued a set of executive orders and proclamations, most importantly E.O. 11615 and Proclamation 4074, which imposed, among other things, a freeze on wages, prices, rents, and salaries and a 10 percent added fee on imports, claiming implied authority from the Economic Stabilization Act of 1970 and the Trade Expansion Act of 1962. Similarly, President Carter's imposition of an oil import fee, later struck down by federal courts, was also based upon a broad reading of the trade act.

Legal Challenges

Despite the fact that the judiciary has struck down a variety of orders over time, it is very difficult to mount a legal challenge to such a presidential action. Some of the most celebrated cases, like the *Youngstown Sheet & Tube Co.* v. *Sawyer* (1952) ruling striking down President Harry S Truman's Executive Order 10340 directing the Secretary of Commerce to take over steel mills in order to keep them in operation during a labor dispute and the challenges to Nixon's wage-price freeze and Carter's oil import fee, involved cases where there was an immediate and direct effect upon specific property claims. There the parties were clear and the basis for a legal challenge was obvious. However, in many cases, the situation is considerably more complex. Thus, when the Office of Management and Budget began to delay issuance of regulations by agencies obligated by statute to produce them, it became very difficult for frustrated critics to get the issue of the validity of the executive order into court. It was only when regulators like the Environmental Protection Agency, caught between congressional mandates and the OMB, provided information to such critics that a suit charging violations of statutory obligations in the name of regulatory review was made.

Where there has been a lack of formal congressional opposition, courts tend to defer to the President.

Even assuming that presidential critics can develop a case that will survive procedural roadblocks, the larger problems remain. Where there has been a lack of formal congressional opposition, courts tend to defer to the President. That is particularly, though not universally, true with respect to executive orders affecting foreign policy questions. The Supreme Court, for example, upheld the executive order issued by President Carter, E.O. 12283 (1981), and reaffirmed by President Reagan, suspending claims pending in United States courts involving Iranian assets affected by the agreement reached between the two countries for release of American hostages ending the Iranian hostage crisis. Even though there were obvious parties with clear property interests at stake, and despite the fact that Congress had taken no action on the presidential move, the Court concluded that there was legislative acquiescence in the Iran settlement that should be understood as congressional support. Coupled with the general judicial deference to presidential foreign policy decisions, that acquiescence was enough to sustain a dramatic presidential action.

More often, the nature of limits on executive orders is less obvious and direct. For example, the Reagan regulatory review orders asserted that the OMB was to proceed "to the extent permitted by law" but the mechanics and politics of the situation made it virtually impossible for the rulemaking process to meet both the substantive and procedural requirements of all of the applicable legislation. In some cases, the orders themselves do not contain language that suggests a problem of authority but other accompanying documents may. Thus, the full implications of E.O. 12498, the second Reagan regulatory review order, did not become clear to those outside government until they saw the White House memoranda to executive-branch agencies that were issued along with the executive order. These implementation guidelines defined terms and processes discussed in E.O. 12498 in such a way as to give the Office of Management and Budget a great deal more power than would be understood from a simple reading of the order itself.

If challenges to orders are difficult with respect to presidential actions purportedly based upon statutes, they are all the more problematic where the President grounds an executive order on a broad claim of constitutional authority. Historically, periods of war and national emergency have prompted some Presidents to issue large numbers of orders relying upon assumed powers that the Congress later ratified. Franklin Delano Roosevelt, for example, issued 3,727 executive orders during his years in the White House. However, in most instances modern Presidents have relied upon some kind of claim to statutory authority for their actions. During the Carter administration, however, the White House regularly made both particular assertions of statutory authority, either direct or implied, and more general claims that the President was acting under the authority "vested in me as President of the United States." Since then the President has more often asserted broad constitutional claims alone or with limited claims of statutory authority as the basis for action. Thus, the regulatory review process established by E.O. 12291 is grounded only on President Reagan's assertion of "the authority vested in me as President by the Constitution and Laws of the United States of America." The same was true of the executive orders on the family (E.O. 12606 [1987]) and federalism (E.O. 12612 [1987]).

Where the President's order is considered to be directed at internal management functions and supervision of executive-branch employees, as in President Bush's E.O. 12674 (1989) setting forth "Principles of Ethical Conduct for Government Officers and Employees," there is often acceptance of a broad constitutional claim on grounds that the President is responsible for the operation of the executive branch under Article II. However, when the President ranges beyond that kind of action, the complexities grow. It is often uncertain just what provision of the "Constitution and laws" the President is asserting.

Hence, executive orders are flexible tools that offer the President a variety of options. At the same time, they are complex and sometimes dangerous in both legal and political terms. They have occasionally tempted Presidents to abuse powers conferred by statute or to claim constitutional powers they do not rightly possess.

[See also (II) Congress, White House Influence on.]

BIBLIOGRAPHY

Cash, Robert. "Presidential Power: Use and Enforcement of Executive Orders." *Notre Dame Lawyer* 39 (1963): 44–55.

Hart, James. *The Ordinance Making Powers of the President of the United States.* 1925.

Keenan, Hugh S. "Executive Orders: A Brief History of Their Use and the President's Power to Issue Them." In U.S. Senate. Report of the Special Committee on National Emergencies and Delegated Emergency Powers. *Executive Orders in Times of War and National Emergency.* 93d Cong., 2d sess. 1974. Committee Print.

Morgan, Ruth P. *The President and Civil Rights: Policy-Making by Executive Order.* 1970.

Office of the Federal Register. *Codification of Presidential Proclamations and Executive Orders, April 13, 1945–January 20, 1989.* 1990.

Rosenberg, Morton. "Beyond the Limits of Executive Power: Presidential Control of Agency Rulemaking under Executive Order 12,291." *Michigan Law Review* 20 (1981): 193–247.

U.S. House of Representatives. Committee on Government Operations. *Executive Orders and Proclamations: A Study of a Use of Presidential Power.* 85th Cong., 1st sess. 1957. Committee Print.

— PHILLIP J. COOPER

EXECUTIVE PREROGATIVE

The power of a monarch or chief executive officer of government to act, in certain areas, outside the bounds authorized by constitutions and laws is called the executive prerogative. The description of it that was familiar to most of the Framers of the U.S. Constitution was probably that contained in John Locke's *Second Treatise of Civil Government* (1690). The prerogative, Locke wrote, was "Power to act according to discretion, for the public good, without the prescription of the Law, and sometimes even against it." Such a power was necessary because legislative bodies though "supream" were too slow to act, because the law could not foresee and provide for every contingency that might affect the public, because it was impossible to frame laws that would do no harm if executed "with inflexible vigor," and because a legislature that sat all the time would be "burthensome to the People" whereas the need for the executive was continuous.

The English Background

The concept of the prerogative that Americans inherited from England grew out of the late medieval distinction, formulated by Henry Bracton, Sir John Fortescue, and other commentators, between two channels through which royal authority was exerted. Bracton called them *jurisdictio* ("jurisdiction") and *gubernaculum* ("governance"); Fortescue wrote of a *dominium politicum et regale* ("political and regal domain"). What they meant was that in those areas of governance that concerned the preservation of domestic order and the defense of the realm from foreign enemies, the power of the crown was absolute and unrestrained; in matters that concerned the life, liberty, and property of free subjects, however, the king was bound by the law of the land. In other countries, the English believed, there was no such distinction, for in them whatever pleased the king had the force of law.

Over time, constitutional evolution changed the form but not the substance of the distinction. Earlier, the king had administered justice directly through courts over which he personally presided. By Bracton's time (late thirteenth century) the king's courts, though still acting in his name and though the judges were still appointed and removed at his pleasure, had become substantially independent. By Fortescue's time (mid to late fifteenth century), Parliament had emerged as a lawmaking body, under the king and subject to his dismissal. These two developments gave the law a more definite and predictable quality, and in time the term prerogative came into general usage to describe the specified royal powers that were exercised outside the law as defined by the common-law courts and Parliament.

The royal prerogative grew enormously in the sixteenth century under the Tudor monarchs, especially Henry VIII and Elizabeth I. It was extended to a broad range of subjects, from minute regulation of domestic commerce to the granting of charters giving a monopoly of trade. Most of this growth was in violation of the law, but it was justified under the dispensation power, the prerogative to dispense with the execution of particular laws in particular cases. There were two important new exercises of the royal prerogative. One was the issuance of proclamations that had the force of law. In 1539 Parliament enacted the Statute of Proclamations, giving such declarations the force of law except in regard to life or limb and the forfeiture of property, but when the statute was repealed a few years later, the effect was to do away with the exceptions, not to prevent proclamation law. The other major change was the creation of prerogative courts in which the king and his council participated directly and in which accused parties were denied the procedural protections afforded in the common-law courts. As a result of all this, by the time of Elizabeth's death England had moved a long way from being a *dominium politicum et regale* toward being purely a *dominium regale.*

The aggrandizement of the prerogative by the Tudors ensured troubles for their seventeenth-century successors, the Stuarts, for it made enemies—or at least rivals—of two potent groups, parliamentarians and common-law lawyers. The unhappy reigns of James I, Charles I, Charles II, and James II, marked by repeated constitutional crises, can be fairly characterized as struggles between champions of the prerogative and champions of power in the hands of Parliament and the common-law courts. Except for the interregnum between the execution of Charles I in 1649 and the restoration of Charles II in 1660, the prerogative party had the better part of the battle the better part of the time.

It was the short reign of James II that brought an end to the struggle and, for practical purposes, to the prerogative itself. James, although a professed Roman Catholic, had sworn in his coronation oath to "defend the faith," meaning the established Anglican Church, but he was nonetheless determined to see England return to the papacy. To that end, he issued a Declaration of Indulgence in 1687 and another the next year, in effect suspending the Test Act, which prohibited Catholics from holding civil or military offices. He then began to appoint Catholics to various high posts. The English, though alarmed, might have been disposed to wait for James to die, for he was fifty-five, he had no male heirs, and his eldest daughter, Mary, was Protestant; but then his wife had a son, opening the prospect of a Catholic line of succession. A group of highly placed Englishmen invited Mary and her husband, William of Orange, to invade England and assume the throne as joint sovereigns. They accepted, and James fled the country.

As part of the Revolution Settlement (1688–1689) William agreed to severe limitations on the prerogative, including the abolition of the dispensing power, and during William's reign most of the remaining prerogative powers were, as Sir William Blackstone put it, "lopped off." During the eighteenth century Britain developed the system of government by cabinet ministers who also served as members of Parliament. In effect the Parliament and the ministers had arrogated the old prerogative unto themselves.

The American Adaptation

American political leaders were thoroughly versed in English constitutional history, and their knowledge as well as their experience with colonial governors (who were nominally vested with the prerogatives that kings had had before 1689) conditioned them to distrust executive power. They did venerate the person and regal office of the king, and as the imperial crisis of 1763–1776 unfolded they not only absolved him of blame, protesting that the oppressive measures were the work of wicked ministers, they also repeatedly petitioned the king to reexert the prerogative to rein in Parliament. When the king instead declared them in rebellion and hired German mercenaries to put them down, their sense of betrayal was profound. The body of the Declaration of Independence, itemizing a long list of "injuries and usurpations," attributes those evils personally to George III. Moreover, in the Articles of Confederation and in the revolutionary state constitutions, Americans almost completely rejected executive authority.

By the time of the Constitutional Convention of 1787, a good many political leaders had come to realize that government without a tolerably strong executive was no government at all, but uneasiness persisted. A third or more of the delegates preferred a plural executive, and until nearly the end of the convention the proposed plan made the President elected by and subordinate to Congress. In the final arrangements, instead of either dividing the presidency or making it dependent, the delegates sought to make the executive safe, though energetic, by fragmenting the prerogative itself.

Part of the traditional prerogative is vested exclusively in the President. Most important, the President is Commander in Chief of the armed forces; in addition, he has the power to grant reprieves and pardons, to receive foreign ministers, to call Congress into special session, and to adjourn Congress when the two houses disagree over adjournment.

Other parts of the prerogative are shared with one or both houses of Congress or conferred exclusively on Congress. Traditionally the crown was the fountain of all positions of honor or authority; in America the President's power to appoint judges, ambassadors, and other high officers is subject to the approval of the Senate (and the power to grant titles of nobility is absolutely prohibited). Traditionally the crown had the power to conclude treaties with foreign governments or sovereigns;

in America that power is subject to senatorial approval. Historically, the crown had power to coin money, grant patents, regulate commerce, create courts, and construct forts and other military facilities; in America these powers belong to Congress, subject only to the presidential veto. And though the crown had the power to declare war, under the Constitution that power rests exclusively with Congress.

Finally, the Constitution departs from tradition in that the President is subject to impeachment and removal upon conviction, whereas the king was beyond the reach of the law personally, though his ministers were not.

Practical Adaptations

In making these arrangements the Framers provided an effective set of barriers against executive tyranny. In trying to bring the prerogative under the rule of law, however, they were attempting the impossible. Virtually every presidential administration has found it necessary or expedient to transgress the boundaries of the Constitution and laws by resorting to the prerogative in the interest of what is deemed to be the public good.

By 1787, many political leaders had come to realize that government without a tolerably strong executive was no government at all.

A few examples will illustrate the point. Nowhere in the Constitution is the President authorized to issue proclamations, but in 1793 George Washington issued a neutrality proclamation—over the strong protests of Secretary of State Thomas Jefferson, who insisted that, inasmuch as only Congress could declare war, only Congress could declare neutrality. In 1794, Congress enacted the Neutrality Act and prosecutions were brought for violations under that statute. Jefferson himself, when President, repeatedly went outside the Constitution and laws, justifying his actions by saying that "the laws of necessity . . . are of higher obligation" than "scrupulous adherence to written law." Lincoln stretched the Constitution in the interest of the "higher obligation" of preserving the Union.

Twentieth-century administrations have exercised a discretionary, extraconstitutional prerogative in myriad ways. Every President since Theodore Roosevelt has employed executive agreements to deal with matters not covered by senatorially ratified treaties (the Supreme Court has ruled that such agreements have the force of treaties, unless they conflict with a treaty or with a statute passed pursuant to congressional authority). Jimmy Carter granted a blanket amnesty to those who dodged the draft during the Vietnam War. What is most telling of all, Presidents have despatched American troops into combat situations more than two hundred times without a declaration of war. Often these have been trivial affairs, but sometimes they have been enormous, as when President William McKinley sent seventy thousand troops to suppress a rebellion in the Philippines (they fought there for three years), or as in the Korean and Vietnam wars.

In sum, prerogative power inheres in the presidential office, a situation that is dangerous but necessary. The restraints upon it are not constitutional but political: the Congress, the bureaucracy, the news media, and public opinion.

[See also (II) Commander in Chief, Executive Agreements.]

BIBLIOGRAPHY

Arnhart, Larry. " 'The God-Like Prince' John Locke, Executive Prerogative, and the American Presidency." *Presidential Studies Quarterly* 9 (1979): 121–130.

Holdsworth, W. S. *A History of English Law.* 2d ed. Vol. 6. 1937.

McDonald, Forrest. *The American Presidency: Roots, Establishment, Evolution.* 1993.

Schlesinger, Arthur M., Jr. *The Imperial Presidency.* 1974.

Scigliano, Robert. "The President's 'Prerogative Power.' " In *Inventing The American Presidency.* Edited by Thomas E. Cronin. 1989.

– FORREST MCDONALD

EXECUTIVE PRIVILEGE

The concept of executive privilege is not mentioned in the Constitution. As the Supreme Court observed in 1974, however, it does have "constitutional underpinnings." The principle emerged out of the more fundamental constitutional concept of Separation of Powers. As Archibald Cox has written, "The controversy over executive privilege arises from our constitutional separation of government into coordinate legislative, executive, and judicial branches." In 1787, the Framers, fearful of creating a political system that would encourage tyranny, conceived a federal political system that emphasized separate institutions that would share power. Separation of powers, along with other concepts such as checks and balances, federalism itself, and the concept of judicial review, were ideas incorporated explicitly or implicitly into the Constitution to reduce the risk of tyranny in the new republic.

The Constitutional Framework

Separation of powers, while also not mentioned explicitly in the Constitution, is implicit in the form of the distribution of powers among the three coordinate branches of the national government and between the central and state governments. Congress, the President, and the federal courts have sets of powers, enumerated in Articles I through III, that define the powers of each branch of government. The concept of separation of powers seems to suggest that none of the coordinate branches will intrude into areas of power reserved to the other coordinate branches. The legislature legislates; the executive implements legislation; and the federal courts judge the constitutionality of the legislation itself or of the way in which the legislation has been implemented by the executive.

In reality, however, the coordinate branches share power to some extent. Since the early days of the Republic an interactive relationship has developed between the coordinate branches of the national government. Because of this interaction and overlap of powers, there is no possibility that any of the branches will be absolutely insulated "within its own sphere," divorced from the actions of the other two branches. As the Supreme Court said in *United States* v. *Nixon* (1974), the "separated powers were not intended to operate with absolute independence."

Given the fact that no formalistic separation of powers is possible or even desired, the reality of separate institutions sharing power leads to occasional conflict. Occasionally, the conflict between the Congress and the President over refusal to release executive information leads to a threat by the chair of an investigating congressional committee to hold the executive officer in contempt of Congress. If either house of Congress holds an executive official in contempt, the U.S. attorney convenes a grand jury to seek an indictment. In *United States* v. *House of Representatives* (1983), the Supreme Court was faced with the request to resolve a confrontation between the Republican President, Ronald Reagan, and the Democrat-controlled House. The Justices urged the two coordinate branches to seek compromise rather than confrontation. Judicial intervention in such confrontations, the Court said, "should be delayed until all possibilities for settlement have been exhausted."

The concept of executive privilege must be viewed in this context. In his battles with Congress and with federal judges over the release of information and audiotapes in his possession, for example, President Richard M. Nixon maintained that the only recourse to his use of presidential privilege to deny documents to congressional investigators and the courts would be "by impeachment and through the electoral process." Viewing presidential-congressional relations since 1789, however, one sees grudging accommodation and compromise more often than the type of confrontation suggested by Nixon.

A President and his staff must be free to examine alternative strategies in the process of formulating policy for the nation. The conversations that take place among executive policy makers must be robust, free-wheeling, and confidential for the President to solicit frank views on controversial public policy matters. Furthermore, it may be necessary to keep certain national security secrets from the courts. Congress, of course, has its own constitutional responsibilities in military and national security affairs. It is recognized that the national security rationale for refusing to release information may conceal a less honorable motivation, such as protecting the administration from embarrassment.

Executive privilege, then, is a derivative concept that emerges from the separation of powers idea and the need for the executive to encourage frank conversations and to protect the national security. As the Justices said in *Nixon,* the privilege "is fundamental to the operation of government and inextricably rooted in the separation of powers under the Constitution."

What happens, however, if these conversations (tape-recorded or transcribed) or papers and other materials are requested by the courts or Congress? Can an investigating committee of Congress looking into claims of fraud and malfeasance in a federal agency request papers and other materials from the executive in order to carry out the legislature's investigative function? Can a subpoena be issued, in line with rule 17(c) of the Federal Rules of Criminal Procedure, that requires a member of the executive branch, even the President, to turn over needed information so that the prosecution can adequately prepare its case for presentation to a federal grand jury investigating a criminal activity or to a petit jury in a criminal trial in a federal district court?

Conflict among the Branches

A presidential claim of executive privilege, that is, a claim made by the executive that information held by the executive will not be given to Congress or to a court, encourages a clash between coordinate branches. The President's power to withhold information conflicts with the power of a federal court to issue a subpoena and with the congressional power to call witnesses in the course of a legislative investigation.

While the term *executive privilege,* or *presidential privilege,* is of recent vintage, President George Washington had to wrestle with the concept as early as 1792. He met with his Cabinet to discuss a request for information from the executive branch from a congressional committee investigating General Arthur St. Clair's ill-fated expedition against the Indians. According to

Thomas Jefferson's notes of the meeting, Washington said that "the Executive ought to communicate such papers as the public good would permit, and ought to refuse those, the disclosure of which would injure the public." On that occasion, the Cabinet concluded that there would be no injury to the public if Washington turned over material to the legislative investigating committee.

That working definition of executive privilege has become a primary foundation block for Presidents and presidential advisers. Since 1792, Presidents have asserted executive privilege to deny Congress sensitive information dealing with foreign policy and national security matters. While the privilege is not an unqualified one, both the federal courts and Congress acknowledge that, under certain conditions, the executive should not have to turn over papers and other materials to the federal courts, nor should key members of the executive branch be compelled to testify before Congress. The question that plagues members of the coordinate branches is this: Under what circumstances can and should the claim of executive privilege be used by the President to avoid exposure of executive-branch discussions and decision making?

EXECUTIVE PRIVILEGE IN THE COURTS. During the Watergate affair, President Nixon acknowledged in a brief presented to the Supreme Court that executive privilege "cannot be claimed to shield executive officers from prosecution for crime." As the Court's *Nixon* decision clearly indicates, when a prosecutor preparing a criminal case for argument before a federal grand jury or before a trial jury in federal district court needs information held by the executive, then a subpoena can be issued to the President or any other and any member of the executive branch.

In *Nixon,* a unanimous Court ordered the President to turn over sixty-four tapes to the federal judge. An absolute, categorical executive privilege, which is what Nixon's attorneys argued for, would mean that criminal proceedings in federal courts would in some cases have to be based on incomplete evidence. Given the adversarial nature of the U.S. justice system, relevant information is necessary to determine guilt or innocence. Prosecuting and defense attorneys' need for compulsory means to obtain information—including the use of the subpoena to force persons to present vital information—overrides the presidential use of privilege. Federal prosecutors, however, must convince trial judges that the specific information sought is relevant, cannot be found elsewhere, and will be admissible as evidence. If persuaded, the judge makes an in camera inspection of the information to determine whether it is indeed relevant to the criminal proceedings. In *Nixon,* the general executive privilege to retain the tapes fell before the argument presented by the Watergate special prosecutor, Leon Jaworski.

EXECUTIVE PRIVILEGE IN THE CONGRESS. Although clashes have frequently occurred between Congress and the President over executive privilege, the federal courts, including the Supreme Court, have never created constitutional limits on the use of executive privilege to deny Congress information. Viewing these conflicts over history, one can see a pattern whereby this type of political dispute is resolved by the political process itself.

The President's power to withhold information conflicts with the congressional power to call witnesses in the course of a legislative investigation.

In certain political conflicts—as, for example, impeachments—Congress has had good access to materials and personnel in the executive branch. The Constitution gives the House of Representatives the "sole power of Impeachment," so it must have complete access to the materials it needs to conduct impeachment investigations. As President James K. Polk noted in 1846, the House has "the right to investigate the conduct of all public officers under the Government. . . . It could command the attendance of any and every agent of the Government, and compel them to produce all papers, public or private, official or unofficial, and to testify on oath to all facts within their knowledge."

Presidential privilege is also deemed inappropriate when employed in an effort to cover up official misconduct. The Supreme Court, in *Watkins* v. *United States* (1957), noted that the power of Congress to conduct investigations "comprehends probes into departments of the Federal Government to expose corruption, inefficiency, or waste." President Reagan's Attorney General, William French Smith, said publicly in 1982 that he would never "shield documents which contain evidence of criminal or unethical conduct by agency officials from proper review." And Reagan himself, after the Iran-contra affair broke in 1986, allowed two top former national security advisers to testify before Congress.

Further, Congress has been successful in obtaining information regarding nominees put forward by the President. The Supreme Court, however, has tried to place some modest restrictions on the scope of the congressional investigatory power. A committee must demonstrate the relevance to its investigation of the information it seeks. However, the Court, as stated in *Barenblatt* v. *United States* (1959), as long as a legislative investigating committee "acts in pursuance of its constitutional power, the judiciary lacks authority to intervene on the basis of the motives which spurred the exercise of that power."

Generally, Congress recognizes the critical value of confidentiality of discussions in the executive branch. The President and his key staff must be able to discuss policy alternatives frankly, and the documents and preliminary drafts of policy statements prepared for such conversations are entitled to presidential privilege protection. Committee members acknowledge that presidential advisers and intimates have the shield of presidential confidentiality and should not be asked to reveal to Congress the substance of confidential discussions with the President.

Executive Privilege and National Security

The most sensitive area, which has occasionally been the basis for serious confrontation between the executive and the other two branches of national government, is that of national security and foreign affairs. In the 1974 *Nixon* decision, a unanimous Supreme Court deferred to executive privilege in controversies involving "a claim of need to protect military, diplomatic, or sensitive national security secrets." For the Justices, even in camera inspection by a federal district judge of papers and documents involving military, diplomatic, or national security matters amounted to too great an interference by the judiciary into political matters.

Even when secret military or diplomatic information is needed for a trial, the Justices have deferred to the President when he employs executive privilege to justify nondelivery of presidential information. In *United States* v. *Reynolds* (1952), the Justices concluded that the federal courts "should not jeopardize the security which the [executive] privilege is meant to protect by insisting upon an examination of the evidence, even by the judge alone, in chambers." Since that time, however, Congress has explicitly authorized judges to inspect sensitive materials in camera.

While the Court has largely relinquished its review of national security materials, Congress, because of its constitutional responsibilities, cannot. Article I gives Congress the enumerated powers to declare war, to raise and support armies and navies, to provide for the common defense, and, through the necessary and proper clause, to create instrumentalities such as the Selective Service System to effectively implement their enumerated powers. Further, Congress has general oversight responsibility over the executive agencies responsible for implementing military and foreign policy. In the critically important areas of military, diplomatic, and national security policy, as the Court noted in *Japan Whaling Association* v. *American Cetacean Society* (1986), Congress and the President jointly play a premier role in the formulation and execution of foreign policy. Courts have continually urged Congress and the executive to resolve their disputes regarding the availability of executive information about military and foreign policy.

As Louis Fisher writes, the scope of executive privilege is shaped by vying claims by the three coequal branches of the national government. Fisher claims, "The integrity of the judicial process requires evidence; the executive branch needs a measure of confidentiality in its deliberations; and Congress depends on information to carry out its responsibilities." Accommodation among the three institutions sharing power is essential. The Supreme Court, very cautious when controversies come close to being nonjusticiable, is reluctant to referee such clashes and instead has consistently encouraged compromise between Congress and President.

[See also (II) Separation of Powers.]

BIBLIOGRAPHY

Ball, Howard. *"We Have a Duty": The Supreme Court and the Watergate Tapes Litigation.* 1992.

Berger, Raoul. *Executive Privilege.* 1973.

Casper, Gerhard. "An Essay on Separation of Powers: Some Early Versions and Practices." *William and Mary Law Review* 30 (1989): 30–78.

Cox, Archibald. "Executive Privilege." *University of Pennsylvania Law Review* 122 (1974): 1383–1424.

Fisher, Louis. *Constitutional Conflicts between Congress and the President.* 3d rev ed. 1991.

Freund, Paul A. "Foreword: On Presidential Privilege." *Harvard Law Review* 88 (1974): 30–107.

Kurland, Philip. *Watergate and the Constitution.* 1978.

Winter, Ralph K., Jr. "The Seedlings for the Forest." *Yale Law Journal* 83 (1974) 1730–1795.

— HOWARD BALL

F

FAITHFUL EXECUTION CLAUSE

The provision of Article II, Section 3, of the Constitution of the United States that directs the President to "take Care that the Laws be faithfully executed" is best understood in broader terms of the rule of law. Government under law is the sustaining principle of constitutional empowerment. In short, authoritative power is derived from and enhanced by acceptance of legal constraints consistent with standards of reasonableness expected of government in a constitutional democracy.

Related fundamentals are also crucial: most specifically that, while separate institutions are created by the Constitution, the three branches share the authority and responsibilities of one national government. The faithful execution of the laws clause has sometimes been viewed, however, in terms of a system of competing branches, increasingly characterized by presidential aggrandizement.

The traditional perspective on faithful execution of the laws is more constrained, and the limits are urgently relevant to basic conditions of American government. Public confidence in political institutions and leaders has often been shaken by corruption, partisan spoils, and failures to collaborate as one government to achieve reasonable public purposes. Government has often been weakened by diminished popular trust. That is a crucial context in which faithful execution of the laws needs to be understood. It is a practical perspective, and in that sense it is much like the situation that prevailed when the clause was written into the Constitution, although contemporary problems of nonobservance of law are significantly different.

Constitutional Origins

Prior to implementation of the new Constitution in 1789, acts of the United States government could only be executed by the Continental Congress—and that could only be accomplished with great difficulty. The states under the Articles of Confederation retained their separate sovereignty and jealous independence. The United States, as a "congress assembled," as provided for by the Articles of Confederation, was relatively impotent to enforce compliance by the states with financial requisitions and other national actions. Delegates to the Philadelphia Convention sought to remedy that condition.

A national executive was conceived by many of the Framers as a necessary extension of the United States government. The purpose was to provide practical means for the national government to implement its decisions, giving rise to the faithful execution of the laws clause and related provisions. The initial language of the Virginia Plan demonstrated this practical orientation. It proposed creation of a "National Executive" to be chosen by Congress, with general authority to execute national laws. Proposed responsibilities of the executive were phrased at the Constitutional Convention on 1 June 1787 by James Madison in these words: "with power to carry into execution the national laws, . . . and to execute such powers, not legislative or judiciary in their nature, as may from time to time be delegated by the national legislature." Roger Sherman said he considered the Executive "as nothing more than an institution for carrying the will of the Legislature into effect." The New Jersey Plan, phrased in terms of a plural executive system, proposed that "the Executives" should have general authority to execute federal acts. The Hamilton Plan, favoring the greatest authority of the executive, simply provided authority to execute all laws passed. Following deliberations and stylistic drafting, the provision emerged in its final version: "take Care that the Laws be faithfully executed."

The faithful execution of the laws clause has sometimes been viewed in terms of a system of competing branches, increasingly characterized by presidential aggrandizement.

In short, enhanced authority of the national government was a great concern in the processes of writing and ratification of the proposed, new constitution. Structuring of the United States government into three branches by the new charter was justified in The Federalist as a means to limit chances of tyranny that might more easily result from concentrated power. Clearly, the institutional arrangement was not aimed at creating an executive with authority to act independently as the government. Creation of an executive branch was quite simply a practical decision to facilitate action, within limits, by the one national government of the United States. Means were previously lacking to enforce laws; the new arrangement was designed to remedy that.

Interpretations in Conflict

Constitutional authority of the President under the faithful execution of the laws clause has been interpreted throughout American history as constrained, particularly by authority assigned by Congress to other governmental officers. But while limited, the authority has been understood as providing for crucial oversight by the President to assure faithful execution of laws, specifically with respect to executive-branch matters. Conflicts over presidential authority under the provision have arisen in recent decades, however, including some over assertions that executive acts can only be done under direction and control of the President. Associated with this activist theory of presidential power are interpretations that stress separation of powers and ignore shared authority and responsibilities. This activist theory at its extreme nearly defines an executive branch that is subordinate to the President as the United States government.

Historical origins of the constitutional language, as summarized above, and practices throughout American history support a more constrained interpretation. Madison in the First Congress stated that the President's responsibility is to ensure "good behavior" and to "superintend" executive officers for that purpose (*Annals of Congress,* 1789, vol. 1, pp. 379 and 387). In 1823, during James Monroe's presidency, Attorney General William Wirt responded as follows to a request for his opinion on the President's authority to alter decisions of Treasury Department auditors and comptrollers: "The Constitution assigns to Congress the power of designating the duties of particular officers: the President is only required to take care that they execute them faithfully" (I Op. Att'y Gen. 625). With respect to ministerial functions and quasi-judicial functions, presidential control is limited.

Chief Justice William Howard Taft, following his service as President, espoused active presidential authority. Specifically, in *Myers* v. *United States* (1926), he found authority for the President to remove a postmaster, without cause, before expiration of his term of office, and the Court held contrary provisions of the Tenure of Office Act of 1867 unconstitutional. Nine years later, in the equally well-known case, *Humphrey's Executor* v. *United States* (1935), the President was held to lack authority to remove a member of the Federal Trade Commission, who was found to exercise no part of executive power but to function under quasi-legislative and quasi-judicial powers.

Taft's support in *Myers* of a "strong" presidency represented a mild brand of activism by contrast with a few later interpretations. In *United States* v. *Nixon* (1974) for example, it was argued on behalf of the President, caught up in the Watergate affair, that the judiciary lacked jurisdiction because the matter was an in-house dispute within the executive branch. The Supreme Court rejected that view, however, and allowed the special prosecutor, an employee of the executive branch, to sue his hierarchical superior, the President. Later, the Reagan administration sometimes argued the view that the President has separate authority and responsibility to interpret the Constitution, Supreme Court decisions to the contrary notwithstanding. While such positions have rarely garnered much support, actions consistent with doctrines of separate and overriding presidential power have concerned careful observers of the national government. For example, persistent Reagan administration interventions into agency rulemaking and adjudications, under the guise of coordination, were seen by experts as troubling violations of traditional, constitutionally based limits.

Contrary to constitutional law, extensive literature of American public administration from the 1930s forward has supported aggrandizement of presidential power in a system characterized by a relatively strict separation of powers rather than by shared authority and responsibility. Many early public-administration leaders deliberately divorced themselves from the field of law. In his influential textbook first published in 1926, for example, Leonard White enjoined the field of public administration to leave aside concerns of law and to embrace, instead, those of the American Management Association. In 1936, the seminal report of the President's Committee on Administrative Management (the Brownlow Committee) established the doctrine of American public administration for the next forty years under the banner of executive leadership and hierarchical conformation and control. The two Hoover Commissions (1947–1949, 1953–1955) forcefully persisted in a similar vein.

Despite such sustained support of aggrandizement of presidential power, constitutional interpretation strongly supports the view that the three branches of United States government share authority and responsibilities. Congress can and does distribute ministerial and adjudicative duties among executive-branch officials without observing the hierarchical principles of public administration orthodoxy. Executive-branch officers, in turn, do implement the laws themselves, except that, in broad areas in which discretion is allowed, the President may exert direction and control.

Failures of a Rule of Law

Questions about the faithful execution of the laws clause most commonly have concerned means of enforcement of national laws and institutional conflicts among the three branches of the national government. Since the late 1960s, however, concerns have focused increasingly on whether governmental officials may properly place self-interests and partisan loyalties, especially to the President, above responsibility to a rule of law. Chronic failures to observe reasonable standards of law have so come to characterize the national government that traditional concerns of constitutional interpretation no longer suffice in analysis of the faithful execution of the laws clause.

Chronic failures to observe reasonable standards of law have so come to characterize the national government that traditional concerns of constitutional interpretation no longer suffice.

Historically, despite such earlier scandals as territorial land-development schemes, shoddy Civil War procurements, crimes in dealing with Indian affairs, corruption of elections, and the Teapot Dome Scandal, it was generally assumed in public affairs that standards of a rule of law as well as reasonable compliance with specific laws would characterize conduct of national government officials. Although successes in maintaining government under law have continued to outnumber failures by far, since the 1960s increasingly destructive violations of reasonable standards have shaken public confidence. Spoils and corruption have ranged among public officials from Vice President Spiro T. Agnew to numerous presidential appointees of the Reagan administration and from former Speaker of the House of Representatives Jim Wright to a multitude of members of Congress in the House bank and post office scandals in the early 1990s. Official national government failures have included the Bay of Pigs invasion, the Vietnam War, the Watergate affair, the Iranian hostage crisis, the Iran-contra affair, and numerous violations in defense and foreign-assistance contracting. Such failures demonstrate a deficiency of shared understanding and acceptance of the discipline of the rule of law.

Constitutional government under the rule of law requires the following conditions:

First, a culture of respect for law. Examples at the top and at all levels of government who do in fact take care that the laws are faithfully executed are essential to facilitate both the substance and image of integrity.

Second, responsible exercise of latitude in interpretation and applications of laws. Both professional expertise and political sensitivity are required to deal effectively with the complexities of public affairs, making shared responsibility among career civil servants and political officials in all branches of government essential.

Third, practices that reach well beyond obedience to specific laws. Most fundamentally, such practices involve a "search for reasonableness," building on experience that reaches back to such teachings as Plato's allegory of the cave. In administrative processes, for example, minimum guidelines that are accepted as basic to a rule of law include actions consonant with disciplined processes, experience, and knowledge; actions accessible to open inquiry; opportunities for fair hearings; and authoritative purposes, the "ends of the law," always weighed positively in the balance.

[See also (II) Separation of Powers.]

BIBLIOGRAPHY

Fisher, Louis. *The Politics of Shared Power: Congress and the Executive.* 1993.

Ledewitz, Bruce. "The Uncertain Power of the President to Execute the Laws." *Tennessee Law Review* 46 (1979): 757–806.

Miller, Arthur S. "The President and Faithful Execution of the Laws." *Vanderbilt Law Review* 40 (1987): 389–406.

Miller, Arthur S., and Jeffrey H. Bowman. "Presidential Attacks on the Constitutionality of Federal Statutes: A New Separation of Powers Problem." *Ohio State Law Journal* 40 (1979): 51–80.

Newland, Chester A. "Faithful Execution of the Law and Empowering Public Confidence." *Presidential Studies Quarterly* 21 (1991): 673–686.

– CHESTER A. NEWLAND

FEDERAL BUREAU OF INVESTIGATION (FBI)

Since its founding in 1908, the FBI has been one of the most controversial institutions in American life. Its history can be divided into three parts: the years before J. Edgar Hoover, Hoover's years as director (1924–1972), and the post-Hoover period.

Before 1908, investigations of violations of federal crimes were handled by Secret Service agents from the Treasury Department lent to the Justice Department (or to other agencies with problems needing investigation). When Theodore Roosevelt investigated land frauds in Idaho involving members of the Idaho Republican

Party, Congress tried to stop the investigation by prohibiting the loan of Secret Service personnel to other departments, so Roosevelt set up the Bureau of Investigation within the Justice Department. Initially, the Bureau was staffed by nine former Secret Service agents and twenty-five other investigators.

A pattern emerged during these early years: when the public became aroused over a real or perceived danger, Congress or the President would respond with new federal laws or executive orders, and the Bureau would be thrown into action, characteristically emerging with a few high-profile arrests to demonstrate federal concern. During public hysteria over the so-called white slave menace in 1910, the Bureau arrested the controversial black heavyweight boxing champion, Jack Johnson, for a violation of the Mann Act. During World War I, the Bureau brought the weight of the government down on draft resisters and antiwar activists, particularly members of the Industrial Workers of the World and the Socialist Party. After the war, the Bureau organized the Palmer raids to round up and deport alien communists.

During the Teapot Dome scandal of 1923 and 1924, the Bureau's efforts to intimidate critics of the Warren G. Harding administration instead discredited the Bureau. As a result, Calvin Coolidge's Attorney General, Harlan F. Stone, put the Bureau under guidelines that restricted it to investigations of federal crimes, a policy adhered to by its new director, J. Edgar Hoover, with few exceptions, until the Franklin D. Roosevelt administration. From 1924 to 1933, Hoover turned the Bureau into a model progressive law enforcement agency, making the Bureau indispensable to local forces by developing fingerprint files, establishing crime laboratories, collecting crime statistics, and providing advanced training facilities in police science.

President Warren G. Harding's administration led the FBI's attempts to intimidate critics of the administration during the Teapot Dome Scandal of 1923 and 1924. (Library of Congress, Prints and Photographs Division)

But under Herbert Hoover the Bureau also began to perform rather innocuous political services for the President at his request—providing information on individuals and groups wishing to meet with the President, for example—that evolved into a regular routine of acting as the President's personal political intelligence agency, furnishing information to Roosevelt on rivals like Huey Long, the Liberty League, and the isolationist movement, to Harry S Truman on Tommy Corcoran, and to the Kennedys on Martin Luther King, Jr., and on the implications of their romances. During the 1964 Democratic Convention, the Bureau kept Lyndon B. Johnson informed on anything that might disrupt his control of the event. The Bureau's need to be ready to service presidential inquiries undoubtedly was one of the motives—or excuses—for its tireless acquisition of information on public figures, a practice that unnerved political Washington during Hoover's lifetime and has fascinated the media ever since.

In 1933 the Bureau received a new mandate from Franklin Roosevelt's Attorney General, Homer Cummings. The news media and Hollywood had made celebrity gangsters a symbol of national demoralization during the early Depression. Cummings put Hoover and the Bureau on the trail of outlaws such as Machinegun Kelly, Pretty Boy Floyd, Baby Face Nelson, and John Dillinger, and the impact of these cases was enormous: they propelled through Congress a package of federal laws vastly increasing the jurisdiction of the Bureau (renamed the Federal Bureau of Investigation in 1935) and touched off a "G-man" boom of FBI entertainment in the movies, radio, the comics, and pulp magazines. In addition, Roosevelt secretly put Hoover and the Bureau back in the business of investigating extremist organizations and individuals, especially communists and fascists. With the outbreak of World War II in Europe, Roosevelt proclaimed a state of emergency and made the FBI publicly responsible for collecting information on espionage, sabotage, and subversive activities. After Pearl Harbor, the FBI publicized its activities on the home front to prevent vigilante loyalty investigations of the World War I variety.

With the outbreak of the cold war, Hoover's FBI embarked on the highly controversial task of investigating

Soviet espionage activities and prosecuting the Communist Party U.S.A. under the Smith Act. The Bureau also provided assistance to congressional internal security investigative committees, notably the House Un-American Activities Committee, the Internal Security Subcommittee of the Senate Judiciary Committee and, eventually, Sen. Joseph McCarthy's investigative subcommittee. The FBI also worked with anticommunist journalists, politicians, and organizations and cooperated with the entertainment industry to create a climate of popular anticommunism and ensure support for the Bureau's plans to detain communists and other persons who represented security risks should hostilities break out between the United States and the Soviet Union.

Throughout the 1950s and 1960s and into the 1970s the FBI continued to raise the alarm about domestic communism, long after most observers felt the danger had passed. During the 1960s the Bureau was criticized for failing to enforce civil rights laws aggressively and for not protecting the safety of civil rights activists. Hoover was also faulted for maintaining a force of agents who were exclusively white and male and for permitting the Bureau to be a stronghold of institutional racism despite changes in the nation's standards of race relations. The FBI's hostility toward the civil rights movement and radical political protest culminated in the notorious COINTELPRO (Counter-Intelligence Program) of the 1960s, which was directed against the black power and student antiwar movements, and in the Bureau's outrageous harassment of Martin Luther King, Jr. (motivated by Hoover's personal hatred of the civil rights leader).

When Hoover died in 1972 the Bureau had become a focus for national fury over the Vietnam War and the Watergate affair, and revelations of illegal FBI activities by Senate and House investigations in 1975 destroyed the Bureau's hard-won reputation as the country's bulwark against crime and communism, replacing it with the image of having itself been a criminal conspiracy against civil liberties and the constitutional political process. After 1978 two former federal judges, William H. Webster and then William S. Sessions, served as directors and moved the FBI into investigations of political corruption and white-collar crime. Recognizing the public and media distrust of the Bureau, they tried to keep away from the kind of publicity-generating activities favored by Hoover. In 1993 the Bureau had about eighty-seven hundred special agents across the country and was continuing to evolve, not without growing pains, into an organization reflecting the pluralistic character of American society.

[See also (II) Justice, Department of.]

BIBLIOGRAPHY

Garrow, David J. *The FBI and Martin Luther King, Jr.* 1983.
Lowenthal, Max. *The Federal Bureau of Investigation.* 1950.
Powers, Richard Gid. *G-Men: Hoover's FBI in American Popular Culture.* 1983.
———. *Secrecy and Power: The Life of J. Edgar Hoover.* 1987.
Theoharis, Athan G., and John S. Cox. *The Boss: J. Edgar Hoover and the Great American Inquisition.* 1988.
Ungar, Sanford J. *FBI.* 1976.

– RICHARD GID POWERS

FEDERAL ELECTION COMMISSION (FEC)

The Federal Election Commission was established by the 1974 amendments to the Federal Election Campaign Act (FECA) to administer the FECA, disburse public financing to presidential (and vice presidential) candidates and political party conventions, enforce the contribution and expenditure limitations and the PAC (political action committee) and political party committee provisions, provide the means for comprehensive disclosure of political receipts and expenditures relating to federal candidacy, and preside over other aspects of federal election law.

The FEC is composed of six voting members appointed by the President and confirmed by the Senate. The terms of the appointments are staggered and are for six years each. No more than three of the appointees may be affiliated with the same political party. The commission elects from among its members a chair and a vice-chair—each of a different political party—and the officers serve a term of only one year, in order to prevent a particular party or interest from dominating agency decisions and actions.

The FEC is empowered to promulgate necessary rules and regulations, conduct audits and investigations, subpoena witnesses, and make reports to the Congress and the President.

The FEC has jurisdiction over civil enforcement of federal laws; it does not have authority to act as a court of law nor to deal with criminal enforcement, though it may refer such cases to the Attorney General. The FECA specifically mandates the commission to encourage voluntary compliance with the law, and the commission has committed itself to correct or prevent violations by seeking conciliation before resorting to civil enforcement actions. Candidates and committees may agree to conciliation for a variety of reasons, such as the pressures of time, cost, and adverse publicity. Although the FEC does not formally adjudicate, the commission does interpret matters of law, determine matters of fact, and publicly declare violations of law. It may sue or be sued in civil actions and constitutional cases.

The FEC has within its jurisdiction a Clearinghouse on Election Administration. Unlike the FEC's main focus, which is on the flow of money in federal elections, the clearinghouse provides information services and studies to state and local governments in the administrative conduct of elections.

The FEC's mission as overseer of the election process requires it to strike a reasonable balance between enforcing the law and the goals of not chilling free speech nor inhibiting citizen participation in the electoral process.

[See also (II) Campaign Finance.]

BIBLIOGRAPHY

Alexander, Herbert E. *Financing Politics: Money, Elections and Political Reform.* 4th ed. 1992.

Jackson, Brooks. *Broken Promise: Why the Federal Election Commission Failed.* 1990.

– HERBERT E. ALEXANDER

FEDERAL RESERVE SYSTEM

The Federal Reserve System consists of two major decision-making bodies, the Federal Reserve Board (or the Board of Governors of the Federal Reserve System) and the Federal Open Market Committee, which includes representatives from twelve Federal Reserve district banks. The Federal Reserve was established in 1913 to perform classic tasks of economic stabilization: serving as lender of last resort to the banking system, correcting periodic regional imbalances in the money supply, and guaranteeing a stable money supply to accommodate the needs of commerce, agriculture, and industry.

The borrowing of banks from the Federal Reserve district banks has little impact on the money supply, but it can be vital in addressing financial crises.

The Federal Reserve took its current institutional form in 1935. Reforms that year removed the Secretary of the Treasury from the board, made the Board of Governors the voting majority of the Federal Open Market Committee for the first time, and lengthened the term of board members to fourteen years. This structure has often been interpreted as ensuring political independence, but the view at the time was more mixed. Franklin D. Roosevelt's appointee as chairman, Marriner Eccles, intended the reforms to make the Federal Reserve an unambiguously public agency so that private financial interests could not block key portions of the New Deal program. Subsequently, Eccles led the Federal Reserve in cooperating closely with White House policy.

This cooperation was reinforced by the demands of financing World War II. Following the war, a conflict arose with the Truman administration when the Federal Reserve, then chaired by Thomas B. McCabe, proposed to fight inflation by permitting more variation in interest rates. This conflict was resolved in 1951 in an "accord" between the Department of the Treasury and the Federal Reserve to the effect that interest rates would vary more widely and that the Federal Reserve would enjoy a wider range of independence.

The Federal Reserve Board has seven members, each appointed for fourteen years by the President with the advice and consent of the Senate. The long terms, together with budgetary independence, are believed to be essential to the system's political independence. The chairman is appointed from among board members to a four-year term. The board has authority for a number of important decisions affecting monetary policy and the regulation of financial institutions. Because these decisions are central to the financial health of the nation, Presidents have a keen interest in Federal Reserve policy.

One important set of decisions involves the discount rate, the rate of interest at which banks, savings and loan institutions, and credit unions can borrow, short-term, directly from the Federal Reserve district banks. Typically this borrowing has little impact on the money supply, but it can be vital in addressing financial crises. For example, the Federal Reserve signaled unusual willingness to lend through the discount window following the Penn Central Railroad failure in 1970, the collapse of the Continental Illinois Bank in 1984, and the stock market crash of October 1987.

A second important set of decisions involves reserve requirements for virtually all depository institutions. Reserve requirements specify how much cash financial institutions must have immediately available in their own vaults or on deposit with the Federal Reserve. Other financial regulatory decisions made by the Federal Reserve involve consumer protection, the behavior of bank holding companies, and the behavior of state-chartered banks that are Federal Reserve System members.

The Federal Open Market Committee has twelve voting members: the members of the Federal Reserve Board plus five of the twelve district bank presidents. One of the five is always the president of the New York Federal Reserve Bank, which is responsible for implementing open market policy—that is, the buying and selling of government bonds in financial markets. The other four voting seats are rotated among the other district banks (all district bank presidents participate in all meetings even when not voting). The district bank presidents are appointed by the district bank boards of directors subject to approval by the Board of Governors.

It has been argued that high-level policymakers such as the district bank presidents should be presidential appointees, subject to Senate confirmation. The importance of these appointments is underscored by the observation that district bank presidents have generally favored more restrictive monetary policy than have members of the Board of Governors, who are direct presidential appointees. By implication, if the President appointed all the members of the FOMC, monetary policy might be marginally more stimulative. However, court challenges to the method of appointment have not succeeded.

The decisions that the Federal Open Market Committee makes about monetary-growth and interest-rate targets are now regarded as the most important decisions made by the Federal Reserve. The White House watches these decisions closely, and when the President or members of his administration call on the Federal Reserve to change interest rates, their comments are directed to the Federal Open Market Committee.

[See also (II) Appointment Power.]

BIBLIOGRAPHY

Clifford, A. Jerome. *The Independence of the Federal Reserve System.* 1965.

Kettl, Donald. *Leadership at the Fed.* 1986.

Maisel, Sherman. *Managing the Dollar.* 1973.

Woolley, John T. *Monetary Politics: The Federal Reserve and the Politics of Monetary Policy.* 1984.

– JOHN T. WOOLLEY

FINDING, PRESIDENTIAL

A formal approval by the President authorizing a covert action abroad by the Central Intelligence Agency (CIA) or some other entity is called a presidential finding. From the administration of Harry S Truman through that of Gerald Ford, the approval process for covert actions—that is, the secret use of propaganda, political activity, economic disruption, or paramilitary operations against foreign countries—was relatively informal and excluded Congress. The CIA, the agency usually employed for covert actions, did not wish to inform legislators about these sensitive activities, and, conveniently, neither did legislators wish to know about them. The political risks might have been too high for members of Congress if an operation went awry and became public; it was safer to remain outside this decision loop.

Nor did the National Security Council (NSC) within the White House approve, or even know of, every significant covert operation carried out by the CIA. The tendency during these years was for the CIA to ask the NSC for broad grants of authority ostensibly covering large numbers of subsidiary operations—a good many arguably warranting separate and specific approval by the NSC.

In December 1974 Congress—in the wake of the Watergate affair and troubled by media revelations alleging domestic spying and unsavory covert actions in Chile—formally confronted this lack of accountability and took the first step toward reining in secret intelligence operations. In a flurry of last-minute legislative activity, Congress approved the Hughes-Ryan Act (1974), sponsored by Senator Harold E. Hughes (D-Iowa) and Representative Leo J. Ryan (D-Calif.). This legislation required the President to approve all important covert actions (approval was assumed to be in writing) and established a procedure for informing Congress of each approval. The law's key provision required that "no funds appropriated under the authority of this or any other act may be expended by or on behalf of the [CIA] for operations in foreign countries, unless and until the President *finds* that each such operation is important to the national security of the United States and reports, in a timely fashion, a description and scope of such operation to the appropriate committees of the Congress" [emphasis added].

The Hughes-Ryan legislation was a bold attempt by Congress to replace the so-called doctrine of plausible denial (by which a President could deny knowing about a covert action and thereby save face) with a clear trail of accountability for covert action that would lead straight to the Oval Office. The law formally forbade all covert actions—from placing false stories in foreign newspapers to overthrowing governments abroad—unless directly approved by the President.

From 1947 to 1974, the CIA decided on and conducted covert actions with only limited accountability.

From the verb *finds* in the statute comes the term *finding,* that is, the anticipated written document bearing the President's signature of approval. The "appropriate committees" to which the finding was to be delivered "in a timely fashion" (understood to be within twenty-four hours) were initially three in the House of Representatives and three in the Senate: the committees on appropriations, armed services, and foreign affairs. In 1976, legislators added the Senate Select Committee on Intelligence and, in 1977, the House Permanent Select Committee on Intelligence. Then, in 1980, with the passage of the Intelligence Accountability Act (known less formally as the Intelligence Oversight Act), Congress trimmed the list back to include only the two intelligence oversight committees.

This 1980 law, the most important formal measure taken by legislators to tighten their control over intelligence operations, also required that the executive branch report a finding to the two oversight committees prior to the implementation of a covert action, replacing the ex post facto "timely fashion" standard. In emergency situations, the statute allowed the President to limit prior notice to eight leaders in Congress: the chairs and ranking minority members of the intelligence committees, the Speaker and minority leader of the House of Representatives, and the majority and minority leaders of the Senate—the so-called Gang of Eight.

In 1991 Congress passed another Intelligence Oversight Act, allowing the President to delay "for a few days" the report on a finding to Congress in emergency situations, thereby relaxing the prior-notice standard by not even requiring a report to the Gang of Eight. President George Bush said at the time, though, that he would honor the concept of prior notice in all but the most pressing circumstances. The 1991 Intelligence Oversight Act also made explicit the understanding (violated by President Ronald Reagan during the Iran-contra affair of 1986–1987) that each finding had to be in written, not oral, form. This law also prohibited the use of retroactive findings, that is, covert action approvals made by the President after an operation was already underway or perhaps even completed. (This had also occurred during the Iran-contra affair; indeed, the belatedly signed and retroactive finding for the covert sale of arms to Iran during the scandal explicitly forbade the CIA from honoring the reporting requirement of the 1980 act.)

From 1947 to 1974, the CIA decided on and conducted covert actions with only limited accountability. With the Hughes-Ryan Act, Congress insisted on a much more formal decision process. For better or worse, covert action had been democratized, with the President and members of Congress now more intimately involved in its supervision.

[See also (II) Central Intelligence Agency, National Security Council.]

BIBLIOGRAPHY

Jeffreys-Jones, Rhodri. *The CIA and American Democracy.* 1989.

Johnson, Loch K. *America's Secret Power: The CIA in a Democratic Society.* 1989.

Ransom, Harry Howe. "The Politicization of Intelligence." In *Intelligence and Intelligence Policy in a Democratic Society.* Edited by Stephen J. Cimbala. 1987.

Treverton, Gregory F. "Covert Action and Open Society." *Foreign Affairs* 65 (1987): 995–1014.

Turner, Stansfield. *Secrecy and Democracy: The CIA in Transition.* 1985.

– LOCH K. JOHNSON

FIRST LADIES

From the ceremonial role played by Presidents' wives in the early days of the republic, the job of First Lady has grown to one of considerable clout, involving campaigning, speaking out on issues, heading a project or cause that complements the President's program, serving as one of the nation's emissaries abroad, and overseeing the White House's management and its use as a national cultural center. The emphasis placed on any particular part of the job remains for each First Lady to define for herself in line with her own interests and personality, her relationship with the President, and her perception of what public attitudes will endorse.

Explanations for the growth in the distaff side of the presidency are numerous and complex, some of them tied up with the willingness of the women to play a public role and some with the wide latitude left to the chief executive to choose his advisers as he wishes—without the constraints of his party, as in a parliamentary system. As the public relations aspect of the presidency increased, incumbents turned to members of their families to augment their effectiveness, and spouses began to play a more prominent part.

The Early Republic

George Washington helped pave the way for spouses to participate in the presidency when he arranged for Martha Washington to arrive with some fanfare in New York City a month after his inauguration. She had remained in Virginia while he took the oath of office partly because her responsibilities had not yet been defined. By the time she joined her husband in late May 1789, he had made additional decisions that tended to magnify her role: his official residence would also serve as his workplace, thus drawing his entire household into the government process. Within days of her arrival in the temporary capital, Martha Washington had assumed the role of a public personage, hosting a dinner and a party that mixed politicians with friends. Newspaper columns debated what her title should be and how much attention she merited.

While Martha Washington and most of her immediate successors refused to acknowledge any role in making presidential decisions, Abigail Adams became known for her sharp wit and partisan views. Dubbed

Mrs. President by some of her critics (who had tacitly approved the nonpartisanship of her predecessor by calling her Lady Washington), Abigail Adams wrote many letters attacking her husband's political enemies and lamenting the pro-French bent of the opposition. She complained that criticism of her husband and son was excessive and suggested limiting such criticism by law. Abigail Adams's strong partisan stance, following the relatively mild-mannered Martha Washington, met a mixed reaction. Her husband's enemies found such intervention unwarranted and wrong while proponents of opinionated women lauded her as an excellent model.

For much of the nineteenth century, First Ladies followed the pattern set by Martha Washington rather than that of Abigail Adams. Most accepted that their husbands' elections propelled them into a public role, one that included entertaining at receptions and dinners, calling on other women in Washington, and overseeing the White House domestic staff—but all this without involving themselves in partisan disputes or taking sides in debates on public policy.

Dolley Madison perfected the role of First Lady as social leader, showing in the process how a popular hostess could help win votes for her husband. Known for her charm and tirelessness, she attempted to call on everyone in the capital who expected a visit and she opened the White House for weekly public receptions. She is sometimes credited with helping her husband win reelection in 1812. Although Elizabeth Monroe and Louisa Adams were less popular than Dolley Madison (and both refused to make the number of social calls that she had made), they persevered in the nonpartisan, hostess role. Louisa Adams pointed to the contradiction in the job: on the one hand she was deemed ignorant of politics simply because she was a woman, and at the same time, she reported that she was scrutinized at each public appearance for some hint as to her husband's opinions.

The Jacksonian Style

After 1829, the arrival in the nation's capital of women from the new western states helped set the stage for a different kind of White House woman. Rachel Jackson did not live to see her husband inaugurated, but she had suffered many verbal attacks from the capital's social arbiters and announced that she had no desire to live in the White House. Her death in December 1829 left her husband bitter, convinced that her critics had hastened her demise. Historians have concluded that Rachel Jackson exercised from the grave more influence over the White House than did some other women who actually resided there. Andrew Jackson's loyalty to his wife's memory is offered as the most plausible explanation for his support of Peggy O'Neal, the woman whose marriage to Jackson's ally and friend, John Eaton, split Washington into opposing camps.

The Jackson presidency coincided with a new emphasis in America on youth, and for much of the next half century, Presidents' wives were often absent or willing to abdicate their public roles, turning to young substitutes (daughters, daughters-in-law, and nieces less than thirty years of age) whose youth protected them from the criticism of the capital's social leaders. Widowers and bachelors relied on young relatives rather

FIRST LADIES

	President	First Lady
1	Washington	Martha Dandridge Custis Washington
2	J. Adams	Abigal Adams
3	Jefferson	Widower
4	Madison	Dolley Madison
5	Monroe	Elizabeth Kortright Monroe
6	J. Q. Adams	Louisa Johnson Adams
7	Jackson	Widower
8	Van Buren	Widower
9	W. H. Harrison	Anna Symmes Harrison
10	Tyler	Letitia Christian Tyler; Julia Tyler
11	Polk	Sarah Childress Polk
12	Taylor	Margaret Mackall Smith Taylor
13	Fillmore	Abigal Powers Fillmore
14	Pierce	Jane Means Appleton Pierce
15	Buchanan	Never married
16	Lincoln	Mary Todd Lincoln
17	A. Johnson	Eliza McCardle Johnson
18	Grant	Julia Dent Grant
19	Hayes	Lucy Webb Hayes
20	Garfield	Lucretia Rudolph Garfield
21	Arthur	Widower
22	Cleveland	Frances Folsom Cleveland
23	B. Harrison	Caroline Scott Harrison
24	Cleveland	France Folsom Cleveland
25	McKinley	Ida Saxton McKinley
26	T. Roosevelt	Edith Kermit Carow Roosevelt
27	Taft	Helen Herron Taft
28	Wilson	Ellen Louise Axson Wilson Edith Bolling Galt Wilson
29	Harding	Florence Kling De Wolfe Harding
30	Coolidge	Grace Goodhue Coolidge
31	Hoover	Lou Henry Hoover
32	F. D. Roosevelt	Anna Eleanor Roosevelt Roosevelt
33	Truman	Elizabeth Wallace ("Bess") Truman
34	Eisenhower	Mamie Doud Eisenhower
35	Kennedy	Jacqueline Bouvier Kennedy
36	L. B. Johnson	Claudia Alta Taylor ("Lady Bird") Johnson
37	Nixon	Thelma Catherine ("Pat") Ryan Nixon
38	Ford	Betty Bloomer Warren Ford
39	Carter	Rosalynn Smith Carter
40	Reagan	Nancy Davis Reagan
41	Bush	Barbara Pierce Bush
42	Clinton	Hillary Rodham Clinton

than mature sisters or colleagues' spouses to oversee social events at the Executive Mansion.

An obvious exception to this pattern is Sarah Polk who, at a time when campaigning for one's husband had not yet become acceptable behavior, wished that it had. Educated at one of the better women's academies in the South, she chafed at being constrained to home while her husband was out trying to win votes; and in a letter to him, she confided that she had attempted (unsuccessfully) to influence local Democrats. In the White House she made a point of subjugating domestic responsibilities to political discussions, and she refused to hide her interest in questions of public policy. Although she escaped the strong criticism that Abigail Adams encountered, she was widely rumored to have influence in her husband's decisions.

Sarah Polk was not unique among nineteenth-century women in experimenting with the job of First Lady and testing the borders of its potential power. Julia Gardiner Tyler, the young, publicity-conscious second wife of John Tyler, paid an assistant to improve her public image; and Julia Grant cooperated with the press by supplying information about the Grant children's weddings, the youngest son's pets, and other family matters. Mary Todd Lincoln's letters indicate that she used her position in the White House to gain special favors from merchants and jobs for friends and acquaintances.

Development of a Public Role

With Lucy Hayes, the job of First Lady took a slightly different turn. Although the term *first lady* had occasionally been used in the 1860s, it began to appear in print in the 1870s, and the President's wife was referred to as "the first lady of the land." Lucy Hayes, whose plain style contrasted with her predecessor's extravagance, became a popular national figure as a result of many newspaper and magazine articles about her. The Hayeses' trip across the continent—the first by a President and his wife—revealed the extent of her popularity, and temperance advocates continued to pressure her to speak up on their behalf. Although her biographer later concluded that Lucy Hayes (who abstained from alcoholic beverages herself) did not hold strong feelings about others' drinking, her ban on alcohol in the White House found wide public support. Rutherford Hayes acknowledged in his diary that his wife's advocacy had helped bring temperance votes into the Republican column.

As national magazines increased their attention to White House occupants in the late nineteenth century, Presidents' wives were singled out as favorite topics, and their relationships with their husbands were scrutinized for some indication as to the President's character. Frances (Frankie) Folsom Cleveland, the only bride of a President to be married in the White House, became enormously popular, and her face was used in commercial advertisements (a move lamented by one Congressman, who introduced legislation to make such use illegal). When unfounded charges were made public about Grover Cleveland's physical abuse of his wife, she replied in a public statement testifying to his good behavior.

Sarah Polk made a point of subjugating domestic responsibilities to political discussions, and she refused to hide her interest in questions of public policy.

This national attention focused on the First Lady helped increase the number of requests she received for help—from writers who explained that they would have communicated directly with the President had not they believed his wife to be kinder, more accessible, or more likely to respond. Lucy Hayes received letters from advocates of polygamy; Frances Cleveland heard from people who wanted her to promote various products; and Caroline Harrison responded to requests for all sorts of souvenirs: quilt patches cut from her discarded dresses and even locks of her hair.

The White House

Part of the public role for First Ladies developed out of their association with the Executive Mansion. Since the first occupancy of the White House in 1800, Presidents' wives had worked at furnishing and maintaining it. Their selections were taken as an indication of their taste, and their expenditures were carefully watched for hints of extravagance or frugality. Dolley Madison solidified the association of Presidents' wives with the mansion when she prevailed on Congress for an $11,000 appropriation and turned to the Surveyor of Public Buildings for assistance in outfitting the President's House. Elizabeth Monroe contributed to the shopping list compiled by her husband for the rebuilt White House when it reopened after being burned in 1814.

By the end of the nineteenth century, First Ladies were taking a larger public role in maintaining the mansion as a public monument. Lucretia Garfield set out to research the mansion's history at the Library of Congress because, as her husband wrote, "so little is known," and Caroline Harrison worked closely with an architect to develop plans for enlarging the White House into a horseshoe-shaped palace with separate wings for museum and office functions. When Congress refused to appropriate the necessary funds, she had to make do with a general cleanup.

This concern with the White House, as something more than a residence and office, would continue to preoccupy Presidents' wives in the twentieth century when the mansion's management would become one of their primary responsibilities. Edith Roosevelt conferred with architects and decorators about the 1902 renovation and helped engineer a change from the Victorian rococo-revival interior with its dark colors, heavy fabrics, and many fringes to rooms with a light, sparsely furnished look. She also originated the idea of displaying portraits of Presidents' wives ("myself included," she said) in the ground-floor corridor. Edith Wilson arranged for china from previous Presidents' purchases to be displayed in a specially designated room on the lower level. Grace Coolidge appointed the first advisory committee ever formed to oversee the mansion's furnishings and decoration, and she prevailed on Congress to pass legislation permitting her and the committee to seek donations of furnishings and artwork much as boards of museums operate. When a public debate erupted about what styles were appropriate for the nation's most famous home, Calvin Coolidge called a halt to the whole project and thus only a few pieces of furniture were donated.

In 1961 Jacqueline Kennedy showed how valuable a popular First Lady can be to an administration when she embarked on a project to turn the White House into a showcase for the nation's finest art and furniture. That same year Congress passed legislation making the mansion's contents public property so that future residents could not discard items according to their personal whims. Jacqueline Kennedy brought a curator on loan from the Smithsonian and appointed an advisory committee to help in the refurbishing. Guidebooks about the house and its occupants went on sale to help finance the project.

Jacqueline Kennedy's enormous personal appeal helped draw attention to the White House and imprint on the public's mind a strong connection between it and the First Lady. After Pat Nixon turned to a new White House curator, Clement Conger, to help encourage donations of art and furniture, many gifts arrived. The emphasis during the Nixon years was on acquisitions that had once been in the White House (such as the chairs ordered by the Monroes for the Blue Room in 1817) rather than on reproductions or period pieces. Pat Nixon also endorsed the idea of making the White House a showcase for American workmanship rather than for the French styles that Jacqueline Kennedy had favored. Nancy Reagan became embroiled in controversy when she announced a project to upgrade the family quarters with more than one million dollars that came from private donations.

Their association with the Executive Mansion's furnishings exposed First Ladies to criticism (and praise) that reflected on their husbands. Opinion is almost unanimous that Jacqueline Kennedy enhanced her husband's record with her refurbishing, which was highlighted in a nationally televised tour that she conducted of the White House public rooms. But Nancy Reagan's project to upgrade the family quarters brought unfavorable attention to the President, partly because it coincided with the administration's announced cuts in social programs.

As the White House took on more and more importance as a cultural showcase for the nation, First Ladies took responsibility for scheduling entertainment. Musicales, held first at the mansion during the Hayes administration, became common in the twentieth century, and concerts that had begun as gatherings of a few dozen people in the East Room were eventually carried on television to the entire nation because, Rosalynn Carter explained, "Jimmy and I knew there were so many people who had never been to the White House and would be so thrilled to be able to come."

In their choice of performers, a selection process in which they have the help of advisers, First Ladies have often gone beyond their own personal preferences to please popular tastes and thus add to the President's following or color his image. Eleanor Roosevelt brought in many different ethnic groups and gave unknown performers, such as the conductor Antonia Brico, a chance to be seen and heard. Mrs. Roosevelt's defense of Marian Anderson's right to sing at the Lincoln Memorial (when the Daughters of the American Revolution refused her the right to perform in Constitution Hall) also earned her support in many areas. Mamie Eisenhower's choice of groups led by Lawrence Welk and Fred Waring was credited by her husband with making Americans feel good about the White House and convincing them that it reflected popular tastes. Jacqueline Kennedy preferred more classically oriented programs, and Nancy Reagan often turned to Hollywood friends.

Causes and Campaigns

In addition to responsibility for overseeing the White House; choosing its china, glassware, and other furnishings; and arranging entertainment; the job of First Lady gradually came to include direction of a project or cause complementary to the President's agenda but separate from it. Hints of this development were already evident in the nineteenth century when Americans appealed to Harriet Lane, James Buchanan's niece, for help on matters relevant to artists or to American Indians. As mentioned, Lucy Hayes's valuable association with the temperance movement revealed the potential value of a President's wife taking on a cause, but not until the twentieth century did First Ladies select their own projects rather than simply respond to public pressure to champion a cause.

Mrs. Roosevelt's defense of Marian Anderson's right to sing at the Lincoln Memorial earned her support in many areas.

This particular way of contributing to the presidency, by spearheading a reform, got a firm start with Ellen Wilson in 1913. Before her death the following August, she had lent her name to slum-clearance projects and invited reformers to meet legislators at White House socials. Using official vehicles to transport observers around Washington, she showed how decrepit and inadequate some housing, within blocks of the President's home, had become. Her association with this cause became so popular that on the day she died, the Senate passed a housing bill in her honor. Her immediate successors linked their names with causes that found wide support, such as the Girl Scouts or the Red Cross.

Eleanor Roosevelt enlarged on these precedents by speaking out on many matters on which a national consensus had not yet formed. Citing her husband's partial paralysis as the reason for her traveling as his "eyes and ears," she eschewed a social leadership role for herself and turned to investigating problems that affected how people lived. She descended into mines, toured poverty-stricken areas, inspected troops in the Pacific, and then reported back to the White House and testified before a congressional committee. Although she insisted that she merely conveyed information and did not attempt to influence her husband on solutions, her own accounts belie this claim. She was widely believed to attract a more liberal following than did her husband (and thus increase his popularity with a particular segment of the population) on issues involving civil rights, women's rights, federally subsidized housing, youth programs and artists' projects. Her regular meetings with the press and her own newspaper columns increased access to her and her views.

Not all her successors followed Eleanor Roosevelt's lead. Neither Bess Truman nor Mamie Eisenhower adopted a project as her own, preferring to follow older models that featured the First Lady as social leader. But each President's wife after 1961 selected a cause as her own; its value to the President depended on how the project was perceived and whether or not the First Lady's concern seemed genuine. Lady Bird Johnson was sometimes ridiculed for her enthusiasm about "beautifying" the nation by tearing down billboards and planting trees, but her actions coincided with a new interest in protecting the environment. Indeed, on balance, her contribution was considered an asset to the administration. Pat Nixon championed volunteerism, traveling thousands of miles and speaking to dozens of audiences about how they could donate time and effort to helping others and their nation. Because the President's staff chose not to publicize her efforts, her work did little for her husband's popular standing. Betty Ford won some votes for her husband and endangered others because of her efforts to support the Equal Rights Amendment and her candor concerning her views on a woman's right to abortion. Rosalynn Carter, who also favored passage of the Equal Rights Amendment, concentrated the energies of her staff on mental health projects and on resettling Cambodian refugees. Nancy Reagan staked out a Foster Grandparents program early in her husband's presidency. When her ratings fell, however, thus causing some concern about a negative effect on the President's popularity, she turned to a program to discourage drug abuse. Billed as "Just Say No," her campaign included many public appearances and a White House conference attended by spouses of other nations' leaders. Barbara Bush sought to bolster her husband's initiative to be the "education president" by setting her own aims on raising literacy.

This increasingly prominent role as the leader of a project or cause coincided with the public acceptance of an important part for wives in the presidential campaign. Well into the twentieth century, women eschewed openly partisan speeches in their husbands' behalf, preferring to keep in the background in a subtle, supporting role. In 1928 Lou Hoover objected to wearing a campaign button for her husband, and later Eleanor Roosevelt expressed some doubts about the propriety of a woman's speaking out in her husband's favor. Bess Truman accompanied her husband on train campaigns but limited her appearances to smiling acknowledgment of her husband's introduction of her as "The Boss." Mamie Eisenhower put her name on an article in a major woman's magazine urging voters to "Vote for my husband or for Governor Stevenson but *please vote.*"

After 1960 spouses undertook increasingly partisan campaigning, and eventually their participation became an expected part of each election. Jacqueline Kennedy traveled and spoke for her husband until she announced her pregnancy and retired to Massachusetts to await the election results. Lady Bird Johnson, who set new records in 1964 when she toured the South in a train dubbed the Lady Bird Special, gave forty-seven speeches to crowds gathered along the way and she invited Democratic Party leaders to come on board for portions of the trip. Rosalynn Carter expanded the idea of spouse as campaigner when she went out on the campaign trail more than a year before the 1976 Democratic Party convention and talked to hundreds of groups, both large and small, in behalf of Jimmy Carter's nomination. She continued this very prominent and separate role in the general election and in the unsuccessful bid for reelection in 1980, explaining that by traveling separately she and her husband could cover more territory. By the 1980s, candidates' wives were accepting invitations for television interviews and for debates with the wives of other candidates.

The Public Role

Since the First Lady's duties have never been fully defined and funding for her efforts is made on an ad hoc basis, each woman experiments with the job's potential. In the twelve years that Eleanor Roosevelt served as First Lady, she enlarged the scope of the position considerably. Yet it is important to realize that she built on the foundations laid by her twentieth-century predecessors, who had attempted in different ways to bolster their husbands' standings and effectiveness.

Edith Wilson, who came to the White House as Woodrow Wilson's bride in December 1915, took on special importance after his paralyzing stroke in the fall of 1919. The Wilsons spent considerable time together after their wedding, and he admitted that he enjoyed working more when he was in her presence. He went less willingly to the West Wing office, and she often sat alongside and assisted him as he read confidential communications relevant to the war. She accompanied him to the peace conference at Versailles and made a triumphant tour of Italy—the first such international tour by a First Lady. After their return to the United States and his illness, she monitored all his visitors and all communications addressed to him, resulting in cries that she had become the "Assistant President" or "petticoat government."

Historians have disagreed on the extent of Edith Wilson's influence during the six months or so that her husband was severely incapacitated. That she limited access to him is undisputed but that she actually made other decisions is questionable. For much of the winter of 1919–1920, few decisions came out of the White House. A miners' strike, a steel workers' strike, and controversy over the deportation of aliens evidently received little presidential attention. Edith Wilson is generally credited, however, with influencing her husband to dismiss appointees who did not meet with her approval, an intervention that is difficult to document because of the privacy that surrounds it. Her lack of interest in politics after leaving the White House lends credence to her claim that she was merely acting as a supportive wife in the White House—attempting to protect her husband's health and well-being—and that she took little interest in government.

Edith Wilson's successor, Florence Harding, had been an ardent promoter of her husband all through their marriage, and she continued to work hard in the White House to bolster his popularity. Staff members noted that she made frequent trips to the public rooms of the mansion to greet tourists and to have her photograph taken with delegations of sorority sisters, Masons, and whatever groups wanted to pose. She met informally with women reporters, although these meetings were not the publicized and well-attended meetings that Eleanor Roosevelt had with the press.

Grace Coolidge took no stands on public issues, but her enormous personal popularity helped soften her husband's image as cool and distant. The White House released photographs showing her with her dog, Rob Roy, and her pet raccoon, Rebecca, thus revealing her as an animal lover and endearing her to the public. Visitors to the White House would remark that she, rather than the President, remained their strongest memory.

By the 1980s, candidates' wives were accepting invitations for television interviews and for debates with the wives of other candidates.

Although she shrank from publicity and refused to be interviewed as First Lady, Lou Hoover worked hard for her husband's program and spoke on national radio urging Americans to fight the Great Depression with volunteerism. Her attempt to refurbish the Executive Mansion with authentic American antiques had little success in those economically bad times, but she did initiate a project to compile a record of the furniture and art in the White House collection.

The stage was thus set in 1933 for Eleanor Roosevelt to reconsider the role of First Lady and to enlarge the public role in its substantive (rather than merely social or decorative) aspects. Taking advice from friends who were more feminist than she, Eleanor Roosevelt expanded the job of First Lady in several ways. She agreed to meet regularly with members of the press, scheduling her first news conference within days of moving into the White House and well before her husband got around to his first encounter with the Fourth Estate. For the rest of her tenure, Eleanor Roosevelt met weekly with women reporters. She lifted her ban on men during World War II and permitted them to attend as well. Reporters could question her on any subject, including those that were political, although she had initially put a ban on such topics. News services that had not employed women felt obliged to hire them so as to have a representative present. These press conferences and her other public statements and writings that revealed her as more liberal than her husband on matters of civil rights and women's rights helped enlarge the President's following in some quarters.

Bess Truman chose not to continue regular meetings with the press, and she refused to take stands on matters of public policy. Except for her statement that she thought the White House should be repaired rather than torn down and replaced when it was found to have structural weaknesses, she issued few public announcements. Harry Truman insisted that he consulted her before making important decisions, including that of whether to use the atomic bomb in Japan in 1945, but supporting evidence (including the recollections of their daughter Margaret) is inconclusive on this matter. Bess Truman refused to answer questions, except some of those directed to her secretaries in writing, and she destroyed many of her papers before she died.

Mamie Eisenhower followed the Truman rather than the Roosevelt model in most respects, and none of Bess Truman's successors agreed to regular press conferences. When Presidents' wives met with reporters, the subject was generally limited to social matters: menus for state dinners, clothing to be worn for special events, guest lists, and new furniture or art acquisitions for the White House.

Betty Ford's press conference, held within weeks of moving into the White House in 1974, broke new ground. She announced that she did not always agree with her husband on important matters, including the recent Supreme Court decision concerning a woman's right to terminate a pregnancy. In staking out her own separate turf and attracting a following that was not necessarily in her husband's camp, she won some followers and antagonized others. Her candor following surgery for breast cancer was even more remarkable. First Ladies had generally kept their medical conditions private, but the Ford White House released details of her surgery, encouraging American women to go for checkups. In the process, Betty Ford came to realize the enormous potential in the job of First Lady.

Although Presidents had usually refused to acknowledge that their wives played any part in important decisions, Gerald Ford admitted that he talked over with his wife major questions and that she had been influential in his controversial decision to pardon Richard Nixon. The Carters continued this trend by emphasizing Rosalynn's role in the presidency. She attended Cabinet meetings, publicized her weekly "working lunches" with the President in the Oval Office, and acted as her husband's emissary abroad. Taking the first trip ever made by a presidential spouse on an international tour of a substantive (rather than ceremonial or investigative) nature, she spoke with leaders of seven nations in the Caribbean and Latin America on matters of defense and trade policy. Yet the criticism leveled at her on her return, since she traveled as an unelected and unappointed representative of the United States, is generally cited as the reason that she made no more such trips and that her successors limited themselves to goodwill

First Lady Hillary Rodham Clinton became the first presidential spouse to have had an extensive professional career of her own. (Library of Congress, Prints and Photographs Division)

missions when they traveled abroad in behalf of their husbands.

The Reagan presidency focused new attention on the President's wife as adviser. By the time Nancy Reagan left the White House in 1989, one major newspaper credited her with raising the job of First Lady to that of "Associate Presidency." Although she downplayed her part in any official decisions, observers were nearly unanimous in insisting that she participated actively, especially in her husband's selection of personnel and in his scheduling. Her prominence was no doubt affected by her husband's being temporarily disabled, first by an assassination attempt in March 1981 and then by subsequent surgeries. But a long list of evidence compiled by the press and by White House insiders suggests her involvement: her visible prompting of the President when he replied to reporters' questions; Chief of Staff Donald Regan's version of how she vetoed certain dates for the President's travels or meetings; various accounts of how she worked to ease out Cabinet members, campaign managers, and others on the Reagan team.

Barbara Bush did not continue this trend toward a more opinionated, involved First Lady. Her literacy project was more in line with a traditionalist role for wives, and she kept most of her views to herself. Observers ventured that her opinions on important questions differed from those held by the President—particularly on gun control and on a woman's right to terminate a pregnancy—but she refused to reveal her views to the public.

The Bush presidency rounded out two centuries in which the job of First Lady evolved from its ceremonial base to become deeply involved in the presidency. In the process a large office in the East Wing became the center of the First Lady's activities. Each woman's account of her years in the White House was read for information about how decisions had been made, and the autobiographies of Lady Bird Johnson, Betty Ford, Rosalynn Carter, and Nancy Reagan were especially revealing. In January 1993, Hillary Rodham Clinton became the first presidential spouse to bring an extensive professional career of her own to the job of First Lady. Graduate of Yale Law School and partner in an Arkansas law firm, she was repeatedly singled out as one of her husband's most trusted advisers, thus illustrating once again that the job of First Lady is one that each administration defines for itself.

BIBLIOGRAPHY

Anthony, Carl Sferrazza. *First Ladies.* 2 vols. 1990–1991.
Boller, Paul. *Presidential Wives.* 1988.
Caroli, Betty Boyd. *First Ladies.* 1987.
Furman, Bess. *White House Profile.* 1957.
Gould, Lewis. "First Ladies and the Presidency." *Presidential Studies Quarterly* 20 (1990): 677–684.
Gutin, Myra. *The President's Partner: The First Lady in the Twentieth Century.* 1989.
Means, Marianne. *The Woman in the White House.* 1963.
Smith, Nancy Kegan, and Mary C. Ryan, eds. *Modern First Ladies: Their Documentary Legacy.* 1989.

– BETTY BOYD CAROLI

FIRST LADY'S OFFICE

Although the origins of the First Lady's office can be found in the nineteenth century in the ceremonial appearances of Presidents' spouses and in their management of the White House, its development as a distinct segment of the executive branch occurred in the twentieth century. Edith Roosevelt paved the way when, in 1901, she brought on loan from the War Department a clerk, Isabella Hagner, to work as her social secretary and assist in answering correspondence, dealing with the press, and handling other tasks that came to the President's wife. Hagner remained throughout the Theodore Roosevelt presidency, working first out of Edith Roosevelt's bedroom on the second floor and then, after the 1902 White House renovation, setting up a desk in the West Hall.

Provisions for Staff and space for the First Lady's office were made on an ad hoc basis until the 1940s. Presidents' wives paid out of their own funds for one or more social secretaries and relied on friends to assist them in answering letters, greeting well-wishers, arranging parties, promoting causes, improving the White House's appearance, and keeping a record of its furnishings and of the guests invited to each official event. Social secretaries compiled the materials that became "White House Social Files" for each administration. Because of the unstructured nature of the operation—involving high turnover, many volunteers, and a paid staff that came on loan from some other part of the executive branch and then left when a particular job was done—it is difficult to document the exact size and personnel of the First Lady's office.

After its construction in 1942, the East Wing of the White House became headquarters for the First Lady's office and whatever staff she chose to name. The East Wing also housed a correspondence division that handled the large volume of mail in and out of the Executive Mansion, including invitations to official events, greeting cards at holiday time, and unsolicited mail to any member of the President's family. The correspondence office grew considerably as more and more Americans reached out to their chief executive for help—in 1988 six million communications were received. Presidents also sought to bolster their popularity by sending out individual cards to acknowledge birthdays, anniversaries, and the Christmas season. In 1990 the Bush White House reported it had sent 750,000 of these messages. Some actual addressing of cards was done by volunteers, but the entire correspondence office is under the First Lady's direction.

In 1953 the *Congressional Directory* made its first public acknowledgment of the First Lady when it listed Mary McCaffree as "Acting Secretary to the President's wife." In the following decade, the office of First Lady would take on an entirely new look. Lady Bird Johnson shaped the operation into its modern version: a professionally trained, paid staff of about thirty people working out of the East Wing. In many ways the First Lady's staff mirrors the organization of the President's West Wing operation, with its own chief of staff (sometimes called staff director), press secretary, speech writers, project directors, and various other assistants for particular assignments.

As demands increased for information about the President's family, the First Lady's press secretary became an important part of the White House operation.

Although Eleanor Roosevelt served as her own press secretary, meeting with women reporters every week, her two immediate successors relied on their husbands' press secretaries to deal with the media. In 1961 Jacqueline Kennedy named her own press secretary—Pamela Turnure. Pierre Salinger, John Kennedy's Press Secretary, estimated that he controlled 90 percent of the access reporters had to Mrs. Kennedy and her children, but the job of a separate press person for the First Lady became accepted. Lady Bird Johnson turned to a seasoned Washington reporter, Elizabeth Carpenter, who doubled as staff director and worked hard to show her employer in the most favorable light, teaching her how to get the most advantageous news coverage and thus enhance her husband's record. Carpenter's success showed the potential value of an activist First Lady and inspired attempts to imitate her. As demands increased for information about the President's family, the First Lady's press secretary became an important part of the White House operation and the sole source for photographs of the presidential family. (Photos of the President and official visitors came from his press office.)

Since 1963 a specially designated project director coordinates the activities intended to promote the First Lady's association with whatever project she has announced as her own: beautification (Lady Bird Johnson); volunteerism (Pat Nixon); support for the arts and passage of the Equal Rights Amendment (Betty Ford); mental health reforms (Rosalynn Carter); Foster Grandparents and fighting drug abuse (Nancy Reagan); literacy (Barbara Bush). The project director and other staff members schedule speaking trips and other public appearances, arrange conferences, and generally work to highlight the First Lady's project as a positive contribution to the President's record.

Each First Lady arranges her own office as she chooses. Rosalynn Carter maintained headquarters in the East Wing and made a point of announcing that she went there regularly to work. Betty Ford kept an office in the residence on the second floor, installing her own telephone for lobbying and partisan pursuits. Nancy Reagan and Barbara Bush also worked out of the residence, but both of them downplayed the "office" aspect of being First Lady.

In her role as manager of the White House, the First Lady has the help of several experts, although they do not technically fall under the rubric of her "office." The Chief Usher, presiding out of a room just inside the north entrance, oversees a staff of slightly more than one hundred and works closely with the First Lady to monitor upkeep of the Executive Mansion and all traffic through it. Since 1961, a White House curator has advised the First Lady regarding exhibition of furniture and artworks in the State Rooms. Barbara Bush described herself as the unpaid guide to the second floor, but she had a sizable, knowledgeable staff to assist her.

Coordination between the First Lady's office and that of the President is not always smooth, and lines of authority frequently overlap. Rules for operation are developed by each administration, and personnel designations shift with each incumbent. Typically, however, the President's spouse heads a large office that figures prominently in each administration's plans for success.

[See also (I) Congressional Directory.]

BIBLIOGRAPHY

Anthony, Carl Sferrazza. *First Ladies.* 2 vols. 1990–1991.

Caroli, Betty Boyd. *First Ladies.* 1987.

Gould, Lewis. "Modern First Ladies: An Institutional Perspective." In *Modern First Ladies: Their Documentary Legacy.* Edited by Nancy Kegan Smith and Mary C. Ryan. 1989.

———. "Modern First Ladies and the Presidency." *Presidential Studies Quarterly* 20 (1990): 677–683.

Gutin, Myra. *The President's Partner: The First Lady in the Twentieth Century.* 1989.

– BETTY BOYD CAROLI

FOREIGN AFFAIRS: AN OVERVIEW

The term *foreign affairs* is not in the United States Constitution. The Constitution does not assign authority to "conduct foreign relations" or to "make foreign policy," and the powers allocated to the different branches of government do not coincide neatly with such categories of responsibility. To understand the constitutional dispositions for what we call foreign affairs it is necessary to examine the Constitution—its blueprint, design, and history.

The President's Foreign Affairs Powers

"The transaction of business with foreign nations is Executive altogether," Thomas Jefferson wrote. Alexander Hamilton read the constitutional provision that "the executive Power shall be vested in a President" as a general grant of all executive power, understood to include the control of foreign relations (subject only to conditions and limitations expressed or implied). The Supreme Court of the United States, building on a statement by John Marshall, referred in *United States* v. *Curtiss-Wright Export Corp.* (1936) to "the very delicate, plenary and exclusive power of the President as the sole organ of the federal government in the field of international relations."

Presidents have cited those and other statements to support a "plenary and exclusive" power over U.S. foreign affairs. If those assertions were an accurate description of the President's constitutional authority, this essay could be a brief sentence. Authoritative pronouncements, however—and even presidential claims—are not as extravagant as those terms may suggest. John Marshall (then still a member of Congress) spoke of the President as the "sole organ of the Nation in its external relations, and its sole representative with foreign nations"—an exclusive organ of communication and representation, not a sole repository of power to determine the foreign policy of the United States. For Hamilton, the Constitution gave the President authority that today might be described as power to conduct foreign relations and execute foreign policy; even for Hamilton the Constitution did not vest in the President exclusive authority to determine foreign policy. The Supreme Court's later dictum confirmed only what Marshall had said, that the President was "sole organ"; it did not suggest that the President had "plenary and exclusive power" to make all the decisions and to take all the actions that add up to the foreign policy of the United States.

Presidential claims, too—even at their most extravagant—have respected limitations on presidential power expressed in the Constitution (for example, the need for the Senate to consent to treaties and appointments); some limitations implicit in grants of authority to other branches (such as the power to declare war [*see* war, declaration of] given to Congress); and other limitations that may be implied in the structure of the Constitution and of the system of government it created.

After two hundred years, however, the President dominates American foreign affairs—far beyond what the Constitution expresses or plausibly implies, far beyond what the Framers contemplated or might have foreseen. Two hundred years of national history have given the presidency a virtually exclusive role in the conduct of foreign relations and a paramount role in the making of foreign policy. Congress honors the President's primacy; the courts defer to it. But the President's part can be understood only in relation to that of Congress, which retains "the power of the purse," its essential legislative role in foreign as in domestic affairs, and other designated responsibilities in foreign affairs, notably the power to decide for war or peace.

The Presidency in Constitutional Text

In constitutional principle, the exercise of political power has to be justified in the constitutional text or by implication. The President's express powers in foreign affairs are few and appear to be meager. According to Article II, Section 2, he has power to make treaties, but only with the advice and consent of the Senate, and provided two-thirds of the Senators present concur. He can appoint ambassadors, but only with the advice and consent of the Senate. He receives foreign ambassadors, but that seems to be a constitutional "assignment" rather than an important source of power.

In time, Presidents began to make much of the clause declaring that "the President shall be Commander in Chief of the Army and Navy of the United States." As written, and as originally conceived, that clause appears to be a designation of function rather than an independent grant of important power. Learning the lessons of the American Revolution, the Framers sought to create a single command (to avoid command by Congress or by congressional committee) and they sought to assure civilian control; but they did not consider the office of Commander in Chief to be a repository of any independent political authority. If Congress maintained an army and navy, the President would be their commander; if Congress declared war, or if the United States were attacked, the President would command the forces provided by Congress to prosecute the war or defend the United States. Nothing in the text or in the history of its promulgation suggests that the Commander in Chief was to have authority to deploy the armed forces for political purposes determined by him.

On the face of the Constitution, that is the sum of presidential power. Alexander Hamilton's argument that the clause providing "the Executive Power shall be vested" in the President was an explicit grant of power to conduct and control foreign relations, is less than obvious, was sharply rejected by James Madison, and has not been authoritatively accepted. (Justice Robert H. Jackson in *Youngstown Sheet & Tube Co.* v. *Sawyer* [1952] failed to see in that clause "a grant in bulk" of all executive power, but only "an allocation to the Presidential office of the generic powers" specified later in that article of the Constitution.)

Traditional modes of constitutional interpretation might find in the spare allocations of the text more than appears. The power to appoint ambassadors and authority to receive ambassadors [*see* ambassadors, receiving and appointing] can plausibly be read to imply authority to recognize (or not to recognize) governments, to maintain (or not to maintain) relations with a particular country. But constitutional interpretation is not an exact science. Some authority that might be claimed by the President as implied in one of his powers might be claimed by Congress by implication from one of its enumerated powers. For example, the power to terminate a treaty may be implied in the President's power to make treaties, but Congress may claim it as within its authority to regulate commerce with foreign nations, or to decide for war or peace. And much of what has been claimed for the President seems to be beyond the reach of plausible constitutional interpretation.

In *Curtiss-Wright,* Justice George Sutherland offered a bold essay with a bold thesis: in foreign affairs the powers of the United States derive not from the Constitution but from this country's international sovereignty, and the U.S. government therefore has many powers not enumerated in the Constitution. The Court did not proceed to indicate how that extra-constitutional authority of the United States is distributed between Congress and President.

Intent and Grand Design

Beyond text and its implications, Presidents have sometimes resorted to larger principles of constitutional construction. A favored source of constitutional meaning is the intent of the Framers. As regards presidential power in foreign affairs, however, there has been little resort to what the Framers intended, perhaps because what they intended is not easy to determine, perhaps because what they intended is not the large presidential power that proponents of presidential power have favored.

It is far from clear where authority in foreign affairs lies in the grand design of the Constitution. The overall constitutional division between recommending legislation and enacting it, between passing laws and executing them, between appropriating money and spending it, was designed to apply in foreign as in domestic affairs. In foreign affairs, however, the Constitution expressly allocates important powers that do not conform neatly to those divisions. For a major and blatant example, Congress was given the power to decide for war or peace, not a legislative act as commonly understood, in 1787 or now. On the other hand, the President was given the power to make treaties, which frequently have a legislative dimension and are, according to Article VI, the law of the land. Moreover, neither the specific grants of the Constitution nor its grand design clearly allocates authority of continuing importance and controversy (e.g., the power to introduce the armed forces into hostilities that are not war, or to engage in covert intelligence activities).

It is far from clear where authority in foreign affairs lies in the grand design of the Constitution.

The debate between Pacificus (Hamilton) and Helvidius (Madison) was essentially a sharp disagreement as to the grand design of the Constitution that both had helped shape (and for the ratification of which both had labored in the *Federalist*). Hamilton saw the clause vesting the executive power in the President as an explicit grant to him of the control of foreign relations except in so far as the Constitution imposed conditions on this power (such as the requirement of Senate consent to treaties or to the appointment of ambassadors), or insofar as the Constitution expressly allocated authority to Congress, as in the power to regulate foreign commerce or to declare war. For Madison, on the other hand, Congress had the principal authority, legislative as well as other policy-making authority, in foreign as in domestic affairs. The President had only the authority expressly bestowed upon him, notably the power to make treaties and to appoint ambassadors, both subject to the advice and consent of the Senate.

Which of these was the grand design of the Framers can be deduced only from the text they produced and the record of their deliberations and other writings, but the Framers were not wholly explicit (or candid), were not always in agreement, and were at times uncertain of their own intentions. They were committed to separation of powers as a principle of good government, and to checks and balances to prevent the concentration of power, but the political thought in which the Framers were educated provided no conclusive guidance as to the appropriate roles of executive and legislature in foreign affairs; nor did the Framers have a firm idea as to the distribution they desired in the new kind of government they were creating. They began with a legislature, growing out of the Continental Congress, and apparently saw Congress as primary: there is no indication they intended to deny to Congress any legislative or other policy-making authority, other than the treaty-making power. The presidency was a new office, and the Framers were divided and uncertain about it. They recognized the need for an executive and wanted one capable of initiative and planning. But they also feared autarchy and tyranny.

By the text they wrote, surely, the authors of the Constitution evinced no intent to create a powerful presidency. They did not make the President a republican, nonhereditary facsimile of the king of England. Above all, the President was not to have the king's power to go to war. The President was entrusted with the royal power to make treaties, but only subject to the advice and consent of the Senate, indeed of an extraordinary majority—two-thirds—of the Senators present.

What emerged from the Constitutional Convention was in some respects compromise, in some perhaps purposeful ambiguity. In substantial measure, the Framers seemed content to allow the office to be shaped by events, and by George Washington, the man it was generally assumed would be the first incumbent.

The Growth of Presidential Power

On balance, the language of the Constitution, the history of its framing, and the intent of the Framers, appear to support Madison's conception of its grand design, but the experience of the nation has tilted toward Hamilton's vision. From the beginning, the nature of the presidential office and the character of foreign relations and of diplomacy contributed to the growth of presidential authority. Unlike Congress, the President is always in session. Unlike Congress, he can act informally, expeditiously, secretly. Early on it was established that the President represented the United States and was the "sole organ" for official communication between the United States and other countries. The President appointed ambassadors and they were his ambassadors, his organs for diplomatic representation and communication, instructed by him and reporting to him. His power to appoint and his authority to receive ambassadors soon translated into power to recognize (or not to recognize) governments, to maintain (or not to maintain) diplomatic relations with them. Congress, for its part, early accepted the President's role as sole organ, recognizing his diplomatic expertise as well as his need for secrecy, which nurtured a sense of congressional inadequacy. Presidents did not attempt to exercise legislative power expressly committed to Congress, or to spend money not authorized and appropriated by Congress, but they readily asserted authority not expressly conferred upon them by the Constitution, and Congress acquiesced. From the beginning of the Republic, Congress began to delegate to the President much of its own undoubted authority. What earlier Presidents did with congressional acquiescence, or even by congressional delegation, later Presidents claimed to be within their own constitutional power.

Encouraged by the growth of Presidential power in foreign affairs generally, Presidents began to place the forces Congress had put under their command at the service of their foreign policy: in several hundred instances Presidents deployed U.S. forces for their own foreign policy purposes, short of war. And Congress generally acquiesced. Later, a growing practice of informal consultations between the President and congressional leaders discouraged congressional objections and served to confirm presidential authority to act without formal congressional participation. On occasion, Congress quickly ratified what the President had already done, as in 1950 when Truman sent U.S. forces to fight in the Korean War and Congress promptly adopted supportive resolutions and appropriations to finance the war. Sometimes Congress delegated its own war powers to the President in terms so broad that he could later claim to have acted under Congress's authority as well as his own, as in the Gulf of Tonkin Resolution of 1964 that gave constitutional legitimacy to the Vietnam War.

Presidential authority in foreign affairs has grown steadily during more than two hundred years. Understandably, perhaps, the President's role grew with the power of the United States. Early in the nineteenth century the international relations of the United States were modest and Presidents were still cautious politically as well as constitutionally. Thomas Jefferson doubted his own authority to do more than deploy the navy for defensive measures to safeguard U.S. shipping against predations by the Barbary Pirates. President James Monroe pronounced his famous Monroe Doctrine in 1823 but did not press its implications. James Polk, it was later charged, manipulated relations with Mexico and maneuvered Congress to declare war, but he did not fight the Mexican War until after Congress had declared it.

Opportunities for asserting extraordinary presidential authority became more frequent later in the nineteenth century and early in the twentieth century. With manifest destiny, President Theodore Roosevelt claimed power as "surrogate" of the people to do whatever was not explicitly forbidden to him by the Constitution or by the laws: he dispatched troops, annexed territory, and made international agreements on his own authority. President Woodrow Wilson armed merchant vessels against German submarine warfare, even in the face of congressional neutrality laws; later he made an armnistice agreement effectively terminating World War I. President Franklin D. Roosevelt, without seeking Senate consent, concluded an agreement with Maksim Litvinov, the foreign minister of the Soviet Union, to settle claims of U.S. nationals (as a condition of recognizing the government of the U.S.S.R.). Later Roosevelt led efforts to help Great Britain resist Adolph Hitler's aggression, by an executive agreement to exchange U.S. destroyers for bases on British territory. During World War II, Roosevelt, and later President Harry S Truman, charted the postwar peace. Truman approved the Nuremberg Charter, planned the United Nations, and promoted the Marshall Plan; he fought the Korean War and pursued a Korean armistice, which President Dwight D. Eisenhower later concluded. President John F. Kennedy blockaded Cuba in the Cuban missile crisis. President Lyndon B. Johnson sent marines to the Dominican Republic. He and President Richard M. Nixon prosecuted the Vietnam War despite growing opposition in Congress. President Jimmy Carter sent marines to Iran in an attempt to extricate American hostages during the Iranian hostage crisis. President Ronald Reagan concluded an agreement to resolve the crisis, sent Marines to Lebanon, invaded Grenada, mined Nicaraguan waters, and bombed targets in Libya. President George Bush invaded Panama and claimed powers to pursue the Gulf War against Iraq without congressional authorization, although before initiating military force against Iraq, he sought and obtained congressional authorization.

Treaties and Executive Agreements

The Constitution expressly confers upon the President the power to make treaties. The President's treaty power is subject to general constitutional restraints, such as the Bill of Rights, but the scope and content of treaties are not otherwise subject to important limitations. He can make treaties "by and with the Advice and Consent of the Senate . . . provided two thirds of the Senators present concur." Originally the Senate's "advice" function atrophied, and since then formal advice has not been asked and has been rarely given; though the executive branch sometimes consults individual Senators, advice and consent has been essentially reduced to consent. The Senate can refuse consent, or consent on conditions, commonly on conditions of change in or reservations to the treaty. Even after Senate consent, the President may decide not to make the treaty, for example, if he finds conditions imposed by the Senate unacceptable. If the President makes the treaty he is bound by its provisions as the Senate understood them and by any conditions the Senate imposed. A treaty is law of the land and the President "shall take care" that it be faithfully executed. But he can terminate a treaty in accordance with its terms, or denounce a treaty even if by doing so he puts the United States in violation of its international obligations [*see* treaty termination].

Practice has developed an alternative method of concluding international agreements by "Congressional executive agreement," made by the President with the approval of both houses of Congress. Congressional executive agreements have no explicit constitutional underpinnings but they are not controversial and their use in some areas (notably international trade) is established.

There is no agreed principle to distinguish agreements that the President can make on his own authority from those requiring the consent of the Senate.

From the beginning, Presidents have claimed also power to make some sole executive agreements, international agreements on their own authority. The Supreme Court has confirmed the President's authority to make agreements incidental to recognition of a foreign government (as in the agreement between President Roosevelt and Soviet Foreign Minister Maksim Litvinov), and agreements settling international claims (such as that by President Reagan resolving the Iran hostage crisis). In general, however, there is no agreed principle to distinguish agreements that the President can make on his own authority from those requiring the consent of the Senate (or the approval of Congress).

Periodically, the Senate has sought to curtail the President's authority to make sole executive agreements. In 1969, the Senate adopted the nonbinding National Commitments Resolution declaring that the President had no authority to make a national commitment involving "the use of the armed forces of the United States on foreign territory, or a promise to assist a foreign country . . . by the use of the armed forces or financial resources of the United States" without the consent of the Senate to a treaty or the approval of Congress. Periodically, Congress has threatened to limit executive agreements by statute and even by constitutional amendment. In the end, however, Congress enacted only the Case Act (1972) requiring the executive branch to transmit to Congress copies of every executive agreement concluded, where necessary under injunction of secrecy. It is difficult to determine whether the obligation to report to Congress has discouraged Presidents from making executive agreements, which the Senate might insist require its consent.

Presidents have not admitted limitations on their power to make executive agreements but they are not unaware that agreements that purport to make law in the United States are subject to challenge in the courts. An agreement that requires implementation by act of Congress or by appropriation of funds depends on the willingness of Congress to accept the authority of the President to conclude that agreement. A President would be rash to conclude an agreement obligating the United States if Congress might decide that it was beyond his authority to make such a promise; but a bold President might make the commitment hoping to force Congress's hand.

President and Congress

The President's role in foreign affairs cannot be understood in isolation from that of Congress. In some respects their roles are mutually exclusive, in some they may overlap, in several respects each depends on the other. Principles of separation of powers, and checks and balances pertain in foreign as well as in domestic affairs.

EXCLUSIVE POWERS. In principle, the powers vested by the Constitution in the Congress and the President respectively were to be exclusive of each other: Congress alone had legislative power, the President alone had executive power. Congress alone exercises the powers conferred upon it, principally in Article I of the Constitution, the President alone exercises the powers vested in him in Article II. In foreign as in domestic affairs the President cannot make law or take action of legislative character. For example, in 1952 the Supreme Court ruled in *Youngstown Co.* v. *Sawyer* that President Truman could not direct the U.S. Army to seize private steel mills in order to settle a labor dispute, though the President insisted that steel production was essential to the prosecution of the Korean War. On another occasion, a lower court declared the President lacked authority to impose a tariff on imports without congressional authorization, because the power to regulate commerce with foreign nations is vested in Congress exclusively. The President cannot coin money, raise an army, or maintain a navy. He cannot appropriate funds or expend money even for foreign affairs purposes except pursuant to authorization and appropriation by act of Congress (Article I, Section 9.). In turn, the President alone speaks for and represents the United States, appoints and receives ambassadors, recognizes governments, conducts diplomatic relations, negotiates with foreign governments, makes, receives, and resolves claims, makes treaties, and commands the armed forces. [*See* diplomat in chief.]

In the 1980s and 1990s, there was some confusion as to the authority of the President to take the United States to war. The constitutional allocation to Congress of the power to declare war has been understood to give Congress the power to decide whether the United States shall go to war or remain at peace. Like other express powers of Congress, the authority to decide for war or peace lies with Congress alone. The Framers recognized that if the country were attacked the United States would be at war without any decision by Congress and the President should have authority to defend the United States; if congressional authorization were deemed necessary it could be assumed.

No President has claimed authority to go to war on his own authority. Arguments that the war power of Congress was not exclusive, that the President had a concurrent, independent power to go to war have not been pressed and have not been taken seriously. In 1950, when President Truman sent armed forces to defend the Republic of Korea, he claimed authority pursuant to the United Nations Charter, which was signed and ratified by the President with the advice and consent of the Senate as a treaty of the United States. In 1991, President Bush claimed that resolutions of the U.N. Security Council authorizing the United States to go to war to liberate Kuwait gave the President constitutional authority to do so without congressional authorization, because he had authority to carry out U.S. treaty obligations under the U.N. Charter. The prevailing view is, however, that Truman and Bush did not have authority to go to war, that the U.N. Charter, though a treaty of the United States, did not confer such authority, and that a Security Council Resolution that was permissive only and did not create a legal obligation upon the United States to go to war could not provide Constitutional authority.

The exclusive power of Congress to declare and make war, and the authority Presidents have claimed to deploy armed forces for foreign-policy purposes short of war, require difficult distinctions and have raised sharp issues as to the power of Congress to regulate presidential deployments.

CONCURRENT AUTHORITY OF PRESIDENT AND CONGRESS. In general, the respective powers of President and Congress are exclusive, but Justice Robert H. Jackson in 1952 had suggested that "there is a zone of twilight in which [the President] and Congress may have concurrent authority—or in which its distribution is uncertain." Foreign affairs is the principal occupant of that twilight zone.

At the end of the twentieth century constitutional jurisprudence accepts the President's power to make foreign-policy decisions and take foreign-policy actions other than those of legislative character or that are otherwise within powers expressly vested in Congress. But the powers of Congress have also grown large, and some matters as to which Presidents have exercised authority may also be within the powers of Congress—under its commerce power, its power to define offenses against the law of nations, its war power, under other enumerated powers including its power to make laws to carry out its powers or those of the other branches, or under an unenumerated foreign-affairs power deriving from the international sovereignty of the United States.

History has given the President large powers in foreign affairs as executive and as Commander in Chief beyond the few expressly provided.

Concurrent authority for the President and Congress inevitably brings the possibility of competition for initiative or for conflicting actions. For a long time that danger remained academic as Congress remained inactive giving the President free rein, but in the wake of the Watergate affair and evidence of other executive abuse of authority such as the Iran-contra affair, Congress became "activist." Beginning in the 1970s, Congress adopted the War Powers Resolution, enacted legislation to regulate covert intelligence activities (dirty tricks, as distinguished from intelligence gathering), and tightened restrictions on executive discretion—in the sale of arms or in granting financial assistance to governments thought to be involved in terrorism or drug smuggling, or guilty of consistent patterns of gross violations of internationally recognized human rights.

With the rise of congressional activism in the 1970s, the President sought to move the focus of constitutional debate: Presidents no longer thought it necessary to argue that they had the unenumerated powers they had been exercising; they insisted that such powers were exclusive, and that Congress did not have power to monitor and regulate them. The issue was no longer the President's power, but the power of Congress. Presidents charged Congress with being "imperial," implying that congressional regulation was improper, usurping, unconstitutional.

Such presidential claims and arguments are generally difficult to sustain. History has given the President large powers in foreign affairs as executive and as Commander in Chief beyond the few expressly provided; it has not recognized those powers as exclusive. History has not limited congressional authority. It has not recognized the President's authority to flout acts of Congress or to refuse to take care that the laws be faithfully executed. Authority to disregard acts of Congress has no support in the classic sources claimed for broad presidential authority. Hamilton argued for presidential authority to act (in one instance, to proclaim neutrality in foreign wars) when Congress is silent; he did not suggest that the President could act contrary to congressional legislation, or even that the powers of Congress should be narrowly construed so as to allow for greater executive power. Neither John Marshall nor the Supreme Court in *Curtiss-Wright* said or implied anything that would warrant the President to flout congressional legislation unless it sought to invade his authority as "sole organ" for representation and communication. In *Youngstown Co.* v. *Sawyer,* Justice Jackson wrote "When the President takes measures incompatible with the expressed or implied will of Congress, his power is at its lowest ebb, for then he can rely only upon his own constitutional powers minus any constitutional powers of Congress over the matter."

In the War Powers Resolution, Congress declared its view that the President has no independent constitutional authority to introduce U.S. armed forces "into hostilities, or into situations where imminent involvement in hostilities is clearly indicated by the circumstances," except in response to an attack on the United States or its armed forces. In the absence of a declaration of war or authorization by statute, the resolution requires the President to consult Congress before introducing U.S. armed forces into hostilities, to report to Congress whenever he had done so, and to terminate the involvement after sixty days (or after ninety days in emergency and unavoidable military necessity), unless Congress authorized the involvement to continue. President Nixon vetoed the resolution claiming it was unconstitutional, but Congress passed it over his veto. Presidents have continued to challenge the constitutionality of the resolution and have sometimes flouted its provisions.

The War Powers Resolution has been criticized for poor drafting and deep ambiguity, but except for its "legislative veto" provision it is difficult to fault it on constitutional grounds. In his veto message Nixon challenged the resolution's validity because it "would attempt to take away . . . authorities which the President has properly exercised under the Constitution for almost 200 years." But whether they were in fact exercised "properly" has not yet been authoritatively determined. In any event, Presidents exercised those powers when Congress was silent; there was no precedent for the introduction of U.S. forces into hostilities by the President in the face of congressional prohibitions or limitations, or for any other unilateral executive actions contrary to congressional legislation.

If the President presses his resistance to congressional regulation of his concurrent authority, Congress will usually prevail, in constitutional principle and in political practice, if only because it holds the purse strings. Under the Constitution the President cannot spend a dollar unless Congress has authorized and appropriated the money. Where the President has independent, exclusive authority to act, Congress is constitutionally bound to implement his actions, notably by appropriating the necessary funds. For example, Congress may not properly refuse to appropriate funds for the salary of the Secretary of State or for the costs of an embassy in a foreign country. But when the President seeks funds for purposes that Congress is persuaded are beyond his constitutional authority, it can properly frustrate the presidential purpose by withholding appropriations. (It can also resist such presidential action by threat of impeachment.)

USURPATION, INTERFERENCE, AND FAILURE OF COOPERATION. Issues that have bedeviled the separation of powers in domestic matters have application in foreign affairs. In general, Congress cannot retain for itself a legislative veto to withdraw authority delegated to the President or to interfere with the President's execution of the laws; it can do so only by statute, by an act of Congress adopted by both houses subject to presidential veto. The power of Congress to investigate is subject to the uncertain limitation of the President's executive privilege, though that privilege is probably not as immune from congressional probing as he would like it to be. For his part, the President cannot refuse to execute the laws, and he must spend and may not impound or defer the expenditure of funds that Congress directed the President to spend. (Congress has adopted anti-impoundment legislation, and Presidents have acquiesced.)

Constitutionalism and Democracy

Much has changed since governmental authority in foreign affairs was allocated in 1787. The President has become "the presidency," with a large executive bureaucracy. The Congress of the Framers' generation has grown and has been transformed into a complex of numerous committees and subcommittees and a huge staff. Over the centuries, each branch of the federal government has aggrandized its constitutional powers and has developed large extraconstitutional powers, the consequence of political parties and patronage, of size and complexities, of the growth of the United States and of a changing world.

Constitutional ideology and national interest require improved processes and procedures that will assure that major decisions are based on the full political authority of the United States, on the powers of Congress and the President. The principle of checks and balances suggests that war and peace and other powers of major national import should not be in the hands of the executive alone. Since the Constitution was adopted, the United States has become a more authentic democracy, its government more authentically representative. Principles of constitutionalism, democracy, and representative government require that important decisions have the consent of both branches, each differently democratic, each differently representative.

[See also (I) Concurrent Powers, Congress, article on Powers of Congress, Treaties; (II) Separation of Powers, War, Declaration of.]

BIBLIOGRAPHY

Corwin, Edward S. *The President, Office and Powers, 1787–1984: History and Analysis of Practice and Opinion.* 1984.

Glennon, Michael J. *Constitutional Diplomacy.* 1990.

Fisher, Louis. *Constitutional Conflicts between Congress and the President.* 3d ed. 1991.

Henkin, Louis. *Constitutionalism, Democracy, and Foreign Affairs.* 1990.

———. *Foreign Affairs and the Constitution.* 1972.

Koh, Harold Hongju. *The National Security Constitution: Sharing Power after the Iran-Contra Affair.* 1990.

Pyle, Christopher H., and Richard M. Pious. *The President, Congress, and the Constitution: Power and Legitimacy in American Politics.* 1984.

Sofaer, Abraham D. *War, Foreign Affairs, and Constitutional Power: The Origins.* 1976.

– LOUIS HENKIN

G

GENERAL ACCOUNTING OFFICE (GAO)

Created by the Budget and Accounting Act of 1921 to give Congress an independent capacity to audit the executive branch, the General Accounting Office is under the control and direction of the Comptroller General of the United States. Over time, Congress has increased the powers and responsibilities of the GAO. Presidents and their Attorneys General have frequently raised constitutional objections to the activities of the GAO, especially when it appears that the Comptroller General is carrying out executive duties without being subject to the direct control of the President.

The history of the GAO has important antecedents in the years before the drafting of the Constitution. In 1781, the Continental Congress created a number of executive officers to handle administrative matters. The positions of Secretary for Foreign Affairs and Secretary at War were accepted by Congress as essentially executive in nature. The question of finance proved much more divisive. Robert Morris accepted the new post of Superintendent of Finance, but his request for total control over his subordinates met with legislative opposition. Congress decided to restrict his power to remove subordinates to cases where he had good cause ("incapacity, negligence, dishonesty or other misbehavior"). Moreover, Congress itself appointed the Comptroller rather than allow the Superintendent to make that selection. The Comptroller was a quasi-judicial officer because he superintended the settlement of public accounts and his decision was "conclusive" on all appeals related to the auditing of accounts. Because of these institutional qualities, the Comptroller of 1781 is clearly a forerunner of the Comptroller General.

When Congress created the Department of the Treasury in 1789, it continued the office of Comptroller. Although James Madison argued strongly in favor of giving the President the power to remove the secretaries of Foreign Affairs, War, and Treasury, he insisted that the Comptroller needed a measure of independence from presidential control. The properties of the Comptroller were not "purely of an Executive nature" and seemed to "partake of a Judiciary quality as well as Executive." Because of the mixed nature of this office, Madison said that there might be "strong reasons why an officer of this kind should not hold his office at the pleasure of the Executive branch of the Government." Only by understanding the history of the Comptroller during the Continental Congress could Madison have offered such remarks.

Legislation in 1795 made the Comptroller's decision on certain claims "final and conclusive." In 1817, Congress abolished the offices of accountant in the War and Navy departments and placed the authority to settle all accounts and all claims and demands by or against the United States within the Treasury Department. To discharge these new duties, the statute created four new auditors and an Assistant Comptroller. Other duties were assigned to the Comptroller over the years, but the major organizational change came in 1921, when Congress created the General Accounting Office. In effect, Congress lifted the Comptroller, Assistant Comptroller, and six auditors out of the Treasury Department—literally transferring people, files, furniture, office equipment, and other property to the newly created GAO. The establishment of the GAO was intended to give Congress an institutional capacity to compete with the President's Bureau of the Budget, also created by the 1921 statute.

The GAO audits the executive branch to ensure that funds are spent efficiently.

The Budget and Accounting Act of 1921 describes the GAO as "independent of the executive departments and under the control and direction of the Comptroller General of the United States." The Comptroller General and Assistant Comptroller General are both appointed by the President with the advice and consent of the Senate and both hold office for fifteen years and may be removed only by a joint resolution of Congress or by impeachment.

The GAO audits the executive branch to ensure that funds are spent efficiently and that expenditures are consistent with statutory authority. The 1921 law directed the Comptroller General to report to Congress "every expenditure or contract made by any department or establishment in any year in violation of law." Moreover, the Comptroller General investigates "all matters relating to the receipt, disbursement, and application of public funds." Balances certified by the Comptroller

General "shall be final and conclusive upon the executive branch of the Government." Claims and demands by the government or against it are settled and adjusted by the GAO.

The statutory responsibilities assigned to the GAO by the 1921 law have been greatly enlarged over the years. The GAO was strengthened significantly by the Budget and Accounting Procedures Act of 1950 and the Legislative Reorganization Act of 1970. As a result of these statutes and internal reforms, GAO now directs more of its resources to broad program evaluation instead of narrow auditing of agency vouchers. The Central Intelligence Agency (CIA) is exempt from GAO audits.

GAO's exercise of statutory powers frequently results in collisions with the executive branch, especially the Department of Justice. Comptrollers General have insisted that their opinions regarding the legality of government expenditures are binding on the executive departments, but ever since 1921 Comptrollers General and Attorneys General have disagreed on statutory interpretations, jurisdiction, and the application of public funds. The Attorney General has regularly placed limits on the binding nature of GAO decisions. Orders given by the GAO to the executive departments affecting the performance of executive functions have been submitted to the Attorney General for his independent opinion. In some cases the executive departments have refused to comply with GAO decisions.

Occasionally a President has intervened to challenge a GAO decision. In 1944 the Comptroller General ruled that the Committee of Fair Employment Practice, created by executive order and lacking any statutory support, did not have the powers it claimed. This ruling was overridden by a letter written by President Franklin D. Roosevelt. Congress, however, passed legislation to prohibit the use of any appropriation to pay the expenses of any agency established by executive order unless Congress specifically authorized funds for the agency. Disputes between GAO and the executive branch have also been litigated and resolved in federal court.

[See also (I) General Accounting Office.]

BIBLIOGRAPHY

Mosher, Frederick C. *The GAO: Quest for Accountability in American Government.* 1979.

Smith, Darrell. *The General Accounting Office: Its History, Activities, and Organization.* 1927.

Walker, Wallace Earl. *Changing Organizational Culture: Strategy, Structure, and Professionalism in the U.S. General Accounting Office.* 1986.

– LOUIS FISHER

H

HEALTH AND HUMAN SERVICES, DEPARTMENT OF

The Department of Health and Human Services (HHS) is responsible for providing health care and social services to millions of Americans. HHS runs 250 separate programs. Its fiscal 1993 budget of $585 billion is the largest of all federal departments and accounts for almost 40 percent of all that the federal government spends. Indeed, the HHS budget exceeds the combined budgets of all fifty states (excluding federal funds they receive) and is larger than the budgets of all countries in the world, except the United States, Germany, and Japan. Each time the consumer price index rises 1 percent, the HHS budget rises almost $4 billion. HHS directly employs about 120,000 people and indirectly pays the salaries of another one million people, in state and local government and on private payrolls, who operate its programs.

History

The department was established as the Department of Health, Education, and Welfare (HEW) by President Dwight D. Eisenhower in 1953. President Lyndon B. Johnson turned HEW into the government's largest department when he placed most of his Great Society social programs and the heavy social artillery of his War on Poverty there. During Johnson's presidency (1963–1969), HEW was given responsibility to execute the following programs and laws: Head Start for preschool children; the Elementary and Secondary Education Act, which provides billions of dollars of aid to help schools with high concentrations of poor children; a series of higher education measures that provides grants and loans to help college students defray the cost of their education; Medicare, which provides health care for Americans over sixty-five years of age and those who are permanently disabled; Medicaid, which provides health care for millions of "medically indigent" Americans, largely single-parent mothers and their children who receive benefits under the Aid For Dependent Children (AFDC) program and poor senior citizens in nursing homes; laws to establish community health centers and regional medical centers for heart, cancer, and stroke; funds that substantially increased the federal government's investment in biomedical research; laws that prohibit discrimination on the basis of race, creed, sex, or ethnic origin in federally funded health and education programs.

In 1979, at President Jimmy Carter's recommendation, the Congress took the "E" out of HEW and created a separate Cabinet-level Department of Education. The Department of Health and Human Services, as it exists in the early 1990s, was established at that time.

Sections of HHS

HHS is formally divided into four sections: the Social Security Administration, which administers social security and welfare programs; the Public Health Service, which includes the National Institutes of Health and Food and Drug Administration; the Health Care Financing Administration, which administers Medicare and Medicaid; and the Administration for Children and Families, which administers service programs for older Americans, children, and families.

President Lyndon B. Johnson turned HEW into the government's largest department when he placed most of his Great Society social programs there.

The Public Health Service (PHS) studies infectious diseases, control of epidemics, and care of American Indians on their reservations. The members of PHS are doctors, nurses, and a variety of paramedicals and other professionals, headed by the Surgeon General of the United States.

The Food and Drug Administration, established in 1906, is responsible for assuring that the nation's food supply is safe and properly labeled and that pharmaceutical and medical devices like prostheses are safe and effective before they are marketed. FDA's regulations and actions affect products that account for 25 cents of each dollar American consumers spend.

The National Institutes of Health (NIH) started with a budget of less than $50,000 in 1930. The NIH comprises the world's largest and greatest medical research complex. The first institute dedicated to a specific disease was the National Cancer Institute created in 1937. Since then a number of mission-oriented institutes have been established, including: the National Heart, Lung, and Blood Institute, the National Eye Institute, and the National Institutes of Dental Research; Mental Health; Neurological and Communicative Disorders and Stroke; Arthritis, Diabetes, Digestive, and Kidney Diseases; Allergy and Infectious Diseases; Child Health and Human Development; Environmental Health Services; Alcohol Abuse and Alcoholism; and Drug Abuse. Since the late 1970s, the national government, almost entirely through these institutes, has been funding 90 percent of the basic biomedical research performed in America.

HHS also houses the Center for Disease Control, which is headquartered in Atlanta, Georgia. CDC is the nation's nerve center to keep track of infectious diseases and collect many health statistics. It monitors all infectious diseases, from children's ailments like measles, to sexually transmitted diseases like AIDS, gonorrhea, and syphilis, and provides data essential to protect the public health and to assist biomedical research efforts.

HHS programs directly serve one in every five Americans, and they touch virtually every citizen at one time or another during his or her life. The department provides cash payments to the elderly, poor, blind, and disabled; kidney dialysis to any who need it; runaway youth shelters; assistance for blind vendors; rescue for abused children; treatment for heroin and cocaine addicts; immunization against childhood diseases like measles, mumps, and whooping cough; rehabilitation for the disabled.

Through its Older Americans program, HHS annually serves more than 150 million meals to almost four million senior citizens at more than 10,000 senior centers it supports across the country, and in the homes of shut-ins. Medicare, the HHS program to provide health services to Americans over 65 and the permanently disabled, pays 25 million bills each month; Medicaid, the program for poor people, pays another 70 million, including many for drug prescriptions. Each day HHS's Social Security Administration receives 25,000 claims; each night the system's computers make millions of entries on individual wage files so workers will receive the proper benefit upon retirement.

Programs and Controversies

Because HHS touches so many Americans personally, its actions have provoked wide-ranging and intense controversies that often embroil the President. Just before Thanksgiving in 1959, the HEW Secretary, Arthur Fleming, stopped the sale of canned cranberries and cranberry products in the United States because of concern about adulteration. To execute the law banning any food additive that caused cancer when ingested by animals, Secretary Robert Finch, in 1970, removed the artificial sweetener cyclamates from the market and almost destroyed the soft drink industry in the United States. In 1976, Secretary David Matthews pressed President Gerald Ford to mount the program to protect the nation against the killer swine flu, an unprecedented and ill-starred attempt to inoculate the entire American population. In the 1960s and 1970s, HEW's Civil Rights division placed the presidency at the center of bitter racial controversies as it sought to carry out its congressional mandate to integrate the nation's school systems. In 1978, Secretary Joseph A. Califano, Jr., mounted a major antismoking campaign, which marked the start of the steady decline in smoking among American adults, but which also embroiled the President in political controversy with tobacco-producing states and the cigarette industry. In 1979, the department issued the first Surgeon General's Report on Health Promotion and Disease Prevention, setting goals for a healthier America. The antismoking campaign continued under Surgeon General C. Everett Koop during the 1980s, and HHS set new goals for a healthy America in 1990, thus making health promotion and disease prevention one of the department's central responsibilities.

During its history, HHS provided the funds to start the television program "Sesame Street."

The department's funding of health programs has put it at the center of controversies such as abortion, whether to fund heart transplants, whether to fund expensive neonatal health centers for premature babies, whether to reimburse hospitals for use of expensive life-extending equipment on terminally ill patients, and how to conduct fetal research. Many of these controversies, notably abortion, have engaged Presidents and presidential candidates.

HHS administers the Aid For Dependent Children program, the welfare payments to poor single parents and children that has been a center of controversy since the 1950s. The political and legislative battles have focused on the need to put welfare parents to work and to get absent fathers to pay support for their children. The program's Child Support Enforcement Administration, which was begun in the 1970s, now leads a nationwide effort to locate fathers who are not making support payments and get them to fulfill their responsibility to support their children.

Accomplishments of HHS

HHS programs are directed in good measure at America's most vulnerable citizens—the poor, the sick, the old, the disabled, the minorities.

During its history, HHS provided the funds to start the television program "Sesame Street"; financed research that led to cures for some children stricken with leukemia; helped minority students become doctors, lawyers, and professors; spearheaded the World Health Organization's successful effort to eradicate smallpox; furnished social, health, and educational services to Southeast Asian refugees in the wake of the Vietnam War and to Jews escaping from the Soviet Union; and funded the expansion of American medical schools.

BIBLIOGRAPHY

Davis, Karen, and Cathy Schoen. *Health and the War on Poverty.* 1978.

Marmor, Theodore. *The Politics of Medicare.* 1977.

– JOSEPH A. CALIFANO, JR.

HIGH CRIMES AND MISDEMEANORS

The constitutional grounds for impeachment are generally termed high crimes and misdemeanors. Article II, Section 4 of the Constitution provides that the President, as well as the Vice President and all civil officers, "shall be removed from Office on Impeachment for, and Conviction of, Treason, Bribery, or other high Crimes and Misdemeanors." "Treason" is defined in Article III, Section 3; "bribery" has an established meaning both at common law and under federal criminal statutes. "High crimes and misdemeanors" is a less familiar term, whose origin is traceable to the British parliamentary common law of crimes.

President Andrew Johnson was faced with impeachment after the House of Representatives passed a resolution in 1868 to impeach him for "high crimes and misdemeanors." (Library of Congress, Prints and Photographs Division)

According to James Madison's notes on the Constitutional Convention, the term was added to the impeachment provision at the suggestion of George Mason of Virginia. As reported by the committee of eleven, the draft constitution limited the grounds for impeachment to treason and bribery. Mason objected that the provision was too limited: "Treason as defined in the Constitution will not reach many great and dangerous offenses," including "attempts to subvert the Constitution." Mason proposed adding "maladministration," then included as a basis for impeachment and removal in a number of state constitutions. Madison responded that "so vague a term will be equivalent to a tenure during pleasure of the Senate," and Mason substituted "other high crimes & misdemeanors . . . agst. the State." To avoid ambiguity, the last phrase was later amended to "against the United States," and then finally deleted by the Committee on Style and Arrangement.

While British impeachments provided "the model from which the idea of this institution has been borrowed," as Alexander Hamilton wrote in *Federalist* 65, impeachment in Britain played a different role. Impeachment convictions could lead to criminal penalties, and impeachments could be directed at ordinary citizens—for "high crimes" against the system of government—as well as public officials. Impeachment was a substitute for trial in the criminal courts for high officers of the government and could reach ordinary, as well as high crimes.

In the American system, impeachment is a mechanism for removing officers of the government, including the President; it cannot be used to impose criminal sanctions on officers or citizens. There is no congressional common law of crimes, and since 1812 no federal common law of crimes at all.

The subjects of impeachment, Hamilton wrote, "are those offences which proceed from the misconduct of public men, . . . from the abuse of public trust"—offenses that are "of a nature which may with peculiar propriety be denominated political, as they relate chiefly to injuries done immediately to the society itself." Impeachment proceedings "can never be tied down by such strict rules, either in the delineation of the offence by the prosecutors, or in the construction of it by the judges, as in common cases serve to limit the discretion of the courts in favor or personal security."

Nonetheless, at least since the impeachment trial of Supreme Court Justice Samuel Chase in 1804, it has been argued that "high crimes and misdemeanors" means indictable criminal offenses, specific violations of known law. Lawyers for Presidents Andrew Johnson and Richard M. Nixon made this argument in their defense.

The more widely held view, consistent with past American impeachment cases and with constitutional history, is that impeachment is not restricted to cases of criminal wrongdoing. The crucial consideration, at least in presidential impeachment proceedings, is not whether conduct would be criminal if engaged in by a private citizen but the effect of the conduct on the functioning of government. A President is subject to impeachment, under this view, for conduct that is seriously incompatible with either the constitutional form and principles of government or the proper performance of the constitutional duties of the presidential office.

[See also (II) Impeachment.]

BIBLIOGRAPHY

Farrand, Max, ed. *The Records of the Federal Convention of 1787.* 1937. Pp. 64–69, 550.

Labovitz, John R. *Presidential Impeachment.* 1978. Pp. 1–131.

Story, Joseph. *Commentaries on the Constitution of the United States.* 1833. sections 749, 763.

U.S. House of Representatives. Committee on the Judiciary. *Constitutional Grounds for Presidential Impeachment: Report by the Staff of the Impeachment Inquiry.* 93d Cong., 2d sess., 1974.

– JOHN R. LABOVITZ

HONEYMOON PERIOD

The presidential honeymoon is the interval between the election of a new President and the point at which disenchantment is voiced by substantial segments of the public, the press, and Congress. When President Gerald R. Ford declared to a joint session of Congress that, "I do not want a honeymoon with you. I want a good marriage," he was seeking to extend this auspicious period.

With a newly elected President, there is excitement, and the initial evaluation of public opinion is positive. The press typically treats a new Chief Executive favorably. The news is primarily about appointments and general plans for the future, and the opposition is relatively silent so as not to appear to be sore losers. Thus, the cues on which the public may base its evaluations of the President are supportive of the White House.

Other factors buttress this favorable start to a presidency. Americans tend to have approving opinions of people. They have a general disposition to prefer, to learn, and to expect positive relationships more than negative relationships and to perceive stimuli as positive rather than negative. This orientation provides the foundation for the predisposing factor called the positivity bias.

The causes of the positivity bias are not well known, but it seems to have the greatest potential for influence in ambiguous situations, such as the beginning of a President's term. New occupants of the White House are unknown to the public as chief executives and therefore may receive the benefit of the doubt in the public's evaluation of them.

Some authors have found evidence of a bandwagon effect in which, after an election, people, especially those who had voted for the loser, tend to view the winner more favorably than they did before the election. This depolarization of politics and the positivity bias itself probably help to give most Presidents a boost in the polls early in their terms.

As a President performs his duties, the public may begin to perceive more implications of presidential policies for their own lives. If people view these policies unfavorably, they may be more receptive to negative information about the President. The conventional wisdom is that the honeymoon period is a short one, with the rest of the term characterized by a decline in the polls.

Presidential honeymoons with the public are not always short-lived, however. Declines do take place, but they are neither inevitable nor swift. President Dwight D. Eisenhower maintained his standing in the public very well for two complete terms. President John F. Kennedy held his public support for two years, as did Ford, once he suffered his sharp initial decline following his pardon of Richard Nixon after only a month in office. Both Presidents Ronald Reagan and George Bush experienced considerable volatility in their relations with the public, but their records certainly do not indicate that the loss of public support is inexorable or that it cannot be revived and maintained. Richard M. Nixon's approval levels were also quite resilient for his entire first term. Lyndon B. Johnson's and Jimmy Carter's approval losses were more rapid, although Johnson's initial ratings were inflated due to the unique emotional climate at the time he assumed office following the assassination of Kennedy. The same was true, of course, for Ford, who assumed office after Nixon resigned.

Thus, honeymoons are not necessarily fleeting phenomena in which new occupants of the White House receive a short breathing period from the public. Instead, the President's constituents seem to be willing to give a new chief executive the benefit of the doubt for some time. It is up to each President to exploit the goodwill provided by the public's predisposition and use it as a foundation on which to build solid support for his administration.

Perhaps the most important consequence of a honeymoon period is for the President's ability to lead Congress. First-year proposals have a considerably better chance of passing Congress than do those sent to the Hill later in an administration. Thus, Presidents are frequently advised to be ready to send legislation to the Hill early in the first year of their terms to exploit the honeymoon atmosphere that typically characterizes this period. President Lyndon B. Johnson explained, "You've got to give it all you can in that first year. . . . You've got just one year when they treat you right and before they start worrying about themselves." Kennedy, Johnson, Reagan, and to some extent Carter took advantage of this opportunity, whereas Eisenhower, Nixon, and Bush did not.

The President might choose simply to propose a policy without thorough analysis to exploit the favorable political climate of his honeymoon.

Although the prospects of passage are enhanced if legislation moves quickly, there are good reasons why many Presidents are not able to ensure that it does. For example, Carter's proposals for energy, welfare reform, and the containment of hospital costs were complex and controversial policies that took a long time to draft and to clear relevant offices in the White House. He could not turn to a well-established party program as Kennedy and Johnson could.

There is of course an alternative to the methodical, time-consuming drafting of legislation. The President might choose simply to propose a policy without thorough analysis to exploit the favorable political climate of his honeymoon. This appears to have been the strategy of Reagan's White House regarding the budget cuts passed by Congress in 1981. The departments (including Cabinet members) and their expertise were kept at a distance during decision making. According to the Budget Director, David Stockman, "None of us really understands what's going on with all these numbers." Lyndon Johnson's legislation to establish the War on Poverty in 1964 is often faulted for having been understood by virtually no one.

Although the strategy of "move it or lose it" may increase the probability of a bill's passage and not affront the sensibilities of someone with Ronald Reagan's lack of concern for details, it is not difficult to understand why someone with the temperament of Jimmy Carter may eschew such a process.

Presidential honeymoons, then, can play an important role in a presidency. But neither their duration nor their significance should be exaggerated.

[See also (II) Chief Executive.]

BIBLIOGRAPHY

Brody, Richard A. *Assessing the President.* 1991.
Edwards, George C., III. *Presidential Approval.* 1990.
Light, Paul C. *The President's Agenda.* Rev. ed. 1991.
Mueller, John E. *War, Presidents, and Public Opinion.* 1970.

– GEORGE C. EDWARDS III

HOUSING AND URBAN DEVELOPMENT, DEPARTMENT OF

The first presidential policy initiatives in the field of housing and urban development were relatively straightforward and modest both in program and organizational arrangements. They were about housing per se—not urban development—and they were advanced in pursuit of the grander objectives of peace and prosperity. Programs were lodged in agencies, not departments, and Presidents gave them only sporadic attention.

Federal Housing Programs

Publicly supported federal housing first appeared during World War I under the auspices of the U.S. Housing Corporation, whose mandate was first to build and then to liquidate housing for war workers (the corporation endured until 1942). Later, in the New Deal years, the Federal Housing Administration (FHA) was created (1934) to direct federal mortgage insurance programs (the Farmers Home Administration and the Veterans Administration would subsequently carry out similar programs). In 1937 the U.S. Housing Authority was established to provide grants and loans to local public housing authorities. In 1942 Franklin D. Roosevelt created the National Housing Agency in a partly successful effort to unify these scattered efforts, and a few years later Harry S Truman undertook a similar reorganization, establishing the Housing and Home Finance Agency (HHFA). Throughout these years, however, housing remained the principal mission assigned to these agencies, and federal involvement in housing was justified principally on the grounds of war needs or economic recovery.

The impetus for the establishment of the Cabinet-level Department of Housing and Urban Development (HUD) was different. The 1950s witnessed a growing concern for cities, their fiscal stability, and the health of urban communities. Creating decent housing remained a central part of HUD's program, but a broader set of urban concerns was now surfacing. Strong and vigorous leadership by the mayors of major American cities, for the first time in league with downtown business executives, was stimulated to action by the 1954 Housing Act, which authorized the federal urban renewal program. The mayors' and business leaders' calls for federal attention were supported by the analyses of social scientists, who in the 1950s "discovered" cities and, using new empirical methods of research, forecast that the quality of urban life was at risk. These two forces—the new breed of politically powerful and policy-oriented big city mayors and business leaders and the new breed of articulate, policy-oriented academics—combined forces to lobby for the cities' having a place at the Cabinet table. During the 1960 campaign, they persuaded John F. Kennedy to commit himself to a new urban program and a new department to carry it out.

At the recommendation of his pre-inauguration task force, President Kennedy tried to keep his commitment. He overrode objections from the professional staff in the Executive Office of the President and proposed the new department to Congress. But Kennedy had appointed Robert Weaver, an African American, as the administrator of HHFA (Weaver was at that time the highest-ranking black in the executive branch). Chiefly because of this, southern members of Congress, anticipating that Weaver would be named thus the first black Cabinet member, killed the Kennedy proposal. It remained for Lyndon B. Johnson to persuade Congress to agree to the establishment of HUD, which he did in 1965—in the euphoric early period of the Great Society.

A Confusion of Purposes

HUD's establishment, however, did not make clear its central purpose. Rather, it confused it. Senator Abraham Ribicoff, the leader of the Senate fight to establish the department, under pressure from mortgage bankers and home builders insisted that housing programs maintain a separate identity. They were to be "coordinated" with other urban programs. Mayors and community and academic leaders pressed for the primacy of general urban interests, going so far as to propose the elimination of the word *housing* from the department's title. (They dropped this proposal when a White House task force pointed out the acronym would then be DUD.)

HUD's departmental structure reflected its conflict of purposes and the ambivalence over its goals. HUD absorbed the same constituent units of HHFA, with the FHA accorded quasi-autonomous status, plus two new programs of rent supplements as well as the Model Cities program. Rather than HUD's being a coordinating office, as the legislation had mandated, a presidential executive order authorized the department to be a "convenor" of other departments with urban interests. HUD did not absorb the fledging antipoverty program (the Office of Economic Opportunity), then an Executive Office agency. Neither were urban environmental programs nor the farm and veteran home loan guarantee programs transferred to the new department.

With an incomplete portfolio, insufficient to convey the image of an organization equally concerned with social as well as physical urban issues, HUD remained bifurcated. Its early years were marked by continuing presidential interest and concern, by major legislative victories, especially in the 1966 and 1968 Housing and Urban Development Acts, and by vigorous program execution (although this was hamstrung by dwindling appropriations as the Vietnam War escalated). But in the tumultuous events of the late 1960s HUD had neither a honeymoon cruise nor a shakedown.

The administrations that followed Johnson's were ideologically and rhetorically hostile to the Kennedy-Johnson emphasis on cities. Yet, somewhat ironically, HUD fared well. Richard M. Nixon's first HUD Secretary, George Romney, embraced and energetically executed the main provisions of the 1968 act, although some of the private housing construction authorized proved ill advised. Romney's successors maintained relatively low profiles, but a substantial pipeline of projects kept the major programs active, albeit with new names, until well into the Carter administration. Even as the department dropped from public view, congressional appropriations continued to increase. What constrained HUD in the Carter years was not ideology but inflation, the oil crisis, and the Iranian hostage crisis, all of which diverted attention from domestic programs.

The Reagan administration, which had neither ideological nor program sympathy for HUD, savaged the department. Ideologically, the New Federalism, which mandated the devolution of formerly federal responsibilities to the states, left little room for a national role in urban affairs. Programmatically, HUD's operating budget fell 57 percent, the largest cut suffered by any federal department during the Reagan years. Program cuts in federally assisted housing, community block grants, and urban development action grants were similarly reduced. Even worse for the department's reputation, a series of scandals lost an estimated $2 billion to fraud and mismanagement. The department's record of passivity in legislative initiatives and low visibility throughout the tenure of Secretary Samuel Pierce compounded the pattern of failure.

HUD's Cabinet Status

During the Bush administration Secretary Jack Kemp brought vigorous leadership to the department, and the 1990 Housing and Urban Development Act represented the first comprehensive strategy in a generation to provide affordable housing, encourage home ownership, and undertake to empower the poor. The central issue, as throughout the 1980s, was whether appropriations sufficient to respond to the needs of cities would be forthcoming. In 1992, even after the Chicago flood and the Los Angeles riots, that issue remained unresolved.

With more than twenty years of departmental experience to review and the tenures of nine secretaries to appraise, what reckoning can be made of the tenth Cabinet department? As far as HUD's organizational status is concerned, the department never received sustained presidential attention except during the Johnson administration. Not only was its secretary never a member of the "inner" Cabinet (i.e., the counselors to the President), but, in terms of political power, Washington observers rank HUD close to the bottom of the "outer" Cabinet, where secretaries are often reduced to being advocates of particularistic interests—pleaders not counselors—and are frequently written off as mere captives of their clienteles.

Washington observers rank HUD close to the bottom of the "outer" Cabinet, where secretaries are reduced to being pleaders not counselors.

Judged internally, HUD was still beset by internal controversy: housing programs still vied with more general urban development programs for the attention of the secretary and to secure a priority position in budget and staffing. Unlike the staffs of the State, Defense, and Health and Human Services departments, HUD's senior professional staffs could claim no particular expertise nor superior knowledge of problems or prescriptions for their solution. The Foreign Service, the military, and government health professionals all enjoy such status, but HUD's knowledge of housing and urban affairs, mostly resting in the disciplines of economics and sociology, is challenged by its clients in the housing industry and local governments and by experts in think tanks and universities. Neither the statistics HUD produces nor the reports it issues enjoy a special stamp of superiority.

Moreover, HUD's jurisdiction is limited, as other housing and community facility programs are assigned to the departments of Agriculture, Interior, Labor, Health and Human Services, and Transportation. The loss of the mass transportation programs, which HUD originally administered, to the Department of Transportation sharply restricted HUD's capacity for strategic urban planning. Moreover, the Treasury Department, in setting interest rates, has a critical impact on the prosperity of the housing industry but is often indifferent to it. When the Treasury assumed responsibility for President Nixon's revenue-sharing program, HUD's prestige again suffered severely.

HUD's clienteles do not compensate for the department's low status. The building industry, comprising homebuilders, realtors, mortgage financiers, unions, and building goods manufacturers, is the most potent, but even these interests lose out when the well-being of the national economy is at stake. Further, they tend to tilt HUD toward housing policy and away from urban development. The mayors, community development leaders, housing consumers, and representatives of the urban poor are much less influential, inside or outside Washington.

In the early 1990s, HUD remained a department that had not succeeded in establishing clear and mutually reinforcing goals. It aided housing chiefly by subsidizing interest rates, not by addressing the problems of spiraling land costs or the potential of new technology to transform the building industry. It had lost ground in jurisdictional turf battles within the executive branch, just as the cities had lost ground to the states in the receipt and management of federal grants. Without a President willing to back a new urban initiative and reorganization plan to pull the fragmented urban programs together, HUD faced the prospect of a continuing long, cold slide toward mediocrity in the quality of its leadership and administrative skill and the relevance of its programs to the urban ills it was created to alleviate.

BIBLIOGRAPHY

Hanson, Royce. *The Evolution of National Urban Policy, 1970–80: Lessons from the Past.* 1982.

Kaplan, Marshall, and Franklin James. *Federal Housing Agencies and National Housing Policies.* 1988.

Orlebeke, Charles J. "Chasing Urban Policy: A Critical Retrospect." In *The Future of National Urban Policy.* Edited by Marshall Kaplan and James Franklin. 1990.

Peterson, George E., and Carol W. Lewis, eds. *Reagan and the Cities.* 1986.

Redford, Emmette S., and Marlan Blisset. *Organizing the Executive Branch: The Johnson Presidency.* 1981.

Weaver, Robert C. "The First Twenty Years of HUD." *American Planning Association Journal* 51 (1985): 463–474.

– ROBERT WOOD

I

IMMUNITY, PRESIDENTIAL

The Constitution does not specify whether the President possesses any immunity from the judicial process. It does accord members of Congress explicit privileges from arrest and from suits for their legislative conduct. The absence of a parallel set of textual immunities for the President may imply that he possesses none. Yet concern was expressed at the Constitutional Convention that subjecting the President even to impeachment could impair his capacity to perform the duties of the office. Hence it is unlikely that the Framers thought that the President could be treated like an ordinary individual by the courts. Congress has not legislated on the subject. A statute purporting to regulate the President's exposure to compulsory process, civil damages, or criminal sanctions might be invalidated on separation of powers grounds. Consequently, delineation of presidential immunities has been left to the courts.

The question of a President's immunity is sensitive for several reasons. First, his office is owed the respect due to the head of a coequal branch of government. Second, if the President must respond in any way to judicial process, and especially if he is amenable to trial, there is potential for interference with his constitutional duties. And third, fear of civil or criminal liability could deter a President from vigorously pursuing the public interest. Yet powerful competing considerations exist as well. If ours is truly to be a government "of laws, and not of men," no one should be above the law. Presidents have power to do great harm as well as good—it would be unfortunate if either affected individuals or the general public were unable to obtain redress for presidential wrongdoing. The courts have tried to balance these values.

Immunity in History

For most of the history of the United States it was unclear that the President could be directly subjected to any kind of compulsory court process. In the treason trial of Aaron Burr in 1807, Chief Justice John Marshall, sitting as a circuit judge, directed a subpoena for evidence to President Thomas Jefferson. Jefferson complied "voluntarily," protesting any obligation to do so, and there the matter rested for many years. In *Mississippi* v. *Johnson* (1867), the Court refused to forbid President Andrew Johnson to enforce Reconstruction legislation. The decision rested, though, on the discretionary nature of the President's statutory duties and the consequent inappropriateness of enjoining his exercise of those duties in advance, rather than on his amenability to suit. Effective legal control of presidential actions was routinely maintained by reviewing the actions of subordinates. For example, in *Youngstown Sheet & Tube Co.* v. *Sawyer* (1952), the Court enjoined the Secretary of Commerce from carrying out the President's order to seize the steel mills to prevent a wartime strike. *Youngstown* confirmed the principle first established in *Marbury* v. *Madison* (1803), that the courts can compel high executive officers to comply with statutory limitations on their power.

Finally, in *United States* v. *Nixon* (1974), the Supreme Court enforced a subpoena directly against the President for evidence in a criminal trial of several of his closest aides. The Court recognized a qualified executive privilege to refuse to reveal presidential discussions and records. This privilege, based on general separation-of-powers concepts, stemmed from the functional need of the President for candid advice in policy formulation. Nevertheless, the Court held that the needs of the courts overrode the privilege in this specific case. It emphasized the narrowness of the subpoena and the power of the trial court to prevent unnecessary intrusion into presidential confidentiality by reviewing pertinent records in camera. In other situations involving military and foreign affairs secrets, the privilege has been treated as absolute, as in *United States* v. *Reynolds* (1953).

Article I, Section 3, of the Constitution does provide that impeached officers may be prosecuted. As applied to the President, this may mean that impeachment must precede any prosecution. (Some other officers have been prosecuted first and impeached afterwards, however.) It is also unclear whether a sitting President may be indicted and prosecuted for crime. None has ever been indicted, although President Nixon was named as an unindicted coconspirator by the grand jury investigating the Watergate affair.

Before the 1970s, civil damages actions against Presidents were extremely rare, and none ever proceeded to trial. *Livingston* v. *Jefferson* (C.C. Va. 1811) was the best-known early attempt to sue a President for damages. Chief Justice Marshall, sitting as a circuit judge, dismissed on a technicality a damages suit against Thomas

Jefferson for an action taken pursuant to his presidential duties. The Supreme Court eventually erected a general barrier to successful civil actions against executive officers by holding that these officers possessed complete immunity from common law tort claims for actions taken in their official capacity. In *Spalding* v. *Vilas* (1896), the Court, granting immunity to the Postmaster General, emphasized that the public interest required the immunity in order to assure that officials would fearlessly execute their duties. The Court reaffirmed *Spalding* in *Barr* v. *Matteo* (1959) by holding a federal officer immune for acts taken within the "outer perimeter" of the line of duty. In *Westfall* v. *Erwin* (1988), however, the Court required that an official must have been exercising government discretion when taking action for which immunity was claimed. Congress subsequently amended the Federal Tort Claims Act (28 U.S.C. 2680) to substitute the United States as defendant and to waive sovereign immunity for the new liability created by *Westfall.*

The potential for civil actions against Presidents became real when the Supreme Court held in *Bivens* v. *Six Unknown Named Agents of Federal Bureau of Narcotics* (1971), that the Constitution directly authorizes civil actions against federal officers who violate constitutional rights of individuals. After *Bivens,* citizens possessed a claim to assert against Presidents who had injured them, but the question remained whether defendants in *Bivens* suits could assert any immunity from damages. In *Butz* v. *Economou* (1978), the Court granted a Secretary of Agriculture a qualified immunity from damages, if the action taken was neither malicious nor clearly illegal.

In *Nixon* v. *Fitzgerald* (1982), involving President Richard M. Nixon's removal of a civilian from the air force, the Court decided that the President possesses an absolute immunity from civil damages when he acts within the "outer perimeter" of his official duties. In justifying the extension of complete immunity to the President, the Court emphasized the likelihood that the prominence of the presidency would draw lawsuits, the existence of other checks on presidential behavior (such as congressional and press scrutiny of his actions), and the possibility of other relief for injured individuals. The breadth of the decision appears to make the President immune in any civil case. A companion case, *Harlow* v. *Fitzgerald* (1982), involved the extension of presidential immunity to his immediate aides. The Court decided that these aides are entitled only to the qualified immunity that is available to other executive officers. It modified that immunity, however, to eliminate the element of subjective malice. The Court thought that too many baseless claims could proceed to trial where allegations of malice were made, because an officer could not readily negate them. The net effect of the two cases is to permit some checking of a President through his aides.

[See also (II) Executive Privilege, Impeachment, Separation of Powers.]

BIBLIOGRAPHY

Carter, Stephen. "The Political Aspects of Judicial Power: Some Notes on the Presidential Immunity Decision." *University of Pennsylvania Law Review* 131 (1983): 1341–1399.

Fisher, Louis. *Constitutional Conflicts between Congress and the President.* 3d ed. 1991.

Ray, Laura K. "From Prerogative to Accountability: The Amenability of the President to Suit." *Kentucky Law Journal* 80 (1991–1992): 739–790.

Shane, Peter M., and Harold H. Bruff. *The Law of Presidential Power.* 1988.

Tribe, Laurence H. *American Constitutional Law.* 2d ed. 1988.

— HAROLD H. BRUFF

IMPEACHMENT

The constitutional procedure for removing a President from office is called impeachment. Article II, Section 4 of the Constitution provides that the President (as well as the Vice President and all civil officers) "shall be removed from office on Impeachment for, and conviction of, Treason, Bribery, or other high Crimes and Misdemeanors." The House of Representative initiates the procedure by voting an accusation—an impeachment—that it then prosecutes in the Senate. Just as the House has "the sole Power of Impeachment" (Article I, Section 2), the Senate has "the sole Power to try all Impeachments" (Article I, Section 3). When sitting for the purpose of an impeachment trial, members of the Senate "shall be on Oath or Affirmation"; when the President is tried, the Chief Justice presides. Conviction requires a two-thirds vote of the members of the Senate who are present. "Judgment in Cases of Impeachment shall not extend further than to removal from Office, and disqualification to hold and enjoy any Office of honor, Trust or Profit under the United States; but the Party convicted shall nevertheless be liable and subject to Indictment, Trial, Judgment and Punishment, according to Law" (Article I, Section 3).

The Framers' Debates

The Framers of the Constitution tailored the impeachment provisions with a view to the removal of the President. They followed the procedural model of English impeachments, which had been adopted in most of the states. The power of originating the inquiry—preferring an impeachment—was placed in the hands of a legislative body because, Alexander Hamilton wrote, impeachment is a legislative remedy, "an essential check in the hands of that body upon the encroachments of the executive." It was lodged in the House, "those who represent the great body of the people," James Iredell told the North Carolina ratifying convention, "because the occasion for its exercise will arise from acts of great injury to the community, and the objects of it may be such as cannot be easily reached by an ordinary tribunal."

House Judiciary Committee Chairman James F. Wilson contended that Johnson was "the worst of Presidents," but he should not be impeached for "a bundle of generalities."

The Framers had difficulty deciding how impeachments should be tried. They rejected trial by the Supreme Court because it might try the President on a criminal charge after the impeachment trial and because the Court, as Gouverneur Morris said, "were too few in number and might be warped or corrupted." The Senate was considered to be the only body that would be unbiased by an accusation brought by the House. Any other tribunal, Iredell said, might "be too much awed by so powerful an accuser." But there was concern that the Senate would be too lenient. For example, James Monroe complained to the Virginia ratifying convention: "To whom is he responsible? To the Senate, his own council. If he makes a treaty, bartering the interests of the country, by whom is he to be tried? By the very persons who advised him to perpetrate the act. Is this any security?"

The impeachment procedure was criticized because the President was not suspended from office during the trial. "[W]hen he is arraigned for treason," George Mason warned the Virginia convention, "he has the command of the army and navy, and may surround the Senate with thirty thousand troops." Impeachments will come too late, Fisher Ames of Massachusetts told the House in 1789: "[W]hile we are preparing the process, the mischief will be perpetrated, and the offender will escape." Impeachment was a "dilatory and inefficient process," John Vining of Delaware said. "[W]hat delays and uncertainty with the forms of trial, details of evidence, arguments of counsel, and deliberate decision!" Theodore Sedgwick of Massachusetts concurred: impeachment was a "tardy, tedious, desultory road."

Impeachments of Other Officials

These representatives were endorsing the President's power to remove executive officers. Just one subordinate executive officer has ever been impeached, Secretary of War William W. Belknap in 1876 for bribery. He resigned hours before the House voted unanimously to impeach him; the Senate acquitted him, with twenty-two of the twenty-five senators who voted not guilty expressing the view that the Senate lacked jurisdiction as a result of his resignation. Senator William Blount was impeached in 1797 for sedition and conspiracy. The Senate, which had already expelled Blount, dismissed the impeachment.

Impeachment has been used principally against federal judges. Thirteen have been impeached, and a number of others were subject to impeachment resolutions and investigations in the House that did not lead to impeachment. Of the thirteen, seven were convicted, four were acquitted, and two resigned. In the three most recent cases—all convictions—a committee of the Senate heard the evidence, and only closing arguments were made to the full Senate.

The most significant of the judicial impeachments involved Supreme Court Justice Samuel Chase. A partisan Federalist, Chase was impeached in 1804 by a Republican House. He was charged, in the words of one of the House managers prosecuting the impeachment at his Senate trial in 1805, with "perverting the high judicial functions of his office for the purposes of individual oppression, and of staining the pure ermine of justice by political party spirit." Eight articles of impeachment charged judicial misconduct while sitting as a circuit justice in 1800 and 1803. During the trial, Chase's defense counsel emphasized that the articles alleged no indictable crime or known wrong and that the impeachment was itself a partisan use of judicial process. The Senate acquitted him on each article, although a majority voted guilty on three of them. The outcome led Thomas Jefferson to reflect, some years later, that "impeachment is an impracticable thing, a mere scarecrow."

Andrew Johnson

Only two Presidents, a century apart, have been the subject of impeachment proceedings—Andrew Johnson in 1868 and Richard M. Nixon in 1974.

In December 1867, after a ten-month investigation, the House Judiciary Committee reported a resolution of impeachment against President Johnson. Five Radical Republicans on the committee voted for the resolution; two moderate Republicans and two Democrats voted against. For the committee majority, George S.

Boutwell acknowledged to the House that "no specific, heinous, novel offense" was charged against President Johnson but rather "a series of acts, . . . a succession of events" all pointing to the charge that "he used as he had the opportunity, and misused as necessity and circumstances dictated, the great powers of the nation with which he was intrusted, for the purpose of reconstructing this Government in the interest of the rebellion." For the Republican minority of the committee, Chairman James F. Wilson contended that the House "must be guided by some rule in this grave proceeding." Johnson was "the worst of the Presidents," but he should not be impeached for "a bundle of generalities" such as those reported by the committee. The House rejected the impeachment resolution by a vote of 57 to 108.

Two and one-half months later, in February 1868, President Johnson ordered the removal from office of Secretary of War Edwin M. Stanton and authorized Maj. Gen. Lorenzo Thomas to act as interim secretary. The Tenure of Office Act, which Congress passed in 1867 over Johnson's veto, provided that officers appointed with the advice and consent of the Senate would hold office until their successors were similarly appointed. Cabinet officers were subject to removal with the advice and consent of the Senate. When the Senate was in recess, the President could suspend an officer and appoint a temporary replacement until the Senate met again and decided whether the officer could be removed. In August 1867, President Johnson had suspended Stanton; in January 1868, the Senate refused to concur in the suspension. The Tenure of Office Act carried a criminal penalty for violations, which it declared to be "high misdemeanors."

The same day President Johnson ordered Stanton's removal, the Senate passed a resolution stating that "under the Constitution and laws . . . the President has no power to remove the Secretary of War and to designate any other officer to perform the duties of that office *ad interim*." The following day, the House Committee on Reconstruction reported a resolution of impeachment. Two days later, the House impeached Johnson by a vote of 126 to 47. "The logic of the former case is made plain, not to say perfect, by the sequence in the present one," James F. Wilson told the House. President Johnson "has presented to us . . . a high misdemeanor known to the law and defined by statute."

The House appointed a select committee to draft articles of impeachment against Johnson. It reported back charges based entirely upon the events surrounding the orders for the removal of Stanton and the designation of Thomas as interim secretary. The House adopted nine articles, each pleading a legal variant of a "high crime" or a "high misdemeanor" from these events.

After the House elected managers to prosecute the impeachment in the Senate, they proposed two broader charges, which the House added to the articles. Article 10 alleged that Johnson had made "intemperate, inflammatory, and scandalous harangues" against Congress and laws enacted by it, by which he brought the office of President "into contempt, ridicule, and disgrace, to the great scandal of all good citizens." Article 11 charged that President Johnson had declared that the Thirty-ninth Congress was not authorized to execute legislative power, but was a Congress of only part of the states, and that, in pursuance of this declaration, he had attempted to prevent the execution of the Tenure of Office Act by preventing Stanton from resuming the functions of Secretary of War after the Senate refused to concur in his suspension, to prevent the execution of the Army Appropriations Act, and to prevent the execution of the Reconstruction Act. (The Thirty-ninth Congress had passed all three laws in 1867.)

The trial focused on the removal of Stanton and the interim appointment of Thomas. Johnson's defense counsel made a number of arguments, not all of them consistent: He had not violated the Tenure of Office Act because there was only an attempt to remove, not a removal. The Tenure of Office Act did not apply to Stanton or the temporary designation of Thomas. The act was unconstitutional. If the act did apply and was constitutional, Johnson should not be removed for a mistaken interpretation of law, made in good faith and with the advice of his Cabinet. Furthermore, Johnson intended to test the constitutionality of the law, which he had a right—even a duty—to do. If he had no such right, he should not be removed for a good faith mistake in construing his constitutional duties and powers. Finally, there was no public injury; it was at best a technical crime, insufficient cause to remove the President from office.

The House managers, having found their "perfect" case in what they thought was an easily proved statutory "high misdemeanor," were constrained by the pretextual charge they chose to prosecute. The Tenure of Office Act simply would not bear the intense scrutiny to which it was put during the trial. The defense, not the managers, was able to invoke the responsibilities, powers, and duties of the presidential office. Having pleaded specific crimes, the managers were hampered in arguing that President Johnson had committed great constitutional wrongs.

The Senate ultimately voted on only three articles—Article 11 and two articles concerning the Thomas appointment. Each failed by a single vote, with thirty-five

Republicans voting guilty and twelve Democrats and seven Republicans voting not guilty. The defense arguments clearly bore fruit with the Republicans voting for acquittal. In written opinions, six of these Senators explained their votes on the basis of statutory construction, Johnson's intent, the supposed justification for his conduct, and the lack of gravity of the offense. Senator Charles Sumner, who declared Johnson guilty of all the articles "and infinitely more," wrote that one of these opinions, by Senator P. G. Van Winkle of West Virginia, treated the impeachment "as if it were a prosecution for sheep-stealing in the police court of Wheeling."

The Johnson impeachment, wrote Clinton L. Rossiter in the 1950s, was "vengefully political in motivation and purpose"; his acquittal "made clear for all time that impeachment is not . . . a political process for turning out a President whom a majority of the House and two-thirds of the Senate simply cannot abide." Presidential impeachment was considered to be a constitutional dead letter.

Richard M. Nixon

The revelation of the Watergate affair and President Nixon's order to fire Special Prosecutor Archibald Cox, who was investigating it, changed this perception. The House Judiciary Committee began an inquiry in November 1973 to determine whether grounds existed to impeach President Nixon. The investigation lasted some eight months. It focused on evidence of wrongdoing by Nixon, including information provided by the federal grand jury investigating the Watergate cover-up, which ultimately named President Nixon an unindicted co-conspirator in an obstruction of justice.

President Richard M. Nixon was the subject of impeachment proceedings in 1974, but he resigned to avoid the trial and probable removal from office. (Library of Congress, Prints and Photographs Division)

In July 1974, the Judiciary Committee voted to report three articles of impeachment to the House. Each of the articles charged that President Nixon had violated his constitutional oath faithfully to execute the office of President and to preserve, protect, and defend the Constitution and his constitutional duty to take care that the laws be faithfully executed.

Article 1 focused on the Watergate cover-up. It charged that President Nixon had prevented, obstructed, and impeded the administration of justice by engaging personally and through his subordinates and agents in a plan or course of conduct to obstruct investigation of the Watergate break-in; to cover up, conceal, and protect those responsible; and to conceal the existence and scope of other unlawful covert activities. It specified nine means used to implement the course of conduct or plan. The Committee voted 27 to 11 to adopt this article.

Article 2 alleged abuse of presidential power. It charged that President Nixon had repeatedly engaged in conduct violating the constitutional rights of citizens, impairing the due and proper administration of justice and the conduct of lawful inquiries, or contravening the laws governing executive agencies and the purposes of these agencies. Included in specifications were misuse of the Internal Revenue Service; improper electronic surveillance by the Federal Bureau of Investigation and Secret Service; creation of a secret investigative unit (the "plumbers") within the Executive Office of the President; failure to act when he knew that close subordinates were impeding investigations; and interference with the FBI, the Justice Department, the Special Prosecutor, and the Central Intelligence Agency. The Committee adopted this article by a vote of 28 to 10.

Article 3 dealt with President Nixon's refusal to produce tape recordings of his private conversations and other materials subpoenaed by the committee for its impeachment investigation. It alleged that he had "interposed the powers of the Presidency against the lawful subpoenas of the House of Representatives, thereby assuming to himself functions and judgments necessary to the exercise of the sole power of impeachment vested by the Constitution in the House of Representatives." The committee voted 21 to 17 to report this article.

The committee rejected two other proposed articles by votes of 26 to 12. One alleged that President Nixon authorized, ordered, and ratified the concealment of information from Congress and supplied Congress with false and misleading statements about American bombing operations in Cambodia during the Vietnam War. The other charged that President Nixon fraudulently failed to report income and claimed unauthorized deductions on his federal tax returns and that he received unconstitutional emoluments in the form of government expenditures on his privately owned homes.

During the deliberations of the committee, both proponents and opponents of President Nixon's impeachment agreed that grounds for impeachment would exist if he had engaged in serious violations of his constitutional duties, as defined by the constitutionally prescribed oath and the constitutional provision that the President "shall take Care that the Laws be faithfully executed." Even those who voted against the impeachment articles acknowledged that "high crimes and misdemeanors" need not be violations of criminal law, although some contended that proof of criminal or wrongful intent was required. The minority of the committee that opposed impeachment asserted that the evidence was inadequate to support the charges and that the allegations were insufficiently grave to warrant the extreme step of impeachment and removal from office.

The committee conducted its inquiry more like an adjudication than the preparation of an accusation for prosecution before the Senate. It permitted counsel for President Nixon to argue his case and to examine witnesses. It required clear and convincing evidence of the allegations included in articles of impeachment.

Six days after the Judiciary Committee finished its deliberations on articles of impeachment, President Nixon released transcripts of three recorded conversations that were among those he had withheld from the committee. The Supreme Court had ordered production of these and other recordings for use in Watergate cover-up prosecutions, rejecting Nixon's claim of executive privilege in a unanimous opinion. Even those who had voted against the impeachment articles considered one of the newly released recordings to be a "smoking gun," proving Nixon's early involvement in the cover-up. Nixon's remaining support evaporated, and he conceded that the new evidence made his impeachment by the House "virtually a foregone conclusion." Three days later, he resigned from office.

An Assessment

In the aftermath of the Nixon resignation, there was consensus that the constitutional system had worked. Like the Johnson trial, the Nixon impeachment seemed to demonstrate that the outcome of a presidential removal proceeding depends much more upon establishing guilt of serious wrongdoing than on partisanship. The constitutional requirement of a two-thirds vote by the Senate necessitates, as a practical matter, that members of the President's own political party support impeachment and removal. "The security to innocence" from this requirement is, as Alexander Hamilton wrote, "as complete as itself can desire."

But the Nixon proceeding again demonstrated that the procedure for removing a President is cumbersome and time-consuming. The first impeachment investigation of Andrew Johnson took ten months. When it voted to impeach Johnson, the House acted quickly—his orders to remove Stanton and install Thomas were issued on a Friday afternoon, the House impeached the following Monday. Even in that case, however, the Senate trial was not completed for nearly three months. In Nixon's case, it took eight months before the Judiciary Committee was able to recommend articles of impeachment; had the impeachment gone forward, it would have taken several months more for trial.

The Supreme Court held in 1982 that a President or former President is absolutely immune from civil suit for conduct while in office.

Nor, because impeachment is such a rare event, have the procedures been modernized or tailored to the constitutional purpose of the undertaking. Articles of impeachment, each considered and voted upon separately, are anachronistic and may obscure the crucial issue in an impeachment proceeding—whether the wrongful conduct of the President, taken as a whole, is sufficiently serious to warrant removal from office. Other elements of the process similarly reflect formalities of the eighteenth century, long obsolete elsewhere in the law, and tend to impart an inappropriate aura of a criminal prosecution to the proceeding.

Presidential impeachment is an uncomfortable enterprise for legislators and citizens alike. It poses fundamental questions about the nature of American government, which it forces Congress to address in the midst of a governmental crisis, without much guidance from precedent. It requires clear-cut choices—to accuse or not, to adjudge guilty or not—by the branch of government most prone to compromise or defer controversial decisions.

The Framers of the Constitution viewed the President's eligibility for reelection every four years as the principal mechanism for ensuring responsibility in the office. James Madison described it as "an impeachment before the community, who will have the power of punishment by refusing to re-elect him." This accountability has been attenuated by the two-term limitation of the Twenty-second Amendment. The President's amenability to criminal prosecution and civil suit has likewise been reduced. Although the Framers envisioned that the President, even while in office, would be subject to legal process, the Supreme Court held in 1982 that a President or former President is absolutely immune from civil suit for conduct while in office. And the Watergate criminal case, in which President Nixon was not indicted but merely named as a conspirator, suggests that prosecution of an incumbent President, although constitutionally permissible, is unlikely to be pursued.

Impeachment itself has proved to be an unwieldy weapon. Its presence in the constitutional arsenal, however, undoubtedly serves as a deterrent to presidential malfeasance. No President would want to face the obloquy of being the first to be convicted upon an impeachment, of having "his very name . . . become a word to frighten children with throughout the land," as one of Andrew Johnson's defense counsel put it. From this perspective, the most important precedent concerning presidential impeachment may prove to be an extraconstitutional one: President Nixon's resignation to avoid impeachment, trial, and probable removal from office.

[See also (II) High Crimes and Misdemeanors; (III) The Judiciary.]

BIBLIOGRAPHY

Benedict, Michael Les. *The Impeachment and Trial of Andrew Johnson.* 1973.

Bushnell, Eleanore. *Crimes, Follies, and Misfortunes: The Federal Impeachment Trials.* 1992.

Hoffer, Peter Charles, and N. E. H. Hull. *Impeachment in America, 1635–1805.* 1984.

Labovitz, John R. *Presidential Impeachment.* 1978.

Rehnquist, William H. *Grand Inquests: The Historic Impeachment of Justice Samuel Chase and President Andrew Johnson.* 1992.

Smith, Samuel H., and Thomas Lloyd, eds. *Trial of Samuel Chase, An Associate Justice of the Supreme Court of the United States, Impeached by the House of Representatives for High Crimes and Misdemeanors before the Senate of the United States,* 2 vols. 1970. Reprint of 1805 ed.

U.S. House of Representatives. *Impeachment of Richard M. Nixon, President of the United States: Report of the Committee on the Judiciary.* 93d Cong., 2d Sess., H. Rept. No 93-1305. 20 August 1974.

U.S. Senate. *Trial of Andrew Johnson, President of the United States, before the Senate of the United States, on Impeachment by the House of Representatives for High Crimes and Misdemeanors.* 40th Cong., 2d Sess. 2 vols. 1970. Reprint of 3 vol. 1868 ed.

– JOHN R. LABOVITZ

IMPLIED POWERS

Because the Constitution does not purport to be an exhaustive catalog of powers, the problem of discovering implied powers in its interstices is frequently encountered. It is met, as are other problems of constitutional construction, by the examination of experience in the light of constitutional principle. In this article the term *implied powers* will be used in a comprehensive sense, to include all powers not enumerated in the constitutional text.

Many judges and other writers on constitutional problems find the source of such powers in one or another of the enumerated powers, or in a combination of several. In other cases, implied powers are derived from the nature and sovereignty of the nation, the grand design of its polity, or similar axioms of political theory deemed to be embodied in the Constitution.

Some argue that implied powers are less legitimate than those mentioned in the constitutional text. They would confine the authority of government strictly to the enumerated powers, especially in the case of the President, whom they view with suspicion as a potential tyrant. This position is clearly untenable. *In re Neagle* (1890) declares that "any obligation fairly and properly inferrible" from the Constitution and the statutes is a law within the meaning of the word "law" as if it were absolutely expressed therein.

Three factors make the task of attributing implied powers to the President particularly complex: the importance of the presidency in the political strategy of the Constitution; the fact that the President is endowed with extensive and rather vaguely defined authority in the sphere of international relations; and the fact that the President is often said to possess inherent powers, or the residual powers, of sovereignty, sometimes identified with the prerogative powers of the British crown.

In his important study of the presidency, Charles C. Thach, Jr., concludes that Article II "admits an interpretation of executive power much wider than that outlined by the enumerated powers." This result, he concludes, was intended by the Framers because the Constitutional Convention was dominated by a fear of unbridled legislative power and by the conviction that a strong and accountable national executive was needed "to counterbalance legislative predominance. The state legislatures' excesses and the incompetency of Congress as an administrative body produced the Presidency." Thach's view encourages the implication of Presidential powers rather freely in order to keep the self-aggrandizing propensities of Congress within tolerable limits.

The bills that established the first four departments of the executive branch required Congress to confront the question whether the Constitution gave the President the implied power to remove officials of the government as well as to appoint them. After extensive debate, Congress left the matter largely to practice and the Courts. James Madison argued forcefully that the President could not be expected faithfully to execute the laws unless he could dismiss subordinates. Madison's view was sustained in *Myers* v. *United States* (1926), which gave a broad reading of the President's removal power.

In general, history has accepted Madison's view that the President has an implied power to remove at least his Cabinet officers and other high-ranking officials with policy-making responsibilities. They serve at the President's pleasure. On the other hand, Congress has established civil service systems of various kinds; they all involve limitations on the President's power to dismiss. Congress has authorized appointments for fixed terms as well. And the President's removal power does not extend to members of independent commissions, as the Supreme Court held in *Humphrey's Executor* v. *United States* (1935).

Article II, Section 3, prescribes that the President shall receive ambassadors and other public ministers, a provision sometimes understood as a routine ceremonial duty as head of state. The duty of receiving ambassadors and other public ministers, has, however, been read to imply the President's sole power of diplomatic recognition, for example; the sole power to conduct foreign relations; the sole power to negotiate treaties which are mentioned in the Constitution, and executive agreements, which are not mentioned [*see* recognition power].

Executive agreements are frequently used in the conduct of international relations. Some, such as trade agreements, are authorized by statutes, but other executive agreements are entered into solely on the President's constitutional authority. In *United States* v. *Pink* (1942), the Supreme Court declared that an assignment of property claims incidental to agreement on the terms of recognition was part of the "supreme law of the land," as if an executive agreement were a treaty. And *Goldwater* v. *Carter* (1979) did not reject President Jimmy Carter's power to abrogate a defense treaty with Taiwan as incident to his decision to establish diplomatic relations with the People's Republic of China.

Other executive agreements are made by the President alone in the course of diplomatic negotiations. In 1957, for example, the United States acted as a secret mediator in helping to persuade Israel to evacuate the Sinai Desert after the Suez Crisis of 1956. To achieve agreement between Egypt and Israel, President Dwight D. Eisenhower guaranteed that the United States would, if necessary, use force to keep the Straits of Tiran open to Israeli shipping. That promise was treated as binding by President Lyndon B. Johnson in the Six-Day War of 1967.

The importance of the President's special responsibility for the conduct of foreign affairs is again illustrated by an episode during President Ulysses S. Grant's administration. It involved granting permission to land international submarine cables on American soil. In the absence of legislation, President Grant authorized a French company to connect by cable a town in Massachusetts to the French city of Brest. The President was reluctant to act without a statute but finally yielded to an Attorney General's opinion and granted the license. The Attorney General explained that the President's implied power to issue the license was based on the fundamental rights that "grow out of the jurisdiction of the nation over its own territory and its international rights and obligations as a distinct sovereignty." For these reasons, the Attorney General concluded, "the President is not limited to the enforcement of specific acts of Congress" (22 *Ops. Att'y Gen.* 13).

No President has claimed that the President's powers over cable connections or international electronic transmission facilities are exclusive. Clearly, the regulation of such activities comes well within any definition of Congress's power to legislate on matters of interstate and foreign commerce. But both constitutional usage and judicial opinions recognize presidential power to act and even to take military action without prior statutory authority in the conduct of foreign relations, so long as he does not trespass on Congress's exclusive authority to declare war or violate any other principle of constitutional law. For example, the President cannot "dispose of the liberty" of a fugitive from justice by extraditing him to another country in the absence of a statute or treaty conferring the power (*Valentine* v. *United States* [1936]).

The President's constitutional authority to respond to national emergencies and threats to public order raises similar issues. Cases such as *In re Debs* (1895) and *In re Neagle* (1890) can be explained only if one accepts as a major premise the doctrine that the President's executive power conferred by Article II is not a mere designation of status but a grant of authority, including emergency powers that may go well beyond the enumerated powers, depending on circumstance. The same principle, on a much larger scale, is required to justify the constitutional propriety of what President Abraham Lincoln did between the time of the attack on Fort Sumter and Congress's meeting to ratify his actions, and some of the initiatives of Presidents Woodrow Wilson and Franklin D. Roosevelt before the United States formally entered World War I and World War II.

[See also (I) Implied Powers; (II) Recognition Power, Removal Power.]

BIBLIOGRAPHY

Corwin, Edward S. *The President: Office and Powers, 1787–1984.* 1940. 5th rev. ed. by Randall W. Bland, Theodore T. Hindon, and Jack W. Pelstson, 1984.

Schwartz, Bernard. *A Commentary on the Constitution of the United States, The Powers of Government.* Vol. 2: *The Powers of the President.* 1962.

Thach, Charles C., Jr. *The Creation of the Presidency, 1775–1789.* 1922.

Van Alstyne, William W. "The Role of Congress in Determining Incidental Powers of the President and of the Federal Courts: The Horizontal Effect of the Sweeping Clause. *Law and Contemporary Problems* (1976): 102–134.

– EUGENE V. ROSTOW

INAUGURAL ADDRESSES

An inaugural address is the first public expression that a President makes after taking the simple thirty-five-word presidential oath of office. It is a unique moment in the American experience when political differences are momentarily put aside as the nation listens intently to the philosophy, aspirations, themes, and goals that will shape the next four years.

Only a few inaugural addresses have been universally acclaimed as being truly memorable, but all afford a picture window on history.

Although not constitutionally required, every ceremony since George Washington's 30 April 1789 inauguration has included an address. Washington's initial speech as President was delivered in the Senate Chamber of Federal Hall in New York City. Between 1793 and 1813, inaugural addresses were delivered either in the House or Senate chamber. Outdoor public inaugurations began with James Monroe in 1817. Only on four occasions since has the inaugural address been given in the warm confines of the Capitol.

Inaugural addresses were initially carried by horseback or stage to an awaiting nation, and then later by train and telegraph. Not until Calvin Coolidge's 1925 inauguration was an address broadcast by radio. Live television coverage began in 1949 with Harry S Truman.

The shortest inaugural speech, George Washington's second, was only 135 words and contained but four sentences. William Henry Harrison's 8,445 word address was the longest, taking nearly two hours to deliver. A month later, Harrison died of pneumonia that started with the cold he caught during the snowy ceremony.

On the average, inaugural addresses have run about 2,400 words. Only a few have been universally acclaimed as being truly memorable, but all afford a picture window on history. Their story lines have covered the faith of Presidents, the special destiny of the American Republic, the nation's growth and expansion, the development of foreign policy, the treatment of ethnic minorities, economic fluctuations, and the evolution of the presidency, as well as numerous other issues. It is after all, as George Bush aptly observed in 1989, "democracy's big day."

Economic Fluctuations

One of the most closely observed aspects of American life noted in inaugural addresses has been the state of the economy. At his second inauguration, Thomas Jefferson announced that the elimination "of unnecessary offices, of useless establishments and expenses," had enabled his administration to discontinue "internal taxes." Although the nation was deep in debt by James Monroe's 1817 inauguration, he maintained that the "great amount of our revenue and the flourishing state of the Treasury are full proof of the competency of the national resources for any emergency."

Martin Van Buren's glowing description of "an aggregate of human prosperity" found nowhere else in the world proved to be misplaced optimism as the entire nation, within months, faced a financial panic. Ulysses S. Grant promised that the "great debt" incurred in preserving the Union would be paid off as quickly as possible.

Amidst prosperity "without parallel in our history," James A. Garfield took office in 1881. "Ample employment," however, soon gave way to the Panic of 1884. Five years later, Benjamin Harrison promised, and then worked to deliver, an administration in which expenditures were "made with economy and only upon public necessity."

For William McKinley, the "best way for Government to maintain its credit is to pay as it goes—not by resorting to loans, but by keeping out of debt—through an adequate income secured by a system of taxation, external or internal, or both." William Howard Taft also felt government had a responsibility "to be as economical as possible, and to make the burden of taxation as light as possible."

As the Great Depression deepened in early 1933, Franklin D. Roosevelt's first inaugural address offered hope to the disillusioned nation. Within the first paragraph was the line destined to be among his most famous: "The only thing we have to fear is fear itself," he said. "This great nation," he counseled the American people, "will endure as it has endured, will revive and will prosper."

In 1937, Roosevelt still saw "one third of a nation ill-housed, ill-clad, ill-nourished." These bleak conditions were not, however, in his mind a picture of despair. He had painted this picture "in hope—because the Nation, seeing and understanding the injustice in it, proposes to paint it out."

Ethnic Minorities

A prominent concern of newly inaugurated Presidents during the nineteenth century was the acculturation of ethnic minorities. Prior to the Civil War, the plight of American Indians and the question of slavery were of particular interest. Jefferson acknowledged that the Indians had been overwhelmed by an "overflowing population from other regions" and "reduced within limits too narrow for the hunter's state." James Monroe called on Congress to develop a plan to care appropriately for them, while Andrew Jackson promised "humane and considerate attention to their rights." Yet, nearly half a century later, Ulysses S. Grant admitted little had changed. Grover Cleveland challenged the American people to treat the Indians "honestly" and "with forbearance," but then the Indians were forgotten.

The question of slavery was even more challenging. Martin Van Buren, James K. Polk, Franklin Pierce, and James Buchanan gave support to the institution of slavery in their inaugural remarks. South Carolina had already seceded when Abraham Lincoln renounced any "purpose, directly or indirectly, to interfere with the institution of slavery in the States where it exists." The Civil War freed the slave to become a citizen, but Ulysses S. Grant did not feel social equality was a "subject to be legislated upon." He was unwilling to do anything "to advance the social status of the colored man, except to give him a fair chance to develop what there is good in him."

Government, Rutherford B. Hayes stressed, had a moral obligation "to employ its constitutional powers and influence to establish the rights of the people it emancipated." The "advance of 4,000,000 people from a condition of servitude to that of citizenship," however, "could not occur without presenting problems." Four years later, James A. Garfield called emancipation the "most important political change since the adoption of the Constitution." Yet in 1909, William Howard Taft concluded it was "not the disposition or within the province of the Federal Government to interfere with regulation by Southern States of their domestic affairs."

Following the Civil War, inaugural addresses also began to contain expressions of concern about the growing number of foreign immigrants. We need rigidly enforced laws, Grover Cleveland argued, prohibiting Chinese immigrants from competing with American labor when they had no intention of acquiring citizenship and insisted on retaining repugnant habits as well as customs. Benjamin Harrison sought the exclusion of all races, "even the best, whose coming is necessarily a burden upon our public revenues or a threat to social order. These should be identified and excluded." President Taft focused on minimizing the "evils likely to arise from" the admission of Asian immigrants.

"Justice," Lyndon B. Johnson told his fellow countrymen in 1965, "requires us to remember that when any citizen denies his fellow, saying: 'His color is not mine,' or 'his beliefs are strange and different,' in that moment he betrays America, though his forebears created this nation." Jimmy Carter hoped his presidency would be remembered as one that "had torn down the barriers that separated those of different race and region and religion, and where there had been mistrust, built unity, with a respect for diversity."

Foreign Affairs

Presidents talked of foreign relations, which had held their attention since the beginning. While Thomas Jefferson sought "honest friendship with all nations, entangling alliances with none" in his first inaugural speech, James Madison was not so generous in 1813. His second inaugural provided justification for war against Great Britain.

Although Ulysses S. Grant vowed to "respect the rights of all nations," he made it clear in 1869, that if "others departed from this rule in their dealings with us, we may be compelled to follow their precedent." Similarly, William McKinley spoke in 1897 of pursuing "a firm and dignified foreign policy." In 1905, Theodore Roosevelt confidently declared that the United States had "become a great nation, forced by the fact of its greatness into relations with the other nations of the earth, and we must behave as beseems a people with such responsibility." Americans had also become, as Woodrow Wilson observed, "a composite and cosmopolitan people." America stood "firm in armed neutrality," but, Wilson warned, it could still be drawn into World War I because our "fortunes as a nation are involved whether we would have it so or not." While

Warren G. Harding wanted "no part in directing the destinies of the Old World" following the war, Calvin Coolidge conceded, "we cannot live to ourselves alone."

Franklin Roosevelt's fourth address, a mere 573 words, delivered near the end of World War II, emphasized that Americans had "learned to be citizens of the world, members of the human race. We have learned the simple truth, as Emerson said, that 'The only way to have a friend is to be one.'"

A combative Harry S Truman accused the communists of trying to prevent "world recovery and lasting peace." His speech outlined four points of action: continued use of the Marshall Plan, creation of an Atlantic defense pact, technical and scientific assistance to underdeveloped nations, and grants or loans to those countries.

Dwight D. Eisenhower stressed that he was willing to use force to deter aggression, saying: "In the final choice a soldier's pack is not so heavy a burden as a prisoner's chains." John F. Kennedy was also willing to "pay any price, bear any burden, meet any hardship, support any friend, oppose any foe, in order to assure the survival and the success of liberty."

As the communist world began to crumble in 1989, George Bush enthusiastically announced that "great nations of the world are moving toward democracy through the door of freedom."

Calls for Reform

A democracy, on occasion, is in need of reform. It was the earnest desire of Ulysses S. Grant in 1873, to correct civil service abuses. Four years later, Rutherford B. Hayes appealed for both civil service reform and "a change in the system of appointment itself." Using even stronger language, James A. Garfield called for the regulation of the civil service by law. Grover Cleveland saw civil service reform as a way of protecting the American people from incompetency, while William McKinley felt reform was necessary to "retaining faithful and devoted public servants in office."

Benjamin Harrison used his 1885 address to challenge the nation's great corporations to "more scrupulously observe their legal limitations and duties," and suggested that Congress should enact more adequate pension laws. A myriad of reform proposals were espoused by William Howard Taft, including calls for relieving the railroads from certain antitrust restrictions, reorganization of the Department of Justice, the Department of Commerce and Labor, and the Interstate Commerce Commission, as well as revision of the antitrust and interstate commerce laws "which shall secure the conservation of our resources."

After four years as President, Woodrow Wilson confidently declared at the outset of his second term that "no equal period in our history has been so fruitful of important reforms in our economic and industrial life or so full of significant changes in the spirit and purpose of our political action." Under his leadership, there had been tariff reductions, banking reforms, stronger antimonopoly legislation, assistance to agriculture, and conservation legislation. Herbert Hoover's 1929 address focused on the need for dealing with crime and the abuses under the Eighteenth Amendment (prohibition) because of the failure of many state and local officials to enforce the law zealously.

Faith in Greater Power

Virtually every President in inauguration remarks has professed a belief in, and reliance on, a Supreme Being. Washington emphasized that every step by which the American people "have advanced to the character of an independent nation seems to have been distinguished by some token of providential agency." Thomas Jefferson sought the "favor of that Being in whose hands we are, who led our fathers, as Israel of old, from their native land and planted them in a country flowing with all the necessaries and comforts of life."

Virtually every President in inauguration remarks has professed a belief in, and reliance on, a Supreme Being.

Humbly invoking God for "wisdom and firmness," James Buchanan hoped to avoid civil war and restore harmony and friendship among the several states. Looking upon the blood and ruin of the Civil War, Abraham Lincoln read perhaps the single most moving paragraph of all inaugurations: "With malice toward none, with charity for all, with firmness in the right as God gives us to see right, let us strive on to finish the work we are in, to bind up the nation's wounds."

As World War II entered its final stages, Franklin D. Roosevelt prevailed on "Almighty God . . . for the way to see our vision clearly—to see the way that leads to a better life for ourselves and for all our fellow men—to the achievement of His will, to peace on earth." By remaining steadfast "in our faith in the Almighty," Harry S Truman declared four years later, "we will advance toward a world where man's freedom is secure."

If we failed as a nation, Lyndon B. Johnson said, "then we have forgotten in abundance what we learned in hardship: that democracy rests on faith, that freedom asks more than it gives, and that the judgment of God is harshest on those who are most favored." "Ours was," Jimmy Carter reminded us, "the first society openly to define itself in terms of both spirituality and human liberty."

Growth and Expansion

When "George Washington, placed his hand upon the Bible" in 1789, Ronald Reagan recalled on the occasion of the fiftieth inaugural, he "stood less than a single day's journey by horseback from raw, untamed wilderness. There were four million Americans in a union of thirteen colonies. Today, we are sixty times as many in a union of fifty States." The excitement, as well as the apprehension that accompanied that expansion, is a well-recorded inaugural theme.

The Louisiana Purchase, Jefferson explained in his second inaugural, had "been disapproved by some from a candid apprehension that the enlargement of our territory would endanger its union." He reasoned, however, that it was "better that the opposite side of the Mississippi should be settled by our own brethren and children than by strangers of another family." In 1821, James Monroe boasted of the acquisition of Florida that opened "to several States a free passage to the ocean" and secured the United States "against all future annoyance from powerful Indian tribes."

After James K. Polk took his oath in 1845, he excitedly announced that the number of states had grown from thirteen to twenty-eight, two having joined the Union within the past week. Polk was somewhat premature in granting Texas statehood, as that did not actually occur for another ten months. In his mind, however, annexation of the territory had settled the issue. He also felt it a "duty to assert and maintain" the Oregon Territory by constitutional means.

Franklin Pierce, like Polk, argued that concern about the ability of the American system to survive territorial expansion and an augmented population had proven unfounded. Instead, the country, he felt, had experienced "an additional guaranty of strength and integrity of both" at both the state and federal level.

Lincoln's anxiety, understandably was quite different, as he spoke directly to southerners in 1861. "We can not remove our respective sections from each other," he reminded them, "nor build an impassable wall between them."

Greatness of America

"Preservation of the sacred fire of liberty and the destiny of the republican model of government," Washington proclaimed at his first inauguration, has been "entrusted to the hands of the American people." His successors have carried that message forward with great regularity on inauguration day.

The "existence of such a government as ours for any length of time," John Adams reasoned, "is a full proof of a general dissemination of knowledge and virtue throughout the whole body of the people." James Monroe was convinced the American system had "shunned all the defects which unceasingly prey on the vitals and destroyed the ancient Republics."

"Our Government," Martin Van Buren proudly declared, "quietly but efficiently performs the sole legitimate end of political institutions—in doing the greatest good to the greatest number—we present an aggregate of human prosperity surely not elsewhere to be found." For James K. Polk, the American system of "well-regulated self-government" was the "most admirable and wisest . . . ever devised by human minds."

On the eve of the twentieth century, James A. Garfield found it inspiring "to remember that no great emergency . . . has ever arisen that has not been met with wisdom and courage by the American people." Theodore Roosevelt stressed that "no people on earth have more cause to be thankful" than Americans. "Much has been given us, and much will rightfully be expected from us."

"Nowhere else in the world," Woodrow Wilson said in 1913, "have noble men and women exhibited in more striking forms the beauty and energy of sympathy and helpfulness and counsel in their efforts to rectify wrong, alleviate suffering, and set the weak in the way of strength and hope." "Because of what America is and what America has done," Calvin Coolidge reminded his countrymen, "a higher hope inspires the heart of all humanity."

Americans, Franklin Roosevelt cautioned in 1941, must never let the "sacred fire of liberty," as our first President proclaimed, "be smothered with doubt and fear." If we do, "then we shall reject the destiny which Washington strove so valiantly and so triumphantly to establish."

America's role as a defender of freedom, John F. Kennedy believed, was a responsibility the citizenry should not shirk. "My fellow Americans," he told us, "ask not what your country can do for you: Ask what you can do for your country. My fellow citizens of the world: Ask not what America will do for you, but what together we can do for the freedom of man."

Few inaugural addresses have better explained the relationship of the presidency to the American people in preserving freedom than James K. Polk's eloquent remarks of 4 March 1845:

Although in our country the Chief Magistrate must almost of necessity be chosen by a party and stand pledged to its principles and measures, yet in his official action he should not be the first President of a part alone, but of the whole United States. While he executes the laws with an impartial hand, shrinks from no proper responsibility, and faithfully carries out in the executive department of the government the principles and policy of those who have chosen him, he should not be unmindful that our fellow-citizens who have differed with him in opinion are entitled to the full and free exercise of their opinions and judgments and that the rights of all are entitled to respect and regard.

BIBLIOGRAPHY

Campbell, Karlyn Kohrs, and Kathleen Hall Jamieson. "Inaugurating the Presidency." *Presidential Studies Quarterly* 15 (Spring 1985): 394–411.

Lott, Davis Newton, ed. *The Presidents Speak: The Inaugural Addresses of the American Presidents from Washington to Nixon.* 1969.

Schlesinger, Arthur M., Jr. and Fred L. Israel. *The Chief Executive: Inaugural Addresses of the Presidents of the United States from George Washington to Lyndon B. Johnson.* 1965.

– STEPHEN W. STATHIS

INAUGURATION

"I do solemnly swear [or affirm] that I will faithfully execute the office of President of the United States, and will to the best of my ability, preserve, protect, and defend the Constitution of the United States." With these words, prescribed by the Constitution, each American President since George Washington has assumed the mantle of Chief Executive. The quadrennial thirty-five-word swearing-in ceremony takes only two minutes. All other activities associated with inaugurals—the receptions, concerts, spectacular parades, lofty addresses, and grand balls—are products of custom and tradition rather than law.

In 1817, Clay refused to allow the Senators to bring their forty "fine red chairs" into the House Chamber for James Monroe's first oath-taking.

When Vice Presidents succeed to the presidency on the death or resignation of an incumbent, all ceremonial formalities are dispensed with except the presidential oath. On four of the six occasions when inauguration day has fallen on a Sunday, Presidents chose to be sworn in twice—first, without fanfare, at the White House and then, on the following Monday at a public ceremony at the Capitol.

On the morning of the first inauguration—30 April 1789—cannons thundered in salute, church bells rang for nearly half an hour, and many people began their day in their places of worship praying for the new government and new President. The first inauguration was eight weeks late because the House of Representatives did not have a quorum to count the electoral votes until 6 April. It then took another week for a messenger to carry the news of Washington's election from New York to Mount Vernon. The ceremony took place on the portico of New York City's Federal Hall.

Washington's second inauguration was held in the Senate Chamber of Independence Hall in Philadelphia. John Adams's 1797 installation as President took place in the House Chamber. Thomas Jefferson, the first President to be inaugurated in Washington, took his oath of office in the Senate Chamber in 1801 and 1805. The scene shifted to the House for James Madison's 1809 and 1813 ceremonies.

Speaker of the House Henry Clay's stubbornness made inaugurals an outdoor affair. In 1817, Clay refused to allow the Senators to bring their forty "fine red chairs" into the House Chamber for James Monroe's first oath-taking, and the ceremony simply moved outside. Although rain and snow forced Monroe's second inaugural back to the House chamber in 1821, the outdoor swearing-in at his first inaugural set a precedent that with few exceptions, has been followed ever since. Beginning in 1981, the ceremony was shifted from the East to the West Front of the Capitol, where it would be visible to a larger number of spectators.

Since the third inauguration, the oath has been administered by the Chief Justice of the United States, except for the half-dozen men who succeeded by death and chose the nearest judge for their emergency ceremonies. John Marshall holds the record of nine inaugural ceremonies (1801–1833), followed by Roger B. Taney with seven (1837–1861), and Melville Fuller with six (1889–1909).

Franklin D. Roosevelt's second inaugural, in 1937, was the first to be held on 20 January, following adoption of the Twentieth Amendment in 1933. The official date for the inaugural was changed from 4 March (originally set by the Continental Congress and confirmed by the Second Congress), because it was felt that too much time lapsed between the election and inauguration, especially in the case of lame-duck Presidents. Also, prior to 1937, the new Vice President had taken his oath of office in the Senate Chamber and not with the President. On 20 January 1945, Roosevelt was sworn-in for his fourth term in a simple ceremony on the south portico of the White House, the only inaugural to be held there. Roosevelt's departure from the traditional pomp and pageantry was prompted by a behind the scenes disagreement with the congressional inaugural committee over what amount of money was to be appropriated for the ceremony. Ultimately, Roosevelt decided to hold the ceremony at the White House. The result was one of the most austere ceremonies in history.

Although inaugural addresses often have been characterized as less than inspiring, they have on occasion accurately captured the unique demands of an era and have moved the nation: Abraham Lincoln's masterful second inaugural address ("With malice toward none, with charity for all, with firmness in the right . . ."), Franklin D. Roosevelt's assurance that "the only thing we have to fear is fear itself," and John F. Kennedy's "ask not what your country can do for you"—each holds an honored place in history and not for eloquence alone.

George Washington, who started the precedent of delivering an inaugural address, also gave the shortest—135 words—in 1793. In addition, he began the tradition of professing a belief in, and reliance on, a Supreme Being in his address, and taking the oath of office with his hand on a Bible.

The first official inaugural ball, according to most historians, was hosted by James and Dolley Madison in 1809 at Long's Hotel on Capitol Hill. Four hundred people made the select guest list. At Madison's second inauguration in 1813, eight thousand clamored to get into the ball at the Davis Hotel on Pennsylvania Avenue.

Between 1913 and 1929, and during World War II, there were no official balls. President Woodrow Wilson asked that there be no inaugural balls for both his first (1913) and second (1917) oath taking. President Warren G. Harding (1921) planned initially to revive the custom but subsequently changed his mind and a charity ball was held instead. Charity balls were also given to launch the Coolidge (1925) and Hoover (1929) administrations. In 1937, an Inaugural Concert served as a substitute for a ball. Inaugural balls made a comeback following the war. In 1969, there were six, and in 1981, for the first time, a ball was held overseas, honoring Ronald Reagan in Paris, and satellite balls were held across the country. For the 1985 and 1989 inaugurations, there were nine balls.

Inaugural parades down Pennsylvania Avenue following the swearing in ceremony began in 1889. Earlier parades had started at the White House and escorted the President to the Capitol. The parades have included everything from a float with a weaving mill (1841), a hot air balloon (1857), ten thousand lantern-bearing marchers singing campaign songs (1877), and Buffalo Bill (1889), to a calliope playing "I'm Just Wild About Harry" (1949), and a reproduction of the LBJ Ranch (1965). Dwight D. Eisenhower was even lassoed by a cowboy at his 1953 parade.

Although Theodore Roosevelt did not follow his daughter Alice's suggestion in 1905 to have the Democratic losers march down Pennsylvania Avenue in chains, there were coal miners with lights on their helmets, American Indians in headdress, the black troops of the famous 9th Cavalry that had ridden with him at Santiago, and his beloved Rough Riders. President John F. Kennedy's PT-109 boat and the eight surviving members of the crew he commanded in World War II, together with thirty thousand other participants passed by the White House reviewing stand in 1961.

Instead of riding at the head of the inaugural parade to the White House, a jubilant Jimmy and Rosalynn Carter, with their daughter Amy, startled parade officials and delighted the crowds in 1977 when they walked the entire sixteen blocks to the White House. The coldest day in inaugural history, 20 January 1985, forced cancellation of the parade for the first time in history, and Ronald Reagan began his second term in the Capitol Rotunda. Although it was not quite as cold in 1873, it was frigid enough for the champagne to freeze at the reception for Ulysses S. Grant. When John F. Kennedy became President, an estimated one million people braved a chilling twenty-two-degree temperature, a nineteen-mile-per-hour wind, and eight inches of snow to see the 1961 inaugural parade.

It was not snowing on 4 March 1841, but it was chilly and overcast when William Henry Harrison, at age sixty-eight, wearing neither overcoat nor hat, rode a white charger in a two-hour procession from the White House to the Capitol. After delivering the longest inaugural address (8,445 words), Harrison returned in another slow-moving parade, shook hands with thousands of well-wishers, and then attended three balls. What started as a cold shortly after the inauguration quickly became pneumonia and Harrison died one month later.

Though the trappings have changed and the ceremony now is witnessed by thousands of spectators and watched on television by millions around the world, inaugurations continue to symbolize the permanence of the nation and the peaceful transfer of power in the world's greatest democracy. Inaugurations play a legitimating role in the American democratic process and offer the best affirmation available of Lincoln's view that "when an election is past, it is altogether fitting a people that until the next election they should be one people."

An inauguration represents a healthy middle ground between a coronation and a coup d'état.

BIBLIOGRAPHY

Durbin, Louise. *Inaugural Cavalcade.* 1971.

Hughes, Patrick. "Inaugural Day Weather." *NOAA* (National Oceanic and Atmospheric Administration) 15 (Winter 1985): 4–8.

The Inaugural Story 1789–1969. 1969.

– STEPHEN W. STATHIS

INDEPENDENT COMMISSIONS

Independent commissions are multimembered bodies that perform regulatory and adjudicatory functions outside the executive branch and not under the direct control of the President. Their virtues are that, ideally, they can carry out their responsibilities in an unbiased manner and can implement regulatory legislation through the application of expert knowledge and group deliberation by a body relatively stable in its membership because of staggered terms. Their clearest drawback is their insulation from political accountability and from the political protection that the President can provide.

At first, the constitutional validity of the commissions was attacked on the ground that they united the powers of lawmaker, prosecutor, and judge in the same entity. Frequently, this attack was leveled by those subject to regulation, but not all the criticism was self-serving, and for a long time it cast a shadow over the commissions' legitimacy. This conjunction of powers, however, is not unique to the commissions; it characterizes regulatory agencies within the executive branch as well. The need for general administrative reform was an important aspect of antiregulatory arguments in the 1930s, and, following the report of the Attorney General's Committee on Administrative Procedure in 1941, Congress, after World War II, passed the Administrative Procedure Act to segregate regulatory and adjudicatory functions without requiring the division of agencies into separate bodies. The constitutionality of this arrangement is now generally accepted.

A distinct separation-of-powers attack on the commissions is that their independence impermissibly creates a fourth branch of government and undercuts the President's constitutional powers. Because Article II, without qualification, vests the executive power in the President, it is argued that no executive power may validly be exercised except by those who are under his direct control, for only in this way will he be able to discharge the constitutional responsibility to "take care that the laws be faithfully executed."

The independence of the first regulatory commission—the Interstate Commerce Commission (ICC), created in 1887 to regulate railroads—did not result from a conscious congressional desire to insulate it from the authority of the President. What Congress wished to guarantee was independence from partisan bias, and it did so through a requirement that not more than a bare majority of the commissioners could belong to the same political party (a stipulation applied to several subsequent commissions). Independence from the President, as such, was not an apparent subject of legislative concern. In fact, Congress initially placed the ICC within the Department of the Interior, but the Secretary requested termination of this arrangement, which was ended in 1889, perhaps to prevent domination of the commission by the incoming President, Benjamin Harrison, previously a railroad lawyer. The commission form was chosen after the model commonly employed for railroad regulation by the states, which alone had been engaged in regulation until the Supreme Court, in *Wabash, St. Louis and Pacific Railway* v. *Illinois* (1886), suddenly forced this responsibility on the federal government by ruling that the states were constitutionally forbidden to regulate interstate railroad rates. The President was given authority to remove members of the ICC for inefficiency, neglect of duty, or malfeasance in office, but this measure was intended as a means by which incompetent commissioners could be removed prior to the completion of their statutorily specified terms rather than as a deliberate curtailment of an unlimited presidential removal power.

Although the regulatory commission was an important instrument during the New Deal, Franklin D. Roosevelt was unprepared to tolerate policy implementation by agencies outside his control.

But Presidents soon began to look upon commissions as diminishing their authority. In 1908 Theodore Roosevelt sent a message to Congress insisting that executive functions should only be carried out by entities answerable to the President. Congress showed little inclination to accede to such a request. The first chairman of the ICC was the renowned constitutional scholar Thomas M. Cooley, who made sure that the commission operated under sound procedures and brought it substantial prestige. As the need for regulation of other types of business activity became apparent early in the twentieth century, Congress chose to make further use of the commission form. Four new commissions were established during the administration of Woodrow Wilson, who supported them but made clear that he believed he had the authority to direct their efforts and sought ex officio membership on them for executive-branch officials. Presidents Warren G. Harding, Calvin Coolidge, and Herbert Hoover also anticipated being able to influence the work of the commissions, either by personal contacts with commissioners or by forcing their resignations. Commissions were required to submit their budgets to Congress through the executive branch.

Although the regulatory commission was an important instrument in the vast expansion of federal authority during the New Deal, Franklin D. Roosevelt was unprepared to tolerate policy formulation and implementation by agencies outside his control. His power to appoint the entire membership of the commissions created during his presidency served to insure that their actions would conform to his desires, but he had no such ability to control the older commissions. In 1933 he summarily removed William Humphrey from the Federal Trade Commission, citing no reason except policy disagreement, even though the Federal Trade Commission Act only authorized removal for inefficiency, neglect of duty, or malfeasance in office. Roosevelt's action was challenged in the Supreme Court, which, in *Humphrey's Executor* v. *United States* (1935), unanimously held that restriction of the President's removal power was constitutionally permissible. The Court distinguished *Myers* v. *United States* (1926), in which it had been held that Congress could not constitutionally require that the Senate concur in the President's dismissal of a postmaster because such a restriction was an improper interference with the constitutional power and responsibilities of the President. It declared that *Myers* only applied to limitations on the President's authority to remove officials exercising purely executive power, and, since independent commissions were bodies whose duties were "quasi-legislative" and "quasi-judicial," the power to remove commissioners was validly subject to congressional restriction.

The reasoning of *Humphrey's Executor* was highly dubious. The duties of a Federal Trade Commissioner are surely executive in large part and are in no way different from those of many executive-branch officers who, under *Myers,* are removable by the President at will. But the controversy over Humphrey's removal underscored the plain fact that the actual independence of the commissions turns not on whether they are located inside or outside the executive branch, or on what their duties are, but on whether the President can remove commissioners without cause. If a President can do so, the commissions are not independent.

Certainly, for Roosevelt and his supporters, the notion that the effectuation of New Deal programs could be obstructed by commissioners who were hold-overs from the past was unacceptable, and the commissions, like the courts, became targets of the administration. Following his landslide reelection in 1936, Roosevelt appointed a committee of distinguished students of government and administration under the chairmanship of Louis Brownlow to prepare a report for submission to Congress advocating centralized presidential control over all administrative activities of the federal government. The Brownlow Committee, formally designated the President's Committee on Administrative Management, took dead aim at the independent commissions. It declared that it would be more accurate to describe them as the "irresponsible" commissions, and condemned them as "a headless 'fourth branch' of the Government, a haphazard deposit of irresponsible agencies and uncoordinated powers," which "enjoy power without responsibility" and "leave the President with responsibility without power."

But the Brownlow report, like the Court-packing plan, was rejected by Congress, which not even in the heyday of the New Deal was prepared to accept the dramatic shift in the balance of political power that would result from granting the President absolute authority over the execution of all federal laws and policies. However, keeping the commissions free from presidential control leaves them, as many commentators have noted, with little protection against congressional influence through the appropriations process, oversight by committees, and personal contacts by members of Congress and their staffs. Political accountability through the President may be replaced by accountability to a small number of strategically situated members of Congress. And because regulated groups can concentrate their efforts at lobbying and persuasion on a single locus of regulation, there has been evidence of "capture" of commissions by those who are supposedly subject to their regulatory authority. Nevertheless, despite their shortcomings, independent commissions offer a promise of fairness and consistency in the administration of regulatory legislation that cannot be quickly dismissed by those who are uneasy about the complete concentration of administrative authority in the executive branch. Thus, the first Hoover Commission, making recommendations in 1949 to Harry S Truman on executive organization, and James Landis, reporting to John F. Kennedy in 1960 on administrative agencies, declared that their retention was appropriate and desirable.

But such a spirit of accommodation has not been shared by all administrations, even though it is obvious that the duties of some regulatory entities, such as the Federal Election Commission, necessitate that they be entirely free from political influence. Richard Nixon's Advisory Council on Executive Organization, chaired by Roy Ash (the Ash Council), recommended in 1971 that the majority of existing commissions be replaced by agencies headed by a single individual removable at the will of the President. Although Congress remained unwilling to accede to such recommendations, the administration of Ronald Reagan saw an apparent opportunity to end the independence of the commissions through judicial action when, for a time in the 1980s, the Supreme Court seemed willing to place strict limits on Congress's power to interfere with the exercise of executive authority. The Reagan administration was no less anxious than the Roosevelt administration had been to bend all government agencies to its will, although for altogether different purposes, and thus sought to take advantage of this emerging judicial attitude. In 1985 Attorney General Edwin Meese III announced that "we should abandon the idea that there are such things as 'quasi-legislative' or 'quasi-judicial' functions that can be properly delegated to independent agencies or bodies." The Solicitor General, while disavowing any intent to call into question the constitutionality of the independent commissions, argued before the Supreme Court in *Bowsher* v. *Synar* (1986) that the President possesses illimitable constitutional authority to remove at will any federal officer appointed by him who is responsible for the administration of the law except where the officer's administrative responsibilities are ancillary to the performance of adjudicatory functions; he also questioned the continued vitality of *Humphrey's Executor* as a precedent.

Although the original draft of Chief Justice Warren Burger's majority opinion in *Bowsher* seemed to endorse these contentions, the Court carefully noted in its final opinion that its holding disallowing the assignment of executive duties to the Comptroller General did not implicate the validity of the independent commissions because it turned on the fact that the Comptroller General was removable by Congress, not that he was not removable by the President. And the Court categorically rejected the administration's position on the commissions in *Morrison* v. *Olson* (1988), where it sustained the constitutionality of an independent counsel over the lone dissent of Justice Antonin Scalia, who argued for absolute presidential removal power. Speaking for the majority, Chief Justice William H. Rehnquist confined the holding in *Myers* to the proposition that Congress could not give itself a role (except through the impeachment process) in the removal of executive officials, and he reaffirmed the result, but not the reasoning, of *Humphrey's Executor*. The Court agreed with the holding that Congress can limit the President's power to remove a commissioner, not because the commission does not exercise executive power, as *Humphrey's Executor* reasoned, but because the Constitution does not require that the President have uncontrolled removal power over every officer with administrative responsibilities.

The *Morrison* decision would appear to settle beyond doubt the constitutional validity and viability of independent commissions. It establishes that the President's ability to remove commissioners is subject to reasonable restrictions not involving actual congressional participation in the removal decision, and that the commissions' independence may be protected by statute. As Justice Byron R. White has observed, "the Court has been virtually compelled to recognize that Congress may reasonably deem it 'necessary and proper' to vest some among the broad new array of governmental functions in officers who are free from the partisanship that may be expected of agents wholly dependent upon the President."

[See also (II) Executive Power, Separation of Powers.]

BIBLIOGRAPHY

Bernstein, Marver H. *Regulating Business by Independent Commission.* 1955.

Cushman, Robert E. *The Independent Regulatory Commissions.* 1941.

Miller, Geoffrey P. "Independent Agencies." *Supreme Court Review* (1986): 41–97.

Steele, Charles N., and Jeffrey H. Bowman. "The Constitutionality of Independent Regulatory Agencies under the Necessary and Proper Clause: The Case of the Federal Election Commission." *Yale Journal on Regulation* 4 (1987): 363–392.

Strauss, Peter L. "The Place of Agencies in Government: Separation of Powers and the Fourth Branch." *Columbia Law Review* 84 (1984): 573–669.

U.S. Senate Committee on Governmental Affairs. *Study on Federal Regulation,* Vol. 5: *Regulatory Organization.* 95th Cong., 2d Sess., 1977. S. Doc. No. 95–91.

U.S. Senate. Committee on the Judiciary. *Separation of Powers and the Independent Agencies: Cases and Selected Readings.* 91st Cong., 1st Sess., 1969. S. Doc. No. 91-49.

Verkuil, Paul R. "The Purposes and Limits of Independent Agencies." *Duke Law Journal* (1988): 257–279.

Verkuil, Paul R. "The Status of Independent Agencies after *Bowsher v. Synar.*" *Duke Law Journal* (1986): 779–805.

– DEAN ALFANGE, JR.

INDEPENDENT COUNSEL

Originally called a special prosecutor, an independent counsel is an official appointed under the Ethics in Government Act of 1978 (28 U.S.C. secs. 591 et seq.) to investigate allegations of serious wrongdoing by the President, Cabinet officials, and certain other high-level executive-branch and presidential campaign personnel.

In the wake of the Watergate affair, Congress created the independent-counsel process to prevent the underprosecution of executive-branch malfeasance that could occur because of the conflict of interest inherent in leaving the policing of the executive to the Justice Department alone.

Appointment, Powers, and Removal

Under the act, the Attorney General has ninety days to investigate, once specific information is presented suggesting that an official covered by the statute has committed a serious federal offense. If the Attorney General determines within that time that no further investigation is warranted, then no action occurs. If, however, the Attorney General refuses or is unable to make that determination, the matter is referred to a special panel of the U.S. Court of Appeals for the District of Columbia Circuit, which appoints an independent counsel. The order of appointment specifies the scope of the counsel's investigation, which may be amended on petition of the counsel or at the initiative of the Attorney General.

It is customary to seek prestigious members of the bar, often from the same political party as the person being investigated, to act as independent counsel.

It is customary for the court to seek prestigious members of the bar, often from the same political party as the person being investigated, to act as independent counsel. Prominent independent counsels in the late 1980s included Laurence Walsh, a retired federal judge and former head of the American Bar Association, appointed to investigate the Iran-contra affair, and another distinguished retired judge, Arlin Adams, appointed to investigate a financial scandal in the Department of Housing and Urban Development (HUD). Once appointed, an independent counsel has powers comparable to those of a U.S. attorney or other Justice Department prosecutor charged with a similar investigation. These include the ability to conduct a grand jury investigation, to pursue all necessary evidence and witnesses, and ultimately to decide whether matters assigned to the counsel warrant prosecution.

The relative independence of the independent counsel is secured not only by his or her judicial appointment but also by statutory protection against discharge. Independent counsels ordinarily have job tenure until they determine that all matters within their jurisdiction are adequately resolved. They may be removed only by personal action of the Attorney General, and then only for "good cause, physical disability, mental incapacity, or . . . other condition that substantially impairs" the independent counsel's job performance. As a consequence, the Attorney General—and, thus, the President—is without power to threaten an independent counsel with removal because of disagreements about the conduct of an investigation or prosecution. Decisions regarding the sufficiency of evidence for an indictment, the appropriateness of alternative investigative techniques, witness selection, and so on, are entirely within the independent counsel's discretion.

[See also (II) Attorney General, Executive Privilege, National Security Council.]

BIBLIOGRAPHY

Bruff, Harold. "Independent Counsel and the Constitution." *Willamette Law Journal* 24 (1988): 539–563.

Carter, Stephen. "The Independent Counsel Mess." *Harvard Law Review* 102 (1988): 105–141.

Eastland, Terry. *Ethics, Politics, and the Independent Counsel: Executive Power, Executive Vice, 1789–1989.* 1989.

Harriger, Katy Jean. *Independent Justice: The Federal Special Prosecutor in American Politics.* 1992.

Shane, Peter M. "Independent Policymaking and Presidential Power: A Constitutional Analysis." *George Washington Law Review* 57 (1989): 596–626.

– PETER M. SHANE

INFORMATION SECURITY OVERSIGHT OFFICE (ISOO)

The Information Security Oversight Office is responsible for monitoring, reviewing, making recommendations, and issuing rules and regulations for classifying and declassifying national security information in the executive branch. Its jurisdiction covers approximately eighty agencies—including the Department of Defense and the Central Intelligence Agency (CIA)—which generate approximately seven million classification actions annually. The office, which reports annually to the President, is located in the General Services Administration (GSA) but takes its policy and program direction from the National Security Council (NSC), a part of the Executive Office of the President.

ISOO is a relatively small organization, with a staff of fifteen and a budget of $1.24 million in fiscal year 1992. It requested an increase for an additional five positions and $600,000 in fiscal year 1993, to oversee the National Industrial Security Program, which covers private contractors who handle classified information.

There have been proposals in Congress that have focused on strengthening ISOO's independence, authority, and resources, in order to increase further its oversight capabilities and, in turn, improve controls over the classified information system.

The office's heritage dates to President Richard M. Nixon's 1972 executive order on classified information (E.O. 11652), which first created an oversight body in this field, the now-defunct Interagency Classification Review Committee. The committee, composed of representatives of the major classifying agencies, was originally housed in the Executive Office of the President and later in the National Archives and Records Service (then a part of GSA) when the Archivist headed it. These two predecessor locations help to explain ISOO's current dual position (still located in GSA but receiving policy direction from the NSC). The Information Security Oversight Office itself was officially established by President Jimmy Carter in 1978 (E.O. 12065)—as a separate office within GSA—in order to increase oversight over the classification system.

ISOO currently operates under President Ronald Reagan's executive order (E.O. 12356) on National Security Information, which replaced Carter's in 1982. ISOO issued the directive that implemented Reagan's order later in the same year. The Director, charged with monitoring agency compliance with the President's order, can also review agency declassification guidelines and regulations and require them, subject to appeal to the NSC, to be changed if not consistent with Executive Order 12356 or ISOO's directive. The Director also has authority to conduct on-site reviews of the information security program of each agency. He can be denied access by the head of the agency to certain categories of information, however, if such access would pose an exceptional national security risk; in that event, the Director may appeal the denial to the NSC.

The Director, moreover, prescribes standard personnel forms to implement the information security program. In 1987, one of the secrecy agreements—because it included the vague term "classifiable information"—generated a substantial amount of controversy, court challenges by federal employees, and congressional restrictions on its implementation. Later, the term was dropped and new language inserted.

ISOO's Director convenes and chairs interagency meetings to study and make recommendations to improve the security classification system. The Director also oversees an ongoing effort to develop a new executive order on the classification system.

BIBLIOGRAPHY

Fisher, Louis. "Congressional-Executive Struggles over Information: Secrecy Pledges." *Administrative Law Review* 42 (1990): 89–107.

Garfinkel, Steven. "Executive Coordination and Oversight of Security Classification Administration." *Government Information Quarterly* 1 (1984): 157–164.

Kaiser, Frederick M. "The Amount of Classified Information: Causes, Consequences, and Correctives of a Growing Concern." *Government Information Quarterly* 6 (1989): 247–266.

U.S. Information Oversight Office. *Annual Reports* (1978).

– FREDERICK M. KAISER

INHERENT POWERS

In the contest over the control of American government, predicted in the *Federalist,* Presidents have claimed several forms of power. Least controversial are those powers expressly granted in Article II, such as the power to receive ambassadors. More controversial, but well established, are the powers implied from specific grants, especially those broad responsibilities expressly conferred, such as the function of Commander in Chief, or executing the laws.

To have separate meaning, arguments based on "inherent power" should be understood as those claims to authority that have no express basis from which such powers can be fairly implied. Claims to implied powers may be so tenuous that they, too, should be equated with claims that certain authority is "inherent" in cer-

Thomas Jefferson disagreed with the idea of inherent powers. He believed that all power vested in the President must be expressly written in the Constitution. (Library of Congress, Prints and Photographs Division)

tain presidential functions—or overall combinations of functions.

Claims of inherent powers have arisen most often in connection with the conduct of foreign policy and national security affairs. The most frequent bases for claiming inherent powers are Article II, Section 1, providing "the executive Power shall be vested in a President of the United States of America," and Section 3, directing the President to "take Care that the Laws be faithfully executed." According to the argument based on this theory, by vesting the executive power in a President, Article II grants the officeholder all the powers that are naturally vested in a sovereign nation. The office possesses a "residuum" of power, independent of the specific powers and duties assigned to it by the Constitution and federal statutes.

In 1936, the Supreme Court in *United States* v. *Curtiss-Wright Export Corp.* identified sovereignty as the basis of the President's inherent power to conduct foreign affairs, tracing the power not to the Constitution, but to the British Crown. "Sovereignty is never held in suspense. When, therefore, the external sovereignty of Great Britain in respect to the colonies ceased, it immediately passed to the union." The foreign policy power, according to the Court, is a "very delicate, plenary and exclusive power of the President as the sole organ of the federal government in the field of international relations—a power which does not require as a basis for its exercise an Act of Congress." The need for a single voice, expertise, and secrecy properly make foreign affairs the domain of the executive.

Adherents of the "delegated" or "formal" powers theory dispute the existence of powers beyond those identified in the Constitution. William Howard Taft wrote, "the President can exercise no power which cannot be fairly and reasonably traced to some specific grant of power or justly implied and included within such grant as proper and necessary." Under this view, Article II, Section 1, only creates the office of the President, while the rest of Article II delineates its functions. Any other reading, according to this theory, makes superfluous the enumerated powers in Sections 3 and 4.

The *Curtiss-Wright* opinion has been vigorously criticized as vague, unnecessary, and lacking proper judicial restraint. Subsequent decisions, such as *Youngstown Sheet & Tube Co.* v. *Sawyer* (1952), have signaled less sympathy toward claims of inherent powers in the domestic arena, even during wartime. *New York Times Co.* v. *United States* (1971) disallowed prior restraint of publication and *United States* v. *United States District Court* (1972) disallowed warrantless national-security searches. Particularly vulnerable to attack are claims that the President is authorized to rely on "inherent" power to act contrary to a legislative determination based on clearly expressed or implied legislative authority. As Justice Robert Jackson wrote in his famous concurring opinion in *Youngstown,* "When the President takes measures incompatible with the expressed or implied will of Congress, his power is at its lowest ebb, for then he can rely only upon his own constitutional powers minus any constitutional powers of Congress over the matter." Alexander Hamilton, in his famous argument as Pacificus, wrote that the President could cause war by refusing to accept an ambassador, but not where Congress has required otherwise. If an express grant of power to the President may in some circumstances be overridden by Congress, so too could a power claimed to "inhere" in the executive function.

While the Constitution does not explicitly incorporate residual powers for the Chief Executive, Presidents have occasionally claimed an inherent emergency power to act in the nation's essential interests, at their own risk. Examples of such claims are Thomas Jefferson's explanation for purchasing naval supplies without legislative authority to defend against an expected British attack on the *Chesapeake,* James Madison's explanation of Andrew Jackson's declaration of emergency after the Battle of New Orleans, and Abraham Lincoln's explanation for curtailing civil liberties upon the outbreak of the Civil War. As Arthur M. Schlesinger, Jr., a critic of the inherent powers theory, has observed, even if the "idea of prerogative was not part of presidential power as defined in the Constitution . . . there is reason to believe that the doctrine that crisis might require the executive to act outside the Constitution in order to save the Constitution remained in the back of [the Framers'] minds." John Locke in his *Second Treatise on Government* argued for an executive power, particularly during emergencies, to act "according to discretion for the public good, without the prescription of law and sometimes even against it." While Taft advocated a system based on enumerated powers, for example, he said that executive power should be limited "so far as it is possible . . . consistent with that discretion and promptness of action that are essential to preserve the interests of the public in times of emergency, or legislative neglect or inaction."

The claim to an inherent power to exceed the Constitution in emergencies differs significantly, however, from the claim that such actions are in fact authorized by the Constitution. Each exercise of the emergency power, as understood by Locke, Jefferson, Lincoln, and others, by definition exceeded authority conferred by the Constitution, and therefore subjected the President's conduct to legislative, judicial, and public review, including possible impeachment.

[See also (II) Emergency Power.]

BIBLIOGRAPHY

Corwin, Edward S. *The President: Office and Powers 1787–1957.*
Fisher, Louis. *Constitutional Conflicts between Congress and the President.* 3d ed. 1991.
Pious, Richard M. *The American Presidency.* 1979.
Schlesinger, Arthur M., Jr. *The Imperial Presidency.* 1973.
Sofaer, Abraham D. "Emergency Power and the Hero of New Orleans." *Cardozo Law Review* 2 (1981): 233.
———. *War, Foreign Affairs, and Constitutional Power: The Origins.* 1976.

– ABRAHAM D. SOFAER

INSPECTORS GENERAL

Offices of inspector general (IG) consolidate authority over auditing and investigations within a federal department or agency. The contemporary effort to create such units by public law—as permanent, nonpartisan, independent offices—began in 1976 with a single office. The concept and constructs have since been extended to sixty-one current federal organizations, including all Cabinet departments and the largest agencies as well as a wide variety of commissions, government corporations, boards, and foundations. The IGs in the departments and largest agencies are nominated by the President and confirmed by the Senate; they can be removed only by the President and not the agency head. The appointment power and removal power over IGs in the smaller entities, by comparison, are held by the agency head.

Establishment of the Offices

Significant legislative initiatives to establish these offices occurred in 1976, when the first IG was created; in 1978, when the Inspector General Act was passed; and in 1988, when major amendments to the act were approved. These efforts reflected substantial bipartisan support in both chambers of Congress, usually in the face of opposition from the affected departments and agencies. Conflicts between the executive and legislative branches have also arisen over IG reporting requirements to Congress and removal of the IGs by the President.

All but one of the sixty-one IGs fall directly or indirectly under the Inspector General Act of 1978, as amended (5 U.S.C. Appendix 3). Fifty-nine are expressly under the act; and the Inspector General in the Government Printing Office, a legislative branch organization, follows its basic provisions (44 U.S.C. 3901). The only exception is the Inspector General in the Central Intelligence Agency (CIA). Although modeled after the IGs under the 1978 Act, the CIA Inspector General has less authority and autonomy than its counterparts (P.L. 100-193).

The President's Council on Integrity and Efficiency (PCIE), established by Ronald Reagan in 1981 (Executive Order 12301), and the Executive Council on Integrity and Efficiency (ECIE) by George Bush in 1992 (Executive Order 12805), serve as coordinating mechanisms for the IGs and other officials. Both headed by the deputy director of the Office of Management and Budget, the two Councils issue annual reports on IG activities and sponsor a number of committees that deal with matters affecting the IG community.

On the day Ronald Reagan became President, he summarily dismissed all the confirmed statutory IGs and one confirmed deputy IG.

The effort to establish statutory OIGs was designed to replace a system that was deficient in detecting and preventing waste, fraud, and abuse in federal programs and operations. The preexisting system relied on administratively created units that had proved defective because of inherent limitations on their stability, independence, resources, and authority. These units, moreover, had no direct or immediate reporting mandates to the agency head let alone to Congress or to the Attorney General (if they uncovered suspected illegalities).

The IG effort arose in the aftermath of the Watergate affair and other abuses in the executive that eroded trust and confidence in it. Along with this, major financial scandals affected the agencies in question and thus served as catalysts for several important legislative developments. The first of the contemporary IGs, created in 1976 in the Department of Health, Education, and Welfare (now Health and Human Services), for instance, followed revelations of widespread fraud in medicare and medicaid programs, which had become a campaign issue in the presidential election that year. Two years later, the Inspector General Act of 1978 was approved during the exposure of pervasive, longstanding violations of procurement laws and policies in the General Services Administration (GSA), one of twelve departments or agencies covered by the new act. The best efforts of the Carter administration, including the creation of an administrative OIG in GSA, had proven inadequate. A more powerful, permanent office was seen as necessary to correct the underlying defects in detecting and preventing such abuses.

Two major enactments—the Inspector General Act of 1978 and its 1988 amendments—established the majority of the offices and standardized the powers, duties, and responsibilities of the IGs. The 1978 IG Act (P.L. 95-452) set up offices in twelve departments and agencies and provided for the basic purposes, authorities, duties, and responsibilities of the IGs. A decade later, the 1988 amendments to the Inspector General Act (P.L. 100-504) extended the offices to the few remaining Cabinet departments and major agencies without them, standardized their powers and authorities, and added specific items to the semiannual reports from the IGs (and companion reports from the head of the agency). The amendments also created a new set of IGs in the mostly smaller federal entities.

Duties and Powers

The inspectors general have been granted broad authority "to promote economy, efficiency, and effectiveness in the administration of, and to prevent and detect fraud and abuse in the [agency's] programs and operations." These include the power to: conduct audits and investigations throughout their respective establishments; have direct access to all information, documents, records, reports, audits, and reviews throughout the establishment; issue subpoenas under their own authority for information and documents; receive complaints from employees, whose confidentiality is to be protected; administer oaths for taking testimony; have direct and prompt access to the head of the agency; hire and control their own personnel and resources; and request assistance directly from any federal, state, or local government agency.

The statutory inspectors general have also been given a substantial amount of independence from political pressures and agency officials, who might be subject to an IG investigation or audit. Protection of the IGs' independence—as well as the integrity of their audits and investigations—is built into the requirements for their appointment and removal; restrictions on agency supervision; prohibitions on IGs assuming program operating responsibilities; protections surrounding their resources and appropriations; and obligations to report to the Attorney General, agency head, and Congress.

Independence

The IGs are to be selected without regard to partisan affiliation and on the basis of integrity and demonstrated ability in accounting, auditing, financial analysis, law, management analysis, public administration, or investigation. Making the IGs presidential nominees confirmed by the Senate (in the Cabinet departments and larger federal agencies), moreover, gives them the same status as the head and other top agency officials who hold confirmed positions.

If the President (or agency head, where appropriate) removes an IG, the President (or head) must communicate the reasons to Congress. The severest challenge to the IGs' independence in this regard occurred in 1981, less than three years after passage of the 1978 act. On the day Ronald Reagan became President, he summarily dismissed all the confirmed statutory IGs (fourteen at the time) and one confirmed deputy IG. This action was criticized—by both Republicans and Democrats in Congress—for undercutting the independence and nonpartisan nature of the inspectors general, thereby politicizing the offices. Eventually, about half of the fired officers were reinstated to IG posts.

Under the IG act, the inspectors general serve only under the "general supervision" of the head of the agency. No agency official can "prevent or prohibit the Inspector General from initiating, carrying out, or completing any audit or investigation, or from issuing any subpoena during the course of any audit or investigation." Exceptions to this exist only for the Departments of Defense, Justice, and Treasury. In these cases, the department head may interfere only for certain specified reasons, dealing mostly with national security or ongoing criminal investigation. And Congress must be notified of the action.

The IGs are precluded from assuming "program operating responsibilities" and from putting their own recommendations for corrective action into effect. This prohibition prevents them from being placed under the direction of other agency officials. It also prevents a conflict of interest from arising as it would if an inspector general investigated or audited a program or activity that his or her own office was carrying out.

All the statutory IGs are granted control over their resources, including authority to hire their own staff and to request assistance directly from other federal agencies. The offices of inspector general in the larger federal establishments (where the IGs are presidential appointees) also have a separate appropriations account.

The IGs' reporting requirements—to the Attorney General, the agency head, and Congress—not only support their autonomy and the integrity of their operations but also contribute to the ability of other government organizations to oversee and investigate executive activities. The IGs, for instance, are directed to "report expeditiously to the Attorney General whenever the Inspector General has reasonable grounds to believe there has been a violation of Federal criminal law."

Inspectors general are also required to keep the head of the establishment and Congress fully and currently informed by specific reports—semiannual and immediate reports—and such other means as testimony at congressional hearings. The IG reports to the agency head (who transmits them to Congress) are not to be cleared or censored by the head, though the head may append comments. This protection is fundamental to the independence and integrity of the IG, who may discover wrongdoing by the head or other agency officials. In addition to semiannual reports, the IGs can issue immediate reports concerning particularly serious or flagrant problems. These reports also go to the agency head who must transmit them, along with any comments, to Congress within seven days. IGs, however, have rarely issued these immediate reports. They are sometimes characterized as "silver bullets," because, if shot, they could terminate the IG's relationship with agency management.

[See also (II) Appointment Power, Removal Power.]

BIBLIOGRAPHY

Adair, John J., and Rex Simmons. "From Voucher Auditing to Junkyard Dogs: The Evolution of Federal Inspectors General." *Public Budgeting and Finance* 8 (1988): 91–100.

Dempsey, Charles L. "The Inspector General Concept: Where It's Been, Where It's Going." *Public Budgeting and Finance* 5 (1985): 39–51.

Gates, Margaret J., and Marjorie Fine Knowles. "The Inspector General Act in the Federal Government: A New Approach to Accountability." *Alabama Law Review* 36 (1985): 473–513.

Kaiser, Frederick M. "The Watchers' Watchdog: The CIA Inspector General." *International Journal of Intelligence and Counterintelligence* 3 (1989): 55–75.

Moore, Mark H., and Margaret Jane Gates *Inspectors-General: Junkyard Dogs or Man's Best Friend.* 1986.

U.S. Department of the Treasury. Office of Inspector General. *Agents for Preventing and Detecting Fraud and Waste: A Report on the Tenth Anniversary of the Inspector General Act of 1978.* 1988.

U.S. House of Representatives. Committee on Government Operations. *The Inspector General Act of 1978: A Ten-Year Review.* 100th Cong., 2d Sess., 1988.

– FREDERICK M. KAISER

INTERIOR, DEPARTMENT OF THE

On 3 March 1849, the last day of James Knox Polk's administration, Congress enacted legislation to create a fifth Cabinet agency, to be called the Home Department, or the Department of the Interior. The idea for such an agency was almost as old as the nation. A department for domestic affairs was considered in 1789, but, instead, both domestic and foreign concerns were lodged in the Department of State. Proposals for a Home Department continued to be discussed for more than half a century.

The vast land acquisitions resulting from the Mexican War enormously enlarged the domestic responsibilities of the federal government and gave the idea new impetus, and Polk's Secretary of the Treasury, Robert J. Walker, championed it. The General Land Office, which oversaw and disposed of lands in the public domain, had been placed in the Department of the Treasury because of the revenues generated from land sales. In his 1848 annual report, Walker pointed out that the duties of the Land Office had little to do with his department's other functions. The functions of the Patent Office in the State Department, the Indian Affairs office in the War Department, and the pension offices in the War and Navy departments were equally remote from the primary responsibilities of those departments, he added. All, he declared, should be brought together in a new Department of the Interior. These ideas were incorporated in the 1849 bill creating the department.

For the first Secretary of the Interior, President Zachary Taylor turned to Thomas Ewing, a colorful son of rural Ohio. A frontier lawyer, a U.S. Senator, and Secretary of the Treasury under Presidents William Henry Harrison and John Tyler, Ewing had long been a force in Ohio's Whig councils. One of Ewing's tasks was to locate satisfactory office space to house his department. Completion of the east wing of the Patent Office building in 1852 finally provided the Secretary with suitable quarters, and the two remaining wings, finished in 1856 and 1867, provided additional space. Although some personnel worked elsewhere in the city, the Patent Office building remained the headquarters of the Department of the Interior until 1917.

Because western issues stimulated the Interior Department's birth, the West has always been the scene of many of its activities.

Interior commanded a huge patronage reservoir and Secretary Ewing launched such a wholesale replacement of officeholders in the bureaus he inherited that opposition newspapers branded him "Butcher Ewing." Heated controversies with congressional Democrats over his use of the spoils system prevented him from devoting much attention to organizing his department, and the task of setting an administrative course for the fledgling Cabinet agency fell to subsequent secretaries.

Interior lacked the clear role definition other departments enjoyed, but it nevertheless played a role in national affairs larger than the sum of its parts. In one way or another, all the responsibilities entrusted to it had to do with the internal development of the nation or the welfare of the American people. It was this fundamental responsibility that united the large, permanent bureaus with smaller transitory offices. The former gave the department strength and continuity, while the latter dramatized its versatility as a force in government. By offering a repository for functions that did not fit elsewhere, Interior enabled Congress more easily to accept and to discharge responsibilities for the internal needs of a rapidly growing nation. Some bureaus, charged with missions of growing importance to the nation, matured and later split off to become independent Cabinet departments and agencies. Among these were the agricultural division of the Patent Office, which became the Department of Agriculture in 1862; the Bureau of Labor, established in Interior in 1884, which became the Department of Commerce and Labor in 1903; and the Department of Energy, formed in 1977.

A sampling of tasks assigned the Interior Department suggests the scope of its cares in the last half of the nineteenth century. Responsibilities ranged from the conduct of the decennial census to the colonization of freed slaves in Haiti, from the exploration of western wilderness to oversight of the District of Columbia jail, from the regulation of territorial governments to the construction of the national capital's water system, from management of hospitals and universities to maintenance of public parks. Such functions, together with basic responsibilities for Indians, public lands, patents, and pensions, gave Interior officials an extraordinary array of concerns.

Because western issues stimulated the department's birth, the West has always been the scene of many of its activities. Two of its major bureaus, Indian Affairs and the General Land Office, operated chiefly in the West and performed duties vital to western interests. Between 1850 and 1857, in cooperation with the U.S. Army, Interior's Mexican Boundary Commission surveyed the new international boundary agreed upon in the treaties ending the Mexican War and formalizing the 1853 Gadsden Purchase. In 1858–1860, Interior commissioners fixed and marked the disputed boundary between Texas and New Mexico.

Rivalries between Interior and the War Department over exploring and mapping the West in the post–Civil War years raised concerns in the scientific community, as well as in official Washington. As a result, in 1879, all the western surveys were consolidated within the Interior Department in the newly formed United States Geological Survey. The department assumed special responsibility for the West's scenic treasures as well. In 1872 Congress established the world's first national park—Yellowstone—under Interior jurisdiction. Others, including Sequoia, Yosemite, and Mount Rainier, were created during the 1890s.

Despite its western emphasis, Interior from its outset conducted major programs of nationwide application. One such program, which assumed enormous magnitude and consequences in the 1880s, was the pensioning of the Union army and navy veterans. (In 1885 there were 1.5 million such veterans.) By 1890 Interior's Pension Bureau employed more than six thousand agents, medical examiners, and clerks.

Interior's fourth major bureau from its inception until 1925 was the Patent Office. Reflecting the burgeoning technology of the industrial revolution, the protection of inventions by government patents assumed growing importance in the latter half of the nineteenth century. By 1890 patent officials received more than 41,000 applications and issued more than 26,000 patents annually.

From its first days Interior bore a special relationship to the District of Columbia. At one time or another, the secretary's federal city responsibilities have covered public buildings, parks, police, the jail, a street railway linking Washington and Georgetown, a railroad bridge across the Potomac, and the city's water supply. The secretary also supervised various institutions serving the capital's health, education, and welfare needs.

As the twentieth century opened, the Department of the Interior became increasingly concerned with efforts to reorient the nation's traditional practices of handling natural resources—land, timber, water, minerals, and wildlife. Most nineteenth-century Americans assumed these resources to be inexhaustible and believed government regulation of their exploitation to be alien to democratic principles. In the prevailing view, Interior's mission was to dispose of government resources to private enterprise, both individual and corporate. A few people of vision, however, dissented from this philosophy. One was Secretary Carl Schurz, who fought to halt the devastation of forests in the public domain. The Forest Reserve Act of 1891, promoted by President Benjamin Harrison's Interior Secretary, John W. Noble, and the creation of the first national parks marked a modest shift in the traditional philosophy. But not until Theodore Roosevelt's administration (1901–1909) did the doctrine of Schurz and his sympathizers become a national crusade. The crusaders gave it a label that has endured: conservation.

Among the results of this movement was legislation providing for construction of dams and aqueducts to water arid and semiarid lands in the West, to be carried out by the Reclamation Service of the Geological Survey. Later Bureau of Reclamation projects, including such world-famous works as the Hoover and Grand

Coulee dams, the All-American Canal in California, and the Alva Adams Tunnel beneath the Continental Divide in Colorado, brought water and flood control, electric power, and recreational resources to vast areas formerly incapable of sustaining major settlement, crop production, and industrial development.

Most nineteenth-century Americans assumed the nation's natural resources to be inexhaustible and believed government regulation of their exploitation to be alien to democratic principles.

The conservation crusade of the early twentieth century and the formation of other departments to address other concerns resulted in a sharper focus in Interior on natural resources and a drift away from the grab-bag "home department" concept. Interior is no longer the "Department of Miscellany," but primarily a land-managing agency, controlling one third of all U.S. land. As of 1992, it had under it ten bureaus: the National Park Service, the Office of Surface Mining Reclamation and Enforcement, the Minerals Management Service, Land Management, the Fish and Wildlife Service, the Bureau of Indian Affairs, Territorial and International Affairs, Mines, Reclamation, and the U.S. Geological Survey.

For most of its life, Interior has been relatively anonymous among Cabinet departments. Its very name, conveying only the vaguest impression of its functions, has contributed to its indistinct image. Occasionally during the twentieth century, however, forceful or colorful Interior secretaries—including Franklin K. Lane, Albert B. Fall, Harold L. Ickes, Stewart L. Udall, and James Watt—and controversies have brought unaccustomed publicity and prominence to the department.

BIBLIOGRAPHY

Forness, Norman O. "The Origins and Early History of the United States Department of the Interior." Ph.D. dissertation, Pennsylvania State University, 1964.

Learned, Henry B. "The Establishment of the Secretaryship of the Interior." *American Historical Review* 16 (1911).

Trani, Eugene. "The Secretaries and Under Secretaries of the Department of the Interior." Typescript, Department of the Interior Library, 1966.

United States Government Manual 1991/92, 1992.

Utley, Robert M., and Barry Mackintosh. *The Department of Everything Else.* 1989.

– E. C. BEARSS

INVESTIGATIONS, CONGRESSIONAL

Congressional investigations have left an indelible mark on the course of American history. Phrases such as "Teapot Dome," "Watergate," and "Iran-contra" have become part of the popular vernacular as a result of congressional investigations. And a number of well-known figures in American political history—Charles Evans Hughes, Hugo Black, Harry S Truman, Joseph McCarthy, and Sam Ervin, to name a few—first obtained national prominence through their involvement in such investigations. Indeed, it is not exaggeration to say that the political rise ("Mr. Hiss, are you now or have you ever been a member of the Communist Party?") and fall ("What did the President know and when did he know it?") of one American President, Richard M. Nixon, were directly linked to congressional investigations.

Congress's power to investigate, recognized as an implicit element of its authority to legislate under Article I, Section 1, of the Constitution, draws its historical foundation from early British parliamentary practice. The first congressional investigation dates back to 1792, when a special committee of the House of Representatives was formed to investigate the military defeat of Major General Arthur St. Clair and his troops by Indians in the Ohio frontier.

High-profile congressional investigations, like those during the Watergate affair and the Iran-contra affair, often undertaken by select investigative committees, generate the most public attention. Far more common, however, are the scores of investigations conducted each year by standing committees of Congress in furtherance of their continuing legislative and oversight responsibilities.

Oversight Investigations

Congressional committees carry on these investigations for a variety of reasons, none more important than congressional oversight of the administration of the laws by the executive branch. Implicit in our tripartite system of government is the need for some mechanism through which Congress can assess the adequacy of existing laws and the efficacy of their administration. Congress's investigatory powers supply this mechanism. William Pitt the elder stated in 1742, "[W]e are called the Grand Inquest of the Nation, and as such it is our duty to inquire into every step of public management, either abroad or at home, in order to see that nothing has been done amiss." Although Pitt's words were directed at the parliamentary system, a similar view was expressed by Senator Sam Ervin about the American system of government based on the separation of powers, "Of considerable importance is Congress's power to investigate the executive branch. We do not live in a monarchy but in a democracy where governmental functions are shared by three equal branches. The White House is the people's house, not an imperial palace. The executive branch is not above the law."

In the latter part of the twentieth century, two examples of these types of oversight investigations were Watergate and Iran-contra. Watergate involved an investigation into the 17 June 1972 break-in of the offices of the Democratic National Committee by five individuals with ties to the Republican National Committee. Suspicions that prominent members of the Nixon administration either knew of or participated in the crime prompted the Senate to establish the Select Committee on Presidential Campaign Activities, chaired by Senator Ervin, to investigate the break-in and any subsequent cover-up. The investigation and hearings resulted in the conviction of high-ranking members of the administration and impeachment proceedings by the House Judiciary Committee, prompting Richard Nixon to become the first President in the history of the United States to resign.

Congress cannot probe into purely private affairs or expose private activity solely for the sake of doing so.

The Iran-contra affair involved the investigation of joint House and Senate committees into a covert operation conducted by the administration of President Ronald Reagan. The operation involved a series of arms sales to the government of the Ayatollah Khomeini in Iran in an effort to secure the release of American hostages, and the transfer of the proceeds of those sales to the contras—the armed resistance movement opposing the communist government in Nicaragua—at a time when Congress had voted to deny them military aid. The investigation revealed that retired military officers, senior members of the National Security Council, and the Central Intelligence Agency Director, William Casey, were all implicated in the operation and subsequent cover-up effort.

History will probably view the Iran-contra investigation less favorably than it has Watergate. To a remarkable degree, the Iran-contra hearings were dominated by some of the witnesses, in particular the "can do" lieutenant colonel, Oliver North. Additionally, the two most important criminal convictions arising from the scandal, those of North and the national security adviser, John Poindexter, were ultimately thrown out as a direct result of Congress's decision to grant them limited immunity for their congressional testimony.

Powers of Inquiry

Congress has a number of tools at its disposal to carry out its investigations, including the power to require by subpoena the attendance of witnesses and the production of documents, the power to punish for contempt of Congress the refusal to comply with a subpoena, the threat of criminal prosecution for giving "perjured" or false testimony, and the power to compel a witness who has asserted his Fifth Amendment privilege against self-incrimination to testify under a grant of limited immunity. These tools play a prominent role in the investigatory process.

Although broad, Congress's powers of inquiry are not unfettered. There must be a valid legislative purpose for conducting an investigation. Congress cannot probe into purely private affairs or expose private activity solely for the sake of doing so. Nor can it usurp the functions of the executive and judicial branches by prosecuting, trying, and convicting individuals for criminal offenses. Furthermore, the fundamental freedoms guaranteed by the Constitution cannot be infringed. The Fifth Amendment privilege against self-incrimination, the Fourth Amendment protection against unreasonable search and seizure, and the First Amendment freedom from forced revelations of thoughts and beliefs or unwarranted intrusions into past associations all apply in the context of congressional investigations. Finally, the procedural rules of each house and its committees and subcommittees that affect the rights of witnesses—for example, open versus closed hearings, protection of confidential materials, broadcasting of hearings, questioning of witnesses, and the role of counsel—are judicially cognizable and also must be observed.

Executive Branch Resistance

Congressional investigations of the executive branch have not infrequently given rise to a "clash of absolutes" between the two political branches; the executive can assert a right to withhold from disclosure information Congress deems necessary to execute its oversight responsibilities. The executive branch has advanced a number of grounds, often grouped together under the rubric executive privilege, to justify its refusal to provide the requested information. These grounds include national security, confidentiality of presidential communications, protection of predecisional intragovernmental opinions, and the secrecy of law enforcement investigatory files.

Since the Watergate affair of the 1970s, courts have become involved, albeit in a limited fashion, in attempting to referee these interbranch skirmishes. The 1974 decision of the United States Supreme Court in *United States* v. *Nixon* recognized for the first time a constitutional basis for executive privilege. The *Nixon* case, however, involved the special prosecutor's subpoena of the tape recordings of President Richard M. Nixon's conversations, for use in a criminal trial, and not the assertion of the privilege in response to a congressional demand for information. The scattered judicial precedents that have addressed this latter question have set forth no clear rules of law, and thus the scope of the privilege is largely undefined.

As a result, the resolution of executive privilege disputes with Congress has largely been the product of the politics of the moment. Typically, both sides stake out intractable positions, a test of political will ensues, and after some period of time, a political compromise is fashioned. These compromises are often extremely complex, as illustrated by the 1982 inquiry of a Senate select committee into Abscam and other law enforcement activities of the Federal Bureau of Investigation, a scandal that in the period 1978–1980 had resulted in the criminal conviction of one Senator and six Representatives. Under the terms of the elaborate access agreement negotiated between the committee and the Department of Justice, the committee was provided access to more than twenty thousand pages of FBI documents generated during the covert stage of the Abscam operation. However, the Department of Justice, under which the FBI operates, was permitted to withhold grand jury materials and certain prosecutorial memoranda (although oral briefings on the factual material contained in the memoranda were provided). The department was also permitted to withhold documents that might compromise ongoing investigations or reveal confidential sources of investigative techniques (although it was required to describe each document and the basis of the refusal to disclose, in addition to providing the committee an opportunity to propose conditions under which such documents might be disclosed). For its part, the committee retained its right to subpoena and seek access judicially to all restricted categories of documents. And the committee agreed to a "pledge of confidentiality" whereby it could use and publicly disclose in its hearings and final report information derived from the Department of Justice documents but could not publicly identify the specific documents from which the information was obtained.

The rise in instances of conflict between the two political branches, as well as the increasing size of the legislative bureaucracy, suggest that congressional investigations will continue to play a prominent role in the future. In the right hands, congressional investigations can be an effective instrument for exposing government corruption and maladministration, and for providing the electorate with a better education about the American system of government than any civics textbook. If abused, witnesses' reputations can be irreparably damaged, public confidence undermined, and the credibility of Congress itself diminished.

[See also (I) Oversight, Subpoena Power.]

BIBLIOGRAPHY

Dash, Sam. *Chief Counsel: Inside the Ervin Committee—The Untold Story.* 1976.

Grabow, John C. *Congressional Investigations, Law and Practice.* 1988.

Hamilton, James. *The Power to Probe: A Study of Congressional Investigations.* 1976.

Schlesinger, Arthur M., Jr. and Roger Burns. *Congress Investigates: A Documented History 1792–1974.* 1975.

Taylor, Tolford. *Grand Inquest: The Story of Congressional Investigations.* 1955.

– JOHN C. GRABOW
COURT E. GOLUMBIC

J

JOINT CHIEFS OF STAFF

The concept of a Joint Chiefs of Staff, to coordinate the military services, is a twentieth-century development. During the eighteenth and nineteenth centuries the army and the navy were wholly independent in terms of plans and, usually, operations. Inadequacies revealed in the Spanish-American War led to the first effort to improve coordination, the Joint Board, created in 1903. However, interservice cooperation remained uneven.

The requirements and pressures of planning for World War II—including the need for a U.S. group to meet regularly with the British Chiefs of Staff—underscored the need for better coordination. In February 1942, the heads of the military services (Army Chief of Staff General George Marshall, Chief of Naval Operations Admiral Ernest King, Army Air Force Commander General Henry Arnold) constituted themselves as the Joint Chiefs of Staff (JCS), albeit without any formal charter or approval. Admiral William Leahy joined when he was named by President Franklin Roosevelt as Chief of Staff to the Commander in Chief. The JCS served as a unified strategic planning unit and commanded all U.S. forces throughout the world.

Secretary of Defense McNamara was always skeptical of JCS and CIA estimates of Soviet capabilities, believing they largely served to promote increased U.S. defense spending.

Toward the end of the war various plans surfaced for overhauling the entire national security structure, emerging finally as the 1947 National Security Act. This act separated the air force from the army and formally created the JCS as "the principal military advisers" to both the President and new Secretary of Defense. In 1949, the position of a nonvoting chairman was created.

Relations between Presidents and the JCS have varied greatly, but are always dominated by the concept of civilian control of the military. Running somewhat counter to this is the provision of law allowing JCS members to dissent publicly from official policy—a right that has rarely been used to its full extent.

Presidential interaction with the JCS was most intense during the height of the cold war, roughly from 1947 through 1975, the end of the Vietnam War. President Harry S Truman relied heavily on the first Chairman, General Omar Bradley. Truman sought JCS concurrence before relieving General Douglas MacArthur in 1951. Truman also relieved Chief of Naval Operations Admiral Louis Denfeld in 1949 after the so-called "revolt of the admirals" over the future of air power and a dispute with the air force about service "roles and missions." President Dwight D. Eisenhower, given his military background, felt better qualified to make defense decisions in a proper policy context than his JCS, and continually worried about JCS pleas for additional resources. Eisenhower also objected to public JCS dissents, believing they should simply comply with the Commander in Chief's decisions.

President John F. Kennedy felt he had been mislead by both the Central Intelligence Agency and the JCS on planning for the ill-fated Bay of Pigs invasion against Fidel Castro and failed to reappoint any incumbent JCS members when their current terms expired. Kennedy's Secretary of Defense, Robert S. McNamara, was always skeptical of JCS and CIA estimates of Soviet capabilities, believing they largely served to promote increased U.S. defense spending. McNamara also kept very tight control over JCS dissents. President Lyndon B. Johnson got involved in a very detailed level of operational planning during the Vietnam War, and relied heavily on Chairman General Earle Wheeler. During President Richard M. Nixon's term, there was a certain degree of tension between the JCS and national security adviser Henry Kissinger, especially over arms control with the U.S.S.R.

In 1986 Congress passed the Goldwater-Nichols Act, which increased the authority (and visibility) of the Chairman within the JCS and made him, rather than the corporate group, the President's principal military adviser.

Finally, in 1990, during the Operation Desert Shield build-up before the Gulf War, President George Bush relieved Air Force Chief of Staff General Michael Dugan for revealing to the press the likely parameters of an air campaign against Iraq.

[See also (II) Air Force, Army, Marine Corps, Navy.]

BIBLIOGRAPHY

Betts, Richard K. *Soldiers, Statesmen, and Cold War Crises.* 1977.

Joint Chiefs of Staff (Historical Division). *History of the Joint Chiefs of Staff.* Edited by Robert J Watson. Vols. I–VI. 1979–1992.

Office of the Secretary of Defense (Historical Office). *History of the Office of the Secretary of Defense.* Edited by Alfred Goldberg Vol. I: *The Formative Years.* 1984. Vol. II: *The Test of War.* 1988.

– MARK M. LOWENTHAL

JUDGES, APPOINTMENT OF

The Constitutional Convention of 1787 adopted the compromise recommendation of a special committee of eleven delegates, which suggested that federal jurists be appointed "by and with the Advice and Consent of the Senate." This recommendation evolved to become Article II, Section 2, clause 2 of the Constitution, which states, "The President . . . shall have Power, by and with the Advice and Consent of the Senate, to . . . nominate . . . Judges of the Supreme Court, and all other Officers of the United States, whose Appointments are not herein otherwise provided for, and which shall be established by Law." Under the terms of these provisions Presidents have nominated, and a majority of the Senate has confirmed, thousands of judges at all levels of the federal judiciary. (In 1992, there were eleven hundred active or senior federal judges, not including bankruptcy and administrative law judges, commissioners, and magistrates.)

The President's responsibility to nominate federal judges has often been largely delegated to the Attorney General and the Deputy Attorney General. This was noticeably true during the later years of the administration of President Dwight D. Eisenhower, when the selection of members of the federal judiciary was left almost exclusively to Attorney General William P. Rogers and Deputy Attorney General Lawrence E. Walsh. On the other hand, President Lyndon B. Johnson gave John C. Macy, Jr., Chairman of the U.S. Civil Service Commission and a trusted fellow Texan, the crucial role in the judicial selection process. During the administration of Ronald Reagan a formal committee was established, chaired by the President's counsel, Fred F. Fielding, and including the Attorney General plus seven other Department of Justice and White House officials. That committee reviewed recommendations for vacancies, submitted these to checks by the Federal Bureau of Investigation and judgments by the American Bar Association (ABA), and then forwarded its recommendation to the President.

The Senate's Role in Selecting Nominees

Whichever mode a President employs for selecting candidates for federal judgeships, three crucial factors enter into the decision making. First is the obvious need to consult with the U.S. Senator(s) and possibly with other powerful political figures in the home state of the candidate for judicial office, provided these political figures are of the same party as the President. Care must be taken that the appointee not be "personally obnoxious" to a home-state Senator, on pain of having the latter invoke the age-old, almost invariably honored, custom of senatorial courtesy—an almost certain death knell to confirmation by the Senate. The custom is based on the assumption that the President will, as a matter of political patronage, practice, and courtesy, engage in such consultation prior to the nominee's designation. If the President fails to adhere to this custom, the aggrieved Senator's colleagues will almost certainly support his or her call for the nominee's defeat.

William Henry Harrison was among the few Presidents who did not see at least one of his Supreme Court nominees become a federal judge. (Library of Congress, Prints and Photographs Division)

Sometimes, powerful Senators of a President's political party will insist not only on the right of prior approval of presidential candidates but will demand the right to designate particular candidates of their own. This was the case in 1974–1975, when Republican Senator Lowell P. Weicker, Jr., of Connecticut insisted that Connecticut's ex-governor, Thomas J. Meskill, be nominated to the federal appellate bench. Meskill was confirmed by the Senate by a vote of 54 to 36 despite the American Bar Association's unanimous "not qualified" rating. This tendency of some Senators to insist on the nomination of candidates of dubious merit has been offset, somewhat, since the establishment of President Jimmy Carter's Circuit Judge Nomination Commission in 1977 (abolished in 1981), coupled with Carter's Executive Order 12097 (1978), which established guidelines and stipulated qualification standards for individuals nominated to federal judgeships. The late 1970s witnessed a burgeoning—in states such as Virginia, Pennsylvania, Iowa, Georgia, Florida, Colorado, and New York—of Senator-created merit advisory groups and commissions charged with recommending nominees to the federal bench to the Senators. By early 1984, fifty Senators in thirty-five states had agreed to choose federal district judges on a merit basis only, aided by commission recommendations. Other Senators, however, had categorically declined to do so, among them Democrats Adlai E. Stevenson (Ill.), Thomas F. Eagleton (Mo.), Paul S. Sarbanes (Md.), and Lloyd M. Bentsen (Tex.); Bentsen went so far as to say, "I am the merit commission for Texas." Yet more than one-half of Reagan's 290 federal district court appointees emerged from selection panels voluntarily sponsored by Senators.

ABA Evaluation

A second factor that has played an increasingly significant role in the federal judiciary appointment process, especially since the last months of the Truman administration, is the American Bar Association's fifteen-member Committee on Federal Judiciary. This committee, established in 1946, was widely utilized at the pre-formal-nomination stage during Eisenhower's term, a practice continued under all subsequent Presidents, although Richard M. Nixon, following the ABA committee's disapproval of his 1970–1971 list of dubiously qualified candidates, refused to submit nominees' names to it until after he had selected and publicized them. The committee's work has generally produced good results and is understandably popular with the legal profession—although there is no unanimity on that evaluation. There are those who deeply believe that the selection of members of the federal judiciary must rest, in fact as well as in name, with the executive branch, its head being specifically charged to do so under Article III of the Constitution. For such critics, the apparent delegation of important aspects of the President's authority (i.e., approval of, or at least judgment on, candidates) to a private body, no matter how qualified or representative, is at best questionable and at worst a dereliction of duty. Nor is the bar free from political or personal biases, as the committee's handling of the Supreme Court nominations of Abe Fortas and Clement Haynsworth in 1969 and those of Robert Bork in 1987 and Clarence Thomas in 1991 demonstrated. To cite an earlier case, had President Woodrow Wilson heeded the ABA's advice, Justice Louis D. Brandeis—one of the nation's greatest jurists—would never have been nominated. Furthermore, as Joel Grossman's intriguing study of the committee's activities over a period of two decades demonstrated rather convincingly, its membership was initially dominated by the "legal establishment."

Had President Woodrow Wilson heeded the American Bar Association's advice, Justice Louis D. Brandeis —one of the nation's greatest jurists— would never have been nominated.

The ABA committee has become a powerful and generally respected vehicle in the vital initial stage of the nominating process—at least below the Supreme Court level. It does not generate names for judicial vacancies but rather evaluates the qualifications of actual or potential nominees. After an investigation, customarily lasting from six to eight weeks, it reports to the Justice Department on the qualifications of the nominee and rates him or her as well qualified (WQ), qualified (Q), or not qualified (NQ). (Similar, but not identical labels are provided for Supreme Court nominees.) Its final report is a one-sentence judgment by the full membership. In a number of cases the consideration of nominees for the federal bench has been dropped after the ABA committee found them not qualified, and no NQs were approved between 1965 and 1975. Moreover, its reports have enabled the Justice Department to rule out certain names recommended by home-state Senators—though "senatorial courtesy" may prevail in the end. It should be noted that the committee also sends its ratings independently to the Senate Judiciary Committee, and does not route them through the Justice Department.

No alert and prudent Chief Executive would nowadays attempt to designate members of the judiciary purely on the basis of political considerations. Too much is at stake, and the ABA is a powerful factor in the selection process. Yet, granting the trend to make appointments on the basis of overall merit and excellence, political pressures must nevertheless be reckoned with and are disregarded only at the appointing authority's peril. Moreover, a federal judgeship is viewed as a "plum" by all concerned, in that it represents a potent patronage-whip in the hands of the executive vis-à-vis state politicians as well as Congress.

Supreme Court's Role in Selecting Nominees

There is a third crucial factor in selecting federal bench nominees: the unquestionably significant influence that sitting and retired members of the Supreme Court, especially the Chief Justice, have on nominations to the Supreme Court itself. Among Chief Justices, William Howard Taft, Charles Evans Hughes, Harlan Stone, Frederick M. Vinson, Earl Warren, and Warren Burger and, among Associate Justices, the first John M. Harlan, Samuel F. Miller, Willis Van Devanter, Louis D. Brandeis, and Felix Frankfurter have all been involved in consultations with Presidents and Attorneys General in selecting Supreme Court nominees. Taft's participation in the selection process was the most open and active of all—followed at some distance by Stone, Hughes, Harlan, and Miller (in that order). Taft's role in President Warren G. Harding's nomination of Pierce Butler is a classic example of the Chief Justice's influence: Harding's Attorney General, Harry M. Daugherty, told Henry Taft (William's brother) that "the President would not approve anybody for appointment who was not approved by the Chief Justice."

Judicial Terms and Salaries

At the federal level, all judges of the constitutional courts—that is, those appointed under the provisions of Article III of the Constitution (the judicial article)—hold their position during "good behavior," which in effect means for life or until they choose to retire. The other federal judges—those of legislative courts created under a provision of Article I (the legislative article)—occupy their positions for whatever period Congress may have prescribed at the time it established the court or in subsequent legislation. In some instances this has meant "good behavior" tenure for them, too, or, frequently, terms of office ranging between four and fifteen years. The constitutional judges have the additional safeguard, stated in Article III, that their "compensation . . . shall not be diminished during their continuance in office." Hence, although their salaries may be increased during their incumbency, they may not be lowered, short of constitutional amendment.

Judicial salaries, although perhaps not commensurate with the responsibilities and prestige of the offices and often lower than comparable positions in private enterprise, are adequate. In 1991 the annual salary range was from $125,000 for district court judges to $160,000 for the Chief Justice of the United States, with the Associate Justices receiving $7,000 less. But people hardly aspire to high judicial office for financial gain.

To enable aging jurists to step down from the bench with dignity and, concurrently, to render their replacement by younger personnel more palatable, Congress in 1937 enacted a vastly improved retirement statute. Under its provisions, federal judges may retire outright on full pay equal to their last year's salary at the age of seventy after having served ten years on the federal bench or at sixty-five after having served fifteen. These requirements are waived in the presence of physical disability, in which case retirement pay is computed in accordance with length of service. A more financially advantageous arrangement, of which many retirees have availed themselves, is to opt for a "senior judge" status upon retirement. That status assumes a judge's ability to serve when called on (although only about 20 to 25 percent actually do serve), but it also means an increase in the judge's pension whenever the sitting members of any federal court receive a raise. A deceased jurist's surviving spouse and dependents receive an annual purse equivalent to 37.5 percent of the judge's average salary—if the jurist elected to participate in a contributory judicial survivor's annuity plan.

Qualifications for Nomination

Today, there is only one standard prerequisite for qualification as a federal judge—an LL.B. or J.D. degree. The possession of a law degree is neither a constitutional nor a statutory requirement for appointment, yet custom would automatically exclude from consideration anyone who did not have one, and the legal profession would remonstrate so determinedly were a nonlawyer nominated that the appointing authority would surely acquiesce. Historically, however, only 58 of the 106 Justices on the U.S. Supreme Court attended law school, and it was not until 1922 that a majority of the sitting Justices were law school graduates and not until 1957 that every sitting Justice was a law school graduate.

Theoretically, any graduate of an accredited law school may hope for an eventual appointment to the federal judiciary—provided that he or she is politically "available" and acceptable to the executive, legislative, and private forces that determine the selection, nomination, and appointment process. In the final analysis, it is the President and his immediate advisers—usually the Attorney General and Deputy Attorney General—who take the crucial step of submitting the nominee's name to the Senate. All Presidents except William Henry Harrison, Zachary Taylor, Andrew Johnson, and Jimmy Carter have succeeded in seeing at least one nominee attain membership on the highest court of the land. Of these four exceptions, the first two were removed too quickly by death; Johnson was the victim of congressional machinations that successfully prevented him from filling several Supreme Court vacancies; and fate simply never presented Carter with an opportunity to make a nomination. The 106 individual Justices who had served on the Court as of the end of the 1991–1992 term provided thirty-six Presidents (counting Cleveland only once) with 110 successful appointments (four Associate Justices were promoted to Chief Justice).

In view of the minimal basic need of a law degree, it is hardly astonishing that many newly appointed jurists lack practical judicial experience. This has been especially true of Supreme Court designees; those of the court level immediately below, the Court of Appeals, have often had some lower court experience in federal district court. Of the 106 Justices who served on the Supreme Court between 1789 and the end of 1991, only twenty-four (not counting the prior service of E. D. White, Hughes, Stone, and Rehnquist, Associate Justices who were promoted to Chief Justices) had had ten or more years of previous judicial experience on any lower level, federal or state, at the time of their appointment, and forty-two had no judicial experience whatsoever. The list of the totally inexperienced, however, contains many of the most illustrious names in the judicial history of the United States, including five Chief Justices—Roger B. Taney, Salmon P. Chase, Morrison R. Waite, Melville W. Fuller, and Earl Warren—and notable Associate Justices Miller, Brandeis, Frankfurter, Joseph Story, Joseph P. Bradley, William O. Douglas, and Lewis F. Powell, Jr., to name a few. (Before his appointment, the great Chief Justice John Marshall had spent a mere three years in the very minor city hustings court of Richmond, Virginia.)

The only person who knows with certainty why someone is appointed is the President of the United States. The record indicates, however, that four basic reasons have been the most important in selecting nominees: objective merit, personal friendship, balancing representativeness on the Court, and political and ideological compatibility. Of the four reasons, the desire to balance representation of religion, geography, race, and sex was by the 1990s playing the major role in presidential choice of nominees. The emphases on gender and racial balance, especially, are here to stay, no matter how controversial they may be.

Political and ideological compatibility often strongly influence presidential choices for the Supreme Court. Among the points a President is almost certain to consider are whether or not the choice will be popular with influential interest groups, whether the nominee has been a loyal member of the President's party, whether the nominee favors presidential programs and policies, whether the nominee is acceptable to his or her home-state Senators, whether the nominee's judicial record (if any) meets the President's criteria of constitutional construction, whether the President is indebted to the nominee for past political services, and finally, whether the President feels "good" or "comfortable" about the nominee.

A comparison of the 106 people who, up to 1992, had sat on the U.S. Supreme Court yields the following "average" profile: a Supreme Court Justice is likely to be native-born (only six Justices, including Frankfurter, originally an Austrian, and George Sutherland, from England, were born outside the United States), male (Sandra Day O'Connor was, by the early 1990s, the only woman to have served on the Court; Ruth Bader Ginsburg was nominated in 1993), white (with Thurgood Marshall and Clarence Thomas the only exceptions), of Anglo-Saxon ethnic stock (all but fifteen), Protestant (there had been only eight Catholic and five Jewish Justices), fifty to fifty-five years of age at the time of appointment, firstborn (fifty-six, or 62 percent), of upper-middle to high social and economic status, reared in a nonrural (but not necessarily urban) environment, civic-minded and politically active (or at least politically aware), possessing a B.A. and a law degree (one-third from Ivy League institutions) with an excellent academic record, and having held some type of public office.

Confirmation Process

That the Senate has taken its confirmation role seriously is documented by its refusal to confirm 40 of the 143 Supreme Court nominees forwarded to it over more than two centuries of U.S. history. Eleven of these nominees were not rejected per se, but their nominations were not acted on by the Senate. True, even counting the Senate's refusal to vote in the Fortas promotion, only five nominees were formally voted down during the twentieth century (and two others not acted upon); but, as the experiences of the Nixon, Reagan, and Bush administrations demonstrate, the possibility is ever present. A return to the nineteenth-century record of one rejection or refusal to act for every three nominees would, however, appear to be highly unlikely.

Among the more prominent reasons for the forty rejections have been the following: senatorial opposition to the nominating President; the nominee's involvement with a contentious issue of public policy; opposition to the record of the incumbent Court, which the nominee was presumed to have supported; senatorial courtesy (closely linked to the consultative nominating process); a perceived "political unreliability" of the nominee; the evident lack of qualifications or limited ability of the nominee; concerted, sustained opposition by interest or pressure groups; and fear that the nominee would dramatically alter the Court's jurisprudential philosophical "lineup." Often, several reasons have figured in the rejection of a nominee.

By the 1990s the desire to balance representation of religion, geography, race, and sex on the Court played a major role in presidential choice of nominees.

In general, opposition to the confirmation of a federal jurist, especially a Supreme Court nominee, seems to reflect the existence of deep-seated concern in the nation. In the early years of the Court's history, relatively little interest was shown in the potentially unfortunate effects of judges of uncertain—or certain—convictions. Such interest became more frequent and noticeable as the influence of the judiciary grew. By the 1980s and 1990s, when there were so many issues with which large numbers of people were deeply concerned, almost every nominee was made to run the gauntlet. The nomination and confirmation procedure had become a battleground on which large issues were fought out before the public eye.

Impeachment

Involuntary removal of federal judges can be effected only by the process of impeachment and conviction. It has long been legal, however, for the judicial council of a U.S. circuit to discipline a judge by stripping him or her of duties and authority while permitting the retention of both title and salary, and in 1980 Congress enacted the Judicial Councils Reform and Judicial Conduct and Disability Act, which gave the judicial councils of the thirteen circuits authority to discipline for misconduct all federal judges except those of the Supreme Court. (Judicial councils cannot, however, remove judges from office.) In accordance with constitutional requirements, impeachment for "Treason, Bribery, or other high Crimes and Misdemeanors" may be voted by a simple majority of the House of Representatives, there being a quorum on the floor. Trial is then held in the Senate, which may convict by a vote of two-thirds if a quorum is present.

As of early 1992 the House of Representatives had initiated a total of sixteen impeachment proceedings, of which thirteen were directed against federal judges. (Nine other judges resigned before formal charges were lodged against them.) Of the thirteen impeachment proceedings involving federal judges, eleven went to trial. (U.S. District Court Judge Mark H. Delaney, who was impeached in 1873 by voice vote, resigned before the articles of impeachment were prepared for Senate action, and, in the other case that did not go to trial, George W. English (a district court judge impeached in 1926) resigned before the Senate could vote.) Of the eleven cases that progressed to trial, four resulted in acquittals and seven in removals. The four acquittals are headed, both chronologically and in importance, by the only impeachment trial (as of early 1993) involving a Justice of the Supreme Court—that of Associate Justice Samuel Chase in 1804–1805.

[See also (I) Judiciary and Congress; (III) Judicial Selection.]

BIBLIOGRAPHY

Abraham, Henry J. *The Judicial Process.* 6th ed. 1993.

———. *Justices and Presidents.* 3rd ed. 1992.

Bronner, Ethan. *Battle for Justice: How the Bork Nomination Shook America.* 1989.

Grossman, Joel B. *Lawyers and Judges: The ABA and the Process of Judicial Selection.* 1965.

Harris, J. P. *The Advice and Consent of the Senate.* 1953.

Massaro, John. *Supremely Political: The Role of Ideology and Presidential Management in Unsuccessful Supreme Court Nominations.* 1991.

Schmidhauser, John R. *Judges and Justices.* 1979.

Twentieth Century Task Force on Judicial Selection. *Judicial Roulette.* 1988.

– HENRY J. ABRAHAM

JUDICIARY, FEDERAL

A coequal branch of the national government, the federal judiciary is independent of the President yet is also dependent on the Chief Executive for the recruitment of its personnel and the enforcement of its rulings. Occasionally, federal courts and the executive branch have been embroiled in major conflicts—as in the 1930s, when the federal judiciary, led by the Supreme Court, struck down progressive economic legislation and much of Democratic President Franklin D. Roosevelt's early New Deal program. But the federal courts more often offer Presidents opportunities to advance their own legal policy agenda through litigation and the President's power to appoint federal judges.

Article III of the Constitution vests the judicial power "in one supreme Court, and in such inferior Courts as the Congress may from time to time ordain and establish." Besides guaranteeing federal judges basically lifetime tenure (subject only to impeachment), Article III extends the judicial power to all cases in law and equity arising under the Constitution and the laws of the United States.

Though it set out the Supreme Court's original jurisdiction and authorized Congress to establish its appellate jurisdiction, the Constitution was silent concerning the structure of the federal judiciary and the power of judicial review.

Structure

It was left to the First Congress to establish the federal judiciary and to define its power. The Judiciary Act of 1789 authorized five Associate Justices and one Chief Justice of the Supreme Court and created two "inferior" courts: district courts, which serve as the trial courts in the federal judicial system, and circuit courts of appeals, which are located in different geographical regions. Along with thirteen district judgeships the Judiciary Act of 1789 required members of the Supreme Court to ride circuit twice a year and to sit with district judges to hear appeals in the circuit courts instead of providing for additional appellate court judges. Although members of the Supreme Court complained about their workload throughout the nineteenth century, there were no permanent appellate court judges until after the passage of the Circuit Court of Appeals Act in 1891.

As the country expanded westward and grew in population, the size of the federal bench gradually grew as well. The number of Justices and circuits grew from three in 1789, to nine in 1837, and then to ten in 1863. During Reconstruction, Congress's antagonism toward President Andrew Johnson led it to reduce the number of Justices from ten to seven in order to deny Johnson the opportunity to make appointments to the Court. After Ulysses S. Grant was elected President, Congress in 1869 again authorized nine Justices—the number that has since prevailed.

From the original 19 federal judges, the number grew to more than 1,000 in 1992, including 709 full-time judges and another 340 who have senior status but continue to hear cases. In 1992 there were ninety-four district courts, with at least one or more in each state, depending on caseloads. District judges sit alone and preside over trials, with or without juries, and over other criminal and civil proceedings. They also approve plea bargains, supervise settlements, monitor remedial decrees, and manage the processing of cases. The number of federal circuit courts of appeals has grown to thirteen. Eleven geographical regions, or circuits, have one appellate court each, with general appellate jurisdiction over appeals from the district courts, rulings by independent regulatory commissions, and appeals of federal administrative agencies' enforcement decisions. In addition, the Court of Appeals for the District of Columbia Circuit has general jurisdiction over federal cases, but by statute also handles most challenges to federal agencies' regulations. In 1982 Congress added the Court of Appeals for the Federal Circuit, which is also located in the District of Columbia and primarily hears tax, patent, and international trade cases and appeals. Unlike district courts, federal appellate courts have twenty or more judges who hear cases in rotating three-judge panels. Occasionally, in important or especially divisive cases (particularly cases that present issues on which two or more three-judge panels have reached opposite results in similar cases), the entire circuit court sits as a panel, or *en banc,* to reach a decision and resolve conflicting interpretation of the law within the circuit.

As the country expanded westward and grew in population, the size of the federal bench gradually grew as well.

Along with the increasing number of federal judges, there has been a significant growth in the number of law clerks, secretaries, support staff, magistrate and bankruptcy judges, and probation and pretrial workers—that is, in the size of the entire judicial branch. In 1900 the federal judiciary had 2,770 employees; by 1960, 4,992 employees; in 1980, 14,500; and more than 24,600 in 1991.

Role

These changes in the size and complexity of the judiciary reflect the increasing flow of litigation into the federal courts and magnify basic tensions in the highly decentralized, three-tiered judicial system. In 1991 federal district courts faced more than 200,000 civil cases and more than 45,000 criminal cases, while federal appellate courts handled more than 42,000 civil and criminal appeals. Because the bulk of federal litigation takes place in district courts and only about 10 percent of their decisions are appealed, district courts function as courts of both first and last resort for the overwhelming majority of federal cases. Moreover, as the size and caseloads of federal courts of appeals grew after World War II, there has been a greater propensity for more intracircuit conflicts (conflicts over the law among three-judge panels within each circuit) and for more intercircuit conflicts among the appellate courts around the country. Together, these trends push toward greater discretionary justice in the district courts, with less supervision and error correction by appellate courts, and indicate a pull away from uniformity, stability, and certainty in national public law and policy.

The increased amount of federal litigation has also affected the Supreme Court's role in the federal judicial system and diminished its capacity for appellate review of the lower federal courts. Whereas in 1920 there were just 565 cases on the Court's docket, the number has grown incrementally during each decade since World War II, from 1,300 in 1950 to more than 2,300 cases by 1960, 4,200 by 1970, 5,300 in 1980, and more than 6,000 cases by 1990. In response to these increases in the size of the docket, Congress expanded the Court's discretionary jurisdiction, giving it the power to deny review to the vast majority of cases and thereby enabling it not only to manage the docket but to set the Court's substantive policy agenda as well. As a result, the Supreme Court reviews only about 140 cases annually (less than 3 percent of the cases arriving on its docket) and takes only those cases that pose major questions of national importance. The present-day Court thus no longer serves primarily to supervise or correct the errors of lower courts. Instead, the Court functions as a "superlegislature," reviewing major issues of public law and policy of interest to the President, Congress, the national government, and the states.

No less significant than the growth in caseload has been the changing nature of the business coming into federal courts. Broad social and economic forces continue to affect the business of the federal courts, but so do the legal policy goals and priorities of the President and administration. The district courts, for example, have gradually taken on fewer criminal cases and more civil litigation. In the late nineteenth century, 61 percent of the work of federal trial courts involved criminal cases, which dominated dockets until the mid-1930s. The filing of criminal cases rapidly increased during the 1920s and early 1930s, when it leveled off. Another surge occurred in the late 1960s, followed by a decline from 1975 on. In 1980, criminal cases amounted to only 15 percent of federal district courts' caseload; this percentage declined farther, to less than 1 percent by 1991, due to a dramatic increase in civil litigation. Despite not keeping pace with the increasing rate of civil litigation, the number of criminal cases did steadily climb throughout the 1980s—the number of drug-related criminal cases alone more than doubled between 1981 and 1991.

The changing nature of the business coming before the Supreme Court further underscores how the federal judiciary's role in shaping national public law and policy grew more significant in the twentieth century. During much of the early nineteenth century, more than 40 percent of the Court's business consisted of admiralty and prize cases; matters of common law accounted for approximately 50 percent. By the 1880s admiralty cases dropped to less than 4 percent. While common law disputes and jurisdictional questions continued to account for almost 40 percent of the Court's business by the 1880s, more than 43 percent involved issues of statutory interpretation and only about 4 percent concerned matters of constitutional law. This change registered the federal government's assertion of powers to regulate interstate commerce and the executive branch's enforcement of antitrust laws and other kinds of new economic regulation. In the twentieth century, the trend toward a Court that principally decides issues of national importance for federal law and public policy continued. In the 1980s, about 47 percent of the cases annually decided by the Court raised questions of constitutional law, 38 percent dealt with the interpretation of congressional statutes, and the remaining 15 percent involved controversies over federal taxation, administrative law, and federal agencies' regulations.

The Judiciary and the Presidency

The executive branch thus plays a large role in determining the business of the federal judiciary and of the Supreme Court in particular. The litigation strategies of the executive branch, moreover, register the changing social- and economic-policy agendas of Presidents. During the administration of Democratic President Jimmy Carter, for instance, the Department of Justice promoted affirmative action by bringing litigation in the federal courts aimed at forcing businesses and state and local governments to hire African Americans and women. That litigation policy was reversed when Republican President Ronald Reagan was elected. Reagan's Department of Justice attacked the constitutionality of affirmative action programs in federal courts and aimed to return power to state and local governments, as well as to cut back on the enforcement of antitrust law and other economic regulation.

The Department of Justice is uniquely positioned to advance a President's social and economic policies in the federal courts. The department not only decides what kinds of litigation to pursue, but it also may relitigate issues in different federal courts. If one circuit court rejects the government's interpretation of a statute or regulation, the Department of Justice may relitigate the issue in another case in another appellate court. The department's relitigation policy foments intercircuit conflicts among the federal appellate courts and thereby creates a basis for appealing a case (and the policy issue it embodies) to the Supreme Court, which tends to hear cases posing intercircuit conflicts and deemed by the government to present "substantial questions of federal law."

Within the Department of Justice, the office of the Solicitor General is responsible for screening all appeals and petitions to the Supreme Court by federal agencies (except for those made by the Interstate Commerce Commission). The Solicitor General decides which cases should be taken to the Court and advances the substantive legal-policy agenda of the President in petitions, briefs, and oral arguments before the Court. Because the Solicitor General screens out a large number of federal cases that might be appealed to the Court and has earned a reputation for high-quality work, the Justices are predisposed to hear cases in which the Solicitor General participates.

Although the federal judiciary generally supports the executive branch and has served to legitimate the legal policies of the President, federal courts have not invariably done so. Democratic President Harry S Truman, for instance, claimed an inherent power to seize the nation's steel mills in order to avert a nationwide strike that, he argued, threatened the country's effort in the Korean War. But his claim was rejected by a federal district court and a majority of the Supreme Court in *Youngstown Sheet & Tube Co.* v. *Sawyer* (1952). Likewise, Republican President Richard M. Nixon's claim of executive privilege to withhold confidential White House communications from disclosure in a criminal trial was rebuffed in *United States* v. *Nixon* (1974). Although Truman and Nixon disagreed with the Court's rulings, they nonetheless respected the federal judiciary's independence and complied with the rulings.

The federal courts have generally served to legitimize the legal policies of the executive branch and to strengthen presidential power.

At times in the history of U.S. politics, Presidents have attacked the federal judiciary in speeches and campaigns. In the early 1930s, President Roosevelt campaigned against the Court's conservative economic philosophy and overturning of early New Deal legislation. After his landslide reelection in 1936, Roosevelt proposed a judicial reform that would have expanded the number of Supreme Court Justices from nine to fifteen, thus enabling him to secure a majority favorable to his social and economic programs. But, while the Senate was debating his Court-packing plan, the Court abruptly upheld major pieces of New Deal legislation, and Roosevelt's proposal was eventually defeated in the Senate. Thirty years later, President Nixon attacked the liberal social philosophy and decisions of the Warren Court and promised to appoint only conservative "strict constructionists" to the federal bench. In the 1980s President Reagan repeatedly attacked the legitimacy of the Court's rulings upholding a woman's constitutional right to abortion, and his Solicitor General took cases to the Court that enabled him to ask the Justices to overturn their rulings on abortion.

While Presidents and their administrations may either enforce or attempt to thwart compliance with controversial rulings of the federal judiciary, in the long run their major influence over the federal courts remains contingent on their appointments to the federal bench. Although Roosevelt's Court-packing plan failed, he and his successor, Harry Truman, appointed more than 80 percent of the federal bench. The federal judiciary in turn became gradually more liberal in the areas of civil liberties and the rights of the criminally accused. In the 1970s, Republican Presidents Nixon and Gerald Ford were moderately successful with their judicial appointments in moving the federal courts back to more conservative directions. In the 1980s and 1990s, Reagan and George Bush achieved even greater success, filling more than 80 percent of the federal bench and strongly carrying their conservative social and economic philosophy into the federal courts.

The size, business, and role of the federal judiciary have evolved along with changes in the national government and American politics. Although an independent branch of the national government, the federal courts have (with some exceptions as in the 1930s) generally served to legitimize the legal policies of the executive branch and to strengthen presidential power. The ideological swing of presidential elections and the President's power to appoint federal judges have generally tended to keep the federal courts in line with the dominant political coalition and to make them democratically accountable.

[See also (II) Solicitor General; (III) The Judiciary.]

BIBLIOGRAPHY

Bator, Paul, Paul J. Mishkin, David L. Shapiro, and Herbert Wechsler, *Hart and Wechsler's The Federal Courts and the Federal System.* 1981.

Caplan, Lincoln. *The Tenth Justice: The Solicitor General and the Rule of Law.* 1987.

Carp, Robert A., and C. K. Rowland. *Policymaking and Politics in the Federal District Courts.* 1983.

Goldman, Sheldon, and Austin Sarat, eds. *American Court Systems.* 2d rev. ed 1989.

Howard, J. Woodford, Jr. *Courts of Appeals in the Federal Judicial System.* 1981.
O'Brien, David M. *Storm Center: The Supreme Court in American Politics.* 3d rev. ed. Forthcoming.
Posner, Richard. *The Federal Courts: Crisis and Reform* 1985.

– DAVID M. O'BRIEN

JUSTICE, DEPARTMENT OF

The executive branch department with primary responsibility for handling the legal work of the federal government, including the enforcement of federal law, is the Department of Justice. The department was created by the Judiciary Act of 1870 and is headed by the U.S. Attorney General, whose office has existed since 1789.

The department is composed of the offices of the Attorney General, Deputy Attorney General, Associate Attorney General, Inspector General, and Solicitor General. The Attorney General, in addition to serving as department head, is also a member of the Cabinet and a presidential adviser. The Deputy Attorney General is the second-highest position in the department, although the Associate Attorney General, created in 1977, is often considered on par. The deputy and associate divide departmental administrative responsibilities, including both lawyering and nonlawyering functions. The Inspector General conducts internal audits of the Department's programs and investigates allegations of misconduct by the Department's employees. The Solicitor General's office conducts government litigation before the Supreme Court.

Organization

The government's legal business has been divided into six subject areas, with an Assistant Attorney General heading each division. The assistants handle litigation below the Supreme Court level. The oldest, with roots going back to 1868, is the Civil Division. It represents the interests of the federal government in civil claims. The Environment and Natural Resources Division, organized in 1910 as the Land and Natural Resources Division and reorganized twenty years later, handles civil actions that relate to acquiring, owning, and managing public land and natural resources. The Criminal Division was formed in 1928 to enforce federal criminal statutes. Five years later, the Tax Division was added to specialize in civil and criminal tax litigation. That same year, 1933, the Antitrust Division was established to oversee enforcement of antitrust laws. In 1957, the Civil Rights Division was created to enforce federal civil rights law.

An Assistant Attorney General also heads the Office of Legal Counsel (OLC), created in 1933 to assist the Attorney General in preparing formal and informal legal opinions for government agencies and departments. The office's biggest client, according to one recent OLC head, is the President, usually through the White House Counsel's office. Under some administrations, the OLC has communicated directly with the White House without going through the Attorney General.

The Justice Department is also responsible for the ninety-five U.S. attorneys and their staffs, although by tradition they operate with some independence and autonomy. Each federal judicial district has a U.S. attorney, appointed by the President and confirmed by the Senate to a four-year term. The U.S. Marshals Service, with ninety-five marshals and their deputies, also comes under the Justice Department. Two investigative units reside at Justice as well: the Federal Bureau of Investigation (FBI) and the Drug Enforcement Administration (DEA). The FBI grew out of a small detective staff formed in 1908; after a bureau scandal, it was reorganized in 1924 under the directorship of a young lawyer named J. Edgar Hoover, who served as its director for the next forty-eight years. The FBI director is appointed to a ten-year term by the President with senatorial confirmation. The bureau is the largest unit in Justice. The DEA, which investigates illicit manufacturing and trafficking in controlled substances, was added to the department in 1973.

The Civil War had brought

a monumental increase in government litigation,

with cases involving questions

ranging from property titles to personal rights.

In addition to the more traditional lawyering and investigatory activities, the Justice Department houses several nonlawyering offices. Among them is the Immigration and Naturalization Service (INS), which enforces laws that relate to admission, exclusion, removal, and naturalization of non-U.S. citizens. The quasi-judicial Board of Immigration Appeals, independent of the INS, also operates out of the department through the Executive Office for Immigration Review. Also part of the Department of Justice are the Bureau of Prisons, which administers the federal prison system; the U.S. Parole Commission, which grants or revokes paroles for federal prisoners and sets parole policies; and the Office of Pardon Attorney, which makes recommendations on clemency to the President.

Other Justice Department programs include the Office of Justice Programs, which supports research in criminal justice, particularly on the state level; the Office of Policy and Communication, which assesses the entire system of justice and makes recommendations for change; and the Community Relations Service, which provides mediation and technical assistance to handle local problems that arise under federal civil rights laws. The Executive Office for United States Trustees operates out of the department as well, providing a nationwide network to handle the administrative processing of bankruptcies. The Office of Intelligence Policy and Review represents the government before the Foreign Intelligence Surveillance Court, and the Interpol—U.S. National Central Bureau serves as a communications conduit with other Interpol member nations.

The housekeeping responsibilities of the department rest primarily with the Justice Management Division, which develops budget requests, handles personnel matters, and oversees department finances. Other internal duties are handled by the Office of Public Information and the Office of Legislative Affairs. The Office of Professional Responsibility investigates charges of misconduct of Justice employees.

Origins and Growth

While the Judiciary Act of 1789 created the office of Attorney General, no department was formally attached to that office until 1870, after the Civil War had brought a tremendous growth in government litigation. Edmund Randolph, the first Attorney General, attempted to centralize the nation's legal affairs when he requested legislation to bring the U.S. attorneys under his control, which, he argued, would help him secure the government's legal interests. The U.S. district attorneys and marshals had been created by the Judiciary Act of 1789, and statutorily they were under presidential supervision, but in reality they operated with few checks. The legislation recommended by Randolph failed to pass, however.

Debates over the establishment of a formal law department began as early as 1829, when President Andrew Jackson sent a proposal to Congress to increase the Attorney General's responsibilities and salary. The bill's supporters claimed that the current system allowed incompetent U.S. district attorneys—who were without adequate federal supervision—to injure financial interests of the country. But there was considerable congressional resistance to the legislation. The opposition was led by the famous orator Daniel Webster, who asserted that the bill would make the Attorney General into "a half accountant, a half lawyer, a half clerk, in fine, a half everything and not much of any thing" (U.S. Senate, *Register of Debates,* 26 March, 13 April, and 30 April 1830). Webster succeeded in replacing Jackson's plan with his own, which created the post of Solicitor of the Treasury.

Presidents James K. Polk and Franklin Pierce also battled Congress in an effort to extend the Attorney General's authority and to increase his salary and staff. Polk recommended the formation of a justice department in 1845, but Congress did not respond. Eight years later, Pierce won a salary increase and two more clerk positions for his Attorney General. In 1861, the U.S. attorneys and marshals were nominally brought under the Attorney General's control. Later, two Assistant Attorneys General were added, along with a law clerk. But the trend in Congress was toward fragmenting, not consolidating, legal offices within the government. Law posts were added to the Internal Revenue Service, War Department, Navy, and Post Office. Other executive departments soon agitated for legal staffs of their own and for the right to supervise their own litigation.

Despite the lack of a formal justice department, Attorneys General began to speak of themselves as heading a "law department": this is how, for example, the office was described by Attorney General Caleb Cushing in 1856. Finally, in the years following the Civil War, the need for a larger, consolidated law department became apparent. The war had brought a monumental increase in government litigation, with cases involving questions ranging from property titles to personal rights. The federal government had to be represented in courts all across the country. The Attorney General's office did not have the staff to handle the demand, nor did it have adequate supervision over the U.S. attorneys. Instead, outside counsel had to be hired by the various executive departments at prevailing professional rates. The enormous costs incurred—estimated at close to half a million dollars over four years from 1862 to 1866—came to the notice of the Thirty-ninth Congress. Legislation to establish a department of justice was introduced in the following two Congresses. Proponents argued for it as a cost-cutting measure and as a resolution to a problem that had long plagued the nation's legal affairs—that of contradictory opinions being issued by the law officers of different departments. The bill was finally passed on 20 June 1870, and the Department of Justice came into existence on 1 July 1870. The staff was increased by two assistants and a Solicitor General, whose responsibility was to share with the Attorney General the duty of conducting cases for the United States before the Supreme Court. The act also gave the Attorney General a positive grant of authority over the U.S. attorneys and marshals.

Legislative fiat alone, however, could not create a department, especially given two seemingly minor congressional oversights. The first was the failure to provide the department with centralized office space. Without such space, the law officers of the other departments—nominally transferred to Justice—remained located at their respective departments, where they continued in much the same manner as before. The other oversight was the failure to repeal the old statutes that had originally established and defined these law officers' positions.

Further pleas to Congress in 1903 and 1909 failed to alter the divided control of and multiple responsibility for the nation's legal system. By 1915, solicitors who were largely independent of Justice operated in State, Treasury, Interior, Commerce, Labor, Agriculture, Navy, Post Office, and Internal Revenue. Each one claimed the right to conduct litigation; each rendered legal advice to his department. With World War I, President Woodrow Wilson issued an executive order that required all government law officers to operate under the supervision and control of the Department of Justice. He also reiterated the binding nature of the Attorney General's opinions on executive officers. Through the war, departmental law officers could continue to render advice for their departments, but they had to leave litigation to the Department of Justice. As the emergency ended, however, the authority of the executive order lapsed and the old system reemerged. Chaos had returned by the 1920s. The consolidation of the government's legal work began again in 1933 under Attorney General Homer Cummings, when President Franklin D. Roosevelt issued another executive order. Department heads, however, continued to resist.

Role

The practice of executive departments maintaining their own law offices continues today. A department's attorneys are generally restricted to rendering legal advice on matters of concern to that department alone. Most of the government's litigation is now placed under Justice Department control, although the department may choose to recognize the litigating authority of particular agencies in particular cases. Independent agencies, such as the Tennessee Valley Authority, continue to maintain their right to conduct their own litigation if they so choose. Although the Justice Department is widely recognized as the appropriate representative for the federal government in court, conflicts do arise. One potential source of conflict exists when executive departments take opposing positions in a case. The Solicitor General and Attorney General must then decide which departmental position will be defended. Occasionally, departments challenge their authority to make this determination, and the issue must be resolved by the President. More serious conflicts can occur when the White House challenges the position taken by the Justice Department before the Supreme Court. Attorneys General recognize that constitutional authority rests with the President, yet on occasion they have resisted White House instructions to switch positions on a case.

Attorneys General recognize that constitutional authority rests with the President, yet on occasion they have resisted White House instructions to switch positions on a case.

In the nineteenth century, congressional fragmentation of the nation's law business derived in part from many states' long-standing fear of a centralized national law office. Many in Congress were suspicious of a strong Attorney General serving a strong President. This concern is evident in the debates over the Justice Department in 1866 and 1870: some members questioned the Attorney General's independence from the President, charging that law officers were mere tools of the White House and that they manipulated their legal advice to advance their Presidents' political agendas. This charge continued to be leveled at Attorneys General, including Robert Jackson for justifying Franklin Roosevelt's destroyers for bases deal with Britain during World War II, and Robert F. Kennedy for describing, contrary to international law, the Cuban quarantine during the 1962 Cuban missile crisis as an act short of war. The criticism resurfaced during John Mitchell's tenure, particularly regarding the Richard M. Nixon administration's response to domestic dissent and civil rights enforcement.

To address this concern, Congress has occasionally considered removing the Department of Justice from presidential control, most recently in 1974, when the Senate Judiciary Committee held hearings on a bill sponsored by Senator Sam J. Ervin. Opponents, though sympathetic to Ervin's goals, argued that the Attorney General must be held accountable by an elected chief executive, who has the constitutional responsibility to "take care that the laws be faithfully executed." The bill did not pass. But Congress and the Watergate affair special prosecution force in 1975 stressed the necessity of removing politics from the administration of justice. Partly in response to concern about the politicization of Justice, Congress created the Office of Independent Counsel by the Ethics in Government Act of 1978.

[See also (II) Attorney General, Federal Bureau of Investigation.]

BIBLIOGRAPHY

Baker, Nancy V *Conflicting Loyalties: Law and Politics in the Attorney General's Office, 1789–1990.* 1992.

Bell, Griffin. *Taking Care of the Law.* 1982.

Clayton, Cornell. *The Politics of Justice: The Attorney General and the Making of Legal Policy.* 1992.

Cummings, Homer, and Carl McFarland. *Federal Justice: Chapters in the History of Justice and the Federal Executive.* 1937; rpt 1970.

Harris, Richard. *Justice: The Crisis of Law, Order, and Freedom in America.* 1970.

Huston, Luther. *The Department of Justice.* 1967.

Langeluttig, Albert. *The Department of Justice of the United States.* 1927.

Learned, Henry B. *The President's Cabinet.* 1912.

Meador, Daniel J. *The President, the Attorney General, and the Department of Justice.* 1980.

– NANCY V. BAKER

L

LABOR, DEPARTMENT OF

The Department of Labor was born on 4 March 1913, the day President Woodrow Wilson took office. It was a product of the progressive movement and of a half-century campaign by organized labor for a voice in the Cabinet. In the words of its organic law, the department's main purpose is "to foster, promote, and develop the welfare of working people."

From Wilson to Hoover

In many ways the history of the department is the history of its secretaries. William B. Wilson, the first Secretary of Labor, had been secretary-treasurer of the United Mine Workers of America and later a Congressman who led the legislative drive to create the Department of Labor. Initially the department consisted of the preexisting bureaus of Labor Statistics, Immigration, and Naturalization, and the Children's Bureau, plus a new Conciliation Division for labor disputes. Most staff and resources, however, were devoted to immigration functions.

Under James P. Mitchell, the "conscience" of the Eisenhower administration, the department began to study the problem of employment discrimination against women, minorities, and the handicapped.

During World War I the department administered the national war-labor program. Secretary Wilson molded a labor policy that included an eight-hour day, grievance mechanisms, and collective bargaining. The department maintained industrial peace, placed 4 million people in jobs, raised living standards, and improved working conditions. Its war programs provided many ideas and models for the New Deal. One immediate by-product was the Women's Bureau, a successor to one of the few wartime agencies to survive into peacetime.

In the Republican era from 1921 to 1933 the department reflected the isolationism and xenophobia of the times and the desire of three administrations for less government. James J. Davis, secretary from 1921 to 1930, was of working-class origins and had become a fund-raiser for the Moose order. Under Davis, administration of tough new immigration laws became the primary activity of the department. At the same time, the Children's Bureau led an unsuccessful fight for a constitutional amendment to protect child labor that paved the way for federal legislation. After the start of the Great Depression, William Doak, of the Brotherhood of Railroad Trainmen, replaced Davis and served from 1930 to 1933. Davis was elected to the United States Senate and, with the cooperation of Secretary Doak, helped enact the Davis-Bacon Act, which prevented wage-slashing on federal construction projects by setting wages at the prevailing local rates.

The New Deal

President Franklin D. Roosevelt appointed Frances Perkins, who had served as New York State Commissioner of Labor while he was governor, to succeed Doak. She was the first woman Cabinet member and served until 1945. Perkins, one of the most creative of Roosevelt's counselors, believed strongly that government had a major role to play in regulating the economic order to promote social justice.

Perkins was a prime shaper of the New Deal. The social security law, enacted in 1935, was to a large extent a product of her efforts. She had accepted her post on the condition that the President would back her in seeking this goal. Her other main contribution was the Fair Labor Standards Act of 1938. Administered by the department, the act set a minimum wage of twenty-five cents per hour and required time-and-a-half after forty hours a week for most, though not all, workers. Perkins supported the National Labor Relations Act of 1935, which sanctioned the right of workers to organize and bargain collectively. She resigned shortly after Roosevelt's death to serve on the Civil Service Commission.

In 1945, President Harry S Truman appointed Lewis B. Schwellenbach, a former Senator and a committed New Dealer. A massive wave of strikes broke out as unions sought catch-up gains after wartime wage freezes. This contributed to the passage of the antiunion Taft-Hartley Act, which separated the Conciliation Service from the department and created the independent Federal Mediation and Conciliation Service. Congress also ordered crippling cuts in the department's budget because it was considered pro-union. When Schwellenbach died in office in June 1948, Truman appointed Maurice J. Tobin, governor of Massachusetts, to fill the vacancy. The department's fortunes quickly turned around. Truman was reelected, the new Democratic Congress raised the minimum wage, and the budget cuts were largely restored.

From Eisenhower to Nixon

In January 1953, President Dwight D. Eisenhower surprised many by appointing Martin P. Durkin, a Democrat and president of the International Brotherhood of Boilermakers. Durkin surprised few when he resigned in September 1953 over a disagreement on labor policy, but in his brief tenure he started a process that led to stronger centralized control within the department. Eisenhower replaced him with James P. Mitchell, a labor-relations executive. Prodded by cold war concerns, Mitchell set up a research office to develop policies for increasing the country's supply of trained workers. These efforts laid the basis for later employment and training programs. Under Mitchell, known as the "conscience" of the Eisenhower administration, the department began to study the problem of employment discrimination against women, minorities, and the handicapped.

To promote equal job opportunity in the construction industry, the labor department set minority hiring goals under the controversial Philadelphia plan.

In 1961, President John F. Kennedy appointed Arthur J. Goldberg, special counsel to the AFL-CIO. Secretary Goldberg mediated labor disputes involving the transportation and aerospace industries, and even settled a strike at New York's Metropolitan Opera. He worked to protect the rights of African Americans and vigorously enforced an executive order on equal employment opportunity. Two new laws gave the department an increased role in employment and training: the Area Redevelopment Act (ARA) of 1961 and the Manpower Development and Training Act (MDTA) of 1962. Under the ARA the department provided retraining and allowances in areas of high unemployment. The MDTA gave the department broader responsibilities for identifying labor shortages and providing training.

When Goldberg resigned in 1962, Under Secretary W. Willard Wirtz, a politically active labor law professor from Illinois, succeeded him. Wirtz believed in the Johnson administration's Great Society and under him the department developed a wide range of education and training programs to help high school dropouts, other unemployed youths, older people, and the hard-core adult unemployed. The most important single program was the Neighborhood Youth Corps (NYC), which enabled needy unemployed youths to earn income while completing high school. By 1968 over 1.5 million young people had benefitted from NYC. After the passage of the Civil Rights Act of 1964 an Office of Federal Contract Compliance was established to promote equal treatment of minorities.

A succession of five secretaries served short terms during the Nixon and Ford administrations: George Shultz, a labor economist, James D. Hodgson, a corporate personnel executive, Peter Brennan, a trade unionist, John Dunlop, an economist and government adviser on labor, and Willie Usery, a unionist and labor mediator. The department's budget and responsibilities increased in this period and many programs to protect the physical and economic welfare of workers were added or expanded by Congress, though others were cut. The Comprehensive Employment and Training Act (CETA) of 1973 replaced existing programs with block grants to local government. The Emergency Employment Act of 1971 provided 170,000 temporary public service jobs. The Job Corps was shifted to the department, though half of the training centers were closed. The department began enforcement of the Occupational Safety and Health Act of 1970. To promote equal job opportunity in the construction industry the department set minority hiring goals under the controversial Philadelphia Plan. The Employee Retirement Income Security Act (ERISA) of 1974 gave the department the responsibility of protecting retirement plans.

From Carter to Bush

In 1977, President Jimmy Carter appointed Ray Marshall, an activist labor economist. Marshall played a major role in planning the administration's economic stimulus program and the department received $8 billion for CETA programs and public service jobs. Workers' safety and health programs were redirected by a new policy of "Common Sense Priorities" that focused on eliminating serious health hazards. In 1978, Congress transferred mine safety and health enforcement from the Department of the Interior to the Department of Labor. Like Wirtz, Marshall minimized his involvement in labor-management disputes, and he promoted more cooperative relations between labor and management. Marshall also worked with Congress to raise the minimum wage to $3.35 an hour.

President Ronald Reagan appointed Raymond J. Donovan, a construction company executive active in Republican politics, in 1981 to help carry out his economic recovery and "regulatory relief" programs. Regulations and enforcement were curtailed to reduce the compliance burden on businesses. CETA authorizations were cut sharply. It expired in 1983 and was replaced by the more limited Job Training and Partnership Act. The department also expanded on Carter administration efforts to promote better labor-management relations.

In 1985, Secretary Donovan resigned and was replaced by William E. Brock, a former Senator then serving as U.S. Trade Representative. Brock emphasized improving manufacturing productivity through education and training programs. He also strengthened enforcement of regulatory programs within the constraints of regulatory relief. When Brock resigned in 1987, Ann Dore McLaughlin, a public relations expert with experience in private industry and government, served until the Bush administration came in. She continued Brock's policies and added efforts to deal with family issues such as child day care.

President George Bush continued Reagan's conservative approach to government and made few major changes at the department. He appointed Elizabeth Hanford Dole, a former Cabinet officer with extensive government experience, as Secretary. When a departmental commission called for government action to improve workers' skills, Dole supported legislation to implement the commission's recommendations. Under her, the department stepped up development and enforcement of job safety and health regulations, worked to improve protection of private employer pension plans, and attempted to deal with the "glass ceiling" faced by women trying to advance into executive positions in private industry. When Dole left in 1990, Lynn Martin, a former U.S. Representative, became Secretary and served until the end of the Bush administration in January 1993. Martin continued most of Secretary Dole's policies, but in 1992 regulatory programs were restrained by a presidentially ordered moratorium on development of federal rules.

[See also (II) Rulemaking Power.]

BIBLIOGRAPHY

Grossman, Jonathan. *The Department of Labor.* 1973.
Lombardi, John. *Labor's Voice in the Cabinet.* 1942.
MacLaury, Judson. *The U.S. Department of Labor: The First 75 Years, 1913–1988.* 1988.
Martin, George. *Madam Secretary, Frances Perkins.* 1976.
U.S. Department of Labor. *The Anvil and the Plough: A History of the United States Department of Labor.* 1963.

– JUDSON MACLAURY

M

MARINE CORPS

Congress and the U.S. Marine Corps have enjoyed an association of mutual respect and collaboration for almost two centuries. Certainly the Marine Corps expects Congress to protect it from its detractors within the executive branch and to respect its military professionalism, combat valor, and affectionate ties with the American people. In almost every challenge to the existence and functions of the Marine Corps, Congress has emerged as the marines' savior.

Matters concerning the Marine Corps and the navy were within the jurisdiction of the Senate and House Naval Affairs committees until 1947, when they were shifted to the unified Armed Services committees. The military budget subcommittee of the two Appropriations committees also reviews marine policies.

Although it approved of the navy's plan to place marines on warships in the Frigate Act of 1794, Congress made its first real contribution when it passed the Marine Corps Act of 11 July 1798. This act created a "Corps of Marines" distinct from the army and navy and established the marines' right to maintain a separate headquarters and staff, headed by the commandant of the Marine Corps, at the seat of the federal government. Congress allowed the Corps to be governed by either the Naval Regulations or the Articles of War, depending on whether the marines were serving at sea as ships guards or ashore as a navy-yard security force or performing "such other duties as the President may direct." This arrangement gave the commandant special flexibility in managing the Corps so long as he had congressional support. No commandant missed that lesson.

Establishing its headquarters and barracks in Washington in 1804, the Marine Corps cultivated Congress by providing the services of its exceptional band, by training a ready force close to the Capitol that was available to protect Congress, and by ingratiating itself by drawing officers from the sons (often failed entrants to the service academies) of the Washington political-professional elite. Its social and political elitism caused it some trouble in the Jacksonian period, when the Treasury and Navy departments found officers at the marine barracks in several navy yards involved in financial irregularities. The serving commandant, Archibald Henderson, had some responsibility for the situation, since he encouraged creative interpretation of both the Articles of War and Naval Regulations, focusing on whichever provisions favored marines in authority, pay, and living conditions.

Congress rushed to the rescue with the Marine Corps Act of 1834, which made the marines clearly an independent military service within the Navy Department. According to the act, however, marine officers fell under the command of navy officers ashore (yard commanders) and at sea (ships captains) and would conduct their affairs under Navy Department instructions, unless the marines were specifically attached to the army for temporary duty (e.g., strike duty or land defense of the Capitol). This legislation stood the test of a Supreme Court decision in *U.S. vs. Freeman* (1845), a case in which a marine barracks commander challenged the authority of a navy-yard commander.

World War II brought the Marine Corps to a new peak of congressional and media popularity.

Congress again proved itself a friend of the Corps when it forced President Theodore Roosevelt to withdraw his executive order removing marine ships guards from navy warships. Acting on behalf of navy officers who saw no need to have marines enforce ship regulations, Roosevelt abolished the ships guards in 1908; but Congress, responding to marine officers' claims that such an act would destroy the Corps, refused to fund any new battleships unless Roosevelt reversed his decision, which he did.

After 1898, the marines assumed a new function, providing colonial infantry and civil administrators in the Caribbean and the Pacific. Marines performed in combat with admiring press attention at Guantánamo Bay, Cuba (1898); Beijing, China (1900); and Veracruz, Mexico (1914). But derring-do in the tropics also imperiled relations between the Corps and Congress. In its 1902 investigations of affairs in the Philippines, members of the Senate found evidence of atrocities by marines against Filipinos, and in 1921 and 1922 the Senate Select Committee on Haiti and Santo Domingo concluded that similar abuses had occurred during the occupation of those Caribbean countries by two marine brigades.

World War II brought the Marine Corps to a new peak of congressional and media popularity. The new bonds of affection were put to their ultimate test in the years 1945 to 1947, when Congress considered the question of postwar defense organization and management. The Truman administration advocated centralized control of the armed forces by a single cabinet secretary and a joint general staff headed by a powerful military chief of staff. This plan would have allowed the executive branch to determine service roles and missions, negating the similar function performed by Congress in the budget process. Dogged Marine Corps opposition to this plan, with equivocal support from the navy, produced the National Security Act of 1947, which provided legislative protection of service roles and missions. The functions written into law covered all the services, but they were especially important to the Marine Corps. The authors of the provisions were marine officers then advising the House Committee on Government Expenditures, which had reviewed the legislation because the Senate managers of the original legislation were afraid to refer it to the pro-Marine House Armed Services Committee.

Impressed by the performance of the First Marine Division and the First Marine Aircraft Wing in the Korean War, Congress exercised its right to determine field organization structure as well as roles and missions by passing the Douglas-Mansfield Act of 1952. This act required the Department of Defense to maintain three divisions and three aircraft wings in the Fleet Marine Force (the largest part of the Marine Corps operating forces), even in peacetime. The sense of Congress was that the Fleet Marine Force would provide a "force in readiness," deployed to trouble spots on amphibious ships and ready to spearhead almost any form of military intervention, large or small. The law also provided that the commandant of the Marine Corps might attend meetings of the Joint Chiefs of Staff (JCS) on all issues that he decided affected the Corps. This provision was expanded in 1979 to make the commandant a full statutory member of the JCS and, thus, eligible to become chairman.

Congress also proved the depth of its commitment to the Fleet Marine Force in the 1970s and 1980s. In the face of civilian and military opposition in the Department of Defense, it supported a number of weapons and equipment innovations for the Marine Corps. In personnel matters, Congress cooperated from 1975 to 1980 with two favorites, Commandants Louis H. Wilson, Jr., and Robert H. Barrow, to purge the Marine Corps of those whom they grouped together as undesirables—malcontents, drug addicts, thugs, homosexuals, racial agitators, and the mentally deficient. Congress made the crusade to restore a quality enlisted force possible by stating it would not penalize the Corps for failing to maintain its budgeted enlistment strength. The only issues on which Congress questioned the Corps involved its conduct of recruiting and recruit training in the mid 1970s and the conduct of the Lebanon intervention in 1983. Congress may, however, have loosened its support for the Marine Corps with the Goldwater-Nichols Defense Reorganization Act of 1986, which gave the chairman of the Joint Chiefs of Staff power to influence interservice affairs well beyond the boundaries envisioned in 1947. The Marine Corps cast a wary eye at the new law and urged Congress to do so, too, since a forceful chairman might use his power, especially during a budgetary or an international political crisis, to change roles and missions—for instance, by not supporting funding for a particular function. The Marine Corps thus serves as a watchdog for Congress within the armed forces while exploiting its ties with Congress to preserve its own identity and functions.

[See also (I) Committees, article on Committee Jurisdiction.]

BIBLIOGRAPHY

Millett, Allan R. *Semper Fidelis: The History of the United States Marine Corps.* Rev. ed. 1990.

Millett, Allan R., ed. *Commandants of the Marine Corps.* Forthcoming.

Heinl, Robert D., Jr. *Soldiers of the Sea: The United States Marine Corps, 1775–1962.* 1962.

Keiser, Gordon W. *The U.S. Marine Corps and Defense Unification, 1944–1947.* 1982.

– ALLAN R. MILLETT

MEDALS, PRESIDENTIAL

Medals have been used to commemorate American Presidents since 1790, when privately struck pieces were sold in Philadelphia in honor of George Washington's election the previous year. Official U.S. government medals bearing the likeness of Washington began to appear shortly thereafter. Today, the U.S. Mint's presidential series includes a medal honoring each of the nation's Chief Executives.

Initially, most of the medals in the series honoring Presidents prior to 1869 (Thomas Jefferson to Andrew Johnson) were made for presentation to American Indian chiefs as symbols of peace, friendship, and special recognition. The Indian peace medals, as they are commonly known, bore a portrayal of the President on the obverse and the inscription "Peace and Friendship" on the reverse, with clasped hands and a crossed tomahawk and peace pipe. Presenting medals to the Indians bearing the likeness of the incumbent President was the

Millard Fillmore's administration changed the reverse side of the presidential medal from images symbolizing peace with the Indians to pictures showing elements of American culture. (Library of Congress, Prints and Photographs Division)

continuation of a practice initially observed by the Spanish, the French, and the British. It was considered an extremely important part of American Indian policy. Over time, the Indian peace medals also began to be regarded as presidential medals.

Beginning with the administration of Millard Fillmore (1850–1853), the reverse sides of the medals began depicting the transformation of American culture. Although Indian peace medals continued to be produced through Benjamin Harrison's administration, they ceased to be included as part of the presidential series after Ulysses S. Grant's election in 1869. Instead, medals not made for Indians began to be struck by the Mint in honor of Presidents. The lone non-Indian medal included in the series prior to this time was a medal commemorating both Lincoln inaugurations (1861 and 1865). Subsequently, two medals modeled after the Indian peace medals were added to the series for Washington and John Adams. Bronze duplicates of the presidential medal series are currently available through the U.S. Mint.

Presidents have also been honored with a second type of medal—special inaugural medals. The first inaugural medal commemorated Thomas Jefferson's initial ceremony in 1801. It was struck by John Reich, a German-born die-maker. Twenty-four years later, a second inaugural medal was struck for John Quincy Adams' 1825 inauguration. A third medal was privately struck for Andrew Jackson's second inauguration (1833).

Between 1837 and 1853, presidential inaugural medals were produced by the U.S. Mint. For much of the remainder of the nineteenth century, inaugural medals were privately made. Since 1889, official inaugural medals have been authorized by the inaugural committee of the winning presidential candidate shortly after the quadrennial November election. On three occasions (1909, 1957, and 1973), images of Vice Presidents (James S. Sherman, Richard M. Nixon, and Spiro T. Agnew) also appeared on the medals.

Initially, these medals were attached to the cloth badges used to identify individuals involved in the various inaugural festivities. The 1901 committee was the first to have official medals struck for inaugural workers.

Since 1929, souvenir bronze replicas of the official inaugural medal have been sold to the public to help defray the expenses of the fireworks, parade, balls, and various social events sponsored by the committee. In 1953, silver replicas were offered for public purchase for the first time.

Only a limited quantity of medals were issued for the inaugurations of Herbert Hoover (1929) and Franklin D. Roosevelt (1933, 1937, 1941, 1945). Beginning with Harry S Truman's 1949 oath taking, however, the quantity of medals produced has continued to increase as their popularity has grown.

[See also (I) Awards and Prizes.]

BIBLIOGRAPHY

Failor, Kenneth M. *Medals of the United States Mint.* 1972.
MacNeil, Neil. *The President's Medal 1789–1977.* 1977.
Prucha, Francis Paul. *Indian Peace Medals in American History.* 1971.

– STEPHEN W. STATHIS

MEDIA AND THE PRESIDENT

A President of the United States performs his leadership techniques on a stage set for news organizations. A President and his advisers set this stage in the hope that news organizations will convey the images, sounds, and words that will persuade the public to endorse his initiatives. Through persuasion, a President kneads his constitutional and political resources into materials that influence the process of governing. The ability to persuade provides a President with those qualities that Woodrow Wilson described as "a dignifying and elevating sense of being trusted, together with a consciousness of being in an official station so conspicuous that no faithful discharge of duty can go unacknowledged and unrewarded."

For most of American history, as Richard Neustadt suggested, the benefit of "the power to persuade [has been] the power to bargain." Since the 1960s, as Samuel Kernell has pointed out, Presidents have used their persuasive powers in another manner. Presidents have "gone public," using the media as the channel to sell their image and their programs to the people. Persuasion is a fungible resource of the presidency. During periods of national crisis, such as those involving economic or foreign policy changes, a President may be made or destroyed by forces beyond his influence. A President needs to have established his ability to persuade the public at these times so that he can take credit for the good news and avoid long-term damage from the bad.

The White House Media Staff

White House publicity operations evolved as part of the White House bureaucracy. The President's aides developed tactics to enhance his image as portrayed by news organizations. During the fifty years beginning with Grover Cleveland's administration and ending with Herbert Hoover's, the evolving White House institutionalized a number of ad hoc roles performed by the President's secretary and other assistants into the permanent position of White House Press Secretary, whose most conspicuous role is as the President's spokesperson. In the twentieth century, the White House bureaucracy has evolved in a manner that has made it possible for a President to maintain, stabilize, and at times exploit his relations with the media.

By the twentieth century four essential features emerged that continue to affect the relationship between the President and the press. First, news about the White House was transmitted to the public by independent nonpartisan news organizations. Second, these organizations were heavily dependent on the White House staff for most of the information they received about the President's activities and policies. Third, the transition from an episodic to a regular relationship between the President and the press required the development of procedures to provide reporters with information on a regular basis. And fourth, the increase in both the amount and the diversity of White House publicity activities made it necessary for the President to seek specialized assistants with skills as promoters and with knowledge of the media.

The economic and technological expansion of publishing and broadcasting enterprises in the last decades of the nineteenth century made it possible for the media to respond to the enlarged prominence of the presidency. In the following decades the continuing expansion of the resources of both news organizations and the White House staff made the relationship between President and press a recognizable feature of the Washington landscape. White House officials decided to create a structure for news operations in response to the growing organizational and technological complexity of the news media as well as to their own ongoing publicity requirements. Since the administration of Theodore Roosevelt, an increasingly important factor in determining the success of a President's communications strategies has been the sophistication with which White House officials approached the job of creating and coordinating White House offices that have responsibilities for communicating the President's image and messages to the public.

By the 1950s, the White House used news organizations as their major conduit for their political communications.

Since 1933, Presidents have developed specific offices within the White House to provide resources that would enable them to develop and implement communications policies that would help increase the support they would receive from the political leadership and the public. The offices created between the 1930s and 1980s that exist at the end of the twentieth century include the West Wing Press Office, the Office of Media Liaison, the Office of Public Liaison, the presidential speechwriters, and special technical advisers. In the Reagan and Bush administrations a Director of Communications coordinated the activities of these offices and advised the President on how to utilize them to maximize the President's success in coordinating his political communications.

By the 1950s, the White House used news organizations as their major conduit for their political communications. James Hagerty, Press Secretary to Dwight D. Eisenhower, managed White House media relations to the benefit of his President. The pace of organizational development increased beginning with the administration of Richard M. Nixon. During the presidencies of Gerald R. Ford, Jimmy Carter, Ronald Reagan, and George Bush, the White House established institutions that administer and coordinate administration publicity, White House staff members who channel the President's message to Congress and interest groups. Throughout this period, administrations responded to fundamental changes involving press and public expectations of the presidency.

The Nixon presidency established the Office of Communications and the Office of Public Liaison. Nixon used both offices to build support for presidential programs and actions. In the following administrations, the Presidents took an organizational as well as a personal role. In order to make good appointments, a President has to understand how the operations of each office fulfills an essential part of his communications strategy. Presidents may not learn this lesson until after they are in office. For example as a candidate Jimmy Carter talked of abolishing the Office of Public Liaison, which he described as an example of the bloated White House staff. Later in his term, Carter realized that the Office of Public Liaison was essential to his ability to persuade. He then appointed Anne Wexler, a knowledgeable Washington insider, to the job. Wexler transformed the office into an effective instrument of political communications. In Ronald Reagan's and George Bush's administrations, the White House Director of Communications was given the specific charge of coordinating these activities for the President.

Relations with the Media

In the period from the administration of Franklin D. Roosevelt through that of Dwight D. Eisenhower, the relationship between the White House and news organizations was conducted with as much cooperation as conflict. In spite of occasional periods when news organizations and the White House treated the other as an enemy force, the more typical pattern of behavior could best be described as one of continuity and stability. For the thirty years since Eisenhower, many major news organizations grew in size, resources, and well-trained personnel. During the same period, technological change evolved so that news organizations are thought of as the media rather than as the press because of the new forms of rapid communications emphasizing the visual, not only in television but in print.

The President's personal relations with the media also changed after Eisenhower. From the White House perspective, the representatives of news organizations, and sometimes the organizations themselves, were regarded as the President's adversary. In contrast to what the White House expected was due to the President, favorable coverage could not be taken for granted. Instead, the administration had to fulfill the high standards and expectations of journalists who were not predisposed to present the Chief Executive or his policies as a success, who had more ability to uncover his mistakes, and who had a more receptive audience to convey their impression of the failures and contradictions of the administration. During the decade between 1965 and 1975, the years when the Vietnam War and the Watergate affair diminished the public's approval of Presidents Johnson and Nixon, both Presidents' supporters regarded the media as an enemy. From the perspective of the White House, news organizations contributed a harsh and unflattering view of an administration, and when a President appeared to fail, their attacks seemed relentless.

Presidents have attempted to use television to provide the appropriate public image to accompany their policies.

An analysis of a segment of the media suggests that, in fact, although the adversarial aspects of the relationship grew throughout this period, the White House advantages were maintained except in response to the most dramatic crises and failures. A survey of White House stories from 1953 to 1978 in the *New York Times* and *Time* and from 1968 to 1978 on the CBS Evening News suggests that there has been a gradual decrease in the number of favorable stories and an increase in unfavorable stories, but that when the Vietnam-Watergate era is excluded, the change is relatively small. The percent of favorable stories in the print media declined from close to 60 percent in the Eisenhower administration to near 50 percent during Kennedy's term and the first part of Johnson's term. They fell near 40 percent for Johnson and close to 25 percent at the time of Nixon's resignation in all three media, but returned to the high 40s for Ford and the first two years of Carter. Similarly unfavorable stories increased from below 20 percent of the total for Kennedy to slightly above 20 percent for the Ford-early Carter years. However, throughout this period the news organizations surveyed continued to produce more favorable than unfavorable stories.

The major change in the approach of the President and his White House advisers to the media during the 1980s and 1990s came in response to the increased importance of television as the main channel of information and images to the public. Some writers have been touting the "rule of television" since the 1950s, but until the late 1970s, television news was a recreation of events whose importance was determined by the print media, especially major national newspapers such as the *New York Times,* the *Washington Post,* and the *Wall Street Journal.* By the 1980s, print journalism published stories that assumed that the reader had already learned of them through television. The reaction of Presidents and their advisers has been to provide "television opportunities" more frequently than news conferences.

Thus Presidents have attempted to use television to provide the appropriate public image to accompany their policies. Nixon, for example, wanted to provide the public with a clear image of his policies of opening relations with China and of détente with the Soviet Union. His trips to China and the Soviet Union in 1972 brought approval to these policies as well as a significant boost to his status in the polls. Television became the key resource for Reagan's success as a persuader. In the last quarter of the twentieth century, the persona of the President as transmitted in his television appearances was the key factor for the public's evaluation of an administration.

[See also (II) White House Bureaucracy, White House Office of Communications, White House Press Secretary.]

BIBLIOGRAPHY

Cornwell, Elmer E., Jr. *Presidential Leadership of Public Opinion* 1965.

Edwards, George C. III. *The Public Presidency.* 1983.

Grossman, Michael Baruch, and Martha Joynt Kumar. *Portraying the President: The White House and the Media.* 1981.

Kernell, Samuel *Going Public: New Strategies of Presidential Leadership.* 1986.

Neustadt, Richard. *Presidential Power.* 1990.

Pollard, James E. *The President and the Press.* 1947.

Tulis, Jeffrey K. *The Rhetorical Presidency.* 1987.

– MICHAEL BARUCH GROSSMAN

N

NATIONAL ECONOMIC COUNCIL (NEC)

Shortly after assuming office in January 1993, President Bill Clinton established by Executive Order 12835 the National Economic Council. The tasks of the council are to coordinate the economic-policy making process with respect to domestic and international economic issues, to coordinate economic-policy advice to the President, to ensure that economic-policy decisions and programs are consistent with the President's stated goals, and to monitor implementation of the President's economic-policy agenda.

The council includes the President; the Vice President; the Secretaries of State, Treasury, Agriculture, Commerce, Labor, Housing and Urban Development, Transportation, and Energy; the Administrator of the Environmental Protection Agency; the Chair of the Council of Economic Advisers (CEA); the Director of the Office of Management and Budget (OMB); the United States Trade Representative; the Assistant to the President for Economic Policy; the Assistant to the President for Domestic Policy; the National Security Adviser; the Assistant to the President for Science and Technology Policy; and such other officials of executive departments and agencies as the President may from time to time designate. The President serves as the chairman of the council, with the Vice President or Assistant to the President for Economic Policy presiding in his absence.

In making these changes in the policy-making process, the executive order also outlines and reaffirms the roles to be played by the key members of the President's economic team. The Secretary of the Treasury will continue to be the senior economic official in the executive branch and the President's chief economic spokesperson. The Director of OMB will continue to be the President's principal spokesperson on budget matters. The CEA will continue its traditional analytic, forecasting, and advisory functions. Under previous administrations, economic policy was largely developed and coordinated by the so-called troika (the Secretary of the Treasury, the Director of OMB, and the Chairman of the CEA). Another high-ranking official has been added to the President's policy team: the Assistant to the President for Economic Policy. It remains to be seen how this appointment and the establishment of the NEC will affect the manner in which economic advice is given to the President and economic policies are formulated and implemented by the administration.

BIBLIOGRAPHY

Carnegie Endowment for International Peace. Institute for International Economics. *Memorandum to the President-elect: Harnessing Process to Purpose.* 1992.

Cuomo Commission on Competitiveness. *America's Agenda: Rebuilding Economic Strength.* 1992.

– EDWARD KNIGHT

NATIONAL SECURITY ADVISER

The national security adviser (formally the assistant to the President for National Security Affairs) is an extremely influential position in national security policy and a key support for direct action in that area by the President. The national security adviser's influence derives from his role as director of the National Security Council (NSC) staff. Given the central role of the NSC

President Dwight D. Eisenhower's national security advisers reflected Eisenhower's own management style by managing the National Security Council as an elaborate bureaucratic structure. (Library of Congress, Prints and Photographs Division)

in coordinating various aspects of national security policy (diplomacy, military, intelligence, economics), the importance of the national security adviser becomes evident.

Interestingly, the position is not a statutory part of the National Security Act, which in 1947 created the NSC. The act created an executive secretary for the NSC, which is how it functioned under President Harry S Truman. The shift away from the executive secretary came under President Dwight D. Eisenhower, who created the position of special assistant for National Security Affairs. Under varying titles, this has been what is commonly called the national security adviser.

The role of the national security adviser has varied with each President, reflecting both their individual management styles and the extreme malleability of the NSC staff structure. Eisenhower's advisers, Robert Cutler and Gen. Andrew Goodpaster, concentrated on managing the strictly delineated NSC staff under him, with its very elaborate structure and paper flow. McGeorge Bundy served both Presidents John F. Kennedy and Lyndon B. Johnson; Bundy was the first adviser to serve as a policy advocate in his own right, rather than simply a coordinator of the views brought to the NSC by the various departments and agencies. Purists have felt that this latter role, an "honest broker" among the agencies responsible for forming and executing policy, was the proper one for the national security adviser. Walt Rostow succeeded Bundy under Johnson and spent most of his tenure dealing with the Vietnam War.

President Richard M. Nixon chose Henry Kissinger as his national security adviser. The elaborate NSC structure was much like that under Eisenhower and totally dominated by the bureaucratically adept and aggressive Kissinger, much to the discomfort of Secretary of State William Rogers. This suited Nixon, who distrusted the State Department. In 1973, Kissinger became Secretary of State while retaining his NSC role. This unique situation continued under President Gerald Ford until 1975, when Kissinger relinquished his NSC slot to Brent Scowcroft, his deputy, as part of a larger reorganization. Scowcroft never challenged Kissinger's primacy, and probably came closest to epitomizing the honest-broker role.

President Jimmy Carter took office hoping to minimize the role of the NSC. However, Zbigniew Brzezinski, his adviser, saw his role akin to Kissinger's and came into frequent conflict with Secretary of State Cyrus Vance.

President Ronald Reagan, who delegated a great deal of authority to subordinates, had six advisers in eight years. Richard Allen, who had unexpectedly lost the job to Kissinger in 1969, resigned under a financial cloud. William Clark was a Reagan confidant but national security neophyte, who never mastered the NSC staff and process. He was succeeded by his deputy, Robert McFarlane, a veteran of the Kissinger NSC; he was succeeded in turn by his deputy, Vice Admiral John Poindexter, who left office as a result of his involvement in the Iran-contra affair, a series of intelligence operations run in his NSC staff. Frank Carlucci took over and impressed many as being the best adviser since Scowcroft. Finally, Gen. Colin Powell served and received high marks as well.

The national security adviser position

is defined solely by the President,

and redefined with each new administration.

Scowcroft returned to the job under President George Bush, but functioned more individually as the President's close friend and adviser, leaving his deputy to run the staff and policy process.

Critics have often commented on the conflict that has arisen between some advisers and the Secretary of State, usually decrying the loss of status. However, this ignores the fact that such rivalries can only continue with the acceptance of the President, for whatever reason. As noted, Nixon used it to cut out the State Department; in Carter's case, it reflected his inability and unwillingness to impose discipline on the system.

The national security adviser position has also posed problems for Congress. As it has no statutory basis, the Senate cannot vote for confirmation. Some believe this should be remedied, given the importance of the job. Moreover, as an assistant to the President, the adviser does not testify before Congress as do the heads of departments and agencies, although advisers have customarily made themselves available to the media for interviews. The debate over the "proper" role of the adviser is unlikely ever to be settled, the nature of the job, perhaps more so than any other position in the national security field, is defined solely by the President, and redefined with each new administration.

[See also (II) National Security Council.]

BIBLIOGRAPHY

Lowenthal, Mark M., and Richard A. Best. *The National Security Council: An Organizational Assessment.* 1992.

Shoemaker, Christopher C. *The NSC Staff: Counseling the Council.* 1991.

– MARK M. LOWENTHAL

NATIONAL SECURITY COUNCIL (NSC)

The National Security Council is a presidential agency responsible for integrating domestic, foreign, and military policies. One of the most difficult demands of national security policy in the twentieth century has been the ability to coordinate, initially, its diplomatic and military aspects, and then such other facets as economics as they became important. There was no such coordination to speak of in the United States through the eighteenth and nineteenth centuries, save in the person of the President himself to the degree that he chose to do so.

Establishment of the NSC

After the Spanish-American War it became evident that better coordination was needed. In 1903, the army and navy created the Joint Board to improve inter-service coordination. Over the next few decades the military tried to include the State Department in some larger group, largely to have some access to foreign policy decisions. A military proposal in the Taft administration for such a Council of National Defense was vetoed by Secretary of State Philander Knox. Such a council was created during the Wilson administration (1916), but largely to coordinate industrial mobilization. It included the two services and the departments of the Interior, Agriculture, Commerce and Labor, but not State, and turned out to be rather ineffective even within its own field.

Concerns over Axis activities in pre-World War II Latin America led Secretary of State Cordell Hull to propose to President Franklin D. Roosevelt in 1938 that a Standing Liaison Committee (SLC) of State, War, and Navy's second-ranking officers be created. The SLC's work was uneven, geographically limited, and solely coordinative, but it served as a precedent. So did informal weekly wartime meetings among the three secretaries, initiated by Secretary of War Henry Stimson. Before the end of World War II, these had evolved into the State, War, Navy Coordinating Committee (SWNCC), made up of assistant secretaries, but with a staff and a mandate to coordinate on "politico-military matters."

The National Security Council (NSC) evolved out of a larger late war and postwar reexamination of the entire national security apparatus and a study overseen by Ferdinand Eberstadt, a protégé of Secretary of the Navy James Forrestal. Eberstadt's plans largely became the National Security Act (1947), which created the NSC, along with a unified Defense establishment and the Central Intelligence Agency, which was subordinated to the NSC. The NSC was given the mandate to advise the President on integrating "domestic, foreign and military policies relating to the national security." The membership of the NSC, as designated by 1949 amendments to the act, are the President, Vice President, the secretaries of State and Defense. The Joint Chiefs of Staff (JCS) were designated the principal military advisers; this was amended in 1986, making the chairman of the JCS the principal military adviser.

Two NSC adjuncts not mentioned in legislation, but which became increasingly important were the NSC staff, largely drawn from other agencies, and the Assistant to the President for National Security Affairs (usually referred to as the national security adviser), who customarily runs the staff and has become a key player in national security policy deliberations and potent rival to secretaries of State.

Reshaping the NSC

The NSC is one of the most malleable of the national security entities, its methods and activities being constantly reshaped to fit the working methods of each President. President Harry S Truman defined the NSC's role as purely advisory, a forum for working out recommendations, but not for making policy, which remained his prerogative.

President Dwight D. Eisenhower greatly expanded the rudimentary NSC structure he inherited into an elaborate and formal committee structure. The NSC staff took on a greater role in coordinating policy among agencies, resolving differences and preparing options and implementation papers. Robert Cutler and General Andrew Goodpaster were key to making this NSC staff function as well as it did, although some felt it was overly layered and too mechanistic.

President John F. Kennedy eliminated virtually all of Eisenhower's apparatus, meeting regularly with NSC members, but not in formal session. Critics felt this system was too ad hoc. During the Cuban missile crisis, for example, Kennedy created an expanded group of advisers, the Executive Committee, also referred to as Ex Comm. McGeorge Bundy, Kennedy's national security adviser, had far greater say in policy deliberations than his Eisenhower predecessors and moved from their "honest broker" role among agencies to be an advocate in his own right. President Lyndon B. Johnson largely followed the same course, again relying heavily on personal meetings with Secretary of State Dean Rusk and Secretary of Defense Robert S. McNamara. The interagency process was controlled, albeit fitfully, by State via a Senior Interdepartmental Group and subordinate Interdepartmental Regional Groups.

President Richard M. Nixon reinvigorated the NSC, largely based on the Eisenhower model he knew well. Under national security adviser Henry Kissinger an elaborate committee structure again emerged for the NSC staff. Kissinger dominated the committees and the committees in turn dominated virtually all policy, much to the discomfit of Secretary of State William Rogers. In 1973, Kissinger was given Rogers's position while keeping his White House post, underscoring the personal nature of the policy process. It was in fact the relationship between Nixon and Kissinger rather than the NSC staff's role that was prominent in this process. Kissinger, even more so than Bundy, was a forceful policy advocate. Critics felt that his "dual hat" role undercut the purposes of the NSC, as its staff director could not be an honest broker if he was also a principal policymaker from one agency. This continued under President Gerald Ford until 1975. As part of a major national security shake-up, Kissinger relinquished his NSC job to his deputy, Brent Scowcroft. Scowcroft clearly could not overshadow the Secretary of State and played an exemplary role as an honest broker.

Investigations revealed that arms were sold to Iran to help free hostages, with profits being used to arm the contras.

Having campaigned against the Nixon-Ford-Kissinger foreign policy, President Jimmy Carter planned to reduce the NSC staff's role. The structure was greatly reduced and simplified, going from seven committees to two. However, national security adviser Zbigniew Brzezinski was eager to play a role similar to Kissinger's. He became an intense and often successful bureaucratic rival to Secretary of State Cyrus Vance. Critics, including some in the administration, later faulted Carter for not imposing greater discipline on the process, believing that the infighting ultimately undermined policy.

Under Reagan and Bush

The Reagan administration was a tumultuous period for the NSC. President Ronald Reagan had six national security advisers (Richard Allen, William Clark, Robert McFarlane, John Poindexter, Frank Carlucci, and Colin Powell) in eight years. None ever rivaled Secretaries of State Alexander Haig or George Shultz, each adviser largely serving a coordinative role again. Reagan's preference was for option papers from which he selected his chosen policy.

But the role of the NSC staff became controversial. Much of this centered on the fact that NSC staff members were given much latitude and some became involved in policy implementation, including intelligence operations. The Iran-contra affair that broke in 1986 centered on two issues: covert support for the contra rebels in Nicaragua, despite congressional bans; and efforts to free U.S. hostages in Lebanon. NSC staffer Oliver North was central to both and the bridge between them. Poindexter was faulted for not keeping NSC members informed about policy decisions taken by Reagan; NSC members Shultz and Secretary of Defense Caspar W. Weinberger were faulted for not being forceful enough about policies with which they disagreed.

Subsequent investigations revealed that arms were sold to Iran to help free hostages, with profits being used to arm the contras. A Special Review Board (the Tower Commission: former Senator John Tower; Brent Scowcroft; former Secretary of State Edmund Muskie) faulted NSC staff operations and suggested improvements, but basically supported the NSC's traditional role given its unique flexibility. Special congressional committees were harsher on the NSC staff's activities. In reaction to the Tower Commission Report, Reagan issued a national security decision directive that specifically forbade the national security adviser or NSC staff from undertaking intelligence operations.

President George Bush's NSC was uncontroversial. Given Bush's own familiarity with national security issues, the NSC was clearly in an advisory and coordinative role again. Scowcroft returned to his old job and was a close adviser, largely based on his long friendship with Bush. Some critics said, however, that Scowcroft was less active in terms of managing the NSC staff than he was under Ford, operating more on a personal rather than institutional basis.

[See also (II) National Security Adviser.]

BIBLIOGRAPHY

Draper, Theodore. *A Very Thin Line.* 1991.
Lowenthal, Mark M., and Richard A. Best. *The National Security Council: An Organizational Assessment.* 1992.
Lowenthal, Mark M. *U.S Intelligence Evolution and Anatomy.* 1984.
President's Special Review Board. *Report of the President's Special Review Board.* 1987.
Senate Select Committee on Secret Military Assistance to Iran and the Nicaraguan Opposition/House Select Committee to Investigate Covert Arms Transactions with Iran. *Report of the Congressional Committees Investigating the Iran-Contra Affair.* 1987.
Shoemaker, Christopher C. *The NSC Staff: Counseling the Council.* 1991.

– MARK M. LOWENTHAL

NAVY

Beginning in November 1775, a committee of the Continental Congress supervised a wartime Continental

Navy. That navy was liquidated after the Revolutionary War, and no attempt was made to rebuild it until Barbary piracy on U.S. ships and the violation of American neutrality during the French Revolution necessitated the construction of U.S. warships. While Vice President Thomas Jefferson's followers in Congress preferred to have the Department of War administer naval affairs, partisans of Secretary of the Treasury Alexander Hamilton demanded a separate small navy to support maritime interests and national honor. The result was a compromise: six large superfrigates—including the forty-four-gun *Constellation, Constitution,* and *United States*—would be built, but construction would stop if peace was obtained with the Barbary powers. Because of Barbary and British intransigency and continued French spoliations, on 30 April 1798 Congress enacted legislation creating a separate, cabinet-level Navy Department under the direction of a secretary of the Navy.

The first change in naval organization was the creation by Congress of a Board of Navy Commissioners in 1815 to advise the secretary of the Navy. In 1842 Congress again revised the navy's management system by establishing five bureaus, each with responsibility over a different part of the navy's operations. The bureau system remained largely unchanged until the office of Chief of Naval Operations was added in 1915. In 1942 Congress established the Joint Chiefs of Staff to improve coordination between the services and to advise the president and secretary of Defense. In the 1960s the bureaus became commands. Since the end of World War II, geographical unified commands have included all operating forces within a certain geographical area, with command exercised by the senior officer present, regardless of the officer's service.

The navy was liquidated after the Revolutionary War, and no attempt was made to rebuild it until Barbary piracy on U.S. ships necessitated the construction of U.S. warships.

The navy has long been known on Capitol Hill as a staunch protector of its traditions and independence. During World War II, demands for an independent air force that would assume control of all airborne military activities and for a Department of Defense came from the U.S. Army Air Forces and those who believed that unifying the services would save money. The navy disputed the air forces' assertion that strategic air bombing would reduce the will of an enemy, citing experiences of World Wars I and II. It also opposed demands for a single chief of staff, a proposal to shift control of the Marine Corps from the navy to the army (Congress had created the Marine Corps and placed it under the navy's jurisdiction on 11 July 1798), a plan for the air forces to take over naval aviation, and a movement toward reliance solely upon atomic bombs—a single weapons system that, for example, could not be tailored to amphibious operations or defense of ocean trade. On the other hand, over the opposition of the air forces, the navy sought authority from Congress to build aircraft carriers capable of handling aircraft that would carry nuclear weapons.

Largely following the suggestions of Secretary of the Navy James V. Forrestal, the National Security Act of 1947 eschewed a single chief of staff and created a civilian secretary of Defense, a National Military Establishment of three coordinated service departments, and various supporting agencies. The Defense secretary replaced the navy and army secretaries in the cabinet. The navy retained its aviation corps and the Marine Corps. In March 1948 Forrestal also revised roles and missions by assigning the services primary and collateral functions, the latter being ways in which each service can help the others. The navy, however, received the broad mandate to "attack any targets, inland or otherwise, which appear necessary for the accomplishment of its missions." Roles and missions have not basically changed since then, but the air force especially has had to be reminded several times to carry out missions designed to help the army and navy.

In 1949 Forrestal obtained amendments to the National Security Act that changed the name of the National Military Establishment to Department of Defense, of which he became its secretary. When his naval secretary sought to build a large carrier to serve strategic bombers, the army and air force objected. At hearings held by the House Armed Services Committee, chaired by Carl Vinson (D-Ga.), a staunch navy defender, the air force's best bomber, the B-36, was deemed inefficient because it lacked the range to strike Soviet targets. Although the new secretary of Defense, Louis A. Johnson, scrapped the building of a supercarrier, Vinson's report, dated 12 March 1950, recommended that one be built when funds became available. With the first *Forrestal*-class carrier in 1952, the navy verged upon breaking the air force's monopoly on strategic air power.

Congress often opposed a large navy, as from 1801 to 1815, 1865 to the days of Theodore Roosevelt, and during the 1920s, 1930s, and 1970s. Congress supported four naval disarmament conferences in the 1920s and 1930s, especially the one held in Washington in 1921 and 1922, which reduced capital ships by about half. Congress fully funded wartime expenses, but with peace restored, it customarily cut back quickly and hard. For example, the 700-ship navy of the Civil War had been reduced to 63 wooden steamers, 48 monitors, and 29 sailors by 1873. An exception was the funding of President Ronald Reagan's requests between fiscal year 1980 and fiscal year 1985 for a 600-ship navy to counter the Soviet Union during the Cold War. That navy played significant roles during the conflicts in Vietnam, Panama, Grenada, and the Persian Gulf and in other emergencies. In fiscal year 1987, however, Congress began to reduce the defense budget. The defense budget for fiscal year 1992 was 24 percent lower than that for fiscal year 1985 and represented only 3.6 percent of the gross national product, the lowest since before World War II. Early in 1993, the Clinton administration asked Congress for cuts in defense expenditures that, if approved, would shrink the navy from a 450-ship, 13-carrier fleet to 340 ships and 12 carriers by 1998.

Until 1946 a naval affairs committee in each house of Congress oversaw naval matters, but funding was entrusted to the Appropriations committees. In 1946 the military and naval committees were merged into House and Senate Armed Services committees. The House Armed Services Committee in 1994 had fifty-five members, a professional staff of forty-eight, and a clerical force of twenty-four. The most important subcommittees are Procurement and Military Nuclear Systems, Seapower and Strategic and Critical Materials, Research and Development, Military Installations and Facilities, Military Personnel and Compensation, Investigations, and Readiness. The Senate committee, twenty strong, has subcommittees substantially parallel to those of the House panel. The annual cost of each committee is about $3 million. In the 103d Congress (1993–1995), Ronald V. Dellums (D.-Calif.) became the chairman of the House committee, and Sam Nunn (D-Ga.) became chairman of the Senate committee. These committees help shape military policy, and the Senate passes nominations onto the officer corps and also to those selected for flag rank, that is, for admiral and general.

[See also (II) Defense, Department of.]

BIBLIOGRAPHY

Albion, Robert G. "The Naval Affairs Committees, 1816–1947." *Proceedings* 78 (1952): 1227–1237.

Coletta, Paolo E. *The United States Navy and Defense Unification, 1947–1953.* 1981.

Coletta, Paolo E., Robert G. Albion, and K. Jack Bauer, eds. *American Secretaries of the Navy.* 2 vols. 1981.

– PAOLO E. COLETTA

NEGOTIATION, POWER OF

The President's power to negotiate treaties and other international agreements with foreign sovereigns derives from the treaty clause in the Constitution. Article II, Section 2, gives the President the "Power, by and with the Advice and Consent of the Senate, to make Treaties, provided two thirds of the Senators present concur." Although the President must share most of his powers as diplomat in chief with the legislative branch (e.g., receiving and appointing ambassadors and regulating the armed forces), his treaty-making power arguably means that his power of negotiation is exclusive. Perhaps the most famous support for the President's exclusive negotiation power comes from the Supreme Court's opinion in *United States* v. *Curtiss-Wright Export Corp.* (1926). Writing for the Court in broad strokes, Justice George Sutherland opined that the federal government's international authority derives not just from the Constitution, but more generally from the nation's status of sovereignty. Sutherland continued that only one branch of the federal government, the executive, could represent the sovereign internationally: "In this vast external realm, with its important, complicated, delicate and manifold problems, the President alone has the power to speak or listen as a representative of the nation." Congress, moreover, may delegate whatever international authority it has to the President, who is the nation's "sole organ" in foreign relations. Under the sole organ theory, then, the President or his representatives may unilaterally negotiate with foreign leaders and create both formal and informal agreements, though the Senate's consent is needed for treaties to come into force.

The President or his representatives may unilaterally negotiate with foreign leaders and create both formal and informal agreements.

On the other hand, the treaty clause refers not only to senatorial consent, but also to the executive receiving the Senate's advice on treaties. The records of the Constitutional Convention do not support the notion that the Senate has no role in treaty-making until after the executive branch has concluded its treaty negotiations; in fact, the executive branch would have been completely omitted from the treaty-making process under preliminary versions of the treaty clause. By neglecting to seek the Senate's advice during treaty negotiations, the President may face unreceptive and even contentious Senators by the time he finally transmits the treaty for their consent. A prominent example is the Treaty of Versailles (1919), ending World War I and calling for the establishment of the League of Nations. President Woodrow Wilson excluded important members of the Senate from the Versailles Treaty's negotiation. The Senate thereafter refused to give its consent to the treaty, and the United States never joined the League of Nations. In certain other instances when the Senate has not given advice during treaty negotiations, the Senate has responded by placing reservations upon or revising the instrument. Whether or not constitutionally required to do so, some modern Presidents have sought senatorial input while negotiating a treaty, with the goal of eventually receiving the Senate's swift and efficient ratification of the accord. Examples of such presidential-senatorial cooperation include the negotiation of both the NATO Treaty following World War II and the proposed United States free-trade accord with Mexico.

[See also (II) Diplomat in Chief.]

BIBLIOGRAPHY

Berger, Raoul. "The Presidential Monopoly of Foreign Relations." *Michigan Law Review* 71: 1, 4–33 (1972).

Fisher, Louis. *Constitutional Conflicts between Congress and the President.* 3d ed. 1991. Chapter 8.

Fisher, Louis. *The Politics of Shared Power: Congress, and the Executive.* 3d ed. 1993.

– KENNETH C. RANDALL

O

OATH OF OFFICE, PRESIDENTIAL

Article II, Section 1, clause 8, of the Constitution provides that before a President "enter on the Execution of his Office, he shall take the following Oath or Affirmation:—'I do solemnly swear (or affirm) that I will faithfully execute the Office of President of the United States, and will to the best of my Ability, preserve, protect and defend the Constitution of the United States.' " At the first inauguration, George Washington added the words "so help me God" at the conclusion of the oath, a practice that has since been followed by almost every President. The oath prescribed for all other federal officials, including the Vice President, was approved by the First Congress.

During the Constitutional Convention of 1787, the drafting of the President's oath generated little debate. The Committee on Detail proposed the first half of the oath on 6 August. Three weeks later, George Mason and James Madison successfully moved to add the phrase "and will to the best of my judgment and power preserve, protect and defend the Constitution of the United States" to the oath. On 15 September the delegates substituted "to the best of my abilities" for "to the best of my judgment and power" without discussion.

In 204 years (1789–1993), the presidential oath has been administered fifty-two times. On four occasions, when inauguration day fell on a Sunday, the President chose to be sworn into office privately at the White House, and then repeated the oath on Monday, at the public ceremony on Capitol Hill. Although the Constitution makes no provision regarding who shall administer the oath, the Chief Justice of the United States has sworn in every President-elect since John Adams (1797). The Chief Justice could not administer the oath at either of George Washington's inaugurations since the Supreme Court had not yet been selected in 1789, and Chief Justice John Jay was out of the county in 1793.

The precedent for succeeding Vice Presidents taking the presidential oath on assuming office was begun by John Tyler in April 1841, after William Henry Harrison became the first President to die in office. Each of the eight Vice Presidents who have since assumed the presidency due to the death or resignation of the President have followed the Tyler Precedent. Among the individuals administering the oath to succeeding Vice Presidents have been three Chief Justices, four federal judges, a state supreme court justice, and a local justice of the peace.

The Constitution makes no mention of the elaborate pageantry, pomp, and celebration that accompanies the swearing in of the President, which has become one of America's most significant traditions.

[See also (II) Vice President.]

BIBLIOGRAPHY

Durbin, Louise. *Inaugural Cavalcade.* 1971.

The Inaugural Story, 1789–1969. 1969.

Stathis, Stephen W. "Our Sunday Inaugurations." *Presidential Studies Quarterly* 15 (Winter 1985): 12–24.

– STEPHEN W. STATHIS

OFFICE FOR EMERGENCY MANAGEMENT (OEM)

A unit of the Executive Office of the President, the Office for Emergency Management was created by President Franklin D. Roosevelt to help the President deal with the emergency posed by World War II. Roosevelt had created the Executive Office of the President in 1939 with Reorganization Plan No. 1. That office was formally organized 8 September 1939 by Executive Order 8248, which defined five operative bodies, including, "in the event of a national emergency, such office for emergency management as the President shall determine." That same day the President declared a "limited" national emergency in response to the German invasion of Poland in early September; the United States maintained a policy of official neutrality, although Britain and France declared war on Germany. Thus, conditions were set for the establishment of the Office for Emergency Management by a presidential administrative order on 25 May 1940.

The administrative order chartered the OEM to "assist the President in the clearance of information with respect to measures necessitated by the threatened emergency," to serve as a liaison between the President and other agencies involved in "meeting the threatened emergency," and "to perform such additional duties as the President may direct." The OEM was headed by one of the President's administrative assistants, known as the Liaison Officer for Emergency Management, who were successively William H. McReynolds, Wayne Coy, and James F. Byrnes. On 3 November 1943, Roosevelt accepted Byrnes's resignation from this position and appointed no successor, thereby terminating the liaison functions of the OEM.

The emergency character of the agency made it difficult for neutralists and pacifists to attack.

As war enveloped Europe and Asia, the OEM became the President's vehicle for U.S. mobilization. A 7 January 1941 administrative order assigned the OEM important new duties. Significantly, the order directed the OEM to advise and assist the President "in the discharge of extraordinary responsibilities imposed upon him by any emergency arising out of war, the threat of war, imminence of war, flood, drought, or other condition threatening the public peace or safety." The emergency character of the agency made it difficult for neutralists and pacifists to attack. Furthermore, with the Reorganization Act of 1939 due to expire automatically in a short time, Roosevelt needed a way to continue mobilization and knew he could not depend on Congress for it. What he chose to do was to make the OEM a holding company for various agencies presidentially created as its subunits. By the end of 1941, America was at war, and the OEM continued to provide the framework for the establishment of a number of wartime agencies, such as the Office of Production Management, the Office of Price Administration, the Office of War Information, and the Office of Economic Stabilization. By mid-1943, the OEM's administrative and coordinative activities began to be reduced and the Office of War Mobilization, another OEM subunit, assumed a leadership role. One of the last OEM subunits to survive was the Philippine Alien Property Administration, which was terminated in 1951. By that time, the OEM had been inactive for several years; it has never been formally abolished.

[See also (II) Executive Office of the President.]

BIBLIOGRAPHY

McReynolds, William H. "The Office for Emergency Management." *Public Administration Review* 1 (1941): 131–138.

U.S. Bureau of the Budget. *The United States at War.* 1946.

Wann, A.J. *The President as Chief Administrator.* 1968.

– HAROLD C. RELYEA

OFFICE OF ADMINISTRATION

The White House Office of Administration was established within the Executive Office of the President (EOP) in 1977. President Jimmy Carter proposed this office, initially referred to as the Central Administrative Unit, to Congress on 15 July 1977 in section 2 of his Reorganization Plan No. 1 of 1977 (42 FR 56101). The proposal took effect on 12 December 1977 via Executive Order 12028.

Before the creation of the Office of Administration, 380 (or 22 percent) of the full-time, permanent EOP personnel performed administrative support services in the various EOP units. This dispersion resulted in a duplication of effort, uneven quality, and poor coordination of administrative support and services. Through the consolidation of administrative functions in a single office, Carter hoped to increase the efficiency of the EOP, improve services, and create a base for more effective management of the budget and planning of all EOP units.

Skeptics saw the formation of the office as an effort to respond to criticism concerning the growth of the White House staff under President Richard M. Nixon. Creating the Office of Administration enabled Carter to shift a number of employees off the White House payroll, thus appearing to reduce the size of the staff without losing support services.

Section 3 of Executive Order 12028 states that the Office of Administration "shall encompass all types of administrative support and services that may be used, or be useful to, units within the Executive Office of the President." Mandated services include personnel management services; financial management services; data processing; library, records and information services; and office services and operations. As of 1992, the Office of Administration was the third-largest unit in the EOP, with a full-time staff of 159.

The Office of Administration is headed by a director, who is appointed by, and directly responsible to, the President. The director is accountable for ensuring that the Office of Administration provides common administrative support and services to institutional units of the Executive Office of the President. The first director, Richard Harden, was appointed by President Carter on 28 December 1977.

The Office has five functional divisions: Administrative Operations, Financial Management, Information Resources Management, Library and Information Services, and Personnel Management. Each is headed by a division director. The Administrative Management Division encompasses general administrative services such as mail, messenger, printing and duplication, graphics, word processing, procurement, and supply services.

Through the Financial Management Division, the Office of Administration maintains accounts, payrolls, and budgeting for all EOP offices. Information Resources Management and Library and Information Services manage the three EOP's nonpublic libraries (general reference, reference, and law), provide data processing and information services, and maintain official records for all units. The Personnel Management Division handles the placement, transfer, and interagency detailing of all EOP staff, with the exception of presidential appointments.

The Office of Administration plays a very small role in EOP politics, as its functions are essentially those of institutional maintenance rather than policy coordination or political liaison. As John Hart points out in *The Presidential Branch,* however, the office could form a strong base for an executive-branch management unit if this responsibility were ever to be removed from the Office of Management and Budget (OMB).

[See also (II) Executive Office of the President.]

BIBLIOGRAPHY

Bonafede, Dom. "Administering the EOP." *National Journal* (31 December 1977): 2017.
Hart, John. *The Presidential Branch.* 1987.
Patterson, Bradley H., Jr. *Ring of Power.* 1988.

– MARGARET JANE WYSZOMIRSKI

OFFICE OF INTERGOVERNMENTAL RELATIONS (OIR)

Established by President Richard M. Nixon by Executive Order 11455 on 14 February 1969, the Office of Intergovernmental Relations was created as part of Nixon's Reorganization Plan No. 2 to provide a way to strengthen relationships between the federal, state, and local governments. The office was charged with expediting the resolution of problems pertaining to intergovernmental relations and increasing local-government power over federal decisions. The location of the office in the Executive Office of the President reflected Nixon's desire to draw local-government perspectives closer to the Oval Office. The OIR's establishment early in the Nixon administration reflected the administration's priority concern with reordering matters related to federalism.

The office consisted of three people: a director, a deputy director, and an assistant director, all under the immediate supervision of Vice President Spiro T. Agnew. This represented one of several administrative responsibilities given to Agnew in the first months of the Nixon administration. In addition to serving as Nixon's stand-in as chair of the Cabinet, Agnew was given a key administrative role in the National Aeronautics and Space Administration (NASA), the Marine Resources and Engineering Development Council, the Council on Recreation and Natural Beauty, the Rural Affairs Council, the Council on Youth Opportunity, the Indian Opportunity Council, the Cabinet Committee on Desegregation, and the Council on Physical Fitness and Sports. Agnew had, as Nixon said, a "full plate" of activities. His appointment to coordinate the OIR was considered especially appropriate because Agnew's political experience as a former county executive and governor of Maryland suited the OIR mission well.

The creation of the OIR also reflected a broader priority of the Nixon administration, labeled the New Federalism. In his order creating the OIR, Nixon said that he was seeking to move government closer to the people, reflecting his view that control over the spending of federal dollars should rest more directly at the local level than had been true during the presidency of Lyndon Baines Johnson, when much federal spending was earmarked for specific purposes defined in Washington (through categorical grants, for example). Nixon's plans for spending at the state and local levels centered on a principle of revenue sharing. As Nixon said, the office was set up to "facilitate an orderly transfer of appropriate functions to State and local government." Nixon also directed that the OIR work closely with the Advisory Commission on Intergovernmental Relations, a commission established by Congress in 1959 to improve intergovernmental cooperation and coordination. Nixon named Nils A. Boe, a former governor of South Dakota, as the OIR's first director. At the end of 1969, Congress appropriated $290,000 for the office's operation.

After more than two years of operation, the OIR was dissolved on 14 December 1972. By Executive Order 11690, Nixon transferred the functions of the OIR to the Domestic Council. According to his statement, Nixon did so on Agnew's recommendation, but the elimination of the OIR reflected two important changes in administration politics. First, it reflected Agnew's declining influence in the administration. (Before the 1972 Republican convention, for example, there had been much talk of dumping Agnew from the ticket.) Second, it reflected the administration's effort to centralize and to place greater emphasis on administrative activities to achieve policy ends—a trend labeled the administrative presidency by the political scientist Richard P. Nathan.

[See also (II) Executive Office of the President.]

BIBLIOGRAPHY

Nathan, Richard P. *The Administrative Presidency.* 1983.
Public Papers of the Presidents of the United States: Richard Nixon. 1971.
Witcover, Jules. *White Knight.* 1972.

– ROBERT J. SPITZER

OFFICE OF LEGAL COUNSEL (OLC)

When President Richard M. Nixon announced the appointment of William H. Rehnquist, then Assistant Attorney General, Office of Legal Counsel, to the Supreme Court, he commented: "He is, in effect, the President's lawyer's lawyer." There is no more apt description of the role of the Office of Legal Counsel.

The Judiciary Act of 1789 provided for the appointment of a "meet person, learned in the law" as Attorney General. From the outset, providing legal advice and opinions to the President and the executive branch was a primary function of the Attorney General and one he performed personally, even after creation of the Department of Justice in 1870.

In June 1933 the appropriation act for the Department of Justice created an Assistant Solicitor General position, to be appointed by the President with the advice and consent of the Senate. His primary responsibility was to prepare opinions of the Attorney General and provide legal advice to the President and the heads of executive agencies. The title was changed to Assistant Attorney General in 1951 and the staff was designated the Executive Adjudications Division. Two years later, the name was changed to Office of Legal Counsel, a more accurate description of its essential role—helping the Attorney General provide legal advice to the President and the executive branch.

The core functions of the Office of Legal Counsel have remained the same for almost sixty years: preparing opinions of the Attorney General, providing written and oral informal advice and opinions, reviewing executive orders and proclamations for form and legality, and reviewing legislation for constitutionality. Other responsibilities have been assigned to the office as the demands on the Department of Justice have varied. Following enactment of the Administrative Procedure Act in 1946, for example, an Administrative Law Section was established within the Office of Legal Counsel to provide guidance to agencies and to conduct studies relating to administrative law. Its foremost recommendation was the creation of the Administrative Conference of the United States, which ultimately replaced the section. Another section of the office carried out the Department of Justice role in making recommendations to the Selective Service System on the validity of conscientious objector claims. The Conscientious Objector Section was eliminated with the ending of the draft.

The President and the Attorney General have also called upon the OLC to undertake special assignments in areas of unique legal complexity. In the 1970s, for example, the office prepared several legal opinions and analyses concerning the reform of the intelligence community.

While formal litigation responsibilities are assigned elsewhere in the Department of Justice, the OLC, from time to time, becomes involved in the preparation of briefs and even in the argument of cases. Usually this occurs because of the expertise of the office in areas of constitutional law, such as the separation of powers doctrine. Thus, the office was directly involved in *INS* v. *Chadha* (1983), dealing with the issue of legislative veto of executive action. Lawyers from the office were also called upon to assist the Solicitor General's Office in the preparation of the government's amicus curiae brief in *Brown* v. *Board of Education* (1954). The office is usually involved in any case before the Supreme Court that has a significant constitutional issue.

The OLC advised President Dwight D. Eisenhower that he had the authority to employ troops to ensure the safe desegregation of schools.

The President has consistently called upon the Attorney General and the Office of Legal Counsel for advice and assistance in times of crises. The opinion advising Franklin D. Roosevelt that he could enter into lend-lease arrangements with Great Britain, prior to entry of the United States into World War II, was prepared by the Assistant Solicitor General. It was the Office of Legal Counsel that advised President Dwight D. Eisenhower he had the authority to employ troops to ensure the safe desegregation of schools during the Little Rock crisis. President John F. Kennedy called upon the office, as well as the Department of State, for advice on the appropriate response to the Cuban missile crisis. The office has long advised Presidents regarding claims of executive privilege vis-à-vis Congress. The necessary proclamations and orders to impose sanctions on Iran, during the Iranian hostage crisis, were prepared by the office, and it later assisted the Attorney General in his legal arguments at the International Court of Justice on Iranian claims.

The Attorney General regularly calls upon the office to provide advice to the President that is fully candid. This advice may range from detailed recommendations on specific conflict-of-interest or other ethics issues to matters of great constitutional import. In 1973 Attorney General Elliot Richardson commissioned the office to conduct an impartial and extensive study of the law of presidential impeachment, which was furnished to the President in 1974 and subsequently made public. President Jimmy Carter received from Attorney General Griffin Bell an opinion notifying him that his campaign promise to remove the Department of Justice from political influence by having the Attorney General appointed for a fixed term of years and removable by the President only for specific cause was unconstitutional.

When constitutional issues are pending in Congress the Office of Legal Counsel is called upon to prepare testimony, to furnish legislative analysis, and, occasionally, to testify. It provides the legal analysis on claims of executive privilege and other matters related to the separation of powers doctrine. Attorney General Robert F. Kennedy's testimony on the constitutional underpinnings of the Civil Rights Act of 1964 was prepared by the OLC. Testimony opposing the War Powers Resolution (1973) as unconstitutional and challenging constraints on the President's authority to collect intelligence and conduct foreign affairs is prepared by, or reviewed by, the office.

While the extent to which the OLC provides routine advice to the President has varied with the closeness of the Attorney General to the President and the size and preferences of the White House Counsel's Office, major issues of executive prerogative and power have always been the unique responsibility of that office.

BIBLIOGRAPHY

Bell, Griffin B., with Ronald J. Ostrow. *Taking Care of the Law.* 1982.

Cummings, Homer Stille, and Carl McFarland. *Federal Justice.* 1937.

Department of Justice. *200th Anniversary of the Office of the Attorney General: 1789–1989.* 1991.

Houston, Luther A. *The Department of Justice.* 1967.

Meador, Daniel J. *The President, the Attorney General, and the Department of Justice.* 1980.

– MARY C. LAWTON

OFFICE OF MANAGEMENT AND BUDGET (OMB)

Responsible for advising the President on government-wide budget and management policies, the Office of Management and Budget is generally regarded as the most institutionalized and powerful of the units in the Executive Office of the President (EOP). This prominence does not arise simply by serving the President with what is by White House and EOP standards a uniquely large and professional staff. The President's budget office is powerful because it manages a decision-making process of inescapable importance to so many people—the executive budget.

Origins

The lineage of OMB dates back to the beginning of the twentieth century. At that time federal and state government bureaus went directly to legislative committees for funds. A major plank in the Progressive reform platform was to change this process to require a unified executive budget put together by a chief executive (mayor, city manager, governor, or president) and presented as a coordinated whole for legislative consideration. In the federal government, this movement resulted in the Budget and Accounting Act of 1921 and the creation of the Bureau of the Budget (BOB), which was renamed the Office of Management and Budget in 1970. Though located in the Treasury Department, BOB was directly responsible to the President. This 1921 reform was aimed, however, not so much at augmenting presidential power as at recognizing the inability of a pluralistic Congress to produce a coordinated budget without executive leadership. The bureau was to be nonpolitical and focused on economy and efficiency in government operations. The orienting idea was that by helping the President prepare and execute a single executive-branch budget, the professional budget staff would enhance the power of Congress to effect its will. As Charles G. Dawes, the first budget director, put it in 1923:

> We have nothing to do with policy. Much as we love the President, if Congress in its omnipotence over appropriations and in accordance with its authority over policy passed a law that garbage should be put on the White House steps, it would be our regrettable duty, as a bureau, in an impartial, nonpolitical and nonpartisan way to advise the Executive and Congress as to how the largest amount of garbage could be spread in the most expeditious and economical manner.

The shift toward the bureau's becoming a more strictly presidential agency began in the 1930s. In 1939, President Franklin D. Roosevelt transferred the BOB to the newly created EOP. Under Directors Harold Smith (1939–1946) and James Webb (1946–1949) the bureau developed a strong esprit de corps as the main institutional arm of the presidency composed almost entirely of career civil servants. Bureau personnel in the Administrative Management Division played a major role in the organization of emergency during World War II and the postwar implementation of the Marshall Plan. From the 1930s and beyond, the bureau's Legislative Reference Division grew to become the center for determining whether or not agencies' legislative proposals were in accord with the President's program. Throughout all this history, the heart of the bureau's activity lay with its budget examiners and the detailed knowledge about programs, organizations, and people that they gained through the annual examination of all agency spending requests.

The 1960s saw the Bureau of the Budget increasingly cross-pressured between its self-conception as the institutional source of presidential advice and executive leadership, on the one hand, and demands for more immediate responsiveness to aggressive policy leadership from the White House, on the other. In seeking new ideas and quick action, John F. Kennedy and especially Lyndon Baines Johnson often bypassed the BOB in developing their New Frontier and Great Society programs. Distrusting the federal bureaucracy and the civil service, Richard M. Nixon sought to increase presidential control over governmentwide policy management

Distrusting the federal bureaucracy and the civil service, Richard M. Nixon sought to increase presidential control over governmentwide policy management.

and in 1970 adopted the recommendations of the Ash Council. Under Reorganization Plan No. 2, the Bureau of the Budget was reorganized to highlight presidential management concerns and renamed the Office of Management and Budget. Since then a variety of management initiatives have occurred under different administrations, but budgeting remains the core of the OMB's power and usefulness to the President.

Organization

The Director and Deputy Director of OMB are presidential appointees subject to Senate confirmation; the Director serves as a member of the Cabinet. Since 1970 the Director has generally functioned not only as head of the budget agency but also as a personal political adviser to the President. New positions have also been created since 1970 to give political appointees the leadership positions for managing OMB and representing its views to the outside world. In 1964 there were three noncareer positions in BOB below the Deputy Director level and none in line-supervisory positions; by 1992 there were about forty political appointees, of whom about fifteen had supervisory responsibility over the various operating divisions (whose staffs are mainly composed of career civil servants).

Throughout the postwar period the BOB/OMB maintained its staff size at roughly five hundred to six hundred people, with the large majority devoted to various aspects of the budget-making process. Budget examiners are the backbone of the organization; they are grouped in four broad program divisions: National Security and International Affairs; Human Resources, Veterans, and Labor; Natural Resources, Energy, and Science; and Economics and Government. The subdivisions, or branches, of these four groups review the proposed budgets and their execution for each of the departments and agencies of the executive branch. A separate Budget Review Division analyzes and keeps track of the budget numbers as a whole while it develops procedures for formulating and presenting the budget.

Since 1970 the OMB staff concerned with federal management issues have successively been separated, merged, reseparated and then remerged with the budget branches. As of 1992 a separate Management Office was responsible for reorganization and management-improvement initiatives. During the administrations of Ronald Reagan and George Bush, the Management Office's size varied from about thirty-five to about seventy persons. The OMB's management activities were supplemented in 1974 with the statutory establishment of the Office of Federal Procurement Policy and in 1980 with the Office of Information and Regulatory Affairs.

The Legislative Reference Division screens executive agencies' submissions to Congress through a process known as legislative clearance. Every department's communication to Congress on proposed legislation, testimony, and reports on pending bills must be cleared through OMB. Communications thought to conflict with important aspects of the President's program will not be cleared. Proposed legislation that is cleared carries an OMB cover statement expressing the degree of presidential support. (In descending order of support, the proposed bill may be "in accord with the President's program," or "consistent with the Administration's objectives" or cleared with "no objection.") Likewise, any pending legislation in conflict with the President's program will, when it is taken up in the House or Senate, receive an OMB statement listing the administration's objections and signaling a possible veto. For passed legislation, the Legislative Reference Division compiles the views of affected agencies, and OMB sends its recommendation to sign or veto to the President.

In addition to these units, a cluster of offices provides staff support to OMB's Director. The General Counsel handles the fifteen to twenty-five lawsuits in which OMB is involved at any one time, as well as coordinating the issuance of executive orders and proclamations by the President. A Legislative Affairs staff—in operation since the late 1970s—helps the Director lobby Congress on behalf of the President's budget program. The Office of Economic Policy provides short- and long-range economic forecasts to help guide budget negotiations, assesses the effects of tax proposals, and conducts special economic analyses of various issues. Offices for public relations and for internal administration round out the OMB organization chart.

Developments in the 1980s and 1990s

Important changes occurred in OMB's operations in the 1980s. In part, these were a function of the personalities involved. Presidents Reagan and Bush seemed to care little about the agency's work except for its ability to reduce domestic spending and regulation. Directors David Stockman, James Miller, and Richard Darman responded vigorously, using the budget agency to push that agenda publicly. But changes at OMB reflected a deeper shift in the political context that went beyond questions of personality. That shift had to do with a growing concern over total government spending levels and mounting deficits. To deal with those concerns, OMB's changes expressed the fact that the budget process was an increasingly interactive and continuous bargaining process between the President and Congress, where the emphasis was on spending totals and not the details of agency programs.

Prior to the Reagan and Bush years, BOB and OMB operated according to what might be termed a modified, bottom-up budget process. The President, in making budget decisions, largely worked from spending requests put forward by the agencies. This process was combined, with broad economic guidelines that were established in the budget agency's spring preview. In this spring stage, estimates of the fiscal policy requirements for managing the economy, agency spending demands, and estimates of likely revenues were brought together by OMB staff to provide general spending ceilings to guide agency budget requests. These requests began to come in during the late summer and early fall. During the fall, OMB staff held hearings with the agencies and examined their proposed budgets in detail. At the end of this process, the Director's Review scrutinized the agency requests and the recommendations of his budget staff and settled on the figures to be proposed to the President. The recommended ("mark" or "passback") funding levels were also given to the agencies. Finally, in December or so, any agency appeals were made to the President and he decided any major outstanding issues. The President's budget proposals were then presented to the various committees of Congress as their starting point to determine the funding for the particular agencies under their jurisdiction. The annual repetition of this cycle gave spending agencies a predictable idea of what their resources would be a year in advance and gave the President's budget staff (after the hectic pace of fall budget reviews) time to pay field visits, read the policy literature, and otherwise delve into the substance of agency programs.

While these stages formally remained in place, much else began to change in the 1970s. As U.S. economic performance deteriorated and federal spending grew, the Budget Impoundment and Control Act of 1974 placed new emphasis on aggregate budget ceilings and on reconciling these totals with projected revenues. New congressional reporting deadlines on these totals were added to OMB's work load. At the end of the Jimmy Carter administration, worries in financial markets about the proposed deficit (then $16 billion) led the President quickly to withdraw what was to have been his final budget and to negotiate a new budget with congressional leaders so as to produce a more acceptable bottom line on total spending and the deficit. The bureau, through Director James T. McIntyre, Jr., and an enlarged congressional liaison staff, played a central role in these then novel negotiations.

These early changes were dramatically reinforced and amplified in the Reagan and Bush administrations. In the first place, budgeting became more of a top-down process in that the focus of most decision making—ranging from the Director's and White House's overall strategy to the work of individual budget examiners—was on aggregate spending levels. Much more attention was devoted to using the budget to attain a preferred, limited spending sum rather than to determining how

George Bush's administration oversaw changes in the Office of Management and Budget that reflected a growing concern over total government spending levels and mounting deficits. (Library of Congress, Prints and Photographs Division)

the budget funded agency operations or related to their programs' merits.

Secondly, OMB staff were routinely and heavily involved in negotiating and advocating the White House budgetary position throughout all stages of the legislative process. Bills with budgetary implications were closely tracked by OMB personnel through the multiple phases of the congressional budget process. A sophisticated computer routine (the Central Budget Management System) kept score of the projected spending results as bills wended their way through Congress and as executive-legislative bargains were made and remade.

Finally, the annual budget cycle, with its neat stages, was overlaid with an OMB budget-making process that was virtually continuous. It could hardly have been otherwise, given the constant rounds of negotiations with Congress, the frequently changing signals on the state of the economy, and the ongoing reactions of the financial community to budget deals and projections. In this setting the OMB's role provided little of the predictability for agencies that it once had. Neither was there an annual rhythm that allowed budget examiners the luxury of in-depth policy and program analysis. (Their compensation was that the Director's key position in setting the overall political strategy for the Administration and its dealings with Congress added luster to their work at OMB.)

In addition to these changes, OMB has gained important powers over federal regulatory activities. Regulations have little direct impact on the budget, but they can impose significant costs elsewhere in society. The 1980 Paperwork Reduction Act established the Office of Information and Regulatory Affairs (OIRA) within OMB. In 1981 President Reagan through Executive Order 12291 expanded the office's mandate to include review of proposed federal regulations. Thus, OIRA not only oversaw and decided on government paperwork requirements (such as reports and information forms) placed on the public, but it was also charged with reviewing each proposed government regulation and requiring agencies to show that the benefits of a regulation exceeded its costs. In response, advocacy groups increasingly used the courts to challenge OMB reviews that delayed the promulgation of particularly controversial regulations. Congress also responded by inventing new procedures that can bypass OMB and force agencies to issue timely regulations.

Enduring Debates

Certain controversies have been a perennial feature of OMB's existence. One such debate has to do with the role of a budget agency in determining management policy. Some have argued that efforts to improve governmentwide management are inevitably shortchanged and distorted by an organization that is preoccupied with the budget. In this view, management advice to the President should, at a minimum, be organized separately within OMB and, at best, be vested in a separate EOP unit or merged with the Office of Personnel Management (OPM). Defenders contend that OMB's control of the budget process can give powerful leverage to management improvement efforts. They argue that, with the carrots and sticks available through this government-wide, action-forcing process, management initiatives have a hope of being taken seriously. Regardless of one's view of this debate, what does seem clear is that since the 1940s management improvement has been interpreted to mean centralized pressure to achieve economy rather than advice and support to help agency managers accomplish their statutory missions.

A related, long-standing debate concerns OMB's role in the budget process itself. Those mainly interested in the content of policies have warned against the tendency of the President's budget agency to become exclusively concerned with narrow concepts of economy and efficiency ("bean counting"). They contend that without detailed knowledge of agency programs and the effects of funding changes on agency operations, OMB staff will fail to offer the sitting President the deep and broad advice required or to build up the intellectual capital for advising his successor. Opponents argue that under late-twentieth-century circumstances it is only realistic for OMB to be primarily concerned with the implications of programs for the size of government, spending totals, and potential deficits. Given the immense time constraints and the need to be directly responsive to the President's central political concerns, leisurely program analysis is said to be a thing of the past for OMB.

Far and away the most prominent controversy is the question of OMB's alleged politicization. As noted earlier, leadership throughout the budget agency has become centered in the hands of temporary political appointees. Nor is there any doubt that since 1970, at an accelerating pace, OMB and its leaders have become much more politically visible in lobbying Congress, advising on political strategy in White House councils, and serving as public advocates of the President's agenda. When latter-day OMB staff invoke the agency's lore and refer to the Dawes quotation at the beginning of this article, they typically misremember it to say that OMB must smartly respond to the President's (rather than Congress's) demand that garbage be dumped on the White House steps.

Thus critics contend that on a variety of counts, OMB's growing political prominence and clout actually weaken it as an institution of the presidency. First, this political visibility and advocacy are said to weaken OMB's credibility as a nonpartisan, impartial source of information and analysis. Since 1980, OMB's periodic use of dubious economic projections favorable to presidential promises on deficit reduction and other budget developments has reinforced those concerns. It has also strengthened the credibility of estimates issuing from the Congressional Budget Office, which contain less political "spin." Second, critics worry that a concern to be responsive to a President's immediate political needs may fail to produce the full range of critical, though loyal, advice that a President should hear. Third, they contend that by becoming so identified with advocating a particular White House political agenda, the OMB may become suspect to successor administrations, thus harming continuity and reducing institutional memory for the presidency over time. Finally, one line of argument sees the OMB's growing political role as a dangerous contribution to nonconstitutional, exclusive presidential rule, both in the public eye and within an executive branch that, after all, derives its statutory missions from Congress, not the President.

Since 1970, OMB and its leaders have become much more politically visible in lobbying Congress.

There are also strong arguments on the other side. One is that trends toward management and budget centralization and politicization simply reflect the incongruence between growing expectations on Presidents to produce results and their difficulty in meeting these expectations within the United States' system of fragmented powers. Another argument is that, in an era of heightened concern over public spending, deficits, and governmental interference in the American economy and society, the President needs OMB's help in responding to those concerns. This view would have the OMB develop a stronger profile as the advocate and negotiator of the President's political position or have it fade into the background. A faded OMB is of little use to current or future Presidents. These debates are important because the fate of OMB says much about the changing nature of the Presidency and thus of American government itself.

[See also (II) Budget Policy.]

BIBLIOGRAPHY

Berman, Larry. *The Office of Management and Budget 1921–1979.* 1979.

Heclo, Hugh. "Executive Budget Making." In *Federal Budget Policy in the 1980s.* Edited by Gregory B. Mills and John L. Palmer. 1984.

Heclo, Hugh. "OMB and the Presidency—The Problem of Neutral Competence." *The Public Interest* 38 (1975): 80–98.

Johnson, Bruce. "From Analyst to Negotiator: The OMB's New Role." *Journal of Policy Analysis and Management* 3 (1984): 501–515.

Moe, Terry. "The Politicized Presidency." In *The New Direction in American Politics.* Edited by John E. Chubb and Paul E. Peterson. 1985.

Pfiffner, James P. "OMB: Professionalism, Politicization, and the Presidency." In *Executive Leadership in Anglo-American Systems.* Edited by Colin Campbell, S.J., and Margaret Jane Wyszomirski. 1992.

U.S. Senate Committee on Governmental Affairs. *OMB: Evolving Roles and Future Issues.* Hearings. 100th Cong., 1st sess., 1986.

Wildavsky, Aaron. *The New Politics of the Budgetary Process.* 1988.

– HUGH HECLO

OFFICE OF PERSONNEL MANAGEMENT (OPM)

Reorganization Plan No. 2, which accompanied the passage of the Civil Service Reform Act (CSRA) of 1978, created the Office of Personnel Management. The act and reorganization plan were the first major overhaul of the federal personnel management system since its creation by the Civil Service Act of 1883 (Pendleton Act) that established the Civil Service Commission (CSC).

The commission was established as a bipartisan commission whose three members would manage and oversee the newly established civil service merit system. The Pendleton Act provided that hiring for the government would be open to all and based on merit as determined by competitive examinations. It prohibited the making of personnel decisions on the basis of partisan political factors. Civil servants could thus only be fired for reasons relating to job performance. Over the next century, as more protections against political abuse were added to CSC rules and regulations, some criticized the commission for making the personnel function cumbersome and for not being responsive enough to new needs of the government and the federal workforce. The reaction against the cumulative rules that protected federal workers contributed to passage of the 1978 CSRA.

Many personnel specialists also thought that the CSC had centralized personnel recruiting and hiring too tightly. They felt that many CSC classifications were out of date and that delays in hiring caused departments and agencies to lose good job candidates who got better offers while waiting to hear from the government.

One of the major problems with the CSC lay in its conflicting functions. The commission was responsible both for providing the leadership of the executive-branch workforce and for protecting the merit system. The conflict between the two roles was personified in the chairman of the commission, who at times served as a primary adviser to the President on personnel matters while simultaneously overseeing the civil service for possible abuse of executive political power. Though no personal impropriety was alleged, the role conflict was evident during the administration of Dwight D. Eisenhower, when Philip Young was Chairman of the CSC and at the same time was invited to Cabinet meetings and held the title of Presidential Adviser on Personnel Management. A similar potential conflict of roles was evident when John Macy was Lyndon Baines Johnson's primary staffer on presidential personnel appointments at the same time that he chaired the CSC.

The Pendleton Act provided that hiring for the government would be open to all and based on merit as determined by competitive examination.

When the CSC was abolished in 1978 its functions were divided among several new organizations. Most of the functions were inherited by the new Office of Personnel Management, but the watchdog function of protecting the merit system from abuse was transferred to the new Merit Systems Protection Board (MSPB) and to the Office of Special Counsel, a semi-independent organization within the MSPB. Two other organizations took over some CSC responsibilities: the Federal Labor Relations Authority (FLRA) took over the functions of the Federal Labor Relations Council, and the Equal Employment Opportunity Commission (EEOC) took over most of the CSC's equal employment opportunity responsibilities.

One of the purposes of the 1978 act was to make the personnel function more responsive to executive leadership. The premise was that agency personnel directors had been too insulated from agency heads and had sometimes been more concerned with abiding by the rules of the merit system than with accomplishing agency missions. Thus the structure of the personnel agency was changed from a bipartisan commission, which is necessarily semi-independent of the President, to an agency with one director reporting directly to the President. The director of OPM, as an Executive Level II presidential appointee, would now be the primary adviser to the President on personnel management matters. The new law did, however, prohibit the OPM director from being the President's political recruiter.

Besides making the personnel function more responsive to political leadership, the framers of the CSRA intended that personnel testing and recruiting would be decentralized to the agency level. The expectation was that tests could be tailor-made for each agency's special needs and that the agencies could move more quickly in hiring than the centralized CSC system. The role of OPM would primarily be to serve as an expert consultant to help agencies with their personnel systems and to monitor the general integrity of agency personnel systems.

The first OPM director, appointed by President Jimmy Carter, was Alan K. Campbell, who had been Chairman of the Civil Service Commission and Carter's main lobbyist on Capitol Hill in getting the CSRA passed. The first mission of the new OPM was to ensure that the CSRA was implemented throughout the government.

The OPM leadership intended the new agency's role to change from the CSC's twin role of overseer and enforcer of the merit system to one of actively assisting other agencies. Along with the new role came the decision to delegate many of the former CSC's functions—particularly recruitment, examination, and staffing—to individual agencies rather than keeping them in the central personnel agency. The OPM was also charged with the implementation of other provisions of the CSRA, including performance appraisal systems, merit pay, and the newly created Senior Executive Service (SES).

With the election of President Ronald Reagan and his appointment of Donald Devine to be director of OPM came a reorientation of the agency's mission. The previous effort to decentralize personnel powers was reversed. Devine led the OPM to concentrate on personnel fundamentals, and OPM began to recentralize control of personnel actions for the federal government. This was in line with the Reagan administration's intention to reduce federal employment on the domestic side of the government by attrition and by reductions in the workforce throughout the domestic agencies. During the early 1980s Devine reorganized OPM several times as funding for the agency was cut by 45 percent and personnel levels were reduced by 54 percent.

Devine was not renominated for a second term as OPM director, and Reagan replaced him with Constance Horner. In 1989 President George Bush appointed Constance B. Newman to direct the agency. Newman returned OPM to the task of delegating personnel functions to agencies and revitalizing federal recruitment. The OPM also moved to take federal leadership in research on productivity improvement and worker motivation.

BIBLIOGRAPHY

Ingraham, Patricia W., and Carolyn Ban. *Legislating Bureaucratic Change: The Civil Service Reform Act of 1978.* 1984.

U.S. General Accounting Office. *Managing Human Resources: Greater OPM Leadership Needed to Address Critical Challenges.* 1989.

U.S. Merit Systems Protection Board. *U.S. Office of Personnel Management and the Merit System: A Retrospective Assessment.* 1989.

– JAMES P. PFIFFNER

OFFICE OF POLICY DEVELOPMENT (OPD)

Since Herbert Hoover, Presidents have established units to help them deal specifically with domestic policy. The Office of Policy Development, one link in this chain of devices for coordinating domestic policy, was created by President Ronald Reagan in 1981.

Hoover was the first President to recognize the need for coordinated domestic policy advice in the White House, and in 1929 he formed the Committee on Social Trends. This committee included economists, sociologists, and political scientists and was charged with assessing social change and development in all domestic policy areas.

The work of President Hoover's committee served as a precedent for Franklin D. Roosevelt's National Emergency Council and National Resources Planning Board as well as Dwight D. Eisenhower's Commission on National Goals. Presidents have also turned to White House assistants and experts for ad hoc domestic policy advice and assistance. Presidents Lyndon B. Johnson and Richard M. Nixon assembled issue-specific task forces for domestic policy advice. Such temporary measures proved ineffective, however, for ongoing policy development, coordination, and planning across the broad scope of domestic issues.

DIRECTORS OF POLICY DEVELOPMENT

President	Director, Office of Policy Development
37 Nixon	John D. Ehrlichman, 1970–1973
	Kenneth R. Cole, Jr., 1973–1974
38 Ford	Kenneth R. Cole, Jr., 1974–1975
	James M. Cannon, 1975–1977
39 Carter	Stuart E. Eizenstat, 1977–1981
40 Reagan	Martin Anderson, 1981–1982
	Edwin L. Harper, 1982–1983
	John A. Svahn, 1983–1986
	Gary L. Bauer, 1987–1988
	Franmarie Kennedy-Keel, 1988–1989
41 Bush	Roger B. Porter, 1989–1993
42 Clinton	Carol Rasco, 1993–

The Domestic Council

In 1970, Nixon created the Domestic Council (DC) in the Executive Office of the President (EOP) by Executive Order 11541, pursuant to Reorganization Plan No. 2 of 1970. It was charged with advising the President on all aspects of domestic policy and with integrating policy into a coherent whole. The DC was a two-tiered organization. The first tier, the council, was chaired by the President; its membership included the Vice President, the Attorney General, and secretaries of Cabinet departments involved in domestic policy issues. The second tier consisted of a support staff under the direction of the Assistant to the President for Domestic Affairs. John D. Ehrlichman, the first person named to this position, served from 1970 until his implication in the Watergate affair prompted his resignation in December 1972.

Presidents have turned to White House assistants and experts for ad hoc domestic policy advice and assistance.

The formal role of the DC staff was to coordinate domestic policy and to follow up on the decisions of the council and the President. In practice, however, Nixon delegated to the DC staff substantial policymaking power and de facto ability to oversee and direct the performance of department and agency executives. Policy formulation and advice were coordinated through a set of issue-oriented committees. Each committee was chaired by a member of the DC staff and included representatives of relevant executive departments and agencies, who examined and recommended possible courses of administrative action. The DC staff and the Assistant for Domestic Policy himself were policy generalists, drawing on the knowledge of experts in the various branches to develop targeted policy information. As the DC evolved, its staff grew quickly, reaching a high of sixty in 1972.

In practice, the DC isolated Cabinet heads from the President and insulated Nixon from most interagency debate on domestic policy issues. As a result, considerable domestic policy power came to reside in the White House Assistant for Domestic Affairs. In turn, the Domestic Council's effectiveness was dependent on the assistant's access to and influence with the President.

Under President Gerald Ford, two important changes were made to the council's organization. First, the Vice President was named vice chairman of the council and given authority for the direction of the staff. This change reflected the extensive domestic policy experience of Vice President Nelson A. Rockefeller. The delay in Rockefeller's confirmation as Vice President, however, allowed the development of other White House domestic policy mechanisms, which hindered Rockefeller's ability to fully realize the potential of this arrangement. Second, President Ford called for a renewed emphasis on policy planning and, to further this, divided the responsibilities for long-term and day-to-day planning between two deputy directors of the DC. Despite these changes, the DC's staff size dropped precipitously, from sixty in 1972 to a low of fifteen in 1975, as the domestic policy unit failed to find a stable role in the Ford's administration.

Carter's Reorganization

In 1977, the DC was one of the first agencies President Jimmy Carter reorganized via Reorganization Plan No. 1. Although the agency maintained its mission to manage the process that coordinated the making of domestic policy and its integration with economic policy, its structure was changed. The council-level tier was abolished, and the remaining (formerly second) tier was renamed the Domestic Policy Staff (DPS) and placed under the direction of the Assistant to the President for Domestic Affairs and Policy. DPS's role, as set out by Domestic Policy Assistant Stuart Eizenstadt, was to coordinate the presentation of views to the President rather than to screen advice from the Cabinet or other agencies. The DPS focused on advice and analysis functions in a multiphase policy coordination process that ranged from formulation to strategic planning for legislative enactment but that avoided involvement in the implementation of policy.

The DPS developed a stable staff of between forty and fifty people and an organizational structure that allowed staff members to develop substantive expertise in assigned issue areas. Director Eizenstadt had both domestic policy experience (having served as a speechwriter for Johnson, research director for the campaign of Hubert H. Humphrey, and issues director for the Carter campaign) and the respect of the President and the Cabinet. He was able to serve as an honest broker between the players, representing the opinions of each to the other while also exercising an advisory role by assessing information as it passed his way.

The DPS brought together representatives from various agencies concerned with given issues areas to form interagency task forces that examined and analyzed policy options. The DPS took an active, although not always leading, role in each of these committees and coordinated their findings for presentation to President Carter. This approach enabled the DPS to play an important role as an administrator and adviser to the President.

Reagan's System

In 1981, President Reagan again reorganized the function of the domestic policy unit, renaming it the Office of Policy Development. Consistent with his declared preference for Cabinet government, President Reagan's domestic policy system aimed at fully involving department and agency heads through a system of Cabinet councils. Five such councils, organized along functional lines, were originally established, each chaired by the President or, in his absence, by the Cabinet secretary who was designated as chairman pro tempore. At first, the frequent council meetings were regularly attended by six to ten Cabinet members, the Vice President, and members of the senior White House staff.

In association with two other EOP offices, the newly formed Office of Cabinet Administration (OCA) and Office of Planning and Evaluation (OPE), OPD was cast in a supporting administrative role to the councils. The OCA was charged with the task of assigning and tracking issues, while OPE helped on strategic planning activities; both offices reported directly to presidential counselor Edwin Meese III. OPD provided staff to the Cabinet councils as well as to OCA and OPE, leaving OPD itself with depleted staff resources and shifting staff assignments. Furthermore, while OPD was headed by the Assistant to the President for Domestic Policy, he did not have direct access to President Reagan but was forced to relay information through Meese. The influence of OPD was further weakened by the frequent turnover of domestic policy assistants: Martin Anderson (1980–1982), Edwin Harper (1982–1983), John Svahn (1983–1987), Gary Bauer (1987–1988), and Franmarie Kennedy-Keel (1988–1989). None of these had the access or stature of an Ehrlichman or an Eizenstadt.

During the Reagan years, other EOP units preempted aspects of the role OPD might have played in domestic affairs. Office of Management and Budget director David Stockman was a driving intellectual force behind the domestic policy agenda of the Reagan administration, capitalizing on both the organizational resources of OMB and his close relationship with the President. Meanwhile, political advice on policy initiation was coordinated by the White House Chief of Staff, James A. Baker III, through his legislative strategy council. During the second Reagan administration, Chief of Staff Donald Regan centralized White House power in his office, thus effectively distancing OPD from the President.

Throughout the Reagan administration, the President's commitment to Cabinet government, his conservative policy agenda, the rapid personnel turnover at OPD, and competition from other executive units limited the office's ability to play a strong role in domestic policy development, formulation, or coordination.

President George Bush continued Reagan's pattern of reliance on Cabinet officials while also assembling a team of trusted policy advisers in the White House. This team included Roger Porter, an alumnus of the Ford and Reagan policy teams, who was given the title of Assistant for Economic and Domestic Policy and, in coordination with OMB director Richard Darman, became the primary White House domestic policy adviser to Bush throughout his presidency.

President George Bush continued Ronald Reagan's pattern of reliance on Cabinet officials while also assembling a team of trusted policy advisers in the White House.

Porter delegated the direction of OPD to his deputy, William Roper, a former administrator of health care financing at the Department of Health and Human Services. Although Roper took a lead role on policy in a number of health-care issues, the office was generally relegated to a supporting role in the domestic-policy hierarchy of the Bush administration, behind Porter, Darman, and domestically oriented Cabinet councils such as the Domestic Policy Council and the Economic Policy Council.

Roper was succeeded as Deputy Assistant in 1990 by Charles E. M. Kolb, a former deputy undersecretary for planning, budget, and evaluation at the Department of Education. In the last year of the Bush administration, Porter took over the directorship of OPD, adding this job to his duties as domestic and economic policy assistant.

Clinton's Focus

As of April 1993, the future of the OPD under President Bill Clinton was unclear. On the positive side, the administration had an electoral mandate for action on domestic issues and the new Assistant for Domestic Policy, Carol Rasco, was a longtime Clinton aide and domestic policy adviser. However, initially, the President used a number of other administrative devices to address particular domestic policy issues. In the instance of health care reform, Hillary Rodham Clinton and senior White House aide Ira Magaziner head a task force to formulate policy. In other cases, economic considerations led to the prominence of various economic policy units such as the Council of Economic Advisers, the new National Economic Council, the Office of Management and Budget, and the Department of the Treasury. These initial policy-development experiences seemed to indicate that OPD would have considerable competition in the domestic policy realm.

[See also (II) Executive Office of the President.]

BIBLIOGRAPHY

Burke, John. *The Institutional Presidency.* 1992.

Cronin, Thomas E. *Presidents and Domestic Policy Advice.* 1975.

Hart, John. *The Presidential Branch.* 1987.

Wyszomirski, Margaret Jane. "The Roles of a Presidential Office of Domestic Policy: Three Models and Four Cases." In *The Presidency and Public Policy Making.* Edited by George Edwards III, Steven Shull, and Norman Thomas. 1985.

– MARGARET JANE WYSZOMIRSKI

OFFICE OF PRESIDENTIAL PERSONNEL (OPP)

The story of the Office of Presidential Personnel has been one of increasing size, greater professionalism, and more centralized control of political appointments in the White House. In the nineteenth century and the first third of the twentieth century, appointments to the executive branch were dominated by the political parties. But with Franklin D. Roosevelt and the beginning of the modern presidency the function of political recruitment slowly began to be taken over by the White House. The Roosevelt administration provided the beginnings of the modern White House staff, and the Executive Office of the President (EOP) was created in 1939. Harry S Truman was the first President to designate one member of his staff to coordinate all political personnel matters. Dwight D. Eisenhower created the position of Special Assistant to the President for Personnel Management.

John F. Kennedy brought the beginnings of a personnel recruitment system (the talent hunt) to the White House, with a small section for political patronage and another section for searching out administrative talent. Lyndon Baines Johnson brought John Macy to the White House to act as his political personnel adviser in addition to Macy's duties as Chairman of the Civil Service Commission. Macy established a computerized talent bank of two thousand names, a figure that grew to thirty thousand by the end of Johnson's term.

Richard M. Nixon's administration began with a small personnel section, but in 1970 Frederic Malek came to the White House to head the newly created White House Personnel Office (WHPO). He developed a professional executive recruitment capacity and brought in professional private-sector head hunters. In previous administrations, the selection of sub-Cabinet-level appointments, even though they technically are presidential appointments, had often been delegated to departmental secretaries. But Malek effectively centralized control of presidential appointments in the White House and carefully protected presidential prerogatives from patronage pressures from Congress. While the number of White House staffers in the two previous administrations had never exceeded twelve, Malek had more than thirty people working for him, and there were sixty in the WHPO by the end of the administration. Malek created the most sophisticated presidential recruitment operation in the White House up to that time.

John F. Kennedy brought the beginnings of a personnel recruitment system to the White House.

President Gerald Ford distinguished his administration from Nixon's by changing the name of the WHPO to the Presidential Personnel Office (PPO) and reducing its size to about thirty-five staffers, who emphasized governmental rather than private-sector recruiting experience. Jimmy Carter began personnel recruitment planning by designating Jack Watson to set up the Talent Inventory Program (TIP) before the election in the summer of 1976. While Watson's team assembled thousands of names, much of that effort was ignored after the election, when Hamilton Jordan, who ran Carter's campaign, dominated the early personnel recruitment efforts of the administration. Carter also reversed the increasing centralization of recruitment of presidential appointees. In accord with his commitment to Cabinet government he delegated the selection of most sub-Cabinet-level appointees to Cabinet secretaries.

President Ronald Reagan assigned preelection planning for personnel recruitment to Pendleton James, a professional private-sector recruiter with experience in the Nixon administration. In a conscious decision to learn from the experience of the Nixon and Carter administrations, the Reagan administration decided to centralize in the White House all recruitment of presidential appointments requiring advice and consent of the Senate (PAS). But in a major departure from precedent they also insisted on White House control of political appointments that are technically agency-head prerogatives—for example, noncareer Senior Executive Service appointments and Schedule C positions. As an indicator of the importance attributed to his position, James had the title of Assistant to the President for Presidential Personnel and controlled a staff of approximately one hundred workers in the early years of the administration.

Vice President George Bush designated Chase Untermeyer to begin planning his personnel operation early in his 1988 campaign for the presidency. Bush, however, stipulated that Untermeyer could not recruit any staff or set up an office until after the election so as not to appear too confident or distract attention from the campaign. With the Bush victory in 1988 some expected that many Reagan appointees would stay in their current positions since no large change in policy or direction was indicated in the campaign. But the Bush White House let it be known that it anticipated a 90 percent turnover in political appointees and that Bush loyalists would be running the new administration. Eventually the turnover approached 70 percent in a personnel transition that was more bitter than had been expected.

The presidential appointment process, and thus the work of the Office of Presidential Personnel (OPP), is becoming more elaborate and time-consuming. This is partly due to the increasing number of presidential appointees in key executive-branch positions (with about one thousand presidential appointments requiring Senate confirmation in the executive branch and about two thousand part-time PAS appointments to boards, commissions, and councils) and the increasing scope of White House control of political appointments. But it is also due to the increasingly close scrutiny of potential personnel by the Federal Bureau of Investigation (FBI) as well as to internal political clearances in the White House. These delaying factors are exacerbated by the lengthening time that the Senate takes to confirm nominees (from seven weeks during the Johnson administration to more than fourteen weeks during the Bush administration). The combination of delays makes it difficult for a new administration to hit the ground running.

In addition to the recruitment and placement function, the OPP in the Reagan and Bush administrations also took on the task of systematically orienting new political appointees to their positions in the federal government. Many new appointees have no federal experience, and the orientation helps to bridge more quickly the gap between the professional context in business, academia, or the law and the much more treacherous environment of a political appointment in the federal government. Congressional relations, press relations, personnel constraints, and rigid ethical strictures are all covered in these orientation sessions.

[See also (II) Executive Office of the President.]

BIBLIOGRAPHY

Mackenzie, G. Calvin. *The Politics of Presidential Appointments.* 1981.

Mackenzie, G. Calvin, ed. *The In-and-Outers.* 1987.

National Academy of Public Administration, *America's Unelected Government.* 1983.

Patterson, Bradley H., Jr. *The Ring of Power.* 1988.

Pfiffner, James P. *The Strategic Presidency.* 1988.

– JAMES P. PFIFFNER

OFFICE OF PUBLIC LIAISON (OPL)

One of several White House staff units established to strengthen the President's position with outside coalitions and interest groups, the Office of Public Liaison was created in 1974. The office is one of several aimed at long-range planning and communication. It was used in a variety of ways by Presidents Gerald Ford, Jimmy Carter, Ronald Reagan, and George Bush.

The office was created in response to changes in the political environment of the presidency. The rise of single-issue interest groups brought increasing pressure on Presidents, whose ability to formulate policy was weakened by the decline of party organization. Presidents began to use interest groups as a resource in getting programs adopted by Congress and implemented by the bureaucracy.

Historically, there had been people on the White House staff who were assigned to maintain liaison with groups important to a President's electoral coalition, but until recently those staff members had close ties to the national party committees or were senior staff with many other duties to perform. Their liaison activities were to some extent viewed as electoral duties.

The contemporary Office of Public Liaison represents the central point of contact in the White House for most interest groups. It responds to groups' requests for information and action. The office also initiates action by bringing together people it believes will prove useful to the President as he makes policy. But the office must walk a fine line: the Lobbying with Appropriated Money Act, passed in 1919, prohibits the use of public money for lobbying. Anne Wexler, who headed the liaison office during the Carter administration, explained how they handled the dilemma: "We never ask a person to call a Congressman, [but] we will tell him when a vote is coming up or when a markup is due and give him a lot of information about it. We can say, 'This is the program and the President would like your help and these are the committee members involved.' "

The White House often has limited resources in trying to push legislation through a reluctant Congress, especially when the President and the Congress are controlled by different parties. The President needs interest groups as much as they need him: interest groups offer not only the numerical strength of their membership but also information on potential supporters that the White House can enlist. When President Reagan sought congressional approval of his tax increase proposal in 1982, the Office of Public Liaison, through Wayne Valis, the staffperson assigned to deal with business groups, worked with a steering committee of business organizations. These groups provided information on supporters and potential opponents and also sent mailings to their members. Their members, in turn, urged their Representatives and Senators to pass the legislation.

The contemporary Office of Public Liaison represents the central point of contact in the White House for most interest groups.

The idea of having a White House office to develop contacts with outside interest groups originated with President Richard M. Nixon, but the Watergate affair prevented him from formally organizing it. Shortly after Ford became President, he announced the office's creation and appointed William J. Baroody as its first head. Subsequent Presidents have almost uniformly appointed women to head the office; these women have been the highest-ranking women on the White House staff.

The office is organized along the lines of interest-group activity. Staff members have portfolios on specific issues and groups needed for a President's electoral and legislative coalition. The liaison unit emphasizes the interest groups and individuals useful for galvanizing support for a program. At its best, the office proves useful to a President in organizing outside support.

[See also (I) Interest Groups, Lobbying.]

BIBLIOGRAPHY

Kumar, Martha Joynt, and Michael Baruch Grossman. "The Presidency and Interest Groups." In *The Presidency and the Political System.* Edited by Michael Nelson. 1984.

Patterson, Bradley H. *The Ring of Power: The White House Staff and Its Expanding Role in Government.* 1988.

Pika, Joseph. "Interest Groups and the White House under Roosevelt and Truman." *Political Science Quarterly* 102 (1987): 647–668.

– MARTHA KUMAR

OFFICE OF SCIENCE AND TECHNOLOGY POLICY (OSTP)

The Office of Science and Technology Policy (OSTP) was formally established in 1976 within the Executive Office of the President (EOP) by the National Science and Technology Policy, Organization, and Priorities Act of 1976 (42 USC 6611). This action marked the most recent incarnation of a White House science and technology unit.

The act provides that "the office shall serve as a source of scientific and technological analysis and judgment for the president with respect to major policies, plans and programs of the Federal Government." The economy, national security, health, foreign relations, and the environment are noted as issue areas in which the OSTP could provide valuable scientific advice to the President.

As early as World War II, it was clear that advances in aircraft, weaponry, and radar technology required that science and technology policy be a component of national-security policy. The Office of Science Research and Development (OSRD) provided wartime advice and support for science. The OSRD awarded contracts for federal war-related science projects and helped to determine the scope of these projects. During the same period, the Office of Naval Research (ONR) in the Department of the Navy served as a de facto national science foundation, providing contracts for general, rather than directed, research in a variety of disciplines.

In 1950 President Truman moved the ONR function into a separate, congressionally established non-military agency, the National Science Foundation (NSF). The NSF was given two main responsibilities: to support basic scientific research and to act as an adviser in the formulation of a coherent national science policy for the United States.

President Truman also empaneled a Science Advisory Committee in the EOP as part of the Office of Defense Mobilization. Under President Eisenhower, this committee evolved into the Presidential Science Advisory Committee (PSAC), which gained prominence after the launch of Sputnik threatened American technological competitiveness. Eisenhower used the PSAC to provide unbiased, expert opinions on changing technologies in defense and space. The chairman of the PSAC was given the title of Special Adviser to the President on Science and Technology.

The PSAC was part of the White House establishment and, therefore, largely insulated from congressional oversight. President Kennedy changed this on the recommendation of the Senate, in his Reorganization Plan No. 2 of 1962, which created the Office of Science and Technology (OST) in the EOP and transferred the coordination and advisory roles of the NSF to this new office. Although separate from the White House staff, the OST served as science adviser to the President. The influence of the science adviser on presidential decision making waned during the terms of Presidents Johnson and Nixon. At this time, the focus of science was changing from a national-security emphasis on military and space to more domestic issues involving environmental and social concerns. This meant that science was dealing with politically sensitive issues, rather than predominantly technological ones. In addition, both NASA and the NSF had developed into other sources for science information and advice.

As early as World War II, it was clear that science and technology policy be a component of national-security policy.

President Nixon's quest for strong administrative control and his tendency to politicize the EOP led to the abolition of the OST in Presidential Reorganization Plan No. 1 of 1973. The advisory function of the OST was combined with that of disburser of federal research grants under the director of the NSF. The abolition of the OST provoked opposition from the scientific community, which argued that scientific advice merited more formal representation in the structure of the Executive Office.

President Ford expressed an interest in changing the presidential science advisory structure and was receptive to recommendations from Congress and from the scientific community concerning the proper function of a new science office. The 1975 legislation establishing the Office of Science and Technology Policy, provided for a single science adviser appointed by the President with the advice and consent of the Senate, a small staff, and the development of "working relationships" with the Office of Management and Budget, the National Security Council, and the Domestic Council.

The OSTP, under the terms of this legislation, is housed in the EOP. Its director once again serves as chief policy adviser to the President on science and technology. Four associate directors, responsible for life sciences, industrial technology, policy and international affairs, and physical sciences and engineering, are also appointed by the President, subject to Senate confirmation. The OSTP was originally assigned the responsibility for producing a five-year outlook and annual reports to the President and Congress. In 1977, a portion of this reporting responsibility shifted to the NSF in order to enable the OSTP to focus on advising the President.

In addition, the OSTP coordinates federal research and development efforts and assists the Office of Management and Budget with analysis of funding proposals for research and development in the budgets of all federal agencies. Frank Press, OSTP director under President Carter, also provided advice on appointments to research and development positions.

In 1981 President Reagan considered abolishing the OSTP, but the scientific community and Congress again rallied in support of the office.

[See also (II) Executive Office of the President.]

BIBLIOGRAPHY

Burger, Edward J., Jr. *Science at the White House: A Political Liability.* 1981.

Smith, Bruce L. R. *The Advisers: Scientists in the Policy Process.* 1992.

– MARGARET JANE WYSZOMIRSKI

OFFICE OF THE U.S. TRADE REPRESENTATIVE (USTR)

Established in January 1980 by President Jimmy Carter, pursuant to a reorganization plan approved by Congress, the Office of the U.S. Trade Representative is responsible for leading the federal government in international trade negotiations and in trade policy coordination. Its head, the U.S. Trade Representative, holds both ambassadorial and Cabinet rank.

USTR is the successor to the President's Special Representative for Trade Negotiations (STR), a position created, at congressional insistence, by President John F. Kennedy in 1963. At that time, the United States was about to embark on a major round of trade talks aimed at achieving major reciprocal reductions in tariff barriers, and key Representatives and Senators feared that the State Department, which had previously led such negotiations, would be overly responsive to other nations' needs and insufficiently attentive to the circumstances facing U.S. industry and agriculture. They therefore insisted that the U.S. delegation be led by an official housed in the Executive Office of the President (EOP) and reporting directly to the President. The STR was responsible for the successful completion of the so-called Kennedy Round in 1967 and helped win congressional authorization for the Tokyo Round of talks of 1973 to 1979 and the enactment of legislation implementing the Tokyo Round agreements.

Originally a small office (about twenty-five professional staff) involved mainly in major multilateral negotiations, STR had by the mid 1970s become the lead U.S. agency for bilateral talks as well. Creation of USTR reinforced this trend. The office's permanent staff was increased in 1980 from 59 to 131 positions (by 1991 the number was 168). Staff tends to be relatively short-term (few officials spend most of their careers there) and not particularly partisan.

USTR plays a unique role as trade policy "broker." Housed in the EOP, it is unusually responsive to congressional concerns, reflecting that branch's constitutional authority to "regulate Commerce . . . with foreign Nations." It also maintains balances between foreign governments and U.S. commercial interests, between American producers that benefit from trade expansion and those that suffer from import competition, and among the several executive branch agencies with strong interests in trade policy—the departments of Commerce, Agriculture, State, and Treasury; the National Security Council; and the Council of Economic Advisers. USTR has consistently leaned toward a liberal, barrier-reducing stance. But it has been more pragmatic and more responsive to producer and congressional concerns than have the economic policy agencies, and it has repeatedly negotiated import-restraining arrangements for sensitive products such as automobiles, steel, textiles, and apparel.

The Office of the U.S. Trade Representative plays a unique role as trade policy "broker."

The USTR (like its predecessor) has usually benefited from high-quality leadership from Kennedy's trade representative, former Secretary of State Christian Herter to George Bush's USTR, Carla A. Hills. Other effective Trade Representatives have included William Eberle under Richard M. Nixon and Gerald Ford, Robert Strauss under Carter, and William Brock and Clayton Yeutter under Ronald Reagan. As foreign commercial competition grew, the Trade Representative took an increasingly aggressive posture in international negotiations. In the multilateral Uruguay Round (1990s), for example, Hills insisted on substantial reductions in agricultural trade barriers imposed by the European Community, whereas in previous rounds USTRs settled for token concessions.

The USTR also exerted more pressure on other nations to open their markets unilaterally. Trade Representatives from Robert Strauss (in 1977) on have pressed Japan for major steps to reduce its formal and informal barriers to imports. In the 1980s, similar pressure was extended to newly industrialized countries such as Korea, Brazil, Taiwan, Singapore, and Thailand. The purpose was both substantive and political. Easing of these nations' import barriers could (and did) result in greater U.S. exports. This in turn broadened support in the United States for continuation of trade-expanding policies.

Throughout its existence, USTR has given priority to global, multilateral trade arrangements under the General Agreement on Tariffs and Trade (GATT). But its pragmatism led the office to seek barrier reduction wherever possible. Hence, when multilateral talks stalemated in the early and mid 1980s, William Brock encouraged development of talks with Canada, resulting in the bilateral free-trade agreement signed and implemented in 1988. During the Bush administration, USTR pushed in both the GATT Uruguay Round and in talks with Mexico and Canada to establish a North American Free Trade Area (NAFTA).

As an operating agency within the President's Executive Office that is particularly responsive to Congress, USTR is an organizational anomaly. This has created problems in transitions between administrations; for example, Reagan counselor Edwin Meese III tried to abolish USTR in the name of organizational tidiness. The office has nonetheless flourished because of its congressional base, its key role, and the substantive and political skill of its leadership.

[See also (II) Office of Management and Budget.]

BIBLIOGRAPHY

Destler, I. M. *American Trade Politics.* 2d ed. 1992.

Winham, Gilbert R. *International Trade and the Tokyo Round Negotiation.* 1986.

– I. M. DESTLER

OPTION PAPERS

The only professional and systematic method of presenting an important, complicated, and controversial proposal to a President is to put it in writing in the form of an option paper. Such a paper describes the issue, gives the background facts, sets forth alternative choices for presidential decision and the pro and con arguments for each, identifies the Cabinet and senior White House staff officers who are proponents and opponents of each alternative, and ends with a recommendation. Inasmuch as policy issues reach the President for action because they are important, complicated, and controversial, the White House has developed a technique for dealing with them.

The option-paper process works in the following way. First, the question and any subquestions to be addressed must be identified. This assignment memorandum is almost always drafted by a White House staff officer; often it is issued over that officer's own signature. The assignment memo will typically name the primary action officer, list the Cabinet or staff officers to be consulted, and specify a deadline; it may also establish an ad hoc working group.

The second step is the tedious process of drafts, meetings, redrafts, and interagency negotiations with the aim of producing a paper ready in every sense for the President's decision. Contrary to stereotype, the drafters of an option paper do not merely produce sycophantic guff, full only of good news and pandering to what they think the President's predilections are. While the policy process of the White House requires brevity and dispatch, it also demands candor and fairness. It would be egregious disservice to any President to present an option paper that is slanted, distorted, or conceals information or that is not balanced by opposing argument.

Third, the draft option paper goes back to the White House officer who made the original assignment, who will judge it to see whether the terms of the assignment have been fulfilled. The paper itself is likely to be brief, but it may also be accompanied by tabbed attachments—in the form, for example, of signed memoranda from individual cabinet officers.

A special category of option paper, called an Enrolled Bill Memorandum and drafted by the Office of Management and Budget (OMB), accompanies every enrolled bill (i.e., a bill that has been passed by both houses of Congress) awaiting presidential action. Such an option paper (prepared within the ten-day limit) analyzes the bill, recommends signature or veto, and always includes the views of each affected Cabinet officer.

If an option paper is particularly lengthy, complicated, or controversial, the White House officer with primary responsibility will then draw up what has been called a road map memorandum—that is, a cover note to the President. The road map memo highlights the issue, summarizes the pro and con discussions, identifies parts of the full package that the President should study carefully, warns the President of traps, points out particularly strong personal views expressed by any of the President's advisers, and alerts the President to any attempts to paper over real differences through the use of mushy compromise language. It may itself suggest compromises and may recommend one of the options for approval.

Finally the option-paper package is then sent to the Staff Secretary, who is not only the last officer to check on the coordination of the paper but is also the person who decides when it should be presented to the President. For example, it may be required just prior to the visit of some important personage or in preparation for a high-level conference.

In reviewing an option paper, some Presidents will convene meetings of the various options' protagonists to discuss the arguments therein; a few Presidents, for example, Richard M. Nixon, are uncomfortable with heated, ego-tinged debate and prefer to read option papers quietly and alone. The President's decision may appear simply as a checked box or may be put in the form of a record of action of a meeting or as a decision memorandum initialed by the President. Presidents have been known to fill the margins of option papers with enthusiastic, angry, or even profane comments. Today, because of the problem of leaks, neither the full text of the decision memorandum nor the original paper with the President's personal comments is (ever) circulated; the decision itself is often orally conveyed down the line. The original copy of the package is put among the President's personal papers for attention by future archivists.

BIBLIOGRAPHY

Patterson, Bradley H., Jr., *The Ring of Power: The White House Staff and Its Expanding Role in Government,* 1988.

– BRADLEY H. PATTERSON, JR.

OUTSIDE INCOME, EXECUTIVE

Officers and employees of the executive branch are limited in the amount and type of income they may accept while in the employ of the federal government. Outside income includes money and gifts received by an executive-branch employee while he or she is receiving a federal salary. Those who support major revisions in policies concerning outside earned income and honoraria consistently support changes in the salary systems for federal officials as well.

Outside income includes money and gifts received by an executive-branch employee while he or she is receiving a federal salary.

The year 1989 was a watershed for the issue of ethics in government. On 25 January 1989, President George Bush issued Executive Order 12668, establishing the President's Commission on Federal Ethics Law Reform. The commission reported on 9 March. Subsequently, Executive Order 12674, issued in April 1989, banned all outside earned income by political appointees and White House staff. In November Congress enacted the Ethics Reform Act of 1989 (P.L. 101-194). Pursuant to these efforts, all officers and employees in the executive branch have since 1991 been prohibited from accepting honoraria. An honorarium is defined (5 USC app. 505) as a "payment of money or any thing of value for an appearance, speech or article by a Member, officer or employee, excluding any actual and necessary travel expenses incurred by such individual (and one relative) to the extent that such expenses are paid or reimbursed by any other person." This ban applies to all political appointees, as well as career officials, and is in effect for legislative and judicial officers and employees, including members of Congress and Justices of the Supreme Court. It is acceptable to allow a sponsoring organization to make a donation of up to $2,000, in lieu of an honorarium, to a charitable organization, but neither the person in whose honor the donation is made nor any dependent relative may derive any financial benefit from that charitable organization.

The total ban on honoraria has proved to be more restrictive than originally intended under the Ethics Reform Act. For example, a person working as a federal employee in the lower pay scales may have been supplementing that income by submitting occasional articles or stories for publication or by performing in occasional musical or theatrical presentations. After the act's passage, income from any such outside activity would generally be considered an honorarium and would be banned. As of 1993, remedies for these restrictions were being sought.

Besides being forbidden to receive honoraria, noncareer executive-branch officers and employees are subject to restrictions on earned outside income. Any such personnel whose basic salary level is equal to or exceeds an established base rate (120 percent of the base rate for a GS-15 pay level; GS stands for General Schedule) must honor that restriction. The limitation amounts to allowable earned income equal to or below 15 percent of the rate of base pay for Level II of the Executive Schedule pay system (Level II is equal to the rate at which members of Congress are compensated).

Generally, accepting gifts is considered inappropriate. In an effort to avoid placing federal officials and employees in compromising positions, Congress has acted to limit the value of gifts and services provided by outside interests. Provisions of the 1992 Legislative Branch Appropriations Act (P.L. 102-90), set a "minimal value" or $250 level, whichever is greater, as the basis for reporting tangible gifts and gifts of food, lodging, and transportation. "Minimal value" is established under the provisions of the Foreign Gifts Act. The travel reimbursement disclosure threshold is also $250 or "minimal value," whichever is greater. The Legislative Branch Appropriations Act also established $100 as the minimum value above which gifts must be disclosed, with the dollar limitation to be adjusted every three years. No gifts of any type may be solicited or received by a federal officer or employee in return for the performance of any official act.

The Office of Government Ethics, an independent organization within the executive branch, is responsible for the issuance and promulgation of rules and regulations relating to outside income.

BIBLIOGRAPHY

Hartman, Robert W., and Arnold R. Weber, eds. *The Rewards of Public Service: Compensating Top Federal Officials.* 1980.

President's Commission on Federal Ethics Law Reform. *To Serve with Honor.* 1989.

U.S. House of Representatives. *Report of the Bipartisan Task Force on Ethics.* 1989.

– SHARON STIVER GRESSLE

OVAL OFFICE

The original Oval Office was built in 1909 by President William Howard Taft, when he doubled the size of the Executive Office Building, known today as the West Wing. Theodore Roosevelt had built the West Wing in 1902 to house the presidential offices, which he moved from the White House, where the office functions had occupied the entire east end of the second floor. The West Wing was built as a staff office in actuality, not the President's office; the chief of state merely had a "President's room" there. On an axis with the front door and in an elegant, bow-ended office was the President's secretary, seated in the dominant position in the building. All bills were signed in the White House, where Roosevelt had what he called the study.

Taft demanded a larger staff than Roosevelt and ordered the officials in charge to create a presidential office central to the West Wing. Congress authorized an expenditure of $40,000. A limited competition of selected architects gave the job to Nathan C. Wyeth; it was he who signed the first Oval Office, which may have been his idea. President Taft was involved and loved architecture, but the extent of his participation is uncertain. Wyeth's design was simplicity itself. The inspiration obviously came from the Blue Room, one of the state rooms inside the White House.

This Oval Office eventually became the main office of the President, although Taft himself signed no bills there; such an event did not take place until 1914, with Woodrow Wilson. The West Wing and the Oval Office burned at Christmas 1929 and were reconstructed exactly within the ruins. In 1934, President Franklin D. Roosevelt needed to expand the West Wing to house a greatly enlarged presidential staff. The idea for such an expansion had been proposed by President Herbert Hoover, but after the fire, with the overpowering presence of the Depression, he had decided merely to reconstruct.

After considerable controversy among the President, the Corps of Army Engineers, the American Institute of Architects, and the Fine Arts Commission, the expansion plan emerged. Eric Gugler of New York was the architect, and he set up his drafting room in the nearby Octagon House on New York Avenue. The work was accomplished between August and November 1934. Taft's earlier office was demolished and the new Oval Office was built on the east end of the West Wing, adjacent to the Rose Garden, which it adjoined by a columned porch. It was near the new Cabinet Room, which also looked out into the garden. The interior was more flamboyant than Wyeth's Oval Office of 1909 and suggested the art moderne style then current in architecture. Gugler surmounted the doors with whimsical pediments and built niches for books, crowned with seashells.

Except for intermittent redecoration, the Oval Office is that completed by Gugler in 1934. While the remainder of the West Wing is in a state of continual rearrangement, the Oval Office has stayed architecturally the same.

BIBLIOGRAPHY

Seale, William. *The President's House: A History.* 1985.

Seale, William. *The White House: History of an American Idea.* 1992.

– WILLIAM SEALE

OVERSIGHT, CONGRESSIONAL

Congressional oversight of the presidency and of the executive branch of government derives from the legitimate involvement of Congress in executive activity. The President is titular head of the executive branch and is ultimately responsible for its actions, but he is not its sole master. The President may be called the Chief Executive, but he actually shares legal authority over the executive branch with Congress. The President is charged with the faithful execution of the laws as well as with the executive power, terms that are never precisely defined in the Constitution or in statutes. From these grants of legal authority emerges the conclusion that Presidents dominate the bureaucracy. What is ignored is that Congress legally determines many things about the bureaucracy.

Areas of Congressional Authority

One of the things Congress determines is the structure of the executive branch. If, for instance, there is to be a department of education, Congress has to create it. Another thing Congress determines is almost all the programs that the executive branch administers, which are created through congressional authority; Social Security, agricultural subsidies, highway improvement programs, and the space program are only a few examples. In addition, the basic outlines of personnel policy in the executive branch are created by Congress through statutes. The senior civil service, executive-compensation formulas, and the scope of the merit system are usually congressionally determined. Finally, the money to run the executive branch and its programs comes out of the congressional budget and appropriations process. Legally then, Congress and the President share in controlling the executive branch; exclusive presidential authority is a myth.

The President may be called Chief Executive, but he actually shares legal authority over the executive branch with Congress.

Congress shares power over the executive branch from a political perspective as well as a legal one. Bureaucrats realize that authority over them is divided between the President and Congress. Understandably they want to please both. Presidential and congressional constituencies differ. Different political parties can control the presidency and Congress. Historically, party control has been divided about 40 percent of the time since 1789 and about 80 percent of the time from 1968 to 1992. Bureaucrats may find it most difficult to satisfy completely both their legal and their political masters. Presidents and some members of Congress may have different priorities and emphases; if they agree on goals, they may still clash over what is the better way to achieve them. Even if there is consensus on ends and means, disputes may arise over timing—how quickly money should be spent and for which programs.

These legal and political factors provide an invitation to struggle. The outcomes of this struggle are predictably mixed. In some situations, Presidents and their close advisers may dominate executive decision making. In other areas, power may be genuinely shared.

That Congress has substantial legal and political power in dealing with the executive branch is not a matter of dispute. Through most of U.S. history the legal basis for legislative oversight has been inferred from the legal powers of Congress over the bureaucracy previously mentioned. In the Legislative Reorganization Act of 1946, the legal basis for legislative oversight of the bureaucracy was clearly and directly stated when each standing committee was instructed to "exercise continuous watchfulness of the execution by the administrative agencies concerned of any laws, the subject matter of which is within the jurisdiction of such committee."

This authority is quite sufficient to justify any oversight that Congress wishes to conduct. Nonetheless, Congress has periodically added to its legal authority to oversee. For example, see the Legislative Reorganization Act of 1970 and the Congressional Budget and Impoundment Control Act (1974). If the legal basis for legislative oversight is broad and all-embracing, its actual exercise and impact seem far more circumscribed. The general impact of legislative oversight on the presidency and the executive branch shows that authority over the bureaucracy is in fact divided. Moreover, oversight is selectively exercised, and its impact is difficult to trace because its significance varies with the situation.

Ways of Asserting Congressional Authority

Congress has a multitude of tools and techniques to influence executive behavior. Its control over structure, program, policy, personnel, and money sets the boundaries. It can exercise that control formally through official investigations, as part of serving constituents by means of casework, through required reports, and in hearings designed to determine the shape of legislation and appropriations.

Congress can exercise its power informally in discussion and negotiation. Congress, its committees, and individual members have many ways of finding out what the executive branch is doing. Committee staff persons regularly consult with relevant persons in the executive branch. A rather constant querying process takes place on the telephone, in memoranda, and over luncheon. There are also many opportunities to attempt to influence executive behavior.

By looking at what Congress does formally and why it does it, one can gain substantial insight into the problems of legislative oversight of the presidency. Probably the most visible oversight technique is that of committee and subcommittee investigations to see that executive programs are being implemented. What is most notable here is that only a small percentage of departments, agencies, and programs are regularly subject to scrutiny through investigations. What accounts for this seemingly insufficient supervision is that while the obligation to oversee the executive branch is general and inclusive, the actual efforts to do so are based less on that obligation than on more concrete motives. The pressure to oversee comes primarily from the pursuit of political advantage. Many investigations also involve a desire to promote good public policy and to create more efficient and responsible bureaucratic behavior, but political advantage is typically the sharpest spur.

An ongoing oversight technique is dealing with the complaints and inquiries from constituents that congressional offices receive on a daily basis. These concern such matters as executive action or inaction, a government check that has not been delivered, a government contract that has been delayed or awarded to another company, a form that has been lost, a permit that has not been granted, or a host of other matters involving interactions between government and individuals. Congressional offices, concerned with serving their constituents, promptly check with the relevant department or agency in the executive branch to clarify the problem or to seek remedies for it. Communications from constituents to Congress provide a vast body of evidence concerning what is going on, or is not going on that should be going on, in the executive branch. This motherlode of data is underutilized within Congress. Valiant efforts are indeed made to satisfy constituents, but mainly that is all that happens. Efforts to collect and synthesize these data as a basis for more systematic congressional action are rare. Congressional routines concerning casework are only occasionally translated into effective, broad oversight activity.

By looking at what Congress does formally and why it does it, one can gain substantial insight into the problems of legislative oversight of the presidency.

Another formal technique that members of Congress use to oversee the executive branch is to require regular reports from the President, his department, and agencies on a wide variety of topics. In 1991 more than two thousand such reports were required. This vast expenditure of executive time and energy supposedly leads to effective oversight from Congress. The correlation, however, is spurious. Most of the reports required by Congress are routinely dispatched to the circular file. Only a few become the basis for action. The gap between appearance and reality is large.

Still another technique of oversight is for congressional committees to hold hearings on proposed legislation or when appropriations are being considered. At such hearings the questions are likely to be, How have these or similar programs worked before? How much money has been spent and for what purposes? Were these expenditures worth the cost? Legislative hearings frequently deal with oversight even if their stated purpose is something else.

If one examines congressional investigations, casework, required reports, and hearings, few will deal explicitly with the President and his behavior. But because the bureaucracy is legally and politically under both presidential and congressional supervision and because the President as the titular head is ultimately responsible, even if he knows nothing about specific bureaucratic actions, almost all congressional oversight of the executive branch of government in some way, mainly indirectly, affects the president.

Relatively few bureaucratic behaviors are directly subject to congressional scrutiny, and of these, even fewer involve direct presidential actions. Presidential responsibility extends far beyond presidential knowledge, and legislative authority to oversee extends far beyond congressional behavior. The direct impact of most efforts of congressional oversight on presidents is neither extensive nor substantial. Precisely what difference oversight makes for Presidents is difficult to specify partly because what impact there is is so largely indirect.

Problems in Executive-Legislative Relations

If precise impacts are difficult to measure, some of the problems in executive-legislative relations when Congress oversees the bureaucracy are easier to specify. One of these is what information concerning the executive branch Congress is entitled to seek and obtain. From the perspective of most members of Congress the answer is whatever information members of Congress want. Legislators point to their extensive legal powers over the bureaucracy and infer from these that there are few limits to the information they can rightfully obtain. From the perspective of the President, however, there are clear limits to what information members of Congress are entitled to receive. Whatever the language used to justify presidential positions, the characteristic presidential interpretation is that Presidents should provide only what information they deem to be appropriate irrespective of congressional requests. Since law seldom provides absolute answers in these disputes, political strength and bargaining tend to determine outcomes. Congressional committees and subcommittees press for what they desire; Presidents resist when they feel requests are legally excessive or politically damaging. On occasion, Presidents even invoke executive privilege, that is, they claim a constitutional right to withhold sensitive information. Members of Congress rail against such executive assertions and can sometimes force the executive to back down through political pressure.

The courts studiously avoided defining executive privilege or establishing its limits until the 1970s, when President Richard M. Nixon claimed that he could withhold tape recordings made during the Watergate affair from Congress and the courts. The Supreme Court ruled that while Presidents did have the right of executive privilege, they could only use it subject to limits. The limit defined here was that claims to executive privilege could not stand when executive-held materials were needed as evidence in criminal proceedings. The Court seemed to be saying that while the doctrine of executive privilege has legal status, its use cannot be determined by the President alone. Although cast in legal terms, the Court decision embodied an astute political compromise.

The few examples of congressional oversight directly related to the presidency tend to be dramatic incidents. In recent years, the Watergate controversy in the Nixon administration and the Iran-contra affair during the administration of Ronald Reagan quickly come to mind.

The Iran-contra investigation reveals a great deal about congressional oversight as it relates to the presidency. When the news reached the public that the U.S. government had been selling arms to the Iranians, allegedly to build good will that would lead to the release of U.S. hostages, and that the profits from these sales had been diverted to the aid of the contras in Nicaragua, Congress mounted an intense investigation. Charges of violations of U.S. policy by the executive branch and of illegal acts (Congress had banned military aid to the contras) resounded through these investigations. The gravity of what had occurred was revealed, and the public was made aware of misbehavior by the executive branch. In these senses, these hearings seemed to be an example of the fruits of diligent congressional oversight.

Limits to Congressional Oversight

The limits to this effort at congressional oversight remain obvious. Neither congressional investigations nor any other source fully established the role of President Reagan in these events. Since that answer has not been forthcoming, one can assert that these congressional attempts to oversee presidential behavior substantially failed. Also, the absence of conclusive evidence linking President Reagan to these machinations in foreign policy stands in the way of effective congressional action to remedy existing problems. If the President personally violated the law, impeachment could have resulted. If the President had been shown to be excessively casual or careless in supervising the bureaucracy, he could have been politically condemned. If problems of bureaucratic organization had been basic, Congress could have acted to correct these, but such problems were never clearly demonstrated. The utility of this major effort at oversight remains unclear partly because the President and the executive branch were not fully forthcoming with what they knew; in fact they could be seen as impediments to successful legislative oversight.

Efforts at legislative oversight aimed at dealing directly with presidential behavior are commonly limited by executive efforts to prevent the full disclosure of relevant facts. Banking scandals in the Reagan and Bush administrations provide another example. Few persons in or out of the executive branch gain joy in wallowing in their own errors of judgment, their failures to act expeditiously, or their apparent protection of vested interests. Other than the complexity of problems themselves, executive intransigence stands as a major barrier to successful legislative oversight.

Presidents have been known to reconsider what they are about to do because they anticipate that congressional oversight with a battery of questions will follow.

There is, of course, a record of some successful congressional oversight of presidential behavior, but that is not the dominant theme. Mainly, Congress tries in a rather fitful manner to oversee some selected portion of presidential activities, as has been noted. The impact of these efforts is a function of specific circumstances. Perhaps the major impact can never be precisely measured. Nevertheless, Presidents have been known to reconsider what they are about to do because they anticipate that congressional oversight with a battery of questions will follow. Presidents consider how, if called upon, they will justify what they have done. No one can prove that the "law of anticipated reactions" works. Yet fragmentary evidence suggests that the process of anticipating possible reactions and preparing defensible answers may be the most significant fruit of congressional oversight.

Since the federal bureaucracy is under the supervision of both the President and Congress, efforts at congressional oversight of the executive branch are at least indirectly oversight of the presidency. The record of congressional oversight of the bureaucracy is more difficult to evaluate. Conclusions vary with perspectives. If the standard is whether Congress systematically oversees all aspects of bureaucratic behavior, then the record of accomplishment is dismal. If the standard is whether Congress looks into basic problems as they are revealed, then the record is more mixed. If the standard is whether Congress regularly checks into a vast variety of executive behavior, then the record of Congress assuredly is good. Conclusions then depend on one's frame of reference. Some would even argue that the relatively small amount of oversight that Congress performs is entirely functional. Congress, these scholars argue, does not waste its time and energy on useless routine checks but gets involved only when its attention is brought to problems of consequence.

[See also (I) Oversight.]

BIBLIOGRAPHY

Aberbach, Joel D. *Keeping a Watchful Eye: The Politics of Congressional Oversight.* 1990.

Dodd, Lawrence, C., and Richard L. Schott. *Congress and the Administrative State.* 1979.

Foreman, Christopher H., Jr. *Signals from the Hill: Congressional Oversight and the Challenge of Social Regulation.* 1988.

Harris, Joseph P. *Congressional Control of Administration.* 1964.

Johnson, Loch K. *A Season of Inquiry: The Senate Intelligence Investigation.* 1985.

Ogul, Morris S. *Congress Oversees the Bureaucracy: Studies in Legislative Supervision.* 1978.

Ripley, Randall B., and Grace A. Franklin. *Congress, the Bureaucracy, and Public Policy.* 5th ed. 1991.

Smist, Frank John. *Congress Oversees the United States Intelligence Community, 1947–1989.* 1990.

– MORRIS S. OGUL

P

PARDON POWER

Article II, Section 2, of the Constitution states: "The President . . . shall have Power to grant Reprieves and Pardons for Offenses against the United States, except in Cases of Impeachment." The authority to grant pardons, the roots of which are traceable to the royal prerogative of the English monarchy, is at once the most imperial and delicate of the President's powers. A presidential pardon precludes the punishment of a person who has committed an offense against the United States. In view of the fact that the impeachment exception is the only explicit textual limitation on the exercise of the power, scholars have described the authority as unfettered and immune to the doctrine of checks and balances. In dictum, the Supreme Court has characterized the power as "unlimited." The apparently untrammeled power always has carried with it a great potential for abuse. The Framers of the Constitution were steeped in English history; the king frequently used pardons as partisan indulgences for friends and supporters. In spite of their familiarity with absolutist Stuart claims and their fear of a power-hungry executive with a proclivity for usurpation, the Framers opted, by the pardon clause, to vest the President with a broad discretion to correct miscarriages of justice and to restore tranquillity in the wake of rebellion.

The Constitutional Framework

The presidential pardon power was forged by the Constitutional Convention in light of English practice. Executive mercy, found in ancient Mosaic, Greek, and Roman law, was introduced into English jurisprudence in the seventh century, according to Blackstone, on the grounds that all offenses are committed against the king's peace, and since it is the king who is injured by fighting in his house, it is reasonable that he alone should possess the power of forgiveness. The act of mercy, then, would be dispensed by the king in his grand role as the "fountain of justice." The historical record suggests, however, that the grant of a pardon was not so much an act of grace as it was the tool of pecuniary and political aggrandizement. Pardons often were sold for fees and used as an instrument of conscription to entice convicted felons and murderers to support military adventures. Evidently, pardons were so easily obtainable for persons who had committed such crimes as homicide, larceny, and robbery that law-abiding subjects who had accused them feared retribution, a prospect that also discouraged others from making accusations. The systematic abuse of the pardon power across several centuries provoked numerous complaints from Parliament, which feared for its statutes, and eventuated in a constitutional crisis in the late seventeenth century between the House of Commons and the Crown. The bold attempt by Charles II to use the pardon power as a means to preempt the impeachment in 1678 of the earl of Danby, lord high treasurer of England, triggered a constitutional crisis that would have resounding implications for the presidential pardon power: May a royal pardon prevent an impeachment? For members of the Commons, who viewed the impeachment power as a means of bringing corrupt ministers to heel, the act of executive clemency could not be tolerated. It was feared that a pardon before trial would stifle testimony and therefore bury the facts surrounding the plot. Had the Commons acquiesced in the pardon, the pretended accountability of the ministers would have ceased, for the king would have been free to exercise the prerogative to screen them from parliamentary inquiry. Charles did not want to lose his trusted aide, but Danby was not worth another civil war. Therefore, in spite of the pardon, Danby spent five years in the Tower of London without trial. In legislation that effectuated the arguments and sentiments expressed by the Commons during the Danby affair, Parliament passed the Act of Settlement in 1700, which declared that an impeachment could not be impeded by a pardon.

A pardon may be conferred absolutely or conditionally, provided the conditions are constitutional.

English practice was constantly before the eyes of those who drafted the state constitutions during the revolutionary war period. For most states, it was the norm: a pardon may not be pleaded to ban impeachment. Exceptions to this practice were more restrictive of the pardoning authority, as reflected, for example, in the absolute denial to the governor of a pardon power, in the requirement that pardons were contingent upon approval from the legislature, or in the prohibition of preconviction pardons.

The Constitutional Convention refused to embrace these restrictions. The debate on the pardon power was framed by a proposal from Charles Pinckney of South Carolina that mirrored the English practice. The impeachment exception evoked no controversy since the Framers were familiar with the Danby affair and they had no desire to vest the President with a power that had been denied to the Crown. The convention focused principally on the question of whether the President should be empowered to grant pardons for treason, an issue that occasioned an impassioned debate. Some delegates, including Alexander Hamilton, would have permitted pardons for treason but only if the Senate approved. In rhetoric that stirred images of a presidential coup and that sharply echoed the concerns of the Commons a century before, George Mason warned that a President might issue pardons "to screen from punishment those whom he had secretly instigated to commit the crime, and thereby prevent a discovery of his own guilt." In the end, in spite of their fear of the subversion of the Republic by pardons, the Framers could not bring themselves to fashion an exception for treason. From history and first-hand experience in the form of Shays' Rebellion, the Framers were familiar with the seductive potential of a well-aimed and well-timed pardon to quell rebellions and restore tranquillity. Without such an option, rebels might just as well die on the battlefield than by the gallows. The wisdom and potential benefits of that policy, however, would not have overcome fears of presidential complicity in treasonous activities without assurances from James Wilson of the availability of impeachment to curb abuse of the pardon power. In fact, every warning that a President might use the pardon power to exonerate accomplices, to forestall investigations, and generally to subvert law and government was met with assurances that the threat of impeachment would prevent such misconduct.

The debate on treason focused attention on the presidency, and not Congress, as the repository of the pardon power. Since the timing of a pardon offered to rebels was critical and since Congress was not expected to be in continuous session, there was little choice but to vest the power in the President. But the Framers' reluctance was alleviated by Wilson's reassuring remarks about the restraining impact of impeachment, and by the rationale, as explained by Hamilton in Federalist 74, that the President's realization that the very fate of an individual might rest on his shoulders would assure a scrupulous exercise of the authority in order to avoid accusations of weakness or connivance.

The convention's creation of a virtually unlimited presidential pardon power has been confirmed by the judiciary. A pardon may be issued before conviction, but not before an offense has been committed, for such an act would amount to the power to dispense with the laws, the claim to which led to King James II's forced abdication. A pardon may be conferred absolutely or conditionally, provided the conditions are constitutional. However, whether a pardon may be conferred over the objections of the recipient is not clear since the acceptance of a pardon is generally considered an admission of the commission of a crime. The power to pardon also includes the authority to commute sentences, and to remit fines, penalties, and forfeitures. It has been held that the pardon power, which includes authority to issue a general amnesty, may not be restricted by congressional legislation, but since Congress also has authority to grant general amnesties, the exercise of its power may confer clemency in terms more generous than the President's.

While the Supreme Court has viewed the President's pardon power as virtually unfettered, it also has held that the abuse of the power is vulnerable to judicial review and impeachment. Two decisions have established a foundation, however slim, for judicial review of the pardon power, in light of considerations of due process and separation of powers. In 1925, in *Ex parte Grossman,* Chief Justice William Howard Taft allowed for the possibility that excessive abuses of the pardoning power might provoke a test of its validity in federal court, but he noted that sufficient abuses had not yet occurred. In 1974, in *Schick* v. *Reed,* Chief Justice Warren Burger stated that under the right circumstances, conditions to pardons could be declared invalid.

Granting Pardons

Presidents have granted pardons for various offenses since the dawn of the Republic. With few exceptions, the country has been well served by exercise of the power. President George Washington initiated the use of the pardon authority in 1795 when he issued a proclamation of amnesty to participants in the Whiskey Rebellion. Since then, pirates who have assisted United States military causes, participants in insurrections, deserters, federal officials, and polygamists, among others, have received clemency. An occasional pardon—to Jefferson Davis and the Confederate soldiers, or to Richard M. Nixon, or to Vietnam War draft evaders, for example—has excited intense controversy and heightened public interest in the power; but a great many pardons have been issued without fanfare to federal prisoners

President Gerald R. Ford's unconditional pardon of Richard M. Nixon stirred intense controversy and heightened public interest in pardon power. (Library of Congress, Prints and Photographs Division)

who have reached the late stages of their lives and are near death. The frequency and volume of pardons granted, moreover, are perhaps greater than most Americans would suppose. During the Civil War and its aftermath, Presidents Abraham Lincoln and Andrew Johnson issued amnesties to some 200,000 persons. In 1933, President Franklin D. Roosevelt exercised the power to restore the civil rights of about 1,500 persons who had completed prison terms for violating the draft or for espionage acts during World War I, and in 1945 he restored citizenship rights to several thousand former convicts who had served at least one year in the military and subsequently had earned an honorable discharge. In 1946, President Harry S Truman granted pardons to more than 1,500 people who had been sentenced to prison for violating the Selective Service Act, and on Christmas Day, 1952, he restored civil rights to 9,000 people who had been convicted of desertion during peacetime. In addition to the more than 10,000 beneficiaries of the Vietnam War clemency and amnesty programs of Presidents Gerald Ford and Jimmy Carter, some 4,600 pardons and 500 commutations were granted between 1953 and 1984 by Presidents from Dwight D. Eisenhower to Ronald Reagan. Reagan issued about 380 pardons during his eight years in the White House.

Until the Civil War, the exercise of the pardoning authority had not provoked controversy or question. But the stresses of that war, the vindictive mood of many Northerners, and the desire for retribution among some in Congress raised concerns about the use of the power. Some members of Congress objected to the inconsistent consideration of requests for pardons and to the preferential treatment accorded Kentuckians; the influence peddling of pardon brokers; and the insincerity of the recipients, who were required to take a loyalty oath to the Union. Congress even undertook an examination of Johnson's bank account pursuant to allegations that he had been bribed to issue pardons. To some Americans, it seemed that the administration of the pardon power was as arbitrary as it had been in England.

The exercise of the pardon power and the consideration of its use in more recent times have perhaps excited more public dissatisfaction with and curiosity in the scope of the power and its political and legal dimensions than at any other point in our history. In particular, Americans have witnessed the possibility that President Nixon might pardon himself and more than thirty aides involved in Watergate affair offenses, the unconditional pardon that President Ford granted to Nixon, and in December 1992 the pretrial pardon that President George Bush issued to former Secretary of Defense Casper Weinberger for charges stemming from his role in the Iran-contra affair. These episodes have revealed the darker ways in which a power to temper justice with mercy might be transformed into a political tool to be exploited and abused for partisan causes.

Befitting its royal heritage, the presidential pardoning power is subject to few constitutional restraints, and only then in rare and unlikely circumstances. In theory, judicial review and impeachment are available to restrain the pardon power, but in practice they are not apt to be invoked unless the President abuses the power excessively or otherwise administers it in a grossly arbitrary manner. Contrary, therefore, to Supreme Court dictum and scholarly assertions of an illimitable power to pardon, there are boundaries that fence the exercise of executive clemency. Nevertheless, it is easier to speak of abuses, as opposed to illegal uses, of the pardon authority. The principal restriction on the power remains political, to be exercised by Americans on Election Day.

BIBLIOGRAPHY

Adler, David Gray. "The President's Pardon Power." In *Inventing the American Presidency.* Edited by Thomas E. Cronin. 1989.

Corwin, Edward S. *The President: Office and Powers, 1787–1984: A History and Analysis of Practice and Opinion.* 5th rev. ed. 1984.

Dorris, Jonathan T. *Pardon and Amnesty under Lincoln and Johnson.* 1953.
Duker, William. "The President's Power to Pardon: A Constitutional History." *William and Mary Law Review* 18 (1977): 475–535.
Humbert, W. H. *The Pardoning Power of the President.* 1941.
Kurland, Philip. *Watergate and the Constitution.* 1978.

– DAVID GRAY ADLER

PARTY LEADER, PRESIDENT AS

The relationship between the presidency and the American party-system has always been a difficult one. The architects of the Constitution established a nonpartisan President who, with the support of the judiciary, was intended to play the leading institutional role in checking and controlling the virulent party conflict that the Framers feared would destroy the fabric of representative democracy. An ideal executive would stand above the "merely" political conflicts of factions and rule benevolently in the public interest.

Like most of the Framers of the Constitution, George Washington, the first Chief Executive, disapproved of factions, and he did not regard himself as the leader of any political party. Washington believed that Article II of the Constitution encouraged the President to stand apart from the jarring party conflict that was inherent to the legislative body. As such, the President could provide a strong measure of unity and stability to the political system. This was a task that, by temperament and background, Washington was well suited to perform. Although he insisted on being master of the executive branch, it was contrary to his principles to try to influence congressional elections or the legislative process. The primary duty of the President, he believed, was to execute the laws.

The Origins of Parties

Washington's conception of the presidency did not survive even his own administration, however. Ultimately, disagreements among his brilliant constellation of advisers led to the demise of the nonpartisan presidency. Party conflict arose from the sharp differences between Alexander Hamilton, Secretary of the Treasury, and Thomas Jefferson, Secretary of State, differences that began during Washington's first term and became irreconcilable during the second term. Hamilton favored a strong, dynamic national government, anchored by an independent and active President; Jefferson professed not to be a friend of energetic central government. Jefferson was especially opposed to Hamilton's proposal for a national bank, which was contained in the Treasury Secretary's December 1790 report to Congress. According to Jefferson, Hamilton's plan would establish national institutions and policies that transcended the powers of Congress and the states. Furthermore, Hamilton favored domestic and international initiatives that presupposed a principal role for the President in formulating public policies and carrying them out. This view, Jefferson believed, made the more decentralizing institutions—Congress and the states—subordinate to the executive, thus undermining popular sovereignty and pushing the United States toward a British-style monarchy.

In the 1824 election, four candidates so divided the electoral votes that no one received the necessary majority to be President.

Ultimately these constitutional disagreements made inevitable an open outbreak of party conflict between the Federalists, who shared Hamilton's point of view, and the Democratic-Republicans, who shared Jefferson's. The full implications of this conflict became clear with the election of Jefferson as the third President in 1800. Jefferson's predecessor John Adams, who occupied the vice presidency during Washington's term, was clearly identified with the Federalist Party. But he shared Washington's disdain for party leadership and any claims he might have made on his party were thwarted by Hamilton's ongoing influence. Jefferson too held an antiparty position; by the time he ascended to the presidency, however, partisan conflict and institutions had evolved to a point that demanded presidential party leadership. Moreover, party leadership offered a means by which he could lead the nation without violating the Democratic-Republican fear of executive usurpation, and thus make the executive office more democratic.

The Democratic-Republican Party [*see* Democratic Party] helped to introduce and, by its example, helped to legitimize the idea of a presidential candidate as the head of a party ticket. The concept of a candidate as a party leader necessitated a formal change in the balloting arrangements of the electoral college. Originally, the Electoral College, which was conceived without political parties in mind, required presidential electors to cast a single ballot with the name of two presidential candidates on it. After the counting of the assembled ballots, the candidate with the most votes, provided the number was a majority, would become President, and the runner-up would become Vice President.

Under this procedure, the election of 1800 produced a tie. A caucus of each party's members of Congress had been held to choose nominees for President and Vice

President; the caucus's decision then was coordinated with party organizations in the various states so electors were selected as instructed agents, pledged to cast their two ballots for the party's presidential and vice-presidential candidates. The party effort was too successful. Seventy-three Democratic-Republican electors were chosen (to sixty-five for the Federalists), and each voted for Jefferson and his running mate, Aaron Burr. According to the Constitution, it thus fell to the lame-duck Federalist majority in the House of Representatives to decide which Democratic-Republican—Jefferson or Burr—would become President. After thirty-five ballots, the Federalist majority finally consented to the choice of Jefferson.

By 1804, the Twelfth Amendment was adopted, which implicitly acknowledged the existence of political parties and provided for separate balloting by the electors for President and Vice President. This amendment ratified a fundamental shift in the status of electors. They quickly lost the independent status envisioned by the Framers. Instead, they became instruments of party will. Moreover, the parties' dominance of presidential selection added a new, extraconstitutional presidential eligibility requirement, a party nomination. Party affiliation and nomination thus became a decisive criteria for selection, and the idea that electors should possess discretion was rejected as undemocratic.

In turn, the presence of a party's candidate at the head of a party ticket for elected offices conferred on that individual the status of party leader. Once elected, that figure assumed responsibility beyond the leadership of the executive branch. Unlike Washington and Adams, Jefferson deemphasized the constitutional powers of the office, governing instead through the role of party leader. The Jefferson administration encouraged the development of disciplined organization in Congress, with the President relying on floor leaders in the House and Senate to advance his program. Another source of presidential influence was the party caucus: during Jefferson's tenure as President, conclaves of leaders from the executive and legislative branches formulated policy and encouraged party unity.

Despite the assumed party division during his two terms in office, Jefferson never viewed a party system, consisting of two parties contending peacefully against each other in mutual tolerance, as a solution to the constitutional challenge posed by Hamiltonianism. Instead, Jefferson, as well as his Democratic-Republican successors in the White House, James Madison (1809–1816) and James Monroe (1818–1825), hoped to overcome the Federalists at the polls and restore a nonpartisan system dedicated to popular rule, that is, joined to a more democratic executive that would be respectful of legislative power and states' rights.

Monroe's ascendance to the presidency in 1817 signaled the complete triumph of the Democratic-Republicans. During Monroe's first term as President, the Federalist Party disappeared as a national organization; in fact, Monroe was unopposed for reelection in 1820. With the Federalists vanquished, the 1824 election became a contest of individuals rather than parties. Rival and sectional leaders, each supported by his own organization and following, ran for President in one of the most bitter and confusing campaigns in American history.

For the second time in twenty years, an election was decided not by the voters but by the House of Representatives. William H. Crawford was the nominee of the Democratic-Republican caucus; but the party machinery had run down badly by 1824, and its support was no longer tantamount to election. Four candidates (Crawford, Andrew Jackson, John Quincy Adams, and Henry Clay) so divided the electoral votes that no one received the necessary majority to be President. In accordance with the Twelfth Amendment, the House of Representatives narrowly elected Adams despite the fact that Jackson had obtained the greater number of popular and electoral votes. The controversial election of 1824 ensured the demise of what had come to be called "King Caucus," thus precipitating reforms that significantly transformed the link between Presidents and their parties.

Presidents and Party Government

With Jackson's election in 1828, the confused political situation that had underlain the previous presidential campaign was replaced by a new party alignment. Jackson and John C. Calhoun, who was Vice President during Adams's administration, formed the Democratic Party, which dedicated itself to the traditional Democratic-Republican principles of states' rights and a narrow interpretation of the national government's constitutional powers. Adams and Clay, who stood for strengthening the role of the federal government, formed the opposition Whig Party.

The advent of the Jackson presidency was accompanied by important party reforms that significantly enhanced the President's party leadership role. The demise of "King Caucus" left a vacuum in the presidential nominating process that was filled by the national party convention. Conventions were used by the Democrats in 1832 and were accepted by the Whigs after the presidential campaign of 1836. National convention delegates were selected by conventions in the states, which consisted in turn of local organizations of party members. Taken together, the new and elaborate Whig and Democratic organizations reached far beyond the halls of Congress and eventually penetrated every corner of the Union. Sustained by his party's far-reaching political network, Jackson became the first President in American history to appeal to the people over the heads of the legislative representatives. Meanwhile, under the astute direction of Jackson's Vice President and successor in the White House, Martin Van Buren, Jackson also implemented a system of rotation into government personnel practices, using the President's power of removal to replace federal employees for purely partisan reasons [*see* patronage].

Although the major elements of presidential party leadership as developed during the Jacksonian era would endure to the twentieth century, an important shift in the character of President-party relations occurred in the immediate aftermath of the Civil War. Abraham Lincoln made skillful use of his position as leader of the new Republican Party (the Whigs disintegrated in the face of the slavery controversy) to hold together the Union and maintain the initiative in conducting the war. But Lincoln's assertive wartime leadership surprised and disconcerted most of his partisan brethren in Congress, who acted forcefully to weaken the presidency after his assassination; thereafter, the presidential nominee was usually beholden to the party leaders, who, fortified by patronage and the strong partisan loyalties among the electorate, dominated national conventions.

The national party chairman firmly linked the President and party. The Democrats had created the first national party committee headed by a party chair in 1848 to conduct the presidential campaign and to guide the party's fortunes between conventions. With Mark Hanna's reign of the Republican national committee from 1896 to 1904, the national party chair emerged as a figure of imposing political stature. As William McKinley's national chairman for the 1896 election, Hanna transformed the Republican national committee into a formidable campaign machine, distributing 120 million pieces of campaign literature, keeping 1,400 speakers on the road, and maintaining good relations with the press. Once elected, McKinley relied heavily upon Hanna, who served as the administration's principal political strategist and patronage agent.

Yet developments were under way in the country that would soon render the Republican model of party government obsolete. Massive social and economic changes were increasing the scale and complexity of American life, producing jarring economic dislocations and intense political conflicts. In the face of change, pressures mounted for a new style of governance, one that would require a more expansive national government and a more systematic administrative of public policy. The limited, nineteenth-century polity, which could accommodate decentralized party organizations, political patronage, and a dominant Congress, began to give way to a new order that depended upon consistent and forceful presidential leadership.

Executive Leadership

The rise of the modern presidency during the first half of the twentieth century signified the emergence of the President, rather than Congress or party organizations, as the leading instrument of popular rule. Acting on this modern concept of presidential leadership, Theodore Roosevelt (1901–1909) and Woodrow Wilson (1913–1921) inaugurated the practices during the Progressive Era that strengthened the President as popular and legislative leader. It fell to Franklin D. Roosevelt, however, to consolidate or institutionalize the changes in the executive office that were initiated during the first two decades of the twentieth century. His long tenure in the White House, 1933–1945, transformed presidential-party relations, placing executive leadership at the heart of the ascendant Democratic Party's approach to politics and government. Roosevelt's New Deal program, developed in response to the Great Depression, brought the welfare state to the United States, years after it had become a fixture in European nations. His extraordinary leadership in expanding the federal government to meet the domestic crisis of the 1930s, and later an international one, Wold War II, effected a dramatic increase in the size and scope of the federal executive.

Under John F. Kennedy,

television became an essential determinant

of a President's ability to lead the nation.

Roosevelt pursued a personnel policy to build up a national organization rather than allowing patronage to be used merely to build senatorial and congressional machines. Although the President followed traditional patronage practices during his first term, the recommendations of James A. Farley, chairman of the Democratic Party, were not followed so closely after his reelection. Instead, Roosevelt turned more and more frequently to a loosely knit, but well defined group of individuals—the so-called New Dealers—whose loyalties were to the New Deal rather than the Democratic

Party. As a result, many appointments in Washington went to individuals who were supporters of the President and believed in what he was trying to do but were not Democrats in many instances, and in all instances were not organization Democrats.

Moreover, whereas Presidents since Jefferson had taken care to consult with legislative party leaders in the development of their policy programs, Roosevelt relegated his party in Congress to a decidedly subordinate status. He offended legislators by his use of press conferences to announce important decisions and eschewed the use of the party in Congress. Though Roosevelt used Farley and Vice President John Nance Garner, especially during the first term, to maintain close ties with Congress, legislative party leaders complained that they were called into consultation only when their signatures were required at the bottom of the page to make the document legal.

The most dramatic moment in Roosevelt's challenge to traditional party practices was the "purge" campaign of 1938. This involved Roosevelt directly in one gubernatorial and several congressional primary campaigns in a bold effort to replace conservative Democrats with candidates who were "100 percent New Dealers." Such intervention was not unprecedented. William Howard Taft and Wilson had made limited efforts to remove recalcitrant members from their party. But Roosevelt's campaign was unprecedented in scale, and unlike previous efforts, it made no attempt to work through the regular party organization. The degree to which his action was a departure from the norm is measured by the press labeling it the "purge," a term associated with Adolf Hitler's attempt to weed out dissent in Germany's National Socialist Party and Joseph Stalin's elimination of "disloyal" party members from the Soviet Communist Party.

In the final analysis the "benign dictatorship" that Roosevelt sought to impose on the Democratic Party was more conducive to corroding the American party system than reforming it. Roosevelt, in fact, felt that a full revamping of party politics was impractical, given the obstacles to centralized party government that are so deeply ingrained in the American political experience. The immense failure of the purge reinforced this view—all but two of the Democrats whom Roosevelt opposed were renominated. Moreover, the purge campaign, which was widely condemned as an assault on the constitutional system of checks and balances, galvanized the political opposition to Roosevelt, apparently contributing to the heavy losses that the Democrats sustained in the 1938 elections. Ironically, then, Roosevelt's campaign only strengthened the conservative Democrats.

As the presidency evolved into a large and active institution, it preempted party leaders in many of their significant tasks: linking the President to interest groups, staffing the executive branch, developing, and most important, providing campaign support. Presidents no longer won election and governed as head of a party but were elected and governed as the head of a personal organization they created in their own image.

The Roosevelt administration obtained legislative authority in the Ramspeck Act (1940) to extend civil service protection over the New Deal loyalists who were brought to Washington to staff the newly created welfare state. Beginning with Roosevelt, Presidents came to rely on executive-branch personnel to perform many of the political and social services that had traditionally been the province of the political party.

Disengagement and Isolation

Since the 1930s, further advancements in communications technology, especially television, served to connect the President even more directly with the public. Although Dwight D. Eisenhower (1953–1961) had been the first President to appear on television regularly, it was under and because of John F. Kennedy (1961–1963) that television became an essential determinant of a President's ability to lead the nation. Kennedy's effective use of television further weakened the party's traditional position as intermediary between the President and the public. In addition and indeed in response, party loyalties in the electorate began to decline.

The 1968 election and its aftermath dramatized the decay of party politics and organization. The Democratic nominee, Vice President Hubert H. Humphrey, led a party that was bitterly divided by the Vietnam War. Its convention in Chicago was ravaged by controversy, both within the hall and out on the streets, where antiwar demonstrators clashed violently with the Chicago police. Without entering a single primary, Humphrey was nominated by the regular party leaders, who still controlled a majority of delegates and who preferred him to the antiwar candidate, Sen. Eugene McCarthy.

Humphrey's controversial nomination and the failure of his general election campaign against the Republican candidate, former Vice President Richard M. Nixon, gave rise to important institutional reforms. The rules of the Democratic Party were revised to make its presidential nominating conventions more representative. The new rules eventually caused a majority of states to change from selecting delegates in closed councils of party regulars to electing them in direct presidential primaries. Although the Democrats initiated these changes, many were codified in state laws that affected the Republican Party almost as much.

The declining influence of the traditional party organizations was apparent not only in the new nominating rules but also in the perceptions and habits of the voters. The 1968 election marked the beginning of an increased tendency for voters to "split their tickets," that is, to divide their votes among the parties. The trend toward ticket splitting continued into the 1990s. The electorate has tended to place the presidency in Republican hands and Congress under the control of Democrats, an historically unprecedented pattern of divided government in national politics.

Lacking his predecessor's popular support and conservative convictions, Bush's term in office exposed the weakness of the Republican Party.

Divided government profoundly affected the course of the Nixon administration, exacerbating the alienation of the White House from party politics. Nixon sought congressional support to achieve policy goals during the first two years of his presidency. But faced with few legislative achievements, he later attempted to carry out his policies through the powers and personnel of the executive branch. Nixon intensified his efforts to strengthen presidential government after 1972, reflecting the more conservative position on domestic issues that characterized his presidency during the second term.

Nixon's attempt to achieve his political and policy objectives unilaterally has been widely regarded as an unprecedented usurpation of power and, ultimately, as a direct cause of the Watergate affair, which forced him to resign from office. The improprieties of Nixon's personal reelection organization, the Committee to Re-elect the President (CREEP), particularly its attempt to tap telephones in the offices of the Democratic national committee and the subsequent efforts by the President and his aides to cover up the break-in, brought down the Nixon presidency.

But Nixon's approach to modern presidential leadership was not entirely new; in important respects it was a logical extension of the evolving modern presidency. CREEP's complete autonomy from the regular Republican organization was merely the culmination of presidential preemption of the traditional responsibilities of national party committees. Nixon's attempt to concentrate managerial authority in the hands of a few White House aides and Cabinet "supersecretaries" simply extended the contemporary practice of reconstructing the executive branch to be a more formidable instrument of presidential government.

Nixon's presidency had the effect of strengthening opposition to the unilateral use of presidential power, while further attenuating the bonds that linked Presidents to the party system. The evolution of the modern presidency now left it in complete political isolation. This isolation continued during the administrations of Gerald R. Ford (1974–1977), a Republican, and Jimmy Carter (1977–1981), a Democrat, so much so that by the end of the 1970s statesmen and scholars were lamenting the demise of the presidency as well as the party system.

Presidential Parties

The erosion of old-style politics allowed a more nationalized party system to develop, forging new links between Presidents and their parties. The Republican Party, in particular, developed a strong institutional apparatus; since the 1970s, its organizational strength in national politics has been unprecedented. Because the reconstituted party system has been associated less with patronage than with political issues and sophisticated fund-raising techniques, it may not pose as much an obstacle to the personal and programmatic ambitions of Presidents as did the traditional system. Indeed, the nomination and election of Ronald Reagan in 1980 were the culmination of nearly two decades of organizational efforts by Republican conservatives. Reagan's candidacy added a firm philosophical commitment and political skill to the partisan recipe. Not only did the Republicans capture the White House, but they won a majority in the Senate for the first time since 1952.

Significantly, it was Reagan who broke with the tradition of the modern presidency and identified closely with his party. The spirit of the relationship between the party chair, Frank Fahrenkopf, and the White House was much more positive than it had been since the advent of the modern presidency. Cooperation and good will prevailed as Reagan worked hard to strengthen the Republican's organizational and popular base, surprising even his own White House political director with his total readiness to make fund-raising appearances for the party and its candidates.

Despite the recent changes in the party system, any celebration of the dawn of a new era of disciplined party government would be premature. Reagan's personal popularity never was converted into Republican control of the government. His landslide in 1984 did not prevent the Democrats from maintaining a strong majority in the House of Representatives; and despite his plea to the voters to elect Republicans in the 1986 congressional elections, the Democrats recaptured control of the Senate.

Thus, the closer ties the Reagan administration tried to forge between the modern presidency and the Republican Party did not alter the unprecedented partisan and electoral divisions that characterize the era of divided government. Furthermore, the persistence of divided government itself retards the restoration of partisanship in the presidency.

The 1988 election, in which Vice President George Bush defeated his Democratic opponent, Governor Michael Dukakis of Massachusetts, seemed to indicate that divided government had become an enduring characteristic of American politics. Indeed, never before had voters given a newly elected President fewer fellow partisans in Congress than they gave Bush. The 1988 campaign and its aftermath, moreover, confirmed the disassembling of the partisan and presidential realms in American politics.

The 1992 presidential election, in which the Democratic candidate, Gov. Bill Clinton of Arkansas, defeated the incumbent President, George Bush, seemed to underscore, if not provide an escape from, the disturbing political and constitutional developments of the previous quarter century. Lacking his predecessor's popular support and conservative convictions, Bush's term in office exposed the weakness of the Republican Party—indeed, his unhappy stay in the White House threatened the modern presidency with the same sort of isolation and drift that characterized the Ford and Carter years. The Democratic Party took surprising advantage of Bush's misfortune; mindful of how intractable factiousness had denied them control of the presidency for twelve years, the Democrats ran a rather effective campaign that not only captured the White House, but left them in control of both congressional chambers. Clinton's victory thus promised to ameliorate the partisan and electoral divisions that had prevailed since 1968.

Still, the meaning of the 1992 election was somewhat ambiguous. In a three-candidate race between Clinton, Bush, and an independent, Ross Perot, Clinton won a landslide in the electoral college, sweeping thirty-two states with 370 electoral votes. Yet he won only 43 percent of the popular vote, roughly the same percentage of the total vote Dukakis won in 1988.

The strong showing of Perot, who won 19 percent of the popular vote, reflected the continuing decline of the electorate's partisan loyalties. Fearful of alienating its already fragile support among a public that has very little inclination to identify with partisan causes, the Clinton administration might resort to the same sort of executive leadership, dominated by plebiscitary appeals and institutional confrontation, that have diminished the place of party in American politics.

As America approached the twenty-first century, the decline of party reopened the old problem of how to constrain presidential ambition. The "emancipation" of the President from the constrictive grip of partisan politics has been closely linked to the transformation of the executive office from an institution of modest size and authority into a formidable institution invested with formal and informal powers that short-circuit the legislative process and judicial oversight. Yet, paradoxically, this more powerful and prominent Chief Executive has been reduced to virtually complete political isolation, deprived of the stable base of popular support once provided by political parties. Presidents must now build popular support on the uncertain foundation of public opinion and a diverse, as well as demanding, constellation of interest groups. The corrosion of presidential party politics also makes the nation vulnerable to the unchecked play of ambition the Framers of the Constitution feared, risking the dangers of "image" appeals and increased divisions among different political groups, exacerbated if not created by leaders operating under weakened restraints.

[See also (I) Political Parties; (II) Primaries, Presidential.]

BIBLIOGRAPHY

Bass, Harold F., Jr. "Chief of Party." In *Guide to the Presidency.* Edited by Michael Nelson. 1989.

Ceaser, James W. *Presidential Selection: Theory and Development.* 1979.

Cronin, Thomas E. "Presidents and Political Parties" In *Rethinking the Presidency.* Edited by Thomas E. Cronin. 1982.

Harmel, Robert, ed. *Presidents and Their Parties: Leadership or Neglect?* 1984.

Ketcham, Ralph. *Presidents Above Party, 1789–1829.* 1984.

Milkis, Sidney M. "The Presidency and Political Parties." In *The Presidency and the Political System.* 3d ed. Edited by Michael Nelson. 1990.

Ranney, Austin. "The President and His Party." In *Both Ends of the Avenue: The Presidency, the Executive Branch, and Congress in the 1980s.* Edited by Anthony King. 1983.

Wattenberg, Martin P. *The Rise of Candidate-Centered Politics: Presidential Elections in the 1980s.* 1991.

– SIDNEY M. MILKIS

PATRONAGE

The appointment of people to government jobs as a reward for past service and with the expectation of future political support is known as political patronage. Its widespread use in the federal government was introduced by Andrew Jackson, who argued that all government jobs were essentially simple and that incumbent government officials tended to abuse their power.

Though Jackson's use of patronage did not lead to the wholesale replacement of federal workers, he did provide the rationale for the transformation of limited patronage into the spoils system and its development over the next half-century.

The Spoils System

The spoils system, in which each newly elected President replaced government workers with political supporters, flourished in the mid nineteenth century and played an important role in the development of political parties in the United States. Reformers criticized the spoils system, arguing that it led to incompetence, inefficiency, corruption, and the need to train a new cadre of compaigners to do government jobs every four years. Further, the system's critics argued that the atmosphere created by the exchange of jobs for political support discouraged the best young people from serving in the government. Rather than representing a conflict over political principles, partisan political competition was reduced to a fight between those in office and those who wanted their jobs.

The argument of the reformers was moral as well as practical. As Theodore Roosevelt said in 1895, "The spoils system was more fruitful of degradation in our political life than any other that could possible have been invented. The spoils-monger, the man who peddled patronage, inevitably bred the vote-buyer, the vote-seller, and the man guilty of misfeasance in office." Presidents complained that they were reduced to petty job-brokers and that too much presidential time was taken up in making patronage decisions. In addition, many of the positions were effectively controlled by partisans in Congress, a reality that undercut the President's control of the executive branch.

One element of the patronage system was the practice of political assessment, in which an officeholder was expected to return a portion, often a fixed percentage, of the annual pay for the position to party coffers. Patronage not only provided government jobs but often conferred other benefits, including government contracts, land grants, and franchises. The modern counterparts of these benefits include grants, contracts, military bases, demonstration projects, and other public works and expenditures.

Defenders of the spoils system argued that it was crucial to the health of political parties and, in turn, that parties were essential to democracy. They also argued that lifetime tenure in government jobs led to arrogance and that frequent turnover in official positions was essential to a republican form of government. The patronage system also performed the important function of recruiting people to work for the government at a time when there was no other practical mechanism for doing so. Contemporary defenders of patronage argue that loyalists in the executive branch are necessary to ensure that the president's policy preferences are faithfully implemented.

Civil Service Reform

The arguments of the reformers came to fruition when Charles Guiteau, a disappointed office-seeker, assassinated President James A. Garfield in 1881. This act galvanized Congress to pass the Civil Service Act of 1883 (Pendleton Act), which created the merit system under which civil servants would be chosen on the basis of ability rather than party affiliation. The act also forbade executive-branch officials from making personnel decisions (hiring, firing, promotions, demotions) on a partisan basis. It also created the Civil Service Commission to run personnel recruitment for the government and act as a watchdog for the protection of merit principles.

Initially, the Pendleton Act covered only 10 percent of the civil service, giving Presidents the option of using executive orders to include (blanket in) other categories of workers, thus protecting their own political appointees from being dismissed by the next President. By the 1930s more than 70 percent of government workers were in the civil service, and by the 1980s well over 80 percent were covered.

The spoils system, however, continued to flourish in state and local governments, giving rise to the infamous political machines of the early twentieth century (which continued well into the century). But when federal aid became conditioned on the presence of merit criteria in state and local civil-service systems, state and local governments became much more professionalized. In the 1970s several Supreme Court cases limited the ability of political officials at the state level to remove government workers only on the basis of partisan affiliation unless it could be shown that partisanship was essential to the performance of the job.

As the merit system was extended in the twentieth century, patronage and political machines began to decline in importance. And in the mid-twentieth century political parties themselves began to decline as government began to be more professionalized. The widening scope of government's role and the increasing complexity of its functions demanded people with high levels of technical skills who were not traditional partisans. The domination of national politics by political parties was undercut by the growing importance of primary elections in the presidential nominating system. Party bosses no longer controlled presidential nominations, and the functions of organizing compaigns and raising money were taken over by individual candidate organizations and professional consultants.

White House Control

With the rise of the modern presidency the number of patronage appointments continued to shrink and the control of patronage began to shift from party organizations to the White House. This process began during the New Deal but accelerated as the White House staff expanded and took on increasingly important functions.

During the 1952 presidential campaign the Republican Party hired a consulting firm to advise Dwight D. Eisenhower on filling high-level political jobs, and in 1961 President John F. Kennedy began to reach beyond partisan politics with his talent hunt. The administration of Richard M. Nixon began the real professionalization of the Office of Presidential Personnel by bringing in professional executive recruiters from private-sector search firms.

The definition of loyalty shifted from partisan loyalty to ideological loyalty, especially in the Reagan administration.

The size of the White House personnel operation also increased, so that the job of handling patronage or political recruitment, which had been performed by a single staffperson in the Truman and Eisenhower administrations, was done by between thirty and sixty staffpeople in the Nixon administration. During the early years of the administration of Ronald Reagan, the presidential recruitment office employed about a hundred people. More than just size and degree of professionalism had changed however. The process of centralizing control of the executive branch in the White House was solidified by the policy of controlling all patronage or political appointments—agency heads as well as presidential appointments—from the White House.

The control of the government also shifted from partisan control by the Democratic or Republican Party to an emphasis on policy control. To gain policy control, competence as well as loyalty was necessary. The definition of loyalty also shifted from partisan loyalty to ideological loyalty, especially in the Reagan administration. In the administration of George Bush, personal loyalty and past service to the President were emphasized more than ideological loyalty. Under both Reagan and Bush there was also the growing realization that technical and managerial competence was also necessary for a successful presidential administration.

The increasing need for professional experts and managers to run the government constrained the use of patronage for purely political purposes. In the late twentieth century, the spoils system amounted to about two thousand honorary and part-time appointments to boards and commissions where political loyalty was a principal criterion for appointment.

At the highest level, the major political appointments available to each President include in the executive branch (including Cabinet secretaries and ambassadors) about 828 presidential appointments requiring confirmation by the Senate (PAS). Other full-time PAS appointments include about 187 U.S. attorneys and marshals and 956 federal judges, though a President would probably appoint only about 200 judges during a single term, since judges hold lifetime tenure. The immediate White House staff who serve at the pleasure of the President number about 438. Part-time Presidential appointments to commissions, boards, and councils number about 2,089.

At the next level down are noncareer (political) members of the Senior Executive Service (SES), which was created by the Civil Service Reform Act of 1978. These can number up to 10 percent of a total of seven thousand SES positions. Finally, there are about eighteen hundred Schedule C positions (at GS level 15 and below) available to each presidential administration. Noncareer SES and Schedule C positions are legally agency head appointments, but in practice the White House has heavily influenced who gets these appointments in recent administrations.

Some scholars distinguish between policy-determining positions, which must be filled by the President in order to control the executive branch, and those positions that are used merely to reward political supporters. They argue that the latter political patronage positions undermine the competence and continuity of government and are thus incompatible with the needs of a modern, technocratic government. In practice, however, it is extremely difficult to distinguish the needs of executive leadership and the desire to reward political supporters. Patronage has had a long history, and despite its shrinkage in the twentieth century, it will continue to play an influential role in politics.

BIBLIOGRAPHY

Henry, Laurin L. *Presidential Transitions.* 1960.

Mackenzie, G. Calvin. *The Politics of Presidential Appointments.* 1981.

Patterson, Bradley H., Jr. *The Ring of Power.* 1988.

Tolchin, Martin, and Susan Tolchin. *To the Victor: Political Patronage from the Clubhouse to the White House.* 1971.
Van Riper, Paul P. *History of the United States Civil Service.* 1958.
White, Leonard D. *The Republican Era.* 1958.

– JAMES P. PFIFFNER

PEACE CORPS

The Peace Corps was founded by President John F. Kennedy in 1961. It was established on the principle of people-to-people contact, the exchange of skills and ideas, and the hope that the individual experiences of Americans in developing countries can make the world a healthier, safer, and better place to live. Working at subsistence allowances, volunteers were to serve as teachers, health workers, community developers, agricultural advisers, childcare workers, nurses, physicians, and thirty-seven other job categories.

The actual program was presaged by a statement made on 14 October 1960 during the presidential campaign at the University of Michigan by the then Senator Kennedy. He was received enthusiastically by a student audience when he announced his intention to create a group of volunteers who would "serve a larger cause, the cause of freedom and the cause of a peaceful world. Peace Corps volunteers will demonstrate their interest in people who may live on the outside of the globe, who may live in misery but who, because of the presence of these Americans, live in hope."

Sargent Shriver, brother-in-law of the President, was appointed the director of the organization, which was initially created as an office in the White House. On 30 August 1961 the first group of American Peace Corps volunteers arrived in Ghana. Under the aegis of the Lyndon Johnson administration, the organization grew to encompass more than fifty countries with more than fifteen thousand volunteers, a number never again reached during the succeeding years. Though the organization became the single most lasting monument to the Kennedy administration, its numbers eroded considerably during the Vietnam War when Americans sought other ways to express their national and patriotic sentiments.

Under Executive Order 11603 of 1 July 1971 (36 Fed. Reg. 12675), the Peace Corps was transferred to the agency created by Reorganization Plan No. 1 of 1971 and designated as ACTION by President Richard M. Nixon. The ACTION Agency was established by law under Title IV of the Domestic Volunteer Service Act of 1973. Executive Order 12137 of 16 May 1979 superseded Executive Order 11603 but continued the policy of the Peace Corps operating as an agency within ACTION. Section 601 of the International Security and Development Cooperation Act of 1981 (Public Law 97–113), in amending the Peace Corps Act, removed the Peace Corps from ACTION and established the Peace Corps as an independent agency within the executive branch, effective 29 December 1981.

In the 1990s, six thousand volunteers, including large numbers of minorities and senior citizens, continued to serve in nearly ninety countries. Upon the collapse of the Eastern bloc nations in the late twentieth century, President George Bush assigned Peace Corps volunteers to Poland, Yugoslavia, and Czechoslovakia.

BIBLIOGRAPHY

Ashabranner, Brent. *A Moment in History: The First Ten Years of the Peace Corps.* 1971.

– JOSEPH F. MURPHY

POLICY, PRESIDENTIAL

A formal response to a specific problem that a President chooses to solve is known as *presidential policy.* Presidential policy is separated into three broad interest areas—economic, domestic, and foreign. Each policy area includes a number of specific programs administered by a variety of agencies of government.

Three Broad Categories

Economic policy includes policy on taxes, employment, inflation, money supply, economic development, public works and job training (which overlap the domestic policy area), trade policy (which overlaps the foreign policy area), and budget (which is sometimes separately treated as a fourth policy area). Economic policy is generally developed by three major policy-making bodies: the Department of the Treasury, the Council of Economic Advisers (CEA), and the Department of Commerce. Other institutional players become involved in specific subareas of economic policy—for example, the Federal Reserve Board on monetary policy, and the Secretary of Labor on employment and job-training policy.

Obviously, economic policy affects domestic and foreign policy, and vice versa. Rising unemployment may create pressure for protectionist trade policy even as it pushes health and welfare costs upward. Because such impacts are felt more directly on domestic income-support programs, economic policy is sometimes considered a subset of presidential domestic policy. However, the administrative hosts are sufficiently balkanized by professional ties and bureaucratic cultures that it is reasonable to think of economic and domestic policy as separate areas.

Even without economic policy in the mix, domestic policy represents a very broad category. In budget impact alone, domestic policy can be said to occupy almost three-quarters of the federal budget, including programs in areas as diverse as agriculture, aging, social security (which is sometimes considered an economic-policy area), aid to families with dependent children, health (which contains strong elements of economic policy in its price controls), veterans, children and youth, education, housing, occupational health and safety, transportation, environmental protection, food and drug regulation, consumer protection, criminal justice, drug control, national forests and parks, Indians, and oceans.

Aside from the departments of Defense, State, and Treasury and the parts of the Department of Commerce that are solely engaged in economic policy, virtually every other agency of government has a role in setting domestic policy, as do the White House domestic policy staff and the Office of Management and Budget (OMB). Domestic policy also engages the largest number of federal civilian employees, with the departments of Agriculture, Health and Human Services, Veterans Affairs, and Interior being the largest providers of policy advice and administration.

Because of the breadth of domestic policy, many presidential scholars break the area down into three subsets: health policy (including veterans programs, Medicare, and Medicaid), income security policy (including all welfare programs, veterans benefits, job-training programs, and sometimes Medicaid), and natural resources policy (including many programs administered by the departments of Interior and Agriculture as well as regulations enforced by the Environmental Protection Agency and the Occupational Health and Safety Administration). This kind of grouping led Richard M. Nixon to propose a "super-cabinet" that would have condensed the then-eleven Cabinet departments into four: natural resources, human resources, economic resources, and national security (Nixon's proposal failed).

Of the three broad policy areas, foreign policy may be the easiest to define. It includes defense and national security issues, human rights, international cooperation, foreign assistance and development, and trade. Foreign-policy programs are more neatly divided up than are those that fall under either domestic or economic policy. The lion's share of foreign-policy responsibility is located in three centers of advice and administration: the Department of Defense, the Department of State, and the National Security Council (NSC). As with economic policy, other institutional players come into the decision-making process on specific programs—for example, the Central Intelligence Agency (CIA) on national security policy and the National Security Agency on more specialized intelligence estimates.

As with both economic and domestic policy, overlaps are notable and frequent in the foreign-policy area. Thus, even though these three policy areas retain their descriptive value, it is important to note that the lines between the three have blurred substantially. International events have profound domestic impacts, and the solutions to domestic problems are increasingly international in reach. In addition, economic problems appear to influence virtually every decision made in either domestic or foreign policy, either because of budgetary constraints or international implications. Thus, it may be increasingly appropriate to refer to presidential policy as a singular phenomenon that, depending on the subject, will have primary impacts on one or more of the three policy areas.

Types of Programs

The three functional categories can be combined with descriptions based on the nature of the specific program or proposal in order to provide a more detailed understanding of presidential policy. As Mark Peterson argues in *Legislating Together,*

> If we are to understand fully the processes by which the President and Congress make legislative choices, and if we are to evaluate the policy-making capacity of both institutions, including giving meaning to the notion of presidential 'success,' then it is essential that careful efforts be made to distinguish among various kinds of policy initiatives.

Thus, in addition to sorting presidential policy by genus (economic, domestic, and foreign) and species (aging, national security, tax, etc.), scholars also describe policy by reference to at least seven additional categories.

Domestic policy can be said to occupy almost three-quarters of the federal budget.

First, presidential policy can be described as either *substantive* or *symbolic.* Presidents are under no obligation to solve a given problem in economic, domestic, or foreign affairs with a new program, or, for that matter, to take any action at all. They can and sometimes do let history take its own course, weighing in with symbolic gestures—among which commissions, studies, and task forces are time-honored devices—in lieu of programmatic action.

Second, policy can be described by its intended effects, whether to *distribute* a set of benefits to all citizens and/or groups, *redistribute* a set of benefits from one class or group of citizens to another, or *regulate* the behavior of citizens, groups, corporations, and other actors in a given policy area through rules and the threat of sanctions. The 1983 social security reform package might be considered an example of another type of policy in which almost all citizens lost benefits, whether through reduced benefits and delays in cost-of-living adjustments for retirees or higher taxes for corporations and workers.

Third, policy can be described by its enactment mechanism—that is, whether it is to be adopted through the legislative, administrative, or judicial channel. Some presidential policies are adopted through executive orders or another administrative strategy; others must be enacted by Congress; and still others move through the courts. Presidential domestic policy, for example, is heavily focused on Congress, since so much of the President's agenda must be enacted to have impact.

Fourth and fifth, policy can be described by its size (large- or small-scale) and scope (is it a new, untested initiative or a modification of an old idea that already has constituents?). All presidential policies are not created equal: some programs have greater scale, others are relatively limited experiments. Ultimately, descriptions of programs' size and scope are most telling when they are combined, characterizing given proposals as large-new, large-old, small-new, or small-old. As John Campbell argues,

> Large-new decisions are the sort one reads about in cases studies and the agenda-setting literature; a good example for the aging policy area in America is Medicare. . . . At the extreme, these decisions have a large fiscal impact and they significantly alter the relations among social groups or between state and society.

Sixth, policy can be described by its implementation focus—that is, whether it is to be managed by federal, state, or local government, by the nonprofit sector, or by individuals who are required to report to government, whether as citizens who file tax returns or corporations that file hazardous waste permits. Implementation focus is particularly important for explaining who the public will hold accountable for how a certain policy fares. By devolving responsibility to state and local governments, for example, a President can distance his administration from direct responsibility while at the same time, however, losing some control over outcomes and diminishing his ability to claim credit should the program succeed.

Seventh, policy can be described by the tool it employs to achieve its desired ends. Presidents have a number of different options at their disposal—grants, tax expenditures, direct provision of services, and so on. Each tool carries both strengths and weaknesses. Cash assistance (as in welfare, for example) is easy to administer but much less attractive politically than some other tools.

Ultimately, policy is best viewed as a concrete expression of the President's goals, which can in turn be separated into three general categories: reelection, historical achievement, and good policy. In searching for policy ideas to match those goals, Presidents pay attention to a variety of different sources but rely primarily on Congress, current events, and the agencies and departments of government.

[See also (II) Foreign Affairs: An Overview.]

BIBLIOGRAPHY

Campbell, John. "Japanese Policy and the Old People Boom." *Journal of Japanese Policy Studies* 5(1981): 329–350.
Peterson, Mark. *Legislating Together.* 1991.
Salamon, Lester. *Beyond Privatization. The Tools of Government.* 1989.

– PAUL C. LIGHT

POLLS AND POPULARITY

Public opinion polls of the American electorate have become the dominant way of assessing the popularity of the President of the United States. These polls are conducted regularly by news organizations such as the joint efforts of the *New York Times* and CBS News or ABC News and the *Washington Post* as well as by polling outfits such as the Gallup Organization. Typically, these polls ask Americans their general opinion of the performance of the President and often ask more specific questions about presidential performance in the realms of the domestic economy and foreign policy. For example, a *New York Times*-CBS News poll asked the following battery of questions about the popularity of President George Bush: "Do you approve or disapprove of the way George Bush is handling his job as President?" "Do you approve or disapprove of the way George Bush is handling foreign policy?" and "Do you approve or disapprove of the way George Bush is handling the economy?"

With such questions, the President's popularity rating is simply the percentage of the citizenry that approves of his performance. Other questions that have been used to measure presidential popularity include "How would you rate the job that is doing as President? Excellent, good, only fair, or poor?" Here the percentage of respondents who replied "excellent" or "good" are combined to produce the measure of presidential popularity.

There are a number of points to be made about patterns and trends in presidential popularity. First, approval levels can change dramatically over a short period of time. For example, the onset of an international crisis in which the President exercises dramatic leadership, addresses the American public on television, holds a televised press conference, and the like is sometimes associated with a sharp increase in presidential popularity, an increase that often fades as the crisis ebbs. There is a marked tendency for Americans to support the President in the face of a foreign threat or challenge.

There is a marked tendency for Americans to support the President in the face of a foreign threat or challenge.

Second, Americans may give the President good grades on one issue, yet strongly disapprove of his performance in regard to another. For example, in March 1991, during the height of the Gulf War, Americans overwhelmingly approved of George Bush's overall performance by a margin of 88 percent to 8 percent with 4 percent unsure in a poll conducted by the *New York Times* and CBS News. Not surprisingly, 83 percent of the people polled in that same survey also approved of the President's handling of foreign policy. But when it came to the handling of the economy, 43 percent of Americans disapproved of the President's performance and only 42 percent approved. In this example, it is clear that citizens' overall evaluations of the President were determined by the issue most salient to them at the time—the Gulf War. But as the war receded in the public's consciousness and the condition of the economy became the prominent issue, the public's assessment of George Bush changed dramatically. Thus, in another *New York Times*-CBS News poll conducted a year later, the President's overall approval rating had plummeted to 39 percent (with 50 percent disapproving), his economic performance was evaluated even more negatively (21 percent approval versus 73 percent disapproval), while his handling of foreign policy still enjoyed support, though diminished (50 percent approval versus 41 percent disapproval).

Third, Americans are not homogeneous in their evaluations of Presidents. That is, different subgroups of Americans are more likely or less likely to be supportive of the President. For example, when Americans are examined according to their political party preferences, strong differences emerge. Throughout the Reagan and Bush Administrations, Americans who identified themselves as Republicans were most supportive of the President, Democrats were least supportive, and independents were somewhere in between. Other breakdowns such as by gender and race are routinely done and differences in presidential support are often observed. For example, blacks during the Reagan and Bush administrations were less supportive of the President than whites (in part because blacks are heavily Democratic in their partisan orientations) and women were less supportive than men.

While many observers welcome the opportunity that public opinion polls provide for citizens to voice their views about the performance of their leaders and their government, other observers worry that the presidential popularity polls distort politics and government in a number of ways. First, the results of the polls have become a major news story in and of themselves. This is especially worrisome since in many instances the media that report the news are also generating it through their sponsorship of polls. More attention becomes devoted to the President's political standing as measured in the polls and less is given to an analysis of the substantive activities of government. Some observers worry that the polls are too influential with respect to presidential decision making. They argue that Presidents who carry the latest polls in their pockets are more likely to govern with an eye toward what is popular rather than what is sound. They worry that the heavy emphasis on presidential popularity polls may lead administrations to be overly dependent on political ploys and gimmicks designed to increase poll ratings in the short term to the detriment of long range problem solving that may entail risks of unpopular decisions. Finally, observers worry that the polls may give a misleading portrait of the condition of the country and the performance of the President; they argue that popularity is not synonymous with successful leadership and that other indicators of performance ratings may encourage leaders to ignore that part of the American public whose dissatisfaction with the President and the government is rooted in deep and fundamental policy concerns. Despite these concerns about how surveys of presidential popularity are used and interpreted, it is clear that public opinion polling is so central to the fabric of American political life and discourse that analyses of presidential popularity will inevitably depend largely on the results provided by polls.

[See also (II) Media and the President.]

BIBLIOGRAPHY

Asher, Herbert B. *Polling and the Public.* 2d ed. 1992.

Kernell, Samuel. *Going Public: New Strategies of Presidential Leadership.* 1986.

Mueller, John E. *War, Presidents, and Public Opinion.* 1973.

— HERBERT B. ASHER

POSTMASTER GENERAL

From 1789 until 1971 the Postmaster General was appointed by, and reported to, the President. Their relationship after 1829, when Andrew Jackson became President and made Postmaster General William T. Barry a member of his Cabinet, was a close one. Not only did the Postmaster General often serve as the President's chief political adviser, he also had more jobs to award to party supporters than any other Cabinet member. Often, the person appointed Postmaster General had chaired the President's political party.

After 1836, the President directly appointed postmasters in larger post offices and the Postmaster General named postmasters of the smaller offices. Postmasters were valuable "agents for disseminating information," according to President James Buchanan. He believed in rotating postmasterships, so one position could be used to reward several supporters. Removals and resignations of postmasters sometimes took place at a dizzying rate, although a few Presidents and Postmasters General preferred to remove postmasters only for cause.

The story is told that Postmaster General John McLean was asked by the third President under which he served, Jackson, whether he objected to removing postmasters who had been active politically in the last campaign. McLean replied that he did not if the removal policy operated against Jackson's supporters as well as Adams's. Jackson offered McLean a seat on the Supreme Court instead. McLean accepted.

Andrew Jackson's presidency marked the beginning of a close relationship between the Postmaster General and the President. Jackson's Postmaster General became a member of his Cabinet. (Library of Congress, Prints and Photographs Division)

During Andrew Johnson's Presidency and over his veto, the Tenure of Office Act was passed, making it illegal to remove certain postmasters from their positions without the consent of the Senate. The act was also interpreted to mean that heads of departments should hold office during the term of the appointing President and for one month thereafter, subject to the Senate's advice and consent. The act was repealed in 1869 but a postal code adopted in 1872 continued that provision for the Postmaster General. It remained in effect until the Postal Reorganization Act of 1970.

Theodore Roosevelt's presidency marked an end to the nineteenth century's postal purges, but the positions of postmasters and, later, rural carriers remained political appointments until 1969 when President Richard Nixon and Postmaster General Winton M. Blount jointly announced an end to political appointments in the Post Office Department. A year later, the Postal Reorganization Act was passed and the appointment of the Postmaster General was depoliticized.

The act removed the Postmaster General from the President's Cabinet and his appointment. Instead, the Postmaster General is selected by nine presidentially appointed postal governors, no more than half of them of the same political party, and the Postmaster General serves at the governor's discretion. To date, the governors have chosen business leaders or postal officers to serve as the chief executive officer of the nation's largest civilian organization, the United States Postal Service.

[See also (II) United States Postal Service.]

BIBLIOGRAPHY

Fowlser, Dorothy Ganfield. *The Cabinet Politician.* 1943.

– MEGAERA HARRIS

PRESENTATION CLAUSE

The Constitution's presentation clause is one of several provisions that ensure presidential involvement in the legislative process. According to Article I, Section 7, "Every Bill which shall have passed the House of Representatives and the Senate, shall, before it becomes a Law, be presented to the President of the United States." Upon a bill's presentation, the President may either approve the bill by signing it within ten days, veto the bill and return it to the house of origin, veto the bill by withholding the executive signature if Congress has made return impossible by adjourning in the intervening time. Or, if Congress is still in session, allow the bill to become law after ten days by not signing it.

Article I, Section 7, further stipulates that "every Order, Resolution, or Vote to which the Concurrence of the Senate and House of Representatives may be necessary . . . shall be presented to the President . . . before the Same shall take Effect." This paragraph was added to avoid a situation in which Congress might seek to avoid presidential review of legislation by giving it some other name.

At the Constitutional Convention there was general agreement that the President should retain final say over legislation. Even though the President must deal with legislation within ten days of presentation, considerable flexibility exists regarding the actual presentation process. After a bill is passed by both houses of Congress, actual presentation may be delayed if the President is out of the country or otherwise indisposed. The U.S. Court of Claims, in *Eber Bros. Wine and Liquor Corp.* v. *United States* (1964), ruled that during a presidential absence Congress can present bills to the President abroad, hold them for presentation until the President's return, or present bills at the White House as though the President were there.

The question of presentation played a key role in a constitutional challenge of the legislative veto. The Supreme Court ruled in *INS* v. *Chadha* (1983) that the congressional practice of using simple and concurrent resolutions to control executive-branch actions was unconstitutional. Despite the fact that legislative vetoes were previously created in bills passed through the regular legislative process, including presentation to the President, the Court held that this power unconstitutionally avoided presentation.

Presentation is not required for congressional enactments that are expressions of opinion or that involve internal administrative matters. Article V of the Constitution also avoids presentation by allowing Congress to propose constitutional amendments by a two-thirds vote in both chambers, at which point proposed amendments are sent directly to the states for ratification.

[See also (I) Veto, article on Presidential Veto; (II) Veto, Pocket; Veto, Regular.]

BIBLIOGRAPHY

Craig, Barbara Hinkson. *Chadha: The Story of an Epic Constitutional Struggle.* 1988.

Fisher, Louis. *Constitutional Conflicts between Congress and the President.* 3d rev. ed. 1991.

Spitzer, Robert J. *The Presidential Veto: Touchstone of the American Presidency.* 1988.

— ROBERT J. SPITZER

PRESIDENT (TITLE)

At the Constitutional Convention of 1787 the Framers wrestled with the thorny issue of creating and titling the office of Chief Executive of the United States. Much attention was paid to determining the nature of the office, the manner of election, term of office, and whether the executive should be a collegial body or a single person and, if the latter, whether there should be a mandated advisory council. Little discussion was devoted to the title of the office and its incumbent.

The presiding officers of the Continental Congress and the Constitutional Convention were called presidents.

What emerged from some sixteen weeks of deliberation (25 May–17 September) was a single executive whom the Constitution denominates as "President of the United States of America" (Article II, Section 1). This presidency is unique in that the incumbent is vested with full executive power and authority, is responsible to the people rather than to Congress, and serves as both chief of state and head of government, whereas in most other countries these are two separate offices and in democratic systems the head of government is responsible to the legislature.

In the process of designing this office, the Framers drew titular precedents from sources such as the American colonial and state governments, the Continental Congress, and the Articles of Confederation. The presiding officers of the Continental Congress and the Constitutional Convention were called presidents. At the time, however, no national executive bore this title, and subsequently only governments that employed the American model, such as Latin American republics and the Philippines, possess a similar executive office and title.

During the deliberations of the Convention—in the Virginia Plan (29 May), the Report of the Committee of the Whole (13 June), the New Jersey Plan (15 June), and the Resolution Referred to the Committee of Detail (26 July)—the office was generically referred to as a national or federal executive, or simply as the executive. Alternative expressions suggested during these considerations and in commentary were "Supreme Executive," "Magistracy, Executive Magistracy, or Magistrate," and "Governor of the United States of America."

It was not until 6 August, when the Committee of Detail—which prepared the actual draft of the Constitution—submitted its report, that the executive was designated the "President of the United States of America" (in Article II). It appears that this title is attributable to James Wilson, who prepared the draft, and that it was not debated at the Convention.

From documentation and analysis it may be inferred that the decision on this title may have been influenced by several factors. First, there was the desire to avoid any semblance of monarchism or aristocracy. Second, until late in the convention's deliberations, the collegial executive proposed may have consisted of a presiding officer, or president, and a council. Third, the emerging executive office in four states (Delaware, New Hampshire, Pennsylvania, and South Carolina) bore the title president instead of governor. Fourth, there was the precedent of the presiding officer of the Continental Congress employing the title "President of the United States of America" for certain purposes. And, finally, there was the simple fact that George Washington, who was universally expected to become the first chief executive under the Constitution, already held the title president as presiding officer of the Constitutional Convention.

In practice, the title of the presidency is expressed in three forms. It is generally specified as "the President," as evidenced by some fifteen references in the Constitution. In some cases it is formally designated as "President of the United States," as in the presidential oath of office. When used in foreign affairs, it is the "President of the United States of America," as in the presidential signing of international instruments such as the Treaty of Versailles (Woodrow Wilson, 1919), the United Nations Declaration (Franklin D. Roosevelt, 1942), and certain arms control treaties (beginning with Richard M. Nixon, 1972) and when it is necessary to distinguish this country from other federations, such as Brazil or Mexico.

The final aspect of the presidential title is the fashion in which the President is addressed. Various forms were discussed during the Constitutional Convention and the First Congress (including "Elective Majesty," "Elective Highness" or "Serene Highness," and "Protector of the Rights of the United States"). Wilson, in his draft constitution, denominated the President as "His Excellency," but this was not included in the final version of the Constitution. As a consequence, the President is officially addressed as "Mr. President." As far as formal protocol is concerned, in correspondence the President's title is simply "The President" (or, in foreign relations, "The President of the United States of America") and orally the President is addressed as "Mr. President."

[See also (II) Chief Executive, Executive Power.]

BIBLIOGRAPHY

Farrand, Max. *The Framing of the Constitution.* 1926.
Farrand, Max, ed. *The Records of the Federal Convention of 1787.* 4 vols. 1966.
Hart, James. *The American Presidency in Action, 1789.* 1948.
Rossiter, Clinton. *1787—The Grand Convention: A Study in Constitutional History.* 1948.
Thach, Charles C., Jr. *The Creation of the Presidency, 1775–1789: A Study in Constitutional History.* 1969.

– ELMER PLISCHKE

PRESIDENT'S FOREIGN INTELLIGENCE ADVISORY BOARD (PFIAB)

The President's Foreign Intelligence Advisory Board is the highest-level advisory committee in the U.S. government. The PFIAB was first established in February 1956 by President Dwight D. Eisenhower and was then called the President's Board of Consultants on Foreign Intelligence Activities. Dr. James R. Killian, Jr., president of the Massachusetts Institute of Technology, was its first chairman. When John F. Kennedy was elected President in 1960, he initially decided to abolish the board as a "useless impediment." But after the fiasco of the Bay of Pigs invasion in April 1961 he quickly reestablished the board, giving it its current name. The President's Foreign Intelligence Advisory Board has played an important role in guiding America's intelligence policy ever since—except for the four-year hiatus after President Jimmy Carter abolished it in 1977. President Ronald Reagan, by Executive Order 12331, reestablished the board on 20 October 1981.

The board's duties and responsibilities are broad. As spelled out in the executive order establishing it, the "Board shall assess the quality, quantity, and adequacy of intelligence collection, of analysis and estimates, of counterintelligence, and other intelligence activities. The Board shall have the authority to continually review the performance of all agencies of the Government [including the Central Intelligence Agency, the Department of Defense, and the Federal Bureau of Investigation] that are engaged in the collection, evaluation, or production of intelligence or the execution of intelligence policy." The board also is given the authority to assess the "adequacy of management, personnel, and organization in the intelligence agencies."

As set forth in Executive Order 12331 the members of the board, who serve without compensation, are appointed directly by the President and are supposed to be chosen from "trustworthy and distinguished citizens outside the Government who are qualified on the basis of achievement, experience, and independence." The board reports directly to the President, although as a practical matter much of the work of the board is conducted with the President's top national security and intelligence advisers. The board is authorized to directly "advise and make recommendations to the Director of Central Intelligence, the CIA, and other Government agencies engaged in intelligence." All members of the board have access to all information necessary to carry out its duties in the possession of any agency in the Government.

The PFIAB, like its smaller sister, the President's Intelligence Oversight Board (PIOB), derives most of its power and influence from its ability to access highly classified information and to deal directly with the President. While it shares with the PIOB the weaknesses of not having a large investigative staff or subpoena powers, it does have a much larger membership, often twenty or more, and a substantially larger staff. Moreover, the domain of PFIAB, unlike that of PIOB, is policy, not policing. In the area of intelligence policy, a board of twenty or more highly competent people, backed by a half a dozen or so professional staff members, can be a formidable force.

During the 1980s the board included such distinguished men and women as Frank Borman, the former astronaut; W. Glenn Campbell, the director of the Hoover Institution; John B. Connally, former governor of Texas; Alan Greenspan, noted economist; Leon Jaworski, the former director of the Office of the Watergate special prosecutor; Claire Booth Luce, former ambassador to Italy; H. Ross Perot, chairman of Electronic Data Systems Corporation; and Edward Bennett Williams, the noted lawyer.

The PFIAB is the classic example of an outside group of private citizens, not on the public payroll, directly advising the President on important policy matters.

While the work that PFIAB has done is unusually highly classified and every member is required on appointment to sign an agreement "never to reveal any classified information obtained by virtue of his or her service with the Board except to the President or to such persons as the President may designate," there have been a few published studies that give some clues concerning the type of issues and problems with which the board is concerned. Some of the things that PFIAB has dealt with in the past include control and coordination of the intelligence community, particularly in the area of covert operations; improved strategic warning systems of a possible nuclear attack on the United States; management of the National Security Agency; the general development and improvement of U.S. intelligence capabilities; improvement of methods of handling sensitive intelligence; more effective coordination and evaluation of covert action; review of CIA paramilitary operations; investigations into satellite reconnaissance systems; and analysis of deficiencies in the collection and analysis of intelligence from Southeast Asia.

To a certain degree the PFIAB does for U.S. intelligence what civilian control in the Department of Defense does for the military. The board is only a part-time board and it has no power of command, but its presence has proved to be a healthy one for U.S. intelligence.

The power and influence of the PFIAB has risen and fallen under different administrations. It was strong under Eisenhower. After a shaky start with Kennedy it regained its foothold and continued strong through Lyndon B. Johnson, Richard M. Nixon, and Gerald Ford. After its demise under Carter, it was resurrected by Reagan and from 1981 to 1985 it regained the kind of influence it had had under Eisenhower. But in October 1985, President Reagan, on the advice of staff, sharply reduced the membership of the board from twenty-one to fourteen, cutting its effectiveness. President George Bush, a former Director of the CIA, went even further and slashed the membership back to six people early in his first term.

The PFIAB is the classic example of an outside group of private citizens, not on the public payroll, directly advising the President on important policy matters. Such a group of outside advisers can be a bracing tonic for any President, helping him to keep from becoming insulated and isolated from the bad news that White House staff is often reluctant to deliver. Unfortunately, outside advisory groups of private citizens are often seen as threats by the President's closest advisers, especially the insecure ones, and these advisory groups are perpetually the subject of abolition attempts.

[See also (II) Central Intelligence Agency.]

BIBLIOGRAPHY

Anderson, Martin. *Revolution.* 1988
Cline, Ray S. *The CIA under Reagan, Bush, and Casey.* 1981
The President's Foreign Intelligence Advisory Board (PFIAB). 1981.

– MARTIN ANDERSON

PRESIDENT'S INTELLIGENCE OVERSIGHT BOARD (PIOB)

The President's Intelligence Oversight Board was first established by President Gerald Ford on 17 February

1976 by Executive Order 11905. Its creation was a direct result of a series of allegations and revelations of improper activity by elements of the U.S. intelligence community. This small, virtually unknown board of three people appointed by the President is charged with the daunting task of keeping U.S. intelligence agencies honest and operating within the law. Reporting directly to the President, the board has potential access to the most secret intelligence information. This combination of knowledge and access to the President gives the Board its potential power.

The formal duties of the Intelligence Oversight Board are to inform the President of intelligence activities that any member of the board believes are in violation of the Constitution or of the laws governing the United States, executive orders, or presidential directives; to forward to the Attorney General reports received concerning intelligence activities that the board believes may be unlawful; to review the internal guidelines of each agency within the intelligence community concerning the lawfulness of intelligence activities; to review the practices and procedures of the inspectors general and general counsel of the intelligence community for discovering and reporting intelligence activities that may be unlawful or contrary to executive order or presidential directives; and to conduct such investigations as the board deems necessary to carry out its function under this order.

The idea of an independent presidential advisory group, acting as a watchdog on the U.S. intelligence community, has enjoyed broad support since its inception in 1976, even though the results have not been as desirable as hoped for. The events that led up the Iran-contra affair in the mid 1980s entirely escaped the attention of the Intelligence Oversight Board until the scandal burst into public view. In hindsight this should not have been unexpected. Although the PIOB does have the authority to request classified material of any nature and reports directly to the President, its powers do not match its responsibilities.

The PIOB operates with a tiny staff, essentially a secretary and an executive director, and does not have the administrative support to conduct thorough, comprehensive investigations on its own. Nor does it have the power to subpoena witnesses and compel testimony, even in cases of national security. As presently constituted, the board must rely primarily on what others report and on its own judgment regarding the questions it puts to high-ranking members of the intelligence agencies. To a great degree the board relies on moral suasion and the reflected authority of the President.

[See also (II) Central Intelligence Agency.]

BIBLIOGRAPHY

Anderson, Martin. *Revolution.* 1988.

Sciaroni, Bretton G. "The Theory and Practice of Executive Branch Intelligence Oversight." *Harvard Journal of Law & Public Policy* 12 (Spring 1989): 397–432.

– MARTIN ANDERSON

PRESS CONFERENCES

The presidential press conference is a permanent feature of the modern presidency. It is a forum of executive presentation that has proved to be a fixed aspect of presidential leadership, yet it is flexible in that a President may choose to use it in different ways. Each President since Franklin D. Roosevelt has felt the need to publicly respond to the queries of newspeople, but Presidents have varied widely in the degree to which they have enjoyed the experience and found it a useful tool.

Even though reporters choose the questions, Presidents and their staffs make fairly accurate predictions about the nature of the questions that will be posed.

Both Presidents and reporters grouse about press conferences, but these events work to the advantage of both sides in Presidents' press relations. Both find them useful forums for explanations of presidential policy, goals, and actions. Such forums are to the President's advantage because he can meet with the press in a place of his choosing and at a time of his liking. He can choose to answer questions as he wishes, with reporters unable to force him to respond to unwanted queries. On the other side, the news media regard news conferences as events worth covering. Unlike many other events, the press conference is one in which news organizations play a significant role. Their reporters have the opportunity to shape the questioning without guidance or control from the White House.

Development of Press Conferences

The routine relationship between reporters and the President crystalized during the administration of Theodore Roosevelt. He set aside a room for the use of the press and spoke regularly with a select group of reporters. In the afternoons he would regularly meet with half a dozen reporters while he was being shaved by the White House barber. Roosevelt's remarks to reporters were off the record; their value lay in reporters' gaining a greater understanding of the President's policies and actions. The opportunity to query the President regularly proved useful for both sides: it produced better-informed news stories, and, from the President's viewpoint, those stories were more favorable than they might otherwise have been.

Even after the dynamic Roosevelt left office, reporters remained very interested in presidential news. If the President did not provide it, people on his staff had to. While William Howard Taft met sporadically with groups of reporters during his years in the White House, Woodrow Wilson formally established the regularly scheduled press conference. Wilson decided that he would rather direct the distribution of information than let others do it for him. In 1913 and 1914, he met with reporters on Mondays and Thursdays; in 1915, he met with them once a week, on Tuesdays. After 1915 the conferences dropped off due to increasing international tension, as evidenced by the sinking of the British luxury liner *Lusitania.*

Two central features of the format established by Wilson remain: press conferences are open to reporters who are eligible to cover the President, and the reporters lead the questioning. Present practice differs, however, in that the President can call a conference whenever he likes rather than on a predetermined day of the week. Too, press conferences are now broadcast live on television, as they have been since the John F. Kennedy administration. Obviously, at formal press conferences the President's remarks are for direct attribution. As an instrument of policy making, particularly domestic policy, which relies heavily on Congress for its enactment, the press conference has continued to be an important element of presidential leadership of public opinion. Press conferences have been especially important when the President is actively promoting a legislative agenda and experiencing good political weather. Thus it became a central part of Franklin Roosevelt's publicity strategies when he was pushing congressional enactment of the New Deal agenda. During World War II, however, Roosevelt's conferences fell off from their earlier twice-weekly schedule.

Roosevelt's successors have found that the press conference has become an indispensable event on the presidential calendar. The average number of press conferences per month from the administration of Franklin Roosevelt through the third year of the George Bush administration, however, fell from 6.9 (for Roosevelt) to around 2 (for Eisenhower, Kennedy, and Johnson), to a low of 0.5 (for Richard M. Nixon). Gerald Ford (1.3) and Jimmy Carter (1.2) met more frequently with the press, but Ronald Reagan matched Nixon's low. George Bush (3.3) nearly matched Harry S Truman's frequency (3.4). While each President has felt the need to have press conferences, not all have done so on a regular basis. In the period since Eisenhower was President, when an average of two conferences were held per month, only Presidents Johnson and Bush have met that standard.

Difficulties with Press Conferences

Right from the beginning of his presidency, President Nixon was loath to hold press conferences because he and his staff believed that reporters were hostile to him and his programs. His press conferences were consistently contentious. Fed by antagonisms that had built up over the years of the Vietnam War and the Watergate affair, when the White House was less than forthcoming with information the press sought, relations between the President and the press hit a low point that was reached in the Carter years. Reporters' questioning was viewed by officials (and by the public) as rude. Ultimately, the contentiousness lessened during President Bush's first term because of the frequency of his press conferences. Reporters knew they would be able to ask Bush questions and stopped competing for the President's attention in an indecorous manner.

Press conferences are just one strategy in a President's publicity arsenal. He chooses those forums in which he is most comfortable. President Reagan appeared best in settings that were scripted. His finest public hours were speeches in which he captured and articulated the public mood, such as the speech marking the anniversary of the Normandy landing and the speech memoralizing the astronauts killed in the explosion of the *Challenger* space shuttle. His habit of summarizing programs and goals in terms of particular cases and anecdotes caused him trouble in press conferences and left his White House Press Office staff with considerable work to explain and refine his statements. Presidents Carter and Ford were quite adept at handling their press conferences, but both avoided using them when they faced severe criticism, such as when Ford pardoned Nixon and, similarly, when Carter was criticized for his mishandling of the Iranian hostage crisis.

Advantages and Disadvantages

Even though reporters choose the questions, Presidents and their staffs are able to make fairly accurate predictions about the nature of the questions that will be posed. White House staff members keep briefing books to make sure that the President is familiar with administration policy and actions. Before a conference, time is spent going over possible responses to the anticipated questions. Yet many Presidents regard such work a waste of time. For example, in the summer of 1979, President

Carter stopped holding frequent conferences despite his proficiency in answering questions. Presidents find other disadvantages to them as well. There is always the danger that the President will misstate himself in a way that will have important policy, particularly foreign policy, implications. Presidents fear they will lose more than they gain through their appearances with reporters. They do not like being put in a position of having to deal with questions they would prefer not to.

For most Presidents, however, the advantages of press conferences outweigh the disadvantages. By scheduling and location, a President can control whether a press conference constitutes a high- or low-profile event. If a President wants to appear in command and with the full trappings of the office, as President Reagan preferred, he will schedule his conferences in the East Room of the White House at an evening hour when he is most likely to get the largest audience. If, on the other hand, the President wants to make his conferences low-profile events, as President Bush chose to do in his first term, he may schedule them very frequently and hold them in the Press Room of the White House or in the auditorium in the Executive Office Building.

The press conference has served as an excellent forum for the President to command national attention. When the President wants to explain a policy or action but does not want to do so in a formal speech before Congress or to the nation, a press conference is often a suitable arena. He can explain policy in his own terms, deciding how he wants to answer questions and free from the pressure of being forced to discuss something he would rather not. He can establish the conference's agenda and, hence, to some extent, the news media's agenda for the following day. The press conference represents one important way for him to dominate the national political scene. When he calls a conference, news organizations and the public generally listen.

[See also (II) Media and the President.]

BIBLIOGRAPHY

Cornwell, Elmer. *Presidential Leadership of Public Opinion.* 1965.

Grossman, Michael Baruch, and Martha Joynt Kumar. *Portraying the President: The White House and the News Media.* 1981.

Kernell, Samuel. *Going Public: New Strategies of Presidential Leadership.* 1986.

Lammers, William. "Presidential Press Conference Schedules: Who Hides, and When." *Political Science Quarterly* 96 (1981): 261–278.

Maltese, John. *Spin Control: The White House Office of Communications and the Management of Presidential News.* 1992.

Manheim, Jarol. "The Honeymoon's Over: The News Conference and the Development of Presidential Style." *Journal of Politics* 41 (1979): 55–75.

Pollard, James E. *Presidents and the Press.* 1964.

Smith, Carolyn. *Presidential Press Conferences: A Critical Approach.* 1990.

— MARTHA KUMAR

PRIMARIES, PRESIDENTIAL

While state presidential primaries are today the major determinant in deciding who will become the nominees of the major political parties for the nation's highest office, their major influence is a relatively recent development. In the first two presidential elections, in 1789 and 1792, there were no nominations separate from the general election process. The members of the political elite from the various states, acting through the mechanism of the Electoral College, chose George Washington by unanimous vote. People of different political persuasions believed that the nation's revered military leader would take the interests of all American citizens into account.

Early Nominating Procedures

Cleavages soon appeared, however, that led to the formation of two major political parties. The Federalist Party, led by Washington and Alexander Hamilton, represented mercantile interests that favored the creation of a national bank (the Bank of the United States) and created a tariff to protect our manufacturers and merchants from competition from abroad. The rival Democratic-Republicans, represented by Thomas Jefferson and James Madison, opposed the Federalist program on the grounds that it benefited only mercantile interests and not the nation's farmers, with whom they had close ties. By the mid-1790s the two blocs were voting against each other in Congress, and congressional candidates were in effect running as Federalists and Democratic-Republicans. Washington stepped down from the presidency in 1797, and party politics spread from the Congress to the nation's highest office. Since that date the major political parties have experimented with a number of mechanisms designed to nominate the presidential candidates who will run against each other in the general election.

As late as 1968, only seventeen states used presidential primaries to select convention delegates.

The first such mechanism was the congressional caucus. In this mechanism, members of the national legislature from the two parties formed caucuses, each of which nominated its own presidential candidate. Already convened in the nation's capital, with a knowledge of potential presidential candidates from all over the country, these caucuses provided peer review by members of Congress, who assessed the skills and abilities of persons seeking the presidency. The method had some serious faults. It violated the separation of powers principle of the constitution by giving members of the legislative branch a major role in choosing the President. Moreover, a party's caucus did not represent those areas that that party had lost in the previous congressional election, not to mention excluding interested and involved citizens who participated in party activities, particularly campaigns. It became impractical for the Federalists when their congressional delegation was so reduced that it ceased to provide adequate geographical representation. The Republicans utilized it between 1800 and 1820 to nominate three Virginians—Jefferson, Madison, and James Monroe—each of whom served as President for two terms. In 1824, however, when the Democratic-Republicans (as the party was now known) attempted to nominate Secretary of the Treasury William H. Crawford three-fourths of the Democratic-Republican members of Congress who were friends of Andrew Jackson boycotted the meeting.

For a short period the nomination of presidential candidates was vested primarily in the states, where legislators and conventions chose favorite sons such as Andrew Jackson and John Quincy Adams as presidential candidates. In 1824, four candidates were nominated, and, although Jackson won more popular votes than any of the others, he did not secure a majority of the electoral votes, and the election was thrown into the House of Representatives, which chose from the top three electoral-vote winners; Jackson lost to John Quincy Adams, who benefited from a political deal with Henry Clay (one of the four nominees but not included in the top three electoral-vote winners) in which Clay gave his support to Adams purportedly in return for being named Secretary of State. Thus, while the congressional caucus system was too centralized to represent state and local political units properly, the method of allowing individual states to nominate candidates was too decentralized to select a common party candidate. Some method was required that would represent party interests from throughout the country and that would also produce the nomination of a single candidate from each party.

The nomination method that soon developed to meet these joint requirements was a national convention composed of party delegates from all the states. By the early 1830s it had become the means by which parties nominated their presidential and vice-presidential candidates. The national convention remains in place today, but it, like the entire nomination process, has undergone major changes.

The selection of delegates to the national convention is determined by states and is also affected by decisions made by the national political parties. Three methods of selection have been used. One is selection by party leaders, such as members of the state central committee, the party chairperson, and the governor (if the party controls that office). The second is choice by state conventions composed of people who are themselves elected at party caucuses and conventions in smaller geographical areas, such as precincts, wards, counties, and congressional districts. The third method is election by the voters themselves in presidential primaries.

The Rise of State Primaries

For most of the century and a half since the institution of the national convention, selection of delegates by party leaders or by state conventions dominated the nomination process. In the early twentieth century, as part of the Progressive movement designed to take government out of the control of political bosses and to place it in the hands of the people, a number of states instituted presidential primaries. This method, unlike the *direct primary* used to vote directly for party nominees for other political offices, selects national-convention delegates, who, in turn, choose the party presidential nominees. After enjoying popularity for a brief period, the use of state presidential primaries became more limited. During the New Deal period, an average of fifteen states had presidential primaries; together, they chose between 33 and 45 percent of the national-convention delegates. As late as 1968, only seventeen states used presidential primaries to select convention delegates, together constituting 38 percent of the convention total.

The acrimonious debates over the Vietnam War at the 1968 Democratic national convention, together with Vice President Hubert H. Humphrey's presidential nomination despite the fact that he failed to enter a single primary (party leaders favoring him dominated the delegations of caucus-convention states) led to great dissatisfaction with the nomination process. In the years that followed, a series of party commissions were appointed to work with states to change the nomination rules to make the process less dominated by party leaders and more open to the influence of rank-and-file Democrats. One of the major outcomes of the movement was a dramatic increase in the number of state presidential primaries—a trend that affected Republicans as well.

By 1980 the number of states holding primaries had more than doubled. After a small decrease in 1984 in the number of states using presidential primaries, the number rose again in 1988. During that campaign year, thirty-five Republican state primaries selected about three-fourths of that party's national convention delegates, and thirty-four Democratic primaries chose about two-thirds of Democratic convention delegates.

State primaries work in a number of different ways. For instance, the selected delegates may be required to vote for the particular candidate with whom they are associated or they may be free to vote their own presidential-candidate preferences at the national convention. Another difference has to do with candidate choice: in some primaries, a candidate's name will appear on the ballot only if he or she officially enters the contest; in others, the candidate's name may automatically be placed on the ballot if the candidacy is recognized by the national news media. A third difference concerns the selection of state delegates: they may be chosen statewide, by district, or by a combination of the two; moreover, a state may award all the delegates to the statewide or district-vote winner or they may be allocated proportionally (though not always exactly) according to the relative size of the votes for the various candidates. In addition, in some states all the delegates are chosen in the primary while in others some are chosen in the primary and some in state conventions. Yet another difference involves who may vote in a primary: the election may be closed to those who are not registered members of a particular party or open to all registered voters. Finally, state presidential primaries are held on different dates, beginning in mid February and ending in June of the presidential year. On some dates, only one primary occurs; on others several are held. In recent years, major changes have occurred in state presidential primaries. Not only have there been more primaries, but they have been scheduled earlier in the election year. New Hampshire has retained its tradition of holding the nation's first primary, but other states have moved their primaries up on the calendar so that they are conducted before mid March. The most dramatic change in this respect was the creation in 1988 of "Super Tuesday." On the first Super Tuesday, 8 March 1988, sixteen states held their presidential primaries. There was a distinctive regional cast to this development: of the sixteen Super Tuesday primaries, fourteen were in southern and border states (the other two were in Massachusetts and Rhode Island). In 1992, eight primaries were held on Super Tuesday (10 March), six of which were in southern and border states and the other two in Massachusetts and Rhode Island. Presidential primaries have thus become the dominant method of choosing delegates to the national conventions of both major political parties. In 1988, however, about one-third (about fifteen of the fifty states) used the caucus-convention system to select their delegates. Moreover, 16 percent of the Democratic convention votes were allocated to "super delegates"—that is party leaders, including Democratic governors, members of the Democratic National Committee, and about 80 percent of the Democratic members of Congress. The process of selecting delegates to the national conventions has therefore remained a mixed system.

General Nature of the Nomination Campaign

The nomination campaign is a long winnowing process in which each of the two major parties chooses a nominee from a pool of potential candidates (the pool is typically much larger in the party that is out of power). As the political scientist Austin Ranney has pointed out, the nomination phase is more important than the general election stage of the campaign because "the parties' nominating processes eliminate far more possibilities than do the voters' electing processes."

The nomination campaign is much more loosely structured than the general election campaign. Instead of contending with one known opponent representing the other major political party, an aspirant for a party's nomination typically does not know how many opponents he or she will face or who they will be. Unlike the general election campaign, which typically begins after the national conventions and accelerates around Labor Day, the nomination campaign has no set starting date. Also, once selected, a presidential nominee can use his or her party label to attract votes and has access to the help of traditional party leaders in waging the campaign; candidates for a party's nomination, however, must develop other types of political appeals to attract the support of what the political scientist Hugh Heclo has termed the "selectorate"—that is, those who take part in the nomination phase of the presidential campaign—as well as personal political organizations to advance their candidacies.

The "Invisible Primary"

Although the nomination process normally does not officially start until early in the election year, political maneuvering may begin long before that time. Indeed, the journalist Arthur Hadley has called the interval between the election of one President and the first primary of the next presidential election the "invisible primary." During that time, would-be candidates test the viability of their candidacies. They try to determine, for example, whether they have the desire and stamina to endure extended absences from home and long hours on the campaign trail. (Democratic hopeful Walter Mondale withdrew two years before the 1976 election when he decided he did not.) A candidate must also find out whether he or she can assemble a personal staff to plan campaign strategy and a larger group to do the advance work necessary to organize the upcoming campaign in the various states.

The media can also be an important factor for the would-be candidate. Massachusetts Senator Edward Kennedy's 1980 campaign for the Democratic nomination, for example, was severely damaged by a 1979 interview with CBS commentator Roger Mudd in which he seemed unable to explain his actions in a 1969 automobile accident in which a young woman, Mary Jo Kopechne, had drowned. In 1988, former Colorado Senator Gary Hart's quest for the Democratic nomination suffered a similar fate when the *Miami Herald* reported his extramarital affair with model and actress Donna Rice. On the other hand, candidates can take action to enhance their name-recognition and to garner favorable publicity from the media. Early in Jimmy Carter's 1976 campaign, for example, his staff recommended that he curry favor with *New York Times* columnist Tom Wicker and *Washington Post* publisher Katherine Graham by commenting favorably on their newspapers and, if possible, scheduling visits with them.

One of the major factors determining the amount of effort a candidate will devote to a given primary is when that primary is held.

Another important factor affecting a would-be candidate's decision to run is his or her ability to raise funds for the long campaign ahead. Since the 1970s legislation has favored the raising of moneys in comparatively small amounts; there is a limit of $1,000 on individual contributions and $5,000 on those by pacs (political action committees); moreover, only contributions of $250 or less may be matched by federal funds. In the 1988 race, nationally recognized candidates such as Republicans George Bush and Robert Dole, as well as those with access to special fund-raising constituencies (e.g., televangelist and Republican candidate Pat Robertson, whose "700 Club" TV show provided a ready-made direct-mail constituency, and Democrat Michael Dukakis, who benefited from Greek-Americans' contributions from all over the country) were advantaged in the fund-raising process. By the end of 1987, Bush had raised $18.1 million; Robertson, $14.2 million; Dole, $13.2 million, and Dukakis, $10.2 million—funds that enabled them to compete in early primaries and caucuses.

During the period preceding the actual state contests, candidates can gather additional political support, name-recognition, and favorable publicity in other ways as well. One way is to gain the endorsement of interest groups, as Walter Mondale did in 1984, when he won the early endorsement of the AFL-CIO, the National Education Association, and the National Organization for Women. (Reacting to criticism that Mondale had been a "special interest" candidate, the Democrats in 1988 avoided such all-out endorsements so early in the campaign.) Another method is to enter contests that have no effect on the composition of the state delegations: for example, in 1979 Carter forces worked hard to defeat Kennedy in the Florida state convention straw poll. A third possibility is to engage in debates with other candidates, hoping to be declared the winner by the media.

The Official State Primaries

Whatever may transpire before the formal state contests, they are the mechanisms that actually select the delegates to the national conventions that will choose the party nominees. In recent years most major candidates have been on the ballots of all or virtually all the primaries. This does not mean, however, that each candidate will expend an equal effort in each primary.

One of the major factors determining the amount of effort a candidate will devote to a given primary is when that primary is held. Since 1952, a pledged-delegate primary in New Hampshire has been the first primary (only the Iowa caucuses have preceded it). Although the number of delegates from New Hampshire is small (in 1992, 18 of 4,288 Democratic delegates and 23 of 2,209 Republicans) a victory there focuses immediate attention on the winner—as it did for John F. Kennedy in 1960, Carter in 1976, and the two eventual nominees in 1988, Bush and Dukakis. Moreover, if a candidate loses in New Hampshire but draws a greater percentage of the votes than is expected, the media may interpret the result as a "moral" victory, a judgment that benefited Democrats Eugene McCarthy in 1968 and George McGovern in 1972.

As previously noted, in 1988 a number of states, primarily in the South, held their primaries in early March. These had a major effect on the nomination campaigns, particularly for the Republicans, who had winner-take-all contests. In 1988 Bush swept all sixteen Republican primaries on Super Tuesday and essentially wrapped up the nomination. In contrast, three candidates—Dukakis, Jesse Jackson, and Tennessee Senator Albert

Gore—divided up the Democratic primaries, which generally used the proportional rule to award delegates.

Besides timing, other factors help determine how candidates focus their efforts. They typically enter state contests in which they expect to do well. In 1984 Mondale chose to concentrate on Pennsylvania and Illinois because both states had many Catholic, Jewish, and union voters—groups among whom the Minnesota politician had long been popular. That same year Hart focused on Massachusetts and Wisconsin because of their academic communities, with which he shared liberal political views. At times, however, candidates may select states that are not considered advantageous to prove that they have a broader appeal than is generally thought. In 1960 Kennedy entered the West Virginia primary to demonstrate that a Catholic could win in a state that was 95 percent Protestant; in 1976 Carter chose the Pennsylvania primary to show that a Southern Baptist could do well in a northern industrial state with a large Catholic population. Both calculations were excellent and greatly advanced their respective candidacies.

The number of delegates a state has at the national convention is also a factor that determines the amount of effort expended there. In 1988, of the ten most populous states, only one, Michigan, did not hold a primary. Thus, unless the nomination has been virtually decided by the time of a large state primary, most, if not all candidates, may be expected to focus their efforts there.

Of the factors that affected presidential nominations in the 1970s, 1980s, and early 1990s, the date of the state contest was the most important. Between 1976 and 1988, every Democratic or Republican nominee won at least one of the two small states of Iowa and New Hampshire and finished no lower than third in the other. Of the two, New Hampshire appeared to be the more important. After winning the Iowa caucuses in 1980, Bush declared he had "Big Mo" (momentum), but it suddenly evaporated a week later when he lost to Ronald Reagan, the eventual nominee, in the New Hampshire primary. In 1988, Bush had the reverse experience: he lost to Dole in Iowa but recovered with a victory in New Hampshire that sent him on the way to the Republican nomination. The same was true for the Democratic contest: Missouri Representative Richard Gephardt won the 1988 Iowa caucuses but was defeated in the New Hampshire primary by Dukakis, the eventual Democratic nominee.

One final point should be made about the presidential primaries. Although the situation differs from election to election, there has been a definite trend to decide the nominations in both parties fairly early. From 1976 to 1988, the candidate who won the most delegates by mid March went on to win the party's nomination. It is significant that during the same general period presidential primaries became the dominant force in presidential nomination policies.

[See also (II) Electoral College.]

BIBLIOGRAPHY

Aldridge, John. *Before the Convention: A Theory of Presidential Nominations.* 1980.

Asher, Herbert. *Presidential Elections and American Politics.* 5th ed. 1992.

Bartels, Larry M. *Presidential Primaries and the Dynamics of Public Choice.* 1988.

Crotty, William, and John S. Jackson III. *Presidential Primaries and Nominations.* 1985.

Grassmuck, George, ed. *Before Nomination: Our Primary Problems.* 1985.

Greer, John. *Nominating Presidents: An Evaluation of Voters and Primaries.* 1989.

Hadley, Arthur. *The Invisible Primary.* 1976.

Kessel, John. *Presidential Campaign Politics.* 4th ed. 1992.

Schaefer, Byron E. *Quiet Revolution: The Struggle for the Democratic Party and the Shaping of Post-Reform Politics.* 1983.

Wayne, Stephen. *The Road to the White House.* 4th ed. 1992.

– RICHARD A. WATSON

PRIVATE ENVOYS

A major summit practice, introduced early in U.S. history, is the President's utilization of private envoys as personal agents to represent the country abroad. Initially called secret agents, they also are known as executive agents, presidential special envoys, or personal emissaries. Private envoys are appointed without Senate confirmation (and sometimes without consulting the State Department) for particular, limited assignments. Their authority, duties, and compensation are determined by the President, and generally they are responsible only to the President and report directly to the White House.

The Envoys' Role

Such special envoys supplement traditional diplomatic missions. Besides representing the United States at state ceremonies abroad, they are commissioned to represent the President directly to foreign leaders, keep the President informed, convey official policies and positions, confer and negotiate on the President's behalf, engage in troubleshooting and mediation, and extend the President's influence abroad. They bypass established bureaucracies, elevate matters to the highest level, and expedite relations.

Today, the missions of such envoys are rarely clandestine. Originally they were commissioned only on exceptional occasions and usually for restricted periods, but over time usage was broadened to include any assignment the President elects to handle outside conventional diplomatic channels.

Approximately four hundred presidential special emissaries were appointed during the century following the Revolution, and by the time of World War I some five to six hundred had been commissioned, evidencing that this practice had become commonplace. At present more than two dozen may be accredited in a single year, and, while their total number and the quantity of their missions can only be surmised, they may well aggregate in the thousands.

Many prominent statesmen and distinguished diplomats have served as executive agents. Prior to the Constitution these included John Adams, William Carmichael, Charles Dumas, Benjamin Franklin, John Jay, and Thomas Jefferson. President George Washington appointed David Humphreys, James Monroe, Gouverneur Morris, Thomas Pinckney, and others to such assignments. The list has embraced ranking statesmen (Dean Acheson and John J. McCloy), professional diplomats (William C. Bullitt, Ellsworth Bunker, and Norman Davis), career Foreign Service officers (Hugh Gibson, Robert J. McCloskey, and Llewellyn E. Thompson), and a few military officers (Generals Maxwell Taylor and Vernon Walters and Colonel William Donovan).

Private envoys are commissioned to represent the President directly to foreign leaders and extend the President's influence abroad.

Presidential personal emissaries may be classified according to the position they occupied prior to appointment, the nature of the tasks assigned, and the extent to which they actually represent the President. Under the first classification, they are of two types: those who otherwise occupy no official position in the government and those government agents, such as Vice Presidents, members of Congress, and the Secretary of State, who are sent abroad on special missions. The trend has been to rely more frequently on current and former government officials for these tasks.

Types of Envoys

Under the second classification, based on assignment, special envoys may be grouped in the following categories: *ceremonial agents,* such as Theodore Roosevelt, who was sent to the funeral of King Edward VII in 1910, and George C. Marshall, sent to the coronation of Queen Elizabeth II in 1953; *goodwill envoys,* such as Milton Eisenhower, who made visits to Latin America during the 1950s, and Robert F. Kennedy, who made a globe-girdling tour in 1962; *special messengers for obtaining information and conveying presidential views,* such as Joel R. Poinsett, who made trips to South America from 1810 to 1814, several emissaries during the crises in Panama and the Dominican Republic in the 1960s, and a series of agents promoting President Lyndon Baines Johnson's "peace offensive" during the Vietnam War; *mediators,* such as Vice President Henry A. Wallace, General Patrick Hurley, and General George C. Marshall, who were sent by Presidents Franklin D. Roosevelt and Harry S Truman to try to ameliorate the conflict between the Nationalist and Communist Chinese, as well as a number of Secretaries of State and other high-ranking State Department officials dispatched to deal with Arab-Israeli and other Middle East crises (including Joseph J. Sisco, Philip Habib, and James A. Baker III); *other troubleshooters,* such as career diplomat Robert Murphy (who served Presidents Roosevelt, Truman, and Dwight D. Eisenhower) and Cyrus Vance (whom President Johnson relied on during the Cyprus, South Korean, Dominican, and Vietnam crises); *roving emissaries* such as W. Averell Harriman (appointed by Presidents Roosevelt, John F. Kennedy, and Johnson) and Secretaries of State Dean Rusk, Henry Kissinger, and Baker; and, on rare occasions, a *resident emissary,* for example, Myron C. Taylor, who was commissioned resident representative to the Vatican during World War II.

A good many emissaries have been appointed as special negotiators. A sampling includes Robert Livingston and James Monroe (Louisiana Purchase, 1803), Secretary Richard Rush (Rush-Bagot Agreement, 1817), Nicholas P. Trist (Treaty of Guadalupe Hidalgo ending the Mexican War, 1848), Admiral Matthew C. Perry and Townsend Harris (commercial treaties with Japan, 1854 and 1868), Secretary William Seward (Alaska Purchase Treaty, 1867), former Secretary William R. Day (Treaty of Paris ending the Spanish-American War, 1898), William W. Rockhill (Open Door policy for China and Peking Protocol, 1901), John Foster Dulles (Japanese Peace Treaty ending World War II, 1951), Deputy Secretary Warren Christopher (settlement of Iranian hostage crisis, 1980–1981), and Max Kampelman (East-West arms limitation, Geneva, 1985–1987). Other twentieth-century special envoys of note include Chief Justice Fred M. Vinson (mission to Moscow, 1948), former Senator Walter F. George (special representative to NATO, 1957), and former Congressman James P. Richards (to promote the Eisenhower Doctrine in the Middle East, 1957).

There are two exceptional categories of executive agents who represent the President in a special way. The first is the *ambassador-at-large.* President Franklin D. Roosevelt commissioned Norman Davis as his ambassador-at-large, sending him to several international conferences. In 1949 this office was formalized, and since then more than thirty emissaries have borne this title, including Arthur J. Goldberg, U. Alexis Johnson, George C. McGhee, and Paul Nitze. The second category embraces those who function as the intimates of the President, possess the President's personal confidence, and are accepted abroad as genuine presidential surrogates. This unique role has been filled by Woodrow Wilson's envoy Colonel Edward M. House; Franklin D. Roosevelt's envoy Harry Hopkins; W. Averell Harriman, who served several Presidents and was twice designated ambassador-at-large; and Henry Kissinger, who served Presidents Richard M. Nixon and Gerald Ford.

Constitution Questions

The appointment of presidential special agents raises both constitutional and political issues.

The practice has been held to violate the spirit, if not the letter, of the Constitution. The matter of constitutionality—including the use of members of Congress for such missions—was debated most vigorously during the period from 1880 to World War I. Aside from expediency and the fact that such envoys have been used throughout U.S. history, two considerations are used to justify their use: the legal fiction that these emissaries are "employees" rather than "officers" of the United States and that such agents on special assignments have temporary duties of limited duration.

The critical legal-political issues are whether such appointments are not overtly prohibited by the Constitution, whether they are necessary for the President to fulfill his responsibilities effectively, and whether they produce acceptable consequences. So many precedents have been set, however, that the use of such envoys may be said to be constitutional by prescriptive practice. Despite the objections raised, the President, as diplomat in chief, is ultimately accountable for the conduct of American foreign relations. So long as he is inclined to assume personal direction over diplomatic affairs, he will appoint individuals he deems able to surmount the constraints of ordinary diplomatic practice in promoting the objectives and policies of the nation.

BIBLIOGRAPHY

Burke, Lee H. *Ambassador at Large: Diplomat Extraordinary.* 1972.

Grieb, Kenneth J. "Executive Agents." In vol. 1 of *Encyclopedia of American Foreign Policy.* Edited by Alexander de Coude. 3 vols. 1978.

Plischke, Elmer. *Diplomat in Chief: The President at the Summit.* 1986. Chapter 3.

Thorpe, Francis N. "Is the President of the United States Vested with Authority under the Constitution to Appoint a Special Diplomatic Agent with Paramount Power without Advice and Consent of the Senate?" *American Law Register and Review* (April 1984): 257–264.

Waters, Maurice. "Special Diplomatic Agents of the President." *Annals of the American Academy of Political and Social Science* 307 (September 1956): 124–133.

Wriston, Henry M. *Executive Agents in American Foreign Relations.* 1929.

Wriston, Henry M. "The Special Envoy." *Foreign Affairs* 38 (1960): 219–237.

– ELMER PLISCHKE

PROCLAMATIONS

Ever since the administration of George Washington, Presidents have issued proclamations having the force of law. These proclamations set boundaries for the behavior of private citizens as well as government officials. Despite their impact, proclamations have not been gen-

George Washington made the first presidential proclamation in 1793 with his Proclamation of Neutrality. The action triggered debate over the proper range of presidential powers. (Library of Congress, Prints and Photographs Division)

erally well understood. The confusing processes by which they have been developed, promulgated, and integrated with other policy tools as well as the controversial claims to authority on which they have sometimes been based have not made proclamations a popular subject for presidential scholars.

The Nature of Proclamations

Presidents have issued more than six thousand proclamations since George Washington's Proclamation of Neutrality of 1793. The number is approximate because, as with executive orders, there was historically no system for identifying, listing, and publishing in one authoritative location all proclamations. Even after the enactment of the Federal Register Act, in 1935, there were difficulties. First, considerable effort was required to construct a codification of proclamations and executive orders that would be comprehensive and current. The Office of the Federal Register has developed the *Codification of Presidential Proclamations and Executive Orders* but it presents only those proclamations issued since World War II. Second, apart from the general requirements for publication of new proclamations in the *Federal Register,* the only guidelines that govern their promulgation are two executive orders, E.O. 10347 (1952) and E.O. 11030 (1962), which themselves do little more than describe the process, format, and routing for the production of the documents. Since Presidents have issued the equivalent of proclamations under many titles and in many forms not covered by existing publication laws, it can be difficult to identify and integrate them into a coherent set of presidential policy statements.

Presidential proclamations issued under a proper claim of authority are legally binding. They may be ratified or nullified by legislative action after their issuance, unless they are based on a valid claim by the executive to independent constitutional authority. Legislative failure to block presidential action or the defeat of resolutions opposing White House actions are considered evidence of support. Of course, proclamations may not violate existing statutes or constitutional constraints.

Proclamations have even been used, and upheld, as the basis for criminal prosecutions. Judge James Wilson charged a grand jury that it could indict a violator of Washington's Neutrality Proclamation even though there was no statute authorizing such an indictment. A man who refused on principle to register for the draft as required by President Jimmy Carter's Proclamation 4771 was convicted and his conviction upheld.

Formally, the distinction between executive orders and proclamations is that orders are issued by the President to government agencies or officials while proclamations are directed to persons outside government. Thus, President Carter's Proclamation 4771 (1980) directed all eighteen-year-old males to register for the military draft. On the other hand, proclamations may be issued together with executive orders. For example, President Gerald R. Ford simultaneously issued Proclamation 4483 in 1973 granting pardons under certain circumstances to Vietnam War-era draft evaders and Executive Order 11967, outlining the implementation actions to be taken by the Attorney General under the program.

The Supreme Court has held that there is no legal distinction between proclamations and executive orders. The internal versus external dichotomy used to distinguish between them is not particularly helpful in practical terms, since many executive orders directing action by government agencies clearly have a major impact on those outside government. In the case of Ford's amnesty program, for example, men who had presumably violated the selective service laws could not obtain the pardon set forth in the proclamation unless the process established by the executive order determined that they were eligible for it.

In general, proclamations have been issued in a number of general categories. Most are hortatory, designating a period of recognition, celebration, or concern, like Proclamation 6407 proclaiming 1992 the Year of the American Indian. Others, like Carter's selective service proclamation, are effectively ordinances, rules of general applicability. Particularly in the area of trade and foreign policy, the President issues a third type of proclamation, which renders an authoritative finding of fact and sets forth the response triggered by the situation. Thus, President George Bush issued Proclamation 6413 (1992) finding that the Peoples' Republic of China had implemented the memorandum of understanding between the PRC and the United States on the protection of intellectual property by recognizing the copyrights of American authors. Therefore, Proclamation 6413 granted copyright protection in the United States to works produced by PRC authors. The President may also make authoritative findings of fact and announce responses in domestic matters. These are often rendered in what are found to be emergency situations such as natural disasters.

Legal Authority

Of course, presidential lawmaking by proclamation depends for its force on the legal authority that supports it. Unlike executive orders, which Presidents have often insisted can rest at least partly on the President's claim of general executive powers to supervise subordinate officials and agencies, proclamations that are directed to those outside government face a demanding challenge.

Historically, the concept of presidential proclamations derives from the crown prerogative. However, many of the Framers of the Constitution, including James Wilson, James Madison, and even Alexander Hamilton, rejected the elements of the crown prerogative as the price for support in creating an effective presidency. Moreover, as the Proclamations Case of 1611 indicated, even the British king did not have unlimited powers to issue any proclamation the crown desired. When Washington issued his Neutrality Proclamation in 1793, it triggered the Helvidius-Pacificus debates over the proper range of presidential powers under the Constitution.

In most cases Presidents rely in issuing proclamations on authority specifically granted or at least implied by statute, even in matters of foreign policy and even where purely hortatory proclamations are involved. In fact, many hortatory proclamations are issued in response to calls from Congress in the form of a public law or joint resolution, as in the case of Public Law 102-188 authorizing and requesting the issuance of the Year of the American Indian.

Because they are directed at private citizens and businesses, presidential proclamations are easier to challenge than executive orders.

The most important proclamations have often been issued in matters of economic policy, international trade and tariffs, national security, or foreign policy. In these fields, Presidents have usually relied on statutes that specified their authority to make a finding that a problem exists and to respond to it. Some statutes authorize the president to undertake a decision-making process. Proclamations are then employed to implement the policy produced by that process. For example, President Carter entered into negotiations with Mexico for a trade agreement under the authority of the Trade Act of 1974. As a result of that negotiation process, the President issued Proclamation 4707 (1979) implementing concessions granted by the United States under the agreement, but, when the Mexican government was not forthcoming on mutual actions expected as part of the process, Carter suspended the U.S. concessions with his Proclamation 4792 (1980).

When Presidents rely on authority they consider to be implied by existing statutes or act under extremely broad delegations of statutory authority, there can be conflict. For example, Carter issued Petroleum Import Adjustment Program Proclamations 4744, 4748, and 4751 (1980), which imposed a 10 percent oil import fee under authority he thought was implied by the Trade Expansion Act of 1962. His actions were later struck down in a legal challenge in which the court observed that the President had erred in attempting to use legislation for something never considered by Congress and in a manner that flew in the face of the intent with which the law was originally adopted.

However, President Richard M. Nixon fared much better in an even more dramatic exercise of power in 1971. Claiming authority from the Trade Expansion Act of 1962, and the Economic Stabilization Act of 1970, the administration suspended exchange of U.S. currency, set limits on domestic spending and foreign aid, imposed a freeze on wages and prices, suspended a variety of trade-related proclamations then in force, and placed a 10 percent surcharge on all dutiable imports. Although the court that reviewed Proclamation 4074 found the legislative delegation of power to the President to be incredibly broad, possibly unwise, and even potentially dangerous, it nevertheless concluded that the President's action on the import fee fit the delegation and that the delegation was permissible in light of its intention to permit presidential response to economic emergencies.

Indeed some of the most important controversies over proclamations have arisen in situations in which Presidents have justified their actions by reference to a state of emergency, usually related to national security or economic crises. President Nixon based his actions in 1971 on the proclamation of a state of economic emergency brought on by serious deficits in balance of payments, instability in trading on the dollar, and related tariff practices that exacerbated the trade imbalance.

Where Presidents act in matters of foreign policy and national security, there is often an assertion of combined statutory and constitutional authority under the Commander in Chief and foreign affairs powers.

Challenges to Proclamations

Because they are directed at private citizens and businesses, presidential proclamations are easier to challenge than executive orders. Since executive orders are directed to agencies or government officials, it is more difficult for citizens to meet procedural requirements and establish a proper basis for a suit that would challenge the President's authority. Still, even if a citizen is able to mount a legal challenge to a presidential proclamation, it may be very difficult to prevail in light of the tradition of deference by the judiciary to foreign policy and national security decisions.

Notwithstanding their usefulness as policy-making tools for a President, proclamations have weaknesses as well. Despite their record of success in court, proclamations may fall in a legal challenge. They are even more likely to be overturned by a later administration. The President who invests the time and energy to move legislation through the Congress is more likely to establish enduring policy than one who relies on proclamations. For example, one of the last proclamations issued by President Carter was Proclamation 4813 (1981), which extended the "Emergency Building Temperatures Restrictions" imposed by Proclamation 4667 (1979) intended to protect the U.S. against further oil crises in the light of unrest in the Middle East. Less than a month later, Ronald Reagan issued Proclamation 4820 (1981) revoking Carter's orders on grounds that his action imposed an "excessive regulatory burden" that would be achieved by "voluntary restraint and market incentives."

Presidential proclamations, like executive orders, are potentially useful tools. However, given their vulnerability as policy statements over time, the sometimes dubious authority on which they may be based, and the closed process by which they are developed and promulgated, they are limited and possibly dangerous tools for many presidential tasks.

[See also (II) Executive Orders.]

BIBLIOGRAPHY

Friedelbaum, Stanley H. "The 1971 Wage-Price Freeze: Unchallenged Presidential Power." *Supreme Court Review* (1974):33–80.

Hart, James. *The Ordinance Making Powers of the President of the United States.* 1925.

Office of the Federal Register. *Codification of Presidential Proclamations and Executive Orders, April 13, 1945–January 20, 1989.* 1990.

U.S. House of Representatives. Committee on Government Operations. *Executive Orders and Proclamations: A Study of a Use of Presidential Power.* 85th Cong., 1st sess., 1957. Committee Print.

U.S. Senate. Committee on Government Operations and the Special Committee on National Emergencies and Delegated Emergency Powers. *The National Emergencies Act: Sourcebook.* 94th Congress, 2d sess., 1976. Committee Print.

– PHILLIP J. COOPER

PROTOCOL, PRESIDENTIAL

Since George Washington's day, the President, serving as both chief of state and head of government, has been the ceremonial head of the country and the operational chief executive of the government respecting both internal and external affairs, comparable to the combined roles of foreign monarchs (and other chiefs of state) and government chief executives. The manner in which the President performs these dual responsibilities depends not only on the President's personal qualities and the temperament but also on the rules that guide his demeanor and actions. Such rules—national and international—constitute the essence of presidential protocol.

Definition of Protocol

As chief of state the President greets and plays host to foreign dignitaries and a procession of American visitors, tours the country to meet with groups of citizens, proclaims holidays, bestows medals and honors, and entertains a variety of White House guests. He is officially received by other governments, confers with their leaders, issues policy declarations, and occasionally signs treaties and agreements. These and similar actions are governed by established, sometimes mandated, procedures. As a consequence, the President has been called a one-person epitomization of America or, as President William Howard Taft put it, the personal embodiment and representative of the people's dignity and majesty.

Protocol applies to all official procedure, ceremony, precedence, and etiquette. It governs not only presidential relations with foreign chiefs of state, heads of government, and other high-level officials but also many aspects of diplomatic affairs and a variety of domestic functions. It regulates diverse features of the international treaty process, the handling of official messages to and from other governments, the accrediting of American diplomats and consuls, and the reception of envoys assigned to Washington. It also controls many national formalities and ceremonies, such as the presidential inauguration and presidential messages to Congress, the signing of legislation, the issuance of presidential proclamations and executive orders, and the conferral of national recognition and awards.

Defined as procedure, deportment, and courtesy, or as the "rule book" by which official relations are conducted, protocol is called a body of "social discipline," a mixture of "good manners and common sense," a set of "rules of conduct," and a prescription of "hierarchical order." Presidential protocol has its supporters and its detractors. Some hold that protocol preserves the symbolism of American sovereignty, continuity, grandeur, and dignity for the President. Others have called it a conspicuous thief of the President's precious time or a device for gaining release from the routine tasks and hard decisions required by the presidential office. Some view it as undemocratic, pretentious, patrician, and unnecessary. But those who utilize it generally regard it as useful, if not essential, in the handling of official relations.

Because of widespread sentiment that ceremonious protocol was not in keeping with the American tradition and spirit, it was not until 1893, in the last days of the Benjamin Harrison administration, that Congress permitted the appointment of American diplomats and reception of foreign diplomats accorded the rank of ambassador. Previously such emissaries had held the inferior rank of minister. Similarly, for more than a century the same sentiment precluded the designation of a State Department official to serve as master of ceremonies for official receptions, dinners, and other occasions.

Only in 1919, during the Woodrow Wilson administration, was an officer empowered to head a Ceremonial Section in the Department of State. In 1928, during the Calvin Coolidge administration, a full-fledged Division of Protocol was created, which twice (1929–1931 and 1933–1937) was amalgamated with and later separated from the Division of International Conferences. Soon after World War II, under President Harry S Truman, the Secretary of State elevated the Division of Protocol to the Office of the Chief of Protocol, who bears the personal status of ambassador.

The Chief of Protocol is the principal adviser to the President, Vice President, Secretary of State, and other officials on diplomatic procedure, precedence, and other matters of protocol. The Protocol Office, as officially prescribed, is responsible for arranging visits of foreign chiefs of state, heads of government, and other leaders; monitoring official White House ceremonial and other high-level functions and public events; operating the President's guest house (Blair House); sending delegations to represent the President at public ceremonies abroad; accrediting thousands of foreign embassy, consular, and international-organization personnel stationed in the United States; and determining entitlement to—and resolving many, sometimes thorny problems respecting—diplomatic and consular privileges and immunities. The office also compiles and publishes diplomatic, consular, and mission employee lists and prescribes ranking within them and deals with many other status, procedural, social, and related matters. In short, this office is responsible for the government's obligations relating to all aspects of national and international protocol.

Practice of Protocol

Whereas protocol was initially regulated by national and international custom and usage, many important aspects have come to be determined by international treaties, congressional statutes, executive orders, and administrative regulations. For example, the Vienna conventions on Diplomatic Relations (1961) and on Consular Relations (1963) prescribed common international principles concerning diplomatic and consular officers accredited to this country and Americans commissioned for service abroad. These treaties, subscribed to by some 150 governments, deal with the mutuality of relations; the manner of establishing, suspending, and terminating foreign missions; determining persona grata (acceptability) status of individual officers and their staffs; and setting the procedure for presenting letters of credence and official reception of diplomats and the issuing of exequaturs to consuls authorizing the performance of their duties. They also stipulate rules respecting precedence, including delineation of categories of diplomatic and consular officials and individual ranking within them; inviolability of persons, premises, and communications; privileges and immunities; the parameters of diplomatic and consular functions; and the public display of national flags, coats of arms, and emblems.

For years the precedence order of diplomats in Washington, D.C., and other capitals was founded on principles established at the congresses of Vienna (1815) and Aix-la-Chapelle (1818), which based rank on titles of individual emissaries and their personal seniority or length of service at that rank in that capital. The four ranks of diplomats, in order of priority, included ambassadors extraordinary and plenipotentiary (and papal legates or nuncios), envoys extraordinary and ministers plenipotentiary (and papal internuncios), ministers resident, and two classes of chargés d'affaires. By the Vienna Convention of 1961 this order was modified to embrace papal nuncios in Catholic countries, ambassadors extraordinary and plenipotentiary, ministers plenipotentiary, and three classes of chargés d'affaires. In each capital the dean of the diplomatic corps is the most senior foreign diplomat, the spokesperson for and representative of the entire diplomatic corps.

Failure to recognize precedence and proper procedure may insult individuals and their governments.

U.S. protocol prescribes that the President head the order of precedence, followed by the Vice President, Speaker of the House of Representatives, Chief Justice, former Presidents, Secretary of State, and foreign ambassadors accredited to Washington. Overall, there are more than forty American precedence categories comprising several hundred individuals and groups, such as cabinet secretaries, Senators, Congressmen, deputy and assistant secretaries of Cabinet departments, and state governors. Each of these categories has its own order of priority. Also included are heads of international organizations, the mayor of Washington, the Director of the Mint, the Librarian of Congress, and many others. Potentially, this order of precedence embraces some two to three thousand individuals and their spouses.

Protocol also applies to such domestic matters as ceremonies for presidential appearances before Congress, swearing in of officials, and the hosting of meetings with foreign leaders and numerous other luncheons, dinners, receptions, and social events, as well as the use of the Great Seal of the United States. It also governs the form of White House invitations and responses, individual positions in reception lines, and the shape and seating arrangements at conference and dinner tables (seating differs depending on whether the table is round, square, rectangular, or C-, E-, or U-shaped). Protocol also prescribes rules for dress (whether formal or informal attire) and forms of address: the President is simply addressed as "Mr. President," whereas other officials bear noble titles, such as "Excellency" (for ranking foreign diplomats) and "Honorable" (for Cabinet officers, Supreme Court Justices, members of Congress, governors, mayors, and American ambassadors).

Failure to recognize precedence and proper procedure may insult individuals and their governments. In inviting foreign leaders to visit the United States, and in receiving them, attention must be paid to the nature, frequency, timing, and duration of each visit in relation to the interests and expectations of other governments. Special protocol difficulties arise when a number of ranking foreign leaders come to Washington for collective ceremonies—as when seventeen attended President John F. Kennedy's funeral in 1963 and when twenty-nine—embracing one emperor, eleven presidents, and seventeen prime ministers—were welcomed by President Richard M. Nixon at a White House dinner to celebrate the United Nations' twenty-fifth anniversary in 1970. In such cases sensitivities are aroused whether precedence is based on titles and ranks of the individuals or on an alphabetical arrangement of the countries they represent.

Practicalities of Protocol

Issues of protocol have inspired many anecdotes. One joke relates how a President, boarding a naval vessel, fell overboard and in keeping with proper procedure was given a forty-three-gun salute—the customary twenty-one for boarding, twenty-one for departing, and one for "man overboard"! It has also been recounted that when President Washington undertook a coach trip to New England in 1790, he avoided Rhode Island because it had not ratified the Constitution and was therefore foreign territory.

American tradition initially eschewed the official and social pageantry common in European societies. Benjamin Franklin appeared at the Versailles court wigless, sporting an old coat and a wooden cane, but learned that it was diplomatically advantageous to adopt the customary dress. During the Franklin Pierce administration, Secretary of State William Marcy issued a dress circular advising U.S. diplomats abroad to limit themselves to the "simple dress" of American citizens, which was applauded at home but created embarrassing difficulties overseas. Since those days traditional attire for state ceremonies and diplomatic relations has transmuted from lace, satin, and buckled shoes to striped trousers, black morning coats, spats, and homburgs, and eventually to worsted and tweed working garb and occasional tuxedos and tails for special occasions. When asked his opinion of full dress at White House dinners, President Truman responded that although it posed a protocol problem, he himself would never wear tails.

When Queen Elizabeth II of Great Britain came to the United States on a formal four-day state visit in 1957, her itinerary included four state dinners, three state luncheons, four receptions, a royal investiture ceremony, an American football game, and a traditional reciprocal state dinner. President Dwight D. Eisenhower later commented that he would have fired any aide who dared devise such a schedule for him. Years earlier Eleanor Roosevelt had cautioned that state guests should be given more time to "put their feet up and relax."

Illustrating the problem of precedence, a troublesome issue was thrust into the lap of protocol experts during the Herbert Hoover administration: they were required to decide whether Vice President Charles Curtis's half-sister outranked Speaker Nicholas Longworth's wife at a White House dinner. In another instance, an American ambassador stationed abroad decided to give a dinner in honor of the newly arrived ambassador of another country but was advised that he could not invite any other ambassadors because they all outranked the guest of honor. In preparing for her first official reception, Mrs. George C. Marshall sought guidance on certain protocol graces and was told always to ask the senior officer's wife to pour the coffee, not the tea, because "coffee outranks tea."

Sometimes protocol preparations are upset by unplanned and embarrassing events. In 1954, President William Tubman of Liberia, arriving at New York by ship a day ahead of schedule, had to remain at anchor in the Upper Bay for a day in order to dock at the prescribed time. When Soviet leader Nikita Khrushchev flew to Washington for a summit meeting in 1959, his plane arrived an hour late and, when it landed, its exit faced in the wrong direction, so that Khrushchev emerged on the side away from the reception party and had to crouch under the plane to be welcomed by President Eisenhower.

BIBLIOGRAPHY

Buchanan, Wiley T., Jr. *Red Carpet at the White House: Four Years as Chief of Protocol in the Eisenhower Administration.* 1964.

McCaffree, Mary Jane, and Pauline Innis. *Protocol: The Complete Handbook of Diplomatic, Official, and Social Usage.* 1989.

Miller, Hope Ridings. *Embassy Row: The Life and Times of Diplomatic Washington.* 1969.

Moreno, Salcedo L. *A Guide to Protocol.* Rev. ed. 1959.

Radlovic, I. Monte. *Etiquette and Protocol: A Handbook of Conduct in American and International Circles.* 1957.

Symington, James W. *The Stately Game.* 1971.

U.S. Department of State, Historical Office. *The Protocol Function in United States Foreign Relations: Its Administration and Development, 1776–1968.* Research Project no. 767. October 1968.

Wood, John R., and Jean Serres. *Diplomatic Ceremonial and Protocol: Principles, Procedures, and Practices.* 1970.

– ELMER PLISCHKE

Q

QUALIFICATIONS FOR PRESIDENT

The Constitution provides that "No Person except a natural born Citizen, or a Citizen of the United States at the time of the Adoption of this Constitution, shall be eligible to the Office of President; neither shall any Person be eligible to that Office who shall not have attained to the Age of thirty five Years, and been fourteen Years a Resident within the United States." The Twenty-second amendment, which was added to the Constitution in 1951, further disqualifies any person who already has been elected to two terms as President, or who has been elected once and, through succession, has served more than half of another President's four-year term.

In the constitutional theories that prevailed during the late eighteenth century, stated qualifications for office were widely regarded as necessary to prevent certain kinds of people from even coming before the voters. Several state constitutions required that the governor meet a minimum property-owning (often land-owning) standard, the idea being that voters should be restricted to choosing among candidates with a substantial economic stake in the community. Some states specified that a profession of Christianity, or even Protestantism, was a minimum constitutional requirement for election, perhaps in accordance with the then-widespread common law rule that only Christians could be relied upon to swear to affirm a valid oath of office. Age and residency requirements for governor were less prevalent.

The Constitutional Convention

The qualifications for President that were included in the plan of government that the Framers wrote at the Constitutional Convention of 1787 do not accord with the common theory and practice of the time. Religious qualifications were, with little debate, explicitly rejected; indeed, Article VI of the Constitution provides that "no religious Test shall ever be required as a Qualification to any Office or public Trust under the United States."

The issue of property qualifications was more vexing to the delegates. On 26 July, two months after the opening of the convention, they approved a motion that "the President of the US[,] the Judges, and members of the Legislature should be required to swear that they were respectively possessed of a clear unencumbered Estate to the amount of in the case of the President &c&c." But the delegates retreated from that decision when John Rutledge of South Carolina, who chaired the committee that was charged to come up with a specific figure for property ownership, confessed that he was "embarrassed by the danger on one side of displeasing the people by making them [the property qualifications] too high, and on the other of rending them nugatory by making them low."

In the late eighteenth century, some states specified that a profession of Christianity, or even Protestantism, was a minimum constitutional requirement for election.

No statement of the age, citizenship, and residency requirements that eventually were included in the Constitution was made until 7 September, when the convention, unanimously and without debate, approved a committee recommendation that the President be at least thirty-five years old, a natural-born citizen (or a citizen at the time of the Constitution's adoption), and a resident of the United States for at least fourteen years. Prior to that late date (the Convention ended just ten days later), the delegates seem to have been operating on the principle that qualifications for an office were unnecessary if qualifications for those who choose the person to fill the office already had been established. Thus, qualifications for judges and other appointed officials were never included in the Constitution because they were to be selected by other government officials for whom qualifications were stated. Conversely, because qualifications were not stated for voters, they were established for members of Congress as early as James Madison's Virginia Plan, which was proposed during the first week of the convention.

Throughout most of the Convention, the majority of delegates remained wedded to the idea that Congress, a body of constitutionally "qualified" members, would elect the President. Thus, no need was seen to include qualifications for President in the Constitution. When, in September, the delegates decided that a constitutionally "unqualified" Electoral College should choose the

President, they added a presidential qualifications clause as well.

The Qualifications

Because no debate accompanied the delegates' decisions on presidential qualifications, any explanation of why they chose the age, residency, and citizenship requirements that are in the Constitution must be somewhat speculative.

AGE. An age requirement of thirty-five years was included in the qualifications clause for two apparent reasons. First, the delegates presumed that age would foster maturity in a President. As George Mason of Virginia said in the debate concerning the minimum age for members of the House of Representatives, "every man carries with him in his own experience a scale for measuring the deficiency of young politicians, since he would if interrogated be obliged to declare that his political opinions at the age of twenty-one were too crude & erroneous to merit an influence on public measures." Second, it was believed, the passage of years in a candidate's life left in its wake a public record for the voters to assess. According to John Jay, the author of Federalist 64, the age requirement "confines the electors to men of whom the people have had time to form a judgment, and with respect to whom they will not be liable to be deceived by those brilliant appearances of genius and patriotism which, like transient meteors, sometimes mislead as well as dazzle."

RESIDENCY. The stipulation that the President must be at least fourteen years a resident of the United States was designed to eliminate from consideration both British sympathizers who had fled to England during the American Revolution and popular foreign military leaders, notably Baron Frederick von Steuben of Prussia, who had emigrated to the United States to fight in the revolution. As for the fourteen-year length of the residency requirement (which was substituted for an initial proposal of twenty-one years), it is worth noting that although the latter length would have excluded three of the delegates from eligibility to the presidency, the former excluded none.

CITIZENSHIP. The reason for requiring that the President must be a natural-born citizen was also tied to contemporary politics. Rumors had spread while the convention was meeting that the delegates were plotting to invite a European monarch to rule the United States. To refute these rumors, the delegates issued the only press release of their otherwise secret deliberations, telling the *Pennsylvania Journal* that "though we cannot, affirmatively, tell you what we are doing, we can, negatively, tell you what we are not doing—we never once thought of a king." More tangibly, they also added the natural-born citizen requirement to the Constitution so that no critic could plausibly charge during the ratification debates that the presidency was a latent European monarchy.

Constitutional Amendments

The two-term limit on Presidents, which was established by the Twenty-second Amendment in 1951, bespoke the politics of its time as surely as the citizenship and residency requirements in the original Constitution bespoke the politics of 1787. From 1932 to 1944, Franklin D. Roosevelt, a liberal Democrat, was elected to four consecutive terms as President. The Republicans, who took control of Congress in 1947 for the first time since 1930, banded with conservative southern Democrats to enact a constitutional amendment that would disqualify any future Roosevelt from serving more than twice. Ironically, the only two Presidents whom the two-term limit has really restricted have been the Republicans Dwight D. Eisenhower and Ronald Reagan, both of whom opposed the amendment.

The Twelfth Amendment, which became part of the Constitution in 1804, applied the President's age, residency, and citizenship requirements to the Vice President.

Constitutional Ambiguities

A number of thorny legal questions attend the Constitution's provisions for presidential qualifications, for example, whether the residency requirement entails fourteen *consecutive* years in the United States prior to the election. Some challenged Herbert Hoover's eligibility to be President in 1929 by arguing that much of his time during the preceding fourteen years had been spent abroad. Hoover's defenders prevailed on the narrow ground that he had maintained a legal domicile in the United States throughout this period.

An even more unsettled issue is whether the "natural born Citizen" requirement disqualifies those who are born of American parents on foreign soil. As the legal scholar Charles Gordon has argued, the principle of *jus sanguinis,* "under which nationality could be transmitted by descent at the moment of birth," was more a part of the common law in 1787 than the old doctrine of *jus soli,* which determined a person's nationality according to the place of birth. But a controversial statement by Justice Horace Gray in the 1898 case of *United States* v.o *Kim Ark* seemed to restrict natural-born citizenship to those born "within the United States." The case did not concern presidential qualifications, however, and Gray's remark was not legally binding.

The legal complexities of the citizenship requirement aside, many have criticized its wisdom. In the late

1970s, the Secretary of State Henry A. Kissinger, a naturalized U.S. citizen of German birth, was barred by the presidential qualifications clause from his office's legal place in the line of succession to the presidency. In 1983, Senator Thomas Eagleton of Missouri proposed a constitutional amendment to repeal the citizenship and residency qualifications for President in favor of a requirement that the President must be a citizen for eleven years.

[See also (II) Vice President.]

BIBLIOGRAPHY

Gordon, Charles. "Who Can Be President of the United States?: The Unresolved Enigma." *Maryland Law Review* 28 (Winter 1968): 1–32.

Nelson, Michael. "Constitutional Qualifications for President." In *Inventing the American Presidency.* Edited by Thomas E. Cronin. 1989. Pp. 13–32.

– MICHAEL NELSON

R

RECESS APPOINTMENTS

Under Article II, Section 2, of the Constitution, "The President shall have Power to fill up all Vacancies that may happen during the Recess of the Senate, by granting Commissions which shall expire at the End of their next Session."

The Framers empowered the President to make recess appointments, without Senate confirmation, because they anticipated long periods each year when the Congress would be in adjournment. It would have been difficult to operate the federal government had it been necessary to wait for the next session of the Senate, which might be a half year or more away, before nominations could be made and confirmed and vacancies filled.

A recess appointee may continue to hold office, without Senate confirmation, until the end of the session following the one in which the appointment was first made. Even in the 1990s, that could be a period of a year or more.

The ambiguous constitutional phrase, "Vacancies that may happen during the Recess of the Senate," was long a subject of controversy. Did it mean simply vacancies that may occur during a recess or all vacancies that happen to exist during a recess even though they may have occurred while the Senate was in session? President George Washington adopted a narrow view of this provision and employed recess appointments only when a vacancy occurred during a Senate recess. Most of his successors have taken a more expansive approach. Since President James Madison's time, despite Senate opposition, Presidents have given this language a broad construction and used recess appointments to fill any existing vacancies, even those that first occurred while the Senate was in session.

Before the lengthening of congressional sessions, Presidents often found some political leverage in the use of recess appointments and would sometimes wait until after adjournment to fill a vacancy. When the Congress returned to session, the name of the individual who had received the recess appointment would then be sent to the Senate for confirmation. By this time, however, the nominee would have accumulated months of experience on the job. This made it difficult for the Senate to oppose the nomination on the grounds of inexperience.

The principal current use of recess appointments is for the strategic purpose of circumventing the confirmation process. President Ronald Reagan used recess appointment powers as part of his effort to undermine the Legal Services Corporation (LSC), a government agency that provides legal assistance in civil cases for the poor. Reagan made no appointments to the board of directors of the LSC for most of his first year in office. Then, to prevent holdovers who were Jimmy Carter's appointees from determining the 1982 grants of the LSC, Reagan made seven recess appointments on the last day of 1981. Over the next few years, Reagan made several regular nominations to the LSC board, then withdrew them before a Senate confirmation decision. At the same time, he continued to fill vacancies with recess appointments. Reagan appointees were thus able to control the LSC between 1981 and 1984, even though not a single one was confirmed by the Senate.

Presidents often found some political leverage in the use of recess appointments and would sometimes wait until after adjournment to fill a vacancy.

Many of the people who served on the LSC board during these years were fundamentally hostile to its purpose and policies. Reagan himself had long sought the abolition of the LSC. But Congress was not likely to follow the President's lead on the matter of abolition, nor to confirm many of the people who received recess appointments to the board. So Reagan used recess appointments to juggle board members, and thus deny Senate control through the confirmation process, in order to impose his own restrictive view of LSC functions.

Recess appointments of federal judges have posed a special concern because they raise the possibility of litigants facing a judge who does not have a lifetime appointment and who will soon be reviewed for confirmation by the Senate. Impartiality and objectivity may be less reliable under those circumstances.

But the federal courts have upheld the President's authority to make recess judicial appointments. The U.S. Court of Appeals for the Second Circuit took that position in an important 1962 case, *United States* v. *Allocco.* In 1983, the full U.S. Court of Appeals for the Ninth Circuit, finding that there was no reason to favor the constitutional guarantee of lifetime tenure for judges over the constitutional language providing for recess appointments, also concluded, in the case of *United States* v. *Woodley,* that Presidents had constitutional authority to make recess appointments to the federal courts.

There have been fifteen recess appointments in the history of the Supreme Court to Potter Stewart, who was named in 1959. Of the fifteen, only five actually participated in the work of the Court before Senate confirmation. Of the five who did take their seats before confirmation, four were later confirmed by the Senate and one, John Rutledge, was denied confirmation by the Senate in 1795. In 1960, however, the Senate passed a sense of the Senate resolution, introduced by Senator Philip A. Hart, which stated that recess appointments should not be made to the Supreme Court "except under unusual circumstances and for the purpose of preventing or ending a demonstrable breakdown in the administration of the Court's business." The Hart Resolution is not legally binding on Presidents, but there have been no recess appointments to the Supreme Court since its passage.

As early as 1863, Congress sought to control the use of recess appointments by enacting a statute that read in part "nor shall any money be paid out of the Treasury of the United States, as salary, to any person appointed during the recess of the Senate, to fill a vacancy in any existing office . . . until such appointee shall have been confirmed by the Senate." That was a broad restriction, preventing payment of any salary to any recess appointee.

Current law applies this restriction more narrowly to any recess appointee selected to fill a vacancy that "existed while the Senate was in session and was by law required to be filled by and with the advice and consent of the Senate." The restriction does not apply if the vacancy arose within thirty days before the end of the session of the Senate; or if, at the end of the session, a nomination for the office, other than the nomination of an individual appointed during a previous recess of the Senate, was pending before the Senate; or if a nomination for the office was rejected by the Senate within thirty days before the end of the session and an individual other than the one whose nomination was rejected thereafter receives a recess appointment. This does not prevent the use of recess appointments to fill vacancies that could be filled by regular appointments, but it does prevent payment of salary to the appointee under the circumstances described here.

The ambiguity of the recess appointments clause of the Constitution has left much room for subsequent—and still continuing—interpretation and debate.

[See also (II) Appointment Power.]

BIBLIOGRAPHY

Congress and the Nation, 1981–1984. 1985.

Corwin, Edward S. *The Constitution and What It Means Today.* 1978.

Fisher, Louis. *Constitutional Conflicts between Congress and the President.* 3d ed. 1991.

Mackenzie, G. Calvin. *The Politics of Presidential Appointments.* 1981.

– G. CALVIN MACKENZIE

RECOGNITION POWER

It is well established that the President as diplomat in chief has the implied power to recognize foreign nations and foreign governments. At the outset, a distinction must be made between recognizing nations and recognizing governments, although the President possesses both recognition powers. The recognition of a nation simply refers to the executive branch's affirmation that a new country has come into existence. To become a nation, an entity must have a defined territory; a permanent population; some domestic regulation or control of that population; and the ability to conduct relations with other countries. Some have argued that the executive must recognize as a new nation any entity having those attributes; but others have argued that an entity attains statehood only if the executive formally recognizes the entity as a nation. Under either theory, a nation's recognition is significant, since only nations can possess all of the sovereign rights and duties available under international law. For example, only nations can usually enter into treaties and join most international organizations. The President's recognition of a nation is the starting point of foreign affairs and is part and parcel of his control over international matters. The executive branch must determine whether to establish diplomatic relations with a new nation.

Nation or Regime?

The President's recognition of a nation may overlap with his recognition of a government in that nation, but not always. When only one governmental regime claims to control a new nation, the President's recognition of that foreign state may occur simultaneously with his recognition of the governmental regime. However, when more than one government contends for a new nation's leadership, or when a revolutionary force challenges a government's control in an existing country, the President must decide which of those entities to recognize. In such instances, the President's decision whether to recognize a foreign government may be more complex and more politicized than his decision to recognize a nation. When faced with a choice between two competing forces, the President may recognize the governmental regime that is more committed to American values and democracy; during the cold war, the United States and the Soviet Union each wanted to recognize and support the particular regime with which it was most compatible. The President may make his recognition decision only after seeing which of the competing regimes actually takes firm and prolonged control of the foreign country. Like the power to recognize a nation, the President's power to recognize a particular foreign government is essential to his foreign affairs authority.

From the earliest days of the Republic, the executive branch has exerted the power to recognize other nations and governments.

The Constitution says nothing explicit about the power to recognize other nations or governments. Instead, the recognition power is said to derive impliedly from one of the President's few explicit international powers—his power of receiving and appointing ambassadors. Article II, Section 2, of the Constitution provides that the President "shall nominate, and by and with the Advice and Consent of the Senate, shall appoint Ambassadors, other public Ministers and Consuls." Article II, Section 3, provides that the President "shall receive Ambassadors and other public Ministers." By implication, if the President is empowered to appoint and receive ambassadors, he can determine which countries and which governments to recognize in conducting those ambassadorial relations. In other words, the President's recognition power is an implied precondition to his authority to appoint and receive ambassadors.

Exclusive Executive Power

The President's recognition power is assumed to reside exclusively in the executive branch, without senatorial oversight. Supreme Court decisions have directly and indirectly validated the President's exclusive recognition power. For example, in *United States* v. *Belmont* (1937), the Supreme Court upheld an agreement between the executive branch and the Soviet Union that settled and assigned monetary claims and counterclaims between the two governments. That executive agreement was made in connection with the President's recognition of the Soviet government. Justice George Sutherland's opinion clearly stated that the executive branch alone possessed the power to recognize the Soviet government: "The recognition, establishment of diplomatic relations, the assignment . . . were all parts of one transaction, resulting in an international compact between the two governments. That the negotiations . . . and agreements and understandings . . . were within the competence of the President may not be doubted." He concluded that "in respect of what was done here, the Executive had authority to speak as the sole organ of [the national] government." Although the federal courts have regularly supported the President's recognition practices, they have established a distinction between de jure recognition and de facto recognition. Even when the executive has not formally accorded recognition to a government by law (de jure recognition), the courts may give some privileges (e.g., immunity) to a government that clearly and realistically exists on a factual basis (de facto recognition).

From the early days of the Republic, the executive branch has exerted the power to recognize other nations and governments. In Federalist 69, Alexander Hamilton initially doubted the significance of the executive's power to receive ambassadors. But when later debating James Madison, Hamilton argued strongly for executive supremacy in foreign affairs, including the recognition power. Hamilton reasoned: "No objection has been made to the President's having acknowledged the republic of France, by reception of its minister, without having consulted the Senate." Presidents have since recognized many countries and governments without consulting with Congress. Nevertheless, even if not constitutionally required, it may be politically prudent for the President to consult with the Congress when recognition issues arise; after all, congressional appropriations may be needed to support the President's recognition of a new country or government.

President Jimmy Carter angered the Congress when he unilaterally terminated the Mutual Defense Treaty with the Republic of China (Taiwan) and shifted the United States' recognition from Taiwan to the People's Republic of China in 1978. In so doing, President Carter contravened a congressional resolution that had sought "prior consultation between the Congress and the executive branch on any proposed policy changes affecting the continuation in force of the Mutual Defense Treaty." Members of Congress sued the politically unsavvy Carter, but the Supreme Court held the suit to be unjusticiable.

[See also (II) Ambassadors, Receiving and Appointing; Diplomat in Chief.]

BIBLIOGRAPHY

American Law Institute. *Restatement (Third) of the Foreign Relations Law of the United States, Section 201–205.* 1987.

Corwin, Edward S. *The President.* 5th ed. 1984.

Franck, Thomas M., and Michael J. Glennon. *Foreign Relations and National Security Law.* 1987.
Henkin, Louis. *Foreign Affairs and the Constitution.* 1972.
McClure, Wallace. *International Executive Agreements.* 1967.

– KENNETH C. RANDALL

REMOVAL POWER

The power to remove executive-branch officials whose appointments require Senate consent is not mentioned in the Constitution. This silence invites four competing theories. According to the first theory, the power of removal is given to Congress by the necessary and proper clause of Article I, Section 8, clause 18, and may be delegated by Congress to the President or other officials with such conditions or limitations as Congress determines necessary. The second theory says that the power to remove is contained in the appointment power and therefore requires the Senate's consent. In the third theory, executive-branch offices are expected to serve through the term of the President who appointed them and to resign at the end of that term, subject only to impeachment by the House and conviction by the Senate. Finally, according to the fourth theory, the removal power—though not explicitly mentioned—is a functional necessity for the President in the exercise of the executive power and therefore exists as one of the inherent powers.

The Federal Period

In *Federalist* 77 Alexander Hamilton argued that the Senate's advice and consent to presidential nominations also extended to removals, unless Congress legislated otherwise. But James Madison, in the debates in 1789 over a removal clause in the statute creating the Department of Foreign Affairs, argued for an unrestricted removal power for the President. Madison warned that providing the Senate with a share in such power would create a "two-headed monster" superintending the departments. Following Madison's argument, the statutes creating the departments of Foreign Affairs, War, and the Treasury acknowledged the removal power of the President.

From the very first, Presidents began to assert their power to remove officials. George Washington secured the resignation of Edmund Randolph as Secretary of State in 1795 after an intercepted letter implied that Randolph would pursue a pro-French policy in exchange for a bribe. Washington also removed seventeen officials whose appointments had been consented to by the Senate. John Adams was the first President to remove a Cabinet secretary without going through the formalities of a resignation: incensed at Secretary of State Timothy Pickering's interference with his French policy and Pickering's failure to support Adams's nomination of his son-in-law for adjutant general, Adams fired him. Adams removed nineteen other civil officers as well. Only one removal, that of Tenche Coxe in 1797 from his post as Commissioner of Revenue, involved party politics.

President Thomas Jefferson removed the Surveyor General of the United States, Rufus Putnam, who disagreed with the President's policies on western lands. He fired John Adams's son-in-law, Col. William Smith, surveyor of the port of New York, for taking part in a plot against Spanish possessions in South America, a violation of U.S. law. Jefferson removed a total of 109 officers, including Adams's midnight appointments at the end of his term, and several lawyers and collectors of customs. James Madison fired his Secretary of State, Robert Smith, for incompetence, claiming that whatever talents Smith had he did not "possess those adapted to his station." During the War of 1812, he also obtained the resignation under pressure of Gen. John Armstrong as Secretary of War after Armstrong failed to prepare the nation's capital against the arrival of British troops and Washington was occupied and sacked. Madison removed twenty-seven officers altogether, most of them revenue collectors. James Monroe also removed only twenty-seven civil officers, one-third of whom were from the foreign service and one-third of whom were collectors of revenue. President John Quincy Adams removed only twelve.

For the most part removals by the Presidents through the 1820s involved wrongdoing in office and not partisan politics.

For the most part removals by the Presidents through the 1820s involved wrongdoing in office and not partisan politics. In 1820, Congress passed a Tenure of Office Act (3 Stat. 582) that established four-year terms for officers handling funds. It also made such officers removable "at pleasure," which presumably empowered the President. Officials covered by the 1820 law included U.S. attorneys, collectors of customs, receivers of moneys for public lands, registrars of land offices, paymasters in the army, and commissary officers in the military.

The Jacksonian and Whig Periods

Controversy over the removal power erupted during the administration of Andrew Jackson, who established the principle of rotation in office on partisan grounds. Although Jackson's slogan "to the victor belong the spoils" seems to imply wholesale removals, the historian Erik McKinley Eriksson has calculated that fewer than one-tenth of the lower-ranking officers of the United States had been removed after Jackson's first year in office, with perhaps one-fifth gone by the end of Jackson's term—a total of 180 removals. Jackson, however, also claimed the power to remove Cabinet officials who asserted an independent judgment on the statutory powers given them by Congress. Jackson removed Secretary of the Treasury William J. Duane for refusing to remove the funds from the Bank of the United States and deposit them in state banks. He then appointed Roger B. Taney during a congressional recess, and Taney implemented Jackson's policy. When it reconvened, the Senate retaliated by blocking Taney's appointment as Secretary of the Treasury, forcing him to give up his post, and then by rejecting his nomination for Associate Justice of the Supreme Court. (In 1836 a more cooperative Senate approved Jackson's nomination of Taney for Chief Justice of the United States.)

The Whig-dominated Senate passed a resolution of censure against Jackson in 1834, stating that the President had "assumed upon himself authority and power not conferred by the constitution and laws, but in derogation of both." Jackson sent a vigorous rebuttal, claiming that he possessed the right of "removing those officers who are to aid him in the execution of the laws." Three years later the Senate expunged the resolution of censure.

In 1838 the Supreme Court observed in *Ex parte Hennen* (1839) that it had "become the settled and well-understood construction of the Constitution that the power of removal was vested in the President alone," but, since the case involved the removal of a clerk by a federal judge, this statement was an obiter dictum. Abel P. Upshur, in his classic *A Brief Inquiry into the Nature and Character of Our Federal Government* (1840), specifically warned of the "great and alarming defect" that the removal power was held by the President.

The Civil War and After

The removal power became unsettled in the years during and after the Civil War. The Currency Act of 1863 (12 Stat. 665) established the office of Comptroller of the Currency, giving the officer a five-year term and authorizing his removal only with the consent of the Senate. In 1864 Congress passed the Consular and Diplomatic Appropriation Act (13 Stat. 137), which required the President to submit reasons for removal of consular clerks to Congress.

In the aftermath of the Civil War, Congress passed measures to protect its Reconstruction policies from President Andrew Johnson. Legislation in 1866 forbade dismissals of military officers in time of peace without sentence by courts martial (14 Stat. 92). The Command of the Army Act of 1867 provided that "the General of the Army shall not be removed, suspended, or relieved from command, or assigned to duty elsewhere than at said headquarters, except at his own request, without the previous approval of the Senate" (14 Stat. 487). The Tenure of Office Act of 1867, passed the same day, provided that the heads of certain departments, including the Secretary of War, would hold office during the term of the President by whom they had been appointed and for one month thereafter, subject to removal by consent of the Senate. It also provided that "every person holding any civil office to which he has been appointed by and with the advice and consent of the Senate . . . shall be entitled to hold such office until a successor shall have been in like manner appointed and duly qualified" (14 Stat. 430). During a Senate recess the President could suspend an official for reason of misconduct in office, criminal activity, incapacity, or legal disqualification, but he would be restored to his office if the Senate refused to endorse the President's action. Both the Command of the Army Act and the Tenure of Office Act were passed over Johnson's veto.

In 1867, after Congress adjourned, Johnson asked Secretary of War Edwin M. Stanton to resign. When Stanton refused, the President, seemingly acting in accordance with the law, suspended him and authorized Gen. Ulysses S. Grant to act as Secretary of War. Johnson had outmaneuvered Congress, for he used the provision in the law that permitted him to suspend a department secretary until the Senate reconvened. But when the Senate did so, it reinstated Stanton. Now Johnson acted for the first time in apparent violation of the Tenure of Office Act by removing Stanton while the Senate was in session and appointing Gen. Lorenzo Thomas as his Secretary of War. The House thereupon voted articles of impeachment against the President in February 1868. At his Senate trial Johnson argued that the Tenure of Office Act was unconstitutional. He also argued that even if the act was constitutional his removal of Stanton did not violate it. Stanton had been appointed by Abraham Lincoln, and Johnson argued that the law covered only those nominations a President himself had made and could not prevent him from removing an official nominated by his predecessor. Johnson escaped removal himself by just one vote in the Senate, and Stanton surrendered his office. Congress repealed the Tenure of Office Act in 1887 after a confrontation with President Grover Cleveland.

The Twentieth Century

In a series of cases the Supreme Court chipped away at legislative removal powers. In *Shurtleff* v. *United States* (1903), the Court recognized a presidential removal power in the absence of explicit statutory language controlling removals. In *Wallace* v. *United States* (1922), Chief Justice William Howard Taft ruled that Senate confirmation of a successor (to the person the President intended to remove) nominated by the President would invalidate legislative restrictions that might otherwise have applied to the removal of an official. Finally, in the landmark case of *Myers* v. *United States* (1926) Chief Justice Taft recognized the removal power as an inherent presidential prerogative and declared unconstitutional statutory procedures that gave the Senate authority to review removals and suspensions.

Congress has continued to protect commissioners of certain agencies from presidential removals.

The acts that established regulatory agencies—the Interstate Commerce Act of 1887, the Federal Trade Commission Act of 1914, the Federal Tariff Commission Act of 1916, and Federal Power Commission Act of 1920—all provided fixed terms for commissioners, whom the President could remove for "inefficiency, neglect of duty or malfeasance in office." In creating the Railroad Labor Board in 1920, Congress provided that the members should be removable by the President "for neglect of duty or malfeasance in office, but for no other cause" and applied a similar provision to the Board of General Appraisers in 1922 and Board of Tax Appeals in 1924. Such provisions were upheld by the Supreme Court in *Humphrey's Executor* v. *United States* (1935), which distinguished between officials performing executive tasks and those engaged in quasi-legislative and quasi-judicial duties. The Court held that the latter could be insulated from the presidential removal power by legislation. Moreover, in *Wiener* v. *United States* (1958), the Court held that the presidential removal power could be restricted even in the absence of statutory provisions.

Agencies that Congress considered its own were also insulated from the removal power. In establishing the General Accounting Office in 1921, Congress provided that the Comptroller General could be removed only by impeachment or a joint resolution of Congress. While a joint resolution requires the President's signature and can be vetoed, clearly such an officer is accountable to Congress and not to the President. Congress has continued to protect commissioners of certain agencies from presidential removals. The U.S. Commission on Civil Rights, for example, was reconstituted in 1983 when Congress added language to the effect that commissioners could be removed by the President "only for neglect of duty or malfeasance in office."

Courts and Congress have also protected special prosecutors and independent counsels who investigate high-level scandals involving the presidency, such as the Watergate affair. President Richard M. Nixon ordered Attorney General Elliot Richardson to dismiss Special Prosecutor Archibald Cox, who pursued the inquiry further than Nixon wished; Richardson promptly resigned along with Deputy Attorney General William Ruckelshaus. Finally, Solicitor General Robert Bork, who had become Acting Attorney General, did fire Cox. The political activist Ralph Nader and several members of Congress filed suit. In *Nader* v. *Bork* (1973), a district court agreed that Cox had been illegally removed from office because the removal violated the department's regulations regarding the special prosecutor. The Ethics Act of 1978 prohibited the removal of a special prosecutor (now called the independent counsel) except for cause, and that statutory restriction was upheld by the Supreme Court in *Morrison* v. *Olson* (1988).

By asserting their prerogative to use the removal power, Presidents throughout the history of the office have transformed their role into that of Chief Executive, exercising broad control over the administrative establishment. Presidents can make departmental officials do their bidding because they have the ultimate sanction to employ against the officials if they refuse.

[See also (II) Executive Prerogative, Inherent Powers.]

BIBLIOGRAPHY

Corwin, Edward S. *The President's Removal Power under the Constitution.* 1927.

Fisher, Louis. *Constitutional Conflicts between President and Congress.* 3d ed. 1991. Chapter 3, "Theory in a Crucible: The Removal Power."

White, Leonard D. *The Federalists: A Study in Administrative History, 1789–1801.* 1948.

White, Leonard D. *The Jacksonians: A Study in Administrative History, 1829–1861.* 1954.

White, Leonard D. *The Jeffersonians: A Study in Administrative History, 1801–1829.* 1951.

White, Leonard D. *The Republican Era: A Study in Administrative History, 1869–1901.* 1958.

– RICHARD M. PIOUS

REORGANIZATION POWER

The delegated authority whereby the President can effect change in executive-branch organization, subject to qualifications imposed by Congress, is known as the reorganization power. Typically, this power has been delegated to Presidents for limited periods. The legislative veto made its first appearance as a qualification on the delegation of reorganization power to the President. The power and accompanying veto appeared for the first time in the Economy Act of 1932; it ended in 1983 with the Supreme Court case of *INS* v. *Chadha.*

Without reorganization power, the President has little capacity to affect administrative organization. With this power, the President has primary responsibility for organization within the executive branch.

Origin of the Reorganization Powers

In the 1920s President Warren G. Harding and the congressional Joint Committee on Reorganization cooperated in creating a reform plan for government. The joint committee's report proposed that genuine reform would require ongoing executive reorganizations. According to the committee, reorganization was a continuing process of change in which the most important job would remain to be accomplished after the initial wave of organizational reforms.

In 1932 President Herbert Hoover requested that Congress grant him reorganization authority. Congress passed the Economy Act of 1932, which gave the President the power to transfer whole agencies or parts of agencies to departments or independent agencies. The act also initiated a mechanism to check presidential use of reorganization power, the legislative veto. It specified that the President's orders for reorganization were subject to a resolution of disapproval by either house of Congress within sixty days after their issuance.

In early December 1932, Hoover issued eleven orders specifying reorganizations. He had, however, been beaten by Franklin D. Roosevelt in the November election, and the House of Representatives passed a resolution of disapproval for all eleven orders, blocking the lame-duck President's action.

Routinization of the Reorganization Power

As Roosevelt entered office, Congress passed the Economy Act of 1933. The act empowered the President to abolish agencies as well as to reorganize them and also gave the President greater leeway by requiring that congressional disapproval of a presidential reorganization order proceed through a bill that had to pass both houses of Congress and achieve the President's signature. That is, the President could veto the very bill meant to block his reorganization action. Congress did qualify this grant by specifying that it would expire in two years.

Roosevelt gave primary attention to the crisis of the Great Depression and spent relatively little effort trying to fix administrative inefficiencies through reorganization. The lapse of the reorganization authority in 1935 therefore meant little to him. The Brownlow Committee and its 1937 report, however, convinced Roosevelt that executive reorganization could be a tool for managing the executive branch. In 1939, Congress passed a reorganization act renewing the President's reorganization power for two years. The act introduced the concept of the President issuing reorganization plans rather than executive orders as means of implementing reorganization power. The act's legislative veto provision specified that a presidential reorganization plan could be killed by a concurrent resolution in which both houses passed expressions of disapproval (not requiring presidential signature).

In early 1937, the Brownlow Committee had proposed a number of reforms at which Congress had balked. The Reorganization Act of 1939 contained few of those recommendations, but with the reorganization power granted in the act, Roosevelt created the Brownlow-recommended Executive Office of the President and transferred agencies to it.

During World War II the President gained reorganization powers (as part of his war powers) through the First War Powers Act of 1941. Peacetime, however, left President Harry S Truman without reorganization authority, and on 24 May 1945 he sent Congress a message requesting the renewal of reorganization power. Congress was slow to respond to Truman's request, and there were some in Congress who advocated a one-house legislative veto to make it even easier for Congress to block a presidential reorganization plan. Congress, however, ended up retaining the concurrent-resolution requirement for the legislative veto in the Reorganization Act of 1945. The 1945 act renewed the delegation of authority for two years only.

Truman issued three reorganization plans in 1946. Plans nos. 1 and 3 addressed rather small-scale reforms without effecting any interdepartmental shifts of agencies, and both survived legislative veto attempts. In Reorganization Plan No. 2, however, the President attempted to transform the Federal Security Administration into a Cabinet-level human services department. That plan was vetoed by Congress.

The postwar years saw increasing recognition of the need for an increased presidential managerial capacity. Many observers saw the reorganization power as a necessary instrument for management. But some members of Congress were increasingly uneasy about both the delegation of legislative authority to Presidents and the constitutional propriety of the legislative veto.

The Reorganization Act of 1949 renewed the reorganization authority but eased the requirements for the legislative veto, making it a one-house resolution of disapproval by a constitutional majority (a majority of all members of the House or of the Senate). The act extended the reorganization power for four years, twice what had become the typical extension period. The first of the two Hoover Commissions was the main beneficiary of the 1949 renewal of the reorganization power. President Truman sent forty-one reorganization plans to Congress, most of which implemented the commission's recommendations, saving them from the riskier pathway of statutory implementation.

In 1953 Congress came close to weakening the reorganization power even further by specifying a one-house veto by a simple majority vote. At first it had seemed that President Dwight D. Eisenhower endorsed that change, but the administration quickly clarified its intentions to Congress, and the Reorganization Act of 1953 extended the 1949 act for two years. In 1955 it was extended for an additional two years. Eisenhower presented twelve reorganization plans to Congress in his first year in office, none of which were vetoed. Several of these effected major changes in departments and one of them created a new department—Health, Education, and Welfare.

A Weakened Reorganization Power

The Reorganization Act of 1957 extended the reorganization power for two years but changed the requirement for the legislative veto to a one-house simple majority. Only two reorganization plans were submitted under the 1957 act, one of which was disapproved by Congress. The reorganization authority was renewed early in the Kennedy administration for a two-year period, with the same one-house, simple-majority veto as the 1957 act. In Reorganization Plan No. 1 of 1962, President John F. Kennedy proposed to establish a department of urban affairs and housing. Congress had rejected a bill to create that department just a year earlier. Kennedy attempted to use the more direct route of a reorganization plan, only to have it killed by legislative veto. In part because of congressional dissatisfaction with the effort to create a new Cabinet department through reorganization, the reorganization power was not renewed during the Kennedy administration, but it was renewed in 1965 at President Lyndon Baines Johnson's behest. Johnson requested permanent renewal, but Congress was only willing to extend the grant of power for four years.

Once it was renewed, Johnson made active use of the reorganization power. In 1965 he sent twelve reorganization plans to Congress, only one of which was vetoed. These addressed diverse subjects, such as shifting all water pollution controls to the Department of the Interior, reorganizing the District of Columbia government, and restructuring the Public Health Service. Johnson also created two new Cabinet-level departments through statute during his term: the Department of Housing and Urban Development and the Department of Transportation.

In 1971, restrictions on reorganization power were designed to protect congressional committees from being overwhelmed by presidential reorganization plans.

Early in the presidency of Richard M. Nixon the reorganization authority was renewed for a two-year term. Two years later, Congress renewed the authority but added a new restriction on its use. According to the 1971 act the reorganization power could only be used to introduce one reorganization plan within a thirty-day period, and each reorganization plan could deal with only one subject. The restrictions were designed to protect congressional committees from being overwhelmed by presidential reorganization plans. The reorganization authority lapsed on 1 April 1973, in a context of worsening presidential-congressional relations, and it was not extended. Nixon did, however, effect significant changes through the reorganization power. In 1969 he reorganized the Interstate Commerce Commission, giving more power to its presidentially appointed chairperson. In 1970 he reorganized the Bureau of the Budget, renaming it the Office of Management and Budget. At the same time he also ordered creation of a new Domestic Policy Council within the Executive Office of the President.

The reorganization power was not again granted to a President until 1977, when it was given to Jimmy Carter. Carter requested a grant of reorganization authority for a four-year period and proposed a presidential right of amendment for reorganization plans. In the Reorganization Act of 1977 new requirements for congressional action were specified, aiming to force a vote in each house on every reorganization plan. The act granted the President the right to amend a reorganization plan within thirty days after it was sent to Congress. A new qualification included in this act prohibited reorganization plans from addressing independent regulatory commissions.

Carter actively sought government reorganization. His largest initiatives were enacted through statutes, but he sought some significant reforms through reorganization plans. Among the more important targets of these plans were reorganization of the Executive Office of the President to reduce the size of its staff, the shift of federal personnel functions from the defunct Civil Service Commission to the Merit Systems Protection Board and the Office of Personnel Management, and creation of the Office of the U.S. Trade Representative.

From its beginning in the Economy Act of 1932, the presidential reorganization power depended on the legislative veto. Without that legislative check, Congress could not justify the delegation of its authority to the President. The alternative to this arrangement was the normal constitutional pattern of presidential submission of proposals to Congress for positive legislative action. In 1983, in the case of *INS* v. *Chadha,* the Supreme Court settled the half-century-old argument about the constitutionality of the legislative veto, ruling that it was unconstitutional in any form and thereby erasing the basis for the delegation of presidential reorganization power. From then on, presidential efforts at reorganizing the executive branch required positive legislative action. Following the Court's decision, Congress passed legislation in 1984 that gave the President reorganization authority subject to congressional approval by joint resolution. The difficulty of gaining the approval of both houses within a fixed period of days resulted in the Ronald Reagan administration not seeking future authority after the 1984 statute expired on 31 December 1984.

[See also (II) Separation of Powers.]

BIBLIOGRAPHY

Berg, Clifford L. "Lapse of Reorganization Authority." *Public Administration Review* 35 (1975). 195–199.

Fisher, Louis, and Ronald Moe. "Delegating with Ambivalence: The Legislative Veto and Executive Reorganization." *Studies on the Legislative Veto.* By Committee on Rules, U.S. House of Representatives. 1980.

Seidman, Harold, and Robert Gilmour. *Politics, Position, and Power.* 1986.

– PERI E. ARNOLD

RULEMAKING POWER

Presidents in the late twentieth century have attempted to influence rulemaking in federal agencies in order to achieve overall policy coordination. In doing so, Presidents have asserted their constitutional powers over the executive branch and have taken advantage of certain indirectly related statutory powers. Congress has not enacted a statute specifically controlling this aspect of presidential supervision of the agencies. Nevertheless, Presidents have established some important programs by executive order.

The Administrative Procedure Act of 1946 (APA) established general policy-making procedures for the executive branch but did not discuss the President's relationship with rulemaking agencies. The Supreme Court in *Franklin* v. *Massachusetts* (1992) held that the APA does not apply directly to the President.

The APA specifies a simple process for federal rulemaking. Agencies must give public notice of proposed rules, receive and consider written comments on the proposals, and then publish final rules in the *Federal Register.* Over the years, this process has become a somewhat more formal interchange with affected interests. The result for most final rules is a record of fact and opinion that undergoes judicial review. The courts seek a reasonable basis for the agency's decision in fact, law, and procedure, but avoid invading the agency's policymaking discretion.

Presidents attempt to impose a measure of coordination on the sprawling executive establishment.

Presidents have a combination of constitutional and statutory powers through which they influence federal rulemaking. First, they have constitutional powers to propose and to veto the statutes that authorize regulation. Second, the Constitution provides that the President or his subordinates, and not Congress, may appoint federal regulators (although often with the Senate's advice and consent). Third, the President has constitutional powers to ensure the faithful execution of the laws and to require his subordinates to furnish him opinions in writing on the performance of their duties. These powers imply the capacity to remove regulators whose performance is disappointing. The Supreme Court upheld the President's authority to remove subordinate executive officers in *Myers* v. *United States* (1926). For the independent regulatory agencies, however, Congress restricts presidential removal power to the presence of cause. In *Humphrey's Executor* v. *United States* (1935), the Court upheld the authority of Congress to do so. In practice, this has meant far greater policy autonomy for independent agencies than for executive agencies.

Presidents have statutory power to formulate the federal budget for congressional consideration and passage. This power applies not only to the executive agencies but also to most of the independent ones. An agency's funding level critically affects its capacity to regulate. Because the President's Office of Management and Budget (OMB) both formulates the budget and exercises most presidential supervision of rulemaking, agencies are reluctant to oppose its preferences. Presidents also often possess statutory power to reorganize existing agencies.

Occasionally a President has taken interest in a particularly important pending regulation and has consulted with the administrator who is responsible for issuing it. The Supreme Court has never decided the permissible extent of this presidential participation in rulemaking. Since a particular regulation of one agency can affect many related policy responsibilities of other agencies, it is important for the President to play some coordinating role. For example, an environmental regulation of power-plant emissions can affect energy and economic policy. The lower courts have struggled to accommodate two competing values. One of these is executive privilege—the need for policy debate in the executive branch to be confidential, so that it will be candid. The other is the need to abide by administrative law requirements that rules be based on known administrative records that fully support them. Thus, it may be permissible for the President or his immediate advisers to consult privately with an administrator, as long as the final rule is supported by the agency's record.

More often, Presidents take a generalized interest in the performance of federal rulemaking. They issue executive orders and other less formal directives to the agencies, stating principles and policies that administrators must follow when regulating. Here, Presidents attempt to impose a measure of coordination on the sprawling executive establishment, within statutory limits. Statutory delegations of regulatory power ordinarily contain enough discretion to allow compliance with such presidential commands.

Since the early 1970s, all Presidents have created interagency review procedures that balance health, safety, and environmental goals of statutes with the administration's economic goals. President Richard M. Nixon instituted "quality of life" review of environmental and other health and safety regulations. Proposed rules were submitted to OMB and other agencies for review and comment. In practice, this program focused on rules of the Environmental Protection Agency. President Gerald Ford issued an executive order requiring executive agencies to prepare an "inflation impact statement" for each proposed major regulation. These were reviewed by the Council on Wage and Price Stability. Agency compliance with the program was quite uneven. The analyses were performed too late in the rulemaking process to affect policy significantly. President Jimmy Carter sought to remedy these deficiencies by issuing an executive order that required agency heads to prepare agendas of proposed actions, to review their own rules early in the process of formulation, and to assure that the most cost-effective approaches were taken for significant rules. President Carter established a Regulatory Analysis Review Group to review analyses prepared for major rules and to comment on them. He also created a Regulatory Council, composed of the heads of rulemaking agencies, to coordinate policy and to avoid conflict or duplication of effort.

A pair of related executive orders that were issued by President Ronald Reagan have had the most far-reaching impact on rulemaking. Executive Order 12291 requires executive agencies, to the extent permitted by statute, to observe cost-benefit principles when promulgating regulations. (The order does not apply to the independent agencies.) Proposed rules must be sent to OMB, which reviews them and discusses them with the agencies. This function has been placed partly in the Office of Information and Regulatory Affairs (OIRA) within OMB and partly in the President's Council on Competitiveness. Executive Order 12291 is not based on statutory authority. It rests on the President's constitutional powers to supervise the executive branch. Congress has repeatedly considered applying statutory controls to the program, but has yet to do so.

Executive Order 12498, promulgated by President Reagan in 1985, established a "regulatory planning process" to be implemented through formulation of an annual regulatory program for the executive agencies of the federal government. (Again, independent regulatory agencies are not included.) The head of each executive agency must send OMB a draft regulatory program containing a description of all significant regulatory actions to be undertaken in the next year. When these are combined into the federal government's program for the year, a single document exists to give an overview of the direction of federal rulemaking.

Other executive orders have required agencies to consider the impact of their rules on such values as federalism. Thus, whenever a President regards an issue as important enough to merit special consideration by the executive agencies, he possesses a mechanism to ensure that the bureaucracy will share his sense of priorities.

[See also (II) Executive Orders, Executive Privilege.]

BIBLIOGRAPHY

Fisher, Louis. *The Constitution between Friends.* 1978.

National Academy of Public Administration. *Presidential Management of Rulemaking in Regulatory Agencies.* 1987.

Pierce, Richard A., Jr., Sidney A. Shapiro, and Paul R. Verkuil. *Administrative Law and Process.* 2d ed. 1992.

Shane, Peter M., and Harold H. Bruff. *The Law of Presidential Power.* 1988.

Strauss, Peter L., and Cass R. Sunstein. "The Role of the President and OMB in Informal Rulemaking." *Administrative Law Review* 38 (1986): 181–207.

Symposium. "Cost-Benefit Analysis and Agency Decision-Making: An Analysis of Executive Order No. 12,291." *Arizona Law Review* 23 (1981): 1195–1298.

– HAROLD H. BRUFF

S

SCIENCE ADVISER

The institution of the function of science adviser to the U.S. President ranks among the most important innovations in governmental organization. At the first science ministerial of the twenty-four-member Organization for Economic Cooperation and Development in 1962, the United States was the only country to be represented by a full-time science adviser to the head of government. Thirty years later, almost all member countries were represented by science advisers of corresponding rank at the OECD science ministerial meeting in 1992.

Since World War II, Presidents recognized the importance of having a science adviser to provide independent advice. President Franklin D. Roosevelt looked to Vannevar Bush as head of the wartime Office of Scientific Research and Development. Following a report by William T. Golden President Truman established the first science advisory mechanism in the Executive Office of the President (EOP) with a science advisory committee reporting to the President through the Director of the Office of Defense Mobilization (ODM). Its chairman, Oliver Buckley, also had direct access to the President, although he seldom used such access. This arrangement was continued during the first Eisenhower Administration, when Lee A. DuBridge and Isidor I. Rabi served as part-time chairmen.

The launching of Sputnik in 1957 moved President Eisenhower to recognize the need for independent counsel in matters involving science-and-technology. Such an adviser would work with senior White House staff groups to handle science-and-technology issues relating to policy and program priorities and budgetary choices and mobilize the best science-and-technology expertise in support of presidential decision making.

President Eisenhower elevated the ODM Science Advisory Committee (chaired by the science adviser) to report directly to him. He sought its advice in responding to Sputnik and to the competing proposals of the military services. The adviser and the President's Science Advisory Committee (PSAC) played a key role in the organization of the National Aeronautics and Space Administration, the Arms Control and Disarmament Agency, and the establishment of the Director of Defense Research and Engineering and the Advanced Research Projects Agency in the Department of Defense. They advised on crucial questions regarding technical intelligence and the possibilities for a nuclear-test ban.

President Kennedy institutionalized the presidential science-advisory function by establishing the Office of Science and Technology (OST) in the EOP, adding the title of Director of OST to that of Special Assistant to the President. The portfolio of his science adviser, Jerome B. Wiesner, was broadened to include health, civilian science and technology, and the environment.

The launching of Sputnik in 1957 moved President Eisenhower to recognize the need for independent counsel in matters involving science-and-technology.

During the Johnson and Nixon administrations, the science adviser was deeply involved in national-security issues particularly as related to the Vietnam War, arms control, and the treaty to eliminate biological weapons. After his reelection in 1972, President Nixon abolished both OST and PSAC, an action attributed to opposition by PSAC members to the President's positions on ballistic missile defense and the development of the supersonic transport, as well as the general disaffection of the academic community toward the Vietnam War. The science adviser's duties were added to those of the director of the National Science Foundation, who concentrated on energy research and development, industrial research and development, and agricultural research.

The OST function was resurrected in the EOP by an act of Congress in 1976 in the form of the Office of Science and Technology Policy, and President Ford reestablished the position of Special Assistant to the President for S&T. President Carter's science adviser dealt with questions such as the MX missile, the test ban, space policy, and air-quality standards. President Reagan's advisers addressed issues concerning support of basic research, the aerospace plane, Stealth technology, and the Strategic Defense Initiative.

President Bush elevated the position to Cabinet rank as Assistant to the President for S&T. Bush reestablished the science advisory committee as the President's Council of Advisers on Science and Technology (PCAST). His science advisor, D. Allan Bromley was instrumental in revitalizing the Federal Coordinating Council for Science and Technology, in framing national technology policies, and in forging government-wide research-and-development programs having presidential priority, including high-performance computing, global climate change, advanced materials, and biotechnology. In the Clinton administration, the importance of the science-advisory role was signified by the appointment of the science adviser very early in the administration at the same time as the appointment of Cabinet officers.

Although the science adviser's role as a senior member of the presidential staff was firmly reinforced during the Bush administration, the vicissitudes in science advising during the past fifty years underscore the fragility of the function and its critical dependence on the direct interest and involvement of the President.

[See also (II) Office of Science and Technology Policy.]

BIBLIOGRAPHY

Beckler, David Z. "A Decision Maker's Guide to Science Advising." In *Worldwide Science and Technology Advice to the Highest Levels of Governments.* Edited by William T Golden. 1991

Bronk, Detlev W. "Science Advice in the White House: The Genesis of the President's Science Advisers and the National Science Foundation." *Science* 186 (11 October 1974): 116–121. Reprinted in *Science Advice to the President.* Edited by William T. Golden. 2d ed. Forthcoming.

Golden, William T., ed. *Science and Technology Advice to the President, Congress, and Judiciary.* 2d ed. Forthcoming.

Killian, James R. *Sputnik, Scientists, and Eisenhower.* 1977.

Kistiakowsky, George B. *A Scientist at the White House.* 1976.

Wiesner, Jerome. *Where Science and Politics Meet.* 1965.

– DAVID Z. BECKLER
WILLIAM T. GOLDEN

SECRET SERVICE

The United States Secret Service, now well known for its function of protection of Presidents, originated as a small anticounterfeiting organization in the Department of the Treasury near the end of the Civil War. It was established by Secretary of the Treasury Hugh McCulloch on 5 July 1865, based on an earlier decision made at the last Cabinet meeting held by Abraham Lincoln.

From extremely modest origins, the Secret Service has grown to an organization of 4,600 employees with a budget of $475 million (in fiscal year 1992). In addition to anticounterfeiting, it is responsible for detecting and suppressing forgery and for investigating frauds connected with Treasury electronic funds transfers, credit cards, computer access, and federally insured financial institutions. Its protective duties, which started a century ago, were initially either authorized by the Secretary of the Treasury or acquired directly on an ad hoc basis at the request of Presidents or their advisers. The specific assignments were ratified in annual appropriations acts usually only after the detail was already in place. These short-term arrangements were finally given statutory permanency in 1951, when Congress first codified the service's authority (18 U.S.C. 3056).

Secret Service protection of the President and others began with President Grover Cleveland and his family in 1894. The service acquired this responsibility in part because of its nationwide investigative and intelligence-gathering capability and the absence of competing organizations at the time (a Bureau of Investigation, for instance, did not exist in the Department of Justice until 1908). Presidential protection was regularized for Theodore Roosevelt following the assassination of William McKinley in 1901 and was first given statutory recognition in 1906.

The protective assignments, which have been added piecemeal over the years, now include: the Vice President (or other officer next in order of succession if the vice presidency is vacant); the President's and Vice President's immediate families; President-elect and Vice

President Grover Cleveland and his family became the first presidential family to receive Secret Service protection. The Secret Service had originated as an anticounterfeiting organization. (Library of Congress, Prints and Photographs Division)

President-elect and their immediate families; major candidates for the presidency and vice presidency (and their spouses within 120 days of the election); and former Presidents, their spouses (until remarriage), and their minor children (until the age of sixteen). In addition, the service provides security for visiting heads of foreign states or governments (and their spouses) and other distinguished visitors as well as official representatives of the United States performing special missions abroad.

As part of the Secret Service, the Uniformed Division—which superseded the Executive Protective Service and its predecessor, the White House Police—has its own protective mandate in public law (2 U.S.C. 202). It is charged with protecting the President, Vice President, and members of their immediate families; the White House and any building in which presidential offices are located; the Vice President's official residence; the Treasury building and grounds; and foreign diplomatic missions located in the Washington, D.C., metropolitan area.

Collectively, these protective assignments account for an estimated 40 percent of the Secret Service's budget in most years, rising to about 60 percent during presidential election years, when the number of protectees and extent of security details increase substantially.

[See also (II) Benefits to Former Presidents; Benefits, Presidential.]

BIBLIOGRAPHY

Bowen, Walter S., and Harry Edward Neal. *The United States Secret Service.* 1960.

Jeffreys-Jones, Rhodri. *American Espionage: From Secret Service to CIA.* 1977.

Kaiser, Frederick M. "Origins of Secret Service Protection of the President." *Presidential Studies Quarterly* 18 (1988): 101–127.

U.S. President's Commission on the Assassination of President John F. Kennedy (Warren Commission). *Report.* 1964.

U.S. Secret Service. *Moments in History, 1865–1990.* 1990.

– FREDERICK M. KAISER

SENIOR EXECUTIVE SERVICE (SES)

The centerpiece of President Jimmy Carter's Civil Service Reform Act of 1978 (CSRA) was the Senior Executive Service. Modeled on both the British higher civil service and the top management level in the private sector, the SES was intended to create a mobile, flexible, and elite cadre of government managers.

Reforms such as the SES had been proposed for a number of years. The second of the Hoover Commissions reported in 1955, for example, that senior managers in the career civil service should be assigned a broader, more flexible role in government. It was left to Carter's Personnel Management Project, however, to create a formal proposal for such a group. To move from the rigidities of the traditional civil service system to this more flexible cadre, the CSR Act proposed to eliminate most of the "supergrade" (GS 16–18) and executive schedule positions in the federal service. In their place would be the Senior Executive Service, a group entered only by contract, whose members would not be covered by many of the traditional civil-service protections and securities.

The problem that the SES was intended to address was complex. Solutions to some aspects of the problem conflicted with solutions to other components. For example, the presidential desire for improved political responsiveness was in tension with the "higher civil service" concept of expanded flexibility and discretion for senior managers. Other aspects of the problem addressed by the SES included a too-narrow, program-linked view of policy and management objectives and the lack of generalized management skills within the civil service. In addition, reformers wished to rectify the problem created by the link between the salaries of top managers in government and those of members of Congress. As managers advanced up the career ladder, they quickly—often at a relatively early age—reached a pay ceiling imposed by Congress that prevented them from receiving appropriate pay. While managers' pay remained capped at this level, that of their subordinates continued to advance, creating serious pay compression problems.

Title IV of the Civil Service Reform Act, which created the Senior Executive Service, contained the following provisions: First, all persons in a supergrade or executive schedule position at the time the legislation was passed were eligible for membership in the SES (about eight thousand positions). Second, government-wide, 10 percent of the positions were reserved for political appointments. Third, members entered the SES through a contract that committed them to increased opportunity for mobility and flexibility but removed some career civil service protections. Fourth, SES members were eligible to compete for financial bonuses and awards based on individual performance; the legislation provided that 50 percent of any agency's SES members would be eligible to receive an award each year. Fifth, the SES would be a rank-in-person system, rather than the rank-in-position system then in place throughout the civil service, meaning that SES members would carry their rank to whatever positions they accepted or were assigned. Sixth, SES members would also be eligible for increased training and development opportunities as well as sabbatical leaves.

The SES was implemented quickly. Nearly 98 percent of those eligible for initial membership in the SES joined, but this high number reflected dissatisfaction with pay restrictions rather than enthusiasm for the reform. The SES encountered difficulties almost at once. Congress was dissatisfied with the outcomes of the first performance review and award process; within six months of the SES's implementation Congress cut the number of SES members eligible for annual awards by half, and the Office of Personnel Management (OPM), using its discretionary authority, reduced the total by another 5 percent.

In the early years of the SES, the often-negative experiences of its members caused many junior members to become disenchanted.

In addition, the budget cuts and staff reductions of the early years of the administration of Ronald Reagan created a turbulence in the federal government that quickly overshadowed efforts at civil-service reform. The SES continued to play a key role in efforts to improve presidential management of the career bureaucracy, however. Presidential management strategies such as "jigsaw puzzle management," advocated by presidential advisers from the Heritage Foundation, utilized the political appointees in the SES to control decision points inside the bureaucracy that had previously been inaccessible to political appointees. The mobility provisions of the SES were utilized to move career managers to different—and generally less influential—positions. Very few career members of the SES moved into policy-making positions, and those who did left government service after brief policy stints.

Of equal significance, a large number of career members of the SES retired or resigned from government in the years 1979 to 1984. Some chose to retire at the end of the "high three" years of benefit calculations. This permitted retirement benefits to be based on the three highest-salary years of the SES member. Many scientific and technical experts left government for better-paying jobs in the private sector. Others, however, left because of the "bureaucrat bashing" so pervasive in Washington and because of a perceived politicization of the top levels of the career bureaucracy. In the early years of the SES, the often-negative experiences of its members caused many junior members of the career bureaucracy to become disenchanted as well. The formation of the Senior Executive Association, which functioned as a quasi union for senior executives, was further evidence that the CSRA had not created an elite cadre of senior policy advisers.

The experience of the SES in the late 1980s and early 1990s was more positive. This was due, in part, to a move away from what one observer termed the "halcyon promise" of the legislation to more realistic expectations for performance and progress. It was also due to a decision by the Office of Personnel Management to take more direct responsibility for the success of the SES. Perhaps most significantly, however, pay increases for senior executives were approved in 1987 and again in 1990 (the latter becoming effective in 1991). Changes also occurred in the bonus system. In 1984, the OPM increased the number eligible for awards in each agency to 35 percent of that agency's total SES membership. In 1987 that limit was removed, and in 1989 40 percent of the total membership received a bonus.

Important changes occurred in other areas as well. One of President George Bush's first speeches was to members of the SES in Washington; in that speech Bush affirmed the importance of excellent career civil servants to good government. Partly because of difficulties in recruiting political appointees, the Bush administration relied more heavily on career civil servants to fill important management positions.

Nonetheless, in the early 1990s problems remained for the SES. Compensation levels remain tied to those of Congress; despite pay increases, agencies employing large numbers of top-level scientific and technical personnel asked to be removed from the SES to increase compensation levels for these critical employees. Provisions of the Ethics Reform Act of 1989 provided for recertification of SES members' performance qualifications every four years. There were also lingering fears of potential for increased politicization.

BIBLIOGRAPHY

Harper, Kirke. "The Senior Executive Service after Twelve Years." In *The Promise and Paradox of Civil Service Reform.* Edited by Patricia W. Ingraham and David Rosenbloom. 1992.

Huddleston, Mark. *The Government's Managers.* 1987.

Huddleston, Mark. "To the Threshold of Reform: The Senior Executive Service and America's Search for a Higher Civil Service." In *The Promise and Paradox of Civil Service Reform.* Edited by Patricia W Ingraham and David Rosenbloom. 1992.

Rosen, Bernard. "Uncertainty in the Senior Executive Service." *Public Administration Review* 42 (March–April 1981): 203–206.

– PATRICIA W. INGRAHAM

SEPARATION OF POWERS

The separation of powers is the principal theory that informs the allocation of powers among the branches of the national government. Its centrality to the government's structure is indicated by the opening phrases of the first three articles of the Constitution, each of which vests a basic category of power (legislative, executive, and judicial) in a distinct and independent branch (a Congress, a President, and a Supreme Court).

The Theory of Separation

As understood by the major authors of the Constitution, the theory of the separation of powers contains two basic elements. First, it holds that political power is divided naturally into fairly distinct powers, each of which can be defined according to a general function. In the evolution of the theory from Locke to Montesquieu, there were debates on exactly what these powers are. But by the time of the founding of the Republic, it was accepted that there were three powers: a legislative power, meaning a power to make laws; a judicial power, meaning a power to assess penalties (criminal or civil) and apply law (including the Constitution) in cases and controversies; and an executive power, meaning a power to carry out law and, more broadly, to act with discretion for the nation, especially in crises or in foreign affairs, where laws either cannot apply or would conflict with the national interest.

Separation of powers theory assisted the Founders in understanding the character of these powers and their respective roles in governing. In particular, the great expositors of the theory had stressed the importance of the executive power, showing that good government requires a command institution capable of exercising broad discretion. This teaching stood in sharp contrast to the prevailing Whig, or antiexecutive, view that informed most of the state constitutions. Separation of powers theory for the Founders was thus directly connected to the establishment of a strong and independent executive office.

The second element of the separation of powers theory holds that there are fundamental benefits that derive from housing the core of each power in a distinct institution that has a capacity to act on its own. One benefit is safety for liberty and freedom from despotism, which results from avoiding a concentration of power in the hands of a single person or institution. Separation of powers provides a rationale for dispersing power. Above all, the separation of the judicial power of determining punishment from the powers of legislating and executing affords an essential protection for individual rights. Unlike the Anti-Federalists, the Founders were willing to grant broad powers to the national government because they were confident that the division of powers inside the government was an adequate check against despotism.

Another benefit of separating powers is governmental efficiency, at least in one respect. Because the powers are different in character, exercising them well requires different qualities. Separation allows each institution to be structured to carry out its own function. Thus, the bulk of the legislative power can be placed in a body that provides for broad representation and that ensures deliberation, while the core of the executive power can be housed in an institution that is headed by a single individual and is capable of "decision, activity, secrecy, and dispatch" (Federalist 70).

The Founders' use of the theory of separation of powers has been widely misunderstood. Contrary to the simpler and more rhetorically satisfactory arguments of their opponents, the Founders insisted that nothing in the theory demanded a total or complete separation. The theory is not a mathematical formula that aims, in James Madison's words, at "beauty or the symmetry of form," but a political doctrine designed to secure important benefits. These benefits require a basic, but not a total, separation.

Shared Powers

The separation of powers, while it is fundamental to the whole constitutional design, is not the only theory that governs the allocation of powers. The Founders relied on other, supplemental considerations to justify placing parts of certain powers outside of their "home" institution. Powers were shared for four reasons: to enable each branch to maintain its independence (as in the President's veto power); to assure conformity to the basic spirit of popular government (as in the Congress's power to declare war; to encourage temperate governmental decisions (as in the Senate's power to confirm judges and other federal officers); and to endow the government as a whole with a greater capacity for coherent action (as in the President's power to inform Congress, make recommendations, and employ the veto). The first three of these reasons rely on a notion of checks and balances to impose further restraints on power, but the last one provides the structural possibility for presidential leadership and is designed to enhance the energy of the government.

Congress's powers are not the exact equivalent of the legislative power, and the President's powers are not the exact equivalent of the executive power. Certain parts of the traditional executive power have been removed from the exclusive control of the President (such as declaring war and making appointments, while parts of other powers have been given to the President. The fact that powers are shared, however, does not reduce the significance of the separation of powers as the foundation on which the national government rests. Both the structure of the government (three distinct branches with no overlapping personnel) and the principal vesting of power in each branch derives from the theory of the separation of powers. That theory remains essential to an understanding of the powers of each institution. Thus Article II, Section 1, which vests "the executive power" in the President, constitutes a positive and meaningful grant of power. As interpreted by many Presidents, this grant gives the President the full executive power, that is, including a power to act for the nation in foreign affairs and in emergencies, qualified only insofar as parts of that power have been explicitly removed or assigned elsewhere.

Reinterpretations

The theory of the separation of powers has been a source of profound controversy. The Founders' view of the theory survives in and through interpretation of parts of the Constitution, but their overall understanding of the theory has been obscured, if not lost, over the course of American history. It has been largely replaced by the very different understandings of the theory of two other schools of thought: the Anti-Federalists and the progressives.

ANTI-FEDERALISTS. The Anti-Federalists claimed to have opposed the Constitution in part because it violated the separation of powers. For the Anti-Federalists, the theory of separation of powers demanded a complete separation. All of each power and only each power had to be placed in its "home" institution. If separation was good, then strict separation must be better.

The Anti-Federalists invoked the theory, however, only when objecting to a strong and independent presidency. Although they were true to their own logic in those instances where the President was granted parts of the legislative power, their overriding concern was less to separate powers than to limit the power of the presidency. It is here, in fact, that one reaches the heart of the debate, for which the separation of powers theory was employed as a stalking horse. The fundamental division was less over the strictness of the separation than over the nature and respective importance of the three powers.

For the Anti-Federalists, the key to the allocation of power was to assure legislative supremacy. The legislative branch, in their view, was the only true representative of the people. All "motion" in government should derive from the legislature. They conceived the executive power very narrowly as a ministerial power to carry out the legislature's will. Any discretionary power the President might exercise should come from explicit grants accorded to him by statute. For them, the separation of powers was another name for legislative supremacy.

PROGRESSIVES. Woodrow Wilson developed the other major school of thought on the separation of powers, which was embraced at the beginning of the twentieth century by many progressive thinkers. Wilson began by accepting the new orthodoxy that the Constitution embodied a pure theory of the separation of powers. "The government of the United States," he wrote, "was constructed upon the whig theory of political dynamics." But whereas the Whig Party celebrated this fact, Wilson declared it to be the fatal flaw of the whole design. The separation of powers impedes strong, effective, and democratic government, which is synonymous with unified leadership under a powerful executive. The Constitution must be changed to overcome the separation of powers. Varying this position slightly for practical reasons, Wilson later argued that while the Constitution was based on Whig theory, it has been written in a way that allowed it to be stretched and reinterpreted. A theory of strong presidential leadership, though contrary to the spirit of the separation of powers, could nevertheless be grafted onto the Constitution.

Congress's powers are not the exact equivalent of the legislative power.

Most theoretical discussions of the separation of powers in the twentieth century have accepted one or the other of Wilson's views about the character of the Constitution and its relationship to the separation of powers. Even those who quibble with the notion of pure separation accept the more fundamental point that the constitutional allocation of powers is incompatible with a strong presidency. The Constitution was intended to fracture power, which makes governance difficult under modern conditions. What has changed since Wilson's time, however, is the judgment of whether the Constitution so understood is good or bad. In the aftermath of the Vietnam War, many abandoned their preference for a Wilsonian presidency in favor of the Whig-like idea of the separation of powers.

Maintaining Separation

A final issue about the constitutional allocation of powers relates to the question of how a balance among the institutions can be maintained over time. Who or what will police the separation? The American tradition has supplied three answers.

The first was Thomas Jefferson's curious idea that no policing system internal to the government is feasible and that therefore a balance can only be assured by the people acting through a constitutional convention every generation. Dismissed by most as too radical, this idea nevertheless reemerged in modified form during the election of 1800. Jefferson established the precedent that major issues relating to the balance of power among the institutions can be submitted to the people during a presidential election, and that some kind of mandate can be claimed by the victor to reduce or enlarge the power of one of the institutions. This approach has been used on several occasions in American history when the constitutional balance of powers has been an important campaign issue.

A second answer, favored by the founders, is to rely on the structure of the government and the incentives those in each branch have to protect their institutional power. As Madison wrote, "Ambition must be made to counteract ambition." (*Federalist* 51) The solution to conflicting claims among the branches is the outcome of their struggle, a struggle in which each institution has the words of the Constitution, its specific powers, and its base of influence with the American people. This method of resolving conflicts has probably been the predominant one, having prevailed in such areas as the war power and executive privilege.

A final answer is judicial review, where the Supreme Court serves as the umpire and resolves constitutional disputes according to a definitive, legal interpretation of the meaning of the Constitution. This method has played an important role in a few instances, such as matters relating to the removal power and the so-called legislative veto, although even in these areas the conflicts between Congress and the President are resolved primarily outside the courts through a sophisticated system of political accommodations. Those who believe that judicial decisions are (or should be) the principal means of resolving constitutional questions relating to the allocation of powers have an overly legalistic understanding of the Constitution. The historical record clearly demonstrates the greater importance, and perhaps the greater flexibility, of the other two mechanisms for resolving constitutional disputes. Both of these mechanisms view the Constitution as a document to be interpreted and enforced through the political process.

[See also (I) Congress, article on Powers of Congress; President and Congress, An Overview; (II) Executive Power.]

BIBLIOGRAPHY

Bessette, Joseph, and Jeffrey Tulis, eds. *The Presidency in the Constitutional Order.* 1981.

Fisher, Louis. *Constitutional Conflicts between Congress and the President.* 3d ed. 1991.

Mansfield, Harvey. *Taming the Prince.* 1989.

Vile, M. J. C. *Constitutionalism and the Separation of Powers.* 1967.

– JAMES CEASER

SIGNING STATEMENTS, PRESIDENTIAL

Approval of major legislation is usually accompanied by a signing statement in which the President gives his reasons for approval. When bills passed by Congress are presented to Presidents for final consideration, Presidents usually issue messages to explain their decisions. Article I, Section 7 of the Constitution requires Presidents to include written explanations with vetoed bills when they are returned to the house of origin in Congress. Even though pocket-vetoed bills are not returned to Congress, Presidents have traditionally issued a memorandum of disapproval explaining their decision. When Presidents approve of legislation submitted to them, however, they are only required to sign the bill into law. According to Section 7, when the President is presented with a bill, "if he approve he shall sign it." For important legislation, however, Presidents often prepare signing statements to publicize, explain, or justify their decisions. These statements may praise or criticize the legislation in question, and they are important primarily for their political, rather than legal, significance. As the Supreme Court noted in *La Abra Silver Mining Co.* v. *United States* (1899), "It has properly been the practice of the President to inform Congress by message of his approval of bills, so that the fact may be recorded." In the twentieth century, bill-signing ceremonies have been used as occasions to recognize the efforts of key members of Congress or others with particular interest in the legislation in question.

One ambiguity regarding bill signing persisted throughout the nineteenth century. During the country's first hundred years, the prevailing belief and consequent practice was that Presidents did not possess the authority to sign bills when Congress was not in session, since bill signing was considered a part of the legislative process. This belief led Presidents to travel to the Capitol on the last day of a congressional session to sign those bills that were not to be vetoed. Abraham Lincoln was the first president to violate this practice, although Congress later objected and repassed the bill in question during the following session. Grover Cleveland became the first President to refuse to travel to Capitol Hill during the final days of congressional sessions, but the issue was not finally resolved until the Supreme Court ruled in the *La Abra* case that Presidents could indeed sign bills after a congressional recess as long as signing occurred within ten days of bill presentation. This ruling was extended to all adjournments in *Edwards* v. *United States* (1932).

In the 1980s, a significant controversy arose concerning the legal significance of presidential signing statements. Prior to the 1980s, Presidents who maintained doubts about some aspect of a bill they planned to sign would usually note their disapproval in their signing statement and perhaps urge further legislative or other action. On occasion, they would use signing statements to impose their interpretation of a statute. Under President Ronald Reagan this practice became systematic. He argued that signing statements could serve as a basis of statutory interpretation—that is, he sought to use signing statements to reinterpret the meaning of the legislation he was signing into law. For

The Constitution requires Presidents to include written explanations with vetoed bills when they are returned to Congress.

example, in his signing statement accompanying enactment of the Immigration Reform and Control Act of 1986, he attempted to reinterpret the statute's standards concerning when an alien would be eligible for permanent citizenship. Reagan made a similar effort by proposing in the signing statement accompanying the Safe Drinking Water Act of 1986 that the Environmental Protection Agency was in fact not required to enforce provisions of the act, even though the bill stipulated such enforcement. Symptomatic of this view was the successful effort of Reagan's Attorney General, Edwin Meese III, to have signing statements included in the *U.S. Code Congressional and Administrative News*—something that had never been done before. This effort spawned criticism that the President was intruding improperly on Congress's exclusive power to assign meaning to the legislation it drafts, since the examination of legislative intent is a frequent means used by courts to interpret statutes. To grant legal or constitutional weight to presidential signing statements, according to critics, would in effect grant the President the power to substitute presidential judgment for that of Congress and to rewrite legislation after it had been passed by Congress. Critics also argue that this practice usurps the judicial power to interpret the laws passed by Congress. This Reagan administration practice was continued by George Bush, who also tried to impose his constitutional interpretation on legislation in signing statements.

[See also (I) Bills.]

BIBLIOGRAPHY

Alston, Chuck. "Bush Crusades on Many Fronts to Retake President's Turf." *CQ Weekly Report,* 3 February 1990, pp. 291–295.

Garber, Marc N., and Kurt A. Wimmer. "Presidential Signing Statements as Interpretations of Legislative Intent." *Harvard Journal on Legislation* 24 (1987): 363–395.

Rogers, Lindsay. "The Power of the President to Sign Bills after Congress Has Adjourned." *Yale Law Journal* 30 (1920): 1–22.

– ROBERT J. SPITZER

SOLICITOR GENERAL

The Office of Solicitor General in the Department of Justice was created, along with the Department itself, in 1870. Before that time, the Attorney General was not the head of a department; rather, he functioned as an individual who for many years had his own private practice in addition to his responsibilities as the government's legal representative. As those responsibilities grew, the Attorney General had to rely increasingly on outside counsel. After the Civil War, the burden of the office and the annual expense of outside counsel had increased to the point that Congress decided to create the Department of Justice and to provide for the appointment of "a Solicitor General, learned in the law to assist the Attorney General in the performance of his duties." From 1870 to the present day, the Solicitor General is the only person in the federal government required by statute to be "learned in the law."

Since the creation of the office, thirty-nine persons have served as Solicitor General, including one who later became President (William Howard Taft), several who later served on the Supreme Court (Taft, Stanley Reed, Robert Jackson, and Thurgood Marshall), or who held other important federal offices in the executive and judicial branches (Francis Biddle, Charles Fahy, and Simon Sobeloff), and many other prominent lawyers, such as John W. Davis, Erwin Griswold, and Archibald Cox.

The duties of the Solicitor General have never been spelled out in detail in the governing statutes. Rather, they have evolved over the years, and are now made more specific in regulations issued by the Attorney General. Most important among these duties is the Solicitor General's responsibility for the representation of the United States, its officers and agencies, in the Supreme Court of the United States. Thus, with few exceptions applicable to certain independent agencies, the Solicitor General must give his approval before a case that the government has lost in a lower court may be taken to the Supreme Court for review. The Solicitor General is also responsible for the briefing and oral argument of cases accepted for review in that Court. Other important duties include the requirement of authorization for appeal from any decision in a federal court that is adverse to the government, for the filing by the United States (or any officer or agency) of a brief amicus curiae (friend of the court) in any court, of a petition for rehearing *en banc* (before the full appeals court rather than before a three-judge panel) in a federal court of appeals, or of a petition for intervention in any judicial proceeding.

Since the Solicitor General's Office is relatively small—totaling in 1992 some twenty lawyers and additional support staff—the office invariably draws on the work of lawyers in other divisions of the Justice Department or other government agencies. But at least two lawyers in the Solicitor General's Office work on almost every matter before it is brought to the Solicitor General for decision or review. With the exception of one of the deputies who serves as counselor to the Solicitor General, these lawyers are career civil servants selected solely on the basis of professional ability and without regard to political views or affiliation.

The Solicitor General is called on by the nature of his position and authority to play a number of roles, and the range and variety of his responsibilities is a source of some tension. One of his tasks, which is of low visibility but of great importance to the working of government, is to deal with intragovernmental conflict with respect to the positions to be taken, and the arguments made, in the Supreme Court. On some occasions, such a conflict arises wholly between divisions in the Department of Justice itself, but the conflict may be broader and many sided, embracing other executive departments or one or more of the independent agencies. These conflicts are often resolved through a process in which all sides are heard and every effort to reach accommodation is explored. Sometimes, the disagreement is one of policy that cannot be resolved without executive action at a higher level. And sometimes, especially when one of the independent agencies is a party to the disagreement, the conflict will not be fully resolved at the executive level but will be disclosed to the Court. This may be done through the use of an amicus curiae brief, either on behalf of the independent agency or, if the agency itself is a party to the case, on behalf of the United States. On at least one occasion—in *St. Regis Paper Co.* v. *United States* (1961)—the disagreement was disclosed to the Court by the Solicitor General himself, who presented both the argument for the Department of Commerce on one side of the issue and for the Federal Trade Commission on the other.

Another source of tension—and one that in the 1980s and 1990s engendered considerable debate—arises from the Solicitor General's role as an advocate and his role as an "officer of the court." To some extent, this tension exists for every lawyer, but in the case of the Solicitor General, it is intensified by the difficulty of identifying the "client" and by the significance of the continuing relationship between the Solicitor General and the courts, and particularly the Supreme Court. Although the Solicitor General is appointed by the President, and may be overruled or removed by him, and also reports to the Attorney General, he is at the same time charged with representing the United States as a professional "learned in the law." The Supreme Court not only relies heavily on the accuracy and completeness of his submissions but also on his judgment and discretion in selecting the cases in which review is sought. And Congress looks to his office to defend the constitutionality of its legislation and to see that the laws it has enacted are applied in accordance with their expressed purposes, even when the executive may be reluctant to do so.

On rare but significant occasions, these responsibilities have led the Solicitor General to confess to the Supreme Court that a lower court has committed an error in the government's favor, to refuse to sign a brief that the Attorney General or an independent agency wishes to submit, or to disagree with the desire of others in the executive branch to take a position that he believes is unwarranted in law. More frequently, it has led him to refuse requests to seek Supreme Court or lower court review because he does not view the cases as worthy of the reviewing court's attention.

From 1870 to the present day, the Solicitor General is the only person in the federal government required by statute to be "learned in the law."

The tension between the Solicitor General's role as advocate and his broader responsibilities can never be fully resolved, and indeed the existence of that tension serves important purposes. The processes and professionalism of the Solicitor General's Office tend to moderate the more extreme views that are part of every administration. Even (or especially) at a time when the line between law and policy is increasingly viewed as indistinct, the Solicitor General's insistence on full and accurate disclosure, and on observing the bounds of appropriate argument, carries many benefits. It serves both the judiciary by helping the judges to evaluate the cases worthy of review and by assuring that the arguments made will be responsible and useful to the court, and the executive by increasing the likelihood that the courts will respond favorably to the government's petitions and arguments. Finally, the duty of the Solicitor General to represent the United States, and not simply his superiors in the executive branch, helps to assure that the interest of the legislative branch will be effectively presented to the Court without the need for separate representation, except in those rare instances when legislative action is viewed as threatening the constitutional prerogatives of the executive itself.

[See also (II) Justice, Department of.]

BIBLIOGRAPHY

Caplan, Lincoln. *The Tenth Justice.* 1987.
Fried, Charles. *Order and Law.* 1991.
Griswold, Erwin N. *Ould Fields, New Corne.* 1992
Salokar, Rebecca Mae. *The Solicitor General: The Politics of Law.* 1992.
"Symposium: The Role and Function of the United States Solicitor General." *Loyola of Los Angeles Law Review* 21 (1987): 1047–1272

– DAVID L. SHAPIRO

SPEECHWRITERS, PRESIDENTIAL

In an age when Presidents must generate public support to achieve legislative and administrative goals, the message of the President matters. Policy success depends on a President's ability to articulate themes that will attract public interest. Because speeches are an important resource for galvanizing presidential electoral and policy support, a White House unit is devoted to preparing the spoken (and written) presidential word.

Presidential speechwriters have been a regular feature of the White House staff since Judson Welliver joined the administration of Warren G. Harding. While Presidents since Harding's time have varied their use of speechwriters, they have all turned to them for assistance. Prior to the development of a White House speechwriting staff in the 1920s, persons working in the departments were detailed to the White House to prepare presidential remarks, although they remained on their departmental payrolls.

The organization of the speechwriting operation generally reflects the type of organization found in a particular White House. If a President prefers a loosely structured White House, speechwriters are likely to report directly to him, as was true during the Lyndon B. Johnson administration. A tightly organized staff structure, as seen in the early Ronald Reagan White House, integrates speechwriting with other staff units. There is a partisan component to the speechwriting operation. In Republican administrations the unit is more likely to be tied to the long-range communications planning operations, while in Democratic administrations the unit tends to be more loosely tied either to the President directly or to the daily communication operations.

When the Brownlow Committee recommended the appointment of several presidential assistants—a recommendation that led to the creation in 1939 of the Executive Office of the President (EOP) and an enhanced White House staff—it spoke of presidential assistants having to have "passion for anonymity." While for many years assistants maintained a low profile, they ultimately became more conspicuous. Speechwriters are among the White House staff members who have made the transition from behind-the-scenes players to front-stage personalities. When President Reagan was leaving office and George Bush was preparing to take over, both had the same speechwriter, Peggy Noonan. She is generally credited with writing the farewell address of Reagan and the inaugural address of Bush. Several Reagan speechwriters left office to take visible communications positions: Patrick Buchanan became a television commentator and a 1992 presidential candidate; David Gergen took an editorial position at *U.S. News and World Report* and became a frequent guest on television news programs.

There is a partisan component to the speechwriting operation.

The speechwriting operation is responsible for preparing major addresses, such as the annual state of the union message, as well as shorter remarks at Rose Garden ceremonies held outside the Oval Office. The material prepared by speechwriters falls into three basic categories: major speeches, remarks delivered at ceremonial appearances, and written statements. The critical speeches of an administration, such as the inaugural address(es), annual state of the union messages, United Nations speeches, and addresses delivered to joint sessions of Congress, involve the work of staff in the speechwriting office and throughout the White House, who review drafts for policy implications. The state of the union address also has to contend with the contributions of members of the Cabinet, who seek to advance their own policy interests. Speechwriters often specialize, with some writing the ideological speeches (as was the case with Tony Dolan in the Reagan years) and others tapped for their particular policy specialty or their ability to write humorous remarks (e.g., Peter Benchley in the Johnson administration).

While Presidents are responsible for the remarks contained in a speech, individual speechwriters can play a significant role in developing content. It is almost impossible to separate policy from the words used to promote it. Bryce Harlow, a senior staff member in the Dwight D. Eisenhower White House, observed, "The speechwriters in the White House can have a very, very substantial influence on policy, either by the methodology of presentation of the material or by the inclusion or exclusion of ideas, and by the fact that he has to work so intimately with the President." A memorandum in the Carter Library illustrates the point. In the Jimmy Carter administration, speechwriter James Fallows used his position to lobby senior administration staff on policy questions. In April 1978 he urged Press Secretary Jody Powell to alter the position of the State Department toward a settlement in Southern Rhodesia, even though he recognized that his effort represented an end run around the White House staffing system.

The usefulness of the speechwriting operation depends upon the President and the message he has to offer. Speechwriters can make a President appear more articulate, but the effectiveness of the speech depends on the President's delivery. In 1986 Peggy Noonan produced a moving speech to honor the astronauts killed in the destruction of the space shuttle *Challenger,* yet that speech had a special impact because of Reagan's capacity to understand and convey the depth of national mourning.

BIBLIOGRAPHY

Anderson, Patrick. *The President's Men.* 1968.

Cornwell, Elmer. *Presidential Leadership of Public Opinion.* 1965.

Deaver, Michael K., with Mickey Herskowitz. *Behind the Scenes.* 1987.

Fallows, James. "The Passionless Presidency." *Atlantic Monthly* 239 (January 1979): 33–47; 243 (May 1979). 33–48.

Grossman, Michael Baruch, and Martha Joynt Kumar. *Portraying the President: The White House and the News Media.* 1981.

Kernell, Samuel. *Going Public: New Strategies of Presidential Leadership.* 1985.

Noonan, Peggy. *What I Saw at the Revolution: A Political Life in the Reagan Era.* 1990.

Patterson, Bradley H., Jr. *The Ring of Power: The White House Staff and Its Expanding Role in Government.* 1988.

Safire, William. *Before the Fall: An Inside View of the Pre-Watergate White House.* 1975.

Tulis, Jeffrey. *The Rhetorical Presidency.* 1987

– MARTHA KUMAR

STATE, DEPARTMENT OF

The Secretary of State is the first-ranking Cabinet member. Though small in size relative to other Cabinet agencies, the State Department performs the critically important services of implementing the foreign policy of the United States.

History of the Department

The State Department was the first executive department created after adoption of the Constitution. The act creating the Department of Foreign Affairs and the Office of Secretary was signed into law on 27 July 1789 and directed the secretary to run the department "in such manner as the President of the United States shall, from time to time order or instruct." Two months later, Congress added important domestic functions, chiefly correspondence with the states, publication of acts of Congress (and later the census), maintenance of a library (forerunner of the Library of Congress), registration of copyrights and patents, and the keeping of the Great Seal of the United States. The addition of these domestic responsibilities (most long since assigned to other agencies) led in 1789 to the changing of the Department's name to the Department of State.

Thomas Jefferson, the first secretary of the department, instituted some of the department's most enduring functions. He dispatched consuls abroad and required them to report on commercial, political, and military developments and to alert American merchants and vessels to the same. Jefferson was also responsible for distinguishing between diplomatic and consular functions: the former involving the conduct of political relations with other countries and the latter concerned with commercial matters and the affairs of U.S. citizens abroad. The diplomatic and consular services functioned separately until they were joined in 1924.

The department grew slowly during the nineteenth century because of U.S. policies of isolation and neutrality toward both Europe and the Americas. In 1833, the first departmental reorganization led to the appointment of a chief clerk, who was given responsibility for managing the department on a daily basis, and the creation of seven bureaus including a diplomatic and a consular bureau to communicate with overseas posts. A second reorganization in 1870 established four geographic bureaus (two diplomatic and two consular) and five functional bureaus.

At the turn of the century, U.S. interventions abroad and American territorial acquisitions expanded the department's duties. The two world wars further increased departmental responsibilities, chiefly in the areas of assistance to American citizens aboard; political, military, and economic reporting; acting as representatives of other states fighting as belligerents in enemy countries; refugee aid; and POW exchanges.

In 1944, a major reorganization was began by Edward Stettinius, then Undersecretary of State. Later, as

Secretary of State, Stettinius issued a departmental order grouping similar functions together and assigning responsibility for related offices to the undersecretary or one of the six assistant secretaries. A number of new functional bureaus were created for trade relations, cultural diplomacy, and public information, and new offices responsible for management and policy planning were added. The Interim Research and Intelligence Service, now the Bureau of Intelligence and Research, was established in 1945. The increasing importance of economics in foreign relations was reflected in the department's absorption of several temporary wartime economic agencies and the addition of an Undersecretary for Economics in 1946.

Thomas Jefferson, the first secretary of the State Department, instituted some of the department's most enduring functions.

Beginning at the turn of the century, efforts were made to professionalize the Foreign Service. Competitive exams for the consular service were initiated in 1895, and a merit system (including competitive entrance exams for all diplomatic and consular positions except minister and ambassador) followed in 1906. The Lowden Act of 1911 allowed the U.S. government to purchase buildings overseas to house foreign missions, relieving the financial strain on envoys and ensuring functional and dignified quarters for all officials irrespective of private wealth. The Rodgers Act of 1924 and the Foreign Service Act of 1946 continued improvements in the conditions affecting foreign service personnel, especially in the areas of entrance and promotion within the service, rotations from post, expenses and benefits, home leave, and retirement.

A number of developments since World War II have had major impact on the department. First, the National Security Act of 1947 concentrated responsibility for coordination of national security policy in the White House under the direction of a national security adviser. Since then, while the influence of the department has varied, it clearly no longer has exclusive executive authority for foreign affairs. Despite this development, or perhaps in response to it, the role of the Secretary of State expanded as many holders of the office personally committed themselves to diplomatic initiatives, heightening the U.S. profile in the Middle East, for example, or focusing on U.S.-Soviet relations.

In 1949, President Harry S Truman launched a new era in U.S. foreign assistance when he announced a large aid package aimed at helping underdeveloped countries expand their economies and participate in international markets. In the 1990s, foreign economic and military aid made up the largest portion of the foreign-affairs budget. While in absolute terms the United States gave more foreign aid than any other country, the absolute amount given has declined steadily and as a percentage of gross national product is smaller than that given by any of the other major noncommunist donors. Foreign-affairs spending declined from 12 percent of federal expenditures in the years immediately after the war to less than 2 percent in 1993.

Finally, the dramatic rise in international terrorism had a profound impact on the department. From 1965 to 1992, eighty-six State Department personnel were killed, including U.S. ambassadors to Guatemala, Sudan, Cyprus, Lebanon, Afghanistan, and Pakistan. The department became increasingly involved in efforts to combat international terrorism through intelligence, coordination with other governments, security measures, and legal proceedings such as the indictment of two suspects in the bombing of Pan Am Flight 103 over Lockerbie, Scotland, in 1988 and subsequent efforts to gain their extradition and trial.

Relationship with Congress

The struggle among the branches for control of the U.S. government, anticipated by the Framers, has been very evident in the area of foreign affairs. Foreign affairs were originally conducted by committees and single executives under the close control of the Continental Congress. The Constitution made the direction of foreign affairs predominantly the province of the President. Article II designated the President as Commander in Chief, with the power to make treaties, to nominate executive officials (including the Secretary of State and all U.S. ambassadors), and to receive foreign ambassadors. To prevent absolute executive power over foreign affairs, the Constitution gave Congress several powers, including the power to regulate foreign commerce, declare war, appropriate funds, ratify treaties, and approve executive appointments. Through the exercise of these powers, Congress has always been able to exercise control over the Department of State and its activities by limiting spending, creating (and abolishing) positions, confirming nominations to high positions within the department, investigating activities, and legislating national polices.

Throughout American history, Congress has sporadically utilized all these powers. In the late twentieth century, however, Congress systematically utilized its powers to control the department. Among the most significant features of Congress's control are (1) specific approval of the number and description of all high-ranking jobs, including creation of an Inspector General, independent of the Secretary of State, to investigate misconduct; (2) predesignation of recipients for the majority of all U.S. foreign aid—as high as 96 percent in one foreign-aid program—leaving the department with discretion over the allocation of a very small portion of such funds; and (3) prohibitions on the extension of humanitarian or military assistance aimed specifically at countries found to engage in activities considered by Congress to be detrimental to U.S. interests (such as terrorism or development of a nuclear device).

Department officials continue to have control over day-to-day diplomacy, which permits the exercise of broad discretion in seeking settlements of disputes or advancement of U.S. interests. Congress has even exercised power, however, over these aspects of department activity. On virtually every issue of public note, for example, negotiators must routinely keep interested legislators and committees informed of their actions and plans. Congress and individual legislators use their power over legislation, appointments, and investigations to demand information about diplomatic activities, including communications with foreign officials and internal deliberations. These demands are routinely resisted, but such information is obtained in many cases. Finally, in some areas of great public visibility, legislators have became observers at negotiating sessions, particularly in arms control but also increasingly in environmental and trade issues. While department personnel continue to control such negotiations, Congress has become a real presence, not merely in the final approval or implementation of policies or treaties but also in their development. Although these trends pose difficulties for the department, they also carry advantages: interested legislators become more informed, contribute to the solutions ultimately adopted, and are more likely to grant approval when called on to do so.

Executive-Branch Competition

Historically, the State Department's control over the management and implementation of foreign policy has cut across all areas of governmental concern. Presidents since George Washington have used private envoys, special agents, or designated negotiators to handle specific problems. Most negotiations as well as ongoing relationships with foreign governments have been handled, however, by the State Department through its control of diplomatic posts and communications.

Over the years, various circumstances have caused control over important areas of foreign affairs to shift from the State Department to other executive agencies. Revolutionary improvements in communications and travel have deprived the State Department of the virtual monopoly it once possessed over contact with foreign officials abroad. In addition, the handling of specific areas of diplomatic activity has become increasingly complex, demanding specialization and expertise. The executive agencies responsible for such subjects as commerce, taxation, defense, intelligence, crime, and the regulation of specific areas such as communication, securities, and environment have been faced with the increasing globalization of their areas of concern. Domestic economic planning, for example, requires an understanding of foreign trends and policies and results in plans for international coordination, cooperation, and negotiation. Similarly, domestic crime, especially federal crime, increasingly contains international sources or components in such areas as narcotics trafficking, terrorism, and financial fraud. Finally, in competing with one another, executive-branch officials are no less prone to pursue their personal ambitions and the aggrandizement of their positions than are executive and legislative officials in competition with each other. Consequently, executive officials in departments other than State have competed for influence and control over the foreign aspects of their areas of responsibility.

The amount of foreign aid that the United States has given has declined steadily.

These trends and activities have significantly shifted foreign-affairs responsibility from the State Department to the executive agencies, especially the National Security Council and the Office of the U.S. Trade Representative. Several agencies have direct liaison with their counterparts in foreign countries.

The effects of multiagency involvement in foreign affairs are offset to a considerable extent by State Department participation in many of the foreign activities of other agencies. But the effects of this dispersal of foreign affairs authority go beyond the mere shift of responsibility from one set of executive officials to another. Agencies with specialized responsibility tend to take positions that are driven strongly by their own special, sometimes relatively narrow, responsibilities, whereas State Department officials tend to take a broader view of the nation's interests. Criminal law enforcement provides one example. Prosecutors understandably seek to prosecute all crime, without regard to the political consequences, as, for example, when U.S.

prosecutors pursued Manuel Noriega of Panama. In such situations, the State Department tends to give greater weight than does the Justice Department to other factors, such as diplomatic immunity and respect for the sovereignty and sensibilities of foreign states and the United Nations. The President, the NSC Adviser and staff, have increasingly become the arbiters of such conflicting agendas.

[See also (II) Cabinet; Foreign Affairs: An Overview.]

BIBLIOGRAPHY

Bemis, Samuel Flagg. *A Diplomatic History of the United States.* 1936.

Eberstadt, Nicholas. *Foreign Aid and American Purpose.* 1988.

Stuart, Graham H. *The Department of State: A History of Its Organization, Procedure and Personnel.* 1949.

Trask, David F. *A Short History of the U.S. Department of State, 1781–1981* 1981.

– ABRAHAM D. SOFAER

STATE OF THE UNION MESSAGES

Article 2, Section 3 of the Constitution stipulates that the President "shall from time to time give to the Congress information of the State of the Union and recommend to their Consideration such Measures as he shall judge necessary and expedient."

So uncontroversial was this notion that the Chief Executive should offer Congress his assessment of the state of the union and recommend legislation for its consideration that it had occasioned no debate in the Constitutional Convention. "No objection has been made to this class of authorities," wrote Alexander Hamilton in *Federalist* 77, "nor could they possibly admit of any."

Although the Constitution specifies that the state of the union message be delivered "from time to time," Presidents read that as an invitation to transmit the President's agenda to Congress each year. For all of the nineteenth and most of the twentieth century, the resulting rhetorical form was known as the President's annual message. Taking its name from its constitutional function, in the mid 1940s, Presidents and presidential scholars began identifying the address as the "state of the union" message.

On 8 January 1790, faced with an unprecedented rhetorical situation, George Washington responded to the constitutional enjoinder by delivering a speech rooted in the monarch's speech from the throne. So obvious was Washington's dependence on the "king's speech" that an observer wrote: "It is evident from the President's speech that he wishes everything to fall into the British mode of business." (The monarch's statement of "cause of summons," known as the "King's Speech," was delivered after a majority of the members of Parliament had been sworn in. In the hands of a powerful ruler, the address constituted a legislative mandate.)

The Congress, which had rejected as too monarchial the title "His Highness the President of the United States of America and Protector of the Rights of the Same" reacted to Washington's first annual message as parliament traditionally had responded to the king's speech, and drafted, debated, and designated a delegation to deliver an echoing speech in response. After repeating the President's requests, the echoing speech pledged congressional cooperation. Should fortune eradicate the annual messages of Washington and Adams, scholars could reconstruct them from their mirror images, the reply speeches. "No man can turn over the Journals of the First Six Congresses of the United States," noted John Randolph, "without being fairly sickened with the adulation often replied by the Houses of Congress."

As the state of the union messages became more controversial, debate over the content and tone of the replies increased. Nonetheless, the practice continued through the Sixth Congress in 1800. In 1801, Thomas Jefferson assumed the presidency and pledged a "return to simple, republican forms of Government." His messages, delivered by messenger in writing, invited no congressional response. "By sending a message, instead of making a speech at the opening of the session," he confided to a colleague, "I have prevented the bloody conflict [to] which the making an answer would have committed them. They consequently were able to set into real business at once."

As the state of the union messages became more controversial, debate over the content and tone of the replies increased.

So interwoven was the oral delivery of the state of the union message and the distasteful British tradition, however, that Woodrow Wilson, a student of history and the first President to deliver the address orally since John Adams, felt the need to divorce the delivered address from its monarchical past. Wilson let it be known that he did not expect a formal answer from Congress except in enactment of the legislation he proposed.

"I am very glad indeed to have this opportunity to address the two Houses directly and to verify for myself the impression that the President of the United States is a person, not a mere department of the Government hailing Congress from some isolated island of jealous power, sending messages, not speaking naturally and with his own voice—that he is a human being trying to cooperate with other human beings in a common service," Wilson told the assembled members of Congress.

Until the advent of radio, the message was transmitted to the public by the print press. Partisan papers reprinted the message in toto. Opponents of the President attacked each address with vigor. These exchanges occasioned the historian Charles Beard to observe that the annual message was "the one great public document of the United States which is widely read and discussed. Congressional debates receive scant notice, but the President's message is ordinarily printed in full in nearly every metropolitan daily, and is the subject of general editorial comment throughout the length and breadth of the land. It stirs the country: it often affects Congressional elections; and it may establish grand policy."

In the state of the union message, the President has the opportunity to exercise legislative leadership by linking national history to present assessments and to make recommendations for future policy. The address affords him the opportunity to appeal for popular and congressional support of his legislative agenda. At the same time, in the television age, the address provides the public with a view of two of the three branches of government each acknowledging the prerogatives of the other, and thus maintaining institutional integrity.

The addresses differ in the number and kind of recommendations they marshall. Some have outlined only general programs, leaving the legislative details to Congress; others have laid out specific policy proposals. Some are lengthy catalogs of unrelated topics; others are focussed discussions of a handful of legislative priorities.

But throughout the presidency, these addresses have, in the words of the historian Arthur M. Schlesinger, Jr., functioned as "both an instrument and an index of presidential leadership." In the hands of a forceful President, the address shapes the country's sense of itself. So, for example, in state of the union messages James Monroe promulgated the Monroe Doctrine, Abraham Lincoln prophesied that "in giving freedom to the slave we assure freedom to the free," Franklin D. Roosevelt committed the country to Four Freedoms, and Lyndon B. Johnson forecast the Great Society. But the addresses also have served venal ends. Ulysses S. Grant's final annual message is a sometimes snivelling apologia; Andrew Johnson used the message to whine and inveigh about Reconstruction. More recently, the 1984 speech was employed by Ronald Reagan as a de facto announcement of his candidacy for reelection.

The issues addressed in the state of the union messages reflect the development of the nation. The messages of the Founders focused on constituent policies, such as abiding entangling alliances and encouraging manufacturing and policies to build the nation state. Throughout the nineteenth century, the messages centered on such distributive issues as development of land and harbors. In the late nineteenth century, questions of regulating resources emerged, with the creation, for example, of the Interstate Commerce Commission in 1887. During the New Deal, the messages took on social and economic themes. After Roosevelt's time, the four types coexisted in various combinations.

Although their content and form vary widely, most of the state of the union messages embody the structure implied in the Constitution: they assess the state of the union and offer either general or specific recommendations in response to that assessment. These functions increase the likelihood that the speech will shape the national agenda.

For Wilson, the address was a powerful vehicle of presidential leadership. "If the President has personal force and cares to exercise it," he wrote, "there is a tremendous difference between his message and the views of any other citizen either outside Congress or in it; . . . the whole country reads them and feels the writer speaks with an authority and a responsibility which the people themselves have given him."

[See also (I) Joint Sessions and Meetings.]

BIBLIOGRAPHY

Campbell, Karlyn Kohrs, and Kathleen Hall Jamieson. *Deeds Done in Words: Presidential Rhetoric and the Genres of Governance.* 1990.

Gilbert, Sheldon, et al. "The State of the Union Address and the Press Agenda." *Journalism Quarterly* 1980: 584–588.

Jamieson, Kathleen M. "Antecedent Genre as Rhetorical Constraint." *Quarterly Journal of Speech* 61 (1975): 406–415.

Schlesinger, Arthur M., ed. *The State of the Union Messages of the Presidents, 1790–1966.* 3 vols. 1966.

– KATHLEEN HALL JAMIESON

SUCCESSION, PRESIDENTIAL

Between October 1973 and December 1974, the United States underwent a series of unprecedented political experiences. A concerned citizenry viewed the events accompanying Spiro T. Agnew's resignation as Vice President, Gerald R. Ford's nomination and appointment as his successor, the sad, swift transition from Richard M. Nixon to Gerald Ford, and then Nelson A. Rockefeller's selection as Vice President. Few if any Americans, however, doubted that the transfer of power in each instance would come about in an orderly manner. Nor was the legitimacy of these transitions at issue.

Still, hardly any aspect of the American presidency has proved more challenging to lawmakers than succession. The Constitution, as well as three constitutional amendments (the Twelfth Amendment, 1804; the Twentieth Amendment, 1933; and the Twenty-fifth Amendment, 1967), the Presidential Succession Act of 1947, and political-party rules govern different succession possibilities.

The importance of the process is evidenced by the nine Vice Presidents who reached the White House through succession. Four—John Tyler (1841), Millard Fillmore (1850), Calvin Coolidge (1923), and Harry S Truman (1945)—assumed the presidential mantle when the incumbent died. Four others—Andrew Johnson (1865), Chester A. Arthur (1881), Theodore Roosevelt (1901), and Lyndon B. Johnson (1963)—became President following a presidential assassination. A unique resignation occasioned Gerald R. Ford's (1974) occupancy of the White House.

In the Constitution

At the Constitutional Convention in 1787, the question of succession was discussed late in the proceedings and given relatively little consideration. Alexander Hamilton offered a proposal on 18 June calling for a successor to the President as part of his plan for a national executive who would serve for life, but it was never debated.

Hardly any aspect of the American presidency has proved more challenging to lawmakers than succession.

Hamilton's idea was revived by the Committee of Detail in its report of 6 August, which provided that if a President was removed from office, died, resigned, or was disabled, the President of the Senate would exercise those duties until another President was chosen or the disability removed. Dissatisfaction with the provision was voiced when it was discussed on 27 August, and the question was delayed until 4 September, when the Committee on Postponed Matters offered a revised proposal. The new language had the Vice President for the first time exercising the duties of Chief Executive in the case of removal, death, absence, resignation, or inability of the President, "until another President could be chosen, or until the inability of the President be removed." Subsequent amendments, approved three days later, provided additional details concerning both presidential and vice presidential vacancies, including as well a provision for a special election.

Most delegates apparently wanted both provisions to be included in the Constitution. Sometime between 8 and 12 September, however, while the Committee on Detail worked to produce a final draft, that intention was lost. The merging of the 4 September motion for the Vice President to succeed the President, and the subsequent motions of 7 September resulted in grammatical ambiguities. The committee's final draft, which, with minor modifications by the Convention, became Article II, Section 2, clause 6, of the Constitution, provided that:

> In case of the Removal of the President from Office, or of his Death, Resignation, or Inability to discharge the Powers and Duties of the said Office, the Same shall devolve on the Vice President, and Congress may by Law provide for the Case of Removal, Death, Resignation, or Inability, both of the President and Vice President, declaring what Officer shall then act as President, and such Officer shall act accordingly, until the Disability be removed, or a President shall be elected.

Left unclear was whether "the Same" in this provision referred to "the said Office" (the presidency) or, as the delegates intended, only its "Power and Duties." Also uncertain was whether there was to be a special election.

Fifty-two years later, when President William Henry Harrison died just one month after his 4 March 1841 inauguration, the Cabinet and many others felt Vice President John Tyler should only be an acting President until a special election could be held. Tyler, however, acted quickly and decisively, assuming both the duties and powers of the office. After arriving in Washington, he took the presidential oath, delivered a message to the American people on the constitutionality of his succession and policies that would guide his administration, and moved into the White House.

When Congress convened in mid May 1841, both Houses by "overwhelming majorities," resolved, in the words of the *New York Daily Express,* that "John Tyler, late vice president [had] become, by the death of General Harrison, 'President of the United States,' and not vice president exercising the office of president." The Tyler precedent paved the way for all future Vice Presidents to complete the unexpired portion of a President's term in instances of death, impeachment, or resignation. In 1967, Congress confirmed this historical practice with the Twenty-fifth Amendment.

Succession Acts

The Framers also left unanswered what would happen when both the President and Vice President were unable to discharge their duties. This responsibility was left to Congress to handle by law. The Presidential Succession Act of 1792, the first attempt to extend the succession line called for the president pro tem of the Senate, followed by the Speaker of the House, to "act as President" when both the presidency and vice presidency were vacant. A special election for a full four-year term was to be held the following November if the double vacancy occurred prior to the last six months of a presidential term. Opponents of the act thought the Secretary of State, rather than a congressional officer, was a more appropriate successor.

On 18 April 1853, when William R. King became the third of seven Vice Presidents to die in office, a month-and-a-half after taking the oath, considerable attention was directed at the unsatisfactory nature of the Succession Act. Concern focused principally on the fact that for periods of considerable length there was neither a president pro tem of the Senate nor a Speaker of the House available as a successor if something happened to the President and Vice President.

The Senate Judiciary Committee in 1856 recommended extending the succession line to include the Chief Justice of the Supreme Court and Associate Justices of the Court, but nothing came of the proposal. President Andrew Johnson's 1868 plea for a revision of the act, shortly after he narrowly escaped removal from office, likewise attracted little attention. Chester A. Arthur, shortly after becoming President following James A. Garfield's death in September 1881, asked Congress to address the uncertainties associated with succession, but a lengthy Senate debate produced no action. Twice in 1883 the Senate approved legislation establishing succession by Cabinet officers.

Not until Vice President Thomas A. Hendricks died in 1885, however, was the House prompted to concur. Hendrick's death on 25 November was especially troublesome because Congress was not in session and there was neither a president pro tem nor Speaker to act as a successor if something happened to President Grover Cleveland. A new Speaker and president pro tem were not chosen until 7 December, when the Forty-ninth Congress convened. Had Cleveland died during the interim, a special session of Congress could not have been called since there would be no Chief Executive to call it or sign legislation addressing the emergency.

President Cleveland in his first annual message on 8 December stressed that such a possibility was intolerable and needed immediate resolution. Congress acted quickly. The Senate after vigorous debate, approved by voice vote a new succession act sponsored by Senator George F. Hoar on 17 December 1885. The House followed suit on 15 January 1886, by a 186 to 72 vote.

President James A. Garfield was incapacitated by an assassin's bullet for over two months, but his Cabinet gave little consideration to a presidential succession. (Library of Congress, Prints and Photographs Division)

The Succession of Act of 1886 provided that in case of the impeachment, death, resignation, or inability of both the President and Vice President, the line of succession then passed to the Secretary of State and other Cabinet officers in the order of the creation of the departments. Although the act did not make provision for a new election, as was done in the 1792 act, a clause was included that allowed Congress to call such an election if it was deemed appropriate.

Two primary factors—the danger of not having a presidential successor and the desirability of assuring continuity in policy—brought about adoption of the act. While it was under consideration, there was no Vice President and the president pro tem, John Sherman, a Republican, stood next in line for the presidency, which the Democrats had recently won. Arguments against the act stressed that it violated democratic principles by allowing the President to appoint his potential successors, and it was unclear if the succession was temporary or permanent.

When Harry S Truman became President in April 1945, following Franklin D. Roosevelt's death, he inherited as potential successors a Secretary of State, followed by a Secretary of the Treasury, who had never held an elective office. Truman was particularly concerned about the nation being without a Vice President for almost four years.

Two months after he assumed office, and again in early 1947, Truman sent special messages to Congress calling for a revision of the 1886 act. Congress responded in mid 1947 by approving a new law incorporating virtually all Truman's suggestions. It placed the Speaker of the House and then the president pro tem in the succession line, followed by officers of the Cabinet. Only Truman's recommendation that a special election be held for the remainder of the unexpired term failed to gain approval.

Presidential Disability

The nature of the Vice President's role when the President was physically or mentally unable to discharge the duties of his office remained unaddressed until 1958. When Presidents James A. Garfield, Grover Cleveland, and Woodrow Wilson suffered serious disabling illnesses, little consideration was given to having the Vice President act as President.

Garfield was incapacitated by an assassin's bullet for two and a half months before his 19 September 1881 death. During the interim, the Cabinet concluded that a presidential disability did not exist, despite the fact that he was prohibited by his physician from conducting any official business.

Congress could declare that the candidate who received a majority of the votes for President was elected, even if he had died or resigned.

On 1 July 1893, President Cleveland secretly underwent a major operation for cancer of the mouth on board the yacht *Oneida.* Cleveland spent the next two months recuperating. Even though a severe financial crisis gripped the nation, neither Vice President Adlai E. Stevenson (1835–1914) nor most of the Cabinet were ever apprised of the seriousness of Cleveland's disability. After President Wilson suffered a stroke on 2 October 1919, he remained a semi-invalid for the remaining seventeen months of his second term. During most of that period, the President's wife, Edith Wilson, his personal physician, and private secretary ran the government. Presidential disability became an issue again early in 1958 when President Dwight D. Eisenhower suffered his third serious illness in three years, any one of which could have been seriously disabling if not fatal. Eisenhower became convinced, he wrote in *The White House Years,* that "specific arrangements" needed to be made "for the Vice President to succeed to [the presidency] if [he] should incur a disability that precluded proper performance of duty over any period of significant length."

At a 26 February 1958 press conference, Eisenhower disclosed that he had a "clear understanding" with Vice President Richard M. Nixon on what to do if he became unable to perform his duties. The arrangement called for Nixon "to serve as Acting President, exercising the powers and duties of the Office until the inability had ended." Determination of inability would be made "if possible," by the President. If the inability prevented the "President from so communicating with the Vice President," Nixon would make the determination "after such consultation as seems to him appropriate under the circumstances." In each instance, the President "would determine when the inability had ended." Presidents John F. Kennedy and Lyndon B. Johnson entered into similar agreements with their potential successors prior to the ratification of the Twenty-fifth Amendment on 10 February 1967.

The Twenty-fifth Amendment

Under the Twenty-fifth Amendment, the Vice President assumes the President's power and responsibilities if the President informs Congress that he is unable to perform his duties. The Vice President then is acting President until the President informs Congress that he is capable of resuming his duties, or if the Vice President and a majority of the "principal officers of the executive branch," or any other body designated by Congress, determine that the President is incapacitated, the Vice President then becomes acting President until the President informs Congress that the disability has been removed. In the latter instance, if the group determining the existence of a disability informs Congress within four days that the disability still exists contrary to the President's opinion, the Vice President continues as acting President and Congress has twenty-one days to resolve the issue, the decision to be made by a two-thirds majority of each House.

It also authorizes the President, whenever there is a vacancy in the office of Vice President, to nominate a replacement, who becomes Vice President when confirmed by a majority of both Houses of Congress. Gerald R. Ford was nominated to be Vice President under this clause in 1973, and when Ford succeeded Richard M. Nixon as President in 1974, he nominated Nelson A. Rockefeller to be his successor. For the first time in the nation's history, there was a President and Vice President neither of whom were elected by the people.

Between Election and Inauguration

Despite three different succession acts, and three constitutional amendments, the selection process is still dependent, to a certain extent, upon political-party rules. Neither the Constitution nor federal statutes provide for the contingency of a presidential or vice presidential candidate dying, withdrawing, or being disqualified between election day and the day the Electoral College meets five weeks later. The rules of the Democratic and Republican parties, however, empower their national committees to fill such vacancies. If the presidential candidate dies, the elevation of the vice presidential candidate would be likely but not certain.

Constitutional scholars have differing opinions on the question of succession between the time the electors meet and the counting of electoral votes by Congress on 6 January. They suggest at least two possible scenarios that might occur if a presidential candidate selected by a majority of the electors dies, withdraws, or is disqualified during this period.

Congress could declare that the candidate who received a majority of the votes for President was elected, even if he had died or resigned, and then the Vice President-elect would assume the presidency under the Twentieth Amendment. It could also declare that no qualified candidate for President had received a majority of the votes cast and the election would accordingly be determined by the House of Representatives under the provisions of the Twelfth Amendment.

If the President-elect dies between 6 January and Inauguration Day (20 January), the Vice President-elect becomes President-elect under the Twentieth Amendment. In the event a President has not been chosen, or a President-elect is disabled, found to be constitutionally unqualified, or refuses to accept the office, the Vice President in the meantime acts as President.

[See also (II) Disability, Presidential; Vice President.]

BIBLIOGRAPHY

Feerick, John D. *The Twenty-fifth Amendment.* 1976.

Silva, Ruth. *Presidential Succession.* 1951.

Stathis, Stephen W. "Presidential Disability Agreements Prior to the 25th Amendment." *Presidential Studies Quarterly* 12 (1982): 208–215.

Thompson, Kenneth W. *Papers on Presidential Disability and the Twenty-fifth Amendment.* 2 vols. 1991.

– STEPHEN W. STATHIS

T

TERM AND TENURE

Issues concerning the President's term and tenure have vexed the nation since the first week of the Constitutional Convention of 1787. Among the longstanding and recurring debates are: How long should the President's term be? How many terms should the President serve? When should the President's term begin and end?

The convention was consumed by questions of presidential term and tenure. Afterward, dissatisfied with the delegates' decision to allow the President unlimited eligibility for reelection, President Thomas Jefferson managed to establish a two-term limit as a matter of tradition. In the twentieth century, two of the four constitutional amendments that have modified the presidency (the Twentieth and Twenty-second) deal with issues of term and tenure. Other possible amendments, such as a single six-year term for the President, have been proposed throughout American history.

The Constitutional Convention

Delegates to the Constitutional Convention began their labors in May 1787 by making one set of decisions about the President's term and tenure and, after numerous twists and turns, ended in September by making an entirely different set.

The delegates initially proposed to establish congressional election of the President to a seven-year term with no possibility of reelection. In the minds of most delegates, these three conditions were carefully connected. For example, if Congress was to choose the President, then the President should only serve one term. The reason, as George Mason of Virginia stated, was that if legislative reelection were permitted, there would exist a constant "temptation on the part of the Executive to intrigue with the Legislature for a reappointment," using political patronage and illegitimate favors in effect to buy votes.

As the convention wore on, the advantages delegates saw in eligibility for reelection became steadily more numerous. Not only would the country have a way to keep a good President in office, but reeligibility would give the President what Gouverneur Morris of Pennsylvania called "the great motive to good behavior, the hope of being rewarded with a re-appointment." Morris also noted the dangers of not allowing the President to stand for reelection: "Shut the Civil road to Glory & he may be compelled to seek it by the sword."

To complicate their task further, the delegates' need to choose between election by Congress and presidential reeligibility implied a related choice between a longer term and a shorter one, seven years or four years. If the President was to be chosen by Congress for a single term only, the delegates believed, the term should be long. If the President was eligible for reelection, a shorter term was preferable.

In September, the convention resolved its dilemma by creating the Electoral College. Having taken presidential selection out of the hands of Congress, the delegates felt free to remove all restrictions on the President's right to run for an unlimited number of four-year terms.

The Constitutional Convention did not establish a starting date for the President's term. Instead, after the Constitution was ratified in 1788, the "old Congress" of the Articles of Confederation declared 4 March 1789 as the date "for commencing proceedings under the said Constitution." Congress passed a law in 1792 that codified the 4 March after each presidential election as the date on which the President's term would begin and end.

The Two-term Tradition

Thomas Jefferson, who was minister to France at the time of the Constitution Convention, had always opposed unrestricted presidential reeligibility. In 1807, as the end of Jefferson's second term as President drew near, the legislatures of eight states petitioned him to run for a third term. Jefferson refused in a letter to the Vermont legislature:

> If some termination to the services of the Chief Magistrate be not fixed by the Constitution, or supplied by practice, his office, nominally four years, will in fact become for life, and history shows how easily that degenerates into inheritance. . . . I should unwillingly be the person who, disregarding the sound precedent set by an illustrious predecessor [George Washington] should furnish the first example of prolongation beyond the second term of office.

Although Jefferson's invocation of Washington was not altogether accurate (Washington retired from the presidency after two terms, he wrote in his Farewell Address because he longed for "the shade of retirement"), the two-term limit quickly and securely took root in the American political tradition. Each of the first nine Presidents sought two terms but no more.

In 1840, the Whig Party took Jefferson's precedent one step further, arguing that one four-year term was all that a President should serve. Most voters, including many Democrats, seem to have agreed: from 1840 to 1860 no President was even nominated to run for a second term. Although Abraham Lincoln restored the two-term tradition to respectability by winning reelection in 1864, he was more the exception than the rule. Of the first thirty-one Presidents (Washington to Herbert Hoover), twenty served one term or less and none served more than two terms. Even so, congressional discontent with the Constitution's provision for unlimited reeligibility simmered steadily on the legislative back burner. More than two hundred resolutions to limit the President's tenure were introduced between 1789 and 1928.

Roosevelt became steadily more frustrated as his second term wore on with congressional resistance to his programs and policies.

The two-term tradition was broken by the thirty-second President, Franklin D. Roosevelt. Elected in 1932 and reelected in 1936, Roosevelt became steadily more frustrated as his second term wore on with congressional resistance to his programs and policies. In 1939, World War II broke out in Europe and Asia, posing a variety of risks to American security that made the argument for keeping a steady hand at the tiller of the ship of state uniquely persuasive. Waiting until the Democratic convention in July 1940 to signal his intention, Roosevelt finally agreed to be nominated for a third term. The delegates overwhelmingly approved his decision.

Roosevelt's Republican opponents emblazoned "No Third Term!" on their campaign banners, and public opinion polls found that the voters were deeply divided over the propriety of Roosevelt's candidacy. Wartime insecurity won him reelection against the Republican nominee, business leader Wendell Willkie, but by a much narrower margin than in 1936—5 million popular votes, compared with 11 million. In 1944, with the United States and its allies nearing victory in the war, Roosevelt won a fourth term, by 3 million votes. He died on 12 April 1945 less than three months after his inauguration.

The Twenty-second Amendment

Republicans and conservative southern Democrats had chafed under Roosevelt's twelve-year reign as President; in the mid-term elections of 1946, the Republican Party took control of Congress for the first time since 1930. On 6 February 1947, less than five weeks after the opening of the Eightieth Congress, the House of Representatives passed a strict two-term-limit amendment to the Constitution by a vote of 285 to 121. Republicans supported the amendment unanimously (238–0); Democrats opposed it by 121 to 47, with most of the yea votes coming from southerners.

Five weeks later, on 12 March, the Senate passed a slightly different version of the amendment by a vote of 59 to 23. (The Senate version allowed a President who had served one full term and, because of succession, less than half of another, to run for reelection one time.) Again, the Republicans were unanimous (46–0); Democrats opposed the amendment by a vote of 23 to 13. On March 24, after the differences between the two houses' versions were ironed out in favor of the Senate, Congress officially sent the amendment to the states for ratification. The Twenty-second Amendment became part of the Constitution three years and eleven months later, in February 1951—the longest time any constitutional amendment has taken to be ratified. Harry S Truman, the incumbent President at the time, was exempted from the term limit.

Although the voting in Congress on the Twenty-second Amendment was partisan, the public debate was framed in philosophical terms. Supporters contended that the limit would protect Americans against the threat of an overly personalized presidency; opponents rejoined that if the people thought the President had been in office too long, they could simply vote the incumbent out. Virtually no attention was given to the careful and thoughtful debates at the Constitutional Convention that underlay the original Constitution's lack of a restriction on presidential reeligibility. Nor did Congress foresee the effects of the two-term limit on the vice presidency. With second-term Presidents barred from seeking reelection, their Vice Presidents were free to campaign openly for the party's presidential nomination virtually from the start of the President's second term, as Richard M. Nixon and George Bush successfully did in 1960 and 1988, respectively.

So few Presidents have served two full terms since the Twenty-second Amendment was enacted that its effects on the presidency are hard to measure. One President was assassinated (John F. Kennedy), one resigned

(Richard Nixon), one declined to run (Lyndon B. Johnson), and three were defeated in their bids for reelection (Gerald R. Ford, Jimmy Carter, and George Bush). The constraints of the constitutional two-term limit, then, have been felt by only two Presidents, both of them Republicans: Dwight D. Eisenhower in 1960 and Ronald Reagan in 1988.

Eisenhower publicly expressed "deep reservations" about the Twenty-second Amendment while in office; according to John Eisenhower, his son and deputy chief of staff, the President would have liked to run for a third term. During Reagan's second term, he unsuccessfully campaigned for a constitutional amendment that would repeal the two-term limit. Public opinion polls have consistently shown that although Americans thought at the time that Eisenhower and Reagan were good Presidents, they have consistently wanted to preserve the Twenty-second Amendment.

The Twentieth Amendment

The inauguration date that was instituted by Congress in 1792 left a four-month interregnum between the presidential election on the first Tuesday after the first Monday in November and the President's inauguration on the following 4 March. In the 1920s, Sen. George W. Norris of Nebraska, arguing that the March date was an artifact of the horse-and-buggy days of travel and communication and that four months was too long a time to have, in effect, two Presidents, campaigned for a constitutional amendment that would advance the start of the term.

Congress passed the Twentieth Amendment on 2 March 1932. One section of the amendment provided that the President's term would begin at noon on the January 20 following the election. It was ratified without controversy and became part of the Constitution in 1933.

Proposed Reforms

Issues of presidential term and tenure, which were the subject of extensive deliberation at the Constitutional Convention and have already prompted two amendments to the Constitution, remain unresolved in American political discussion. As noted earlier, a campaign was launched by Republicans in the late 1980s to repeal the Twenty-second Amendment and restore the original Constitution's provision for unlimited reeligibility. A different, more longstanding and widely discussed idea is to limit the President to a single six-year presidential term. Advocates, including Presidents Andrew Jackson, Woodrow Wilson, Eisenhower, Johnson, and Carter, traditionally have claimed that awarding the President one long term would free him from the unwelcome pressures of reelection and grant the administration more time to accomplish its long-term objectives. Critics point out that under a single six-year term, an unpopular President would serve two years longer than under the current system and a popular President would be forced out two years sooner. In any event, despite the ongoing discussion, no proposed amendment affecting the President's term and tenure has gained widespread public support.

[See also (II) Two-Term Tradition.]

BIBLIOGRAPHY

Milkis, Sidney M., and Michael Nelson. *The American Presidency: Origins and Development, 1776–1990.* 1990.

Sundquist, James L. *Constitutional Reform and Effective Government.* 1982.

Willis, Paul G., and George L. Willis. "The Politics of the Twenty-second Amendment." *Western Political Quarterly* 5 (September 1952):469–482.

– MICHAEL NELSON

TRANSPORTATION, DEPARTMENT OF

After several efforts to rationalize federal transportation policy, President Lyndon B. Johnson submitted legislation to Congress on 6 March 1966, to establish a Cabinet-level department of transportation. Johnson's administration designed the department to provide guidance in resolving transportation problems and to develop national transportation policies. Johnson's aim was to solve the following dilemma: while the United States had one of the best-developed transportation systems in the world, the system lacked the coordination that would let travelers and goods move conveniently and efficiently from one mode of transport to another, using the best characteristics of each. Johnson maintained that a modern transportation system was critical to the national economic health and well-being, including high employment, a high standard of living, and national defense.

The Johnson administration was not alone in seeking a Cabinet-level Department of Transportation. This new department was the result of a combination of factors, ranging from suggestions that had long been made by government reorganization teams such as the Hoover Commission to the realization by the administrator of the Federal Aviation Agency that he needed representation at the Cabinet table.

The Enabling Legislation

The White House framed the legislation to combine agencies involved in transportation enterprises scattered throughout the federal government. The bill, however, avoided matters of transportation policy.

Johnson signed the Department of Transportation Enabling Act on 15 October 1966. By this act, thirty-eight agencies or functions and ninety thousand employees came under the control of the department. Various congressional compromises had made the final version of the bill less than what the White House had wanted. Even in its watered-down form, however, the act produced the most sweeping reorganization of the federal government since the National Security Act of 1947, which, among other things, set up the Department of Defense. Johnson endorsed the compromise measure as the most acceptable piece of legislation that could be pushed through Congress, the first step toward bringing efficiency and rationality to federal transportation policy.

The new department would do more than simply set in motion aviation policies, or say, surface transportation policies. Rather, it would develop coordinated transportation policies to meet the continuing needs of the nation. For instance, Secretary-designate Alan Boyd maintained that, with the Department of Transportation (DOT) in place, specific bills such as the National Traffic and Motor Vehicle Safety Act of 1966 would in some manner have an impact on other modes of transportation besides the automobile. The National Transportation Safety Board (established by the 1966 DOT act) would investigate many kinds of transportation-related accidents, whatever the mode of transportation, and use the gathered data to start what Boyd claimed would be a national approach to transportation safety. In his message to Congress on 2 March 1966, President Johnson claimed that no function of the new department and no responsibility of its secretary would be more important than safety.

Planners designed the department with a view to combining the experience of the various agencies regulating different modes of transportation with the general skill of the Office of the Secretary of Transportation to devise long-range plans and policies. A diverse group of agencies were to be brought under the new department's umbrella, including the Maritime Administration (made part of the department in 1981), the Car Service Division, the Saint Lawrence Seaway, the Federal Aviation Agency, and the Bureau of Public Roads. Because these agencies' operating characteristics had so little in common in terms of skills required, clients served, problems faced, and general system character, planners called for decentralized operations with DOT staff control limited to testing the effectiveness of the various systems. From the start, the department functioned with as much of a sense of purpose as the planners could have expected. Five and a half months after Johnson signed the enabling legislation, the Department of Transportation—the twelfth Cabinet department and suddenly the fourth-largest department—had a combined annual budget of nearly $5 billion.

Post-1967 Organization

Conceding the link between transportation needs and the needs of urban areas—where more than 70 percent of the U.S. population lived—the White House transferred most urban mass-transportation functions to the Department of Transportation from the Department of Housing and Urban Development, effective 1 July 1968. Responsibility for these was placed in the newly established Urban Mass Transportation Administration (now the Federal Transit Administration).

Johnson's administration designed the Transportation Department to provide guidance in resolving transportation problems and to develop national transportation policies.

By the end of the Johnson administration, the Department of Transportation embraced the U.S. Coast Guard, the Federal Aviation Administration, the Federal Highway Administration, the Federal Railroad Administration, the Saint Lawrence Seaway Development Corporation, the Urban Mass Transportation Administration, and, tangentially, the National Transportation Safety Board.

In 1970, Boyd's successor, John Volpe, proposed to separate functions involving the safety of highway construction (under the Bureau of Public Roads) from those of the National Highway Safety Bureau (NHSB), which was responsible for enforcing the National Traffic and Motor Vehicle Safety Act. Volpe approved the transfer of the NHSB to the Office of the Secretary. To emphasize the high-level commitment to preventing traffic fatalities, Volpe separated the NHSB from the Federal Highway Administration completely. The Highway Safety Act formally separated the safety bureau from the highway administration and created a new administration, the National Highway Traffic Safety Administration.

In moves to limit the President's powers, Congress gave the NTSB full autonomy in the early 1980s, having begun to move toward this in 1976. Congress now feared that the loose autonomy that the Department of Transportation Enabling Act had given the NTSB made it too vulnerable to executive pressure.

On 23 September 1977, Jimmy Carter's first Transportation Secretary, Brock Adams, established the Research and Special Programs Administration (RSPA), an institutional development of major import. When Adams created RSPA, he combined the Transportation Systems Center, the hazardous materials program, and diverse activities that did not readily fit under any of the existing operating administrations. RSPA moved cross-cutting research and development pursuits from the Office of the Secretary to an autonomous operating administration.

The Inspector General Act of 1978, created an inspector general for the Department of Transportation as well as for other executive agencies. The mission of this officer, appointed by the President and confirmed by the Senate, was to help the secretary cope with waste, fraud, and abuse. Though housed in the department and given the rank of Assistant Secretary, the inspector general was autonomous.

President Carter's second Secretary of Transportation, Neil Goldschmidt, established the Office of Small and Disadvantaged Business Utilization in the Office of the Secretary. OSDBU was responsible for implementing procedures, consistent with federal laws, to provide policy guidance for minority-owned, woman-owned, and disadvantaged businesses that joined the department's procurement and federal financial-assistance activities.

President Ronald Reagan's first Transportation Secretary, Drew Lewis, succeeded in moving the Maritime Administration from the Department of Commerce to Transportation, providing the department with the maritime element it needed to frame national transportation policy. While Elizabeth Dole, Reagan's second secretary, held the post, the Commercial Space Launch Act of 1984 gave the department a new mission: the promotion and regulation of commercial satellite launches. As none of the department's existing operating administrations had a mission compatible with this, Dole housed the Office of Commercial Space Transportation in the Office of the Secretary.

BIBLIOGRAPHY

Burby, John. *The Great American Motion Sickness: Or Why You Can't Get from There to Here.* 1971.

Davis, Grant Miller. *The Department of Transportation.* 1970.

Dean, Alan L. "The Organization and Management of the Department of Transportation." Paper. National Academy of Public Administration. 1991.

Hazard, John L. "The Institutionalization of Transportation Policy: Two Decades of DOT." *Transportation Journal* 26 (Fall 1986): 17–31.

– R. DALE GRINDER

TREASURY, DEPARTMENT OF THE

The second-oldest of the current Cabinet departments (after the State Department), the Department of the Treasury is the branch of the federal government charged with the management and supervision of the nation's finances. Because most governmental functions overlap with financial and economic issues, the Treasury, with its broad responsibilities, is among the most important of the executive departments, and the Secretary of the Treasury is necessarily a key adviser to the President in the formation and execution of economic policy.

Origins

The Department of the Treasury was created by an act of Congress on 2 September 1789 as the third of the original Cabinet departments, following the departments of State and War. Treasury became the second-ranking department in the Cabinet when the Department of War was eliminated in 1948 and its functions subsumed under the Department of Defense. In creating the Treasury in the first session after the ratification of the Constitution, Congress recognized the critical importance of national finance to the success of the new government.

The Treasury grew out of the old Treasury Office of Accounts, which was created to manage funds necessary to finance the War of Independence.

The Department of the Treasury grew out of the old Treasury Office of Accounts, which was created by the Continental Congress in 1775 to raise and manage funds necessary to finance the then-impending War of Independence. In this capacity, the Office of Accounts issued bills of credit for sale to the public with the promise that they would be redeemed at some point in the future.

The new department was given far broader powers by the Congress than had been held by the Office of Accounts. The Treasury, in the original legislation, was charged with the following responsibilities: preparing plans for the improvement and management of the nation's revenue and support for the public credit, supervising the collection of government revenue, preparing and reporting estimates of the public revenue and expenditures, enforcing tariff and maritime laws, overseeing the sale of public lands, making reports on all matters pertaining to the Treasury, and receiving, keeping, and distributing the moneys of the United States. These broad financial powers have remained with the Treasury down to the present day, with appropriate adjustments and additions in response to changing circumstances in the nation.

Treasury, though created in conjunction with the State and War departments, was given a unique and ambiguous status by Congress. State and War were clearly identified as executive departments in the original legislations, but Treasury was not so clearly identified. The Secretary of the Treasury was required by the statute to provide periodic reports on finance to Congress and to respond in writing and in person on any matter referred to him by Congress. No similar requirements were imposed on the other departmental secretaries.

The statute suggested that Congress intended Treasury to be affiliated with it in some way, either as the agent of Congress or as the agent jointly of Congress and the President. Congress, jealous of its own powers in the area of finance, may have expected to exercise influence over the Treasury that it did not seek in relation either to State or War with their responsibilities in foreign affairs. However, the first Treasury Secretary, Alexander Hamilton, immediately acted as the agent of the executive branch, exactly as did the secretaries of the other departments. The status of the Treasury remained controversial until 1833, when President Andrew Jackson succeeded, despite initial opposition from the Senate, in removing a Treasury Secretary who defied his orders concerning the Bank of the United States. Jackson's successes in this confrontation with the Congress thus solidified executive control over the Treasury and ended this controversy.

Functions

The principal functions of the Treasury are to manage the financial and economic affairs of the United States government. Within this mandate, the Treasury has a unique package of responsibilities that cut across both domestic policy and foreign affairs. On the domestic side, the Treasury collects revenue for the government, disburses funds for approved purposes, manages the public debt, keeps government accounts, oversees national banks and insures the soundness of the national banking system, and manufactures coins and currency. On the international side, the Treasury works on dollar exchange, trade, Group of Seven meetings, the International Monetary Fund (IMF), the World Bank, and many other issues dealing with international finance and economic policy.

Both on the domestic and international fronts, Treasury also carries out important law-enforcement functions, including the enforcement of tax and tariff laws, interdicting illegal narcotics traffic into the United States, and conducting antifraud and anti-counterfeiting operations. Following the assassination of President William McKinley in 1901, the Secret Service, a bureau within Treasury that had earlier been established to stop counterfeiting of U.S. currency, began to provide protection for the President. Its functions were later expanded to include the protection of the President-elect, the President's immediate family, the Vice President, former Presidents, presidential candidates, and other high-ranking officials and foreign diplomats. The Department of the Treasury is thus not only the chief financial institution of the U.S. government but also one of its most important law enforcement agencies.

Congress has seen fit over the years to broaden the scope of the Treasury's responsibilities to keep pace with the expansion of the country and the ever-growing size and complexity of the nation's financial system. Despite these growing responsibilities, there is a fundamental continuity in the history of the department from Hamilton's time to the present; indeed, when I first assumed the office of Secretary of the Treasury in 1974, I was struck by how similar the problems confronting me were to those facing Hamilton when he took his post as the first Treasury Secretary in 1789.

The Treasury was once solely responsible for most of the President's economic forecasts, budgets, and economic proposals.

While most government departments are preoccupied with spending funds on programs assigned to them, Treasury has a broader mandate. It must concern itself with raising needed revenue, keeping the government's accounts, financing deficits, and assessing the effects of federal policy on the economy as a whole. These responsibilities have been faced by all secretaries since Hamilton, and though the department itself has grown, it has done so out of the basic structure and functions assigned to it more than two hundred years ago.

Office of the Secretary

Appointed by the President with the consent of the Senate, the Secretary of the Treasury is the chief financial officer of the federal government, responsible for the smooth functioning of revenue collection and disbursement of federal funds, management of the public debt, and the operation of the various Treasury bureaus. The Secretary is also the President's chief economic spokesman and the chief architect to the administration's economic policy. As the second-ranking Cabinet official, the secretary is the key adviser to the President on a range of issues involving government finance.

As the chief financial officer and economic spokesman, the Secretary of the Treasury represents the U.S. government in trade, monetary policy, and economic policy negotiations with foreign governments. He represents the United States as a governor of the International Bank for Reconstruction and Development, the Inter-American Development Bank, and the International Monetary Fund. The Secretary is an ex officio member of various governmental boards concerned with domestic and international financial issues. The Secretary also has chief fiduciary responsibility for the Social Security trust funds.

The Treasury was once solely responsible for most of the President's economic forecasts, budgets, and economic proposals. Today, however, the Department works with the Council of Economic Advisers (CEA), the Office of Management and Budget (OMB), and the Bureau of Economic Analysis in the Department of Commerce to develop the forecasts that serve as a basis for the administration's budget projections. The Secretary also chairs the "troika" meetings to establish such economic forecasts. These meetings are attended by the Chairman of the CEA, the Director of the OMB and, informally, by the Chairman of the Federal Reserve Board.

The Secretary of the Treasury frequently consults with the Chairman of the Federal Reserve Board on a host of financial questions that concern both institutions. The Federal Reserve is an independent agency charged with regulating the money supply, with powers delegated to it by the Congress. Coordination between the Treasury and the Federal Reserve is critical, because the Treasury issues and manages the federal debt, and the Federal Reserve regulates the money supply through its open market operations and the sale of federal debt instruments. The Treasury no longer dictates policy to the Federal Reserve, but the Secretary meets often on an informal basis with the Chairman of the Federal Reserve Board to exchange views on the economy and on regulatory issues concerning the financial industry and credit markets.

Organization

The Treasury in 1991 had an annual operating budget of approximately $11 billion and employed more than 160,000 people, making its workforce third in size among Cabinet departments (behind the departments of Defense and Veterans Affairs) and meaning that, in sheer size, it is the largest law-enforcement agency in the U.S. government. The department has its headquarters in Washington, D.C., but maintains field organizations in every state and offices in nearly every major city.

The government's financial activities were at one time concentrated exclusively within the Treasury, but in the last fifty years, several other institutions and agencies have been created to perform functions that had previously been reserved for the Treasury alone. These institutions include, most notably, the Bureau of the Budget (which later became the Office of Management and Budget), the Council of Economic Advisers, and the Federal Reserve Board.

Treasury itself has also experienced much internal diversification in the postwar years. It is currently organized into thirteen departmental offices, which are responsible for making policy and managing the department, and thirteen bureaus, which perform the specific operating functions of the department. The Secretary is aided by a Deputy Secretary, two Undersecretaries, and thirteen Assistant Secretaries who head the various departmental offices. The key assistant secretaries manage the offices for Economic Policy, Tax Policy, International Affairs, and Domestic Finance.

Each of the bureaus is managed by a director who reports to the Secretary through one of the assistant secretaries. Many of the operating bureaus within the Treasury are well known in their own right, independent of their relationship to the Treasury. The thirteen existing operating bureaus are the Bureau of Alcohol, Tobacco, and Firearms; the Internal Revenue Service; the Mint; the Secret Service; the Customs Service; the Comptroller of the Currency; the Bureau of the Public Debt; the U.S. Savings Bond Division; the Financial Management Service; the Federal Law Enforcement Training Center; the Bureau of Government Financial Operations; the Bureau of Engraving and Printing; and the Office of Thrift Supervision.

Treasury Building

Completed in 1842, the Treasury Building is an imposing, five-story, Neoclassical structure, located immediately east of the White House. In addition to the main building, three wings were constructed between 1860 and 1869 to accommodate the growing department.

The existing building was constructed after the building that had previously housed the department was destroyed by fire in 1833 (arson was suspected). Construction of the new building was to have begun in 1836, but work was delayed when builders and architects could not agree on a location for the cornerstone. Legend has it that President Jackson, frustrated by the haggling, walked over to the site one day, planted his cane in the ground, and declared, "Right here is where I want the cornerstone." Thus was established the location of the building, which, because of Jackson's haste, blocks the view of the Capitol Building from the White House.

Taxes have grown along with government expenditures, though at a somewhat slower rate, and they now represent about one-fifth of gross domestic product.

The proximity of the Treasury Building to the White House is a clear sign of the importance of the Treasury to the President, and because of its location the building has been the scene of many important historical events. Indeed, President Andrew Johnson even had to keep his offices in the Treasury Building for a time after Abraham Lincoln's death when Mary Todd Lincoln refused to leave the White House.

Treasury's Changing Role

Since the department's beginnings, the scope and magnitude of the Treasury's functions and responsibilities have grown enormously. In large part, this growth has resulted from the continuing expansion of the federal government's presence in nearly every aspect of the nation's life. Government expenditures in the early days of the Republic represented a very small fraction of the total income produced in the country. These expenditures now amount to one-quarter of the nation's gross domestic product. Taxes have grown along with expenditures, though at a somewhat slower rate, and they now represent about one-fifth of gross domestic product. The accumulated difference between the growth in expenditures and taxes is the national debt, which in 1992 totaled $3.9 trillion, of which $2.7 trillion was held by the public. These facts and figures significantly understate the pervasive role of the federal government, however. Government regulations and mandates apply to virtually every type of economic activity and exert a major and, not infrequently, harmful influence on the conduct of all aspects of the daily economic affairs of every household and business in the country.

This imposing array of government activities must be financed. As the scope of government activities has increased, so too has the federal government's claim on the income of the American people. The federal tax system, especially the income tax, has become ever more complex and demanding; the Internal Revenue Code now consists of hundreds of sections and thousands of pages, defying comprehension by even the most skillful and experienced tax experts.

We need to remind ourselves that our government has no power except that granted to it by the American people. As I maintained throughout my tenure as Treasury Secretary and in my 1978 book *A Time for Truth,* much of the cynicism and negativism in late twentieth-century America is the result of the demonstrated failure of collectivist approaches to national problems that have promised so much and delivered so little. In the process, a mood of dependence on government has increased, feeding on itself and creating still more demands for benefits without recognizing that the bills must be paid—either directly in higher taxes and growing debt burdens or indirectly through accelerating inflation and economic disruption.

We ignore at our peril the fundamental truth that our personal, political, and economic freedoms are inextricably linked and that loss of economic freedom invariably leads to loss of political and personal freedoms. Our basic challenge, then, is to determine how much personal freedom, if any, we are willing to give up in seeking security through government. It is not easy to live with the uncertainties of a free society, but the real personal benefits it creates are far superior to those created in any other system. In short, it is America's faith in a free economy, more than anything else, that is in need of revitalization if we are going to remain the freest and most prosperous nation into the twenty-first century.

BIBLIOGRAPHY

Simon, William E. *A Time for Action.* 1980.
Simon, William E. *A Time for Truth.* 1978.
U.S. Treasury Department. *The Treasury Story.* 1966.
Walston, Mark *The Department of the Treasury.* 1989.
White, Leonard D. *The Federalists: A Study in Administrative History.* 1948.
———. *The Jacksonians: A Study in Administrative History,* 1829–1861. 1954.
———. *The Jeffersonians A Study in Administrative History,* 1801–1829. 1951.
———. *The Republican Era: A Study in Administrative History,* 1869–1901. 1958.

– WILLIAM E. SIMON

TREATY-MAKING POWER

Article II of the Constitution gives the President the "Power, by and with the Advice and Consent of the

Senate, to make Treaties, provided two thirds of the Senators present concur." The President serves as the nation's diplomat in chief and the authority to make treaties is one of the President's most significant foreign-affairs powers. This presidential power includes making the United States' bilateral and multilateral treaties with other countries on a variety of topics (for example, treaties on tariffs, economic relations, nuclear arms, mutual defense, human rights, and terrorism). Through his treaty-making capacity, the President or his designees conduct communications and negotiations with other foreign leaders. The President's treaty-making authority, however, is subject to the Senate's advice and consent; this requirement often has led to disputes between the executive branch and the Senate over treaties that the President has negotiated with another country. Such disputes are part of a broader separation of powers controversy between the political branches over the treaty power.

In the Constitution

Framers of the Constitution established the treaty power so that it would be centralized in the new national government, rather than dispersed among the several separate states of the Union. Indeed, a major impetus for forging the Constitution was to avoid the individual states' embarrassing international forays under the weak Confederacy following the War for Independence. James Madison wrote that the Confederacy's main defect was its inability to "cause infractions of treaties, or of the law of nations to be punished," and thus "particular states might by their conduct provoke war without control." The Articles of Confederation conferred upon Congress "the sole and exclusive right and power of . . . entering into treaties and alliances," although the states could still enter into a treaty with another nation with the Congress's consent. The Articles of Confederation, moreover, created neither an executive nor a judiciary of which to speak; the Confederacy lacked an effective enforcement mechanism to stop the individual states from rambunctiously entering into treaties and from conducting foreign affairs on their own. It was important for the United States to coordinate successful foreign relations, particularly given the wary existence of a country in its infancy. As a result of these concerns, the new Constitution placed the treaty power in the new national government and expressly says that "No State shall enter into any Treaty, Alliance or Confederation." This and other constitutional prescriptions helped to ensure that the treaty power is centralized, and more generally that foreign relations are federal relations.

The Framers, however, still had to decide how to distribute the treaty-making power (and other foreign affairs powers) among the three branches of the new federal government. In July 1787, the Constitutional Convention appointed a Committee of Detail to create a draft constitution, pursuant to the Convention's prior resolutions. That committee's draft placed the treaty-making power exclusively in the Senate; it did not provide any presidential involvement in the treaty-making process. The draft clause simply read: "The Senate of the United States shall have power to make treaties, and to appoint Ambassadors." The committee of Detail's delegation of the treaty power to the legislative branch was reminiscent of the Articles of Confederation, which, as noted, also had conferred the treaty power exclusively upon Congress. The committee's draft proposal stirred controversy at the Convention, although the initial negative reaction had little to do with the President's absence from the treaty-making process. Instead, the controversy stemmed from the fact that the House of Representatives would not participate in making treaties; that debate involved the more general issue of how the states should be represented (equally or proportionate to their populations) when regulating various federal powers. Relatedly, the committee draft also engendered discussion about the fact that a simple majority of Senators could make a treaty, since the proposal did not contain any special voting requirement for a treaty's passage (e.g., a two-thirds or other "super majority" rule).

The President and the Senate

have not balanced treaty power easily.

Of course, the Constitutional Convention adopted a treaty clause markedly different from the Committee of Detail's version. The treaty clause does still preclude the "fluctuating" and "multitudinous" House of Representatives from making treaties (*Federalist* 75). As Alexander Hamilton reasoned in that essay: "Accurate and comprehensive knowledge of foreign politics; . . . a nice and uniform sensibility to national character; decision, secrecy, and dispatch, are incompatible with the genius of a body so variable and numerous." Unlike the committee version, however, the Constitution's treaty clause requires not just a simple majority, but a two-thirds majority of the Senators voting to adopt a treaty. And the most significant difference between the proposed and adopted treaty clauses is that the Framers gave the treaty-making power to the President. Why did they empower the President to make treaties, while the committee had given him absolutely no role in treaty making? Unfortunately, the records from the Constitutional Convention inadequately illuminate this dramatic shift in the treaty power. According to James Madison's notes, one speaker, John Francis Mercer of Maryland, strongly favored presidential domination of treaty making, following the British model: Mr. Mercer "contended . . . that the Senate ought not have the power of treaties. This power belonged to the Executive department" (2 M. Farrand, *The Records of the Federal Convention of 1787,* at 297). This was the case of treaties in Great Britain. But it should be noted that Mercer was not one of the most influential or significant convention delegates.

Interpreting the Constitution

Certain essays in the *Federalist* (published to support the Constitution's ratification) argue for the President's authority over foreign affairs, including the treaty-making power. For example, in *Federalist* 75, Alexander Hamilton asserts that if the President played only a "ministerial" role in treaty making, he "could not be expected to enjoy the confidence and respect of foreign powers in the same degree with the constitutional representative of the nation, and, of course, would not be able to act with an equal degree of weight or efficacy." Those who argue for executive supremacy over treaty making cite such passages, as they do John Marshall's later, much-quoted remark: "The President is the sole organ of the nation in its external relations, and its sole representative with foreign nations" (10 *Annals of Cong.* 613 [1800]). But the significance of Marshall's stanza should not be exaggerated or taken out of context; he actually uttered it in a speech before the House of Representatives on an extradition matter. Moreover, those who argue for a greater sharing of the treaty power between the President and the Senate can also cite *The Federalist.* In fact, also in *Federalist* 75, Hamilton himself writes that the treaty-making power "does not seem strictly to fall within the definition of either" the executive or legislative authority. And "the history of human conduct does not warrant the exalted opinion of human virtue which would make it wise . . . to commit interests of so delicate and momentous a kind, as those which concern its intercourse with the rest of the world, to the sole disposal of . . . [the] President." Given the fact that Article II subjects presidential treaty making to the Senate's advice and consent—and given the lack of historical evidence for trivializing the senatorial role in treaty making—it is reasonable to conclude that the Framers simply intended for some balancing of the treaty power between the President and the Senate.

The Role of the Senate

The President and the Senate, however, have not balanced the treaty power easily. In 1789, President George Washington initiated a meeting with the Senate to seek its advice on the terms of a treaty that he wanted to negotiate with southern Indians. The President was displeased when the Senate then referred the matter to a committee, causing him to return to the Senate for a second meeting on the treaty. No President (including Washington) has ever again so personally sought the Senate's advice on a treaty before its negotiation. Thereafter, during the early 1790s, Washington dealt with the Senate on such matters only in writing. But in 1794, Washington did not at all seek (even in writing) the Senate's advice on Jay's Treaty before concluding negotiations with Great Britain. Not having had the opportunity previously to give advice on Jay's Treaty, the Senate retaliated by revising one article of the treaty as part of its decision to consent to the treaty; Washington was then forced to seek Great Britain's agreement to the revised article. This reduction or postponement of the Senate's advice function was not limited to Jay's Treaty. Only rarely over the next two hundred years have Presidents solicited the Senate's advice prior to concluding treaty negotiations. Since the Senate does not usually participate in treaty making until its consent to ratification is solicited, the Senate is more likely to reject a treaty than might otherwise be the case. At a minimum, the Senate is more likely to seek treaty amendments or reservations, causing the President either to reopen negotiations with the other sovereign, or to decide himself to shelve a treaty if the Senate's amendments are too substantial. In short, the treaty-making process is inefficient, controversial, and potentially embarrassing and adverse to the President's dealings with foreign sovereigns. Without its more timely advice on treaties, the Senate has indeed become the graveyard of treaties.

Despite these significant problems, the executive branch has not tried to improve the Senate's advice function. A President apparently would rather risk the rejection of his treaty than to give the Senate a more meaningful role in treaty making—which might be taken as a concession that he is not the sole organ of foreign affairs but a copartner with the Senate in shaping the nation's international commitments. Presidents occasionally have appointed a few key Senators to a treaty's negotiating team, ostensibly seeking their advice during a treaty's formulation. But such a practice may violate the Constitution's prohibition in Article I against a Senator being "appointed to any civil office under the authority of the United States, which shall have been created, or the emoluments whereof shall have been increased during such time." A cynic, moreover, might suggest that the executive branch has appointed Senators as treaty negotiators not really to gain their wise advice but to make them feel superficially that they are part of the treaty-making process, so that they will later work to gain the Senate's consent to a treaty. That practice does not meaningfully enhance the advice function of the Senate as a whole. Presidents, however, might contend that most Senators lack the foreign-affairs expertise to provide helpful advice during a treaty's negotiation. In addition, soliciting the Senate's advice throughout the treaty-making process might itself be inefficient, time-consuming, and counterproductive. It is arguable that the United States should speak in one, unified voice (the President's) when negotiating with another nation's executive branch; this argument recommends postponing the Senate's input until the President has concluded his treaty negotiations.

Executive Agreements

It is thus not surprising that Presidents have tried to circumvent the treaty-making process. Presidents historically have established certain international agreements without following the treaty clause's procedures. Such instruments are called executive agreements and are classified by three categories: a treaty-authorized executive agreement, which is an agreement that the President establishes with another nation pursuant to a treaty to which the Senate earlier consented; a congressional-executive agreement, to which the President procures a majority of both Houses' consent (rather than two-thirds of the Senate's consent) before or after making the agreement with the other nation; and a sole-executive agreement, which the President establishes with another nation without any senatorial or congressional consent.

Treaty negotiations are regulated by diplomatic protocol and international law, not constitutional law.

The first category, the treaty-authorized executive agreement, has not been problematic because the President originally received the Senate's consent when the initial compact (the treaty) was created; so the Senate essentially preapproved the subsequent compact (the executive agreement) by which the President executes the initial compact (the treaty). However, the second and third categories, the congressional-executive agreement and the sole-executive agreement, have been very controversial. Since Article II of the Constitution mentions only treaties and not other international compacts, it is arguable that all compacts must be made pursuant to the treaty clause's procedures or are otherwise unconstitutional. Apart from this textual argument that all nontreaty agreements are invalid, sole-executive agreements raise more difficult separation-of-powers issues than do congressional-executive agreements.

Although they can be approved by a simple majority (not a two-thirds majority), congressional-executive agreements do involve the Congress in checking and balancing presidential power. The Framers may have intended for just the Senate and not the House of Representatives to participate in making international compacts, but actually democracy might be better served when the entire Congress plays a representational role in ratifying congressional-executive agreements, as compared with the more elite Senate representing the people in ratifying treaties. Sole-executive agreements, however, are particularly problematic because they are made exclusively by the President and without any congressional input or oversight. The President's creation of sole-executive agreements is inconsistent with the Framers' view that the Senate and President should share the treaty-making power.

In the final analysis, congressional-executive agreements are probably too entrenched in the political system for them to be discarded as an alternative to treaties; but sole-executive agreements should not be created unless they concern either mundane matters or substantive topics clearly within the President's exclusive Article II powers. Furthermore, the executive and legislative branches should try to find mutually acceptable criteria for determining when an accord may be cast as an executive agreement and when it must be cast as a treaty. Until the political branches (or the courts) establish such criteria, executive agreements will continue to be a controversial alternative to the treaty-making process.

The Treaty Process

Within the executive branch, the President (or usually his designees in the White House or the State Department) decides whether and how to negotiate both treaties and executive agreements with other nations. The President or his designee identifies and instructs the individuals who will negotiate the accord. The nature and significance of a particular agreement dictates both who will represent the United States in the negotiations and how long the negotiations will take. The treaty negotiations are regulated by diplomatic protocol and international law (not constitutional law). Once the executive branch is satisfied with the agreement, it will transmit the agreement to the Senate in the case of treaties—which is where the dispute begins about the Senate's advice and consent. Presidents later decide, one last time, whether the United States should sign the formal documents obligating the country to follow treaties to which the Senate has consented.

But even if the President signs such documents and the United States becomes a party to the treaty, the executive and legislative branches may argue further about the President's interpretation of the treaty, and whether that interpretation is consistent with the Senate's original understanding of the treaty. For example, the Senate disagreed with the Sofaer Doctrine, which President Ronald Reagan invoked to reinterpret nuclear-arms agreements with the Soviet Union to allow for the deployment of new technology. And the political branches may also argue about whether the President alone can terminate a treaty without any congressional consent, as they did when President Jimmy Carter unilaterally terminated the Mutual Defense Treaty with Taiwan. Such controversies about interpreting and terminating international agreements are linked with the historic controversy about treaty making; all of these debates essentially concern balancing the power to shape the nation's treaty obligations. The Framers committed that power to two branches of government, so that they could oversee each other. Although such oversight has advantages, it certainly has caused treaty making to be disputatious.

[See also (I) Treaties; (II) Diplomat in Chief, Separation of Powers.]

BIBLIOGRAPHY

Bestor, Arthur. "Respective Roles of Senate and President in the Making and Abrogation of Treaties—The Original Intent of the Framers of the Constitution Historically Examined." *Washington Law Review* 55 (1979): 1–135.

Franck, Thomas M., and Michael J. Glennon. *Foreign Affairs and National Security Law.* 1987. Chapter 3.

Franck, Thomas M., and Edward Weisband. *Foreign Policy by Congress.* 1979. Chapter 6.

Henkin, Louis. *Foreign Affairs and the Constitution.* 1972.

Randall, Kenneth C. "The Treaty Power." *Ohio State Law Journal* 51 (1990): 1089–1126.

– KENNETH C. RANDALL

TREATY TERMINATION

The question of whether the President is constitutionally empowered to terminate treaties is the subject of a long-standing debate. The uncertainty, which stems from the fact that the Constitution is silent on the repository of the power to denounce treaties, has engendered doctrinal confusion on the point and variety in practice. The Supreme Court bypassed an opportunity to resolve the controversy in *Goldwater* v. *Carter* (1979), when it dismissed as nonjusticiable a challenge to President Jimmy Carter's termination of the 1954 Mutual Defense Treaty with Taiwan. While the decision, technically, did not establish a precedent, it left Carter's act undisturbed, and it was invoked in 1986 as authority for President Ronald Reagan's termination of a treaty of commerce and friendship with Nicaragua.

The locus of authority to terminate treaties presents serious ramifications for constitutional doctrine and the course of American foreign policy, as measured by the mutual security treaties, treaty alliances, and nuclear-weapons agreements that expressly govern United States security matters, and other international arrangements that have an important effect on economic, environmental, and commercial interests. Apparently, the Constitutional Convention did not address the issue of treaty termination. It seems likely, however, that the Framers' fear for unilateral executive power in foreign affairs, their commitment to collective decision making, and the policy concerns that impelled them to create a treaty power shared by the President and Senate would have precluded the possibility of a unilateral presidential power to terminate treaties. This shared power regarding the treaty power satisfied the southern states, which feared that their regional, economic, and security interests would be ignored by northern states. It was made clear at the convention that without these accommodations, including Senate approval of a treaty by a two-thirds vote, the treaty power would not have been accepted. Manifestly, the termination of a treaty could do as much harm to the jealously guarded sectional and state interests as the negotiation of a treaty, and its denunciation by one person could hardly maintain the delicate balance of this carefully crafted system. In fact, writings at the time suggest that the Framers assumed that the power to make treaties implied the power to terminate them. This principle of symmetrical construction was endorsed by John Jay who wrote in *Federalist* 64 that "they who make treaties may alter or cancel them," and by James Madison, who stated: "That the contracting parties can annul a treaty cannot, I presume, be questioned, the same authority, *precisely,* being exercised in annulling as in making a treaty" [emphasis added].

Nevertheless, a unilateral presidential power to terminate treaties has been adduced on constitutional, historical, and policy grounds. Various commentators and Presidents, including Franklin D. Roosevelt and Jimmy Carter, have invoked the sole-organ doctrine advanced by Justice George Sutherland's bizarre opinion in

United States v. *Curtiss-Wright Export Corp.* (1936), as a foundation for a unilateral presidential power to terminate treaties. In dicta, Sutherland stated that the external sovereignty of the nation is vested in the presidency and is neither derived from nor restrained by the Constitution. Foreign-affairs powers were essentially executive, which Sutherland explained as "the very delicate, plenary, and exclusive power of the President as the sole organ" of American foreign policy. Sutherland's theory of inherent presidential power rests on the premise that domestic and foreign affairs are different. Domestic affairs are confined by the Constitution, but authority over foreign affairs is not dependent upon a grant from the Constitution since the powers of external sovereignty were somehow transferred directly from the Crown to the Continental Congress and then to the federal government in a way that bypassed the Articles of Confederation and the Constitutional Convention.

Treaty power is not executive in character, but legislative.

Sutherland's historical thesis is untenable. Under the Articles of Confederation, states were sovereign entities that delegated foreign-affairs powers to Congress. Moreover, the Supreme Court has consistently held that foreign-affairs powers are derived from and limited by the Constitution. Sutherland's sole-organ doctrine, moreover, rests on a distortion of Representative John Marshall's statement in 1800 that the President was solely responsible for communicating with foreign nations. Sutherland infused this purely communicative role with a substantive policy-making power, an assumption that finds no foundation in the text or architecture of the Constitution. Indeed, the constitutional design for foreign policy rests on the premise of shared powers and responsibilities, but the Framers clearly vested the bulk of foreign-affairs powers in Congress. At bottom, the sole-organ argument cannot be reconciled with the policy concerns that determined the nature of the treaty-making power.

Other commentators have attempted to forge an exclusive presidential termination power through analogy to the removal of executive officers. Since Article II of the Constitution vests the President with the power to make treaties and appointments, with the advice and consent of the Senate, treaty termination and the removal power, neither of which is mentioned in the text of the Constitution, are analogous powers. Because the President may remove a subordinate executive officer without the consent of the Senate, and in defiance of an act of Congress, it is argued that he may likewise terminate treaties without the consent of the Senate. The argument is fragile and the analogy is weak. The removal power is derived from the President's obligation to see that the laws are faithfully executed. By contrast, the treaty power is not executive in character, but legislative, as Alexander Hamilton and James Madison explained, and treaty termination is a contradiction rather than a corollary of the President's enforcement obligation. A third argument for exclusive presidential termination is grounded in the claim that the Framers were concerned only to check the President from "entangling" the United States with foreign powers. "Disentangling" is less risky and may have to be done quickly by various means or acts, and Senate approval, therefore, should not be required. This view ignores the Framers' paramount concerns surrounding the treaty power, which included a commitment to collective decision making and, as Hamilton noted in *Federalist* 22, the rehabilitation of the United States' reputation abroad as an unreliable treaty partner, a reputation attributable to the states' frequent violations of the nation's international obligations under the Articles of Confederation. These concerns hardly could have been satisfied by placing an unchecked termination power in the hands of a single officer.

The United States has terminated approximately two dozen treaties, either by the President acting alone, by Senate directive, or by joint resolution. The Constitution provides no role for the House of Representatives in the treaty-making process. It would seem incongruous then to suppose that the Framers intended the House to participate in the termination of treaties. The case for a congressional role is rooted in the supremacy clause of the Constitution. Since treaties are the supreme law of the land, it should take a legislative act to repeal a law. That argument ignores the fact that the provision in Article VI that treaties "are the supreme Law of the Land" is addressed principally to the courts and is designed to assure the supremacy of treaties over state laws. The first treaty termination effectuated at international law occurred in 1856 as a result of a directive from the Senate to President Franklin Pierce to provide notice of termination of a commercial treaty with Denmark. William Howard Taft was the first President to invoke a unilateral executive power of termination when he denounced in 1911 a commercial treaty with Russia. While Taft acted alone, he exhibited concern for constitutional procedure by seeking, and obtaining, Senate ratification of his action. The trend toward unilateral presidential authority to terminate treaties probably began in 1927 when President Calvin

Coolidge denounced an antismuggling treaty with Mexico in the mist of badly strained relations. President Franklin D. Roosevelt independently terminated several commercial treaties, some of which were dictated by the circumstances of World War II. In 1939, for the first time, Roosevelt invoked the sole-organ doctrine as a basis for a unilateral power to terminate treaties, in this case a commerce and navigation agreement with Japan. Presidents Dwight D. Eisenhower, John F. Kennedy, and Ronald Reagan also asserted an independent termination power. Historically, Presidents have complied with Senate instructions and joint resolutions that have directed them to denounce treaties in accordance with their provisions, but in the past half-century Presidents have captured the termination authority, much as they have aggrandized other foreign-policy powers.

[See also (I) Treaties.]

BIBLIOGRAPHY

Adler, David Gray. *The Constitution and the Termination of Treaties.* 1986.

Berger, Raoul. "The President's Unilateral Termination of the Taiwan Treaty." *Northwestern University Law Review* 75 (1980): 577–634.

Bestor, Arthur. "Respective Roles of Senate and President in the Making and Abrogation of Treaties—The Original Intent of the Framers of the Constitution Historically Examined." *University of Washington Law Review* 55 (1979): 1–135.

Emerson, J. Terry. "The Legislative Role in Treaty Abrogation." *Journal of Legislation* 5 (1978): 46–80.

Glennon, Michael J. *Constitutional Diplomacy.* 1990.

Henkin, Louis. "Litigating the President's Power to Terminate Treaties." *American Journal of International Law* 73 (1979): 647–654.

– DAVID GRAY ADLER

TWO-TERM TRADITION

Delegates to the Constitutional Convention considered both four-year and six-year terms for the office of the President. When they decided on a four-year term, reeligibility was assumed. At the close of his second term, President George Washington declined a third term, which he undoubtedly could have had. His refusal was based primarily on reasons of personal convenience. But when President Thomas Jefferson announced in 1807 that he would withdraw after two terms, he stressed Washington's example and raised the issue to a principle, arguing that indefinite reeligibility might undermine the elective system and turn the presidency into a life-tenure post. The subsequent two-term administrations of James Madison, James Monroe, and Andrew Jackson gave the tradition almost unassailable validity.

The first concerted attack on the two-term tradition came in 1876 from a group of Republicans who wanted Ulysses S. Grant to run for a third term, but the resistance was overwhelming. In 1908 Theodore Roosevelt, having served three and one-half years of William McKinley's term and one term in his own right, stated that "the wise custom which limits the President to two terms regards the substance and not the form" and announced flatly that "under no circumstances will I be a candidate for or accept another nomination." By 1912, however, he had changed his mind, and he unsuccessfully sought a third term. Calvin Coolidge found himself in somewhat the same situation in 1928, but he never definitely stated his view on the application of the two-term tradition in his case, merely announcing that he did not "choose to run for President in 1928."

President Franklin D. Roosevelt was elected to an unprecedented third and fourth term because the electorate wanted his experienced leadership while the world was at war. (Library of Congress, Prints and Photographs Division)

It was left for Franklin D. Roosevelt definitely to breach the tradition in 1940, when the electorate concluded that maintenance of the two-term limit was less important than retaining his experienced leadership in a world at war. Roosevelt's election to a precedent-shattering fourth term in 1944 was quickly followed by his death on 12 April 1945. The tragic denouement of this experience with unlimited reeligibility, combined with pent-up Republican frustration over four successive defeats by the same candidate, quickly resulted in a campaign to write the two-term limit into the Constitution. When the Republicans won control of the

Eightieth Congress, they immediately pushed through such an amendment, which was ratified in 1951.

The Twenty-second Amendment provides that no person shall be elected to the office of President more than twice and that no person who has held the office of President, or acted as President, for more than two years of a term to which another person was elected President shall be elected more than once. The terms of the Twenty-second Amendment would have made Theodore Roosevelt ineligible in 1912 and Coolidge ineligible in 1928 but would not have prevented Lyndon Baines Johnson from seeking reelection in 1968, since he had served for less than two years after the assassination of John F. Kennedy. It is ironic that the Republican-sponsored two-term limitation eliminated potential third terms for two Republicans, Dwight D. Eisenhower and Ronald Reagan.

It has been argued against the two-term limit, that the electorate should not be foreclosed from complete freedom of choice in selecting the President. Alexander Hamilton wrote, "How unwise must be every . . . self-denying ordinance as serves to prohibit a nation from making use of its own citizens, in the manner best suited to its exigencies and circumstances." A second objection is that the two-term limitation creates the possibility of lame-duck Presidents, since a President's constitutional inability to seek reelection could conceivably handicap him as he tries to maintain party support during the second term.

The idea of a single six-year presidential term, though rejected by the Constitutional Convention, has occasionally been revived. President Jackson in each of his annual addresses invited consideration of a single-term amendment. The Progressive movement of the late nineteenth and early twentieth century alleged that Presidents manipulated second-term elections and supported the single term, as did the Democratic national convention of 1912. But its nominee, Woodrow Wilson, promptly rejected the idea and served two terms.

[See also (II) Term and Tenure.]

BIBLIOGRAPHY

Corwin, Edward S. *The President: Office and Powers, 1787–1957.* 1957.

– C. HERMAN PRITCHETT

U

UNITED STATES POSTAL SERVICE

After considering bills that proposed scrapping the Post Office Department and creating a "government-owned postal system," an "independent Postal Service wholly owned by the Federal Government," "a public authority," or a "body corporate and an instrumentality of the United States," the Ninety-first Congress in 1970 opted for "an independent establishment of the executive branch of the Government of the United States, the United States Postal Service." It was to be operated as a "basic and fundamental service provided to the people by the Government of the United States . . . and supported by the people." People, in this case, referred to postal customers, not taxpayers.

Symbolized by a post rider on a galloping horse, the old Post Office Department might better have been represented by a great, broad-backed horse spurred by many riders headed in different directions. Postage rates, pay rates, postal facilities and, to a large degree, use of transportation were determined outside the organization. That the department carried the mail in spite of these crippling conditions pays tribute to its strength and determination.

But, in 1966, post rider and horse stumbled to a halt in the country's largest postal facility, the Chicago Post Office. Postal management could no longer push mail through a decrepit physical plant.

The President and the Congress agreed on the need for postal reform and in 12 August 1970, President Richard M. Nixon signed the Postal Reorganization Act into law. On 1 July 1971, the United States Postal Service began to function—an organization that could be managed, not merely administered.

The changes were dramatic. First, authority to determine policy and rates was vested in nine governors, appointed by the President and approved by the Senate, with no more than five of any one political party. The governors select the Postmaster General, the Postal Service's chief executive, who serves at their pleasure.

The President no longer directly appoints the Postmaster General and, in turn, the Postmaster General no longer serves in the President's Cabinet. By moving the Postmaster General away from the political arena, the President and the Congress hoped to stabilize postal management and establish a career service based on performance, not partisanship.

Postal operations are financed solely by the sale of stamps and postal services.

Second, the Postal Reorganization Act authorized collective bargaining on wages and working conditions. Strikes remain outlawed, but binding arbitration ends impasses between postal management and unions.

Third, the Postal Service received authority to issue public bonds to finance postal buildings and equipment. In the past, when the Post Office Department had to compete with other national interests for building funds, it usually came in last. Not knowing whether funding would be granted made planning impossible.

Once it could operate in a more businesslike manner, the United States Postal Service needed less of a tax subsidy and, in 1983, announced it no longer needed any subsidy. Postal operations are financed solely by the sale of stamps and postal services, and the United States Postal Service is symbolized by the stylized profile of the bald eagle, a more independent, nationally recognized image.

[See also (II) Postmaster General.]

BIBLIOGRAPHY

Towards Postal Excellence: The Report of the President's Commission on Postal Organization. 1968.

– MEGAERA HARRIS

V

VETERANS AFFAIRS, DEPARTMENT OF

Two-thirds of American Presidents—twenty-five of the forty-one through George Bush—had some prior military service, ranging from high command (George Washington, Ulysses S. Grant, Dwight D. Eisenhower), to wounded or decorated heroism in combat (James Monroe, Rutherford B. Hayes, John F. Kennedy, George Bush), to three months of volunteer service in 1832 in the Indian Wars (Abraham Lincoln).

The compassion of the pledge in Lincoln's second inaugural address in 1865—"to care for him who shall have borne the battle, and for his widow and his orphan"—is cast in metal plaques at both sides of the entrance to the massive headquarters of the Department of Veterans Affairs (DVA) in Washington, D.C. Lincoln's inspiring words, turned into sprawling bureaucracy by the demands of five subsequent wars and influenced by partisan politics, set the stage for more than a century of enormous government growth.

Through the "GI Bill," nearly 2 million veterans of World War II were supported while enrolled in colleges and universities.

In 1992, thirty-six children of Civil War veterans were still receiving benefits from the DVA. They were among nearly 3.5 million others cared for under veteran's expenditures that totaled $16 billion a year in tax-free monthly benefit checks. Separately, to run the world's largest medical care network, the DVA spent another $14 billion a year.

About 10 percent of the 26.6 million living U.S. veterans and 820,000 of their widows, children, and dependents received ongoing veterans' benefits. At a time when the U.S. Census counted about 248.7 million Americans, the 3.5 million beneficiaries were between 1 and 2 percent of the total population. But serving them involved a DVA staff approaching a quarter million.

In 1989 the DVA was set on a course to further growth by its elevation from an independent agency, the Veterans Administration (VA) to a Cabinet-rank department. The VA had been created in 1930, mid-way through the administration of President Herbert Hoover, by the consolidation of various small veterans' bureaus, until then established on a war-by-war basis. In the aftermath of World War II, the Korean War, and Vietnam War, the low-profile agency grew to such massive proportions that its $32 billion annual budget exceeds all but that of the Defense Department.

In 1944 the Roosevelt administration greatly broadened veterans' benefits by creating what is widely believed to have been the most enlightened and successful veterans' compensation program ever enacted, the Serviceman's Readjustment Act of 1944 or "GI Bill of Rights." In a program which created a new middle-class, nearly 2 million veterans of World War II were supported while enrolled in colleges and universities.

President Ronald Reagan personally arranged the elevation of the VA to the Department of Veterans' Affairs. At a time when the veteran population was declining because aging veterans were expiring at nearly twice the rate of discharge from the armed forces, Reagan proposed, on Veterans' Day 1987, elevating the VA to the Cabinet. (In practical terms, giving a Secretary of Veterans Affairs the fourteenth seat at the Cabinet table was an elevation already effectively granted de facto by President Jimmy Carter's 1977 executive order appointing the VA Administrator, then Max Cleland, a wheelchair-bound amputee, as a regular participant in Cabinet meetings.) The House of Representatives approved the VA's Cabinet status within a week. The Senate approved departmental status despite the advice of a negative report prepared for it by a panel of management experts at the National Academy of Public Administration. The panel warned that the grant of Cabinet status imposed no requirements for reform of the VA's seemingly unremediable administrative mismanagement and programmatic failures.

At the time, the agency's reputation was in decline because thousands of Vietnam veterans, disenchanted and alienated from civilian society in the 1960s and 1970s, felt estranged and rejected. Their problems were not then widely reported by the press, an abdication that helped perpetuate the broad array of bureaucratic abuses disclosed later in congressional investigations and by the DVA's strengthened in-house Inspector General.

In 1988 a new U.S. Court of Veterans' Appeals was created. Judicial review of denials of claims gives DVA applicants for the first time the due process afforded all other citizens. Veterans have standing to sue to rectify the mistakes of a historically paternalistic, assertedly nonadversarial bureaucracy.

Given the choice of the first Secretary of Veterans Affairs in 1989, President Bush chose Edward J. Derwinski, until 1982 an unchallengeable twelve-term Republican member of the House of Representatives. Derwinski proved to be a surprisingly apolitical incumbent, gaining from Congress added billions of dollars for deteriorating DVA hospitals, and suggesting limited access to them for the nonveteran poor in Appalachia and elsewhere. In proposing that opening, Derwinski so deeply offended the Veterans of Foreign Wars that President Bush, by then fearing a reelection defeat, sacrificed him to VFW demands by summarily dismissing him six weeks before election day.

In 1992, the DVA's quarter-million employees dispensed $16 billion a year in monthly checks—no longer "charity," but firmly established as "entitlements," which are periodically increased based on the cost-of-living index.

To run its 58 regional offices; 171 veterans' hospitals and 350 out-patient, community, and outreach clinics; 128 nursing homes and old soldiers' domiciliaries, 196 storefront veterans' outreach centers, and 114 national cemeteries in thirty-eight states and Puerto Rico, the new Secretary of Veterans Affairs has more moderately to well-paid employees in the fifty states than the United States Postal Service.

BIBLIOGRAPHY

Department of Veterans Affairs. *Survey of Disabled Veterans.* 1989.

National Academy of Public Administration. *Evaluation of Proposals to Establish a Department of Veterans Affairs.* 1988.

Severo, Richard, and Lewis Milford. *The Wages of War: When America's Soldiers Came Home—From Valley Forge to Vietnam.* 1989.

Stewart, Anne C. *Proposals in the 100th Congress to Make the Veterans Administration a Cabinet-Level Department: Background Information and Analysis of Issues.* 1987.

U S. House of Representatives. Committee on Government Operations. *Investigation of Disability Compensation Programs of the Veterans' Administration.* 100th Cong., 2d Sess. 1988. H. Rept. 100-886.

– BEN A. FRANKLIN

VETO, POCKET

Provided for in Article I, Section 7, of the Constitution, the pocket-veto power allows the President to withhold approval of a bill sent to the Chief Executive for signature after Congress has adjourned. The Constitution's wording is deceptively simple: "If any Bill shall not be returned by the President within ten Days (Sundays excepted) after it shall have been presented to him, the Same shall be a Law, in like manner as if he had signed it, unless Congress by their Adjournment prevent its Return, in which case it shall not be a Law." A regular, or return, veto is exercised when the President vetoes a bill by returning it to the house of origin. The pocket-veto power was inserted to guard against the possibility that Congress could pass a bill but then, as a way of avoiding a veto, quickly adjourn before the President had a chance to return the bill. Since pocket-vetoed bills cannot be returned to Congress, they are in effect absolute-vetoed—that is, Congress has no opportunity to override a pocket veto. Congress's only alternatives are to stay in session for at least ten days after the passage of a bill that may be subject to veto or to start from scratch and repass the bill when Congress reconvenes.

During the Constitutional Convention of 1787, no debate was recorded concerning the pocket veto. But the Framers did discuss and emphatically reject efforts to give the President an absolute veto—that is, one not subject to override. That the pocket veto operates as an absolute veto is explainable by the Framers' concern that the President needed this power to defend against any congressional effort to duck the regular veto. Unlike the regular veto, the pocket veto is carefully circumscribed by the fact that it may only be used when "Congress by their Adjournment prevent [a bill's] Return."

The Constitution allows for the pocket veto when congressional adjournment prevents a bill's return, but what constitutes adjournment?

The first two pocket vetoes were exercised by President James Madison; they aroused little attention. The next President to use the power, Andrew Jackson, aroused considerable controversy by exercising the power seven times (out of a total of twelve bills vetoed in his two terms), although his opponents' objections were founded mostly in their general dissatisfaction with his aggressive political style. The term "pocket veto" was apparently coined during Jackson's term.

Early concern about use of the pocket veto centered on two principles. First, the Framers wanted to ensure that Presidents would have adequate time to consider legislation sent to them. The pocket veto would come into play at the end of a congressional session, when Congress would be likely to present the President with a rush of last-minute bills, and would ensure that Presidents would not be forced into signing what they considered to be imprudent legislation. The second principle was to ensure that Congress would have time to consider and, if it chose, override the President's objections. Since the pocket veto does not allow for any reconsideration or override, the return veto is the preferred option, if such return can occur.

Persisting ambiguities have surrounded the pocket-veto power. For example, the Constitution allows for the pocket veto when congressional adjournment prevents a bill's return, but what constitutes adjournment? When does adjournment prevent bill return? May proxies for Congress or the President serve as legal stand-ins to receive veto messages or enrolled bills (bills passed by Congress but not yet signed by the President)? Some of these questions have been addressed in court cases.

In the *Pocket Veto Case* (1929), the Supreme Court ruled on a challenge to a pocket veto by President Calvin Coolidge that occurred between sessions at the start of a six-month congressional break in 1926. In grappling with the key question of the meaning of adjournment, the Court noted that "the determinative question . . . is not whether it is a final adjournment of Congress or an interim adjournment . . . but whether it is one that 'prevents' the President from returning the bill to the House in which it originated within the time allowed." The Court rejected the idea that a bill could be returned to a designated agent when Congress was not in session, both because Congress had never actually done this and because the Court feared that this might cause bills to hang in limbo for many months.

In *Wright* v. *United States* (1938), the Court considered a challenge to a regular veto of a bill returned to the Secretary of the Senate during a three-day Senate recess. The court said that it did not consider the three-day period an adjournment, but it also contradicted its previous conclusion in the *Pocket Veto Case* by saying that Congress could indeed designate agents on its behalf, rejecting what it now considered in the earlier ruling "artificial formality" by saying that the "Constitution does not define what shall constitute a return of a bill or deny the use of appropriate agencies in effecting the return." The Court also dismissed the potential delay problem mentioned in the *Pocket Veto Case* as "illusory."

In 1974, the U.S. Court of Appeals upheld a lower court ruling that struck down a 1970 pocket veto by Richard M. Nixon that occurred during a six-day Christmas recess (*Kennedy* v. *Sampson* [1974]); in this case, the tenth day had lapsed during the six-day break. The Court noted that bill return could have been effected, consistent with *Wright,* and cast doubt on pocket vetoes applied during any intra- or intersession adjournment as long as appropriate arrangements were made for bill receipt, suggesting that a pocket veto was now only possible after Congress adjourned *sine die* (literally, "without a day") at the end of a two-year Congress. The Court also noted that congressional practices had changed dramatically since the 1920s, in that Congress was now in session nearly year-round. The Nixon administration declined to appeal the ruling to the Supreme Court.

During the 1970s, Presidents Gerald Ford and Jimmy Carter abided by the principle of avoiding pocket vetoes during intra- and intersession adjournments, and Congress formalized procedures for receiving presidential messages during adjournments, just as Presidents have long delegated to agents the authority to receive enrolled bills on their behalf. Ronald Reagan backtracked on this arrangement, however, when he pocket-vetoed a bill between the first and second sessions of the Ninety-eighth Congress in 1983. Members of Congress took the President to court, but the Supreme Court refused to hear the case on its merits, vacating it as moot in *Burke* v. *Barnes* (1987).

George Bush went even farther than Reagan, arguing that a pocket veto may be used whenever Congress recesses for longer than three days. Critics have taken issue with this interpretation, citing the weight of court precedent, the workability of bill-receipt procedures during adjournments, the fact that this interpretation would allow pocket vetoes even during long weekends in the middle of a session, and the desirability of interbranch comity. Presidents' temptations to use pocket vetoes will continue to be great, as pocket-vetoed bills avoid any override fight. In 1990, the House Judiciary and Rules committees reported legislation to restrict pocket vetoes to the end of a Congress.

Presidents' temptations to use pocket vetoes

will continue to be great,

as pocket-vetoed bills avoid any override fight.

One other constitutional ambiguity surrounds the pocket veto. While the Constitution mandates that the President include written objections to vetoed bills returned to Congress, it says nothing about the necessity of written messages for pocket vetoes. Presidents from Madison to Andrew Johnson did prepare written messages for pocket vetoes, but the practice lapsed with Ulysses S. Grant, probably because of the vast increase in pocket vetoes. The practice of issuing no public message (the so-called silent pocket) persisted until 1934, when Franklin D. Roosevelt announced that he would resume preparing written messages—something all Presidents have done since. In this instance, constitutional ambiguity was resolved amicably.

[See also (I) Bills; Veto, Presidential.]

BIBLIOGRAPHY

Antieau, Chester J. *The Executive Veto.* 1988.

Dumbrell, John W., and John D. Lees. "Presidential Pocket-Veto Power: A Constitutional Anachronism?" *Political Studies* 28 (1980): 109–116.

Spitzer, Robert J. *The Presidential Veto: Touchstone of the American Presidency.* 1988.

———. "Presidential Prerogative Power." *PS: Political Science and Politics* 24 (1991): 38–42.

U.S. House of Representatives. Rules Committee. Subcommittee on the Legislative Process. *Hearings on H.R. 849, A Bill to Clarify the Law Surrounding the President's Use of the Pocket Veto.* 101st Congress, 1st sess., 1989.

Zinn, Charles J. *The Veto Power of the President.* 1951.

– ROBERT J. SPITZER

VETO, REGULAR

The power to veto legislation is one of the few explicit powers granted to the President that formally involves the Chief Executive in legislative affairs. Described in Article I, Section 7, of the Constitution, the veto is a capstone decision, the final leg of the legislative gauntlet before a bill becomes a law.

When presented with a bill by Congress, the President faces four possible choices: the executive may approve the bill by signing it into law; the executive may exercise the regular, or return, veto by refusing to sign the bill and returning it to the house of origin, including a statement of objections; the President may do nothing, in which case the bill automatically becomes law after ten days (Sundays excepted); and, lastly, if Congress adjourns within ten days of having presented a bill to the President, the President may choose to do nothing, in which case the bill is killed by pocket veto if, according to the Constitution, "Congress by their Adjournment prevents its Return." A return veto is subject to override by a two-thirds vote of both houses of Congress; a pocket veto is not.

The veto power is indisputably a presidential power, yet its location in Article I, the article otherwise devoted to the legislative branch, reflects the fact, first, that it is a legislative power possessed by the executive and, second, that the Constitution's system of checks and balances permits some sharing of powers between the branches of government.

The Framers' Purposes

Fears of the baneful consequences of strong executives motivated the new nation's leaders to create a governing system without an independent executive branch under the Articles of Confederation. But by the time the Constitutional Convention met in 1787, the prevailing sentiment favored an independent executive. Even though many still remembered the oppressive veto practices that the British king and his appointed colonial governors had exercised before the Revolution, there was little disagreement that the new President should have a qualified veto power. The Framers were adamant, however, that the President's veto not be absolute, as was that of the British monarch.

A central reason for granting the President this power was the Framers' realization that the executive would need such a power to protect the executive branch against legislative encroachments on executive power—a tendency observed in many state governments during the time the nation was governed by the Articles of Confederation. The Framers expected that the veto would be used to block legislation that was hastily conceived, unjust, or of dubious constitutionality. The power was not considered to be a purely negative action. Often called the revisionary power, the veto was conceived as a creative, positive device whereby the President could bring a bill back to Congress for a final round of debate and consideration. This constructive purpose of the veto has mostly been lost in the intervening years.

Early Presidents used the veto power cautiously and sparingly, giving rise to claims that the Constitution somehow countenanced restrictions on the numbers or kinds of bills vetoed. Neither claim is substantiated by the Constitution itself or the debates of the time. George Washington, who had presided over the Constitutional Convention, used the veto twice in his two terms as President—once for constitutional reasons and once for policy reasons. Andrew Jackson aroused deep antipathy by invoking the veto twelve times. His veto of a bank bill in 1832 infuriated his foes and was the pivotal issue for that year's presidential election. Jackson's sweeping reelection victory was viewed, at least in part, as a referendum on the bank veto. Some of Jackson's vetoes also focused attention on another major issue of the time—government involvement in public works and other internal improvement projects.

Among early Presidents seeking to use the veto, the greatest difficulties were faced by John Tyler. During Tyler's term of office (1841–1845), he vetoed a total of ten bills. While his political problems sprang primarily from his maladroit political leadership, controversy surrounding his use of the veto contributed directly to the effort to impeach him in 1843. Indeed, the two central impeachment charges brought against him centered on his alleged improper use of the veto. Tyler also bears the distinction of being the first President to have a veto successfully overridden by Congress (in 1845).

From the 1820s to the 1840s, Congress frequently entertained proposals to modify or to strip the President of the veto power. Yet, after Tyler's term, complaints over the terms and conditions of the veto subsided. For example, despite the many problems faced by Andrew Johnson, none of his opponents charged him with improper use of the veto, even though he vetoed twenty-nine bills from 1865 to 1869, a record number up to that time. Use of the veto exploded after the Civil War. From the first veto to 1868, Presidents vetoed eighty-eight bills. From that time to 1990, more than two thousand bills were vetoed.

Franklin D. Roosevelt holds the record for the most vetoes, blocking a total of 635 bills in his four terms. On a per-year basis, Roosevelt comes in second behind Grover Cleveland, who averaged seventy-three vetoes per year (584 total). Most of these two Presidents' vetoes involved private bills sponsored by members of Congress trying to obtain relief for specific individuals seeking pensions and other private benefits that only Congress could authorize.

As use of the veto increased, its importance seemed to recede as Presidents acquired a wide array of political powers that enabled them to influence virtually every aspect of the legislative process. Yet the veto power provided a key means by which Presidents inserted themselves into the legislative process. Early in the nineteenth century, many in Congress considered it improper for Presidents to express public opinions about legislation pending before Congress, based on the fear that such expressions might taint or alter the congressional deliberations. As the veto was used more often, however, Senators and Representatives began openly to solicit Presidents' opinions as to whether they might be planning to veto legislation. These informal inquiries opened the door to more formal requests that Presidents submit statements of their legislative preferences to Congress—a process that now takes the form of extensive legislative agendas presented to Congress annually by the President.

Consequences of the Veto

Although use of the veto has expanded the power of the presidency, the delicate politics of that power are demonstrated by the fact that vigorous use of the veto has usually been politically detrimental to the Presidents involved. Americans tend to view the veto as a negative, reactive move and to reward Presidents for assertive, positive leadership. Cleveland's prolific vetoes certainly contributed to his defeat in his first bid for reelection in 1888. Franklin Roosevelt, who used a large number of vetoes, seems to be an exception to this rule. His repeated use of the veto was symptomatic of a powerful President who felt free to use all the tools at his disposal. Moreover, most of Roosevelt's vetoes involved bills of little importance. Cleveland was compelled to rely heavily on the veto; Roosevelt could influence legislation in a variety of ways before legislation reached his desk.

Vigorous use of the veto has usually been politically detrimental to the Presidents involved.

In more recent times, Gerald Ford found reliance on a veto strategy to be both necessary and damaging to his presidency. Appointed Vice President by Richard M. Nixon after the resignation of Spiro T. Agnew in 1973, Ford suddenly found himself sitting in the Oval Office when Nixon resigned the following year. Ford had neither won an electoral mandate nor had time to develop a legislative program of his own. As a result, Republican Ford and his aides felt compelled to rely heavily on the veto to try to control the actions of a headstrong post—Watergate affair Democratic Congress. In his two and one half years in office, Ford vetoed sixty-six bills. Taken together, these vetoes helped encourage the attitude that Ford was unable to engage in affirmative governance and the kind of positive leadership the country had come to expect—an attitude that contributed to his defeat in 1976.

George Bush was also criticized by some for overreliance on the veto and an apparent failure to produce positive policy alternatives, but Bush was careful in his use of the veto. (In his first three years in office, for example, he vetoed twenty-five bills; all the vetoes were sustained.)

For Presidents, one appealing trait of the veto is its effectiveness. Of the 1,436 regular vetoes applied by Presidents from 1789 to 1991, only 103 have been overridden by Congress. When that figure is broken down between public and private bills, the record is somewhat less impressive: public bills have been overridden 19.3 percent of the time, private bills 0.8 percent. Still, a presidential success rate of more than 80 percent for important legislation poses a daunting challenge to anyone seeking to overturn a veto.

Various studies of the veto have helped to delineate conditions of its use. Presidents are more likely to use a veto when the executive and legislative branches are controlled by different parties, when the President lacks congressional experience, when the President's public standing is low, and during the second and fourth years of a presidential term. Congress is more likely to override a veto when party control is split between the two branches, when the President's popular support is low, after a midterm election, and in times of economic crisis. In short, a veto is most potent when it is least needed by a President—that is, at the beginning of a term.

A related tool stemming from the veto power is the veto threat. Discussed by Alexander Hamilton in *Federalist* 73, the veto threat has been an important, if underrecognized, attribute of the veto power. As early as 1789, Washington's expression of displeasure over the passage of a tonnage bill prompted Congress to pass a second bill more to the President's liking. A veto threat forces congressional proponents of a bill to contemplate the task of having to rouse an extraordinary two-thirds majority to ensure the bill's eventual passage—even before the bill has arrived on the President's desk. Such threats may alone be sufficient to modify or deter legislation the President opposes. Threats can also have the effect of an item veto, in that the President may (and indeed often does) threaten to veto a bill because of an offensive provision. Such occurred frequently in the latter part of the nineteenth century. Rutherford B. Hayes, for example, complained loudly and often about Congress's penchant for attaching objectionable riders to appropriations bills. Congress ignored Hayes's objections on most occasions; nevertheless, Hayes vetoed several bills because of riders and successfully fought override attempts.

Both Ronald Reagan and George Bush were prolific and relatively successful users of the veto threat. For example, of twenty-nine veto threats issued by Reagan from 1981 to 1986, Congress either backed down or modified the legislation in question nineteen times.

Yet the veto threat is not without costs. A threat applied too often is likely to lose credibility, and if threats are followed by too many actual vetoes, Presidents risk being criticized for being too negative and reactive. Resort to frequent veto threats may also be viewed as a sign of presidential weakness, since such threats probably reflect the President's failure to influence the course of legislation in other, more subtle or substantive ways.

Deciding When to Veto

Presidents rarely act alone in making important decisions, and since Washington they have sought advice on whether to veto bills. Washington often solicited opinions from Cabinet members such as Hamilton and Thomas Jefferson and from members of Congress such as James Madison.

As the presidency became more institutionalized in the twentieth century, so did the handling of veto decisions. The drive to institutionalize the process stemmed from the volume of legislation and the constitutionally mandated ten-day period within which the veto decision must be made. In typical nineteenth-century practice, when an enrolled bill (passed by Congress but not yet signed into law) reached the White House, a presidential aide would guess which agency or agencies would be affected, have the bill delivered to them, and then wait for a reply. This process yielded inadequate, ill-considered veto decisions.

The effort to deal more systematically with enrolled bills began with the 1921 creation of the Bureau of the Budget (known after 1970 as the Office of Management and Budget [OMB]). The Budget Bureau was asked to render its views of enrolled appropriations bills as part of the larger effort to enhance executive authority over the budget process. This led naturally to occasional veto recommendations from the bureau. The examination of enrolled bills was expanded by Roosevelt in 1934 to include private bills. By 1938, the Budget Bureau was assessing all enrolled bills, a procedure that included contacting affected departments and compiling views on the bills under scrutiny. Since the 1930s, these procedures have varied little, except that ever greater attention has been focused on the President's priorities as distinct from the independent opinions of affected agencies. Indeed, one of the first actions of the OMB after receiving an enrolled bill is to draft a memorandum summarizing the background, purposes, and relation of the bill to the President's program. This information, along with any agency reactions, is sent to the White House, usually by the fifth day of the ten-day period. There, presidential aides add their own recommendations to assist the President in the final decision. Since the 1960s, the number of White House Staff devoted to the consideration of enrolled bills has increased. Still, the OMB continues to exert decisive influence over the veto-versus-sign decision. Although an OMB recommendation to veto does not assure a veto, the President rarely vetoes a bill when OMB does not make such a recommendation.

[See also (I) Bills; Veto, Presidential; (II) Veto, Pocket.]

BIBLIOGRAPHY

Antieau, Chester J. *The Executive Veto.* 1988.
Jackson, Carleton. *Presidential Vetoes, 1792–1945.* 1967.
Mason, Edward C. *The Veto Power.* 1890.
Presidential Vetoes, 1789–1976. U.S. Senate Library. 1978.
Spitzer, Robert J. *The Presidential Veto: Touchstone of the American Presidency.* 1988.
Zinn, Charles J. *The Veto Power of the President.* 1951.

– ROBERT J. SPITZER

VICE PRESIDENT

The American vice presidency has always been a somewhat anomalous office. Its awkward nature has provided rich stores for satirists and a source of lingering concern for students of American political institutions. Unlike other major offices, the legitimacy of the vice presidency has always been controversial; whereas other offices undergo attack at the margins, the questions about the vice presidency are more basic and address the very character of, and need for, the office.

The Vice President's Situation

During the twentieth century, particularly since the 1940s, the vice presidency was transformed into a position of greater importance. The development of the office has followed changes in American politics and government, particularly the growth of the presidency since the New Deal. These changes have drawn the vice presidency into the executive branch and made it attractive to competent people with presidential ambitions. Yet this progress has not resolved all problems inherent in the office or eliminated skepticism regarding its ultimate merit.

The doubts about the vice presidency have related to three characteristics that have, to varying degrees, defined the office during its history. First, there is a huge discrepancy between what the Vice President is and what he may become. "I am nothing," recognized John Adams, the first Vice President. "But I may be everything." In eight words Adams expressed a dilemma that has persisted for two hundred years. The office, Adams recognized, was a modest position. Yet as the designated successor in case of the death, resignation, disability, or removal of the President, he may be "everything." Indeed, Vice Presidents become everything with unhappy frequency. Nine have become President following the death or resignation of the Chief Executive; they have served as President for twenty-six years during terms to which someone else was elected. Put differently, up to 1992, 20 percent of Vice Presidents have been Presidents by succession for 13 percent of the history of the presidency.

If the most evident rationale for the vice presidency is to provide a competent successor ready to assume the presidency following an unscheduled vacancy, the vice presidency must be structured to attract able persons and to prepare them to be President. Yet that plausible purpose falls victim to the huge disparity between the power of the presidency and the power of the vice presidency. For how can a "nothing" office routinely attract persons of presidential caliber? How can a sinecure engage its occupant sufficiently to prepare him to assume the presidency?

The vice presidency seems to deviate from basic premises of American government in a second impor-

VICE PRESIDENTS OF THE UNITED STATES

President	Vice President
1 Washington	John Adams, 1789–1797
2 J. Adams	Thomas Jefferson, 1797–1801
3 Jefferson	Aaron Burr, 1801–1805
	George Clinton, 1805–1809
4 Madison	George Clinton, 1809–1813
	Elbridge Gerry, 1813–1814
5 Monroe	Daniel D. Tompkins, 1817–1825
6 J. Q. Adams	John C. Calhoun, 1825–1829
7 Jackson	John C. Calhoun, 1829–1832
	Martin Van Buren, 1833–1837
8 Van Buren	Richard M. Johnson, 1837–1841
9 W. H. Harrison	John Tyler, 1841
10 Tyler	None
11 Polk	George M. Dallas, 1845–1849
12 Taylor	Millard Fillmore, 1849–1850
13 Fillmore	None
14 Pierce	William R.D. King, 1853
15 Buchanan	John C. Breckinridge, 1857–1861
16 Lincoln	Hannibal Hamlin, 1861–1865
	Andrew Johnson, 1865
17 A. Johnson	None
18 Grant	Schuyler Colfax, 1869–1873
	Henry Wilson, 1873–1875
19 Hayes	William A. Wheeler, 1877–1881
20 Garfield	Chester A. Arthur, 1881
21 Arthur	None
22 Cleveland	Thomas A. Hendricks, 1885
23 B. Harrison	Levi P. Morton, 1889–1893
24 Cleveland	Adlai E. Stevenson, 1893–1897
25 McKinley	Garret T. Hobart, 1897–1899
	Theodore Roosevelt, 1901
26 T. Roosevelt	Charles W. Fairbanks, 1905–1909
27 Taft	James Schoolcraft Sherman, 1909–1912
28 Wilson	Thomas R. Marshall, 1913–1921
29 Harding	Calvin Coolidge, 1921–1923
30 Coolidge	Charles D. Dawes, 1925–1929
31 Hoover	Charles Curtis, 1929–1933
32 F. D. Roosevelt	John Nance Garner, 1933–1941
	Henry A. Wallace, 1941–1945
	Harry S Truman, 1945
33 Truman	Alben W. Barkley, 1949–1953
34 Eisenhower	Richard M. Nixon, 1953–1961
35 Kennedy	Lyndon B. Johnson, 1961–1963
36 L. B. Johnson	Hubert Humphrey, 1965–1969
37 Nixon	Spiro Agnew, 1969–1973
	Gerald R. Ford, 1973–1974
38 Ford	Nelson A. Rockefeller, 1974–1977
39 Carter	Walter F. Mondale, 1977–1981
40 Reagan	George Bush, 1981–1989
41 Bush	Dan Quayle, 1989–1993
42 Clinton	Al Gore, 1993–

tant respect. Certainly the belief that decision makers should be elected by or accountable to the populace remains a fundamental tenet of American democracy. Notwithstanding the survival of the Electoral College, most Americans would no doubt apply that principle most rigorously to the presidency. Yet the Vice President is not separately elected, and has not been since 1804. He comes as part of a package under circumstances that limit greatly the ability of the electorate to vote based upon the relative merits of the vice presidential candidates. Nonetheless Vice Presidents may serve as President following the premature departure of the elected Chief Executive for as much as four years without being elected directly. Indeed, on seven occasions presidential successions have occurred with more than half of the four-year term remaining; in five instances more than three years and five months lay ahead.

Finally, the constitutional scheme places the vice presidency in an ambiguous position. By design it is something of a hybrid between the executive and legislative branches. The Vice President is elected with the President, becomes President or Acting President upon the death, resignation, removal, or disability of the President and has acquired some prerogatives within the executive branch such as membership in the Cabinet by custom and in the National Security Council by statute. Yet his sole constitutional function of an ongoing nature is to preside over the Senate, a role that, though seldom performed, allows him to break tie votes and to make parliamentary rulings. Over time the vice presidency has migrated between the two branches in search of a home. Yet the manner in which Vice Presidents have been selected and the security of their tenure have complicated their quest to find a place where they are welcomed. Until recently presidential candidates played little or no role in the selection of their running mate; once in office, the President could not remove the second man until the end of the term. Accordingly, Presidents historically have been reticent to entrust executive powers to their Vice President. Similarly, unlike other legislative officers the Vice President is not chosen by the body over which he presides; the Senate can remove him only if the House of Representatives first goes to the extraordinary means of impeaching him. Not surprisingly, the Senate has not assigned much power to an officer not responsible to it.

The Constitutional Design

The reasoning that inspired the creation of the office is somewhat obscure. The position was an afterthought conceived in the closing days of the Constitutional Convention and devised despite the misgivings of prominent members including Alexander Hamilton who observed that "the appointment of an extraordinary person, as Vice President, has been objected to as superfluous, if not mischievous." Although much discussion addressed the need for a presiding officer who was not a Senator (otherwise the Senate might deadlock and some state would be underrepresented if one of its two delegates relinquished his vote to chair the sessions), this consideration did not lead to the invention of the office. These difficulties were susceptible to other solutions. Moreover, some observed that the Vice President "would be without employment" unless he presided over the Senate, an argument that suggests that the role was an expedient to occupy the Vice President.

Since the 1940s, the vice presidency has been transformed into a position of greater importance.

The Founders spent little time discussing presidential succession, making that factor an unlikely explanation for the office. More likely, the office was invented to facilitate the election of a national President. Fearing that electors would favor citizens from their home state for President, the Founders gave electors two votes but required that they cast at least one for a citizen of a different state. They expected the electors' second-choice votes to identify a national consensus President; the second office, the Founders apparently reasoned, would ensure that electors voted seriously. The office, said delegate Hugh Williamson, "was introduced only for the sake of a valuable mode of election which required two to be chosen at the same time."

Inasmuch as the electoral scheme offered electors the opportunity to vote for two persons of presidential caliber, it seemed destined to produce Vice Presidents of real stature. Indeed, the first two Vice Presidents—John Adams and Thomas Jefferson—were men of unquestioned ability who brought impeccable credentials to the office. Adams established cordial relations with President George Washington and acted as one of his chief advisers. He occasionally met with the Cabinet, though apparently Jefferson, as Secretary of State, not Adams, presided in Washington's absence. Yet Adams was essentially a legislative officer who regularly presided over the Senate and indeed broke twenty-nine deadlocks, the most by any Vice President.

The office was not unduly taxing; Adams found it "too inactive and insignificant" and, during his first term, wrote that "[m]y country has in its wisdom contrived for me the most insignificant office that ever the invention of man contrived or his imagination conceived; . . . I can do neither good nor evil." Adams hoped Jefferson would follow him "for . . . if he could do no good, he could do no harm." Jefferson viewed the office as "honorable and easy" and admitted to some ambivalence regarding whether he would rather be Vice President or not. Jefferson insisted that the Vice President was a legislative officer and accordingly refused proffered assignments from Adams.

The initial system, then, provided for a truly elected Vice President and filled the office with eminent figures. Separate election raised the specter of a Vice President at odds with the Chief Executive on fundamental issues of policy. The office was essentially a creature of the legislative branch, particularly when President and Vice President represented different parties.

The Nineteenth-Century Vice Presidency

The office underwent fundamental change in 1804. Parties had begun to form and to designate a ticket; electors would cast their votes for the two men their party had designated. In 1800 the Republican-Democratic presidential nominee, Thomas Jefferson, and the vice presidential nominee, Aaron Burr, received an equal number of votes. Although Jefferson was clearly intended for the presidency, the election was thrown into the House of Representatives, which held thirty-six ballots before Jefferson prevailed. The traumatic events caused dissatisfaction with the electoral system. Accordingly, the Twelfth Amendment to the Constitution was ratified in 1804; it provided that electors would vote separately for President and Vice President

The amendment worked a dramatic change in the vice presidency. Some legislators anticipated that the new electoral procedure would jeopardize the ability of the office to provide high caliber successors. Their fears were prophetic.

The remainder of the nineteenth century witnessed a sharp decline in the vice presidency. Inasmuch as the Vice President was no longer the runner-up for President the quality of Vice Presidents suffered. The running mate was chosen based on partisan considerations rather than merit. Occasionally, the office still attracted someone of presidential stature, John C. Calhoun and Martin Van Buren being two examples. Most occupants fell far short of that standard. George Clinton (1805–1812), Elbridge Gerry (1813–1814), William R. King (1853), and Thomas A. Hendricks (1885) had served in important positions but were in failing health when they became Vice President. Others brought lackluster credentials to the office. Chester A. Arthur's prior public service consisted of seven years as collector of customs for the port of New York; Garret A. Hobart had served as presiding officer of the New Jersey assembly and state senate but had never held statewide or national office. Millard Fillmore had served in the House of Representatives but had not been considered presidential timber before becoming Zachary Taylor's running mate. Levi P. Morton (1889–1893) served in the House and as minister to France but had generally been unsuccessful when he ran for office. His successor, Adlai E. Stevenson (1893–1897), was Assistant Postmaster General in President Grover Cleveland's first term before becoming Vice President in his second.

The conduct of nineteenth-century Vice Presidents often fell below the deportment that would have been expected. Daniel D. Tompkins spent most of his term responding to charges that he had improperly used public funds as governor of New York. Richard M. Johnson kept a series of slave mistresses and preferred presiding over his tavern to the Senate. Andrew Johnson appeared intoxicated at his inauguration. Schuyler Colfax was nearly impeached for questionable financial transactions.

Election as a ticket promoted, but did not ensure, compatibility. Party leaders, not the presidential candidate, typically filled the second spot. Accordingly, the Vice President was not beholden to the Chief Executive for his position. Moreover, the vice presidential nomination was often used to unify the party by selecting a candidate who disagreed with the standard-bearer on important issues to placate a faction not enchanted with the head of the ticket. Occasionally, harmonious relations did exist, most notably between James Madison and Gerry Andrew Jackson and Van Buren, James Polk and George Dallas, and William McKinley and Hobart. More often, acrimony characterized dealings between the occupants of the two positions. Clinton refused to attend Madison's inauguration and was contemptuous of him. Calhoun openly opposed Jackson on important matters. Arthur denounced President James Garfield in a newspaper article.

The early electoral system provided for a truly elected Vice President and filled the office with eminent figures.

The nineteenth-century vice presidency was a legislative office. Although an occasional President involved his running mate in business of the executive branch—Polk consulted Dallas and McKinley conferred with Hobart—they were exceptions. Rarely did Presidents enlist the assistance of their Vice President. The second man was not included in Cabinet meetings or sent on international missions. His sole governmental function was to chair sessions of the Senate. Although some—Dallas, Morton, and Hobart for instance—discharged that task with skill, others were indifferent to that role. Tompkins frequently absented himself, Richard Johnson preferred his tavern, Henry Wilson spent his term writing a three-volume history of slavery in America.

On four occasions, nineteenth-century Vice Presidents succeeded to the presidency upon the death of the Chief Executive. When President William Henry Harrison died in 1841, John Tyler became the first Vice President to confront questions relating to presidential succession. The Constitution provided that in case of the President's death, resignation, removal, or inability "to discharge the powers and duties of the said office, the same shall devolve on the Vice President." The clause was ambiguous as to whether what devolved was the "office" or merely its "powers and duties." The issue had more than academic significance. If the "powers and duties" only passed to the Vice President, a disabled President could, upon termination of the inability, resume his position. If, on the other hand, the office itself was transferred, the elected Chief Executive would apparently be displaced permanently even if temporarily disabled. Although informed opinion was divided, Tyler insisted that he became President, not merely a Vice President acting as President. Tyler probably mistook the Framers' intent; records of the Constitutional Convention suggest that they intended that the powers, but not the office, pass to the Vice President. Nonetheless, the Tyler precedent prevailed and when Fillmore, Andrew Johnson, and Arthur were faced with an unscheduled presidential vacancy they each claimed that they became, and they were accepted as, President.

Several features characterized the four instances of presidential succession in the nineteenth century. On each occasion the Vice President came either from a different party or faction than his predecessor. Major upheavals in policy and personnel ensued. All but one member of the Cabinet that Tyler inherited resigned within five months. Arthur replaced six of seven Cabinet members in five months; Fillmore discharged Taylor's entire Cabinet in approximately two months. Each President by succession occupied a position of weakness for the remainder of his term. None won a term of his own.

Finally, the nineteenth-century vice presidency became a poor stepping stone to the presidency. Of the twenty-one Vice Presidents in the nineteenth century after the Twelfth Amendment only one (Van Buren) was elected Chief Executive. Six were not nominated for a second term with the Chief Executive. The four who became President by succession were not reelected. Of the twenty-one Vice Presidents from 1805 to 1899, only three (Clinton, Calhoun, and Hendricks) had been plausible presidential candidates before seeking at least one term as Vice President; only Van Buren and John C. Breckinridge of those who did not succeed to the presidency subsequently became a serious candidate.

In short, the nineteenth-century vice presidency was a hollow shell. The office and the quality of its occupants declined precipitously after 1804. In *Congressional Government,* first published in 1885, Woodrow Wilson devoted less than a page to the vice presidency because "the chief embarrassment in discussing his office is, that in explaining how little there is to be said about it one has evidently said all there is to say."

The Twentieth-Century Office

The new century began a slow, but discernible rise in the office. McKinley's Vice Presidents, in different ways, revealed long latent possibilities in the office. Owing to his rapport with the Chief Executive, Hobart gained real influence beyond what would have been anticipated for someone whose résumé was so modest. Conversely, Theodore Roosevelt lacked a close relationship with McKinley but elevated the office by his prominence, his energy, and by becoming the first President by succession to win his own term.

To be sure, the office did not suddenly become robust. From 1900 until 1940, party leaders, not the presidential candidate, filled the second spot on the ticket. Accordingly, the running mate was not beholden to the Chief Executive. The two generally came from different wings of their party; often they were not personally or politically compatible. Presidents Theodore Roosevelt, William Howard Taft, and Herbert Hoover opposed the selections of Vice Presidents Charles W. Fairbanks (1905–1909), James S. Sherman (1909–1913), and Charles Curtis (1929–1933) respectively; once in office, the second man was ignored. Thomas Marshall (1913–1921) was more involved but he, too, found himself often excluded.

Yet the office underwent some change during the first half century. First, the quality of Vice Presidents improved. From the anonymous figures of the nineteenth century, the office began to attract persons of stature. Roosevelt, Fairbanks, Curtis, John Nance Garner (1933–1941), and Alben W. Barkley (1949–1953) were leaders in their parties before becoming Vice President; Charles G. Dawes (1925–1929) had received the Nobel Peace Prize; Henry A. Wallace (1941–1945) had served in the Cabinet.

Second, the office handled presidential succession more efficiently. Whereas nineteenth-century Vice Presidents quickly jettisoned the Cabinets they inherited, Roosevelt and Calvin Coolidge essentially retained top administration officials, thereby lending stability to government. Whereas those who became President in the nineteenth century following the death of their predecessor failed to be reelected or even renominated, Roosevelt, Coolidge, and Harry S Truman won terms.

Moreover, the vice presidency was no longer a dead end for the ambitious. In addition to the three Vice Presidents who succeeded to the presidency and won election in their own right, others made credible, though unsuccessful attempts. Fairbanks campaigned to follow Roosevelt but failed largely due to the President's active opposition. Marshall and Dawes enjoyed some support for the presidential nomination. Garner was the most popular Democrat in preference polls from 1937 to 1940, excluding Franklin D. Roosevelt; his ambitions fell victim to Roosevelt's desire for a third term.

Finally, the duties of the vice presidency underwent subtle change. Whereas nineteenth-century Vice Presidents presided over the Senate and did little else, some Vice Presidents assumed duties in the executive branch. The change began with Hobart, who became a close adviser to President McKinley, and continued during the tenure of some of his successors. Roosevelt, Fairbanks, and Curtis, for instance, had little, if any, discernible involvement and Dawes refused to meet with the Cabinet before he was invited to do so. Yet during Wilson's absence from the country Marshall became the first Vice President to preside over Cabinet meetings, a task he undertook diffidently and surrendered eagerly. Coolidge attended Cabinet meetings, as did Garner, Wallace, and Barkley. Garner advised Roosevelt on legislative and other matters; Wallace chaired the Economic Defense Board, an entity that included seven Cabinet members. By statute, Vice Presidents from Barkley on became members of the National Security Council.

Vice President Calvin Coolidge brought stability to government when, unlike Vice Presidents of the nineteenth century, he retained top administration officials in the Cabinet he inherited. (Library of Congress, Prints and Photographs Division)

The Modern American Vice Presidency

The real growth in the vice presidency began during the New Deal and continued at an accelerated rate in the following decades. The New Deal and World War II worked fundamental changes in government. In essence, those events drew power to the federal government generally and to the presidency in particular, increasing the influence of its occupant with respect to Congress and political parties.

These changes transformed the vice presidency. First, the office was in effect pulled into the executive branch. No longer did Vice Presidents define themselves, as had Jefferson and Dawes, as legislative officers precluded from participating in the executive branch. Rather, they began to receive presidential assignments. As the President became responsible for offering a legislative agenda, Vice Presidents, especially those with congressional experience, became active as liaisons to Capitol Hill. Garner, for instance, advised Roosevelt on legislative strategy and lobbied for the New Deal. Richard M. Nixon brought legislative background to the Eisenhower administration. Even after Presidents developed their own professional legislative staffs, a Vice President like Walter F. Mondale could help with Congress.

As the presidency became the fulcrum of government and its occupant became expected to address a range of issues, Presidents often appointed Vice Presidents to head executive commissions. Nixon chaired the President's Committee on Government Contracts and Lyndon B. Johnson headed the President's Committee on Equal Employment Opportunity, both of which had some responsibilities in combatting racial discrimination. Nelson A. Rockefeller chaired the Domestic Council and an investigation into the Central Intelligence Agency.

Although many Vice Presidents embraced such "line" assignments, and some had significance, they also posed real dangers. The direct responsibilities Vice Presidents accepted normally invaded the province of some other player. Accordingly, each such assignment risked antagonizing other administration officials, often for little real power. Vice Presidents had to move cautiously to avoid an embarrassing reversal by the Chief Executive. Many assignments were so trivial they demeaned the vice presidency; Hubert H. Humphrey, for instance chaired presidential committees on marine resources, Indian opportunity, and domestic travel, issues not high on the nation's agenda in the 1960s, or since. Yet Vice Presidents typically lacked sufficient staff support to handle true administrative tasks. Moreover, line assignments took time that could better have been spent on more urgent issues.

Vice Presidents also assumed some role in international affairs. From Barkley on, they were members of the National Security Council, which, depending on the extent to which the President used that body, afforded some opportunity to learn about and participate in foreign and strategic policy. Vice Presidents also began to make frequent trips abroad. Trips served a variety of purposes including fact finding, building goodwill, and discharging ceremonial functions the President or Secretary of State were too busy to perform. They gave Vice Presidents exposure and the semblance of participation.

Vice Presidents also became active as administration spokespersons, able to exploit the podium their office guaranteed to raise issues that shaped the nation's political discourse. Nixon, for instance, spoke widely on the threat of communism. Johnson delivered a series of addresses on civil rights. Humphrey became a leading salesperson of the Vietnam War. Spiro T. Agnew and Dan Quayle accused diverse elites of corrupting societal values.

Moreover, Vice Presidents devoted time to partisan work—raising funds, appearing for administration allies, campaigning for the President's renomination—particularly under Presidents who cultivated a nonpolitical image. Nixon, for instance, performed especially well in this task for the Eisenhower administration. As presidential primaries proliferated and the President suddenly became subject to challenge for renomination, Vice Presidents like Mondale and Quayle undertook much of the campaign role for Presidents Jimmy Carter and George Bush respectively.

Finally, Vice Presidents became presidential advisers. Attendance at Cabinet meetings symbolized the office's migration toward the executive branch where some achieved some influence. Garner advised Roosevelt during their first term before their relationship deteriorated. Rockefeller persuaded Ford to undertake some initiatives early in his tenure before his position eroded as the term continued.

Mondale, more than any other Vice President, achieved real influence in that role. He lunched alone with Carter once a week during which he could raise any topic. He was granted access to the same documents Carter received and was given the right to attend any meeting Carter held. The Vice President's staff, which had been relatively small during the 1960s, exceeded sixty persons during Mondale's tenure. Mondale was given an office in the White House close to the Oval Office and Carter's other top advisers; physical proximity encouraged involvement. Mondale was able to place associates in important administration positions and formed alliances with key members of Carter's staff. He participated in virtually all significant decisions during the Carter years and his counsel was valued.

Those who became President in the nineteenth century following the death of their predecessor failed to be reelected or even renominated.

Bush and Quayle retained many of these amenities—the lunch, the staff, the office. Bush's experience in foreign policy and in Washington, D.C., were important assets in the Reagan White House, populated as it initially was with outsiders. Quayle participated actively in debates in the Bush White House though it is not clear that he had the clout Mondale and, to some extent, Bush had had. Vice President Al Gore played a prominent role as presidential adviser in choosing personnel for the Clinton administration.

Selecting Vice Presidents

The rise of the presidency also changed the manner of selecting vice presidential candidates. Beginning in 1940, the presidential nominee, not party leaders, filled the second spot on the ticket. In that year, Roosevelt forced the convention to accept Wallace despite its misgivings. To be sure, presidential candidates continued, in most cases, to solicit advice from other party leaders and rarely ignored strong sentiment. Still, presidential candidates began to submit a nominee who invariably was selected with little or no opposition. Presidential candidates followed many of the same strategies conventions had long employed in selecting vice presidential candidates. They sought to balance the ticket geographically (e.g., Dewey-Warren, Dukakis-Bentsen) or ideologically (e.g., Carter-Mondale) or to placate a defeated wing of the party (e.g., Kennedy-Johnson, Reagan-Bush). They chose running mates to appeal to an important state (e.g., Earl Warren, Johnson), to emphasize a particular issue (e.g., Nixon) or to place an effective campaigner on the ticket. Yet these strategies were rarely pursued to the extremes common in the nineteenth and early twentieth centuries. The exigencies of a national campaign with many competitive states made it impractical to pick a running mate with one state's electoral votes in mind. The need to preserve national credibility made it difficult for presidential candidates to select running mates whose views on important issues diametrically opposed their own. The ideological balance that occurs tends to be much more subtle. Finally, the scrutiny vice presidential candidates receive provided some incentive to select a running mate of presidential quality. On rare occasions, presidential candidates ignored ticket-balancing criteria and selected a running mate with similar characteristics to the standard-bearer in order to emphasize particular issues or themes. The most successful examples of this strategy were the Truman-Barkley ticket of 1948 and the Clinton-Gore ticket of 1992. With few exceptions, vice presidential candidates on winning tickets have generally brought imposing credentials to the office.

The President has some incentive to involve the Vice President at least to some degree to deter speculation that he regretted his choice.

The increased presidential role in vice-presidential selection has had implications for the vice presidency. First, the President has become responsible for the selection of his running mate. Accordingly he has some incentive to involve the second man at least to some degree to deter speculation that he regretted his choice. Moreover, the new method has increased the likelihood that the two top officers would be compatible politically and personally. Theoretically the candidate for the top spot could make certain that his running mate shared similar views. Although some Presidents and Vice Presidents have disliked each other—Nixon and Agnew, for instance—other relationships have been harmonious (Carter and Mondale, Reagan and Bush come to mind).

The succession of Vice Presidents to the presidency has changed also. The Truman, Johnson, and Ford successions operated relatively smoothly under quite different circumstances; Truman and Johnson won terms of their own and Ford lost but narrowly even while inheriting the baggage of the Watergate affair. Owing to the vast responsibilities of the President, it has become far more difficult to select a running mate totally unsuited to office. With rare exceptions modern Vice Presidents have brought to office impressive credentials. Since 1952 every Vice President except Agnew and Quayle had either been considered presidential timber prior to his selection or else subsequently won his party's nomination. Presidents particularly since Carter have taken steps to ensure that the second man would be knowledgeable regarding administration programs and pressing issues. Sections 3 and 4 of the Twenty-fifth Amendment, which provide relatively clear guidelines for handling situations of presidential disability, enhanced the ability of the Vice President to act temporarily to avoid a hiatus in the exercise of presidential power.

Finally, during the latter half of the twentieth century the vice presidency has become the best springboard to a presidential nomination. Virtually every Vice President since Nixon has either become President, been nominated by his party, or been a serious contender for the nomination. Ratification of the Twenty-fifth Amendment, which includes a mechanism for filling vice presidential vacancies, reflected the new respectability of the job. Presidential candidates with a serious chance of winning have found that virtually all leading figures in their party will make themselves available for the ticket.

Although the vice presidency has achieved new stature its growth has not resolved all of the problems that historically afflicted it. The office remains devoid of any ongoing function other than to inquire regularly regarding the President's health. The Vice President depends on the President for the assignments that give his service meaning and make his office something. But, as Hubert Humphrey observed, "He who giveth can taketh away and often does."

Accordingly, the success of a vice presidency depends on the relationship between the President and Vice President, the relationship between the Vice President and the White House staff, and the ability of the second man to offer resources the administration needs. All factors become important in determining a Vice President's success. Rockefeller clearly had skills and experience that the Ford administration needed and enjoyed cordial relations with the President. Yet, the animosity that developed between Rockefeller and the White House staff, particularly Chief of Staff Donald Rumsfeld, undermined his effectiveness. Agnew's standing with the Republican right wing provided an asset for the Nixon administration but Nixon excluded his running mate due to his low regard for him. Certainly the most successful vice presidency was Mondale's; he developed a close rapport with the President and his staff that enabled him to be a player in all significant decisions. His experience in Washington and ties to traditional Democratic groups with which the administration was weak enhanced his position as did the manner in which he and Carter shaped his role and their sensitivities to each other.

The rise of the vice presidency has neither satisfied the skeptics nor muted the calls for reform. Professor Arthur M. Schlesinger, Jr., has forcefully advocated abolition of the vice presidency. He argues that the office is a "maiming" rather than a "making" job whose incumbent devotes his time to insignificant makework. He objects that the Vice President is not truly elected; he would favor having a caretaker succeed temporarily following a presidential vacancy with a special election to follow. Others favor expanding the office to assign its occupant meaningful roles in the executive branch, such as requiring him to hold a Cabinet position, or giving him a vote or powers in the Senate. Finally, a third reform impulse focuses on the selection of the Vice President. The preferred solutions range from having tickets run together in presidential primaries to voting separately for the two offices to voting not at all for the Vice President but instead allowing the President to nominate him after the election subject to approval by each house of Congress as is done under the Twenty-fifth Amendment.

It seems unlikely that any of these reforms will be enacted or that they would improve the overall performance of government. The changes that have enhanced the office in recent decades seem likely to continue. Further growth in the vice presidency will follow larger changes in American politics and government and will depend upon the relation between future Presidents and Vice Presidents.

[See also (I) Senate.]

BIBLIOGRAPHY

Feerick, John D. *From Failing Hands.* 1965.

Goldstein, Joel K. *The Modern American Vice Presidency: The Transformation of a Political Institution.* 1982.

A Heartbeat Away. Report of the Twentieth Century Fund Task Force on the Vice Presidency. 1988.

Light, Paul C. *Vice-Presidential Power: Advice and Influence in the White House.* 1984.

Milkis, Sidney M., and Michael Nelson. *The American Presidency: Origins and Development, 1776–1990.* 1990. Chapter 14, "The Vice Presidency."

Pika, Joseph A. "Bush, Quayle and the New Vice Presidency." In *The Presidency and the Political System.* Edited by Michael Nelson. 3d ed. 1990.

Schlesinger, Arthur M., Jr. "On the Presidential Succession." *Political Science Quarterly* 89 (1974): 475–505.

"Symposium on the Vice-Presidency." *Fordham Law Review* 45 (1977): 707–799.

Williams, Irving G. *The Rise of the Vice Presidency.* 1956.

Witcover, Jules. *Crapshoot: Rolling the Dice on the Vice Presidency.* 1992.

Young, Donald. *American Roulette: The History and Dilemma of the Vice Presidency.* Rev. ed. 1972.

– JOEL K. GOLDSTEIN

W

WAR, DECLARATION OF

The Constitution explicitly places the President in command of all military forces belonging to the United States. Article II, Section 2, states that "The President shall be Commander in Chief of the Army and Navy of the United States, and of the Militia of the several States, when called into the actual Service of the United States." The President's power to initiate military action, however, is limited by Article I, Section 8, which states that "Congress shall have Power . . . to declare War, grant Letters of Marque and Reprisal, and make Rules concerning Captures on Land and Water." Therefore, the Constitution places the decision to engage in hostilities with other nations in the hands of Congress.

Constitutional Context

These limitations may best be understood in historical context. In the eighteenth century the United States had no standing army. With no ability to wage war, a President would clearly have no recourse but to turn to Congress. The President may initiate hostilities only when swift action is necessary to repel a sudden attack. Otherwise, Congress is granted the sole authority to "raise and support Armies," "provide and maintain a Navy," "make Rules for the Governance and Regulation of" the armed forces, and "provide for calling forth the Militia to execute the Laws of the Union, suppress Insurrections and repel Invasions." In short, the armed forces may be used only to pursue legislatively authorized goals. As Attorney General Caleb Cushing stated in an 1853 legal opinion, the President is like a "commander in command of a squadron or a general in the field." Any orders issued by the President "must be within the range of purely executive or administrative action."

Those who drafted the Constitution considered the war clause to be a comprehensive ban against presidential warmaking. From the outset of the debate on the Constitution's structure, the Framers expressed the fear that executive war power would lead to the "evils of elected Monarchies." Subsequent debate on the precise phrasing of the war clause itself shows that the drafters of the clause originally sought to bar the President from "making" any war but drafted the clause to bar the President from "declaring" war so that the President could legally respond to a surprise attack on the United States without congressional approval.

The Framers' interpretation of their own document as a comprehensive check on executive war power is reflected in a statement made by Thomas Jefferson regarding the war clause: "We have already given . . . one effectual check to the dog of war by transferring the power of letting him loose, from the executive to the legislative body." The Framers consciously repudiated the European concept of monarchical war power. The U.S. Constitution is a product of the Enlightenment, and the Framers, aspiring to achieve the Enlightenment ideal of republican government, drafted a Constitution that allowed only Congress to loose the military forces of the United States on other nations.

Those who drafted the Constitution considered the war clause to be a comprehensive ban against presidential warmaking.

The war clause's injunction against executive warmaking was respected by Presidents Jefferson and James Madison, both of whom participated in framing the Constitution, though Jefferson was not at the Constitutional Convention. Moreover, the U.S. Supreme Court also recognized and affirmed the war clause's exclusive grant of war power to the Congress in such early cases as *Bas* v. *Tingy* (1800), *Talbot* v. *Seeman* (1801), and *Little* v. *Barreme* (1804). Those decisions recognized that Congress must either declare war or explicitly authorize it, as it did with the Quasi-War with France.

Under the constitutional model of war power, there is no question that the Commander in Chief clause allows the President to engage U.S. military forces after war is declared. Full declarations of war have occurred at five points in United States history: the War of 1812, the Mexican War of 1846, the Spanish-American War of 1898, World War I, and World War II. In each instance, Congress declared by joint resolution that the United States was at war with other nations, thus empowering the President to wage war against those nations named. Congress can also empower the President by issuing a conditional declaration of war, consisting of an ultimatum to another nation. Interestingly, while conditional declarations of war have been issued several times in U.S. history, only the 1898 ultimatum that Spain relinquish its claim to Cuba actually led to violence.

Congressional Authorization

Short of a declaration of total war, the President can obtain limited war power where Congress by statute authorizes the President to use military force limited to certain means or objectives. Statutory authorization to wage limited war was one of the earliest exercises of constitutional war power. The Congressional authorizations for naval actions against the Barbary states of North Africa from 1794 to 1815 are examples of constitutional delegation of limited war power to the President. Presidential war power only exists within the limits established by the authorization.

Congressional grants of limited war power have routinely been abused in the modern era. The Gulf of Tonkin Resolution of 1964 (originally referred to as the Southeast Asia Resolution) authorized the President to repel North Vietnamese attacks on U.S. armed forces and allowed the President to provide military support for any nations that were signatories of the SEATO Treaty. The Tonkin Gulf Resolution's ambiguous phrasing and nearly limitless delegation of war power frustrated the constitutional constraints on executive warmaking and resulted in the escalation of the Vietnam War, a war that in many ways resembled the long, bloody, and inclusive wars of Europe that the Framers had sought to avoid.

More recently, the 1991 resolution authorizing the President to use armed forces in the Gulf War came only after President George Bush had massed troops and equipment for the offensive against Iraqi forces. To be in accordance with the constitutional model of war-power delegation, congressional resolutions for limited warfare must be carefully tailored, narrowly construed, and made a prerequisite before the commitment of any U.S. forces to a conflict.

With the advent of nuclear-war strategies, defense against nuclear attack included the President's authority to launch America's entire arsenal of nuclear weapons without congressional approval. The events surrounding the Cuban Missile Crisis, when the United States moved dangerously close to nuclear confrontation without full congressional approval, demonstrated the extent of presidential war power in the cold war era. Nevertheless, many commentators believe that any first use of nuclear weapons demands congressional authorization.

Despite the Constitution's injunction against executive war power, the executive branch now seems to possess the ability to initiate military action without congressional approval or even congressional consultation. The expansion of presidential war power paralleled the perception that the United States was threatened with imminent attack from communist forces in virtually every corner of the world. This fear led to increasing judicial deference to aggressive executive foreign policy.

The Courts Defer

The creation of the so-called fluctuating powers doctrine bolstered judicial deference toward executive foreign-policy decisions. In his concurrence in *Youngstown Sheet & Tube Co.* v. *Sawyer* (1952), Justice Robert Jackson said that "presidential powers are not fixed but fluctuate, depending on their disjunction or conjunction with those of Congress." In other words, if Congress has not clearly expressed its will on a matter relating to foreign policy, the courts will allow the President successfully to exercise a certain degree of power, including war power. Both the Korean War and the Vietnam War demonstrated the executive branch's newfound ability to wage undeclared war under the rubric of containing communism.

The confusion over where foreign-policy power ends and war power begins was exacerbated by the judiciary's refusal to adjudicate war power disputes. The tendency of the courts to avoid war power issues emerged during the Vietnam era, when several suits were brought by members of Congress and other citizens to halt the undeclared war in Indochina. Despite the Supreme Court's ruling in *Baker* v. *Carr* (1962) that "it is error to suppose that every case or controversy which touches foreign relations lies beyond judicial cognizance," the federal courts consistently invoked the political question doctrine to avoid addressing the constitutionality of the Vietnam War.

The judiciary's refusal to address war power issues continues to frustrate attempts by Congress to restore the constitutional delegation of war powers. In 1990, several members of Congress sought to reestablish congressional control over the decision whether to attack Iraqi forces in the Persian Gulf. Their suit, *Dellums* v. *Bush,* was dismissed as not ripe for adjudication by a federal district judge.

Covert Warmaking

After Vietnam, the executive branch resorted to large-scale covert military actions in order to free military activity from the constraints of the war clause of the Constitution and the War Powers Resolution of 1973. The executive branch contended that covert activity was constitutionally authorized, but that argument is flawed. The Constitution does require congressional approval for covert military actions. The war clause gives Congress the exclusive power to grant "Letters of Marque and Reprisal"—the eighteenth-century equivalents of authorization for private acts of war and covert military activities. Nonetheless, examples of covert operations engineered by agencies in the executive branch abound. U.S. sponsorship of the Nicaraguan contra rebels during the 1980s is an example of presidential sponsored covert warfare that clearly violates constitutional war power.

Though large-scale, decisive use of armed force represents a trend in executive use of war power, the practice nonetheless violates constitutional separation of powers.

The executive branch also resorted to warfare that was covert only in the sense that the decision to engage U.S. forces was made without informing Congress. This practice reached its height during the 1980s; the tactic that emerged was a quick and decisive use of military force without congressional approval. By adopting blitzkrieg-type tactics, the executive branch could complete a military campaign before Congress could assert constitutional constraints. Military operations such as the invasion of Grenada in 1983 and the invasion of Panama in 1989 involved commitments of military force. The war clause surely applied. Nonetheless, the executive branch was able to evade a constitutional challenge because the rapid conclusion of the activity rendered the question moot. So, while it is true that large-scale, decisive use of armed force represents a trend in executive use of war power, the practice nonetheless violates constitutional separation of powers.

Perhaps in a period when the specter of communism no longer haunts foreign policy makers, American foreign policy will retreat from the perpetual state of emergency that existed for more than forty years. If this occurs, the power to engage U.S. forces in warfare may return to the constitutional model and a congressional declaration or authorization of war will again be a prerequisite to the use of armed force by the President. While it remains to be seen what practical war powers will remain with the presidency after the cold war, the constitutional constraints on executive warmaking cannot be denied. According to the war clause of the Constitution, a congressional declaration of war or its equivalent is required before the President may engage U.S. military force.

[See also (II) Commander in Chief.]

BIBLIOGRAPHY

Firmage, E. B. "Rogue Presidents and the War Power of Congress." *George Mason Law Review* 11 (1988): 79.

Firmage, E. B., and J. E. Wrona. "The War Power." *George Washington Law Review* 59 (1991): 1684.

Glennon, M. J. *Constitutional Diplomacy.* 1990.

Keynes, E. *Undeclared War.* 1982.

Lobel, J. "Emergency Power and the Decline of Liberalism." *Yale Law Journal* 98 (1989): 1385.

Wormuth, F. D., and E. B. Firmage. *To Chain the Dog of War.* 2d ed. 1989.

– EDWIN B. FIRMAGE

WHITE HOUSE ADVISERS

A modern President has several hundred men and women who are personal advisers and assistants—comprising the senior and central part of the much larger White House staff community. Despite labels in the annual Budget Appendix such as "Office of Policy Development" and "National Security Council," which imply that these units are part of the professional Executive Office of the President, the policy assistants in those sections, like the others in the "White House Office" itself, are in reality part of the President's personal staff; they all serve without tenure and at the President's pleasure.

The Need for Advisers

In the late twentieth century the American nation is a cacophonous, no-consensus society; not only are its dissensions reflected in Congress and throughout the federal system, but its pluralism is mirrored in the President's own enormously diverse executive branch. Demarcations between matters "foreign" and "domestic" are disappearing, and boundaries separating cabinet departments are increasingly irrelevant. The principal policy issues facing a modern President—for example, the eradication of illegal drugs—stretch across all those borders; they are interdepartmental, intergovernmental, and international.

Article II of the Constitution, however, remains unchanged: in the executive branch, ultimate responsibility still rests in one person's hands. The President's personal White House staff bridges this gap between a raucously plural executive establishment and a determinedly singular President and manages the now-indispensable coordination of the President's business. It is not clear that cabinet officers or budget directors could ever have performed these very personal political functions, but nowadays they certainly could not. The Cabinet is a diverse bunch; its members, who are typically assembled to bind up the wounds of the presidential primaries, include the erstwhile feuding factions of the President's party and also encompass representatives of both sexes, of several racial and/or ethnic groups, various professions, ages, states, and religions. Cabinet officers are (and should be) antagonists: often, they not only differ vociferously with one another but also mix their considerable egos into their disputes. It is too much to expect any one of them to be a central coordinator to whose signals the others will defer.

Furthermore, department and agency heads have divided loyalties: they are always deferential—sometimes even hostage—to congressional committees, outside support constituencies, and their own bureaucracies. If, for instance, a major presidential speech is in the works, agency heads are likely to behave as supplicants rather than as integrators for the President.

Functions

Personal presidential advisers in the modern White House have five core functions. First, they coordinate the policy process across the spectrum of departments and agencies. Meetings of "task forces" or Cabinet councils (rarely of the full cabinet because of its size, pluralism, and propensity for leaks) are a frequently used technique. The White House staff sets the agenda of any White House meeting, composes whatever formal record is made of the proceedings (especially of the presidential decision), and performs the follow-up surveillance over departmental compliance. Some Presidents, however, distrust or even detest meetings; they prefer to work from option papers. Here, too, a White House adviser specifies the assignment for the paper and drafts either the last version of the option paper or the "road map" memorandum that guides the President through the paper's attachments and alerts the President to traps and pitfalls. White House advisers draft or record the chief executive's decision and mount the follow-up.

Second, policy issues occasionally arise that are of extreme sensitivity. Sometimes they must be kept secret for national security reasons, or they may be potentially politically explosive, or they may be of such great import that the President is determined to capture the initiative by issuing a major presidential statement. The President will want absolutely no leaks, no premature dribbling out of bits and snippets of his program to be attacked piecemeal before his comprehensive argument is set forth. In such cases, the President will instruct that the preparatory work be kept deep in his advisers' pockets, from start to finish, with little or no reaching out to his Cabinet subordinates. (Examples include Richard M. Nixon's March 1970 statement on school desegregation and busing, Jimmy Carter's 1977 energy package, and Ronald Reagan's 1982 "new federalism" proposals). The President may direct one or more personal advisers to drop everything else and concentrate all their time on a single undertaking—a mandate no Cabinet officer could handle.

Third, a President cannot get through his early press conferences without being rudely asked, for example, about what he is doing to fix an operational goof-up in such-and-such an agency or about whether he agrees with yesterday's speech by Secretary So-and-so. If he confesses ignorance it is doubly embarrassing. Presidents have thus come to demand the establishment of information systems that will make sure that the White House knows about where things are going off the track. He and his staff insist on acquiring a very rare commodity in big institutions: anticipatory information. At least five such systems have been put in place: the situation rooms into which raw and processed information of all kinds flows from the entire national security community; the daily News Summary, a twenty-page digest of important items from all U.S. television networks, wire services, East Coast newspapers (and others coming in by mail), foreign papers and foreign radio and TV stations (once a week a "Friday Follies" supplement of some sixty cartoons is appended); the regular Cabinet Report compiled by the secretary to the cabinet from individual submissions dragooned from the respective department and agency heads; weekly written reports from principal staff members summarizing all their and their subordinates' activities; and, supplementing all this, the informal, word-of-mouth networks that are maintained by each of the President's advisers and that reach throughout the bureaucracy and across the country.

White House advisers are a brainy, aggressive, egotistical coterie, intolerant of mistakes and impatient for results.

Fourth, White House staffs have discovered that they must do more than assist in the development of policy; they must also mount a surveillance over the implementation, by the departments and agencies, of those presidential decisions that break new ground. Presidents are, after all, change-makers and are impatient to "turn the ship around." Although government bureaucrats, career or noncareer, do not often dig in against a President (though this does occasionally happen), 180-degree corrections in course may give rise to so many alterations in so many past practices that inertia is very difficult to overcome.

Fifth, crisis management is a special form of White House administration. Crises are always handled by the White House, usually in close detail, although the intensity of the supervision from the top is often masked at the time. In crises, all the aforementioned practices are redoubled. The staff taxes its information systems to wrest data from the very front lines of the crisis (often bypassing intermediate points); policy development is vastly accelerated but with an even higher degree of personal input from White House advisers.

The Work of Advisers

White House advisers are a brainy, aggressive, egotistical coterie, intolerant of mistakes and impatient for results. Most come from the campaign apparat, but they are not cut from the same mold, and the group is likely to include civilians and military people, young and old, men and women, whites and members of minorities, and ideologues and pragmatists. A few may be famous, most will be unknown. Out of this variety spring correspondingly different viewpoints on issues of public policy. When they are kept within the White House perimeter, staff debates are beneficial to the President, but they can be harmful if leaked to the always-encircling newspeople and columnists. With very few exceptions White House advisers are men and women of high intellectual integrity, insisting that the policy processes they manage be honest and fair; crusaders and sycophants are unwelcome and scarce. But White House advisers are not merely process-managers; they have strong convictions and are expected to express them. This means they must guard against letting their personal predilections skew their commitment and must make sure that all sides of a debate get through to the President.

White House advisers live tension-filled lives; they work such sacrificial hours that there are family strains and high divorce rates; many staffmembers quit short of the President's own four or eight years. When their President does leave office, they all depart abruptly, and while some experts recommend that there be continuity in senior White House staff ranks, these proposals hardly coincide with the reality of a new Chief Executive's housecleaning proclivities.

The most frequent accusation hurled at White House advisers is that they are not accountable. They have been called "29-year-old wimps" and accused of riding their own hobbyhorses and not representing the President. In almost every case such charges are wrong. Though it is unrecognized by the recipients of their queries or requests, they are in fact relaying or acting on the President's own general—and sometimes very specific—instructions. In fact, junior and middle-level White House advisers, who most commonly suffer from such accusations, are constantly subject to challenge and are instantly disciplined if they are caught out on a limb.

BIBLIOGRAPHY

Hess, Stephen. *Organizing the Presidency.* 2d ed. 1988.

Patterson, Bradley H., Jr. *The Ring of Power: The White House Staff and Its Expanding Role in Government.* 1988.

Pfiffner, James P. *The Managerial Presidency.* 1991.

– BRADLEY H. PATTERSON, JR.

WHITE HOUSE BUREAUCRACY

The real character of the White House staff is cloaked by two widely held but incorrect assumptions: that it is small and that the men and women who compose it function as generalists with broad, undifferentiated responsibilities. In fact, the White House staff community is large and the policy staff is subdivided into twenty specialized offices with firmly staked-out jurisdictions. These twenty, in turn, are undergirded by a sizable technical support staff. The White House (quite apart from the rest of the Executive Office of the President) is indeed a bureaucracy.

Offices and Functions

The twenty principal offices in the contemporary White House are the embodiments of the twenty major staff functions supporting the modern President. They are as follows:

1. THE ASSISTANT FOR NATIONAL SECURITY AFFAIRS. Though the specific position of Assistant for National Security Affairs was created in 1953 by Dwight D. Eisenhower, the national security staff office itself began earlier, in 1947. This unit of nearly two hundred people is the secretariat for the National Security Council and manages the President's entire national security decision-making process and apparatus, including flows of intelligence materials, policy cables to and from posts abroad, the "hot line," and two White House situation rooms. As instructed by the President, the Assistant himself will meet and deal with foreign ambassadors in Washington, undertake personal negotiating missions to hot spots in far corners of the world, and appear on national television talk shows. He is expected to add his own policy advice into the decision system but must guard against skewing the whole process to favor his own leanings.

2. THE ASSISTANT FOR DOMESTIC POLICY. This office was created de jure under Richard M. Nixon, but its antecedents go back at least as far as Franklin D. Roosevelt's administration. The staff in this office performs the same review and coordinating functions for domestic affairs that the National Security Affairs office does for national security.

3. THE COUNSEL. Franklin Roosevelt wanted a personal legal/policy adviser in addition to his Attorney General; so has each succeeding President. Since almost every policy matter in the White House has a legal dimension, the White House Counsel and a staff of nearly thirty are involved in many different areas. All bills passed by Congress cross the Counsel's desk before the final decision to sign or veto; so do all proclamations, executive orders, pardons, and drafts of major speeches. The Counsel is the ethics officer for the staff and the principal coordinator for judicial appointments. The Counsel reviews the Solicitor General's briefs on ultrasensitive Supreme Court cases, guards the President's executive privilege, and heads off challenges to the President's constitutional powers, advises the President about his will, his papers, and, whenever he is facing surgery, about the applicability of the Twenty-fifth Amendment.

A modern President is never unaware

that the White House is a splendid theater.

---

4. THE ASSISTANT FOR LEGISLATIVE AFFAIRS. A few staff members dabbled in this role during the administrations of Roosevelt and Harry S Truman, but it was Eisenhower who elevated the head of this office and enlarged and strengthened its corps. Every later President has copied the Eisenhower model. This unit is the President's personal link with Congress—"an ambulatory bridge across a constitutional gulf," as one White House assistant put it. All congressional mail addressed to the President goes first to this office for logging and control. Using the legislative assistants in each of the departments as a network, the office of the Assistant for Legislative Affairs tracks the President's priority legislation and nominations and tries to round up the needed votes for passage or confirmation.

5. THE ASSISTANT FOR POLITICAL AFFAIRS. This officer is the link between the White House and the national party and with the party's local committees in the states and territories. Under Truman, the Appointments Secretary had this responsibility, but it has become more institutionalized under later Presidents. Everything in the White House is political: a major speech, an unpopular veto message, and a presidential trip as well as plans for the reelection campaign.

6. THE ASSISTANT FOR INTERGOVERNMENTAL AFFAIRS. The federal system is exceedingly plural: there are 50 states, some 3,050 counties, 19,200 cities, 17,000 townships, 15,000 school districts, 30,000 special districts, and 500 Indian tribes—the total governed by some 320,000 elected officials. Major domestic programs (drug control, education, environmental protection) involve coordination across all those governmental boundaries. The intergovernmental affairs office is the White House's contact point and ombudsman with the governors, mayors, and other principal officeholders among those 80,000-plus units of local government.

7. THE DIRECTOR OF COMMUNICATIONS. A modern President is never unaware that the White House is a splendid theater—playing to both a nationwide and worldwide audience. The Director of Communications is in effect the theater manager. Every presidential trip, speech, visit, or photo opportunity is prearranged and exploited to make the boss appear favorably in the print media and especially on the evening television news programs. The White House "theater director" makes sure that good news is released from the White House, while unwelcome announcements come from the agencies. No Cabinet officer appears on the Sunday morning talk shows without White House approval.

8. THE PRESS SECRETARY. The President meets the press occasionally, but the White House Press Secretary faces reporters' insistent questioning every working day. Close to two thousand people hold White House press passes; some fifty regulars have labeled seats in the West Terrace Briefing Room. With rare exceptions, the Press Secretary is the only responsible, on-the-record spokesperson on the White House staff. The Press Secretary consults constantly not only with the President and with staff colleagues but also with the press secretaries in the various departments (whose appointments he controls). The staff that prepares the daily White House News Summary is often attached to the Press Secretary's office, but then the News Summary editor must take care not to make his product merely the echo of the Press Secretary's pronouncements.

9. THE ASSISTANT FOR PUBLIC LIAISON. Of the twenty thousand nationwide nonprofit public-interest organizations in the United States, many have Washington, D.C., headquarters staffed by power-brokers eager to present their views to the White House. At least since Nixon's time, the Public Liaison office has been their door-opener; it arranges strategically timed White

House sessions at which they may set forth their views and petitions. The President gains by this arrangement as well: those same nationwide nongovernmental organizations, when they are persuaded to support his legislative initiatives, can be potent lobbying forces on the Congress.

10. SPEECHWRITERS AND THE RESEARCH OFFICE. Except at press conferences, modern Presidents make hardly any extemporaneous remarks. Speeches by the Chief Executive are often great theater and major policy simultaneously; they are accordingly the product of meticulous staff creativity. Even "Rose Garden rubbish"—for example, greeting the Turkey of the Year—is crafted ahead of time. There have been designated presidential speechwriters since Harding.

11. THE ASSISTANT FOR APPOINTMENTS AND SCHEDULING. The President has 1,461 days in his four-year term. The Appointments Secretary bestrides the voluminous flow of invitations and, sometimes backstopped by a senior-level internal White House committee, screens out low-priority requests and helps the President focus on those events that will strengthen his policy program. Once the schedule is set (though it is usually reworked every few hours), the Scheduling Office sees to it that all the other White House offices (Secret Service, photographer, speechwriters, Press Secretary, Director of Communications, etc.) are reminded of their roles in the upcoming event. Attached to the Scheduling Office is the Presidential Diarist, who gleans from the cooperating offices (the Chief Usher, White House telephone operators, the Secret Service, and so on) the details of every moment of the President's waking life: who was with him, or talked with him, for how long, and on what subject.

12. OFFICE OF PRESIDENTIAL PERSONNEL. In addition to the White House staff (which this office does not handle), a modern President can control some five thousand political jobs, including roughly nine hundred full-time senior executive-branch positions, the two hundred judicial vacancies that will typically occur during a presidential term, more than fifteen hundred part-timers on boards and commissions, and some twenty-three hundred Schedule C positions or noncareer Senior Executive Service jobs in various agencies. The Presidential Personnel Office has a forty-person staff that catalogues, recruits, and helps the President select appointees for this patronage universe.

13. THE ADVANCE OFFICE. There is practically no extemporaneous presidential travel; every trip is planned in minute detail. The Advance Office staff comprises the planners and coordinators who mobilize and synchronize the efforts of many of the existing White House units (the Press Office, the Secret Service, the First Lady's office, communications, medical, Air Force One, speechwriters, etc.) for presidential journeys. Advance staffers visit all sites ahead of time.

14. WHITE HOUSE "CZARS." If a momentous problems slams itself onto the presidential agenda, making the nation apprehensive, provoking calls for swift response, and cutting widely across departmental jurisdictions, a President will be tempted to take quick, and at least symbolic, action—often appointing a "czar" right in the White House. Eisenhower used this technique often, and his successors have done likewise. Some positions, such as the "Drug Czar," have been authorized by Congress.

15. THE FIRST LADY. Students of the American presidency should never underestimate the policy role of the President's spouse. Eleanor Roosevelt traveled widely and wrote a newspaper column; Rosalynn Carter attended Cabinet meetings; Nancy Reagan hosted a world summit conference of first ladies; and Barbara Bush had an active schedule of public appearances. First Ladies have some thirty-five assistants to help them.

16. THE VICE PRESIDENT. After Harry S Truman's experience of becoming President without any executive branch experience in 1945, Vice Presidents have increasingly become advisers to the President and participants in the work of the administration. Under John F. Kennedy, Lyndon Baines Johnson became the first Vice President to move his office and staff into the White House environs. Under Jimmy Carter, Vice President Walter Mondale was the first whose advice was truly welcomed; the Ronald Reagan and George Bush presidencies followed the Carter-Mondale model. In the early 1990s the Vice President's staff numbered about one hundred, and even the Vice President's spouse had a staff. Most of the President's information is shared with the Vice President, who has been made a statutory member of the National Security Council and participates in important White House meetings.

17. THE STAFF SECRETARY. First created under Eisenhower in 1953, the Staff Secretary regulates the flow of papers into the Oval Office, enforcing the internal system of circulating draft speeches and papers for staff comment.

18. THE OFFICE OF CABINET AFFAIRS. This office handles external coordination with the departments and agencies, sending option memoranda and speech drafts out for comment and issuing the periodic "Cabinet Report" to which agency heads contribute. The full Cabinet meets rarely, but Cabinet councils and subgroups convene constantly, and the Cabinet Secretary and assistants provide the executive secretariat services to these groups. This office also began under Eisenhower in 1953.

19. THE PERSONAL OFFICE ASSISTANTS. One or two secretaries and a personal assistant sit outside the President's door, the former performing standard secretarial duties, the latter handling the myriad daily personal details for the boss: making sure that the schedule is being followed, that people whose presence the President is going to acknowledge will in fact be on hand, and that a presidential request, made while walking to or from the office, is put into the action system.

20. THE CHIEF OF STAFF. Most centripetal of all, the Chief of Staff is the system manager, "boss of none but the quarterback of everything." The Chief of Staff does not command any other senior White House staff officer, but his personal antennae reach into every corner of the place. He enforces the indispensable coordination across all of the sixteen principal offices described above. Since it is the Chief of Staff who so often has to say "no"—to inadequate papers, beseeching visitors, or proposed appointees—he swiftly makes many more enemies than friends.

Support Staff

Undergirding these twenty offices are the professional support units of the contemporary White House, including the Secret Service details (involving eight hundred personnel, with others borrowed as needed), the thirteen-hundred-person Military Office (with ten specialized subunits, e.g., Air Force One, the doctor, the mess, Camp David, and the eight-hundred-person White House Communications Agency), the Chief Usher (who manages the mansion), the Executive Clerk, and the Correspondence, Gifts, Telephone, and Visitors offices. The number of people in the entire White House Staff community totals some thirty-four hundred. Many are assigned or detailed from other agencies. In addition, five hundred volunteers help out part time.

Every White House staff will inevitably reflect the style and working habits of the President. The offices are often renamed and the lines of supervision rejiggered. But these twenty principal functions are such basic responsibilities of the White House that future Presidents are not likely to abolish any of them outright.

[See also (II) White House Chief of Staff.]

BIBLIOGRAPHY

Hess, Stephen. *Organizing the Presidency.* 2d ed. 1988.

Kernell, Samuel, and Samuel L. Popkin. *Chief of Staff: Twenty-Five Years of Managing the Presidency.* 1986.

Patterson, Bradley H., Jr. *The Ring of Power: The White House Staff and Its Expanding Role in Government.* 1988.

Pfiffner, James P. *The Managerial Presidency.* 1991.

– BRADLEY H. PATTERSON, JR.

WHITE HOUSE CHIEF OF STAFF

Up until the advent of World War II the White House still served primarily as the President's residence. White House staff maintained informal relations with President Franklin D. Roosevelt: formal staff meetings did not occur, but rather key advisers often met with Franklin Roosevelt at breakfast to discuss the agenda for the day. Advisers who needed to see him during the day could readily gain access to Roosevelt in his office by going through the President's appointment secretary or his personal secretary. Roosevelt was also typically available during the afternoon cocktail hour, and he frequently spent evenings with his speechwriters.

The expanding role of the federal government in the domestic sphere can be traced back to the Great Depression.

The war increased demands on the presidency, as did the expanded role of the federal government, both internationally and domestically, after the war. By the time the war ended, the staff within the White House reporting personally to the President had grown considerably, and the White House had become a locus for policy development and decision making as well as a residence. These intensifying pressures contributed to the creation of the post of White House Chief of Staff during the Dwight D. Eisenhower administration.

Eisenhower's predecessor, Harry S Truman, had initially intended to cut the White House staff back to its prewar size. The cold war, however, expanded the role of the United States in global military and diplomatic affairs. The expanding role of the federal government in the domestic sphere can be traced back to the Great Depression of the 1930s, which had launched the country into an era of Keynesian fiscal policy, with greater government intervention in the economy. From the 1930s on, government regulation had expanded incrementally (but seemingly inevitably) to encompass regulation of business practices, management-labor relations, and consumer protection. Government's greater role, in turn, had generated greater demands by various constituencies to pursue their cases before the President. Truman therefore reversed himself and expanded the White House staff, without, however, creating a chief of staff. (One assistant did serve as a route to the President for minor agencies without other direct presidential access.)

Drawing on his military experience of managing complex and sometimes competing units in unfamiliar circumstances, Eisenhower replicated the military role of chief of staff in the White House. Although Sherman Adams retained the previously used title of Assistant to the President, his role was vastly expanded. Adams functioned in a way similar to how General Walter Bedell Smith had functioned as Eisenhower's chief of staff during the war. Eisenhower saw his Chief of Staff as his personal "son of a bitch": Adams served as a gatekeeper for all activities, issues, and constituencies (except for those involving foreign policy) wanting to reach the President. He oversaw patronage and personnel decisions, appointments and scheduling, presidential speechwriters, and press relations. He also served as the liaison to the Cabinet, headed up special projects, and managed presidential-congressional relations. Adams held staff meetings as frequently as three times a week to coordinate White House work. Under his management the White House staff gained a valued reputation for efficiency and a less-valued reputation for rigidity. Adams wielded immense power as Chief of Staff until he was forced out in 1958 after having been accused of accepting favors from a Boston industrialist.

There was no formally appointed White House Chief of Staff under Presidents John F. Kennedy and Lyndon B. Johnson. Kennedy was more attracted to the informal managerial techniques of Roosevelt than to Eisenhower's formal organizational structure, which had been designed to meld relative strangers into an efficient working team. In contrast, most of the staff Kennedy appointed had worked with him previously and were personally loyal to him. Johnson, too, preferred personal control and informal organization. Richard M. Nixon, however, reinstituted the Chief of Staff position, appointing H. R. Haldeman to fill it. Haldeman's mismanagement of the considerable powers he was given as Chief of Staff played a major role in the disastrous Watergate affair. In response to this, Gerald Ford did not appoint a formal Chief of Staff, although Donald Rumsfeld, who had headed up the Ford transition team, served as a de facto Chief of Staff. At the end of the Ford Administration, Dick Cheney was the Chief of Staff.

Jimmy Carter also initially eschewed the formal appointment of a Chief of Staff, preferring to serve as his own. This overburdened the President with minor details, however, and, by 1979, Hamilton Jordan was appointed to the position. Ronald Reagan, likewise, chose not to appoint a single Chief of Staff during his first term, instead splitting the Chief of Staff's functions among three advisers. At the beginning of his second term, he appointed a single Chief of Staff, Donald Regan. In contrast to his two immediate predecessors, George Bush embraced the Chief of Staff concept and appointed the bright but contentious John Sununu, former governor of New Hampshire, to the post. Both Regan and Sununu were unpopular with the public, and both were replaced before the ends of their respective Presidents' terms. Bill Clinton followed in the tradition of Eisenhower, Nixon, and Bush and appointed a chief of staff (Thomas F. McLarty) on first assuming office.

The Chief of Staff requires no Senate approval and serves at the pleasure of the President with few formal constraints. The Chief of Staff wields considerable power from serving daily at the President's elbow and may be the second most important person in an administration.

The Chief of Staff performs several functions. One primary duty is to organize the information flowing to the President. The Chief of Staff must make sure that important issues receive adequate attention and enough staff to handle their workload. Further, the Chief of Staff coordinates policy development and work across various issues. Another important function of the Chief of Staff is to take the heat for the President, serving as a buffer between the President and angry constituencies. For example, appointments are often announced by the President personally, but personnel who are dismissed will likely receive the news from the White House Chief of Staff.

The Chief of Staff manages White House-department relations, negotiating with members of the Cabinet over budget and personnel matters. As the President's surrogate, the Chief of Staff may be called on to massage egos and soothe hurt feelings. Besides these functions, a Chief of Staff may be asked to orchestrate policy issues, cutting across several Cabinet departments to develop policies on issues of particular interest to the President, to uncover information (sometimes embarrassing) that Cabinet officers may be reluctant to report, and to intervene in and monitor foreign and domestic crises in which the White House has a role.

[See also (II) White House Bureaucracy.]

BIBLIOGRAPHY

Dwight D. Eisenhower. *The White House Years: Waging Peace, 1956–1961.* 1965.

Hess, Stephen. *Organizing the Presidency.* 2d ed. 1988.

Kernell, Samuel, and Samuel L. Popkin. *Chief of Staff: Twenty-five Years of Managing the Presidency.* 1986.

Pffifner, James P. *The Strategic Presidency.* 1988.

– MARCIA LYNN WHICKER

WHITE HOUSE COUNSEL

The key legal adviser to the President is known as the White House Counsel. The Counsel works in the

White House Office and provides legal advice to the President on a wide array of issues; legal services performed by the Counsel and staff include legal clearance of documents for the President's signature, assistance on legal problems not provided by the Justice Department, and liaison between the President and the Justice Department. The position of White House Counsel is located in the personal office of the President. White House Counsel staff and facilities allow the President to communicate with Congress, the press, the public, and appointed department and agency heads.

In administrations that have employed a central-management model, counsels have had less-frequent contact with the President and have worked through the White House Chief of Staff.

Even during the Franklin D. Roosevelt and Harry S Truman administrations, when members of the White House office were mostly generalists, the position of legal counsel was somewhat functionally specialized, although the counsel did not yet have a large staff at his disposal. Despite this relative specialization, the legal counsel continued to perform many nonlegal duties as late as the Truman administration.

Functional specialization within the White House became more pronounced during the Dwight D. Eisenhower administration. Specialized staff units were formed to handle functions (including Cabinet affairs, legislative liaison with Congress, and liaison with the President's party) previously handled by the legal counsel as well as other staff members. Under Richard M. Nixon, Gerald Ford, and Jimmy Carter, additional specialized units were created to deal with communications and to provide liaison with state and local governments and interest groups.

Some administrations have taken on additional legal advisers within the White House. By the Lyndon B. Johnson administration, the President's legal staff had grown to include not only a counsel and four special counsels but also a deputy special counsel, assistant special counsel, associate counsel, and associate special counsel. Besides serving the legal unit, these special counsels provided advice to White House speechwriting, appointments, and legislative program development units. Counsel staff were also active in executive guidance and control. More recent administrations have followed Johnson's lead, employing a number of legal counselors on the President's personal staff.

The White House Counsel facilitates White House coordination with the Justice Department, headed by the U.S. Attorney General, who is the chief law enforcement officer in the federal government. Unlike the White House Counsel, who represents the interests of the President personally, the Attorney General represents the legal interests of the United States. As a personal adviser to the President, the White House Counsel is not subject to confirmation by the U.S. Senate, and here, too, the Counsel position differs from that of the Attorney General, who as a department head and Cabinet member must be confirmed by the Senate. Moreover, the White House Counsel cannot be forced to testify before congressional committees, whereas the Attorney General is expected to appear regularly at congressional hearings and to respond to legislators' requests for information.

The White House Counsel does not appear in court on behalf of the President, but informally provides advice on litigation. By contrast, the Attorney General may appear in person in court to represent the United States in particularly important cases. (More commonly, the Solicitor General represents the U.S. government in cases before the U.S. Supreme Court.)

The relation of the White House Counsel to the President has varied from administration to administration. In administrations that have employed a central-management model, such as the Nixon presidency and to a lesser extent the Ronald Reagan and George Bush presidencies, counsels have had less-frequent contact with the President and have worked mainly through the White House Chief of Staff. In collegially managed White Houses (the model used by John F. Kennedy and attempted by Carter), the Counsel has had more direct contact with the President. In a competitive advisory system—the staffing arrangement preferred by Franklin Roosevelt—the President's legal counsel may have frequent access to him, but duties are more ambiguously defined and no member of the staff has proprietorship of any particular advisory role.

Organizational problems may occur when a President encounters legal difficulties in an area that has not been defined as belonging to the realm of the White House Counsel, as when legal problems arise over matters of substantive policy or electoral politics. Such problems are more likely to arise when the White House follows a central-management model than when it uses a collegial or competitive model. For example, some of the legal problems Nixon encountered during the Watergate affair involved election tactics rather than the legal suitability of routine government documents or laws. Similarly, the legality of actions of Reagan and

Bush in the Iran-contra affair were subsequently questioned, but the decisions made in the arms-for-hostages deal with Iran to fund contra activities in Nicaragua were kept from the White House Counsel.

[See also (II) Attorney General, Solicitor General.]

BIBLIOGRAPHY

Burke, John P. *The Institutional Presidency.* 1992.

Edwards, George C., and Stephen J. Wayne. *Presidential Leadership: Politics and Policy Making.* 2d ed. 1990.

Groner, Jonathan. "Counseling Clinton." *Legal Times* (1 February 1993): 1, 22–23. On Bernard Nussbaum.

Moore, W. John. "The True Believers." *National Journal* (17 August 1991): 2018–2022. On C. Boyden Gray.

Redford, Emmette S., and Richard T. McCulley. *White House Operations: The Johnson Presidency.* 1986.

– MARCIA LYNN WHICKER

WHITE HOUSE OFFICE

One of the five original divisions of the Executive Office of the President (EOP) established by Franklin D. Roosevelt's Executive Order 8248 of 8 September 1939, the White House Office is the formal home of the personal staff of the President. The White House Office was intended, in the words of the executive order, "to serve the President in an intimate capacity in the performance of the many detailed activities incident to his immediate office."

Although the White House Office officially dates from 1939, there has, in effect, been a White House Office ever since President George Washington appointed Tobias Lear as his private secretary 150 years earlier. By 1937, when the Brownlow Committee recommended formalizing the President's personal staff as a division of the proposed EOP, the White House staff was already institutionally well established.

WHITE HOUSE OFFICE

Chief of Staff
Office of the Staff Secretary
Office of Communications
  Office of Speechwriting
  Office of Research
  Office of Public Liaison
  Office of Intergovernmental Affairs
Office of Media Affairs
Press Secretary
Office of Management and Administration
White House Counsel
National Security Adviser
Office of Legislative Affairs [Congressional Liaison]
Office of Policy Planning
Office of Political Affairs
Office of the Cabinet Secretary
Presidential Personnel
First Lady's Office

Executive Order 8248 envisaged three kinds of staff in the White House Office. One group consisted of the secretaries to the President—those senior presidential staff positions that had existed prior to the Brownlow Report. They were "to facilitate and maintain quick and easy communication with the Congress, the heads of executive departments and agencies, the press, the radio and the general public"—a job description that merely recognized what the post of Secretary to the President had become by the early twentieth century. The second group comprised the institutional support staff in the White House Office and included those, like the Executive Clerk and his assistants, who were responsible for clerical services and the official routines of the presidency. The third category covered the six new administrative assistants that the Brownlow Report had recommended adding to the presidential staff. Their role was described, and circumscribed, in much the same way as it had been in the Brownlow Report, which is not surprising given that Louis Brownlow also drafted Executive Order 8248 for President Roosevelt. The administrative assistants were "to assist the President in such matters as he may direct, and at the specific request of the President, to get information and to condense and summarize it for his use." These positions were clearly intended to be of less importance than the secretaries to the President, and the role prescribed for the administrative assistants in the both the Brownlow Report and the executive order envisioned them as information-gatherers and messengers, but little else.

Those titles have long gone, and the functional distinction between the secretaries to the President and the administrative assistants has been eroded over time. Today, a substantial number of White House Office staff carry senior positions as Assistant, Deputy, or Special Assistant to the President. In fact, the growth of senior positions in the White House Office, and the high salaries that went with them, so disturbed some members of Congress that in 1978 Congress passed the White House Personnel Authorization Act, imposing a ceiling on the number of senior staff a President would be permitted to employ in the White House Office.

The clerical and support staff still remain as a distinct group, largely because they are not considered political appointees (although they are not protected under civil service regulations) and they continue to serve in the White House Office irrespective of who is President. Their number has been declining over the last three decades, however, as successive Presidents have been inclined to bring more of the institutional support services under political direction. Today, the institutional memory of the White House Office resides largely in the offices of the Executive Clerk and the Records Manager, but even their existence as nonpolitical, professional staff is vulnerable to any incoming administration's failure to make the distinction between institutional and personal staff within the White House Office.

One other aspect of Brownlow's blueprint for the White House Office also went unrealized. In proposing the six additional administrative assistants, Brownlow suggested that some might be recruited from executive branch departments, do a tour of duty in the White House Office, and then return to their former assignments. This was analogous to the recruitment method used for staffing the secretariat in the British Cabinet Office—an institution Brownlow much admired and had hoped to imitate, at least in part, in the White House Office.

Presidents have preferred to staff their personal office with loyal, devoted, and highly political individuals who often possess little or no prior experience of Washington.

But the attempt to give the White House Office a professional, career civil-service staff was not to be. Presidents have preferred to staff their personal office with loyal, devoted, and highly political individuals who often possess little or no prior experience of Washington and who see their role as serving the interests of their President rather than satisfying the longer-term concerns of an institutional presidency. The staff in the White House Office are an extension of the President himself. Their appointments are not subject to Senate confirmation (as are a number of senior posts in other EOP units); they do not usually testify before congressional committees; and they are answerable to no one but the President. When the President's term is over, so is theirs. Furthermore, Congress does not normally interfere with the structure and functions of the White House Office, whereas it has shown a remarkable propensity to intervene in the development of the rest of the EOP and to tell the President what staff units he needs to have, or ought not to have, irrespective of his wishes. In that sense, the White House Office is marked off from the other EOP units as a highly personal staff that is subject to congressional scrutiny only in the most exceptional circumstances.

The nature and size of the White House Office have developed far beyond the scope of Executive Order 8248. Successive post-Brownlow Presidents have made the White House Office into a highly responsive, politically powerful, personal staff unit that has become the directing force of the EOP and the hub of the presidential policy-making process. Therein lies its strength. The White House Office extends the reach of the President into the executive branch and Congress, which are not always inclined to respond to presidential leadership and direction without persuasion or pressure. But the intensely personal nature of much of the White House Office is also its institutional weakness. Institutional memory and continuity are at risk each time the presidency changes hands, and the collective lack of experience in a new White House Office can be a potential source of weakness, even damage, in the early days of a new administration. Most staff in the White House Office have to learn while on the job—and learn very quickly. What is surprising is that this institutionally weak body, located at the very center of presidential government, generally performs as well as it does.

[See also (II) Executive Office of the President.]

BIBLIOGRAPHY

Burke, John P. *The Institutional Presidency.* 1992.
Hart, John. *The Presidential Branch.* 1987.
Hess, Stephen. *Organizing the Presidency.* 2d ed. 1988.
Kernell, Samuel, and Samuel L. Popkin. *Chief of Staff: Twenty-five Years of Managing the Presidency.* 1986.
Patterson, Bradley H., Jr. *The Ring of Power: The White House Staff and Its Expanding Role in Government.* 1988.

– JOHN HART

WHITE HOUSE OFFICE OF COMMUNICATIONS

Although the precise structure and jurisdiction of the White House Office of Communications, created by President Richard M. Nixon in 1969, have changed from administration to administration, its functions have remained constant. The office develops long-term public relations planning, coordinates news flow from the entire executive branch, and orchestrates direct appeals to the public through television, radio, town meetings, surrogate speakers, and outreach to local media.

The goal of the Office of Communications is to set the public agenda, to make sure that all parts of the presidential team (the White House staff, Cabinet officers, and other executive-branch officials) adhere to that agenda, and to promote the public agenda through aggressive mass marketing. Communications Office staff use data drawn from focus groups and polls to fashion presidential messages, make sure that the public pronouncements of the President and his underlings contain sound-bites that clearly articulate those messages, choreograph public appearances so that the messages are reinforced by visual images, and enforce the White House viewpoint through the "line of the day," to prevent the articulation of conflicting messages. Technological developments have made such efforts easier. For instance, communications satellites allow the office to target messages to specific media markets in congressional districts where the White House needs support. Similarly, presidential spokespeople around the country can use their personal computers to obtain the line of the day before talking with reporters.

The Office of Communications is primarily proactive, while the Press office is primarily reactive.

The Office of Communications' functions are different from those of the more visible White House Press Office, which is primarily concerned with providing information from the White House itself, not the entire executive branch. Also, the Press Office avoids long-term public relations management, seldom moving beyond disseminating the news of the day and responding to reporters' queries. And rather than targeting local media outlets and engaging in other tactics to circumvent the elite media, the Press Office caters almost exclusively to the needs of the White House press corps. Thus, the Office of Communications is primarily proactive, while the Press Office is primarily reactive. The two offices have often been completely distinct entities, but in the Bill Clinton White House, as during parts of the Gerald Ford and Ronald Reagan administrations, the Press Office has fallen under the jurisdiction of the Office of Communications.

Before the Office of Communications was created, its functions were carried out either in a sporadic, ad hoc manner by the White House Press Secretary or by a few formal structures for coordinating the flow of news from the executive branch. The most notable of these structures was the Committee on Public Information, chaired by George Creel, that was established during World War I. Such structures were short-lived and were almost always created in response to national emergencies.

By the 1960s it was obvious that communications functions needed to be institutionalized through the creation of a permanent office. With the rise of electronic media, Presidents were no longer as dependent on newspaper reporters to convey their messages to the public. Increasingly, Presidents and their surrogates took messages directly to the people in an effort to mold mandates for their policy initiatives. The strategy for increasing presidential power via such appeals is known as "going public." As defined by Samuel Kernell, this understanding of presidential power assumes that the elite bargaining community that implements policy is neither as insulated from public pressure nor as tightly bound together by established norms of elite behavior as it used to be. According to this scenario, policymakers became increasingly susceptible to the influence of public opinion, and the ability to harness or manufacture that opinion became a key to presidential power. This atmosphere created new institutional demands on the White House that were filled by the Office of Communications.

During the earlier years of the Nixon administration, under its first director, Herbert G. Klein, the Office of Communications was a respected, professional operation. During the Watergate affair, however, the office degenerated into a hard-line political operation designed to shore up the image of the embattled President. At times, the office stepped over the line that separates legitimate appeals for public support from illegitimate tactics to induce or fabricate that support through the use of administration-sponsored letters and telegrams, the creation of supposedly independent citizens' committees to praise administration policy, and even threats of Internal Revenue Service investigations and antitrust suits against media organizations that painted the White House in an unfavorable light.

The discredited Office of Communications was significantly cut back when Nixon resigned in 1974, but in 1976, during the Gerald Ford administration, it reemerged as a powerful and professional office under the direction of David Gergen. Jimmy Carter, as part of his effort to create an "open" White House, all but abolished the office in 1977, but he was forced by his sinking approval rating to recreate the office a year later under the direction of Gerald Rafshoon. The office played a major role in the Ronald Reagan administration, especially under the directorships of Gergen, who returned as director of communications in 1981, and of Patrick Buchanan, and it became even more visible in the Clinton White House, largely because of the high profile of Clinton's first communications director, George Stephanopoulos, and the highly publicized restaffing of the office when Gergen unexpectedly joined the Democratic administration as Counselor to the President in June 1993.

Increasingly, the Office of Communications has become an umbrella term for a variety of offices that fall under its jurisdiction. The Press Office, the Planning Office, the Speechwriting Office, the Advance Office, the Public Liaison Office (which handles outreach to special interest groups), the Media Affairs Office (covering outreach to local media), and the Public Affairs Office (serving as liaison with public information officers throughout the executive branch), among others, have all fallen under the purview of the Office of Communications.

[See also (II) Media and the President.]

BIBLIOGRAPHY

Grossman, Michael Baruch, and Martha Joynt Kumar. *Portraying the President.* 1981.

Kernell, Samuel. *Going Public: New Strategies of Presidential Leadership.* 2d ed. 1993.

Maltese, John Anthony. *Spin Control: The White House Office of Communications and the Management of Presidential News.* 1992.

Tulis, Jeffrey K. *The Rhetorical Presidency.* 1987.

– JOHN ANTHONY MALTESE

WHITE HOUSE PRESS SECRETARY

The first White House aide to have press relations as his sole responsibility—the equivalent of being Press Secretary to the President—was George Akerson, who served (not very successfully) from 1929 to 1931 under Herbert Hoover. Presidential press relations, of course, predated the institution of a full-time Press Secretary, and some earlier White House assistants, notably William Loeb during Theodore Roosevelt's administration and Joseph Tumulty during Woodrow Wilson's administration, had been skillful at explaining their Presidents' actions to reporters.

Theodore Roosevelt's administration came before the institution of a full-time Press secretary. Roosevelt used White House assistant William Loeb to explain his actions to reporters. (Library of Congress, Prints and Photographs Division)

The role of the Press Secretary came of age during the administration of Franklin D. Roosevelt; Stephen Early ran Roosevelt's press office. While later changes in the office resulted from new communications technologies and the growth of the White House press corps, the Press Secretary's basic functions remained relatively constant, and included conducting daily briefings for reporters on the White House beat, helping the President prepare for press conferences, handling press arrangements for presidential trips and vacations, responding to reporters' individual requests for interviews and information, and putting out press releases and the texts of presidential speeches and messages.

Strictly speaking, the Press Secretary is not a policy adviser, although the law of propinquity—the power that can emanate from being close to the powerful—has from time to time affected staffers who have occupied the press relations slot. For example, Bill Moyers, Press Secretary to Lyndon Baines Johnson, was one of six officials composing what was known as the Tuesday Cabinet, which held weekly Vietnam War decision-making sessions.

The Press Secretary's domain largely involves the handling of Washington-based reporters, with other media relations handled by other White House offices. The Press Office staff had grown to seventeen by 1991, with three Deputy Press Secretaries, one of whom was in charge of foreign policy issues and also served as the spokesperson for the national security adviser. Junior staff, responsible for turning out press releases, are housed in what is called the Lower Press Office, which is adjacent to the White House Briefing Room. During Richard M. Nixon's first term the White House swimming pool, located between the President's residence and his office in the West Wing, was decked over to create this working area for reporters.

There were eighteen presidential Press Secretaries from Akerson through Marlin Fitzwater, who served under Ronald Reagan and George Bush. All were white males, usually of early middle years. The average age at time of appointment was forty-two; the youngest, Ronald Ziegler, who served under Nixon, was thirty; the oldest, Charles Ross, sixty, died in office during the presidency of Harry S Truman. Half had served as Washington correspondents; five had never been journalists. Interestingly, those whose entire careers had been in journalism were among the least successful Press Secretaries. The most successful, on the other hand, were either very close to the Presidents they served regardless of their previous occupations or had had some previous experience in public affairs or political press relations.

Perhaps the most successful was James Hagerty, who served under Dwight D. Eisenhower. Hagerty had been a *New York Times* reporter, press secretary to a governor of New York, and spokesman for the 1952 Republican presidential campaign. Hagerty is credited with creating new rules for frankness when Eisenhower suffered a heart attack in 1955. For three weeks he held five briefings a day, releasing such intimate details as the number of bowel movements recorded on the President's medical chart. (At the other extreme, press secretaries do not always offer the whole truth; for example, Ronald Reagan's Press Secretary Larry Speakes said that an invasion of Grenada was "preposterous" on the day before the United States invaded that island in 1983.)

At Hagerty's first meeting with White House reporters in 1953, he told them, "When I say to you, 'I don't know,' I mean I don't know. When I say, 'No comment,' it means I'm not talking, but not necessarily any more than that. Aside from that, I'm here to help you get the news. I am also here to work for one man, who happens to be the President. And I will do that to the best of my ability." Being between President and press creates what Walter Wurfel, a Deputy Press Secretary under President Jimmy Carter, has called "the fundamental duality to the role of the White House press secretary." Wurfel wrote that the Press Secretary is "a government official paid by the taxpayers and is responsible for supplying information to the public. On the other hand, he is a political appointee answerable only to the president, and the president views the spokesman's job to be that of putting the most favorable light on his administration." Some of the Press Secretaries who came directly from journalism were the most conflicted by this "fundamental duality." Jerald terHorst, who left the Washington bureau of the *Detroit News* to become Gerald Ford's first Press Secretary, lasted only thirty days, resigning when he could not support Ford's decision to pardon former President Nixon.

Thirty-nine White House reporters, interviewed in the summer of 1991 about their preferences among the Press Secretaries they had known, often mentioned desirable personal and professional qualities. Among the personal qualities they appreciated were friendliness, an unwillingness to embarrass reporters, a sense of humor, and honesty. Professional qualities they admired included an understanding of journalists' needs, a lack of favoritism, and good briefing skills. But overwhelmingly what they wanted in a White House Press Secretary was confidence that what he told them came from an intimate and immediate knowledge of what the President was thinking. They appreciated, for example, the almost father-son relationship between Carter and Press Secretary Jody Powell. Reporters also enjoyed Pierre Salinger's company, but they knew that John F. Kennedy had kept him in the dark in advance of the Bay of Pigs invasion, and they respected George Reedy's intelligence, but they knew that Lyndon Johnson withheld information from him. Ultimately, then, as George Christian, another of Johnson's Press Secretaries, once said, Press Secretaries' "style will be shaped by the Presidents they work for, or they won't be there long."

[See also (II) Media and the President.]

BIBLIOGRAPHY

Hess, Stephen. *The Government/Press Connection: Press Officers and Their Offices.* 1984.

Spragens, William C., with Carole Ann Terwoord. *From Spokesman to Press Secretary: White House Media Operations.* 1980.

Wurfel, Walter. "The White House: Center Stage for Government." In *Informing the People.* Edited by Lewis M. Helm, Ray Eldon Hiebert, Michael R. Naver, and Kenneth Rabin. 1981.

– STEPHEN HESS

PART THREE

Judicial Branch

THE FEDERAL COURT SYSTEM

This essay will examine the growth of the federal judicial system, in particular, the United States district courts, the courts of appeals and the United States Supreme Court, from the Constitutional Convention and the First Congress (1789) to the activities of the Reagan administration and the Ninety-eighth Congress. An examination of the development of the federal judicial system is an examination of controversial political issues pitting federalism and states' rights against each other. From the beginning of the Republic, the issue has been whether there was a justification for the federal judicial system, given the existence of an energetic state court system with a fairly well developed common law in each state. Through political compromise, the federal judiciary was created in 1787 and 1789. After the Civil War and again after the Great Depression there were dramatic expansions of federal judicial power and authority. The essay describes these various periods of growth and stability in the federal judicial system.

Historical Evolution

The evolution of the federal court system to its present jurisdictional and organizational shape and authority is a reflection of the general growth of central powers in a federal system. In the beginning of the Republic, there was dramatic mistrust of the federal judicial system, and from 1789 to 1875, the lower federal courts did not have very much authority. However, after the Civil War, with its clear resolution of the question of an organic versus a compact form of government, the growth of the federal judiciary, like the growth of the federal system generally, was inexorable.

CONSTITUTIONAL CONVENTION OF 1787. Throughout the period of the Articles of Confederation, an active state judiciary and viable state judicial systems provided adjudicative relief for persons with conflicts in need of resolution. Article III of the Constitution of 1787 created a second federal judicial system: "The judicial power of the United States shall be vested in one supreme Court and in such inferior courts as the Congress may from time to time ordain and establish." The creation of this separate federal court system inspired a great deal of contemporary controversy. During the Constitutional Convention in Philadelphia in the summer of 1787, heated debate took place over the necessity for a national court system. According to the noted constitutional historian Charles Warren, Article III was the subject "of more severe criticism and greater apprehension than any other portion of the Constitution."

There were serious concerns, especially among the Antifederalists (later called Jeffersonians) at the Constitutional Convention, that such a federal court system, with its obvious commitment to adjudication as the basic form of conflict resolution in the new social and political system, would dampen efforts that were under way in the states to develop nonlegalistic approaches to conflict resolution. Among Antifederalists, the legal profession was not the most popular vocation and the lawyer was not seen as the best or only person to act energetically to resolve conflicts in the community. Furthermore, as states'-rights advocates, they favored decentralized government, shorter tenure for judges, and an easier removal process and so were extremely concerned about the "monstrous appearance" of a new system of federal courts. Such a federal court system, even though its exact parameters were not worked out in 1787, was a manifest threat to those at the Constitutional Convention who believed in the dominance of state power in the new system of government. The Antifederalists felt that the state courts could continue the business of dispensing justice under the watchful eyes of the local populations. Luther Martin, one of the delegates opposed to the creation of the federal court system, said that the creation of these federal courts "would create jealousies and oppositions in the state tribunals with the jurisdiction of which they will interfere."

The Antifederalists felt that the state courts could continue dispensing justice under the watchful eyes of the local populations.

At the Constitutional Convention, the Antifederalists were opposed by the Federalists, or Hamiltonians, who believed that a strong, central government and a national commercial economy—with a strong federal judicial system to enforce the national government's rulings—were important for the continued viability of the new nation. The nationalists argued that the success of the new political system, federalism, "depended on the existence of a supreme national tribunal, free from local bias or prejudice, vested with power to give an interpretation to Federal laws and treaties which should be uniform throughout the land . . . and to control State aggression on the Federal domain" (Warren, vol. 1, 9). The Federalists did not trust the state courts to act objectively regarding property issues that would come into the court involving citizens of the local community. Said Warren, "The Courts of the states cannot be trusted with the administration of the national laws. The objects of jurisdiction are such as will often place the general and local policy at variance."

The 1787 Constitution finally incorporated two articles that attempted to satisfy both Federalists and Antifederalists: Article III vests "the judicial power . . . in one supreme Court, and in such inferior courts as the Congress may from time to time ordain and establish," and Article VI contains the supremacy clause, which states that the Constitution and the federal laws and treaties are the "supreme Law of the Land" and that "the judges in every state shall be bound thereby, any thing in the Constitution or laws of any state to the contrary notwithstanding." In the end the general concept of a federal, or national, court system was accepted in 1787–1788; it would be for the new national legislature to develop the specifics of the new court system.

JUDICIARY ACT OF 1789. To the First Congress, meeting in 1789, was given the delicate task of determining the composition of the Supreme Court, erecting those inferior federal courts referred to in Article III, and establishing the jurisdiction of the Supreme Court and the inferior federal courts because, as a check on federal judicial power, Article III gave the Congress the power to limit the appellate jurisdiction of these federal courts. The fundamental differences of opinion between the Antifederalists and the Federalists that had existed in 1787 came out sharply during the debates from April to September 1789. Out of this intensely partisan discussion emerged the Judiciary Act of 1789.

For the Antifederalist legislator of 1789, such as James Jackson of Georgia, the creation of a federal court system "swallows up every shadow of a state judiciary." But, for the Federalist, such as Roger Sherman of Connecticut, "it is necessary that the National tribunal possess the power of protecting those [federally developed] rights from such [state court] invasion." Two basic questions were addressed by the national legislators in the First Congress: Should inferior federal courts be created at all? If so, should there be narrow jurisdictional limits so that federal courts will not "swallow up" the state court systems?

Two politically astute legislators, Oliver Ellsworth of Connecticut and William Patterson of New Jersey, led

George Washington presides over debate at the 1787 Constitutional Convention in Philadelphia. Delegates argued such concerns as the need for a national court system balanced against their desire for decentralized government. (Library of Congress/Corbis)

the fight in the First Congress for the creation of a federal court system. Political compromise ensued in the Congress, and the result was a federal court system that was structurally acceptable to the Federalists and functionally tolerable to the Antifederalists. Section 34 of the 1789 Judiciary Act was a basic restriction on the new federal courts' jurisdiction. It stated that the laws of the states "shall be regarded as rules of decision in trials at common law in the courts of the United States in cases where they apply." In effect, this meant that the state common law controlled the decisions of the federal courts in all cases except those involving "federal questions." State law controlled the actions of federal judges in cases heard in federal district courts, primarily diversity and maritime litigation. Furthermore, "federal question" jurisdiction—that is, the judicial power to hear cases involving clashes between a federal statute and a state law—was left with state courts in the first instance. While the Supreme Court could review these state actions, as is evident from Section 25 of the 1789 Judiciary Act and *Cohens* v. *Virginia* (1821), lower federal courts did not have jurisdiction to hear these types of cases until 1875. And, in 1793, Congress passed legislation that barred the new federal courts from enjoining proceedings in the state courts. This was a major bar to federal judicial power until the post-Civil War congressional statutes gave power to the three-judge federal district courts to remove certain civil rights cases from state courts.

The system of inferior federal trial courts established at that time placed severe restrictions on the jurisdiction of those courts. Although the federal trial courts, called United States district courts, were created to hear cases and controversies, the federal judges had to apply state law, the boundaries of the district courts followed state lines, the federal district court judges were given very limited jurisdiction by the First Congress, and the federal judges who would sit on these trial benches would be nominated by the president but the chief executive's selections would have to receive the advice and consent of the United States Senate.

As passed by the Congress, the Judiciary Act of 1789 established the structure of the federal court system that still exists today. There were thirteen federal district courts created by Congress in the 1789 legislation, with a federal district court judge assigned to each district. There was one federal district court in each of the eleven states in the federal Union at that time. Two other district courts were placed in Maine, then a part of Massachusetts, and in Kentucky, then still part of Virginia. (North Carolina and Rhode Island, after they ratified the Constitution, each received a federal district court and judge.)

Additionally, the Congress created three federal circuit courts—the southern, middle, and the eastern circuits. There were, however, no permanent circuit court federal judges. Instead, two justices of the United States Supreme Court and one judge from a federal district court would ride circuit to hear appeals from the district courts. The Congress also determined that the Supreme Court, the only federal court specifically mentioned in the Constitution, would have one chief justice of the United States and five associate justices.

A removal act allows defendants in state courts to request a removal of their case from the state to the local federal district court.

Finally, much of the Judicary Act's language focused on congressional development of the appellate power of the federal courts. For example, Section 25 of the 1789 act gave the United States Supreme Court the jurisdiction to review, on writ of error, certain actions of the state supreme courts that involved federal questions. This section was very controversial and led to a number of interesting Supreme Court opinions, notably *Martin* v. *Hunter's Lessee* (1816) and *Cohens* v. *Virginia* (1821). Section 13 of the 1789 statute led to the famous case of *Marbury* v. *Madison* (1803).

ORGANIZATIONAL DEVELOPMENT, 1789–1891. By 1791, Federalists in Congress had begun attempts to expand the organization and the power of the federal court system. In 1799 the Federalists introduced legislation, passed and signed into law by Federalist President John Adams in February 1801. In addition to expanding the jurisdiction of the federal courts, the Judiciary Act of 1801 eliminated the burdensome circuit-riding responsibilities of the Supreme Court justices, created six circuit courts of appeals, and created sixteen federal circuit court judges to sit permanently on these newly created circuit courts.

However, as soon as the new Antifederalist President Thomas Jefferson took office in 1801, along with a Jeffersonian-Republican Congress, that body passed the Circuit Court Act of 1802, which effectively repealed the 1801 Federalist legislation. Jefferson's repeal argument was simple and political: "The Federalists have retired into the Judiciary as a stronghold . . . and from that battery all the works of republicanism are to be beaten down and erased." In 1803 the solidly Federalist Supreme Court, with Chief Justice John Marshall writing the opinion in *Stuart* v. *Laird,* validated the 1802 repeal statute. Charles Warren commented of this opinion that "no more striking example of the nonpartisanship of the American Judiciary can be found than this decision by a Court composed wholly of Federalists, upholding, contrary to its personal and political views, a detested Republican measure." It was also, however, the better part of wisdom for the outgunned Federalist judges to withdraw from this battle; the Republicans were on the ascendancy politically and it would have been political suicide for the Federalist judges to have fought the Republicans on that issue.

Franklin D. Roosevelt would ultimately appoint a total of nine men to the Supreme Court.

With the validation of the 1802 repeal act, no further change in the structure of the federal court system occurred until 1891. Periodically, bills were introduced in Congress to change the organization of the federal court system. Essentially, these changes revolved around concepts of a viable intermediate federal court of appeals with permanent sitting federal judges given substantive jurisdiction to hear cases and controversies and thereby reduce the reviewing burden of the Supreme Court. Friedman notes, "In Congress, a strong states-rights bloc was hostile to the federal courts. . . . Again and again, reform proposals became entangled in sectional battles or battles between Congress and the President, and went down to defeat" (p. 126).

The Removal Act of 3 March 1875 was the first major breakthrough in the nationalists' efforts to give more power and responsibility to the federal court system. A removal act enables defendants in state courts to request a removal of their conflict from the state court into the local federal district court. Earlier removal act legislation had, in Warren's words, been introduced "out of a fear of prejudice in state courts against the national government." The successful 1875 Removal Act accomplished the following: Any action asserting a federal right could begin in a federal district court or, if begun in a state court, could be removed through a writ of habeas corpus to the federal courts. Functionally, after 1875, the federal courts took on a new, vastly important role in the federal system. Organizationally, however, it was not until 1891 that legislation was passed creating the new intermediate appellate courts with permanent sitting federal judges presiding over the appeals process.

Friedman has stated that the creation of the federal court of appeals was the outcome of "one of the most enduring political struggles in American political history." By 1890 the Supreme Court had a docket of over eighteen hundred cases. (By contrast, the Supreme Court's case load in 1950 was less than fifteen hundred cases.) The Court's case load was high because in the absence of an intermediate federal appellate court system, it had to hear all appeals from the district courts. As a result of this case-load problem, the nationalists prevailed in Congress and legislation was passed creating nine new intermediary federal circuit courts of appeals. Each of these new courts would have three federal judges sitting permanently on these appeal courts. Under the legislation passed in 1891, most appeals from the federal trial courts (the district courts) would end in these courts, subject to discretionary review by the Supreme Court.

ORGANIZATIONAL DEVELOPMENT, 1891–1937. In 1903 the three-judge United States district court was created by Congress to hear the Interstate Commerce Commission or Sherman Antitrust Act cases on appeal. All cases involving violations of this substantive legislation were to be heard by the special district court—made up of two court of appeals judges and one judge from the district court in that area—with appeals as of right directly to the Supreme Court. In 1910 the Mann-Elkins Act empowered these courts to hear cases brought by private individuals involving the constitutionality of state or federal statutes and to issue injunctions to prevent enforcement of these challenged statutes. In the 1960s these three-judge courts would play an important role in the resolution of civil rights clashes in the South.

Prior to 1960 these three-judge district court hearings were a rarity. However, civil rights litigation groups such as the National Association for the Advancement of Colored People (NAACP) began using these courts to remove hard cases from state courts. In 1956 there were 50 three-judge district court hearings; in 1976, there were 208 cases heard in these courts, including 161 civil rights cases. Given criticism of the use of these courts, Congress, in 1976, passed legislation that greatly restricted the use of these three-judge district courts, to lighten the burden of the federal judges. Additionally, during the early years of the Burger Court, the Supreme Court justices themselves took action to limit the activities of the three-judge district court, as in *Younger* v. *Harris* (1971). By 1983 the number of three-judge district court cases had dropped to a low of 27 cases.

By 1911, with passage by Congress of the Judicial Code, the basic contours of the federal system were established. There were the federal trial courts (the district courts), the intermediate-level appellate courts (the courts of appeals), and the Supreme Court. In 1925, Congress passed the Judge's Act. Prodded by the national organized bar and Chief Justice William Howard Taft, the national legislature, in a purely Hamiltonian move, expanded the jurisdiction of the federal courts, especially the Supreme Court, and dramatically improved the administration of a very decentralized federal court system. Congress accomplished this by authorizing the Supreme Court to have total control of its appellate docket by allowing the Court to use its certiorari power in a purely discretionary manner. With this very important change, the Court has had broad discretion to decide which cases it will resolve on the merits. In addition, the chief justice was allowed to assign federal judges to temporary duty anywhere in the federal court system, and he could create the Conference of Senior Circuit Judges (later called the Judicial Conference), which would meet annually in Washington, D.C., to discuss common federal court problems.

ROOSEVELT'S COURT-PACKING PLAN. When Franklin D. Roosevelt became president in 1933, he confronted a Supreme Court of nine elderly justices. Characteristically conservative (Chief Justice Taft had derisively referred to President Herbert Hoover as a "bolsheviki"), the federal justices on the High Bench did not like Roosevelt's energetic brand of governing. This was especially true of a handful of the justices known as the "Four Horsemen"—Justices Willis Van Devanter, James C. McReynolds, George Sutherland, and Pierce Butler. These "direct descendents of Darwin and Spencer," according to Henry Abraham, "were totally antagonistic to the New Deal, and they could usually count on support in their antagonism from Justice [Owen] Roberts and Chief Justice [Charles E.] Hughes."

By 1937 the Supreme Court, led by the Four Horsemen, had struck down over a dozen major pieces of New Deal legislation. Roosevelt was extremely frustrated because of these judicial actions and because he had not yet had a single occasion to select his first justice to sit on the Court. Consequently, on 5 February 1937, President Roosevelt sent to Capitol Hill his plan to enlarge the Supreme Court. His plan was simple: for every justice over seventy years of age who had served ten years on the federal bench and who had failed to retire within six months after reaching his seventieth birthday, the president would be allowed to appoint a new federal judge, up to a maximum of fifty such appointments in the entire federal court system and fifteen on the Supreme Court.

The public justification for the plan was that the elderly men on the High Court needed the assistance of younger jurists to reduce the burdens on these federal courts. If successful, the Roosevelt plan would have given the president six new Supreme Court seats to fill. It would have given the country a new Court, a Court that would not invalidate New Deal legislation. Indignant letters from Chief Justice Charles Evans Hughes and Justice Louis D. Brandeis to influential senators helped kill the legislation in the Senate.

However, two critical events made such a draconian change of the federal court system unnecessary. First, two of the justices who had voted with the Four Horsemen, Hughes and Owen J. Roberts, switched their votes in key New Deal cases, thereby validating these controversial measures, notably in *West Coast Hotel* v. *Parrish* (1937) and *National Labor Relations Board* v. *Jones & Loughlin Steel Corp.* (1937). Second, in May 1937, the oldest of the Four Horsemen, Justice Van Devanter, announced his retirement effective 1 June 1937. Roosevelt's first appointee was a loyal New Deal legislator, Senator Hugo L. Black, a Democrat from Alabama. Roosevelt would ultimately appoint a total of nine men to the Supreme Court. As a consequence of vote switches, retirements, and death, Roosevelt did not have to push through his "organizational" reform of the federal system.

GROWTH OF THE SYSTEM AFTER 1939. The case load of the federal court system has increased dramatically in the years since the New Deal. Another section will examine the reasons for the growth of this case load; for now, it is enough to note its existence and to examine the response by Congress to these new developments. Ideally, in an adjudicative conflict resolution environment, "a litigant should have his case heard and decided within a reasonable time by an unhurried, highly qualified judicial officer" (Comment).

The reality of the federal court system is that since the Roosevelt administration, it has moved away from a purely deliberative, and toward a bureaucratic, response to increased litigation pleadings. As a recent United States Department of Justice Commission on the Revision of the Federal Judicial System report entitled *Needs of the Federal Courts* (1977) indicated, "We are creating a workload that is even now changing the nature of Courts, threatening to convert them from deliberative institutions to processing institutions, from a judiciary to a bureaucracy."

ADMINISTRATIVE OFFICE OF THE UNITED STATES COURTS. In 1939, at the behest of the Judicial Conference, the Administrative Office of the United States Courts was created by the Congress. The basic function of the office, reflecting this growing federal court system tendency toward "bureaucratization," was to collect statistics on the case load and related judicial activities of the federal courts. Its director was charged with the responsibility for issuing *Management Statistics for United States Courts for the Chief Justice of the United States.*

This annual report provides the federal judges and the federal judicial administrators with extremely useful data to be used to deal with problems associated with the rise of the case load.

OFFICE OF UNITED STATES MAGISTRATES. In 1961 the case load for the district court judges across America totaled 98,000 criminal and civil filings. By 1976 the total number of filings was almost double the 1961 figure: 171,000 filings. One congressional response to this dilemma, which forced courts to choose between careful and efficient justice, was to free up the federal district court judge by providing relief in the form of better use of the United States magistrate.

In 1968, Congress passed the Federal Magistrate Act, which formally established the office of United States magistrate. According to Steven Puro, the office was created to "provide a first new echelon of judicial officers in the federal judicial system and to alleviate the increased work load of U.S. District Courts." Magistrates, appointed and supervised by the federal district court judges, relieve the federal judges of certain routine duties. Consequently, the federal judges are free to hear and monitor the cases that go to trial, while magistrates handle the various pretrial activities in both civil and criminal filings. Rather than enlarging the federal court system with another layer of federal courts, the 1968 legislation attempted to ease the work-load problem by enabling federal judges to get away from performance of purely administrative functions.

In 1996 over 500 full- and part-time magistrates served in the federal court system. The magistrate performs certain pretrial and posttrial functions in civil and criminal cases. These duties are ministerial (taking depositions, administering oaths), advisory, adjudicative, and quasi-judicial (hearing petty offenses cases, issuing search warrants, receiving prisoner petitions, disposing of motions, conducting postindictment arraignments). Magistrates must be members of the state bar; they are appointed by the federal judges in the United States district court for an eight-year term during which they can only be removed for "good cause."

A NATIONAL COURT OF APPEALS. As the case load handled by the judges in the federal court system increased in the middle decades of the twentieth century, there were increased demands by federal judges and others for organizational changes and substantive modifications in federal appellate court jurisdiction to parallel the kind of assistance the trial court judges of the federal court system received with the creation of the office of United States magistrate. In the 1960s and 1970s, renewed concern over the increased work load of the appellate federal judges, especially the United States Supreme Court justices, led to a debate over the creation of another federal court that would be situated, organizationally, between the federal courts of appeals and the Supreme Court.

There are over 26 million cases that are initiated annually in the fifty state court systems.

In December 1972 a seven-person panel appointed by Chief Justice Warren Burger, an advocate of some kind of plan to relieve the justices of the work-load dilemma, presented its findings. In arguments reminiscent of the nineteenth-century arguments for a federal court of appeals, the *Federal Judicial Center Report of the Study Group on the Case Load of the Supreme Court,* chaired by Professor Paul A. Freund (the report is commonly referred to as the *Freund Report*), said that "relief is imperative" and called for the creation of a new tribunal, a national court of appeals, to ease the work load of the Supreme Court. The *Freund Report* envisioned a special appellate court, composed of seven United States court of appeals judges sitting in Washington, D.C., for (staggered) three-year terms, that would receive all cases (except original jurisdiction pleadings) presently petitioned to the United States Supreme Court. It recommended that this seven-judge appellate court "screen all petitions . . . and hear and decide on the merits of many cases of conflicts between circuits. . . . The great majority . . . would be finally decided by that court. Several hundred would be certified annually to the Supreme Court for further screening and choice of cases to be heard and adjudicated there."

Once certified to the Supreme Court, the justices would use their discretionary powers to grant, to dismiss, or to deny. In addition, the report recommended that the Supreme Court be given the power to "make rules governing the practice in the National Court of Appeals." By mid-1975, five of the nine Supreme Court justices had indicated their support for the Freund plan—the four Nixon appointees (Chief Justice Burger, Justices Harry A. Blackmun, Lewis F. Powell, and William H. Rehnquist) and Justice White.

In 1975 a report was published by the Commission on Revision of Federal Court Appellate System, chaired by United States Senator Roman Hruska. It, too, recommended that a national court of appeals be created, but its vision of the relationship between the Supreme Court and the national court of appeals differed radically from the Freund committee's vision. The Hruska Commission urged that the new court "furnish additional authoritative decisions on issues of national law through the adjudication of cases referred to it by the Supreme Court."

Neither report was enthusiastically received. Supreme Court justices such as William O. Douglas, Potter Stewart, and William J. Brennan were highly critical. Douglas' response to these proposals: "It's about a four-day-a-week job." Stewart's comment was that "the very heavy caseload is neither intolerable nor impossible to handle." Other constitutional scholars pointed out that the concept of a national court of appeals, if implemented, would take away the Supreme Court's critically important power to review, to select the cases it wished to hear, and to decide them definitively as the final court of the federal system.

As a consequence of these criticisms, those who have been calling for an easing of the work load of the appellate courts, especially the Supreme Court's work load, including Justices White, Stevens, and Blackmun, have refocused their lobbying efforts in two directions. First is remedial legislation that would, in Chief Justice Burger's language, "reduce the load on nine mortal justices," including Burger's recommendation that the three-judge federal district courts be eliminated entirely by Congress. Second is a narrowing of the jurisdictional doors of the appellate process to litigants, which, according to Burger, could be done by eliminating the abolition of the federal courts' diversity of citizenship jurisdiction.

In December 1978, in an opinion attached to a Supreme Court denial of certiorari, in the case of *Brown Transport* v. *Atcom* (1978), Chief Justice Burger pointed out that the Court was "accepting more cases for plenary review than [we] can cope with in the manner they deserve." Burger, in his opinion, called for a national reexamination of the Freund Committee recommendations. Referring to the fact that there were additional judgeships created recently, Burger concluded by stating that they "may solve short-term problems, but the long-term problems of the Supreme Court analyzed by the Freund committee . . . remain as they were a decade ago." In his *Brown* dissent, Justice White noted omi-

Chief Justice Warren Burger swears in President Richard M. Nixon on January 20, 1973. Nixon's second term brought on many difficult challenges to America's legal system and ended in his resignation in 1974. (Library of Congress/Corbis)

nously "There is grave doubt that the appellate system has the capacity to function in the manner contemplated by the Constitution." Justice Brennan, however, in that same case, indicated that he was "completely unpersuaded . . . that there is any need for a new National Court."

Organizational changes in the federal court system will continue to take place. The debate does not have the same sharpness of focus that the Jeffersonians and Hamiltonians brought to the Congress about the role and function of the federal judiciary. There is an acceptance of the important role of the federal court system in the larger society. The discussion surrounding the creation of a national court of appeals centers around the need for such a body and the effect it might have in eroding the discretionary power of the Court.

Contemporary Federal Court System

Since the Roosevelt New Deal, we live in the age of the Leviathan. Consequently, the federal courts have expanded to deal with the litigation that has developed as a consequence of new responsibilities that the central government has taken since 1933. More than 300,000 cases are heard annually in the federal judicial system, involving constitutional issues as well as commercial ones. The case load per judge in the federal district court has increased to over 508 per judge in the 94 district courts and the Supreme Court receives over 5,000 petitions annually. There is clearly a dramatic growth in the federal judicial case load. However, to place matters in perspective, there are over 26 million cases that are initiated annually in the fifty state court systems. Thus, while the federal judicial personnel are struggling to deal with the increased case load, the state judicial personnel are still, much as in 1789, handling the bulk of the litigation in the federal system.

The federal court system in the 1980s (Fig. 1) is essentially the same one envisioned by the Federalists in 1787. There are the trial courts, an intermediate layer of appellate courts, and the Supreme Court. In addition, over the past century a small number of specialized, Article I federal courts, such as the Tax Court, the Court of Military Appeals, the Court of Claims, and the Court of Customs and Patent Appeals, have been created by Congress to handle special kinds of controversies that arise in America.

PROCESS IN THE FEDERAL COURTS. An overview of the legal process in the federal court system (Fig. 2) emphasizes the point that adjudication in the system is essentially a time-consuming, procedural flow from trial court to appeal court. Most civil and criminal cases are settled prior to the formal trial, but most of the remaining transactions end at the trial level. The remaining sections will focus on the process in each of the three Article III courts in the federal court system: the district courts, the courts of appeal, and the Supreme Court.

THE FEDERAL DISTRICT COURT AS AN ORGANIZATION. Federal district courts have become organizations that administer justice in a bureaucratic manner. This change from pure adjudication to "jurocracy" has led many people to review the process in an effort to return to the judicial process. The difficulty lies with the case load that the federal district courts have had to shoulder since the end of World War II. Jack Weinstein, a federal district court judge, summarized the development of the problem: "As the law has become more compassionate and the guarantees of equality and due process have begun to be realized, the quantitative problems of the courts have increased. The increased load on the courts because of the fact that we are doing more than merely paying lip service to the Constitution and our democratic ideals is great" (p. 145).

Because of the renewed legal emphasis by the Warren Court on "fundamental fairness" and on "equal protection of the laws" and because of the character of federal legislation that has created the additional load (that is, statutes creating civil rights and legislation providing more social and remedial-type legislation, with judicial review sections built into these statutes), the federal judge has become, in effect, a managing partner in a small law firm. On average, filings for district court judges were 77 in 1964 but almost 200 in 1980. In 1958, the staff-judge ratio in federal district courts was 11-1; by 1982, it had risen to 17-1.

In the federal district court, there exists an organized network of relationships centering about the federal judge. The judge has, minimally, two secretaries, two law clerks, a docket clerk, a court reporter, and several United States magistrates and probation officers as intimate support mechanisms in the effort to administer justice. In addition, in each district court system there is the office of the United States attorney, a chief clerk, private counsel (officers of the court), bailiffs, United States marshalls, and others.

THE DISTRICT COURT JUDGE. The federal district court judge is the trial judge in the federal court system. The judge is also responsible for making that small federal court system function effectively. As Flanders and Sager put it, "the responsibility of the judge is to be superintendent of the production of justice" in the courtroom environment. Judicial bureaucratization occurs because the federal district court judge has begun to perform a great many administrative functions in addition to the judicial function.

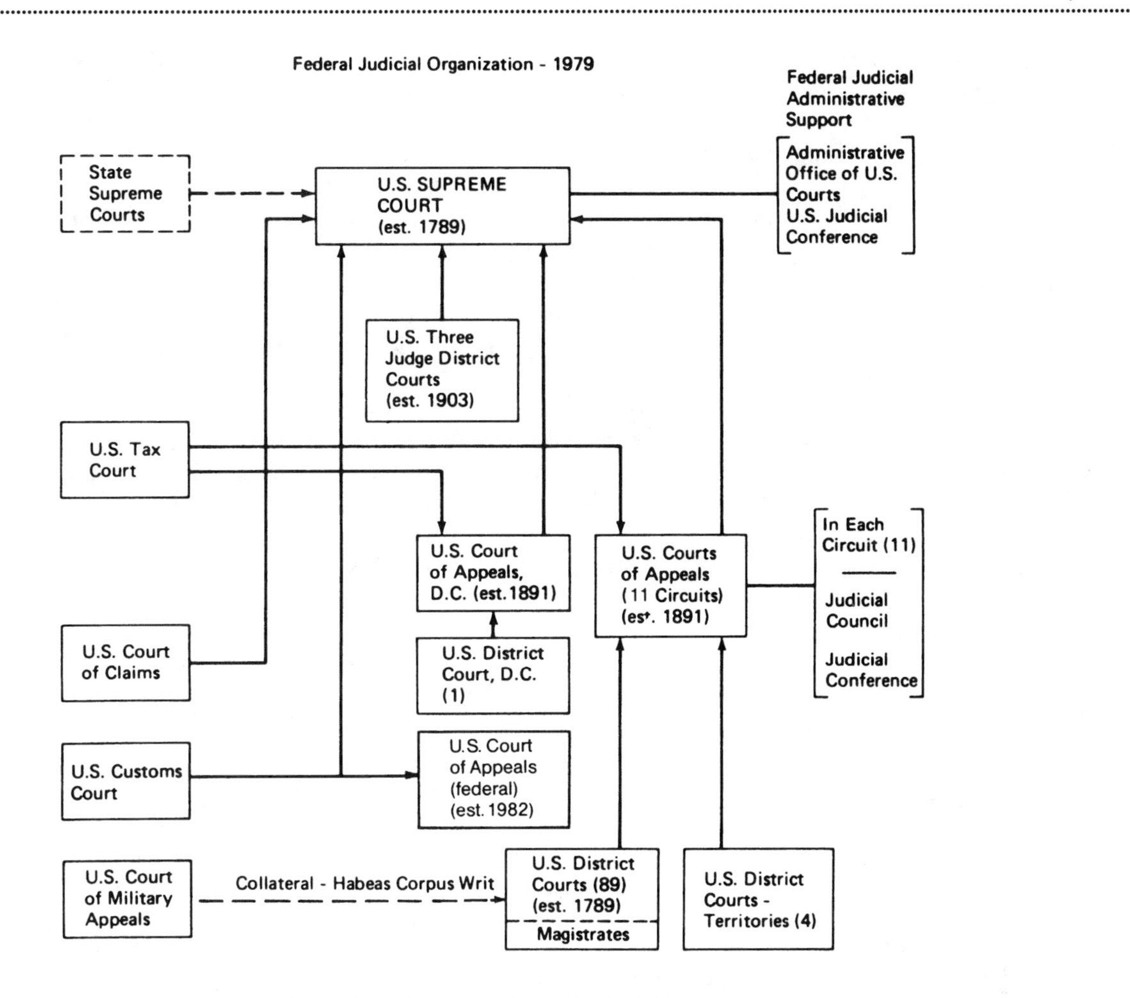

Figure 1: Federal Court System in the 1980s.

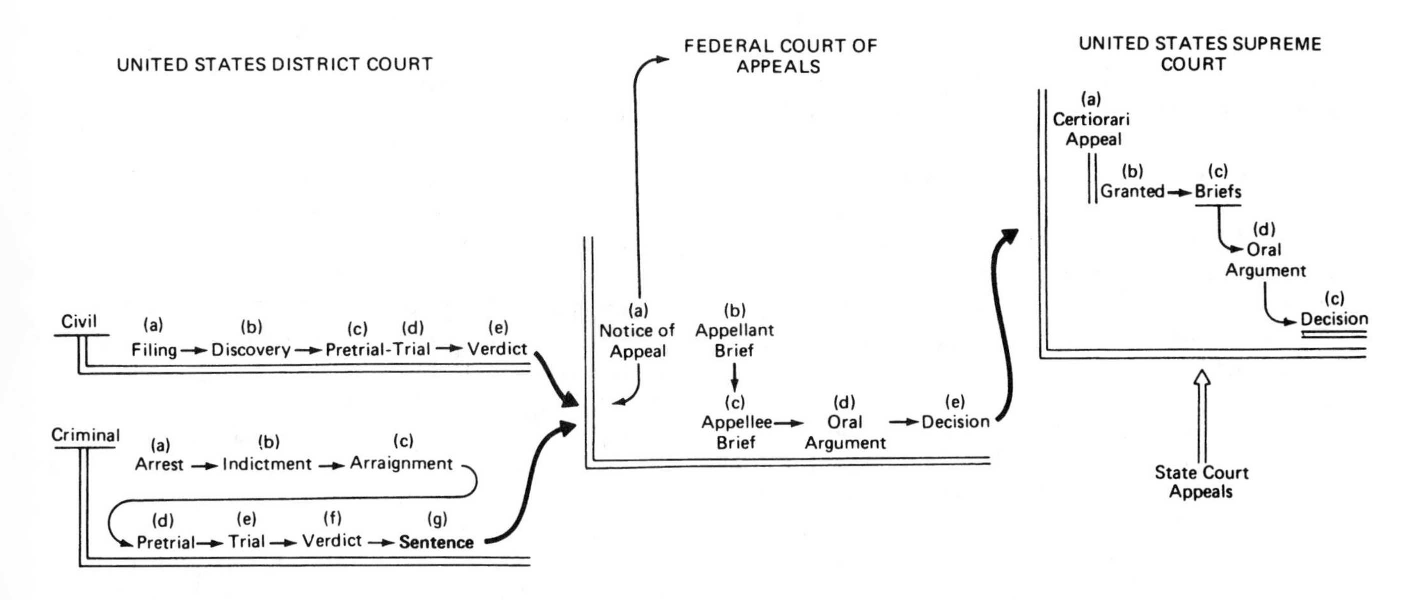

Figure 2: Federal Judicial Process from Trial to Final Appellate Review.

As trial judge, the district court judge occasionally has to judge in an emotionally charged trial atmosphere. In sharp contrast to the serenity of the federal appellate courts, the federal trial judge must make instantaneous decisions on points of law during the trial itself. Most of the district court judge's judicial career is spent enforcing technical, procedural, and legal rules about which there is little disagreement. Even a policy-oriented district court judge spends a great deal of time issuing rulings on motions brought to him by attorneys involved in the litigation.

The trial judge must know the rules of federal civil and criminal procedure, as interpreted by the court of appeals and by the Supreme Court, and must also control the trial-court flow and personnel so that things get done in the organization. In this regard, the trial judge is assisted by major sets of subordinates: personal law clerks, court clerk, United States magistrate, United States attorneys, and private counsel.

The Federal Rules of Civil Procedure were developed by Congress to assist the parties in a civil suit in federal court.

At least two law clerks work for each federal district court judge. These young men and women assist the federal judge by working with the judge on legal briefs and requests for motions. The court clerk, appointed by the federal judge, is responsible for case management in the courtroom. The clerk maintains the judge's calendar and handles scheduling communications with the attorneys. In sum, the clerk is responsible for making sure that the basic court operations run smoothly and that things happen in the trial court when they are supposed to happen. The magistrates relieve the judge of administrative chores such as dealing with pretrial motions and prisoner petitions and trying minor cases. The United States attorney is responsible for prosecuting defendants in these district court trial proceedings, while the defense attorneys provide the legal counsel for those charged with violation of federal civil or criminal statutes.

CASE FLOW IN THE DISTRICT COURTS. Over 300,000 cases are filed annually in the federal district courts; these filings have increased by as much as 10 percent annually in recent years. There are essentially two broad types of cases that make up the work docket of the federal trial judges: private cases involving tort liability suits and diversity of citizenship; and public cases in which the United States attorney initiates criminal actions against individuals or in which the federal government is a defendant in a civil proceeding.

CIVIL CASE FLOW. As noted in Figure 3, the civil process begins in federal trial court with a plaintiff filing a complaint against the defendant. In 1938 the Federal Rules of Civil Procedure were developed by Congress to assist the parties in a civil suit in federal court. Two very important elements in this process are discovery and the pretrial conference. The former practice, carried on extensively under the guidance of the United States magistrate, allows both parties to a dispute to engage in a thorough review of the facts and an examination of the witnesses in order to find out the dimensions of the controversy. The pretrial conference between the judge (or the magistrate in many cases) and both parties to the dispute is carried on with the hope that out-of-court settlement will result. Most civil suits (90 percent nationally) are settled without going to trial.

CRIMINAL CASE FLOW. The criminal-suit case flow was streamlined by virtue of congressional passage of the Speedy Trial Act of 1973. Criminal cases seldom reach the trial stage; generally, there is either dismissal of charges or a guilty plea through the mechanism of plea bargaining. Fewer than 10 percent of the criminal prosecutions initiated in the federal trial courts ever get to the trial stage. Figure 4 highlights the process since the passage of the 1973 legislation.

The 1973 federal law calls for the commencement of trial in criminal proceedings no more than one hundred days after the arrest. Between arrest and trial, there is the indictment phase, wherein the grand jury finds probable cause that a defendant has committed the act. This is followed by the arraignment phase, wherein the defendant formally responds, in the federal court, to the charges against the person. Within ten days there is a pretrial hearing, where the lawyers review the charges and evidence and attempt to settle the case prior to formal trial. If the charges have not been dismissed and if there has not been a successful plea bargaining, then the criminal case goes to trial before the federal district court judge.

APPEALS OF DISTRICT COURT JUDGMENTS. Federal law provides persons with the opportunity to appeal final decisions of the federal district courts to the United States courts of appeals. In addition, the federal courts of appeals hear appeals from federal administrative-agency or commission judgments. These intermediate appellate courts are required to hear all appeals brought to them from the federal trial courts, although the judges do not devote equal time to all cases. Every case that comes into the court of appeals from the trial courts or from the federal agencies is an attempt to, in the

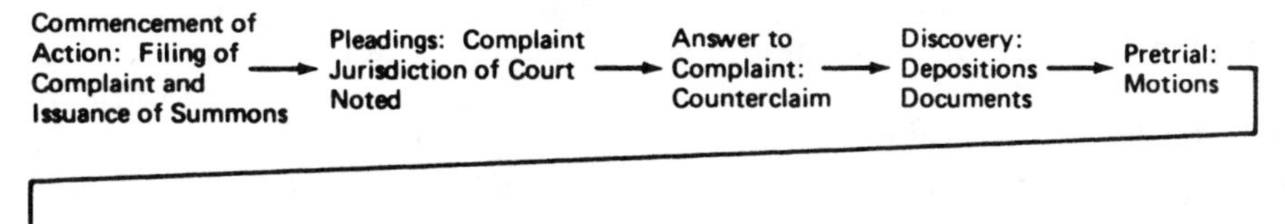

Figure 3: United States District Court: Civil Case Flow.

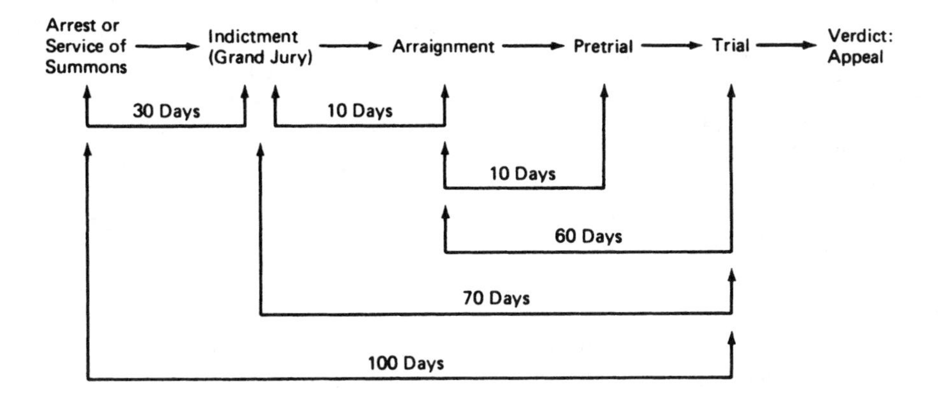

Figure 4: United States District Court: Criminal Case Flow.

words of Richardson and Vines, "undo a previous judicial or administrative determination" (p. 115). Generally, less than 4 percent of the federal trial court judgments are appealed to the federal courts of appeals; most of the courts of appeals judgments end at that level.

THE COURT OF APPEALS AS AN ORGANIZATION. Each of the courts of appeals, covering the entire federal system, including those lands that are the nation's territorial responsibility, consists of a number of judges who do most of their work in panels of three judges randomly selected by the chief judge of the circuit. The First Circuit has four judges and meets in Boston. The Second has eleven jurists and meets in New York. The Third has ten and meets in Philadelphia. The Fourth has ten and meets in Richmond, Virginia, and Asheville, North Carolina. The redrawn Fifth has fourteen and meets in New Orleans; Fort Worth, Texas; and Jackson, Mississippi. The Sixth has eleven judges and meets in Cincinnati, Ohio. The Seventh has nine judges and meets in Chicago. The Eighth has nine judges and convenes in Saint Louis, Missouri; Kansas City, Missouri; Omaha, Nebraska; and Saint Paul, Minnesota. The Ninth Circuit has twenty-three judges and meets in San Francisco and Los Angeles; Portland, Oregon; and Seattle, Washington. The Tenth has eight judges and convenes sessions in Denver; Wichita, Kansas; and Oklahoma City, Oklahoma. The new Eleventh Circuit has twelve jurists and meets in Atlanta; Jacksonville, Florida; and Montgomery, Alabama. In addition, there is the District of Columbia Circuit, with eleven judges, which meets in Washington, D.C., and the new Federal Circuit, with twelve judges, which meets in the District of Columbia and "in any other place listed above as the court by rule directs."

Each court of appeals, as a small organization, has its support staff to assist these judicial panels. Included in the support picture are the court clerk and the clerk's staff assistants, the law clerks that each federal appeals judge brings into the judge's chambers to assist the judge with case preparation (at least two for each federal judge and three for the chief judge of a circuit), librarians, bailiffs, messengers, criers, marshalls, United States attorneys, and the private counsel, considered officers of the court. A recent personnel addition to the federal courts of appeal support staff reflects the growing "bureaucratization" of the federal courts: each chief judge of a circuit court of appeals may appoint a senior staff attorney as well as a senior technical assistant to further assist the court in the management of the case flow in the federal courts of appeals.

The chief judge of each circuit is a senior judge, which means a judge who is at least sixty-four years of age, has served at least one year in a circuit court role, and has not previously been a chief judge. He presides at en banc sessions of the circuit court and is responsible for the administration of the circuit's legal responsibilities. In addition, he plays a major role in the assignment of the other federal judges in the circuit to the three-judge panels, which hear the vast majority of appeals. The court, through the judgment of the chief judge, authorizes "the hearing and determination of cases and controversies by separate panels, each consisting of three judges."

CASE FLOW IN COURTS OF APPEALS. In 1940 the courts of appeals received 3,446 filings; in 1964 the filings rose to 6,000; in 1984 there were 28,000 appeals taken to the courts of appeals. In addition to the quantitative increase that has confronted federal court of appeals judges, there are the qualitative differences. Many of these appeals to the federal appellate court are highly complex cases that, unlike the one- or two-issue appeals of the 1940s, involve dozens of legal issues.

While judges have been added to the courts of appeals and the size and number of courts have increased to deal with the increased case flow into the federal courts of appeals, these changes have not kept pace with the case-load increase. Much like the explosion of the case load at the district court level, the explosion at the court of appeals level has had a qualitative impact on the amount of time a federal judicial panel can give to the multi-issue case before that small group.

The new Federal Circuit Court of Appeals, with its large contingent of federal judges, is available for relocation to the most crowded and burdened of the other circuits. Consequently, the process provides for short-circuiting of the full appellate review process. Figure 5 suggests that all appeals have oral arguments scheduled before the court's decision is announced. However, due to the case-load crunch, one-third to one-half of these appeals are not argued orally before the court of appeals.

EN BANC PROCEEDINGS IN COURTS OF APPEALS. When, in the estimation of the chief judge, a case raises major policy issues, the chief judge will convene an en banc panel of that circuit. The en banc panel consists of all the judges sitting on that circuit. A classic example of a chief judge convening the court en banc was the 1973 litigation involving then-President Richard M. Nixon and the Watergate tapes. Judge John Sirica's decision in the district court was appealed by both the president's attorneys and the special prosecutor in the Court of Appeals for the District of Columbia. Because of the historic nature of the constitutional and political and policy issues, the chief judge convened that court of appeals en banc.

FILING THE BRIEFS IN THE COURT OF APPEALS. After an adverse judgment in a federal trial court or a federal administrative agency, a person must file papers in both the trial court and in the court of appeals informing the courts of the intent to appeal. The appeal brief (stating the reason for the appeal and suggesting certain remedies that the court of appeals may apply to the case) must be filed in the court of appeals. The appeal brief must be accompanied by a transcript of the trial proceedings so that the court of appeals panel of judges will know with certainty what took place at the trial and will have the record to pore over as they and their clerks examine the legal points raised by counsel.

Informal discussions are then conducted between counsel for both parties to the dispute and officers of the court of appeals, including the staff attorney or an assistant staff attorney. The presubmission screening in a federal court of appeals, done by the court staff, sets aside those appeals called consensual—that is, those where there is general agreement on how the case ought to be disposed of by the court of appeals. These cases are disposed of summarily by the court of appeals without oral argument. Many cases, between a third and one-half of the total that begin this process, are screened out of the appellate process at this stage. Wheeler and Whitcomb note that "attorneys may 'settle' the case before court consideration, or they may withdraw the appeal, or the court may dismiss it on one party's motion that the court does not have jurisdiction."

ORAL ARGUMENTS. Appellate oral argument is older than the written brief. It assists the federal appellate judge in a number of ways; the human connection between the bench and the bar is one important function of the oral argument. (Cases not settled or summarily decided are then scheduled for oral argument before a three-judge panel.)

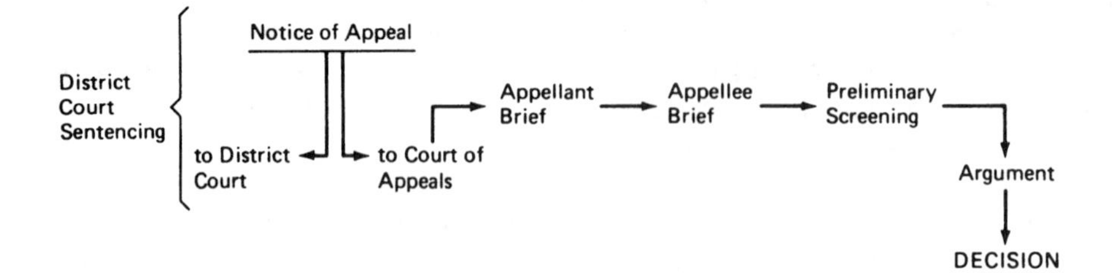

Figure 5: Case Flow: United States Courts of Appeals.

During oral argument, counsel for both parties to the dispute elaborate upon points developed earlier in their written briefs and respond to questions by the sitting judges. These cases are the most difficult ones to be heard by the federal court and the resolution of these conflicts occasionally leads to intracourt conflict. (Statistically, J. W. Howard's study of three courts of appeals found that these middle-level appellate courts upheld the lower federal trial court judgment about 67 percent of the time.)

APPELLATE DECISIONS. On many occasions, a court of appeals panel will render its judgment immediately after oral argument has ended, without meeting in conference session to vote and to assign someone to write the opinion. There is also the per curiam opinion, a short written opinion that announces the judgment without an elaborate judicial justification for the decision. The balance of the cases are discussed in conference session after oral argument, a formal vote is taken, and then the opinions are written, based on the law of the circuit and the precedents of the Supreme Court. After the opinion has been written, printed, and approved by the panel, it is announced by the court of appeals.

COURTS OF APPEALS AS FINAL REVIEWERS. Congress' purpose in creating the courts of appeals in 1891 was to alleviate some of the federal appellate burden that rested solely with the Supreme Court justices. The courts of appeals have fulfilled that purpose. They have relieved the Supreme Court of that burden. The federal courts of appeals, to the extent that very few appeals go from them to the Supreme Court, have functionally become the "court of last resort" for many claimants. What justice a person receives when appealing an adverse district court or administrative-agency ruling will be found generally in the federal court of appeals in that person's geographical area.

APPEALS TO THE SUPREME COURT. Appeals to the Supreme Court come from federal courts of appeals, three-judge district courts, and state supreme courts. To be considered by the Supreme Court, these appeals must fall into the Court's constitutionally and statutorily defined jurisdiction and the case must be seen by the justices as justiciable.

By the mid-1990s the Supreme Court was receiving around 5,000 petitions yearly from these various sources. Annually, the justices of the Supreme Court decide between 130 and 150 cases. The rest, almost 95 percent of the number, are either denied the writ of certiorari or their appeals are dismissed for want of a substantial federal question.

The important point here is that the Supreme Court virtually controls its docket, for it hears only those petitions it wants to hear. The Supreme Court is not an appellate court in the traditional sense. The fact that the Court has decided to grant certiorari in a particular case means that the federal justices have decided to use that particular litigation as a vehicle for making known their policy preferences on one of the issues raised in the litigation and in the briefs.

Summary

The development of the federal court system over two centuries of American history mirrors the tensions and dynamics of the growth of American society. The early years of the Republic were stressful ones; even after the Civil War, federal-state conflicts inhibited the full development of a functioning national judiciary. Not until 1891, with the creation of a fully functioning court of appeals network, did the federal court system begin to realize its potential—perceived a century earlier by the Federalists.

An example of a chief justice convening the court en banc was the 1973 litigation involving Richard Nixon and the Watergate tapes.

The development of the federal court system since 1891 has come full circle. In 1973, Chief Judge Irving H. Kaufman, of the United States Court of Appeals for the Second Circuit, sardonically said, "I submit that we [federal judges] are being smothered with confidence." By that decade, the federal court system was in the process of turning into a jurocracy—that is, a judicial bureaucracy. Because of the activism of the Warren Court and several Congresses, the jurisdiction of the federal courts has grown geometrically. The federal courts were being "smothered," but it was the paperwork—the thousands and thousands of pages of complex filings, the jurisdictional briefs, the briefs on the merits, the amicus curiae briefs—that was choking the federal jurists.

It is a great paradox that the system finds itself trying to build more federal courthouses and hire more federal judges—trial and appellate—and continuing to increase the jurisdiction of these federal courts. What was labeled a "monstrous appearance" in 1787, the federal courts, has become the very basic foundation of America's functioning republican system of self-government. Hamiltonianism has finally triumphed: there is a strong, independent, somewhat overworked federal judicial system in place, providing the citizens of a great nation with the opportunity to resolve conflicts in the context of a national court system.

[See also (I) Judiciary and Congress; (III) Certiorari, Discovery, Jurisdiction, Plea Bargaining, Supreme Court of the United States.]

CASES

Brown Transport v. Atcom, 439 U.S. 1014 (1978)
Cohens v. Virginia, 19 U.S. 264 (1821)
Marbury v. Madison, 1 Cranch 137 (1803)
Martin v. Hunter's Lessee, 14 U.S. 304 (1816)
National Labor Relations Board v. Jones & Loughlin Steel Corp., 301 U.S. 1 (1937)
Stuart v. Laird, 1 Cranch 299 (1803)
West Coast Hotel v. Parrish, 300 U.S. 379 (1937)
Younger v. Harris, 401 U.S. 37 (1971)

BIBLIOGRAPHY

Henry J. Abraham *The Supreme Court in the Governmental Process* (1975), provides the reader with a good view of the functions of the Supreme Court and its interactions with other political agencies in Washington, D.C.; and *Justices and Presidents* (1985), is a chronological political study of all presidential appointments to the Supreme Court from Washington to Reagan. Howard Ball, *Courts and Politics* (1980), examines roles, functions, and organization of the federal court system as well as the processes of decision-making in each of the three major federal constitutional courts. Warren Burger, "Annual Report on the State of the Judiciary," in 96 *U.S. Reports,* no. 9 (1 March 1976), focuses on the problems facing the federal judiciary and suggests organizational and management improvements. Comment, "An Expanding Civil Role for U.S. Magistrates," in *American University Law Review,* 26 (1975), describes the rapid growth of the responsibilities of United States magistrates in the district courts. James Eisenstein and Herbert Jacob, *Felony Justice* (1977), explores the organizational and policy relationships between the federal judge and his or her staff.

Steven Flanders and Alan Sager, "Case Management Methods and Delay in Federal District Courts," in Russell Wheeler and Howard Whitcomb, eds., *Judicial Administration* (1977), carefully examines and explains the rapid growth of the case load problem in the federal courts. Lawrence M. Friedman, *A History of American Law* (1973), is a well-written history of the development of the American legal profession. Sheldon Goldman and Thomas Jahnige, *The Federal Courts as a Political System* (1971), is a very good collection of essays focusing on the Supreme Court's judicial behavior as a part of the larger political process. J. Woodford Howard, "Role Perceptions and Behaviors in Three U.S. Courts of Appeals," in *Journal of Politics,* 39, no. 4 (1977), is a perceptive essay that analyzes judicial self-perceptions relative to the role and function of a federal judge. Roman Hruska, *Commission on Revision of Federal Court Appellate System* (1975), is the report that recommended the creation of a national court of appeals and was one of a number of proposals developed in the mid- and late 1970s that called for organizational modifications of the federal judicial system in order to deal with the increasing case load. Steven Puro, "U.S. Magistrates: A New Federal Judicial Officer," in *Justice System Journal,* 2 (1976), is a fine essay that examines the growth of the powers and responsibilities of magistrates.

Richard J. Richardson and Kenneth N. Vines, *The Politics of Federal Courts* (1970), is an early, yet still valuable, examination of the nature of federal judicial decision-making processes. United States Department of Justice, *Needs of the Federal Courts* (1977), is a government report that reflects on the growing case load dilemma of the federal courts. Charles Warren, *The Supreme Court in United States History,* 3 vols. (1922), is the classic recording of the history of the United States Supreme Court up to the early 1920s. Jack Weinstein, "The Role of the Chief Judge in a Modern System of Justice," in Russell Wheeler and Howard Whitcomb, eds. *Judicial Administration* (1977), written by a federal judge, clearly illuminates the role and functions of the federal judge who handles the administrative chores for his or her federal district court. Charles Wright, *Federal Courts* (1972), is an excellent examination of the federal court system from a legal perspective.

– HOWARD BALL

A

THE ADVERSARY SYSTEM

The term *adversary system* refers to certain features of Anglo-American legal systems that are sometimes contrasted with European inquisitorial systems, socialist systems, and some so-called primitive law systems. The term has no fixed and precise meaning and in different contexts refers to different features of a legal system. At best it refers to a constellation of factors, not all of which are present in any one legal system and absent in others. Notwithstanding this ambiguity, it is a useful term for identifying a distinctive set of features and style of decision-making that is most fully developed in Anglo-American legal systems and particularly in the American criminal justice system.

The theory of the adversary system of adjudication is perhaps most clearly distinguished by its sharply defined roles for litigants and judge. Normally the system of judicial decision-making in an adversarial proceeding envisions two contestants—or, more precisely, their representatives—arguing their cases before a neutral and largely passive judge. The adversary process proceeds by pitting the two partisan advocates against each other and having their differences resolved by the judge, who bases his or her decision upon legal principles and the evidence presented by the adversaries. The judge has no staff or resources to make extended, independent investigation, and the norms associated with the adversary system require that the judge's decision be based upon the evidence presented by the contesting parties. What they do not present the judge cannot consider, and what they stipulate the judge cannot easily question. This same passive role extends to juries as well. Because of this the adversary system has often been likened to a battle or sporting event in which the litigants are the players and the judge and jury are the umpires.

Correlative to this, it is the task of the advocates to present their clients in the best possible light. Extending the analogy of the sporting event, the goal of the advocate is focused and limited. In the adversary system the goal of the advocate is not to determine truth but to win, to maximize the interests of his or her side within the confines of the norms governing the proceedings. This is not to imply that the theory of the adversary process has no concern with truth. Rather, the underlying assumption of the adversary process is that truth is most likely to emerge as a by-product of vigorous conflict between intensely partisan advocates, each of whose goal is to win. Thus, the duty of the advocate in the adversary system is to present his or her side's position in the very best possible light and to challenge the other side's position as vigorously as possible.

Although often criticized for elevating partisan interests above the search for truth and justice, the adversary process is also defended as the most effective means of getting at the truth and rendering justice. Defenders argue that the clash of limited and partisan interests—through the making of claims and counterclaims, challenges and counterchallenges, examinations and cross-examinations—is most likely to yield the maximum of relevant information and subject it to careful scrutiny and, in so doing, be most likely to expose falsehood and reveal truth. The sharply defined and antagonistic roles, it is felt, foster thoroughness and vigor that might be absent in a more cooperatively organized process.

Judges in adversarial systems have an extremely limited capacity to oversee mediation or to foster bargaining.

In his defense of the adversary system in *Economic Analysis of Law* (1973), Richard Posner likens the adversary system to competition in the market. Just as customers, he argues, are most likely to make the best choices if they have the benefit of fiercely competitive salesmen, each of whom extols the virtues of his or her own product and raises questions about the other's, so too a judge is most likely to gain the most and best information for making the fairest decision after listening to the arguments of two vigorous and fiercely partisan advocates.

The distinctive features of the theory of the adversary system are perhaps best appreciated when contrasted to other styles of adjudication. In general, the norms that govern inquisitorial systems more directly assign truth-seeking roles to each of the central actors in the process. Rather than being a by-product of the activities of fierce partisans whose conflict is umpired by a passive judge, inquisitorial systems envision a more active role for the judge and, correspondingly, a less active role for the advocates, at least in courtroom proceedings. In theory, the judge dominates the formal proceeding by actively questioning witnesses, requesting information, and in some systems—for example, the French judge d'instruction—actually supervising the pretrial investigation and marshaling the evidence. If the judge in an adversarial system can be likened to a consumer assessing the positions of competitive salesmen, the judge in an inquisitorial system might be likened to a leader of a seminar, the collective goal of which is to get at the truth and each of whose members is expected to volunteer what they know. In the criminal process, where practices in adversarial and inquisitorial systems are distinguished most sharply, this difference is underscored by the fact that in inquisitorial systems there are fewer safeguards of a defendant's interests and the judge assumes a more active role in questioning witnesses.

The adversary system of adjudication, which squarely pits parties against one another and expects passive decision-makers to resolve their disputes according to established rules, can also be contrasted to mediation, often associated with so-called primitive law systems but also gaining popularity among advocates of informality in both Europe and the United States. In mediation, a third party, the mediator, assumes the role of a broker whose task it is to try to reunite the parties or repair the damage they have done one another. The mediator may best be understood as a facilitator of compromise. As we shall see, adversary theory does allow for, if not indirectly encourage, bargaining and compromise. However, one of the features that sharply distinguish adversarial adjudication from mediation is that the adjudicative judge is more or less passive and reactive and his or her decisions are likely to be formulated in either/or terms.

In contrast, the mediator, also a neutral third party, plays an active part in trying to reconcile the contending parties. The central task of the mediator is to act as a go-between for the two hostile parties, getting each to see the issues from the other's point of view and attempting to find areas of agreement between the two parties in order to find a formula for bringing an end to the hostilities between them. Judges in adversarial systems have an extremely limited capacity to oversee mediation or to foster bargaining, and when they do engage in this behavior, they are frequently criticized for betraying one of the central tenets of their judicial role.

Historians of the adversary process often trace its roots to early Anglo-Saxon proceedings in which legal disputes would be resolved by means of an ordeal of fire or water from which the victor would emerge unscathed or by means of a contest of strength between the disputants or their representatives. The noted jurist Jerome Frank argued that the adversary system was only a slight advance from the earlier system of resolving conflicts by means of recourse to physical prowess: once, disputes were resolved by means of physical strength; in the adversary system, words have been substituted for swords. His point was that in both instances, it is all too likely that those with the most resources in the struggle—rather than those with the most compelling cause—are likely to be judged the victors by passive and reactive judges.

However, defenders of the adversary system bridle at the allegation that it is a vestige of an early system in which actual physical combat was used to decide disputes; they point to what they see as the untenable dual roles that inquisitorial systems force upon advocates and judges. We explore these issues here as a way of identifying some of the salient features of adversary systems and to contrast them with features of other systems of adjudication.

Defenders of the adversary system claim that in an inquisitorial system an advocate's dual role as representative of client interests and coseeker of truth conflict with one another. If one is to be a zealous advocate, they maintain, he or she cannot simultaneously be an active participant in the cooperative and joint venture of discovering the whole truth. Zealous advocacy, they insist, requires that an advocate refrain from doing anything that hurts a client and requires that the advocate emphasize only those things that advance a client's interests. Perhaps the classic expression of this limited and highly focused role of the advocate in an adversary system is found in Lord Brougham's well-known observation made in the course of defending Queen Caroline:

> An advocate, in the discharge of his duty, knows but one person in all the world, and that person is his client. To save that client by all means and expedients, and at all hazards and costs to other persons, and, amongst them, to himself, is his first and only duty; and in performing this duty he must not regard the alarm, the torments, the destruction which he may bring upon others. Separating the duty of a patriot from that of an advocate, he must go on reckless of the consequences, though it should be his unhappy fate to involve his country in confusion.
>
> (quoted in Freedman, 9)

Origins of the Anglo-American Adversary System

Since the adversary system cannot be defined with precision and since elements of it are found in virtually all legal systems, no concise history is possible. However, to the extent that the adversary system is associated with Anglo-American common-law systems, the history of the adversary system is in large a history of the development of the machinery of justice under the common law. In medieval and early modern England this meant the development of crown courts, which over a period of several centuries came to displace a variety of local feudal and ecclesiastical courts. But it also meant recognizing the importance and transformation of a distinctively English institution, the jury, a decision-making body comprised of laymen from the community.

Today the most vigorous defenses and the most fully developed adversary institutions are found in American criminal law.

In brief, the adversary system is a process dominated by the parties themselves and stands in contrast to judge-dominated proceedings. Thus, the history of the adversary process is in large the history of the transformation of the jury and later the judge from an instrument of active official inquiry into a neutral and passive fact finder. Similarly it is found in the evolution in the role of the judge from that of agent of the crown who actively made inquiries and conducted proceedings in order to protect and promote the interests of the crown to that of neutral and disinterested fact finder. While there is no logical necessity requiring that a jury be an element in the adversary system, the jury appears to have been an important catalyst in the development of the culture of the adversary system, and it is for this reason that we briefly review its origins.

British legal historians disagree among themselves as to the origins of the first juries in England. Some suggest that the jury was an ancient indigenous institution in use even before the Saxon conquest of England in the fifth and sixth centuries. Others suggest that it was imported from the Continent in the eighth or ninth century. Whatever the case, the earliest known juries in England were around the ninth century and were quite different institutions from what we know today. Until well into the fifteenth century, jurors were selected precisely because they were knowledgeable about facts and issues in the controversy they were asked to decide. Indeed, juries were often selected well in advance of trial so that they could have time to gather additional evidence and make inquiries of the parties themselves. Under such conditions trials were essentially inquisitorial, in that the proceedings—to the extent that there even were any—allowed knowledgeable decision-makers to share information with each other. However, by the fifteenth century the character of the jury had evolved; jurors were no longer expected to rely upon privately obtained knowledge but on what they learned in court. This transformation was later reinforced by rules that prohibited pretrial contact between litigants and jurors and excluded people with prior knowledge from serving on juries.

This evolution of the jury had its parallel in later developments of the role of the judge. As the jury emerged into an independent and disinterested fact finder and decision-making body, so, too, did judges in those systems in which the jury was used. Initially, it appears that the shared fact-finding and decision-making responsibilities of the judge and jury allowed the judges, who were also representatives of the crown, to distance themselves somewhat from jury findings adverse to crown interests. This distancing appears to have fostered a desire among judges to insulate themselves still further from pressures of the crown. A series of clashes between the crown and its judges during the seventeenth century saw the crown eventually rebuffed in its efforts to remove judges who ruled against its interests. This established the independence of the judiciary and secured two important elements of the adversary system: a neutral and passive jury and a disinterested judiciary who presided over party-controlled proceedings.

The eighteenth and early nineteenth centuries saw further refinements in the adversary system, as newly developed rules of evidence spelled out in great detail the process by which parties could present evidence to judge and jury. It was perhaps during this period that a self-conscious theory of the adversary process was first articulated.

The adversary system was embraced with even greater enthusiasm and self-consciousness in the American colonies, a practice that continued after their independence. The jury, independent judiciary, and party dominance of proceedings reinforced the impulse for decentralization and served as a check on colonial authorities. The experience with summary criminal proceedings employed by royal officials during the struggle for independence served to reinforce American enthusiasm for juries and a passive, independent judiciary. Many institutions closely associated with the adversary system, especially those dealing with criminal matters, were elevated to constitutional status. It is not surprising then that today the most vigorous defenses and the most fully developed adversary institutions are to be found in American criminal law.

Distinctive Features of the Adversary System

In American criminal law the stakes are high, the interests of the two parties are clearly divergent, and the lone defendant faces two agents of the state—the prosecutor and the judge. Indeed, even vigorous critics of the battle or sporting model admit that their greatest vulnerability to criticism is in the prosecution of the criminal law, in which the entire weight of the state is thrown against the individual defendant (Simon). To counterbalance this obvious disadvantage, Anglo-American systems (and many nonadversarial systems as well) have erected a variety of barriers to prosecution and surrounded the criminally accused with a host of legal protections in an effort to offset the obvious advantages of state, as opposed to private, prosecution. Several of the more salient features of adversarial criminal justice systems are examined below: the standard of proof in criminal cases, the presumption of innocence, the right to confront adverse witnesses, the right to have compulsory process for obtaining witnesses, the right to silence, exclusionary rules, and the right to counsel. While none of these provisions is unique to adversary systems, taken together and in the extreme forms they often assume they do distinguish the distinctive adversarial features of the American criminal justice process.

The standard of proof in a criminal case is "beyond a reasonable doubt," a standard markedly higher than that used in civil cases ("the preponderance of the evidence") in both inquisitorial and adversarial legal systems. This high standard underscores the divergence of interests of the two parties: the state is intent on curtailing the life or liberty of the accused, and the accused in turn has an interest in avoiding or minimizing the stigma of conviction and the sting of the sanction. Given such clear-cut and opposed interests, proponents of the adversary system maintain that it is difficult, if not impossible, to imagine a proceeding in which all participants share in a search for the truth.

This divergence of interests between the parties in the criminal process is underscored by a number of other procedures as well. The presumption of innocence

Opposing political forces sometimes face off in court. These defendants, (L to R) Jerry Rubin, Abbie Hoffman, and Rennie Davis, were three of seven men charged with conspiring to riot at the 1968 Democratic Convention. (UPI/Corbis-Bettmann)

places total responsibility on the prosecution for proving guilt and therefore further underscores the antagonism between the state and the accused. This presumption is made meaningful by a variety of procedures, many of which in the United States have been incorporated into constitutional law. Both the Sixth Amendment's right to confront adverse witnesses and right to have compulsory process for obtaining favorable witnesses are designed to facilitate the interests of the accused in his or her battle against the state.

Perhaps the fullest and most significant expression of the inherent conflict between the accused and the state is manifest in the constitutional right of the criminally accused to remain silent, both in the courtroom and, since *Escobedo* v. *Illinois* (1964), in a variety of pretrial settings involving law enforcement officials. In the United States, the antagonistic relationship between the accused and the state has been carried to an extreme found in no other country in the world, and elements of the adversary system have been introduced early in the criminal process. Since *Miranda* v. *Arizona* (1966), not only do suspects have a right to remain silent when questioned by police, but police officers have an affirmative obligation to warn suspects of their rights to remain silent, to receive free legal assistance, and to be warned that whatever they say may subsequently be used against them. In effect, the police must alert suspects that they may soon be engaged in a battle with the state and to prepare for this battle. Failure of the police to warn suspects of these rights can lead to the exclusion at trial of whatever information the police may obtain from the suspect. Nowhere is the antagonism of interests and the adversarial nature of relationships so clearly demonstrated as in the right to be warned of the right to silence.

Exclusionary rules further underscore the battle model inherent in adversary systems. While many criminal justice systems—both inquisitorial and adversarial—exclude coerced confessions, such exclusions are generally justified on the lack of truth value of confessions obtained through coercion. That is, a coerced—whether by physical or psychological methods—confession is likely to be unreliable (Kamisar). However, in the United States this is not the only ground on which exclusionary rules rest. In *Weeks* v. *United States* (1914) and *Mapp* v. *Ohio* (1961), the Supreme Court ruled that evidence illegally obtained is excluded, regardless of its reliability. Indeed, indisputably accurate physical evidence is inadmissible at trial if it is illegally obtained by the police. Since reliability is not an issue, this exclusion must rest on other grounds, and these grounds, so the Supreme Court has ruled, are important components of the adversary process. Without an exclusionary rule, the Court majority reasoned first in *Weeks* and later in *Mapp,* the integrity of the judicial process and the ability to require meaningfully the police to follow the law would be in jeopardy. In other words, the exclusionary rule is justified as a device to assure that the contest between the state and the accused is fair and takes place according to the established rules of the game. To this end, evidence not obtained according to the rules is inadmissible even it is indisputably accurate and even if its exclusion results in a factually guilty person going free. Such a policy is highly controversial; beginning in the 1970s a series of Supreme Court decisions began to circumscribe the scope of earlier exclusionary-rule cases, and some justices are on record as favoring abandonment of the rule altogether.

Limitations of the Adversary System

Even the most vigorous defenders of the adversary system acknowledge some constraints upon partisan advocacy. The norms of the profession forbid advocates from fabricating evidence, encouraging their clients to lie, pursuing frivolous lawsuits, and the like. In this sense, the adversary process is more like a game in which contestants must compete within a prescribed set of rules, which limits their options, than it is like a battle, which presumably is an all-out fight to win.

Still, even the analogy to a game causes many people to question the value and ethics of the adversary system. They argue that the administration of justice is too important to be determined by a process organized like a contest and animated by the singular goal to win. This form of organization, critics continue, places too much responsibility for pursuing public interests in the hands of individual participants who are motivated by their own personal interests rather than public concerns. And perhaps more important, outcomes in adversarial contests, like those in games, are likely to be determined by the luck, skill, and resources of the contestants rather than legal merits alone. If resources are unevenly distributed between the contestants—as they often are in the criminal process, where the state opposes a sole and often poor individual, or in many civil cases when an individual must confront a large and powerful organization—outcomes will be a function of these differences rather than legal merit. As a consequence, over the years the adversary process has been modified.

Adversary theory, like the theory of the market in economics, assumes active viable participants—that is, that the adversaries are in the best position to know and pursue their own interests and that they have the capacity to do so. But just as economists recognize that there are areas in which the market does not work well, so, too, it is recognized that there can be weaknesses in the adversary system that are the equivalent of a market failure. In such instances, rather than abandoning the adversary process for something else, defenders have sought to shore up its weaknesses. We explore two such prominent efforts here: appointment of free counsel for the poor and use of pretrial discovery.

APPOINTMENT OF FREE COUNSEL. To the extent that the adversarial system is like a battle or sporting event, there is the danger that the outcome may be determined not by who has the most convincing case but by who has the most resources. If this is so, the adversary system cannot easily be defended. Hence, any gross imbalance of resources available to the competing parties is likely to be viewed with suspicion. This concern is at its height in the criminal process, and particularly in the modern criminal process, where the state has considerable resources to do battle with the criminally accused, typically a sole individual and often poor.

The expansion of the right to counsel was constitutionally guaranteed in a series of cases handed down by the Supreme Court.

During the formative years of the adversary system, in sixteenth-century to early-nineteenth-century England, criminal prosecution was by and large a private affair, initiated by, and left in the hands of, the victim, usually an individual who had to mount and pay for the prosecution personally. Throughout this period both the accused and the accusor were roughly equal before the law in that both were private parties who had to pay their own legal costs. But the later eighteenth and early nineteenth centuries witnessed a shift from private to public prosecution, and with it there emerged an increasing and systematic imbalance of resources between prosecution and defense. The former had the vast resources of the state to call upon, while the latter was often without the means of obtaining even rudimentary legal advice. Rather than abandoning the adversarial process in the face of such an imbalance, Anglo-American reformers chose to try to restore (or create) some degree of balance between the parties through a variety of procedural rules and by expanding the opportunity for right to counsel to defendants of limited means.

In the United States the expansion of the right to counsel was constitutionally guaranteed in a series of cases handed down by the Supreme Court. In its landmark decision *Powell* v. *Alabama* (1932), the Court took an important first constitutional step in trying to equalize access to legal resources by interpreting the Sixth Amendment's guarantee of fair trial and the Fourteenth Amendment's due process clause to require that counsel be appointed for poor people accused of capital offenses when "exceptional circumstances" were present. Over the years the Court expanded its list of exceptional circumstances and in 1963 held that the Constitution required appointment of free counsel in all serious criminal cases in which the accused wanted counsel but could not afford to pay for one *(Gideon* v. *Wainwright).* This ruling was later broadened to include all persons accused of offenses in which there was a possibility of a jail term being imposed (*Argersinger* v. *Hamlin,* 1972). Rather than repudiating the adversary system because of obvious disparities of resources of the participants, this line of decisions celebrates the adversary system and seeks to shore up—in the form of subsidies to one party—one of its weakest components.

This same logic has been argued with much less success in areas of civil law. With only a few exceptions, the Supreme Court has not embraced a constitutional right to counsel in civil matters, no doubt in part because the Bill of Rights does not express the same degree of concern with parties in civil suits. Still an imbalance in the civil adversary process has been recognized and has led Congress to adopt provisions providing for free counsel for the poor in a variety of areas.

RULES OF PRETRIAL DISCOVERY. Games often involve strategic use of the element of surprise and lore of the legal profession is filled with stories of surprise witnesses and unanticipated evidence the introduction of which caught a formidable adversary off guard and led to victory. This sporting theory of justice, as Roscoe Pound contemptuously referred to it, was modified in significant ways during the early twentieth century. With the adaption of the Federal Rules of Civil Procedure in 1938, federal courts assumed the responsibility for supervising early pretrial disclosure of evidence by both sides in a lawsuit, in order to allow each the opportunity to scrutinize the central features of its opponent's case. These pretrial discovery rules have affected the adversary system in two ways: they have reduced the likelihood that important outcomes will be the consequence of surprise or pure chance, and they have aided and facilitated the process of adjudication by clarifying issues and narrowing the scope of controversy in advance of the trial itself.

However, this reform has had important side effects that reveal the importance of resources and the protean character of the adversary system. Opposing parties can now try to "outdiscover" each other, and as a result, the party unable or unwilling to pay for the most extensive pretrial discovery may be at a disadvantage in preparing a case. Further, since discovery requires that opposing parties cooperate with one another, the party willing to invest most heavily in the process of discovery may be able to force the other to invest in the process as well and, in so doing, can significantly increase the cost of litigation and wear his or her adversary down. Some observers, such as Judith Resnick, have pointed to still another problem with pretrial discovery. Because discovery may involve close judicial supervision of the pretrial process (that is, overseeing the scope and nature of each party's inquiry to see that it remains within the bounds set by the court and setting timetables for proceedings to be completed), there is a very real potential that the neutrality and disinterestedness of the judge will be undermined. While there are ways to guard against this to the extent that judges do become actively involved in scrutinizing evidence and discussing the case with parties, the integrity of the adversary system may be damaged. Indeed, a number of scholars have argued that a new type of court proceeding has emerged, one that is neither inquisitorial nor adversarial. They label it "bureaucratic" and use the term to express their concern that judges have unwittingly abandoned their neutral and disinterested stance and now take too active a role in bringing cases to a close. Thus, justice, critics maintain, is being sacrificed to the bureaucratic concern of efficiency. Despite these concerns, there are probably very few who in the name of the integrity of the adversary system would do away entirely with some form of judicially supervised pretrial discovery and case management.

Continuing Criticisms of the Adversary System

The American adversary system, then, has been strengthened in order to overcome some of its obvious deficiencies or modified in order to eliminate some of its worst features. But many thoughtful observers point to still other problems and press for still more modifications to curb what they see as continuing and widespread abuses. Some critics focus upon the criminal process and argue that the barrier of protections erected around the criminally accused frustrate the ends of justice in that they exclude solid and reliable evidence. Others argue that many provisions in fact are little more than a web of technicalities that foster innumerable appeals challenging technical errors and hence frustrate finality. In both instances, critics continue, adversaries intent on winning can use such rules for strategic advantage, which has nothing to do with the quest for material truth. The implications of such criticisms are that legal—and particularly criminal—procedure needs to be drastically simplified.

Still another line of criticism argues that in the effort to be fair, so many safeguards and protections have been built into the adversary process that it has become inefficient and self-defeating. For instance, Feeley has found that in lower criminal courts, where the harshest punishment is likely to be a few days in jail, a suspended sentence, or a small fine, the very process of going through the proceeding is often more of a sanction than the final punishment itself. Others, like Fleming, have argued that we have constructed such an elaborate and expensive adversary trial system that only very few are in fact able to take advantage of it.

Still others are skeptical of the extension of adversarial hearings to grievance mechanisms in a variety of settings when traditionally they were not used, such as welfare rights hearings, social security disability hearings, and school disciplinary hearings. Here, critics say, the use of adversary procedures has fostered hostility between clients and officials and, in so doing, undercut the capacity of officials to pursue their work effectively. Some critics maintain that the heightened and expanded use of adversarial proceedings are self-defeating in that officials will find ways to subvert or avoid them.

There is certainly considerable evidence to support these views. Despite the fact that American culture celebrates the adversary trial in criminal cases, only a very small proportion of all criminal cases—perhaps no more than 4 percent or 5 percent in misdemeanor cases and no more than 10 percent or 15 percent in felony cases—are disposed of by means of a jury trial. Similarly, very few civil cases filed in court are actually disposed of by trial, perhaps no more than 5 percent to 10 percent. And in some settings administrators of social-service programs are accused of pursuing their objectives indirectly in order to avoid cumbersome and time-consuming proceedings. However, it is problematic whether the figures on trial rates are evidence of the weaknesses of the adversary system, since in fact nothing in the theory of the adversary system precludes the possibility of negotiation, and as we shall see, the adversary process, especially in criminal matters, actually facilitates it.

A frequently voiced criticism of the adversary system is that it too easily fosters a desire to win at all costs.

Another frequently voiced criticism of the adversary system is that it too easily fosters an unreasonable zealousness that leads to a desire to win at all costs. Just as some athletes and athletic programs have been criticized for putting the goal of winning above good sportsmanship, fairness, and safety, so critics of the adversary system can point to innumerable examples where attorneys, in the words of Judge Marvin Frankel, engage in a "free-for-all" well beyond the bounds of propriety. Any number of lawyers' and judges' memoirs are replete with long catalogs of tricks used by zealous advocates. Among them are how in the process of "interviewing" clients, lawyers can "prepare" them for testimony by subtly suggesting how they can lie, withhold information, and conveniently "forget" pertinent information. Attorneys can purposefully engineer delays in hopes that witnesses will die, move out of town, lose patience, or forget. And they employ a host of rhetorical tricks to intimidate and confuse witnesses and curry favor with impressionable jurors.

In recent years the issue of the limits of the extent to which counsel can use such techniques has been vigorously debated within the legal profession as it continues to attempt to reformulate its Code of Professional Responsibility. However these issues are ultimately resolved, two factors should be remembered. First, the debate within the legal profession is relatively narrow; even the most restrictive proposals still allow attorneys considerable room for zealous advocacy. This perhaps is illustrated by the fact that one of the issues seriously considered in this debate is whether the adversary system not only permits but compels a lawyer to help his or her client lie on the witness stand if it is to the client's advantage to do so. With issues such as this being debated in all seriousness, there is little likelihood that the code will impose significant restrictions on the zealousness of advocates. Second, regardless of the provisions in the code, there is no real means to enforce them, and lawyers, motivated by the desire to maximize the interests of their clients, are likely to continue to have strong incentives to employ whatever they think will help their clients and perhaps even cut corners if they think such action poses no risks to themselves and is beneficial to their clients. This attitude is what critics of the adversary system find most frustrating: once a fight or sporting theory of justice is set into motion, it is difficult to assure that the contest is played according to acceptable rules rather than fought in gladiator fashion.

One reform that has been put forward to curb the worst features of overly zealous advocacy is to invigorate the traditionally passive judiciary. That is, some reformers propose to modify the traditional party control of the lawsuit by having the judge take a more active role in managing the cases; overseeing the questioning of witnesses; and, in the criminal process, reviewing the guilty-plea process. For instance, Abraham Goldstein argues that judges have the authority, and should embrace the opportunity, to oversee more actively the exercise of the prosecutor's discretionary authority to charge and negotiate pleas of guilt. More generally, and particularly in the federal courts, judges have begun to take an active role in overseeing cases before them. While some of this has arisen as a consequence of the concern for greater efficiency, this increasing assumption of an active role by judges is also motivated by their desire to trim some of the abuses that result from the overzealousness of advocates, the imbalance of resources of parties, and public concerns not necessarily of interest to the parties themselves. It remains to be seen how many such proposals will be adopted, but it should be emphasized that few such proposals suggest any significant modification of the structure of the adversary system itself.

Political Theory, Culture, and the Adversary System

Although the connection between political theory and ideology, on the one hand, and institutional structure and behavior, on the other, is rarely direct and immediate, social and legal institutions are shaped by theories, and in turn theories are influenced by prevailing social practices and institutions. Thus, there are strong, if not always clear, links between political theories and institutional practices. These links become discernible when we locate both the theory and practice of the adversary process in broad cultural context and compare them with the theory and practices of legal systems in other political cultures. We can demonstrate this by examining the different theoretical traditions of two distinct cultures and then contrasting them with the legal systems associated with each.

Commentators on the adversary system have frequently noted its affinity with the theory of the market and with classical liberalism. In his extended treatment of the American courts, in *Courts on Trial,* Judge Jerome Frank criticized the adversary system precisely because it took a laissez-faire approach to decision-making and, in so doing, systematically frustrated the quest for truth and justice. Conversely, Judge Richard Posner, a defender of the adversary system and of the value of a market economy, likened the adversary system to the market and extolled its virtue precisely because it operates like a market system. Thus, despite their differences, they agree that the adversary system is closely akin to the market.

Similarly, many commentators have seen a connection between the adversary, system and classic liberal political theory in that both envision an essentially passive and reactive state. Classic liberalism celebrates the autonomy of the individual and justifies a political system that maximizes individual choice and minimizes governmental control. The state, in liberal theory, is an institution with a primary function to ensure that individuals have maximum opportunity to pursue their own private interests; to provide certain public goods that are not easily pursued by individual private initiative (providing for common defense, roads, and law enforcement); to establish a framework of laws (that is, establish the frameworks through which private affairs are conducted); and to provide a mechanism to see that they are enforced. The public interest or public good in liberal theory is understood as the aggregate of individual interests.

The connection of the theory of the adversary system with liberal political theory should be apparent. Both the state and the court are reactive institutions, responding to claims brought to them. Voters (politics) and litigants (the adversary system) are expected to pursue their own personal interests rather than subsume them for some larger community good or sense of justice. And as in the market, both the political process and the adversary system celebrate the clash of interests. In politics the public good is understood to be the resultant shaped by the various vectors of personal preferences or interests, and in the adversary system justice is likely to emerge as a by-product of intense partisan struggle. Both distrust the power of the state and of officials who act in behalf of others. In politics this is manifest in theories of limited government and fragmentation and decentralization of power; in the legal process this is manifest in the passive role assigned to the judge and the importance given to the litigants in presenting their cases and in the criminal law theory that views the public prosecutor as the agent for the individual victim. While the quest for justice is not wholly eliminated in either system, neither is it of central concern to the most active participants. Both systems define justice as the by-product of the pursuit of individual interests.

Perhaps the central feature that links liberal political theory with the adversary system is an intense skepticism concerning the power of the state. Liberal theory

Information gathered by coercion, such as suggested in this shadowy rendering of a police interrogation, is deemed not only unreliable but inadmissible as evidence in United States courts. (Frank McMahon/Corbis)

embraces limited government on the grounds that public power distorts and corrupts, and the adversary system questions the ability of disinterested parties to be sufficiently motivated to strive for complete understanding. To this end, both rely heavily upon private initiative and the intensity of self-interest. The Anglo-American adversary system provides an extensive role for lay jurors in both grand and petit juries, just as liberal political theory celebrates a wide array of opportunities for citizen participation in political life.

There are limits to this comparison. Although liberal theory expects that individual legislators, like individual voters, will represent selected interests and not the community as a whole, the judge and jury, as distinct from the parties in adversarial theory, are expected to be motivated by the pursuit of justice and not particular interests. This difference is reflected in the process of argumentation. While both voting and litigation presume ample opportunity for thorough airing of issues, it is permissible—indeed desirable—for candidates in elections to appeal to voters' self-interests. By contrast, litigants must make principled arguments, and judges must articulate principled reasons for their decisions. Still, the mobilization of facts and the clarification of principles in the adversary system are believed to best be produced by means of the vigorous pursuit of limited interests.

The affinity of classical liberalism and the adversary process becomes apparent when compared with European inquisitorial systems and the major traditions in continental political theory and institutions. European traditions of political theory are much more diffuse than the liberal British tradition of John Locke, Jeremy Bentham, and John Stuart Mill and their modern pluralist variants in the United States. Nevertheless the dominant theoretical traditions in Europe do tend to place considerably more emphasis on the importance of community and relatively less on the interests and rights of individuals. As a consequence, European traditions of political theory have been more willing to embrace the notion of an active and positive state, an institution that embodies something considerably more than, and quite distinct from, the aggregate of citizen interests. This concern with community informs traditions of European political theory, both liberal and conservative, and this concern stands in sharp contrast to the British and American traditions, which are preoccupied with the individual and individual rights. Thus, for instance, the Hegelian tradition elevates the state to central concern and gives it an autonomous status. Similarly, while the various strains of Marxism have all predicted the withering away of the bourgeois state, they all also emphasize the centrality of the community, which is separate and distinct from the aggregation of individual interests. These various traditions of continental political philosophy are reflected in both the theory and practice of continental inquisitorial legal systems.

The structure and administration of the criminal law will serve to illustrate the impact of these traditions. The continental philosophical tradition links law quite closely with morality. A violation of law is understood as a breach of the moral order, and the community has a right—indeed, an obligation—to respond to this breach. In contrast, English philosophical tradition tends to draw a sharper distinction between law and morality, thus giving law a more limited sphere of importance. While this tradition acknowledges that the two realms often overlap, it nevertheless emphasizes that they are distinct concepts and that the state and its legal system are not to be confused with morality.

English philosophical tradition draws a sharp distinction between law and morality.

These differences are reflected in the structure of the administration of criminal justice in the two systems. In the continental tradition, where the state, law, and morality are more closely linked, there has been a longer tradition of strong centralized state authority and full prosecution. For instance, as Langbein has shown, centralized, state responsibility for criminal prosecution emerged in Germany and France in the sixteenth century, but in England responsibility for criminal prosecution long remained the responsibility of individual victims. Indeed, in England until well into the nineteenth century, complainants had to bear the cost of criminal prosecution, just as victims of torts still must. Private prosecution was justified by the theory that crime was primarily a wrong to the victim and only secondarily an affront to the integrity of the state. This view placed considerable discretion in the hands of the victim, for if he or she did not want to prosecute, the state could not easily intervene.

While private prosecution in England and the United States has long been superseded by a system of public prosecution, important residues of the earlier theory and practice of private prosecution still remain and are reflected in the adversary system. In England and Wales until 1985, there was no formal system of public prosecutors, and although prosecutions have long been paid for from public funds, important aspects of private prosecution have been retained. Prosecutors were appointed for individual cases and theoretically were representatives of the victim. While a system of public prosecution was embraced much earlier in the United

States, here, too, important features of private prosecution were retained. In particular, prosecutors still have considerable discretion to set charges and prosecute, and while crime is now seen primarily as an offense against the public, in practice prosecutors often take their cues from complainants, agreeing to drop or reduce charges according to the victim's inclination.

This discretion, while not a central tenet of the theory of adversarial justice, nevertheless has an affinity to the adversary system, since both place responsibility for initiating the judicial process upon the involved private parties and view the state as a largely reactive institution. In the criminal process, not only is the judiciary largely passive, waiting for the case to be brought to it, but so is the other state agency, the prosecutor's office, which often takes its cues from complainants. All this is of course relative; prosecutors often do pursue cases irrespective of the wishes of victims, and continental prosecutors also often take their cues from complainants. Still, when British and American prosecutors are contrasted to their European counterparts, significant differences stand out. For instance, a much higher proportion of cases are dropped by prosecutors in the United States and England than on the Continent, a pattern that cannot be accounted for entirely by evidentiary problems.

Furthermore, political cultures with more pronounced political traditions of strong state authority are more likely to have stronger judges and weaker litigants, while cultures in the liberal tradition are likely to have adversary systems, which have a more restricted role for judges and a more active role for litigants. Similarly, many socialist and so-called primitive societies are likely to have a legal process that depends less heavily on the self-interest of disputants to guide the proceedings and that emphasizes communal concerns as well as the interest of the individual participants. All of these differences must be understood as matters of degree. Still, there is clearly a very real affinity between political culture and legal systems.

Finally, the theory of the adversary system encourages parties to circumvent adjudication and seek alternatives to full-fledged trials if it is in their own interests to do so. Since initiation of the suit and mobilization of the relevant facts are left to the litigants and their agents, what they do not present the court is not likely to consider. The style of decision-making in adversary systems, then, encourages this judicial passivity in civil and criminal matters. In Anglo-American systems, for example, the vast majority of criminal convictions are obtained through guilty pleas, many of which are the result of plea bargaining, or negotiation in which the accused pleads guilty in exchange for some assurance of lenient treatment, through either the reduction of charges or the promise of a shorter sentence. Roughly 90 percent to 95 percent of all criminal convictions in the United States are obtained in this manner. This mode of decision-making is in sharp contrast to the way criminal cases are handled in inquisitorial systems. On the Continent, while a great many criminal defendants plead guilty, there appears to be no appreciable amount of plea bargaining or negotiation over charges.

While a great many factors no doubt are required to explain these differences, the point to be stressed here is how easily the practice of plea bargaining can fit within the standard theory of the adversary process. Since the adversary system is animated by the interests of the parties themselves and permits them considerable discretion to pursue these interests, it easily tolerates, if not actually fosters, negotiation and bargaining. Certainly once the parties agree as to how to resolve the conflict among themselves, the judge, who is largely dependent upon the parties themselves for information, has little choice but to ratify that decision. That is, if the accused reports to the judge that he or she has accepted the charges set by the prosecution, in a very real sense there is no "contest" to umpire—hence, the adversary system's encouraging stance toward plea bargaining.

In inquisitorial systems, by contrast, a trial is not understood as a contest but is seen as an inquiry (hence, the term *inquisitorial*) in which the court is expected to gather and independently assess the evidence and make a judgment. In such a system, in a very real sense it does not matter to the court whether the defendant has pleaded guilty or not, or what, if anything, the prosecution has promised in return. The inquiry can be conducted regardless of the attitude or plea of the accused; it is not dependent upon a real contest between the parties.

In practice, at least in serious cases in adversarial systems, judges often require that the prosecution reveal its case against the accused and warn the accused of his or her right to trial. Conversely, in inquisitorial systems judges often make no sustained independent investigation if the accused does not challenge the prosecutor's case. Still, there are important differences between the two systems, the most significant one being the prevalence of plea bargaining in adversarial systems and its virtual absence in many, if not most, inquisitorial systems. These differences, it appears, are due in large part to the theories that underlie each system.

Alternatives to the Adversary System

Not even the most vigorous advocates of the adversary system argue that all types of disputes can or should be resolved through adversarial adjudication. As already noted, the costs associated with adversary proceedings suggest that in at least some situations a different type of proceeding might be appropriate. In this section we examine some other issues that have long posed problems in adversary proceedings. Many of these issues involve parties who have prior, and possibly continuing, relationships.

Judges often require that the prosecution reveal its case against the accused and warn the accused of his right to trial.

Almost everyone who has written on the topic has emphasized the winner-take-all or zero-sum aspects of adversarial decision-making and has emphasized that adversary proceedings tend to exacerbate differences between disputants. For these reasons, certain disputes between intimates and those who anticipate close and continuing relationships may best be dealt with in non-adversarial proceedings. Perhaps the classic example of such a situation is the process of awarding custody of a child following a divorce. The either/or approach typical of adversary proceedings squarely pits one parent against the other and thus may not foster the best interests of either the parents or child. For this reason, most family-law experts support mediated settlement of custody issues, in which the decision is made through a process in which each party is expected to pursue his or her own interests in a spirit of cooperation and both disputants are encouraged to share the common goal of reducing the trauma to the child involved. Similarly, in labor disputes, mediation is often preferred to adjudication, in order to minimize the rift between labor and management and to facilitate harmonious continuing relations. More generally, the distinctive aim of mediation is to foster compromise, often for the purpose of healing or repairing the tears in the fabric of continuing social relations.

In this sense, there may be no difference in objectives between mediation and negotiation; in both, disputants are expected to pursue their own interests and a decision must be voluntarily accepted by the involved parties. However, the introduction of the third party—the mediator—gives mediation a superficial resemblance to adjudication. The comparison, however, is erroneous in that a mediator's role is to encourage parties to see that their best interests are served by compromise and to help facilitate agreement between the parties. In contrast, the judge in adjudication is charged with imposing a solution upon the parties based upon an authoritative interpretation of rules governing their dispute.

Some argue that the mediation model is intrinsically desirable and more conducive to fostering communal development than is adjudication or, more particularly, adversarial adjudication. For instance, in a wide-ranging critique of the adversary process in the criminal justice system, John Griffiths attacks the basic premises of the adversary system, labeling it the "battle model," which serves to alienate and separate still further the criminal suspect from the community. In his opinion, those most in need of being reintegrated into the community are subjected to a process that achieves precisely the opposite result, further alienating them. In contrast, he envisions replacing the adversary system with a system of dispute resolution that emphasizes the effort to deal with the "whole person," that tries to reconcile those who have grievances with one another, and that generally makes the effort to bring persons accused of offenses back into the fold of the community. Indeed something of this philosophy had long informed juvenile court proceedings.

Conclusion

This review has identified the salient features of adversary systems. It has also revealed that there is no clear and precise understanding of the term. At times it refers broadly to common-law systems, and at others it refers to distinctive features of American criminal procedure. Further, no clear set of characteristics unambiguously sets adversary systems apart from other types of legal systems. Still, Anglo-American legal systems are distinguishable by certain of their emphases, allowing an overall contrast with other types of legal systems. The essence of this distinctiveness can be captured in what has been called the adversary system's "by-product of truth." In adversary theory, disputants are expected to vigorously pursue their own interests before a largely passive judge who acts as umpire, and truth is expected to emerge as a by-product of this clash of interests.

The adversary system's emphasis on individual interests is reinforced in the Anglo-American culture and political philosophy, which emphasizes individual interests and is skeptical of state power. It stands in contrast to other cultures and philosophies that emphasize community and communal obligations and view government as an expression of these concerns. Thus, like so many other areas of law, the structure of the legal process reflects the larger society of which it is a part.

[See also (III) Criminal Justice System, Discovery, Trial Courts and Practice.]

CASES

Argersinger v. Hamlin, 407 U.S. 25 (1972)
Escobedo v. Illinois, 378 U.S. 478 (1964)
Gideon v. Wainwright, 372 U.S. 335 (1963)
Mapp v. Ohio, 367 U.S. 643 (1961)
Miranda v. Arizona, 384 U.S. 436 (1966)
Powell v. Alabama. 287 U.S. 45 (1932)
Weeks v. United States, 232 U.S. 383 (1914)

BIBLIOGRAPHY

Richard Abel, "A Comparative Theory of Dispute Institutions in Society," in *Law and Society Review,* 8 (1973), is a theoretical analysis of the structure of various types of dispute-processing systems. Henry J. Abraham. *The Judicial Process: An Introductory Analysis of the Courts of the United States, England, and France,* 4th ed. (1980), examines the basic structure of three legal systems in a way that reveals differences between adversary and inquisitorial systems. Mauro Cappelletti and John Anthony Jolowicz, *Public Interest Parties and the Active Role of the Judge in Civil Litigation* (1975), studies the role of judges in large "public interest" cases. George F. Cole, Stanislaw J. Frankowski, and Marc G. Gertz, eds., *Major Criminal Justice Systems* (1981), is a collection of essays describing criminal justice systems in common-law, civil law, and socialist law systems. Mirjan Damaska, "Structures of Authority and Comparative Criminal Procedure," in *Yale Law Journal,* 84 (1975), compares American and European inquisitorial systems with special reference to the role of the judge in criminal procedure. Alan Dershowitz, *The Best Defense* (1982), is a lively account of cases handled by a well-known Harvard law professor and a caustic evaluation of the problems of the American judicial process.

Malcolm M. Feeley, *The Process Is the Punishment* (1979), studies the by-product costs of being a defendant in a criminal case. Macklin Fleming, *The Price of Perfect Justice* (1974), is an essay by a California judge arguing that many of the high standards of the adversary system lead to counterproductive results and miscarriages of justice.

Jerome Frank, *Courts on Trial: Myth and Reality in American Justice* (1949), is a classic critical examination of the adversary system from a reformer's perspective. Marvin Frankel, *Partisan Justice* (1980), presents a wide-ranging analysis of the strengths and limits of the adversary system by a well-known judge and scholar. Monroe H. Freedman, *Lawyers' Ethics in an Adversary System* (1975), is a thoughtful examination of legal ethics, including a spirited defense of vigorous advocacy in the adversarial system. Lon Fuller, "The Forms and Limits of Adjudication," in *Harvard Law Review,* 92 (1978), studies the role of judges in the adversary system, contrasting it with other types of decision-making systems; and "The Adversary System," in Harold J. Berman, ed., *Talks on American Law* (1961), is a brief introduction to the adversary system by a leading legal philosopher.

Abraham S. Goldstein, *The Passive Judiciary: Prosecutorial Discretion and the Guilty Plea* (1981), examines the role of prosecutors and judges in the adversary system, ending with an argument that judges should take a more active role in supervising prosecutorial discretion. Edward L. Greenspan, "The Future Role of Defence Counsel," in Anthony N. Doob and Edward L. Greenspan, eds., *Perspectives in Criminal Law* (1985), examines and vigorously defends the role of defense counsel in the adversarial system. John Griffiths, "Ideology in Criminal Procedure, or A Third 'Model' of the Criminal Process," in *Yale Law Journal,* 79 (1970), offers a wide-ranging critique of the underlying ideology of the American adversary process and a proposal for a new and different system based upon principles of mediation or what the author terms the family-law model. E. A. Hoebel, *The Law of Primitive Man* (1954), is a review of several primitive legal systems, showing their variation, by a major anthropologist of law. Yale Kamisar, *Police Interrogation and Confessions: Essays in Law and Policy* (1980), a review of the history of the law excluding confessions from trial, is by a vigorous defender of a broad approach to the exclusionary rules. Stephan Landsman, *The Adversary System: A Description and Defense* (1984), is a brief and easy to read history and overview of the adversary system, along with a strong defense of it. John Langbein, *Prosecuting Crime in the Renaissance* (1974), provides a comparative study of criminal prosecution in England, France, and Germany, pointing out their differences during formative periods in the development of the inquisitorial and adversarial systems.

John H. Merryman, *The Civil Law Tradition* (1969), is the standard treatment of civil law systems and includes a discussion of the distinctive features of the inquisitorial system. John B. Mitchell, "The Ethics of the Criminal Defense Attorney—New Answers to Old Questions," in *Stanford Law Review,* 32 (1980), examines the role of defense counsel in the adversary system. Herbert L. Packer, *The Limits of the Criminal Sanction* (1968), studies the structure and rationale of the American criminal justice system. Richard Posner, *Economic Analysis of Law* (1973), is a treatise examining substantive law and legal procedure from an economic perspective, which reveals the affinity between the market and the adversary system. Judith Resnick, "Managerial Judges," in *Harvard Law Review,* 96 (1982), is a wide-ranging critique of judges who abandon their traditional passivity and become active in managing cases before them in order to speed up processes.

Ellen Ryerson, *The Best-Laid Plans: America's Juvenile Court Experiment* (1978), studies the history, philosophy, and failure of the nonadversarial system of juvenile justice in the United States. William H. Simon, "The Ideology of Advocacy: Procedural Justice and Professional Ethics," in *Wisconsin Law Review,* 29 (1978), is a thoughtful analysis of the ethics of the adversary system. Kawashima Takeyoshi, "Dispute Resolution in Contemporary Japan," in A. T. Von Mehren, ed., *Law in Japan* (1963), relates the Japanese preference for mediation to Japanese culture.

– MALCOLM FEELEY

APPEALS AND APPELLATE PRACTICE

One of the few aspects of the American judicial process about which there is a consensus is that every loser in a trial court should have a right to appeal to a higher court. This principle is best expressed by the statement, often made by real-life litigants as well as fictional ones, "I'm going to take this all the way to the Supreme Court"—a statement indicating that the matter is of such importance that the person will not rest until all efforts to obtain justice have been exhausted. Notwithstanding the unanimous agreement on the importance of the right to appeal, the Supreme Court of the United States has held that the right to appeal is not mandated by due process. There are in fact two states, Virginia and West Virginia, in which there is no right to appeal; appellate review is at the discretion of the appellate court. The right to seek appellate review is thus dependent solely upon statute. If a legislature decided to abolish either the right to appeal or even the right to seek discretionary review in an appellate court, it could do so without violating the requirements of due process. In spite of this anomaly of constitutional principle, the fact remains that there is, in the federal system and in every state, a process by which an action of a trial court is reviewable in an appellate court. It is the purpose of this article to explain how this process developed and how it works.

Development of Concept of Appellate Review

In examining the history of the development of appellate review, it is important to understand that appellate review as it now exists in the United States reflects to a substantial degree the structure of government, which divides governmental power into the legislative, executive, and judicial branches, each having a particular role. The separation of powers as a basic element of governmental structure dates back only to the eighteenth century, but the concept of a judicial process and appellate review goes back much further. Appellate review originated in the civilizations that developed around the Mediterranean Sea. During the Middle Ages in Europe the development of a structured legal system with an appeal process depended upon the existence of a central governmental structure. As power became centralized in an individual sovereign, procedures developed whereby a person dissatisfied with the decision of a judicial official could have the decision reviewed by one or more higher judicial officers. The sovereign, as the repository of all governmental authority, was the final judicial authority.

In England, as in the continental countries, an increase in royal power resulted in the development of a national legal system. In the thirteenth and fourteenth centuries, appellate review was initiated by the filing of a new lawsuit in the reviewing court by the losing party against the judge whose decision was contested. By the time of Edward I, however, the prevailing party rather than the judge was required to defend the judgment of the trial court. During this same period the formal record in the lower court became established, as did the jury as the finder of fact and the distinction between finding of facts and discovering and applying legal principles to those facts.

At the beginning of the eighteenth century there were two principal procedures for appellate review in the English legal system, writ of error and appeal. The writ of error was a common-law writ that grew out of the earlier procedures under which the losing party filed suit against the judge who rendered the original decision. The writ of error initiated a new lawsuit with the parties, known as the plaintiff in error (the losing party in the lower court) and the defendant in error (the winning party in the lower court). The writ of error could be obtained as a matter of right. When it was obtained, it automatically stayed the enforcement of the judgment of the lower court if a bond was posted to secure the amount of the judgment and any costs or damages that would be caused by delaying enforcement of the judgment. The plaintiff in error arranged for a copy of the record in the lower court to be sent to the reviewing court. The record consisted of the writ of error, the pleadings, the judge's notes of the trial, the verdict, the proceedings after the verdict, and the judgment.

In the American colonies, appellate review was virtually nonexistent until the eighteenth century because there were no well-developed legal systems.

To raise any matter in the appellate court not included in the original record, the plaintiff in error had to prepare a bill of exceptions recording alleged errors of law made at the trial but not shown on the record. A record had to be made of each exception in writing at the time that the adverse ruling was made. At the end of the trial all the exceptions were put together to constitute the bill of exceptions. This bill, once approved by the trial judge, was then appended to the record.

After the record and bill of exceptions were transmitted to the appellate court, the plaintiff in error prepared an assignment of the errors, which in the appellate court served the same function as a complaint in the trial court. The defendant in error then filed a plea in response to the assignment of errors. Review was limited to errors of law made by the judge. Any factual errors made by the jury could not be reviewed. Oral argument was heard at the request of either side, and a copy of the record was given to each judge.

There also existed in England during this time another legal system called equity. Proceedings in this system were held in the Court of Chancery. The decisions of the Court of Chancery were subject to review in the House of Lords. An unsuccessful litigant in the Court of Chancery desiring to challenge the decision filed a petition and appeal with the House of Lords. That document recited the proceedings in the lower court and presented the grounds for appeal. The successful party in the Court of Chancery then filed an answer. The papers were printed, and oral argument was held in the

House. The House could review any matter in the case, whether or not it was in the record and whether it was a factual or legal issue, and could render any judgment it thought appropriate. After 1873 the House of Lords could even accept new evidence.

In the American colonies, appellate review was virtually nonexistent until the eighteenth century because there were no well-developed legal systems. Usually the colonial legislature or the governor and his council were the highest court of review except for the privy council in England. The review was similar to that in the House of Lords in an equity matter; the legislature or the governor and his council had the power to render any judgment thought appropriate. During the eighteenth century the colonies began to develop legal systems with an appellate review procedure that increasingly resembled the English writ of error rather than the equity appeal. This change developed in large part because larger numbers of colonial lawyers obtained their legal training in England. They brought back with them the common-law concept of appellate review as reflected in the writ of error rather than the equity appeal. Although there was continuing conflict between the two approaches to appellate review, the writ of error system clearly prevailed. This continued to be true in the states after the Revolution began in 1776 and in the federal system after the Constitution became effective in 1789.

Because the technical writ-of-error procedure became generally applicable rather than the more flexible equity appeal procedure, the appellate process as it developed in both the federal and state systems became overridden with procedural technicalities. As a result, at least six separate steps were required before an appellate court would review an issue on the merits: (1) making a timely objection; (2) taking an exception; (3) preserving the objection, the ruling on the objection, and the exception to the exception in the bill of exceptions; (4) moving for a new trial; (5) specifying the overruling of the objection in the assignment of errors; and (6) specifying the issue in a "brief." The same insistence on procedural technicalities affected every step in the appellate process.

Even though the procedural requirements of the writ of error became applicable to the equity appeal, the appeal in equity was nonetheless preserved. The major difference between it and the writ of error was in the scope of review. Following the English practice, under the writ of error only errors of law could be reviewed. In an equity appeal, however, both questions of law and questions of fact could be reviewed, and the appellate court had full authority to render any judgment it thought justice required. The appeal in equity was thus considered a trial de novo rather than a review of the lower court judgment, even though no new evidence was admissible in the appellate court. Even in equity appeals during the nineteenth century, however, appellate courts began to give such deference to the factual findings of the judge that the scope of review in the equity appeal became very similar to that of the writ-of-error review.

The result at the end of the nineteenth century was a very formalistic procedure. Appellate review was to be denied if any of the technical procedural requirements had not been complied with completely. To the extent that there was appellate review, it was of a very limited nature. Since early in the twentieth century, there has been a continuing effort to reform the appellate process. The objective has been to make the procedure for appeals more simple, to make sure that appellate courts review cases on the merits, and to expand the scope of review from the narrow review of errors of law as shown by the record to include a broader review of both questions of law and questions of fact.

Nature of the Appellate Process

Beginning in the 1960s, the increase in the number of cases being brought to the trial courts and the simplification of the appellate process have created what has been termed a "crisis of volume" for appellate courts. The increased burden on appellate courts has prompted a wide range of responses. In most jurisdictions the initial steps were to add additional judges to existing courts and to create new appellate courts. These remedies, however, were not long-range solutions. Furthermore, the creation of intermediate appellate courts made it easier for persons to appeal, thereby increasing the appellate court case load. The most dramatic fact of the appellate process in the federal courts of appeals has been the growth in the number of appeals from decisions of the federal court. The number of appeals increased from 4,204 in 1961 to 29,630 in 1983, an increase of 705 percent. During the same period, the number of circuit judges increased by only 100 percent. The growth in appeals at the state level has been almost as dramatic as at the federal level. Although statistics for the same period are not available, between 1972 and 1983 the number of appeals filed in the state appellate courts grew by 151 percent, whereas the number of judges increased by only 33 percent.

A whole range of techniques designed to reduce a court's backlog and to reduce the time for a case to move from judgment in the trial court to judgment in the appellate court were also implemented. It was recognized that if courts continued to do business as usual, appellate review would become an empty remedy because the delay in obtaining it would make review ineffectual in many, if not most, cases. There was also recognition, however, that speed and efficiency were not ends in themselves and that an undue emphasis on them could deny litigants the thoughtful review traditionally characteristic of the appellate process. For these reasons the appellate process since the 1960s has been in an evolutionary state. On the one hand, there have been efforts to preserve the essential features of appellate review, while on the other hand, the process has been adjusted to accommodate the demands of an ever-expanding case load. The consensus on the essentials to be preserved include prompt review, by a group of judges, of the merits of a final judgment of the trial court; a statement of reasons by the appellate court; and, after the parties have submitted their views on the issues, consideration by the judges as dictated by the complexity of the appeal.

Structure of Federal Appellate Systems

In Article III of the United States Constitution, only the Supreme Court of the United States is specifically mentioned. All other federal courts, trial and appellate, are created by act of Congress pursuant to a grant of power under Article III. The basic court of original jurisdiction in the federal system is the United States district court. In almost all cases, appeals from the district court are taken to one of the United States courts of appeals and thereafter, by appeal or petition for certiorari, to the United States Supreme Court. There is a right to appeal every final judgment to a court of appeals. To obtain further review in the Supreme Court requires a vote of at least four justices of the Supreme Court. As a practical matter, the Supreme Court is not required to review any decision of a court of appeals; thus, in all but a relatively small percentage of cases, the decision of the court of appeals is final.

The United States is divided into twelve geographic circuits, eleven comprising various states and one for the District of Columbia. There is a United States court of appeals in each circuit and another in the District of Columbia. There is also the United States Court of Appeals for the Federal Circuit, which sits in Washington, D.C. An appeal is taken from a district court to the court of appeals for the circuit in which the district is located, except for certain types of cases such as patent, trademark, and copyright cases, which go to the Court of Appeals for the Federal Circuit. Each court of appeals has a number of judges specified by statute, based upon the size of the circuit and its case load. In 1985 there were 168 circuit judges, assigned on the basis of the case load of the circuit and historical circumstance, as follows: First, 6; Second, 13; Third, 12; Fourth, 11; Fifth, 16; Sixth, 15; Seventh, 11; Eighth, 10; Ninth, 28; Tenth, 10; Eleventh, 12; District of Columbia, 12; and Federal, 12.

The court of appeals' decisions are usually made by three-judge panels. If a majority of the active judges so vote, however, the court of appeals may hear a case either initially or on rehearing while sitting en banc—that is, with all the active judges of the circuit plus any senior judge who participated in the original decision. The chief judge of each court of appeals is the judge senior in commission under seventy years of age.

Justification for Appellate Review

The most basic justification for appellate review is stated in terms of the desire for uniformity of decisions among the trial courts. Chief Judge John J. Parker expressed this position in the following terms:

> The judicial function in its essence is the application of the rules and standards of organized society to the settlement of controversies, and for there to be any proper administration of justice these rules and standards must be applied, not only impartially, but also objectively and uniformly through the territory of the state. This requires that decisions of trial courts be subjected to review by a panel of judges who are removed from the heat engendered by the trial and are consequently in a position to take a more objective view of the questions there raised to maintain uniformity of decisions throughout the territory.

There are additional justifications for appellate review. Appellate review aids in creating the appearance of providing justice—often just as important as actually providing justice. It protects against outside interference because it permits the judicial system both to correct itself and to develop as society changes. It offers psychological relief by providing the aggrieved party with a way to save face, at least temporarily, by taking additional steps to assert the justice of his or her cause.

Functions of Appellate Courts

Although there is general agreement as to the necessity for appellate review, there is less agreement as to an accurate description of the functions of appellate courts. Error correction and law development are the two functions most often set forth. Some authorities also include "doing justice" as one of the functions of appellate courts.

The most obvious function of appellate review is to correct errors made by the trial court. It is inevitable that mistakes will be made in any process that depends upon humans to ascertain facts and law and to apply one to the other in thousands of cases involving adverse parties. The potential for error is high, and it is perhaps remarkable that the system produces as few appeals as it does. Error correction is concerned primarily with the effect of the judicial process in the trial court upon the individual litigants; it is intended to protect those persons from arbitrariness in the administration of justice. In most cases the error-correction function will be exercised only when the law is clear and the action of the trial court is inconsistent with the demands of the law. The issues often involve a ruling on a matter of procedure or evidence, the application of the wrong legal principle, or the misapplication of the correct legal principle. In any case, the function will be exercised only if the error is not harmless; that is, the impact of the error upon the losing party must be such as to deny something to which the party is clearly entitled.

The basic court of original jurisdiction in the federal system is the United States district court.

As noted, error correction is concerned with the impact of the lower court's decision on the parties in the case. An equally important concern of appellate review is the impact of the lower court's decision upon the law and the legal process. Review so concerned has been termed "institutional review." Its purpose is to provide an opportunity for the common law to develop, thereby permitting it to reflect the demands of the individuals and institutions the law serves, as well as to accommodate factual situations substantially different from those in prior cases. The development function is crucial in a common-law jurisdiction, which has a body of judge-made law as well as law declared by a legislative body or in a constitution.

The functions of error correction and law development have uniformity as their ultimate objective. Yet appellate judges neither can nor should forget that their decisions are not rendered on abstract legal questions but have a direct and immediate effect upon the parties before them. They also cannot forget that their decisions should not be good only for one case and irrelevant to all other cases. Precedent and stare decisis are essential features of a common-law legal system, and appellate courts, like trial courts, cannot ignore the requirements of the law in deciding individual cases. Judge Albert Tate, Jr., of the United States Court of Appeals for the Fifth Circuit expressed the principle in the following terms: "The result that seems 'just' for the present case must be a principled one that will afford just results in similar conflicts of interest. The judge has an initial human concern that the litigants receive common sense justice, but he also realizes that the discipline of legal doctrine governs his determination of the cause."

Doing justice, if it means having the most deserving party prevail, cannot be divorced from doing justice in the context of the entire legal system. Obviously the legal system does not exist for the purpose of doing injustice. But justice is not done by ignoring the applicable substantive and procedural law to achieve a particular result in an individual case. In every case, consequently, the judge's function can be summarized as doing justice in accordance with the law. This means that the judge should try to treat the parties fairly, in accordance with the equities reflected by the facts of the case, and not simply to apply the law mechanically, without regard to the effect upon the persons before the court. At the same time, the judge is not free to disregard the law simply to do what he or she thinks is right as between the parties. There is a tension involved in virtually every case between these two interests, and the judge must try to balance them. When the judge goes too far in the interest of justice and bends the law to accommodate the individual case, he or she gives rise to the type of result that is characterized by the maxim "Hard cases make bad law."

Preserving Issues for Appeal

One of the basic features of the appellate process is that it begins not when the notice of appeal is filed but at the very start of the litigation process when consideration is first given to filing suit. The principal reason for this is one of the basic rules of appellate procedure: only those issues raised in the trial court can be raised on appeal.

The origin of the requirement that issues be raised first in the trial court goes back to the development of the writ of error in England and its subsequent influence on appellate procedure in the United States. If the appeal is looked at from the perspective of the original form of the writ of error—that is, as a new lawsuit filed by the losing party in the trial court against the trial judge and attacking the errors made by him—then the necessity for having the issues presented to the trial judge is obvious. The trial judge cannot be charged with making a wrong decision on an issue if it was never presented to him.

Even though the appeal is no longer considered a separate suit against the trial judge, the requirement that issues be presented at the trial level has been retained primarily because the rule has several important justifications beyond the merely historical. If the function of the appellate court is considered to be error correction, error can be committed only on an issue raised in the trial court. If the losing party can raise a matter on appeal for the first time, he may be able to build in an error to ensure a successful appeal by failing to make a timely objection; that is, had the objection been presented in the trial court, it is possible that no error would ever have been committed. Allowing new issues on appeal also may diminish the need to be fully prepared for the trial itself, a result contrary to the current concern over the competency of trial attorneys. Finally, the requirement also promotes efficient judicial administration because it results in fewer new trials or remands for further proceedings.

Even though the rule requiring issues to be raised first in the trial court is applied by almost every appellate court, there are many refinements or exceptions to the rule. These include fundamental or plain error, particularly if it involves constitutional questions; questions that first arise after the judgment appealed from was entered; jurisdiction of the trial court over the subject matter; failure to plead a claim upon which relief can be granted; and new arguments or theories to support the position of a party originally presented to the trial court.

These exceptions or refinements are usually discussed in terms of issues that a party can raise in the appellate court even though they were not presented to the trial court. It is also generally accepted that an appellate court can and will on occasion consider certain types of issues on its own motion even though they were not raised by either party in the trial court or the appellate court. The subject-matter jurisdiction of the trial or appellate court is always open to question by the appellate court. In addition, two other issues are considered under this principle: the appellate court may wish to review an error committed by the trial court that is not recognized by the appellant, or the appellate court may decide to consider a change in the controlling legal rule that had been accepted by the parties and the trial court.

In addition to the rule that an issue first be presented to the trial court, there are a number of other requirements for preserving an issue for appeal. Some jurisdic-

The losing side in a trial has the right to appeal their case. Long hours of research in a law library such as this one often form the basis for a successful appeal. (Dan Lamont/Corbis)

tions require that an issue, even if originally presented at the trial, must also be presented to the trial court in a posttrial motion to give the judge an opportunity to correct his or her own error. Although this was once the general rule, very few jurisdictions continue this requirement, because posttrial motions usually build in additional delay and are seldom granted. Another important requirement is that the alleged error be reflected in the record on appeal. There is also a requirement that the issue be raised and discussed in the brief.

In summary, the basic requirements for appellate review are that issues initially be presented to the trial court, that this fact be reflected in the record, and that the issue be submitted to the appellate court in the brief filed in that court. These requirements will be enforced, absent one or more of the circumstances set forth above.

Appealability

Probably the best-known rule of appellate procedure is that a judgment must be final before it can be appealed. A final judgment is defined as one that determines all the issues as to all parties in a case, leaving only execution of the judgment to be completed. Although most jurisdictions have adopted the final-judgment rule, the application of the rule is a source of great difficulty for both federal and state appellate courts. The final-judgment rule has several goals. A single appeal that consolidates all issues is economic in that it prevents "piecemeal adjudication" of intermediate orders. It prevents potential harassment of opponents, reduces the cost to the parties and the courts, prevents delay in the trial court, and reduces congestion in appellate courts. The ultimate goal is efficient judicial administration.

Unfortunately, the application of the final-judgment rule has not been as simple as the statement of the rule may imply. Competing with the goals of the rule is the litigants' need for effective review of intermediate rulings that may irreparably harm them, such as revealing information claimed to be confidential or defending a case in a foreign jurisdiction. To avoid arbitrary harshness in particular cases or classes of cases, the finality requirement has been refined or exceptions created by either legislative or judicial action. Each refinement or exception has reduced the effectiveness of the final-judgment rule, with the result that it is often unclear when the rule will be enforced or ignored.

The final-judgment rule as it is applied in the federal judicial system is representative. The rule is embodied in section 1291 of Title 28 of the United States Code, which provides that "the courts of appeals shall have jurisdiction of appeals from all final decisions of the district courts." The Supreme Court has interpreted the statute to mean that a decision is final if it "ends the litigation on the merits and leaves nothing for the court to do but execute the judgment" (*Catlin* v. *United States,* 1945).

A judgment must meet two provisions of the Federal Rules of Civil Procedure before it will be declared "final": it must be set forth separately (Rule 58), and it must be entered by the clerk of the district court in the civil docket (Rule 79[a]). Even after a final judgment has been properly entered, the time limitation on appealing it may be tolled by the timely filing of postjudgment motions such as a motion for judgment notwithstanding the verdict, a motion to amend or make additional findings of fact, a motion for a new trial, or a motion to alter or amend the judgment. A judgment's appealability is restored only when such a motion is denied.

In every case, the judge's function can be summarized as doing justice in accordance with the law.

The Supreme Court has said that the finality requirement of section 1291 should be construed in a pragmatic rather than a technical sense (*Cohen* v. *Beneficial Industrial Loan Corp.,* 1949). The pragmatic approach has resulted in three major refinements or exceptions to the final-judgment rule. One is in a statute, one in a court rule, and one in judicial decision. Under section 1292 of Title 28 of the United States Code, Congress has provided for the appeal of certain types of interlocutory orders. These include orders concerning injunctions and orders that present "controlling questions of law" about which there is a "substantial ground for difference of opinion" and whose immediate review will "materially advance the ultimate termination of the litigation." (An example would be the applicability of a statute to the facts of a case.) For the latter the trial judge must certify that the requirements of the section are met, and the appellate court must agree. Both courts have wide discretion in making these determinations.

Another exception to the final-judgment rule is Federal Rule of Civil Procedure 54(b). This rule applies only when a case involves multiple claims or multiple parties. The rule permits the trial court to direct entry of a final judgment "as to one or more but fewer than all of the claims or parties only upon an express determination that there is no just reason for delay" in entering judgment. The principal difficulty in applying this rule is determining when a claim is separate. Under the most common approach, a claim is considered separate when it arises from a legal theory different from that under which the other claims arose.

The most significant judicially created exception to the final-judgment rule is the collateral-order rule. This rule makes final, for purposes of section 1291, certain orders that do not finally determine the entire controversy between the parties. Under the rule the order must conclusively determine the issue and not be subject to revision; resolve an important issue completely separate from the merits of the action; and be effectively unreviewable upon appeal of the final judgment. An example would be whether the defendant is immune from suit under the facts alleged by the plaintiff. Some courts of appeals have tended to use the collateral-order rule as a basis on which to review any order they have deemed important to review immediately rather than waiting for the final judgment, even though the order did not technically fit any of the other exceptions to the final-judgment rule. The Supreme Court in recent years, however, has rendered several decisions that reject these efforts, beginning with *Coopers and Lybrand* v. *Livesay* (1978).

Although most states, in theory at least, follow the final-judgment rule, there are, as in the federal system, many exceptions to its universal application created by statutes, rules, and judges. In addition, some states either enforce the final-judgment rule strictly or ignore it almost completely. An example of the first is Wisconsin, where an appeal of right can be taken only from a true final judgment. Wisconsin does provide, however, that an appellate court has discretion to review almost any order made by a trial court. New York, in contrast, allows an appeal of right from virtually every kind of intermediate order.

The Wisconsin approach is based upon the Standards of Judicial Administration of the American Bar Association, which recognize the significant distinction between an appeal of right and an appeal within the discretion of the appellate court. Given the tendency of both legislatures and courts to create exceptions to the final-judgment rule to avoid hardship in individual cases or to treat special-classes cases differently, the standards reflect the position that it is better to give the appellate court discretion to review any order when it thinks it appropriate. This restricts the final-judgment rule to appeals of right but allows discretionary review for all other orders.

Parties

Almost as important as determining what can be appealed is the question of who can appeal, who defends the judgment rendered by the trial court, and what special problems are created when there are multiple parties and multiple claims on each side of the case in the trial court. These issues suggest that the status of parties in the appellate courts is extremely complicated. An analysis must be made to determine the status of persons affected by the judgment of the trial court and their rights and duties in the appellate court.

The first and most basic question is who can appeal. The general rule is that only a person who is aggrieved by a judgment can take an appeal from it. The rule is often contained in the statute that provides for the right to appeal, but even without a statutory provision the courts apply the rule. Essentially the rule is one of standing. To bring a lawsuit, a person must have a legally recognized interest that is claimed to be harmed by the defendant. So, too, must a person have an interest adversely affected by the judgment to be able to take an appeal from the judgment.

The person who files the initial appeal is designated as the appellant. If other persons with the same interest as the first appellant also appeal, they are designated as coappellants. Those persons who are not designated as appellants become appellees. Usually their role is to defend the judgment rendered by the trial court. On some occasions the appellee will also seek to challenge some order or ruling of the trial court. In such a case the appellee files a cross-appeal and becomes both an appellee and a cross-appellant; the appellant acquires the additional status of cross-appellee.

As with almost every other rule in appellate practice, the rule that permits only an aggrieved party to appeal has some exceptions. One is on the question of subject-matter jurisdiction. The winning party in the trial court can always appeal to attack the jurisdiction of the trial court over the subject matter of the case. The winning party can also appeal if the party has not recovered all that it sought as relief in the trial court. A party receiving less than the full amount requested is technically aggrieved by the judgment and thus can appeal. A successful party accepting the benefits of the judgment, even though less than requested, cannot appeal. The court treats the person who accepts the benefit of a judgment as though he or she consented to the judgment and thus is prevented from challenging it. For the same reason, the unsuccessful party who voluntarily pays the judgment cannot appeal from it.

There often are persons who are not formal parties in the trial but who may be adversely affected by the judgment. These persons can appeal the judgment if they petition the trial court to intervene in the case for the purpose of taking the appeal. A trustee or other fiduciary who is a formal party in the proceeding can appeal to protect the interest of the estate but not the interests of individual beneficiaries. An attorney does not have a right to appeal in his own name a judgment adverse to his client, even if the fee of the attorney is dependent upon recovery by the client or even when the attorney's fee is an item of recovery and includable in the judgment. This rule does not apply, however, in those cases in which the attorney files a fee petition in his own name. In those situations the attorney can appeal an adverse decision on the fee petition.

Initiating and Perfecting the Appeal

The single most important procedural step in the appellate process is the filing of the notice of appeal. Most appellate courts treat timely filing as mandatory and jurisdictional. The failure to file a timely and proper notice of appeal results in dismissal of the appeal.

The most significant judicially created exception to the final-judgment rule is the collateral-order rule.

Most jurisdictions have placed minimal formal requirements upon the filing of the notice of appeal. Usually the notice of appeal is filed with the clerk of the court from which the appeal is taken, although in some jurisdictions it is filed with the court to which the appeal is taken. The content of the notice of appeal usually requires only the name of the party taking the appeal, the judgment or order from which the appeal is taken, and the name of the court to which the appeal is taken. Most courts are very liberal in construing a notice of appeal. The absence of some of the required information is not fatal so long as the opposing party has a reasonable notice of the intent of the appellant to appeal.

Every jurisdiction has established a time limit within which the notice of appeal must be filed. Sometimes the time limit will vary with the nature of the case or the type of party involved. Time limits are strictly enforced because they are treated as though they are statutes of limitations. A typical rule provision is that an appellate court can waive any failure to comply with the appellate rules except the timely filing of the notice of appeal. Trial courts are often given limited authority to extend the time in which to file the notice of appeal. In addition, the filing of certain types of postjudgment motions, such as a motion for a new trial, delay the time for filing the notice of appeal until the motion is acted upon by the trial court.

In addition to the filing of the notice of appeal, there are several other requirements for perfecting the appeal. These include the payment of the required filing fee, the docketing of the appeal in the appellate court, the filing of a bond to guarantee payment of court costs if required, and the filing of the appeal record in the appellate court.

Cross-Appeal

If an appellee desires only to support the judgment entered by the trial court, the appellee may make any argument in support of the judgment, even that the trial court was correct in entering the judgment but for the wrong reason. The appellee must file a cross-appeal, however, if the appellee seeks to change the judgment of a lower court.

The notice of cross-appeal must follow the same form as the notice of appeal. The cross-appeal must be filed within a limited period specified in the appellate rules.

Relief Pending Appeal

When an appeal is taken, it is not automatic that the enforcement of the judgment appealed from is stayed—that is, unenforced temporarily—while the appeal is pending. Most jurisdictions provide that a money judgment is stayed if a bond is filed, the amount of bond being either specified by statute or rule or as established by the trial court. In all other cases a stay is granted only if the trial court so directs and only under the terms and conditions specified by the trial court. In many situations a stay is absolutely necessary to preserve the status quo while the appeal is pending. Otherwise, the matter may become moot before the appeal is decided. This can occur whenever the lawsuit involves the doing or the not doing of an act, such as the demolition of a building.

In considering whether to grant a request for relief pending appeal, the trial court normally considers four factors: the likelihood that the appellant will prevail upon appeal; the probability that the appellant will suffer irreparable harm in the absence of relief; the harm that the appellee may suffer if relief is granted; and the public interest. The trial court must balance all four of these factors, no one of which is controlling. The action of the trial court in granting or denying the relief requested can be challenged in the appellate court by either party.

Record on Appeal

The general rule is that a reversible error must appear in the record on appeal and that, for the purposes of the appeal, if it is not in the record, it did not happen. The record on appeal can consist either of all the papers and exhibits filed in the trial court plus the transcript of testimony or of only those items in the trial court record designated as the appeal record by the parties. In either case, the record on appeal is crucial to the appellate process because it is the only means by which the appellate court may ascertain what happened in the trial court. Appellate rules generally provide that within a specified period of time, usually thirty days after notice of appeal is filed, the clerk of the trial court or the appellant must have the record on appeal transmitted to the appellate court. Appellate rules also provide for an agreed-upon statement of facts as a substitute for the record on appeal, but this procedure is not often followed.

An important part of the record in most cases is the transcript of testimony at the trial. A major cause of delay in the appellate process traditionally has been the preparation of the transcript of testimony. This transcript is prepared by the court reporter who was present in the courtroom during the trial and recorded the testimony by stenographic, mechanical, or electronic means. The court reporter often has difficulty finding time to transcribe the notes into a typewritten record because when one case is finished, the reporter usually must begin working immediately on the next case. Preparation of the transcript has been one of the major focuses of efforts to expedite the appellate process. Probably the most significant step has been for the appellate court to supervise the preparation of the transcript and to ensure that it is filed within the time period allowed by the rules. Disputes over the content of the record on appeal or the accuracy of the transcript of testimony are decided by the trial court, which retains jurisdiction for this purpose. Only in rare circumstances will this matter reach the appellate court.

The Brief and Appended Materials

The brief is the principal written communication from each party submitting the factual and legal basis on which the appellate court should decide in the party's favor. The relative importance of the brief and the oral argument in the appellate process has been changing slowly over the past two centuries and has changed dramatically since the mid-1960s. In late eighteenth-century England and the United States, communication from the attorneys for the parties to the court was almost exclusively oral. Arguments often lasted several days. Briefs, to the extent that there were any, were merely summaries or outlines of the oral argument and were not of major consequence. In the middle of the nineteenth century, courts became busier, and so they began to impose limitations on the length of the oral argument. At first each side was allowed several hours, then one hour, and then thirty minutes; arguments of fifteen or twenty minutes per side are now common. Written briefs became the substitute for lengthy oral argument. The shortened oral argument became primarily an opportunity for lawyers to emphasize principal points made in their briefs. Since the mid-1960s it has become the opportunity for judges to ask attorneys questions about issues raised in the briefs. In most busy appellate courts, oral argument is heard only in a portion of the cases—sometimes in even less than 50 percent of all appeals. In these courts the brief affords the primary, and perhaps the only, opportunity for the attorney to present arguments on behalf of the client to the appellate court.

The brief is a formal document usually limited in length and following a format specified by the appellate rules. Most jurisdictions allow only three types of briefs as a matter of right: an appellant's brief, an appellee's brief, and an appellant's reply brief. Other briefs may be filed only with the consent of all the parties or by leave of court.

Every jurisdiction has established a time limit within which the notice of appeal must be filed.

A brief usually includes a table of contents and authorities; a statement of the issues; a statement of the case; a statement of facts; an argument; and a conclusion. Each part of the brief plays a particular role. The table of contents is simply a listing of each of the sections of the brief and the page on which it is found. The table of authorities is an alphabetical listing of all the cases, statutes, and other authorities cited in the brief. This is followed by a statement of the issues or questions presented. These are the issues that in the opinion of the party will determine the outcome of the case. Usually only the two or three most important issues are presented, and they are framed in such a way as to incorporate the essential factual and legal elements in the case. The statement of each issue is usually only one sentence long.

The next section, the statement of the case, gives in one or two paragraphs the procedural history of the case, including the status of the parties in the trial court, the relief sought, and how the matter was resolved by the trial court. Essential dates of the most significant procedural events are also given.

After the statement of the case comes the statement of facts. This is supposed to be a neutral statement written in narrative form and giving the essential facts of the dispute between the parties as revealed by the record. Each statement of fact must be supported by a reference to the place in the appendix or the record that supports it. Facts are presented in chronological order rather than in the order presented at the trial. Facts that are in dispute should also be noted.

Next follows the argument, which has as many sections as there are issues presented, with one section of the argument addressed to each issue presented. It is here that the attorney must relate the relevant law to the facts as set forth in the statement of facts and show why both the facts and the law compel a decision in favor of the attorney's client. This is usually the longest section of the brief and the one in which the art of persuasion comes to the fore. The final section of the brief is a conclusion, which is nothing more than a short paragraph stating the precise relief sought. (The appellee's brief follows the same format except that the statement of the case, the statement of facts, or the statement of issues can be omitted when the appellee agrees with the appellant's statement.)

The brief must be prepared in accordance with the appellate rules, which specify the size of paper, whether it is to be printed or typewritten, and, most important, the maximum length. Each brief must be filed within a specified time. For the appellant this is usually thirty days after the appeal record is filed, and for the appellee it is usually thirty days after the appellant's brief is filed.

An appendix is filed at the same time as the appellant's brief. This is a document prepared in the same manner as a brief. It includes the items in the record that both parties think are essential to a decision in the case. Because of the expense of preparing the appendix, some courts have dispensed with it and require only photocopies of portions of the record.

Oral Argument

After the briefs are filed, the case is then scheduled for oral argument or, if oral argument is not heard in every case, a decision is made as to whether oral argument is necessary. Cases are usually scheduled either in the order in which the record is filed or in the order in which the last brief is filed.

As noted above, the relative importance of the brief and the oral argument has changed dramatically since the 1960s. Oral argument in most cases now plays a subsidiary role to the brief, and its primary function is to allow the judges to ask questions about the case that have occurred to them in reading the briefs. Judges prepare for oral argument not only by a careful reading of the briefs but also by having a memorandum prepared by a law clerk or staff attorney and, in some courts, by discussing the case with the other judges on the panel.

Oral argument in an appellant court has a very stylized protocol. The court sits on a raised bench facing the attorneys; the chief or presiding judge sits in the middle, and the other members of the panel alternate to the right and the left of the presiding judge in the order of their seniority. The attorneys sit at a table or tables facing the court with a lectern in the middle. Thirty minutes per side is usually the maximum, but in many courts only fifteen or twenty minutes per side is allowed. The appellant always speaks first and usually will save a few minutes of the allotted time for rebuttal. Each attorney starts off with the statement "May it please the court" and then identifies himself or herself and the client. At one time it was traditional for the appellant to give a shortened version of the statement of the case and the statement of the facts, but because of the advance preparation for oral argument undertaken by most judges, this is no longer necessary. The attorney begins to address the most significant issues in the case but often spends most of the time responding to questions from the bench. By their questions the judges make known to the attorneys the issues that they think are the most important.

The appellee's argument follows the same format except that the appellee has no opportunity for rebuttal. When the appellee is finished, the appellant uses whatever time was reserved to respond to points made by the appellee or simply emphasizes one or two points made in the main argument. At the conclusion of the argument, the presiding judge thanks the attorneys and advises them that the court takes the case under advisement.

The Decisional Process

Following oral argument or, if there is no oral argument, when the court begins to consider the case on its merits, the decisional process of the court starts. The first step is a conference of the members of the panel, usually held immediately following the last oral argument of the day. A tentative decision is reached, and the case is assigned to a member of the panel to write the opinion.

The judge to whom the case is assigned then proceeds to prepare a draft opinion, assisted by the judge's law clerks. After a draft opinion has been prepared, it is circulated to the other members of the panel for their comments. Draft opinions are subject to substantial or little criticism, depending upon their acceptability to the other judges. When the opinion is finally approved by the entire panel, it is filed with the clerk of the court, who sends copies to the parties. A second conference may be held in some courts for final approval of the opinion. The number of conferences may depend upon whether the judges have their offices in the same building. If the court decides that the case is not significant enough to warrant the writing of an opinion, it may simply enter an order disposing of the case.

The decision of the court is not implemented immediately when the opinion and judgment are filed. The parties usually have a certain period, ordinarily fourteen days, in which to petition the court for a rehearing or reconsideration. If the panel that heard the court is less than the full court, the party may also request that the matter be reheard by the entire court rather than just the panel. It is rare for either type of rehearing to be granted, but if one is, supplemental briefs may be called for and the case may be argued again.

Oral argument in an appellant court has a very stylized protocol.

Seeking Review in Higher Courts

If the first appellate court that decided the case was an intermediate rather than a supreme court, it is also possible to seek review in the higher court. There is usually a limited time in which to seek review. The normal procedure is to file a petition with the supreme court along with a copy of the opinion of the intermediate court. There are three common grounds for seeking review in the supreme court. First, the decision of the intermediate appellate court may be in conflict with prior decisions of the supreme court or with decisions of other panels of the intermediate appellate court. Second, if the decision is consistent with prior decisions, the supreme court should consider changing the law. Third, if there are no prior decisions on the issue, the supreme court should give an authoritative decision. If the supreme court accepts the case, oral argument is almost always heard.

Judgment and Mandate

After all appellate proceedings have been completed, whether after rehearing or after the matter has been taken to a higher court, the final appellate court issues its judgment. It will either affirm or reverse the trial court's judgment or vacate it. The case is then returned to the lower court for execution of the original judgment, entry of another judgment as directed by the appellate court, or any other action ordered by the appellate court, such as conducting a new trial. The formal communication from the appellate court is called the mandate, which notifies the trial court of the judgment of the appellate court and returns the record in the case.

Upon receipt of the mandate, the trial court must then take action as directed by the appellate court. If further proceedings are required, they must be consistent with the appellate court's decision. There are, however, certain circumstances under which the trial court can reconsider a matter decided by the appellate court. This can occur when a new trial establishes facts different from those found at the first trial or when the statutory or case law is changed retroactively before the trial court acts in accordance with the mandate.

[See also (III) Certiorari, Federal Court System, Supreme Court of the United States.]

CASES

Catlin v. United States, 324 U.S. 229 (1945)
Cohen v. Beneficial Industrial Loan Corp., 337 U.S. 541 (1949)
Coopers and Lybrand v. Livesay, 437 U.S. 463 (1978)

BIBLIOGRAPHY

American Bar Association Commission on Standards of Judicial Administration, *Standards Relating to Appellate Courts* (1976), is a report with standards and commentary on most aspects of the appellate process from functions of appellate courts to internal operating procedures. American Bar Association Task Force on Appellate Procedure, *Efficiency and Justice in Appeals: Methods and Selected Materials* (1977), is an anthology of pieces on various aspects of the appellate process. Paul D. Carrington, Daniel J. Meador, and Maurice Rosenberg, *Justice on Appeal* (1976), is a general overview of the appellate justice systems, with special emphasis on problems created by the crisis of volume in appellate courts. Frank M. Coffin, *The Ways of a Judge: Reflections from the Federal Appellate Bench* (1980), is a highly introspective analysis of the work of an appellate judge written by a federal court of appeals judge. Commission on Revision of the Federal Court Appellate System, *Structure and Internal Procedures: Recommendations for Change* (1975), is a study of the problems of the federal courts of appeals in coping with an ever-increasing case load with some recommendations.

J. Woodford Howard, Jr., *Courts of Appeals in the Federal Judicial System* (1981), is a study of the federal courts of appeals written from a political science perspective, with concentration on three circuits. Robert A. Leflar, *Appellate Judicial Opinions* (1974), is a collection of excerpts from articles and books on the role of the opinions of appellate courts and how they are crafted; and *Internal Operating Procedures of Appellate Courts* (1980), describes how appellate courts function internally and provides a broader review of the appellate justice system. Robert J. Martineau, *Modern Appellate Practice: Federal and State Civil Appeals* (1983), a text for practicing attorneys covering all aspects of the appellate practice, is a general treatise on the appellate process; and *Fundamentals of Modern Appellate Advocacy* (1985), a text written for use by law students in courses on brief writing and oral argument, gives additional material on the appellate process. Thomas B. Marvell et al., *State Appellate Caseload Growth: Documentary Appendix* (1983), a documentary summary of appellate court statistics for thirty-eight states from 1970, includes filings, reversal rate, time to decision in intermediate court, pending and disposed cases, and trial-court case loads. Marlin O. Osthus and Mayo H. Stigler, *State Intermediate Appellate Courts* (1980), surveys varieties in jurisdiction and structure of state intermediate appellate courts, with compilations of arguments for and against their creation.

John J. Parker, "Improving Appellate Methods," in *New York University Law Review,* 25 (1950), describes prevailing procedures in appellate courts in the 1940s and efforts to improve them. Roscoe Pound, *Appellate Procedure in Civil Cases* (1941), is an historical examination of the appellate process from earliest times, with concentration on development of the English and American appellate systems through the 1930s. Albert Tate, Jr., "The Art of Brief Writing: What a Judge Wants to Read," in *Litigation,* 4 (1978), is an article on the changes in brief-writing technique caused by the greatly increased case load of appellate courts, written by a federal appellate judge. Stephen L. Wasby, Thomas B. Marvell, and Alexander B. Aikman, *Volume and Delay in State Appellate Courts: Problems and Responses* (1979), is a report on statistical data on appellate court delay and the responses to delay, including adding of new resources and more efficient use of existing resources.

– ROBERT J. MARTINEAU

C

CERTIORARI

Certiorari is the name of a writ, or order, that an appellate court can issue to require a lower tribunal to certify and send up the record in a case for review. Literally translated from the Latin, it means "to make more certain," a phrase that suggests the purpose of the writ: careful review of a case by a higher court to ensure that the judgment below is consistent with governing law. The writ developed early in the history of English law, but that fact should not obscure its modern significance. Certiorari is an enormously important aspect of modern appellate procedure in America, for reasons that will become clear in this article.

With the passage of the Judiciary Act of 1925, the Court gained authority to refuse review in most types of cases.

A court exercises its certiorari power when it accepts petitions filed by litigants disappointed with the outcome of their cases in the court below and selects a fraction of these cases for review "on the merits"—that is, reconsideration of the law applied below. This petitioning process should be distinguished from "appeal," another route to reconsideration of a case by a higher court. Litigants generally enjoy a right to at least one appeal, usually from the original decision at trial; the filing of an appeal obliges the appellate court to evaluate and respond to the legal arguments litigants put forward. Litigants enjoy no such right when they petition for certiorari.

In the Supreme Court, certiorari petitions are accepted all year long, but most decisions regarding review occur during the term (October to July) in the midst of the oral argument, voting, and opinion writing associated with the resolution of fully considered cases. The public is only vaguely aware of the agenda-setting process, though, because the Court makes its selection decisions in secret.

Yet, while certiorari decisions are much less visible than the Court's decisions on the merits, they are no less important, either for litigants or for those concerned with the causes they represent. The denial of certiorari is, practically speaking, the end of a lawsuit in most cases that come to the Supreme Court; the disappointed litigant is usually without further recourse to review and must accept the decision of the court below as final. Over 90 percent of the cases that come to the Supreme Court each year meet this fate, the Court granting full review to 150–200 cases a year out of about 4,000 applications.

Rejected litigants can only speculate about why the Court denied review. The Court issues no opinions in making these decisions, though individual justices do occasionally publish dissents from denials. Nor does the Court release the individual votes of the justices or vote totals for and against review, as it does with nearly all votes when the Court actually decides a case on the merits. The public learns who voted for review only if a published dissent from a denial makes this clear. The certiorari power, in short, gives the Supreme Court complete, unreviewable authority to select from among the cases brought to it those which it wants to decide on the merits, and it makes these selections without creating a body of precedent that might narrow its discretion in future cases.

The Supreme Court has not always had authority to set its own agenda. It had no discretion at all over its docket until Congress created the United States courts of appeals in 1891 in response to growing demands on the Supreme Court's capacity for appellate review. These new appellate courts provided a forum for hearing appeals from trial-court decisions and helped make mandatory review in the Supreme Court seem less necessary. Congress gave the Supreme Court some power over its docket at that point, but not until the passage of the Judiciary Act of 1925 did the Court gain authority to refuse review in most types of cases, Supreme Court justices wrote this legislation, which became known as the Judge's Bill. A delegation of justices, led by Chief Justice Taft, then campaigned hard for its passage.

The 1925 act did not give the Court complete discretion over its docket. Some types of cases brought to the Court for review remained mandatory—that is, the Court was obliged to decide them. This bifurcation of review powers remains in effect today. Cases come to the Court via the mandatory route of appeal when a lower court has held a federal statute unconstitutional, when a state court has upheld a state statute against the claim that it violates the federal Constitution, and in certain other limited circumstances. Its certiorari jurisdiction is much broader, extending to any civil or criminal case from the courts of appeal and to questions from state courts involving federal constitutional or statutory law or treaties.

The mandatory cases, or appeals, now constitute about 5 percent of the cases that reach the Court. The Court has three choices in dealing with them: if it believes the appeal to be frivolous or outside its jurisdiction, it can "dismiss for want of a substantial federal question" or affirm summarily; it can overturn the result below at this stage by reversing summarily; or it can note probable jurisdiction and schedule the case for further consideration, as it does when it grants certiorari.

The justices give short shrift to most appeals, processing them much as they do certiorari cases. But the Court has not entirely eliminated the distinction between certiorari and appeal. It selects a disproportionate number of them for full, or plenary, review. Appeals make up approximately one-quarter of the cases scheduled for oral argument. These cases, together with the appeals reversed or affirmed summarily, made up approximately half of the cases the Court decided on the merits that term.

The Court's summary disposition of many appeals inevitably creates some uncertainty in the legal community, because technically speaking, these decisions

The Supreme Court of the 1990s included members of varied social backgrounds, but the justices' ability to reach a high level of consensus comes from their mutual experience in the American court system. (Ronald Reagan Library/Corbis)

have significance as precedent. But it is often unclear just what a summary decision signifies, for it occurs before oral argument or full briefing of the questions raised by the appeal. Signed opinions are rare in these cases; usually the Court simply states its result, sometimes citing the cases it deems controlling in an anonymous (per curiam) opinion.

Denials of certiorari cause no such uncertainty for the practicing bar or the lower courts. The Court issues no opinions in these cases either, but the reasons why the Court decided as it did are, legally speaking at least, not important. Denials of certiorari do not have any official significance as precedents and cannot be cited for this purpose. This does not mean that denials have no significance at all in the eyes of the attentive public. Most observers interpret repeated denials as an indication of judicial indifference to an issue.

The certiorari power is not limited to the United States Supreme Court. It exists, to varying degrees, in about half the states. In some, like California and Illinois, discretionary jurisdiction predominates. Other state supreme courts, like that of Colorado, have a case load almost evenly balanced between mandatory and discretionary cases, but in others, like those of Alabama and Georgia, mandatory cases predominate. In almost all of the states whose supreme courts have certiorari power, there is an intermediate appellate court (or courts) to handle some or all direct appeals from trial-court judgments. But appellate capacity at an intermediate level does not always spawn discretionary review at the top, as it did in the federal system. Thirty-two states have intermediate appellate courts, but only twenty-four of these states have any significant discretionary jurisdiction in their state supreme courts.

The particular arrangements by which mandatory and discretionary cases come to the state supreme court vary from state to state. A few states allow appeals directly from trial courts. In at least two others, the supreme court screens cases, deciding some appeals itself and referring others to a lower court for decision there. States attach different names to the case-selection process too. What would be a petition for certiorari in the federal setting is a petition for leave to appeal or a petition for review in some state courts.

The evidence we have suggests that the considerations involved in case selection at the state level bear a strong resemblance to those that influence certiorari decision-making in the United States Supreme Court. Judges at both levels agree on how to dispose of many review requests but differ among themselves on a significant minority, their differences following patterns that transcend specific subject matter and persist over long periods of time. Because research on certiorari at the state level is still at an early stage and because of space limitations, the remainder of this article will focus on certiorari in the United States Supreme Court.

Criteria for Granting the Writ

The certiorari power is obviously important to the litigants, whose lives are directly affected by review decisions, but it is also important to the American political community as a whole, for the Supreme Court helps set the nation's political agenda as it sets its own agenda. The cases the Court selects and then decides on the merits become the focus of attention in the mass media, scholarly journals, law schools, and the lower courts. The cases denied review are more likely to sink into relative obscurity, for it is not definite whether they represent nationally binding law.

It would be misleading to imply that the Supreme Court sets its agenda with no help from anyone. Disputants and their lawyers play important roles in the process. They determine the universe of cases from which the Court chooses, and they decide how vigorously and fully the issues raised will be pursued. The reality in all phases of the Supreme Court's work is clearly shared power.

The standards the justices use to select the tiny minority of cases they review on the merits are undefined. Some claim that they simply weed through the incoming cases and choose the most important or worthy, and others, that they grant review to correct the most egregious errors they perceive in lower-court decisions. The Court offers some guidance on its criteria for review in rules it has written and published regarding its operations. Supreme Court Rule 17 lists the following as "the character of reasons that will be considered" in granting or denying certiorari:

> *a.* When a federal court of appeals has rendered a decision in conflict with the decision of another federal court of appeals on the same matter; or has decided a federal question in a way in conflict with a state court of last resort; or has so far departed from the accepted and usual course of judicial proceedings, or so far sanctioned such a departure by a lower court, as to call for an exercise of this Court's power of supervision.
>
> *b.* When a state court of last resort has decided a federal question in a way in conflict with the decision of another state court of last resort or of a federal court of appeals.
>
> *c.* When a state court or a federal court of appeals has decided an important question of federal law which has not been, but should be, settled by this Court, or has decided a federal question in a way in conflict with applicable decisions of this Court.

Rule 17 indicates that conflict among the lower courts in interpreting federal law is an important criterion in the review decisions. Litigants shape their petitions for review to take account of this preference, alleging many more conflicts than an objective observer guided by the spirit of Rule 17 would find. A study conducted by Floyd Feeney, for example, found no genuine conflicts, direct or indirect, in 708 of the 966 cases that claimed them. Feeney showed, however, that the Court does not take up every single genuine conflict that it could. Review was denied in 66 cases presenting direct conflicts in the 1971 term and in 70 cases in the 1972 term. Sidney Ulmer has discovered that the Court has varied over time in the extent to which it makes conflicts the basis for review on the merits. The Burger Court apparently put less emphasis on resolving either conflicts between lower courts or conflicts between a lower court and the Supreme Court than the Warren Court did.

The certiorari power allows the Court to conserve its resources for the most important cases that come to it each term.

The question such statistics cannot resolve is whether the Court really should review every conflict between judicial interpretations that is brought to its attention. To allow some conflicts to stand is to permit local variation in interpretations of federal statutes and the Constitution. Such tolerance seems unfair to the individuals and organizations whose rights vary by region. Regional variation can also make legal planning difficult for litigants who operate across jurisdictions.

Yet differences between lower courts may allow some conflicts to "ripen," providing helpful guidance to the Court when it finally (perhaps years later) does resolve the issue. The existence of conflicts, Justice John Paul Stevens has argued, can "illuminate" matters for the Court and "may play a constructive role in the lawmaking process," thus making complex cases easier to resolve. Philosophically, too, Stevens is opposed to reaching out too quickly to resolve inconsistent outcomes in the lower courts: "The doctrine of judicial restraint teaches us that patience in the judicial resolution of conflicts may sometimes produce the most desirable result."

The Court's sense of what constitutes a significant legal issue also plays a role in these decisions. The Court denies review in the face of some legitimate conflicts, apparently because it is not persuaded that the claim is important enough to merit full review. Challenges to the constitutionality of school regulations concerning student hair length, for example, seem to have fallen into this category when they first began to come before the Court: for a time, the justices failed to grant review despite a five-to-five split among the federal circuit courts.

Rule 17 does not mention errors in decisions below as an independent ground for review. The omission is no accident; simple error-correction, the justices have noted from the outset, is not the purpose of certiorari. As Chief Justice William Howard Taft described the Court's role in 1925, just after Congress had provided it with the broad certiorari power it enjoys today, "The function of the Supreme Court is conceived to be, not the remedying of a particular litigant's wrong, but the consideration of cases whose decision involves principles, the application of which are of wide public or governmental interest" (p. 2).

The certiorari power, Taft and other justices have argued over the years, allows the Court to conserve its resources for the most important cases that come to it each term. The litigant's right to appeal perceived errors at the trial level is satisfied by resort to the courts of appeals and to state appellate tribunals. It is this reasoning that lies behind the Court's frequent reminder that the denial of certiorari implies nothing as to its view of the actual merits of a petitioner's arguments.

The impact of the Court's policy of rejecting apparent error in the decision below as the sole basis for review is evident in the certiorari decisions it makes. The justices generally deny petitions that simply allege a mistake or abuse of discretion in the application of existing law to the particular facts of a controversy. Such cases, whatever their significance to individual litigants, raise no broader issues that call out for the Supreme Court's attention. Capital cases are something of an exception to this rule; the Court has always been much more generous in reviewing these cases than other types of criminal cases. In noncapital cases, though, the Court looks for indications that the matter in dispute involves an interpretation of federal law that is bound to arise (or has arisen) elsewhere.

The perception that the results below were wrong does seem to have some impact on the Court's evaluation of the significance of the question, however. This can be seen in the preponderance of reversals in cases accepted for review: on the average, the Court reverses or remands for further proceedings about two-thirds of the cases it decides on the merits each term. The same pattern was evident at the individual level as well during the one period in the Court's history for which we have access to the certiorari and appeals votes of the justices. Justice Harold H. Burton, who sat on the Court between 1945 and 1958, released these votes to the Library of Congress upon his death. They are an invaluable resource for understanding how the Court sets its agenda.

Justice Burton's docket books indicate that all of the justices apparently took their views of the proper outcome of a case into account in voting for or against review. Each of the fifteen justices who sat during Burton's tenure on the Court was more likely to vote to reverse the cases he voted to review than the ones that came up for review on the merits despite his negative vote. These justices varied, however, in the extent to which they linked votes to review with the merits of the controversy. Justice Charles E. Whittaker, for example, voted to reverse 93 percent of the cases he voted to review but only 43 percent of those that came to him for a final decision despite his negative case-selection vote. Justice Burton, in contrast, voted to reverse only 56 percent of the cases he voted to review and 39 percent of the others. There is no reason not to expect similar differences in sensitivity to error below among the current members of the Supreme Court.

Even if the justices were alike in their propensity to vote for review to correct error below, they would still differ over what they perceived to be error. Even the most casual Court watcher is aware of this difference between justices. The tradition of releasing the on-the-merits votes of each justice and publishing both majority and minority opinions (and sometimes more than one of each) ensures that these differences will be obvious to everyone.

A final limiting factor in the review decision is quasi-jurisdictional. If the Court perceives a case as lying outside its competence or appropriate sphere, it will generally deny review, even where the consequences for the litigants involved are serious. The Court has been quite consistent in denying review to petitions turning on the interpretation of state statutes or case law, for example. The Court leaves these matters to the state courts. The Court also avoids correcting errors of trial courts not properly noted in the original appeal from the trial-court judgment. When, for example, a petitioner claims for the first time at the Supreme Court level that trial counsel was incompetent, the justices will not ordinarily respond. Petitioners are expected to raise their issues in a timely way in a lower appellate court to preserve them in petitioning for certiorari.

Evaluation of Petitions

Requests for certiorari arrive as petitions shortly after the entry of final judgment in the court below. The Court regulates the form in which they must be filed through its rules. Absent Court permission to file in forma pauperis, petitioners must frame their arguments within the highly structured form of a legal brief no more than thirty pages long, have forty copies of this document printed for distribution to the justices and staff, and pay a filing fee. Copies of the opinion and judgment below are attached as appendices. Respondents (those parties who won in the court below and therefore would like to avoid review) have thirty days from receipt of notice of petitioner's filing to submit a brief in opposition. Petitioners are then entitled to respond with a reply brief. The rules for cases that come to the Court as appeals are similar, the principal difference being that appellants file a jurisdictional statement, rather than a petition for certiorari.

The extent to which justices rely on the recommendations of law clerks can only be a matter of speculation.

A petitioner or appellant can avoid the formality of filing and the financial outlay it involves by asking the Court's permission to file in forma pauperis. If the Court grants the motion, the litigant need not comply with the standard format, printing, reproduction, and filing-fee requirements. The number of persons who claimed that they could not comply with standard filing requirements began to increase drastically in the late 1950s and has continued to grow since then. In forma pauperis cases now constitute approximately half of the total number filed each year. Prisoners and persons proceeding without lawyers *(pro se)* often choose this option.

The decision to proceed in forma pauperis used to have important implications for the way a case was considered by the Court. The in forma pauperis, or "unpaid," cases were recorded separately on the miscellaneous docket, while the regular, or "paid," cases went on the appellate docket. The chief justice's clerks briefed the miscellaneous docket cases and distributed their memos to the rest of the Court. Appellate docket cases, on the other hand, entered the chambers of each justice to be briefed by the designated clerk in each office. (Capital cases were the only exception to the rule of diminished consideration in in forma pauperis cases.) This two-track system ended in the mid-1960s: all requests for review now receive the same type of preconference analysis. Only the numbering system the Court uses preserves the distinction between them. Docket entries in paid cases, after a two-digit prefix denoting the year, begin at 1 each term. In forma pauperis cases begin at 5,000.

Despite the similarity in processing, unpaid cases do not have nearly as high a rate of review as paid cases do.

The in forma pauperis litigants are less successful in getting review, in large part because they tend to raise issues the Court perceives as confined closely to the facts of particular cases; that is, they are often unimportant in the legal sense discussed earlier. But lack of financial resources inevitably takes a toll too. These litigants cannot afford to hire the legal help necessary to shape their cases to the standards the Court applies in case selection.

The rules discussed so far assume that the only way the justices have to determine the legal significance of the cases they screen is to assess the materials provided by those proposing and opposing review. This is usually the situation, but sometimes other interested individuals or groups want to make known to the Court their views concerning the worthiness of a case for certiorari. The Court regulates their participation through its rules regarding participation amicus curiae (that is, as "a friend of the court").

The requirements are very similar to those the Court applies to potential friends of the court in fully considered cases. Private individuals and organizations who want to participate must secure the permission of the named parties or get the permission of the Court itself before filing a brief in support of, or, less often, in opposition to, review. Such requests are usually granted. Government, whether state or federal, can file without asking permission.

Amicus participation at the case-screening stage has grown increasingly frequent since the mid-1960s. Before then, briefs focused on the screening decision were almost unheard of. The change is due not so much to liberalization of the Court's rules regarding an amicus as to the increasing difficulty litigants face in getting Supreme Court review. People concerned with shaping public policy through litigation have come to realize that the Court, with a fixed capacity for on-the-merits review, must be quite selective.

The Court has developed certain routines to keep the time involved in deciding review requests to a minimum. These routines have changed as the case load has increased and the justices have received more staff support. All the justices, for example, once scanned all petitions and jurisdictional statements themselves. In the 1980s, Justice William J. Brennan was the only one who still did, and even he was unable to do this over the summer months. The rest of the Court has come to rely on law clerks to summarize these materials. The clerks produce short memos outlining the facts, decision below, contentions on appeal, and recommended disposition of the case.

The law clerks are young lawyers, most of whom graduated from elite law schools and then clerked a year or two in a lower court. The chief justice currently has five law clerks, and six of the associate justices employ four each, while of the two justices remaining, one has three and the other has two. Each of the clerks works independently for a justice on opinions in fully decided cases, but the situation is not quite the same where case screening is involved. Since the mid-1970s, some of the justices have pooled law clerks for memo-writing purposes. The clerks involved produce a memo on each case, which is then shared among justices in the pool. This practice reduces the work load of the clerks; its impact on case selection has not been assessed.

The extent to which the justices rely on the recommendations of the law clerks can only be a matter of speculation. Clerks who have written on the subject generally deny that they have a significant influence on their justice's decision, but some litigators are not so sure. Philip Kurland, for example, has complained that the Court's reliance on law-clerk summaries in case-selection decisions reduces carefully drafted petitions to pap for quick judicial consumption.

Justice Burton's records indicate that he agreed with his clerks about 85 percent of the time. Agreement does not tell us who was following whose lead or whether similar judgments were arrived at independently. It seems fair to assume, though, that it is the clerks who respond to the views of their justices, rather than the reverse. The one- or two-year tenure of most clerks, the vast difference between justice and clerk in age and experience, and the inequality of their positions all point toward clerk accommodation to judicial views in case selection.

The Court convenes as a body to consider review requests and other business on most Fridays throughout the term and occasionally on a Wednesday or Thursday. These Friday conferences, which occur after a week of oral argument, are multipurpose; the Court generally devotes the morning to review requests and the afternoon to argued cases. It disposes of review requests that arrive over the summer in a series of several all-day sessions early in the Court's term.

The justices are able to dispose of large numbers of certiorari requests quickly because they have developed certain decision-making conventions, the most important of which is the "discuss list," a listing of cases that will be voted upon in the conference. The chief justice and his clerks prepare the discuss list and circulate it, though any justice is free to add cases to it. The justices can also request a delay in the disposition of any case on the conference list. All cases on the much longer conference list for that date, but not on the discuss list, are automatically denied review without discussion.

Certiorari and appeals decisions thus have two phases: an individual phase, in which each judge, usually with assistance from clerks, decides whether a case might be worthy of review and therefore should be among the minority of cases that make up the discuss list; and a group phase, in which the Court scrutinizes and rejects many of the cases that survive the first cut. In Justice Burton's day, roughly 60 percent of the cases were cut at the first phase, and another 25–30 percent in the conference. Members of the Supreme Court in the late 1980s estimated that about 70 percent of all cases brought before them were utterly frivolous, which suggests that this may be the proportion that failed to make the discuss list at that time.

Two-thirds of the cases the Court reviews are constitutional claims and one-third are statutory.

The conferences in which certiorari petitions are considered are rather formal meetings. They begin with a shaking of hands all around, and the justices then arrange themselves around the table in order of their seniority. The chief justice starts the discussion by summarizing the case and stating his own views. After a general discussion, the voting occurs, reportedly also in order of seniority. Evidence about these conferences is scanty because they include no one except the justices themselves, and the justices tend to be very close-mouthed about conference proceedings.

It seems clear, however, that chief justices have an important opportunity for leadership at this stage. Their use of the certiorari decision-making process as an opportunity to try to push their views on the others or to seek consensus varies with the individual. Chief Justice Hughes, according to several of the justices who served with him, dominated the discussion, as much because of his preparation and formidable intellectual powers as because of the opportunity to speak first.

Other chiefs have apparently interpreted their leadership responsibilities differently. The Burton materials contain evidence on the voting patterns of three chief justices: Harlan F. Stone, Fred M. Vinson, and Earl Warren. None of these chiefs voted alone, for or against review, as often as most of their colleagues. These chiefs were also more likely than most members of the Court to contribute the crucial vote necessary for granting review in close cases. This pattern suggests that these chief justices used certiorari voting as an occasion to promote consensus on the Court, checking their own views in the process.

Four affirmative votes are required to grant petitions for certiorari and to note probable jurisdiction in appeals cases. The origins of this rule are unclear, but it appears to have been in operation even before the passage of the 1925 Judiciary Act, when certiorari cases were relatively rare. The rule could be avoided if the majority who voted against review at the certiorari stage voted, after oral argument, to dismiss the petition as improvidently granted. The justices have always felt bound, however, to honor the rule of four and give full consideration to cases that pass the screening stage, unless most or all of the Court comes to feel the petition was mistakenly granted.

The four-vote requirement obviously gives a minority of the Court the chance to force the majority to consider a case it would prefer to avoid deciding on the merits. But the evidence is strong that most certiorari decisions are not this close. In the Burton era, over half of the cases considered in conference received no votes at all for review, and a significant proportion of the rest were unanimous grants. Taking account of the cases eliminated even before the conference (through the discuss-list procedure), the rate of unanimity about review-worthiness becomes truly impressive, reaching 82 percent. The overall level of agreement at the certiorari stage may be even greater today, given the Court's much larger case load.

The justices of the Supreme Court, whose tendency to disagree with each other on the merits is well known, reach such a high level of consensus in certiorari voting because they share a basic understanding of the role the Court should play in superintending the nation's judicial system. The justices, after all, have in common their professional education and a lifetime of daily experience with the traditions and presuppositions of the profession. It is easy to lose sight of this shared intellectual tradition because so much attention is devoted to the Court's work on the merits, where close questions of law and policy often divide their votes.

Within the boundaries of fundamental agreement about the types of cases that deserve Supreme Court review, the available data suggest that the justices differ among themselves along three dimensions: in how frequently they vote for review, in the extent to which they take their disagreement with the outcome below into account in voting to review (discussed earlier), and in their interpretation of the merits of the underlying controversies. Differences along the first dimension are probably the most dramatic and certainly the least well understood of the three.

The extent to which justices might differ in their propensity to vote for review can be gauged by comparing Justices Felix Frankfurter and Harold Burton with two justices of much different persuasion, Hugo Black and William O. Douglas. Burton and Frankfurter rarely voted alone for review, each casting less than fifty votes alone in the course of ten years; they were only slightly more likely to vote with one other justice for review. During the same period, Black and Douglas each cast over two hundred lone votes for review and over three hundred apiece with one other justice.

The jurisprudential writings of these justices offer some assistance in explaining the difference in voting patterns between the two pairs. Frankfurter described his own approach in unambiguous terms in a letter to Chief Justice Warren (26 January 1956): "I am, in the main, alert against taking cases except those that obviously call for determination by this Court. By 'obviously' I mean cases about which there can hardly be a difference of opinion around the table." Black and Douglas, on the other hand, shared the view that the lower courts must be closely supervised. These justices were also less worried than many of their colleagues about the burdens a large plenary docket imposes at the argument and opinion-writing stage.

Who Wins Review and Why

Chances of review vary dramatically from one type of case to another. Some types, as noted earlier, have little chance of review: cases not ripe for Supreme Court decision on technical grounds, those based on competing interpretations of state law, and those of little concern to anyone beyond the parties to the action. But even among cases without such deficiencies, chances of review vary tremendously. The Court does not, for example, review many patent or bankruptcy cases, even though they raise federal questions of real significance to petitioners and others concerned with these statutes.

The Court's sense of the importance of a suit obviously operates to the benefit of some causes and petitioners and to the disadvantage of others. A comparison of the cases the Court selected for review in a given period with those eligible can help explain how the Court arrives at a sense of what is important and what that operational definition includes.

In general, the Court prefers constitutional claims to those based on the interpretation of a statute: roughly two-thirds of the cases it reviews are constitutional claims and one-third are statutory. In 1955 the proportions were just the opposite. In the constitutional realm, the court favors claims of infringed personal rights over property rights, a preference it has demonstrated since the 1930s, when it began to distinguish the level of scrutiny it would give each type of claim on the merits. Since then, the Court's understanding of what is included in the realm of personal rights has grown broader.

Changing public attitudes and legislation have been important in altering the Court's view of significance where personal rights are concerned. But the numbers of cases that come to the Court for review and the energy and imagination with which they are litigated also play important roles in altering judicial sensitivities. "Each age," Justice Douglas once noted, "brings the Court its own special worries, anxieties, and concerns. The main outlines of the life of the nation are mirrored in the cases filed with us."

Allegations of sex discrimination provide a useful example of how events, litigation, and legal development can combine to cause the Court to change its mind about "certworthiness." The Court did get occasional petitions alleging sex discrimination in the administration of the tax laws and other statutes before 1970, but it almost invariably denied them. In the Burton period, these cases did not even survive the first cut to discussion at the weekly conference. The number of filings began to grow in the early 1970s as the women's movement gained momentum and state antiabortion laws and other laws allegedly disadvantaging women came under constitutional attack. Grants of review soon began to grow at an even faster rate, in part because conflicts over the constitutional protections available to women developed among the lower courts.

The passage of far-reaching federal legislation can have a similar effect on filings and chances of review. A new law inevitably creates disputes over its meaning, some of which are likely to become lawsuits. These lawsuits are likely to spawn some petitions to the Supreme Court, and the Court may well feel the obligation to grant them to resolve significant ambiguities. The likelihood of review will diminish, though, as the broader questions are resolved.

The sophistication of the party who brings the case to the Court is also relevant to its chances for on-the-merits review. Nowhere is this more obvious than in cases brought by the United States. About 70 percent of the federal government's petitions gain review. This extraordinary grant rate is not simply an artifact of subject matter, for when the federal government's opponents are the petitioners, the grant rate does not rise much above the overall average, now less than 10 percent. Nor can the current rate at which the federal government wins review be explained in terms of the politics of the current configuration of justices, for the

United States has always enjoyed enormous success in gaining review.

The federal government is successful largely because the solicitor general, who handles cases destined for the Supreme Court, is an expert and selective petitioner. The solicitor general allows only 10 percent to 15 percent of the cases the government lost below to go forward for Supreme Court review, and in those already select cases, petitions are prepared with care. The justices can thus rely on the solicitor general's sense of self-restraint in petitioning, and he or she in turn enjoys a special status with the Court. The solicitor general is, for example, the only petitioner who has an office in the Supreme Court itself.

A few law firms have become expert in filing for Supreme Court review, but most other petitioners have no expertise at all in petitioning for certiorari, for the United States has no tradition of limiting practice before its highest court to an elite bar, as Britain does with its select corps of barristers. In the United States admission to practice before the Supreme Court is required, but this is not difficult for a lawyer with some experience in the practice of law. The negative side of this policy is that the Court is inundated with cases that have little prospect of review. The positive side is that the Court can maintain an image of openness to anyone with a legitimate grievance and thereby keep alive the often-repeated threat "I'll take this matter all the way to the Supreme Court."

The impact of the Court's policy of easy access on criminal filings is striking. Nothing prevents large numbers of prisoners from petitioning the Court, sometimes repeatedly. Unlike the solicitor general, however, these petitioners cannot afford to be selective. The result is that the Court grants only a tiny proportion of the prisoner petitions it receives each term, though the total it receives is so large that criminal cases constitute a significant fraction of the cases the Court considers on the merits each year.

The power of the Court to pass over some types of petitioners and issues entirely raises another question about who wins review and why: Does the Court sometimes use its certiorari power to dodge issues that, if resolved on the merits, might jeopardize the Court's institutional resources? Consider, for example, the problem of the enforceability of decrees. Might the Court sometimes be better advised to dodge the occasional conflict that threatens to open the Court to widespread public criticisms or open defiance? At least one constitutional scholar, Alexander Bickel, has advocated the "passive virtue" of nondecision in such circumstances.

The justices seem to have rejected the call to what one of them has described as "political self-protection" at the review-granting stage. The indirect evidence is the infrequency with which the Court is accused, even by its critics, of ducking important policy issues. Direct evidence that the Court rejects the idea of using case selection instrumentally is available in the Burton files. The files reveal that Burton's clerk recommended denials of review in several important race-discrimination cases, including *Shelley* v. *Kraemer* (1948) and *Holmes* v. *City of Atlanta* (1955), on the grounds that the public would not accept an integrationist result. In *Shelley,* which challenged judicial enforcement of racially restrictive housing covenants, Burton's clerk argued that "an abrupt and sweeping judicial invalidation of all restrictive covenants might well create about as many problems as it would solve." The clerk closed by recommending that the Court deny the petition. The Court rejected this advice, all but Justice Robert H. Jackson voting in favor of review.

Proposals to Modify Certiorari Power

The certiorari power gives a busy Court tremendous scope to shape its own agenda each term, but at a potentially significant cost in its time and resources for considering argued cases on their merits. Time spent on review requests is obviously time not available for on-the-merits decision-making; these two aspects of the Court's work are inevitably interdependent. As the case load of the Court has increased from less than two thousand cases a year up until the mid-1960s to over triple that number in the mid-1990s, the question has been raised more and more often whether the Court can adequately discharge both functions without assistance. Erwin Griswold, for example, has warned that under current arrangements "we have been unduly rationing justice." As solicitor general from 1967 to 1973, Griswold claims to have seen at least twenty cases a year that deserved review by an appellate court with national jurisdiction but did not get it.

Others who have observed the Court closely disagree with this assessment. According to Arthur D. Hellman, "There has been a lot of attention paid to intercircuit conflicts that the Court supposedly does not resolve. In my research thus far, I have not found very many square conflicts, or even side-swipes . . . that the Court doesn't resolve. For the most part, a conflict comes up and the Court seizes the case" (Greenhouse et al., 397).

The first full-fledged report addressed to the issue of the Supreme Court's work load was commissioned by Chief Justice Burger. This report, named after its chairman, Harvard law professor Paul Freund, appeared in 1972. It recommended that the Court be relieved of case selection, which it characterized as a burdensome chore of little significance to the primary mission of the Court, which is "to give direction to the law, and to be as precise, persuasive, and invulnerable as possible in its exposition" (Federal Judicial Center, 1). The commission proposed to locate the case-selection responsibility in a new national court of appeals. The new court would certify some cases to the Supreme Court, resolve certain conflicts between the regional courts of appeals on its own, and deny review to the rest. This drastic proposal for relieving the Court's work load met with considerable hostility, both on and off the Court, and the proposal died under the weight of adverse comment and lukewarm endorsements. Another proposal, drafted by the congressionally appointed Commission on Revision of the Federal Court Appellate System, chaired by Senator Roman Hruska, was released in 1975. It recommended a new federal court with "reference" jurisdiction. The new court would take up cases referred to it by the Supreme Court; these would be cases too important to be denied review but too unimportant to absorb the Court's limited time for on-the-merits review. Case selection would remain entirely in the Supreme Court's hands under the Hruska proposal, which may explain why it was better received than the Freund Commission report. Despite the more positive reception accorded the Hruska approach, the idea has so far failed to win congressional approval, and its prospects do not appear very bright.

The certiorari power gives a busy Court tremendous scope to shape its own agenda each term.

Chief Justice Burger was enthusiastic about establishing a new court. He proposed a temporary court staffed with judges from around the country presently on the various courts of appeal. This court would resolve issues referred to it by the Supreme Court, most of which would involve conflicts between the courts of appeals on questions of statutory construction. Losers at this level would retain the right to petition the Court for further review.

Members of the Court did not rally behind the chief justice's proposed emergency court of appeals, though some justices do favor a new court in some form. Others propose different remedies, such as changing the rule of four to a rule of five. Nearly everyone on the Court, though, has complained of the burdens imposed by the current work load. As long as the Court remains divided about what to do about its work load, however, the chances of major structural reform are slim.

Congress is more likely to take a less controversial (and less effective) approach to the workload issue than that proposed by the chief justice or other proponents of a new court. House and Senate committees are considering bills to eliminate the Court's jurisdiction over so-called diversity cases, cases concerning the application of state law that arrive in the federal courts because an earlier era feared prejudice against out-of-state plaintiffs in state courts. This reform would have relatively little effect on the Supreme Court because the Court already disfavors diversity cases. Rule 17 emphasizes the Court's interest in federal, as opposed to state, legal questions.

Congress is also considering eliminating all types of jurisdiction that are still mandatory. All of the justices and many legal scholars have encouraged this reform, and Congress has already taken some small steps in this direction. In the mid-1970s it eliminated a few types of appeal in favor of certiorari jurisdiction. The elimination of all mandatory jurisdiction would be helpful to the Court, but it is unlikely to have a profound impact, because the justices have already developed ways to expedite their consideration of mandatory cases.

Congress could reduce the number of cases the Court gets by limiting the number of federal grounds for relief, thus eliminating some kinds of cases from the federal court system. Every grant of federal jurisdiction, however, has its defenders. These constituencies would resist any effort to eliminate federal causes of action. Major changes are unlikely to come from this direction.

The Court would benefit from a Congress more attentive to its case-management problems, but it is not necessarily harmed by Congress' unwillingness to create a new national appellate court, especially one that would lessen the Court's control over its own docket. The issues involved in evaluating and altering appellate capacity are complex, but the desirability of maintaining certiorari in the Court should be clear: the certiorari power gives the Court the opportunity to remain involved with the changing face of litigation and sensitizes it to new claims and causes. Certiorari also helps maintain the Court's image as an available forum, for it can deny review without necessarily denying the validity of a claim. The certiorari power also creates an important buffer for the Court, allowing it to time its interventions with their impact in mind. The important right-to-counsel case *Gideon* v. *Wainwright* (1963) furnishes a useful example. According to Nathan Lewin, a law clerk who served in the period, the justices chose this case from among many raising the same issue with the idea of making the result as palatable as possible:

> Justice Harlan—for whom I worked—would ask, as to each case that might be resolved on the ground ultimately taken in *Gideon,* whether there were . . . unsatisfactory elements in the case that would cause greater popular resentment to the decision than it deserved. One case which seemed perfect in all other re-

spects was rejected because it involved a charge of molesting little girls.

(p. 18)

Whatever the ultimate significance of Court-controlled case selection to the institutional power of the Supreme Court, it need not remain as secret as it has been in the past. The paucity of data about how case selection actually works has limited understanding of the work of the Supreme Court and has contributed to the tendency to view the Court solely in terms of disagreement among the justices in decisions on the merits. Voting data from the now-secret conferences where certiorari decisions are made could enable students of the Court to gain a better appreciation of how review decisions occur.

This is not to suggest that the Court should open its conferences to the public or publish its review votes as they occur. Such openness would undoubtedly inhibit the free flow of ideas in conferences and force the justices to spend much more time than they currently do in making review decisions. A better approach would be to follow Justice Burton's lead and release voting records after an interval of several years. Case selection is an important dimension of Supreme Court power, and the public deserves the opportunity to learn more about how that process proceeds.

[See also (III) Federal Court System, Judicial Review, Jurisdiction, State Court Systems, Supreme Court of the United States.]

CASES

Gideon v. Wainwright, 372 U.S. 335 (1963)
Holmes v. City of Atlanta, 350 U.S. 879 (1955)
Shelley v. Kraemer, 334 U.S. 1 (1948)

BIBLIOGRAPHY

Lawrence Baum, "Decisions to Grant and Deny Hearings in the California Supreme Court," in *Santa Clara Law Review,* 16 (1976), is the first empirical analysis of how certiorari works in a state court. Alexander Bickel, *The Least Dangerous Branch: The Supreme Court at the Bar of Politics* (1962), is a wide-ranging analysis of the Court's political role. Gerhard Casper and Richard Posner, *The Workload of the Supreme Court* (1976), analyzes the growth in the Court's case load and includes possible remedies. Commission on Revision of the Federal Court Appellate System, *Structure and Internal Procedures: Recommendations for Change* (1975), is the Hruska Commission report suggesting a new national appellate court. William O. Douglas, "The Supreme Court and Its Case Load," in *Cornell Law Quarterly,* 45 (1960), argues that there is no case-load crisis in the Supreme Court. Editors of the Harvard Law Review, "The Supreme Court," *Harvard Law Review,* is an annual survey of the Supreme Court's work and includes statistics on dispositions useful to anyone interested in numbers of grants. Sam Estreicher and John E. Sexton, "New York University Supreme Court Project," in *New York University Law Review,* 59 (1984), reanalyzes the work of the 1982 term to ascertain the Court's effectiveness in case selection.

Federal Judicial Center, *Report of the Study Group on the Caseload of the Supreme Court* (1972), is the Freund Commission report suggesting the establishment of a national court of appeals. Floyd Feeney, "Conflicts Involving Federal Law: A Review of Cases Presented to the Supreme Court," in Commission on Revisions of the Federal Court Appellate System, A-50, analyzes the extent of unresolved conflicts in certiorari petitions. Victor E. Flango, "Court Control of Access: Which Appeals Are Heard?" in *State Court Journal,* 8 (1984), briefly describes the incidence and operation of certiorari in the state courts. Linda Greenhouse et al., "Rx for an Overburdened Supreme Court," in *Judicature,* 66 (1983), discusses the Court's case load and how to reduce it and summarizes current justices' views. Erwin N. Griswold, "Rationing Justice: The Supreme Court's Caseload and What the Court Does Not Do," in *Cornell Law Review,* 60 (1975), argues for a national court of appeals. Arthur D. Hellman, "Caseload, Conflicts, and Decisional Capacity," in *Judicature,* 67 (1983), is a well-informed analysis of the Court's case-load issues. Philip Kurland, "Jurisdiction of the United States Supreme Court: Time for a Change?" in *Cornell Law Review,* 59 (1974), discusses reform proposals. Nathan Lewin, "A Response to Goldberg and Bickel," in *New Republic,* 3 March 1973, offers a former clerk's support for the current power of Court over review.

Doris Marie Provine, *Case Selection in the United States Supreme Court* (1980), is the only book-length treatment of the subject; and "Deciding What to Decide: How the Supreme Court Sets Its Agenda," in *Judicature,* 64 (1981), briefly describes criteria the justices use in granting and denying review. Robert L. Stern and Eugene Gressman, *Supreme Court Practice,* 5th ed. (1978), is a "how-to" for lawyers, full of information on the nuts and bolts of applying for review. John Paul Stevens, "Some Thoughts on Judicial Restraint," in *Judicature,* 66 (1982), gives the justice's view that case-selection discretion should be exercised with restraint. William Howard Taft, "The Jurisdiction of the Supreme Court Under the Act of February 13, 1925," in *Yale Law Journal,* 35 (1925), discusses the certiorari power from the perspective of the chief justice who drafted the legislation. S. Sidney Ulmer, "Selecting Cases for Supreme Court Review: An Underdog Model," in *American Political Science Review,* 72 (1978), stresses the relationship between judicial attitudes toward litigants and selection behavior; and "Conflict with Supreme Court Precedent and the Granting of Plenary Review," in *Journal of Politics,* 45 (1983), analyzes the significance of different outcomes below to the review decision.

– DORIS MARIE PROVINE

CIRCUIT COURTS

The Judiciary Act of 1789 fashioned a decentralized circuit court system. The boundaries of the three circuits coincided with the boundaries of the states they encompassed, a practice that opened them to state and sectional political influences and legal practices. The act assigned two Supreme Court Justices to each circuit to hold court along with a district judge in the state where the circuit court met. (After 1794, a single Justice and a district judge were a quorum.) The circuit-riding provision brought federal authority and national political views to the new and distant states, but also compelled the Justices to imbibe local political sentiments and legal practices.

For a century questions about the administrative efficiency, constitutional roles, and political responsibilities of these courts provoked heated debate. In the Judiciary Act of 1801, Federalists sought to replace the Justices with an independent six-person circuit court judiciary, but one year later the new Jeffersonian Republican majority in Congress eliminated the circuit judgeships and restored the Justices to circuit duties, although they left the number of circuits at six. Subsequent territorial expansion prompted the addition of new circuits and new Justices until both reached nine in the Judiciary Act of 1837. Slave state interests opposed further expansion because they feared the loss of their five-to-four majority on the high court. Congress in 1855 did create a special circuit court and judgeship for the Northern District of California to expedite land litigation.

Significant structural and jurisdictional changes accompanied the Civil War and Reconstruction. The Judiciary Act of 1869 established a separate circuit court judiciary and assigned one judge to each of the nine new circuits that stretched from coast to coast. Justices retained circuit-riding duties although the 1869 act and subsequent legislation required less frequent attendance.

Historically, these courts had exercised original and appellate jurisdiction in cases involving the criminal law of the United States, in other areas where particular statutes granted jurisdiction, and in cases resting on diversity of citizenship. The Judiciary Act of 1869 strengthened the appellate responsibilities of the circuit courts by denying litigants access to the Supreme Court unless the amount in controversy exceeded $5,000. The Jurisdiction and Removal Act of 1875 established a general federal question jurisdiction and made it possible for, among others, interstate corporations to seek the friendly forum of the federal as opposed to the state courts. The 1875 measure also transferred some of the original jurisdiction of the circuit courts to the district courts. However, because the circuit courts were given increased appellate responsibilities, along with only modest adjustments in staffing, their dockets became congested. The resulting delay in appeals, combined with similar congestion in the Supreme Court, persuaded Congress in 1891 to establish the Circuit Courts of Appeals which became the nation's principal intermediate federal appellate courts. Although the old circuit courts became anachronisms, Congress delayed abolishing them until 1911.

Throughout the nineteenth century Supreme Court Justices held ambivalent attitudes toward circuit duty.

The United States is divided into 12 circuits, or districts, each of which has a court of appeals. This is the federal court house located in New Mexico's capital, Santa Fe. (Jan Butchofsky-Houser/Corbis)

The Justices complained about the rigors of circuit travel and the loss of time from responsibilities in the nation's capital, but most of them recognized that circuit judging offered a unique constitutional forum free from the immediate scrutiny of their brethren on the Court. "It is only as a Circuit Judge that the Chief Justice or any other Justice of the Supreme Court has, individually, any considerable power," Chief Justice Salmon P. Chase observed in 1868.

Circuit court judges contributed to the nationalization of American law and the economy. Justice Joseph Story, in the First Circuit, for example, broadly defined the federal admiralty and maritime jurisdiction. In perhaps the most important circuit court decision of the nineteenth century, Story held, in *De Lovio* v. *Boit* (1815), that this jurisdiction extended to all maritime contracts, including insurance policies, and to all torts and injuries committed on the high seas and in ports and harbors within the ebb and flow of the tide. This decision, coupled with Story's opinion eight years later in *Chamberlain* v. *Chandler* (1823), expanded federal control over admiralty and maritime-related economic activity and added certainty to contracts involving shipping and commerce.

The circuit courts extended national constitutional protection to property, contract, and corporate rights. Justice William Paterson'S 1795 decision on circuit in *Van Horne's Lessee* v. *Dorrance* was the first significant statement in the federal courts on behalf of vested rights. But in 1830 Justice Henry Baldwin anticipated by seven years the public use doctrine later embraced by the Supreme Court. In *Bonaparte* v. *Camden* & A. R. Co. he held that state legislatures could take private property only for public use, and that creation of a monopoly by a public charter voided its public nature. As new forms of corporate property emerged in the post-Civil War era, the circuit courts offered protection through the contract clause. In the early and frequently cited case of *Gray* v. *Davis* (1871) a circuit court held, and the Supreme Court subsequently affirmed, that a legislative act incorporating a railroad constituted a contract between the state and the company, and a state constitutional provision annulling that charter violated the contract clause.

Circuit court judges contributed to the nationalization of American law and the economy.

The circuit courts' most dramatic nationalizing role involved commercial jurisprudence. Through their diversity jurisdiction the circuit courts used Swift V. Tyson (1842) to build a federal common law of commerce, thus encouraging business flexibility, facilitating investment security, and reducing costs to corporations. After the Civil War these courts eased limitations on the formation and operation of corporations in foreign states (*In Re Spain,* 1891), supported bondholders' rights, allowed forum shopping (*Osgood* v. *The Chicago, Danville, and Vincennes R. R. Co.,* 1875), and favored employers in fellow-servant liability cases.

Ambivalence, contradiction, and frustration typified circuit court decisions involving civil and political rights. In 1823 Justice Bushrod Washington, in *Corfield* v. *Coryell,* held that the privileges and immunities clause guaranteed equal treatment of out-of-state citizens as to those privileges and immunities that belonged of right to citizens of all free governments, and which had at all times been enjoyed by citizens of the several states. After 1866 some circuit judges attempted to expand this narrow interpretation. Justice Joseph P. Bradley held, in *Live-Stock Dealers' & Butchers' Ass'n* v. *Crescent City Live-Stock Landing & Slaughter-House Co.* (1870), that the Fourteenth Amendment protected the privileges and immunities of whites and blacks as national citizens against state action. In 1871 the Circuit Court for the Southern District of Alabama, in *United States* v. *Hall,* decided that under the Fourteenth Amendment Congress had the power to protect by appropriate legislation all rights in the first eight amendments. And in *Ho Ah Kow* v. *Nunan* (1879) Justice Stephen J. Field struck down as cruel and unusual punishment, based on the Eighth Amendment and the equal protection clause of the Fourteenth Amendment, a San Francisco ordinance that required Chinese prisoners to have their hair cut to a length of one inch from their scalps.

These attempts to nationalize civil rights had little immediate impact. The Supreme Court in 1873 rejected Bradley's reading of the Fourteenth Amendment, and in 1871 the Circuit Court for the District of South Carolina in *United States* v. *Crosby* concluded that the right of a person to be secure in his or her home was not a right, privilege, or immunity granted by the Constitution. Neither the Supreme Court nor any other circuit court adopted the theory of congressional power to enforce the Fourteenth Amendment set forth in *Hall.* Justice Field's *Nunan* opinion was most frequently cited in dissenting rather than majority opinions.

Political rights under the Fifteenth Amendment fared only slightly better. In *United States* v. *Given* (1873) the Circuit Court for the District of Delaware held that the Fifteenth Amendment did not limit congressional action to cases where states had denied or abridged the right to vote by legislation. In the same year, however, Justice Ward Hunt, in *United States* v. *Anthony,* concluded that the right or privilege of voting arose under state constitutions and that the states might restrict it to males.

Despite a regional structure and diverse personnel, these circuit courts placed national over state interests, reinforced the supremacy of federal power, promoted national economic development, and enhanced the position of interstate corporations. However, in matters of civil and political rights they not only disagreed about the scope of federal powers but also confronted a Supreme Court wedded to a traditional state-centered foundation for these rights.

[See also (I) Districts.]

BIBLIOGRAPHY

Frankfurter, Felix and Landis, James M. 1927 *The Business of the Supreme Court: A Study in the Federal Judicial System.* Pages 3–86. New York: Macmillan.

Hall, Kermit L. 1975 The Civil War Era as a Crucible for Nationalizing the Lower Federal Courts. *Prologue: The Journal of the National Archives* 7:177–186.

Swisher, Carl B. 1974 *The Taney Period, 1836–1864.* Volume IV of *The Oliver Wendell Holmes Devise History of the Supreme Court of the United States.* Pages 248–292. New York: Macmillan.

– KERMIT L. HALL

CLAIMS COURT

The Claims Court hears actions for money damages against the United States, except for tort claims. The court thus hears claims for contract damages, tax refunds, and just compensation for property taken. With the consent of all parties to an action against the government under the Federal Tort Claims Act, the court can substitute for a court of appeals and review the decision of a federal district court.

Under the doctrine of sovereign immunity, the United States cannot be sued without its consent. At first, persons with claims against the government had to ask Congress for relief under private acts. This practice became burdensome, and in 1855 Congress established the Court of Claims to hear nontort money claims against the United States, and report its recommendations to Congress. Much of the congressional burden remained; thus, in 1863, Congress empowered the court to give judgments against the government. In 1866 the process became fully "judicial" when Congress repealed a provision delaying payment of such a judgment until the Treasury estimated an appropriation.

The Court of Claims retained the nonjudicial function of giving advisory opinions on questions referred to it by the houses of Congress and heads of executive departments. However, its judges from the beginning had life tenure during good behavior. In 1933 the question arose whether the Court of Claims was a constitutional court. Congress, responding to the economic depression, reduced the salaries of federal employees, except for judges protected by Article III against salary reductions. In *Williams* v. *United States* (1933), the Supreme Court, taking the preposterous position that claims against the government fell outside the judicial power of the United States, held that the Court of Claims was a legislative court whose judges' salaries could constitutionally be reduced.

In 1953 Congress declared explicitly that the Court of Claims was established under Article III. In *Glidden* v. *Zdanok* (1962) the Supreme Court accepted this characterization on the basis of two separate (and incompatible) theories, pieced together to make a majority for the result. Two Justices relied on the 1953 Act; three others would have overruled *Williams* and held that the court had been a constitutional court since 1866 when Congress allowed its judgments to be paid without executive revision, and its business became almost completely "judicial." (The same decision confirmed that the court of customs and patent appeals was a constitutional court.) The Court of Claims transferred new congressional reference cases to its chief commissioner, and Congress ratified this practice. The court's business became wholly "judicial."

Under the doctrine of Sovereign Immunity, the United States cannot be sued without its consent.

In the Federal Courts Improvement Act (1982) Congress reorganized a number of specialized federal courts. The Court of Claims disappeared, and its functions were reallocated. The commissioners of that court became judges of a new legislative court, the United States Claims Court. They serve for fifteen-year terms. The Article III judges of the Court of Claims became judges of a new constitutional court, the United States Court of Appeals for the Federal Circuit. That court hears appeals from a number of specialized courts, including the Claims Court.

The availability of a suit for damages in the Claims Court serves to underpin the constitutionality of some governmental action that might otherwise raise serious constitutional problems. Some regulations, for example, are arguable takings of property; if the regulated party can recover compensation in the Claims Court, however, the constitutional issue dissolves (*Blanchette* v. *Connecticut General Insurance Corps., 1974*).

BIBLIOGRAPHY

Symposium: The Federal Courts Improvement Act 1983 *Cleveland State Law Review* 32:1–116.

– KENNETH L. KARST

THE CRIMINAL JUSTICE SYSTEM

The criminal justice process is marked by five characteristics. First, it consists of many closely interconnected segments and may be thought of as a system in which one part affects every other. These segments also enjoy a high degree of autonomy; thus, the second characteristic is fragmentation. Third, all major participants in the process enjoy a high degree of discretion in making their decisions. That discretion is in every case limited by the fourth characteristic, an intricate set of legal rules. Fifth, the process is marked by intense conflict between two sets of competing values. On the one hand, a lively distrust of governmental authority pervades the process and displays itself in elaborate rights for those accused of crime; on the other hand, criminal justice officials feel a strong commitment toward promoting public safety by dealing swiftly and, if necessary, harshly with those who have committed crimes. These five characteristics are evident in every phase of the criminal justice process. Before exploring the separate elements of the process, we shall briefly discuss each of these fundamental characteristics.

First, the criminal justice process consists of many segments that are connected to each other in intricate ways. The police, prosecutors, defense counsel, courts, judges, and prisons each respond to actions one of the others undertakes; their actions affect, and are affected by, every other element of the criminal justice process. For instance, although the police are responsible for making arrests, they sometimes modify their actions to accommodate pressure from prosecutors and judges who want them to direct their energies toward different types of crimes or to observe legal technicalities more carefully. These modifications may entail, for example, a shift in police attentions from prostitution to illegal gambling, or the exercise of greater diligence in obtaining search warrants. And although prisons are filled through court convictions, judges ration prison sentences when penitentiary facilities become overcrowded. The systems metaphor has become the conventional way to conceptualize the criminal justice process since the President's Commission on Law Enforcement and Administration of Justice adopted it in its report in 1967. Yet it remains mostly a metaphor. Scholars rarely succeed in examining the entire set of interrelationships. Most research on the criminal justice process focuses on single segments, with some attention being paid to their links to other elements of the system.

The criminal justice process is constantly engaged in seeking to balance two conflicting values: maintaining defendants right's and promoting public safety.

Second, the system paradigm is difficult to execute, because the criminal justice process is in reality only a loosely coupled system of many autonomous fragments. Most criminal justice agencies operate with independent grants of authority based on a statute or constitutional provision. For instance, elected mayors usually control the police, but they have little influence and no control over prosecutors, judges, and prisons. Similarly, judges only control their own bailiwick, the courtroom, but they have no control over police, prosecutors, or prisons. The same is true of prosecutors and prison administrators. There is no true hierarchy among criminal justice agencies; one is not the superior of others, but all are more or less coequal. Moreover, every institution exists in triplicate—at the local, state, and national levels. No other large nation has such a decentralized, fragmented criminal justice system as the United States. Nevertheless, these agencies constitute a loosely coupled system because they remain interdependent.

Third, decisions to invoke the law must fit an enormous array of situations. For instance, while the police have rules governing the firing of handguns, every officer must make a split-second judgment when confronted with a dangerous situation on the street about whether the rule governs. Such judgmental decisions permeate the criminal justice process. Officials constantly must use their judgment to determine whether to invoke a rule or to choose among alternative rules. Many such discretionary decisions are barely visible to outside observers and often are scarcely checked by higher authorities. Thus, the process entails a high degree of discretion.

Fourth, law dominates the criminal justice process in the United States. It limits allowable discretion, and sometimes it may override discretionary decisions. The rule of law in criminal proceedings is reinforced in the United States by the deep commitment to it by the principal decision-makers in the process, all of whom are lawyers: prosecuting and defense attorneys, judges, and the legal counselors of the police and prisons. These officials do not view the law as a mere technicality that hinders appropriate action. Rather, they are usually imbued with the lawyer's view that constitutional rights establish overriding obligations.

Finally, a constant tension between individual rights and community protection marks the criminal justice process. On the one hand, an elaborate set of procedures has been designed to protect the rights of persons accused of crimes. Those procedures seek to protect persons against self-incrimination and unfair police practices and require that the accused be allowed to face their accusers at trial. These and other safeguards are usually encompassed in the term *due process of law.* On the other hand, every important criminal justice official feels the heat of public opinion and the public's fear of crime. Public opinion polls often reveal a desire for safer streets and better protection of private property. Officials fear being accused of coddling criminals. Consequently, the criminal justice process is constantly engaged in seeking to balance two conflicting values: maintaining defendant's rights and promoting public safety.

These five characteristics will be evident in our discussion of the separate elements of the criminal justice process. The process itself consists of six parts. First, laws must be passed that define which acts are to be considered criminal. Second, someone must commit such an act. Third, the police must intervene and label the act as illegal and press charges against the perpetrator. Fourth, a prosecutor must decide to take these charges to a court for adjudication. Fifth, the court must decide on the innocence or guilt of the alleged offender. Sixth, if the court convicts, the offender is punished, often with some form of incarceration in a jail or prison. The remainder of this article will examine each of these segments and show how the overriding characteristics pervade each of them.

The Adoption of Criminal Laws

Congress may pass criminal laws effective for the entire nation, but most criminal laws in the United States are the product of the legislatures of the fifty states and are valid only within each state's borders. In addition, local legislative bodies, such as city councils and county boards, enact ordinances defining minor offenses for their jurisdictions. No empirical study has encompassed all three of these levels of lawmaking.

Criminal laws are complex, providing many opportunities for legislative tinkering as well as for fundamental policy shifts. Criminal codes in the first instance define activities that are considered illegal. That, however, is not enough. They may also need to define the persons who are prohibited from engaging in the activities, the occasions on which activity is prohibited, and the circumstances in which it is outlawed. Finally, the penalty must be specified. Consider, for instance, killing. All killing is not criminal. A soldier may kill at the front line; mentally ill persons may not be convicted of killing if their lawyers can prove that they did not know what they were doing. Penalties may vary with the particular mix of characteristics that happen to exist. The penalty is greater for intentional killing than for accidental deaths. It may be different for killings committed by adults and those committed by youths. It may be different if committed with a weapon than with a car.

Another example is the crime of carrying a concealed weapon. The law must first define which weapons are to be included (rifles as well as handguns; pocket knives as well as daggers). It must distinguish between persons who carry weapons as part of their trade, such as policemen and bank guards, and those for whom carrying concealed weapons is illegal. It must distinguish places where weapons are carried, differentiating between hunters in the field and criminals in urban alleyways. It may distinguish between minors and adults. Once more, a whole range of penalties may be provided in order to accommodate varying circumstances.

Since World War II, state legislators have adopted many minor and major changes in their state's criminal codes. One major change has been legislative attention to "the drug problem," which has been exhibited in many ways. Laws have been revised to include entirely new narcotic substances. In many states, legislatures have mandated harsh sentences for narcotics suppliers and sometimes for users. On the other hand, possession of small quantities of marijuana has been decriminalized by some state legislatures. Legislatures have not treated all narcotic substances in identical ways. They have paid no attention to caffeine or nicotine abuse. Alcohol abuse in the form of public drunkenness has been decriminalized in most states, although drunk driving has attracted increasingly severe penalties.

Because crime statistics are inherently unreliable, it is very difficult to discern whether harsher laws or more vigorous law enforcement makes a difference.

Another area of major legislative action has involved the adoption of laws that constrain the discretion of judges when they hand out sentences to persons convicted of crimes. The range of prison time that can be given has been severely limited in many states, with some adopting "flat," or determinate, sentences and other states adopting legislatively mandated sentencing guidelines that specify not only the range of discretion but also the factors that may be considered in exercising that discretion. Those actions reflected a loss of confidence in the possibility of rehabilitating offenders. Prison increasingly became considered an instrument of punishment rather than an opportunity to rehabilitate. Consequently, legislatures have deprived both judges and parole officials of much of their discretion to alter sentences on the basis of prisoner behavior.

These and other changes in criminal law were the product of the intricate play of political forces. An important factor in determining the content of legislation and the time of its adoption was the interplay of interest groups in state legislatures. Law enforcement agencies and their officials often played a prominent role in lobbying for changes in criminal codes. Arrayed against them were groups representing defense attorneys and civil liberties groups, such as the American Civil Liberties Union (ACLU). Occasionally, a dominating personality such as Harry J. Anslinger, a long-term commissioner of the Federal Bureau of Narcotics, seemed to have a substantial impact on the development of the law. Political parties had notably little interest in such legislation, with the legislative coalition in favor of or opposed to particular changes usually crossing party lines. However, during the 1960s and 1970s, Republicans on the national level were widely perceived to be more concerned about "law and order" than their Democratic rivals and Republican administrations generally provided more national funds for law enforcement activities than their Democratic counterparts.

Legislative changes in state criminal codes appeared to reflect general unease in the American population about the rise in official crime rates that characterized most of the period between the end of World War II and the late 1970s. However, no direct relationship existed between changes in the official crime rate and the adoption of changes in the criminal code. The existence of model laws and exemplars appears to have been important in the legislative process. For instance, the prominent abandonment of indeterminate sentences by California in 1976 played a large role in convincing other state legislatures to reconsider their own state's commitment to such practices. The Uniform Controlled Substances Act, as proposed by the National Conference of Commissioners on Uniform State Laws, also was influential in the adoption of revised narcotics laws by the states in the 1970s.

A major result of legislative revision of state codes and of city-council actions regarding ordinances was to reduce the variability of criminal law in the United States. Provisions of the criminal code still vary considerably from place to place, but the differences were narrowed during the thirty years before 1978. Their administration, however, continued to show great diversity from place to place.

A police officer making an arrest becomes the first point of contact between an offender and the criminal justice system. (Karl Weatherly/ Corbis)

Criminal Behavior

The effect of criminal law depends in the first instance upon the behavior of violators. While it is true that without criminal acts, there is no crime, the relation between law and criminal behavior is at best a subtle one.

Crime and *criminals* are generic terms, for they include a wide variety of phenomena. In a technical sense, a crime is any act that violates a law that provides for criminal sanctions such as a fine or imprisonment. It not only includes common offenses such as murder, assault, and theft but also the sale and use of some narcotics (but not all), "unnatural" sex acts, gambling in certain circumstances, and the pollution of air and water. Scholars commonly distinguish between three categories of crimes: those involving violence and principally directed against persons; those principally aimed at property; and so-called victimless crimes, in which the "victim" (for instance, the buyer in a drug transaction) is a willing participant. According to the 1984 Uniform Crime Reports, property crimes known to the police are more common than violent crimes, by a ratio of approximately 8 to 1. However, violent crimes are generally more feared and considered more serious by the general public than are property or victimless crimes.

Another important distinction separates crimes committed calculatingly and those committed as the result of uncontrolled passion. Calculating crimes are often considered to be instrumental in the sense that they are planned and the result of a calculation that the gain is likely to outweigh the cost. Many crimes against property fall into this category; they are committed in order to enrich the offender. In contrast, other crimes occur on the spur of the moment as the result of anger or unexpected opportunity. They are often committed while under the influence of alcohol. Many violent crimes fall into this category.

The law is likely to have a greater direct deterrent effect on instrumental crimes. When legislatures impose severe penalties on some actions, they may deter calculating offenders because the possible costs have been raised far beyond the expected benefit. However, most of those who commit crimes unthinkingly will not be deterred. Nevertheless, laws may create a deterrent climate indirectly by stigmatizing certain actions and mobilizing social pressures to prevent illegal actions.

Deterrence is also considered to be the result of the probability of swift enforcement. Criminals in the United States face a low likelihood of arrest and imprisonment and can often count on long delays between arrest (when it comes) and punishment (if it comes).

Much controversy exists over the real deterrent potential of law. Most of the research has centered on the deterrent effect of the death penalty on homicides. Some researchers, most notably Ehrlich, believe that they have detected a substantial deterrent effect; many others doubt it (Blumstein, Cohen, and Nagel). In any case, one would expect less deterrent effect for homicides, which are mostly committed in the heat of passion, than for burglary and theft, which are often planned. However, even property crimes are not prevented by extraordinary safeguards and harsh laws, as can be inferred from the regular occurrence of bank robberies, a serious federal offense that usually leads to arrest, conviction, and imprisonment.

Persons committing crimes represent a broad spectrum of the American population. Most are men, although the participation of women in crime has increased since World War II. Most are youthful; involvement in crime drops markedly when people get beyond their mid-thirties. Many are minorities; the proportion of known offenders who are black is much larger than their share of the general population. Most, but not all, identified offenders have low incomes and poor educations. Some are career criminals in the sense that they do little else for a living. However, a substantial number of offenders are moonlighters; they hold full-time jobs in the legitimate world, but when they need additional cash or when an unusual opportunity beckons, they rob or burglarize. We possess little reliable information about these patterns of behavior because our knowledge rests entirely on research about criminals who have been caught and are studied in prison. More successful criminals may possess quite different characteristics.

Two sources exist in the United States for counting crime. The most widely used is the count of offenses known to the police made by the Federal Bureau of Investigation (FBI) and published annually under the title *Uniform Crime Reports*. Although the FBI and other agencies have vigorously sought to standardize these counts, they remain dependent on factors that are beyond their control. These factors are of two kinds. The first are the habits of citizens in calling the police when something that might be a crime has occurred. Citizens call the police only in the minority of such occurrences, although the proportion varies by kind of offense, apparently being higher in violent crimes than in property crimes. People have a variety of reasons for not calling the police. Some do not trust the police; many believe that no benefit will come from reporting an offense. There is reason to believe that the number of people reporting crimes may have risen during the period that official crime rates rose, because new telecommunications technologies (such as the simple 911 telephone number to reach the police) came into widespread use and dramatically increased the calls for service received by the police.

The second factor affecting the reliability of official crime rates is the manner in which police record offenses. Some cities have been known to be much more lax than others, with the result that changes in recording practices have periodically produced substantial jumps in city crime rates. For instance, in Chicago a television station discovered that the police were "unfounding" about one-third of all crimes originally recorded by patrol officers, thereby artificially reducing the city's crime rate. That practice was halted in 1983, but for that year Chicago was excluded from the FBI's crime statistics. Consequently, an unknown but substantial error exists in official crime rates. Small differences between cities or from one year to the next are as likely to be the result of changes in counting practices as they are to reflect changes in criminal behavior.

The second source for crime statistics in the United States is the annual victimization survey conducted by the Census Bureau and known as the National Crime Survey. The survey identifies victimizations by asking a random sample of residents in the United States whether anything that might be considered a crime happened to them during the previous six months. It also suffers from problems. It does not cover such crimes as homicide, where the victim obviously cannot be interviewed, or victimless crimes, where the ostensible victim will not report his own behavior. It is likely to be unreliable for offenses where the assailant is a relative or friend, as in the case of child or spouse abuse. The most serious shortcoming of the National Crime Survey, however, is that it provides information only about the nation as a whole and not for individual cities, where most law enforcement activities occur and are controlled.

Because crime statistics are inherently unreliable, it is very difficult to discern whether harsher laws or more vigorous law enforcement makes a difference. It appears that many policymakers disregard the unreliability of the statistics. When crime rates rise, they point with alarm to that statistic; when rates fall, they point with pride to their past efforts to pass harsher laws or to provide more funds for law enforcement activities.

The Police

The application of criminal laws depends almost entirely on local police in the United States. Police activity responds to many factors within the criminal justice process and outside it.

Discretion is the key characteristic of police actions. The police are in fact first-instance judges of the citizen actions they encounter. If a police officer thinks citizen behavior warrants an arrest, he sets in motion the criminal justice process, from which the alleged offender cannot escape without considerable trouble and cost. If a police officer decides to ignore the behavior or deal with it by some action short of an arrest or summons, no one is likely to second-guess that decision, and the citizen will escape all the consequences of being accused of a crime.

These discretionary powers are routinely exercised by officers with little legal training and no immediate supervision. Unlike judges, police officers are not graduates of law school; many are only high school graduates. Their police academy training covers only the rudiments of criminal law. They work out of sight of their immediate supervisors. When they encounter a situation on their beat, they must immediately make decisions on which their lives and the lives of bystanders sometimes hinge. Consequently, although patrol officers are the foot soldiers of the police, they work with considerable autonomy and make many discretionary decisions.

The police officer's discretion is affected by many elements of his or her environment. Some of those elements expand or support police discretion; many of them constrain it. The most important of them include the degree of citizen involvement, the requirements imposed by courts, the political environment, the available technology, and the degree of professionalization.

In some situations the police are fully in charge, while in others they depend on citizen initiative to involve them. The difference is one between "proactive" and "reactive" police patrolling. When the police engage in proactive patrol, they search for violations and themselves initiate any action. Typical proactive activities involve "sting" operations, such as when the police open a fencing operation to trap burglars into selling their stolen goods before hidden cameras, which will lead to their later arrest. Many narcotics investigations depend on proactive undercover operations in which police officers act the role of drug dealers in order to obtain evidence against real narcotics traffickers. Proactive policing is particularly important for combating victimless crimes because such offenses usually occur with the compliance of those who are victimized. Few outside constraints govern proactive patrolling. The police determine their target and the means for snaring their prey. Only after an arrest has been made do external constraints begin to impose themselves on the results of proactive patrolling.

Reactive patrolling, by contrast, depends on the cooperation of ordinary citizens. It is triggered by a call from either the victim or a bystander. Police have little choice about responding to such calls, because they risk severe public criticism if they ignore a call that turns out to have involved a serious crime. When the police respond, they encounter citizens, who must be accommodated. Although the police retain discretion founded on their authority and expertise, they must also often justify its use to those who called them to the situation. Consequently, they may make an arrest when confronted with disorder, to mollify neighbors, even though they might prefer to handle the situation through a warning. However, in many instances, they cannot make an arrest, for the simple reason that the offender has already escaped because the victim delayed in calling the police. For instance, a householder who finds his house burglarized often conducts a search of the premises himself and then confers with neighbors before calling the police. Such a delay, even when it takes only half an hour, usually makes it impossible for the police to find the burglar. In reactive policing, the police are also constrained by social relationships in the situation. Being themselves mostly of working-class or lower-middle-class origins, they tend to treat the poor with brusque authority and the rich with inordinate respect. Finally, they cannot ignore the interpretation that citizens have imprinted on the situation to which they are called. If the caller considers the matter a very serious one, police have difficulty in downgrading it. Thus, reactive patrolling places many more constraints on the use of police discretion than does proactive patrolling.

The choice between proactive and reactive patrolling is to a large degree dictated by the resources of a police department and its technology. Since the mid-1960s, most large police departments have installed communications systems that permit citizens to call the police quickly and easily through the installation of the 911 telephone number. That has greatly increased the number of calls for service. Most departments have not obtained commensurate increases in resources, so that patrol time that might once have been devoted to proactive patrol now must be committed to reacting to calls for service.

The Miranda *warning has forced the police to share the questioning of suspects with defense attorneys.*

Police behavior is also subject to constraints of the law as interpreted by the courts. During the 1960s the United States Supreme Court issued a series of decisions intended to control abuse of police discretion. One set of decisions was based on the Fourth Amendment's prohibition of illegal searches and seizures. In *Mapp* v. *Ohio* (1961), the Court extended the exclusionary rule, which had already applied to federal courts, to state courts. That rule required the exclusion of evidence in criminal trials if it was illegally seized. In practice, the exclusionary rule required a police officer to obtain a search warrant from a judge before searching for evidence or seizing it. To obtain a search warrant, police officers had to show reliable evidence of a probable crime, thus sharing discretion with judges. The number of situations covered by *Mapp* and subsequent rulings of the Supreme Court has been the subject of continuing controversy. The fact that searches and seizures are the object of continuing litigation indicates that police compliance with these rulings has been far from complete. Searches and seizures, however, do not apply equally to all crimes. They are most important in narcotics and weapons offenses; they are rarely invoked in crimes of violence or ordinary property crimes. Thomas Davies suggests that the bulk of empirical evidence collected seems to indicate that compliance with the exclusionary rule has not substantially reduced the number of persons convicted of crime.

A second set of court rules involves the interpretation of the Fifth Amendment's prohibition against involuntary self-incrimination. The police may not force a person to testify against himself. The Supreme Court in *Miranda* v. *Arizona* (1966) extended this rule by requiring that police warn persons whom they arrest that anything they say may be held against them and by forbidding police interrogation until the detained person has been informed of his right to obtain a lawyer and, if he or she wants an attorney, until the lawyer has arrived and is present during the questioning. This has led to the formulation of the "*Miranda* warning," which almost all police officers now read to persons whom they arrest. As with the exclusionary rule, the *Miranda* warning has constrained police discretion by forcing the police to share the questioning of suspects with defense attorneys. The warning has reduced the number of spontaneous, "voluntary" confessions, but because few convictions depend entirely on confessions, it, like the exclusionary rule, has not substantially reduced the number of convictions obtained after an arrest.

The exclusionary rule and the *Miranda* warning are only two examples of the ways in which the criminal law attempts to control police discretion. They operate only to control abuse of the arresting power of the police. If the police abuse their discretion by not intervening in some situations, the courts rarely intervene.

The political environment might be thought to constitute the most appropriate constraint on inactivity by the police, as well as affording additional constraints on the active abuse of police powers. In fact, it does not consistently do so. One reason is that the police are not centrally controlled. Control over the police in the United States is scattered among thousands of municipalities, counties, states, and federal agencies. In most metropolitan areas, dozens of police agencies vie with each other. It is not easy for the public to identify the official they should hold responsible for police actions; public officials often cannot control police who violate priorities and standards.

In addition, city politics are themselves too difuse to render effective control over the police in many cities. Although the police chief is often a key mayoral appointee, in many cities a city manager appoints the chief. Control over the police budget is shared with the city council. However, the principal obstacle to effective political control over police activities is the obscurity of most police operations. Knowledge of police operations comes mostly from the police department itself.

Police departments cannot be readily penetrated. They are often more autonomous than other city agencies because the police are a socially isolated group operating under a quasi-military discipline. Police harbor an intense distrust of "civilians." Consequently, they have worked hard and successfully in avoiding the establishment of civilian review boards that might investigate and punish instances of police abuses. In addition, supervisory personnel are almost entirely recruited from the department itself or from similar departments in other cities.

Therefore, although a mayor or city-manager appointee, the chief is usually the only political appointee in the department and is still more representative of the department than of the political leadership of the city. Police departments that avoid major scandals usually evade political supervision.

Still another factor affecting the exercise of police discretion is the technology employed by the police. Two characteristics of American police forces have particularly strong effects on the use of patrol discretion. The first is the deployment of most patrol officers in motor vehicles. Few patrol on foot. Their use of cars insulates patrol officers from citizens. It would also insulate them from supervisors, were it not for another technology—sophisticated radio communications systems. Radio systems permit supervisors to contact patrol officers in their cars and direct them to locations where they are needed. The radio may even allow headquarters to keep silent track of the location of police cruisers. Consequently, the command echelon of the police can direct the deployment of their officers, but that fact does not yet permit control over officers' actions when they have stepped out of their cars.

Finally, increasing professionalization of the police has both increased their autonomy and subjected them to a new set of external standards. The more the police manage to convey an impression of possessing arcane skills and professional ethics, the more they can resist control by civilians and politicians. On the other hand, professional ethics themselves may constrain use of police discretion. Thus far, few instances of internal professional control exist among American police forces. Professionalization has usually meant resistance to political control by increasing the civil service protection available to police officers and opposition to the creation of civilian review boards.

Criminal Courts

After the police have made an arrest, the case moves to the courts. However, police share control over access to the courts with prosecutors. Together the police and prosecutors may be considered the gatekeepers of the criminal courts.

Except for minor offenses (such as traffic violations), where the police act in the prosecutorial role, police charges must be brought into the courts by prosecutors. Once prosecutors have decided to accept some version of the police charges, the criminal prosecution process begins. Prosecutors play a major role in the process, but it is not dominated by any single participant. At various decision points, defense counsel, defendants, judges, and jurors exercise considerable influence over the proceedings. Rarely can a single participant ramrod a verdict through the criminal courts; rather, verdicts of innocence or guilt are the product of intricate interactions between these participants.

To clarify the criminal justice process, we will examine each participant separately. However, their close dependence upon each other needs to be kept in mind.

PROSECUTORS. Every criminal courtroom in the United States except those handling the most minor matters has a prosecutor assigned to it. These prosecutors, however, are not part of a single hierarchy. They work for different superiors with different policies and priorities.

In many cities, the local prosecutor's offices rival in size the largest private law firms and the United States attorney's office.

When a federal police agency, such as the FBI, charges someone with violating a federal criminal statute, the offender is brought to a federal magistrate and prosecution is brought by a federal prosecutor, the United States attorney, before the federal district court. United States attorneys are presidential political appointees who must be confirmed by the United States Senate, just as federal judges must be. They serve for a term of four years and generally resign when a new president takes office. Consequently, federal prosecutors are usually aligned with the party controlling the White House. The office is a patronage appointment. However, United States attorneys operate under the bureaucratic control of the Department of justice, which controls their budgets and guides their actions. These prosecutors generally handle routine violations of federal laws, such as narcotics probes; prosecution of labor-law violations; interstate crime, such as racketeering and kidnappings; and tax fraud. Unusually important or sensitive prosecutions, such as those involving prominent officials or crimes affecting national security, may not be initiated without approval from Washington.

Because the office of United States attorney is under presidential patronage and has the potential for focusing public attention on official corruption as well as on routine crimes, it possesses considerable visibility and prestige. Appointees usually have close political connections with congressional as well as executive party leaders. They often later seek high elective office themselves. Because of the high prestige of the office, United States attorneys also frequently succeed in recruiting extremely able young attorneys as their assistants. In many places, the office has a very large staff of attorneys, many of whom serve for only a few years before moving on to private-sector legal positions.

When local police bring charges against someone for violating state or local criminal statutes, they do not take those charges to the federal court or to the United States attorney. Rather, they go to local criminal courts and local prosecutors, who operate independently of the United States attorneys. In most areas prosecutors are county officials elected on a partisan ballot for a term of four years. In only a few states do they serve larger areas than counties or are chosen by some method other than election. Such county prosecutors—usually holding the title of state's attorney or district attorney—handle the bulk of police arrests. There are many more state's attorneys offices than United States attorneys. Many operate in rural areas with part-time personnel. In metropolitan areas, however, the local prosecutor's offices are large, full-time, professional establishments. In many cities, they rival in size the largest private law firms and the United States attorney's office. Most of the staff consists of assistant prosecutors who are appointed in most jurisdictions through a civil service examination system.

While the elected prosecutor in a large office is almost always an important political figure in his locale, assistants are usually anonymous civil servants or beginning lawyers. Young attorneys seek appointment to the local prosecutor's office because it provides good trial experience and a way to begin a legal career if the lawyer has not succeeded in obtaining a position in a private law firm. For many assistants the prosecutor's office is only the first step of their legal career. They remain in the office just long enough to obtain a better position. Consequently, assistant prosecutors often work hard to build good reputations among local lawyers, with an eye toward getting an offer to join a local firm. Such rewards are as significant for young assistants as those offered through internal promotions in the prosecutor's office.

The local prosecutor's office is not part of a larger bureaucratic hierarchy, as is the United States attorney's office. Each state's attorney is accountable only to the electorate. No superior office formulates policy or priorities for an entire state, and important cases are not referred to some superior officer. In terms of formal authority, the local prosecutor is an independent official who does not need to coordinate actions with local police, local judges, or the United States attorney.

Nevertheless, many informal forces lead to considerable collaboration between prosecutors and the police. They have a common interest in controlling crime. The police depend upon prosecutors to convict those whom they arrest, and prosecutors rely on the police to collect evidence that they need for successful prosecutions.

Circumstances constantly force police and prosecutors to respond to each other. The largest police department in a jurisdiction generally controls the prosecutor's work load. That means that it not only sets the number of cases that prosecutors process, but it also determines the kinds of cases that prosecutors must handle. The most serious charges simply arise because the crimes have been committed. But even with such serious charges as murder, police and prosecutors have discretion to charge intentional homicide or accidental manslaughter. In most cases, charges can be upgraded or downgraded by the police. When the police regard them as serious incidents, they place a greater burden on the prosecutor. When they treat incidents as minor crimes, the prosecutor's office can handle them with less effort.

The police also control the quality of the evidence with which prosecutors must work. Most evidence is collected at the crime scene by the responding officers. They take down the names of eyewitnesses and gather physical evidence, such as shell casings, guns, narcotics substances, or stolen goods. When the prosecutor receives these bits of evidence a few days or weeks later, it is usually impossible to supplement them. Much of the prosecutor's success depends on the quality of initial police work. When police are thorough and careful, the task of the prosecutor is eased. However, if the police miss significant pieces of evidence, make mistakes in recording the names and addresses of witnesses, or are careless in handling the evidence, so that it cannot be clearly linked with the offender, the prosecutor may be unable to obtain a conviction. This organizational interdependence sometimes leads to conflict as when the police and prosecutor exchange charges of incompetence. On the one hand, the police often do not appreciate the need for attention to the details of evidence collection; they generally dislike the paperwork required. It is often more important to them to control offenders or victims at the scene of the crime. On the other hand, prosecutors have little sense of the situation on the street but must face the threat of a courtroom challenge to the evidence they must present to a judge. Consequently, although the police and prosecutor normally work together, they often do so with considerable tension.

Constituency differences between the two agencies add to those tensions. One significant difference in constituency is geographical. Police serve municipalities that usually are much smaller than the county. Prosecutors work with police from cities and towns with varying degrees of commitment toward combating the kinds of crime that the prosecutor's office is presently targeting. Neither a mayor (or the police chief) nor the prosecutor can set law enforcement priorities for the entire community. The mayor may be most concerned about vice, while the prosecutor may see child abuse as the number-one priority. In such an instance, the police may find that the vice arrests they make get dismissed by the prosecutor's office but the prosecutor tries to obtain indictments about child abuse through office-based investigations. Another source of conflict lies in the different electoral base of mayors (who control the police) and prosecutors. It is not unusual for the mayor of a large city to be the political rival of the prosecutor serving the same area. They occasionally try to embarrass each other with charges of inefficiency or corruption.

In felonies, prosecutors must demonstrate that probable cause exists to believe that a crime was committed and that the defendant committed it.

Another potent source of conflict between police and prosecutors lies in their social and intellectual roots. Police generally come from working-class and lower-middle-class backgrounds and possess at most a college education. Most prosecutors come from middle- or upper-middle-class backgrounds and have a law school education in addition to their college degrees. Prosecutors are always lawyers and have the lawyer's respect for judicial procedures and legal technicalities, matters that simply seem irksome to many police officers. Moreover, while police officers must deal with the reality of life on the street, prosecutors must deal with the reality of life in the courtroom. Thus, they begin with different perceptions of what is proper and necessary and respond to different imperatives.

The first task facing the prosecutor is to determine whether to accept the charges brought by the police. The prosecutor's mandate in the United States is to see that justice is done. That means that prosecutors must dismiss charges if evidence is insufficient. Alternatively, prosecutors may alter the charges originally brought by the police so that they accord more closely to the situation as reflected by police reports and the evidence forwarded to the prosecutor. Consequently, prosecutors enjoy enormous discretion. That discretion is exercised by decisions to change charges and to drop charges as well as to control the speed with which charges are processed.

If a prosecutor decides to proceed, formal charges are drawn up. The defendant is then notified of the charges before a judge. That hearing, called an arraignment, must generally take place within twenty-four hours after the defendant's arrest. At arraignment, the defendant is notified of the formal charges and is given an opportunity to obtain legal counsel and to post bail. Both are crucial to the later outcome of the case. As we shall see below, defendants may have several choices about which defense attorneys will represent them. The bail decision determines whether a defendant awaits the outcome of the case in jail or at home.

Prosecutors play a major role in the bail decision. The level of bail ordinarily is closely related to the seriousness of the charge facing a defendant. Consequently, when prosecutors decide on a charge, they also influence the range of bail that might be set. In addition, prosecutors normally make specific recommendations about bail, which in many instances influence the presiding judicial officer. Bail is usually an amount of money that the defendant must post (or get someone else like a bail bondsman to post) before he or she may be released from jail. However, in some instances, defendants are released on their own recognizance (known as an ROR release) on the basis of their roots in the community. Usually, ROR defendants have lived a long time at their current address, are married, have a job, and do not possess long arrest records. While the prosecutor's recommendations about bail do not always prevail, they usually receive serious consideration. Thus, the prosecutor has considerable influence over whether defendants are free or sit in jail while awaiting their trial. Defendants who await disposition of their case in jail are in fact punished before trial and are seriously disadvantaged in their attempts to defend themselves.

When the charges are minor (usually called misdemeanors), trials occur almost immediately after arraignment and usually end with guilty pleas. Elaborate plea bargaining rarely occurs in such matters. Sentence is pronounced by the presiding judge—but once again, the prosecutor plays an important role in recommending a sentence. In these cases, as Feeley has shown for New Haven, Connecticut, the prosecutor and police possess inordinate influence because their joint decision about the charge against a defendant usually determines the punishment. Relatively few defendants contest minor charges; an overwhelming proportion result in a conviction resulting from the defendant's guilty plea.

Prosecutors exercise less influence when serious charges are involved, because the procedure is more elaborate and involves other participants more actively. In serious cases (called felonies), prosecutors must generally first demonstrate that probable cause exists to believe that a crime has been committed and that the defendant committed it. Probable cause is a lighter burden of proof than the standard of "beyond a reasonable doubt," which is ultimately required for conviction. However, prosecutors must present sufficient evidence to a judge in a preliminary hearing or to a grand jury to meet the standard of probable cause. Failure to do so means that the charge will be dismissed. Such dismissals are a common outcome for criminal charges because prosecutors find that they lack sufficient proof to proceed further. That occurs when an eyewitness fails to identify the defendant in the courtroom, when a complaining witness decides not to testify, or when the powder the police seized on the assumption that it was heroin turns out to be sugar. The preliminary hearing requires prosecutors to share decision-making with police, witnesses, defense counsel, and judge. Unless the coordinated effort of all of these leads to a ruling of probable cause, the charges are dismissed.

Dismissal of charges does not mean that the person involved escapes without punishment. The arrest, the loss of time, the expense of defense (even at this stage), and the embarrassment of being involved in a criminal proceeding may be a substantial price for whatever behavior led the police to make the initial arrest. In all but extreme cases of police harassment, persons whose charges are dismissed have no possibility of recovering damages or costs incurred.

When prosecutors have obtained a ruling that probable cause exists, the case proceeds to a trial. However, few cases actually get to trial. Most are plea-bargained. In exchange for a guilty plea by the defendant, prosecutors may promise to dismiss some charges (when multiple charges face the defendant), reduce the charge upon which the guilty plea is made, or make a recommendation for a sentence that might be more lenient than that which might be given after a trial. As Eisenstein and Jacob have shown, negotiations leading to guilty pleas take place in a variety of conditions. In some jurisdictions, all such negotiations are centralized in a single bureau of the prosecutor's office. Cases routinely flow through that bureau. The attorneys who work

Prison becomes the final stop in the criminal justice system for many offenders, such as these male prisoners in the Dade County Men's Correction Facility. (Joseph Sohm; ChromoSohm Inc./Corbis)

there do nothing but negotiate plea bargains with defense counsel. In other jurisdictions, bargains are struck in the courtroom, in adjoining hallways, or in the judge's chambers. A much larger portion of the prosecutor's office is involved when the negotiations are decentralized. Even judges may be explicitly drawn into the negotiations.

In all plea negotiations prosecutors hold the controlling cards. They do so because they possess more information about the offense than anyone else in the negotiations. Prosecutors possess the police report and have information about the prior record of the defendant. They also have the results of any interrogations conducted by the police or prosecutor. Defense counsel may obtain similar information, but in ordinary cases they do not have sufficient funds to finance independent investigations. Moreover, the prosecutor's information has the authority and imprimatur of the police, while the defense counsel's information usually consists of undocumented assertions by defendants and their friends or relatives, assertions that can easily be depicted as being self-serving.

Plea negotiations usually proceed informally. No one testifies under oath; no one is cross-examined. Rather, prosecutors typically present a narrative description of the incident and give their characterization of the defendant. Defense counsel then attempt to counter some or all of the assertions made by the prosecutor. When judges participate, they may hasten agreement by suggesting particular sentence or charge reduction, an arrangement that carries the weight of prior approval by the judge. Even with judicial participation, however, prosecutors retain their dominant position in plea negotiations. Defendants rarely join these negotiations. Only after an agreement is struck must the defense counsel present it to the defendant for his or her approval.

If a bargain is struck and the defendant agrees to it, the accused pleads guilty and is sentenced accordingly. If no bargain is reached, a trial must be held. At trial the dominant position of the prosecutor is diminished by the larger role that defense counsel, witnesses, and judges play.

DEFENSE COUNSEL. The conventional view of the criminal justice process puts defense counsel on an equal plane with prosecutors. Defense attorneys are, in that view, simply the defense counterparts of the prosecuting team. In reality, however, substantial differences exist between the resources and roles of defense lawyers and prosecuting attorneys.

Whereas all prosecutors are members of a government office, only some defense attorneys are. Defendants in the United States may be represented by attorneys from various sources. If defendants can afford to pay legal fees, they must hire their own private lawyer. In practice, the means test imposed is whether the defendant can afford to make bail. Many courts require that defendants who can afford to buy their pretrial liberty by making bail must also pay for their own attorney. In some jurisdictions, that arrangement is promoted by directing the bail refund (when the case is finished) directly to the attorney rather than to the defendant. Attorneys hired by defendants vary considerably in their characteristics. Most come from small partnerships or individual practices rather than from large law firms. Many are attorneys who hang out around criminal courts to seek clients from among those just arraigned. Such defense attorneys are particularly expert in the folkways of the courthouse, even though they may not be highly sophisticated in legal doctrine. Since they normally defend routine accusations of common crimes, their organizational expertise is often quite appropriate to the task. They ordinarily take cases for set fees (called retainers), which they often require in advance. Such payment up front is important to these lawyers because clients who are convicted and sent to prison (and most are) usually cannot and will not pay their fee.

Many defendants cannot afford a private attorney. If they win pretrial release, they do so on personal recognizance rather than on a monetary bail payment. Under Supreme Court decisions dating from *Gideon* v. *Wainwright* in 1963, almost all defendants must be offered an attorney if they cannot afford to retain one themselves. Most use their opportunity. Such lawyers come from two sources. In some jurisdictions, the trial court assigns private attorneys to defend the accused with the county or state paying their fee. Those fees are generally less than the going rate charged by private attorneys. In some places, every attorney must take such cases when his or her turn comes up. In most places, however, attorneys volunteer to accept these cases. Some of these attorneys are young lawyers just beginning their practice and eager for some paying cases and experience; others are courthouse regulars who also take many paying clients.

Defense attorneys may also be provided by the public defender's office. Public defenders are government employees funded from local taxes and supervised by the court or by the county board. In most cases, the chief public defender is appointed, as are the other members of the office. Only in a few jurisdictions does the public defender run for election like the prosecuting attorney. The public defender's office rarely offers the political advantages of the prosecutor's office. Defense of accused criminals is often an unpopular task; a successful office boasting a high acquittal rate is unlikely to obtain favorable public notice. Consequently, the office attracts fewer politically ambitious lawyers. In many places, it is an alternative to the prosecutor's office for young lawyers who want a steady income and an opportunity to develop the skills and contacts needed to develop a private trial practice. Assistants in the public defender's office, like those in the prosecutor's, are mostly civil service appointees who serve for three to five years before moving on to a private legal career.

Public defenders are government employees funded from local taxes and supervised by the court or by the county board.

Defense attorneys work with far more meager resources than the prosecutor's office. Whereas the police serve as a rich source of information for prosecutors, defense counsel have no counterpart. In most routine cases they conduct no independent investigation of the incident that led to the arrest of their client. Rather, defense attorneys generally rely on the same police reports that the prosecutor holds. They obtain those reports from the prosecutor rather than directly from the police. Often they only gain access to the reports just before trial, and thus, there is insufficient time to resolve any contradictions between their client's story and the police report through additional investigation. Consequently, the plea-bargaining session or trial ordinarily becomes a credibility contest between police officers and defendants, with the police usually winning because they come with better reputations. Unusual cases are handled differently. When the defendant is well-off, he or she can finance independent investigations. Moreover, in the most notorious cases, such as those involving mass murderers, defense counsel are given more resources to conduct a more vigorous defense, lest the accused be released upon appeal because the trial was judged to have been unfair. The public knows much more about such cases because they receive far more publicity than routine ones, where defense counsel operate under severe resource constraints.

Defense attorneys exercise less discretion in the criminal justice process than do prosecutors. Prosecutors are in the driver's seat and control the pace of the proceedings; defense attorneys usually respond only to prosecutorial initiatives. However, in a few instances, the rules of the courtroom give defense lawyers considerable influence. In the many jurisdictions where a time limit is set for conducting a prosecution, defense attorneys gain bargaining power as the time limit approaches. When a prosecutor is on the verge of losing a case simply because it was not processed according to schedule, a more lenient bargain may be reached. Defense counsel can also delay cases by asking for continuances on the ground that they are not yet prepared, that they have to try another case in a different courtroom, or because "Mr. Green" is not in the courtroom. Mr. Green is not a witness but a reference to the fact that the attorney has not yet been paid by his client. Such continuances are not always granted, and when they are, they do not count against the prosecutor's deadline for finishing the case. Delay creates problems for prosecutors because it provides a way through which defense attorneys can prolong a case until witnesses become forgetful or unwilling to appear in court. Nevertheless, the defense lawyer's ability to delay is a meager weapon compared to all of the information at the disposal of prosecutors.

A final difference between prosecutors and defense counsel is that defense lawyers must defer to their clients' preferences. Those wishes are often less predictable than the policy directives that prosecutors must obey. When a prosecutor and defense attorney have agreed upon a plea bargain, it must be accepted by the defendant before becoming binding. He or she may refuse. Refusals are not common, because defense attorneys can exert considerable psychological pressure upon clients. Clients often possess only a fragmentary knowledge of the alternatives available to them. They may be frightened by the prospect of a trial and by the uncertainties of the sentence that may await them upon conviction at trial. Clients may not fully understand that they are in charge. Yet despite such considerations, some clients give considerable trouble to defense lawyers.

The defense counsel's role is not entirely unique; defense attorneys share some important characteristics with prosecutors. When defense lawyers work for the public defender's office or when they are criminal law specialists, they face much the same work-load strain as do prosecutors. Ordinarily defense attorneys have too many cases to give each of them individual attention. Public defenders cannot afford to try every case before a jury or judge because that would take too much time. Private attorneys also cannot afford trials in every instance, because the fees that they have collected are insufficient. Private attorneys who have collected only $1,000 will then be reluctant to devote more than $1,000 worth of their time to the case. If they commit more time, they are unlikely to be reimbursed. The constraints that lead defense attorneys to prefer plea bargains are quite similar to those we described for prosecutors. Neither attorney has enough time or money to go to a full-fledged trial in every case.

Moreover, like the prosecutor, defense counsel in most jurisdictions are courthouse regulars. That means that they intermittently confront the same prosecutors over a long period of time. Prosecutors and defense counsel become associates in the same task—disposing of cases. Although defense lawyers have a fundamental commitment to their clients, they also share with prosecutors a commitment to keep the process viable. They cannot treat each case in total isolation from the flow of cases they handle. Today's negotiations with a prosecutor are likely to reflect the relationship established in previous negotiations and must be conducted with an eye on future interactions with a prosecutor. Similar constraints impinge on prosecutors. Consequently, the actions of defense attorneys cannot be understood solely from the perspective of their obligation to their clients. While that responsibility is primary, the secondary obligations incurred through their contacts with prosecutors and other persons working in the courthouse exert some influence on their decisions.

While most judicial decisions are not appealed, appeals occur much more frequently in criminal matters than in civil ones.

Thus, courtroom encounters are not simply contests between two equal contenders, the prosecution and defense. The prosecution enjoys a considerable advantage, and in many instances the process is not a contest at all but rather a joint venture in which both prosecutor and defense counsel seek to dispose of pending cases expeditiously. But they are not the only participants in the process. They must share that concern and their power with judges.

JUDGES. Judges are conventionally thought to control the criminal justice process. It is true that they preside over trials, but as we have already seen, judges are only one of several officials with considerable influence on the outcome of criminal prosecutions. In a few instances judges are truly in charge; in many they must take into account what other officials want done.

The power of judges is greatest in formal proceedings; it is least when discretion is exercised before a trial is scheduled. Thus, although the Supreme Court has fashioned many decisions to constrain abuse of police discretion, the effectiveness of those decisions is questionable. Judges never see the potential defendants whom the police fail to arrest. Likewise, judges rarely can intervene if prosecutors decide not to press charges, and they do not have much influence on the nature of the charges that prosecutors choose when they proceed against a defendant. When plea bargaining centers on dismissal of concurrent charges rather than on the promise of a specific sentence, judges usually remain powerless to intervene. Only when a defendant stands before the judge at trial or for sentencing do judges assume the power that the public associates with their title.

Nevertheless, it would be inaccurate to portray judges as powerless in the preliminary stages of the criminal justice process. Their influence is indirect rather than direct; it is exerted in subtle ways. Judges are part of the same courtroom work group as prosecutors and defense attorneys. Through many informal contacts, they convey their preferences without seeming to command compliance. Judges obtain compliance in part out of respect for their superior position. But they also possess powers to enforce compliance. Judges possess the formal power (which they rarely invoke) to speed up or slow down proceedings. They can insist that a case begin or continue at a time that is very inconvenient to the others. Judges can compel attention to the minutiae of court proceedings or wink at minor lapses. Judges not only control appointments of defense attorneys in some cases but also may publicly praise or chide an attorney before a full courtroom. All of these powers make prosecutors and defense attorneys attentive to the judges' preferences. In the normal course of courtroom proceedings, judges do not intervene in matters that they cannot directly control; rather, they rely on the informal deference that is paid them, to maintain their influence.

During formal proceedings the judge appears to be clearly in charge. The judge makes all important decisions as to the admissibility of evidence, the length of a sentence, and the guilt or innocence of the defendant in juryless trials. However, even at formal proceedings, the other participants have considerable influence. While judges make the formal decisions, the information on which those decisions are based usually comes from prosecutors, defense counsel, or other participants. A judge's sentence, for instance, is normally heavily influenced by the prosecutor's recommendation (itself often the result of a plea bargain) and information about the defendant supplied by the prosecutor, defense counsel, and probation officer. Decisions on the admissibility of the evidence depends on testimony submitted to the judge and on legal briefs on which trial judges heavily rely. Even instructions to a jury are the result of negotiations in the judge's chambers at which prosecuting and defense lawyers present alternative versions of disputed instructions. Judges normally choose one or the other rather than drafting their own.

Moreover, judges also respond to pressures from their hierarchical superiors—the appellate bench. While most judicial decisions are not appealed, appeals occur much more frequently in criminal matters than in civil cases. Judges are sensitive to being overruled by appellate courts, especially because it occurs infrequently. However, appellate courts do not usually directly supervise the actions of trial judges in their jurisdiction. Trial judges do not wait to have their decisions overturned. Rather, they pay attention to the drift of appellate decisions and respond to legal arguments citing those decisions.

On the other hand, judges are much less responsive to local political pressures than are elected prosecutors or police departments under the control of mayors. In many jurisdictions, judges win office by a gubernatorial appointment process called merit selection, in which the bar association has more influence than local politicos. Under this plan, candidates for judgeships must win endorsement from a selection panel composed of lawyers and judges rather than from local government officials. Judges so appointed usually face retention elections in which they run only against their record rather than against an opponent. Where such merit-selection schemes are not used, trial judges are elected either on a party ballot (as congressmen are) or on a nonpartisan ballot. In both cases their campaigns attract little attention from the electorate, and few judges lose office because of decisions they have made. Moreover, judicial ethics and the culture surrounding the judicial office stigmatize judicial behavior that responds to public opinion. Instead, judges are supposed to be above partisan politics. Consequently, judges are much more insulated from day-to-day fluctuations in public opinion. Because they typically have deep roots in their communities and many social ties to them, they are not entirely isolated from community pressures, but political responsiveness is not their strong suit.

OTHER PARTICIPANTS. Private citizens play an important part in many criminal court proceedings. They may serve as witnesses or as jurors. Both are important roles, because they significantly break into the professional monopoly held by prosecutors, defense attorneys, and judges. They also contribute a large degree of uncertainty in the proceedings in which they take part.

As witnesses, private citizens provide testimony either for the prosecution or defense about charges facing a defendant. During a trial their task is to respond to questions that attorneys put to them. First, they testify in direct examination by the prosecutor (or defense attorney, if a defense witness) and then under cross-examination by the other attorney. Judges occasionally intercede in the questioning and make their own queries. The experience can be an intimidating and frightening one for witnesses. In some cases, it can be degrading, as when a rape victim is asked to testify about her own virtue as well as about the assault that occurred. Witnesses introduce a considerable degree of uncertainty into trials because their performance can vary greatly. In many routine criminal trials, attorneys spend little time preparing them and may be surprised by the answers they give. Sometimes witnesses become confused under the pressure of testifying in court; often they are not very articulate.

Jurors participate in fewer cases than witnesses. Only a tiny proportion of all cases are decided by juries in the United States; the remainder are tried by judges alone or result in guilty pleas. If a defendant wants a jury trial, he or she can obtain it, but most attorneys will advise against it. Jury trials tend to occur in cases where there is considerable doubt about guilt; in very serious cases, where the defendant has nothing to lose; and in cases involving very prominent defendants.

Juries listen passively to the presentation of evidence and to the summations presented by defense and prosecuting attorneys. They are then instructed by the presiding judge about the applicable law on such matters as how to weigh the evidence, what outcomes they may choose, and what vote is required for a decision. When all these proceedings have been completed, the jury withdraws to its room to deliberate. Jury deliberations are entirely private; no outsider is permitted to observe them. Sometimes, a jury reaches its decision almost immediately; on more rare occasions, a jury may deliberate for days. When its decision is reached, the jury reports to the judge and announces its decision in open court.

Juries are notoriously unpredictable. Each jury is different. None belong to the web of relationships that composes the courtroom work group. Few courtroom professionals feel confident that they can accurately guess the outcome of jury trials, because it is difficult to gauge the impression testimony made on jurors or the dynamics of jury decision-making.

Conviction and Prison

The final institutional actors in the criminal justice process are those involved in punishing the guilty. Prisons and other correctional agencies resemble the police more than courts in many respects. They are organizationally independent of courts in most instances. Their staffs do not share the legal training common to key court personnel. They respond to different imperatives than do courts.

Two entirely different kinds of agencies handle persons who are convicted of a crime. First are parole and probation agencies, which supervise persons who are convicted but not incarcerated. Second are jails and prisons, which house those who are. Both are as fragmented as all the other agencies of the criminal justice system.

Probation and parole agencies exist at the local, state, and national levels. At each level, agencies are often autonomous from those at higher levels. The local agencies generally work under the supervision of local courts, although their staffs generally consist of persons with backgrounds in law enforcement or social work rather than in law. State-and national-level agencies usually are part of the prison system rather than of the courts. Their autonomy makes coordinated policy as unlikely in the field of probation and parole as in other segments of the criminal justice system.

The work of probation and parole agencies share many similarities, although they intervene at different stages of the process. Probation is generally an alternative to prison or jail. Parole occurs after part of a prison or jail sentence has been served. In both cases, convicted persons must subject themselves to supervision of their daily activities. They must periodically report to their parole (or probation) officer. That report may be no more than a phone call indicating that they still live at the same address. It may, however, involve a detailed probing into their lives, with orders to avoid certain friendships of which the officer disapproves, to maintain a job, or to reside in a particular section of the city. Serious violations of parole or probation—generally involving an arrest for a new offense—may result in revocation proceedings and in the subsequent jailing of the probationer or parolee.

Intrusive as parole or probation may be, incarceration is far more severe. It involves the total control of prisoners from the moment they enter the institution until they leave it. Violations of institutional regulations may result in severe punishment such as solitary confinement, in which all social contact with other prisoners becomes impossible.

Prisons are expensive, highly labor-intensive institutions. It costs as much or more to incarcerate someone in the United States for a year as to send a college student to a private university. Most of the prison staff are relatively unskilled persons serving as guards. They work under close supervision by the prison warden. While regulations vary considerably from one institution to another, the warden ordinarily provides detailed guidance for guards and inmates. But like others in the criminal justice process, prison officials exercise considerable discretion over inmates because much of their work is out of sight of supervisors and out of the limelight of public attention.

Prisons are not simply the passive recipients of court decisions. All prisoners come to them because of court decisions. But while one set of courts may be increasing the number of prisoners, another set may be setting limits on the numbers prisons may hold. That was particularly true during the 1970s and 1980s when prison populations increased dramatically in the United States while the size and number of state and federal penitentiaries has hardly changed. Consequently, in response to prisoner complaints that the increasingly crowded conditions violated the Constitution's ban on "cruel and unusual punishments," courts imposed limits on the number of inmates that could be housed in existing facilities. Such court decisions typically also established minimal food and health conditions that state and local authorities had to establish and maintain. Therefore, in many places, trial-court decisions to impose a prison sentence on those convicted could be accommodated only by a parallel decision by prison authorities to release some other person. Often such releases come many months or years before the expiration of inmates' formal sentences. As long as most sentences were of indeterminate length, prison authorities or parole boards enjoyed considerable discretion about the actual length of sentences to be served. Whereas a robber might be sentenced with considerable fanfare to a ten- to thirty-year prison term in court, the actual sentence served was often as little as four years. With the passage of determinate sentence laws by many states in the 1970s, much of this discretion disappeared. Yet, even in states with determinate sentences, early-release programs existed in order to make room for new prisoners. Alternatively, new prisoners were kept in local jails until there was room in the state penitentiary or until the local jail also became overcrowded.

It costs as much or more to incarcerate someone in the United States for a year as to send a student to a private university.

It is at this final stage of the criminal justice system that its lack of coordination becomes most evident. Both police and courts make decisions with little regard for the ability of prisons to accommodate the persons sent there. Often indeed, police and courts lack information about the level of available prison capacity. Decisions to build more prisons or to staff them differently are made at the state level by gubernatorial appointees and by state legislatures. Proposals to expand prisons must compete for funds with highways, schools, mental health, and all other programs, many of which have much more powerful political support than do prisons. At the national level, prisons are administered by the United States Department of Justice; they usually receive little attention amidst the many programs and agencies that the federal government administers.

Prisons incur much of the wrath of the public about the apparent ineffectiveness of the criminal justice system. The police often point to persons whom they have arrested and whom the courts have convicted but who reappear in the community in a few months to commit new crimes. Prosecutors often recommend long sentences, and judges impose them only to find the prisoner on the street a little while later in order to make room for new inmates. Indeed, as stated by Martinson, studies of the rehabilitative function of prisons indicate that they more often fail than succeed. At most, prisons appear to be warehouses for those adjudged guilty. In some instances they teach crime; in a few cases they provide an occasion for reform. In most, the persons leaving are no better than when they entered. Uniformly they are worse off because of employment difficulties they normally encounter, because of their difficulty in readjusting from the regimented life of prison to the free life outside its walls, and because of the fractured families to which they return.

Conclusion

The principal characteristics of the criminal justice process should now be apparent. The process is a system—albeit a loosely coupled one—because each of the many agencies involved in criminal justice affect the others. It is also one marked by a high degree of fragmentation and decentralization. Each of the major participants enjoys a high degree of discretion in making decisions, but that discretion is contained by intricate legal rules. Finally, each portion of the criminal justice process is marked by the tension between a desire to control crime and a distrust for excessive governmental authority. These characteristics make criminal justice in the United States unique and difficult to reform.

[See also (I) Enforcement; (III) Judicial Selection, Plea Bargaining, Prosecutors, Sentencing Alternatives, Trial Juries and Grand Juries.]

CASES

Gideon v. Wainwright, 372 U.S. 335 (1963)
Mapp v. Ohio, 367 U.S. 643 (1961)
Miranda v. Arizona, 384 U.S. 436 (1966)

BIBLIOGRAPHY

Richard A. Berk, Harold Brackman, and Selma Lesser, *A Measure of Justice: An Empirical Study of Changes in the California Penal Code, 1955–1971* (1977), is the most comprehensive existing study of the political activity leading to change in parts of the criminal law; however, it deals only with the situation in California. Donald Black, *The Manners and Customs of the Police* (1980), a collection of articles about policing, is by one of the leading sociological scholars of the police in the United States. Alfred Blumstein, Jacqueline Cohen, and Daniel Nagin, eds., *Deterrence and Incapacitation: Estimating the Effects of Criminal Sanctions on Crime Rates* (1978), addresses the deterrence question in this collection of papers by eminent criminologists and statisticians that was commissioned by the National Academy of Sciences. Greg A. Caldeira and Andrew T. Cowart, "Budgets, Institutions, and Change: Criminal Justice Policy in America," in *American Journal of Political Science,* 24 (1980), examines the politics of budgeting for criminal justice activities in the United States. William J. Chambliss, ed., *Crime and the Legal Process* (1968), is standard but critical criminology text. Thomas Y. Davies, "A Hard Look at What We Know (and Still Need to Learn) about the 'Costs' of the Exclusionary Rule," in *American Bar Foundation Research Journal* (1983), analyzes the effects of the exclusionary rule.

Isaac Ehrlich, "Participation in Illegitimate Activities: An Economic Analysis," in G. S. Becker and W. M. Landes, eds., *Essays in the Economics of Crime and Punishment* (1977), is regarded as the opening salvo in the dispute between conventional criminologists and economists about the efficacy of the death penalty and is considered a classic by some and a seriously faulted piece of research by others. James Eisenstein and Herbert Jacob, *Felony Justice: An Organizational Analysis of Criminal Courts* (1977), describes and analyzes felony case processing in Baltimore, Chicago, and Detroit in the early 1970s; particularly noted for its application of organizational analysis to criminal court processes. Malcolm M. Feeley, *The Process Is the Punishment: Handling Cases in a Lower Criminal Court* (1979), is an account of misdemeanor processing in New Haven, Connecticut. David F. Greenberg, ed., *Corrections and Punishment* (1977), is an excellent collection of articles on various elements of the work of correctional agencies. Anne M. Heinz, *Legislative Responses to Crime: The Changing Content of Criminal Law* (1982), analyzes the politics of criminal legislation at the state and local level in the United States. Anne M. Heinz, Herbert Jacob, and Robert L. Lineberry, *Crime in City Politics* (1983), analyzes the politics of crime control between 1948 and 1978 in ten large American cities.

Alfred R. Lindesmith, *The Addict and the Law* (1965), studies the interaction of drug addiction and legal prohibitions. William F. McDonald, ed., *The Defense Counsel* (1983), is a useful and up-to-date collection of articles on various modes of providing counsel for criminal defendants. Robert Martinson, "What Works? Questions and Answers about Prison Reform," in *Public Interest* 35 (1974), is a scathing critique of the rehabilitative potential of prisons. Jonathan Rubenstein, *City Police* (1973), offers a study of the police in Philadelphia by a participant-observer. Jerome H. Skolnick, *Justice Without Trial* (1966), gives sociological study of the use of discretion by the police and is considered by many to be a classic.

United States Department of Justice, Bureau of Justice Statistics, *Career Patterns in Crime* (1983), one of a series of reports by the bureau, summarizes current research on participation in criminal activities by various elements of the American population; "Prisoners in 1983," *Bulletin,* April 1984, is a statistical summary of distribution of prisoners within American prisons, published annually; and *Criminal Victimizations in the United States,* published annually, reports a sample survey estimating the number of criminal victimizations in the United States. United States Department of Justice, Federal Bureau of Investigation, *Uniform Crime Reports,* published annually, is the most frequently cited count of crime in the United States. Franklin E. Zimring and Gordon J. Hawkins, *Deterrence* (1973), examines empirical evidence on the deterrent effect of criminal laws and analyzes the potential for empirical research on this effect.

— HERBERT JACOB

D

DISCOVERY

The word *discovery* refers to a set of procedures used by lawyers to gather information that is controlled by other parties to a lawsuit or by people who are not parties to the suit. The vast bulk of discovery is conducted well before the date on which the case is scheduled to go to trial. Thus, the principal purposes of discovery are to provide lawyers and clients with access to the relevant evidence before trial so that they can evaluate their position in the litigation; decide whether they want to attempt to negotiate a settlement and, if so, on what terms; and, if no settlement is reached, be well prepared for what will occur at trial.

It is important to understand at the outset that discovery in civil cases is quite different from discovery in criminal matters. In civil litigation (that is, in cases other than those brought by government to punish someone for violating criminal laws) discovery is very broad, meaning that most kinds of evidence that have some bearing on the suit can be discovered, and all parties (plaintiffs and defendants) are under the same kinds of obligations to disclose information that is properly requested. In current civil practice, discovery is the most important and time-consuming part of litigation.

In criminal cases, by contrast, there are more-strict limits on what kinds of information one party can discover from another. The prosecution (government) generally has a much broader duty to disclose the evidence that it has developed than does the defendant, who is protected by the right not to be forced to incriminate himself or herself (a right guaranteed by the Fifth Amendment to the United States Constitution as well as by provisions in many state constitutions). Because of these substantial differences we will describe separately the two discovery systems. Because there is substantially more civil than criminal litigation in the United States and because the discovery system is broader and more elaborate in civil suits, we will devote more attention to civil discovery than to its narrower counterpart in criminal prosecutions.

Before turning to more detailed descriptions of procedures, we must emphasize one dominant fact about discovery in both civil and criminal litigation: discovery takes place in an adversary system, a system in which the parties exercise a great deal of control over the course of events and assume responsibility for much that does or does not occur. The tools of discovery are used by advocates; they are used against opponents. Discovery itself is an adversary process. In virtually all discovery systems the courts have until very recently played a largely passive role. It is the parties who use discovery tools, who ask the questions of one another, who demand that opponents disgorge information relevant to the suit before trial. A party with relevant information is generally under no obligation to disclose it unless and until another party properly asks for it. Thus, if lawyers do not use the tools of discovery well or do not respond in good faith to requests for information, significant evidence can remain hidden, and the courts generally have taken no action to be sure that all the relevant data has been brought forward. These basic facts of life about discovery have significant implications for how the system works and for the character of the problems that it has developed.

Discovery in Civil Lawsuits

To understand the purposes and problems of modern civil discovery, it is helpful to know something about the system's history. That history is complex; the generalizations that follow do not do justice to its dense texture and convolutions.

Nineteenth-century courts expected the parties to use pleadings to present a great deal of information about their positions.

Well before the American Revolution the English had developed two court systems, one called courts of law and the other called courts of equity. The law courts developed first, but they were rather narrow and inflexible. They did not recognize some kinds of rights and generally would enter only one kind of judgement: that some party did or did not owe some other party a specified sum of money. This kind of money judgement was not an adequate solution to some kinds of problems. Sometimes what a party really needed was an order from a court commanding someone to stop behaving in a certain way or to deliver a specified piece of property. Law courts generally refused to enter such orders. Occasionally someone would secure a money judgement by fraudulent representations, but law courts were not always responsive to efforts to get such judgments set aside. For these and many other reasons (some of which had to do with political power struggles), the king established a second system of courts—courts of equity—that would recognize new rights, offer more flexible kinds of relief, and correct errors made by the courts of law.

The colonists who settled America brought both kinds of court systems with them. Law courts remained relatively rigid. As court procedures evolved during the nineteenth century they provided parties with relatively few means for learning before trial what evidence other parties had developed. Thus, trial in the law courts remained to a considerable extent a game of chance; each party tried to "ambush" or surprise the other by introducing unanticipated evidence. A party who had no idea that some document or testimony would be used at trial had no opportunity to determine whether the document or testimony was reliable and thus could not help the jury or the judge determine what the truth really was. In this important respect the use of "surprise" evidence at trial undermined the adversary system: since both sides did not have a chance to explore and test its reliability, there could be no fair contest about how persuasive the evidence was. Limiting the parties' pretrial access to opponents' evidence also made it difficult to negotiate settlements rationally prior to trial. A party who knew little about the strength of the evidentiary support for his opponent's version of the facts could not rationally determine what the likelihood of winning at trial was or what the size of the judgment might be. Thus, when cases were settled before trial, it was often fear of the unknown, rather than carefully considered assessments of all the relevant information, that led to the negotiated dispositions.

During the nineteenth century, pressure from reformers led to only modest expansion of the discovery system in law courts, but equity courts developed more meaningful discovery procedures. In an equitable action, for example, a party could demand that the opponent spell out in considerable detail facts on which he or she was relying in pursuing the suit; these demands were called "bills of particulars." Equity courts also permitted parties to submit written questions to other parties and to inspect an opponent's documents. Finally, a party in an action in an equity court could "depose" another party before trial (that is, orally ask the party questions and have the party respond under oath). Such depositions could be used only to capture the testimony of someone who would not be present at the trial; they could not be used for the broader purpose of learning what someone who would be called as a witness at trial would say and how credible that person might be.

One reason American courts limited discovery in the nineteenth century is that "pleadings" performed much more substantial functions than they have come to play in twentieth-century litigation. Pleadings are the formal papers through which parties present their claims and their defenses. Nineteenth-century courts expected the parties to use pleadings to present a great deal of information about their positions in the suit. Law courts, in particular, expected the parties to go through a series of exchanges of pleadings in order to clarify and narrow the dispute between them so that by the time the case was ready for trial only a few issues would be left to be resolved.

Critics of nineteenth-century practice had harsh words for the way pleading practice had evolved, saying it had become extremely complicated and highly stylized. They argued that pleadings failed to serve their intended purpose of providing each side with essential information about the proposition being taken by the other and had become unduly expensive instruments of injustice.

It was against this backdrop that reformers, around the beginning of the twentieth century, began pushing for basic changes in the system. The upshot of the reformers' work, which climaxed with the adoption of the Federal Rules of Civil Procedure in 1938, was the merger of courts of law and courts of equity into one unified system and a dramatic shift in the functions that pleadings and discovery were expected to perform. Federal courts and most state courts no longer viewed pleadings as vehicles for exchanging detailed information about parties' positions. Under the new regime, pleadings came to serve very modest purposes. For plaintiffs, pleadings became the vehicle for giving opponents "notice" (hence the phrase "notice pleading") that a suit had been commenced and for pointing, often in very general terms, to the circumstances in the real world out of which the claims arose. Defendants used pleadings simply to announce that the matter would be contested and to reserve the right to develop a myriad of affirmative defenses. In most lawsuits the pleadings consist of no more than a simple complaint and a generalized answer, neither of which communicates a great deal about the bases for the parties' contentions. The reformers who designed this system simply abandoned the idea that pleadings could effectively serve more ambitious purposes.

Court reformers turned next to discovery. They decided that discovery should be used to perform many of the functions that pleadings had not been able to perform well. The discovery system was expanded so that lawyers could use it to learn the evidence that supported opponents' positions. The modern system was intended to equip both sides to understand fully the case before the trial. Reformers hoped that this full knowledge would result in negotiated settlements in a higher percentage of cases, would improve the fairness of those settlements, and, for cases in which no agreement could be negotiated, would make the trial more orderly and less likely to be marred by surprises. Before examining the fate of those expectations, we should describe the tools that make up most contemporary discovery systems.

The Scope of Contemporary Discovery

From the 1930s until the last quarter of the century the trend in the law governing discovery had been in one direction: to expand the subject area that parties can use discovery to explore and to give probing parties great freedom to decide which discovery devices to use and how often to use them. In the early 1980s the drafters of proposed amendments to the Federal Rules of Civil Procedure took potentially significant steps that might signal the beginning of a reversal of this trend. Because it is not clear how much these changes will affect established practices, we will examine the discovery system as it has been operating in most jurisdictions before we describe the 1980s amendments and assess their implications for the future.

Under rules in effect in most states and in federal courts, the scope of discovery is very broad. Parties can use discovery not only to seek information about issues actually raised in the pleadings but also to explore material that is "relevant to the *subject matter* involved in the pending action," according to Federal Rule of Civil Procedure 26(b)(1) (emphasis added). A party may pursue information even if he or she cannot show that it would be admissible as evidence at trial. It is sufficient if it can be shown that the information sought "appears reasonably calculated to lead to the discovery of admissible evidence." This right to probe broadly into information an opponent controls is designed to reduce the likelihood that a party will fail to learn something significant because of not knowing exactly what to ask for or because the kinds of documents an opponent might generate cannot be anticipated.

In most jurisdictions there are two principal sources of limits on the scope of the matters into which a discovering party may probe. One source is the law of "privilege." The second is the power of judges to enter "protective orders."

Privilege doctrine reflects policy judgments made by legislatures or courts that have decided that in order to vitalize certain relationships, it is necessary to assure the parties to those relationships that their private communications will be kept confidential. Of the relationships protected by privilege law, the one that has the greatest effect on litigation is between attorney and client. Policymakers have decided that it is very important for clients to feel that they can talk freely to their lawyers. If lawyers could be forced to disclose everything their clients told them, clients would be forced to decide what things to tell their lawyers and what things to keep to themselves. The effect of such a system would be to force clients to act as their own lawyers; that is, clients would be compelled to make judgments about what the legal and tactical consequences would be of disclosing different kinds of information. Thus, in virtually all jurisdictions the law preserves the confidentiality of private communications between lawyer and client when the purpose of the communication is to secure legal advice. It follows that during pretrial discovery a party may refuse to disclose to an opponent these kinds of communications, even if their content is relevant to the issues in the case and would be quite helpful to the other side.

The courts use protective orders to guard against unjustifiable intrusions and to impose restraints on a process that needs discipline.

Many state and federal courts recognize privileges in additional kinds of relationships that encourage openness, such as between a doctor or psychiatrist and a patient, between a member of the clergy and a penitent, and between a husband and wife. Unlike the attorney-client privilege, most of these privileges are "qualified" rather than absolute, meaning that there are some circumstances in which a party can be forced to disclose things that were communicated in confidence to a physician, priest, or spouse. To overcome an assertion of one of these privileges, an opponent must make a persuasive showing that the information sought is not available from another source and that a serious injustice would be done if access to the information were denied.

Another doctrine that lawyers often invoke to protect information from discovery is called the "work-product" doctrine. This law is designed to encourage attorneys to do their own work, to investigate their own client's cases thoroughly, and to think independently about the legal issues. To promote these ends, the work-product doctrine generally prohibits a party from discovering documents that opposing counsel has generated while preparing a case for trial. In many jurisdictions, documents that reflect an attorney's mental impressions, legal research, or strategies about the case never can be discovered. Other kinds of documents that counsel prepare in anticipation of litigation might be discoverable if an opponent could show that the information contained in them could not be acquired elsewhere and was very important. For example, federal law would include in the concept "attorney's work product" a report prepared by an expert who was hired by a lawyer to help the lawyer prepare for trial (for example, an accountant who analyzed complex financial data for the lawyer or a scientist who conducted tests on a product that was involved in the litigation). A party could force the disclosure of this kind of work product, for example, if he could show that the opponent's expert had destroyed or significantly altered important evidence when the expert conducted the analysis.

As noted above, the second important source of limits on the scope of discovery is the judiciary's power to enter "protective orders." Courts use such orders for a wide range of purposes, but most commonly to prevent sensitive information from being disclosed or to protect a party from being harassed or unduly burdened by needlessly intrusive or expensive discovery demands. In a lawsuit between two competing businesses, for example, a judge might grant the defendant's request for an order prohibiting the plaintiff from asking questions about secret manufacturing techniques if the court had concluded that the plaintiff could adequately develop her side of the case without that information, even though it would otherwise fall within the scope of discovery because technically it was "relevant to the subject matter" of the suit. Another kind of protective order permits a party to discover specified information but prohibits him from disclosing it to anyone who is not directly involved in the suit. Courts also use protective orders to prevent parties from repeatedly asking the same questions of an opponent or from needlessly protracting discovery events (especially depositions). In short, the protective order is a device that courts use to guard against unjustifiable intrusions and to impose common sense restraints on a process that sometimes reflects too little discipline.

The Tools of Discovery

In most jurisdictions rules of court or statutes provide parties with several different tools through which to conduct discovery. Of these, three are the most commonly used: interrogatories, oral depositions, and requests for production of documents and other tangible evidence.

Interrogatories are written questions that one party asks another party to answer in writing. In most jurisdictions, parties may use interrogatories to seek a wide range of information, from such discrete data as the names of witnesses or the location of important documents to such general matters as the facts on which an opponent bases a claim. The latter are called "contention interrogatories" and are controversial; many lawyers resent having to answer this kind of question and insist that responses to contention interrogatories often are of little value because they are vague. When intelligently used, interrogatories can serve as an inexpensive and effective means to learn useful information from an opponent; they can be especially useful for identifying sources of information that an attorney can then use other discovery tools to explore.

Until the early 1980s, most jurisdictions imposed no limits on the number of interrogatories a party could serve on an opponent. Thus, lawyers could periodically send large sets of written questions. Word processors enable lawyers to serve long lists of questions at very little expense to themselves. The burden of answering these questions can be severe. Moreover, some lawyers are not careful to tailor questions to the specific needs of given cases; instead, they use their word processors to produce standard sets of stock questions. Inevitably, some of these questions have little or nothing to do with some of the cases in which they are used. These kinds of problems have led some courts to impose presumptive limits on the number of interrogatories a party can serve without the consent of the opponent or special permission from the court. Other courts have attempted to control these problems by restricting the kinds of information parties may seek through interrogatories; for example, some courts prohibit use of contention interrogatories until the end of the pretrial period. Because unrestricted use of interrogatories has provoked so many complaints, the trend seems to be toward imposing some limit on the use of this particular discovery tool. In the debates about imposing such limits, policymakers are pressed to keep in mind that interrogatories are the least expensive means of acquiring many kinds of information. Thus, rigid restrictions could force parties to use more-expensive means of gathering evidence and might impose unfair disabilities on clients with limited resources. On the other hand, presumptive limits on the number of interrogatories that each party can serve can protect the poor litigant from the burden of having to answer waves of only marginally useful questions.

A second commonly used discovery tool is the deposition. This device normally consists of questions posed orally by a lawyer to a party or a witness. Occasionally attorneys submit their questions in writing. In either case, the person being deposed answers under oath, and a court reporter or tape recorder captures both the questions and the answers. Unlike interrogatories, which can be served only on a party to the lawsuit, a deposition can be taken of anyone who might know something useful, such as witnesses to an important event or experts who will be called to testify at trial. Depositions usually are taken out of court, in the office of one of the lawyers or the certified court reporter. Occasionally a judge or a special officer of the court will be present to make sure that the participants follow the rules, but in the vast majority of instances the deposition takes place in a private and informal setting. Some jurisdictions permit depositions to be taken over the telephone. This procedure can be economical, especially if the person to be deposed lives a great distance from the lawyers who want to ask the questions. Many lawyers, however, prefer to take depositions in person so that they can observe the demeanor and appearance of the witness and assess his credibility. Sometimes depositions are videotaped, especially if counsel are concerned that the deponent might not appear at the trial, for example, because of health problems or because the deponent resides outside the area where the court could compel attendance at the trial.

A person being deposed is required to answer only questions that are relevant to the subject matter of the suit.

Depositions can serve several purposes. They can be used to preserve the testimony of a person who will not appear at trial; the transcript of what the person said can then be introduced at trial as part of the evidence. Historically, the deposition was first developed for this purpose. In modern litigation practice, however, depositions are more commonly taken of people who will testify at trial. The purpose is not to preserve their testimony but to find out what they will say, to see how they stand up under cross-examination, and to uncover leads to other information that might be useful to the lawyer asking the questions. Lawyers occasionally use depositions to educate the person being deposed or the lawyer representing that person. This educational mission is accomplished by asking the deponent questions that will force him and his lawyer to confront the weaknesses of their case. Another purpose of taking a deposition can be to force a party to take a position on important disputed matters. If the party offers testimony at the trial that is inconsistent with what he or she said during the pretrial deposition, the transcript of the deposition can be read to the jury for the purpose of raising doubts about the party's honesty or accuracy of memory.

Expert witnesses can play a particularly important role in many kinds of litigation; for example, in some personal injury matters analysis offered by medical experts determines the value of the case. Nonetheless, not all jurisdictions permit parties to depose another party's expert in advance of trial. In the federal courts, for example, an expert who merely offers pretrial advice to another party but will not be called to testify at trial cannot normally be deposed. Even experts who will testify at trial may be deposed only if the party who wants to take their depositions can persuade the court that he cannot prepare adequately if he is given only a written description of the substance of what the expert will say. (Parties are entitled to these written statements.) In other jurisdictions, such as California, the rules permit parties to depose any expert who will testify at trial, without any showing of special need.

During depositions, lawyers pose the questions. Parties themselves are generally not permitted to ask questions. A person who is being deposed is required to answer only questions that are relevant to the subject matter of the suit and need not disclose communications that are protected by a privilege. If a lawyer representing the person being deposed believes that a line of questions probes an area that is irrelevant to the subject matter of the lawsuit or attempts to penetrate communications that are protected by a privilege, the lawyer will state a basis for objection and sometimes will order a client not to answer the questions. Some jurisdictions permit counsel to block testimony in this manner until a judicial officer can decide whether the objection is well made. Another source of tension at a deposition can be the so-called speaking objection. A lawyer who engages in this practice uses objections to questions as a means to coach his witness about how to testify. The lawyer representing the deponent might say, for example, that he objects to the form of the question being posed and proceed to rephrase the question in a manner that suggests to his own client how he should answer. There is no jurisdiction that condones this practice, but it is not uncommon.

The third discovery tool that lawyers use in many cases is the request for production of documents. In most jurisdictions a party can request permission to inspect not only documents but also other kinds of physi-

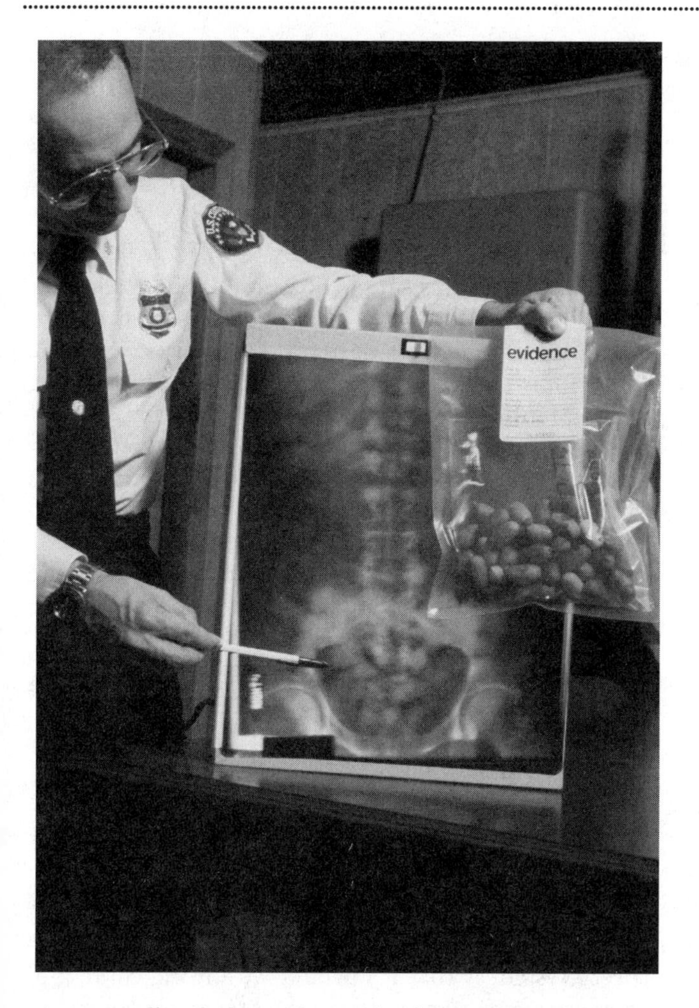

A customs officer displays evidence gathered from a drug smuggler: an x ray of the offender's stomach as well as drugs recovered from the stomach. (Jacques M. Chenet/Corbis)

cal evidence. Parties also may request permission to enter real property to examine the places where relevant events occurred. But in the vast majority of instances, requests for production focus on documents and photographs, such as medical records and X rays. The normal document-production scenario proceeds relatively informally and without the intervention of a judicial officer. A party who wants to examine documents controlled by another party simply sends a request specifying the categories of documents to be examined; then counsel for both sides work out a time and a place where the documents will be made available so that the requesting party can study them and decide whether copies are to be made. In many instances, the party responding to the request simply makes copies and sends them to the lawyer for the requesting party. A party who insists on seeing the originals has a right to do so.

Several kinds of problems can arise in connection with document-production requests. Sometimes such requests are drafted carelessly or with ulterior motives in mind and result in imposing a huge burden on the responding party, either because of the volume of material requested or because the material is difficult to gather. Over-broad requests usually provoke an objection from the responding party, which in turn leads to negotiations that ultimately result in a narrower, more focused demand. But sometimes the over-broad request evokes an overwhelming response: a party responding to a broad request may simply open the warehouse where all its records are kept and invite the propounding party to start looking for material. If the warehouse is large, lawyers refer to this tactic as the "Hiroshima defense," meaning that the objective is to dump so much information on the requesting party that the cost of sifting through it will be immense and the odds of finding anything useful will be small.

Another kind of problem can arise when a party in effect "shuffles" documents before producing them. Instead of producing documents organized according to the categories in the request or as the documents are kept in the normal course of business, responding parties occasionally mix them up, hoping to make the process of examining them more onerous and less fruitful. In some jurisdictions, including the federal courts, concern about this problem has provoked rule makers to prohibit expressly such document shuffling and to compel responding parties either to produce materials as maintained in the normal course of business or to organize the documents to conform to the categories in the request.

There is one additional source of friction that may impede an exchange of documents: a dispute about whether a privilege or the work-product doctrine protects materials that otherwise fall within the scope of a request. When one party invokes a privilege as a ground for refusing to disclose requested documents, the other party usually has the right to demand that the party asserting the privilege provide sufficient information about the documents (for example, who wrote them, when they were written, and to whom they were sent) to permit an independent determination that the privilege in fact applies. Occasionally a judicial officer is forced to examine the disputed documents in the judge's office to determine whether they are protected by privilege doctrine.

The kinds of problems described in the preceding paragraphs tend to arise more often in large, complex cases than in smaller, more straightforward matters. In routine cases, the document-exchange process often goes forward with little difficulty and contributes meaningfully to the parties' ability to negotiate a rational settlement without going through a trial.

Many jurisdictions provide parties with two additional important, but less frequently used, tools for discovery. One of these is a physical or mental examination of a party who has made his or her own physical or mental condition an issue in the litigation. In many jurisdictions a plaintiff who sues to recover for injuries suffered as a result of an auto accident may be compelled to submit to a physical examination by a doctor hired by the defendant. The purpose of this requirement is to assure that the expert medical evidence about the plaintiffs condition will be fairly balanced. Similarly, if a party alleges psychological harm he or she may be compelled to undergo psychiatric examination or testing by an expert. Because physical or mental examinations are intrusive, courts sometimes impose strict conditions on how, when, and by whom they may be conducted. In many jurisdictions, including California and the federal courts, a party who has submitted to an examination by a doctor retained by an opponent has a right to a copy of a detailed written report from that physician, setting forth the findings and the results of any tests. In California a plaintiff who demands such a report incurs a reciprocal obligation to make available to the defendant any reports generated by physicians hired by the plaintiff.

The other significant discovery tool that most jurisdictions make available to litigants is the written "request for admissions." Such requests often resemble interrogatories, but this discovery tool was designed to serve an independent function and to have a more telling effect. Interrogatories are primarily used as devices for gathering information from an opponent, information about sources of evidence and bases for positions asserted. Requests for admissions, by contrast, are used primarily to narrow the scope of a dispute, to remove the need to formally prove facts about which the parties are in essential agreement. Requests for admissions are especially useful for establishing the genuineness of documents that will be used as evidence at trial. In the absence of admissions or stipulations (less formal agreements), a party who wants to introduce a document at trial must go through an expensive ritual to prove that the document is what it purports to be and has not been altered. In most situations it is a waste of the resources of both the parties and the court to go through this proof ritual. Thus, admissions of the genuineness of documents can streamline the trial.

In theory, requests for admission can be used to establish much more important facts, even such "ultimate facts" as whether a party was negligent, or whether a contract had been entered. In practice, however, it is the unusual case where requests for admission are used successfully to eliminate truly significant fact issues from the trial. Understandably, parties are reluctant to admit facts that would substantially improve their opponent's position.

How Well Does the Discovery System Work?

Since the 1970s this simple question has been the subject of heated debate and of a modest amount of empirical research. There does not seem to be a simple answer. In smaller cases where the parties are proceeding in good faith, the system generally works well. In larger cases the system is more cumbersome and afflicted with greater problems, even when the parties comply with the rules. But a lawyer or litigant who decides not to abide by the spirit of the rules can cause a virtual breakdown of the entire process unless a judge intervenes and plays such a vigilant monitoring role that there is little room for misbehavior.

Critics charge that some lawyers use discovery to snoop around to see if there is a basis for asserting new claims.

Perhaps the principal source of problems for the discovery system is that it operates within the context of an adversary system of litigation. The principal goal of an adversary litigator is to win. He is inclined to cooperate only when he believes that cooperation will advance his client's interests and is only secondarily concerned about the health of the system, as such. These adversarial instincts often are inconsistent with the purposes of the Federal Rules of Civil Procedure, whose goals, as stated in Rule 1, are "to secure the just, speedy, and inexpensive determination of every action."

In theory, when a party launches his discovery there are two straightforward objectives: to gather information that might help support a claim or defense and to explore the quality of the evidence that supports the opponent's position. Sometimes, however, discovering parties have subtler, ulterior motives. Critics charge, for example, that some lawyers use discovery for "fishing expeditions"—that is, to snoop around in information controlled by another entity to see if there is a basis for asserting new claims. These critics contend that contemporary procedural rules permit parties to file vague, unsubstantiated complaints and then use discovery to determine whether there really is a foundation for a legitimate claim or to expand what starts out as a relatively simple suit into a more intimidating, complex piece of litigation. How often parties use discovery for these kinds of purposes is not at all clear, but liberal rules of pleading make it possible for a party who begins a suit with one claim to add many others if some basis for doing so is exposed during the course of discovery.

Occasionally parties use discovery for clearly illegitimate purposes. For example, lawyers have admitted using discovery in one suit for the purpose of laying the foundation for an entirely different action against a third person (Brazil, 236). Commercial entities have been accused of filing suits against competitors in order to use discovery to try to learn trade secrets. It is not likely, however, that discovery is often used for this purpose. The potential victims of such tactics frequently are sophisticated businesses that will fight hard to get the courts to protect the secrecy of confidential material.

It probably is more common for litigants to use discovery as an economic weapon. Responding to discovery requests can be expensive and can disrupt normal business operations. Moreover, defendants in large commercial litigation usually are forced to conduct expensive discovery of their own. The cost of litigation can be so substantial (and most of it is incurred in the discovery phase) that some defendants accuse some plaintiffs of filing suits as a form of ransom—that is, of filing complaints and then threatening to launch burdensome discovery campaigns unless the defendants offer early in the case to pay a settlement, which can amount to many thousands of dollars.

It would be misleading to suggest that only plaintiffs are accused of economic abuse of the discovery system. Some plaintiffs' lawyers contend that some defendants launch massive discovery campaigns as part of a strategy of pressuring economically weaker opponents into accepting settlements that do not reflect the real value of the plaintiffs' rights. Short of such coercive strategies, lawyers sometimes use discovery to send tactical messages to an opponent; for example, early in a suit a party might decide to make a demanding discovery request for the purpose, in part, of letting an opponent know that he intends to fight hard in the suit and to make it expensive for his opponent to get the case to trial. How often motives like these affect the use of discovery is not clear, but litigants must be tempted to consider such tactics because it is so obvious that responding to, and conducting, discovery can be so expensive. Such temptations may be even greater when one party to a suit is much wealthier than the opponent.

There is another economic reason why the discovery system sometimes does not function as smoothly as its designers anticipated. Many lawyers, especially those who represent defendants, are paid by the hour. The more hours they work on a case, the more money they make. This fact gives attorneys an economic incentive to make discovery more elaborate, more thorough, and more time-consuming than the needs of the case might otherwise dictate. This economic incentive can be reinforced by a lawyer's fear of a malpractice suit. That fear provides an additional impetus to conduct discovery exhaustively and to contest discovery requests that might yield information useful to an opposing party. There is no empirical data that shows how much either of these incentives affects lawyers' behavior during discovery. At this juncture all that is known is that some lawyers perceive these factors at work in other lawyers' conduct.

Adversarial instincts also account for what many lawyers believe is the biggest single problem in the discovery system: evasive or incomplete responses to discovery requests. In one survey, lawyers reported that this kind of problem makes discovery more difficult in 60 percent of their cases. Lawyers who primarily handle large, complex matters report experiencing this problem in 80 percent of their cases; the comparable figure for small-case litigators is 40 percent (Brazil). According to the same group of lawyers the next most troublesome problem with discovery is dilatory responses. Lawyers from a wide range of practices complain that in at least half of their cases they are forced to endure "extended delays" before receiving responses to discovery requests.

It is clear that lawyers often are not forthcoming and diligent in providing information sought by opponents through the discovery process. There is no rush to disclose evidence that might be helpful to an adversary. And the knowledge that an opposing party will provide as little useful information as possible plays an important role in the vicious circle that dominates the discovery process in many larger cases: a lawyer who expects his opponent to play artful dodger will cast a wide discovery net, asking as many questions as possible in order to reduce the odds that a clever adversary will be able to avoid disclosing the key material. Thus, evasive responses spawn over-broad demands, and the process becomes more expensive, less productive, and more frustrating to all concerned.

There is one additional major source of difficulty for the system. Unlike the others, it is not directly a product of adversary instincts. Instead, it is a product of the economics of law practice, especially law practice that revolves around litigation. Litigation is unpredictable. Cases that look like they will consume substantial lawyer resources settle or are dismissed almost without notice. Moreover, no lawyer can control the pace of cases; decisions by clients, by opposing counsel, by opposing parties, by judicial officers, and by people involved in other cases that compete for the court's time all affect the pace at which cases move toward disposition, Without warning, the lawyer may face long hiatuses in several suits.

Given these facts of litigation life, lawyers feel the need to work simultaneously on many files so that they will be able to maintain a flow of income when some of their cases settle unexpectedly or are placed by someone else on the back burner. But in their effort to take on enough cases to assure a constant flow of work, many litigators accept responsibility for more cases than they can comfortably handle. They end up dashing from crisis to crisis in different cases. They have relatively little time to plan the orderly development of individual matters or to craft specific discovery requests to fit peculiar needs of individual cases. Therefore, they often resort to form interrogatories and stock responses to discovery requests. Moreover, they postpone thorough investigation of their own clients' positions, so that when they respond to discovery requests, they cannot provide all the relevant information. Eventually they have to come to more complete terms with each case, but they tend to devote their most intense energy to the cases that have the most imminent trial dates and to let the others meander along.

This picture of litigators' practices may be somewhat exaggerated, but there is truth at its center. What it means for the system of discovery is plain enough: there is too little planning and too little order, especially in the early stages of case development. Discovery often is not done well: information exchanges are not coordinated, and depositions and document productions are handled piecemeal and often need to be repeated or cleaned up. In short, inefficiency abounds.

In smaller, relatively simple cases the toll taken by these problems consists mostly of delay in reaching a final disposition. In larger suits, however, discovery can consume vast resources and leave parties feeling unsure whether they have learned all the potentially important information. This feeling may well be justified. A research team recently asked a sizable group of litigators how often they settled cases in the belief that their opponents had not discovered arguably significant information. Lawyers who primarily handle larger suits indicated that this occurred in about half of their cases (Brazil, 811–812). If this perception is accurate, discovery is failing to achieve its principal objective in a large percentage of big cases. It is not providing the interested parties with that "mutual knowledge of all the relevant facts . . . [that] is essential to proper litigation" (*Hickman* v. *Taylor,* 1947).

Efforts to Correct Problems of Discovery

As described in the preceding paragraphs, many of the problems that encumber the discovery process are deeply rooted in the adversary system. Because these problems are in some measure products of basic human instincts, reinforced by competitive institutions, it is unrealistic to think that they can be corrected completely. Since 1976, however, concern about the inefficiency of the discovery process and about abuse of discovery tools has become so widespread that it has inspired major efforts to improve the way the discovery machinery operates. Among these efforts, the most visible and the most ambitious has been in the federal courts. It is appropriate to conclude by describing these recent corrective measures.

The amendments to the Federal Rules of Civil Procedure that the United States Supreme Court and Congress approved in 1983 attack the discovery problem in several ways simultaneously. They discourage lawyers from unjustifiably expanding the scope of lawsuits by asserting baseless claims or defenses, and they encourage judges to play more active roles in monitoring and managing the pretrial process. They also discard the notion that parties have a right to use discovery tools as often and as extensively as they choose. In addition, the new rules attempt to create an environment in which courts will be more likely to punish those who breach discovery duties.

Taken together, these changes reflect a perception by the rule makers that in the past neither the courts nor the parties have assumed sufficient responsibility for the operation of the system as such. The people who introduced modern discovery into the federal courts in the 1930s expected the system to be largely self-executing and self-policing. They thought lawyers would make responsible, reasonable discovery demands, would forthrightly disclose properly sought material, and would be quick to detect and report violations of the rules. As the discussion in the preceding pages makes clear, these expectations have not been fulfilled, especially in large, complex, or hotly contested lawsuits.

The 1983 amendments to the Federal Rules of Civil Procedure begin by imposing responsibilities for case management, in the pretrial period, on federal judges. Rule 16, which for decades had simply authorized pretrial conferences, now actively encourages judges to hold scheduling and planning conferences early in the life of most litigation. The new version of the rule encourages judges to help the parties narrow the scope of their dispute, to establish a discovery plan that focuses on the key issues, and to keep the case-development process moving efficiently by setting deadlines for completion of important pretrial work. The theory is that if judges get more thoroughly involved in their cases from the outset they will be in a better position to deter misbehavior and to encourage litigants to come to terms promptly with their situations, thus facilitating earlier settlements.

Prior to 1983 the Federal Rules conferred on litigants a right to use the tools of discovery as frequently as they chose, subject only to the right of an opponent to seek a protective order to block abuses. The rules did not explicitly compel counsel to exercise restraint in conducting discovery. The 1983 amendments dramatically changed this situation by introducing the concept of "proportionality" and requiring lawyers to limit discovery to the real needs of the case. Rule 26(b)(1) expressly commands judges to impose limits on the frequency or extent of the use of discovery tools if they determine that the discovery sought is "unreasonably cumulative or duplicative, or is obtainable from some other source that is more convenient, less burdensome, or less expensive," or if "the discovery is unduly burdensome or expensive, taking into account the needs of the case, the amount in controversy, limitations on the parties' resources, and the importance of the issues at stake in the litigation." Rule 26(g) compels lawyers to certify that each of their requests for, or responses to, discovery is "not interposed for any improper purpose, such as to harass or to cause unnecessary delay or needless increase in the cost of litigation," and is "not unreasonable or unduly burdensome or expensive, given the needs of the case, the discovery already had in the case, the amount in controversy, and the importance of the issues at stake in the litigation."

Modern discovery,

introduced into the federal courts in the 1930s,

was expected to be self-executing and self-policing.

The other major component of the rule makers' attack on discovery problems is designed to assure that federal judges and magistrates are more vigorous in enforcing the discovery rules. Studies conducted in the late 1970s showed that judges were reluctant to impose sanctions on lawyers who breached duties imposed by the discovery laws and that many litigators believed that this reluctance was one major reason the system did not work as well as it could (Brazil; Ellington). The rule makers responded by adding new provisions designed not only to make lawyers' duties clearer but also to increase the likelihood that breaches of those duties would result in sanctions. An added paragraph in Rule 16 empowers judges to impose financial penalties or other kinds of sanctions on counsel who fail to prepare adequately for, appear at, or participate in good faith in a conference called to plan discovery or other pretrial aspects of a case. Another paragraph in the discovery rules now compels judges to impose sanctions whenever they conclude that a lawyer has requested or responded to discovery in a manner that is inconsistent with the rules—for example, by interposing an objection in order to cause delay or to annoy an opponent or making a discovery demand that is unreasonably burdensome or expensive.

There is evidence that some judges are becoming more assertive about managing the pretrial development of cases assigned to them and about imposing sanctions when counsel fail to comply with the letter and spirit of the new rules. This new assertiveness by judicial officers is causing at least some lawyers to make more responsible decisions about how they handle the discovery aspects of their litigation. These trends should significantly improve the efficiency and efficacy of the system.

Discovery in Criminal Prosecutions

Discovery in criminal prosecutions fulfills functions similar to discovery in civil lawsuits. Criminal discovery is designed to promote fairness and the efficient use of judicial resources. It fosters more informed decision-making during plea bargaining and helps reduce the number of issues that must be resolved in cases that end up in trial. It also reduces the incidence of surprise evidence at trial. In most jurisdictions, however, there are striking differences between the way the discovery system operates in civil and in criminal actions. These differences have two principal sources: the constitutional privilege against compulsory self-incrimination that protects defendants in criminal actions and special concerns about restraining the power of the state.

Pretrial discovery was introduced into criminal procedure more recently and more cautiously than into civil litigation. For example, Federal Rule of Criminal Procedure 16, which gives defendants limited rights to inspect documents held by the prosecution, became law in 1948—ten years after the adoption of the corresponding Federal Rule of Civil Procedure. Moreover, the discovery rights conferred by the original version of Criminal Rule 16 were quite narrow. Document discovery, by defendants in criminal actions did not approach the scope and informality of document discovery in civil suits until the late 1960s and early 1970s.

During most of the history of the American system of criminal justice, defendants had no right to pretrial discovery. In the heyday of the common law in the United States (the nineteenth century), opponents of discovery by defendants successfully argued two points. First, they asserted that pretrial production of the prosecution's evidence would equip defendants to develop perjured testimony, to harass and intimidate prosecution witnesses, or to fabricate evidence in advance of trial. Second, they insisted that since the constitutional privilege against self-incrimination prevented the prosecution from discovering much of the evidence gathered by defendants, permitting defendants to discover the prosecution's evidence would give them an unfair advantage.

During most of the history of the American criminal justice system, defendants had no right to pretrial discovery.

Today, most states and the federal courts have rejected the common-law ban on discovery. Law-makers generally have decided that the benefits of at least some discovery in criminal cases outweigh the risks that discovery entails. They have concluded that giving defendants access to the prosecution's evidence improves the likelihood that the results of criminal cases will be fair and that a higher percentage of these cases will be settled without going to trial. Fear that broad discovery will equip defendants to prepare false evidence has not wholly disappeared, however, and vestiges of common-law restrictions on discovery rights remain in effect in most jurisdictions.

The remainder of this section describes the essential rights and procedures by which prosecution and defense may discover the evidence necessary to prepare their cases. Rules vary considerably from jurisdiction to jurisdiction. In the limited space here we can do no more than present examples of typical provisions. We focus primarily on rules developed for state court systems rather than their federal court counterparts. Unlike the situation on the civil side, where federal rule makers played a leadership role in liberalizing (broadening) discovery, on the criminal side certain states have led the movement toward expanding discovery rights.

This discussion emphasizes the scope of the parties' rights to compel pretrial disclosure. In many areas, much pretrial discovery occurs as a result of informal agreements between prosecution and defense. This is particularly true in federal courts, where the rules formally confer only limited discovery rights on defendants. Under federal law, for example, a defendant has a formal right to see pretrial statements by government witnesses only after the witnesses have testified at trial. Nevertheless, in order to prevent the delays during trial that would be necessary to permit defendants to study such statements, many federal prosecutors will disclose the statements in advance of trial. This type of informal discovery occurs most frequently where the prosecution believes that it has a very good case and wishes to encourage plea bargaining. But even when the evidence is not overwhelming, many prosecutors make disclosures in advance of trial that no statute or rule requires.

Discovery generally occurs in criminal actions only when a party makes a discovery request. There are only a few instances in which the prosecution or the defense has a duty to make disclosures without first being asked by the opposing party or ordered by a judge. In criminal matters discovery is circumscribed by the requirement of relevance and by the operation of privilege doctrines. Moreover, most jurisdictions distinguish material a party may discover merely by making a request from material that may be discovered only after demonstrating that "good cause" exists for the court to order his opponent to make the disclosure. In a few states, all discovery requests require prior court approval.

Some states impose additional restrictions on discovery in criminal matters. Some jurisdictions, for example, require a party seeking discovery to show not only that the information is "relevant" to the case but also that it is "material." The relevancy requirement merely limits discovery to items having some, even minor, connection to a case; the materiality requirement, by contrast, limits discovery to evidence that would make a difference in a juror's evaluation of the case. Some states also require the discovering party to demonstrate that the information sought will be admissible as evidence at trial.

As a further general limitation on pretrial criminal discovery, some jurisdictions, including the federal courts and Florida, refuse to permit the prosecution to discover some kinds of material unless the defendant has already asked the prosecution to disclose similar information. In these jurisdictions the prosecution has no right to compel document production from the defense unless the defense has previously requested document production from the government. And in some jurisdictions the prosecution has no formal discovery rights at all.

Discovery by the Defense

In addition to the kinds of general requirements described in the preceding section, all jurisdictions have developed special rules governing the discoverability of specific items.

WITNESS STATEMENTS. Most jurisdictions permit defendants to discover written or recorded statements they have made to government agents. Many jurisdictions also compel the prosecution to disclose its version of oral conversations between the defendant and government agents. In cases where the government is simultaneously prosecuting two or more people, each defendant usually has a right to obtain copies of statements made by the codefendants.

The kind of material that defense lawyers often want most to discover consists of statements that prospective witnesses for the prosecution have made prior to trial. These statements give the defense its best single opportunity to learn before trial the exact contours of the government's case. They also equip defense counsel to impeach a witness whose story changes. Jurisdictions with the broadest discovery provisions, such as the state of Washington, permit discovery of such statements. Other jurisdictions expressly preclude the discovery of government witnesses' statements. The rule in federal courts falls between these two positions: it compels prosecutors to disclose pretrial statements by their witnesses but only after their witnesses have testified at trial. This provision enables prosecutors to protect any witnesses whom they fear a defendant might harass or attempt to intimidate before trial.

States that compel the government to disclose prospective witnesses' identities and pretrial statements generally impose special requirements when a defendant tries to team the identity of a confidential informant. For example, in California the court conducts a closed hearing at which the defendant must demonstrate a reasonable possibility that the informant will give testimony tending to exonerate the defendant. Unless the defendant can make such a showing, the court will not order the prosecutor to disclose the informer's identity. Courts also take great care to prevent intimidation of confidential informants. The greater the likelihood of harm to an informant, the more demanding courts are of defense lawyers.

Another controversial issue revolves around whether the government should be compelled to make available to a defendant a transcript of testimony he or other witnesses offered to a grand jury. In many states and in the federal courts, a defendant has a right only to a transcript of his own grand jury testimony. Some jurisdictions require the defendant to show a "special need" for the prior testimony. This rule usually blocks defendants' access to grand jury testimony. In contrast, Vermont—the state with the broadest discovery in criminal cases—compels the government to disclose the entire grand jury proceedings that culminated in the defendant's indictment.

PRIOR CONVICTION RECORD. In most jurisdictions the prosecution must disclose information it has about the defendant's prior convictions. Jurisdictions differ about whether a defendant may discover the prior conviction records of prosecution witnesses. The jurisdictions that require the government to disclose the identity and prior statements of prospective trial witnesses generally also require the disclosure of those witnesses' past conviction records.

OTHER DOCUMENTS AND TANGIBLE OBJECTS. Most jurisdictions authorize fairly broad discovery of relevant books, papers, documents, photographs, and other tangible objects. The defendant must usually demonstrate that the items are material to his case, were obtained from him, or will be used by the government at trial. In many jurisdictions defendants also are permitted to enter and inspect government property if they can show that doing so would assist their defense.

EXPERTS' REPORTS. Most jurisdictions specifically authorize the discovery of test results and other reports made by government experts. Defendants most frequently utilize these provisions to obtain results of chemical, blood, physical, or mental examinations. In theory, the work-product doctrine might protect such material, but in practice prosecutors rarely assert this privilege. They know that defendants usually could make a showing of need sufficient to gain access to this kind of material.

DEPOSITIONS. Jurisdictions differ widely over the availability of depositions in criminal pretrial discovery, unlike in civil cases, where depositions occur frequently. Many jurisdictions only allow depositions in criminal cases in exceptional circumstances. A defendant in a federal prosecution will be permitted to take a deposition only if he or she can show that the deponent is unlikely to testify at trial, for example, because the deponent is very ill or about to leave the country. By contrast, rules in effect in Vermont permit parties to take depositions as freely in criminal matters as in civil suits.

POTENTIALLY EXONERATING EVIDENCE. Under the landmark ruling of *Brady* v. *Maryland* (1963), a defendant's conviction may be overturned if, before trial, he or she sought discovery of exculpating evidence that the government controlled but failed to disclose. The *Brady* rule is based on a defendant's right to a fair trial. By itself, the holding in that case does not create discovery rights. Instead, it sets forth what the penalty can be if the government fails, in this way, to treat a defendant fairly. Nonetheless, a number of states have incorporated the *Brady* principle into their discovery rules. In Vermont, for example, the prosecution must disclose any evidence tending to disprove the defendant's culpability or to reduce his punishment. In the state of Washington, the prosecutor also must disclose any evidence tending to show that the government entrapped the defendant.

Discovery by the Prosecution

A prosecutor's right to discover information from a defendant is circumscribed to a considerable extent by the defendant's constitutional right not to be compelled to testify against himself. This right, commonly known as the privilege against self-incrimination, extends solely to testimony—that is, to statements made under oath by the defendant. Thus, it does not prevent the prosecution from forcing a defendant to be fingerprinted and then using those fingerprints at trial. Similarly, the privilege against self-incrimination does not protect a defendant from being compelled to produce other non-testimonial evidence, such as samples of hair, bodily fluids, or handwriting. Most jurisdictions also compel defendants to take part in lineups, to speak for voice-identification purposes, to pose for photographs, and to submit to reasonably necessary medical examinations.

The states (fewer than half) that allow the defense to discover the names and prior statements of prospective prosecution witnesses generally also require the defense to disclose to the prosecution the names and prior statements of prospective defense witnesses.

There are many differences among the states with respect to whether to permit the prosecution to force disclosure of the theories on which the defendant intends to base his or her defense. Many jurisdictions compel disclosure of certain kinds of defenses, in order to prevent unfair surprise of the prosecution. These states require a defendant to notify the prosecution of intent to assert a defense based on alibi, insanity, or incompetency.

Discovery Procedures

While the various time frames created by criminal discovery rules strongly resemble their civil counterparts, the discovery phase of criminal litigation usually proceeds expeditiously. Thus, while civil discovery may stretch over years, most discovery in criminal prosecutions occurs over a period of a month or less. The limits imposed on the scope of criminal discovery and the requirement that defendants receive a speedy trial prevent the kinds of delays that afflict the discovery system in civil litigation.

All jurisdictions authorize their courts to regulate discovery in order to prevent abuse and injustice. In many jurisdictions, all discovery requests require prior court approval. Other jurisdictions require court supervision of only particular aspects of discovery. Vermont, for example, does not require the defendant to seek a court order to initiate discovery; the prosecution, however, must get approval from a court for all its discovery.

The prosecutor's right to discover information is circumscribed by the defendant's privilege against self-incrimination.

Because of the limits on the scope and duration of criminal discovery, criminal prosecutions generally involve far fewer discovery disputes than civil suits. Most disputes about discovery occur after trial. It is at this stage, for example, that defense attorneys are most likely to contend that the prosecution failed to disclose potentially exculpatory information.

As in civil cases, all jurisdictions allow their courts to issue protective orders to limit the discovery of otherwise relevant material after a showing that disclosure would unduly harass, embarrass, or intimidate the party from whom disclosure was sought. Also as in civil cases, where argument in open court of the reasons a party opposes discovery would itself require relevation of privileged or unduly embarrassing material, the court will hear the argument in private.

All jurisdictions give their courts broad power to enforce discovery rights and court orders. Penalties for discovery violations or abuses range from verbal reprimands to dismissal of the prosecution's case or reversal of a conviction. Courts generally have great discretion in deciding whether to sanction a party and, if so, how. In making such decisions courts consider the reasons offered as to why disclosure did not occur; the extent of the prejudice, if any, to the opposing party; the feasibility of rectifying the prejudice by a continuance (postponement) of trial; and the general circumstances surrounding the dispute.

Rules governing sanctions in criminal cases usually do not specifically authorize courts to compel one party to reimburse another for the expenses it incurred, including attorney's fees, as a result of a breach of a discovery duty. This kind of monetary sanction, which is becoming relatively common in civil litigation, is imposed only rarely in criminal matters. Criminal courts are much more likely to sanction serious discovery abuses by prohibiting the offending party from introducing certain evidence or calling certain witnesses.

Perhaps because the discovery system is expected to do less and to be completed in a shorter period in criminal matters, it seems to cause fewer problems and to function more efficiently than the discovery process in civil litigation. In civil suits, discovery has come to play the dominant role in the entire adjudicatory process. In criminal cases, by contrast, that role continues to be played by the trial itself.

[See also (III) Criminal Justice System, Trial Courts and Practice.]

CASES

Brady v. Maryland, 373 U.S. 83 (1963)
Hickman v. Taylor, 329 U.S. 495 (1947)

BIBLIOGRAPHY

American Bar Association, *Standards for Criminal Justice,* vol. 3 (1980), earlier editions of which served as the model for many states' efforts to revise their criminal discovery system, provides some good background authorities and analysis; and "Second Report of the Special Committee for the Study of Discovery Abuse," 92 F.R.D. 137 (1982), analyzes the problems of abuse and recommends solutions, some of which have been incorporated into the Federal Rules. Barbara Babcock, "Fair Play: Evidence Favorable to an Accused and Effective Assistance of Counsel," in *Stanford Law Review,* 34 (1982), reviews *Brady* and its progeny. Wayne Brazil, "Civil Discovery: Lawyers' Views," in *American Bar Foundation Research Journal* (1980), surveys 180 Chicago litigators' views about how the discovery system is working and what its principal problems are.

Paul Connolly, Edith Holleman, and Michael Kuhlman, *Judicial Controls and the Civil Litigation Process: Discovery* (1978), studies the volume of discovery activity and judicial efforts to contain abuses in several federal district courts. C. Ronald Ellington, *A Study of Sanctions for Discovery Abuse* (1979), is an empirical study of the frequency with which federal judges impose sanctions after alleged violations of discovery duties. Marvin Frankel, "The Search for Truth: An Umpireal View," in *University of Pennsylvania Law Review,* 123 (1975), challenges some basic premises of the adversary system.

David Louisell, "Criminal Discovery: Dilemma Real or Apparent?" in *California Law Review,* 49 (1961), discusses in depth the policies behind criminal discovery. National Conference on Discovery Reform, "Proceedings," in *Review of Litigation,* 3 (1982), reports and comments on the discovery system and proposed reforms offered by the ABA Special Committee for the Study of Discovery Abuse and about eighty federal judges, senior litigators, and scholars. Charles Renfrew, "Discovery Sanctions: A Judicial Perspective," in *California Law Review,* 67 (1979), is an important essay by a former federal trial judge about the need for vigorous judicial enforcement of discovery rules. Charles Wright, *Federal Practice and Procedure: Criminal,* vol. 2 (1982), provides one of the best single sources of material on federal criminal discovery. Charles Wright and Arthur Miller, *Federal Practice and Procedure: Civil,* vol. 8 (1970), is an annually updated treatise offering a thorough, readable, and reliable description of current procedural law in federal courts.

— WAYNE D. BRAZIL
GREGORY S. WEBER

DUE PROCESS OF LAW

The concept of due process of law is firmly lodged in the text of the Constitution of the United States. The Fifth Amendment of the Constitution provides that "no person shall . . . be deprived of life, liberty, or property, without due process of law." This provision applies only to the national government (*Barron* v. *Baltimore,* 1833). The states, however, are limited by the express language of the Fourteenth Amendment, which stipulates "nor shall any State deprive any person of life, liberty, or property, without due process of law." Thus, the due process guaranty, which is part of the supreme law of the land, is binding upon all public officials, national and state.

The due process clauses must be understood in the light of several basic doctrines of American constitutional theory. The first is that the Constitution is a law and not a mere collection of theoretical or abstract political principles. The second is that the Constitution, as declared in Article VI, is the supreme law of the land, binding upon all public officials at every level of authority. The third is that the United States Supreme Court is the final judge of the meaning of that supreme law. That the courts have the authority to hold unenforceable any statutes or executive acts that they find in contravention of the Constitution (the power of judicial review) is the key to the American system of public law.

In addition, every state of the American union has a bill of rights, most of which include due process clauses stated in much the same language as that employed in the federal Constitution. Indeed, even where a state constitution does not explicitly contain a due process clause (as in the case of Wisconsin), the concept is embraced within the state's constitutional law.

The definition of due process is one of the chief problems in American constitutional law, for its character is such that it qualifies most other constitutional guaranties. Due process applies to a wide range of issues, including the administration of justice, criminal law, police power, taxation, administrative procedures, corporate enterprises, and eminent domain. It has been observed that the study of due process is *de rebus omnibus* (Hough, 222). American constitutions do not spell out the meaning of due process of law. The problem of definition has been left to the courts as they decide specific cases.

English Origins and Usages

The origin of the phrase "due process of law" is generally assigned to the Magna Charta, which the rebellious English nobility compelled King John to accept at Runnymede in 1215. In the Great Charter, the king was compelled to agree to respect certain ancient and important rights and privileges of the feudal nobility. The Great Charter contained an important guaranty that was destined to develop into a mighty doctrine: the king agreed that "no freeman shall be taken or imprisoned or disseised or exiled or in any way destroyed, nor will we go upon him nor send upon him, except by the lawful judgment of his peers and by the law of the land." Since the expression "by the law of the land" *(per legem terrae)* was merely part of a treaty between king and nobles guaranteeing certain procedural rights of a technical character—that is, judicial proceedings according to the nature of the case—there was no suggestion of trial by jury or any other popular liberty. But with time, Magna Charta acquired greater significance as successive kings reissued or reconfirmed its principles.

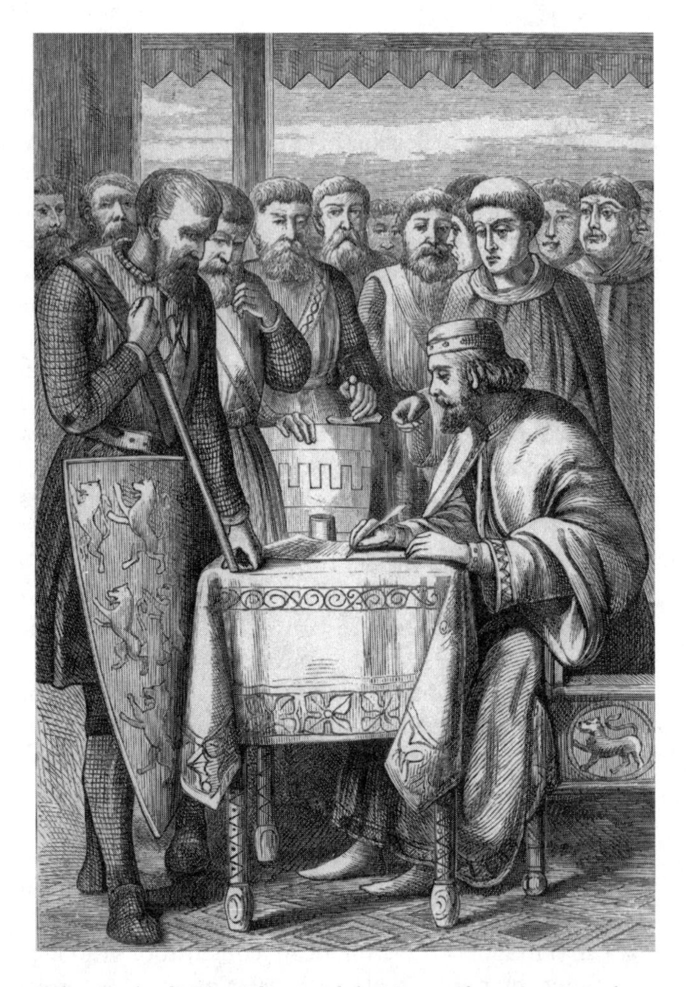

When England's King John signed the Magna Charta in 1215, the legal rights of ordinary citizens began to develop, including the right to "due process of law." (Corbis-Bettmann)

The phrase "due process of law" was first used in 1354, in the Statute of Westminster. There Edward III affirmed "that no man of what estate or condition that he be, shall be put out of land or tenement, nor taken, nor imprisoned, nor disinherited, nor put to death, without being brought to answer by due process of law." Thus, "due process of law" and "law of the land" came to mean the same thing.

The British constitution was transformed by the revolutions of 1640 and 1688. It was this new constitution that was so masterfully expounded by Sir William Blackstone, who published his influential *Commentaries on the Laws of England* in 1765–1769. In that great treatise, the due process clause acquired a firm position in the English legal system. Blackstone said, "It were endless to enumerate all the affirmative acts of parliament wherein justice is directed to be done according to the law of the land: and what that law is, every subject knows, or may know if he pleases; for it depends not upon the arbitrary will of any judge, but is permanent, fixed, and unchangeable, unless by authority of parliament."

The limitations of Magna Charta applied to the king and not to Parliament. Since Parliament is legally omnipotent, its decisions are not amenable to the judgment of the courts, and even today the courts do not have the power to refuse to enforce acts of Parliament on any constitutional ground, including due process grounds.

Even so, English judges can and do resort to the concept of natural justice, which is an aspect of natural law, especially where the absence of specific statutory directives affords them scope for the affirmation of general principles of justice. Of course, English judges are bound by what Parliament declares, but as A. L. Goodhart has observed, "By a convenient fiction it [the House of Lords] assumes that Parliament always intends that its statutes will accord with natural justice; no statute will therefore be construed to be retrospective or to deprive a person of a fair hearing or to prevent freedom of speech unless Parliament has so provided in the most specific terms."

The concept of natural justice serves various due process purposes in English courts. It is well established, for example, that the principle of natural justice requires administrative boards to give hearings to affected parties. The concept of natural justice has also been applied by English judges in criminal cases.

In many ways, the concept of natural justice is comparable to the American doctrine of due process of law. The English barrister E. B. Simmons wrote that the concept comes to three points essentially: "(1) No man may seem to act as judge in his own cause. (2) Every accused person has a right to hear the whole case against him. (3) No man may be condemned unheard." Of course, this is not the whole of due process as construed by American courts, but it is a good part of it. What gives the doctrine of due process of law greater force in the United States than in England is that American courts may employ it to declare federal and state statutes and administrative acts to be unenforceable because of their unconstitutionality. To be sure, these courts do not repeal or expunge an unconstitutional statute; they merely refuse to enforce it.

The Rise of Due Process in American Courts

It is settled beyond question that the principle of due process came from England to America as part of the common law and has been a fundamental rule in the judicial system of every state. It is clear that in their legislation, the American colonists gave evidence of the importance they attached to the due process notion, for particularly in the later days of the colonial empire, the words of Magna Charta were closely paraphrased. Later on, in the more controversial stage of the prerevolutionary debate, the due process concept was frequently restated and emphasized. Thus, in 1774, the First Continental Congress declared "that the respective colonies are entitled to the common law of England, and more especially to the great and inestimable privilege of being tried by their peers of the vicinage, according to the course of that law."

While no specific mention was made of the right to due process of law in the Declaration of Independence, which was drawn up by the Second Continental Congress in 1776, the "due process of law" clause received specific treatment in the first state constitutions. Thus, the Virginia Bill of Rights, which was drafted by George Mason in 1776 and afterward made a part of the first Virginia Constitution, provided "that no man be deprived of his liberty, except by the law of the land or the judgment of his peers." Seven other states followed suit. By the time the federal Bill of Rights was added to the Constitution with the adoption of the first ten amendments in 1791, eight of the thirteen states had constitutions that contained due process clauses. Today almost all state constitutions include such clauses.

Section 1 of the Fourteenth Amendment added a new weapon to those available to American courts involved in cases dealing with the limits on governmental power, by providing that no state shall "deprive any person of life, liberty, or property, without due process of law." However, despite its enormous importance today, Section I was little debated in Congress.

Not only did the members of the Thirty-Ninth Congress who participated in the debate on Section 1 of the Fourteenth Amendment fail to spell out the specific meaning of due process of law, but it is equally true that the United States Supreme Court has never committed itself to a precise, all-embracing definition. In the leading case of *Davidson* v. *New Orleans* (1878), Justice Miller expressed the conviction that it was neither possible nor wise to attempt a definition of due process "at once perspicuous, comprehensive and satisfactory." He went on to say, "There is wisdom, we think, in the ascertaining of the intent and application of such an important phrase in the Federal Constitution, by the gradual process of judicial inclusion and exclusion, as the cases presented for decision shall require, with the reasoning on which such decisions may be founded."

The "due process of law" clause received specific treatment in the first state constitutions.

As Justice John Marshall Harlan wrote in a distinguished dissenting opinion in *Poe* v. *Ullman* (1961), the Fourteenth Amendment was intended "to embrace those rights 'which are . . . *fundamental;* which belong . . . to the citizens of all free governments.'" He went on to say,

> Due Process has not been reduced to any formula; its content cannot be determined by reference to any code. The best that can be said is that through the course of this Court's decisions it has represented the balance which our Nation, built upon postulates of respect for the liberty of the individual, has struck between that liberty and the demands of organized society.

Similarly, Justice Felix Frankfurter, who thought deeply on this subject, once declared that "due process of law is a summarized constitutional guarantee of respect for those personal immunities which, as Mr. Justice Cardozo twice wrote for the Court, are 'so rooted in the traditions and conscience of our people as to be ranked as fundamental,' . . . or are 'implicit in the concept of ordered liberty.'" As Justice Harlan argued, so Justice Frankfurter pointed out that "the vague contours of the Due Process Clause do not leave judges at large. We may not draw on our merely personal and private notions and disregard the limits that bind judges in their judicial function. Even though the concept of due process of law is not final and fixed, these limits are derived from considerations that are fused in the whole nature of our judicial process" (*Rochin* v. *California,* 1952).

Clearly, American courts, in deciding concrete cases, have construed due process of law by the judicial process of gradual inclusion and exclusion on the basis of traditional values, philosophy, logic, ethical principles, and a large measure of social expediency. The courts have always maintained that this approach conforms with the elastic nature of the common law. In a case involving the problem of self-incrimination, *Twining* v. *New Jersey* (1908), the Court held that due process is to be construed in the light of the circumstances of each case, without reference to a particular status of the law in the past. Justice William H. Moody wrote,

> It does not follow that a procedure settled in English law at the time of the emigration, and brought to this country and practiced by our ancestors, is an essential element of due process of law. If that were so, the procedure of the first half of the seventeenth century would be fastened upon the American jurisprudence like a straight-jacket, only to be unloosed by constitutional amendment.

Manifestly, the sheer weight of long-established historical practice makes a difference, but history is an aid to construction and does not supply an imperative guide. Due process of law is basically a flexible process because conditions change. Thus, as a general rule, American judges do not attempt to define the concept of due process of law with any precision. It is considered an impracticable thing to try to do. Indeed, the New Jersey Supreme Court once observed that "it certainly would be presumptuous, to attempt to frame a definition of 'due process of law,' which shall embrace all and only all the cases which a just mind will perceive to be included in it" (*Moore* v. *State,* 1881).

Unquestionably, the due process clause of the Fifth Amendment got off to a slow start.

Even so, there have been a number of attempts to define due process of law, at least in a general way, although their very generality seems to substitute vagueness for vagueness. Thus, in a famous statement expressed as counsel in presenting *Dartmouth College* v. *Woodward* (1819), Daniel Webster asserted, "By the law of the land is most clearly intended the general law; a law which hears before it condemns; which proceeds upon inquiry, and renders judgment only after trial. The meaning is, that every citizen shall hold his life, liberty, property, and immunities, under the protection of the general rules which govern society." To be sure, this is by no means a definition utterly devoid of meaning, but its lack of specificity reduces its value in a considerable measure.

The position that has found the largest measure of acceptance by the justices of the nation's highest court was that which Justice Frankfurter spelled out so eloquently in his concurring opinion in *Joint Anti-Fascist Refugee Committee* v. *McGrath* (1951):

> Representing a profound attitude of fairness between man and man, and more particularly between the individual and government, "due process" is compounded of history, reason, the past course of decisions, and stout confidence in the strength of the democratic faith which we profess. Due process is not a mechanical instrument. It is not a yardstick. It is a process. It is a delicate process of adjustment inescapably involving the exercise of judgment by those whom the Constitution entrusted with the unfolding of the process. . . . The precise nature of the interest that has been adversely affected, the manner in which this was done, the reasons for doing it, the available alternatives to the procedure that was followed, the protection implicit in the office of the functionary whose conduct is challenged, the balance of hurt complained of and good accomplished—these are some of the considerations that must enter into the judicial judgment.

Due Process as Fair Procedure

Unquestionably, the due process clause of the Fifth Amendment got off to a slow start. The early legal history of the United States bears out the fact that little importance was attached to the due process clause during the formative period of its institutions. All that Justice Joseph Story had to say about the clause when he published the first edition of his treatise on the Constitution in 1833 was the following: "This clause in effect affirms the right of trial according to the process and proceedings of the common law" (vol. 3, 661). Had the clause attained more significance, undoubtedly it would not have escaped the attention of such a learned legal scholar. Thus, in the early years under the Constitution, the due process concept was applied only to secure procedural regularity or fairness and had nothing to do with the adjudication of substantive rights. The early cases dealt with questions of notice, personal service, the right to a hearing, and taxation procedures. Accordingly, the Supreme Court found it easy to define due process in 1855 as merely implying "regular allegations, opportunity to answer and a trial according to some settled course of judicial proceedings" (*Murray* v. *Hoboken Land and Improvement Co.*). Furthermore, since the national government, in the years prior to the Civil War, rarely enacted legislation affecting the basic liberties of the citizen, there was little occasion to invoke broader protection of the Fifth Amendment.

From the point of view of the process considered as a guaranty of procedural regularity or fairness, the principal requirements are adequate notice and a fair hearing. For example, in 1969, in the case of *Sniadach* v. *Family Finance Corp.,* the United States Supreme Court ruled that for a state to permit the freezing of wages in a garnishment proceeding without first giving the debtor notice and a hearing is a violation of fundamental principles of due process. It was asserted that a prejudgment garnishment of this type constituted a taking of property that may impose tremendous hardship on wage earners and their families. In other words, a debtor has a right to notice and a hearing before he can be deprived of the unrestricted use of his property. There are situations, however, where summary action by government may be justified, as in the case of the summary destruction by public officials of spoiled food on the ground that in the case of such a dangerous nuisance, the protection of public health is a more compelling interest than the property owner's right to prior notice and a hearing. Of course, he can get a judicial hearing afterward, but in such cases the public officials involved have very strong good-faith defenses in damage suits (*North American Cold Storage Co.* v. *Chicago,* 1908).

Procedural due process was thoroughly reviewed by the Supreme Court in 1967, in the case of *In re Gault.* This case involved a challenge to the juvenile-court proceedings of the state of Arizona. A fifteen-year-old boy was taken into custody by the police on the charge of having made obscene telephone calls. The Supreme Court ruled that in this case due process had clearly been denied. There had been no notice of charges to the boy or his parents; no counsel was offered or provided; the accused was not warned of his privilege against self-incrimination, and the privilege of silence was not knowingly waived. Moreover, because no witnesses were sworn, the accused had been denied the right of cross-examining his accusers (that is, the right of confrontation), so vitally required to validate a judicial hearing. Said Justice Abe Fortas, "Due process of law is the primary and indispensable foundation of individual freedom. It is the basis and essential term in the social compact which defines the rights of the individual and delimits the powers which the state may exercise." He insisted that the constitutional domestication of juvenile-court proceedings will not damage the procedure for handling juveniles, since it is still possible to deal with juveniles separately from adults under the supervision of the "kindly judge."

The meaning of due process as a guaranty of fundamental fairness in criminal cases involving adults has been explored by the Supreme Court in numerous important decisions. Thus, it is a violation of due process to permit a conviction for a crime where the courtroom was under mob domination (*Moore* v. *Dempsey,* 1923). Similarly, due process means that an accused has a right to be present at every stage of the proceedings, although he may forfeit that right by disorderly, disrespectful, and disruptive behavior in the courtroom (*Illinois* v. *Allen,* 1970) or by voluntary absence from the courtroom (*Taylor* v. *United States,* 1973). Furthermore, a defendant has been denied due process if he was tried by a judge who had a direct financial stake in the outcome of the case (*Tumey* v. *Ohio,* 1927).

The right to an impartial judge is an essential ingredient of the due process guaranty of fundamental fairness. Similarly, it is a violation of due process to convict a defendant on the basis of no corroborative evidence at all (*Thompson* v. *Louisville,* 1960). Due process also protects the defendant's right to an impartial jury (*Irvin* v. *Dowd,* 1961).

In the celebrated case of *Mooney* v. *Holohan* (1935), the Supreme Court ruled that due process has been denied if the prosecution presented testimony that it knew was perjured. Due process is also violated if the prosecution suppresses evidence in its possession that is favorable to the accused (*Brady* v. *Maryland,* 1963). In short, the prosecution may strike hard blows, but not foul blows.

Whatever else due process assures to the accused, it stands for the proposition that a defendant is entitled to a fair hearing, and the concept of a fair hearing has many dimensions. For example, before being punished for disrupting a legislative sitting, the accused is entitled to a notice of charges and a hearing on the charges (*Groppi* v. *Leslie,* 1972). While there is no mechanical formula for due process, the Court agreed that all the rights accorded to a defendant in a criminal trial are not necessary in legislative contempt proceedings. Even so, notice of charges and an opportunity to reply to them are absolutely fundamental. It was pointed out in *Groppi* that if given a hearing, the putative contemnor might prove mistaken identity or mental incompetence or might offer mitigating circumstances.

Similarly, it is established that an accused is constitutionally entitled to a hearing on the issue of his mental competence to stand trial (*Pate* v. *Robinson,* 1966). Since it is a violation of due process for a state to convict an accused person while he is legally incompetent, the

Court held that it follows that state procedures must be adequate to protect this right. The Court has also ruled that it is a denial of due process to revoke a parole without a hearing (*Morrissey* v. *Brewer,* 1972). In addition, a fair hearing means that the presiding judge in a criminal trial has denied due process if, through threatening remarks from the bench, he in effect drove a witness from the stand (*Webb* v. *Texas,* 1972).

The due process requirement of a fair trial is denied if there has been such a clear buildup of prejudice in the community through massive adverse publicity as to raise serious doubts regarding the impartiality of the jury (*Irvin*). Thus, in a notorious case where a socially prominent doctor was convicted of murdering his wife, the Supreme Court reversed the conviction because, prior to the trial, there had been massive newspaper, radio, and television publicity, which included many matters unfavorable to the defendant that were never presented in court (*Sheppard* v. *Maxwell,* 1966). The Supreme Court ruled that the trial judge had failed to fulfill his duty to protect the defendant from the inherently prejudicial publicity that had saturated the community and to control disruptive influences in the courtroom, which had created an atmosphere of bedlam. Finally, it is to be noted that the right to a fair trial implies the right to a public trial, since due process frowns on the dangers inherent in holding secret trials, which in the past have been instruments for the suppression of political and religious heresies (*In re Oliver,* 1948).

It is well understood, however, that an accused may waive his right to a full trial by entering a plea of guilty, and many defendants do in fact waive their trial rights by making such a plea. But due process has been violated if the plea was not voluntary, and a plea may be regarded as involuntary if the accused did not understand the nature of the constitutional rights he was waiving or the nature of the charge against him (*Henderson* v. *Morgan,* 1976).

A basic requirement of procedural due process is that a court that has given judgment in a case must have had jurisdiction of the case. Lack of jurisdiction clearly negates any decision the court may have made. Thus, in *Kinsella* v. *United States ex rel. Singleton* (1960), the Supreme Court set aside the conviction of a woman who was married to an American soldier and who had been convicted of murder under the Uniform Code of Military Justice by a court-martial sitting in Germany. The Court held that since the accused was not a member of the armed forces, she was not triable by a court-martial, whose jurisdiction has always been based on the status of the accused rather than the nature of the offense.

In addition to the requirement that a court must have proper jurisdiction over cases it tries, procedural due process also assures to a defendant specific notice of charges so that he may know in advance precisely what he has to respond to. Thus, on several occasions the Supreme Court has set aside convictions for violating statutes that were so vaguely worded as not to give adequate notice of just what was forbidden. In the famous case of *Lanzetta* v. *New Jersey* (1939), the Court ruled unconstitutional, on the grounds of vagueness, a state statute that made it a crime to be a "member of a gang." The Court has ruled a number of times that where a statute is so vague that persons of ordinary intelligence can only guess as to its meaning, the statute is invalid for lack of adequate notice. For example, in *Coates* v. *Cincinnati* (1971) the Court ruled unconstitutionally vague a city ordinance that made it a criminal offense for "three or more persons to assemble . . . on any of the sidewalks . . . and there conduct themselves in a manner annoying to persons passing by." It was held that the statute was invalid because it was based upon "an unascertainable standard": because conduct that annoys some people does not annoy others, the ordinance does not specify any standard of conduct at all.

Procedural due process requires that a court that has given judgment in a case must have had jurisdiction of the case.

Although most statutes survive the challenge of vagueness, the doctrine that statutes must not be so vague as to provide no ascertainable standard of conduct for individuals, the police, and trial judges still has some vitality. For example, the Supreme Court of Massachusetts ruled invalid a statute making it an offense for one "known to be a thief or a burglar" to act "in a suspicious manner around a store" (*Alegata* v. *Massachusetts,* 1967). However, statutes forbidding "disorderly conduct" are usually upheld by the courts on the grounds that the phrase has acquired a well-established meaning through "common usage and our legal tradition" (*State* v. *Reynaldo,* 1954).

Just as courts and legislative bodies are obliged to observe the fundamental notice and fair-hearing requirements of due process, so are administrative agencies required to observe the amenities of due process of law. For example, before welfare payments can be discontinued by an administrative official, he is obliged to conduct an evidentiary hearing (*Goldberg* v. *Kelly,*

1970). Similarly, students may not be suspended from a public school without some sort of hearing appropriate to the circumstances (*Goss* v. *Lopez,* 1975), and a tenured professor may not be dismissed from the faculty of a state college without a hearing (*Perry* v. *Sindermann,* 1972). It has also been established in many cases that an occupational or professional license may not be revoked by administrative act without due notice and a fair hearing. Speaking generally, administrative agencies must observe various procedural rights, including rights to specific notice of charges, to present evidence and argument, to challenge adverse evidence through cross-examination, to appear with counsel, to have the decision based upon the evidence in the record, and to have a complete record of the proceedings.

In conclusion, it would be appropriate to take note of an observation that Justice Harlan F. Stone made in *Missouri ex rel. Hurwitz* v. *North* (1926):

> The Fourteenth Amendment is concerned with the substance and not with the forms of procedure. . . . The due process clause does not guarantee to a citizen of a state any particular form or method of state procedure. Its requirements are satisfied if he has reasonable notice, and reasonable opportunity to be heard and to present his claim or defense, due regard being had to the nature of the proceedings and the character of the rights which may be affected by it.

Substantive Due Process

As long as the courts construed due process as a guaranty only of procedural rights, particularly those rights which had achieved a well-defined place in the common law, the judicial interpretation of due process did not stir up much public controversy. In fact, it has always been felt that judges are especially competent experts insofar as procedural law is concerned. As Justice Robert H. Jackson explained in his dissenting opinion in *Shaughnessy* v. *United States ex rel. Mezei* (1953),

> Procedural fairness, if not all that originally was meant by due process of law, is at least what it most uncompromisingly requires. Procedural due process is more elemental and less flexible than substantive due process. It yields less to the times, varies less with conditions, and defers much less to legislative judgment. Insofar as it is technical law, it must be a specialized responsibility within the competence of the judiciary on which they do not bend before political branches of the Government, as they should on matters of policy which comprise substantive law.

Due process of law serves to protect two important sets of rights, the right to procedural fairness and the right to be free from arbitrary or unreasonable regulations by government. The latter right is called a substantive right, since no procedural question may be involved. For example, even where there had been no procedural flaw, a holding that the rates imposed on a public utility by a regulatory commission or legislative body are so low as to amount to taking of private property involves a substantive right.

A new point of view that extended the concept of due process to include judicial scrutiny of the substantive content of law as well as procedural rights appeared gradually in the state courts. The New York Court of Appeals, one of the nation's most prestigious state appellate courts, began to break new ground in the mid-nineteenth century in several important decisions. In 1856, in *Wynehamer* v. *New York,* the New York Court of Appeals ruled that a statute that established prohibition constituted an unconstitutional taking of the property of those already in the liquor business, contrary to due process of law. In other words, the court ruled that the substantive right to own and sell property lawfully acquired was protected by the due process clause of the state constitution. The court held that the legislature does not have an absolute discretion to subvert property rights, that all property rights are inviolable, and that while the legislature may regulate the liquor business, it cannot confiscate and destroy property lawfully acquired. "All property," the court declared, "is equally sacred in the view of the constitution." The legislature is not omnipotent, the court observed, and the due process clause forbids it to exercise arbitrary power.

When the United States Supreme Court was first called upon to construe the due process clause of the Fourteenth Amendment, in the celebrated *Slaughterhouse Cases* (1873), the Court backed away from construing due process broadly, by ruling constitutional an act of the New Orleans City Council that gave a virtual monopoly to one slaughterhouse, thus putting many independent butchers and slaughterers out of business. In denying their appeal, the Court ruled that Section 1 of the Fourteenth Amendment was designed to uphold only the newborn rights of blacks, not those of anyone else.

This position had a short life. The rapid increase of the population and the growth of the economy, particularly after the panic of 1873 had run its course, created the need for more social control by means of governmental regulation through the expansion of the state's police power. Judicial intervention was soon to follow, and in 1884, in *Hurtado* v. *California,* wherein the Court sustained the validity of a state statute that abolished indictment by grand jury in the state courts over due process objections, the Court warned, "But it is not to be supposed that these legislative powers are absolute and despotic, and that the amendment prescribing due process of law is too vague and indefinite to operate as a practical restraint. It is not every act, legislative in form, that is law. Law is something more than mere will exerted as an act of power."

The floodgates opened a few years later, when cases arose that challenged as arbitrary the decisions of the burgeoning state railroad or public utility commissions. In the *Railroad Commission Cases* (1886) the Supreme Court served notice that it is not to be inferred that the power of regulation is without limit:

> This power to regulate is not a power to destroy, and limitation is not the equivalent of confiscation. Under pretence of regulating fares and freights, the State cannot require a railroad corporation to carry persons or property without reward; neither can it do that which in law amounts to a taking of private property for public use without just compensation, or without due process of law.

In the earliest railroad rate cases, while the Court asserted the power of judicial review of rates, it exercised that power only as to those rates which were so low as to be regarded as confiscatory in their effect upon the railroads. The next logical step was taken in *Chicago, Milwaukee & St. Paul Railway v. Minnesota* (1890), wherein the Court declared invalid a certain rate that, although it allowed a net profit to the railroad, did not permit a profit large enough to constitute what the justices thought was a fair return on the investment. Above all, the Court made it clear that "the question of the reasonableness of a rate of charge for transportation by a railroad company, involving, as it does, the element of reasonableness both as regards the company and as regards the public, is eminently a question for judicial investigation, requiring due process of law for its determination." The Court therefore held that because the statute, as construed by Minnesota's highest court, made rates determined by the state railroad commission final, conclusive, and unreviewable by the courts, it denied due process of law. To put it somewhat differently, the right of a judicial investigation of rates determined by an administrative agency is assured to the railroad by due process of law. A flood of appeals began to pour into the calendars of the United States Supreme Court. From then on, the courts were willing to look into the underlying reasons for statutes and to make judgments regarding the substantive quality of legislation. In the years 1890–1900, the United States Supreme Court heard 197 appeals that invoked the due process clauses.

Thus, due process of law became something more than a guaranty of procedural regularity. The Supreme Court opened the door to independent judicial review of the reasonableness of legislation in the light of conditions and values as understood by the judges. In short, the courts became the judges of legislative wisdom. In a sense, the Supreme Court became, in fact if not in theory, a third branch of the legislature—indeed, a sort of perpetual constitutional convention. In the due process cases, the judicial veto became judicial supremacy. A striking example of the construction of due process to defeat important social legislation was the decision of the New York Court of Appeals in 1911, in *Ives* v. *South Buffalo Railway*, which held the state's workman's compensation law unconstitutional. Because the statute imposed upon employers liability without fault for injuries occurring to workers in the course of employment, the Court ruled that this constituted an unreasonable taking of private property without due process of law.

It was in the area of labor legislation that the United States Supreme Court exercised its widest discretion in ruling on statutes on the basis of substantive due process. A majority of the Court soon began to rule corrective labor legislation invalid on such grounds. Thus, in 1908, the Court held that a statute that outlawed a "yellow dog" contract for railroad employees (a contract of employment in which the worker had to pledge not to join a union) was unconstitutional on the ground that such a restriction was an "arbitrary interference with the liberty of contract" of both employers and employees *(Adair* v. *United States).* There soon followed a series of cases in which the Court ruled unconstitutional state statutes that sought to regulate a wide variety of commercial transactions.

The decisions that stirred up the greatest controversy were *Lochner* v. *New York* (1905), which, by a 5–4 vote, invalidated a state statute that provided for a ten-hour work day and a sixty-hour work week for bakers, on the ground that these regulations were "mere meddlesome interferences with the rights of the individual," and two later cases that, by 5–4 votes, held unconstitutional on substantive due process grounds a minimum-wage law for women, *Adkins* v. *Children's Hospital* (1923) and *Morehead* v. *Tipaldo* (1936).

However, responding to the pressures generated by the Great Depression, legislative bodies, state and federal, began to enact various price-fixing statutes, and the Supreme Court slowly modified its views on the due process issue. Thus, in 1934, by a 5–4 vote, the Court upheld the regulation of milk prices as being "a reasonable exertion of governmental authority" *(Nebbia*

v. *New York).* Soon thereafter, the Court sustained the validity of statutes that regulated maximum warehouse charges (*Townsend* v. *Yeomans,* 1937), minimum prices for milk sold in interstate commerce (*United States* v. *Rock Royal Co-Operative, Inc.,* 1939), and price-fixing for coal moving in interstate commerce (*Sunshine Anthracite Coal Co.* v. *Adkins,* 1940). Reversing two recent precedents, the Supreme Court ruled in 1937 that a minimum-wage law for women was consistent with due process *(West Coast Hotel Co.* v. *Parrish)* and in 1941 the Court sustained the constitutionality of the Fair Labor Standards Act of 1938 (the so-called Wages and Hours Bill) enacted under the commerce power of Congress *(United States* v. *Darby Lumber Co.).* In 1963, in upholding a state statute that provided that only lawyers may engage in the business of "debt adjustment," Justice Black declared, "It is up to the legislatures, not courts, to decide on the wisdom and utility of legislation" *(Ferguson* v. *Skrupa*). The notion that due process authorizes courts to hold statutes unconstitutional when they believe that legislatures have acted unwisely, said Justice Black, has long since been discarded: "We have returned to the original constitutional proposition that courts do not substitute their social and economic beliefs for the judgment of legislative bodies, who are elected to pass laws."

The Survival of Substantive Due Process

The United States Supreme Court is no longer willing to substitute its judgment regarding the reasonableness of economic legislation for that of the legislative bodies. To this extent, the concept of substantive due process, as a basis for the exercise of judicial review, has lost its vitality. But substantive due process is still invoked by the courts, for in a considerable variety of cases involving what are regarded as "fundamental rights" the Supreme Court has established on a wide front the judicial power to strike down restrictive legislation.

One of the earliest decisions to take this line of thought was *Meyer* v. *Nebraska* (1923), wherein the Court ruled unconstitutional a state statute that required that all instruction through the eighth grade, in all schools, whether private or public, be in the English language. Although it was conceded that the state may regulate various aspects of schooling, such as the certification of teachers, "fundamental rights," such as that involved in this instance, are protected by due process. Justice James McReynolds, who spoke for the Court, declared that the liberty protected by the Fourteenth Amendment includes

> not merely freedom from bodily restraint, but also the right of the individual to contract, to engage in any of the common occupations of life, to acquire useful knowledge, to marry, establish a home and bring up children, to worship God according to the dictates of his own conscience, and generally to enjoy those privileges long recognized at common law as essential to the orderly pursuit of happiness by free men.

In fact, Justice Stone set the intellectual tone for the "fundamental rights" approach to due process in a famous footnote he wrote into the opinion in *United States* v. *Carolene Products Co.* (1938). In that case, the Court upheld the constitutionality of a federal statute that forbade the shipment of filled milk in interstate commerce on the ground that the wisdom of this sort of legislation is a matter for the judgment of the legislature and not that of the courts. But Justice Stone went on to explain that there "may be narrower scope for operation of the presumption of constitutionality" in several situations: (1) when the legislation on its face appears to be within a specific prohibition of the Constitution; (2) when legislation restricts those political processes which can ordinarily be expected to bring about repeal of undesirable legislation, such as the right to vote or to disseminate information, interference with political organizations, or prohibition of peaceable assembly; and (3) when legislation is directed against particular religious or racial minorities, or embodies prejudice against "discrete and insular minorities . . . which tends seriously to curtail the operation of those political processes ordinarily to be relied upon to protect minorities." In these situations, a more searching judicial inquiry than is usually appropriate is called for.

In the due process cases,

the judicial veto became judicial supremacy.

The concept of fundamental rights as a basis for activist judicial review of substantive legislation was greatly strengthened in 1942, in *Skinner* v. *Oklahoma,* wherein a statute that provided for the sexual sterilization of certain classes of habitual criminals was ruled unconstitutional. The Court based its decision on the equal protection clause rather than the due process clause but said that the statute in question denied a "basic liberty," because "marriage and procreation are fundamental to the very existence and survival of the race." Since a fundamental right was involved, the statute could not survive the "strict scrutiny" to which such statutes are subjected by reviewing courts.

In a series of cases the Supreme Court developed the concept of a right to privacy as one that falls within the scope of substantive due process. In *Griswold* v. *Con-*

necticut (1965) the Court ruled invalid a state statute that prohibited the use of contraceptives or the giving of advice as to their use, as an interference with the right of privacy, a right that Justice Douglas asserted was "older than the Bill of Rights." Although he was reluctant to revive substantive due process language and preferred to link the idea of privacy to other sections of the Bill of Rights, such as the Third, Fourth, and Ninth Amendments, two other justices of the Court, Harlan and White, thought that the statute clearly violated due process of law.

The newly developed concept of the right of privacy was expanded in 1973 in *Roe* v. *Wade,* which ruled unconstitutional a state statute forbidding abortions at any stage of pregnancy except to save the life of the mother. Speaking for the Court, Justice Harry A. Blackmun argued that the right at stake was founded in the personal liberty concept of the due process clause of the Fourteenth Amendment.

The Court has also judged the substantive merit of legislation regarding voting. In *Baker* v. *Carr* (1962) the Supreme Court ruled unconstitutional state legislative apportionments that result in unequal voting power for various citizens. The concept of "one man, one vote" became the watchword of a long series of decisions that sought to protect equality of voting power. The Court chose to rest its decision on the equal protection clause, but the result was the same as that which invocation of substantive due process would have produced. Indeed, many constitutional law writers now speak of substantive equal protection, according to which discriminations based on sex, race, financial status, or youth are ruled invalid. A good example is a series of decisions that ruled invalid legislation hostile to the interests of illegitimate children. For example, in 1983 the Court ruled unconstitutional a Tennessee statute that barred paternity suits or child-support actions brought on behalf of illegitimate children more than two years after birth *(Pickett* v. *Brown).* The Court thought that the state's asserted interest in preventing the litigation of stale or fraudulent claims was outweighed by the importance of providing children an adequate opportunity to secure support.

The continuing vitality of the principle of due process of law is strikingly reflected in the Supreme Court's gradual expansion of the thrust of the due process clause of the Fourteenth Amendment with regard to various forms of state action. It must be recalled that this amendment provides that no *state* shall "deprive any person of life, liberty, or property without due process of law." It should also be recalled that the first eight amendments to the Constitution are not addressed to the states but only to the national government.

However, the adoption of Section 1 of the Fourteenth Amendment in 1868 drastically changed the legal picture with regard to civil liberties. Initially, the provision was read restrictively when, in the *Slaughterhouse Cases,* the Court refused to hold that a citizen who had lost his employment because of a state-created monopoly was protected by a federal right or privilege. The Court's determination during Reconstruction to limit the thrust of the Fourteenth Amendment was underscored ten years later when, in the *Civil Rights Cases* (1883), it ruled that the legislative power of Congress to enforce Section I of the Fourteenth Amendment was limited to action by a state and did not extend to ordinary relations between private individuals, such as racial discrimination by innkeepers, theater owners, and public conveyances.

The Court developed the concept of a right to privacy as one that falls within the scope of substantive due process.

The "liberty" phrase in the due process clause did nonetheless generate the possibility of reading various provisions of the Bill of Rights into Section 1 of the Fourteenth Amendment. The Supreme Court took a first hesitant step in the direction of incorporating provisions of the Bill of Rights into the demands of the Fourteenth Amendment in 1897, when it decided that the Fifth Amendment requirement of just compensation for private property taken by a state for a public use applied to the state through the due process clause *(Chicago, Burlington & Quincy Railroad* v. *Chicago).* Above all, in 1925, in the celebrated case of *Gitlow* v. *New York,* the Court ruled squarely, without even arguing the point, that the freedom of speech protected by the First Amendment from abridgment by Congress was one of the fundamental personal liberties protected by the due process clause of the Fourteenth Amendment from impairment by the states. Gitlow lost his appeal from a conviction in the New York courts for violating a state criminal anarchy statute, but the long-term significance of the case lies in the fact that the Supreme Court was willing to take jurisdiction of the appeal. Since then, decisions have underscored the proposition that a state denial of liberty of speech and press presented questions of federal constitutional law, over which the Supreme Court may take jurisdiction. In 1940 the Court held that the liberty secured by Fourteenth Amendment due process included the First Amendment guaranty of religious freedom *(Cantwell* v. *Connecticut).* Today all parts of the First Amendment, relating to freedom of speech, the press, religion, assembly and petition, and the prohibition of an establishment of religion, now apply as federally enforceable limitations on the states.

Most of the provisions of the federal Bill of Rights deal with the rights of persons accused of crime, and until 1923 the Supreme Court was unwilling to review state appellate court decisions in criminal matters. In the leading case of *Moore* v. *Dempsey* (1923), however, the Supreme Court ruled that where a person convicted in a state court petitions for a writ of habeas corpus in a federal district court on the ground that the trial court had been dominated by overwhelming mob pressures, the district judge must make an independent evaluation of the facts, even though the state appellate court had previously reviewed the facts and upheld the verdict. This decision opened the door to a significant expansion of federal control over state criminal procedures, through review by the Supreme Court on the basis of the due process clause. Most, though not all, of the provisions of the Bill of Rights have now been incorporated into the due process clause, but a few have not been regarded as essential to justice and remain unincorporated, such as the Fifth Amendment guaranty of indictment by grand jury.

While the Court has not read into the due process concept all of the guaranties of the federal Bill of Rights, it has also not limited the meaning of due process to principles specifically enumerated in the Constitution, for due process is construed as a guaranty of a fair trial, in accordance with the principles of fundamental justice, and thus the due process clause is read as including rights not stated in the Constitution. An important example is the famous 1935 case of *Mooney* v. *Holohan,* wherein the Court ruled that where the prosecution has deliberately deceived the court and jury by presenting testimony known to be perjured, the state has denied due process. Later, the Court extended the *Mooney* rule to include the suppression by the prosecution of evidence favorable to the accused.

The net result of the decisions rendered in the twentieth century has been to constitute the United States Supreme Court as a veritable court of criminal appeals. While the states still handle most criminal litigation and are deeply involved in the area of basic human rights, there is now available a considerable array of corrective federal judicial remedies, largely under the rubric of due process of law, as well as a growing body of federal civil rights legislation.

[See also (III) Judicial Review.]

CASES

Adair v. United States, 208 U.S. 161 (1908)
Adkins v. Children's Hospital, 261 U.S. 525 (1923)
Alegata v. Massachusetts, 335 Mass. 287, 23, N.E.2d 201 (1967)
Baker v. Carr, 369 U.S. 186 (1962)
Barron v. Baltimore, 7 Peters 243 (1833)
Brady v. Maryland, 373 U.S. 83 (1963)
Cantwell v. Connecticut, 310 U.S. 296 (1940)
Chicago, Burlington & Quincy Railroad v. Chicago, 166 U.S. 226 (1897)
Chicago, Milwaukee & St. Paul Railway v. Minnesota, 134 U.S. 418 (1890)
Civil Rights Cases, 109 U.S. 3 (1883)
Coates v. Cincinnati, 402 U.S. 611 (1971)
Dartmouth College v. Woodward, 4 Wheaton 518 (1819)
Davidson v. New Orleans, 96 U.S. 97 (1878)
Ferguson v. Skrupa, 372 U.S. 726 (1963)
In re Gault, 387 U.S. 1 (1967)
Gitlow v. New York, 268 U.S. 652 (1925)
Goldberg v. Kelly, 397 U.S. 254 (1970)
Goss v. Lopez, 419 U.S. 565 (1975)
Griswold v. Connecticut, 381 U.S. 479 (1965)
Groppi v. Leslie, 404 U.S. 496 (1972)
Henderson v. Morgan, 426 U.S. 637 (1976)
Hurtado v. California, 110 U.S. 516 (1884)
Illinois v. Allen, 397 U.S. 337 (1970)
Irvin v. Dowd, 366 U.S. 717 (1961)
Ives v. South Buffalo Railway, 201 N.Y. 271, 94 N.E. 439 (1911)
Joint Anti-Fascist Refugee Committee v. McGrath, 341 U.S. 123 (1951)
Kinsella v. United States ex rel. Singleton, 361 U.S. 234 (1960)
Lanzetta v. New Jersey, 306 U.S. 451 (1939)
Lochner v. New York, 198 U.S. 45 (1905)
Meyer v. Nebraska, 262 U.S. 390 (1923)
Missouri ex rel. Hurwitz v. North, 271 U.S. 40 (1926)
Mooney v. Holohan, 294 U.S. 103 (1935)
Moore v. Dempsey, 261 U.S. 96 (1923)
Moore v. State, 43 N.J.L. 203 (1881)
Morehead v. Tipaldo, 298 U.S. 587 (1936)
Morrissey v. Brewer, 408 U.S. 471 (1972)
Murray v. Hoboken Land and Improvement Co., 18 Howard 272 (1855)
Nebbia v. New York, 291 U.S. 502 (1934)
North American Cold Storage Co. v. Chicago, 211 U.S. 306 (1908)
In re Oliver, 333 U.S. 257 (1948)
Pate v. Robinson, 383 U.S. 375 (1966)
Perry v. Sindermann, 408 U.S. 593 (1972)
Pickett v. Brown, 462 U.S. 1 (1983)
Poe v. Ullman, 367 U.S. 497 (1961)
Railroad Commission Cases, 116 U.S. 307 (1886)
Rochin v. California, 342 U.S. 165 (1952)
Roe v. Wade, 410 U.S. 113 (1973)
Shaughnessy v. United States ex rel. Mezei, 345 U.S. 206 (1953)
Sheppard v. Maxwell, 384 U.S. 333 (1966)
Skinner v. Oklahoma, 316 U.S. 535 (1942)
Slaughterhouse Cases, 16 Wallace 36 (1873)
Sniadach v. Family Finance Corp., 395 U.S. 337 (1969)

State v. Reynaldo, 243 Minn. 196, 66 N.W.2d 868 (1954)
Sunshine Anthracite Coal Co. v. Adkins, 310 U.S. 381 (1940)
Taylor v. United States, 414 U.S. 17 (1973)
Thompson v. Louisville, 362 U.S. 199 (1960)
Townsend v. Yeomans, 301 U.S. 441 (1937)
Tumey v. Ohio, 273 U.S. 510 (1927)
Twining v. New Jersey, 211 U.S. 78 (1908)
United States v. Carolene Products Co., 304 U.S. 144 (1938)
United States v. Darby Lumber Co., 312 U.S. 100 (1941)
United States v. Rock Royal Co-Operative, Inc., 307 U.S. 533 (1939)
Webb v. Texas, 409 U.S. 95 (1972)
West Coast Hotel Co. v. Parrish, 300 U.S. 379 (1937)
Wynehamer v. New York, 13 N.Y. 378 (1856)

BIBLIOGRAPHY

Daniel A. Farber and John E. Muench, "The Ideological Origins of the Fourteenth Amendment," in *Constitutional Commentary,* 1 (1984), is a scholarly analysis of the theoretical background of the Fourteenth Amendment in its formative historical period. A. L. Goodhart, "Legal Procedure and Democracy," in *Cambridge Law Journal* (1964), is an analysis of the concept of natural justice as employed by English judges. Charles M. Hough, "Due Process of Law—Today," in *Harvard Law Review,* 32 (1919), examines the concept of due process. Sanford H. Kadish, "Methodology and Criteria in Due Process Adjudication—A Survey and Criticism," in *Yale Law Journal,* 66 (1957), is a scholarly analysis of due process adjudication. James Kent, *Commentaries on American Law,* 14th ed. (1896), is one of the leading treatises on American constitutional law.

Rodney L. Mott, *Due Process of Law* (1926), the first large-scale treatise on the concept of due process, although dated, is still valuable for background material. E. B. Simmons, "Natural Justice," in *Justice of the Peace and Local Government Review,* 127 (1963), summarizes the concept of natural justice as employed by English judges. Virginia Wood, *Due Process of Law, 1932–1949* (1972), is a learned text covering the history of due process in an important formative period.

– DAVID FELLMAN

J

JUDICIAL CONFERENCE OF THE UNITED STATES

The Judicial Conference of the United States is a legacy of William Howard Taft's chief justiceship. Its establishment in 1922 constituted a part of the former President's broad campaign against progressives' demands for changes in the substance of then-prevailing federal law. Taft responded with a structural reform proposal: unprecedented administrative integration of a geographically dispersed court system manned by virtually autonomous judges. Thus, the third branch as a whole would achieve enhanced independence coincident with, and protective of, the uniqueness of the essential judicial function.

The Judicial Conference remains the linchpin of national judicial administration. From its beginnings as an annual meeting of the presiding judges of the United States Courts of Appeals chaired by the Chief Justice, the organization's membership has grown to include a representative from one of the United States District Courts in each of the eleven numbered circuits and the District of Columbia and the chief judges of those circuits, the United States Court of Appeals for the Federal Circuit, and the Court of International Trade. Biennial meetings at Washington, held in executive session, are largely repositories for reports from an extensive committee system involving the participation of approximately two hundred federal judges. This system provides status differentiation among the more than 700-member federal judiciary, but more significantly responds to a work load spawned both by the brevity of conference sessions and by a voluminous and complex agenda associated with the growth of judicial business and personnel.

Further structural changes in the conference-related administrative organization originated in causes both within and without the third branch. Congress in 1939 established the Administrative Office of the United States Courts and provided for regional administrative units: circuit judicial councils and circuit judicial conferences. Chief Justice Charles Evans Hughes promoted the Administrative Office Act as a response to Franklin D. Roosevelt's 1937 "Court-packing" bill, perceived by conference members as threatening executive-branch domination of the judiciary.

The new act vastly increased the functions performed by the Judicial Conference and its committees. Although the director and deputy director are appointed by the Supreme Court, the Office acts under "the supervision and direction" of the conference. Consequently, housekeeping, personnel, aud budgetary duties once performed by the attorney general and Department of Justice now fall within the oversight of the conference. These and subsequent congressionally mandated duties, some of which affected the district judges, ignited trial judge demands for conference representation, achieved in 1957, and led to establishment in 1967 of the Federal Judicial Center. This research, development, education, and training arm of the courts is directed by a governing board whose members are appointed by the conference.

The separation of powers makes the federal judiciary dependent on Congress for support.

The Judicial Conference has from its inception promoted administrative centralization, a functional tendency enhanced by the information-gathering and supportive services available from the Administrative Office. Consonant with the 1922 act's charge "to promote uniformity of management procedures and expeditious conduct of court business," the conference formulates policies for allocating budgetary, personnel, and space resources. It similarly addresses administrative questions raised in areas such as legal defenders, bankruptcy, probation, magistrates, and rules of practice and procedure.

The Judicial Conference promulgates standards of judicial ethics. Its role in disciplining wayward judges received explicit congressional authorization in 1980. The Judicial Councils Reform and Judicial Conduct Act empowered the circuit judicial councils to certify intractable misbehavior problems to the conference for "appropriate action." Remedies include referral of such cases to the House Judiciary Committee upon finding "that consideration of impeachment may be warranted," a procedure followed in three instances from 1986 through 1988.

The separation of powers makes the federal judiciary dependent on Congress for support. Since Taft's chairmanship and later with congressional authorization, the Judicial Conference has developed and promoted legislative programs. Additional judgeships, appropriations, judicial salaries, court organization, jurisdiction, procedural rules, and impeachment recommendations have been among the proposals brought to Capitol Hill, usually by conference committee chairmen. Thus, judges do and must lobby Congress to obtain necessary resources. Yet, legislative liaison may embroil the judiciary in visible political conflict, as occurred when Chief Justice Warren E. Burger lobbied against portions of the 1978 Bankruptcy Act.

The strategic position of the Judicial Conference, its policymaking functions, and its implementation responsibilities pose dilemmas. A quest by the conference for efficiency, uniformity, and equity has induced intrabranch policies favorable to development of "managerial" judges and has produced unavoidable tensions between centralized policymaking and individual court administration. Conference recommendations to Congress permit submission of proposals freighted with substantive public policy implications packaged in the wrappings of judicial administration, a characteristic that marked the struggle to divide the Fifth Circuit.

BIBLIOGRAPHY

Barrow, Deborah J. and Walker, G. Thomas 1988 *A Court Divided: The Fifth Circuit Court of Appeals and the Politics of Judicial Reform.* New Haven, Conn.: Yale University Press.

Fish, Peter Graham 1973 *The Politics of Federal Judicial Administration.* Princeton, N.J.: Princeton University Press.

– PETER GRAHAM FISH

JUDICIAL REVIEW

Although not limited today to the United States, judicial review is the unique American contribution to the art of governance. It has no historical counterpart, and other modern nations have not carried the process nearly as far as has the United States. Often considered the principal means of resolving disputes over constitutional boundaries, in recent years judicial review has taken on a significant new dimension—that of judges filling in the interstices of statutes written in general terms or giving meaning to ambiguous statutory terms. In both roles, judges have a significant policymaking function; by no means are they passionless recipients of data presented by litigants. Justice Robert H. Jackson once wrote, "The political nature of judicial review generally is either unrecognized or ignored. But it is that which gives significance to constitutional litigation and which makes it transcend mere legal proceedings" (p. 311).

Although some mention will be made of other courts, this essay discusses judicial review principally as exercised by the Supreme Court of the United States. The Supreme Court may, and does, propose, but other courts (and administrators) may, and do, dispose. In this respect, there are lower-court and administrative checks on Supreme Court power. Because most law cases begin and end at the trial level, with the Supreme Court ruling definitively on only 150–200 out of the more than 4,000 cases filed each year, trial-court rulings become a significant aspect of judicial review. The Supreme Court interprets the Constitution and statutes, but lower courts, both federal and state, and administrators interpret the Court.

"The judiciary, from the nature of its functions, will always be the least dangerous to the political rights of the Constitution."—Federalist 78

No commonly accepted definition of judicial review exists. To add focus to the ensuing discussion, judicial review is here defined as a process by which lawyer-judges, sitting as official organs of the state, determine the constitutional validity of actions of other governmental officers, at all levels and in all departments, and construe statutory language. This definition is based upon the following assumptions: courts are part of the governing coalition of the nation; in interpreting both the Constitution and statutes, judges cannot avoid being lawmakers; and to some extent, all judges bring their personal philosophies to the judging process, and these philosophies guide their determinations. Each of these assumptions is to some extent controversial, but the intellectual disputes over them are less over their validity than over the legitimacy of judicial review itself or the desirability of what is judicially decided—the results reached rather than the process. Leonard Levy wrote, "Much of the literature on the Supreme Court reflects the principle of the gored ox. Attitudes toward the Court quite often depend on whether its decisions are agreeable" (p. 1).

Judicial review was an inevitable consequence of the coincidence of three historical factors: a new nation with a written constitution; a federal system (that is, with the powers of government divided between those allocated to the national government and those retained by, or denied to, the states); and a tradition of judge-made law in both Great Britain and the American colonies. A written constitution requires, at least in most instances, one body to give ultimate meaning to its terms, and a federal system needs an umpire to settle the unavoidable conflicts that arise between local and national powers. However much disliked—and often they have been and are—judges have lent a sense of continuity to the American experience.

In the United States the Supreme Court, not without stout opposition, assumed the roles of determining the limits of constitutional powers generally and of arbitrating the federal system. The latter is perhaps the more important. Justice Oliver Wendell Holmes once asserted that he did not believe the United States would be seriously damaged if the Supreme Court lost its power to invalidate congressional statutes, but the nation would be imperiled if the Court could not determine the validity of the laws of the several states. It is worth mentioning that most constitutional questions that the Supreme Court decides today derive from actions of state, rather than national, governmental officers. The contrary is true for statutes, with the Court sitting as a supreme tribunal of interpretation of the growing number of federal statutes.

The Constitution and Judicial Powers

Although the question of judicial review was debated in the Constitutional Convention of 1787, no provision was made for it in the Constitution. At best, the evidence is inconclusive as to whether the framers assumed the general propriety of judicial review, however much they may have disagreed on details.

What can be said with certainty is that the idea was far from unknown in pre-1787 America. Some trace its beginning to England and Sir Edward Coke's famous, albeit questionable, statement in *Bonham's Case* (1610): "When an act of parliament is against common right and reason, or repugnant, or impossible to be performed, the common law will controul it, and adjudge such act to be void." The actual intent of Coke's decision, however, is still debated in Great Britain (although modern versions may still be found in cases where British judges rely on "natural justice" in deciding cases).

Relatively little attention was paid to the powers of the judiciary in the *Federalist Papers,* the essays by Alexander Hamilton, James Madison, and John Jay that were designed to sway public opinion in favor of the new constitution. Of the eighty-five papers, the final six, all written by Hamilton, deal in part with the courts. *Federalist* no. 78 is the most important; in it Hamilton seems to go out of his way to allay fears of an all-powerful judiciary:

> Whoever attentively considers the different departments of power must perceive that, in a government in which they are separated from each other, the judiciary, from the nature of its functions, will always be the least dangerous to the political rights of the Constitution; because it will be least in a capacity to annoy or injure them. The executive not only dispenses the honors but holds the sword of the community. The legislature not only commands the purse, but prescribes the rules by which the duties and rights of every citizen are to be regulated. The judiciary, on the contrary, has no influence over either the sword or purse; no direction either of the strength or of the wealth of the society; and can take no active resolution whatever. It may truly be said to have neither FORCE nor WILL, but merely judgment; and must ultimately depend upon the aid of the executive arm even for the efficacy of its judgments.

Hamilton either did not foresee the ways in which the powers of the judiciary would develop or was disingenuous in some of that statement—or both, which is likely.

However much serious scholars may disagree about particular decisions, all acknowledge today that judges have more than mere "judgment" and that they often exercise "will," if not "force." Although it has been asserted that judicial review was not imposed by the Court on an unwilling people, it is also fair to say that had the framers foreseen what the Supreme Court and judicial review were to become two centuries later, they probably would have taken steps to ensure that judicial power could not be—as it has been—aggrandized.

As in all its litigable provisions, the Constitution speaks in general, even vague, terms about the judiciary. Article III, Section 2 states in part,

> The judicial Power shall extend to all Cases, in Law and Equity, arising under this Constitution, the Laws of the United States, and Treaties made, or which shall be made, under their Authority;—to all Cases affecting Ambassadors, other public Ministers and Consuls;—to all Cases of admiralty and maritime Jurisdiction;—to Controversies in which the United States shall be a party;—to Controversies between two or more States;—between a State and Citizens of different States;—between Citizens of the same State claiming Lands under Grants of different States, and between a State, or the citizens thereof, and foreign States, Citizens or Subjects.
>
> In all Cases affecting Ambassadors, other public Ministers and Consuls, and those in which a State shall be a Party, the supreme Court shall have original jurisdiction. In all other Cases before mentioned, the supreme Court shall have appellate Jurisdiction, both as

> to Law and Fact, with such Exceptions, and under such Regulations as the Congress shall make.

Two aspects of Article III merit mention. First, the framers wanted to create an independent judiciary; that is the substance of Section 1. But they also wished to check judicial power—hence, the provision in the second clause of Section 2 concerning Congress's power to regulate the appellate jurisdiction of the Supreme Court. Because all but a handful of the cases that the Court decides come to it by some form of appeal, this clause is—at least it could be, for its exact meaning is yet to be determined—an important limitation on the High Bench. Furthermore, by not mentioning judicial review, the framers at least implicitly rejected the idea, advanced in the Convention of 1787, that the Supreme Court should act as a "council of revision" of congressional enactments. Two centuries later, a perhaps persuasive case can be made for the Court's having become a type of de facto "council," not in the original sense of having prior scrutiny of statutes but by virtue of the fact that the Court's decisions on the meanings to be given statutory language are often difficult for Congress to alter.

The only other important constitutional provision concerning the judiciary, and then only inferentially, is in the second clause of Article VI:

> This Constitution, and the Laws of the United States which shall be made in Pursuance thereof, and all Treaties made, or which shall be made, under the Authority of the United States, shall be the supreme Law of the Land; and the Judges in every State shall be bound thereby, any Thing in the Constitution or Laws of any State to the Contrary notwithstanding.

This, in brief, is a constitutional provision for the principle of federal supremacy, a principle that has had great significance for the legal relationships within the federal system.

The spare terms of the Constitution concerning the courts obviously pose more questions than they provide answers for. Perhaps most significant among those questions is how Article III is to be executed. Only when Congress, on 24 September 1789, passed "An Act to establish the Judicial Courts of the United States" was flesh put on the bare constitutional bones. The powers that federal courts, particularly the Supreme Court, exercise today are thus the result of a combination of ambiguous constitutional provisions and the greater specificity of the Judiciary Act of 1789. That statute is one of the most important ever enacted by Congress—so much so that it should be viewed as at least a quasi-constitutional pronouncement.

For present purposes, Section 25 of the Judiciary Act is the most significant. It provided for Supreme Court review of final judgments or decrees "in the highest court of law or equity of a State in which a decision in the suit could be had," in three situations:

> where is drawn in question the validity of a treaty or statute of, or an authority exercised under the United States, and the decision is against their validity; or where is drawn in question the validity of a statute of, or an authority exercised under, any State, on the ground of their being repugnant to the constitution, treaties, or laws of the United States, and the decision is in favor of such validity; or where is drawn in question the construction of any clause of the constitution, or of a treaty, or statute of, or commission held under, the United States, and the decision is against the title, right, privilege or exemption specially set up or claimed [thereunder].

Although subsequent statutes amended the Judiciary Act of 1789, its principal thrust has remained intact. The importance of the statute, considered together with the constitutional provisions, cannot be overestimated—particularly when one realizes that it is the judiciary itself that gives ultimate meaning to what the constitutional framers (and Congress) intended. In that sense, judges are permitted to judge their own causes.

The Experience of Judicial Review

Although judicial review is taken for granted today, with little dissent except over specific decisions, it is indeed extraordinary for one organ of the state to sit in judgment on acts of other organs of the governing apparatus of the state. That this is tolerated is best explained by the fact that as a part of the governing coalition of the nation, the judiciary cannot long be out of phase with the other parts of the coalition. Supreme Court justices assert the power to say what the law is, but their power is attenuated in fact. There is only a superficial validity to justice Jackson's well known comment about the Supreme Court: "We are not final because we are infallible, but we are infallible only because we are final" (*Brown* v. *Allen,* 1953). Finality is not the language of politics, and the Court cannot avoid being deeply immersed in the political process.

Judicial review is therefore politics carried on under another name and in different forums. As lawmakers, the courts are targets of pressure-group tactics. This is seen, to mention the outstanding example, in the way in which black Americans employed the judiciary in the

1940s, 1950s, and 1960s as a means of enhancing their status. If they were to work "within the system," they had to seek a judicial remedy because the avowedly political branches of government completely failed to comply with the spirit and promise of the Constitution's guarantee of equal protection under the laws.

Americans are notoriously litigious—much more so than people in other nations—and they have made judicial review the linchpin of the American legal order. Other means of dispute settlement are, of course, available and are used, but the ultimate resort is to invocation of the state's judicial arm. In addition, this means that Supreme Court decisions on the affirmative powers of government—as distinguished from the negative limitations on government—serve to lend constitutional legitimacy to those powers.

Americans are notoriously litigious, and they have made judicial review the linchpin of their legal order.

In the last analysis, judicial review is what the Supreme Court says it is. It is important to realize that although the process began slowly and has been highly discontinuous, in that different issues are prominent in different periods of time, the years since 1789 have seen a steady aggrandizement of power in the judiciary. In the 1830s, Alexis de Tocqueville asserted in his classic *Democracy in America* that almost all political questions in the nation are sooner or later presented to the courts as judicial questions—a statement that was not completely accurate when made and is only apparently true today. Many political questions simply did not receive judicial cognizance in the nineteenth century—for example, the question of the exploitation of the nation's resources in accordance with principles early stated by Hamilton in such influential state papers as his *Report on Manufactures* (1791).

In recent decades, for reasons not yet fully studied or understood, the Supreme Court has carved out larger areas of judicial concern, as in the belated enforcement of the Bill of Rights and the Civil War Amendments. Even so, much that is political today does not become judicial, either because the justices eschew ruling because they observe a number of self-imposed restrictions or because the pervasiveness and complexity of government make it difficult and often counterproductive to trigger the judicial process. In a society characterized by rapid and continuing social change, the delays inherent in the judicial system militate against even greater use of courts. Of course, some benefit from delay and readily resort to the judiciary, as is clear from the numerous appeals filed by the more than 3,200 men and women on Death Row.

Moreover, a tension has always existed in the United States between the idea of popular sovereignty (the view that ultimate power rests in the people) and of a Constitution that in certain designated instances places limits on the power of the people. Majoritarianism thus conflicts with the purportedly immutable principles of limited government. President Abraham Lincoln, among others, drew attention to these tensions when in his first inaugural address he criticized the Supreme Court, which had assumed the task of reconciling the disputes emanating from two apparently irreconcilable polar opposites:

> The candid citizen must confess that if the policy of the government upon vital questions affecting the whole people is to be irrevocably fixed by decisions of the Supreme Court, the instant they are made in ordinary litigation between parties in personal actions the people will have ceased to be their own rulers, having to that extent practically resigned the government into the hands of that eminent tribunal.

In the end, judges making constitutional (and other) decisions are not passive instruments of objective justice. Their rulings, as Theodore Roosevelt remarked to the dismay of many conservatives, depend upon their economic and social philosophies. All serious students of the judicial process concede the point—as do presidents when they are filling Supreme Court vacancies. They search for men and women whose political philosophies parallel their own. However much judges may strive to be invincibly disinterested, they are, like all people, prisoners of their heredity and their environment. There is a pervasive myth of neutrality in constitutional decision-making. In the words of Judge Learned Hand,

> [Judges] do not, indeed may not, say that taking all things into consideration, the [governmental act] is too strong for the judicial stomach. On the contrary, they wrap their veto in a protective veil of adjectives such as "arbitrary," "artificial," "normal," "reasonable," "inherent," "fundamental," or "essential," whose office usually, though quite innocently, is to disguise what they are doing and impute it to a derivation far more impressive than their personal preferences, which are all that in fact lie behind the decision.
>
> (p. 70)

Judges, it must be stressed, are hardly as innocent as Hand stated. Holmes once commented that judges tend to be naive, unsophisticated people who needed a touch of Mephistopheles. One wonders what company he and Hand kept. Judges are generally hard-nosed realists, fully aware of what they are doing.

In the American system judges are not self-starters. They must await the accident of litigation before making decisions. The astonishing consequence is that portentous problems of public policy are made into legal-constitutional questions by fortuitous litigation. Yet, the fact that judges are not self-starters emphatically does not mean that they are fettered by what lawyers present to them in their briefs and oral argument. Supreme Court justices routinely do independent research into the legal issues involved in a case—not personally, it should be noted, but through their law clerks. Moreover, they make extensive use of "judicial notice," by which that which is said to be "common knowledge" becomes a part of the information considered by the Court. Both independent research and judicial notice are discretionary, although limits supposedly, but not actually, exist on use of the latter. In *Roe* v. *Wade* (1973), for example, Justice Harry Blackmun, writing for the majority in the decision validating consensual abortions, cited numerous medical data not presented to the Court by the lawyers. Chief Justice Warren Burger, in a concurring opinion, observed that Blackmun had taken judicial notice to its outermost limits (which he did not define) but had not gone beyond them.

Acceptance of judicial review by the populace apparently rests on a myth of judicial independence and a belief in the sovereignty of the "rule of law." The idea of an independent judiciary "is simply an elaborate rationalization for the substitution of coercion for consent. . . . The myth of judicial independence is designed to mollify the loser" (Shapiro, 1981, 65). The myth thus has a functional utility. The same may be said for the conventional notion of the rule of law, which purportedly binds even the sovereign. A "government of laws and not of men," as the shibboleth goes, is an ideal construct, often far from the actuality. It, too, is a myth, one that serves to hide the realities of the exercise of power.

The Mechanics of Judicial Review

The institution of judicial review has several distinct characteristics. Initially at least, it is adversarial. The cases that the Supreme Court accepts for decision "on the merits"—about one out of twenty-five of the four thousand to five thousand that are filed each year—are chosen not because of the litigants but in the interests of development of the law. Litigants are important because only they can start the process. Once the Court takes a case for full-dress examination, the litigants usually fade into the background, as the justices routinely promulgate general rules in specific decisions. Although it is logically impossible to infer a general principle from one particular, the practice is accepted by bench, bar, and professoriat alike. Here again the justices have discretion: they can, and sometimes do, limit the effect of a decision to the facts and the particular litigants before them. But the usual practice is to state a general rule—which makes the Supreme Court a de facto third (and at times apparently the highest) legislative chamber. This is true even though, as a matter of technical law, only the parties before the Court are bound by the decision. In sum, most Supreme Court decisions on constitutional questions are essentially "class actions," with an individual or small group suing on behalf of himself or itself and "all others similarly situated." For example, *Brown* v. *Board of Education* (1954), the school desgregation case, was a class action brought by Linda Brown for herself and all other black schoolchildren who were kept in racially separated schools.

The great majority of petitions for certiorari are summarily denied, with no reason given for denial.

Yet, the adversary system is flawed. For instance, it is assumed that lawyers are of approximately equal competence. They are not: a wide disparity in ability may be seen in the legal profession. For that matter, the level of advocacy before the Supreme Court is often depressingly low. Furthermore, the flow of information to the Court is faulty, in that much information relevant to a case is not presented by counsel for the litigants. This leads, as previously noted, to independent research and use of judicial notice—and also to participation of "friends of the court" *(amici curiae),* individuals or groups who do not have a direct interest in a case but are thought to be able to be of help in sorting out the complexities of the case. Even then, the justices frequently issue rulings in cases where considerable relevant information simply is not available—particularly on the social consequences of decisions. Moreover, judges are often narrow-minded lawyers whose background gives them little experience in dealing with significant governmental affairs.

All but a few cases come to the Supreme Court from some other court. Within the national government there is a three-tiered system of courts: the district (trial) courts, the courts of appeal, and the Supreme Court.

In addition, there are some specialized courts, such as the Temporary Emergency Court of Appeals (dealing mainly with energy problems) and the Foreign Intelligence Surveillance Court (a highly secret body that passes on requests for eavesdropping for foreign intelligence purposes). The federal Supreme Court also reviews decisions of state supreme courts but only when federal questions are involved. Justice Felix Frankfurter once remarked that the Supreme Court is not a super legal-aid bureau. A federal question is one that concerns litigation in which the Constitution, a congressional statute, or a treaty is at issue. Americans thus are governed by two sets of courts and have recourse to two constitutions—national and state—when their rights are concerned. (State courts must decide federal constitutional questions when properly presented by a litigant.)

Litigants who lose in a lower federal or a state court have two principal avenues to the Supreme Court—appeal and writ of certiorari. (A third route, certification, is seldom used, and then not by a litigant but by a court of appeals that considers some issue so important that the Supreme Court should decide it at once. The Court may at its discretion send it back to the court of appeals to get the benefit of that tribunal's reasoning.) *Appeal* is a word of art, theoretically meaning that the Supreme Court must rule on the merits—that is, give the case the complete treatment of briefs and oral argument. Generally, this avenue is limited to instances in which a federal action has been declared unconstitutional in the lower court. In practice, the Court handles an appeal much the same as a petition for certiorari (what lawyers call "cert"). Such a petition is a request that the record of the proceedings in the lower court be transmitted to the Supreme Court for its review. Most cases come to the Court through the cert process. And the great majority are summarily denied, with no reason given for denial (although on occasion a justice will write a dissent to a denial). For cert to be granted, the "rule of four" applies: four justices must agree that the case merits full-dress treatment. Whatever the avenue followed, only 150–200 cases receive consideration on the merits each year. (In theory, denial of cert means neither approval nor disapproval of the decision below, although many nonlawyers believe to the contrary. The same applies to appeals that are dismissed, often "for want of a substantial federal question," although some argue that such dismissals are rulings on the merits.)

Opinions are routinely written on cases decided on the merits. Increasingly in recent years, opinions are written by several justices, which makes it difficult and at times impossible for lawyers to determine the exact meaning of the decision. Most opinions are signed by the justices who wrote them, although "per curiam" (unsigned) opinions are issued from time to time. The office of the opinion is supposedly to explain the reasoning that led to the conclusion. Often, however, opinions are more rationalizations than explanations, and at times the "reasoning" is circular, with the justice restating the question being decided and using it as a reason for the decision. The methodology of judicial reasoning is one of the more controversial aspects of judicial review. Although most observers agree that opinions should be "principled," it is fair to say that there is a high degree of disagreement over the meaning of that word.

It is clear that judges consider the social consequences of their decisions; that is, they attempt, however imperfectly (because the relevant information is not always available), to forecast the impact of a given decision on the social order. They thus tend to be forward-looking rather than applying, as the myth would have it, the law as it has been received and understood. This means that judges are "result-oriented" to some degree. *Result-orientation* is a Frankfurter neologism; it is a term of opprobrium in some circles, used to castigate some judges, such as Chief Justice Earl Warren, for paying what some commentators believe is excessive attention to who the litigants are rather than to "the law."

Judicial review is instrumental. Judge Benjamin Cardozo once correctly remarked that the teleological conception of the judge's function must always be in his or her mind. Judicial review thus is purposive, with the justices seeking to further their personal value preferences. This may be seen in the way in which judicial review has evolved since 1789.

Historical Development

Judicial review was the first major constitutional silence filled by judicial decree. Always controversial, it has now achieved legitimacy simply because almost two centuries of practice have solidified the claim of lawyer-judges on the highest tribunal to be a constituent part of the governing process. Those two hundred years may usefully be divided into several segments: the establishment of the authority of the courts to rule; the period to the end of the Civil War, when considerations of nationalism and localism were high on the Supreme Court's agenda; the three-quarters of a century leading up to 1937, during which protection of corporate capitalism was the ultimate judicial goal; and the period since 1937, during which several developments may be seen, including the protection of human rights and liberties for the first time in American history, the Supreme Court's "abdication" as czar of national economic policy, and the approval of aspects of the emergent "national security state." The dates, of course, are approximate; the Supreme Court has never announced sharp shifts in doctrine in so many words. Only hindsight enables one to perceive patterns of development. Moreover, there were, and are, aberrations in each period.

By no means was it clear in 1789 that the Supreme Court or any other organ of government would have the authority to say what the law is with respect to the Constitution. The Court had so little prestige that John Jay declined reappointment as chief justice to be governor of New York. Jay told President John Adams that he doubted that the Court would ever acquire enough energy, weight, and dignity to be important in the governing structure. Perhaps because judges were aware both that inherent limitations to their power existed and that there was an endemic dislike of the judiciary, the edifice of judicial review was constructed slowly. These fears were verified for many when *Chisholm* v. *Georgia* (1793) was decided: a furor erupted when the Court held that a citizen of South Carolina could sue Georgia in federal court. For the first, but not the last, time, a Supreme Court decision was reversed by constitutional amendment (the Eleventh, in 1798).

In the famous decision of Marbury *v.* Madison, *Marshall began to construct the foundation of judicial review under the Constitution.*

Chisholm is an early example of the interplay of politics and law in the judicial process. The members of the Supreme Court were to a man ardent Federalists; they believed in a strong central government at the expense of state "sovereignty," and they saw in the courts one means of furthering that goal. By erring politically in *Chisholm,* they learned a hard lesson—that they had to proceed circumspectly. When Adams named John Marshall, as canny a politician as ever sat on the High Bench, to be chief justice, he chose a man thoroughly wedded to Hamiltonian principles of nationalism. Marshall knew that caution was the best strategy. Thomas Jefferson had won the 1800 presidential election, and he and his party had a fervent desire to undo what they considered to be outrages by Federalist judges.

Marshall took office in 1801 and served for thirty-four years. By 1803 he felt confident enough to seize upon an otherwise trivial dispute—whether William Marbury was entitled to his commission as a justice of the peace in the District of Columbia—to assert judicial preeminence in constitutional interpretations. Adams had appointed Marbury at the last moment but failed to deliver his commission; Jefferson and Secretary of State James Madison refused to do so. Marbury then asked the Supreme Court to order Madison to hand it over. The result was the famous decision in *Marbury* v. *Madison* (1803). Marbury relied on a part of the Judiciary Act of 1789 that seemed to permit the Court to issue such orders as part of its "original" jurisdiction. Marshall was confronted with a dilemma. If he ordered Madison to deliver the commission, Jefferson and Madison doubtless would refuse, and the Court would suffer a grievous blow. But if he did not sustain Marbury's claim, he would give aid and comfort to his political enemies, who were determined to purge the federal judiciary of Federalist judges.

Marshall's decision in *Marbury* was Solomonic: he gave a little to both parties and then, with a remarkable display of political shrewdness, lofted the banner of judicial supremacy. After conceding that the commission was being illegally withheld, he went on to say that even so, Marbury did not have a remedy in the Supreme Court. The reason for this was that Congress cannot constitutionally enlarge upon the original jurisdiction of the Supreme Court. Congress's attempt to allow the Court to issue mandatory writs had failed because such a power was not listed in Article III; it was therefore void.

In an opinion that is a masterpiece of judicial casuistry, Marshall began to construct the foundation of judicial review under the Constitution. The nominal victory of Jefferson—he now could appoint the person of his choice to the office—was far overshadowed by the astute Marshall's willingness to absorb a minor "defeat," all the while keeping his eye on his long-term objectives: to increase judicial power in general and simultaneously diminish the constitutional powers of the several states.

Jefferson, however, was not appeased; he and his party soon began a process of impeachment of Federalist judges. Choosing their targets carefully, they began with the hopelessly insane District Judge John Pickering of New Hampshire. Successful there, they chose as their next target the savage and vindictive Justice Samuel Chase of the Supreme Court. The House of Representatives impeached him, but the Senate refused to convict. The idea of an independent judiciary was saved, at least in theory, although independence from the governing coalition of the nation has always been more apparent than real. But the episode so alarmed Marshall that he wrote an amazing letter to a friend, proposing to give Congress appellate jurisdiction over Supreme Court decisions as an alternative to impeachment. Chase's acquittal obviated the need for this alternative. Marshall, however, paid a small price for (theoretical) judicial independence: for a time he ruled cautiously, thus giving the Jeffersonians no overt cause for complaint. By voluntarily giving up some power, Marshall paradoxically gained more power for the Supreme Court.

The chief justice bided his time, awaiting an opportunity to realize his twin goals of judicial supremacy and diminution of state power. It came in 1810, when for the first time the Court declared a state law unconstitutional. The case, *Fletcher* v. *Peck,* dealt with the so-called Yazoo land fraud. The Georgia legislature had sold most of what is now Alabama and Mississippi at about one cent an acre. It soon became known that the legislators had been bribed, and a subsequent legislature canceled the grant. In the meantime, much of the land had been sold to allegedly innocent third parties. Was the rescission of the grant valid? The answer from the Supreme Court: No. In a classic example of scrambled judicial rhetoric, Marshall did not seem to know why the cancellation was invalid, only that it was. His turgid opinion concludes that the "state of Georgia was restrained, either by general principles, which are common to our free institutions, or by the particular provisions of the Constitution" from rescinding the fraudulent grant. Justice William Johnson went even further. In the only instance in which a Supreme Court justice asserted that the writ of the Court could run against the Supreme Being, he said that the rescinding law was invalid on "the reason and nature of things: a principle which will impose laws even on the Deity."

John Marshall in effect rewrote the contract clause of the Constitution in *Fletcher* by first calling the legislative grant a contract and, more important, holding that a state is bound by its own contracts, thus chipping away at the foundation of state sovereignty. *Marbury* and *Fletcher* laid the foundation for the development of judicial review. But it was not merely review for the sake of review: Marshall had in mind the larger goal of constructing the legal basis for making the national government supreme.

Several decisions are especially noteworthy in what was to become the second important historical period: *Martin* v. *Hunter's Lessee* (1816), *Cohens* v. *Virginia* (1821), *McCulloch* v. *Maryland* (1819), and *Gibbons* v. *Ogden* (1824). Together with *Marbury* and *Fletcher,* these decisions are the pillars of national supremacy. To the extent that law can alter human affairs, itself a difficult and complex question, they helped to make a united state out of the United States. In addition, during this second period Chief Justice Marshall went far toward making "vested rights"—the protection of property rights—the basic doctrine of American constitutional law.

The meaning to be given to Section 25 of the Judiciary Act of 1789 was the focus of judicial attention in *Martin* and *Cohens.* Could the Supreme Court review decisions of state supreme courts in civil matters *(Martin)* and in criminal law cases *(Cohens)* when a federal question was involved in the litigation? The Court answered both questions in the affirmative. Again a furor erupted. A truly basic question of American federalism was at issue: Who was to have the ultimate word in such problems—state supreme courts or the Supreme Court of the United States? Attacking neither the Constitution itself nor the Judiciary Act, Virginia insisted in both cases that its highest court was as capable of interpreting the Constitution and statutes as the United States Supreme Court—a point that Justice Joseph Story cheerfully conceded in *Martin.* (Story wrote the opinion because Marshall had disqualified himself.) But Story knew that how the question of ultimate power was resolved would be crucial to the formation of American nationalism. If each state could say what the Constitution meant, the result would be a balkanized United States. Story and Marshall prevailed, not without difficulty, and the law is clear today. Judge Spencer Roane of Virginia, among others, waxed apoplectic at the decision in *Cohens;* he called it monstrous, unexampled, and motivated by a grasping for power that history had taught corrupts all who wield it.

Martin and *Cohens* thus settled the questions of judicial supremacy and national supremacy, with the Supreme Court acting as a vital part of the federal government. The other legs of the four-legged stool are *McCulloch* and *Gibbons,* which dealt not with judicial power as such but with the range and nature of congressional powers. *McCulloch's* significance cannot be overestimated, both for its specific holding—that Congress had the implied power to create a national bank free from the taxing power of the state of Maryland—and for Marshall's theory of constitutional interpretation.

The shrewd chief justice varied his methodology to suit the case before him. In *Marbury,* for example, he treated the Constitution as a simple legal instrument, such as a contract or a will, and refused to add to Article III's listing of the original jurisdiction of the Court. Because the framers had not given the Court the power to issue mandatory writs, Congress could not do so by statute. Had Marshall employed his *McCulloch* technique, by which he read the Constitution expansively (saying that the justices should never forget that they were expounding a constitution), the result in *Marbury* would likely have been different. But that would not have suited Marshall's long-range goals. In 1819, Marshall considered the Constitution to be something far greater than a simple legal document: it was an instrument designed for the ages and to deal with the various crises in human affairs. This neat bit of intellectual footwork makes *McCulloch* the most important decision in American history insofar as constitutional interpretation is concerned. It paved the way for later expansive readings of the document. The larger point is truly significant: there is no one way to interpret the Constitution. The method chosen in any given case, as in the result reached, depends upon the personal preferences of the justices.

Gibbons is the other leg of the stool of judicial monopoly on constitutional interpretation and for national supremacy. Congress has express power "to regulate Commerce . . . among the several States." As usual, the phrase was not defined by the framers. *Gibbons* provided a prime opportunity for the Court (and Marshall) to say what the phrase meant. At issue was a monopoly granted by New York for steamboat navigation in the waters of New York. Did that grant unconstitutionally infringe upon the congressional power over commerce? In a decision that is cited to this day, Marshall first defined *commerce* (following his *McCulloch* lead, quite expansively) and then said that the congressional power was plenary. But with characteristic casuistry he did not go the full mile and invalidate the New York statute because it was at odds with the constitutional commerce clause; rather, he determined that New York's action conflicted with a federal coastal licensing statute. He thus achieved long-lasting results while cleverly sidestepping the area of greatest controversy—the nature and reach of the federal power over commerce. Not until 1851 did the Court, this time under Chief Justice Roger B. Taney, finally rule that the commerce power by itself could prevail over state laws even in the absence of federal action.

Marshall's contributions to the establishment of judicial review and national supremacy were so firmly embedded in the law and in the mores of the people that they have remained viable to this day. If success is a criterion of greatness, then John Marshall must be given the mantle of the greatest chief justice.

When President Andrew Jackson named Taney to succeed Marshall, some thought that the clock would be turned back and that the Supreme Court would begin to follow Jeffersonian principles. But that was not to be. If anything, judicial review became even more secure in the public mind. Marshallian principles were in general still followed. Marshall's strong edifice of judicial review even survived Taney's dreadful decision in *Dred Scott* v. *Sandford* (1857), declaring void the Missouri Compromise, only the second federal statute to meet that end. Taney denied blacks the right to citizenship and Congress the power to control slavery in the territories, relying on what he said were the intentions of the framers.

The Taney Court, spanning the years 1836–1865, consolidated principles first enunciated by the Marshall Court. But it failed miserably in coping with the slavery question, as did the other branches of government, state and national. Only a sanguinary war would determine, seemingly permanently, that the United States was both one nation indivisible (Lincoln's primary goal) and a nation in which the "peculiar institution" of slavery was outlawed. The Taney Court's judicial failure meant that the very idea of judicial review, for a time at least, hung in the balance.

Judicial review was saved by a strategic judicial retreat during the Civil War, with the Court validating some of President Lincoln's extraconstitutional actions taken at the beginning of the war. Again, the paradox: the Court relinquished power only soon to become more powerful. The landmark decision came in the *Prize Cases* (1863), in which Lincoln's order to blockade Southern ports in the early part of the war was challenged. For the first time, the Court considered what John Locke called the "executive prerogative," or reason of state. Does the president have inherent power to take action he considers necessary in times of emergency? As the Supreme Court has often done in times of national emergency as perceived by the executive, it in effect became an arm of the executive and constitutionalized the prerogative. Said Justice Robert C. Grier in the *Prize Cases:*

> Whether the President in fulfilling his duties, as Commander-in-Chief, in suppressing an insurrection, has met with such armed hostile resistance, and a civil war of such alarming proportions as will compel him to accord to them the character of belligerents, is a question to be decided *by him,* and this Court must be governed by the decisions and acts of the political department of the Government to which this power was entrusted. "He must determine what degree of force the crisis demands."
>
> (emphasis in original)

With that decision the Court either neatly amended the Constitution—if for no other reason than that the Constitution probably would not have been ratified had the thirteen original states thought they were not free to leave the Union—or, at the very least, added constitutional reason of state to what the framers wrote. (The prerogative or reason of state is the principle that those responsible for the survival of the state can take actions to save it, even in the absence of permissive legislation—or, indeed, even if such action is against the law.)

Far from being an aberration, the *Prize Cases* set a precedent for numerous extraordinary, even extraconstitutional, actions by subsequent presidents. The outstanding example is *Korematsu* v. *United States* (1944), in which the Court lent its imprimatur to incarcerating in concentration camps tens of thousands of Japanese-Americans, many of whom were native-born citizens of the United States. It is proof positive that the Supreme Court, during times of all-out emergency, becomes a part of the executive juggernaut. This is a large chink in the armor of judicial supremacy.

With the end of the Civil War, the third period of judicial review was ushered in. Three important amendments were added to the Constitution—the Thirteenth, Fourteenth, and Fifteenth—mainly to protect the newly freed slaves. But government, including the Supreme Court, was much more interested in promoting economic growth than in enforcing the Bill of Rights and the Civil War Amendments during the period that followed.

The war had given an immense forward thrust to capitalism. After the war, judicial review became a de facto arm of the propertied (business) class. To be sure, this was by no means a major realignment of judicial interest: judges and the law they promulgate have always been class-oriented and far from neutral, as Holmes acknowledged in 1873. Noting the criminal penalties imposed on laborers striking in England, Holmes maintained that the idea that the law is neutral, impartially imposed by judges, presupposed an identity of class interests that did not actually exist. The lack of social unity was eventually transmuted into a similar lack of unity in law. To Holmes, the decisions of courts represented the interests of the strongest in society: "Whatever body may possess the supreme power for the moment is certain to have interests inconsistent with others which have competed unsuccessfully. The more powerful interests must be more or less reflected in legislation [and judicial decisions]: which, like every other device of man or beast, must tend in the long run to aid the survival of the fittest" (quoted in Miller, 1982, 198). That early statement of social Darwinism epitomized a judicial system that neatly turned the Civil War Amendments into protections of corporate industry; the Fourteenth Amendment soon became a barrier behind which corporate officers could hide from the onslaught of regulatory measures.

Nationalism having become triumphant, business protectionism became the polestar of judicial review. This was accomplished in two ways: the Court invented a new constitutional principle, substantive due process, and cavalierly rewrote such statutes as the Sherman Antitrust Act of 1890. The Court thereby helped the few against the many who would do to the few, via legislation, what the few had done to them. No abrupt shift was announced. If there is a major turning point, it came in 1886 when Chief Justice Morrison Waite casually announced for a unanimous Court, without hearing argument on the question, that the business corporation was a person within the meaning of the Fourteenth Amendment's due process clause. Soon thereafter, the justices became the final arbiters of what they considered to be sound national economic policy.

McCulloch *v.* Maryland *paved the way for later expansive readings of the Constitution.*

During that same three-quarters of a century, the Supreme Court interpreted the Civil War Amendments in ways that ensured that blacks would be consigned to a condition of virtual peonage. The Court invented the concept of "state action," which means that the Constitution runs against governments only. This meant that corporations had the protection of the Constitution (as of 1886) but had no concomitant duty to adhere to constitutional norms. The status of black Americans became starkly clear with the Court's invention of the "separate but equal" doctrine in *Plessy* v. *Ferguson* (1896), a case that tolled the end of the first Reconstruction.

As for business protectionism, two strands of judicial review may be discerned in the third historical period. First, the justices discovered, through an intuition belonging only to them, that the liberty protected by the due process clause included not only a guarantee of procedural safeguards when governments took action—the historical understanding—but also a requirement that the regulation itself not be arbitrary. Substantive due process was born, a lusty infant that established the Court as a little lunacy commission sitting to determine whether state legislation was "reasonable" in particular circumstances. The content (substance) of legislation was reviewed to determine if it was arbitrary. Reasonableness or arbitrariness were ascertained not by objective criteria but by the personal philosophies of the justices. Moreover, when Congress did enact statutes aimed at regulating railroads and other corporate entities "affected with a public interest," its efforts were sabotaged by the judiciary. Again, reasonableness became the magic formula to test the specifics of statutes.

This breathtaking intervention into the very center of government was accomplished by judges who, in contrast to John Marshall, struck out boldly and forcefully. Judicial hegemony in socioeconomic matters of course met opposition, but not from those who wielded effective control over the levels of power in the political order. Thus, for three-quarters of a century the justices ruled on the wisdom of economic legislation—all the while denying that they were doing so.

The status of blacks became starkly clear with the Court's invention of the "separate but equal" doctrine in Plessy *v.* Ferguson.

Constitutional judicial review in the 1865–1937 period was paralleled by like actions when the justices dealt with federal statutes. Realizing that invalidating too many statutes on the grounds of substantive due process could lead to public disapproval, the justices cannily played fast and loose with statutory programs, all to the same end of protecting corporate capitalism. But along with the Great Depression came the introduction of the American version of the welfare state. Not without difficulty, however, for the Court still stood like King Canute commanding the tides of social discontent to stop. And halt they did, at least at the legislative level, but only for a brief time. After a series of decisions early in the 1930s that eviscerated much of President Franklin Roosevelt's New Deal, the justices saw a new light in 1937. Without announcement or fanfare, they came to see that legislation that was unconstitutional prior to 1937 was now within constitutional boundaries. The fourth period of historical judicial review emerged.

Abdication of economic policymaking responsibility marks a major turning point in the history of judicial review. Since 1937, the Court has been quick to defer to Congress in economics. A Constitution that popular wisdom had called one of rights or limitations became a Constitution of powers. The "positive state" was born, one in which the Court constitutionalized the affirmative powers of government in social-welfare matters.

Abdication of economic sovereignty left the Supreme Court with an obvious task: to be a Court of statutory interpretation of the many laws passed in the 1930s and 1940s. The Court also began to search for a new constitutional role. This role was found, after some pulling and hauling, in judicial protection of civil rights and liberties. The "revolution" in civil rights and civil liberties that has occurred since 1937 is essentially one concerned with egalitarianism. Suddenly human rights and liberties became a preeminent concern as the Court dealt with cases involving racial discrimination, legislative reapportionment, and more protection for those caught in the toils of enforcement of the criminal law.

Attacks on judicial review have always characterized the American policy, from Thomas Jefferson down to the present day. Academics today argue over the legitimacy of an appointed body of judges making policy decisions; some maintain that this violates the principles of democracy. These attacks have a subtle but significant impact upon the manner in which the Court acts. As political actors, Supreme Court justices are fully aware of the ebb and flow of public opinion. Judicial review will doubtless continue, at least in form, although it is more than a little odd to think in terms of government by lawsuit in a complex technological society. A fast-changing society with planetary interests, such as the United States, simply cannot—indeed, will not—permit policy that really matters to be settled by an eighteenth-century institution using ancient methods of operation (the adversary system). The modern debate over the legitimacy of judicial review is curiously unsatisfactory: it argues yesterday's problems when today's and tomorrow's should be first on the agenda. Much of the debate is reminiscent of medieval Scholasticism, and like the Scholastics, the contestants in today's intellectual controversy over judicial review may be passed by. The Supreme Court and judicial review are—at least for the moment—important parts of American governance, but they are not sovereign. This is the age of the administrative or bureaucratic state as well as the national security state. All but a handful of the millions of governmental decisions never receive judicial scrutiny, a condition not at all likely to change.

[See also (III) Appeals and Appellate Practice, Due Process of Law, Federal Court System, Jurisdiction, Legal Reasoning, Supreme Court of the United States.]

CASES

Bonham's Case, 77 Eng. Rep. 646 (1610)
Brown v. Allen, 344 U.S. 443 (1953)
Brown v. Board of Education, 347 U.S. 483 (1954)
Chisholm v. Georgia, 2 Dallas 419 (1793)
Cohens v. Virginia, 6 Wheaton 264 (1821)
Dred Scott v. Sandford, 19 Howard 393 (1857)
Fletcher v. Peck, 6 Cranch 87 (1810)
Gibbons v. Ogden, 9 Wheaton 1 (1824)
Korematsu v. United States, 323 U.S. 214 (1944)
McCulloch v. Maryland, 4 Wheaton 316 (1819)

Marbury v. Madison, 1 Cranch 137 (1803)
Martin v. Hunter's Lessee, 1 Wheaton 304 (1816).
Plessy v. Ferguson, 163 U.S. 537 (1896)
Prize Cases, 2 Black 635 (1863)
Roe v. Wade, 410 U.S. 113 (1973)

BIBLIOGRAPHY

Paul M. Bator, Paul J. Mishkin, David L. Shapiro, and Herbert Wechsler, eds., *Hart and Wechsler's The Federal Courts and the Federal System,* 2nd ed. (1973), is a valuable collection of cases and materials dealing with judicial review, with emphasis on the procedural side. Raoul Berger, *Government by Judiciary* (1977), is a leading but tendentious attack on modern judicial review, focusing on the Fourteenth Amendment. Alexander Bickel, *The Least Dangerous Branch* (1962), is an important account of the development of judicial review; and *The Supreme Court and the Idea of Progress* (1970), is an attack on decisions of the Warren Court. Charles L. Black, *The People and the Court* (1960), is a defense of judicial review by a thoughtful scholar. Jesse Choper, *Judicial Review and the National Political Process* (1980), is a valuable study.

John Hart Ely, *Democracy and Distrust* (1980), presents the argument that judicial review should be limited to decisions "reinforcing voter representation" at the polls. Stephen C. Halpern and Charles M. Lamb, *Supreme Court Activism and Restraint* (1982), is a collection of articles by leading scholars on the pros and cons of judicial review. Learned Hand, *The Bill of Rights* (1958), is a prominent federal judge's discussion of the merits of judicial review. Robert H. Jackson, *The Struggle for Judicial Supremacy* (1941), is a well-written account of the development of judicial review; although somewhat out of date, it is still useful. Leonard W. Levy, ed., *Judicial Review and the Supreme Court* (1967), offers nine especially useful articles on judicial review.

Robert G. McCloskey, *The American Supreme Court* (1960), one of the best shorter accounts of the development of judicial review, is particularly useful when read with the Black volume. Arthur Selwyn Miller, *The Supreme Court: Myth and Reality* (1978), is a collection of the author's articles questioning the conventional wisdom about the Supreme Court and judicial review; *Democratic Dictatorship: The Emergent Constitution of Control* (1981), presents an argument that the United States is moving into an era of authoritarianism; and *Toward Increased Judicial Activism: The Political Role of the Supreme Court* (1982), is an astringent view of the history of judicial review, coupled with a suggestion for an even greater judicial role in the political order. Michael J. Perry, *The Constitution, the Courts, and Human Rights* (1982), a forceful argument for judicial protection of human rights, is an antidote to the John Hart Ely book above.

Martin M. Shapiro, *The Supreme Court at the Bar of Politics* (1964), is an interesting analysis of the political role of the Court; and *Courts: A Comparative and Political Analysis* (1981), is a groundbreaking study of the role of courts in several legal systems. Symposium, "Constitutional Adjudication and Democratic Theory," in *New York University Law Review,* 56 (1981); Symposium, "Judicial Review Versus Democracy," in *Ohio State Law Journal,* 42 (1981); and Symposium, "Judicial Review and the Constitution—The Text and Beyond," in *University of Dayton Law Review,* 8 (1983), cover the entire range of the modern debate about judicial review, with articles written by leading scholars. Laurence H. Tribe, *American Constitutional Law* (1978), is the leading text treatment of the ways in which the Supreme Court has interpreted the Constitution.

— ARTHUR S. MILLER

JUDICIAL SELECTION

The question of how American judges are selected might be thought a relatively simple one to answer, but this is decidedly not so. At the surface level there are five principal methods of judicial selection, or recruitment, as it is sometimes called. Yet, for most intents and purposes the formal process does not reflect behavioral and political realities or their transactional complexities. Let us first examine the formalities of the selection methods in use before considering their empirical dimensions. We will subsequently turn to a consideration of a variety of issues that surround judicial selection and finally focus our attention on the subject of judicial tenure and the disciplining of judges, including removal from office.

Five Selection Methods

There are five methods for selecting judges in use in the United States. They are legislative election; executive (gubernatorial or presidential) appointment with the approval of another body; partisan election; nonpartisan election; and merit selection. Of the five appointment methods, the oldest are legislative election and executive appointment with the advice and consent of another body.

The move to elect judges on a nonpartisan ballot dates back to the progressive era at the beginning of the twentieth century.

Legislative election, still in use in Rhode Island (for state supreme court judges only), South Carolina (for most judges), and Virginia, was the method adopted by a majority (seven) of the states after the former colonies won their independence from Great Britain. Under this method both houses of the legislature must vote to elect judges to judicial office. The governor has no constitutionally mandated role in the process. This selection method was a reaction to one of the grievances held by the colonists, that the King of England unilaterally appointed and removed colonial judges. Indeed, among the list of "repeated injuries and usurpations" found in the Declaration of Independence is the charge that the king "has made judges dependent on his will alone, for the tenure of their offices, and the amount and payment of their salaries." Election by legislators as representatives of the people was considered to be a major step toward democratizing the selection of judges.

Gubernatorial appointment with the approval of another body, typically the executive council or the state senate, is the method used in eight states (nine, if Rhode Island, which appoints most lower court judges this way, is included). This method dates back to the years following the Revolution, when five of the thirteen states chose this scheme and one, Connecticut, adopted a variation, still used, whereby the governor nominates and the legislature (both houses) appoints. The federal Constitution also provides for the President to appoint federal judges with the approval ("advice and consent") of the Senate. Delaware, Maine, Maryland, New Jersey, and Rhode Island have their governors appoint some or all judges with the consent of the state senate. In Massachusetts and New Hampshire the executive (or governor's) council is the body that is authorized to approve judicial appointees, while in California the Commission on Judicial Appointments must give its approval.

The age of Jacksonian democracy, with its democratic and egalitarian impulses, gave rise to some dissatisfaction concerning the ways judges were chosen. The judiciary was seen as being drawn from too narrow an economic and political base and too far removed from democratic accountability. Although "reform" was gradual, by the mid-nineteenth century the move to have the voters directly elect judges in normal partisan elections was well under way. The partisan election method has voters elect judges who run for office under a party label that has been designated by the party primary or convention. There are generally no special restrictions on the conduct of judicial campaigns, which means that they are conducted in as partisan a manner as campaigns for other public offices. Partisan election at one time was used by a majority of states. Today twelve states (thirteen if New York, which chooses most lower court judges this way, is included) use partisan elections to select most or all of their judges.

The move to elect judges on a nonpartisan ballot—that is, without any party designation—dates back to the progressive era at the beginning of the twentieth century. Progressives saw urban political machines dominate the electoral process, and they were determined to end what they saw as an insidious pattern of corruption reaching from city hall to the local courthouses. One way to achieve this objective was to alter the election law so that political parties would no longer be designated on the local election ballot. The assumption was that candidates for local office would no longer need the political machine to be elected to office and therefore would not be beholden to the party bosses. As for judicial elections, progressives argued that there was no valid reason to elect judges on a partisan ballot and no justification for judicial candidates to conduct a partisan campaign. The result of this movement, primarily in the Midwest and West, was the adoption of the nonpartisan election method to select judges. Today ten states use nonpartisan ballots to elect most or all of their judges.

The newest of the selection methods is the merit plan, which is sometimes called the Missouri plan because it was first established there, in 1940. Merit selection is the method favored by the organized bar and, since the early 1960s, has been the subject of extensive campaigns for its adoption. The merit scheme is simply that a nominating commission submits to the governor a list of names to fill a particular judicial post. The governor is legally required to make the appointment from that list. The heart of this method is the selection by the nominating commission of those who are presumably best qualified, chosen on their professional merits. Under the original nominating commission concept of the Missouri plan, the commission consists of lawyers selected by the bar (elected or appointed), gubernatorial appointees who are not lawyers, and one or more members of the judiciary. Today seventeen states have established by constitutional or statutory law some form of the merit plan for selecting their highest judicial officials. Most of these states select their lower-level judges in a similar way.

The names and composition of merit-selection nominating commissions vary; for example, Alaska and Idaho call it the Judicial Council, Arizona calls it the Commission on Appellate Court Appointments, and Vermont's is the Judicial Nominating Board. Some statutes specify that the nominating commission must be bipartisan or nonpartisan. In three states (New York, Utah, and Vermont) the state senate must still approve the governor's selection from the list provided by the commission.

Merit plans were adopted by three states during the years 1940–1961. Eight states adopted it during the 1962–1971 period, and six states from 1972 through 1983. In some states (notably Delaware, Maryland, and Massachusetts) and localities, governors and mayors have, by executive order, established nominating commissions similar to the merit plan, but they do not have the force of constitutional or statutory law; that is, the commissions are not binding on the executives' successors in office and even the originators can return the list of names and ask for others if the original list is unsatisfactory. Further, the nominating commission can be dissolved at any time by the public official who created it. In contrast, where merit selection has been established in the state constitution or by statute, the governor can neither unilaterally dissolve the commission nor reject its nominees.

Complicating the picture of judicial selection is the fact that only twelve states initially select all their judges by one method. In a large majority of states there are different selection methods for different court levels. For example, in New York the highest state court's membership is selected by a variation of the merit plan: the bipartisan Judicial Nominating Commission is required to present the governor with from three to five names for associate judge and seven for chief judge, and the governor must select from the list of names provided by the commission. The state senate must then approve the choice. Selection of other New York Judges utilizes the partisan election method. However, the gubernatorial appointment method is used for the selection of judges of courts of claims and the appellate division of the state trial court. The mayor of New York City appoints judges of the city criminal and family courts but has voluntarily used a merit process.

Another complicating factor is that the formal selection methods discussed here are for initial selection. In the forty-seven states in which judgeship tenure is for a fixed term of office, there is the possibility of an interim appointment when a judge dies or resigns. However, only twelve states use the same method to fill interim vacancies as they do the initial selection. Proponents of the merit plan have achieved some success in persuading states that initially select judges by other methods to use the merit plan to fill interim appointments. Kentucky, Montana, Nevada, and North Dakota have formally adopted the merit plan for the filling of interim appointments. In five other states governors have issued executive orders to establish a merit plan by which to make interim appointments.

The Politics of Selection

To understand why one particular individual received an appointment and not another, similarly qualified person, it is necessary to be privy to the series of backstage transactions that propelled the appointee to the judgeship. To understand how a specific judicial recruitment method works in practice, it is necessary to study the actual process as it has concerned numerous appointments. Fortunately, the subject of judicial recruitment has received so much scholarly attention that we are in a position to make reasonably accurate generalizations about how the process works. It should be understood that generalizations apply in most but not necessarily all instances and that there are occasional exceptions to the rule. We will examine first the political reality of judicial selection in the states and then federal judicial selection.

STATE JUDICIAL SELECTION. Common to all selection methods regardless of the intent of their proponents is that judicial selection is a political process. This is not to say that all methods have the same form of politics or necessarily the same extent or mix of the various forms of politics. There is the most obvious form of party organizational politics, and at the local level it is most felt with the electoral methods for selecting judges. This is obviously true for party-label ballots where the party designation has been obtained during the party primary or convention. In some states and localities where the nonpartisan ballot is used, local party leaders even endorse a candidate and otherwise make it known that a person running for judicial office has party backing. At the state level, party organizational politics have a hand in both the legislative and gubernatorial selection methods. Judicial appointments can be viewed then as rewarding the faithful who have been active in behalf of the party. Also, appointments can be seen as "rewarding" certain party constituency groups, such as ethnic minorities.

Aspiring judges need to mobilize bar support as well as political support and public backing such as newspapers.

Akin to party organizational politics is the politics of personal patronage, best manifested in those methods involving the governor. Governors at times seek to appoint close associates and supporters (presumably otherwise qualified) to the state bench. Obviously, the gubernatorial appointment method is the most straightforward way for a governor to secure a judgeship, but even with merit selection the governor's friends and appointees on the nominating commission can influence the selection of the names to be presented to the governor.

One can also consider the politics of policy—that is, judicial appointments being made because of the policy views or orientation of the appointees. Interest groups have been known to be concerned about appointments to the bench, particularly at the highest court levels. Civil rights and civil liberties groups are sensitive to the views of potential appointees and can be counted on to actively oppose the appointment of one with a poor record on those issues. Conservative or right-wing groups are alert to the policy or ideological perspective of appointees. This concern of interest groups exists under all five methods but potentially can be most effective with electoral selection methods. Methods involving the governor also may involve the politics of policy, with the governor taking the initiative or responding to group pressures.

Still another form of politics is bar association politics, and while the involvement of the organized bar cuts across all selection methods (for example, the bar may rate or even endorse candidates for judgeships), it is clearly most involved with merit selection. The judicial nominating commissions under the Missouri plan include members of the bar elected by the bar associations. A study of such elections in Missouri found that a quasi-party system emerged with contested elections between distinctly different groupings of lawyers with different interests and outlooks. Some merit plans leave the means of selection of the bar representatives on the commissions up to the bar groups themselves, but there is a political type process at work there, too.

All selection methods involve negotiation. With electoral methods much of the activity is concerned with obtaining backing for the placement of the name on the ballot and achieving electoral support. For the merit plan the negotiation occurs in the legal community and concerns pressures, however subtle, that are brought to bear on the nominating commissions. This may include not only personal contact with commission members but also the mobilization of bar groups and individual lawyers and judges who send to the commission letters of support in behalf of candidates. For gubernatorially involved methods, negotiations may include state legislators, party leaders, interest-group representatives, bar association leaders, and judges—all of whom may also be involved in one form or another with the other selection methods. It is also of interest to observe that for the most part those who want to become judges have to wage a campaign. This is obviously true for the electoral methods but also for the other methods. Aspiring judges need to mobilize bar support as well as political support and other forms of public backing, such as newspapers and civic organizations.

A variety of considerations have been seen as playing a part in judicial selection, regardless of formal method. First, particularly for the highest state court bench, the legal credentials of potential judges come into play. Governors do not relish being attacked in the newspapers or by bar associations for nominating clearly unqualified persons. Similarly, bar associations will be highly sensitive to the professional qualifications of potential or actual judicial nominees and will wage campaigns against the clearly incompetent.

Second, partisan considerations are present with every selection method—not only with electoral, gubernatorial, and legislative selection but also with merit selection. Under the merit scheme the governor appoints most or all members of the commission, which assures at the very least that commission members will be minimally sensitive to his or her political needs (for example, the need to make some or most appointments to members of the governor's party). Under merit selection the governor selects from the names presented by the commission, and unless the commission deliberately stacks the panel with people not belonging to the governor's party (which has been known to happen), the governor is free to select along partisan lines. As to political considerations, those selection methods in which the governor has a role may have the governor making selection decisions on the basis of what may best enhance reelection or even what may best enhance passage of legislation favored by the governor (for example, selection of a close associate of a key state legislator whose legislative support is needed).

Finally, policy considerations can be seen as playing a part in all selection methods. The policy orientation of a candidate for a judgeship may surface during an electoral campaign as well as at different points with the other selection methods. The governor may consider the policy outlook of judicial candidates, particularly when constituent groups from within the governor's party take a lively interest in policy views. For example, a conservative Republican governor in a conservative state will generally not appoint a liberal reformer to the highest state bench.

Electoral methods of judicial selection have received some scholarly attention, and it has been found that in practice judicial elections tend to be largely ignored by the electorate, with low voter interest and turnout at the polls. Another significant aspect of the electoral method of judicial selection is that research findings reveal that the majority of judges are initially selected by the governor to fill vacancies that occur between elections. When judges resign, retire, or die in states whose formal method of judicial selection is by the partisan or nonpartisan ballot, the governor is authorized to make interim appointments. This means that at the next election such judges are able to run as incumbents with all the advantages of that position, such as name recognition and whatever mystique surrounds the occupants of judicial office. It has also been found that with partisan elections, the party label is the most significant factor in the voter's choice. Normally, judicial elections are uncontested; but on relatively few occasions there are contested elections, particularly for the highest state court positions, and invariably the organized bar strenuously objects to the conduct of such campaigns. In New York State, after several contested high-court elections, the state switched to a merit plan. Similarly, the Missouri plan was adopted in Missouri

Belva Ann Lockwood, a lawyer, won the right for women to practice before the Supreme Court in the late 1800s. About 100 years later, Sandra Day O'Connor became the first female Supreme Court justice. (Library of Congress/Corbis)

after several acrimonious contested elections to the state supreme court.

Merit selection plans have been examined by scholars. It has been found that gubernatorial politics is inherent in the merit selection method because of the provision for the governor to select some or even all (depending on the state plan) of the membership of the judicial selection commission and to make the final selection from the names submitted by the commission. Bar association politics is also institutionalized by merit plans that provide for bar association selection of bar representatives for service on the commissions. In the major study of how the merit plan has worked in Missouri, it was found that rival bar associations with contrasting socioeconomic interests contested the elections for the slots on the nominating commissions. The commissions were also found to be characterized by intense negotiation and internal politicking, and in some instances the commissions sought to dictate the selection outcome by stacking the list of names so that the commission favorite would be the likely person to be picked by the governor. In other cases, the governor quietly let be known a preference for certain individuals being included on the lists. It has also been found that the partisan makeup of the commissions has at times resulted in partisan considerations being taken into account in preparing the lists.

FEDERAL JUDICIAL SELECTION. There are a number of similarities between state and federal judicial selection. Federal judicial selection involves a negotiation process in which the varying types of politics discussed earlier can be seen at work. Party-organizational politics, the politics of personal patronage, the politics of policy, and bar association politics all come into play, as do the considerations examined previously.

Federal judges are nominated by the president after a recommendation from the attorney general. This has meant that the center of selection activity lies in the Justice Department and in practice today is located in the Office of Legal Policy. Participants in the negotiations, particularly for lower-court judgeships include not only Justice Department officials but also United States Senators and other major leaders of the president's party from the state in which there is a federal judgeship or the state that is "entitled" (that is, as a matter of expectation but not as a legal requirement) to be represented on a federal court of appeals. In addition, since 1953 the American Bar Association (ABA) Standing Committee on Federal Judiciary has investigated and rated leading candidates for judgeships as part of its informal working relationship with Justice officials during the prenomination stage. The Justice Department officials request a preliminary or tentative report, and the ABA committee if given more than one name can potentially influence the selection process by a finding of "not qualified" for one candidate as opposed to an "exceptionally well-qualified" rating for another. (The other ratings used by the ABA committee are "qualified" and "well-qualified.")

A senator of the president's party expects to be able to influence heavily the selection of a federal district judgeship in the senator's state; indeed, most such senators insist on being able to pick these judges, and they expect judgeships on the federal courts of appeals going to persons from their states to be "cleared" by them—that is, to meet with their approval. Judgeships in the federal territories, including the District of Columbia, on specialized courts, and especially on the United States Supreme Court are considered more within the prerogative of the president, and free from such senatorial pressures. When a senator from the president's party promotes a candidate not acceptable to the Justice Department, when a state has two senators of the president's party and they are in disagreement over the filling of a judgeship, or when senators and state party leaders are at odds, extensive negotiations may result. The senators are of such importance in the prenomination stage because the president's nomination must be sent to the Senate to be voted on and approved (confirmed) by a majority of those voting. Once a nominee has been confirmed, the president makes the formal appointment.

There are at least four major categories of considerations that tend to be of great relevance in the selection of federal judges. First are the professional qualifications of the candidates. This is so not only because of the active participation of the ABA and intense interest on the part of other bar groups but also because senators and presidents can be damaged politically if they are seen as promoting or choosing clearly unqualified persons for federal judgeships. Justice Department officials, furthermore, normally take pride when the administration is able to select people with outstanding legal records.

Second are partisan considerations. The political reality of federal judicial selection is that from the administration of George Washington to the present, the large majority of judicial appointments has gone to members of the president's party. Typically, the proportion has been more than 90 percent.

A third consideration from the standpoint of the administration is approval of the senator or senators of the president's party from the state of the prospective nominee. No administration deliberately seeks to alienate senators of their own party or to run the risk of a senator's sabotaging a nomination once it has been sent to the Senate. Although rarely invoked, a senator can claim senatorial courtesy, which would mean that the senator's colleagues would refuse to confirm.

The creation of selection panels resulted in a unique opening up of the recruitment process to women and minorities.

A fourth principal consideration is the policy or even ideological outlook of judicial candidates. The Republican Reagan Administration, for example, shied away from political liberals or those who were publicly identified as supporters of a woman's right to choose abortion. The Democratic Carter Administration placed a considerable number of political liberals on the bench and few political conservatives. In assessing the relative importance of these four considerations, one can say that in general, political considerations have taken priority over the ideological or policy views of the candidates, which in turn have tended to be more important than the recruitment of the best legal talent available.

During the Carter Administration there was an attempt to bolster the relative importance of legal qualifications by the introduction of presidentially appointed merit selection commissions to recommend to the president the best available candidates for judgeships on the federal courts of appeals. By executive order President Carter established the Judicial Selection Commission. When a vacancy on an appeals court occurred, the eleven-member selection panel for that circuit was given sixty days in which to choose five persons qualified to fill the position. The selection panel was authorized to advertise for applicants, and the only way to be considered for the judgeship was for the aspiring judge to file an application and be investigated and interviewed by the panel. President Carter was pledged to select the nominee from the list of five names submitted by the selection panel.

In practice, the commission panels, whose membership was chosen by the White House, consisted of primarily Democrats, a large chunk of them active Carter supporters prior to his winning the Democratic party presidential nomination in 1976. Studies of the panels found that a majority of the panelists were political liberals and that approximately 40 percent were women and approximately 30 percent were black. It was also found that the selection panels were not only concerned with the professional qualifications of prospective nominees but also their policy outlook.

The creation of these selection panels resulted in a unique opening up of the recruitment process to women and minorities in terms of being able to choose potential nominees and being chosen as nominees. Of the fifty-six courts-of-appeals appointments by the Carter Administration, an unprecedented eleven appointments went to women, nine to blacks, two to Hispanics, and one to an Asian-American. They were also primarily Democrats. The selection panels used by the Carter Administration established merit selection of Democrats regardless of sex or race.

The Carter Administration also encouraged senators to establish similar selection commissions for federal district judgeships, and in a majority of states, such commissions were created. However, when Ronald Reagan became president, he eliminated use of the selection commission and reverted to the traditional negotiation process centered in the Justice Department. Nevertheless, some Republican senators have still retained their versions of selection commissions, although the result has typically been the merit selection of Republicans.

A change in the federal judicial selection process that carried through the Reagan years is the change in procedures within the Senate Judiciary Committee. Since 1979 the committee has utilized its own investigatory apparatus to help it independently determine whether the nominees are qualified for office. Each judicial nominee is required to complete an extensive questionnaire on his or her personal, professional, and financial background. There is also a section on the nominee's views on the proper scope of the exercise of judicial power. The questionnaire is the starting point for the committee's investigation. A further change since 1979 is that the chairman of the Senate Judiciary Committee no longer automatically buries the nomination of someone opposed by the senator from the nominee's state. Under the changed procedures the nomination is discussed by the full committee, with the possibility that the nomination will be reported out of committee to the full Senate.

Any consideration of federal judicial selection should devote special attention to appointments to the Supreme Court. These appointments generally hold the greatest interest for the general public. The Supreme Court is widely acknowledged to be the leading judicial policymaker for the nation; thus, appointments to the Court are the subject of keen concern and occasional controversy. Since the 1960s, a frequent presidential campaign issue has been what sorts of people will be named by the person elected president.

Supreme Court nominations, it should be clear, are in a class by themselves and are considered to be the personal choice of the president. Presidents have made their selections on the basis of a variety of considerations, including the personal, the political (such as party affiliation and effect on constituent groups in the president's coalition), and the ideological. Sometimes these considerations coalesce and reinforce each other. This was true, for example, with President John F. Kennedy's appointments of Byron White and Arthur Goldberg and with President Lyndon B. Johnson's appointment of Abe Fortas. Political considerations, as well as ideological or policy orientation, governed President Johnson's selection of Thurgood Marshall, the first black American to serve on the Court and President Reagan's appointment of Sandra Day O'Connor, the first female Supreme Court Justice and Antonin Scalia, the first Italian-American. It should also be mentioned that the Senate does not necessarily rubber-stamp presidential nominations. During the nineteenth century close to one out of three nominations were not confirmed by the Senate. In the twentieth century there have been several occasions when nominations died in the Senate. Thus, appointments to the Supreme Court must be handled with some care by the White House and with a sensitivity to the concerns of senators.

Issues in Judicial Selection

The subject of judicial selection has been a source of continuing controversy. Some of the issues have been of long standing; others, such as affirmative action for the judiciary, are of more recent vintage. Without attempting to be exhaustive, several issues and questions surrounding judicial selection will be briefly discussed.

PARTISANSHIP. The organized bar and the American Judicature Society have long decried the partisan aspects of judicial selection. Party affiliation has no place, they have argued, in the selection of judges and is, or should be, irrelevant to the administration of justice. It is demeaning for those with judicial ambitions to have to court party bosses or otherwise play the political game. The best selection process, they insist, is one in which party affiliation and party connections are minimized, if not eliminated altogether, and professional qualifications are maximized, so that they become the decisive factors.

Those on the other side of the issue have argued that for every judicial vacancy there are many individuals who have similar legal credentials and are qualified to serve. Party affiliation and partisan activity are legitimate concerns on the part of those who select judges and ought to play a role in the method of selection. They argue further that the party system is crucial to American democracy and that service on behalf of the party and its candidates for public office helps to maintain the system. If political parties are to remain viable institutions, it is important that men and women of talent, skill, and commitment be active in politics. A selection method that rewards an individual on the basis of party activism, if not party affiliation, over a similarly qualified individual without such political credentials is a method that provides incentives necessary for viable political parties. Moreover, by choosing partisans, the party makes it reasonable for voters to hold the party responsible for the judges' performance in office. Political considerations of this sort, it is argued, thus foster a responsible party model of American politics and should be encouraged, rather than discouraged, by anyone concerned with the health of American democracy.

PERSONAL PATRONAGE. Similar to the debate over partisan considerations is that over the use by governors and presidents of their selection powers to advance their friends and associates. Again, legal reformers argue that personal patronage as a selection variable demeans the bench and, at least initially, stigmatizes those chosen. The determinants should be not "who you know" but "what you know" about law and the administration of justice and whether you possess the professional skills necessary to be a successful judge. Courts should not be the repository of cronyism; while some close personal associates of governors, senators, and presidents have distinguished themselves, others have been pedestrian, or worse, on the bench.

The counterargument is that a personal association or relationship with a key participant in the selection process should not disqualify an otherwise qualified person from judicial office. To do so would penalize individuals who already may have made personal sacrifices to serve in public office, and that would not only be unfair but also cause dysfunction in the workings of government. When a governor, senator, or president turns to a close associate, that should be taken as a sign of confidence in the caliber of the individual. It should be recognized that the judicial performance of an individual so chosen will reflect more on the politician responsible for the appointment than if there were no prior personal relationship. Substituting a Missouri plan will not eliminate personal variables. Rather, it has been argued, these considerations are shifted to a different sphere, the bar association. Instead of party politics, there is bar association politics. Instead of politicians' associates having the inside track, bar leaders' associates are in that enviable position.

POLICY, OR IDEOLOGICAL, SCREENING. When the Republican platform of 1980 contained a provision that pledged a future Republican administration not to appoint to the federal bench anyone who favored the right to have an abortion, opponents of the plank offered several criticisms. First, they argued that it is not right to have an ideological or policy litmus test for prospective judges. A judge is called on to handle a wide variety of matters and to single out only one of a multitude of legal issues before the federal courts for ideological screening distorts the nature of the judicial process and is unfair.

Second, they argued that an individual's personal views on a controversial question of public policy should play no part in the decisions that an individual will make as a judge. As such, one's private views are irrelevant to judicial decision-making, and to suggest otherwise is to undermine the professional integrity of the judiciary.

Third, it was argued that to specify a preferred policy position on a controversial issue and to seek out individuals sympathetic to that position means that the courts are being stacked with biased persons. Even if these individuals conduct themselves in a thoroughly professional manner and decide on the basis of law and not their personal predilections, they will have come to the bench with an image of being biased and already committed on the particular issue. Each judicial action will then be suspect and placed in the most damaging light, and the confidence of the public will be undermined.

And finally, on the specific issue of a woman's right to choose abortion of a nonviable fetus rather than childbirth, the Supreme Court has already spoken and has established that right as a constitutional one and the law of the land. To search for active opponents of that right and the Supreme Court's constitutional determination in that sphere is to search for potential saboteurs of the very court that in theory heads the judicial system. This cannot be good for the workings of the system nor for the public image of the courts.

The debate over whether judicial selection should permit the ideological stacking of a court is bound to continue.

The counterargument is that courts, particularly at the higher levels but also at the trial level, cannot help but make policy by their interpretations of precedents, statutes, and the Constitution. Where there is room for judicial discretion, a judge's personal values and judicial philosophy come into play. A concern with a judge's policy or ideological orientation is then a concern with how the judge will use the very discretion that is inevitable and is inherent in the judicial function. What is wrong, these rebutters ask, with a political administration or body that is responsible for choosing judges being concerned with how prospective judges will behave when faced with alternative, if not conflicting, solutions to the judicial questions before them? Should a political official ignore the overwhelming evidence that from among viable alternatives, judges choose those consistent with their judicial philosophies and ideological or policy outlook? Should a political official appoint judges who stand for that which the official is publicly committed to oppose?

This issue is a particularly sensitive one with regard to appointments to the Supreme Court. President Eisenhower apparently regretted that he had not been concerned with the policy outlook of Earl Warren when Eisenhower named him to the chief-justiceship of the Supreme Court. Presidents Nixon and Reagan, on the other hand, were quite pleased with their appointees because they had been ideologically screened before being named. Senators, however, may be uneasy about Supreme Court nominations of those whose views are diametrically opposed to theirs. But senators usually recognize that more than ideological opposition is needed to oppose successfully a Supreme Court nomination. The debate over whether judicial selection should permit the ideological stacking of a court is bound to continue, particularly concerning the Supreme Court.

AFFIRMATIVE ACTION FOR THE JUDICIARY. The Carter Administration introduced the concept of affirmative action for the judiciary, a determined effort (in the words of the executive order establishing the circuit judge nominating commission) "to seek out and identify well-qualified women and members of minority groups as potential nominees." Carter's selection commission panels, particularly with their women and minority membership, were thought to constitute a useful means for accomplishing this goal. However, the application of affirmative action to the judiciary was met with severe criticism that included the arguments also applicable to efforts at the state level.

First, it has been argued, affirmative action in practice means the imposition of quotas to achieve a sexual and racial balance on the bench and that use of quotas is incompatible with merit selection and can result in the appointment of marginally qualified or unqualified persons.

Second, affirmative action promotes reverse discrimination in that persons of the "wrong" sex or race are not seriously considered and are thereby discriminated against because of their sex or race.

Third, by ignoring individual merit and focusing on group affiliation in the initial screening for a judicial position, affirmative action places the government in the position not of being neutral but of playing favorites. Rather than simply ending racial and sexual discrimination, the government perpetuates a new form of sexual and racial favoritism.

Fourth, by engaging in affirmative action, the government—meaning government bureaucrats—must classify people by their race, which in turn requires clumsy and arbitrary definitional standards such as how many black parents or grandparents are necessary in order to classify a person as black.

Finally, it has been posited that affirmative action is inappropriate for the judiciary because the need for highly skilled legal practitioners requires that the best people be selected and so a person's race, sex, or national origin is totally irrelevant to job performance as a judge.

Answers have been offered to these objections. First, the supporters of the Carter Administration's affirmative-action efforts and similar programs elsewhere emphasize that they never intended to implement rigid quotas but rather wished to widen the recruitment net and actively seek out qualified women and minorities. Rather than being incompatible with merit selection, affirmative action assures that all potential candidates will be considered on their individual merits. There is no evidence at all that affirmative action applied to judicial selection has resulted in marginally qualified or unqualified appointments. To the contrary, at least for the appointments of women, blacks, and Hispanics by the Carter Administration, the evidence suggests that these nontraditional appointees were as qualified, if not more so, as traditional, white male appointees.

Second, proponents of affirmative action stress that white males have not been discriminated against and in fact still constitute the large majority of appointments. During the Carter Administration there was no reverse discrimination, but instead, all other things being roughly equal, preference was given to the person belonging to the group that was victimized by past discrimination.

Third, affirmative-action supporters argue that individual merit is still the most important consideration and that government's role in ending racial and sexual discrimination and becoming truly neutral is enhanced by its active recruitment of women and minorities. Neutrality is not the same as indifference, and a meaningful end to past practices of discrimination must be heralded by vigorous and conspicuous attempts to open up the judicial recruitment process.

Fourth, while supporters of affirmative action are generally not enthusiastic about bureaucratic procedures to classify people as to their race and ethnicity, the fact that this is being done with benign, positive, antiracist motives and for antidiscriminatory purposes justifies this excursion into racial classification.

Last, defenders of affirmative action vigorously deny that sex or race are irrelevant to the judicial process. Issues of sexual and racial discrimination have come before the courts in relatively large numbers since the early 1960s. Women and minorities personally familiar with discrimination bring to the bench life experiences and sensitivities that the typical white male does not. There are certain qualities of the heart and mind that, when brought to bear on issues of discrimination, may well add a new dimension of justice to the courts. The visibility of women and minority judges on the bench may inspire confidence in the courts within those groups in the population. And on the bench these judges cannot help but educate and sensitize their colleagues. Indeed, given the wide range of variables and personal attributes associated with judicial selection, the deliberate recruitment of qualified women and minorities may indeed result in the "best" people to fill certain judgeships.

DEFINING AND FINDING GOOD JUDGES. A perennial issue surrounding judicial selection is how to define and then find "good" judges. There are certain traits associated with being a good judge that most observers seem to agree on, although they might describe them somewhat differently. They include neutrality toward the parties in litigation; fair-mindedness in the conduct of a trial, with special emphasis on a scrupulous concern for procedural due process; knowledge of, and experience in, the law; an ability to think and write clearly and logically; great personal integrity; good physical and mental health; a judicial temperament (being even-tempered, courteous, cooperative, patient); and the capacity to handle judicial power sensibly. This last characteristic is the most controversial as it is open to more widely differing interpretations than the others. Some believe that a good judge will defend and promote human rights and personal freedom and be particularly sensitive to the plight of the racially, sexually, and economically oppressed. Others believe that a good judge will recognize the place of the judiciary in a democratic society and not arrogate power and behave imperiously (as a philosopher-king).

How to find good people for the judiciary, assuming that the qualities of a good judge have been adequately defined, is an exceedingly difficult task for at least two reasons. First, it is hard to establish an objective indicator for each quality, with a precise measurement rather than a subjective evaluation. Second, the selection methods in practice are concerned with factors other than those that define a good judge; thus, considerations of what makes a good judge are rarely given close attention.

Nevertheless, it is essential to make every attempt to be thorough in assessing these qualities and to use such methods as surveys of the bar, former clients, and sitting judges, along with close analysis of briefs written by the candidate. If the candidate is already a lower-court judge or has had previous judicial experience, a qualitative and quantitative assessment of the candidate's judicial record may be in order. For federal judgeships, the Federal Bureau of Investigation (FBI) conducts extensive background investigations as does the staff of the Senate Judiciary Committee. There is considerably less extensive investigation for most state judgeships. Despite the likelihood of some errors of evaluation, a systematic evaluation of the qualities previously mentioned can identify those who are clearly suitable for judicial office, as opposed to those clearly unsuited. Undoubtedly, the success of judicial selection depends upon the intelligence, perceptiveness, skill, and sensitivity of those involved in the choosing and the wisdom of their subjective evaluations.

EVALUATION OF SELECTION METHODS. To evaluate the five principal selection methods, it is first necessary to establish the criteria according to which the selection methods are to be assessed. There are a variety of standards that bar groups offer, such as the desirability that the selection method results in the "best" available people being chosen and minimizes "politics" as a factor in selection. Four basic principles are useful in efforts to maximize the likelihood of selecting good judges.

First, the selection process should be an open one in at least two ways: compilation of information about all possible candidacies and provision for expansion of the recruitment net to include all those who wish to be considered.

Second, the selection process should provide for the active recruitment of women, blacks, and other ethnic groups that have been the victims of discrimination. By actively seeking out those who may have been shut out of the system, it is likely that there will be an increase in the numbers of well-qualified people from which to choose. Furthermore, a sincere effort to recruit more women and minorities can reassure certain segments of the population of the neutrality and fairness of the judicial process. The presence and interaction of women and minorities on the bench can enhance other judges' sensitivity to issues of race and sex discrimination thereby enhancing further the judiciary's qualities of neutrality and fair-mindedness.

Third, a thorough investigatory apparatus of the leading candidates is necessary to ensure that all relevant facets of these individuals are consistent with the qualities that constitute a good judge. The investigators should do more than compile allegations: They should follow through and evaluate the information collected.

Fourth, some form of political accountability may be useful in the quest to maximize the possibility of selecting good judges. It is taken for granted that judges exercise discretion and by so doing can act as policy-makers. The challenge is to place the judiciary within a democratic framework of accountability so that judges' choices of policy and other aspects of their performance in office will be subject to review either directly at the polls or indirectly (that is, holding those who selected them responsible), while at the same time not compromising their independence while they sit.

Taking these four selection principles as the basis for evaluation, we can suggest that on the surface the electoral methods seem to provide for the most open selection process in that anyone can choose to run for judicial office. Those running for office are subject to the scrutiny of bar groups, the media, and citizens' organizations, so that theoretically a great deal of investigation of the candidates occurs. Direct election of judges would appear to be the highest embodiment of the democratic process and to provide for the greatest accountability when limited terms of office require judges to run for reelection. Of the four principles of selection, only that of affirmative action appears inadequately addressed. In reality, electoral methods fall far short of the idealized portrait, although partisan elections do ensure a rough sort of political accountability.

The success of judicial selection depends upon the intelligence, perceptiveness, skill, and sensitivity of those involved in the choosing.

The legislative and gubernatorial appointment methods hold legislators and particularly governors accountable. In the case of gubernatorial appointment, governors have the opportunity to appoint those in tune with their own overarching values, if not more specific policy perspectives. Accordingly, gubernatorial appointment can produce a "responsible party model," whereby policy coordination among the branches of government occurs and the party takes the credit or the blame at the next election. Gubernatorial appointment is also a selection method potentially flexible enough to employ the openness principle and the use of affirmative action. Whether or not there is openness and affirmative action depends on the particular individuals in office and the political pressures they face. The executive appointment method appears to allow the complete investigatory resources of the state to be made available for investigating judicial candidates, and this may be more systematic and reliable for the gathering of information about candidates than reliance on bar groups and the print and broadcast media (as is the case with electoral selection methods). In practice, however, there is a heavy reliance on political processes that do not place much of an emphasis on the qualities that make for a good judge.

Merit selection in theory would seem to embody all four of the principles suggested earlier and to result in good judges being chosen. The selection commission is supposed to be concerned with precisely the sorts of considerations suggested earlier as being the indispensable qualities of the good judge. The process is thought to be an open one, whereby any interested individual can apply. The commission can also try to interest people in applying and herein lies the potential for affirmative action. It could also be argued that emphasis on merit and searching for the best available candidates should overcome the racial and sexual biases of the past and bring well-qualified women and minorities before the commissions. Both the merit commission and the governor who must make the formal appointment will have had the opportunity to investigate the backgrounds of the candidates. And last, the merit tenure concept, whereby the judge periodically goes before the electorate in what is essentially a plebiscite, is consistent with the principle of accountability.

In practice, as seen earlier, merit selection fails to live up to the goals of its founders in that political considerations and bar association politics can be seen at work. It has not automatically guaranteed affirmative action absent a vigorous commitment on the part of the governor. The selection commission, consisting largely or entirely of gubernatorial appointees, can be shaped so that certain outcomes are more likely than others. Yet, in the public's eye the governor is not held politically accountable because the process was ostensibly based on merit.

Federal judicial selection, like gubernatorial appointment, has the virtues of political accountability and the potential for openness, affirmative action, and thorough investigation. Under President Carter the Judicial Service Commission had a mandate to open up the process and to vigorously proceed with affirmative action. The Senate's more independent investigatory role also enhanced the fact-finding aspects of the process. It can be argued that judicial selection during the Carter administration came closer to satisfying the four selection principles than any other method. In that respect the Reagan administration's abandonment of the Judicial Selection Commission, its explicit rejection of affirmative action, and its reversion to the more closed selection process of the past can be seen as a move away from the principles suggested earlier.

Nonetheless, there is no evidence that any one selection method produces more good judges than any other method. In terms of state judicial selection, while the merit concept has become increasingly favored, there has yet to be any definitive evidence that any one method produces superior judges or judges with vastly different backgrounds or qualifications. Given the available evidence, no one selection method can be said to be a superior method for the appointment of judges with the qualities that make for good judges or judges whose on-the-bench performance is adjudged to be of the highest caliber. There is no hard evidence linking the method of judicial selection with judicial decision-making trends.

One final point to keep in mind is that the methods currently in use are not the only possible methods of judicial selection. For example, the Constitution suggests in Article II that Congress could authorize the Supreme Court or the attorney general to appoint lower-court judges. Similarly, state supreme courts or attorneys general could be given the responsibility for state judicial selection. Article II also indicates that lower-court judges could be appointed by the president alone if Congress so provided. Still another method of judicial selection could be modeled after the process used in Europe, which essentially considers the judiciary a specialized type of civil service. Would-be judges complete a special course of study, take special examinations, and work their way up the judicial hierarchy—all outside the political appointment process. It is not appropriate here to evaluate these alternative methods, but it is relevant to observe that there is no movement in the United States to adopt any of these alternative judicial selection methods.

Judicial Tenure and Judicial Discipline

The mirror image of judicial selection is judicial tenure, with the subsidiary issue of judicial discipline. Once a judge comes on the bench, how does he or she retain office and what means are there for disciplining gross misconduct?

Most judges serve for as long as they wish or until a mandatory retirement age, usually seventy, is reached.

There are six principal provisions for tenure in current use. First, three states and the federal government appoint most or all their judges for life tenure or its close approximation, tenure to age seventy. Second, in six states tenure for most or all judges depends upon reappointment by the governor with the consent of the state senate. In Connecticut, the governor nominates and the full legislature elects. The terms of office vary from six to fourteen years. Periodic partisan or nonpartisan elections are the third and fourth methods of tenure with terms of office ranging from four to ten years. (Appellate court judgeships tend to have the longest tenure, with terms of office at least six years.) Ten states, eight of them southern, use partisan elections to determine tenure in judicial office. Twelve states, eleven of them midwestern or western, use nonpartisan elections for establishing tenure. Two states, South Carolina and Virginia, use legislative reappointment, the fifth tenure method. Sixth, in seventeen states the tenure provisions of the merit plan or a close facsimile are in effect. Terms of office vary, but the ranges are similar to those in states with other than life tenure.

Under merit tenure, judges run unopposed "on their records" in nonpartisan retention elections. Typically the question on the ballot is "Shall Judge X be retained in office" and the electorate votes yes or no. Of the seventeen states that use merit selection, thirteen use merit tenure. (In Hawaii, the Judicial Selection Commission, not the electorate, makes the retention decision.) Of the other four states that use merit tenure, Illinois and Pennsylvania use partisan elections for selection while California and Maryland use gubernatorial appointment with the advice and consent of the Commission on Judicial Appointments and of the state senate, respectively.

In practice, most judges serve for as long as they wish or until a mandatory retirement age, usually seventy, is reached, regardless of the formal method for tenure. Most judicial incumbents running for reelection run without opposition. Those who do run against opposition are seldom defeated, although on rare occasions an upset has been known to occur. In states that use the merit plan's provisions for tenure, it is almost a certainty that judges win retention. In Missouri, for example, in the two decades or so following the adoption of merit selection and tenure, only one judge failed to win the retention election. Even where there is a concerted effort to oust a judge by voting no at the retention election, as has happened on several occasions with the justices of the California Supreme Court, it has been difficult (but not impossible as the 1986 elections showed) to defeat an incumbent judge. The fact remains that a judge who does not conspicuously court notoriety will be reappointed, reelected, or retained in office. This has meant that it has been extraordinarily difficult to discipline, if not remove, judges who are unwilling or unable to perform their duties satisfactorily. Until the 1960s the difficult process of impeachment and conviction begun during the term of office (rather than other efforts at reelection or reappointment time) was the only potential means of disciplining the judiciary. Only the most serious and public offenses triggered such extreme action, and as a consequence, such removal machinery has been infrequently employed.

The problem of the lack of judicial disciplinary institutions began to be faced in the early 1960s, and within two decades all states had established or strengthened judicial qualifications commissions or otherwise named investigatory and disciplinary boards. At the federal level Congress enacted the Judicial Councils Reform and Judicial Conduct and Disability Act of 1980, which authorizes each of the circuit judicial councils to exercise disciplinary authority, short of removal from office, over federal judges within their respective circuits.

That disciplinary machinery now exists does not mean that all methods are equally effective or that the machinery will necessarily be used. A few states seem to have made little better than token gestures in this regard. For example, in 1977 the state of Arkansas enacted legislation establishing a judicial ethics committee with the authority to investigate allegations of judicial misconduct and to report its recommendation to the state legislature. However, the removal from office of the major state judicial officials, including judges of trial courts with general jurisdiction, must be done through the traditional process of impeachment or by the governor upon the joint address (vote) of two-thirds of each house of the legislature.

A somewhat stronger method exists in Massachusetts, where the Commission on Judicial Conduct was established by state statute in 1978 and given authority to investigate allegations of misconduct. However, it can only recommend disciplinary action to the Supreme Judicial Court, which in turn can discipline, short of removal from office. Removal from office must be accomplished either through impeachment (only six states do not make this provision) or upon the address of both houses of the legislature to the governor (seventeen states have such provisions), with the governor needing the consent of the executive council. Another method used in several other states is the recall election, whereby a retention election is held upon the signing of a petition by a certain number or percentage of registered voters. These are cumbersome methods.

By contrast, in Michigan the Judicial Tenure Commission was established by an amendment to the state constitution in 1968. Under its provisions the Michigan Supreme Court, upon recommendation of the commission, may censure, suspend with or without salary, retire, or remove from office a judge convicted of a felony, found to have a physical or mental disability, found to have persistently failed to perform duties or to have engaged in other misconduct in office, or found to have engaged in conduct clearly prejudicial to the administration of justice. In fact, thirty-nine states have similar strong disciplinary mechanisms that permit removal from office by a commission or the highest state court. In the District of Columbia the local judges (with a fixed term of office) may be removed from office by the Commission on Judicial Disabilities and Tenure. However, federal judges appointed for life under the authority of Article III of the Constitution may only, according to the Constitution, be removed by impeachment in the House of Representatives and conviction after trial in the Senate, a rarely used method (although used successfully in 1986 to remove convicted felon Harry Clairborne from the federal district bench).

The qualifications commissions vary in membership, but they generally consist of judges, lawyers, and lay persons. How they operate in practice and how effective they have been are questions that must await systematic empirical investigation, although the anecdotal evidence suggests that in some states, such as New York, they have had some impact.

Conclusion

The problems posed by judicial selection, tenure, and discipline are not easy to resolve for several reasons. First, there are fifty different state governments and the federal government, each with its own laws and unique combination of methods and machinery. Second, the formal methods do not necessarily suggest what happens in practice. Finally, there are numerous issues of some degree of complexity that surround judicial selection. What might superficially seem to be a process that ought to be straightforward is not in reality and for good reason. The people who are selected to serve on the American bench determine the course of the administration of justice. Particularly at the higher levels of the judiciary but even at the trial level, these judges, in their rulings, formulate public policy that may affect the lives and fortunes of many people. That is why there has been, and will continue to be, a lively interest in the processes of judicial selection and in the people selected. That is also why there will continue to be controversy.

[See also (II) Judges, Appointment of; (III) Federal Court System, Judiciary, Judicial Review; State Court Systems.]

BIBLIOGRAPHY

Henry J. Abraham, *Justices and Presidents* (2nd ed., 1985), provides a comprehensive descriptive account of appointments to the Supreme Court from Washington to Reagan. Burton Atkins and Henry Glick, "Formal Judicial Recruitment and State Supreme Court Decisions," in *American Politics Quarterly,* 2 (1974), puts the relationship between formal judicial recruitment and judicial decisions to an important test. Griffin Bell et al., *Whom Do Judges Represent?* (1981), offers differing views on the issues surrounding judicial selection in this edited transcript of a television panel discussion.

Larry C. Berkson and Susan B. Carbon, *The United States Circuit Judge Nominating Commission: Its Members, Procedures, and Candidates* (1980), extensively examines the nominating commission created by President Carter. Harold W. Chase, *Federal Judges: The Appointing Process* (1972), analyzes and discusses in rich detail federal judicial selection from Eisenhower to Johnson. Nancy Chinn and Larry Berkson, *Literature on Judicial Selection* (1980), is a valuable annotated bibliography of the judicial selection literature.

John H. Culver, "Politics and the California Plan for Choosing Appellate Judges," in *Judicature,* 66 (1982), analyzes California's method of judicial selection and examines alternative methods in use in the states. David J. Danelski, *A Supreme Court Justice Is Appointed* (1964), analyzes the events leading to the appointment of Pierce Butler to the Supreme Court and is still the best theoretical work on the transactional nature of selection. Phillip L. Dubois. *From Ballot to Bench: Judicial Elections and the Quest for Accountability* (1980), provides a systematic analysis of judicial election and related data and draws many important insights and conclusions.

W. Gary Fowler, "Judicial Selection Under Reagan and Carter," in *Judicature,* 67 (1984), systematically analyzes comparisons between the two administrations, including the use of selection commissions. Sheldon Goldman, "Judicial Selection and the Qualities That Make a 'Good' Judge," in *Annals of the American Academy of Political and Social Science,* 462 (1982), considers various aspects of the linkage between judicial selection methods and the recruitment of "good" judges and considers the challenge of determining and applying objective criteria to particular individuals; and "Reaganizing the Judiciary," in *Judicature,* 68 (1985), offers an analysis of the selection process of lower federal court judges during President Reagan's first term. Sheldon Goldman and Thomas P. Jahnige, *The Federal Courts as a Political System* (1985), examines federal judicial selection and places it within the context of the workings of the federal judicial system.

Kenyon N. Griffin and Michael J. Horan, "Patterns of Voting Behavior in Judicial Retention Elections for Supreme Court Justices in Wyoming," in *Judicature,* 67 (1983), provides a valuable analysis of the problems associated with merit tenure. Joel B. Grossman, *Lawyers and Judges* (1965), although dated, is the most thorough book-length account available of the workings of the ABA Standing Committee on Federal Judiciary. Kermit L. Hall, *The Politics of Justice: Lower Federal Judicial Selection and the Second Party System, 1829–61* (1979), offers a valuable, methodologically sophisticated, historical perspective on federal judicial selection from the Jacksonian period to the outbreak of the Civil War.

Alan Neff, *The United States District Judge Nominating Commissions: Their Members, Procedures and Candidates* (1981), has written a comprehensive account of selection commissions used by senators during the Carter Administration. Charles Sheldon, "Influencing the Selection of Judges: The Variety and Effectiveness of State Bar Activities," in *Western Political Quarterly,* 30 (1977), scrutinizes the role of state bar associations in judicial selection. Elliot E. Slotnick, "Judicial Selection: Lowering the Bench or Raising it Higher?: Affirmative Action and Judicial Selection During the Carter Administration," in *Yale Law and Policy Review,* 1 (1983), provides a systematic and insightful empirical analysis of the backgrounds and professional qualifications of the affirmative-action appointees of the Carter Administration; and "The ABA Standing Committee on Federal Judiciary: A Contemporary Assessment," in *Judicature,* 66 (1983), gives an up-to-date, extensive, and excellent survey of the workings of the ABA committee.

Mary L. Volcansek, "Money or Name? A Sectional Analysis of Judicial Elections," in *The Justice System Journal,* 8 (1983), is an analysis of certain variables and their effect on the outcomes of judicial elections. Richard A. Watson and Rondal G. Downing, *The Politics of the Bench and the Bar* (1969), is the classic study of the Missouri plan.

– SHELDON GOLDMAN

THE JUDICIARY

The judiciary, as it evolved in the Western legal tradition, is often described as an institution that resolves conflicts on the basis of fair, predictable, and objective principles and procedures. It achieves its purposes by developing and maintaining its independence from external institutional influences, such as governmental leaders and bureaucracies, political parties, and religious leaders and organizations. Its judges and supporting legal personnel are trained and socialized to develop and apply doctrines and procedures that are rational and predictable. Such legal officials are selected on the basis of merit, professional training, and experience. Ascriptive criteria, such as race, caste, tribe, socioeconomic status, or gender, are rejected.

The judiciary serves as a neutral arbiter of relations between equals before the law. It assumes the responsibility for safeguarding economic rights, such as contract or property, and protecting noneconomic rights and liberties, such as freedom of speech and religion. Its decision-making procedures and customs are characteristically objective and nonpartisan with respect to individuals, groups, political parties, and ideologies. These attributes contain fundamental components of the ideal conception of a judiciary. Most elements of this ideal conception are embodied in the analyses of a number of perceptive scholars of the Western legal tradition, such as Max Weber and Harold J. Berman.

These characteristics of a model or ideal judicial system may not, of course, be fully attained in the actual judicial and legal systems of nations under most circumstances. For example, it is generally recognized that a judicial system is not likely to maintain its independence and objectivity in periods of dangerous political unrest. Neither can such a judicial system maintain fair standards and render objective doctrines in a nation driven by bribery, nepotism, and conflicts of interest. Nor can a judicial system function fairly in a nation that abides bitterly divisive class or caste societal distinctions. Thus, it is not surprising that in a revolution, a national judicial system and its judicial and legal elite may be considered significant contributors to the oppressions and grievances which led to the revolt. This is, in part, what occurred in the 1776 revolution of colonists in the portions of British North America that became the original thirteen American states.

Origins of the American Judiciary

Convinced that their rights and privileges as Englishmen had been tyrannically denied them, many Americans fought for independence from Great Britain. While broad issues such as taxation without representation were salient, other conflicts involving the legal and judicial system controlled by Great Britain were very important. Chief among the latter were issues involving corrupt use of the legal system and the arrogant manner in which the British chose unqualified individuals for judicial posts sought by able Americans. For example, John Jay, destined to become the first Chief Justice of the United States, was outraged by British selections of "needy ignorant dependents [of] great men . . . to the seats of justice, and other places of trust and importance" (Wood, 78). Another colonial was less restrained. He resented the advancement "to the most eminent stations men without education and of dissolute manners . . . sporting with our persons and estates, by filling the highest seats of justice with bankrupts, bullies, and blockheads" (Wood, 145). Their experiences and disillusionment with British corruption and legal imperialism during the events that led to the American Revolution sharpened their ideas about judicial organization and the need for judicial independence.

When the former colonials succeeded in winning their national independence, they were confronted by a dilemma. Their entire legal culture was based upon the English common law. When the founders of the new American constitutional system met to create a stable foundation for their federal governmental system, would they totally reject the fundamentals of the British legal system under which they had been nurtured as British colonials and denied equality and fair play as transatlantic subjects? What emerged after the momentous sessions of the Philadelphia Convention of 1787 was not only a Constitution that delineated the powers of the new federal government but also specified limitations on those powers as well. A new judicial system was developed to fulfill a central role in defining those powers and enforcing limitations. The entire American legal cultural foundation remained fundamentally within the framework of the English common law tradition, but the organization and structure of the new federal judicial system represented a departure from the eighteenth-century British model. The key elements of the new system were significantly influenced by the prevailing notion of the separation of powers and checks and balances as safeguards of the independence of the three branches of the national government and by the notion of federalism as a determinant of the relationship of the national government to the governments of the states. The new judiciary was also the product of political compromise in the protracted meetings of the Philadelphia Convention of 1787.

Because the members of the convention vividly remembered the undue influence of the crown, safeguards against excessive executive authority were provided. The president nominated justices of the new Supreme Court and the judges of such inferior federal courts as the Congress chose to create. But presidential nominations and appointments were subject to the advice and consent of the Senate. Justices of the Supreme Court and judges of the regular federal judiciary were provided two very important protections for judicial independence—life tenure on good behavior and a prohibition of the reduction of their salaries.

The powers of the federal judiciary, spelled out specifically in Article III, Section 2 of the Constitution as jurisdictional authority, ensured that the new system would play a determinative role as interpreter of the safeguards of the separation of powers and as final arbiter in conflicts between the states and the national government. The founders of the American constitutional system were keenly aware of the intimate relationship between a sound and independent judiciary, political and economic stability, and individual freedom.

The founding fathers were keenly aware of the relationship between a sound and independent judiciary, political and economic stability, and individual freedom.

The first decade of the new national American judicial system was very significant for the future development and expansion of judicial powers. The First Congress passed the seminal Judiciary Act of 1789, in which the appellate jurisdiction of the new Supreme Court was given statutory substance. Significantly, there was enacted the framework of a complete organization for an inferior federal judiciary consisting of courts of first instance, denominated district courts, and three initial intermediate appellate courts, the federal circuit courts for the three major regions of the new nation, New England, the Middle Atlantic states, and the South. Provision was made for regular federal district judges, but not for separate judges for the circuit courts, which were manned during congressionally designated periods each year by federal district judges serving as circuit judges and by members of the United States Supreme Court serving as chief judges or members of the circuit to which they were assigned. The Supreme Court members and district judges chosen by the first president, George Washington, were all Federalists, thus establishing partisan selection as the general appointing policy of subsequent presidents. The justices of the 1790s did not receive the recognition accorded to Chief Justice John Marshall, but they did contribute in a number of significant ways to judicial supremacy and the sanctity of contracts—two principles central to Federalist and neo-Federalist doctrinal judicial influences.

Judicial Independence and Political Pressure

When John Marshall was appointed chief justice of the United States by President John Adams, the Supreme

Court was destined to face major tests of the independence and stability of the judicial system. The Jeffersonian Republicans, enraged by Adam's selection of many Federalists for new circuit judgeships created by the Judiciary Act of 1801 (a product of the lame-duck Federalist Congress), promptly repealed the act in 1802. Since the Federalist circuit judges were protected by the constitutional provisions providing life tenure on good behavior, the question arose whether Congress could constitutionally remove regular federal judges by the exercise of its power "to ordain and establish" or disestablish "inferior courts." When the repealing act came before the Supreme Court in *Stuart* v. *Laird* (1803), the Federalist justices (Marshall abstaining) provided a cryptic yes to the question. The major companion decision, *Marbury* v. *Madison* (1803), by contrast, contained Marshall's articulation of the power of judicial review, establishing the principle in American constitutional law that the Supreme Court possessed the authority to determine the constitutionality of congressional enactments and executive decisions.

The intense partisanship of some of the early Federalist judges and justices and the lame-duck partisanship of the first Adams administration stimulated strong Jeffersonian Republican reactions. The conflicts involving the judiciary in the Jacksonian era were occasionally intense but did not result in institutional setbacks as direct and severe as in both the era of Jefferson and the era of President Abraham Lincoln. Several clear patterns of political-judicial conflict and interaction emerged by the end of the nineteenth century. Particularly after the great, albeit contemporaneously controversial, era of Chief Justice John Marshall, the Court's institutional independence emerged in fact as well as in constitutional clause. But such institutional independence was subject to at least two practical political limitations and had been threatened by others. In rare instances, a politically controversial Supreme Court decision could be overturned by the complex but occasionally politically responsive amending process. Significant amending-process reversals of Supreme Court decisions followed *Chisholm* v. *Georgia* (1793); *Dred Scott* v. *Sandford* (1857), and *Pollock* v. *Farmers' Loan and Trust Company* (1895).

The first decision had held, contrary to Philadelphia Convention understandings, that a state could be sued by a citizen of another state. The decision aroused strong Antifederalist reactions. The initial call for a constitutional amendment to overturn the *Chisholm* decision came in 1795, two years after the Court had acted. On 8 January 1798, after the requisite three-fourths of the states had ratified the amendment, President Adams formally announced that the Eleventh Amendment was part of the Constitution.

The reaction to the *Dred Scott* decision of 1857 was perhaps the most intense adverse response, because of the intimate relationship of the case to the bitter decisions that ultimately led to the Civil War. The Thirteenth Amendment, ratified in 1865, makes major portions of the *Dred Scott* decision irrelevant because the amendment's prohibition of slavery and involuntary servitude repudiates the portions of the decision that upheld the concept of slaves as property and the doctrine that slavery could not be territorially limited in the United States. The Fourteenth Amendment, adopted in 1868, similarly repudiates the *Dred Scott* decision's doctrine that national citizenship is contingent upon state citizenship. Section 1 holds that "all persons born or naturalized in the United States and subject to the jurisdiction thereof, are citizens of the United States and of the States wherein they reside." The Pollock decision struck down a congressionally passed federal income tax statute on the ground that it was a direct tax requiring apportionment among the states in accordance with state population distributions determined by the decennial census. In 1913, with the impetus of Progressive legislators, the Sixteenth Amendment was ratified, eighteen years after the Pollock decision was handed down. Repudiation of Supreme Court decisions by constitutional amendment obviously does not occur frequently and is often a slow and politically complex procedure. But it is important to note that the amending process has been invoked successfully in periods of great political tension and thus represents a constitutionally valid source of restraint on the judiciary.

While twentieth-century Supreme Court crises have been fewer and less intense, the institutional weapons to mount attacks are still intact.

The most direct political weapons available to antagonistic Congresses or presidents are the impeachment process, the removal of judges of inferior federal courts by abolishing their courts, and the occasional, politically motivated withdrawal of appellate jurisdiction. After the bitter conflicts of the Federalists and Jeffersonian Republicans that resulted in the removal of Federalist District Judge John Pickering in 1804, and the near impeachment of Justice Samuel Chase, impeachment has not been successfully invoked as a method of political removal of judges or justices, although the threat of the impeachment process has stimulated judicial resignations, such as those of Circuit Judge Martin Manton and Associate Justice Abe Fortas. The abolition of courts with the resultant removal of their judges could not constitutionally be applied to the Supreme Court of the United States but has been utilized on two separate occasions in the nineteenth century—first, to abolish the Federalist-created circuit court system of 1801 and, second, during the Civil War, to abolish the circuit court for the District of Columbia. The latter was replaced immediately by President Lincoln and the Republican Congress with a new court with virtually the same jurisdiction called the Supreme Court for the District of Columbia.

Adjustments of the appellate jurisdiction of the Supreme Court of the United States have been generally made for straightforward legal purposes unrelated to conflicts between the branches of the national government. But the precedent created by the Radical Republican Congress in the hasty repeal of a provision of the statute of 1867 affirming the appellate jurisdiction of the Supreme Court in cases involving habeas corpus, the writ providing that a person held in custody be brought before the court to establish whether he or she is being detained lawfully, is instructive. In acknowledging the power of Congress to repeal portions of its appellate jurisdiction in *Ex parte McCardle* (1869), Chief Justice Salmon P. Chase summed up the effect of such denial of jurisdiction: "Without jurisdiction the court cannot proceed at all in any cause. Jurisdiction is power to declare the law, and when it ceases to exist, the only function remaining to the court is that of announcing the fact and dismissing the cause."

After the unpopularity of President Franklin D. Roosevelt's Court-packing plan of the 1930s, it was commonly assumed that the Court enjoyed an attitude of reverence in Congress and support among the public. But the main portion of the congressional opposition to Roosevelt's plan consisted of a conservative coalition composed of conservative southern Democrats and northern Republicans. When the balance of Supreme Court appointments shifted to the New Deal and its successor, Harry Truman's Fair Deal, the conservative coalition became the political center of anti-Supreme Court political activity. By the 1980s, many elements of an anti-Court conservative coalition had shifted further to the right, augmented by younger conservatives elected to the House of Representatives and the Senate with the support of the Moral Majority and its political-action committee, which was controlled by Senator Jesse Helms of North Carolina. The "social agenda" goals of the new right included repudiation of a number of Supreme Court decisions, such as the key abortion ruling in *Roe* v. *Wade* (1973). Senator Helms, with the support of President Ronald Reagan, recommended selective statutory curtailment of the appellate jurisdiction of the Supreme Court to accomplish Moral Majority legislative goals. One such Helms bill was only narrowly defeated in the Senate in 1982. In short, direct political action against the Supreme Court is not merely a nineteenth-century phenomenon.

In sum, the independence of the Supreme Court and regular federal judiciary against direct political attacks by Congress or the president has generally been maintained. But while twentieth-century Supreme Court crises have been fewer and less intense, the institutional weapons to mount such attacks, from the cumbersome amending process to statutory manipulation of the appellate jurisdiction of the Supreme Court, are still intact and have tempted some contemporary critics of the doctrines and personnel of the Supreme Court.

The Relationship of the Federal and State Courts

One of the most interesting and initially unpredictable aspects of the adoption of the Constitution of 1787 was the creation of an entirely new court system that operated as the judicial arm of the new nation upon individuals who were used to utilizing the court systems of their respective states. The initial conflict between the two systems occurred even before the national court system was created. There was little disagreement over the establishment of a Supreme Court of the United States with jurisdiction sufficiently broad to encompass cases and controversies that involved the scope of national authority or the violation by states of claimed federal rights. The Philadelphia Convention of 1787 left to the Congress the question of whether a system of inferior federal courts would be created or not. The First Congress was controlled by Federalists, who wanted to create a complete federal court system. They succeeded in passing a comprehensive framework, but as the comments above about the first circuit court system indicate, no separate federal circuit judges were included. In Section 25 of the Judiciary Act of 1789, Congress provided for a means by which any state court challenge to federal powers or rights could be finally decided by the Supreme Court of the United States. The section stated that final judgment in any suit in the highest court of law or equity of a state,

> where is drawn in question the validity of a treaty or statute of, or an authority exercised under the United States, and the decision is against their validity; or where is drawn in question the validity of a statute of, or an authority exercised under any State, on the

> ground of their being repugnant to the Constitution, treaties or laws of the United States, and the decision is in favour of their validity, or where is drawn in question the construction of any clause of the Constitution, or of a treaty, or statute of, or commission held under the United States, and the decision is against the title, right, privilege or exemption specially set up or claimed by either party, under such clause of the said constitution, treaty, statute, or commission, may be re-examined and reversed or affirmed in the Supreme Court of the United States [upon writ of error].

The Antifederalists argued that Supreme Court oversight was enough and also argued on states' rights and economic grounds that inferior federal courts were not needed. The Federalists prevailed, and the two judicial systems were paired in every state.

The most dramatic confrontations between the two systems occurred in situations in which the highest court of a state directly challenged the authority of the Supreme Court of the United States. Chief Justice Marshall firmly rejected such assertions of state judicial authority in *Cohens* v. *Virginia* (1821), as did Justice Joseph Story in *Martin* v. *Hunter's Lessee* (1816). Both invoked the supremacy clause as the ultimate source of federal judicial authority. But it should be noted that the relationship and relative positions of the federal and state courts were not determined by dramatic constitutional confrontations alone, although such conflicts ultimately established the subordinate positions of the state courts when valid federal judicial authority was at stake. As the relative positions of the federal and state judicial systems changed over the nineteenth and early twentieth centuries, other factors, such as the prestige and relative independence of the two sets of courts, were important. For example, a notable and very conservative New York state jurist, James Kent, concerned about the successes of the Jacksonians in gaining state approval of public election of judges, suggested that

> the judiciary of the United States has an advantage over many of the state courts, in the tenure of the office of the judges, and the liberal and stable provision for their support. The United States are, by these means, fairly entitled to command better talents, and to look to more firmness of purpose, greater independence of action, and brighter displays of learning. The federal administration of justice has a manifest superiority over that of the individual states, in consequence of the uniformity of its decisions, and the universality of their application. Every state court will naturally be disposed to borrow light and aid from the national courts, rather than from the courts of other individual states, which will probably never be so generally respected and understood.

Perhaps more important, the Supreme Court of the United States and the inferior federal courts became, especially during and after the era of John Marshall, rather clearly identified as the legal tribunals that reliably sustained property rights via the contract clause. Commercial and banking interests increasingly avoided state courts in favor of federal courts where the jurisdictional requirements could be met. Chief Justice William Howard Taft candidly and accurately summed up some of the reasons for such forum preference. Addressing the American Bar Association, Taft stated that

> litigants from the eastern part of the country who are expected to invest their capital in the West or South, will hardly concede the proposition that their interests as creditors will be as sure of impartial consideration in a western or southern state court as in a federal court. . . . No single element in our governmental system has done so much to secure capital for the legitimate development of enterprises throughout the West and South as the existence of federal courts there, with a jurisdiction to hear diverse citizenship cases.
>
> (Parker)

It should be noted that jurists of several of the highest appellate courts of the states have, over the nearly two centuries of dual court systems, achieved notable reputations. These include Chief Justice Lemuel Shaw and Chief Justice Oliver Wendell Holmes of the Supreme Judicial Court of Massachusetts, Chief Justice Benjamin N. Cardozo of the Court of Appeals of New York, Chief Justice Roger Traynor of the Supreme Court of California, and Chief Justice Arthur Vanderbilt of New Jersey. The prestige and doctrinal influence of some of the highest state courts have been rather substantial and contribute a degree of diversity and intellectual stimulation that would be lacking in a single judicial system. Just as several conservatively oriented Midwestern state supreme courts doggedly opposed New Deal Supreme Court doctrine when the jurisdictional properties permitted, so did contemporary liberally oriented state supreme courts, such as California's, provide doctrinal counterpoint to the Burger Court's narrowing of the rights of criminal defendants.

The Sociopolitical Characteristics of Federal Appellate Jurists

Federal appellate judicial selection has, since 1789, involved characteristics that in a number of important respects have contributed both to the strength and stability of the American national judiciary and, on occasion, to the political controversies that have engulfed the system. In sociopolitical terms, such selection has not generally been very responsive to the democratization of American politics and society, which purportedly has progressed since the era of government by gentry class of the late eighteenth and early nineteenth centuries. Particularly, by the twentieth century, ethnic and religious groups in the United States began to indicate greater interest in a concept of judicial representation. This concept resembles the suggestion of Walter F. Murphy and Joseph Tanenhaus that many "national constitutional courts typically display a large element of representation" because the political authorities making judicial selections may "consciously try to staff constitutional courts with personnel of diverse background characteristics that are more or less shared by the various politically relevant groupings within the polity." Another characteristic of the American selection process that has occasionally contributed to political conflict is the age of appointees and the possibility that justices or judges chosen in an earlier political generation may, under the system of life tenure on good behavior, be doctrinally at odds with legislative and executive leaders of a totally different political generation.

An ideal model of a judicial recruitment system would presumably be based upon attributes such as professional training, educational proficiency, and, as in the continental European system from which it was derived, judicial training and experience. The American system of national judges and justices (and the systems of the numerically increasing states, for that matter) did not evolve in accordance with the continental European model. The selection of federal appellate judges and justices has usually combined partisanship with an interesting composite of judicial skill and practical experience. The importance of background and careerist attributes has changed in certain respects with political eras, but in certain matters they have remained remarkably consistent. One key indication of social status, parental occupation, is a good example. Approximately 90 percent of the members of the Supreme Court have been products of economically comfortable families, largely the prestigious and politically powerful gentry class in the late eighteenth and early nineteenth centuries and the professionalized upper middle class thereafter. The circuit court judges come from the same sorts of families.

A special type of occupational heredity includes the transmission of a family tradition of political participation, which generally entails the prestige of a political name, and a family apprenticeship in political education. Two-thirds of all the justices have come from such

John Marshall, the fourth chief justice of the Supreme Court, raised the court to a level equal to that of the executive and legislative branches of the government. (Library of Congress/Corbis)

a background, but after the Civil War few of the circuit court judges came from such families. One-third of the justices came from an even more unusual type family, those with a tradition of judicial service, a relationship generally not present for circuit court judges.

Ethnicity and sex have become factors of increasing importance in the politics of judicial selection in the twentieth century. For more than the first hundred years of the Supreme Court, it was a complete monopoly of white men and a virtual monopoly of white men of western European background. Indeed, throughout the entire history of the Court, approximately 85 percent of the appointees have been of English, Welsh, Scotch, or Irish heritage. It was not until the 1960s that a black, Justice Thurgood Marshall, was nominated and appointed. The first woman chosen, Justice Sandra Day O'Connor, was selected in the 1980s. The federal circuit courts were ethnically diversified earlier than the

Supreme Court, with President Truman selecting the first black circuit judge, William H. Hastie, in 1949; President Richard M. Nixon chose the first circuit judge of Asian extraction, Herbert Y. C. Choy, in the early 1970s. President Franklin D. Roosevelt chose the first female circuit judge considerably earlier, nominating and appointing Ohio Supreme Court Justice Florence E. Allen in 1934.

By the twentieth century, ethnic and religious groups in the United States began to indicate greater interest in a concept of judicial representation.

Religion has often proved a complex issue for presidents because religious issues and attitudes occasionally stimulate serious political conflict. Historically, Roman Catholics and Jews have been subjected to nativist and religious criticism, and as a result, few of either denomination have been chosen, with most selected in the twentieth century. The overwhelming number of nominations made were of Protestants, with high-status denominations such as Episcopalian, Presbyterian, and Congregationalist constituting most of the selections. The nineteenth-century nominations of Roman Catholics and Jews did not involve the beginning of a tradition of such denominational choices but were made for contemporary political reasons largely unrelated to religion. President Andrew Jackson's choice of Chief Justice Roger B. Taney had little to do with Taney's Roman Catholicism, but Taney was the very first of his denomination on the Court. President Millard Fillmore's offer to nominate Louisiana senator-elect Judah P. Benjamin also was primarily political and had little to do with Benjamin's Jewish faith. Like the choice of Taney, this was the first such denominational choice. Benjamin preferred to keep his newly won Senate seat. Thus more than six decades lapsed before President Woodrow Wilson nominated and, after a bitter Senate fight, appointed Louis D. Brandeis as associate justice, an appointment accepted by Brandeis.

It was not until the twentieth century that political controversy arose over the concept of a Catholic seat or a Jewish seat on the Court. For example, President Truman was asked after the death of Justice Frank Murphy whether the Court "should have at least one representative of each major minority religious community?" Truman replied that he did "not believe that religions had anything to do with the Supreme Bench." This certainly appeared to be the case when Republican President Herbert Hoover selected New York Court of Appeals Justice Benjamin N. Cardozo as associate justice despite the fact that he would be the second member of the Jewish faith currently on the Court (Brandeis was still serving), the second New Yorker, and a moderately liberal Democrat as well. However, the political controversies over alleged failures to fulfill a custom of maintaining a Roman Catholic and Jewish seat on the Court are likely to intensify as group consciousness increases in American society. In fact, a considerable number of smaller and more unusual religious groups in the United States have never been represented on the Court. Of the members of major religions that have on occasion experienced discrimination, only three have been represented—Catholics, Jews, and Quakers—and throughout the entire history of the Court they have collectively constituted only 16 percent of all appointments. The proportion for circuit judges has been similar.

Because geographic representation has often been an important political consideration for presidents making judicial nominations, states having greater electoral-college significance have had more selections and those states entering the Union most recently have generally produced fewer justices and judges. A small number of foreign-born jurists have been chosen, the greatest number having been selected in the early decades of the Republic.

The framers of the Constitution did not specify that members of the federal appellate judiciary be lawyers. In practice, all the justices and circuit judges have been lawyers, although a number of the selectees in the earliest periods were primarily politicians and a few in the New Deal era were drawn from the ranks of law professors, notably Felix Frankfurter, William O. Douglas, and Wiley Rutledge. But most nominees to the Supreme Court after the 1870s have been former corporate lawyers. The New Deal interrupted the trend, but it was reinstated at the levels of the Supreme Court and the circuit courts after Truman's presidency and was particularly important under the presidencies of Eisenhower, Nixon, Ford, and Reagan.

Education, both undergraduate and professional, has been one of the most important background variables in the American judicial selection process. While the educational backgrounds of justices and circuit judges of the late eighteenth century and early nineteenth century were frequently superior to those of most contemporary lawyers, this dimension of the qualitative relationship of the public and private sectors of America's legal culture has changed. Perhaps the most significant changes took place after a frequently close relationship evolved between the emergent corporate law firms and the law schools that largely supplanted other modes of legal education by the late nineteenth century. An analysis of legal-educational background of the young associates hired by two large prototype law firms, the Cravath firm of New York City and O'Melveny and Myers of Los Angeles, indicates that in comparison to the Supreme Court justices and circuit judges who attended law schools, a far higher proportion of associates graduated from highly ranked law schools located in states that were highly industrialized, commercially active, and culturally influential. Such schools and regions do not, of course, have a monopoly on legal talent, as Thurman Arnold indicated in his witty and perceptive autobiographical chapter entitled "Law and Politics in Wyoming and Why I Left." Differences in salaries had been a source of dispute over the relative positions of state and federal courts in the nineteenth century. For example, a federal judicial salary increase proposed in 1838 was defeated on the ground that higher salaries would lure many state judges to the federal judiciary. But the most significant salary differential in the late twentieth century was between the public and private sectors. Judge Henry J. Friendly of the U.S. Court of Appeals for the Second Circuit provided an unusually candid commentary on the problem while arguing against substantial increases in the number of federal judges. He pointed out that

> prestige is a very important factor in attracting highly qualified men to the federal bench from much more lucrative pursuits. Yet the largest district courts will be in the very metropolitan areas where the discrepancy between uniform federal salaries and the financial rewards of private practice is the greatest, and the difficulty of maintaining an accustomed standard of living on the federal salary the most acute. There is real danger that in such areas, once the prestige factor was removed, lawyers with successful practices, particularly young men, would not be willing to make the sacrifice.

The trends in private-sector and public-sector legal and judicial salaries, especially when the incomes of corporate law firm partners are measured against those of federal judges and justices, have steadily enhanced the position of the private sector with consequences for the federal appellate judicial system still largely unexplored.

Of all the background and career factors that may influence the federal appellate judiciary, chronological age appears at first glance to be the simplest and least important. But when age is assessed in relation to stage of career at judicial selection and at termination of service, it assumes considerable importance because of the constitutional provision for life tenure on good behavior. This complex of age and constitutional factors practically ensures periodic policy conflict and doctrinal dissonance in the American political system. In elementary terms, the House of Representatives is totally renewed every two years, although in modern times renewal has often been a matter of course for congressmen who combine a strong instinct for survival and a "safe" one-party district. The Senate, similarly, is renewed regularly with one-third of the members up for election for a six-year term every two years. The most important potential generator of fundamental political change is the election for renewal of the presidency every four years. Unlike the House and Senate, where politically entrenched members may seek reelection as often as their health or constituents permit, the presidency was subjected to a two-term limitation in 1951 by the Twenty-second Amendment, in reaction to the four-term Roosevelt administration. The prospect of a conflict between political generations is considerably diminished in periods of political stability and concomitant legislative seniority but is especially likely in the aftermath of critical elections in which a long-controlling political party loses the White House, the House, and the Senate, and a new or rejuvenated party takes electoral control of those three institutions for a long period of time.

Most nominees to the Supreme Court after the 1870s have been former corporate lawyers.

Major conflicts involving the federal appellate judiciary have occurred in connection with four of the five critical elections. In the first such election, that of 1800, the Federalist-controlled federal courts were the only remaining party positions after the victory of the Jeffersonian Republicans. Despite the effective elimination of the "midnight" circuit judges created by the lame-duck Federalist Congress, Federalists controlled the Supreme Court and the single remaining circuit court, that for the District of Columbia. The persistence of Federalist doctrinal influence is dramatically underscored by John Marshall's thirty-five years as Chief Justice and by Federalist William Cranch's astonishing fifty-five years of service as a member of the Circuit Court for the District of Columbia. The Federalist party never captured the White House, the House, or the Senate after 1800, but the Federalists' conservative judicial principles were perpetuated in the federal appellate judiciary in doctrines such as judicial review, broad constructionist interpretations of the commerce clause, the implied-powers clause, and the contract clause. The Federalist justices had a numerical majority for twelve years after Jefferson's first presidential election and maintained effective doctrinal influence well into the Jacksonian era because of the ideological defection of Joseph Story and the neo-Federalism of Thomas Todd and Robert Trimble.

The critical election of 1828 did not directly involve the federal appellate judiciary, but the incoming president, Andrew Jackson, soon found himself in disagreement with Chief Justice Marshall and with his congressional opponents, the political successors to the Federalists, the Whigs. Their leaders, Henry Clay and Daniel Webster, frequently invoked Federalist judicial arguments in defense of the Bank of the United States. The bitter congressional battles over the Bank and the senatorial confirmation fights over Jackson's nominations of Roger B. Taney and other Jacksonian judicial nominees made clear the importance attached to control of the Supreme Court by both parties in the 1830s, 1840s, and 1850s. During the latter two decades especially, Court-related controversies shifted more and more away from the economically oriented battles that began to dominate political controversy. By the late 1850s Jacksonian justices and judges controlled the federal appellate judiciary. On a number of slavery-related issues, they became identified, generally correctly, as proslavery jurists. The *Dred Scott* decision catapulted the Supreme Court fully into the mounting slavery controversy. Chief Justice Taney's references to blacks as individuals who "had for more than a century before been regarded as beings of an inferior order . . . [having] no rights which the white man is bound to respect" inflamed abolitionists. His decision to declare unconstitutional the Missouri Compromise on the ground that Congress could not constitutionally exclude slaveholders and their property in slaves from any territory of the United States aroused wide opposition. Indeed, Taney asserted that the "only power conferred [upon Congress] is the power coupled with the duty of guarding and protecting the [slave] owner in his rights." This portion of the decision eliminated the major plank of the new Republican party—free soil. As a result, the Jacksonian Court majority found itself pitted against not only the abolitionists but also the Republican party, which achieved victory under the leadership of its presidential standard-bearer, Abraham Lincoln.

The critical election of 1860 not only included the Court-president confrontation but was soon followed by a bitter, divisive, and violent revolution by the secessionist Southern states. The Jacksonian Democratic majority, which held all but one of the nine seats of the Court on the eve of the election, lost control of the Court in an astonishingly short period. Unlike the Federalists of 1800, the Jacksonians did not extend their influence beyond the era of Jacksonian electoral ascendancy. Justice Peter V. Daniel died in 1860, Justice John A. Campbell resigned to join the Confederacy in 1861, the Republicans increased the size of the Court to ten members in 1863, Chief Justice Taney died in 1864, and Justice John Catron died in 1865. President James Buchanan's only appointee, Justice Nathan Clifford, died in 1881 after vainly hanging on to his seat awaiting election of a Democratic president. Had the full Jacksonian Democratic judicial majority of 1859 remained on the Court throughout the Civil War years, a very serious confrontation with the new Republican president and Congress would have been highly likely. Most of the Jacksonians had been proslavery in doctrinal orientations and the non-Southerners on the bench had been accurately identified as "Northern men with Southern principles."

When President Lincoln was confronted with the prospect that the three proslavery judges for the circuit court for the District of Columbia were likely to apply Chief Justice Roger B. Taney's *Merryman* doctrine of habeas corpus, Lincoln ordered the judges placed under house arrest. In order to maintain the military authority he deemed vital to the defense of the capital city, he then successfully asked Congress to abolish the circuit court, thus eliminating the judges. His Congress soon replaced the circuit court with a larger judiciary, denominated the Supreme Court for the District of Columbia, and granted similar judicial authority over the District of Columbia.

As in 1860, the critical election of 1896 was in part fought over issues related to the Supreme Court. This time the controversies related to the conservative doctrinal tendencies limiting the capacity of Congress to curb monopolies in restraint of trade and to the power of state legislatures and state regulatory agencies to regulate the rates of grain elevators and railroads. The Court also managed to limit congressional regulatory power over railroads, too. It struck down the income tax and upheld racial segregation in public transportation, adopting the separate-but-equal doctrine, which was destined to dominate public education for decades. Overall, the Court substantially broadened constitutional protections for corporations and minimized protections for individuals' noneconomic rights and liberties under the equal protection and due process clauses of the Fourteenth Amendment. At the Democratic convention of 1896, the nominee, William Jennings Bryan, adopted the strong anti-Supreme Court plank of the Populist party as a Democratic party plank, thus making the Court a major issue in the presidential campaign. Bryan's Republican opponent, William McKinley, won, and the Court's conservatism seemed electorally vindicated.

However, within a few years, progressive Republican Theodore Roosevelt and progressive Democrat Woodrow Wilson were both critical of the Court's conservatism and sought by appointments and public exhortation to change the Court's doctrinal direction, efforts that only achieved limited successes. These progressive efforts at liberalizing the Court failed in part because both Roosevelt and Wilson each made one serious error in selection—Day, by the former, and McReynolds, by the latter. And, more important, both progressive presidents were totally overshadowed by the conservative appointment opportunities available to Presidents William Howard Taft, Warren G. Harding, and Calvin Coolidge.

At the convention of 1896, William Jennings Bryan adopted the strong anti-Supreme Court plank of the Populist party as a Democratic party plank.

A dramatic change occurred after the last critical election, in 1932. Although little serious discussion of a possible confrontation took place before the election, the presence of a majority of conservative justices who had been chosen largely during more than a decade of solid Republican presidential and congressional control provided the foundation for the major constitutional crisis of the mid-1930s. The conservative majority struck down a number of key New Deal economic recovery statutes. By the end of President Franklin D. Roosevelt's first term, not a single justice had left the Court. Although conservative justices had served for decades, McReynolds since 1914, and Sutherland since 1922, there was no indication of a possible resignation or retirement. Roosevelt was confronted by a situation similar to that which apparently prompted Thomas Jefferson to state resignedly that "judges never die, and seldom resign." After the beginning of his second term, Roosevelt urged passage of the most direct legislative effort at neutralizing a Court majority short of impeachment based on political orientation. The statute, generally referred to as the Court-packing plan, would have enlarged the Court to as many as fifteen members by in effect matching new members with sitting members of the Court who were more than seventy years of age and had served ten years. The plan was not successful in Congress, but by 1937 the two most flexible of the conservatives had changed their positions abruptly, thereafter generally supporting the very forms of New Deal legislation that they had earlier deemed unconstitutional. The year 1937 also proved to be the one in which President Roosevelt, for the first time in his long tenure, could fill a vacancy on the Supreme Court. Thereafter, the transformation was rapid. After the appointment of Hugo Lafayette Black in 1937 came those of Stanley Reed in 1938; William O. Douglas and Felix Frankfurter in 1939; Frank Murphy in 1940; James Byrnes, Robert H. Jackson, and the promotion of Harlan Fiske Stone to chief justice in 1941; and Wiley Rutledge in 1943.

The high tide of positive judicial policy-making by the Supreme Court came with the unique combination of Eisenhower nominees for chief justice and associate justice plus enough New Deal Democrats to fashion a working liberal majority. Chief Justice Earl Warren, chosen in 1953, and Associate Justice William Brennan, selected in 1956, were the two important additions in this development. The defeat of President Lyndon Johnson's effort to name Associate Justice Abe Fortas as Chief Justice Warren's successor set the stage for resurgent conservatism on the Court. On the eve of the 1984 presidential election, only a few members of the old liberal coalition remained on the Court, all elderly, several in reported poor health. Associate Justice William Brennan, a nominal Democrat, who was chosen after a distinguished career on the Supreme Court of New Jersey, was the last Eisenhower appointee remaining on the Court. Moderate Associate Justice Byron White, chosen from a western corporate law firm in 1962, is the last of only two Kennedy selectees. Former civil rights attorney and NAACP legal strategist Thurgood Marshall is similarly the last of only two Johnson appointees. Marshall has served since 1967.

To Johnson's successor, President Richard M. Nixon, fell the most significant prize, the chief justiceship, and with the resignation of Associate Justice Abe Fortas in May 1969, a second vacancy. Nixon chose a sitting court of appeals judge, chosen for the District of Columbia circuit by President Eisenhower. The new chief justice, Warren E. Burger, had a visible track record as a strong 'law and order' judge on the circuit court, thus fitting Nixon's criteria established in the 1968 campaign. After the defeats of his nominees Haynsworth and Carswell, President Nixon chose another circuit judge and friend of Burger, Harry A. Blackmun. In 1971, President Nixon chose two corporate lawyers to replace Justices Black and Harlan. Former American Bar Association President and Richmond, Virginia, firm member Lewis F. Powell, and former corporate law firm member and Assistant Attorney General William H.

Rehnquist were often described as advocates of judicial restraint but were in the forefront with Chief Justice Burger as conservative judicial activists. After Nixon's resignation and presidential pardon, President Gerald R. Ford chose moderate circuit judge John Paul Stevens in 1975. Stevens became a severe critic of the conservative judicial activism of some of his colleagues in August 1984. President Jimmy Carter did not have a vacancy on the Court to fill. In 1981, when Associate Justice Potter Stewart resigned, President Ronald W. Reagan chose a former corporate law firm member serving on an Arizona appellate court, Sandra Day O'Connor. She was the first woman chosen for the Supreme Court.

An overview of the significance of the background and career factors in the selection of members of the Supreme Court suggests that the highest appellate court of the United States embodies a relatively unique institution. The Court does not completely conform to the ideal model often associated with the contributions of the sociologist Max Weber. Its members in modern times have conformed to the main attributes of American social stratification, with upper-middle-class professional family backgrounds predominating. Education in general and legal training in particular have generally screened out most lower socioeconomic class potential candidates, yet the quality of education has not matched that of corporate law firm members nor has the salary and lifestyle. The selection process makes it highly likely that most justices are political activists of some sort. This factor, in combination with jurisdictional grants of judicial authority in subject-matter areas of great political sensitivity, such as federalism, virtually ensures that the Supreme Court normally renders constitutional decisions of major political importance. This political emphasis is generally enlarged in those periods of fundamental political change when an entrenched Court majority, safeguarded by life tenure on good behavior, thwarts judicially the executive and legislative purposes of a different political generation.

The Internal Procedures and Customs of the Supreme Court

A countervailing institutional factor is summed up in Justice Felix Frankfurter's argument that the role changes the man. The extent to which such an institutional tradition has influenced Supreme Court or circuit court voting behavior varies by individual. There is no question that the procedures and customs of such higher appellate courts are related to the internal performance of an appellate court as a collegial body, while the broader political policy issues are external in certain respects. The line between external political purposes and internal institutional goals is, of course, not very precise. Chief Justice John Marshall's major change in the mode of rendering Supreme Court decisions is a good example. For the first decade of the Supreme Court, under the chief-justiceships of John Jay and Oliver Ellsworth, the justices followed the practice of writing separate opinions, technically referred to as seriatim opinions. Marshall was chosen as chief justice of the United States after the defeat of the Federalists in 1800. As a matter of fact, Marshall continued to fulfill his duties as Secretary of State after he assumed the chief justiceship, an example of dual office-holding that would not be permitted under modern standards. Soon after becoming chief justice, Marshall persuaded his fellow Federalists to adopt modes of procedure that would enable the Court to present a unified front. The practice of writing seriatim opinions was completely abandoned, dissent was discouraged, and the writing of concurring opinions was virtually eliminated. During the first four years of Marshall's leadership, Marshall himself wrote every majority opinion except two coming from his own circuit court.

In eras of great national political divisions, individual justices tended to assert their independence by accentuating their differences.

President Jefferson's first appointee, William Johnson, eventually succeeded in getting a compromise procedural arrangement. A return to seriatim opinions was not accepted, but a compromise procedure, majority opinion-writing, with the concept of dissents and concurring opinions, was established. In the initial years of Marshall's chief-justiceship, Court unity was essentially Federalist unity. After the compromise procedure was adopted, the greatest internal pressure was still against dissents and concurrences. But in eras of great national political divisions, individual justices tended to assert their independence by accentuating their differences. The crises of slavery and states' rights in the decades immediately preceding the Civil War; the late nineteenth-century and early twentieth-century public and judicial disputes over the power of corporations and the scope of state and federal regulatory authority; and the contemporary societal and judicial dissonances regarding such matters as police behavior related to criminal defendants, pornography, racial desegregation, and abortion provide the best examples of divided decisions.

Throughout much of the history of the Supreme Court, the mainstream of American legal culture held a rather conservative opinion on the matter of a divided Court. Through much of the most bitter post-Civil War judicial eras, very strong conservative professional opinions on the question were stated by a number of judges and by leaders of the American Bar Association. The association itself adopted Canon 19 of the Canons of Judicial Ethics, which provides that

> it is of high importance that judges constituting a court of last resort should use effort and self-restraint to promote solidarity of conclusion and the consequent influence of judicial decision. A judge should not yield to pride of opinion or value more highly his individual reputation than that of the court to which he should be loyal. Except in case of conscientious difference of opinion on fundamental principle, dissenting opinions should be discouraged in courts of last resort.

It was not until the flowering of dissent and concurring opinions of the 1940s, 1950s, and 1960s that a clearly stated countervailing body of liberal legal opinion began to emerge. One of the most direct of the advocates of separate opinion-writing was Justice William O. Douglas. Douglas not only wrote rationales for dissents in some of his own dissenting opinions (as did several of his colleagues) but he also contributed to the debate in journals. For example, in response to a veritable flood of critical articles about an allegedly divided Court, Douglas not only argued that justices were often divided because they were dealing with issues over which society was divided but he also equated dissent with the Jeffersonian conception of the role of judges in a democracy. It may be noted that although the practice of writing separate opinions was attacked as a procedural shortcoming of liberal justices in the 1940s and 1950s, members of the conservative majority headed by Chief Justice Warren E. Burger continued the practice with undiminished intensity.

The disagreements among the justices are usually muted by the use of language that tempers the degree of dissonance. On the rare occasions when sharp disagreement becomes public, such as in the aftermath of the *Dred Scott* decision or the period of deep divisions between New Deal chief justices, considerable public and professional interest is aroused. But there are other institutional practices, many developed under the chief justiceship of John Marshall, that militate against frequent public disagreement. The chief justice presides at the conferences in which individual cases are discussed. When, after each justice has freely discussed the issues, a vote on the outcome of the case is called for, each justice responds in reverse order of seniority. If the chief justice is with the Court's majority, he designates the associate justice (or himself) who will write the majority opinion. If not, the senior justice with the majority makes the assignment.

These procedural matters and the incidence of dissents and concurring opinions have created far fewer problems than those associated with the burgeoning case load of the Supreme Court and the federal circuit courts of appeal. Since the Court has not appreciably increased since 1925 the number of cases that are actually decided annually, the case load pressures are serious for the institution and for the individual justices themselves. Justice Harry Blackmun's moving commentary about the effects of the huge case load ably sums up the problem for the justices as individuals. He pointed out that

> the question is how long we can continue so to function and to do our work adequately. The heavier the burden, the less the possibility of adequate performance and the greater is the probability of less-than-well considered adjudication. Personally, I have never worked harder and more concentratedly than since I came to Washington just five years ago. I thought I had labored to the limits of my ability in private practice, in my work for a decade as a member of the Section of Administration of the Mayo organizations, and as a judge of the Court of Appeals. Here, however, the pressure is greater and more constant, and it relents little even during the summer months. One, therefore, to a larger degree, relies on experience and an innate and hopefully already developed proper judicial reaction. One had better be right! Good health is an absolute requisite. The normal extracurricular enjoyments of life become secondary, if it can be said that they exist at all. What I am saying, I suppose, is that there is a breaking point somewhere at which one's capacity will be exceeded or at which one's work becomes second-rate. The nation, in my opinion, deserves better than this.

Considerable attention has been given in Congress, the legal profession, and the federal judiciary to a variety of suggested solutions. The recommendations have ranged from adding more inferior federal judges to the creation of yet another appellate court with authority greater than the courts of appeals of the circuits but less than that of the Supreme Court. A commonly accepted solution has not been found.

Conclusion

The Supreme Court of the United States is unique in the manner in which it often exercises policy-making authority, which on occasion thwarts the purposes of the politically elective branches of the national government. To be sure, the Court has on occasion suffered serious setbacks in its policy-making endeavors.

In the context of an ideal Weberian conception of a judiciary based upon nonpartisan professionalism, the highest appellate judiciary of the United States does not totally fulfill the criteria, nor do any other judiciaries throughout the world. The Founding Fathers quite consciously anticipated a political role for the Court, especially as final arbiter of federalism. They could not have fully anticipated its generally consistent commitment to corporate power. Perhaps the greatest test to be anticipated by the American appellate judiciary is that of reconciling such corporate preference with the more objective requirements of equal justice.

[See also (II) Judiciary, Federal; (III) Federal Court System, Judicial Review, Judicial Selection, Legal Profession and Legal Ethics, State Court Systems.]

CASES

Chisholm v. Georgia, 2 Dallas 419 (1793)
Cohens v. Virginia, 6 Wheaton 264 (1821)
Dred Scott v. Sandford, 19 Howard 393 (1857)
Ex parte McCardle, 7 Wallace 506 (1869)
Marbury v. Madison, 1 Cranch 137 (1803)
Martin v. Hunter's Lessee, 1 Wheaton 304 (1816)
Pollock v. Farmers' Loan and Trust Company, 157 U.S. 429; 158 U.S. 601 (1895)
Roe v. Wade, 410 U.S. 113 (1973)
Stuart v. Laird, 1 Cranch 299 (1803)

BIBLIOGRAPHY

Thurman Wesley Arnold, *Fair Fights and Foul: A Dissenting Lawyer's Life* (1965). Harold J. Berman, *Law and Revolution: The Formation of the Western Legal Tradition* (1983). Testimony of Associate Justice Harry Blackmun, Report of the Commission on the Revision of the Federal Court Appellate System, U.S. Government Printing Office (1973). William O. Douglas, "The Dissent: A Safeguard of Democracy," in *Journal of the American Judicature Society,* 32 (1948) and "Stare Decisis," in *Columbia Law Review,* 49 (1949). Henry J. Friendly, *Federal Jurisdiction: A General View* (1973).

James Kent, *Commentaries on American Law,* 1 (1844). Walter F. Murphy and Joseph Tanenhaus, "Constitutional Courts and Political Representation" in Michael N. Danielson and Walter F. Murphy, eds., *Modern Democracy* (1969). John J. Parker, "The Federal Judiciary," in *American Bar Association Journal,* 24 (1938). C. Herman Pritchett, *The American Constitution* (1977). Guenther Roth and Claus Wittich, eds., *Max Weber: Economy and Society: An Outline of Interpretive Sociology* (1968). Gordon Wood, *The Creation of the American Republic, 1776–1787* (1969).

– JOHN R. SCHMIDHAUSER

JURISDICTION

In its broadest sense, *jurisdiction* refers to the authority by which a court takes cognizance of, and decides, matters brought to its attention. To establish this authority, the court must consider whether it is the proper forum for resolution of the dispute; whether the person who invokes the court's authority is a proper plaintiff; and, if so, whether the court has jurisdiction over the parties, especially the defendant.

Proper Forum

Determination of whether a court is the proper forum for resolution of the matter to be adjudicated depends on whether the court has subject matter, geographical, and hierarchical jurisdiction over the controversy.

SUBJECT JURISDICTION: FEDERAL QUESTIONS. The sources of a court's subject matter jurisdiction are constitutional provisions and statutes enacted pursuant thereto. In the case of the federal courts, Article III of the Constitution specifies the heart of this power, as "all Cases . . . arising under this Constitution, the Laws of the United States, and Treaties." Cases so arising are known as federal questions. To invoke federal question jurisdiction, a party must demonstrate to the court's satisfaction that the case substantially concerns a constitutional provision, an act of Congress (or administrative actions pursuant thereto), or a treaty of the United States.

Article III also gives the federal courts jurisdiction over disputes to which the federal government is party; disputes between states; admiralty and maritime cases; disputes involving foreign diplomatic personnel accredited to the United States; and disputes between residents of different states. For all practical purposes, when the federal government is party to litigation, the case may be considered to arise as a federal question. The other listed subjects either do not occur very frequently (for example, those involving foreign diplomatic personnel, because of diplomatic immunity to suit) or typically involve purely private disputes (such as cases in which a resident of one state sues a resident of another state, and cases involving admiralty and maritime jurisdiction). Suits between states arise infrequently also; they usually concern boundaries, water rights, or financial obligations. Accordingly, cases of national, rather than local, import surface as federal questions. That is not to say that every federal question is of earthshaking proportions but, rather, that nonfederal questions have an effect largely limited to the parties involved in the litigation.

Because the federal courts are empowered by the Constitution to hear only those cases within the judicial power of the United States, they are considered to be courts of limited jurisdiction. As such, subject matter jurisdiction is presumed not to exist. Therefore, the party who seeks access to federal court must affirmatively demonstrate that the court has subject matter jurisdiction. Insofar as federal questions are concerned, this means that the plaintiff must show that a right or immunity "arising under" federal law (Constitution, statute, or treaty) is a basic element in his cause of action and not merely a collateral issue (not involving the merits of the controversy) or introduced as a defense or in response to the defendant's counterclaim. The requirement that the plaintiff's claim show its federal basis stems from the view that if a federal court decided a case not within its jurisdiction, it would necessarily—and unconstitutionally—invade the reserved powers of the states.

If the facts alleging federal jurisdiction are challenged, the burden of proof falls on the party claiming federal jurisdiction.

Two additional results flow from the limited jurisdiction of the federal courts. First, if the facts alleging federal jurisdiction are challenged, the burden of proof falls on the party claiming federal jurisdiction. Second, each and every federal court is obligated to notice a lack of jurisdiction and to dismiss any case on its own motion if either party fails to so move.

SUBJECT JURISDICTION: DIVERSITY OF CITIZENSHIP. Apart from federal questions, the other major source of federal subject matter jurisdiction is diversity of citizenship—controversies between residents of different states or between a resident of a state and an alien. Needless to say, such cases contain no federal questions; rather, they consist of the ordinary, garden-variety litigation that is the staple of the state judicial systems: tort (private injury) actions. The reason for assigning federal courts diversity jurisdiction was the fear that a state court might be biased against the out-of-state litigant. Thus, to protect nonresidents from potential prejudice in the local courts, access to the federal courts is provided if certain conditions are met.

First, the amount in controversy must be more than $10,000, exclusive of interest and costs. This jurisdictional amount is set by Congress and is pegged sufficiently high so that the federal courts will not be inundated with a flood of petty lawsuits. Doubts about the adequacy of the jurisdictional amount redound to the plaintiff's benefit, however. If the sum claimed is made in good faith and if it is not a legal certainty that the plaintiff will not recover more than $10,000, the amount in controversy is met. The amount claimed, rather than the amount recovered, controls. And once the amount claimed is established, subsequent events cannot destroy jurisdiction. When the plaintiff's cause of action does not allege a dollar amount, as in a request for an injunction, the abatement of a nuisance, or specific performance of a contract, the court will determine either the value to the plaintiff of the relief sought or the cost to the defendant if the requested relief is granted.

The major complication regarding jurisdictional amount concerns the aggregation of claims. A plaintiff may aggregate even unrelated claims against a single defendant (such as two $6,000 claims), but the defendant's counterclaims against the plaintiff may not be aggregated to meet the jurisdictional amount. In multiple-party litigation, aggregation is permitted if the plaintiffs or defendants have a joint and common interest in the subject matter of the lawsuit (for example, a $12,000 painting owned by two persons) rather than an individual interest. (An example of the latter is two passengers in an auto accident each with a $6,000 injury; however, if one of the passengers suffers a $12,000 injury and the other a $6,000 one, federal jurisdiction lies only for the former.)

Second, the "citizenship" to which diversity jurisdiction pertains is a party's domicile in a state or status as an alien. If both parties are aliens or if one party is a United States citizen who is not domiciled in a state, the federal courts lack jurisdiction. (A "state," for this purpose, includes the District of Columbia and Puerto Rico.) "Domicile," however, does not mean "residence." A person may have several residences but only one domicile. The latter requires an initial physical presence within the state, plus the intent to remain there, whether temporarily or permanently. Hence, students and military personnel can establish a domicile so long as they have no immediate intention of moving elsewhere. As with the amount in controversy, diversity is established at the time a legal action commences. A person may change domicile in order to create diversity, but once established it cannot be lost because of movement during the course of litigation.

Third, in *Strawbridge* v. *Curtiss* (1806), the Supreme Court ruled that the diversity of parties must be complete. In multiparty lawsuits, therefore, no plaintiff may have the same "citizenship" as a defendant. Complete diversity is not required in class actions. The domicile of the class is that of the named plaintiff (the person who represents the class); the domiciles of the other class members are irrelevant. Neither do interpleader actions require complete diversity. Interpleader is a remedy by which a person (the "stakeholder," typically an insurance company) who admits an obligation but is unsure to whom it is owed deposits the money or property with the court and notifies the claimants that he has done so, thereby washing his hands of the matter. The claimants are required to dispute ownership among themselves. So long as at least two claimants reside in different states, diversity obtains. The amount in controversy in such actions need only be $500. Deviation from the prevailing rules is permitted because of the equitable nature of interpleader.

Federal district courts have subject matter jurisdiction over virtually all cases the federal courts may hear.

To overcome the difficulties that complete diversity posed to corporations, the United States Supreme Court created two remarkable legal fictions. It first asserted, in *The Louisville, Cincinnati & Charleston R. Co.* v. *Letson* (1844), that a corporation was a "citizen" of the state in which it was chartered. It subsequently reversed itself and said that inasmuch as a corporation is an artificial entity it cannot be a citizen, and that the citizenship of its stockholders must control. The Court thereupon irrebuttably presumed that each stockholder is a citizen of the state of incorporation, notwithstanding the patent falsity of the presumption. The Court's reasoning makes Delaware, the home of many major corporations, by far the most populous of the states.

A corporation has dual citizenship if its principal place of business is located in a state other than the one in which it is chartered. Regardless of the breadth of a corporation's activities, it may have only one principal place of business. This may either be corporate headquarters or wherever the bulk of the corporation's activity occurs. Each option has its judicial adherents, and the choice is made generally by that court's precedent. Unincorporated associations (partnerships, labor unions, and the like) do not enjoy the entity fiction. Instead, the domicile of each of its human members controls. As a result, national organizations (for example, the Teamsters Union) cannot avail themselves of diversity jurisdiction, because they have at least one member in every state.

Diversity jurisdiction as a means of access to the federal courts has come under serious attack since the 1960s. Its original justification—to prevent bias against out-of-state litigants—has faded as mobility has weakened parochialism. Increases in the docket of the federal courts, with resulting delay and congestion, have caused many to advocate its limitation, if not outright abolition, as the most expendable aspect of the federal courts' subject matter jurisdiction. The reformist appeal is enhanced by two considerations: diversity concerns disputes that, absent diversity, the state courts regularly resolve; and federal judges, in deciding such controversies, apply state law.

SUBJECT JURISDICTION: ANCILLARY AND PENDENT. The federal courts exercise a third type of subject matter jurisdiction, ancillary and pendent jurisdiction, even though no statute authorizes them to do so. Ancillary jurisdiction enables claims of persons other than the original plaintiff that arise out of the same transaction to be joined together in a single proceeding (for example, the defendant's counterclaim or the interest of a third party in property that is the subject of dispute). Pendent jurisdiction permits a plaintiff to join a state claim to a federal-question claim if both stem from "a common nucleus of operative fact" (*United Mine Workers of America* v. *Gibbs,* 1966). Both ancillary and pendent jurisdiction arise in multiple-claim litigation to permit federal courts to try an entire dispute instead of just the federal portion of it, thereby promoting judicial economy and precluding piecemeal litigation. Invocation of either recognizes the presence of at least one claim sufficient to establish either federal-question or diversity jurisdiction. Both ancillary and pendent jurisdiction lie within the discretion of the presiding judge. Their exercise is appropriate if economy and fairness to the parties will result.

HIERARCHICAL AND GEOGRAPHICAL JURISDICTION. Jurisdiction is defined not only by subject matter but also by geography and hierarchy. The last distinguishes trial courts (courts of first instance) from those that hear appeals. The latter are divided into intermediate appellate courts and courts of last resort. Geographical jurisdiction pertains to the reach of a court's jurisdiction: the state court systems organize themselves along county lines, while the federal courts do so on a state basis. The federal court structure is much simpler and displays less internal diversity than the state systems. The federal district courts, at least one of which is located in every state, are the trial courts of the federal system. They are identified by state and, if the state has more than one, by the geographical region within the state—thus, the District of North Dakota, the Southern District of New York, the Central District of California.

Appeals from the federal district courts are heard by the courts of appeals. The United States is divided into eleven numbered circuits, with an additional circuit having geographical jurisdiction over the District of Columbia. The numbered circuits have jurisdiction over the district courts in specific states. Thus, the First Circuit hears appeals from the district courts in Maine, Massachusetts, New Hampshire, Rhode Island, and Puerto Rico, and the Eleventh Circuit, created by Congress in 1980, reviews those from Alabama, Florida, and Georgia. At the top of the federal hierarchy, with jurisdiction over the whole of the United States, is the Supreme Court.

A marked difference between the federal and state court systems is that federal district courts have subject matter jurisdiction over virtually all cases the federal courts may hear. Major exceptions are monetary claims against the United States, which the Court of Claims hears, and disputes involving customs duties, which the Customs Court decides. State trial courts, by contrast, tend to have specialized subject matter jurisdiction, such as criminal cases or those concerning juveniles. In this sense, then, the federal district courts are describable as courts of general jurisdiction, while most state courts are of limited jurisdiction. Specialized subject matter tends not to exist at appellate levels. Federal exceptions are the Temporary Emergency Court of Appeals, which hears appeals pertaining to price and wage controls, and the Court of Appeals for the Federal Circuit, which includes the Court of Claims and the Court of Customs and Patent Appeals. The most unusual state exceptions are Oklahoma and Texas, each of which has two courts of last resort, one dealing with civil matters and the other with criminal cases.

Limitations on the subject matter jurisdiction of state trial courts are diverse. One court may exclusively try civil cases, while another has exclusive jurisdiction over criminal offenses; other courts may be limited to probate jurisdiction (wills, estates, and juveniles). Some states, such as New York, divide probate among more than one court. Typically, states further divide the subject matter jurisdiction of their courts on the basis of the amount in controversy and the seriousness of criminal charges. Thus, a court of common pleas may be authorized to hear only cases in which the amount in controversy is less than a specified dollar value. Or a small-claims court may have jurisdiction where the amount is less than, say, $600. On the criminal side, one court may try felonies, another misdemeanors, and a third only traffic violations. If the state contains a large city, separate trial courts may have specialized jurisdiction only within municipal boundaries. Elsewhere, the minor trial courts may have jurisdiction only over a municipality or a township, rather than throughout the county.

The foregoing divisions do not exhaust the subject matter limitations that the states impose on their trial courts. On the other hand, no state utilizes all the listed limitations.

Proper Party

Even though a particular court may be the proper forum for the resolution of a dispute, that court's jurisdiction also depends on whether or not the person who invokes the court's decision-making capability is a proper party—in other words, whether the plaintiff deserves access to the court, or whether he or she has standing to sue. Resolution of this matter turns on a number of factors. Insofar as the federal courts are concerned, some criteria are mandated by the Constitution; others are viewed as prudential considerations. Questions about standing to sue rarely arise in the context of private law disputes. In such cases, whether the plaintiff is a proper party tends to be self-evident. This is not so when an interested bystander raises a public law issue, such as the constitutionality of governmental action. Hence, rules governing access primarily concern the federal, rather than the state, courts.

CASE OR CONTROVERSY. Paramount is the case or controversy requirement. The words of Article III of the Constitution limit federal judicial power to cases or controversies. The difference between a "case" and a "controversy" lacks practical importance. The latter is narrower in scope than the former and includes only civil suits. Like the other elements of standing to sue, the case or controversy requirement does not admit of precise definition. It requires a bona fide dispute between two or more persons whose interests conflict. As such, the federal courts have no power to decide hypothetical questions, collusive cases, or questions demanding advisory opinions. These matters are nonjusticiable.

Hypothetical questions typically result when a formerly live controversy becomes moot because of changes affecting a litigant's contentions. Thus, an out-of-court settlement moots further court proceedings. Similarly, a party's challenge to the constitutionality of a law ends with the repeal of the statute. The United States Supreme Court refused to decide the constitutionality of affirmative action programs when the issue first reached it in *DeFunis* v. *Odegaard* (1974) because the student who challenged the practice had been admitted to the educational institution in question and was assured of graduation regardless of any decision the Court might have made. Mootness does not govern criminal convictions as rigorously as other types of proceedings. The release of a convict after sentence has been served does not preclude the possibility of adverse collateral consequences. Rearrest may warrant more severe charges; reconviction may warrant a stiffer sentence. Such possibilities save the case from mootness. On the other hand, a challenge to visitation privileges would not survive the prisoner's release from custody.

The requirement that a plaintiff's dispute remain live throughout the course of litigation is perhaps most problematic in situations "capable of repetition, yet evading review." Here courts apply mootness less rigorously. Thus, short-lived controversies, such as the right of a pregnant woman to an abortion or the right of someone to vote in an election, may be addressed. Class-action suits, in which an individual sues on her own behalf as well as on behalf of all others similarly situated, also minimize the chance of mootness. Even though the status of the named plaintiff changes, the lawsuit continues. Thus, an employer's settlement with the plaintiff in an employment discrimination action, or the graduation of a child or the moving of the family to another district in a school desegregation suit, does not moot a class action.

The rule against advisory opinions (in the absence of lawsuits) to resolve legal issues dates from 1793, when Secretary of State Thomas Jefferson, at President George Washington's request, submitted to the Supreme Court twenty-nine questions of international law. Advisory opinions are considered objectionable not only because they lack liveliness but also because they have an impact on the separation of powers. If the federal courts accepted hypothetical disputes, the hypothesized questions would likely concern presidential conduct and congressional statutes, thereby increasing the potential for conflict between the judiciary and the coordinate branches of government. Nonetheless, a number of states do permit advisory opinions if requested by the governor or the attorney general.

The prohibition of hypothetical questions does not prevent courts from rendering declaratory judgments. These obviate the need for an individual to break a law in order to obtain judicial determination of his rights and duties. Although under the common law such determinations could be had only if a breach occurred, the Supreme Court reasoned that Article III of the Constitution defines and limits judicial power, not the manner in which it is exercised.

Collusive actions fail to meet the case or controversy requirement because the parties lack adversariness. Plaintiff and defendant possess a common interest—hence the labels "friendly suit" and "feigned litigation." The absence of adversariness is not always apparent. A number of landmark Supreme Court decisions appear to have been collusive cases. They commonly manifest themselves as suits by stockholders against their corporations to enjoin payment of taxes or compliance with governmental regulations. Note that the rule against collusive litigation does not necessarily require disagreement between the parties. Courts may enter default judgments and accept guilty and nolo contendere pleas. But where one party controls or finances the litigation, courts deem the case collusive.

LEGAL INJURY. Mere dispute does not establish access to court. A conflict must concern a legal claim—a statutory or constitutional right, or some personal or property interest. That is, a proper plaintiff must demonstrate entitlement to rights prescribed by law. Ordinary commercial competition, for example, undeniably produces economic injury, but no legal injury results therefrom. One looks to legislative enactments, constitutional provisions, and the common law to identify the rights and interests that receive legal protection; and traditionally, protected interests were those on which a dollar value could be placed. Currently, aesthetic, conservational, and recreational interests may also suffice.

The personal injury requirement is judicially created and not constitutionally mandated.

Thus, persons interested in a river's scenic beauty may object to the installation of overhead power lines; an organization to preserve a park may challenge highway construction through it; and conservationists may seek to enjoin the sale of timber from a national forest. If, however, "injury" results from governmental action—as when persons are subsequently found innocent of crimes for which they were convicted, or property values decline because of changes in zoning ordinances—judicial redress may not be available. Neither does the quantum of injury necessarily affect its legal character. Trifles may be legally protected. Under the common law, a single footstep on another's land, an unwanted touching, or the pointing of a gun, respectively, constitute trespass, battery, and assault—notwithstanding that the resulting damage is not discernible.

PERSONAL INJURY. A third element of standing to sue is the requirement that the legal injury complained of be suffered by the plaintiff personally. One may not bring suit solely on behalf of a third party except in the case of a legal guardian or next of kin when the injured person is legally incompetent for one reason or another. This element focuses on the party and not the issue she wishes to litigate. The question, rather, is whether the plaintiff is the proper party to litigate a particular issue, not whether the issue itself is justiciable.

Accordingly, physicians may not sue on behalf of their patients, and persons may not enjoin enforcement of a law where the statute has long existed but no prosecutions have occurred. On the other hand, organizations have been permitted to litigate their members' rights: a parochial school attacked a statute requiring compulsory public education even though the right inhered in the children and their parents; and a school board obtained an injunction prohibiting conduct that interfered with students' civil rights.

The reason for exceptions to the direct personal injury rule is that the constitutional standing requirements do not mandate its application; rather, prudential considerations are allowed to guide adjudication in the federal courts. The rule ought not apply if a substantial relationship exists between the plaintiff and the third parties, if the rights of the third parties would otherwise not be presented, or if their rights risk dilution.

The classic example of rigorous adherence to the personal injury requirement is taxpayer's suits. In the states, taxpayers have used this device to challenge governmental expenditures, bond issues, and special assessments. In the federal courts, by contrast, taxpayers, with one exception, have lacked standing to sue. The rationale is that personal injury requires that the plaintiff suffer in a peculiar and more severe fashion than the public generally, but a federal taxpayer merely suffers in an indefinite way along with millions of others. If the taxpayer can show that the challenged expenditure exceeds specific constitutional limitations on the taxing and spending power, he has standing to sue. Thus, a plaintiff successfully alleged that congressionally appropriated monies disbursed to parochial schools violated the establishment of religion clause of the First Amendment, in *Flast* v. *Cohen* (1968).

The personal injury requirement, as noted, is judicially created and not constitutionally mandated. Consequently, where a dispute is otherwise justiciable, Congress is free to authorize plaintiffs to function as "private attorneys general" who seek to vindicate the public's rights. If Congress is silent or unclear, the federal courts may infer access to private parties desiring to vindicate congressionally established rights. Thus, in *Cannon* v. *University of Chicago* (1979), the Supreme Court granted a plaintiff the right to sue an educational institution for violating a federal statute that prohibits sex discrimination in federally funded programs. The statute itself, Title I of the Education Amendments of 1972, does not expressly authorize a private remedy. Four factors, formulated in *Cort* v. *Ash* (1975), determine if a private remedy should be inferred: (1) whether Congress enacted the law to benefit a special class, one in which plaintiff holds membership; (2) whether evidence exists that Congress intended to create a private remedy; (3) whether such a remedy comports with the statute's purpose; and (4) whether a private remedy is inappropriate because the statute's subject is primarily a state responsibility. Application of this test provides courts with wide discretion.

POLITICAL QUESTIONS. Judges will not decide those questions that they deem more suitable for resolution by legislators or executive officials, calling them political questions. Courts have applied the label to a diverse range of issues; as a result, the only meaningful, though inadequate, definition is that a political question is whatever a court says it is. The label itself is a misnomer. All judicial decisions allocate society's resources, which is what politics is. Nonetheless, the label has utility. The designation of a question as political places a limit on judicial policymaking and suggests that judicial decisions qualitatively differ from those of other governmental officials. Examples of political questions include whether a constitutional amendment was ratified, the legitimacy of two competing state governments, the length of time the United States could rightfully occupy enemy territory, the deportation of an enemy alien whom the attorney general considered dangerous to the public peace and safety, the status of Indian tribes, and the termination of a treaty. One issue that originally was considered a political question but is no longer is legislative districting and apportionment. Beginning with *Baker* v. *Carr* in 1962, the Supreme Court ruled that the matter was justiciable and that private citizens have standing to sue for disparities in the population of state and local legislative districts as well as congressional districts.

Ironically, in this first decision to hold districting and apportionment a justiciable, rather than a political, question, the Supreme Court presented a set of criteria to determine whether a question is political. The list is treated as definitive, even though the criteria contain words and phrases of a markedly murky character: (1) a "textually demonstrable" commitment of the issue to the legislative or executive branch of government; (2) a "lack of judicially discoverable and manageable standards" for its resolution; (3) the need for an initial policy determination of a kind "clearly for nonjudicial discretion"; (4) a judicial resolution that would indicate "lack of the respect due" a coordinate branch of government; (5) an "unusual need" for "unquestioning adherence" to a previously made political decision; (6) the "potentiality of embarrassment" because of "multifarious pronouncements by various departments" on a single issue.

FINALITY OF DECISION. To preserve their coordinate status with the president and Congress, the federal courts refuse to decide controversies if the decision will not be final and binding on the litigants. Except for the Supreme Court's original jurisdiction, the lower federal courts and the Supreme Court receive their jurisdiction as a result of acts of Congress. Congress, however, has not seen fit to give to the courts subject matter jurisdiction over all matters that fall within the constitutionally specified judicial power of the United States. Instead, Congress has authorized various nonjudicial officials and agencies to make the final and binding decision. The classic example concerns the eligibility of a veteran for pension and disability benefits. An eighteenth-century statute vested this power in the secretary of war; today the authority lodges in the Veterans Administration.

The capability of a court to reverse the decision of a lower court does not negate this element of standing; neither does the possibility that the legislature may amend a statute already construed by a court and thereby overturn the court's decision. The same applies to a proposed constitutional amendment. The rule merely requires that, at the time of decision, the court's judgment bind the litigants and not be susceptible to review by bureaucratic or administrative officials.

ESTOPPEL. Peripherally related to the foregoing element of standing is that pertaining to the binding effect of judicial decisions themselves. Res judicata, or claim estoppel, is the assertion that a claim has already been litigated and so cannot be made the subject of a second lawsuit. Similarly, collateral estoppel bars relitigation of an issue in a second trial. Claim and issue preclusion are based on the principle that a litigant should get only one bite of the apple—that once individuals have had their day in court, further proceedings are precluded. The principle serves several purposes: it lessens the courts' burdens; it enables litigants to rely on a court's initial decisions and thereby plan for the future; and it prevents the judicial system from being used as a tool of harassment.

To assert res judicata, a party must show that the same claim or cause of action between the same parties was resolved by a final judgment and that the final judg-

A national corporation, such as Tupperware, with these headquarters in Florida, may have divisions of their business under different jurisdictions around the country. (Nik Wheeler/Corbis)

ment was based on the merits of the controversy. Accordingly, where an initial cause of action was dismissed for want of subject matter jurisdiction, res judicata does not bar relitigation in the proper forum. The interests of judicial economy cause many jurisdictions to define causes of action broadly, thereby requiring a litigant to join all his claims against his opponent. Multiple suits are avoided inasmuch as these "transaction test" jurisdictions effectively define as res judicata claims that should have been litigated in the original proceeding even if they actually were not. Such claims remain unlitigated. The same party requirement of res judicata encompasses those who are in privity with an original litigant (for example, agency and employment relationships, as well as successors in interest). In short, res judicata binds persons whose interests are so wedded to those of an existing party that it would waste judicial time to allow a second action merely because they were not named in the initial suit.

Invocation of collateral estoppel requires showing that the identical issue was actually decided in an earlier proceeding and that deciding it was necessary to resolve the original dispute. Whether identity of issue obtains and whether it was a decided issue pose far less difficulty than a determination that the issue was necessary to the original proceeding. Because due process of law prevents use of collateral estoppel against non-parties who were given no opportunity to be heard, nonparties may be allowed to assert it. Historically, the doctrine of mutuality prevented its assertion—that collateral estoppel applied only where the parties to the second action had both been parties to the first suit. But today many jurisdictions disregard mutuality to varying degrees.

Consider an auto accident in which three passengers were injured. Passenger A establishes the driver's liability. If the jurisdiction allows collateral estoppel to be asserted offensively, passengers B and C may move for summary judgment on the issue of the driver's liability. Conversely, nonmutual defensive collateral estoppel occurs when a defendant seeks to prevent a plaintiff from relitigating an issue plaintiff previously lost against another defendant. To determine whether a previous nonparty may assert collateral estoppel against a party, courts focus on whether the party had a full and fair opportunity to litigate the issue in the first action. Increasingly, courts are tending to apply collateral estoppel only where the subsequent action was reasonably foreseeable at the time of the initial adjudication. If so, estoppel applies; if not, it does not.

EXHAUSTION OF ADMINISTRATIVE REMEDIES. In order to avoid encroaching on alternative methods of dispute resolution, courts typically require plaintiffs to exhaust any administrative remedies that the law affords. Accordingly, a plaintiff charging unfair labor practices must exhaust the remedies provided by the National Labor Relations Board, and a federal taxpayer challenging the amount of taxes owed must initially utilize the procedures provided by the Internal Revenue Service. Only thereafter will a federal court entertain the cases. Exceptions to exhaustion exist: when an agency acts ultra vires (beyond the scope of its authority); when an agency's action will produce irreparable injury; when an agency behaves in a deliberately dilatory manner; or when pursuit of an administrative remedy is obviously futile. The plaintiff bears the burden of proving an exception. Courts regularly require exhaustion when the question presented clearly falls within the agency's expertise and when the remedy sought is as likely as judicial action to provide the wanted relief.

In summary, the elements of standing—the determination of whether the litigants are proper parties—effectively limit the types of controversies courts will hear, in order that judges may avoid hypothetical, officious, and redundant questions and unnecessary conflicts with other policymakers. The rules governing standing also provide judges with a tactical flexibility that enables them to avoid issues they prefer not to resolve and to cite good legal form as their justification for doing so.

Conflicts of Law

The constitutionally prescribed division of power between the national government and the states, which made the United States a federal system, is a primary source of legal conflict. Such conflicts concern federal-state relationships and interstate relationships. Conflicts between the state and federal courts result because of overlapping, or concurrent, jurisdiction. For example, a question that is within the subject matter jurisdiction of the federal courts will frequently arise in the course of state court proceedings. Thus, a person accused of violating state law is tried without representation by counsel or is convicted as a result of illegally seized evidence; or a state law allegedly abridges First Amendment freedoms or unconstitutionally dispossesses a person of her property. Interstate conflicts occur because individuals and corporations do not limit their activities to the confines of a single state. State courts, however, traditionally reached only those persons and things within their geographical jurisdiction. How, then, could a state bring to the bar of its justice nonresidents? Is a victim denied judicial remedy in his own state courts because his injuries result from the negligence of an out-of-state business?

NATIONAL SUPREMACY. The Constitution, in the supremacy clause of Article VI, unequivocably establishes federal law as supreme over that of the states and requires that state court judges give effect to federal law, "any thing in the Constitution or laws of any State to the contrary notwithstanding." To make this language operative, Congress, in the Judiciary Act of 1789, gave the Supreme Court jurisdiction to review state court decisions that involved a federal question. Supreme Court review was not triggered until the litigant pleading the federal question had exhausted all avenues of appeal open to him in the state court system—typically a final judgment rendered by the state supreme court. This jurisdictional grant did not settle matters. The state courts were markedly involved in deciding federal questions because Congress did not see fit to give the federal district courts first-instance jurisdiction over federal questions until after the Civil War. Only state courts could try these controversies.

Courts typically require plaintiffs to exhaust any administrative remedies that the law affords.

To ensure the supremacy of federal law, it was especially important that the Supreme Court have jurisdiction to review state court decisions. State court judges, however, maintained that inasmuch as they were bound by the supremacy clause of the Constitution, they, as well as the Supreme Court, had the right to ultimately decide federal questions. In a landmark decision, *Martin* v. *Hunter's Lessee* (1816), which was aptly described as "the keystone of the whole arch of federal judicial power," the Supreme Court rejected the states' argument and affirmed its own power to review and authoritatively resolve federal questions.

Several results flow from *Martin* v. *Hunter's Lessee* and the facts from which it arose. First, the major link between the state and federal judiciaries is that which connects the courts at the top of each hierarchy. Second, absent this link, each state's supreme court would have been left to decide for itself the meaning of constitutional provisions, acts of Congress, and treaties of the United States. And if that were the situation, the United States would be no more united than the United Nations. Each state would long since have become a separate, sovereign entity—a nation. The meanings of due process, interstate commerce, and the First Amendment would vary from one state to another, with the likely result that any given constitutional guarantee or statutory provision would have fifty different meanings, depending on the state. Third, the link that the Judiciary Act provides is, for all practical purposes, the only glue that effectively unites the states as governmental entities. Congress provided this link, and what Congress gives, Congress may take away. Indeed, until a decade or two after the Civil War, bills to do just that were introduced on at least ten separate occasions.

COMITY AND THE ABSTENTION DOCTRINE. Mindful of the tender sensibilities of the states and their judges (which sensibilities are markedly less than those of pre-Civil War states' righters), the Supreme Court has devised a system of comity to minimize conflict between the state and federal courts. The most popular description of comity dates from a 1971 Supreme Court decision, *Younger* v. *Harris:*

> a proper respect for state functions, a recognition of the fact that the entire country is made up of a Union of separate state governments, and a continuance of the belief that the National Government will fare best if the States and their institutions are left free to perform their separate functions in their separate ways. . . . The concept does not mean blind deference to "States' Rights" any more than it means centralization of control over every important issue in our National Government and its courts. . . . What the concept does represent is a system in which there is sensitivity to the legitimate interests of both State and National Governments, and in which the National Government, anxious though it may be to vindicate and protect federal rights and federal interests, always endeavors to do so in ways that will not unduly interfere with the legitimate activities of the States.

The major instrument for effectuating comity is the abstention doctrine, formulated in a 1941 decision, *Railroad Commission of Texas* v. *Pullman Co.,* "whereby the federal courts, 'exercising a wise discretion,' restrain their authority because of 'scrupulous regard for the rightful independence of the state governments' and for the smooth working of the federal judiciary." Abstention thus requires the federal courts to avoid intruding themselves into ongoing state court proceedings or otherwise duplicating litigation previously commenced in a state's courts. Accordingly, litigants must exhaust state remedies, administrative as well as judicial, before gaining access to the federal courts. This gives the courts of each state priority in determining the constitutionality of their state's statutes and regulations and may obviate the need for federal court involvement if a state court's resolution of the federal question is compatible with federal law. On the other hand, abstention precludes prompt federal court protection of federal rights.

Occasioning federal-state judicial conflict has been the expansion of the subject matter jurisdiction of the federal courts to encompass virtually all federal questions and the increased authority of the federal district courts to enjoin state court proceedings, to issue writs of habeas corpus, and to remove cases from the state to the federal courts. Inasmuch as the abstention doctrine does not flatly require federal courts to stay their hands in all circumstances, the Supreme Court has formulated additional criteria for specific forms of federal relief.

Injunctions to stop criminal prosecutions will be granted only on a showing of "great and immediate" danger of "irreparable injury." The same difficult-to-meet standard applies to efforts to enjoin state civil proceedings. As a result, injunctions are largely limited to bad-faith prosecutions or official harassment.

Writs of habeas corpus will be granted to state prisoners by a federal district court only if they "seasonably" (that is, contemporaneously) raised their federal question at the appropriate stage of state judicial proceedings and, in addition, the state court failed to provide "an opportunity for full and fair litigation" of the federal claim. Although the quoted test is applied in the context of violations of the search-and-seizure clause of the Fourth Amendment, most habeas petitions are based thereon. Neither would it be surprising if the Court, as cases arose, extended its "full and fair litigation" standard across the full range of federal questions.

The statutory provision permitting removal of cases from the state to a federal district court that bears most directly on the system of comity concerns state denial or refusal to enforce federally protected civil rights. The Supreme Court has construed such rights extremely narrowly: the federal rights must be expressly specified, and they must grant freedom not only to engage in the protected conduct but also freedom from state arrest and prosecution. The Supreme Court has imposed an additional limitation that applies to at least one civil right—namely, removal only for violent interference with the exercise of the specified right, not merely freedom from arrest and prosecution (*Soliusou* v. *Mississippi,* 1975).

As the foregoing discussion suggests, the abstention doctrine applies most forcefully when state judicial proceedings have commenced and when one of the parties is the state itself. If the former condition is absent, no duplication of proceedings occurs; in such a situation, according to the Court, "principles of federalism not only do not preclude federal intervention, they compel it." If the latter condition is absent, the dispute concerns private persons and, as a result, removal of the case from state to federal court may be appropriate. In such cases, federal law permits defendants to remove if the controversy is one that could have been brought in federal court originally. This precludes removal when the defendant relies on federal law as a defense to plaintiff's nonfederal action. Federal-question jurisdiction extends only to plaintiff's claims. The major limitation on removal prohibits such in diversity-of-citizenship cases if any defendant is a resident of the state in which the action was brought. A minor limitation prohibits removal in certain classes of tort (private injury) actions where Congress wishes to give the plaintiff an unrestricted choice of forum.

SOVEREIGN IMMUNITY. Although Article III of the Constitution provides the Supreme Court with original jurisdiction in suits between states, the Eleventh Amendment immunizes the states from suit in federal court brought by nonresidents. The amendment, ratified in 1798 in reaction to the Supreme Court decision *Chisholm* v. *Georgia* (1793) that held that federal jurisdiction extended to such suits, lessens federal-state conflicts by denying federal-court access to those who would sue a state for damages. Even prior to the Eleventh Amendment, federal jurisdiction did not extend to suits against a state brought by its own residents. A state may waive its immunity from suit, either expressly or by implication. Waiver, however, is not required where one state sues another, but a foreign nation may not sue a state without its consent. Of course, sovereign immunity does not prevent any person—resident or not—from appealing an adverse state court decision in a suit that the state itself commenced.

Supreme Court decisions have narrowly construed the Eleventh Amendment. Immunity applies only to the states as states; it does not apply to state officials or to local governments. In general, only suits seeking to recover money from the state treasury are barred. Finally, the last section of the Fourteenth Amendment, which gives Congress the power to enforce the amendment's provisions (most especially, the rights of persons not to be deprived of due process or denied equal protection), overrides the Eleventh Amendment. Congress, therefore, may authorize the federal courts to entertain damage suits brought by persons whose civil rights a state has abridged.

ENFORCEMENT OF JUDGMENTS. The full faith and credit clause of Article IV of the Constitution requires each state to give to the judgments of any other state's courts the same effect that those judgments would have in the states which rendered them. As such, full faith and credit also causes the courts of one state to give the decisions of other states' courts at least as much res judicata effect as they would have in the rendering state. Although the full faith and credit clause binds only the states, federal law requires the federal courts to enforce state court judgments. If a federal court makes the initial decision, res judicata decrees that the state court, in turn, enforce the federal decision.

The utility of the foregoing is obvious. If losing litigants could avoid liability merely by moving out of state, unity and good interstate relations would be lost. As it is, where a litigant has won a judgment that is unenforceable because the defendant has removed his property from the state whose court rendered judgment, said litigant may commence suit in a state wherein defendant does have property. Upon proof of the original judgment, the second state's court must enter an identical judgment on the basis of which the plaintiff may attach or levy on defendant's property. The second court may not reexamine the merits of the original judgment, even if that judgment misinterpreted a law of the second state.

Assume, for example, that state A construes B's laws (as applicable to the case) to permit enforcement of antenuptial contracts or imposition of strict liability in certain circumstances. In a proceeding in B's courts to enforce the wrongfully awarded damages, B's judges have no option but to grant full faith and credit to A's decision. The only exception to automatic enforcement permits B to examine A's jurisdiction over the person or property of the defendant. If such jurisdiction is lacking or has not been waived, B may refuse to enforce A's judgment.

The use of full faith and credit to establish a claim as res judicata benefits the defendant, rather than the plaintiff, in the initial lawsuit in trial court. Assume, for example, that state A renders a judgment that, by its laws, may not be relitigated. The original plaintiff then seeks to avail himself of the laws of B that permit relitigation of the claim in question. State B may not apply its law; rather, it must give A's decision the res judicata effect it would have had if plaintiff had brought a second suit in state A.

CHOICE OF LAW. In cases in which federal and state law conflict, the Constitution mandates that preference be accorded to federal law. In cases in which no controlling federal law exists—typically, diversity-of-citizenship cases—Congress has, since 1789, required the federal courts to apply the "laws of the several states." Does this phrase apply only to constitutional provisions and legislation, or does it extend to the "common law" of a state (that is, that made by judges)? Before the twentieth century, legislatures enacted few laws. Then, as now, constitutions only outlined the scope of governmental power and, in actuality, paid more attention to limitations on government rather than the exercise of power.

Consequently, if the "laws of the several states" meant only constitutions and statutes, the federal courts would need to fashion their own common law to resolve disputes based on diversity jurisdiction. The Supreme Court so held in the definitive nineteenth-century decision *Swift* v. *Tyson* (1842). Nearly a century, later, in *Erie R. Co.* v. *Tompkins* (1938), the Court overruled *Swift* and held that the refusal of federal courts, sitting in diversity, to follow state common law occasioned an unconstitutional assumption of power. Nothing in the Constitution confers on either Congress or the federal courts the power to formulate and apply to the states substantive common law rules. Rather, this power is reserved to the states under the Tenth Amendment.

The practical effect of the *Erie* decision terminated the bias in favor of out-of-state litigants. Previously, rights varied according to whether relief was sought in state or federal courts. The selection of the court to resolve the dispute was made by the nonresident. He, consequently, would "forum shop" for the court most favorable to himself. *Erie,* however, required federal courts to apply the law—written, as well as judge-made—of the state in which the federal court sat, "except in matters governed by the Federal Constitution or by acts of Congress."

One matter so governed is the authority of Congress to prescribe rules of procedure for the federal courts. In 1934, Congress enacted an "Enabling Act" that delegated to the Supreme Court such power so long as the resulting rules did not "abridge, enlarge, or modify the substantive rights of any litigant." Four months prior to the *Erie* decision, the Court adopted the Federal Rules of Civil Procedure, which provided a uniform system of procedure for the federal courts. These took effect in September 1938, less than five months after *Erie.* The problem, of course, is that rules are never neutral and, as a result, invariably affect "substantive" rights.

Mindful of "the twin aims of the Erie rule, discouragement of forum-shopping and avoidance of inequitable administration of the laws," the Court, in a series of decisions, has provided guidance for the resolution of problems that the federal courts exercising diversity jurisdiction faced in the aftermath of *Erie:* (1) Federal courts are to apply the "substantive" law of the state in which they sit and federal "procedural" rules. (2) A rule is "substantive" if it is "outcome determinative"—for example, a state statute of limitations shorter than that provided by federal law, or a law barring an out-of-state corporation the right to bring a lawsuit because it had failed to comply with the state's corporation law. (3) If, however, the issue is covered by the Federal Rules of Civil Procedure, the matter is considered procedural and the federal rule applies. To date, none of the Federal Rules have been held to violate the "substantive" language of the 1934 legislation that authorized the enactment of the Federal Rules. Hence, if the Federal Rules address a matter, that matter is by definition procedural, notwithstanding the fact that it may completely frustrate the state's substantive concerns and determine the outcome of the litigation. (4) If a matter is not covered by the Federal Rules but nonetheless affects an important federal interest, the matter is to be treated as procedural, notwithstanding its outcome-determinative character. For example, the federal interest in disposing of complicated multiparty litigation in a single trial overrides a state law that prohibits suits against out-of-state corporations by nonresidents, and the "very strong federal policy" supporting jury determination subordinates a state law requiring a judge rather than a jury to determine certain factual matters pertaining to employment relationships.

Injunctions to stop criminal proceedings are granted only on a showing of "great and immediate" danger of "irreparable injury."

Although the federal courts since *Erie* have shown sensitivity to considerations of federalism in their choice of law, no set of rules can provide clear-cut guidance. Whereas state court judges confronted by a conflict between state and federal law have no choice but to follow federal law as the supremacy clause of the Constitution requires, federal judges must attempt to weigh and balance the interests of both state and nation.

Jurisdiction Over Parties

The ability of a court to render a binding, enforceable judgment in a lawsuit depends on the court's jurisdiction over the specific parties to the litigation or the property at stake. By bringing a lawsuit, the plaintiff submits himself to the court's jurisdiction. Not so the defendant. To exercise jurisdiction over a defendant's person or property, a court must meet the requirements of due process of law. Defendants are clearly entitled to notice and hearing, but those alone do not suffice. The court must also have the power to act on the defendant or his property. Whether such power exists depends on whether there have been sufficient "minimum contacts" with the forum state. Individuals having substantial contacts with the forum state subject themselves to "general" personal jurisdiction; a binding judgment may be entered against them on any claim. "Limited" personal jurisdiction, by comparison, permits binding judgments only on claims arising out of the specific minimal contacts or relationships that the defendant has with the forum state.

MINIMUM CONTACTS. If a person is domiciled or resides in the forum state, minimum contacts and general personal jurisdiction may be presumed, the rationale being that a state which affords protection to a person and his property may exact reciprocal duties. Persons may also consent to jurisdiction and thereby establish minimum contacts, either expressly or by implication. A plaintiff, for example, by initiating suit, subjects himself to a possible counterclaim brought by the original defendant. Jurisdiction attaches even though the plaintiff dismisses his action or fails to prosecute it. Persons may expressly subject themselves to the jurisdiction of a particular court even before a controversy has arisen. Thus, individuals may agree that the terms of their contract may be enforced against them only in the courts of the other party's state of domicile, and they may, in addition, even waive their rights to notice and hearing.

Obviously, application of the minimum-contacts test is much more crucial when the defendant is an unconsenting nonresident. If the defendant is within the state's boundaries, limited personal jurisdiction applies to the defendant's "contacts." Persons whose contacts involve transacting business may be sued in connection therewith; thus, motorists may be sued for the accidents they cause, and corporations, for injuries their products produce. But if the unconsenting nonresident is outside the state, jurisdiction does not attach unless, as a threshold matter, the forum state has a "long-arm statute" authorizing its courts to assert extraterritorial jurisdiction.

Long-arm statutes are of two types. One type lists in detail the kinds of intrastate activity that permits assertion of extraterritorial jurisdiction. Every state, for example, authorizes jurisdiction over nonresident motorists who cause accidents within the state. Other common acts include contracting to provide goods or services, owning land, and out-of-state acts that produce injuries within the state. The other type of long-arm statute avoids a detailed listing and grants to the state courts jurisdiction over the defendant whenever he has the necessary minimum contacts. The undefined language of the latter type allows the state to stretch its jurisdiction to the limits allowed by due process. As such, that type is readily applicable to an increasingly mobile society and its expanded business and commercial activities. On the other hand, its vagueness invites defendants to challenge the constitutionality of its reach as applied to them.

Application of the minimum-contacts test involves certain considerations: whether the defendant has minimum contacts with the forum state sufficient to ensure that maintenance of the lawsuit does not offend "traditional notions" of "fair play" and "substantial justice"; whether defendant's contacts with the forum state were voluntary; and whether defendant benefited by his contacts with the forum state. The foregoing considerations, needless to say, do not admit of precise application. They are, at best, rough guidelines.

Although the minimum-contacts test was formulated in a case involving personal jurisdiction over an out-of-state corporation, *International Shoe Co.* v. *State of Washington, Etc.* (1945), it applies to individuals as well. Inasmuch as it was established in reaction to the nineteenth-century test that virtually limited jurisdiction to personal presence within the forum state, it presumably governs defendants who were temporarily in the state when served with notice of the pending lawsuit. In addition to personal jurisdiction over individuals and corporations (that is, in personam), the minimum-contacts test also applies to jurisdiction over property (in rem).

JUDGMENTS IN PERSONAM. The policy-oriented character of the minimum-contacts test allows courts to exercise considerable discretion in determining whether in personam jurisdiction exists. Nonetheless, certain general considerations apply. If an individual or corporation regularly and voluntarily enters the state for beneficial purposes and if the cause of action also arose within the state, jurisdiction exists. Defendant's contacts exceed a minimal level; the court will be convenient as the witnesses, evidence, and applicable law are at hand. If entry is irregular, voluntary, and without particular benefit but the cause of action occurred within the state, jurisdiction likely lies, as when a traveler passing through a state in order to get to a destination in another state causes an accident in the interim state. Where defendant has more than minimum contacts with a state the specific cause of action need not be forum-related, as when a California-licensed trucker who hauls $400,000 worth of cargo into California during twenty trips per year, while en route to California, kills a California resident in Nevada. However, if defendant's activities are sporadic, then the cause of action likely needs to have occurred within the forum state.

Perhaps the outer limit of minimum contacts was reached in a case involving a life insurance policy written by a Texas company that apparently neither solicited nor did any other business in the forum state. The insurer refused to pay, claiming that the insured's death was a suicide. The insured, his beneficiary, and all witnesses resided in the forum state. The Supreme Court held that entering into this contract was sufficient to establish jurisdiction because of the state's interest "in providing effective means of redress for its citizens when insurers refuse to pay claims." Fairness to the insurer was subordinated.

To exercise jurisdiction over a defendant, a court must meet the requirements of due process of law.

Where, however, the cause of action occurred outside the forum state, fairness to the defendant receives heavier, and perhaps controlling, weight. In any event, minimum contacts between the defendant and the state must have existed. A court's convenient location or the fact that it may be the "center of gravity" of a particular controversy does not establish jurisdiction. However minimal the burden of defending in an out-of-state tribunal, "territorial limitations on the power of the respective states" preclude requiring a defendant to do so unless the requisite contacts exist.

Other considerations being equal, minimum contacts are more difficult to establish when the cause of action concerns a contract dispute rather than a tort action. In the latter situation, state interest in public safety, health, or welfare may tip the jurisdictional balance in favor of its own courts. Witnesses and evidence may not be easily moved to an out-of-state court. In contract actions, however, the defendant's contacts with the forum state may have been involuntary—for example, when a buyer must enter the state to purchase goods, or when the plaintiff is a major corporation and thus has ready access to a convenient out-of-state forum and the defendant is an individual who would be unfairly burdened traveling to the forum state.

Nonetheless, application of the minimum-contacts test remains problematic even where torts are concerned. Consider an Ohio company that made valves which it sold to another company who incorporated them into boilers. Plaintiff purchased a boiler that exploded in Illinois. Illinois' courts had jurisdiction over the valve maker on the basis that the tort was committed when the damage occurred rather than when the product was manufactured. Similarly, an Indiana company manufactured golf carts that it sold to another Indiana company. The latter sold a defective one to an Illinois country club. The manufacturer was held subject to Illinois' jurisdiction, notwithstanding the absence of any other contacts, so long as the plaintiff could show that defendant intended to use interstate channels of commerce and that defendant could reasonably have foreseen entry of golf carts into states other than that of manufacture.

From a policy standpoint, the main concern has been the use of minimum contacts to establish jurisdiction based on a single out-of-state tort with in-state consequences, even though the consequences were foreseeable. If, for example, a retailer or other small business can be forced to defend in a distant state's courts for injuries occurring therein, availability to suit would travel with every item sold. As a result, sellers might refuse to do business with nonresidents, thereby deterring interstate commercial activity. The Supreme Court allayed such fears in *World-Wide Volkswagen Corp.* v. *Woodson* (1980). New York residents who had purchased an automobile from a New York dealer brought a product-liability action in Oklahoma against the dealer and his New York distributor for injuries suffered in an accident in Oklahoma. The Court held that the defendants' only contact with Oklahoma was "the fortuitous circumstance that a single . . . automobile, sold in New York to New York residents, happened to suffer an accident while passing through Oklahoma." Defendants closed no sales and performed no services in Oklahoma; they solicited no business there either through salespersons or media; neither did they avail themselves of the benefits of Oklahoma law, nor did they regularly sell or seek to serve, directly or indirectly, the Oklahoma market. The record therefore displayed "a total absence of those affiliating circumstances that are a necessary predicate to any exercise of state-court jurisdiction." And while foreseeability is not wholly irrelevant, the foreseeability "critical to due process analysis is not the mere likelihood that a product will find its way into the forum State. Rather, it is that the defendant's conduct and connection with the forum State are such that he should reasonably anticipate being haled into court there."

Insofar as the federal courts are concerned, their in personam jurisdiction is limited to the state in which they sit and anyplace else that that state's law permits. Congress, of course, could enact legislation governing the assertion of personal jurisdiction, but for the most part Congress has not done so. Major exceptions include suits brought under the federal antitrust and securities laws, and interpleader actions. The latter gives the district courts jurisdiction over claimants to the funds in the stakeholder's possession regardless of where they are in the United States. Causes of action involving joinder of parties other than the original plaintiff and defendant extend jurisdiction 100 miles from the federal courthouse.

JUDGMENTS IN REM AND QUASI IN REM. It happens, particularly where real estate is involved, that a lawsuit does not impose personal liability on anyone but, rather, seeks to litigate the interests of persons in a specific thing (the res). On the theory that a state's "sovereignty" gives it power over all property within its borders, its courts could therefore render valid and enforceable judgments concerning ownership and title to instate property. The same rationale applied to the status of persons domiciled within a state. Accordingly, a state's courts could issue binding decrees concerning such matters as marital status or the custody of children. The status is considered the res, and domiciliaries may commence in rem actions to alter their status, as in divorce.

Jurisdictional questions rarely arise for in rem actions. If it is established that the property is within the state or that the person seeking a change in status is domiciled therein, the state's courts may proceed. Although the minimum-contacts standard applies, it is typically met because the property or status is voluntarily acquired and protected by the state. Insofar as the federal courts are concerned, federal law allows the district courts to reach defendants nationwide "to enforce any lien upon or claim to, or to remove any incumbrance or lien or cloud upon the title to, real or personal property within the district" (28 U.S.C. 1655).

Considerably greater difficulty attends the exercise of *quasi in rem* jurisdiction. In such actions, defendant's property within the state is seized as a vehicle to adjudicate personal rights that are unrelated to the seized property; in other words, because jurisdiction over the defendant's person cannot be had, his property is attached instead, not as the subject of litigation but rather as a means of satisfying a possible judgment or establishing jurisdiction. A typical example concerns a nonresident's indebtedness to someone, here called A. A sues debtor in state X, which has no relationship with the debt and in which the debtor has no contacts, minimum or otherwise. Debtor, however, does own property in state X. To establish jurisdiction in the courts of X, A attaches debtor's property therein. If A wins his suit to collect on the debt, the attached property constitutes payment.

Quasi in rem jurisdiction, which typically involves money damages, may be viewed as a halfway house between in rem and in personam jurisdiction: it is in rem in the sense that the court can adjudicate the case only because the defendant has in-state property and in personam in the sense that the dispute really concerns a personal dispute between the plaintiff and defendant, not title to the attached property.

The Federal Rules allow federal district courts to exercise *quasi in rem* jurisdiction compatibly with the law of the state in which the court sits. Hence, if the state's long-arm statute reaches the defendant, so also may the district court. Of course, federal courts, no less than those of the states, must meet the minimum-contacts standard to perfect jurisdiction.

Quasi in rem proceedings have unusual features. First, if the plaintiff wins, his judgment may be satisfied only out of the attached property. If, for example, defendant has a $10,000 obligation to the plaintiff but the value of the attached property is only $5,000, a new action must be brought and litigated on its merits for plaintiff to recover further—even if other unattached property exists within the forum state. Second, *quasi in rem* judgments have no res judicata effect. If plaintiff wins in one state, he may not use that judgment to escape having to litigate his claim in a second state. Similarly, if the defendant wins, she cannot use that result to bar plaintiff from initiating a new action elsewhere. Furthermore, judicial actions without res judicata effects are not enforceable by way of the full faith and credit clause except insofar as the specifically attached property is concerned. Third, if a defendant to *quasi in rem* action appears in court, he subjects himself to in personam jurisdiction and, if the plaintiff wins, the court may enter a binding judgment with res judicata effect for the full amount claimed rather than just for the value of the attached property.

The in personam jurisdiction of a federal court is limited to the state in which it sits and anyplace else the state's law permits.

To alleviate defendant's dilemma about appearing, a number of states authorize defendants to make a limited appearance. This enables defendants to contest cases on their merits but limits liability to the property attached by the court. Alternatively, some states permit defendants to make a special appearance. This allows a defendant to object to the court's jurisdiction over either his person or his property without subjecting himself to the exercise of the jurisdiction to which he objects. With regard to limited appearances, a federal court follows the law of the state in which it sits. In place of a special appearance, the Federal Rules of Civil Procedure allows a defendant to move to dismiss for lack of jurisdiction. The making of such a motion does not subject the mover to the jurisdiction he is protesting.

So long as *quasi in rem* jurisdiction was limited to real property, controversy surrounding its exercise remained limited. But with its twentieth-century extension to movable property, intangibles, and contingent obligations, quarreling intensified. Legal fictions and presumptions divorced from reality were created to identify the location of certain kinds of property: bank deposits were deemed to be located in the bank where they were made; stock where the stock certificates were held; and debts wherever the debtor happened to be. These developments, plus the alleged unfairness of *quasi in rem* jurisdiction to many defendants, have caused the Supreme Court to revamp it in recent years.

In a major decision, *Shaffer* v. *Heitner* (1977), the Court initially applied the minimum-contacts test to *quasi in rem* jurisdiction. A stockholder sued a corporation's nonresident officers and directors in Delaware, the state of incorporation. None of the activities complained of had occurred in Delaware; neither did any of the defendants have other contacts with the state. The corporation itself was headquartered in Arizona and conducted most of its activities there. The plaintiff gained jurisdiction via a statute which provided that the stock of any Delaware corporation could be attached because its stock was irrebuttably presumed to be located within the state. More than $1 million worth of stock was thereby attached. Because Delaware does not allow limited appearances, the defendants confronted a Hobson's choice: fail to defend and forfeit their stock, or defend and subject themselves to unlimited personal liability.

In its opinion, the Court focused on reality, not fiction, and ruled that all judicial action concerning "things" actually adjudicates the rights and interests of people; nowhere is that truer than in *quasi in rem* proceedings where the "thing" is merely a means to get at people. The fact that liability is limited is irrelevant. "Fairness . . . does not depend on the size of the claim." The Court concluded that "if a direct assertion of personal jurisdiction . . . violate[s] the Constitution . . . an indirect assertion . . . should be equally impermissible." Therefore, all assertions of state-court jurisdiction must meet the minimum-contacts standard. The Court also rejected various arguments supporting *quasi in rem* jurisdiction, most important, the contention that defendants ought not be able to avoid their obligations by placing their assets in states where minimum contacts preclude suit. Such attempts, the Court noted, may be countered by suing defendants in their domicile state—regardless of the presence of assets—or where minimum contacts do exist, securing a judgment, and enforcing it under the provisions of full faith and credit.

As for the application of minimum contacts in a *quasi in rem* context, the Supreme Court in *Rush* v. *Savchuk*

(1980) again ignored legal fictions and emphasized a focus on fairness. *Savchuk* concerned an Indiana resident who injured another resident in an Indiana auto accident. Indiana law barred the injured party's claim. The claimant then domiciled himself in Minnesota and brought suit in a Minnesota court, claiming that *quasi in rem* jurisdiction attached because of an insurance policy issued to the defendant in Indiana by a company doing business in Minnesota, as well as the other forty-nine states. Plaintiff alleged that insurance companies are obliged to defend their policyholders (here the defendant), that such obligations are debts, and that debts may be garnisheed. The Court, however, held that the only link Minnesota's courts had to the suit was the business done by the insurer in Minnesota. The assignment of a site to the insurance company's "debt" is a legal fiction, as is the view that a corporation is present, for jurisdictional purposes, wherever it does business. Combining these two fictions makes the debt present in all fifty states, and "it is apparent that such a 'contact' can have no jurisdictional significance" under the minimum-contacts test. Furthermore, defendant's contacts may not be aggregated together. Minimum contacts "must be met as to each defendant over whom a state court exercises jurisdiction." As a result of *Savchuk,* jurisdiction over conditional obligations resulting from indebtedness shrank substantially.

On the basis of *Shaffer* and *Savchuk* one might conclude that *quasi in rem* jurisdiction has lost all utility and become merged with in personam jurisdiction. Because *quasi in rem* actions must meet minimum contacts, they will not do anything for plaintiffs that in personam jurisdiction cannot do better. This argument, however, overlooks two considerations. First, in personam jurisdiction requires a long-arm statute, in addition to minimum contacts, for the assertion of extraterritorial jurisdiction. In those states whose long-arm statutes do not go to the limits of due process, a statute authorizing attachment of in-state property may permit *quasi in rem* action. Second, courts may view minimum contacts as a sliding scale whose requirements vary depending on the protections each type of proceeding—in personam, in rem, and *quasi in rem*—provides out-of-state defendants.

[See also (I) Oversight; (III) Federal Court System, Judicial Review, State Court Systems, Supreme Court of the United States.]

CASES

Baker v. Carr, 369 U.S. 186 (1962)
Burger King Corp. v. Rudzewicz, 85 LEd2d 528 (1985)
Cannon v. University of Chicago, 44 U.S. 677 (1979)
Chisholm v. Georgia, 2 Dall. 419 (1793)
Cort v. Ash, 422 U.S. 66 (1975)
DeFunis v. Odegaard, 416 U.S. 312 (1974)
Erie R. Co. v. Tompkins, 304 U.S. 64 (1938)
Flast v. Cohen, 392 U.S. 83 (1968)
Hanna v. Plumer, 380 U.S. 460 (1965)
Hanson v. Denckla, 357 U.S. 235 (1958)
International Shoe Co. v. State of Washington, Etc., 326 U.S. 310 (1945)
Louisville & Nashville R. Co. v. Mottley, 211 U.S. 149 (1908)
The Louisville, Cincinnati & Charleston R. Co. v. Letson, 2 Howard 497 (1844)
Marshall v. The Baltimore & Ohio R. Co., 16 Howard 314 (1853)
Martin v. Hunter's Lessee, 1 Wheaton 304 (1816)
Railroad Commission of Texas v. Pullman Co., 312 U.S. 496 (1941)
Rush v. Savchuk, 444 U.S. 320 (1980)
Shaffer v. Heitner, 433 U.S. 186 (1977)
Soliusou v. Mississippi, 421 U.S. 213 (1975)
Stone v. Powell, 428 U.S. 465 (1976)
Strawbridge v. Curtiss, 3 Cranch 267 (1806)
Swift v. Tyson, 16 Peters 1 (1842)
United Mine Workers of America v. Gibbs, 383 U.S. 715 (1966)
World-Wide Volkswagen Corp. v. Woodson, 444 U.S. 286 (1980)
Younger v. Harris, 401 U.S. 37 (1971)

BIBLIOGRAPHY

American Jurisprudence, 2nd ed. (1982), details the case law on federal court jurisdiction. "Federal Practice and Procedure," §§ 1–2609. *Corpus Juris Secundum* (1960–1961) details the case law on federal court jurisdiction, §§ 1–360. Kenneth Culp Davis, *Administrative Law Text* (1972), gives a detailed treatment on the subjects of proper parties and sovereign immunity. John P. Frank, *Justice Daniel Dissenting* (1964), is a biography of the United States Supreme Court's champion dissenter; Daniel's dissents substantially concerned the jurisdiction of the federal courts.

Lawrence M. Friedman, *A History of American Law* (1973), works jurisdictional issues into a scholarly yet fascinating account. John A. Garraty, ed., *Quarrels That Have Shaped the Constitution* (1962), includes the jurisdictional features of sixteen lawsuits that produced landmark Supreme Court decisions. James Willard Hurst, *The Growth of American Law* (1950), discusses the structure and jurisdiction of the state and federal courts in chapters 5 and 6. Anthony Lewis, *Gideon's Trumpet* (1964), is a journalist's account of the celebrated case of *Gideon* v. *Wainwright.*

Lewis Mayers, *The American Legal System* (1964), discusses aspects of jurisdiction in the first four chapters. Richard Neely, *How Courts Govern America* (1981), includes a state supreme court justice's assessment of the uses to which courts put jurisdiction; and *Why Courts Don't Work* (1982), explains the reasons for judicial inefficiency, including that relating to jurisdiction. Robert L. Stern and Eugene Gressman, *Supreme Court Practice* (1978), details, in chapters 2–4, the Supreme Court's jurisdiction. Alan Westin, *The Anatomy of a Constitutional Law Case* (1958), includes an account of the jurisdictional aspects of the famous steel seizure case of 1952. Charles A. Wright, *Law of Federal Courts* (1976), is a standard treatise on federal-court jurisdiction.

– HAROLD J. SPAETH

L

THE LEGAL PROFESSION AND LEGAL ETHICS

The very term *profession* implies a high level of social prestige, to which many occupational groups aspire and which lawyers clearly enjoy in American society. Such high social status emerges in part out of the special skills and knowledge that are allegedly peculiar to a profession. Affirmation of these special competencies is found in licensing requirements and laws that grant the designated group an exclusive right to perform certain tasks. In the case of the legal profession, licensing in almost every state requires graduation from a law school accredited by the American Bar Association (ABA), successful completion of a state bar examination, and approval by a character and fitness committee. In an increasing number of states, membership in the state bar association is also required. A monopoly is granted to the legal profession for a wide range of services, from such clearly defined ones as representing a client in court to those ambiguously labeled the practice of law. Bar associations, particularly at the state level, work actively to protect the monopoly granted by the state. In a majority of states, membership is a mandatory condition of practice.

Another aspect of professionalism to which many groups aspire is self-regulation. Given that only members of the profession have the special skills and knowledge that are the core of their work, it follows that only other lawyers are in a position to evaluate and regulate lawyers' conduct. Such independence is also presumed by the profession to be necessary if it is to operate autonomously so as to perform its social role. In the case of the legal profession, this entails two sometimes conflicting roles: the representation of client interests and the representation of the legal system as officers of the court. The latter implies some professional responsibility to serve the society at large. In recent years questions have been raised about the professionalism of lawyers. Has the profit motive overtaken the commitment to service? Does working as a so-called hired gun representing any and every point of view conflict with the obligation to act as an officer of the court committed to improving the system of justice?

The privileged status of lawyers implies a uniformity within the profession that is difficult to substantiate. Not only is the legal profession very heterogeneous, but there are direct conflicts of interest between different segments of the bar. For example, trial lawyers who generally represent plaintiffs in personal injury cases may have a view of what would qualify as an improvement in the judicial system very different from that of lawyers who represent insurance companies. The former argue that justice would be best served by creating rules that would make it easier for plaintiffs to succeed in their claims; the latter argue just the opposite.

Lawyers in Society

Beyond the status enjoyed by professions generally, the legal profession derives great power from its control over the law that is central to the American political and social system. The tendency for basic social issues to become questions of law in the United States implies an obvious role for lawyers in the determination of public policy. This was recognized early in the twentieth century in a study of legal education in which the practice of law was distinguished as "a public function, in a sense that the practice of other professions, such as medicine, is not. Practicing lawyers do not merely render to the community a social service. . . . They are part of the governing mechanism of the state. Their functions are in a broad sense political" (Reed, 3).

While courtroom advocacy is lawyer's work, it constitutes but a small part of what lawyers do.

Lawyers are the primary gatekeepers to the administration of justice. This means that to get a case before the courts, it is generally necessary to have a lawyer present it. Although lawyers are available for a fee to take a case to court, there are a number of reasons they might decline to do so. Examples include the lack of valid legal claims, the settlement of the case more expeditiously without going to court, and a claim insufficient to justify the costs of litigation. Without a lawyer's agreement to take a case to court, there will be no public decision in the case. By screening cases, lawyers thus influence which laws will be enforced and which will be challenged. The highly structured educational and licensing requirements of the bar give lawyers control of what enters the courts and what is therefore subject to judicial decision.

Lawyers' advice also determines how economic exchanges are arranged and whether legal rights are pursued. A national survey found that in addition to the extensive use of lawyers by businesses, nearly two-thirds of the adult population had consulted a lawyer at least once about a personal nonbusiness legal problem (Curran, 1977, 186). Indeed, lawyers appear to be ubiquitous in American society.

The United States has long had more lawyers per capita than any other nation. In the decades since 1950, the number of lawyers both absolutely and in relation to the population as a whole has increased dramatically.

Growth of the profession has been greeted with a mixed response. Some believe that the more lawyers there are, the more they will be available to do the less remunerative work of the middle- and lower-income populations. This will, it is argued, increase the access to justice that is required in a democratic society. Others argue that the increase of lawyers only means more litigation, which will further clog the courts. These two arguments are of course not unrelated. Almost by definition, the more access there is, the more litigation there will be. Whether this is good or bad depends on one's views as to the cases that should be heard by the courts.

The Work of Lawyers

The public's image of the lawyer at work is the courtroom advocate arguing a client's case before a jury. While courtroom advocacy is lawyer's work, it constitutes but a small part of what lawyers do. The legal profession is in fact quite heterogeneous. Lawyers differ in workplace and specialty; they also differ in how they spend their time and in the skills needed to do their jobs. With the focus of legal education almost exclusively on legal rules, there has been continuing concern over how, when, and where lawyers learn to do their work. A prominent law professor wrote,

> Meantime, what pictures should we of today be making about the actual workings of "the" heterogeneous Bar? *Not rules, but doing, is what we seek to train men for.* Rules our men need. Rules do in part control or shape, do in still greater part set limits to, their doing. But the thing remains the doing. What is this doing of lawyers? Whither we are to head our students? We do not know.
>
> (Llewellyn, 1935, 654)

Practicing lawyers, whether in the office or the courtroom, are in the business of representing the legal status of others. Although law schools concentrate on the analysis of rules, practicing lawyers consider facts the more important in their work. For most situations the rules are a given; what is important to preparing the individual case or document is the facts of a situation. Lawyers who practice different specialties, however, also tend to use different skills. Thus, selection of a specialty is critical to determining the actual tasks in which a lawyer will be engaged. In the larger law firms, one's status within the firm may also determine the nature of one's work, with younger associates doing the research and more-senior members dealing more directly with clients.

Although analytic skills are most characteristic of the practice of law, more-generalizable skills like fact-gathering, effective oral expression, and interviewing are at the core of much of the practice of law. Many of these competencies are, of course, equally important to other occupations and may be learned in a variety of contexts. In the practice of law these skills are used to write contracts that will be enforceable in court, to help collect debts, to give tax advice, to write wills, to arrange a real estate transaction, or to reach a divorce settlement. The same skills and many of the same tasks apply to the lawyer's special preserve: the representation of clients before courts and other government agencies.

With the exception of prosecutors, public defenders, and attorneys working for organizations who are specifically seeking judicial rulings, only a very small percentage of lawyers ever argue a case in a courtroom. A somewhat larger proportion file cases in court but settle most of them outside of court. In fact, the filing of a case in court is often a strategic move to encourage an opponent to settle a case. Even the categories of cases that require a judicial decision, such as divorce and probate, only rarely are actually litigated; in most cases the judge merely affirms arrangements entered into by the affected parties. Lawyers employed or retained on an ongoing basis are more likely to be engaged in anticipating and avoiding legal problems in such activities as negotiating contracts or writing wills. If problems do develop, it becomes their job to reach the best possible result within the confines of the law and legal process. The work of lawyers who largely serve individuals on a case-by-case basis is not very different except that since they are not engaged until a client perceives a need for legal assistance, they are usually not in a position to anticipate and therefore assist the client in avoiding legal trouble.

There are, of course, many lawyers admitted to practice in one or more states who do not practice law. Some enter completely different, nonlegal careers. Others, though not practitioners, pursue alternative legal careers in academia, on the bench, or in judicial administration. Still others serve as legislative staff, government examiners, trust officers of banks, lobbyists, and policymakers and executives at all levels of government. These last two positions, while often filled by lawyers, do not require legal training and background, and there is some debate as to whether the lawyer credential should in fact be an advantage, as it clearly now is, to obtaining such a position. Many lawyers, of course, have chosen to enter politics. Indeed, young people attracted to politics often enter law school as a step toward building a political career. While few offices require candidates to be lawyers (district attorneys and attorneys general who are legal counsel to governmental entities are obvious exceptions), the representation of lawyers in political office is out of proportion to their numbers in the society at large.

The dominance of lawyers as public office holders and advisers is well documented by Peter Irons, among others. They are prominent in both elective and appointive office. Most United States presidents and vice-presidents have been lawyers, and the majority of United States senators are lawyers, as they have been since the 1940s. The United States House of Representatives has also been historically dominated by lawyers, although not to the same extent as the Senate. Lawyers are not nearly so prominent in state governments. At the end of the 1970s, in only one state legislature was the proportion of members who were lawyers as much as 40 percent; most states had substantially fewer. It can be said that lawyers are prominent in politics but do not predominate. Although many lawyers enter local politics to develop a reputation and clientele and to secure business relationships, most lawyers in political office have made a career out of politics. Except for their ability to begin political careers as state or federal prosecutors, lawyer-politicians are in most ways quite similar to those who are nonlawyers.

Aside from the power that accrues to roles with obvious political influence, the public power of the legal profession stems largely from the part lawyers play in applying and interpreting the law, in advising private clients in the settlement of legal matters, and thereby in the shaping of the law in action. Lawyers effectively

Most lawyers work in private practices, many in association with one or two other lawyers. (Kevin R. Morris/Corbis)

transform real-life events into a legal formulation. Issues are narrowed to fit into legal categories and to meet required standards of evidence. The legal profession sets the policy agenda of the third branch of government by filing cases in court and influences judicial decisions and the development of the law by formulating (framing) the issues in legal arguments. It influences which laws will be enforced by virtue of advising clients to seek the benefits of their legal rights. Lawyers decide which cases to pursue as a means of changing the laws. Thus, it is in allegedly private capacities that the greatest public power of the legal profession is exercised.

Structure and Organization

The traditional image of the lawyer has been that of the solo practitioner who represents individual clients on a case-by-case basis. It implied a knowledgeable client who could recognize a legal problem and seek the services of a lawyer, who could then provide independent professional advice in the client's best interests. Even though most of the adult population have sought a lawyer's services, businesses rather than individuals are the major consumers of legal services.

Individuals generally use lawyers intermittently. Writing a will, buying or selling a house, and suing one who has caused an injury (as in an automobile accident) are discrete events not often repeated in the average individual's life. Businesses, by contrast, seek legal assistance on a more continuous basis, often to prevent legal problems from developing. The relationship between the lawyer and the individual client more closely approximates the traditional lawyer-client relationship, in which professional services were sought in connection with a particular event or difficulty. The relationship between the lawyer and the business client is much more likely to be ongoing; many lawyers are kept on retainer for general legal counsel, with additional work billed on an hourly fee basis. That relationship makes the lawyer more knowledgeable of the client's affairs and better able to provide legal advice, absent a discrete legal event. Such relationships raise questions as to how independent the lawyer's advice is, particularly if the client accounts for a substantial proportion of the lawyer's income. This problem is further exacerbated in those situations in which lawyers and clients become business partners or the lawyer sits on the client's board of directors.

Questions have been raised as to the degree of independence that counsel can exercise under such circumstances. On the other hand, there has been criticism of the legal profession for exerting too much control in the lawyer-client relationship where the client is an individual and the relationship is on a one-time-only basis (Rosenthal). Of particular concern has been the degree of control exercised by the lawyer over the client's affairs and whether the interests of the client rather than the lawyer remain paramount.

Businesses rather than individuals are the major consumers of legal services.

Even if it is agreed that the lawyer owes loyalty to the client and must represent the client's interests, in contemporary America it is sometimes difficult to determine exactly who is the client. Identification of the client is complicated by work settings that include lawyers working for other lawyers, for legal-services organizations, for interest groups, and for business corporations whose management and stockholders may be in conflict.

Still, most lawyers (68 percent) are in private practice (that is, not employees of government, industry, or other organizations), and about two-thirds of those still practice alone or in association with one or two other lawyers. There has, however, been a growth in both the number and size of large law firms, particularly in large cities. This trend has developed during a period when the legal profession as a whole has become increasingly urban both as a reflection of population trends and as a response to the concentration of economic activity in urban areas. At the same time, solo practice has been on the decline.

While most lawyers are still private practitioners, law firms have many associates (the larger the firm, the greater the proportion of associates) who are employees, not partners. Partnership is typically granted after five to eight years of associate status. Promotion to partnership was once nearly automatic, but it has become more competitive, with disassociation from the firm usually the only alternative to partnership. (A new job category, the permanent associate, has so far been limited to a small number of the largest law firms.) Traditionally, once a lawyer was elevated to partnership, particularly in large firms, it meant that an entire career would be spent in that firm. This is less true today, with more movement between firms by individuals and groups of attorneys. Movement by a group sometimes results in the spin-off and creation of a new firm. At the same time, large firms are getting larger, not only by hiring new lawyers but also by merging with other firms. In addition, since the mid-1970s the multioffice law firm has become more common. Firms are increasingly opening branch offices in major cities around the

United States, enabling them to serve the national legal needs of their clientele. This trend, while much examined in the legal media, is confined to large law firms located in major metropolitan areas.

Since 1960, the proportion of the bar in private practice has been on the decline, in large measure because of the increase in the number of lawyers working for government or private industry. Among government lawyers, the greatest number work for the federal government, most for the Department of Justice; at the state and local levels, the largest number work as prosecutors. Most industry lawyers work for very large corporations, which are increasingly conscious of the cost-savings of employing in-house counsel and which have become more selective about the aspects of their legal work that they refer to private attorneys. This trend has been in response to the recognition by corporations that their outside legal fees were growing at a faster rate than their profits and that lawyers, by virtue of their orientation to asserting rights, are often counterproductive to the furtherance of business relationships and interests. An executive with a major corporation put it this way:

> I think lawyers too often assume a combative posture best likened to gladiators in an arena, a fight to the death . . . victory at all costs. The client's interests may be ignored consciously or unconsciously as the highs and lows of battle ensue.
>
> I think that the combative nature of some lawyers converts important litigation into personal episodes for counsel, which tends to cloud opportunities for amicable disposition. I think this tends to extend the litigation and certainly increases the cost of litigation.
>
> ("A Businessman's View of Lawyers," 834)

In addition to employment arrangements, lawyers are also often characterized by the specialty or area of the law in which they practice. Corporate law, family law, tax law, and criminal law are among the areas identified as legal specialties. Greater specialization has occurred in virtually all facets of American society, but despite similar trends, the legal profession is not nearly as specialized as other occupational groups, particularly the medical profession. Even those lawyers who consider themselves specialists only rarely practice exclusively in one area of law. With the exception of prosecutors and public defenders who practice only criminal law, specialization among lawyers typically means that a large share or most of one's time, not the whole of it, is devoted to a particular area of the law.

In private practice, specialization varies with both the context of practice and the nature of the clientele, which are interrelated. Although specialization is often identified as characteristic of lawyers in firms, rather than of solo attorneys, the difference is really between lawyers in large firms, who tend to be highly specialized, and lawyers who practice in other settings.

The precise area in which a lawyer practices is largely the result of the expertise needed by the firm early in one's career.

The larger the law firm, the greater the degree of specialization in the individual lawyer's work. With members of large law firms specializing in different areas of the law, the firms can provide for all the legal needs of their business clientele. These include corporate law, securities, antitrust, and tax. In some areas, such as antitrust, the bar is further divided, with some lawyers specializing in plaintiff work (that is, representing those bringing suit) and others specializing in defending the corporations being challenged. It has in fact been argued that the emergence and rise of large law firms was a result of the development of large corporations that demand specialized legal services (Ladinsky). As such, the trend toward specialization was noted at least as early as the 1930s in a commentary on the modern metropolitan bar: "Most of its best brains, most of its inevitable leaders, have moved masswise out of court work, out of a general practice akin to that of the family doctor, into highly paid specialization in the service of large corporations" (Llewellyn, 1933).

Individuals' legal needs are serviced by quite a distinct segment of the bar, one that tends to be less specialized. To the extent that lawyers who handle legal work for individuals do specialize, it is a function of their clientele; specialties include family law, real estate, wills and estates, criminal law, and personal-injury work. These are the areas in which individuals are most likely to seek legal services, and so they are often practiced together.

Among lawyers who do legal work mostly for businesses, a single attorney may do corporate, tax, and securities work. Some specialties, such as tax and real estate, are practiced by all segments of the bar, but while the large firm is engaged in corporate tax work and real estate development, the solo attorney is more likely to be involved in individual estate and tax planning and the sale of individual homes. These distinctions, however, are most likely to occur in large cities; in small towns, lawyers are more likely to do many varieties of legal work.

Although the substantive specialty that a lawyer practices may determine the skills used in practice (Zemans and Rosenblum), the clientele served, and the lawyer's status within the bar (Heinz and Laumann), very little is known about the factors that influence who will practice which specialty. With the exception of engineering graduates entering patent law and of accounting and business students practicing tax law, there is little predictability as to who will specialize in what legal areas. Law students do not major in a particular area of the law; in fact, law schools pride themselves on training generalists. Determination of specialization generally occurs after the lawyer enters the practice of law. This is particularly curious because of the importance of specialty in defining the actual nature of one's practice.

In most cases the context within which one practices appears to be the most important determinant of both the degree of specialization and the areas of specialization. The precise area in which a lawyer practices is largely the result of the expertise needed by the firm early in one's career. There may be a general need in the tax area, or the firm may require work on a particular case. A firm that is handling a very large case is likely to assign to it many junior members of the firm. In the course of that case, some of the lawyers will become the firm experts in that area of the law. This applies particularly to younger lawyers not only because they have not yet developed an area of expertise but also because firms are structured to assign them as the need arises. In private practice, expertise and therefore specialization is developed in response to client demand. In contrast to the medical profession, which requires substantial formal training in a self-selected specialty, lawyers almost universally develop their specialty on the job in the course of representing clients. Thus, the determination of the tasks in which a lawyer is engaged are to a substantial degree determined by others. To the extent that the specialty practiced determines one's prestige within the bar, the same can be said of a lawyer's professional status.

Prestige within the Profession

Although the bar as a whole enjoys a high level of prestige within American society, there is a hierarchy of prestige within the profession. Since formal requirements for entry to the profession are nearly universal (graduation from an ABA-accredited law school and passage of a state bar examination), more subtle distinctions are made. At the point of hiring, the law school attended and class standing in law school are the most important criteria. Those who obtain judicial clerkships upon graduation from law school have an additional credential. This is particularly important for those seeking a teaching position in a law school.

The difference in the jobs obtained and specialties practiced by graduates of different law schools has been recognized at least since the publication of Reed's 1921 study of legal education. The more prestigious the law school attended and the higher one's class standing, the more likely a law graduate is to join a larger, more prestigious firm and to do law work for high-status clients. Clients with higher social status tend to use lawyers in selected specialties. It has been argued that lawyers who mainly practice in areas of the law such as securities and antitrust are accorded high status within the bar by virtue of the nature of their clientele (Heinz and Laumann). The lower end of the bar's status hierarchy is occupied by criminal lawyers, whose clients are almost all of lower social status.

Appropriate social, religious, and ethnic credentials have also played an important role in the distribution of lawyers within the bar (Auerbach). Many of the most prestigious firms were for many years the bastions of white, Anglo-Saxon, Protestant males. Catholics, Jews, those of southern and eastern European ancestry, and, more recently, blacks and women have entered the most prestigious and powerful big-city law firms, although in most cases they remain decided minorities. To some extent, exclusions in the early days could be based simply on the allegedly objective criterion of law school attended. In practice, immigrants, the children of immigrants, women, and minorities had only limited access to the very law schools whose attendance was a prerequisite for consideration for hiring.

It should be made clear, however, that access to the profession has been quite open to those seeking upward mobility. This was reflected in the conscious decision in the early part of the century to maintain part-time night law schools, thereby maintaining variations in legal educational opportunities. This contrasts with the policies adopted by the medical profession. Still, those coming from low-status backgrounds often attend law school at night because they cannot afford to be full-time students.

In the distribution of law school graduates, it is the largest law firms (more than fifty lawyers) that are most likely to recruit graduates from the more prestigious law schools. Although class standing plays a significant role, in the metropolitan bar the law school attended is the best single predictor of both the size of the firm in which one practices and the prestige of the specialty practiced. Despite the importance of law school attended to legal career, it must be noted that lawyer markets are relatively localized; with a half dozen exceptions, so are the reputations of law schools. That is to say that even law schools unknown outside of their own locale get their graduates hired by the most prestigious firms within their own geographic area. Most lawyers attended law school in the same general locale in which they practice.

Preparation for the Practice of Law

In the colonial era, one aspiring to a legal career sought an apprenticeship with a practicing lawyer. The nineteenth-century emergence of university-based study of the law did not supplant the need for an apprenticeship if one was to practice law. Such university-based instruction was tied to philosophy, political economy, and ethics and linked law with the broader social order; it prepared men for prominent positions of leadership. Concurrently, the practicing bar began to establish its own schools to train future lawyers. These trends merged as law schools were established within universities. Still, apprenticeship was the major route to the profession and remained so well into the twentieth century.

The most radical change in the preparation of lawyers was instituted in 1870 at Harvard Law School by the new dean Christopher Columbus Langdell. For him the study of law was a science whose tools were housed in the library. The case method, as it came to be called, based instruction exclusively on the examination of appellate court opinions and was aimed at developing analytic skills. This mode of instruction was distinct from both the philosophical approach and the apprenticeship model; it was to become the basic model of instruction in law schools nationwide. This uniformity became particularly important as the organized bar successfully encouraged states to require law school attendance as a prerequisite for admission to the bar. By 1970, less than half a dozen states allowed admission to the bar by apprenticeship without law school training. The preparation of lawyers is almost universally oriented to learning to "think like a lawyer," with neither the philosophy of early university training nor the skills of apprenticeship given much attention.

One indicator of the limits of legal education in preparation for the practice of law is the success of what are known as bar review courses. These entail short intense training to prepare law school graduates to pass state bar examinations, a requirement if one is to be licensed to practice law. Although law schools have more recently given greater attention to skills training and the relationship of law and society, the legal profession as a whole is a product of the strictly analytic training introduced by Langdell more than a century ago. The historic changes in the prerequisites to practice are arguably linked to access to the profession.

Access to the Profession

There is a difference of opinion as to the effects that changes in prerequisites to the practice of law have had on access to the profession. Alexis de Tocqueville, in his 1835 description of *Democracy in America,* observed that "if I were asked where I place the American aristocracy, I should reply without hesitation . . . that it occupies the judicial bench and bar" (vol. 1, 278). Later studies confirm the high status of the legal profession as an occupational group. Indeed, it has been portrayed as a path to higher status in a society that lauds upward mobility.

At the same time, it has been described as a profession likely to draw its members from high-status backgrounds. This is a matter of some concern, for, as noted by Reed, "the interests not only of the individual but of the community demand that participation in the making and administration of the law shall be kept accessible to Lincoln's plain people" (p. 418). As preparation for the practice of law, a college degree and three years of high-tuition professional schooling (often, if not typically, to the exclusion of income-generating employment during the school year) have been viewed by some as restricting access to the profession and denying a route of upward mobility that was used particularly by the children of immigrants in the early part of the twentieth century. At that time the only requirement was an apprenticeship with a practicing lawyer. Although comparative figures are not available, there is still a significant number of members of the bar, at least in the cities, whose fathers had substantially lower-status occupations. For many, the law is still seen as a path of upward mobility; evidence suggests that prestige and above-average income are important attractions to those seeking careers in the law. Given the geometric rise in admissions to the practice of law in the 1970s, the absolute numbers attaining higher status have no doubt increased. It should be noted that the growth in the profession beyond what would be predicted by population has, since 1974, been largely the result of the entrance of women. Through the 1960s, only 3 percent of new entrants to the bar were women; by 1983, the figure had risen to approximately 34 percent.

There are contradictory views on the effects of the movement of legal training from law offices to law schools. Some argue that given the costs of law school and the prerequisite college degree, the law is less accessible than it once was. Others contend that the apprentice system demanded that personal connections to an established lawyer were necessary to obtain an apprenticeship, thereby excluding those without such connections. It should also be noted that at least in urban areas many law schools have maintained evening programs for students who need to work while attending school. However much opportunities may or may not have changed, upward mobility continues to be a strong attraction of a legal career.

The Cost of Legal Services

The cost of legal services is perceived as limiting access to the legal process for many Americans. Although most lawyers probably do not turn away potential clients because they are unable to pay, such questions are only rarely raised, for consumers do not seek the services they do not think they can afford. It should be noted that available evidence indicates that those who want an attorney to represent them usually find one with the assistance of family, friends, or associates who recommend particular lawyers (Curran, 1977; Mayhew and Reiss). In addition, irrespective of one's ability to pay, there is the question of whether the benefit that may be gained will be worth the cost of pursuing a case. For example, let us say that a neighbor damages your $500 electric lawnmower beyond repair. Despite admitting fault, the neighbor refuses to pay for the lawnmower. Although you may have the evidence necessary to win a case in court and can even afford to hire a lawyer to represent you, if it costs more than $500 or even somewhat less, it is not worth the trouble to pursue the amount legally due you.

While some lawyers have incomes of hundreds of thousands of dollars a year, they are a distinct minority in the legal profession.

The hypothetical case just described includes the expectation that each party to the dispute will pay his or her own attorney. This practice is so unique that it is known as the American rule. In British law, from which much of the American legal system is derived, the loser is generally required to pay the winner's costs, including lawyer's fees. In the United States, judicial awards collected are in fact diminished by the cost of bringing the claim. If the value of the potential award is insufficient to cover the expected lawyer's fee, no case will be brought. As in the hypothetical case, the owner of damaged property has no effective legal recourse. The defendant in a lawsuit may similarly determine that it is less costly to pay a claim than to pursue the case to a judicial decision, even if he or she might ultimately win the case.

The contingent fee substantially diminishes the negative social impact of the apparent inability of many people to pay for the legal services needed to bring a valid legal claim. Under this arrangement, a lawyer agrees to represent a claimant in return for a percentage of the award (usually 30 percent to 40 percent). This has been an effective means of providing representation in damage cases, particularly involving personal injury to the claimant, where the amount claimed is sufficient to make the lawyer's percentage fee cover the time anticipated to pursue the case. Although the lawyer gets nothing if the case is unsuccessful, experienced lawyers know which cases are likely to be successful.

There are three limitations on the applicability of the contingent-fee arrangement. First, only legal claims likely to result in a monetary award are covered by contingent-fee arrangements. Cases that involve equitable relief are thus excluded. (Equitable relief cases involve actions intended to force defendants to fulfill acts for which they are legally responsible, such as completing a theatrical performance for which they have legally contracted. Other examples are cases seeking to stop defendants from actions that are prohibited, such as denying a divorced parent visitation rights with his or her children.) The second limitation on the contingent-fee arrangement is its applicability only to claims of sufficient size to make the lawyer's percentage worth the required time necessary to bring the case to a successful conclusion. The $500 lawnmower in our hypothetical case would, for example, be of insufficient size to attract a lawyer to the case. Finally, since the claims of the poor are often too small to be represented on a contingent-fee basis, that segment of the population may be largely excluded from gaining representation at all, even if their claims are meritorious. For cases in excess of several thousand dollars, the contingent-fee arrangement can work well.

Although consumers generally like the idea that they pay their lawyers only from proceeds recovered in a successful suit, in some areas of the law, such as medical malpractice, there has been some negative reaction to the size of lawyers' contingent fees. An example would be a case in which the lawyer gets $4 million of a $10 million award to a mentally retarded paraplegic whose condition is the result of medical negligence.

Availability of Legal Services

As part of the emergence of demands for expanded social justice in the 1960s, there was a push for greater availability of legal services, particularly for those unable to afford a lawyer on the usual fee-for-service basis. The argument was, and still is, that without a lawyer to represent you, or at least the realistic expectation that one could be engaged if necessary, legal rights have little meaning. The classic "So sue me" response to a recognized violation of a legal right carries an underlying message that a lawsuit is not expected to follow. For one without access to legal counsel, it is a particularly harrowing message. Although cost is not the only factor affecting the use of legal services, it became the major focus of reform efforts.

The development of free and low-cost legal services was not, however, a new idea. Legal-aid societies for immigrants existed before the turn of the century, and some free and low-fee representation has always been done by individual lawyers or firms *pro bono publico* ("for the public good"). Although this is consistent with a lawyer's obligation under the Code of Professional Responsibility to make legal counsel available, the amount of *pro bono* work has always been limited.

The demand for greater availability of legal representation has focused particularly on civil cases. This is largely because of the involvement of government in providing legal representation to the poor in criminal cases. This, too, has been a relatively recent development. Unlike civil cases, representation in criminal cases has been based on the Sixth Amendment to the United States Constitution, which guarantees the right to counsel in a criminal trial. Although some states provided legal counsel to indigents in criminal cases before it was required, over recent decades all states have been mandated to do so by a series of United States Supreme Court decisions that made the guarantees of the Sixth Amendment applicable to the states via the due process clause of the Fourteenth Amendment. First for capital cases in which the death penalty was threatened (*Powell* v. *Alabama*) in 1932, then for all felony cases (*Gideon* v. *Wainwright*) in 1963, and finally for misdemeanor cases that result in a jail sentence (*Argersinger* v. *Hamlin*) in 1972, the United States Supreme Court has required states to provide or to pay for legal representation of the indigent. Almost all of the largest counties in the United States currently provide free counsel to indigents through a public-defender program, with lawyers serving as full-time or part-time salaried staff. Other counties use an assigned-counsel system, by which private attorneys are appointed by the courts, or a contract system, in which law firms, bar associations, or individual lawyers contract to represent the indigent for a specified dollar amount. Although an assigned-counsel or contract system may offer representation by a lawyer with little or no experience with the criminal law, professional legal counsel is provided. With counsel in criminal cases essentially guaranteed, since the mid-1960s the concern and debates over legal fees and the availability of legal services has occurred largely in the civil arena.

In 1966 the Legal Services Program was created within the Office of Economic Opportunity (OEO), as part of the War on Poverty. The congressional legislation that created the program reflected two goals: to "provide legal advice and representation . . . [and] to further the cause of justice among persons living in poverty." The latter goal encouraged a strong law-reform and social-change orientation, but the actual work funded by the program largely served poor clients with immediate problems (often divorce and landlord-tenant disputes) and little interest in social change. Many of the young lawyers attracted to the Legal Services Program were committed to seeking and achieving social change through the legal process, and their work generated sufficient political opposition to the program that the independent Legal Services Corporation was created with restrictions on the kinds of cases it could accept. Despite this change, the Legal Services Corporation continues to be the object of political debate, with its proponents arguing that it is the only means by which the poor and disadvantaged can begin to obtain the rights guaranteed them by law and its opponents continuing to object to the use of public funds to challenge public procedures and decisions (such as a cutoff of social security benefits) and to clog the courts with litigation over minor cases.

All states have been mandated to provide legal counsel to indigents in criminal cases by a series of Supreme Court decisions.

Whatever the success or failure of legal-services programs, they have all been limited to the very poor. A large portion of the population has had too high an income to qualify for government assistance but insufficient financial means to pay for legal representation on a fee-for-service basis. There followed substantial demand for greater availability of legal services for middle-income Americans.

Since the 1960s, new free-market efforts have emerged to meet the legal needs of this middle-income population. In particular, prepaid legal-services programs and legal clinics have grown substantially. Legal-services plans only began to achieve any level of significance in the United States in the 1970s. As with all insurance, the governing principle of prepaid legal-services plans is the distribution of cost among many individuals over a long period of time, thereby limiting the chance of any one person having to bear extremely high costs. Although based on the same model as medical insurance, thus far legal insurance plans have been developed largely to cover members of preexisting groups, such as labor unions. It is unclear, given the greater predictability of the need for legal services as compared to medical services and the availability of legal services on a contingency-fee basis, whether legal insurance will ever be a major mechanism for payment of legal fees in the United States.

Legal clinics may present a more widely available alternative. The emergence of legal clinics that are typically low-fee, high-volume operations has been closely tied to the lifting of prohibitions on lawyer advertising. Early proponents of legal clinics argued that low-cost services would be possible only with a high volume of cases, most particularly uncontested divorces or simple wills, for which the service could be readily standardized. The necessary volume of cases, it was argued, was possible only if the clinics could advertise. Under traditional lawyer ethical codes, advertising was explicitly prohibited. It was not until 1977, when a legal clinic successfully challenged a state ban on lawyer advertising, that clinics became a real possibility. The United States Supreme Court held that prohibitions on advertising constituted an unconstitutional restriction on free speech *(Bates* v. *State Bar of Arizona).* Since then legal clinics have proliferated, including the development of chains and franchises that can share the benefits of a single advertising campaign. As yet there is little systematic evidence detailing the productivity of these clinics. Whether they are serving a clientele that would have otherwise remained unrepresented is not known. It is also unknown whether lawyer advertising and the emergence of legal clinics have expanded the demand for legal services or whether legal work now done by clinics was previously done by other lawyers.

In addition to these mechanisms for providing legal representation, many individuals have chosen to pursue their legal claims *pro se* ("for themselves"). In many jurisdictions this has been facilitated by the creation of special procedures and even special courts designed for use by the layperson. In particular, small monetary claims and uncontested divorces are now being settled without the assistance of legal counsel. The creation of these *pro se* procedures and courts has been part of the official response to public demand for access to the courts for cases too small to interest most lawyers. At the same time, segments of the bar have been concerned that cases that once accounted for a portion of their business are now being handled without them.

Legal Ethics

Codes of professional ethics are formal mechanisms that announce to the public that a profession is self-regulating and thus worthy of the autonomy granted to it by the state. These ethical standards set the profession apart from, if not above, the standards of the larger society. Although words like *responsibility* and *integrity* are used to describe "professional" conduct, they are accompanied by disclaimers that terms like *legal ethics* and *professional responsibility* have very precise meanings that are applicable only within the context of the practice of law.

This alleged distinctiveness of legal ethics from general moral standards is credited by some with contributing to the traditional public hostility to lawyers. For example, it is generally considered inappropriate and unfair to impugn another person's integrity by implying lack of truthfulness when you know otherwise. Yet, in the context of defending an accused in a criminal trial, it may be deemed appropriate for a lawyer to cross-examine a truthful witness with the intent of giving the appearance that the witness is being less than totally honest or even lying. Another example is the lawyer's obligation not to reveal anything divulged by the client. Since a good defense requires that the lawyer be as informed as possible, a relationship of trust and confidence between lawyer and client must be encouraged. Client candor is assured by guaranteeing confidentiality. Thus, all communication between client and lawyer is privileged information.

The extremes to which this obligation can lead were revealed in a highly publicized case in the 1970s in which a defendant in a case told his lawyers that he had killed two people in a separate crime and identified the location of the bodies. Although the lawyers subsequently saw and photographed the bodies, they kept their existence secret even after information was requested by the parents of one of the victims. When the lawyers' failure to reveal this information became public after a confession many months later, there was great public outrage. Although there was disagreement within the bar as to the appropriateness of the lawyers' actions, the defense that was offered argued that if client revelations are not kept in confidence, clients will not reveal all the information that is needed to best represent them.

These distinctive professional standards are closely tied to, and in fact justified by, the requirements of the adversary system. If each side is to receive the best defense, then the lawyers must consider only the interests of their clients. An advocate who considers the good of society rather than the good of the client does damage to the adversary process, which is itself presumed to contribute to the social good. Professional norms thus may dictate behavior that would otherwise be considered inappropriate.

The question frequently asked of criminal defense counsel as to how they can defend someone that they know is guilty illustrates the point. The same, of course, could be asked of the counsel representing toxic-waste companies whose disposal practices have contaminated a town's water supply. In both cases, and in many others, the lawyers' response is that their obligation as lawyers is to represent their clients to the best of their ability because the American system of justice is based on an adversarial process that in the long run will give the most just results.

Critics of this perspective on legal ethics point out that the essence of professionalism—indeed, the basis for granting any profession the right to self-regulation—is its responsibility to the social good. That responsibility is called into question by events like the Watergate scandal, in which a large number of lawyers were implicated in burglary, perjury, and the obstruction of justice on behalf of the Nixon administration.

There is in fact often an inherent tension between obligation to client and obligation to society, as noted by Karl Llewellyn:

> Duty to client reads in terms of taking advantage of each technicality the law may show, however senseless. It reads in terms of distortion of evidence and argument to the utter bounds of the permissible. Duty to court reads in terms of shaping every piece of the machinery that can be made to give, toward better functioning. It reads in terms of trying issues of fact to reach the probable truth.
>
> (1933, 181–182)

According to Llewellyn, the tension has been resolved in favor of the client. Critics argue further that even if total obligation to client were essential to an actual trial, such an obligation is much less persuasive in the context within which most lawyers practice.

The inherent conflict between obligations to client and obligations as officers of the court committed to promoting justice has remained through the continuing development of professional codes of conduct. In addition, such model codes have been unable to reflect the great diversity in law practice. As a result, the codes have continued to be more relevant to some practice contexts than to others.

The first code of professional ethics was passed by the Alabama State Bar Association in 1887. That code, like others that followed, was based on George Sharwood's *Essay on Professional Ethics* (1854), originally delivered as lectures at the then new law school of the University of Pennsylvania. The ABA promulgated its first code, the Canons of Professional Ethics, in 1908, also along the lines suggested by Sharwood. This ABA code and those it has since passed have served as models for adoption by state bar associations, courts, and disciplinary bodies. Since lawyers are licensed to practice in the states (with additional licensure required to practice in the federal system), it is the states that largely determine the rules of conduct. Over the years, most states have adopted some form of the ABA standards, with local variations.

Sharwood's essay and the early codes emphasized the high moral principles and dignity required of the profession. The traditional duties of the bar were in part derived from English practices. These included the duty to police the bar, the duty to represent the indigent, the duty not to stir up litigation, and the duty not to aid in the unauthorized practice of law (Drinker, 59–66). These duties have continued to appear with varying degrees of emphasis throughout the various reformulations of codes of conduct.

The emergence of the ABA Canons and subsequent state formulations of them came at a time when the practice of law was undergoing significant change. The growth of the American corporation was accompanied by changes in law practice to meet corporate needs. Many lawyers after the turn of the century moved away from small-town practice, in which they represented individuals, to urban practice, with its increasing representation of business corporations.

According to Drinker, the motivating force behind the 1908 ABA Canons was "the realization by thoughtful leaders of the bar of the growing commercialism all over the country. The consequent weakening of an effective professional public opinion clearly called for a more definite statement by the bar of the accepted rules of professional conduct" (p. 25). Negative reaction by the leaders of the bar to increased commercialization in the practice of law was reflected in the Canons' prohibition on lawyer advertising. The traditional view was that

> advertising, solicitation, and encroachment on the practice of others does not tend to benefit either the public or the lawyer in the same way as in the case of the sale of merchandise. While extensive advertising would doubtless increase litigation, this has always been considered as against public policy. Also, many of the most desirable clients, imbued with high respect both for their lawyer and his calling, would have no

use for a lawyer who did not maintain the dignity and standards of his profession.

(Drinker, 211–212)

Others have argued that "the Canons were part of an attempt to defend the better element in the bar from the inroads of a commercial spirit and the practice of those who were not gentlemen" (Macaulay, 16). This view recognizes the fact that the prohibition on advertising was particularly felt by young immigrant lawyers who were largely excluded from the developing urban firms and who at the same time did not have the established connections of the traditional small-town lawyers. Their problems were further exacerbated by their dependence on a continuing stream of individual clients to sustain their practices while the firms dealt largely with a continuing clientele. Exhortations of professional codes to await clients were thus much easier for higher-status firm lawyers to follow.

All communication between client and lawyer is privileged information.

This easier applicability to one segment of the bar is not limited to the ABA Canons' prohibition on advertising. There are a number of professional ethical norms that are affected by the nature of one's practice and clientele. A study of legal ethics among practicing lawyers found that higher-status firm lawyers exhibited greater adherence to the ethical norms of the ABA Canons than did solo practitioners, who do the divorces and personal injuries that constitute much of the legal work of individual clients (Carlin). Critics have long charged that these codes of professional conduct contain both class and ethnic biases (Auerbach). It is also clear that although significant change has occurred in the distribution of lawyers in various practice contexts, ethnic and class differences have not disappeared.

The ABA's 1908 Canons of Ethical Conduct were amended over the years in response to changes in society and a series of Supreme Court decisions that reflected those changes. Developments eventually demanded a new code. During the 1960s there was increasing concern over the limited availability of legal services despite the ethical requirement to make legal services available. Indeed, some efforts to deal with this problem were opposed by the organized bar. One mechanism developed was group legal representation. Under such a plan, an individual would receive legal representation by virtue of membership in the organization. However, unlike the traditional lawyer-client relationship, an individual was represented by a lawyer chosen by the group. States and bar associations fought these plans until a series of United States Supreme Court decisions sustained their validity (*National Association for the Advancement of Colored People* v. *Button,* 1963; *Brotherhood of Railway Trainmen* v. *Virginia,* 1964; *United Mine Workers District 12* v. *Illinois Bar Assn.,* 1967; *United Transportation Union* v. *State Bar,* 1971). At about the same time, the creation of the Office of Economic Opportunity's Legal Services Program called attention to the failure of the traditional duty to provide legal services to those who could not afford it.

In 1969 the new Code of Professional Responsibility was adopted by the ABA. The new code included the same traditional duties of the bar but appeared to shift its emphasis. Canon 2 provided that "a lawyer should assist the legal profession in fulfilling its duty to make legal counsel available." Although this canon constituted approximately 25 percent of the code, it continued to prohibit all advertising and to permit the establishment of minimum-fee schedules until barred by the *Bates* decision in 1977 and the *Goldfarb* decision in 1975, respectively. It has in fact been argued that the code establishes a hierarchy of interests, putting the lawyer's interest first, then the client's, and then society's (Morgan). For example, although a client's confidences are privileged, they can be disclosed when necessary to collect a fee. In addition, the protection of the public that is to flow from prohibitions on the unauthorized practice of law often appears more like protectionism.

Particular subjects of controversy have been do-it-yourself books and nonlawyer assistance in completing legal forms required in divorce, adoption, name-change, and other proceedings. The books are generally written by lawyers and even those that are not have been acknowledged as having the right to publication. Of much greater concern to the legal profession have been the nonlawyers who have established themselves in business to complete legal forms. Some are former paralegals or legal secretaries. They claim that they are doing precisely the same work they did when working for a lawyer, only now they are being paid directly and the client is charged only a fraction of what it would cost to purchase the same service through a lawyer. It is argued that requiring the use of a lawyer for these simple tasks would exclude many from using the legal process. For the legal profession these practices constitute "unauthorized practice of law," which is prohibited by every state.

Such conflicts are not unique to the contemporary scene. There has, for example, long been conflict between lawyers and real estate brokers over who should be advising home buyers and sellers and who should be drafting their sale agreements. Legislatures have granted tasks that have been defined as "the practice of law" exclusively to those licensed by the state to do so. However, the practice of law is not as clearly defined as one might assume. While there is broad agreement that arguing a case for a client in a court of law constitutes the practice of law, much of the actual work of lawyers does not so obviously fall within the strict definition of that term. The work of lawyers includes advising, interviewing, and negotiating—tasks that are part of many occupational pursuits. In addition, there is the work of lobbyists, politicians, and government officials, who are often trained as lawyers and licensed to practice law. Yet it is clear that these roles are not the exclusive preserve of the legal profession, nor should they be in a democratic society. What constitutes legal services is therefore a subject of some disagreement.

The work of lawyers includes advising, interviewing, and negotiating— tasks that are part of many occupational pursuits.

The tendency to resolve conflicts between obligations to clients and obligations to the court and society in favor of the former is reinforced by the actual disciplinary practices used to enforce professional codes of conduct. The threat of actual sanction under the ABA code is quite small, with only a minute proportion of complaints against lawyers for unprofessional conduct resulting in any unfavorable action. Carlin's study of New York from 1951 to 1969 shows an average of only 4 percent of complaints going to a formal hearing, and fewer resulting in the imposition of any sanction. Carlin's figures are not unique. Another study compared official reports of four jurisdictions and found the same pattern; 91 percent to 97 percent of all complaints were dismissed without investigation, with fewer than 3 percent resulting in a sanction in any of the jurisdictions (Steele and Nimmer, 982).

Enforcement of the code is also more likely to relate to some kinds of prohibited behavior than others. Although each state has its own disciplinary agency, they are all basically reactive institutions, relying strongly on third-party complaints. Client complaints are the most common. As a result, allegations of wrongdoing are skewed toward contract disputes rather than activities that constitute more serious misconduct. Also eliminated from investigation is behavior of which the client is unaware or which is in the client's interest. Thus, for example, the bribing of a judge is not likely to be reported to a disciplinary body. Most complaints concern fees, performance not meeting expectations, delay, lack of representation, rudeness, and conflicts of interest.

Continuing criticism of the code and of the behavioral standards of the profession led to another major rewriting of the profession's code of conduct. The new Model Rules of Professional Conduct were adopted by the ABA in 1983. Like the earlier Canons of Professional Ethics and the Code of Professional Responsibility, this is a model for the states to adopt, with or without local variations.

There are both similarities and differences between the new and old codes. Unlike the 1969 code, the 1983 code no longer contains the "ethical considerations" that were aspirational statements encouraging the highest standards of professional conduct. For example, the 1983 code omitted statements such as these from the 1969 code: "Neither [a lawyer's] personal interests, the interests of other clients, nor the desires of third persons should be permitted to dilute his loyalty to his client" (Ethical Consideration 5-1) and "The professional responsibility of a lawyer derives from his membership in a profession which has the duty of assisting members of the public to secure and protect available legal rights and benefits" (Ethical Consideration 7-1). The new code is more oriented to rules that delineate minimal standards defining behavior that can give rise to disciplinary action; these had been defined as the "disciplinary rules" under the former code.

Although the new code does not answer critics' concerns that the social good is not a sufficiently high priority of the legal profession, it does take into account some of the changes that have occurred in the nature of law practice. Thus, for example, it considers different roles of lawyers (such as counselor versus advocate) and different practice settings (such as relationships within law firms) than those previously addressed, and it recognizes the reality of lawyer advertising. In addition, the 1983 code responds to some criticisms regarding lawyer-client relations, particularly those areas that had been the basis of many client complaints. Rule 1.4(a), for example, states that "a lawyer shall keep a client reasonably informed about the status of a matter and promptly comply with reasonable requests for information." Since enforcement of the new code relies on the same disciplinary mechanisms used previously, it is likely to suffer from the same limitations. Thus, the actual impact of the new rules remains unknown.

The Public and the Profession

Although lawyers have enjoyed consistently high social standing, their public image has not been particularly positive. Underlying much of the criticism has been the view that the law has become curiously dissociated from justice and that lawyers are more concerned with monetary gain than with the public good. Instead of being committed to justice and the rule of law, they are, it is said, merely "hired guns."

Although contemporary criticism implies that earlier in American history lawyers were somehow more concerned with justice and the social good, there is substantial contrary evidence. For example, even before the American Revolution, colonial statutes were written in an attempt to restrict lawyers' activities. Indeed, criticism of lawyers in the early years of the Republic have a very contemporary ring; alleged offenses were malpractice, excessive fees, promotion of litigation, and the accumulation of great wealth.

Public discomfort with the bar is probably as old as the profession and is no doubt related to the power it exerts. Negative images of lawyers also appear in popular literature, including Swift's reference to lawyers in *Gulliver's Travels* as "a society of men among us, bred up from their youth in the art of proving by words multiplied for the purpose, that white is black, and black is white, according as they are paid" (Pt. IV, Chap. 5). A more contemporary example is found in the refrain from Carl Sandburg's poem "The Lawyers Know Too Much": "Tell me why a hearse horse snickers hauling a lawyer's bones."

Even so, lawyers are frequently lauded as defenders of the downtrodden and pursuers of justice willing to guarantee an individual's day in court and to protect modern-day Davids from their Goliaths. We often object to the intrusion of law and lawyers in our lives; at the same time, we look to them as a last resort to protect us. In addition, there is evidence that members of the public who have employed attorneys on their own behalf are generally pleased with the representation provided. Among individuals who have retained legal counsel, between 80 percent and 90 percent rate their lawyers good or excellent in honesty, promptness, and reasonableness of fees.

Even so, modern pollsters document the low level of public confidence in the legal profession as the love-hate relationship between lawyers and laypersons continues unabated. In particular, there seems to be a growing awareness of the limits of the law and lawyers in curing social ills. Yet Americans seem unwilling to give up any legal advantage and seek to protect and promote their rights under the law. In so doing, they commit themselves to the legal professionals.

CASES

Argersinger v. Hamlin, 407 U.S. 25 (1972)
Bates v. State Bar of Arizona, 433 U.S. 350 (1977)
Brotherhood of Railway Trainmen v. Virginia, 377 U.S. 1 (1964)
Gideon v. Wainwright, 372 U.S. 335 (1963)
Goldfarb v. Virginia State Bar, 421 U.S. 773 (1975)
National Association for the Advancement of Colored People v. Button, 371 U.S. 415 (1963)
Powell v. Alabama, 287 U.S. 45 (1932)
United Mine Workers District 12 v. Illinois Bar Assn., 389 U.S. 217 (1967)
United Transportation Union v. State Bar, 401 U.S. 376 (1971)

BIBLIOGRAPHY

American Bar Association, *ABA Canons of Ethics* (1908), formed the first set of ethical standards for lawyers that were intended to be applicable nationally; *ABA Code of Professional Responsibility* (1969), constituted the major midcentury overhaul of the canons; and *ABA Model Rules of Professional Conduct* (1983), is the most recent revision of ABA standards of conduct for lawyers. American Bar Association Special Committee on Evaluation of Disciplinary Enforcement, *Problems and Recommendations in Disciplinary Enforcement,* Final Draft (June 1970), approaches ethical questions from the standpoint of enforcement. Jerold S. Auerbach, *Unequal Justice: Lawyers and Social Change in Modern America* (1976), is a critical examination of the legal profession and its efforts to contain social change. "A Businessman's View of Lawyers," in *Business Lawyer,* 33 (January 1978), is the transcript of a panel discussion of corporate executives at the Program of the Section of Corporation, Banking and Business Law, American Bar Association 1977 Annual Meeting.

Jerome E. Carlin, *Lawyer's Ethics* (1966), examines how the social organization of the profession affects adherence to codes of ethics. Barbara A. Curran, *The Legal Needs of the Public* (1977), reports on a national survey of nonbusiness use of lawyers' services by adults in the United States; and *1984 Lawyers' Statistical Report* (1985), reports on national statistics on the legal profession based on 1980 data and includes demographics and nature-of-practice information.

Henry S. Drinker, *Legal Ethics* (1953), is the most extensive treatment of the historical development of standards of legal ethics, written by a longtime chairman of the ABA Standing Committee on Professional Ethics and Grievances. Monroe H. Friedman, *Lawyers' Ethics in an Adversary System* (1975), points out the conflicting values in codes of ethics for lawyers and argues the overriding importance of obligations to client in an adversary system. Cynthia Fuchs, *Women in Law* (1981), is a study of women lawyers in the 1960s and 1970s that documents their increased opportunities in the legal profession.

John P. Heinz and Edward O. Laumann, *Chicago Lawyers: The Social Structure of the Bar* (1983), provides a sociological analysis of the Chicago bar based on interviews with more than seven hundred lawyers, with particular attention on the relationship between lawyers' demographic characteristics and the nature of their legal practice. Peter H. Irons, *The New Deal Lawyers* (1982), describes and examines the central contribution of lawyers to the dramatic change in

American public policy and the role of the federal government that occurred in the 1930s.

Jack Ladinsky, "The Impact of Social Backgrounds of Lawyers on Law Practice and the Law," in *Journal of Legal Education,* 16 (1963), is a study of solo and firm lawyers in the Detroit area that examines the relationship between their family origins and education and their work situations. Karl Llewellyn, "The Bar Specializes—With What Results?" in *Annals of the American Academy of Political and Social Science,* 167 (1933), is a well-known law professor's examination of the impact of specialization within the legal profession, written at a time when specialization was quite minimal compared with today; and "On What Is Wrong with So-called Legal Education," in *Columbia Law Review,* 35 (1935), is his critique of legal education, focusing on what it is that law schools do not do to prepare their students for the actual practice of law.

Stewart Macaulay, "Lawyer Advertising, Yes, but . . . ," University of Wisconsin Institute for Legal Studies, Working Paper No. 1–2, 1985, supports lawyer advertising but cautions limits. Martin Mayer, *The Lawyers* (1967), is a popular account of the legal profession, the work of lawyers, and the world in which they operate. Leon Mayhew and Albert J. Reiss, "The Social Organization of Legal Contacts," in *American Sociological Review,* 34 (1969), reports on a study of use of lawyers by residents of the Detroit area. Thomas D. Morgan, "The Evolving Concept of Professional Responsibility," in *Harvard Law Review,* 90 (1977), examines the conflicting norms within the Code of Professional Responsibility and which goals take primacy over others.

Alfred Z. Reed, *Training for the Public Profession of the Law* (1921), is an early analysis of the various modes of preparation of lawyers for practice. Douglas E. Rosenthal, *Lawyer and Client: Who's in Charge?* (1974), describes two models (traditional and participatory) of lawyer-client relationships and examines their impact on the results in personal-injury cases. H. Laurence Ross, *Settled Out of Court* (1970), an examination of automobile accident cases in which the major actors are not lawyers but insurance adjusters and layperson claimants, is an excellent presentation of the law in action and how it differs from the law on the books.

Erwin O. Smigal, *The Wall Street Lawyer* (1969), discusses recruitment, background characteristics, career patterns, and work of lawyers in large law firms in New York City, examining the internal structure of those firms. Eric Steele and Raymond T. Nimmer, "Lawyers, Clients and Professional Responsibility," in *American Bar Foundation Research Journal* (1976), reports on the enforcement of codes of professional conduct, including consideration of the nature of complaints and the frequency of sanctions. Alexis de Tocqueville, *Democracy in America,* H. Reeve, trans. (1976), is the classic examination of American society and government by a Frenchman who visited the United States in the 1830s, in which he noted the central importance of the judicial system and judges and lawyers to the system of government.

United States Department of Commerce, Bureau of Industrial Economics, *U.S. Industrial Outlook* (1984), describes the status and prospects for more than three hundred industries. Richard Wasserstrom, "Lawyers as Professionals: Some Moral Issues," in *Human Rights,* 5 (1975), considers the complexities of determining appropriate behavior when lawyers' professional rules of conduct conflict with general social rules of conduct. Frances Kahn Zemans and Victor G. Rosenblum, *The Making of a Public Profession* (1981), analyzes legal education and the professional development of lawyers, using data from more than five hundred practicing lawyers.

– FRANCES KAHN ZEMANS

LEGAL REASONING

When rules of law provide no single dispositive solution to a legal dispute, judges choose a solution. The term *legal reasoning* refers to the theory and practice by which judges justify their choices. To understand legal reasoning one must appreciate that judges do choose what the law means. Legal reasoning is the process by which judges persuade us that these discretionary choices are impartial.

Impartiality and Legal Reasoning

All complex human systems contain institutions and routines for resolving conflicts between people. In most organized sports, umpires and referees resolve the conflicts and disagreements that inevitably arise in the play of the game. In commercial life, employment contracts, often negotiated through a union representing employees, establish grievance procedures for settling disputes about conditions of employment. In government and public affairs, legal institutions have the responsibility for preventing and resolving conflicts.

All institutions that solve conflicts rely in varying degrees on rules. In simple systems and relationships, a few clear rules (such as the order of winning hands in a poker game) prevent or resolve conflicts almost automatically. However, in complex, institutionalized conflict control, the rules cannot anticipate and govern unambiguously in advance the many different conflict situations that occur. Thus, people—judges—must be prepared to exercise "judgment" in order to resolve conflicts. These people—umpires, arbitrators, judges, and so forth—must act impartially if they wish to keep conflict within acceptable bounds. Impartiality ensures that losers in disputes trust the fairness of the decision, at least in the minimal sense that they do not rebel against the regime the judge represents. Martin Shapiro concludes that when the decider appears simply to take on the winner's side against the loser, the dispute-settling mechanism becomes "politicized." Individual cases become "causes" in escalating political conflicts that can destroy the structure of institutions and polities. The failure of trust in conflict-resolving mechanisms has with some frequency contributed to the collapse of political regimes not only in developing nations but also in the United States during the Civil War era.

Impartial decisions must appear to be consistent with rules, procedures, and values that the institution and therefore the conflicting parties within it have previously accepted as applicable to the dispute. In Herman Melville's great story *Billy Budd,* the innocent hero, Billy, so trusts the rightness of the rules and the impartiality of his ship's captain that he calmly accepts his own hanging for striking and killing a ship's officer, Claggart. The ship's company, which reveres Billy, does the same. That Claggart was an evil bully, that he provoked Billy's blow, that the unforeseeable way he fell after receiving the blow contributed to his death, that the sentence of hanging could have been mitigated—none of these facts destroys Billy's faith in the captain's impartiality. Hence, impartiality depends upon the capacity of the judge and the formal trappings of the judgmental process to persuade the audience that the decisions are made not on the basis of the judge's own will but in terms of broader rules, customs, and values that the community shares. Short of the brutal use of force and coercion, only this maintenance of trust can keep social conflicts within manageable bounds.

The legal systems of the American nation, the fifty states, and thousands of local governmental units are all highly developed. That is, these systems all purport to govern with reference to a complex network of rules applied by people with political authority to do so—hence, the popular slogan "We live under the rule of law, not under the rule of men." Legislatures, executive and administrative agencies, and courts all make, and purport to follow, the literally millions of rules that fill law libraries. The impartiality of judges who decide cases depends on their honoring these rules in application.

Legal reasoning *refers to the justifications of choices that judges express in their opinions.*

The vast majority of potential human conflicts do not, however, become publicly visible lawsuits. Clear and authoritative legal rules permit citizens and their lawyers to anticipate and resolve most problems privately and usually in their early stages. Lawsuits cost money, and when a rule speaks unambiguously to a case, the involved parties have little incentive to pay a judge to tell them what they already know. Thus, the very success of governance through rules—rules concerning estates, insurance, business and financial dealings, liability for negligently hurting others, and so on—screens cases from the courts and prevents students of the judicial process from seeing the power of "the rule of law" firsthand.

In the main, two kinds of disputes do get to court. The first is a factual dispute between parties. A plaintiff injured in an automobile accident insists that the defendant hit him after running a red light. The defendant insists the light was green or perhaps that he ran a red light while rushing a choking child to the hospital. Such factual disputes often raise no conflict about the interpretation of legal rules, and no judicial justification is required. The rules of trial procedure and evidence are very detailed and specific so as to minimize the chances for judicial error. The other kind of dispute involves the meaning of the legal rules themselves. Granting, for the sake of argument, that a certain set of facts is true, the plaintiffs and defendants make contradictory legal arguments, each arguing that a rule or legal principle related to the presumed facts dictates that his or her side should win.

And so a fascinating paradox in legal reasoning emerges: if political stability depends in part on judicial impartiality, but if impartiality depends on decisions consistent with rules, how can judges decide impartially if the rules in fact give no answer or give conflicting and inconsistent answers? If rules conflict or are worded ambiguously, then the judge must choose among them. Precisely because the tension is so great between the ideal of impartiality, on the one hand, and the reality of legal indeterminacy, on the other, judges (particularly appellate judges) provide published reasons, or "opinions," for their choices. *Legal reasoning,* therefore, refers to the justifications of choices that judges express in these opinions. Ultimately, judicial impartiality and the efficacy of the judicial system itself depend on the persuasiveness of legal reasoning.

Legal reasoning, in theory and practice, does not deal directly with the actual psychological process by which judges choose legal solutions. The neurobiology of human decision-making is still in many ways mysterious to experts in psychology, and how judges decide remains at bottom just as mysterious. In an oft-quoted passage from 1929, Judge Joseph Hutcheson wrote, "The judge really decides by feeling and not by judgment, by hunching and not by ratiocination, such ratiocination appearing only in the opinion" (Golding, 15). Hutcheson used the metaphor of an "intuitive flash" of electric current that makes the connection between a legal question and a judicial decision.

Behavioral studies of the American legal system have established through empirical research that judicial backgrounds, values, role models, and political aspirations do influence judges' legal choices, but this descriptive research hardly specifies how individuals actually make particular choices. The term *legal reasoning* thus will here be used for the observable characteristics of the reasons judges give for their choices. Legal reasoning thus provides an ideal model of how judges ought to decide, but it does not describe how judges actually decide.

Jerome Frank went so far as nearly to divorce the psychological process of choice from its justification, as if a judge who chose a solution by flipping a coin would commit no sin as long as he or she could provide an adequate justification for the choice after the fact. More recently, however, Richard Wasserstrom has pointed out that the forms of justifications influence the way people search for their decisions. Because experimental reproducibility is the test of justification in science, scientists search for truth by doing experiments; they do not flip coins. Discussions of legal reasoning can directly describe and analyze only published judicial justifications. These discussions may in turn affect the way judges reach their hunches through processes we do not yet understand.

Legal reasoning operates at both analytical and theoretical levels. It analyzes the logical patterns that judges seem frequently to use when they publish reasons for their decisions. It also differentiates between more and less desirable techniques of reasoning that judges ought theoretically to follow. The theoretical and necessarily ethical level at which legal reasoning operates is part of the field of political philosophy. It is considerably more controversial than the empirical workings of this kind of reasoning.

Ambiguity in Law

Legal reasoning occurs whenever rules of law, in their practical operation, fail to provide judges and lawyers with obvious and automatic solutions to factual disputes. Ronald Dworkin has argued that courts must act as if there were one correct solution to each legal dispute and that in a world of cost-free, completely available information, such solutions presumably exist. In practice, however, many forces work against the judge who tries to deduce from principles, rules, and facts the correct solution in each case. Appellate courts, as opposed to trial courts, hear and review questions of law—they do not retry the facts of cases—and litigants on both sides invest their money in the costs of an appeal because they believe they have a chance to win. In appellate courts the principles and rules of law are arguably ambiguous at the outset. It is certainly true that to reach legal closure in a case, a judge must appeal to something, but the something often turns out to be a principle of the judge's own making. Sometimes the judge does no more than give hints in his or her opinion as to the nature of that principle.

In the American system legal rules originate in all branches of national, state, and local governments. Legislatures make statutes; city councils and county commissions make ordinances; and executive agencies and independent regulatory agencies make rules to further the policies they are created to execute. Moreover, the American practice of following precedent, the most prominent characteristic of modern common-law systems, gives judicial decisions themselves the force of law in future cases that seem factually to resemble earlier cases.

Each of these kinds of law have characteristics that engender legal uncertainty. Statutes and similar rules tend by their nature to create ambiguous applications. A statute is a political command that attempts to provide a solution to a class of problems, not a unique conflict. In defining this class, questions inevitably arise about the location of its boundaries. Thus, in one famous case, *McBoyle* v. *United States* (1931), Congress had made it criminally punishable to transport knowingly a stolen motor vehicle across state lines. The statute, the National Motor Vehicle Theft Act, defined *motor vehicle* to "include an automobile, automobile truck, automobile wagon, motor cycle, or any other self-propelled vehicle not designed for running on rails." The defendant had knowingly transported a stolen airplane across state lines. He argued in the Supreme Court that because all the vehicles specifically mentioned in the statute ran on the ground, it was not fair to punish him for transporting an airplane, something the statute might not cover. Justice Oliver Wendell Holmes agreed with him: "Although it is not likely that a criminal will carefully consider the text of the law before he murders or steals, it is reasonable that a fair warning should be given to the world in language that the common world will understand, of what the law intends to do if a certain line is passed." Had McBoyle knowingly transported a stolen automobile, the rule would have covered him unambiguously, but he argued successfully that it did not cover airplanes.

For every choice an appellate judge makes, there exist prior judicial decisions (precedents) that arguably govern the result.

Another possibility is a hypothetical case of a Federal Bureau of Investigation (FBI) agent who recovers a stolen automobile and drives it back to its owner across a state line. He has fallen within the letter of the law, but he does not represent the class of problems the statute tries to resolve. Must the law apply to him anyway?

Statutes may also speak in language that raises doubts about the application of the words in any context. Words are inherently crude and inexact communicative tools. Statutes may speak so uncertainly that judges cannot distinguish the statutory core from its periphery. Thus the 1970 Occupational Safety and Health Act defines an "occupational safety and health standard" as a standard that is "reasonably necessary or appropriate to provide safe or healthful employment." It directs the setting of standards for toxic materials and substances that "most adequately assures, to the extent feasible, on the basis of the best available evidence, that no employee will suffer material impairment of health or functional capacity." But what do phrases such as "reasonably necessary," "extent feasible," and "material impairment of health or functional capacity" mean? The Supreme Court justices could not agree on the statute's meaning in cases involving benzene, in *Industrial Union Department, AFL-CIO* v. *American Petroleum Institute* (1980) and *American Textile Manufacturers Institute* v. *Donovan* (1981).

Constitutional rules, particularly in the Constitution of the United States, address fundamental questions about the nature of the polity at a more general and abstract level than do statutes. Therefore, constitutional rules are even more open-ended and uncertain in their application than are statutory rules. It is inevitable that the Supreme Court, not the Constitution, shapes constitutional meaning in practice. Thus, Charles Evans Hughes remarked, "We are under a Constitution—but the Constitution is what the Judges say it is."

The primary reason judges face the inevitability of choice concerns the nature of judicial precedent. For every choice an appellate judge makes, there exist prior judicial decisions (precedents) that arguably govern the result. This happens both in case-law situations (tort and contract law, for example) and when judges choose between competing applications of constitutional, statutory, and administrative rules.

To reason from a precedent is to reason by example. The judge must decide whether the case or issue put before him or her factually resembles a prior case that a party has argued resolves the current dispute. Unfortunately, the legal system provides no clear formula telling judges how to decide whether a prior case is factually similar enough to the current case to serve as precedent (Levi). A judge faced with a decision in the case of a hypothetical defendant charged under the National Motor Vehicle Theft Act with the transportation of a motor boat across state lines might find the airplane precedent determinative. If so, the judge would hold the accused not punishable under the terms of the statute by the authority of *McBoyle.* But nothing in the law obligates this judge to treat *McBoyle* that way. He or she is free to articulate a factual difference. If the stolen boat was either driven across a lake or river or transported on a truck across state lines, the judge could freely argue that *McBoyle* did not cover this defendant because the act of transport did not take place in the air.

Reasoning from precedents is the primary source of legal indeterminacy. This form of reasoning by example makes judicial choices inevitable. It is therefore particularly necessary for judges to justify their choices persuasively in order to maintain judicial impartiality.

The Logical Structure of Judicial Justifications

Judges do not make choices by "doing" statutory, common-law, or constitutional reasoning. These phrases merely describe the outer contours of legal reasoning; they denote categories of reasoning problems, not the logical structure of the justifications themselves.

Martin Golding provides a useful dissection of the varying forms of the logic of judicial justification. He reviews the common logical forms that most arguments take. These include both determinate and indeterminate forms. The standard deductive syllogism ("If all A are B and all B are C, then all A are C") is a determinate argument. An argument by inferential observation ("All observed cases of A are B; therefore, the next observed case of A will be B") is not determinate.

Four important observations stand out in Golding's analysis. First, it is possible to find judicial opinions that appear to take the form of any and all conceivable logical forms, including fallacious ones. Second, most judicial opinions are indeterminate. They do not meet the criteria of what logicians call a "sound deductive argument," which is one in which all the premises are true; the premises are arranged in valid form (not, for example, "If all Americans are humans and all French are humans, then all Americans are French"); and no other premises need be asserted to establish the truth of the conclusion. Reasoning by example is inferential and indeterminate ("The new case is more like precedent 1 than precedent 2; therefore, precedent 1 governs"). In cases where judges do not resort to precedent, it is difficult, if not impossible, for them to prove either the truth or the exhaustiveness of an opinion's stated premises.

Third, judicial opinions frequently fail to state and support a premise on which the logical structure of the argument depends. (A logical statement that leaves unstated or implicit a premise on which the conclusion depends is an "enthymeme.") Although it is often possible to analyze an opinion in such a way that the analyst supplies a plausible implicit premise, judges by no means necessarily make plain the logic of their opinions.

Finally, the most common single form of judicial argument does not meet standards of determinate logic. Judges tend to engage in an assertive and implicitly ethical form of logic known as "practical reasoning."

Judges rarely receive formal training in logic, and the legal community (including the bar and law-school associations) has not seriously demanded of judges that their decisions meet the criteria of determinate logic. The flawed syllogisms and reductiones ad absurdum should not surprise anyone, nor do they necessarily constitute failures in impartiality. The elements of practical reasoning suggest how legal reasoning may be impartial at the same time that it employs a technically illogical structure.

Consider first the well-known 1954 desegregation case, *Brown* v. *Board of Education.* Its legal question was, Does the equal protection clause of the Fourteenth Amendment ban racial segregation of public school children? The Court's answer runs, in effect, as follows: Racial equality is a desirable social goal and a protected individual right as well. Racially segregated schools impede progress toward racial equality. Therefore, the law ought to bar public racial segregation in schools. Note that this argument does not prove deterministically that the equal protection clause, either by its words or by prior precedents applying it, prohibits racial segregation. Instead, the Court argued that the law ought to do so.

This is the essence of practical reasoning. It is, as Golding points out, value-laden and action-oriented. Practical reasoning asserts that the law ought to say something in order to achieve in action a desired state. Often the court contents itself with asserting the desirability of the asserted state, not proving it by either deductive or inferential means. Thus, the legal reasoning that the mix of ambiguity in law and the political demand for impartiality makes mandatory becomes on close inspection an operation in which judges articulate their beliefs about the way society works and how it ought to work.

The observable structure of judicial justifications thus takes many forms. These justifications tend, however, to have important normative assertions at their cores. The remainder of this essay therefore describes the normative issues, often controversial ones, that commonly arise in judicial justifications.

The Doctrine of Stare Decisis

Lay people—and, for that matter, more than a few lawyers and judges—have more misunderstandings about the nature and role of precedents than about any other aspect of legal reasoning. As many people understand it, when primary rules do not on their own terms resolve a specific conflict, the judge should find a previous application of the rule in a case whose facts most resemble the facts of the current case and then decide the current case in the same way. This is the conventional but incomplete doctrine of stare decisis.

The perception of factual similarity or difference between the conflict in court and any prior case depends, as we have seen, on the judge's perception of which facts in the cases are pertinent. In making comparisons, the judge may already have decided, at least roughly, how the case should come out. It may serve the cause of impartiality for a judge to assert that his or her decision is consistent with at least one prior decision, but this does not mean that the new decision proceeds from the past case or that the past case is, when compared to other cases that the opinion may ignore, a more persuasive or dispositive precedent. Hence, the doctrine of stare decisis cannot merely involve "following" precedent.

Stare decisis is indeed a useful legal reasoning tool, but its role is very different from the conventional perception of it. Specifically, *after* a judge concludes from reasoning by example that the holding of a previous case does determine the result, the judge should then ask whether this holding must be followed. He will of course want to follow the precedent if doing so would achieve the "right" result. Indeed, he may well choose one factual similarity as opposed to others precisely because that choice produces the outcome he desires.

Nevertheless, cases arise where a well-developed line of precedents states a rule that is so clear and well known that judges cannot ignore it, *and* the judge feels that the original rule, as a matter of practical reasoning, produces the "wrong" result—that is, it serves no useful public purpose or protects no valid individual rights. To illustrate, the Supreme Court held in 1922 and again in 1953 that the business of professional baseball did not need to comply with the antitrust laws, laws prohibiting unfair and monopolistic competition in commerce. Everyone in the baseball business knew these precedents, and in 1972 the Court reiterated the position for a third time *(Flood* v. *Kuhn).* Yet, many doubts existed about the wisdom of the precedents. In the interim, the Court had held that all other professional sports did need to comply with the antitrust laws, and the commercial character of baseball had expanded tremendously.

Thus, the doctrine of stare decisis really provides reasons for judges to follow precedents that state "bad law," precedents whose practical reasoning the judge, unburdened by the weight of precedents, would question or reject. There are two kinds of circumstances under which judges should do so. First, whenever a lower-court judge establishes that an authoritative precedent from a higher court in the same jurisdiction disposes unambiguously of the case in court, he is in nearly all circumstances normatively obligated to follow it. This strong norm of "vertical stare decisis" follows from the hierarchic nature of judicial systems. But the same judge is not similarly obligated to follow a precedent from a court in another jurisdiction or from a court on the same level in the same jurisdiction.

Second, when (as in the baseball cases) a state or federal supreme court is tempted to overturn an outmoded precedent of its own making, one or more of the following five social norms, each itself a statement of practical reasoning, may justify "horizontal stare decisis." The first is the preservation of the stability of social institutions. The second is the protection of specific reliance on law; individuals actually do make plans (business arrangements, tax investment decisions, wills, deeds to property, and so forth) on the basis of announced law. The third is the promotion of efficient judicial administration; the judicial work load would become overwhelming if judges had to decide each and every legal issue anew. Fourth is the protection of equality, and fifth is the promotion of the image of justice. Impartiality depends on giving the appearance of treating people equally and justly by deciding on general, not individual, grounds. Following precedent helps maintain the appearance of impartiality.

Impartiality depends on giving the appearance of treating people equally and justly by deciding on general, not individual, grounds.

It is often said, as the Supreme Court did in the baseball cases, that when these norms apply, legal changes should come from the legislature because the legislature can act without upsetting plans made in honest reliance on past law. However, there is a growing consensus that in many cases the five reasons just given for following outmoded precedents apply only weakly, or not at all. In such cases, courts should embrace opportunities for change. Viewed in the light of these five principles, the baseball cases should probably have come out the other way (Carter, 1984).

Statutory Interpretation in the First Instance

A statute or local ordinance is an attempt by an elected lawmaking body to remedy some perceived evil. Such rules solve problems by a variety of means. Some rules command people to behave in a particular way in certain circumstances; for instance, most Americans who earn over a certain number of taxable dollars in a year must file a federal tax return. Other rules prohibit certain behaviors; as an example, certain statutes prohibit the willful taking of another's life in the absence of a legally recognized defense. Some statutes command the expenditure of public funds for certain programs in the hope that these programs will better the human condition.

Although statutory commands vary widely, important political norms underlie their application. In a democracy it is presumed that elected lawmaking bodies are the primary source of law. Absent conflicts with constitutional commands, statutory rules ought to determine how courts should apply them to concrete situations.

Where a statute speaks clearly to a situation, conflicts about statutory meaning do not arise. When a statute fails in its own terms to resolve a problem, because of the generality of its language, because it conflicts with other statutory commands, or because of any of the causes of legal uncertainty noted above, then judges must choose what the statute means. If precedents exist, the judge may conclude that they are wise in themselves or that the doctrine of stare decisis requires that precedents be followed, despite doubts about their wisdom. If, however, the judge finds no dispositive precedents or concludes that the existing precedents need not be followed, then the statute itself must be examined. This process is called statutory interpretation in the first instance. To interpret a statute in a manner that is consistent with the democratic norm, the judge must ask and answer these questions: What is the social evil the statute (or statutes) bearing on this case seeks to remedy? What remedy has the statute commanded? Is the case before me an instance of the problem the statute seeks to remedy?

Judges in recent English and American practice have developed an astonishing array of theories about statutory interpretation. Many of them seek to evade the issues just posed. Judges are uncomfortable with these questions because they believe that judges have no lawmaking authority in a democracy. Judges often believe that once a legislature has spoken, they ought to have no choice in the matter. The solution to the legal problem must somehow exist in the statute itself and in the legislative action that brought the statute into being. The judge must discover that solution, not choose it; to choose would substitute the decisions of less democratically responsive judges for those made by more democratically responsive elected officials.

One technique for evading the obligations of legal reasoning in the application of ambiguous statutes is to apply statutory language literally whenever possible. A literalist judge would thus hold the hypothetical FBI officer liable under the National Motor Vehicle Theft Act for returning the stolen car to its owner by driving it across a state line. Such a judge might agree that the result is absurd and that to so apply the act does not serve any discernible public purpose. This judge would also argue, however, that a statute is a statute and that once courts assume the power to say what statutory words do not say, undemocratic courts can say anything they like. The practical reasoning implicit in this argument would hold that legislatures ought to make clear laws and that courts should reach absurd decisions so as to teach legislatures to make clear laws.

Fortunately, American judges have tended not to follow the literal approach as often as English judges have. Unfortunately, American judges have more frequently employed a second approach, called the plain-meaning rule, which is not much better. This rule holds that when the words of a statute do not produce an absurd result in application and when one reading of the words seems more direct and less tortured than others, then statutory commands must be followed according to that reading.

The plain-meaning rule is an unworkable concept in both theory and practice. In theory it cannot work because words have no plain meaning except in context. A basketball player who says to a teammate during timeout, "I can get free underneath. When I do, feed me the ball," is not asking his teammate to place a spherical rubber snack in his mouth during play. The judge who invokes the plain-meaning rule without looking at the problem-solving context of the statute makes no better than a stab in the dark. Judicial invocations of the plain-

This suspect undergoes an early version of the lie detector test. Many experts believe that lie detector evidence is not accurate enough, but it can be used in court if all parties agree. (Hulton-Deutsch Collection/Corbis)

meaning rule have proved neither coherent nor consistent.

A third method for pretending that ambiguous statutory language is certain allows a judge to invoke one or more "canons" of statutory interpretation. The judge can say that the legislature intended its language to be read with the canons in mind. These rules for interpreting rules, like the plain-meaning rule, seem sensible from a safe distance. For example, the canon of ejusdem generis holds that where a statute contains both general and specific language (for instance, "vehicle" and "automobile" in *McBoyle*), the general language covers only those things which possess the characteristics that all the specifically mentioned things have in common.

The list of canons is, however, a lengthy one. Karl Llewellyn listed fifty-six of them in twenty-eight pairs and showed how, in a given case, for each pair the two canons yielded opposite results. Like the plain-meaning rule, canons disguise judicial choices but do not eliminate the fact that judges make them.

The fourth and most common method by which judges pretend that uncertain statutes are certain is to attempt to discover how the legislature intended the courts to apply the statute in practice. Judges explore statements made in legislative debate, the reports of committees that drafted the legislation, statements in the record of the sponsors of the bill, and so forth.

The concept of legislative intent suffers from severe logical and practical defects. First, the question before the court always concerns a unique case. In all likelihood, the legislature never intended anything regarding the unique case because the facts of the unique case never crossed any legislator's mind. The late-nineteenth-century authors of the Sherman Antitrust Act almost surely did not anticipate the growth of the sport of baseball into a major commercial enterprise in the twentieth century. To hold that baseball is not covered because Congress did not intend to cover it belies the very generality of statutory problem-solving commands.

Second, only a duly constituted majority of a legislative body possesses the legal power to enact a law, and only the bill duly passed and enacted has the force of law. One sponsor or one committee constitutes a legislative minority that lacks any lawmaking power of its own. To hold that such a sponsor's or committee's intent governs is to admit lawmaking by minority. Put another way, if intent counts, it is the intent of the legislative majority. But the only measure or poll of this majority's intent is its vote to convert the words of a bill into law. This merely returns a judge back to the starting point: the words in the context of the unique case are ambiguous.

Third and finally, legislatures are political and practical places. Ambiguity in statutes often reflects political compromises necessary to get a bill passed. In effect, the legislative process creates bounded ambiguities and then transfers the responsibility of clarifying what the words really mean to the courts.

The core of the difficulty in much modern statutory interpretation arises from the assumption that legislatures, not courts, "make" statutes. Judges are tempted to grasp any concept that reaffirms at least the appearance that judges honor this democratic norm. This practice, however, cannot logically coexist with a central feature of the American legal system: that each appellate case represents a potential precedent for future similar cases. If, in the literal reading of statutory words, the mechanistic application of a canon, or the superficial assertion of legislative intent, an appellate court produces a result that does not promote the social goals of the statute, then such a court, probably without appreciating the fact, creates case law for the future that undercuts the "will of the people" expressed in the statute. Ironically, the techniques for giving legislative acts the appearance of clarity and primacy in reality have precisely the opposite effect. They undermine legislative primacy in favor of judicial face-saving. Because common-law political systems traditionally accept judicial lawmaking, the effect is even more ironic. A legislature unhappy with a judicial application of its statute remains politically free to rewrite or amend the legislation.

When statutory language does not resolve a problem,

judges must interpret not the statute

but the context in which the statute arose.

When statutory language does not resolve a problem, judges must interpret not the statute but the context in which the statute arose. Interpretation is a practice that Clifford Geertz calls "thick description." To interpret a statute in the first instance, judges must explore the social history surrounding the passage of an act. In 1890 the monopolization of businesses was perceived to cause higher prices and lower wages than would competitive business conditions. When the National Motor Vehicle Theft Act was passed, it had become clear that the jurisdictional boundaries of states prevented state law enforcement officials from acting swiftly against crimes carried on through movement from state to state. Federal officials, who could cross state boundaries without losing their legal authority to enforce, could therefore assist in the apprehension of those taking easily moved items across state lines.

Statutory words, canons, the statements of sponsors, committee reports, and the like may assist in the thick-textured effort to diagnose the targeted social evil, but these are rarely conclusive. Justice Holmes, in the airplane theft case, did not really inquire into the purpose of the statute. He did not ask the following questions: Are stolen airplanes easily moved from state to state, like stolen cars? If so, on what basis would the purpose of the act not cover airplanes? If airplanes fall within the act's purposes, on what basis should we excuse McBoyle? Does McBoyle have a moral claim that what he did was otherwise lawful? Similarly, if the two major baseball leagues conspire to prevent the development of competition from a third league in the twentieth century, on what basis does this conspiracy differ from the monopolization of sugar or steel in the nineteenth century? These are precisely the questions judges frequently evade despite the fact that the common-law political system presumes that the courts will resolve them.

Two further points about judicial articulation of statutory purposes deserve mention. First, not even exhaustive interpretive efforts, efforts far greater than those which judges have time in their daily schedules to undertake, reveal one, and only one, correct decision in a given case. Judges may honestly disagree about the nature of statutory purposes. Thus, Justice Holmes might have argued in *McBoyle* that the statutory exclusion of trains must have some purposive significance. Presumably the significance lies in the easy traceability of stolen trains by following their tracks. He might then have cited a general norm favoring localism in law enforcement and pointed out that one can easily trace airplanes to airports. If so, he would have reached the same result (excusing McBoyle), but he would have done so by reasoning about statutory purpose.

Second, the misunderstandings about the legislative process just described have led some scholars, including Edward Levi, to advocate a more rigid adherence to stare decisis in statutory interpretation. Levi argues that if courts have freedom to reinterpret legislation, legislatures will be relieved of the pressure to update and improve their statutes. Legislatures and courts must cooperate in the lawmaking effort, and a clear-cut division of labor makes that cooperation possible.

Indeed, there are instances in which legislators heave a sigh of relief that courts have taken a delicate political problem off their hands. But the assumption that most interpretive problems raise highly charged public issues that deserve legislative rather than judicial responses is inaccurate. Most statutory interpretations lie either at the margins of a policy problem, where busy legislatures concerned with general policymaking will not really care which way courts go, or the issue will be so intertwined with the never-ending pulling and tugging of lobbyists, bureaucratic agencies and legislators, and their committees that it will receive occasional reexamination, regardless of judicial decisions in specific cases.

Of course, there are exceptions, but the better rule, when a judge is satisfied that the five reasons for horizontal stare decisis listed above do not apply, is to ignore precedent and treat the problem as a new one; Guido Calabresi has elaborated this position.

Normative Problems in Common-Law Reasoning

In 1881, in a book entitled *The Common Law,* Oliver Wendell Holmes wrote:

> The life of the law has not been logic: it has been experience. The felt necessities of the time, the prevalent moral and politcal theories, intuitions of public policy, avowed or unconscious, even the prejudices which judges share with their fellow-men, have had a good deal more to do than the syllogism in determining the rules by which men should be governed.
>
> (p. 1)

Holmes was reporting his understanding of centuries of common-law history. Throughout its development from the Battle of Hastings on, common-law principles and the methods by which judges reach them mirror the thought patterns of their times. Earlier common-law thinkers, whose work culminated in the treatises of Blackstone, attempted to codify principles of common law into "correct" legal principles. Pervasive religious beliefs made the absence of "correct principles" unthinkable. But that era has given way, as Holmes predicted, to a more rational and pragmatic, hence open-ended and indeterminate, approach to law.

The Supreme Court's constitutional rulings

have throughout American history

helped to shape political and social events.

In the twentieth century, common law has become, according to Karl Llewellyn, not a reservoir of "right rules for human conduct" but a process that permits a healthy compromise between legal predictability and legal change. Ambiguities in law seem not merely inevitable but desirable. Ambiguities encourage those with opposing interests to go to court with arguments about what the law ought to say. Ambiguity, in other words, provides the necessary incentive for people to bring new ideas and factual information to court. Contestants invest in the presentation of a believable case because they have a chance to win. The normative principles that guide judicial thinking may thus change with the times.

One dramatic illustration of a change in legal doctrine that appears to mirror broader social and political changes is the shift toward protecting personal liberty and physical safety in contests pitting the claims of business interests against those of individuals. The common-law tendency to "let the buyer beware" had in the nineteenth century produced a variety of holdings that protected the interests of businesspeople in the youthful days of corporate capitalism. A person injured by a product purchased from a retailer but made negligently by the manufacturer had, with the exception of things the courts found "inherently dangerous," no cause of action against the manufacturer because his contract was with the retailer. But the retailer was rarely a negligent party, so the retailer was liable only to the extent he guaranteed the product.

Courts today, however, are much more likely to protect the consumer in such instances. Owners of shopping centers have been held liable for damages to the nighttime victims of muggers and pursue snatchers, on the theory that the shopping center parking lots were not so well illuminated as to prevent the crime. It is possible to associate these changes in law with changes in democratic ideology, with the growing realization that losses of health and property can be spread across society through insurance coverage, and with increasing technological and economic complexity, which necessitates increased reliance on the care exercised by those with whom the public has no direct contact.

These modern common-law dynamics—incremental legal changes in relation to changing social conditions and ideologies—apply in theory to all judicial decisions, statutory and constitutional as well as judge-made common law. Because judges accept both the inevitability and propriety of judicial lawmaking in a common-law framework, judicial justifications in common-law cases often articulate with candor and clarity the ethical assertions and factual assumptions, the practical reasoning, on which the legal conclusions rest. In a particularly compelling example, *Soldano* v. *O'Daniels* (1983), an intermediate appellate court in California held, contrary to more than a century of common-law rulings, that one citizen with no relationship to a second citizen may in certain circumstances be liable in tort for failing to aid the second. In *Soldano* the court held a bar owner potentially liable to the heirs of a man who died from injuries suffered in a fight across the street when the owner's bartender refused to allow a Good Samaritan to use the bar's telephone to call the police.

The principal debate in modern common-law reasoning involves the extent to which, in a legislative age, courts should cease extending common-law principles of tort, contract, and the like, in deference to the legislature's presumably superior lawmaking position. Judges hotly debate the issue. In *Tarasoff* v. *Regents of the University of California* (1976), California Supreme Court Justice William Clark, later prominent in the administration of President Ronald Reagan, argued in dissent that a psychiatrist has no legal duty to warn the potential victims of his patients: "The Legislature obviously is more capable than is this court to investigate, debate and weigh potential patient harm through disclosure against the risk of public harm by nondisclosure. We should defer to its judgment."

This primary question in contemporary common-law reasoning becomes, on close inspection, a variation on the themes discussed above in the section on statutory interpretation. Is a legislature in fact a superior fact-finding body? Levi wrote, "Despite much gospel to the contrary, a legislature is not a fact-finding body. There is no mechanism, as there is with a court, to require the legislature to sift facts and to make a decision about specific situations" (p. 22). The key to Levi's statement is the word *require.* Legislative committees often make thorough and complete analyses of the arguments for and against pending legislation, but they are not required to do so. The slower but more orderly and public exchange of information and debate of ideas, and particularly the custom of justification in judicial but not legislative policymaking, make courts relatively effective fact-finding bodies. (Indeed, in the *Tarasoff* case Justice Clark rather effectively refuted his claim of legislative superiority by digesting in considerable depth the professional literature analyzing the dynamics and consequences of confidentiality in the doctor-patient relationship.)

Thus, the real issue is neither one of political or constitutional deference by courts to legislatures nor one of comparative institutional capacity. Whether courts ought with some confidence to venture to initiate legal innovations, common-law or otherwise, really depends on the nature of the issues before the court. If the issues and the language that expresses them fall within areas of traditional judicial training, competence, and experience, there seems little reason for courts to abandon the common-law tradition (Horowitz; Carter, 1977).

Reasoning About the Constitution

The United States Supreme Court's constitutional rulings have throughout American history helped to shape political and social events. Of all judicial decisions, the Court's receive the widest press coverage. In the belief that judges at this most powerful and most public level must, in order to preserve political trust, be particularly impartial, both the press and scholars pay a disproportionate amount of attention to the quality of constitutional reasoning.

Despite, or perhaps because of, the Supreme Court's prominence, constitutional reasoning is highly controversial. The legal reasoning perspective adds some important insights to this debate. Chief among them is the observation that the very nature of the Constitution inevitably induces judges to justify constitutional decisions in ways that tend to differ, in theory and in practice, from legal reasoning in other areas of law.

The Constitution consists of a set of legal commands. Indeed, it claims to create "the supreme law of the land," and the legal system has come to accept it as the law that governs the government. Many of these commands—"Congress shall make no law respecting an establishment of religion, or prohibiting the free exercise thereof," for example—are general, ambiguous, and capable of colliding with each other in specific application. Indeed, the two phrases within the amendment just quoted do collide if, for instance, a public schoolteacher who wishes to exercise his religious commitment to evangelism asks all his students to pray in the classroom with him. Because the Constitution articulates the fundamental values of the nation—values that potentially apply to an unimaginably broad range of specific conflicts—constitutional generality, ambiguity, and the potential for collision among rules should not be surprising.

Since the Constitution has a statutory form—its clauses are rules made by a "constitutional" legislature—judges often attempt to interpret it by using statutory interpretation techniques. Often enough, judges pretend that they need not choose what the Constitution means at all. They claim to read the words literally or to discover the intent of the framers, for example. They pretend, as Max Lerner once put it, that constitutional decisions are delivered by "constitutional storks." When judges reason this way, they hide from their audience the reality that they have chosen, not discovered, the result. Given the paramount importance of constitutional impartiality, the temptation to so hide is understandably great. But if judges in fact choose, then, as in statutory interpretation, their method of justifying their choices should reflect that reality.

Because practical reasoning involves, implicitly or explicitly, an estimation of the consequences of certain choices, the judge content with a legalistically determined "discovery" may not pay adequate attention to the consequences of his or her choice. This, we have seen, is true for all kinds of legal reasoning; however, constitutional reasoning here takes a twist. Although in statutory interpretation the judge ought to seek out the purpose of statutory language—the class of social problem that the statute has historically seemed to address—and then determine if the issue in court belongs to that class, judges should not, and usually do not, do so when they reason about the Constitution. Whereas the statute in its historical context defines the problem for the judge, in constitutional law the judge may change the definition of the problem altogether.

Three forces produce this twist. First, some judges and scholars believe that constitutional clauses ought to change meaning with the times. Chief Justice John Marshall's opinion in *McCulloch* v. *Maryland* (1819) said as much. Thus, assuming even conclusive proof that the First Amendment's religion clauses did not react to the mischief of prayer by officials in government in the eighteenth century, it would not follow that a modern court must, as a matter of law, deny that the amendment prohibits prayer in public schools today. Second, the political realities of constitution-making obscure beyond reconstruction either what a majority of founders may have intended a given clause to mean or, more deeply, the scope of the purpose of that clause. Third, the machinery for amending the Constitution operates so infrequently and unpredictably that courts cannot "defer" judgment on constitutional questions to other governmental institutions. When citizens present an appealing constitutional claim, such as a claim that their tax monies should not be spent to support schools operated by a religious denomination, as in *Flast* v. *Cohen* (1968), the courts cannot defer to the legislature. The constitutionality of its statute is the very issue in question.

Scholars have recently escalated the debate over whether the phrase "constitutional interpretation" has any meaning—that is, whether the Court does, or should, interpret the Constitution at all. The technical definition of the interpretive act—"thick description"—suggests that courts rarely interpret in any legal area. In the looser legal sense of interpretation the weight of scholarly opinion seems to tip toward the proposition that courts should justify constitutional conclusions in terms of normative propositions about the character of contemporary American social and political life. However, in 1985 Attorney General Edwin Meese and other conservative politicians argued the opposite view that courts should decide according to the historical context in which a specific clause was drafted and adopted.

No doubt this debate will continue indefinitely. As an empirical matter, however, there is little doubt that the Supreme Court throughout constitutional history has justified its landmark constitutional decisions primarily in relation to contemporary values and experience, and not to history. For example, from about 1880 to the middle of the Great Depression the Court believed that societal well-being depended upon minimizing the power of government to affect private decisions about the use of property and labor in commerce. The Court therefore struck down or severely limited the scope of statutes that sought to correct perceived commercial abuses. The Warren and Burger Courts' emphasis on individual rights and liberties follows from a different and partially incompatible set of premises, according to John H. Ely. Organized commercial interests are well represented in the pluralistic, money- and vote-driven processes of political policymaking and implementation; and individuals and insulated minorities deserve access to the courts because they lack the resources to be heard elsewhere.

Neither approach is demonstrably correct or incorrect in any absolute sense. The point, rather, is that Holmes's "felt necessities of the time, the prevalent moral and political theories, [and] intuitions of public policy" stand out prominently in constitutional reasoning.

Conclusions

This essay began by emphasizing the importance of judicial impartiality and, hence, of legal reasoning within a larger political framework. Subsequent descriptions, however, seemed at every turn paradoxically to underscore the political realities of legal reasoning, realities that raise doubts that judges can decide impartially after all. Judges do not regularly honor the criteria for determinate logic. Judicial justifications tend to take the form of practical reasoning, but even here judicial opinions often fail to state their premises clearly. Analysts must supply the missing premises, and they may themselves disagree. Judicial obscuring of logic, if deliberate, seems motivated to hide from the audience the political and, hence, partial character of many judicial decisions. Indeed, the internal compromises necessary to get different appellate court judges on the same bench to agree with each other enough to sign a common opinion resolving a case can obscure key premises in the opinion (Murphy).

Furthermore, judicial justifications exhibit little patterned consistency in the theories that judges employ. Judges follow prior precedents blindly in the face of powerful evidence that the five reasons given for horizontal stare decisis pose no obstacle to a decision to overrule. Judges also speak of legislative intent or the "plain meaning" of statutory words as if these phrases denoted some reality. Few formal norms consistently guide the justification process. Judges disagree about when, whether, and how actively courts should intervene on behalf of a constitution in legislative matters. They do not even agree about the role either a constitution or a legislature ought to play in lawmaking. It would seem that theories and norms of legal reasoning amount to no more than a hegemonic device to maintain the political power of the legal profession.

Such an assessment is misguided. Legal reasoning does indeed possess all the characteristics just described. Holmes's description is apt, yet the system seems to persist, and despite occasional criticisms, complaints about the quality of appellate court justifications are not very widely shared.

The political culture widely endorses the proposition of equality, that differential treatment of individuals should have a rational basis.

Perhaps we overestimate the political importance of legal reasoning. If only lawyers, judges (and their clerks), and a few professors (and their students) pay serious attention to opinions, then the substance of the result—which interests win and which lose—will shape the public's assessment of appellate court impartiality more than the fine points of the opinion. No matter how well reasoned it is, large segments of the public will oppose a ban on voluntary public school prayer. No matter how poorly reasoned it is, large numbers of the public will approve the reintroduction of the death penalty. Perhaps trust in the judiciary rests on only a minimal kind of impartiality. As long as the courts do not, over many cases and jurisdictions, appear to take sides consistently with one political party or one political ideology, as long as a "Nixon Court" votes to bring down President Nixon, as long as free-speech doctrines protect Ku Klux Klansmen and Communists alike, legal reasoning will pass public muster.

The public unquestionably knows little or nothing of the reasons courts give in opinions. Yet, if judges believe it is their job to justify within an isolated framework of legal language but in reality their decisions significantly affect policy, then their chosen forms of legal reasoning will prevent them from attempting effective practical reasoning about the consequences of their choices. Furthermore, a merely minimal impartiality will suffer the long-term consequences of professional and scholarly criticism. If the legal and academic professions increasingly condemn the judicial process wholesale, that condemnation will spill over—as criticism of the Supreme Court spilled over during the Great Depression—into overtly politicized reactions.

Perhaps political satisfaction with legal reasoning arises from the fact that judges are nobody's fools. If most appellate judges know quite well that they are part of the political process, if they consider as carefully as their resources permit the practical consequences of their choices, then we should not object if they couch justifications in an artificial language of political impartiality so as to preserve public trust.

This approach might suffice in a one-court world, a world of only horizontal stare decisis; but in a common-law system, lower courts and private parties do base plans on what they believe the law permits and requires. The political culture seems widely to endorse the proposition of equality, that differential treatment of individuals should have a rational basis. Planning, particularly by trial judges and practicing attorneys, seeks to predict the consequences of specific actions through reasoning by example. Judicial opinions must therefore contain reasons that permit planning and preserve some sense of equal treatment. Reasons proffered only cosmetically, without real relation to the substance of the decision, increase political and social unpredictability. Ultimately, too, they risk increasing unnecessarily the number of costly lawsuits.

In the 1980s a solution to these paradoxes of legal reasoning began to emerge, in part through the much publicized work of a group of liberal law professors loosely designated "the critical legal studies movement." The solution offered by many critical and noncritical scholars in the 1980s makes the following assertions about the legal process and legal reasoning. First, Holmes not only described correctly the character of legal reasoning but also prescribed, without intending to do so, how legal reasoning ought to operate. Impartiality means acting so as to satisfy audience expectations of the decision-making process. Since by definition legal rules have failed to resolve conflicts in their own terms, it is entirely proper, indeed inevitable, for judges to justify results by resorting to deeper cultural beliefs and values that provide a coherent resolution of the case (Gusfield).

Second, one central criterion of a "good" practically reasoned judicial justification is that it expresses as accurately and candidly as possible both assumptions about empirical reality and assertions about what society ought to resemble (Nonet and Selznick). Third, "good" justification must also claim to reach normative or moral closure on the issue at hand. Unlike scientific research, legal reasoning must resort to such devices as theatrical staging (robes, judicial benches, and the like) and the poetic use of language to persuade its audience, if only temporarily, that it has achieved closure (Ball; White).

Finally, each instance of judicial practical reasoning should seek to contribute to an ongoing ethical narrative about the nature of the American polity. It is not possible, desirable, or necessary for any one justification to end the narrative. Rather, the social value of good judicial justifications lies in keeping the narrative alive. Justifications should, by harmonizing rules, empirical data, and cultural values within the facts of a given case, reassure the polity that it possesses a coherent and enduring character (Carter, 1984 and 1985; Cover).

If this view is correct, it is (except for those who believe in natural law) no rebuttal to argue that an opinion's substantive accuracy and normative attractiveness amount to no more than the "felt necessities" of the late twentieth century. If they amount to no more, they nevertheless provide a framework for understanding and accepting many important legal justifications since World War II. To take perhaps the most significant example, *Brown,* the issue is not whether the framers of the Fourteenth Amendment intended to proscribe separate-but-equal racial discrimination; rather, the question is whether the Court accurately appreciated the human costs of segregation and whether, through such affective phrases as "we cannot turn back the clock to 1868" and "separate educational facilities are inherently unequal," it helped prolong the public conversation about the meaning of equality in American life.

[See also (III) Judicial Review.]

CASES

American Textile Manufacturers Institute v. Donovan, 452 U.S. 490 (1981)
Brown v. Board of Education, 347 U.S. 483 (1954)
Flast v. Cohen, 392 U.S. 83 (1968)
Flood v. Kuhn, 407 U.S. 258 (1972)
Industrial Union Department, AFL-CIO v. American Petroleum Institute, 448 U.S. 607 (1980)
McBoyle v. United States, 283 U.S. 25 (1931)
McCulloch v. Maryland, 4 L. Ed. 579 (1819)
Soldano v. O'Daniels, 190 Cal. Rptr. 310 (1983)
Tarasoff v. Regents of the University of California, 551 P.2d 334 (1976)

BIBLIOGRAPHY

Milner S. Ball, *The Promise of American Law* (1981), is a provocative argument for recovering law's poetic and spiritual dimensions by an author trained in law and theology. Raoul Berger, *Government by Judiciary* (1977), offers the conservative argument for constitutional interpretation in terms of the original historical meaning of constitutional clauses. Guido Calabresi, *A Common Law for the Age of Statutes* (1982), argues for greater judicial willingness to change and update interpretations of statutes. Benjamin N. Cardozo, *The Nature of the Judicial Process* (1921), is the classic statement of the inevitably creative and discretionary character of judicial decision-making.

Lief H. Carter, "When Courts Should Make Policy: An Institutional Approach," in John Gardiner, ed., *Public Law and Public Policy* (1977), calls for varying degrees of judicial activism depending on characteristics of the policy environment of the case at hand; *Reason in Law,* 2nd ed. (1984), provides further elaboration of all points in this essay; and *Contemporary Constitutional Lawmaking* (1985) reviews competing theories of constitutional interpretation and proposes evaluating the work of the Supreme Court in explicitly aesthetic terms. Robert Cover, "Foreword: *Nomos* and Narrative," in *Harvard Law Review,* 97 (1983), chastises the Supreme Court for failure to acknowledge the power and significance of myths and non-rational beliefs in private communities.

Alfred Rupert Cross, *Statutory Interpretation* (1976), and F. Reed Dickerson, *The Interpretation and Application of Statutes* (1975), are comprehensive critical analyses of standard issues in statutory interpretation. Ronald Dworkin, *Taking Rights Seriously* (1977), makes a widely discussed and controversial philosophical justification for active judicial protection of fundamental human rights. John Hart Ely, *Democracy and Distrust* (1981), attempts to explain the circumstances in which judicial activism is consistent with democratic political theory. Jerome Frank, *Law and the Modern Mind* (1930; repr. 1963), uses early psychological theory to criticize many conventions and procedures in courts and in the legal profession.

Clifford Geertz, *The Interpretation of Cultures* (1973), explores the nature of interpretation in the social sciences. Martin Golding, *Legal Reasoning* (1983), gives precise descriptions of the various forms judicial logic (and illogic) can take. Joseph R. Gusfield, *The Culture of Public Problems* (1981), reveals how unexamined moral assumptions determine the funding and credibility of scientific research. Oliver Wendell Holmes, Jr., *The Common Law* (1881), cleared the way for positivists, realists, and pragmatists in jurisprudence. Donald Horowitz, *The Courts and Social Policy* (1977), is an important early study of institutional weaknesses of courts as policymakers. Edward Levi, *An Introduction to Legal Reasoning* (1949), raised many fundamental questions in modern legal reasoning theory for the first time.

Karl Llewellyn, *The Common Law Tradition* (1960), is an excellent integration of legal realism and traditionalism by one of the great law teachers of the twentieth century. Walter Murphy, *Elements of Judicial Strategy* (1964), describes the negotiating and compromising necessary to generate agreement among United States Supreme Court judges. Philippe Nonet and Philip Selznick, *Law and Society in Transition* (1978), states a sociological case that law should move away from abstract legal formalities and concern itself more directly with the substantive rationality of policy. Michael J. Perry, *The Constitution, the Courts, and Human Rights* (1982), argues that the Constitution can be interpreted to permit the Supreme Court to decide in terms of modern values and social conditions.

Martin Shapiro, *Courts: A Comparative and Political Analysis* (1981), provides an excellent comparative analysis of courts in different cultures. Richard A. Wasserstrom, *The Judicial Decision* (1961), carefully analyzes the procedures of justification courts should follow within a utilitarian philosophical framework. James Boyd White, *When Words Lose Their Meaning* (1984) and *Heracles' Bow* (1985), assert that we can understand judicial opinions best by treating them as literary and poetic expressions.

– LIEF H. CARTER

P

PLEA BARGAINING

Plea bargaining is the process of negotiation by which the defendant in a criminal case agrees to give up his or her right to go to trial in return for a reduction in charge or a real or anticipated reduction in sentence. Although it is a major mode of disposition of most criminal cases in most courts in the United States, plea bargaining continues to be the subject of much scholarly, policy, and legal debate. Opponents call for its outright abolition; proponents include those who view it as a necessary case-management expedient in the nation's always overwhelmed courts as well as those who go further in endorsing it in the belief that it is a preferable way to resolve many of the disputes that work their way into the criminal justice system.

This essay does not take a specific position in the debate about the propriety of plea bargaining but, instead, adopts a descriptive analytical approach to help inform judgments on the costs and benefits of plea bargaining. Moreover, by describing the process of plea bargaining in some detail, we will be able to consider its implications for sentencing reform, an issue of much current concern.

The Actors

In the typical image conjured up by the term *plea bargaining,* a prosecutor and a defense attorney haggle over a case's disposition in a corridor, a courtroom, or occasionally an office. These attorneys work something out and sell it to both the client and the judge, and the deal is thus completed. As a rough approximation of the pattern of plea bargaining, this is accurate; however, there are a substantial number of exceptions to this model as well as refinements that need to be made if we are to accurately appreciate the way plea bargaining works in the court.

First, it is useful to identify who is doing the bargaining. On one side, at least in instances in which explicit bargaining takes place, there is a representative of the prosecutor's office, usually an assistant prosecutor. The amount of discretion allowed the assistant prosecutor depends on the size of the office, its policies, and probably traditions within the jurisdiction as well. In some prosecutors' offices the assistant is given complete discretion to negotiate a case. The assistant prosecutor is considered a professional who will make responsible decisions by weighing all the competing values at stake. These offices afford the professional staff maximum latitude. In contrast, some offices prohibit assistant prosecutors from indiscriminate plea bargaining. This increasingly fashionable posture, in turn, takes several forms. In the strictest version, neither the assistant prosecutor nor the chief prosecutor engages in plea bargaining; the office adopts a "no plea bargaining" policy. However, even within this model, prosecutors and attorneys discuss a case—indeed, even "negotiate," "reappraise," or "reevaluate" it. It is only the actual bargaining that they are not doing, or so they claim. Other jurisdictions adopt more moderate restrictions on plea bargaining, such as forbidding the assistant to bargain but allowing his superior to do so, allowing limited forms of plea bargaining that are severely circumscribed by prosecutorial policies and directives and reserving plea bargaining for a designated unit of the prosecutor's office and/or the chief prosecutor. The point here is that even in the straightforward "prosecutor plea bargains" model, the nature and extent of the prosecutor's participation is not a simple matter.

Some judges feel it inappropriate to get involved in plea bargaining, whether it is charges, sentences, or both under consideration.

Similar complexity is evident when we consider the defense attorney side of the model. Too often the popular literature stereotypes the plea-bargaining defense attorney as either a harried public defender without the time or motivation to devote to a case or as an unscrupulous private attorney whose practice depends on turning over a large number of cases quickly. Though these stereotypes may sometimes comport with reality, on balance they are unfairly critical of public defenders in particular and many private practitioners as well. It is true that many public-defender organizations and other offices set up to represent indigent defendants (the bulk of the defendants processed in the courts) are overworked and may have to dispense with some of the "handholding" commonly associated with a lawyer-client relationship. It is also true that the defendants themselves, perhaps because they have little choice in selecting assigned counsel, tend to view public defenders as less than full-fledged attorneys. (In an oft-quoted response to an interviewer, one defendant replied, when asked if he had an attorney when he went to trial, "No, I had a public defender.") But the data do not generally support the proposition that when comparable cases are examined in terms of outcomes, public defenders on average provide inferior representation. Similarly, it is wrong, though easy, to stereotype unfavorably the private attorney who plea bargains. Suffice it to say that elite defense attorneys, not just struggling criminal practitioners, end up negotiating the dispositions for most of their clients' cases.

Not all defense attorneys plea bargain in the same way. Styles of plea bargaining vary quite substantially. On the one hand, some attorneys file extensive formal criminal motions prior to the plea sessions or raise substantial legal issues during plea negotiations. On the other hand, there are attorneys who argue their motions orally and do not devote a great deal of time to case preparation and research.

Other matters affect the defense side of plea bargaining. As is the case in some prosecutors' offices, assistant public defenders may be assigned to cases on either a "zone" or a "person-to-person" basis. In the latter, a defendant receives counsel when he first appears in court, and the assigned attorney is normally his for the duration of the proceedings. In the zone defense, a defendant receives different attorneys at different stages of the proceedings. Although typically one public defender will handle the plea bargaining, it is possible for a different member of the office to attempt to reach a disposition. Again, the important point is that even in a very simple model of prosecutor-defense attorney plea bargaining, very different patterns of plea bargaining are possible depending on the particular prosecutor-defense attorney mix.

If we move beyond the simple model, the two major additional actors who need to be introduced are the judge and the defendant. The assumption in the simple model (often one that is not unwarranted) is that if the prosecutor and the defense attorney reach an agreement, the judge will in almost all instances ratify it. Departures from this model and this assumption arise in terms of the extent of judicial participation in generating the particular plea or pleas in general. Some judges feel it inappropriate to get involved in plea bargaining, whether it is charges, sentences, or both that are being discussed. These judges feel that this is a task appropriately left to the adversaries and inappropriately participated in by judges, though these judges will acquiesce in plea bargains offered by the prosecutors and defense. Other judges take a more active posture in generating pleas. Some allow prosecutors and defense attorneys to speak to them in chambers about the difficulties they are encountering in reaching agreement; others call counsel in to encourage the plea-bargaining process. Finally, some judges plea bargain (even in felony cases) on the bench in court (though off the record) at the time cases are called.

Most plea agreements are now put on the record and the defendant no longer needs to falsely state that he or she is pleading with no expectation of charge or sentence reduction. A judge now informs the defendant that if, upon reading the probation report (prepared before formal sentencing in felony cases), he cannot abide by the terms of the agreement, the judge will allow the defendant to withdraw his plea of guilty. This commendable openness in the rules of plea bargaining certainly marks a significant step forward; however, beyond these changes, judges continue to differ rather drastically in the extent to which they inquire about the details of the plea-bargaining process and, more important, about the details of the offense. Does the plea fit the facts the defendant is willing to admit to? Must the plea fit the facts? Must the defendant admit to the facts of other offenses with which he was charged? These are questions that remain open about the plea-bargaining process generally and about judicial inquiry specifically. There has been little systematic research on differences between judges with regard to the extent to which they make inquiries and the amount of time they devote to accepting pleas (whether or not various inquiries are undertaken). Some judges do pride themselves on being able to take pleas in under two minutes, assuring observers (quite correctly) that their inquiries of the defendant meet all state and federal constitutional requirements. Other judges engage in a far more deliberative process, some communicating sincerely that they want defendants to understand what rights they are waiving; still others seem determined to make the record immune to subsequent challenge. A systematic survey of these practices, particularly in light of the attention given to the matter of the factual inquiries that ought to be included as part of the plea canvass, remains one of the most pressing research needs in the plea-bargaining field.

The final and, curiously, often overlooked participant in the plea-bargaining process is the defendant. Critics of plea bargaining address what they believe to be the coercive forces that encourage defendants to plead, notably the fear of a substantially higher penalty if defendants do not plead and go to trial. While acknowledging that the final choice of a disposition is the defendant's, proponents of plea bargaining focus on the professional judgments of the defense attorney and the prosecutor about the strengths and weaknesses of the case. What is often lost in these discussions is the issue of the pressure defendants put on attorneys to "work out a deal." It is certainly true that the way defense attorneys frame the choices when presenting plea bargains to defendants can substantially affect a defendant's calculus. But defendants are often learned in the ways of the criminal court (particularly those defendants who have committed felonies) and are not naive buffoons who can be easily misled by an attorney, especially since defendants often mistrust assigned attorneys to begin with. They have a sense of what is "a good deal." This is not to say that their choices are unaffected by a fear that they will be penalized with a higher sentence simply for going to trial. It is to say, however, that the independent input of a defendant is a factor—occasionally a major factor—that affects the plea-bargaining system. Defendants often want to plead; the sections that follow will examine some of the reasons why this is so.

Reasons for Plea Bargaining

Traditionally, plea bargaining has been explained as the practice of crowded urban courts, courts in which case loads were too large to be processed by trials. Plea bargaining was viewed as an unattractive, quasi-legitimate expedient necessary for processing the volume of cases but not really an appropriate means of case disposition in an adversary system. This conception of the nature of the criminal justice system and of the development and role of plea bargaining within it is not totally inaccurate. It is indeed the way plea bargaining has been perceived, and to an extent it remains a popular perception. However, the social science research of the past two decades, along with a number of notable developments on the appellate level, have done much to debunk the mythical components of the model and to suggest alternate explanations for the centrality of plea bargaining in the criminal courts.

The first problem with the hypothesis that case pressure explains plea bargaining is that the data do not support it. Both crowded and uncrowded, urban and rural courts dispose of most of their cases by pleas. And it appears that reliance on nontrial disposition is not a new, "crowded urban court" phenomenon at all but one that has characterized most American courts at least since the Civil War. A number of alternative explanations have been developed for why plea bargaining appears to dominate the disposition practices of most criminal courts. A cornerstone of these explanations is the argument that adopting an adversary posture in court is not likely to be fruitful. It is simply the fact—and an encouraging fact if one reflects on what would exist were it otherwise—that most of the defendants brought to court are factually guilty of the charge or of some related charge. Of course, in a system in which procedural protections loom large, factual guilt does not always equate with legal guilt. The burden is on the state to establish the defendant's guilt, and if the state is unable to do so because of procedural defects (illegal searches and seizures, involuntary confessions, and the like), the consideration that the defendant is factually guilty is in a sense irrelevant. The argument against adopting an adversary posture suggests that of the many cases in which defendants are factually guilty, few contain realistically contestable legal issues. Although one can never be sure about claims of contestability either in a particular case or across a range of cases, research does support the proposition that there are many cases without meaningful factual or legal issues to be contested. Such cases are said to be "born dead." The collective task of the prosecutor, defense attorney, judge, and defendant is to negotiate a disposition; the guilty plea itself is almost a foregone conclusion. Under this conception of the disposition process, the frequency of pleas is a function not of case volume but of the contestability of cases. Advocates of this view hold that it is futile to go through the motions on cases in which the outcome is clear; and there is widespread agreement that everyone's time is best spent on cases that raise real factual or legal questions.

In addition to this general understanding of plea bargaining, there are several actor-specific explanations for plea bargaining that have been advanced by various court scholars. Some of these are related to the theme of reducing uncertainty for the parties in the plea-bargaining process. Specifically, prosecutors, defense attorneys, and defendants are well aware that their expectations about trial outcomes can go awry; plea bargaining affords these actors the opportunity to reduce the uncertainty of trial. The prosecutor does not run the risk of an acquittal; the defense attorney and the defendant do not run the risk of conviction on the highest charge (when they are able to charge bargain) or an uncertain sentence (when they are able to sentence bargain). Similarly, the judge, by acquiescing in the negotiated disposition, can appear to manage his docket efficiently, a concern of judges in crowded and uncrowded courts alike. Also, although the argument is probably overstated in some of the popular literature, there is more than a kernel of truth to the notion that judges do not like to be reversed on appeal. A plea bargain in most circumstances immunizes a judge against appeal, thus increasing the judge's confidence in the finality of the decision. Some judges stress this finality in outcome, along with the swiftness potentially afforded by the plea-bargaining process in contrast to the trial process, as important additional arguments in favor of the criminal justice system's reliance on pleas. Some judges believe that certainty and celerity of punishment are related to the efficacy of criminal sanctions with respect to individual deterrence and that plea bargaining allows the system to achieve its goals more successfully than would a greater reliance on trials.

Prosecutors often work with defense attorneys to tailor general laws to particular defendants—in effect, to seek "substantive justice."

A host of other role-specific explanations for plea bargaining are found in the literature. Prosecutors are said to be able to maximize "batting averages" for pleading (the ratio of convictions to total cases) and perhaps even to maximize total person-years that convicted defendants must serve in prison. (Even if a "discount" is given for pleading, as discussed below, the expected value of cases after trial would include those cases in which the defendant was acquitted.) Similarly, prosecutors are portrayed as being concerned about individualizing dispositions. Whether the concern stems from their sense that legislative penalties are too high (particularly in mandatory-sentencing cases) or just from a more general tendency to feel that they are "close to the case" and as capable as (maybe more capable than) the judge in tailoring dispositions need not concern us here. What is of importance is that prosecutors often work with defense attorneys to tailor general laws to particular defendants—in effect, to seek "substantive justice" while at the same time disposing of the business.

It is of course in the defense attorney's interest to work with the prosecutor who wants to individualize dispositions by mitigating the potential punishment. It is also in the defense attorney's interest to not become an annoyance to the prosecutor. An adversarial relationship can exist within a framework of mutual accommodation, up to a point. For example, both prosecutors and defense attorneys will occasionally need a postponement in a case. The prosecutor's witness may not have shown up, or the private defense attorney's fee might not be forthcoming. (Judges can call postponements to await the arrival of "Mr. Green" or "pursuant to Rule Number 1 of this court" to give private attorneys time to collect their fees.) On any given day, one side could make it difficult for the other in terms of a particular motion. However, because it is likely that these same attorneys will be adversaries in many cases, it is in the interests of each to cooperate as long as neither is sacrificing professional obligations (to the state or to the client).

These are, then, some of the more persuasive or at least justifiable reasons for participation in the plea-bargaining system. No discussion of the reasons for plea bargaining would be complete, however, if it did not at least note some of the other, far less defensible reasons that some argue animate the plea-bargaining system. In the views of those who advance these explanations, judges are seen as lazy and eager to get cases out of the way as quickly as possible and with a minimum of effort; prosecutors are portrayed alternatively as overwhelmed, lazy, or too accommodating. The overwhelmed prosecutor is eager to plead simply to manage a large case load or the lazy prosecutor wants to dispose of cases because he or she has something better to do; the accommodating prosecutor is eager to obtain the support of defense attorneys who may be helpful when the prosecutor attempts to become a judge. The prosecutor, in these arrangements, adjusts professional responsibilities to realize none too laudatory goals. Finally, the defense attorney, if a public defender, is depicted as not very competent, very overwhelmed, or both. Plea bargaining allows the public defender to process a heavy case load, notwithstanding minimal skills and limited time. If the attorney is in private practice, by plea bargaining he can carry a heavy case load through the courts, generating far more in fees than would be possible even with the higher charges that could be levied for trials. Although there may be a kernel of truth to these explanations for some judges, prosecutors, and defense attorneys in some courts, they do not usefully or accurately explain why plea bargaining characterizes the courts, nor do they do justice to the majority of attorneys practicing in the courts.

Central Concerns of Plea Bargaining

In this section, four themes from the plea-bargaining literature are discussed. Two of these—the issue of discounts for pleas and the question of the inevitability of plea bargaining—are currently being actively debated by social scientists who study plea bargaining as well as by attorneys concerned about the propriety of discounts in the first instance, and about the feasibility of abolishing plea bargaining in the second. The other two issues—the actual sentences associated with plea dispositions and the relationship between plea bargaining and the recent flurry of sentencing innovations in the states—are less frequently discussed and are presented here precisely because of their centrality and the fact that they have often been overlooked.

PLEA DISCOUNTS. The issues raised in connection with discounts for pleading guilty are both normative and empirical. Should defendants be rewarded for waiving their right to go to trial and opting to plead guilty? In other words, should defendants who go to trial receive higher sentences (be penalized) for going to trial? Answers to these normative questions vary. A principled case is made by some that the exercise of a constitutional right should never be associated with a penalty, here a higher sentence for exercising the right to trial. At the other extreme, some argue that it is perfectly appropriate to reward defendants who plead guilty with a discount from the sentence that the defendant would be expected to receive after trial. The justifications for this reward, however, vary among its proponents. Some argue that pleading guilty is the first step to rehabilitation and that the defendant who so pleads should receive a shorter sentence than the defendant who is found guilty after a trial. Also, the case of the defendant who goes to trial may simply look worse after its details are revealed in open court. Further, if defendants take the stand in their own defense, they may, upon conviction, be viewed as having perjured themselves during the trial. Others defend the discount for a plea because of the time and money it saves the state or because of what is termed a "provability discount": with pleading, problems of proof for the state are removed. A middle position argues that only for the defendant who opts to pursue a "frivolous trial"—one in which provability for the state is easy—should the penalty for trial loom large. By this argument, it is not that the defendant is using the state's time and resources; rather, he or she is wasting them. Plea bargaining helps send a message for these kinds of cases.

The perception that the defendant who pleads fares better than the defendant who goes to trial is widely shared in most courts. Marshaling empirical evidence to support this perception is a different matter. The case characteristics or prior record of defendants who plead as compared to those who go to trial may be different in systematic ways. (For example, some argue that only the weakest state cases go to trial, whereas others argue that the state only takes it strong cases to trial and pleads the rest.) Because assignment to trial or plea is not random and because it is possible to argue that systematic differences do exist, one must be cautious in comparing groups of defendants. Of the comparisons that have been made, most support the notion of some plea-trial differential, although at least one prominent study has questioned these findings (Heumann). What does seem unarguable is that most court actors do believe that there is a difference, that defendants who plead generally do better than defendants who do not plead. The extent to which this belief is fueled by the reality of systematic differences, by some isolated cases of dramatic disparities between plea offers and trial sentences, by differences in some categories of offenses but not in others, or by some other dynamic remains an important question for future research.

THE INEVITABILITY OF PLEA BARGAINING. Most plea-bargaining research since the 1960s falls squarely on the side of the argument that maintains that plea bargaining of some sort is likely to remain a cental means of case disposition in the criminal courts for the foreseeable future. This argument does not rest on the notion that overburdened courts must plea bargain to survive. This is accurate for some courts but inaccurate for others; low-volume, well-staffed courts seem to plea bargain at a fairly high rate. Some plea bargaining may be a product of habit and tradition. But more important are notions that have already been touched upon—namely, the widely shared perception that many defendants are both factually and legally guilty, that they have few plausible issues to contest, and that they expect to benefit from a plea. Included in this understanding are pleas entered with an expectation of a reward even if no explicit negotiations take place. This kind of implicit plea bargaining seems to be different in degree but not in kind from the explicit variant.

Support for the proposition that plea bargaining, either implicit or explicit, will persist into the foreseeable future comes from several different bodies of research. First, a number of studies have evaluated the success of various efforts to abolish plea bargaining. These studies teach several lessons. When prosecutors have strictly adhered to proscriptions on charge bargaining, judges typically have gotten more involved in the plea-bargaining process and increasingly have negotiated sentences with the defense attorney. In those few jurisdictions that have imposed further restrictions on this kind of judicial plea bargaining (for example, the Alaska Supreme Court prohibited judicial sentence bargaining, which increased dramatically after the Alaska attorney general prohibited prosecutors from charge bargaining), the guilty-plea rates remained high despite the prohibitions on explicitly negotiated dispositions. Although trial rates have increased slightly in some of these jurisdictions, for the most part defendants continue to plead. Their pleas are animated by implicit plea bargaining, by the general expectation that they will fare better by pleading than by contesting their cases. Moreover, with knowledge of a jurisdiction's preprohibition norms, defendants can make reasonably good guesses about what sentences they will receive with a plea before particular judges. They or their attorneys are aware of the "going rates," or sentencing norms, of a jurisdiction and of a judge; and even without the preferred option of explicit negotiation to ensure that the case is correctly handled, defendants apparently still plead under the reasonable expectation that they will receive a particular going rate or, at a minimum, that what they will receive will be a benefit compared to the possible sentence after trial.

A second part of the argument about the centrality and inevitability of plea bargaining derives from the results of a number of studies outside the United States. Plea bargaining or functional equivalents thereof seem to be quite common in England, Scotland, Israel, and perhaps (there have been heated debates about this) on the Continent as well.

Additional findings of import for the theme of plea bargaining's centrality and inevitability are those from studies that have examined jurisdictions purported not to rely extensively on plea bargaining. The results of a number of these studies suggest that often, but not always, what looks like a greater reliance on adversary procedures, most notably bench (nonjury) trials, is illusory. The high rate of bench trials is not conclusive evidence of a more adversarial system, for it has been found that in many of these jurisdictions many of the bench trials are nothing more than "slow pleas of guilty." They seem to serve as a means for defendants to plead before a judge in a truncated procedure that may not, and often does not, take longer than a guilty-plea hearing. It is important to qualify these findings in two ways. First, even in jurisdictions in which the bench trial commonly serves as a functional equivalent of a guilty plea, not all bench trials are necessarily slow pleas. There are circumstances in which contesting a case before a judge alone, without a jury, is preferable to the parties. Also, there may be jurisdictions—there is some evidence suggesting that Philadelphia is one such example—where real bench trials are used at a fairly high rate and consequently the percentage of plea bargains is substantially lower than in most jurisdictions (Alschuler, 1981).

Some observers of such bench-trial practices use the existence of these trials to raise questions about the centrality and inevitability of plea bargaining. Lest anyone

An attorney meets with her jailed client. The defendant and the judge must both agree to the terms for a plea bargain to take place. (Shelley Gazin/Corbis)

make too much of these bench trials, several things about them ought to be noted. At least in Philadelphia, one factor responsible for the high bench-trial rate is the seeming pattern in the assignment of judges: "harder" sentencing judges to jury trials, "softer" judges to bench trials. The coerciveness of this practice of directing defendants away from jury trials is obvious and troublesome. Furthermore, the bench trials that are held, even if they are not slow pleas, are often brief, truncated proceedings. It may be that adjudicating a disposition in this manner is different, perhaps importantly so, from the plea process. Indeed, some may well prefer this more adversarial practice, but in light of the coercive context in which such bench trials are generated (at least in some jurisdictions), it is a preference with which not many informed observers would readily join.

The perception that the defendant who pleads fares better than the defendant who goes to trial is widely shared in most courts.

Nonetheless, these "real" bench trials are legitimately introduced as a limit on the inevitability hypothesis. Cases are plea bargained in some communities but at a rate significantly below that in most others. And it is interesting to speculate why these communities opt for abbreviated trials rather than following the usual plea-bargaining pattern. Notwithstanding plea bargaining's centrality in most American courts and in many other countries as well, its perseverance in the face of efforts to abolish it, and its close kinship to many "functional equivalents," it is possible to point to settings that do function without a heavy reliance on plea bargaining. It remains far from certain, however, whether these exceptions are exportable practices or whether it would be desirable to export them.

THE OUTCOMES OF PLEA BARGAINING. To the chagrin of many of its proponents, plea bargaining suggests by its very name that defendants receive a bargain. Indeed, it is this specter of "bargain-basement justice" that makes plea bargaining, when raised in a political campaign, a potent issue to use against its practitioners and advocates. The problem with this view is that the link of plea bargaining to "bargain" justice may often be incorrect in practice, and it is certainly wrong in principle. To appreciate the relation of plea bargaining to its outcome, the sentence, one must begin by asking about the origins of the sentences imposed. Legislative indeterminate-sentencing schemes typically define penalties in terms of wide ranges of years of imprisonment for particular offense classes. Thus, judges and prosecutors have traditionally been left with the responsibility to choose a sentence from within these broad ranges. Many factors guide this sentencing decision, and we would need to range far afield to cover them all here. But it is clear that different court actors emphasize different goals (rehabilitation, deterrence, and so on) and that personal proclivities and hunches about defendants and about the efficacy of different sanctions are also at work. What is important to emphasize is that no single sentence is necessarily the right one for a defendant.

Whatever sentence is meted out by a typical plea-bargaining or trial system is neither required nor right. The sentence could be higher or lower, and the differential in plea and trial sentences in most cases could be large, small, or even nonexistent. Clearly, some defendants' sentences are lower than they would be if they had gone to trial. But is this a bargain objectively, and must it be set at a particular price? The answer is no. Because no price is right, the plea-bargain price may be harsh or lenient, fair or unfair, and it might be raised or lowered without having a substantial effect on plea rates in a specific jurisdiction.

Recent attempts to raise criminal sentences have not been accompanied by a decrease in pleas. New and more severe prices have been set in jurisdictions, and defendants still plead. But as long as uncertainty can be removed, as long as the court continues to process many clear-cut cases, and perhaps as long as actors continue to believe there is a plea-trial differential, plea bargaining will continue to characterize many courts' dispositional processes, however harsh the sentences in the particular jurisdiction.

SENTENCING AND PLEA BARGAINING. The years since the mid-1970s have been a period of great change for the sentencing codes of the states. Indeterminate-sentencing schemes, which afford judges wide latitude in sentencing, have been replaced, piecemeal or as a whole, by various less discretionary systems. No state has adopted a complete mandatory-sentencing plan, but some have passed mandatory sentences for a fairly wide range of crimes (for instance, firearms use) or criminals (such as repeat offenders). Other, somewhat less severe sentencing changes that impose constraints on judicial discretion include those based on empirical or prescriptive sentencing guidelines as well as those that include determinate or presumptive sentences that call for a specific sentence rather than a range of years.

What is important here is the focus reformers accord judicial discretion. To decrease discretion in sentencing, they decrease judicial discretion; to decrease the perceived leniency in sentences, they sometimes remove judicial discretion altogether. To the extent that judges sentence—a not surprising perception that legislatures have of the judicial role—these reforms, for better or worse, ought to achieve their objectives. The problem is, of course, that in many systems judges do not sentence or at least do not have the control over the sentencing process assumed by the reformers. It is the prosecutor who, through the initial charging decision and subsequent charge and sentence bargaining, controls in large measure the sentences that defendants receive. If prosecutors and judges disagree with the aims of a new sentencing code, they can use the plea-bargaining process to undermine the reform's intent.

Plea bargaining is the Achilles' heel of sentencing reform. Narrowing judicial discretion simply and directly enhances prosecutorial power as it shifts more discretion to the prosecutor's office. Although some prosecutors claim to have eschewed this power to charge- and sentence-bargain (particularly vis-à-vis cases directly affected by new reforms in the jurisdiction) and some have promulgated voluntary guidelines for assistants within their offices, for the most part prosecutors have remained silent about their enhanced prerogatives under the new sentencing codes. Whether this silence reflects an acceptance of the new order or indicates that prosecutors and judges are quietly circumventing these new sentencing schemes is a question that we can set aside. It is sufficient to note that plea bargaining remains the Achilles' heel of efforts to reform sentencing by focusing only on reducing judicial discretion. Although prosecutors and judges may indeed feel obligated to observe both the letter and the spirit of the new sentencing schemes—and many do—plea bargaining lurks as a potent and tempting means to adjust a new code's strictures to former practices and norms.

A Look Ahead

What directions for future research and reforms of plea bargaining practices are suggested by these observations? There is, first, a need for more research on how case pressure affects plea bargaining. Earlier this essay argued that plea bargaining did not result from case pressure, that it was not caused by overworked and understaffed courts. This is different from saying that case pressure does not affect plea bargaining. It seems clear that case pressure beyond some point may well affect the way some or all cases are processed in a court. This relationship may be straightforward: in a system that begins with no case pressure, as the number of cases increases, plea bargaining increases to cope with the new imbalance of cases and resources. Or the relationship might be far more complicated: a penalty for trial might be introduced, or the former penalty for trial might be increased in an effort to ensure that defendants are aware of the gap between plea and trial results. Interestingly, since the plea price can be kept the same, there is no reason for prosecutors to reduce the sentence associated with a plea by "giving away the store" when case pressure increases. Alternatively, screening of cases for trial may increase through outright dismissals, more diversion programs, or other such mechanisms. The general point is that more research is needed into how different case loads affect plea-bargaining practices.

A second matter in need of more research is the issue of differences between plea-bargaining systems. Plea bargaining can mean very different things in different jurisdictions. In some, it can be quite adversarial, a process in which defense attorneys vigorously contest, perhaps informally in the prosecutor's office or more formally in the context of pretrial motions, the state's claims; in others it can be a far more cooperative system in which working out a solution or "doing substantive justice" is given primacy and the adversary process is simply not used as often and perhaps not valued as highly. In certain jurisdictions, as some have suggested, plea bargaining may be likened to a bazaar in which prices fluctuate with demand; in others (probably most), a supermarket metaphor might be more appropriate. Prices for the different products are on the shelves, and these prices, or "going rates," more than the haggling of the bazaar, are what lead to the settling of cases with particular sentences.

Some states have passed mandatory sentences for a wide range of crimes (i.e., firearms use) or criminals (such as repeat offenders).

Finally, with respect to understanding these differences in jurisdictions, we need to devote more attention to the elusive but important notions of courtroom culture, courthouse culture, and local legal culture. Court participants seem to share a set of values, norms, perceptions, and beliefs about the way a community's courts should operate. Whether these beliefs are simply the product of tradition or reflect a more complex interplay of courtroom, courthouse, and community values and expectations shaped by the criminal code, case types, crime rates, case load, and so on is a question that merits further study.

The agenda for work on plea bargaining ought not be limited to social science research. More attention needs to be given to the abuses of plea bargaining and to legal and policy reforms of plea-bargaining practices. Since the mid-1960s the United States Supreme Court has brought plea bargaining out of the closet, recognizing it as a common method of case disposition, legitimizing it as an appropriate practice, and, in the eyes of some, applauding it as a preferable means of dispute resolution. It is not yet evident what limits if any the Court will impose, nor is there a consensus as to what these limits ought to be.

More research must also be done on the question of "truth in plea bargaining." The days of the guilty-plea charade, when defendants were forced to deny in open court the promises just made to them behind closed doors, are largely over; plea agreements are put now on the record. However, there remains some ambiguity about the extent to which a factual basis for the guilty plea must be established before a judge can accept the plea. Should a plea be accepted only for the real offense, or should artificial pleas to decreased charges be acceptable even when they conflict with the facts of the offense, such as allowing pleas to unarmed robbery despite assertions in the record that a gun was used? To what extent should a defendant be afforded an opportunity to contest specific facts at the sentencing stage even though the defendant chose to plead guilty to the charge? With the narrowing of judicial discretion through guideline-sentencing schemes and determinate sentencing, plans that are sometimes coupled with the abolition of parole, defendants can be less assured that judges will tailor sentences to particular facts in the file and that parole boards will use case facts to individualize sentences. Thus, the opportunity for a defendant to set the factual record straight while still having the opportunity to plead seems all the more important.

The policy components of the plea-bargaining agenda ought to include efforts to develop prosecutorial guidelines or some other method of rationalizing and regularizing prosecutorial discretion. Other policy matters worthy of new or increased attention include according victims and/or defendants a larger role in the plea-bargaining process; working on ways to make explicit the sentencing norms of a jurisdiction so that novice attorneys do not lose out on the "standard discount" generally given to experienced attorneys and so that defendants are not misled by their attorneys or by the prosecutor into believing that they are obtaining an unusually good deal (which the attorneys or prosecutor can use to justify an unusually high fee); and continuing the trends toward increased discussion of plea bargaining and more training in negotiation skills in law schools.

Much has been accomplished by the research since the 1960s into plea bargaining and the criminal justice system. We have learned about plea-bargaining dynamics, and we have become increasingly sophisticated and realistic with respect to our ability to frame the questions in need of further research and thought. The challenge that confronts us in the decades to come is to work on informed responses to these research questions and related policy issues.

[See also (III) Sentencing Alternatives.]

CASES

Blackedge v. Allison, 431 U.S. 63 (1977)
Bordenkircher v. Hayes, 434 U.S. 357 (1978)
North Carolina v. Alford, 400 U.S. 25 (1970)
Santobello v. New York, 404 U.S. 257 (1971)

BIBLIOGRAPHY

Albert Alschuler, "Implementing the Criminal Defendant's Right to Trial," in *The University of Chicago Law Review*, 50 (1983), vigorously opposes plea bargaining; and "The Changing Plea Bargaining Debate," in *California Law Review*, 69 (1981), discusses the bench trial alternatives to plea bargaining. John Baldwin and Michael McConville, *Negotiated Justice* (1977), discusses plea bargaining in Great Britain. David Brereton and Jonathan Casper, "Does It Pay to Plead Guilty? Differential Sentencing and the Functioning of Criminal Courts," in *Law and Society Review*, 16 (1981–1982), is the best summary of existing research on the issue of a penalty for going to trial. Jonathan Casper, *American Criminal Justice* (1972), presents the very mixed views that defendants have about plea bargaining.

Thomas Church, Jr., "Plea Bargaining, Concessions and the Courts: Analysis of a Quasi-Experiment," in *Law and Society Review*, 10 (1976), evaluates attempts to abolish selectively plea bargaining in the United States. James Eisenstein and Herbert Jacob, *Felony Justice* (1977), and Martin A. Levin, *Urban Politics and the Criminal Courts* (1977), are two valuable comparative studies of felony courts containing important insights into plea bargaining. Malvina Halberstam, "Toward Neutral Principles in the Administration of Criminal Justice: A Critique of Supreme Court Decisions Sanctioning the Plea Bargaining Process," in *The Journal of Criminal Law and Criminology*, 73 (1982), critically summarizes the case law on plea bargaining.

Milton Heumann, *Plea Bargaining* (1978), develops the argument that prosecutors and defense attorneys believe that defendants who plead guilty fare better than those who go to trial. *Law and Society Review*, 13 (1979), published as part of a National Conference on Plea Bargaining held in June 1978, is an excellent collection of articles reporting on studies of plea bargaining in different jurisdictions and on the attempts to reform or abolish plea bargaining. William F. McDonald and James Cramer, eds., *Plea Bargaining* (1980), also treats these issues. Lynn Mather, *Plea Bargaining or Trial?* (1979), Arthur Rosett and Donald R. Cressey, *Justice By Consent* (1976), and Pamela Utz, *Settling the Facts* (1978), are book-length empirical studies of plea bargaining in felony courts. William M. Rhodes, *Plea Bargaining: Who Gains? Who Loses?* (1978), articulates the view that the state gives away little and gains much in the plea-bargaining process.

– MILTON HEUMANN

PROSECUTORS

Prosecutors in the United States, as public officials responsible for the initiation and conduct of criminal proceedings, are central actors in the American criminal justice system. They screen arrests made by police and complaints made by private citizens through their decision to proceed with formal criminal charges against defendants. Prosecutors also interact regularly with defense attorneys, grand juries, and judges in the process of setting bail, establishing probable cause, negotiating guilty pleas, arguing cases at trial, and recommending sentences for those convicted. As the linkage between enforcement and adjudication, interacting closely with private citizens and diverse criminal justice personnel, the prosecutor is often seen as the pivotal figure in the criminal justice process.

A fundamental characteristic of the prosecutor is the possession of largely unchecked discretion to shape the outcome of criminal cases, especially through decisions on charges, dismissals, and plea bargaining. This discretion has been questioned periodically and attempts have been made to limit it, but discretionary decision-making remains an essential component of the prosecutor's job. As political officials (usually elected), prosecutors also represent the views of their local constituency in setting priorities on issues of criminal and, sometimes, civil law enforcement. Moreover, prosecutors often lobby the legislature regarding statutory changes in criminal law, and they press for particular rulings in appellate litigation.

While the prosecution function in the United States is defined as a public one, this was not true in early American history, nor does it hold in many other legal cultures today. Most countries use a system that combines public and private prosecution. In such a system, the public prosecutor's responsibility for initiating criminal actions is shared with private citizens, who can also initiate their own criminal proceedings. Provision for private prosecution is especially important in situations in which the public prosecutor decides not to prosecute.

There is an important difference between a private prosecutor, who is hired by the victim to represent his or her interests by pursuing criminal action, and a public prosecutor, who is paid by the state to represent it in the pursuit of criminal proceedings that were originally initiated by the victim. Not only does the role of the victim decrease in public prosecution, but the public prosecutor confronts two serious and interrelated dilemmas in doing his or her job.

The first dilemma is found in the conflict between the prosecutor's role as chief law enforcement officer and as officer of the court. As a law enforcement official, the prosecutor acts in an adversary mode to seek conviction of those suspected of crime; like the police, the prosecutor's primary obligations are to control crime and maintain public order. In contrast, the prosecutor's quasi-judicial role is quite different. As an officer of the court, the prosecutor is sworn to uphold legal values and to see that justice is done; in this role the official must interpret the law and apply principles of due process. The tension that arises is between order and law as reflecting conflicting responsibilities of a prosecutor.

Following the American Revolution, private prosecution was still an integral aspect of local criminal justice systems.

Although law and order are commonly spoken of in one phrase, the juxtaposition is misleading. Jerome Skolnick aptly commented that " 'law' and 'order' are frequently found to be in opposition, because law implies rational restraint upon the rules and procedures utilized to achieve order" (p. 7). The dilemma for a prosecutor is how to mediate between the public demand for order and the principles of legality, as articulated in judicial forums.

A second dilemma for prosecutors emerges from the conflict between the general legal rule and the needs of an individual case. Criminal laws are written in broad, abstract language, leaving to legal officials the task of matching concrete facts with general legal categories. Prosecutors, in particular, routinely choose between competing legal frameworks in their decision-making. For example, given a fistfight between acquaintances in a bar in which one party was the aggressor, should the prosecutor pursue the most serious criminal charge or consider all mitigating circumstances and file a lesser charge or none at all? To prosecute at the maximum level publicly reinforces the importance of the legal norm against physical assaults and may act as a deterrent to others in similar situations. However, full prosecution may not resolve the underlying conflict between the offender and the victim, nor may it best serve the interests of justice. The tasks of individual conflict resolution and general social control are intertwined in the criminal law. To the extent that prosecutors pursue one task, they risk compromising the other.

These tensions in the role of prosecutor should be borne in mind as we review the history of the modern prosecutor, the organizational context, decision-making and discretion, and recent trends in prosecution. Prosecutors have addressed the conflicts differently in offices throughout the country and during different historical periods.

Development of the Modern Prosecutor

In 1929, in his classic study *Politics and Criminal Prosecution,* Raymond Moley wrote that the "significance of the American prosecuting attorney has been strangely neglected by institutional commentators and historians" (p. 48). Research since that time has shed more light on the history of the prosecutor, but the origin and development of this key public official remains a matter of controversy. Records from the colonial period show various officers of government, such as deputy attorneys general and sheriffs, performing the duties of prosecutor. In 1704 the colony of Connecticut formally created the first office of prosecutor, calling for the appointment of an "attorney for the Queen to prosecute and implead in the law all criminals and to do all other things necessary or convenient . . . to suppress vice and immorality" (Jacoby, 16). The colony of Virginia followed with the establishment of county attorneys in 1711. After the founding of the Republic, the Judiciary Act of 1789 officially designated United States attorneys as prosecutors for the federal government.

Based on records about these early prosecutors, some scholars have argued that the system of public prosecution was "firmly established" throughout the colonies by the end of the American Revolution. Other, more recent research suggests that public prosecutors existed alongside the older system of private prosecution; further, there was considerable local variation in the handling of criminal matters, with private prosecution still commonplace in some colonies but rare in others.

The specific historical origin of the public prosecutor in America is unclear. Several different theories have been advanced, but none has complete support. Some writers point to the influence of the English common-law tradition on legal development in the colonies, using this tradition to explain the derivation of the public prosecutor. What is puzzling, however, is that eighteenth-century England had no public prosecutor, and even today England operates on the principle of private prosecution. Thus, in theory at least, all English criminal proceedings were, and are, initiated by individual citizens. (In practice, police officials play a major role.) Hence, it is difficult to argue that the American public prosecutor is a direct product of the English system. Indirect evidence provides some support for an English ancestry from either the king's attorney general or from the justices of the peace, who performed limited prosecutorial functions as far back as the sixteenth century.

Another line of argument proposes that the American colonists turned not to England but to the civil law system of France or Holland for the office of public prosecutor. In France the *procureur publique,* a state-appointed official, investigates and prosecutes criminal offenses. While the American prosecutor is somewhat similar to the French *procureur,* there is no specific historical evidence to connect the two, although several reports have attempted to do so. More persuasive evidence of a civil law derivation comes from the early Dutch administration of New York and surrounding areas. According to this theory, the American prosecutor can be traced to a Dutch official, the *schout,* who was responsible for apprehending and prosecuting criminal offenders. These competing views of the origins of the prosecutor will no doubt continue to be debated and refined with further research. They will also be compared with the view that the office of public prosecutor is itself an American invention.

Regardless of the historical origin of the public prosecutor, it is important to examine the substantial changes in the office since its beginning and to understand the changing context of the criminal justice system. Following the American Revolution, private prosecution was still an integral aspect of local criminal justice systems. Victims—or their families—were responsible for securing arrest warrants, gathering witnesses, and attending pretrial hearings. Often, too, the victims hired a personal lawyer to argue the case at trial.

Judges, especially the justices of the peace, played a major role in the criminal process, frequently arranging informal settlements after interviewing the defendant. There is some question as to how common jury trials were in the early nineteenth century, but when trials were held, they were extremely rapid proceedings without defense lawyers or the extensive procedures we have today. The public prosecutor was a minor actor in the criminal process. He worked part-time, as an adjunct to the judge, presenting cases to grand and trial juries or simply expediting private prosecution. He exercised no discretion and was paid a fee for each case by the court. There was no correctional system as such. Restitution to victims was common, as was hanging, banishing, flogging, and other corporal punishment.

During the course of the nineteenth century, American criminal justice underwent a fundamental transformation, which included a much greater role for the public prosecutor. The biggest shift was in the rise of a professional police force. Urbanization and industrialization led to problems of public order that were no longer effectively handled by a private system of law enforcement. Modern police departments were formed during the 1840s and 1850s, first in big cities and then throughout the country. Police took over the responsibility for arrest and investigation of crime that earlier had been held by private victims. The victim's role was further reduced by a shift in the punishment of offenders away from restitution and toward incarceration in the newly created prison system.

Most states provide for the election of the prosecutor, typically with a term of office of four years.

Concurrently, the public prosecutor's position increased in importance. The prosecutor began making decisions about charges, possible dismissals, and the handling of dispositions. The legality of such prosecutorial discretion was initially a matter in question, with numerous lawsuits filed to challenge prosecutorial decisions. Appellate courts, however, upheld the power of the prosecutor, so that by the end of the nineteenth century the central actors in the criminal process were officers of the state (police, prosecutors) rather than individual citizens.

The professional prosecutor was further institutionalized in the nineteenth century by a change in selection. By the Civil War most states had shifted to a system of election for public prosecutors rather than appointment. The prosecutor became part of the executive branch of government, with his own source of political support, distinct from courts and the judicial branch. One means of exercising his greater power was through the prosecutor's filing of an "information" to formally charge offenders with felonies, thus displacing the once-powerful grand jury in many states. The Constitution requires grand jury indictment for accused felons in federal cases, but in the key 1884 decision of *Hurtado* v. *California* the Supreme Court ruled that the requirement did not extend to the states.

Another illustration of the increase in prosecutorial power was through the rise of plea bargaining. Case screening by full-time police and prosecutors means that evidence that once emerged at trial was now available earlier in the process. By 1880, defendants were often convicted by guilty pleas rather than by jury trial. It is not clear how much actual bargaining accompanied these guilty pleas, but surely the defendant's guilty plea in at least some of the cases was influenced by prosecutorial promises of leniency.

The prosecutor's interest in plea bargaining was aided by two factors. First, a trend in sentencing philosophy toward reformation of offenders was evident at the turn of the century. Sentencing laws were revised to introduce probation, parole, and indeterminate sentences. The emphasis was on the individualization of punishment, fitting the sentence to meet the needs of each offender. This new sentencing goal was facilitated by plea bargaining, where prosecutors could justify discretionary acts of charge reduction by reference to considerations of appropriate punishment. Second, the criminal law itself expanded tremendously at this time, as states criminalized acts that earlier had been legal or had been civil law violations. Frequent dismissals and plea bargaining by prosecutors were ways to mitigate the impact of these new laws.

That the public prosecutor had, over the course of one hundred years, achieved such a dominant and powerful position in the criminal process was a largely unnoticed fact until the 1920s. Spurred by a concern about urban crime following World War I, government officials and legal scholars initiated major surveys of criminal justice in cities such as Cleveland, Chicago, and New York. Moley's 1929 summary of these reports shows the frequency of dismissals, the high proportion of guilty pleas, and the minor role for jury trials. Writers of the 1920s expressed shock and outrage at these facts and decried the political influences and corruption that characterized many prosecutorial decisions.

Oddly, after this huge outpouring of interest in the prosecutor, little was written or done further until the late 1960s and 1970s. In those years, crime and criminal justice processes once again became political issues, leading to government commission reports and numerous scholarly studies. Each of these newer works provided valuable empirical data about prosecutors, while also offering different perspectives.

Organizational Context

Prosecution at the state level is highly decentralized. Although the attorney general is the highest legal officer of each state, the attorney general rarely has control over the prosecution of crime. That official instead deals primarily with civil-law matters. State criminal law is enforced by a locally selected prosecutor. There are about twenty-seven hundred autonomous prosecutor's offices in the United States, each serving a county or other local geographic district. The states of Alaska, Delaware, and Rhode Island are exceptions to this; the attorney general in those states also acts as local prosecutor.

The job of a local prosecutor, commonly called district attorney, state's attorney, or county attorney, varies tremendously according to the size of the community served. In rural or small-town areas, the district attorney may work only part-time as prosecutor while also maintaining a private law practice. The rural prosecutor has little or no supporting staff; decision-making tends toward the personal and informal; and there is often a substantial share of civil law work for local government in addition to the duties of criminal prosecution. According to a 1972 national survey, 37 percent of the nation's local prosecutors worked alone, with no assistant attorneys, while another 37 percent had one to three staff assistants (Jacoby).

The job of the urban prosecutor stands in stark contrast to that of the small-town prosecutor with his or her few assistants. In metropolitan areas with a tremendous volume of crime, the district attorney oversees an office with dozens or even hundreds of assistant attorneys. In 1986, Los Angeles County had the largest prosecutor's office in the country with more than seven hundred attorneys, while Cook County (Chicago) was second with about six hundred prosecuting attorneys. Attorneys in an urban prosecutor's office typically have supporting staff such as investigators, paralegals, and public relations officers to aid in their work. Procedures are institutionalized and decision-making is often specialized in these large urban offices.

The vast majority of states provides for the election of the prosecutor, typically with a term of office of four years. Where local elections are partisan, the political parties dominate in recruiting and organizing the contest for prosecutor. Even in nonpartisan elections, however, the influence of political parties is sometimes seen through the involvement of key party individuals or special-interest groups. Election as prosecutor has long been a stepping-stone to higher political office in state or national government. The public visibility of the office provides excellent exposure for those with political ambitions. Indeed, a rather large number of state judges, governors, and representatives in Congress have had prior experience as prosecutors.

Assistant, or deputy, prosecuting attorneys are appointed by the prosecutor. In some areas selection is based on political connections, and in other areas, on legal credentials and competitive examinations. Most deputies are young and just out of law school. They seek the responsibility, professional contacts, and courtroom experience that come with prosecution. After several years, most assistant prosecutors leave the office for private law practice. Some deputies do stay on to become career prosecutors, while others leave the office to pursue political ambitions in local or state politics.

Prosecutors for the federal government are organized and selected differently. First, the Department of Justice in Washington provides some centralized control and sets broad policies for the United States attorneys who work in the ninety-four federal judicial districts. Thus, the federal prosecutor does not have complete autonomy, as does his or her local counterpart. Nevertheless, as Eisenstein's detailed study shows, United States attorneys and their assistants do possess considerable independence. Their degree of autonomy depends on the size of the judicial district, their relations with federal judges in the district, issues involved in a specific case, and the pattern of interaction between particular United States attorney offices and the Department of Justice in Washington.

Second, United States attorneys are appointed, not elected, to office. The president nominates, and the Senate confirms, prosecutors for the federal government for a term of four years. United States attorneys are nearly always of the same political party as the president, and by custom they all resign when a president of the opposing party is elected. Both the deputy attorney general's office and the senators from the state where a vacancy occurs exert great influence on the process of recruitment for United States attorneys. Those ultimately selected as federal prosecutors tend to have active political backgrounds, strong local support, some prior governmental experience, and an average age of about forty-two years (Eisenstein).

While the excitement and focus for any prosecutor revolves around the criminal process, these officials also handle civil law matters. For example, when the United States government is sued in a tort action or contract dispute, a United States attorney (or assistant) will handle the defense. United States attorneys also represent the government as plaintiff in cases of land condemnation, debt collection, and civil fraud. Indeed, Eisenstein estimates that civil law work accounts for about 40 percent of the activity in the United States attorney offices. While the comparable figure would be far lower for local prosecutors, they, too, handle civil cases.

In about one-quarter of the states, the prosecutor has only criminal law duties, but in the remainder the prosecutor is charged with both criminal and civil law enforcement. In these states the prosecutor may represent local governments in an array of civil matters ranging from adoption, mental health, and paternity proceedings to sewers, taxes, and zoning. However, both federal and local offices give priority to their criminal case loads over their civil law matters. Prosecution in criminal cases commands the greatest visibility and provides the greatest opportunity for influence within the courts and for political impact beyond the courts. For these reasons, prosecutorial decision-making has been examined very little in the civil process as compared to the criminal process. Discussion of decision-making in the next section will be limited to prosecution of criminal cases.

Decision-Making

Decisions by prosecutors affect the processing of criminal cases in fundamental ways. Central to any empirical study of the criminal process today is the finding of widespread attrition of cases following the initial complaint or arrest. Much of this attrition can be explained by prosecutorial screening or motions for dismissal. In addition, only a small fraction of cases that do reach court are resolved by adversary trial. The remainder are handled through plea bargaining—that is, implicit or explicit negotiations between the prosecutor, defense attorney, and sometimes the judge.

Prosecutors engage in screening and negotiation for several different reasons. On the one hand, they are charged with evaluating facts and evidence according to the law to make a preliminary assessment of the likelihood of guilt or innocence. Hence, they weed out cases with weak or inadequate evidence. Yet prosecutors also must decide which crimes—both in general terms and in individual cases—warrant the most serious attention, given the inevitable limit on resources in the criminal justice system. Every violation of criminal law cannot be prosecuted (because of resource constraints), nor, many would argue, would this be the ideal policy to achieve the broader interests of justice. Consequently, prosecutors, in interaction with other criminal justice actors, make decisions that give shape and operational meaning to the formal criminal law categories. Following an overview of key decision points in the criminal process, specific factors that influence prosecutorial discretion will be analyzed.

Prosecutors have wide authority in deciding what level of charge to file or whether to file charges at all.

After police make an arrest or a citizen files a complaint, the prosecutor decides whether or not to file criminal charges, and if so, which ones. The importance of this decision cannot be overstated, for it is the entry point for defendants into the criminal courts. While prosecutors and police work together in law enforcement, they also operate in very different environments with quite distinct organizational goals. Police seek primarily to maintain order. Arrests are devices that may be used toward that end. But whether or not an arrest leads to conviction is not a high priority for the patrolman maintaining order on the street. In contrast, obtaining convictions is of paramount importance to prosecutors. Knowing that the process of securing a conviction in court is bound by formal legal rules, prosecutors make charging decisions so as to avoid losing cases later on. Consequently, less than one-half of all felony arrests in many areas result in felony charges filed by the prosecutor. In the federal courts, fewer than one-quarter of all complaints result in prosecution by United States attorneys.

This pattern of prosecutorial dominance of the charging decision does not characterize all courts, however. There is great variation in how discretion is exercised, by whom, and at which stage in the process. Indeed, one of the most valuable and least appreciated lessons of empirical scholarship on criminal justice is the wide range of differences from one community to the next. All communities share an overall pattern of high attrition of cases from arrest to conviction. But the bulk of dismissals and charge reductions may occur anywhere in the charging stage, the preliminary hearing, the grand jury, or the final court hearing.

Likewise, the ones who exercise the most power over cases vary from jurisdiction to jurisdiction. For example, while the prosecutor dominates the charging process with very strict screening of arrests in Los Angeles and Detroit, there is no prosecutorial screening in some other cities; where police file cases directly with the courts, it is the local magistrates who dismiss or reduce the bulk of the felonies at the preliminary hearing. This and other variations are due to differences in local traditions, state laws, organizational resources, and relationships among police, prosecutors, judges, and others in the community.

In formulating an initial criminal charge, prosecutors have wide authority in deciding what level of charge to file or whether to file charges at all. Alschuler first wrote of the problem of overcharging, whereby prosecutors are said to inflate the initial charges in anticipation of later plea negotiations. Vertical overcharging occurs when prosecutors file charges on a single offense at a higher level than seems warranted by the facts of the case. For example, first-degree burglary may be charged in expectation of a later plea bargain to the lesser included, second-degree burglary. Horizontal overcharging refers to a set of multiple charges, or sometimes multiple counts of the same charge, filed for every possible criminal transaction that occurred. Thus, if a defendant allegedly wrote twenty bad checks, he or she could be charged with twenty counts of check forgery (or even twenty counts of forgery and twenty counts of receiving stolen property). A typical disposition in this type of case, however, would be a guilty plea to one count with dismissal of the other nineteen. Defense attorneys argue that these charging practices are unfair devices used simply to add bargaining leverage to the prosecutor's position in later dispositions. Most prosecutors, in contrast, defend charging the "highest and most" permitted by the evidence as purely part of their professional duty in law enforcement, and they deny that this would be considered "overcharging."

Prosecutors also vary greatly in their philosophy of charging. For instance, Utz (1978) found a policy of strategic overcharging in the San Diego district attorney's office but a policy of undercharging by the district attorney in Alameda County, California. Similar differences between offices can be seen in the decision whether to file criminal charges at all. Whereas prosecutors in one midwestern city file charges only "if the case will probably win at trial" (Neubauer), prosecutors in other cities follow a much looser standard and defer more to police views of the case. Interestingly, if a prosecutor chooses not to file criminal charges, it is extremely difficult to challenge the decision. Attempts to obtain a court order to compel prosecution have rarely been successful.

Once charges are filed in court, the defendant is informed by a judge of the official accusation against him or her, and bail is set. This initial court appearance occurs soon after the arrest, usually within forty-eight hours. The amount of bail in many areas is determined by a schedule that sets bail according to the type of offense. Prosecutors frequently have input into this schedule, and they also often testify at, or else informally influence, defense motions for bail reduction and for release of defendants on their own recognizance.

In misdemeanor cases defendants may plead guilty at this initial court hearing, or they may wait for a trial date. The prosecutor engages in discussion and/or negotiation with the defense during this process about the possibility of dismissing charges, reducing charges, or recommending a lesser sentence if the defendant pleads guilty. A high proportion of misdemeanor charges are dismissed. Of those convicted throughout the country, well over 90 percent are convicted by guilty plea rather than by trial. Decision-making in lower criminal courts tends to be rapid and informal, as prosecution offices typically conserve their resources for the more serious cases.

Felony cases are those in which defendants face a possible prison term, most often of at least one year. Procedures for handling felonies are more formal and complex than for misdemeanors. Most important, ad-

An urban district attorney oversees dozens or hundreds of assistant attorneys. He or she often has a high community profile as spokesperson for the actions of prosecutors. (Robert Maass/Corbis)

ditional screening of charges occurs after the initial filing of a complaint. This screening is done by a lower-court judge in a probable-cause hearing and/or by a grand jury. It is only after these hearings that the prosecutor or grand jury enters an official felony accusation in the higher court—that is, in the county or superior court in which the disposition will occur.

The probable-cause hearing (also called preliminary hearing or preliminary examination) allows a lower-court judge to review the evidence in a case to determine whether it is sufficient to proceed with felony prosecution. The legal standard used in the hearing is one of probable cause: Is there probable cause to believe that a crime occurred and that the defendant committed it? The prosecutor presents evidence and calls witnesses in an effort to establish probable cause, but rarely does the defense introduce evidence of its own. In some areas the probable-cause hearing is a formal adversary proceeding with considerable cross-examination of witnesses and a written transcript made of the hearing. Elsewhere, the probable-cause hearing is rapid, informal, and indeed, often waived by the defendant. Finally, some courts (especially federal trial courts) rarely hold probable-cause hearings, relying instead on the grand jury to screen felonies.

At the conclusion of a probable-cause hearing the magistrate holds the defendant for felony prosecution, reduces charges to the misdemeanor level, or dismisses the charges altogether. Lower-court judges in some cities use the probable-cause hearing as the major disposition point, screening out many weak cases and encouraging prosecutors to confer with defense to arrange guilty pleas to reduced charges at this stage. But in other cities, especially where there is considerable prosecutorial screening of initial arrests, relatively few felonies are weeded out at the probable-cause hearing.

If probable cause is found at the preliminary hearing, then the prosecutor either takes the case to a grand jury or files felony charges in court, depending on the jurisdiction. About one-half of the states, and the federal government, require grand jury indictment for felonies or capital offenses. The remaining states use grand juries on occasion, but most commonly rely on a bill of information to commence prosecution. An information is simply a formal accusation of felony charges issued by the prosecutor. It is the equivalent of an indictment by the grand jury.

By the time a felony case reaches the trial court for final disposition, a number of key decisions have been made: on the specific charges, on the amount of bail, and on the sufficiency of evidence to establish probable cause. The prosecutor has either made or heavily influenced these decisions, often working in close cooperation with police, lower-court judges, and the grand jury. Most important, a large proportion of cases has been screened out during the pretrial process, so that the felonies left for trial are typically quite strong. Defense attorneys in Connecticut (Heumann) and in Los Angeles (Mather) estimate that 90 percent of their felony clients in superior court are factually guilty and that for most of these, the cases present no disputable legal issues. Although some questions of guilt or innocence remain, the primary task of the criminal court lies in the determination of proper punishment for guilty offenders. As new court personnel learn this reality of their job, they adapt to the existing pattern of frequent plea bargaining.

With plea bargaining, defendants plead guilty, rather than insisting on a trial, because of an expectation of a lesser sentence or reduced charge. An explicit plea bargain involves a specific promise by the prosecutor about the sentence or charge agreement, while an implicit bargain relies on a tacit understanding of leniency in sentencing that accompanies a guilty plea. When prosecutors engage in plea bargaining, they assure themselves a criminal conviction while also influencing the sentence imposed. Cases settled by trial require more time and resources and, even more important, may represent risks to the prosecution of a possible acquittal. Prosecutors thus evaluate their cases to assess their seriousness and the likelihood of conviction. Defendants whose cases are not "worth" much can expect easy agreements to charge or sentence leniency, but prosecutors will often refuse to bargain in very serious cases.

In most jurisdictions, the prosecutor is the central actor in the plea-bargaining process. By controlling the charge, and sometimes the sentence recommendation as well, the prosecutor is the one that defense must convince about leniency in disposition. In some jurisdictions, however, judges exercise the more dominant role.

For those cases not settled by guilty plea, the prosecutor must prepare witnesses, organize the evidence, and develop an argument for trial. During the trial, the prosecutor participates in the selection of jurors, presents the case against the defendant, and cross-examines defense witnesses. Although the trial is typically viewed as a purely adversarial process, there are also opportunities at trial for cooperation between prosecutor and defense. Depending upon the case, the prosecutor may decide, for example, not to use all his or her possible challenges to potential jurors, to stipulate to certain facts alleged by defense rather than to force proof of the facts at trial, or not to cross-examine certain defense witnesses as aggressively as possible. Following conviction at trial, the prosecutor then decides whether to recommend a sentence to the judge and, if so, what kind. Here, for example, the prosecutor's decision may be influenced by sympathy for the defendant resulting from facts that emerged at trial or by desire to punish the defendant for needlessly wasting the court's (and prosecutor's) time with a frivolous or fabricated defense.

The above discussion of prosecutorial decision-making points to several notable themes: the centrality of the prosecutor in most stages of the criminal court process (with the exception of certain jurisdictions in which the prosecutor's power is substantially shared with others); the importance of organizational interactions and interpersonal relationships (such as relations with police, judges, and defense attorneys) that shape the prosecutor's working environment; and the great breadth of discretion available to prosecutors in making decisions.

Prosecutorial Discretion

Kenneth Culp Davis, in his book *Discretionary Justice,* states that a "public officer has discretion whenever the effective limits on his power leave him free to make a choice among possible courses of action or inaction" (p. 4). Other scholars have refined or modified this definition—for example, by distinguishing between authorized and unauthorized discretion. Prosecutors may be said to exercise discretion when there are no clear rules guiding their decisions and when those decisions are not subject to review. The most obvious examples of prosecutorial discretion are the decisions to charge, to dismiss charges once made (nolle prosequi), and to reduce charges or recommend leniency in exchange for a guilty plea.

Recognizing the importance of these decisions for the entire criminal process, numerous scholars have attempted to explain empirically how prosecutors exercise their discretion; that is, what factors influence prosecutors' decisions? Given the diversity of research methodologies and in view of basic differences between prosecutors and between jurisdictions, it is not surprising that the research results are not entirely consistent. Variation lies primarily in the emphasis or importance accorded different explanatory factors. With this qualification in mind, we can summarize the general themes that have emerged from the recent literature.

Prosecutorial decisions are made on the basis of evaluation of the strength of evidence, severity of offense, defendant's background, and victim characteristics. These evaluations, in turn, are shaped by the general policies of a given prosecutor's office and by an individual prosecutor's interaction with other criminal justice actors.

Consideration of evidence is a primary factor in all prosecutorial decisions, especially initial decisions on charging and nolle prosequi. This factor exemplifies the traditional legal judgment of prosecutors to screen out cases with weak or inadequate evidence and to dismiss or to reduce charges that rest on a shaky legal foundation. In assessing the strength of a case, prosecutors ask a number of questions. Is there physical evidence such as fingerprints, stolen goods, illegal drugs, a weapon? Did the defendant confess during police examination? If so, is the confession admissible in court? Are there any search-and-seizure problems? Were there witnesses to the crime? How positive is their identification of the defendant? How credible and cooperative is the victim? Does the defendant have a credible explanation for the event that would raise reasonable doubts in the minds of jurors? In answering these questions, prosecutors decide whether the evidence is sufficient to proceed with formal charges. Analysis of the reasons given for case drop-off (screening and dismissals) suggests the significance of evidentiary or witness problems in a large number of cases (for example, in 45 percent of the declinations to prosecute studied by Frase). Prosecutorial willingness to plea-bargain is also influenced by case strength, with most research concluding that prosecutors are more inclined to bargain in weak cases.

When prosecutors engage in plea bargaining, they assure themselves a criminal conviction while also influencing the sentence imposed.

Decisions on charges, reductions, and plea bargains are, in nearly all studies, closely related to type of offense. Typical evidentiary differences between crimes account for some of the effects of offense type, but differences in perceived severity may account for a good deal more. The seriousness of the offense, a second factor explaining prosecutorial discretion, reflects both individual judgments and office policies on the relative importance of prosecuting various crimes. Crimes of violence are seen as more serious than property crimes, and crimes between strangers, more serious than those between relatives or acquaintances. Nearly every prosecutor's office also has a group of crimes that they consider "petty," "junk," or "garbage," in which dismissals or plea bargains are quite common. Mather found severity of offense strongly related to method of case disposition; serious felonies were more likely to be settled by adversary trial, in part because of the prosecutor's reluctance to plea bargain in these cases. Note that offense seriousness is only partially determined by statutory penalties; prosecutors also use their own values and knowledge of typical circumstances of offenses to determine what a crime is "worth."

Defendant characteristics constitute a third factor for prosecutors. In view of widespread concern about the discriminatory aspects of discretion, scholars have tried to pinpoint the effect of social characteristics of the defendant, such as prior record, race, ethnicity, gender, age, and economic status. With the exception of prior criminal record, these personal attributes have not been shown, by themselves, to be major influences on prosecutorial discretion (Eisenstein and Jacob). Testing this relationship is admittedly difficult, however, and the research findings are not entirely consistent. Most studies do suggest the importance of prior record, with prosecutors less likely to dismiss and less generous with bargains according to the severity of the defendant's record.

Finally, the identity of the victim and the relationship between the victim and the defendant influence prosecutorial discretion. The victim's role has been discussed far less than the three factors above but is increasingly the focus of greater scholarly attention. Disposition patterns have clearly shown a much higher proportion of dismissals and reductions in cases involving acquaintances or family members. Studies by Miller, Neubauer, and the Vera Institute of Justice all discuss the reluctance of prosecutors to pursue criminal cases involving prior personal relationships. Sometimes this reluctance is defended on evidentiary grounds; that is, it is sometimes said that victims in such relationships make poor witnesses or that juries will never convict in such a case. Other explanations include the availability of alternatives to prosecution (for example, telling the battered wife to "get a divorce") and the belief that the criminal sanction is simply not appropriate to resolve conflicts between those with a prior relationship.

In addition to the victim's relation to the defendant, various social attributes of the victim may also come into play to influence prosecutorial assessment of case strength and seriousness. Stanko's study of screening decisions in New York, for example, demonstrates the important role played by victim credibility, as shaped by stereotypes based on gender, race, and occupation. Thus, higher-status victims were more likely to have their complaints result in the filing of felony charges. A similar conclusion has emerged from recent research on death-penalty cases, which suggests that racial differences in the imposition of the death penalty may be explained by more vigorous prosecution and sentence severity against those who commit crimes with white victims, as against those who commit crimes with black victims.

Evaluation of these various factors may depend upon the personal views of individual prosecutors. Especially in small offices, the personal values of the elected prosecutor affect fundamentally the assessment of strength and seriousness of cases. However, in larger offices and especially in many of the huge urban prosecutors' offices, there are clear priorities or even guidelines that shape the decisions of individual deputies.

The variation in office policies affects evidentiary considerations and is illustrated by the different charging standards used by prosecutors throughout the country. McDonald found that 39 percent of the offices he surveyed used a probable-cause standard, 11 percent looked for a "50–50 chance of conviction," 14 percent looked for a "high probability of conviction," and 19 percent used a standard of "beyond a reasonable doubt." Utz integrated data on decisions about charging and plea bargaining to distinguish two models of prosecution, the "adversary" and the "magisterial," which she found characterized the office policies and behavior in San Diego and Oakland, respectively.

Such broad differences in office policy also shape the assessment of offense, defendant, and victim attributes. Thus, for example, office policy may dictate vigorous prosecution of habitual offenders and/or special leniency for those with no prior criminal background. Certain criminal offenses may be targeted in response to public outcry, leading to a policy of no dismissals or plea bargains in those cases. Another common office policy is to decline prosecution for certain cases where there are alternatives to criminal processing, such as mediation or informal settlement following restitution to the victim. Frase observed a general pattern for federal prosecutors, who frequently declined to prosecute where state prosecution was available.

In establishing or modifying office policies, prosecutors respond to a host of factors, such as case-load pressure, availability of resources, type of crime problem, expectations and power of other criminal justice actors, and local geographic and political context. Relations with others, besides affecting general office priorities, may also affect prosecutorial discretion in specific cases. For instance, police pressure to file charges may override a prosecutorial judgment of insufficient evidence. Or, if the victim is prominent and well respected, the prosecutor may hesitate to dismiss or reduce charges, even if weaknesses develop in the case. The identity of the opposing defense attorney has also been found to influence prosecutors' decisions, through a personal working relationship between attorneys, knowledge of a particular defense attorney's reputation, or a perceived difference between public and private defense attorneys. Other actors who sometimes affect decisions by prosecutors include judges, court clerks, probation and parole officers, and representatives of community publics.

Recent Trends in Prosecution

Greater understanding and public awareness of the extent of prosecutorial discretion have led to calls for limits or checks on that discretion. Changes in prosecution since the 1970s can be explained largely as an effort to control discretion in decision-making. Not only were legal scholars unhappy with unbridled discretion, but prosecutors themselves discovered the political vulnerability that could result from discretionary decisions. Consequently, there has been a trend toward limiting discretion by internal measures within prosecutors' offices and by external action by judges and legislatures.

Prosecutors have attempted to structure and check the decisions of their deputies by several different means. Some require written records of discretionary actions with justification provided for each action. Others formalize procedures—for example, by encouraging explicit rather than implicit plea bargaining. Prosecutors have also begun to formalize policies and procedures by providing written guidelines and informal training sessions in an effort to establish some uniformity in decisions. Finally, some prosecutors have restricted the discretion available to deputies by centralizing decision-making or by increasing supervision. For example, offices might designate a few attorneys to be solely responsible for plea bargaining or else require that no deputy dismiss or reduce charges without the prior written approval of a supervisor. These efforts by prosecutors to monitor decision-making through internal management have been aided by technological and bureaucratic changes adopted by many offices throughout the 1970s. Offices shifted from paper record keeping on cases to systems like PROMIS, an automated case-tracking system that allows management to easily research discretional issues in charging or disposition.

Trial courts have provided an occasional external check on prosecutors' actions through informal or formal challenge to prosecutorial decisions. New judges, for example, may refuse to cooperate in an ongoing system of plea bargaining either by rejecting guilty pleas where bargains are involved or by rejecting recommendations of sentence leniency from the prosecutor.

Appellate court decisions represent the most well known judicial limit on prosecutors. At the initiation of defense counsel frustrated by what they consider abuses of prosecutorial discretion, numerous cases have challenged actions by prosecutors. The few resulting decisions from the United States Supreme Court have struck down certain prosecutorial strategies while legitimating others. In *Santobello* v. *New York* (1971), the Court implicitly supported prosecutorial discretion in plea bargaining, calling the process of plea bargaining "an essential component of the administration of justice," but the Court admonished the prosecutor of the need to respect the terms of the bargain; the defendant in *Santobello* was thus entitled to relief because of the prosecutor's failure to follow through on the agreed-upon sentence recommendation.

Several other Supreme Court cases in the last decade have led to the development of a doctrine of prosecutorial vindictiveness, although the contours of that doctrine are not entirely clear. In *Blackledge* v. *Perry* (1974), the Court prohibited the prosecutor from increasing charges against a defendant who had invoked his statutory right to appeal. While the court noted there was no evidence of actual vindictiveness in *Blackledge,* they held that due process of law required the defendant to be free even of the appearance of such vindictiveness. In the next two cases, however, *Bordenhircher* v. *Hayes* (1978) and *United States* v. *Goodwin* (1982), the Court seemed to retreat from that position, allowing prosecutors to increase charges or file a habitual-offender charge against defendants who insisted on a jury trial after the failure of plea negotiations. The distinction between these three cases seems to be that the prosecutor's actions in *Blackledge* occurred in a posttrial context (where they were disallowed), while *Bordenkircher* and *Goodwin* occurred in a pretrial setting (where the Court gave prosecutors more latitude).

As a result of extensive public criticism of plea bargaining and a general cry for harsher sentencing, some states have enacted legislation to restrict or abolish plea bargaining and to increase penalties for certain offenses. Other sentencing reforms have included the passage of mandatory minimums and presumptive sentences. All of these legislative actions attempt to restrain or influence from the outside the decisions of prosecutors and others within the criminal justice process. While conclusions on the effectiveness of such measures are tentative and research is still ongoing, many studies point to the remarkable self-adjusting capacity of the court system, which allows discretion to be shifted from one stage of the criminal justice process to the next when confronted by external influences. As an example, restricting the discretion exercised by prosecutors in plea negotiation may simply result in greater discretion in the formulation of charges by prosecutors.

Another trend in prosecution has been an increased role for victims of crime. As an outsider to the criminal court, the victim has generally had negligible impact on decisions. Out of frustration and anger at their treatment by the criminal justice process, victims have lobbied successfully for greater participation and respect. In response, Congress passed the Victims of Crime Act of 1984, authorizing funds to help states establish programs for victim assistance and compensation. Whether these and other such programs will really result in a more active influence by victims on decisions by prosecutors remains to be seen.

Certain criminal offenses may be targeted in response to public outcry, leading to a policy of no dismissals or plea bargains.

Of particular importance in generating support for consideration of the victim's viewpoint has been lobbying and litigation by women's groups, especially in major cities. These political efforts have persuaded prosecutors to prosecute more fully defendants arrested for crimes against women, such as rape and domestic violence. These two offenses have often been downgraded in the eyes of criminal justice personnel, with a much higher than average rate of dismissal and reduction of charges. Prosecutors now are more politically sensitive in these cases, and some offices have established special task forces or charging units for rape, other sexual crimes, and crime within families.

A final trend in prosecution has been the development of informal alternatives to criminal processing. This idea was instituted through programs of pretrial diversion whereby defendants with social problems (who may also have committed criminal offenses) were diverted away from the criminal courts into social agencies that specialize in mental health, alcohol, or drug treatment. While the direct impact of diversion programs was minimal, they may have encouraged further thought about a range of informal alternatives to criminal punishment. Current programs, spurred by congressional legislation (the Dispute Resolution Act), include community (or neighborhood) justice centers, mediation, and arbitration. Those supporting alternative dispute resolution for criminal cases stress the cost savings for courts with the removal of minor offenses and the more appropriate and flexible processes afforded, for example, cases of interpersonal conflict.

The movement toward informal alternatives to criminal court is, oddly enough, somewhat like the movement toward increasing the severity of formal punishment: both represent efforts from the wider community to influence the policies of prosecutors and others in the criminal process, and both speak to the fundamental conflict facing prosecutors between the need to resolve disputes in the interests of justice and the need to maintain order and social control.

[See also (III) Criminal Justice System, Plea Bargaining, Trial Juries and Grand Juries.]

CASES

Blackledge v. Perry, 417 U.S. 21 (1974)
Bordenkircher v. Hayes, 434 U.S. 357 (1978)
Hurtado v. California, 110 U.S. 516 (1884)
Santobello v. New York, 404 U.S. 257 (1971)
United States v. Goodwin, 457 U.S. 368 (1982)

BIBLIOGRAPHY

Albert W. Alschuler, "The Prosecutor's Role in Plea Bargaining," in *University of Chicago Law Review,* 36 (1968), discusses plea bargaining, compares prosecutorial behavior in ten cities, and argues forcefully for the abolition of plea bargaining. Keith O. Boyum and Lynn Mather, eds., *Empirical Theories About Courts* (1983), includes recent articles discussing police-prosecutor relationships, courts as organizations, and other topics. Lief H. Carter, *The Limits of Order* (1974), presents a detailed case study of prosecutorial decision-making in California, with analysis of variation in prosecuting styles and of problems in establishing uniformity of decisions. George F. Cole, *Politics and the Administration of Justice* (1973), is an overview of the criminal justice system that draws heavily on the author's own research on prosecution in Seattle. Kenneth Culp Davis, *Discretionary Justice* (1969), emphasizes the injustices to individual parties from the exercise of discretionary power and suggests ways of confining, checking, and reducing discretion.

James Eisenstein, *Counsel for the United States* (1978), is an excellent study of the organization, politics, and behavior of the federal prosecutor. James Eisenstein and Herbert Jacob, *Felony Justice: An Organizational Analysis of Criminal Courts* (1977), analyzes and compares the disposition of felony cases in three cities, stressing the importance of the courtroom work group in decision-making. Malcolm M. Feeley, *The Process Is the Punishment* (1979), studies in detail a misdemeanor court, focusing especially on pretrial processes. Richard S. Frase, "The Decision to File Federal Criminal Charges," in *University of Chicago Law Review,* 47 (1980), presents a quantitative analysis of prosecutorial discretion in the filing of charges by federal prosecutors.

Milton Heumann, *Plea Bargaining: The Experiences of Prosecutors, Judges, and Defense Attorneys* (1978), questions the importance of case overload and shows how and why newcomers to the court learn to plea bargain. Joan E. Jacoby, *The American Prosecutor: A Search for Identity* (1980), is a comprehensive work on prosecutors, noted for its discussion of variation in prosecutors' offices and policies. Jack M. Kress, "Progress and Prosecution," in *Annals of the American Academy of Political and Social Science,* 423 (1976), summarizes current and historical material on prosecutors. *Law and Society Review,* 13 (1979), a special issue on plea bargaining, is an oversized collection of articles with various pieces on prosecutors.

William F. McDonald, *Plea Bargaining: Critical Issues and Common Practices* (1985), is a research report on plea bargaining, especially useful for the comparisons drawn between the author's findings and the diverse results in the current literature; and, as ed., *The Pros-*

ecutor (1979), is an excellent collection of diverse articles on prosecutors. Lynn M. Mather, *Plea Bargaining or Trial? The Process of Criminal Case Disposition* (1979), describes and analyzes felony dispositions in Los Angeles from the attorneys' point of view, emphasizing the factors determining trial or guilty-plea disposition. Frank W. Miller, *Prosecution: The Decision to Charge a Suspect with a Crime* (1969), studies the charging decision, exploring the many reasons prosecutors have for not filing charges. Raymond Moley, *Politics and Criminal Prosecution* (1929), a classic early work on the politics of prosecution, presents fascinating material on criminal courts of the 1920s. David W. Neubauer, *Criminal Justice in Middle America* (1974), is a very readable and thoughtful overview of the criminal process, based on a study of a small midwestern city.

Jerome H. Skolnick, *Justice Without Trial* (1966), discusses police-prosecutor interactions. Elizabeth Anne Stanko, "The Impact of Victim Assessment on Prosecutor's Screening Decisions," in *Law and Society Review,* 16 (1981–1982), presents data on New York City prosecutors, demonstrating the importance of the victim to the decision to charge. Allen Steinberg, "From Private Prosecution to Plea Bargaining," in *Crime and Delinquency,* 30 (1984), presents new historical research on the early public prosecutors and the extent of private prosecution. W. Randolph Teslik, *Prosecutorial Discretion: The Decision to Charge* (1975), is a thorough, annotated bibliography on prosecutorial discretion. Pamela J. Utz, *Settling the Facts: Discretion and Negotiation in Criminal Court* (1978), compares prosecution in two California offices and analyzes the very different styles of decision-making. Vera Institute of Justice, *Felony Arrests: Their Prosecution and Disposition in New York City's Courts* (1977), describes the processing of felony cases in New York after initial arrest and explores why there is such extensive attrition.

– LYNN MATHER

S

SENTENCING ALTERNATIVES

The sentence is the penalty society exacts from an offender who has been found guilty of a crime after a public trial conducted in conformity with various rights guaranteed defendants by the Constitution. What sentence is given a particular offender depends on a variety of factors, including the objectives of the criminal justice system, constitutional and statutory limitations, the seriousness of the offense, and characteristics of the offender.

Condemnation, retribution, incapacitation, deterrence, and rehabilitation are generally asserted to be objectives of the criminal justice system. However, these objectives usually have not been specified in legislation or court decisions because there is no public consensus on which objective is paramount. In contrast to today's objectives, restitution to the victims was the primary goal in ancient civilization. Later, retribution became the principal objective. But in the eighteenth century, deterrence was advanced as the most appropriate goal and remained so until the twentieth century, when rehabilitation increasingly became recognized as the major, if not the only, appropriate goal of the criminal justice system. Since the mid-1970s, however, because of a large increase in reported crime, especially violent crime, and the belief that efforts to rehabilitate offenders had been unsuccessful, increasing emphasis has been placed on the objectives of retribution, incapacitation, and deterrence. Concurrently, there is also increased interest in the victim's needs, and so, for the first time in several hundred years, restitution is increasingly mentioned as a sentencing objective.

Actors in the Sentencing Process

Most people think of the judge as the person responsible for sentencing. However, there are a host of other actors—the legislature, victim, prosecutor, jury, probation officer, and clinicians—who either make a contribution to the initial sentencing decision or have the power to subsequently modify that decision. Legislatures initiate the sentencing process by deciding what activities are to be considered criminal. By denominating those activities that are criminal, legislatures determine whether any criminal sanction can be imposed for engaging in, or refraining from, that behavior. Provisions in the state or federal constitution may limit the legislature's power to enact criminal laws. For example, a legislature cannot make it a crime to criticize the government, because the law would violate the First Amendment guarantee of freedom of speech. A second limit on the freedom of the legislature to criminalize or increase or reduce penalties from various activities is public opinion. The decriminalization of sexual relations between consenting adults and the relaxation of marijuana laws have been responses to such public pressures, as has the adoption of more severe penalties for drunk driving.

The overwhelming majority of defendants plead guilty, often as the result of a plea bargain.

Legislatures also play a major role in sentencing by setting the limit for the sanctions that may be applied to various crimes. It is the legislature that decides whether an offense is punishable by incarceration or a fine or whether capital punishment may be imposed for murder. Similarly, the legislature decides whether the sanction of probation can be used for a particular offense or for recidivists. The legislature also decides, at least in the first instance, whether sentences for multiple offenses are to be served concurrently or consecutively.

How much sentencing authority judges should exercise is also a legislative decision. The legislature may delegate a great deal of authority to the judge. For example, the judge may be allowed to impose a sentence of from one to twenty years for robbery. On the other hand, the legislature may arrogate most of the sentencing power to itself, allowing the judge to decide only whether the offender is to serve four, five, or six years in prison. Still another alternative used by some legislatures is to divide sentencing responsibility between the judge and an administrative agency. Under this type if system, the judge sets the maximum sentence within the legislative guidelines, but the sentence may be shortened by a parole agency.

Although it was commonplace during the nineteenth century for juries to impose sentences, juries now sentence in noncapital cases in only a handful of states. The American Bar Association (ABA) and many other national legal groups have strongly protested the practice of jury sentencing, because jurors have no chance to acquire sentencing expertise. In capital cases, however, this practice is preferred, but not required, by the United States Supreme Court.

By choosing whether or not to report a crime, the victim is instrumental in determining whether an offender will receive any sanction for the crime. The crime of rape, for example, may be undetected or unpunished because many victims do not notify the police or are unwilling to testify. In the past, victims had no role after guilt was determined. Now, however, a number of jurisdictions permit victims to testify at the sentencing hearing.

The prosecutor may influence the sentence before and after the trial. If an offender is charged with several offenses, the prosecutor may seek convictions on one, two, or all of them. Also, the prosecutor selects the exact crime with which the suspect is to be charged. Choosing between a prosecution for murder and manslaughter may make a significant difference in the penalty imposed upon conviction. Recommending a sentence to the judge after conviction of the offender is a third way in which the prosecutor can influence the sentence.

But perhaps the most influential role that prosecutors play in the sentencing process is in plea bargaining. The overwhelming majority of defendants plead guilty, often as the result of a plea bargain. The defendant frequently is willing to admit responsibility for an offense for which a lighter penalty is imposed, instead of taking the risk of being convicted of a more serious crime. The prosecutor may accept the plea to the lesser charge in preference to a time-consuming trial and the always present chance of an acquittal. This process is called charge bargaining. Charge bargaining also occurs when the defendant pleads guilty to one charge in return for an agreement to dismiss other charges. A third type of plea bargaining involves the situation in which an offender admits guilt to the offense charged in exchange for the prosecutor's recommendation for a light sentence.

The probation officer usually compiles information about the offender's criminal record, background, and personal characteristics for the judge's consideration in designing the sentence. In some jurisdictions the report also contains the probation officer's opinion about the appropriate sentence.

If an offender is placed on probation, a probation officer monitors his activities. If the probationer violates any of the conditions of probation, the officer decides whether the violation should be reported to the judge. Accordingly, the probation officer may stimulate a change in the offender's sentence because the report may result in the revocation of the probation and the imposition of a jail or prison sentence by the judge.

Increasingly, judges request a psychiatric or psychological evaluation of an offender in order to obtain information about the type of rehabilitative program an offender needs and about his "dangerousness." Consequently, the opinion expressed by the clinician may influence the choice of sanction, probation, imprisonment, the death penalty, or the length of the sentence the offender receives.

The president of the United States, governors, and parole boards usually are not thought of as having a role in sentencing, because they do not make initial sentencing decisions. However, they are able to modify the decision. For example, the president has the power to pardon federal offenders. He also has the power to remit fines, penalties, and forfeitures and the power to commute sentences. A commutation moderates a sentence, while a pardon completely absolves the offender of guilt and restores him to the legal position of a defendant who has been acquitted. Governors have similar clemency powers over persons convicted of violating state laws. Although clemency powers were once exercised frequently, they have been replaced to a large extent by the practice of parole.

The final and most recent actor in the post-sentencing process is the offender. In many states the offender may have his prison term reduced substantially by complying with "good time" policies. In some states the offender can earn the reduction simply by maintaining good behavior, but in others he must participate in educational or training programs to accrue good time.

Sentencing Procedures

Criminal trials, where guilt or innocence is determined, are governed by a variety of rules required by the Constitution, legislation, or court rules of criminal procedure. Most of these rules, however, do not apply at the sentencing stage. For example, in most jurisdictions the defendant has the right to exclude illegally obtained evidence and to cross-examine witnesses at trial but not at sentencing. Sentencing procedures can be best examined by dividing them into three stages: the presentence investigation, the sentencing hearing, and postsentence review.

The belief that the sentence should be designed to "fit the offender," as well as "fit the crime," is the reason for the presentence investigation. Typically, immediately after a verdict or plea of guilty, the judge asks a probation officer to investigate the offender's criminal and social history and to present a report of the results. The goal of this report is to assist the judge in evaluating the risk of allowing the defendant to remain in the community or in determining the length of the period of incarceration. The typical report contains the defendant's criminal history, with all official records of prior convictions; details of the offense, including the police version (from police records), the defendant's version, and statements of the victim, witnesses and codefendants; biographical information, including family, school, employment, military, and marital data obtained from records and statements of the offender's friends, acquaintances, and relatives; treatment plan resources, especially if probation is the recommended or likely sentence; and recommendation of the probation officer.

A judge may choose from a variety of sanctions, including death, incarceration, probation, restitution to the victim, and fines.

In the past the defendant was not entitled to know the contents of a presentence report. However, an increasing number of jurisdictions now require its partial or complete disclosure. In the federal system, for example, disclosure is required, but information obtained by a promise of confidentiality, information diagnostic in nature, and information that if disclosed could be harmful to the offender or others may be withheld, but the defendant must be given a summary of any withheld information upon which the judge expects to rely in determining the sentence.

After the presentence report has been submitted to the judge, the sentencing hearing takes place. In the past, it was a brief, informal proceeding. The offender merely was asked if he had anything to say before the sentence was announced, and the offender's lawyer, if he had one, made an appeal for leniency. Then the judge would announce the sentence.

The sentencing phase of the trial is now more structured and formalized. Representation by counsel at the sentencing hearing has been recognized as a constitutional right (*Mempa* v. *Ray*, 1967), and counsel now take a more active role at this stage than they did in the past. It is now common for the offender's attorney to present witnesses and offer a treatment plan. The prosecutor also has a more extended role at sentencing and may present witnesses and make a sentencing recommendation to the judge. Victims, too, now more often participate in the sentencing hearing.

Offenders have more rights at sentencing when the death penalty is a possible sanction. For example, in capital cases the Supreme Court has held that the presentence report must be disclosed to the offender or the offender's counsel prior to the sentencing hearing, the offender must be allowed to introduce any mitigating evidence, and appellate review of death sentences is required (*Gardner* v. *Florida*, 1977; *Bell* v. *Ohio*, 1978; and *Gregg* v. *Georgia*, 1976).

In addition to requiring the probation officer's presentence report, some states authorize a psychiatric evaluation of the offender as part of the presentence procedure. At least in death penalty cases, where the defendant's dangerousness is at issue, the Supreme Court has determined that due process entitles the defendant to a presentence psychiatric evaluation on this issue, the assistance of a psychiatrist in preparing for the sentencing hearing, and the psychiatrist's testimony at the hearing (*Ake* v. *Oklahoma*, 1985).

The third stage of sentencing, the postsentence review, was unavailable in most jurisdictions before 1970. Extensive criticism of sentencing disparity during that decade produced a significant change in the law. More than half of the states now authorize appellate review of sentences in at least some circumstances, and in the remaining jurisdictions, the failure to develop such measures seems to be the result of inertia, not opposition.

There has been considerable controversy over the issue of whether the government as well as the defendant should be allowed to appeal a sentence. However, the ABA, whose views have been influential with legislatures and courts in criminal justice matters, has taken the position that the prosecution should not be able to appeal a sentence on the grounds that it is too lenient. Nor would the ABA permit the reviewing court to increase a sentence, only to reduce or affirm it.

Types of Sentences

A judge may choose from a variety of sanctions, including death, incarceration, probation, restitution to the victim, and fines, when designing a sentence. The judge's choice of a penalty is limited by the applicable statute, and both the judge and the legislature are restricted in their choice of sanction by the state and federal Constitution. For example, the Constitution specifically prohibits the passage of bills of attainder and ex post facto laws. A bill of attainder is a legislative act that inflicts punishment without a judicial trial, while an ex post facto law is one that imposes punishment for an act that was not a crime at the time it was committed. A law that imposes more severe punishment than that permitted at the time of the crime would also be an ex post facto law.

Cruel and unusual punishments also are prohibited by the Constitution. There are three ways in which this prohibition affects sanctions. First, it limits the method of punishment that may be imposed. Branding an offender, cutting off his hand, or depriving him of citizenship would be considered cruel and unusual punishment.

The second way in which the Eighth Amendment affects sanctions is that it limits the amount of punishment that may be used. For example, six years in prison for cutting flowers in a public park would be out of all proportion to the offense committed.

The third restriction is a prohibition against any penalty in some circumstances. This was illustrated by the Supreme Court when it said that even one day in prison would not be allowed as punishment for having a cold (*Robinson* v. *California*, 1962).

CAPITAL PUNISHMENT. The most severe sanction, the death penalty, cannot be imposed for most offenses. Thirty-eight states and the federal government allow imposition of a death sentence for certain types of murder, currently the only offense that the Supreme Court has recognized as warranting the death sentence, which therefore cannot be said to violate the cruel and unusual punishment clause (*Gregg*). Two sentencing objectives, retribution and deterrence, justify this sanction.

Most states allow the death penalty for persons who have been convicted of murder as minors; between 1975 and 1985, at least eighteen youngsters received this sentence, and at least one of those sentences was carried out. By 1985 the Court had not decided the constitutionality of this penalty for minors.

Although a few states authorize capital punishment for other crimes, such as kidnapping, the constitutionality of such statutes is doubtful because in 1977 the Supreme Court forbade the use of the death penalty for rape on the grounds that the victim did not die (*Coker* v. *Georgia*, 1977). Under this reasoning, treason and

This electric chair at Sing Sing state prison in New York stands as a grim testament to the ultimate sentencing alternative. (Library of Congress/ Corbis)

espionage, when they result in death, may be the only offenses other than murder for which the death penalty will be approved.

INCARCERATION. Incarceration is the most frequently imposed sanction for serious criminal offenses. There are four rationales for its employment: deterrence of other potential offenders, protection of society by the incapacitation of offenders, rehabilitation of the offender, and retribution for the crime.

Authorized periods of incarceration or confinement vary from a few months to life imprisonment. Historically, confinement was always in a correctional facility and was a full-time penalty. Since the 1960s, there have been variations both in the place and the extent of confinement. It is now not uncommon to hear of "confinement in the community" and "partial confinement."

Although it is generally agreed that the length of incarceration should correspond to the seriousness of the crime, it is well known that the penalty structure of many states does not meet this goal. Some states have revised their laws to rectify this situation, and others will undoubtedly follow their lead. One method is to divide all the offenses into five or six groups, each group containing crimes of similar seriousness, and to assign sanctions accordingly. Table 1 illustrates this approach.

It is also well documented that the length of confinement imposed by sentences in the United States is longer than the rest of the Western world. However, this disparity may be reduced because of the extensive use in America of parole and "good time" to shorted the incarceration period.

Life imprisonment, which frequently means a period of twenty or thirty years instead of the actual life of a particular offender, is normally reserved for violent offenses, such as murder, rape, and kidnapping. However, in many states life imprisonment may also be imposed on offenders who have been sentenced on three or more occasions, even if their crimes were neither violent nor involved a substantial amount of property. The propriety of imposing this severe penalty for the repetition of other than serious crimes is beginning to be questioned both on policy and constitutional grounds. The sanction of life imprisonment for three thefts of less than $100, for example, may be found to be disproportionate and thus offend the Constitution's prohibition against cruel and unusual punishment.

The states employ a variety of systems to determine the length of the prison term to be imposed. The legislature, the courts, and the parole authorities have differing degrees of control over whether the offender must be imprisoned, and, if so, the length of the sentence, depending on which type of system is in operation in that state.

TABLE 1

OFFENSE LEVELS AND PENALTIES

Class of Offense	Maximum Term
A level	Life
B level	20 years
C level	10 years
D level	5 years
E level	1 year
F level	6 months

In some instances a judge may be required to sentence an offender to prison. Forty-three states mandate a prison term for certain violent crimes, such as murder and rape. Other common mandatory prison laws include the use of a gun while committing a crime (in 1985, thirty-seven states and the District of Columbia) and narcotics offenses (twenty-nine states and the District of Columbia). In addition, these mandatory-imprisonment laws frequently specify a minimum term of imprisonment.

Some states use an indeterminate sentencing system. In those states, the judge sets a minimum and maximum term to be served (for example, five to ten years). Within the range set by the judge, the parole agency decides the actual time of release and therefore determines the actual time to be served. Instead of the judge speculating at the time of the sentencing when the offender will be sufficiently rehabilitated to deserve release, the correctional authorities make this determination, presumably on the basis of prison behavior.

If a state has a determinate sentencing system, the judge sets a fixed term, which must be served in full. Under this system, parole officials do not have the authority to release the prisoner before the expiration of the sentence. One form of determinate sentencing is called presumptive sentencing. In presumptive sentencing, a convicted offender always will receive a particular sentence assigned to the offense committed, unless the judge finds that specified aggravating or mitigating factors exist that should lengthen or shorten the sentence by a specific amount. Any deviation from this pattern must be justified by the sentencing judge in a written opinion, which is subject to review by an appeals court. In 1985 nine states used determinate sentencing.

Some states employ a sentencing guideline system, under which the judge is to consider both the severity of the offense committed and the offender's criminal history in designing the sentence. These guidelines are used to form tables, which provide recommended sentences to the judge. Approximately ten states have such guidelines.

An offender sentenced to a term of imprisonment is usually able to serve a portion of that term outside the prison, by means of either parole or good-time reduction. All but the nine determinate-sentencing states allow the parole authorities to release an offender prior to the expiration of his sentence. During the remainder of the sentence, paroled offenders remain subject to the parole system and under the supervision of a parole officer. Parole may be revoked and the offender returned to prison if any of the conditions of the parole release are violated.

Of the states that allow parole, about one-fourth allow it at any time during the sentence, within the discretion of the parole board. Other states require that a specified portion of the sentence be served before the prisoner can be considered for parole. Still others require a minimum term to be served before the prisoner is eligible for parole. Fifteen jurisdictions use parole guidelines, similar to sentencing guidelines, to assist the parole authorities in making the parole decision.

Time actually spent in prison may also be reduced by involving other policies, collectively referred to as good-time programs. Even states that do not allow for early release on parole reduce the period of incarceration through good time. The maximum amount of good time that can be awarded varies widely from state to state, with extremes ranging from five to forty-five days for each month served.

PARTIAL INCARCERATION. Partial incarceration is a relatively new sanction, lying between total incarceration of the offender and leaving him free to live in the community. It has several forms. In one, the offender is never totally incarcerated but is placed in jail or prison only in the evening and/or on weekends. The purpose of this sanction is to allow the offender to support himself and his family or to enable him to earn money to make restitution for his offense. A variation of this sanction would permit the offender to be placed in a halfway house in the community, which is supervised by correctional personnel. Although not free to live where he chooses, the offender has more freedom than if he were in jail or prison.

Some states allow partial incarceration only after the offender has spent some time in total incarceration. Still another variation is sentencing the offender to prison but allowing him, usually after having served some of his sentence, to leave the correctional facility for a part of each day to work, receive employment training, or to attend school.

PROBATION. Probation is a sanction that does not involve confinement but imposes conditions and allows the judge to retain authority over the offender, to modify the conditions of the sentence, or to resentence the offender if its conditions are violated. It is essentially a twentieth-century development.

Two separate rationales are offered for the use of probation sanctions. For one group of offenders, probation is imposed primarily for symbolic reasons, while for the second group, probation putatively serves rehabilitative goals. For the first group, a judge uses probation because no further criminal conduct is anticipated, yet considerations of restitution and deterrence require some sanction. The judge will use probation for the second group when it is thought that the offender needs some supervision and treatment, which in the opinion of the judge can be provided in the community.

During the term of probation, which seldom exceeds five years, the offender must abide by all of the conditions set down by the sentencing judge. These conditions are usually related to the crime for which the offender was convicted. For example, those convicted of drug abuse may be required to participate in a clinic or hospital treatment program. If the conditions are violated or another crime is committed, the judge may revoke probation and impose another sentence.

The probationer remains under the supervision of a probation official to whom the offender usually must make regular visits. Ideally, the probation officer is to aid in the rehabilitation of the offender. The official is also responsible for notifying the court of any probation violations which warrant the court's attention. Probation is often combined with other types of sentences, such as a fine or restitution.

RESTITUTION. Restitution is another sentencing alternative available to a judge. Restitution can be defined as court-ordered compensation to the offender's victim for damage caused by the offender's criminal conduct. Most often, restitution entails actual financial compensation to the victim. It may involve returning stolen property or donating services to the victim, to a value equivalent to the loss sustained. Restitution is commonly limited by statute to the amount of actual loss suffered by the victim and does not compensate for pain and suffering or provide a vehicle for punitive damages. Actual loss may include destroyed or stolen property, services fraudulently obtained, medical expenses incurred as a result of an injury caused by the offender's crime, and wages lost because of time absent from work as a result of victimization. Although some suggest that restitution be combined with incarceration, with funds being taken from the inmate's earnings from work in prison industry, restitution is usually coupled with a sentence of probation.

COMMUNITY SERVICE. Sentencing an offender to perform services benefiting the community, rather than an individual victim, is relatively new. In many instances this sanction is more appropriate than either a fine or restitution, the other nonincarcerative sanctions that require the offender to make amends for his criminal act.

Community service may be a more effective penalty than a fine for the middle-class offender, for whom the sum involved may have little significance. It may also be a better alternative for indigent offenders or those who have only moderate means, because the unintended consequence of fines on offenders with low incomes may be to penalize their families.

Ordering an offender to perform community service also may be a better disposition at least in some circumstances than restitution. For some offenses, such as selling liquor to a minor or drunken driving, there is no appropriate action the offender can take that will benefit the victim, while for other offenses, such as white-collar crime, often no individual can be identified. Even when the victim is known and a specific amount of money that would repay the loss can be established, the objectives of deterrence and rehabilitation may be better served by having the offender perform some noncompensated service for a segment of the public.

States allow the parole authorities to release an offender prior to the expiration of his sentence.

Service projects vary widely and may involve work to improve public parks and highways or services to charitable and civic organizations. The following are examples of community service sentences: A self-employed cleaner convicted of petty larceny charges agreed to provide $250 worth of services to a home for the elderly. A judge assigned graffiti scrawlers to clean-up chores. A president of a college, convicted of manslaughter for killing a pedestrian while driving under the influence of alcohol, was sentenced to lecture for a stipulated period of time on the consequences of drinking and driving.

FINES. Fines are the most commonly employed of all criminal sanctions, making up as much as 75 percent of all sentences. Like other sanctions, fines may be the sole sentence given an offender or may be combined with other penalties such as imprisonment or probation. Most frequently a fine is the only sanction imposed. Fines differ from restitution in that they are paid to the government rather than to the victim of crime and therefore serve as a source of revenue for the state.

Usually the court may exercise some discretion in setting the fine. Statutes usually set only the upper limits on the amount of the fine that may be imposed for a particular offense. The only constitutional limit on the judge's discretion to impose a fine of a lesser amount is that the fine may not be so grossly excessive that it amounts to a deprivation of property without due process of law.

Theoretically a fine is due as soon as it is imposed by the court. However, the court usually sets a reasonable time, which varies depending on the circumstances of the case, within which the fine is to be paid. In recent years, some states have started to permit payments of fines in installments, which helps avoid defaults and financial hardship in the case of poorer offenders.

If the offender does not make a reasonable effort to pay the fine within the required time, he may be jailed until payment. Imprisonment in this situation is not part of the sentence for the offense but is only a means of enforcing the sentence of the fine. The offender may secure his release at any time by paying the fine. Some states set a maximum time limit on imprisonment resulting from failure to pay a fine.

Trends in Sentencing

The task of devising a sentencing system that will achieve the goals of deterrence, retribution, incapacitation, and rehabilitation and will also function with fairness to offenders, victims, and the community is an old one. However, public recognition that this is an extremely difficult goal to achieve is relatively recent. Throughout most of the first two-thirds of the twentieth century the underlying premises of the sentencing system were that offenders should be given a sanction that would reform them and that they should be under state control until reformation was achieved. The indeterminate sentence was developed to facilitate this aim. It was based on the beliefs that most criminals could be rehabilitated, judges could determine which criminals could be reformed and by what sanction, and correctional officials could determine when offenders were "cured."

In the late 1960s all of these beliefs came under attack. The view that we do not know how to rehabilitate offenders has become dominant. Many people who have come to this conclusion argue that rehabilitation should be abandoned as a sentencing objective and that more emphasis should be place on retribution, deterrence, and incapacitation.

In addition, there is considerable controversy about the ability of judges, correctional officials, or clinicians to identify offenders who will or will not commit crimes again. Consequently, the indeterminate sentence is considered to be unfair, no matter what its length, because similar offenders may be incarcerated for different periods of time.

The following practices have been suggested for implementing more evenhanded sentencing practices: offenders committing similar offenses and who are equally blameworthy should receive the same punishment; offenders should know the duration of their punishment when they are sentenced; sentences based on prediction of future criminality and expectations of cure should be abolished; parole should be abolished; and treatment programs should be available to offenders but not required.

Not everyone subscribes to these views. There are those who argue that the resources necessary to achieve the rehabilitative objective have not been available. Instead of the abandonment of the rehabilitative ideal, they seek a new commitment to this goal and an increase in the amount and kind of rehabilitative services for offenders, especially for those offenders who can remain in the community without threatening public safety. Proponents of this view often are convinced that the sanction of imprisonment is used too often and for too extensive a period. Members of both groups seem to agree that offenders should be given increased procedural protections at the sentencing stage and that sentencing review should be made available to reduce sentencing disparity.

[See also (III) Criminal Justice System, Plea Bargaining, Prosecutors.]

CASES

Ake v. Oklahoma, 105 S. Ct. 1087 (1985)
Bearden v. Georgia, 461 U.S. 660 (1983)
Bell v. Ohio, 438 U.S. 637 (1978)
Coker v. Georgia, 433 U.S. 584 (1977)
Gardner v. Florida, 430 U.S. 349 (1977)
Gregg v. Georgia, 428 U.S. 153 (1976)
Mempa v. Ray, 389 U.S. 128 (1967)
Robinson v. California, 370 U.S. 660 (1962)
Solem v. Helm, 463 U.S. 277 (1983)

BIBLIOGRAPHY

Francis A. Allen, *The Decline of the Rehabilitative Ideal* (1981), discusses the decline and the future of the role of rehabilitation in sentencing. American Bar Association, *Standards for Criminal Justice* (1980 and 1982 Supplement), provides model sentencing procedures, extensive commentary, and references. Marvin E. Frankel, *Criminal Sentences: Law Without Order* (1972), is the seminal book on sentencing reform. Nicholas N. Kittrie and Elyce H. Zenoff, *Sanctions, Sentencing and Corrections* (1981), contains articles, cases, statutes, statistics, and commentary on sentencing objectives, procedures, types of sanctions, and proposed reforms.

Norval Norris, *The Future of Imprisonment* (1974), analyzes the problems and expectations of imprisonment as a sanction. Charles Renfrew, "The Paper Label Sentences: An Evaluation," in *Yale Law Journal,* 86 (1977), describes the reasons for and reactions to Judge Renfrew sentencing five corporate executives convicted of price-fixing to make twelve oral presentations about their offense to civic and business groups. Twentieth Century Fund, Task Force on Criminal Sentencing, *Fair and Certain Punishment* (1976), describes the merits of presumptive sentencing. United States Department of Justice, Bureau of Justice Statistics, *Sourcebook, Criminal Justice Statistics* (1983), contains comprehensive statistics on criminal justice, including the number of offenders imprisoned, executed, and paroled. Franklin E. Zimring, "Making the Punishment Fit the Crime," in *Hastings Center Report,* 6 (1976), criticizes presumptive sentencing and other determinate sentencing proposals.

– ELYCE ZENOFF

STATE COURT SYSTEMS

When people think of the three branches of state government—the executive, the legislature, and the judiciary—they usually think of a single institution of government located in the state capital. The state legislature, for example, is usually composed of a senate and a house of representatives and typically is located in a single building. The judicial branch, however, does not involve just one institution; the state's highest court in the capital is only one of many courts in that state. The judiciary is a system of courts, located in towns, cities, and counties throughout a state and in the state capital. In a court system, various courts are connected to each other through decision-making procedures and legal policy. Therefore, understanding a state judiciary involves understanding the structure, behavior, and interrelationships of a variety of courts in a state court system.

Many states have separate divisions of the same trial court to process civil and criminal cases.

Most crimes and civil disputes that occur in the United States become the subject of state, not federal, court cases. Compared with the states, the scope of decision-making (jurisdiction) of the federal courts is very limited, so most litigation falls to the state courts. The chances are extremely high that when Americans go to court, they go to a state court.

Each of the fifty states has its own separate system of courts with legal authority over people within the state. State courts make legal decisions in a wide variety of criminal law violations and in private (civil) disputes between people within the state. In some instances, state courts are affected by federal law and the decisions of federal courts, but in most ways they are substantially independent and separate systems of courts. Although they also are independent of each other, the fifty state court systems have much in common with each other. They all have similar levels and types of courts, with roughly comparable functions. For example, a murder trial or a serious business-contract dispute involving thousands of dollars would be heard in a state's major trial court and probably could be reviewed by the state's highest appellate court. There are variations in state law, but in general, a crime or a civil dispute in one state probably would be a crime or a dispute in another, with a comparable court available to decide it.

While the fifty state court systems share certain overall similarities, a closer look shows that there also are many important differences between them. For example, some states have relatively simple sets of courts with clear and distinct functions, while other states have many complex types of courts, which creates considerable confusion about their functions. The idea of a court system also oversimplifies the actual relationships among the courts in a state. The official role of appellate courts is to review and correct trial-court errors. However, appellate courts do not have continuous or predictable opportunities to provide legal guidance for the trial courts, since most trial-court decisions are not appealed to higher courts. Most losing litigants end their litigation with the trial courts because it is too expensive for them to continue the fight or because they believe that the chances of winning a reversal are not very good. This means, then, that most trial-court decisions are the final decisions.

There also are strong traditions of localism in American courts that prevent appellate courts from controlling local justice. Historically, the states did not create a system of multilevel courts all at once. Most early courts were local trial courts, and the few appellate courts were far away and had little authority. Today, even though trial judges are parts of state court systems and receive state salaries, most of them continue to think of themselves as providers of local justice. Consequently, even when appellate judges make general rules that they expect trial courts to follow, local judges are often reluctant to fully support them if the rules conflict with local judicial policy or traditional ways of managing the work of the courts. Traditions of local control and the value of judicial independence are strong. Therefore, a diagram of an official court hierarchy that places appellate courts on top does not fully

This old Court House of Queen Anne's County, built in 1708, stands in Queenstown, Maryland. (Lee Snider/Corbis)

describe the reality of how state judicial systems exercise authority or create judicial policy.

The Structure of Courts

There are two key elements to understanding court organization: the structure of court systems (the number and types of courts) and court jurisdiction (their legal authority to hear different kinds of disputes that people bring to court). Both the structure and jurisdiction of courts are determined by state constitutions and by statutes passed by state legislatures. These basic organizational features of courts are important because they determine the role that various courts have in state policymaking. Organization and jurisdiction affect judicial authority to deal with important state issues.

Approximately two-thirds of the states have four basic types of courts: a supreme court, intermediate courts of appeal, trial courts of general jurisdiction, and trial courts of limited jurisdiction. About one-third of the states have no intermediate appellate courts. Courts also have different names in the states. For instance, New York calls its highest court the Court of Appeals and refers to its major trial courts as supreme courts. In many states, however, intermediate appellate courts are called courts of appeals. Trial courts have many different designations. They may be called district courts, circuit courts, superior courts, or the like. Although particular courts often have different names, their functions are roughly similar. Table 1 lists the major types of courts that are found in the fifty states.

TRIAL COURTS. Trial courts are the points of entry into the judicial process. Each side in a lawsuit or a criminal case has an opportunity to state its claim or complaint, to present witnesses to prove its version of the facts and circumstances, and to cite the law relevant to the conflict. Each of the opponents hopes the judge or jury will decide that his position is the correct one. Court cases involve either criminal or civil conflicts. Criminal cases occur when a person has committed an act that is forbidden by state law and is punishable, possibly by a fine payable to the government or by a jail term. Crimes are illegal acts against "the people" or the state. Civil cases include all other cases and do not involve jail terms. Civil cases often pit a government against an individual or a group, but the issues usually concern the enforcement of government policy. Civil cases not involving the government are conflicts between private parties and usually involve personal injury, property damage, debts, or some other conflict and claims for the payment of money from one side to the other. Many states have separate divisions of the same trial court to process civil and criminal cases, respectively.

Trial courts are divided into two groups: those with general jurisdiction and those with limited jurisdiction. "Limited jurisdiction" means that the particular court may hear only certain narrowly defined categories of cases. Many states have specialized trial courts that hear, for example, only traffic violations cases (traffic court), divorce and child-custody cases (family court), cases involving youthful criminal offenders (juvenile court), or cases involving small amounts of money (small-claims court). Although states are increasingly inclined to reduce the number and variety of these courts, some states have ten or more of them. Trial courts of "general jurisdiction" have broader authority to hear a large variety of cases. Any dispute involving more than a specific amount of money (for example, more than the $1,500–$2,500 limit in many state small-claims courts) may be heard by a state trial court of general jurisdiction. Most criminal cases involving serious crimes also are heard by these courts.

APPELLATE COURTS. A person found guilty in a criminal case or a party in a civil suit who is unhappy about the outcome of a trial may appeal to another court for review of the decision of the trial court. Everyone is entitled to one appeal. Supreme courts and intermediate courts of appeals are the main appellate courts. Appellate courts do not hold new trials; they only review the written record of the lower court and hear the arguments of opposing attorneys. Appeals courts determine if the trial judge made an important error in procedure or interpretation of law that would require the appeals court to reverse the decision or to order a new trial. Exceptions sometimes occur in cases appealed from trial courts of limited jurisdiction. Appeals from these courts may require new trials in trial courts of general jurisdiction. Certain other appeals are heard by intermediate appeals courts, while others—often those involving more serious crime and more money—are reviewed by the highest court.

TABLE 1

THE STRUCTURE OF STATE COURTS

Court type	Examples
Highest Appellate Courts	State supreme court
Intermediate Courts of Appeals	Superior court, district or circuit court of appeals, etc. (found in about two-thirds of the states)
Trial Courts of General Jurisdiction	District court, circuit court, court of common pleas, etc.
Trial Courts of Limited Jurisdiction	Small-claims court, traffic court, family court, juvenile court, county court, justice of the peace, etc.

The formal purpose of intermediate courts of appeals is to hear certain types of cases that are considered to be less important and to take on some of the work of the highest appellate court. Some state supreme courts, for example, review criminal cases only when the death penalty is imposed. Others hear cases if the prison term handed down by the trial court is five years or more.

Federal courts have the power to hear only certain types of cases, and few of them affect most people.

Lesser penalties are reviewed by intermediate appellate courts. Cases involving less than certain amounts of money, perhaps $10,000, will be reviewed only by the intermediate appellate courts in certain states. Cases involving more money go to state supreme courts. In a few states, supreme courts have substantial powers to decide for themselves which cases they will decide. This is called the power of certiorari. It is similar to, but usually not as extensive as, the power of the United States Supreme Court to accept or reject most cases. Where state supreme courts may choose the cases they will decide, the importance of intermediate appellate courts is greatly increased because these courts become the last stop for most cases in the state appellate process.

DISTRIBUTION OF COURTS. Trial and intermediate appellate courts are distributed geographically throughout individual states, and consequently they often are viewed by local residents, judges, and lawyers as "local" courts, even though they are parts of state court systems. Trial courts have the greatest local flavor. All of the states are divided into various judicial districts, with state trial courts of limited and general jurisdiction serving local populations throughout the state. Small or sparsely populated states such as Alaska, Rhode Island, and Delaware have less than a half dozen judicial districts. Many other states have several dozen: Texas has more than 250 separate judicial districts. With few exceptions, cases are brought to courts in the area where the dispute or violation of criminal law occurs. This usually is a great convenience for local people involved in court cases, but it also means that out-of-towners who become involved in a dispute, such as a traffic accident, have to travel from their homes to a court in a distant county to participate in the case. Deciding local cases in the immediate area also means that getting justice is likely to be affected by local differences in attitudes and beliefs.

State intermediate courts of appeals usually are found in the more heavily populated and urban states, which produce many more cases than rural and sparsely populated states. However, the trend is toward the creation of more intermediate appellate courts, and we can expect more states to have them in the future. About 60 percent of the states with intermediate appellate courts have a single court with statewide jurisdiction. In the remainder, the state is divided into various geographic regions with each having its own independent branch of the intermediate appellate court. Illinois and Florida, for example, are divided into five regions, each with its own branch of the intermediate appellate court. The large state of Texas has fourteen separate intermediate appellate courts. As in the trial courts, cases are appealed to the intermediate appellate court located in the same section of the state as the trial court that first decided the case.

Court Jurisdiction

As mentioned earlier, state courts hear most of the cases that arise in the United States. The federal courts have the power to hear only certain types of cases, and few of these affect most people. A common type of federal case is one in which people from different states sue each other for money exceeding $10,000. Because the parties to the suit are from diverse jurisdictions, such actions are called diversity cases. Few people ever become involved in these kinds of lawsuits. Other federal civil cases involve conflicts over federal law or major constitutional questions. Again, few people become litigants in such cases. There are also some (though relatively few) federal crimes, usually involving specialized and rare types of violations, such as counterfeiting, illegal immigration, and bank robbery. In contrast, the jurisdiction of the state courts is much larger and more general, and the state courts decide many everyday types of disputes.

The jurisdiction of individual courts within particular states often is very complex. Laws describing jurisdiction designate the precise types of disputes that must be heard by one court or another, but a state may permit more than one court to hear the same kind of case. The legal term for this overlapping of powers is *concurrent jurisdiction.* Where there are many different types of state courts with concurrent jurisdiction, it often is very difficult for citizens and even their lawyers to decide which court ought to hear a particular case.

We can get a clearer picture of the jurisdiction of various state courts by looking at examples of state court systems and the kinds of cases the individual courts are expected to decide. Figure 1 and Figure 2 are models of the state court systems of California and Indiana. The California system is an example of relatively simple state court systems, and Indiana represents complex and often confusing systems.

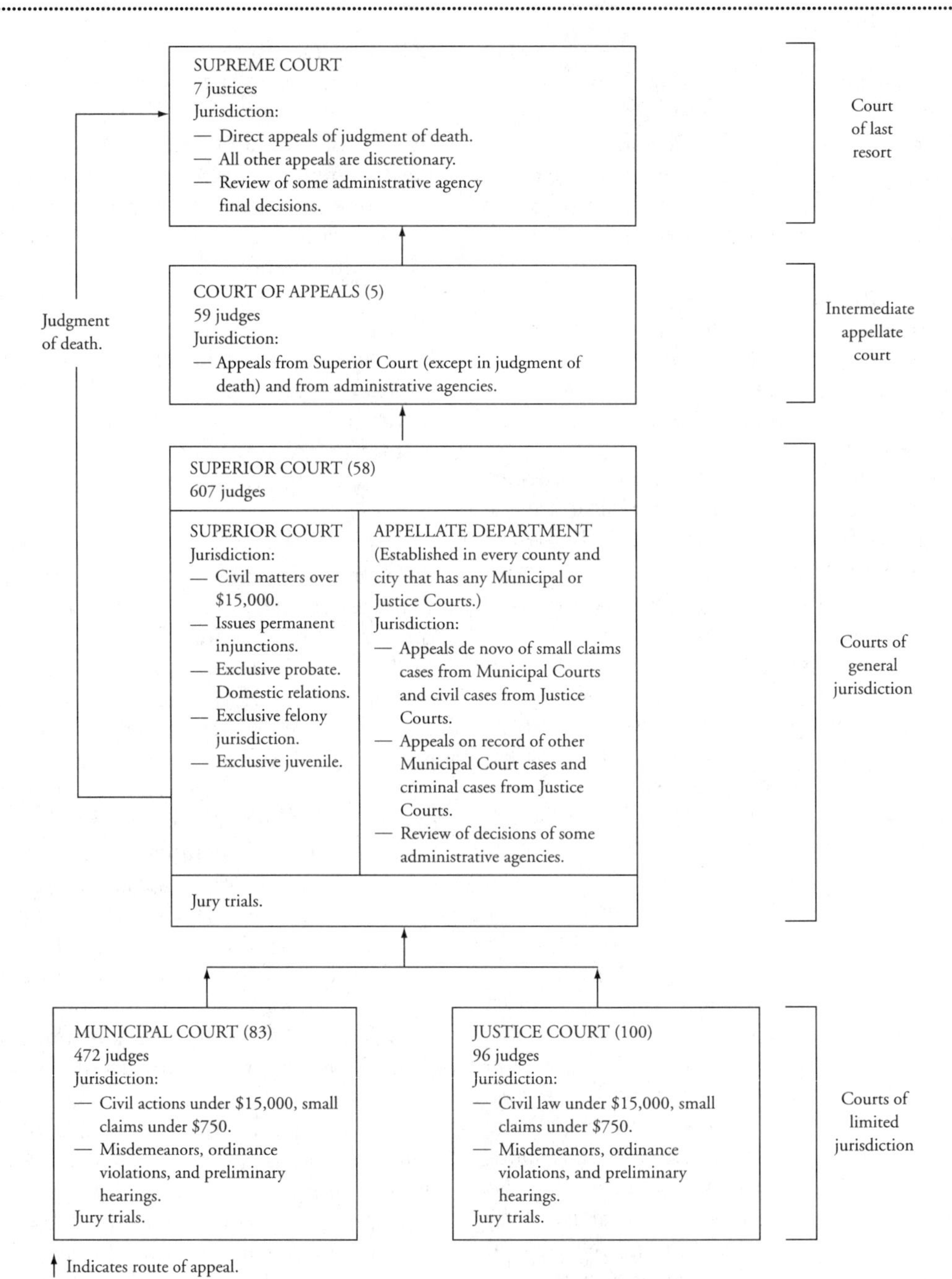

Figure 1. California Court System, 1980. (United States Department of Justice, Bureau of Justice Statistics, State Court Organization 1980. *1982)*

California has a state supreme court, five divisions of an intermediate appellate court distributed regionally throughout the state, a single type of trial court of general jurisdiction located in local districts (superior court), and two types of trial courts of limited jurisdiction found in cities and towns (municipal court and justice court). The two trial courts of limited jurisdiction have exactly the same powers but different locations. The main difference between the two is that municipal courts are found in larger cities, while the justice courts are located in smaller towns and rural areas. The main role of these two courts is to conduct trials in civil cases involving less than $15,000, and the courts have separate, simplified procedures for small-claims disputes of less than $750. They also hear any criminal case designated by state law as a less serious crime (misde-

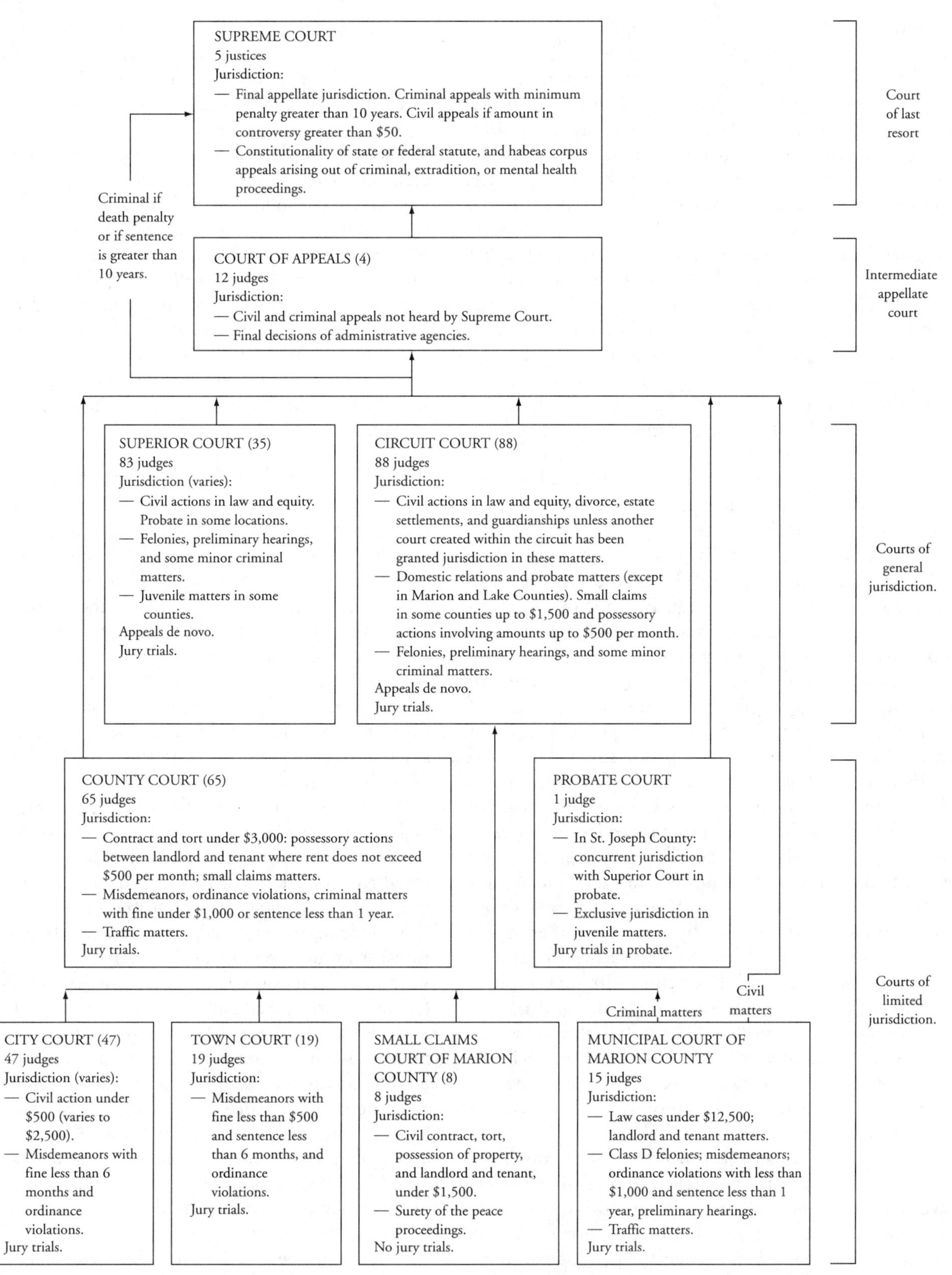

Figure 2. Indiana Court System, 1980. (United States Department of Justice, Bureau of Justice Statistics, State Court Organization 1980. *1982)*

meanor). A conviction for a misdemeanor usually results in a fine or very short jail sentence.

The state trial court of general jurisdiction hears civil disputes involving more than $15,000 and all criminal cases that the state has classified as serious crimes (felonies). Convictions for felonies often result in long prison terms or, in the case of murder, the death penalty. These courts also hear divorce and juvenile criminal cases. In California, and most other states, trial courts of general jurisdiction hear appeals from the trial courts of limited jurisdiction. In Figure 1, the arrow from the trial court of general jurisdiction to the courts of appeals signifies that nearly all cases decided by the major trial court may be appealed to, and must be heard by, the intermediate appellate court. An important exception is a criminal conviction carrying the death penalty. These are heard only by the state supreme court. With few other exceptions, the state supreme court has discretionary power to determine for itself which other cases it will decide. If it refuses to hear a case, the intermediate appellate court has the last word.

The Indiana court system, depicted in Figure 2, is much more complex. As in California, there is a single state supreme court and several divisions of the intermediate appellate court. However, the Indiana Supreme Court is required to hear many more cases than the California Supreme Court. In Indiana, there are two trial courts of general jurisdiction and six trial courts of limited jurisdiction. There are also special courts for particular counties as well as separate small-claims and probate courts, which deal exclusively with wills, trusts, estates, and various juvenile cases. However, a careful reading of the jurisdiction summarized in the boxes in the diagram reveals that the jurisdiction of the same type of court often varies around the state and the jurisdiction of one court often overlaps that of another court. In particular, the jurisdiction of the superior and city courts varies from place to place. Also, the powers of the superior court and the circuit court are very similar in civil cases, and the superior courts and county courts may hear some of the same types of cases. An Indiana lawyer familiar with the courts only in his home county would have to study the court system elsewhere in the state before he could comfortably take a case out of his usual territory.

The organization and jurisdiction of state courts is a major issue of judicial politics. Many legal reformers favor consolidating and streamlining state courts to obtain systems that are more like the California than the Indiana model. They believe that the presence of many different kinds of trial courts with overlapping jurisdiction is confusing and frustrating to lawyer and layman alike. It also leads, they believe, to inefficiency and disrespect for state courts. However, some lawyers and judges oppose change, because they are satisfied and familiar with the courts as they are and are reluctant to learn new law and procedures. Lawyers who specialize in trial work sometimes oppose change because their intimate knowledge of intricate local courts gives them an advantage over others in processing cases. Nevertheless, court consolidation is the current trend, and we can expect to find more consolidation in the future. About twenty states follow a system similar to California's including about a half dozen that have systems even simpler and easier to understand, and ten states have systems similar to Indiana's. The twenty remaining states have systems that lie between the two models; they usually have somewhat fewer trial courts of limited jurisdiction than Indiana but have systems that are more complex than California's.

Links Between State and Federal Courts

Although the federal courts frequently decide certain specialized kinds of cases that rarely come up in the state courts, there are several ways that state and federal courts are tied to each other. First, there are various types of cases that may be heard in either state or federal court. It is also possible for certain cases to move from the state courts into the federal courts. Various links between state and federal courts add to the complexity of the American legal system. For a complete picture, state and federal judicial policymaking have to be considered together and within the broader context of federal-state political relations.

There are several areas of law in which state and federal courts have concurrent jurisdiction. An important one is diversity cases. As explained earlier, these are cases in which opposing litigants live in different states and the amount of money in contention is $10,000 or more. Both federal and state courts may hear these kinds of cases. Another type of case that may be heard in either state or federal court is one that involves a substantial federal question. Federal questions concern federal statutes and/or the United States Constitution. There are many cases involving federal questions that are begun in the federal courts, although litigants may decide to start these cases in the state courts. A third area of overlap is in certain kinds of criminal cases. Certain criminal acts violate both state and federal laws, and a suspect could be prosecuted in either court. Examples of these kinds of laws are robbery and larceny, embezzlement, interstate auto theft, forgery, and narcotics violations. The odds are that federal officials will defer to local police and prosecutors if they begin prosecution for one of these crimes, but frequently, state and local officials are not as proficient in detecting and investigating certain crimes, such as organized drug trafficking, embezzlement, and interstate auto theft, so the Federal Bureau of Investigation (FBI) or other federal agency usually investigates and prosecutes these crimes in the federal courts.

Certain criminal acts violate both state and federal laws, and a suspect could be prosecuted in either court.

Aside from the possibility that certain kinds of cases may be initiated in either state or federal court, the courts are linked through the movement of state cases into the federal court system. A major way in which this occurs is through petitions by litigants from decisions of state supreme courts directly to the United States Supreme Court. State litigants who petition the United States Supreme Court for a hearing argue that certain of their rights guaranteed by the United States Constitution have been violated and that they have not received a remedy in the state courts. Frequently, these cases involve state and local officials, such as police or other government administrators who carry out state and local law. Issues in these cases often involve the rights of criminal defendants, students' rights concerning dress codes and free speech, apportionment of state legislatures, the right to an abortion, prayer and Bible reading in the public schools, and racial and sex discrimination.

The United States Supreme Court has declared about a thousand state and local laws unconstitutional since 1800 through cases that came to the Court from state supreme courts. About one-third of these declarations have occurred since 1960. Probably the greatest impact that the United States Supreme Court has had on promoting personal freedom has occurred through its review of state cases. State and local courts and other officials are expected to support these decisions and to implement them in their own areas of policymaking. This does not always occur, nor is it usually a smooth process, but there is little doubt that the United States Supreme Court has had a lasting effect in many areas of public policy by overturning state judicial policy and by implementing its own policies at state and local levels.

Another frequent link between state and federal courts occurs when convicted criminals held in state or local jails or prisons petition federal trial courts for a review of their conviction and imprisonment, arguing that state actions have violated their constitutional rights. Their cases are based on federal habeas corpus laws. *Habeas corpus* means "you have the body," and it requires state officials to show good reason for the imprisonment. The practical purpose of these cases is to find some way of getting out of jail or getting an order for a new trial. The number of these petitions has increased over the years from approximately fourteen thousand in 1975 to more than twenty-three thousand in 1981. However, less than 5 percent are successful. These cases are last-chance attempts to overturn state court decisions, and federal judges find very few reasons to overturn most state court convictions and sentences. Despite the important role of the United States Supreme Court in setting national judicial policy through several landmark cases, most decisions of the state courts continue to stand as the final word on judicial policy.

Effects of Structure and Jurisdiction

The existence of fifty separate state court systems, a separate federal court system, and strong traditions of localism and judicial independence have a number of important consequences for American justice. First, since state and federal courts may hear some of the same kinds of cases, there always is a strong possibility that state and federal judicial policy will differ on important and controversial issues. For example, for many years since the 1950s, the federal courts were substantially more liberal in supporting individual rights than most state courts. The United States Supreme Court in particular was severely criticized by many state and local government officials, including state judges, when it began to make controversial decisions granting greater constitutional rights to criminal defendants and requiring racial integration of public schools. Many state judges refused to apply these decisions to their own cases. However, judges in some states supported the Supreme Court and made similar liberal decisions. By 1986 some state supreme courts had become even more liberal than the Supreme Court.

Just as there are differences between state and federal judicial policy, so there are many differences between the decisions of the fifty state court systems as well as differences in judicial policy within each of the fifty states. The existence of many levels and types of courts distributed locally practically guarantees variations in judicial policy. For example, prison sentences for similar crimes often vary widely. It is common for trial judges in large cities, where crime is routine and thousands of similar cases flood the courts every year, to sentence defendants to relatively short prison terms. In contrast, in smaller towns and rural areas, where serious crime is more unusual and a more significant event, criminals are likely to face prison terms that are twice as long as those imposed in bigger cities or even longer. Variations like these can be found throughout the United States.

Appellate courts rarely control which cases are appealed, so there is generally no continuous or logical flow of cases that might stimulate appellate judges to create clear and well-developed judicial policies on many subjects. In states that have several divisions of intermediate appellate courts located in different geographic regions of the state, the chances of finding differences in judicial policy are even greater. Since these courts have taken on much of the work previously handled by state supreme courts, many cases brought to them go no further in the judicial system. The chances are good that they will develop different interpretations of law and settle similar kinds of cases in different ways. State supreme courts resolve some of these differences, but many conflicts on policy continue to exist.

Another effect of the overlap of courts is to provide litigants with certain alternatives in going to court. Decisions to use one set of courts or another usually hinge on cost and calculations about where the most favorable decisions can be found. Diversity cases give lawyers and litigants valuable options to choose the most favorable courts. The civil rights movement also discovered through using both state and federal courts over the years that federal judges generally were more supportive of civil rights. Consequently, the civil rights movement has concentrated its litigation efforts in the federal courts. If state courts had been more responsive, civil rights groups would have used them more. Overlapping jurisdiction within a state also provides litigants with some opportunities to shop for courts where judges have reputations for being more sympathetic to the legal claims brought by litigants. This sometimes occurs in large cities, where several criminal courts have citywide jurisdiction and prosecutors and defense lawyers jockey with each other to get their case decided by judges with harsh or lenient reputations.

The potential of courts to differ in judicial policy indicates that the actual operation of the legal system is closely tied to local social and political environments and is related to the characteristics of people who run the system. Courts are integral parts of the larger society in which they operate.

The Work of State Courts

Despite the greater visibility of state appellate courts, especially the supreme court, only a tiny fraction of all state cases get beyond the trial level. As indicated earlier, most appeals also stop with intermediate appellate courts. The flow of cases drops sharply at each higher level of court within the state court system. Therefore, even the trial courts of limited jurisdiction are important because they decide the most cases and hear the kinds of disputes and problems that are most likely to affect the most people.

A more precise picture of the work of state trial courts is presented in Table 2, which shows the number of cases filed in trial courts of limited and general jurisdiction in all fifty states and the special federal courts for the District of Columbia. The total number of cases contained in Table 2 for 1981–1982 is more than 82 million, and the trend is toward more cases. Filings in state courts have increased about 20 percent since 1977. However, not all cases decided in the state courts are included in Table 2, because some states do not keep accurate records of the cases decided by the trial courts of limited jurisdiction. There probably are several million more cases decided in the states, but no exact totals are available. Many of the cases handled by the state trial courts are for very minor offenses, particularly traffic cases. Traffic cases account for about two-thirds of the total number of cases in Table 2. Nevertheless, even with these cases removed from the total, the state courts decide more than 27 million other kinds of civil and criminal cases.

The importance of the state courts in dealing with most litigation in the United States becomes even clearer when we compare the work of the state courts with that of the federal courts. All of the federal courts, from the United States Supreme Court to the special federal trial courts of limited jurisdiction, decide fewer than 250,000 cases per year. Therefore, in terms of the probable direct impact on citizens, the state courts are much more significant than the federal courts.

There are important differences between the states in the number of cases decided and how types of cases are treated. The most heavily populated states have very large court systems and decide many more cases than the more rural, sparsely populated areas. For example, California courts hear more than 18 million cases per year, although 16 million of them are traffic cases. But even with the traffic cases removed, California courts decide more civil and criminal cases than any other state. New York has about the same number of civil and criminal cases as California, but many fewer traffic cases. Texas, which has a population roughly two-thirds that of California, has a very heavy case load, particularly in criminal cases. Texas also has one of the largest prison populations in the United States. In contrast to these larger states, small-population states such as Montana, North Dakota, and Wyoming have fewer cases and smaller judicial systems.

TABLE 2

FILINGS IN COURTS OF GENERAL AND LIMITED JURISDICTION, CY 1981 OR FY 1981/82

	Civil	Criminal	Juvenile	Total excluding traffic	Traffic	Total including traffic
Alabama*	216,408	140,170	46,866	403,444	227,722	631,166
Alaska	30,728	22,355	1,270	54,353	86,729	141,082
Arizona	138,621	148,395	1,076	288,092	1,153,217	1,441,309
Arkansas	99,452	147,428	13,907	260,787	479,106	739,893
California	1,639,518	923,834	102,333	2,665,685	15,599,845[a]	18,265,530[a]
Colorado*	202,775	59,578	26,153	288,506	181,873	470,379
Connecticut	212,240	109,539	14,255	336,034	303,281	639,315
Delaware	49,728	56,822	9,870	116,420	128,425	244,845
Dist. of Columbia	145,911	36,597	4,765	187,273	10,403	197,676
Florida	553,574	447,754	113,841	1,115,169	2,287,888	3,403,057
Georgia*	257,173	45,286	34,482	436,941	361,167	798,108
Hawaii	47,382	52,537	8,913	108,832	871,916[a]	980,748[a]
Idaho	52,347	32,632	7,661	92,640	209,904[a]	302,544[a]
Illinois	647,096	712,379	32,642	1,392,117	6,582,043[a]	7,974,160[a]
Indiana	388,301	144,960	26,315	559,576	354,232	913,808
Iowa	133,484	113,667	5,570	252,721	661,254	913,975
Kansas*	118,187	30,093	10,607	158,887	275,828[a]	434,715
Kentucky	187,210	217,193	36,445	440,848	274,788	715,636
Louisiana*	238,609	536,856	30,117	805,582	467,506	1,273,088
Maine*	57,938	96,449	13,404	167,791	88,372	256,163
Maryland*	590,887	171,781	29,750	792,418	646,313[a]	1,438,731[a]
Massachusetts*	465,987	657,551	118,876	1,242,414	3,243,585[a]	4,485,999[a]
Michigan*	263,863	538,014	22,131	824,008	1,313,532[a]	2,137,540[a]
Minnesota	251,062	114,986	44,672	410,720	1,448,626[a]	1,859,346[a]
Mississippi	NA	NA	NA	NA	NA	NA
Missouri	220,643	148,155	14,935	383,733	656,011	1,039,744
Montana*	6,533	1,340	576	8,449	NA	NA
Nebraska*	81,199	173,844	3,118	258,161	189,089	447,250
Nevada	81,874	52,822	2,777	137,473	225,953	363,426
New Hampshire	65,476	39,175	7,287	111,938	202,218	314,156
New Jersey*	573,166	31,719	109,881	714,766	NA	NA
New Mexico*	66,325	69,355	4,342	140,022	382,177[a]	522,199[a]
New York*	793,896	1,209,061	37,005	2,039,962	460,260	2,500,222
North Carolina	378,688	487,783	19,900	886,371	677,247	1,563,618
North Dakota	25,765	21,719	1,249	48,733	119,662[a]	168,395[a]
Ohio*	619,043	406,403	202,835	1,228,281	1,598,165[a]	2,826,446[a]
Oklahoma*[b]	208,088		8,063	NA		483,691
Oregon	155,362	149,695	NA	NA	671,893	NA
Pennsylvania	515,014	745,308	47,979	1,308,301	4,540,269[a]	5,848,570[a]
Rhode Island*	40,175	38,940	7,275	86,390	NA	NA
South Carolina	182,336	469,894	9,633	661,863	416,184	1,078,047
South Dakota	35,911	136,471	NA	NA	NA	NA
Tennessee*	94,631	37,213	NA	131,844	NA	NA
Texas	679,107	1,316,709	11,761	2,007,577	4,226,529	6,234,106
Utah*	92,894	37,366	34,848	165,108	444,421	609,529
Vermont	24,856	16,599	1,616	43,071	85,750	128,821
Virginia	770,693	399,209	133,471	1,303,373	1,014,304[a]	2,317,677[a]
Washington	218,446	170,557	24,424	413,427	1,650,194[a]	2,063,621[a]
West Virginia*	89,608	117,493	7,514	214,615	114,787[a]	329,402[a]
Wisconsin	326,920	161,645	28,336	516,901	230,680	747,581
Wyoming*	11,513	1,772	975	14,260	NA	NA

Source: United States Department of Justice. Bureau of Justice Statistics. *State Court Caseload Statistics* (1983).

* These figures represent virtually all cases filed in general-jurisdiction courts and between 70% and 80% of cases filed in limited-jurisdiction courts.

NA These data were not available and therefore are not included in the total filing figures.

[a] Parking tickets are included in the traffic case load reported for these states.

[b] Civil cases only.

Differences in the case loads of the state trial courts are not accounted for only by differences in population. Local traditions and values also probably play a part. For example, perhaps in California, where the population is very mobile and there is a constant stream of newcomers, there are more impersonal and transitory relationships. Perhaps conflicts lead to court cases rather than to informal negotiated settlements. Several states, such as Texas, have many more criminal cases, which may reflect a tougher law-and-order political environment.

Despite the greater visibility of state appellate courts, only a tiny fraction of all state cases get beyond the trial level.

The work of state appellate courts is described in Table 3. The total number of cases filed for hearings in all of the state appellate courts is about 160,000 per year. About three-quarters of them are heard by intermediate appellate courts. These figures underscore the importance of intermediate appellate courts as the final appellate courts for most state cases. The overall totals in Table 3 also reinforce the point that few cases get beyond the trial-court stage. Table 3 also reveals that there are differences between the appellate courts similar to the differences between the state trial courts. California courts hear more appeals than courts in any other state, and New York and Texas also score high on the number of appeals channeled through the judicial system. The smaller, rural states have fewer appeals, and many of the small states have no intermediate appellate courts. All of the appeals heard in these states go directly to state supreme courts.

It is clear that state courts deal with most of the litigation in the United States. They also decide the cases that are most likely to involve the most citizens. This is demonstrated by the figures in Table 4, which presents a description and an approximate distribution of the kinds of civil and criminal cases that appear in most state courts. In most types of cases, there is a wide range of percentages because there are no national or even statewide totals for the types and number of issues brought to the courts.

The figures show that among the civil cases, with the exception of divorce cases, which are plentiful in some courts, those with which state trial courts deal most involve financial and commercial issues. State supreme courts also hear a significant number of cases involving the regulation of business, although a majority of state supreme court cases involve appeals concerning private economic disputes. The trial courts of limited jurisdiction (small-claims courts) also deal with a variety of commercial litigation. These courts were created to provide low cost and simplified procedures so that average citizens could go to court to recover relatively small amounts of money from other individuals or small businesses. Small-claims cases involve appliance and auto repairs, landlord-tenant disputes, and similar types of issues. While the courts do hear cases involving these issues, they are used most heavily and repeatedly by large businesses, such as banks, hospitals, and building contractors, to collect small loans and debts for goods and services. These kinds of cases range from 15 percent to 90 percent of the total case load, but in most small-claims courts in the United States the percentage of debt-collection cases probably is closer to 70 percent.

Table 4 shows that in the criminal case category the trial courts of limited jurisdiction hear relatively minor criminal cases, mostly traffic violations. Traffic cases constitute from 30 percent to 85 percent of the total case load in these courts, with the national average at about 67 percent. Precise figures are not available for other kinds of minor criminal cases. Estimates from various sources indicate that cases involving drunkenness and other liquor violations, such as possession of alcohol by minors, and disorderly conduct, which usually means rowdiness and fighting, are at the top of the list. Cases involving prostitution are common in some cities, but not in others. The percentages for drunkenness also vary from zero to 25 percent of the total, since some cities have decriminalized drunkenness, so that arrests no longer result in court cases. Instead, people intoxicated from alcohol or drugs are referred to detoxification facilities.

The state trial courts of general jurisdiction deal with most types of more serious crime. More research has been done on these courts than on others, and so we have more reliable figures for these kinds of cases. The percentages are estimates based on various sources, but they provide a reasonably accurate overview of the work of the major trial courts. Property crimes are highest on the list, and burglary, theft, and armed and unarmed robbery are common in nearly all courts. Cases involving the sale of narcotics vary widely, depending upon the size of the drug problem and upon local law enforcement capabilities and priorities. Crimes against persons, including assault, murder, and rape, are not as plentiful as the other types. Even though these kinds of cases make the headlines most often because they are so serious and are directed against individuals, they constitute a relatively small percentage of the work of the state trial courts.

TABLE 3

APPELLATE COURT FILINGS, CY 1981 OF FY 1981–1982

	Courts of last resort	Intermediate appellate courts	All appellate courts
Alabama[a]	1,018	496[a]	
Alaska	417	463	880
Arizona	1,143	2,436	3,579
Arkansas	446	1,194	1,640
California	4,325	14,933	19,258
Colorado	1,052	1,512	2,564
Connecticut	595	191	786
Delaware	337	—	337
Dist. of Columbia	1,663	—	1,663
Florida	1,456	13,795	15,251
Georgia	1,617	2,152	3,769
Hawaii	387	127	514
Idaho	455	—	455
Illinois	1,803	6,516	8,319
Indiana	409	1,095	1,504
Iowa	1,733[b]	(b)	1,733
Kansas	188	1,060	1,248
Kentucky	1,150	2,689	3,839
Louisiana	3,337	2,878	6,215
Maine	571	—	571
Maryland	867	1,983	2,850
Massachusetts	773		
Michigan	1,949	6,318	8,267
Minnesota	1,609	—	1,609
Mississippi		—	
Missouri	1,059	2,964	4,023
Montana	574	—	574
Nebraska	956	—	956
Nevada	732	—	732
New Hampshire	558	—	558
New Jersey	289	5,993	6,282
New Mexico	610	505	1,115
New York	708	11,638	12,346
North Carolina	989	1,994	2,983
North Dakota	309	—	309
Ohio	2,134	8,915	11,049
Oklahoma[c]	2,543	1,080[b]	2,543[b]
Oregon	812	3,403	4,215
Pennsylvania	2,254	12,830	15,084
Rhode Island	592	—	592
South Carolina	1,173	—	1,173
South Dakota	363	—	363
Tennessee	885	1,723	2,608
Texas[c]	3,395	6,151	9,546
Utah	700	—	700
Vermont	601	—	601
Virginia	2,257	—	2,257
Washington	863	2,799	3,662
West Virginia	1,549	—	1,549
Wisconsin	737	2,479	3,216
Wyoming	198	—	198

Source: United States Department of Justice, Bureau of Justice Statistics, *State Court Caseload Statistics* (1983).
Note: All available data are included in the table. Blank spaces indicate that the data were not available.
— These states did not have intermediate appellate courts in 1981.
[a] Data are incomplete: Alabama has two intermediate appellate courts, but only one, the Court of Civil Appeals, reported data in 1981.
[b] All appellate cases in Iowa and Oklahoma are filed in the courts of last resort. A portion of this case load is transferred to the intermediate appellate court for disposition.
[c] Both Oklahoma and Texas have two courts of last resort.

TABLE 4

TYPES OF CASES DECIDED IN SELECTED STATE COURTS

Trial courts of limited jurisdiction[a,d]	Trial courts of general jurisdiction[b]	Supreme courts[c]
Civil Cases		
Payments for goods and services (15%–90%)	Divorce and family (10%–60%)	Government regulation of business (4%–64%; average = 23%)
Unsatisfactory goods and services (25%)	Debts and loans (10%–25%)	Private economic disputes (wills, estates, real estate) (6%–77%; average = 46%)
Landlord-tenant (20%–30%)	Contracts (10%–20%)	Personal injury and other liability (2%–50%; average = 14%)
Property damage-auto (15%–30%)	Liens (15%)	Other (average = 18%)
Other property damage (3%–15%)	Personal injury and property damage (10%–25%)	
Debts, loans (10%)	Property foreclosures (2%–5%)	
Wages (3%–5%)	Evictions (3%)	
Other (10%)	Government regulation (1%–3%)	
	Other (1%–3%)	
Criminal Cases		
Traffic (30%–85%; average = 67%)	Burglary (15%)	Trial court error in a variety of felony cases (5%–70%; average = 31%)
Drunkenness (0%–25%)	Theft (15%)	Constitutional claims (0%–5%; average = 1.7%)
Other liquor laws (5%)	Armed Robbery (10%–15%)	
Disorderly conduct (5%–10%)	Robbery (3%–10%)	
Prostitution (1%–6%)	Assault (5%–7%)	
Other (25%)	Sale of narcotics (1%–20%)	
	Use of narcotics (2%–8%)	
	Weapons possession (4%–15%)	
	Murder (2%–4%)	
	Rape (1%–5%)	
	Gambling (1%–5%)	
	Other (7%–15%)	

[a] Adapted from Austin Sarat, "Alternatives in Dispute Processing: Litigation in a Small Claims Court," in *Law and Society Review* (Spring, 1976); John C. Ruhnka and Steven Weller, *Small Claims Courts* (1978); Robert J. Hollingsworth et al., "The Ohio Small Claims Court: An Empirical Study," in *Cincinnati Law Review,* 42 (1973); Herbert Jacob, *The Frustration of Policy* (1984); *Statistical Abstract of the United States, 1982–1983.*

[b] Adapted from Craig Wanner, "The Public Ordering of Private Relations," in *Law and Society Review* (Spring, 1974); Lawrence M. Friedman and Robert V. Percival, "A Tale of Two Courts: Litigation in Alameda and San Benito Counties," in *Law and Society Review* (Winter, 1976); *Felony Arrests,* rev. ed. (1981); James Eisenstein and Herbert Jacob, *Felony Justice* (1977).

[c] Adapted from Burton Atkins and Henry R. Glick, "Environmental and Structural Variables as Determinants of Issues in States Courts of Last Resort," in *American Journal of Political Science,* 20 (1976).

[d] The trial court of limited jurisdiction in the civil case category is the small-claims court.

State supreme courts hear appeals from a variety of criminal cases. The range in the percentage of criminal appeals is from 5 percent to 70 percent, with a national average of about 30 percent. These cases involve a variety of issues raised during the trial or as the case was processed by police and prosecutors. However, criminal defendants do not assert many constitutional claims in their appeals, as is common in the federal courts. Most criminal appeals are based on state sentencing laws and other court procedures. They do not involve major constitutional issues. The crimes involved in cases that reach state supreme courts vary widely, according to the social characteristics of the states, the presence or absence of an intermediate appellate court below the supreme court, and the jurisdiction of the state supreme court. Generally, serious felonies involving heavy sentences are appealed most often.

Policymaking in State Courts

A major function of courts is to impose legal settlements in various individual disputes and cases of crime. However, both appellate and trial courts also make policies through court decisions that have broader significance and consequences for society. "Policymaking" is governmental action designed to solve or cope with various social, economic, or political problems. Therefore, "judicial policymaking" comprises those decisions that have greater social significance than the settlement of individual cases.

Courts generally make policy in two ways. The first involves single court cases that present new, unusual, and often controversial issues. Court decisions in these cases attract news attention and reactions from other public officials and interested groups of citizens. This kind of policymaking occurs most often in appellate courts for several reasons. One important reason is that appellate courts, especially state supreme courts, have the final authority to interpret state law and constitutions and to correct errors made by state trial courts. Therefore, their decisions directly affect the policymaking of other state officials and serve as guidance for trial courts when they decide similar cases in the future. Furthermore, decisions of appellate courts are often explained in written legal opinions, so that the reasons behind the decision are set out. Written opinions also state what other officials and judges are supposed to do in current and future similar cases. Examples of these kinds of cases are state supreme court decisions that have required state governments to revise state tax laws and financing of public schools to assure greater equality among school districts, decisions on whether proposed constitutional amendments that are scheduled for a public vote meet state constitutional requirements, decisions affecting the way that police and prosecutors treat defendants in criminal cases, and rules concerning when hospitals may disconnect life-support systems to terminally ill patients. All of these individual case decisions are controversial and have major effects on society.

Courts also make policies in more subtle ways that rarely capture as much public attention or create much controversy. But the decisions still reveal how the judiciary copes with social and economic problems. This is called cumulative policymaking. It occurs when courts repeatedly make similar decisions in a long series of similar cases. Courts often develop consistent patterns of decision-making that accumulate over time and reveal court policy toward problems that repeatedly come to court. Examples of this kind of policymaking are the sentencing decisions of trial courts. Many judges in the same city tend to sentence defendants convicted of similar crimes to roughly similar jail terms, while judges in other cities often produce sentences more lenient or more harsh. Sentencing decisions reflect the policies of the courts because they demonstrate how judges have decided to cope with the crime problem. Another example concerns awarding and collecting child support in divorce cases. Some judges have recently changed from showing leniency toward fathers who have not paid court-ordered child support to imposing jail terms until fathers obtain the money needed to pay off all of their unpaid support. Both the early patterns of leniency and the change to stringent enforcement of divorce agreements are examples of court policy toward child support.

CIVIL RIGHTS AND LIBERTIES. A major concern in judicial policymaking concerns civil rights and liberties. These refer to a number of constitutional rights that guarantee individual freedom and equality in the United States. Two of the most controversial policy areas in civil liberties are racial discrimination and the rights of criminal defendants and convicted criminals. However, other civil liberties involve the freedoms of speech, press, and religion; age and sex discrimination; and rights to privacy. Civil rights and liberties have become major controversial issues in the United States and in the courts in particular because of liberal interpretations of the Constitution by the United States Supreme Court beginning in the 1950s.

Criminal defendants do not assert many constitutional claims in their appeals, as is common in the federal courts.

Civil rights and liberties are important in the state courts for two major reasons. The first is that the state courts are directly affected by decisions of the United States Supreme Court because many of its liberal policies were created by overruling conservative decisions of various state supreme courts. As part of the hierarchy of courts and law in the United States, the state courts are obligated to change their own policies to conform to the policy of the Supreme Court. Second, the state courts have opportunities to interpret provisions of state constitutions that affect individual rights. Provisions of state constitutions often are identical or similar to those of the national constitution. In recent years, a few state supreme courts have created liberal interpretations of constitutional liberties that go beyond United States Supreme Court policy. However, the large majority of the state courts have resisted past liberal Supreme Court interpretations of the Constitution, have welcomed recent conservative policies of the Supreme Court, and have interpreted their own state constitutions in ways that do not broaden interpretations of civil rights and liberties in the states.

A prominent example of the way that state courts deal with these issues involves the rights of criminal defendants. Prior to the 1960s, nearly all state supreme courts interpreted the rights of criminal defendants very narrowly. For instance, confessions and evidence seized as a result of police searches were admitted as evidence in criminal cases without much concern for how they had been obtained. Defendants had no right to attorney, and the states provided few protections against police pressure in interrogations. This began to change in 1964 when the United States Supreme Court, under the leadership of Chief Justice Earl Warren, decided *Escobedo* v. *Illinois.* This decision required that when suspects become the focus of a police investigation they must be allowed to consult with an attorney. But the decision did not specifically require police, prosecutors, or trial judges to inform defendants of this new right. State judges not sympathetic to the plight of criminal defendants refused to expand the decision to help defendants obtain lawyers. Consequently, in practice, many poor, uneducated, and uninformed defendants had no access to lawyers, despite this new ruling.

Torts concern rules for recovering financial awards in court for civil wrongs committed by one person or organization against another.

In 1966 the Supreme Court required that police explicitly inform defendants of their right to an attorney, their right to remain silent during police questioning, and their right to a court-appointed attorney if they were too poor to hire one *(Miranda* v. *Arizona).* This decision was much clearer and more specific than *Escobedo* and gave state courts and police much less opportunity to ignore the rights of criminal defendants than the earlier decision. Most state supreme courts have followed the requirements of the Supreme Court in *Miranda.* However, even this decision did not cover all situations that arise after a suspect has been arrested and is on the way to the police station. For example, the Court's opinion did not state exactly when the police had to inform a suspect of his rights, which might give ample time for a defendant to incriminate himself through voluntary statements made upon his arrest. The decision did not automatically apply to defendants already convicted and serving jail time or to retrials of those already convicted. Generally, the large majority of the state courts did not expand the *Miranda* ruling beyond the Supreme Court's specific policy. If anything, they interpreted it narrowly so that few defendants could make full use of the Supreme Court decision. For example, in order to obtain a reversal of a conviction before a state supreme court, a defendant had to have objected to a violation of his rights during his original trial. If he had not done so, it was assumed that he had waived his rights.

In recent years, as conservative Republican justices have replaced many of the Warren Court liberals, the United States Supreme Court has become more conservative as regards the rights of criminal defendants. Like the conservative state judges, the newer justices on the Supreme Court have narrowed the interpretation of past Court decisions concerning the admissibility of evidence at a trial. Much incriminating evidence now can be admitted into court with fewer limitations on how the police obtained it. Most of the state courts have welcomed these new conservative decisions and embrace the new leadership of the Supreme Court because the decisions generally go in the direction that most state judges always have favored.

There are a few exceptions to these generally conservative state court policies. Some supreme courts in states with heterogeneous and heavily urban populations have produced liberal policies concerning the rights of criminal defendants and other personal liberties. They frequently rely on earlier, liberal Supreme Court rulings and a legal doctrine called independent state grounds, which provides a way for state rather than federal court interpretations of the Constitution to become the basis for civil liberties decisions.

State court treatment of civil liberties policy is a good illustration of the powers of all courts to make important policy and the likelihood that judicial policy will differ throughout the United States. In most areas of law, including civil rights and liberties, there are large numbers of state and federal court cases that can serve as precedent or guidance to the state courts. There are the liberal decisions of the Warren Court era and the conservative decisions of the Burger Supreme Court. Both national and state constitutions contain general provisions concerning individual rights that can be interpreted differently by judges throughout the country. There also are various general legal doctrines or principles that judges may select as the legal basis for their decisions. Doctrine supporting the supremacy of federal law clearly provides a way for national Supreme Court policy to stand in place of state law and state court decisions. But other legal doctrines, particularly independent state grounds, provide opportunities for state law to become the basis of judicial decisions. Options in legal doctrine enhance the power and significance of the separate state court systems.

OTHER STATE POLICIES. Although civil liberties cases attract most news media and public attention, the state courts make policy in many other areas of law that affect more people more of the time than civil liberties policies. As indicated earlier, state courts make millions of decisions involving traffic accidents and other criminal cases, as well as a wide variety of personal disputes involving financial transactions. Few of these are affected by federal law or federal courts.

A major policymaking area in which the state courts have had a major impact on social and economic life is

This court house, built in 1767, is the oldest court house in North Carolina that has been in continuous use. (Raymond Gehman/Corbis)

tort law. Torts concern rules for recovering financial awards in court for a variety of civil wrongs committed by one person or organization against another. Examples of torts involve personal injuries resulting from badly manufactured products, injuries suffered by workers on the job, and injuries sustained by patients in hospitals or by passengers in cars or on public transportation. There are about as many examples of torts as there are possibilities for injuries in a modern technological society.

Two important and similar issues in tort law concern sovereign immunity and charitable immunity. Until the 1960s, sovereign immunity prevented citizens in most states from suing a state or local government for injuries caused by negligent public employees or while using public facilities. Individuals could not sue for injuries suffered while a patient was in a public hospital or as a result of badly maintained streets and sidewalks, public utilities, or other public services. Charitable immunity prevented citizens from suing nonprofit organizations that operate schools or hospitals, such as religious organizations. By the end of the 1970s, more than three-quarters of the states had abandoned the doctrine of sovereign and charitable immunity, so that people can now recover damages for injuries. Many of these changes occurred through state supreme court decisions. Sometimes, however, the state legislatures imposed maximum dollar limits that an individual can recover from a state or local government, and some states still impose serious restrictions on suing the state government.

Another judicial policy in tort law concerns products liability. Until the 1950s, state court decisions generally prevented successful suits for injuries caused by badly manufactured products unless an individual could clearly show negligence by the manufacturer. Even then, liability was limited to the business that sold the product to the consumer. Therefore, manufacturers were successfully insulated against claims, since most products are sold through retailers. The major change in this policy occurred in 1960 when the New Jersey Supreme Court created a new policy that held manufacturers liable and made it unnecessary for consumers to prove negligence. Incurring an injury from normal use of a product was sufficient grounds for a lawsuit. Later court decisions established a policy stating that manufacturers created implied warranties in their products that guaranteed them as safe to consumers. Consequently, manufacturers became directly and strictly liable for injuries. Similar changes have occurred in suits concerning defects in construction. Before the 1950s, building contractors were held blameless for any injuries caused by faulty construction after a new owner paid his final bill and accepted the property. More recent policies permit owners to sue later if injuries caused by defects in construction are not uncovered immediately.

A third area of change in the law of torts concerns the ability of members of the same family to sue each other for injuries. This policy began to change from a complete prohibition on intrafamily suits to allowance for them in the early 1900s. But it did not become a common policy in the states until after World War II. This area of policy is important because in the past it was difficult for a member of a family to recover financial losses from an insurance company when the injury occurred in an automobile accident in which a spouse or parent was at fault.

There are many other areas of state judicial policymaking in which courts can have a significant impact on society. State constitutions are very long and complex. Therefore, state supreme courts frequently receive cases in which individuals or groups challenge the constitutionality of state laws. In most cases, supreme courts approve of legislative and other governmental action, but some laws are overturned or require legislative rewriting before they become valid. Controversial cases coming to state supreme courts include no-fault insurance plans, medical malpractice laws, the legality of special local tax districts, approval of local taxes and special fees on the sale of utilities, government licensing of professions, and government regulation of business. No exact figures on the important policymaking decisions of state supreme courts exist, but there probably are a dozen or more such decisions in most of the states every year.

LOCAL JUDICIAL POLICIES. Since nearly all cases originate in trial courts, local judicial policy sometimes involves issues similar to those found in state supreme courts. Local trial courts hear cases involving zoning regulations; the conduct of elections; school board policy concerning budgets, public hearings, teacher demands, and the like; local tax laws and procedures; and other issues involving local government and politically active local interest groups. Like state appellate courts, trial courts generally approve the decisions of other local government authorities. The process of going to court and obtaining a judicial hearing frequently delays the implementation of a local government policy, but trial courts rarely stand in the way of other government action.

Although trial courts sometimes make policy in single controversial cases, they have more opportunities to affect social and economic conditions through cumulative policies. The most common types of cases involve crime, divorce, alimony and child support, creditor-debtor cases, and real estate and other financial transactions. As indicated earlier, the pattern of decisions in these cases defines the policy of local courts. Several examples will illustrate local judicial policymaking.

Local criminal justice policy is usually very different from appellate policy because relatively few defendants claim violations of their constitutional rights. It is common nearly everywhere for defendants to be protected to the extent that they are assured of having lawyers to aid in their defense and police advise them of their rights. The presence of lawyers and other constitutional safeguards, however, does not alter the fact that most defendants seem obviously guilty of having committed a crime and are willing to plead guilty in exchange for a promise of leniency in sentencing. Consequently, local criminal justice almost always results in convictions. Furthermore, the odds are high nearly everywhere in the United States that most criminal defendants are poor, disproportionately nonwhite, and accused of assault, robbery, or other theft. Relatively few white-collar crimes are detected or prosecuted.

The lengths of prison terms in some cities are twice as long as those imposed by courts in other cities.

The key differences in local criminal justice policy concern the sentences imposed by the courts. State criminal law is determined by state legislatures, which frequently allow judges broad discretion in choosing the appropriate penalty for a large variety of crimes. Therefore, it is possible for judges to impose suspended sentences, probation, or long prison terms for the same crime. State law invites and practically guarantees variation in local sentencing policy. Research on cities of similar size and with similar types of crime, often within the same state, reveals that there is enormous variation in the type and length of sentences. Judges in some cities sentence defendants in similar criminal cases to prison terms twice as often as judges in other cities. The length of prison terms in some cities also are twice as long as, or longer than, those imposed by courts in other cities.

Appellate courts sometimes develop sentencing guidelines for trial judges in their state so that sentencing policies will become more uniform, but local trial judges, jealously guarding their traditional independence and power to determine appropriate sentences, often resist efforts to standardize sentencing. Compromise guidelines frequently contain vague or general language that permits local judges to continue to do as they see fit.

Local judicial policies in economic disputes also develop predictable patterns. Generally, most economic cases are brought by individuals or businesses to collect loans and to enforce contracts and rental agreements that have been duly signed by businesses and their clients and customers. Businesses are repeat players in the judicial process. They go to court frequently in the same kinds of disputes, they seek the same kind of results, and they are experienced and able to hire legal talent to press their many routine, repetitive claims. Defendants in these cases usually are individuals who have not been to court before, are unsophisticated about the legal process, and may not have the ability or finances to hire capable lawyers to defend them. Often in these cases, they have no good defense because they signed legal agreements and have become unable, or are unwilling, to pay. Judges are normally concerned only with proof of their indebtedness, and the businesses who are repeat players normally win their cases. Local courts rarely examine the background of legal contracts to determine whether they were arrived at fairly or whether the business could have predicted that a customer would not be able to meet his or her financial obligations. If a person has entered into an agreement, the courts normally enforce collections.

Judicial policy in family law varies and is undergoing a great deal of change. Traditionally, divorces have not been very easy to obtain. It was necessary for the husband or wife seeking the divorce to prove in court that the other party had been at fault in some major way, such as committing adultery, before a court could grant a divorce. Once granted, judges would require the major wage earner, usually the husband, to pay support to his wife (alimony) and child support for his dependent children. Children typically lived with their mothers, and fathers had visitation rights. Since the 1970s, divorce has been much easier to obtain. No-fault divorce laws in many states permit divorce if the judge determines that a marriage is irretrievably broken. This very vague rule provides almost automatic grounds for granting divorces to either party seeking a divorce. Payment for alimony and child support is still common, but since larger numbers of women are in the work force, alimony is more doubtful, and levels of child support and which parent should pay is less certain.

State laws are very vague concerning alimony, child support, and child custody and visitation. Laws typically permit judges to make their own best guess about what are appropriate or fair arrangements and what is in the best interest of the children. Consequently, decisions in these cases vary enormously depending upon the values and beliefs of individual judges and informal local policies that judges may develop together concerning proper family arrangements. In most cases, mothers continue to obtain custody of their children when both parents agree, but some fathers have successfully claimed that they are the better parent. Joint custody, in which mothers and fathers share care and visitation with their children, is becoming a new judicial policy in many states.

Conclusion

This discussion of state court systems has described the structure and roles of state courts in the American judicial process. The structure and jurisdiction of state courts and the links between the state and federal court systems demonstrate the importance of state courts in handling most judicial business in the United States. Most crime and most interpersonal disputes that affect most people are dealt with by the state courts. State supreme courts are most visible in state judicial policymaking, and they have made important changes over the years in several major areas of law. However, state trial courts also are extremely important because they control many cumulative policies that affect most people and most aspects of life. The general independence of state court systems from each other and from the federal system also indicate that state courts have many important opportunities to make policy that affects the decisions of the other branches of government and the lives of most Americans.

[See also (III) Federal Court System, Sentencing Alternatives.]

CASES

Escobedo v. Illinois, 378 U.S. 478 (1964)
Miranda v. Arizona, 384 U.S. 436 (1966)

BIBLIOGRAPHY

Larry C. Berkson and Susan B. Carbon, *Court Unification: History, Politics and Implementation* (1978), describes the history and implementation of major changes in state court systems and includes illustrations of individual state experiences. Malcolm M. Feeley, *Court Reform on Trial* (1983), a survey of the adoption and effects of trial-court reform, including bail reform, pretrial diversion, sentencing reform, and speedy-trial rules, concludes that most reforms fail to affect how courts process cases and defendants. Henry R. Glick, *Courts, Politics and Justice* (1983), a current and comprehensive social science text on the American judicial process that includes discussion of all levels and types of courts and judicial processes in the United States; and *Supreme Courts in State Politics* (1971), examines judicial roles in four state supreme courts, using research based on interviews with supreme court judges and examining how they view their positions and functions. Henry R. Glick and Kenneth N. Vines, *State Court Systems* (1972), is an early description of the structure and behavior of state court systems.

Herbert Jacob, *Justice in America,* 4th ed. (1984), is a short but valuable summary of major judicial institutions and processes in the United States. Fannie J. Klein, *Federal and State Court Systems: A Guide* (1977), is an overview of American judicial systems. Richard Neely, *Why Courts Don't Work* (1983), an appraisal and criticism of the performance of state trial courts, although written by a state supreme court judge, is nonlegalistic and directed to nonlawyers. Mary Cornelia Porter and G. Alan Tarr, *State Supreme Courts: Policymakers in the Federal System* (1982), includes eight essays on the importance of state supreme courts as state policymaking institutions, with much useful discussion of innovations in state judicial policymaking. G. Alan Tarr, *Judicial Impact and State Supreme Courts* (1977), discusses the responses of state supreme courts to decisions of the United States Supreme Court and how Supreme Court decisions are implemented in the states.

– HENRY R. GLICK

SUPREME COURT AT WORK

In its first decade, the Supreme Court had little business, frequent turnover in personnel, no chambers or staff, no fixed customs, and no institutional identity. When the Court initially convened on February 1,

1790, only Chief Justice John Jay and two other Justices arrived at the Exchange Building in New York City. They adjourned until the next day, when Justice John Blair arrived. With little to do other than admit attorneys to practice before its bar, the Court concluded its first sessions in less than two weeks. When the capital moved from New York City to Philadelphia in the winter of 1790, the Court met in Independence Hall and in the Old City Hall for ten years, until the capital again moved to Washington, D.C. Most of the first Justices' time, however, was spent riding circuit. Under the Judiciary Act of 1789, they were required twice a year to hold circuit court, in the company of district judges, to try some types of cases and to hear appeals from the federal district courts. Hence, the Justices resided primarily in their circuits rather than in Washington and often felt a greater allegiance to their circuits than to the Supreme Court.

The Supreme Court is a human institution that has adapted to changing conditions. The Justices no longer ride circuit and the caseload now keeps them in Washington most of the year. As the caseload increased, sessions became longer, and an annual term was established. Throughout the nineteenth century, Congress moved the beginning of each term back in stages to the present opening day on the first Monday in October; the term now runs through to the following June or July. These and other changes in the Court's conduct of its business have been shaped by American society and politics. The Justices' chambers have come to resemble "nine little law firms," and the Court has become a more bureaucratic institution.

When the capital moved to Washington, D.C., in 1800, no courtroom was provided. Between 1801 and 1809, the Justices convened in various rooms in the basement of the Capitol. In 1810, they shared a room

The African-American lawyer pictured here became the first African-American to be admitted before the Supreme Court, in 1880. (Library of Congress/Corbis)

in the Capitol with the Orphans' Court of the District of Columbia. This room was destroyed when the British burned the Capitol on August 24, 1814, and for two years, the Court met in the Bell Tavern. In 1817, the Court moved back into the Capitol, holding sessions in a small dungeon-like room for two years. In 1819, it returned to its restored courtroom, where it met for almost half a century.

For most of the nineteenth century, the Justices resided in their circuits and stayed in boardinghouses during the Court's terms. Chief Justice Roger Brooke Taney (1836–1864) was the first to reside in the Federal City, and as late as the 1880s most Justices did not maintain homes there. Lacking offices and sharing the law library of Congress, the Justices relied on a single clerk to answer correspondence, collect fees, and to locate boardinghouse rooms for them.

Coincident with the 1801 move into the Capitol, John Marshall assumed the Chief Justiceship. During his thirty-four years on the Court, Marshall established regularized procedures and a tradition of collegiality. He saw to it that the Justices roomed in the same boardinghouse and, thereby, turned the disadvantage of transiency into strategic opportunity for achieving unanimity in decision making. After a day of hearing oral arguments, the Justices would dine together, and around 7:00 PM they would discuss cases.

After 1860, the Court met upstairs in the old Senate Chamber, between the new chambers of the Senate and those of the House of Representatives. The Justices still had no offices or staff of their own. After the Civil War, however, the caseload steadily grew, the Court's terms lengthened, and the Justices deserted boardinghouses for fashionable hotels along Pennsylvania Avenue. Instead of dining together and discussing cases after dinner, they held conferences on Saturdays and announced decisions on Monday.

By the turn of the century, the Justices resided in the capitol and for the most part worked at home, where each had a library and employed a messenger and a secretary. The Court's collegial procedures had evolved into institutional norms based on majority rule. The Chief Justice assumed a special role in scheduling and presiding over conferences and oral arguments. But the Court's deliberative process was firmly rooted in the Justices' interaction as equals. Each Justice was considered a sovereign in his or her own right, even though the Justices decided cases together and strove for institutional opinions.

After becoming Chief Justice in 1921, William Howard Taft persuaded four Justices to support his lobbying Congress for the construction of a building for the Court. Taft envisioned a marble temple symbolizing the modern Court's prestige and independence. Yet, when the building that houses the Court was completed in 1935, none of the sitting Justices moved in, although sessions and conferences were held there in the later years of the Hughes Court (1930–1941). Upon his appointment in 1937, Hugo L. Black was the first to move in, leading the way for President Franklin D. Roosevelt's other appointees. Even when Harlan Fiske Stone was elevated from Associate to Chief Justice, he still worked at home. The Vinson Court (1946–1953) was the first to see all nine Justices regularly working in the Supreme Court building.

The marble temple stands for more than a symbol of the modern Court. Once again, the institutional life of the Court changed. As Taft hoped, the building buttressed the Court's prestige and reinforced the basic norms of secrecy, tradition, and collegiality that condition the Court's work. The Justices continued to function independently, but the work of the Court grew more bureaucratic. Along with the rising caseload in the decades following World War II, the number of law clerks more than tripled and the number of other employees dramatically increased as well. The Justices in turn delegated more and incorporated modern office technology and managerial practices into their work. The Warren Court (1953–1969) started delivering opinions on any day of open session, and the Burger Court (1969–1986) moved conferences back to Fridays.

When Potter Stewart joined the Court in 1958, he expected to find "one law firm with nine partners, if you will, the law clerks being the associates." But Justice John Marshall Harlan told him, "No, you will find here it is like nine firms, sometimes practicing law against one another." Even today, each Justice and his or her staff works in rather secluded chambers with little of the direct daily interaction that occurs in some appellate courts. Nor do recent Justices follow Felix Frankfurter's practice of sending clerks ("Felix's happy hotdogs") scurrying around the building to lobby other clerks and Justices.

A number of factors isolate the Justices, but most important is the caseload. The Justices, in Justice Byron R. White's view, "stay at arm's length" and rely on formal printed communications because the workload discourages them "from going from chamber to chamber to work things out." Each chamber averages about seven: the Justice, three to four law clerks, two secretaries, and a messenger. As managing chambers and supervising paperwork consumes more time, the Justices talk less to each other and read and write more memoranda and opinions. Each chamber now has a photocopying machine and four to five terminals for word processing and legal research.

Law clerks became central to the work of the Court. In 1882, Justice Horace Gray initiated the practice of hiring a "secretary" or law clerk. When Oliver Wendell Holmes, Jr. succeeded Gray, he continued the practice, and other Justices gradually followed. By Chief Justice Stone's time it was well established for each Justice to have one clerk. During the chief justiceships of Fred M. Vinson and Earl Warren, the number increased to two. In the 1970s, the number grew to three and to four. The number of secretaries likewise increased—initially, in place of adding clerks and, later, to assist the growing number of clerks. A legal office, staffed by two attorneys, was created in 1975 to assist with cases in the Court's original jurisdiction and with expedited appeals.

Although the duties and functions of clerks vary with each chamber, all share certain commonly assigned responsibilities. Most notably, Justices have delegated to them the task of initially screening all filings for writs of certiorari. This practice originated with the handling of indigents' petitions by Chief Justice Charles Evans Hughes and his clerks. Unlike the "paid" petitions that are filed in multiple copies, an indigent's petition is typically a handwritten statement. Except when an unpaid petition raised important legal issues or involved a capital case, Hughes neither circulated the petitions to the other Justices nor discussed them at conference. Stone, Vinson, and Warren, however, circulated to the chambers their clerks' memoranda, which summarized the facts and questions presented, and recommended whether the case should be denied, dismissed, or granted a review. But Chief Justice Warren E. Burger refused to have his clerks shoulder the entire burden of screening these petitions. And in 1972, a majority of the Justices began to pool their clerks, dividing up all paid and unpaid filings and having a single clerk's certiorari memo circulate to those Justices participating in what is called "the cert. pool." With more than a hundred filings each week, even those Justices who objected to the "cert. pool" have found it necessary to give their clerks considerable responsibility for screening petitions. Justice John Paul Stevens describes his practice: "[The clerks] examine them all and select a small minority that they believe I should read myself. As a result, I do not even look at the papers in over 80 percent of the cases that are filed."

Law clerks have also assumed responsibility for the preliminary drafting of the Justices' opinions. Chief Justice William H. Rehnquist's practice, for instance, is to have one of his clerks do a first draft, without bothering about style, in about ten days. Before beginning work on an opinion, Rehnquist goes over the conference discussion with the clerk and explains how he thinks "an opinion can be written supporting the result reached by the majority." Once the clerk finishes a draft and Rehnquist works the draft into his own opinion, it circulates three or four times among the other clerks in the chambers before it circulates to the other chambers.

Justices have delegated to law clerks the task of initially screening all filings for writs of certiorari.

In addition to law clerks, five officers and their staffs also assist the Justices. Central to the Court's work is the Office of the Clerk. For most of the Court's history, the clerk earned no salary, but this changed in 1921 when Taft lobbied for legislation making the clerk a salaried employee. The clerk's office collects filing and admission fees; receives and records all motions, petitions, briefs, and other documents; and circulates those necessary items to each chamber. The clerk also establishes the oral-argument calendar and maintains the order list of cases granted or denied review and final judgments. In 1975, the office acquired a computer system that automatically notifies counsel in over ninety-five percent of all cases of the disposition of their filings.

There was no official reporter of decisions during the first quarter-century of the Court, and not until 1835 were the Justices' opinions given to the clerk. Early reporters worked at their own expense and for their own profit. In 1922, Congress established the present arrangement (at Chief Justice Taft's request): the reporter's salary is fixed by the Justices and paid by the government, and the Government Printing Office publishes the *United States Reports.* The reporter has primary responsibility for supervising the publication of the Court's opinions, writing headnotes or syllabi that accompany each opinion, and for making editorial suggestions subject to the Justices' approval.

Order in the courtroom was preserved by U.S. marshals until 1867, when Congress created the Office of Marshal of the Supreme Court. The marshal not only maintains order in the courtroom and times oral arguments but also oversees building maintenance and serves as business manager for the more than two hundred Court employees, including messengers, carpenters, police and workmen, a nurse, physiotherapist, barber, seamstress, and cafeteria workers.

The Justices acquired their first small library in 1832. It was run by the clerk until the marshal's office took over in 1884. In 1948, Congress created the Office of the Librarian, which employs several research librarians to assist the Justice.

Unlike other members of the Court, the Chief Justice has special administrative duties. Over fifty statutes confer duties ranging from chairing the judicial conference and the Federal Judicial Center to supervising the Administrative Office of the U.S. Courts and serving as chancellor of the Smithsonian Institution. Unlike Taft and Hughes, Stone felt overwhelmed by these duties. His successor, Vinson, appointed a special assistant to deal with administrative matters, whereas Warren delegated such matters to his secretary. By contrast, Burger became preoccupied with administrative matters and pushed for judicial reforms. In historical perspective, he brought Taft's marble temple into the world of modern technology and managerial practices. Burger also lobbied Congress to create a fifth legal officer of the Court, the administrative assistant to the Chief Justice. While also employing an administrative assistant, Chief Justice Rehnquist has less interest in judicial administration, and his assistant is less occupied with liaison work with organizations outside the Court.

The caseload remains the driving force behind the Court's work; its increase has changed the Court's operations. After Taft campaigned for relief for the Court, Congress passed the Judiciary Act of 1925, which enlarged the Court's discretionary jurisdiction and enabled it to deny cases review. Subsequently, on a piecemeal basis, the Court's discretion over its jurisdiction was further expanded, and in 1988, virtually all mandatory appeals were eliminated. As a result, the Court has the power to manage its docket and set its agenda for decision making.

The cornerstone of the modern Court's operation, in Justice John Harlan's words, "is the control it possesses over the amount and character of its business." The overwhelming majority of all cases are denied review; less than three percent of the more than 5,000 cases on the Court's annual docket are granted and decided by fully written opinion.

When a petition is filed at the Court, the clerk's staff determines whether it satisfies the rules as to form, length, and fees. After receiving opposing papers from respondents, the clerk circulates to the chambers a list of cases ready for consideration and a set of papers for each case. For much of the Court's history, every Justice reviewed every case, but this practice no longer prevails. Since the creation of the "cert. pool" in 1972, most of the Justices have delegated to their clerks much of this initial screening task. Moreover, the Court has found it necessary to hold its initial conference in the last week of September, before the formal opening of its term. At this conference, the Justices dispose of more than 1,000 cases, discussing less than two hundred. Before the start of the term, the Court has thus disposed of approximately one-fifth of its entire docket, with more than four-fifths of those cases effectively screened out by law clerks and never collectively considered by the Justices.

In conference, attended only by the Justices, the Court decides which cases to accept and discusses the merits of argued cases. During the weeks in which the Court hears oral arguments, conferences are held on Wednesday afternoons to take up the four cases argued on Monday, and then on Fridays to discuss new filings and the eight cases argued on Tuesday and Wednesday. In May and June, when oral arguments are not heard, conferences are held on Thursdays, from 10:00 AM to 4:00 PM, with a forty-five-minute lunch break around 12:30 PM.

Summoned by a buzzer five minutes before the hour, the Justices meet in their conference room, located directly behind the courtroom itself. Two conference lists circulate to each chamber by noon on the Wednesday before a conference. On the first list are those cases deemed worth discussing; typically, the discuss list includes about fifty cases. Attached is a second list, the "Dead List," containing those cases considered unworthy of discussion. Any Justice may request that a case be discussed, but over seventy percent of the cases on the conference lists are denied review without discussion.

Since the Chief Justice presides over conferences, he has significant opportunities for structuring and influencing the Court's work. Chief Justices, however, vary widely in their skills, style, and ideological orientations. Hughes is widely considered to be the greatest Chief Justice in this century because of his photographic memory and ability to state concisely the relative importance of each case. "Warren was closer to Hughes than any others," in Justice William O. Douglas's view, and "Burger was closer to Vinson. Stone was somewhere in between." Rehnquist, by all accounts, is an effective Chief Justice because he moves conferences along quickly and has the intellectual and temperamental wherewithal to be a leader.

For a case to be heard by the Court, at least four Justices must agree that it warrants consideration. This informal Rule of Four was adopted when the Justices were trying to persuade Congress that important cases would still be decided after the Court was given discretionary control over much of its jurisdiction under the Judiciary Act of 1925. Unanimity in case selection, nevertheless, remains remarkably high because the Justices agree that only a limited number of cases may be taken. "As a rule of thumb," Justice White explains, "the Court should not be expected to produce more than

150 opinions per term in argued cases." The rule of four, however, also permits an ideological bloc to grant review in cases it wants to hear and, thus, to influence the Court's agenda.

Immediately after conference, the Chief Justice traditionally had the task of reporting to the clerk which cases were granted review, which were denied review, and which were ready to come down. Burger, however, delegated this task to the junior Justice. The clerk then notifies both sides in a case granted review that they have thirty days to file briefs on merits and supporting documents. Once all briefs (forty copies of each) are submitted, cases are scheduled for oral argument.

The importance of oral argument, Chief Justice Charles Evans Hughes observed, lies in the fact that often "the impression that a judge has at the close of a full oral argument accords with the conviction which controls his final vote." Because the Justices vote in conference within a day or two of hearing arguments, oral arguments come at a crucial time. Still, oral arguments were more prominent in the work of the Court in the nineteenth century. Unlimited time was allowed, until the Court began cutting back on oral argument in 1848, allowing eight hours per case. The time has been reduced periodically, and since 1970, arguments have been limited to thirty minutes per side. The argument calendar permits hearing no more than 180 cases a year. For fourteen weeks each term, from the first Monday in October until the end of April, the Court hears arguments from 10:00 to 12:00 and 1:00 to 3:00 on Monday, Tuesday, and Wednesday about every two weeks.

Justices differ in their preparation for oral arguments. Douglas insisted that "oral arguments win or lose a case," but Chief Justice Earl Warren claimed that they were "not highly persuasive." Most Justices come prepared with "bench memos" drafted by their law clerks, identifying the central facts, issues, and possible questions. On the bench, they also vary in their style and approach toward questioning attorneys. Justices Sandra Day O'Connor and Antonin Scalia, for example, are aggressive and relentless in the questioning of attorneys, while Justices William J. Brennan and Harry A. Blackmun tend to sit back and listen.

Conference discussions following oral arguments no longer play the role they once did. When the docket was smaller, conferences were integral to the Court's work. Cases were discussed in detail, differences hammered out, and the Justices strove to reach agreement on an institutional opinion for the Court. As the caseload grew, conferences became largely symbolic of past collective deliberations. They currently serve only to discover consensus. "In fact," Justice Scalia points out, "to call our discussion of a case a conference is really something of a misnomer. It's much more a statement of the views of each of the nine Justices."

Most of the time spent in conference is consumed by the Justices deciding which cases should be granted review. Moreover, less time is spent in conference (now about 108 hours) each term. The caseload and conference schedule permits on average only about six minutes for each case on the discuss list and about twenty-nine minutes for those granted full consideration. Perhaps as a result, the Justices agree less often on the opinion announcing the Court's decision and file a greater number of separate opinions. In short, the combination of more cases and less collective deliberation discourages the compromises necessary for institutional opinions and reinforces the tendency of the Justices to function independently.

All votes at conference are tentative until the final opinion comes down. Voting thus presents each Justice with opportunities to negotiate which issues are to be decided and how they are to be resolved. Before, during, and after conference, Justices may use their votes in strategic ways to influence the outcome of a case. At conference, a Justice may vote with others who appear to constitute a majority, even though the Justice may disagree with their reasoning. The Justice may then suggest changes in draft opinions to try to minimize the damage, from his or her perspective, of the Court's decision.

Because conference votes are tentative, the assignment, drafting, and circulation of opinions is crucial to the Court's work. Opinions justify or explain votes at conference. The Opinion of the Court is the most important and most difficult to write because it represents a collective judgment. Writing the Court's opinion, as Justice Holmes put it, requires that a "judge can dance the sword dance; that is he can justify an obvious result without stepping on either blade of opposing fallacies." Because Justices remain free to switch votes and to write separate opinions, concurring in or dissenting from the Court's decision, they continue after conference to compete for influence on the final decision and opinion.

The power of opinion assignment is the Chief Justice's "single most influential function," observed Justice Tom C. Clark, and an exercise in "judicial-political discretion." By tradition, when the Chief Justice votes with the majority, he assigns the Court's opinion. If the Chief Justice is not with the majority, then the senior Associate Justice in the majority either writes the opinion or assigns it to another Justice.

Chief Justices may keep the Court's opinion for themselves, especially when a case is unanimously decided. Since Vinson, however, Chief Justices have generally sought parity in their opinion assignments. Opinions may be assigned to pivotal Justices to ensure or expand the size of the majority joining the opinion for the Court. But the Chief Justice may also take other factors into account, such as a Justice's expertise or what kind of reaction a ruling may engender. Hughes, for example, was inclined to assign the opinions in "liberal" decisions to "conservative" justices.

The assignment, drafting, and circulation of opinions is crucial to the Court's work.

The circulation of draft opinions among the chambers has added to the Supreme Court's workload and changed its deliberative process. The practice of circulating draft opinions began around 1900 and soon became pivotal in the Court's decision-making process, especially with the Justices spending less time in conference discussing and reconciling their differences. Occasionally, proposed changes in a draft opinion will lead to a complete recasting or to having the opinion reassigned to another Justice. To accommodate the views of others, the author of an opinion for the Court must negotiate language and bargain over substance. At times, however, Justices may not feel that a case is worth fighting over; as Justice George Sutherland noted on the back of one of Stone's drafts, "probably bad—but only a small baby. Let it go."

Final published opinions for the Court are the residue of compromises among the Justices. But they also reflect changing norms in the work of the Court. Up until the 1930s, there were few concurring or dissenting opinions. But individual opinions now predominate over opinions for the Court. When the Court's practice in the 1980s is compared with that of forty years ago, there are roughly ten times the number of concurring opinions, four times more dissenting opinions, and seven times the number of separate opinions in which the Justices explain their views and why they concur and dissent from parts of the Court's opinion. Even though the business of the Court is to give institutional opinions, as Justice Stewart observed, "that view has come to be that of a minority of the Justices."

The Justices are more interested in merely the tally of votes at conference than in arriving at a consensus on an institutional decision and opinion. As a result, whereas unanimity remains high on case selection (around eighty percent), unanimous opinions for the Court count for only about thirty percent of the Court's written opinions. The number of cases decided by a bare majority also sharply grew in the 1970s and 1980s, and frequently, no majority could agree on an opinion announcing the Court's rulings.

A Justice writing separate concurring or dissenting opinions carries no burden of massing other Justices. Concurring opinions explain how the Court's decision could have been otherwise rationalized. A concurring opinion surely is defensible when a compromised opinion might be meaningless or impossible to achieve. The cost of concurring opinions is that they add to the workload and may create confusion over the Court's rulings.

A dissenting opinion, in the words of Chief Justice Hughes, appeals "to the brooding spirit of the law, to the intelligence of a future day, when a later decision may possibly correct the error into which the dissenting judge believes the Court to have been betrayed." Even the threat of a dissent may be useful in persuading the majority to narrow its holding or tone down the language of its opinion.

The struggles over the work of the Court (and among the Justices) continue after the writing of opinions and final votes. Opinion days, when the Court announces its decisions, may reveal something of these struggles and mark the beginning of larger political struggles for influence within the country.

Decisions are announced in the courtroom, typically crowded with reporters, attorneys, and spectators. Before 1857, decisions came down on any day of the week, but thereafter they were announced only on Mondays. In 1965, the Court reverted to its earlier practice, and in 1971, the Justices further broke with the tradition of "Decision Mondays." On Mondays, the Court generally releases memorandum orders and admits new attorneys to its bar. In weeks when the Justices hear oral arguments, opinions are announced on Tuesdays and Wednesdays and then on any day of the week during the rest of the term. By tradition, there is no prior announcement of the decisions to be handed down. In 1971, the practice of reading full opinions was abandoned; typically, only the ruling and the line-up of the Justices is stated.

Media coverage of the Court's work has grown since the 1930s, when fewer than a half-dozen reporters covered the Court and shared six small cubicles on the ground floor, just below the courtroom, where they received copies of opinions sent down through pneumatic tube. In 1970, the Court established a Public Information Office, which provides space for a "press room" and makes available all filings and briefs for cases on the docket, as well as the Court's conference lists and final opinions. More than fifty reporters and all major television networks currently cover the Court, although cameras are still not allowed in the courtroom.

When deciding major issues of public law and policy, Justices may consider strategies for winning public acceptance of their rulings. When holding "separate but equal" schools unconstitutional in 1954 in *Brown* v. *Board of Education,* for instance, the Court waited a year before issuing its mandate for "all deliberate speed" in ending school segregation. Some of the Justices sacrificed their preference for a more precise guideline in order to achieve a unanimous ruling, and the Court tolerated lengthy delays in the implementation of *Brown,* in recognition of the likelihood of open defiance.

Although the Justices are less concerned about public opinion than are elected public officials, they are sensitive to the attitudes of their immediate "constituents": the solicitor general, the attorney general and Department of Justice, counsel for federal agencies, states' attorneys general, and the legal profession. These professionals' responses to the Court's rulings help determine the extent of compliance. With such concerns in mind, Chief Justice Warren sought to establish an objective bright-line rule that police could not evade, when holding, in *Miranda* v. *Arizona* (1966), that police must inform criminal suspects of their Fifth Amendment right against self-incrimination and their Sixth Amendment right to counsel, which included the right to consult and have the presence of an attorney during police interrogation. The potential costs of securing compliance may also convince the Justices to limit the scope or application of their decisions.

Compliance with the Court's decisions by lower courts is uneven. They may extend or limit decisions in anticipation of later rulings. Ambiguities created by plurality opinions, or 5–4 decisions invite lower courts to pursue their own policy goals. Differences between the facts on which the Court ruled and the circumstances of a case at hand may be emphasized so as to reach a different conclusion.

Major confrontations between Congress and the Court have occurred a number of times, and Congress has tried to pressure the Court in a variety of ways. The Senate may try to influence the appointment of Supreme Court Justices, and Justices may be impeached. More frequently, Congress has tried to pressure the Court when setting its terms and size and when authorizing appropriations for salaries, law clerks, secretaries, and office technology. Only once, in 1802, when repealing the Judiciary Act of 1801 and abolishing a session for a year, did Congress actually set the Court's term in order to delay and influence a particular decision. The size of the Court is not preordained, and changes generally reflect attempts to control the Court. The Jeffersonian Republicans' quick repeal of the act passed by the Federalists in 1801, reducing the number of Justices, was the first of several attempts to influence the Court. Presidents James Madison, James Monroe, and John Adams all claimed that the country's geographical expansion warranted increasing the number of Justices. Congress, however, refused to do so until the last day of Andrew Jackson's term in 1837. During the Civil War, the number of Justices increased to ten. This was ostensibly due to the creation of a circuit in the West, but it also gave Abraham Lincoln his fourth appointment and a chance to secure a pro-Union majority on the bench. Antagonism toward Andrew Johnson's Reconstruction policies, then, led to a reduction from ten to seven Justices. After General Ulysses S. Grant's election, Congress again authorized nine Justices. In the nineteenth century at least, Congress rather successfully denied Presidents additional appointments in order to preserve the Court's policies, and increased the number of Justices so as to change the ideological composition of the Court.

Under Article III, Congress is authorized "to make exceptions" to the Court's appellate jurisdiction.

More direct attacks are possible. Under Article III, Congress is authorized "to make exceptions" to the Court's appellate jurisdiction. This has been viewed as a way of denying the Court review of certain kinds of cases. But Congress succeeded only once in affecting the Court's work in this way; an 1868 repeal of jurisdiction over writs of habeas corpus was upheld in *Ex Parte McCardle* (1869).

Court-curbing legislation is not a very viable weapon. Congress has greater success in reversing the Court by constitutional amendment, which three-fourths of the states must ratify. The process is cumbersome, and thousands of amendments to overrule the Court have failed. But four rulings have been overturned by constitutional amendment. *Chisholm* v. *Georgia* (1793), holding that citizens of one state could sue another state in federal courts, was reversed by the Eleventh Amendment, guaranteeing sovereign immunity for states from suits by citizens of other states. The Thirteenth Amendment and Fourteenth Amendment, abolishing slavery and making blacks citizens of the United States, technically overturned *Dred Scott* v. *Sandford* (1857). With the ratification in 1913 of the Sixteenth Amendment, Congress reversed *Pollock* v. *Farmers' Loan and Trust*

Company (1895), which had invalidated a federal income tax. In 1970, an amendment to the Voting Rights Act of 1965 lowered the voting age to eighteen years for all elections. Although signing the act into law, President Richard M. Nixon had his attorney general challenge the validity of lowering the voting age in state and local elections. Within six months, in *Oregon* v. *Mitchell* (1970), a bare majority held that Congress had exceeded its power. Less than a year later, the Twenty-Sixth Amendment was ratified, thereby overriding the Court's ruling and extending the franchise to eighteen-year-olds in all elections.

Even more successful are congressional enactments and rewriting of legislation in response to the Court's rulings. Congress, of course, cannot overturn the Court's interpretations of the Constitution by mere legislation. But Congress may enhance or thwart compliance with its rulings. After the landmark ruling in *Gideon* v. *Wainwright* (1963) that indigents have a right to counsel, for instance, Congress provided attorneys for indigents charged with federal offenses. By contrast, in the Crime Control and Safe Streets Act of 1968, Congress permitted federal courts to use evidence obtained from suspects who had not been read their *Miranda* rights if their testimony appeared voluntary based on the "totality of the circumstances" surrounding their interrogation.

Congress may also openly defy the Court's rulings. When holding in *Immigration and Naturalization Service* v. *Chadha* (1983) that Congress may not delegate decision-making authority to federal agencies and still retain the power of vetoing decisions with which it disagrees, the Court invalidated over two hundred provisions for congressional vetoes of administrative actions. Congress largely responded by deleting or substituting joint resolutions for one-House veto provisions. However, in the year following *Chadha,* Congress passed no less than thirty new provisions for legislative vetoes.

Congress indubitably has the power to delay and undercut implementation of the Court's rulings. On major issues of public policy, Congress is likely to prevail or at least temper the impact of the Court's rulings.

The Court has often been the focus of presidential campaigns and power struggles as well. Presidents rarely openly defy particular decisions by the Court, and in major confrontations, they have tended to yield. Still, presidential reluctance to enforce rulings may thwart implementation of the Court's rulings. In the short and long run, Presidents may undercut the Court's work by issuing contradictory directives to federal agencies and assigning low priority for enforcement by the Department of Justice. Presidents may also make broad moral appeals in response to the Court's rulings, and those appeals may transcend their limited time in office. The Court put school desegregation and abortion on the national political agenda. Yet John F. Kennedy's appeal for civil rights captivated a generation and encouraged public acceptance of the Court's ruling in *Brown* v. *Board of Education.* Similarly, Ronald Reagan's opposition to abortion focused attention on "traditional family values" and served to legitimate resistance to the Court's decisions.

Presidential influence over the Court in the long run remains contingent on appointments to the Court. Vacancies occur on the average of one every twenty-two months, and there is no guarantee as to how a Justice will vote or whether that vote will prove the key to limiting or reversing past rulings with which a President disagrees. Yet through their appointments, Presidents leave their mark on the Court and possibly align it and the country or precipitate later confrontations.

The Supreme Court at work is unlike any other. It has virtually complete discretion to select which cases are reviewed, to control its work load, and to set its own substantive agenda. From the thousands of cases arriving each year, less than two hundred are accepted and decided. The Court thus functions like a superlegislature. But the Justices' chambers also work like nine separate law offices, competing for influence when selecting and deciding those cases. The Justices no longer spend time collectively deliberating cases at conference. Instead, they simply tally votes and then hammer out differences, negotiating and compromising on the language of their opinions during the postconference period when drafts are circulated among the chambers. When the final opinions come down, the Court remains dependent on the cooperation of other political branches and public acceptance for compliance with its rulings. The work of the Court, in Chief Justice Edward D. White's words, "rests solely upon the approval of a free people."

BIBLIOGRAPHY

Abraham, Henry J. 1986 *The Judicial Process,* 5th ed. New York: Oxford University Press.

Choper, Jesse 1980 *Judicial Review and the National Democratic Process.* Chicago: University of Chicago Press.

Congressional Quarterly 1989 *Guide to the U.S. Supreme Court,* 2nd ed. Washington, D.C.: Congressional Quarterly Press.

Diamond, Paul 1989 *The Supreme Court & Judicial Choice: The Role of Provisional Judicial Review.* Ann Arbor: University of Michigan Press.

Fisher, Louis 1988 *Constitutional Dialogues.* Princeton, N.J.: Princeton University Press.

Johnson, Charles and Cannon, Bradley 1984 *Judicial Policies: Implementation and Impact.* Washington, D.C.: Congressional Quarterly Press.

O'Brien, David M. 1990 *Storm Center: The Supreme Court in American Politics,* 2nd ed. New York: W. W. Norton.
Stern, Robert and Gressman, Eugene 1987 *Supreme Court Practice,* 6th ed. Washington, D.C.: Bureau of National Affairs.

– DAVID M. O'BRIEN

THE SUPREME COURT OF THE UNITED STATES

A century and a half ago, Alexis de Tocqueville wrote in *Democracy in America* that the "judicial organization of the United States is the institution which the stranger has the greatest difficulty in understanding." And by European and Latin American standards the United States Supreme Court remains a peculiar institution.

First, it operates within a system of judge-made "common law" as opposed to codes of legislatively created "civil law." In Europe, Latin America, and many developing nations colonized by the Dutch, French, Portuguese, or Spanish, the national legislature has created a systematic body of law—codes of criminal law, civil law, and procedural law with supposedly clearly written, logically arranged rules to cover all problems likely to arise. The function of judges is to apply these rules to a controversy and, if interpretation is necessary, to construe them according to principles laid down within the codes themselves. (In fact, because no "code" can be perfectly clear or cover all eventualities, the judicial function under the civil law is much more complex.)

Common-law systems—the term *system* is misleading, for common law is by nature unsystematic—are found only in Britain and its former colonies. In contrast to the civil law's ideals of a comprehensive set of rules made by legislators, common-law judges made most of the rules that they applied and interpreted, and they did so on a case-by-case basis, using experience more than abstract logic and narrowly focusing on each problem rather than constructing broadly applicable principles.

For centuries the British king and Parliament mainly concerned themselves with such over-arching matters of public policy as war, peace, and taxes, and by and large left to judges the task of formulating rules to govern day-to-day activities of life. And in this context common-law judges proceeded cautiously, deciding one case at a time and citing earlier cases as authorities for decisions. They gradually built up rules by tinkering rather than by conceiving and executing a grand design.

Today legislatures in common-law countries do make rules about minute as well as broad aspects of public life; but except in areas like Quebec and Louisiana, which were originally settled by the French, these legislatures almost never try to enact comprehensive codes on the European model. What Americans call "codes" are often little more than efforts to put some order into statutes enacted over many decades. Even the "uniform codes" that have become popular among the states are seldom either uniform or all-encompassing.

Judicial review,

a peculiarity of the United States Supreme Court,

distinguishes it from its ancestral institutions,

the British courts of common law.

The ordinary piece of legislation in common-law countries deals with a particular problem—monopoly, for example—and even then rarely claims to be complete within itself. To understand the typical statute, one has to know the earlier judge-made rules it attempts to abolish, alter, or reinforce as well as the later rules judges have made to fill in the statute's general language. An intelligent, educated citizen in a civil law system can read the appropriate code and have an accurate idea of his or her rights and duties. A similar exercise in a common-law country is a sure recipe for trouble, unless one also reads dozens of judicial opinions "explaining" the statute.

The principal point of this first distinction is that the Supreme Court, as heir to a common-law tradition, operates within a framework in which wide judicial discretion and creativity have been normal and legitimate. It is a system in which judges rely on previous decisions, on precedents, at least as much as—and usually far more than—on general legislative pronouncements.

Judicial review, a second peculiarity of the United States Supreme Court—one shared by almost all American courts, state and federal—distinguishes it from its ancestral institutions, the British courts of common law. Those tribunals fashioned and refashioned the rules of the common law as well as interpreted statutes, but they lacked authority to declare that any act of Parliament, no matter how outrageous, violated the British Constitution.

Like the "constitutional courts" of Austria, Italy, and West Germany, the United States Supreme Court plays the extraordinary role of authoritative interpreter of the national constitution, exercising the power to declare invalid acts of coordinate branches of government. But even here the Supreme Court differs from European constitutional courts. Those are specialized tribunals whose jurisdiction is largely limited to disputes involving constitutional interpretation. They cannot review and correct any other form of judgment. They do not sit at the apex of a judicial hierarchy but alongside other courts of specialized jurisdiction. Unlike those tribunals, and much more like the supreme courts of Canada and Japan and the High Court of Australia, the United States Supreme Court is also the highest court of general jurisdiction for a national legal system, with authority to interpret that government's treaties, statutes, common law, and administrative orders.

A third peculiarity stems from the federal nature of the United States and of a decision of Congress to create a separate system of national courts. Article III of the Constitution reads, "The judicial Power of the United States, shall be vested in one supreme Court, and in such inferior Courts as the Congress may from time to time ordain and establish." Congress might have provided, as the Australians, Canadians, and West Germans later did, that cases involving national law would start in state courts and have given the Supreme Court appellate jurisdiction over such issues. Instead, Congress chose to establish a federal judicial system parallel to state courts and to make the Supreme Court responsible for overseeing the administration of justice in those tribunals.

One effect of a dual set of courts is that both often apply laws relating to similar matters. A single act may violate state as well as federal statutes and result in a double prosecution—not a violation of the prohibition against double jeopardy because, the Supreme Court has ruled, federalism makes people in the United States subject to two governments.

Causing more confusion is the fact that a private citizen often has the option of starting in a state or federal court, for while Congress has provided that trials for most federal crimes will be conducted in federal courts, it has given federal courts exclusive jurisdiction over few areas of civil law. Thus, for instance, a citizen hurt by a law that she thinks violates the federal Constitution may challenge the statute in either a state or federal court. In effect, then, the Supreme Court presides not only over a national system of courts but also over fifty state systems insofar as they rule on controversies involving the United States Constitution, statutes, treaties, administrative orders, or, in very rare instances, federal common law.

Further complicating matters, if the challenged statute is that of a state and the litigant chooses to begin in a state court, he or she may allege that the statute also violates the state constitution. On that point, however, the judgment of the state's highest court is final. When the justices hear cases from state courts, they are not supposed to interpret state law, whether statutory, common, or constitutional. When state law is involved, the Court's sole task is to decide whether that law, as interpreted by state judges, is compatible with national regulations and the national Constitution. As the justices explained in *Herb* v. *Pitcairn* (1945),

> This Court from the time of its foundation has adhered to the principle that it will not review judgments of state courts that rest on adequate and independent state grounds. The reason is so obvious that it has rarely been thought to warrant statement. It is found in the partitioning of power between the state and Federal judicial systems and in the limitations of our own jurisdiction. Our only power over state judgments is to correct them to the extent that they incorrectly adjudge federal rights.

These peculiarities are surrounded by an apparent anomaly. Although officials of the United States often proclaim that the country is a democracy, with government chosen by, and responsible to, the people, members of the Supreme Court, like all other federal judges, are not popularly elected; and like most federal judges, they serve "during good Behaviour." Impeachment by the House of Representatives followed by conviction by a two-thirds vote of the Senate is the only formal way of removing a federal judge. In two hundred years of the Constitution's operation, only once has the House impeached a justice, and on that occasion the Senate refused to convict. One other justice voluntarily left the bench because of questionable private financial dealings. For all practical purposes, "good Behaviour" means as long as a justice cares to remain in office.

Personnel and Procedures

The Constitution provides for the establishment of "one supreme Court" but says nothing about how many judges shall staff it. The number of justices, set by statute at six in 1789 and periodically changed during the nineteenth century, has ranged from five to ten and has remained at nine since 1869, a chief Justice and eight associate justices. They are nominated by the president, and their appointment is subject to confirmation by the Senate.

SELECTION OF JUDGES. Although neither the Constitution nor any statute imposes restrictions on who is eligible for selection, a president does not have a free hand. Common-law systems do not have a cadre of professional judges, as do those under the civil law; but by tradition all justices have been lawyers. There are also expectations of geographic representation. Normally, there will be at least one justice from the major

Within this massive edifice of the Supreme Court, momentous and authoritative interpretations of the United States Constitution take place. (Kelly-Mooney Photography/Corbis)

regions of the country: New England, the Middle Atlantic states, the Deep South, the Midwest, and the Far West.

There are now also expectations of ethnic representation. During most of this century there has been a Catholic on the Court, and since 1916, there has usually been a Jew. The appointment of Thurgood Marshall in 1967 probably marked the beginning of a tradition of having at least one black justice; and Sandra Day O'Connor's appointment in 1981 makes it unlikely that the High Bench will ever again be an all-male sanctuary.

The power of the Court imposes additional restrictions on presidential choices. Given judicial review and the invitation to discretionary interpretation that Congress opens in many statutes, only a fool or a madman would nominate a person who disagreed with the legitimacy of his policies. Richard Nixon was only being candid when he described his principal criterion for selecting judges: "First and foremost, they had to be men who shared my legal philosophy." Thus, presidents have typically chosen people from their own political party—and people whose views they think they know well. Many justices have been governors, senators, or attorneys general; and, whether or not they have held public office, the vast majority have been sufficiently active in politics to make a record that the president can assess. As Lincoln put it to George Boutwell, "We cannot ask a man what he will do [if appointed], and if we should, and he should answer us, we should despise him for it. Therefore we must take a man whose opinions are known."

Several factors have kept the Court from becoming the mirror of a president's constitutional views. First, on the average a vacancy occurs only about once every two and a half years, making it difficult for a president, even in two four-year terms, to select a majority of the justices.

Second, presidents often make mistakes about the views of the people they nominate. Woodrow Wilson, an economic liberal, nominated James C. McReynolds, who turned out to be among the most economically conservative judges in American history. Dwight Eisenhower once referred to his choice of Earl Warren as chief justice as "the biggest damn fool mistake I ever made." Moreover, the past is not an infallible indicator of the future, for what a person thinks is constitutional when a senator or cabinet official may, when he or she views the matter from the perspective of a judge, seem unconstitutional.

A third factor limiting presidential influence is that the nature of pressing political problems and their social contexts may change radically. For instance, President Franklin D. Roosevelt fought a bitter battle against the Supreme Court from 1934 until 1937, when the justices, stubbornly insisting that the Constitution required laissez-faire, invalidated many of the president's most important economic policies. As one would expect, Roosevelt nominated only justices who fervently believed that governmental regulation of the economy was constitutional. But very quickly that issue faded in importance. Replacing economic regulation was a myriad of questions about racial justice, freedom of speech and press, electoral districting, privacy, and fairness in criminal procedure—none of which Roosevelt had even remotely considered in picking judges.

THE JUSTICES. A total of 103 people sat on the Supreme Court between 1788 and 1986. Although their disagreements with each other have been frequent, public, and acerbic, most of the justices have come from remarkably similar social, economic, and professional backgrounds. All have been lawyers and most have been political activists. More than half had served as judges on other courts, but only about a quarter had spent much of their professional careers on the bench and many of those had earlier been in partisan politics. With the single exception of Sandra Day O'Connor, all have been males and, with the sole exception of Thurgood Marshall, white. Seven have been Catholics, and five, Jews. The other ninety-one have been at least nominal Protestants.

The Court's jurisdiction is divided into two categories, original, as a trial court, and appellate, as a reviewer of the rulings of other courts.

Most of the justices have come from politically active families of the upper middle or upper class; received educations at the best universities; and, when practicing law, tended to handle corporate and financial problems rather than less genteel divorce and criminal cases. When appointed they have usually been in late middle age, and curiously, they tend to outlive by a considerable margin their contemporaries, even those of the same social class.

JURISDICTION. The Court's jurisdiction—that is, its authority to hear and decide cases—is divided into two categories, original, as a trial court, and appellate, as a reviewer of the rulings of other courts. The Constitution specifies that the Supreme Court, sitting as a trial court, shall hear cases involving foreign diplomats and those to which a state is a party. Since diplomats cannot be sued and it is undiplomatic for them to sue, states tend to monopolize the Court's original jurisdiction.

In most years the Court hears several disputes between states over such matters as the location of a boundary or allocation of water from a river that flows through both. These cases could tie up the justices for many months, but the Court has devised an efficient procedure. When one of these cases is filed, the justices appoint a "special master," a retired judge or an eminent attorney, to call witnesses, examine documents, hear arguments, and report findings and recommendations. After receiving the special master's report, the Court treats the case just as it does those that come up under its appellate jurisdiction: it allows the states to present written briefs and oral arguments contesting or supporting the master's report.

It is as an appellate tribunal that the Court does the bulk of its business. Cases come to the Court from both state and federal tribunals. But, again, the losing party in the highest state court may ask the Supreme Court to review the case only if that dispute raises questions of the interpretation of a federal statute, treaty, or the Constitution.

Below the Supreme Court in the federal judicial system are two tiers of tribunals: district courts and courts of appeals. There is at least one United States district court in each state, and its jurisdiction is limited not only by subject matter but also by territory. That is, a federal district court in New York cannot hear disputes, even about issues of federal law, that arise in New Jersey.

For supervision of district courts, the country is divided geographically into twelve circuits, each headed by a court of appeals. As a matter of right, the loser in the district court may ask the court of appeals in that circuit to review the decision. (Appeals from three-judge district courts go directly to the Supreme Court.) Usually, each court of appeals sits in panels of three judges, though, as with district courts, many more judges may be attached to the tribunal.

Although no new factual evidence may be introduced in an appeal, on occasion judges at all levels will take what is called "judicial notice" of certain kinds of notorious facts, for example, the existence of a war, a depression, or even, as in *Roe* v. *Wade* (1973), in holding that a woman has a constitutional right to an abortion at least during the first three months of pregnancy, of advances in medical technology, such as antibiotics. Furthermore, some judges—especially on the Supreme Court—have gone beyond the argument and written record to do their own homework so that they might better understand both the factual issues and the implications of certain lines of reasoning. This practice has angered some jurists, because they believe it unfair in not allowing opposing counsel to respond to what the judge has read in private. The usual response is that to depend completely on counsel would mean that issues affecting the entire country would often be determined by a single litigant's wisdom in choosing a lawyer.

The Supreme Court has appellate jurisdiction over all decisions of the courts of appeals as well as over several specialized national tribunals that hear only disputes about taxes, customs, patents, and courts martial. Much of the Court's business arises out of state supreme court decisions on federal issues.

There are three avenues to the Supreme Court. First is "certification." Here a court of appeals certifies a question to the justices for their decision; in effect, the judges of a court of appeals say that the issue is of such importance and difficulty that they should not decide it. Not unexpectedly, given judicial egos, certification is rare, and even when a court of appeals certifies a question, the Supreme Court sometimes refuses to respond, asking instead that it first have the benefit of that court's wisdom.

The second avenue is an "appeal," in a narrow, technical sense. According to federal statutes, a losing litigant can appeal to the Supreme Court and the justices must take the case when a United States court of appeals or a special three-judge district court declares a state or federal act unconstitutional or the highest court of a state invalidates a federal act or sustains the constitutionality of a state statute. In fact, because of the number of cases the justices are asked to review—more than four thousand a year—they treat appeals as being within their discretion to hear or refuse to hear.

The third and most commonly used avenue is "certiorari." The losing litigant in cases not covered by appeal may petition the justices to review a decision by a United States court of appeals or a state supreme court that has ruled on a federal issue. The next subsection describes how the Court handles these petitions; here we note only that it takes a vote of four of the justices, one less than a majority, to agree to hear the case.

The justices refuse to review more than 95 percent of all the cases brought to them, and rarely does the Court offer any useful explanation of its action. When it declines to take an appeal from a state supreme court, it typically says only, "Appeal dismissed for want of a substantial federal question." When it refuses to grant a petition for certiorari, it usually does so with a one-word opinion: "Denied." These statistics do not mean, however, that the justices treat such matters lightly.

PROCEDURES. When a petition for review arrives at the Supreme Court, it goes to the office of the clerk of the Court. He sends a copy to each justice. From then on, practice varies, depending on the justice's preferences. Some read all or most of these petitions themselves; others divide them among their own clerks; and some have agreed to share their clerks' recommendations. Each justice may choose as many as four clerks. They work for the justice, not for the clerk of the Court, and are almost always young men or women who have recently graduated at or near the top of their classes at the most prestigious law schools. They usually serve for only one year, acting as research assistants and perhaps critics, but they have no formal authority.

Every week or so the chief justice circulates a "discuss list"—the petitions for certiorari and the appeals that he recommends the justices debate at the Court's next conference. Unless a justice objects, all other petitions received during the period covered by the list are automatically denied. If a justice wishes to discuss any petitions not included on the list, he or she merely so notes and those items are added. Refusal to review means that the lower court's decision stands; but it does not imply that the Supreme Court approved either that ruling or the principles behind it.

During the term—which begins on the first Monday in October and for all practical purposes ends sometime in July—the Court sits for two weeks, then recesses for several weeks to allow the justices to think, research, and write. During the weeks the Court is sitting, the justices hear oral arguments on Mondays, Tuesdays, and Wednesdays from 10 A.M. until noon, and from 1 P.M. until 3 P.M. Later on Wednesday afternoons and all day Friday, the justices meet in conference to debate petitions on the discuss list and cases just argued on their merits.

When the Court agrees to hear a case, each side may submit a "brief," more fully stating its arguments, and a "reply brief," responding to the other's arguments. At this stage or when the petition for review is filed, any other person or group may also present a brief to the Court as an *amicus curiae,* or "friend of the court." Those wishing to submit an *amicus* brief must either obtain the consent of the parties or special permission from the Court by showing a real interest at stake in the litigation and an intention to present arguments different from those of either side. On occasion, the Court will invite someone to appear as an *amicus,* most often the solicitor general of the United States or a state attorney general.

After the justices have granted review, the Court sets a date for oral argument. Each side is allowed thirty minutes, although in cases whose impact is likely to be especially far-reaching, the Court may permit additional time. Normally, an *amicus* is not allowed to participate in oral argument, though the Court frequently allows the solicitor general and, less often, state attorneys general to do so.

Counsel stands at a lectern facing the bench and begins, "Chief Justice, may it please the Court. . . ." These may well be the lawyer's last prepared words. The justices want a discussion, not a lecture. Most attorneys who have a case before the Court are there for the first time and erroneously assume that the justices want to hear explanations of their own previous decisions. Counsel find themselves constantly interrupted, as two or three justices simultaneously push for responses to questions that range from a decision's potential effects on public policy to more details about the case's factual background.

When five minutes remain, a white light flashes on the lectern. When time is up, a red light goes on. Counsel must stop instantly. There is a story that Chief Justice Charles Evans Hughes once cut a famous lawyer off in the middle of the word *if.* The enormousness of the Court's work load makes every second precious.

When the justices meet in conference, no one except the nine members of the Court is allowed into the room. If there is a message for one of the justices or much-needed coffee, the junior justice serves as doorkeeper and relieves the caller of his or her burden.

The chief justice opens discussion by summarizing the case and explaining his views. Then the justices speak in order of seniority. The Court keeps no formal record of these debates, but some justices take notes either to refresh their memories or to enlighten history. What Justices Frank Murphy, Harold Burton, and William O. Douglas scribbled provide the same general picture of intense, informed, and wide-ranging debate that takes place during oral argument.

Justices use the conference either to try to persuade their colleagues or, if undecided, to learn from them. Some justices make eloquent pleas; others play devil's advocate. Some sit passively, taking notes or staring out the window to relieve boredom. At times tempers flash. "We take our jobs seriously," one justice said in private, "and we do get angry. Any judge who didn't get angry when he saw the Constitution misinterpreted ought to be impeached."

The style of conferences has varied with the personality of the chief justice. Charles Evans Hughes and Harlan Stone represent extremes. Hughes disciplined himself to speak only a few minutes, and he expected similar self-control from his colleagues. He would cut off a speech with a curt "Thank you" and nod to the justice next in seniority to begin. He preferred rapid disposition of cases to give-and-take. Stone had bridled under Hughes's management; and when he became chief, he tried to turn the conference into a seminar. His colleagues sometimes turned it into a shouting match. Business that took several hours under Hughes might consume several days under Stone, but no one complained that issues were not thoroughly debated.

When the chief believes that more discussion would be fruitless, he calls for a vote. The justices vote in the same order as they speak, with the chief voting first and the junior justice last. This procedure, begun under Earl Warren, marked an important change. At least from the time of John Marshall the justices had spoken in order of seniority and then voted in reverse order, allowing the chief justice to vote last and to side with the majority.

Being in the majority is important, for one of the few prerogatives the chief has is that of assigning the task of writing the opinion of the Court if he is in the majority. If he is in the minority, the senior associate justice in the majority makes the assignment. The person who assigns the opinion may keep it himself or pass it on to the justice whom he thinks most likely to reflect the views that he wants to prevail.

Some chief justices almost never dissented. John Marshall and Charles Evans Hughes, for example, almost always found it expedient to stifle their own views when they saw they would lose, to vote with the majority, and sometimes even to assign the opinion of the Court to themselves so as to damage as little as possible the principles that they supported. Others, like Warren Earl Burger and Earl Warren, seldom suppressed their own views.

When the justices meet in conference,

no one except the nine members of the Court

is allowed into the room.

Being assigned the task of writing the Court's opinion does not guarantee that the opinion written will be that of the Court. To be so labeled and so to carry the institutional authority of the Supreme Court rather than be an expression of personal views, an opinion must have the approval of at least five justices; and all justices are free to write their own opinions, either concurring or dissenting, and to change their votes up to the minute the Court announces its decision. (If that happens, the Court does not announce its decision until the justices write new opinions.) Even later, if the losing party asks for a rehearing, justices can change their minds.

The opinion writer prepares a manuscript and circulates it to the rest of the Court. Few justices have been bashful about making suggestions for change. Sometimes these are minor; sometimes they involve recasting the entire reasoning; and sometimes suggestions from different justices are mutually incompatible. If the last is true, the opinion writer has to convert others or decide which colleague's vote to lose.

At the same time, the dissenters, acting alone or together, may circulate their opinion(s), although they may wait until the majority's opinion has approached final form. Dissents are also circulated to every member of the Court, and sometimes they persuade justices to change their votes. It is unusual, but not unheard of, for what began as a dissent to become the opinion of the Court. It is more usual for the Court's opinion writer to try to accommodate justices who plan to write separate concurring or dissenting opinions and win them over to a modified version of the Court's opinion.

In civil law systems, no matter how sharply judges disagree among themselves, decisions are reported as if they were unanimous and authors of the court's opinions are not identified. Except in the Constitutional Court of West Germany, dissents and concurrences are not allowed. The United States Supreme Court uses a somewhat similar method when it denies petitions for review; that is, it merely issues a one-word or, at most, one-sentence order. Still, justices sometimes publish dissents against denials, and others may respond. In the past, when the justices were unanimous and either thought that the issue before them was settled or, for tactical reasons, wished to give the impression that the issue was settled, they used opinions labeled *per curiam* ("by the court"). These were terse, often only a line or two and usually no more than a paragraph, basically citing previous rulings that, the Court said, controlled the matter. Over the past few decades, however, per curiam opinions have often been much longer—that sustaining the constitutionality of most but not all of the Federal Election Campaign Act of 1971 ran to 138 pages, with an appendix that added another 90 (*Buckley* v. *Valeo,* 1976). If it takes that much space to explain the resolution of an issue, it can hardly have been settled before the Court spoke. Under such circumstances, a per curiam opinion probably indicates only that the opinion reflects, even more than is typically true, the work of a group of justices rather than a single author. Moreover, recent per curiam practice frequently involves equally long dissents and concurring opinions.

More generally, separate opinions are normal aspects of the common-law tradition; and these individual opinions sometimes propel barbed attacks on the likely effects of a decision, as well as on the majority's logic. Justice Brennan's dissent in *Paul* v. *Davis* (1976) branded the majority's opinion as "inconsistent with our prior case law," "dissembling," using "irrelevant" arguments, proceeding "by mere fiat and with no analysis," and "frightening for a free people." The decision was, he added, "a saddening denigration of our majestic Bill of Rights" and "a regrettable abdication" of the Court's role in "providing a formidable bulwark against governmental violation of constitutional safeguards securing in our free society the legitimate expectations of every person to innate human dignity and sense of worth."

In one sense, publication of a separate opinion is an appeal to history—and sometimes it turns out to be a successful appeal, for, when later justices review similar cases, they may find the minority's reasoning more convincing than the majority's and overrule the previous case. Such an overruling does not usually affect the earlier litigants, but it does mean the Court will no longer apply the principles controlling that decision.

The whole intra-Court process encourages negotiation, even bargaining of a sort. The justice who refuses to compromise seldom writes for the Court in important cases. Strong-willed, intelligent, experienced people usually have powerful views of their own and are not likely to be awed by colleagues. Sometimes the price of compromise is high. Oliver Wendell Holmes complained that "the boys generally cut one of the genitals" out of his opinions. Although he accepted such surgery with good humor, other justices have refused, allowing the case to be decided without an opinion of the Court.

A second factor encouraging compromise is the justices' knowledge that they will be working together over a long period. The average tenure on the Court is almost twenty years. The person who graciously concedes a point today can expect similar treatment tomorrow; just as the person who today refuses to compromise when in the majority can face a similar stonewall next week when he is in the minority.

Writing an opinion for the Court involves what Justice Felix Frankfurter called "an orchestral and not a solo performance." It puts a premium not only on good judgment and sound legal craftsmanship but also on skill in interpersonal negotiation—in short, on leadership rather than on command.

Scope of Judicial Power

"Scarcely any question arises in the United States," de Tocqueville observed in 1835, "that is not resolved, sooner or later, into a judicial question." That observation was, and remains, only partially accurate. American judges have been sufficiently astute to avoid most issues of foreign policy, and in domestic policies, it is usually only government's action, not its inaction, that comes before judges. Still, what is left constitutes "a stately jurisdiction."

Partly because of the country's long history under the common law and its reliance on judicial lawmaking, legislators tend to speak in broad phrases, announcing general policy rather than carving specific regulations. More or less deliberately, they allow, and sometimes even invite, creative interpretation from judges and administrators.

Other factors reinforce this inclination. Fragmentation of power and diversity of interest groups make it difficult for Congress to enact politically significant legislation unless there are webs of compromises and sharings of benefits. What begins as a coherent attack on a problem often ends as a jumble of mutual accommodations of competing interests concealed through fuzzy language.

The constitutional document speaks in even more grandiose terms. It, too, is a bundle of compromises. Fundamentally, two different and not always compatible purposes compete for dominance within that basic law: providing for effective government and providing for limited government. As James Madison, the Constitution's principal architect, explained in the pamphlet *Vices of the Political System,* which he circulated shortly before the Constitutional Convention met, "The great desideratum of Government is such a modification of the sovereignty as will render it sufficiently neutral between the different interests and factions, to controul one part of the society from invading the rights of another, and at the same time sufficiently controuled itself from setting up an interest adverse to that of the whole Society." After the Convention, Madison described the two competing objectives as "combining the requisite stability and energy in government, with the inviolable attention due to liberty and the republican form."

A factor encouraging compromise is the justices' knowledge that they will be working together over a long period.

Thus, the framers tried to limit power at the same time as they conferred power. Restrictions operate both by the document's "thou shalt nots" and, even more important, Madison thought, by overlapping grants of power that require public officials to share authority. Article I, for instance, confers "all legislative powers" on Congress, while Article II gives the president an independent and influential role in the legislative process. Article II makes the president the chief executive, but Article I forces him to share executive authority with Congress.

Similarly, the Constitution's divisions of authority between the nation and states are less than clear. Article VI says that congressional acts "made in pursuance of" the Constitution are, like the Constitution itself, "the supreme law of the land"; and the so-called sweeping clause of Article I, Section 8, gives Congress power "to make all laws which shall be necessary and proper" to carry out any power the Constitution delegates to any branch of the national government. On the other hand, the Tenth Amendment reads, "The powers not delegated to the United States by the Constitution, nor prohibited by it to the States, are reserved to the States respectively, or to the people." In the context of the "necessary and proper clause," that restriction means nothing at all or else it means a great deal. The words themselves do not reveal the meaning.

Because of these crosscutting grants of power, seldom can one set of public officials try to act without arousing jealousy and suspicions among others. In sum, the American Constitution separates institutions, makes them share powers, and connects the interest of the officeholder with the power of the office. The system operates precisely as Madison claimed it would: it pits "ambition against ambition" and "power against power." Whether or not judges are natural arbiters of such political disputes and whether or not the framers intended judges to act in that capacity, in fact the Supreme Court has frequently played that role, deciding where the boundaries of power run, whether between state or nation or between the branches of the federal government.

Where rights of individual citizens are more immediately involved, judges are apt to be even more active. And the relevant constitutional clauses are no more precise. The Fourth Amendment, for instance, forbids only "unreasonable" searches and seizures; the Fifth and Fourteenth forbid the taking of "life, liberty, or property, without due process of law"; and the Eighth forbids "excessive bail" as well as "cruel and unusual punishments." The Ninth Amendment is the most general of all. It forms a counter-weight to the "sweeping clause": "The enumeration in the Constitution, of certain rights, shall not be construed to deny or disparage others retained by the people."

Broad public access to courts provides judges with frequent opportunities to interpret the Constitution, and the general terms of its clauses give judges a wide range of discretion in that interpretation. The charge of "government by judiciary" has echoed down the decades. Always critics allege that judges have "legislated." And always there is a considerable measure of truth in such assertions: Congress often refuses to be very precise in writing statutes and the Constitution speaks in what Ronald Dworkin refers to as broad "concepts rather than specific conceptions." The words of the constitutional document, Frankfurter once commented, "are so unrestricted by their intrinsic meaning or by their history or by prior decisions that they leave the individual Justice free, if indeed they do not compel him, to gather meaning, not from reading the Constitution, but from reading life" (p. 30).

Access to the Supreme Court

The Constitution limits the jurisdiction of national courts, including the Supreme Court, not only to the matters of federal law discussed earlier but also to "cases and controversies." These are words of art. To have a case or controversy, one must show that he or she is suffering or is in imminent danger of suffering a real injury to a legally protected right. This restriction means that federal courts are supposed neither to give advisory opinions nor adjudicate the rights and obligations of those, whether private citizens or governmental officials, who are not parties to the case being decided. (An opinion might say a great deal about the rights of others, but the actual decision will not bind them.) As the Supreme Court explained in *Massachusetts* v. *Mellon* (1923), "We have no power *per se* to review and annul acts of Congress on the ground that they are unconstitutional. That question may be considered only when the justification for some direct injury suffered or threatened, presenting a justiciable issue, is made to rest upon such an act."

There are four principal ways in which a person may bring a constitutional issue before a state or national court. First, when sued by another private citizen or by a governmental official the defendant may set up as a defense a claim that the statute, order, or treaty under which the plaintiff is proceeding violates some provision of the Constitution. Second, in a criminal prosecution, the defendant may use a similar defense, but one which may include an allegation that before the trial the police did not follow the procedures outlined in the Constitution. (It is by no means unknown for a person deliberately to violate a law that he or she believes is unconstitutional so as to provoke a criminal prosecution and then attack the provision's validity.)

Third, a litigant may directly challenge a governmental policy by asking a trial court to issue a declaratory judgment (a judgment that defines the legal rights of two parties who have a real dispute about those kinds of rights but does not order a specific action) and/or an injunction to protect a legal—here a constitutional—right. If the court is satisfied that the action complained of would violate such a right, the judge will issue the injunction. Fourth—and sometimes together with request(s) for a declaratory judgment and/or an injunction—a person may sue a public official for monetary damages because of allegedly unconstitutional action that has injured the plaintiff.

In all of these instances, a judge is supposed to interpret the Constitution and apply that interpretation in deciding the case. Nevertheless, American courts, especially the Supreme Court, shy away from constitutional issues. They do so partly because of the political checks on their power discussed below and partly because of the apparent anomaly of their position in a country that proclaims itself a democracy. As Justice Frankfurter once reminded an attorney during oral argument, "This Court reaches constitutional questions last, not first." Usually, if there is any way of disposing of a case without reaching constitutional problems, the justices will seize it.

In addition, especially if the person who instituted the suit is challenging the legitimacy of a governmental policy, the Court applies rather strict and extremely complex rules regarding what is called "standing to sue." The justices have created these rules to determine if the litigant not only meets jurisdictional criteria but also is asserting, in the context of a real controversy in which his or her personal rights are being injured or threatened with immediate injury, a question on which the Constitution authorizes courts to pass judgment.

If there is any way of disposing of a case without reaching constitutional problems, the justices will seize it.

Organized interest groups, like private citizens and public officials, may obtain access to judicial power. Under many circumstances, groups may be sued for civil damages or prosecuted under the criminal law, and they, too, may utilize the Constitution in their defense. Where the standing rules permit, associations may also sue in their own name. They may also assist someone who is already involved in litigation by paying court costs and lawyers' fees—which in the United States can bankrupt even the wealthy. Or, an organized group may ask a court to be heard as an amicus curiae. In addition, a group may actively recruit litigants who have standing to start a lawsuit, with the organization paying all expenses of litigation and directing the strategy.

Sources of the Supreme Court's Power

Max Weber, the great German sociologist, distinguished three "pure" types of authority: (1) legal, based on a set of normative rules accepted by the community as binding and the right of persons operating under those rules to issue commands; (2) traditional, "resting on an established belief in the sanctity of immemorial traditions and the legitimacy of the status of those exercising authority under them"; and (3) charismatic, resting on a peculiar personal magnetism, of being "touched with grace."

Like that of most governmental agencies that endure, the authority of the Supreme Court partakes of all three types of legitimacy. Legally, the justices base their authority on the specific words of the Constitution, most particularly Articles III and VI, and, what are to judges at any rate, the logical implications of those words. The justices' authority is also rooted in tradition in that they were, in the early days of the Republic, the heirs to a long line of common-law judges, men of some wisdom, wide discretion, and much power. In more modern times the justices have been able to reinforce that tradition by appealing to the record of great American jurists.

There is also more than a pinch of charisma behind judicial power. The notion of the judge as endowed with special talent for understanding the sacred and mysterious texts of the law, inscrutable to mere laymen in common-law systems—all enhanced by black robes and the templelike atmosphere that the architect of the Supreme Court's building (ably prodded by Chief Justice William Howard Taft, under whom planning began) succeeded in conveying—has contributed to a picture of judges as a group whom fate, if not the Deity, has set above the grit and grind of the world's ugliness.

The three specific sources of the Supreme Court's power depend on, and are related to, Weber's types of authority: its legal authority to interpret statutes and the Constitution, its prestige, and the system's need for an umpire. These are connected with each other. Without, for instance, a high level of prestige, it is improbable that the Court could fulfill its role as umpire; without authority to interpret the Constitution, it is likely the Court would lose some prestige. We should also note that these particular and more general sources of judicial power occur in the context of a blend of political theories, constitutionalism and democracy, that infuses the entire American political system. We shall look at the more specific sources and examine the underlying political theories.

STATUTORY AND CONSTITUTIONAL INTERPRETATION. As noted above, to be able to interpret statutes, especially where legislatures tend to speak in general rather than specific terms, bestows considerable power on the interpreter. Statutory interpretation had long become a routine function of British courts, and their judicial nephews in colonial America continued the practice. When it came into existence, the Supreme Court carried on such work as a matter of course. Particular interpretations might have aroused dismay or even anger, but the function itself was not controversial.

Constitutional interpretation poses entirely different problems. First of all, if Congress disapproves of the Court's interpretation of a statute, it need only enact a new one by a simple majority and secure the president's approval. Changing the Court's constitutional interpretation by amending the Constitution is much more complicated and difficult, however. Not only do opponents need a two-thirds vote in each house of Congress, they also need the approval of three-quarters of the states.

The cumbersomeness of the amending process vastly increases the importance of the question of who shall authoritatively interpret the Constitution. The text of the document is silent on this critical point. It does not mention any power of judges to invalidate an act of Congress or of the president. Neither does it, in so many words, authorize courts to strike down state statutes, although the argument that the words of Article VI plainly imply the latter power is compelling:

> This Constitution, and the Laws of the United States which shall be made in Pursuance thereof; and all treaties made, or which shall be made, under the Authority of the United States, shall be the supreme Law of the Land; and the Judges in every State shall be bound thereby, any Thing in the Constitution or Laws of any State to the Contrary notwithstanding.

In Section 25 of the Judiciary Act of 1789, the First Congress conferred on the Supreme Court jurisdiction to review and reverse state judges' interpretations of the Constitution. The justices asserted this prerogative during the 1790s, but it was not until *Fletcher* v. *Peck* (1810) that they actually held a state statute invalid.

Charges that Congress and the Court had usurped authority were both loud and frequent, with Thomas Jefferson being among the protesters. Before the Civil War, states' righters made persistent efforts to repeal Section 25, and occasionally state officials physically resisted the Court's orders. Although the Civil War should have put the issue to rest, after *Brown* v. *Board of Education* in 1954 eight southern state legislatures passed resolutions "nullifying" the Court's actions, and in 1957 the governor of Arkansas called out the national guard to prevent integration of a high school in Little Rock. President Eisenhower dismissed the guard and sent federal troops to execute the district judge's order.

Afterward, when the justices reviewed the case from Little Rock (*Cooper* v. *Aaron,* 1958), they reiterated what had long become accepted constitutional jurisprudence on the Court's relations with the states:

> The interpretation of the Fourteenth Amendment enunciated by this Court in the *Brown* case is the supreme law of the land, and Art. VI of the Constitution makes it of binding effect on the States "any Thing in the Constitution or Laws of any State to the Contrary notwithstanding." Every state legislator and executive and judicial officer is solemnly committed by oath taken pursuant to Art. VI. cl. 3 "to support this Constitution." . . . No state legislator or executive or judi-

cial officer can war against the Constitution without violating his undertaking to support it.

The question of the Court's authority to annul acts of president and Congress has even less basis in the constitutional document than its authority to review state action. *Marbury* v. *Madison* (1803) was not the first instance in which the justices had claimed such authority, but it was the first in which they offered a lengthy justification. That power, as it has evolved over time, is immense, though it remains controversial and limited.

PRESTIGE. Prestige can be a vital source of power. Because they do not command physical force, judges ultimately have to depend on the feeling that a party ought to obey a court's decision and that if one of the parties does not, then other public officials ought to use their power to compel obedience. Here charisma ties in with the claim to interpret the Constitution. "Among holy things," Walton Hamilton and Irene Till asserted, "likeness passes by contagion," and some of the Constitution's sacredness might have rubbed off on the justices. "Since the Constitution is America's covenant," Max Lerner has claimed, "its guardians are . . . touched with its divinity."

It is difficult, however, to gauge precisely how much (or little) prestige the Court actually enjoys. From time to time, scholars, journalists, lawyers, elected politicians, and judges themselves make statements about the Supreme Court's prestige. Unfortunately, there are few hard data to gauge the relative popularity of the Court in different periods. Some decisions irritate some groups, while those same decisions please yet others. The correlation between general public opinion and the noisy praise or condemnation of specific interest groups is doubtful. What does seem clear, is that if we were fully to believe what critics have been saying since 1789, the justices began with no prestige whatever and have fallen steadily in public esteem. With gentle irony, C. Herman Pritchett remarked that "the Supreme Court is not what it used to be, and what's more it never was."

Mass polling promises some clarification, but its use on a scientific basis goes no further back than the 1930s, and even since then, there has been scant sampling of public attitudes on judicial issues. One systematic study reveals some awareness of the Court's work. About 45 percent of national samples of voting-age adults in 1964, 1966, and 1975 could recall a recent Supreme Court action—names of cases were not asked. When a respondent could recollect a decision, it was likely that he or she disapproved of what the Court had done. Yet more than two out of three of the people who had an opinion—including 40 percent of those who had expressed only critical views of particular decisions—thought that the Court was doing its basic job very well. This difference between criticism of individual decisions and approval of the Court as an institution indicates that the justices have a reservoir of public support on which they can draw in emergencies. Other surveys of practicing attorneys and professional politicians, as well as views expressed by better-educated people in national samples, indicate that this support runs deep and is widely shared among those who might be identified as political activists and opinion leaders.

Yet three pieces of evidence from this study imply that the justices' reservoir of public support is not unlimited. First, and perhaps most significant, replies showed emotions ranging from respect, admiration, and approval, on the one hand, to disapproval, anger, and contempt, on the other. But there was no evidence of adulation that would remotely imply automatic acceptance of decisions.

Second, variations in evaluations of the Court were closely associated with respondents' overall political views, usually lumped under liberalism and conservatism. This connection indicates a complex relationship. In part, public approval of certain policies may be due to Supreme Court decisions—which is another way of saying that the Court's rulings about the constitutionality of public policies can affect the way people evaluate those policies. But, because the Court's decisions are not the only factors influencing public attitudes, this connection may also mean that certain kinds of decisions can severely drain the Court's reservoir of support and that, as general political attitudes change, so may those toward the Court if the Court's rulings do not change in the same direction as public opinion.

Third, a large portion of the public either is unaware of the Court's work or so slightly aware as to be unable to answer simple questions. As a result, we do not know how deeply, if at all, the support of this silent minority runs. Moreover, ignorance or apathy may occur among those who benefit most from judicial decisions and whose political support the Court would most need in time of crisis. In the mid-1960s, for example, one would have expected blacks to be among the most ardent defenders of the Court, and so knowledgeable blacks were. But proportionately far fewer blacks than whites had much knowledge of the Court in particular or politics in general.

THE NEED FOR AN UMPIRE. We have already discussed a third source of judicial power: a federal system that divides power among state and national units of government, denies some power to each, and then further fragments power among units of the national government needs some kind of umpire. Governmental officials may also need the Court to help legitimize controversial decisions. In a pluralistic society any important public policy is likely to hurt the interests of many individuals and groups. Opposition will be based in part on the wisdom of a policy; but, especially when a broadly worded constitutional clause is involved, challenges to the policy's validity will occur.

To survive, every governmental structure must provide means of quieting basic constitutional doubts of this kind. In American politics the campaign speech, the ballot box, and the constitutional amendment may perform this legitimizing function, and as the discussion of the Court and public opinion indicated, so may a judicial decision. In fact, the justices are far more likely to declare a contested congressional act constitutional than unconstitutional. From 1789 to 1986 the Supreme Court invalidated federal laws in only 111 instances.

Limitations on Supreme Court Power

TECHNICAL CHECKS. A series of interlocking restrictions limit the Supreme Court's power. As judges, the justices must follow certain formal procedures. These are flexible, but not infinitely so. First and most important, judges lack a self-starter. Unlike administrators, judges cannot initiate action. Someone must bring a case to them and in a form that meets jurisdictional and standing requirements. The justices can, for instance, sustain the conviction of a brutal sheriff under a civil rights law, but they cannot start such a prosecution themselves.

A second restriction limits the effect of a decision. A judicial order legally obligates only the parties to that case, those who cooperate with them, and those who succeed to their office or status. A decision that the legislature of Tennessee is gerrymandered does not, of itself, legally oblige the government of any other state, even one using exactly the same representational formula. A separate suit must be brought, although the existence of the first judgment might well move the second state to act on its own.

Federal statutes and those of most states now allow a suit called a class action, a procedure that allows one litigant or a small group of litigants to sue for themselves and all others similarly situated. These kinds of options widen access to the courts, but the resulting order still binds only the specific defendants in the case. With this much said, however, the real, as contrasted with the technical, reach of any ruling by the Supreme Court is likely to be wide. As soon as a decision is announced, governmental officials, leaders of interest groups, and even private citizens are apt to use the general principles in the Court's opinion as legal weapons in fresh lawsuits or moral weapons in other arenas of policymaking.

Judges are also restricted in the kinds of orders they can issue. In general, they can far more easily forbid action than they can command action, especially where public officials are involved. The justices can hold a civil rights statute or social security law constitutional, but they cannot compel Congress to pass such a statute. To be sure, sometimes they can loosely interpret existing statutes and surprise members of Congress by discovering more policy than legislators thought they had set. In 1956, for example, Representative Howard Smith, author of the Smith Act, which punishes advocacy of violent overthrow of the United States government, expressed stunned disbelief at the Court's decision in *Pennsylvania* v. *Nelson* that this statute forbids states to adopt similar laws to protect the United States. Still, one should not be misled: Despite occasional opportunities to reap a bigger harvest than Congress has thought it has sown, limitations on the kinds of orders a court can issue are very real.

About 45 percent of voting-age adults could recall a recent Supreme Court action.

PUBLIC OPINION. If the Court draws much of its power from public esteem, popular attitudes can also check judicial power—unless the public considers the Court incapable of error, and as we have seen, there is no evidence of such adulation. Like the Lord, the public taketh away as well as giveth, and it may act considerably more capriciously than the Deity.

INTERNAL RESTRICTIONS. The justices are also limited by their own and others' ideas of how they, as judges, ought to act. Because they come to the bench after a long period of legal training and usually a far longer period of apprenticeship in public service, the justices probably have absorbed many prevailing norms about judicial action. These norms may be vague, yet they do broadly distinguish between behavior perfectly proper for legislators and administrators but improper for judges. For instance, a legislator who, when faced with a difficult decision about how to vote on a bill, consults with experts would be looked on as imaginative and enterprising. In contrast, a judge who discusses a pending case with a person not a member of the court or his or her staff, such as a law clerk, unless attorneys for both sides are present, is skirting, and probably crossing, the edge of unethical conduct.

In addition, the justices cannot help being aware that they are appointed officials serving what amounts to life terms in a government that is in many respects democratic. The apparent oddity of this situation has caused justices to hesitate to substitute their own judgment for that of popularly elected officials.

INSTITUTIONAL LIMITATIONS. The simple fact that the Supreme Court is staffed by nine justices constitutes a further check. To hear a case requires a vote of four members, and to decide it requires five votes. Since nine is an uneven number, one might expect clear-cut decisions in all cases where every justice sat; but complex litigation often presents more than two options.

Furthermore, for an opinion to be labeled that of the Court, it must win the assent of a majority of the justices. It is no easy matter to persuade five or more justices to agree on a closely reasoned document based on controversial assumptions of political philosophy that may have immediate as well as long-term effects on public policy. The Court's internal procedures make it likely that a justice who is determined to write exactly as he or she wishes will write for himself or herself alone.

There are ample incentives and sanctions for bargaining within the Court. A justice's main incentive is to enshrine as those of the Supreme Court of the United States the principles he or she thinks best cover this and similar situations. The major sanction available to the opinion writer is to ignore a colleague's wishes—if he or she can still muster five votes. The sanction of those who disagree is to write separate opinions and persuade other justices to join them or to appeal to history to vindicate them.

The effectiveness of either sanction depends on the closeness of the vote and the intellectual powers of individual justices. A 5–4 division puts the opinion writer at a considerable disadvantage in dealing with other members of the majority, just as an 8–1 judgment gives the writer great latitude. So, too, a threat to circulate a separate opinion means much more from a Holmes or a Brandeis than from a less skillful judge.

That the Supreme Court rarely makes either the first or the final decision in a case imposes another set of institutional checks. As noted above, the Court's jurisdiction is almost totally appellate. It reviews a lower-court decision, reverses or affirms it, writes an opinion explaining the principles behind choices, and usually sends ("remands") the case back to the court where it began for final disposition. Thus, like the president, the justices operate through a bureaucracy, but they have even less control over their bureaucracy than does the president over his. The justices can exercise very little influence in appointing, retaining, or promoting lower federal judges and probably none whatever in state judicial selection.

The sheer volume of business, the frequency with which new issues arise, the generality of many legal rules, and the compromises within the Court that may have further blurred concepts and language mean that the justices are at most leaders of their branch of government, not its masters. The analogy of bureaucracy—judicial or administrative—to international politics, where independent and semi-independent leaders negotiate, is apt. The military model of disciplined subordinates saluting and unquestioningly carrying out orders is one that presidents and justices may sorely envy but never see.

POLITICAL RESTRAINTS. The Supreme Court can interpret statutes and executive orders; it can even declare them unconstitutional. These are great powers, but Congress and the president have weapons they can turn against the justices. Impeachment may be, as Jefferson branded it, "a scarecrow," but Congress can, and has, changed the number of justices, withdrawn some of the Court's appellate jurisdiction (although how much it can validly withdraw remains an open question), denied funds to execute decisions, enacted new statutes to "correct" judicial interpretations of old law, and proposed constitutional amendments to counter the effects of a judicial decision, as the Fourteenth, Sixteenth, and Twenty-sixth Amendments did, or even to strike at judicial power itself, as the Eleventh Amendment did.

During Jefferson's administration, Congress abolished a whole tier of federal courts and turned the judges out without salaries.

During Jefferson's administration, Congress, although its action was flagrantly unconstitutional, abolished a whole tier of federal courts and turned the judges out without salaries. After the Civil War, when the justices seemed ready to uphold individual rights against the martial law that formed the heart of Radical Republicans' plans for the South, several Radical legislators threatened to abolish the Supreme Court itself, arguing that while the Constitution called for "one supreme Court," it did not command that there always be "one and the same Supreme Court."

For his part, the president may refuse to enforce judicial decisions. Jefferson and Lincoln were prepared to do so, and Andrew Jackson actually did refuse. They argued that the president was independent of the Supreme Court. As Jackson put it in 1832 in a message drafted by Roger Brooke Taney, who would soon succeed Marshall as chief justice,

> Each public officer who takes an oath to support the Constitution swears that he will support it as he understands it, and not as it is understood by others. . . . The opinion of the judges has no more authority over Congress than the opinion of Congress has over the judges, and on that point the President is independent of both.

Today it is unlikely that a president would openly defy the Court unless he were extraordinarily popular or Congress and public opinion perceived the Court as extraordinarily wrong in its decisions. These qualifying clauses mean that there are important limits on the Court's power. Moreover, although a situation like Little Rock in 1957 when Eisenhower used federal troops rarely occurs, it is not uncommon for the Court to need at least the president's tacit acquiescence in executing its rulings.

The president has other weapons. If he decides to do battle with the justices or merely to drag his heels, he can pardon his subordinates or anyone else convicted of criminal contempt of court for disobeying judicial orders.

Selection of new justices gives the president an additional opportunity to influence future decisions, as it does senators in confirming or rejecting a nominee. The president can also try to persuade Congress to use any of its powers against the Court, and like senators and representatives, he can draw on his own prestige to attack the justices.

Although the national-supremacy clause of Article VI of the Constitution puts state officials on a lower level than federal officers, state officials can still challenge the Court. They, too, can pass new statutes or issue fresh orders to force apparent winners back to court for additional and expensive litigation. Like federal officials, state officers may try to undermine the justices' prestige. And because the decentralized structure of both political parties makes presidents, senators, representatives, and even federal administrators to some, and often a great, extent dependent on local politicos, state officials may pressure federal officials to oppose Supreme Court decisions. Efforts to impede implementation of the Court's rulings regarding segregation and school prayers demonstrate how effectively states may retard judicial action.

The Supreme Court in a Constitutional Democracy

Earlier we referred to an apparent anomaly that affects judges' estimates of the way they should function in the American system of government. In a somewhat perverse sense, this anomaly, properly understood, helps explain both some of the Court's power and some of the psychological limitations on that power.

Many United States officials frequently and vociferously proclaim that their nation is a democracy, with a government chosen by, operating for, and responsible to the people. Yet the justices of the Supreme Court, like most federal judges, serve for what amounts to life tenure and are not elected. More significantly, the power they exercise in nullifying decisions of Congress, the president, and elected state officials, while not unlimited, is still immense. It would seem that the judiciary—and the Supreme Court in particular—is incongruent with the rest of the political system.

Indeed, the argument is sometimes made that judges should not have the power of judicial review at all or, even if it is legitimately theirs, they should exercise it only to keep democratic processes open. That is, they should only protect the rights to speak, publish, assemble, vote, and ensure the right to equal treatment by government for minorities who lack significant representation in policymaking bodies.

These arguments, no less than the proclamations of many public officials, fundamentally mistake the nature of the polity. It is not a democracy, not even a representative democracy. Rather, like most nations of Western Europe and like Japan since the end of World War II, the United States is a political hybrid, a "constitutional democracy." Formal political structures and the ideas on which they are based combine, on the one hand, popular rule by elected representatives and, on the other, limited government. The notion that the people should govern through those whom they elect blends—sometimes lumpily—with the notion that there are critical limitations on both what government can do and how it can carry out its authority.

Although the American political system's failings by either democratic or constitutionalist standards have been frequent and obvious, when viewed as a constitutional democracy, that system takes on more logical coherence. Popular election of senators, representatives, presidents, and their counterparts at the state level—and often at the state level of judges as well—combines with protection of the freedoms of speech, press, and assembly and a right to vote to meet, albeit far from perfectly, the institutional criteria for representative democracy.

On the other hand, federalism and equal representation of states in the Senate; staggered terms of office for presidents, senators, and congressmen; sharings of power among governmental departments; removal of some matters, such as religious belief, from all governmental control; requirements that government accord those suspected of crime certain procedural rights; and judicial review to allow nonelected officials to oversee these provisions, all reflect constitutionalist theory.

The Court, then, is limited in its power, not only by a series of institutional checks but also by gnawing reminders from democratic theory that appointed officials should be silent on many questions of public policy. On the other hand, not only the Court's institutional sources of power but also reminders from constitutionalism that human dignity and autonomy take precedence over transient popular demands make the justices important political actors.

In this intellectual and institutional context, the Court plays a series of critical roles in formulating national goals and ideals as well as more specific public policies. First, as a successor to common-law courts, it operates within a system accustomed to much judicial discretion and, in the common-law tradition, interprets and applies rules and decides specific cases falling within its jurisdiction. Although usually these cases directly involve only a few people, the principles the Court announces—such as that racial segregation has no valid place in public education or that "one person, one vote" is a constitutionally mandated requirement for electoral districting—can affect the entire nation.

Second, in interpreting the Constitution, the justices define boundaries of authority between governmental institutions and between government and individual citizens, and those rulings might also affect the entire citizenry. In a third and related fashion, in interpreting the broad concepts of the Constitution and the often equally open-ended terms of statutes, the Court must legislate. If the constitutional document does not and if Congress and the president will not formulate specific rules, that task falls to judges.

Fourth, as the head of a national judiciary, the Supreme Court must also oversee the administration of justice in that system, a duty imposed by statute as well as by logical inference from a hierarchical arrangement. Fifth, because of expectations about the composition of the Court, it also performs a representative function. It does not represent in the sense of being "chosen by" but in the looser sense of being "chosen from." Obviously, a group of nine cannot be a cross section of the population; but today, a bench composed of only white male Protestants would be as unthinkable as a bench staffed completely by men from the East was fifty years ago.

Sixth, as part of its constitutional interpretation, the Court also helps stabilize the larger political system. It offers a means of peaceful change that those who lost in the political processes may utilize to challenge the legitimacy of public policies that touch on their vital interests. Sometimes the challengers win, and that chance makes the Court an attractive alternative to violence or to abandoning the political system. More often, the challengers lose, and the Court affirms the legitimacy of the policy and the system's normal rules for making policy. But even that decision may help cool the losers' resentment and quiet their objections.

In all of this work, the Court performs its seventh and most important function: It educates. Its decisions and opinions directly instruct the litigants, other judges, members of the legal profession, public officials, and those who follow the Court's work closely. Indirectly, insofar as news of the Court's rulings infiltrates mass media of communication and finds its way into writing and thinking about politics, the Court teaches the rest of the country. The real substance of the message relates not to technical matters of law but to visions of American society, its ideals and goals and means that are congruent with those ends. That the justices may perform this or any of their functions well or poorly may change the amount and direction of their influence; but their potential for shaping the country's present and future is an integral part of the political system.

[See also (II) Separation of Powers; (III) Federal Court System, Judicial Review, Judiciary, Jurisdiction.]

CASES

Brown v. Board of Education of Topeka, 347 U.S. 483 (1954)
Buckley v. Valeo, 424 U.S. 1 (1976)
Cooper v. Aaron, 358 U.S. 1 (1958)
Fletcher v. Peck, 6 Cranch 87 (1810)
Herb v. Pitcairn, 342 U.S. 117 (1945)
Marbury v. Madison, 1 Cranch 137 (1803)
Massachusetts v. Mellon, 262 U.S. 447 (1923)
Paul v. Davis, 424 U.S. 693 (1976)
Pennsylvania v. Nelson, 350 U.S. 497 (1956)
Roe v. Wade, 410 U.S. 113 (1973)

BIBLIOGRAPHY

Henry J. Abraham, *The Judicial Process* (1980), offers a general introduction that helps put the Supreme Court in the context of a larger judicial system. Jesse H. Choper, *Judicial Review and the National Political Process* (1980), attempts in this interesting but controversial effort to prescribe a set of functions for the Supreme Court "proper" to the political system. Edward S. Corwin, *Liberty Against Government* (1948), written by the dean of American constitutional scholars, explores the idea of limited government and its role in American constitutional development. Archibald Cox, *The Role of the Supreme Court in American Government* (1976), presents a set of introductory lectures about the Court, originally given to a British audience.

David J. Danelski, "The Influence of the Chief Justice in the Decisional Process," in Walter F. Murphy and C. Herman Pritchett, eds., *Courts, Judges and Politics* (1985), gives a close analysis of the capacity of the chief justice to shape the Court's course. Ronald Dworkin, *Taking Rights Seriously* (1977), probes the problems of judicial decision-making in general and constitutional interpretation in particular. John Hart Ely, *Democracy and Distrust* (1980), presents an elegant but controversial effort to carve out a more limited set of functions for the Supreme Court than those prescribed by Choper. Felix Frankfurter, *Law and Politics,* edited by E. F. Pritchard, Jr., and Archibald MacLeish (1962), contains a series of insightful articles that the justice wrote while a professor at Harvard. Paul A. Freund and Stanley N. Katz, eds., *History of the Supreme Court of the United States* (1971–), was financed by a gift from Justice Oliver Wendell Holmes to the United States; as of early 1985 six of the projected nine volumes had been published: vol. 1, covering the years from 1789 to 1801, by Julius Goebel, Jr. (1971); vol. 2, 1801–1815, by George Haskins and Herbert A. Johnson (1981); vol. 5, 1835–1864, by Carl B. Swisher (1974); vols. 6–7, 1864–1868, by Charles Fairman (1971 and 1985); vol. 9, 1910–1921, by Alexander M. Bickel and Benno Schmidt, Jr. (1984).

M. Judd Harmon, ed., *Essays on the Constitution of the United States, 1978* (1978), has assembled a collection of lectures by leading scholars on the work of the Supreme Court in interpreting the Constitution. Robert G. McCloskey, *The American Supreme Court* (1960), presents an excellent, though brief, history of the Court through the early years of the Warren Court. Alpheus Thomas Mason, *Harlan Fiske Stone* (1956), a premier scholar's classic judicial biography, has become the model for such studies, and perhaps more than any other single work, it illuminates the Court not only during the critical years 1925–1946 but more generally as an institution. Walter F. Murphy, *Congress and the Court* (1962), uses a case study to analyze efforts in the 1950s to curb the Supreme Court; and *Elements of Judicial Strategy* (1964), analyzes the Court's place in the political system by utilizing the private papers of several justices. Walter F. Murphy, James E. Fleming, and William F. Harris, II, *American Constitutional Interpretation* (1986), presents an overall view of constitutional interpretation and the varying roles of the Supreme Court and other institutions in those processes. Walter F. Murphy and C. Herman Pritchett, eds., *Courts, Judges, and Politics* (1985), presents a collection of cases, articles in professional journals, and essays by the editors outlining the political functions of judges in the American political system. Walter F. Murphy and Joseph Tanenhaus, "Patterns of Public Support for the Supreme Court," in *Journal of Politics,* 43 (1981), is a systematic study of public attitudes and awareness.

David M. O'Brien, *Storm Center: The Supreme Court in American Politics* (1986), updates and goes beyond Murphy's *Elements of Judicial Strategy.* Lewis F. Powell, Jr., "What Really Goes On at the Supreme Court," in *American Bar Association Journal,* 66 (1980), describes the internal operations of the Court and implicitly denies some of the allegations in the book by Woodward and Armstrong cited below. C. Herman Pritchett, *The Roosevelt Court: A Study in Judicial Politics and Values, 1937–1947* (1948) and *Civil Liberties and the Vinson Court* (1954), two path-breaking studies, reveal the decision-making process of the Supreme Court, as well as the Court's roles in the political system. John R. Schmidhauser, *The Supreme Court* (1960), gives a collective portrait of the justices. Bob Woodward and Scott Armstrong, *The Brethren* (1979), discloses an "inside" account of the Court's workings from 1969 to 1976, heavily based on gossip among, and leaks from, law clerks, some of which are accurate.

– WALTER F. MURPHY

SUPREME COURT'S WORK LOAD

With the growth of population and the enormous expansion of federal law in the post-New Deal period, the business of the federal courts has mushroomed. This increase is most striking in the first two tiers of the federal judicial pyramid. In the years 1960–1983, cases filed in United States District Courts more than tripled, from 80,000 to 280,000, but cases docketed in the United States Courts of Appeals during the same period increased eightfold, from 3,765 to 25,580. To cope with this rise in appeals, Congress more than doubled the number of appellate judgeships. Not surprisingly, a similar growth can be found in Supreme Court filings: decade averages have increased in units of a thousand, from 1,516 per term in the 1950s to 2,639 in the 1960s, to 3,683 in the 1970s, to 4,422 in the 1981 term and 4,806 in the 1988 term.

The time allotted for oral argument

is thirty minutes on each side,

and additional time is rarely granted.

The contrast between this explosion in federal judicial business and the fixed decisional capacity of the Supreme Court—the nine Justices sitting as a full bench hear an average of 150 argued cases per year—has led to persistent calls for enhancing the appellate capacity of the federal system. A number of proposals have emerged since 1970, none resulting in legislation. In 1971 the Study Commission on the Caseload of the Supreme Court, chaired by Paul A. Freund of the Harvard Law School, recommended creation of a National Court of Appeals (NCA) that would assume the Supreme Court's task of selecting cases for review. The Freund committee believed that the selection process consumed time and energy the Justices might better spend in deliberation and opinion writing. This proposal died at birth. In 1972, Congress created the Commission on Revision of the Federal Court Appellate System, chaired by Senator Roman Hruska. The Hruska commission envisioned a mechanism for national resolution of open intercircuit conflicts, recommending an NCA that would hear cases referred to it by the Supreme Court or the United States Courts of Appeals. This NCA was to be a permanent tribunal, with its own institutional identity and personnel. In 1983, Chief Justice Warren E. Burger publicly endorsed proposed legislation to create on an experimental basis an Intercircuit Tribunal of the United States Courts of Appeals (ICT), which would decide cases referred to it by the Supreme Court. The ICT would be comprised of judges drawn from the current courts of appeals who would sit for a specified number of years. This proposal drew faint support.

Other proposals have sought to enhance national appellate capacity without establishing new tribunals. The most recent recommendation of this type can be found in the 1990 report of the Federal Courts Study Committee, chaired by Judge Joseph F. Weis, Jr. The report urges Congress to give the Supreme Court authority, for an experimental period, to refer cases presenting unresolved intercircuit conflicts to a randomly selected court of appeals for a ruling by that court's full bench. These en banc determinations would be binding on all other courts, save the Supreme Court.

Many of these proposals are conceived as measures to alleviate the Supreme Court's work load. The work load problem is, however, not one of obligatory jurisdiction; the Court's appellate jurisdiction has been largely discretionary as far back as the Judiciary Act of 1925, but even more so after 1988 legislation repealing virtually all mandatory appeals. The Justices do have to screen all of the petitions filed. It is doubtful, though, that any of the recent proposals promise much relief on this score. The Freund committee's NCA did, but received widespread criticism for suggesting delegation of

With the vast expansion of federal law in the aftermath of President Roosevelt's New Deal, the work load of the courts grew in direct proportion. (Library of Congress/Corbis)

the selection function. It is hard to believe referral to an NCA or a randomly selected court of appeals would reduce the Court's screening burden, for the losing party would still be free to appeal to the High Court. Moreover, the Justices will not likely tolerate nationally binding resolutions with which they disagree. Indeed, the Court's case selection process may be significantly complicated by adoption of any of these proposals.

If the Court's overload is not a function of its mandatory jurisdiction and if its selection burden cannot be alleviated (under current proposals), what function is the Court failing to perform that it ought to perform?

Critics claim that the Court is unable to ensure uniformity in federal law, because 150 appeals a year must leave unresolved an intolerable number of intercircuit conflicts. The evidence for this contention is largely anecdotal, and what little empirical work exists is sharply contested in the literature. Significant disagreement exists as to what constitutes a "conflict." Are conflicts clear disagreements over a governing issue of law or simply different approaches to a legal issue that are capable ultimately of being reconciled? Much also depends on one's view of the costs and benefits of leaving particular conflicts unresolved for a time. Does the absence of a rule of inter-circuit stare decisis in the federal system reflect a deliberate policy of allowing disagreements to percolate? The continuing conflicts may aid the Court's selection process by highlighting legal issues requiring national resolution. Through the process of multicourt consideration, the conflicts may improve the final decision of the Supreme Court when it does intervene. Moreover, some conflicts do not require immediate resolution, because they involve questions of local procedure, or do not frustrate planning concerns of multicircuit actors, or are not capable of being exploited by litigant forum shopping.

A broader claim, one not dependent upon the incidence of intercircuit conflict, is also made: that the problem is fundamentally one of insufficient supervision of the panel rulings of the courts of appeals. That conflicts are appropriately left unresolved does not matter, the argument goes. Given the sheer number of appeals, the practical inability of many of the circuits to engage in en banc review, and the infinitesimal probability of Supreme Court review, the panels operate as a law unto themselves. This version of the case for enhancing appellate capacity does have some force. It is undeniable that the Court can no longer engage in the kind of direct oversight of the courts of appeals that was possible in the 1920s, when it reviewed one in ten appellate rulings.

Whether this inability to supervise creates a problem requiring new institutional arrangements is, however, debatable. At present the Supreme Court appears not to have on its docket enough cases warranting plenary review to fill its argument calendar. Moreover, whether the panels operate as such wayward institutions is not clear. Many a circuit has, for example, adopted a "mini" en banc procedure to ensure uniformity of law within the circuit and to promote reconciliation of intercircuit splits. Even if one concedes that the Supreme Court has a work load problem (or that there is a need for additional appellate capacity), will the oversight benefits of an additional layer of review in, say, another 150 cases outweigh the attendant costs? Or will these otherwise nationally binding rulings be irresistible candidates for immediate plenary review by the Supreme Court—and hence a new category of practically mandatory jurisdiction?

The expansion of federal judicial business is the result of an explosion in federal law. Creating new layers of appeals creates more law, but not law enjoying the peculiar finality of a Supreme Court resolution. Improvements can be made. They are more likely to be found, however, in legislation reducing forum choice in federal statutes and imposing sanctions for unwarranted appeals; better management by the courts of appeals of panel disagreements and a greater willingness to reconsider circuit law in light of developments elsewhere; and strategic deployment by the High Court of its scarce decisional resources.

BIBLIOGRAPHY

Baker, Thomas E. and McFarland, Douglas D. 1987 The Need for a New National Court. *Harvard Law Review* 100:1401–1416.

Estreicher, Samuel and Sexton, John E. 1986 *Redefining the Supreme Court's Role: A Theory of Managing the Federal Judicial Process.* New Haven, Conn.: Yale University Press.

Ginsburg, Ruth Bader and Huber, Peter W. 1987 The Intercircuit Committee. *Harvard Law Review* 100:1417–1435.

Posner, Richard 1985 *The Federal Courts: Crisis and Reform.* Cambridge, Mass.: Harvard University Press.

Strauss, Peter L. 1987 One Hundred Fifty Cases per Year: Some Implications of the Supreme Court's Limited Resources for Judicial Review of Agency Action. *Columbia Law Review* 87:1093–1136.

– SAMUEL ESTREICHER

T

TRIAL COURTS AND PRACTICE

Courts are public institutions whose principal purpose is to resolve legal disputes. With very few exceptions, all disputes (cases) coming before American court systems begin in a trial court. Because no appeal is made to a higher court in the vast majority of these cases, the decision of the trial court is usually the final decision. Thus, the functions performed by trial courts are crucial to the orderly administration of justice in American society.

The Functions of Trial Courts

The primary function of the trial court is to conduct trials. The trial is an adversarial process governed by regularized rules of procedures and evidence. The trial court resolves cases at trial by deciding disputed factual issues and applying legal rules. For most cases, the parties have the option of having the case tried by a judge (bench trial) or a judge and jury (jury trial). At a bench trial the judge decides the facts, determines the law applicable to the case, applies the law to the facts, and reaches a decision. At a jury trial the jury decides the facts and reaches a decision by applying the law to the facts but only after being instructed on the applicable law by the judge.

Besides conducting trials, trial courts perform other, equally important, functions. In approximately 90 percent of the criminal cases filed in American trial courts, for example, there is no trial. For those cases that are not dismissed, the factual issue—whether the accused is guilty of having committed the crime with which he or she is charged—is resolved by the accused person pleading guilty. In these cases, the trial court's sentencing function is predominant and is normally performed by the trial judge. (A notable exception in some states is jury sentencing in death-penalty cases.) In fixing sentence, the trial judge considers such factors as the nature of the crime and the background of the accused and imposes an appropriate sanction such as a fine or a prison term.

Trial courts also perform remedial functions in cases involving juveniles, family matters such as child-custody hearings, and the commitment of the mentally ill. In fashioning appropriate remedies in these cases, the trial court normally relies on information obtained through such sources as diagnostic examinations or social evaluations. The trial court also performs a remedial function when it issues an injunction to prevent a threatened wrong or injury.

In addition to their trial, sentencing, and remedial functions, trial courts are sometimes required to perform supervisory functions.

To perform these sentencing and remedial functions, trial courts are invested with a great deal of discretion. Because the exercise of this discretion often results in widely disparate sentences or remedies in apparently similar cases before different courts or even before different judges in the same court, trial courts have come under a good deal of criticism in recent years. To rectify this situation, trial courts have been urged to experiment with certain innovations that ostensibly would establish greater uniformity and equality of treatment of similar cases. Among the recommendations are the formulation of guidelines to be followed by judges in exercising discretion, the review of judicial dispositions by panels of other judges prior to making a disposition in a case. Such recommendations or reforms aimed at reducing trial-court discretion and achieving greater uniformity have not met with universal approval. David Neubauer, for example, worries that "there will not be as much flexibility in the system and not as much individualization of justice" (p. 486). This tension between trying to do uniform justice on the one hand and individualized justice on the other is a persistent concern in the literature on trial courts.

In addition to their trial, sentencing, and remedial functions, trial courts are sometimes required to perform what has been characterized as supervisory functions. As stated by the American Bar Association, these include "monitoring of adult probationers, juveniles under the court's wardship, persons under orders for care and treatment for mental conditions, children under custody orders, and control of the estates of decedents and incompetents over which the court has jurisdiction" (1976, 10). Normally, a trial court places great reliance on nonjudicial personnel, such as probation officers, to carry out these supervisory reponsibilities.

Since the mid-1950s, some courts have employed their remedial and supervisory functions in more expansive ways to deal with extended impact cases. Extended impact cases usually involve violations of individual rights in public institutions such as prisons, mental hospitals, and schools. To help them address the conditions that are violating these rights, judges often use individuals with special expertise or insight into the problem, called "special masters." In addition to assisting the court in fashioning an appropriate remedy—such as providing for additional facilities to relieve prison overcrowding—the special master often is called upon to assist the court in its supervisory role by monitoring compliance with the judge's remedial order.

The willingness of some trial-court judges to use the remedial and supervisory functions of their courts in extended impact cases has evoked considerable controversy. Those who oppose judicial intervention in these cases claim that the courts have usurped functions of the legislative or executive branch of government in directly intruding into the operations of state-run institutions. They also argue that trial courts have neither the expertise nor the resources to correct the alleged deficiencies. Those who favor judicial intervention claim that the courts must intervene to make up for the legislative- and executive-branch shortcomings that led to the problem in the first place.

In a broader sense, the controversy over the extent of judicial intervention in extended impact cases reflects a more general debate over the proper role and functions of the courts in American society. The Council on the Role of Courts identified a "traditionalist" view and an "adaptationist" view in this debate. Traditionalists are concerned that the functions of courts are expanding so much that soon courts will no longer be recognizable as such. The traditionalist "seeks to define the appropriate limits of court function within the traditional boundaries of the adversary process." The adaptationist, on the other hand, argues that the adjudicative functions of courts are more expandable and should be continually changing to accommodate the needs of a changing society.

In furtherance of their adjudicative (trial, sentencing, remedial, and supervisory) functions, trial courts perform administrative functions. Concern over burgeoning case loads and delay in America's trial courts since midcentury has led to a heightened awareness of these administrative functions and an increased emphasis on "case-flow management." Maureen Solomon has defined case flow as "the continuum of activities through which cases move within a court." In setting forth the elements of effective case-flow management, Solomon stresses that "commitment of the judges to *court control* of caseflow is the cornerstone upon which improvements in case processing can be built" (p. 30). For many trial courts the notion that the court, rather than the attorneys, should accept the primary responsibility for such management functions as scheduling cases and monitoring their progress was a new one. In many trial courts, for example, the local prosecutor traditionally assumed responsibility for scheduling criminal cases. More radical still were the suggestions that the trial courts adopt restrictive continuance policies, which would limit the parties' ability to postpone case-related hearings and the trial itself, and case-processing time standards. Yet, such case-flow management policies have been widely adopted in American trial courts in recent years largely in response to increased public pressure to reduce case delays and backlogs.

Some commentators have become concerned over this increased emphasis on judicial management. Judith Resnik raises the specter of the "managerial judge" and argues that overemphasis on a trial court's administrative responsibilities may have an adverse effect on its adjudicative functions. She is particularly concerned that trial judges may abuse their discretionary powers in restricting the amount of time that parties will be allowed to prepare their cases and in encouraging settlement of cases prior to trial at pretrial conferences with the parties.

Organization and Jurisdiction

Increased emphasis on the administrative functions of trial courts has been encouraged by structural and organizational changes in American court systems. Grouped under the general rubric of "court unification," these changes were developed and promoted by individual reformers such as Roscoe Pound and Arthur Vanderbilt and encouraged by various national commissions (American Bar Association, 1974; President's Commission on Law Enforcement and Administration of Justice, 1967; and National Advisory Commission on Criminal Justice Standards and Goals, 1973).

These reform proposals were prompted by an increasing concern during the first half of the twentieth century that the courts were inefficient, inaccessible, and unaccountable. Many reformers argued that these conditions were occasioned by the fact that in most states there was no semblance of an organizational or administrative scheme among the various courts. Shortcomings were most apparent at the local level, where the bewildering array of autonomous trial courts with overlapping jurisdictions made it difficult for citizens and lawyers alike to know where to bring certain kinds of cases. Before the judicial reforms in Illinois in 1964, for example, there were 208 separate courts in Cook

County (Chicago). Many judges ran their courts as little fiefdoms, treating those who came before them with a distinct lack of impartiality.

Proposals for the unification of court systems have been part of a larger movement during the twentieth century to make agencies of government more efficient and businesslike. Court unification calls for a centralized management scheme whereby overall administrative authority is vested in the highest appellate court with a chief or presiding judge exercising administrative control over a consolidated trial-court system in each judicial district. Arguably, such an arrangement would not only make judges accountable for their actions to others within the judicial hierarchy but would also lead to a heightened managerial consciousness within the judiciary, ultimately resulting in greater administrative efficiency.

Although many state court systems now have centralized administrative schemes, only a few have completely consolidated their trial courts into a single trial court of general jurisdiction. In this regard, the model of the state courts is the federal system, which employs a single-level trial court—the United States district court.

There are ninety-four federal trial-court districts. The size of the districts vary, depending on population and judicial business. The geographic jurisdiction of some of the federal trial-court districts is an entire state (for example, the United States District Court for the District of Maine), while others have jurisdiction over only a portion of a state (for example, the United States District Court for the Central District of California). The federal district courts hear both criminal and civil cases. Their criminal cases involve violations of federal criminal law, ranging from lesser offenses (misdemeanors) to more serious crimes (felonies). Many "white-collar crimes," such as crimes involving politicians or business executives for violations of tax or corporate securities laws, are heard in the federal trial courts.

There are several different types of civil cases that may be heard in the federal trial courts. These include cases involving diversity jurisdiction, federal questions, and suits against the federal government. "Diversity jurisdiction" cases involve those lawsuits between citizens of different states in which the amount in controversy is more than $10,000. These are cases in which there is an option between filing the case in a federal court or a state court. An example of a situation giving rise to a diversity jurisdiction case is one in which a resident of state A is driving through state B and is involved in an accident with a resident of state B. The resident of state A is given the option of suing in federal court to avoid any potential bias that a state court in state B might have in favor of a resident of its own state. "Federal question" cases are those arising under federal (rather than state) law, such as cases involving copyright or patent infringement. Finally, a common suit against the federal government would be one to establish or reinstate benefits under the social security laws.

The United States district courts exist side by side with the state trial courts. In other words, every locale in the United States is within the jurisdiction of at least two trial courts—one federal and one state. While all state court systems have a trial court of general jurisdiction that resembles the neighboring United States district court in certain operational respects (for example, regularized rules of procedure and evidence), most state court systems also have one or more trial courts of limited jurisdiction. The state trial courts of general jurisdiction are variously named district courts, circuit courts, superior courts, and courts of common pleas. The limited-jurisdiction courts, sometimes referred to as the "lower" or "minor" trial courts, are usually named county courts, municipal courts, city courts, justice of the peace courts, magistrate courts, and police courts.

On the criminal side of their dockets, the state trial courts of general jurisdiction generally handle cases involving felonies, while the trial courts of limited jurisdiction handle misdemeanors. Many limited-jurisdiction courts also perform a screening function for the general-jurisdiction trial courts by handling preliminary hearings in felony cases. The purpose of the preliminary hearing is to ensure that there is a good reason for holding the accused. At the preliminary hearing the prosecutor must show that there is probable cause to believe that a crime has been committed and that the person accused committed the crime.

The civil case loads of the state general-jurisdiction trial courts include a wide variety of case types. Some of the more common are automobile accident lawsuits, disputes over contracts, divorces, will contests, and suits challenging the actions of state or local agencies, such as zoning commissions or transportation authorities. Some of these lawsuits can be very complex and the trials can last for several weeks. There is no limit to the amount of money that a plaintiff can sue for in these courts. The civil jurisdiction of the limited-jurisdiction trial courts, on the other hand, is generally limited to cases involving lesser claims, most commonly where the amount in controversy is less than $5,000. Civil cases that are common in these courts include disputes between landlords and tenants and between consumers and local businesses.

The vast majority of the cases filed in state courts are handled by the limited-jurisdiction courts, with the great bulk of their case loads consisting of traffic cases.

The Council on the Role of Courts estimated that less than 2 percent of the cases filed in state trial courts actually go to trial. The vast majority of criminal cases are disposed of through guilty pleas or dismissals and most civil cases through settlements or default judgements (cases in which one of the parties fails to appear in court).

Although a much smaller number of cases are filed in the federal district courts than in the state trial courts, a higher percentage of the federal cases are tried.

Trial Courts of General Jurisdiction

In their handling of both civil and criminal cases, the state and federal trial courts of general jurisdiction follow specific, regularized practices at both the pretrial and trial stages. These regularized practices are known as rules of procedure and rules of evidence. Since their adoption in 1938, the Federal Rules of Civil Procedure have governed practice in the United States district courts and have served as a model for state court rules of civil procedure. The federal rules have been particularly influential in providing for simplified pleadings and broadened discovery.

The pleadings are the formal claims of the parties to a civil lawsuit. The parties, or litigants, to a civil lawsuit are referred to as the plaintiff (the person suing) and the defendant (the person being sued). In the federal trial courts and most state trial courts, a civil case is initiated or commenced by the plaintiff's filing a complaint with the court. The complaint contains the plaintiff's statements or allegations setting forth his or her claim against the defendant. The defendant is advised of the plaintiff's lawsuit against him or her when the defendant is served with a summons and a copy of the complaint. In many states, the local sheriff delivers the summons to, or "serves process on," the defendant. In other states, private process servers are commonly used.

After being served with the complaint, the defendant may attack the plaintiff's complaint for errors of either form or substance. In states using what is known as code pleading, the defendant attacks the complaint for errors of form by means of a special demurrer. The defendant may, for example, object that the complaint is too vague or ambiguous. Under the federal rules, the corresponding procedural device to the special demurrer is the more descriptive "motion to make more definite and certain." If the defendant detects an error of substance in the complaint, a general demurrer would be used to attack the complaint in a code-pleading state, but a "motion to dismiss for failure to state a claim on which relief may be granted" would be used in a trial court operating under the federal rules or their equivalent. An example of an error of substance would be the failure to allege in a contract dispute that the defendant breached (broke) the contract by his or her actions.

Motions are requests by either the plaintiff or the defendant that the trial court do something. They are used throughout the pretrial and trial stages of a lawsuit. With the motion to dismiss for failure to state a claim on which relief may be granted, for example, the defendant is asking the trial court to end the lawsuit at this early stage because the plaintiff has made substantive errors in the complaint. If the trial court rejects (overrules) this motion (general demurrer) but accepts (sustains) the motion to make more definite and certain (special demurrer), the court may allow the plaintiff to amend the complaint to correct its errors.

State trial courts of general jurisdiction are variously named district courts, circuit courts, superior courts, and courts of common pleas.

The defendant responds to the allegations in the plaintiff's complaint in an answer, which is the pleading used by the defendant to admit some of the facts alleged in the complaint and to deny others. The defendant may also set forth affirmative defenses in the answer. These are additional facts that would prevent the plaintiff's recovery even if all the facts in the complaint could be proven. Affirmative defenses in a case in which the plaintiff is suing to enforce a contract, for example, might be the defendant's allegation that he entered the contractual relationship under duress or was induced by the plaintiff's fraud. The plaintiff's alleged fraud might also form the basis of a counterclaim, by which the defendant seeks to recover from the plaintiff in the same lawsuit.

Just as the defendant has the right to attack the complaint, the plaintiff may attack the answer by means of a demurrer or the equivalent federal-rules motion. The plaintiff may also refute allegations in the answer through the use of a third pleading known as a reply. In many jurisdictions the reply is seldom used, because the defendant's allegations in the answer are assumed to be denied by the plaintiff.

Because the allegations in the pleadings usually are stated in general terms and do not deal with the actual evidence that will be introduced at trial, federal and state procedural rules specify a process for finding out more about an opponent's case prior to trial. This process is called discovery. The federal rules of civil procedure and subsequently adopted state procedural rules have broadened the scope of discovery on the theory that arming each side with the relevant facts through pretrial disclosures would make the trial more of a search for truth and less of a sporting event.

The most frequently used discovery device is the deposition. Both the plaintiff and the defendant may take their opponent's deposition, which consists of answers to questions under oath. The questions are posed to the plaintiff or defendant by the opposing lawyer before a court reporter. The opponent may also be required to respond to interrogatories, or written questions asking the plaintiff or defendant for certain information, including the names and addresses of their witnesses. These witnesses may subsequently be deposed as well.

Broadened discovery, a welcome reform in the 1930s, was a cause of some concern by the 1980s. Studies and scholarly commentary have identified certain problems generally referred to as discovery abuse. These problems include the unnecessary use of discovery and the improper withholding of discoverable information, resulting in increased delay and expense to the litigants. Many of the United States district courts have experimented with local rules to improve the discovery process, such as imposing time limits on the discovery process, limiting the number of interrogatories, and calling for mandatory pretrial conferences.

The federal rules of civil procedure and many state rules provide for a pretrial conference. The lawyers for each side usually attend the conference in the judge's chambers. The conference affords an opportunity to discuss possibilities for settling the case without trial and, failing that, to get the case ready for trial. At the conference, the judge attempts to refine the issues, identify and decide points of law that might be raised at trial, and deal with other matters that can be decided beforehand.

Trial may also be avoided by seeking to have the judge grant a "motion for summary judgment." This motion asks the judge to decide that there is no need for a trial because there is no genuine issue of fact. It may be made any time after the complaint is filed.

Most civil cases may be tried before either a judge or a jury. If the demand for a jury trial is not made within the time limits specified in the court's rules, it is considered to be a waiver of the right to a jury trial. The jury trial begins with a jury-selection procedure known as voir dire. This process involves the questioning of the jurors by the lawyers or the judge. In some jurisdictions the jurors are examined during voir dire exclusively or primarily by the judge, while in other jurisdictions the lawyers conduct the voir dire examination. Some argue that judge-conducted voir dire is less time-consuming and more efficient than lawyer-conducted voir dire. They point in particular to well-publicized cases, in which it may take weeks to pick a jury because many potential jurors may be subjected to lengthy questioning by the lawyers and then excused for the reason that the news coverage before the trial may have prejudiced them against one of the parties. Trial lawyers, on the other hand, argue that the lawyers must be allowed to question the jurors to ensure that their clients' right to an unbiased jury is preserved.

Federal and state procedural rules specify a process—discovery—for finding out more about an opponent's case prior to trial.

If it appears during the questioning of a juror that the juror cannot fairly or impartially judge the case, the juror may be challenged for cause. In addition to being able to challenge a juror for cause, each party is allowed to exercise peremptory challenges which allow a party to excuse jurors without having to state a reason. Each side is allowed a specified number of peremptory challenges (for example, some states allow twelve in a noncapital felony case). Lawyers usually excuse jurors by peremptory challenge based on their intuition that the particular juror will not favor their client. However, many lawyers have recently been using social scientists to assist them in selecting juries. Usually, the social scientists conduct surveys of the local population to determine the characteristics of potential jurors who would be most sympathetic and those who would be least sympathetic toward their client.

The use of peremptory challenges has become a source of concern in criminal cases. Most notably, prosecutors have been criticized for apparently using peremptories to eliminate minorities from juries on the theory that they would be too sympathetic to minority defendants. Although the United States Supreme Court has condemned this practice, it has made it very difficult for a minority defendant to prove racial discrimination in the use of peremptories (*Swain* v. *Alabama,* 1965). In recent years, however, some state supreme courts and lower federal courts have established less burdensome criteria for finding racial discrimination.

Once the jury is selected, the trial begins with the opening statements of the lawyers. In the opening statement, the plaintiff's lawyer explains the plaintiff's case and tells what their evidence will show. The defendant's lawyer may follow with an opening statement or wait until after the plaintiff has introduced his or her evidence. In his case, the plaintiff must introduce evidence to prove the allegations in the complaint. A principal means of introducing evidence is to offer the testimony of witnesses. The process by which the plaintiff's lawyer questions the plaintiff's witnesses is known as direct examination. When the defendant's lawyer questions the plaintiff's witnesses, it is known as cross-examination.

During the direct examination or the cross-examination of a witness, the lawyer not engaged in the questioning of the witness may offer an objection to certain testimony. An objection is a device used by either lawyer to bring an impropriety to the attention of the trial court. The objection may focus not only on the actions of the opposing lawyer but also on the actions of a litigant, a juror, a witness, or even the judge. By objecting, the lawyer is asking the court to correct or prevent an impropriety that is adverse to the interests of the lawyer's client. In deciding whether to overrule or sustain the objection, the judge may first ask the lawyer to state the grounds on which the objection is based. Permissible grounds usually include violations of evidentiary rules, such as the attempted introduction of hearsay testimony or a privileged communication. Hearsay testimony reports an out-of-court statement that the witness overheard and although such statements are considered to be unreliable as a general rule, they often are allowed if they were overheard under exceptional circumstances. A privileged communication is one occurring between individuals whose confidential relationship the law recognizes as deserving of special protection, such as that between an attorney and a client. The lawyer may offer an objection for a number of reasons—to keep certain information from the jury, to modify the manner of questioning ("counsel is badgering the witness"), or even to gain a tactical advantage.

After the plaintiff has offered his evidence, the plaintiff rests his case. In effect, the plaintiff is saying that he has proved the case against the defendant and deserves a favorable verdict. The defendant, on the other hand, may believe that the plaintiff has failed to offer sufficient evidence and may ask for a *nonsuit* or, under the federal rules, move for a dismissal or a directed verdict (in a jury trial). This motion says that even if all the facts offered by the plaintiff are correct, the law would not permit the plaintiff to recover against the defendant.

In presenting the plaintiff's case to the judge or jury, the plaintiff's lawyer is seeking to meet the plaintiff's burden of producing ("going forward with") the necessary evidence. This means that the plaintiff must meet the burden of presenting enough evidence to avoid a motion for dismissal or a directed verdict. The plaintiff's evidence must establish an issue of fact that can be sent to the jury. If the plaintiff has accomplished this, the burden shifts to the defendant, so that the defendant must now establish his case.

If the judge denies the motion for a dismissal or directed verdict, the defendant will proceed with his case by offering evidence that refutes that of the plaintiff. The defendant will also offer evidence in support of affirmative defenses set forth in the answer or in support of a counterclaim. At the end of the defendant's case, either the defendant or the plaintiff may move for a dismissal or a directed verdict.

Throughout the trial, the plaintiff and defendant will be bound by the "rules of evidence," which set forth a method by which relevant information may be presented to the trier of fact (the judge or the jury). They deal with such problems as relevancy, privilege, hearsay, competency of witnesses, opinion testimony, expert testimony, impeachment of witnesses, and objections. In most jurisdictions, these evidence rules are an amalgam of case law and state statutes. The Federal Rules of Evidence, adopted in 1975, reflect well-established evidence principles and are applicable in both civil and criminal cases in the United States district courts.

In offering closing arguments, the plaintiff's lawyer once again goes first, followed by the defendant's lawyer. Both will stress the evidence that is most favorable to their side of the case and will seek to convince the jury that they have met their burden of proof. Sometimes referred to as the "burden of persuasion," the burden of proof becomes crucial at this stage of the trial. Each side must have persuaded the jury of its version of the truth of the disputed facts by a specified standard. In most civil cases, the standard is "a preponderance of the evidence." The plaintiff, for example, must have convinced the jury that the facts alleged in the plaintiff's complaint are more probably true than not. In criminal cases, the prosecution is held to a higher standard. The defendant's guilt must be established by the prosecution "beyond a reasonable doubt."

After counsel conclude their closing arguments, the judge instructs the jury on the law applicable to the case. In some jurisdictions, the judge may also summarize the evidence for the jury. The judge's instructions to the jury have often been criticized for being so steeped in legal jargon as to be virtually incomprehensible. Some states have recently tried to improve on this situation by creating "pattern instructions," uniform instructions that may be used in all the trial courts of the state and are written in understandable language. Some states also permit jurors to take copies of the instructions with them into the jury deliberation room. Those jurisdictions that allow individual jurors to take notes during the trial also allow them to bring their notes with them to the deliberation room. Note taking by jurors, however, has not met with widespread approval. Those that oppose note taking argue that the note taker will be distracted during the trial, will record irrelevant evidence, and will have too much influence in the deliberation room.

In civil cases, juries usually return from their deliberations with a general verdict, in which they indicate whether they are finding in favor of the plaintiff or the defendant and the amount that should be recovered in damages. Sometimes, the jury is asked to return a special verdict, whereby they are given a list of questions relating to the facts at issue that they must answer.

Even after the jury returns a verdict, the trial court may entertain motions. The most common posttrial motions are the motion for judgment notwithstanding the verdict—sometimes referred to by its Latin abbreviation, judgment n.o.v.—and the motion for a new trial. The motion for judgment notwithstanding the verdict is similar to both the motion for a directed verdict and the general demurrer in that it once again raises the question of the legal sufficiency of the evidence introduced by either side. The motion for a new trial, on the other hand, identifies procedural or evidentiary errors that took place during the trial and seeks a retrial that would avoid these allegedly prejudicial errors.

In criminal cases, the defendant's guilt must be established by the prosecution "beyond a reasonable doubt."

The Federal Rules of Civil Procedure and their state counterparts are inapplicable in criminal cases. Although there are important similarities between the procedures employed in the trial of criminal cases and those used in civil cases, there are also significant differences. Moreover, there is less uniformity in criminal procedure than in civil procedure across American jurisdictions. Criminal procedure has no analogue to the Federal Rules of Civil Procedure in terms of the scope of the influence of the civil rules. Indeed, more recently adopted rules of criminal procedure—such as the Federal Rules of Criminal Procedure, adopted in 1975—would appear to have been influenced at least in part by experience with the federal rules of civil procedure (for example, with respect to broadened discovery provisions).

Among the ways in which the criminal trial differs from the civil trial are the presumption of innocence, the requirement of proof beyond a reasonable doubt, the right of the accused not to take the stand, and the exclusion of evidence obtained by the state in an illegal manner. In other respects, the criminal trial is much like the civil trial, particularly with regard to the means of introducing evidence and making objections.

Until relatively recently, there were very few empirical studies of the operational realities of trial courts of general jurisdiction. However, empirical research on America's trial courts became a growth industry in the 1970s and 1980s. Most studies of trial courts have concentrated on their handling of criminal cases, because of the greater availability of federal and state research grants tied to the "war on crime."

Comparative studies of the handling of felony cases in different locales reveal significant differences in operating practices and substantive outcomes. Researchers have advanced various explanations for this diversity. Martin Levin focuses on differences in community politics and values to explain the diversity in sentencing severity in the trial courts in Pittsburgh and Minneapolis, while Eisenstein and Jacob develop the concept of the "courtroom work group" to help explain differences in adjudication and sentencing practices in the trial courts of Baltimore, Chicago, and Detroit. Work-group members include those with shared tasks and goals within the courtroom—prosecutors, defense attorneys, clerks, and bailiffs. In examining the ways in which the interactions of work-group members influence the outcomes of criminal cases, Eisenstein and Jacob introduce an organizational approach to studying trial courts.

The seemingly ageless concern over delay in the trial courts has also spawned studies that suggest new theoretical approaches. For example, Thomas Church and his associates attempt to explain differences in both civil and criminal case-processing time (delay) in large city trial courts by pointing to the "local legal culture." They argue that judges and lawyers in a particular locale become used to a certain pace of litigation and adapt themselves accordingly. Thus, local practices and expectations will have to be overcome in attempts to reduce delay. Included among recent delay-reduction innovations are simplification of procedural rules, improved case-flow management techniques, and technological innovations (for example, telephone conferencing and videotaping).

Managerial innovations have become increasingly important in handling the massive, complex cases that are becoming more prevalent in American trial courts. Because these cases often involve violations of the federal antitrust laws, they are more frequently litigated in the federal courts. Perhaps the most prominent example of complex litigation is the case brought by the United States government to restructure the American Telephone and Telegraph Company (AT&T) for alleged antitrust violations. The AT&T case lasted approximately eight years from filing to disposition and generated tens of millions of pages of documents. A key ingredient in managing this mammoth litigation was the federal judge's appointment of two special masters (lawyers acting as quasi-judicial officers) to assist in supervising certain aspects of the case, such as the discovery process, which involved more than five hundred document subpoenas and two hundred depositions. The case was settled in the eleventh month of trial.

Some believe that juries are not competent to handle such complex litigation. They argue that there should be a "complexity exception" to the right to a jury trial in civil cases. In a few recent cases, certain federal courts have denied a party's jury demand on complexity grounds and allowed the case to proceed without a jury. Although the United States Supreme Court has never upheld the denial of a jury demand, it has not foreclosed this possibility in future cases (*Ross* v. *Bernhard,* 1970).

Trial Courts of Limited Jurisdiction

Unlike the trial courts of general jurisdiction, the limited-jurisdiction trial courts handle large numbers of uncomplicated civil and criminal cases quickly. Delay is usually not seen to be a problem in these courts. Indeed, they are often criticized for processing cases too quickly and failing to give adequate consideration to the rights of those who come before them.

Approximately 75 percent of American courts are trial courts of limited jurisdiction. Sometimes referred to as the "inferior," "lower," or "minor" trial courts, they process the vast majority of cases, and are the average citizen's most frequent point of contact with the judicial system. However, in contrast to the trial courts of general jurisdiction, there has been relatively little attention paid to these courts by legal scholars and researchers.

In the forty-six states that have limited-jurisdiction courts, these courts are officially titled county courts, municipal courts, city courts, justice of the peace courts, police courts, magistrate courts, and district courts. A majority of states have more than one type of limited jurisdiction court. Although Idaho, Illinois, Iowa, Missouri, and South Dakota do not have limited-jurisdiction courts, these states include separate divisions or classes of judges in their general trial court to handle the kinds of cases normally handled by limited-jurisdiction courts. Within the federal court system, federal magistrates perform somewhat similar functions.

The principal business of the limited-jurisdiction trial court is the handling of misdemeanor cases. Indeed, states use the term *misdemeanor* most often to describe the criminal jurisdiction of the limited-jurisdiction court. Most states define a misdemeanor as an offense punishable either by imprisonment for less than one year or by imprisonment other than in a penitentiary.

In addition to misdemeanor cases, all of the limited-jurisdiction courts handle cases in one or more of the following areas: minor civil cases, felony preliminary hearings, traffic offenses, local ordinance violations, juvenile matters, and (in four states) certain felonies. Among the more common civil cases handled by the limited-jurisdiction courts are those involving disputes between landlords and tenants and between consumers and businesses.

Because most limited-jurisdiction trial courts are much less formal than general-jurisdiction courts and less likely to fit traditional notions of how a court of law should operate, they have frequently been criticized for providing "rough justice" or "assembly-line justice" (Robertson). However, some commentators have been more generous in their assessment of these courts. Susan Silbey explains that in being "more particularistic, empirical, individualized, and responsive to local communities" than the general-jurisdiction courts, the lower courts perform an important function as "official gatekeepers" for the judicial system.

What is perhaps most distinctive about the limited-jurisdiction courts is their diversity. These courts display considerable differences with regard to jurisdictional authority, case loads, available sanctions and remedies, and their case-handling practices. A good example of these differences may be seen in the various methods these courts use to handle small civil claims.

Many limited-jurisdiction courts are referred to as "small-claims courts" because they have established a simplified procedure for handling a certain range of smaller civil disputes. Although the maximum dollar amount for invoking the small-claims process varies considerably from state to state, the most common limits are between $500 and $1,000. Developed in the early part of the twentieth century, small-claims procedures were viewed as an efficient and less costly means of settling minor disputes. In particular, it was assumed that the simplified procedures would eliminate the need for a lawyer.

In their comparative study of small claims practices in fifteen limited-jurisdiction courts across the United States, Ruhnka and Weller found significant differences.

Some of the courts, for example, prohibited the use of small-claims procedures by collection agencies. These courts, not surprisingly, had the highest percentage of individual plaintiffs (consumers) in their case loads, whereas in those courts that permitted collection-agency practice, business plaintiffs predominated. Ruhnka and Weller also found considerable differences in the use of attorneys in these courts by both plaintiffs and defendants. Among the fifteen courts surveyed, the percentage of plaintiffs who contacted attorneys about their claim ranged from 18 percent to 67 percent, while the percentage of defendants was from 29 percent to 61 percent. The lower percentages tended to be concentrated, predictably, in the five courts that prohibited attorneys at trial. They also found considerable differences in jurisdictional limits, the mix of cases, the size of awards as a percentage of the claims, and plaintiff and defendant satisfaction with small-claims procedures.

Although some of the trial courts of limited jurisdiction now operate within a statewide administrative system as a result of court-unification efforts, many of the limited-jurisdiction courts have retained a large degree of local autonomy, even in states in which other aspects of the court-unification movement have taken hold. This autonomy apparently has led to the development of specialized work loads among courts and judges in particular locales. Although all state limited-jurisdiction trial courts ostensibly have jurisdiction to try both civil and criminal cases, only 61 percent of the 13,221 state courts of limited jurisdiction identified by the United States Census Bureau in 1972 reported handling both civil and criminal cases, while 11 percent reported handling only civil and 28 percent only criminal (United States Department of Justice). Within those courts handling at least some criminal matters, the Census Bureau survey revealed wide variation with regard to the percentage distribution of judge time spent on nontraffic criminal cases. Although the survey indicates that state misdemeanor cases are the predominant case type (in terms of distribution of judge time), in many of these limited-jurisdiction courts, civil, traffic, or juvenile cases appear to be the predominant case type in at least an equal number of courts.

In addition to this general-jurisdictional diversity, these courts differ with regard to the mix of offenses included within their misdemeanor case loads. In particular, there is a good deal of variation with regard to the incidence of the following most frequently tried crimes: traffic offenses, public intoxication, drunk driving, disorderly conduct, narcotics offenses, petty theft, disturbing the peace, assault and battery, prostitution, and writing a bad check. The incidence of certain of these crimes may be affected by such factors as the varying success of decriminalization efforts, community mores, local politics, and community size.

Even where the incidence of certain crimes within these courts is similar, the range and severity of sanctions that may be imposed vary. Although the maximum jail sentence that may be imposed by the limited-jurisdiction courts in the majority of states is one year (with maximum fines ranging from $250 in Arkansas to $3,000 in Oregon), the maximum permissible sentence in the Minnesota courts is three months, and in the lower courts in seven states the maximum jail sentence ranges from two to seven years.

Two studies that have carefully examined sentencing practices in these courts come to very different conclusions. In his study of the handling of cases in the lower court in New Haven, Connecticut, Malcolm Feeley found that the primary sanctions were meted out in the pretrial process and that the sentences were relatively inconsequential. Feeley argues that the economic and psychological costs involved in making bail, hiring an attorney, appearing in court, and preparing the defense are the major punishment, since jail terms are unlikely and fines relatively slight in the type of cases studied. In contrast to Feeley's finding that "the process is the punishment," John Paul Ryan found that sentences in the Columbus (Ohio) Municipal Court were much more substantial and that process costs were relatively low. Ryan concludes that "the outcome is the punishment."

In the limited-jurisdiction courts, there is also considerable variation with regard to case-processing practices, the presence of prosecution and defense attorneys, the incidence of plea negotiation, the use of probation, and the legal training of judges. Many limited-jurisdiction courts support the popular notion of these courts as dispensing assembly-line justice. Cases are handled in a perfunctory, nonadversarial fashion, with the vast majority of criminal cases being disposed of by guilty plea at the first appearance. Defendants in many of these courts are seldom represented by counsel and some are prosecuted by police officers. The judges in these courts often are nonlawyers. Postverdict services such as the preparation of presentence reports and probation are either unavailable or seldom used. Practices in other limited-jurisdiction courts, on the other hand, suggest a paradigm that is closer to the popular notion of the general-jurisdiction trial court. Few cases are disposed of at initial appearance in these courts. In fact, a case may move through numerous stages with the defendant represented by counsel and prosecuted by an attorney before a lawyer judge. Presentence reports and probation are available and frequently used.

A number of legal scholars have been concerned that the assembly-line justice of many of the limited-jurisdiction courts does not give full effect to the rights of criminal defendants and have called for reforms that would inject a greater degree of procedural fairness in lower-court proceedings. These scholars have contended that there is a need for procedural reform—such as an expansion of the right to counsel—not only for theoretical but also for practical reasons. For example, Francis A. Allen explains that improvements in the administration and operation of the misdemeanor courts may be late in coming because these courts have enjoyed a "freedom from scrutiny." More specifically, those in the best position (lawyers) to analyze and critique administrative and operational shortcomings have not been present in large numbers in these courts until quite recently.

Many limited-jurisdiction courts are referred to as "small-claims courts" because they have established a simplified procedure for handling small civil disputes.

It has been argued that the few lawyers who traditionally have practiced in these courts generally lack the influence or are too corrupt to constitute a force for reform. Yet, procedural reformers have exercised a good deal of caution in calling for an expansion of the due process rights of misdemeanor defendants. They have emphasized a need to reconcile "administrative imperatives" or "problems of feasibility" with procedural changes that ostensibly would give greater effect to these rights (Allen). Recent United States Supreme Court decisions indicate a sensitivity to such "administrative imperatives" and illuminate the need to develop a better sense of how differences in adjudication practices may influence substantive rights and outcomes. In the 1970s the Supreme Court issued major decisions concerning the right to counsel in misdemeanor cases. It also decided cases relating to a defendant's right to an impartial judge, to a law-trained judge, and to a jury trial in the limited-jurisdiction courts.

In *Argersinger* v. *Hamlin* (1972), the Supreme Court held that no person can be imprisoned for any offense unless, absent a knowing and intelligent waiver, the defendant was represented by counsel. In effect, *Argersinger* extended the right to counsel, established in *Gideon* v. *Wainwright* (1963) nine years earlier, to indigent misdemeanor offenders. In the majority and three separate concurring opinions in *Argersinger,* six of the justices attempted to assess the extent of the additional administrative burdens that the decision would place on the limited-jurisdiction courts and suggested ways of easing these burdens, Chief Justice Burger, for example, pointed out that counsel need be provided to an indigent defendant only if the defendant is actually imprisoned, and suggested that the prosecutor assist the judge in predicting whether the defendant would be sent to jail if convicted. Such an approach to the provision of defense counsel to the indigent was supported by the Court's later decision in *Scott* v. *Illinois* (1979). In a 5–4 decision in *Scott,* the Court ruled that the right to counsel mandated by *Argersinger* did not extend to all cases in which there was a possibility of imprisonment but only to cases in which the defendant was actually imprisoned.

Although the impact of the defense attorney on misdemeanor court proceedings is problematic, a preliminary study suggests that the increased use of counsel in the lower trial courts has not contributed to their woes in the ways that many have assumed (Alfini and Passuth). More research is needed to examine the effect of procedural and administrative reforms on such factors as guilty-plea rates, the incidence and nature of plea negotiations, the pretrial process, and delay in the limited-jurisdiction courts.

In *Ward* v. *Monroeville* (1972), *Ludwig* v. *Massachusetts* (1976), and *North* v. *Russell* (1976), the Supreme Court ruled on the constitutionality of other limited-jurisdiction court procedures and practices. In each case, the Court considered the impact of these procedures on a defendant's substantive rights and considered the constitutional relevance of the availability of an appeal from the limited-jurisdiction trial court to a general-jurisdiction trial court.

In *Ward,* the Supreme Court ruled that the defendant was unconstitutionally deprived of his right to a trial before a disinterested and impartial judge where he was tried by the village mayor, who was responsible for village finances and whose court provided a substantial portion of village funds through fines, forfeitures, costs, and fees. The Court based its decision on principles it had laid down in a 1927 case, *Tumey* v. *Ohio.* In *Tumey,* the Court reversed the convictions when it appeared that the judge (also the village mayor) received part of the court fees and costs levied by him, in addition to his regular salary. The Court stated that "it certainly violates the Fourteenth Amendment, and deprives a defendant in a criminal case of due process of law, to subject his liberty or property to the judgment of a court the judge of which has a direct, personal, substantial, pecuniary interest in reaching a conclusion against him in his case." In *Ward,* the Supreme Court ruled that the fact that the defendant had a right to a trial de novo in the general-jurisdiction court (and that any unfairness might therefore be corrected at this level) had no constitutional significance. The Court stated that the defendant was "entitled to a neutral and detached judge in the first instance."

A trial de novo is a new trial or retrial in a higher court, as if there had been no trial in the lower court.

A trial de novo is a new trial or retrial in a higher court. The case is handled as if there had been no trial in the lower court. Historically, it was invented as a procedural device to prevent abuses in the lower courts.

Although the Supreme Court decisions in *Tumey* and *Ward* have encouraged many states to do away with fee-based compensation systems for these courts, recent studies indicate that a few states are still using a fee system. Some commentators (following the Court's reasoning in *Tumey* and *Ward*) have argued that this system of compensation results in a judge's having a financial interest in the outcome of a case, which destroys his impartiality and thus results in a denial of due process. The principal justification for retaining a fee system, particularly in rural areas, appears to be that relating the judge's compensation to his work load will give him the necessary incentive to work full-time as a judge. In states retaining some form of a fee-based compensation system, it has been argued that their systems have eliminated the constitutional objections by removing the judge's financial interest in the outcome of a case. One such system has been characterized as the "salary fund fee system," whereby the judge is paid a set salary, which is derived solely from a designated fund consisting of fines and fees imposed by the judge.

Even in courts where judges receive fixed salaries, important economic issues concerning the administration of justice in urban as well as rural misdemeanor courts remain to be addressed through systematic research. As long as judges must look to limited local funds to run their courts, the extent to which judges can remain impartial and unbiased in deciding cases and administering justice is problematic. Unlike general trial courts, limited-jurisdiction courts generate substantial revenues. Even though fines and fees may be mixed, as in many locales, with general county funds and the judge's compensation may be fixed by state statute, the judge is still required to look to local officials in most jurisdictions for the funding of court facilities and services. They may thus be encouraged to overexploit the revenue-generating potential of their courts or, conversely, discouraged from doing anything (particularly using certain sentencing alternatives) that would have an adverse effect on the amount of revenue generated by their courts. As of 1986 there had been no empirically based studies that sought to determine the effect of these and other local economic incentives and disincentives on the administration of justice in the lower courts.

Contrary to its decision in *Ward,* the Supreme Court ruled in *Ludwig* v. *Massachusetts* (1976) and *North* v. *Russell* (1976) that certain procedural shortcomings in state limited-jurisdiction courts would be tolerated as long as a de novo appeal is available in a general trial court where these shortcomings can be remedied. In *Ludwig,* the Supreme Court upheld the constitutionality of Massachusetts' two-tier trial-court system, where no trial by jury is available in the first-tier (limited-jurisdiction) court, because a de novo jury trial is available on appeal to the second-tier (general-jurisdiction) court. In *North,* the Supreme Court similarly upheld the constitutionality of Kentucky's two-tier trial-court system, where the defendant faces the possibility of incarceration by a nonlawyer judge in the first-tier court. The Court upheld the constitutionality of incarceration by a nonlawyer judge as long as the defendant has an opportunity for a trial de novo before a lawyer judge in the second-tier court.

Although the twenty-four states that utilize a two-tier trial-court system (that is, trial court systems in which the defendant has a right to a de novo appeal to the second-tier) differ with regard to the procedural rights accorded defendants in the first-tier court, the effect of the Court's decisions in *Ludwig* and *North* is to encourage the perpetuation of two-tier trial-court systems in which certain procedural rights are unavailable to the defendant in the first-tier. In other words, these decisions may encourage the continued diversity among limited-jurisdiction courts on procedural matters.

Of relevance to the *Ludwig* decision is the question of whether and how a defendant's right to a jury trial in a limited-jurisdiction court affects substantive outcomes. Available research suggests that very few defendants are actually tried before a jury in misdemeanor courts where a jury trial is available. However, in some of these courts the number of jury demands is very high. This suggests the possibility that the mere availability of a jury trial may affect negotiation and adjudication strategies in these courts and thus affect substantive outcomes.

The *North* decision raises the question of whether and how misdemeanor courts staffed by nonlawyer judges differ from those staffed by lawyer judges. The impressionistic literature suggests that nonlawyer judges (particularly in rural areas) have a greater potential for bias in deciding cases insofar as they look to others (particularly the local prosecutor) for legal assistance and may rely more on personal knowledge than the law in deciding cases.

The persistence of the nonlawyer justice courts in rural areas of the United States would argue in favor of the need for more research on these courts. Silberman's 1979 study reveals that nonlawyer judges are still authorized in an estimated 20,280 state judicial positions (approximately two-thirds of all state judicial positions) and that 13,217 of these positions were in fact filled by nonlawyers. Certainly, the *North* decision does not encourage any reduction in their number.

Although they have been subjected to a great deal of criticism, primarily for their procedural irregularities, limited-jurisdiction courts serve an important function in the judicial system. Each year, they resolve disputes involving millions of citizens. However, at a time when many of these courts are adopting long-awaited procedural reforms and formal practices, there is a newer reform movement calling for alternate (generally less formal) dispute resolution (ADR) mechanisms for handling many of the kinds of disputes processed in these courts (Council on the Role of Courts). ADR proponents argue that the adversarial process employed in court cases discourages other than win/lose outcomes, often frustrates the search for truth, encourages delay, and is too costly. As an alternative to formal adjudication, they propose mechanisms such as arbitration and mediation. The future role of the limited-jurisdiction courts, and indeed of trial courts generally, will be largely determined by their willingness and ability to respond to these changing societal concerns and demands.

[See also (III) Criminal Justice System, Discovery, Federal Court System, Judiciary, Jurisdiction, Sentencing Alternatives, State Court Systems.]

CASES

Argersinger v. Hamlin, 407 U.S. 25 (1972)
Gideon v. Wainwright, 372 U.S. 335 (1963)
Ludwig v. Massachusetts, 427 U.S. 618 (1976)
North v. Russell, 427 U.S. 328 (1976)
Ross v. Bernhard, 396 U.S. 531 (1970)
Scott v. Illinois, 440 U.S. 367 (1979)
Swain v. Alabama, 380 U.S. 202 (1965)
Tumey v. Ohio, 273 U.S. 510 (1927)
Ward v. Village of Monroeville, 409 U.S. 57 (1972)

BIBLIOGRAPHY

Administrative Office of the United States Courts, *Federal Court Management Statistics* (1983), is a statistical breakdown of the work load of the federal courts from 1978 to 1983. James J. Alfini, "Introductory Essay: The Misdemeanor Courts," in *Justice System Journal,* 6 (1981), argues that efforts in improving the lower criminal courts will be more likely to succeed if full consideration is given to their diversity; and Alfini, ed., *Misdemeanor Courts: Policy Concerns and Research Perspectives* (1981), contains articles identifying lower-court policy issues and possible research strategies for addressing these issues. James J. Alfini and Patricia M. Passuth, "Case Processing in State Misdemeanor Courts: The Effect of Defense Attorney Presence," in *Justice System Journal,* 6 (1981), reports on the results of a questionnaire survey aimed at assessing the effect of counsel on case processing in lower trial courts. Francis A. Allen, "Small Crimes and Large Problems: Some Constitutional Dimensions," in C. H. Whitebread, ed., *Mass Production Justice and the Constitutional Ideal* (1970), examines constitutional issues related to case processing in the lower criminal trial courts. American Bar Association, *Standards Relating to Court Organization* (1974), sets forth standards on court-organization topics such as unified court systems, selection and tenure of judges, rule making, and administrative authority; and *Standards Relating to Trial Courts* (1976), sets forth standards for case handling in the trial courts.

Ralph Cavanagh and Austin Sarat, "Thinking About Courts: Toward and Beyond a Jurisprudence of Judicial Competence," in *Law and Society Review,* 14 (1980), reviews arguments over the competence and capacity of courts to handle certain kinds of cases. Thomas Church, Alan Carlson, Jo-Lynn Lee, and Teresa Tan, *Justice Delayed: The Pace of Litigation in Urban Trial Courts* (1978), argues that trial-court delay can best be understood by examining the "local legal culture." Council on the Role of Courts, *The Role of Courts in American Society* (1984), gives the results of a study aimed at shaping the future role of American courts. James Eisenstein and Herbert Jacob, *Felony Justice: An Organizational Analysis of Criminal Courts* (1977), examines adjudication and sentencing practices in the felony trial courts in Baltimore, Chicago, and Detroit. Malcolm M. Feeley, *The Process Is the Punishment: Handling Cases in a Lower Criminal Court* (1979), examines criminal case processing in the lower trial court in New Haven, Connecticut, and finds, among other things, that "process costs" are high and sentences relatively inconsequential. Jerome Frank, *Courts on Trial* (1949), is a classic critique of the courts in operation, by a prominent judge and legal philosopher. Sheldon Goldman and Thomas P. Jahnige, *The Federal Courts as a Political System* (1985), contains important information on the federal courts and reviews recent research. Sheldon Goldman and Austin Sarat, *American Court Systems* (1978), is a collection of readings on various facets of American state and federal courts.

Herbert Jacob, *Justice in America* (1972), is regarded as the classic treatment of the operational realities of America's justice system; and "Trial Courts in the United States: The Travails of Exploration," in *Law and Society Review,* 17 (1983), reviews twelve years of research on trial courts. James W. Jeans, *Trial Advocacy* (1975), is a handbook on trial practice with detailed advice on the various stages of preparing for and conducting the trial. Harry W. Jones, ed., *The Courts, the Public, and the Law Explosion* (1965), is a collection of essays focusing on the courts and their problems prepared for an American assembly program of Columbia University. Yale Kamisar,

Wayne R. La Fave, and Jerold H. Israel, *Basic Criminal Procedure* (1974), contains basic materials on criminal procedure. Norbert L. Kerr and Robert M. Bray, eds., *The Psychology of the Courtroom* (1982), is a collection of essays reviewing empirical and experimental research on trial-court procedures and key actors, with emphasis on the jury trial.

Martin A. Levin, *Urban Politics and the Criminal Courts* (1977), examines differences in the handling of felony cases in the trial courts in Pittsburgh and Minneapolis. David W. Louisell and Geoffrey C. Hazard, *Cases and Materials on Pleading and Procedure: State and Federal* (1979), contains cases and materials on state and federal civil procedure. National Center for State Courts, *State Court Caseload Statistics: Annual Report, 1980* (1984), reports comprehensive case load statistics for state trial and appellate courts on an annual basis. David W. Neubauer, *America's Courts and the Criminal Justice System* (1979), is an undergraduate textbook on America's criminal courts, focusing on "the dynamics of the courthouse." President's Commission on Law Enforcement and Administration of Justice, *The Challenge of Crime in a Free Society* (1967), makes two hundred specific recommendations for improving the criminal justice system.

Judith Resnik, "Managerial Judges," in *Harvard Law Review,* 96 (1982), argues that the recent emphasis on trial-court management may have adverse effects on the adjudicative responsibilities of trial courts. John Robertson, ed., *Rough Justice: Perspectives on Lower Criminal Courts* (1974), is a collection of articles on criminal case handling in the limited-jurisdiction courts. H. Ted Rubin, *The Courts: Fulcrum of the Justice System* (1976), is a primer on the American judicial system. John C. Ruhnka and Steven Weller, *Small Claims Courts: A National Examination* (1978), assesses small-claims procedures in fifteen limited-jurisdiction trial courts. John Paul Ryan, "Adjudication and Sentencing in a Misdemeanor Court: The Outcome Is the Punishment," in *Law and Society Review,* 15 (1980), examines adjudication and sentencing practices in the limited-jurisdiction trial court in Columbus, Ohio. John P. Ryan, Allan Ashman, Bruce Sales, and Sandra Shane-DuBow, *American Trial Judges: Their Work Styles and Performance* (1980), reports the results of a national survey of judges in state general-jurisdiction trial courts.

Linda J. Silberman, *Non-Attorney Justice in the United States: An Empirical Study* (1979), examines the use of nonattorney judges in American court systems. Susan S. Silbey, "Making Sense of the Lower Courts," in *Justice System Journal,* 6 (1981), argues that even though the limited-jurisdiction trial courts do not adhere strictly to a rule of law model, they have a distinct capacity for providing responsive justice for the kinds of cases they are asked to handle. Maureen Solomon, *Caseflow Management in the Trial Court* (1973), argues for increased judicial control of the flow of cases through a trial court. United States Department of Justice, *National Survey of Court Organization* (1973), contains the results of a survey of American courts conducted by the Census Bureau as a preliminary step to establishing a national program of judicial statistics. United States National Advisory Commission on Criminal Justice Standards and Goals, *Courts* (1973), sets forth standards relating to the role of the courts in the criminal justice system.

– JAMES J. ALFINI

TRIAL JURIES AND GRAND JURIES

The panels of common citizens assembled to serve as grand juries and trial juries are among the most democratic of American institutions. The idea itself—that ordinary citizens without experience in judicial decision-making should be brought together to decide issues of great importance—is an unusual one in the world today. The jury developed as part of a long struggle against centralized power in Britain and later in those countries that inherited the British traditions of justice. But the jury is unusual even in democracies. Most institutions of democratic governments draw their power from the people, who elect their representatives to decision-making bodies, but in the American courtroom it is the people themselves, as jurors, who make the decisions. No wonder, then, that the jury continues to be the object of controversy.

The democratic features of the jury have evolved slowly, and when juries and grand juries first began to be used in Britain and the United States, they were not selected according to the democratic principles that hold sway today. The jury has been affected by changes in society and has helped change society as well. After almost a thousand years of experience with the jury, persons raised in the Anglo-American tradition have come to view a jury trial as the right of every defendant accused of a serious crime and the jury as a body consisting of a cross section of the community, randomly selected. But the jury was originally a creation of the crown, made up of landowners. Concepts of its form and function have evolved over the centuries along with democratic government.

English Origins

The roots of the jury date back to Anglo-Saxon England, but its modern development began with William the Conqueror, who determined the countryside's wealth and population through "inquests" or "inquisitions." The king sent his barons to the villages and townships, where they summoned the important men from the neighborhood, placed them under oath, and questioned them about the community's financial affairs. The sworn men were fundamentally witnesses, supplying the information to the royal officers that eventually produced the Domesday Book, a massive census conducted around 1086. They were primarily interested in financial affairs but occasionally examined criminal matters as well.

Henry II, who ruled from 1154 to 1189 and was concerned with strengthening the crown's presence in the countryside, can probably be credited more than any other single individual with laying the foundation for the modern jury. He developed the system of inquests begun by William into the direct ancestor of the grand jury, by impaneling the "most lawful men" of every community to review the evidence against those suspected of committing crimes.

During this early period, most civil disputes over land ownership were decided by "assizes," in which a group of carefully selected men studied the case and gave a verdict. In criminal cases, however, guilt or innocence was usually determined either by trial by battle, proof by oath or compurgation (see below), or trial by ordeal, an ancient and brutal form of settling controversies that involved dunking the accused in water or forcing him to carry hot irons in his hands. These ordeals were supervised by the clergy, who would evaluate the dunking or burning to give divine sanction to the decision of guilt or innocence. The jury was used erratically according to the king's wishes until 1215, when a group of barons exacted the promise from King John, in Article 39 of the Magna Charta, that "no freeman shall be taken or imprisoned or [dispossessed], or outlawed or exiled or in any way destroyed . . . except by the lawful judgment of his peers and the law of the land." The jury of 1215 was still more like the modern grand jury than a trial jury because its role was to decide whether the evidence justified further proceedings against a defendant—further proceedings in the nature of an ordeal. But in the same year as the Magna Charta, Pope Innocent III prohibited participation by priests in trials by ordeal, and the way was opened for trials by jury to take their place. A decline of religious values had in any case already brought into question the validity of the oaths taken in ordeals as well as the motives of the clergy, who were found to manipulate some of the ordeals and to profit from fees collected from them.

In the first half of the fourteenth century, the trial jury and the grand jury were finally separated. The trial jury began to be recognized as a body whose task was to evaluate the evidence and come up with a definitive verdict as to guilt or innocence, as differentiated from the grand jury, which had brought the charges. In 1352 a statute was passed stating explicitly that grand jurors could not also sit on the trial jury. After that date, when one of the king's traveling justices arrived to hear disputes, the local sheriff would choose twelve men from the immediate surrounding community to serve as jurors and would then select an additional group of twenty-four men (usually knights) from a larger area to serve as an accusing body for the entire county. After these twenty-four eliminated one member so that they could act by majority vote, they investigated incidents and soon took over the entire burden of filing indictments.

It is not known for certain why juries of twelve developed. Theorists frequently refer to the twelve prophets or the twelve disciples and to the proof by compurgation, which had frequently called on twelve men to swear that the accused's oath was trustworthy. The real reason probably was that twelve is a number large enough to ensure some reliability and impartiality and yet small enough to function with some degree of efficiency. In any case, by the middle of the fourteenth century the requirement of twelve was fixed.

As the concept of the trial jury emerged, so did the rule of unanimity. For a time, decisions reflecting an eleven-to-one split were accepted, with the dissenting juror fined for perjury on the theory that he must have been wrong if the eleven others disagreed with him. Another technique involved adding additional jurors when the original twelve were split until a group of twelve could be assembled that would agree on a verdict. But these alternatives did not satisfy the true purpose of the jury—to provide a reliable decision reflecting the view of the community in as authoritative a manner as trial by ordeal had earlier reflected the views of the divinity. Nothing short of a unanimous verdict would supply this level of reliability.

The supremacy of the jury's verdict was established in 1670 in a celebrated case involving William Penn and William Mead.

Although the Magna Charta had taken the right to use a jury out of the hands of the crown and given it to the barons, the crown retained considerable control over the jury's decisions for several more centuries. Until the early sixteenth century, jury verdicts could be overturned by a larger, specially selected, and generally more elite "jury of attaint." The original jurors were then frequently imprisoned and their lands confiscated by the crown, because they were viewed as having committed perjury in returning an "erroneous" verdict. After juries of attaint were discredited because of the harshness of their penalties, verdicts were still sometimes rejected by a judge, and jurors could still be imprisoned or fined.

In the late seventeenth century, the supremacy of the jury's verdict, and thus its independence, was finally established in a celebrated case involving William Penn and William Mead. Penn (who was then twenty-six) and Mead (another young Quaker activist) were charged in 1670 with conducting an unlawful assembly after they had held a meeting of Quakers in London that had been disrupted by others. The jury refused to return a guilty verdict, even though the judges pressured them heavily for several days to do so. Edward Bushell, leader of the dissenting jurors, was soundly scolded by the magistrate. After a series of deliberations and verdicts that were rejected by the court, the jury eventually found Penn and Mead not guilty. The magistrate then imposed a stiff fine on the jurors and ordered them imprisoned until they paid the money.

The undaunted jurors, insisting on their right to return a verdict free from judicial coercion, applied for a writ of habeas corpus. Ten weeks later, Chief Justice Vaughan, speaking for himself and ten other sitting appeals judges of the Court of Common Pleas, freed the jurors and stated decisively that jurors cannot be punished for their decision. Vaughan's historic opinion in *Bushell's Case* emphasized that the purpose of the jury is to obtain persons from the location of the alleged crime so that they can evaluate the evidence according to their own understanding, reasoning, and conscience. Why, he asked, insist on careful selection procedures—to ensure that jurors come from the site of the incident and are unbiased—unless the verdict of the jury is to stand as the final decision on the question? The Vaughan decision articulates a principle that is now fully accepted: that if the jury is to play its intended role as an impartial fact finder to express the community's decision, it must be independent. Otherwise, it is not really the community's voice but the voice of the crown (or state), and the entire rationale for using a jury is undercut.

In 1681, eleven years after the trial jury's independence was established in *Bushell's Case,* a grand jury asserted the same power. In that year a London grand jury refused to return an indictment against the earl of Shaftesbury, who was accused of treason. After hearing the prosecution's witnesses and questioning them in private, the grand jury returned the bill presented by the prosecutor with the word *ignoramus* ("we do not know") written on the back. The royal authorities then presented the same evidence before the Oxford grand jury, which apparently did not share the politics of its counterpart in London and which indicted the earl. Despite the Oxford action, the principle that a grand jury could stand between the king and the accused was established, and the London grand jurors were not punished.

The American Jury

The independence of the jury from the crown was also an important aspect of the North American drive for independence from Britain in the eighteenth century. The people who settled in the original thirteen colonies considered jury trial a fundamental right, as indeed it had been in England for centuries. Most of the colonies specifically guaranteed trial by jury in their charters, although the methods of selection, size of the vicinage (the area from which jurors are selected), and the extent of use differed both within colonies over time and from colony to colony.

The First Continental Congress in 1774 stressed the importance of the jury by declaring that "the respective colonies are entitled to . . . the great and inestimable privilege of being tried by their peers of the vicinage, according to the course of [common] law." The Declaration of Independence specifically included among the grievances against the king deprivation "in many cases of the benefits of trial by jury." One such deprivation was an edict by the governor of colonial New York in 1765 that jury verdicts could be appealed to the governor and his council and overruled by them if deemed incorrect. Such a claim obviously ran counter to the recognition of the jury's independence in William Penn's case one hundred years earlier. Another deprivation was the Port Bill of 1773, which gave the royal governor of Massachusetts the power to transfer trials to another colony or back to England—a move that denied the accused a jury from the community, another right that had been recognized in the Penn controversy.

Prior to 1776, jurors and grand jurors were generally handpicked by the sheriff, who was appointed by the British crown.

The importance of jury trial was also expressed in the constitutions of the thirteen original states. Many employed phrases similar to Maryland's Declaration of Rights, which stated that "the trial of facts where they arise, is one of the greatest securities of the lives, liberties and estates of the people," among whose rights is "a speedy trial by an impartial jury, without whose unanimous consent he ought not to be found guilty." Some state constitutions borrowed language directly from the Magna Charta in their provisions on jury trial.

The great variation in practice among the thirteen colonies probably explains why the only provision relating to jury trial in the original 1787 Constitution was in Article III, Section 2, which states that "the Trial of all Crimes, except in Cases of Impeachment, shall be by Jury; and such Trial shall be held in the State where the said Crimes shall have been committed." The vagueness of this provision was one reason for opposition to the Constitution during the ratification period of 1787–1789. Many people expressed fears that jury verdicts might be reversed by appellate judges, that the vicinage requirement was too broad (calling for juries drawn within a state, rather than from smaller areas), and that no provision specifically guaranteed the right to challenge prospective jurors.

These fears were largely answered by the Bill of Rights, which was adopted as the first ten amendments to the Constitution in 1791 and refers to trial by jury in three different places: the Fifth Amendment declaration that no person can be criminally charged "unless on a presentment or indictment of a Grand Jury"; the Sixth Amendment guarantee that persons so accused shall have the right to a trial "by an impartial jury of the State and district where in the crime shall have been committed"; and the Seventh Amendment guarantee of the same right in civil cases, which says that "in Suits at common law, where the value in controversy shall exceed twenty dollars, the right of trial by jury shall be preserved, and no fact tried by a jury, shall be otherwise re-examined in any Court of the United States, than according to the rules of the common law." The Constitution thus firmly establishes an individual's right to demand the community's sanction—expressed in the jury's verdict—before he or she can be convicted of a crime and denied freedom.

The modern meaning of the constitutional protection of trial by jury was summed up by Justice Byron R. White in the 1968 case of *Duncan* v. *Louisiana:*

> The guarantees of jury trial in the Federal and State Constitutions reflect a profound judgment about the way in which law should be enforced and justice administered. *A right to jury trial is granted to criminal defendants in order to prevent oppression by the Government. . . . Providing an accused with the right to be tried by a jury of his peers gave him an inestimable safeguard against the corrupt or overzealous prosecutor and against the compliant, biased or eccentric judge.* If the defendant preferred the common-sense judgment of a jury to the more tutored but perhaps less sympathetic reaction of a single judge, he was to have it. Beyond this, the jury trial provisions in the Federal and State Constitutions reflect a fundamental decision about the exercise of official power—a reluctance to entrust plenary powers over the life and liberty of the citizen to one judge or to a group of judges.
>
> (Emphasis added.)

The American commitment to the use of citizen panels for juries and grand juries is thus firm and based on sound policy reasons. Many disputes nonetheless remain about what roles these panels should play and how they should be structured and should operate.

The Grand Jury

The grand jury has been a particularly controversial body because it operates in secret and has frequently been manipulated by the prosecutor to reach a preordained result. American history contains numerous examples of independent grand juries that have confronted and exposed governmental corruption but also contains many other examples of docile, controlled grand juries that have sat idly by while elected officials enriched themselves at the expense of the public.

Prior to 1776, jurors and grand jurors were generally handpicked by the sheriff, who was appointed by the British crown, and as a result, only the largest landholders became members of these largely passive bodies. In Virginia, however, grand jurors were selected in a more random fashion, and these more independent panels frequently made unusually probing and embarrassing examinations of governmental activities. The royal governor, Francis Nicholson, became upset at this activity and issued a proclamation in 1690 instructing the local sheriffs to select grand jurors only "from the most substantial inhabitants of your counties." Nine years later, the Virginia General Assembly defined more particularly the requirements for jury service, saying that jurors in the General Court must be freeholders whose real and personal property are visibly of the reputed value of £100. These decrees substantially ended the independence of the Virginia juries and reduced the potential for embarrassment to the crown.

In the colony of Massachusetts the sheriff originally selected all grand jurors, but in the early eighteenth century the colonists were able to wrest away the sheriff's power and assign it to the town meetings held in all communities. This change became particularly important during the turbulent years before the American Revolution. When the royal governor asked the grand jury to investigate the frequent disturbances connected with anti-British activity, the colonists were able to thwart the investigation by selecting as grand jurors persons who had played leading roles in the disturbances. After the Boston Tea Party of 1773, the British House of Commons passed an elaborate statute called the Port Bill, which revised local government in Massachusetts and required that the king's sheriff choose grand and trial jurors from a list of freeholders. This move was protested vehemently, and the few token persons opposing British rule who were selected for the grand jury—men like Paul Revere and John Hancock's brother Ebenezer—refused to take their oaths as grand jurors.

Examples of abuses in the selection of grand jurors can be found throughout United States history. One instance occurred at the beginning of the twentieth century in San Francisco. A political boss named Abraham Ruef had gained control of city government through various corrupt maneuvers, and a special prosecutor was finally appointed to investigate his activities. Ruef sought to derail this investigation by controlling the 1906 grand jury, which was selected through a nominating process: each of the 12 trial judges nominated 12 persons, and then 19 grand jurors were selected by lot from the pool of 144. Several of these judges were subject to the influence of Ruef, including at least one who was directly under his control.

The grand jury secretary, Myrtile Cerf, was a confederate of Ruef. He determined the nineteen most favorable nominees before the drawing, and folded the slips bearing their names together in a packet, which he was able to feel when he placed his hand in the box at the official drawing. He was thus able to draw the names of nominees most favorable to Ruef in a process that appeared to be impartial. The editor of the *San Francisco Bulletin* later discovered this fraudulent selection process and eventually persuaded the presiding judge to discharge the panel and select a new one. Free of Ruef's influence and finally independent, the new grand jury promptly indicted Ruef; he was convicted and served a prison term with several of his confederates.

Many states have now eliminated the requirement of grand jury indictments.

The California grand juries continued to be selected through a judicial nominating process until the 1970s, when most counties moved to a system of selecting names randomly from the voters' registration list in order to avoid the discrimination that almost inevitably results from a personal selection scheme. The specific impetus for this change in San Francisco was a 1975 ruling by a federal judge who examined the statistics of the grand jurors by racial categories and sex and ruled that the "substantial underrepresentation" of nonwhite ethnic groups and women could be "the basis for a *prima facie* case of unconstitutional discrimination in selection" (*Quadra* v. *San Francisco Superior Court*).

FUNCTION OF THE GRAND JURY. In over half the states, the grand jury has evolved from a body that reviews all criminal charges and issues formal indictments ordering accused persons to appear for trial to a body whose primary responsibility is to investigate governmental activities and major criminal schemes. This change began in the nineteenth century, and in those states that have moved in this direction, most criminal charges are reviewed by a judge in a public "preliminary hearing," in which the accused can be present and participate.

The United States Supreme Court considered this innovation in the 1884 case of *Hurtado* v. *California*. The Court tested the California change by asking whether the preliminary hearing satisfied the requirements of the due process clause of the Fourteenth Amendment of the Constitution. The Court concluded that the minimum requisites of liberty and justice were in fact preserved by a preliminary hearing in which the district attorney was obliged to establish probable guilt before a neutral magistrate. In certain respects the accused is given more protection in a preliminary hearing than by a grand jury indictment because the accused, who is barred from grand jury proceedings, can appear at the hearing with counsel and cross-examine the government's witnesses. Justice John M. Harlan, writing the single dissenting opinion, complained that an essential element of liberty was being sacrificed by this process:

> In the secrecy of the investigations by grand juries, the weak and helpless—proscribed, perhaps, because of their race, or pursued by an unreasoning public clamor—have found, and will continue to find, security against official oppression, the cruelty of mobs, the machinations of falsehood, and the malevolence of private persons who would use the machinery of the law to bring ruin upon their personal enemies.

But this concern did not convince those who preferred a more public procedure, and many states have now followed California's lead in eliminating the requirement of grand jury indictments. The grand jury may in theory be a body of citizens designed to protect people from being falsely accused; but because the grand jury meets in secret and because the potential defendant has no right to appear or refute the government's case, it provides an uncertain protection. The British, in fact, found the grand jury to be totally unnecessary and discarded the institution in 1933.

In the United States, grand juries are still active bodies, but their main role in many states is the investigation of major governmental scandals and elaborate criminal conspiracies that require extensive investigation and a greater-than-usual need to obtain private information. Colorado and Wyoming view the grand jury as such a useful investigating body that they have passed legislation authorizing statewide grand juries to be impaneled to examine wrongs that transcend county borders.

The grand jury has continued to be viewed as a useful institution, because it has a unique power to obtain evidence. A grand jury has an authority to demand answers from government officials and private citizens that go far beyond the power given to any other law enforcement body. The constitutional privileges and protections that can be asserted to avoid responding to the inquiries of the police, the Federal Bureau of Investigation, or any other law enforcement body do not shield one from a grand jury inquiry. In 1972 the Supreme Court stated that the "longstanding principle that 'the public . . . has a right to every man's evidence' . . . is particularly applicable to grand jury proceedings" (*Branzburg* v. *Hayes*), and in 1974 the Court applied that rule to the president of the United States (*United States* v. *Nixon*).

GRAND JURY ABUSES AND REFORM EFFORTS. The romantic image of the grand jury involves a body of citizens who gather together to investigate the crimes of the community. In fact, however, grand jurors all too often follow the prosecutor's lead completely and return indictments whenever requested to do so. Because they meet behind closed doors, are carefully guided by the prosecutor, and have almost unlimited power to demand evidence, the potential for abuse is great. During the Nixon administration, abuses of federal grand juries occurred with some regularity, causing Supreme Court Justice William O. Douglas to write in a dissenting opinion in 1973, "It is, indeed, common knowledge that the grand jury, having been conceived as a bulwark between the citizen and the Government, is now a tool of the Executive" (*United States* v. *Mara*).

Efforts to reform the grand jury have faltered because most victims of grand jury abuse are isolated, with little ability to generate public attention to the problems that exist. Except during periods like the Nixon and Vietnam era, when the victims of grand jury abuse were part of a larger political movement, this institution has not been the subject of concerted political focus.

One important reform priority—as mentioned above—is to ensure that the membership of grand juries accurately reflects the composition of the population at large. When the grand jury first became a body separate and distinct from the trial jury, those selected to serve as grand jurors were wealthier and of a higher social class than their trial jury counterparts, because their jurisdiction was broader and their potential power was greater. This tradition remains intact in some areas, and, although the statutes in most states say that grand jurors are to be selected in the same manner as trial

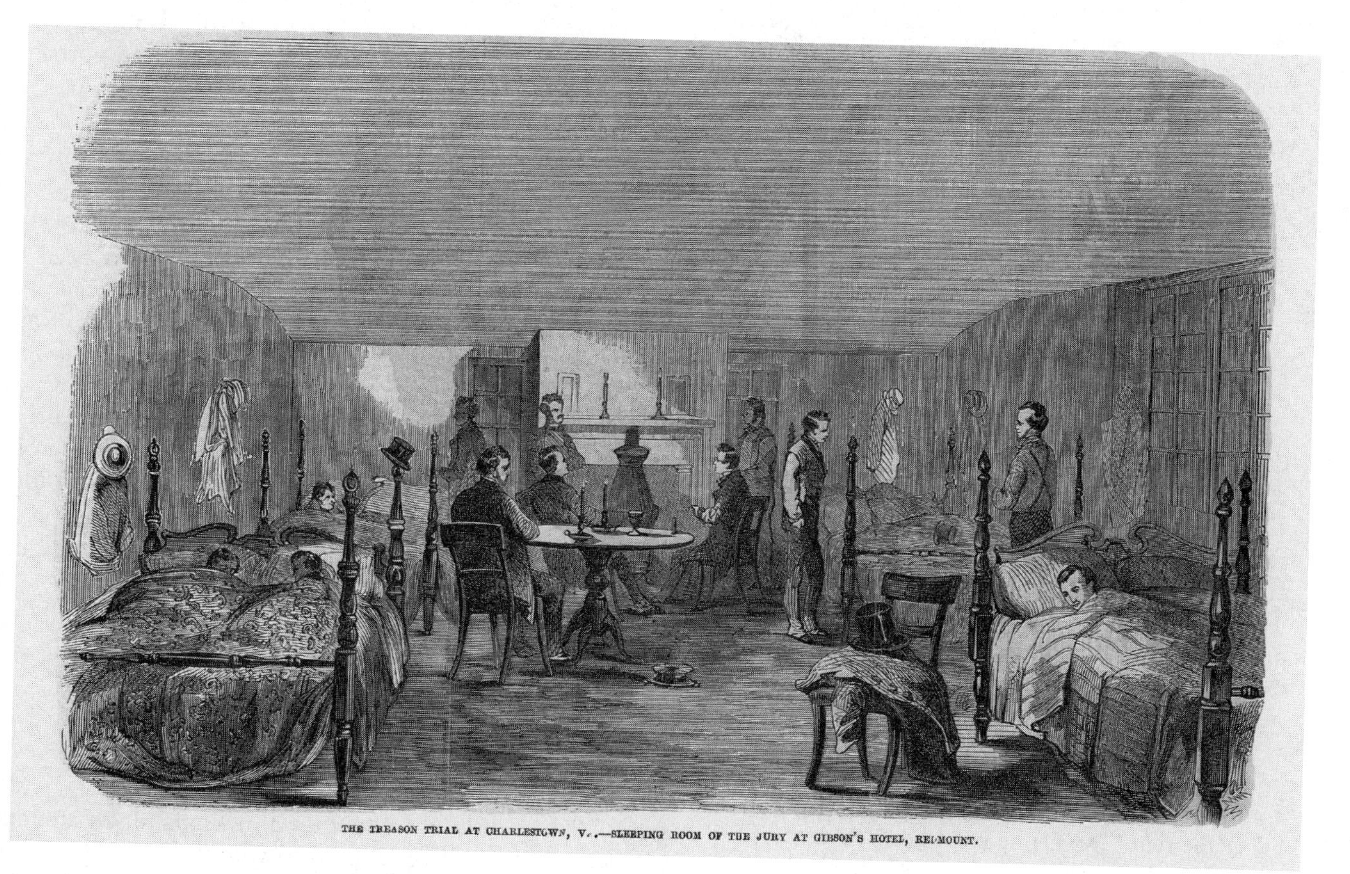

THE TREASON TRIAL AT CHARLESTOWN, V.—SLEEPING ROOM OF THE JURY AT GIBSON'S HOTEL, REDMOUNT.

Jurors serving on the trial of radical abolitionist John Brown share sleeping quarters. Brown was convicted of treason and hanged on December 2, 1859. (Frank Leslie's Illustrated Newspaper/Corbis)

jurors, substantial differences nonetheless sometimes exist in practice and result. A "blue-ribbon" grand jury composed of elite and influential citizens may be particularly vulnerable to governmental abuse and is unlikely to protect the interests of less powerful groups in society.

Another reform proposal would allow a witness to have an attorney with him in the grand jury room. At present, a witness is permitted to leave the grand jury after a question is asked and consult with an attorney outside in the corridor, but such a procedure is awkward and seems inconsistent with the right to counsel that exists in all other phases of the American judicial process.

An accused should have greater access to the grand jury's deliberations and some right to participate in the proceeding. In some states (California, for instance), an accused will automatically receive a copy of the grand jury transcript after an indictment is filed; and, in others (New York, for instance), the trial judge is required to examine the transcript upon request by the accused. In federal courts the accused must demonstrate a special need before being shown even a partial transcript. Recent United States Supreme Court rulings require prosecutors to present "exculpatory" evidence (evidence that would tend to show the accused's innocence) to the grand jury if such evidence is in the prosecutor's possession. It is difficult to enforce such an obligation, particularly when the grand jury operates in secret.

One reform that has been introduced in the Hawaii state courts could provide the foundation for returning the grand jury to its original role as "the people's panel" elsewhere. In 1978 the Hawaii Constitution was amended to require the court to appoint a lawyer to serve as "independent grand jury counsel"—to advise the grand jurors directly about legal issues so that they can perform their jobs more fully without relying on the prosecutor for legal advice. The independent lawyer does not participate in the questioning of grand jury witnesses or in the grand jury's deliberations but does respond to questions posed by the grand jury and discusses difficult legal issues with them when appropriate. This device has worked quite well and has given the grand jurors more confidence about how to evaluate evidence and when and how they should question witnesses themselves. The presence of an independent lawyer in the grand jury room appears also to have encouraged the prosecutors to present their evidence with somewhat more care and thoroughness to ensure that all elements of the crime have been covered. This is a modest and relatively inexpensive reform that appears to have helped to restore the grand jury as a neutral panel of citizens standing between the government and the accused and protecting the accused from governmental oppression.

If the grand jury could be modernized, it could once again be a proud part of the American democratic tradition. When confronted with governmental overreaching, a grand jury can refuse to indict persons that the government wishes to prosecute. The grand jury also has the power to investigate the activities of governmental agencies and uncover abuses of power in a uniquely probing and thorough manner. Because the grand jurors are independent citizens who fade anonymously back into the community when their job is done, they need not fear future job reprisals or face other pressures that inevitably occur when the investigators are part of the system being investigated. Special Prosecutor Leon Jaworski, in his July 1974 brief before the Supreme Court demanding President Nixon's tapes and defending the action of the grand jury in naming Nixon a coconspirator, described the grand jury as "this body of citizens, randomly selected, beholden neither to court nor to prosecutor, trusted historically to protect the individual against unwarranted government charges, but sworn to ferret out criminality by the exalted and powerful as well as by the humble and weak." The grand jury does not always play this important role, but when it does, it reminds one anew of its importance to American democracy.

The Trial Jury

The trial jury has been subjected to the same kind of exacting scrutiny as the grand jury, but the result of this scrutiny—at least in the United States—has been to reaffirm the central role of the jury in the judicial process and to underscore again the role of jurors in bringing common-sense wisdom into the legal system. The United States Supreme Court has repeatedly stressed the importance of the jury, and reforms have occurred in the state and federal systems to make it more probable that juries will be representative of their communities.

Most states now use random selection systems of jury selection, drawing names from lists of voters or holders of driver's licenses or both.

When juries were first used in England, an attempt was made to impanel persons who were the "peers" of the litigants, but this frequently meant that only men of property served as jurors. In the twelfth century, jurors were selected on the basis of their loyalty to the crown, as well as their reputed honesty and familiarity with local conditions. At the time, only freemen, and not serfs (who outnumbered freemen by about ten to one), were permitted to serve on juries. In land disputes, juries had to include four knights as well as twelve freemen, with a majority of twelve required for a verdict. Blue-ribbon juries of landowners handled appeals from other juries and disputes considered particularly complex. Until 1972, in fact, an individual had to own property to serve as a juror in England.

Many colonial courts in North America had strict property requirements for jurors as well. Even after independence, juries consisted of the more elite members of the population. Property qualifications existed for both voting and jury duty. Likewise, women were not eligible to serve as jurors, just as they were not eligible to vote. During the 1800s many states dropped their property requirements, but at least a dozen still retained them in the last quarter of that century. Some states selected their jurors from voter rolls and some from tax rolls (which automatically limited them to property owners); some jurors were selected by judges, town officials, or county supervisors, and some through a "key-man" system, wherein jury commissioners consulted prominent members of the community ("key men") for suggestions of jurors.

The federal courts impaneled elite juries through the key-man system until 1968, when Congress passed the Jury Selection and Service Act, which requires federal courts to select jurors randomly from the list of registered voters (supplemented by other lists when appropriate). Congress took this action specifically to ensure jury independence and impartiality. In the hearings preceding passage of the reform bill, Judge Irving R. Kaufman of the Court of Appeals for the Second Circuit responded to the argument that jurors should continue to be carefully selected by key men to ensure that they would have sufficient intelligence and common sense:

> Long experience with subjective requirements such as "intelligence" and "common sense" has demonstrated beyond any doubt that these vague terms provide a fertile ground for discrimination and arbitrariness, even when the jury officials act in good faith. . . . We have learned that at the present time a prospective juror may be considered unfit for jury service because he is not very articulate, or speaks with an accent, or appears nervous (something all of us experience in strange or new settings). But all these considerations are arbitrary. They have nothing to do with "intelligence," "common sense," or, what is more important, ability to understand the issues in a trial. *And they are discriminatory—usually against the poor.*
>
> The end result of subjective tests is not to secure more intelligent jurors, but more homogeneous jurors. If this is sought in the American jury, then it will become very much like the English jury—predominately middle-aged middle-class and middle-minded. . . .
>
> But, I submit, such a goal is not in harmony with our historic jury tradition. *If the law is to reflect the moral sense of the community, the whole community—and not just a special part—must help to shape it.* If the jury's verdict is to reflect the community's judgment—*the whole community's judgment*—jurors must be fairly selected from *a cross section of the whole community,* not merely a segment of it.
>
> (Emphasis added.)

As a result of the 1968 legislation, all litigants in federal courts entitled to trial by jury have the right to juries "selected at random from a fair cross section of the community." The act further states that all citizens have the opportunity to serve on juries, and strengthens this commitment by pledging that "no citizen shall be excluded from service as a . . . juror . . . on account of race, color, religion, sex, national origin, or economic status."

Most states also now use random selection systems, drawing names usually from lists of voters or holders of driver's licenses or both. It is preferable to use more than one list and to experiment to determine which lists work best to provide a cross section of the community, because no one list is likely to be adequate and different communities will require different approaches. For example, nonwhites, the poor, the less educated, and the young register to vote at substantially lower rates than the rest of the population, and so the exclusive use of the voter list is unlikely to produce a representative jury in many communities. It is also important to use recent lists in order to ensure that persons who have recently moved are not excluded from the source of names.

If a litigant challenges a jury selection process as being discriminatory, the reviewing court will require the challenger to show both that some clearly identifiable group has been deprived of its fair share of seats on jury panels and that this deprivation occurred not by chance but through governmental design at some level. Ethnic minorities and women are examples of identifiable groups that must not be underrepresented under this test. Some courts have also heard challenges relating to the underrepresentation of young adults, daily-wage earners, the less educated, and members of specific religious groups.

THE EXCUSING PROCESS. Underrepresentation can also creep into the jury-selection process at the stage when excuses are granted to prospective jurors. Although jury service is a right and privilege of citizenship, many persons consider it a nuisance. Being a juror is time-consuming, inconvenient, and frequently a financial hardship. In some jurisdictions, jurors may be required to serve for several weeks or even months.

In those areas requiring long service, about 60 percent of all persons whose names are pulled from the master wheel return their questionnaires asking to be excused (or do not return them at all). How the court clerks and trial judges respond to requests for excuses and pursue those who do not answer can play a major role in determining the makeup of the panels. Some jury commissioners grant all requests automatically, because they believe that any person who does not want to serve will not be a good juror. Especially likely to be excused are women (because they are presumed to be needed for child-care duties), blue-collar workers (because their employers are less likely to continue to pay them during jury service), the young (because they are in school), and the old (because they often have health and transportation problems).

Federal jurors receive $40 a day, or $5.00 an hour, which is only slightly below the minimum wage. State courts generally pay even less, averaging slightly above $20 a day. Many employees, but not all, continue to receive their normal salaries during jury duty. White-collar professionals are much more likely to continue to receive their pay than blue-collar workers. And the larger the employer, the more likely it is that employees will be paid during their jury duty. Housewives, students, retired persons, daily-wage earners, and the self-employed are essentially asked to donate their time to the jury system.

Aside from monetary considerations, the prospect of a long period of service discourages many persons from willingly serving as jurors. Jurors in some federal courts are on call for four months and report for duty on thirty separate court days. To counter this problem, an increasing number of progressive courts have been moving to a "one day, one trial" system. Under this system, each juror is called only for one day and sent into one trial. If selected, the juror serves for the duration of the trial. (Most trials are over in a day, but some are longer.) If not selected, the person goes home and is not called again until drawn from the jury wheel at some future time. Such a system makes it much harder for a prospective juror to claim hardship and request an excuse from service, and the resulting jury panels are more likely to reflect the diversity of the community.

The states that have moved in this direction have also frequently abandoned the long list of occupational groups that are entitled to automatic excuses. These states now require an individual showing of "undue hardship, extreme inconvenience, or public necessity" before a person will be excused from service. In many states, police officers, lawyers, and even judges have served as jurors without causing any significant problems.

VOIR DIRE AND CHALLENGES. The final stage in the selection of the jury, which involves the questioning of jurors by the judge and attorneys, may also introduce unsatisfactory procedures. A prospective juror will be removed from the jury panel "for cause" if the judge determines that he or she has some deep-seated bias or partiality that would interfere with a fair evaluation of the evidence. The court's acceptance of a challenge for cause will depend upon a finding of specific bias (for example, a potential juror's relationship to the defense, prosecution, or a witness) or nonspecific bias (for example, prejudicial views on race or religion) that might play a part in the case.

Litigants can also exercise a set number of "peremptory challenges" to remove prospective jurors who appear unsympathetic to their cause, without giving any reason whatsoever. The number of these peremptory challenges varies from two to twenty-six, depending on the jurisdiction and seriousness of the crime.

Challenges can sometimes serve to restore balance when the process of selecting jurors has distorted the demographic profile of the jury panel, as is often the case. They may, however, make the jury less representative than the original jury wheel, even to the point of removing all members of a race or group from the jury. If the jury panel sent into the courtroom is indeed representative and does fairly reflect the community's diverse biases, challenging certain jurors because of their prejudices may alter the cross section of views represented.

Prior to the exercise of challenges, the attorneys, the judge, or both, question the prospective jurors about their backgrounds and their views. This questioning procedure is known as *voir dire,* an ancient term variously translated as "to speak the truth" or "to see what is said." The process of questioning varies widely from court to court. In federal courts judges tend to control the questioning, but in many states the attorneys question the jurors directly.

Court observers have engaged in heated debate over which system of questioning best serves the judicial process. Trial attorneys prefer to question the jurors directly, because they feel that their own familiarity with the case enables them to ask questions that will elicit hidden prejudices and because they want to establish personal rapport with the jurors. Judges sometimes respond that trial attorneys abuse this process by trying to persuade the jurors about the merits of the case and that questioning by attorneys takes too much court time. The proper resolution of this debate is probably to have some questioning by both the judge and the attorneys. The judge can ask the general questions, followed by more-specific questioning by the attorneys subject to judicial guidance so that the process does not become endlessly prolonged.

The right to question jurors for nonspecific bias was established in 1807 in the treason trial of Aaron Burr.

In the early English courts, prospective jurors could be questioned and challenged only for specific bias; this limitation survives in the United Kingdom and Canada. In the colonies that became the United States, however, litigants demanded the right to question jurors about their general prejudices or nonspecific biases as well. This issue was an important one during the revolutionary era. The right to question jurors for nonspecific bias was finally established in 1807 by Chief Justice John Marshall in the trial of Aaron Burr for treason. Marshall ruled that preconceived notions about the dispute were grounds for a challenge for cause and that the jurors should therefore be questioned to determine their feelings on the evidence. Marshall reasoned that a person who has preconceived ideas about the matter, like a person who has some relationship with a litigant, cannot be expected to be impartial. Because of the persuasiveness of this decision, virtually all state courts authorized the questioning of jurors in areas of nonspecific bias.

The voir dire must strike a balance to separate those few whose inflamed passions result in bias from those who can conscientiously concentrate on the evidence presented at trial, even though they are somewhat familiar with certain aspects of the case. In *Murphy* v. *Florida* (1975), the Supreme Court stated that "qualified jurors need not . . . be totally ignorant of the facts and issues involved" and that the governing standard was whether the prospective juror exhibited "a partiality that could not be laid aside." In that case, the Court sustained the conviction of a notorious figure in Florida known as Murph the Surf, even though some of the seated jurors had stated during voir dire that they remembered the press reports of the robbery incident and the defendant's prior criminal record.

The trial judge has broad discretion to decide which questions should be asked of prospective jurors to discover prejudices relevant to the facts at issue, and appellate courts will only rarely reverse a trial judge's decision. In 1973 the Supreme Court examined the case of Gene Ham, a young, bearded black who was active in the civil rights movement in South Carolina and who had been convicted of possessing marijuana and sentenced to eighteen months' imprisonment. Prior to the trial, the judge had asked the prospective jurors whether they were conscious of any bias for or against Ham and whether they could be fair and impartial. The judge refused, however, to ask whether the jurors were prejudiced against blacks, whether they would be influenced by the term *black,* whether they could disregard the defendant's beard, and whether they had been influenced by local publicity involving the drug problem. The Supreme Court ruled that the trial judge had erred by not posing the racial-prejudice question but that the Constitution does not require that questions about beards be asked because it is too difficult to "constitutionally distinguish possible prejudice against beards from a host of other possible similar prejudices" (*Ham* v. *South Carolina*).

In the late 1970s and early 1980s, some judges ruled that jurors should be questioned behind closed doors in order to protect the defendant's right to a fair trial and the privacy of prospective jurors. In 1984 the Supreme Court ruled that these concerns had to give way in most cases to the First Amendment rights of access of the public and press to all aspects of a criminal proceeding. This presumption of openness can be overcome "only by an overriding interest based on findings that closure is essential to preserve higher values and is narrowly tailored to serve that interest" (*Press-Enterprises Co.* v. *Riverside County Superior Court*).

Another controversy concerning peremptory challenges centers on whether a pattern of the use of challenges against a single ethnic group constitutes a constitutional violation. For almost a century after the Civil War, blacks rarely appeared on jury lists at all in the South. When, after years of litigation, they were finally included on lists of qualified jurors, the prosecution frequently used its peremptory challenges to exclude them completely from the jury box. This pattern of prosecutorial challenges was attacked in *Swain* v. *Alabama* (1965), but the Supreme Court ruling put only theoretical limits on the government's power.

In *Swain,* a black who had been convicted and sentenced to death for raping a white woman complained that although an average of six or seven blacks appeared on the trial-jury lists for criminal cases, not a single black person had served on a jury since 1950. Eight black men were among the prospective jurors called for Swain's trial, but none served; two were excused, and the prosecutor peremptorily challenged the other six. Despite these figures, the Supreme Court held that the defendant had not proved that the prosecution systematically and deliberately used its challenges to deny black persons the right to participate in the jury system and therefore affirmed Swain's death sentence.

The Batson *decision was significant in reaffirming the importance of juries that are representative of a cross section of the community.*

The *Swain* decision was attacked by many commentators who viewed this heavy burden of proof—and the continued prosecutorial practice of challenging minority-race jurors—as inconsistent with the strong constitutional commitment to impartial, and thus representative, juries. State courts and some federal courts began adopting their own approaches to this problem in the late 1970s, and finally, in 1986, the Supreme Court reexamined the issue and reversed the *Swain* burden of proof. *Batson* v. *Kentucky* involved a black man who was convicted of second-degree burglary and receipt of stolen goods by an all-white jury selected after the prosecutor peremptorily challenged all four black persons on the venire. The trial judge followed the *Swain* approach in ruling that the prosecutors could "strike anybody they want to."

The Supreme Court reversed the conviction, establishing a new rule to govern this situation. If a member of "a cognizable racial group" shows that "the prosecutor has exercised peremptory challenges to remove from the venire members of the defendant's race," in circumstances that indicate that the prosecutor took this action "on account of their race," then "the burden shifts to the State to come forward with a neutral explanation" for its challenges. The prosecutor cannot justify the challenges by stating "that he challenged jurors of the defendant's race on the assumption—or his intuitive judgment—that they would be partial to the defendant because of their shared race." Instead, "the prosecutor must give a 'clear and reasonably specific' explanation of his 'legitimate reasons' for exercising the challenges."

Justice Thurgood Marshall went further in his concurring opinion and argued that the use of peremptory challenges should be abolished altogether, because their use inherently works to defeat the goal of impaneling representative panels and because the standards offered by the majority are subjective and difficult to apply. The majority declined to take this step because it felt that the use of peremptory challenges has historically "served the selection of an impartial jury" and that prosecutors and trial judges would be able to conform their behavior to the Court's new standard.

The majority's approach in *Batson* should prove effective in curbing prosecutorial abuses. States using a similar test have found that it is workable in most cases and that it establishes a new mood during the jury-selection process. The *Batson* decision is significant in reaffirming the importance of juries that are representative of a cross section of the community and in indicating that the Supreme Court will continue to monitor jury selection to ensure that all racial groups are fairly represented on jury panels.

JURY SIZE. As mentioned above, twelve became the fixed size of juries in England in the mid-fourteenth century. Although some of the North American colonies experimented with smaller juries in less important trials, by the eighteenth century twelve was the universally accepted number in the United States as well. In 1970, however, the Supreme Court declared that the number twelve was a "historical accident . . . wholly without significance 'except to mystics' " and not required by the Constitution (*Williams* v. *Florida*). The Court ruled that the constitutional definition of a jury should be determined by examining the function of the jury, which is to ensure that the commonsense judgment of the community stands between the state and the accused. This function, the Court explained, was served if the number of jurors was "large enough to promote group deliberation, free from outside attempts at intimidation, and to provide a fair possibility of obtaining a representative cross-section of the community." Applying these principles to the six-person jury used in Florida in all but capital cases, the Court concluded that the smaller size did not impair the function of the jury, because there was "no discernible difference between the results reached by the two different-sized juries" and because the "reliability of the jury as a factfinder hardly seems likely to be a function of its size." The Court did not, however, make any real attempt to examine relevant social science data to test this hypothesis.

Eight years later, the Court ruled that juries with fewer than six were unconstitutional (*Ballew* v. *Georgia*). The court reviewed the extensive literature on jury size that had developed since *Williams* and concluded that a jury's size may well affect the reliability of its verdicts.

Social scientists writing after *Williams* tended to criticize both the Court's result and its use of social science data. The Court summarized the literature and concluded from it that "progressively smaller juries are less likely to foster effective group deliberation," that "the data now raise doubts about the accuracy of the results achieved by smaller and smaller panels," that "the verdicts of jury deliberations in criminal cases will vary as juries become smaller, and that the variance amounts to an imbalance to the detriment of one side, the defense," and that decreases in jury size reduce the representation of minority groups of juries.

The reduced reliability of a smaller jury should be the central concern. With fewer jurors, some details in the evidence may be missed or forgotten. Studies also show that a smaller jury in civil cases rules in favor of the defendant more often than a larger jury. Apparently a larger group is needed to legitimize departures from the status quo. The decrease in minority representation on six-person juries was dramatically illustrated in Florida in the early 1980s when a series of all-white six-person juries were assembled to adjudicate charges against white police officers charged with abusing blacks. The acquittals by the all-white juries were followed by extensive rioting in the black communities and substantial dissatisfaction with the jury system.

The Court in *Ballew* also examined contentions that smaller juries saved time and money; it concluded that these savings were small or nonexistent. In sum, the Court held that criminal juries of fewer than six would violate the guarantees of an impartial jury and the equal protection of the laws found in the Sixth and Fourteenth Amendments. The Court refused, however, to take the next logical step and reexamine its 1970 decision in *Williams,* which permitted juries of fewer than twelve.

Only a few states have in fact reduced the size of their criminal juries since 1970, and most of those that have done so have reduced jury size for trials of misdemeanors only. Most state systems and the federal judicial system have remained committed to the criminal jury of twelve.

The federal courts have since the early 1970s used six-person juries for civil cases, and many important cases have been decided by only six citizens, including the multimillion-dollar defamation suit won in 1974 by Robert Maheu against Howard Hughes in Los Angeles; the $12 million damage suit won by the American Civil Liberties Union in Washington, D.C., in 1975 on behalf of 1,200 antiwar demonstrators who had been unlawfully arrested on the steps of the Capitol in 1971; and the case brought by the County of Honolulu against the city's two daily newspapers for allegedly violating the federal antitrust laws (which incidentally ended in a 3–3 hung jury).

Serious questions exist as to whether juries of only six can adequately serve the purpose of representing the community to make the sensitive judgments required in cases such as these with broad public implications. The Hawaii jury mentioned above consisted, for instance, of six women and no men, and no matter how carefully a six-person jury is selected in Hawaii, it cannot contain representatives of all the ethnic groups that make up the state's diverse population. Should a decision that could have led to the demise of one of the city's two daily newspapers have been made by a body that did not contain members of both sexes and represent the different ethnic communities in the islands? Similar questions are raised when a jury is permitted to reach a decision by a less-than-unanimous verdict.

THE UNANIMITY REQUIREMENT. The requirement that a jury reach its decision unanimously became a firm rule in England during the fourteenth century, and the North American colonies accepted the unanimity requirement with virtually no dissent. Agreement by all of the jurors in a judgment served to legitimize the decision, giving the community a sense that the conclusion must be correct. When experimenting communities permitted a less-than-unanimous verdict and one or more jurors recorded a disagreement with the result, doubts would continue that perhaps the opposite conclusion might have been the proper one. These early experiments were therefore always short-lived.

The unanimity requirement has been criticized as wasteful and time-consuming, because it sometimes leads to a "hung jury" (a jury that cannot reach a unanimous verdict) and thus to an expensive retrial or the dismissal of charges. Louisiana, whose law is based more on the French system than on the English tradition, has permitted 9–3 verdicts in all felony cases except capital cases. In 1934, Oregon voted to permit 10–2 jury judgments in all but capital cases. The United Kingdom moved in 1967 to a system permitting a trial judge to accept a 10–2 verdict, but the British judge can do so only after the jury has deliberated together for at least two hours without reaching agreement.

Until 1972, the United States Supreme Court consistently recognized that unanimity was an essential component of the Sixth Amendment's guarantee of trial by jury in criminal cases. (*Thompson* v. *Utah,* 1898; *Patton* v. *United States,* 1930). In 1972, however, the Court upheld (over strong dissent) the Louisiana and Oregon laws as constitutional (*Johnson* v. *Louisiana; Apodaca* v. *Oregon*). The Court also implicitly ruled that less-than-unanimous verdicts would not be permitted in federal courts. When faced seven years later with the question of whether a less-than-unanimous verdict is constitutionally permissible in state courts if only six jurors are utilized, the Court said no, concluding unanimously that a 5–1 jury decision violates the safeguards that the jury is designed to provide in criminal trials (*Burch* v. *Louisiana*).

Even though the Court now permits states to use nonunanimous verdicts with juries of twelve, no other states have joined Louisiana and Oregon in allowing them in felony trials, and only a few have adopted the less-than-unanimous approach for misdemeanor trials. Strong policy arguments favor retaining the unanimity requirement. Unanimity is essential to the legitimacy of verdicts and to confidence in the legal system, because it supports the fairness of verdicts. Losing parties are much less apt to complain if their defenses have failed to convince even a single juror.

The unanimity requirement ensures careful weighing of the evidence in dispute. In a nonunanimous system, the jurors stop deliberating sooner and the majority jurors pay less attention to the jurors arguing minority viewpoints. Judge Lois G. Forer of the Philadelphia Court of Common Pleas kept records when her court system moved from a unanimous system to a five-sixths requirement for civil verdicts in the early 1980s, and she noted that the average time for deliberations dropped from four to two hours. In addition, she found that she disagreed with many of the five-sixths verdicts but found the unanimous verdicts to conform to her judgments ("Split Verdicts in Pennsylvania"). Unanimity thus reinforces the requirement that juries be selected from a representative cross section of the community, because it gives each juror, even members of small minorities, a voice.

In addition, unanimity sustains the delicate power balance between the government and the defendant. To prevent oppression by the government, which has awesome power and resources that the individual defendant cannot hope to match, the defendant is protected by certain rights and procedures. Unanimity is one of those rights. Finally, unanimity supports the constitutional requirement that no defendant be convicted except by proof beyond a reasonable doubt and the social decision that "it is far worse to convict an innocent man than to let a guilty man go free" (*In re Winship,* 1970, Justice Harlan concurring).

A number of arguments have been made for abolishing the unanimity requirement. Its abolition would arguably reduce the time and expense of trials by lowering the number of trials that result in hung juries, deal with the problem of jury tampering and juror corruption, and reduce the possibility of one stubborn juror thwarting the majority. These arguments are not convincing. Efficiency gains would be minimal, because the number of hung juries is small in general and some occur even in the less-than-unanimous systems. Although jury tampering is not unknown in the United States, not enough of this type of criminal conduct occurs to warrant preventive measures as drastic as elimination of the unanimity principle. Less drastic alternatives, such as stricter enforcement of laws against jury tampering, are certainly available. Finally, the premise that a single stubborn juror irrationally upsets the reasoned views of other jurors was disproved by the Chicago Jury Project, which found that juries that begin with a large majority in either direction almost never hang. Only if a sizable minority—four or five jurors—disagrees with the other jurors on the first vote will a hung jury result. For one or two jurors to hold out to the end, they must have had companionship at the beginning of deliberations (Kalven and Zeisel, 462–463).

These arguments are somewhat less persuasive in the context of civil trials, where the jury must determine the verdict by a "preponderance of the evidence" instead of by the "beyond a reasonable doubt" standard used in criminal trials. Over three-fifths of the states now permit less-than-unanimous verdicts in civil cases, allowing the jury to return a judgment by a three-fourths or five-sixths margin.

No enthusiasm has developed for such experimentation in criminal cases. The legitimacy of the jury's verdict as an expression of the conscience of the community is brought into question by juries of fewer than twelve and by less-than-unanimous verdicts. The ability of juries to reflect minority viewpoints is hampered by smaller juries and will be erased in many cases in which unanimity is not required. The jury is a preserver of independence and freedom as well as a fact finder. Both functions are threatened by the Supreme Court's removal of the constitutional barriers to juries of less than twelve and less-than-unanimous verdicts. But the ultimate determination of the wisdom of abandoning these safeguards rests in the hands of the legislators and the people, and thus far they have resisted making any major changes.

CASES THAT REQUIRE JURIES. The Sixth Amendment guarantees a trial by an "impartial jury" to all persons accused of serious crimes. The Supreme Court has interpreted this provision to apply to all criminal charges that could lead to an imprisonment of six months or more (*Duncan* v. *Louisiana,* 1968). Some states, such as California, guarantee a jury trial to anyone facing any criminal charges whatsoever, including traffic offenses.

As mentioned above, the Seventh Amendment requires that civil cases in federal courts be decided by juries (unless the litigants agree to a decision by the judge alone) if the dispute involves $20 or more. This requirement has not been imposed on the states, and each state has established its own rules on which types of civil disputes warrant a jury trial.

Unanimity supports the constitutional requirement that no defendant be convicted except by proof beyond a reasonable doubt.

In 1980 the Court of Appeals for the Third Circuit ruled that certain civil cases—involving protracted antitrust violations, for instance—are too "complex" for lay juries and should instead be decided by a judge who is better equipped to sort out evidence presented over a months-long trial (*Matsushita Electric Industrial Co.* v. *Zenith Radio Corp.*). This view has also been championed by Chief Justice Warren Burger, who said in a lecture at Loyola University, New Orleans, in November 1984 that extremely technical cases should be heard by a three-judge panel or by a jury of highly qualified people. The most competent members of a community do not serve on juries, he contended, because they do not have time for such service and because lawyers are afraid of jurors who know too much.

Most other judges have, however, rejected this view. Although it is certainly true that some modern trials do present difficult technical data, most observers have been reluctant to abandon a centuries-long commitment to the common-sense verdict of lay jurors, and suggestions that "complex" trials be given instead to "experts" for decision have not been received with enthusiasm. Chief Justice Burger's concern about the unrepresentative quality of juries should, of course, be addressed by appropriate reforms such as moving to the one-day, one-trial approach, limiting excuses, and guiding voir dire and the use of peremptory challenges as discussed above, rather than by wholesale alteration of the traditional role played by civil juries in the American judicial system.

Conclusion

The use of the jury and the grand jury as institutions of self-governance for eight hundred years are powerful statements of commitment to democratic institutions. Decision-making by citizens provides a level of common sense and a stamp of democratic legitimacy that cannot be attained by "experts," no matter how skilled they may be. Discretion and sound judgment must be exercised by some group, and American society has found that these decisions are made in the most reliable fashion if made by a representative group of ordinary persons with no personal ambition or stake in the matter. Only such a random sample of community members can render judgments that are truly impartial, reflecting the community's norms and collective conscience.

[See also (III) Adversary System, Criminal Justice System, Trial Courts and Practice.]

CASES

Apodaca v. Oregon, 406 U.S. 404 (1972)
Ballew v. Georgia, 435 U.S. 223 (1978)
Batson v. Kentucky, 106 S. Ct. 1712 (1986)
Branzburg v. Hayes, 408 U.S. 665 (1972)
Burch v. Louisiana, 441 U.S. 130 (1979)
Bushell's Case, 6 St. Tr. 999 (1670)
Duncan v. Louisiana, 391 U.S. 145 (1968)
Ham v. South Carolina, 409 U.S. 524 (1973)
Hurtado v. California, 110 U.S. 516 (1884)
Johnson v. Louisiana, 406 U.S. 356 (1972)
Matsushita Electric Industrial Co. v. Zenith Radio Corp., 631 F.2d 1069 (3d Cir. 1980)
Murphy v. Florida, 421 U.S. 794 (1975)
Patton v. United States, 281 U.S. 276 (1930)
Penn and Mead's Case, 6 St. Tr. 951 (1670)
Press-Enterprises Co. v. Riverside County Superior Court, 464 U.S. 501 (1984)
Quadra v. San Francisco Superior Court, 403 F. Supp. 486 (1975)
Swain v. Alabama, 380 U.S. 202 (1965)
Thompson v. Utah, 170 U.S. 343 (1898)
United States v. Gometz, 730 F.2d 475 (7th Cir. 1984)
United States v. Mara, 410 U.S. 19 (1973)
United States v. Nixon, 418 U.S. 683 (1974)
Williams v. Florida, 399 U.S. 78 (1970)
In re Winship, 397 U.S. 358 (1970)

BIBLIOGRAPHY

Leroy Clark, *The Grand Jury: The Use and Abuse of Political Power* (1975), provides a history of the grand jury and then focuses on the abuses that occurred during the Nixon administration. Patrick Devlin, *Trial by Jury* (1956), is a useful historical survey of the jury combined with an analysis of certain issues about its use. Ann Fagan Ginger, *Jury Selection in Civil & Criminal Trials,* 2 vols., 2nd ed. (1985), examines the practical problems facing lawyers who are selecting juries, with many examples of strategies that have been used.

Reid Hastie, Steven D. Penrod, and Nancy Pennington, *Inside the Jury* (1983), is a fine social science analysis of how juries operate in their deliberations, which complements Harry Kalven and Hans Zeisel, *The American Jury* (1966), a path-breaking study of the process of jury decision-making. Lloyd E. Moore, *The Jury: Tool of Kings, Palladium of Liberty* (1973), is a lively and informative survey of how juries have been used over the years. John Profatt, *A Treatise on Trial by Jury* (1877), is an earlier classic study on the subject. Rita J. Simon, *The Jury: Its Role in American Society* (1980), is a good analysis of both the social science literature on juries and policy questions about its role. "Split Verdicts in Pennsylvania," in *Center for Jury Studies Newsletter,* 3, no. 6 (1981), reports the findings of Judge Forer's study. Lysander Spooner, *An Essay on the Trial by Jury* (1852; repr. 1971), is another classic study, which focuses on the jury's power and its lawmaking role.

Jon M. Van Dyke, *Jury Selections Procedures: Our Uncertain Commitment to Representative Panels* (1977), focuses in particular on how juries are formed and the types of discrimination that still exist in the selection process; this volume also looks at questions of jury size and unanimity and jury nullification. Richard D. Younger, *The People's Panel: The Grand Jury in the United States, 1634–1941* (1963), is a useful study of the historical role of the grand jury.

– JON M. VAN DYKE

U

UNITED STATES COURT OF APPEALS FOR THE FEDERAL CIRCUIT

This court was created by the Federal Courts Improvement Act (1982), to take over the Jurisdiction of the Court of Customs and Patent Appeals and the Court of Claims. Its first judges were the judges of the superseded courts. It is a constitutional court, whose twelve judges serve for life during good behavior.

The Federal Circuit, like the other United States Courts of Appeals, is an intermediate appellate court; its jurisdiction, however, is defined not by region but by subject matter. It has nationwide jurisdiction to hear appeals in cases chiefly of the types previously heard by the superseded courts: customs and patent matters, and claims against the United States. In the future, however, other types of cases may be added to the Federal Circuit's jurisdiction—tax appeals, for example. Such developments might relieve some of the pressure on the Supreme Court's docket, effectively removing certain technical and specialized areas from the Court's work load. Many proponents of the 1982 act regard the creation of this opportunity as the act's most important achievement.

– KENNETH L. KARST

UNITED STATES COURTS OF APPEALS

The United States Courts of Appeals form the intermediate component of the three-tiered federal judiciary, lying between the United States District Courts and the Supreme Court of the United States. As such, they normally serve as the first courts of review in the federal judicial system. But because of the natural limitations upon the Supreme Court's capacity, the Courts of Appeals are often also the final courts of review.

Article III, section 1, of the Constitution provides: "The judicial power of the United States, shall be vested in one supreme Court, and in such inferior Courts as the Congress may from time to time ordain and establish." Thus, in contrast to the Supreme Court, inferior federal courts were not required by the Constitution; rather, their creation was left to the discretion of Congress. Such treatment reflected a compromise between two views, one favoring the mandatory creation of inferior courts, and the other completely opposed to the existence of any such courts.

The Courts of Appeals are relative newcomers to the federal judicial system, having been born with the Circuit Courts of Appeals Act (Evarts Act) of 1891. The Courts of Appeals were created to solve an acute crisis in the federal judiciary stemming from the limited capacity of the existing system, which had remained largely unchanged since the Judiciary Act of 1789. That act had established a bilevel system of inferior federal courts. There were, first of all, single-judge "district courts," generally one per state. The Union was also divided into several "circuits." Circuit court was to be held twice a year in each of the districts encompassed by a given circuit. At these sittings, cases would be heard by a three-judge panel consisting of two Supreme Court Justices and the district judge for the district in which the circuit court was being held.

The seeds of the modern federal courts of appeals were planted by the first Judiciary Act.

Having determined to avail itself of its constitutional prerogative to establish inferior federal courts, Congress faced the further issue of those courts' appropriate function and jurisdiction. In the debates over Article III, there had been substantial support for giving Congress the power to create only admiralty courts, rather than inferior courts of general jurisdiction. No such limitation was adopted, however. It has therefore been generally assumed that Congress is constitutionally free to define the role of the inferior federal courts however it chooses.

The manner that Congress selected in the 1789 act is of some interest. The district courts were, and remain today, trial courts or courts of first instance. The circuit courts, in distinct contrast to today's middle-tier courts, also functioned primarily as trial courts. In the area of private civil law, the circuit courts' jurisdiction was largely concurrent with that of the district courts: it encompassed cases within the diversity jurisdiction, but not federal question cases. (Original federal jurisdiction was not extended to federal question cases until 1875.) Similarly, with respect to civil suits by the United States, both circuit and district courts were given original jurisdiction, the only difference being that the requisite amount in controversy was higher for circuit court jurisdiction.

The circuit courts even had certain original jurisdiction that the district courts lacked. The first removal jurisdiction was vested in the circuit courts alone. And the circuit courts had exclusive jurisdiction over most federal crimes.

Nonetheless, the seeds of the modern federal courts of appeals were planted by the first Judiciary Act. The early circuit courts had appellate jurisdiction in civil cases involving disputes over amounts exceeding $50, and in admiralty cases exceeding $300. (A district judge sitting as a circuit judge was not, however, permitted to vote on appeals from his own decisions.) Unlike the modern courts of appeals, however, the circuit courts were the final federal forum for many of these cases. In civil suits, circuit court judgments were reviewable only when the amount in dispute exceeded $2,000. Judgments in criminal cases were categorically unreviewable.

The early circuit courts proved problematic, in the main because of the burden that circuit riding placed on the Supreme Court Justices. Congress attempted to alleviate that hardship by reducing from two to one the number of Justices required to sit on a circuit court, but the benefit of the reduction was more than outweighed by several important augmentations of the High Court's jurisdiction that were enacted by Congress during the century following the 1789 Judiciary Act. Most notable of such legislation was the Judiciary Act of 1875, which granted the lower courts, as well as the Supreme Court, nearly the full scope of Article III jurisdiction, including original federal question jurisdiction in the district and circuit courts. The federal courts, already vastly overloaded with cases, were virtually submerged after this act. Reform was inevitable.

Indeed, attempts to improve the judicial system had more than once been made. In 1801 Congress had enacted the Judiciary Act of 1801 (the "Law of the Midnight Judges"), which among other things had established permanent circuit judgeships, three to a circuit. When political tides shifted the following year, however, the act was repealed, and the system reverted essentially to its original condition, except that Congress permitted circuit court to be held by a single judge, rather than three. Much later, in 1869, Congress partially restored the plan of 1801 by creating a single permanent circuit judgeship for each of the nine circuits then in existence. And in 1887 and 1888 Congress passed a series of measures aimed at pruning the expanded jurisdiction of the lower federal courts.

But it was not until the Evarts Act that Congress provided structural reforms adequate to the crisis of judicial overload. The act established three-judge courts of appeals for each of the nine circuits, and increased the number of permanent circuit judgeships to two per circuit. The third appeals judge would in most instances be a district judge (though Supreme Court Justices remained eligible), but the act, following the rule set down by the Act of 1789, barred district judges from reviewing their own decisions.

Curiously, the Evarts Act left the old circuit courts standing, although it did remove their appellate jurisdiction. Until these courts were abolished in 1911, there thus functioned two sets of federal trial courts.

The vast majority of important constitutional precedents are produced not by the courts of appeals but by the Supreme Court.

The Evarts Act provided for direct review by the Supreme Court of the decisions of the district courts and the old circuit courts, in some important cases. The new circuit courts of appeals would review the remainder. Under the act, a circuit court's decision in an admiralty or diversity case would be final, unless that court certified a question to the Supreme Court or the Supreme Court granted a writ of certiorari in order to review the circuit court's decision. In most other cases, circuit court decisions were appealable as of right.

Since the Evarts Act, only a few significant alterations have been made to the federal judicial system in general, and the courts of appeals in particular. The rules governing Supreme Court review are perhaps the most important arena of change. In 1925, Congress replaced appeal as of right with discretionary review for all circuit court judgments except those holding a state statute unconstitutional. In 1937, Congress passed a law permitting appeal to the Supreme Court from any judgment by a federal court holding an act of Congress unconstitutional in any civil case to which the United States is a party.

In 1948 the circuit courts established by the Evarts Act were renamed; each court is now known as the United States Court of Appeals for the ____ Circuit. The number of circuits has also been increased; and there is now a "Federal Circuit" court to hear appeals from the Claims Court and from district courts in patent cases or in cases arising under the Tucker Act. Finally, procedures in the various courts of appeals were standardized in 1968 in the Federal Rules of Appellate Procedure. Each circuit, however, retains its own rulemaking power for matters not covered by the Federal Rules.

The chief work of the courts of appeals is the review of final judgments of the United States district courts. The courts, however, are also empowered to review certain orders that are not strictly final, essentially when the benefit of such review clearly outweighs any attendant disruption and delay of district court proceedings. In addition, Congress has enabled the appeals courts to issue the extraordinary writ of mandamus and writ of prohibition in cases in which district courts may abuse their constitutional powers. Finally, the statutes governing many of the various federal administrative agencies provide for direct review of agency adjudication and rule-making in the court of appeals for the circuit in which the party seeking review resides, or in the Court of Appeals for the District of Columbia Circuit. The latter circuit court has been a frequent forum for challenges, constitutional and otherwise, to federal agency action.

To understand the role of the courts of appeals in the development of constitutional law, it is necessary to understand the relationship between the appeals courts and the Supreme Court. As was noted above, since the Judiciary Act of 1925, the "Judges Bill," the Supreme Court has had a discretionary power of review of most circuit court decisions. Again, however, appeal as of right lies in cases in which the appeals court has held a state statute to be repugnant to the Constitution, laws, or treaties of the United States, and in civil cases in which either a court of appeals or a district court has held an act of Congress unconstitutional and the United States is a party. Nonetheless, neither type of case in which appeal is of right bulks very large in the overall volume of appeals from circuit courts, and of those, many are denied Supreme Court review for want of a substantial federal question.

Accordingly, the Supreme Court has the discretion to review or not to review the vast majority of decisions by the courts of appeals. Not surprisingly, because of the limited capacity of the High Court, its discretion is much more often exercised to deny review than to grant it. As a general rule, in fact, the Supreme Court tends not to review appeals court decisions unless the issues involved either have an urgent importance or have received conflicting treatment by different circuits, or both.

One might conclude that, because the Supreme Court does review important cases, the appeals courts have no significant role in the development of constitutional law. Constitutional law, however, is not the product solely of the Supreme Court.

To begin, the Supreme Court can only review a decision that a party seeks to have reviewed; not every losing party in the court of appeals may do so. For example, in *Kennedy* v. *Sampson* (1974) the District of Columbia Circuit construed the pocket veto clause of the Constitution (Article 1, section 7, clause 2) to bar the President from exercising the pocket veto power during brief, intrasession adjournments of Congress. The President then declined to seek review in the Supreme Court; he chose instead to acquiesce in the rule laid down by the appeals court. The court's decision thus became a cornerstone of the law respecting the presentation of laws for presidential approval.

Of course, as a glance at any constitutional law textbook or casebook reveals, the vast majority of important constitutional precedents are produced not by the courts of appeals but by the Supreme Court. Decisions like *Kennedy* are thus the exception, not the rule. Nonetheless, in several ways the appeals courts contribute significantly to the development of constitutional law.

Before a constitutional issue is decided by the Supreme Court, it will often have received a thorough ventilation by one or more circuit courts. The Supreme Court thus has the benefit of the circuit judges' consideration of difficult constitutional matters, and may sometimes explicitly adopt the reasoning of the court of appeals. For example, in *United States* v. *Dennis* (1950) the Second Circuit faced the difficult issue of whether, and if so, how, the clear and present danger test applied to a conspiracy to advocate the overthrow of the government by force and violence and to organize a political party for the purpose of such advocacy. The Court of Appeals, in an opinion by Judge Learned Hand, held that such advocacy was unprotected by the First Amendment even though the actual forceful overthrow of the government was not imminent. The Supreme Court affirmed the decision in *Dennis* v. *United States* (1951), and its opinion adopted much of Judge Hand's analysis, including Judge Hand's "clear and present danger" formula, namely, "whether the gravity of the 'evil,' discounted by its improbability, justifies such invasion of free speech as is necessary to avoid the danger."

The role of the courts of appeals in resolving novel issues of constitutional law, however, is only half of the picture. Equally important is the appeals courts' adjudication of cases raising issues on which the Supreme Court has already spoken. Because the High Court can only sketch the broad outlines of constitutional doctrine, it remains for the lower courts to apply precedent, elaborate or clarify it, and extrapolate from it. Because appeal from the district courts to the appeals court is of right, and because most litigation never reaches the Supreme Court, it is in the courts of appeals that the Supreme Court's sketch is worked into a fully drawn landscape.

When the Supreme Court decides not to give plenary review to a case arising from an appeals court, what implication should be drawn concerning the value of the appeals court's opinion as a precedent? By denying a petition for certiorari or dismissing an appeal as of right for want of jurisdiction, the Court formally indicates no view of the merits or demerits of the appeals court's decision. Nonetheless, it is commonly thought that the Supreme Court generally does not decline to review an appeals court decision that it finds clearly incorrect. Similarly, when the Supreme Court summarily affirms an appeals court's decision, it is formally signaling its agreement with the result only, and not necessarily the reasoning of the lower court. Yet, such affirmances are popularly thought to indicate at least the Court's tentative agreement with the substance of the lower court's opinion.

Since the early 1960s, the federal courts at all three levels have experienced a dramatic and continuing increase in their workload. At the district and circuit levels, Congress has responded by adding judges to existing courts. When the number of judges in a circuit has become sufficiently great, Congress has divided the circuit into two. That course is not entirely satisfactory, however, because it tends to push the appeals courts in the direction of being regional, rather than national courts, and increases the likelihood of inter-circuit conflict.

At the Supreme Court level, Congress has made no significant changes. Various proposals for reducing the Court's workload would also affect adjudication at the appeals court level. A frequent suggestion has been to establish a national court of appeals. In one version, the national court would sit only to resolve conflicts among the circuits, thereby eliminating a significant share of the Supreme Court's annual docket. In another version, the national court would screen cases to determine those worthy of Supreme Court review. Another proposal would reduce the Supreme Court's workload by eliminating appeal as of right. One effect of such a measure, of course, would be to increase the number of appeals court decisions that are effectively final.

BIBLIOGRAPHY

Bator, Paul M.; Mishkin, Paul J.; Shapiro, David L.; and Wechsler, Herbert 1973 *Hart and Wechsler's The Federal Courts and the Federal System,* 2nd ed. Mineola, N.Y.: Foundation Press.

Wright, Charles A. 1983 *Handbook of the Law of Federal Courts.* St. Paul, Minn.: West Publishing Co.

– CARL MCGOWAN

UNITED STATES DISTRICT COURTS

In enacting Article III, the Framers of the Constitution authorized the establishment of a federal judicial system consisting of a Supreme Court and such inferior courts as Congress might decide to establish. In the Judiciary Act of 1789 Congress created a Supreme Court, divided the country into three circuits, authorized a circuit court to sit in each circuit, and established a federal district court in each of the states. The Supreme Court was the only truly appellate court in the system. Unlike the modern courts of appeal, the old circuit courts, while exercising some appellate jurisdiction, were intended to be the chief federal trial courts. A Supreme Court Justice riding the circuit and judges of the district courts in the circuit manned each of these circuit courts.

The federal district courts were empowered to sit at various times in specified locations within the states where they were located. They were tribunals of very limited jurisdiction and originally had as their main function the adjudication of admiralty and maritime matters. It was anticipated that the state trial courts or federal circuit courts would handle, as trial courts, the most important legal issues facing the new nation. The federal district courts were empowered to try minor criminal cases. In addition, they had concurrent jurisdiction with the circuit courts over suits by aliens for tort violations of a treaty or the law of nations, suits against consuls, and disputes in which the federal government initiated the proceeding and the matter in controversy was $100 or less. However, district court jurisdiction was exclusive in admiralty, over seizures of land for violation of federal statutes, and over seizures under import, navigation, and trade statutes.

This limited and specialized jurisdiction has steadily expanded. Today the district court is the only federal nonspecialized court, handling both criminal and civil matters. Among the latter are admiralty cases, federal question cases, and cases within the diversity jurisdiction (cases between different states). In a diversity case the matter in controversy must exceed $10,000. No jurisdictional amount is normally required for the other exercises of the district court's civil jurisdiction. Appeals from a district court go to the United States Court of Appeals.

The first district court to be organized was the district court of New York. That court began functioning on November 3, 1789, and was the predecessor to the current district court for the Southern District of New York. Even today judges of the Southern District refer to theirs as the "Mother Court."

As the system was originally conceived, each state was to contain at least one federal district and one federal court. There has been no deviation from this pattern as the country has expanded from thirteen to fifty states. In addition, the District of Columbia and the federal territories (the Virgin Islands, Puerto Rico, and Guam) are each organized as a federal district with a district court. In over half the states, although there may be a number of federal district judges who sit in separate locations throughout the state, there is only one federal district. Twelve states are divided into two federal districts; some states have three federal districts; and California, New York, and Texas are subdivided into four federal districts.

As the country has expanded, the number of federal district judges has increased. Since 1954 the roster of federal judges has grown through enactment of legislation authorizing additional judgeships for federal district courts nationwide. The Omnibus Judgeship Act of 1978 raised the number of authorized district judges from 399 to 516. The Southern District of New York has twenty-seven authorized judgeships, the largest number of any district in the country.

Federal district judges are nominated by the President and appointed with the advice and consent of the Senate. The prevailing practice is for the selection of the nominee to come to the President from the Department of Justice. If one or both of the senators from the state in question belong to the President's party, the candidate for nomination is proposed by one or both senators and submitted to the Department of Justice for approval and recommendation to the President for nomination. Today few candidates are nominated and sent to the Senate for confirmation without first being found qualified by the American Bar Association. When the President decides to nominate a candidate, the Federal Bureau of Investigation undertakes a security check. If the candidate is cleared, the President announces the nomination and sends the name to the Senate. The Senate Judiciary Committee holds hearings, which are usually one-day affairs for candidates for federal district courts. If the Senate Judiciary Committee approves, the nomination is voted on by the full Senate.

An Article III judge has life tenure during good behavior, and his salary cannot be diminished while he is in office. The only way to remove a federal district judge from office is by impeachment. Of course, a federal judge, like any other person, may be prosecuted for criminal law violations. Bribery has been the most frequent charge, but criminal prosecutions of federal judges are rare and attempts to remove them by impeachment have been infrequent.

When the first change of political power occurred in the United States at the national level, from the Federalist party to the Republican party of Thomas Jefferson, the Jeffersonians commenced impeachment proceedings against two judges appointed by the Federalists and disliked by the Republicans: John Pickering, a judge of the district court in New Hampshire, and Samuel Chase, an Associate Justice of the Supreme Court. Pickering was convicted by the Senate in 1803, but the requisite two-thirds Senate majority could not be mustered to convict Chase. Since that time impeachment to unseat a federal judge has not been a successful political weapon. Partisan politics has from time to time generated unsuccessful calls for impeachment of various judges.

The first woman to be confirmed as a federal judge was Florence Allen, who was appointed to the Court of Appeals in 1934.

A federal district court judgeship carries considerable prestige. It is a presidential appointment; it is a national rather than a local office; and federal district court judgeships are limited in number. District judges in the main have had prior careers as prominent or distinguished lawyers before going on the bench. They are drawn for the most part from the middle and upper strata of our society. They are generally alumni of the best known law schools of the nation or of the state in which they will serve. They have generally had successful careers in private practice, often with backgrounds as federal, state, or local prosecutors. A few are former academics, and some come to court from public service careers outside government.

Until the twentieth century, all federal district judges were white males. The first woman to be confirmed as a federal judge was Florence Allen, who was appointed to the Court of Appeals for the Sixth Circuit in 1934. The first woman appointed to the district court was Burneta Matthews, who was given an interim appointment to the District of Columbia bench in 1949. She was confirmed by the Senate in 1950 for a permanent appointment. Constance Baker Motley was the first black woman to be appointed to the federal bench. She was appointed to the District Court for the Southern District of New York in 1966, and in 1982 became chief judge of that court.

William Hastie was the first black to be made a federal judge. He was appointed to the District Court of the Virgin Islands in 1937 and in 1949 was named to the Court of Appeals for the Third Circuit. James Parsons, appointed judge of the Northern District of Illinois in 1961, was the first black named a district judge in the continental United States. Since these initial appointments the number of blacks, women, and members of other ethnic minorities has grown steadily.

The first Judiciary Act authorized each court to make rules for conducting its own business, and in 1842 the Supreme Court was empowered to regulate process, pleading, proof and discovery in equity, admiralty, and law cases in the district and circuit courts. In 1938 uniform rules for conducting civil cases, entitled the Federal Rules of Civil Procedure, were adopted for the federal system. In 1946 the Federal Rules of Criminal Procedure were enacted. These rules have achieved uniformity of procedure and practice in the federal district courts throughout the nation.

It is not unusual for a judge who decides a case contrary to the majority's view to face public criticism and even social ostracism.

The typical calendar of civil cases in a federal district court contains a plethora of complex cases involving patent, trademark, and copyright infringement claims; federal securities law violations; civil rights infractions; private antitrust claims; shareholders' derivative suits; immigration and naturalization cases; employment, age, and housing discrimination claims; and claims under a variety of other federal statutes, such as the Freedom of Information Act, Investment Advisers Act, Commodities Exchange Act, Fair Labor Standards Act, and Federal Employers' Liability Act. In addition, there are seamen's injury and cargo damage claims, habeas corpus petitions by both state and federal prisoners, and litigation based on diversity jurisdiction. The criminal case load involves a variety of infractions defined in the United States criminal code.

Among the primary functions of the federal district courts are the vindication of federal rights secured by the Constitution and laws of the United States. The federal district court is often called upon to hold a state law or act unconstitutional because it violates federal constitutional guarantees or has been preempted by federal legislation. Obviously, the exercise of this power by federal district courts has the potential for creating friction and disharmony between state and federal courts. A lower federal court's power to strike down a state law on federal constitutional grounds, in the face of a contrary ruling by the highest court of the state, is not an easy pill for state judges to swallow. Federal courts have devised doctrines of comity and abstention to ease the friction. A growing number of federal judges, recognizing that state judges, too, have a duty to protect and enforce federal rights, have been inclined to give increasing deference to state court determinations of federal constitutional questions.

A burgeoning federal caseload undoubtedly promotes this inclination toward accommodation and also promotes a tightening of limitations on federal habeas corpus review of state court criminal convictions. A habeas corpus petition enables a state prisoner, after unsuccessfully appealing his conviction through the state court system, to have the matter reviewed by the federal district court to determine whether the trial and conviction violated the defendant's federal constitutional rights. Not surprisingly, habeas corpus petitions have inundated the federal courts. While most are without merit, the few petitions of substance that succeed are another cause of federal-state court friction. Rules of limitations have been imposed requiring exhaustion of state remedies and forbidding review if the state court's denial of the appeal of the criminal conviction rests on the defendant's failure to conform to state governing procedure absent a showing of cause and prejudice. (See *Wainwright* v. *Sykes,* 1977.)

Diversity jurisdiction brings to the federal courts issues of state law that would ordinarily be tried in the state courts. The initial justification for giving federal courts jurisdiction over such cases was concern that parochialism would put the out-of-state complainant at a disadvantage in seeking redress in state court against a resident of the forum state.

Exercise of federal diversity jurisdiction was at one time a cause of federal-state confusion if not friction. The district courts in diversity cases have been required to follow applicable state statutes, but until 1938 they were free to disregard state decisional law and decide on the basis of their own notions of what the common law was or should be. With the Supreme Court's decision in *Erie Railroad* v. *Tompkins* (1938) federal courts were no longer free to disregard state court decisions. Federal courts may apply their own rules as to pleading and practice but on substantive issues must function as adjuncts of the state judiciary.

Erie v. *Tompkins* has made clear that the diversity jurisdiction is a wasteful use of federal judicial resources. State court parochialism is no longer a justifiable basis for federal diversity jurisdiction. Because the federal court must apply state law, apart from federal procedural rules, the litigant is seldom better off in federal court than he would be if relegated to state courts, where increasing numbers of federal judges feel such cases belong. Congress, however, has shown little interest in divesting federal district courts of the diversity jurisdiction.

The federal district court is the place where litigation usually commences to test the constitutional validity of state or federal governmental action with national implication. These test cases usually seek injunctive relief or declaratory judgments. These are suits in equity; thus no jury is empaneled, and the district judge must determine both the facts and the law. The judge will articulate his or her findings of the facts and legal conclusions as to the constitutional validity of the governmental action being tested. The trial record and the district court's analysis are thus extremely important for appellate courts, particularly in cases of first impression.

It is the district court that decides in the first instance whether the government is violating a newspaper's First Amendment rights, an accused's right against self-incrimination, or a minority citizen's right to the equal protection of the laws. Organizations such as the American Civil Liberties Union, the National Association for the Advancement of Colored People, Jehovah's Witnesses, environmental groups, corporations, and individuals initiate litigation in the district court to test the constitutionality of some federal, state, or local legislation or practice.

Such a case was *McLean* v. *Arkansas Board of Education* (D. Ark., 1982). The American Civil Liberties Union sought to challenge an Arkansas law requiring that creationism—a biblical story of man's and the world's creation, as opposed to Darwin's evolutionary theory for explaining the genesis of mankind—be taught in the public schools. The issue was tried first in the federal district court, which framed the issue in these terms: is creationism a religious doctrine or a valid scientific theory? The court heard and weighed testimony, chiefly from experts on both sides, and held that the Arkansas statute was an unconstitutional establishment of religion.

Sometimes prior doctrine has forecast the outcome. For instance, although the separate but equal doctrine on which school segregation had been founded was not overruled until *Brown* v. *Board of Education* (1954), earlier decisions such as *Sweatt* v. *Painter* (1950) and *McLaurin* v. *Oklahoma State Regents* (1950) pointed to that overruling. Nonetheless, the record amassed by several district courts, showing the psychological and education deprivation inflicted by segregation on black children, was crucial in enabling the Supreme Court to take the final step of overruling *Plessy* v. *Ferguson* (1896) and holding that segregated schools violated the right of minority school children to equal protection of the law.

Similarly, a federal district court facing a constitutional challenge to the Hyde Amendment, a congressional provision largely denying Medicaid funds for the cost of abortions, held hearings for about a year. The trial record contained some 400 exhibits and 5,000 pages of testimony. The judge was required to digest this mountain of testimonial and documentary evidence and prepare cohesive findings of facts and conclusions of law. (See *Harris* v. *McRae,* 1980.)

The need for so long a trial and the condensation of so voluminous a record into a coherent decision is not commonplace. However, it is not unusual for a district judge to be required to master the facts in a complex trial lasting many months, and to set forth the facts found and legal conclusions in a comprehensive fashion.

In some cases the district court, as a supplement to its own adjudicative fact-finding, must make findings as to legislative facts as well. For instance, in *Fullilove* v. *Klutznick* (1980) Congress had required at least ten percent of federal funds granted for local public works projects to be set aside for minority businesses. This legislation was attacked as unconstitutional racial discrimination. The district court framed the issue as the power of Congress to remedy past discrimination. The district judge relied on congressional findings that minorities had been denied access to entrepreneurial opportunities provided in building construction works financed by public funds. Based on this legislative finding and Congress's purpose to take remedial action, the district court found the set-aside to be a legitimate remedial act. The Supreme Court adopted this rationale, and upheld the quota.

At times, in a constitutional controversy, the district court, although adhering to judicial precedent requiring it to dismiss the constitutional challenge, may help to bring about a reversal of precedent by recognizing that a wrong exists which should be remedied. *Baker* v. *Carr* (1962) was a challenge to Tennessee's malapportioned legislature. The district court, in its opinion, carefully and sympathetically tracked the contentions of the plaintiffs that the legislators had condoned gross inequality in legislative representation and debased the voting rights of a large number of citizens. The court, however, relied on *Colegrove* v. *Green* (1946) and dismissed the action. On review of this order, the Supreme Court ruled that the plaintiffs' allegations had stated a case within the district court's jurisdiction. Subsequently, *Reynolds* v. *Sims* (1964) embodied the Supreme Court's famous one-person, one-vote principle, requiring legislative districts to be constructed as nearly as possible of an equal number of voters.

Issues of such magnitude are highly charged; it is not unusual, in these controversial circumstances, for the judge who decides a case contrary to the majority's view to face public criticism and in some cases even social ostracism.

Judge Waties Waring's unpopular decision in favor of blacks in voting and school cases led to his social ostracism in Charleston, South Carolina; Judge Skelly Wright became anathema to many whites in New Orleans for the same reason, and escaped that environment through appointment to the Court of Appeals of the District of Columbia Circuit. Similarly, Judge William Ray Overton, who decided the creationism case adversely to local sentiments, and Judge James B. MacMillan, who ordered a complex program of school busing in Charlotte, North Carolina, were subjected to severe community criticism.

Although not so dramatic as the examples given, public criticism meets almost every district judge at one time or another for rendering an unpopular decision. Because most public controversies have a way of ending up in the federal courts, district judges must decide whether seniority systems must be modified to prevent the employment gains of minorities and women from being wiped out; whether regulations requiring physicians to report to parents abortions performed on teenagers are valid; whether the overcrowding and the rundown conditions of a prison require it to be closed; or whether permitting school authorities to provide for prayer or meditation violates the separation of church and state. The district judge normally sits alone, and does not share decision with others, as do federal appellate judges—and therefore is singularly exposed to abuse and pressure.

Life tenure helps secure the independence of the district judge in facing such issues. This independence is crucial, not only for the judge but also for a constitutional system that seeks to secure the rights of the unpopular and despised.

BIBLIOGRAPHY

Administrative Office of the United States Court. *Annual Report of the Director.* Washington, D.C.: Government Printing Office.

Clark, D. S. 1981 Adjudication to Administration: A Statistical Analysis of Federal District Courts in the 20th Century. *Southern California Law Review* 55:65–152.

Hall, Kermit 1976 The Antebellum Lower Federal Judiciary, 1829–1861. *Vanderbilt Law Review* 29:1089–1129.

——— 1981 California's Lower Federal First Judicial Appointments. *Hastings Law Journal* 32:819–837.

Henderson, Dwight F. 1971 *Courts for a New Nation.* Washington, D.C.: Public Affairs Press.

Hough, Charles M. 1934 *The U.S. District Court for the Southern District of New York.* New York: Maritime Law Association.

Management Statistic for United States Courts. 1981.

Steckler, William E. 1978 Future of the Federal District Courts. *Indiana Law Review* 11:601–620.

Surrency, Erwin C. 1963 History of Federal Courts. *Missouri Law Review* 28:214–244.

Thompson, Frank, Jr. 1970 Impeachment of Federal Judges: A Historical Overview. *North Carolina Law Review* 49:87–121.

– ROBERT L. CARTER

Appendix

CONSTITUTION OF THE UNITED STATES

PREAMBLE. WE THE PEOPLE of the United States, in Order to form a more perfect Union, establish Justice, insure domestic Tranquility, provide for the common defence, promote the general Welfare, and secure the Blessings of Liberty to ourselves and our Posterity, do ordain and establish this Constitution for the United States of America.

ARTICLE I. *Section 1.* All legislative Powers herein granted shall be vested in a Congress of the United States, which shall consist of a Senate and House of Representatives.

Section 2. The House of Representatives shall be composed of Members chosen every second Year by the People of the several States, and the Electors in each State shall have the Qualifications requisite for Electors of the most numerous Branch of the State Legislature.

No Person shall be a Representative who shall not have attained to the age of twenty five Years, and been seven Years a Citizen of the United States, and who shall not, when elected be an Inhabitant of that State in which he shall be chosen.

Representatives and direct Taxes shall be apportioned among the several States which may be included within this Union, according to their respective Numbers, which shall be determined by adding to the whole Number of free Persons, including those bound to Service for a Term of Years, and excluding Indians not taxed, three fifths of all other Persons. The actual Enumeration shall be made within three Years after the first Meeting of the Congress of the United States, and within every subsequent Term of ten Years in such Manner as they shall by Law direct. The Number of Representatives shall not exceed one for every thirty Thousand, but each State shall have at Least one Representative; and until such enumeration shall be made, the State of New Hampshire shall be entitled to chuse three, Massachusetts eight, Rhode-Island and Providence Plantations one, Connecticut five, New-York six, New Jersey four, Pennsylvania eight, Delaware one, Maryland six, Virginia ten, North Carolina five, South Carolina five, and Georgia three.

When vacancies happen in the Representation from any State, the Executive Authority thereof shall issue Writs of Election to fill such Vacancies.

The House of Representatives shall chuse their Speaker and other Officers; and shall have the sole Power of Impeachment.

Section 3. The Senate of the United States shall be composed of two Senators from each State, chosen by the Legislature thereof, for six Years; and each Senator shall have one Vote.

Immediately after they shall be assembled in Consequence of the first Election, they shall be divided as equally as may be into three Classes. The Seats of the Senators of the first Class shall be vacated at the Expiration of the second Year, of the second Class at the Expiration of the fourth Year, and of the third Class at the Expiration of the sixth Year, so that one third may be chosen every second Year; and if Vacancies happen by Resignation, or otherwise, during the Recess of the Legislature of any State, the Executive thereof may make temporary Appointments until the next Meeting of the Legislature, which shall then fill such Vacancies.

No Person shall be a Senator who shall not have attained to the Age of thirty Years, and been nine Years a Citizen of the United States, and who shall not, when elected, be an Inhabitant of that State for which he shall be chosen.

The Vice-President of the United States shall be President of the Senate, but shall have no Vote, unless they be equally divided.

The Senate shall chuse their other Officers, and also a President pro tempore, in the Absence of the Vice-President, or when he shall exercise the Office of President of the United States.

The Senate shall have the sole Power to try all Impeachments. When sitting for that Purpose they shall be on Oath or Affirmation. When the President of the United States is tried, the Chief Justice shall preside: And no Person shall be convicted without the Concurrence of two thirds of the Members present.

Judgment in Cases of Impeachment shall not extend further than to removal from Office, and disqualification to hold and enjoy any Office of honor, Trust or Profit under the United States: but the Party convicted shall nevertheless be liable and subject to Indictment, Trial, Judgment and Punishment, according to Law.

Section 4. The Times, Places and Manner of holding Elections for Senators and Representatives, shall be prescribed in each State by the Legislature thereof; but the Congress may at any time by Law make or alter such Regulations, except as to the Places of chusing Senators.

The Congress shall assemble at least once in every Year, and such Meetings shall be on the first Monday in December, unless they shall by Law appoint a different Day.

Section 5. Each House shall be the Judge of the Elections, Returns and Qualifications of its own Members, and a Majority of each shall constitute a Quorum to do Business; but a smaller Number may adjourn from day to day, and may be authorized to compel the Attendance of absent Members, in such Manner, and under such Penalties as each House may provide.

Each House may determine the Rules of its Proceedings, punish its Members for disorderly Behaviour, and, with the Concurrence of two thirds, expel a Member.

Each House shall keep a Journal of its Proceedings, and from time to time publish the same, excepting such Parts as may in their Judgment require Secrecy; and the Yeas and Nays of the Members of either House on any question shall, at the Desire of one fifth of those Present, be entered on the Journal.

Neither House, during the Session of Congress, shall, without the Consent of the other, adjourn for more than three days, nor to any other Place than that in which the two Houses shall be sitting.

Section 6. The Senators and Representatives shall receive a Compensation for their Services, to be ascertained by Law, and paid out of the Treasury of the United States. They shall in all Cases, except Treason, Felony and Breach of the Peace, be privileged from Arrest during their Attendance at the Session of their respective Houses, and in going to and returning from the same; and for any Speech or Debate in either House, they shall not be questioned in any other Place.

No Senator or Representative shall, during the Time for which he was elected, be appointed to any civil Office under the Authority of the United States, which shall have been created, or the Emoluments whereof shall have been encreased during such time; and no Person holding any Office under the United States, shall be a Member of either House during his Continuance in Office.

Section 7. All Bills for raising Revenue shall originate in the House of Representatives; but the Senate may propose or concur with Amendments as on other Bills.

Every Bill which shall have passed the House of Representatives and the Senate, shall, before it becomes a Law, be presented to the President of the United States; If he approve he shall sign it, but if not he shall return it, with his Objections to that House in which it shall have originated, who shall enter the Objections at large on their Journal, and proceed to reconsider it. If after such Reconsideration two thirds of that House shall agree to pass the Bill, it shall be sent, together with the Objections, to the other House, by which it shall likewise be reconsidered, and if approved by two thirds of that House, it shall become a Law. But in all such Cases the Votes of both Houses shall be determined by Yeas and Nays, and the Names of the Persons voting for and against the Bill shall be entered on the Journal of each House respectively. If any Bill shall not be returned by the President within ten Days (Sundays excepted) after it shall have been presented to him, the Same shall be a Law, in like Manner as if he had signed it, unless the Congress by their Adjournment prevent its Return, in which Case it shall not be a Law.

Every Order, Resolution, or Vote to which the Concurrence of the Senate and House of Representatives may be necessary (except on a question of Adjournment) shall be presented to the President of the United States; and before the Same shall take Effect, shall be approved by him, or being disapproved by him, shall be repassed by two thirds of the Senate and House of Representatives, according to the Rules and Limitations prescribed in the Case of a Bill.

Section 8. The Congress shall have Power To lay and collect Taxes, Duties, Imposts and Excises, to pay the Debts and provide for the common Defence and general Welfare of the United States; but all Duties, Imposts and Excises shall be uniform throughout the United States;

To borrow Money on the credit of the United States;

To regulate Commerce with foreign Nations, and among the several States, and with the Indian Tribes;

To establish an uniform Rule of Naturalization and uniform Laws on the subject of Bankruptcies throughout the United States;

To coin Money, regulate the Value thereof, and of foreign Coin, and fix the Standard of Weights and Measures;

To provide for the Punishment of counterfeiting the Securities and current Coin of the United States;

To establish Post Offices and post Roads;

To promote the Progress of Science and useful Arts, by securing for limited Times to Authors and Inventors the exclusive Right to their respective Writings and Discoveries;

To constitute Tribunals inferior to the supreme Court;

To define and punish Piracies and Felonies committed on the high Seas, and Offences against the Law of Nations;

To declare War, grant Letters of Marque and Reprisal, and make Rules concerning Captures on Land and Water;

To raise and support Armies, but no Appropriation of Money to that Use shall be for a longer Term than two Years;

To provide and maintain a Navy;

To make Rules for the Government and Regulation to the land and naval Forces;

To provide for calling for the Militia to execute the Laws of the Union, suppress Insurrections and repel Invasions;

To provide for organizing, arming, and disciplining, the Militia, and for governing such Part of them as may be employed in the Service of the United States, reserving to the States respectively, the Appointment of the Officers, and the Authority of Training the Militia according to the discipline prescribed by Congress;

To exercise exclusive Legislation in all Cases whatsoever, over such District (not exceeding ten Miles square) as may, by Cession of particular States, and the Acceptance of Congress, become the Seat of the Government of the United States, and to exercise like Authority over all Places purchased by the Consent of the Legislature of the State in which the Same shall be, for the Erection of Forts, Magazines, Arsenals, Dock-Yards, and other needful Buildings;—And

To make all Laws which shall be necessary and proper for carrying into Execution the foregoing Powers, and all other Powers vested by this Constitution in the Government of the United States, or in any Department or Officer thereof.

Section 9. The Migration or Importation of such Persons as any of the States now existing shall think proper to admit, shall not be prohibited by the Congress prior to the Year one thousand eight hundred and eight, but a Tax or duty may be imposed on such Importation, not exceeding ten dollars for each Person.

The Privilege of the Writ of Habeas Corpus shall not be suspended, unless when in Cases of Rebellion or Invasion the public Safety may require it.

No bill of Attainder or ex post facto Law shall be passed.

No Capitation, or other direct Tax shall be laid, unless in Proportion to the Census or Enumeration herein before directed to be taken.

No Tax or Duty shall be laid on Articles exported from any State.

No Preference shall be given by any Regulation of Commerce or Revenue to the Ports of one State over those of another; nor shall Vessels bound to, or from, one State, be obliged to enter, clear, or pay Duties in another.

No Money shall be drawn from the Treasury, but in Consequence of Appropriations made by Law; and a regular Statement and Account of the Receipts and Expenditures of all public Money shall be published from time to time.

No Title of Nobility shall be granted by the United States: And no Person holding any Office of Profit or Trust under them, shall, without the Consent of the Congress, accept of any present, Emolument, Office, or Title, of any kind whatever, from any King, Prince, or foreign State.

Section 10. No State shall enter into any Treaty, Alliance, or Confederation; grant Letters of Marque and Reprisal; coin Money; emit Bills of Credit; make any Thing but gold and silver Coin a Tender in Payment of Debts; pass any Bill of Attainder, ex post facto Law, or Law impairing the Obligation of Contracts, or grant any Title of Nobility.

No State shall, without the Consent of the Congress, lay any Imposts or Duties on Imports or Exports, except what may be absolutely necessary for executing its inspection Laws; and the net Produce of all Duties and Imposts, laid by any State on Imports or Exports, shall be for the Use of the Treasury of the United States; and all such Laws shall be subject to the Revision and Controul of the Congress.

No State shall, without the Consent of Congress, lay any Duty of Tonnage, keep Troops, or Ships of War in time of Peace, enter into any Agreement or Compact with another State, or with a foreign Power, or engage in War, unless actually invaded, or in such imminent Danger as will not admit of delay.

ARTICLE II. *Section 1.* The executive Power shall be vested in a President of the United States of America. He shall hold his Office during the Term of four Years, and, together with the Vice-President, chosen for the same Term, be elected, as follows:

Each State shall appoint, in such Manner as the Legislature thereof may direct, a Number of Electors, equal to the whole Number of Senators and Representatives to which the State may be entitled in the Congress: but no Senator or Representative or Person holding an office of Trust or Profit under the United States, shall be appointed an Elector.

The Electors shall meet in their respective States, and vote by Ballot for two Persons, of whom one at least shall not be an Inhabitant of the same State with themselves. And they shall make a List of all the Persons voted for, and of the Number of Votes for each; which List they shall sign and certify, and transmit sealed to the Seat of the Government of the United States, directed to the President of the Senate. The President of the Senate shall, in the Presence of the Senate and House of Representatives, open all the Certificates, and the Votes shall then be counted. The Person having the greatest Number of Votes shall be the President, if such Number be a Majority of the whole Number of Electors appointed; and if there be more than one who have such Majority, and have an equal Number of Votes, then the House of Representatives shall immediately chuse by Ballot one of them for President; and if no Person have a Majority, then from the five highest on the list the said House shall in like Manner chuse the President. But in chusing the President, the Votes shall be taken by States, the Representation from each State having one Vote; a quorum for this Purpose shall consist of a Member or Members from two thirds of the States, and a Majority of all the States shall be necessary to a

Choice. In every Case, after the Choice of the President, the Person having the greatest Number of Votes of the Electors shall be the Vice-President. But if there should remain two or more who have equal Votes, the Senate shall chuse from them by Ballot the Vice President.

The Congress may determine the Time of chusing the Electors, and the Day on which they shall give their Votes; which Day shall be the same throughout the United States.

No Person except a natural born Citizen, or a Citizen of the United States, at the time of the adoption of this Constitution, shall be eligible to the Office of President; neither shall any Person be eligible to that Office who shall not have attained to the Age of thirty five Years, and been fourteen Years a Resident within the United States.

In Case of the Removal of the President from Office, or of his Death, Resignation, or Inability to discharge the Powers and Duties of the said Office, the Same shall devolve on the Vice-President, and the Congress may by Law provide for the Case of Removal, Death, Resignation or Inability, both of the President and Vice-President, declaring what Officer shall then act as President, and such Officer shall act accordingly, until the Disability be removed, or a President shall be elected.

The President shall, at stated Times, receive for his Services, a Compensation, which shall neither be encreased nor diminished during the Period for which he shall have been elected, and he shall not receive within that Period any other Emolument from the United States, or any of them.

Before he enter on the Execution of his Office, he shall take the following Oath or Affirmation:—"I do solemnly swear (or affirm) that I will faithfully execute the Office of President of the United States, and will to the best of my Ability, preserve, protect, and defend the Constitution of the United States."

Section 2. The President shall be Commander in Chief of the Army and Navy of the United States, and of the Militia of the several States, when called into the actual Service of the United States; he may require the Opinion, in writing, of the principal Officer in each of the executive Departments, upon any Subject relating to the Duties of their respective Offices, and he shall have Power to grant Reprieves and Pardons for Offences against the United States, except in Cases of Impeachment.

He shall have Power, by and with the Advice and Consent of the Senate, to make Treaties, provided two thirds of the Senators present concur; and he shall nominate, and by and with the Advice and Consent of the Senate, shall appoint Ambassadors, other public Ministers and Consuls, Judges of the supreme Court, and all other Officers of the United States, whose Appointments are not herein otherwise provided for, and which shall be established by Law; but the Congress may by Law vest the Appointment of such inferior Officers, as they think proper, in the President alone, in the Courts of Law, or in the Heads of Departments.

The President shall have power to fill up all Vacancies that may happen during the Recess of the Senate, by granting Commissions which shall expire at the End of their next Session.

Section 3. He shall from time to time give to the Congress Information of the State of the Union, and recommend to their Consideration such Measures as he shall judge necessary and expedient; he may, on extraordinary Occasions, convene both Houses, or either of them, and in Case of Disagreement between them, with Respect to the Time of Adjournment, he may adjourn them to such Time as he shall think proper; he shall receive Ambassadors and other public Ministers; he shall take Care that the Laws be faithfully executed, and shall Commission all the Officers of the United States.

Section 4. The President, Vice-President, and all civil Officers of the United States, shall be removed from Office on Impeachment for, and Conviction of, Treason, Bribery, or other high Crimes and Misdemeanors.

ARTICLE III. *Section 1.* The judicial Power of the United States, shall be vested in one supreme Court, and in such inferior Courts as the Congress may from time to time ordain and establish. The Judges, both of the supreme and inferior Courts, shall hold their Offices during good Behavior, and shall, at stated Times, receive for their Services, a Compensation, which shall not be diminished during their Continuance in Office.

Section 2. The judicial Power shall extend to all Cases, in Law and Equity, arising under this Constitution, the Laws of the United States, and Treaties made, or which shall be made, under their Authority;—to all Cases affecting Ambassadors, other public Ministers and Consuls;—to all Cases of admiralty and maritime Jurisdiction;—to Controversies to which the United States shall be a party;—to Controversies between two or more States:—between a State and Citizens of another State;—between Citizens of different States;—between Citizens of the same State claiming Lands under Grants of different States, and between a State, or the Citizens thereof, and foreign States, Citizens or Subjects.

In all Cases affecting Ambassadors, other public Ministers and Consuls, and those in which a State shall be Party, the supreme Court shall have original jurisdiction. In all other Cases before mentioned, the supreme Court shall have appellate Jurisdiction, both as to Law and Fact, with such Exceptions, and under such Regulations as the Congress shall make.

The trial of all Crimes, except in Cases of Impeachment, shall be by Jury; and such Trial shall be held in the State where the said Crimes shall have been committed; but when not committed within any State, the Trial shall be at such Place or Places as the Congress may by Law have directed.

Section 3. Treason against the United States, shall consist only in levying War against them, or in adhering to their Enemies, giving them Aid and Comfort. No Person shall be convicted of Treason unless on the Testimony of two Witnesses to the same overt Act, or on Confession in open Court.

The Congress shall have Power to declare the Punishment of Treason, but no Attainder of Treason shall work Corruption of Blood, or Forfeiture except during the Life of the Person attainted.

ARTICLE IV. *Section 1.* Full Faith and Credit shall be given in each State to the Public Acts, Records, and judicial Proceedings of every other State. And the Congress may by general Laws prescribe the Manner in which such Acts, Records and Proceedings shall be proved, and the Effect thereof.

Section 2. The Citizens of each State shall be entitled to all Privileges and Immunities of Citizens in the several States.

A Person charged in any State with Treason, Felony, or other Crime, who shall flee from Justice, and be found in another State, shall on Demand of the executive Authority of the State from which he fled, be delivered up, to be removed to the State having Jurisdiction of the Crime.

No Person held to Service or Labour in one State, under the Laws thereof, escaping into another, shall, in Consequence of any Law or Regulation therein, be discharged from such Service or Labour, but shall be delivered up on Claim of the Party to whom such Service or Labour may be due.

Section 3. New States may be admitted by the Congress into this Union; but no new State shall be formed or erected within the Jurisdiction of any other State; nor any State be formed by the Junction of two or more States, or Parts of States, without the Consent of the Legislatures of the States concerned as well as of the Congress.

The Congress shall have Power to dispose of and make all needful Rules and Regulations respecting the Territory or other Property belonging to the United States; and nothing in this Constitution shall be so construed as to Prejudice any Claims of the United States, or of any particular State.

Section 4. The United States shall guarantee to every State in this Union a Republican Form of Government, and shall protect each of them against Invasion; and on Application of the Legislature, or of the Executive (when the Legislature cannot be convened) against domestic Violence.

ARTICLE V. The Congress, whenever two thirds of both Houses shall deem it necessary, shall propose Amendments to this Constitution, or, on the Application of the Legislatures of two thirds of the several States, shall call a Convention for proposing Amendments, which, in either Case, shall be valid to all Intents and Purposes, as Part of this Constitution, when ratified by the Legislatures of three fourths of the several States, or by Conventions in three fourths thereof, as the one or the other Mode of Ratification may be proposed by the Congress; Provided that no Amendment which may be made prior to the Year One thousand eight hundred and eight shall in any Manner affect the first and fourth Clauses in the Ninth Section of the first Article; and that no State, without its Consent, shall be deprived of its equal Suffrage in the Senate.

ARTICLE VI. All Debts contracted and Engagements entered into, before the Adoption of this Constitution, shall be as valid against the United States under this Constitution, as under the Confederation.

This Constitution, and the Laws of the United States which shall be made in Pursuance thereof; and all Treaties made, or which shall be made, under the Authority of the United States, shall be the supreme Law of the Land; and the Judges in every State shall be bound thereby, any Thing in the Constitution or Laws of any State to the Contrary notwithstanding.

The Senators and Representatives before mentioned, and the Members of the several State Legislatures, and all executive and judicial Officers, both of the United States and of the several States, shall be bound by Oath or Affirmation, to support this Constitution; but no religious Test shall ever be required as a Qualification to any Office or public Trust under the United States.

ARTICLE VII. The Ratification of the Conventions of nine States, shall be sufficient for the Establishment of this Constitution between the States so ratifying the Same.

done in Convention by the Unanimous Consent of the States present the Seventeenth Day of September in the Year of our Lord one thousand seven hundred and eighty seven and of the Independence of the United States of America the Twelfth

In witness whereof We have hereunto subscribed our Names,

George Washington—President and deputy from Virginia

New Hampshire—John Langdon, Nicholas Gilman

Massachusetts—Nathaniel Gorham, Rufus King

Connecticut—William Samuel Johnson, Roger Sherman

New York—Alexander Hamilton

New Jersey—Wil. Livingston, David Brearley, William Paterson, Jona. Dayton

Pennsylvania—B. Franklin, Thomas Mifflin, Robt Morris, Geo. Clymer, Thomas Fitzsimons, Jared Ingersoll, James Wilson, Gouv Morris

Delaware—Geo. Read, Gunning Bedford jun, John Dickinson, Richard Bassett, Jaco. Broom

Maryland—James McHenry, Dan of St. Thomas Jenifer, Daniel Carroll

Virginia—John Blair, James Madison Jr.

North Carolina—William Blount, Richard Dobbs Spaight, Hu. Williamson

South Carolina—J. Rutledge, Charles Cotesworth Pinckney, Charles Pinckney, Pierce Butler

Georgia—William Few, Abr. Baldwin

Amendments to the Constitution

Resolved by the Senate and House of Representatives of the United States of America, in Congress assembled, two thirds of both Houses concurring, that the following Articles be proposed to the Legislatures of the several States, as Amendments to the Constitution of the United States, all, or any of which Articles, when ratified by three fourths of the said Legislatures, to be valid to all intents and purposes, as part of the said Constitution, viz.

ARTICLE I. Congress shall make no law respecting an establishment of religion, or prohibiting the free exercise thereof; or abridging the freedom of speech, or of the press; or the right of the people peaceably to assemble, and to petition the Government for a redress of grievances.

ARTICLE II. A well regulated Militia, being necessary to the security of a free State, the right of the people to keep and bear Arms, shall not be infringed.

ARTICLE III. No Soldier shall, in time of peace, be quartered in any house, without the consent of the Owner, nor in time of war, but in a manner to be prescribed by law.

ARTICLE IV. The right of the people to be secure in their persons, houses, papers, and effects, against unreasonable searches and seizures, shall not be violated, and no Warrants shall issue, but upon probable cause, supported by oath or affirmation, and particularly describing the place to be searched, and the persons or things to be seized.

ARTICLE V. No person shall be held to answer for a capital, or otherwise infamous crime, unless on a presentment or indictment of a Grand Jury, except in cases arising in the land or naval forces, or in the Militia, when in actual service in time of War or public danger; nor shall any person be subject for the same offence to be twice put in jeopardy of life or limb; nor shall be compelled in any criminal case to be a witness against himself, nor be deprived of life, liberty, or property, without due process of law; nor shall private property be taken for public use, without just compensation.

ARTICLE VI. In all criminal prosecutions, the accused shall enjoy the right to a speedy and public trial, by an impartial jury of the State and district wherein the crime shall have been committed, which district shall have been previously ascertained by law, and to be informed of the nature and cause of the accusation; to be confronted with the witnesses against him; to have compulsory process for obtaining witnesses in his favor, and to have the Assistance of Counsel for his defence.

ARTICLE VII. In Suits at common law, where the value in controversy shall exceed twenty dollars, the right of trial by jury shall be preserved, and no fact tried by a jury, shall be otherwise re-examined in any Court of the United States, than according to the rules of the common law.

ARTICLE VIII. Excessive bail shall not be required, nor excessive fines imposed, nor cruel and unusual punishments inflicted.

ARTICLE IX. The enumeration in the Constitution, of certain rights, shall not be construed to deny or disparage others retained by the people.

ARTICLE X. The powers not delegated to the United States by the Constitution, nor prohibited by it to the States, are reserved to the States respectively, or to the people.

ARTICLE XI. The Judicial power of the United States shall not be construed to extend to any suit in law or equity, commenced or prosecuted against one of the United States by Citizens of another State, or by Citizens or Subjects of any Foreign State.

ARTICLE XII. The Electors shall meet in their respective states, and vote by ballot for President and Vice-President, one of whom, at least, shall not be an inhabitant of the same state with themselves; they shall name in their ballots the person voted for as President and in distinct ballots the person voted for as Vice-President, and they shall make distinct lists of all persons voted for as President, and of all persons voted for as Vice-President, and of the number of votes for each which lists they shall sign and certify, and transmit sealed to the seat of the government of the United States, directed to the President of the Senate;—The President of the Senate shall, in the presence of the Senate and House of Representatives, open all the certificates and the votes shall then be counted;—The person having the greatest number of votes for President, shall be the President, if such number be a majority of the whole number of Electors appointed; and if no person have such majority, then from the persons having the highest numbers not exceeding three on the list of those voted for as President, the House of Representatives shall choose immediately, by ballot, the President. But in choosing the President, the votes shall be taken by States, the representation from each state having one vote; a quorum for this purpose shall consist of a member or members from two thirds of the states, and a majority of all the states shall be necessary to a choice. And if the House of Representatives shall not choose a President whenever the right of choice shall devolve upon them, before the fourth day of March next following, then the Vice-President shall act as President, as in the case of the death or other constitutional disability of the President.—The person having the greatest number of votes as Vice-President, shall be Vice-President, if such number be a majority of the whole number of Electors appointed, and if no person have a majority, then from the two highest numbers on the list, the Senate shall choose the Vice-President; a quorum for the purpose shall consist of two thirds of the whole number of Senators, and a majority of the whole number shall be necessary to a choice. But no person constitutionally ineligible to the office of President shall be eligible to that of Vice-President of the United States.

ARTICLE XIII. *Section 1.* Neither slavery nor involuntary servitude, except as a punishment for crime whereof the party shall have been duly convicted, shall exist within the United States, or any place subject to their jurisdiction.

Section 2. Congress shall have power to enforce this article by appropriate legislation.

ARTICLE XIV. *Section 1.* All persons born or naturalized in the United States, and subject to the jurisdiction thereof, are citizens of the United States and of the State wherein they reside. No State shall make or enforce any law which shall abridge the privileges or immunities of citizens of the United States; nor shall any State deprive any person of life, liberty, or property, without due process of law; nor deny to any person within its jurisdiction the equal protection of the laws.

Section 2. Representatives shall be apportioned among the several States according to their respective numbers, counting the whole number of persons in each State, excluding Indians not taxed. But when the right to vote at any election for the choice of electors for President and Vice-President of the United States, Representatives in Congress, the Executive and Judicial officers of a State, or the members of the Legislature thereof, is denied to any of the male inhabitants of such State, being twenty-one years of age, and citizens of the United States, or in any way abridged, except for participation in rebellion, or other crime, the basis of representation therein shall be reduced in the proportion which the number of such male citizens shall bear to the whole number of male citizens twenty-one years of age in such State.

Section 3. No person shall be a Senator or Representative in Congress, or elector of President and Vice-President, or hold any office, civil or military, under the United States, or under any State, who, having previously taken an oath, as a member of Congress, or as an officer of the United States, or as a member of any State legislature, or as an executive or judicial officer of any State, to support the Constitution of the United States, shall have engaged in insurrection or rebellion against the same, or given aid or comfort to the enemies thereof. But Congress may by a vote of two thirds of each House, remove such disability.

Section 4. The validity of the public debt of the United States, authorized by law, including debts incurred for payment of pensions and bounties for services in suppressing insurrection or rebellion, shall not be questioned. But neither the United States nor any State shall assume or pay any debt or obligation incurred in aid of insurrection or rebellion against the United States, or any claim for the loss or emancipation of any slave; but all such debts, obligations and claims shall be held illegal and void.

Section 5. The Congress shall have power to enforce, by appropriate legislation, the provisions of this article.

ARTICLE XV. *Section 1.* The right of citizens of the United States to vote shall not be denied or abridged by the United States or by any State on account of race, color, or previous condition of servitude.

Section 2. Congress shall have power to enforce this article by appropriate legislation.

ARTICLE XVI. The Congress shall have power to lay and collect taxes on incomes, from whatever source derived, without apportionment among the several States, and without regard to any census or enumeration.

ARTICLE XVII. *Section 1.* The Senate of the United States shall be composed of two Senators from each state, elected by the people thereof, for six years; and each Senator shall have one vote. The electors in each State shall have the qualifications requisite for electors of the most numerous branch of the State legislatures.

Section 2. When vacancies happen in the representation of any State in the Senate, the executive authority of such State shall issue writs of election to fill such vacancies: Provided, that the legislature of any State may empower the executive thereof to make temporary appointments until the people fill the vacancies by election as the legislature may direct.

Section 3. This amendment shall not be so construed as to affect the election or term of any Senator chosen before it becomes valid as part of the Constitution.

ARTICLE XVIII. *Section 1.* After one year from the ratification of this article the manufacture, sale, or transportation of intoxicating liquors within, the importation thereof into, or the exportation thereof from the United States and all territory subject to the jurisdiction thereof for beverage purposes is hereby prohibited.

Section 2. The Congress and the several States shall have concurrent power to enforce this article by appropriate legislation.

Section 3. This article shall be inoperative unless it shall have been ratified as an amendment to the Constitution by the legislatures of the several States, as provided in the Constitution, within seven years from the date of the submission hereof to the States by the Congress.

ARTICLE XIX. *Section 1.* The right of citizens of the United States to vote shall not be denied or abridged by the United States or by any State on account of sex.

Section 2. Congress shall have power to enforce this article by appropriate legislation.

ARTICLE XX. *Section 1.* The terms of the President and Vice-President shall end at noon on the 20th day of January, and the terms of Senators and Representatives at noon on the 3rd day of January, of the years in which such terms would have ended if this article had not been ratified; and the terms of their successors shall then begin.

Section 2. The Congress shall assemble at least once in every year, and such meeting shall begin at noon on the 3rd day of January, unless they shall by law appoint a different day.

Section 3. If, at the time fixed for the beginning of the term of the President, the President elect shall have died, the Vice-President elect shall become President. If a President shall not have been chosen before the time fixed for the beginning of his term, or if the President elect shall have failed to qualify, then the Vice-President elect shall act as President until a President shall have qualified; and the Congress may by law provide for the case wherein neither a President elect nor a Vice-President elect shall have qualified, declaring who shall then act as President, or the manner in which one who is to act shall be selected, and such person shall act accordingly until a President or Vice-President shall have qualified.

Section 4. The Congress may by law provide for the case of the death of any of the persons from whom the House of Representatives may choose a President whenever the right of choice shall have devolved upon them, and for the case of the death of any of the persons from whom the Senate may choose a Vice-President whenever the right of choice shall have devolved upon them.

Section 5. Sections 1 and 2 shall take effect on the 15th day of October following the ratification of this article.

Section 6. This article shall be inoperative unless it shall have been ratified as an amendment to the Constitution by the legislatures of three fourths of the several States within seven years from the date of its submission.

ARTICLE XXI. *Section 1.* The Eighteenth Article of amendment to the Constitution of the United States is hereby repealed.

Section 2. The transportation or importation into any State, Territory, or possession of the United States for delivery or use therein of intoxicating liquors, in violation of the laws thereof, is hereby prohibited.

Section 3. This article shall be inoperative unless it shall have been ratified as an amendment to the Constitution by conventions in the several States, as provided in the Constitution, within seven years from the date of the submission hereof to the States by the Congress.

ARTICLE XXII. *Section 1.* No person shall be elected to the office of the President more than twice, and no person who has held the office of President, or acted as President, for more than two years of a term to which some other person was elected President shall be elected to the office of the President more than once. But this Article shall not apply to any person holding the office of President when this Article was proposed by the Congress, and shall not prevent any person who may be holding the office of President, or acting as President, during the term within which this Article becomes operative from holding the office of President or acting as President during the remainder of such term.

Section 2. This article shall be inoperative unless it shall have been ratified as an amendment to the Constitution by the legislatures of three fourths of the several States within seven years from the date of its submission to the States by the Congress.

ARTICLE XXIII. *Section 1.* The District constituting the seat of Government of the United States shall appoint in such manner as the Congress may direct: A number of electors of President and Vice-President equal to the whole number of Senators and Representatives in Congress to which the District would be entitled if it were a State, but in no event more than the least populous State; they shall be in addition to those appointed by the States, but they shall be considered, for the purposes of the election of President and Vice-President, to be electors appointed by a State; and they shall meet in the District and perform such duties as provided by the Twelfth Article of amendment.

Section 2. The Congress shall have power to enforce this article by appropriate legislation.

ARTICLE XXIV. *Section 1.* The right of citizens of the United States to vote in any primary or other election for President or Vice-President, for electors for President or Vice-President, or for Senator or Representative in Congress, shall not be denied or abridged by the United States or any State by reason of failure to pay any poll tax or other tax.

Section 2. The Congress shall have power to enforce this article by appropriate legislation.

ARTICLE XXV. *Section 1.* In case of the removal of the President from office or of his death or resignation, the Vice-President shall become President.

Section 2. Whenever there is a vacancy in the office of the Vice-President, the President shall nominate a Vice-President who shall take office upon confirmation by a majority vote of both Houses of Congress.

Section 3. Whenever the President transmits to the President pro tempore of the Senate and the Speaker of the House of Representatives his written declaration that he is unable to discharge the powers and duties of his office, and until he transmits to them a written declaration to the contrary, such powers and duties shall be discharged by the Vice-President as Acting President.

Section 4. Whenever the Vice-President and a majority of either the principal officers of the executive departments or of such other body as Congress may by law provide, transmit to the President pro tempore of the Senate and the Speaker of the House of Representatives their written declaration that the President is unable to discharge the powers and duties of his office, the Vice-President shall immediately assume the powers and duties of the office as Acting President.

Thereafter, when the President transmits to the President pro tempore of the Senate and the Speaker of the House of Representatives his written declaration that no inability exists, he shall resume the powers and duties of his office unless the Vice-President and a majority of either the principal officers of the executive department or of such other body as Congress may by law provide, transmit within four days to the President pro tempore of the Senate and the Speaker of the House of Representatives their written declaration that the President is unable to discharge the powers and duties of his office. Thereupon Congress shall decide the issue, assembling within forty-eight hours for that purpose if not in session. If the Congress, within twenty-one days after receipt of the latter written declaration, or, if Congress is not in session, within twenty-one days after Congress is required to assemble, determines by two thirds vote of both Houses that the President is unable to discharge the powers and duties of his office, the Vice-President shall continue to discharge the same as Acting President; otherwise, the President shall resume the powers and duties of his office.

ARTICLE XXVI. *Section 1.* The right of citizens of the United States, who are eighteen years of age or older, to vote shall not be denied or abridged by the United States or any State on account of age.

Section 2. The Congress shall have power to enforce this article by appropriate legislation.

ARTICLE XXVII. No law, varying the compensation for the services of the Senators and Representatives, shall take effect, until an election of Representatives shall have intervened.

Index

K

O

S